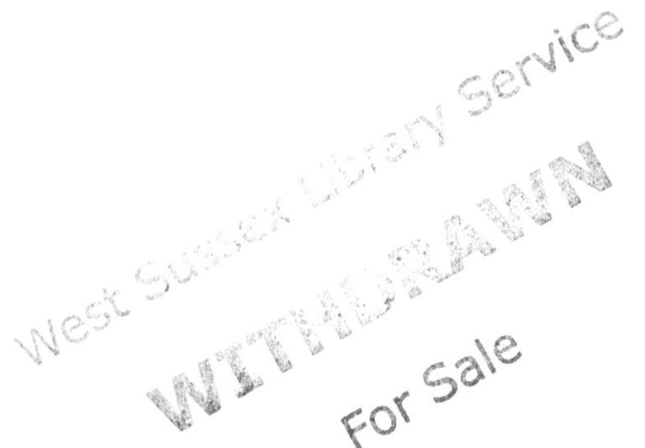

THE NATIONAL ROLL OF THE GREAT WAR.

The National Roll of the Great War

One of the most sought-after sets of reference books of the First World War is the *National Roll of the Great War*. The National Publishing Company attempted, shortly after hostilities ceased, to compile a brief biography of as many participants in the War as possible. The vast majority of entries refer to combatants who survived the Great War and the *National Roll* is often the only source of information available. Fourteen volumes were completed on a regional basis; **the Naval & Military Press has compiled a fifteenth volume which contains an alphabetic index to the fourteen now republished volumes**.

The National Roll - complete 15 vol. set	ISBN: 1 847340 33 4	£285.00
Section I - London	ISBN: 1 847340 34 2	£22.00
Section II - London	ISBN: 1 847340 35 0	£22.00
Section III - London	ISBN: 1 847340 36 9	£22.00
Section IV - Southampton	ISBN: 1 847340 37 7	£22.00
Section V - Luton	ISBN: 1 847340 38 5	£22.00
Section VI - Birmingham	ISBN: 1 847340 39 3	£22.00
Section VII - London	ISBN: 1 847340 40 7	£22.00
Section VIII - Leeds	ISBN: 1 847340 41 5	£22.00
Section IX - Bradford	ISBN: 1 847340 42 3	£22.00
Section X - Portsmouth	ISBN: 1 847340 43 1	£22.00
Section XI - Manchester	ISBN: 1 847340 44 X	£22.00
Section XII - Bedford & Northampton	ISBN: 1 847340 45 8	£22.00
Section XIII - London	ISBN: 1 847340 46 6	£22.00
Section XIV - Salford	ISBN: 1 847340 47 4	£22.00
Section XV - Index to all 14 volumes	ISBN: 1 847340 48 2	£22.00

The Naval & Military Press Ltd

Unit 10, Ridgewood Industrial Park, Uckfield,
East Sussex, TN22 5QE, England
Tel: 01825 749494 Fax: 01825 765701

www.naval-military-press.com
www.military-genealogy.com

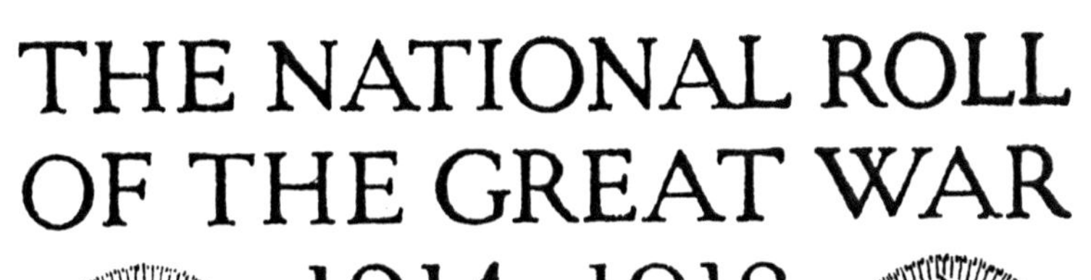

THE NATIONAL ROLL OF THE GREAT WAR 1914-1918

CONTAINED WITHIN THE PAGES OF THIS VOLUME WILL BE FOUND THE NAMES AND RECORDS OF SERVICE OF THOSE WHO HELPED TO SECURE VICTORY FOR THE EMPIRE DURING THE GREAT WAR OF 1914-1918.

THE
NAVAL &
MILITARY
PRESS LTD
2006

Published by

The Naval & Military Press Ltd

Unit 10, Ridgewood Industrial Park,

Uckfield, East Sussex,

TN22 5QE England

Tel: +44 (0) 1825 749494

Fax: +44 (0) 1825 765701

www.naval-military-press.com

www.military-genealogy.com

FOREWORD

AND SHORT OUTLINE OF THE PART PLAYED BY BRITAIN IN THE GREAT WAR.

WHEN we quietly consider what the Great War, with its gains and losses, its cares and anxieties, has taught us, we are at once struck by the splendid heroism of all who took part in it. Many by reason of special qualities of mind or soul stand out more prominently than the rest; but the names and deeds of others, who toiled no less meritoriously, are officially left unsung.

Yet it is well, if only for purely personal and family reasons, that there should be some abiding record of the self-sacrificing services of all men and women who answered their Country's call in her hour of need, and who, whether on land, or sea, or in the air, in hospital, or camp, or workshop, were ready to lay down life itself, if need be, that Britain might live and Right prevail over Might.

It is for this reason primarily that the present "National Roll of the Great War" was projected. In these pages will be found records of devotion and patriotism of which the individual, the family, and the nation have every reason to be proud.

1914. This foreword, besides recording our gratitude to all who toiled for the Empire, may also serve a subsidiary purpose by providing a sketch of the part which Britain played in the war which burst on the World in the Summer of 1914. Space does not allow us to follow the course of the negotiations which preceded the outbreak, or to explain the aims of Germany. Suffice it to say that her long projected design of rushing through Belgium on France in one overwhelming flood was foiled by the gallantry of the Allies in August and September. Our share in that struggle is told in the records of "The Contemptible Little Army" that fought at Mons, the Marne, the Aisne and Ypres.

1915. Our campaign in 1915 opened with the Battle of Neuve Chapelle, and in quick succession followed those at St. Eloi, Hill 60, Ypres and Festubert. In the Autumn we gained a temporary success at Loos, and at one time Lens was almost ours, but when Winter set in, our lines were much the same as they had been a year before. We now began to realize, in a way we had not done hitherto, the greatness of the task to which we had set our hands. Our failure in the East had taught us the lesson that in the West and on the Sea lay our hopes of victory.

1916 Early in 1916 the fortune of war swayed for and against us at Loos, Ypres and Vimy Ridge, while the Germans were making their great effort at Verdun. Their protracted attack on that fortress failed, while their attempt to take command of the Sea was crushed by our Naval victory in the Battle of Jutland. Our great effort in 1916 was the Somme Offensive, which opened in July, and continued with varying success until November.

1917. Early in 1917 we reaped to some extent the benefit of our efforts of the preceding year, and a German retirement on a long line of the front took place, which by the middle of March gave us Bapaume and Péronne. On Easter Monday we attacked along the Vimy Ridge, and before Arras. Monchy-le-Preux was captured, Bailleul and several villages near Lens fell into our hands, and by May 17th we had taken Bullecourt. In June came our victory at Messines, and from July to November we fought the series of engagements round St. Julien, Pilkem, Hooge, Polygon Wood and Passchendaele, which go by the name of the third Battle of Ypres. At the same time severe fighting was going on near Lens, and this was followed in November and December by the first Battle of Cambrai, which opened auspiciously, but left us with little gained in the end.

1918. The year 1918 opened with the great German Offensive, which was designed to end the struggle before the full weight of the American help could tell in our favour. It broke upon the Allied lines between the Scarpe and the Oise on March 21st, and for a time carried everything before it; but Arras and Amiens remained in our possession. On April 9th the Germans made another effort on the Lys front, from La Bassée to Armentières. Desperate fighting occurred around Bailleul, Passchendaele, Kemmel and Givenchy, but in spite of our severe losses, Ludendorff failed to break through.

At the end of May the Germans made yet another attempt along the Aisne, and captured Soissons, Dormans and many villages. Their last effort began on July 15th along the Marne, east and west of Rheims. They achieved some success at first, but on July 18th the Allied counter-stroke began. Blow followed blow in quick succession, and Soissons and Beaumont-Hamel, that had been lost in the Spring, were now recovered. On August 21st the Battle of Bapaume opened, and concurrently with it the Battle of the Scarpe was going on. Towards the end of September the Battles of Cambrai and Ypres began, and our victories began seriously to jeopardise the enemy's lines of communication Eastwards. Le Cateau was entered on October 10th; Ostend, Lille and Douai fell into Allied hands and within a few days the Belgian coast was freed. In November our successes still continued in the Battle of the Sambre, and the enemy retreated rapidly towards Mons and Maubeuge. Mons was entered at dawn on November 11th, 1918, and at 11 a.m. fighting ceased.

GALLIPOLI. During 1915 we anxiously followed the course of our venture in the Dardanelles. Weighty reasons prompted it, and we hoped that our combined forces would be able to make their way to Constantinople, and by so doing would relieve the pressure on Russia, as well as remove the danger that threatened Egypt.

Unhappily, however, the successes at Anzac and Krithia and the later landing at Suvla Bay could not be followed up; the Naval forces could not force their way through the Narrows; and reluctantly we had to admit failure and evacuate the Peninsula.

EGYPT. Early in the war the Turks made several unsuccessful attacks on the Canal Zone, while on the Western Frontiers of Egypt the Senussi were repulsed at Mersa, Matruh and Agagia. In August 1916 another Turkish attack was crushed at Romani, and six months later the enemy were again defeated at Magdhaba and Rafa. Henceforward Egypt became the base for offensive operations against the Turks in Palestine. Gaza was first attacked in March 1917, and again in April, but it was not captured until November, after General Allenby had previously taken Beersheba. Shortly afterwards Jaffa fell into our hands, and on December 9th Jerusalem surrendered, to be followed by Jericho in February. Hostilities were resumed in September, 1918, and by the end of October we were masters of Acre, Haifa, Damascus, Tripolis and Aleppo.

MESOPOTAMIA. Indian detachments reached Mesopotamia in November 1914, and occupied Basra and Kurma on the Tigris. Amara, higher up the river, was captured in June 1915, and Kut-el-Amara in September. General Townshend's forces then proceeded towards Baghdad, but their way was barred at Ctesiphon, and finding it impossible to break through the Turkish lines they retired on Kut, where in April 1916 they surrendered. In December 1916 a better organised offensive began, which in 1917 and 1918 captured Kut, Baghdad, Tekrit and Mosul.

SALONIKA Our troops on this front came from Gallipoli in December 1915, too late to stem the Bulgarian Advance against Serbia, but in August 1916 they began a general offensive along the Doiran front, and in September advanced across the Struma. Before the close of the year Monastir was recovered. In 1917 we were mainly concerned in the Doiran Advance, and in 1918 in a similar operation along the Vardar, which on September 30th ended in the victory of the Allies and the Armistice with Bulgaria.

AFRICA. The Germans in Togoland were overcome by August 27th, 1914, while those in the Cameroons held out only one month longer. German South-West Africa proved more difficult to reduce owing to political complications, but it eventually surrendered to General Botha in July 1915. In East Africa the Germans kept up the struggle with success whilst hostilities continued in Europe, and ceased fighting on November 14th, 1918, in compliance with the terms of the Armistice.

THE NAVY. The work of the Navy throughout the war was of boundless importance. Not only did she take command of the Seas in August 1914, but she kept it to the end. Of the Battles of Heligoland, Coronel and the Falkland Islands in 1914, the Dogger Bank and the Dardanelles in 1915, Jutland in 1916, the bombardments of Zeebrugge and Ostend in 1917, and the raids on Zeebrugge and Durazzo in 1918 the public have full information; but of the smaller engagements in almost all waters of the globe, few have as yet any accurate knowledge.

ROYAL AIR FORCE. Still less do we know, except in a general way, of the work of the Royal Air Force, which arose in 1918 from the union of the R.F.C. and the R.N.A.S. Handicapped at first by lack of men and material, they soon became a highly efficient body, and proved of incalculable value to both the Army and the Navy. The heroic deeds of Major McCudden, Captain Leefe Robinson, Captain Ball, Lieutenant Warneford and many others, will for ever live in our memory.

The National Roll makes no claim to being a complete book of reference—in fact no such record could be compiled—but it may safely claim to supply a wonderful memorial of splendid services, truly worthy of the thankful remembrance of a grateful Empire.

To all who, by their Faith and Courage, helped to bring Victory to our Arms, we dedicate this book.

THE EDITOR.

1, York Place, Baker Street,
London, W.1.

THE NATIONAL ROLL OF THE 1914 GREAT WAR 1918

SECTION XII.

PART I.

A

ABBOTT, A. E., Driver, Royal Field Artillery.
Mobilised at the outbreak of hostilities, he served at various stations until embarking for Egypt in 1917. On the Palestine front he fought in many engagements, including the Battle of Gaza, the operations resulting in the capture of Jerusalem and was engaged in heavy fighting throughout the final British Advance into Syria. Returning to England, he was demobilised in April 1919, and holds the General Service and Victory Medals. 38, Public Road, Cople, Bedford. Z1001.

ABBOTT, A. J., Private, Queen's Own (Royal West Kent Regiment).
He joined in 1916, and in the following year was drafted to France, where he was in action in the Battles of Ypres, Lens and Cambrai. He gave his life for the freedom of England at Cambrai on August 9th, 1918, during the final Allied Advance. He was entitled to the General Service and Victory Medals.
"He joined the great white company of valiant souls."
Marston, near Bedford. Z1002/C.

ABBOTT, E. V., Private, R.A.M.C.
Mobilised at the commencement of hostilities, he proceeded to Egypt in 1915, and was engaged on important ambulance duties in many engagements during the Advance across the Sinai Peninsula and in Palestine. He was present at the Battle of Gaza, at the operations resulting in the capture of Jerusalem and saw heavy fighting in the Jordan Valley. Transferred to France in March 1918 he served throughout the Retreat and Advance, and returning home after the Armistice was demobilised in February 1919. He holds the 1914–15 Star, and the General Service and Victory Medals.
23, St. John's Place, Bedford. X1003.

ABBOTT, G. C., Private, R.A.S.C.
Volunteering in June 1915, he completed his training and served at various stations on important duties with his unit. Owing to ill-health he was unsuccessful in obtaining his transfer overseas, but rendered excellent services until invalided out of the Army in August 1918. 81, George Street, Bedford. Z1000.

ABBOTT, H., Private, Essex Regiment.
He joined in March 1916, and was sent to Egypt in the following July. He was in action at Gaza, in the operations resulting in the capture of Jerusalem, and on the Jordan, and was twice wounded. Returning home he served for some time in Ireland, and was demobilised in September 1919, holding the General Service and Victory Medals.
14, Prospect Place, Cambridge Street, St. Neots, Hunts. Z1005.

ABBOTT, J. W. C., Gunner, Tank Corps.
Volunteering in 1915, he was drafted to the Western Front in the following year and was in action in many parts of the line, including the Loos, Albert and Somme sectors. He was killed in action at Kemmel Hill on April 25th, 1917, and was buried at Wytschaete. He was entitled to the General Service and Victory Medals.
"A costly sacrifice upon the altar of freedom."
The Gardens, Great Barford, Bedfordshire. Z1004/C.

ABBOTT, W., Pte., Royal Inniskilling Fusiliers.
He volunteered in 1915, and, landing in France later in that year, was in action at Ypres, Hill 60, Loos, Vimy Ridge and the Somme, and was wounded. On his recovery he was drafted to Egypt in 1917, and fought at Gaza, in the operations resulting in the fall of Jerusalem, throughout the final British Advance into Syria and was twice wounded. Returning home, he was demobilised in February 1919, and holds the 1914–15 Star, and the General Service and Victory Medals.
The Gardens, Great Barford, Bedfordshire. Z1004/B.

ABBOTT, W., Private, R.M.L.I.
Volunteering in September 1914, he was posted to H.M.S. "Campania," which acted as a seaplane carrier. He saw much service in this ship in the North Sea, and later, transferred to the Dover patrol, was engaged on patrol, escort, and other important duties until the close of hostilities. He was demobilised in April 1919, and holds the 1914–15 Star, and the General Service and Victory Medals. Marston, near Bedford. Z1002/A.

ABBOTT, W. J., Private, 8th Bedfordshire Regt.
Volunteering in 1915, he was drafted to the Western Front and was in action at Albert and Vimy Ridge. Owing to ill-health he was invalided home for hospital treatment, and on his recovery returned to France and fought in various parts of the line. He was reported missing on April 19th, 1917, and later was presumed to have been killed on that date. He was entitled to the General Service and Victory Medals.
"His life for his Country, his soul to God."
Marston, near Bedford. Z1002/B.

ABEL, J. E., Air Mechanic, Royal Air Force.
He joined in August 1917, and, after undergoing a period of training, was retained at various stations, where he was engaged on duties of a highly important nature. He was not successful in obtaining his transfer to a theatre of war, but, nevertheless, rendered valuable services with his Squadron until March 1919, when he was demobilised.
Greens Norton, Towcester, Northants. Z2859.

ABRAHAM, A., Private, 5th Bedfordshire Regt.
He volunteered in November 1914, and, completing his training was engaged on guard and other important duties at various stations. Owing to ill-health he was unsuccessful in obtaining his transfer overseas, but rendered excellent services until demobilised in January 1919.
28, Church Square, Bedford. X1008.

ABRAHAM, A. J., Private, R.A.S.C. (H.T.)
He joined in June 1918, and in the following August was drafted to France, where he was engaged on important transport duties in the forward areas. He served at Cambrai and Ypres and in many other parts of the line during the German and Allied Offensives of 1918. Owing to an accident he was invalided home in January 1919, and after receiving hospital treatment was demobilised in the following month. He holds the General Service and Victory Medals.
81, Brickyard, Olney, Bucks. Z1010/B.

ABRAHAM, E. A., Sergeant, Bedfordshire Regt.
Volunteering in September 1914, he went through a course of training and served at various depôts on important duties with his unit. Owing to ill-health he was unsuccessful in obtaining his transfer overseas, and after a period of hospital treatment was invalided out of the Service in November 1915.
5, Bardolphs Court, St. Germain Street, Huntington. Z1007/A.

ABRAHAM, E. P., Pte., Royal Warwickshire Regt.
Joining in September 1918, he completed his training and served at various military centres with his unit. He was not sent to a theatre of war prior to the close of hostilities, but in February 1919, was drafted to the Army of Occupation in Germany. He was stationed at Cologne on guard and other important duties until he returned to England and was demobilised in March 1920.
81, Brickyard, Olney, Bucks. Z1010/C.

ABRAHAM, F., Private, Machine Gun Corps.
He joined in March 1917, and, proceeding to the Western Front later in that year, was in action in the Battles of Vimy Ridge, Ypres and Cambrai. He was engaged in heavy fighting during the Retreat of 1918, and was wounded in June. Returning home he received hospital treatment, and on recovery was sent to Russia in December 1918, and served in that country for three months. In 1920 he was stationed in India, and holds the General Service and Victory Medals.
81, Brickyard, Olney, Bucks. Z1010/D.

ABRAHAM, H. W., Cpl., South Wales Borderers.
He joined in March 1916, and in the following June was sent to India and thence to Mesopotamia. He was in action at Kut, Amara, and in the operations resulting in the capture of Baghdad, but in January 1919 was invalided to India, suffering from malaria. On recovery he served at various stations on the North Western Frontier on garrison duties. Returning home, he was demobilised in January 1920, and holds the General Service and Victory Medals.
81, Brickyard, Olney, Bucks. Z1010/A.

ABRAHAM, W., Pte., Buffs (East Kent Regt.)
Joining in June 1916, he was drafted to the Western Front in the following October, and was engaged in heavy fighting in many parts of the line. He laid down his life for the freedom of England at Albert on November 19th, 1916. He was entitled to the General Service and Victory Medals.
New Town, Kimbolton, Hunts. Z1009.

ABRAHAMS, E., Sergeant, Bedfordshire Regt.
Volunteering at the commencement of hostilities, he completed his training and was stationed at various depôts with his unit. He was not successful in obtaining his transfer to a theatre of war, but rendered excellent services until demobilised in March 1919. Buckden Road, Brampton, Hunts. Z1011/A.

ABRAHAMS, E. R. G., Rifleman, Rifle Brigade.
He volunteered in August 1914, and in June of the following year was drafted to France, where he took part in the Battles of Neuve Chapelle, Festubert, the Somme, Arras, Ypres and Cambrai. He was demobilised in March 1919, and holds the 1914–15 Star, and the General Service and Victory Medals.
16, Dunville Road, Queen's Park, Bedford. Z1012.

ABRAHAMS, J., Sergeant, Northants. Regiment.
He volunteered in 1915, and after completing his training was sent to France. In this theatre of war he was in action at Festubert, Loos, Albert, Vimy Ridge, the Somme, Arras, Messines, Ypres, Passchendaele and Cambrai. He was demobilised in March 1919, and holds the 1914–15 Star, and the General Service and Victory Medals.
Buckden Road, Brampton, Hunts. Z1011/C.

ABRAHAMS, W. G., Quartermaster-Sergeant, 17th (Duke of Cambridge's Own) Lancers.
He was mobilised in August 1914, and was immediately afterwards sent to France. He took part in the Retreat from Mons and the Battles of the Marne the Aisne, Albert, Festubert, Loos, Vimy Ridge, the Somme, Ypres, Lens and Cambrai. He was discharged in March 1919, and holds the Mons Star, and the General Service and Victory Medals.
Buckden Road, Brampton, Hunts. Z1011/B.

ACKROYD, G. E., Sergeant, Machine Gun Corps.
He was mobilised in 1914, and in the following year was sent to France, where he took part in the fighting at Ypres, Loos, Vimy Ridge and the Somme, and was wounded in April 1916. He was later sent to hospital at Rouen suffering from shell-shock. He was demobilised in March 1919, and holds the 1914–15 Star, and the General Service and Victory Medals.
39, All Hallows Lane, Bedford. X1013.

ADAMS, A. (Miss), Worker, Land Army.
She joined in January 1916, and, after completing a period of training served at Byfield, Northamptonshire. There she was engaged on ploughing and general farm work and rendered very valuable services until December 1918, when she was demobilised.
Green's Norton, Towcester, Northants. Z2860/B.

ADAMS, D., Sergeant, R.A.V.C.
He volunteered in January 1915, and in the following May was drafted to France. Throughout his service there he was engaged in attending to sick and wounded horses in the Loos, Somme, Ypres and Cambrai sectors. He was on leave pending demobilisation when he was taken ill and unfortunately died on May 15th, 1919. He was entitled to the 1914–15 Star, and the General Service and Victory Medals.
"His memory is cherished with pride."
15, Trevor Street, Bedford. Z1019.

ADAMS, D. H., Corporal, Northants. Dragoons.
He volunteered in June 1915, and, on completing his training in the following year, was drafted to the Western Front, where he saw severe fighting in various sectors. He took part in the Battles of the Somme, Ypres and Cambrai, and many other important engagements, and also fought in the Retreat and Advance of 1918. He afterwards served with the Army of Occupation at Cologne, finally returning home for demobilisation in March 1919. He holds the General Service and Victory Medals. Green's Norton, Towcester, Northants. Z2860/A.

ADAMS, E. J., Private, 1st Bedfordshire Regiment.
He volunteered in June 1915, and in February of the following year was drafted to France, where he was in action on the Somme and at Ypres. Wounded on the Somme in March 1918, he was invalided home, and after a year's hospital treatment was demobilised in June 1919. He holds the General Service and Victory Medals.
Weston Underwood, Bucks. Z1015/A.

ADAMS, E. T., 2nd Lieutenant, Royal Air Force.
He volunteered in May 1915, and later proceeded to the Western Front with the Balloon Section. Returning home, he was granted a commission and was afterwards engaged as an Instructor at Pulham. After doing excellent work, he was demobilised in March 1919, and holds the General Service and Victory Medals. Park Lane, Sharnbrook, Bedford. Z1021.

ADAMS, F., Private, 1st Bedfordshire Regiment.
Joining in March 1916, he was in the following month sent to France, and took part in July 1916 in the Battle of the Somme, where he was severely wounded. After a long period in hospital, he was discharged owing to his injuries in April 1918, and holds the General Service and Victory Medals.
Weston Underwood, Bucks. Z1015/B.

ADAMS, H., L/Cpl., 1st Oxford & Bucks. L.I.
He volunteered in September 1914, and in March 1916 was drafted to France, where he took part in the fierce fighting in the Somme and Ypres sectors. In November 1917 he proceeded to Italy and was in action on the Piave and in numerous other engagements. He was demobilised in February 1919, and holds the General Service and Victory Medals.
Weston Underwood, Bucks. Z1016.

ADAMS, H. W., Pte., 1/8th R. Warwickshire Regt.
He joined in February 1916, and later in the same year was drafted to France, where he took part in important engagements. He was unhappily killed in action on the Somme on July 1st, 1916, and was entitled to the General Service and Victory Medals.
"A costly sacrifice upon the altar of freedom."
22, Oxford Street, Wolverton, Bucks. Z1017/B.

ADAMS, J. G., Gunner, Royal Garrison Artillery.
He volunteered in March 1915, and in August of the following year was sent to France, where he served on the Somme and at Arras. In January 1917 he was transferred to Italy and took part in the Piave Offensive. He was demobilised in June 1919, and holds the General Service and Victory Medals.
8, Weston Road, Olney, Bucks. Z1014/B.

ADAMS, J. H., Pte., 2/5th R. Warwickshire Regt.
He joined in January 1918, and in the following June was drafted to France, where he took part in the fighting at Cambrai and Ypres. After the Armistice he proceeded with the Army of Occupation to Germany, and served at Cologne for a long period. He was demobilised in December 1919, and holds the General Service and Victory Medals.
2, Weston Road, Olney, Bucks. Z1014/A.

ADAMS, O. G., Private, Durham Light Infantry.
Volunteering in September 1915, he was early in the following year drafted to France and took part in the Battles of the Somme, Arras and Ypres. He was unfortunately killed in action near Passchendaele on October 25th, 1917. He was entitled to the General Service and Victory Medals.
"His life for his Country, his soul to God."
15, Howbury Street, Bedford. Z1022/A.

ADAMS, T., Sapper, Royal Engineers.
Having joined in May 1916, he was drafted to France in the following month and was engaged at the Base on important duties in connection with engineering. After doing excellent service, he was demobilised in February 1919, and holds the General Service and Victory Medals.
22, Oxford Street, Wolverton, Bucks. Z1017/A.

ADAMS, W., Sick Berth Attendant, R.N.R.
He was mobilised in August 1914, and was stationed at Plymouth and Chatham, where he was engaged on important hospital duties. He also served in H.M.S. "China," hospital ship, plying between Southampton and France. He was discharged in March 1919, and holds the 1914–15 Star, and the General Service and Victory Medals.
Olney Road, Lavendon, Bucks. Z1018.

ADAMS, W., Private, Royal Naval Division.
He was mobilised in August 1914, and shortly afterwards was sent to France, where he took part in numerous engagements, including those at Oppy Wood, Ypres and Cambrai. He was discharged in March 1919, and holds the 1914 Star, and the General Service and Victory Medals.
34, Ouse Walk, Huntingdon, Bucks. Z1020.

ADDICOTT, A., Gunner, Mercantile Marine.
He was already in the Merchant Service at the outbreak of war, and served in H.M.T. "Crown of Toledo," engaged on patrol duties in the North Sea, Atlantic, Pacific and Mediterranean. On one occasion his vessel was torpedoed, but fortunately he was saved. Holding the General Service and Mercantile Marine War Medals, he was still serving in 1921.
71, Strathnairn Street, Roath Park, Cardiff. Z1023.

AIRD, C. J., L/Corporal, 4th Queen's Own Cameron Highlanders.
Volunteering in August 1914, he proceeded in the following February to France, where he served in many notable engagements until January 1917. He then returned to England and was engaged on work of an important nature at Woolwich until demobilised in March 1919. He holds the 1914–15 Star, and the General Service and Victory Medals.
28, Russell Street, Bedford. TX1024.

ALBAN, F. V., Stoker, Royal Navy.
Already in the Navy at the outbreak of war, he did duty during the course of hostilities in H.M.S. "Aquarius." He served principally off the coast of Greece and also took part in the Naval operations at the Dardanelles and in covering the landing of the troops. He was invalided home through ill-health and in March 1919, was discharged as medically unfit. He holds the 1914–15 Star, and the General Service and Victory Medals. 42, St. Germain Street, Huntingdon. Z1026/B.

ALDERMAN, W., Sapper, R.E. (R.O.D.)
Joining in November 1916, he served after a course of training on important duties at various stations with his unit. He was not successful in obtaining his transfer overseas before the end of the war, but rendered valuable services throughout. In December 1919 he was demobilised.
158, High Street, Stony Stratford, Bucks. Z1027.

ALDRIDGE, W. (M.S.M.), A.B., Royal Navy.
Already in the Navy when war broke out, he served throughout on board H.M.S. "Tenedos," and did escort duty in the North Sea and off the coasts of China and Russia. His ship also escorted the King to France on his visits there during the war. He was awarded the Meritorious Service Medal for devotion to duty, and in addition holds the 1914–15 Star, and the General Service and Victory Medals, and in 1921 was still in the Navy.
25, Tavistock Place, Bedford. X1028.

ALLEN, A. F., Private, 3rd Royal Sussex Regt.
Joining in 1918, he served, after a brief training, on important duties at various stations with his unit. Owing to physical unfitness he was not successful in obtaining a transfer overseas, but rendered valuable services until his demobilisation in 1919.
Upper Dean, near Kimbolton, Hunts. Z1035/B.

ALLEN, A. G. (M.S.M.), Sergt., 7th Wiltshire Regt.
Volunteering in September 1914, he embarked in July of the following year to France, where he served for about six months. Transferred to Salonika he experienced much fighting on the Vardar and Doiran fronts, but, returning to France early in 1918, took part in the Battles of Ypres and Cambrai and in other engagements until the Armistice. He was awarded the Meritorious Service Medal for good work and devotion to duty, and also holds the 1914–15 Star, and the General Service and Victory Medals. He was demobilised in April 1919.
20, Elm Street, Buckingham, Bucks. Z1034/A.

ALLEN, A. H., Pte., 5th Northamptonshire Regt.
Volunteering in August 1914, he crossed to France in May of the following year and took part in the Battles of Festubert, Loos, the Somme, Ypres and Cambrai. During the Advance of 1918 he was wounded, and after receiving hospital treatment was demobilised in July 1919. He holds the 1914–15 Star, and the General Service and Victory Medals.
The Green, Goldington. Z1039/C.

ALLEN, B., Private, 1/5th Bedfordshire Regt.
He volunteered in August 1914, and, drafted to the East in March 1916, experienced much fighting in Egypt and Palestine. He took part in the operations in the Suez Canal zone and at Jaffa and Gaza, and on his return to England in August 1919 was demobilised, holding the General Service and Victory Medals.
55, Hassett Street, Bedford. X1036/B—X1037/B.

ALLEN, C. C., Trooper, Bedfordshire Lancers; and Private, Machine Gun Corps.
He volunteered in September 1914 and in June of the following year was drafted to France. After fighting at Ypres, the Somme, and at Arras, he was invalided home through ill-health, but on recovery in 1917 returned to the Western Front and saw service at Cambrai and the subsequent engagements until the Armistice. Demobilised in March 1919, he holds the 1914–15 Star, and the General Service and Victory Medals.
Silver Street, Stevington, near Bedford. Z1040/A.

ALLEN, E., Sapper, Royal Engineers.
Volunteering in January 1915, he proceeded in January of the following year to Egypt and thence to Palestine. He took part in the operations on the Suez Canal and in the fighting at Gaza and Jaffa. Returning home, he was demobilised in July 1919, and holds the General Service and Victory Medals.
55, Hassett Street, Bedford. X1036/A—X1037/A.

ALLEN, F. E., Sapper, Royal Engineers.
He volunteered in January 1915, and was shortly afterwards sent to the East, where he did much valuable work in Egypt and Palestine. He served in the operations at Gaza, Jaffa, Damascus, Haifa and in many minor engagements. He was demobilised on his return to England in April 1919, and holds the General Service and Victory Medals.
16, Canning Street, Bedford. X1029/C.

ALLEN, F. H., Bombardier, R.G.A.
Volunteering in October 1915, he proceeded on the completion of his training to France and fought in many battles, notably those on the Somme and at Cambrai. In 1917 he was gassed, but after receiving treatment at the Base was able to return to the trenches and he took part in the fighting until the end of war. Demobilised in April 1919, he holds the General Service and Victory Medals.
22, Well Street, Buckingham. Z1034/C.

ALLEN, G. L., Sergeant, Bedfordshire Regiment.
Volunteering in December 1914, he sailed for France in the following year and fought at Ypres, Arras and Cambrai. He was unhappily severely gassed, and as a result was invalided home and discharged as unfit for further service in January 1917. He holds the 1914–15 Star, and the General Service and Victory Medals.
16, Canning Street, Bedford. X1029/A.

ALLEN, H., Private, 7th Suffolk Regiment.
He joined in July 1917, and, landing in France in the following November, was in action in many engagements, including those at Cambrai and Albert. During his service he was twice wounded, but on his recovery rejoined his unit. Demobilised in January 1919, he holds the General Service and Victory Medals. 29, Salisbury Street, Bedford. X1042.

ALLEN, H., Driver, Royal Field Artillery.
Joining in March 1917, he proceeded to France two months later and there saw severe fighting in various sectors of the front. He took part in the Battles of Arras, Vimy Ridge, Ypres and Cambrai, and in many minor engagements, fought also in the Retreat and Advance of 1918, and was gassed on the Somme in that year. He was demobilised in May 1919, and holds the General Service and Victory Medals.
54, Duncombe Street, Bletchley, Bucks. Z2861.

ALLEN, H., Private, 1st Northamptonshire Regt.
Already in the Army when war broke out, he quickly proceeded to France, but was taken prisoner in the memorable Retreat from Mons. He was held in captivity until December 1918, and was later sent to Ireland, where in 1920 he was still serving. He holds the Mons Star, and the General Service and Victory Medals. 16, James Street, Bedford. Z1038.

ALLEN, H. J., Private, Buffs (East Kent Regt.)
He joined in May 1918, and in the following September crossed to France, where after only a month's service he was unhappily killed in action in the St. Quentin sector on October 28th, 1918. He was entitled to the General Service and Victory Medals.
"Whilst we remember, the sacrifice is not in vain."
35, Northwood End, Haynes, near Bedford. Z1033

ALLEN, H. R., Private, 9th West Yorkshire Regt.
Joining in September 1916, he was sent in July of the following year to the Western Front, and took part in the fighting at Ypres. During the Battle of Cambrai he was seriously wounded, and unfortunately succumbed to his injuries on April 24th, 1918. He was entitled to the General Service and Victory Medals.
"A costly sacrifice upon the altar of freedom."
The Green, Goldington, Bedford. Z1039/A.

ALLEN, J., Gunner, Royal Field Artillery.
Volunteering in September 1914, he was drafted after a course of training to France. There he was in action in many notable battles, including those at Festubert, Loos and Vimy Ridge, and was wounded on the Somme. On recovery he returned to the fighting line and served on until the Armistice. On his return to England in March 1919 he was demobilised, and holds the 1914–15 Star, and the General Service and Victory Medals. West End, Brampton, Huntingdon. Z1032.

ALLEN, J. W., Driver, Royal Field Artillery.
He joined in April 1916, and in the following December crossed to France, where he experienced much heavy fighting. He was engaged on important transport work in the Arras, Ypres, Somme and Cambrai sectors, and on his return to England in March 1919 was demobilised, holding the General Service and Victory Medals.
Upper Dean, Kimbolton, Hunts. Z1035/A.

ALLEN, L. S., A.B., R.N., H.M.S. "President."
He joined the Royal Navy in September 1916, and, after completing his training at the Crystal Palace, was posted to H.M.S. "President." In this vessel he was engaged on important duties in the Mediterranean Sea, and was wounded. Returning to shore, he was demobilised in May 1919, and holds the General Service and Victory Medals.
3, Elm Street, Buckingham, Bucks. Z1034/B.

ALLEN, T., Sergeant, 11th Essex Regiment.
He volunteered in December 1915, and in July of the following year proceeded to France, where he took part in the fighting at Beaumont-Hamel, Arras, Passchendaele and Cambrai and in the Retreat and Advance of 1918. Returning home, he was demobilised in January 1919, and holds the General Service and Victory Medals.
55, Hassett Street, Bedford. X1036/C—X1037/C.

ALLEN, W., Private, 2nd Bedfordshire Regiment.
Volunteering in August 1914, he embarked in the same year for France, and during his service there took part in many engagements, and was wounded at Neuve Chapelle in March 1915. On recovery he fought at Arras, on the Somme, and in the Retreat and Advance of 1918. In March 1919 he was demobilised, holding the 1914 Star, and the General Service and Victory Medals.
39, Woburn Road, Kempston, Bedford. X1031.

ALLEN, W., Corporal, R.A.S.C.
He volunteered in April 1915, and after his training served at various stations on important duties in a Remount Depôt. He was not successful in obtaining his transfer overseas before hostilities ceased, but rendered valuable services until demobilised in March 1919.
2, Cromwell Walk, Huntingdon. Z1041.

ALLEN, W. A., Gunner, Royal Field Artillery.
He joined in August 1916, and three months later proceeded to France in time to take part in the final engagements of the Somme Offensive. Later he was in action at Albert, Armentières and Vimy Ridge, before being badly gassed at the Battle of Ypres in July 1917. Twelve months later he was invalided home with both arms broken, and was in hospital in the Isle of Wight. Demobilised in February 1919, he holds the General Service and Victory Medals.
Foscott, Buckingham. Z3176.

ALLEN, W. C., Private, 2nd Bedfordshire Regt.
He volunteered in November 1914, and in June of the following year landed in France, where he experienced much heavy fighting. He fought and died for the freedom of England in the Battle of Loos on October 18th, 1915, and was entitled to the 1914–15 Star, and the General Service and Victory Medals.
"A valiant Soldier, with undaunted heart he breasted life's last hill."
Silver Street, Stevington, near Bedford. Z1040/B.

ALLEN, W. E., Private, R.A.M.C.
Joining in June 1918, he served, after a brief training, as Orderly in military hospitals at various stations. He was not able to obtain a transfer overseas before the conclusion of hostilities, but rendered valuable services until demobilised in February 1920. The Green, Goldington. Z1039/B.

ALLEN, W. J., Trooper, Bedfordshire Lancers.
Volunteering in November 1915, he was retained for a time on duties of an important nature in England. In 1917, however, he was drafted to the East, and saw service in Egypt and Palestine, and was present in the fighting at Gaza and Jaffa, and at the capture of Jerusalem. Returning home in February 1919, he was demobilised, and holds the General Service and Victory Medals.
Luke Street, Eynesbury, St. Neots, near Huntingdon. TZ1030.

ALLEN, W. S., Private, 4th Bedfordshire Regt.
He volunteered in September 1914, and in the same year embarked for France. There he fought at Hill 60, Ypres and Vimy Ridge, but after fighting at Arras was reported missing, and later presumed killed in action on August 29th, 1917. He was entitled to the 1914 Star, and the General Service and Victory Medals.
"Whilst we remember, the sacrifice is not in vain."
55, Hassett Street, Bedford. X1036/D—X1037/D.

ALLIN, G., Private, R.A.S.C. (M.T.)
Joining in May 1916, he was shortly afterwards sent to France, and was engaged on important duties in connection with the Field Ambulance in various sectors, including Cambrai and St. Quentin, where he was wounded in 1917. He was demobilised in August 1919, and holds the General Service and Victory Medals. 4, Green Street, St. Ives, Hunts. Z1043.

ALLSOPP, C., Air Mechanic, Royal Air Force.
He joined in June 1917, and in the following month was drafted to France, where he served at Rouen, Boulogne and many other places. He was attached to the General Headquarters of the Independent Air Force, and was engaged as telephone operator, and on other important duties. He was demobilised in March 1919, and holds the General Service and Victory Medals. Emberton, Bucks. Z1044

ALSOP, J., Private, R.A.S.C.
He was mobilised in August 1914 and was immediately afterwards sent to the Western Front, where he was engaged on important transport duties in the Retreat from Mons and at La Bassée, the Marne, the Aisne, Ypres, Loos, the Somme, Arras and Cambrai, and was gassed. He was discharged in May 1919, and holds the Mons Star, and the General Service and Victory Medals.
6, Marne Street, Kempston, Bedford. Z1045.

AMBROSE, A., Gunner, Royal Field Artillery.
He volunteered in 1915, and was sent to German South-West Africa. In 1916 he proceeded to France, where he took part in numerous engagements, including those at Arras, Armentières and the Somme, and was both wounded and gassed. He was invalided home and discharged as medically unfit for further service in March 1919, holding the 1914–15 Star, and the General Service and Victory Medals.
4, Paggs Court, Silver Street, Newport Pagnell. Z1046.

AMBROSE, A., Private, 7th Northants. Regt.
He was mobilised in August 1914, and sent to France in October of the same year. After taking part in the Battles of La Bassée and Ypres, he was wounded and invalided home. On his recovery, however, he returned to France and was again in action at Neuve Chapelle, Ypres, Hill 60 and Festubert, where he was a second time wounded. He was sent home, but returning in September 1915, fought at Loos, the Somme, Arras, Ypres and Cambrai, and was unhappily killed in action on March 25th, 1918. He was entitled to the 1914 Star, and the General Service and Victory Medals.
"The path of duty was the way to glory."
7, Cumberland Place, St. Ives, Hunts. Z1047/A.

AMES, A. J., Private, 1st Leicestershire Regiment.
He was serving at the outbreak of war, and was immediately sent to France, where he took part in the Battles of Mons, La Bassée, Ypres, Hill 60, Vimy Ridge and Arras. He also served in the Retreat of 1918, and was released in July 1918 for work of National importance at the General Post Office. He holds the Mons Star, and the General Service and Victory Medals. 60, Bunyan Road, Kempston. X1049/B.

AMES, C. J. A., Corporal, Bedfordshire Regiment.
He was mobilised in August 1914, and in the following year was drafted first to Egypt and thence to the Dardanelles, where he was wounded in the Landing at Suvla Bay. In 1916 he returned home and was discharged as time-expired, but shortly afterwards re-enlisted in the Royal Army Ordnance Corps, and was sent to Mesopotamia, where he was still serving in 1920. He holds the 1914–15 Star, and the General Service and Victory Medals. 17, Union Street, Bedford. X1048.

AMES, C. T., Trooper, Bedfordshire Lancers.
He volunteered in December 1914, and in September of the following year was drafted to France. In this theatre of war he took part in the Battles of Loos, Vimy Ridge, Arras, Ypres and Cambrai, and also served in the Retreat and Advance of 1918. He was demobilised in March 1919, and holds the 1914–15 Star, and the General Service and Victory Medals.
60, Bunyan Road, Kempston. X1049/A.

AMES, F. C., Rflmn., 16th King's Royal Rifle Corps.
Joining in April 1917, he was sent to France in September of the same year, and took part in the fighting in numerous engagements, including the Battle of Ypres. Wounded near Arras in November 1917, he was invalided home, and was afterwards engaged on important duties with his unit, until he was demobilised in March 1919, holding the General Service and Victory Medals. 4, Grey Friars Walk, Bedford. X1052/A.

AMES, R. S., Bandsman, 2nd Cheshire Regiment.
He joined in May 1917, and after his training was engaged at Chester on important duties with his unit. He rendered valuable services, but was not successful in obtaining his transfer overseas before the cessation of hostilities owing to his being under age, and was demobilised in August 1919.
4, Grey Friars Walk, Bedford. X1052/B.

AMES, W. A. J., L/Corporal, Bedfordshire Regt.
He volunteered in November 1914, and was later transferred to the Royal Fusiliers and afterwards to the Machine Gun Corps. In 1916 he was sent to France and took part in the fighting on the Somme and at Arras, Lens, Cambrai and Loos. He was demobilised in April 1919, and holds the General Service and Victory Medals.
16, Marne Street, Kempston. Z1050.

AMES, W. H., Private, Highland Light Infantry.
He joined in 1916, and after completing his training was drafted to France later in the same year. He took part in the severe fighting at Ypres and in other important engagements, including the Battle of Cambrai, during which he was engaged as stretcher-bearer. He was demobilised in February 1919, and holds the General Service and Victory Medals.
13, Grey Friars Walk, Bedford. X1051.

AMOS, C. T. B., Air Mechanic, Royal Air Force.
He joined the Royal Navy in August 1914, and was stationed at Devonport until early in 1917, when he was transferred to the Royal Air Force, with which he was employed as a fitter. His duties, which demanded a high degree of technical skill, were carried out in a most efficient manner. He rendered valuable services, but was not successful in obtaining his transfer overseas before the cessation of hostilities. He was still serving in 1920. Moulsoe, Bucks. Z1053.

ANDERSON, E. S., Pte., R. Warwickshire Regt.
He volunteered in September 1914, and in the following year was drafted to Egypt, and thence to Palestine, where he was in action at Gaza and Haifa. He was afterwards engaged on important duties with his unit, and remained in this area till the end of the war. Returning home, he was demobilised in April 1919, and holds the 1914–15 Star, and the General Service and Victory Medals.
10, King Street, Stony Stratford, Bucks. Z1055/A.

ANDERSON, F. T., Private, South Wales Borderers.
Volunteering in April 1915, he was sent to France later in the same year, and took part in the Battles of the Somme, Arras and Ypres, and in other important engagements. During his service he was at first engaged as a pioneer and afterwards as a Lewis gunner. He was demobilised in February 1919, and holds the 1914–15 Star, and the General Service and Victory Medals. 10, King Street, Stony Stratford, Bucks. Z1055/B.

ANDERSON, J. T., Pte., Royal Berkshire Regt.
He was mobilised in August 1914, and in the following November was sent to France, where he fought in the Battle of Ypres. He was unfortunately killed in action at La Bassée on January 29th, 1915. He was entitled to the 1914 Star, and the General Service and Victory Medals.
"Thinking that remembrance, though unspoken, may reach him where he sleeps."
Near White Lion, Eaton Socon, near St. Neots, Hunts. Z1056.

ANDERSON, W. H., Private, 5th Yorkshire Regt.
He joined in August 1916, and later in the same year was drafted to France, where he took part in numerous engagements. He unhappily fell fighting on the Somme on January 12th, 1917, and was entitled to the General Service and Victory Medals.

"Nobly striving,
He nobly fell that we might live."

Church Street, St. Neots, Hunts. Z1054/B.

ANDERTON, S., Private, Bedfordshire Regiment.
He volunteered in November 1915, and in the following August was drafted to the Western Front. Whilst overseas he fought in the vicinity of Ypres and Cambrai, and was wounded in October 1916, sustaining the loss of his left eye. He was invalided home, and after six months' treatment in hospital in London was transferred to the Labour Corps, and engaged on agricultural duties until September 1919, when he was demobilised. He holds the General Service and Victory Medals.
3, Priory Court, Newport Pagnell, Bucks. Z1057.

ANDREWS, B., Sapper, Royal Engineers (R.O.D.)
He joined in August 1916, and in the following October was drafted to Egypt. After being engaged on important duties at Kantara for about 2½ years he was sent home in February 1919 and demobilised in the following month. He holds the General Service and Victory Medals.
15, Jubilee Terrace, Stony Stratford, Bucks. Z1064/A.

ANDREWS, C., Rifleman, 5th London Regiment (London Rifle Brigade).
He joined in March 1916, and in the following July was drafted to France. During his service on the Western Front he fought in the Battles of the Somme, Arras, Ypres and Cambrai, but was gassed in action in April 1918. On recovery he was again fighting in the Advance at Le Cateau. He returned home and was demobilised in March 1919, and holds the General Service and Victory Medals.
40, London Road, Stony Stratford, Bucks. Z1066/B.

ANDREWS, F., Sergeant, 1st (Royal) Dragoons.
He was serving in the Regular Army in Africa at the outbreak of hostilities, and was drafted to France in January 1915. Whilst on the Western Front he took part in various engagements in the Ypres salient, and gave his life for King and Country in the second Battle of Ypres on May 13th, 1915. He had previously fought in the South African Campaign, and in addition to the medals for that war was entitled to the 1914–15 Star, and the General Service and Victory Medals.
4, West Lane, Emberton, Bucks. Z1067/B.

ANDREWS, F., Pte., 7th Oxford. & Bucks. L.I.
Volunteering in August 1914, he was drafted to France on the completion of his training in September of the following year, and fought in the Albert sector. He was then sent to Salonika, and was in action in many operations on the Vardar and Doiran fronts, but was wounded in April 1917 and invalided to Malta. After about six months in hospital he returned to Salonika, and served until the conclusion of hostilities. Returning home, he was demobilised in May 1919, and holds the 1914–15 Star, and the General Service and Victory Medals.
40, London Road, Stony Stratford, Bucks. Z1066/A.

ANDREWS, F. C. M. (M.M.), Private, 5th Bedfordshire Regiment.
He enlisted in May 1914, and was drafted to Gallipoli in August of the following year. Wounded in action at Suvla Bay, he was sent to Egypt in December 1915, and served with General Allenby's Forces in the Advance through Palestine. He took a prominent part in all the Battles of Gaza and Jaffa, and was awarded the Military Medal for distinguished bravery at the third Battle of Gaza. He was demobilised after his return to England in June 1919, and holds in addition to the Military Medal the 1914–15 Star, and the General Service and Victory Medals.
Chapel Lane, Weston Underwood, near Olney, Bucks. Z1061.

ANDREWS, G., Special Constable.
He volunteered as a Special Constable in November 1914, and for over four years devoted the whole of his available time to this responsible work, and rendered valuable services which were highly appreciated. He did not relinquish his position until January 1919.
Weston Underwood, near Olney, Bucks. Z1060/A.

ANDREWS, H., Private, R.A.S.C. (M.T.)
He joined in May 1917, and in the following August was drafted to France. During his service on the Western Front he was engaged on important duties in driving anti-aircraft lorries, and was present at operations in the Albert, Cambrai, Amiens and Le Cateau sectors, and in the entry into Mons at dawn on Armistice Day. Afterwards he proceeded to Germany with the Army of Occupation, and was stationed at Bonn until October 1919, when he returned to England. He was demobilised in the following month, and holds the General Service and Victory Medals.
40, London Road, Stony Stratford, Bucks. Z1066/D.

ANDREWS, H., Private, R.A.M.C.
He joined in April 1917, and after his training served at various military hospitals on important duties as an Orderly. He rendered valuable services, but was not successful, owing to medical reasons, in obtaining a transfer overseas before the cessation of hostilities, and was demobilised in October 1919.
20, Weston Road, Olney, Bucks. Z1062/B.

ANDREWS, H. J., Sapper, R.E. (R.O.D.)
He joined in June 1916, and later in the same year was drafted to France, where he was engaged on important duties with the Railway Operative Division, and was present at the Battles of the Somme, Arras, Ypres and St. Quentin, and at many later engagements. He was demobilised in March 1919, and holds the General Service and Victory Medals.
Old Stratford, Bucks. Z1065/C.

ANDREWS, H. T., Drummer, 4th Seaforth Highlanders.
He volunteered in December 1914, and after his training served at various stations on important duties until January 1917, when he was drafted to France. Whilst in this theatre of war he fought in the Battles of the Somme and Ypres, and was wounded at La Bassée. He holds the General Service and Victory Medals, and was demobilised in March 1919.
Weston Underwood, near Olney, Bucks. Z1060/B.

ANDREWS, J. C., Private, Royal Fusiliers.
He joined in May 1917, and later in the same year was drafted to France. After taking part in heavy fighting at Arras, Passchendaele Ridge and Albert, he was wounded in the vicinity of Cambrai in March 1918, and invalided to hospital in Wales. He holds the General Service and Victory Medals, and was not demobilised until March 1920.
Old Stratford, Bucks. Z1065/A.

ANDREWS, T., Private, Bedfordshire Regiment.
He volunteered in January 1915, and in July of the following year was drafted to France. During his service on the Western Front he fought in the Battles of the Somme and the Ancre, and in April 1917 was severely wounded at Arras. He was invalided home, and after nine months in hospital was discharged as medically unfit for further service in January 1918. He holds the General Service and Victory Medals.
72, East Street, Olney, Bucks. Z1059/B.

ANDREWS, T. G., L/Cpl., Royal Bucks. Hussars.
He joined in October 1916, and in the following December was drafted to France. Whilst overseas he took part in the severe fighting at Arras, Ypres and Cambrai, and was wounded in action. After the Armistice he proceeded to Egypt in December 1918, and was stationed at Cairo on important garrison duties. He returned to England and was demobilised in January 1920, holding the General Service and Victory Medals.
109, High Street, Olney, Bucks. Z1063.

ANDREWS, T. W., Company Quartermaster-Sergeant, Bedfordshire & Hertfordshire Regt.
He was serving at the outbreak of hostilities, and was shortly afterwards drafted to France. Whilst overseas he took part in heavy fighting at Ypres, Loos, Vimy Ridge, Arras and Passchendaele, and in many subsequent engagements in the Retreat and Advance of 1918, and was wounded during this period. He was discharged in May 1920, and holds the 1914 Star, the General Service, Victory and Long Service and Good Conduct Medals.
30, Castle Lane, Beds. X1058.

ANDREWS, W., Private, 10th Hampshire Regt.
He joined in October 1916, and in May of the following year proceeded overseas. Whilst in France he took part in the engagements at Arras, but was severely gassed and invalided home. After his recovery he served in Ireland, and when hostilities ceased proceeded to Constantinople, and was stationed there on important duties until his return home for demobilisation in December 1919. He holds the General Service and Victory Medals.
20, Weston Road, Olney, Bucks. Z1062/A.

ANDREWS, W., Private, 5th Devonshire Regt.
He joined in July 1918, and was trained in Ireland, where he afterwards served on important duties until February 1919, when he proceeded to Germany with the Army of Occupation. He was stationed near Cologne, and rendered valuable services for about a year, returning home for demobilisation in February 1920. 40, London Road, Stony Stratford, Bucks. Z1066/C.

ANDREWS, W., Private, Oxford. & Bucks. L.I.
He volunteered in December 1915, and after his training proceeded overseas in May of the following year. Whilst on the Western Front he took part in many important engagements, including the Battles of the Somme, Arras and Cambrai. Returning to England, he was demobilised in March 1919, and holds the General Service and Victory Medals.
Hollington Cottage, Petsoe, Emberton, Bucks. Z1067/A.

ANDREWS, W. G., Sapper, Royal Engineers.
He was mobilised at the outbreak of hostilities and in the following December was drafted overseas. During his service on the Western Front he was engaged on important duties in connection with the operations and was frequently in the forward areas, notably at Hill 60, Ypres and Loos, and was wounded in June 1915. After his recovery he again served on the Somme, at Passchendaele, Cambrai and many subsequent operations until the Armistice was signed. He then proceeded to Germany with the Army of Occupation and was stationed on the Rhine, returning to England to be demobilised in February 1919. He holds the 1914–15 Star, and the General Service and Victory Medals. 5, New Fenlake, Beds. TZ1068.

ANGIER, G. T., Pte., 1st Northamptonshire Regt.
Mobilised on the outbreak of war, he was drafted to France soon afterwards and fought in the Retreat from Mons and the Battles of the Aisne and the Marne. Severely wounded at Ypres in November 1914, he was invalided home, and after treatment served on Police duties in Gillingham, Kent. He was discharged as medically unfit for further service in February 1916, and holds the Mons Star, and the General Service and Victory Medals. Cow and Hare Yard, St. Ives, Hunts. Z1069/C.

ANNIS, E., Private, 8th Bedfordshire Regiment.
He volunteered in April 1915, and crossing to the Western Front in the following January, was in almost continuous action during heavy enemy attacks at Loos. He fell fighting near Albert on April 19th, 1916, and was entitled to the General Service and Victory Medals.
"Honour to the immortal dead, who gave their youth that the world might grow old in peace."
Upper Dean, Kimbolton. Z1071/B.

ANNIS, W. G., Private, Norfolk Regiment.
Volunteering in October 1915, he completed his training, and owing to medical unfitness for active service was transferred to the Labour Corps. Engaged with his company on agricultural work at Earith he rendered valuable services in connection with the increase of food supplies, and in 1921 was still serving.
Earith, Hunts. Z1070.

ANSTEY, C. J., Gunner, Royal Garrison Artillery.
He volunteered in 1915, and in the following year landed in France, where he served for three years. During this period he took part in the Battles of the Somme, Arras, Ypres, Cambrai, and was gassed. He did good work with his Battalion in several engagements until the close of the war, and returned to England for demobilisation in January 1919. He holds the General Service and Victory Medals.
Cranfield, Bedfordshire. Z1072.

APPLEBY, A. R., Private, Royal Fusiliers.
He joined in July 1918, and on the conclusion of his training was engaged on important duties with his unit at various depôts. He rendered valuable services, but was unable to secure his transfer overseas before the termination of hostilities. After the Armistice, however, he was sent into Germany and served with the Army of Occupation until his return to England for demobilisation in February 1920.
3, Greenhill Street, Bedford. X1073/A.

APPLEBY, J. E., Private, Essex Regiment.
Joining in 1917, he was sent overseas in the same year and saw service in various sectors of the Western Front. There he was engaged in heavy fighting in the Battle of Cambrai and in the Retreat and Advance of 1918, and was wounded near Albert. Returning home after the Armistice, he was demobilised in February 1919, and holds the General Service and Victory Medals. 3, Greenhill Street, Bedford. X1073/C.

ARCHER, W. J., L/Corporal, Lancashire Fusiliers.
Volunteering in January 1916, he sailed for Egypt in the same year, and after a period of service there took part in the British Advance through Palestine. In the course of this campaign he fought in the Battles of Gaza, Jaffa, and was present at the capture of Haifa, and on the conclusion of hostilities was stationed in Egypt for several months. He returned home for demobilisation in June 1919, and holds the General Service and Victory Medals. Wistow, Hunts. Z1074.

ARMES, H. A., Private, 6th Bedfordshire Regt.
He joined in February 1917, and after completing his training served at home on special duties until drafted to France in January of the following year. In that theatre of war he fought in engagements at Ypres, Arras and the Somme, and gave his life for the freedom of England during heavy fighting at Lens on April 8th, 1918. He was entitled to the General Service and Victory Medals.
"A valiant Soldier, with undaunted heart he breasted life's last hill."
2, Oxford Road, St. Ives, Hunts. Z1078.

ARMOUR, J., Driver, R.A.S.C.
Mobilised when war broke out, he proceeded to France in September 1914, and took part in the final operations of the Retreat from Mons. He was engaged on important transport duties in the Battles of La Bassée, Ypres, the Somme, Arras, Cambrai and in several other engagements until the signing of the Armistice. Discharged on account of service in December 1918, he holds the Mons Star, and the General Service and Victory Medals.
2, Castle Hill Lane, High Street, Huntingdon. Z1075.

ARMSTRONG, F., Sergeant, R.A.V.C.
He joined in November 1916, and after serving at Woolwich and other stations embarked for the Western Front in December 1917. Engaged with his Corps in the forward areas he did good work whilst heavy fighting was in progress, and was present at the Battles of the Somme, Albert, Ypres and Cambrai. He returned home for demobilisation in April 1919, and holds the General Service and Victory Medals.
30, Bletsoe, Bedford. Z1077/B.

ARMSTRONG, T., Private, 1/5th Bedfordshire Regiment and Royal Irish Fusiliers.
Volunteering in August 1914, he sailed for Salonika in the following year and took part in various operations in the Balkans, including the Serbian Retreat in which he was wounded. Invalided to Malta he was later evacuated to England in March 1917, and was under hospital treatment in Kent and Hampshire. In the following November he was drafted to France, and was gassed and wounded at Cambrai. Rejoining his unit on recovery he was killed in action near Le Cateau on October 12th, 1918, and was entitled to the 1914–15 Star, and the General Service and Victory Medals.
"He passed out of the sight of men by the path of duty and self-sacrifice."
30, Bletsoe, Bedford. Z1077/A.

ARMSTRONG, W., Private, R.M.L.I.; and Air Mechanic, Royal Air Force (late R.N.A.S.)
He was mobilised when war was declared and was posted to H.M.S. "Heart," which ship was engaged on important patrol duties in the North Sea and off the coasts of France and Belgium. She was in action at Dunkirk and assisted in operations during the raid on Zeebrugge. He was demobilised in May 1919, and holds the 1914–15 Star, and the General Service and Victory Medals.
16, Castle Lane, Bedford. X1076/B.

ARMSTRONG, W. (jun.), A.B., Royal Navy.
Joining in May 1916, he was posted to H.M.S. "Constance," which vessel was engaged on patrol duties in the North Sea and was in action in the Battle of Jutland and in the raid on Zeebrugge. He was later stationed at Scapa Flow and was present at the internment of the surrendered German Fleet. Transferred to a trawler he served in Russian and other waters, and in 1921 was stationed at Milford Haven. He holds the General Service and Victory Medals.
16, Castle Lane, Bedford. X1076/A.

ARNOLD, A., Tpr., 4th (Royal Irish) Dragoon Guards.
He volunteered in August 1914, and after a brief training was drafted to the Western Front, where he fought in the concluding operations of the Retreat from Mons, and was wounded and taken prisoner. Owing to neglect and ill-treatment he died whilst in captivity in Germany in August 1915. He was entitled to the Mons Star, and the General Service and Victory Medals.
"His life for his Country, his soul to God."
15, Shakespeare Place, Huntingdon. Z1084/A.

ARNOLD, A., Cpl., 4th (Royal Irish) Dragoon Guards.
A serving soldier, he was mobilised at the outbreak of hostilities, and proceeded to France shortly afterwards. He took part in the Retreat from Mons, during which he was seriously wounded and taken prisoner. He unfortunately died from the effects of his injuries whilst a prisoner of war in Germany on May 24th, 1915, and was entitled to the Mons Star, and the General Service and Victory Medals.
"Whilst we remember, the sacrifice is not in vain."
8, Princess Street, Huntingdon. Z1085/B.

ARNOLD, A. J., Private, R.A.S.C. (M.T.)
He joined in July 1917, and two months later embarked for France. Whilst in this theatre of war he was engaged in transporting ammunition and supplies to the forward areas, and was present at the Battles of Ypres, Cambrai, the Somme, Albert and other actions until hostilities ceased. He then remained on the Western Front and served on special duties for a year. He was demobilised in December 1919, and holds the General Service and Victory Medals.
46, Great Brickhill, Bletchley. Z1080/A

ARNOLD, G. J., Sapper, Royal Engineers.
Volunteering in December 1914, he was employed at home, after completing his training, and crossed to France in 1916. There he served on special duties in connection with operations, and was in action at the Battles of the Somme, Ypres and Arras. Suffering from shell-shock he was evacuated to England in 1917, and received prolonged treatment at Chichester Hospital. He was discharged unfit for further service in July 1919, and in 1921 was still in hospital. He holds the General Service and Victory Medals.
64, Westbourne Road, Bedford. Z1079/A.

ARNOLD, H. T. G., Sergeant, Machine Gun Corps.
He volunteered in October 1915, and at the conclusion of his training served at various stations in England on special duties until 1917, when he proceeded to France. Fighting in various parts of the line he was in action at the Battles of Arras, Ypres, Passchendaele, the Somme (II.), Le Cateau (II.), and in the Retreat and Advance of 1918. After the Armistice he returned to England and was later sent to Mesopotamia, where in 1921 he was still serving. He holds the General Service and Victory Medals.
46, Great Brickhill, Bletchley. Z1080/B.

ARNOLD, R., Private, New Zealand Canterbury Light Infantry.
He volunteered in October 1914, and after completing his training, embarked for the Dardanelles in the following year. He served with his Battalion in heavy fighting at the Landing at Suvla Bay, and was severely wounded in action at Anzac in September. Invalided to hospital at Malta, he unhappily died there from the effects of his injuries on October 18th, 1915. He was entitled to the 1914–15 Star, and the General Service and Victory Medals.
"Great deeds cannot die:
They with the sun and moon renew their light for ever."
18, Beaconsfield Street, Bedford. X1086.

ARNOLD, R., Private, Bedfordshire Regiment.
He volunteered in November 1915, and at the conclusion of his training, served on guard and other duties at various stations with his Battalion. He did good work, but owing to medical unfitness, was not successful in securing his transfer overseas, and he was invalided out of the Army in September 1916.
Goldington, Beds. Z1082.

ARNOLD, R. C., Rifleman, Rifle Brigade.
Joining in September 1917, he underwent a course of training at Winchester, and was there engaged on special duties with his regiment. Contracting illness, he was admitted into hospital at Hampstead, where he unfortunately died in January 1918.
"Thinking that remembrance, though unspoken, may reach him where he sleeps."
64, Westbourne Road, Bedford. Z1079/C.

ARNOLD, S. G., Sapper, Royal Engineers.
A serving soldier, he was mobilised when war broke out, and drafted to France soon afterwards, served in the Retreat from Mons. He was later engaged in wiring, tunnelling and trench digging whilst operations were in progress at Ypres, Arras, the Somme and Cambrai. Returning to England in 1919, he was discharged in April of that year, and holds the Mons Star, and the General Service and Victory Medals.
64, Westbourne Road, Bedford. Z1079/B.

ARNOLD, T. A., Private, Hunts. Cyclist Battalion.
Joining in 1916, he was drafted to France later in that year, and took part in operations at Vimy Ridge and in the Somme Offensive. Transferred to Egypt in the following year, he fought in engagements at Gaza, Jaffa and those resulting in the fall of Jerusalem, during the Advance through Palestine and Syria. He holds the General Service and Victory Medals, and was demobilised after returning to England in 1919.
5, St. Germain Street, Huntingdon. Z1083/C.

ARNOLD, W. T., Rifleman, 3rd Cameronians (Scottish Rifles).
Volunteering in December 1914, he served at Home for a time and in March 1916 embarked for France. He fought in many fiercely contested engagements, and was wounded at Guillemont Farm in September 1916. Evacuated to England he was treated at Chester Hospital, and returned to the Western Front in June 1917. He was in action on the Ypres front, and was wounded for the second time at Passchendaele in the following November. Invalided home he received hospital treatment at Sheffield, and returned to France in March 1918. After serving for a short time with the Balloon Section, Royal Air Force, he was sent back to England suffering from trench fever and shell-shock, and was a patient in Nottingham Hospital for some months. He holds the General Service and Victory Medals, and was demobilised in February 1919.
The Hollow, Great Brickhill, Bletchley. Z1081.

ARPINO, A., Private, K.O. (Y.L.I.)
He joined in June 1917, and after completing his training crossed to France six months later. He served with his Battalion in many parts of the line, and fought in the German Offensive and subsequent Allied Advance. He died gloriously on the Field at the second Battle of Cambrai on September 24th, 1918, and lies buried at Bapaume. He was entitled to the General Service and Victory Medals.
"A costly sacrifice upon the altar of freedom."
108, Grey Friars Walk, Bedford. X1087.

ARTHUR, F. W., Sergeant, Royal Engineers.
A Reservist, he was mobilised at the declaration of war, and proceeded to France in December 1914. He was engaged on special work in connection with operations, and was present at the Battles of Neuve Chapelle and Hill 60. In April 1915 he returned to England, and served as an Instructor at Bedford and Maidenhead until the following year, when he again crossed to the Western Front. He rendered valuable services in the Somme Offensive, and at the Battles of Arras, Ypres and Cambrai, and in the Retreat and Advance of 1918. He was demobilised in April 1919, and holds the 1914–15 Star, and the General Service and Victory Medals.
11, York Street, Bedford. Z1088.

ASHCROFT, P., Shoeing-Smith, R.A.V.C.
He joined in July 1916, and in the following month landed in France, where he was engaged on farriers' duties, and in attending to sick and wounded horses behind the lines. Owing to an accident he was invalided to hospital in England in May 1917, and after treatment served at Winchester in a similar capacity until discharged on account of service in May 1919. He holds the General Service and Victory Medals.
Croxton, near St. Neots. TZ1089.

ASHLEY, A., Sergeant, 1st Bedfordshire Regt.
He volunteered in September 1914 in the Huntingdonshire Cyclists' Battalion, and in the following year was drafted to France after being transferred to the Bedfordshire Regiment. He was in action in the Battles of Festubert and Loos, and was badly gassed at Albert in September 1917. Sent to England he received hospital treatment, and was eventually invalided out of the Service in May 1918. He holds the 1914–15 Star, and the General Service and Victory Medals.
West Street, Godmanchester, Hunts. Z1090.

ASHLEY, C. H., Air Mechanic, Royal Air Force.
Joining in October 1917, he was sent overseas in the same year, and served in various parts of France. Engaged on duties calling for a high degree of technical skill he did good work with his Squadron in the Ypres, Lens and Cambrai sectors, and in July 1918 was injured in an accident. On recovery he saw heavy fighting in the concluding stages of the war, and returned to England in February 1919 for demobilisation. He holds the General Service and Victory Medals.
28, Marne Street, Kempston, Beds. Z1091/A.

ASHLEY, G. E., Private, Machine Gun Corps.
He joined in March 1917, and in April of the following year crossed to the Western Front. There he took part in several engagements, including those on the Somme and at Cambrai in the final operations of the war, and after the Armisitice was employed as an Instructor under the Army Education Scheme. Returning home in February 1919, he was demobilised four months later, and holds the General Service and Victory Medals. Thrapston Road, Brampton, Hunts. Z1093.

ASHLEY, G. H., Private, R.A.M.C.
He joined in September 1916, and on the conclusion of his training, served with his unit at Home. Engaged as an orderly he rendered valuable services at Tidenworth, Mansfield and other military hospitals, but was unable to obtain his transfer overseas owing to medical unfitness, and in consequence he was discharged in June 1919.
3, St. Benedict's Court, Huntingdon, Hunts. Z1092.

ASHLEY, H., Sergeant, 6th Bedfordshire Regt.
Volunteering in September 1914, he sailed for the Western Front in the following August, and took an active part in the Battles of Loos, the Somme, Ypres, Cambrai, Dickebusch, Albert and St. Quentin. He was gassed near Cambrai on April 28th, 1918, and, evacuated to England, was under treatment at Brighton for some months. Discharged as medically unfit in September of that year, he holds the 1914–15 Star, and the General Service and Victory Medals.
8, St. Clement's Passage, Huntingdon. Z1094.

ASHLEY, S. H., Private, R.A.S.C.
Joining in 1916, he was engaged in the Bakery at Aldershot until his embarkation for France in the following year. Whilst overseas he was engaged on important duties in connection with the transport of ammunition and supplies to the forward areas, and did good work in the Ypres salient, on the Somme, and in other sectors. He was demobilised in April 1919, and holds the General Service and Victory Medals.
28, Marne Street, Kempston, Beds. Z1091/B.

ASHPOLE, B., Private, Bedfordshire Regiment; Labour Corps.
He volunteered in August 1914, and after completing his training was drafted overseas in the following year. Serving on the Western Front, he was stationed at Etaples and other places, and did good work in attending to sick and wounded horses. Returning home for demobilisation in 1919, he holds the 1914–15 Star, and the General Service and Victory Medals.
18, Marne Street, Kempston, Beds. Z1095/A.

ASHPOLE, E., Private, 5th Northants. Regt.
Volunteering in August 1914, he sailed for Egypt in the following December, and after a period of service there, proceeded to Gallipoli. He was in action in several engagements on the Peninsula, and after the Evacuation returned to Egypt and took part in the British Advance through Palestine. He fought in the Battle of Gaza, and in operations resulting in the fall of Jerusalem, and served in the Holy Land for several months after hostilities were concluded. He returned to England for demobilisation in November 1919, and holds the 1914–15 Star, and the General Service and Victory Medals.
Keeley Lane, Wootton, Bedford. Z1096/A.

ASHPOLE, F., L/Corporal, Machine Gun Corps.
He volunteered in September 1915, and, crossing to France in December of the following year, fought in the Battles of Arras, Vimy Ridge, Messines and was seriously wounded at Ypres. Removed to hospital he died from the effects of his injuries on October 27th, 1917, and was entitled to the General Service and Victory Medals.
"A valiant Soldier, with undaunted heart he breasted life's last hill."
Keeley Lane, Wootton, Bedford. Z1096/C.

ASHPOLE, F. J., Gunner, Royal Horse Artillery.
Volunteering in 1915, he served with his Battery at home until 1917, when he sailed for the Western Front. In this theatre of war he was in action in several engagements in the Ypres salient and in the Retreat and Advance of 1918, and was at Mons the day the Armistice was signed. After hostilities were ended he proceeded into Germany with the Army of Occupation and was stationed on the Rhine until June 1919, when he returned to England for demobilisation. He holds the General Service and Victory Medals.
32, West Street, Newtown, Huntingdon. Z1097/C.

ASHPOLE, G., Driver, Royal Engineers.
He volunteered in August 1914, and was sent to Egypt in the following December. A few months later he proceeded to Gallipoli, where he served with his unit until the Evacuation of the Peninsula and then returned to Egypt. He did good work in connection with the operations during the British Advance through Palestine, and was present at the Battle of Gaza and the Entry into Jerusalem. Demobilised on his return home in April 1919, he holds the 1914–15 Star, and the General Service and Victory Medals.
Keeley Lane, Wootton, Bedford. Z1096/B.

ASHPOLE, G. W. (M.M.), Sergeant, 1/6th Royal Warwickshire Regiment.
Volunteering in 1915, he landed in France in the same year and was engaged in heavy fighting in the Battles of the Somme and Passchendaele, where he was wounded. On recovery he was sent to Italy in November 1917, and in the course of operations there was wounded on the Asiago Plateau. He was awarded the Military Medal for conspicuous gallantry and devotion to duty in the Field. He also holds the 1914–15 Star, and the General Service and Victory Medals, and was demobilised in March 1919.
32, West Street, Newtown, Huntingdon. Z1097/A.

ASHPOLE, R. T., Private, Royal Fusiliers.
He volunteered in 1915, and at the conclusion of his training was engaged on defence duties on the North East Coast until drafted overseas in 1917. Serving in various parts of the line in France, he was in action in the Battles of Messines, Lens and Ypres, and was wounded and taken prisoner at Poilcourt on September 17th, 1917. Repatriated after the termination of hostilities, he was demobilised in March 1919, and holds the General Service and Victory Medals.
32, West Street, Newtown, Huntingdon. Z1097/B.

ASHPOLE, W. E., Corporal, Bedfordshire Regt.
Volunteering in August 1914, he embarked for Egypt in the following year and served in that theatre of war until the Armistice. During this period he took part with his Battalion in heavy fighting in the Battles of Gaza and Jaffa, and in other engagements in the British Advance through Palestine, and did very good work. He was demobilised in 1919, and holds the 1914–15 Star, and the General Service and Victory Medals.
18, Marne Street, Kempston, Bedford. Z1095/B.

ASHTON, D., Private, Bedfordshire Regiment.
He joined in October 1916, and in the following May proceeded to the Western Front. Serving in various sectors he was engaged in the Battles of Arras and Ypres until September 1917, when he was sent home owing to illness. After treatment at Halifax he returned to France in June 1918, and, severely wounded at Merville a month later, was evacuated to England and admitted to Orpington War Hospital for treatment. He was demobilised in March 1919, and holds the General Service and Victory Medals.
London Lane, Great Paxton, St. Neots. Z1098/A.

ASHWELL, C., Private, Yorkshire Regiment.
Mobilised on the outbreak of war, he landed in France soon afterwards and fought in several engagements during the Retreat from Mons. He was also in action in the Battles of the Marne, Festubert, Hill 60, Albert, Vimy Ridge, the Somme, Messines, Ypres and Cambrai. He returned to England and was discharged on account of service in February 1918, and holds the Mons Star, and the General Service and Victory Medals.
Eaton Socon, Beds. Z1099.

ASHWELL, C. W., Trooper, Bedfordshire Lancers; Private, Machine Gun Corps.
He volunteered in May 1915, and in the following year embarked for Egypt. Serving there for a time he was afterwards in action in the Battle of Gaza and other engagements in General Allenby's victorious Advance through Palestine and was drafted to France in 1918. Transferred to the Machine Gun Corps, he did good work with his section at Cambrai and other places in the final operations of the war. Returning home for demobilisation in March 1919, he holds the General Service and Victory Medals. 97, Marlborough Road, Bedford. Z1101.

ASKEW, C. C., L/Corporal, 1st Connaught Rangers.
A Regular, he was mobilised when war broke out, and landing in France in September 1914, was in action in several engagements until severely wounded on November 21st of the same year at La Bassée. Sent home on account of his injuries he was under treatment for some months, and in July 1915 was invalided out of the Army. He holds the Mons Star, and the General Service and Victory Medals.
37, Greenhill Street, Bedford. X1104.

ASKEW, G. V., Private, Queen's (Royal West Surrey Regiment).
Joining in November 1918, he underwent training at St. Albans and was then engaged on special duties with his Battalion. He was unable to secure his transfer overseas owing to illness which necessitated his removal to hospital, and after prolonged medical treatment was discharged as medically unfit for further service in August 1919.
7, St. Leonard's Street, Bedford. X1103/B.

ASKEW, J., Private, 1/3rd Bedfordshire Regt.
He joined in August 1916, and, on completion of his training, sailed for India, where he served at Delhi on garrison and other duties for some time. He was then sent to Mesopotamia and did good work with his Battalion at Baghdad. Returning home for demobilisation in May 1919, he holds the General Service and Victory Medals.
7, St. Leonard's Street, Bedford. X1103/A.

ASPLEY, A. E., Rifleman, K.R.R.C.
He joined in April 1918, and, after completing his training, proceeded to France, where he was engaged with his Battalion in heavy fighting in the final operations of the war. After the Armistice he went into Germany with the Army of Occupation, and was stationed at Cologne. Returning to England in 1920, he was demobilised in February of that year, and holds the General Service and Victory Medals.
Silver Street, Stevington, Beds. Z1105/B.

ASPLEY, H. G., L/Corporal, Bedfordshire Regt.
Volunteering in September 1914, he was engaged on Coastal Defence duties for a time, and crossed to the Western Front in the following year. In this theatre of war he served as a bomb-thrower and fought in many fiercely contested battles, including those at Ypres and Loos. He gave his life for the freedom of England whilst on night patrol in the Loos sector on January 8th, 1916. He was entitled to the 1914–15 Star, and the General Service and Victory Medals.
"He died the noblest death a man may die,
Fighting for God and right and liberty."
Silver Street, Stevington, Beds. Z1105/A.

ASPLIN, H. F., Private, R.A.S.C. (M.T.)
He joined in February 1917, and, after completing his training embarked for Mesopotamia in the following November. In this theatre of war he was engaged in the workshops and on convoy work at Baghdad, Beyrout and Mosul, and did very good work. After the Armistice he served on special duties for a time, and, returning to England in March 1920, was demobilised two months later. He holds the General Service and Victory Medals.
2, Little Thurlow Street, Bedford. X1107.

ASPLIN, H. J., Private, Labour Corps.
He joined in July 1916, and in the following month proceeded to France, where he was engaged in conveying ammunition to the forward areas during the period of hostilities. He was frequently under shell-fire and served in the Ypres salient, and other parts of the line, and throughout rendered valuable services. He holds the General Service and Victory Medals, and was demobilised in January 1919.
Wyboston, Beds. Z1106.

ATHOW, F. H. J., Corporal (Shoeing-Smith), 8th (King's Royal Irish) Hussars.
A serving soldier, he was mobilised at the outbreak of war and embarked for France early in the following year. During his service in this theatre of operations he was in action at the Battles of Loos, the Somme, Arras, Ypres and Albert. He also did good work in the Retreat and Advance which concluded hostilities in November 1918. Returning to England in 1919, he was discharged in March of that year, and holds the 1914–15 Star, and the General Service and Victory Medals.
George Town, Sandy. Z1108.

ATKINS, A. C., Bandsman, Oxfordshire and Buckinghamshire Light Infantry.
A serving soldier, having enlisted in April 1912, he was mobilised at the outbreak of hostilities and subsequently served at various depôts with his Battalion. He did good work in the Band, but was not successful in securing his transfer overseas owing to medical unfitness, and was discharged in consequence in March 1916.
6a, Silver Street, Stony Stratford. Z1110.

ATKINS, F. J., Private, Machine Gun Corps.
Volunteering in August 1914, he underwent a course of training on Salisbury Plain, and in the following March embarked for Gallipoli. There he took part in the first Landing at Cape Helles and the engagements which followed until wounded at Suvla Bay in August 1915. Evacuated to England, he received treatment at Bristol Hospital and was drafted to Egypt six months afterwards. In this theatre of war he fought in operations during the British Advance through Palestine, including the Battles of Gaza. In June 1918 he was transferred to the Western Front, and served at Cambrai in the Allied Offensive which brought the war to a close. He was demobilised in March 1919, and holds the 1914–15 Star, and the General Service and Victory Medals.
32, Mill Street, Newport Pagnell. Z1112.

ATKINS, G. B., Private, King's Own Scottish Borderers.
Volunteering in March 1915, he embarked for Egypt in the following month, and, stationed at Kantara and Alexandria, was engaged on special duties as a shoeing-smith. Owing to illness he was invalided to No. 1 Stationary Hospital, Kantara, where he unfortunately died on November 11th, 1917, and lies buried in the British Cemetery there. He was entitled to the 1914–15 Star, and the General Service and Victory Medals.
"Thinking that remembrance, though unspoken, may reach him where he sleeps."
2, Fredreca Cottages, Newport Pagnell. 1109/A.

ATKINS, T. W. (D.C.M.), Corporal, Oxfordshire and Buckinghamshire Light Infantry.
Volunteering in August 1914, he completed his training, and, crossing to France in the following February, fought in many fiercely contested battles, including those at Ypres and the Somme, and was awarded the Distinguished Conduct Medal for conspicuous bravery and devotion to duty in the Field. Severely wounded in action in July 1916, he was invalided to England, and after receiving treatment at Reading Hospital was discharged as medically unfit for further service in October of that year. He also holds the 1914–15 Star, and the General Service and Victory Medals.
2, Fredreca Cottages, Newport Pagnell. Z1109/B.

ATKINSON, F., Private, 2/5th Lincolnshire Regt.
He joined in March 1916, and, crossing to France four months later, was shortly afterwards in action in the Somme Offensive. He was also engaged in heavy fighting in the Battles of Ypres, Arras and Albert, and was taken prisoner at Cambrai in March 1918 and held in captivity in Germany. Repatriated in December of that year, he was discharged on account of service in the following May, and holds the General Service and Victory Medals. Moggerhanger, Sandy. Z1115/B.

ATKINSON, H. G., Gunner, R.G.A.
He volunteered in July 1915, and in the following year was drafted to India. During his service there he was attached to a Mountain Battery and engaged on garrison and other important duties at Bombay and Rawal Pindi. He did good work throughout his service, and, returning home for demobilisation in September 1919, holds the General Service Medal.
17, St. Leonard's Street, Bedford. X1113.

ATKINSON, J., Private, Bedfordshire Regiment.
He was mobilised on the outbreak of war, and, landing on the Western Front early in 1915, was engaged in severe fighting in the Battles of Hill 60, Ypres and Festubert. He was unhappily killed in action at Loos in September 1915, and was entitled to the 1914–15 Star, and the General Service and Victory Medals.
"A costly sacrifice upon the altar of freedom."
Chalton, near Sandy. Z1115/A.

ATKINSON, J., L/Corporal, Oxfordshire and Buckinghamshire L.I.; and A.B., Royal Navy.
Mobilised on the declaration of war, he was sent to France in March 1915, and took part in many engagements in the Ypres salient. Returning home in March 1916 for discharge as time-expired, he later joined the Royal Navy and was posted to H.M.S. "Europa," in which vessel he served until the close of hostilities. His ship was engaged in important patrol duties in the North Sea and also in escorting troopships to the various theatres of war. He was demobilised in September 1919, and holds the 1914–15 Star, and the General Service and Victory Medals.
7, Station Terrace, Great Linford, Bucks. Z1114/A.

ATKINSON, W., Sapper, Royal Engineers.
Joining in July 1916, he proceeded to the Western Front in the following month and served there for upwards of three years. Stationed at Abbeville and Etaples, he was engaged on important duties in the railway workshops and did good work as a coach-builder and repairer. He returned home for demobilisation in May 1919, and holds the General Service and Victory Medals. 7, Station Terrace, Great Linford, Bucks. Z1114/B.

AUDLEY, P. W., Private, 3rd London Regiment (Royal Fusiliers).
He joined in November 1917, and, after his training was completed, embarked for France. In the course of his service he was in action in several engagements in the Ypres salient, and was wounded on the Somme in July 1918. Sent home on account of his injuries, he was admitted to the V.A.D. Hospital at Hull, and after treatment was discharged as medically unfit in February 1919. He holds the General Service and Victory Medals. Church Lane, Buckden, Hunts. Z1116.

AUSTIN, G., Private, Northumberland Fusiliers.
He was mobilised when war was declared, and, embarking for France almost immediately afterwards, was engaged in severe fighting in the Retreat from Mons and the engagements which followed. He made the supreme sacrifice on December 2nd, 1914, and was entitled to the Mons Star, and the General Service and Victory Medals.
"He died the noblest death a man may die,
Fighting for God and right and liberty."
Mill Green, Warboys, Hunts. Z1117.

AUSTIN, W., Private, R.A.S.C. (M.T.)
Volunteering in August 1914, he was drafted overseas in the following year and saw service in various sectors of the Western Front. Serving as a motor-driver, he was engaged on important duties in connection with the transport of ammunition and supplies to the firing-line and did good work in the Battles of Loos, the Somme, Arras, Ypres and Cambrai. He was wounded in the course of operations, but, rejoining his unit on recovery, was in action until hostilities ceased. He was demobilised in July 1919, and holds the 1914–15 Star, and the General Service and Victory Medals. 37, Cavendish Street, Bedford. X1118.

AVERIES, H., Private, 1st Wiltshire Regiment.
He joined in October 1916, and in July of the following year was drafted to the Western Front, where he took part in the Battles of Ypres and Passchendaele and many other engagements. He died gloriously on the Field of Battle at Cambrai on March 22nd, 1918, during the Retreat. He was entitled to the General Service and Victory Medals.
"A valiant Soldier, with undaunted heart he breasted life's last hill."
West Street, Moulton. Z2862/A.

AVERY, G. A., Driver, Royal Engineers.
Mobilised on the outbreak of war, he crossed to France soon afterwards and served in several engagements in the Retreat from Mons. He also did excellent work during the Battles of Festubert, Loos, Albert, and was wounded at Merville. On recovery he rejoined his unit, with which he was engaged in various sectors until the conclusion of hostilities. Demobilised in June 1919, he holds the Mons Star, and the General Service and Victory Medals.
9, Victoria Terrace, St. Ives, Hunts. Z1120/B.

AVERY, J. W., Driver, Royal Field Artillery.
He volunteered in August 1914, and, landing on the Western Front in the same month, took part in the Retreat from Mons and the Battles of Festubert, Loos and several other engagements. In 1917 his Battery was transferred to Italy, in which theatre of war he was engaged in operations on the Asiago Plateau and during the British Offensive on the Piave. Demobilised on his return home in 1919, he rejoined for a further term of service in the same year, but unfortunately died at Colchester in June 1920. He was entitled to the Mons Star, and the General Service and Victory Medals.
"He joined the great white company of valiant souls."
9, Victoria Terrace, St. Ives, Hunts. Z1120/A.

AVERY, W. A., Private, 7th Northants. Regiment.
Joining in September 1917, he was sent to France three months later and shortly afterwards took part in heavy fighting in the Albert sector, where he was thrice slightly wounded—in January 1918 and in March of the same year. Taking part in the German Offensive, he was unhappily killed in action near St. Quentin on June 8th, 1918, and was entitled to the General Service and Victory Medals.
"The path of duty was the way to glory."
3, St. Clement's Passage, Huntingdon. Z1119.

AXTELL, A., Bombardier, R.G.A.
A Territorial, he was mobilised when war broke out, and in April 1915 proceeded to the Western Front. There he fought in the Battles of Ypres (II.), Festubert, Loos, Albert, and was gassed and wounded on the Somme in 1916. Invalided home in consequence of his injuries, he received treatment in Sunderland War Hospital, and on recovery returned to France. He was in action at Ypres (III.) and Cambrai, and at Amiens, Le Cateau and other places in the German Offensive and subsequent Allied Advance of 1918. He holds the 1914–15 Star, and the General Service and Victory Medals, and was demobilised in February 1919.
2, Spencer Street, New Bradwell, Bucks. Z1121.

AYLOTT, G., Sapper, Royal Engineers.
Mobilised on the outbreak of hostilities, he was drafted to France later in 1914, and served there for upwards of five years. Engaged with his unit in wiring, tunnelling, mining and trench-digging in the forward areas, he was present at heavy fighting in the Ypres salient, on the Somme and at Arras, Cambrai and other places until hostilities were concluded. He returned home for demobilisation in February 1919, and holds the 1914 Star, and the General Service and Victory Medals.
8, Marlborough Road, Bedford. Z1122/B.

AYLOTT, J. (M.M.), Pte., 7th Bedfordshire Regt.
He volunteered in December 1914, and, crossing to the Western Front in the following year, did excellent work as a stretcher-bearer in several engagements in the Ypres salient and on the Somme. He was awarded the Military Medal for conspicuous bravery and devotion to duty in bringing in wounded under heavy fire. He was unfortunately killed in action at Vimy Ridge on October 1917, and was entitled to the 1914–15 Star, and the General Service and Victory Medals.
"Great deeds cannot die:
They with the sun and moon renew their light for ever."
8, Marlborough Road, Bedford. Z1122/A.

AYRES, A., Corporal, 26th Royal Fusiliers.
Volunteering in September 1914, he was engaged on Home Service duties for two years, and landed in France in September 1916. In the course of his service on the Western Front he was in action in the Battles of Beaumont-Hamel, Vimy Ridge and Bullecourt. He fell fighting near Messines on June 7th, 1917, and was entitled to the General Service and Victory Medals.
"His life for his Country, his soul to God."
89, Pilcroft Street, Bedford. X1123.

AYRES, J. C., Private, Bedfordshire Regiment.
He volunteered in December 1914, and was stationed at home until 1916, when he was sent overseas. Serving on the Western Front, he saw heavy fighting in the Arras and Ypres sectors until sent to the Base owing to illness. On recovery he was engaged on important duties at the Fat Factory at Calais and rendered valuable services. He was demobilised in January 1919, and holds the General Service and Victory Medals.
Park Hall Road, Somersham, Hunts. Z1124.

AYRES, W. (M.M.), Corporal, Royal Engineers.
Volunteering in January 1915, he sailed for France three months afterwards and served with distinction for over four years. Engaged on important duties in connection with operations in the forward areas, he did excellent work in the Battles of Loos, Arras, Ypres and Cambrai, and was awarded the Military Medal for conspicuous gallantry and devotion to duty in the Field. He was severely gassed in the course of his duties, and after treatment rejoined his unit and served until the close of the war. He was demobilised in February 1919, and holds the 1914–15 Star, and the General Service and Victory Medals.
8, East Street, St. Neots. TZ1125.

B

BACKHOUSE, F. W., Driver, R.F.A.
Having enlisted in March 1905, he was drafted to the Western Front immediately on the outbreak of war in August 1914, and there fought in the Retreat from Mons. After taking part in the Battles of the Marne, La Bassée and Ypres, he was blown up by an explosion in May 1915 and invalided to hospital at Liverpool. On his recovery, however, he returned to France, where he served at Armentières, Givenchy and the Somme before being transferred to Salonika in 1916. There he saw severe fighting on the Struma and Doiran fronts until sent home and invalided from the Army in April 1917, suffering from shell-shock. He holds the Mons Star, and the General Service and Victory Medals. Wyton, near Huntingdon. TZ1126.

BACON, A., Private, 13th Essex Regiment.
Volunteering in April 1915, he was drafted to the Dardanelles in July of that year and there saw much severe fighting, being twice wounded in action at Suvla Bay. He afterwards served in Mesopotamia until transferred in August 1916 to the Western Front, where he took part in many engagements during the Somme Offensive. He was again twice wounded in action—at Vimy Ridge in September and on the Ancre in December 1916—and as a result has lost his right arm. He was invalided from the Army in July 1917, and holds the 1914–15 Star, and the General Service and Victory Medals.
1, Queen's Row, Bedford. Z1127/B.

BACON, T., L/Cpl., Oxford. & Bucks. L.I. (T.F.)
He volunteered in September 1914, and, on completing his training in the following year, was drafted to the Western Front. After taking part in the Battles of Albert, the Somme, Arras, Ypres, Passchendaele and Cambrai, and many minor engagements in various sectors, he was transferred to Italy, where he was again in action on the Asiago Plateau, the Piave, and Trentino until the cessation of hostilities. Demobilised on his return home in February 1919, he holds the 1914–15 Star, and the General Service and Victory Medals.
Weston Underwood, near Olney, Bucks. Z1128.

BADHAM, W., Private, 20th Middlesex Regt.
He volunteered at the outbreak of war in August 1914, and was retained on important duties in England until February 1918, being medically unfit for active service. He was then drafted to the Western Front, however, and there took part in many engagements, including the Battle of Cambrai, and fought also in the Retreat and Advance of 1918. He was demobilised in July 1919, and holds the General Service and Victory Medals.
20, Muswell Road, Bedford. Z1129/D.

BADRICK, T., Private, Royal Engineers.
Joining in July 1916, he proceeded to France four months later and was there engaged on important duties in various sectors of the Front. After taking an active part in the Battles of Arras and Bullecourt and many other engagements he was invalided home suffering from trench-fever, and was for a time in hospital at Bath. He was finally demobilised in March 1919, and holds the General Service and Victory Medals.
2, Elm Street, Buckingham. Z1130.

BAGNALL, A., Private, North Staffordshire Regt.
He joined in May 1916, and in the following October was drafted to the Western Front, where he saw severe fighting in various sectors. He took part in the Battles of Arras, Bullecourt and Passchendaele and many other important engagements in this theatre of war, and was gassed whilst in action at Cambrai. Demobilised in February 1919, he holds the General Service and Victory Medals.
29, Priory Street, Bedford. Z1131.

BAGSTAFF, B. B., Pte., 1st Cambridgeshire Regt.
He volunteered in August 1914, and, on completing a period of training, in the following year proceeded to the Western Front. Whilst in this theatre of war he took part in many important engagements, including the Battles of Festubert, Loos, Albert, Vimy Ridge, Passchendaele, Cambrai and the Marne, and was wounded in action on the Somme in July 1916 and on one other occasion. He was demobilised in January 1919, and holds the 1914–15 Star, and the General Service and Victory Medals. Earith, Hunts. Z1132/B.

BAILEY, A. C., Driver, Royal Field Artillery.
Mobilised in August 1914, he was immediately drafted to the Western Front, where he took part in the fighting at Mons. After serving also through the Battles of La Bassée, Ypres, Festubert, Loos, the Somme and Cambrai and other engagements he was transferred in November 1917 to Italy, where he was again in action on the Piave. He returned to France, however, in March 1918, but in September of that year was invalided home suffering from shell-shock. He was discharged in March 1919, and holds the Mons Star, and the General Service and Victory Medals.
65, Bunyan Road, Kempston, Bedford. X1138.

BAILEY, A. H., Pioneer, Royal Engineers (R.O.D.)
He joined in July 1915, and in the following year proceeded to the Western Front, where he was engaged on road-making, rail transport and other important duties. He also took an active part in the Battles of Albert, the Somme, Arras, Ypres and Cambrai and other engagements in various sectors until the cessation of hostilities. Returning home in 1919, he was demobilised in October of that year, and holds the 1914–15 Star, and the General Service and Victory Medals.
Oak Villa, Water Lane, Sherrington, Newport Pagnell, Bucks. Z1139/B.

BAILEY, A. L., Pte., 11th Somerset Light Infantry.
He joined in May 1917, and underwent a period of training prior to being drafted to the Western Front in October of the same year. There he saw much severe fighting during the final stages of the Advance of 1918, and, after the cessation of hostilities, was sent with the Army of Occupation into Germany, where he was stationed at Cologne. He was demobilised on his return in March 1919, and holds the General Service and Victory Medals. Castle Road, Lavendon, Bucks. Z1133.

BAILEY, E., Driver, R.A.S.C. (M.T.)
Shortly after volunteering in 1915, he was drafted to the Western Front, where he was engaged on important transport duties in various sectors. He also took an active part in the Battles of Festubert and Loos and many minor engagements until invalided home and discharged from the Army in June 1916. He holds the 1914–15 Star, and the General Service and Victory Medals.
3, Green Street, St. Ives, Hunts. Z1140.

BAILEY, F. B., Private, Oxford. & Bucks. L.I.
He volunteered in September 1914, and in January of the following year proceeded to the Western Front, where he took part in the Battles of Neuve Chapelle and Ypres and other engagements. Invalided home in 1915 suffering from trench-fever, he returned to France, however, on his recovery and was again in action at Loos and Albert. He fell fighting on the Somme on July 1st, 1916. He was entitled to the 1914–15 Star, and the General Service and Victory Medals.
"His life for his Country."
Oak Villa, Water Lane, Sherrington, Newport Pagnell, Bucks. Z1139/C.

BAILEY, F. G., Gunner, Royal Field Artillery.
He joined in May 1916, and, on completing a period of training in the following October, proceeded to the Western Front, where he saw severe fighting in various sectors. He took part in the Battles of Arras, Ypres Cambrai and the Somme and other important engagements until the cessation of hostilities, and was then sent with the Army of Occupation into Germany. He was demobilised on returning home in October 1919, and holds the General Service and Victory Medals.
Turvey, Beds. Z1134.

BAILEY, G., Gunner, Royal Field Artillery.
Mobilised in August 1914, he was immediately drafted to the Western Front, where he served through the Retreat from Mons. He also took part in many minor engagements until severely wounded in action in November 1914, and admitted to hospital at Bath. He was finally invalided from the Army in November 1916, and holds the Mons Star, and the General Service and Victory Medals.
Mill Cottage, Turvey, Beds. Z1135/A—Z1136/A.

BAILEY, M., Petty Officer, R.N.A.S.
He joined in July 1917, and, after undergoing a period of training, was retained at various stations, where he was engaged on important duties of a highly technical nature. He was medically unfit for active service, and was consequently unable to obtain his transfer overseas, but nevertheless rendered valuable services with his Squadron until February 1919, when he was demobilised.
14, Churchville Road, Bedford. Z1137.

BAILEY, P. J., Private, Sherwood Foresters.
After volunteering in 1915, he underwent a period of training prior to being drafted to the Western Front in March 1918. There he took part in several important engagements, including the Battle of Cambrai, and was gassed during the Advance. Mortally wounded in action near Ypres, he unhappily died on October 15th, 1918. He was entitled to the General Service and Victory Medals.
"Whilst we remember, the sacrifice is not in vain."
Oak Villa, Water Lane, Sherington, Newport Pagnell, Bucks. Z1139/A.

BAILEY, R., Sapper, Royal Engineers.
Volunteering in August 1914, he was sent to France after a period of training, and whilst on the Western Front played an important part in the Battles of Loos, Albert, the Somme, Messines Ridge and Cambrai. He was chiefly engaged as a driver of ration and pontoon wagons, and did consistently good work. He holds the 1914–15 Star, and the General Service and Victory Medals, and was demobilised in 1919.
Mill Cottage, Turvey, Beds. Z1135/C—Z1136/C.

BAILEY, R. C., Driver, R.A.S.C.
He volunteered in August 1914, and, proceeding to the Western Front in the following year, rendered valuable services with his unit in the forward areas during the Battles of Loos, the Somme, Lens and Cambrai. His duties were principally in connection with the transport of supplies to troops in the line. He was demobilised in 1919, and holds the 1914–15 Star, and the General Service and Victory Medals.
Mill Cottage, Turvey, Beds. Z1135/B—Z1136/B.

BAILEY, S., Private, 10th Queen's (Royal West Surrey Regiment).
He volunteered in 1915, and in the following year was drafted to France. During his service on the Western Front he took part in the Battles of the Somme, Albert, Arras and Cambrai, and in severe fighting during the Retreat and Advance of 1918. Returning to England in 1919, he was then demobilised, and holds the General Service and Victory Medals.
Mill Cottage, Turvey, Beds. Z1135/D—Z1136/D.

BAISLEY, C., Private, 1/6th Essex Regiment.
He joined in March 1916, and later in the same year was sent to Egypt, but after a period of heavy fighting there advanced into Palestine and took part in the Battles of Gaza and Jaffa and the capture of Jerusalem. He was also in action in the Balkans, Albania and Italy. He holds the General Service and Victory Medals, and was demobilised in April 1919.
Shepard's Terrace, Somersham, Hunts. Z1141.

BAKER, A. J., Private, Oxford. & Bucks. L.I.
Volunteering in September 1914, he was drafted to France twelve months later and took part in many important engagements, including the Battle of the Somme. He was wounded in action whilst on the Western Front, and was eventually demobilised in February 1919. Unfortunately he contracted pneumonia, and died on April 15th, 1920, and was entitled to the 1914–15 Star, and the General Service and Victory Medals.
"His memory is cherished with pride."
2, Priory Court, Newport Pagnell, Bucks. Z1144.

BAKER, C., Gunner, Royal Field Artillery.
He joined in 1916, and proceeded to the Western Front later in the same year. After taking part in many important engagements, including the Battles of the Somme, Ypres and Cambrai, he was unhappily killed in action at Douai on August 22nd, 1918. He was entitled to the General Service and Victory Medals.
"A valiant Soldier, with undaunted heart he breasted life's last hill."
The Bank, Somersham, Hunts. Z1149.

BAKER, E. J., 2nd Lieutenant, Royal Engineers.
He joined in January 1916, and, after completing his course of instruction, was engaged on important duties at Gravesend. He was unsuccessful in obtaining his transfer overseas, but rendered valuable services with the Searchlight Section of the Royal Engineers, and was demobilised in April 1919.
4, College Street, Kempston. Z1145/A

BAKER, G. E., Guardsman, Welch Guards.
He volunteered in September 1914, and was drafted to France in the following year. During his service on the Western Front he played a prominent part in the Battles of Hill 60, Loos, Vimy Ridge, Ypres and Passchendaele, and was wounded in action no less than seven times. He was discharged in 1918 as medically unfit for further service, and holds the 1914–15 Star, and the General Service and Victory Medals.
5, Britannia Place, Bedford. X1142.

BAKER, G. W., Corporal, 1/5th Bedfordshire Regt.
He volunteered in 1915, and early in the following year was drafted overseas. Whilst on the Western Front he served with distinction at the Battles of the Somme, Arras, Ypres and Cambrai, and in minor engagements in various other sectors. He was demobilised in February 1919, and holds the General Service and Victory Medals.
4, College Street, Kempston. Z1145/B.

BAKER, J., L/Cpl., Loyal North Lancashire Regt.
He volunteered in 1915, and on completion of his training was drafted to France, where he played a prominent part in many important engagements, including the Battles of the Somme, the Ancre, Vimy Ridge, Messines and Cambrai. He laid down his life for King and Country at the second Battle of Le Cateau on October 22nd, 1918, and was entitled to the General Service and Victory Medals.
"Honour to the immortal dead, who gave their youth that the world might grow old in peace."
Bank Houses, Somersham, Hunts. Z1146/B.

BAKER, R. A., Sergeant, 2/4th Cheshire Regt.
He volunteered in September 1914, and on completion of his training rendered valuable services as a Bombing Instructor at various home stations. On proceeding to France early in 1917 he played a prominent part in severe fighting, particularly in the Arras, Cambrai and Somme sectors. He was demobilised in February 1919, and holds the General Service and Victory Medals.
29, Newham Street, Bedford. X1147.

BAKER, S., Private, Royal Fusiliers.
He joined in March 1916, and was drafted to the Western Front. Whilst in this theatre of war, he took part in the Battles of Vermelles, the Somme, Vimy Ridge, Messines, Passchendaele and Cambrai, where he was badly wounded in action in November 1917. He was invalided home and spent six months in hospital before being sent to Eastbourne for convalescence. He holds the General Service and Victory Medals, and was demobilised in February 1919.
Warboys, Huntingdonshire. Z1148.

BAKER, T., Air Mechanic, R.A.F. (late R.N.A.S.)
He volunteered in 1915, and on completion of his training was retained on special duties in connection with the construction of aeroplanes at Eastbourne and in London. He rendered valuable services which called for a high degree of skill, but was unsuccessful in obtaining his transfer overseas and was demobilised in 1919.
Bank Houses, Somersham, Hunts. Z1146/A.

BAKER, W. H., Private, R.A.S.C.
Volunteering in June 1915, he was sent to France 12 months later, having been employed on special duties as a wheeler in the workshops during this period. Whilst on the Western Front he took an active part in the Battles of the Somme, Arras, Ypres, Cambrai and the Marne, being chiefly engaged on the transport of supplies to the forward areas. He was demobilised in March 1919, and holds the General Service and Victory Medals.
Sherington, near Newport Pagnell, Bucks. Z1143.

BALDOCK, D. L., L/Corporal, Machine Gun Corps.
He joined in 1916, and after a brief period of training with the Middlesex Regiment was transferred to the Machine Gun Corps, and proceeded to France in 1917. During his service on the Western Front he took part in the Battles of Ypres, Cambrai (where he was wounded in action), and the Somme (II.). He was demobilised on his return to England in February 1919, and holds the General Service and Victory Medals.
Mill Green, Warboys, Hunts. Z1150.

BALDOCK, E. A., Private, Bedfordshire Regiment and 6th Queen's (Royal West Surrey Regt.)
He volunteered in August 1914, and was retained for some time on important duties at various home stations. In 1916, however, he was drafted to the Western Front, and was in action at many important engagements, including the Battles of the Somme, Arras, Ypres and Cambrai. He was unfortunately killed on October 9th, 1918, and was entitled to the General Service and Victory Medals.
"Nobly striving:
He nobly fell that we might live."
36, Russell Street, St. Neots, Hunts. Z1151/A.

BALDOCK, J. W., Pte., Canadian Overseas Forces.
Prior to the outbreak of war he had served in the Bedfordshire Regiment, but in August 1914 volunteered in Canada, and was sent to France early in the following year. After taking part in the Battles of Ypres (II.) and Loos, he was badly wounded in action during the Somme Offensive in 1916, and was invalided to England. On his recovery he was transferred to the Machine Gun Corps, and returned to the Western Front, where he fought at the Battles of Messines, Lens and Cambrai. He was demobilised in 1919, and holds the 1914–15 Star, and the General Service and Victory Medals.
36, Russell Street, St. Neots, Hunts. Z1151/B.

BALDOCK, T., Private, Bedfordshire Regiment.
Mobilised in August 1914, he was immediately drafted to the Western Front, where he took part in the Retreat from Mons and the Battles of Ypres. He also saw heavy fighting at Arras, and was badly wounded in action at the Battle of Hill 60 in May 1915. Invalided to England, he was discharged as medically unfit for further service in January 1916, and holds the Mons Star, and the General Service and Victory Medals.
27, Muswell Road, South End, Bedford. Z1152.

BALDREY, F. G., Private, East Surrey Regiment and Labour Corps.
He volunteered in August 1914, and after his training was retained on important duties in England until 1917. Proceeding to France in September of that year, he took part in heavy fighting at Ypres, Cambrai and St. Quentin, but was badly wounded in action in June 1918 and invalided home. He was eventually demobilised in March 1919, and holds the General Service and Victory Medals.
Wilsted Road, Elstow, Bedford. X1153.

BALDWIN, C. H. R., C.S.M., 1st Bedfordshire Regiment and Royal Engineers.
A serving soldier, he proceeded to France with the 1st Bedfordshire Regiment in August 1914, and played a conspicuous part in the Retreat from Mons and the Battles of the Aisne, Ypres, Neuve Chapelle, Festubert, Loos, Arras, Vimy Ridge and Cambrai. In 1917 he was transferred to the Royal Engineers, and rendered valuable services with this unit until his discharge in March 1919. Whilst in France he was twice wounded in action in September 1914, during the Retreat from Mons, and two years later on the Somme. He holds the Mons Star, and the General Service and Victory Medals.
7a, Beauchamp Row, Bedford. X1156.

BALDWIN, W. F., Pte., 2nd Oxford. & Bucks. L.I.
He enlisted in March 1914, and was sent to France four months after the outbreak of war. Whilst on the Western Front he played a prominent part in the Battles of Richebourg, Givenchy, Loos, the Somme, Arras, Vimy Ridge, Passchendaele and Cambrai. He was gassed in action in July 1916, and was invalided home, but returned to the Western Front and was again gassed at Cambrai in April 1918. He was once more sent to hospital in Wales and eventually received his discharge in March 1920, holding the 1914–15 Star, and the General Service and Victory Medals.
4, White Horse Yard, Stony Stratford, Bucks. Z1155.

BALDWIN, W. J., Private, Border Regiment and 1st and 4th Essex Regiment.
He volunteered in October 1915, and in July of the following year was sent to Egypt, but later proceeded to Palestine. After taking part in engagements at Jaffa and Haifa, he was reported missing at the Battle of Gaza on March 27th, 1917. He is now presumed to have been killed in action on that date, and was entitled to the General Service and Victory Medals.
"He died the noblest death a man may die,
Fighting for God and right and liberty."
Northcroft, Cambridge Road, Sandy, Beds. Z1154.

BALL, F., Private, Bedfordshire Regiment.
He joined in 1916, and on completion of his training was engaged on important guard duties at various Home depôts. Although unsuccessful in obtaining his transfer overseas, he nevertheless rendered very valuable services with his unit until his demobilisation in 1919.
"The Jetty," London Road, Girtford, Sandy, Beds. Z1157.

BALL, J., Private, Royal Welch Fusiliers.
Although under military age, he volunteered in the Bedfordshire Regiment in 1914, and completed his training with this unit. In July 1915 he was transferred to the Royal Fusiliers, and drafted to France, where he was badly wounded in action in September of the same year. Invalided to England, he was in hospital at Woolwich for 10 months, and was then discharged as medically unfit for further service in July 1916. He holds the 1914–15 Star, and the General Service and Victory Medals.
Ellington, Hunts. Z1159.

BALL, R. S., Private, 2nd Bedfordshire Regiment.
Mobilised at the outbreak of hostilities, he was sent to France in August 1915, and played a prominent part in the Battles of Givenchy and Loos, and in heavy fighting at Ypres. He laid down his life for King and Country on July 5th, 1916, shortly after the commencement of the Somme Offensive, and was entitled to the 1914–15 Star, and the General Service and Victory Medals.
"And doubtless he went in splendid company."
Rose Cottage, Eaton Ford, St. Neots, Hunts. Z2976/B—Z2977/B.

BALL, S., Private, Machine Gun Corps.
He volunteered in November 1914, and eight months later was drafted to the Western Front, where he took part in the Battles of the Somme, Arras, Ypres and Cambrai. He was also in action throughout the Retreat and Advance of 1918, and was gassed at Ypres in June 1917. After the cessation of hostilities he proceeded to Germany with the Army of Occupation and was stationed at Cologne. He returned home for demobilisation in June 1919, and holds the 1914–15 Star, and the General Service and Victory Medals.
34, Salisbury Street, Bedford. X1158/B.

BALLARD, C. H., Private, Royal Defence Corps.
Being too old for service in the fighting forces, he volunteered in the Royal Defence Corps in May 1915, and during the remaining period of hostilities was engaged on special guard duties at prisoners of war camps and at ammunition dumps and aerodromes on the coast. He did excellent work with his unit until his demobilisation in December 1919.
Upper Dean, Beds. Z1160.

BALLM, C. L., Pte., 1/5th Royal Warwick. Regt.
A Reservist, he was called to the Colours in August 1914, and was first engaged on important duties on the East Coast. In 1916, however, he was drafted to the Western Front, where he served as a stretcher-bearer and took part in the Battles of the Somme and Vimy Ridge. He was transferred to Italy in December 1917, and was in action during severe fighting on the Asiago Plateau, and the Piave. He holds the General Service and Victory Medals, and was demobilised in February 1919.
11, Princess Street, Huntingdon. Z1161.

BAMBRIDGE, W. T., Private, Cheshire Regiment; and Sapper, Royal Engineers.
Volunteering in May 1915, he was drafted to France on completion of his training and took part in the Battles of the Somme and Arras before being badly wounded in action at Ypres in September 1917. He was invalided home, and, after hospital treatment at Newcastle, was discharged in May 1918 as medically unfit for further service, holding the General Service and Victory Medals.
10, Roxton, Beds. Z1162.

BAMBRIDGE, W. T., Cpl., 1/8th Middlesex Regt.
He joined in March 1916, and three months later was sent to France, where he served with distinction at the Battles of the Somme, Arras, Messines, Bullecourt and Ypres before being badly gassed in action near Cambrai in March 1918. He was invalided to hospital in England, and, after a period of treatment, was demobilised in August 1919, holding the General Service and Victory Medals.
River Lane, Roxton, Beds. Z1163/B.

BANDY, C. J., Stoker Petty Officer, Royal Navy.
Already in the Royal Navy at the outbreak of war in August 1914, he immediately proceeded to the North Sea on board H.M. Submarine "H.29," and was engaged on important duties hunting for German submarines. He also served with distinction at the Battle of Jutland, and in the raids on Zeebrugge and Ostend, and for a time patrolled the English Channel and Russian Waters. He holds the 1914–15 Star, and the General Service and Victory Medals, and received his discharge in February 1920.
39, Bunyan Road, Kempston. X1165.

BANDY, L. J., Corporal, Bedfordshire Regiment and Royal Army Medical Corps.
He joined in June 1917, and, after a period of training, was engaged at various stations on important duties with his unit. He was unable to obtain a transfer overseas owing to his being under military age, but rendered valuable services until his demobilisation in November 1919.
3, Spring Road, Kempston, Bedford. Z1164.

BANES, F. J., L/Corporal, 1st Bedfordshire Regt.
He volunteered in September 1914, and, in the following year, was drafted to the Western Front, where he took part in several engagements, including the Battles of Thiepval (where he was wounded), the Somme, Arras and Ypres. He died gloriously on the Field of Battle on October 26th, 1917, and was entitled to the 1914–15 Star, and the General Service and Victory Medals.
"A valiant Soldier, with undaunted heart he breasted life's last hill."
Ivel Road, Sandy, Beds. Z1166.

BANFIELD, C. J., Sapper, Royal Engineers.
He joined in October 1916, and underwent a period of training prior to his being drafted to Salonika. Whilst in this seat of operations he was engaged on many important duties and took part in much fighting. He returned home and was demobilised in March 1919, holding the General Service and Victory Medals.
6, Gawcott Road, Buckingham, Bucks. Z1167.

BANKS, C., Private, Oxford. & Bucks. L.I.
He volunteered in July 1915, and, on completing his training in the following January, was drafted to the Western Front, where he took part in the Battles of Delville Wood, Albert, Vimy Ridge and the Somme, and was wounded. He was unfortunately killed in action on the Arras front on April 16th, 1917, and was entitled to the General Service and Victory Medals.
"The path of duty was the way to glory."
80, Spencer Street, New Bradwell, Bucks. Z1168/A.

BARBER, F., Private, 1st Bedfordshire Regiment.
He was mobilised in August 1914 and almost immediately drafted to France, where he took part in much heavy fighting at the Battles of Ypres, Loos, Neuve Chapelle and St. Eloi. He made the supreme sacrifice, being killed in action at Hill 60 on April 21st, 1915, and was entitled to the 1914 Star, and the General Service and Victory Medals.
"Whilst we remember, the sacrifice is not in vain."
12, Edward Road, Bedford. Z1169/B.

BARBER, P., Sapper, Royal Engineers.
He was mobilised in August 1914, and shortly afterwards drafted to the Western Front, where he took part in much severe fighting at Loos. He died gloriously on the Field of Battle at Neuve Chapelle on February 20th, 1915, and was entitled to the 1914–15 Star, and the General Service and Victory Medals.
"A costly sacrifice upon the altar of freedom."
12, Edward Road, Bedford. Z1169/A.

BARBER, S., Gunner, Royal Garrison Artillery.
Volunteering in October 1915, he was drafted overseas after a period of training. Whilst on the Western Front he took part in many engagements, including the Battles of the Somme, Arras, Ypres and Cambrai. He was demobilised in June 1919, and holds the General Service and Victory Medals.
56, High Street, Kempston, Bedford. X1170/A.

BARCOCK, A. G., Sapper, Royal Engineers.
He volunteered in 1915, and underwent a period of training prior to his being drafted to Egypt. He took part in the Advance into Palestine and saw much fighting at Gaza and at the fall of Jerusalem. In August 1919 he returned home, and was demobilised, holding the General Service and Victory Medals. 68, Wellington Street, Bedford. X1171.

BARCOCK, H. W., Pte., 31st Training Reserve Bn.
He joined in March 1917, and underwent a period of training at Dover. After only four weeks' service with the Colours, he unfortunately died on April 6th, 1917, of spotted fever, contracted whilst in the Army.
"Thinking that remembrance, though unspoken, may reach him where he sleeps."
High Street, Sharnbrook, Bedford. Z1172.

BARDELL, W., Private, Herefordshire Regiment.
He volunteered in August 1914, and after his training was retained at home for a time before being drafted to France. There he took part in several engagements, including the Battles of Ypres (III.), the Somme, Cambrai and Ypres (IV.), where he was wounded in action in 1918. He was demobilised in April 1919, and holds the General Service and Victory Medals.
73, High Street, New Bradwell, Bucks. Z1173.

BARDEN, F. H., Corporal, Oxford. & Bucks. L.I.
He volunteered in May 1915, and in the following year was drafted to France. There he took part in severe fighting at the Battle of the Somme, during which he was unfortunately killed in action in July 1916, after only a month on active service. He was entitled to the General Service and Victory Medals.
"Great deeds cannot die:
"They with the sun and moon renew their light for ever."
52, Napier Street, Bletchley, Bucks. Z1174.

BARDEN, F. H., Private, Hampshire Regiment.
He joined in March 1917, and, after undergoing a period of training was engaged on duties of great importance at various stations. He was unable to obtain his transfer to the front on account of ill-health, but, nevertheless, rendered valuable services with his unit until invalided from the Army. He unhappily died of consumption after his discharge in September 1918.
"Steals on the ear the distant triumph song."
69, Napier Street, Bletchley, Bucks. Z2863/B.

BARDEN, H. G., Sapper, Royal Engineers.
Two months after joining in March 1917, he proceeded to the Western Front, where he served in various sectors. He was engaged on important duties on the railways whilst in this theatre of war, and did much useful work with his Company until his return to England for demobilisation in April 1919. He holds the General Service and Victory Medals.
69, Napier Street, Bletchley, Bucks. Z2863/A.

BARDEN, W. G., Private, Royal Scots.
He joined in August 1917, and underwent a period of training prior to his being drafted to Russia. In this seat of operations he was engaged on important duties and saw much active service as a machine gunner. He returned home and was demobilised in August 1919, holding the General Service and Victory Medals.
28, Abbey Road, Old Bradwell, Bucks. Z1175.

BARFOOT, A. L., Private, 11th Essex Regiment.
Volunteering in October 1914, he proceeded to the Western Front in the following year. During his service overseas he took part in several engagements, including the Battles of Neuve Chapelle, Ypres, Loos and Arras, and was wounded three times. He was demobilised in December 1919, and holds the 1914–15 Star, and the General Service and Victory Medals.
18, Gladstone Street, Bedford. X1176/A.

BARFOOT, E. G., Pte., 5th Seaforth Highlanders.
Volunteering in January 1915, he was drafted overseas in the following year. Whilst on the Western Front he took part in many engagements, including the Battles of Arras, Vimy Ridge, Ypres and Cambrai, and was wounded once and gassed three times. He was demobilised in April 1919, and holds the General Service and Victory Medals.
18, Gladstone Street, Bedford. X1176/B.

BARFOOT, H. S., Gunner, Royal Garrison Artillery.
He volunteered in January 1916, and later in the same year proceeded to France, where he was stationed at Abbeville and employed on important duties. After hostilities ceased he went to Germany with the Army of Occupation and served with the anti-aircraft sector of the Royal Garrison Artillery, until his demobilisation in November 1919. He holds the General Service and Victory Medals.
High Street, Sharnbrook, Bedford. Z1177.

BARKER, A. G., Private, 1st Bedfordshire Regt.
He was mobilised in August 1914, and immediately drafted to France, where he took part in the Battles of Mons, Ypres, Festubert, Loos and the Somme. He made the supreme sacrifice, being killed in action at Ypres on October 5th, 1917, and was entitled to the Mons Star, and the General Service and Victory Medals.
"He died the noblest death a man may die,
Fighting for God and right and liberty."
26, Beaconsfield Street, Bedford. X1178/A

BARKER, E. C., Private, Labour Corps.
He joined in August 1917, and was retained at various stations, chiefly on agricultural work in Scotland, and with the Army Remount Department near London. After the cessation of hostilities he proceeded to Germany with the Army of Occupation, and was there engaged in tending sick horses. He was demobilised in April 1920.
258, Bedford Road, Kempston, Bedford. X1179.

BARKER, F., Private, Queen's Own (Royal West Kent Regiment).
He joined in April 1916, and three months later was drafted to the Western Front, and immediately sent into action on the Somme. There he died gloriously on the Field of Battle on August 27th, 1916, and was entitled to the General Service and Victory Medals.
"Honour to the immortal dead, who gave their youth that the world might grow old in peace."
26, Beaconsfield Street, Bedford. X1178/C.

BARKER, H., Private, 1st Bedfordshire Regiment and Hertfordshire Regiment.
Volunteering in August 1914, he was drafted to the Western Front in the following year, and there saw severe fighting in various sectors. After taking part in many important engagements, including the Battles of Arras, Ypres, Cambrai and the Somme, he was taken prisoner in 1918 and held in captivity until after the cessation of hostilities. He was invalided from the Army in December 1919, and holds the 1914–15 Star, and the General Service and Victory Medals.
Carter Street, Girtford, Sandy, Beds. Z1184.

BARKER, J., Sapper, Royal Engineers.
He volunteered in January 1916, and on completing a period of training, later in that year was drafted to the Western Front. Whilst in this theatre of war he was engaged on important duties on the railways in various sectors, and also took an active part in the Battles of Ypres, Cambrai and the Somme and other engagements. He was demobilised in March 1919, and holds the General Service and Victory Medals.
Presevine Cottages, Clapham, Bedford. Z1186.

BARKER, J. A., Private, Bedfordshire Regiment.
He volunteered at the outbreak of war in August 1914, and in the following year was drafted to France, where he saw severe fighting in various sectors of the front. He took part in the Battles of Loos, Vermelles, Vimy Ridge, Arras, Ypres and Cambrai, and many other important engagements, and also served through the Retreat and Advance of 1918, and was wounded in action. He was invalided from the Army in March 1919, and holds the 1914–15 Star, and the General Service and Victory Medals.
52, Gwyn Street, Bedford. X1185/A.

BARKER, P., L/Corporal, Royal Fusiliers.
He joined in April 1916, and was retained on important duties in England into November of the following year, when he was drafted to the Western Front. There he saw severe fighting in various sectors and took part in the Battles of Cambrai and the Somme, and many other important engagements until the cessation of hostilities. Returning home in January 1919, he was demobilised in the following month, and holds the General Service and Victory Medals.
26, Beaconsfield Street, Bedford. Z1178/B.

BARKER, P., Driver, Royal Field Artillery.
Joining in October 1916, he was drafted to the Western Front in June of the following year, and there saw much heavy fighting. He took part in the Battles of Ypres, Passchendaele, Cambrai and the Marne, and other important engagements in various sectors, and served also through the Retreat of 1918. He was invalided home in August of that year suffering from appendicitis, and after his recovery served at Edinburgh until his demobilisation in March 1919. He holds the General Service and Victory Medals.
Hail Weston, near Huntingdon. Z1183.

BARKER, W., Driver, Royal Engineers.
He volunteered in August 1915, and in March of the following year proceeded to the Western Front, but in April was invalided to England. He was then retained on home duties until March 1918, when he was again drafted to France in time to take part in the Battles of Kemmel Hill, Cambrai and Ypres, and other important engagements. He afterwards served with the Army of Occupation in Germany, finally returning home in April 1919 for demobilisation in the following month. He holds the General Service and Victory Medals.
16, Russell Street, Bedford. Z1180.

BARKER, W. A., L/Cpl., 1st Bedfordshire Regt.
Already in the Army when war was declared in August 1914, he was immediately drafted to the Western Front, where he fought in the Retreat from Mons and in the Battles of Ypres and Loos, and was twice wounded—at Neuve Chapelle in 1915 and on the Somme in the following year. He was unhappily killed in action on September 25th, 1916, during the Somme Offensive. He was entitled to the Mons Star, and the General Service and Victory Medals.
"His memory is cherished with pride."
5, Beauchamp Row, Bedford. Z1181/B.

BARKER, W. A., Sergeant, Royal Sussex Regt. and Machine Gun Corps.
Three months after volunteering in December 1915, he proceeded to Salonika with the Machine Gun Corps, and there took a prominent part in many important engagements. After seeing much severe fighting, he was invalided to hospital at Malta and thence home, suffering from malaria. He was retained, after his recovery, on important duties as an Instructor at Grantham until July 1919, when he was demobilised. He holds the General Service and Victory Medals.
1, Tickford Court, Priory Street, Newport Pagnell. Z1182.

BARKER, W. C., Private, Sherwood Foresters.
He joined in May 1916, and underwent a period of training prior to being drafted to the Western Front in October of the following year. There he saw severe fighting in various sectors, and took part in the Battles of Cambrai and Ypres, and many other important engagements until the cessation of hostilities. Demobilised in February 1919, he holds the General Service and Victory Medals.
26, Beaconsfield Street, Bedford X1178/D.

BARLEY, A., Private, R.A.O.C.; 5th Bedfordshire Regiment and Devonshire Regiment.
He joined in March 1916, and on completing a period of training in the following year was drafted to the Western Front, where he saw severe fighting in various sectors. He took part in the Battles of Messines, Ypres, Cambrai and the Somme, and many other important engagements in this theatre of war. Returning home in 1919, he was still with his unit in the following year, and holds the General Service and Victory Medals.
32, Russell Street, Bedford. Z1187/B—X1188/B—X1189/B.

BARLEY, B., Private, Queen's (Royal West Surrey Regiment).
He joined in December 1916, and after four months' training proceeded to the Western Front, where he took part in the Battles of Arras, Vimy Ridge and Messines, and many minor engagements. He died gloriously on the Field of Battle near Ypres on October 4th, 1917. He was entitled to the General Service and Victory Medals.
"Courage, bright hopes, and a myriad dreams, splendidly given."
32, Russell Street, Bedford. Z1187/C—X1188/C—X1189/C.

BARLEY, F., Sergeant, 2nd Bedfordshire Regt. and Royal Irish Fusiliers.
Mobilised in August 1914, he was immediately drafted to the Western Front, where he fought in the Retreat from Mons. He also took a prominent part in the Battles of La Bassée, Neuve Chapelle and Hill 60, and other important engagements, and was wounded in action at Ypres in May 1915. In October of that year he was transferred to Salonika, where he fell fighting on December 8th, 1915. He was entitled to the Mons Star, and the General Service and Victory Medals.
"The path of duty was the way to glory."
32, Russell Street Bedford. Z1187/E—X1188/E—X1189/E.

BARLEY, J., Private, 1st Bedfordshire Regiment.
Already in the Army when war broke out in August 1914, he was immediately drafted to France, and there, after serving through the Retreat from Mons, took part in the Battles of the Marne, the Aisne, La Bassée, Ypres and Neuve Chapelle, and many minor engagements. He fell fighting at Hill 60 on June 3rd, 1915. He was entitled to the Mons Star, and the General Service and Victory Medals.
"A costly sacrifice upon the altar of freedom."
32, Russell Street, Bedford. Z1187/D—X1188/D—X1189/D.

BARLEY, T. L., Corporal, 1st Bedfordshire Regt.
He volunteered in April 1915, and in December of the same year was drafted to the Western Front, where he took part in the Battles of Albert, Vimy Ridge and the Somme, and other engagements in various sectors. In 1917 he was transferred to Italy, and was there again in action on the Piave until the cessation of hostilities. He was demobilised on his return home in January 1919, and holds the 1914–15 Star, and the General Service and Victory Medals.
71, Muswell Road, Bedford. Z1187/A—X1188/A—X1189/A.

BARLOW, C. W. J., Sapper, Royal Engineers.
He volunteered in 1915, and in the following year proceeded to France, where he was engaged on important duties in various sectors of the front. He also took an active part in the Battles of Arras, Ypres and Cambrai, and other engagements, and was wounded in action in December 1917. After the cessation of hostilities he served with the Army of Occupation in Germany, finally returning home for demobilisation in April 1919. He holds the General Service and Victory Medals.
Rectory Lane, Somersham, Hunts. Z1190.

BARLOW, G., Corporal, Royal Horse Guards.
Volunteering in January 1915, he proceeded to the Western Front in October of that year, and there saw severe fighting in various sectors. He took part in the Battles of Loos, Vimy Ridge, the Somme and Ypres, and many other important engagements in this theatre of war, and was gassed. He holds the 1914–15 Star, and the General Service and Victory Medals, and in 1920 was still serving.
Park Hall Road, Somersham, Hunts. Z1191.

BARNES, A. V., Private, Bedfordshire Regiment and Royal Scots.
After volunteering in 1914, he underwent a period of training prior to being drafted to the Western Front in 1916. There he saw much severe fighting in various sectors, and took part in the Battles of Vimy Ridge and the Somme and many other important engagements, until invalided home in 1918 suffering from fever. Later in that year, however, he proceeded to Russia, finally returning home for demobilisation in June 1919. He holds the General Service and Victory Medals.
Baker's Lane, Tempsford, near Sandy, Beds. Z1192/C.

BARNES, F., Private, Bedfordshire and Essex Regiments; and Sapper, Royal Engineers.
Volunteering in 1914, he was drafted to the Western Front in September of the following year, and there, after seeing much severe fighting, was wounded in action at Loos and invalided home in October 1915. On his recovery in 1916, however, he proceeded to Palestine, where he served at various stations until 1918, when he was again sent to England, having been severely injured in an accident. He unhappily died in 1918. He was entitled to the 1914–15 Star, and the General Service and Victory Medals.
Baker's Lane, Tempsford, near Sandy, Beds. Z1192/B.

BARNES, H., Sergeant, 5th Bedfordshire Regt.
A Reservist, he was called to the Colours in August 1914, and in the following year was drafted to the Dardanelles, where he saw severe fighting at Suvla Bay, and was wounded in action in August 1915. He afterwards served in Egypt, and, taking part in the Advance into Palestine, fought in the Battles of Gaza and at the capture of Jerusalem and Jaffa. He was discharged on his return home in March 1919, and holds the 1914–15 Star, and the General Service and Victory Medals.
Baker's Lane, Tempsford, near Sandy, Beds. Z1192/A.

BARNES, H. G., Private, 1st Bedfordshire Regt.
He was called up from the Reserve in August 1914, and after a few days at home was drafted to the Western Front. There he saw much severe fighting at the Battle of Mons, but later died gloriously on the Field of Battle on October 17th, 1914. He was entitled to the Mons Star, and the General Service and Victory Medals.
"A valiant Soldier, with undaunted heart he breasted life's last hill."
39, Russell Street, St. Neots, Hunts. Z1193.

BARNES, T., Corporal, Bedfordshire Regiment.
He volunteered in August 1914, and, after a period of training, was engaged at various stations on important duties with his unit. He was unable to obtain a transfer overseas owing to his being medically unfit, but rendered valuable services until his demobilisation in February 1919.
Montague Street, Eynesbury, St. Neots, Hunts. Z1194/B.

BARNETT, E. E., Private, Royal Fusiliers.
He joined in October 1916, and in the following year was drafted to France. In this theatre of war he was in action at the Battle of Ypres (III.), and was taken prisoner in September 1917. Whilst in captivity in Germany he was stationed at Gustrow Camp in Westphalia, and suffered many privations. He was repatriated after the Armistice and returned home for his demobilisation in October 1919. He holds the General Service and Victory Medals.
Hail Weston, near Huntingdon, Hunts. Z1195/A—Z1196/A.

BARNETT, P. J. T., Private, 7th Bedfordshire Rgt.
He volunteered in February 1915, and later in the same year was drafted to France. There he took part in much heavy fighting at the Battles of Loos, the Somme, Albert (where he was slightly wounded), Arras, Vimy Ridge and Messines. He was unfortunately killed in action during the Battle of Ypres (III.) on August 10th, 1917, and was entitled to the 1914–15 Star, and the General Service and Victory Medals.
"The path of duty was the way to glory."
Hail Weston, near Huntingdon, Hunts. Z1195/B—Z1196/B.

BARNWELL, C. T., Cpl., 1/5th Bedfordshire Regt.
He was mobilised in August 1914, and almost immediately drafted to the Western Front, where he served with the Machine Gun Corps, and took part in many engagements, including those at Ypres and on the Somme. He suffered severely from trench feet, and was consequently invalided home and finally discharged in June 1917. He holds the 1914 Star, and the General Service and Victory Medals.
High Street, Sheringham, Bucks. Z1197/B.

BARNWELL, D. J., L/Cpl., Oxford. & Bucks. L.I.
Volunteering in September 1914, he was drafted overseas in the following year. During his service in France he took part in the Battle of Loos, and was later transferred to Salonika. There he saw much severe fighting on the Vardar and Doiran fronts, and was severely wounded. He unfortunately died from the effects of his wounds on May 9th, 1917, and was entitled to the 1914–15 Star, and the General Service and Victory Medals.
"Nobly striving:
He nobly fell that we might live."
104, High Street, Newport Pagnell, Bucks. Z1198/B—Z1199/B.

BARNWELL, W. C. (M.M.), Pte., 7th Wilts. Regt.
He joined in September 1917, and, on completing his training in the following March, proceeded to France. There he played a distinguished part in the Battles of Cambrai, Ypres, Epéhy and Le Cateau, and was slightly wounded in action. He was awarded the Military Medal for conspicuous bravery in the Field. After hostilities ceased he went to Germany with the Army of Occupation and served there until his demobilisation in October 1919. He also holds the General Service and Victory Medals.
104, High St., Newport Pagnell, Bucks. Z1198/C—Z1199/C.

BARNWELL, W. G., (D.C.M., M.M.), Sergt., R.E.
He volunteered in September 1914, and six months later was sent to France with the 1st Oxfordshire and Buckinghamshire Light Infantry (T.F.). He served with distinction as a Lewis Gunner at the Battles of Ypres, Festubert, Loos, St. Eloi and the Somme, during which last engagement he was wounded in action at Pozières in July 1916. Invalided to England, he spent some time in hospital, but, on his recovery, was transferred to the Royal Engineers (R.O.D.) and sent to Ireland. After a short period of service there, however, he returned to the Western Front and did much excellent work in the workshops at Etaples. He was awarded the Distinguished Conduct Medal, the Military Medal and the Russian Order of St. George (2nd Class), for conspicuous gallantry in action on several occasions, and, also holding the 1914–15 Star, and the General Service and Victory Medals, was eventually demobilised in April 1919.
104 High Street, Newport Pagnell, Bucks. Z1198/A—Z1199/A.

BARRATT, A., Private, 10th Suffolk Regiment.
He volunteered in December 1915, but on completion of his training was found to be unfit for service overseas. He was stationed at Colchester and Harwich, where he performed excellent work in the cook-house. In July 1916 he was discharged from the Army as medically unfit for further military duties. 41, Garfield Street, Bedford. Z1200.

BARRATT, A. W., Private, Royal Fusiliers.
He joined in February 1916, and on completion of his training was two months later drafted overseas. During his service on the Western Front he took an active part in many important engagements, including the Battles of the Somme, Albert, Messines and Bapaume. He was wounded in action at Ypres in 1917, and was invalided to England, where he served until demobilised in October 1919, holding the General Service and Victory Medals. 43, Garfield Street, Bedford. Z1201.

BARRATT, F., Private, Queen's (Royal West Surrey Regiment).
Joining in May 1916, he was retained on important duties at home until September 1917, when he received his transfer to the war zone. Whilst serving on the Western Front he experienced fierce fighting, principally in the Ypres sector, and was severely wounded in action at Passchendaele in November 1917. In consequence he was invalided out of the Army in August 1918, holding the General Service and Victory Medals.
40, St. Leonard's Street, Bedford. X1202.

BARRATT, R., Private, 2nd Bedfordshire Regt.
In January 1915 he volunteered, and four months later was drafted to the Western Front. There he was in action in important engagements at Ypres, Festubert and Loos, and was severely wounded at Hill 60 in July 1915. After protracted hospital treatment at Boulogne and Edmonton, he was discharged as unfit for further service in August 1917. He holds the 1914–15 Star, and the General Service and Victory Medals. 82, Howbury Street, Bedford. Z1203/B.

BARRATT, W., Private, 3/5th Bedfordshire Regt.
He volunteered in February 1915, and in the following year proceeded overseas. On reaching France he was transferred to the 1st Leicestershire Regiment, and did good work with that unit in various sectors of the front. He fought in the Battles of Albert and the Somme, and was unhappily killed in action on September 16th, 1918. He was entitled to the General Service and Victory Medals.
"His life for his Country."
82, Howbury Street, Bedford. Z1203/A.

BARRINGER, A. B., Sapper, Royal Engineers.
He volunteered in August 1914, and in 1915 was sent to Gallipoli, where he was wounded in the Suvla Bay Landing. He was invalided to England, and in 1917 was drafted to Palestine, where he saw heavy fighting at Gaza and Haifa. During his service in this theatre of war he performed excellent work driving ammunition and Red Cross trains. On his return home in 1919 he was demobilised, holding the 1914–15 Star, and the General Service and Victory Medals.
Eaton Ford, Bedford. Z1205/B.

BARRINGER, A. G., Private, Hussars.
Volunteering in June 1915, he was later in the same year sent to the Western Front. There he took part in fierce fighting in various important engagements, chiefly in the Ypres, Cambrai and the Somme sectors. After the close of hostilities he proceeded to Germany with the Army of Occupation, and in 1919 contracted trench fever. He was demobilised in the same year, holding the 1914–15 Star, and the General Service and Victory Medals.
The Crown, Luke St., Eynesbury, St. Neots, Hunts. Z1204/B.

BARRINGER, G. T., Tpr., Bedfordshire Lancers; and Private, 12th Lancers.
A month after the outbreak of war he volunteered, and in February 1915 proceeded overseas. During his service on the Western Front he was in action at the Battles of Neuve Chapelle, Ypres, Loos, the Somme, Passchendaele and Cambrai, and in the Retreat and Advance of 1918. After the Armistice he proceeded into Germany with the Army of Occupation and was stationed at Cologne until demobilised in November 1919. He holds the 1914–15 Star, and the General Service and Victory Medals.
3, Luke Street, Eynesbury, St. Neots, Hunts. Z1208.

BARRINGER, H. J., Private, East Surrey Regt.
He joined in May 1916, and after training at Felixstowe, was in the following September drafted overseas. Whilst serving on the Western Front he did good work with his unit in the Battles of Ypres, Passchendaele, Messines and Cambrai, and in the final engagements of the war. After the cessation of hostilities he served in Germany with the Army of Occupation until demobilised in October 1919, holding the General Service and Victory Medals.
Berrick Yard, St. Mary's Street, Eynesbury, St. Neots. Z1207.

BARRINGER, J. T., Private, Machine Gun Corps.
Joining in 1917, he proceeded in the same year to the Western Front, where he was wounded and taken prisoner in November 1917. He was kept in captivity until February 1919, and on his release returned to England. He was drafted to Egypt and served at Cairo for six months, rendering valuable services in connection with the transport of ammunition. On his return home in January 1920 he was demobilised, holding the General Service and Victory Medals.
Eaton Ford, Bedford. Z1205/A.

BARRINGER, W., Private, 7th Leicestershire Rgt.
He joined in March 1916, and later in the same year was sent to the Western Front, where he was wounded at Epéhy in 1917. He also took part in the Battles of the Somme, Ypres, Arras, Cambrai, the Marne, and was gassed at Hamel in October 1918 during the Allied Advance. He was sent to hospital in Boulogne, and on his recovery served in France until demobilised in March 1919, holding the General Service and Victory Medals.
4, Harringay Terrace, Eaton Socon, St. Neots. Z1206.

BARTHOLMEW, T., Pte., 2nd Bedfordshire Regt.
When war broke out he was already serving in Africa, and at once proceeded to the Western Front. There he fought in the Battles of Mons, the Marne, the Aisne and La Bassée, and was severely wounded in the Battle of the Somme in July 1916. He was invalided to England, and three months later was discharged from the Army as medically unfit for further military duties. He holds the Mons Star, and the General Service and Victory Medals.
6, Church Passage, Newport Pagnell, Bucks. Z1209.

BARTON, G. A., Private, Queen's Own (Royal West Kent Regiment).
He volunteered in September 1914, and in February of the following year was drafted overseas. Whilst serving on the Western Front he saw heavy fighting in engagements at Ypres, Loos, Albert, Arras, Cambrai, Combles, and was present during the triumphal entry into Mons. He remained in France until March 1919, when he was demobilised, holding the 1914–15 Star, and the General Service and Victory Medals.
78, Spencer Street, New Bradwell, Bucks. Z1210.

BARTON, R. H., Private, Dorestshire Regiment.
Joining in April 1917, he served on Salisbury Plain and at Aldershot, and a year later was sent to the Western Front. There, after a month's service, he was wounded in an engagement on the Somme, and in consequence was discharged in August 1918 as medically unfit for further duty. He holds the General Service and Victory Medals.
58, Spencer Street, New Bradwell, Bucks. Z1211.

BARTON, T., Private, Oxford. & Bucks. Light Infantry; and Pioneer, Royal Engineers.
He volunteered in September 1914, and on being drafted to France in the following April, saw heavy fighting at Gommecourt, Bullecourt and Armentières. He was invalided to England in 1916, but in 1917 returned to the Western Front, and was again sent to hospital in October 1918. On his recovery he was transferred to the Royal Engineers, and during the remainder of his service was engaged on the construction of roads at Wareham. Demobilised in May 1919, he holds the 1914–15 Star, and the General Service and Victory Medals.
4, Spencer Street, New Bradwell, Bucks. Z1212.

BARTRAM, A. T., Sapper, R.E.; and Suffolk Regt.
Volunteering in November 1915, he was attached to the Suffolk Regiment, but was discharged as medically unfit in April 1916. In May 1917, however, he rejoined as a Sapper in the Royal Engineers, and on being sent overseas in January 1918, served on the Western Front for 16 months. During that time he did good work with his unit at Cambrai, Dunkirk and Amiens, and was eventually demobilised in July 1919, holding the General Service and Victory Medals.
24, Melbourne Street, Bedford. X1214/B.

BARTRAM, E., Guardsman, 2nd Grenadier Guards.
At the outbreak of war in August 1914, he was already serving, and at once proceeded with the first Expeditionary Force to France. There he fought in the Battle of Mons and was unfortunately killed in action at the Battle of the Ancre in September 1914. He was entitled to the Mons Star, and the General Service and Victory Medals.
"A valiant Soldier, with undaunted heart he breasted life's last hill."
5, Dane Street, Bedford. X1215.

BARTRAM, F. W., Private, Royal Fusiliers and 16th Royal Sussex Regiment.
He joined in July 1916, and after training at Dover was in the following year sent to Egypt, where he served at Alexandria and Cairo. On being drafted to Palestine, he was in action at Jerusalem, and in March 1918 was transferred to France. There he took an active part in severe fighting on the Somme and the Aisne, and at Bapaume and Cambrai. He was demobilised in February 1919, holding the General Service and Victory Medals. 48, Russell Street, St. Neots. Z1213.

BARTRAM, R. J., Sapper, Royal Engineers.
Volunteering in December 1914, he was, on completion of his training in July 1915, drafted to Gallipoli. During the campaign on the Peninsula he was in action at Suvla Bay and subsequent engagements. In March 1918 he was sent to France, where he performed excellent work with No. 1 Light Railway Company on the Ypres and Cambrai fronts. He was demobilised in June 1919, holding the 1914–15 Star, and the General Service and Victory Medals.
24, Melbourne Street, Bedford. X1214/A.

BASFORD, A., Private, R.A.S.C. (M.T.)
Volunteering in September 1914, he was drafted to the Western Front early in the following year, and was there engaged in conveying food and ammunition to the forward areas. Serving in various sectors, he was also present at many important engagements until the cessation of hostilities, finally returning home for demobilisation in February 1919. He holds the 1914–15 Star, and the General Service and Victory Medals.
Green's Norton, Towcester, Northants. Z2864.

BASS, A. (Miss), Navy and Army Canteen Board.
This lady served with the Navy and Army Canteen Board for several months at Folkestone before being sent to France in 1917. She worked for the Canteen Board at Boulogne and Abbeville, and was engaged on important clerical duties, which she carried out with great ability. During the Retreat of 1918 she rendered valuable services in the hospitals, and relinquished her position in 1919.
New Town, Kimbolton, Hunts. Z1219/D.

BASS, A., Private, Bedfordshire Regiment.
He volunteered in 1914, and in July 1915 was sent to the Western Front, where he fought in engagements at Ypres and Vimy Ridge. In July 1916 he was wounded in the Battle of the Somme and invalided to England. On his recovery two months later he was drafted to Palestine, and saw heavy fighting at Gaza and Jerusalem. He returned home in 1919 and was demobilised, holding the 1914–15 Star, and the General Service and Victory Medals.
Mill Green, Warboys, Huntingdonshire. Z1217/A.

BASS, A. E., Sapper, Royal Engineers.
At the outbreak of hostilities in August 1914 he volunteered, and after a course of training was in the following year sent to Egypt, thence to Palestine. In this theatre of war, he took part in severe fighting at Gaza, Jerusalem and Jaffa, and also performed good work as an officer's servant. He returned to England in March 1919, when he was demobilised, holding the 1914–15 Star, and the General Service and Victory Medals.
33, Woburn Road, Kempston, Bedford. X1216/A.

BASS, C. F., Sapper, Royal Engineers.
When war was declared in August 1914 he volunteered, and after a period of training proceeded overseas in the following year. Whilst serving on the Western Front he fought in the Battles of Vimy Ridge and the Somme, and was wounded at Ypres in 1916. He was also in action in the Retreat and Advance of 1918, and was demobilised in January 1919, holding the 1914–15 Star, and the General Service and Victory Medals. 33, Woburn Road, Kempston, Bedford. X1216/B.

BASS, D. J., Private, Labour Corps.
He joined in 1916, but was unsuccessful in procuring a transfer to the fighting area before the cessation of hostilities. He did good work as a cook at St. Albans, Felixstowe and Bedford, and after the Armistice proceeded to Germany with the Army of Occupation, and rendered valuable services until demobilised in 1919. Newtown, Kimbolton, Hunts. Z1219/B.

BASS, F. W., Private, 13th Essex Regiment.
Joining in 1916, he was sent overseas in November of that year, on completion of his training. During his service on the Western Front he was engaged in severe fighting in the Somme, Ypres and Vimy Ridge sectors. In April 1917 his health broke down, and he was invalided to England. On his recovery he was transferred to the Royal Engineers, and served with this unit at Felixstowe and Richborough. Demobilised in January 1919, he holds the General Service and Victory Medals.
Eaton Socon, Bedfordshire. Z1218.

BASS, J. A., Private, Bedfordshire Regiment.
He joined in August 1916, and in the following year proceeded to the Western Front, where he was in action at Ypres and Arras. Shortly afterwards he was invalided to England suffering from dysentery, and on his return to France in April 1918, rendered valuable services as a clerk in the post office in the Cambrai and Somme sectors. He was demobilised in April 1919, holding the General Service and Victory Medals.
Shaftsbury Avenue, St. Neots, Hunts. Z1221.

BASS, O. C. E. B., Tpr., Bedfordshire Lancers, and Private, 20th Hussars.
At the outbreak of hostilities in August 1914 he volunteered, and in April of the following year was drafted overseas. During his four years' service on the Western Front he took part in numerous engagements in different sectors, including those at Ypres, Festubert, Albert, Vimy Ridge, the Somme and Cambrai. He was demobilised in 1919, and holds the 1914–15 Star, and the General Service and Victory Medals.
Newtown, Kimbolton, Hunts. Z1219/C.

BASS, W. J., Private, Northamptonshire Regt.
He joined the Army in 1916, and after a period of training at Northampton and Farnborough, was sent overseas in the same year. Whilst serving on the Western Front he did good work with his unit at the Battles of Arras, Ypres, Messines and Cambrai, and was wounded and gassed on the Somme in 1918. He remained in France until September 1919, when he was demobilised, holding the General Service and Victory Medals.
Newtown, Kimbolton, Hunts. Z1219/A.

BASSON, E. J., Corporal, 1st Leicestershire Regt.
Joining in March 1916, he was later in the same year drafted to the Western theatre of war. There he was engaged in fierce fighting in numerous engagements of importance, especially in the Somme, Arras and Ypres sectors. He was wounded in action in the Battle of the Somme in March 1918, and was eventually demobilised in February 1919, holding the General Service and Victory Medals.
3, East Street, St. Neots, Hunts. Z1220/B.

BASSON, G. A., A.B., Royal Naval Division.
He volunteered in June 1915, and on completion of a course of training was in the following year ordered overseas. Throughout the period of his service in France he was stationed at Calais, where he fulfilled the duties assigned to him with the greatest ability. He was wounded in December 1917, during an air-raid, and was eventually demobilised in March 1919, holding the General Service and Victory Medals.
3, East Street, St. Neots, Hunts. Z1220/A.

BATCHELOR, F., Sapper, R.E. (Signals).
Volunteering in December 1914, he proceeded to France in the following February, and, during his service on the Western Front, was present at engagements at Ypres and in the Somme sector. In January 1916 he was drafted to Salonika, and, whilst in this theatre of war, was engaged on important duties in the forward areas, notably on the Vardar, Doiran and Struma fronts. He returned to England and was demobilised in September 1919, and holds the 1914–15 Star, and the General Service and Victory Medals.
2, Mill Lane, Stony Stratford. Z1223/B.

BATCHELOR, J. A., Private, Hampshire Regt.
He volunteered in June 1915, and trained in the Royal Army Service Corps, but was later transferred to the Hampshire Regiment and drafted to France in August 1917. He then served in various engagements, including those on the Somme, at Ypres and Cambrai, and in many of the later operations in the Retreat and Advance of 1918. He returned home and was demobilised in July 1919, and holds the General Service and Victory Medals. 2, North End Square, Buckingham. Z1222.

BATCHELOR, W., Gunner, Royal Field Artillery.
Volunteering in March 1915, he was drafted to France in the following September and was in action in the Somme sector. In January 1916 he proceeded to Salonika, where he did good work as a gunner on the Vardar, Struma and Doiran fronts. He returned home and was demobilised in March 1919, holding the 1914–15 Star, and the General Service and Victory Medals.
2, Mill Lane, Stony Stratford. Z1223/A.

BATES, J., Pioneer, Royal Engineers.
He volunteered in October 1915, and in the following month was drafted to France. Whilst overseas he was engaged on important duties in connection with the operations, and was in the forward areas at Ypres and on the Somme. He sustained a spinal injury in an accident, and was invalided to England and subsequently discharged suffering from shell-shock in January 1917. He holds the 1914–15 Star, and the General Service and Victory Medals.
Church End, Sherington, Newport Pagnell, Bucks. Z1225.

BATES, J. W., Sapper, R.E.; Private, Cheshire Regiment; and Air Mechanic, R.A.F.
Volunteering in February 1915, he was drafted to France in the following November, and during his service on the Western Front was in action at the Battles of Vimy Ridge, Ypres, Arras, Passchendaele and Cambrai. After the Armistice he advanced into Germany with the Army of Occupation, and was stationed for about five months on the Rhine. He holds the 1914–15 Star, and the General Service and Victory Medals, and was demobilised after his return to England in May 1919.
38, Melbourne Street, Beds. X1224/B.

BATES, W. G., Trooper, Northants. Dragoons.
Volunteering in September 1914, he proceeded to the Western Front after two months' training and there saw severe fighting in various sectors. He took part in the Battles of Neuve Chapelle, Arras and Cambrai and many other important engagements, and served also through the Retreat and Advance of 1918. Demobilised in February 1919, he holds the 1914 Star, and the General Service and Victory Medals.
Church End, Paulerspury, Towcester Northants. Z2865.

BATTAMS, E. C., Corporal, Oxford. & Bucks. L.I.
He volunteered in February 1915, and after the completion of his training, was drafted to France in May of the following year. He died gloriously on the Field of Battle on the Somme a few weeks later in July 1916, and was entitled to the General Service and Victory Medals.
"Nobly striving:
He nobly fell that we might live."
29, Tavistock Street, Fenny Stratford, Bucks. Z1226/B.

BATTAMS, J. H., Sapper, R.E. (R.O.D.)
He joined in January 1917, and in July of the same year was drafted overseas. During his service in France he was engaged on important duties in connection with the operations, and was frequently in the forward areas, notably on the Somme and at Ypres and Cambrai. He returned to England and was demobilised in March 1919, and holds the General Service and Victory Medals.
29, Tavistock Street, Fenny Stratford, Bucks. Z1226/A.

BATTAMS, W. J., L/Corporal, Duke of Cornwall's Light Infantry.
He joined in June 1917, and, after his training, proceeded to Ireland, where he rendered valuable services at Londonderry attached to the Military Police. He was not successful in obtaining a transfer overseas before hostilities ceased and was demobilised in November 1919.
49, Tavistock Street, Fenny Stratford, Bucks. Z1226/C.

BATTLE, F. W., Private, Royal Fusiliers.
He joined in February 1916, and in October of the same year embarked for France. Whilst on the Western Front he took part in the heavy fighting at the Battle of the Somme, and was severely wounded near Ypres in June 1917. He was invalided home to hospital, and was demobilised in January 1919, and holds the General Service and Victory Medals.
Park Lane, Blunham, Beds. Z1227.

BATTLE, P. S., Private, Bedfordshire Regiment.
Volunteering in October 1915, he proceeded to France in January of the following year, and, whilst on the Western Front took part in many important engagements. He fought at Richebourg, Arras, Givenchy and Bullecourt, and was very severely wounded in the third Battle of Ypres on July 16th, 1917. Two days later he unfortunately died from his wounds, and was buried at Hazebrouck Cemetery. He was entitled to the General Service and Victory Medals.
"A valiant Soldier, with undaunted heart he breasted life's last hill."
High Street, Blunham, Beds. Z1228.

BAXTER, B., Sergt., Canadian Royal Highlanders.
He volunteered in Canada in August 1915 and embarked for England, where he completed his training and was then drafted to France. During his service on the Western Front he fought at Festubert, Albert, Loos, and on the Somme, and was wounded at Lens and admitted to hospital. After his recovery he was again in action at Vimy Ridge and Messines, and in many subsequent engagements, and was demobilised in February 1919. He holds the 1914–15 Star, and the General Service and Victory Medals. Church Street, Buckden, Hunts. Z1229.

BAXTER, B., Corporal, R.A.S.C. and Royal Irish Fusiliers.
Volunteering in April 1915, he was drafted to France in the following September, and whilst overseas rendered valuable services in connection with the supply of rations to the troops at Le Havre and Boulogne. Later he was transferred to the Royal Irish Fusiliers and was in action on the Somme and at Ypres, Passchendaele and Cambrai. He holds the 1914–15 Star, and the General Service and Victory Medals, and was demobilised in March 1919.
Church Street, Eynesbury, St. Neots, Hunts. Z1230.

BAXTER, G., Private, 2nd Bedfordshire Regiment.
He joined in March 1916, and six months later embarked for France. Whilst in this theatre of war he took part in the Battles of the Somme, Arras, Ypres and Cambrai. He gave his life for the freedom of England in the second Battle of the Somme on March 21st, 1918, and was entitled to the General Service and Victory Medals.
"He passed out of the sight of men by the path of duty and self-sacrifice."
Abbots Ripton, Hunts. Z1232/A.

BAXTER, G. A., Private, 8th Bedfordshire Regt.
He volunteered in June 1915, and in the following February was drafted to the Western Front. During his service in France he took part in severe fighting at Trônes Wood, Delville Wood, Gommecourt, and Bullecourt. He was badly wounded in action on the Somme on September 28th, 1916, and was invalided home to Edmonton Military Hospital, where he died of his injuries on December 24th of the same year. He was entitled to the General Service and Victory Medals.
"He joined the great white company of valiant souls."
Graveley, near Huntingdon, Hunts. TZ1231.

BAXTER, H., A.B., Royal Navy.
He joined in November 1916, and was later sent to the North Sea on board H.M.S. "Dragon," with which vessel he was engaged on important patrol duties. He was also on board H.M.S. "Conqueror" when she was mined, and was severely gassed during the course of his service. Demobilised in January 1919, he holds the General Service and Victory Medals.
Abbots Ripton, Hunts. Z1232/B.

BAXTER, J., Private, East Yorkshire Regiment.
He joined in August 1916, and in the following year was drafted to the Western Front. Whilst overseas he was attached to the Labour Battalion of his Regiment and was engaged on important duties in road repairs in the Somme, Arras and Cambrai sectors. After the Armistice he advanced into Germany with the Army of Occupation and was stationed at Cologne. He returned home and was demobilised in April 1920, and holds the General Service and Victory Medals.
2, Brookland Terrace, Huntingdon. Z1234/B.

BAXTER, J. W., Private, Labour Corps.
He joined in June 1917, and two months later proceeded to France. Whilst overseas he was engaged on special duties, including transport work, and was present at the Battles of Ypres, Cambrai, the Somme and Péronne. He returned to England and was demobilised in November 1919, and holds the General Service and Victory Medals.
5, Luke Street, Eynesbury, St. Neots, Hunts. Z1233.

BAXTER, W. W., Private, Northamptonshire Regt.
Volunteering in November 1915, he served at various stations on important duties of a special nature. He was medically unfit for transfer overseas, but did very valuable work at home, and was demobilised in January 1919.
19, Russell Street, St. Neots, Hunts. Z1235.

BEAL, W., Corporal, 2nd Bedfordshire Regiment and Hertfordshire Regiment.
He volunteered in October 1914, and in April 1916 was drafted to France. During his service on the Western Front he was gassed at the Battle of the Somme in July 1916, and was invalided home to hospital. He rejoined his unit in the following year and fought at Arras, Ypres and Cambrai, and in June 1918 was engaged on special duties in connection with Army stores. Demobilised in March 1919, he holds the General Service and Victory Medals.
7, Jubilee Terrace, Eaton Ford, St. Neots. Z1236.

BEARD, B., Sapper, Royal Engineers.
He volunteered in October 1915, and six months later was drafted to Egypt, where he did much excellent work. Later he was transferred to Palestine and took part in the Battles of Gaza, the capture of Jerusalem and Jaffa, and in other important engagements during the Advance of General Allenby's Forces. He was demobilised in September 1919, and holds the General Service and Victory Medals
19, Woburn Road, Kempston, Beds. X1239.

BEARD, C., Private, Royal Fusiliers.
Volunteering in January 1915, he proceeded to France in September of the following year on the completion of his training. Whilst overseas he took part in severe fighting at the Battles of the Somme, Arras and Ypres, but was invalided home with fever in August 1917. After spending several months in hospital, he was discharged as medically unfit for further service in March 1918, and holds the General Service and Victory Medals. 76, Bunyan Road, Kempston, Beds. X1237.

BEARD, E. J., Sergeant, Bedfordshire Regiment.
A serving soldier, at the outbreak of war he was sent to the Western Front early in 1915, and took part in the Battles of Neuve Chapelle and Festubert. He was afterwards drafted to the Dardanelles, and served at the Landing at Suvla Bay and in subsequent operations until the Evacuation of the Peninsula. Proceeding then to Italy, he was in action in various engagements on the Piave and the Asiago Plateaux until the cessation of hostilities. He advanced into Germany with the Rhine Army and was stationed at Cologne, where he was still serving in 1920. He holds the 1914–15 Star, and the General Service and Victory Medals. 28, Great Butt Street, Bedford. X1240.

BEARD, H., Guardsman, Grenadier Guards.
He joined in January 1916, and later in the same year proceeded to France, where he took part in severe fighting at Arras and Ypres and in the Battle of the Somme. He was reported missing on September 25th, 1916, after an engagement at Combles, and was later officially presumed to have been killed in action on that day. He was entitled to the General Service and Victory Medals.
"A costly sacrifice upon the altar of freedom."
Stagsden, Beds. Z1241.

BEARD, H. R., C.Q.M.S., 5th Oxford. & Bucks. L.I.
He volunteered in September 1914, and nine months later was drafted to the Western Front, where he served with distinction at the Battles of the Somme, Arras, Ypres and St. Quentin, took part in the Retreat and Advance of 1918, and was wounded in action. In May 1919 he was sent to the East, and was stationed at Cairo in Egypt, and at Damascus in Palestine. He was demobilised in May 1920, and holds the 1914–15 Star, and the General Service and Victory Medals.
26, London Road, Stony Stratford, Bucks. Z1238.

BEASLEY, H., Private, 2nd Bedfordshire Regt. and Labour Corps.
A serving soldier at the outbreak of war, he was retained on important duties at home for some time owing to an attack of nephritis. In October 1916, however, he was sent to France, and played a prominent part in the Battles of the Somme, Arras, Ypres and Cambrai. He received his discharge in February 1919, and holds the General Service and Victory Medals. 40, St. Leonard's Street, Bedford. X1242.

BEATTIE, A., Corporal, 7th Argyll and Sutherland Highlanders.
Mobilised in August 1914, he proceeded to the Western Front in December and served with distinction at the Battles of Ypres (II.) (where he was wounded in action), Hill 60, Loos, the Somme, Arras, Messines and Cambrai. He also took part in the Retreat and Advance of 1918, and was eventually discharged on his return to England in March 1919, holding the 1914–15 Star, and the General Service and Victory Medals.
12, Bower Street, Bedford. Z1243/C.

BEAUCHAMP, A. J., Private, 20th Hussars.
He volunteered in June 1915, and landing in France a year later fought in many sectors of the front. He was in action at the Battles of the Somme, Arras, Ypres and Cambrai, and, during the Advance in June 1918, was wounded. Demobilised in March 1919, he holds the General Service and Victory Medals.
13, Trevor Street, Bedford. X1244.

BEAUMONT, R. A., Private, 2nd Bedfordshire Regiment and Hertfordshire Regiment.
Volunteering in September 1914, he landed in France two months later and took part in the Battles of Ypres, the Somme and Arras. During his service on the Western Front he was twice wounded and was invalided home, later being sent to India, where in 1920 he was still serving. He holds the 1914–15 Star, and the General Service and Victory Medals.
Tempsford, near Sandy, Bedford. Z1245.

BEAUMONT, P. V., Private, Leicestershire Regt.
Volunteering in March 1915, he was drafted in the following December to the Western Front, where he took part in much of the severe fighting, but was unhappily killed in action at Vermelles on March 16th, 1917. He was buried at Philosophe, and was entitled to the General Service and Victory Medals.
"His life for his Country, his soul to God."
5, Farrer Street, Bedford. X1246.

BEDFORD, P., Private, 5th Yorkshire Regiment.
Joining in July 1916, and landing in France in June of the following year, he saw service in may sectors of the front. He did much good work as a driver with the transport of his unit in connection with supplies, and was present during the fighting on the Somme, and at Ypres and Cambrai. Demobilised in 1919, he holds the General Service and Victory Medals.
West Street, Godmanchester, Hunts. Z1247.

BEDFORD, S., Private, Bedfordshire Regiment.
He volunteered in September 1914, and in the following February crossed to France, and fought in many notable engagements, including the Battles of Festubert, Loos, Arras, Ypres and Cambrai. On his return to England in March 1919 he was demobilised, holding the 1914–15 Star, and the General Service and Victory Medals.
8, Victoria Terrace, St. Ives, Hunts. Z1248.

BEETHAM, B. P. A., Pte., R. Warwickshire Regt.
He volunteered in August 1914, and for a time was retained for duties of an important nature in England. Transferred to France in January 1916, he fought in numerous engagements, and was wounded on the Somme in 1917. After receiving hospital treatment he was able to return to the line, and took part in the fighting in the Cambrai sector until the Armistice. Demobilised in March 1919, he holds the General Service and Victory Medals.
Sapley Lane, Hartford, Hunts. Z1249/B.

BEETHAM, R. A., Gunner, R.G.A.
He volunteered in August 1914, and in June of the following year proceeded to France, where he took an active part in the heavy fighting on the Somme. He was severely gassed, and after being in hospital some considerable time, unfortunately died in May 1920. He was entitled to the General Service and Victory Medals.
"His memory is cherished with pride."
Sapley Lane, Hartford, Hunts. Z1249/A.

BEGLEY, F. A., Pte., Royal Warwickshire Regt.
He joined in March 1916, and landing in France four months later, took part in the severe fighting on the Somme. He was unhappily killed in action at Ovillers on August 19th, 1916, and was entitled to the General Service and Victory Medals.
"He died the noblest death a man may die,
Fighting for God and right and liberty."
90, Tickford Street, Newport Pagnell, Bucks. Z1250/B.

BEGLEY, W. J., Pte., Royal Warwickshire Regt.
He joined in June 1916, and a month later was sent to India, where he rendered very valuable services at various stations. He took part in the fighting during the Afghanistan risings, and remained in the East until January 1920, when he was demobilised. He holds the General Service and Victory Medals, and the India General Service Medal (with Clasp, Afghanistan North West Frontier, 1919).
90, Tickford Street, Newport Pagnell. Z1250/A.

BEGRAVE, A. C., Private, 4th Bedfordshire Regt.
He joined in 1916, and in the following year proceeded to France, where he saw much active service. He fought and was wounded at Ypres, and after receiving hospital treatment, was discharged as medically unfit in December 1919. He holds the General Service and Victory Medals.
Alconbury Weston, Huntingdon. Z1251.

BEHAGG, F. H., Private, 4th Bedfordshire Regt.
He was mobilised in August 1914, and proceeded to France early in the following year. During his service on the Western Front, he was in action at the Battles of Loos, Albert, the Somme (at Delville Wood), Arras, Bullecourt, Ypres and Epéhy, and throughout the Retreat and Advance of 1918. He holds the 1914–15 Star, and the General Service and Victory Medals, and was discharged in March 1919.
Pidley, Hunts. Z2966/B—Z2967/B.

BELL, J., Driver, R.A.S.C.

He volunteered in April 1915 and, landing in France a month later, did valuable work in transporting ammunition and supplies to the forward areas. He was present during the fierce fighting on the Somme, and at Ypres, Arras and Cambrai, and after the cessation of hostilities proceeded with the Army of Occupation into Germany. Demobilised in September 1919, he holds the 1914–15 Star, and the General Service and Victory Medals. 51, Coventry Street, Bedford. Z1252

BELL, W., Private, R.M.L.I.

He volunteered in September 1914, and in April of the following year proceeded to Gallipoli, where, after taking part in the Landing at Cape Helles, he saw severe fighting, especially at Suvla Bay, until the Evacuation of the Peninsula. He was then transferred to the Western Front, but was shortly afterwards wounded in action at Loos and admitted to hospital at Northampton. He was invalided from the Army in September 1917, and holds the 1914–15 Star, and the General Service and Victory Medals.
Hog Lane, Church End, Towcester, Northants. Z2866.

BELLAMY, A., Corporal, 7th Bedfordshire Regt.

Volunteering in September 1914, he proceeded in the following year to France. Whilst there he took part in the fighting at the Battles of Loos, Vimy Ridge and the Somme, where he was unfortunately wounded. After receiving hospital treatment, he was discharged as medically unfit in September 1917, and holds the 1914–15 Star, and the General Service and Victory Medals.
Berckley Street, Eynesbury, St. Neots, Hunts. Z1258.

BELLAMY, A., Private, Royal Irish Fusiliers.

Mobilised in August 1914, he was shortly afterwards drafted to France, and fought in the memorable Retreat from Mons, and was shell-shocked. He returned home, and six months later was drafted to the East, and saw service in Salonika, Egypt and Palestine, taking part in the fighting at Gaza and in many minor engagements. In 1918 he was transferred to the Western Front, and was in action during the Retreat and Advance of that year. He holds the Mons Star, and the General Service and Victory Medals, and in February 1919 was discharged.
27, Russell Street, St. Neots, Hunts. Z1256/B.

BELLAMY, B., Sergeant, R.A.S.C.

Mobilised on the outbreak of war, he at once proceeded with his unit to France and did valuable work in the Retreat from Mons and in the Battles of Le Cateau, the Marne and the Aisne. He was severely wounded at Ypres in November 1914, and returning to England, was invalided out of the Service in March of the following year. He holds the Mons Star, and the General Service and Victory Medals.
C1234.

BELLAMY, C., Corporal, 1st Bedfordshire Regt.

Mobilised in August 1914, he quickly proceeded to France, and was in action during the Retreat from Mons, and at the Battles of the Marne, Festubert and Hill 60. He was wounded on the Somme in July 1916 and invalided home, but on recovery returned to the Western Front, and was shortly afterwards transferred to Italy, where he served for about five months. Rejoining his unit on the Western Front, he remained there until discharged in February 1919, and holds the Mons Star, and the General Service and Victory Medals.
27, Russell Street, St. Neots, Hunts. Z1256/A—Z1257/A.

BELLAMY, E. A., 2nd Lieut., 1st Northants. Regt.

Volunteering in September 1914, he proceeded in the following year to France, and amongst other engagements was in action at Ypres, on the Somme and at Arras. He was wounded at Cambrai in 1918, and was invalided home, and on recovery was retained on light duties at Sheerness before being sent to Ireland. Demobilised in August 1919, he holds the 1914–15 Star, and the General Service and Victory Medals.
65, Ford End Road, Bedford. Z1254/A.

BELLAMY, F., Sapper, Royal Engineers.

Volunteering in March 1915, he embarked in the same year for France, and served in many sectors of the front. He was present during the fighting at Vimy Ridge, Arras, Ypres, Passchendaele, Cambrai, and in other engagements until hostilities ceased. He then proceeded to Germany with the Army of Occupation, and was stationed on the Rhine. Demobilised in April 1919, he holds the General Service and Victory Medals. 25, Greenhill Lane, Bedford. X1255.

BELLAMY, F. H., Private, Queen's (Royal West Surrey Regiment).

He joined in 1917, and in March of the following year crossed to France, and took part in the Retreat and Advance of that year. After the Armistice he proceeded with the Army of Occupation to Germany, and was engaged on clerical duties at Cologne. On his return home in November 1919 he was demobilised, holding the General Service and Victory Medals.
15, Avenue Road, Huntingdon. Z1253.

BENBOW, C. J., Driver, Royal Field Artillery.

Joining in February 1918, he proceeded after a brief course of training to France, and took part in the fighting in the Cambrai sector until the end of the war. Afterwards he was sent with the Army of Occupation into Germany, and served at Cologne. Returning home in October 1919 he was demobilised, holding the General Service and Victory Medals.
Bow Brick Hill, near Bletchley, Bucks. Z1259.

BENNELL, E. E., Private, King's Own (Royal Lancashire Regiment).

Volunteering in December 1915, he was drafted in the following year to the East. During his service in Salonika he took part in much of the fighting on the Vardar, Doiran and Struma fronts, and was also in action at Monastir. On his return home in March 1919 he was demobilised, and holds the General Service and Victory Medals.
63, Commercial Road, Bedford. Z1260.

BENNETT, C. A., Driver, Royal Engineers.

He joined in 1916, and later in the same year crossed to France, where he saw much heavy fighting. He was present during the Battles of the Somme, Arras, Ypres and Cambrai, and did important transport work in various sectors. Demobilised in February 1919, he holds the General Service and Victory Medals. Broad Green, Cranfield, Bedford. Z1271.

BENNETT, C. L., Sapper, Royal Engineers.

Volunteering in July 1915, he was drafted a month later to Gallipoli, and took part in the Landing at Suvla Bay and in many minor engagements throughout that campaign. After the Evacuation of the Gallipoli Peninsula he was drafted to Palestine, and whilst attached to the Camel Corps did very valuable work at Gaza, Jerusalem and Aleppo. On his return to England in June 1919 he was demobilised, holding the General Service and Victory Medals.
30, Greenfield Road, Newport Pagnell. Z1269/B.

BENNETT, F., Private, 1/5th Bedfordshire Regt.

He volunteered in September 1914, and, proceeding in the following year to the East, saw much service in Egypt and Palestine. He was in action at Gaza, Haifa, Jaffa and in many minor engagements with General Allenby's Forces. Returning home in 1919 he was demobilised, and holds the 1914–15 Star, and the General Service and Victory Medals.
Keeley Green, Wootton, Bedford. Z1272/D.

BENNETT, F. A., Private, 2nd Essex Regiment.

He joined in February 1917, and after a course of training proceeded to France. Whilst in this theatre of war he fought in many notable engagements, including that of Arras, where he was taken prisoner. On March 28th, 1918, he was reported missing, but is now presumed to have been killed. He was entitled to the General Service and Victory Medals.

"His memory is cherished with pride."

29, Foster Street, Bedford. X1265/B.

BENNETT, G., Corporal, 1/5th Bedfordshire Regt.

Volunteering in April 1915, he embarked in the same year for Egypt, and whilst in the East saw much fighting. He later proceeded to Palestine, and took part in the operations at Jaffa, Haifa, Gaza and Aleppo, and in various other engagements, until hostilities ended. Returning home in May 1919 he was demobilised, holding the 1914–15 Star, and the General Service and Victory Medals.
Keeley Green, Wootton Bedford. Z1272/B.

BENNETT, H., Private, 2nd Bedfordshire Regt.

He joined in January 1917, and, after a course of training, served at various stations as Band Boy, and did much useful work. Owing to his being under military age, he was not able to obtain a transfer overseas, but rendered valuable service until demobilised in May 1919.
Keeley Green, Wootton, Bedford. Z1272/A.

BENNETT, H. J., Private, Oxford. & Bucks. L.I.

He volunteered in September 1914, and in the following year crossed to France and fought at Ypres and in other sectors of the front. Transferred to Salonika, he took part in the operations on the Vardar and Doiran fronts, remaining in that seat of war until after the Armistice. Demobilised in April 1919, he holds the 1914–15 Star, and the General Service and Victory Medals.
30, Greenfield Road, Newport Pagnell. Z1269/C.

BENNETT, H. J., Tpr., Bedfordshire Lancers.

He volunteered in December 1915, and after having completed his training served at various stations on important duties. Later he was drafted to Ireland, where he did much valuable work. Owing to medical unfitness, he was not able to obtain a transfer to a fighting area, but rendered valuable services until demobilised in April 1919.
Tilbrook, Kimbolton, Hunts. Z1263.

BENNETT, J. W., Sapper, Royal Engineers.

Volunteering in August 1914, he proceeded in the following year to France, and served with a Tunnelling Company on various sectors of the front on mine-laying and other important duties. He was in action at the Battles of Ypres, Loos, the Somme and Cambrai and whilst abroad was twice wounded. On his return to England in March 1919 he was demobilised, holding the 1914–15 Star, and the General Service and Victory Medals. 1, Hills Yard, Sherington, Newport Pagnell. Z1261/B.

BENNETT, M., Private, 1/4th Somerset L.I.
He joined in January 1917, and in November of the same year was sent to India and served on important duties at various stations. Transferred to Mesopotamia, he took part in the operations at Baghdad, but contracted malaria and returned to India, later proceeding to Salonika, where he remained until December 1919, when he was demobilised. He holds the General Service and Victory Medals.
Northampton Terrace, Newport Pagnell, Bucks. Z1267.

BENNETT, M. F., Corporal, R.G.A.
Joining in October 1916, he served, after having completed his training at various stations, on important Police and other duties. Owing to medical unfitness he was not able to obtain a transfer overseas, but rendered valuable services until demobilised in August 1919.
45, Greenfield Road, Newport Pagnell, Bucks. Z1266.

BENNETT, P., Private, Suffolk Regiment.
Joining in 1916, he proceeded in the same year to France, but after a short period of service was invalided home. On recovery he returned to the Western Front, and was in action at Ypres, Cambrai and on the Somme. After the conclusion of hostilities he went with the Army of Occupation into Germany. Demobilised in September 1919, he holds the General Service and Victory Medals.
Cambridge Street, St. Neots, Hunts. Z1264.

BENNETT, P. J., Sapper, Royal Engineers.
Volunteering in July 1915, he embarked in the following November for France and served in many sectors of the front. Amongst other engagements, he was present at the Battles of the Somme, Arras, Ypres, Passchendaele (where he was wounded) and Cambrai. Demobilised in February 1919, he holds the 1914–15 Star, and the General Service and Victory Medals. 29, Foster Street, Bedford. X1265/A.

BENNETT, V. B., A.B., Royal Navy.
Volunteering in December 1915, he underwent a course of training at Devonport. He was then posted to H.M.S. "Warspite," with which he was engaged on important patrol and escort duties and also in the transport of supplies to Egypt and Russia. He later served on board H.M.S. "Centaur," but returned to port and was demobilised in March 1920, and holds the General Service and Victory Medals.
30, Greenfield Road, Newport Pagnell. Z1269/A.

BENNETT, W. C., Private, Oxford. and Bucks. L.I.
Joining in January 1916, he proceeded in the following July to France. There he fought in many notable engagements, including those of the Somme, Cambrai, and in the Retreat and subsequent Allied Advance of 1918. Afterwards he was sent with the Army of Occupation into Germany, serving on the Rhine until March 1919, when he was demobilised. He holds the General Service and Victory Medals.
14, Greenfield Road, Newport Pagnell. Z1268.

BENNETT, W. H., Rifleman, K.R.R.C.
Mobilised at the outbreak of war, he quickly proceeded to France and was in action in the Retreat from Mons and the subsequent battles. He was wounded at La Bassée in October 1914, but on recovery returned to the line and fought at Ypres, Loos, Vimy Ridge and on the Somme. In December 1916 he was transferred to Salonika, and saw much fighting on the Vardar and Doiran fronts until hostilities ceased. Returning home in March 1919 he was then discharged, and holds the Mons Star, and the General Service and Victory Medals.
6, Pattershall Street, Bedford. X1270.

BENNETT, W. J., Private, Machine Gun Corps.
Joining in 1917, he crossed in the same year to France, where he served until November 1919. During this period he took an active part in many notable battles, including those of Arras, Ypres, Cambrai and the Somme. He holds the General Service and Victory Medals, and in 1920 was still in the Army.
Keeley Green, Wootton, Bedford. Z1272/C.

BENNETT, W. J. S., Private, R.A.S.C. (M.T.)
Two months after volunteering in November 1915 he was drafted to Egypt, where he was engaged on important duties in the workshops at various stations. He afterwards proceeded into Palestine and there, employed on similar duties, rendered valuable services with his Company until his return home for demobilisation in July 1919. He holds the General Service and Victory Medals.
7, Newton Road, Far Bletchley, Bucks. Z2867.

BENSON, F. W., Private, Machine Gun Corps.
He joined in January 1917, and after a period of training was drafted to the Western Front. There he played a prominent part in heavy fighting at Arras, Ypres and Cambrai, and was wounded in action at Kemmel Hill in August 1918. As a result he was invalided home, sent to East Suffolk Hospital and eventually demobilised in January 1919, holding the General Service and Victory Medals. Wootton, Bedford. Z1274.

BENSON, G., Private, 1st Bedfordshire Regiment.
Mobilised in August 1914, he was at once ordered to France, where he participated in the Battle of Mons and in the Retreat. He later took part in the Battles of the Marne, Ypres, Festubert, Loos, the Somme and Arras, and in November 1917 was transferred to Italy, where he was in action on the Piave front and Asiago Plateau. Returning to France, he saw further service during the final Advance, and was wounded at Cambrai in October 1918. Invalided home, he was eventually discharged in April 1919, and holds the Mons Star, and the General Service and Victory Medals.
Crickets Lane, Goldington, Bedford. Z1273.

BENTON, J. W., Corporal, Queen's (Royal West Surrey Regiment).
Mobilised in August 1914, he was shortly afterwards discharged as medically unfit for military duty. He, however, rejoined in February 1917, and in the following month was sent to France, where he was in action at Arras, Messines, Ypres, Cambrai, on the Somme front, and at Albert. Later, whilst in charge of working parties of prisoners of war, he did good work until March 1919. He was demobilised a month later, and holds the General Service and Victory Medals.
Woolpack Lane, St. Ives, Hunts. TZ1275.

BERRILL, A., Sapper, Royal Engineers.
Called up from the Reserve at the outbreak of war in August 1914, he was drafted in the following June to the Dardanelles, and, after serving at the Landing at Suvla Bay, was admitted to hospital suffering from malaria and dysentery. On his recovery he was transferred to France, and whilst stationed on the Somme and Ancre fronts was employed with his Company in building bridges and in other important duties. After the Armistice he proceeded with the Army of Occupation to Germany, and remained there until February 1920, when he returned home. Discharged in the following month, he holds the 1914–15 Star, and the General Service and Victory Medals.
29, Patteshall Street, Bedford. X1277.

BERRILL, G., Private, 1st Bedfordshire Regiment and Tank Corps.
He was mobilised in August 1914, and, proceeding a month later to the Western Front, took part in the Retreat from Mons. He subsequently played a prominent part in many important engagements, including the Battles of Ypres, Festubert, Loos, the Somme, Arras and Cambrai, and performed excellent work. Returning home after the Armistice, he was discharged in January 1919, and holds the Mons Star, and the General Service and Victory Medals.
River Terrace, Eynesbury, St. Neots, Hunts. Z1276.

BERRINGER, A. H., Staff-Sergeant, R.A.O.C.
Mobilised in August 1914, he was at once drafted to France, where he served until after the termination of hostilities. During his service overseas he performed consistently good work engaged on important duties, and after serving through the Retreat from Mons, was present during the Battles of the Marne, Festubert, Lens, Albert, Ypres and the Somme. Discharged in April 1919, he holds the Mons Star, and the General Service and Victory Medals.
Earith, Hunts. Z1278.

BERRINGER, A. R., Gunner, R.G.A.
Serving at the outbreak of war in August 1914, he was sent to France early in the following year. In this theatre of war he took part with his Battery in many important engagements, including the Battles of Festubert, Albert, Vimy Ridge, the Somme, Messines Ridge, Cambrai, Ypres and the Aisne, and did excellent work. Returning home after the Armistice, he was discharged in 1919 after six years with the Colours, holding the 1914–15 Star, and the General Service and Victory Medals.
Eaton Socon, Beds. Z1279/A.

BERRINGTON, A. G., L/Corporal, Middlesex Regiment and Labour Corps.
He joined in October 1916, and, after a period of service at Bedford and Crawley, was drafted in the following year to France, where he was employed on various duties of an important nature in the Arras, Passchendaele, Cambrai and Bapaume sectors. Subsequently, proceeding to Germany, he served with the Army of Occupation at Cologne, and was eventually demobilised in October 1919, holding the General Service and Victory Medals.
Old Harrowden, near Bedford. Z1280.

BERRINGTON, R. R., Sapper, Royal Engineers.
He joined in December 1916, and proceeding in the following September to the Western Front, was employed on various duties of an important nature. He served on the Somme and Cambrai fronts until 1918, when he was transferred to Italy, where he remained until the following year. During his service overseas he did excellent work with his unit, and was demobilised in March 1919, holding the General Service and Victory Medals.
97, Bower Street, Bedford. Z1281.

BERRY, G. D., Air Mechanic, Royal Air Force.
Joining in August 1917, he was not successful in obtaining a transfer to a theatre of war. Retained on Home Service, he was stationed in Shropshire and employed on duties which demanded a high degree of technical skill. He rendered services of a valuable nature until he was demobilised in March 1919.
26, Abbey Road, Old Bradwell, Bucks. Z1282.

BERRY, H. E., Private, 7th Wiltshire Regiment.
He volunteered in September 1914, and 12 months later proceeded to France. After two months' service on the Western Front he was drafted to Salonika, where he took part in several actions on the Struma and Vardar fronts, and was awarded the Serbian Cross of Kara George. Returning to France in May 1918, he took part in further fighting and was wounded at the Battle of Le Cateau (II.) in the following October. Invalided home as the result, he was eventually demobilised in June 1919, and holds the 1914–15 Star, and the General Service and Victory Medals.
25, York Road, Stony Stratford, Bucks. TZ1283.

BERRY, J. G., Private, 1st Northants. Regiment.
Having enlisted in October 1911, he proceeded to the Western Front shortly after the outbreak of war in August 1914, and there served through the Retreat from Mons. After taking part also in many minor engagements, he was severely wounded in action at Ypres in November 1914, and admitted to hospital at Manchester. He was finally invalided from the Army in June 1915, and holds the Mons Star, and the General Service and Victory Medals.
Sargent Yard, Towcester, Northants. Z2868.

BERWICK, A. J., Sapper, Royal Engineers.
Volunteering in June 1915, he was sent to Egypt in the following January, and proceeded later into Palestine. In this theatre of hostilities he served at Gaza, Jerusalem, Jaffa, and on the River Jordan, and was employed in road-making and building pontoon bridges. He did good work until he returned home for demobilisation in March 1919, holding the General Service and Victory Medals.
Wilsted Road, Elstow, near Bedford. X1284.

BESTER, H. A., Corporal, 11th Suffolk Regiment and Middlesex Regiment.
He joined in 1916, and in July of the same year was drafted to France. There he played a prominent part with his unit in strenuous fighting on the Somme front, also at Messines Ridge, Ypres and Cambrai. He did excellent work until he was evacuated to England suffering from shell-shock, and, after spending some time in hospital, was eventually invalided out of the Service in March 1919, holding the General Service and Victory Medals. Melchbourne, Beds. Z1285.

BETTLE, J., Sapper, Royal Engineers.
He volunteered in November 1915, and was drafted to France in the following year, remaining there until after the termination of hostilities. During his services overseas he was employed constructing bridges, and in other important duties at Kemmel Hill, Ypres, Vimy Ridge, on the Somme front, and at Cambrai. He performed excellent work until returning home for demobilisation in January 1919, holding the General Service and Victory Medals.
High Street, Cranfield, Beds. Z1287.

BETTLE, J. W., Driver, R.E. and R.F.A.
Volunteering in 1915, he was retained at home on important duties, and was stationed at Peterborough and Newmarket, and in Essex until 1917, when he was transferred to the Royal Field Artillery. After a further period of service at Aldershot, he was sent to France, and was in action at Arras, Messines Ridge, Lens and Cambrai. He was demobilised in June 1919, and holds the General Service and Victory Medals.
West End, Cranfield, Beds. TZ1286/B.

BETTLE, W., Rifleman, 16th London Regiment (Queen's Westminster Rifles).
He joined in August 1918, but was not successful in obtaining a transfer overseas before the termination of hostilities. He, however, proceeded to Germany in November 1918, and was employed on various duties of an important nature whilst serving with the Army of Occupation on the Rhine, until February 1920, when he returned home for demobilisation.
West End, Cranfield, Beds. TZ1286/C.

BETTLES, A., Private, Labour Corps.
Joining in March 1916, he was sent a month later to the Western Front, where he served in the Somme, Ypres and Arras sectors. He was employed with his company on transport duties and later in road-making, and remained overseas for some months after the Armistice. Demobilised in March 1919, he holds the General Service and Victory Medals.
2, Spring Gardens, Castle Road, Bedford. X1288.

BEWELL, J. R., Private, Labour Corps.
He volunteered in January 1915, and later in the same year was drafted to France. There he took part in the heavy fighting on the Somme and other fronts, and did good work until 1916, when he was evacuated to England on account of ill-health. On his recovery he served at Dover and Brighton, and was employed on duties of an important character until he was demobilised in February 1919, holding the 1914–15 Star, and the General Service and Victory Medals.
29, Bower Street, Bedford. Z1289.

BICHENER, E., Driver, R.A.S.C.
Joining in August 1918, he was not successful in securing a transfer to a theatre of war before the signing of the Armistice. After being employed on transport duties at Crowborough, he was later sent to Germany and served with the Army of Occupation. He was demobilised on his return home in April 1920, having rendered valuable services.
1, College Street, Kempston. Z1292/B.

BICHENER, F. H., Guardsman, Grenadier Guards.
He was mobilised in August 1914, and two months later proceeded to France, where he took part in the Battles of the Aisne and Ypres, and was wounded at the latter place in November 1914. Invalided home he returned to France in the following year, was again in action at Festubert, and was wounded for the second time in September 1915 during the Battle of Loos. Evacuated to England, he was eventually discharged in July 1916 as unfit for further military service, and holds the 1914 Star, and the General Service and Victory Medals.
6, Ford End Cottages, Queen's Park, Bedford. X1291.

BICHENER, H. F., Driver, Royal Engineers.
Volunteering in August 1914, he was drafted in the following year to Egypt, and was later sent to Palestine. There he served at Gaza and Jerusalem, engaged on transport and other duties of an important character. During his service overseas he performed consistently good work, and was demobilised on returning home in June 1919, holding the 1914–15 Star, and the General Service and Victory Medals.
1, College Street, Kempston. Z1292/A.

BICHENER, J. L., Sapper, Royal Engineers.
He volunteered in September 1914, and three months afterwards proceeded to the Western Front. In this theatre of war he served in the Ypres, Neuve Chapelle and Loos sectors and at Givenchy, where he was severely wounded in February 1915. As a result he was invalided home and spent a considerable time in hospital, being eventually discharged in 1919. He holds the 1914–15 Star, and the General Service and Victory Medals. 10, College Road, Bedford. Z1290.

BICK, L. E., Tpr., Bedfordshire Lancers and Lincolnshire Lancers.
He volunteered in March 1915, and later in the same year proceeded to the Western Front. After fighting in the Battles of Loos and the Somme, his health broke down, and he was invalided to England in 1916. On his recovery he served in Ireland for a short time, but in November 1917 was drafted to Palestine. There he took an active part in fierce fighting at Gaza and Jaffa. On his return home in March 1919 he was demobilised, holding the 1914–15 Star, and the General Service and Victory Medals.
63, Westbourne Road, Queen's Park, Bedford. Z1293/A.

BICK, W. R., Driver, Royal Naval Air Service.
He joined in January 1918, but was unsuccessful in obtaining a transfer to the war zone. After his period of training he was stationed at Eastbourne, where he was engaged on important transport work, which he performed in a highly capable manner. He was eventually demobilised in February 1919.
63, Westbourne Road, Queen's Park, Bedford. Z1293/B.

BIGG, F., Private, 12th East Surrey Regiment.
Joining in June 1916, he was, on completion of his training three months later, drafted overseas. Whilst serving on the Western Front he saw heavy fighting in the Somme, Ypres, Arras and Messines sectors, but was taken prisoner at Cambrai in March 1918. He remained in captivity until the following December, and was subsequently demobilised in August 1919, holding the General Service and Victory Medals.
5, Bunyan Road, Kempston, Bedford. X1294.

BIGGS, F. E., Private, 6th Oxford. & Bucks. L.I.
In November 1914 he volunteered, and in the following year was sent to France, where he was in action at Ypres, Laventie, Neuve Chapelle, Fleurbaix and St. Quentin. He was wounded at Ypres in June 1916, and invalided to England, but returned to the Western Front in February 1917. He was again wounded in action at Cambrai, and on his recovery was transferred to Italy, where he served until demobilised in February 1919. He holds the 1914–15 Star, and the General Service and Victory Medals.
57, High Street, New Bradwell, Bucks. Z1295.

BIGGS, F. J. S., Private, Oxford. & Bucks. L.I.
Volunteering in April 1915, he proceeded overseas in February 1916. During his service in France he took part in engagements at Ypres, the Somme, Péronne, Passchendaele and Arras, before being transferred to the Italian front. There, whilst engaged in heavy fighting on the Asiago Plateau in June 1918, he was taken prisoner, and kept in captivity for six months. On his release in December 1918 he was demobilised, holding the General Service and Victory Medals.
Simpson, near Bletchley, Bucks. Z1296.

BIGGS, J. T., L/Corporal, Royal Berkshire Regt.
He joined in March 1917, and on completion of his training on Salisbury Plain, was drafted to France. On this front he was in action in numerous engagements, especially in the Somme and Cambrai sectors. In November 1918 he was sent back to England suffering from trench fever, and was in hospital at Nottingham until demobilised in December 1918. He holds the General Service and Victory Medals.
Simpson, near Bletchley, Bucks. Z1297.

BIGNELL, A. J., Private, 3rd Worcestershire Regt.
Joining in March 1916, he was trained at Ipswich and Dublin, and five months later proceeded to the Western Front. There he took an active part in fierce fighting in the Somme and Cambrai sectors, and was unfortunately killed in action at Cambrai in September 1918. He was entitled to the General Service and Victory Medals.
"A valiant Soldier, with undaunted heart he breasted life's last hill." Moulsoe, Bucks. Z1298/B.

BIGNELL, G. W., Sergt., 7th Gloucestershire Regt.
He volunteered in September 1914, and in January of the following year was drafted overseas. Whilst serving in France he took a prominent part in numerous important engagements until wounded in action at Ypres in 1915. He was sent to hospital in England, and on his recovery in March 1916 proceeded to Mesopotamia. After ten months' service in this theatre of war, he fell fighting at Kut on January 25th, 1917. He was entitled to the 1914–15 Star, and the General Service and Victory Medals.
"Whilst we remember, the sacrifice is not in vain."
Moulsoe, Bucks. Z1298/A.

BIGNELL, H., Bombardier, Royal Field Artillery.
Volunteering in December 1915, he was trained at Northampton and Salisbury Plain, and in June 1916 was sent to France On this Front he did excellent work with his Battery in important engagements, including the Battles of the Somme and Cambrai, but was unhappily killed at Cambrai on November 9th, 1917. He was entitled to the General Service and Victory Medals. "His life for his Country."
Moulsoe, Bucks. Z1298/C.

BIGNELL, J. H., Private, 7th Northants. Regiment.
A month after the outbreak of war he volunteered, and in January 1915 was ordered to the Western Front, where he served for over three years. During that time he was in action in different sectors of the line, and was wounded and taken prisoner at Cambrai in March 1918. He remained in captivity until the close of hostilities, and on his release was demobilised in March 1919, holding the 1914–15 Star, and the General Service and Victory Medals. Moulsoe, Bucks. Z1298/D.

BIGNELL, S. J., Private, 8th Leicestershire Regt.
Volunteering in August 1914, he was drafted to the Western Front on completing his training in January of the following year, and there saw severe fighting in various sectors. After taking part in the Battles of Ypres, the Somme and Arras, and many other engagements, he was wounded in action and taken prisoner near Ypres in May 1917, and was held in captivity in Germany until December of the following year. Demobilised in March 1919, he holds the 1914–15 Star, and the General Service and Victory Medals.
7, New Row, Pauler's Pury, Towcester, Northants. Z2869.

BILLING, E. W., Private, Essex Regiment.
He joined the Army in March 1916, and on conclusion of a period of training was later in the same year drafted to Egypt. There he was engaged in guarding prisoners of war at Cairo, until transferred to Palestine. In this theatre of war he took part in numerous engagements and saw fierce fighting at Gaza. On returning to England he was demobilised in July 1919, holding the General Service and Victory Medals.
Wootton, Bedford. Z1300/A.

BILLING, T., Sergeant, 5th Bedfordshire Regt.
When war was declared in August 1914, he volunteered, and after serving at Bury-St.-Edmunds and Norwich, was sent to Gallipoli in the following year. He took a conspicuous part in various engagements on the Peninsula, and whilst engaged in heavy fighting at Suvla Bay was killed on August 15th, 1915. He was entitled to the 1914–15 Star, and the General Service and Victory Medals.
"Great deeds cannot die."
Wootton, Bedford. Z1300/B.

BILLINGHAM, E. A., Sapper, Royal Engineers.
He volunteered in September 1914, and three months later proceeded to the Western Front, where he served for over four years. During that time he took part in numerous important engagements, including the Battles of Neuve Chapelle, Hill 60, Loos, the Somme, Ypres, Arras and Cambrai. He was eventually demobilised in February 1919, and holds the 1914–15 Star, and the General Service and Victory Medals.
36, Muswell Road, Bedford. TZ1301/C.

BILLINGHAM, T. W., Sergeant, Royal Engineers.
A month after the declaration of war in August 1914, he volunteered, and in July 1915 was sent to Gallipoli. There he fought with distinction at Suvla Bay and Anzac, but unfortunately contracted dysentery and died at Malta on November 25th, 1915. He was entitled to the 1914–15 Star, and the General Service and Victory Medals.
"His memory is cherished with pride."
36, Muswell Road, Bedford. TZ1301/B.

BILLINGS, T., Private, 7th Buffs (East Kent Regt).
He volunteered in January 1916, and later in the same year was drafted overseas. During his service on the Western Front he was in action at Vimy Ridge and Passchendaele, and was badly wounded at Ypres in October 1917, which wound resulted in the loss of a leg. In consequence he was discharged from the Army in November 1918, holding the General Service and Victory Medals. Hemingford Abbots, Hunts. Z1302.

BILLINGTON, E., Private, 2nd Bedfordshire Regt.
Volunteering in January 1915, he was on completion of his training sent overseas later in the same year. Whilst on the Western Front he participated in severe fighting at Trônes Wood, and was wounded in action in the Battle of the Somme in 1916. On his recovery he rendered valuable services in connection with agricultural work, until demobilised in March 1919, holding the 1914–15 Star, and the General Service and Victory Medals. Church Row, Cranfield, Bedford. Z1299.

BILLINGTON, F., Shoeing-Smith, 133rd R.F.A.
When war broke out in August 1914, he was already in the Army, and was stationed in India. Whilst proceeding to the scene of activities in Mesopotamia he contracted dysentery, and was invalided to England in 1915. On his recovery he was sent to the Western Front, and, after taking part in many important engagements, was taken prisoner at Cambrai in March 1918. After the cessation of hostilities he was released, and in 1920 was still serving, holding the General Service and Victory Medals. The Common, Aspley Guise, Bedford. Z1303.

BILLINGTON, F. E. (M.M.), L/Corporal, Warwickshire Regiment.
At the outbreak of hostilities in August 1914, he volunteered, and five months later was ordered to the Western Front. There he was in action in important engagements at Neuve Chapelle, Ypres, Loos, the Somme, Messines, Arras and Cambrai. He was awarded the Military Medal for conspicuous gallantry in the Field, and was demobilised in December 1919, also holding the 1914–15 Star, and the General Service and Victory Medals.
35, York Street, Bedford. Z1492/B.

BILLINGTON, S., Private, Labour Corps.
He volunteered in August 1914, and in the following year was drafted to Gallipoli, where he was in action at Suvla Bay. He was then transferred to the Western Front, and took part in heavy fighting at Loos and Festubert, and was wounded in action. In 1916 he was sent to Salonika, and served in that theatre of war until the termination of the war. On his return home he was demobilised in July 1919, holding the 1914–15 Star, and the General Service and Victory Medals.
Cross Hall Ford, Bedford. Z1304.

BINT, F. G. W., Corporal, 6th Northants. Regt.
In October 1914 he volunteered, and after a period of training was drafted overseas in September 1915. During his service in France he was engaged in severe fighting at Loos, Festubert, Ypres and Vimy Ridge. He was wounded in October 1915, and twice during the operations on the Somme in 1916, and was unhappily killed in action at St. Quentin on March 22nd, 1918. He was entitled to the 1914–15 Star, and the General Service and Victory Medals.
"A costly sacrifice upon the altar of freedom."
22, Duke Street, Aspley Guise, Bedford. Z1305/B—Z1306/B.

BINT, W. H., A.B., R.N.V.R., H.M.S. "Sabre."
He joined the R.N.V.R. in March 1917, but on completion of his training was not successful in procuring a transfer to the fighting areas. He was retained on home defence and served at Scapa Flow and Portsmouth, where he performed excellent work in connection with guarding the coast from enemy attacks. He was eventually demobilised in January 1919.
22, Duke Street, Aspley Guise, Bedford. Z1305/A—Z1306/A.

BIRCH, A., L/Corporal, 7th Leicestershire Regt.
Volunteering in August 1914, he was retained on important work at Halton Camp until 1916, when he was ordered to France. On this front he performed excellent work as a machine gunner in the Ypres, the Somme, Arras, Cambrai, Loos, Lens and La Bassée sectors. He served in France until August 1919, when he was demobilised, holding the General Service and Victory Medals.
34, Bunyan Road, South End, Bedford. Z1307/A.

BIRCH, A. G., Private, 2/1st London Regiment (Royal Fusiliers).
He volunteered in November 1915, and served at Huntingdon and Scarborough, with the Huntingdonshire Cyclist Corps until 1917, when he was drafted to the Western Front. There he was in action in the Ypres sector until wounded and taken prisoner in September 1917. He was released from captivity in December 1918, and was demobilised two months later, holding the General Service and Victory Medals.
20, Princess Street, Huntingdon. Z1308.

BIRD, A. E., Corporal, R.A.S.C.
He volunteered in November 1915, and, in June of the following year, was drafted to the Western Front, where, attached to the 63rd Royal Naval Supply Column, he served in the Somme and Arras sectors until August 1917, when he was invalided home. After three months in hospital, however, he returned to France, where he did much useful work until after the cessation of hostilities. He was demobilised in March 1919, and holds the General Service and Victory Medals.
26, Park Street, Bletchley, Bucks. Z2870.

BIRD, A. J., Sapper, R.E. (486th Field Company).
Volunteering in January 1915, he was later in the same year drafted to Gallipoli, where he was in action at Suvla Bay and was wounded. After the Evacuation of the Peninsula he proceeded to Palestine, and was engaged in severe fighting at Gaza, Jerusalem, Jaffa and Haifa. On his return to England he was demobilised in March 1919, holding the 1914–15 Star, and the General Service and Victory Medals.
35, Woburn Road, Kempston, Bedford. X1314.

BIRD, B. J., C.S.M., R.A.S.C. (M.T.)
He joined in April 1916, and in the following August was drafted to the Western Front, where he rendered valuable services conveying ammunition and supplies to the forward areas. He also took part in fierce fighting at the Somme, Arras, Ypres and Cambrai, and in the final decisive engagements of the war. Demobilised in October 1919, he holds the General Service and Victory Medals. Oakley, Bedford. Z1310.

BIRD, B. R., Private, Labour Corps.
In November 1915 he volunteered, and was sent to the Western Front in June 1917. During his service in France he was engaged in making roads, and also took an active part in engagements at Albert, Ypres, the Somme and St. Quentin. He was gassed at Cambrai in November 1917, and was demobilised in February 1919, holding the General Service and Victory Medals. In September 1919 he re-enlisted, but died from enteric whilst *en route* to India on February 28th, 1920.
"His memory is cherished with pride."
King John's Terrace, London Street, Godmanchester, Hunts. Z1317/B.

BIRD, C., Private, The Buffs (East Kent Regt.).
He joined in December 1917, but on account of his youth was unable to secure a transfer to a theatre of war. Whilst stationed at Dover he was engaged on Coast Defence duties and later was employed on agricultural work at Folkestone and Maidstone. In 1919 he proceeded to India, and in 1920 was still serving in the Army.
King John's Terrace, London Street, Godmanchester, Hunts. Z1317/A.

BIRD, F., Corporal, 1st Bedfordshire Regiment.
At the outbreak of hostilities in August 1914 he was already serving, and at once proceeded with the first Expeditionary Force to the Western Front. There he was engaged in fierce fighting at Mons, Loos, Ypres, Arras, Cambrai, Lille and Armentières, and in various other sectors of the line. In 1920 he was still serving in the Army, and holds the Mons Star, and the General Service and Victory Medals.
Wootton, Bedford. Z1316/A.

BIRD, G., Private, Labour Corps.
He joined in 1916, and after a period of training was employed on agricultural work, which he performed in a very able manner. Owing to ill-health he was not successful in his efforts to secure a transfer to the war zone, but nevertheless rendered valuable services until demobilised in March 1919.
Blunham Terrace, London Road, Sandy, Bedford. Z1315/B.

BIRD, H. R., Gnr., R.F.A.; and Pte., Leinster Regt.
Joining in May 1916, he served at Woolwich and in Ireland, and proceeded in 1917 to Salonika. He saw heavy fighting there, chiefly on the Doiran front, until transferred to Palestine later in the year. On that front he was in action at Gaza and Jerusalem, and after the Armistice served with the Royal Army Service Corps for a few months. On returning home he was demobilised in September 1919, holding the General Service and Victory Medals. King's Ripton, Hunts. Z1311.

BIRD, J., Driver, R.E. (Signal Section).
He volunteered in October 1915, and was retained on important duties at Hitchin until June 1916, when he was drafted overseas. During his service on the Western Front he took part in many important engagements, including those on the Somme and at Albert and Pozières. He remained in France until March 1919, when he was demobilised, holding the General Service and Victory Medals.
9, Park Street, Bletchley, Bucks. Z1312/A.

BIRD, J. W., Private, Queen's Own (Royal West Kent Regiment).
Volunteering in December 1914, he proceeded in June 1915 to France, and after fighting at Ypres, Festubert and Givenchy, was wounded at Loos in September 1915. On his recovery he was sent to Afghanistan and served on the North-West Frontier for nine months. In November 1916 he was transferred to Mesopotamia, where he was in action at Baghdad, Amara, Kut, and Basra. After the Armistice he returned home and re-enlisted for a further period of service, but was discharged as medically unfit in March 1920. He holds the 1914–15 Star, and the General Service and Victory Medals.
King John's Terrace, London Street, Godmanchester, Hunts. Z1317/C.

BIRD, S., Air Mechanic, Royal Air Force.
He joined in 1916, and was engaged on work demanding great technical knowledge at Farnborough, Bradford and Sheffield until 1917, when he was sent overseas. During his service on the Western Front he did good work with his Squadron on the Somme front and at Namur. He was demobilised in March 1919, and holds the General Service and Victory Medals.
9, West Street, Newtown, Huntingdon. Z1318.

BIRD, S., Private, 2nd Bedfordshire Regiment.
When war was declared in August 1914 he volunteered, and in the following year was drafted to the Western theatre of war. There he saw much severe fighting, principally in the Loos, Festubert, the Somme, Ypres, Messines, Passchendaele, Albert and Cambrai sectors. He served in France until March 1919, when he was demobilised, holding the 1914–15 Star, and the General Service and Victory Medals.
Blunham Terrace, London Road, Sandy, Bedford. Z1315/A.

BIRCH, S. J., Private, 2nd Bedfordshire Regiment.
He volunteered in 1914, and on completion of his training was retained on important duties at various stations. Later he proceeded to France and took part in many important engagements, including the Battles of Loos, the Somme and Cambrai, where he was wounded. As a result he was invalided to England and finally discharged as medically unfit for further service in May 1918. He holds the 1914–15 Star, and the General Service and Victory Medals.
Keysoe, Bedfordshire. Z1313.

BIRCH, W. J., Sergt., 1/4th Oxford. & Bucks. L.I.
He volunteered in April 1915, and was retained on very important duties at various stations, and did good work. In 1917 he was drafted to France, where he played a prominent part in many important engagements in various sectors of the front. Later he was transferred to Italy, and was in action on the Piave front, and was wounded and invalided to hospital. Returning to England, he was demobilised in March 1919, and holds the General Service and Victory Medals.
7, Simpson Road, Fenny Stratford, Bucks. Z1312/B.

BISHOP, G. W., Private, 1st East Surrey Regiment.
Joining in November 1917, he proceeded to France in the following April. During his service in this theatre of war he took part in many important engagements in various sectors of the front. In April 1918 he was wounded during heavy fighting, and as a result was sent to England. On his recovery he was engaged on important agricultural work in Huntingdonshire until demobilised in November 1919. He holds the General Service and Victory Medals.
2, Albert Terrace, St. Neots, Hunts. Z1319/A.

BISHOP, H., Private, Bedfordshire Regiment.
He volunteered in June 1915, and shortly afterwards was drafted to France. In the course of his service in this seat of war he took part in the engagements on the Somme and Ypres fronts. He was buried by an explosion, and, owing to his injuries, was invalided home, and, after receiving hospital treatment, was discharged as medically unfit for further service in September 1916. He holds the General Service and Victory Medals. Southoe, Hunts. Z1320.

BIZZELL, F. A., Guardsman, Grenadier Guards.
He joined in March 1917, and in the following December was drafted to the Western Front, where he took part in the engagements at Arras and Albert, and in the Advance at Cambrai. He was reported missing on April 17th, 1918, and is now presumed to have been killed in action on that date. He was entitled to the General Service and Victory Medals.
"His memory is cherished with pride."
8, Churchville Road, Bedford. Z1321.

BLACK, H. E., Corporal, Buffs (East Kent Regt.)
He joined in 1916, and in the same year proceeded to France, where he took part in many important engagements in various sectors of the front. He was in action during the heavy fighting at the Battles of Arras, Ypres and the Somme, and remained in this seat of war until after the Armistice. In April 1920 he was demobilised, and holds the General Service and Victory Medals. Later he re-enlisted and served with the Army of Occupation on the Rhine.
132, Coventry Road, Queen's Park, Bedford. Z1322/B.

BLACK, W. E., Private, R.A.M.C.
He volunteered at the outbreak of hostilities in August 1914, and in the following year was wounded in action on the Gallipoli Peninsula. He was then transferred to Egypt, but later proceeded to Palestine, where he took part in the three Battles of Gaza, and was also present at the capture of Jerusalem and Jaffa. He contracted black fever through risking his life whilst attending to others. He was demobilised in February 1919, and holds the 1914–15 Star, and the General Service and Victory Medals.
132, Coventry Road, Queen's Park, Bedford. Z1322/A.

BLACKWELL, E., Private, 10th King's Liverpool Regiment.
He joined in September 1916, and, on completion of his training in the following year, was drafted to France. In the course of his service in this seat of war he took part in many important engagements. He served at the capture of Vimy Ridge and the Battle of Ypres, and later in the Retreat and Advance of 1918. In March 1919 he was demobilised, and holds the General Service and Victory Medals.
62, Clarence Road, Stony Stratford, Bucks. Z1324/B.

BLACKWELL, G., Private, R.A.V.C.

He volunteered in February 1915, and after a period of training with the Royal Buckinghamshire Hussars was transferred to the Army Veterinary Corps, and was engaged in attending to the sick horses. Later he was drafted to France and served in various sectors of the front, and saw heavy fighting at Arras and Ypres. In August 1917 he was gassed, and as a result was invalided to England, and finally discharged as medically unfit for further military service in March 1918. He holds the General Service and Victory Medals.

2, Rumbolds Lane, Buckingham. Z1325.

BLACKWELL, J. S., Private, Essex Regiment.

He joined in 1916, and, after completing a period of training, was drafted to France, where he took part in many important engagements in various sectors of the front. He was wounded at Loos in 1917, and as a result was invalided to England, and, after a period of treatment, was discharged as medically unfit for further military service in June 1918. He holds the General Service and Victory Medals.

London Road, Girtford, Sandy, Bedfordshire. Z1326.

BLACKWELL, L. F., Private, Bedfordshire Regt.

He volunteered in November 1914, and early in the following year was drafted to France, where he took part in the Battle of Ypres (II.), and was wounded and invalided to hospital. Returning to the Western Front on his recovery, he was again in action throughout many important engagements, and was present at the first and second Battles of the Somme, Arras, Ypres and Cambrai. In March 1919 he was demobilised, and holds the 1914–15 Star, and the General Service and Victory Medals.

9, Bury Avenue, Newport Pagnell, Bucks. Z1323.

BLAIN, A., Gunner, Royal Garrison Artillery (Anti-Aircraft Section).

He joined in 1916, and on completion of his training was engaged on important duties with his Battery at Dover. Owing to his being medically unfit, he was unable to obtain his transfer to a theatre of war, and was finally discharged in June 1918, after a period of valuable services.

Carter Street, Girtford, Sandy, Bedfordshire. Z1328.

BLAIN, P. W., Signaller, Royal Navy, H.M.S. "Dartmouth."

He joined in July 1916, and was posted to H.M.S. "Dartmouth," which ship was engaged on important patrol and escort duties in the North and Mediterranean Seas. He was also present at the bombardment of Durazzo in the Adriatic Sea, and did excellent work until the close of hostilities. In July 1919 he was demobilised, and holds the General Service (with four Clasps) and Victory Medals.

Brick Hill Road, Sandy, Bedfordshire. Z1327.

BLANCHARD, R. J., Chief Stoker, Royal Navy, H.M.S. "Princess Royal."

He was already in the Navy at the outbreak of hostilities, was posted to H.M.S. "Princess Royal," and took part in the Battles of Heligoland Bight, the Dogger Bank and later in the Battle of Jutland. He was afterwards engaged on important patrol duties, attached to the Grand Fleet in the North Sea until the close of war, when he proceeded to Russia on special service. In January 1919 he returned to home waters, and served until discharged in October 1919. He holds the 1914–15 Star, and the General Service (with nine Clasps) and the Victory Medals, and Long Service and Good Conduct Medal.

C1329.

BLAND, A. E., Guardsman, Coldstream Guards.

He joined in March 1917, and, after completing a period of training, was drafted overseas. During his short service on the Western Front he fought in many sectors. He made the supreme sacrifice on November 4th, 1918, being killed in action at Villers-Pol, and was entitled to the General Service and Victory Medals.

"His life for his Country, his soul to God."

High Street, Stoke Goldington Bucks. Z1330/B.

BLAND, C. A., L/Cpl., 1st Bedfordshire Lancers.

Volunteering in December 1914, he was drafted to France in the following year, and during the course of his service in this theatre of war took part in many important engagements in various sectors. He served at the Battles of Hill 60, Ypres and Festubert, and later was in action on the Cambrai front, where he was badly wounded and unfortunately died on January 16th, 1917. He was entitled to the 1914–15 Star, and the General Service and Victory Medals.

"A valiant Soldier, with undaunted heart he breasted life's last hill."

Rabanna Terrace, Clapham, Bedfordshire. Z1331/B.

BLAND, H., Private, Warwickshire Regiment.

He joined in August 1918, and after completing a period of training was retained on important duties. Owing to the early cessation of hostilities, he was unable to proceed overseas but in October 1919 was sent to Ireland, where he was still serving in 1920.

High Street, Stoke Goldington, Bucks. Z1330/C.

BLAND, W. G., Private, Royal Fusiliers.

He volunteered in May 1915, and, after completing a period of training, was drafted to the Western Front, where he was wounded and taken prisoner whilst fighting at the Battle of Vimy Ridge in May 1916. He suffered many hardships in Germany, and was released from captivity after the cessation of hostilities, and, returning to England, was demobilised in September 1919, holding the General Service and Victory Medals. Rabanna Terrace, Clapham, Bedfordshire. Z1331/A.

BLENCOWE, F., Private, Tank Corps.

He was mobilised in 1914, and was retained on important duties at various home stations until early in 1917, when he was drafted to France. There he saw much heavy fighting on the Somme, but was shortly afterwards invalided home and was in hospital for some time. On his recovery he served at Catterick until demobilised in March 1919, and holds the General Service and Victory Medals.

High Street, Gawcott, Buckingham, Bucks. Z1333.

BLENCOWE, J. H., Private, R.A.V.C.

He volunteered in the Oxfordshire and Buckinghamshire Light Infantry in October 1914, but, after a period of training, was discharged as medically unfit in March 1915. In June 1917 he re-enlisted under the Derby Scheme and was drafted to Mesopotamia, where he was engaged in attending to sick and wounded horses at Baghdad, Kut, Amara, Basra, and on the River Tigris. He contracted malaria and was finally discharged in July 1919, and holds the General Service and Victory Medals.

Main Street, Gawcott, Buckingham, Bucks. Z1332.

BLENCOWE, W., Private, Oxford. & Bucks. L.I.

He volunteered in September 1914, and in the following June was drafted to France. In this theatre of war he took part in the Battles of Ypres, the Somme, Arras and Cambrai, and in the Retreat and Advance of 1918. He was demobilised in April 1919, and holds the 1914–15 Star, and the General Service and Victory Medals.

Preston Road, Gawcott, Buckingham, Bucks. Z1334.

BLISS, B. B., Private, 2nd Northants. Regiment.

Already stationed at Alexandria when war broke out in August 1914, he was transferred in October to the Western Front, where he took part in the first Battle of Ypres and many minor engagements. He made the supreme sacrifice, falling in action at Neuve Chapelle in March 1915. He was entitled to the 1914 Star, and the General Service and Victory Medals.

"He died the noblest death a man may die :
Fighting for God and right and liberty."

Heathencote, Towcester, Northants. Z2871.

BLOOM, A. P., Private, Suffolk Regiment.

He joined in April 1917, and during his training was engaged at various home stations. In 1918 he was drafted to India and served on important garrison duties there until hostilities ceased. He was still in India in 1920, and holds the General Service and Victory Medals.

15, Beatrice Street, Kempston, Bedford. Z1335.

BLUNT, A. J., Mechanic, Royal Air Force.

He joined in August 1916, and after a period of training was engaged at various stations on duties which demanded a high degree of technical skill. He was unable to obtain a transfer overseas, but rendered valuable services in connection with the repair and manufacture of aero-engines until his demobilisation in November 1919.

42, Spencer Street, New Bradwell, Bucks. Z1336/C.

BLUNT, F., Private, 4th Oxford. & Bucks. L.I.

Volunteering in August 1914, he was drafted overseas after completing his training. Whilst on the Western Front he took part in several engagements, including those in the Somme, Ypres and Cambrai sectors, and was twice wounded in action. He was demobilised in March 1919, and holds the General Service and Victory Medals.

42, Spencer Street, New Bradwell, Bucks. Z1336/B.

BLUNT, H., Private, Machine Gun Corps.

He joined in April 1916, and in the following year proceeded to the Western Front. Whilst in this seat of war he took part in several engagements, including the Battles of Messines, Ypres and Cambrai, and was badly wounded in action. As a result he was finally discharged in March 1918 as medically unfit for further service. He holds the General Service and Victory Medals.

42, Spencer Street, New Bradwell, Bucks. Z1336/A.

BODLE, C., Private, 1/5th Bedfordshire Regt.

He volunteered in September 1914, and in the following July was drafted to the Dardanelles, where he saw much heavy fighting and was wounded in action. After the Evacuation of the Gallipoli Peninsula he was sent to Egypt and thence proceeded into Palestine, took part in engagements at Jaffa and Gaza, and was present at the fall of Jerusalem. Whilst in the East he also suffered severely from malaria. He returned home and was demobilised in April 1919, and holds the 1914–15 Star, and the General Service and Victory Medals.

38, Littledale Street, Kempston, Bedford. Z1337.

BODLE, R. A., Sergt., 15th (The King's) Hussars.
He was mobilised in August 1914 and almost immediately drafted to the Western Front. There he took part in much heavy fighting at the Battles of Mons, Neuve Chapelle, the Somme, Arras, Ypres and Cambrai. He quickly gained promotion and did continuously good work throughout hostilities, and in 1920 was serving in Ireland. He holds the Mons Star, and the General Service and Victory Medals.
38, Littledale Street, Kempston, Bedford. Z1338.

BODSWORTH, L. B., Private, R.A.O.C.
He volunteered in September 1914, and was retained at various home stations until 1916, when he was drafted to Egypt. In this seat of operations he was stationed at Alexandria and engaged on important clerical work and duties connected with the stores. He returned home for his demobilisation in June 1919, and holds the General Service and Victory Medals.
Court Lane, Stevington, near Bedford. Z1339.

BOLTON, D., Private, Bedfordshire Regiment.
He volunteered in March 1915, and was sent to Shoreham for a period of training, and for three months did consistently good work. Owing to his being found medically unfit he returned home and was discharged in June 1915.
High Street, Carlton, Beds. Z1340/A.

BOLTON, H., Private, Labour Corps.
He joined in February 1916, and in the following July was drafted to the Western Front. In this theatre of war he saw much service in the Somme, Ypres and Cambrai sectors and was engaged on various important duties connected with guarding ammunition dumps and digging trenches. He was demobilised in 1919, and holds the General Service and Victory Medals.
High Street, Carlton, Sharnbrook, Beds. Z1340/B.

BONE, A. E., Gunner, Royal Field Artillery.
Mobilised in August 1914, he proceeded to the Western Front in time to fight in the Retreat from Mons, and took part also in the Battle of Festubert and many other important engagements. He died gloriously on the Field of Battle on August 21st, 1915. He was entitled to the Mons Star, and the General Service and Victory Medals.
"Whilst we remember, the sacrifice is not in vain."
Chapel Lane, Sharnbrook, Bedford. Z1362.

BONESS, F., Private, 5th Bedfordshire Regt.
He volunteered in August 1914, and in the following year proceeded to Egypt. In this seat of operations he saw much service and took part in the Advance into Palestine and was in action at Haifa and Gaza. After hostilities ceased he returned home and was demobilised in 1919, holding the 1914–15 Star, and the General Service and Victory Medals.
Queen's Terrace, Sandy, Beds. Z1341/B.

BONESS, H. W., Private, 4th Bedfordshire Regt.
Joining in July 1916, he proceeded overseas later in the same year. Whilst on the Western Front he took part in several engagements, including the Battles of the Somme, the Ancre and Arras, where he was badly wounded in May 1917. As a result he was invalided home and finally discharged in September 1918 as medically unfit for further service. He holds the General Service and Victory Medals.
37, Princes Street, Bedford. X1342.

BONESS, P. J., Private, Bedfordshire Regiment.
He was mobilised in August 1914, and quickly drafted to France, where he took part in much heavy fighting at Mons and on the Marne. He made the supreme sacrifice, being killed in action at Ypres on March 12th, 1915, and was entitled to the Mons Star, and the General Service and Victory Medals.
"A valiant Soldier, with undaunted heart he breasted life's last hill."
Queen's Terrace, Sandy, Beds. Z1341/A.

BONHAM, A. G., Rifleman, 9th London Regiment (Queen Victoria's Rifles).
He joined in April 1916, and, on completing his training in the following December, was drafted to France, where he saw much heavy fighting in various sectors. He was unfortunately killed in action whilst on patrol near Arras on April 14th, 1917, and was entitled to the General Service and Victory Medals.
"The path of duty was the way to glory."
Milton Ernest, Bedford. Z1345.

BONHAM, J., Private, Queen's Own (Royal West Kent Regiment).
He joined in June 1916, and, after completing his training in the following year, was drafted to France. Whilst in this theatre of war he was engaged on various important duties at General Headquarters and also saw service in the Somme, Ypres and Cambrai sectors. He was demobilised in June 1920, and holds the General Service and Victory Medals.
High Street, Milton Ernest, near Bedford. Z1343.

BONHAM, W. W., Private, R.A.M.C.
Volunteering in September 1915, he was drafted overseas two months later. During his service on the Western Front he acted as a stretcher-bearer and took part in several engagements, including those at Ypres, Albert, the Somme, Messines, Cambrai, Amiens and Le Cateau (II.). He was demobilised in March 1919, and holds the 1914–15 Star, and the General Service and Victory Medals.
4, Coronation Road, Stony Stratford, Bucks. Z1344.

BONNETT, W. H., Private, Suffolk Regiment.
He joined in May 1918, and, after a short period of training, was engaged at various stations on important clerical duties. He was unable to obtain a transfer overseas owing to his being medically unfit, but rendered valuable services until his demobilisation in September 1919.
Rose Cottage, High Street, Stagsden. Z1346.

BOON, A. E., Private, 1st Bedfordshire Regiment.
He was mobilised in August 1914, and quickly proceeded to the Western Front, where he took part in the Retreat from Mons and in the Battles of the Marne and La Bassée. He died gloriously on the Field of Battle at Ypres on January 10th, 1915, and was entitled to the Mons Star, and the General Service and Victory Medals.
"Whilst we remember, the sacrifice is not in vain."
Willoughby Cottages, Great Barford, Bedford. Z1347/B.

BOON, B. J., Pte., 51st Royal Warwickshire Regt.
He joined in August 1918 on attaining military age, and underwent a period of training at various home stations and rendered valuable services. He contracted influenza and was in hospital for some time, finally being discharged in January 1919 as medically unfit for further duty.
30, Mill Street, Newport Pagnell, Bucks. Z1349.

BOON, F., Private, 2nd Bedfordshire Regiment.
Volunteering in November 1914, he was drafted overseas in the following year. Whilst on the Western Front he took part in much heavy fighting on the Somme, and was badly wounded in action in December 1915. As a result he was invalided home and finally discharged in September 1916 as medically unfit for further service. He holds the 1914–15 Star, and the General Service and Victory Medals.
35, Water Eaton, near Bletchley, Bucks. Z1348.

BOON, O. J., Private, 4th Bedfordshire Regiment.
He volunteered in 1915, and, on completing his training in the following year, was drafted to the Western Front. There he was engaged as a runner with his Battalion, and took part in much heavy fighting at Ypres, on the Somme and at Messines. He was unfortunately killed in action at Passchendaele on October 30th, 1917, and was entitled to the General Service and Victory Medals.
"Honour to the immortal dead, who gave their youth that the world might grow old in peace."
Willoughby Cottages, Great Barford, Bedford. Z1347/A.

BOOTH, R. W., L/Corporal, R.M.L.I.
He joined in February 1916, and was retained for a time at various home stations on important duties. He was then posted to one of H.M. ships, and took part in the raid on Zeebrugge and was wounded in action. In 1918 he served on duties in the stores at Calais and Etaples, until his demobilisation in June 1919. He holds the General Service and Victory Medals.
2, Railway Cottages, Oakley, Bedford. Z1350.

BORHAM, F., Private, 9th East Surrey Regiment.
He joined in February 1917, and was shortly afterwards drafted to the Western Front. In this seat of war he took part in many engagements, including those at Ypres, Cambrai, Lens, and in the Retreat and Advance of 1918. He suffered from shell-shock and was in hospital for some time, but on his recovery served with the Army of Occupation in Germany until his demobilisation in December 1919. He holds the General Service and Victory Medals.
St. Neots Road, Sandy, Beds. TZ1351.

BORTON, A., Private, 2nd Wiltshire Regiment.
He joined in April 1918, and, after a period of training with the Somersetshire Light Infantry in Ireland, proceeded to the Western Front. There he saw much heavy fighting in the Somme, Arras, Ypres and Cambrai sectors until the cessation of hostilities. He was demobilised in June 1919, and holds the General Service and Victory Medals.
Church End, Sherington, Bucks. Z1352/A.

BORTON, A. W., Gunner, Royal Field Artillery.
He joined in January 1917, and three months later was drafted to France. Whilst in this theatre of war he took part in several engagements, including the Battles of Arras, Ypres, Cambrai and Amiens, and, after the cessation of hostilities, served with the Army of Occupation in Germany. He was demobilised in October 1919, and holds the General Service and Victory Medals.
Church End, Sherington, Bucks. Z1352/B.

BOSTON, A. F., Pte., Northamptonshire Regt.
He volunteered in 1915, and underwent a short period of training prior to his being drafted to the Western Front. In this seat of war he saw much heavy fighting during the Battles of Ypres, the Somme (where he was wounded), Arras and Cambrai. He was demobilised in April 1919, and holds the General Service and Victory Medals.
27, Dane Street, Bedford. X1353/B.

BOSTON, E. (M.M.), Pte., 15th Lancashire Fusiliers.
He joined in May 1916, and later in the same year was drafted to France. During his service overseas he played a prominent part in the heavy fighting at the Battles of the Somme, Ypres, Arras, Passchendaele and Cambrai, and was wounded in action. He was awarded the Military Medal for conspicuous gallantry and devotion to duty in the Field. He was demobilised in February 1919, and holds also the General Service and Victory Medals. 6, Chandos Street, Bedford. X1354.

BOSTON, P., Private, 1/5th Bedfordshire Regt.
He volunteered in January 1915, and underwent a period of training prior to his being drafted to Egypt. In this seat of operations he took part in the Advance into Palestine, and was in action at Gaza, Jaffa and in the capture of Jerusalem. After hostilities ceased he returned home and was demobilised in April 1919, holding the General Service and Victory Medals.
6, Chandos Street, Bedford. X1355.

BOSTON, W. S., Private, R.E. (Postal Section).
He joined in March 1916, and underwent a period of training prior to his being drafted overseas. Whilst on the Western Front he served with the Loyal North Lancashire Regiment on the Somme, and was engaged on important duties with the Postal Section and rendered valuable services. He was demobilised in September 1919, and holds the General Service and Victory Medals.
30, Russell Street, Bedford. TX1356.

BOSWELL, W. A., Private, 1st Royal Warwickshire Regiment.
Volunteering in January 1916, he proceeded overseas in the following year. Whilst on the Western Front he took part in many engagements, including those at Vimy Ridge, Arras, Ypres, Passchendaele and Cambrai, where he was badly wounded. As a result he was invalided home and later demobilised in February 1919, holding the General Service and Victory Medals. 15, Church Street, Olney, Bucks. Z1357.

BOUD, H. J., Driver, Royal Army Service Corps.
He joined in May 1916, and was shortly afterwards drafted to Mesopotamia. Whilst in this seat of operations he took an active part in several engagements, including the capture of Kut and Baghdad, and was also employed on various important duties. He returned home and was demobilised in June 1919, and holds the General Service and Victory Medals.
21, Marne Street, Bedford. Z1358.

BOUGHTON, H., Pte., 2/4th Oxford. & Bucks. L.I.
He volunteered in August 1914, and, on completing his training in the following year, was drafted to France, where he took part in the Battles of Festubert, Loos, the Somme and Arras. He was severely wounded at the Battle of the Somme (II.), and unfortunately died through the effects on August 28th, 1918. He was entitled to the 1914–15 Star, and the General Service and Victory Medals.
"His life for his Country, his soul to God."
86, Tickford Street, Newport Pagnell, Bucks. Z1359/A.

BOUGHTON, H., Private, Somerset L.I.
He joined in May 1918, and underwent a short period of training prior to his being drafted to the Western Front. There he was engaged on important duties guarding German prisoners, and, after hostilities ceased, proceeded to Germany, where he served until his demobilisation in October 1919. He holds the General Service and Victory Medals.
86, Tickford Street, Newport Pagnell, Bucks. Z1359/B.

BOWD, A., Gunner, Royal Field Artillery.
Mobilised in August 1914, he was immediately drafted to the Western Front, where he served through the Retreat from Mons. He also took part in the Battles of the Marne, Festubert, Loos, the Somme, Arras, Ypres, Passchendaele and Cambrai, and many other important engagements in various sectors until the cessation of hostilities. He was discharged in September 1919, and holds the Mons Star, and the General Service and Victory Medals. Station Road, Warboys, Hunts. Z1360.

BOWDEN, E. A. (M.S.M.), S.S.M., R.A.S.C.
He was mobilised in August 1914, and in the following year was drafted to the Dardanelles, where he saw much severe fighting until the Evacuation of the Peninsula. He was then transferred to Salonika and was there engaged on important duties on various fronts until the cessation of hostilities, when he was sent with the Army of Occupation to Constantinople. He was awarded the Meritorious Service Medal for continuously good work, and a Serbian Order for distinguished service in the Field, and holds also the 1914–15 Star, and the General Service and Victory Medals. He was still with his Company in 1920.
102, George Street, Bedford. Z1361.

BOWDEN, T. J., Officers' Steward, Royal Navy.
He joined in March 1917, and, after a period of training, was posted to H.M.S. "Walleroo." On board this vessel he was engaged on important duties attached to the Home Fleet at Grimsby, where he rendered very valuable services until March 1919, when he was demobilised.
10, Tree Square, Far Bletchley, Bucks. Z2872.

BOWEN, R., Private, King's Own (Y.L.I.)
Already in the Army when war was declared in August 1914, he was immediately drafted to the Western Front, where, after fighting in the Retreat from Mons, he took part in the Battles of La Bassée, Ypres, Hill 60 and Festubert, and was wounded. He made the supreme sacrifice, falling in action at Loos in September 1915. He was entitled to the 1914–15 Star, and the General Service and Victory Medals.
"His memory is cherished with pride."
2, Tower Gardens, Bedford. X1363/A.

BOWERS, E., Tpr. (Saddler), Bedfordshire Lancers.
Volunteering in September 1914, he was drafted to Egypt in the following year, and served at various stations. He took part in the Advance into Palestine, where he fought in the Battles of Gaza, and was also present at the fall of Jerusalem, and was for some months in hospital suffering from malaria during 1917. He also served in Mesopotamia, where he was stationed at Baghdad before returning home for demobilisation in April 1919. He holds the 1914–15 Star, and the General Service and Victory Medals. 4, Gladstone Street, Bedford. X1364.

BOWES, C., Private, 8th Oxford. and Bucks. L.I.
He volunteered in August 1914, and, on completing his training in March of the following year, proceeded to the Western Front, where he took part in the Battle of Ypres and many minor engagements until October 1915. He was then transferred to Salonika, where he was again in action, seeing much heavy fighting on the Vardar and Doiran fronts until the cessation of hostilities. Demobilised on his return home in April 1919, he holds the 1914–15 Star, and the General Service and Victory Medals.
184, Simpson Road, Fenny Stratford, Bucks. Z1365.

BOWLER, E. W., Corporal, Machine Gun Corps.
Volunteering in September 1915, he was drafted to the Western Front, on completion of a period of training, in the following year and there took part in the Battles of Vimy Ridge and Vermelles and many minor engagements. He fell fighting on the Somme in November 1916, and was buried at Bailleul. He was entitled to the General Service and Victory Medals.
"A costly sacrifice upon the altar of freedom."
Elstow, near Bedford. X1369/B.

BOWLER, F. J., Pte., 2/1st Oxford. & Bucks. L.I.
He volunteered at the outbreak of war in August 1914, and in March of the following year was drafted to the Western Front. There he saw severe fighting in various sectors, and, after taking part in the Battles of Ypres, the Somme, Arras and Cambrai and other engagements, was wounded in action on the Somme two days before the cessation of hostilities and admitted to hospital in England. He was finally demobilised in March 1919, and holds the 1914–15 Star, and the General Service and Victory Medals.
Bow Brickhill, near Bletchley, Bucks. Z1367.

BOWLER, F. R., L/Corporal, Royal Warwickshire Regiment.
After volunteering in August 1914 he underwent a period of training prior to being drafted to the Western Front in 1916. He saw much severe fighting in this theatre of war, and took part in the Battles of the Somme, Arras and Ypres, and many other engagements before being transferred to Italy. There he was again in action on the Piave and the Asiago Plateaux until the cessation of hostilities, finally returning home for demobilisation in April 1919. He holds the General Service and Victory Medals.
3, Crown Yard, St. Ives, Hunts. Z1370.

BOWLER, G., Gunner, Royal Garrison Artillery.
Four months after joining in May 1916, he was drafted to France, where he saw severe fighting in various sectors of the front. After taking part in the Battle of the Somme and other important engagements he was transferred in November 1917 to Italy, where he was again in action on the Piave until the signing of the Armistice. He was demobilised on his return home in March 1919, and holds the General Service and Victory Medals. Bridge House, Simpson, Bucks. Z1366.

BOWLER, R. W., Corporal, Royal Engineers.
Joining in August 1916, he was drafted to the Western Front on completing a period of training in the following year and there saw severe fighting in various sectors. After taking part in the Battles of Arras, Ypres and Cambrai and other important engagements he was invalided home in 1918, and admitted to hospital at Netley. He was discharged in December 1918 as medically unfit for further service, and holds the General Service and Victory Medals.
Elstow, near Bedford. X1369/A.

BOWLER, W. C. (M.M.), Sergeant, R.A.V.C.
He volunteered in August 1914, and in May of the following year proceeded to the Western Front. Whilst in this theatre of war he was engaged on important duties in various sectors, and also took a prominent part in the Battles of Arras, Cambrai and the Somme and other engagements. He was awarded the Military Medal for conspicuous gallantry in the Field in October 1917, and, holding also the 1914–15 Star, and the General Service and Victory Medals, was demobilised in May 1919.
Church Lane, Sharnbrook, Beds. Z1368.

BOWLES, C. R., Private, 11th Essex Regiment and 1st Hertfordshire Regiment.

Joining in August 1916, he was drafted to the Western Front in January of the following year, and there took part in the Battles of Arras and Vimy Ridge and many minor engagements. He died gloriously on the Field of Battle at Loos on June 24th, 1917. He was entitled to the General Service and Victory Medals.

"Honour to the immortal dead, who gave their youth that the world might grow old in peace."

Offord D'Arcy, Huntingdon. Z1371.

BOWYER, A., Private, Bedfordshire Regiment.

Having previously served with the Colours, he re-enlisted in June 1915, and, after a period of training, was drafted to the Western Front. There he saw severe fighting in various sectors and took part in the Battles of Albert, the Somme, Arras and Ypres and other engagements, and was twice wounded in action at Passchendaele. He was demobilised in March 1919, and holds the General Service and Victory Medals.

33, Priory Street, Bedford. X1372.

BOWYER, A. G., Private, Northants. Regiment.

Having enlisted in 1907, he proceeded to France shortly after the outbreak of war in August 1914, and there saw much severe fighting. After taking part in the first Battle of Ypres and other important engagements, however, he was sent home and invalided from the Army in January 1915, on account of deafness. He holds the 1914 Star, and the General Service and Victory Medals. Olney Road, Lavendon, Bucks. Z1373/A.

BOWYER, A. H., Private, Machine Gun Corps.

He joined in November 1917, and, after two months' training, proceeded to the Western Front. Whilst in this theatre of war he saw much severe fighting in various sectors, and took part in the Battles of the Somme and Cambrai and other important engagements during the Retreat and Advance of 1918. Returning home in January 1919, he was demobilised in the following month, and holds the General Service and Victory Medals. 75, Oakley, near Bedford. Z1374/A.

BOWYER, F. T., Private, 7th Bedfordshire Regt.

He volunteered in May 1915, and in June of the following year proceeded to the Western Front, where he took part in the Battles of the Somme, Arras, Ypres and Cambrai and many other important engagements. He made the supreme sacrifice, falling in action on the Somme in April 1918. He was entitled to the General Service and Victory Medals.

"He died the noblest death a man may die,
Fighting for God and right and liberty."

Olney Road, Lavendon, Bucks. Z1373/B.

BOWYER, H., Sapper, Royal Engineers.

Volunteering in January 1915, he was drafted to the Western Front on completing a period of training later in the same year, and was there engaged on road-making and other important duties. He also took an active part in the Battles of Ypres, Loos, the Somme, Arras and Bapaume and other engagements in various sectors, finally returning home for demobilisation in 1919. He holds the 1914–15 Star, and the General Service and Victory Medals. 3, Leys Cottages, Clapham, Bedford. Z1375.

BOWYER, H. F., Private, 1st London Regiment (Royal Fusiliers).

A Reservist, he was called to the Colours in August 1914, and was immediately drafted to the Western Front, where he took part in the Battle of Mons and the subsequent Retreat and many minor engagements. He was unhappily killed in action at the first Battle of Ypres on November 24th, 1914. He was entitled to the Mons Star, and the General Service and Victory Medals.

"The path of duty was the way to glory."

Olney Road, Lavendon, Bucks. Z1373/C.

BOWYER, S. J., Private, 7th Norfolk Regiment.

Three months after volunteering in November 1915 he was drafted to France, where he saw much severe fighting and took part in the Battles of the Somme, Arras, Messines, Ypres and Cambrai and other engagements in various sectors of the front. He fell in action near Ribecourt on August 8th, 1918. He was entitled to the General Service and Victory Medals.

"A valiant Soldier, with undaunted heart he breasted life's last hill."

75, Oakley, near Bedford. Z1374/B.

BOWYER, W. (M.S.M.), Sergeant, Middlesex Regt.

Mobilised in August 1914, he proceeded to the Western Front in time to take part in the Retreat from Mons. He also fought with distinction in the Battles of La Bassée, Ypres, Festubert and the Somme, and many other important engagements in various sectors, and served through the Retreat and Advance of 1918. He was awarded the Meritorious Service Medal for continuously good work and, holding also the Mons Star, and the General Service and Victory Medals, was discharged in March 1919. 47, Union Street, Newport Pagnell, Bucks. Z1377.

BOWYER, W. H., Tpr., Bedfordshire Lancers and Nottinghamshire Hussars (Sherwood Rangers).

He volunteered in September 1914, and was retained on important duties at various stations in England until 1916, when he proceeded to Egypt. He was sent thence into Palestine and there took part in the Battles of Gaza and the entry into Jaffa and Jerusalem, fought also in many other important engagements, and was twice wounded in action in 1917. He was finally sent home, and in August 1919 was invalided from the Army, holding the General Service and Victory Medals.

Church Road, Stevington, near Bedford. Z1376.

BOYCE, C., Private, 8th Bedfordshire Regiment.

Shortly after volunteering in January 1915 he was drafted to the Western Front, where he saw severe fighting in various sectors. He took part in the Battles of Festubert, Loos, Albert, Vimy Ridge, Ypres, Cambrai and Amiens, and many other important engagements, and was wounded in action in the Somme Offensive of July 1916. Demobilised in January 1919, he holds the 1914–15 Star, and the General Service and Victory Medals. Thrapston Road, Brampton, Hunts. TZ1378.

BOYD, E. G., Sapper, Royal Engineers.

He volunteered in 1914, and, on completion of a period of training in the following year, was drafted to Egypt, where he served at various stations. He proceeded thence into Palestine and was there in action at the Battles of Gaza and took part also in the capture of Jaffa, Jerusalem, and Haifa. He was demobilised on returning home in February 1919, and holds the 1914–15 Star, and the General Service and Victory Medals. 160, Bower Street, Bedford. Z1379.

BOYLES, W. J., Gunner, Royal Garrison Artillery.

He joined in August 1918, and, after undergoing a period of training, served at various stations, where he was engaged on duties of great importance. Owing to the early cessation of hostilities he was not successful in obtaining his transfer overseas, but nevertheless rendered valuable services with his Battery until February 1919, when he was demobilised.

Wootton, Bedford. Z1380.

BOZEAT, F., L/Corporal, Royal Fusiliers and 2nd Queen's (Royal West Surrey Regiment).

He joined in 1916, and, after a period of training, proceeded to the Western Front, where he saw much severe fighting. He took part in the Battles of the Somme and Arras and many minor engagements until gassed at Messines Ridge and invalided home. On his recovery, however, in October 1918, he returned to France and was again in action in various sectors. Demobilised on his return home in 1919, he holds the General Service and Victory Medals.

Station Road, Warboys, Hunts. Z1381.

BRACE, A. F., Private, R.A.S.C.

He volunteered in April 1915, and, after completing a term of training, was retained at various stations on duties of a highly important nature. Unable to obtain his transfer to a theatre of war, he was, nevertheless, employed in conveying horses to and from France, and rendered very valuable services with his Company. He was demobilised in April 1919, and holds the General Service and Victory Medals.

Chapel Yard, Goldington, Bedford. Z1384.

BRACE, F., Private, Bedfordshire Regiment.

He joined in April 1917, and, after a period of training, proceeded to France, where he saw severe fighting in various sectors of the front. He took part in the Battles of the Marne and Cambrai and many other important engagements until invalided home suffering from septic poisoning and admitted to hospital in England. He was finally demobilised in 1919, and holds the General Service and Victory Medals.

Roxton, Beds. Z1385.

BRACE, G., L/Corporal, 1st Lincolnshire Regt.

Volunteering in January 1915, he was drafted to the Western Front in September of that year and was there wounded in action in the Somme Offensive twelve months later. Invalided to hospital at Devonport, he returned to France, however, on his recovery in March 1917, and was again in action at the Battles of Arras, Vimy Ridge, Ypres and Cambrai and many minor engagements. Taken prisoner in April 1918, during the Retreat, he unhappily died whilst still in captivity on October 21st of that year. He was entitled to the 1914–15 Star, and the General Service and Victory Medals.

"His life for his Country, his soul to God."

New Street, St. Neots, Hunts. Z1382.

BRACE, W. J., Private, 1/5th Bedfordshire Regt.

He volunteered at the outbreak of war in August 1914, and in the following year was drafted to the Dardanelles, where he was wounded in action in the Landing at Gallipoli. He afterwards served in Palestine, where he was again in action at the Battles of Gaza and was present also at the fall of Jaffa and Jerusalem. He returned home in 1919, and in July of that year was demobilised, holding the 1914–15 Star, and the General Service and Victory Medals.

32, Marlborough Road, Bedford. Z1383/A.

BRADBURY, A., Corporal, Royal Engineers.

Volunteering in April 1915, he proceeded to France in the following month and was there engaged on important duties with the Railway Transport Section in various sectors of the front. He was stationed chiefly at Rouen, where he rendered very valuable services with his Company until his return home for demobilisation in June 1919. He holds the 1914–15 Star, and the General Service and Victory Medals.

44, Napier Street, Bletchley, Bucks. Z1386/C.

BRADBURY, H., Sergeant-Major, R.A.S.C.
Volunteering in May 1915, he was drafted to Gallipoli in August of that year and there, after taking part in the Landing at Suvla Bay, saw much severe fighting until the Evacuation of the Peninsula. He was then transferred to Egypt, where stationed at Alexandria, he rendered valuable services at the Supply Depôt until his return home. Demobilised in August 1919, he holds the 1914–15 Star, and the General Service and Victory Medals.
44, Napier Street, Bletchley, Bucks. Z1386/B.

BRADLEY, C. F., Private, Sherwood Foresters.
Shortly after joining in 1916 he was drafted to the Western Front, where he saw severe fighting in various sectors. He took part in the Battles of Arras, Ypres and Cambrai and many minor engagements in this theatre of war until invalided home suffering from trench-fever. On his recovery, however, in 1918 he proceeded to Egypt and thence into Palestine, where he was stationed at Gaza and Jaffa. Returning home in 1919, he was demobilised in July of the following year, and holds the General Service and Victory Medals.
16, St. John's Street, Huntingdon. Z1387.

BRADSHAW, A., Pte., Royal Warwickshire Regt.
After volunteering in January 1915, he underwent a period of training prior to being drafted to the Western Front in July of the following year. There he took part in many important engagements during the Somme Offensive, and in December 1916 was severely wounded in action on the Ancre and invalided home. He was retained in England on his recovery until June 1919, when he was discharged as medically unfit for further service. He holds the General Service and Victory Medals.
11, Station Road, Warboys, Hunts. Z1389.

BRADSHAW, J. H., Private, Hampshire Regt.
Volunteering at the outbreak of war in August 1914, he proceeded to the Western Front on completing a period of training in the following year and there saw much heavy fighting. He took part in the Battles of Ypres, the Somme, Messines and Passchendaele and many other important engagements in various sectors until the cessation of hostilities. He was demobilised on his return home in 1919, and holds the 1914–15 Star, and the General Service and Victory Medals.
Wyboston, Beds. Z1391.

BRADSHAW, W., Pte., 2/6th Royal Sussex Regt.
He joined in 1916, and, on completing his training later in the same year, was drafted to India. There he saw active service on the North-West Frontier and was also engaged on garrison duties at Bombay, where he did much useful work with his unit. He returned home for demobilisation in December 1919, and holds the General Service, Victory and India General Service Medals (with Clasp, "Afghanistan, N.W. Frontier, 1919").
Baker's Lane, Tempsford, near Sandy, Beds. Z1388.

BRADSHAW, W. G., Private, 2nd Bedfordshire Regiment and Hertfordshire Regiment.
He joined in May 1916, and in the following year was drafted to the Western Front. Whilst in this theatre of war he saw severe fighting in various sectors, took part in the Battles of Arras, Messines, Ypres and Cambrai and other important engagements, and was wounded in action during the Retreat of March 1918. After the cessation of hostilities he served with the Army of Occupation at Cologne, and in 1919 proceeded to India, where he was still with his unit in the following year. He holds the General Service and Victory Medals.
The Green, Milton Ernest, near Bedford. Z1390.

BRANDON, E. G., Private, R.A.M.C.
Volunteering in September 1914, he was drafted to the Dardanelles in the following year and there, after taking part in the Landing at Suvla Bay, saw severe fighting until the Evacuation of the Gallipoli Peninsula. He was then transferred to Salonika, where he was again in action, and was later sent to Egypt, whence he proceeded into Palestine. He was afterwards transferred to the Western Front, where he took an active part in many engagements until the cessation of hostilities, then proceeding with the Army of Occupation into Germany, where he was stationed at Berlin. He was wounded in action whilst overseas and was finally demobilised in July 1919, holding the 1914–15 Star, and the General Service and Victory Medals.
Carlton, Beds. Z1393/A.

BRANDON, F., Sapper, Royal Engineers.
Joining in June 1916, he was drafted to the Western Front on completing a period of training in the following December, and was there engaged on important duties in various sectors. He served at Etaples, Calais and other stations and suffered from trench-fever whilst overseas. Returning home in 1919, he was demobilised in October of that year, and holds the General Service and Victory Medals. Carlton, Beds. Z1392.

BRANDON, W. G., Bombardier, R.G.A.
He volunteered in October 1915, and, in June of the following year, proceeded to France, where he saw severe fighting in various sectors of the front. He took part in many important engagements in this theatre of war, including the Battles of Arras, Ypres and Cambrai, and was wounded in action. He was demobilised in February 1919, and holds the General Service and Victory Medals. Carlton, Beds. Z1393/B.

BRANSON, E., Driver, R.A.S.C.
Volunteering in February 1915, he was drafted to Salonika in the following year, and there saw much severe fighting. Later in 1916, however, he was transferred to Egypt, where he was present at engagements at Sollum, Katia and many other places, and was for some time in hospital suffering from fever. Invalided home in 1918, he was finally demobilised in September 1919, holding the General Service and Victory Medals.
Church End, Biddenham, Bedford. Z1394.

BRANSON, W., Sapper, Royal Engineers.
Three months after volunteering in September 1914 he proceeded to the Western Front, where he served as a blacksmith and on other important duties in various sectors. He was also present at the Battles of Ypres, the Somme, Arras and Cambrai, and many minor engagements, and was wounded in action near Ypres in January 1915. Demobilised in February 1919, he holds the 1914–15 Star, and the General Service and Victory Medals. 42, St. Paul's Road, Bedford. Z1395.

BRASHIER, J. J., Leading Stoker, Royal Navy.
Having enlisted in 1905, he was already in the Navy when war was declared in August 1914, and afterwards served in H.M. Submarine "E.49." On board this vessel he was engaged on various important duties in the Mediterranean Sea and other waters, and took part in the Battle of Jutland and many minor actions. He unhappily lost his life when the "E.49" was sunk in the North Sea on March 12th, 1917. He was entitled to the 1914–15 Star, and the General Service and Victory Medals.
"Great deeds cannot die:
They with the sun and moon renew their light for ever."
St. Neots Road, Sandy, Beds. Z1396/A.

BRASHIER, S. M., Private, 22nd Royal Fusiliers.
He volunteered in September 1914, and, after a period of training, was drafted to the Western Front. In this theatre of war, he took part in the Battles of Neuve Chapelle, Ypres and the Somme and was wounded. As a result he was invalided home, but, returning to France in April 1917, participated in further fighting, prior to being killed in action at Ypres on May 3rd, 1917. He was entitled to the 1914–15 Star, and the General Service and Victory Medals.
"Whilst we remember, the sacrifice is not in vain."
St. Neots Road, Sandy, Beds. Z1396/B.

BRASON, A. J., L/Corporal, Royal Engineers.
He joined in December 1916, and in the following month proceeded to France. There he served with his Company in the Loos sector, and did excellent work whilst engaged on various duties of an important character, but was subsequently killed on May 30th, 1917. He was entitled to the General Service and Victory Medals.
"His life for his Country, his soul to God."
3, Spencer Street, Bradwell, Bucks. Z1397/A.

BRAY, J. A., Private, 1/5th Bedfordshire Regt.
Volunteering in October 1914, he was sent four months later to France, where he took part in many important engagements, including the Battles of Neuve Chapelle, Hill 60, Ypres, the Somme and Passchendaele. He was twice wounded, the second time whilst in action on the Somme in March 1918, when he was invalided home and sent to hospital in Manchester. Eventually demobilised in January 1919, he rejoined in the following May for service in Russia, and was finally discharged in October 1919, holding the 1914–15 Star, and the General Service and Victory Medals. London Road, Harrowden, Bedford. Z1398.

BRAYBROOK, F., Private, Bedfordshire Regt.
He was serving at a foreign station when war broke out, in August 1914, and was at once sent to France. There he took part in the Retreat from Mons, and the Battles of the Marne, the Aisne and La Bassée, where he was wounded in October 1914. Evacuated to England, he was subsequently invalided out of the Service in February 1915, holding the Mons Star, and the General Service and Victory Medals.
Pertenhall, near St. Neots. Z1402/A.

BRAYBROOKS, B., Sergeant-Major, Highland Light Infantry.
Mobilised in August 1914, he was drafted early in the following year to the Western Front. In this theatre of war he played a prominent part with his unit in strenuous fighting at Ypres and on the Somme, performing very good work until he was killed in action on August 15th, 1916. He was entitled to the 1914–15 Star, and the General Service and Victory Medals.
"Great deeds cannot die."
High Street, Sandy, Beds. Z1399/A.

BRAYBROOKS, C.W., Pte., 1st Bedfordshire Regt.
He was mobilised from the Reserve at the outbreak of hostilities in August 1914, and at once proceeded to France, where he was in action during the Retreat from Mons. He subsequently fought in the Battles of the Marne, the Aisne and La Bassée, but was unfortunately killed in action on November 7th, 1914. He was entitled to the Mons Star, and the General Service and Victory Medals.
"His memory is cherished with pride."
13, Poplar Cottages, Longfield Road, Sandy, Beds. Z1401/A.

BRAYBROOKS, E., Pte., 2nd Bedfordshire Regt.
He joined in March 1916, and in the following November was sent to the Western Front. During his service overseas he took part in many important engagements, including those at Arras, Albert, Messines Ridge and Ypres, and was wounded. He performed consistently good work and was demobilised on his return home in January 1919, holding the General Service and Victory Medals. Carter Street, Sandy, Beds. Z1400 /A.

BRAYBROOKS, F. J., Pte., 7th Bedfordshire Regt.
Volunteering in September 1914, he was drafted in the following July to the Western Front. In this theatre of war he took part in the Battles of Festubert and Loos, and was wounded on the Somme in September 1916. On his recovery he participated in further fighting at Messines Ridge and Arras before he fell in action at Ypres on December 8th, 1917. He was entitled to the 1914–15 Star, and the General Service and Victory Medals.
"A costly sacrifice upon the altar of freedom."
13, Poplar Cottages, Longfield Road, Sandy, Beds. Z1401 /B.

BRAYBROOKS, G., Private, Essex Regiment.
He joined in January 1917, and, after completing his training in the following April, proceeded to France. There he participated in strenuous fighting at Messines Ridge and Ypres, and did excellent work until he died gloriously on the Field of Battle at Arras on July 11th, 1917. He was entitled to the General Service and Victory Medals.
"The path of duty was the way to glory."
13, Poplar Cottages, Longfield Road, Sandy, Beds. Z1401 /C.

BRAYBROOKS, H., Private, Queen's (Royal West Surrey Regiment).
Serving at the outbreak of war in August 1914, he was immediately drafted to the Western Front. In this theatre of hostilities he participated in the Battle of Mons and in the subsequent Retreat, and was unhappily killed whilst taking part in heavy fighting at Menin Road in October 1914. He was entitled to the Mons Star, and the General Service and Victory Medals.
"Thinking that remembrance, though unspoken, may reach him where he sleeps."
Carter Street, Sandy, Beds. Z1400 /B.

BRAYBROOKS, S., 2nd Lieutenant, Labour Corps.
He volunteered in August 1914, and in the following year proceeded to France. During his service in this theatre of hostilities he was engaged on important duties in the Arras, Ypres, Cambrai and other sectors, and was wounded on two occasions. He performed exceedingly good work until he unfortunately contracted pneumonia, from the effects of which he died in hospital in France on February 3rd, 1919. He was entitled to the 1914–15 Star, and the General Service and Victory Medals.
"Courage, bright hopes, and a myriad dreams splendidly given."
High Street, Sandy, Beds. Z1399 /B.

BREDGER, N. E., Sapper, Royal Engineers.
He volunteered in November 1915, and in the following year was sent to the Western Front, where he was transferred to a Pioneer Battalion. He took part in several engagements and in 1917 was wounded, as a result of which he was evacuated to England. On his recovery he was retransferred to the Royal Engineers, and rendered valuable services until he was demobilised in March 1919, holding the General Service and Victory Medals. Cambridge Street, St. Neots, Hunts. Z1408.

BREED, A. W., Private, 22nd London Regiment (The Queen's).
He joined in October 1917, and on the completion of his training was drafted to Egypt. After serving for some time at Cairo, he was sent into Palestine, where he took part in severe fighting at Jaffa, Haifa and Damascus. He remained in this theatre of war after the termination of hostilities, and was eventually demobilised in May 1920, holding the General Service and Victory Medals.
39, Priory Street, Bedford. X1403.

BREED, E. G., Corporal, Royal Engineers.
Volunteering in October 1915, he was afterwards sent to France, where he participated in severe fighting at Ypres, Zillibeke and in the Somme and Arras sectors, and did excellent work. After the signing of the Armistice he proceeded to Germany with the Army of Occupation and served on the Rhine. until July 1919, when he returned home and was demobilised, holding the General Service and Victory Medals.
34, New Fenlake, Bedford. TZ1406 /B.

BREED, G., L/Corporal, Bedfordshire Regiment.
He volunteered in February 1915, but was not medically fit for transfer to a theatre of war. After completing his training he was stationed at Ampthill, and rendered valuable services whilst employed guarding bridges and railways. He was invalided out of the Army in March 1916 as unfit for further military duty. 7, Station Road, Sandy, Beds. Z1405.

BREED, G. E., Corporal, Royal Fusiliers.
He joined in March 1916, and later in the same year was sent to the Western Front. There he played a prominent part with his unit in many important engagements, and was in action during the Battles of Arras, Cambrai and the Somme. Returning home after the signing of the Armistice, he was demobilised in March 1919, and holds the General Service and Victory Medals. 34, New Fenlake, Bedford. TZ1406 /A.

BREED, O. A., Private, 5th Bedfordshire Regt.
Volunteering in September 1914, he was retained at home on important duties and did good work whilst stationed at Bury St. Edmunds and Bedford until September 1916, when he proceeded to France. In this theatre of war he participated in heavy fighting at Albert, Arras, Vimy Ridge, Cambrai and on the Somme, and was twice wounded. He was demobilised in March 1919, holding the General Service and Victory Medals.
High Street, Wootton, Beds. Z1404.

BREEN, M., Gunner, Royal Garrison Artillery.
He was mobilised at the outbreak of war in August 1914, and a month later was drafted to France, where he took part with his Battery in the Battle of the Aisne and in subsequent engagements. He was severely wounded at Ypres in May 1915, his wound unfortunately involving the loss of his left leg. Invalided home, he was eventually discharged in August 1916, and holds the 1914 Star, and the General Service and Victory Medals.
Damerstown, Castlecomer, Co. Kilkenny, Ireland. TZ1407.

BRIARS, H., Gunner, Royal Field Artillery.
Volunteering in August 1914, he was employed on important duties at various home stations until November 1915, when he was drafted to France. There he participated with his Battery in heavy fighting at Loos and Albert, and in the Battles of the Somme, Ypres and Cambrai. Returning to England after the Armistice, he was demobilised in 1919, and holds the 1914–15 Star, and the General Service and Victory Medals.
Hemingford Grey, Hunts. Z1409 /B.

BRIARS, R., Petty Officer, Royal Naval Division.
He joined in 1916, and in the following year proceeded to Mesopotamia. In this theatre of war he did excellent work with the Armoured Car Corps on various fronts. Later, invalided home on account of ill-health, he spent some time in hospital at Grantham, and was eventually demobilised in April 1919, holding the General Service and Victory Medals.
6, Oxford Road, St. Ives, Hunts. Z1410.

BRIARS, W., Rifleman, King's Royal Rifle Corps.
Joining in January 1916, he was sent five months later to the Western Front. During his service in this theatre of hostilities, he was in action on the Somme front, also at Vimy Ridge, Passchendaele, Ypres and Cambrai. He subsequently took part in heavy fighting in various sectors during the Retreat and was killed in action on April 18th, 1918. He was entitled to the General Service and Victory Medals.
"Nobly striving,
He nobly fell that we might live."
Hemingford Grey, Hunts. Z1409 /A.

BRICE, A. B., A.B., R.N., H.M.S. "Shark."
Serving in the Royal Navy at the outbreak of war in August 1914, he was posted to H.M.S. "Shark," and, whilst attached to the Chatham Division, was engaged on patrol and escort duty. He subsequently served in the North Sea, and did good work until he made the supreme sacrifice, losing his life on May 31st, 1916, when his vessel was sunk during the Battle of Jutland. He was entitled to the 1914–15 Star, and the General Service and Victory Medals.
"He passed out of the sight of men by the path of duty and self-sacrifice."
Lathbury, Newport Pagnell, Bucks. Z1412 /B.

BRICE, C. W., Pte., Bedfordshire Regt. and M.G.C.
He volunteered in June 1915, and later in the same year was drafted to the Western Front, where he took part in heavy fighting at Loos, Ypres and Armentières. Wounded in action at Ypres in 1916, he was invalided home and admitted to hospital in Cardiff, but on his recovery served at various home stations on important duties until 1918, when he was sent to Russia. There he took part in several important engagements and performed good work. Demobilised on returning home in October 1919, he holds the 1914–15 Star, and the General Service and Victory Medals.
68, Priory Street, Newport Pagnell, Bucks. Z1411.

BRICE, J., Private, Royal Fusiliers.
He joined in 1917, and on completion of his training proceeded in March 1918 to France. In this theatre of war he participated in strenuous fighting at Albert and St. Quentin, and was gassed in action at Cambrai during the Advance of 1918. Remaining on the Western Front until after the Armistice, he was demobilised in 1919, holding the General Service and Victory Medals. Goldington Green, Goldington, Beds. Z1413.

BRICE, P., A.B., R.N., H.M.S. "Hannibal."
He was already serving in the Royal Navy at the outbreak of hostilities in August 1914, and was posted to H.M.S. "Hannibal." In this vessel he did good work whilst engaged on patrol and other important duties in the North Sea and home waters until November 11th, 1914, when he was found dead in his bed, having died from the effects of carbonic gas poisoning. He was entitled to the 1914–15 Star, and the General Service and Victory Medals.
"His life for his Country."
Lathbury, Newport Pagnell, Bucks. Z1412 /A

BRIDGE, C. J. J., Private, 4th Northants. Regt.
Volunteering in September 1914, he proceeded in the following July to the Dardanelles. There he was in action at the Landing at Suvla Bay and in subsequent engagements. After the Evacuation of the Gallipoli Peninsula he was transferred to Egypt, and later sent into Palestine, where he took part in further fighting at Gaza and Jerusalem. He was demobilised on returning home in March 1919, and holds the 1914–15 Star, and the General Service and Victory Medals.
166, Simpson Road, Fenny Stratford, Bucks. Z1415/C.

BRIDGE, G. F., Private, 3rd Northants. Regt.
He volunteered in September 1914, and was drafted in July 1915 to the Dardanelles, where he took part in the Landing at Suvla Bay, and was wounded. In the following November he was invalided home suffering from dysentery, but, on his recovery, two months later, was sent to France. There he was in action at Ypres and on the Somme front, where he was wounded and taken prisoner in July 1916. Interned in Germany until the signing of the Armistice, he was then repatriated and was eventually demobilised in March 1919, holding the 1914–15 Star, and the General Service and Victory Medals.
166, Simpson Road, Fenny Stratford, Bucks. Z1415/B.

BRIDGE, H. C., Private, 3rd Hampshire Regiment.
Volunteering in December 1915, he was sent in the following July to the Western Front. In this theatre of hostilities, he took part with his unit in several important engagements, and was wounded on the Somme in October 1916. Evacuated to England, he spent some time in hospital at Fulham, undergoing many operations, prior to being invalided out of the Service in August 1917. He holds the General Service and Victory Medals. 166, Simpson Rd., Fenny Stratford, Bucks. Z1415/A.

BRIDGES, A. E., Sapper, Royal Engineers.
Mobilised in August 1914, he was immediately drafted to the Western Front, where he served through the Retreat from Mons. He also took an active part in the Battles of the Marne, Ypres and Festubert, and many other important engagements in various sectors. Admitted to hospital at Liverpool, he was finally invalided from the Army in April 1916, suffering from shell-shock, and holds the Mons Star, and the General Service and Victory Medals. 10, Bridge Road, Bedford. Z1414.

BRIDGES, G., C.Q.M.S., Royal Engineers (R.O.D.)
Mobilised in August 1914, he was retained at various stations in England until June 1917, when he proceeded to Egypt. He was there engaged on important railway transport work, and, proceeding into Palestine, took a prominent part in the Battles of Gaza and the entry into Jaffa. After the cessation of hostilities he was transferred to France, where he served for six months, returning home for discharge in June 1919. He holds the General Service and Victory Medals.
39, Bletsoe, near Bedford. Z1416.

BRIEN, H. J. F., Sapper, Royal Engineers.
Volunteering in August 1914, he underwent a period of training prior to being drafted to Salonika in the following year and was there engaged on important duties on the Doiran front. In October 1916 he was transferred to Egypt and thence proceeded into Palestine, where he fought in the Battles of Gaza, in the Jordan Valley and at the capture of Jerusalem. Demobilised on his return home in July 1919, he holds the 1914–15 Star, and the General Service and Victory Medals.
8, Gawcott Road, Buckingham. Z1417.

BRIGGS, J. W., Private, Essex Regiment.
He volunteered in 1915, and, on completing his training in the following year, was drafted to Egypt, where he served at various stations. Taking part in the Advance into Palestine, he fought in the three Battles of Gaza, at the capture of Haifa and in many other important engagements until the cessation of hostilities. Transferred in July 1919 to Malta, he was still with his unit in 1920 with the Army of the Black Sea. He holds the General Service and Victory Medals.
Hardwick, Buckden, Hunts. Z1418.

BRIGHT, F. H., Air Mechanic, Royal Air Force.
He joined in January 1917, and, after undergoing a period of training, was retained at various stations, where he was engaged on duties of a highly technical nature. He was employed also in conveying aeroplanes to and from France, but was not successful in obtaining his transfer to a theatre of war. He, nevertheless, rendered very valuable services, and in 1920 was still with his Squadron, holding the General Service and Victory Medals.
77, Marlborough Road, Bedford. Z1430.

BRIGHTMAN, F. G., Corporal, Royal Engineers.
A Reservist, he was called to the Colours in August 1914, and in February of the following year proceeded to the Western Front, where he was present at the Battles of Ypres and Festubert, and other engagements. Returning home, he was discharged, time-expired, but shortly afterwards re-enlisted, and was again drafted to France, where he served in various sectors. He took part in the Battles of the Somme, Arras, Ypres and Cambrai, and was gassed during the Advance of 1918. Demobilised in March 1919, he holds the 1914–15 Star, and the General Service and Victory Medals.
35, St. Giles Street, New Bradwell, Bucks. Z1419.

BRIGHTMAN, F. T., Private, Machine Gun Corps.
Joining in October 1916, he was drafted to the Western Front after three months' training, and there served as a machine-gunner in various sectors. He took part in much severe fighting in this theatre of war, and served through the Battles of Arras, Vimy Ridge, Cambrai and the Somme, and many other important engagements. He was demobilised in October 1919, and holds the General Service and Victory Medals
Houghton Conquest, near Ampthill, Beds. Z1420.

BRIMLEY, F. C., Private, 6th Bedfordshire Regiment and Essex Regiment.
He volunteered in May 1915, and, in February of the following year, was drafted to the Western Front. Whilst in this theatre of war he saw severe fighting in various sectors, and after taking part in the Battles of Albert, the Somme and Arras and other important engagements, was wounded in action in April 1917. Invalided home, he was for three months in hospital, and on his recovery was retained on clerical duties in England. He was demobilised in May 1919, and holds the General Service and Victory Medals.
7, Leys Cottages, Clapham, Bedford. Z1421.

BRINKLOW, G., Private, Oxford. & Bucks. L.I.
Volunteering in May 1915, he was drafted to France in September of the following year, and there saw severe fighting in various sectors of the front. After taking part in engagements at Ypres, he was wounded in action at Arras in April 1917 and invalided to hospital at Birmingham. He returned to the Western Front, however, on his recovery six months later, and was again in action at Cambrai, and on the Somme. Demobilised in September 1919, he holds the General Service and Victory Medals.
27, Water Eaton, Bletchley, Bucks. Z1423.

BRINKLOW, W., Pte., 2/4th Oxford. & Bucks. L.I.
He volunteered in November 1915, and, on completing his training in July of the following year, was drafted to the Western Front, where he saw much severe fighting. After taking part in engagements at Armentières and many other places, he was gassed and wounded in action in June 1918, and was for four months in hospital at Boulogne. On his recovery, however, he rejoined his unit, and was again in action until the cessation of hostilities. He was demobilised in December 1919, and holds the General Service and Victory Medals.
8, Stratford Road, Buckingham. Z1422.

BRINNAND, T. T., Private, 7th Wiltshire Regt.
Shortly after volunteering in September 1914, he was drafted to the Western Front, where he took part in the Battle of Ypres and many other engagements until October 1915. He was then transferred to Salonika, and there fought on the Doiran front, and was severely wounded in action on the Struma in November 1917. Invalided home, he was for a considerable period in hospital before being discharged in 1918 as medically unfit for further service. He holds the 1914–15 Star, and the General Service and Victory Medals.
19, Aylesbury Street, Wolverton, Bucks. Z1424.

BRITTAIN, A., Private, 2nd Bedfordshire Regt.
Volunteering in November 1914, he proceeded to the Western Front on completing his training in the following year and there took part in the Battles of Ypres, the Somme and Arras and many minor ngagements. He made the supreme sacrifice, falling in action near Ypres in June 1917. He was entitled to the 1914–15 Star, and the General Service and Victory Medals.
"Steals on the ear the distant triumph song."
14, Hartington Street, Bedford. X1427/A.

BRITTAIN, B. E., Pte., 1/5th Bedfordshire Regt.
Volunteering in January 1915, he proceeded to the Western Front in September of that year, and there saw much heavy fighting. After taking part in several important engagements, he was severely wounded in action at Loos in December 1915, and was admitted to hospital in England. He was finally invalided from the Army in December 1916, and holds the 1914–15 Star, and the General Service and Victory Medals.
3, Featherstone Buildings, Bedford. X1426.

BRITTAIN, G., Private, 2nd Bedfordshire Regt.
He volunteered in November 1915, and, on completing a period of training in the following year was drafted to the Western Front, where he saw severe fighting in various sectors. He took part in many important engagements in this theatre of war, and was five times wounded in action, on the Somme, at Arras, Vimy Ridge, Ypres and Cambrai. Demobilised in April 1919, he holds the General Service and Victory Medals.
Eaton Ford Green, Eaton Ford, Beds. Z1425.

BRITTAIN, W., Private, R.A.M.C.
Mobilised in August 1914, he was drafted to Gallipoli in April of the following year, and there, after taking part in the Landing at Suvla Bay, saw much severe fighting. On the Evacuation of the Peninsula, however, he was transferred to Egypt and proceeded thence into Palestine, where, acting as a stretcher-bearer, he was present at the Battles of Gaza and the fall of Jerusalem. He was discharged on his return home in May 1919, and holds the 1914–15 Star, and the General Service and Victory Medals. 14, Hartington Street, Bedford. X1427/B.

BRITTEN, R. G., Private, 2nd Northants. Regt.
He volunteered in July 1915, and, after undergoing a period of training, was retained at various stations, where he was engaged on duties of great importance. Unable, on account of ill-health, to obtain his transfer to a theatre of war, he nevertheless rendered valuable services with his unit until his demobilisation in December 1918.
Brook Cottage, Chawston, St. Neots, Beds. Z1428.

BRITTON, F., Corporal, Royal Engineers.
He was mobilised in August 1914, and, in July of the following year, proceeded to the Dardanelles, where he was wounded in action at Suvla Bay. Invalided home, he was finally discharged in October 1917 as medically unfit for further service, and holds the 1914–15 Star, and the General Service and Victory Medals. He afterwards served with the London Fire Brigade.
123, Marlborough Road, Queen's Park, Bedford. Z1429.

BROADWAY, A., Pte., Royal Warwickshire Regt.
Three months after volunteering in October 1915, he was drafted to Egypt, where he served at various stations. Proceeding thence into Palestine he saw much severe fighting, and took part in the Battles of Gaza and the entry into Jaffa and Jerusalem. Invalided home in October 1917, he unhappily died on November 9th of that year. He was entitled to the General Service and Victory Medals.
"He joined the great white company of valiant souls."
119, Marlborough Road, Queen's Park, Bedford. Z1431/E.

BROADWAY, J. H., 1st Class Gunner, Royal Navy.
Already in the Navy when war was declared in August 1914, he afterwards served in H.M.S. "Vimiera," attached to the Grand Fleet in the North Sea. He was engaged chiefly on patrol duties in these waters, and took part in the Battle of Heligoland and many minor actions, being present also at the bombardment of Zeebrugge. He holds the 1914–15 Star, and the General Service and Victory Medals, and in 1920 was still at sea.
119, Marlborough Road, Queen's Park, Bedford. Z1431/B.

BROADWAY, S., Gunner, Royal Field Artillery.
Having previously served in the Royal Navy in H.M.S. "Antrim" in the North Sea, he enlisted in the Royal Field Artillery in October 1915, and, in the following month, proceeded to the Western Front. There he saw severe fighting in various sectors, took part in the Battles of Albert, Ypres, Passchendaele, Cambrai and St. Quentin, and was wounded in action on the Somme in October 1916. Demobilised in May 1919, he holds the 1914–15 Star, and the General Service and Victory Medals.
119, Marlborough Road, Queen's Park, Bedford. Z1431/C.

BROADWAY, W., Sapper, Royal Engineers.
Volunteering in October 1914, he was drafted to the Western Front two months later and there saw much severe fighting. After taking part in the Battles of Festubert, Loos and the Somme and other important engagements in various sectors, he returned home in August 1916, and was afterwards employed on munition work at Messrs. Allen's, Bedford. He was finally demobilised in February 1919, and holds the 1914–15 Star, and the General Service and Victory Medals.
119, Marlborough Road, Queen's Park, Bedford. Z1431/D.

BROCKETT, A. A. V., Sapper, Royal Engineers.
Mobilised in August 1914, he was retained on important duties in England until 1916, and was then drafted to the Western Front. Whilst in this theatre of war he took part in important engagements in various sectors, including the Battles of the Somme, Arras, Ypres and Cambrai, and was wounded in action at Ypres in 1917. He was discharged in May 1919, and holds the General Service and Victory Medals.
36, College Street, Kempston, Bedford. Z1433/A.

BROCKETT, J. W., Rflmn., King's Royal Rifle Corps.
Joining in November 1917, he proceeded to France in the following month, and there saw severe fighting in various sectors of the front. He took part in the Battles of the Aisne, Amiens and Cambrai, and many other important engagements in this theatre of war, served also through the Retreat and Advance of 1918, and was wounded in action in the second Battle of the Somme. He was demobilised in November 1919, and holds the General Service and Victory Medals.
10, Beckett Street, Bedford. X1432.

BROCKETT, W. J., Sapper, Royal Engineers.
Already in the Army when war broke out in August 1914, he was retained on important duties at various stations in England until 1917, when he proceeded to the Western Front. There he served in various sectors, took part in the Battles of Messines, Ypres and the Somme, and many other engagements, and was twice wounded in action at Arras in 1917 and at Cambrai in the following year. He was discharged in March 1919, and holds the General Service and Victory Medals.
36, College Street, Kempston, Bedford. Z1433/B.

BROOKER, H., Staff-Sergeant, R.F.A.
Mobilised at the outbreak of war in August 1914, he was immediately drafted to the Western Front, where he fought in the Retreat from Mons. He also took a prominent part in the Battles of Ypres, Neuve Chapelle, Festubert, Loos, the Somme and Cambrai, and many other important engagements in this theatre of war. Returning home in 1919 he was discharged in March of that year, and holds the Mons Star, and the General Service and Victory Medals.
Elexandra Place, St. Ives, Hunts. Z1434.

BROOKER, J., Rifleman, Rifle Brigade.
He was mobilised in August 1914, and was immediately drafted to the Western Front, where, after serving through the Retreat from Mons, he was wounded in action on the Aisne in October 1914, and admitted to hospital at Norwich. On his recovery, however, he returned to France and fought in the Battle of Neuve Chapelle. He fell in action at Ypres on May 14th, 1915. He was entitled to the Mons Star, and the General Service and Victory Medals.
"Courage, bright hopes and a myriad dreams splendidly given."
Walnut Tree Terrace, Luke St., Eynesbury, St. Neots, Hunts. Z1437.

BROOKER, J., Corporal, 2nd Bedfordshire Regt.
He volunteered in January 1915, and, after his training, was retained on important duties at various stations in England until 1918. He was then drafted to the Western Front, where he saw much severe fighting and was wounded in action. He was invalided home, and was for a considerable period in hospital before being discharged in September 1919 as medically unfit for further service. He holds the General Service and Victory Medals.
Great Northern Street, Huntingdon. Z1436.

BROOKER, R., Gunner, Royal Garrison Artillery.
Joining in March 1916, he was drafted to the Western Front in August of that year, and there saw severe fighting in various sectors. He took part in the Battles of the Somme, Arras and Cambrai, and many other important engagements, and was wounded in action near Ypres. After the cessation of hostilities he served with the Army of Occupation in Germany, finally returning home for demobilisation in September 1919. He holds the General Service and Victory Medals.
Elexandra Place, St. Ives, Hunts. Z1435.

BROOKES, A. S., Driver, Royal Engineers.
Volunteering in September 1914, he was drafted to Gallipoli in June of the following year, and there saw much severe fighting, particularly at Suvla Bay. On the Evacuation of the Peninsula he was transferred to Egypt, where he served at various stations until invalided home in July 1918, suffering from malaria. He was finally discharged in January 1919 as medically unfit for further service, and holds the 1914–15 Star, and the General Service and Victory Medals.
Harrowden Road, Cardington, Bedford. Z1438.

BROOKS, A. J., Private, 1st Hampshire Regiment.
Volunteering in February 1915, he proceeded to the Western Front in June of that year, and there took part in the Battles of Ypres, Loos and Albert, and many other important engagements in various sectors. He was unfortunately reported missing and presumed to have been killed in action on July 1st, 1916, in the Somme Offensive. He was entitled to the 1914–15 Star, and the General Service and Victory Medals.
"He joined the great white company of valiant souls."
1, Hill's Yard, Sherington, Newport Pagnell, Bucks. Z1261/A.

BROOKS, E., Driver, Royal Engineers.
He volunteered in March 1915, and, twelve months later, was drafted to Salonika, where he was engaged on important duties on the lines of communication with the Signal Section. He also took an active part in many engagements on the Vardar, Doiran and Struma fronts until the cessation of hostilities, and finally returned home for demobilisation in May 1919. He holds the General Service and Victory Medals.
Biddenham, Beds. Z1443.

BROOKS, F., Guardsman, Grenadier Guards.
Mobilised in August 1914, he was immediately drafted to the Western Front, where he fought in the Retreat from Mons. He also took part in the Battles of La Bassée, Festubert, the Somme, Vimy Ridge and Cambrai, and many other important engagements in various sectors, and was wounded in action at Arras in 1917. He was discharged in October 1918, and holds the Mons Star, and the General Service and Victory Medals.
262, Bedford Road, Kempston, Bedford. X1441.

BROOKS, H. C., Leading Stoker, Royal Navy.
Already in the Navy when war was declared in August 1914, he afterwards served in H.M.T.B.D. "35," attached to the Chatham Division. He was engaged chiefly on patrol duties in the North Sea, where his ship was torpedoed on several occasions and was instrumental in sinking three German cruisers. He was still at sea in 1920, plying between England and America, and holds the 1914–15 Star, and the General Service and Victory Medals.
12, Near Town, Olney, Bucks. Z1444.

BROOKS, H. E., Private, R.A.S.C. (M.T.)
Shortly after volunteering in January 1915 he proceeded to the Western Front, where he was engaged on duties of great importance in various sectors. He was also present at the Battles of Ypres, the Somme, Arras and Cambrai, and many other engagements until the cessation of hostilities, and was then sent with the Army of Occupation into Germany. Demobilised on his return home in May 1919, he holds the 1914–15 Star, and the General Service and Victory Medals.
29, Bury Avenue, Newport Pagnell, Bucks. Z1439.

BROOKS, T. E., Q.M.S., 1st Essex Regiment.
At the outbreak of war in August 1914 he was already serving in the Army, and in the following year proceeded overseas. He was stationed at Alexandria throughout the period of hostilities and engaged on very important clerical work on the Headquarters' Staff. He returned to England in 1919, after rendering valuable services, and was discharged in April 1920, holding the 1914–15 Star, and the General Service and Victory Medals. 3, Tower Gardens, Bedford. X1442.

BROOKS, W. C., Private, 19th (Queen Alexandra's Own Royal) Hussars.
A month after the declaration of war he volunteered, and five months later was ordered to the Western Front. There he took part in severe fighting at Neuve Chapelle, Ypres, Festubert, Loos, the Somme, Albert and Messines, and was unfortunately killed in action at Cambrai on October 8th, 1918. He was entitled to the 1914–15 Star, and the General Service and Victory Medals.
"The path of duty was the way to glory."
2, Ouse Walk, Huntingdon. Z1440/A.

BROOKS, W. H., Private, Labour Corps.
He joined in February 1917, and in the following June was drafted to the Western Front. There he rendered valuable services in connection with salvage and canteen work in the Ypres, Cambrai, Albert and Amiéns sectors. After the Armistice he was sent to Calais, and worked in the Officers' Mess until demobilised in December 1919. He holds the General Service and Victory Medals. 2, Ouse Walk, Huntingdon. Z1440/B.

BROUGHTON, A. E., Pte., 1/1st Beds. Regt.
Volunteering in November 1915, he was employed on important duties in England until 1917, when he was sent to the Western Front. He fought in engagements at Arras, Vimy Ridge and Cambrai, and was wounded in action on the Somme, and also at Hill 60. In consequence he was invalided out of the Army in March 1918, and holds the General Service and Victory Medals.
90, Grey Friars Walk, Bedford. X1446/C.

BROUGHTON, W. C., Tpr., Bedfordshire Lancers.
He volunteered in May 1915, and in the following year proceeded to the Western Front. He took an active part in severe fighting in numerous engagements of importance, including the Battles of the Somme, Passchendaele, Ypres, Arras and Cambrai. He was wounded in action which resulted in the loss of one eye. Demobilised in February 1919, he holds the General Service and Victory Medals.
90, Grey Friars Walk, Bedford. X1446/B.

BROUGHTON, W. M., Pte., Royal Defence Corps.
Volunteering in April 1915, he was unable to obtain a transfer to a fighting unit on account of his age. He served at various important home stations, and was also engaged in guarding railways. In 1917 his health broke down, and he was discharged as medically unfit for further military duties in September of that year. 90, Grey Friars Walk, Bedford. X1446/A.

BROWN, A., 1st Air Mechanic, Royal Air Force.
He volunteered in September 1915, and in the following year proceeded to the Western Front. During his period of service there he was stationed at St. Omer, where he was engaged in the responsible work of repairing aircraft. He was demobilised in February 1919, but seven months later, on August 6th, 1919, he unhappily died, and was entitled to the General Service and Victory Medals.
"His memory is cherished with pride."
19, Bury Avenue, Newport Pagnell, Bucks. Z1476.

BROWN, A., Sapper, R.E.; and Pte., Cheshire Regt.
He joined in February 1916, and after a period of training was ten months later drafted overseas. Whilst on the Western Front he rendered valuable services in tunnelling, and did good work with his unit in engagements at Arras, Passchendaele, Bray and Cambrai, and was wounded in action. He was later transferred to the Cheshire Regiment and served with that unit until demobilised in February 1919, holding the General Service and Victory Medals. 5, Priory Street, Bedford. X1466/A.

BROWN, A. C., Private, 3rd East Surrey Regiment.
On attaining military age in July 1918, he joined the Army, and a month later was ordered to the Western Front, where he served for 15 months. During that period he saw much fierce fighting in the Cambrai and St. Quentin sectors, and in the final victorious engagements of the war. He was demobilised in November 1919, and holds the General Service and Victory Medals. 11, St. Leonard's Street, Bedford. X1455/C.

BROWN, A. S. (D.C.M.), Sergt., 2nd Beds. Regt.
When war was declared he was already in the Army, and accordingly at once proceeded overseas with the First Expeditionary Force. Whilst on the Western Front he served with distinction in the Battles of Mons, Ypres (I.), Hill 60, Ypres (II.), and fell fighting at Festubert on May 17th, 1915. He was awarded the Distinguished Conduct Medal for conspicuous bravery in the Field, and was also entitled to the Mons Star, and the General Service and Victory Medals.
"Great deeds cannot die:
They with the sun and moon renew their light for ever."
1, Ram Yard, Bedford. X1467/C.

BROWN, A. T., Pte., 2nd Bedfordshire Regiment.
In October 1914 he volunteered, and in the following year was sent to France, where he fought at Festubert and Loos, and was wounded in action on the Somme in August 1916. On returning to the firing line he served at Bullecourt, Delville Wood, Arras and Vimy Ridge, and was wounded and taken prisoner in April 1917. He was released from captivity in December 1918, and demobilised two months later, holding the 1914–15 Star, and the General Service and Victory Medals.
Cross Hall Ford, St. Neots, Hunts. Z1472.

BROWN, C., Private, 2/1st London Regiment (Royal Fusiliers).
On the declaration of war in August 1914, he volunteered, but was retained on home service until 1917, when he proceeded to France. On this front he saw heavy fighting in the Arras and the Somme sectors, and was wounded in action on two occasions. In March 1918 he was taken prisoner, and kept in captivity until the close of hostilities. He was demobilised in 1919, and holds the General Service and Victory Medals.
8, Green Street, St. Ives, Hunts. Z1475/B.

BROWN, C., Private, 1st East Surrey Regiment.
He joined the Army in February 1917, and on completion of his training, was six months later sent to the Western Front. There he was engaged in fierce fighting in different sectors of the line, and was in action at Cambrai, the Somme, Amiens, and in the Retreat and Advance of 1918. He was wounded on one occasion, and served in France until demobilised in May 1919, holding the General Service and Victory Medals.
5, Priory Street, Bedford. X1466/C.

BROWN, C., Private, Bedfordshire Regiment.
He was already serving at the outbreak of war, and at once proceeded to the Western Front. Whilst serving in that theatre of war, he took an active part in the Battles of Mons, La Bassée, Ypres, Hill 60 and Loos. He was severely wounded in action, and consequently was discharged from the Army as medically unfit in January 1916. He holds the Mons Star, and the General Service and Victory Medals.
6, Brace Street, Bedford. X1454.

BROWN, C. E., Sergeant, Royal Field Artillery.
At the outbreak of hostilities in August 1914, he was already serving, and immediately proceeded to the Western Front. He saw heavy fighting in the Battles of Mons, the Marne, the Aisne, Ypres, the Somme and Cambrai, and took a prominent part in the Allied Advance of 1918. In March 1919 he was discharged from the Army, and holds the Mons Star, and the General Service and Victory Medals.
27, Mill Street, Newport Pagnell, Bucks. Z1463/D.

BROWN, C. H., Private, 2/5th Bedfordshire Regt.
At the outbreak of hostilities he was mobilised and immediately ordered to France, where he fought in the Battles of Mons, La Bassée and Festubert. He was wounded in action at Neuve Chapelle and Ypres, and in 1916 was transferred to Palestine. There he did good work with his unit at Gaza, Jaffa, Haifa and Jerusalem. He was discharged on his return to England in February 1919, and holds the Mons Star, and the General Service and Victory Medals.
3, Britain's Yard, Hitchin St., Biggleswade, Beds. Z1460/B.

BROWN, E., Air Mechanic, Royal Air Force.
He joined in February 1918, and on completion of his training at Bangor, served at various important home stations. He was unable to procure a transfer overseas, but nevertheless rendered valuable services in carrying out work requiring great technical knowledge and skill. He was eventually demobilised in January 1919. 22, School St., New Bradwell, Bucks. Z1448/B.

BROWN, E., Pte., 1st Highland Light Infantry.
Having enlisted in 1906, he was already serving in India when war broke out in August 1914, and three months later proceeded to the Western Front. After taking part in the Battle of Ypres, he was wounded in action and taken prisoner at La Bassée, and was held in captivity in Germany until after the cessation of hostilities. He was discharged in April 1919, and holds the 1914 Star, and the General Service and Victory Medals. Green's Norton, Towcester, Northants. Z2873/C.

BROWN, E. E. (M.M.), Driver, R.A.S.C.
He joined in April 1916, and shortly afterwards was drafted to the Western Front, where he took part in many engagements. He saw heavy fighting at the Battles of the Somme, Arras, Ypres and Passchendaele, and was gassed as Cambrai in October 1918. He was awarded the Military Medal for conspicuous bravery in repairing motor lorries under very heavy shell-fire. Demobilised in December 1919, he also holds the General Service and Victory Medals.
London End, Milton Ernest, Bedford. Z1450.

BROWN, F., A.B., Royal Naval Division.
He volunteered in November 1914, but was retained on important duties at Blandford and Alford until 1917, when he succeeded in obtaining a transfer to the fighting area. During his service on the Western Front he was engaged in severe fighting in the Somme, Ypres and Arras sectors, and remained in France until after the cessation of hostilities. He was demobilised in July 1919, and holds the General Service and Victory Medals. 1, Oxford Road, St. Ives, Hunts. Z1477.

BROWN, F., Corporal, Royal Engineers.
Joining in 1916, he was on completion of his training sent overseas in the same year. During his service in France he performed excellent work with his unit in making roads through the devastated areas. He also served as a Cook in the Officers' Mess in the Arras, Ypres, Cambrai and the Somme sectors. He was demobilised in 1919, and holds the General Service and Victory Medals. 8, Green Street St., Ives, Hunts. Z1475/A.

BROWN, F., Private, 7th Northamptonshire Regt.
He volunteered in August 1914, and in September of the following year proceeded to the Western Front, where he saw much severe fighting. He was unfortunately reported missing and later killed in action in the Battle of Loos on September 27th, 1915, after only a few days in France. He was entitled to the 1914–15 Star, and the General Service and Victory Medals.
"A costly sacrifice upon the altar of freedom."
Pury End, Paulerspury, Towcester, Northants. Z2874.

BROWN, F. C., Gunner, Royal Garrison Artillery.
He was mobilised when war was declared and proceeded to France in January 1915. Whilst on the Western Front he took an active part in severe fighting in engagements at Hill 60, Ypres, Loos, Vimy Ridge, Passchendaele and Cambrai. In November 1918 he was discharged as a time-expired man, and holds the 1914–15 Star, and the General Service and Victory Medals. 1, Ram Yard, Bedford. X1467/D.

BROWN, F. C., Driver, Tank Corps.
He volunteered in August 1914, and in January of the following year proceeded to the Western Front. There he was in action at Festubert, Loos, Albert, the Somme, Arras and Cambrai, and was wounded on three occasions. In consequence he was invalided out of the Army in December 1918, holding the 1914–15 Star, and the General Service and Victory Medals.
The Green, Cardington, Beds. Z1451.

BROWN, F. H., Private, 2/5th Bedfordshire Regt.
Volunteering in 1915, he proceeded in the following year to Palestine, where he was in action at Gaza. Later he was sent to Italy, contracted fever and was eventually sent to hospital in England. On his recovery he was drafted to France, and saw heavy fighting at Cambrai and the Somme. In May 1918, however, his health broke down, and he was invalided to England and discharged from the Army suffering from heart disease in February 1919. He holds the General Service and Victory Medals. 25, Bletsoe, Bedford. Z1458.

BROWN, G., Private, Machine Gun Corps.
He volunteered in January 1916, and on conclusion of a period of training was drafted overseas later in the same year. He served on the Western Front for over three years, and during that time was in action in important engagements on the Somme and at Arras, Ypres, Messines and Cambrai. In July 1919 he was demobilised, holding the General Service and Victory Medals. Cople, Bedford. Z1452.

BROWN, G., Sapper, Royal Engineers.
Volunteering in May 1915, he proceeded in the same year to the Western Front, and after serving at Ypres and Arras was wounded in action at Delville Wood in August 1916. He was invalided home, and on his recovery, in June 1917, was sent to Palestine. On this front he was engaged in fierce fighting at Gaza, and performed excellent work with his unit in tunnelling and trench-digging. In 1920 he was still serving in the Army, and holds the 1914–15 Star, and the General Service and Victory Medals. 39, Chandos Street, Bedford. X1465.

BROWN, G., Private, 9th Leicestershire Regiment and Labour Corps.
He joined in March 1916, and five months later was sent to the Western Front. There he was engaged in severe fighting in different sectors of the line, and served on the Somme and at Arras, Ypres and Cambrai. He was wounded in action, and, on being transferred to the Labour Corps, was employed in guarding prisoners of war. Demobilised in October 1919, he holds the General Service and Victory Medals.
2, Tickford Court, Priory St., Newport Pagnell, Bucks. Z1468.

BROWN, G. E., Private, R.A.M.C.
He volunteered in September 1914, and in April 1915 was drafted to Gallipoli. There he served as a stretcher-bearer at Krithia and Suvla Bay, and in the subsequent engagements of the campaign. After the Evacuation of the Peninsula he was invalided home with enteric fever, and on his recovery was sent to India, where he was employed as a hospital Orderly at Doulah. He was demobilised on his return to England in November 1919, and holds the 1914–15 Star, and the General Service and Victory Medals.
22, School Street, New Bradwell, Bucks. Z1448/A.

BROWN, G. E., Rifleman, Rifle Brigade.
A Reservist, he was called up in August 1914, and a month later was sent to France. On this front he was in action at Festubert, Loos, Messines, Vimy Ridge and the Somme. He was wounded in the Battles of the Aisne and Ypres, and gassed at Cambrai. He served in France until January 1918, and a year later was discharged, holding the 1914 Star, and the General Service and Victory Medals.
Woodside Cottages, Aspley Hill, Woburn Sands, Beds. Z1453.

BROWN, G. F., Private, Labour Corps.
He joined the Army in March 1916, but on completion of his training proved to be unfit for service overseas. Throughout the period of hostilities he was stationed at Norwich, and employed as a carpenter, which duties he fulfilled with great ability. He was eventually demobilised in June 1919.
8, Green Street, St. Ives, Hunts. Z1471/A.

BROWN, H., Private, Bedfordshire Regiment.
He volunteered in April 1915, and, on completing his training later in the same year, was drafted to Egypt. In this seat of operations he took part in the Advance into Palestine, and was in action at Gaza and Jaffa. He suffered from shell-shock and was in hospital for a time, but on his recovery was engaged on important duties until his return home for his demobilisation in March 1919. He holds the 1914–15 Star, and the General Service and Victory Medals.
18, Green Street, St. Ives, Hunts. Z1469.

BROWN, H., Sapper, Royal Engineers.
He joined in June 1916, and after a period of training was drafted to the Western Front. In this theatre of war he was engaged on important duties in connection with the construction of bridges, pill-boxes and water posts in various sectors, including those at Ypres, Arras, and Cambrai. He was demobilised in February 1919, and holds the General Service and Victory Medals. 5, Priory Place, Bedford. X1466/B.

BROWN, H., Private, R.A.S.C. (M.T.)
Volunteering in January 1916, he was drafted overseas later in the same year. He was engaged with the Mechanical Transport in Egypt, and later took an active part in the Advance into Palestine and served at Gaza, Jerusalem and Jaffa. In August 1919 he returned home and was demobilised, holding the General Service and Victory Medals.
36, Argyll Street, Bedford. X1464

BROWN, H. A., Private, 5th Warwickshire Regt
He joined in March 1917, and underwent a period of training prior to his being drafted to France. There he was stationed at Etaples, and was engaged in guarding German prisoners, in which capacity he rendered valuable services. He was demobilised in October 1919, and holds the General Service and Victory Medals.
11, School Street, New Bradwell, Bucks. Z1448/C.

BROWN, H. E., Cpl., 5th Royal Warwickshire Regt.
He volunteered in 1914, and was retained for a time on important duties at various home stations. In 1916, however, he was drafted to France, and took part in the Battle of the Somme, where he was wounded in August 1916. On August 24th, 1917, he was unfortunately killed in action at St. Julien whilst serving as a bomber. He was entitled to the General Service and Victory Medals.
"Great deeds cannot die:
They with the sun and moon renew their light for ever,"
8, Station Road, Warboys, Hunts. Z1474/B.

BROWN, H. H., Private, 4th Northants. Regt.
Joining in March 1916, he proceeded to the Western Front on completing his training in the following July, and there took part in many important engagements in the Advance on the Somme He died gloriously on the Field of Battle at Bapaume on March 20th, 1917. He was entitled to the General Service and Victory Medals.
"Nobly striving,
He nobly fell that we might live."
Green's Norton, Towcester, Northants. Z2873/A.

BROWN, H. S., Corporal, 1st Royal Berkshire Regt.
Volunteering in 1914, he was drafted overseas after completing his training. During his service on the Western Front he took part in engagements at Albert, Vimy Ridge and on the Somme. He made the supreme sacrifice, being killed in action at Beaumont-Hamel on November 5th, 1916, and was entitled to the General Service and Victory Medals.
"A valiant Soldier, with undaunted heart he breasted life's last hill."
8, Station Road, Warboys, Hunts. Z1474/A.

BROWN, J., Private, 2nd Bedfordshire Regiment.
He was mobilised in August 1914, and was shortly afterwards drafted to the Western Front, where he took part in many engagements. He was severely wounded at Neuve Chapelle and unfortunately died of his wounds on November 13th, 1915. He was entitled to the Mons Star, and the General Service and Victory Medals.
"He passed out of the sight of men by the path of duty and self-sacrifice."
Church Path, Sandy, Beds. TZ1459.

BROWN, J. G., Private, 1st Northamptonshire Rgt.
He joined in August 1917 as a Drummer Boy at the age of 15 years and was engaged at various stations on important duties with his unit. He was not successful in obtaining his transfer overseas owing to his youth, but rendered valuable services throughout hostilities, and in 1920 was still in the Army.
High Street, Carlton, Sharnbrook, Beds. Z1449/A.

BROWN, J. J., L/Corporal, 2nd Northants. Regt.
He was already in the Army in Egypt when war broke out in August 1914, but was quickly drafted to France and took part in the Battles of the Marne and Ypres. He died gloriously on the Field of Battle at Vimy Ridge on May 9th, 1915, and was entitled to the 1914 Star, and the General Service and Victory Medals. "His life for his Country, his soul to God."
High Street, Carlton, Sharnbrook, Beds. Z1449/B.

BROWN, J. J., Private, 8th Northants. Regiment.
He joined in June 1916, and in February of the following year was drafted to the Western Front, where he saw much severe fighting. He took part in the Battles of Arras, Ypres and the Somme and many other important engagements in various sectors whilst in this theatre of war. He was demobilised on his return home in April 1919, and holds the General Service and Victory Medals.
Mount Pleasant, Green's Norton, Towcester, Northants. Z2873/B.

BROWN, J. S., Private, R.A.S.C.
He joined in February 1916, and underwent a short period of training before proceeding to the Western Front Whilst in this theatre of war he was engaged on various important duties, and took an active part in the Battles of Ypres and Cambrai. He unfortunately met with an accident which resulted in his discharge in December 1918 as medically unfit for further service. He holds the General Service and Victory Medals.
Alconbury Weston. Z1462

BROWN, J. W., Private, Labour Corps.
Joining in March 1916, he was drafted overseas in the following October. During his service on the Western Front he was engaged on transport duty, and saw much service in the Somme, Ypres, Arras and Cambrai sectors. He was demobilised in March 1919, and holds the General Service and Victory Medals.
Vicarage Lane, Somersham, Hunts. Z1473.

BROWN, L., Pte., 7th Royal Warwickshire Regt.
He enlisted in January 1917, and a month later was drafted to the Western Front, where he took part in much fighting in the Vimy Ridge, Passchendaele and Cambrai sectors. He made the supreme sacrifice, being killed in action in October 1917, and was entitled to the General Service and Victory Medals.
"A costly sacrifice upon the altar of freedom."
11, St. Leonard's Street, Bedford. X1455/B.

BROWN, P., Private, Northamptonshire Regiment.
He volunteered in November 1915, and on completing his training in the following year was drafted to France, where he saw much heavy fighting at the Battles of the Somme and Arras. He died gloriously on the Field of Battle at Messines on May 3rd, 1917, and was entitled to the General Service and Victory Medals.
"Honour to the immortal dead, who gave their youth that the world might grow old in peace."
8, Station Road, Sandy, Beds. Z1460/A.

BROWN, R., Gunner, Royal Garrison Artillery.
Joining in May 1916, he proceeded overseas in the following November. Whilst on the Western Front he took part in many engagements, including those on the Somme and at Ypres, Arras and Cambrai, and was also in action with his Battery throughout the Retreat and Advance of 1918. He was demobilised in 1919, and holds the General Service and Victory Medals.
8, Green Street, St. Ives, Hunts. Z1471/B.

BROWN, S. W., Sapper, Royal Engineers.
He joined in June 1916, and underwent a period of training prior to his being drafted to France. There he took part in engagements on the Somme, at Ypres, Arras and Cambrai, and was attached to the break-down gang on the light railways, with which he served until after the cessation of hostilities. He was demobilised in July 1919, and holds the General Service and Victory Medals.
3, Bletsoe, Bedford Z1457.

BROWN, T. M., Private, Bedfordshire Regiment.
He volunteered in October 1915, and in the following July was drafted to the Western Front. In this theatre of war he took part in engagements on the Somme, at Gommecourt and Arras, and was wounded and gassed in action. As a result he was invalided home, but on his recovery returned to France and served on important duties until his demobilisation in August 1919. He holds the General Service and Victory Medals.
1, Ram Yard, Bedford. X1467/A.

BROWN, V. H., Private, 19th London Regiment.
He joined in October 1917, and underwent a period of training prior to his being drafted to the Western Front. There he was engaged on many important duties, and took part in heavy fighting at Lille and Tournai and in many other sectors. He was demobilised in January 1919, and holds the General Service and Victory Medals.
Station Road, Warboys, Hunts. Z1474/C.

BROWN, W., Private, Royal Defence Corps.
He volunteered in 1915, and, after a period of training, was engaged at various stations on important duties with his unit. He rendered valuable services whilst employed in guarding bridges and railways, and later worked on a farm until he was discharged in September 1918 as medically unfit for further duty. Station Road, Tempsford, near Sandy, Beds. Z1470.

BROWN, W., Gunner, Royal Field Artillery.
Volunteering in April 1915, he was drafted overseas in the following year. Whilst in Mesopotamia he took part in much heavy fighting at Kut and Baghdad, but later contracted black fever. He unfortunately died from its effects on November 8th, 1917, and was entitled to the General Service and Victory Medals.
"Thinking that remembrance, though unspoken, may reach him where he sleeps."
Opposite Schools, Blunham, Sandy, Beds. Z1461.

BROWN, W., Driver, R.A.S.C.
He was already in the Army when war broke out in August 1914, and in the following year was drafted to Salonika, and thence to Egypt. In this seat of operations he saw much service, and took part in the Advance into Palestine and was in action at Gaza. He contracted fever, from which he unfortunately died in November 1918. He was entitled to the 1914–15 Star, and the General Service and Victory Medals.
"His memory is cherished with pride."
Bourne End, Cranfield, Beds. Z1447/A.

BROWN, W., Private, Canadian Overseas Forces.
He was already in the Army when war broke out in August 1914, and was retained for a time on important duties at various home stations. In February 1916 he was drafted to France, and fought at Loos, Vimy Ridge and on the Somme. He was reported missing on September 16th, 1916, and is now presumed to have been killed in action. He was entitled to the General Service and Victory Medals.
"A valiant Soldier, with undaunted heart he breasted life's last hill."
11, St. Leonard's Street, Bedford. X1455/A.

BROWN, W., Trooper, Northamptonshire Dragoons.
Having enlisted in 1911, he was drafted to the Western Front three months after the outbreak of war in August 1914, and there saw heavy fighting in various sectors. After taking part in the Battles of Ypres, Neuve Chapelle, Festubert, Loos, Vimy Ridge, the Somme, Arras, Passchendaele, Cambrai and minor engagements, he was transferred in November 1917 to Italy. There he was again in action on the Piave and the Asiago Plateaux until the cessation of hostilities, returning home for demobilisation in January 1919. He holds the 1914 Star, and the General Service and Victory Medals.
Green's Norton, Towcester, Northants. Z2873/D.

BROWN, W. J. (D.C.M.), Sergeant, Queen's (Royal West Surrey Regiment).
A Regular soldier, he was sent to France with the first Expeditionary Force in August 1914, and, after taking part in the Retreat from Mons, served with distinction at the Battles of Ypres, Loos and the Somme and in heavy fighting at Arras. He laid down his life for King and Country on September 3rd, 1916. He had been awarded the Distinguished Conduct Medal for conspicuous gallantry and devotion to duty in the Field, and was also entitled to the Mons Star, and the General Service and Victory Medals.
"Whilst we remember, the sacrifice is not in vain."
1, Ram Yard, Bedford. X1467/B.

BROWN, W. J., Sergt., 6th York & Lancaster Regt.
Volunteering in September 1914, he first saw heavy fighting at the Suvla Bay Landing in August 1915, and was in action on Gallipoli until the Evacuation of the Peninsula in January 1916. He then proceeded to Egypt, but, after taking part in engagements on the Suez Canal, was transferred to the Western Front six months later. Whilst in France he served with distinction at the Battles of the Somme and Ypres, and was three times wounded. On the last occasion, in October 1917, he unfortunately had to have his left leg amputated, and was eventually invalided from the Army in November 1918, holding the 1914–15 Star, and the General Service and Victory Medals.
17, Rose Villa, Bletsoe, Beds. Z1456.

BROWN, W. J., Sapper, Royal Engineers.
Volunteering in April 1915, he was drafted to the Western Front after three months' training and was there engaged on important duties in various sectors. He returned home, however, in October 1915, and was retained in England until September 1919, when he was demobilised. He holds the 1914–15 Star, and the General Service and Victory Medals.
Carey Row, Pury End, Pauler's Pury, Towcester, Northants Z287

BRUCE, A., Private, 7th Northamptonshire Regiment and Royal Sussex Regiment.
Volunteering in December 1915, he was drafted overseas in the following year. Whilst on the Western Front he took part in many engagements, including those at Ypres and Passchendaele. He was taken ill and consequently invalided home, but on his recovery returned to France and was employed on escort duty to prisoners of war. He was demobilised in March 1919, and holds the General Service and Victory Medals.
Southoe, Hunts. Z1478

BRUCE, F., Private, 1st Bedfordshire Regiment.
He volunteered in September 1914, and was retained for a time at various home stations before proceeding to France. There he took part in the Battles of Loos, Ypres and Lens, in heavy fighting at Béthune, and was twice wounded in action. He also saw service in Italy for about six months, during which time he was in action in many engagements. Returning home, he was demobilised in May 1919, and holds the General Service and Victory Medals.
Pipers Lane, Godmanchester, Hunts. Z1479

BRUCE, T., Private, 8th Bedfordshire Regiment.
He was mobilised in August 1914, and, after a period of training, was engaged at various stations on important duties with his unit. He was unable to obtain a transfer overseas owing to his being medically unfit, but rendered valuable services on pioneer work until his discharge in March 1918.
Eaton Socon, Beds. Z1480.

BRUMMELL, H. (D.C.M.), Corporal, 1/5th South Staffordshire Regiment.
He joined in July 1917, and a month later was drafted to the Western Front. In this theatre of war he played a prominent part in the Battles of Ypres, Cambrai (I. and II.) and in the Retreat and Advance of 1918. He was awarded the Distinguished Conduct Medal for conspicuous gallantry and devotion to duty in the Field during a bombing attack by the enemy, and also in putting a trench mortar gun out of action. He was demobilised in December 1919, and also holds the General Service and Victory Medals.
22, Tavistock Place, Bedford. TX1481.

BRUMMELL, W. H., L/Cpl., Bedfordshire Regt.
He volunteered in July 1915, and in the following year was sent overseas. During his service on the Western Front he took part in many important engagements, including the Battles of the Somme, Arras and Cambrai. Later he was in action during the second Battle of the Somme, and was wounded. He returned to England and was demobilised in February 1919, and holds the General Service and Victory Medals.
54, Coventry Road, Bedford. Z1483.

BRUNDLE, S., Trooper, Bedfordshire Lancers.
He volunteered in April 1915, and in the following year proceeded to the Western Front. There he was engaged on important transport work in the forward areas and did consistently good work throughout hostilities. He was demobilised in February 1919, and holds the General Service and Victory Medals 5, Weston Road, Olney, Bucks. Z1482.

BRUTON, F. W., Private, 6th Middlesex Regiment.
He joined in June 1916, and later in the same year was sent to France. There he took part in many important engagements in various sectors of the front. He was in action at the Battles of the Somme, Beaucourt, Arras, Ypres and Cambrai, and was wounded in 1918 and invalided to England. As a result he was discharged as medically unfit for further service in May 1918, and holds the General Service and Victory Medals.
80, Dudley Street, Bedford. Z1484.

BRYAN, C. (D.C.M.), Sergeant, Bedfordshire Regt.
He volunteered at the outbreak of war in August 1914, and was first retained on important duties at various stations. In August 1916, however, he proceeded to the Western Front, where he played a prominent part in many engagements, including those at Beaumont-Hamel, Arras, Ypres and Passchendaele. Later he was in action throughout the Retreat and Advance of 1918 until the close of hostilities. He was awarded the Distinguished Conduct Medal for conspicuous bravery and devotion to duty in the Field. Returning to England, he was demobilised in April 1919, and also holds the General Service and Victory Medals. 12, Dane Street, Bedford. Z1485/B.

BRYAN, H. (D.C.M.), Sergeant, Royal Engineers.
Mobilised at the outbreak of war in August 1914, he was shortly afterwards drafted to France. He did excellent work throughout the Battles of La Bassée, Ypres, Hill 60, Vimy Ridge and the Somme, where he was unfortunately killed in action on July 28th, 1916. He had been awarded the Distinguished Conduct Medal for great gallantry and devotion to duty in the Field at Neuve Chapelle, and was also entitled to the 1914–15 Star, and the General Service and Victory Medals.
"Great deeds cannot die:
They with the sun and moon renew their light for ever."
12, Dane Street, Bedford. Z1485/A.

BRYANT, J., Corporal, Oxford. and Bucks. L.I.
He volunteered in the 2/1st Buckingham Battalion in June 1915, and twelve months later was drafted to France, but after only a short period of service overseas, during which he played a prominent part in the Somme Offensive, he was badly wounded in action at Beaumont-Hamel, and unfortunately died on November 28th, 1916. He was entitled to the General Service and Victory Medals. "A costly sacrifice upon the altar of freedom." Maids Moreton, Bucks. Z3177/B.

BUCK, E., Air Mechanic, Royal Air Force.
He joined in January 1917, and later in the same year was drafted to France, where he served with his Squadron in various sectors of the front. Later he was transferred to the Labour Corps, and was engaged during the heavy fighting at Messines and Ypres, and was wounded in action. As a result he was discharged as medically unfit for further service in October 1918, and holds the General Service and Victory Medals.
7, Boswell Place, Bedford. X1487.

BUCK, H., Sapper, Royal Engineers.
He joined in June 1918, and on completion of his training was retained on important duties with his unit at various stations. He was not successful in obtaining his transfer to a theatre of war, but, nevertheless, rendered valuable services with the Inland Water Transport, until discharged in March 1919.
27, Russell Street, Bedford. X1488.

BUCKINGHAM, D., Private, 13th Essex Regt.
Joining in July 1916, he proceeded to France later in the same year, and took part in many important engagements in various sectors of the front. He was in action during the heavy fighting on the Somme, and was wounded and taken prisoner. Whilst in captivity he unfortunately died from the effects of his wounds on April 28th, 1918, and was entitled to the General Service and Victory Medals.
"A costly sacrifice upon the altar of freedom."
Earith, Hunts. Z1489.

BUCKINGHAM, G., Private, Queen's (Royal West Surrey Regiment).
He joined in February 1917, and in the following August was sent overseas. In the course of his service in this seat of war he saw much heavy fighting in various sectors of the front, and was in action at the Battles of Cambrai, the Somme (II.) and Amiens. Later he was engaged in guarding prisoners of war until demobilised in August 1919. He holds the General Service and Victory Medals. Little Staughton, Hunts. Z1491.

BUCKINGHAM, R. S., Corporal, 1st Oxfordshire and Buckinghamshire Light Infantry.
He volunteered in January 1915, and later in the same year was drafted to Mesopotamia. During his service in this theatre of war he took part in many important engagements. He was in action during the capture of Amara and the Battle of Kut, but was unfortunately killed on April 6th, 1916, and was buried at Sanna-i-Yat. He was entitled to the 1914–15 Star, and the General Service and Victory Medals.
"He died the noblest death a man may die:
Fighting for God and right and liberty."
56, Priory Street, Newport Pagnell, Bucks. Z1490/A.

V.C. BUCKINGHAM, W., Sgt., 2nd Leicestershire Regiment
Enlisting in November 1901, he was sent to France with the first Expeditionary Force in August 1914. He was in action during the Retreat from Mons, and served with distinction at the Battles of Ypres and Neuve Chapelle, where he was badly wounded. For great gallantry and absolute disregard of personal safety in this last engagement on March 22nd, 1915, he was awarded the Victoria Cross in rescuing a wounded comrade, and a badly wounded German, in the face of heavy rifle and shell fire, and for capturing two enemy machine guns single-handed. He was invalided to England, and, on his recovery, rendered valuable services by obtaining many recruits for the Army. In February 1917, however, he returned to his old unit on the Western Front, but, after taking a prominent part in further heavy fighting, died gloriously on the Field of Battle on the Somme on September 15th, 1917. In addition to the Victoria Cross he was also entitled to the Mons Star, and the General Service and Victory Medals.
"He died the noblest death a man may die:
Fighting for God and right and liberty."
35, York Street, Bedford. Z1492/A.

BUCKLE, F., Bandsman, 2nd Bedfordshire and Hertfordshire Regiments.
He joined in 1918, and after completing a period of training was retained on important duties with his unit at various stations. Later he proceeded to India and was stationed at Wellington, where in 1920 he was still serving.
28, St. John's Street, Kempston, Bedford. X1494/B.

BUCKLE, F., Private, Royal Defence Corps.
Volunteering in October 1914, he was retained at various stations on important duties with his unit. He was chiefly engaged in the guarding of bridges and also prisoners of war, and rendered valuable services. On November 22nd, 1918, he unfortunately died from effects of his military service.
"His memory is cherished with pride."
22, Ombersley Road, Bedford. Z1493.

BUCKLE, J., Sapper, Royal Engineers.
He volunteered in February 1915, and on completion of his training served at Harrogate on important duties. He was chiefly engaged as an officers' servant and did good work until December 1917, when he was discharged as medically unfit for further military service.
28, St. John's Street, Kempston, Bedford. Z1494/A.

BUFTON, E., Pte., 1/4th Shropshire Light Infty.
He volunteered in August 1914, and on completion of his training was at first retained on important duties with his unit at various stations. In January 1918, however, he proceeded to France, and took part in many important engagements in various sectors of the Front. He fought at the Battles of Cambrai, Albert and the Marne, where he was wounded in June 1918. On returing home he was demobilised in February 1919, and holds the General Service and Victory Medals.
41, Grey Friars Walk, Bedford. Z1495/B.

BUFTON, W. H., Private, 1st Herefordshire Regt.
He volunteered at the outbreak of war in August 1914, and in the following July was drafted to the Dardanelles. In the course of his service in this theatre of war he was present at the Landing at Suvla Bay, and took part in other engagements until the Evacuation of the Gallipoli Peninsula. He then went to Egypt and later was in action throughout many important engagements in Palestine, including the Battles of Gaza and the capture of Jerusalem. Returning to England in October 1918 he was invalided from the Army, but unfortunately died of consumption, due to his military service, on February 15th, 1919, and was entitled to the 1914–15 Star, and the General Service and Victory Medals.
"Steals on the ear the distant triumph song."
41, Grey Friars Walk, Bedford. Z1495/C.

BUGDEN, G. G., Sapper, Royal Engineers (R.O.D.)
Three months after joining in August 1916, he proceeded to Salonika, where he was engaged on important duties on the railways. Serving chiefly on the Vardar and Doiran fronts, he did much useful work with his Company, until sent home and invalided from the Army in December 1919, suffering from dysentery. He holds the General Service and Victory Medals. 62, Duncombe Street, Bletchley, Bucks. Z2876.

BUGGINS, D. E., Ship's Carpenter, R.N., H.M.S. "St. Vincent."
He volunteered in September 1914, and was engaged as a carpenter at Portsmouth Dockyard. Later he saw service at Scapa Flow and in the North Sea, where he was engaged on important patrol and escort duties until July 1918. He was then transferred to the Royal Air Force, and was stationed at Farnborough, where he did good work until demobilised in March 1919, holding the General Service and Victory Medals.
4, Spring Gardens, Newport Pagnell. Z1496.

BULL, A. A., Private, Northamptonshire Regt.
Mobilised at the outbreak of hostilities in August 1914, he was immediately sent to France, where he fought in the Battle of, and in the Retreat from, Mons, also in the Battles of the Marne and the Aisne, and was wounded at Festubert in December. On his recovery he was transferred to the Royal Engineers, and was engaged in trench-digging in various sectors of the front. After the Armistice he returned home, and was discharged in March 1919, holding the Mons Star, and the General Service and Victory Medals.
65, Caldecote Street, Newport Pagnell, Bucks.
Z1503/B—Z1504/B.

BULL, A. J., Private, Northamptonshire Regt.
He was mobilised in August 1914, and shortly afterwards was drafted to the Western Front, where he was engaged in severe fighting in the Retreat from Mons. He also took part in the Battle of the Marne, but was wounded in September 1914 on the Aisne. He was invalided to England, and after a protracted hospital treatment at York was discharged as medically unfit in March 1916, holding the Mons Star, and the General Service and Victory Medals
65, Caldecote Street, Newport Pagnell, Bucks.
Z1503/A—Z1504/A.

BULL, B. J., C.S.M., Royal Sussex Regiment.
A month after the outbreak of war he volunteered, and in 1915 proceeded overseas. During his service in France he fought with distinction in engagements at Ypres, Givenchy, Loos, the Somme, Arras and Cambrai, and in the Retreat and Advance of 1918. He was wounded in action and gassed, and was mentioned in Despatches for bravery in the Field. In March 1919 he was demobilised, holding the 1914–15 Star, and the General Service and Victory Medals, and the Italian Bronze Medal. 16, York Road, Stony Stratford, Bucks. TZ1499.

BULL, C. D., Private, Oxford. and Bucks. L.I.
He volunteered in September 1914, and six months later was sent to the Western Front. There he took an active part in many engagements of importance, particularly in the Ypres, Arras, and the Somme sectors, but was unfortunately killed in action on the Somme in September 1918. He was entitled to the 1914–15 Star, and the General Service and Victory Medals.
"His life for his Country, his soul to God."
65, Caldecote Street, Newport Pagnell, Bucks.
Z1503/E—Z1504/E.

BULL, F. J., Sergeant, 2nd Northamptonshire Regt.
He was serving in the Army when war was declared, and immediately proceeded to the Western Front. He took a prominent part in many important engagements, including those at Mons, La Bassée, Ypres, the Somme, Arras and the 1918 Retreat. Whilst engaged in fierce fighting in the Allied Advance he was unhappily killed on October 8th, 1918. He was entitled to the Mons Star, and the General Service and Victory Medals.
"A costly sacrifice upon the altar of freedom."
65, Caldecote Street, Newport Pagnell, Bucks.
Z1503/D—Z1504/D.

BULL, F. P., Private, R.A.S.C. (M.T.)
He volunteered in December 1915, and after a course of training was drafted overseas in June of the following year. Whilst in France he served at St. Omer, and was employed on important transport work until sustaining injuries whilst driving a motor lorry. He was invalided to England, and on his discharge from hospital served at various important depôts. In November 1917, however, he was discharged as medically unfit for further military duties, and holds the General Service and Victory Medals. 3, Britannia Place, Bedford. Z1505

BULL, F. W., Gunner, Royal Garrison Artillery.
Volunteering in September 1915, he was sent overseas on completion of his training in March 1916. He served on the Western Front for over three years, and during that time saw fierce fighting at Ypres and Vimy Ridge, and in the engagements prior to the cessation of hostilities. He was demobilised in September 1919, and holds the General Service and Victory Medals. 106, Church Street, Wolverton, Bucks. Z1502.

BULL, G., Private, 7th Buffs (East Kent Regiment).
He joined in June 1918, and after a period of training, was four months later sent to the Western Front. After only three weeks' active service he was wounded whilst taking part in severe fighting at Cambrai. He was sent to hospital in England, and was demobilised in February 1919, holding the General Service and Victory Medals.
Milton Ernest, Bedford. Z1506.

BULL, G. H., Gunner, Royal Garrison Artillery.
When war was declared in August 1914 he was serving in India, and in October 1915 was drafted to the Western Front. He saw heavy fighting in many sectors of the line, and did excellent work as a gunner in engagements at Ypres, the Somme, Arras, Neuve Chapelle and Cambrai. He was twice wounded in 1916, and again in 1917, and was discharged from the Army in May 1919, holding the 1914–15 Star, and the General Service and Victory Medals.
High Street, Stoke Goldington, Bucks. Z1501/B.

BULL, J. A., Private, 7th Bedfordshire Regiment.
In September 1914 he volunteered, and in the following February was drafted overseas. During his service in France he fought in the Battles of Neuve Chapelle, Hill 60, Ypres, and Festubert, but was unfortunately killed in action at Loos on October 17th, 1915. He was entitled to the 1914–15 Star, and the General Service and Victory Medals.
"Whilst we remember, the sacrifice is not in vain."
Great Staughton, Hunts. Z1500.

BULL, R. J., Private, 7th Oxford. and Bucks. L.I.
He volunteered in September 1914, and a year later proceeded to France, and served at Albert for a few weeks, before being drafted to Salonika. In that theatre of war he took an active part in numerous engagements, and experienced severe fighting on the Vardar and Doiran fronts. On returning to England in April 1919 he was demobilised, holding the 1914–15 Star, and the General Service and Victory Medals.
13, Slated Row, Old Wolverton, Bucks. Z1498.

BULL, T. (D.C.M.), Private, 2nd Northants. Regt.
At the outbreak of war he was already serving in the Army, and in September 1914 proceeded to the Western Front. There he fought with distinction in numerous important battles, and was awarded the Distinguished Conduct Medal for great bravery in the Field, and also a French decoration for conspicuous gallantry. During the Battles of the Somme in 1916 he was gassed, and unfortunately died from the effects in London in September 1917. He was also entitled to the 1914 Star, and the General Service and Victory Medals.
"Great deeds cannot die:
They with the sun and moon renew their light for ever."
65, Caldecote Street, Newport Pagnell, Bucks.
Z1503/F—1504/F.

BULL, T., Private, 3rd Oxford. and Bucks. L.I.
He joined the Army in June 1917, and after a period of training at Dover, was nine months later ordered to France. On this front he did good work with his unit at Ypres, and also in the Retreat and final decisive engagements of the war. He served in France until November 1919, when he was demobilised, holding the General Service and Victory Medals.
High Street, Stoke Goldington, Bucks. Z1501/A.

BULL, W. J., Private, Northamptonshire Regt.
At the outbreak of hostilities in August 1914 he volunteered, and in the following March proceeded overseas. Whilst serving in France he was in action at Neuve Chapelle and Ypres, and was wounded at Festubert in April 1915. He was invalided to England, and on his recovery returned to the Western Front, but was again wounded at the Somme in August 1916. He was sent to hospital at Taplow, where he received treatment, until discharged as medically unfit for further military duties in September 1918. He holds the 1914–15 Star, and the General Service and Victory Medals.
65, Caldecote St., Newport Pagnell, Bucks. Z1503/C—Z1504/C.

BULL, W. J. R., Corporal, 1st Wiltshire Regiment and 13th Devonshire Regiment.
He volunteered in December 1914, and in June 1915 proceeded to France, where he was in action at Ypres and Vimy Ridge. He was wounded in the Battle of the Somme in August 1916, and sent to hospital in England. After prolonged treatment there, he returned to the Western Front in July 1917, and served in the Ypres sector until the close of hostilities. Demobilised in March 1919, he holds the 1914–15 Star, and the General Service and Victory Medals.
High Street, Stoke Goldington, Bucks. Z1497.

BULLARD, A. H. E., Artificer, R.N., H.M.S. "Kilcock."
He joined in March 1918, and on being posted to his ship was engaged in conveying troops to Egypt and Port Said. During the latter period of his service he performed excellent work in mine-sweeping off the Dutch Coast, and in the North Sea. He was eventually demobilised in November 1919, and holds the General Service and Victory Medals.
24, Marlborough Road, Bedford. Z1507.

BUND, H. F., L/Corporal, 1st Essex Regiment.
Mobilised in August 1914, he was a month later drafted to the Western Front, and after fighting in the Battle of La Bassée, was wounded in action at Ypres. He was invalided to England, and, after 12 months' treatment in hospital, was sent to back France, but was unfortunately killed at Albert on April 14th, 1916. He was entitled to the 1914 Star, and the General Service and Victory Medals.
"His life for his Country."
Pertenhall, near St. Neots, Hunts. Z1508.

BUNDY, A., Private, Bedfordshire Regiment.
He volunteered in September 1914, and, after serving at Aldershot for ten months, was drafted to the Western Front, where he served for four years. During that period he took part in numerous important engagements, including the Battles of Loos, the Somme, Ypres, Arras and Cambrai. He was eventually demobilised in August 1919, and holds the 1914–15 Star, and the General Service and Victory Medals.
Montague Street, Eynesbury, St. Neots, Hunts. Z1194/A.

BUNDY, J., Driver, R.A.S.C.
He joined in March 1917, and on conclusion of his training was later in the same year sent to the Western Front, where he was wounded at Ypres. On his recovery he rejoined his unit in 1918, and was for the remainder of his period of service employed on important transport work in the Ypres, Cambrai and the Somme sectors. He was demobilised in January 1919, holding the General Service and Victory Medals.
Near George Bridge, Eaton Socon, Beds. Z1509.

BUNKER, J., Private, 8th Bedfordshire Regiment.
Volunteering in 1915, he was, on completion of his training in the following year, drafted to the Western Front. Whilst in this theatre of war he saw much severe fighting, took an active part in engagements on the Somme, at Arras and Ypres, and was gassed at Cambrai. He was demobilised in January 1919, and holds the General Service and Victory Medals.
Marston Shelton, Beds. Z1510.

BUNNAGE, A. W., Pte., Buffs (East Kent Regt.)
He volunteered in September 1915, and after completing his training, did good work with the Military Police at Dover until drafted overseas in 1916. During his service on the Western Front he was engaged in severe fighting in the Battles of the Somme, Vimy Ridge, Arras and Ypres, and remained in France until demobilised in September 1919. He holds the General Service and Victory Medals. 32, Russell St, St. Neots, Hunts. Z1511.

BUNTING, E. G., Private, 4th Northamptonshire Regiment; and 1st Air Mechanic, R.A.F.
He volunteered in January 1915, and, in April of that year, proceeded to Gallipoli, where, after taking part in the Landing at Cape Helles, he saw much severe fighting until the Evacuation of the Peninsula. He was then transferred to Egypt, whence he proceeded into Palestine and was engaged on duties of a highly technical nature near Gaza. He was finally demobilised on his return home in February 1919, and holds the 1914–15 Star, and the General Service and Victory Medals.
Green's Norton, Towcester, Northants. Z2877/A.

BUNTING, J. A., Private, 2nd Northants. Regt.
He joined in September 1916, and, on completion of a period of training in March of the following year, proceeded to the Western Front. Whilst in this theatre of war he took part in important engagements in various sectors, including the Battles of Arras and Ypres, and was twice wounded in action. He was demobilised in October 1919, and holds the General Service and Victory Medals.
Green's Norton, Towcester, Northants. Z2877/B.

BUNYAN, C., Private, 2nd Bedfordshire Regiment.
At the outbreak of hostilities in August 1914 he was serving in the Army, and two months later proceeded to the Western Front. There, after fighting in the Battle of La Bassée, he was unfortunately killed in action at Ypres on November 7th, 1914. He was entitled to the 1914 Star, and the General Service and Victory Medals.
"Great deeds cannot die."
42, Bunyan Road, Kempston, Bedford. X1512/B.

BUNYAN, H. G., Private, 1st Leicestershire Regt.
He volunteered in 1915, but was retained on important duties at home until 1917, when he obtained a transfer to a theatre of war. Whilst serving on the Western Front he took part in fierce fighting at Ypres, Arras, St. Quentin and Albert, but was unhappily killed in action at Cambrai on October 22nd, 1918. He was entitled to the General Service and Victory Medals.
"A costly sacrifice upon the altar of freedom."
42, Bunyan Road, Kempston, Bedford. X1512/A.

BUNYAN, W. A., Private, Labour Corps.
In January 1916 he volunteered for active service, and on completion of his training was two months later ordered to the Western Front. Whilst serving there he was engaged in road-making, and also saw much severe fighting in numerous engagements, including the Battles of the Somme, Arras, Ypres, and Cambrai. He was demobilised in February 1919, and holds the General Service and Victory Medals.
42, Bunyan Road, Kempston, Bedford. X1512/C.

BURBIDGE, H. E., Corporal, R.A.M.C.
When war broke out in August 1914, he was called up from the Reserve, and in the following year proceeded to the Western Front. He was at first stationed at Rouen, and rendered valuable services in No. 10 General Hospital there. Later he served at Arras and Amiens, where he was employed as a cook to the medical officers. He was discharged in May 1919, holding the 1914–15 Star, and the General Service and Victory Medals. 12, School Street, New Bradwell, Bucks. Z1513.

BURBRIDGE, J. W., Driver, Royal Engineers.
He volunteered in February 1915, and in the following August proceeded to the Western Front. During his service there he was engaged on important transport duties at Armentières, Ypres, the Somme, Loos and Albert, and was wounded in action at Ypres in 1916. He was demobilised in February 1919, holding the 1914–15 Star, and the General Service and Victory Medals. Hamerton, Hunts. Z1534.

BURDEN, G., Driver, R.A.S.C.
Joining in November 1916 he was, on conclusion of a period of training, found to be medically unfit for service overseas. He was therefore stationed at Bedford, where he was employed as a cook, which work he performed in a highly capable manner. He was eventually demobilised in January 1920.
9, Tower Gardens, Bedford. X1514.

BURGESS, J. J., Private, Essex Regiment.
He joined in February 1916, and after completing his training, was later in the same year ordered overseas. He served on the Western Front for nearly three years, and during that time saw fierce fighting in engagements on the Somme, and at Albert, Arras, Ypres, Passchendaele, and St. Quentin. He was demobilised in February 1919, and holds the General Service and Victory Medals. 6a, Nelson St., Buckingham, Bucks. Z1515.

BURGG, A., Private, 2nd Lincolnshire Regiment.
He was already serving in India when war was declared in August 1914, and was transferred in the following December to the Western Front, where he saw much severe fighting at Neuve Chapelle and Hill 60. He died gloriously on the Field of Battle near Ypres on February 15th, 1915. He was entitled to the 1914–15 Star, and the General Service and Victory Medals.
"He passed out of the sight of men by the path of duty and self-sacrifice."
106, Coventry Road, Queen's Park, Bedford. Z1538/B

BURGOYNE, G. F., Cpl., King's Royal Rifle Corps.
He volunteered in December 1914, and 11 months later was sent to France. On this front he took an active part in the Battles of Loos, Vermelles and Vimy Ridge, and was gassed whilst fighting in the Somme sector in June 1917. He was invalided to England, and on his recovery was retained on Home Defence until demobilised in January 1919, holding the 1914–15 Star, and the General Service and Victory Medals.
17, Grey Friars Walk, Bedford. X1516.

BURKETT, J. T., Private, Royal Army Service Corps (attached Tanks Corps).
Joining in November 1916, he trained at Grove Park until January 1917, when he was sent overseas. During his service in France he saw heavy fighting in the Battles of Arras, Cambrai and the Somme, and was also engaged on important transport work, conveying supplies to the forward areas. In June 1919 he was demobilised, and holds the General Service and Victory Medals. 1, Cromwell Walk, Huntingdon. Z1517.

BURKITT, A., Assistant Steward, H.M.S. "St. George."
He volunteered in June 1915, and after a course of training at Portsmouth, was in the following year posted to H.M.S. "St. George." In this ship he proceeded to the East, and rendered very valuable services whilst conveying troops to and from Egypt and Salonika. He was demobilised in March 1919, holding the General Service and Victory Medals.
86, Windsor Street, Wolverton, Bucks. Z1518.

BURKITT, L. F., 2nd Writer, Royal Navy.
Volunteering in November 1915, he was not successful in obtaining a transfer to the fighting area on account of bad health. Nevertheless, during the period of his service he performed very excellent work, and was employed on important clerical duties at Fort Blockhouse until demobilised in May 1919. 12, Windsor Street, Wolverton, Bucks. Z1519.

BURLEY, C., Private, 20th Canadian Infantry (Canadian Overseas Forces).
He volunteered in February 1915, and in May of the following year proceeded overseas. During his three years' service on the Western Front he took an active part in numerous important engagements in different sectors of the line. He also saw fierce fighting in the Battles of the Somme, Vimy Ridge and Ypres, and served in France until demobilised in April 1919, holding the General Service and Victory Medals.
Stagsden, Beds. Z1522.

BURLEY, F. S., Sapper, Royal Engineers.
Joining in May 1916, he received his training at Maidenhead, and in the following year was drafted to the Western Front. There he was engaged in severe fighting, and did good work with his unit in the Battles of Arras, Ypres, Cambrai and the Somme. He remained in France until December 1919, when he was demobilised, holding the General Service and Victory Medals. 14, Gladstone Street, Bedford. TX1520.

BURLEY, G. W., Driver, Machine Gun Corps.
He volunteered in May 1915, and served with the Bedfordshire Regiment at Ampthill for 11 months, and, on being transferred to the Machine Gun Corps, was stationed at Grantham before proceeding overseas in July 1916. Whilst serving in France he was in action on the Ancre front, and at Ypres and Cambrai. After the Armistice he proceeded into Germany with the Army of Occupation, and was eventually demobilised in February 1919. He holds the General Service and Victory Medals. 22, Melchbourne, near Sharnbrook, Beds. Z1521.

BURNAGE, A., Private, Royal Defence Corps.
He volunteered in March 1915, but on account of his age was unsuccessful in his efforts to procure a transfer to the war zone. He was retained on home defence, and served at various important stations, where he was engaged in guarding prisoners of war until demobilised in March 1919.
70, Wellington Street, Bedford. X1524/B.

BURNAGE, F., Drummer, East Yorks. Regt.
When war broke out in August 1914 he was already serving, and accordingly at once proceeded with the first Expeditionary Force to the Western Front. He took an active part in fierce fighting in the Battles of Mons and Ypres, and was severely wounded in action, and unfortunately succumbed to his injuries at Versailles on March 1st, 1915. He was entitled to the Mons Star, and the General Service and Victory Medals.
"His life for his Country, his soul to God."
70, Wellington Street, Bedford. X1526/C.

BURNAGE, G., Private, 5th Bedfordshire Regiment.
He volunteered in September 1914, and on completing his training in the following year, was drafted to Egypt, where he served at various stations. He afterwards proceeded into Palestine, and there fought in the Battles of Gaza, and also took part in the capture of Jaffa, Jerusalem and Damascus. He returned home for demobilisation in August 1919, and holds the 1914–15 Star, and the General Service and Victory Medals. 70, Wellington Street, Bedford X1524/A.

BURNAGE, G. H., Private, Bedfordshire Regiment.
Mobilised in August 1914, he was immediately drafted to the Western Front, where he served through the Retreat from Mons. He also took part in the Battles of the Aisne, La Bassée, Ypres, Arras, Passchendaele and Cambrai, and many other important engagements in various sectors, and was wounded in action at Hill 60 in April 1915, and on one other occasion. He holds the Mons Star, and the General Service and Victory Medals, and in 1920 was still with his unit.
7, Hassett Street, Bedford. X1530.

BURNAGE, H., Private, 2nd Bedfordshire Regt.
He was already serving in Africa when war broke out in August 1914, and in October of that year was drafted to the Western Front, where he took part in the Battle of La Bassée. After seeing much severe fighting in this theatre of war, he fell in action at Ypres on November 5th, 1914, only four weeks after landing in France. He was entitled to the 1914 Star, and the General Service and Victory Medals.
"And doubtless he went in splendid company."
70, Wellington Street, Bedford. X1526/B.

BURNAGE, W., Driver, Royal Engineers.
Volunteering in September 1914, he proceeded to the Western Front on completion of a period of training in the following year and there served in various sectors. He took part in the Battles of Neuve Chapelle, Festubert, Loos, the Somme, Arras, Vimy Ridge and Cambrai, and many other important engagements, and on his return to England in July 1919 was demobilised. He holds the 1914–15 Star, and the General Service and Victory Medals.
19, Dunville Road, Queen's Park, Bedford. Z1525/A.

BURNAPP, C. W. H., Air Mechanic, Royal Air Force (late Royal Naval Air Service).
He joined in November 1917, and after undergoing a period of training, served at Plymouth and other stations, where he was engaged on important patrol duties with the sea-planes. He was not successful in obtaining his transfer to a theatre of war, but, nevertheless, rendered valuable services with his Squadron until November 1918, when he was demobilised. He holds the General Service and Victory Medals.
24, Hartingdon Street, Bedford. TX1531.

BURNHAM, A. E., Sapper, Royal Engineers.
He joined in November 1916, and in May of the following year was drafted to France, where he served as a telephone operator with the Signal Section in various sectors of the front. He also took an active part in the Battles of Ypres, Passchendaele, St. Quentin Amiens, Le Cateau, and other important engagements until the cessation of hostilities. Demobilised in November 1919, he holds the General Service and Victory Medals.
87, Duncombe Street, Bletchley, Bucks. Z1528.

BURNHAM, E. B., Sapper, R.E. (R.O.D.)
Shortly after joining in March 1917 he was drafted to the Western Front, where he was engaged on important duties at the control boxes on the railways. Serving in various sectors, he took part also in the Battles of Arras, Cambrai and the Somme, and many minor engagements, finally returning home for demobilisation in March 1919. He holds the General Service and Victory Medals.
49, Tavistock Street, Fenny Stratford, Bucks. Z1527.

BURNS, J., Sapper, Royal Engineers.
Already in the Army when war broke out in August 1914, he was drafted to the Western Front in the following year, and there saw severe fighting in various sectors. After taking part in the Battles of Ypres, Festubert and the Somme, and other engagements, he was transferred in 1916 to German East Africa, where he was again in action. Invalided home in 1918 suffering from malaria, he was discharged in May of the following year, and afterwards served for four months on board a mine-sweeper in the North Sea. He holds the 1914–15 Star, and the General Service and Victory Medals.
7, Bell Court, Bedford. X1529.

BURR, C. R., Private, 11th Queen's (Royal West Surrey Regiment).
He joined in June 1918, and after a period of training was retained on important duties at various stations. He was unable to obtain his transfer overseas before the cessation of hostilities, but in March 1919 was drafted with the Army of Occupation to Germany, where he served at Cologne. He was for over three months in hospital there suffering from pleurisy and diphtheria, and was finally demobilised on his return home in April 1920.
93, Cople, near Bedford. TZ1532/C.

BURR, F., Private, R.A.S.C. (M.T.)
After joining in 1916, he underwent a period of training prior to being drafted to the Western Front in March 1918. There he was engaged in conveying food and ammunition to the forward areas in the Cambrai and other sectors, and also took an active part in the Allied Retreat and Advance He afterwards served with the Army of Occupation at Cologne before returning home for demobilisation in October 1919, and holds the General Service and Victory Medals.
93, Cople, near Bedford. TZ1532/A.

BURR, G., Private, 19th Canadian Light Infantry.
Volunteering in February 1915, he proceeded to the Western Front in January of the following year, and there saw heavy fighting in various sectors. After taking part in the Battles of the Somme, Arras and Messines, and many other important engagements, he was severely wounded in action at Ypres in July 1917, and admitted to hospital at Bromley. He was invalided from the Army in 1918, and holds the General Service and Victory Medals.
93, Cople, near Bedford. TZ1532/B.

BURRAWAY, A., Gunner, R.G.A.
Shortly after joining in March 1916 he was drafted to the Western Front, where he saw severe fighting in various sectors. He took part in the Battles of Albert, Vimy Ridge, the Somme, the Ancre, and many minor engagements until invalided home in 1918 and admitted to hospital at Liverpool. He was demobilised in June 1919, and holds the General Service and Victory Medals. Tag's End, Wootton, Bedford. Z1533.

URRIDGE, G., Private, 9th Royal Fusiliers.
He joined in June 1916, and shortly afterwards was drafted to the Western Front, where he took part in many important engagements during the Advance on the Somme. He made the supreme sacrifice, falling in action at the Battle of Arras on April 9th, 1917. He was entitled to the General Service and Victory Medals.
"Courage, bright hopes, and a myriad dreams, splendidly given."
11, Farrer Street, Kempston, Bedford. X1536.

BURRIDGE, J., Private, 1st Bedfordshire Regt.
Volunteering in September 1914, he was drafted to the Dardanelles in the following year and there saw much severe fighting, particularly at Suvla Bay. On the Evacuation of the Gallipoli Peninsula he was transferred to Egypt, and proceeded thence into Palestine, where he fought in the Battles of Gaza and also took part in the entry into Jaffa and Jerusalem. Demobilised on returning home in March 1919, he holds the 1914–15 Star, and the General Service and Victory Medals. 83, Woburn Road, Kempston, Bedford. X1535.

BURROWS, W., Private, 2nd Monmouthshire Regt.
Mobilised with the Territorials in August 1914, he was retained on important duties in England until 1917, when he proceeded to the Western Front. There he was engaged on transport duties in various sectors, took part also in the Battles of the Somme, the Marne, Bapaume and Havrincourt, and was wounded in action. He afterwards served with the Army of Occupation in Germany, before returning home for discharge in June 1919, and holds the General Service and Victory Medals. Biddenham, Bedford. Z1537.

BURT, W. G., Private, R.A.M.C.
Joining in March 1916, he was drafted to France in October of that year, and there served as a stretcher-bearer in various sectors of the front. He took an active part in the Battles of Arras, Ypres and the Somme, and many other important engagements, and served also through the Retreat and Advance of 1918. He was demobilised in March 1919 and holds the General Service and Victory Medals.
20, Vicarage Walk Stony Stratford, Bucks. Z1539.

BURTON, A., Trooper, Bedfordshire Lancers; and Private, Royal Fusiliers.
He volunteered in November 1915, but in March of the following year was discharged as under age. He re-enlisted, however, in February 1917, and, 12 months later was drafted to the Western Front, where he saw much severe fighting. Taken prisoner during the Retreat of March 1918, he unhappily died whilst in captivity in Germany on August 3rd of that year. He was entitled to the General Service and Victory Medals.
"Honour to the immortal dead, who gave their youth that the world might grow old in peace."
20, Muswell Road, Bedford. Z1129A.

BURTON, A. H., Sapper, Royal Engineers.
Three months after volunteering in September 1914 he was drafted to the Western Front, where he was engaged on road making, pontoon bridge building and other important duties. He served in various sectors and took part in the Battles of Ypres, Festubert, Loos, the Somme, Arras and Cambrai, and many other engagements in this theatre of war. Demobilised in November 1919, he holds the 1914–15 Star, and the General Service and Victory Medals.
Church End, Biddenham, Beds. Z1540.

BURTON, E. A., Pte., Essex Regt. and R.A.S.C.
He joined in June 1918, and, after undergoing a period of training, was retained at various stations, where he was engaged on duties of a highly imporant nature. Owing to ill-health he was not successful in obtaining his transfer to a theatre of war, but nevertheless rendered valuable services with his unit until January 1919, when he was demobilised.
18, Coventry Road, Bedford. Z1541/B.

BURTON, G. R., Private, 2nd Northants. Regt.
He volunteered in September 1914, and on completing his training in the following year was drafted to the Western Front, where he saw much heavy fighting. After taking part in the Battle of St. Eloi he was severely wounded in action at Hill 60 in May 1915, and was admitted to hospital in England. He was finally invalided from the Army in September 1916, and holds the 1914–15 Star, and the General Service and Victory Medals.
18, Coventry Road, Bedford. Z1541/A.

BURTON, J. W., Private, 6th Bedfordshire Regt.
Joining in October 1916, he proceeded to the Western Front after three months' training and there saw much heavy fighting on the Ancre and at Vimy Ridge. Severely wounded in action in the Battle of Arras, he contracted pneumonia whilst at the dressing station, and unhappily died on April 24th, 1917. He was entitled to the General Service and Victory Medals.
Thinking that remembrance, though unspoken, may reach him where he sleeps."
Rose Cottage, Spaldwick, Hunts. Z1542—Z1543.

BURTON, T., Corporal, 7th Royal Dublin Fusiliers.
Already in the Army when war broke out in August 1914, he was immediately drafted to the Western Front, where he took part in the Retreat from Mons. He also fought in the Battles of the Marne, the Aisne, Ypres and Neuve Chapelle and was wounded in action at Hill 60 in May 1915. In November of that year he was transferred to Salonika, where he was again in action on the Vardar and Doiran fronts until sent to Egypt in 1917. He was invalided home in the following year suffering from malaria, and in February 1919 was discharged. He holds the Mons Star, and the General Service and Victory Medals. 20, Muswell Road, Bedford. Z1129/C.

BURTON, T. P., Private, Army Cyclist Corps.
He volunteered in September 1915, and in May of the following year was sent to France, where he saw severe fighting in various sectors of the front. He took part in the Battles of Loos, Arras and Ypres and many other important engagements in this theatre of war, and was wounded in action at Hulluch. Demobilised in February 1919, he holds the 1914–15 Star, and the General Service and Victory Medals.
23, Islington Road, Towcester, Northants. Z2878.

BURTON, W., Driver, Royal Engineers.
He was mobilised in August 1914, and was retained on important duties in England until February 1916, when he was drafted to Egypt. He proceeded thence into Palestine, and whilst in this seat of operations took part in many important engagements, including the Battles of Gaza, and was also present at the fall of Jaffa and Jerusalem. Discharged on his return home in April 1919, he holds the General Service and Victory Medals. 20, Muswell Road, Bedford. Z1129/B.

BUSWELL, J., Corporal, East Surrey Regiment.
He joined in April 1916, and in January of the following year was drafted to the Western Front, where he saw much severe fighting, and was wounded in action in the Battles of Arras and Ypres. Later, in 1917, he was transferred to Italy, and there took part in many engagements on the Piave and Asiago Plateaux before returning to France for service in the Advance of 1918. Demobilised in September 1919, he holds the General Service and Victory Medals.
1, Coronation Road, Stony Stratford, Bucks. Z1544.

BUTCHER, B., Driver, Royal Engineers.
He volunteered in May 1915, and, later in that year, was drafted to Salonika, but was shortly afterwards invalided home suffering from malaria. He returned to the Macedonian front, however, on his recovery, and there saw severe fighting until transferred to Egypt. He proceeded thence into Palestine and fought in the Battles of Gaza and at the capture of Jerusalem and Jericho. Wounded in action whilst overseas, he was demobilised on his return home in July 1919, and holds the 1914–15 Star, and the General Service and Victory Medals.
Earith, Hunts. Z1545.

BUTCHER, F., Sapper, Royal Engineers.
He volunteered in 1915, and later in the same year proceeded to Egypt, where he served for some time. Afterwards sent to Palestine, he was employed on various duties at Jaffa, Haifa and Damascus, and performed consistently good work. He remained overseas until after the signing of the Armistice, and was demobilised on returning home in July 1919, holding the 1914–15 Star, and the General Service and Victory Medals.
37, Howbury Street, Bedford. Z1547/B.

BUTCHER, P., Private, Gloucestershire Regiment.
He joined in February 1916, and, after a period of training was drafted to the Western Front. There he took part in several important engagements, including the Battles of the Somme, Arras and Cambrai, and was wounded at Passchendaele. As a result, he was invalided home, and was eventually discharged in August 1918 as unfit for further military service. He holds the General Service and Victory Medals.
37, Howbury Street, Bedford. Z1547/A.

BUTCHER, S., Driver, R.A.S.C. (M.T.)
Volunteering in October 1914, he was sent in the following year to France. In this theatre of war he served at Festubert, Loos, on the Somme front, also at Cambrai and Arras, and was engaged on important duties in connection with motor transport. He remained in this theatre of war until the cessation of hostilities, and was demobilised in January 1919, holding the 1914–15 Star, and the General Service and Victory Medals.
37, Howbury Street, Bedford. Z1547/C.

BUTCHER, W. J., Private, Labour Corps.
He joined in July 1916, but was physically unfit for transfer to a theatre of war. Retained on home service, he was stationed in the Reading district, and did excellent work whilst employed on agricultural and other important duties until August 1918, when he was invalided out of the Army as unfit for further military duty.
Brickyard Cottages, Woburn Sands, Beds. Z1546.

BUTLER, A., Rifleman, King's Royal Rifle Corps.
Joining in January 1918, he was not successful in obtaining a transfer overseas before the termination of hostilities owing to being under age. Whilst stationed at Colchester and at Rugeley Camp, he was employed on garrison and other duties of an important character, and rendered valuable services until demobilised in December 1918.
Main Street, Hartford. Z1548/C.

BUTLER, C., Pte., Canadian Expeditionary Force.
He volunteered in October 1914, and left Canada with the first Canadian Expeditionary Force. After a period of service in England he was drafted to the Western Front, where he took part in strenuous fighting at Messines Ridge and on the Arras and Ypres fronts. He did excellent work overseas until he was unfortunately killed in action at Passchendaele on October 12th, 1917. He was entitled to the General Service and Victory Medals.
"Whilst we remember, the sacrifice is not in vain."
8, Ouse Walk, Huntingdon, Hunts. Z1549.

BUTLER, E., Private, 19th (Queen Alexandra's Own Royal) Hussars.
Serving at the outbreak of war in August 1914, he was drafted a month later to the Western Front, and during his service in this theatre of hostilities took part in numerous important engagements in France and Belgium. After the Armistice he was sent to Germany, and served with the Army of Occupation on the Rhine until March 1919, when he returned home and was discharged, holding the 1914 Star, and the General Service and Victory Medals. Main Street, Hartford. Z1548/B.

BUTLER, H., Private, 8th (Prince of Wales') Leinster Regiment.
He volunteered in August 1914, and early in the following year was sent to France. There he participated with his unit in severe fighting on many fronts, and was in action during the Battles of Festubert, Loos, Albert, Vimy Ridge, the Somme, Messines and Cambrai, being wounded on two occasions. He was demobilised in March 1919, and holds the 1914–15 Star, and the General Service and Victory Medals.
St. Neots Road, Sandy, Beds. Z1553/A.

BUTLER, J., Private, Royal Marine Light Infantry.
He joined in March 1918, and was sent to undergo his training at Deal. Owing to being under age, he was not successful in obtaining a transfer to a theatre of hostilities before the signing of the Armistice, but was later posted to H.M.S. "Egmont," and was still serving in 1920, stationed at Malta.
St. Neots Road, Sandy, Beds. Z1553/B.

BUTLER, T. J., Private, Royal Irish Fusiliers.
Called up from the Reserve in August 1914, he proceeded two months later to France. After taking part in the Battle of Ypres, he was wounded at Neuve Chapelle in March 1915, and as a result was invalided home. On his recovery he was drafted to Salonika and was in action on the Vardar and Struma fronts. In 1916 he was evacuated to England suffering from an illness attributed to his wounds, and unfortunately died in hospital at Lewisham on August 17th, 1916. He was entitled to the 1914 Star, and the General Service and Victory Medals.
"His life for his Country."
2a, Britannia Place, Bedford. X1550.

BUTLER, W. G., Private, Bedfordshire Regiment.
He volunteered in September 1915, and in the following December was sent to Egypt. After serving there for some time he proceeded to Palestine, where he took part in heavy fighting at Gaza and at other places, and did excellent work until May 1918, when he was invalided home suffering from pneumonia. He spent four months in hospital at Netley, after which he was stationed at Rugeley Camp until demobilised in May 1919, holding the 1914–15 Star, and the General Service and Victory Medals. Main Street, Hartford. Z1548/A.

BUTLER, W. L., Sergeant, R.A.M.C.
He joined in 1916, and was later drafted to the Western Front. During his service in this theatre of war he was stationed on the Somme front, also at Vimy Ridge, Messines, Ypres and Cambrai, and did excellent work whilst engaged on various duties. He remained in France for some time after the termination of hostilities, and was eventually demobilised in December 1919, holding the General Service and Victory Medals. 23, Russell Street, St. Neots, Hunts. Z1551.

BUTTRUM, A. H., Private, 7th Border Regiment.
Serving at the outbreak of war in August 1914, he was sent in the following July to the Dardanelles, where he took part in severe fighting at Suvla Bay. After the Evacuation of the Gallipoli Peninsula he was transferred to France, and in this theatre of hostilities took part in many important engagements, being four times wounded. He was later admitted to hospital suffering from influenza, from which he unhappily died on November 20th, 1918. He was entitled to the 1914–15 Star, and the General Service and Victory Medals.
"Great deeds cannot die."
13, Ampthill Street, Bedford. X1554.

BYATT, P., Private, 1st Hunts. Cyclist Battalion.
He volunteered in January 1915, and was employed on important duties at Whitby and Sutton-on-Sea until 1916, when he proceeded to France. There he took part with his unit in the Battles of the Somme, Arras, Messines, Ypres and Cambrai. Later he was in action in many sectors during the Retreat and Advance of 1918, and was wounded in May and October. He was demobilised on returning home in February 1919, and holds the General Service and Victory Medals.
Rectory Cottages, Huntingdon. Z1556.

BYATT, P. E., Private, Bedfordshire Regiment.
Volunteering in 1915 he was drafted in the following year to the Western Front. In this theatre of war he was in action at Albert, Vimy Ridge and on the Somme front, and did good work until he fell gloriously on the Field of Battle at Arras on April 23rd, 1917. He was entitled to the General Service and Victory Medals.
"A costly sacrifice upon the altar of freedom."
North Road, St. Ives, Hunts. Z1555.

BYE, G. F., 1st Air Mechanic, Royal Air Force.
He joined in February 1917, and was retained at home on important duties until September 1918, when he was sent to France. There he was stationed at the Base, and rendered valuable services whilst employed on duties which demanded a high degree of technical skill. In 1920 he was still in the Royal Air Force, and was serving in Malta, holding the General Service and Victory Medals.
35, Hartington Street, Bedford. X1558.

BYGRAVE, E. H., Private, 3rd Bedfordshire Regt.
He was mobilised at the outbreak of war in August 1914, and immediately ordered to the Western Front. In this theatre of hostilities he participated in the Battle of Mons, fought through the subsequent Retreat, and was unfortunately killed in action near Ypres on November 7th, 1914. He was entitled to the Mons Star, and the General Service and Victory Medals.
"The path of duty was the way to glory."
"Elms," Elstow, near Bedford. X1557/A.

BYGRAVES, J. C., L/Corporal, Royal Engineers.
Serving when hostilities broke out in August 1914, he was drafted in the following year to France. There he served with his Company on the Somme front, also at Arras, Ypres, Passchendaele and Cambrai, and was wounded in action. He did good work whilst engaged on important duties, and after the Armistice served in Germany with the Army of Occupation. He was eventually discharged in February 1920, and holds the 1914–15 Star, and the General Service and Victory Medals.
1, All Hallows Lane, Bedford. X1559.

C

CADD, J., Private, Oxford. and Bucks. L.I.
He volunteered in December 1914, and in the following year was drafted to France and served for a time in the Albert sector. In November 1915 he was transferred to Salonika, and took part in many engagements on the Vardar and Doiran fronts, and was wounded in action three times. Later he contracted malarial fever and was invalided home, where he remained until his demobilisation in February 1919. He holds the 1914–15 Star, and the General Service and Victory Medals. 50, Great Brickhill, near Bletchley, Bucks. Z1560.

CADE, F. H., L/Corporal, Machine Gun Corps.
Volunteering in June 1915, he was drafted overseas almost immediately. Whilst in Salonika he took part in many engagements on the Doiran front, but later suffered from frost bite, and was invalided to Malta, thence to Alexandria. On his recovery he returned to Salonika, where he served until he came home, and was demobilised in May 1919. He holds the General Service and Victory Medals.
2, Silver Street, Eynesbury, St. Neots, Hunts. Z1562.

CADE, H., Guardsman, 1st Scots Guards.
A serving soldier, he was drafted to the Western Front with the First Expeditionary Force in August 1914. He played a conspicuous part in the Battle of Mons, but was reported missing during the subsequent Retreat, and, as nothing has since been heard of him, he is now presumed to have been killed in action. He was entitled to the Mons Star, and the General Service and Victory Medals.
"He died the noblest death a man may die:
Fighting for God and right and liberty."
Huntingdon Street, St. Neots, Hunts. TZ1561/B.

CADE, L., Private, 1/4th London Regiment (Royal Fusiliers).
He volunteered in October 1914, and on completing his training in the following year was drafted to the Western Front. In this theatre of war he took part in many engagements, including the Battles of Hill 60, Festubert, Ypres, the Somme, Arras, Vimy Ridge, Passchendaele and Cambrai, where he was wounded and taken prisoner in April 1918. He was held in captivity in Germany and suffered many privations. After the Armistice he was repatriated and returned home for his demobilisation in January 1919. He holds the 1914–15 Star, and the General Service and Victory Medals.
Huntingdon Street, St. Neots, Hunts. TZ1561/A.

CADMAN, J., Private, R.A.S.C. (M.T.)
He volunteered in November 1914, and in the following month was drafted to France, where he was engaged on important duties with the mechanical transport in the Ypres, Béthune and Lille sectors. He was taken ill and invalided home to hospital, and was finally discharged in October 1915 as medically unfit for further service. He holds the 1914–15 Star, and the General Service and Victory Medals.
West Perry, near Huntingdon, Hunts. Z1563.

CAHILL, B., Sergeant, R.E. (Signal Section).
Volunteering in August 1914, he was drafted overseas after a period of training. During his service on the Western Front he did consistently good work in the forward areas as Sergeant Operator. He was demobilised in February 1919, and holds the General Service and Victory Medals.
103, Anson Road, Wolverton, Bucks. Z1564.

CALDWELL, W., Corporal, 1st Hampshire Regt.
Having previously served with the Cheshire Regiment during the Boer War, he re-enlisted in August 1914, and was sent to France in the following May. He played a prominent part in the Battles of Ypres (II.), Hill 60, Loos, the Somme and Arras, but was taken ill with pneumonia, and unfortunately died in the casualty clearing station at Arras in March 1918, having completed 14 years' service with the Colours. He already held the Queen's and King's South African Medals, and was entitled to the 1914–15 Star, and the General Service and Victory Medals.
"He joined the great white company of valiant souls."
84, Duncombe Street, Bletchley, Bucks. Z2879.

CALLABY, P., Private, 1st Bedfordshire Regiment.
He was mobilised in August 1914, and almost immediately drafted to the Western Front. Whilst in this theatre of war he took part in the Retreat from Mons, the Battles of Hill 60, Ypres, Festubert, Vimy Ridge, the Somme and Passchendaele, and in the Retreat and Advance of 1918. He was discharged in March 1919, and holds the Mons Star, and the General Service and Victory Medals. 4, Dane Street, Bedford. X1565.

CAMBERS, A. C., Private, Northants. Regt.
He joined in April 1918, and underwent a short period of training prior to his being drafted to France. There he took part in the Advance at Cambrai and many engagements until the Armistice. He afterwards proceeded to Germany with the Army of Occupation and served on important guard duties. He was demobilised in November 1919, and holds the General Service and Victory Medals.
7, St. Paul's Road, Queen's Park, Bedford. X2092.

CAMBERS, E., Private, Leicestershire Regiment.
He was mobilised in August 1914, and quickly proceeded to the Western Front, where he fought at Mons, Ypres, Loos, Armentières and Arras. Later he was transferred to Mesopotamia and saw much heavy fighting at Kut and in the Advance on the Tigris. He was wounded in action on five occasions, and was discharged in March 1919, holding the Mons Star, and the General Service and Victory Medals.
2, Little Butts Street Bedford. X1568/A.

CAMBERS, F. J., Private, Royal Fusiliers and Labour Corps.
He joined in May 1916, and in the following month was drafted overseas. During his service on the Western Front he was engaged on important duties in the Somme, Ypres, Albert and Cambrai sectors and did good work throughout. He was demobilised in October 1919, and holds the General Service and Victory Medals.
Ford End Cottages, Biddenham, Bedford. Z1567.

CAMBERS, F. W., Corporal, R.A.S.C. (M.T.)
He volunteered in 1915, and in the following year was drafted to Mesopotamia. In this seat of operations he took an active part in many engagements and was also employed on various important duties. He was in hospital for a time suffering slightly from dysentery. He returned home and was demobilised in February 1920, and holds the General Service and Victory Medals. Eaton Ford, Beds. Z1572.

CAMBERS, H., Pte., Royal Army Service Corps; and Mechanic, Royal Air Force.
He volunteered in June 1915, and was retained for a time at Aldershot on important duties. Later he was transferred to the Royal Air Force, and proceeded to France, where he was attached to a Kite Balloon Section and did good work on observation duties on the Western Front. He was demobilised in January 1919, and holds the General Service and Victory Medals. 2, Little Butts Street, Bedford. X1568/B.

CAMBERS, J. W., Sapper, Royal Engineers.
He joined in February 1916, and later in the same year was drafted to the Western Front. Whilst in this theatre of war he took part in many engagements, including the Battles of the Somme, Ypres and Cambrai. He contracted rheumatism and was consequently invalided home and finally discharged in August 1918 as medically unfit for further service. He holds the General Service and Victory Medals. Eaton Ford, Beds. Z1573.

CAMBERS, P. C., A.B., Royal Navy.
He joined in November 1917, and underwent a period of training at Devonport before proceeding to the North Sea on board H.M.S. "Canada." He was engaged with the Grand Fleet on important patrol duties, and did continuously good work until his discharge in October 1918 as medically unfit for further service. He holds the General Service and Victory Medals. 28, Church Walk, Kempston, Bedford. X1570.

CAMBERS, W., Gunner, Royal Field Artillery.
He volunteered in January 1915, and later in the same year was drafted to the Western Front, where he took part in the Battles of Ypres, Festubert, Loos and on the Somme. He was unfortunately killed in action in the Ypres sector on October 1st, 1917. He was entitled to the 1914–15 Star, and the General Service and Victory Medals.
"Whilst we remember, the sacrifice is not in vain."
13, Cobden Street, Bedford. X1571/A.

CAMBERS, W. J., Private, 2nd Bedfordshire Regiment and Middlesex Regiment.
He volunteered in November 1914, and, on completing his training in the following year, was drafted to France, where he fought at Loos and on the Somme. He was badly wounded at Delville Wood, and consequently invalided home in August 1916. On his recovery he was retained on important agricultural work until his discharge in January 1918 as medically unfit for further service. He holds the 1914–15 Star, and the General Service and Victory Medals.
15, Church Road, Cople, Bedford. Z1566.

CAMBURS, A. T., Sapper, Royal Engineers.
He volunteered in August 1914, and in the following year was drafted to Egypt, where he took part in the Advance into Palestine and was in action at Gaza and Jaffa. Later he was transferred to German East Africa, and served there until his demobilisation in 1919. He holds the 1914–15 Star, and the General Service and Victory Medals.
11, Beatrice Street, Kempston, Bedford. Z1569.

CAMPBELL, W., Private, R.A.V.C.
He volunteered in January 1916, and two months later was drafted to the Western Front. In this theatre of war he was stationed at Etaples and engaged in attending wounded and sick horses, in which capacity he rendered valuable services. He was demobilised in March 1919, and holds the General Service and Victory Medals. Moulsoe, Bucks. Z1298/E.

CAMPION, W., Private, R.A.M.C.
He joined in July 1917, and underwent a period of training prior to his being drafted to Salonika. Whilst in this seat of operations he was engaged on many important duties, and after hostilities ceased went to Turkey with the Army of Occupation and served there until he returned home for his demobilisation in June 1919. He holds the General Service and Victory Medals. Church Row, Cranfield, Beds. Z1574/A.

CAPEL, S. E., Gunner, Royal Garrison Artillery.
He joined in April 1917, and, after a period of training, was engaged at various stations on important duties with his unit. After hostilities ceased he proceeded to Germany with the Army of Occupation and served there until his demobilisation in September 1919. 2, Silver St., Stony Stratford, Bucks. Z1575.

CARDER, G., Private, Oxford. and Bucks. L.I.
He volunteered in August 1914, and in May of the following year was drafted to the Western Front, where he took part in the Battles of Ypres, the Somme and Arras, and was wounded in action at each of these engagements. On the third occasion the serious nature of his wound necessitated the amputation of his left arm, and after hospital treatment at York he was invalided from the Army in September 1918. He holds the 1914–15 Star, and the General Service and Victory Medals.
Chackmore, Bucks. Z3175.

CARESS, A., Pte., 5th Bedfordshire Volunteer Regt.
He joined in December 1916, and after his training was engaged at various stations on important duties with his unit. He was unable to obtain a transfer overseas owing to his being medically unfit, but rendered valuable services until his discharge in October 1919. 42, College Road, Bedford. Z1576/C.

CARESS, F., Private, Bedfordshire Regiment.
He volunteered in December 1914, and was engaged on various important duties at many home stations, where he rendered valuable services. He was discharged in December 1915 as medically unfit for further duty, but unfortunately died through the effects of his service in June 1916.
"His memory is cherished with pride."
42, College Road, Bedford. Z1576/A.

CARESS, G. C., Private, 1st Lincolnshire Regiment.
He was mobilised in August 1914, and almost immediately drafted to France, where he took part in the Retreat from Mons and in the Battle of the Marne. He made the supreme sacrifice, being killed in action near the Marne in September 1914, and was entitled to the Mons Star and the General Service and Victory Medals.
"He died the noblest death a man may die:
Fighting for God and right and liberty."
Pertenhall, near St. Neots. Z1578.

CARESS, R., Private, 5th Bedfordshire Regiment.
He volunteered in December 1914, and in the following July was drafted to the Dardanelles, where he took part in the Landing at Gallipoli and Suvla Bay, and, after the Evacuation of this Peninsula, saw service in Egypt on the Suez Canal. He was invalided home in 1916, and was in hospital for some time, but on his recovery was sent to France, and saw much fighting on the Somme and at Passchendaele. Later he was transferred to Italy, and served there until after the cessation of hostilities. He was three times wounded in action, and was discharged in February 1919. He holds the 1914–15 Star, and the General Service and Victory Medals. 42, College Rd., Bedford. Z1577.

CARESS, S., Private, Queen's Own (Royal West Kent Regiment).
He volunteered in January 1916, and later in the same year proceeded to France. Whilst in this theatre of war he took part in many engagements, including those at Ypres, the Somme, Vimy Ridge, Albert and Cambrai, and was twice wounded in action. He was discharged in May 1919 owing to the effects of his wounds, and holds the General Service and Victory Medals.
42, College Road, Bedford. Z1576/B

CARPENTER, A. E., Fireman, Merchant Service.
He joined in July 1916, and after completing his training proceeded to sea on board the S.S. "Northland." He was engaged on important duties transporting supplies from America to England, and on one occasion his ship was torpedoed in the Atlantic, but he was fortunately rescued. He was demobilised in February 1919, and holds the General Service and the Mercantile Marine War Medals.
18, Oxford Street, Stony Stratford, Bucks. TZ1579/A.

CARPENTER, W. H., Driver, Oxford. & Bucks. L.I.
He was mobilised in August 1914, and almost immediately proceeded to the Western Front, where he took part in the Retreat from Mons and the Battles of the Marne, La Bassée, Ypres, Festubert, Loos, the Somme, Arras and Cambrai, and was wounded in August 1917. He was badly gassed in March 1918, and consequently invalided home. He was discharged in March 1919, and holds the Mons Star, and the General Service and Victory Medals.
18, Oxford Street, Stony Stratford, Bucks. TZ1579/B.

CARR, A., Sergeant, 28th Bedfordshire Hussars.
He volunteered in August 1914, and underwent a period of training prior to his being drafted to France. In this theatre of war he played a prominent part in the Battles of Hill 60, Ypres, Loos, the Somme, Vimy Ridge, Passchendaele, Cambrai and Lens, and quickly gained promotion. He was demobilised in April 1919, and holds the 1914–15 Star, and the General Service and Victory Medals.
Wootton, Bedford. Z1580/D.

CARR, C., Private, 2nd Bedfordshire Regiment.
He joined the Army in 1908, and when war broke out in August 1914 was immediately drafted to the Western Front. There he took part in the Retreat from Mons, the Battles of La Bassée, Festubert, the Somme, Arras and Cambrai, and was gassed in action. He made the supreme sacrifice, being killed at Ypres on December 7th, 1917, and was entitled to the Mons Star, and the General Service and Victory Medals.
"A costly sacrifice upon the altar of freedom."
19, Dunville Road, Queen's Park, Bedford. Z1525/B.

CARR, T., Sergeant, Bedfordshire Regiment.
Volunteering in May 1915, he was drafted overseas later in the same year. During his service on the Western Front he played a prominent part in many engagements, including those at Vimy Ridge, Ypres, Messines, Cambrai and Lens, and was wounded in action. He was demobilised in January 1919, and holds the 1914–15 Star, and the General Service and Victory Medals.
Hilton, Hunts. Z1581.

CARTER, A., Gunner, Royal Horse Artillery.
He volunteered in August 1914, and on completing his training in the following year proceeded to France. There he took part in much heavy fighting on the Somme, at Arras and Cambrai, and was wounded in action. As a result he was invalided to hospital in Boulogne, but on his recovery returned to his unit. After hostilities ceased he went to Germany with the Army of Occupation, and served there until his demobilisation in September 1919. He holds the General Service and Victory Medals.
4, Shakespeare Place, Huntingdon. Z1584/B.

CARTER, A. C., Private, 8th East Yorks. Regt.
He volunteered in 1914, and in the following year was drafted to France. Whilst in this theatre of war he took part in the Battles of Festubert, Loos, Albert, Vimy Ridge, the Somme, Ypres and Messines, and was badly wounded in September 1917. As a result he was invalided home, and finally discharged in June 1919 as medically unfit for further service. He holds the 1914–15 Star, and the General Service and Victory Medals. Hemingford Grey, Hunts. Z1590.

CARTER, A. E., L/Corporal, Labour Corps.
Having previously served with the Colours before the war, he re-enlisted in June 1918, and was retained on important defence and guard duties with his unit on the East Coast. Owing to his being over age he was not successful in obtaining a transfer overseas, but, nevertheless, rendered valuable services until discharged in March 1919.
3, Great Northern Street, Huntingdon, Hunts. Z1582.

CARTER, A. E., Corporal, Royal Engineers.
Mobilised at the outbreak of war in August 1914, he was early in the following year drafted to France. Serving in various sectors of the Western Front, he was engaged on important trench digging and bridge building during the Battles of the Somme, Arras, Ypres and Cambrai. He continued serving in France after the Armistice, and returning home for discharge in March 1919, holds the 1914–15 Star, and the General Service and Victory Medals. 20, Millbrook Road, Bedford. Z1583.

CARTER, A. G., Private, 1/5th Royal Warwickshire Regiment.
He volunteered in August 1915, and on completion of his training in the following year was sent to France. During his service in this seat of war he took part in many important engagements in various sectors of the front. He was in action during the Somme Offensive, and was wounded in November 1916 and invalided to England. After a period of hospital treatment he was finally discharged as medically unfit for further military service in February 1918, and holds the General Service and Victory Medals.
16, St. Germain Street, Huntingdon. Z1586/A.

CARTER, A. T., Sergt., North Staffordshire Regt.
Joining in April 1916, he proceeded in the same year to France. In the course of his service in this seat of war he played a prominent part in many important engagements in various sectors of the front. He was in action on the Somme, and in December 1916 was invalided to hospital suffering from trench feet. Returning to France on his recovery, he did good work in engagements at Ypres and Loos, and was again invalided home. Later he once more saw further service on the Western Front, taking part in the heavy fighting at Cambrai. In September 1918 he was wounded and gassed, and returned to England. He was finally demobilised in March 1919, and holds the General Service and Victory Medals.
3, Dilleys Yard, Huntingdon. Z1593.

CARTER, A. W., A.B., Royal Naval Division.
He volunteered in the Huntingdonshire Cyclist Battalion, but was later transferred to the Royal Naval Division, and sent to France early in 1917. Whilst in this theatre of war he took part in the Battles of Vimy Ridge, Ypres, Passchendaele, Cambrai and the Somme. He was taken prisoner during the Retreat in March 1918, and suffered many hardships in captivity. After his release he went into hospital at Cambridge, and was eventually discharged as medically unfit for further service in March 1919, holding the General Service and Victory Medals.
16, Germain Street, Huntingdon. Z1587.

CARTER, B. L. (Miss), Special War Worker.
During the war this lady volunteered for work of National importance, and for a period of four years acted as a postwomen in Huntingdon, thus releasing a man for the Army. She rendered valuable services whilst carrying out her strenuous duties in a highly commendable manner.
5, Orchard Lane, Huntingdon. Z1588/E.

CARTER, C. D., Private, 1/5th Bedfordshire Regt.
He joined in 1916, and on completion of his training in the following year was drafted to the East. Whilst in this seat of war he saw service in Palestine, particularly at the Battles of Gaza and the capture of Jerusalem. Returning to England after the close of hostilities, he was demobilised in 1919, and holds the General Service and Victory Medals.
Silver Street, Buckden, Hunts. Z1595/A.

CARTER, E. E., Private, 7th Royal Fusiliers.
He joined in October 1916, and was retained on important duties with his unit at various stations. In 1917 he proceeded to the Western Front, where he was in action during the heavy fighting at Messines and Ypres. He made the supreme sacrifice on April 5th, 1918, and was entitled to the General Service and Victory Medals.
"Thinking that remembrance, though unspoken, may reach him where he sleeps."
16, St. Germain Street, Huntingdon. Z1586/B.

CARTER, G., Sapper, Royal Engineers.
He volunteered in November 1914, and after completing a period of training was drafted to the Dardanelles, where he took part in the Landing on Gallipoli and other important engagements until the Evacuation of the Peninsula. Later he saw service in Egypt and Malta. In 1916 he was transferred to the Western Front, and took part in the heavy fighting at the Battles of Vimy Ridge, Messines, Ypres, Marne (II.), and Bapaume. After the cessation of hostilities he returned to England, and was demobilised in April 1919, holding the 1914–15 Star, and the General Service and Victory Medals.
32, Sandhurst Road, Bedford. Z1591.

CARTER, G. E., A/Sergeant, Bedfordshire Regt.
He volunteered in September 1914, and after completing a period of training was retained on important duties with his unit. In 1916 he proceeded to the Western Front, where he did excellent work in many important engagements in various sectors. He took an active part in the heavy fighting at the Battles of the Somme, Ypres and Passchendaele, where he was badly wounded. As a result he unfortunately died from the effects of his wounds in 1917. He was entitled to the General Service and Victory Medals.
"He died the noblest death a man may die,
Fighting for God and right and liberty."
10, Sayer Street, Huntingdon. Z1585/B.

CARTER, G. W., Gunner, Machine Gun Corps.
He volunteered in November 1915, and on completing his training in the following year, was drafted to France, where he served as a Gunner with his Battery in the Battles of the Somme, Arras and Cambrai. In May 1918 he was wounded in action and invalided to England, and after a period of hospital treatment was discharged and sent to Purfleet, remaining on home duties until demobilised in November 1919, holding the General Service and Victory Medals.
4, Shakespeare Place, Huntingdon. Z1584/A.

CARTER, H., Trooper, Bedfordshire Lancers.
Volunteering in August 1914, he landed in France four months later. During his service in this seat of war he took part in much heavy fighting in various sectors of the front. He fought at the Battles of Festubert, Loos, the Somme and other important engagements until the close of hostilities. In February 1919, he was invalided to England suffering from influenza, and was demobilised, holding the 1914–15 Star, and the General Service and Victory Medals.
5, Orchard Lane, Huntingdon. Z1588/D.

CARTER, H. S., Private, Army Cyclist Corps.
He volunteered in October 1914 in the Huntingdonshire Cyclist Corps, but was later transferred to the Royal Berkshire Regiment, and sent to France early in 1917. Whilst in this theatre of war he saw much severe fighting during the Battles of the Somme, Ypres and Cambrai. Returning to England after the conclusion of hostilities, he was demobilised in March 1919, and holds the General Service and Victory Medals.
10, Sayer Street, Huntingdon. Z1585/A

CARTER, J., L/Corporal, Army Cyclist Corps.
Volunteering in October 1914, in the Huntingdonshire Cyclist Battalion, he was drafted to France on completion of his training. There he served during many important engagements in various sectors of the front, and was in action at the Battles of the Somme, Beaumont-Hamel, Ypres and Cambrai. After the Armistice he returned home and was demobilised in March 1919, holding the General Service and Victory Medals.
10, Sayer Street, Huntingdon. Z1585/C.

CARTER, J. F., Private, Bedfordshire Regiment.
He was called up from the Reserve at the outbreak of war in August 1914, and was retained on important guard and other duties at York and Stafford. He was also engaged on farm work in Bedfordshire, and rendered valuable services until demobilised in February 1919.
Church End, Wilden, near Bedford. Z1592.

CARTER, J. H., Pte., Hussars (Machine Gun Cavalry).
He joined in June 1918, and, after completing a period of training, was sent to Germany and stationed at Cologne, where he was engaged on important guard and other duties until September 1919. He was then sent to Ireland and served there until demobilised in November 1919.
2, Hartford Place, Hartford Road, Huntingdon. Z1589/A.

CARTER, J. W., L/Corporal, 8th Canadian Mounted Rifles.
He volunteered in 1915, and, after completing a period of training in Canada, was sent to France in the following year. During his short service in this seat of war he took part in the heavy fighting on the Somme front, where he was unfortunately killed in action on October 1st, 1916. He was entitled to the General Service and Victory Medals.
"The path of duty was the way to glory."
5, Orchard Lane, Huntingdon. Z1588/A.

CARTER, P., Private, R.A.S.C. (M.T.)
He volunteered in January 1917, and shortly afterwards proceeded to Salonika. Whilst in this seat of war he was engaged in conveying supplies to the forward areas during many important engagements, including those on the Doiran and Struma fronts. Later he was invalided to hospital suffering from typhoid fever, and unfortunately died in August 1917. He was entitled to the General Service and Victory Medals.
"He passed out of the sight of men by the path of duty and self-sacrifice."
41, Beaconsfield Street, Bedford. X1594.

CARTER, R. W., Private, 7th Norfolk Regiment.
He joined in February 1916, and in the following year was drafted to France. During his service in this theatre of war he took part in the heavy fighting at Ypres, and was badly wounded in action on October 14th, 1917, at Armentières, and, as a result, had both legs amputated and unfortunately died four days later. He was entitled to the General Service and Victory Medals.
"A costly sacrifice upon the altar of freedom."
2, Hartford Place, Hartford Road, Huntingdon. Z1589/B.

CARTER, S. R., Private, Army Cyclist Corps and 13th London Regiment.
He volunteered in August 1914 in the Huntingdonshire Cyclist Battalion, and after a period of training was drafted to the Western Front, where he took part in many important engagements, including the Battles of the Somme, Arras and Ypres. Later he was transferred to Egypt, and was afterwards in action in Palestine and also at the capture of Jerusalem. He was demobilised in March 1919, and holds the General Service and Victory Medals. 5, Orchard Lane, Huntingdon. Z1588/A.

CARTER, W., Private, Buffs (East Kent Regt.)
He joined in 1917, and, after completing a period of training, served at Dover and other stations until 1918, when he proceeded to France. After taking part in engagements on the Western Front he was taken ill and invalided to hospital. On his recovery he was sent to Ireland, and served there until demobilised in 1919, holding the General Service and Victory Medals. 5, Orchard Lane, Huntingdon. Z1588/C.

CARTER, W., Private, Army Cyclist Corps and Bedfordshire Regiment.
Volunteering in 1915 in the Huntingdonshire Cyclist Battalion, he was retained on important duties at various stations. In 1917 he proceeded overseas, and took part in many important engagements in various sectors of the Western Front. He was in action during the Battles of Vimy Ridge, Messines, Cambrai and the Somme. After the close of hostilities he returned to England, and was demobilised in April 1919, holding the General Service and Victory Medals.
Silver Street, Buckden, Hunts. Z1595/B.

CASBURN, S. E. V., Sapper, Royal Engineers; and Private, Royal Sussex Regiment.
He joined in July 1918, and on completion of his training, proceeded with the Army of Occupation into Germany, and was stationed on the Rhine. He did good work with his unit on guard and other important duties until demobilised in March 1919.
"The Grovage," Park Hall Rd., Somersham, Hunts. Z1596/B.

CASBY, C. D., Flight-Sergeant, Royal Air Force.
Volunteering in 1915, he was drafted to the Western Front in the following year, where he did excellent work attached to the 22nd Bombing Squadron in the Somme sector. Returning to England in 1918 he was stationed at Wyton Aerodrome, and rendered valuable services until demobilised in July 1919. He holds the General Service and Victory Medals.
King's Ripton, near Huntingdon. Z1597.

CASEY, J., Private, 2/4th Oxford. and Bucks. L.I.
He joined in February 1916, and four months later landed in France. Whilst in this seat of war he took part in many important engagements in various sectors of the front. He served at the Battles of the Somme, Arras, Passchendaele and Cambrai, and was taken prisoner in March 1918. After the cessation of hostilities he was released from captivity in December 1918, and was demobilised on his return to England in February 1919. He holds the General Service and Victory Medals. 12 Spencer Street, New Bradwell, Bucks. Z1599.

CASEY, T., Private, R.A.V.C.
He volunteered at the outbreak of war in the Royal Dublin Fusiliers, but was later transferred to the Royal Army Veterinary Corps, and sent to France in September 1914. Whilst on the Western Front he saw service at Ypres, the Somme, Arras, and was wounded during heavy fighting at Loos in 1917. On his recovery he was engaged on important duties in Huntingdonshire until demobilised in April 1919, and holds the 1914 Star, and the General Service and Victory Medals.
3, St. John's Terrace, Huntingdon. Z1598.

CASSELL, T., Private, Bedfordshire Regiment.
He joined in January 1916, and in the same year proceeded to France, where he was in action in numerous engagements, including the Battles of the Somme (I.), Vimy Ridge, Passchendaele and Cambrai. In March 1918 he was wounded during the heavy fighting at the second Battle of the Somme, but remained in this seat of war until after the close of hostilities. He was demobilised in February 1919, and holds the General Service and Victory Medals. Buckworth, Hunts. Z1600.

CASTLEMAN, F., 1st Class Stoker, R.N., H.M.S. "Jason."
He volunteered at the outbreak of war in August 1914, and was posted to H.M.S. "Jason," in which vessel he first served with the Grand Fleet in the North Sea on important mine-sweeping duties, and later saw much service in the Baltic Sea. On April 3rd, 1917, he was unfortunately drowned when his ship was torpedoed. He was entitled to the 1914–15 Star, and the General Service (with three Clasps) and Victory Medals.
"Thinking that remembrance, though unspoken, may reach him where he sleeps."
30, Church Square, Bedford. X1601.

CATLIN, J., Private, Bedfordshire Regiment.
He volunteered in November 1915, and in the following year was drafted to the Western Front. There he took part in many important engagements in various sectors, and was in action throughout the heavy fighting at the Battles of the Somme and Beaumont-Hamel. On August 24th, 1917, he made the supreme sacrifice, being killed in action near Arras, and was buried at Roclincourt. He was entitled to the General Service and Victory Medals.
"And doubtless he went in splendid company."
36, George Street, Bedford. Z1603.

CATLIN, V., Private, R.A.S.C. (M.T.)
He volunteered in June 1915, and, on completing his training later in that year, was drafted to the Western Front, where he was engaged in conveying ammunition and food to the forward areas. He also took an active part in the Battles of Loos, the Somme, Arras, Ypres and Cambrai, and many other important engagements in this theatre of war. He was demobilised in June 1919, and holds the 1914–15 Star, and the General Service and Victory Medals.
23, Beaconsfield Street, Bedford X1602.

CATMULL, C. W., Private, Royal Fusiliers.
Shortly after joining in February 1917, he proceeded to the Western Front, where he saw severe fighting in various sectors, and was three times wounded in action. He took part in the Battles of Ypres and Cambrai and other important engagements, was admitted to hospital at Le Tréport in June 1918, suffering from trench fever, and, on rejoining his unit, was gassed in October of that year and was again in hospital. He was demobilised in February 1919, and holds the General Service and Victory Medals. Yelling, St. Neots, Hunts. Z1604.

CAVANAGH, E., A.B., Royal Navy.
Already in the Navy when war broke out in August 1914, he was afterwards posted to H.M.S. "Juliet," attached to the Dover Patrol. He also served in the English Channel and the North Sea, and, engaged chiefly on mine-sweeping duties, his ship was blown up by a mine, but he fortunately escaped uninjured. He holds the 1914–15 Star, and the General Service and Victory Medals, and in 1920 was still at sea.
38, Hartington Street, Bedford. X2071/B.

CAVES, C. W., Private, 6th Northants. Regiment.
Joining in May 1916 he was drafted to the Western Front on completing his training in the following August, and there saw severe fighting in various sectors. He took part in many important engagements in this theatre of war, and was twice wounded in action— at Ypres in May 1917 and at Cambrai in March of the following year. He was demobilised in March 1919, and holds the General Service and Victory Medals.
5, Beauchamp Row, Bedford. X1181/A.

CAVES, H., Sapper, Royal Engineers.
He volunteered in December 1914, and in July of the following year proceeded to the Dardanelles, where he saw severe fighting at Suvla Bay. On the Evacuation of the Gallipoli Peninsula he was transferred to Egypt, but in 1916 was invalided home suffering from dysentery. He was drafted, on his recovery in July 1917, to the Western Front, and there took part in the Battles of Ypres and Cambrai, and other engagements. Demobilised in May 1919, he holds the 1914–15 Star, and the General Service and Victory Medals.
17, Hartington Street, Bedford. TX1605/C.

CHALDERLEY, E., Private, 1st Bedfordshire Regt.
He volunteered in November 1914, and after undergoing a period of training with the Huntingdonshire Cyclist Battalion, was retained in England until 1916. He was then drafted to the Western Front, where he took part in many important engagements, including the Battles of Ypres, Albert and Messines, and was twice wounded in action on the Somme in 1916, and at Cambrai in 1918. He was demobilised in February 1919, and holds the General Service and Victory Medals. High Street, Brampton, Hunts. Z1632/C.

CHALDERLEY, J., Private, Bedfordshire Regt.
He enlisted in 1914, and in September of that year proceeded to the Western Front, where he took part in the Battles of the Marne, the Aisne, La Bassée and Ypres, and many other important engagements. Mortally wounded in action in July 1915 he unhappily died on the fifth of that month. He was entitled to the 1914 Star, and the General Service and Victory Medals.

"Nobly striving,
He nobly fell that we might live."

High Street, Brampton, Hunts. Z1632/A.

CHALDERLEY, J., Private, Royal Berkshire Regt.
After volunteering in 1914, he was retained on important duties with the Huntingdonshire Cyclist Battalion at various stations in England until 1916. He then proceeded to the Western Front, where, after taking part in the Battles of the Somme, Ypres and Arras, he was wounded in action in March 1917. Severely wounded a second time in December of that year, he lay for seven days before being discovered, and as a result, had to have both legs amputated. He was invalided from the Army in March 1918, and holds the General Service and Victory Medals. High Street, Brampton, Hunts. Z1632/B.

CHAMBERLAIN, C., Private, Middlesex Regiment.
Four months after joining in March 1916, he proceeded to France, where he saw severe fighting in various sectors of the front. He took part in the Battle of the Somme, and in many minor engagements, and in February 1917 was wounded in action on the Ancre, and was for a considerable period in hospital at Rouen, and in England. Invalided from the Army in December 1918, he was still undergoing treatment in 1920, and holds the General Service and Victory Medals.
London Lane, Great Paxton, Hunts. Z1609.

CHAMBERLAIN, E., Pte, 8th Bedfordshire Regt.
He volunteered in September 1914, and after completing a term of training served at various stations, where he was engaged on important duties in the Quartermaster's Stores. Unable to obtain his transfer to a theatre of war, he nevertheless rendered valuable services with his unit until February 1919, when he was demobilised.
Montague Street, Eynesbury, St. Neots, Hunts. Z1608/A.

CHAMBERLAIN, G., Private, Bedfordshire Regt.
Volunteering in September 1914, he was drafted to Salonika in the following year, and there saw much severe fighting. He took part in many important engagements on the Doiran and Struma fronts whilst in this theatre of war, and finally returned to England for demobilisation in March 1919. He holds the 1914–15 Star, and the General Service and Victory Medals.
Montague Street, Eynesbury, St. Neots, Hunts. Z1608/B.

CHAMBERLAIN, J. W., Pte, Bedfordshire Regt.
Mobilised in August 1914, he was drafted to the Western Front in October of that year, and was wounded in action at Ypres in November, and invalided home. He returned to France, however, on his recovery in January 1915, and was again wounded on the Somme in September 1916, and admitted to hospital at Exeter. Again proceeding to the Western Front in July of the following year, he fought in the Battle of Ypres, and was a third time wounded at Passchendaele in August 1917. He fell fighting at Villers-Bretonneux on April 24th, 1918. He was entitled to the Mons Star, and the General Service and Victory Medals.

"Steals on the ear the distant triumph song."

St. Mary's Street, Eynesbury, St. Neots, Hunts. Z1606/B.

CHAMBERLAIN, W., Private, 1st Oxfordshire and Buckinghamshire Light Infantry.
He volunteered in August 1915, and in March of the following year was drafted to the Western Front, where he saw much severe fighting in the Somme sector. Invalided home in July 1916, he was for seven months in hospital in England, and was finally discharged in May 1917 as medically unfit for further service. He holds the General Service and Victory Medals.
High Street, Great Linford, Bucks. TZ1607.

CHAMBERS, A., Private, 1/5th Bedfordshire Regt.
Shortly after joining in March 1916, he proceeded to Egypt, where he served at various stations. Taking part in the Advance into Palestine, he was there in action in many important engagements, served at the entry into Jaffa and was wounded in action in the third Battle of Gaza in October 1917. He was demobilised on returning home in April 1919, and holds the General Service and Victory Medals.
Wistow, Hunts. Z161

CHAMBERS, A. V., Gunner, Tank Corps.
After joining in June 1916, he underwent a period of training prior to being drafted to the Western Front in 1918. There, after seeing much severe fighting in various sectors, he was wounded in action near Cambrai in August of that year, and was admitted to hospital at Camberwell, where he remained for eight months. He was finally demobilised, and holds the General Service and Victory Medals.
Elms, Elstow, Beds. X1557/B.

CHAMBERS, A. W. R., Corporal, Hertfordshire Regiment and Sherwood Foresters.
He joined in August 1916, and in April of the following year proceeded to the Western Front, where he was wounded in action in the same month. Later, in 1917, he was transferred to Italy, but returned to France in 1918, and there took part in many important engagements. He fell fighting at Gouzeaucourt on October 6th, 1918. He was entitled to the General Service and Victory Medals.

"His memory is cherished with pride."

The Lane, Bromham, Bedford. Z2577/B—Z2578/B.

CHAMBERS, E. E., Pte., 1st & 2nd Leicestershire Regiment.
Having enlisted in November 1912, he was drafted to the Western Front immediately on the outbreak of war in August 1914, and there fought in the Retreat from Mons and was wounded in action in October of that year. After taking part also in the Battles of Armentières and Loos, he was transferred in 1915 to Egypt and thence to Mesopotamia. There he fought at Samaria and many other places, was present at the Relief of Kut, and served also at the capture of Sheikh Saad and Baghdad. Five times wounded in action whilst overseas, he was discharged on his return home in 1919, and holds the Mons Star, and the General Service and Victory Medals.
30, Melbourne Street, Bedford. X1614.

CHAMBERS, E. E., Private, Yorkshire Regiment.
He volunteered at the outbreak of war in August 1914, and was retained on important duties in England until 1916, when he proceeded to the Western Front. Whilst in this theatre of war he saw severe fighting in various sectors, and took part in the Battles of the Somme, Arras, Ypres, Cambrai, the Aisne and the Marne, and many other important engagements. Demobilised in February 1919, he holds the General Service and Victory Medals. 3, Oxford Road, St. Ives, Hunts. Z1613.

CHAMBERS, E. T., Driver, R.A.S.C.
He volunteered in June 1915, and after a period of training, served at various stations in England until drafted to Italy in 1917. There he saw much severe fighting and took an active part in many important engagements until the cessation of hostilities. He unhappily contracted influenza and died in France whilst on his way home on November 21st, 1918. He was entitled to the General Service and Victory Medals.
"His memory is cherished with pride."
25, Chandos Street, Bedford. X1611.

CHAMBERS, L., Sapper, Royal Engineers.
He volunteered in February 1915, and after a period of training was drafted in the following year to the Western Front, where he was engaged in conveying ammunition to the forward areas. He also took an active part in the Battles of the Somme, Arras, Ypres and Cambrai, and other important engagements in various sectors. He was demobilised in August 1919, and holds the General Service and Victory Medals.
32, Tavistock Place, Bedford. X1612.

CHAMBERS, S. C., Private, 17th Middlesex Regt.
Joining in April 1916, he proceeded to the Western Front on completing his training in November of that year, and there saw heavy fighting in various sectors. After taking part in engagements on the Somme, he was severely wounded in action, and taken prisoner at Arras in April 1917, and unhappily died of wounds whilst in captivity in Germany on May 9th of that year. He was entitled to the General Service and Victory Medals.
"His life for his Country, his soul to God."
South View, Blunham, Sandy, Beds. Z1616.

CHAMBERS, W., Private, Labour Corps.
He joined in March 1916, and after undergoing a period of training with the 3/5th Bedfordshire Regiment, proceeded to the Western Front in July of the following year, and there served with the 7th Northamptonshire Regiment in various sectors. He was afterwards transferred to the R.A.M.C. as a stretcher-bearer, attached to the 25th Casualty Clearing Station, and also took part in the Battles of Cambrai, Douai and Valenciennes. He was demobilised in February 1919, and holds the General Service and Victory Medals.
3, Slows Buildings, St. Clement's Passage, Huntingdon. TZ1610.

CHANDLER, A., Air Mechanic, Royal Air Force.
Volunteering in October 1915, he was drafted to the Western Front in the following month, and there, attached to No. 9 Squadron, was engaged on duties of a highly technical nature. He served at Etaples, Rouen, Le Havre and various other stations, and did much useful work until his return home for demobilisation in March 1919. He holds the 1914–15 Star, and the General Service and Victory Medals.
29, Denmark Street, Fenny Stratford, Bucks. Z1620/A.

CHANDLER, C. E., Pioneer, Royal Engineers.
He joined in November 1916, and was retained on important duties in England until March 1918, and was then drafted to the Western Front, where he saw much severe fighting on the Lys. He was unfortunately reported missing, and is believed to have been killed in action, on April 13th, 1918, after only a month's service in France. He was entitled to the General Service and Victory Medals.
"The path of duty was the way to glory."
Great Paxton, Hunts. Z1623/A.

CHANDLER, J. T., Private, 8th Bedfordshire Regt.
Volunteering in September 1915, he proceeded to the Western Front in February of the following year and there saw severe fighting in various sectors. After taking part in the Battles of Albert and the Somme, and other important engagements, he was taken prisoner at Arras in April 1917, and was held in captivity until December of the following year. He was demobilised in February 1919, and holds the General Service and Victory Medals. Toseland, St. Neots, Hunts. Z1618.

CHANDLER, J. T., Private, Army Cyclist Corps.
Already in the Army when war broke out in August 1914, he was drafted to the Western Front in January of the following year and there saw much severe fighting in the Ypres sector. He died gloriously on the Field of Battle at Neuve Chapelle on March 14th, 1915. He was entitled to the 1914–15 Star, and the General Service and Victory Medals.
"A costly sacrifice upon the altar of freedom."
2, Holme Street, Bedford. X1621/A.

CHANDLER, L., Private, East Surrey Regiment.
Volunteering in September 1914, he was drafted to the Western Front in the following month and there saw much heavy fighting. After taking part in the Battles of La Bassée and Neuve Chapelle and many other important engagements, he was sent home and admitted to hospital at Netley in April 1915. Finally invalided from the Army in January 1917, he holds the 1914 Star, and the General Service and Victory Medals. Great Paxton, Hunts. Z1617.

CHANDLER, S. (M.M.), Sapper, Royal Engineers.
Volunteering in September 1914, he was drafted to France on completing his training in April of the following year, and was there engaged on bridge-building and other important duties in various sectors of the front. He also took an active part in the Battles of Ypres, the Somme, Arras and Cambrai and other engagements, and was wounded in action. He was awarded the Military Medal for conspicuous bravery in the Field, and, holding also the 1914–15 Star, and the General Service and Victory Medals, was demobilised in May 1919.
15, Russell Street, Bedford. X1624.

CHANDLER, S. S., A.B., Royal Navy.
Already in the Navy when war was declared in August 1914, he afterwards served in H.M.S. "Blake," attached to the Grand Fleet in the North Sea. He was engaged chiefly on mine-laying duties in these waters and was later transferred to the River Tigris, and was there employed on transport duties. He holds the 1914–15 Star, and the General Service and Victory Medals, and in 1920 was still at sea.
2, Holme Street, Bedford. X1621/B.

CHANDLER, T. J., Sapper, Royal Engineers.
He volunteered in September 1914, and in July of the following year was drafted to Gallipoli, where he saw severe fighting, especially at Suvla Bay, until the Evacuation of the Peninsula. Transferred in November 1915 to Egypt, he was invalided home two months later, suffering from malaria and sunstroke, but, on his recovery in January 1917, proceeded to Salonika. There he fought on the Doiran and Vardar fronts before returning home for demobilisation in March 1919. He holds the 1914–15 Star, and the General Service and Victory Medals.
34, Pilcroft Street, Bedford. X1619.

CHANDLER, W. H., Private, Bedfordshire Regt.
He joined in November 1917, and, on completing his training in the following year, was drafted to the Western Front, where he saw much severe fighting. He took part in the Battles of the Somme, the Marne, Bapaume, Cambrai and Ypres, and other engagements in various sectors until the cessation of hostilities. He then served with the Army of Occupation at Cologne, but returned home, and was admitted to hospital at Manchester in 1919. Invalided from the Army in March 1920, he holds the General Service and Victory Medals.
27, College Road, Bedford. Z1622.

CHANDLER, W. H. J., A.B., Royal Navy.
He volunteered in January 1916, and was stationed for a time at Devonport before being posted to H.M.A.S. "Brisbane" for service in various waters. He was afterwards transferred to H.M.A.S. "Margaret," on board which vessel he was engaged on duties of great importance in Australian waters. He holds the General Service and Victory Medals, and in 1920 was still at sea. Great Paxton, Hunts. Z1623/B.

CHAPLAIN, F., Tpr., City of London Lancers (Rough Riders).
He volunteered in March 1915, and underwent a period of training prior to being drafted to Egypt in August 1917. He proceeded thence into Palestine, and there, after much severe fighting, fell in action in the third Battle of Gaza on November 27th, 1917. He was entitled to the General Service and Victory Medals.
"Great deeds cannot die:
They with the sun and moon renew their light for ever."
Horse Shoe Yard, Lavendon, Bucks. Z1625/B.

CHAPLAIN, W., Private, 8th Bedfordshire Regt.
He volunteered in May 1915, and in February of the following year was drafted to the Western Front, where he took part in heavy fighting at Ypres, and was badly wounded in action on the Somme in September 1916. Invalided to England, he spent some time in hospital at Bristol before being discharged as medically unfit for further service, holding the 1914–15 Star, and the General Service and Victory Medals.
Horse Shoe Yard, Lavendon, Bucks. Z1625/A.

CHAPMAN, A., Private, 3/4th Northants. Regt.
He volunteered in September 1914, and six months later was drafted to France. During his service on the Western Front he played a prominent part in the Battles of Ypres, the Somme (I.) and Cambrai, and was wounded in action during the second Battle of the Somme in March 1918. He was invalided to England, and, after twelve months in hospital at Oxford, was discharged as medically unfit in March 1919, holding the 1914–15 Star, and the General Service and Victory Medals.
Bird's Lane, Stoke Goldington, Bucks. Z1628/C

CHAPMAN, A. E., Corporal, Royal Engineers.
He volunteered in August 1914, and, proceeding to France in the following June, was in action at the Battles of Festubert, Loos, Albert and the Somme, and in heavy fighting at Ypres. In January 1917 he was invalided home suffering from shell-shock, and unfortunately died on May 13th, 1918. He was entitled to the 1914–15 Star, and the General Service and Victory Medals.
"He joined the great white company of valiant souls."
3, Ewelme Terrace, Chalton, Sandy, Beds. Z1626/B.

CHAPMAN, H. F., Sapper, Royal Engineers.
Joining in April 1916, he was drafted to the Western Front five months afterwards and rendered valuable services with his unit whilst engaged on important trench and road construction work in the Somme, Ypres, Arras and Kemmel Hill sectors. He returned to England in April 1919, was demobilised in May, and holds the General Service and Victory Medals.
Spaldwick, Hunts. Z1629

CHAPMAN, J., Private, 1st Northants. Regiment.
A Reservist, he was mobilised in August 1914, and, proceeding to France with the first Expeditionary Force, first took part in the Retreat from Mons. He was also in action at the Battles of the Marne, the Aisne, La Bassée and Ypres, where he was severely wounded in November 1914. Invalided to England he underwent treatment at Cambridge, and was discharged as medically unfit for further service in July 1916, holding the Mons Star, and the General Service and Victory Medals.
The Fields, Stoke Goldington, Bucks. Z1627.

CHAPMAN, J. (sen.), Private, 2nd Northants. Regt.
He was mobilised in August 1914, and within a month was drafted to the Western Front, where he took a prominent part in the Battles of Ypres, Loos and Hill 60. On January 21st, 1916, he was found dead on the Field of Battle, having unhappily succumbed to heart failure. He was entitled to the 1914 Star, and the General Service and Victory Medals.
"A costly sacrifice upon the altar of freedom."
Bird's Lane, Stoke Goldington, Bucks. Z1628/B.

CHAPMAN, J., Private, 2nd Northants. Regiment.
Mobilised at the outbreak of war, he was drafted to France in October 1914, and played an important part in heavy fighting in the Ypres sector. He was very badly wounded in action at the second Battle of Ypres in May 1915, and, on being invalided to England, was in hospital at Shoreham. On his recovery he was retained on special duties at Home stations until eventually discharged as medically unfit in August 1918. He holds the 1914 Star, and the General Service and Victory Medals.
Bird's Lane, Stoke Goldington, Bucks. Z1628/A.

CHAPMAN, J. W., Private, 2nd Devonshire Regt.
He joined in April 1917, and, on completion of his training, was drafted to the Western Front early in the following year. After the Battle of the Aisne (III.) he was reported missing, and is now presumed to have been unfortunately killed in action on May 29th, 1918. He was entitled to the General Service and Victory Medals.
"Honour to the immortal dead, who gave their youth that the world might grow old in peace."
7, North Street, Newtown, Hunts. Z1630/B.

CHARD, E. G. (Miss), Worker, Q.M.A.A.C.
She joined in January 1917, and during the remaining period of hostilities was engaged on special duties at Biggleswade and at the Connaught Club, Seymour Street, London, W. She rendered valuable services as a cook and waitress until her demobilisation in November 1919.
Farr's Yard, Blunham, Beds. Z1631/A.

CHATER, J. H., Sergeant, Royal Garrison Artillery.
He volunteered in January 1915, but owing to his being medically unfit for transfer to a theatre of war was retained on special duties in England. He also rendered valuable services in charge of escorts taking troops to Ireland, and did much excellent work until his demobilisation in December 1919.
5, Berrell's Court, Olney, Bucks. Z1633.

CHATTELL, H., Guardsman, 3rd Grenadier Guards.
Already in the Army at the outbreak of war, he was sent to France in August 1914, and took part in the Retreat from Mons and the Battles of La Bassée and Ypres (I.), after which engagement he was erroneously reported killed. He was badly wounded in action in the Ypres sector in February 1915, and was invalided home. On his recovery in 1916 he was retained on special duties at Wellington Barracks, and remained there until he received his discharge in June 1919. He holds the Mons Star, and the General Service and Victory Medals.
The Causway, Carlton, Beds. Z1634.

CHEESEMAN, J., Corporal, 1st Loyal North Lancashire Regiment.
Enlisting in February 1913, he was sent to France at the outbreak of war, and was first in action in the Retreat from Mons. He then took part in the Battles of the Marne and La Bassée, but was invalided home with bronchitis in October 1914. He returned to the Western Front in January 1915, and served with distinction at the Battles of Neuve Chapelle, Ypres and Loos, where he was wounded in the following September. Once more invalided to England, he spent four months in hospital and was then again drafted to France, but, after serving at the Battles of the Somme, Arras, Messines and Passchendaele, was badly wounded near Cambrai in December 1917. He was then invalided to England for the third time, and was eventually discharged in February 1920, holding the Mons Star, and the General Service and Victory Medals.
Maltmans Villa, Eaton Socon, St. Neots, Hunts. Z1635.

CHELSOM, W. J., Sgt., 2nd Bedfordshire Regt.
Mobilised at the outbreak of hostilties, he was drafted to France in August 1914, and served through the Retreat from Mons. He also played a prominent part in the Battles of La Bassée, Ypres, Neuve Chapelle, Festubert, Albert, the Somme and Cambrai, and was badly wounded in action in 1917, as a result of which he lost a finger. He received his discharge in June 1919, and holds the Mons Star, and the General Service and Victory Medals.
69, Muswell Road, South End, Bedford. Z1636.

CHENEY, J., Private, 7th Oxford. and Bucks. L.I.
Volunteering in September 1914, he was first sent to France eight months later, but, after taking part in the Battle of Loos, was drafted to Salonika in October 1915. Whilst in the Balkan theatre of war he served through the Retreat from Serbia, in heavy fighting on the Doiran front, and was twice wounded in action. On the second occasion, in May 1917, the serious nature of his wounds necessitated the amputation of one of his legs. After hospital treatment in Birmingham he was invalided from the Army in June 1918, and holds the 1914–15 Star, and the General Service and Victory Medals.
2a, Mount Pleasant, Fenny Stratford, Bucks. Z1638/B.

CHERRY, A., Private, 11th Bedfordshire Regt.
He volunteered in December 1915, and, on completion of his training, was engaged on important defence duties on the East Coast. Owing to his being medically unfit he was unsuccessful in obtaining his transfer to a theatre of war, but did excellent work with his unit until invalided from the Service in October 1917.
74, Pilcroft Street, Bedford. X1639/B.

CHESHER, F., Private, 2nd Bedfordshire Regt.
He was mobilised in August 1914, and, proceeding to France with the first Expeditionary Force, took part in the Battle of, and the Retreat from, Mons, and in much of the heavy fighting in the early stages of the war. He laid down his life for the freedom of England at Loos on October 22nd, 1914, and was entitled to the Mons Star, and the General Service and Victory Medals.
"Courage, bright hopes, and a myriad dreams, splendidly given."
The Jetty, London Road, Girtford, Sandy, Beds. TZ1640.

CHESHIRE, B. (M.S.M.), C.S.M., R.A.S.C.
He volunteered in September 1914, and in the following year was drafted to the Western Front, where he first saw heavy fighting in the Ypres and Loos sectors. He also rendered valuable services in the Company Office in the forward areas and at Boulogne, and was awarded the Meritorious Service Medal and mentioned in Despatches for conspicuous work whilst in France. He was demobilised in February 1920, and also holds the 1914–15 Star, and the General Service and Victory Medals.
50, Howbury Street, Bedford. Z1641.

CHESTER, C., Private, Middlesex Regiment.
He volunteered in August 1914, and on completion of his training was engaged on important supply duties with the transport of his unit at Aldershot. He was unsuccessful in obtaining his transfer to a theatre of war owing to medical unfitness, but for a time rendered valuable services whilst acting as escort to German prisoners being brought from France He was demobilised in February, 1919 and holds the General Service and Victory Medals.
39, Marlborough Road, Bradford. Z1642.

CHILDS, A. E., Private, Royal Fusiliers.
He joined in March 1916, and was soon drafted to the Western Front, where he rendered valuable services with a Labour Battalion which was engaged on important duties in connection with the laying of pipes and the construction of roads. He returned to England for his demobilisation in March 1919, and holds the General Service and Victory Medals.
Cambridge Street, St. Neots, Hunts. Z1643.

CHILDS, A. W., Pte., Royal Warwickshire Regt.
He volunteered in the Huntingdonshire Cyclist Battalion in August 1915, and was later transferred to the Royal Warwickshire Regiment. Proceeding to France early in 1916 he saw heavy fighting at Arras, Vimy Ridge and Albert before being invalided home with trench feet. On his recovery he returned to the Western Front, but was unfortunately killed in action on the Ancre on March 5th, 1917. He was entitled to the General Service and Victory Medals.
"A costly sacrifice upon the altar of freedom."
5, Montague Street, Eynesbury, St. Neots, Hunts. Z1645/A.

CHILDS, E. E. (M.S.M.), Flight-Sergeant, R.A.F.
Volunteering in January 1916, he underwent his training and was then engaged on the night defence of London against enemy air-raids. He rendered valuable services, and on one occasion his machine caught fire during an aerial combat, but by great skill was brought safely to the ground, although he himself was wounded. In recognition of this daring work he was awarded the Meritorious Service Medal. He was demobilised in March 1919, and also holds the General Service and Victory Medals.
56, Stanley Road, Bedford. Z1644.

CHILDS, H. C., Driver, R.A.S.C.
He joined in February 1916, and was quickly sent to France, where he was engaged on important transport duties in the forward areas during the Battles of the Somme, Vimy Ridge, Messines, Ypres and the Marne (II.). He was also engaged as a motor-ambulance driver, and was gassed at Vimy Ridge. After rendering valuable services he was demobilised in October 1919, and holds the General Service and Victory Medals.
Mount Pleasant, Milton Ernest, Bedford. Z1646/B.

CHILDS, J., Sergeant, Tank Corps.

He joined in December 1916, and was quickly drafted to the Western Front, where he served with distinction at the Battles of Arras, Ypres, Cambrai and the Somme (II.), and in the Retreat and Advance of 1918. After the cessation of hostilities he proceeded to Germany with the Army of Occupation, and was stationed on the Rhine until his demobilisation in November 1919. He holds the General Service and Victory Medals.
"The Blue Ball," Eynesbury, St. Neots, Hunts. Z1645/C.

CHILDS, S., Private, Duke of Cornwall's L.I.

He was mobilised in August 1914, and, proceeding to France immediately, was in action at the Battle of, and in the Retreat from, Mons. Later he played a prominent part in the Battles of the Somme, Albert, Arras and Cambrai, and in the Retreat and Advance of 1918. He received his discharge in March 1919, and holds the Mons Star, and the General Service and Victory Medals.
5, Montague Street, Eynesbury, St. Neots, Hunts. Z1645/B.

CHILLERY, A. C., A.B., Royal Navy.

He joined in February 1918 on attaining military age, and received his training at Chatham. Owing to the early cessation of hostilities he was not successful in procuring a transfer overseas, but throughout the period of his service fulfilled the various duties assigned to him with great ability. He was demobilised in February 1919. Wilstead Rd, Elstow. X1649./C

CHILLERY, C. W., Cpl., 8th Bedfordshire Regt.

On the outbreak of war in August 1914 he volunteered, and in 1916 was drafted overseas. Whilst on the Western Front he saw fierce fighting in different sectors, and was wounded in action in 1917. On returning to the firing-line he took part in the Battles of Arras and Cambrai, and fell in action at Ypres on September 12th, 1917. He was entitled to the General Service and Victory Medals.
"A valiant Soldier, with undaunted heart he breasted life's last hill."
6, Council Cottages, St. Neots Road, Sandy, Beds. Z1650/A.

CHILLERY, F., Corporal, Royal Engineers.

When war was declared in August 1914 he was already serving, and was retained on important duties with his Battery at home until 1917, when he was sent to Egypt. He was subsequently drafted to Palestine and took part in important engagements at Gaza, Jerusalem and Jericho. He was discharged on his return to England in June 1919, and holds the General Service and Victory Medals. 21, Patteshall Street, Bedford. X1648.

CHILLERY, H. K., Private, Suffolk Regiment.

He joined in July 1916, and proceeded in 1917 to France, where he was wounded at Cambrai in August of that year. He was invalided to England and eight months later returned to the Western Front. After taking part in several important engagements he fell fighting at Cambrai on October 1st, 1918. He was entitled to the General Service and Victory Medals.
"His life for his Country."
Wilstead Road, Elstow. X1649/B.

CHILLERY, J. J., 1st Class Stoker, R.N., H.M.S. "Pembroke."

He joined in May 1918, and, after a period of training at Chatham, was posted to H.M.S. "Pembroke." On board this vessel he served at Gibraltar and in the North Sea, and performed excellent work. In 1920 he was still serving in the Navy, and holds the General Service and Victory Medals.
6, Council Cottages, St. Neots Road, Sandy, Beds. Z1650/B.

CHILLERY, R. F., Corpl., 2nd Bedfordshire Regt.

He volunteered in November 1914, and in the same year proceeded to the Western Front. There, after taking part in the Battles of La Bassée and Ypres, he was unhappily killed in action at Loos on September 25th, 1915. He was entitled to the 1914 Star, and the General Service and Victory Medals.
"He died the noblest death a man may die,
Fighting for God and right and liberty."
Wilstead Road, Elstow. X1649/A.

CHINN, H. A., Leading Seaman, Royal Navy.

He was serving in the Navy at the outbreak of hostilities, and for a time was stationed at the submarine base at Dundee. Later he served with the Grand Fleet in H.M. submarines C. 26, C. 25, E. 16, E. 35, J. 3 and G. 4, and carried out excellent work in the North Sea. He was mentioned in Despatches for bravery and devotion to duty, and was discharged in December 1919, holding the General Service and Victory Medals. Silver Street, Stevington, near Bedford. Z1651.

CHISP, H. P., Sapper, Royal Engineers.

Joining in March 1917, he was trained at Bournemouth, and in the following May was sent to the Western Front. There he saw much heavy fighting at Vimy Ridge, but after only five months' active service was unfortunately killed in action at Ypres on October 19th, 1917. He was entitled to the General Service and Victory Medals.
"Nobly striving:
He nobly fell that we might live."
6, Paggs Court Silver Street, Newport Pagnell, Bucks. Z1652.

CHRISP, C. J., Corporal, R.A.M.C.

A month after the outbreak of war he volunteered, and in May 1915 was drafted to Egypt, where he served at Ismailia for three months. He was then drafted to Gallipoli and fought at Suvla Bay and in the subsequent engagements of the campaign. After the Evacuation he was sent to Palestine and rendered valuable services to the wounded at Gaza, Jerusalem and in the Jordan Valley. On returning home in July 1919 he was demobilised, holding the 1914–15 Star, and the General Service and Victory Medals.
10, Wood Street, New Bradwell, Bucks. Z1653.

CHRISTOPHER, F. J., Private, 1st Royal Bucks. and Essex Regiments.

He volunteered in August 1914, and three months later proceeded overseas. During his service on the Western Front he fought in the Battles of La Bassée, Ypres, Festubert and Vimy Ridge, but, being severely wounded in the last two engagements, was consequently, after prolonged hospital treatment, invalided out of the Army in September 1917. He holds the 1914 Star, and the General Service and Victory Medals.
Longfield Road, Sandy, Beds. Z1654.

CHURCH, A. W., Private, 7th Norfolk Regiment.

He joined in January 1917, and, on conclusion of his training, was eight months later sent to the Western Front. In this theatre of war he experienced very severe fighting, particularly in the Somme, Albert and Epéhy sectors, and was wounded in action at Cambrai in November 1917. After the close of hostilities he served in France until demobilised in October 1919, and holds the General Service and Victory Medals.
8, Beaconsfield Street, Bedford. X1662/A.

CHURCH, E. J. B., Private, Bedfordshire Regt.

Mobilised at the declaration of war in August 1914, he was at once ordered to the scene of activities in France. On this front he took an active part in the Battles of Mons, the Aisne, La Bassée, Ypres and Neuve Chapelle, and fell fighting at Ypres on May 7th, 1915. He was entitled to the Mons Star, and the General Service and Victory Medals.
"Courage, bright hopes, and a myriad dreams, splendidly given."
Wootton, Bedford. Z1658/A.

CHURCH, F., Driver, Royal Engineers.

He volunteered in September 1914, and, after a course of training, was sent overseas in the following year. Whilst serving on the Western Front he saw severe fighting in numerous engagements of importance, and carried out important transport duties in the Loos, Festubert, Somme, Arras and Cambrai sectors. He was demobilised in June 1919, and holds the 1914–15 Star, and the General Service and Victory Medals.
8, Beaconsfield Street, Bedford. X1662/B.

CHURCH, F., Private, 2nd Bedfordshire Regiment.

Joining in March 1916, he was nine months later drafted to France, and on this front was engaged in fierce fighting at Arras and Cambrai, but was wounded at Ypres in February 1917. He was sent to hospital at St. Omer, and subsequently to England. On his discharge from hospital he was employed on agricultural work at Bedford until demobilised in February 1919. He holds the General Service and Victory Medals.
Bromham, near Bedford. Z1655.

CHURCH, G. E., Private, 6th Wiltshire Regiment.

He volunteered in September 1914, and in August 1915 was drafted to France, but after serving at Ypres was transferred in November 1915 to Salonika. He served there for 14 months, but whilst fighting on the Vardar front contracted malaria, and was invalided to England. On his recovery he was again sent to the Western Front and was unhappily killed in action at Messines in June 1917. He was entitled to the 1914–15 Star, and the General Service and Victory Medals.
"He passed out of the sight of men by the path of duty and self-sacrifice."
129, High Street, Stony Stratford, Bucks. TZ1656/B.

CHURCH, G. H., Private, R.A.M.C.

In March 1917 he joined the Army, and, on completion of a perod of training, was engaged on important duties with his unit at various Home stations. Owing to ill-health he was unable to secure a transfer to a theatre of war, but nevertheless rendered valuable services until demobilised in September 1919. 20, East Street, Olney, Bucks. Z1660.

CHURCH, H., Driver, Royal Engineers.

He volunteered in September 1914, and, after a course of training at Bury St. Edmund's and Melton Constable, proceeded in the following year to France. There he fought in engagements at Hill 60, Albert and Vimy Ridge, but received a severe wound which rendered him unfit for further active service. He returned to England in 1916, and served at Maidenhead and Purfleet until demobilised in April 1919, holding the 1914–15 Star, and the General Service and Victory Medals.
36, Littledale Street, Kempston, Bedford. Z1661.

CHURCH, H., Private, Gordon Highlanders.

A month after the declaration of war he volunteered, and, on conclusion of his training at Bedford, was sent overseas in 1915. During his service on the Western Front he saw much severe fighting in different sectors of the line, and took an active part in the Battles of Loos, Albert, the Somme and Arras. He was demobilised in 1919, and holds the 1914–15 Star, and the General Service and Victory Medals.
Mill House, Sharnbrook, Beds. Z1659.

CHURCH, H., Private, 7th Oxford and Bucks. L.I.
He volunteered in September 1914 and in November of the following year proceeded to Salonika. There he took an active part in fierce fighting on the Vardar and Doiran fronts. He was wounded in action in April 1917, and a month later unhappily succumbed to his injuries. He was entitled to the 1914–15 Star, and the General Service and Victory Medals.
"He joined the great white company of valiant souls."
129, High Street, Stony Stratford, Bucks. TZ1656/A.

CHURCH, J., Corporal, Royal Horse Artillery.
He joined the Royal Horse Artillery in January 1916, having previously served with the Huntingdonshire Cyclist Battalion from February 1915 to November 1915, and in July 1917 proceeded to Palestine, where he performed excellent work as a cook at Gaza, Jaffa, the Jordan, Jerusalem and Jericho. He was demobilised on his return to England in December 1919, and holds the General Service and Victory Medals.
2, Slows Buildings, St. Clement's Passage, Huntingdon. TZ1657.

CHURCH, R., Private, 2nd Hampshire Regiment.
Volunteering in January 1916, he was trained at St. Albans and proceeded overseas six months later. Whilst serving in France he was wounded in the Battle of the Somme and invalided to England. On his recovery he was retained on Home Defence until October 1919, when he was sent to India, and in 1920 was still serving there. He holds the General Service and Victory Medals.
129, High Street, Stony Stratford, Bucks. TZ1656/D.

CHURCH, R. F., Pte., 13th London Regt. (Rangers).
He joined in 1918, and was retained on important duties with his unit at Orpington. Owing to ill-health he was not successful in his efforts to obtain a transfer overseas, but fulfilled the duties allotted to him with great ability. He was discharged in February 1919, suffering from consumption.
Wootton, Bedford. Z1658/B.

CHURCH, W., Private, 5th Oxford and Bucks. L.I.
Volunteering in January 1915, he received his training at Bovington Camp, and in the following September was drafted to the Western Front. He fought in the Battle of Loos, but only a month after landing in France was killed in action on October 17th, 1915. He was entitled to the 1914–15 Star, and the General Service and Victory Medals.
"His life for his Country, his soul to God."
129, High Street, Stony Stratford, Bucks. TZ1656/C.

CHURCH, W. C., Private, Royal Fusiliers.
He joined the Army in June 1918, but owing to the early cessation of hostilities was unable to obtain a transfer overseas before the termination of the war. In April 1919 he proceeded to Germany with the Army of Occupation, and was engaged on important guard duties in Cologne until demobilised in February 1920. Biddenham, Beds. Z1663.

CHURCHILL, C. J., Private, 16th Lancers and Machine Gun Corps.
He volunteered in September 1914, and, on conclusion of his training in Ireland, was sent to the Western Front in July 1915. During nearly four years' service in France he took part in many important engagements, saw severe fighting at Loos, Vimy Ridge, the Somme, Messines and Cambrai, and was wounded and gassed at Delville Wood. Demobilised in February 1919, he holds the 1914–15 Star, and the General Service and Victory Medals. 4, York Street, Bedford. TZ1664/B.

CHURCHILL, F. A., Driver, Royal Engineers.
He volunteered in May 1915, and, after a period of training at Maidenhead, was sent in March 1916 to Egypt. Later he was transferred to Palestine and took an active part in severe fighting at Gaza and Jaffa. He was discharged in November 1918 as medically unfit for further military service, and holds the General Service and Victory Medals.
4, York Street, Bedford. TZ1664/A.

CHURCHMAN, E. G., Driver, Royal Engineers and Royal Welch Fusiliers.
He was mobilised when war was declared in August 1914, and in the following year was drafted to the Western Front, where he was engaged on important transport duties. He saw fierce fighting in numerous engagements, including those at Ypres, the Somme, Arras and Passchendaele, and was also employed in guarding prisoners of war. Discharged in March 1919, he holds the 1914–15 Star, and the General Service and Victory Medals. 43, St. Leonards Street, Bedford. X1665/B.

CHURCHMAN, E. S., Cpl., 2nd Bedfordshire Regt.
At the outbreak of hostilities he was mobilised, and immediately proceeded to the Western Front. There he took part in fierce fighting in the Retreat from Mons and in the Battles of Neuve Chapelle, Hill 60, Ypres, the Somme and Arras. His health, however, broke down, and he was discharged as medically unfit for further military service in April 1918. He holds the Mons Star, and the General Service and Victory Medals. 43, St. Leonards Street, Bedford. X1665/C.

CHURCHMAN, F. C., Cpl., 2nd Bedfordshire Regt.
He joined in August 1916, and, after completing his training, was sent overseas in September of the following year. A month later, whilst in action at Passchendaele, he was gassed and sent to hospital at Boulogne. On his recovery he was much severe fighting in many engagements, and also served in the Retreat and Advance of 1918. He was demobilised in September 1919, and holds the General Service and Victory Medals. 138, Bower Street, Bedford. Z1666/B.

CHURCHMAN, W. W., Sapper, Royal Engineers.
Joining in May 1916, he was, on conclusion of a period of training, drafted overseas in June of the following year. During his service on the Western Front he was engaged in severe fighting, particularly in the Passchendaele and Ypres sectors, and was wounded at Ypres in November 1917. In August 1919 he was demobilised, holding the General Service and Victory Medals. 138, Bower Street, Bedford. Z1666/A.

CHUTER, A. O., 1st Air Mechanic, Royal Air Force.
He joined in November 1916, but was not successful in his endeavours to secure a transfer to the war zone. Throughout the period of his service, however, he was employed on work which demanded exceptional technical knowledge and skill in connection with the repair of aircraft. He was stationed at Cranwell and Sleaford, and was eventually demobilised in April 1919.
Raymond Cottages, Cambridge Street, St. Neots, Hunts. Z1667.

CIRCUIT, G., L/Corporal, Bedfordshire Regt.
He enlisted in 1900, and at the outbreak of war was serving in India, but was immediately recalled and sent to France with the first Expeditionary Force. He was in action in the Retreat from Mons and the Battles of the Marne, La Bassée, Ypres, Hill 60, the Somme, Arras and Cambrai, and was twice wounded in engagements on the Somme and at Ypres. In September 1919 he returned to India, and in 1920 was still serving there, holding the Mons Star, and the General Service and Victory Medals. 70, Wellington St., Bedford. X1526/A.

CIRCUIT, P., Pte., 5th Royal Warwickshire Regt.
He volunteered in November 1915, and, on completion of his training, was drafted to the Western Front, where he took part in the Battles of Arras and St. Quentin and was badly wounded in action in March 1918. Invalided to England, he spent five months in hospital at Blackburn, and was then engaged on important duties at Home stations until his demobilisation in March 1919, holding the General Service and Victory Medals.
56, Duncombe Street, Bletchley, Bucks. Z2880.

CLARE, A. W., Private, 4th Dorsetshire Regt.
He joined in March 1918, and, after a course of training at Larkhill, was drafted to Ireland, where he was engaged on important garrison duties. Owing to ill-health he was unable to obtain a transfer to a theatre of war, but nevertheless rendered many valuable services until demobilised in October 1919
5, East Street, Olney, Bucks. Z1668.

CLARE, E., A.B., R.N., H.M.S. "Castor."
Volunteering in June 1915 for a period of twelve years, he was in training at Devonport until posted to his ship, H.M.S. "Castor." In this vessel he served in many waters and performed excellent work on the Italian, Spanish and French coasts, and also at Scapa Flow. Whilst serving at Malta he contracted dysentery and was sent back to England. In 1920 he was still in the Navy, and holds the General Service and Victory Medals.
Green End Road, Great Barford, Beds. Z1670/A—Z1671/A.

CLARE, H. M. (Miss), Worker, Q.M.A.A.C.
She joined in December 1917, and, on completion of her training, served at many important stations, including London, Wendover, Aldershot, Pirbright and Crookham. Throughout the period of her service she was employed as a cook, and fulfilled her duties with the greatest ability. She was demobilised in April 1919.
Green End Road, Great Barford, Beds. Z1670/B—Z1671/B.

CLARE, J. H., Private, 1/5th Bedfordshire Regt.
Volunteering in September 1914, he was trained at Bury St. Edmund's and St. Albans, and in July 1915 was drafted to Gallipoli. There he saw severe fighting in several engagements, and was wounded in action at Suvla Bay in August 1915. He was sent to hospital in Cairo and then to England, and was eventually invalided out of the Army as unfit for further service in March 1916. He holds the 1914–15 Star, and the General Service and Victory Medals.
Simpson, near Bletchley, Bucks. Z1669.

CLARIDGE, A. J., Cook's Mate, Royal Navy.
He joined in February 1916, and whilst in training was attached to H.M.S. "Pembroke" at Chatham. He rendered valuable services before contracting pneumonia, from which he unfortunately died in Gillingham Hospital on April 1st, 1917.
"A costly sacrifice upon the altar of freedom."
Bow Brickhill, Bletchley, Bucks. TZ2881.

CLARK, A., L/Corporal, 8th Bedfordshire Regt.
He volunteered in September 1914, and later in the same year proceeded to the Western Front. In this theatre of war he fought in the Battles of La Bassée, Neuve Chapelle, Hill 60 and Loos, and was unfortunately killed in action at Beaumont-Hamel in September 1916. He was entitled to the 1914 Star, and the General Service and Victory Medals.
"Great deeds cannot die."
Buckden Road, Brampton, Hunts. Z1684/B.

CLARK, A., Private, Royal Warwickshire Regt.
Mobilised in August 1914, he was sent in July 1916 to France, where he was wounded in the Battle of the Somme a month later. On his recovery he was drafted to Italy and served on the Piave and Asiago fronts until March 1918, when he returned to the Western Front. He took an active part in engagements at St. Quentin and Amiens, but was again wounded at Cambrai, and unfortunately succumbed to his injuries at Le Cateau on October 10th, 1918. He was entitled to the General Service and Victory Medals.
"Nobly striving:
He nobly fell that we might live."
1, St. Clement's Passage, Huntingdon. Z1678/A.

CLARK, A., Private, Bedfordshire Regiment.
He volunteered in September 1914, and in the following year was drafted to France, where he took part in the Battles of Hill 60, Festubert, Loos, Albert and Vimy Ridge. Later he was transferred to Mesopotamia, and saw much fighting at Kut and Khan Baghdadie. He returned home and was demobilised in December 1919, and holds the 1914–15 Star, and the General Service and Victory Medals.
Warboys, Hunts. Z1713.

CLARK, B., Corporal, Bedfordshire Regiment.
He joined in 1916, and, after a period of training in Ireland, was engaged at various stations on important duties with his unit. He was unable to obtain a transfer overseas owing to his being medically unfit, but rendered valuable services until his demobilisation in July 1920.
14, Marne Street, Kempston, Bedford. Z1690/A.

CLARK, B. (jun.), Private, 10th London Regt.
He joined in April 1917, and, on completing his training later in the same year, was drafted to France. In this theatre of war he took part in many engagements, including the Battles of Arras, Vimy Ridge, Ypres, Messines and the Somme (II.), where he was wounded in action. He was demobilised in November 1919, and holds the General Service and Victory Medals. 14, Marne Street, Kempston, Bedford. Z1690/B.

CLARK, C., Sapper, Royal Engineers.
He volunteered in November 1914, and in the following year was drafted to the Western Front. During his service overseas he saw much fighting at the Battles of Festubert, Loos, the Somme, Arras, Cambrai and Lens, and was also engaged on important duties. He was demobilised in May 1919, and holds the 1914–15 Star, and the General Service and Victory Medals. 3, Vine Cottage, Bromham, Bedford. Z1703.

CLARK, C., Private, Machine Gun Corps.
He joined in May 1916, and, on completing his training later in the same year, was drafted to France. Whilst in this seat of war he took part in many engagements, including the Battles of Arras, Ypres, St. Quentin, Cambrai and the Somme (II.). He was demobilised in August 1919, and holds the General Service and Victory Medals.
Wyton, Huntingdon. Z1687.

CLARK, CHARLES, Gunner, R.G.A.
He volunteered in August 1914, and was quickly drafted to the Western Front, where he took part in the Battles of Ypres and Loos and was wounded in action. As a result he was invalided home and, on his recovery, served for a time on Home Defence and then returned to France. There he saw much fighting on the Somme, at Ypres, Passchendaele, Cambrai and Le Cateau. He was demobilised in July 1919, and holds the 1914 Star, and the General Service and Victory Medals.
19, Slow's Buildings, St. Clement's Passage, Huntingdon. TZ1683.

CLARK, C., Gunner, Royal Garrison Artillery.
He was mobilised in August 1914, and immediately drafted to the Western Front. Whilst in this theatre of war he took part in many engagements, including the Battles of Mons, Ypres, the Somme, Arras, Albert and Cambrai, and was wounded in action. He did continuously good work throughout hostilities, and was discharged in 1919, holding the Mons Star, and the General Service and Victory Medals. C1673.

CLARK, C. F., Private, Northumberland Fusiliers.
He vounteered in January 1916, and underwent a period of training prior to his being drafted to Italy. Whilst in this seat of operations he took part in much heavy fighting and was wounded. He was unfortunately killed in action on the Piave on October 27th, 1918, and was entitled to the General Service and Victory Medals.
"Honour to the immortal dead, who gave their youth that the world might grow old in peace."
45, Tavistock Place, Bedford. X1689.

CLARK, E., Private, R.A.S.C. and Cadet, R.A.F.
He volunteered in August 1914, and in the following year proceeded to the Western Front. There he took an active part in engagements at Loos, Ypres, the Somme, the Ancre, Arras, Albert, Beaumont-Hamel and Armentières. He returned home in June 1918 and joined the Royal Air Force, with which he served until his demoblisation in March 1919. He holds the 1914–15 Star, and the General Service and Victory Medals.
15, Churchville Road, Bedford. Z1677.

CLARK, F., Private, Army Cyclist Corps.
He volunteered in September 1914, and in the following year was drafted to the Dardanelles, but owing to ill-health was invalided home. On his recovery he was sent to Egypt, where he took part in the Advance into Palestine and was in action at Gaza, Haifa and Jaffa. He returned home and was demobilised in June 1919, and holds the 1914–15 Star, and the General Service and Victory Medals. Stagsden, Beds. Z1675.

CLARK, G., Driver, Royal Horse Artillery.
He volunteered in November 1914 in the Royal Army Veterinary Corps, and served on important duties at Aldershot. Later he was transferred to the Royal Horse Artillery and drafted to Egypt, whence he took part in the Advance into Palestine and saw much fighting at Gaza, on the River Jordan and at the capture of Jerusalem and Jericho. He returned home and was demobilised in March 1919, holding the General Service and Victory Medas.
1, St. Clement's Passage, Huntingdon. Z1678/B.

CLARK, G. A., Private, Huntingdonshire Cyclist Battalion and Royal Warwickshire Regiment.
He volunteered in May 1915 and was retained at various Home stations before proceeding to France in July 1916. He took part in much heavy fighting, and was unfortunately killed in action near Albert on August 18th, 1916. He was entitled to the General Service and Victory Medals.
"Thinking that remembrance, though unspoken, may reach him where he sleeps." Southoe, Hunts. Z1685/A.

CLARK, G. E., Private, Bedfordshire Regiment.
Volunteering in October 1915, he was drafted overseas in the following year. During his service on the Western Front he took part in many important engagements, including the Battle of the Somme, Arras, Ypres and Cambrai, and in the Advance of 1918, and was twice wounded in action. He was demobilised in August 1919, and holds the General Service and Victory Medals. 44, Tavistock Place, Bedford. X1688.

CLARK, J., Corporal, 1st London Regiment (Royal Fusiliers).
He volunteered in August 1915, and underwent a period of training prior to his being drafted overseas. Whilst on the Western Front he took part in the Battles of the Somme, Arras, Ypres, Bullecourt, Passchendaele and Cambrai, and was gassed in action. He was demobilised in July 1919, and holds the General Service and Victory Medals.
6, St. Leonard's Street, Bedford. X1681/A.

CLARK, J. G., Private, 6th Bedfordshire Regiment.
He was mobilised in August 1914, and immediately drafted to France, where he took part in the Retreat from Mons and in the Battles of the Marne, Festubert, Loos and the Somme, and was wounded in action. On his recovery he was transferred to Egypt, thence to India, and was stationed at Bombay and Calcutta, engaged on important duties, until his discharge in November 1919. He holds the Mons Star, and the General Service and Victory Medals.
Buckden Road, Brampton, Hunts. Z1684/A.

CLARK, M., 2nd Corporal, R.E. (Signal Section).
Volunteerng in November 1914, he was drafted to the Western Front eight months later, but after serving in the Somme sector was transferred to Salonika in December 1915. Whilst in the Balkan theatre of war he took part in much severe fighting on the Doiran, Struma and Vardar fronts, and did exceedingly good work as an operator. He was demobilised in March 1919, and holds the 1914–15 Star, and the General Service and Victory Medals.
2, Manor Cottages, Far Bletchley, Bucks. Z2882.

CLARK, R., Sapper, Royal Engineers, and Private, Labour Corps.
He volunteered in 1915, and, after his training, was engaged at various Home stations on important duties before being drafted to France. There he rendered valuable services on the railways at Rouen, Boulogne and in the Ypres sector. He did continuously good work, and was demobilised in 1919, holding the General Service and Victory Medals.
St. Neots Road, Girtford, Sandy, Beds. Z1682.

CLARK, S., Farrier-Sergeant, R.E. (Signal Section).
He was mobilised in August 1914, and in the following year was drafted to the Dardanelles, where he saw much severe fighting. After the Evacuation of the Gallipoli Peninsula he was transferred to Egypt and did consistently good work during the Advance into Palestine, being in action at Gaza, Jerusalem, Jaffa and Aleppo. He returned home and was demobilised in April 1919, and holds the 1914–15 Star, and the General Service and Victory Medals. 7a, Gt. Butts St., Bedford. X1680.

CLARK, S. C., Private, Queen's Own (Royal West Kent Regiment).
He volunteered in August 1914, and underwent a period of training prior to his being drafted to France early in 1916. He took part in the Battle of the Somme and was badly gassed in action, which resulted in his being invalided home. On his recovery he was retained on Home Service until his discharge in March 1919. He holds the General Service and Victory Medals. Main Street, Hartford. Z1679.

CLARK, W., Guardsman, Coldstream Guards.
He joined in April 1917, and three months later proceeded to the Western Front. There he took part in the Battles of Arras, Passchendaele (where he was wounded) and Cambrai, and after hostilities ceased went into Germany with the Army of Occupation. He served at Cologne until his demobilisation in October 1919, and holds the General Service and Victory Medals.
6, St. Leonard's Street, Bedford. X1681/B.

CLARK, W., Private, Queen's Own (Royal West Kent Regiment).
He joined in April 1916, and later in the same year was drafted to France. There he took part in much severe fighting on the Somme, at Arras, Ypres and Bapaume, where he was badly wounded. As a result he was invalided home, and unfortunately had to have his left arm amputated. He was finally discharged in June 1920, and holds the General Service and Victory Medals. King's Ripton, Hunts. Z1686.

CLARK, W., Private, Leicestershire Regiment.
Volunteering in August 1914, he was drafted overseas in the following year. Whilst on the Western Front he took part in several engagements, including the Battles of Ypres, Arras and Cambrai, and was badly wounded in action, losing the sight of his left eye. In consequence he was invalided home and discharged in January 1918. He holds the 1914–15 Star, and the General Service and Victory Medals.
Stagsden, Beds. Z1676.

CLARK, W. G., Private, Bedfordshire Regiment.
He volunteered in September 1914, and in the following July was drafted to France, where he took part in many important engagements. He made the supreme sacrifice, being killed in action on the Somme on July 1st, 1916, and was entitled to the 1914–15 Star, and the General Service and Victory Medals.
"He died the noblest death a man may die,
Fighting for God and right and liberty."
Southoe, Hunts. Z1685/B.

CLARK, W. G., Private, Queen's (Royal West Surrey) Regt.
He joined in July 1917, and in the following month was drafted to the Western Front. There he was attached to the Labour Corps, and did good work conveying supplies and ammunition to the forward areas in the Ypres, Arras and Cambrai sectors. He was demobilised in February 1919, and holds the General Service and Victory Medals.
43, All Hallows Lane, Bedford. X1672.

CLARK, W. T., Driver, R.A.S.C.
He joined in August 1916, and in the following September proceeded overseas. Whilst on the Western Front he rendered valuable services with an Ammunition Column in the Ypres, Vimy Ridge, Loos, the Somme and Arras sectors. After hostilities ceased he went to Germany with the Army of Occupation and served there until his demobilisation in January 1919. He holds the General Service and Victory Medals.
29, St. Germain Street, Huntingdon. Z1674.

CLARKE, A., Private, Sherwood Foresters.
Joining in 1916, he was drafted overseas after completing his training. During his service in France he took part in engagements at Ypres, Arras and the Somme (II.), where he was taken prisoner. He was held in captivity in Germany about nine months, and was then released after the Armistice, and returned home. Demobilised in December 1919, he holds the General Service and Victory Medals.
10, Dunville Road, Queen's Park, Bedford. Z1715

CLARKE, A., Private, 9th Bedfordshire Regiment.
He volunteered in September 1914, and, after a period of training was engaged at various stations on important duties with his unit. He was unable to obtain a transfer overseas owing to his being medically unfit, but rendered valuable services until his discharge in May 1916.
27, Cater Street, Kempston, Bedford. X1709.

CLARKE, A. C., Sergeant, Royal Engineers.
He was mobilised in August 1914, and retained for a time on important duties at various home stations before proceeding overseas. Whilst in Egypt he played a distinguished part in the Advance into Palestine, and was in action at Gaza, Jaffa and the capture of Jerusalem. He returned home and was discharged in July 1919, holding the General Service and Victory Medals.
36, Westbourne Road, Queen's Park, Bedford. Z1716/B.

CLARKE, A. J., Q.M.S., 1/5th Bedfordshire Regiment and Royal Air Force.
He vounteered in November 1914, and was retained at various stations, where he was engaged on duties of a highly important nature. He was not successful in his efforts to obtain his transfer to a theatre of war on account of ill-health, but nevertheless rendered very valuable services with his Squadron until February 1919, when he was demobilised.
43, York Street, Bedford. Z1702/A.

CLARKE, A. W., Private, Oxford. and Bucks. L.I.
He joined in July 1916, and, after completing a period of training, served at various stations, where he was engaged on duties of great importance. In 1917 he was transferred to Class "W" of the Reserve and was afterwards employed on Government work at Newport Pagnell, where he rendered valuable services until March 1919, when he was finally demobilised.
38, Greenfield Road, Newport Pagnell, Bucks. Z1706/B.

CLARKE, A. W., Sapper, Royal Engineers.
Shortly after joining in March 1916 he proceeded to the Western Front, where, attached to the Signal Section, he was engaged on important duties in various sectors. He also took an active part in the Battles of the Somme, Vimy Ridge and Ypres and other engagements in this theatre of war, and finally returned home for demobilisation in October 1919. He holds the General Service and Victory Medals.
24, School Street, New Bradwell, Bucks. Z1695/B.

CLARKE, A. W., L/Cpl., 1st Gloucestershire Regt.
Already in the Army when war broke out in August 1914, he was drafted to Salonika in the following year and there saw much severe fighting. After taking part in many important engagements on the Macedonian front he was transferred to Egypt, where he was again in action until the cessation of hostilities. He holds the 1914–15 Star, and the General Service and Victory Medals, and in 1920 was still with his unit in England. 43, York Street, Bedford. Z1702/B.

CLARKE, B. J. (M.M.), Cpl., 16th Cheshire Regt.
He was mobilised in August 1914, and was retained on important duties in England until December 1916, and was then drafted to the Western Front, where he took part in the Battles of Arras, Ypres and the Somme and other important engagements in various sectors. He was unhappily reported missing, and later killed in action at Cambrai on March 22nd, 1918. He had been awarded the Military Medal for conspicuous gallantry in the Field, and was entitled also to the General Service and Victory Medals.
"Whilst we remember, the sacrifice is not in vain."
36, Westbourne Road, Queen's Park, Bedford. Z1716/A.

CLARKE, C., C.S.M., King's (Liverpool Regiment).
Having enlisted in July 1904, he was immediately drafted to the Western Front on the outbreak of war in August 1914. There, after taking a prominent part in the fighting at Mons, he served through the Battles of La Bassée, Ypres and Neuve Chapelle and many other important engagements before being transferred to the East. Again in action at Salonika and in Egypt, he finally returned home for discharge in May 1919, holding the Mons Star, and the General Service and Victory Medals. 12, Denmark Street, Bedford Z1704.

CLARKE, C. E., Air Mechanic, Royal Air Force.
He joined in October 1917, and, after undergoing a period of training, served at various stations, where he was engaged on duties of a highly technical nature. He was not successful in obtaining his transfer to the front, but nevertheless rendered very valuable services, and in 1920 was still with his Squadron.
40, York Street, Bedford. Z1702/C.

CLARKE, C. H., Gunner, Royal Field Artillery.
Volunteering in August 1914, he proceeded to the Western Front on completing his training in March of the following year, and there saw severe fighting in various sectors. He took part in the Battles of Hill 60, Ypres, Albert, the Somme, Arras and Cambrai and many other important engagements until the cessation of hostilities. He holds the 1914–15 Star, and the General Service and Victory Medals, and in 1920 was still with his Battery. 59, Albert Street, Bedford. X1692/A.

CLARKE, C H., Sapper, Royal Engineers (R.O.D.)
He joined in July 1916, and two months later was drafted to the Western Front, where he was engaged on important transport duties in various sectors. He served at Dunkirk and other stations, and was also present at the Battle of Ypres. He finally returned to England for demobilisation in April 1919, and holds the General Service and Victory Medals.
3, White Horse Yard, High Street, Stony Stratford, Bucks. TZ1699.

CLARKE, C. T., Private, 2nd Bedfordshire Regt.
Mobilised in August 1914, he was immediately drafted to the Western Front, where he saw severe fighting in various sectors. After taking part in the Battles of Ypres, Neuve Chapelle, Festubert, Loos, the Somme and Arras and many other important engagements, he was badly gassed near Cambrai in the Retreat of March 1918. Invalided home, he was discharged in June of that year as medically unfit for further service, and holds the Mons Star, and the General Service and Victory Medals. 33, Tavistock Place, Bedford. X1723.

CLARKE, E., Sapper, Royal Engineers.
Shortly after volunteering in September 1914 he proceeded to the Western Front, where he served in various sectors. He took an active part in the Battles of Hill 60, Ypres, Festubert, the Somme and Arras and many minor engagements until severely wounded in action near Cambrai in September 1918. He was for a considerable period in hospital at Paisley before being invalided from the Army in 1919, and holds the 1914–15 Star, and the General Service and Victory Medals.
15, Bunyan Road, South End, Bedford. Z1708.

CLARKE, F., Gunner, Royal Field Artillery.
Joining in June 1917, he was drafted to the Western Front after three months' training and there took part in the Battle of Passchendaele Ridge before being transferred, in November 1917, to Italy. He was there in action on the Piave and Trentino, but returned to France in time to fight in the Battles of the Somme, Amiens, Ypres and Le Cateau and other engagements in the Retreat and Advance of 1918. He afterwards served with the Army of Occupation in Germany, where he was stationed at Cologne, and in 1920 was still with his Battery in England. He holds the General Service and Victory Medals.
Manor House, Easton, Hunts. Z1712 /B.

CLARKE, F. W., Driver, Royal Engineers.
Mobilised in August 1914, he proceeded to the Dardanelles in July of the following year and was there present at the Landing at Suvla Bay. He also saw heavy fighting at Anzac and various other places, and in November 1915 was severely wounded in action and invalided home. After a considerable period in hospital he was discharged in January 1917 as medically unfit for further service, and holds the 1914–15 Star, and the General Service and Victory Medals.
36, Westbourne Road, Queen's Park, Bedford. Z1716 /C.

CLARKE, F. W., Sapper, R.E. (Signal Section).
He volunteered in May 1915, and later in the same year was drafted to the Western Front, where he rendered valuable services as a telephone operator during the Battles of the Somme, Arras, Ypres and Cambrai. In July 1919 he was invalided from the Army owing to deafness brought about by his war service, and holds the 1914–15 Star, and the General Service and Victory Medals.
13, New Row, Pauler's Pury, Towcester, Northants. Z2883.

CLARKE, G., Private, 1st Worcestershire Regt.
He joined in 1917, and, after undergoing a period of training, was retained at various stations, where he was engaged on farm work and on other important duties. He was unable, on account of ill-health, to obtain his transfer to a theatre of war, but, nevertheless, rendered valuable services with his unit until his demobilisation in June 1919.
Cold Brayfield, Beds. Z1697.

CLARKE, G., Corporal, R.A.S.C.
He was mobilised in August 1914, and was immediately drafted to France, where he was engaged on duties of great importance at Le Havre and various other stations. In December 1917 he was transferred to Italy, and there employed on similar duties, rendered valuable services with his Company until after the cessation of hostilities. Discharged in February 1919, he holds the 1914 Star, and the General Service and Victory Medals.
24, School Street, New Bradwell, Bucks. Z1695 /A.

CLARKE, H., Private, Bedfordshire Regiment.
Mobilised in August 1914, he was shortly afterwards drafted to the Western Front, where he served through the fighting at Mons. He also took part in the Battles of Ypres, the Somme, Arras and Cambrai and many other important engagements in various sectors, and was twice wounded in action. He was discharged in March 1919, and holds the Mons Star, and the General Service and Victory Medals.
Cold Brayfield, Beds. Z1696.

CLARKE, H., Sergeant, Bedfordshire Regiment.
He was mobilised at the outbreak of war in August 1914, and was drafted to the Western Front in time to take part in the Retreat from Mons, and afterwards fought with distinction in the Battles of La Bassée, Ypres and Festubert, and other engagements. He fell in action at Monchy on May 4th, 1916. He was entitled to the Mons Star, and the General Service and Victory Medals.
"Whilst we remember, the sacrifice is not in vain."
3, College Road, Bedford. TZ1701.

CLARKE, H. G. C., Corporal, Royal Engineers.
Mobilised in August 1914, he proceeded in December of that year to France, where he saw severe fighting in various sectors of the front. After taking part in the Battles of Neuve Chapelle, Loos, Vimy Ridge and the Somme and many minor engagements, he was wounded in action near Loos in 1916, and invalided home. Discharged in January 1917 as medically unfit for further service, he holds the 1914–15 Star, and the General Service and Victory Medals.
33, Maitland Street, Bedford. TX1700.

CLARKE, H. H., Private, 2nd London Regiment (Royal Fusiliers).
Joining in February 1916, he proceeded to the Western Front in August of that year, and there saw much heavy fighting. He took part in the Battles of the Somme and Arras and minor engagements in various sectors until wounded in action at Ypres in June 1917, and admitted to hospital in London. He was afterwards retained on important duties in England until his demobilisation in March 1919, and holds the General Service and Victory Medals.
11, Church Passage, Newport Pagnell, Bucks. Z1707 /B.

CLARKE, H. J., Private, 1/8th Hampshire Regt.
He joined in November 1917, and, on completing his training in April of the following year, was drafted to the Western Front. Whilst in this theatre of war he saw severe fighting in various sectors, and, after taking part in several important engagements, was wounded in action at Merville in June 1918. He was invalided home later, suffering from appendicitis, and was finally demobilised in February 1920, holding the General Service and Victory Medals.
5, Russell Street, Stony Stratford, Bucks. Z1698 /A.

CLARKE, M. A., Air Mechanic, Royal Air Force.
He joined in May 1918, and, after undergoing a period of training, served at various stations, where he was engaged on duties of a highly technical nature. He was not successful in obtaining his transfer to the front, but nevertheless rendered valuable services with his Squadron until October 1919, when he was demobilised.
24, School Street, New Bradwell, Bucks. Z1695 /C.

CLARKE, O. G., Private, Royal Berkshire Regt.
He volunteered in January 1915, and, after training with the Huntingdonshire Cyclist Battalion, was drafted in July of the following year to the Western Front, where he took part in the Battles of the Somme, Arras, Vimy Ridge, Ypres and Cambrai, and other engagements. He fell fighting on the Somme on March 25th, 1918, during the Retreat. He was entitled to the General Service and Victory Medals.
"His memory is cherished with pride."
Manor House, Easton, Hunts. Z1712 /A.

CLARKE, R. J., Private, Royal Berkshire Regt.
Volunteering in January 1916, he proceeded to the Western Front six months later, and there saw severe fighting in various sectors, taking part in the Battle of Cambrai and other important engagements. He was three times wounded in action—on the Somme in 1916, at Arras in the following year, and again during the Retreat of 1918, and was on each occasion invalided home. He was finally demobilised in October 1919, and holds the General Service and Victory Medals.
38, Greenfield Road, Newport Pagnell, Bucks. Z1706 /A.

CLARKE, S., Sergeant, 1st Hunts. Cyclist Battn.
Mobilised in August 1914, he was retained at various stations in England, where he was engaged as a machine-gun Instructor and on other important duties. Owing to ill-health he was unable to obtain his transfer to a theatre of war, but nevertheless rendered very valuable services with his unit until June 1919, when he was demobilised.
2, Ambury Road, Huntingdon. Z1691.

CLARKE, S. J. (D.C.M.), C.S.M., 7th Wiltshire Regiment.
He volunteered in September 1914, and in August of the following year proceeded to the Western Front, where he took a prominent part in the Battle of Loos and minor engagements. In October 1915 he was transferred to Salonika and there saw severe fighting on the Vardar front until his return to France in August 1918. He was again in action in this theatre of war, serving through many important engagements in the Allies' Advance. He was awarded the Distinguished Conduct Medal for conspicuous gallantry and devotion to duty in the Field in France, and, holding also the 1914–15 Star, and the General Service and Victory Medals, was demobilised in February 1919.
104, Simpson Road, Fenny Stratford, Bucks. Z1693.

CLARKE, T. S., Private, Yorkshire Regiment.
He joined in July 1916, and in February of the following year was drafted to the Western Front, where, acting as a stretcher-bearer, he saw much severe fighting at Ypres and in various other sectors. He was unhappily killed on October 15th, 1917, whilst rescuing a wounded comrade at Passchendaele Ridge. He was entitled to the General Service and Victory Medals.
"Greater love hath no man than this, that a man lay down his life for his friend."
Silver Street, Buckden, Hunts. Z1714.

CLARKE, W., Gunner, Royal Garrison Artillery.
Joining in 1916, he was drafted to the Western Front on completing his training in December of that year, and there served with the 50th Siege Battery in various sectors. He took part in the Battles of Vimy Rdge and Ypres and many other important engagements, and was twice wounded in action—in October 1917, and at St. Quentin in March of the following year. He was for a time in hospital at Exeter before being invalided from the Army in April 1919, and holds the General Service and Victory Medals.
Below the Green, Renhold, near Bedford. Z1710.

CLARKE, W. F., Private, Middlesex Regiment, Royal Fusiliers and Labour Corps.
He volunteered in 1914, and in the following year proceeded to Mesopotamia, where, after seeing much heavy fighting, he was wounded in action at Kut in December 1915. He was sent home and discharged in 1916 as under age, but re-enlisted, however, in July of the following year, and in March 1918 was drafted to the Western Front. There he took part in many important engagements, and was wounded a second time in May. Demobilised in April 1919, he holds the 1914–15 Star, and the General Service and Victory Medals.
28, St. Leonard's Street, Bedford. X1705.

CLARKE, W. G., Private, Royal Army Medical Corps; and Sapper, Royal Engineers.
A Reservist, he was called to the Colours at the outbreak of war in August 1914, and, after serving with the Royal Army Medical Corps, was drafted, in April of the following year, to Egypt with the Royal Engineers. Taking part in the Advance into Palestine, he served through the Battles of Gaza and engagements on the River Jordan and was also present at the fall of Jerusalem. He was discharged on his return home in January 1919, and holds the 1914-15 Star, and the General Service and Victory Medals.
5, Russell Street, Stony Stratford, Bucks. Z1698/B.

CLARKE, W. J., Private, R.A.O.C. and 3rd Duke of Cornwall's Light Infantry.
He volunteered in December 1915, and was retained on important duties in England until 1918, when he was drafted to the Western Front. There he saw severe fighting in various sectors, took part in the Battle of the Somme and many other engagements, and also served through the Advance of 1918. Returning home in 1919, he was stationed for three months in Ireland before being demobilised in September 1919, and holds the General Service and Victory Medals.
The Hollow, Great Brickhill, Bletchley, Bucks. Z1694.

CLARKE, W. J., Sergeant, 2nd Royal Scots.
Having enlisted in February 1897, he proceeded to the Western Front immediately war broke out in August 1914, and there took part in the fighting at Mons. After serving also through the Battles of the Marne, the Aisne, La Bassée, Ypres and Neuve Chapelle, he was invalided home in March 1915, suffering from eye trouble, and was for some time in hospital at Oxford. In February 1918, however, he returned to France and was there severely wounded in action and taken prisoner at Merville in April, and, whilst in captivity in Germany, had his right arm amputated. He was discharged on his release in December 1918, and holds the Mons Star, and the General Service and Victory Medals. 11, Bury St., Newport Pagnell, Bucks. Z1711.

CLARKE, W. T., Private, Bedfordshire Regiment.
He joined in June 1917, and three months later landed in France, where he took part in the heavy fighting at Ypres and was wounded. Later he was in action at the Battles of Cambrai and the Somme, and was then invalided home, suffering from trench-feet in May 1918. Returning to France on his recovery, he served at other important engagements until the close of hostilities, after which he proceeded with the Army of Occupation into Germany, and was stationed on the Rhine on important duties. He returned home and was demobilised in September 1919, holding the General Service and Victory Medals.
Manor House, Easton, Hunts. Z1712/C.

CLAYDON, E. J., Sapper, Royal Engineers.
He joined in May 1916, and after a period of training was drafted to France. During his service in this theatre of war he was engaged in conveying supplies to the various sectors and was often under heavy shell-fire He did good work until after the close of hostilities, and, returning to England, was demobilised in April 1919, holding the General Service and Victory Medals.
53, Spencer Street, New Bradwell, Bucks. Z1717.

CLAYSON, B., Private, 1/4th Northants. Regt.
He joined in 1917, and in the same year proceeded to Palestine. Whilst in this seat of hostilities he took an active part in the Battles of Gaza and was wounded. On his recovery he was engaged on important duties until 1919, when he returned home and was demobilised. He holds the General Service and Victory Medals. Carlton, Bedford. Z1718.

CLAYTON, F., Private, Bedfordshire Regiment.
He volunteered in November 1915, and early in the following year was sent overseas. During his service on the Western Front he took part in many important engagements in various sectors. He fought at the Battles of the Somme, Arras, Messines, Ypres, and was twice wounded—in April and in August 1918, during the Retreat and Advance. He was demobilised on his return to England in February 1919, and holds the General Service and Victory Medals.
Station Grove, Woburn Sands, Beds. Z1719/B.

CLAYTON, G. T., Private, Bedfordshire Regiment.
A Regular soldier, he was drafted to France in October 1914, and played a prominent part in the Battles of Ypres, La Bassée, Neuve Chapelle and Festubert. He was seriously wounded in action at Loos on October 4th, 1915, and was admitted to hospital at Rouen, where he had one of his legs amputated and unhappily died from lockjaw four days later. He was entitled to the 1914 Star, and the General Service and Victory Medals.
"A costly sacrifice upon the altar of freedom."
Station Grove, Woburn Sands, Beds. Z1719/A.

CLEMENTS, A. A., Cpl., 51st Royal Sussex Regt.
He joined in June 1916, and, on completion of his training in the same year, was drafted to the Western Front. There he was engaged on important transport duties and served in various sectors. He saw heavy fighting at the Battles of the Somme, Arras, Ypres and Cambrai, where he was wounded. After the close of hostilities he went with the Army of Occupation into Germany and was stationed at Cologne on important duties until December 1919, when he returned home and was demobilised in January 1920 He holds the General Service and Victory Medals. 7, High Street, Bletchley, Bucks. Z1720.

CLEMENTS, E. A., L/Corporal, East Surrey Regt.
Volunteering in 1915, he proceeded to France in the same year. During the course of his service in this theatre of war he took part in much heavy fighting in various sectors of the front. He was unfortunately killed in action near Béthune on March 15th, 1917, and was buried at the cemetery at Bully-Grenay. He was entitled to the 1914-15 Star, and the General Service and Victory Medals.
"Thinking that remembrance, though unspoken, may reach him where he sleeps."
4, Green Street, St. Ives, Hunts. Z1721/B

CLEMENTS, H. R., Private, Bedfordshire Regt.
Volunteering at the outbreak of war in August 1914, he was sent to France in the following year. There he took part in many engagements in various sectors of the front. He served at the Battles of Festubert, Loos, Ypres and Lens, and was wounded and gassed in action. He was invalided from the Service in September 1916, holding the 1914-15 Star, and the General Service and Victory Medals.
4, Green Street, St. Ives, Hunts. Z1721/A.

CLEMENTS, W. G., Sapper, Royal Engineers.
He volunteered in May 1915, and on completion of his training was retained on important duties with his unit at various stations. Later in 1918 he was sent to Russia, and was stationed at Murmansk, where he served until returning home for demobilisation in August 1919. He holds the General Service and Victory Medals. 23, Cobden St., Bedford. X1722.

CLIFTON, A. J., Private, 1st Northants. Regt.
He was called up from the Reserve at the outbreak of war in August 1914, and immediately proceeded to France. There he fought during the Retreat from Mons, and also in the Battle of La Bassée, where he was wounded and invalided to England. On his recovery he returned to France and took part in the heavy fighting at Hill 60, Festubert and on the Somme. In October 1916 he was discharged as unfit for further military service, and holds the Mons Star, and the General Service and Victory Medals. 2, Lime Street, Olney, Bucks. Z1727.

CLIFTON, C., Private, Bedfordshire Regiment.
He volunteered in 1915, and on completion of his training in the following year, was drafted to the Western Front. During his short period of service in this seat of war he took an active part in the Battle of Albert and in the heavy fighting on the Somme, where he was unfortunately killed in action on October 6th, 1916. He was entitled to the General Service and Victory Medals.
"He died the noblest death a man may die,
Fighting for God and right and liberty."
Balls Yard, London Street, Godmanchester, Hunts. Z1725/A.

CLIFTON, E., Private, R.A.M.C.
Mobilised at the outbreak of hostilities in August 1914, he was immediately drafted to the Western Front, where he was engaged as a stretcher-bearer. He was in action during the Battle of, and in the Retreat from Mons, and saw service at Ypres, the Somme, Arras, St. Quentin and Cambrai. Later he was engaged on important duties in hospital at Boulogne, and, returning to England, was discharged in January 1919, holding the Mons Star, and the General Service and Victory Medals. 28, Hartington Street, Bedford. TX1724.

CLIFTON, F. G., Sergeant, Royal Field Artillery.
He joined in May 1916, and, on completing a period of training in the following year, was drafted to Egypt. Later he played a prominent part during the British Advance through Palestine and Syria, and fought in the Battles of Gaza and at the capture of Jerusalem. Whilst out of action he was engaged as a riding Instructor, and rendered good services. Returning to England, he was demobilised in November 1919, and holds the General Service and Victory Medals
13, Church Street, Olney, Bucks. Z1726.

CLIFTON, F. W., L/Cpl., R. Warwickshire Regt.
He volunteered in 1915, and, after completing a period of training, was drafted overseas in 1916. In the course of his service on the Western Front he took part in much heavy fighting in various sectors. He was present at the Battles of the Somme, Ypres and Cambrai, and was afterwards transferred to Italy, where he took part in the engagements on the Piave front. After the close of hostilities he returned to England and was demobilised in 1919, holding the General Service and Victory Medals.
West Street, Godmanchester, Hunts. Z1730/B.

CLIFTON, P., L/Corporal, 4th Australian Infantry (Australian Overseas Forces).
He volunteered in 1915, and later in the same year was drafted to the Western Front. During his service in this seat of war he took part in the heavy fighting at the Battles of Ypres, Loos and Albert. In 1916 he made the supreme sacrifice, being killed in action during the Somme Offensive. He was entitled to the 1914-15 Star, and the General Service and Victory Medals.
"Whilst we remember, the sacrifice is not in vain."
Mill Green, Turvey, Bedford. Z1729.

CLIFTON, T., Private, Royal Sussex and East Surrey Regiments.
Volunteering in September 1914, he proceeded to France in the following year and took part in the heavy fighting in various sectors, including the Battles of Festubert and Loos. Later he was transferred to Egypt, and was also in action in Palestine, particularly at the Battles of Gaza, and in the capture of Jerusalem, and was invalided to hospital suffering from malarial fever. On his recovery in 1918 he was sent to Russia, where he served until returning home for demobilisation in September 1919. He holds the 1914–15 Star, and the General Service and Victory Medals.
West Street, Godmanchester. Z1730/A.

CLIFTON, T., Private, 3rd Bedfordshire Regiment.
He volunteered in July 1915, and after completing a period of training was retained on guard and other important duties with his unit at various stations. Owing to his being medically unfit, he was unable to obtain a transfer to a theatre of war, but rendered valuable service until demobilised in February 1919. 6, Royal Oak Passage, Huntingdon, Hunts. Z1728.

CLIFTON, W. F., Private, Middlesex Regiment.
He joined in May 1916, and shortly afterwards proceeded to the Western Front. During his service in this seat of war he fought at the Battle of the Somme, and was unfortunately killed in action near Delville Wood on October 12th, 1916. He was entitled to the General Service and Victory Medals.
"The path of duty was the way to glory."
Balls Yard, London Street, Godmanchester. Z1725/B.

CLINCH, G. E., Sapper, Royal Engineers.
He joined in August 1916, but on completion of his training was retained on special duties with the Searchlight Section at various home stations. In 1918, however, he was sent to France, and whilst at Etaples rendered valuable services with his unit until his demobilisation in January 1919. He holds the General Service and Victory Medals.
Bow Brickhill, near Bletchley, Bucks. Z1731.

COCKINGS, G. H., Gunner, R.G.A.
Joining in September 1917, he completed his training in the following year, and was drafted to France, where he served with his Battery in various sectors of the front. He was in action during the heavy fighting at Lens, and was wounded in April 1918 and invalided to England. After a period of hospital treatment he was discharged as medically unfit for further service in November 1918, and holds the General Service and Victory Medals.
6, Beaconsfield Place, Newport Pagnell. TZ1732.

CODLING, J. T., Bombardier, Royal Field Artillery.
He volunteered in January 1916, and four months later landed in France, where he served with the Royal Army Veterinary Corps, and did good work attending to the sick and wounded horses at the Base. In November 1916 he was invalided to England, and after a period of hospital treatment was discharged, and sent to Scotland, where he served until 1919. He was then sent to India, and in 1920 was still serving there. He holds the General Service and Victory Medals.
11, Shakespeare Place, Huntingdon. Z1733/A.

COE, B. M. O. (Miss), Member, Women's Legion.
This lady volunteered in July 1915, and was employed as cook in the officers' mess at Biggleswade Camp until she was discharged in July 1916. During the period of her employment she rendered valuable services.
12, Great Butts Street, Bedford. X1734/B.

COLBERT, E. J., Private, Huntingdonshire Cyclist Battalion and Royal Warwickshire Regiment.
He volunteered in October 1914, and after a period of training in Yorkshire served with the Huntingdonshire Cyclist Battalion on various duties until 1916, when he was transferred to the Royal Warwickshire Regiment, and drafted to France in July of the same year. He had only served overseas for a few weeks when he made the supreme sacrifice, falling in action at Thiepval on August 18th, 1916. He was entitled to the General Service and Victory Medals.
"He died the noblest death a man may die,
Fighting for God and right and liberty."
Broughton, Hunts. TZ1735/A.

COLBERT, G. H., Gunner, R.G.A.
Volunteering in August 1914, he proceeded in the following May to the Western Front. There he took part with his Battery in the Battles of Festubert, Loos, Albert, Vimy Ridge, Messines, Ypres, Passchendaele and Cambrai. Wounded in action in September 1918, he was evacuated to England and subsequently invalided out of the Service in February 1919. He holds the 1914–15 Star, and the General Service and Victory Medals Croft Lane, Brampton, Hunts. Z1736.

COLBERT, H., Private, 1st Queen's (Royal West Surrey Regiment).
He joined in October 1917, and six months later was sent to France. In this theatre of war he took part in several important engagements during the final Advance, including the Battles of Amiens, Ypres (IV.), and Le Cateau (II.), and did excellent work. He remained overseas until March 1919, and was demobilised a month later, holding the General Service and Victory Medals.
Broughton, Hunts. TZ1735/B.

COLBON, C. B., L/Corporal, R.A.M.C.
After volunteering in November 1915, he was stationed at Eastbourne, Salisbury Plain, and Ripon prior to proceeding to the Western Front in 1916. Whilst overseas he was engaged on various duties of an important nature, and served in the Somme, Arras, Ypres, Lens, Cambrai and other sectors. He subsequently proceeded into Germany with the Army of Occupation, and was demobilised in January 1919, holding the General Service and Victory Medals.
19, West Street, Newtown, Huntingdon. Z1737.

COLBOURN, A. P., Private, Essex Regiment.
He joined in 1916, and in October of the same year was drafted to France. There he participated with his unit in many important engagements, including the Battles of the Somme and Cambrai, and was gassed in action. He performed consistently good work, remaining overseas until after the cessation of hostilities, and was demobilised in May 1919, holding the General Service and Victory Medals.
Thrapston Road, Brampton, Hunts. TZ1738.

COLBURT, C., Rifleman, 10th Rifle Brigade.
Joining in June 1916, he proceeded in the following October to the Western Front, where he was immediately in action on the Somme. After taking part in heavy fighting at Beaumont-Hamel, he was unfortunately killed during a severe engagement at Le Transloy in February 1917, and was buried near Bapaume. He was entitled to the General Service and Victory Medals.
"Thinking that remembrance, though unspoken, may reach him where he sleeps."
1, Russell Street, Bedford. X1739.

COLE, A. J. (M.S.M.), Sapper, Royal Engineers.
He volunteered in October 1914, and four months later was sent to France. There he was employed on important work in connection with the railways, and served in many sectors. He was awarded the Meritorious Service Medal in 1917 in recognition of his consistently good work and devotion to duty. Wounded at La Bassée in October 1918, he was sent to hospital at La Tréport, and was later evacuated to England, being eventually invalided out of the Army in December 1918, holding also the 1914–15 Star, and the General Service and Victory Medals.
Cambridge Street, St. Neots, Hunts. Z1740.

COLE, F., A.B., R.N., H.M.S. "Gibraltar."
Already in the Royal Navy at the outbreak of war in August 1914, he was posted to H.M.S. "Gibraltar," and in this vessel proceeded to the Dardanelles, where he took part in the naval operations. He subsequently served in the Mediterranean, and later was engaged on patrol duty in the North Sea and escorting troops to France. Discharged in July 1920, he holds the 1914–15 Star, and the General Service and Victory Medals.
36, Grey Friars Walk, Bedford. X1743.

COLE, H., Private, 6th Royal Warwickshire Regt.
He volunteered in September 1914, but was medically unfit for transfer to a theatre of war. Retained at home, he was stationed in Essex and at various places on the East Coast, and rendered valuable services, whilst employed as transport driver, until he was demobilised in February 1919.
9, Bell Place, St. John Street, Bedford. X1744.

COLE, J. A., Driver, Royal Engineers.
He was mobilised in August 1914, and in the following July was drafted to the Dardanelles. There he was employed on important duties during the Landing at, and the Battle of, Suvla Bay, and later served at Anzac. He was subsequently sent to Egypt, and, proceeding afterwards into Palestine, served at Gaza, Jaffa and Jerusalem. Demobilised on returning home in July 1919, he holds the 1914–15 Star, and the General Service and Victory Medals.
51, Westbourne Road, Queen's Park, Bedford. X1741.

COLEMAN, C. J., Gnr., 5th Canadian Siege Battery.
He volunteered in January 1915, and having completed his training served at Shoreham and Bury St. Edmunds until December 1916, when he was sent to France. There he was in action at Vimy Ridge and Arras, and was unhappily killed near Vimy Ridge on April 21st, 1917. He was entitled to the General Service and Victory Medals.
"He passed out of the sight of men by the path of duty and self-sacrifice."
Bow Brickhill, near Bletchley, Bucks. Z2884.

COLEMAN, D., Private, Duke of Cornwall's Light Infantry.
He joined in June 1918, but was not successful in obtaining a transfer to a theatre of war owing to the termination of hostilities. Sent for training to Ireland, he was later employed on guard and other important duties at various stations in that country, and rendered excellent service until he was demobilised in January 1919.
Wellmore, Maids Moreton, Buckingham. Z1747.

COLEMAN, E., Private, 8th Suffolk Regiment.
He volunteered in November 1915, and in the following year proceeded to the Western Front. There he took part in several important engagements in France and Belgium, and did good work until he was badly wounded at Ypres in August 1917. Invalided home, he spent a considerable time in hospital at Brighton, and was eventually demobilised in February 1919, holding the General Service and Victory Medals.
Eaton Ford, Beds. Z1746.

COLEMAN, E., Private, Leicestershire Regiment.
Joining in June 1917, he was drafted in the following April to France. In this theatre of war he was in action with his unit on the Marne front and at Bapaume and Cambrai. Evacuated to England as the result of being severely wounded on the Selle in October 1918, he was admitted to hospital and was still an inmate in 1920. He holds the General Service and Victory Medals. 103, Coventry Road, Bedford. Z1751/B.

COLEMAN, E., Sapper, Royal Engineers.
He joined in June 1916, and a month later was sent to France. During his service overseas he was employed with his Company on various duties of an important character on the Somme front and at Arras, Ypres and Cambrai. He performed consistently good work until the termination of hostilities, and was demobilised on his return home in February 1919, holding the General Service and Victory Medals.
52, Spencer Street, Bradwell, Bucks. Z1748/C.

COLEMAN, G., Private, R.A.S.C.
He volunteered in August 1915, and was drafted later in the same year to the Western Front. There he served at Loos, Ypres, Neuve Chapelle, Havrincourt and on the Somme front, and was employed on important duties For some time he was attached to the Labour Corps, working behind the lines. Returning home after the Armistice, he was demobilised in February 1919, and holds the 1914–15 Star, and the General Service and Victory Medals.
103, Coventry Road, Bedford. Z1751/A.

COLEMAN, H., Sapper, Royal Engineers.
Joining in April 1916, he served at Borden Camp until the following February, when he proceeded to France. Whilst stationed at Divisional Headquarters he was employed on special duties in connection with the Railway Operating Department of the Royal Engineers and rendered excellent service until he was demobilised in August 1919, holding the General Service and Victory Medals.
3, Mount Pleasant, Bletchley, Bucks. Z2885.

COLEMAN, S., Rifleman, K.R.R.C.
He joined in September 1918, and during his training was stationed at Northampton. He was unable to obtain a transfer overseas before the termination of hostilities, but, after the Armistice, was sent to Germany and served with the Army of Occupation in Cologne. He was demobilised on returning home in February 1919. 103, Coventry Rd., Bedford. Z1751/C.

COLEMAN, S. E., Sapper, Royal Engineers.
Joining in August 1916, he was sent in the following April to the Western Front. There he served at Arras, Messines, Ypres, Albert and Cambrai, where he was gassed in June 1918. As a result he was invalided home, and, after spending some time in hospital, was eventually demobilised in March 1919, holding the General Service and Victory Medals.
115, Sun Street, Biggleswade, Beds. Z1750.

COLEMAN, W. C., Trooper, City of London Lancers (Rough Riders).
He volunteered in 1915, and, having completed his training, was later sent overseas. Serving in Egypt and Palestine, he participated with his unit in several severe engagements and did excellent work until he was killed in action on November 27th, 1917. He was entitled to the General Service and Victory Medals.
"His memory is cherished with pride."
High Street, Carlton, Beds. Z1749.

COLES, A., Private, 1st Oxford. and Bucks. L.I.
He volunteered in September 1914, and six months later proceeded to France. In this theatre of hostilities he played a prominent part with his unit in the Battles of Ypres and Loos, but, after 12 months' service overseas fell during heavy fighting at Loos on March 28th, 1916. He was entitled to the 1914–15 Star, and the General Service and Victory Medals.
"Honour to the immortal dead, who gave their youth that the world might grow old in peace."
178, Simpson Road, Fenny Stratford, Bucks. Z1753/B.

COLES, B., Private, R.M.L.I.
He joined in November 1916, and after a period of training at Blandford was drafted in the following March to the Western Front. There he at once took part in heavy fighting, and was reported missing after a severe engagement at Cambrai on October 26th, 1917. He was later presumed to have been killed on that day, and was entitled to the General Service and Victory Medals.
"Courage, bright hopes and a myriad dreams, splendidly given."
14, Near Town, Olney, Bucks. Z1757/B.

COLES, C., Trooper, Bedfordshire Lancers.
Volunteering in June 1915, he was sent four months afterwards to France, where he served for 3½ years. During this period he played a prominent part with his unit in many important engagements, including those at Loos, Messines, Arras and Ypres. He was demobilised in April 1919, a month after his return to England, and holds the 1914–15 Star, and the General Service and Victory Medals.
32, Priory Street, Bedford. X1756/A.

COLES, E., Sapper, Royal Engineers.
Volunteering in December 1915, he was drafted overseas after completing his training. Whilst on the Western Front he was engaged on important pontoon and bridge building in the Somme, Arras and Passchendaele sectors, and was gassed in action in 1917. He was demobilised in March 1919, and holds the General Service and Victory Medals.
Cross Street, Moulton. Z2886.

COLES, G., Private, Oxford. and Bucks. L.I.
He volunteered in September 1914, and in the following March proceeded to the Western Front. In this theatre of hostilities he participated in the Battles of Ypres and Loos, and was later wounded in July 1916, during the first Battle of the Somme. Evacuated to England, he was sent to hospital at St. Albans, and was eventually invalided out of the Army in March 1917. He holds the 1914–15 Star, and the General Service and Victory Medals.
178, Simpson Road, Fenny Stratford, Bucks. Z1753/C.

COLES, H., Sergeant, R.A.S.C. (M.T.)
Mobilised in August 1914, he was sent two months later to France. During his service overseas he was stationed for 16 months at Ypres and did excellent work whilst engaged on important duties. He was subsequently attached to the 17th Field Ambulance and later employed in various workshops as an electrical engineer. Demobilised in May 1919, he holds the 1914 Star, and the General Service and Victory Medals.
44, Nelson Street, Buckingham. Z1754.

COLES, H. W., Sergeant, 2nd King's Own (Royal Lancaster Regiment).
Called up from the Reserve at the outbreak of war in August 1914, he was retained at home on important duties until the following April, when he was sent to France. He was taken prisoner a month later during the second Battle of Ypres, and died in captivity at Giessen, Germany, in December 1916. He was entitled to the 1914–15 Star, and the General Service and Victory Medals.
"Whilst we remember, the sacrifice is not in vain."
60, Hatch Green, Olney, Bucks. Z1752.

COLES, M., Gunner, Royal Garrison Artillery.
He volunteered in August 1915, and four months afterwards was drafted to the Western Front. In this theatre of war he served in many sectors and was in action with his Battery at Loos, on the Somme front, and at Ypres, Passchendaele and Cambrai. Returning home after the Armistice, he was demobilised in February 1919, and holds the 1914–15 Star, and the General Service and Victory Medals.
32, Priory Street, Bedford. X1756/B.

COLES, P., Corporal, Royal Air Force.
He joined in April 1917, but was physically unfit for transfer to a theatre of war. Retained at home, he served at Felixstowe and other stations, and was engaged on important duties which demanded a high degree of technical skill. He rendered valuable services until he was demobilised in September 1919.
32, Priory Street, Bedford. X1756/D.

COLES, P. G., Pte., 8th Bedfordshire Regiment.
Volunteering in January 1915, he was employed on various duties at home stations until December of the same year, when he proceeded to France. There he took part in heavy fighting at Festubert and Loos, but had only served overseas for two months when he made the supreme sacrifice, being killed in action at Vermelles on February 11th, 1916. He was entitled to the 1914–15 Star, and the General Service and Victory Medals.
"His life for his Country, his soul to God."
Ellington, Hunts. Z1755.

COLES, R., Private, 1/4th Dorsetshire Regiment.
Two months after joining in July 1917 he was drafted to Mesopotamia, and, during his service in this theatre of hostilities took part in many important engagements on the Euphrates and other fronts. He performed consistently good work, and was demobilised on his return home in March 1920, holding the General Service and Victory Medals.
9, East Street, Olney, Bucks. Z1757/A.

COLES, T., Private, Somerset Light Infantry.
He volunteered in September 1914, and six months later was sent to France, where he was in action during the Battles of Ypres (II.), Loos and the Somme. Wounded during heavy fighting at Cambrai in September 1917, he was sent to hospital in the Isle of Wight, and on his recovery was drafted to India. There he was employed on various duties and served on the Afghan front. Demobilised on his return home in March 1919, he holds the 1914–15 Star, and the General Service and Victory Medals. 178, Simpson Road, Fenny Stratford, Bucks. Z1753/A.

COLES, W. G., Private, 3rd Border Regiment.
He was mobilised in August 1914, and immediately drafted to France. There he took part in the Retreat from Mons, the Battles of the Marne, the Aisne, Ypres, Festubert, Loos and the Somme, and was wounded four times. He unfortunately died on December 24th, 1917, through the effects of war service, and was entitled to the Mons Star and the General Service and Victory Medals.
"A valiant Soldier, with undaunted heart he breasted life's last hill."
32, Priory Street, Bedford. Z1756/C.

COLEY, J. R., A.B., Royal Navy.
He volunteered in November 1914, and after a period of training proceeded to the North Sea on board H.M.S "Arrogant," in which vessel he served until 1916. He was then drafted to France with the Royal Naval Division, and took part in many engagements, including those at Arras, Cambrai and Oppy Wood, where he was wounded in action. He was demobilised in March 1919, and holds the 1914–15 Star, and the General Service and Victory Medals.
15, Althorpe Street, Bedford. X1758.

COLEY, S. W., Sapper, Royal Engineers.
He joined in June 1916, and, on completing his training in the following year, was drafted to France. In this theatre of war he served with the Railway Operative Department and did good work as an engine driver on the troop trains in many sectors. He was demobilised in October 1919, and holds the General Service and Victory Medals.
29, Water Eaton, near Bletchley, Bucks. Z1759.

COLLIE, F., Private, 5th Gordon Highlanders.
He volunteered in 1914, and in the following year was drafted to the Western Front, where he took part in the Battles of Festubert, Loos and Ypres. He made the supreme sacrifice, being killed in action on the Somme on July 11th, 1916. He was entitled to the 1914–15 Star, and the General Service and Victory Medals.
"Whilst we remember, the sacrifice is not in vain."
11, Bunyan Road, Kempston, Bedford. X1760.

COLLING, W. B. C., Sapper, Royal Engineers.
He was mobilised in August 1914, and almost immediately drafted to the Western Front. There he took part in the Retreat from Mons, the Battles of Ypres, Loos, the Somme, and in several other engagements. He was invalided home in 1917, and finally discharged in March 1918. He holds the Mons Star, and the General Service and Victory Medals.
80, Cauldwell Street, Bedford. X1761/A.

COLLINGWOOD, H. (M.S.M.), Sergeant, Royal Field Artillery and Royal Garrison Artillery.
He volunteered in October 1914, and was shortly afterwards drafted to the Western Front. There he quickly gained promotion and played a distinguished part in the Battles of Ypres, Loos and the Somme, and many other engagements. He was wounded in action, but soon returned to his unit, although unfit, and did continuously good work, acting for part of his service as sergeant-major. He was awarded the Meritorious Service Medal for his excellent work throughout, and was later demobilised in February 1919. He also holds the 1914–15 Star, and the General Service and Victory Medals.
106, Coventry Road, Queen's Park, Bedford. Z1538/A.

COLLINS, C. A., Private, Bedfordshire Regiment.
Volunteering in 1915, he proceeded overseas after completing his training. Whilst on the Western Front he took part in many engagements, including the Battles of Hill 60, the Somme, Arras, Ypres, Passchendaele and Cambrai. He was demobilised in February 1919, and holds the 1914–15 Star, and the General Service and Victory Medals.
66, Wellington Street, Bedford. X1762/A.

COLLINS, E. J., Private, 8th (King's Royal Irish) Hussars.
He was mobilised with the Bedfordshire Regiment in August 1914, but later was transferred to the 8th Hussars and proceeded to France. There he took part in several important engagements, including those at Ypres, Festubert, Loos, the Somme, Albert and Cambrai. After hostilities ceased he went to Germany with the Army of Occupation, and served at Cologne until his discharge in May, 1919. He holds the 1914–15 Star, and the General Service and Victory Medals.
Great Paxton, Hunts. Z1763/B

COLLINS, W., Private, Suffolk Regiment.
He joined in April 1917, and in the following month was drafted to Egypt, where he took part in the Advance into Palestine and saw much fighting at Gaza and Jerusalem. He was invalided to the Base suffering from dysentery and diphtheria, but, on his recovery, was transferred to France and was in action in the Advance of 1918. He was demobilised in February 1919, and holds the General Service and Victory Medals.
Great Paxton, St. Neots, Hunts. Z1763/A.

COMPTON, T., Driver, R.A.S.C.
He volunteered in September 1915, and after a period of training was engaged at various stations on important duties as a farrier. He rendered valuable services, but was unable to obtain a transfer overseas owing to his being medically unfit. He was discharged in October 1917.
6, Bell Court, Bedford. X1764.

CONNOR, A., Private, Royal Army Medical Corps.
Joining in September 1916, he was drafted overseas three months later. During his service on the Western Front he took part in many engagements, including the Battles of Arras, Vimy Ridge, Bullecourt, Cambrai and in the Retreat and Advance of 1918. He was demobilised in June 1919, and holds the General Service and Victory Medals.
23, Tavistock Place, Bedford. X1765/A.

CONSTANT, D., Private, 1/5th Bedfordshire Regt.
He volunteered in September 1914, and in the following year was drafted to the Dardanelles, where he saw much heavy fighting at the Landing at Cape Helles and Suvla Bay. After the Evacuation of the Gallipoli Peninsula he was transferred to Egypt and took part in the Advance into Palestine, being in action at Gaza and in the Offensive under General Allenby. He returned home and was demobilised in 1919, holding the 1914–15 Star, and the General Service and Victory Medals.
Near Post Office, Renhold, near Bedford. Z1766/B.

CONSTANT, J., Private, 3rd Norfolk Regiment.
He joined in 1916, and later in the same year was drafted to France, where he took part in the Battles of Albert and the Somme and was wounded and invalided home in July 1917. Later he was sent to Italy, but was invalided home again on account of ill-health, and on his recovery returned to France and saw much fighting at Lens and Cambrai. He was demobilised in 1919, and holds the General Service and Victory Medals. Salph End, Renhold, near Bedford. Z1766/A.

COOK, A., Sapper, Royal Engineers.
He volunteered in September 1914, and in the following January proceeded to France. In this theatre of war, he saw much heavy fighting in the Ypres and Neuve Chapelle sectors, and later served with the Railway Operative Department on important duties in the forward areas. He was demobilised in March 1919, and holds the 1914–15 Star, and the General Service and Victory Medals.
72, Victoria Street, Bletchley, Bucks. Z1859/B.

COOK, A., Private, 1st Cambridgeshire Regiment.
He volunteered in 1914, and underwent a short period of training prior to his being drafted to France. Whilst in this theatre of war he took part in many engagements, including the Battle of Ypres and the Somme, and was badly wounded in action. As a result he was invalided home and finally discharged in 1916 as medically unfit for further duty. He holds the 1914–15 Star, and the General Service and Victory Medals.
St. Neots, Girtford Road, Sandy, Beds. Z1780.

COOK, A., Guardsman, 1st Coldstream Guards.
He was already in the Army when war broke out in August 1914, and was immediately drafted to France, where he fought at Mons and in the subsequent Retreat, the Battles of the Marne, the Aisne and La Bassée, and was wounded. As a result he was invalided to Boulogne, but on his recovery returned to his unit, and was again wounded at Ypres and sent to hospital in Calais. Later he took part in the Battle of the Somme, where he sustained his third wound and was invalided home. He was afterwards retained at various home stations on important duties until his discharge in February 1919. He holds the Mons Star, and the General Service and Victory Medals. Grove Cottage, Great Linford, Bucks. Z1778/A.

COOK, A., Corporal, Oxford. and Bucks. L.I.
Volunteering in August 1914, he was drafted overseas after a period of training. Whilst on the Western Front he took part in several engagements, but was unfortunately reported missing during the Battle of the Somme. He was afterwards reported killed in action in July 1916, and was entitled to the General Service and Victory Medals.
"Honour to the immortal dead, who gave their youth that the world might grow old in peace."
8, Nelson Street, Buckingham, Bucks. Z1767/C.

COOK, A. A. N., Private, Queen's Own (Royal West Kent Regiment).
He joined in May 1917, and, after a short period of training, was drafted to Italy, where he served for about three months, and was then transferred to France. There he took part in the Retreat and Advance of 1918, and was wounded in action near Cambrai, which wound resulted in his being invalided home. He was demobilised in December 1918, and holds the General Service and Victory Medals.
Main Street, Hartford. Z1784.

COOK, A. C., Private, R.A.S.C. (M.T.)
Volunteering in July 1915, he was quickly drafted to France, where he was stationed at Boulogne, Rouen and St. Omer. He did continuously good work whilst engaged in repairing transport lorries and ambulance cars throughout hostilities. He was demobilised in May 1919, and holds the 1914–15 Star, and the General Service and Victory Medals.
74, Spencer Street New Bradwell, Bucks. Z1769/A.

COOK, A. G., Sapper, R.E. (Signal Section).
He volunteered in August 1914, and after two months' training war drafted overseas. During his service on the Western Front he was engaged as a telegraphist, and took part in much heavy fighting in the Ypres, Somme and Cambrai sectors. He was demobilised in January 1919, and holds the 1914 Star, and the General Service and Victory Medals.
7, Western Road, Bletchley, Bucks. Z1773.

COOK, A. G., Private, 13th Middlesex Regiment.
He joined in March 1916, and later in the same year was drafted to France, where he took part in the Battles of the Somme, Albert, Delville Wood, Ypres and Messines, being gassed and blown up three times by shell explosions. Later he was transferred to Italy and saw much fighting on the Piave until 1918, when he returned to France. There he was in action on the Somme (II.), at Lens and Cambrai, and was severely wounded in action and consequently invalided to Boulogne. He was recommended for the Distinguished Conduct Medal for gallantry and devotion to duty in the Field near Messines. He was discharged in 1919 totally blind, and holds the General Service and Victory Medals and an Italian decoration.
35, Sandhurst Road, Bedford. Z1779.

COOK, C., Private, 1/5th Bedfordshire Regiment.
He volunteered in January 1915, and later in the same year was drafted to France, where he took part in much severe fighting at the Battles of Loos, Albert and on the Somme. He died gloriously on the Field of Battle at Arras on April 24th, 1917, and was entitled to the General Service and Victory Medals.
"The path of duty was the way to glory."
West End, Cranfield, Beds. Z1781.

COOK, C. F., Wireless Telegraphist, Royal Navy.
He joined in July 1916, and after a period of training was engaged at Scapa Flow on important coastal duties. He did continuously good work during the war, and in 1920 was still in the Navy, serving at Malta. He holds the General Service and Victory Medals. 2, Pilcroft Street, Bedford. X1771/B.

COOK, C. H., Private, Oxford. and Bucks. L.I.
He was mobilised in August 1914, and shortly afterwards proceeded to France, where he took part in the Retreat from Mons, the Battles of Ypres and La Bassée, and was wounded in action, which resulted in his being invalided home. On his recovery he was sent to Salonika and saw much fighting on the Vardar front, and was again wounded. He returned home and was discharged in March 1919, and holds the Mons Star, and the General Service and Victory Medals.
2, Spring Gardens, Newport Pagnell. Z1775/C—Z1776/C.

COOK, F. C., Private, 1/5th Bedfordshire Regt.
He volunteered in August 1914, and underwent a period of training prior to his being drafted to France, where he took part in the Battles of Ypres, the Somme and Vimy Ridge, and was twice gassed in action. Later he was transferred to Italy and served on the Piave until the end of 1917, when he again proceeded to France. There he fought at the Battles of the Somme (II.) and Cambrai and in many engagements until hostilities ceased. He was demobilised in February 1919, and holds the General Service and Victory Medals.
Church Row, Stagsden, Beds. Z1783/A.

COOK, F. G., Private, 3rd Bedfordshire Regiment.
He was mobilised in August 1914, and quickly drafted to France. In this theatre of war he took part in many engagements, including the Retreat from Mons and the Battle of Ypres. He was buried in a dug-out by a shell explosion, and consequently invalided home. He was finally discharged in April 1916 as medically unfit for further service, and holds the Mons Star, and the General Service and Victory Medals.
2, Pilcroft Street, Bedford. X1771/A.

COOK, H., Private, Cheshire Regiment.
He volunteered in October 1914, and, on completing his training in the following year, was drafted to France. There he took part in many important engagements, including the Battles of Ypres, Vimy Ridge, Arras and Cambrai, and in the Retreat and Advance of 1918. He died gloriously on the Field of Battle near Cambrai in September 1918, and was entitled to the 1914–15 Star, and the General Service and Victory Medals.
"His life for his Country, his soul to God."
51, Queen's Street, Bedford. X1777/A.

COOK, H. C. (D.C.M.), Corporal, Northants. Regt.
He joined in April 1918, and in the following September was drafted to France, where he played a prominent part in much severe fighting at Cambrai, and was awarded the Distinguished Conduct Medal for conspicuous gallantry and devotion to duty on the Sambre-Meuse Canal. He was unfortunately killed in action on November 4th, 1918, and was also entitled to the General Service and Victory Medals.
"Honour to the immortal dead, who gave their youth that the world might grow old in peace."
19, College Road, Bedford. Z1772.

COOK, H. T., Private, Bedfordshire Regiment.
We volunteered in August 1914, and in the following July was drafted to Egypt. In this seat of operations he first saw sevrice on the Suez Canal and at Katia, and later took part in the Advance into Palestine. He made the supreme sacrifice, being killed in action near Gaza in July 1917. He was entitled to the 1914–15 Star, and the General Service and Victory Medals.
"Thinking that remembrance, though unspoken, may reach him where he sleeps."
51, Queen's Street, Bedford. X1777/B.

COOK, J., Private, Royal Army Medical Corps.
Mobilised in 1914, he completed his training and in November 1915 was sent to Mesopotamia, where he took part in the operations at Kut-el-Amara in the early part of 1916. Captured by the Turks in February 1916, whilst attached to the Camel Corps, he was held a prisoner in Constantinople until the end of the war. After his return home he was discharged in April 1919, and holds the 1914–15 Star, and the General Service and Victory Medals.
The Grove, Great Linford, Bucks. Z1778B.

COOK, R. G., Private, 2/4th Oxford. & Bucks. L.I.
He volunteered in November 1915, and eleven months later was drafted to France, where he saw heavy fighting in the Somme sector. In January 1917 his health broke down and he was invalided to England, but five months later returned to the firing-line. He took an active part in important engagements at Ypres, Albert, St. Quentin and Cambrai, and was demobilised in April 1919, holding the General Service and Victory Medals.
74, Spencer Street, New Bradwell, Bucks. Z1769/B.

COOK, S. R., Leading Stoker, Royal Navy.
When war was declared in August 1914 he volunteered, and served in the Baltic and other seas. He also took an active part in fighting off Jutland, and served in U.B. "90." In April 1920 he was invalided to England for a month, and in 1921 was still in the Navy. He holds the 1914–15 Star, and the General Service and Victory Medals.
Silver Street, Buckden, Hunts. Z1768.

COOK, T., Sapper, Royal Engineers.
He volunteered in September 1915, and later in the same year was drafted to the Western Front, where he rendered valuable services laying mines and trench-digging. He also was in action at Hill 60, Loos and Albert, and in 1916 was invalided to England. He was discharged in June of that year as medically unfit for further military duties, and holds the 1914–15 Star, and the General Service and Victory Medals.
31, Priory Street, Newport Pagnell, Bucks. Z1774.

COOK, W. A., Private, Bedfordshire Regiment.
Volunteering in September 1914, he proceeded in the following year to Gallipoli, where he was in action in many engagements, including that at Suvla Bay. He was wounded in August 1915 and sent back to England, and on his recovery in 1916 was drafted to France. On that front he was engaged in severe fighting on the Somme and at Albert, Messines and Cambrai. He was demobilised in 1919, and holds the 1914–15 Star, and the General Service and Victory Medals.
Church Row, Stagsden, Beds. Z1783/B.

COOK, W. A., Private, 12th Middlesex Regiment.
He volunteered in October 1914, and on completion of his training was drafted overseas five months later. During his service on the Western Front he experienced fierce fighting in the Ypres, Loos and Somme sectors, and was unfortunately killed in action on April 25th, 1916. He was entitled to the 1914–15 Star, and the General Service and Victory Medals.
"His life for his Country."
8, Nelson Street, Buckingham, Bucks. Z1767/A.

COOK, W. F. (M.M.), Cpl., 2nd South Staffs. Regt.
When war was declared in August 1914 he volunteered, but was retained on important duties at home until January 1916, when he was ordered overseas. Whilst serving in France he fought with distinction at Albert, the Somme, Gommecourt, Arras, Ypres and Cambrai, and was wounded in the last engagement in September 1918. He was awarded the Military Medal for conspicuous gallantry in the Field, and was demobilised in April 1919. He also holds the General Service and Victory Medals.
2, Spencer Street, New Bradwell, Bucks. Z1770.

COOK, W. J., Private, 7th Oxford. & Bucks. L.I.
He volunteered in August 1914, and shortly afterwards was drafted to the Western Front, where he was wounded in the Battle of Ypres in November 1914. He was sent to hospital in England, and on his recovery in January 1915 rejoined his unit in France. After fighting at Neuve Chapelle, Hill 60, Ypres, Arras, Vimy Ridge and Bullecourt, he was wounded on two occasions in the Battle of the Somme. He was demobilised in March 1919, holding the 1914 Star, and the General Service and Victory Medals.
7, Spencer Street, Bradwell, Bucks. Z1782.

COOKE, A. E., Gunner, Royal Garrison Artillery.
Joining in April 1916, he was sent three months later to the Western Front, where he took part in numerous engagements. He saw much severe fighting in the Somme, Arras, Messines, Ypres, Cambrai, St. Quentin and Amiens sectors, and also in the Retreat and Advance of 1918. In December 1918 he was invalided home suffering from influenza, and in April 1919 was demobilised, holding the General Service and Victory Medals. King's Ripton, Hunts. Z1786/B

COOKE, B. E., Private, 4th Lincolnshire Regiment.
He volunteered in September 1914, and in the following year proceeded to the Western Front. There he took part in many engagements, including the Battles of Ypres, the Somme, Arras and Cambrai, and was twice wounded in action, being invalided home on each occasion. He was demobilised in March 1919, and holds the 1914–15 Star, and the General Service and Victory Medals.
Church End, Paulerspury, Towcester. Z2887.

COOKE, G., Gunner, Royal Garrison Artillery.
He joined in July 1918, but on account of his age was not fit for active service. After a period of training, however, he was drafted to Gibraltar, and was engaged on important garrison duties, which he performed in a very capable manner. On his return to England in January 1919 he was demobilised, and holds the General Service Medal.
4–5, Rose Cottages Castle Hill Court, Huntingdon. Z1788.

COOKE, H., Sergeant, Bedfordshire Regiment and Hertfordshire Regiment.
At the outbreak of hostilities in August 1914 he volunteered, but was retained on important work in England until 1916, when he was drafted to the Western Front. There he played a prominent part in many engagements until he contracted trench fever, and was invalided home. On his recovery he rendered valuable services as an Instructor at Felixstowe, and was not demobilised until October 1919. He holds the General Service and Victory Medals.
15, Bury Avenue, Newport Pagnell, Bucks. Z1785.

COOKE, J. T., Private, Bedfordshire Regiment and Hertfordshire Regiment.
On attaining military age he joined the Army in January 1918, and on conclusion of his training was six months later drafted overseas. During his service in France he was engaged in fierce fighting on the Cambrai front, but was invalided to England suffering from heart trouble. Consequently he was discharged as medically unfit in February 1919, and holds the General Service and Victory Medals.
15, Canning Street, Bedford. X1787.

COOKE, W., Driver, Royal Field Artillery.
He joined in April 1916, and in the following September was sent to France, where he took part in the Battles of the Somme, Arras, Ypres and Cambrai. In November 1917 he was transferred to Italy, but after four months' service on that front was drafted back to the Western Front. Whilst engaged in fierce fighting during the Advance of 1918 he was wounded and invalided home. On his recovery he was employed on agricultural work at King's Ripton. until demobilised in August 1919, holding the General Service and Victory Medals.
King's Ripton, Hunts. Z1786/A.

COOPER, A., Private, 1/5th Bedfordshire Regt.
At the declaration of hostilities in August 1914 he volunteered and after a course of training was sent overseas in the following year. Whilst serving in Palestine he took an active part in important engagements at Gaza, Jerusalem, Beyrout and Jaffa. On his return to England he was demobilised in August 1919, and holds the 1914–15 Star, and the General Service and Victory Medals. Luke Street, Eynesbury, St. Neots, Hunts. Z1795/B.

COOPER, A. J., Private, 1/4th Northants. Regt.
He was mobilised in August 1914, and in April 1915 was drafted to Egypt. On being transferred to the Palestine front he took an active part in many important engagements, and was unhappily killed in action at Gaza on December 2nd, 1917. He was entitled to the 1914–15 Star, and the General Service and Victory Medals.
"Whilst we remember, the sacrifice is not in vain."
18, Berrell's Court, Olney, Bucks. Z1792.

COOPER, A. W., Private, 3rd Queen's Own (Royal West Kent Regiment).
Joining in July 1917, he received his training at Chatham, and in June 1918 proceeded to the Western Front, where he served for three months. During that time he saw heavy fighting in the Cambrai sector, and was wounded in action there in September 1918. He was sent to hospital in England, and was eventually demobilised in March 1919, holding the General Service and Victory Medals.
Castle Road, Lavendon, Bucks. Z1793.

COOPER, C., Private, Northumberland Fusiliers.
He volunteered in November 1914, and was engaged on important duties with his unit at various home stations until 1917, when he was drafted to France. Shortly after going into the firing-line he was taken prisoner, and died in captivity on October 29th, 1918. He was entitled to the General Service and Victory Medals.
"Thinking that remembrance, though unspoken, may reach him where he sleeps."
West End, Somersham, Hunts. Z1799/B.

COOPER, C., Stoker, R.N., H.M.S. "Phæton."
He volunteered in November 1914, and after a period of training was posted to H.M.S. "Phæton." In this vessel he rendered valuable services in patrol and escort work in the North, Mediterranean and Baltic Seas, and also took an active part in the Battle of Jutland and in the bombardment of Zeebrugge. In 1920 he was still serving in the Navy, and holds the 1914–15 Star, and the General Service and Victory Medals.
Cow and Hare Yard, St. Ives, Hunts. Z1069/B.

COOPER, E. J., Private, R.A.S.C. (M.T.)
In May 1917 he joined the Army, and was engaged on important duties with his unit at Woolwich, Norwood and Camberwell. At these stations he rendered valuable services in connection with the repair of motor-cycles, and carried out his responsible work with great ability. He was medically unfit for service overseas, and was eventually demobilised in February 1919.
Keeley Lane, Wootton, Beds. Z1800/B.

COOPER, F., Sergeant, Bedfordshire Regiment.
He volunteered in August 1914, but was retained on important work at home until 1916, when he was drafted to France. On this front he took a conspicuous part in engagements on the Somme and at Arras, and was wounded at the latter place. On his recovery he fought at Ypres, and was gassed at Passchendaele. He was demobilised in February 1919, and holds the General Service and Victory Medals.
Luke Street, Eynesbury, St. Neots, Hunts. Z1795/A.

COOPER, F., Private, 1st Bedfordshire Regiment.
When war broke out he was serving in India, and was at once ordered to the Western Front, where he took part in the Retreat from Mons. He was also engaged in severe fighting at Ypres, Festubert, Vimy Ridge, the Somme and Cambrai, and was wounded in action. In 1919 he returned home and was stationed at Colchester, where in 1920 he was still serving. He holds the Mons Star, and the General Service and Victory Medals.
62, St. Germain Street, Huntingdon. Z1794/F.

COOPER, F., Private, 2nd London Regiment (Royal Fusiliers).
He volunteered in 1914, and was employed on coastguard duties in Yorkshire until 1916, when he was drafted to France. After fighting at St. Eloi and the Somme, he was transferred to Salonika, and was in action on the Struma front. On being transferred to Palestine he took part in important engagements at Gaza and Jaffa. He was demobilised on his return to England in 1919, and holds the General Service and Victory Medals.
62, St. Germain Street, Huntingdon. Z1794/B.

COOPER, G., Private, Queen's (Royal West Surrey Regiment).
Joining in March 1917, he was sent to the Western Front in the following month and there saw severe fighting in various sectors. He took part in the Battles of Bullecourt, Ypres, Cambrai, the Somme and Le Cateau and many other important engagements, serving also through the Retreat and Advance of 1918, and was wounded in action. Returning home in 1919, he was demobilised in April of that year, and holds the General Service and Victory Medals.
14, Grey Friars Walk, Bedford. X1791/B.

COOPER, G. A., Private, 7th Bedfordshire Regt.
When war was declared in 1914 he volunteered, and after completing his training was drafted overseas in June of the following year. Whilst serving on the Western Front he was in action at Festubert and Loos, and fell fighting in the Battle of the Somme in September 1916. He was entitled to the 1914–15 Star, and the General Service and Victory Medals.
"A valiant Soldier, with undaunted heart he breasted life's last hill."
62, St. Germain Street, Huntingdon. Z1794/C.

COOPER, G. W., Corporal, Huntingdonshire Regt. and Warwickshire Regiment.
He volunteered in 1915, and served at Sutton-on-Sea and Scarborough until 1917, when he was sent to the Western Front. There he took part in many important engagements, and did good work with his unit in the Lens and Cambrai sectors. After the Armistice he was engaged on the transport of troops from Italy to France. He was demobilised in 1919, and holds the General Service and Victory Medals.
Southoe, Hunts. Z1789/B.

COOPER, H., Private, 2nd Leicestershire Regiment.
When war was declared in August 1914 he was stationed in India, but was immediately recalled and drafted to France. On this front he was engaged in fierce fighting in numerous engagements, including the Battles of the Marne, La Bassée, Ypres, Vimy Ridge and the Somme. In 1920 he was still serving in the Army, and holds the 1914 Star, and the General Service and Victory Medals.
62, St. Germain Street, Huntingdon. Z1794/E.

COOPER, J., Private, 1st Huntingdonshire Regt.
He joined in June 1917, but was unable to procure a transfer to a theatre of war. He was engaged on important duties with his unit at various stations in Huntingdonshire, and throughout his period of service carried out his work in a highly capable manner. He was demobilised in October 1919.
West End, Somersham, Hunts. Z1798/A.

COOPER, J., Trooper, Bedfordshire Lancers.
He was already serving in the Army at the outbreak of hostilities, and in December 1914 was ordered to the Western Front. There he was in action in important engagements at Loos, Festubert and Albert, and was gassed at Ypres. He was invalided to England, and on his recovery was drafted to Ireland, where he served until discharged in January 1919, holding the 1914–15 Star, and the General Service and Victory Medals. 88, Tickford St., Newport Pagnell, Bucks. Z1797.

COOPER, J., L/Corporal, 16th Middlesex Regiment.
He joined in June 1916, and on conclusion of his training was three months later drafted overseas. He served on the Western Front for 11 months, and during that time saw heavy fighting in different sectors of the line, and was wounded in action. On August 14th, 1917, he was unfortunately killed in action near Poperinghe, and was entitled to the General Service and Victory Medals.
"A costly sacrifice upon the altar of freedom."
Cambridge Street, St. Neots, Hunts. Z1796.

COOPER, J. A. C., L/Corporal, 4th Royal Welch Fusiliers.
He volunteered in November 1914, but, being unfit for active service, was not successful in his endeavours to procure a transfer to the fighting areas. He, however, served at Stroud and Bedford, at which stations he fulfilled the duties allotted to him in a very able manner, until demobilised in March 1919.
28, Russell Street, Bedford. TX1790.

COOPER, J. W., Private, Huntingdonshire and Warwickshire Regiments.
Volunteering in 1915, he trained at Huntingdon, Whitby and Sutton-on-Sea, and in June 1916 proceeded to the Western Front, where he took part in severe fighting in various sectors. He served at Vimy Ridge and Messines, but was wounded in action at Poperinghe, and unhappily succumbed to his injuries on October 9th, 1917. He was entitled to the General Service and Victory Medals.
"His memory is cherished with pride."
Mill Green, Warboys, Hunts. Z1217/B.

COOPER, P., L/Corporal, 2nd Leicestershire Regt.
When war broke out he was recalled from duty in India, and at once ordered to the Western Front, where he took part in the Battle of the Marne. In 1915 he was drafted to Gallipoli, and was in action at Suvla Bay and in the subsequent engagements of that campaign. After the Evacuation he served in Mesopotamia until sent back to India in 1918. He was discharged in June 1919 on his return to England, and holds the 1914–15 Star, and the General Service and Victory Medals.
62, St. Germain Street, Huntingdon. Z1794/A.

COOPER, R. G., Drummer, 1st Bedfordshire Regt.
Joining in September 1917, he was unable to obtain a transfer overseas before the cessation of hostilities, and was engaged on important work with his unit at various stations until January 1920, when he was drafted to Russia and served at Novo Vossiysk. Later he was stationed at Lemnos, Mudros and Malta, and in 1920 was still serving in the Army.
Keeley Lane, Wootton, Beds. Z1800/A.

COOPER, T., Sergeant, Machine Gun Corps.
He volunteered in 1914, and on completion of his training at Grantham, in 1915, was drafted to the Western Front, where he served for four years. During that time he was engaged in severe fighting in various sectors, and played a conspicuous part in the Battles of Ypres, Loos, the Somme and Cambrai. He was gassed on one occasion, and was demobilised in 1919, holding the 1914–15 Star, and the General Service and Victory Medals.
62, St. Germain Street, Huntingdon. Z1794/D.

COOPER, W., Private, Bedfordshire Regiment.
He volunteered in 1914, and, in June of the following year was drafted to the Western Front, where he saw heavy fighting in various sectors. After taking part in the Battles of Loos, Albert, the Somme and Arras, and many minor engagements, he was severely wounded in action near Ypres in August 1917, and as a result has lost the sight of an eye. Invalided from the Army in 1918, he holds the 1914–15 Star, and the General Service and Victory Medals. Southoe, Hunts. Z1789/A.

COOPER, W., L/Corporal, Middlesex Regiment.
He joined in July 1918, and, after a short period of training, was retained on important duties in various sectors. He was not successful in obtaining his transfer to a theatre of war before the cessation of hostilities, but, in December 1918, proceeded with the Army of Occupation into Germany. There he was stationed at Cologne until his return home for demobilisation in December 1919.
Cow and Hare Yard, St. Ives, Hunts. Z1069/A.

COOPER, W. C., Private, 1st Bedfordshire Regt.
Already in the Army when war was declared in August 1914, he was immediately drafted to the Western Front, where, after fighting in the Retreat from Mons, he took part in the Battle of Ypres and other engagements. He died gloriously on the Field of Battle at Hill 60 on April 20th, 1915. He was entitled to the Mons Star, and the General Service and Victory Medals.
"The path of duty was the way to glory."
14, Grey Friars Walk, Bedford. X1791/A.

COOPER, W. C., Private, Bedfordshire Regiment.
He volunteered in December 1914, and six months later was drafted to the Western Front, where he saw heavy fighting in various sectors. After taking part in the Battle of Loos and other important engagements in this theatre of war, he returned home and was invalided from the Army in May 1916. He holds the 1914–15 Star, and the General Service and Victory Medals. Cranfield, Beds. Z1799/A.

COPE, E. A. G., Pte., 14th R. Warwickshire Regt.
He volunteered in April 1915, and, after undergoing a period of training with the Huntingdonshire Cyclist Battalion, was drafted in the following year to the Western Front, where he took part in the Battle of the Somme, and other important engagements. He fell fighting at Vimy Ridge on May 8th, 1917. He was entitled to the General Service and Victory Medals.
"His life for his Country, his soul to God."
Hardwick, Buckden, Hunts. Z1801.

COPE, G., Private, 2nd Bedfordshire Regiment.
Volunteering in August 1914, he was shortly afterwards drafted to the Western Front, where he saw much severe fighting. He took part in many important engagements in this theatre of war, including the Battles of Ypres, the Somme, Arras and Cambrai, and was wounded in action at Neuve Chapelle in 1915. He was demobilised on his return home in 1919, and holds the 1914 Star, and the General Service and Victory Medals.
Church Path, Sandy, Beds. Z1803.

COPE, J., Private, Lancashire Fusiliers.
Joining in July 1916, he proceeded to the Western Front in January of the following year and there took part in the Battles of Arras, Messines and Ypres and many minor engagements. He made the supreme sacrifice, falling in action at Passchendaele on October 22nd, 1917. He was entitled to the General Service and Victory Medals.
"Thinking that remembrance, though unspoken, may reach him where he sleeps."
High Street, Sandy, Beds. Z1802.

COPPERWHEAT, C., Pioneer, Royal Engineers.
He joined in March 1918, and, after completing a period of training, was drafted to the Western Front. There he saw much severe fighting in various sectors and took part in the Battles of Cambrai and Ypres, and many other important engagements until the cessation of hostilities. He was demobilised on his return home in March 1919, and holds the General Service and Victory Medals. Pavenham, near Bedford. Z1804.

COPPERWHEAT, G., L/Corporal, M.G.C.
He volunteered in June 1915, and, on completing a period of training in the following year, proceeded to the Western Front. There he saw much severe fighting in various sectors, and took part in the Battles of the Somme, Arras, Ypres, Cambrai and Valenciennes and many other engagements, and was wounded in action. Demobilised in July 1919, he holds the General Service and Victory Medals. Wootton, Bedford. Z1805.

COPPOCK, J. (M.M.), Sergt., Northamptonshire Regt.
Mobilised in August 1914, he shortly afterwards proceeded to the Western Front, where he took part in the fighting at Mons. He also served with distinction through many other important engagements in various sectors, and was twice wounded in action—at Neuve Chapelle and at Cambrai in October 1918. He was awarded the Military Medal for conspicuous bravery in the Field, and holding also the Mons Star and the General Service and Victory Medals, was discharged in March 1919.
Huntingdon Street, St. Neots, Hunts. Z1806.

COPPOCK, W., Private, 18th Lancashire Regiment.
Two months after joining in June 1917 he was drafted to the Western Front, where he served through the Battles of Ypres, Passchendaele, Cambrai, Amiens and Le Cateau and many other important engagements in various sectors. He fell in action on October 30th, 1918. He was entitled to the General Service and Victory Medals.
"Nobly striving:
He nobly fell that we might live."
35, East Street, St. Neots, Hunts. TZ1807/A.

CORBETT, C., Private, 4th Bedfordshire Regt.
He joined in February 1916, and, four months later, was drafted to the Western Front, but was shortly afterwards invalided home, suffering from trench feet. In August 1916, however, he returned to France and was wounded in action in October of that year at Thiépval during the Somme Offensive. He was again sent to hospital in England but on his recovery rejoined his unit in the firing-line, and was unhappily killed in action at Arras on April 28th 1917. He was entitled to the General Service and Victory Medals.
"He joined the great white company of valiant souls."
Maltman's Villa, Eaton Socon, St. Neots, Hunts. Z1809/A.

CORBY, F. G., Rifleman, 7th Royal Irish Rifles.
He volunteered in June 1915, and, in February of the following year, proceeded to the Western Front, where he saw heavy fighting in various sectors. After taking part in many important engagements in this theatre of war, he was severely wounded in action at Ypres in August 1917, and was admitted to hospital at Norwich, where he remained for two years. Invalided from the Army in September 1919, he holds the General Service and Victory Medals.
16, Park Street, Bletchley, Bucks. Z2888.

CORBY, R. H., L/Corporal, Oxford and Bucks. Light Infantry and 1/1st Herefordshire Regt.
Volunteering in November 1914, he was drafted to the Western Front in the following year, and was there wounded in action near Armentières in February 1915. After taking part also in the second Battle of Ypres, he was again wounded at Loos in September and invalided to hospital at Stockport. Returning to France on his recovery in 1916, he fought in the Battles of the Somme, Arras and Cambrai, and other engagements, and was wounded in action a third time at Ypres in August 1917. He was finally demobilised in March 1919, and holds the 1914–15 Star, and the General Service and Victory Medals.
28, Water Eaton, near Bletchley, Bucks. Z1810.

CORNEY, R. W., Sapper, Royal Engineers.
Shortly after volunteering in 1915 he proceeded to France, where he was engaged on important duties in various sectors of the front. He was also present at the Battles of Loos, the Somme, Arras, Ypres and Cambrai, and many other important engagements until the cessation of hostilities, and was demobilised on his return home in 1919. He holds the 1914–15 Star, and the General Service and Victory Medals.
3, St. Mary's Terrace, Godmanchester, Beds. Z1811/B.

CORWOOD, J., Sergeant, 7th Cheshire Regiment.
Mobilised in August 1914, he was drafted to Gallipoli in July of the following year, and there saw much severe fighting until the Evacuation of the Peninsula. He was then transferred to Egypt, whence he was shortly afterwards invalided home suffering from dysentery. Discharged time-expired in May 1916, he re-enlisted, however, in July 1918, and later in that year proceeded to the Western Front, where he took part in several important engagements in the final stages of the war. He was demobilised in May 1919, and holds the 1914–15 Star, and the General Service and Victory Medals.
Swan Terrace, Goldington, Bedford. Z1812.

COTTERRELL, L. R., A.B., Royal Navy.
He volunteered at the outbreak of war in August 1914, and was posted to H.M.S. "Falcon," on board which vessel he was engaged on various duties in the Atlantic and Pacific Oceans until 1916. He was then attached to the Dover Patrol and took part in bombardments of Ostend and other parts of the Belgian coast. Demobilised in April 1919, he holds the 1914–15 Star, and the General Service and Victory Medals.
1, Leys Terrace, Woburn Sands, Bucks. Z1813.

COTTON, F., Gunner, Royal Field Artillery.
He volunteered in 1915, and, on completing a period of training later in that year, proceeded to France. There he was engaged on important duties at Boulogne and various other stations, being too old for service in the firing line, and did much useful work until demobilised in 1919 at the age of 45 years. He holds the 1914–15 Star, and the General Service and Victory Medals. Roxton Road, Great Barford, Bedford. Z1814.

COTTON, G. T., Sergeant, R.A.V.C
Volunteering in September 1914, he proceeded to Egypt in February of the following year, and was shortly afterwards transferred to Gallipoli. He returned to Egypt, however, on the Evacuation of the Peninsula, and, proceeding thence into Palestine, was present at the Battles of Gaza and the entry into Jerusalem. He was for a time in hospital at Alexandria, before returning home for demobilisation in August 1919, and holds the 1914–15 Star, and the General Service and Victory Medals.
Riverside, Milton Ernest, Bedford. Z1815/D—Z1816/D.

COTTON, L. M. (Miss), Member, W.R.A.F.
Having previously been engaged for over two years on dangerous munition work at Park Royal Shell-filling Factory, she joined in October 1917. After a period of training, she served at Hendon and various other stations, engaged as a tester and examiner of aeroplane parts in the workshops. She rendered valuable services until her demobilisation in July 1919.
Riverside, Milton Ernest, Bedford. Z1815/A—Z1816/A.

COTTON, T., Sergeant, R.A.V.C.
He volunteered in March 1915, and, after undergoing a period of training, was retained at various stations, where he was engaged on duties of great importance. Unable to obtain his transfer to a theatre of war on account of his age, he nevertheless, rendered valuable services with his Company until January 1919, when he was demobilised.
Riverside, Milton Ernest, Bedford. Z1815/C—Z1816/C.

COTTON, W. E., Tpr., 1st Bedfordshire Lancers.
Mobilised in August 1914, he was drafted to the Western Front in October of that year, and there saw severe fighting in various sectors. He took part in the Battles of Ypres, Neuve Chapelle, Loos and Passchendaele and other important engagements, was wounded in action at Arras in 1917, and on the Somme in the following year, and gassed. He was discharged in March 1919, and holds the 1914 Star, and the General Service and Victory Medals.
Riverside, Milton Ernest, Bedford. Z1815/B—Z1816/B.

COURSE, A. C., Private, 2/6th Manchester Regt.
Joining in February 1917, he was drafted to the Western Front in May of that year and there saw much heavy fighting. After taking part in the Battles of Arras and Ypres and other engagements, he was severely wounded in action at Passchendaele in October 1917, and admitted to hospital at Glasgow. He was invalided from the Army in May 1918, and holds the General Service and Victory Medals.
5, New Church Terrace, St. Ives, Hunts. Z1819/B.

COURSE, P., Private, 3rd Bedfordshire Regiment.
He volunteered in November 1914, and in the following January proceeded to France, where he took part in much heavy fighting in various sectors of the Front. He fought at the Battles of Ypres, Albert, Arras and Messines, and was wounded on three occasions—in 1915 at the Battle of Loos, in 1916 during the Somme Offensive and in 1917 at Zillebeke. As a result he was invalided from the Army in September 1918, and holds the 1914–15 Star, and the General Service and Victory Medals.
5, New Church Terrace, St. Ives, Hunts. Z1817.

COURSE, P., Private, Bedfordshire Regiment.
He volunteered in September 1914, and early in the following year proceeded to the Western Front. In the course of his service in this theatre of war he took part in many important engagements, notably those at Festubert and Loos, and was later in action on the Somme, where he was wounded in July 1916. On his recovery he again went into action at the engagement at Passchendaele, and was wounded and invalided to hospital. After a period of treatment he was discharged as medically unfit for further service, and holds the 1914–15 Star, and the General Service and Victory Medals.
5, New Church Terrace, St. Ives, Hunts. Z1819/A.

COURSE, R., Sapper, Royal Engineers.
He volunteered in December 1914, and early in the following year proceeded to France, where he was engaged in trench-digging in various sectors of the front, and was constantly under heavy shell-fire. In December 1915 he was transferred to Mesopotamia, and took part in many important engagements, including the fighting at Kut-el-Amara. After the cessation of hostilities he was sent to Ireland, where he was still serving in 1920. He holds the 1914–15 Star, and the General Service and Victory Medals. 9, St. Paul's Road, Bedford. Z1818.

COVERLEY, A. J., Private, Dorsetshire Regiment.
Volunteering in December 1915, he was at first retained on important duties with his unit at various stations. In 1916, however, he proceeded to the Western Front, and took part in much heavy fighting in various sectors. He served at the Battles of Arras, Ypres, Cambrai and the Somme, where he was wounded, and was invalided to hospital. After a period of treatment he was demobilised in February 1919, and holds the General Service and Victory Medals.
133, High Street, Newport Pagnell. Z1821.

COVERLEY, F., Private, Labour Corps.
He volunteered in December 1915, and after completing a period of training was retained on important duties with his unit at various stations. Later, in 1916, he proceeded to Salonika, where he took part in the fighting on the Vardar and Doiran fronts, and was wounded in October 1916. On his recovery he returned to the fighting area and served on until after the close of hostilities. Returning to England, he was demobilised in July 1920, and holds the General Service and Victory Medals. 5, Beaconsfield Place, Newport Pagnell. Z1820/A.

COVINGTON, H., Air Mechanic, R.A.F.
He volunteered in November 1915, and after completing a period of training, was retained on important duties at various stations. Owing to his being medically unfit, he was not successful in obtaining his transfer to a theatre of war, but rendered valuable services until demobilised in February 1919.
33, Garfield Street, Bedford. Z1822.

COWLEY, C. A., Private, Oxford. & Bucks. L.I.
He joined in February 1918, and after a period of training served in Ireland. In July he was drafted to the Western Front, where he took part in many important engagements in various sectors. He served during the Battles of Cambrai, Le Cateau (II.) and Amiens, and was wounded whilst in action. After the close of hostilities he returned to England and was demobilised in September 1919, holding the General Service and Victory Medals. 13, Wolverton Road, Newport Pagnell, Bucks. Z1826.

COWLEY, G. H., Private, 2nd Northants Regt.
He joined in 1916, and in the same year was drafted to France. In the course of his service in this theatre of war he took an active part in many important engagements. He was in action during the heavy fighting on the Somme, and later in the Battles of Arras, Messines, Ypres and Cambrai, where he was wounded. As a result he was invalided home and discharged as medically unfit for further service in December 1918. He holds the General Service and Victory Medals.
5, Orchard Place, Rushden, Northants. X1823.

COWLEY, H. C., Sergeant, 9th Edmonton Fusiliers (Canadian Overseas Forces).
He was called up from the Reserve in August 1914, and after completing a period of training in Canada was sent to the Western Front. There he took part in much heavy fighting in various sectors, and was in action during the Battles of Ypres, Festubert, Givenchy, and later in the Somme Offensive and the Battle of Cambrai, and others of importance until the close of hostilities. He was demobilised in February 1919, and holds the 1914–15 Star, and the General Service and Victory Medals.
32, Abbey Road, Old Bradwell, Bucks. Z1824 /A.

COWLEY, H. W., Sapper, Royal Engineers.
Joining in April 1918, two months later he landed in France, where he took part in the many important engagements during the Retreat and Advance of 1918, until the close of hostilities, and after the Armistice procceeded with the Army of Occupation into Germany, where he did duties as a carpenter. He was demobilised in October 1919, and holds the General Service and Victory Medals.
32, Greenfield Road, Newport Pagnell. 1825 /A.

COWLEY, O. S., Private, Royal Fusiliers.
He joined in April 1918, and after a period of training was drafted to the Western Front. During his short period of service in this seat of war he was present at many important engagements, and took part in the fighting on the Marne, at Ypres and Cambrai, and later in the final Advance. Returning to England he was demobilised in February 1919, and holds the General Service and Victory Medals.
32, Abbey Road, Old Bradwell, Bucks. Z1824 /B.

COX, A., Private, Royal Marine Light Infantry.
A serving soldier, he was mobilised at the outbreak of war in August 1914, and, after training at Portsmouth, proceeded to Jamaica, where he did good work attached to the Transport Section. Later he was engaged on important duties with the Grand Fleet in the North Sea, where he served until the close of hostilities. He was demobilised in 1919, and holds the General Service and Victory Medals.
Wyboston, Beds. Z1841.

COX, A., Private, Labour Corps.
He joined in May 1916, and in the following month was drafted to France, where he did good work in various sectors whilst engaged in repairing roads. He saw much heavy fighting and was unfortunately killed in action on the Ypres front on July 6th, 1917. He was entitled to the General Service and Victory Medals.
"A costly sacrifice upon the altar of freedom."
Doves Lane, Moulton, Northamptonshire. Z2890 /D.

COX, A., Private, 6th Middlesex Regiment.
He joined in June 1917, and, after a period of training, was engaged at various stations on important duties with his unit. He was unable to obtain a transfer overseas owing to his being medically unfit, but rendered valuable services until his demobilisation in October 1919.
Barlow Street, Moulton, Northants. Z2889 /B.

COX, A. A., Sapper, Royal Engineers.
He volunteered in January 1915, and in the following June proceeded to France. Whilst in this theatre of war he took part in several engagements, including the Battles of the Somme, Arras, Passchendaele, the Aisne (III.) and the Marne (II.). He was demobilised in February 1919, and holds the 1914–15 Star, and the General Service and Victory Medals.
84, Grey Friars Walk, Bedford. X1844 /A.

COX, A. A., Private, 2nd Bedfordshire Regiment.
He volunteered in September 1914, and in the following June was drafted to the Western Front, where he took part in the Battles of Festubert and Loos, and was wounded. As a result he was invalided to Scotland, but on his recovery again proceeded overseas and saw service in Mesopotamia and India. He suffered from malaria and was in hospital for some time in the East. He returned home and was demobilised in April 1919, holding the 1914–15 Star, and the General Service and Victory Medals.
Church Road, Stevington, near Bedford. Z1845 /A.

COX, A. E., Private, 1st Hampshire Regiment.
He joined in April 1917, and, after a period of training, was engaged at various stations on important duties with his unit. He was unable to obtain a transfer overseas owing to his being medically unfit, but rendered valuable services until his demobilisation in December 1919.
29, Princess Street, Bedford. TX1834.

COX, A. J., Private, 1/5th Bedfordshire Regiment.
He volunteered in September 1914, and, on completing his training in the following February, was drafted to the Western Front, where he took part in the Battles of Neuve Chapelle, Ypres, the Somme and Arras. He died gloriously on the Field of Battle in the Arras sector on April 28th, 1917. He was entitled to the 1914–15 Star, and the General Service and Victory Medals.
"He died the noblest death a man may die:
Fighting for God and right and liberty."
The Old Post Office, Renhold, near Bedford. Z1843 /B.

COX, C., Private, 5th Northamptonshire Regiment.
He volunteered in August 1914, and was shortly afterwards drafted to France, where he took part in much heavy fighting at the Battles of Ypres (I. and II.), Loos, the Somme, Arras and Cambrai, and was wounded. He made the supreme sacrifice, being killed in action in the Cambrai sector in November 1917, and was entitled to the 1914 Star, and the General Service and Victory Medals.
"Great deeds cannot die:
They with the sun and moon renew their light for ever."
Doves Lane, Moulton, Northants. Z2890 /C.

COX, E., Private, Bedfordshire Regiment.
He volunteered in October 1914, and in the following July was drafted to France, where he fought at Loos and Vimy Ridge. He was taken ill and consequently invalided home, but, on his recovery, returned to the Western Front and took part in the Battle of Cambrai. He was unfortunately reported missing, and is now presumed to have been killed in action on March 27th, 1918. He was entitled to the 1914–15 Star, and the General Service and Victory Medals.
"A valiant Soldier, with undaunted heart he breasted life's last hill."
Court Lane, Stevington, near Bedford. Z1846.

COX, E. J., Sergeant, 7th Bedfordshire Regiment.
He volunteered in September 1914, and, on completing his training in the following July, proceeded to France. There he quickly gained promotion and played a prominent part in the Battles of Ypres and Loos, and was badly wounded in action. As a result he was invalided home and finally discharged in 1917 as medically unfit for further service. He holds the 1914–15 Star, and the General Service and Victory Medals.
Church Road, Stevington. Z1845 /C.

COX, E. W., L/Corporal, 6th Bedfordshire Regt.
He volunteered in August 1914, and in the following July was drafted to France, where he saw much severe fighting at the Battles of the Somme, the Ancre and Arras. He died gloriously on the Field of Battle on February 14th, 1917, and was entitled to the 1914–15 Star, and the General Service and Victory Medals.
"The path of duty was the way to glory."
Church Road, Stevington, near Bedford. Z1845 /B.

COX, F. J., Private, 1st Bedfordshire Regiment.
He was mobilised in August 1914, and almost immediately drafted to France, where he saw much heavy fighting at the Battles of the Marne, La Bassée, Ypres and Neuve Chapelle. He was unfortunately kiilled in action at Hill 60 on April 28th, 1915, and was entitled to the 1914 Star, and the General Service and Victory Medals.
"Whilst we remember, the sacrifice is not in vain."
Great Staughton, St. Neots, Hunts. Z1837 /A.

COX, F. W. (M.M.), Pte., 23rd Middlesex Regiment.
He joined in April 1916, and in the following July was drafted to France, where he fought on the Somme, at Beaucourt and Arras, and was slightly wounded. Later he saw service in Italy on the Piave, but, in December 1917, returned to the Western Front and took part in the Battles of Cambrai and the Somme (II.). He was awarded the Military Medal for great gallantry and devotion to duty in the Field in saving the life of a wounded comrade, and was himself badly wounded. As a result he was invalided home, and, on his recovery, was demobilised in February 1919, holding also the General Service and Victory Medals.
Harrowden Lane, Cardington, Beds. Z1847.

COX, F. W., Corporal, Bedfordshire Lancers.
He volunteered in September 1914, and was engaged for a time at various home stations on important duties with his unit. Later he was drafted to France and was stationed at Le Havre, where he was employed as a farrier, and rendered valuable services. He was demobilised in February 1919, and holds the General Service and Victory Medals.
21, Priory Street, Bedford. TX1835.

COX, G. E., Sergeant, Royal Garrison Artillery.
He joined the Army in October 1901, and, when war broke out in August 1914, was immediately drafted to France. There he played a distinguished part in the Battles of Mons, Le Cateau (I.), Ypres (I. and.II.), the Somme, Arras, the Somme (II.), Havrincourt and Le Cateau (II), and was twice wounded in action. He received his discharge in March 1920, and holds the Mons Star, and the General Service and Victory Medals.
Dove Lane, Moulton, Northants. Z2890 /E.

COX, G. T., Sergeant, Rifle Brigade.
He was already in the Army when war broke out in August 1914, and was immediately drafted from India to France. There he played a prominent part in the Battles of Neuve Chapelle and Ypres, and in several other important engagements. He sustained a serious injury owing to the collapse of a trench, and was consequently invalided home and finally discharged in 1918 as medically unfit for further service. He holds the 1914 Star, and the General Service and Victory Medals.
2, Bardolph's Court, St. Germain Street, Huntingdon. Z1832.

COX, J., Private, Oxford. and Bucks. L.I.
He joined in November 1916, and, after a period of training, was engaged at various stations on important duties with his unit. He was unable to obtain a transfer overseas owing to his being medically unfit, but rendered valuable services until his discharge in March 1918.
30, Oxford Street, Stony Stratford, Bucks. TZ1836.

COX, J. E., Private, 8th Northants. Regiment.
He volunteered in September 1915, and was engaged at various stations on important duties with his unit. Later he was transferred to the Norfolk Labour Battalion and was employed on agricultural work, but was unable to obtain a transfer overseas. He rendered valuable services until his demobilisation in January 1919.
4, White Horse Yard, Stony Stratford, Bucks. Z1828.

COX, R., Private, 1/8th Middlesex Regiment.
He joined in March 1916, and, after a months' training, was drafted to France, where he took part in much heavy fighting on the Somme. He made the supreme sacrifice, being killed in action on August 17th, 1916, and was entitled to the General Service and Victory Medals.
"Honour to the immortal dead, who gave their youth that the world might grow old in peace."
Barlow Street, Moulton, Northants. Z2889/A.

COX, R. G., Drummer, Seaforth Highlanders.
He volunteered in 1915, and, after a period of training, was engaged in Scotland on various important duties with his unit. He could not proceed overseas owing to his being under military age, but rendered valuable services until his demobilisation in March 1919.
84, Gray Friars Walk, Bedford. X1844/B.

COX, R. H. (M.S.M.), Sergt., R.E. (Signal Section).
He was mobilised in August 1914, and retained for a time at various home stations as an Instructor with the Cable Section. In 1917, however, he was drafted to France, and played a prominent part in the Battles of Arras, Ypres, Cambrai and the Somme. He was awarded the Meritorious Service Medal for continuously good work throughout hostilities, and was demobilised in April 1919, holding also the General Service and Victory Medals. Stagsden, Beds. Z1842.

COX, S. H., L/Corporal, Machine Gun Corps.
He volunteered in the Huntingdonshire Cyclist Battalion in May 1915, and in the following year, proceeded to France with the Machine Gun Corps, and took part in the Battles of the Somme, Arras, Ypres and Cambrai. He was taken prisoner during the Retreat of March 1918, and was held in captivity in Germany at Gustrow Camp, Westphalia. He was repatriated after the Armistice,and returned home for his demobilisation in April 1919. He holds the General Service and Victory Medals.
Hail Weston, St. Neots, Hunts. Z1838.

COX, T., Private, 2nd Northants. Regiment.
Mobilised in August 1914, he was drafted overseas in the following month. Whilst on the Western Front he took part in several engagements, including the Battles of Ypres, Loos, the Somme (I.) and Cambrai, and was wounded in action. He died gloriously on the Field of Battle in the Somme sector on March 26th, 1918, and was entitled to the 1914 Star, and the General Service and Victory Medals.
"A valiant Soldier, with undaunted heart he breasted life's last hill."
Doves Lane, Moulton, Northants. Z2890/B.

COX, W., Private, Northants. Regiment.
He volunteered in August 1914, and underwent a short period of training prior to his being drafted to France. In this theatre of war he took part in many engagements, including the Battles of Ypres (I. and II.), the Somme, Arras and Cambrai, and was twice wounded in action. He was demobilised in January 1919, and holds the 1914 Star, and the General Service and Victory Medals. Doves Lane, Moulton, Northants. Z2890/A.

COX, W. (M.M.), Gunner, R.G.A.
He was called up from the Reserve in August 1914, and immediately drafted to France, where he fought in the Retreat from Mons. He also took part in the Battles of La Bassée, Festubert, Ypres (II. and III.), and was twice wounded in action. He was awarded the Military Medal for conspicuous bravery and devotion to duty in the Field whilst conveying ammunition to the lines. He also holds the Mons Star, and the General Service and Victory Medals, and was discharged in February 1919. 28, Gawcott Road, Buckingham. Z1833.

COX, W., Private, Machine Gun Corps.
He volunteered in November 1915, and, on completing his training in the following year, was drafted to the Western Front. Whilst in this theatre of war he took part in several engagements, including the Battles of Arras, Ypres, Cambrai and the Somme (II.). After hostilities ceased he went to Germany with the Army of Occupation, and served there until his demobilisation in February 1919. He holds the General Service and Victory Medals.
Broad Green, Cranfield, Beds. Z1831.

COX, W., Private, Essex Regiment.
He volunteered in October 1914, and, after completing his training in the following year, was drafted to India. In this country he was engaged on important garrison duty and did continuously good work until after the cessation of hostilities. He then returned home, and was demobilised in December 1919, holding the General Service and Victory Medals.
High Street, Cranfield, Beds. Z1830/A.

COX, W., Private, Cambridgeshire Regiment.
He volunteered in 1914, but proved to be medically unfit for service overseas, and, retained on home defence, was engaged on important guard duties at various stations, including Dartford, Ipswich and Norwich. Throughout the period of his service he carried out his work in a very able manner, and was demobilised in March 1919.
Piper's Lane, Godmanchester, Hunts. Z1840.

COX, W., Private, Royal Warwickshire Regiment.
At the outbreak of hostilities he volunteered, and in 1916 was drafted overseas. During his service on the Western Front he saw heavy fighting in engagements on the Somme and at Arras, Ypres and Cambrai, and was severely wounded at Péronne. In consequence he was discharged from the Army as medically unfit in November 1917, and holds the General Service and Victory Medals. Eaton Ford, Beds. Z1827.

COX, W. H., Private, 1st Bedfordshire Regiment.
He volunteered in December 1914, and in the following year proceeded to France, but after taking part in the Battle of Ypres, was wounded at Loos in September 1915. He was invalided to England, and on his recovery returned to the Western Front, and served on the Ancre and at Beaumont-Hamel, but was unfortunately killed in action on September 6th, 1916. He was entitled to the 1914-15 Star, and the General Service and Victory Medals.
"The path of duty was the way to glory."
Salph End, Renhold, near Bedford. Z1843/C.

COX, W. J., Sapper, R.E.; and Pte., 10th K.O. (Y.L.I.)
Joining in June 1916, he proceeded overseas seven months later. During his service on the Western Front he saw much severe fighting in numerous important engagements, and was unfortunately killed in action at Amiens on March 28th, 1918. He was entitled to the General Service and Victory Medals.
"He died the noblest death a man may die:
Fighting for God and right and liberty."
42, Cavendish Street, Bedford. TX1839.

COX, W. T., Private, Somerset Light Infantry.
He volunteered in January 1915,and a month later proceeded to Ireland, where he was engaged on important duties with his unit in Cork. Early in 1916 he was drafted to India and served there until after the cessation of hostilities. On his return to England in March 1919 he was demobilised, holding the General Service and Victory Medals.
122, Victoria Road, Fenny Stratford, Bucks. Z1829.

COXAN, C. A., Private, 5th Bedfordshire Regt.
He joined in February 1917, and on completion of his training was later in the same year drafted to Egypt. On proceeding to Palestine he took part in fierce fighting in numerous important engagements, including those at Gaza, Haifa and Aleppo. He was demobilised on his return to England in August 1919, and holds the General Service and Victory Medals.
8, Trinity Road, Queen's Park, Bedford. Z1848/B.

COXAN, J. H., L/Corporal, Royal Engineers.
Joining in 1916, he was drafted overseas on completion of his training later in the same year. Whilst serving in Egypt he was attached to the Desert Mounted Corps, and on being transferred to the Palestine theatre of war did good work with his unit in engagements at Gaza, Jaffa, Haifa and Aleppo. Returning to England in May 1919 he was demobilised, and holds the General Service and Victory Medals.
8, Trinity Road, Queen's Park, Bedford. Z1848/A.

COXEN, F. T. C., Lieut., Buffs (East Kent Regt.) and Royal Air Force.
A month after the outbreak of war he volunteered, and in June of the following year proceeded to the Western Front. There he fought with distinction in the Battles of Ypres, Albert, the Somme and Arras, and was wounded in action in the Somme sector. On his recovery he was transferred to Italy in November 1917, and took a prominent part in severe fighting on the Piave and Asiago fronts. He was demobilised in August 1919, and holds the 1914-15 Star, and the General Service and Victory Medals.
26, Albert Street, Bletchley, Bucks. Z2891/A.

COXEN, R. H., Corporal, Royal Engineers.
He joined in December 1916, and on conclusion of his training was drafted overseas eight months later. During his service on the Western Front he took an active part in numerous engagements, principally in the Ypres sector, and performed excellent work with the Light Railway Works Company. He was not demobilised until October 1919, and holds the General Service and Victory Medals.
26, Albert Street, Bletchley, Bucks. Z2891/B.

CRADDOCK, H. J., Private, 32nd M.G.C.
He joined in 1917, and shortly afterwards proceeded to the Western Front, where he fought in various sectors of the line. After taking part in numerous important engagements in the Ypres and Cambrai sectors, he was wounded in action in March 1918. He was demobilised in December 1919, and holds the General Service and Victory Medals.
Ellington, Hunts. Z1849.

CRAKER, E. A., Private, R.M.L.I.
He joined in June 1917, and five months later proceeded overseas. Whilst serving in France he saw much severe fighting in the Somme and Cambrai sectors, and was unfortunately killed in action in August 1918. He was entitled to the General Service and Victory Medals.
"Honour to the immortal dead, who gave their youth that the world might grow old in peace."
9, Beaconsfield Place, Newport Pagnell, Bucks. Z1851/A.

CRANE, A. S., Driver, Royal Engineers.
He volunteered at the outbreak of war at the age of 16, and in September 1914 proceeded to the Western Front, where he served in many sectors. He took an active part in the Battles of the Aisne, La Bassée, Ypres, Hill 60, Festubert, Albert, Vimy Ridge and the Ancre, but whilst on active service contracted trench fever. He was eventually demobilised in 1919, and holds the 1914 Star, and the General Service and Victory Medals. 9, Bridge Road, Bedford. Z1852.

CRANFIELD, J., Private, 2nd Bedfordshire Regt.
In September 1914 he volunteered, and after a period of training was drafted overseas in the following year. Whilst serving on the Western Front he was engaged in severe fighting in the Festubert, Loos and Arras sectors, was wounded in the Battles of the Somme and Ypres, and gassed at Cambrai. He was demobilised in February 1919, and holds the 1914–15 Star, and the General Service and Victory Medals.
51, North End, Bletsoe, Beds. Z1853.

CRANWELL, E. P., Private, 14th London Regiment (London Scottish).
Volunteering in September 1915, he received his training at Richmond and Purfleet, and in January 1916 was sent to France. In this theatre of war he took part in fierce fighting on the Albert front, and was mortally wounded at Arras on June 7th, 1916. He was entitled to the General Service and Victory Medals.
"He passed out of the sight of men by the path of duty and self-sacrifice."
11, Brooklands Road, Bletchley, Bucks. Z1854.

CRASHILL, J. W., Private, Royal Naval Division.
When war was declared in August 1914 he volunteered, and after serving at an important station in Yorkshire was drafted in June 1916 to France. There, after taking part in the fighting at Arras and Passchendaele, he was wounded and taken prisoner at Arras in April 1917. He remained in captivity in Germany until the close of hostilities, and on his release was demobilised in December 1918, holding the General Service and Victory Medals.
2, Brookland Terrace, Huntingdon. Z1234/A.

CRAWLEY, F., Private, 9th Essex Regiment.
He joined in February 1917, and shortly afterwards was sent to the Western Front. There, after taking part in engagements at the Somme, Ypres and Cambrai, he fell fighting at Arras on October 7th, 1917. He was entitled to the General Service and Victory Medals.
"Nobly striving,
He nobly fell that we might live."
London Road, Girtford, Sandy, Beds. Z1856/B.

CRAWLEY, F. J., L/Cpl., 7th Bedfordshire Regt.
Volunteering in September 1914, he was on completion of his training drafted overseas later in the same year. Whilst on the Western Front he was engaged in severe fighting in the Ypres, the Somme, Arras and Cambrai sectors, and was unhappily killed in action at St. Quentin on May 3rd, 1917. He was entitled to the 1914 Star, and the General Service and Victory Medals.
"Great deeds cannot die."
London Road, Girtford, Sandy, Beds. Z1856/A.

CRAWLEY, G., L/Corporal, K.R.R.C.
He enlisted in 1908, and at the declaration of war in August 1914, was at once ordered to France with the first Expeditionary Force. During his service on the Western Front he was in action in the Retreat from Mons, took part in the Battle of Ypres, and was wounded at Vimy Ridge in 1916. Consequently he was invalided out of the Army in December 1916, and holds the Mons Star, and the General Service and Victory Medals. 51, Allhallows Lane, Bedford. X1855.

CREEK, W., Private, 1/5th Bedfordshire Regt.
He volunteered in August 1914, and after a course of training was in the following year drafted to Gallipoli. He served throughout the campaign there, and after the Evacuation of the Peninsula was sent to hospital at Malta, suffering from dysentery. On October 12th, 1916, he died there from fever, and was entitled to the 1914–15 Star, and the General Service and Victory Medals.
"His memory is cherished with pride."
St. Mary's Street, Eynesbury, St. Neots, Hunts. Z1857/A.

CRICK, J. W., Private, Buffs (East Kent Regt.)
He joined in May 1916, and later in the same year was drafted to the Western Front, where he took part in severe fighting in various sectors. After serving in engagements at the Somme, Ypres, Albert, Vimy Ridge and Beaumont-Hamel he was unfortunately killed in action on April 5th, 1917, near Arras. He was entitled to the General Service and Victory Medals.
"Whilst we remember, the sacrifice is not in vain."
Thrapston Road, Brampton, Hunts. Z1858.

CRIPPS, G. H., Private, 52nd Oxford. & Bucks. L.I.
At the outbreak of war in 1914 he was already serving, and at once proceeded with the first Expeditionary Force to the scene of activities in France. Whilst serving there he fought in numerous engagements, including the Battles of Mons, Ypres, Armentières and Amiens, and was wounded in action on two occasions. He was discharged in March 1916, and holds the Delhi Durbar, Queen's and King's South African Medals, Mons Star, and the General Service and Victory Medals.
72, Victoria Road, Bletchley, Bucks. Z1859/C.

CRISP, A., Private, 2nd Royal Sussex Regiment.
He volunteered in 1915, and on completion of his training was drafted in the following year to the Western Front. There he was in action in numerous engagements in the Ypres and Cambrai sectors, and fell fighting at La Bassée on April 18th, 1918. He was entitled to the General Service and Victory Medals.
"He died the noblest death a man may die,
Fighting for God and right and liberty."
71, Grey Friars Walk, Bedford. X1860.

CRISP, C. E., Driver, Royal Army Service Corps.
He was already in the Army when war was declared, and at once proceeded to France, where he was present at the Battles of Mons, Ypres and Loos. In November 1915 he was drafted to Egypt, and after a short period of service there, during which he suffered from malaria, was in the following year sent to Salonika. On that front he took part in numerous engagements on the Doiran before being transferred to Russia in 1918. On his return home in June 1919 he was discharged, holding the Mons Star, and the General Service and Victory Medals. 24, Great Butts Street, Bedford. X1861/B.

CRISP, R. J. W., Private, Bedfordshire Regiment.
He volunteered in September 1915, and after a course of training at Sutton-on-Sea was drafted overseas in the following year. During his service on the Western Front he was engaged in fierce fighting on the Somme and Ancre, and at Beaumont-Hamel, and was unhappily killed in action at Vimy Ridge on April 23rd, 1917. He was entitled to the General Service and Victory Medals.
"A costly sacrifice upon the altar of freedom."
Station Road, Warboys, Hunts. Z1863/A.

CRISP, W., Sapper, R.E.; and Pte., Cheshire Regt.
Volunteering in April 1915, he was on completion of his training sent in the following year to France, and on this front took an active part in many important engagements, including the Battles of the Somme, Arras, Ypres, Passchendaele and Cambrai. He was wounded and gassed in action and served in France until demobilised in February 1919, holding the General Service and Victory Medals.
71, Grey Friars Walk, Bedford. X1862.

CRISP, W. C., Private, Machine Gun Corps.
He joined in February 1917, and after a period of training was later in the same year drafted to Egypt. After serving there for a short time he was transferred to Palestine, and took part in fierce fighting at Gaza, Haifa, Jericho and Tripoli. He was demobilised on his return to England in January 1919, and holds the General Service and Victory Medals.
Station Road, Warboys, Hunts. Z1863/B.

CROFT, A., Private, R.A.V.C.
He joined the Army in June 1916, and after completing a period of training was in the following year ordered to Salonika. In this theatre of war he saw heavy fighting on the Doiran and Struma fronts, and rendered invaluable services in attending to sick and wounded horses. Returning to England in March 1919 he was demobilised, and holds the General Service and Victory Medals.
12, Derby Street, Bedford. X1864/A.

CROMPTON, W. J., Private, R.A.S.C. (M.T.)
Volunteering in January 1916 he proceeded in the following June to the Western Front, where he served for 15 months. During that time he was engaged in driving transport lorries and ambulances, and saw heavy fighting at Albert, the Somme, Arras and Ypres. He was wounded in the last engagement in September 1917, and invalided to England. After prolonged hospital treatment he was demobilised in May 1919, holding the General Service and Victory Medals.
Cambridge Street, St. Neots, Hunts. Z1865.

CROSBY, J. E., Corporal, Royal Engineers.
Mobilised in August 1914, he proceeded with the first Expeditionary Force to the Western Front, where he performed good work in wiring, tunnelling and laying mines. He also took an active part in the Battles of Mons, Ypres, the Somme, Arras and Cambrai, and in the engagements during the Retreat and Advance of 1918. In December 1918 he was discharged, holding the Mons Star, and the General Service and Victory Medals. 123, Tavistock Street, Bedford. X1866.

CROSHAW, H. A., Drummer, 1/5th Beds. Regt.
He was mobilised at the declaration of war in August 1914, and in July of the following year was drafted to Gallipoli. There he saw much severe fighting in several engagements, but was unfortunately killed in action at Suvla Bay on November 17th, 1915. He was entitled to the 1914-15 Star, and the General Service and Victory Medals.
"His life for his Country, his soul to God."
31, King's Place, Bedford. X1867/A.

CROSHAW, S. R., Pte., 1/5th Bedfordshire Regt.
Mobilised in August 1914, he proceeded to Egypt in June 1916, and after a month's service there he was drafted to Gallipoli. On this front he was engaged in fierce fighting, and was wounded at Suvla Bay in August 1915. After the Evacuation of the Peninsula he returned to Egypt, and, on being sent to Palestine, was in action at Gaza, Jerusalem and Jaffa. He was discharged on his return to England in April 1919, and holds the 1914-15 Star, and the General Service and Victory Medals.
31, King's Place, Bedford. X1867/B.

CROSS, C., Private, Huntingdonshire Cyclist Battalion and 3rd London Regiment.
He volunteered in September 1914, and was retained at home on important duties serving at Filey until 1917, when he was transferred to the London Regiment and proceeded to the Western Front. There he participated in strenuous fighting in the Arras, Ypres and Cambrai sectors, and was wounded. Remaining overseas until the termination of hostilities, he was demobilised in 1919, and holds the General Service and Victory Medals.
St. Anne's Lane, Godmanchester, Hunts. Z1871/B—Z1872/B.

CROSS, E. P., Private, 3rd Bedfordshire Regiment.
Volunteering in March 1915, he was found to be medically unfit for transfer to a theatre of war. Retained at home he served at Ipswich and Felixstowe, where he was stationed for 2½ years. He was employed on military police and other important duties, and rendered valuable services until he was demobilised in February 1919.
St. Anne's Lane, Godmanchester, Hunts. Z1871/E—Z1872/E.

CROSS, F. W., L/Corporal, 4th Bedfordshire Regt.
He joined in January 1916, and two months later was drafted to the Western Front, where he served for three years. During this period he took part in many important engagements, including the Battles of the Somme, Arras, Ypres, Passchendaele, Cambrai and Albert. He was demobilised on his return to England in March 1919, and holds the General Service and Victory Medals.
1, Thurlow Street, Bedford. X1870.

CROSS, G. D., Private, Huntingdonshire Cyclist Battalion and Royal Scots.
He volunteered in April 1915, and after a period of service at Filey proceeded to France. In this theatre of war he participated in numerous severe actions and fought in the Battles of Ypres, the Somme and Cambrai. He was demobilised in July 1919, holding the General Service and Victory Medals, and shortly after his demobilisation was unfortunately drowned whilst making a gallant attempt to save life at Godmanchester.
"His memory is cherished with pride."
St. Anne's Lane, Godmanchester, Hunts. Z1871/A—Z1872/A.

CROSS, H. (M.S.M.), Sergeant, Canadian Engineers.
Having volunteered in June 1915, he served on the Western Front from 1916 until July 1919. Stationed with his Company at Albert, Vimy Ridge, on the Somme, Ypres and Cambrai, he was engaged erecting bridges and performed very excellent work, being later awarded the Meritorious Service Medal. When demobilised in July 1919, he was also entitled to the General Service and Victory Medals.
St. Anne's Lane, Godmanchester, Hunts. Z1871/C—Z1872/C.

CROSS, H., Pte., 1/8th Worcestershire Regiment.
He joined in March 1917, and two months later was drafted to France, where he was in action during the Battles of Ypres and Cambrai. In 1918 he was transferred to Italy, and saw further service on the Piave front and the Asiago Plateau. Returning home after the Armistice, he was demobilised in March 1919, and holds the General Service and Victory Medals.
High Street, Spaldwick, Hunts. Z1868.

CROSS, K. E., Drummer, 1st London Regiment.
Joining in 1917, he was too young for transfer to a theatre of war. Stationed at Catterick Camp, Yorkshire, he was employed with the band of his unit and rendered valuable services whilst so engaged until he was demobilised in 1919.
St. Anne's Lane, Godmanchester, Hunts. Z1871/F—Z1872/F.

CROSS, T., A.B., R.N., H.M.S. "Battleaxe."
Already serving in the Royal Navy at the outbreak of hostilities in August 1914, he was posted to H.M.S. "Battleaxe," and in this vessel served with the Grand Fleet in the North Sea. He participated in the Battle of Jutland and was later engaged on patrol duties and mine-sweeping in various waters. In 1921 he was still serving, and was stationed off the Irish coast. He holds the 1914-15 Star, and the General Service and Victory Medals.
St. Anne's Lane, Godmanchester, Hunts. Z1871/G—Z1872/G.

CROSS, W., Sergeant, 1st Canadian Mounted Rifles.
He volunteered in December 1914, and proceeded in the following July to the Western Front. There he participated in strenuous fighting at Festubert, Loos, Albert and Ypres, and was unforunately killed in action on September 23rd, 1916, during the first Battle of the Somme. He was entitled to the 1914-15 Star, and the General Service and Victory Medals.
"A costly sacrifice upon the altar of freedom."
St. Anne's Lane, Godmanchester, Hunts. Z1871/D—Z1872/D.

CROSS, W. C., Gunner, Royal Garrison Artillery.
Serving at the outbreak of war in August 1914, he was immediately drafted to France, where he took part in the Battle of Mons and in the subsequent Retreat. He afterwards participated with his Battery in the Battles of La Bassée, Festubert, the Somme, Ypres, Passchendaele and Cambrai, and was wounded in September 1916 on the Somme front. Remaining overseas for some time after the Armistice, he was demobilised in September 1919, and holds the Mons Star, and the General Service and Victory Medals. 83, Oakley, Bedford. Z1869.

CROSSLEY, C. J., Pte., Beds. Regt. and M.G.C.
He joined in 1916, and in the same year was sent to France. In this theatre of war he was in action on the Somme front, and at Arras, Vimy Ridge and Ypres. Transferred to Italy in November 1917, he was again in action and fought on the Piave front and the Asiago Plateau. He was demobilised on returning home in March 1919, and holds the General Service and Victory Medals. 19, Wellington Street, Bedford. X1873/B.

CROUCH, A., Gunner, Royal Field Artillery.
He was serving in India when war was declared in August 1914, and in the following December was sent to France. After taking part in heavy fighting during the Battles of Ypres and Neuve Chapelle, he was transferred to Mesopotamia, but early in 1917 returned to France, where he participated in further fighting at Lens and Cambrai. He was wounded in action on three occasions, and was some time in hospital at Woolwich prior to being demobilised in January 1919. He holds the 1914-15 Star, and the General Service and Victory Medals.
London Road, Harrowden, Bedford. Z1874.

CROUCH, R. A. G., Sapper, Royal Engineers.
Joining in June 1918, he was drafted to Italy three months later, and served there until January 1919, when he proceeded to Salonika. In the following June he was sent to Russia and stationed at Batoum. During his service overseas he was employed on important clerical duties in the Orderly Room, and did good work until he returned home and was demobilised in March 1920, holding the General Service and Victory Medals.
24, Westbourne Road, Bedford. Z1876.

CROWE, H., Driver, Royal Engineers.
He volunteered in 1915, and later in the same year was drafted to France. There he was engaged on transport duties and served at Givenchy, Neuve Chapelle, the Somme, Arras, Ypres, Messines and Hill 60, and was also stationed for some time in Brussels. During his service overseas he did very good work, and when demobilised in 1919, was entitled to the 1914-15 Star, and the General Service and Victory Medals.
C/o Mrs. Breed, Laburnum Road, Sandy, Beds. Z1877.

CROWE, R. A., Private, 8th Bedfordshire Regt.
He volunteered in September 1914, and in the following June was drafted to the Western Front, where he played a prominent part in the Battles of Ypres, Festubert and Loos. He was buried alive by the explosion of a shell, but was fortunately rescued. In April 1916 he was taken prisoner in the Ypres sector, and during his captivity in Germany suffered many hardships. Released after the cessation of hostilities, he was demobilised in February 1919, and holds the 1914-15 Star, and the General Service and Victory Medals.
Church End, Great Stukeley, Hunts. Z1878.

CROWSLEY, A., Corporal, Durham L.I.
Volunteering in January 1915, he was sent to Ireland on completion of his training, and was engaged on special duties in Dublin. He was unsuccessful in obtaining his transfer overseas, but, nevertheless, rendered valuable services until his demobilisation in January 1919. Potter's Cross, Wootton, Beds. Z1880/A.

CROWSLEY, A. S., Drummer, 1st North Staffordshire Regiment.
He joined in January 1917, and early in the following year was drafted to the Western Front. During his service in this theatre of war he played an important part in the severe fighting in the Retreat and Advance of 1918, and was wounded in action near Cambrai. He returned to England for his demobilisation in March 1919, and holds the General Service and Victory Medals.
Potter's Cross, Wootton, Bedford. Z1880/B.

CROWSLEY, G. W., Sapper, Royal Engineers.
He joined in August 1916, and on completion of his training was engaged on special duties of an important nature in the South-east of England. After rendering valuable services with his unit, he unfortunately contracted influenza, which developed into pneumonia, and caused his death on July 4th, 1918.
"His memory is cherished with pride."
108, Bower Street, Bedford. Z1879.

CUFFE, J. J., Corporal, Bedfordshire Regiment.
He volunteered in June 1915, and in the following year was drafted to the Western Front, where he took part in the Battle of the Somme (during which he was wounded in action) and in heavy fighting at Arras and Ypres. In April 1917 he was taken prisoner in the Ypres sector, and whilst in captivity in Germany suffered many hardships. Released at the close of hostilities, he was demobilised in April 1919, holding the General Service and Victory Medals.
Castle Hill Court, Huntingdon. Z1881.

CULLABINE, C., Tpr., 2/1st Surrey Lancers (Queen Mary's Regiment).
He joined in March 1916, and on completion of his training was engaged on important duties at various home stations. He did consistently good work with his unit, but was unfortunately badly injured through being struck by lightning. After a period of treatment at King George's Hospital in London he was invalided from the Army in November 1918.
23, Dunville Road, Queen's Park, Bedford. Z1882.

CULLOP, W., Private, Bedfordshire Regiment.
Volunteering in August 1914, he was sent to France after a period of training at Bedford, and took part in the Battles of Festubert, Loos, Albert and Vimy Ridge (May 1916). He was badly wounded in action on the Ancre in February 1917, and underwent hospital treatment at Boulogne and in London. In February 1919, after two years' suffering, he was invalided from the Service medically unfit, and holds the 1914–15 Star, and the General Service and Victory Medals.
Yelling, St. Neots, Hunts. Z1883.

CUMBERLAND, R. T., Corporal, 1/7th Royal Warwickshire Regiment.
He volunteered in August 1914, and first rendered valuable services on coast defence duties in Yorkshire. In June 1915 he was sent to France, but two months later was badly wounded in action and invalided home. On his recovery he served in Ireland for a time, but in July 1917 returned to the Western Front and played a prominent part in the Battles of Cambrai before being again badly wounded at St. Julien, and sent to hospital in England. He was discharged in February 1918 as medically unfit for further service, and holds the 1914–15 Star, and the General Service and Victory Medals.
2, St. John's Terrace, Sayer Street, Huntingdon. Z1884.

CUMBERLAND, W. J., Private, Northants. Regt.
Already in the Army at the outbreak of war, he proceeded to France with the first Expeditionary Force in August 1914, and was in action throughout the Retreat from Mons. He also took part in the Battles of Ypres and Hill 60 before being badly wounded in action and invalided home. In May 1916 he was discharged as medically unfit for further service, and holds the Mons Star, and the General Service and Victory Medals.
26, King's Place, Bedford. Z1885.

CUNNINGTON, D. A., Pte., 7th Bedfordshire Regt.
He joined in May 1916, and proceeded to France four months later. He took part in the Somme Offensive, and was also in action at Arras and Vimy Ridge. In January 1917, however, he was invalided home with nephritis and, after hospital treatment, was discharged as medically unfit for further service in May 1917. He holds the General Service and Victory Medals.
Cold Brayfield, Bucks. Z1886.

CURRINGTON, E., Private, 6th Bedfordshire Regt.
Volunteering in January 1915, he was sent to France in July and took part in the Battle of Loos and in heavy fighting at Ypres and Givenchy. He was wounded at Delville Wood during the Somme Offensive in July 1916, and was invalided home. Six months later he returned to the Western Front, but was unhappily killed in action at the Battle of Arras on April 17th, 1917. He was entitled to the 1914–15 Star, and the General Service and Victory Medals.
"His life for his Country, his soul to God."
Yelling, St. Neots, Hunts. TZ1888.

CURRINGTON, J. Z., Pte., 6th Bedfordshire Regt.
He volunteered in January 1915, and in the following November was sent to France, where he took part in the Battle of Albert before being badly wounded at Guillemont during the Somme Offensive in September 1916. After hospital treatment in London he returned to the Western Front in March 1917, and was in action at the Battles of Arras, Vimy Ridge and Ypres, but was again badly wounded in March 1918 and invalided to Manchester. He was discharged as medically unfit in March 1919, and holds the 1914–15 Star, and the General Service and Victory Medals. Yelling, St. Neots, Hunts. Z1887/B.

CURRINGTON, S., Driver, R.A.S.C. (M.T.)
He joined in March 1916, and, on completion of his training, was engaged on important duties with the Mechanical Transport at various home stations. He did much excellent work with his unit, but was unsuccessful in his efforts to obtain a transfer overseas, and was demobilised in April 1919.
Yelling, St. Neots, Hunts. Z1890/B.

CURRINGTON, W., Private, 1st Bedfordshire Regiment and Sherwood Foresters.
Having volunteered in November 1914, he was sent to the Western Front in July of the following year and took part in the Battles of the Somme (I.), Arras, Messines, Ypres (III.) and the Somme (II.). He was three times wounded in action —at Delville Wood in 1916, at Ypres in the following year, and on the Somme in 1918, when he was invalided to hospital at Norwich. He holds the 1914–15 Star, and the General Service and Victory Medals, and was demobilised in March 1919.
Yelling, St. Neots, Hunts. Z1889.

CURRINGTON, W., Private, 1st Bedfordshire Regt.
Five months after volunteering he was drafted to France in June 1915, and took part in the Battles of Loos, Vimy Ridge (May 1916) and the Somme. He laid down his life for King and Country near Delville Wood on July 27th, 1916, and was entitled to the 1914–15 Star, and the General Service and Victory Medals.
"He died the noblest death a man may die,
Fighting for God and right and liberty."
Yelling, St. Neots, Hunts. Z1890/A.

CURRY, A., Private, Bedfordshire Regiment.
He joined in July 1917, but was not successful in obtaining his transfer overseas during the course of hostilities. In December 1918, however, he was sent to the Army of Occupation in Germany, and rendered valuable services with his unit on the Rhine until his demobilisation in September 1919.
34, Coventry Road, Bedford. Z1891.

CURTIS, A. A. H., Private, R.A.M.C.
Mobilised in August 1914, he was immediately drafted to the Western Front and rendered valuable services with his unit during the Retreat from Mons. He also took a prominent part in the Battles of the Marne, the Aisne, Ypres and the Somme, but died gloriously on the Field of Battle in the Cambrai sector on September 19th, 1917. He was entitled to the Mons Star, and the General Service and Victory Medals.
"He joined the great white company of valiant souls."
Old Stratford, Stony Stratford, Bucks. Z1896/A.

CURTIS, C., Leading Aircraftsman, R.A.F.
He joined in November 1916, and two months later was drafted to the Western Front, where he was engaged on important duties which demanded a high degree of skill. He served with a Bombing Squadron principally in the Ypres sector, but was also attached to a Field Artillery Battery and an Ammunition Column. He was demobilised in July 1920, and holds the General Service and Victory Medals.
Old Stratford, Stony Stratford, Bucks. Z1896/B.

CURTIS, F., Private, 4th Bedfordshire Regiment.
He was mobilised at the outbreak of war, and, proceeding to France in August 1914, took part in the Retreat from Mons. He was also in action at the Battles of Ypres, Loos, the Somme, Vimy Ridge and Cambrai, and throughout the Retreat and Advance of 1918, and was gassed. He received his discharge in February 1919, and holds the Mons Star, and the General Service and Victory Medals. Near Elms, Elstow, Beds. X1894.

CURTIS, F. F., Air Mechanic, Royal Air Force.
He joined in August 1917, and, on completion of his training, was engaged on special duties as a fitter in the workshops at Grantham. Owing to the important nature of his work he could not be spared for transfer to the theatre of war, but rendered valuable services until his demobilisation in March 1919. 7, Coronation Road, Stony Stratford, Bucks. Z1895.

CURTIS, F. W., Sergeant, 2nd Bedfordshire Regt.
Already in the Army in August 1914, he was sent to France immediately and took part in the Retreat from Mons. He also served with distinction at the Battles of Ypres, La Bassée, Festubert and Loos, but was badly wounded in action in May 1916. Invalided to England, he spent twelve months in hospital, and was discharged in May 1917 as medically unfit for further service. He holds the Mons Star, and the General Service and Victory Medals.
32, Cater Street, Kempston, Bedford. Z1893.

CURTIS, T. W., Private, Hertfordshire Regiment.
He joined in January 1917, and later in the same year was drafted to the Western Front, where he took part in much severe fighting. On March 23rd, 1918, he was reported missing, but is now presumed to have been killed in action in the Cambrai sector on that date. He was entitled to the General Service and Victory Medals.
"A valiant Soldier, with undaunted heart he breasted life's last hill."
2, Farrar Street, Kempston, Bedford. Z1892/A.

CUTBUSH, F. E., C.S.M., Royal Defence Corps.
Medically unfit for service in a fighting unit, he volunteered in the Royal Defence Corps in September 1914, and was first engaged on important guard duties over bridges and munition works in the London district. He also did excellent work in charge of a prisoners of war camp at Bedford, and was eventually demobilised in May 1919. Park Row, Goldington, Beds. Z1897.

D

DALLEY, A. E., Private, R.A.M.C.
He volunteered in September 1915, and shortly afterwards was drafted to the Western Front. There he was employed on various duties of an important character whilst serving at Vimy Ridge, on the Somme front and at Lens, and performed consistently good work. He spent some time in hospital at Rouen suffering from shell-shock prior to returning home for demobilisation in July 1919. He holds the 1914–15 Star, and the General Service and Victory Medals.
Melchbourne, Beds. Z1898.

DANIEL, A. W. G., Sapper, Royal Engineers.
Volunteering in January 1915, he proceeded later in the same year to France, and in this theatre of war served at Ypres, on the Somme front, also at Arras and Cambrai, whilst employed with his Company wiring, tunnelling and mining, and rendered excellent service. He remained overseas for some time after the Armistice, and was eventually demobilised in November 1919, holding the 1914–15 Star, and the General Service and Victory Medals. 44, Argyll Street, Bedford. X1900.

DANIELLS, C. H., Private, Oxford. & Bucks. L.I.
He volunteered in September 1914, and, after the completion of his training at Salisbury Plain, did exceedingly good work whilst employed on various duties of an important nature. He was later admitted to hospital suffering from fever, and six months afterwards was invalided out of the Army as unfit for further military service.
34, Greenfield Road, Newport Pagnell. Z1900/B.

DANIELLS, J. C., Pte., 2nd Oxford. & Bucks. L.I.
Volunteering in September 1914, he was sent for training to Portsmouth, and in the following November was drafted to France. In this theatre of war he was in action during the Battles of Ypres, the Somme, Arras and Cambrai. Wounded in July 1916 during the Battle of the Somme, he spent a month in hospital in Rouen, but on his recovery rejoined his unit and took part in further fighting. He was demobilised in February 1919, and holds the 1914–15 Star, and the General Service and Victory Medals. 91, Caldecote St., Newport Pagnell. Z1902.

DANIELLS, W. E., Private, Devonshire Regiment.
He volunteered in July 1915, but was physically unfit for transfer to a theatre of war. Retained at home and stationed at Warminster and Sutton-Veny, he rendered valuable services whilst employed on duties of an important nature. He was subsequently discharged in December 1918 as unfit for further military duty.
21, Queen Street, Stony Stratford, Bucks. Z1901.

DANIELLS, W. J., Sapper, Royal Engineers.
He volunteered in July 1915, and in the following June was sent to Egypt. There he was employed for some time laying water-pipes in the desert, but later proceeding into Palestine, served at Gaza and Jerusalem. He was wounded near Gaza in March 1918 and removed to hospital at Port Said, later rejoining his Company. Demobilised on returning home in July 1919, he holds the General Service and Victory Medals.
34, Greenfield Road, Newport Pagnell. Z1903/A.

DANIELS, A. W., Pte., R.A.S.C. & Labour Corps.
Volunteering in August 1915, he was shortly afterwards drafted to the Western Front, where he served at the Base and was employed unloading ships and on other important duties. Invalided home on account of ill-health in June 1916, he was discharged a month later as unfit for further duty, and died on December 23rd, 1919, from an illness attributed to his military service. He was entitled to the 1914–15 Star, and the General Service and Victory Medals.
"His memory is cherished with pride."
38, Priory Street, Bedford. X1908/C.

DANIELS, E. C., Private, Royal Fusiliers; and Drummer, 4th Seaforth Highlanders.
He volunteered in January 1915, and was retained at home on various duties of an important nature until March 1918, a considerable portion of the time being stationed with the 4th Seaforth Highlanders at Bedford. Proceeding to the Western Front, he was in action at Albert and on the Cambrai front, and, returning home in December 1918, was demobilised a month later, holding the General Service and Victory Medals.
38, Priory Street, Bedford. X1908/B.

DANIELS, F., Private, East Surrey Regiment and Labour Corps.
He volunteered in September 1914, and in the following May proceeded to France. There he took part in heavy fighting at Givenchy, Loos, Ypres and Arras, and was wounded on the Somme in September 1916. Invalided home, he was transferred to the Labour Corps when he recovered and was employed on agricultural work at Blunham until he was demobilised in February 1919. He holds the 1914–15 Star, and the General Service and Victory Medals.
Park Lane, Blunham, Beds. Z1907.

DANIELS, H., Private, 3rd East Surrey Regiment.
He joined in January 1917, and, after completing his training, was drafted to the Western Front. In this theatre of hostilities he was in action on the Arras front, and did consistently good work until he was invalided home in 1918, having contracted fever. He was eventually demobilised in March 1919, holding the General Service and Victory Medals.
34, Bury Avenue, Newport Pagnell, Bucks. Z1904.

DANIELS, H. G., Corporal, Coldstream Guards.
Joining in January 1916, he was sent in the following August to France, and served in the Battles of the Somme and at Arras. Admitted to hospital in Cherbourg on account of ill-health, he was later invalided home, sent to hospital in Wales and subsequently to Seaford. In December 1917 he returned to France and took part in further fighting on the Cambrai and other fronts. Demobilised in March 1919, he holds the General Service and Victory Medals.
7, Spencer Street, Bradwell, Bucks. Z1905/B.

DANIELS, H. J., Private, York & Lancaster Regt., R.A.M.C., and Sherwood Foresters.
He joined in April 1916, and was employed at various home stations until June 1917, when he was drafted to France. There he was engaged looking after the wounded in the Ypres, Arras and Somme sectors, and, being later transferred to Italy, was similarly engaged on various fronts in that theatre of war. Returning home in February 1919, he was then demobilised, holding the General Service and Victory Medals.
St. Neots Road, Sandy, Beds. Z1906.

DANIELS, W. A., Private, 9th (Queen's Royal) Lancers; and 1st Air Mechanic, R.A.F.
He volunteered in October 1914, and served in Ireland until the following June, when he was discharged on account of ill-health. He re-enlisted in the Royal Air Force in November 1915, and, after passing the necessary tests, was drafted early in 1916 to France. There he served at Ypres, on the Somme front, also at Arras and Cambrai, and was engaged on important duties which demanded a high degree of technical skill. He rendered valuable services whilst so employed until June 1919, when he was demobilised, holding the General Service and Victory Medals. 38, Priory Street, Bedford. X1908/A.

DARLOW, A. E., Pte., 1/5th Bedfordshire Regt.
Volunteering in October 1915, he was shortly afterwards sent to Egypt, and later proceeded into Palestine. In this theatre of hostilities he took part with his unit in the Battle of Gaza and also participated in the capture of Jaffa and Aleppo. He performed consistently good work whilst serving overseas, and was demobilised on his return home in February 1919, holding the 1914–15 Star, and the General Service and Victory Medals.
50, New Fenlake, Bedford. Z1913/A.

DARLOW, A. E., Private, 1st Essex Regiment.
He volunteered in September 1914, and in the following year was drafted to Egypt. Later sent to Palestine, he participated in the Battle of Gaza and in heavy fighting at Jerusalem and Jaffa prior to the entry into those cities. He remained overseas until December 1918, and, demobilised in the following month, holds the 1914–15 Star, and the General Service and Victory Medals. 95, Bunyan Road, Kempston, Beds. X1912.

DARLOW, A. J., Driver, Royal Engineers.
Called up from the Reserve in August 1914, he was drafted in the following year to Gallipoli, and in this theatre of war was engaged on various duties during the operations at Suvla Bay. He returned home for discharge in January 1916, his period of engagement having expired, and he holds the 1914–15 Star, and the General Service and Victory Medals.
62, St. John's Street, Kempston, Beds. X1914.

DARLOW, C. J., Sergeant, 7th Wiltshire Regiment.
Volunteering in September 1914, he was drafted in the following year to Salonika, where he played a prominent part with his unit in many important engagements on the Doiran and Struma fronts. Wounded in action in 1917, he was invalided home, but on his recovery was sent to France. There he was again in action at Arras, Ypres, Cambrai and Albert, and was wounded for the second time and also sustained shell-shock. Demobilised on his return home in February 1919, he holds the 1914–15 Star, and the General Service and Victory Medals.
5, Lovatt St., Newport Pagnell, Bucks. Z1909/C—Z1910/C.

DARLOW, E. W., L/Corporal, R.A.M.C.
He volunteered in August 1915, and quickly proceeding to France, rendered valuable services as a stretcher-bearer in important engagements in various sectors and also in field hospitals. In 1916, however, he was sent home medically unfit, and then acted as an Orderly at Belmont in Surrey. He was demobilised in May 1919, and holds the 1914–15 Star, and the General Service and Victory Medals.
5, Lovatt St., Newport Pagnell, Bucks. Z1909/B—Z1910/B.

DARLOW, F. J., Private, 1st Bedfordshire Regt.
He volunteered in October 1914, and, after a period of training, proceeded to the Western Front. In this theatre of hostilities he at once participated in very heavy fighting, but had only served overseas for three months when he fell in action at Wulverghem, in Belgium, on February 26th, 1915. He was entitled to the 1914–15 Star, and the General Service and Victory Medals.
"Great deeds cannot die."
56, High Street, Kempston, Beds. X1170/B.

DARLOW, G. L., Staff-Sergeant, R.A.S.C.
Coming from Canada in August 1914, he was sent to France in 1915. There he was engaged on important duties in connection with transport at Ypres, Loos, Givenchy and on the Somme, and was twice wounded. In November 1916 he was transferred to Palestine, served at Gaza, Jerusalem and on the Jordan, and was again wounded. Sent to Salonika in November 1917, he saw further service on the Doiran and Vardar fronts. He did excellent work, was three times mentioned in Despatches, and was demobilised in August 1919, holding the 1914–15 Star, and the General Service and Victory Medals.
5, Lovatt St., Newport Pagnell, Bucks. Z1909/E—Z1910/E.

DARLOW, O. T., Gunner, Royal Garrison Artillery.
A Regular soldier, he was stationed in South Africa at the outbreak of hostilities in August 1914, and served under General Botha in German East Africa. He took part with his Battery in many important engagements, and was wounded. Remaining overseas until after the cessation of fighting, he was eventually discharged in November 1919, and holds the 1914–15 Star, and the General Service and Victory Medals.
5, Lovatt St., Newport Pagnell, Bucks. Z1909/D—Z1910/D.

DARLOW, S., Sapper, Royal Engineers.
He volunteered in October 1915, and was drafted to Egypt, where he was stationed for some time. Proceeding later to Palestine, he served at Gaza, Jaffa, Haifa and Aleppo, and was employed on various duties of an important nature. He did excellent work until April 1919, when he returned and was demobilised, holding the 1914–15 Star, and the General Service and Victory Medals.
50, New Fenlake, Bedford. Z1913/B.

DARLOW, S. W., L/Corporal, R.A.M.C.
Volunteering in August 1915, he was shortly afterwards sent to the Western Front, where he was engaged as a stretcher-bearer and on various duties in Field hospitals until invalided home through ill-health in 1916. On his recovery he served in various home hospitals as an Orderly and did good work until his demobilisation in May 1919. He holds the 1914–15 Star, and the General Service and Victory Medals.
5, Lovatt St., Newport Pagnell, Bucks. Z1909/B—Z1910/B.

DARLOW, W., Private, R.A.S.C.
He joined in 1916, but was medically unfit for transfer to a theatre of war. He was stationed at Peckham and Northampton, and rendered valuable services whilst employed on various duties in connection with supplies until he was demobilised in September 1919. 27, Albert Street, Bedford. X1911.

DARLOW, W. H., Gunner, Royal Field Artillery.
He was mobilised in August 1914 and immediately ordered to France. There he was in action with his Battery in the Battle of Mons and the Retreat, and at the Battles of the Marne, the Aisne, La Bassée, Ypres (I.) and Neuve Chapelle. Wounded during the second Battle of Ypres in May 1915, he was sent to hospital at Rouen and was later evacuated to England. He was eventually invalided out of the Army in January 1919 as unfit for further military service. He holds the Mons Star, and the General Service and Victory Medals.
5, Lovatt St., Newport Pagnell, Bucks. Z1909/A—Z1910/A.

DARNELL, F. P., Sergeant, R.A.V.C.
He volunteered in September 1914, and was drafted early in 1915 to the Western Front. In this theatre of war he served at Hill 60, Loos, on the Somme front and at Albert, and did consistently good work whilst engaged on veterinary duties. He was later invalided home with pneumonia, from which he unhappily died in Cambridge Military Hospital on November 3rd, 1918. He was entitled to the 1914–15 Star, and the General Service and Victory Medals.
"Honour to the immortal dead, who gave their youth that the world might grow old in peace."
High Street, Sharnbrook, Beds. Z1918/A.

DARNELL, G., Private, Bedfordshire Regiment.
He joined in 1916, and, on the completion of his training, was sent to France. After taking part in strenuous fighting at Albert and on the Somme, he was reported missing during the Battle of Arras in April 1917, and is now believed to have been wounded and taken prisoner, dying whilst in German hands. He was entitled to the General Service and Victory Medals.
"Great deeds cannot die."
Seddington, Sandy, Beds. Z1917.

DARNELL, G. H., Leading Telegraphist, R.N.
Volunteering in February 1915, he served as a wireless operator in various vessels with the Grand Fleet in the North Sea, and was engaged on patrol duties. He participated in the Battle of Jutland, in several actions off Heligoland, and in the bombardment of Zeebrugge. Demobilised in 1919, he holds the 1914–15 Star, and the General Service and Victory Medals.
18, Dunville Road, Queen's Park, Bedford. Z1916/A.

DARNELL, H. J., Sapper, Royal Engineers.
He volunteered in August 1914, and, after serving at home for some time, proceeded to the Western Front. During his service in this theatre of war he was stationed at Courtrai and Tournai whilst looking after acetylene-gas plant. He did good work until after the Armistice, and was demobilised in 1919, holding the General Service and Victory Medals.
18, Dunville Road, Queen's Park, Bedford. Z1916/B.

DARNELL, H. W., Cpl., 1st Bedfordshire Regt.
He joined in 1916, and when drafted to France played a prominent part in heavy fighting at Loos, Albert, Vimy Ridge, Arras, Messines, Beaumont-Hamel, Cambrai and on the Marne. He performed consistently good work until the Armistice, after which he proceeded into Germany and served with the Army of Occupation in Cologne. He was demobilised in 1919, and holds the General Service and Victory Medals.
18, Dunville Road, Queen's Park, Bedford. Z1916/C.

DARNELL, J., Sergeant, R.A.M.C.
Serving at the outbreak of war in August 1914, he was quickly sent to the Western Front. In this theatre of hostilities he was employed on various important duties during the Battle of Mons and the subsequent Retreat, and later at Loos and in other sectors. He rendered excellent service whilst overseas, and in 1920 was still in the Royal Army Medical Corps at Warlingham Military Hospital. He holds the Mons Star, and the General Service and Victory Medals.
17, Pilcroft Street, Bedford. X1919/A.

DARNELL, R., Private, East Yorkshire Regiment.
A Regular soldier, he was drafted to France immediately after the outbreak of war in August 1914, and took part in the Battle of Mons and the Retreat. He subsequently participated in heavy fighting, but was unhappily killed in action at Dickebusch, near Ypres, on October 28th, 1914. He was entitled to the Mons Star, and the General Service and Victory Medals.
"His life for his Country."
17, Pilcroft Street, Bedford. X1919/B.

DARNELL, W. G., 2nd Lieutenant, R.F.A.
He volunteered in the Royal Army Veterinary Corps as a Private in September 1914, and was afterwards sent to the Western Front. During his service overseas he did excellent work, and was later awarded a commission in the Royal Field Artillery. He was in action at Arras, Cambrai and on the Somme, and, after being taken prisoner in March 1918, was interned in Germany until the Armistice was signed. He was then repatriated and eventually demobilised in January 1919, holding the 1914–15 Star, and the General Service and Victory Medals. High Street, Sharnbrook, Bedford. Z1918/B.

DARRINGTON, A., Private, Royal Fusiliers.
He joined in 1917, and later in the same year was drafted to the Western Front. In this theatre of hostilities he served at Arras, Ypres, on the Somme front and at Neuve Chapelle, and for some time was employed on garrison and other important duties. He performed consistently good work until his return to England, and was demobilised in August 1920, holding the General Service and Victory Medals. Wyboston, Hunts. Z1920.

DARRINGTON, A., L/Cpl., 5th Bedfordshire Regt.
Volunteering in September 1914, he was sent to France in 1915. Whilst overseas he was transferred to the 5th Gloucestershire Regiment, and took part in the Battles of Loos, the Somme, Ypres and Passchendaele, prior to being killed in action in November 1917. He was entitled to the 1914–15 Star, and the General Service and Victory Medals.
"Courage, bright hopes, and a myriad dreams, splendidly given."
Roxton, Beds. Z1922/C.

DARRINGTON, J., Private, 2nd Bedfordshire Regt.
Mobilised in August 1914, he was shortly afterwards drafted to France, and took part in the Battle of Mons and the subsequent Retreat. He was later in action during heavy fighting in various sectors, and was wounded, but was taken prisoner in March 1917, and released after the Armistice. Eventually demobilised in March 1919, he holds the Mons Star, and the General Service and Victory Medals.
Wyboston, St. Neots, Hunts. Z1924.

DARRINGTON, J. S., Shoeing-Smith, R.F.A.
He joined in June 1916, and was soon afterwards sent to Salonika. There he served on the Vardar and Struma fronts, and did excellent work whilst employed as a shoeing-smith. He subsequently served in Turkey prior to returning home for demobilisation in June 1919, and holds the General Service and Victory Medals. Roxton Road, Great Barford. Z1923.

DARRINGTON, P., Pte., 7th Bedfordshire Regt.
Volunteering in May 1915, he proceeded to the Western Front in December of that year and there saw much severe fighting at Loos, Vimy Ridge and many other places. He made the supreme sacrifice, being killed in action on July 1st, 1916, in the Advance on the Somme. He was entitled to the 1914–15 Star, and the General Service and Victory Medals.
"He joined the great white company of valiant souls."
Roxton, Beds. Z1922/B.

DARTS, A., Private, Bedfordshire Regiment.
He volunteered in November 1915, and in the following month was drafted to the Western Front, where he took part in engagements at Loos and Vimy Ridge and in various other sectors. He died gloriously on the Field of Battle on the Somme in July 1916. He was entitled to the 1914–15 Star, and the General Service and Victory Medals.
"Courage, bright hopes, and a myriad dreams, splendidly given."
19, Greenhill Street, Bedford. X1926/A.

DARTS, F., Private, K.O. (Y.L.I.)
Mobilised in August 1914, he was drafted to the Western Front in January of the following year, and there served through the Battles of Neuve Chapelle and St. Eloi and minor engagements. He unfortunately fell fighting at Hill 60 on April 25th, 1915. He was entitled to the 1914–15 Star, and the General Service and Victory Medals.
"He passed out of the sight of men by the path of duty and self-sacrifice."
19, Greenhill Street, Bedford. X1926/C.

DARTS, J., Guardsman, Grenadier Guards.
Already in the Army when war broke out in August 1914, he was shortly afterwards drafted to the Western Front, where he saw severe fighting in various sectors. He took part in the Battles of Ypres and Hill 60 and many other important engagements, was gassed at Arras, and twice wounded in action. After the cessation of hostilities he served with the Army of Occupation in Germany, finally returning home for discharge in April 1918. He holds the 1914–15 Star, and the General Service and Victory Medals.
19, Greenhill Street, Bedford. X1926/B.

DAVEY, J. W., Private, Suffolk Regiment and Labour Corps.
He was already in the Army when war was declared in August 1914, and was retained at various stations, where he was engaged on duties of great importance in the military hospitals and at a school of instruction. He was unable to obtain his transfer to a theatre of war, but nevertheless rendered valuable services with his unit until June 1919, when he was discharged.
17, St. Leonard's Street, Bedford. X1927.

DAVIES, T., Gunner, Royal Garrison Artillery.
Already in the Army when war broke out in August 1914, he was shortly afterwards sent to the Western Front, where he saw severe fighting in various sectors. He took part in the Battles of Ypres, Neuve Chapelle and Vimy Ridge and many other important engagements, and was gassed and wounded in action. After the cessation of hostilities he served with the Army of Occupation in Germany, and returned home for discharge in January 1919. He holds the 1914 Star, and the General Service and Victory Medals.
19, Church Walk, Kempston, near Bedford. X1929.

DAVIS, A. (M.S.M.), Sergeant, R.A.S.C. (M.T.)
He volunteered in May 1915, and was retained at various stations in England until October 1917, when he proceeded to Mesopotamia. There he was engaged on important transport duties, afterwards serving in Persia and Russia on similar duties. He was awarded the Meritorious Service Medal for his continuously good work, and holds also the General Service and Victory Medals. He was demobilised on his return home in May 1919.
30, York Road, Stony Stratford, Bucks. Z1931.

DAVIS, E. W., Private, East Surrey Regiment.
He joined in May 1916, and in September of the following year proceeded to the Western Front, where he saw much heavy fighting. After taking part in the Battles of Ypres and Passchendaele he was severely wounded in action near Cambrai in December 1917 and admitted to hospital at Newcastle. He was finally invalided from the Army in July 1918, and holds the General Service and Victory Medals.
8, Cobb's Cottages, Olney, Bucks. Z1934.

DAVIS, G., Gunner, Royal Garrison Artillery.
Joining in May 1916, he proceeded to the Western Front in December of that year and there saw heavy fighting in various sectors. After taking part in many important engagements in this theatre of war he was so severely wounded in action near Cambrai in November 1918 as to necessitate the amputation of his right leg. He was invalided from the Army in August 1920, and holds the General Service and Victory Medals.
83, Caldecote Street, Newport Pagnell, Bucks. Z1932/B.

DAVIS, J., Sapper, Royal Engineers.
He volunteered in November 1915, and, on completion of a period of training, was drafted to Egypt, whence he proceeded into Palestine. There he took part in the Battles of Gaza, was present also at the fall of Jaffa, Jerusalem and Haifa, and was wounded in action. He returned home after the cessation of hostilities and unfortunately caught a chill and died on February 9th, 1919. He was entitled to the General Service and Victory Medals.
"Steals on the ear the distant triumph song."
2, Eastville Road, South End, Bedford. Z1935.

DAVIS, J., Private, Worcestershire Regiment.
He joined in November 1917, and, after a period of training, served at various stations, where he was engaged on duties of great importance. He was unable to obtain his transfer to a theatre of war, being medically unfit for active service, but in March 1919 was sent to the Army of Occupation in Germany, where he was stationed at Cologne. He was demobilised on his return home in December 1919.
83, Caldecote Street, Newport Pagnell, Bucks. Z1932/C.

DAVIS, O. E., Driver, Royal Engineers.
He was already in the Army when war was declared in August 1914, and was retained on important duties at various stations. He was not successful in obtaining his transfer to a theatre of war on account of injuries caused by a kick from a horse, but nevertheless rendered valuable services with his Company until July 1916, when he was invalided from the Army.
20, Littledale Street, Kempston, Bedford. Z1937.

DAVIS, P., Ordinary Seaman, Royal Navy.
He joined in July 1916, and, after serving for a time at the Royal Naval Barracks at Chatham, was posted to H.M.S. "Royal Oak." In the following year he was transferred to H.M.S. "Kildorie," on board which vessel he was attached to the Grand Fleet in the North Sea, and was afterwards engaged on convoy duty in the Atlantic Ocean. Demobilised in February 1919, he holds the General Service and Victory Medals. 6, Park Road West, Bedford. Z1928.

DAVIS, S. F., Private, Middlesex Regiment.
He joined in February 1917, and underwent a period of training prior to being drafted to the Western Front in March of the following year. There he took part in the Battles of Cambrai and Le Cateau, and many other important engagements in the Retreat and Advance of 1918, and was gassed in September of that year. Demobilised in November 1919, he holds the General Service and Victory Medals.
24, Tavistock Place, Bedford. X1936.

DAVIS, T. J., Sapper, Royal Engineers (R.O.D.)
He volunteered in December 1914, and in October of the following year proceeded to the Western Front, where he was engaged on important duties as an engine-driver and stoker. Serving chiefly in the Ypres, Somme, Arras and Cambrai sectors, he did much useful work in this theatre of war until his return home in January 1918. Invalided from the Army in the same month, he holds the 1914–15 Star, and the General Service and Victory Medals. 22, Cater Street, Kempston, Bedford. X1933.

DAVIS, W., Private, 3rd (King's Own) Hussars.
Mobilised in August 1914, he was immediately drafted to the Western Front, where he fought in the Battle of Mons and the subsequent Retreat. He also took part in the Battles of the Marne, the Aisne, La Bassée, Ypres, the Somme, Arras, Cambrai and St. Quentin and many other important engagements, and served through the Retreat and Advance of 1918. He was discharged in January 1919, and holds the Mons Star, and the General Service and Victory Medals.
21, Mill Street, Newport Pagnell, Bucks. Z1930

DAVIS, W., Private, 1/22nd London Regiment.
Three months after joining in May 1916 he proceeded to the Western Front, where he took part in many important engagements during the Advance on the Somme. He made the supreme sacrifice, falling in action in October 1916, after only two months in France. He was entitled to the General Service and Victory Medals.
"Honour to the immortal dead, who gave their youth that the world might grow old in peace."
83, Caldecote Street, Newport Pagnell, Bucks. Z1932/A.

DAVIS, W. M., C.S.M., Bedfordshire Regiment.
Already in the Army at the outbreak of war in August 1914, he was retained on important duties as an Instructor at various stations in England until January 1917. He then proceeded to the Western Front, where he took a prominent part in the Battles of Arras, Vimy Ridge and Ypres and many other engagements, and was wounded in action on the Somme. He was discharged in November 1918, and holds the General Service, Victory, and Long Service and Good Conduct Medals.
Keeley Lane, Wootton, Bedford. Z1938.

DAVISON, H. B., Private, Labour Corps.
He joined in March 1916, and in April of the following year was drafted to the Western Front. Whilst in this theatre of war he was engaged on duties of great importance at Dunkirk, Boulogne and various other stations, and after the cessation of hostilities was sent into Germany with the Army of Occupation. He was demobilised on his return home in February 1920, and holds the General Service and Victory Medals.
18, Poplar Houses, Sandy, Beds. TZ1939.

DAWBORN, W., Sergeant, 7th Bedfordshire Regt.
He volunteered in September 1914, and in July of the following year proceeded to the Western Front, where, after taking a prominent part in the Battles of Albert and the Somme, he was wounded in action at Arras in May 1917. Invalided home, he returned to France, however, on his recovery in November of that year, fought at Cambrai, and was again wounded at St. Quentin in March 1918. He was for a considerable period in hospital at Newport before being discharged in August 1919, and holds the 1914–15 Star, and the General Service and Victory Medals. 42, Great Brickhill, Bletchley, Bucks. Z1940.

DAWSON, C., Private, American Army.
He joined in 1916, and, after undergoing a period of training, was retained at various stations in America, where he was engaged on duties of a highly important nature. Although unsuccessful in obtaining his transfer overseas, he rendered very valuable services with his unit until his demobilisation in 1919.
Rose Cottages, Clapham, Bedford. Z1941/B.

DAWSON, C. W., Private, R.M.L.I.
He joined in June 1916, and, after completing a term of training, was sent to sea. He was engaged chiefly in escorting merchant ships to and from America, and served also in many other waters. He was afterwards stationed at Queenstown, Ireland, and in 1920 was still serving, holding the General Service and Victory Medals. Willington, Bedford. Z1942/B—Z1943/B.

DAWSON, E. I., Sapper, Royal Engineers.
He volunteered in May 1915, and, on completing his training in the following year, proceeded to the Western Front, where he served in various sectors. He took an active part in the Battles of Albert, Messines and Ypres and many other important engagements until the cessation of hostilities, and was then sent with the Army of Occupation into Germany. He was demobilised on his return home in May 1919, and holds the General Service and Victory Medals.
Willington, Bedford. Z1942/A—Z1943/A.

DAWSON, F. A., Sapper, Royal Engineers.
Shortly after volunteering in January 1915 he was drafted to Gallipoli, where, after taking part in the Landing at Cape Helles, he saw much severe fighting, especially at Anzac and Suvla Bay. On the Evacuation of the Peninsula he was transferred to Egypt, whence he proceeded into Palestine. There he was again in action, serving through the three Battles of Gaza, and was also present at the entry into Jaffa and Jerusalem. He was demobilised on his return home in April 1919, and holds the 1914–15 Star, and the General Service and Victory Medals. 9, Leys Cottages, Clapham, Bedford. Z1946.

DAWSON, G. T. C., Pte., 1/8th Hampshire Regt.
He volunteered in November 1914, and in September of the following year was drafted to Gallipoli, where he saw severe fighting at Suvla Bay and Anzac. In December 1915 he was transferred to Salonika, and there took part in many engagements on the Vardar, Doiran and Struma fronts until invalided to Malta suffering from malaria and dysentery in 1917. On his recovery, however, he proceeded to Egypt and thence advanced into Palestine, where he took part in the Battles of Gaza and the entry into Jaffa. Returning home in August 1919, he was demobilised in the following month, and holds the 1914–15 Star, and the General Service and Victory Medals.
Moggerhanger, near Sandy, Beds. Z1944/B.

DAWSON, P., Private, Machine Gun Corps.
He joined in May 1918, and, after completing a period of training, served at various stations, where he was engaged on duties of a highly important nature. Being too young for active service, he was unable to obtain his transfer to the front, but nevertheless rendered very valuable services until his demobilisation in March 1919.
Rose Cottages, Clapham, Bedford. Z1941/A.

DAWSON, W. H., Private, 4th Northamptonshire Regiment and Labour Corps.
He joined in June 1917, and, after undergoing a period of training, was retained on important duties at various stations. He was not successful in obtaining his transfer to a theatre of war, but, nevertheless, rendered valuable services with his unit until February 1919, when he was demobilised.
The Warren, Clapham, Bedford. Z1945.

DAY, A. H., Pte., 1/5th Royal Warwickshire Regt.
He joined in April 1917, and shortly afterwards proceeded to the Western Front, where he was stationed for a time at Etaples, and also took part in the Battles of Cambrai and the Somme and other engagements. He also served in Italy, where he was again in action, and was for a considerable period in hospital, suffering from trench-fever, whilst overseas. Demobilised on his return home in December 1919, he holds the General Service and Victory Medals.
19, Maryville Road, Bedford. Z1947.

DAY, A. R., Gunner, Royal Garrison Artillery.
Joining in May 1916, he proceeded to the Western Front in September of that year, and there took part in many important engagements during the Advance on the Somme. Mortally wounded in action near Arras on May 8th, 1917, he unhappily died at the 30th Casualty Clearing Station. He was entitled to the General Service and Victory Medals.
"Nobly striving:
He nobly fell that we might live."
Pertenhall, near St. Neots, Hunts. Z1948.

DAY, C., L/Corporal, 2nd Bedfordshire Regiment.
Mobilised in August 1914, he was immediately drafted to the Western Front, where, after serving through the Retreat from Mons, he took part in the Battles of the Marne, Festubert, Ypres and Loos and many minor engagements. He fell fighting on January 5th, 1917. He was entitled to the Mons Star, and the General Service and Victory Medals.
"A valiant Soldier, with undaunted heart he breasted life's last hill."
Eaton Socon, Beds. Z1950/B.

DAY, E. (M.M.), Sergeant, 15th Essex Regiment.
He joined in September 1916, and later in the same year proceeded to France, where he saw severe fighting in various sectors of the front. He took a prominent part in many important engagements in this theatre of war, and was three times mentioned in Despatches for distinguished service at Morlancourt, Beaucourt and Mormal Forest. He was awarded the Military Medal (and Bar) for conspicuous gallantry and devotion to duty in the Field, and, holding also the General Service and Victory Medals, was demobilised in April 1920.
Piper's Lane, Godmanchester, Hunts. Z1953.

DAY, F., Driver, Royal Engineers.
Mobilised in August 1914, he was drafted to Gallipoli in the following year, and there, after taking part in the Landing at Suvla Bay, saw much severe fighting until the Evacuation of the Peninsula. He was then transferred to Egypt, and advanced thence into Palestine, where he took part in the Battles of Gaza and was present at the fall of Jaffa and Jerusalem. He was discharged on his return home in July 1919, and holds the 1914–15 Star, and the General Service and Victory Medals.
3, Millbrook Street, Bedford. Z1949/A.

DAY, G., Corporal, Bedfordshire Regiment.
He volunteered in 1915, and was retained at various stations in England until June 1917, when he was drafted to the Western Front. There he served as a stretcher-bearer in the Battle of Amiens and many other important engagements in various sectors until wounded in action in 1918 and admitted to hospital at Bedford. He was finally demobilised in 1919, and holds the General Service and Victory Medals.
Eaton Socon, Beds. Z1950/D.

DAY, G. T., Private, 1st Bedfordshire Regiment.
He volunteered in September 1914, and early in the following year proceeded to France. During his service in this seat of war he took part in many engagements in various sectors of the front, particularly in the heavy fighting during the Somme Offensive, and was unfortunately killed in action at Arras on October 2nd, 1916. He was entitled to the 1914–15 Star, and the General Service and Victory Medals.
"Steals on the ear the distant triumph song."
Cambridge Street, St. Neots, Hunts. Z1951/A.

DAY, H., Sapper, Royal Engineers.
He joined in August 1918, and, after completing a period of training, was engaged on important duties in England. Owing to the early cessation of hostilities he was unable to proceed to a theatre of war, but in April 1920 he was sent to Ireland and stationed at Dublin. 17, Newnham Lane, Bedford. Z1952/B.

DAY, H., Private, 6th Essex Regiment.
Joining in December 1916, he completed a period of training in the following year and was sent to Egypt. There he took part in the Advance into Palestine and the Battles of Gaza, and was also present at the capture of Jerusalem. In 1918 he was transferred to Italy, where he fought on the Piave front, and remained in this seat of war until December 1919, when he returned home and was demobilised, holding the General Service and Victory Medals.
17, Newnham Lane, Goldington, Bedford. Z1952/A.

DAY, H., L/Corporal, 3rd Leicester Regiment.
Volunteering at the outbreak of hostilities in August 1914, he proceeded to the Western Front in the following year. There he was in action during many important engagements, including the Battles of Festubert, Loos, the Somme and Arras, where he was wounded in April 1917. On his recovery he returned to the fighting area and took part in other engagements until May 1918, when he was taken prisoner. He was released from captivity in 1919, and, returning to England, was demobilised in March of that year. He holds the 1914–15 Star, and the General Service and Victory Medals.
Eaton Socon, Bedford. Z1950/C.

DAY, J., Private, R.A.S.C.
He joined in 1916, and, after completing a period of training, was drafted overseas in the same year. Whilst on the Western Front he took part in the engagements on the Somme, at Ypres and Albert, and was wounded in May 1917 at Kemmel Hill. After the close of hostilities he proceeded with the Army of Occupation into Germany and was stationed at Cologne, where he was still serving in 1920. He holds the General Service and Victory Medals. Eaton Socon, Bedford. Z1950/A.

DAY, R., Private, Labour Corps.
He volunteered in June 1915, and, on completion of his training, was attached to the 12th Labour Battalion, with which he did good work at the docks near Skegness. Owing to his being medically unfit he was not successful in obtaining his transfer to a theatre of war, but rendered valuable services until demobilised in January 1919.
17, Newnham Lane, Goldington, Bedford. Z1952/C.

DAY, S. W., Private, 1st Black Watch.
Volunteering at the outbreak of hostilities in August 1914, he completed his training in the following July, and proceeded to the Dardanelles. In the course of his service in this seat of war he was present at the Landing at Suvla Bay, and, after the Evacuation of the Gallipoli Peninsula, was drafted to France. There he was in action during the heavy fighting on the Somme, at Arras, Passchendaele, Albert and other engagements of importance until the conclusion of the war. Returning to England, he was demobilised in April 1919, and holds the 1914–15 Star, and the General Service and Victory Medals.
3, Millbrook Road, Bedford. Z1949/B.

DAZLEY, A., Private, 3rd Bedfordshire Regt.
He volunteered in June 1915, and later in the same year proceeded to France, where he served in various sectors of the front, taking part in the engagements at Ypres and on the Somme. Later, in 1917, he was transferred to Egypt and was in action during the Advance in Palestine and in the Battles of Gaza. In March 1919, after his return home, he was demobilised, and holds the 1914–15 Star, and the General Service and Victory Medals. 33, Bunyan Road, Bedford. Z1954.

DEACON, W. J., Private, Middlesex Regiment.
He joined in 1916, and, on completion of his training, was drafted to Egypt, where he saw much heavy fighting and was in action during the British Advance into Palestine. He also took part in the Battles of Gaza and was present at the capture of Jaffa and Haifa. Returning to England, he was demobilised in March 1919, and holds the General Service and Victory Medals. Carter Street, Girtford, Sandy, Beds. Z1955.

DEAMER, J. (M.M.), Corporal, Royal Engineers.
He was called up from the Reserve at the outbreak of war in 1914, and quickly drafted to France, where he took part in much heavy fighting in various sectors of the front. He did good work during the Battles of Neuve Chapelle, Ypres, Loos, Albert and the Somme. In 1916 he was invalided to England, but after a period of hospital treatment returned to France and was in action at Arras, Vimy Ridge, Passchendaele and others of importance until August 1918. He was awarded the Military Medal in June 1918 for conspicuous bravery and devotion to duty in the Field, and was demobilised in February 1919, holding in addition to the Military Medal the 1914–15 Star, and the General Service and Victory Medals.
28, Muswell Road, Bedford. Z1956.

DEAN, A. E., Petty Officer, Royal Navy.
Already in the Navy at the outbreak of war, he was serving on board H.M.S. "Bristol" in the South Pacific, and was in action at the Battle of the Falkland Islands. Later he took part in the Naval operations in the Dardanelles, and, after the Evacuation of the Gallipoli Peninsula, was engaged on patrol duties whilst attached to the Italian Fleet in the Adriatic Sea. He also rendered valuable services in H.M.S. "Broke," and eventually received his discharge in February 1919, holding the 1914–15 Star, and the General Service and Victory Medals.
36, Church Square, Bedford. Z1963.

DEAN, C., Private, 7th Royal Warwickshire Regt.
He volunteered in August 1914 in the Huntingdonshire Cyclist Battalion, and, after completing his training, was transferred to the Royal Warwickshire Regiment and drafted to France. There he was in action in the engagements on the Somme, where he was wounded, and was invalided to hospital. Returning to the fighting area on his recovery, he took part in other important battles, and was again wounded in 1917 near Arras. As a result he was sent to England, and, after a period of treatment, was discharged from hospital and sent to Ireland, where he was engaged on important duties until demobilised in June 1919. He holds the General Service and Victory Medals.
Main Street, Hartford. Z1966/A.

DEAN, E., Pioneer, Royal Engineers.
He joined in June 1917, and, on completion of his training in the following year, proceeded to France, where he was chiefly engaged on important duties in connection with road construction, and did consistently good work. He served in the Ypres, Arras and Cambrai sectors, and was wounded in September 1918 and invalided to hospital. On his recovery he served during the final Advance, and, on his return to England, was demobilised in September 1919, holding the General Service and Victory Medals. Main Street, Hartford. Z1966/B.

DEAN, F. J., Sapper, Royal Engineers.
Joining in September 1916, he was in the same year drafted overseas. During his service on the Western Front he was engaged on important duties with his unit in various sectors and was constantly under heavy shell-fire. He served at Boulogne, on the Somme and at Cambrai, and rendered valuable services until demobilised in January 1919, holding the General Service and Victory Medals. Cambridge Road, Sandy, Beds. Z1957.

DEAN, H., Private, 14th Worcestershire Regiment.
He volunteered in December 1915, and, after completing a period of training in the following year, was drafted to France. In the course of his service on the Western Front he was engaged on important duties and served during the Battles of Loos, the Somme, Arras, Bullecourt, Ypres and Cambrai, and did good work until the close of hostilities. He was demobilised in January 1919, and holds the General Service and Victory Medals. 6, Cobden Street, Bedford. X1958.

DEAN, H. J., Private, 1st Bedfordshire Regiment.
A Reservist, he was called to the Colours in August 1914, and, after a period of training, was drafted to the Dardanelles, where he was present in many important engagements. After the Evacuation of the Gallipoli Peninsula he was transferred to France, was in action during the Somme Offensive and later in the Battles of Arras, Ypres and Cambrai, and was severely wounded. He unfortunately died of his wounds on October 23rd, 1918, and was entitled to the 1914–15 Star, and the General Service and Victory Medals.
"His memory is cherished with pride."
George Town, Sandy, Beds. Z1959/B.

DEAN, J. J., Sergeant, Essex Regiment.
Joining in 1916, in the same year he landed in France, where he served with distinction in many important engagements in various sectors of the front. He took part in the Somme Offensive and later fought at the Battles of Arras, Ypres, Passchendaele and Cambrai. In 1918 he was wounded and gassed during the Advance, and on his recovery did good work in the guarding of prisoners of war. After the Armistice he returned home and was demobilised in October 1919, holding the General Service and Victory Medals.
Near Post Office, Eaton Socon, St. Neots, Hunts. Z1962.

DEAN, T., Private, R.A.M.C.
He joined in 1917 in the Royal Fusiliers, and after a period of training was transferred to the R.A.M.C. and sent to France. During his service in this theatre of war he took part in the memorable Retreat and Advance of 1918 and other engagements until the close of hostilities. After the Armistice he proceeded to Germany with the Army of Occupation and was stationed at Cologne, where he was engaged on important duties until his return for demobilisation in 1919. He holds the General Service and Victory Medals. Eaton Socon, Beds. Z1961.

DEAN, T., Private, Essex Regiment.
He volunteered in January 1915, and, after completing a period of training, was drafted to Egypt. Whilst in this seat of war he was in action during the Advance into Palestine, and also took part in the Battles of Gaza and the capture of Jerusalem and Jericho. After the cessation of hostilities he returned to England and was demobilised in April 1919, holding the 1914–15 Star, and the General Service and Victory Medals.
29, Dane Street, Bedford. X1965/C.

DEAN, V. F., Pte., Queen's (R. West Surrey Regt.)
Volunteering in May 1916, he landed in France three months later and fought in many sectors of the front. He was in action during the heavy fighting at the Battles of Arras, Ypres, Cambrai and the second Battle of the Somme, where he was unfortunately killed on March 25th, 1918. He was entitled to the General Service and Victory Medals.
"Whilst we remember, the sacrifice is not in vain."
High Street, Sandy, Beds. TZ1960.

DEAN, W., Private, Labour Corps.
Volunteering in 1915, he was quickly drafted to the Western Front, where he did good work in various sectors. He was present at the Battles of Festubert, Loos, the Somme and Arras, but in May 1918 he was badly gassed in action near Cambrai, and unfortunately died from the effects of gas-poisoning. He was entitled to the 1914–15 Star, and the General Service and Victory Medals.
"His life for his Country, his soul to God."
2, Queen's Row, Bedford. X1964.

DEAN, W., Private, 19th Canadian Regiment (Canadian Overseas Forces).
He volunteered at the outbreak of war in August 1914, and, after a period of training in England, proceeded to France. During his service in this seat of hostilities he took part in the engagements on the Ypres and Cambrai fronts, and was wounded in 1918. Returning to the fighting area on his recovery, he took part in other important battles until the close of hostilities. In March 1919 he was demobilised, and holds the 1914–15 Star, and the General Service and Victory Medals.
Main Street, Hartford. Z1966/C.

DEAN, W. C., Private, Essex Regiment.
He volunteered in February 1915, and, after completing his training in the following year, proceeded to France, where he took part in much heavy fighting in various sectors of the front. He fought at the Battles of Vimy Ridge, the Somme, Arras, Bullecourt, and was later in action at Cambrai and the Aisne (III.), where he was unfortunately killed in May 1918. He was entitled to the General Service and Victory Medals.
"He died the noblest death a man may die,
Fighting for God and right and liberty."
27, Dane Street, Bedford. X1965/B.

DEAN, W. F., Sapper, Royal Engineers.
Volunteering in 1914, early in the following year he landed in France, and in the course of his service in this theatre of war did good work in various sectors of the front. He took an active part in the Battles of Loos, Vimy Ridge, the Somme, Cambrai and the Aisne (III.). In May 1918 he made the suprema sacrifice, being killed in action. He had been awarded a Divisional Certificate for bravery in the Field, and was also entitled to the 1914–15 Star, and the General Service and Victory Medals.
"Great deeds cannot die:
They with the sun and moon renew their light for ever."
29, Dane Street, Bedford. X1965/A.

DEANE, D., Driver, Royal Engineers.
Volunteering at the declaration of war in August 1914, he was, after a period of training, drafted to France, and took part in many engagements in various sectors of the front. He served at Ypres, Vimy Ridge, the Somme, Bullecourt, Cambrai, and later in the Retreat and Advance of 1918, and after the conclusion of war returned to England. He was demobilised in February 1919, and holds the 1914–15 Star, and the General Service and Victory Medals. 47, Tavistock Place, Bedford. X1967.

DEAR, A., Private, Royal Warwickshire Regiment.
He volunteered in August 1914, in the Huntingdonshire Cyclist Corps, but was later transferred to the Royal Warwickshire Regiment and sent to France, where he took part in the Somme Offensive. In December 1917 he was invalided to hospital with trench feet, and after a period of treatment was discharged and sent to Ireland, where he served until demobilised in March 1919. He holds the General Service and Victory Medals.
13, Sapley Lane, Hartford. Z1972.

DEAR, A., Private, Royal Army Medical Corps.
He volunteered in September 1917, and later in the same year was drafted to Salonika. During his service in this theatre of war he was chiefly engaged as a nursing orderly in the General Hospital on the Vardar, and rendered valuable services until demobilised in April 1920. He holds the General Service and Victory Medals.
26, Foster Street, Bedford. X1969.

DEAR, B., Sergeant, 7th Warwickshire Regiment.
He was mobilised at the outbreak of war in 1914, and after completing a period of training was drafted to France, where he did excellent work in various s ctors of the front, taking an active part in many importan. engagements until March 1917, when he was transferred to Italy. There he saw service on the Piave front and took part in the engagements on the Asiago Plateau. Returning to England, he was demobilised in February 1920, and holds the General Service and Victory Medals. 13, Sapley Lane, Hartford. Z1972/B.

DEAR, C. H., Corporal, R.A.S.C. (M.T.)
Joining in 1915, on completion of his training in the following year he proceeded overseas, and whilst in France did good work in various sectors of the front, being chiefly engaged in conveying supplies to the forward areas, often under heavy shell-fire. He saw service at Vimy Ridge, Arras, Ypres, and was gassed in action. Later he was transferred to Italy and served on the Italian frontier until his returnhome for demobilisation in July 1919. He holds the General Service and Victory Medals. 33, Howbury Street, Bedford. Z1970.

DEAR, F. W., A.B., Royal Navy.
He enlisted in the Royal Navy in 1912, and during the period of hostilities did good work in H.M.S. "Oberon," "Lennox" and "Essex." He was engaged on important duties, and served in many waters. In June 1920 he was invalided from the Navy suffering from neurasthenia, and holds the 1914–15 Star, and the General Service and Victory Medals.
94, Coventry Road, Queen's Park, Bedford. Z1971.

DEAR, H., Private, Bedfordshire Regiment.
Volunteering at the outbreak of war, he completed a period of training in the following year, and was drafted to France. There he took part in many important engagements, including the Battles of Ypres, the Somme, Arras and Cambrai, until the close of hostilities. On his return to England he was demobilised in 1919, and holds the General Service and Victory Medals.
8, Garfield Street, Bedford. X1968/A.

DEAR, J., Sergeant, Loyal North Lancashire Regt.
He was already serving in India at the outbreak of war in August 1914, and was sent to German East Africa, where he took part in heavy fighting. Later, in 1915, he was transferred to the Western Front, and played a prominent part in many important engagements, but was wounded in action at Armentières and invalided to England. After a period of hospital treatment he was discharged, and retained as a Drill Instructor at Felixstowe, where he did good work until demobilised in March. He holds the 1914–15 Star, and the General Service and Victory Medals. 13, Sapley Lane, Hartford. Z1972/A.

DEAR, W., Sapper, Royal Engineers.
He volunteered in September 1914, and after completing a period of training was drafted to the Dardanelles, where he was present during the Landing at Cape Helles, and at other important engagements. Owing to ill-health he was invalided from the Army in June 1916, and has since died of tuberculosis. He was entitled to the 1914–15 Star, and the General Service and Victory Medals.
"His memory is cherished with pride."
8, Garfield Street, Bedford. X1968/B.

DEARDS, R., Private, 10th Essex Regiment.
He joined in August 1916, and two months later landed in France. During his service in this seat of war he was in action in the Somme Offensive, and later at the Battle of Arras, where he was wounded in May 1917. As a result he was invalided to England, and, after a period of hospital treatment, was transferred to the Grenadier Guards and retained on light duties until demobilised in February 1919, holding the General Service and Victory Medals.
38, Marlborough Road, Bedford. Z1973.

DEAS, W. A. F., A.B., Royal Navy.
Joining in 1917, he was posted to H.M.S. "Powerful," and was in training at Devonport. Later he was transferred to H.M.S. "Gobien," in which ship he saw much service, and was chiefly engaged on important patrol duties in the North Sea. He did excellent work until the end of hostilities, and was demobilised in January 1919, holding the General Service and Victory Medals. 12, Clarence Road, Stony Stratford, Bucks. Z1974.

DE-LA-HAYE, H. W., Private, South Wales Borderers.
He volunteered in August 1914, and, on completion of his training, was retained on important transport duties until after the cessation of hostilities. He was not able to proceed to a theatre of war, but rendered valuable services until demobilised in October 1919.
43, Garfield Street, Bedford. Z1975.

DELL, J. L., Private, Oxford. and Bucks. L.I.
Joining in 1917, he proceeded in the following year to France and took part in the final operations of the war. He was in action duringthe Retreat and Advance of 1918, and was gassed. Later he served in Germany and was stationed near Cologne until January 1919, when he returned home for demobilisation, holding the General Service and Victory Medals. He later re-enlisted in the Army, and in 1920 was serving at Lichfield.
33, Brooklands Road, Bletchley, Bucks. Z3024.

DELLAR, R., Corporal, Royal Engineers.
He volunteered in November 1915, but was retained on important duties in England until February 1917, when he proceeded to France, where he did good work in various sectors of the front. He served at the Battles of Arras, Ypres and Cambrai, and, after the end of war, returned home and was demobilised in March 1919, holding the General Service and Victory Medals.
11, Bedesmans Place, Bedford. X1977.

DELLER, F., Private, Royal Warwickshire Regt.
He volunteered in October 1914, and after completing a period of training was drafted overseas. During his service on the Western Front he took part in much heavy fighting in various sectors. He was present at the Battles of Arras, Ypres, Cambrai and others of importance until the close of hostilities, and was wounded on one occasion. Returning home, he was demobilised in June 1917, and holds the General Service and Victory Medals.
Old Court Hall, London Street, Godmanchester. Z1976.

DENNIS, A. J., Private, Machine Gun Corps.
He volunteered in November 1915, and on conclusion of his training was in the same year drafted overseas. During his service on the Western Front he took part in much severe fighting in the Ypres, Arras and Somme sectors, and was unhappily killed in action at Montauban on July 9th, 1916. He was entitled to the 1914–15 Star, and the General Service and Victory Medals.
"His life for his Country."
Cardington, Bedford. Z1978.

DENNIS, F. R., Staff-Sergeant, Royal Engineers.
Volunteering in November 1914, he was engaged on important work at Norwich until January 1916, when he was drafted to Egypt. After serving at Kantara he proceeded to Palestine, where he took a prominent part in the Battles of Gaza and the capture of Jerusalem and Jaffa. On his return to England in June 1919 he was demobilised, and holds the General Service and Victory Medals.
Northwood End, Haynes, near Bedford. Z1979.

DENNIS, W., Private, R.A.S.C. (M.T.)
He joined in February 1916, and two months later he was sent to the Western Front, where he served for nearly two years. During that time he was engaged on important transport work, particularly in the Béthune sector, until wounded near Dunkirk in December 1917. He was invalided to England, and was retained on home service until demobilised in August 1919, holding the General Service and Victory Medals.
9, Bell Court, Bedford. X1980.

DENTON, A., Private, Bedfordshire Regiment.
When war was declared in August 1914, he volunteered, and after a period of training was engaged on important duties with his unit at Shoreham. After only four months' service in the Army he was discharged as medically unfit for further military duties in December 1914.
17, Short Street, Queen's Park, Bedford. Z1984.

DENTON, A., Sapper, Royal Engineers.
He joined in February 1916, and five months later proceeded to the Western Front. There he took part in many engagements of importance, and did good work with his Battery in the Battles of the Somme, Arras, Ypres and Cambrai. He remained in France until February 1919, when he was demobilised, holding the General Service and Victory Medals.
2, Castle Hill, Bedford. X1981/C.

DENTON, A. W. G., Rifleman, K.R.R.C.
In February 1916 he joined the Army, and shortly afterwards proceeded overseas. During his service on the Western Front he was in action in numerous important engagements, and fell fighting in the Battle of the Somme on July 23rd, 1916. He was entitled to the General Service and Victory Medals.
"A valiant Soldier, with undaunted heart he breasted life's last hill."
19, Wellington Street, Bedford. X1873/A.

DENTON, E. H. T., Private, 12th Royal Fusiliers.
He volunteered in November 1914, and in the following year was drafted to Gallipoli. On that front he was engaged in severe fighting and was wounded in action in August 1915. He was invalided home, and on his recovery was sent to France in the following year, but was at first reported missing at Ypres on July 31st, 1917, and subsequently presumed to have been killed on that date. He was entitled to the 1914–15 Star, and the General Service and Victory Medals.
"Whilst we remember, the sacrifice is not in vain."
12, College Street, Kempston, Beds. Z1982.

DENTON, F., Sapper, Royal Engineers.
Volunteering in October 1915, he was four months later ordered to France, where he performed excellent work building bridges on the Arras, Ypres and Cambrai fronts. After the cessation of hostilities he entered Germany with the Army of Occupation, and served at Cologne until demobilised in May 1919. He holds the General Service and Victory Medals.
2, Castle Hill, Bedford. X1981/A.

DENTON, G., Driver, Royal Engineers.
He volunteered in June 1915, and later in the same year was drafted to the Western Front, where he took part in the Battles of Ypres, the Somme, Arras and Cambrai. He also experienced fierce fighting in the Retreat of 1918, and in the final decisive engagements of the war. Demobilised in June 1919, he holds the 1914–15 Star, and the General Service and Victory Medals.
22, Canning Street, Bedford. X1983.

DENTON, H. R., Rifleman, 17th London Regiment (Rifles); and Private, 13th Yorkshire Regiment.
He volunteered in 1915, and was retained on home defence at Bow and Plymouth, at which stations he fulfilled the duties assigned to him in a very able manner. In 1918 he proved to be successful in his efforts to obtain a transfer overseas, and was drafted to Russia, where he rendered valuable services. Returning home in August 1919 he was demobilised, holding the General Service and Victory Medals.
Newtown, Kimbolton, Hunts. Z1985.

DENTON, J. F., Gunner, Royal Field Artillery.
Volunteering in October 1915, he served at Bedford and Felixstowe until 1916, when he was drafted to Mesopotamia. There he saw much severe fighting in many sectors of the front, and took an active part in the capture of Baghdad. In 1918 he was transferred to the Western Front, and served there until demobilised in May 1919. He holds the General Service and Victory Medals. 47, Garfield Street, Bedford. Z1986.

DENTON, S., Private, Royal Sussex Regiment and Bedfordshire Regiment.
He joined in July 1918, but was unable to procure a transfer to a theatre of war before the cessation of hostilities. In April 1919, however, he was drafted to Egypt, and subsequently to Palestine, where he rendered valuable services as a cook whilst stationed at Jerusalem. On returning to England in February 1920 he was demobilised.
27, Tavistock Place, Bedford. X1987.

DENTON, S. J., Private, 1st Hampshire Regiment.
He was mobilised in August 1914, and in the following year was sent to Salonika. There he took an active part in heavy fighting on the Struma and Vardar fronts, until transferred to the Western Front in 1916. After serving in various important engagements he was unhappily killed in action at Cambrai on March 28th, 1918. He was entitled to the 1914–15 Star, and the General Service and Victory Medals.
"Great deeds cannot die."
44, Little Butts Street, Bedford. X1988/A.

DENTON, W., Corporal, Bedfordshire Regiment.
He volunteered in November 1914, and after completing his training was in the following year drafted overseas. After serving in Egypt he proceeded to Palestine, where he saw heavy fighting in important engagements at Gaza, and was present at the capture of Jerusalem and Aleppo. He was demobilised on his return to England in February 1919, and holds the 1914–15 Star, and the General Service and Victory Medals. 44, Little Butts Street, Bedford. X1988/B.

DENTON, W., L/Corporal, Royal Engineers.
Volunteering in May 1915, he completed his training, and in January 1916 proceeded to Egypt. He was subsequently drafted to Palestine, and performed excellent work with his company on the railways there, and also in Syria. Whilst in the East he suffered from malaria, and on his return to England in July 1919 was demobilised, holding the General Service and Victory Medals. 12, Farrer St., Bedford. X1989.

DENTON, W., Sergeant, 1st Bedfordshire Regt.
A Reservist, he was called up at the outbreak of hostilities in August 1914 and at once ordered to France with the first Expeditionary Force. He took a conspicuous part in the Battle of Mons, and was wounded there and invalided to England. In 1916 he was drafted to India, where he was employed on important garrison duties at Delhi. Returning home in May 1919 he was discharged, and holds the Mons Star, and the General Service and Victory Medals.
The Woodlands, Harrowden, Beds. Z1990.

DEVEREUX, A., Private, Bedfordshire Regiment.
He joined in February 1916, and later in the same year was drafted overseas. During his service on the Western Front he was in action in the Battles of Loos, Albert, Vimy Ridge and the Somme, and was wounded at Arras. He was mentioned in Despatches for bravery in the Field, and was demobilised in September 1919, holding the General Service and Victory Medals. 5, Leys Cottages, Clapham, Bedford. Z1991/A.

DEVEREUX, P., Corporal, 2nd Bedfordshire Regt.
A month after the outbreak of war he volunteered, and in 1915 was sent to the Western Front. There he took part in many important engagements, including the Battles of Hill 60, the Somme, Arras and Cambrai, and was twice wounded in action. He remained in France until December 1919, when he was drafted to India, where in 1920 he was still serving. He holds the 1914–15 Star, and the General Service and Victory Medals. 5, Leys Cottages, Clapham, Bedford. Z1991/B.

DEVEREUX, W. F., Private, 11th (Prince of Wales' Own Royal) Hussars.
At the outbreak of hostilities in August 1914 he was serving in South Africa, but was immediately recalled and drafted to the Western Front two months later. After only a few weeks in the firing-line he fell fighting at La Bassée on October 31st, 1914. He was entitled to the 1914 Star, and the General Service and Victory Medals.
"A costly sacrifice upon the altar of freedom."
5, Leys Cottages, Clapham, Bedford. Z1991/C.

DEVERICK, F., Private, Queen's (Royal West Surrey Regiment).
He joined in February 1918, and on completion of a period of training was later in the same year drafted to the Western Front. In this theatre of war he saw much severe fighting in various sectors, and was in action at Albert and Mormal Forest. In November 1919 he was demobilised, holding the General Service and Victory Medals.
24, Eastville Road, Southend, Bedford. Z1992/A.

DEVERICK, W. G., L/Corporal, 5th Beds. Regt.
At the outbreak of war he was already serving, and proceeded to France with the first Expeditionary Force. He was wounded in the Retreat from Mons, and after fighting in the Battles of the Marne and La Bassée, was discharged in December 1914. In June 1915, however, he rejoined, and on being drafted to the Western Front, was in action in engagements at Loos, Albert, Vimy Ridge, the Somme, Arras and Cambrai. He was again wounded on two occasions, and was eventually discharged in January 1919, holding the Mons Star, and the General Service and Victory Medals.
24, Eastville Road, Southend, Bedford. Z1992/B.

DEVERILL, E. (Miss), Worker, Q.M.A.A.C.
She joined in August 1918, and throughout the period of her service was stationed at No. 2 School of Instruction, Bedford. There she was engaged on domestic duties, and carried out her work in a very capable manner until demobilised in October 1919. 44, Southville Road, Bedford. Z1993.

DEWEY, W., Private, 2nd Bedfordshire Regiment.
He volunteered in November 1914, and having completed a period of training at Felixstowe, was seven months later drafted to the Western Front. After only eight days' active service he was unfortunately killed in action in the La Bassée sector on June 16th, 1915. He was entitled to the 1914–15 Star, and the General Service and Victory Medals.
"The path of duty was the way to glory."
Church Street, Somersham, Hunts. Z1994.

DICKENS, A., Pte., Royal Inniskilling Fusiliers.
Mobilised in August 1914, he proceeded a month later to France, where he saw heavy fighting in the final stages of the Retreat from Mons. He also took an active part in the Battles of the Marne, the Aisne, La Bassée, Ypres, the Somme, Arras and Cambrai, and in the Retreat and Advance of 1918. In March 1919 he was discharged, and holds the Mons Star, and the General Service and Victory Medals.
Newton Longville, Bucks. Z1999/A.

DICKENS, C., Trooper, Royal Bucks. Hussars.
He volunteered in April 1915, and 11 months later was drafted overseas, and during his service on the Western Front was in action in engagements on the Somme, and at Albert, Péronne and Ypres. In November 1917 he was transferred to Italy, and took part in severe fighting on the Piave and Asiago fronts. He was demobilised in February 1919, and holds the General Service and Victory Medals.
Heath Road, Great Brickhill, Bletchley, Bucks. Z1997.

DICKENS, E. J., Gunner, R.G.A.
Joining in May 1916, he trained at Plymouth, and two months later was drafted to Egypt, and subsequently to Palestine. There he took part in the Battle of Gaza, and in February 1918 was transferred to France. On that front he was in action at the Somme, and in the Retreat and Advance of 1918, and on the close of hostilities entered Germany with the Army of Occupation. He was demobilised in November 1919, and holds the General Service and Victory Medals.
9, London End, Newton Longville, Bucks. Z1999/D.

DICKENS, E. W., Private, R.A.M.C.
He volunteered in December 1914, and in March of the following year was drafted to the Western Front, where he served for four years. During that time he did good work as a stretcher-bearer at a casualty clearing station and rendered valuable services in the hospitals at Etaples, Cherbourg and Cammes. In May 1919 he was demobilised, and holds the 1914–15 Star, and the General Service and Victory Medals.
7, New Fenlake, Bedford. TZ1995.

DICKENS, F., Private, 1st Oxford. and Bucks. L.I.
Volunteering in December 1914, he was, on conclusion of his training, drafted overseas in May 1915. Whilst on the Western Front he saw much severe fighting in the Battles of Ypres, Festubert, Loos and the Somme, and was unfortunately killed in action at Pozières on August 15th, 1916. He was entitled to the 1914–15 Star, and the General Service and Victory Medals.
"The path of duty was the way to glory."
7, Bedford Street, Wolverton, Bucks. Z2001.

DICKENS, F., Private, Machine Gun Corps.
He volunteered in August 1914, and in April of the following year was ordered to France. On that front he was engaged in fierce fighting in the Ypres and the Somme sectors, but was wounded in action at Cambrai in November 1917, and in consequence was discharged from the Army as medically unfit in June 1918, holding the 1914–15 Star, and the General Service and Victory Medals. Newton Longville, Bucks. Z1999/C.

DICKENS, S., L/Corporal, Machine Gun Corps.
Volunteering in August 1914, he trained at Southampton, and seven months later proceeded to the Western Front, where he took part in fierce fighting, principally in the Ypres sector. In 1916 he was transferred to India, and was engaged on important garrison duties there until after the close of hostilities. He was demobilised on his return to England in September 1919, and holds the 1914–15 Star, and the General Service and Victory Medals. Newton Longville, Bucks. Z1999/B.

DICKENS, T., Sergeant, R.A.S.C.
A month after the declaration of war in August 1914 he volunteered, and after a course of training at Aldershot was three months later sent to the Western Front. Throughout the period of his service he was engaged on important and responsible work at Dieppe, Rouen and Lyons, and fulfilled his duties with the greatest ability. Demobilised in January 1920, he holds the 1914 Star, and the General Service and Victory Medals. Lower Dean, near Kimbolton, Hunts. Z1996.

DICKENS, W. H., Private, 2nd Bedfordshire Regt.
When war was declared in August 1914 he volunteered, but was retained on important duties at home until July 1916, when he was sent to the Western Front. There he saw severe fighting in numerous engagements in the Arras, Ypres, St. Quentin and Cambrai sectors, until he contracted fever. On his discharge from hospital he served with the Military Police at Calais, and was eventually demobilised in May 1919, holding the General Service and Victory Medals.
Kimbolton, Hunts. Z2002.

DICKENS, W. J., Sapper, Royal Engineers.
He volunteered in May 1915, and later in the same year proceeded to the Western Front, and was stationed at Audrique. He rendered many valuable services in connection with the repair of railways, but after the close of hostilities, when on his way home to England for demobilisation, contracted influenza, and died in Belgium on March 2nd, 1919. He was entitled to the 1914–15 Star, and the General Service and Victory Medals.
"His memory is cherished with pride."
Great Brickhill, near Bletchley, Bucks. Z1998.

DICKENS, W. T., L/Corporal, 1st Rifle Brigade.
At the outbreak of hostilities he was mobilised and at once ordered to the Western Front, where he was in action during the Retreat from Mons. He also saw heavy fighting in the Battles of the Marne, the Aisne, La Bassée and Ypres, and was twice wounded—at Loos and also on the Somme. He was invalided home, and on leaving hospital served in England until discharged in March 1919. He holds the Mons Star, and the General Service and Victory Medals.
Great Brickhill, near Bletchley, Bucks. Z2000.

DICKS, T. G., Private, R.M.L.I.
He joined in May 1916, and served at Deal, Blandford and Aldershot, before being drafted overseas a year later. Whilst on the Western Front he took part in many important engagements, including those at Arras and Ypres. In September 1917 he was invalided to England suffering from trench fever, and on his discharge from hospital was demobilised in January 1919. He holds the General Service and Victory Medals.
89, Wolverton Road, Stony Stratford, Bucks. Z2003.

DIEMER, C., Private, Labour Corps.
He joined in January 1917, and after a period of training was employed on barges plying between London, Birmingham and Nottingham. Later he served in Ireland, where he was engaged on important guard duties. He was not successful in procuring a transfer overseas, but nevertheless rendered valuable services before being demobilised in November 1919.
9, St. John's Place, Bedford. X2005/B.

DIEMER, W., Corporal, 1st Bedfordshire Regt.
Volunteering in August 1914, he proceeded in the following year to France, where he was in action at Ypres, Vimy Ridge, Arras and Cambrai. In 1917 he was transferred to Italy, and after taking part in engagements on the Piave returned to the Western Front. He served there until April 1919, when he was demobilised, holding the 1914–15 Star, and the General Service and Victory Medals.
11, St. John's Place, Bedford. X2005/A.

DIGHTON, A. V., Private, Royal Berkshire Regt.
He volunteered in 1914, and whilst training at Sutton-on-Sea served with the Huntingdonshire Cyclist Corps. On being transferred to the Royal Berkshire Regiment, he was drafted to France, and was engaged in severe fighting at Ypres and on the Somme. He was severely wounded at Beaumont-Hamel, and in consequence was invalided out of the Army in 1917, holding the General Service and Victory Medals.
Rose Cottage, Godmanchester, Hunts. Z2008/D.

DIGHTON, E. W., Pte., Royal Warwickshire Regt.
Volunteering in 1914, he served at Filey and Scarborough before being drafted overseas in 1916. During his service on the Western Front he experienced fierce fighting in the Loos, Albert, Vimy Ridge, Somme, Messines, Ypres and Cambrai sectors, and took an active part in the final victorious engagements of the war. Demobilised in March 1919, he holds the General Service and Victory Medals.
Rose Cottage, Godmanchester, Hunts. Z2008/B.

DIGHTON, G. H., Private, Royal Warwickshire Regiment.
He volunteered in March 1915, and on conclusion of his training in the following year proceeded to the Western Front. In this theatre of war he served in many important engagements, including the Battles of the Somme, Arras, Ypres and Cambrai. He was transferred to Italy in 1917, and saw severe fighting on the Piave and Asiago fronts. Demobilised in 1919, he holds the General Service and Victory Medals.
Cambridge Street, Godmanchester, Hunts. Z2006.

DIGHTON, J. H., Private, Huntingdonshire Cyclist Battalion and 1st Bedfordshire Regiment.
Volunteering in 1914, he served at Sutton-on-Sea until 1916, when he was drafted to the Western Front, where he saw heavy fighting in various sectors. After taking part in engagements at Ypres and on the Somme, he was unfortunately killed in action at Vimy Ridge on April 23rd, 1917. He was entitled to the General Service and Victory Medals.
"Nobly striving:
He nobly fell that we might live."
Rose Cottage, Godmanchester, Hunts. Z2008/C.

DIGHTON, R., Private, 7th Bedfordshire Regt.
He volunteered in September 1915, and later in the same year proceeded to the Western Front. There he fought in engagements at Ypres, Arras and Cambrai, and unhappily fell in action at Albert on September 27th, 1916. He was entitled to the 1914–15 Star, and the General Service and Victory Medals.
"Honour to the immortal dead, who gave their youth that the world might grow old in peace."
Nether Dean, Kimbolton, Hunts. Z2007.

DIGHTON, W. T., Sergeant, Huntingdonshire Cyclist Battalion & 1st Bedfordshire Regiment.
Volunteering in December 1914, he was engaged on important duties at Sutton-on-Sea until 1916, when he was ordered to France. On this Front he took a prominent part in engagements at Ypres, the Somme and Cambrai, and fell fighting at Arras on June 27th, 1918. He was entitled to the General Service and Victory Medals.
"He passed out of the sight of men by the path of duty and self sacrifice."
Rose Cottage, Godmanchester, Hunts. Z2008/A.

DILLEY, A., Private, R.A.S.C.
He volunteered in October 1915, and in the following year was drafted to the Western Front, where he was engaged in fierce fighting in the Somme, Arras and Ypres sectors. In November 1917 he was transferred to Italy and saw service on the Piave and Asiago fronts. He remained in Italy until demobilised in July1 919, and holds the General Service and Victory Medals.
45, Woburn Road, Kempston, Bedford. X2009.

DILLINGHAM, G. W., Private, Bedfordshire Regt.
At the outbreak of hostilities he was serving in the Army, and accordingly at once proceeded to France, where he was in action in the Battles of Mons, Ypres, Hill 60, Vimy Ridge and the Somme. After taking part in fierce fighting at Cambrai he was reported wounded and missing on March 18th, 1918, and was subsequently assumed to have been killed on that date. He was entitled to the Mons Star, and the General Service and Victory Medals.
"He joined the great white company of valiant souls."
33a, Pilcroft Street, Bedford. X2011.

DILLINGHAM, W., L/Corporal, R.A.M.C.
He volunteered in November 1915, and, after completing a course of training, was in the following year drafted overseas. During his service on the Western Front he took an active part in severe fighting in important engagements on the Somme, and at Arras, Ypres, Cambrai, Givenchy and Amiens. He was demobilised in April 1919, and holds the General Service and Victory Medals.
47, Pembroke Street, Bedford. Z2010.

DIMMOCK, C. E., Pte., 7th Royal Warwick. Regt.
In March 1915 he volunteered, and six months later proceeded to France, where he was wounded in an engagement at Ypres. He was invalided home, and on his recovery returned to the Western Front, but after taking part in further heavy fighting was taken prisoner at Ypres in 1917. He was released from captivity in December 1918, and a month later was demobilised, holding the 1914–15 Star, and the General Service and Victory Medals. 2a, Mount Pleasant, Fenny Stratford, Bucks. Z1638 /A.

DIMMOCK, F. J., Private, R.A.V.C. and 8th West Yorkshire Regiment.
He volunteered in the Royal Army Veterinary Corps in 1915, but was later transferred to the Tank Corps, with which, in 1916 he proceeded to France, where he took part in the Battles of the Somme, Arras, Lens and Cambrai, and in an engagement at Loos. After the close of hostilities he proceeded to Germany with the Army of Occupation and served with the Military Police on the Rhine. Prior to his demobilisation in January 1919 he served with the 8th West Yorkshire Regiment for a short period in Germany. He holds the General Service and Victory Medals. Church Street, Sharnbrook, Beds. Z2012.

DIMMOCK, M., 1st Air Mechanic, R.A.F.
Joining in December 1917, he trained at Chingford, Norwich and Tregantle before proceeding in March 1918 to the Western Front. There he rendered valuable services in connection with the repair and construction of aircraft, and also did good work with his Squadron on one occasion in a bombing raid over Germany. He was demobilised in February 1919, and holds the General Service and Victory Medals.
16, Queen Anne Street, New Bradwell, Bucks. Z2091.

DIXON, A. C., L/Corporal, Royal Engineers.
When war was declared in August 1914 he volunteered, and later in the same year was sent to France, where he saw heavy fighting in various sectors of the front. In 1915 he was sent to Gallipoli, and served throughout the campaign there. After the Evacuation of the Peninsula he returned to the Western Front and took an active part in engagements at Loos, Ypres, Arras, Passchendaele, Cambrai and Lille. In 1920 he was still serving in the Army, and holds the 1914 Star, and the General Service and Victory Medals.
18a, New Fenlake, Bedford. Z2014 /C.

DIXON, J. H., Sergeant, 1/5th Bedfordshire Regt.
Already in the Army when war broke out in August 1914, he immediately proceeded to the Western Front. There he was in action in the Retreat from Mons, and took a prominent part in the Battles of the Marne, the Aisne, La Bassée, Ypres and the Somme. He was wounded in the last engagement and invalided to England, but on his recovery returned to France, where he fought in engagements at Cambrai and the Somme. He was discharged in March 1919, and holds the Mons Star, and the General Service and Victory Medals.
12, Water Eaton, near Bletchley, Bucks. Z2013.

DIXON, T. G. (D.C.M.), C.S.M., Royal Engineers.
When war was declared in August 1914 he was already serving, and was at once ordered to France. There he fought with distinction in the Battles of Mons, Ypres, Neuve Chapelle, Loos, Beaumont-Hamel, Arras and Cambrai, and played a conspicuous part in engagements at Lille and Armentières. He was awarded the Distinguished Conduct Medal for bravery in the Field, and also the Croix-de-Guerre. In 1920 he was still serving in the Army, and in addition holds the Mons Star, and the General Service and Victory Medals.
18a, New Fenlake, Bedford. Z2014 /B.

DIXON, W. A. (M.S.M.), Sergeant, R.E.
He volunteered in August 1914, and later in the same year was drafted overseas. During his service on the Western Front he took an active part in severe fighting at Ypres, Loos, Vimy Ridge, Arras, Passchendaele, Cambrai, Lille and Armentières, and was awarded the Meritorious Service Medal for his splendid work in the Field. In 1920 he was still serving in the Army, and also holds the 1914 Star, and the General Service and Victory Medals. 18a, New Fenlake, Bedford. Z2014 /A.

DOBNEY, A. F., L/Corporal, 3rd Beds. Regt.
Volunteering in September 1915, was found to be medically unfit for service overseas, and accordingly was unsuccessful in his efforts to procure a transfer to the war zone. However, he was engaged on important work with his unit, and rendered many valuable services before being invalided out of the Army in July 1917. He died from consumption on November 18th, 1917, at Eaton Ford.
"His memory is cherished with pride."
Eaton Ford, Beds. Z2015.

DOBNEY, G., Private, 4th Essex Regiment and Queen's (Royal West Surrey Regiment).
He joined the 4th Essex Regiment in June 1916, and on conclusion of his training was transferred to the Queen's Royal West Surrey Regiment, and drafted in 1917 to France. On that front he saw fierce fighting in various important engagements, particularly in the Ypres and Cambrai sectors. He served in France until February 1919, when he was demobilised, holding the General Service and Victory Medals.
Brook Street, St Neots, Hunts. Z2016.

DOBSON, C. A., Corporal, 11th Hampshire Regt.
At the outbreak of hostilities he was already serving, and proceeded to France with the First Expeditionary Force. He served in the Retreat from Mons, and saw heavy fighting in many other engagements, including the Battles of the Marne and Festubert. He was wounded at Havrincourt in 1918, and invalided to England, and in 1919 was discharged, holding the Mons Star, and the General Service and Victory Medals.
134, Honey Hill Road, Queen's Park, Bedford. Z2017 /A.

DOBSON, E. G., Private, East Kent Regiment.
He joined in January 1918, but owing to his youth was unable to procure a transfer to a theatre of war. During his period of service he was stationed at Crowborough, where he carried out the various duties assigned to him with the greatest ability. He was demobilised in November 1919.
134, Honey Hill Road, Queen's Park, Bedford. Z2017 /B.

DOBY, H. A., Private, 3rd Bedfordshire Regiment.
He joined in August 1916, and underwent a period of training prior to his being drafted to France. There he took part in much heavy fighting in the Battles of the Somme and Cambrai, and was wounded in action in the Hill 60 sector. He was demobilised in January 1919, and holds the General Service and Victory Medals.
11, Greenhill Street, Bedford. X2018 /A.

DOGGETT, G. W., Pte., Royal Warwickshire Regt.
Joining in 1916, he was drafted overseas in the following year. During his service on the Western Front he took part in many important engagements, including those at Arras, Ypres, Cambrai, and the Somme (II.), but contracted typhoid fever and was invalided to hospital in Rouen. He was demobilised in March 1919, and holds the General Service and Victory Medals. Earith, Hunts. Z2019.

DOLTON, E. A., Sapper, Royal Engineers; and Private, Labour Corps.
He volunteered in September 1915, and two months later proceeded to France. Whilst in this theatre of war he took part in many important engagements at Loos, the Somme, Ypres, Albert and in the Advance of 1918, and was gassed in action. As a result he was invalided home, and on his recovery transferred to the Labour Corps, with which unit he served until his demobilisation in April 1919. He holds the 1914–15 Star, and the General Service and Victory Medals.
Brickyard Cottage, Woburn Sands, Beds. Z2020 /A.

DONEGAN, A. J., A.B., Royal Navy.
He joined in August 1918, and after a short period of training was sent to Russia on board H.M.S. "Dunedin." He took part in some heavy bombardments in the Baltic, and was later sent to Ireland to convey Sinn Fein prisoners to England. In 1920 he was still at sea.
2, Station Road, Oakley, Bedford. TZ2021.

DORMER, A., Private, Oxford. and Bucks. L.I.
He volunteered in September 1915, and in the following January was drafted to Egypt, where he took part in the Advance into Palestine, and saw fighting at Gaza, Jerusalem and on the River Jordan, and was wounded. As a result he was invalided to Alexandria, and on his recovery embarked for France. During the voyage his ship was torpedoed, but fortunately he was taken aboard a passing vessel and conveyed to France. There he was again in action and wounded in October 1918. He was demobilised in March 1919, and holds the General Service and Victory Medals.
3, Bath Lane, Buckingham, Bucks. Z2082 /A.

DORRILL, A. R. (M.M.), Corporal, Oxfordshire and Buckinghamshire Light Infantry.
He volunteered in September 1914, and in the following year proceeded to France. After taking part in the fighting in the Somme sector, he was sent to Salonika, and whilst there fought on the Vardar and Doiran fronts, and was wounded. For conspicuous bravery in the former he was awarded the Greek Military Cross (3rd class), and for further gallantry on Lake Doiran the Military Medal. He also holds the 1914–15 Star, and the General Service and Victory Medals, and was demobilised in March 1919 after his return home.
Lathbury, Newport Pagnell, Bucks. Z2022 /A.

DORRILL, W., Private, R.A.V.C.
He volunteered in November 1915, and after a period of training was engaged at various stations on important duties attending sick horses. He was unable to obtain a transfer overseas owing to the important nature of his work, but rendered valuable services until his demobilisation in December 1918.
Lathbury, near Newport Pagnell, Bucks. Z2022 /B.

DORRINGTON, W., Sergeant, Labour Corps.
He volunteered in June 1915 in the Bedfordshire Regiment, and was engaged at various stations on important duties with his unit. He was later transferred to the Middlesex Regiment and afterwards to the Labour Corps, quickly gained promotion, and rendered valuable services throughout hostilities. He was medically unfit to obtain a transfer overseas and was demobilised in March 1919.
Croft Lane, Brampton, Hunts. Z2023.

DOUGHTY, W., Private, Queen's (Royal West Surrey Regiment).
He joined in July 1916, and later in the same year was drafted to France, where he took part in much heavy fighting in the Vimy Ridge and Albert sectors. He was unfortunately killed in action near Albert on March 9th, 1917, and was entitled to the General Service and Victory Medals.
"Thinking that remembrance, though unspoken, may reach him where he sleeps."
24, Muswell Road, Bedford. Z2024.

DOVE, N., Signalman, Royal Navy.
He was already in the Navy when war broke out in August 1914, and quickly proceeded to sea on board H.M.S. "Australia." He was engaged on important duties in the North Sea, and did continuously good work throughout hostilities. In 1920 he was still at sea, and holds the 1914–15 Star, and the General Service and Victory Medals.
63, Wellington Street, Bedford. X2025/A.

DOVE, W., Private, K.O. (Y.L.I.)
He enlisted in August 1916, and was shortly afterwards sent to Ireland, where he was engaged on important duties. He was not successful in obtaining a transfer to a theatre of war, but rendered valuable services until his demobilisation in March 1919. 63, Wellington Street, Bedford. X2025/B.

DOWLER, E., A.B., Royal Navy.
He joined in August 1917, and after a short period of training proceeded to the North Sea on board H.M.S. "Torch." He was engaged on patrol duties and did consistently good work for over two years. In 1920 he was serving in the Black Sea, and holds the General Service and Victory Medals.
Biddenham, Beds. Z2026/A.

DOWLER, R. W., Pte., Q.O. (R. West Kent Regt.)
He volunteered in September 1914, and on completing his training in the following year was drafted to Salonika. There he took part in many engagements on the Vardar, Doiran and Struma fronts, and at the capture of Monastir. He was badly wounded, lost his right arm and his right eye, and was consequently invalided home. He was finally discharged in December 1916, and holds the 1914–15 Star, and the General Service and Victory Medals.
Biddenham, Beds. Z2026/B.

DOWN, F., A.B., Royal Navy.
He was already in the Navy when war broke out in August 1914, and quickly proceeded to sea on board H.M.S. "Vanguard." He took part in the Battles of Heligoland Bight and Jutland, and was also engaged on important duties in the North Sea. He unfortunately lost his life when the "Vanguard" was blown up at Scapa Flow on July 9th, 1917. He was entitled to the 1914–15 Star, and the General Service and Victory Medals.
"Whilst we remember, the sacrifice is not in vain."
East Chadley Lane, Godmanchester, Hunts. Z2027/A.

DOWN, H., A.B., Royal Navy.
He was already in the Navy when war broke out in August 1914, and quickly proceeded to sea on board H.M. Submarine "L.18." He was engaged on important duties as a helmsman, and took part in the Landing at the Dardanelles and in the Battle of Jutland. He did continuously good work throughout hostilities, and in 1920 was still at sea. He holds the 1914–15 Star, and the General Service and Victory Medals.
East Chadley Lane, Godmanchester, Hunts. Z2027/B.

DRACUP, A. F., Sergeant, 1/5th Bedfordshire Regt.
He volunteered in August 1914, and in the following year was drafted to the Dardanelles, where he played a distinguished part in much heavy fighting. He made the supreme sacrifice, being killed in action at Suvla Bay on August 15th, 1915. He was entitled to the 1914–15 Star, and the General Service and Victory Medals.
"A costly sacrifice upon the altar of freedom."
138, Honey Hill Road, Queen's Park, Bedford. Z2028.

DRAGE, G., Private, Duke of Cornwall's Light Infantry.
He joined in July 1918 on attaining military age, and after a short period of training proceeded to Ireland, where he was engaged on important duties with his unit. He rendered valuable services until his demobilisation in November 1919.
Northampton Road, Lavendon, Bucks. Z2029/B.

DRAGE, H., Private, Royal Army Medical Corps.
He volunteered in April 1915, and was quickly drafted to the Western Front. There he acted as a stretcher-bearer and took part in many important engagements, including those at Ypres, the Somme and Bullecourt, and was wounded in action. Later he saw much service in Italy employed in the hospitals until hostilities ceased. He was demobilised in April 1919, and holds the 1914–15 Star, and the General Service and Victory Medals.
Green's Norton, Towcester, Northants. Z3025/A.

DRAGE, T. W., L/Cpl., 6th London Regt. (Rifles).
He joined in April 1916, and later in the same year was drafted to France. In this theatre of war he took part in many engagements, including the Battles of the Somme, Arras and Cambrai, and was wounded in action. As a result he was invalided to Boulogne, but on his recovery returned to his unit and fought in the Retreat and Advance of 1918. He was demobilised in March 1919, and holds the 1914–15 Star, and the General Service and Victory Medals.
Northampton Road, Lavendon, Bucks. Z2029/A.

DRAPER, F., Private, Labour Corps.
He joined in June 1916, and after completing his training was engaged at various stations on important duties with his unit. He was unable to obtain a transfer overseas owing to his being medically unfit, but rendered valuable services until his demobilisation in June 1919.
64, Bridge Street, New Bradwell, Bucks. Z2030.

DRAPER, H. C., 2nd Corporal, Royal Engineers.
He joined in August 1916, and in the following month was drafted overseas. During his service in France he was stationed at Boulogne, and did continuously good work repairing waggons and engaged on other important duties until the cessation of hostilities. He was demobilised in March 1919, and holds the General Service and Victory Medals.
Post Office, Great Linford, Bucks. Z2031/B.

DRAPER, R. J., Air Mechanic, Royal Air Force.
He joined in February 1918, on attaining military age, and underwent a period of training prior to his being engaged at various stations on important duties. In April 1919 he proceeded to Germany with the Army of Occupation, and served on the Rhine attached to No. 12 Squadron until his demobilisation in January 1920.
Post Office, Great Linford, Bucks. Z2031/A.

DRING, H., Private, Bedfordshire Regiment.
Volunteering in 1915, he was drafted overseas in the following year, and whilst on the Western Front took part in many engagements, including those at Arras, Amiens and on the Somme, and was gassed in action. He was in hospital for some time, and was later demobilised in March 1919, holding the General Service and Victory Medals.
Prospect Place, St. Ives, Hunts. Z2032.

DRING, J., Sergeant, 7th Bedfordshire Regiment.
Mobilised in August 1914, he was immediately drafted to the Western Front, where, after taking part in the Retreat from Mons, he fought with distinction in the Battles of Ypres and many other important engagements, and was twice wounded in action. He fell fighting on April 4th, 1918, in the Cambrai sector. He was entitled to the Mons Star, and the General Service and Victory Medals.
"His life for his Country, his soul to God."
3, Castle Hill Cottages, Bedford. X2033.

DUDLEY, A., Private, 1st Bedfordshire Regiment.
Volunteering in September 1914, he proceeded to the Western Front on completing his training in the following year, and there took part in the Battles of Festubert, Loos and Arras and other engagements, and was wounded on the Somme in 1916. He was killed in action at Vimy Ridge on April 23rd, 1917. He was entitled to the 1914–15 Star, and the General Service and Victory Medals.
"The path of duty was the way to glory."
Biddenham, Beds. Z2034/A.

DUDLEY, A., Corporal, Lincolnshire Regiment.
Shortly after volunteering in April 1915 he was drafted to Gallipoli, where he saw much severe fighting at Suvla Bay and Anzac. Invalided home in 1915, he was afterwards retained in England until March 1918, when he proceeded to the Western Front, and was there wounded in action at Cambrai during the Advance. Demobilised in February 1919, he holds the 1914–15 Star, and the General Service and Victory Medals.
Biddenham, Beds. Z2034/B.

DUDLEY, F. W., Sergeant, Bedfordshire Regiment.
He volunteered in September 1914, and in the following year was drafted to the Dardanelles, where he saw much severe fighting and contracted dysentery. He was afterwards transferred to the Western Front, where he was unfortunately killed in action on April 25th, 1917. He was entitled to the 1914–15 Star, and the General Service and Victory Medals.
"Great deeds cannot die:
They with the sun and moon renew their light for ever."
Marston, Beds. Z2035.

DUDLEY, H. J., Private, Bedfordshire Regiment.
He volunteered in 1915, and, in the following year was drafted to the Western Front, where he saw severe fighting in various sectors. He took part in the Battles of the Somme, Arras and Cambrai, and many minor engagements, and was gassed and wounded in action at Ypres. He was finally demobilised in March 1919, and holds the General Service and Victory Medals.
Marston, Beds. Z2036.

DUNBAR, R. J., Private, 1st Norfolk Regiment.
He joined in June 1918, and, after a short period of training, was drafted to the Western Front, where he was stationed at Calais, Le Havre and various other stations until after the cessation of hostilities. He was then sent with the Army of Occupation into Germany, finally returning home for demobilisation in June 1920. He holds the General Service and Victory Medals. 91, Priory Street, Bedford. X2037.

DUNCOMBE, F. J., Sapper, R.E. (R.O.D.)
Two months after joining in June 1917, he proceeded to Egypt, where he was engaged on important duties on the railways at various stations. Proceeding later into Palestine, he took an active part in the Battles of Gaza and other engagements, and was also present at the capture of Jerusalem. He was demobilised on his return home in March 1919, and holds the General Service and Victory Medals.
Drayton Parslow, Bucks. Z2038/A.

DUNHAM, A. J., L/Cpl., 11th Royal Sussex Regt.
He joined in August 1916, and, in September of the following year, was drafted to the Western Front, where he served through the Battles of Passchendaele, Lens, Cambrai and the Somme, and many minor engagements. He died gloriously on the Field of Battle on March 22nd, 1918, during the Retreat. He was entitled to the General Service and Victory Medals.
"A costly sacrifice upon the altar of freedom."
56, York Street, Bedford. Z2041.

DUNHAM, D., Sapper, Royal Engineers.
Shortly after volunteering in 1915, he proceeded to France, where he saw severe fighting in various sectors of the front. He took part in the Battles of Ypres, Loos, Arras, Cambrai and Lille, and many other important engagements in this theatre of war, and was gassed and wounded in action. He was demobilised in October 1919, and holds the 1914–15 Star, and the General Service and Victory Medals.
12, Pembroke Street, Bedford. Z2039.

DUNHAM, M. C. W., Sapper, Royal Engineers.
He volunteered at the outbreak of war in August 1914, and, on completing his training in the following year, proceeded to the Western Front. After taking part in the Battles of Ypres, Festubert and Loos, and many other important engagements in this theatre of war, he was severely gassed and sent home. He was invalided from the Army in March 1916, and holds the 1914–15 Star, and the General Service and Victory Medals.
3, Rope Walk, Bedford. X2040.

DUNHAM, W. C., Private, Royal Fusiliers.
He volunteered in February 1915, and, on completion of a period of training later in that year, was drafted to the Western Front. Whilst in this theatre of war he took part in many important engagements, including the Battles of Neuve Chapelle, Loos, Cambrai and Lille, and was twice wounded in action—on the Ancre and on the Somme in August 1916. Demobilised in January 1919, he holds the 1914–15 Star, and the General Service and Victory Medals.
4, Firbank Road, Bedford. Z2042.

DUNKLEY, A. E. (Mrs.), Special War Worker.
For over three years of the war this lady was engaged as a porter on the Midland Railway, thereby releasing a man for service with the Colours. She did much useful work during the period of hostilities, and her services were highly valued by the Company.
Ellington, Hunts. Z2043/A.

DUNKLEY, C. E., Private, Royal Berkshire Regt.
He joined in August 1916, and was retained on important duties at various stations in England until October of the following year, when he was drafted to the Western Front. There, after much severe fighting at Lens, he fell in action at Cambrai on November 6th, 1917, not four weeks after landing in France. He was entitled to the General Service and Victory Medals.
"His memory is cherished with pride."
23, Mitre Street, Buckingham. Z2081/B.

DUNKLEY, E., Gunner, Royal Field Artillery.
Volunteering in September 1914, he proceeded to Gallipoli in August of the following year and there saw much severe fighting, especially at Suvla Bay. On the Evacuation of the Peninsula he was transferred to the Western Front, where he was again in action at Loos and on the Somme. He fell fighting on December 24th, 1916. He was entitled to the 1914–15 Star, and the General Service and Victory Medals.
"Whilst we remember, the sacrifice is not in vain."
23, Mitre Street, Buckingham. Z2081/C

DUNKLEY, F. C., Air Mechanic, Royal Air Force.
He joined immediately on attaining military age in September 1918, and, after undergoing a period of training, served at various stations, where he was engaged on duties of a highly technical nature. Owing to the early cessation of hostilities he was unable to obtain his transfer overseas, but, nevertheless, rendered valuable services with his Squadron until November 1919, when he was demobilised.
Great Linford, Bucks. Z2044/A.

DUNKLEY, G., Private, Royal Sussex Regiment.
Joining in June 1916, he proceeded to the Western Front in January of the following year and there saw much severe fighting. He took part in the Battles of Arras, Ypres and Cambrai, and many other important engagements until the cessation of hostilities, and was wounded in action on the Somme in March 1918. Demobilised in February 1919, he holds the General Service and Victory Medals.
Doves Lane, Moulton, Northants. Z3027.

DUNKLEY, G., Pte., Royal Warwickshire Regt.
A Reservist, he was called to the Colours in August 1914, and was immediately drafted to the Western Front, where, after fighting at Mons, he took part in the Battle of Ypres and other engagements. In August 1915 he was transferred to Gallipoli, and there took part in the Landing at Suvla Bay, afterwards being sent to Egypt. He was three times wounded in action whilst overseas, and was finally discharged on his return home in March 1919. He holds the Mons Star, and the General Service and Victory Medals.
23, Mitre Street, Buckingham. Z2081/A.

DUNKLEY, G., Private, R.A.S.C.
Joining in April 1917, he was drafted to the Western Front in the following month, and was there engaged on important transport duties. Serving chiefly at Calais and Boulogne, he rendered very valuable services whilst overseas, and finally returned home in October 1919 for demobilisation in the following month. He holds the General Service and Victory Medals. 19, Moreton Road, Buckingham. Z2085.

DUNKLEY, H. T. W., Air Mechanic, R.A.F.
He joined in January 1918, immediately on attaining military age, and, after completing a term of training, was retained at various stations, where he was engaged on duties which required a high degree of technical skill. He was unable to obtain his transfer overseas, but, nevertheless, did much useful work with his Squadron until his demobilisation in April 1919.
Great Linford, Bucks. Z2044/B.

DUNKLEY, J., Driver, Royal Field Artillery.
He volunteered in January 1916, and was engaged on important transport duties in Ireland until drafted to the Western Front in the following year. There he served in various sectors, and, engaged in conveying ammunition to the lines, was present at many engagements until the cessation of hostilities. He was demobilised in May 1919, and holds the General Service and Victory Medals.
Ellington, Hunts. Z2043/B.

DUNKLEY, J. G., L/Corporal, 1/1st Oxfordshire and Buckinghamshire Light Infantry (T.F.)
Volunteering in August 1914, he was drafted to the Western Front in March of the following year and there took part in the Battles of Neuve Chapelle, Ypres and Loos and other engagements, and was wounded on the Somme in August 1916. He fell fighting near Arras on March 10th, 1917, and was buried at Hem. He was entitled to the 1914–15 Star, and the General Service and Victory Medals.
"A valiant Soldier, with undaunted heart he breasted life's last hill."
25, High Street, Buckingham. Z2083/A.

DUNKLEY, J. W., Pte., 5th Oxford. & Bucks. L.I.
He volunteered in April 1915, and, after his training, was retained on important guard duties at Great Linford. Owing to his being over age, he was unsuccessful in obtaining his transfer to a theatre of war, but did much excellent work with his unit until his demobilisation in March 1919.
Great Linford, Bucks. Z2044/C.

DUNKLEY, L., Pte., 1/1st Ox. & Bucks. L.I. (T.F.)
He volunteered in September 1914, and five months later was drafted to the Western Front, where he played a prominent part in much severe fighting. He was in action at the Battle of Ypres (II.), and was seriously wounded in August 1916 during the Somme Offensive. As a result, he unfortunately had his right foot amputated, and, after hospital treatment at Netley, was invalided from the Service in April 1917, holding the 1914–15 Star, and the General Service and Victory Medals.
11, North End Square, Buckingham. Z2084/B.

DUNKLEY, L. (Mrs), Worker, Women's Land Army.
This lady offered her services in May 1918, and was engaged on important agricultural work in Buckinghamshire for nine months. During this time she carried out her arduous duties in a very capable manner and rendered valuable services to her Country. She was demobilised in January 1919.
11, North End Square, Buckingham. Z2084/A.

DUNKLEY, S., Pte., Duke of Cornwall's L.I.
Joining in March 1916, he was drafted to France in July and played a prominent part in the Battles of the Somme, Arras, Ypres and Passchendaele. After the Battle of Cambrai (I.) he was reported missing and is now presumed to have been killed in action on November 6th, 1917. He was entitled to the General Service and Victory Medals.
"A costly sacrifice upon the altar of freedom."
Maids Moreton, Bucks. Z3177/A.

DUNKLEY, W. T., Pte., 1st Cambridgeshire Regt.
He volunteered in September 1914, and five months later proceeded to the Western Front, but was badly wounded in action at the Battle of Neuve Chapelle in March 1915, a few weeks after landing in France. He was invalided home, and, after hospital treatment at Leamington, was discharged as medically unfit for further service in May 1916. He holds the 1914–15 Star, and the General Service and Victory Medals.
Islington Row, Towcester, Northants. Z3026.

DUNKLEY, W. T., Private, Oxford. & Bucks. L.I.
He joined in November 1916, but whilst in training met with a serious accident to his knee, and was therefore retained on important duties in the South West of England. Unfortunately his injury was aggravated by his service, and, after doing consistently good work, he was discharged as medically unfit in May 1918. 3, Bath Lane, Buckingham. Z2082/B.

DUNKLING, A. (sen.), Private, Labour Corps.
He volunteered in September 1915, and was quickly drafted to the Western Front, where he rendered valuable services whilst engaged on important pioneer duties in the Arras and Ypres sectors. He was invalided to hospital owing to a breakdown in health, and was discharged as medically unfit in July 1917, holding the 1914–15 Star, and the General Service and Victory Medals. 6, Oakland Terrace, St. Ives, Hunts. Z2045/B.

DUNKLING, A. (jun.), Pte., Army Cyclist Corps.
He volunteered in the Huntingdonshire Cyclist Corps shortly after the outbreak of hostilities, and was drafted to France in 1916. Whilst in this theatre of war he played a prominent part in the Battles of the Somme, Arras, Ypres and Cambrai, and was badly gassed in March 1918. He was recommended for the Military Medal, but his Commanding Officer was unfortunately killed in action before the recommendation could go through. He holds the General Service and Victory Medals, and was demobilised in February 1919.
6, Oaklands Terrace, St. Ives, Hunts. Z2045/A.

DUNKLING, F. A., Private, 2nd Beds. Regiment.
Volunteering in January 1915, he was drafted to France in August, and took part in much severe fighting, particularly at the Battle of Loos and on Vimy Ridge. He laid down his life for the freedom of England on October 13th, 1916, being killed in action during the Battle of the Somme. He was entitled to the 1914–15 Star, and the General Service and Victory Medals.
"His memory is cherished with pride."
"The Waits," St. Ives, Hunts. Z2046.

DURHAM, A. (M.M.), Pte., 1st Bedfordshire Regt.
Already in the Army when war was declared, he proceeded to France in August 1914, and was in action throughout the Retreat from Mons. He took part in the Battles of the Marne, Ypres, Hill 60, Festubert and the Somme, where he was wounded in 1916. He was awarded the Military Medal for conspicuous braveryand devotion to duty in the Field,and,also holding the Mons Star and the General Service and Victory Medals, was discharged in January 1919.
7, Russell Street. St. Neots, Hunts. Z2048/A.

DURHAM, H. A., Private, 4th Bedfordshire Regt.
Mobilised in August 1914, he was sent to France with the 1st Expeditionary Force, and was in action during the Retreat from Mons. He later took part in the Battles of the Marne, Festubert and the Somme, and was wounded and gassed in action. Receiving his discharge in February 1919, he holds the Mons Star, and the General Service and Victory Medals.
7, Russell Street, St. Neots, Hunts. Z2048/A.

DURHAM, W. F., Bandsman, Royal Scots Fusiliers.
Already serving in August 1914, he was sent to Egypt early in the following year, but, whilst on the voyage out, his ship was torpedoed. Fortunately he was rescued, and, proceeding to the East, took part in the Advance into Palestine, and was present at the Battles of Gaza and at the capture of Jerusalem and Jaffa. He was admitted to hospital at Cairo suffering from malarial fever and dysentery, but, on his recovery, was transferred to the Western Front and was badly wounded in action at Cambrai in June 1918. He was invalided home, and, after hospital treatment at Gosport, was discharged as medically unfit in January 1919, holding the 1914–15 Star, and the General Service and Victory Medals.
The Old Schoolyard, Luke Street, Eynesbury, St. Neots, Hunts. Z2047.

DYNES, W. J., Private, R.A.S.C. (M.T.)
He joined in May 1916, and three months later was drafted to the Western Front, where he was engaged as a driver with the Mobile Repair Unit in the Somme, Ypres, Arras, Loos, Lens, and Festubert sectors. He did consistently good work, and, after the cessation of hostilities, served in Germany for a time with the Army of Occupation. He was demobilised in 1919, and holds the General Service and Victory Medals.
32, Bunyan Road, South End, Bedford. TZ2049.

DYTHAM, L. T., Bandsman, Royal Horse Guards.
He joined in May 1916, and 12 months later was drafted to the Western Front, where he served as a trumpeter and took part in the Battles of Ypres and Cambrai. He was invalided home with trench fever, but, after nine months in hospital, returned to France, and, at the cessation of hostilities, proceeded to Cologne with the Army of Occupation. In 1920 he was still serving, and holds the General Service and Victory Medals.
64, Queen Anne Street, New Bradwell, Bucks. Z2050.

E

EAGLES, R. E., Private, 8th Middlesex Regiment.
He was called up from the Reserve in August 1914 and quickly drafted to France, where he took part in the Retreat from Mons and the Battles of Ypres and Givenchy. He died gloriously on the Field of Battle at Hill 60 on April 30th, 1915, and was entitled to the Mons Star, and the General Service and Victory Medals.
"Great deeds cannot die.:
They with the sun and moon renew their light for ever."
9, Farrar Street, Kempston, Bedford. X2051.

EALES, C., Private, 1st Somerset Light Infantry.
He joined in May 1918, and in the following August was drafted to France, where he took part in much heavy fighting at Amiens, Mormal Forest and Le Cateau (II.). After hostilities ceased he proceeded to Egypt and served there on important duties until his demobilisation in April 1920. He holds the General Service and Victory Medals.
Weston Underwood, near Olney, Bucks. Z2052.

EAMES, F. C., L/Corporal, Royal Field Artillery.
He volunteered in 1915, and underwent a period of training prior to his being drafted to France. There he took part in many engagements, including the Battles of the Somme, Vimy Ridge, Messines, Passchendaele and Cambrai. He was demobilised in 1919, and holds the General Service and Victory Medals. Warboys, Hunts. Z2053.

EAMES, H., Private, 4th Suffolk Regiment.
He joined in September 1916, and after completing his training in the following year proceeded to France. In this theatre of war he was employed on various important duties, and saw much heavy fighting in the Ypres sector. He was demobilised in September 1919, and holds the General Service and Victory Medals. 25, Duncombe Street, Bletchley, Bucks. Z3029.

EAMES, R. J., Sapper, Royal Engineers.
Joining in March 1916, he was drafted overseas in the following July. Whilst on the Western Front he was engaged on many important duties and saw much heavy fighting on the Somme, at Arras, Ypres, Cambrai, and in the Retreat and Advance of 1918. He was demobilised in October 1919, and holds the General Service and Victory Medals
15, Simpson Road, Bletchley, Bucks. Z3028.

EARL, A. W., Private, 13th Middlesex Regiment.
He volunteered in February 1915, and in the following month proceeded to France, where he took part in many engagements, including the Battles of Ypres, the Somme and Cambrai. Wounded on the Somme in April 1918, he was taken prisoner and held in captivity in Germany until after the Armistice. He was then repatriated, returned home and was demobilised in April 1919, holding the 1914–15 Star, and the General Service and Victory Medals.
Chater Street, Moulton, Northants. Z3031.

EARL, D. J., Gunner, Royal Field Artillery.
He volunteered in June 1915, and later in the same year was drafted to France. In this theatre of war he was engaged on many important duties and took part in much heavy fighting, particularly in the Retreat and Advance of 1918. After hostilities ceased he served with the Army of Occupation on the Rhine. He was demobilised in October 1919, and holds the General Service and Victory Medals.
12, Church Passage, Newport Pagnell, Bucks. Z2054/A.

EARL, T. F., Private, R.A.O.C.
He volunteered in August 1914, and in the following month was drafted to France. There he was stationed at Rouen and Calais, and, whilst engaged on important duties in the Stores Department, rendered valuable services throughout hostilities. After the Armistice he went to Germany with the Army of Occupation, and served there until his demobilisation in March 1919. He holds the 1914 Star, and the General Service and Victory Medals.
12, Church Passage, Newport Pagnell, Bucks. Z2054/B.

EARL, W., Corporal, Royal Berkshire Regiment.
He volunteered in December 1914, and in the following year was drafted to France, where he took part in many engagements on the Ypres front. He was reported missing, and is now believed to have been killed in action on October 13th, 1915. He was entitled to the 1914–15 Star, and the General Service and Victory Medals.
"The path of duty was the way to glory."
12, Church Passage, Newport Pagnell, Bucks. Z2054 /C.

EARLE, J. T., Pte., Hunts. Cyclists; A.B., R.N.V.R.
He volunteered in December 1914, and after a period of training proceeded to France, where he saw much heavy fighting in many engagements, including the Battle of Cambrai, and was wounded in action. As a result he was invalided home and later demobilised in March 1919, holding the General Service and Victory Medals.
Silver Street, Buckden, Hunts. Z2055.

EAST, F., Private, 1st Leicestershire Regiment.
He was mobilised in August 1914, and quickly proceeded to France, where he took part in the Battles of La Bassée, Loos, the Somme, Ypres, St. Quentin, and was wounded slightly in September 1915. He was awarded the Croix-de-Guerre for conspicuous bravery in the Field. He died gloriously on the Field of Battle near Cambrai on October 17th, 1918, and was also entitled to the 1914 Star, and the General Service and Victory Medals.
"His life for his Country, his soul to God."
East End Cottages, Goldington, Bedford. Z2056.

EASTWELL, A. F., Sapper, Royal Engineers.
He volunteered in September 1914, and was shortly afterwards drafted to France, where he was engaged on important bridge-building and mining duties, and served in the Ypres, Arras, the Somme and Cambrai sectors. He did continuously good work, and was demobilised in April 1919. He holds the 1914–15 Star, and the General Service and Victory Medals.
10, College Street, Kempston, Bedford. Z2057.

EATON, A. (Miss), Special War Worker.
During the war she worked for the Navy and Army Canteen Board at Bedford Park and Harries Park. She rendered valuable services whilst carrying out her work in a highly commendable way, and relinquished her duties in June 1919.
38, Pilcroft Street, Bedford. X2060 /A.

EATON, C., Private, 1st Bedfordshire Regiment.
He joined in April 1916, and later in the same year proceeded to France, where he took part in much severe fighting on the Somme and at Arras and Vimy Ridge. He was severely wounded in action, and unfortunately died of his wounds at the 22nd Casualty Clearing Station on May 2nd, 1917. He was entitled to the General Service and Victory Medals.
"He died the noblest death a man may die:
Fighting for God and right and liberty."
St. Neots Road, Sandy, Beds. Z2061 /C.

EATON, F. W., Corporal, Royal Engineers.
He volunteered in November 1915, and in the following June was drafted to France, where he was engaged on important wiring and pontoon bridge-building in the Somme, Arras and Ypres sectors, and was gassed in action. In consequence he was invalided home, and, on his recovery, served as a gymnastic Instructor for a short time. Later he proceeded to Egypt, and also saw much service in Palestine and Syria until his demobilisation in August 1919. He holds the General Service and Victory Medals.
4, Queen Street, Stony Stratford, Bucks. Z2058.

EATON, H., Private, R.A.O.C.
He joined in September 1918 on attaining military age, and after a period of training proceeded to France, where he was engaged on various important duties. After hostilities ceased he went to Germany with the Army of Occupation and served there until his demobilisation in April 1920. He holds the General Service and Victory Medals.
38, Pilcroft Street, Bedford. X2060 /B.

EATON, H. J., Private, R.M.L.I.
He joined in March 1918, and proceeded to Deal for his training, but unfortunately met with an accident which necessitated his being invalided to hospital and later discharged as medically unfit. He unfortunately died through the effects of his military service on July 15th, 1919.
"His memory is cherished with pride."
St. Neots, Sandy, Beds. Z2062 /B.

EATON, J., A/Sergeant, Army Cyclist Corps.
He volunteered in September 1914, and in the following year was drafted to France and thence to Salonika. In this seat of operations he served with the 12th Corps and did continuously good work on the Vardar and Doiran fronts. Later he saw service in Russia, being stationed at Tiflis and Batum, and was finally demobilised in May 1919. He holds the 1914–15 Star, and the General Service and Victory Medals.
3, Abbey Terrace, Newport Pagnell, Bucks. Z2059.

EATON, J., Private, R.A.S.C.
He volunteered in November 1914, and was engaged at various stations on important duties as a baker. He was unable to obtain a transfer overseas, but did continuously good work throughout hostilities. He was demobilised in June 1919.
St. Neots Road, Sandy, Beds. Z2062 /A.

EATON, O., Corporal, Royal Engineers.
He joined the Army in March 1912, and, when war broke out in August 1914, was immediately drafted to France. There he took part in the Battles of Mons, the Marne, Neuve Chapelle, Givenchy, Ypres and Loos, and was twice wounded in action. Later he was transferred to Egypt and saw much fighting during the Advance into Palestine, at the Battles of Gaza, Jaffa and the capture of Jerusalem. He returned home, and was still in the Army in 1920. He holds the Mons Star and the General Service and Victory Medals.
St. Neots Road, Sandy, Beds. Z2061 /A.

EATON, W., Private, Machine Gun Corps.
He was mobilised in August 1914, and in the following year was drafted to the Dardanelles, where he saw much heavy fighting at Suvla Bay and Anzac Cove. After the Evacuation of the Gallipoli Peninsula he was transferred to Egypt, and took part in the Advance into Palestine, being in action at Gaza, Jaffa and the capture of Jerusalem. He returned home and was demobilised in March 1919, and holds the 1914–15 Star, and the General Service and Victory Medals.
St. Neots Road, Sandy, Beds. Z2061 /B.

EATON, W. F., Driver, Royal Engineers.
He volunteered in 1915, and early in the following year proceeded to Mesopotamia, where he saw much fighting and was wounded in action. As a result he was invalided to Cairo and Alexandria, and, on his recovery, took part in the Advance into Palestine and was in action at Gaza, Jaffa and Aleppo. He returned home and was demobilised in April 1919, holding the General Service and Victory Medals.
Oakley, Bedford. Z2063.

EATS, T., Sergeant, Royal Engineers.
He volunteered in September, and on completing his training in the following year was drafted to Egypt. In this seat of operations he quickly gained promotion and did consistently good work, wiring, trench-digging and bridge-building during the Advance into Palestine, where he was in action at Gaza and Jerusalem. He returned home and was demobilised in May 1919, holding the 1914–15 Star, and the General Service and Victory Medals. 6, Derwent Place, Bedford. Z2064.

EDGELEY, J., Private, 2nd Bedfordshire Regt.
He joined in March 1916, and later in the same year was drafted to the Western Front, where he took part in the heavy fighting at the Battles of the Somme, Ypres, Passchendaele and Albert. He made the supreme sacrifice, being killed in action near Cambrai on May 8th, 1918, and was entitled to the General Service and Victory Medals.
"A valiant Soldier, with undaunted heart he breasted life's last hill."
36, Pilcroft Street, Bedford. X2065.

EDMUNDS, A., A.B., Royal Navy.
He enlisted in June 1914, and, after a period of training, proceeded to the North Sea on board H.M.S. "Bellerophon," and was engaged on important patrol and escort duties. He took part in the Battle of Jutland and did continuously good work throughout hostilities. In 1920 he was serving in the Mediterranean on board H.M.S. "Emperor of India," and holds the 1914–15 Star, and the General Service and Victory Medals. Emberton, Bucks. Z2066 /A.

EDMUNDS, A., Air Mechanic, Royal Air Force.
Joining in April 1917, he was drafted to the Western Front on completion of a period of training in August of the same year. There he was engaged on important duties in the workshops in various sectors and did much useful work with his Squadron until his return home for demobilisation in February 1919. He holds the General Service and Victory Medals.
Emberton, Bucks. Z2066 /B.

EDMUNDS, J., Pte., 1st Duke of Cornwall's L.I.
He volunteered in May 1915, and, after three months' training, proceeded to the Western Front, where, after much severe fighting, he was wounded in action on the Somme in August 1916, and invalided home. He returned to France, however, on his recovery in December of that year, and, unhappily, fell in action in October 1917, and was buried at Poperinghe. He was entitled to the 1914–15 Star, and the General Service and Victory Medals.
"Whilst we remember, the sacrifice is not in vain."
Emberton, Bucks. Z2066 /E.

EDMUNDS, M., Driver, R.A.S.C.
Already in the Army when war was declared in August 1914, he proceeded to the Western Front in the following month and was there engaged on important transport duties in various sectors, being present also at the Battle of Ypres and other engagements. He unfortunately contracted fever and died in hospital at Etaples on June 2nd, 1916. He was entitled to the 1914 Star, and the General Service and Victory Medals.
"Thinking that remembrance, though unspoken, may reach him where he sleeps."
Emberton, Bucks. Z2066 /C.

EDMUNDS, W., L/Cpl., Oxford. & Bucks. L.I.
Volunteering in August 1914, he was drafted to the Western Front in January of the following year, and there took part in the Battle of Ypres and many other important engagements, and was wounded in action at Loos in September 1915. He was reported missing, and later, killed in action at Guillemont on July 29th, 1916, during the Somme Offensive. He was entitled to the 1914–15 Star, and the General Service and Victory Medals.
"His memory is cherished with pride."
Emberton, Bucks. Z2066/D.

EDNEY, H., Sergeant, Royal Defence Corps.
He volunteered in 1915, and, after his training, was retained at various stations, where he was engaged in guarding prisoners of war, and on other important duties. He was not successful in his efforts to obtain his transfer to a theatre of war, on account of ill-health, but, nevertheless, rendered valuable services with his unit until February 1919, when he was demobilised. 11, Shakespeare Place, Huntingdon. Z1733/B.

EDWARDS, A. S., Sapper, Royal Engineers.
He volunteered in December 1914, and was retained on important duties in England until January 1916, being then sent to Egypt, where he served at various stations. He unhappily contracted fever, and died in hospital on the Suez Canal on September 4th, 1916. He was entitled to the General Service and Victory Medals.
"His memory is cherished with pride."
22, Beatrice Street, Kempston, Bedford. Z2070.

EDWARDS, C. O., Gunner, Royal Field Artillery.
Shortly after volunteering in 1915, he proceeded to France, where he saw severe fighting in various sectors of the front. He took part in the Battles of Ypres, the Somme, Arras, Passchendaele and Cambrai, and many other important engagements until the cessation of hostilities, and, on his return home in 1919, was demobilised. He holds the 1914–15 Star, and the General Service and Victory Medals.
8, Maitland Street, Bedford. X2072/B.

EDWARDS, E. W., Private, Royal Welch Fusiliers.
He volunteered at the outbreak of war in August 1914, and, after completing a term of training, was retained on important duties at various stations, where he did much useful work with his unit. He was unfortunately killed accidentally on January 23rd, 1917.
"Steals on the ear the distant triumph song."
76, Grey Friars Walk, Bedford. X2075.

EDWARDS, G., Sergeant-Major, Royal Engineers.
Already in the Army at the outbreak of war in August 1914, he was shortly afterwards drafted to the Western Front, where he was engaged on important duties as a paymaster at Calais. He also took a prominent part in the Battles of Ypres and Arras, and other engagements, and was wounded in action. Still with his Company in 1920, he holds the 1914 Star, and the General Service and Victory Medals.
38, Hartington Street, Bedford. X2071/A.

EDWARDS, H., Private, 1st Norfolk Regiment.
He joined in May 1918, and, after three months' training, was drafted to the Western Front, where he saw severe fighting in various sectors. He took part in the second Battle of Cambrai and in many other important engagements during the Allies' Advance, and, on returning home in February 1919, was demobilised. He holds the General Service and Victory Medals.
42, St. Paul's Road, Queen's Park, Bedford. Z2073.

EDWARDS, H. F., Sapper, Royal Engineers.
Volunteering in September 1914, he proceeded to the Western Front in May of the following year, and there saw much heavy fighting. He took part in the Battles of Loos, Arras, Ypres and Cambrai and many other engagements, and was gassed and wounded in action on the Somme in 1916, and again gassed on the Somme two years later. He afterwards served with the Army of Occupation in Germany, finally returning home for demobilisation in May 1919. He holds the 1914–15 Star, and the General Service and Victory Medals.
Limes, London Road, Harrowden, Bedford. Z2069.

EDWARDS, J. T., Corporal, R.A.M.C.
He was mobilised in August 1914, and, in May of the following year, proceeded to the Western Front, where he was present at the Battle of Festubert. Invalided home in November 1915, he returned to France, however, on his recovery, and took an active part in the Battles of the Somme, Arras and Cambrai, and other engagements until again sent home in August 1918. He was discharged in November 1919, and holds the 1914–15 Star, and the General Service and Victory Medals.
Rose Cottage, Goldington, Bedford. Z2076.

EDWARDS, M., Corporal, R.A.M.C.
He joined in June 1916, and, after a period of training, was engaged on important clerical duties at various stations in Ireland. He was medically unfit for active service and was consequently unable to obtain his transfer to the front, but did good work with his Company until November 1919, when he was demobilised.
58, Pontypridd Road, Porth Rhondda, Glam. Z2068.

EDWARDS, S. J., Corporal, R.A.O.C.
He volunteered at the outbreak of war in August 1914, and, on completing a period of training in the following year, was drafted to Salonika. There he was engaged on various important duties and also saw severe fighting on the Macedonian front, being wounded in action. He was demobilised on his return home in March 1919, and holds the 1914–15 Star, and the General Service and Victory Medals.
56, Coventry Road, Bedford. Z2074.

EDWARDS, T., Gunner, Royal Garrison Artillery; and Private, Labour Corps.
A Reservist, he was called to the Colours at the outbreak of war in August 1914, and was retained on important duties in England until 1916. He was then drafted to the Western Front, where he took part in the Battles of Vimy Ridge, and the Somme, and many other engagements until invalided to hospital at Colchester. He was afterwards retained in England on land work until his discharge in February 1919, and holds the General Service and Victory Medals.
4, Redbrick Cottages, Wilden, near Bedford. Z2067.

EKINS, F. H., Private, Gloucestershire Regiment.
Volunteering in January 1915, he proceeded to Gallipoli in July of that year and there saw much severe fighting, particularly at Suvla Bay, until the Evacuation of the Peninsula. He was then transferred to the Western Front, where he took part in the Battles of Albert, Vimy Ridge and the Somme, and other engagements. He was killed in action at Arras on April 5th, 1917. He was entitled to the 1914–15 Star, and the General Service and Victory Medals.
"The path of duty was the way to glory."
Great Staughton, Hunts. Z1837/B.

ELFORD, W., Private, Labour Corps.
He joined in June 1917, and, after undergoing a period of training, was retained at various stations on duties of a highly important nature. He was not successful in obtaining his transfer to a theatre of war, but, nevertheless, rendered very valuable services with his unit until April 1919, when he was demobilised. 2, Tower Gardens, Bedford. X1363/B.

ELLIOT, G., Private, Norfolk Regiment.
He joined in August 1918, and, after a short period of training, was drafted to the Western Front, where he saw severe fighting until the cessation of hostilities. He then proceeded with the Army of Occupation into Germany, but returned home for demobilisation in January 1919. He holds the General Service and Victory Medals.
Pury End, Pauler's Pury, Towcester, Northants. Z3030/B.

ELLIOTT, A. J., Air Mechanic, Royal Air Force.
He joined in September 1918, and, after completing a term of training, served at various stations, where he was engaged on duties which required a high degree of technical skill. Owing to the early cessation of hostilities, he was unable to obtain his transfer overseas, but, nevertheless, rendered valuable services with his Squadron until his demobilisation in April 1919.
8, Bedford Street, Wolverton, Bucks. Z2077/B.

ELLIOTT, B. S. J., Air Mechanic, Royal Air Force.
He joined in June 1917, and, after a period of training was engaged on important duties as a rigger at various stations. Unable to obtain his transfer to the front, he nevertheless, rendered very valuable services with his Squadron until his demobilisation in March 1919.
8, Bedford Street, Wolverton, Bucks. Z2077/A.

ELLIS, A. A. C., Private, Royal Berkshire Regt.
He volunteered in June 1915, and in October of the following year proceeded to the Western Front, where he took part in many important engagements in various sectors. Mortally wounded in action on the Somme in the Advance of 1918, he unhappily died on October 10th of that year at a Casualty Clearing Station, and was buried near Bapaume. He was entitled to the General Service and Victory Medals.
"His life for his Country, his soul to God."
37, Caldecote Street, Newport Pagnell, Bucks. Z2089.

ELLIS, F., Sergeant, R.A.S.C. (H.T.)
He joined in February 1916, and was retained at various stations in England until February 1918, and was then drafted to Egypt. There he was engaged on important transport duties at Alexandria, and, proceeding into Palestine, was stationed at Jerusalem, Gaza and various other places, where he did much useful work. Returning home in November 1919, he was demobilised in the following month, and holds the General Service and Victory Medals.
West Perry, near Huntingdon. Z2090/A.

ELLIS, G., Corporal, 1st Northants. Regiment.
Having enlisted in 1905, he was sent to France with the First Expeditionary Force in August 1914, and took part in the Battle of, and the Retreat from, Mons. He also served with distinction in many of the important engagements in the early stages of the war, but was unhappily killed in action at the second Battle of Ypres in May 1915. He was entitled to the Mons Star, and the General Service and Victory Medals.
"A costly sacrifice upon the altar of freedom."
1, Slated Row, Old Wolverton, Bucks. Z2080/B.

ELLIS, G. H., Private, 1/4th Essex Regiment.
Already serving in the 2nd Bedfordshire Regiment in August 1914, he was immediately sent to France and took part in the Retreat from Mons. He was also in action at the Battles of the Marne and Festubert before being wounded and gassed in 1915 and invalided home. On his recovery in 1916 he proceeded to Egypt, but later advanced into Palestine and served at the Battles of Gaza and the capture of Haifa. He received his discharge in June 1919, and holds the Mons Star, and the General Service and Victory Medals.
High Street, Brampton, Hunts. Z2078/A.

ELLIS, G. W., Private, Dorsetshire Regiment.
He volunteered in February 1915, and first served with the Royal Field Artillery, but before proceeding to France in 1916 was transferred to the Dorsetshire Regiment. Whilst on the Western Front he took part in the Battles of Albert, the Somme, Vimy Ridge, Messines, Passchendaele, Cambrai and Havrincourt, and in the Retreat and Advance of 1918. He was demobilised in September 1919, and holds the General Service and Victory Medals. High St., Brampton, Hunts. Z2078/B.

ELLIS, H., Pte., Queen's (Royal West Surrey Regt.)
He joined in February 1917, and was quickly drafted to the Western Front, where he played a prominent part in the Battles of Arras, Vimy Ridge, Messines, Ypres, Cambrai, the Somme and Tournai. He was also in action in other important engagements during the Retreat and Advance of 1918. Returning to England in January 1919, he was demobilised a month later, and holds the General Service and Victory Medals.
8, Pilcroft Street, Bedford. X2094.

ELLIS, H., Private, Bedfordshire Regiment.
Joining in March 1916, he was first sent to Egypt, but later proceeded into Palestine, where he took part in the Battles of Gaza, the capture of Haifa, Jaffa and Aleppo, and in other important engagements during the Advance of General Allenby's Forces. In April 1919 he was transferred to India, and in 1920 was stationed at Secunderabad. He holds the General Service and Victory Medals.
66, Wellington Street, Bedford. X1762/B.

ELLIS, J., Private, Royal Warwickshire Regiment.
Having been mobilised with the Huntingdonshire Cyclist Battalion in August 1914, he completed his training with this unit and was then transferred to the Royal Warwickshire Regiment. Proceeding to France in July 1916, he took part in the Battles of the Somme, Arras, Vimy Ridge and Ypres. In November 1917 he was sent to Italy, but, after taking part in heavy fighting on the Piave and the Asiago Plateaux, returned to the Western Front in March 1918. He was gassed in June of the same year, and was wounded in action at the second Battle of Le Cateau during the Advance. Demobilised in March 1919, he holds the General Service and Victory Medals.
High Street, Somersham, Hunts. Z2093.

ELLIS, J., Driver, Royal Army Service Corps.
He volunteered in December 1915, and in the following year was drafted to the Western Front, where he rendered valuable services with his unit whilst engaged on important transport duties in the Somme, Arras, Ypres and Cambrai sectors. He was demobilised in March 1919, and holds the General Service and Victory Medals. Barham, Hunts. Z2079.

ELLIS, J. E., Private, 1st Royal Welch Fusiliers.
He volunteered in March 1915, and, on completion of his training, was drafted to France, where he took part in the Battles of the Somme, Arras, Bullecourt and Ypres, before being badly wounded in action at Polygon Wood in October 1917. He was invalided home, and, on his recovery, served in Ireland. Demobilised in March 1919, he holds the General Service and Victory Medals. 21, Hartington Street, Bedford. X2088.

ELLIS, T., Sergeant, Rifle Brigade.
Already in the Army at the outbreak of war, he was sent to France in August 1914, and was in action throughout the Retreat from Mons. He also served with distinction at the Battles of the Marne, La Bassée, Ypres, Neuve Chapelle, Loos and Arras, but was unhappily killed in action near Cambrai on March 23rd, 1918. He was entitled to the Mons Star, and the General Service and Victory Medals.
"A valiant Soldier, with undaunted heart he breasted life's last hill."
Church End, Wootton, Bedford. Z2095.

ELLIS, T. W., Sergeant, Queen's (Royal West Surrey) Regiment.
Volunteering in August 1914, he was drafted to France in the following year and served with distinction at the Battles of Festubert, Loos, Vimy Ridge, Messines, Passchendaele and Cambrai, where he was badly wounded in action in November 1917. He was invalided home, and after eleven months in hospital at Bath, was discharged as medically unfit for further service in September 1918. He holds the 1914–15 Star, and the General Service and Victory Medals. Warboys, Hunts. Z2086.

ELLIS, W. J., Staff-Sergeant Saddler, R.F.A.
He volunteered in January 1915, and was retained on special duties with the 321st Brigade at various stations in England and Scotland. Owing to the important nature of his work he was unsuccessful in his efforts to obtain a transfer overseas, but rendered valuable services until his demobilisation in April 1919. Kimbolton, Hunts. Z2087.

ELLIS, W. S., Private, 1st Northants. Regiment.
He enlisted in 1910, and, at the commencement of hostilities in August 1914, was immediately drafted to France, where he served with distinction at the Battle of Mons. He laid down his life for King and Country during the subsequent Retreat in September, and was entitled to the Mons Star, and the General Service and Victory Medals.
"Nobly striving:
He nobly fell that we might live."
1, Slated Row, Old Wolverton, Bucks. Z2080/A.

ELSTOW, T., Sapper, Royal Engineers.
He joined in June 1916, and was quickly drafted to France, where he was attached to the Railway Operative Department. He did excellent work at Andruicq whilst engaged on the repairing of ambulance trains, and was eventually demobilised in September 1919, holding the General Service and Victory Medals. 98, Church Street, Wolverton, Bucks. Z2096.

EMENS, B. E. (Mrs.), Special War Worker.
This lady first volunteered in the Land Army in May 1915, and did excellent work at Bray Fields, Bucks., for some considerable time. Later she was engaged on the manufacture of munitions at the Diamond Foundry, Luton, and rendered valuable services until October 1919. High Street, Lavendon, Bucks. Z2097/B.

EMENS, H., Sergeant, R.A.V.C.
He volunteered in May 1915, and was first engaged on important duties in connection with the treatment of sick and wounded horses on Salisbury Plain. In September 1918 he was sent to France for similar work, and, after the Armistice, proceeded to Germany with the Army of Occupation. He rendered valuable services at Cologne until demobilised in May 1919, and holds the General Service and Victory Medals.
High Street, Lavendon, Bucks. Z2097/A.

EMERY, D. L., Guardsman, 2nd Grenadier Guards.
He enlisted in the 3rd Bedfordshire Regiment in 1911, but was transferred to the Grenadier Guards in March 1913. In August 1914 he proceeded to France and took part in the Retreat from Mons. He was wounded in action at the Battle of the Aisne in September, but on his recovery served with distinction at the Battles of Neuve Chapelle, Ypres, the Somme (during which engagement he fought at Beaumont-Hamel and was wounded at Ginchy in 1916), Arras, Vimy Ridge, and Cambrai. He received his discharge in March 1919, and holds the Mons Star, and the General Service and Victory Medals.
Queen's Terrace, London Road, Sandy, Beds. TZ2098.

EMERY, F., Private, Bedfordshire Regiment.
Volunteering in September 1914, he proceeded to France ten months later and took part in the Battles of Festubert, the Somme, Arras and Ypres before being badly wounded in August 1917. He was invalided home, and on his recovery was transferred to the Labour Corps, with which unit he rendered valuable services at Home stations until his discharge in February 1919. He holds the 1914–15 Star, and the General Service and Victory Medals.
London Road, Sandy, Beds. Z2100/C—Z2101/C.

EMERY, G., Private, Somerset Light Infantry.
He first volunteered in the Bedfordshire Regiment in 1914, but, after a period of training, was discharged as medically unfit later in the same year. In 1915, however, he rejoined in the Somerset Light Infantry, and rendered valuable services until being drafted to India in 1917. There he was engaged on important garrison duties, and was eventually demobilised in 1920, holding the General Service and Victory Medals.
London Road, Sandy, Beds. Z2100/B—Z2101/B.

EMERY, J., Private, Royal Fusiliers.
Volunteering in March 1915, he was drafted to the Western Front on completion of his training. Whilst in this theatre of war he played an important part in the Battles of Albert, the Somme, Arras and Cambrai, and in heavy fighting during the Retreat and Advance of 1918. He was demobilised in 1919, and holds the General Service and Victory Medals.
London Road, Sandy, Beds. Z2100/D—Z2101/D.

EMERY, O. (M.M.), Private, Bedfordshire Regt.
Mobilised in August 1914, he was sent to France with the first Expeditionary Force and served through the Retreat from Mons. Later he took a prominent part in the Battles of the Marne, Hill 60, Festubert and Cambrai, and was twice wounded in action. He was awarded the Military Medal for conspicuous bravery and devotion to duty under heavy fire whilst acting as a stretcher-bearer, and, also holding the Mons Star and the General Service and Victory Medals, was discharged in 1919.
London Road, Sandy, Beds. Z2100/A—Z2101/A.

EMERY, T., Private, 1/5th Bedfordshire Regiment.
Volunteering in August 1914, he was drafted to Mesopotamia in the following year. Whilst in this theatre of war he was in action at Amara, Um-el-Hannah, Kut-el-Amara, Baghdad and Mosul, and was wounded during heavy fighting. He was demobilised on returning to England in February 1919, and holds the 1914–15 Star, and the General Service and Victory Medals. 4, Tower Gardens, Bedford. X2099.

EMERY, W., Private, Bedfordshire Regiment.
Already in the Army at the outbreak of war, he was drafted to France in August 1914, and served through the Retreat from Mons. After taking part in further severe fighting during the early engagements of the war, he was unfortunately killed in action on November 7th, 1914. He was entitled to the Mons Star, and the General Service and Victory Medals.
"He died the noblest death a man may die,
Fighting for God and right and liberty."
London Road, Sandy, Beds. Z2100/E—Z2101/E.

ENDERSBY, E. A., A.B. and Stoker, Royal Navy.
He joined in 1917, and, after his training was posted to H.M.S. "Pembroke." He rendered valuable services whilst engaged on dangerous mine-sweeping duties off the Irish coasts, and was eventually demobilised in May 1919, holding the General Service and Victory Medals.
10, Brace Street, Bedford. Z2103.

ENDERSBY, E. J., Private, 1st Bedfordshire Regt.
Volunteering in April 1915, he was sent to France in the following January, and, after taking a prominent part in much severe fighting, particularly at Delville Wood, was unhappily killed in action on July 31st, 1916, during the Somme Offensive. He was entitled to the General Service and Victory Medals.
"Honour to the immortal dead, who gave their youth that the world might grow old in peace."
Pym's Cottages, Bedford Road, Sandy, Beds. Z2105.

ENDERSBY, F. J., Pte., R.A.M.C. and M.G.C.
After volunteering in July 1915 he underwent a period of training prior to being drafted to the Western Front in March 1918. There he took part in important engagements in various sectors, and was wounded in action near Cambrai in April of that year. Returning home in February 1919, he was demobilised in the following month, and holds the General Service and Victory Medals. 11, Cobden Street, Bedford. X2102.

ENDERSBY, H. W., Sapper, Royal Engineers.
He volunteered in 1915, and, on completing a period of training, proceeded to the Western Front, where he served in various sectors. He took an active part in the Battles of the Somme, Arras, Ypres and Lille, and many other important engagements until the cessation of hostilities, and was then sent with the Army of Occupation into Germany. Demobilised on returning home in April 1920, he holds the General Service and Victory Medals. 29, Howbury Street, Bedford. Z2104.

ENFIELD, A., Private, Machine Gun Corps.
He joined in November 1916, and was retained at various stations with the Bedfordshire Regiment, and later the King's Own Scottish Borderers until 1918. He was then transferred to the Machine Gun Corps and drafted to the Western Front, where, after much heavy fighting, he was severely wounded in action in September 1918. He was invalided from the Army in March 1919, and holds the General Service and Victory Medals. Earith, Hunts. Z2106/A.

ENFIELD, S., L/Corporal, 2nd Bedfordshire Regt.
Volunteering in September 1914, he was drafted to the Western Front in the following year and took part in the Battles of Neuve Chapelle and Hill 60 and many minor engagements. He died gloriously on the Field of Battle at Festubert on May 15th, 1915. He was entitled to the 1914–15 Star, and the General Service and Victory Medals.
"And doubtless he went in splendid company."
Earith, Hunts. Z2106/B.

ENO, A. G., Private, Oxford. and Bucks. L.I.
He volunteered in September 1914, and was retained on important duties at various stations until November 1916, and then proceeded to the Western Front, where he saw much severe fighting in the Somme sector. He died gloriously on the Field of Battle at Arras on February 28th, 1917. He was entitled to the General Service and Victory Medals.
"Whilst we remember, the sacrifice is not in vain."
28, Young Street, Wolverton, Bucks. Z2107/A.

ENO, F., Gunner, Royal Garrison Artillery.
Having enlisted in 1913, he was drafted to the Western Front a month after the outbreak of war in August 1914. There he took part in many important engagements, including the Battles of the Marne, Ypres, Loos, Arras, Passchendaele, Cambrai, Amiens and Le Cateau, fought also in the Retreat and Advance of 1918, and was wounded on the Somme in 1916. In November 1919 he was transferred to Mesopotamia, where he was still with his Battery at Baghdad in 1920. He holds the 1914 Star, and the General Service and Victory Medals.
28, Young Street, Wolverton, Bucks. Z2107/B.

EVANS, B., Pte., 1/7th Royal Warwickshire Regt.
He volunteered in August 1914, and, after training with the Huntingdonshire Cyclist Battalion, proceeded to the Western Front in 1915. There he saw severe fighting in various sectors, and took part in the Battles of Festubert, Loos, Albert, the Somme and Ypres. In 1917 he was transferred to Italy, where he was again in action on the Piave and the Asiago Plateaux, finally returning home for demobilisation in February 1919. He holds the 1914–15 Star, and the General Service and Victory Medals.
33, Russell Street, St. Neots, Hunts. Z2114/C.

EVANS, C., Private, Norfolk Regiment.
He volunteered in 1915, and, on completing a period of training in January of the following year, was drafted to Egypt, where he was engaged on important duties at various stations. He unfortunately contracted dysentery, and died on April 26th, 1916, after only three months' service overseas. He was entitled to the General Service and Victory Medals.
"A valiant Soldier, with undaunted heart he breasted life's last hill."
33, Russell Street, St. Neots, Hunts. Z2114/A.

EVANS, F. J. (M.M.), Sapper, R.E. (R.O.D.)
He volunteered in September 1914, and in October of the following year was sent to France, where he was engaged as an engine-driver on troop trains. He served chiefly in the Ypres, Somme, Arras and Cambrai sectors, and was for three months in hospital at Boulogne suffering from shell-shock. He was awarded the Military Medal for conspicuous bravery displayed in saving a train load of wounded when the Germans broke through at Cambrai in 1917, and holds also the 1914–15 Star, and the General Service and Victory Medals. He was demobilised in June 1919.
12, Berrell's Court, Olney, Bucks. Z2116.

EVANS, G., Private, Royal Warwickshire Regt.
He volunteered at the outbreak of war in August 1914, and, after completing a period of training with the Huntingdonshire Cyclist Battalion was sent to the Western Front, where he saw severe fighting in various sectors. After taking part in the Battles of Festubert, Loos, the Somme, Arras and Ypres, and other engagements, he was transferred in 1917 to Italy, where he was in action on the Piave and the Asiago Plateaux. He was demobilised on his return home in February 1919, and holds the General Service and Victory Medals.
33, Russell Street, St. Neots, Hunts. Z2114/B.

EVANS, G. F., Private, Worcestershire Regiment.
Having previously been rejected on seven occasions, he joined in March 1918, and, after a period of training, was retained on important duties at various stations. He was unable to obtain his transfer overseas before the cessation of hostilities, but in December 1918 was sent with the Army of Occupation to Germany, where he served at Cologne. He was demobilised on his return home in November 1919.
Stoke Goldington, Bucks. Z2108.

EVANS, J., Private, 4th Bedfordshire Regiment.
He joined in March 1916, and underwent a period of training prior to being drafted to the Western Front in November of the following year. There he took part in the Battle of Cambrai and many other important engagements, fought also in the Retreat and Advance of 1918, and was wounded in action. He was demobilised in April 1919, and holds the General Service and Victory Medals. 15, Dane Street, Bedford. X2110/A.

EVANS, J., Private, 2nd Bedfordshire Regiment.
He volunteered in 1915, and in the following year was drafted to the Western Front, where he saw heavy fighting in various sectors. After taking part in the Battles of Albert and the Somme and many other engagements, he was severely wounded in action on the Somme during the Retreat of March 1918, and invalided home. He unhappily died of wounds in hospital at Wolverhampton on February 19th, 1919. He was entitled to the General Service and Victory Medals.
"His memory is cherished with pride."
High Street, Cranfield, Beds. Z1830/B.

EVANS, K. G., Corporal, Yorkshire Regiment.
Volunteering in October 1914, he was drafted to Egypt in the following year, but was shortly afterwards wounded in action and invalided home. Returning to Egypt, however, on his recovery, he was later transferred to France, where he took part in the Battles of Arras, Ypres, Cambrai and the Somme and other engagements, and was again twice wounded. Demobilised in February 1919, he holds the 1914–15 Star, and the General Service and Victory Medals.
Cranfield, Beds. Z2112/B—Z2113/B.

EVANS, P. W., Private, 8th Bedfordshire Regt.
Shortly after joining in 1916, he proceeded to the Western Front, where he saw much severe fighting in the Ypres and Arras sectors. Mortally wounded in action on the Somme in September 1916, he unhappily died on November 7th of that year in the Canadian General Hospital at Etaples. He was entitled to the General Service and Victory Medals.
"A costly sacrifice upon the altar of freedom."
Cranfield, Beds. Z2112/A—Z2113/A.

EVANS, R., Private, Machine Gun Corps.
He volunteered in September 1914, and was retained on important duties in England until January 1917, when he proceeded to the Western Front. There he took part in many engagements, including the Battles of Arras and the Somme, and was twice wounded in action at Cambrai —in 1917 and 1918—and was invalided home. He returned to France, however, in time to fight in the final Advance, and was demobilised in June 1919, holding the General Service and Victory Medals.
Moulsoe, Bucks. Z2109/A.

EVANS, R. W., Corporal, 1st Bedfordshire Regt.
He joined the Army in January 1901, and when war broke out in August 1914, was immediately drafted to France. There he took part in the Retreat from Mons and the Battles of La Bassée and Ypres, but unfortunately met with an accident and was invalided home. On his recovery he was retained at various Home stations on important duties. He was discharged in February 1919, and holds the Mons Star, and the General Service and Victory Medals. 55, Foster St., Bedford. X2117/B.

EVANS, T. C., Private, R.A.S.C.
Volunteering in October 1915, he was drafted overseas in the following year. During his service on the Western Front he took an active part in many engagements, including the Battles of Arras, Ypres, Cambrai and the Somme (II.). He did continuously good work, and was demobilised in August 1919, holding the General Service and Victory Medals.
25, Eastville Road, Bedford. Z2115/B.

EVANS, T. E., Corporal, Royal Air Force.
He volunteered in August 1914, and, after a period of training, was engaged at various stations on important duties which called for a high degree of technical skill. He was unable to obtain a transfer overseas owing to his being over age, but rendered valuable services until his demobilisation in March 1919. 25, Eastville Road, Bedford. Z2115/C.

EVANS, W., Private, Oxford. and Bucks. L.I.
He enlisted in June 1917, and early in the following year proceeded to France, where he took part in the Battle of the Somme (II.), and in heavy fighting during the Retreat and Advance of 1918. After hostilities ceased he went to Germany with the Army of Occupation, and served on the Rhine until his demobilisation in November 1919. He holds the General Service and Victory Medals. Moulsoe, Bucks. Z2109/B.

EVANS, W. A., Private, Essex Regiment.
He was already in the Army when war broke out in August 1914, and in the following year proceeded to Egypt. Later he took part in the Advance into Palestine, and saw much fighting at Gaza, Jaffa, the capture of Jerusalem and at Aleppo. He returned home and was discharged in August 1919, holding the 1914–15 Star, and the General Service and Victory Medals.
15, Dane Street, Bedford. X2110/B.

EVANS, W. C., Cpl., 1/2nd Monmouthshire Regt.
He volunteered in August 1914, and in the following July was drafted to France. In this seat of war he took part in many important engagements, including the Battles of Beaumont-Hamel, Loos, Vimy Ridge, Bullecourt, Passchendaele and Cambrai (II.), and was gassed three times, and eventually invalided home. He was discharged in November 1919, and holds the 1914–15 Star, and the General Service and Victory Medals. 8, Beckett Street, Bedford. X2111.

EVANS, W. G., Private, Royal Defence Corps.
Being over age for active service, he volunteered in the Royal Defence Corps in July 1915, and, after a period of training, was engaged at various stations on important guard duties. Later he worked on the land, and rendered valuable services throughout hostilities. He was demobilised in February 1919.
Cranfield, Beds. Z2112/C—Z2113/C.

EVANS, W. H., Private, R.A.M.C.
He was mobilised in August 1914, and was shortly afterwards drafted to France, where he took part in the Retreat from Mons and the Battles of Ypres, Loos, Givenchy, the Somme and Beaumont-Hamel. He died gloriously on the Field of Battle at Arras on April 9th, 1917, and was entitled to the Mons Star, and the General Service and Victory Medals.
"He died the noblest death a man may die,
Fighting for God and right and liberty."
25, Eastville Road, Bedford. Z2115/A.

EVERETT, R. E., Driver, R.A.S.C. (M.T.)
He volunteered in March 1915, and in the following May was drafted to France, where he served with the Mechanical Transport, conveying supplies to the forward areas in the Ypres, Somme, Albert, Arras and Cambrai sectors. Later he was transferred to Italy, but after a short period of service there was taken ill and eventually invalided home. He was demobilised in March 1919, and holds the 1914–15 Star, and the General Service and Victory Medals.
Main Street, Maids Moreton, Buckingham. Z2118.

EVERETT, W. A., Private, R.A.M.C.
He joined in May 1918, and, after his training, was engaged at various Home stations on important duties, whilst attached to the Royal Fusiliers. In 1919 he proceeded to Germany with the Army of Occupation, and served there as a hospital orderly until his demobilisation in April 1920.
Silver Street, Great Barford, Beds. Z2119/A.

EVERNDON, E., Private, 7th Bedfordshire Regt.
He volunteered in 1914, and underwent a period of training prior to his being drafted to France. There he served as a signaller and saw much heavy fighting in the Arras sector. He made the supreme sacrifice, being killed in action near Ypres on April 24th, 1917, and was entitled to the General Service and Victory Medals.
"Whilst we remember, the sacrifice is not in vain."
Eaton Ford Beds. Z2120/A.

F

FABLE, W. H., Private, 11th Royal Sussex Regt.
Joining in February 1917, he was employed on various duties of an important character whilst stationed at Bedford and Gravesend. In September 1918 he was sent to Russia, where he participated in severe fighting in several sectors and did excellent work until he returned home for demobilisation in October 1919, holding the General Service and Victory Medals.
St. George's Terrace, St. Ives, Hunts. Z2121.

FACEY, A. T., Driver, R.A.S.C. (M.T.)
He volunteered in November 1914, and shortly afterwards was drafted to the Western Front. There he was employed as a motor-transport driver, conveying supplies to the forward areas on various fronts in France and Belgium. He performed consistently good work until after the cessation of hostilities, and was demobilised in January 1919, holding the 1914–15 Star, and the General Service and Victory Medals.
136, Honey Hill Road, Queen's Park, Bedford. Z2124/A.

FACEY, C. E., Pte., Duke of Cornwall's L.I.
Volunteering in February 1915, he proceeded three months later to France, where he took part with his unit in many important engagements, including the Battle of Ypres, and was wounded in 1916 during the first Battle of the Somme. Invalided home, he was sent to hospital at Oswestry, and, returning three months afterwards to France, participated in further fighting at Arras and Cambrai, where he was again wounded. Evacuated to England, he was eventually demobilised in February 1919, and holds the 1914–15 Star, and the General Service and Victory Medals. 32, East Street, Olney, Bucks. Z2122.

FACEY, G. H., Driver, R.A.S.C.
He joined in 1916, and, after a period of service at Grove Park and in Bristol, was sent in 1917 to the Western Front. There he served on the Somme, Arras and Cambrai fronts as a transport driver carrying rations to the troops in the forward areas. He did good work up to the Armistice, after which he returned home and was demobilised in 1919, holding the General Service and Victory Medals.
136, Honey Hill Road, Queen's Park, Bedford. Z2124/C.

FACEY, S. W., Private, 17th (Duke of Cambridge's Own) Lancers.
A serving soldier, he was drafted to France immediately after the outbreak of war, and took part in the Battle of Mons and the subsequent Retreat. He was later in action during the Battles of the Marne, the Somme, Arras and Cambrai, and, when transferred to Palestine in 1917, participated in the Battle of Gaza and the capture of Haifa. Returning home, he was discharged in September 1919, having completed seven years with the Colours, and holds the Mons Star, and the General Service and Victory Medals.
136, Honey Hill Road, Queen's Park, Bedford.
Z2123/B—Z2124/B.

FAIREY, A. C., Gunner, Royal Field Artillery.
He volunteered in January 1915, and six months later proceeded to the Western Front. In this theatre of hostilities he was employed as a signaller and was in action during the Battles of Ypres, the Somme and Cambrai. Early in 1918 he was sent to Russia, and served through several engagements. Demobilised on his return home in March 1919, he holds the 1914–15 Star, and the General Service and Victory Medals.
76, Duncombe Street, Bletchley. Z3032/A.

FAIREY, W., 1st Class Stoker, R.N., H.M.S. "Erebus."
Volunteering in November 1915, he was posted to H.M.S. "Erebus," and did good work in this vessel whilst employed on patrol duties in the North Sea and Home waters. Later he was engaged on escort duty, and in 1918 was sent to Russia, where he was stationed for some time. He was still serving in the Royal Navy in 1920, holding the 1914–15 Star, and the General Service and Victory Medals.
76, Duncombe Street, Bletchley. Z3032/B.

FAITHFULL, E. T., Sergeant, R.F.A.
Having previously taken part in the South African Campaign, he re-enlisted in February 1915, and in the following July was sent to France. There he played a prominent part with his Battery in the Battles of Ypres, the Somme and Cambrai, and in various actions during the Retreat of 1918. Wounded at Wulverghem in April of that year, he was invalided to hospital at Warrington, and remained there for six months. He was then stationed at Newcastle until December 1918, when he was demobilised, holding the 1914–15 Star, and the General Service and Victory Medals, in addition to the Queen's and King's South Africa Medals.
9, Broad Street, Newport Pagnell. Z2125.

FANCUTT, C., Leading Aircraftsman, R.A.F.
He joined in August 1917, and whilst stationed in Scotland was employed as a carpenter making parts for aeroplanes. Owing to the important nature of his work he was unable to obtain a transfer overseas, but nevertheless rendered valuable services until he was demobilised in June 1919.
Slated Row, Old Wolverton, Bucks. Z2126.

FARMER, A. J., Driver, R.A.S.C.
He volunteered in August 1915, and a few weeks later proceeded to France, where he was employed as a transport driver carrying ammunition to the forward areas. He served at Loos, on the Somme front and at Ypres and Cambrai, and, after the Armistice, went with the Army of Occupation to Germany until October 1919, when he returned home and was demobilised. He holds the 1914–15 Star, and the General Service and Victory Medals. Woburn Road, Woburn Sands. Z2129.

FARMER, F., A.B., R.N., H.M.S. " Dragon."
Volunteering in August 1915, he was posted to H.M.S. " Dragon," and in this vessel participated in the Battle of Jutland, in heavy fighting in Heligoland Bight, and in the bombardment of Zeebrugge. He was subsequently employed on patrol duties in the North Sea, and was still serving in the Royal Navy in 1920, holding the 1914–15 Star, and the General Service and Victory Medals.
12, Beauchamp Row, Bedford. X2127/B.

FARMER, T., Corporal, 2nd Bedfordshire Regt.
Mobilised in August 1914, he was at once drafted to the Western Front, where he took part in the Battle of Mons and the subsequent Retreat. He was also in action during the Battles of La Bassée and Ypres, and in many other important engagements, being wounded on three occasions. He was awarded the Croix-de-Guerre, and was discharged in May 1918 as unfit for further service in consequence of his wounds, holding the Mons Star, and the General Service and Victory Medals.
43, Canning Street, Bedford. X2128.

FARMER, T. H., Private, 1st Bedfordshire Regiment; and Air Mechanic, Royal Air Force.
He volunteered in September 1914, but was medically unfit for transfer to a theatre of war. Retained at home, he served with the 1st Bedfordshire Regiment at Halton Park and Bury St. Edmunds, and was later transferred to the Royal Air Force. He rendered valuable services whilst employed on important duties until he was demobilised in February 1919.
12, Beauchamp Row, Bedford. X2127/A.

FARR, F., Corporal, Bedfordshire Regiment.
He was mobilised in August 1914, and, proceeding at once to France, fought in the Battle of Mons and the Retreat, and also participated in heavy fighting on the Marne, at Festubert, Albert and Beaumont-Hamel. Whilst overseas he did excellent work, and after his discharge subsequently re-enlisted in order to complete 21 years' service with the Colours. He holds the Mons Star, and the General Service and Victory Medals.
30, Willington, Bedford. Z2130.

FARRAR, F., Private, 1st Bedfordshire Regiment.
At the outbreak of war in August 1914 he was already in the Army, and was at once ordered to the Western Front. There he took an active part in the Battles of Mons and the Aisne, and was severely wounded in action on the Marne in October 1914. After protracted hospital treatment he was discharged as medically unfit in January 1917, holding the Mons Star, and the General Service and Victory Medals.
34, Muswell Road, Bedford. Z2131/A.

FARRAR, F. T., Corporal, R.E. and Labour Corps.
He joined in August 1916, and, after completing his training, was two months later sent to the Western Front. In this theatre of war he rendered valuable services as a carpenter in the workshops behind the line, and also performed excellent work in connection with road-making. He served in France until March 1919, and was demobilised a month later, holding the General Service and Victory Medals.
20, Newnham Lane, Goldington Road, Bedford. Z2132.

FARRAR, J. F., Private, R.A.M.C.
He was mobilised in August 1914, and in the following November was drafted to the Western Front, where he served for over four years. During that time he performed valuable work as a stretcher-bearer in the Ypres, Loos, the Somme, Albert and Arras sectors, and also as a hospital orderly. He remained in France until his discharge in April 1919, and holds the 1914 Star, and the General Service and Victory Medals.
34, Muswell Road, Bedford. Z2131/C.

FARRAR, J. W., Corporal, Royal Engineers.
Mobilised in August 1914, he proceeded four months later to the Western Front, where he was employed on important transport duties with his unit. He also saw heavy fighting in various sectors, and took an active part in important engagements at Festubert, Loos, the Somme, Vimy Ridge, Arras and Cambrai. In February 1919 he was discharged, holding the 1914–15 Star, and the General Service and Victory Medals.
34, Muswell Road, Bedford. Z2131/B.

FARRER, A. H., Private, 2nd Middlesex Regiment.
He joined the Army in September 1917, and, after a period of training, was later in the same year drafted overseas. During his service on the Western Front he experienced fierce fighting in many important engagements, but was wounded and taken prisoner in 1918, and unfortunately succumbed to his injuries on April 2nd, 1918. He was entitled to the General Service and Victory Medals.
" Whilst we remember, the sacrifice is not in vain."
15, The Grove, Bedford. X2133/B.

FARRER, R. W., Sapper, Royal Engineers.
Joining in October 1916, he was, on completion of a period of training, drafted in the following year to East Africa. There he saw severe fighting in many important engagements, including that at Dar-es-Salaam, and rendered valuable services in the Wireless Section. His health broke down and he was ill for many months, and on his return to England in March 1919 was demobilised, holding the General Service and Victory Medals. 15, The Grove, Bedford. X2133/A.

FARRINGTON, G. H., A.B., Merchant Service.
He joined in November 1916, and, after a period of training, was posted to H.M. hospital ship " Glengorm Castle." In this vessel he did duty in the Mediterranean and Baltic Seas, and rendered invaluable services conveying wounded troops from Egypt and Russia to England. In 1920 he was still in the Merchant Service, and holds the General Service and Victory Medals, and the Mercantile Marine War Medal.
119, Marlborough Road, Queen's Park, Beds. Z1431/A.

FARROW, E., Sapper, Royal Engineers.
He volunteered at the outbreak of war in August 1914, and, after completing his training, was in the following year drafted to Egypt. He subsequently proceeded to Palestine, and in this theatre of war took an active part in important engagements at Gaza, Jerusalem, Jericho and Aleppo. On his return to England in April 1919 he was demobilised, holding the 1914–15 Star, and the General Service and Victory Medals.
8, Patteshall Street, Bedford. X2134.

FAULKNER, A. E., Private, Lincolnshire Regt.
He volunteered in September 1914, but was retained on special duties at Home stations until 1917. Proceeding to France in that year, he saw heavy fighting at Arras and Cambrai before being seriously wounded in action at Ypres. He was invalided home, and eventually discharged as medically unfit for further service in October 1918. Unfortunately he died from his wounds in hospital in London on October 16th, 1919, and was entitled to the General Service and Victory Medals.
" His memory is cherished with pride."
50, New Fenlake, Bedford. Z1913/C.

FAULKNER, B., Air Mechanic, Royal Air Force.
He joined in September 1918, but owing to the early cessation of hostilities was not successful in obtaining a transfer to the fighting area. He was stationed at Halton Camp, Tring and Harpswell, and was engaged on work calling for a high degree of technical knowledge and skill until demobilised in April 1919.
60, Queen Anne Street, New Bradwell, Bucks. Z2137.

FAULKNER, G. S. (M.M.), Cpl., 10th Rifle Brigade.
He joined in June 1916, and three months later proceeded to the Western Front, where he did excellent work as a Lewis gunner in various sectors. He fought in engagements on the Somme and at Ypres, and was severely wounded at Passchendaele in September 1917, which resulted in the loss of a leg. In August 1917 he was awarded the Military Medal for conspicuous gallantry and initiative under heavy fire, and on his discharge from hospital was demobilised in February 1919. He also holds the General Service and Victory Medals.
High Street, Wootton, Beds. Z2136.

FAULKNER, H., Pioneer, Royal Engineers.
Volunteering in March 1915, he was unable to obtain a transfer to a theatre of war owing to ill-health. He was, however, employed on important duties with his unit at various stations, and during the latter period of his service was engaged on agricultural work, which he performed in a very capable manner. In March 1919 he was demobilised.
Church End, Biddenham, Beds. Z2139.

FAULKNER, H. E., Air Mechanic, R.A.F.
He joined the Royal Air Force in March 1918, and after a course of training, was shortly afterwards drafted to the Western Front. There he saw much severe fighting in the Cambrai sector and in the engagements prior to the cessation of hostilities. He was wounded, and, after the Armistice, rendered valuable services in France until demobilised in January 1919, holding the General Service and Victory Medals.
Rose Cottages, Clapham, Bedford. Z2138.

FAULKNER, S., Private, 6th Bedfordshire Regt.
Volunteering in 1915, he served at Bedford and Felixstowe before being sent to the Western Front in the following year. He was engaged in severe fighting on the Somme and at Arras and Ypres, but was unfortunately killed in action on February 17th, 1917. He was entitled to the General Service and Victory Medals.
" His life for his Country."
Montague Street, Eynesbury, St. Neots, Hunts. Z2135/A.

FAULKNER, W., Private, Huntingdonshire Cyclist Battalion and Warwickshire Regiment.
He volunteered in September 1915, and was sent to France on completion of his training in 1916. Whilst on the Western Front he took part in heavy fighting in the Loos and Albert sectors, and was wounded in action and invalided to England. On his discharge from hospital he was employed on agricultural work until demobilised in March 1919. He holds the General Service and Victory Medals.
Montague Street, Eynesbury, St. Neots, Hunts. Z2135/B.

FAULKNER, W., Sapper, Royal Engineers.
Volunteering in December 1915, he was sent to France on completion of his training in the following year. Owing to ill-health he was not sent to the firing-line, but nevertheless rendered valuable services as a crane-driver at Calais until the cessation of hostilities. He was demobilised in November 1919, and holds the General Service and Victory Medals.
1, Station Road, Sandy, Beds. Z2140.

FAVELL, E., Sapper, Royal Engineers.
Joining in October 1916, he was engaged on important duties at home until April 1918, when he succeeded in obtaining a transfer to the Western Front. Whilst serving in that theatre of war he took part in severe fighting in engagements in the Somme and Cambrai sectors. He was demobilised in May 1919, and holds the General Service and Victory Medals.
Thrapston Road, Brampton, Hunts. Z2143.

FAVELL, F. W., Private, Suffolk Regiment.
He volunteered in December 1914, and, after a course of training at Colchester, was four months later sent to the Western Front. There he experienced fierce fighting in many important engagements, including the Battles of Ypres, Loos, the Somme, Arras and Cambrai. He served in France until February 1919, when he was demobilised, holding the 1914–15 Star, and the General Service and Victory Medals.
High Street, Hemingford Grey, Hunts. Z2141/A.

FAVELL, G., Private, Suffolk Regiment.
A month after the outbreak of war he volunteered, and, after training at Colchester, was drafted to France in the following year. Whilst serving on the Western Front he saw heavy fighting, chiefly in the Loos and Ypres sectors, and was unhappily killed in action at Ypres on May 19th, 1916. He was entitled to the 1914–15 Star, and the General Service and Victory Medals.
"His life for his Country."
High Street, Hemingford Grey, Hunts. Z2141/C.

FAVELL, H., Guardsman, Grenadier Guards.
He joined in 1916, and was drafted overseas in the following year. During his service on the Western Front he was in action in the Battles of Ypres, Lens, the Somme and Amiens, and in numerous other engagements of importance. At the close of hostilities he proceeded into Germany with the Army of Occupation, and served on the Rhine until demobilised in 1919. He holds the General Service and Victory Medals.
High Street, Hemingford Grey, Hunts. Z2141/B.

FEARY, E., Driver, Royal Army Service Corps.
He joined the Army in 1917, but, on completion of his training, was not successful in his efforts to secure a transfer to a theatre of war. Throughout the period of his service he was engaged on important transport work at Crowborough, Tring and Hastings, and fulfilled his duties in an exemplary manner. He was demobilised in September 1919.
Robb's Yard, The Waits, St. Ives, Hunts. Z2144/B.

FEARY, J. W., Private, Royal Fusiliers.
Joining in July 1916, he received his training at Dover, and three months later proceeded to the Western Front, where he took an active part in numerous important engagements. He saw fierce fighting on the Somme and at Arras, Lens and Cambrai, and served in France until 1919, when he was demobilised, holding the General Service and Victory Medals.
5, St. George's Terrace, St. Ives, Hunts. Z2144/C.

FEASEY, H. A., Driver, Royal Engineers.
He volunteered in November 1914, and in January 1916 was drafted to the Western Front, where he performed valuable work conveying food and ammunition to the forward areas. He also took an active part in many important engagements, including those at Arras, Ypres and Cambrai. In February 1919 he was demobilised, and holds the General Service and Victory Medals. 76, Cauldwell Street, Bedford. X2145.

FEASEY, J. H., Bombardier, R.G.A.
He joined in August 1916, and four months later proceeded to the Western Front. There he took part in numerous important engagements, including the Battles of the Somme, Arras, Vimy Ridge, Albert, Ypres, Passchendaele and Cambrai, and in the final Allied Advance. After the Armistice he served with the Army of Occupation at Cologne until demobilised in September 1919, holding the General Service and Victory Medals.
7, Northampton Terrace, Newport Pagnell, Bucks. Z2146.

FELCE, F., Private, 3/4th Oxford. & Bucks. L.I. and Labour Corps.
Joining in September 1916, he trained at Cheltenham, and in the following December was drafted to France. On that front he saw service in various sectors, fought in engagements at Péronne, and in August 1918 was sent to England suffering from trench-fever. On his recovery he served in Ireland with the Labour Corps, and was demobilised in February 1919, holding the General Service and Victory Medals.
25, Park Street, Bletchley, Bucks. Z3033.

FELLS, B., Private, 5th Royal Irish Fusiliers.
He volunteered in August 1914, and shortly afterwards was sent to France, but after taking part in heavy fighting at Ypres and Hill 60, he was transferred in December 1915 to Salonika. There he was in action in engagements on the Vardar and Struma fronts, and in 1917 proceeded to Palestine, where he served at Gaza and Jerusalem. In 1918 he returned to the Western Front, and was engaged in severe fighting in the Retreat and Advance. Demobilised in April 1919, he holds the 1914–15 Star, and the General Service and Victory Medals.
15, Cater Street, Kempston, Beds. X2147.

FENABLES, F., Private, 2nd Royal Berkshire Regt.
Volunteering in August 1914, he proceeded overseas in May of the following year. Whilst serving on the Western Front he was in action in numerous important engagements, especially in the Ypres, the Somme, Arras and Cambrai sectors. He also fought in the Retreat of 1918 and in the Allied Advance. He was demobilised in February 1919, and holds the 1914–15 Star, and the General Service and Victory Medals.
26, Gawcott Road, Buckingham. Z2148.

FENELEY, D. J., 2nd Corporal, Royal Engineers.
When war was declared in August 1914 he volunteered, and after a period of training proceeded to France, where he fought in the Battles of the Somme, Arras, Ypres and Cambrai. He also took part in engagements at Loos, and was wounded in action at Neuve Chapelle. He served in France until February 1919, and was demobilised a month later, holding the 1914–15 Star, and the General Service and Victory Medals.
36, Priory Street, Bedford. X2149.

FENN, A. W., Private, Royal Army Ordnance Corps and 10th Hampshire Regiment.
He volunteered in 1915, and, on completion of his training, was in the same year drafted to Salonika. In that theatre of war he took an active part in many engagements, and saw heavy fighting on the Doiran, the Struma and the Vardar fronts. On his return to England he was demobilised in April 1919, holding the 1914–15 Star, and the General Service and Victory Medals. 42, Bunyan Road, Bedford. Z2150.

FENSOM, C. W., Private, Huntingdonshire Cyclist Battalion and Machine Gun Corps.
He volunteered in November 1915, and in the following year proceeded to the Western Front, where he was in action on the Somme, at Dickebusch, Epéhy and Péronne, but was wounded in April 1917 and invalided to England. On his recovery he served with the Military Police at Derby and London until April 1918, when he returned to France. He saw heavy fighting at Cambrai, Le Hamel and Graincourt, and was demobilised in April 1919, holding the General Service and Victory Medals.
West Perry, Huntingdon. Z2152/A.

FENSOM, J. (M.M.), Private, Queen's Royal West Surrey Regiment.
He joined in March 1916, and four months later was drafted to the Western Front, where he fought and was wounded in the Battle of the Somme. He was invalided home and was in hospital for twelve months, after which he returned to France in 1917. He then took a prominent part in engagements at Messines, Ypres, Lens and Cambrai, and was awarded the Military Medal for conspicuous gallantry in the Field in September 1918. He was discharged as medically unfit in August 1920, and also holds the General Service and Victory Medals.
Wilden, near Bedford. Z2154/B.

FENSOM, J., Private, Middlesex Regiment.
Joining in March 1916, he was trained at Cambridge and Purfleet, and in the following August proceeded overseas. Whilst on the Western Front he was engaged in severe fighting at Ypres, and was unfortunately killed in action on the Ancre on November 17th, 1917. He was entitled to the General Service and Victory Medals.
"A valiant Soldier, with undaunted heart he breasted life's last hill."
Wilden, near Bedford. Z2154/A.

FENSOM, W. C., Private, Royal Scots.
He joined in May 1918, and was engaged on important duties with his unit at Tidworth and Salisbury Plain. Owing to the early termination of the war he was unsuccessful in procuring a transfer to a theatre of war, but nevertheless rendered many valuable services before being demobilised in November 1919.
Wilden, near Bedford. Z2154/C.

FENSOME, J., Private, Bedfordshire Regiment.
At the outbreak of hostilities in August 1914 he was already serving in the Army, and at once proceeded with the first Expeditionary Force to the Western Front. There he was engaged in fierce fighting in the Battles of Mons, Hill 60, Loos and the Somme, and owing to shell-shock was discharged as medically unfit for further service in September 1916. He holds the Mons Star, and the General Service and Victory Medals. 146, Bower Street, Bedford. Z2151/A.

FENSOME, W. E., Pte., Royal Inniskilling Fusiliers.
He volunteered in December 1915, and a year later was drafted to Salonika, where he was in action on the Struma and the Doiran fronts. In July 1917 he proceeded to Palestine and saw heavy fighting at Gaza and Jerusalem before being transferred in July 1918 to France. There he served in engagements on the Somme, at Cambrai, Villers-Outreaux and Le Cateau, and, when wounded in action, was invalided to England. On his discharge from hospital he was demobilised in February 1919, holding the General Service and Victory Medals.
East Perry, near Huntingdon, Hunts. Z2153

FERGUSON, T. A., Private, Devonshire Regt.
On attaining military age in March 1918 he joined the Army and rendered valuable services in the defence of the East Coast before being drafted to Ireland. There he was stationed at Dublin, and employed on important duties until demobilised in March 1919. 27, Broad St., Newport Pagnell, Bucks. TZ2155.

FESSEY, G. F., Pte., 1st Royal Warwickshire Regt.
He joined in April 1917, and on completion of a course of training was in the same year drafted to North Russia In that theatre of war he took an active part in numerous engagements and saw fierce fighting at Dvinsk. On his return to England he was stationed at Chatham, and in 1920 was still serving in the Army. He holds the General Service and Victory Medals.
38, Young Street, Wolverton, Bucks. Z2543/B.

FESSEY, J., Private, 2nd Oxford. & Bucks. L.I.
On the outbreak of hostilities in August 1914 he was mobilised with the Territorials, but was engaged on important duties at Aylesbury and Chelmsford until May 1916, when he was sent overseas. Whilst serving on the Western Front he took part in engagements on the Somme, and at Ypres, Bullecourt and Delville Wood, but his health broke down, and in consequence he was invalided out of the Army in February 1917. He holds the General Service and Victory Medals.
38, Young Street, Wolverton, Bucks. Z2543/A.

FESSEY, W. F., Bugler, 2nd Ox. & Bucks. L.I. (T.F.)
He joined in 1916, and, after a period of training at Chelmsford, proceeded in May of that year to France. On this front he fought in the Battle of the Somme and numerous other engagements, but was unhappily killed in action at Ypres on August 22nd, 1917. He was entitled to the General Service and Victory Medals.
"He died the noblest death a man may die,
Fighting for God and right and liberty."
38, Young Street, Wolverton, Bucks. Z2543/C.

FIELD, A., Private, 8th Leicestershire Regiment.
Joining in July 1918, he was quickly drafted to the Western Front, and was in action in the Advance of that year, during which he was taken prisoner and held in captivity until after the Armistice. Returning to England, he was finally demobilised in August 1919, and holds the General Service and Victory Medals. 74, St. John's Street, Kempston, Bedford. X2159/B.

FIELD, A. J., Pte., 2nd Oxford. & Bucks. L.I.
He joined in August 1916, and shortly afterwards proceeded to rance, where he was in action in much heavy fighting. He was present at the Battle of Arras, but was severely wounded, and died from the effects of his wounds on April 30th, 1917. He was entitled to the General Service and Victory Medals.
"Whilst we remember, the sacrifice is not in vain."
87, High Street, Olney, Bucks. Z2157.

FIELD, C., Private, Army Cyclist Corps.
He was mobilised at the outbreak of hostilities in August 1914, and immediately proceeded to France, where he saw much service as a Despatch-rider. He took an active part in the Battles of Mons and Ypres, and was later present at the Battles of Arras, Passchendaele and Cambrai. On his return to England he was discharged in February 1919, and holds the Mons Star, and the General Service and Victory Medals.
19, Derby Street, Bedford. X2158.

FIELD, F., Private, 1/4th Dorsetshire Regiment.
Volunteering at the outbreak of war in August 1914, he proceeded in the following year to Egypt, where he served for some time. He was also present during the British Advance into Palestine and took part in the Battles of Gaza and the capture of Jerusalem. In 1920 he was still serving with the Colours, and holds the 1914–15 Star, and the General Service and Victory Medals. 74, St. John's Street, Kempston, Bedford. X2159/A.

FIELD, H., Corporal, Bedfordshire Regiment.
Mobilised in August 1914, he immediately proceeded to France, where he played a prominent part in the Battles of Mons, Ypres, Hill 60, the Somme, Arras and Cambrai. In March 1918 he was reported missing after heavy fighting in the Cambrai sector and is now presumed to have been killed in action. He was entitled to the Mons Star, and the General Service and Victory Medals.
"He passed out of the sight of men by the path of duty and self-sacrifice."
74, Pilcroft Street, Bedford. X1639/A.

FIELD, H. E., Rifleman, Royal Irish Rifles.
He volunteered in January 1915, and after a period of training was drafted to France. During his service in this seat of war, he took part in many important engagements in various sectors of the front. He was in action during the heavy fighting at Thiepval, Messines and St. Quentin, where he was unfortunately killed in March 1918, and was entitled to the General Service and Victory Medals.
"The path of duty was the way to glory."
74, Bunyan Road, Kempston, Bedford. X2160.

FIELD, W., Ship's Cook, R.N., H.M.S. "Juno."
He volunteered in December 1914, and after a period of training proceeded to sea on board H.M.S. "Juno," in which ship he saw much service in the Persian Gulf, East Indies and the Red Sea. In 1917 he returned to home waters and was engaged on important mine-sweeping duties in the North Sea, and was wounded. He rendered excellent services throughout the period of hostilities, and was discharged medically unfit for further service in December 1919, holding the 1914–15 Star, and the General Service and Victory Medals.
12, Lawrence Street, Bedford. Z2156.

FILBY, W. H., Bombardier, R.G.A.
Joining in June 1916, he completed his training and was drafted to France. In the course of his service in this seat of war, he was in action with his Battery in many important engagements in various sectors of the front, and took an active part in the Battles of Arras, Cambrai and the Somme. Returning home after the Armistice he was demobilised in February 1919, and holds the General Service and Victory Medals.
122, Coventry Road, Queen's Park, Bedford. Z2161.

FINCH, B. A., Private, 5th Oxford. & Bucks. L.I.
Volunteering in 1914, he proceeded in the following year to the Western Front. During his short period of service in this theatre of war he was in action during the heavy fighting at the Battles of Festubert and Loos. He made the supreme sacrifice being killed on September 25th, 1915, and was entitled to the 1914–15 Star, and the General Service and Victory Medals.
"Thinking that remembrance, though unspoken, may reach him where he sleeps."
43, Priory Street, Newport Pagnell, Bucks. Z2163/D.

FINCH, F., Private, Royal Marine Light Infantry.
He joined in April 1918, and was shortly afterwards sent to France. During his service in this theatre of war, he took part in heavy fighting on the Somme and Cambrai fronts, where he was wounded in action and invalided to hospital. He was finally demobilised in February 1919, and holds the General Service and Victory Medals. Cold Brayfield, Beds. Z2162.

FINCH, S. F., Driver, Royal Horse Artillery.
He volunteered in August 1914, and in the following year was sent to France, where he took part in much heavy fighting. He was in action with his Battery in many important engagements, including those in the Ypres, Arras and Somme sectors, and remained in this seat of hostilities until after the Armistice. On his return to England in February 1919 he was demobilised, and holds the 1914–15 Star, and the General Service and Victory Medals. 43, Priory Street, Newport Pagnell. Z2163/B.

FINCH, W. T., Private, Worcestershire Regiment.
He joined in February 1916, and on conclusion of his training, was in the same year drafted to France. In the course of his service on the Western Front, he took part in much severe fighting in various sectors, particularly at the Battles of Arras, Ypres, Cambrai and the Somme, where he was unfortunately killed in action on May 27th, 1918. He was entitled to the General Service and Victory Medals.
"A valiant Soldier, with undaunted heart he breasted life's last hill."
43, Priory Street, Newport Pagnell, Bucks. Z2163/C.

FINCHER, J. G., Gunner, Royal Field Artillery.
Volunteering at the outbreak of war in August 1914, he completed his training and was retained on important duties. Later he proceeded to the Western Front and took part in many important engagements, including the Battles of Arras, Cambrai and the Somme, and was later in action throughout the Retreat and Advance of 1918. After the conclusion of hostilities he returned home and was demobilised in August 1919, holding the General Service and Victory Medals.
Pertenhall, near St. Neots, Hunts. Z2164.

FINDING, C., Private, 7th Bedfordshire Regiment.
He volunteered at the outbreak of hostilities in 1914, and, after a period of training, was drafted to France. There he took part in severe fighting in various sectors of the front, and was in action at the Battles of Albert, the Somme, Arras and Ypres. In October 1917 he was wounded at Passchendaele, and, being invalided to hospital in England, was finally discharged in August 1918. He holds the 1914–15 Star, and the General Service and Victory Medals.
Laburnham Road, Sandy, Bedfordshire. Z2165.

FISHER, A., Driver, Royal Engineers.
Mobilised at the outbreak of war, he was immediately drafted to the Western Front. During his service in this theatre of war he fought at the Battle of, and in the Retreat from, Mons, and also in the Battles of La Bassée and Ypres, and was wounded. In 1916 he proceeded to Egypt, his ship being torpedoed on the way to the East. As a result he was invalided to hospital, and after a period of treatment was finally demobilised in 1919. He holds the Mons Star, and the General Service and Victory Medals. 34, Park Road East, Bedford. Z2166/C.

FISHER, E., Sapper, Royal Engineers.
Volunteering in 1915, he proceeded to France in the following year. In the course of his service on the Western Front he took part in much heavy fighting. He was present at the Battles of Loos, Albert and the Somme, and later saw service at Arras, Lens, the Marne and Bapaume After the cessation of hostilities he was engaged on important duties at the Base, until returning for demobilisation in June 1919, and holds the General Service and Victory Medals.
34, Park Road East, Bedford. Z2166/B.

FISHER, F., Private, Canadian Light Infantry (Canadian Overseas Forces).
He joined in January 1916, and, after completing his training in the same year, proceeded to the Western Front. There he was in action during much heavy fighting, and took part in the engagements in the Somme and Cambrai sectors, and was wounded in November 1917. Returning to the fighting area on his recovery, he was present at other engagements until the close of hostilities. He was demobilised on his return to England in March 1919, and holds the General Service and Victory Medals.
124, Victoria Road, Fenny Stratford, Bucks. Z2168 /A.

FISHER, F., Aircraftsman, Royal Air Force.
He joined in January 1918, and on completion of his training was engaged on important duties in Sheffield. Owing to the early cessation of hostilities he was unable to proceed to a theatre of war, but in 1919 was sent to Egypt, where he was still serving in 1920.
34, Park Road East, Bedford. Z2166 /A.

FISHER, G., Private, Machine Gun Corps.
Volunteering in August 1914, he was first retained on important duties at various stations, but in 1917 he was drafted to Egypt, where he saw much service. Later he took part in the Advance into Palestine, and was in action at the Battles of Gaza and the capture of Jerusalem. He was then transferred to the Western Front and fought in engagements in the Cambrai and Somme sectors. He was demobilised in March 1919, and holds the General Service and Victory Medals.
10, Castle Lane. Bedford. X2169.

FISHER, R., Private, Canadian Light Infantry (Canadian Overseas Forces).
He joined in January 1916, and later in the same year was sent overseas. During his service on the Western Front he took part in much heavy fighting in various sectors. He was in action during the Somme Offensive and later in the Battle of Vimy Ridge, where he was wounded in April 1917. As a result he was invalided to hospital and finally certified as unfit for further military service, and was discharged in June 1918, holding the General Service and Victory Medals.
124, Victoria Road, Fenny Stratford, Bucks. Z2168 /B.

FISHER, T. D., Private, R.A.M.C.
He was called up from the Reserve at the declaration of war in August 1914, and after completing a period of training was retained on important duties at various stations. Later, in 1916, he proceeded to France, where he did good work as a stretcher-bearer, and took an active part in the engagements at Ypres, the Somme and Armentières. On his return to England in January 1919 he was discharged, and holds the General Service and Victory Medals.
63, High Street, New Bradwell, Bucks. TZ2167.

FITZGERALD, A. G., Pte., 6th Bedfordshire Regt.
Volunteering in September 1915, he completed his training and was drafted to France. During his service in this seat of war he took part in many important engagements in various sectors, and was wounded during the heavy fighting on the Somme. As a result he was invalided to England, and, after a period of hospital treatment, was finally demobilised in March 1919. He holds the General Service and Victory Medals.
80, Westbourne Road, Bedford. X2170.

FITZ-JOHN, B. F., Private, Machine Gun Corps.
He volunteered in August 1914, and, after a period of training, in the following year was drafted to Egypt. In the course of his service in the East he took part in many important engagements, including the Advance into Palestine and was in action at the Battles of Gaza. He made the supreme sacrifice, being killed in action on November 22nd, 1917, and was entitled to the 1914–15 Star, and the General Service and Victory Medals.
"And doubtless he went in splendid company."
Earith, Hunts. Z1132 /A.

FLATMAN, F. A., Corporal, R.E. (R.O.D.)
He volunteered in November 1915, and, after completing his training in the following year, was drafted to France, where he did good work as an electrical fitter in various sectors of the front. He served during the fighting on the Somme and in the Retreat and Advance of 1918, and was gassed. Later he was in charge of motor transport lorries, and rendered good services throughout the period of hostilities. He was demobilised in September 1919, and holds the General Service and Victory Medals.
39, Park Street, Bletchley, Bucks. TZ3034.

FLEET, A. F., Private, Royal Berkshire Regt.
He volunteered in October 1915, and, after the conclusion of his training, was drafted to Egypt. During his service in this seat of war he took part in much heavy fighting. He was also in action during the Advance into Palestine, and took part in the Battles of Gaza and the capture of Jerusalem. Later he was transferred to the Western Front and served at Cambrai. Returning to England, he was demobilised in February 1919, and holds the General Service and Victory Medals.
Gun Lane, Sherington, Newport Pagnell. Z2171.

FLEMONS, P. E. F., Private, R.A.S.C.
He volunteered in December 1915, and shortly afterwards proceeded to the Western Front, where he took part in many important engagements in various sectors. He served during the heavy fighting at Loos, the Somme, Arras, Ypres, Lens and Cambrai, and was twice wounded at Ypres. After the conclusion of hostilities, he went with the Army of Occupation into Germany, where he served until returning home for demobilisation in May 1919. He holds the General Service and Victory Medals.
76, Dudley Street, Bedford. Z2172.

FLETCHER, G., Private, Bedfordshire Regiment.
He volunteered early in 1915, and later in the same year proceeded to France, where he took an active part in the Battles of Loos and the Somme, and was wounded and invalided to hospital. After a period of treatment he returned to France, and was in action at the engagements at Arras, Ypres, Passchendaele and Cambrai, and in the Retreat and Advance of 1918. After the close of war he returned home, and was demobilised in February 1919, holding the 1914–15 Star, and the General Service and Victory Medals.
9, Station Road, Warboys, Hunts. Z2173.

FLINT, A., Corporal, Oxford. and Bucks. L.I.
He volunteered in September 1914, and was retained on important duties at various home stations until March 1916, when he proceeded to France. In the course of his service in this seat of war, he took part in the heavy fighting in the Somme and Ypres sectors. He made the supreme sacrifice, being killed in action on August 16th, 1917, and was entitled to the General Service and Victory Medals.
"His life for his Country, his soul to God."
10, School Street, New Bradwell, Bucks. Z2175 /A.

FLINT, F., Gunner, Royal Garrison Artillery.
Volunteering in May 1915, he was sent in the same year to France, where he did good work in various sectors of the front whilst attached to an Anti-Aircraft Section. He served during the heavy fighting at Ypres, Arras, Vimy Ridge and the Somme. After the conclusion of hostilities he returned to England, and was demobilised in February 1919, holding the 1914–15 Star, and the General Service and Victory Medals.
Morehanger, near Sandy, Beds. Z1944 /A.

FLINT, J. T., Sapper, Royal Engineers.
He joined in June 1916, and, on conclusion of his training in the same year, proceeded to France. During his service in this theatre of war, he was engaged on important duties during the Battles of Arras, Cambrai and the Somme, and did good work until the close of hostilities. He was demobilised in March 1919, and holds the General Service and Victory Medals.
27, Queen Street, Stony Stratford, Bucks. Z2174.

FLINT, W., Corporal, Royal Engineers.
Volunteering at the outbreak of war in August 1914, he was sent to France on completion of his training. During his short period of service on the Western Front, he took part in the heavy fighting on the Somme, where he was severely wounded in action. He unfortunately died from the effects of his wounds in July 1916, and was entitled to the General Service and Victory Medals.
"Whilst we remember, the sacrifice is not in vain."
10, School Street, New Bradwell, Bucks. Z2175 /B.

FLUTE, F. E., Private, Bedfordshire Regiment.
He volunteered in November 1914, and, after completing his training in the following year, was drafted to the Western Front. Whilst in this seat of hostilities he took part in the heavy fighting at the Battles of Loos, Somme, Arras, Ypres, Lens and Cambrai, where he was wounded. On his recovery he was present during the Retreat and Advance of 1918, and was demobilised in April 1919, holding the 1914–15 Star, and the General Service and Victory Medals.
Bromham, Bedford. Z2177.

FLUTE, W., Private, 2nd South Wales Borderers.
Joining in October 1916, he proceeded to France in the following March. During his service in this theatre of war, he took part in many important engagements in various sectors of the front. He fought at the Battle of Ypres and was later in action during the Retreat of 1918, where he was reported missing on April 11th, 1918, and finally presumed to have been killed on that date. He was entitled to the General Service and Victory Medals.
"A costly sacrifice upon the altar of freedom."
Chapel Yard, Great Linford, Bucks. Z2176.

FOLKES, F. J., Pte., 1/5th Bedfordshire Regiment.
Volunteering in September 1914, he was immediately drafted to France, where he took part in the Retreat from Mons, and the Battles of the Aisne, Hill 60 and Ypres. He was then transferred to the Dardanelles, and was present during the Landing at Suvla Bay, where he was unfortunately killed in action on August 6th, 1915, and was entitled to the Mons Star, and the General Service and Victory Medals.
"He joined the great white company of valiant souls"
Tags End, Wootton, Bedford. Z2178 /A.

FOLKES, J., L/Corporal, 4th Bedfordshire Regt.
He volunteered in September 1914, and after completing a period of training, in the following year was drafted to the Western Front. There he was in action during many important engagements, including the Battles of Neuve Chapelle, Hill 60, Ypres, Festubert and Loos. Later he took part in the Somme Offensive and the Battle of Arras, where he was reported missing on April 23rd, 1917, and is now presumed to have been killed in action on that date. He was entitled to the 1914–15 Star, and the General Service and Victory Medals.
"Thinking that remembrance, though unspoken, may reach him where he sleeps."
Tags End, Wootton, Bedford. Z2178/B.

FOOKES, F., Private, Bedfordshire Regiment.
He volunteered in September 1914, and on completion of his training in the following January proceeded to France and took part in the Battles of Ypres, Festubert, Loos (where he was gassed in 1915) and the Somme. He was later invalided home and transferred to the Labour Corps, with which unit he served on important agricultural duties, and also in the guarding of prisoners of war. In March 1919 he was demobilised, and holds the 1914–15 Star, and the General Service and Victory Medals. 4, Thurlow Street, Bedford. X2180.

FOOLKES, F., Private, 1st Hampshire Regiment.
He joined in June 1917, and on the conclusion of his training in the following year was drafted to France. After a very short period of active service he was unfortunately killed in action on April 22nd, 1918, during the second Battle of the Somme. He was entitled to the General Service and Victory Medals.
"His life for his Country, his soul to God."
19, Loughton Road, Old Bradwell, Bucks. Z2179/C.

FOOLKES, J., Private, 7th Wiltshire Regiment.
He volunteered in September 1914, and in the following year was drafted to France and served at Albert. In November 1915 he was transferred to Salonika, where he took part in the engagements on the Vardar, Doiran and Struma fronts. Early in 1918 he returned to France, and was in action throughout the closing operations of the war. Returning home, he was demobilised in March 1919, and holds the 1914–15 Star, and the General Service and Victory Medals.
19, Loughton Road, Old Bradwell, Bucks. Z2179/B.

FOOLKES, T. G., Cpl., Oxford. & Bucks. L.I. (T.F.)
Volunteering in September 1914, he was drafted to the Western Front in the following year. There he took part in much heavy fighting in various sectors, and was in action at the Battles of Ypres, Festubert, Loos and the Somme. In April 1917 he was wounded and invalided to England, and, after a period of hospital treatment, returned to France and saw further service. Later he was transferred to Italy, where he was in action during the engagements on the Piave front. On his return to England he was demobilised in March 1919, holding the 1914–15 Star, and the General Service and Victory Medals.
19, Loughton Road, Old Bradwell, Bucks. Z2179/A.

FOOTE, T., Private, 2nd Northamptonshire Regt.
He was already serving in Egypt at the outbreak of war in August 1914, and was quickly transferred to the Western Front, where he took part in the heavy fighting in various sectors. He fought at the Battles of Neuve Chapelle, Hill 60, Ypres, Loos and Passchendaele, and was three times wounded. He did excellent work throughout hostilities and was mentioned in Despatches for devotion to duty in the Field. Returning to England, he was discharged in March 1918, and holds the 1914 Star, and the General Service and Victory Medals.
7, North End Square, Buckingham. Z2181.

FOOTE, W. H., Private, Bedfordshire Regiment.
He volunteered in November 1915, and in the following year embarked for the Western Front. During his service in this theatre of war he took part in the fighting at Beaumont-Hamel, where he was reported missing in July 1916, and is now presumed to have been killed in action. He was entitled to the General Service and Victory Medals.
"And doubtless he went in splendid company."
12, Whitbread Avenue, Bedford. Z2182/A.

FORD, G., Sapper, Royal Engineers; and Private, Cheshire Regiment.
He volunteered in June 1915, and, after completing his training was retained with his unit on important duties until 1917. He then proceeded to France and took an active part in engagements in the Neuve Chapelle and Somme sectors, but was unfortunately killed in action on May 14th, 1917. He was entitled to the General Service and Victory Medals.
"He passed out of the sight of men by the path of duty and self-sacrifice."
West End, Cranfield, Beds. Z2185.

FORD, H. E., Private, 9th Royal Sussex Regiment.
He volunteered in September 1914, and in the following year was drafted to France, where he took part in much heavy fighting at Givenchy and Loos, and was seriously wounded in September 1915. He unfortunately died of his wounds on October 2nd, 1915, and was entitled to the 1914–15 Star, and the General Service and Victory Medals.
"A costly sacrifice upon the altar of freedom."
2, Bridge Street, New Bradwell, Bucks. Z2183/B.

FORD, J. W., Private, 1st Queen's Own (Royal West Kent Regiment).
He was called up from the Reserve in August 1914, and immediately drafted to France, where he took part in the Battle of Mons and in other important engagements. He was eventually sent home and discharged in January 1915 as medically unfit for further service, and holds the Mons Star, and the General Service and Victory Medals.
26, Caledonian Road, New Bradwell, Bucks. Z2184.

FORMSTONE, H., Driver, Royal Field Artillery.
He was already in the Army when war broke out in August 1914, but was retained for a time at various home stations and was engaged on important duties. In 1917 he proceeded to Egypt, took part in the Advance into Palestine, and was in action at Gaza and Jaffa. After hostilities ceased he was sent to India, where in 1920 he was still serving. He holds the General Service and Victory Medals.
High Street, Cranfield, Beds. Z2186.

FOSTER, A., Private, 10th Bedfordshire Regiment.
He volunteered in November 1915, and, after completing his training, was stationed at Colchester. He was unhappily taken ill and succumbed after an operation on his throat on April 30th, 1916, at Colchester Hospital.
"His memory is cherished with pride."
Ewelme Terrace, near Blunham, Beds. Z3850/B.

FOSTER, A. H., Private, 8th Bedfordshire Regiment.
He volunteered in 1914, and, on completing his training in the following year, was drafted to France, where he took part in much heavy fighting in the Ypres sector. He died gloriously on the Field of Battle on the Somme on September 15th, 1916, and was entitled to the 1914–15 Star, and the General Service and Victory Medals.
"The path of duty was the way to glory."
Piper's Lane, Godmanchester, Hunts. Z2187.

FOSTER, A. J., Private, Middlesex Regiment.
He joined in March 1917, and, after a period of training, was drafted to France, where he took part in much heavy fighting on the Somme. He was taken prisoner of war and held in captivity in Germany for several months, during which time he suffered many privations. He was repatriated after the Armistice, and was sent to hospital in England and finally discharged in February 1919, holding the General Service and Victory Medals.
12, Whitbread Avenue, Bedford. Z2182/B.

FOSTER, A. S., Private, West Riding Regiment.
He joined in September 1917, and underwent a period of training prior to his being drafted to France, where he took part in the Battle of Cambrai and was badly wounded. As a result he was invalided home, and on his recovery was engaged on agricultural work until his demobilisation in March 1919. He holds the General Service and Victory Medals.
Piper's Lane, Godmanchester, Hunts. Z2191/E.

FOSTER, F., Private, Bedfordshire Regiment.
Volunteering in 1915, he was drafted overseas in the following year. Whilst on the Western Front he took part in the Battles of Ypres and the Somme, and was wounded and taken prisoner. He was held in captivity in Germany, but was eventually released after the Armistice, and returned home. He was demobilised in 1919, and holds the General Service and Victory Medals. Cranfield, Beds. Z2188.

FOSTER, G., Private, Royal Fusiliers.
He enlisted in March 1917, and later in the same year proceeded to France, where he was wounded at the Battle of Cambrai. As a result he was invalided home, but, on his recovery, returned to his unit and was in action during the Advance of 1918. He was again wounded and sent home, and later was engaged on agricultural work until his demobilisation in August 1919. He holds the General Service and Victory Medals. Piper's Lane, Godmanchester, Hunts. Z2191/D.

FOSTER, H. A., Private, Machine Gun Corps.
He volunteered in November 1915, and, after completing his training in the following year, was drafted to France. There he saw much fighting on the Somme, at Arras, Ypres and Cambrai, and, after hostilities ceased, proceeded to Germany with the Army of Occupation. In 1920 he was serving in India, and holds the General Service and Victory Medals.
Piper's Lane, Godmanchester, Hunts. Z2191/C.

FOSTER, J. R., Driver, Royal Field Artillery.
He joined in July 1916, and in the following November proceeded to France, where he was engaged on important duties and saw much heavy fighting on the Somme and at Arras, Ypres, Amiens and Cambrai. Later he served with the Army of Occupation in Germany until his demobilisation in April 1919. He holds the General Service and Victory Medals.
Piper's Lane, Godmanchester, Hunts. Z2191/F.

FOSTER, M. R., Sergeant, 20th Hussars.
He was already in the Army when war broke out in August 1914, and quickly proceeded to the Western Front. There he took part in the Retreat from Mons, during which he was badly wounded in action and invalided home. On his recovery he was stationed at Colchester, where he did consistently good work as a Gymnastic Instructor. He was discharged in June 1919, and holds the Mons Star, and the General Service and Victory Medals. 7, Grey Friars Walk, Bedford. X2192/A.

FOSTER, R. G., A.B., Royal Naval Division.
He volunteered in December 1914, and after completing his training was drafted to France, where he saw much service at Le Havre and Dunkirk. He is believed to have been killed during an air raid at Dunkirk on December 31st, 1917. He was entitled to the General Service and Victory Medals.
"His life for his Country, his soul to God."
Piper's Lane, Godmanchester, Hunts. Z2190/A.

FOSTER, T. (M.M.), Private, Middlesex Regiment.
He volunteered in 1914, and underwent a period of training prior to his being drafted to France. There he played a distinguished part in the Battles of the Somme, Ypres and Cambrai, but was badly wounded in 1917 whilst saving an officers' life under heavy shell-fire, for which gallant deed he was awarded the Military Medal. He was invalided home, and finally discharged in May 1918 as medically unfit for further service. He also holds the General Service and Victory Medals.
Chadley Lane, Godmanchester, Hunts. Z2189.

FOSTER, T., Private, 4th Bedfordshire Regiment.
He volunteered in August 1914, and in the following year was drafted to France, where he took part in many engagements, including the Battles of Neuve Chapelle, Hill 60, Loos, the Somme, Arras and Ypres. He was badly wounded near Cambrai in 1917, and consequently invalided home and finally discharged in December 1918. He holds the 1914–15 Star, and the General Service and Victory Medals.
Piper's Lane, Godmanchester, Hunts. Z2191/B.

FOSTER, W. J., Private, Bedfordshire Lancers.
He volunteered in August 1914, and in the following June proceeded to France, where he was engaged on important duties. He also took part in the Battles of Festubert, Loos, the Somme, Ypres, Arras and Cambrai, and did continuously good work throughout hostilities. He was demobilised in February 1919, and holds the 1914–15 Star, and the General Service and Victory Medals.
Piper's Lane, Godmanchester, Hunts. Z2191/A.

FOSTER, W. S., Private, Middlesex Regiment.
He joined in May 1916, and later in the same year was drafted to Salonika. In this seat of operations he took part in many engagements on the Vardar and Doiran fronts, but contracted malaria, and unfortunately died on May 29th, 1918. He was entitled to the General Service and Victory Medals.
"Thinking that remembrance, though unspoken, may reach him where he sleeps."
Piper's Lane, Godmanchester, Hunts. Z2190/B.

FOUNTAIN, H., Sapper, Royal Engineers.
He joined in March 1916, and in the following year he was drafted to the East. In this seat of operations he was engaged on important pioneer duties during the Advance into Palestine, and was in action at Gaza, Jaffa, and the capture of Jerusalem. He returned home and was demobilised in December 1919, holding the General Service and Victory Medals.
5, Sandhurst Place East, Bedford. Z2193.

FOWKES, G., Private, Labour Corps.
He joined in May 1916, and after a period of training was engaged at various stations on important duties, and later worked on the land. He was unable to obtain a transfer overseas owing to his being medically unfit, but rendered valuable services until his demobilisation in March 1919.
41, High Street, Olney, Bucks. Z2194.

FOWLER, C. F., Driver, Royal Engineers.
He volunteered in December 1914, and underwent a period of training prior to his being drafted to the East. In this seat of operations he did consistently good work with the transport in Palestine, particularly at Gaza, Jaffa and Jerusalem. He returned home and was demobilised in June 1919, holding the General Service and Victory Medals.
37, Cavendish Street, Bedford. X2195/B.

FOWLER, G. A., Private, 1st Middlesex Regiment.
He joined in April 1916, and later in the same year was drafted to France, where he took part in much heavy fighting in the Messines sector. He was unfortunately killed in action in October 1917, and was entitled to the General Service and Victory Medals.
"Honour to the immortal dead, who gave their youth that the world might grow old in peace."
Corpus Christi, Godmanchester, Hunts. Z1026/A.

FOWLER, H., B.Q.M.S., R.G.A.
Volunteering in January 1915, he was drafted overseas later in the same year. Whilst on the Western Front he took part in several engagements, including the Battles of Loos, Vimy Ridge, the Somme, Arras, Cambrai, and in the Retreat and Advance of 1918. He was demobilised in March 1919, and holds the General Service and Victory Medals.
37, Cavendish Street, Bedford. X2195/A.

FOWLER, H. T., Private, 7th Oxford. & Bucks. L.I.
He volunteered in September 1914, and in the following year proceeded to France, where he took part in the Battle of Loos. Later he was transferred to Salonika and saw much fighting on the Doiran and Struma fronts, and in Macedonia. He returned home and was demobilised in January 1919, holding the 1914–15 Star, and the General Service and Victory Medals.
7, Church Street, Olney, Bucks. Z2196/C.

FOWLER, W. G., King's Sergeant, Motor M.G.C.
He volunteered in August 1914, and was quickly drafted to France, where he played a prominent part in the Battles of Ypres, Neuve Chapelle, Loos, Festubert, Albert, the Somme, Arras, Vimy Ridge, Cambrai, and in the Retreat and Advance of 1918. He was promoted to King's Sergeant for conspicuously good service in the Field. He was demobilised in 1919, and holds the 1914–15 Star, and the General Service and Victory Medals.
7, Church Street, Olney, Bucks. Z2196/D.

FRANCIS, A., Private, Bedfordshire Hussars.
He volunteered in 1915, and, after completing his training, was drafted to France, where he took part in much severe fighting at Hill 60, Ypres and on the Somme. He was seriously wounded at Cambrai, and unfortunately died through the effects of his wounds in 1918. He was entitled to the 1914–15 Star, and the General Service and Victory Medals.
"Great deeds cannot die:
They with the sun and moon renew their light for ever."
5, Dunville Road, Queen's Park, Bedford. Z2230/B.

FRANCIS, E. F. (M.M.), Gunner, R.G.A.
He volunteered in August 1914, and in the following year proceeded to Egypt, where he saw much fighting on the Suez Canal, at Mersa Matruh, and in the Advance into Palestine, being in action at Gaza. In 1917 he was transferred to France, where he played a distinguished part in the Battles of Arras and the Somme, and was wounded. He was awarded the Military Medal for conspicuous bravery in the Field during an Advance. He was demobilised in 1919, and also holds the General Service and Victory Medals.
5, Dunville Road, Queen's Park, Bedford. Z2230/A.

FRANCIS, F., Private, 1st Bedfordshire Regt.
He was already in the Army when war broke out in August 1914, and immediately proceeded to France, where he took part in the Retreat from Mons and the Battle of Ypres, and was badly wounded. As a result he was invalided home, but, on his recovery, was drafted to the Dardanelles and fought at Suvla Bay, being again wounded. Later he was sent to Egypt, and saw much fighting in the Advance into Palestine, at the Battles of Gaza, Jaffa and Haifa, and received his third wound. He was invalided to Alexandria, thence home, and was finally discharged in April 1919. He holds the Mons Star, and the General Service and Victory Medals.
Ivel Road, Sandy, Beds. Z2229.

FRANKLIN, C., Private, Machine Gun Corps.
He joined in October 1916, and in the following year was drafted to France. There he took part in many engagements, including the Battles of Ypres, Passchendaele and the Somme (II.), and was present at the entry into Mons on Armistice Day. Later he served in Palestine until his demobilisation in March 1920. He holds the General Service and Victory Medals.
Gawcott Road, Buckingham, Bucks. Z2233/B.

FRANKLIN, C. T., Private, 11th Northants. Regt.
He volunteered in November 1915, and, on completing his training in the following year, was drafted to the Western Front. In this theatre of war he took part in many engagements, including those at Merville, Vimy Ridge, the Somme, Arras and Armentières, and was gassed and suffered from shell-shock. He was transferred to the Labour Corps and engaged on important duties during the Retreat and Advance of 1918. He was demobilised in September 1919, and holds the General Service and Victory Medals.
Wellmore, Maids Moreton, Buckingham, Bucks. Z2234.

FRANKLIN, G. W., Cpl., 1st Bedfordshire Regt.
Prior to the outbreak of war he saw service in South Africa and India, and in 1914 was quickly drafted to France, where he took part in the Retreat from Mons and the Battles of the Marne and Festubert. He made the supreme sacrifice, being killed in action at Hill 60 on June 5th, 1915, and was entitled to the Mons Star, and the General Service and Victory Medals.
"The path of duty was the way to glory."
George Town, Sandy, Beds. Z1959/A.

FRANKLIN, H., Private, 3rd Suffolk Regiment.
He joined in October 1918 on attaining military age, and was engaged at various stations on important duties with his unit. He was medically unfit to obtain a transfer overseas, but rendered valuable services until his demobilisation in June 1919.
Chapel Yard, Green's Norton, Towcester, Northants. Z3035/B.

FRANKLIN, H. B., Pte., Yorks. Regt. & R.A.S.C.
He joined in 1916, and in the following year proceeded to Egypt. In this seat of operations he also took part in the Advance into Palestine, and saw much fighting at Gaza, Jaffa, and at the capture of Jerusalem. After hostilities ceased he remained overseas until his demobilisation in 1920. He holds the General Service and Victory Medals.
Yelling, St. Neots, Hunts. Z2231.

FRANKLIN, H. J., Private, R.A.S.C. (M.T.)
He joined in May 1917, and in the following August proceeded to France. There he did good work with the Mechanical Transport conveying supplies to the forward areas during engagements at Ypres, Zillebeke, Passchendaele and Armentières. He was demobilised in May 1919, and holds the General Service and Victory Medals.
2, Norton's Place, Buckingham, Bucks. Z2233 /C.

FRANKLIN, J., Private, 6th Dorsetshire Regt.
He joined in November 1917, and early in the following year proceeded to France, where he saw much fighting in the Ypres and Cambrai sectors. He died gloriously on the Field of Battle at Flers on August 24th, 1918, and was entitled to the General Service and Victory Medals.
"Honour to the immortal dead, who gave their youth that the world might grow old in peace."
Gawcott Road, Buckingham, Bucks. Z2233 /A.

FRANKLIN, S. G., Private, Suffolk Regiment.
He volunteered in May 1915, and later in the same year was drafted to France. In this theatre of war he took part in many important engagements, including the Battles of the Somme (I.), Arras, Ypres, Cambrai, Albert and the Somme (II.). He was demobilised in September 1919, and holds the 1914–15 Star, and the General Service and Victory Medals.
The Moor, Carlton, Beds. Z2235.

FRANKLIN, T., Private, R.A.S.C. (M.T.)
He joined in November 1916, and, after a period of training, was engaged at various stations on important transport work. After the Armistice he proceeded to France, and for some time served at Boulogne, where he did consistently good work. He was demobilised in November 1919.
21, Mitre Street, Buckingham. Z2232.

FRANKLIN, T., Private, 1st Northants. Regiment.
In spite of the fact that he had been exempted from military service on account of the vital importance of his occupation, he volunteered in October 1915. After a period of training, however, he was claimed by his employer and was accordingly discharged in February 1916. He then rendered valuable services on work of National importance throughout hostilities.
Chapel Yard, Green's Norton, Towcester, Northants. Z3035 /A.

FRANKS, C., Private, 2nd Bedfordshire Regiment.
Mobilised in August 1914, he immediately proceeded to France and played a prominent part in the Battles of Ypres (I.), Loos, the Somme (I.), Arras and Cambrai, in all of which engagements he was wounded in action. He was also present at the entry into Mons on Armistice Day, when he received his sixth wound. Discharged in March 1919, he holds the 1914 Star, and the General Service and Victory Medals.
19, Patteshall Street, Bedford. X2238.

FRANKS, E., Private, Bedfordshire Regiment.
He was mobilised in August 1914 and immediately drafted to the Western Front. Whilst in this theatre of war he took part in the Battles of Mons (and in the subsequent Retreat), Ypres, Hill 60, Arras and Cambrai, and was wounded in action six times. He was discharged in March 1919, and holds the Mons Star, and the General Service and Victory Medals.
7, Tower Court, Bedford. X2237 /A.

FRANKS, S., Private, R.A.S.C.
He joined in March 1916, and after a period of training was engaged at various stations on important duties with his unit. He was unable to obtain a transfer overseas owing to his being medically unfit, but rendered valuable services until his demobilisation in November 1919.
7, Tower Court, Bedford. X2237 /B.

FRANKS, W. C., Private, Worcestershire Regt.
Joining in March 1917, he was drafted to the Western Front in December of that year, and there saw severe fighting in various sectors. He took part in the Battles of the Marne and Ypres and many other important engagements, and was wounded in action at Ypres in 1917. Returning home in 1918 he was demobilised in February of the following year, and holds the General Service and Victory Medals.
Church Road, Wilden, near Bedford. Z2236 /A.

FRANKS, W. G., Private, 2nd Bedfordshire Regt.
He volunteered in November 1914, and in June of the following year proceeded to the Western Front, where he saw much heavy fighting and was twice wounded in action. After taking part in the Battles of Loos and the Somme and other engagements, he was taken prisoner in the Ancre sector in February 1917, and held in captivity until after the cessation of hostilities. Demobilised in January 1919, he holds the 1914–15 Star, and the General Service and Victory Medals.
East End, Wilden, near Bedford. Z2236 /B.

FRAZER, E. M. (Mrs.), Special War Worker.
During the period of hostilities this lady was engaged on work of National importance at Messrs. Kent's Filling Factory at Luton, where, employed on responsible and dangerous duties, she rendered very valuable services. She unfortunately contracted T.N.T. poisoning and was forced to resign her post in consequence, but whilst convalescent did much useful work for Queen Mary's Guild. 7, Church St., Olney, Bucks. Z2196 /B.

FRAZER, F. C., Pte., Beds. Regt. & Labour Corps.
Volunteering in November 1914, he was drafted to the Western Front after two months' training and there fought in various sectors. He took part in the Battles of Loos and Arras and many other important engagements, and was twice wounded—at Ypres in 1915 and on the Somme in 1917. Invalided home, he afterwards served with the Labour Corps on agricultural work until his demobilisation in March 1919. He holds the 1914–15 Star, and the General Service and Victory Medals.
7, Church Street, Olney, Bucks. Z2196 /A.

FREAME, A. G., Private, 5th Bedfordshire Regt.
He volunteered in August 1914, and was retained on important duties in England until January 1916, when he proceeded to the Western Front. After taking part in heavy fighting at Loos, Vimy Ridge and many other places, he was severely wounded in action on the Somme in September 1916, and admitted to hospital at Manchester. He was invalided from the Army in October 1917, and holds the General Service and Victory Medals. 59, Marlborough Road, Bedford. Z2239.

FREAME, C. P., Private, R.A.M.C.
Mobilised in August 1914, he was immediately drafted to the Western Front, where, after serving through the Retreat from Mons, he was present at the Battles of Ypres and Hill 60, and other engagements. In January 1916 he was transferred to Salonika, and there served on the Vardar and Doiran fronts, until sent home and invalided from the Army in November 1918. He holds the Mons Star, and the General Service and Victory Medals. 65, Ford End Road, Bedford. Z1254 /C.

FREAME, E. A., Trooper, Bedfordshire Lancers.
Shortly after joining in February 1916 he was drafted to France, where he saw severe fighting in various sectors of the front. He took part in the Battles of the Somme, Arras, Ypres and Cambrai, and many other important engagements until the cessation of hostilities, and on his return home in March 1919 was demobilised. He holds the General Service and Victory Medals. 65, Ford End Road, Bedford. Z1254 /B.

FREEMAN, A., Private, 1st Bedfordshire Regt.
Mobilised in August 1914, he was shortly afterwards drafted to the Western Front, where he fought in the Battles of La Bassée and Ypres, and many minor engagements, and was wounded at Hill 60 in 1915. He made the supreme sacrifice, falling in action at Ypres in July of that year. He was entitled to the 1914 Star, and the General Service and Victory Medals.
"Steals on the ear the distant triumph song."
Castle Road, Lavendon, Bucks. Z2542.

FREEMAN, A. E., Private, 2nd Bedfordshire Regt.
He was mobilised in August 1914, and was immediately drafted to the Western Front, where he served through the Retreat from Mons. After taking part also in the Battles of the Marne, the Aisne and La Bassée, he was taken prisoner at Ypres in November 1914, and, whilst in captivity in Germany, was engaged as a telephone operator. Released in December 1918, he holds the Mons Star, and the General Service and Victory Medals, and in 1920 was still with his unit.
The Baulk, Beeston, Beds. Z2241 /A.

FREEMAN, A. H., L/Corporal, Bedfordshire Regt.
He volunteered in August 1914, and in the following year was drafted to the Western Front. Whilst in this theatre of war he saw much heavy fighting, and, after taking part in the Battles of Ypres, Arras and Lens and other engagements, was severely wounded in action on the Somme in April 1918, and admitted to hospital in Scotland. He was invalided from the Army in 1918, and holds the 1914–15 Star, and the General Service and Victory Medals. Kimbolton, Hunts. Z2244 /B.

FREEMAN, C., Private, 4th Bedfordshire Regt.
He volunteered in June 1915, and in the following year was drafted to the Western Front, where he was engaged on pioneer duties in various sectors. He was also present at the Battles of the Somme and Ypres and other engagements, and was later attached to a Labour Battalion. He was demobilised in February 1919, and holds the General Service and Victory Medals. 75, Garfield Street, Bedford. Z2242.

FREEMAN, E., Private, Huntingdonshire Cyclist Battalion and Royal Warwickshire Regiment.
He volunteered in August 1914, and was retained in England until 1916, when he proceeded to the Western Front. After taking part in the Battles of the Somme, Arras and Ypres and minor engagements, he was wounded in action in 1917, and invalided home. He returned to France, however, on his recovery, fought at Passchendaele, Cambrai and the Somme, and was gassed at Lens in October 1918. Demobilised in March 1919, he holds the General Service and Victory Medals.
5 St. George's Terrace, St. Ives, Hunts. Z2522 /A.

FREEMAN, H. H., Private, Oxford. & Bucks. L.I.
He joined in March 1916, and, on completing his training in the following August, proceeded to the Western Front, where he saw much severe fighting. He died gloriously on the Field of Battle during the Somme Offensive in August 1916, after only a month's active service. He was entitled to the General Service and Victory Medals.
"Thinking that remembrance, though unspoken, may reach him where he sleeps."
Green's Norton, Towcester, Northants. Z3036/B.

FREEMAN, H. W., Pte., 5th Oxford. & Bucks. L.I.
Joining in April 1916, he was drafted to the Western Front in December of that year, and was there engaged on important duties as a signaller in various sectors. He was unhappily reported missing, and later, killed in action at Arras on May 3rd, 1917. He was entitled to the General Service and Victory Medals.
Nobly striving :
He nobly fell that we might live."
44, East Street, Olney, Bucks. Z2240.

FREEMAN, J. W., Private, Northants. Regiment.
He volunteered in September 1915, and in the following year was drafted to the Western Front, where he saw severe fighting in various sectors. After taking part in the Battles of Arras, Ypres and Cambrai and many other engagements, he was sent home in 1918, and, attached to the Labour Corps, was engaged on agricultural work until his demobilisation in 1919. He holds the General Service and Victory Medals.
Kimbolton, Hunts. Z2244/A.

FREEMAN, P., Rflmn., King's Royal Rifle Corps.
He volunteered in 1914, but was shortly afterwards claimed from the Army on account of his youth. He re-enlisted, however, in 1916 and, in the following year was drafted to the Western Front, where he saw severe fighting in various sectors. He took part in the Battles of Messines, Cambrai and Amiens, was wounded in action, and after the cessation of hostilities was engaged in escorting prisoners of war to the frontier. Demobilised in 1919, he holds the General Service and Victory Medals.
5, St. George's Terrace, St. Ives, Hunts. Z2522/B.

FREEMAN, W., L/Corporal, Northants. Dragoons.
Having enlisted in 1911, he was drafted to the Western Front three months after the outbreak of war in August 1914. He took part in the Battles of La Bassée and Ypres, and many other important engagements, fought also in the Retreat and Advance of 1918, and, afterwards, attached to the Military Mounted Police, served at Cologne with the Army of Occupation. He was discharged on his return home in June 1919, and holds the Mons Star, and the General Service and Victory Medals.
Green's Norton, Towcester, Northants. Z3036/A.

FREEMAN, W., Corporal, 6th Bedfordshire Regt.
He volunteered at the outbreak of war in August 1914, and in the following year was drafted to the Western Front, where he took part in the Battles of Loos, Vimy Ridge, the Somme, Arras and Messines Ridge and many other engagements. He was killed in action at Ypres on July 22nd, 1917. He was entitled to the 1914–15 Star, and the General Service and Victory Medals.
"He joined the great white company of valiant souls."
The Baulk, Beeston, Beds. Z2241/C.

FREEMAN, W. C., Gunner, Royal Field Artillery.
He volunteered in June 1915, and in the same year proceeded overseas. He saw much severe fighting in Mesopotamia, where he was present at the relief of Kut and the capture of Baghdad, and afterwards served in Palestine, where he was wounded in action at Gaza. He also saw active service in Italy, on the Piave, and in 1918 was transferred to the North West Frontier of India. Demobilised on his return home in September 1919, he holds the 1914–15 Star, and the General Service, Victory, and the India General Service Medals (with clasp, Afghanistan, North West Frontier, 1919).
15, All Hallows Lane, Bedford. X2243.

FREEMAN, W. J., Private, 3rd Norfolk Regt.
He joined in March 1918, and, after completing a period of training, served at various stations, where he was engaged on duties of great importance. Owing to the early cessation of hostilities, he was unable to obtain his transfer to a theatre of war, but, nevertheless, rendered valuable services with his unit until February 1919, when he was demobilised.
The Baulk, Beeston, Beds. Z2241/B.

FRENCH, A. E. M., Rifleman, 18th K.R.R.C.
Volunteering in November 1915, he proceeded to the Western Front after three months' training, and there saw much severe fighting. He made the supreme sacrifice, being killed in action at St. Eloi in 1916, after only a few weeks' service in France. He was entitled to the General Service and Victory Medals.
"He passed out of the sight of men by the path of duty and self-sacrifice."
60, Young Street, Wolverton, Bucks. Z2526.

FRENCH, A. G., Private, 7th Oxford. & Bucks. L.I.
He volunteered in September 1914, and in the following year was drafted to Salonika, where he took part in many important engagements on the Vardar and Doiran fronts. He was unhappily reported missing and believed to have been killed in action on May 9th, 1917. He was entitled to the 1914–15 Star, and the General Service and Victory Medals.
"And doubtless he went in splendid company."
32, York Road, Stony Stratford, Bucks. Z2527.

FRENCH, C. E., Sapper, Royal Engineers.
He volunteered in May 1915, and, in November of that year, proceeded to France, where he was engaged in bridge-building and other important duties. He served at Ypres, the Somme and Cambrai, and in various other sectors of the front, and did much useful work until his return home for demobilisation in January 1919. He holds the 1914–15 Star, and the General Service and Victory Medals.
1, Armdale Cottages, Newport Pagnell, Bucks. Z2529.

FRENCH, F., A.B., Royal Navy.
Already in the Navy when war was declared in August 1914, he afterwards served in H.M.S. "Good Hope" in many waters. He unfortunately lost his life when his ship was sunk at the Battle of Coronel on November 1st, 1914. He was entitled to the 1914–15 Star, and the General Service and Victory Medals.
"Courage, bright hopes, and a myriad dreams, splendidly given."
33, Beaconsfield Place, Newport Pagnell, Bucks. Z2530.

FRENCH, H. G., Guardsman, 2nd Grenadier Guards.
He volunteered in December 1914, and four months later proceeded to France, where he took part in heavy fighting in the Ypres and Somme sectors. Badly wounded in action at Ypres in 1916, he was invalided home, and, on his recovery, was transferred to the Royal Engineers, with which unit he served until his demobilisation in March 1919. He holds the 1914–15 Star, and the General Service and Victory Medals.
81, Victoria Road, Fenny Stratford, Bucks. Z2524.

FRENCH, J., Sapper, R.E. (Signal Section).
Mobilised in August 1914, he was drafted to France immediately and was engaged on important duties in the Somme, Amiens, Givenchy, Loos and Ypres sectors. In February 1917 he was evacuated to England with rheumatic fever, and was in hospital in London. On his recovery he served with the Royal Engineers' Postal Section at home stations, until his discharge in March 1919, holding the 1914 Star, and the General Service and Victory Medals. 24, Well Street, Buckingham. Z2525.

FRENCH, W., Sapper, Royal Engineers (R.O.D.)
He joined in February 1917, and was quickly drafted to the Western Front, where he rendered valuable services with the Railway Operative Department, and was engaged in carrying supplies to the forward areas in the Arras, Cambrai and Somme sectors. He was demobilised in October 1919, and holds the General Service and Victory Medals.
29, Victoria Road, Fenny Stratford, Bucks. Z2523.

FRENCH, W. T., Private, Royal Berkshire Regt.
Joining in June 1916, he was sent to France three months afterwards, and took part in much strenuous fighting. He was seriously wounded in action in the Cambrai sector in March 1917, and unfortunately died from the effects of his wounds on April 6th. He was buried at Etaples Military Cemetery, and was entitled to the General Service and Victory Medals.
"A costly sacrifice upon the altar of freedom."
37, Russell Street, Stony Stratford, Bucks. Z2528.

FRESHWATER, F., Pte., 8th Bedfordshire Regt.
He volunteered in May 1915, and, proceeding to France early in the following year, was first in action at Loos. Later he played a prominent part in the Battles of the Somme, Arras, Vimy Ridge and Cambrai, and in heavy fighting during the Retreat and Advance of 1918, when he was wounded on two occasions. Demobilised in February 1919, he holds the General Service and Victory Medals.
5, Russell Street, Bedford. X2531/A.

FRESHWATER, G., Pte., 13th Royal Sussex Regt.
He joined in October 1916, and was drafted to the Western Front early in the following year. Whilst in this theatre of war he took part in the Battles of Arras (where he was wounded in action in 1917), Bullecourt, Ypres, Passchendaele and Cambrai. He was demobilised on his return home in May 1919, and holds the General Service and Victory Medals.
5, Russell Street, Bedford. X2531/B.

FREW, E. H., Private, Royal Fusiliers.
Volunteering in January 1916, he proceeded to France in July and went straight into action on the Somme, where he saw much severe fighting during the Offensive. He later took part in the Battles of Arras and Ypres, and in the Retreat, but was unfortunately killed near Cambrai on August 31st, 1918. He was entitled to the General Service and Victory Medals.
"His life for his Country, his soul to God."
36, Muswell Road, Bedford. TZ1301/A.

FROST, A. H., Rifleman, 8th London Regiment (Post Office Rifles).
He volunteered in November 1915, and on completion of his training was drafted to the Western Front, where he played an important part in the Battles of the Somme, Ypres and Cambrai and in heavy fighting in various other sectors. He was eventually demobilised in 1919, and holds the General Service and Victory Medals. Ellington, Hunts. Z2532.

FROST, C., Sapper, Royal Engineers.
Having previously served through the Boer war and in India, he was mobilised in August 1914, but, owing to medical unfitness, was not drafted overseas. He nevertheless rendered valuable services whilst engaged on special ship-building work, and was finally discharged in December 1918. He holds the Queen's and King's South African Medals.
Pertenhall, St. Neots, Hunts. Z2699/B.

FROST, G., Gunner, Royal Field Artillery.
He joined in July 1916, and in November was drafted to the Western Front, where he was in action with his Battery on the Somme. Unfortunately he sustained a serious injury in an accident, and, after nine months in hospital at Birmingham, was sent to Fermoy in Ireland, where he was engaged on important duties during the Sinn Fein troubles. He was eventually discharged in April 1919, and holds the General Service and Victory Medals.
6, Riverside, Newport Pagnell, Bucks. Z2533.

FROST, H., Private, Suffolk Regt. and R.A.S.C.
He volunteered in 1914, and in the following year was sent to the Gallipoli Peninsula, where he was badly wounded in action during the Landing at Suvla Bay in August 1915. Invalided to England he spent some time in hospital, and was then transferred to the Royal Army Service Corps, with which unit he did excellent work at home stations until his demobilisation in January 1919. He holds the 1914–15 Star, and the General Service and Victory Medals.
Hemingford Abbots, Hunts. Z2534.

FULLER, A. H., Private, Northants. Regiment.
He joined in 1916, and, on completion of his training, was engaged on special duties at various home stations. Owing to his being medically unfit, he was unsuccessful in obtaining his transfer to a theatre of war, but did excellent work with his unit until his demobilisation in December 1919.
9, Short Street, Queen's Park, Bedford. Z2540/B.

FULLER, B., Private, 1st Bedfordshire Regiment.
Volunteering in September 1914, he was drafted to France six months later and took part in the Battles of Neuve Chapelle, Hill 60, Festubert and Loos. He died gloriously on the Field of Battle on the Somme on July 28th, 1916, and was entitled to the 1914–15 Star, and the General Service and Victory Medals.
"A valiant Soldier, with undaunted heart he breasted life's last hill."
95, Woburn Road, Kempston, Bedford. X2537/B

FULLER, H., 1st Air Mechanic, Royal Air Force.
He volunteered in March 1915, and four months later proceeded to Gallipoli with the 1/5th Bedfordshire Regiment, but was wounded in action at the Landing at Suvla Bay in August of the same year. On his recovery he was drafted to France, and served as a mechanic in the workshops, where he was engaged on work which required a high degree of technical skill. He was demobilised in March 1919, and holds the 1914–15 Star, and the General Service and Victory Medals.
23, Grey Friars Walk, Bedford. X2539

FULLER, H., Private, Suffolk Regiment.
He joined in June 1916, and, on completion of his training, was drafted to France, where he took part in the Battles of Vimy Ridge and Ypres. At the end of 1917 he was transferred to Italy, and was in action on the Asiago Plateau and the Piave. He also served in the Royal Warwickshire Regiment, and was demobilised in February 1919, holding the General Service and Victory Medals.
3, Bedesman's Place, Bedford. X2535.

FULLER, J., Sapper, Royal Engineers.
Mobilised with the Territorials in August 1914, he was eventually drafted to France and took part in the Battles of Neuve Chapelle, Hill 60, Festubert, Loos and the Somme. He died gloriously on the Field of Battle in the Ancre sector on November 14th, 1916, and was entitled to the 1914–15 Star, and the General Service and Victory Medals.
9, Short Street, Queen's Park, Bedford. Z2540/A.

FULLER, R., Private, 4th Bedfordshire Regiment.
Volunteering in November 1915, he was drafted to the Western Front and saw much severe fighting. He took part in engagements at Loos, Vimy Ridge and Beaumont-Hamel, and was unhappily killed in action on November 30th, 1916. He was entitled to the General Service and Victory Medals.
62, Russell Street, Bedford. X2536.

FULLER, S., Corporal, Labour Corps.
He volunteered in November 1914, and, after a period of service in England, was sent to France in September 1916. Whilst on the Western Front he took part in the Battles of the Somme, Arras and Ypres, where he was badly wounded in action in August 1917. On his recovery he was engaged on important guard duties at prisoner of war camps until his demobilisation in March 1919. He holds the General Service and Victory Medals.
95, Woburn Road, Kempston, Bedford. X2537/A.

FULLER, W., Sapper, Royal Engineers.
He volunteered in August 1914, and in December was drafted to the Western Front, where he took part in the Battles of Neuve Chapelle, Hill 60, Festubert and Loos before being wounded in action and invalided home. Returning to France in June 1916, he fought at Vimy Ridge, Beaumont-Hamel and Beaucourt, but was again badly wounded and sent to England. He was discharged as medically unfit for further service, holding the 1914–15 Star, and the General Service and Victory Medals. 34, College Road, Bedford. Z2538.

FURR, W., Private, East Surrey Regiment.
Already in the Army when war was declared, he immediately proceeded to the Western Front and served through the Retreat from Mons. After taking part in other important engagements, including the Battles of La Bassée and Ypres, he was unfortunately killed in action at the Battle of Loos in September 1915. He was entitled to the Mons Star, and the General Service and Victory Medals.
"He joined the great white company of valiant souls."
16, Princess Street, Bedford. X2541/C.

G

GABLE, I. G. H., Private, 1st Hampshire Regt.
He joined in February 1916, and later in the same year was drafted to France. There he took part in many important engagements, including the Battles of the Somme, Ypres and Cambrai. He was later in action in various sectors during the Retreat and Advance of 1918, and did excellent work. Demobilised on his return home in April 1919, he holds the General Service and Victory Medals.
Berkley Cottages, Stoke Goldington, Bucks. Z2544.

GADSBY, F., Private, Bedfordshire Regiment.
He volunteered in September 1915, and in the following July proceeded to the Western Front. In this theatre of war he participated in the Battle of the Somme and in strenuous fighting at Vimy Ridge, and was unfortunately killed in action on April 27th, 1917, during the Battle of Arras. He was entitled to the General Service and Victory Medals.
"Honour to the immortal dead, who gave their youth that the world might grow old in peace."
5, Swan Terrace, Goldington, Beds. Z2545/B.

GADSBY, J., Private, 2nd Bedfordshire Regiment.
Volunteering in March 1915, he was sent early in the following year to France, where he was in action on the Somme front and at Arras. He was wounded in July 1916, and invalided home in 1917 suffering from shell-shock. Returning later to France, he took part in further fighting at Kemmel Hill and Combles, and was wounded for the second time in October 1918. He was demobilised in January 1919, and holds the General Service and Victory Medals.
5, Swan Terrace, Goldington, Beds. Z2545/A.

GADSDEN, J. F., Private, Bedfordshire Regiment.
He volunteered in November 1914, and, after completing his training, rendered valuable service whilst employed as Lewis Gun Instructor at Felixstowe until 1916, when he was drafted to France. There he took part in strenuous fighting on the Somme front and at Vimy Ridge and Arras. Invalided home later on account of ill-health, he was discharged in April 1918, and unhappily died on October 30th, 1918, from an illness contracted on military service. He was entitled to the General Service and Victory Medals.
"His memory is cherished with pride."
East End, Wilsden, near Bedford. Z2546/B.

GAGE, B., Bombardier, Royal Garrison Artillery.
He volunteered in 1914, and in the following year proceeded to the Western Front. In this theatre of hostilities he participated with his Battery in the Battles of Festubert, Loos, Arras and Cambrai, and was also in action at Messines Ridge. He remained overseas until after the Armistice, and was demobilised in April 1919, holding the 1914–15 Star, and the General Service and Victory Medals.
2, Victoria Terrace, Huntingdon. Z2547/B.

GAGE, S. A., Bombardier, Royal Field Artillery.
Joining in 1916, he was sent for training to High Wycombe, and in the following year was drafted to France. There he was in action during the Battles of Ypres (III.), Cambrai and the Somme, and in various sectors during the Retreat and Advance of 1918. Returning home after the termination of hostilities, he was demobilised in April 1919, and holds the General Service and Victory Medals.
2, Victoria Terrace, Huntingdon. Z2547/A.

GAILER, A. J., Bombardier, R.G.A.
Called up from the Reserve in August 1914, he was ordered to the Western Front in the following December, and in this theatre of hostilities took part in heavy fighting during the Battles of Hill 60 and Ypres, and fell gloriously on the Field at Festubert on May 11th, 1915. He was entitled to the 1914–15 Star, and the General Service and Victory Medals.
"Whilst we remember, the sacrifice is not in vain."
1, Cross Street, Newtown, Hunts. Z2548.

GALE, A., Private, Middlesex Regiment.
He joined in 1916, and, after a period of training, proceeded to Salonika. In this theatre of hostilities he took part in many severe engagements on the Doiran and Struma fronts. He was later invalided home suffering from malaria, and sent to hospital at Lincoln, afterwards spending seven months in hospital at Cambridge. He was eventually discharged in September 1919, holding the General Service and Victory Medals.
Mill Road, Buckden, Hunts. Z2549/A.

GALE, J. T., Sapper, Royal Engineers.
Joining in February 1916, he was stationed during his training at Chatham, and in 1917 was drafted to France, where he served in the Ypres sector. Suffering from shell-shock, he was evacuated to England, and was a patient in hospitals at Finchley and Epsom prior to being invalided out of the Service in May 1919 as unfit for further military duty. He holds the General Service and Victory Medals.
Church Street, Buckden, Hunts. Z2550.

GALLOP, W., Private, Royal Welch Fusiliers.
He volunteered in April 1915, and for a considerable period was retained at home on important duties. Eventually proceeding to the Western Front, he was wounded near the Somme in 1917, but upon his recovery rejoined his unit and was in action in various sectors. He did good work until he fell fighting in May 1918, during the third Battle of the Aisne. He was entitled to the General Service and Victory Medals.
"His life for his Country."
124, Bower Road, Bedford. Z2551.

GALTRESS, F., Private, Oxford. and Bucks. L.I.
Mobilised when war broke out in August 1914, he was drafted a month later to France. There he played a prominent part with his unit in the Battles of the Marne, the Aisne, Ypres and Neuve Chapelle, and was also in action at Armentières. He was wounded near Ypres in 1915, evacuated to England, and remained in hospital in Scotland until June 1916, being then discharged as unfit for further service. He holds the 1914 Star, and the General Service and Victory Medals.
80, Spencer Street, New Bradwell, Bucks. Z1168/B.

GALTRESS, G., Pte., 15th R. Warwickshire Regt.
Serving with the Colours since 1912, he proceeded overseas with the first Expeditionary Force shortly after the outbreak of war in August 1914. On the Western Front he participated in the Battle of Mons and the subsequent Retreat, also in the Battles of Ypres, Loos and the Somme, and was unfortunately killed in action near Passchendaele Ridge in October 1917. He was entitled to the Mons Star, and the General Service and Victory Medals.
"Great deeds cannot die."
74, Aylesbury Street, Wolverton, Bucks. Z2552/A.

GALTRESS, H., Private, 12th Royal Fusiliers.
He joined in January 1916, and, after completing his training at Hounslow, was drafted in the following May to France. He had only served overseas for a few weeks when he made the supreme sacrifice, being killed near Corbie in June 1916. He was entitled to the General Service and Victory Medals.
"A costly sacrifice upon the altar of freedom."
74, Aylesbury Street, Wolverton, Bucks. Z2552/B.

GAMAGE, A. E., Private, 1st Bedfordshire Regt.
Volunteering in December 1915, he was retained at home on various duties of an important nature until June 1917, when he was sent to India. Whilst stationed with his unit in Delhi he was employed on garrison and other duties, and did good work until he returned home for demobilisation in March 1919, holding the General Service and Victory Medals.
2, Agusta Road, Stony Stratford, Bucks. Z2553/D.

GAMAGE, A. P., Corporal, Royal Field Artillery.
He volunteered in August 1915, and, after the completion of his training, was stationed at Bulford Camp employed on garrison and other important duties, and also in instructing recruits. Medically unfit for transfer overseas, he nevertheless, rendered valuable services until he was demobilised in March 1919. 2, Agusta Road, Stony Stratford, Bucks. Z2553/B.

GAMAGE, H. H., Pte., 2/4th Oxford. & Bucks. L.I.
Mobilised in August 1914, he was drafted to the Western Front in the following July, and in this theatre of war took part in the Battles of Ypres (II.), Somme (I.), Arras, Cambrai and Somme (II.). He later participated in heavy fighting in various sectors during the Retreat and Advance of 1918, and was wounded near Mons shortly before the Armistice. Sent to the 47th General Hospital, Le Trefort, he died from the effects of his injuries on November 14th, 1918. He was entitled to the 1914–15 Star, and the General Service and Victory Medals.
"His memory is cherished with pride."
2, Agusta Road, Stony Stratford, Bucks. Z2553/A

GAMAGE, W. R., Pte., 2/1st Oxford. & Bucks. L.I.
Volunteering in September 1915, he was sent four months later to France, and there he at once participated in heavy fighting. Invalided home in March 1916, suffering from trench feet, he was sent to hospital in Balham, and unfortunately had to have both legs amputated. He was discharged in December 1918, and holds the General Service and Victory Medals.
3, Agusta Road, Stony Stratford, Bucks. Z2553/C.

GAMBLE, F. W., Sergeant, Royal Engineers.
He volunteered in December 1914, and a month later proceeded to the Western Front. During his service overseas he was stationed in the Hazebrouck region, attached to the Railway Operative Department, and did excellent work employed as a driver. From March 1918 until the Armistice he served at St. Omer. Demobilised in March 1919, he holds the 1914–15 Star, and the General Service and Victory Medals.
16, Duncombe Street, Bletchley, Bucks. Z3037.

GAMMONS, F. C., Driver, Royal Engineers.
He volunteered in May 1915, and two months later proceeded to the Western Front, where he was engaged on important transport work in the Loos, Somme, Arras, Ypres, Cambrai and Lille sectors. In 1917 he was wounded in action and invalided to England, but on his recovery returned to France and served on there until the close of hostilities. He was demobilised in March 1919, and holds the 1914–15 Star, and the General Service and Victory Medals.
Willington, Beds. Z2554/A.

GAMMONS, G. M. (Mrs.), Member, Women's Land Army.
This lady joined the Land Army in 1915, and rendered valuable services in agricultural work at Mill Farm, Willington. She worked there until the close of hostilities in 1918, and carried out her arduous duties with the greatest ability.
Willington, Bedford. Z2555/A.

GAMMONS, L. G., Driver, Royal Engineers.
He joined in October 1916, and, after a course of training, was later in the same year drafted overseas. Whilst serving on the Western Front he took part in many important engagements and did good work with his Battery at Loos, Neuve Chapelle, Lille and Armentières. He was gassed on one occasion, and also suffered from shell-shock, and in consequence was discharged as medically unfit in April 1919, holding the General Service and Victory Medals.
Willington, Beds. Z2554/B.

GAMMONS, M. (Miss), Special War Worker.
In 1916 this lady joined the Land Army and was employed at Mill Farm, Willington, on important agricultural work. Throughout her period of service she performed her duties in a highly capable manner, and rendered great satisfaction to her employer. She relinquished her position in 1918.
Willington, Bedford. Z2555/B.

GARDINER, G. T., Sergeant, R.E. (R.O.D.)
He joined the Army in April 1916, and, on completion of a period of training, was ordered to the Western Front, where he served for over three years. During that time he was stationed at Audrique, and was employed on important duties with the Railway Operative Department. He was demobilised in August 1919, and holds the General Service and Victory Medals.
4, Glyn Square, Wolverton, Bucks. Z2557.

GARDINER, W. G. J. P., Air Mechanic, R.A.F.
He joined in November 1916, and was engaged on work requiring exceptional technical skill at Mullion. From 1917 until the close of hostilities he performed valuable work with his Squadron in the English Channel, escorting convoys and mine-spotting. He was mentioned in Despatches for valuable services in January 1918, and was demobilised in March 1919, holding the General Service and Victory Medals.
12, Bridge Street, New Bradwell, Bucks. Z2558.

GARDNER, A., Private, Bedfordshire Regiment.
Volunteering in January 1915, he completed his training six months later and was drafted to Egypt, where he took part in important engagements. Subsequently he was sent to the Palestine front, and saw much severe fighting at Gaza, Jerusalem and Aleppo. He was demobilised on his return to England in April 1919, and holds the 1914–15 Star, and the General Service and Victory Medals.
23, All Hallows Lane, Bedford. X2559/C.

GARDNER, J., Private, 6th Northamptonshire Regiment and Labour Corps.
He volunteered in September 1914, and ten months later proceeded to the Western Front. After fighting in numerous engagements he was wounded in the Battle of the Somme in September 1916, and invalided to England. On his recovery he was drafted back to France, where he rendered valuable services repairing roads until demobilised in March 1919. He holds the General Service and Victory Medals.
5, South Terrace, Green's Norton, Towcester, Northants. Z3039.

GARDNER, J., 1st Air Mechanic, Royal Air Force.
He joined in February 1916, and, on the completion of his training on Salisbury Plain, was sent overseas four months later. During his service on the Western Front he performed excellent work as a rigger, and rendered valuable services until the termination of the war. He was demobilised in March 1919, and holds the General Service and Victory Medals.
Brackley Road, Towcester, Northants. Z3038.

GARDNER, S. T., Corporal, R.A.S.C.
Two months after the outbreak of war in August 1914, he volunteered for active service, but was retained on important duties at Peterborough, Harrogate and in South Wales. Owing to ill-health he was not successful in his endeavours to secure a transfer to the war zone, but did much valuable work until demobilised in April 1919.
Brackley Road, Towcester, Northants. Z3040.

GARDNER, W. C., Private, 7th Northants. Regt.
He volunteered in June 1915, and, after completing his training at Colchester, was sent overseas in the following September. Whilst serving on the Western Front he fought in the Battles of Loos, the Somme and Cambrai, and in numerous other engagements, and was twice wounded in action. He was eventually demobilised in March 1919, and holds the 1914–15 Star, and the General Service and Victory Medals.
Pauler's Pury, Towcester, Northants. Z3041.

GAREY, A. J., Private, 15th Cheshire Regiment.
He joined the Royal Engineers in May 1916, and when drafted to the front in the same year was transferred to the 15th Cheshire Regiment. During his service in France he saw fierce fighting in the Arras, Ypres, Albert and Cambrai sectors, and was unfortunately killed in action on November 26th, 1918. He was entitled to the General Service and Victory Medals.
"A costly sacrifice upon the altar of freedom."
146, Coventry Road, Queen's Park, Bedford. Z2556/A.

GAREY, R., Sapper, Royal Engineers.
He volunteered in March 1915, and, on completion of his training, was later in the same year drafted to Egypt. After a short period of service on that front he proceeded to Gallipoli, where he served until the Evacuation. He was then sent to Mesopotamia and subsequently to France, and in all these theatres of war performed excellent work in laying cables. Returning home, he was demobilised in February 1919, and holds the 1914–15 Star, and the General Service and Victory Medals.
146, Coventry Road, Queen's Park, Bedford. Z2556/B.

GARNER, A., L/Corporal, Bedfordshire Regiment.
Volunteering in August 1914, he proceeded in the following year to Gallipoli and, after only four days' service there, was wounded in action and invalided to England. On his recovery in 1916 he was sent to the Western Front and fought in the Battle of the Somme and numerous other engagements. In 1917 he was transferred to Italy, where he was in action on the Piave front until drafted back to France in the same year. He saw severe fighting in the Cambrai and Ypres sectors, and in 1919 was demobilised, holding the 1914–15 Star, and the General Service and Victory Medals.
High Street, Cranfield, Beds. Z2560/A.

GARNER, E., Private, Labour Corps.
He volunteered in 1915, and, after a course of training at Thetford, was drafted to France in the following year. During his service on the Western Front he took an active part in the Battles of the Somme, Arras, Vimy Ridge, Ypres and Bapaume, and saw fierce fighting in numerous other important engagements. He was demobilised in 1919, and holds the General Service and Victory Medals.
High Street, Cranfield, Beds. Z2560/B.

GARNER, E. W. F., Trooper, 4th Dragoon Guards.
At the outbreak of hostilities in August 1914 he volunteered, and, after a course of training, was in the following year ordered to the Western Front. There he was engaged in fierce fighting in various sectors of the line, and was in action in the Battles of Hill 60, Ypres, the Somme, Arras and Cambrai. Demobilised in February 1919, he holds the 1914–15 Star, and the General Service and Victory Medals.
16, Foster Street, Bedford. X2562.

GARNER, G. T., Private, Queen's (Royal West Surrey Regiment).
He joined in February 1917, and eight months later was drafted to India, where he was engaged on important garrison duties at Bangalore. In September 1918 he was transferred to Salonika, and in that theatre of war took an active part in engagements on the Vardar front. On his return to England in March 1919 he was demobilised, holding the General Service and Victory Medals.
5, Featherstone Buildings, Newnham Street, Bedford. X2563.

GARNER, H., Private, Bedfordshire Regiment.
He joined the Army in 1917, but after only five weeks' training at Tring his health broke down, and he was sent to hospital. Later in the year he was discharged as medically unfit for further military service, and in August 1917 unhappily died.
"His memory is cherished with pride."
High Street, Cranfield, Beds. Z2560/C.

GARNER, H., Private, 2nd & 12th Cheshire Regt.
Joining in July 1916, he proceeded later in the same year to Salonika, where he took an active part in severe fighting in numerous important engagements. He also carried out important transport work after the Armistice in Turkey, and on his return to England was demobilised in October 1919, holding the General Service and Victory Medals. Cranfield, Beds. Z2561.

GARRETT, B. E., Guardsman, Coldstream Guards.
He joined in May 1917, and, after completing his training, was seven months later drafted overseas. During his service on the Western Front he experienced severe fighting in many engagements, chiefly in the Cambrai and Somme sectors, and was wounded in action in November 1918. He was invalided to England, and in March 1919 was demobilised, holding the General Service and Victory Medals.
78, Aylesbury Street, Fenny Stratford, Bucks. Z2564.

GASCOIN, F., Driver, R.A.S.C.
He volunteered in July 1915, and in the following year was sent to the Western Front, where he was engaged on important transport work, conveying food and ammunition to the forward areas. He also saw heavy fighting in various sectors, and was in action in the Battles of the Somme, Arras, Ypres and Cambrai. In March 1919 he was demobilised, and holds the General Service and Victory Medals.
55, St. John's Street, Bedford. X2565.

GASCOYNE, A. C. J., Pte., 1/5th Bedfordshire Rgt.
Volunteering in May 1915, he proceeded in the following November to Gallipoli, where he served for a short time. In December 1915 he was transferred to Egypt and subsequently to Palestine, and on that front rendered valuable services as a stretcher-bearer in important engagements at Gaza and Jaffa. He was demobilised on his return home in July 1919, and holds the 1914–15 Star, and the General Service and Victory Medals.
23, Church Walk, Kempston, Beds. X2568/A.

GASCOYNE, J., Private, R.A.M.C. and M.G.C.
When war was declared he was already serving in the Royal Army Medical Corps, and in April 1915 was drafted to Gallipoli, where he performed valuable work as a stretcher-bearer until November 1915. In 1916 he was discharged as a time-expired man, but in the following year re-enlisted in the Machine Gun Corps, and was sent to France. There he took an active part in engagements at Ypres, Albert, the Somme and Cambrai, and was gassed at Passchendaele. He was demobilised in March 1919, and holds the 1914–15 Star, and the General Service and Victory Medals.
14, Spencer Street, New Bradwell, Bucks. Z2566/A.

GASCOYNE, P. W. G., Private, Bedfordshire Regiment and Suffolk Regiment.
He joined in October 1916, and after a period of training was in the following year sent to the Western Front. During his service there, he was engaged in severe fighting in various sectors, and was in action in the Battles of Arras, Ypres, Cambrai and the Somme. In 1918 he was transferred to Italy where he served on the Piave front. He was demobilised in October 1919, and holds the General Service and Victory Medals. 23, Church Walk, Kempston, Beds. X2568/B.

GASCOYNE, T. J., Air Mechanic, Royal Air Force.
Joining in July 1918 he was not successful in his efforts to secure a transfer overseas owing to the early cessation of hostilities. He was engaged on important duties with his Squadron at Blandford, Putney and in Devonshire, and performed excellent work on the observation balloons, engaged in the defence of the English coast until demobilised in February 1919. 14, Cater Street, Kempston, Beds. X2567.

GASKIN, O., Sapper, Royal Engineers (R.O.D.)
He joined in March 1917, and on conclusion of his training was six months later ordered to the Western Front. In that theatre of war he served for over a year, and during that time was employed on important work at the Base. After the close of hostilities he returned to England, and in March 1919 was demobilised, holding the General Service and Victory Medals. 2, School Street, New Bradwell, Bucks. Z2569/B.

GASKIN, P. A., Pte., Duke of Cornwall's L.I.
Joining in March 1917, he proceeded on the completion of his training three months later to Egypt, where he saw heavy fighting at Siwa. He was later transferred to Palestine, and took an active part in the operations which led to the capture of Jerusalem, Jericho and Tripoli. Returning to England in January 1920, he was demobilised, and holds the General Service and Victory Medals.
2, School Street, New Bradwell, Bucks. Z2569/A.

GATES, H. E., Private, Bedfordshire Regiment.
At the declaration of war in August 1914 he volunteered, and was employed on important work at Aldershot until 1916 when he proceeded to France. On that front he fought in the Battles of the Somme, Arras, Ypres, Lens and Cambrai, and was also in action in the engagements in the Retreat and Advance of 1918. He was demobilised in May 1919, and holds the General Service and Victory Medals.
34, Bunyan Road, South End, Bedford. Z1307/B.

GATHERGOOD, A. H., Private, 3/4th Northants. and 8th East Yorkshire Regts., and M.G.C.
He volunteered in October 1915, and after training at Northampton and Tring, was in the following year drafted overseas. Whilst serving on the Western Front he took an active part in the Battles of Vimy Ridge, Bullecourt, Messines and Ypres, and fell fighting at Arras on March 31st, 1917. He was entitled to the General Service and Victory Medals.
"Whilst we remember, the sacrifice is not in vain."
27, West Street, Olney, Bucks. TZ2570.

GAUNT, P., Private, 1/4th Oxford. & Bucks. L.I.
Volunteering in July 1915, he proceeded in April of the following year to the Western Front. In that theatre of war he saw much severe fighting in various engagements, including the Battle of the Somme, and was unfortunately killed in action at Le Sars on November 19th, 1916. He was entitled to the General Service and Victory Medals.
"A valiant Solidier, with undaunted heart he breasted life's last hill."
14, Elm Street, Buckingham. Z3571.

GAUNT, W. [illegible], Sergt., 1/5th & 2/5th Beds. Regt.
When war was declared in August 1914 he volunteered, but owing to ill-health was unable to procure a transfer to a theatre of war. He rendered valuable services, however, at Aldershot and Ampthill Park, where he was engaged in instructing recruits. His excellent work soon secured promotion for him, but in July 1917 he was discharged as medically unfit for further military duties.
18, Eastville Road, Bedford. Z2572/B.

GAUNT, W. J., Driver, Royal Army Service Corps.
He joined in May 1916, and after training at Blackpool and Southend, proceeded in the following year to Egypt. Soon after landing there his health broke down, and he was sent to hospital for some time. On his recovery he was drafted to Palestine, where he was engaged in fierce fighting at Gaza, Jerusalem and Jericho. He was demobilised on his return to England in August 1919, and holds the General Service and Victory Medals. 18, Mabel Road, Bedford. Z2573.

GAUNT, W. T., Sapper, Royal Engineers.
Already serving at the outbreak of hostilities, he was immediately drafted to the Western Front, where he was wounded whilst fighting in the Retreat from Mons. On returning to the firing-line he was in action in the Battles of La Bassée, Neuve Chapelle and Festubert, and served in numerous other engagements until the termination of the war. He was discharged in December 1918, and holds the Mons Star, and the General Service and Victory Medals.
18, Eastville Road, Southend, Beds. Z2572/A.

GAYLOR, F., Private, Lancashire Fusiliers.
He joined in October 1917, and after two months' training at Luton was drafted to the Western Front. There he took an active part in severe fighting in several engagements, until wounded in action at Cambrai in February 1918. He was invalided to England, and on his discharge from hospital was demobilised in April 1919, holding the General Service and Victory Medals.
Northcroft, Cambridge Road, Sandy, Beds. Z2574/A.

GAYLOR, H., Private, 4th Seaforth Highlanders.
Volunteering in January 1915, he trained at Bedford, and later in the same year was drafted overseas. Whilst serving on the Western Front he saw heavy fighting in engagements in the Loos, Festubert, Arras and Cambrai sectors, and was unhappily killed in action in the Battle of the Somme on March 28th, 1918. He was entitled to the 1914–15 Star, and the General Service and Victory Medals.
"His life for his Country, his soul to God."
Northcroft, Cambridge Road, Sandy, Beds. Z2574/B.

GAZELEY, F., Corporal, Royal Engineers.
He was already serving in the Army when war was declared in August 1914, and accordingly at once proceeded with the First Expeditionary Force to the Western Front. There he fought in the Battles of Mons, Ypres, the Somme, Arras and Cambrai, and also did good work with his Battery in numerous other important engagements. He was discharged in August 1919, and holds the Mons Star, and the General Service and Victory Medals.
1, Holt Row, Bedford. X2575/A

GAZELEY, H., Private, Queen's (Royal West Surrey Regiment).
He joined in April 1917, and, after a period of training in England, was in July 1918, drafted to the Western Front, where he took part in heavy fighting near Amiens and on the Somme during the Advance of 1918, and was wounded. Remaining in France until late in 1919, he was demobilised in November of that year, and holds the General Service and Victory Medals.
1, Holt Row, Bedford. X2575/B.

GAZELEY, J., Private, 3rd Bedfordshire Regiment.
Three months after joining in June 1916, he was sent to France, and there took part in the later phases of the Somme Offensive. He also fought at Arras, Ypres, Messines, Vimy Ridge, Passchendaele and Cambrai, and concluded his service at Mons in November 1918. He was demobilised three months later, and holds the General Service and Victory Medals.
1, Holt Row, Bedford. X2575/C.

GEARY, R. S., Private, 15th Cheshire Regiment.
He volunteered in February 1915, and after a course of training at Harrogate, was drafted to the Western Front in the following year. After taking part in numerous important engagements in the Ypres sector he fell fighting in 1916. He was entitled to the General Service and Victory Medals.
"He died the noblest death a man may die:
Fighting for God and right and liberty."
58, Garfield Street, Bedford. Z2576.

GEE, W. H., Gunner, Royal Garrison Artillery.
Volunteering in 1915, he was sent later in the same year to France. On that front he fought in the Battles of Loos, the Somme, Ypres, Arras, Lens and Cambrai, and also performed excellent work as a gunner in engagements at Lille. He was demobilised in 1919, and holds the 1914–15 Star, and the General Service and Victory Medals.
The Lane, Bromham, Beds. Z2577/A—Z2578/A.

GEORGE, A., Private, 1st Bedfordshire Regiment.
He volunteered in August 1914, and after a course of training was in the following year drafted to Egypt. Subsequently he was sent to Palestine, and in that theatre of war saw heavy fighting at Gaza and Jerusalem. In December 1917, the ship in which he was returning to Egypt was torpedoed, and he was unfortunately drowned. He was entitled to the 1914–15 Star, and the General Service and Victory Medals.
"He joined the great white company of valiant souls."
11, Cavendish Street, Bedford. X2583.

GEORGE, A. W., Private, 6th Queen's (Royal West Surrey Regiment).
Joining in October 1916, he was six months later drafted to the Western Front, where he was in action in the Battles of Ypres, Passchendaele and Cambrai. He also saw heavy fighting in the Albert sector, and was wounded in action at Passchendaele in August 1917. After the Armistice he was engaged on important guard duties at Boulogne and Rouen until demobilised in September 1919. He holds the General Service and Victory Medals.
Luke Street, Eynesbury, St. Neots, Hunts. Z2582.

GEORGE, C. S., Corporal, Bedfordshire Regiment.
He enlisted in the Huntingdonshire Cyclist Battalion in September 1914 at the age of 17, and was engaged on important duties with his unit at various stations. In 1917 he was transferred to the Bedfordshire Regiment and drafted to the Western Front, where he took an active part in the Battles of Arras, Ypres, Cambrai, the Somme and Bapaume. He was demobilised in January 1919, and holds the General Service and Victory Medals.
3, New Houses, Buckworth, Hunts. Z2581.

GEORGE, O. J. (M.M.), Cpl., East Surrey Regt.
He volunteered in September 1914, and after serving at stations in England, was sent to France in October of the following year. There he fought at St. Eloi and Ypres, but being wounded two months later was invalided home to hospital. Returning to the front in April 1916 he was in action at Messines, but at Guillemont during the Somme Offensive, received a second wound which necessitated his evacuation to England. Early in 1917 he was again in action, this time at Nieuport, and in November was drafted to Italy. Returning to France two months afterwards, he served at Bapaume and on the Somme during the Retreat and Advance, and for conspicuous gallantry whilst in charge of a "mopping-up" section in an operation at Menin in October, which resulted in the capture of 28 prisoners and two officers, was awarded the Military Medal and the Croix de Guerre. Afteralso serving with the Army of Occupation, he was demobilised in March 1919, and holds the 1914–15 Star, and the General Service and Victory Medals.
Adelaide Terrace, Godmanchester, Hunts. Z2579.

GEORGE, S. D., Private, Bedfordshire Regiment.
Volunteering in 1914, he proceeded to the Western Front in the following year, and served there for about four years. During the course of this service he fought at Ypres, Loos, Festubert, Arras, Cambrai and the Somme, and was gassed. Serving on until the end of the war, he was demobilised in March 1919, and holds the 1914–15 Star, and the General Service and Victory Medals.
Piper's Lane, Godmanchester, Hunts. Z2580.

GETHINS, J., Private, Royal Scots Fusiliers.
He volunteered in May 1915, and after completing his training, was in October 1915 drafted to the Western Front. Whilst in that theatre of war he took part in heavy fighting at Festubert, Loos, the Somme, and Ypres, and was wounded at Arras in November 1917. He was demobilised in January 1919, and holds the 1914–15 Star, and the General Service and Victory Medals. 1, Little Butts Street, Bedford. X2584.

GIBBONS, A., Sapper, Royal Engineers (R.O.D.)
He joined in June 1916, and three months later was drafted to the Western Front, where for a time he was employed in the repair of engines in the workshops at Andrique. He also served in the Somme, Ypres, Arras and Cambrai sectors, and was employed on transport duties. He was not demobilised until November 1919, and holds the General Service and Victory Medals.
37, St. Giles Street, New Bradwell, Bucks. Z2585.

GIBBS, A. V., Private, 1st & 2nd Wiltshire Regt.
Joining in May 1917, he was sent to France after a period of training and service in England, in April 1918, with the 4th Hampshire Regiment. Transferred to the Wiltshire Regiment, he fought at Ypres and La Bassée, but in September was sent to hospital in England with fever. He was eventually demobilised in October 1919, after serving at Dublin, and holds the General Service and Victory Medals.
Maids Moreton, Buckingham. Z2586.

GIBBS, C. H., Air Mechanic, Royal Air Force.
He volunteered in August 1915, and after completing his training at various stations in England, was drafted to France in June 1917. Whilst on the Western Front he was employed in photographing the German lines and other duties of a similar nature. Continuing his service, he was demobilised in February 1919, and holds the General Service and Victory Medals. Main Street, Hartford. Z2587/B—Z2588/B.

GIBBS, H., L/Corporal, 2nd Royal Berkshire Regt.
A time-serving soldier, he was stationed at Aldershot before being sent to France in August 1914, and took part in the Battle of Mons and the subsequent Retreat. He also fought in the Battles of the Marne, the Aisne, Ypres, Loos, the Somme, Arras and Vimy Ridge, and during the Retreat and Advance of 1918 served on the Somme. He finished his service at Mons, and was discharged in March 1919, holding the Mons Star, and the General Service and Victory Medals.
Maids Moreton, Buckingham. Z2589.

GIBBS, H. P., Private, 4th London Regiment (Royal Fusiliers).
He volunteered in August 1914, and was at once sent to France, where he fought in the Retreat from Mons. He also played a prominent part in the Battle of the Marne, but was unhappily killed in action near Loos on September 13th, 1915. He was entitled to the Mons Star, and the General Service and Victory Medals.
"A costly sacrifice upon the altar of freedom."
Colne, Hunts. Z2590/B.

GIBBS, W. P., Private, Middlesex Regiment.
He volunteered in July 1915, and was retained in England after completing his training. Engaged in the manufacture of aeroplane parts and similar duties at Bedford and Purfleet, and stations in Norfolk and Surrey, he rendered valuable services, and was eventually demobilised in 1919.
Colne, Hunts. Z2590/A.

GIBLETT, J. W., Pte., Royal Warwickshire Regt.
Mobilised at the outbreak of war, he served with the Huntingdonshire Cyclist Battalion for a time, and was not sent to France until July 1916. He then went into action on the Somme, and also fought at Bullecourt and Arras, but in February 1917 was invalided home with fever. Returning to the Western Front, he fought at Passchendaele Ridge and Cambrai, but was gassed in April 1918, and invalided home again. He was then engaged on agricultural work at Cambridge until July 1919, when he was discharged, holding the General Service and Victory Medals.
Eaton Socon, Bedfordshire. Z2591.

GIDDINGS, H., Corporal, 26th Royal Fusiliers.
He was mobilised in August 1914, but retained in England on special duty, was not sent to France until October 1916. In that theatre of war he took part in the Somme Offensive and heavy fighting at Arras and Messines, but met a soldier's death at Ypres on June 12th, 1917. He was entitled to the General Service and Victory Medals.
"Whilst we remember, the sacrifice is not in vain."
Park Lane, Blunham, Beds. Z2592/A.

GILBERT, A., Private, Hunts. Cyclist Battalion.
He volunteered in August 1914, but was not sent to France until 1916. There, however, he went at once into action on the Somme, and later at Givenchy, where he was wounded in September. Invalided to England a month later, he was in hospital for a time, and was there discharged as unfit in July 1917. He holds the General Service and Victory Medals.
Eaton Ford, Beds. Z2596.

GILBERT, F. J., Private, 2nd Bedfordshire Regt.
Immediately after volunteering in August 1914, he was sent to France and fought in the Retreat from Mons and at Givenchy. He was, however, unfortunately killed in action at Festubert on May 16th, 1915, and was buried at the Guards' Cemetery near Béthune. He was entitled to the Mons Star, and the General Service and Victory Medals.
"His life for his Country, his soul to God."
Church Cottages, Wootton, Bedford. Z2593/A.

GILBERT, G. W., Private, 1st Worcestershire Regt.
Volunteering in March 1915, he was drafted to France a year later, and took part in the Somme Offensive of that summer. He also was in action at La Bassée, Givenchy and Ar as, but was severely wounded and invalided home. After hospital treatment at Newcastle, he was discharged as unfit in December 1917, and holds the General Service and Victory Medals.
21, Market Square, Stony Stratford, Bucks. Z2594.

GILBERT, H. G., Sergeant, Royal Defence Corps.
He volunteered in November 1914 from the National Reserve and for a time served at stations in England. Later, however, he was sent to France, and was employed as a Lewis Gun Instructor with the Essex and Surrey Regiments at Etaples, Amiens and on the Somme. He was demobilised in January 1919, and holds the General Service and Victory Medals.
21, Gratton Road, Queen's Park, Bedford. Z2598.

GILBERT, H. J., Private, 3rd Cheshire Regiment.
He joined in 1916, and after serving for a time at Bedford, was sent to Salonika in the next year. There he was in action on the Doiran front and saw heavy fighting in the Balkan Peninsula. After more than two years in that theatre of war he returned to England, and was demobilised in December 1919, holding the General Service and Victory Medals.
Montague Street, St. Neots, Hunts. Z2601.

GILBERT, J. R., Private, R.M.L.I.
He joined in August 1918, and after training at Deal and Portsmouth, was posted to H.M.S. "Delhi." In this vessel he served in various waters and was employed as watchman on a voyage to Dantzig. He was still in the Marines in 1920, and holds the General Service and Victory Medals.
Church Cottage, Wootton, Bedford. Z2593/C.

GILBERT, S. A., Private, R.M.L.I.
Joining the Red Marines in August 1916, he completed his training at Deal and Plymouth, and was posted to H.M.S. "Resolution," in which vessel he served as a watchman. Whilst hostilities lasted, and after, he was engaged on duties in Chinese waters and at Constantinople. Still serving in 1920, he holds the General Service and Victory Medals.
Church Cottage, Wootton, Bedford. Z2593/B.

GILBERT, S. T., Private, Queen's Own (Royal West Kent Regiment).
He volunteered in February 1915, and in July was sent to the Dardanelles, where he took part in the landing at Suvla Bay, and the Evacuation of the Peninsula. He was then drafted to Egypt, and in March 1916 to France. In that theatre of war he fought in the Somme Offensive, and was invalided home in November owing to ill-health. Returning to the Western Front he served at Ypres, Passchendaele and Cambrai, and was wounded at Monchy on August 23rd, 1918, and invalided home. Owing to his injuries he lost his left hand, and was in consequence discharged in May 1919. He holds the 1914–15 Star, and the General Service and Victory Medals.
4, Oxford Street, Stony Stratford, Bucks. Z2595.

GILBERT, W. T., Sergt., 1/5th Bedfordshire Regt.
Volunteering in August 1914, he was soon sent to Egypt, and took part in the operations in Palestine. Fighting in this theatre of war at Gaza, Jaffa and Haifa, he rendered very valuable services and returned home for demobilisation in September 1919. He re-enlisted a year later for service with the Military Police, and holds the 1914–15 Star, and the General Service and Victory Medals.
Church Cottages, Wootton, Bedford. TZ2597.

GILES, S. R., Sapper, Royal Engineers (R.O.D.)
He joined in May 1917, and after training in the South of England, was drafted in December to Egypt. On his way out, his vessel, H.M.S. "Attack," was twice torpedoed near Alexandria, but he was rescued. Attached to the Palestine Expeditionary Force, he served at Gaza, Jaffa, Haifa and Damascus, and did good work with his section. Returning home he was demobilised in May 1919, and holds the General Service and Victory Medals. 18, Ledsam St., Wolverton, Bucks. TZ2599.

GILL, F., Staff-Sergeant, Royal Garrison Artillery.
A time-serving soldier, he was in India at the outbreak of war and was quickly sent to the Western Front, where he fought in the concluding stages of the Retreat from Mons. After taking part in the Battles of Ypres, Loos and the Somme, he was employed on the postal staff as a censor from 1916 until 1918, and in 1919 was sent back to India. He was still there in 1920, and holds the Mons Star, and the General Service and Victory Medals. Cross Hall Ford, St. Neots, Hunts. Z2602/B.

GILL, J., Leading Seaman, R.N.V.R. and R.N.D.
Volunteering in January 1915, he served in H.M.S. "Lord Nelson," and took part in the landing at Salonika. Transferred to the Royal Naval Division he was sent to France in June 1917, but was almost at once wounded at Arras and invalided to Calais. Re-joining, he went into action at Ypres and Passchendaele, but at Cambrai, in March 1918, suffered from a severe wound and gas-poisoning, which rendered him blind for a week, and he was taken prisoner. He was released in December 1918, returned to England, and was demobilised two months later. He holds the 1914–15 Star, and the General Service and Victory Medals. 16, Ouse Walk, Huntingdon, Hunts. TZ2603.

GILL, J., Private, Essex Regiment.
A time-serving soldier, he served at Aldershot and was then sent to India. After being engaged on garrison duty there for some time he returned to England, and was again stationed at Aldershot. He was discharged in 1919, and holds the General Service Medal.
London Road, Girtford, Sandy, Beds. Z2600.

GILL, W. F., Leading Signalman, R.N., H.M.S. "Recruit."
Having enlisted in the Navy in 1911, he at once went to sea at the outbreak of war, and served in the Mediterranean. He was subsequently with the Grand Fleet in the North Sea, and took part in the Battle of Jutland on May 31st, 1916, but unhappily lost his life when H.M.S. "Recruit" was sunk by a mine on August 9th, 1917. He was entitled to the 1914–15 Star, and the General Service and Victory Medals.
"His life for his Country, his soul to God."
Cross Hale Ford, St. Neots, Hunts. Z2602 /A.

GILLARD, A., Private, 2nd Middlesex Regiment.
He joined in July 1918, and, after training at Oxford, was sent to Ireland. In August 1919 he was drafted to Egypt and stationed at Cairo, where he was engaged on important guard duties. He was still in the Army in Egypt in 1920.
1, School Street, New Bradwell, Bucks. Z2604 /C.

GILLARD, W., Driver, Royal Army Service Corps.
Volunteering in July 1915, he reached France in time to take part in the Battle of Loos in September. After being employed on transport work in the Somme sector, he proceeded to Salonika and was engaged on similar duties on the Doiran front. Invalided home owing to ill-health in August 1916, he was discharged in the following month as unfit, and holds the 1914–15 Star, and the General Service and Victory Medals.
1, School Street, New Bradwell, Bucks. Z2604 /A.

GILLARD, W. J., A.B., Royal Navy.
He joined in August 1916, and completed his training at Chatham before being sent to the North Sea. There, particularly off Zeebrugge, he was engaged on mine-sweepers from 1917 until 1919. In March of the latter year he was demobilised, and holds the General Service and Victory Medals.
1, School Street, New Bradwell, Bucks. Z2604 /B.

GILLETT, A. G., Pte., 1/7th R. Warwickshire Regt.
Volunteering in October 1915, he completed his training with the Huntingdonshire Cyclist Battalion, and was sent to France in the following July. There he served as a Lewis Gunner in the Somme Offensive and the Battles of Ypres, Arras and Cambrai, and was wounded during the Advance of 1918. He was demobilised in March 1919, and holds the General Service and Victory Medals. Great Staughton, Hunts. Z2608 /B.

GILLETT, A. J., Private, Bedfordshire Regiment.
After completing his training, he was sent to France in 1916, and fought on the Ypres, Arras, Somme and Cambrai fronts. On September 29th, 1918, he was unhappily killed during the fourth Battle of Ypres, and was buried near by. He was entitled to the General Service and Victory Medals.
"Thinking that remembrance, though unspoken, may reach him where he sleeps."
Marston, Beds. Z2605.

GILLETT, F. W., Guardsman, Grenadier Guards.
A Regular soldier, he proceeded to France at the outbreak of war, and fought in the Retreat from Mons. He also took a prominent part in the Battles of Ypres, but on May 2nd, 1915, unhappily succumbed to wounds received at Hill 60 shortly before. He was entitled to the Mons Star, and the General Service and Victory Medals.
"A costly sacrifice upon the altar of freedom."
2, Church Walk, Kempston, Bedford. X2606.

GILLETT, I. F., L/Corporal, Bedfordshire Regt.
He volunteered early in 1915, and, after being stationed at Dovercourt, was drafted to Egypt a year later. Serving with the Palestine Expeditionary Force, he was frequently in action, notably at Gaza, but whilst in that sector was reported missing on July 21st, 1917. As no official information has been received, it is presumed that he was killed. He was entitled to the General Service and Victory Medals.
"His life for his Country."
Church Street, Somersham, Hunts. Z2607.

GILLETT, M., Private, Machine Gun Corps.
He joined in May 1917, and was drafted to the Western Front in time to serve throughout the Retreat and Advance of 1918, during which he took part in the Battles of the Somme (II.), Amiens, Cambrai and Le Cateau (II.), and was wounded in action. After the cessation of hostilities, he was sent to Germany with the Army of Occupation and remained on the Rhine until his demobilisation in March 1919, holding the General Service and Victory Medals.
Great Staughton, Hunts. Z2608 /A.

GINN, A. C., Sergeant, Bedfordshire Regiment.
He was mobilised in August 1914, and first rendered valuable services as an Instructor of recruits at various home stations. In 1916, however, he proceeded to France and played a prominent part in the Battles of the Somme, Arras, Ypres and Cambrai, in heavy fighting at Albert and Beaumont-Hamel, and was wounded in action. He was discharged in June 1919, and holds the General Service and Victory Medals.
5a, Tavistock Place, Bedford. X2609.

GINN, W. C., Private, R.A.M.C.
Mobilised in August 1914, he was immediately drafted to the Western Front, and served as a stretcher-bearer during heavy fighting in the Ypres, Somme and Arras sectors. He did excellent work with his unit until his discharge in April 1917, and holds the 1914 Star, and the General Service and Victory Medals. 32, Marlborough Road, Bedford. Z1383 /B.

GLIDDEWELL, J., Private, Bedfordshire Regt.
He volunteered in September 1914, and in the following year was drafted to the Dardanelles, where he saw much severe fighting. After the Evacuation of the Gallipoli Peninsula he was sent to Egypt, but was later transferred to Palestine, and took part in the Battles of Gaza and the capture of Haifa and Jaffa. He was demobilised in May 1919, and holds the 1914–15 Star, and the General Service and Victory Medals.
Stagsden, Beds. Z2610.

GLIDEWELL, W. J., Pte., Royal Berkshire Regt.
He joined in September 1916, and was quickly drafted to the Western Front, where he saw much severe fighting on the Somme, and took part in the Battles of Vimy Ridge, Lens and Amiens, and in the Retreat of 1918. Unfortunately he gallantly fell in action near Courcelles on August 23rd, 1918, and was entitled to the General Service and Victory Medals.
"Nobly striving:
He nobly fell that we might live."
Broad Green, Cranfield, Beds. Z2611.

GOATES, S. E., Private, Queen's (Royal West Surrey Regiment).
Joining in June 1916, he was soon sent to France, and was attached to the transport section of his unit for a time. He was also engaged in guarding ammunition dumps, and did excellent work until invalided home with shell-shock in September of the same year. After hospital treatment at Netley, he was discharged as medically unfit for further service in April 1917, holding the General Service and Victory Medals.
4, New Church Terrace, St. Ives, Hunts. Z2612.

GOATLEY, A. E., Private, 1/6th Essex Regiment.
Volunteering in August 1915, he was drafted to Egypt on completion of his training, but later proceeded to Palestine, where he took part in the Battles of Gaza. He was taken seriously ill with malarial fever and unfortunately died in hospital at Alexandria on July 16th, 1918. He was entitled to the General Service and Victory Medals.
"He joined the great white company of valiant souls."
25, Cavendish Street, Bedford. X2615 /B.

GOATLEY, A. E. (sen)., Private, 1/4th Dorsetshire Regiment.
Volunteering in August 1914, he was sent to the Dardanelles in the following year, and was in action at the Landings at Cape Helles and Suvla Bay. After the Evacuation of the Dardanelles, he was transferred to Mesopotamia, where he took part in the heavy fighting prior to the capture of Kut-el-Amara and Baghdad. He was demobilised in August 1919, and holds the 1914–15 Star, and the General Service and Victory Medals.
25, Cavendish Street, Bedford. Z2615 /A.

GODFREY, A. T., Private, Bedfordshire Regiment.
He volunteered in July 1915, and 12 months later was drafted to the Western Front, where he took part in much severe fighting, particularly in the Somme sector. He was unfortunately killed by a sniper on April 23rd, 1917, and was entitled to the General Service and Victory Medals.
"Honour to the immortal dead, who gave their youth that the world might grow old in peace."
Marston, near Bedford. Z2617.

GODFREY, G., Private, R.A.S.C.
He joined in 1916, and, on completion of his training, was retained on important duties at various home stations. He rendered valuable services with his unit, but, owing to his being medically unfit was unsuccessful in obtaining his transfer overseas, and was demobilised in August 1919.
19, Bunyan Road, South End, Bedford. TZ2616 /A.

GODWIN, H. W., Gunner, Royal Field Artillery.
He volunteered in August 1914, and was first engaged on important duties in England. In 1916, however, he was drafted to Salonika, and whilst in the Balkan theatre of war took part in much severe fighting. Unfortunately he contracted malaria, was invalided home, and in June 1918 discharged as medically unfit for further service. He holds the General Service and Victory Medals.
Vine Cottage, Renhold, near Bedford. Z2618

GOFF, C., Steward, Royal Navy.
He joined in September 1918, and was engaged as a sick-berth attendant at Chatham Royal Naval Barracks. He rendered valuable services for two months, but then contracted influenza whilst nursing others, and unfortunately died in November 1918.
"His memory is cherished with pride."
14, River Street, Bedford. X2620 /A.

GOFF, E. H., Private, 1st Bedfordshire Regiment.
He enlisted in March 1911, and proceeding to France in August 1914, took part in the Retreat from Mons and the Battles of Ypres, the Somme and Oppy Wood. He was also in action during the Retreat and Advance of 1918, and was four times wounded—at Ypres in December 1915, at Longueval in July 1916, at Richebourg-St.-Vaast five months later, and at Oppy Wood in May 1917. Discharged in November 1919, he holds the Mons Star, and the General Service and Victory Medals.
Keeley Lane, Wootton, Bedford. Z2619/C.

GOFF, F. J., Private, Bedfordshire Regiment.
A Reservist, he was called to the Colours in August 1914, and immediately drafted to France, where he took part in the Battles of Mons, the Marne, Neuve Chapelle, Loos and the Somme. He laid down his life for King and Country at Passchendaele on July 28th, 1917, and was entitled to the Mons Star, and the General Service and Victory Medals.
"A costly sacrifice upon the altar of freedom."
14, River Street, Bedford. X2620/B.

GOFF, J., Corporal, Rifle Brigade.
Already in the Army at the outbreak of war, he proceeded to France in August 1914, and took part in the Retreat from Mons and the Battle of Ypres. He was unfortunately killed in action at Armentières on December 17th, 1914, and was buried by his brother. He was entitled to the Mons Star, and the General Service and Victory Medals.
"Great deeds cannot die,
They with the sun and moon renew their light for ever."
Keeley Lane, Wootton, Bedford. Z2619/B.

GOFF, W. G., Sergeant, Rifle Brigade.
He was already in the Army when war was declared in August 1914, and had seen service in India. Proceeding to France with the first Expeditionary Force, he took part in the Retreat from Mons. He laid down his life for King and Country at Armentières on December 18th, 1914, having only the previous day buried his brother. He was entitled to the Mons Star, and the General Service and Victory Medals.
"A costly sacrifice upon the altar of freedom."
Keeley Lane, Wootton, Bedford. Z2619/A.

GOFFE, W., Private, Oxford. and Bucks. L.I.
Volunteering in January 1915, he was first engaged on important duties at various home stations for two years. He then proceeded to France, but after only four months on active service, died gloriously on the Field of Battle at Vimy Ridge on April 28th, 1917. He was entitled to the General Service and Victory Medals.
"And doubtless he went in splendid company."
5, St. Paul's Terrace, Silver Street, Newport Pagnell, Bucks. Z2621/B.

GOLDING, A., Farrier-Sergeant, R.F.A.
Volunteering in March 1915, he was quickly drafted to the Western Front, where he served with distinction at the Battles of the Somme (I.) and Vimy Ridge, and was wounded in action. Invalided to Scotland, he spent some time in hospital at Aberdeen, and then returned to France and took part in the Battles of Ypres, St. Quentin, Cambrai and the Somme (II.). He was twice mentioned in Despatches for conspicuous bravery under heavy fire, and was eventually demobilised in March 1919, holding the 1914–15 Star, and the General Service and Victory Medals.
Hemingford Grey, Hunts. Z2622/A.

GOLDING, A., Sergeant, R.A.S.C.
He joined in 1917, and was first engaged on important duties in England. In 1919, however, he was sent to Russia, and owing to his knowledge of the language, rendered valuable services with the telegraph section, translating messages from Russian into English. He was still in the Army in 1920, and holds the General Service and Victory Medals.
Hemingford Grey, Hunts. Z2622/C.

GOLDING, F. G., Driver, Royal Field Artillery.
He joined in June 1917, and on completion of his training was sent to Ireland, where he did excellent work with his Battery at Bantry and Cork. He was unsuccessful in obtaining his transfer to a theatre of war, and was demobilised in September, 1919.
Tyringham, Newport Pagnell, Bucks. Z2613/B—Z2614/B.

GOLDING, F. W., Corporal, 1st Bedfordshire Regt.
A Regular soldier, who had served in Africa prior to the outbreak of war, he was sent to France in August 1914, and played a prominent part in the Battles of Mons and Hill 60. In 1915 he was invalided home suffering from shell-shock and gas-poisoning, and was discharged in March 1916 as medically unfit for further service. He holds the Mons Star, and the General Service and Victory Medals. Goldington, Beds. Z2623.

GOLDING, R. E., 1st Air Mechanic, R.A.F.
He joined immediately on attaining military age in August 1918, and after his training was engaged on important duties which called for a high degree of technical skill. Owing to the early cessation of hostilities, he was not drafted overseas, but did excellent work with his Squadron until his demobilisation in March 1920.
Tyringham, Newport Pagnell, Bucks. Z2613/A—Z2614/A.

GOLDING, W. H., Private, Labour Corps.
He volunteered in the Infantry in August 1914, but in the following year was discharged as medically unfit. In 1916, however, he joined the Labour Corps, and was retained on special duties in connection with agricultural work at various home stations. He rendered valuable services with his unit until his demobilisation in November 1919.
Hemingford Grey, Hunts. Z2622/B.

GOLDSMITH, C. J., Private, 1st Bedfordshire Regt.
He volunteered in January 1915, and in November was drafted to the Western Front, where he took part in heavy fighting at Loos, Ypres, the Somme and Vimy Ridge before being killed in action at Delville Wood on July 27th, 1917. He was entitled to the 1914–15 Star, and the General Service and Victory Medals.
"He died the noblest death a man may die,
Fighting for God and right and liberty."
Silver Street, Stevington, near Bedford. Z2625.

GOLDSMITH, F., Corporal, King's Own Scottish Borderers.
Mobilised in August 1914, he immediately proceeded to France, but after playing a prominent part in the Battle of Mons, was taken prisoner at Le Cateau on the 26th of that month. During his captivity in Germany he was forced to work in the mines and suffered many hardships. He was repatriated after the Armistice, and was eventually discharged in May 1920, holding the Mons Star, and the General Service and Victory Medals.
31, Pilcroft Street, Bedford. X2624/D.

GOLDSTONE, W., Private, Gloucestershire Regt.
He volunteered in October 1914, and first served with the Hunts. Cyclist Battalion, but was later transferred to the Gloucestershire Regiment, and sent to France in June 1916. He took part in heavy fighting at St. Julien and Ypres before being wounded in action and invalided home in March 1918. On his recovery he was transferred to the Royal Engineers, and engaged on special duties until his demobilisation in March 1919, holding the General Service and Victory Medals.
2, Sapley Lane, Hartford, Hunts. Z2626.

GOODEN, F., Shoeing-Smith, 17th (Duke of Cambridge's Own) Lancers.
At the outbreak of war he was stationed in India, but was quickly drafted to the Western Front and took part in the Battles of Ypres and Loos before being invalided home sick. On his recovery he was sent to Ireland, and served through the Rebellion of 1916, after which he returned to France and fought in the Cambrai sector, and throughout the Retreat and Advance of 1918. At the cessation of hostilities he proceeded to Germany with the Army of Occupation and served at Cologne until his discharge in March 1919. He holds the 1914 Star, and the General Service and Victory Medals.
The Hollow, Hartford, Hunts. Z2628.

GOODES, C. A., Private, 3rd Royal Fusiliers.
Volunteering in August 1914, he proceeded to France five months later and played an important part in the Battles of Neuve Chapelle, Hill 60, Loos and the Somme, where he was wounded in 1916 and admitted to hospital at Boulogne. On his recovery he rejoined his unit and fought at the Battles of Arras, Messines, Ypres and Cambrai, but was badly wounded in action in April 1918 and invalided home. After hospital treatment in Birmingham, he was sent to the Army of Occupation in Germany, and was still serving there in 1920. He holds the 1914–15 Star, and the General Service and Victory Medals. 8, Royal Oak Passage, Huntingdon. Z2627/A.

GOODES, H., Private, Royal Fusiliers.
Volunteering in 1915, he was drafted to France in 1916, but after taking part in the Battles of Albert, Vimy Ridge and the Somme, was badly wounded in nine places and invalided home. On his recovery he returned to the Western Front, was severely gassed in action, and again sent to England, where he unhappily died on December 18th, 1917. He was entitled to the General Service and Victory Medals.
"His memory is cherished with pride."
Park Lane, Sharnbrook, Bedford. Z2629/A.

GOODES, J. E., Private, 6th Essex Regiment.
He volunteered in March 1915, and in February of the following year was drafted to Egypt, but later proceeded into Palestine, where he took part in the Battles of Gaza, the capture of Jerusalem and Jaffa, and in other important engagements during General Allenby's Advance, and was wounded in action. He also suffered severely from malaria and sunstroke, and was eventually invalided from the Army in November 1919, holding the General Service and Victory Medals.
8, Royal Oak Passage, Huntingdon. Z2627/B.

GOODEY, C., Corporal, 1st Essex Regiment.
He volunteered in August 1914, and was first retained on important duties in England. In June 1916, however, he proceeded to France, where he played a prominent part in much severe fighting, particularly at the Battles of the Somme, Ypres and Cambrai, and was three times wounded in action. He was demobilised in March 1919, and holds the General Service and Victory Medals. 21, Great Butts St., Bedford. X2630/A.

GOODGER, C. H., Bombardier, R.G.A.
He volunteered in May 1915, and eight months later was sent to France, where he did excellent work with a heavy Battery in many important engagements. In March 1918 he was badly gassed in the Somme sector, and was invalided home. After five months in hospital at Liverpool he returned to the Western Front, and was in action in the Cambrai sector. He was demobilised in February 1919, and holds the General Service and Victory Medals.
88, Wolverton Road, Stony Stratford, Bucks. Z2631/A.

GOODGER, G. H., Cpl., Royal Warwickshire Regt.
He joined in March 1916, and was drafted to France in the following January. Whilst on the Western Front he played a prominent part in the Battles of Arras, Ypres and Cambrai, and was twice wounded in action. In April 1919 he volunteered to go to Russia, and rendered valuable services there for several months. He was finally demobilised in November 1919, and holds the General Service and Victory Medals.
4, Silver Street, Stony Stratford, Bucks. Z2632.

GOODING, A. G., Private, 8th Bedfordshire Regt.
He volunteered in June 1915, and, in February of the following year, was drafted to the Western Front, where he took part in the Battles of Vimy Ridge, the Somme and Cambrai, and many minor engagements in various sectors, and was wounded in April 1918. He fell fighting at Ypres on September 28th of that year. He was entitled to the General Service and Victory Medals.
"Whilst we remember, the sacrifice is not in vain."
32, Ampthill Street, Bedford. X2633.

GOODMAN, A., Gunner, Royal Field Artillery.
Joining in April 1916, he proceeded to the Western Front in October of the same year, and there saw severe fighting in various sectors. He took part in the Battles of Arras, Ypres and the Somme, and many other important engagements in this theatre of war, and served also through the Retreat and Advance of 1918. He was demobilised in April 1919, and holds the General Service and Victory Medals.
78, St. John's Street, Kempston, Bedford. X2639.

GOODMAN, B., Private, R.A.S.C.
He joined in April 1916, and, after undergoing a period of training, was retained at various stations, where he was engaged on important duties as a blacksmith. Unable to obtain his transfer to the front, he nevertheless, rendered valuable services with his Company until December 1919, when he was demobilised. 17, Greenhill Street, Bedford. X2635.

GOODMAN, E. R., Corporal, Royal Engineers.
He volunteered at the outbreak of war in August 1914, and was retained in England until March 1916, when he proceeded to the Western Front. There he was engaged on bridge-building and other important duties, and from 1917 served as an engine-driver on the railways in various sectors. He was demobilised in June 1919, and holds the General Service and Victory Medals.
31, Broad Street, Newport Pagnell, Bucks. Z2636/B.

GOODMAN, F. W., Pte., M.G.C. & Beds. Regt.
Volunteering in April 1915, he was drafted to France in November of that year, and there saw severe fighting in various sectors of the front. He took part in the Battles of Albert, the Somme, Ypres and Cambrai, and many other engagements, and was wounded in action at Arras in May 1917. He was later transferred to India, where he was still serving with his unit in 1920, holding the 1914–15 Star, and the General Service and Victory Medals. 44, Pilcroft Street, Bedford. X2638/B.

GOODMAN, J., Cpl., Royal Warwickshire Regt.
Volunteering in August 1914, he was drafted to Egypt twelve months later, and proceeded thence into Palestine. There he took part in the Battles of Gaza and many other important engagements, and, wounded in action in 1916, was for two months in hospital in Egypt. He was demobilised on returning home in March 1919, and holds the 1914–15 Star, and the General Service and Victory Medals.
31, Broad Street, Newport Pagnell, Bucks. Z2636/C.

GOODMAN, J. A., Ordinary Seaman, Royal Navy.
He volunteered in March 1915, and was posted to H.M.S. "Marazion," on board which vessel he was engaged on patrol duties with the Grand Fleet in the North Sea. He took part in many actions in these waters, and was wounded at the Battle of Jutland. Later he served in North Russian waters, and was finally demobilised in November 1919, holding the 1914–15 Star, and the General Service and Victory Medals.
44, Pilcroft Street, Bedford. X2638/A.

GOODMAN, J. T., Private, Labour Corps.
He joined in 1916, and, on completion of a period of training, was retained on duties of great importance at various stations. He was unable to obtain his transfer to a theatre of war on account of ill-health, but, nevertheless, rendered very valuable services until his demobilisation in August 1919.
Silver Street, Great Barford, Beds. Z2119/B.

GOODMAN, J. W., Private, Royal Scots Fusiliers.
Three months after volunteering in June 1915, he was drafted to the Western Front, where he saw much severe fighting. He died gloriously on the field of Battle near Ypres on October 19th, 1915, after only a month's service in France. He was entitled to the 1914–15 Star, and the General Service and Victory Medals.
"A valiant Soldier, with undaunted heart he breasted life's last hill."
20, Greenfield Road, Newport Pagnell, Bucks. Z2637/A.

GOODMAN, S. C., Private, 1st Norfolk Regiment.
Volunteering in January 1916, he proceeded to the Western Front in September of that year, and there took part in many important engagements in the Somme sector. Later, however, he was transferred to Italy, where he was again in action on the Piave until the cessation of hostilities. Demobilised on returning home in October 1919, he holds the General Service and Victory Medals.
20, Greenfield Road, Newport Pagnell, Bucks. Z2637/B.

GOODMAN, S. C., Sapper, Royal Engineers.
A Territorial, he was mobilised in August 1914, and shortly afterwards proceeded to the Western Front, where he saw severe fighting in various sectors. He took part in the Battles of La Bassée, Ypres, Hill 60, Loos, the Somme, Arras, Vimy Ridge and Cambrai, and many other important engagements and was gassed. Demobilised in April 1919, he holds the 1914 Star, and the General Service and Victory Medals.
14, Garfield Street, Bedford. X2634.

GOODMAN, W. L., Corporal, Middlesex Regiment.
He joined in April 1918, and, on completing a period of training later in that year, was drafted to the Western Front, where he took part in the final stages of the Advance into Germany. In July 1919 he was transferred to Egypt, where he was still with his unit at Cairo in 1920. He holds the General Service and Victory Medals.
31, Broad Street, Newport Pagnell, Bucks. Z2636/A.

GOODRIDGE, D., Spr., Royal Engineers (R.O.D.)
Joining in April 1916, he proceeded to the Western Front in the following month, and was there engaged on duties of great importance in various sectors. He rendered very valuable services whilst in this theatre of war, and finally returned to England for demobilisation in February 1919. He holds the General Service and Victory Medals.
57, Clarence Road East, Stony Stratford, Bucks. Z2640/A.

GOODRIDGE, J., Private, 1st Worcestershire Regt.
Joining in June 1916, he was drafted to France in the following December and there took part in the Battles of Arras, Vimy Ridge and Messines, and many other important engagements. He made the supreme sacrifice, falling in action on the Menin Road on July 31st, 1917. He was entitled to the General Service and Victory Medals.
"Honour to the immortal dead who gave their youth that the world might grow old in peace."
9, Vicarage Walk, Stony Stratford, Bucks. Z2640/B.

GOODSHIP, B., Private, 6th Bedfordshire Regt.
He volunteered in January 1916, and, in July of that year, was drafted to the Western Front, where he saw much severe fighting. He was unhappily reported missing and believed to have been killed in action on the Somme on August 9th, 1916, only a month after landing in France. He was entitled to the General Service and Victory Medals.
"His memory is cherished with pride."
Park Lane, Blunham, Beds. Z2641/A.

GOODSHIP, F. A., Private, 9th Essex Regiment.
Four months after joining in June 1916, he proceeded to the Western Front, where he was wounded in action on the Somme in December of the same year, and invalided home. He returned to France, however, on his recovery in June 1917, and, after much fighting, was taken prisoner near Albert in March 1918. Held in captivity until after the cessation of hostilities, he was demobilised in August 1919, and holds the General Service and Victory Medals.
Park Lane, Blunham, Beds. Z2641/B.

GOODSHIP, H., Private, Bedfordshire Regiment.
He joined in September 1916, and, in the following year, was sent to the Western Front, where, after taking part in the Battles of Arras and Ypres, he was wounded in action. Invalided home, he returned to France, however, in 1918, and was again wounded at Bapaume in September of that year. He holds the General Service and Victory Medals, and in October 1919, was demobilised.
Station Road, Tempsford, near Sandy, Beds. Z2642/A.

GOODWIN, H. J., Driver, Royal Engineers.
He volunteered in September 1914, and in the following year was drafted to Gallipoli, where he saw much severe fighting, especially at Suvla Bay. Invalided home, suffering from influenza, he proceeded to France in 1916 and there took part in the Battles of the Somme and Arras, and many minor engagements. Demobilised in June 1919, he holds the 1914–15 Star, and the General Service and Victory Medals.
Rosedale, Goldington, Bedford. Z2643/B.

GOODWIN, M. W., Driver, Royal Engineers.
Volunteering in September 1914, he was drafted to the Dardanelles in May of the following year, but after much severe fighting was invalided home suffering from fever. On his recovery, however, in March 1916, he was drafted to the Western Front, where he fought in the Battles of the Somme, Arras and Cambrai. He was demobilised in May 1919, and holds the 1914–15 Star, and the General Service and Victory Medals.
Rosedale, Goldington Road, Bedford. Z2643/A.

GOODYEAR, G., Sapper, Royal Engineers.
He joined in February 1918, and after undergoing a period of training, was retained on duties of great importance in the dockyards at various stations. He was not successful in obtaining his transfer to a theatre of war, but nevertheless, rendered valuable services with his Company until January 1919, when he was demobilised.
20, Melbourne Street, Bedford. X2644.

GOSLING, B. A. J., Sergeant, 1/4th Hants. Regt. and Indian Army.
Volunteering in August 1914, he was drafted to Mesopotamia three months later, and there saw much severe fighting. He took a prominent part in the attempted Relief of Kut, the capture of Baghdad and Mosul, and saw much severe fighting until the cessation of hostilities. Demobilised on his return home in March 1919, he holds the General Service and Victory Medals. 4, Beckett Street, Bedford. X2645.

GOSS, W., Private, 2nd Oxford. and Bucks. L.I.
He volunteered in August 1914, and in December of that year proceeded to the Western Front. There he saw much heavy fighting, and after taking part in the Battle of Neuve Chapelle, was severely gassed at Festubert and admitted to hospital at Southampton. He was invalided from the Army in August 1915, and holds the 1914–15 Star, and the General Service and Victory Medals.
3, School Street, New Bradwell, Bucks. Z2646.

GOSS, W. C., Guardsman, 2nd Grenadier Guards.
He joined in April 1917, and after completing a term of training, served at various stations, where he was engaged on duties of great importance. He was not successful in obtaining his transfer to the front, but nevertheless, rendered valuable services with his unit until his demobilisation in November 1919.
4, Brook Cottages, Water Eaton Rd., Bletchley, Bucks. Z2647.

GOSTICK, J. A., Private, Queen's Own (Royal West Kent Regiment).
He volunteered in 1915, and later in the same year proceeded to the Western Front, where he saw much severe fighting. After taking part in the Battle of Festubert and other engagements, he was reported missing in 1916 and believed to have been killed in action, but was afterwards discovered to be a prisoner of war in Germany. Released by exchange, he was invalided from the Army in March 1918, and holds the 1914–15 Star, and the General Service and Victory Medals.
High Street, Carlton, Beds. Z2648.

GOUGH, C., Gunner, Royal Garrison Artillery.
He volunteered in September 1914, and served with the anti-aircraft section in the Isle of Wight until June 1916, when he was drafted to the Western Front. There he saw much heavy fighting in the Somme sector until gassed and wounded in action in August and admitted to hospital at Newport. He was invalided from the Army in January 1917, and holds the General Service and Victory Medals.
Mount Pleasant, Bletchley, Bucks. Z3042.

GOUGH, F. G., Private, 2nd Bedfordshire Regt.
He was already in the Army when war broke out in August 1914, serving in South Africa, and was quickly drafted to France. He took part in the Battles of La Bassée and Ypres, but was reported missing and was afterwards believed to have been killed in action at Ypres about November 8th, 1914. He was entitled to the 1914 Star, and the General Service and Victory Medals.
"A valiant Soldier, with undaunted heart he breasted life's last hill."
Church Lane, Great Stukeley, Hunts. Z2651/B.

GOUGH, G. H., Private, Machine Gun Corps.
He volunteered in October 1914, and underwent a period of training prior to his being drafted to France. After fighting on the Somme and at Arras, he was transferred to Egypt, and took part in the Advance into Palestine, where he saw heavy fighting at Gaza, Jaffa and in the operations that led to the capture of Jerusalem. He returned home and was demobilised in July 1919, holding the General Service and Victory Medals.
Biddenham, Beds. Z2649.

GOUGH, T. L., Private, R.A.S.C.
He joined in August 1916, and was shortly afterwards drafted to Mesopotamia, where he took an active part in several engagements, including those at Kut and the capture of Baghdad, and also saw service in the Persian Gulf. He later proceeded to India and saw much fighting during the Afghan risings on the North West Frontier. He returned home, was demobilised in December 1919, and holds the General Service and Victory Medals, and India General Service Medal (with Clasp, Afghanistan, North West Frontier, 1919).
104, George Street, Bedford. Z2650.

GOUGH, W., Private, Royal Warwickshire Regt.
He volunteered in the Huntingdonshire Cyclist Battalion in December 1914, but after a period of training was transferred to the Royal Warwickshire Regiment and proceeded to France. There he took part in the Battles of the Somme, Arras, Ypres and Cambrai, where he was badly wounded and consequently invalided home. He was demobilised in 1919, and holds the General Service and Victory Medals.
Great Stukeley, Hunts. Z2651/A.

GOULDING, T. J., Corporal, Royal Engineers.
He volunteered in November 1914, and after serving at various home stations, was transferred to the 21st Lancers, and proceeded to France. There he took part in much heavy fighting in the Ypres, Arras and Cambrai sectors. He was demobilised in February 1919, but re-enlisted shortly afterwards and returned to France, where he was employed on exhumation duties. He unfortunately died through heart failure on October 29th, 1919, and was entitled to the General Service and Victory Medals.
"Thinking that remembrance, though unspoken, may reach him where he sleeps."
Park Lane, Blunham, Beds. Z2652.

GOWLER, E. J. (Miss), Worker, Forestry Corps.
She joined in October 1918, and proceeded to Hinchenbrook Park, Huntingdonshire, where she rendered valuable services with the Forestry Corps. She carried out her work in a commendable manner until her demobilisation in April 1919.
King Street, Somersham, Hunts. Z2653/B.

GOWLER, T. (sen.), Pte., 2nd Bedfordshire Regt.
He was mobilised in August 1914, and was quickly drafted to France. There he took part in many important engagements, including the Battles of Ypres, Neuve Chapelle, Loos, Hill 60, Festubert and the Somme, and was wounded and gassed in action. As a result he was invalided home, and on his recovery was retained on important duties in Liverpool and Wales. He was demobilised in February 1919, and holds the 1914 Star, and the General Service and Victory Medals.
King Street, Somersham, Hunts. Z2653/A.

GOWLER, T. (jun.), Private, Machine Gun Corps.
He volunteered in October 1914, and underwent a period of training prior to his being drafted to Salonika, where he took part in much heavy fighting on the Vardar and Struma fronts, and at Monastir. He made the supreme sacrifice, being killed in action on the Doiran front on April 25th, 1917. He was entitled to the General Service and Victory Medals.
"Honour to the immortal dead, who gave their youth that the world might grow old in peace."
King Street, Somersham, Hunts. Z2653/C.

GRACE, A. F., Sapper, Royal Engineers.
Joining in June 1916, he proceeded overseas two months later. During his service on the Western Front he did good work in the forward areas whilst engaged on the railways, and in repairing waggons. He was demobilised in September 1919, and holds the General Service and Victory Medals.
50, New Bridge Street, New Bradwell, Bucks. Z2654.

GRACE, H. D., Corporal, 7th Wiltshire Regiment.
He volunteered in September 1914, and in the following year was drafted to Salonika. In this seat of operations he took part in much severe fighting on the Vardar and Doiran fronts, and was badly wounded in August 1916. As a result he was invalided to Malta, and, after partial recovery, was sent to Dulwich Hospital. He was demobilised in March 1919, and holds the 1914–15 Star, and the General Service and Victory Medals.
9, Loughton Council Cottages, Loughton, Bucks. Z2655.

GRAHAM, C., Gunner, Royal Field Artillery.
He joined in August 1916, and was retained for some time at various home stations before being drafted to Mesopotamia. Whilst in this theatre of war he took part in many engagements, including that of Kut and the capture of Baghdad. He returned home and was demobilised in September 1919, holding the General Service and Victory Medals.
High Street, Milton Ernest, near Bedford. Z2656/B.

GRAHAM, J. W., Private, Middlesex Regiment.
He joined in March 1918, and after training at Bedford and Purfleet, rendered valuable services for about two months. He was then found to be medically unfit for further service, and was discharged in May 1918.
High Street, Milton Ernest, near Bedford. Z2656/A.

GRANBY, C., Rifleman, King's Royal Rifle Corps.
He joined in March 1918, and underwent a period of training at various home stations. After the cessation of hostilities he proceeded to Germany with the Army of Occupation, and served on the Rhine until his demobilisation in February 1920.
Church Road, Wootton, Bedford. Z2657/B.

GRANBY, F. J., Private, 1/5th Bedfordshire Regt. and 1/2nd London Regiment (Royal Fusiliers).
He volunteered in August 1914, and was retained at various home stations until 1916 owing to his being under age for overseas. He was then drafted to France, and took part in much severe fighting on the Ancre. He died gloriously on the Field of Battle at Arras on April 11th, 1917, and was entitled to the General Service and Victory Medals.
"Honour to the immortal dead, who gave their youth that the world might grow old in peace."
Church Road, Wootton, Bedford. Z2657/A.

GRANGER, E. I., Private, 1/7th Essex Regiment.
He joined in March 1917, and later in the same year proceeded to Egypt. Whilst in this seat of operations he took part in the Advance into Palestine, and saw much heavy fighting at Jaffa and Gaza. He returned home and was demobilised in November 1919, holding the General Service and Victory Medals.
Station Road, Market Bosworth, Leicester. Z2659.

GRANGER, J. W., Corporal, R.A.S.C. (M.T.)
He volunteered in September 1914, and in the following year was drafted to Salonika. There he was engaged on various important duties with the Mechanical Transport, and did good work throughout. He suffered from dysentery and malaria, and was in hospital for some time. He returned home and was demobilised in March 1919, holding the 1914–15 Star, and the General Service and Victory Medals.
7, Montague Road, Huntingdon. Z2658.

GRANT, H. W., Air Mechanic, Royal Air Force.
He joined in 1916, and later in the same year was drafted overseas. Whilst on the Western Front he was engaged on important transport work with the Royal Air Force in many sectors, including those of Albert, the Somme and Cambrai. He did good work throughout, and was demobilised in April 1919, holding the General Service and Victory Medals.
46, Ouse Walk, Huntingdon. Z2660.

GRANT, J. P. D., Private, Machine Gun Corps.
He volunteered in September 1914, and in the following January was drafted to France, where he took part in the heavy fighting at the Battles of Festubert, Hill 60, Loos and the Somme. He made the supreme sacrifice, being killed in action in the Ypres sector on October 4th, 1917. He was entitled to the 1914–15 Star, and the General Service and Victory Medals.
"The path of duty was the way to glory."
1, Queen's Row, Bedford. X1127/A.

GRAVES, G. H., Corporal, K.O. (Y.L.I.)
He was called up from the Reserve at the declaration of war in August 1914, and was immediately drafted to France. He fought through the Retreat from Mons, and also at the Battles of Ypres and the Somme, where he was wounded. Later he served in many other important engagements, and gave his life for his King and Country on March 31st, 1918, being killed in action at Cambrai. He was entitled to the Mons Star, and the General Service and Victory Medals.
"Nobly striving:
He nobly fell that we might live."
11, Greenhill Street, Bedford. X2018/B.

GRAY, A., Private, Machine Gun Corps.
Volunteering at the outbreak of war in August 1914, he completed his training in the following year, and was sent to the Western Front. Whilst in this seat of hostilities he was in action at Loos, Albert, the Somme, Arras, Lens and Cambrai. He was invalided to England suffering from pneumonia, but on his recovery returned to France and saw further service until the close of hostilities. In February 1919 he was demobilised, and holds the 1914–15 Star, and the General Service and Victory Medals. 11, Conquest Road, Bedford. Z2662.

GRAY, C. E., L/Corporal, Machine Gun Corps.
He volunteered in May 1915, and in the following year was drafted to France, where he saw much service in various sectors of the front. He served in the Battles of Ypres, the Somme, Arras and Cambrai, and was twice wounded—at Ypres and the Somme. On his return to England he was demobilised in February 1919, and holds the General Service and Victory Medals. Ellington, Hunts. Z2665.

GRAY, C. H., Private, 1st Northants. Regiment.
A Reservist, he was called to the Colours at the outbreak of war in August 1914, and was quickly drafted to France. In the course of his service in this seat of war he took part in the heavy fighting at Ypres, and was badly wounded in November 1914. As a result he unfortunately died shortly afterwards, and was entitled to the 1914 Star, and the General Service and Victory Medals.
"A costly sacrifice upon the altar of freedom."
9, Wellington Street, Bedford. X2666/B.

GRAY, G. E., Private, Machine Gun Corps.
Volunteering in November 1914, he was immediately sent to the Western Front, where he saw much service in various sectors. He took part in the Battles of Ypres, Festubert, Loos and the Somme, where he was wounded, and later served in the fighting at Arras and Cambrai. Returning home after the cessation of hostilities, he was demobilised in February 1919, and holds the 1914–15 Star, and the General Service and Victory Medals.
16, Green Street, St. Ives, Hunts. Z2661.

GRAY, H., Drummer, 1st Essex Regiment.
Volunteering in November 1914, he soon proceeded to France, but was both wounded and gassed at Hill 60. On his recovery he was sent to Egypt, whence he was drafted to Gallipoli. After serving through the remainder of the campaign there he returned to Egypt, and took part in the Advance into Palestine, being in action in the operations that led to the fall of Jerusalem. Returning home, he was demobilised in March 1919, and holds the 1914–15 Star, and the General Service and Victory Medals.
9, Wellington Street, Bedford. X2666/A.

GRAY, J. P., Corporal, Royal Defence Corps.
He volunteered in August 1914, but owing to his being medically unfit was retained on important home duties at various stations. His duties chiefly consisted in guarding prisoners of war, and he rendered good services throughout the period of hostilities, and was not demobilised until December 1919.
25, Commercial Road, Bedford. Z2663.

GRAY, N., Private (Signaller), Bedfordshire Regt.
Volunteering at the outbreak of hostilities in August 1914, he proceeded in the following year to France. During the course of his service in this theatre of war he was in action at the Battles of Ypres, and was wounded. On his recovery he returned to the fighting area, and took part in the Somme Offensive, and was again wounded. Later he saw further service until the conclusion of war, and was demobilised in 1919, holding the 1914–15 Star, and the General Service and Victory Medals. Kimbolton, Hunts. Z2664/A.

GRAY, S. F., Lieutenant, 3rd Bedfordshire Regt.
Shortly after volunteering in August 1914, he crossed to France, and saw heavy fighting, notably at the Battle of Loos, where he was wounded in 1915. Subsequently he took a conspicuous part in the Battles of Ypres, Arras and Festubert, and after the Armistice served at Cologne and Bonn with the Army of Occupation. Returning home, he was demobilised in May 1920, and holds the 1914 Star, and the General Service and Victory Medals. Kimbolton, Hunts. Z2664/B.

GRAY, S. H. H., Sergeant, Royal Field Artillery.
He volunteered in August 1914, and was quickly drafted to France, where he did excellent work throughout the period of hostilities. He took an active part in the Battle of Mons and in the Retreat, and later served at Ypres, the Somme, Arras and Cambrai. After the conclusion of war he proceeded with the Army of Occupation into Germany, and was engaged as an Instructor. In February 1920 he was demobilised, and holds the Mons Star, and the General Service and Victory Medals.
Kimbolton, Hunts. Z2664/C.

GREAVES, A. J., Private, Royal Berkshire Regt.
He joined early in 1918, and in April proceeded to the Western Front, where he served on the Cambrai front, taking part in the Retreat and Advance. Gassed in October 1918, he spent three months in hospital at Rouen before joining the Army of Occupation in Cologne. He was not demobilised until September 1919, and holds the General Service and Victory Medals.
25, Broad Street, Newport Pagnell. Z2667/A.

GREAVES, H. M. F., Private, Bedfordshire Regt.
Volunteering in May 1915, he was unable to proceed overseas after completing his training, and was retained at Ampthill, Felixstowe, Hastings, Waterford and Salisbury Plain. In spite of ill-health he rendered valuable services whilst employed on guard and clerical duties, and was eventually demobilised in February 1920. 15, Firbank Road, Bedford. Z2668.

GREAVES, W. R., Private, 5th Northants. Regt.
He volunteered in August 1914, and, completing his training at Shorncliffe, was sent to France in June 1915. After only a short period of service in that theatre of war, he was unhappily killed on August 4th in the Armentières sector, and was buried at Ploegsteert. He was entitled to the 1914–15 Star, and the General Service and Victory Medals.
"A valiant Soldier, with undaunted heart he breasted life's last hill."
25, Broad Street, Newport Pagnell. Z2667/B.

GREEN, A., Private, 53rd Bedfordshire Regiment.
He joined in August 1918, and was retained on the coast with the Huntingdonshire Volunteers until March 1919. He was then drafted to Germany and served for over a year at Cologne and on the Rhine with the Army of Occupation, being eventually demobilised in August 1920.
River Terrace, Eynesbury, St. Neots, Hunts. Z2678.

GREEN, A., Trooper, Bedfordshire Lancers.
Volunteering in September 1914, he proceeded to France in January, and saw heavy fighting on the Ypres front. Drafted early in 1916 to Egypt, he joined the Palestine Force and was in action at Gaza and in the operations leading to the capture of Jerusalem. After his return home he was demobilised in May 1919, and holds the 1914–15 Star, and the General Service and Victory Medals.
High Street, Lavendon, Bucks. Z2676/B.

GREEN, A., Air Mechanic, Royal Air Force.
He joined in January 1918, and completed his training. Despite his efforts to proceed overseas he was unable to obtain his transfer, but was employed as a rigger at aerodromes at Hendon, Gillingham and Chingford, where he was engaged on duties of a highly technical nature. He was demobilised in March 1919.
22, Oxford Street, Stony Stratford, Bucks. Z2669.

GREEN, A. (Mrs.), Special War Worker.
This lady offered her services in 1916, and was employed at Godmanchester on important agricultural work, in which she rendered very valuable services. She carried out her duties until the following year, relinquishing in favour of the Women's Land Army.
Chadley Lane, Godmanchester, Hunts. Z2671/B.

GREEN, A. T., Private, R.A.M.C.
Volunteering in December 1915, he completed his training with the Durham Light Infantry and was transferred later to the King's Liverpool Regiment and afterwards to the Scottish Rifles. He then served at Blackpool and Tidworth as an orderly with the Royal Army Medical Corps. Though unfit for active service he rendered valuable services before being demobilised in February 1919.
6, Newton Road, Bletchley, Bucks. Z3043—Z3044.

GREEN, C., Corporal, Royal Engineers.
Mobilised at the outbreak of war, he served at Bedford and Bury St. Edmunds before being sent to France in 1914. During over four years on the Western Front he was in action at La Bassée, Ypres, Hill 60, Loos, Albert, the Somme, Arras, Cambrai, the Marne, Bapaume and Havrincourt. He was discharged in February 1919, and holds the 1914–15 Star, and the General Service and Victory Medals.
Biddenham, Bedford. Z2673/A.

GREEN, C., Private, 1st Leicestershire Regiment.
In July 1917 he joined the Rifle Brigade, and in the same year was drafted to France, where he fought in the Battles of Ypres, Cambrai and the Somme, and was gassed. Demobilised in November 1919, he re-enlisted in January 1920 in the Leicestershire Regiment, and was stationed in Ireland. He holds the General Service and Victory Medals.
3, Victoria Terrace, Huntingdon. Z2672.

GREEN, E. M. (Miss), Member, W.R.A.F.
She joined in June 1918, and was stationed at Porte Holme, Huntingdonshire, and at Scotwick, Lincolnshire. At these places she was employed as a cook, officers' mess waitress, and on general duties, and rendered valuable services before being demobilised in June 1919.
Mill Street, Houghton, Hunts. Z2674/D.

GREEN, F., Air Mechanic, Royal Air Force.
He joined in September and throughout his training and service was stationed on Salisbury Plain, where he was employed on highly technical work in the aeroplane sheds, and was engaged in the cook-house. After doing excellent work, he was demobilised in June 1919.
Biddenham, Bedford. Z2673/B.

GREEN, F. F., Gunner, Royal Garrison Artillery.
He volunteered in the Life Guards in April 1915 at Windsor, but, being under age was discharged in May 1917. Re-enlisting, however, three months later in the Royal Garrison Artillery, he was in action at Cambrai as a gun-layer during the Retreat and Advance of 1918, and was gassed in August. Subsequently he served at Cologne and on the Rhine with the Army of Occupation, and on his return home was demobilised in August 1919, holding the General Service and Victory Medals.
Mill Street, Houghton, Hunts. Z2674/A.

GREEN, H., Private, 1st Bedfordshire Regiment.
He volunteered in August 1914, and in the following year was drafted to France. There he took part in the Battles of Festubert, Loos, the Somme, Arras, Ypres and Cambrai, and was badly wounded in action three times. In consequence he was invalided home, and eventually discharged in 1919 as medically unfit for further service. He holds the 1914–15 Star, and the General Service and Victory Medals.
Chadley Lane, Godmanchester, Hunts. Z2671/C.

GREEN, J., Corporal, Royal Engineers.
He joined in 1916, and later in the same year was drafted to France. In this theatre of war he was engaged on various important duties connected with laying telephone wires and wireless, and saw much service in the Somme, Arras, Ypres, Passchendaele and Cambrai sectors. He was demobilised in 1919, and holds the General Service and Victory Medals.
Barham, Hunts. Z2679.

GREEN, J., Private, Royal Defence Corps.
He volunteered in January 1915, and underwent a period of training, but was retained at various stations on important duties with his unit. He did continuously good work, but was unable to proceed overseas, and was discharged in December 1917 as medically unfit for further service.
Mill Street, Houghton, Hunts. Z2674/B.

GREEN, J. J., Sapper, Royal Engineers.
He volunteered in March 1915, and was retained at various home stations on important duties with the Royal Engineers and Royal Defence Corps until April 1918. He was then drafted to France, and did good work at Dunkirk on transport and clerical duties. He was demobilised in June 1919, and holds the General Service and Victory Medals.
Mill Street, Houghton, Hunts. Z2674/C.

GREEN, R., Private, 53rd Middlesex Regiment.
He joined in July 1918, and, after undergoing a period of training, was retained on important duties at various stations. He was unable to obtain his transfer overseas before the cessation of hostilities, but in 1919 was sent with the Army of Occupation into Germany, where he served at Cologne until invalided to hospital at Sheffield. He was demobilised in June 1919.
Cranfield Road, Wootton, Bedford. Z2675/B.

GREEN, S., Private, 1/5th Bedfordshire Regiment.
He volunteered in November 1915, and in the following June proceeded to Egypt. In this seat of operations he took part in many engagements, including the Advance into Palestine, and saw fighting at Gaza, Jaffa and on the River Jordan. He returned home and was demobilised in September 1919, holding the General Service and Victory Medals.
68, Iddesleigh Road, Queen's Park, Bedford. Z2670.

GREEN, S., Private, R.A.M.C.
He was mobilised in August 1914, and quickly drafted to the Western Front. There he was engaged as a stretcher-bearer, and rendered valuable services at the Battles of Ypres, Givenchy, Loos, the Somme, Albert and Arras, and in the Retreat and Advance of 1918, and was slightly wounded in action. He was discharged in February 1919, and holds the Mons Star, and the General Service and Victory Medals.
43, St. Giles Street, New Bradwell, Bucks. Z2677.

GREEN, V., Private, Royal Warwickshire Regt.
He volunteered in August 1914, and on completing his training was drafted to France, where he took part in the Battles of the Somme, Arras and Ypres. He was then transferred to Italy, and did good work in the fighting on the Piave River and Asiago Plateau. He was awarded the Italian Military Cross for gallantry and devotion to duty in the Field. He returned home and was demobilised in May 1919, but later rejoined in the Bedfordshire Regiment and proceeded to India, where in 1920 he was still serving. He also holds the General Service and Victory Medals.
Chadley Lane, Godmanchester, Hunts. Z2671/D.

GREEN, V. (Miss), Member, W.R.A.F.
She joined the W.R.A.F. in 1917, and after a period of training was engaged at various home stations on important duties. She acted as a waitress in the officers' mess, and carried out her work in a highly commendable manner. She was demobilised in 1919.
Chadley Lane, Godmanchester, Hunts. Z2671/A.

GREEN, W. R. J., Private, Queen's (Royal West Surrey Regiment).
He joined in February 1917, and in the following July was drafted to France, where he took part in the Battle of Arras and was taken prisoner of war near Cambrai in November 1917. He was held in captivity in Germany until December 1918, when he was repatriated and returned home. He was demobilised in November 1919, and holds the General Service and Victory Medals.
High Street, Lavendon, Bucks. Z2676/C.

GREEN, W. W., Private, 1st Gordon Highlanders.
He joined in June 1916, and in the following year proceeded to Italy, where he saw much severe fighting. He took part in many important engagements on the Piave until the cessation of hostilities, and in 1919 was invalided home, and was for a time in hospital at Aberdeen. He was later sent with the Army of Occupation to Turkey, where he was still with his unit in 1920, holding the General Service and Victory Medals.
Cranfield Road, Wootton, Bedford. Z2675/A.

GREENHAM, C., Driver, Royal Horse Artillery.
Already in the Army when war broke out in August 1914, he was drafted two months later to the Western Front, where he saw severe fighting in various sectors. He served through the Battles of Ypres, Festubert, Loos, Albert, the Somme, Vimy Ridge and Cambrai, and many minor engagements, and also took part in the Advance into Germany. Returning home in March 1919, he was demobilised in the following month, and holds the 1914 Star, and the General Service and Victory Medals.
65, Grey Friars Walk, Bedford. X2680.

GREENWOOD, C. R., Guardsman, Grenadier Gds.
Volunteering in September 1914, he proceeded to the Western Front on completing a period of training in the following year, and there saw much heavy fighting. He took part in the Battles of Festubert and Loos and many other important engagements in various sectors, and was wounded in action at Ypres in 1917. He holds the 1914–15 Star, and the General Service and Victory Medals, and in 1920 was still with his unit.
Wennington, near Abbot's Ripton, Hunts. Z2681.

GREGORY, A. G., Private, Oxford. and Bucks. L.I.
He volunteered in September 1915, and, after a period of training, was retained on important duties with the Royal Buckinghamshire Hussars in England. In February 1918, however, he was transferred to the Oxfordshire and Buckinghamshire Light Infantry, and drafted to the Western Front, where he took part in the Battles of Amiens, Cambrai and Le Cateau and other engagements during the Advance. Demobilised in March 1919, he holds the General Service and Victory Medals.
3, Rumbold's Lane, Buckingham. Z2682.

GRIBBLE, A., Private, 5th Bedfordshire Regt.
He volunteered at the outbreak of war in August 1914, and, in the following year, was drafted to the Dardanelles, where he saw much severe fighting. After only five days' service in Gallipoli he fell in action on August 15th, 1915. He was entitled to the 1914–15 Star, and the General Service and Victory Medals.
"He died the noblest death a man may die :
Fighting for God and right and liberty."
45, Hassett Street, Bedford. X2684/A

GRIBBLE, G. F., 1st Air Mechanic, R.A.F.
Three months after joining in January 1917, he proceeded to France, where he was engaged on important duties with the Balloon Section in various sectors of the front. Present at the Battle of Vimy Ridge, Messines and Ypres, and many other engagements in this theatre of war, he did much useful work with his Squadron until his return home in January 1919. He was demobilised in the following month, and holds the General Service and Victory Medals.
40, Greenhill Street, Bedford. X2683.

GRIFFIN, H., Private, 7th Oxford. and Bucks. L.I.
He joined in May 1916, and, in the following November, proceeded to the Western Front, where he saw much severe fighting in the Somme sector. Afterwards transferred to Italy, he was again in action on the Piave, where he was wounded, and was for six months in hospital at Genoa. On his recovery he was engaged on important duties at various stations, until his return home for demobilisation in February 1919, and holds the General Service and Victory Medals.
19, Spring Gardens, Newport Pagnell, Bucks. Z2686.

GRIFFIN, W. J., Private, Oxford. and Bucks. L.I.
Joining in March 1916, he was drafted to the Western Front after four months' training and there took part in the Battles of the Somme and Arras, and was wounded at Guillemont in April 1917. He was for a time in hospital at Manchester and in November of that year was transferred to Salonika, where he fought on the Vardar, Doiran and Struma fronts. Again invalided home suffering from malaria, he was finally demobilised in October 1919, holding the General Service and Victory Medals.
6, St. Paul's Terrace, Newport Pagnell, Bucks. Z2685.

GRIFFITH, A. C., Sergeant, 7th Wiltshire Regt.
He volunteered in September 1914, and, twelve months later, proceeded to France, where he saw much severe fighting. In November 1915, however, he was transferred to Salonika, and there took part in many important engagements on the Vardar and Doiran fronts until invalided home in February 1918, suffering from malaria. Later he returned to the Western Front and fought in the Battles of Amiens and Le Cateau. He was demobilised in April 1919, and holds the 1914–15 Star, and the General Service and Victory Medals.
24, Young Street, Wolverton, Bucks. Z2688/A.

GRIFFITH, J. H., Sapper, Royal Engineers.
Two months after volunteering in July 1915, he was drafted to the Western Front, where he was engaged on trench-digging and other important duties at Loos, Lens, Bullecourt, Gommecourt and many other places. He died gloriously on the Field of Battle on the Somme on November 18th, 1916. He was entitled to the 1914-15 Star, and the General Service and Victory Medals.
"Great deeds cannot die :
They with the sun and moon renew their light for ever."
24, Young Street, Wolverton, Bucks. Z2688/B.

GRIFFITHS, A. L., Tpr., Bedfordshire Lancers.
He joined in 1915, and, on completion of a period of training in the following year, was drafted to Egypt, whence he proceeded into Palestine, and took part in the Battles of Gaza and the entry into Jaffa. In 1917 he was transferred to the Western Front, and there fought in the Battles of Cambrai and the Somme and many other engagements. Demobilised in April 1919, he holds the General Service and Victory Medals.
69, Hassett Street, Bedford. X2687/B.

GRIFFITHS, E., Sapper, Royal Engineers.
Volunteering in February 1915, he proceeded to France after three months' training and was there engaged on important duties with a Railway Construction Company in various sectors of the front. He served at Ypres and Arras and many other places in this theatre of war, and did much useful work until his return home for demobilisation in March 1919. He holds the 1914–15 Star, and the General Service and Victory Medals.
London Lane, Great Paxton, St. Neots, Hunts. Z2689.

GRIFFITHS, J., Private, 1st Royal Welch Fusiliers.
After volunteering in August 1914 he underwent a period of training prior to being drafted to the Western Front two years later. There he saw much heavy fighting, and, after taking part in many important engagements during the Somme Offensive, was severely wounded in action in June 1917 and invalided home. In October 1919 he proceeded to India, where he was still with his unit at Lucknow in 1920, and holds the General Service and Victory Medals.
High Road, Clapham, Bedford. Z2690.

GRIFFITHS, J., Private, Sherwood Foresters.
He volunteered in 1914, and, after his training, was retained on important duties in England until 1917, when he proceeded to the Western Front. Whilst in this theatre of war he saw severe fighting in various sectors, and took part in the Battles of Ypres, Passchendaele, Cambrai, the Somme and Amiens and many minor engagements. He was demobilised in January 1919, and holds the General Service and Victory Medals.
Great Paxton, Hunts. Z2691.

GRIFFITHS, S. A., Corporal, Bedfordshire Regt., and Somerset Light Infantry.
He joined in March 1916, and, after undergoing a period of training, served at various stations, where he was engaged on duties of great importance. Owing to ill-health he was not successful in obtaining his transfer to a theatre of war, but nevertheless rendered valuable services with his unit until December 1919, when he was demobilised.
69, Hassett Street, Bedford. X2687/A.

GRIMWOOD, G., Private, 1st Suffolk Regiment.
He joined in 1918, and shortly afterwards proceeded to Egypt, where he was engaged on important duties at various stations. He also served in Palestine at Jerusalem, Jaffa, Haifa and Gaza, and many other places, and did much useful work until his return home for demobilisation in January 1920. He holds the General Service and Victory Medals.
High Street, Somersham, Hunts. Z2692.

GROVES, O. G., Sapper, Royal Engineers.
He joined in April 1917, and, after completing a term of training, was retained at various stations, where he was engaged on duties of a highly important nature. He was unable to obtain his transfer to a theatre of war, but, after the cessation of hostilities, was sent with the Army of Occupation into Germany where he served at Cologne. He was demobilised on his return home in October 1919. 16, Maitland St., Bedford. X2693.

GUDGEON, A. C., A.B., Royal Navy.
Already in the Navy when war was declared in August 1914, he afterwards served in H.M.S. "Dwarf" and "Pembroke" in many waters. Attached chiefly to the Grand Fleet in the North Sea, he was engaged on submarine-chasing and coastal defence duties, and also took part in the Battles of Heligoland Bight and Jutland and minor actions. He was discharged in April 1919, and holds the 1914–15 Star, and the General Service and Victory Medals.
The Warren, Clapham, Bedford. Z2694/B.

GUDGIN, B., Sapper, Royal Engineers.
He volunteered at the outbreak of war in August 1914, and in May of the following year proceeded to the Western Front. There he was engaged on important duties in various sectors, being unfit for service in the firing-line, and did much useful work during the period of hostilities. He was demobilised on his return home in April 1919, and holds the 1914–15 Star, and the General Service and Victory Medals.
Biddenham, Beds. Z2696.

GUEST, A., Private, Oxford. and Bucks. L.I.
He volunteered in August 1914, and, after his training, served at various stations in England until February 1916. He was then drafted to the Western Front, where he took part in many important engagements, including the Battles of Arras, Ypres and Cambrai, fought also in the Retreat and Advance of 1918, and was gassed on the Somme in 1916. He was demobilised in March 1919, and holds the General Service and Victory Medals. Simpson, near Bletchley, Bucks. Z2698/B.

GUEST, C., Private, Oxford. and Bucks. L.I.
Volunteering in September 1914, he was drafted to the Western Front in January of the following year, and there saw severe fighting in various sectors. After taking part in the Battles of Ypres, the Somme, Arras and Cambrai and many other important engagements he was transferred to Italy, where he was again in action on the Piave. Demobilised on returning home in March 1919, he holds the 1914–15 Star, and the General Service and Victory Medals.
Simpson, near Bletchley, Bucks. Z2697.

GUEST, W., Private, Oxford. and Bucks. L.I.
Four months after volunteering in September 1915, he was drafted to France and served in the Somme and various other sectors of the front. After taking part in several important engagements he was unhappily reported missing, and later killed in action, at Ypres on August 22nd, 1916. He was entitled to the General Service and Victory Medals.
"A valiant Soldier, with undaunted heart he breasted life's last hill."
Simpson, near Bletchley, Bucks. Z2689/A.

GULLIVER, A., Private, 5th Bedfordshire Regt.
He was already in the Army when war broke out in August 1914, and was retained at various stations, where he was engaged on duties of a highly important nature. He was medically unfit for service overseas, and was consequently unable to obtain his transfer to the front, but nevertheless rendered valuable services with his unit until January 1919, when he was demobilised.
15, Pilcroft Street, Bedford. X2695.

GUMBLEY, J., Gunner, Royal Garrison Artillery.
Volunteering in September 1914, he was drafted to Ceylon in the following month, and was there engaged on garrison duties until January 1916. He was then transferred to the Western Front, where he took part in many important engagements, and was three times wounded in action—on the Somme in July 1916, at Cambrai in the following year, and again on the Somme in 1918. He afterwards served with the Army of Occupation in Germany, and in 1920 was still with his Battery in India. He holds the General Service and Victory Medals.
Pertenhall, near St. Neots, Hunts. Z2699/A.

GUNTHORPE, R. R. G. (M.M.), Corporal, 5th Royal Berkshire Regiment.
He volunteered in September 1914, and in March of the following year was drafted to the Western Front, where he saw much severe fighting. He took part in the Battles of Ypres and the Somme and many other engagements, and was wounded in action at Epéhy in 1918 and admitted to hospital at Boulogne. He was awarded the Military Medal for conspicuous bravery in the Field in the same engagement, and holds also the 1914–15 Star, and the General Service and Victory Medals. He was still with his unit in Persia in 1920.
Gawcott Road, Buckingham. Z2700.

GUNTRIP, J., Private, 1st Northants. Regiment.
He was already serving in India when war was declared in August 1914, and was shortly afterwards drafted to the Western Front, where he took part in severe fighting at Ypres and various other places. He made the supreme sacrifice, falling in action at the Battle of Neuve Chapelle on March 11th, 1915. He was entitled to the 1914 Star, and the General Service and Victory Medals.
"Whilst we remember, the sacrifice is not in vain."
120, Victoria Road, Fenny Stratford, Bucks. Z2701/B.

GUNTRIP, J., Leading Stoker, Royal Navy.
He volunteered in June 1915, and was posted to H.M.S. "Patrol," on board which vessel he was engaged on patrol duties with the Chatham Squadron in the North Sea and Home waters. He took part in the Battle of Jutland and many minor actions until the cessation of hostilities, and was finally demobilised in January 1919. He holds the 1914–15 Star, and the General Service and Victory Medals.
124, Victoria Road, Fenny Stratford, Bucks. Z2168/C.

GUNTRIP, J. J., L/Cpl., 1st Oxford. & Bucks. L.I.
He volunteered in September 1914, and in March of the following year was sent to the Western Front, where he saw heavy fighting in various sectors. He took part in the Battles of Ypres, Loos, the Somme and Cambrai and many minor engagements, and was severely wounded on the Somme in 1918 and admitted to hospital at Blackburn. Invalided from the Army in November 1918, he holds the 1914–15 Star, and the General Service and Victory Medals.
120, Victoria Road, Fenny Stratford, Bucks. Z2701/A.

GURNEY, F. W., Private, 9th Norfolk Regiment.
He volunteered in September 1914, and in December of the following year was drafted to the Western Front, where he took part in many important engagements. He fell fighting on September 15th, 1916, during the Advance on the Somme. He was entitled to the 1914–15 Star, and the General Service and Victory Medals.
"He passed out of the sight of men by the path of duty and self-sacrifice."
11, Duncombe Street, Bletchley, Bucks. Z3045/A.

GURNEY, T., Sapper, Royal Engineers.
Shortly after joining in 1917 he was drafted to Egypt, where he was engaged on important duties on the railways at various stations. He also served in Palestine, and was present at the Battles of Gaza and the entry into Jaffa and Jerusalem, finally returning to England for demobilisation in January 1919. He holds the General Service and Victory Medals.
Station Road, Tempsford, Sandy, Beds. Z2702.

H

HACKETT, A., Private, R.A.M.C.
He volunteered in September 1915, and, after a period of training on Salisbury Plain, was two months later drafted overseas. During his service on the Western Front he took an active part in many important engagements, and performed excellent work as a stretcher-bearer. He was demobilised in March 1919, and holds the 1914–15 Star, and the General Service and Victory Medals.
5, Beaconsfield Place, Newton Pagnell, Bucks. Z1820/B.

HACKETT, C. W., Corporal, R.A.S.C.
He joined in October 1916, and, after completion of his training, was employed in transporting horses from Southampton to Boulogne and Le Havre. Throughout the period of hostilities he fulfilled these duties with the greatest ability, and rendered valuable services before being demobilised in November 1919. He holds the General Service and Victory Medals.
The Green, Great Staughton, Hunts. Z2703/D—Z2704/D.

HACKETT, E., Guardsman, Grenadier Guards.
Volunteering in December 1914, he proceeded eight months later to the Western Front, where he fought in important engagements at Festubert and Givenchy, and was severely wounded in action at the Battle of Loos in September 1915. He unfortunately succumbed to his injuries on October 7th, 1915, and was entitled to the 1914–15 Star, and the General Service ad Victory Medals.
"A valiant Soldier, with undaunted heart he breasted life's last hill."
The Green, Great Staughton, Hunts. Z2703/B—Z2704/B.

HACKETT, G., Gunner, Royal Field Artillery.
He volunteered in December 1914, and in July of the following year was ordered overseas. Whilst serving on the Western Front he was engaged in fierce fighting in the Battles of Ypres, Festubert, Loos, the Somme, Albert, Passchendaele, Cambrai, Amiens and Le Cateau. He was wounded in action in October 1918, which resulted in the loss of his left leg. On his discharge from hospital he was invalided from the Army in July 1920, holding the 1914–15 Star, and the General Service and Victory Medals.
The Green, Great Staughton, Hunts. Z2703/A—Z2704/A.

HACKETT, J. T., Private, Labour Corps.
Volunteering in the Queen's (Royal West Surrey Regiment) in December 1915, he was employed as a hospital orderly at Bedford until transferred to the Labour Corps in May 1916, when he proceeded to France. There he saw heavy fighting in various sectors, and was engaged on important transport duties at Ypres, Albert, the Somme and Cambrai. He was demobilised in March 1919, and holds the General Service and Victory Medals.
The Green, Great Staughton, Hunts. Z2703/C—Z2704/C.

HADDON, A., Private, Oxford. & Bucks. L.I.
He volunteered in December 1914, and, on completion of his training, was employed on important defence duties with his unit at Portsmouth and Gosport. His health broke down, however, and he was discharged as medically unfit for further military service in March 1915.
The Lane, Little Brickhill, Bletchley, Bucks. Z2705/A.

HADDON, E., Private, 1st Royal Berkshire Regt.
He volunteered in September 1914, and was engaged on important work at Chelmsford until May 1916, when he was drafted to the Western Front. In that theatre of war he did excellent work as a gunner in the engagements at Albert, the Somme, Arras, Ypres and Cambrai, and was badly wounded in action during the Retreat in March 1918. He was invalided to England and discharged in March 1919, holding the General Service and Victory Medals.
31, Brooklands Road, Bletchley, Bucks. Z2892/A.

HADDON, H. J., Private, Labour Corps.
He volunteered in December 1914, and, after completing his training at Dover, was discharged as medically unfit for further military service three months later. In June 1917, however, he rejoined and was sent to Scotland, where he rendered valuable services in connection with agricultural work until demobilised in March 1919.
The Lane, Little Brickhill, Bletchley, Bucks. Z2705/C.

HADDON, H. V., Sapper, Royal Engineers.
Volunteering in December 1914, he was engaged on important duties with his unit at various stations, including Sheringham, Cromer, Peterborough, Slough and Brightlingsea. He was unsuccessful in his endeavours to obtain a transfer to the fighting area, but nevertheless performed very valuable work until demobilised in February 1919.
Potter's Cross, Wootton, Beds. Z2706.

HADDON, W., Private, Labour Corps.
In January 1917 he joined the Army, and, on completion of a period of training, was drafted later in the same year to the Western Front. Proving to be medically unfit for active service, he was not sent to the firing-line, but notwithstanding rendered valuable services with the Graves Registration Department in France until demobilised in March 1920. He holds the General Service and Victory Medals.
The Lane, Little Brickhill, Bletchley, Bucks. Z2705/B.

HADDOW, A. G., Rifleman, Rifle Brigade.
Joining in July 1918, he was unable to obtain a transfer to a theatre of war before the cessation of hostilities. He was engaged on important garrison duties at home until 1919, when he was drafted to Germany, where he served with the Army of Occupation at Cologne until demobilised in March 1920.
Potter's Cross, Wootton, Beds. Z2707.

HAGGER, E. A., 2nd Lieut., 6th Huntingdonshire Cyclist Battalion and 8th Norfolk Regiment.
He volunteered in February 1915, and in the following year was drafted to the Western Front, where he took a prominent part in severe fighting at Vimy Ridge, the Somme and the Ancre. In October 1917 he returned to England for a short period, and in recognition of his good service at the front was granted a commission. On his return to France he was in action at the Battles of the Somme, Amiens and Bapaume, and was gassed. Demobilised in March 1919, he holds the General Service and Victory Medals.
Ramsey Road, St. Ives, Hunts. Z2708.

HAGGERWOOD, J., Private, Bedfordshire Regt.
Volunteering in February 1915, he was not successful in obtaining a transfer to the war zone owing to ill-health. He was retained on home service and stationed at Lowestoft and Felixstowe, where he fulfilled his various duties in a very able manner until discharged as medically unfit for further service in March 1917. Four months later, on July 7th, 1917, he unfortunately died of consumption.
"His memory is cherished with pride."
4, St. Cuthbert's Street, Bedford. X2709.

HAINES, P. E., Sergeant, York & Lancaster Regt.
At the outbreak of hostilities in August 1914 he was already serving in the Army, but was not successful in his efforts to secure a transfer to a theatre of war. He was stationed at Sunderland, where he performed valuable work as a Musketry Instructor, and was also engaged in escorting troops to France. He was eventually discharged in February 1919, and holds the General Service and Victory Medals.
5, Maitland Street, Bedford. X2710/A.

HALE, J. H., Private, R.A.M.C.
He volunteered in December 1914, and, after a course of training, was engaged on hospital work at Bedford and Northampton until drafted overseas in December 1916. Whilst on the Western Front he carried out excellent work as a stretcher-bearer in the Arras, Messines, Lens and Cambrai sectors until his health broke down. He was then invalided to England and subsequently discharged as medically unfit for further military duties in July 1918, holding the General Service and Victory Medals. Keeley Green, Wootton, Beds. Z2711.

HALES, F., Private, 7th Northamptonshire Regt.
A month after the declaration of war in August 1914 he volunteered, and in September of the following year was drafted to France. During his service on the Western Front he did good work as a machine-gunner in various important engagements, and was unhappily killed by a sniper at Guillemont on August 19th, 1916. He was entitled to the 1914–15 Star, and the General Service and Victory Medals.
"Whilst we remember, the sacrifice is not in vain."
34, Marne Street, Kempston, Beds. Z2712.

HALL, A. W., Private, Huntingdonshire Cyclist Battalion and Royal Warwickshire Regiment.
He volunteered in August 1914, and, after completing his training, was five months later drafted to the Western Front, where he was engaged on important signalling duties in numerous engagements. He took an active part in the Battle of the Somme, and was unfortunately killed in action at Martinpuich on November 11th, 1916. He was entitled to the 1914–15 Star, and the General Service and Victory Medals.
"His life for his Country."
Sapley Lane, Hartford. Z2719/A.

HALL, E. A., Cpl.-Drummer, 11th Suffolk Regt.
Joining in September 1916, he was, on conclusion of his training, drafted overseas in March of the following year. Whilst serving on the Western Front he saw heavy fighting in numerous important engagements and took an active part in the Battles of the Somme, Arras, Ypres and Cambrai. He remained in France until demobilised in October 1919, and holds the General Service and Victory Medals.
New Town, Kimbolton, Hunts. Z2713/A.

HALL, E. A., Private, 13th Hussars.
Mobilised in August 1914, he was at once ordered to the Western Front, where he fought in the Battles of Mons, the Marne, Ypres, Loos and the Somme. In July 1916 he was transferred to Mesopotamia, and, after serving in important engagements at Kut, Amara and Basra, was invalided to India suffering from dysentery. On his return to the firing-line in 1917 he took an active part in the capture of Baghdad. He was discharged on his return to England in July 1919, and holds the Mons Star, and the General Service and Victory Medals.
10, Ouse Walk, Huntingdon, Hunts. Z2715.

HALL, F., Private, Royal Marine Light Infantry.
He volunteered in November 1915, and a month later was drafted to the Western Front. There he was engaged in severe fighting in various sectors of the line, and was in action at the Battles of the Somme, Arras, Ypres and Cambrai, and in the Retreat and Advance of 1918. He was eventually demobilised in May 1919, and holds the 1914–15 Star, and the General Service and Victory Medals.
Old Stratford, Stony Stratford. Z2717/A.

HALL, G., Rifleman, 5th London Regiment (London Rifle Brigade).
Joining in June 1915, he was drafted four months later to France. On that front he experienced fierce fighting in the Loos sector, and was gassed during the Battle of the Somme in July 1916. He was sent to hospital at Boulogne, and later was invalided to England suffering from rheumatic fever. On his recovery he was employed on agricultural work at Ely until demobilised in March 1919, holding the 1914–15 Star, and the General Service and Victory Medals.
Sapley Lane, Hartford. Z2719/B.

HALL, H., Private, Northamptonshire Regiment.
He volunteered in October 1914, and, after completing his training, was drafted to the Western Front in September of the following year. He was unhappily killed in action at Loos on September 10th, 1915, during his first engagement. He was entitled to the 1914–15 Star, and the General Service and Victory Medals.
"A costly sacrifice upon the altar of freedom."
School House, Water Eaton, near Bletchley, Bucks. Z2721/A.

HALL, H. J., Private, 4th Bedfordshire Regiment.
Volunteering in November 1915, he proceeded overseas in the following year. During his service on the Western Front he took an active part in important engagements in the Ypres and Arras sectors, and fell fighting on the Somme on February 11th, 1917. He was entitled to the General Service and Victory Medals.
"He died the noblest death a man may die:
Fighting for God and right and liberty."
New Town, Kimbolton, Hunts. Z2713/B

HALL, J., Private, 5th Bedfordshire Regiment.
He volunteered in March 1915, and, after a course of training, was nine months later drafted to the Western Front. There he fought in numerous important engagements, including those at Loos and Arras, and fell gloriously on the Field of Battle at Vimy Ridge in April 1917. He was entitled to the 1914–15 Star, and the General Service and Victory Medals.
"The path of duty was the way to glory."
1, Marlborough Road, Bedford. Z2720/A.

HALL, J. T., Private, 6th Bedfordshire Regiment.
Volunteering in November 1914, he trained at Aldershot and Salisbury Plain, and in August 1915 proceeded to France, where he saw fierce fighting at the Battles of Loos, Albert, Vimy Ridge and Delville Wood. He was unfortunately killed in action at the Battle of the Somme on August 7th, 1916, and was entitled to the General Service and Victory Medals.
"His life for his Country, his soul to God."
High Street, Pavenham, near Bedford. Z2716.

HALL, R., L/Corporal, Royal Engineers (R.O.D.)
He joined the Army in April 1916, and, on completion of a period of training, was drafted two months later to the Western Front, where he served for over three years. During that time he was engaged on work of an important nature in connection with the railways, and was stationed at Audricque. In October 1919 he was demobilised, holding the General Service and Victory Medals.
School House, Water Eaton, near Bletchley, Bucks. Z2721/B.

HALL, R., Private, Bedfordshire Regiment.
Already serving at the outbreak of war in August 1914, he was at once ordered to the Western Front and saw heavy fighting in the Retreat from Mons. He was also in action in the Battles of the Marne and Festubert, but his health broke down and he was invalided home. On his recovery he was drafted to India and was engaged on important garrison duties there until the close of hostilities. He was discharged on his return to England in December 1919, holding the Mons Star, and the General Service and Victory Medals. 6, Avenue Road, Huntingdon. Z2718/B.

HALL, T., Pte., Queen's Own (R. West Kent Regt.)
He joined in June 1916, and, after a period of service at Sittingbourne, was sent overseas in February of the following year. Whilst on the Western Front he was engaged in severe fighting in various sectors, and did good work with his unit at the Battles of Arras, the Somme and Bapaume. He was eventually demobilised in March 1919, holding the General Service and Victory Medals. Keysoe, Beds. Z2714.

HALL, W. J., Sergeant, 4th Bedfordshire Regiment.
Volunteering in January 1915, he was sent six months later to the Western Front. After taking a conspicuous part in the Battles of Loos and Ypres he was wounded in action in March 1917 and invalided to England, where he was in hospital for three months. He then served at Plymouth and in Ireland, but was subsequently discharged from the Army in August 1918 as medically unfit, holding the 1914–15 Star, and the General Service and Victory Medals.
3, Spencer Street, Bradwell, Bucks. Z1397/B.

HALLARD, P., Private, Bedfordshire Regiment.
When war was declared in August 1914 he volunteered, and in the following year proceeded to the Western Front. There he fought in the Battles of Ypres and Festubert, and was unhappily killed in action at Hill 60 in 1915. He was entitled to the 1914–15 Star, and the General Service and Victory Medals.
"Nobly striving:
He nobly fell that we might live."
1, The Cottages, Tempsford, near Sandy, Beds. Z2722

HALSEY, F., 2nd Lieut., 1st Bedfordshire Regt.
Already in the ranks at the outbreak of war in August 1914, he was quickly drafted to the Western Front, where he served with distinction in much severe fighting, particularly at the Battle of Ypres, and was wounded. In July 1917 he was granted a commission for conspicuous services in the Field, but was unfortunately killed in action at Arras in the same year. He was entitled to the 1914 Star, and the General Service and Victory Medals.
"His life for his Country, his soul to God."
7, Wellington Street, Bedford. X2723.

HAMMOND, C. H., Private, Machine Gun Corps.
He joined in May 1916, and, on proceeding to France in the following March, took part in the Battles of Arras, Bullecourt, Messines, Ypres and Passchendaele. In November 1917 he was transferred to Italy, and saw much severe fighting on the Piave and Asiago Plateaux. He was demobilised in August 1919, and holds the General Service and Victory Medals.
14, Cople, Bedford. TZ2726/A.

HAMMOND, C. W., Sapper, Royal Engineers.
He volunteered in August 1914, and in the following year was sent to Gallipoli, but, after taking part in severe fighting on the Peninsula, was invalided home suffering from dysentery and nervous breakdown. In 1916 he returned to the Western Front, and was in action at the Battles of the Somme, Arras, Ypres and Cambrai, but unfortunately died from influenza and pneumonia on November 24th, 1918. He was entitled to the 1914–15 Star, and the General Service and Victory Medals.
"His memory is cherished with pride."
117, Tickford Street, Newport Pagnell, Bucks. Z2730/A.

HAMMOND, E. E., L/Corporal, Royal Engineers.
Volunteering in October 1914, he trained at Liverpool and Bedford, and in the following year was ordered overseas. During his service on the Western Front he took an active part in numerous important engagements, including the Battles of Neuve Chapelle, Hill 60, Ypres, the Somme, Lens and the Marne. He was demobilised in March 1919, holding the 1914–15 Star, and the General Service and Victory Medals.
1, Raleigh Street, Bedford. Z2725.

HAMMOND, G. W., Private, 1/4th Queen's Own Cameron Highlanders.
At the outbreak of war in August 1914 he volunteered, and, after a period of training at Inverness, was sent overseas. Whilst serving on the Western Front he saw severe fighting in several engagements, but was unfortunately killed on June 16th, 1915, at Givenchy. He was entitled to the 1914–15 Star, and the General Service and Victory Medals.
"He passed out of the sight of men by the path of duty and self-sacrifice."
4, George Street, St. Ives, Hunts. Z2728/B.

HAMMOND, H. T., L/Corporal, Bedfordshire Regiment and Hertfordshire Regiment.
He volunteered in August 1914, and in the following year embarked for France. On that front he was engaged in fierce fighting in various sectors, and was in action at the Battles of the Somme, Arras, Havrincourt and Epéhy. He was wounded and gassed, and was mentioned in Despatches for conspicuous gallantry in capturing 21 German prisoners. Demobilised in 1919, he holds the 1914–15 Star, and the General Service and Victory Medals.
4, George Street, St. Ives, Hunts. Z2728/A.

HAMMOND, J. W., Corporal, R.A.S.C. (M.T.)
Three months after the outbreak of war in August 1914 he volunteered, and in the following year proceeded to Egypt. He was subsequently sent to Palestine, where he saw much severe fighting in numerous engagements and carried out important transport duties at Gaza, Jerusalem and Jaffa. Returning to England in August 1919, he was demobilised, holding the 1914–15 Star, and the General Service and Victory Medals.
14, Cople, Bedford. TZ2726/B.

HAMMOND, L. B., Driver, Royal Field Artillery.
He joined the Army in March 1916, and, after a course of training at Woolwich and Ipswich, was drafted in the following year to Russia, where he served for over two years. During that period he saw much fierce fighting and took an active part in many engagements on the Northern front. He was demobilised on his return to England in October 1919, and holds the General Service and Victory Medals.
11, Raleigh Street, Bedford. Z2724.

HAMMOND, T., L/Corporal, 1st Hampshire Regt.
Volunteering in April 1915, he proceeded overseas later in the same year. Whilst on the Western Front he was engaged in fierce fighting at the Battles of Loos and Albert, and, after being wounded on two occasions, was unfortunately killed in action near Cambrai on September 26th, 1917. He was entitled to the 1914–15 Star, and the General Service and Victory Medals.
"Courage, bright hopes, and a myriad dreams, splendidly given."
117, Tickford Street, Newport Pagnell, Bucks. Z2730/B.

HAMMOND, T. J., Cpl., Royal Warwickshire Regt.
He joined in 1916, and later in the same year was sent to the Western Front, where he fought in engagements at Loos and Vimy Ridge, and was wounded in the Battle of the Somme. In 1917 he was transferred to Italy, and did good work with his unit on the Piave and Asiago Plateaux. He was eventually demobilised in September 1919, and holds the General Service and Victory Medals.
Paggs Court, Silver Street, Newport Pagnell, Bucks. Z2727/B.

HAMMOND, W., Private, Royal Defence Corps.
Being too old for service in the fighting forces, he joined the Royal Defence Corps in 1918 and was engaged on important coast defence duties. He did excellent work with his unit at various home stations, and was eventually demobilised in 1919.
4, George Street, St. Ives, Hunts. Z2728/C.

HAMMOND, W. E., Corporal, Machine Gun Corps.
Joining in April 1917, he proceeded eight months later to the Western Front, where he saw heavy fighting in engagements in the Cambrai and St. Quentin sectors, and was wounded in action at Albert in October 1918. He was sent to hospital in Rouen, and in 1919 was drafted to Egypt and stationed at Alexandria. On his return home he was demobilised in April 1920, holding the General Service and Victory Medals.
6, Priory Court, Priory Street, Newport Pagnell, Bucks. Z2729.

HANCOCK, A. E., Private, Northants. Regiment.
In April 1916 he joined the Army, and in the following July was sent overseas. During his service on the Western Front he was in action at the Battles of the Somme, Arras, Ypres and Passchendaele, saw fierce fighting at St. Quentin, and was taken prisoner at Cambrai in March 1918. He was released from captivity in December 1918, and demobilised in September 1919, holding the General Service and Victory Medals.
Hail Weston, St. Neots, Hunts. Z2731/A.

HANCOCK, H. R., L/Corporal, Queen's (Royal West Surrey Regiment and Labour Corps).
He joined in March 1917, and shortly afterwards proceeded to France, where he was in action in the Battles of Arras, Ypres, Passchendaele and Cambrai, and took an active part in the final Advance. After the Armistice he served in France until September 1919, when his health broke down and he was invalided to England. He was eventually demobilised in March 1920, and holds the General Service and Victory Medals.
Hail Weston, St. Neots, Hunts. Z2731/B.

HAND, F., Private, 8th Lincolnshire Regiment.
Joining in March 1916, he embarked for France six months later. Whilst serving on the Western Front he was engaged in severe fighting at the Battles of the Somme, Arras, Vimy Ridge and Messines, and was wounded and taken prisoner at Ypres in July 1917. He remained in captivity until December 1918, and, on being released, was demobilised a month later, holding the General Service and Victory Medals.
Windmill Terrace, St. Neots, Hunts. Z2732.

HANDS, G. M. (Miss), Special War Worker.
For over two years this lady was engaged on work of National importance with the Machinery Company, Northampton. She was employed on making shells, which work she carried out with great ability, thus rendering valuable services to her Country during the most critical periods of the war.
20, Islington Road, Towcester, Northants. Z2893/A.

HANDS, H., Private, 1st Northants. Regiment.
He volunteered in October 1915, and in January of the following year was sent to the Western Front. There he was in action in the Loos and the Somme sectors, but,, after only seven months' active service, was unfortunately killed in action at Contalmaison on August 18th, 1916. He was entitled to the General Service and Victory Medals.
"He joined the great white company of valiant souls."
20, Islington Road, Towcester, Northants. Z2893/B.

HARCOURT, W. (Miss), Worker, Women's Land Army.
This lady joined the Land Army in June 1915, and throughout the period of her service was employed on a farm at Lathbury. She rendered valuable services, and carried out her arduous and responsible duties to the entire satisfaction of her employers. She was eventually demobilised in December 1918.
Lathbury, near Newport Pagnell, Bucks. Z2733/A.

HARCOURT, W. R., Private, 7th Oxfordshire and Buckinghamshire Light Infantry.
When war broke out in August 1914 he was mobilised, and in the following year proceeded to Salonika. In that theatre of war he took an active part in numerous engagements, and saw heavy fighting on the Vardar and Doiran fronts, but unfortunately contracted malaria and died on September 6th, 1918. He was entitled to the 1914–15 Star, and the General Service and Victory Medals.
"Thinking that remembrance, though unspoken, may reach him where he sleeps."
Lathbury, near Newport Pagnell, Bucks. Z2733/B.

HARDING, A., Private, 2nd Bedfordshire Regt. and Labour Corps.
He volunteered in September 1914, but was retained on important duties in England until January 1917, when he was ordered to France. On that front he served in engagements on the Somme and at Hill 60, and was wounded and buried alive at Ypres. He was invalided home in December 1917, but returned to the Western Front in November 1918, and was engaged in repairing roads in the devastated areas. Demobilised in March 1919, he holds the General Service and Victory Medals. 18, High Street, Kempston, Beds. Z2737.

HARDING, A., Private, Royal Defence Corps.
He volunteered in September 1915, and, after a period of training, was engaged on important guard duties over vital points in Yorkshire. He rendered very valuable services with his unit, and was eventually demobilised in March 1919.
1, Pilcroft Street, Bedford. X2735/B.

HARDING, A. J., Private, Leicestershire Regiment.
At the outbreak of hostilities he was already serving, and accordingly at once proceeded with the first Expeditionary Force to France. There he was in action during the Retreat from Mons and experienced fierce fighting in numerous engagements, including the Battles of La Bassée, Ypres, Festubert, the Somme, Arras and Cambrai. He was discharged in February 1919, and holds the Mons Star, and the General Service and Victory Medals.
16, High Street, Kempston, Beds. Z2734/A.

HARDING, B., Driver, Royal Engineers.
He volunteered in August 1914, but, on completion of his training, was retained on important duties with his unit at various home stations and rendered valuable services. Early in 1918, however, he was sent to France, and was stationed at Albert on transport work. After the cessation of hostilities he served on the Rhine with the Army of Occupation, and was eventually demobilised in July 1919, holding the General Service and Victory Medals.
1, Pilcroft Street, Bedford. X2735/A.

HARDING, F. (M.M.), Pte., 2nd Bedfordshire Regt.
Volunteering in 1914, he was drafted to France in the following year and played a prominent part in the Battles of Festubert, Loos, Albert, the Somme, Arras, Vimy Ridge, Messines, Ypres and Cambrai. He was awarded the Military Medal for conspicuous bravery and devotion to duty in carrying a badly wounded officer to safety whilst under heavy shell-fire. He also holds the 1914–15 Star, and the General Service and Victory Medals, and was demobilised in February 1919.
Grange Road, Blunham, Beds. Z2740/A—Z2741/A.

HARDING, F., Gunner, Royal Field Artillery.
He joined in April 1916, and in October was sent to Mesopotamia, where he took part in the heavy fighting on the Tigris and was present at the capture of Kut-el-Amara and Baghdad. In December 1917 he was transferred to India, and was in action against the Afghans on the North-West Frontier. He was demobilised in December 1919, and holds the General Service and Victory Medals, and the India General Service Medal (with Clasp, "Afghanistan, N.W. Frontier, 1919").
Park Lane, Blunham, Beds. Z2738.

HARDING, G., Private, Machine Gun Corps.
Volunteering in September 1914, he was drafted to the Western Front and took part in the Battles of Loos (where he was wounded in action) and the Somme. Later in 1916 he was transferred to Salonika, and saw much severe fighting on the Doiran, Vardar and Struma fronts before being invalided home with malarial fever in 1918. He was discharged as medically unfit in January 1919, and holds the 1914–15 Star and the General Service and Victory Medals.
Grange Road, Blunham, Beds. Z2740/B—Z2741/B.

HARDING, H. J., Tpr., Bedfordshire Lancers.
Volunteering in January 1916, he was sent to France later in the same year and took part in many important engagements, including the Battles of Arras and Ypres (III.). He was badly wounded in action on the Somme in July 1918, and invalided home. On his recovery he did excellent work until his demobilisation in August 1919, holding the General Service and Victory Medals. Blunham, Sandy, Beds. Z2742.

HARDING, J. B., Private, Bedfordshire Regiment.
He volunteered in January 1916, and four months later was drafted to the Western Front, where he took part in the Battles of the Somme and Vimy Ridge. Unfortunately he was killed in action during a bombing raid at Bullecourt on May 29th, 1917, and was entitled to the General Service and Victory Medals.

"He died the noblest death a man may die,
Fighting for God and right and liberty."

16, High Street, Kempston, Bedford. Z2734/B.

HARDING, L. R., Sapper, Royal Engineers.
Volunteering in June 1915, he was quickly drafted to France, where he did excellent work with the Railway Operative Department. He was chiefly engaged on troop and ammunition trains on the railways in the Somme, Arras, Ypres and Albert sectors. Returning to England in April 1919, he was demobilised in the following month, and holds the 1914–15 Star, and the General Service and Victory Medals.
40, Duncombe Street, Bletchley, Bucks. Z2894/A—Z2895/A.

HARDING, S., Sapper, Royal Engineers.
He volunteered in September 1914, and was first retained on important duties at various home stations. In March 1916, however, he was drafted to France, but, after only a few weeks' active service was unfortunately killed whilst unloading ammunition behind the line on April 25th, 1916. He was entitled to the General Service and Victory Medals.

"His life for his Country, his soul to God."

115, Marlborough Road, Queen's Park, Bedford. Z2736.

HARDING, T. J., Pte., 2/1st Oxford. & Bucks. L.I.
Mobilised in August 1914, he was drafted to France with the Territorials in April of the following year, and played an important part in the Battles of Ypres, Loos, the Somme (I.), Vimy Ridge, Cambrai and the Somme (II.), and in heavy fighting during the Retreat and Advance of 1918. He was present at the entry into Mons on Armistice Day, and was eventually demobilised in February 1919, holding the 1914–15 Star, and the General Service and Victory Medals.
24, King Street, Stony Stratford, Bucks. Z2739.

HARDING, W. H. R., Private, 4th Devonshire Rgt.
He joined in June 1918, and, on completion of his training, served in Scotland and on Salisbury Plain until February 1919 He was then sent to the Army of Occupation in Germany, and did excellent work whilst stationed near Cologne. He was demobilised in October 1919, one month after returning to England.
40, Duncombe Street, Bletchley, Bucks. Z2894/B—Z2895/B.

HARDWICK, A., Corporal, Bedfordshire Regt.
He joined in 1916, and, on completion of his training, was engaged on important guard duties in Bedfordshire. Owing to his being over age he was not drafted to a theatre of war, but rendered very valuable services with his unit. He was also engaged on the clerical staff at Brocton Camp, and was eventually demobilised in 1919. Oakley, Bedford. Z2745/A.

HARDWICK, F. G., Private, Machine Gun Corps.
He joined in March 1916, and was sent to France in August. Whilst on the Western Front he took part in the Battles of the Somme, Arras, Ypres and Passchendaele, and was wounded near Cambrai in March 1918. After hospital treatment in England he returned to France in the following October, but was unhappily killed in action on November 9th, 1918, two days before hostilities ceased. He was entitled to the General Service and Victory Medals.

"A costly sacrifice upon the altar of freedom."

9, Alexandria Court, Old Bradwell, Bucks. Z2744/C.

HARDWICK, H. L., Private, East Yorkshire and Bedfordshire Regiments.
He volunteered in 1914, but was retained on important duties at various home stations before being sent to France in March 1918. He saw heavy fighting at Arras, Cambrai and Armentières, where he was wounded in action. Returning to England in December 1918, he was drafted to India two months later and served at Secunderabad until his demobilisation in January 1920, holding the General Service and Victory Medals. Oakley, Bedford. Z2743.

HARDWICK, R. G., Bandsman, 1st Bedfordshire Regiment and Hertfordshire Regiment.
He joined in 1917, and, after his training, was retained on important duties in England. In November 1918 he was sent overseas, and after taking part in the march into Germany, did excellent work with the Army of Occupation on the Rhine until December 1919. He was then transferred to Ireland, and in 1920 was stationed at Belfast.
Oakley, Bedford. Z2745/B.

HARDY, C. E., Air Mechanic, Royal Air Force.
Joining in August 1917, he passed the necessary tests and was then engaged at various aerodromes on important duties which called for a high degree of technical skill. Although unsuccessful in obtaining his transfer overseas, he did excellent work until his demobilisation in April 1919.
81, Woburn Road, Kempston, Bedford. X2747/B.

HARDY, C. E., Private, R.A.S.C.
He joined in June 1917, and nine months later was drafted to the Western Front. Whilst in this theatre of war he was attached to a Field Bakery at Dieppe, and rendered valuable services there until June 1919. He was then sent home, and a month later demobilised, holding the General Service and Victory Medals.
81, Woburn Road, Kempston, Bedford. X2747/A.

HARDY, G. W., Corporal, 2nd Bedfordshire Regt.
He volunteered in 1915, and, proceeding to France in the following year, played a prominent part in the Battles of Albert, the Somme, Arras and St. Quentin, and in heavy fighting at Hill 60. He also served with the Huntingdonshire Cyclist Battalion, and was twice wounded in action. Demobilised in December 1918, he holds the General Service and Victory Medals. 14, Castle Lane, Bedford. X2746.

HARE, A., Private, York and Lancaster Regiment.
He joined in 1917, and proceeded later in the same year to the Western Front, where he saw severe fighting at Loos. He was also in action at the Battles of Arras, Ypres, Lens, Cambrai and the Somme, and in the Retreat and Advance of 1918. Demobilised on returning to England in 1919, he holds the General Service and Victory Medals.
1, St. Neots Road, Sandy, Beds. Z2748.

HARLOTT, A. C., Private, 1/5th Beds. Regt.
Mobilised with the Territorials in August 1914, he was sent to the Dardanelles in the following July and took part in the Landing at Suvla Bay. In January 1916 he was invalided home with dysentery and enteric fever, but on his recovery proceeded to France, where he was in action at the Battles of the Somme, Arras, Ypres and Cambrai, in the Retreat and Advance of 1918, and was twice wounded. He was transferred to the Labour Corps in October 1918, and did excellent work until his demobilisation in March 1919, holding the 1914–15 Star, and the General Service and Victory Medals.
Cross Hall Ford, St. Neots, Hunts. Z2749.

HARLOW, ALFRED, Bombardier, R.F.A.
A serving soldier, he was sent to France in August 1914, and took part in the Battles of Mons, the Aisne and La Bassée before being invalided home with trench feet in January 1915. On his recovery he returned to his Battery on the Western Front, and was in action at the Battles of the Somme, Arras and Cambrai, and in heavy fighting at Ypres, where he was wounded in November 1915. He received his discharge in July 1919, and holds the Mons Star, and the General Service and Victory Medals.
14, Newnham Lane, Goldington Road, Bedford.
Z2753/C—Z2754/C.

HARLOW, ARTHUR, Private, 2nd Queen's (Royal West Surrey Regiment).
Joining in March 1917, he was drafted to France twelve months later, and, after taking part in heavy fighting in the Cambrai and St. Quentin sectors during the Retreat, was badly wounded in action at Dickebusch in July 1918, and invalided home. He was discharged in the following December, and holds the General Service and Victory Medals.
14, Newnham Lane, Goldington Road, Bedford.
Z2753/D—Z2754/D.

HARLOW, C., Corporal, King's Own (Royal Lancaster Regiment).
A Reservist, he was called to the Colours in August 1914, and quickly proceeded to France, where he played a prominent part in the Battles of the Marne and La Bassée. Seriously wounded in action in October 1914, he was invalided home and unfortunately had to have one of his arms amputated. He was discharged medically unfit in February 1915, and holds the 1914 Star, and the General Service and Victory Medals.
44, York Street, Bedford. TZ2750.

HARLOW, E., Air Mechanic, Royal Air Force.
He joined in June 1918, and, after receiving his training in the workshops, was engaged on important clerical duties with his Squadron in Yorkshire. He was not drafted overseas, but did excellent work until his demobilisation in February 1920.
14, Newnham Lane, Goldington Road, Bedford.
Z2753/E—Z2754/E.

HARLOW, H. A., Private, 2nd Northants. Regt.
He was stationed in Egypt at the outbreak of war, but immediately proceeded to France and took part in the Battles of La Bassée and Ypres. In December 1914 he was invalided home with trench-fever, but, returning to the Western Front on his recovery, fought at the Battles of Loos (where he was wounded in September 1915) and the Somme, and was unhappily killed in action on November 16th, 1916. He was entitled to the 1914 Star, and the General Service and Victory Medals.
"His memory is cherished with pride."
127, George Street, Bedford. Z2752/B.

HARLOW, H. J., Sapper, Royal Engineers.
He joined in January 1917, and was soon drafted to the Western Front, where he rendered valuable services with his unit whilst engaged on important road-construction work. He also took an active part in the Battles of Arras, Ypres and Bullecourt. Demobilised on returning to England in February 1919, he holds the General Service and Victory Medals.
14, Newnham Lane, Goldington Road, Bedford.
Z2753/A—Z2754/A.

HARLOW, H. L., Pte., 3/5th Bedfordshire Regt.
He volunteered in November 1915, but whilst in training was found to be medically unfit for military service, and was accordingly invalided from the Army in February 1916.
14, Newnham Lane, Goldington Road, Bedford.
Z2753/B—Z2754/B.

HARLOW, L. G., Private, 1st Northants. Regt.
Having enlisted in April 1913, he was drafted to France in August 1914, and took part in the Battles of Mons, the Marne, La Bassée and Ypres, where he was badly wounded in November. Invalided home, he was in hospital at Portsmouth, but, returning to the Western Front in May 1915, was in action at the Battles of Loos, the Somme and Arras before being taken prisoner in July 1917. He was repatriated in December 1918, and then served at Tipperary, in Ireland, until his discharge in April 1920, holding the Mons Star, and the General Service and Victory Medals. 127, George Street, Bedford. Z2752/A.

HARLOW, S., Cadet, Royal Air Force.
He joined in September 1918, but owing to the early cessation of hostilities was retained on Home Service. He did much excellent work whilst in training with his Squadron at Blandford, and was eventually demobilised in March 1919.
41, Pembroke Street, Bedford. Z2751.

HARLOW, S. G., Trooper, Bedfordshire Lancers.
Volunteering in April 1915, he was transferred to the Military Mounted Police owing to his being medically unfit for service in a theatre of war. He did consistently good work with his unit at Bedford and Chelmsford, but was invalided from the Army in February 1917.
14, Newnham Lane, Goldington Road, Bedford.
Z2753/F—Z2754/F.

HARPER, A., Rifleman, Rifle Brigade.
Already in the Army, he was stationed in India in August 1914, but immediately left for the Western Front, where he took part in heavy fighting at Ypres, Passchendaele and on the Somme. In 1916 he was transferred to Salonika, and was in action on the Doiran front. Later he saw much service in Russia against the Bolsheviks, and was eventually discharged in April 1919, holding the 1914–15 Star, and the General Service and Victory Medals.
5, Chapel Court, Silver Street, Newport Pagnell, Bucks. Z2759.

HARPER, C., Private, 2nd Bedfordshire Regiment.
He volunteered in November 1914, and six months later proceeded to the Western Front, where he first saw heavy fighting at St. Eloi and Vimy Ridge. He laid down his life for King and Country at Trônes Wood in July 1916 during the Somme Offensive, and was entitled to the 1914–15 Star, and the General Service and Victory Medals.
High Street, Cranfield, Beds. Z2756/B.

HARPER, E. A., 1st Air Mechanic, R.A.F.
He joined in 1916, and later in the same year was sent to France, where he rendered valuable services with the 66th Squadron in the Somme sector. In 1917 he was transferred to Italy and did good work with a bombing Squadron on the Piave front. Unfortunately he died from influenza in October 1918, and was entitled to the General Service and Victory Medals.
"A costly sacrifice upon the altar of freedom."
Carlton, Beds. Z2755.

HARPER, G., Private, 2nd Bedfordshire Regt.
Joining in 1916, he was sent to France in the same year, and took part in the Battles of the Somme, Arras, Messines and Ypres. Badly wounded in the Somme sector in 1918, he was invalided home, and, after hospital treatment in Cambridge, was engaged on important duties at various stations until his demobilisation in March 1919. He holds the General Service and Victory Medals.
Church Row, Cranfield, Beds. Z1574/B.

HARPER, G. H., Driver, Royal Engineers.
Volunteering in September 1915, he was sent to Egypt in the following year, and took part in heavy fighting at Sollum and Katia. Proceeding into Palestine, he served with General Allenby's Forces during the Advance, and was present at the capture of Jerusalem, Jericho and Damascus. Whilst in the East, he was in hospital for some time, and was finally demobilised in August 1919, holding the General Service and Victory Medals. 13, Beatrice Street, Bedford. Z2757.

HARPER, G. W., Sapper, Royal Engineers.
He joined in December 1916, and six months later was drafted to France. During his service on the Western Front, he was engaged on important pioneer duties with his unit in the Somme, Ypres, Arras and Cambrai sectors and did excellent work. Demobilised in April 1919, he holds the General Service and Victory Medals. 6, Holme Street, Bedford. X2794.

HARPER, H., Sergt., 16th (The Queen's) Lancers.
Already in the Army in August 1914, he was at once drafted to France, and fought through the Retreat from Mons. He also served with distinction at the Battles of Ypres, Loos, the Somme, Arras, Messines and Cambrai, but, in October 1918, was invalided home with bronchial-pneumonia. After hospital treatment at Birmingham and Malvern, he received his discharge in March 1919, and holds the Mons Star, and the General Service and Victory Medals. 12, Bower Street, Bedford. Z1243/A.

HARPER, J., Driver, Royal Field Artillery.
Called up from the Reserve in August 1914, he was immediately sent to France, and was in action with his Battery throughout the Battle of, and the Retreat from, Mons. He also played an important part in the Battles of the Aisne, La Bassée, Ypres, Hill 60, Loos, the Somme and Cambrai. He was discharged in 1919, and holds the Mons Star, and the General Service and Victory Medals.
High Street, Cranfield, Beds. Z2756/A.

HARPER, R., Private, 2nd Bedfordshire, and Hertfordshire Regiments.

A serving soldier, he was mobilised in August 1914, but was retained on important work at home stations until early in 1917. He was then drafted to France, and took part in the Battles of Arras, Messines, Ypres and Cambrai, and the Retreat and Advance of 1918. In October 1919 he was transferred to India, and was still serving on garrison duty there in 1920, holding the General Service and Victory Medals.
12, Bower Street, Bedford. Z1243/B.

HARPER, R. W., Sergeant, 1st King's Own (Royal Lancaster Regiment).

Already in the Army in August 1914, he was engaged on important duties in England for five months before proceeding to France. After taking part in the Battles of Hill 60, Ypres and Festubert, he was invalided home with dysentery and frost bite, and was in hospital for some time. Returning to the Western Front in March 1917, he died gloriously on the Field of Battle at Passchendaele on October 26th of the same year. He was entitled to the 1914–15 Star, and the General Service and Victory Medals.
"He joined the great white company of valiant souls."
5, Boswell Place, Bedford. X2760.

HARPER, W. H., L/Corporal, Rifle Brigade.

He joined in May 1916, and four months later was drafted to the Western Front, where he played a prominent part in the Battles of Arras, Messines, Ypres and Cambrai. On August 23rd, 1918, he was reported wounded and missing, and is now presumed to have been killed in action on that date. He was entitled to the General Service and Victory Medals.
"Nobly striving:
He nobly fell that we might live."
3, Redbrick Cottages, Wilden, near Bedford. Z2758.

HARPIN, A. P., Private, Bedfordshire Regiment.

A Reservist, he was mobilised in August 1914, and sent to France in the following year. After taking part in heavy fighting at Loos and Albert, he was seriously wounded in action on the Somme in 1916, and invalided home. In 1920 he was still under hospital treatment in Kent, having undergone 20 operations. He holds the 1914–15 Star, and the General Service and Victory Medals.
256, Bedford Road, Kempston, Bedford. X2762/A.

HARPIN, C. E., Private, Bedfordshire Regiment.

A serving soldier, he was drafted to the Western Front in 1915 and took part in the Battle of Neuve Chapelle, and other important engagements before being invalided home with eye trouble. After hospital treatment he returned to the fighting area and saw service in Italy. Whilst overseas he was twice wounded in action, and eventually received his discharge in April 1919, holding the 1914–15 Star, and the General Service and Victory Medals.
256, Bedford Road, Kempston, Bedford. X2762/B.

HARPIN, R. E., Private, Royal Defence Corps.

He volunteered in 1915, and was engaged at various stations on important duties with his unit, and rendered valuable services. In 1916 he was taken ill, and, after being in hospital for some time, was unfortunately discharged in 1917 as medically unfit for further service. 103, Church End, Haynes, near Beds. Z2763/B.

HARPIN, W., Private, Buffs (East Kent Regt.)

Volunteering in August 1915, he was drafted overseas later in the same year. Whilst in Mesopotamia, he took part in much heavy fighting at Kut. He was unfortunately killed in action on March 14th, 1916, near Kut, and was entitled to the 1914–15 Star, and the General Service and Victory Medals.
"A valiant Soldier, with undaunted heart he breasted life's last hill."
20, Church Walk, Kempston, Beds. X2761/B.

HARPUR, W., Trooper, Bedfordshire Lancers.

He volunteered in 1915, and later in the same year was drafted to France. In this theatre of war he took part in many engagements, including the Battles of Festubert, Loos, the Somme, Arras, Ypres and Cambrai, where he was wounded in action in 1917. As a result he was invalided home, and finally discharged in 1918 as medically unfit for further service. He holds the 1914–15 Star, and the General Service and Victory Medals. Church Row, Cranfield, Beds. Z2764.

HARRADINE, A., Private, 2nd Bedfordshire Regt.

Volunteering in August 1914, he was drafted overseas in the following November. During his service on the Western Front he took part in many engagements, including the Battles of Ypres, Hill 60, Loos, the Somme, Albert and Passchendaele, and was badly wounded at Cambrai. As a result he was invalided home, and on his recovery was transferred to the Labour Corps, and served at various home stations until his demobilisation in March 1919. He holds the 1914 Star, and the General Service and Victory Medals.
Penfold Lane, Godmanchester, Hunts. Z2765.

HARRALD, F. C., Private, Duke of Cornwall's L.I.

He joined in July 1918, and was shortly afterwards sent to Ireland, where he was engaged on various important duties with his unit. Owing to the early cessation of hostilities, he was unable to obtain a transfer to a theatre of war, but rendered valuable services until his demobilisation in December 1919.
44, High Street, Fenny Stratford, Bucks. Z2766/A.

HARRALD, G. W., Sapper, Royal Engineers.

He joined in June 1918, and in the following October was drafted to the Western Front. In this theatre of war he served with the Railway Operative Department in many sectors on important work as a fireman on the railways. He was demobilised in November 1919, and holds the General Service and Victory Medals. 44, High St., Fenny Stratford, Bucks. Z2766/B.

HARRIS, A. J., Private, 1st Northants. Regiment.

He was mobilised in August 1914, and immediately drafted to France, where he took part in the Retreat from Mons. He made the supreme sacrifice, being killed in action at Moulins on September 17th, 1914, and was entitled to the Mons Star and the General Service and Victory Medals.
"A costly sacrifice upon the altar of freedom."
Stoke Goldington, Bucks. TZ2770/A.

HARRIS, A. L., Private, Bedfordshire and 12th Middlesex Regiments.

Volunteering in 1915, he was drafted overseas after completing his training. Whilst on the Western Front, he took part in several engagements, including the Battles of Hill 60, the Somme, Arras, Passchendaele and Cambrai. After hostilities ceased he proceeded to Germany with the Army of Occupation, and served there until his demobilisation in November 1919 He holds the 1914–15 Star, and the General Service and Victory Medals. 32, All Hallows Lane, Bedford. X2769/C.

HARRIS, E. E., Driver, Royal Engineers.

He was already in the Army when war broke out in Augus 1914, and in the following December proceeded to France. There he took part in much fighting at the Battles of Neuve Chapelle, Festubert, Loos, the Somme, Arras and Ypres. H was discharged in 1918, time-expired, and holds the 1914–15 Star, and the General Service and Victory Medals.
Harrowden, near Bedford. Z2772

HARRIS, F., Pte., 6th Beds. Regt. and Royal Scots

He joined in March 1916, and in the following July was drafted to France. Whilst in this theatre of war he took part in much heavy fighting in the Ypres sector, but later contracted trench feet and fever and was consequently invalided home. He wa discharged in March 1918 as medically unfit for further service, and holds the General Service and Victory Medals.
Station Road, Tempsford, near Sandy, Beds. Z2771/A

HARRIS, G., Private, 3rd (King's Own) Hussars.

He joined in January 1917, and in the following July proceeded to the Western Front, where he took part in several engagements. He was badly wounded in action during the Retreat of 1918 on the Somme, and, being invalided home, was finally discharged in October 1918, as medically unfit for further service. He holds the General Service and Victory Medals.
Stoke Goldington, Bucks. TZ2770/C

HARRIS, G. H., Trooper, Bedfordshire Lancers.

He volunteered in May 1915, and later in the same year wa drafted to France. Whilst in this seat of war he took part in many engagements, including the Battles of Hill 60, Ypres, the Somme, Arras and Cambrai, and was twice wounded in action. He was demobilised in March 1919, and holds the 1914–15 Star, and the General Service and Victory Medals.
32, All Hallows Lane, Bedford. X2769/B.

HARRIS, H., Private, 1st Oxford. and Bucks. L.I.

He joined in September 1916, and early in the following year was drafted to Mesopotamia. In this seat of operations he took part in much heavy fighting on the Euphrates, and was present at the capture of Hit in March 1918. He returned home and was demobilised in April 1920, holding the General Service and Victory Medals. Stoke Goldington, Bucks. TZ2770/B.

HARRIS, J., Driver, Royal Field Artillery.

He joined in March 1916, and later in the same year proceeded to Salonika. There he saw much heavy fighting on the Vardar, Doiran and Struma fronts, and took part in many engagements until the cessation of hostilities. He returned home and was demobilised in September 1919, holding the General Service and Victory Medals.
62, Clarence Road, Stony Stratford, Bucks. Z3124/A.

HARRIS, J., Private, Machine Gun Corps.

Volunteering in May 1915, he was drafted overseas in the following year. Whilst on the Western Front he took part in the Battles of the Somme, Arras and Ypres, and saw much fighting at La Bassée, Festubert and Givenchy. He was wounded in action at Ypres in 1917, and was later demobilised in January 1919, holding the General Service and Victory Medals. 75, High Street, New Bradwell, Bucks. Z2767.

HARRIS, T., L/Corporal, 6th Bedfordshire Regt.

He joined in February 1916, and a few months later was drafted to the Western Front, where he took part in much severe fighting on the Somme. He was unfortunately reported missing, and afterwards killed in action, on August 9th, 1916, and was entitled to the General Service and Victory Medals.
"Whilst we remember, the sacrifice is not in vain."
Station Road, Tempsford, near Sandy, Beds. Z2771/B.

HARRISON, B., Private, Royal Berkshire Regt.
He volunteered in January 1915, and, after completing his training in the following year, was drafted to France, where he took part in much fighting at St. Eloi and on the Somme. He died gloriously on the Field of Battle near Albert on October 4th, 1916, and was entitled to the General Service and Victory Medals.
"He died the noblest death a man may die: Fighting for God and right and liberty."
Easton, near Spaldwick, Hunts. Z2775/A.

HARRISON, E. H., Sapper, Royal Engineers.
He enlisted in August 1918, and two months later was drafted to France. There he served with the Railway Operative Department, and was engaged on many important duties connected with ambulance trains. He was discharged in May 1919, and holds the General Service and Victory Medals.
Whaddon Road, Far Bletchley, Bucks. Z2896/A.

HARRISON, F., Private, 15th Cheshire Regiment.
He volunteered in September 1914, and was retained for a time at various home stations before being drafted to France. There he served with the Signal Section, and took part in the Battles of the Somme, Albert, Messines, Cambrai, Bapaume and Havrincourt. He was demobilised in February 1919, and holds the General Service and Victory Medals.
13, Sandhurst Place East, Bedford. Z2774.

HARRISON, L., Private, 1st Queen's (Royal West Surrey Regiment).
He joined in June 1918, and a few months later was drafted to France. In this theatre of war he did good work behind the lines whilst engaged on general duties until after the Armistice. He was demobilised in January 1919, and holds the General Service and Victory Medals.
Easton, Hunts. Z2775/B.

HARRISON, S., Private, R.A.M.C.
He was mobilised in August 1914, and in the following year was drafted to France, where he acted as a stretcher-bearer and took part in much fighting at Neuve Chapelle, Hill 60, Armentières, Ypres, Festubert, the Somme, Arras, Albert and Cambrai. He was severely wounded on June 17th, 1918, and unfortunately died through his wounds the same day. He was entitled to the 1914–15 Star, and the General Service and Victory Medals.
"Great deeds cannot die: They with the sun and moon renew their light for ever."
4, Aylesbury Street, Wolverton, Bucks. Z2773.

HART, A. J., Officers' Steward (1st Class), R.N.
He was already in the Navy when war broke out in August 1914 and immediately proceeded to sea on board H.M.S. "Miranda." He was engaged in the North Sea on patrol duties, and took part in the Battles of Heligoland Bight and Jutland. Whilst serving on board H.M.S. "Formidable," she was torpedoed, but he was fortunately rescued. Later he was engaged off Scotland until his discharge in January 1919. He holds the 1914–15 Star, and the General Service and Victory Medals.
11, Howard Avenue, Queen's Park, Bedford. Z2779C.

HART, C., Private, 2/1st Royal Fusiliers.
He volunteered in August 1914, and, after a period of training, was drafted to France. In this theatre of war he took part in many important engagements, including the Battles of Festubert, the Somme and Ypres, and was badly wounded. As a result he was invalided home and finally discharged in 1918. He holds the 1914–15 Star, and the General Service and Victory Medals. Hemingford Abbots, Hunts. Z2776.

HART, F. R. A., L/Cpl., 1st Cambridgeshire Regt.
He joined in November 1916, and in the following year was drafted to France, where he took part in several engagements, including the Battles of Arras, Ypres, Messines, Albert and Cambrai. He died gloriously on the Field of Battle during the Advance in the Cambrai sector on September 18th, 1918. He was entitled to the General Service and Victory Medals.
"The path of duty was the way to glory."
11, Howard Avenue, Queen's Park, Bedford. Z2779/B.

HART, H. H., Steward, Merchant Service.
He was already in the Merchant Service when war broke out in August 1914, and quickly proceeded to sea on board H.M.S. "Watchful," and was engaged on dangerous mine-sweeping duties in the North Sea. He was also employed in patrol and escort work, and in transporting food supplies from Australia on board the S.S. "Warswan." He did continuously good work, and was discharged in February 1919, holding the General Service and the Mercantile Marine War Medals.
11, Howard Avenue, Queen's Park, Bedford. Z2779/A.

HART, H. J., Sergeant, Bedfordshire Regiment.
He volunteered in December 1914, and on completing his training proceeded to France. In this seat of war he took a prominent part in several engagements and was badly wounded at Ypres in July 1917. As a result he was in hospital for a considerable period, and was finally demobilised in January 1919. He holds the General Service and Victory Medals.
77, Howbury Street, Bedford. Z2777/B

HART, J., Private, Royal Defence Corps.
Having previously served as Quartermaster-Sergeant in the Royal Army Service Corps Volunteers for nine years, being finally discharged as medically unfit, he volunteered in the Royal Defence Corps in April 1915. He did continuously good work throughout hostilities at various home stations, and was engaged on important duties. He was demobilised in October 1919. 140, George Street, Bedford. Z2778.

HART, S. A., Rifleman, 16th London Regiment (Queen's Westminster Rifles).
He joined in April 1917, and underwent a short period of training prior to his being drafted to France, where he saw much heavy fighting at Arras, Ypres, Loos, Beaumont-Hamel and Cambrai. He was badly gassed in action and unfortunately died of gas-poisoning on September 10th, 1918, at Boulogne. He was entitled to the General Service and Victory Medals.
"His life for his Country, his soul to God."
77, Howbury Street, Bedford. Z2777/A.

HART, W., Air Mechanic, Royal Air Force.
He joined in May 1918, and, after completing a short training, proceeded overseas. Whilst in Italy he was engaged on various important duties which called for a high degree of technical skill. He rendered valuable services until his demobilisation in May 1919, and holds the General Service and Victory Medals.
77, Howbury Street, Bedford. Z2777/C.

HARTILL, J. L., Private, 1st Bedfordshire Regt.
Volunteering in September 1914, he proceeded overseas in the following January. Whilst on the Western Front he took part in several engagements, including the Battles of Ypres, Arras and the Somme, and was badly wounded at Morval in September 1916. As a result he was invalided home, and finally discharged in December 1917 as medically unfit for further service. He holds the 1914–15 Star, and the General Service and Victory Medals.
66, Westbourne Road, Bedford. Z2780.

HARTLEY, E. E., Petty Officer, Royal Navy.
He was already in the Navy when war broke out in August 1914, and attached to the Chatham Division. He served throughout hostilities on board H.M. Ships "Lord Clive," "Berwick" and "Lowestoft," took part in the raids on Ostend and Zeebrugge, and was also engaged on important duties in the Atlantic Ocean, the West Indies and the Mediterranean Sea. He did good work during the war, and received his discharge in February 1919, holding the 1914–15 Star, and the General Service and Victory Medals.
52, Park Street, Bletchley, Bucks. TZ2897.

HARTRUPP, W., Pte., 2/5th Lancashire Fusiliers.
He volunteered in January 1916, and in the following June proceeded to the Western Front, where he was in action at the Battles of the Somme and Arras, and was gassed. As a result he was invalided to Boulogne, but, on his recovery, returned to his unit and took part in much fighting at Cambrai, and in the Retreat and Advance of 1918. He was demobilised in March 1919, and holds the General Service and Victory Medals.
Moulsoe, Bucks. Z2781.

HARTUP, E. A., Sapper, Royal Engineers.
He joined in June 1916, and underwent a short period of training prior to his being drafted to France. There he was engaged on important duties in the workshops at Rouen, Calais and Boulogne, and rendered valuable services until his demobilisation in March 1919. He holds the General Service and Victory Medals.
26, Greenfield Road, Newport Pagnell, Bucks. Z2782/B.

HARTUP, H., Private, Royal Warwickshire Regt.
He joined in March 1916, and three months later war drafted to the Western Front, where he took part in much heavy fighting on the Somme. He died gloriously on the Field of Battle near Albert in August 1916, and was entitled to the General Service and Victory Medals.
"Honour to the immortal dead, who gave their youth that the world might grow old in peace."
26, Greenfield Road, Newport Pagnell, Bucks. Z2782/A.

HARTUP, H. H., Private, Royal Defence Corps.
He volunteered in December 1914, and, after a period of training, was engaged on important agricultural work at various farms. He was unable to obtain a transfer overseas owing to his being medically unfit, but rendered valuable services until his demobilisation in March 1919.
128, Victoria Road, Fenny Stratford, Bucks. Z2783.

HARTUP, R. F., 1st Air Mechanic, Royal Air Force (late Royal Naval Air Service).
He joined in November 1916, and was attached to H.M.S. "Phaeton," with the aeroplane carrying ships, in which he was engaged as an electrical fitter. He also served in H.M.S. "Cassandra," which ship was struck by a mine in Riga Bay. Later he was transferred to another vessel, and did good work until demobilised in March 1919, and holds the General Service and Victory Medals.
26, Greenfield Road, Newport Pagnell, Bucks. Z2782/C.

HARTWELL, A. M. C., L/Corporal, Labour Corps.
He joined in November 1916, and on completion of his training in the following year proceeded to France, where he did consistently good work in many sectors. He was chiefly engaged in trench-digging on the Arras front. Later he was engaged on important duties as a cook. In March 1919 he was demobilised, and holds the General Service and Victory Medals.
43, New Fenlake, Bedford. Z2786.

HARTWELL, F., L/Corporal, 2nd Beds. Regt.
Volunteering in September 1914, he completed his training and was drafted to France. During his service in this theatre of war he did good work in various sectors of the front. He took part in the heavy fighting at Vimy Ridge, Arras and Passchendaele. On September 18th, 1918, he was unfortunately killed in action during an attack on the Hindenburg Line. He was entitled to the General Service and Victory Medals.
"Whilst we remember, the sacrifice is not in vain."
29, Marne Street, Bedford. Z2784.

HARTWELL, G., Private, Labour Corps.
He volunteered in 1914 in the Royal Field Artillery, and after a period of training was drafted to France, where he was in action in various sectors of the front. He took part in the Battle of Arras, and was wounded and invalided to England. On his recovery he was transferred to the Labour Corps, and retained on important duties with his unit until demobilised in April 1919. He holds the 1914–15 Star, and the General Service and Victory Medals.
Mill Green, Turvey, Beds. Z2785.

HARTWELL, G. W. J., Sapper, R.E. (R.O.D.)
He was mobilised in 1914 in the Oxfordshire and Buckinghamshire Light Infantry, and after completing a period of training was sent to France, where he was in action during the Somme Offensive. In 1916 he was transferred to the Royal Engineers, and whilst stationed at Rouen was engaged on important railway operations until the conclusion of war. He was demobilised in September 1919, and holds the 1914–15 Star, and the General Service and Victory Medals.
8, Park Street, Bletchley, Bucks. TZ2898.

HARVEY, H., Drummer, Queen's (Royal West Surrey Regiment).
He joined in May 1917, and on conclusion of his training in the following year proceeded to France. During his short service on the Western Front he took part in the heavy fighting at Amiens, where he was unfortunately killed in action on August 9th, 1918, and was entitled to the General Service and Victory Medals.
"Thinking that remembrance, though unspoken, may reach him where he sleeps."
9, Nelson Street, Bedford. Z2788.

HARVEY, H., Sapper, Royal Engineers.
Volunteering at the outbreak of war in August 1914, he completed a period of training, and was drafted to the Dardanelles. Whilst in this theatre of war he took part in the Landing at Suvla Bay and other important engagements until 1916, when he was invalided home suffering from dysentery. On his recovery he was stationed on the East Coast on important duties until demobilised in March 1919, and holds the 1914–15 Star, and the General Service and Victory Medals.
3, Thurlow Street, Bedford. X2787.

HARVEY, H. F., L/Cpl., Royal Warwickshire Regt.
Mobilised at the outbreak of hostilities in August 1914, he was retained on important duties until July 1916, when he proceeded to France, and was in action during the fighting on the Somme, where he was wounded and sent to the Base. On his recovery he was present at the Battles of Arras, Ypres, Passchendaele and Cambrai, but was taken prisoner in March 1918, and held in captivity until after the Armistice. Returning to England he was demobilised in January 1919, and holds the General Service and Victory Medals.
Old School Yard, Lure Street, Eynesbury, St. Neots, Hunts. Z2793.

HARVEY, L. A., Private, Bedfordshire Regiment and Sherwood Foresters.
He volunteered in 1915, and after completing his training in the following year was sent to France, where he took part in the Battle of the Somme. He made the supreme sacrifice, being killed in action on September 27th, 1916, and was entitled to the General Service and Victory Medals.
"And doubtless he went in splendid company."
Station Road, Tempsford, near Sandy, Beds. Z2791.

HARVEY, O., Trooper, Bedfordshire Lancers.
He volunteered in May 1915, and after a period of training was drafted to France, where he was transferred to the 8th King's Royal Irish Hussars. In the course of his service in this seat of war, he took an active part in many engagements, including the Battles of the Somme, Arras, Ypres, Cambrai and St. Quentin, and later in the Retreat and Advance of 1918. He was demobilised in March 1919, and holds the 1914–15 Star, and the General Service and Victory Medals.
6a, Tavistock Place, Bedford. X2792.

HARVEY, S., Sapper, Royal Engineers.
He volunteered in September 1915, and early in the following year was sent to Mesopotamia. During his period of service in this theatre of war, he took part in many important engagements. He served during the heavy fighting on the Tigris, also at Kut-el-Amara, and was later present at the capture of Baghdad. After the conclusion of hostilities he returned home and was demobilised in April 1919, holding the General Service and Victory Medals. 2, Beauchamp Row, Bedford. X2790.

HARVEY, T., Sapper, Royal Engineers.
Mobilised on the declaration of war in August 1914, he was quickly sent overseas. Whilst on the Western Front he was engaged on important duties in connection with the lines of communication, and served at Ypres, Festubert, Loos, the Somme, Arras and Cambrai. He was discharged in April 1919, and holds the 1914 Star, and the General Service and Victory Medals. 9, Hartington Street, Bedford. X2789/B.

HASELDINE, J. H., Pte., 4th Ox. & Bucks. L.I.
Volunteering in November 1915, he was drafted to France in the following July. Whilst in this seat of war he saw much active service in various sectors of the front. He took part in the heavy fighting at the Battles of Albert, the Somme, Arras and Ypres, and was wounded in August 1917. As a result he was invalided to England, and finally discharged as medically unfit for further military service in March 1918. He holds the General Service and Victory Medals.
26, West Street, Olney, Bucks. Z2795/A.

HASKELL, F. H., Private, Oxford. and Bucks. L.I.
He volunteered in September 1914, and after a period of training was drafted to the Western Front. In the course of his service in this theatre of war, he was in action at the Battle of Loos and in the Somme Offensive. Owing to heart trouble he was invalided home, and finally discharged as medically unfit for further service in 1916, and holds the 1914–15 Star, and the General Service and Victory Medals.
8, St. Mary's Terrace, New Town, Huntingdon. Z2796.

HASSIN, U., Private, Royal Army Medical Corps.
He was called up from the Reserve at the outbreak of war in August 1914, and immediately drafted to France, where he served through the Battle of, and the Retreat from, Mons, and at the Battles of Ypres, Festubert, Loos, Vimy Ridge and Cambrai. After the cessation of hostilities he proceeded with the Army of Occupation into Germany, and was stationed on the Rhine, where he did good work until returning home. He was discharged in March 1919, and holds the Mons Star, and the General Service and Victory Medals.
The Glen, Little Stokeley, Huntingdon. Z2797.

HAW, R., Sergeant, Royal Engineers.
He volunteered in September 1914, and was first retained on important duties. Early in 1917 he proceeded to the Western Front, where he was engaged on important duties in connection with the lines of communication. He did excellent work during the Battles of Arras and Ypres, and was unfortunately killed in action in October 1917. He was entitled to the General Service and Victory Medals.
"His life for his Country."
7, Church Passage, Newport Pagnell, Bucks. Z2798.

HAWES, S., Private, Bedfordshire Regiment.
He volunteered in June 1915, and in the same year proceeded to Egypt. He was also in action during the Advance into Palestine and took part in the Battles of Gaza and Jaffa. In 1918 he was transferred to Salonika, where he saw much heavy fighting. After the close of hostilities he proceeded with the Army of Occupation into Turkey, and served there until returning home for demobilisation in December 1919. He holds the 1914–15 Star, and the General Service and Victory Medals. 24, All Hallows Lane, Bedford. X2799.

HAYCOCK, C. R., Cpl., 5th Royal Irish Fusiliers.
Volunteering in August 1914, he completed his training in the following year and proceeded to Salonika, where he took part in many important engagements, including the recapture of Monastir, and was wounded. In 1917 he was transferred to Egypt, and did excellent work as a physical training Instructor until the close of hostilities. He was mentioned in Despatches for devotion of duty in the Field, and in March 1919 was demobilised, holding the 1914–15 Star, and the General Service and Victory Medals. Milton Ernest, Bedford. Z2800.

HAYLLAR, A., Stoker, R.N., H.M.S. "Lowestoft."
He joined in August 1917, and was posted to H.M.S. "Lowestoft," in which vessel he did good work throughout the period of hostilities. He was engaged in the chasing of submarines in Italian waters until the conclusion of war. In April 1919 he was demobilised, and holds the General Service and Victory Medals. 23, Bridge Road, Bedford. Z2801/C.

HAYLLAR, W., Private, 15th Devonshire Regt.
He volunteered in March 1915, and after completing a period of training, was retained on important guard and coastal defence duties at various stations. He was unsuccessful in obtaining his transfer to a theatre of war, but nevertheless rendered valuable services until demobilised in January 1919.
23, Bridge Road, Bedford. Z2801/B.

HAYLLAR, W. B., Pte., 1/5th Bedfordshire Regt.
He volunteered in September 1914, and in the following year proceeded to Gallipoli, where he took part in the Landing at Suvla Bay and other important engagements until the Evacuation of the Peninsula. Later he was transferred to Egypt, and was afterwards in action during the Battles of Gaza and Aleppo, and was recommended for the Military Medal. Returning to England, he was demobilised in July 1919, and holds the 1914–15 Star, and the General Service and Victory Medals.
23, Bridge Road, Bedford. Z2801/A.

HAYLOCK, G. A., Private, Bedfordshire Regt.
He volunteered in the Huntingdonshire Cyclist Battalion in November 1914, but on completion of his training was transferred to the Bedfordshire Regiment and sent to France in July 1916. Two months later he was badly wounded in action during the Somme Offensive and was invalided home. After protracted hospital treatment at Netley he was demobilised in April 1919, holding the General Service and Victory Medals. 9, Green End, Brampton, Hunts. Z2802/B.

HAYLOCK, H., Private, Bedfordshire Regiment.
Volunteering at the outbreak of war in August 1914, he completed his training in the following year and was sent to France. During his service in this theatre of war he took part in the heavy fighting at the Battles of Albert, the Somme, Ypres and Cambrai, and was twice wounded in the Somme sector in 1916 and 1918. After the conclusion of war he returned home and was demobilised in February 1919, holding the 1914–15 Star, and the General Service and Victory Medals.
Thrapston Road, Brampton, Hunts. TZ2803.

HAYLOCK, J. H., Private, Bedfordshire Regiment.
He volunteered in August 1914, and early in the following year proceeded to France, where he served in various sectors of the front. He was in action at the Battles of Festubert, Loos, Albert and the Somme, and was wounded. On his recovery he returned to the fighting area and saw further service, and was again wounded in June 1918 at the Battle of the Aisne (III.). As a result he was invalided to England, and after losing an eye, was finally discharged in March 1919. He holds the 1914–15 Star, and the General Service and Victory Medals.
Green End, Brampton, Hunts. Z2802/A.

HAYNES, A., Bombardier, Royal Horse Artillery.
He volunteered in September 1915, and was quickly drafted to the Western Front. Whilst in this theatre of war he saw much active service in various sectors, and took part in the severe fighting at the Battles of Arras, Ypres, the Somme (II.) and the Marne (II.). He was later invalided to England, and after a period of hospital treatment was finally demobilised in December 1918, holding the 1914–15 Star, and the General Service and Victory Medals.
1, Salisbury Street, Bedford. Z2809.

HAYNES, A., Private, Royal Fusiliers.
He joined in September 1917, and on completion of his training was retained on important duties with his unit at various stations. He was unable to obtain his transfer to a theatre of war, but rendered valuable services until invalided out in February 1918. 220, Bedford Rd., Kempston, Beds. X2807.

HAYNES, B. E., Private, R.A.S.C. (M.T.)
He joined in October 1916, and on completion of his training was retained on important home duties until July 1918, when he proceeded to France. During his service in this theatre of war he was engaged on important transport duties, conveying the supplies to the forward areas under heavy shell-fire. He served on the Somme and at Ypres and Cambrai, and after the close of hostilities proceeded with the Army of Occupation into Germany. On his return to England he was demobilised in November 1919, and holds the General Service and Victory Medals. Dillington, near St. Neots, Hunts. Z2806/B.

HAYNES, C. H., Sapper, Royal Engineers.
He volunteered in November 1914, and was drafted to France. Whilst on the Western Front he took part in many important engagements in various sectors, including the Battles of Arras, Ypres and Cambrai. Early in 1918 he was invalided home suffering from trench fever, and in March 1918 was discharged as medically unfit for further service. He holds the General Service and Victory Medals.
1, Conquest Road, Bedford. Z2808.

HAYNES, H., Private, 2nd Bedfordshire Regiment.
Volunteering in September 1914, he proceeded to the Western Front in January and fought at Neuve Chapelle, Festubert and Givenchy. He was severely wounded at the Battle of Loos in September 1915, and after treatment was invalided out of the Service in July 1916 in consequence. He holds the 1914–15 Star, and the General Service and Victory Medals.
2, Unwin's Place, St. Mary's Street, Huntingdon. Z2805.

HAYNES, H., L/Corporal, R.E. (Signal Section).
He volunteered in April 1915, and during the first part of his service was retained at home. In June 1918, however, he was drafted to France and was employed on the lines of communication in the Ypres and Cambrai sectors. After a year's service on the Western Front he was demobilised in August 1919, and holds the General Service and Victory Medals.
9, Ampthill Street, Bedford. X2810/C.

HAYNES, H. C., Corporal, Military Mounted Police.
Volunteering in 1915, he was sent to Gallipoli, and served there with the Royal Engineers. Later in June 1918 he reached the Western Front, and during the Advance of 1918 was in action at Cambrai and Le Cateau. Until May 1920 he served at Cologne with the Army of Occupation and on his return home was demobilised, holding the 1914–15 Star, and the General Service and Victory Medals. 9, Ampthill St, Beds. X2810/B.

HAYNES, H. E. M., Private, Bedfordshire Regt.
He joined in August 1918, but being unfit to proceed to a theatre of war, was stationed at Catford and Aldershot with his unit. He did good work, but owing to ill-health had to be discharged in December of the same year.
8, Maitland Street, Bedford. X2072/A.

HAYNES, H. G., Private, Royal Fusiliers.
He joined in January 1916, and completed his training with the Loyal North Lancashire Regiment before being transferred to the Royal Fusiliers and sent to France. There he served at Cambrai and on the Somme during the 1918 Offensive. After also serving at Cairo and Alexandria during 1919, he returned home and was demobilised, holding the General Service and Victory Medals. Dillington, near St. Neots, Hunts. Z2806/A.

HAYNES, R. A., Corporal, 1st Norfolk Regiment.
A time-serving soldier, he proceeded to France at the outbreak of war and fought in the Retreat from Mons. He also took a conspicuous part in others of the early engagements, but made the supreme sacrifice on October 24th, 1914, at La Bassée. He was entitled to the Mons Star, and the General Service and Victory Medals.
"His life for his Country, his soul to God."
9, Ampthill Street, Bedford. X2810/A.

HAYNES, S., Private, 6th Dorset Regiment.
Volunteering in August 1914, he proceeded to the Dardanelles, and was wounded at Suvla Bay in August 1915. Drafted to France, he was again in action, fighting at Arras and Ypres, but later was wounded on the Somme in May 1918. He continued his service and was eventually demobilised in March 1919, holding the 1914–15 Star, and the General Service and Victory Medals. Cambridge St., St. Neots, Hunts. Z2804.

HAYWARD, F. C., Tpr., 1/1st Bedfordshire Lancers.
Nine months after volunteering in September 1914 he was sent to France, and fought in the Battles of Ypres, Loos, the Somme, St. Quentin and Passchendaele. In March 1919 he entered Germany with the Army of Occupation and was stationed at Cologne, remaining there until his demobilisation in March 1920. He holds the 1914–15 Star, and the General Service and Victory Medals. 65, Priory Street, Bedford. X2811.

HEAD, F. W., Driver, Royal Field Artillery.
He volunteered in 1915, and in the same year was sent to France. In that theatre of war he fought at Ypres and Neuve Chapelle, but, returning home, was employed on special work with his unit at Newcastle and Leeds. He was demobilised in February 1919, and holds the 1914–15 Star, and the General Service and Victory Medals. 6, The Grove, Bedford. Z2812.

HEARN, A. W., Private, Essex Regiment.
Volunteering in August 1914, he proceeded to the Western Front and fought in the Retreat from Mons and also at La Bassée in October and Ypres in March of the following year, at each of which engagements he received a wound. In August 1915 he was drafted to the Dardanelles, and was in action at the Landing at Suvla Bay. He was discharged as unfit in September 1916, and holds the Mons Star, and the General Service and Victory Medals.
31, Patteshall Street, Bedford. X2813.

HEATHCOTE, E. A., Private, 2nd Hunts. Cyclist Battalion and Bedfordshire Regiment.
He volunteered in February 1915, and, after a year's service with the Huntingdonshire Cyclist Battalion in England, was transferred to the Bedfordshire Regiment and sent to France. There he fought at Arras and Ypres and on the Somme, but taken ill, was operated on at Rouen and invalided to England in 1917. He underwent treatment until February 1919, when he was demobilised, holding the General Service and Victory Medals. The Green, Brampton, Hunts. Z2814.

HEDGE, A., Private, 1st Bedfordshire Regiment.
He joined in February 1916, and five months later embarked for France, where he went straight into action in the Somme Offensive, and was wounded in September. Invalided home, he was under treatment for some months and was transferred to the Labour Corps. After serving on agricultural work, notably driving a tractor, he was demobilised in February 1919, and holds the General Service and Victory Medals.
New Cottages, Toseland, St. Neots, Hunts. Z2815/A.

HEDGE, A., Private, 6th Bedfordshire Regiment.
Volunteering in June 1915, he was drafted to the Western Front in the following February, and during the Somme Offensive fought at Albert and Delville Wood. In October 1916 he was invalided home with fever, and after hospital treatment was discharged as unfit for further service in November 1917. He holds the General Service and Victory Medals.
New Cottages, Toseland, St. Neots, Hunts. Z2815/B

HEDGE, A., Private, Bedfordshire Regiment.
Volunteering in November 1914, he was sent to France in July of the following year, and was in action at Ypres, Festubert, Givenchy and Loos. Invalided home, he spent some time in hospital with fever at Norwood, and was discharged as no longer fit for service in August 1916. He holds the 1914–15 Star, and the General Service and Victory Medals.
The Vines, Toseland, St. Neots, Hunts. Z2816/A.

HEDGE, E., Private, Queen's (Royal West Surrey Regiment).
He joined in June 1917, and at the close of the year crossed to the Western Front, where he took part in engagements at Cambrai and Merville and in the Retreat and Advance of 1918. He also served at Brussels and Calais, and was employed in guarding enemy prisoners of war. He was demobilised in November 1919, and holds the General Service and Victory Medals. The Vines, Toseland, St. Neots, Hunts. Z2816/B.

HEDGE, M., Private, Essex Regiment.
He joined in 1916, and, after being stationed at Felixstowe, was sent to Egypt, where he served at Cairo. Joining the Palestine Expeditionary Force, he took part in the Battle of Gaza, the Occupation of Jaffa and the operations which led to the capture of Jerusalem. Returning home, he was demobilised in 1919, and holds the General Service and Victory Medals.
Station Road, Tempsford, near Sandy, Beds. Z2817.

HEDGE, S., Private, Bedfordshire Regiment.
Volunteering in 1914, he was sent to France in the following February, after training at Ampthill, and served in various sectors. He took part in the Battles of Neuve Chapelle and Hill 60, but during the latter laid down his life for King and Country in April 1915. He was entitled to the 1914–15 Star and the General Service and Victory Medals.
"Nobly striving:
He nobly fell that we might live."
Toseland, St. Neots, Hunts. Z2818/B.

HEDGE, T. J. (M.M.), Corporal, Bedfordshire Regt.
Volunteering in November 1914, he proceeded to France in the following June, and was in action at Ypres, the Battles of Festubert and Loos, and the Somme Offensive. In April 1917 he was awarded the Military Medal for conspicuous gallantry and devotion to duty in the Field at Arras. Later he fought at Passchendaele Ridge, Cambrai and Albert, but was unhappily killed on August 21st, 1918, at Kemmel Hill. He was entitled to the 1914–15 Star, and the General Service and Victory Medals, as well as the Military Medal.
"Whilst we remember, the sacrifice is not in vain."
Yelling, St. Neots, Hunts. TZ2819.

HEDGE, W., Private, Royal Fusiliers.
Two months after volunteering in April 1915 he embarked for France and fought in the Battles of Loos, Ypres and Passchendaele Ridge. He was severely wounded at Ypres in 1918, and was in consequence invalided home. After some months' treatment in hospital and service at home he was demobilised in July 1919, and holds the 1914–15 Star, and the General Service and Victory Medals.
Toseland, St. Neots, Hunts. Z2818/A.

HEMMINGS, F. J., Private, 2nd Bedfordshire Regt.
Volunteering in 1914, he was drafted in the following year to the Dardanelles and took part in the Landing. He was later sent to France, but after taking part in fighting on the Somme and at Arras and Cambrai, was killed in action at Ypres on July 29th, 1917. He was entitled to the 1914–15 Star, and the General Service and Victory Medals.
"A costly sacrifice upon the altar of freedom."
Eaton Socon, Beds. Z2820/A.

HEMMINGS, W. J., Private, Bedfordshire Regt.
He volunteered in September 1914, and in the ensuing year was sent to France, where he served for about four years. During that period he fought at Festubert, Loos, Arras, Ypres, the Somme and Cambrai and in the Retreat and Advance of 1918, and was wounded. He was demobilised in March 1919, and holds the 1914–15 Star, and the General Service and Victory Medals. Eaton Socon, Beds. Z2820/B.

HENLEY, O. J., L/Corporal, Machine Gun Corps.
He joined in January 1917, and in the Summer was sent to the Western Front. After fighting at Ypres and Passchendaele Ridge, he was drafted to Italy and was in action in the Piave and Asiago sectors, but was unhappily killed in action at Gramezzo on June 14th, 1918. He was entitled to the General Service and Victory Medals.
"He died the noblest death a man may die:
Fighting for God and right and liberty."
18, North End Square, Buckingham. Z3017/B.

HENLEY, T., Private, 2nd Lincolnshire Regiment.
He was serving abroad at the outbreak of war, but was almost at once sent to France. There he took part in the Retreat from Mons and the Battles of the Marne, the Aisne, Ypres and the Somme, and was wounded in April 1917, during the Battle of Arras. Invalided to England, he recovered and was retained at home until sent to India, where he was still serving in 1920. He holds the Mons Star, and the General Service and Victory Medals. Bow Brickhill, near Bletchley, Bucks. Z2821.

HENRICK, A. E. S., Sapper, Royal Engineers.
Mobilised in 1914, he was sent to Egypt in the following year and later joined the Palestine Expeditionary Force, with which he fought at Gaza, and was wounded in 1917. He also took part in the occupation of Jaffa, the operations which culminated in the fall of Jerusalem and the capture of Aleppo, and was engaged on trench-digging and the lines of communication. Returning home, he was demobilised in April 1919, and holds the 1914–15 Star, and the General Service and Victory Medals.
38, Melbourne Street, Bedford. X1224/A—Z2824.

HENRICK, C., Corporal, Bedfordshire and 2nd Royal Sussex Regiments.
Having enlisted in April 1914, he was stationed at various places in England before landing in France in 1916. He took part in fighting at Loos, Albert and the Somme, where he was wounded, but recovered and was in action at Lens, Loos and Cambrai. Wounded at Loos in May 1918, he was invalided home and was eventually demobilised in February 1919. He holds the General Service and Victory Medals.
25, George Street, Bedford. Z2825.

HENSON, F. V. (M.S.M.), Sergeant, R.E. (R.O.D.)
He volunteered in July 1915, and after a brief training at Longmoor was sent to France, where he served as an electrician at Abbeville and on various ambulance trains. For his invaluable services he was awarded the Meritorious Service Medal, and also holds the 1914–15 Star, and the General Service and Victory Medals. He was demobilised in May 1919.
4, Wood Street, New Bradwell, Bucks. Z2822.

HENSON, W., Driver, Royal Field Artillery.
He joined in April 1916, and in November crossed to France, where he served at Lens, Arras, Messines, Ypres, Passchendaele and Cambrai. He also took part in the Retreat and Advance of 1918, being in action in the Battles of the Marne (II.), Amiens, Ypres (IV.) and Le Cateau (II . He was demobilised in March 1919, and holds the Genera rvice and Victory Medals.
Station Road, Warboys, Z2823/A.

HEWITT, B., Private, Oxford. and Bucks. L.I.
Volunteering in September 1914, he completed his training at Oxford, and was drafted to France early in the following year. During the course of his service he fought in the Battles of Ypres, Loos, the Somme, Arras and Cambrai, but gave his life for the great cause in February 1918. He was entitled to the 1914–15 Star, and the General Service and Victory Medals.
"Thinking that remembrance, though unspoken, may reach him where he sleeps."
38, Caledonian Road, New Bradwell, Bucks. Z2826/A.

HEWITT, F. J., Private, 7th Oxford. & Bucks. L.I.
He volunteered in September 1914, and at the close of the following year was drafted to Salonika, having completed his training at Oxford. Whilst in the Balkans he took part in the fighting on the Vardar and Doiran fronts and served during the Advance into Bulgaria. Returning home, he was demobilised in February 1919, and holds the 1914–15 Star, and the General Service and Victory Medals.
38, Caledonian Road, New Bradwell, Bucks. Z2826/B.

HICKFORD, F., L/Corporal, Royal Engineers.
Having volunteered in August 1914, he proceeded to France at the close of the year and was engaged in trench-digging and pontoon and bridge-building. He served at Albert, Pozières, Arras and Villers-Brétonneux, and was in action on the Hindenburg Line. After also being employed on transport work for twelve months he was disabled and discharged as unfit in March 1919, holding the 1914–15 Star, and the General Service and Victory Medals.
5, Tickford Court, Newport Pagnell, Bucks. Z2827.

HICKMAN, R., Private, Lincolnshire Regiment.
He joined in May 1917, and in the following December embarked for the Western Front, where he took part in the second Battle of the Somme, the heavy fighting at Havrincourt and the Retreat and Advance of 1918. He also served at Cologne with the Army of Occupation, and was not demobilised until January 1920. He holds the General Service and Victory Medals. Ellington, Hunts. Z2828.

HIGGINS, E. J., Private, 1st Worcestershire Regt.
Volunteering in October 1915, he was drafted to the Western Front in the following year and served in the Somme Offensive. He also took part in heavy fighting at Ypres, Arras, Cambrai and Vimy Ridge, and was wounded in April 1917. After three years' service in France he was demobilised in March 1919, and holds the General Service and Victory Medals.
13, Cobden Street, Bedford. X1571/B.

HIGGINS, F. J., Private, Duke of Cornwall's L.I.
He joined in May 1917, and, after a period of training and service on Salisbury Plain, was sent to France in March 1918. There he took part in the Retreat and Advance of 1918, being in action at Cambrai, Albert and on the Somme. He was demobilised in March 1919, and holds the General Service and Victory Medals.
Sandfield Cottages, Woburn Sands. Z2829/A

HIGGINS, F. W., Private, Bedfordshire Regiment.
He volunteered in November 1915, and seven months later reached France, where he fought at Festubert, Givenchy and Loos. Wounded in January 1916 at Lens, he was invalided to hospital in England, but on his recovery was drafted again to the Western Front in August 1916, and took part in the Somme Offensive and the Battles of Arras, Messines and Ypres. On August 2nd, 1917, he laid down his life for King and Country at Passchendaele Ridge. He was entitled to the 1914–15 Star, and the General Service and Victory Medals.
"Great deeds cannot die.:
They with the sun and moon renew their light for ever."
Eaton Ford, St. Neots, Hunts. Z2831/A—Z2833/A.

HIGGINS, H. C., Private, 2nd Bedfordshire Regt.
Volunteering in August 1914, he proceeded to the Western Front in October, and fought in the Battles of La Bassée, Ypres (I.) and Neuve Chapelle. He was wounded at Ypres (II.) in June 1915, and took part in the Battles of Loos, Lens and the Somme (I.), where in September 1916 he was a second time wounded. He also served in the Battles of Arras, Messines and Vimy Ridge, and received a third wound at Passchendaele Ridge in October 1917. Invalided home, he remained in England until January 1919, when he was demobilised, holding the 1914 Star, and the General Service and Victory Medals.
Russell Street, Woburn Sands, Beds. Z2832.

HIGGINS, J. H., Driver, Royal Engineers.
He volunteered in 1915, and in the same year was drafted to the Dardanelles, where he took part in the first Landing and subsequent fighting at Suvla Bay. After the Evacuation he continued his service, and was eventually demobilised in April 1919, holding the 1914–15 Star, and the General Service and Victory Medals.
1, Little Grove Place, Bedford. X2830/B.

HIGGINS, T., Private, Bedfordshire Regiment.
Volunteering in March 1915, he was sent to the Western Front in May 1916, and went straight into action during the Somme Offensive. He also fought at Arras, but was reported missing and subsequently killed in action on July 27th, 1916. He was entitled to the General Service and Victory Medals.
"He died the noblest death a man may die:
Fighting for God and right and liberty."
Sandfield Cottages, Woburn Sands. Z2829/B.

HIGGINS, W. H., A.B., R.N., H.M.S. "Kildare."
He volunteered at the outbreak of war, and during the first part of his service was employed on patrol and escort duties in the North Sea and to Russia. He was accidentally drowned at night whilst rowing to his ship on May 17th, 1917, and was buried at Bedford. He was entitled to the 1914–15 Star, and the General Service and Victory Medals.
"His memory is cherished with pride."
Eaton Ford, St. Neots, Hunts. Z2831/B—Z2833/B.

HIGGINS, W. M., Private, Bedfordshire Regiment.
Volunteering in 1915, he soon proceeded to the Western Front and took part in the Battles of Ypres, Hill 60, Arras, the Somme and Cambrai. In 1917 he was drafted to Italy, and was in action on the Piave and Austrian frontier. Returning home, he was discharged as unfit in March 1918, and holds the 1914–15 Star, and the General Service and Victory Medals.
1, Little Grove Place, Bedford. X2830/A.

HIGMAN, H., Sergeant, 1st Hampshire Regiment.
Mobilised in 1914, he was retained in England for a time and did not reach France until July 1916, when he went into action during the Offensive on the Somme. He also served with distinction at Ypres, Arras, La Bassée and the Lys, and in the Retreat of 1918. He was discharged in March 1919, and holds the General Service and Victory Medals.
28, Westbourne Road, Bedford. Z2834/A.

HILL, A., Private, 7th Northants. Regiment.
Volunteering in September 1914, he proceeded to France in the following March. He served in the Battles of Loos, Hill 60, Vimy Ridge, the Somme, Bullecourt, Messines, Lens and Cambrai, but, being gassed in the latter engagement, was sent to hospital. He was eventually demobilised in December 1918, and holds the 1914–15 Star, and the General Service and Victory Medals.
16, Near Town, Olney, Bucks. Z2842.

HILL, A. J., Private, 52nd Royal Sussex Regiment.
He joined in September 1918, and, after completing his training, was retained in England until March 1919, when he was sent to the Army of Occupation in Germany, where he was engaged on guard duties at Cologne. He returned home and was demobilised in February 1920.
9, Tower Gardens, Bedford. X1514/B.

HILL, C., Trooper, Hertfordshire Dragoons.
He joined in March 1917, and, after training with the Hertfordshire Dragoons, was transferred to the Lincolnshire Regiment, with which he served in France. After only three months' service on this front he was wounded in September 1918, was invalided home, and, after treatment, was discharged as unfit in February 1919. He holds the General Service and Victory Medals. Mill Road, Buckden, Hunts. Z2836/A.

HILL, E. (Miss), Special War Worker.
In June 1915 this lady offered her services, and was employed until November at Brampton's Nurseries. She there did valuable work as a stitcher on aeroplane wings for four years, and did not relinquish these duties until 1919.
Mill Road, Buckden, Hunts. Z2836/B.

HILL, F. A., Sapper, Royal Engineers (R.O.D.)
He volunteered in January 1915, and six months later, after completing his training, was sent to France, where he was employed as fireman on troop-trains in different parts of the front. In that capacity he served right on until after the Armistice, and was eventually demobilised in March 1919, holding the 1914–15 Star, and the General Service and Victory Medals.
Chew Cottages, Little Brickhill, Bucks. Z2840.

HILL, F. J., Guardsman, 2nd Grenadier Guards.
A Regular soldier, he proceeded to France at the outbreak of war and fought in the Retreat from Mons. He also played a distinguished part in the Battles of the Marne and the Aisne, but was unhappily killed in action at Ypres in October 1914. He was entitled to the Mons Star, and the General Service and Victory Medals.
"The path of duty was the way to glory."
14, Canning Street, Bedford. X2839/A.

HILL, G. H., Corporal, Oxford. and Bucks. L.I.
Volunteering in January 1915, he reached France three months later and fought at Ypres and Loos, where he was wounded. Returning from hospital in England, he took part in the Battle of Cambrai, but there received a second wound in 1917. He continued serving, and was eventually demobilised in March 1919, holding the 1914–15 Star, and the General Service and Victory Medals.
118, Victoria Road, Fenny Stratford, Bucks. Z2837.

HILL, G. W., Private, Bedfordshire Regiment.
Shortly after volunteering in August 1914 he was drafted to France, where he saw severe fighting in various sectors of the front. He took part in the Battles of Ypres, Arras, Vimy Ridge, Passchendaele and Cambrai and many other important engagements in this theatre of war, and was wounded in action. He was demobilised in December 1919, and holds the 1914–15 Star, and the General Service and Victory Medals.
14, Canning Street, Bedford. X2839/B.

HILL, G. W., Private, Bedfordshire Regiment.
A Territorial, he was mobilised at the outbreak of war in August 1914, and was retained on important duties in England until 1916. He was then drafted to the Western Front, where he fought in the Battles of Arras, Ypres and Cambrai, and many minor engagements, and was twice wounded in action—on the Somme and at Hill 60. He was discharged in January 1919, and holds the General Service and Victory Medals.
68, Grey Friars Walk, Bedford. X2838.

HILL, H. J., Driver, R.A.S.C. (M.T.)
A Reservist, he was called to the Colours in August 1914, and later in that year proceeded to the Western Front, where he was engaged on important transport duties in various sectors. He was gassed and wounded in action in 1915, and in April of the following year was invalided from the Army, suffering from heart trouble. He holds the 1914–15 Star, and the General Service and Victory Medals.
22, Farrer Street, Kempston, Bedford. X2841.

HILL, N., Private, 5th Oxford. and Bucks. L.I.
He volunteered in January 1915, and in October was sent to France. There he fought on the Somme front, notably at Delville Wood, and was wounded in April 1917 during the Battle of Arras. Invalided home, he spent some time in hospital and then proceeded to Ireland. Subsequently transferred to the Labour Corps, he returned to England and served in Surrey until January 1919, when he was demobilised, holding the 1914–15 Star, and the General Service and Victory Medals.
Simpson, near Bletchley, Bucks. Z3848/B.

HILL, W. H., Private, R.A.S.C. (M.T.)
He joined in November 1916, and, on completing a period of training in the following year, was drafted to the Western Front. Whilst in this theatre of war he was engaged on transport duties in various sectors, and served at Arras, Ypres, Cambrai and the Somme and many other places until the cessation of hostilities. He was demobilised on his return home in January 1919, and holds the General Service and Victory Medals. 37, Bunyan Road, Kempston, Bedford. X2835.

HILLS, E., Private, 1st Bedfordshire Regiment.
After volunteering in July 1915, he underwent a period of training prior to being drafted to the Western Front in January 1917. After taking part in the Battle of Ypres and minor engagements he was transferred in November of the same year to Italy, where he was again in action on the Piave. He returned to France, however, in April 1918, and fought at St. Quentin and the Somme, and was wounded at Cambrai in September. Demobilised in March 1919, he holds the General Service and Victory Medals.
13, Patteshall Street, Bedford. X2843.

HILLS, F., Private, 1st Northants. Regiment.
Volunteering in February 1915, he proceeded to Gallipoli in October of that year, but in December was transferred to Egypt. He proceeded thence into Palestine, and fought in the three Battles of Gaza and on the River Jordan, and took part also in the entry into Jaffa and Jerusalem. He was invalided home in December 1918, suffering from dysentery and malaria, and was demobilised in March 1919, holding the 1914–15 Star, and the General Service and Victory Medals.
West Perry, near Huntingdon. Z2090/B.

HILLS, H., Private, 11th Suffolk Regiment.
He volunteered in January 1916, and, on completion of a period of training in June of that year, was drafted to the Western Front, where he took part in the Battles of Arras and Ypres, and many minor engagements. He fell in action near St. Quentin on August 26th, 1917. He was entitled to the General Service and Victory Medals.
"Nobly striving:
He nobly fell that we might live."
Earith, near St. Ives, Hunts. Z1445.

HILLS, W. J., Private, Machine Gun Corps.
Already in the Army when war broke out in August 1914, he was retained on important duties in England until Jannuary 1916, when he proceeded to France. There he saw severe fighting in various sectors of the front, and took part in the Battles of Vermelles, the Somme, Arras, Bullecourt, Passchendaele and Cambrai and other engagements. He was discharged in January 1919, and holds the General Service and Victory Medals. 5, All Hallows Lane, Bedford. X2845.

HILLYARD, F., Private, 10th London Regiment.
He joined immediately on attaining military age in November 1918, and, after a short period of training, was engaged on important duties at various stations. Owing to the early cessation of hostilities he was unable to obtain his transfer overseas, but, nevertheless, did much useful work with his unit until March 1919, when he was demobilised.
3, Islington Row, Towcester, Northants. Z2899/B.

HILLYARD, J. W., Private, 11th Suffolk Regt.
Joining in March 1916, he proceeded to the Western Front in the following September and there saw much severe fighting. He took part in the Battles of the Somme, Arras and Cambrai and many other important engagements, and was three times wounded in action—near Béthune, in September 1918, at Merville, where he was also gassed; and near Mons in the following month. He was demobilised in May 1919, and holds the General Service and Victory Medals.
3, Islington Row, Towcester, Northants. Z2899/A.

HILLYARD, T., Private, Queen's Own (Royal West Kent Regiment).
Joining in April 1918, he was drafted to the Western Front on completing his training in August of that year, and there saw much severe fighting during the Allies' Advance. He took part in engagements at Cambrai and the Somme and many other places until the cessation of hostilities, and was wounded in action in October 1918. Demobilised in February 1919, he holds the General Service and Victory Medals.
5, Ford End Cottages, Queen's Park, Bedford. X2846.

HILLYER, F. A., Air Mechanic, Royal Air Force.
He joined in October 1918, and, after undergoing a period of training, was retained at various stations, where he was engaged on duties of a highly technical nature. He was unable to obtain his transfer overseas owing to the early cessation of hostilities, but nevertheless rendered valuable services with his Squadron until July 1920, when he was invalided from the Service.
79, Spencer Street, New Bradwell, Bucks. Z2847—Z2848.

HILLYER, G. L., Private, 6th Northants. Regt.
He joined in May 1918, and, on completing a period of training, in September of that year was drafted to the Western Front, where he saw much severe fighting during the Advance, taking part in the Battle of Cambrai and other important engagements. He afterwards served with the Army of Occupation in Germany, but later returned to Belgium and was engaged in guarding prisoners of war at Ypres. Demobilised in November 1919, he holds the General Service and Victory Medals.
Green's Norton, Towcester, Northants. Z2900.

HILLYER, L. A., Air Mechanic, Royal Air Force.
He joined in July 1917, and, after completing a term of training, served at various stations, where he was engaged on important duties as a shipping-clerk at the docks. He was unable, on account of ill-health, to obtain his transfer to a theatre of war, but, nevertheless, rendered valuable services with his Squadron until February 1919, when he was demobilised.
4, Vicarage Walk, Stony Stratford, Bucks. Z2844.

HILTON, R. J., Private, 1st Northants. Regiment.
Mobilised at the outbreak of war in August 1914, he was drafted to the Western Front in January of the following year, and there saw severe fighting in various sectors. He took part in the Battles of Ypres, the Somme and Arras and many other important engagements in this theatre of war, and served also through the Retreat and Advance of 1918. He was discharged in February 1919, and holds the 1914–15 Star, and the General Service and Victory Medals.
Weston Underwood, Bucks. Z2849.

HINCH, J., Private, 1st Bedfordshire Regiment.
Volunteering in October 1914, he was drafted to the Western Front in the following month, and there took part in the Battles of Festubert and Loos and minor engagements. In October, 1915, however, he was transferred to Egypt, and, proceeding thence into Palestine, fought in the Battles of Gaza and at the capture of Jaffa and Haifa, and was twice wounded. Invalided home in 1919, suffering from malaria, he was demobilised in March of that year, and holds the 1914 Star, and the General Service and Victory Medals.
Piper's Lane, Godmanchester, Hunts. Z2850.

HINDE, C., Corporal, R.A.M.C.
He joined in May 1917, and was retained on important duties in England until the following January, when he was drafted to Egypt. He proceeded thence into Palestine, where he served as a stretcher-bearer in many engagements, and was stationed for a time at Gaza and Jerusalem. He was demobilised on his return to England in March 1920, and holds the General Service and Victory Medals.
54, Russell Street, Bedford. X2851/D.

HINDE, E., Private, Royal Berkshire Regiment.
He joined in June 1917, and in April of the following year proceeded to the Western Front, where he saw much severe fighting in the Cambrai sector. He made the supreme sacrifice, being killed in action at Mailly-Maillet on April 28th, 1918, after just four weeks' service in France. He was entitled to the General Service and Victory Medals.
"Thinking that remembrance, though unspoken, may reach him where he sleeps."
6, Cobb's Cottages, Olney, Bucks. Z2852/D.

HINDE, F., Private, 2nd Oxford and Bucks. L.I.
Volunteering in November 1915, he was sent to the Western Front in August of the following year, and there saw much severe fighting. He took part in the Battles of the Somme, Arras, Ypres and Cambrai and many other important engagements, and also fought in the Retreat and Advance of 1918. He afterwards served with the Army of Occupation in Germany, where he was stationed at Cologne, until his return home for demobilisation in September 1919. He holds the General Service and Victory Medals.
6, Cobb's Cottages, Olney, Bucks. Z2852/C.

HINDE, G. T., Private, Royal Army Medical Corps.
He volunteered in September 1914, and underwent a period of training prior to being drafted to France in February 1916. There he served as a stretcher-bearer in various sectors of the front, and took an active part in the Battles of the Somme, Arras, Ypres and Cambrai and other important engagements. He was demobilised on his return home in May 1919, and holds the General Service and Victory Medals.
54, Russell Street, Bedford. X2851/B.

HINDE, J., Private, 2nd Northants. Regiment.
Mobilised in August 1914, he proceeded to the Western Front three months later, and there saw much severe fighting. He took part in many important engagements in various sectors, including the Battles of Ypres, Neuve Chapelle, Loos, the Somme, Arras, Passchendaele and Cambrai, and served also through the Retreat and Advance of 1918. He was demobilised in February 1919, and holds the 1914 Star, and the General Service and Victory Medals.
6, Cobb's Cottages, Olney, Bucks. Z2852/B.

HINDE, J. W., Private, R.A.M.C.
After volunteering in September 1914 he was retained on important duties in England until October 1916, when he proceeded to the Western Front. There, serving as a stretcher-bearer, he took an active part in the Battles of Arras, Ypres, Cambrai and the Somme and many other engagements, and was gassed. Demobilised on his return home in March 1919, he holds the General Service and Victory Medals.
54, Russell Street, Bedford. Z2851/A.

HINDE, R., Private, 2nd Oxford. and Bucks. L.I.
He volunteered in November 1915, and in August of the following year proceeded to the Western Front, where, after taking part in the Battles of the Somme and Ypres, he was wounded in action in August 1917. Invalided home, he returned to France, however, on his recovery, and, attached to the Transport Section, served through the Advance of 1918, and was afterwards sent with the Army of Occupation to Cologne. He was demobilised on returning home in October 1919, and holds the General Service and Victory Medals.
6, Cobb's Cottages, Olney, Bucks. Z2852/A.

HINDE, W. E. (sen.), Sapper, Royal Engineers.
He joined in July 1918, and, after completing a period of training, was retained on important duties on the searchlights at various stations. Being too old for active service, he was not successful in obtaining his transfer to a theatre of war, but, nevertheless, rendered valuable services with his Company until his demobilisation in February 1919.
54, Russell Street, Bedford. X2851/E.

HINDE, W. E., Private, R.A.M.C.
He volunteered in September 1914, and, after a period of training, was sent in October 1916 to the Western Front. Whilst in this theatre of war he served as a stretcher-bearer in various sectors, and took part in the Battles of Arras, Ypres, Cambrai and the Somme and other important engagements. He was demobilised in July 1919, and holds the General Service and Victory Medals. 54, Russell Street, Bedford. X2851/C.

HINES, J. C., Private, Royal Berkshire Regiment.
Joining in May 1916, he proceeded to France in December of that year, and there saw severe fighting in various sectors of the front. He took part in the Battles of Arras, Vimy Ridge and the Somme, and many other important engagements until the cessation of hostilities, and was wounded in action at Ypres. He was demobilised in February 1919, and holds the General Service and Victory Medals.
2, Meadow Row, Buckingham. Z2854.

HINES, W. G., Air Mechanic, Royal Air Force.
Joining in June 1918, he proceeded to the Western Front in the following month, and there served in various sectors. He was engaged on important duties with a Labour Company whilst in this theatre of war, and rendered very valuable services until his return home for demobilisation in January 1919. He holds the General Service and Victory Medals.
Meadow Row, Buckingham. Z2853.

HIRST, F. J., Stoker, Royal Navy.
He joined in February 1917, and later served in H.M.S. "Danæ" and "Sandhurst." On board these vessels he was engaged on various important duties in Russian and German waters, and also served in the North and Baltic Seas. He was finally demobilised in 1920, and holds the General Service and Victory Medals.
41, Muswell Road, South End, Bedford. Z2855.

HITCH, A., Private, 1st Bedfordshire Regiment.
Volunteering in August 1914, he was drafted to the Western Front in the following December, and there, after taking part in the Battle of Hill 60, was wounded in action at Villers-Brétonneux and admitted to hospital at Boulogne. On his recovery, however, he rejoined his unit, and was again in action in the Cambrai sector until the cessation of hostilities. Demobilised in February 1919, he holds the 1914–15 Star, and the General Service and Victory Medals.
10, Royal Oak Passage, Huntingdon. Z2856.

HIVES, E., Sick Berth Attendant, Royal Navy.
He was mobilised at the outbreak of war in August 1914, and was posted to H.M.S. hospital ship "China," on board which vessel he was engaged in conveying the wounded from France. He was also engaged for a time at Shotley Hospital, where he was engaged on various important duties, assisting also in the operating theatre. He was discharged in May 1919, and holds the General Service and Victory Medals.
Olney Road, Lavendon, Bucks. Z2857.

HIXON, A. A., Private, 3rd Bedfordshire Regt.
Mobilised in August 1914, he proceeded in the following year to the Western Front. In this theatre of war he participated in many important engagements, including the Battles of the Somme, Arras, Ypres and Cambrai. After the Armistice he was employed re-burying the dead and in other duties of an important nature until April 1920, when he returned home and was demobilised. He holds the 1914–15 Star, and the General Service and Victory Medals.
33, Gratton Road, Queen's Park, Bedford. Z2858.

HOBBS, A., Private, Bedfordshire Regiment.
Already serving at the outbreak of war in August 1914, he was at once ordered to the Western Front, where he took part in the Battle of Mons and the Retreat, and also in the Battles of Ypres, the Aisne and Hill 60, and was four times wounded. He was taken prisoner in April 1917, and interned in Germany until after the Armistice, when he was repatriated. He was discharged in March 1920, and holds the Mons Star, and the General Service and Victory Medals.
1, Cauldwell Place, Cauldwell Street, Bedford. X2902.

HOBBS, W., Corporal, Royal Horse Guards.
He joined in May 1916, and was drafted in the following year to France. During his service overseas he participated in the Battles of Arras, Vimy Ridge and the Somme, and in severe fighting in many sectors during the Retreat and Advance of 1918. He was wounded in action at Arras, but remained on the Western Front until February 1919, when he was demobilised, holding the General Service and Victory Medals.
8, Little Grove Place, Bedford. X2901.

HODDLE, W., Corporal, 2nd London Regiment and Labour Corps.
He volunteered in October 1914, and, after completing his training, was employed on various duties at Newmarket until 1917, when he was drafted to the Western Front. There he took part in strenuous fighting in various sectors, and was wounded on two occasions—at Ypres in October 1917, and at Cambrai in April 1918. Invalided home as the result of the latter wound, he spent some time in hospital at Birmingham, and, returning to France in November 1918, was engaged on important duties. He was demobilised in August 1919, and holds the General Service and Victory Medals.
25, Cowper Street, Olney, Bucks. Z2903.

HODGEMAN, W. G., Private, R.M.L.I. and R.A.V.C.; and Gunner, R.F.A.
Serving when war broke out in August 1914, he was at once drafted to the Western Front, where he took part in the operations at Antwerp. He was later sent to East Africa, and served there until October 1916, when he returned to France and was transferred to the Royal Army Veterinary Corps. Employed looking after invalid horses, he did good work until the following year, when he was transferred to the Royal Field Artillery and sent to Salonika. There he was in action with his Battery on the Vardar, Doiran and Struma fronts. He was still serving with the Colours in 1920, and holds the 1914 Star, and the General Service and Victory Medals.
32, Pilcroft Street, Bedford. X2905.

HODGKIN, C. T. M., Private, Bedfordshire Regt. and Royal Army Service Corps (M.T.)
He volunteered in September 1914, but was invalided out of the Army after six months' service, in March 1915, as unfit for military duty. In the following September he re-enlisted, and five months later was sent to France. There he was employed as a motor mechanic and did excellent work in this capacity until June 1919, when he returned home. Demobilised in the following month, he holds the General Service and Victory Medals. 16, Ampthill Street, Bedford. X2904.

HODSON, W., L/Cpl., Hunts. Cyclist Battalion and Royal Fusiliers.
Volunteering in November 1915, he was found to be medically unfit for transfer to a theatre of war. Retained at home, he served at Huntingdon, Sutton-on-Sea, Skegness, St. Leonards and Walton-on-the-Naze, employed on various duties of an important nature. He performed exceedingly good work until he was demobilised in February 1919.
Hardwick, Buckden, Hunts. Z2906.

HOLDEN, J. W., Private, 2nd Bedfordshire Regt.
He joined in June 1918, and during his training served at Bedford, Brocton Camp and Colchester. Later he proceeded to India, where he was employed with his unit on garrison and other duties of an important nature, being stationed for some time in Bombay. In 1920 he was still serving with the Colours.
Buckden Road, Brampton, Hunts. Z2907/A.

HOLDEN, W., Pte., Middlesex Regt. & Labour Corps.
He volunteered in September 1915, and, after completing his training at Aldershot, was transferred to the Labour Corps. Whilst stationed at Royston, Cambridge and other places he was engaged with his unit on duties of an important character. Medically unfit for transfer overseas, he, nevertheless, rendered valuable services until he was demobilised in March 1919.
Buckden Road, Brampton, Hunts. Z2907/B.

HOLDICH, G., Pte., Training Reserve Battalion.
He joined in February 1917, and was sent for training to Dovercourt. After a few weeks' service his health broke down and he was admitted to hospital, his illness unhappily ending in his death on March 30th, 1917.
"His memory is cherished with pride."
Windmill Inn, St. Ives Road, Somersham, Hunts. Z2908.

HOLLAND, A. E., Cpl., 2nd Bedfordshire Regt.
Volunteering in September 1914, he was drafted early in the following year to the Western Front. There he took part with his unit in the Battles of Ypres, Loos, the Somme and Cambrai, and did good work until he was invalided home on account of ill-health. After spending some time in hospitals at Ampthill and Lowestoft he was, on his recovery, sent to Hertford, where he was employed on recruiting duties until February 1919, when he was demobilised, holding the 1914–15 Star, and the General Service and Victory Medals.
5, St. Germain Street, Huntingdon. Z1083/A.

HOLLAND, C., Private, Tank Corps.
He joined in August 1918, and a month later was sent to France. In this theatre of hostilities he was employed on various duties at Amiens, on the Somme front and at Treport, during the final Advance. Returning home in January 1919, he was demobilised a month later, and holds the General Service and Victory Medals.
13, Chicheley Street, Newport Pagnell, Bucks. Z2909/A.

HOLLAND, G. E., Drummer, Hunts. Cyclist Bn. and Royal Fusiliers.
Mobilised with the Territorial Force at the outbreak of war in August 1914, he was retained at home on important duties, serving at Scarborough and other stations until 1916, when he was sent to France. There he was transferred to the Royal Fusiliers, and was in action on the Somme front and at Arras and Ypres. He was for a short period in hospital at Boulogne as the result of being wounded, and on his recovery rejoined his unit. He was later invalided home on account of ill-health and sent to hospital in Lancashire. Eventually demobilised in April 1919, he holds the General Service and Victory Medals.
5, St. Germain Street, Huntingdon. Z1083/B.

HOLLAND, W., Private, Oxford. and Bucks. L.I.
He volunteered in September 1914, and, on the completion of his training, was sent in the following March to the Western Front. There he went into action immediately at Neuve Chapelle, but had only been overseas for a few weeks when he made the supreme sacrifice, being killed at La Bassée on April 8th, 1915. He was entitled to the 1914–15 Star, and the General Service and Victory Medals.
"His life for his Country."
13, Chicheley Street, Newport Pagnell, Bucks. Z2909/B.

HOLLEY, E. J., Cpl., Hunts. Cyclist Battalion and Royal Warwickshire Regiment.
Volunteering in January 1915, he served for some time at Sutton-on-Sea, and was afterwards transferred to the Royal Warwickshire Regiment. In 1916 he was drafted to France, and in this theatre of war played a prominent part with his unit in severe fighting on the Somme and Ypres fronts, and also at Givenchy. Returning home after the termination of hostilities, he was eventually demobilised in December 1919, and holds the General Service and Victory Medals.
Hemingford Grey, Huntingdon. Z2911.

HOLLINRAKE, H., Sapper, Royal Engineers.
He volunteered in August 1914, and four months later proceeded to France. There he served at Mons, Ypres, Loos, Arras, the Somme, Passchendaele and Cambrai, engaged in erecting pontoon-bridges and in other important duties. He performed consistently good work whilst overseas, and was demobilised in March 1919, holding the 1914–15 Star, and the General Service and Victory Medals.
7, St. Leonard's Street, Bedford. X1103/C.

HOLLOWAY, A., Sergeant, Royal Engineers.
A Regular soldier, he was sent to the Western Front immediately after the outbreak of war in August 1914, and served through the Retreat from Mons. He was wounded during the first Battle of the Aisne, and as a result was invalided home and sent to hospital at Plymouth. After recovery he served at Aldershot and Haynes Park, and was still with the Colours in 1920, stationed at Maresfield. He holds the Mons Star, and the General Service and Victory Medals.
Northwood End, Haynes, near Bedford. Z2912.

HOLLOWAY, F., Sapper (Cyclist), R.E.
Volunteering in July 1915, he was sent to the Western Front in February 1917, and attached for duty to the Naval Division. He did good service with his unit at Arras, Vimy Ridge and Ypres, but, wounded in September 1917, was invalided home. After treatment at Cambridge Hospital he was discharged as medically unfit in October 1918. He holds the General Service and Victory Medals. 42, Salisbury Street, Bedford. TX2914/A.

HOLLOWAY, H., Private, Oxford. & Bucks. L.I.
He joined in October 1916, and in the following January was drafted to Mesopotamia, where he served for nearly three years. During this time he took part with his unit in many important engagements, including several on the Tigris front, also at Baghdad and Kut-el-Amara. He returned home in October 1919, and was demobilised a month later, holding the General Service and Victory Medals. West St., Olney, Bucks. Z2913.

HOLLOWAY, R., Farrier-Sergeant, R.E.
He volunteered in January 1915, and was retained at various stations, where he was engaged on duties of great importance in the blacksmiths' shop. Unable to obtain his transfer to a theatre of war, he, nevertheless, rendered valuable services with his Company until January 1919, when he was demobilised. 42, Salisbury Street, Bedford. TX2914/B.

HOLLYOAKE, A. E. (M.M.), Sergeant, Oxford. and Bucks. Light Infantry.
He volunteered in November 1915, and proceeded, after a short period of training, to France. There he was in action at Albert, Vimy Ridge and on the Somme front, taking a conspicuous part in strenuous fighting. Severely wounded near Le Cateau in October 1918, he was invalided home, and unfortunately had to suffer the amputation of his right leg. He was awarded the Military Medal for bravery and consistent devotion to duty in the Field, and when discharged in June 1919 as physically unfit for further service, was also entitled to the General Service and Victory Medals.
143, High Street, Stony Stratford, Bucks. Z2915/A.

HOLLYOAKE, A. G. (M.M.), Private, 1/1st Oxford. and Bucks. Light Infantry.
Mobilised with the Territorial Force in August 1914, he was drafted in the following March to the Western Front. In this theatre of war he played a prominent part with his unit in the Battles of Loos, Ypres, the Somme and Arras, and was awarded the Military Medal for conspicuous bravery and devotion to duty in the Field. In November 1917 he was transferred to the Italian front, and, after taking part in several severe engagements, he was unhappily killed in action on the Asiago Plateau on August 26th, 1918. He was entitled to the 1914–15 Star, and the General Service and Victory Medals, in addition to the Military Medal.
"A costly sacrifice upon the altar of freedom."
143, High Street, Stony Stratford, Bucks. Z2915/B.

HOLLYOAKE, F. H., Private, R.A.M.C. (T.F.)
He was mobilised in August 1914, and seven months later was sent to Egypt, where he served at Alexandria and on the Suez Canal. Transferred to the Dardanelles, he was engaged on important duties at Suvla Bay, and after the Evacuation returned to Egypt. He was later invalided home suffering from fever, and, after spending a considerable time in hospital in Manchester, was sent to France in 1918. Whilst employed on clerical duties in the Indian Hospital at Marseilles he did good work until he returned home for demobilisation in June 1919. He holds the 1914–15 Star, and the General Service and Victory Medals.
30, York Road, Stony Stratford, Bucks. Z2916.

HOLMAN, J. O., Private, 18th Yorkshire Regt.
He joined in December 1916, and was sent for training to Weston-super-Mare and Bedford. He was later stationed at Ipswich and Margate, and was engaged on important duties in the Orderly Room. Medically unfit for transfer to a theatre of war, he, nevertheless, rendered valuable services until he was demobilised in April 1919.
4, Church Street, Stony Stratford, Bucks. TZ2917.

HOLMES, A. H., Private, 5th Royal Warwickshire Regiment.
Joining in October 1918, he was sent to Oxford and shortly afterwards proceeded to Newcastle. There he was admitted to the First Northern General Hospital, suffering from influenza, which developed into pneumonia and caused his death on November 1st, 1918.
"His memory is cherished with pride."
37, High Ash, Great Brickhill, Bucks. Z2919/A.

HOLMES, A. J., Cpl., 3rd Suffolk Rgt., 15th Queen's (Royal West Surrey Regt.), and Labour Corps.
He joined in August 1916, and was drafted in the following December to Salonika. Whilst in this theatre of hostilities he served on the Doiran, Vardar and Struma fronts with the 15th Queen's (Royal West Surrey Regiment), and later with the Labour Corps. He remained overseas until January 1919, and was demobilised twelve months later, holding the General Service and Victory Medals.
41, Grey Friars Walk, Bedford. X1495/A.

HOLMES, F., Corporal, R.A.S.C.
Serving at the outbreak of war in August 1914, he was shortly afterwards drafted to the Western Front, where he was engaged on transport and other duties of an important nature. He served on the Ypres, Arras and Cambrai fronts, and in various sectors during the Retreat and Advance of 1918. Demobilised on returning home in April 1919, he holds the 1914 Star, and the General Service and Victory Medals.
22, Albert Street, Bedford. X2918.

HOLMES, H. F., Private, R.A.S.C. (M.T.)
He volunteered in June 1915, and a few weeks later proceeded to France. There he was stationed at Rouen and Paris, and whilst employed in workshops as fitter and repairer performed exceedingly good work. He was eventually demobilised in September 1919, holding the 1914–15 Star, and the General Service and Victory Medals.
Prospect Place, Emberton, Bucks. Z2920.

HOLMES, P., Private, Royal Army Medical Corps.
Volunteering in December 1914, he served for twelve months at a hospital at Warley, and in December 1915 was drafted to Mesopotamia. There he was employed as a stretcher-bearer and in other duties of an important nature during severe fighting in the attempt to relieve Kut. He rendered excellent service until he returned home for demobilisation in May 1919, and holds the 1914–15 Star, and the General Service and Victory Medals.
Olney Road, Lavendon, Bucks. Z2921/B.

HOLMES, R., Private, Queen's (Royal West Surrey Regiment).
He volunteered in January 1916, and six months later proceeded to the Western Front. In this theatre of war he took part in many important engagements, including the Battles of the Somme, Arras and Cambrai, and was in action in various sectors during the Retreat and Advance of 1918. He was demobilised in February 1919, and holds the General Service and Victory Medals.
Olney Road, Lavendon, Bucks. Z2921/C.

HOLMES, S., Private, Queen's (Royal West Surrey Regiment).
He volunteered in August 1914, and was employed at home on various duties until August 1915, when he was sent to France. There he participated in strenuous fighting on the Ypres front, and was wounded in January 1916. As a result he was evacuated to England, and, after spending some months in hospital at Cheltenham, returned to France, where he took part in further fighting on the Somme and Cambrai fronts, and during the Retreat and Advance of 1918. He was demobilised on his return home in March 1919, and holds the 1914–15 Star, and the General Service and Victory Medals.
Olney Road, Lavendon, Bucks. Z2921/A.

HOLT, J., Private, 1/5th Bedfordshire Regiment.
Volunteering in November 1914, he was drafted in the following July to Gallipoli and took part in operations during the Landing at Suvla Bay. He was wounded during heavy fighting in November 1915, sent to hospital at Cairo, and, later evacuated to England, was eventually invalided out of the Army in July 1916 as unfit for further service. He holds the 1914–15 Star, and the General Service and Victory Medals.
12, Beckett Street, Bedford. X2922.

HOLTOM, F., Private, R.A.M.C.
He was mobilised in August 1914, and served in hospitals at Wokingham and Reading until he was drafted early in 1916 to Egypt. In this theatre of hostilities he was engaged on important duties during heavy fighting, and was wounded and taken prisoner in April 1916, unfortunately dying from the effects of his wounds in captivity in Turkey on December 26th, 1916. He was entitled to the General Service and Victory Medals.
"He passed out of the sight of men by the path of duty and self-sacrifice."
15, King Street, Stony Stratford, Bucks. Z2926/A.

HOLTOM, W. H., Driver, Royal Field Artillery.
He volunteered in January 1915, and, after completing his training at Christchurch, was employed on transport and other important duties. He rendered valuable services whilst so engaged until he was invalided out of the Army on account of ill-health in May 1915.
20, King Street, Stony Stratford, Bucks. Z2926/B.

HOLTON, D., L/Corporal, 8th Bedfordshire Regt.
He volunteered in January 1915, and proceeded six months later to France. There he played a prominent part with his unit in various important engagements on the Somme and other fronts, and did excellent work until he fell in action near Ypres in July 1917. He was entitled to the 1914–15 Star, and the General Service and Victory Medals.
"Nobly striving :
He nobly fell that we might live."
Church End, Sherington, Newport Pagnell. Z2923/A.

HOLTON, G., Corporal, Royal Engineers.
He joined in April 1916, and four months later was drafted to France. There he was engaged as a wireless operator with the Royal Engineers Signal Section, and did excellent work. He served on the Somme front and in other sectors, and was gassed at Havrincourt. Three days after being demobilised in August 1919 he was admitted to hospital in Bedford, suffering from an illness caused by the effects of gas-posioning, and was later transferred to hospital at Lewisham, where he died in January 1920. He was entitled to the General Service and Victory Medals.
"His memory is cherished with pride."
21, Park Street, Bletchley, Bucks. Z2924.

HOLTON, S., Pte., Beds. Regt. & Sherwood Foresters.
Volunteering in September 1915, he proceeded in the following January to the Western Front, and was in action at Albert and on the Somme front. He was wounded at Arras in 1917, evacuated to England and sent to hospital in Birmingham. Returning to France early in 1918, he took part in further fighting, and was taken prisoner at Cambrai in March of that year. Repatriated after the Armistice, he was later transferred to the Sherwood Foresters, and in 1920 was still serving with the Colours, stationed at Blackdown Camp. He holds the General Service and Victory Medals.
Church End, Sherington, Newport Pagnell, Bucks. Z2925/B.

HOMANS, E. J., Private, Worcestershire Regt. and Labour Corps.
He joined in March 1917, and, afterwards transferred to the Labour Corps, was employed on various duties at Southampton. In October 1917 he was sent to France, and whilst stationed at Etaples did good work engaged in road-making and on transport duties. He was later admitted to hospital, suffering from an illness contracted on service, and unfortunately died on April 6th, 1918. He was buried in the British Cemetery at Etaples, and was entitled to the General Service and Victory Medals.
"Honour to the immortal dead who gave their youth that the world might grow old in peace."
33, Priory Street, Newport Pagnell, Bucks. Z2927.

HOOD, D. V., Driver, R.A.S.C.
He attested in December 1915, and was called up for service in February 1917. Proceeding later to the Western Front, he served in the Arras and Ypres sectors, employed taking ammunition and rations to the front line, and also in the transport of anti-aircraft guns. After the Armistice he served in Germany with the Army of Occupation, and was demobilised in December 1919, holding the General Service and Victory Medals.
Roxton Road, Great Barford. Z2928/A.

HOOK, A., Private, 19th (Queen Alexandra's Own Royal) Hussars.
Volunteering in August 1914, he was sent to France in the following year, and participated in many important engagements, including the Battles of Ypres (III.), the Somme and Arras. He was wounded on the Somme front in 1918, and, after treatment at a Base hospital, rejoined his unit and was in further fighting. He afterwards proceeded to Germany and served with the Army of Occupation on the Rhine until February 1919, when he returned home and was demobilised, holding the 1914–15 Star, and the General Service and Victory Medals.
East Street, Kimbolton, Hunts. Z2929.

HOOKHAM, A., Private, East Surrey Regiment.
He joined in March 1918, but was medically unfit for transfer to a theatre of war. After completing his training he served in various stations in Scotland and at Clipstone Camp, and did excellent work engaged on important duties until he was demobilised in November 1919.
26, Filberts Walk, St. Ives, Hunts. Z2932/B.

HOOKHAM, I., Gunner, Royal Garrison Artillery.
Joining in May 1917, he was drafted two months later to the Western Front, and in this theatre of war took part with his Battery in heavy fighting at Arras, Ypres, Cambrai and on the Somme front. He performed uniformly good work until the termination of hostilities, and, demobilised on his return home in February 1919, holds the General Service and Victory Medals.
23, Victoria Terrace, St. Ives, Hunts. Z2930.

HOOKHAM, R. A., Private, Suffolk Regiment.
He volunteered in September 1915, and in the following year proceeded to France. There he was in action at Loos, Arras, Ypres and Cambrai, and was wounded at Loos. Later transferred to Palestine, he took part in further fighting at Gaza and near Jaffa, and was again wounded. He returned home and was demobilised in March 1919, and holds the General Service and Victory Medals.
26, Filberts Walk, St. Ives, Hunts. Z2932/A.

HOOKHAM, R. J., Private, Bedfordshire Regt.
He joined in 1916, and in December of the same year was sent to the Western Front. During his service overseas he participated in various important engagements, including the Battles of Arras, Ypres, Cambrai and the Somme, and was wounded. He remained in this theatre of hostilities until after the Armistice, and was demobilised in March 1919, holding the General Service and Victory Medals.
7, Victoria Terrace, St. Ives, Hunts. Z2931.

HOOKHAM, T. H., Private, Army Cyclist Corps.
Mobilised in August 1914, he was immediately ordered to France, and fought in the Battle of Mons and through the subsequent Retreat. He later took part in the Battles of the Marne, La Bassée, Neuve Chapelle, Hill 60, and Festubert, and was wounded at Ypres. Evacuated to England, he was eventually invalided out of the Army in December 1915 as unfit for further service, and holds the Mons Star, and the General Service and Victory Medals.
8, Filberts Walk, St. Ives, Hunts. Z2933.

HOOTON, H., Private, 2nd Bedfordshire Regiment.
He volunteered in April 1915, and in June of the following year proceeded to the Western Front, where he saw severe fighting in various sectors. After taking part in the Battles of the Somme, Arras, Ypres and Cambrai, and many minor engagements, he was invalided home in January 1918, suffering from trench-fever, and was admitted to hospital at Southampton. Demobilised in January 1919, he holds the General Service and Victory Medals.
Silver End, Olney, Bucks. Z2934.

HOPCRAFT, S., Private, Labour Corps.
He volunteered in December 1915, and, after undergoing a period of training, was retained on important agricultural duties at various stations. He was medically unfit for duty overseas, and was consequently unable to obtain his transfer to the front, but, nevertheless, rendered very valuable services until his demobilisation in October 1919.
Moulsoe, Bucks. Z2935.

HOPKINS, J. T., Private, Bedfordshire Regiment.
Shortly after volunteering in January 1915 he was drafted to the Western Front, where he saw much heavy fighting. After taking part in the Battles of Ypres, the Somme, Arras and Cambrai, and other important engagements, he was wounded in action and taken prisoner on the Somme in March 1918, and was held in captivity until the cessation of hostilities. He was demobilised in September 1919, and holds the 1914–15 Star, and the General Service and Victory Medals.
Luke Street, Eynesbury, St. Neots, Hunts. Z2936.

HOPKINS, W., Private, 2/1st Monmouthshire Regt.
He volunteered in September 1914, and was retained on important duties in England until February 1916, when he was drafted to the Western Front. There he took part in the Battles of the Somme, Arras, Messines and Ypres, and many other engagements, and, taken prisoner at Cambrai in April 1918, was wounded in endeavouring to escape. He was demobilised on his release in December 1918, and holds the General Service and Victory Medals.
115, Bunyan Road, Kempston, Bedford. X2938.

HOPKINS, W. G., Corporal, Machine Gun Corps.
Volunteering in June 1915, he was sent to the Western Front on completing his training three months later, and there saw severe fighting in various sectors. He took part in the Battles of the Somme, Arras, Ypres and Cambrai, and many other important engagements, and also served through the Retreat and Advance of 1918. He was demobilised in March 1919, and holds the 1914–15 Star, and the General Service and Victory Medals.
1, London End, Newton Longville, Bucks. Z2937.

HORNE, A., Stoker, Royal Navy.
He joined in September 1916, and was posted to H.M.S. "Neptune," on board which vessel he served until 1918, and during this period was present at the sinking of H.M.S. "Vanguard." He was later transferred to H.M.S. "Sandhurst," attached to the Grand Fleet in the North Sea, and in 1920 was still serving. He holds the General Service and Victory Medals. Milton Ernest, Bedford. Z2940/C.

HORNE, E., Driver, Royal Field Artillery.
He volunteered in June 1915, and in the following year was drafted to the Western Front. Whilst in this theatre of war he saw severe fighting in various sectors, and took part in the Battles of Arras, Vimy Ridge, the Somme and the Marne, and other important engagements until the cessation of hostilities. He then served with the Army of Occupation in Germany, finally returning home for demobilisation in April 1919. He holds the General Service and Victory Medals.
Milton Ernest, Bedford. Z2940/E.

HORNE, G., Air Mechanic, R.A.F. (late R.N.A.S.)
He joined in September 1916, and, after undergoing a period of training, served at various stations, where he was engaged on duties of a highly important nature. He was unable to obtain his transfer overseas before the cessation of hostilities, but later was sent with the Army of Occupation to Germany. Returning home in 1919, he was still with his Squadron in the following year. Milton Ernest, Bedford. Z2940/A.

HORNE, T., Pte., 6th and 4th Bedfordshire Regt.
Volunteering in August 1914, he was drafted to the Western Front in July of the following year, and, after much severe fighting, was wounded in action on the Somme in July 1916. Invalided home, he returned to France, however, in the following January, and was again wounded at Arras in April 1917, and sent to England. He again rejoined his unit in May 1918, and was unhappily reported missing and later killed in action on August 22nd of that year. He was entitled to the 1914–15 Star, and the General Service and Victory Medals.
"His memory is cherished with pride."
Milton Ernest, Bedford. Z2940/B.

HORNE, W., Private, 1/5th Bedfordshire Regt.
A Reservist, he was called to the Colours in August 1914, and in April of the following year was drafted to Gallipoli, where he saw much severe fighting and was wounded in action. On the Evacuation of the Peninsula, however, he was transferred to Egypt, and thence proceeded into Palestine, where he was again in action at the Battles of Gaza and the capture of Jerusalem. He was discharged on his return home in July 1919, and holds the 1914–15 Star, and the General Service and Victory Medals.
Milton Ernest, Bedford. Z2940/D.

HORNE, W. G., Driver, Royal Army Service Corps.
Two months after volunteering in September 1914, he proceeded to France, where he was engaged on important transport duties in various sectors of the front. He also took part in the Battles of Ypres, Festubert, Loos, Vimy Ridge, Cambrai and Armentières, and many other engagements until the cessation of hostilities. He was demobilised in April 1919, and holds the 1914 Star, and the General Service and Victory Medals.
Bridge End, Chellington, Beds. Z2939.

HORNER, A. E., Private, 1st Devonshire Regiment.
Already in the Army when war broke out in August 1914, he was immediately drafted to the Western Front, where he fought in the Retreat from Mons. After taking part also in the first Battle of Ypres, he was wounded in action in 1915 and invalided home, but returned to France, however, on his recovery in the following year. He served through the Battles of the Somme and Cambrai, and other engagements in the Retreat and Advance of 1918, and in 1920 was still with his unit in Ireland, holding the Mons Star, and the General Service and Victory Medals. 27, Westbourne Road, Bedford. Z2941

HORSBURGH, G., Engine-room Artificer, R.N.
He volunteered in June 1915, and, after training at the Royal Naval Barracks at Chatham, served in H.M.S. "Orpheus" and other vessels. His ship was torpedoed in September 1915, but he was fortunately rescued, and was afterwards engaged on convoy duties in the North Sea and other waters. He took part in the Battle of Jutland, and many minor actions until the cessation of hostilities, and was demobilised in February 1919, holding the General Service and Victory Medals.
21, Stanley Street, Bedford. Z2942.

HORSMAN, J., Private, West Yorkshire Regt.
Mobilised in August 1914, he proceeded to the Western Front in the following year, and there took part in the Battles of Ypres, Festubert and Loos, and many minor engagements. He was sent home in 1916, and, transferred to Class W of the Reserve, was engaged on munition work until the cessation of hostilities. He was discharged in March 1919, and holds the 1914–15 Star, and the General Service and Victory Medals.
34, Melbourne Street, Bedford. X2943.

HORTON, B. A., Sapper, R.E. (R.O.D.)
Volunteering in May 1915, he proceeded to the Western Front on completion of a period of training in September of that year, and there served in various sectors. He was engaged on important duties as a fireman whilst in this theatre of war, and did much useful work until his return home for demobilisation in May 1919. He holds the 1914–15 Star, and the General Service and Victory Medals.
15, Duncombe Street, Bletchley, Bucks. Z2944.

HOTSON, J. R., Private, Bedfordshire Regiment.
Shortly after joining in 1916, he was drafted to the Western Front, where he took part in the Battle of the Somme, and many other important engagements in various sectors. He was reported missing, and later, killed in action on April 25th, 1918, and was buried near Hill 60. He was entitled to the General Service and Victory Medals.
"A costly sacrifice upon the altar of freedom."
Little Stukeley, Hunts. Z2945.

HOUGHTON, C. D., Private, 4th East Surrey and Bedfordshire Regiments.
He volunteered in September 1914, and in the following year proceeded to the Western Front, where he took part in the Battles of Ypres, Loos and the Somme, and was gassed and wounded in action on two occasions. Invalided home, he was drafted to Mesopotamia on his recovery in 1917, and was there present at the Relief of Kut and the capture of Baghdad. Demobilised on his return home in February 1919, he holds the 1914–15 Star, and the General Service and Victory Medals.
Pinfold Lane, Godmanchester, Hunts. Z2948.

HOUGHTON, G., Corporal, 9th Essex Regiment.
He joined in April 1916, and in the following year was drafted to the Western Front, where he saw severe fighting in various sectors. He took part in the Battles of Arras and Ypres, and many other important engagements in this theatre of war, and was for a time in hospital suffering from trench-fever. He was recommended for decoration for conspicuous bravery in the Field in 1918, and holding the General Service and Victory Medals, was demobilised in August 1919.
8, Bunyan Road, Bedford. TZ2949.

HOUGHTON, G., Pte., 7th Oxford. and Bucks. L.I.
Joining in November 1916, he proceeded to Mesopotamia on completing his training in the following June, and there saw much severe fighting. He took part in many important engagements in this theatre of war, and was for a time stationed at Amara, Kut and Baghdad. He also served in Salonika, and finally returned home for demobilisation in May 1919, holding the General Service and Victory Medals.
Gawcott Road, Buckingham. Z2946.

HOUGHTON, G. M., Sapper, Royal Engineers.
He was already in the Army when war was declared in August 1914, and was retained at various stations, where he was engaged on duties of great importance. He was unable, on account of ill-health, to obtain his transfer overseas, and in November 1917 was invalided from the Army. He has unhappily died since of consumption.
"Steals on the ear the distant triumph song."
69, Coventry Road, Bedford. Z2947.

HOUSE, H. A., Private, R.A.V.C.
He joined in February 1916, and in the following year proceeded to the Western Front. There he was stationed for a time at Rouen, and was also engaged on important duties in various sectors, being present at the Battles of Ypres and the Somme. Returning home in 1919 he was demobilised in May of that year, and holds the General Service and Victory Medals.
High Street, Brampton, Hunts. Z2950.

HOWE, A. W., Sergeant, Royal Air Force.
He volunteered in October 1915, and after two months' training proceeded to France, where he served at Rouen, Etaples and various other stations. He was engaged on important duties which demanded a high degree of technical skill whilst overseas, and rendered very valuable services until his return home for demobilisation in March 1919. He holds the 1914–15 Star, and the General Service and Victory Medals.
12, Union Street, Newport Pagnell, Bucks. Z2959/B.

HOWE, C. E., Private, 1/5th Bedfordshire Regt.
Joining in 1916, he was shortly afterwards drafted to Egypt, where he saw much severe fighting on the Suez Canal and at many other places, He took part in the capture of Sollum and Magdhaba, and many other important engagements in this seat of operations. He unhappily died of malaria and pneumonia on November 4th, 1919. He was entitled to the General Service and Victory Medals.
"He joined the great white company of valiant souls."
35, Prebend Street, Bedford. Z2957/C.

HOWE, F. J., Tpr., Bedfordshire Lancers; and Pte., 8th (King's Royal Irish) Hussars.
He volunteered in September 1914, and in June of the following year was drafted to the Western Front, where he saw severe fighting in various sectors. He took part in the Battles of Loos, Albert, Vimy Ridge, the Somme, Arras, Ypres and Passchendaele, and many other important engagements until the cessation of hostilities. Demobilised in April 1919, he holds the 1914–15 Star and the General Service and Victory Medals. 6, Luke Street, Eynesbury, St. Neots, Hunts.
Z2954 /C—Z2955 /C.

HOWE, F. J., Private, 9th Norfolk Regiment.
Joining in June 1916, he was drafted to the Western Front twelve months later and there took part in the Battles of Ypres and Passchendaele, and many other important engagements. Mortally wounded in action at Lens in September 1918, he unhappily died in hospital at Boulogne on October 9th of that year. He was entitled to the General Service and Victory Medals.
"The path of duty was the way to glory."
19, York Street, Bedford. Z2952.

HOWE, F. W., Private, 2nd Bedfordshire Regt.
Volunteering in September 1914, he proceeded to the Western Front after two months' training, and there saw much heavy fighting. He took part in the Battles of Ypres, Loos, the Somme and Arras, and many other important engagements in various sectors and was wounded in action. He was demobilised on his return home in March 1919, and holds the 1914 Star, and the General Service and Victory Medals.
128, High Street, Stony Stratford, Bucks. TZ2958 /A.

HOWE, G. A., Private, 1st Northants. Regiment.
Two months after joining in May 1918 he proceeded to the Western Front, where he served through the Battles of the Marne and Bapaume, and many minor engagements. He was severely wounded in action in the second Battle of Cambrai, and unfortunately died on November 6th, 1918, and was buried at Le Havre. He was entitled to the General Service and Victory Medals.
"His life for his Country, his soul to God."
6, Luke St., Eynesbury, St. Neots, Hunts. Z2954 /B—Z2955 /B.

HOWE, G. E., Gunner, Royal Garrison Artillery.
Shortly after joining in 1916 he was sent to the Western Front, where he saw severe fighting in various sectors. He took part in the Battles of the Somme, Arras and Ypres, and many other important engagements until the cessation of hostilities, and then proceeded with the Army of Occupation into Germany, where he was stationed at Cologne. Demobilised on returning home in 1919, he holds the General Service and Victory Medals.
35, Prebend Street, Bedford. Z2957 /B.

HOWE, G. F., Sapper, Royal Engineers.
He volunteered in May 1915, and in January of the following year was drafted to the Western Front. Whilst in this theatre of war he took part in the Battles of the Somme, Arras, Armentières and Bapaume, and many other engagements, fought also in the Retreat and Advance of 1918, and was gassed near Ypres in 1917. He was demobilised in February 1919, and holds the General Service and Victory Medals.
27, Brooklands Road, Bletchley, Bucks. Z2953 /B.

HOWE, H. C., Petty Officer, Royal Navy.
He was already in the Navy when war was declared in August 1914, and afterwards served in H.M.S. "Paris," attached to the Grand Fleet in the North Sea for mine-laying and patrol duties. He was later transferred to the "Edinburgh Castle," and on board this vessel was engaged in escorting food ships to and from America and France. He holds the 1914–15 Star, and the General Service and Victory Medals, and in 1920 was still as sea.
12, Union Street, Newport Pagnell, Bucks. Z2959 /A.

HOWE, H. T., Corporal, Royal Engineers.
Volunteering in January 1915, he proceeded to the Dardanelles in July of that year, and there, after seeing severe fighting at Suvla Bay was wounded in action two months later. He was invalided to hospital at Malta and thence to England, but on his recovery in September 1916 was drafted to the Western Front, where he took part in the Battles of the Somme and Cambrai and fought also in the Retreat and Advance of 1918. Demobilised in February 1919, he holds the 1914–15 Star, and the General Service and Victory Medals.
29, Denmark Street, Fenny Stratford, Bucks. Z1620 /B.

HOWE, J., Private, 2nd Bedfordshire Regiment.
He volunteered in January 1915, and on completing his training in the following September was sent to the Western Front, where he was wounded on the Somme in July 1916. Invalided home, he returned to France, however, in October, and was in action on the Ancre and at Arras and Ypres, and was again twice wounded—in March and May 1918. He was admitted to hospital at Leeds, and was finally discharged in January 1919 as medically unfit for further service. He holds the 1914–15 Star, and the General Service and Victory Medals.
High Street, Sharnbrook, Bedford. Z2951.

HOWE, J. C., Private, 8th Bedfordshire Regiment.
Six months after volunteering in November 1915 he proceeded to the Western Front, where he took part in engagements at Vimy Ridge, Albert and many other places. Mortally wounded in action on the Somme, he unhappily died on September 14th, 1916, and was buried at Corbie. He was entitled to the General Service and Victory Medals.
"Courage, bright hopes and a myriad dreams, splendidly given."
6, Luke St., Eynesbury, St. Neots, Hunts. Z2954 /A—Z2955 /A.

HOWE, P. L., Gunner, Royal Field Artillery.
He joined in February 1916, and on completing a period of training later in that year was drafted to France, where he saw severe fighting in various sectors of the front. He took part in the Battles of Albert, the Somme, Vimy Ridge, Ypres and Cambrai, and many other engagements until the cessation of hostilities, and was then sent with the Army of Occupation into Germany. He was demobilised on his return home in August 1919, and holds the General Service and Victory Medals. 35, Prebend Street, Bedford. Z2957 /D.

HOWE, S. J., L/Corporal, Oxford. and Bucks. Light Infantry and Worcestershire Regiment.
Joining in April 1918, he proceeded to the Western Front after two months' training and there saw much heavy fighting. He took part in the Battle of Amiens, and in engagements at Mormal Forest, and in many other sectors during the final Advance. Returning home in July 1919, he was demobilised in the following month, and holds the General Service and Victory Medals. 27, Brooklands Rd, Bletchley, Bucks. Z2953 /A.

HOWE, W., Private, 2/5th Lancashire Fusiliers.
After volunteering in October 1914, he underwent a period of training prior to being drafted to the Western Front in 1917. There he saw severe fighting in various sectors, taking part in many important engagements, and was twice wounded in action—at Bapaume and Ypres. He was demobilised on his return home in March 1919, and holds the General Service and Victory Medals. Elm Cottages, Pavenham, Beds. Z2956.

HOWE, W. H., Sapper, Royal Engineers.
Shortly after joining in 1916 he proceeded to the Western Front, where he was engaged on important duties in various sectors. He took an active part also in the Battles of Arras, Ypres, Cambrai and the Somme, and many minor engagements, and was wounded in 1917 by an aerial torpedo. He was demobilised in December 1919, and holds the General Service and Victory Medals. 35, Prebend Street, Bedford. Z2957 /A.

HOWELL, G. J., Private, Norfolk Regiment.
He joined in 1916, and on completing a term of training later in that year was drafted to the Western Front. Whilst in this theatre of war he saw severe fighting in various sectors, and took part in the Battles of the Somme and many other important engagements until the cessation of hostilities. He was demobilised in February 1919, and holds the General Service and Victory Medals. 22, Russell St., St. Neots, Hunts. Z2960 /B.

HOWELL, J., Private, Bedfordshire Regiment.
Volunteering in September 1914, he proceeded to the Western Front twelve months later, and there saw severe fighting in various sectors. He took part in the Battles of Loos, Vimy Ridge and the Somme, and many minor engagements in this theatre of war, and was for a considerable period in hospital at Rouen. Demobilised in March 1919, he holds the 1914–15 Star, and the General Service and Victory Medals.
22, Russell Street, St. Neots, Hunts. Z2960 /A.

HOWES, A., L/Corporal, Royal Fusiliers.
He volunteered in September 1914, and in August of the following year was drafted to the Western Front, where he saw much severe fighting. He made the supreme sacrifice, falling in action in the Battle of Loos on September 28th, 1915, after only four weeks in France. He was entitled to the 1914–15 Star, and the General Service and Victory Medals.
"Thinking that remembrance, though unspoken, may reach him where he sleeps."
4, St. John's Street, Huntingdon. Z2968 /B.

HOWES, A., Private, Royal Army Service Corps.
Joining in September 1916, he was sent to France shortly afterwards, and was there engaged on important duties with an ammunition column in various sectors of the front. He was also present at the Battles of Arras, Vimy Ridge, Ypres and on the Somme, and many minor engagements, and after the cessation of hostilities served with the Army of Occupation in Germany. He was demobilised on his return home in August 1919, and holds the General Service and Victory Medals.
27, St. Germain Street, Huntingdon. Z2964 /B.

HOWES, C., Trooper, Bedfordshire Lancers.
He volunteered in September 1914, and after his training was retained on important duties in England until 1916. He was then drafted to Egypt, and proceeded thence into Palestine, where he took part in the Battles of Gaza and the capture of Jerusalem. In 1918 he was transferred to the Western Front, and there fought in the Battles of the Somme, Cambrai, Ypres and other engagements. Demobilised in February 1919, he holds the General Service and Victory Medals.
4, St. John's Street, Huntingdon. Z2968 /A.

HOWES, C. B., Private, 3rd Bedfordshire and Manchester Regiments.
He joined in 1917, and later in the same year proceeded to France. There he took part in several engagements, including those on the Somme, at Passchendaele and Cambrai, and was wounded in action. After hostilities ceased he proceeded to Germany with the Army of Occupation and served there until his demobilisation in January 1919. He holds the General Service and Victory Medals.
Little Stukeley, Hunts. Z2965.

HOWES, C. W., Shoeing-Smith, M.G.C.
He was mobilised in August 1914, and retained for a time at various home stations before being drafted to Mesopotamia. There he took part in engagements at Kut, in the capture of Baghdad and in the fighting on the Euphrates. He met with an accident which caused the loss of a finger. He returned home and was demobilised in December 1919, holding the General Service and Victory Medals.
Pidley, Hunts. Z2966/A—Z2967/A.

HOWES, E., Private, Hunts. Cyclist Battalion.
He volunteered at the beginning of April 1915, but whilst in training at Huntingdon, unfortunately contracted a chill and died on the 14th of the same month in the military hospital, after only a fortnight in the Army.
"His memory is cherished with pride."
4, St. John's Street, Huntingdon. Z296 /C.

HOWES, F., L/Corporal, Military Foot Police.
He volunteered in December 1914, and after a period of training was engaged at various home stations on important duties with his unit. He was unable to obtain a transfer overseas owing to his being medically unfit, but rendered valuable services until his demobilisation in January 1919.
22, Wallace Street, New Bradwell, Bucks. Z2963.

HOWES, F., Sapper, Royal Engineers.
He joined in June 1917, and underwent a short period of training prior to his being drafted to Egypt. He embarked for the East on board H.M.S. "Osmania," but unfortunately lost his life on December 31st, 1917, when the "Osmania" was sunk by a mine off Alexandria. He was entitled to the General Service and Victory Medals.
"Thinking that remembrance, though unspoken, may reach him where he sleeps."
44, Spencer Street, New Bradwell, Bucks. Z2962/A.

HOWES, H. V., Private, Hunts. Cyclist Battalion and Royal Warwickshire Regiment.
He volunteered in August 1914, and was retained for a time at various home stations before proceeding to France. There he saw much heavy fighting on the Somme, where he was wounded in action, and was consequently invalided home. On his recovery he returned to France, was attached to the Royal Irish Rifles, and took part in engagements in the Cambrai sector. He was demobilised in February 1919, and holds the General Service and Victory Medals.
1, Sapley Lane, Hartford. Z2961/B.

HOWES, J. W., Private, Durham Light Infantry.
Joining in November 1916, he was drafted overseas in the following year. Whilst on the Western Front he took part as a signaller in the Battles of Arras, Ypres, Cambrai and the Somme (II.), and saw much fighting during many engagements. He was demobilised in September 1919, and holds the General Service and Victory Medals.
1, Sapley Lane, Hartford. Z2961/A.

HOWES, R. V. (M.M.), Sergeant, 1/8th Warwickshire Regiment.
He volunteered in August 1915, and completing his training in the following year was drafted to France, where he took part in the Battles of the Somme, Arras, Ypres and Vimy Ridge. Later he proceeded to Italy and saw much heavy fighting on the Piave, being awarded the Military Medal for gallantry and devotion to duty in the Field. He returned home, and was demobilised in January 1919, and holds also the General Service and Victory Medals.
27, St. Germain Street, Huntingdon. Z2964/A.

HOWKINS, A. E., Pte., Royal Warwickshire Regt.
He joined the Army in January 1902, and when war broke out in August 1914 was immediately drafted to France, where he took part in the Retreat from Mons, the Battles of the Marne, the Aisne and Ypres. He was wounded and taken prisoner at Zillebeke in October 1914, and held in captivity in various prison camps in Germany throughout hostilities, during which time he suffered many hardships. He was repatriated in December 1918, returned home, and served at various stations until his discharge in March 1920. He holds the Mons Star, and the General Service and Victory Medals.
49, Greenfield Road, Newport Pagnell, Bucks. Z2969.

HOWSON, F. E., Gunner, Royal Field Artillery.
He joined in January 1917, and underwent a period of training prior to his being drafted to France. In this seat of war he took part in the Retreat and Advance of 1918, and after hostilities ceased served on important duties until his demobilisation in February 1919. He holds the General Service and Victory Medals.
7, West Lane, Emberton, Bucks. Z2970.

HOY, J. A., A.B., Royal Navy.
He was already in the Navy when war broke out in August 1914, and quickly proceeded to the North Sea on board H.M.S. "Columbine." He took part in the Battle of Jutland and was also engaged on patrol duties. Whilst serving on board H.M.S. "Medusa" he lost his life when this vessel was sunk in March 1916. He was entitled to the 1914–15 Star, and the General Service and Victory Medals.
"Thinking that remembrance, though unspoken, may reach him where he sleeps."
6, Tower Court, Bedford. X2971.

HUBBARD, D., Signalman, Royal Navy.
He volunteered in March 1915, and after a period of training was posted to H.M.S. "Canada," in the North Sea. There he served with the Grand Fleet engaged on patrol duties, and took part in the Battle of Jutland. Later he saw service in the Mediterranean until his demobilisation in June 1920. He holds the 1914–15 Star, and the General Service and Victory Medals. 5, Dean Street, Bedford. TZ2972.

HUBBARD, H., L/Cpl., 2nd Bedfordshire Regt.
He volunteered in April 1915, and underwent a period of training prior to his being drafted to France, where he saw much heavy fighting in the Cambrai, Albert and Le Cateau sectors. He was unfortunately killed in action during the Advance near Amiens on September 18th, 1918, and was entitled to the General Service and Victory Medals.
"His life for his Country, his soul to God."
Field Cottage, Chauston, Beds. Z2973/A.

HUBER, A. L., Corporal, 9th Royal Welch Fusiliers.
He was mobilised in August 1914, and quickly drafted to France. During his service on the Western Front he took part in many engagements, including the Retreat from Mons, the Battles of Ypres and the Somme, where he was wounded and made a prisoner of war in March 1918. He was held in captivity in Germany for about eight months, and was released after the Armistice. He returned home and was demobilised in December 1919, holding the Mons Star, and the General Service and Victory Medals.
16, Canning Street, Bedford. X1029/B.

HUCKLE, A., Private, Machine Gun Corps.
He joined in 1916, and after completing his training was drafted to France, where he took part in engagements on the Somme and at Ypres. He was wounded and made a prisoner of war in March 1918, being held in captivity in Germany for many months. Repatriated after the Armistice he returned home, and in 1920 was serving in India. He holds the General Service and Victory Medals.
Eaton Socon, Beds. Z2978.

HUCKLE, A. E., Private, Bedfordshire Regiment.
He volunteered in December 1915, and in the following August proceeded to France. There he took part in many important engagements, including those at Arras, Oppy Wood and the Somme, being twice wounded, and finally invalided home. On his recovery he was engaged on agricultural work until his demobilisation in February 1919. He holds the General Service and Victory Medals.
St. Neots Road, Sandy, Beds. Z2974/C.

HUCKLE, A. F., Trooper, Bedfordshire Lancers.
He volunteered in November 1914, and on completing his training in the following year was drafted to France, where he fought at the Battles of Loos, the Somme, Messines, Albert and Cambrai. He made the supreme sacrifice, being killed in action on November 5th, 1918, and was entitled to the 1914–15 Star, and the General Service and Victory Medals.
"A costly sacrifice upon the altar of freedom."
St. Neots Road, Sandy, Beds. Z2974/B.

HUCKLE, C. S., L/Corporal, Royal Berks. Regt.
He was mobilised in August 1914, and in the following May proceeded to France. There he took part in many engagements, including those at Festubert, Ypres, Loos, the Somme, Arras and St. Quentin, where he was wounded and taken prisoner of war in August 1917. He was held in captivity in Germany and suffered many hardships until his release in December 1918. He holds the 1914–15 Star, and the General Service and Victory Medals, and was demobilised in April 1919.
Rose Cottage, Eaton Ford, St. Neots, Hunts. Z2976/A—Z2977/A.

HUCKLE, E. W., Private, 7th Bedfordshire Regt.
He volunteered in August 1914, and after completing his training in the following year was drafted to France. There he took part in much severe fighting in the Neuve Chapelle, Ypres and Arras sectors. He died gloriously in the Field of Battle near Arras on May 7th, 1917, and was entitled to the 1914–15 Star, and the General Service and Victory Medals.
"The path of duty was the way to glory."
London Road, Girtford, Sandy, Beds. Z2975.

HUCKLE, F. C., Private, R.M.L.I.
He was mobilised in August 1914, and immediately drafted to France, where he took part in the defence of Antwerp. Later he was transferred to the Dardanelles, and saw much severe fighting during the Landing at Gallipoli. He made the supreme sacrifice, being killed in action on April 30th, 1915, and was entitled to the 1914 Star, and the General Service and Victory Medals.
"A valiant Soldier, with undaunted heart he breasted life's last hill."
4, Albert Cottages, Houghton Conquest, near Ampthill, Beds. Z2979/B.

HUCKLE, P. W., Trooper, 5th (Princess Charlotte of Wales') Dragoon Guards.
He joined in February 1916, and after completing his training in the following year, proceeded to France. In this theatre of war he took part in the Battles of Albert, the Somme, Cambrai and Amiens. After hostilities ceased, he went to Germany with the Army of Occupation, and served there until his demobilisation in November 1919. He holds the General Service and Victory Medals.
4, Albert Cottages, Houghton Conquest, near Ampthill, Beds. Z2979/A.

HUCKLE, S. C., Private, Bedfordshire Regiment and 2nd London Regiment (Royal Fusiliers).
He joined the Army in May 1914, and after war broke out in the following August, was retained for a time at home on important duties. In August 1916 he was drafted to France, where he took part in much severe fighting on the Somme, and was unfortunately killed in action on October 9th, 1916. He was entitled to the General Service and Victory Medals.
"Whilst we remember, the sacrifice is not in vain."
St. Neots Road, Sandy, Beds. Z2974/A.

HUDSON, W., Private, Bedfordshire Regiment.
He volunteered in February 1915, and on completing his training later in the same year, was drafted to France, where he took part in many engagements, including the Battles of Festubert, Loos, Albert, Vimy Ridge and Messines. He died gloriously on the Field of Battle near Lens on September 14th, 1917, and was entitled to the 1914–15 Star, and the General Service and Victory Medals.
"The path of duty was the way to glory."
West End, Earith, Hunts. Z2981.

HUFFORD, T., Gunner, Royal Horse Artillery.
He joined in February 1916, and underwent a period of training prior to his being drafted to France. There he took part in many important engagements, including those in the Ypres, Arras, Loos, Cambrai, Vimy Ridge and Somme sectors. He was demobilised in April 1919, and holds the General Service and Victory Medals. Barham, Hunts. Z2982.

HUGHES, P., Trooper, North Somerset Dragoons.
He volunteered in October 1914, and in the following January proceeded to France. Whilst in this theatre of war he took part in many engagements, including the Battles of Ypres, Loos, Arras, the Somme, Messines, Vimy Ridge, Albert and Cambrai, and in the Retreat and Advance of 1918, and was wounded in action in September 1917. He was demobilised in January 1919, and holds the 1914–15 Star, and the General Service and Victory Medals.
Brickyard Cottages, Woburn Sands, Beds. Z2020/B.

HUGHES, W., Private, R.A.S.C. (M.T.)
He joined in May 1917, and five months later proceeded to German East Africa, where he served on important duties with the Mechanical Transport. He did good work, but unfortunately contracted malarial fever, and was finally invalided home. He was discharged in June 1919 as medically unfit for further service, and holds the General Service and Victory Medals.
1, Oxford Street, Stony Stratford, Bucks. Z2983.

HULATT, A. G., Private, Bedfordshire Regiment.
He volunteered in March 1915, and in the following year was drafted to France, where he took part in much heavy fighting on the Somme and at Beaumont-Hamel. He was taken prisoner of war in the Arras sector in February 1917, and was held in captivity in Germany for nearly two years. He was repatriated after the Armistice, returned home, and was demobilised in March 1919. He holds the General Service and Victory Medals. Ra lway Cottages, Oakley, Bedford. Z2987/C.

HULATT, F. W., Rifleman, K.R.R.C.
He joined in February 1918, and after a period of training was engaged at various stations on important duties. After hostilities ceased he proceeded to Germany with the Army of Occupation, and served on the Rhine at Cologne until his demobilisation in June 1920.
24, Gwyn Street, Bedford. X2985/B.

HULATT, G. J., Bombardier, R.G.A.
He volunteered in September 1915, and was retained for a time at home on various duties on the Coast. In June 1918 he was drafted to France and did good work in many sectors whilst attached to the Anti-Aircraft Section. He was demobilised in February 1919, and holds the General Service and Victory Medals. 11, Oakley, near Bedford. Z2986.

HULATT, H. J., Sapper, Royal Engineers.
He volunteered in 1915, and in the following year was drafted to Egypt, where he served with the Railway Operative Department transporting troops and ammunition to the forward areas. In July 1916 he was transferred to France and was employed on similar duties in the Somme, Ypres, Arras and Cambrai sectors. He was demobilised in April 1919, and holds the General Service and Victory Medals.
Railway Cottages, Oakley, Bedford. Z2987/A.

HULATT, H. W., Private, 1/5th Bedfordshire Regt.
He was mobilised with the Territorials in August 1914, and completing his training in the following year was drafted to France, where he took part in much severe fighting in the Somme and Arras sectors. He died gloriously on the Field of Battle at Ypres on August 19th, 1917, and was entitled to the 1914–15 Star, and the General Service and Victory Medals.
"His life for his Country, his soul to God."
24, Gwyn Street, Bedford. X2985/A.

HULATT, J. R. Private, 4th Bedfordshire Regt.
Volunteering in 1915, he was drafted overseas in the following year. During his service on the Western Front, he took part in many important engagements, including the Battles of the Somme, Bullecourt, Arras and Cambrai, and was wounded twice and gassed in action. He was demobilised in January 1920, and holds the General Service and Victory Medals.
24, Gwyn Street, Bedford. X2984.

HULATT, W. A., Sapper, Royal Engineers.
He volunteered in November 1915, and in the following year proceeded to the East. In this seat of operations he took part in the Advance into Palestine, and saw much fighting at Gaza, Jaffa and at the capture of Jerusalem. He returned home and was demobilised in July 1919, holding the General Service and Victory Medals. 23, Cavendish St., Bedford. X2988/B.

HULATT, W. H., Private, Bedfordshire Regiment.
Volunteering in August 1914, he was sent to France eight months afterwards, and after taking part in the Battles of Festubert, Loos, the Somme and Arras, was badly wounded in action at Ypres in 1917. He was invalided home, and was in hospital for a considerable period before being discharged as medically unfit in October 1918, holding the 1914–15 Star, and the General Service and Victory Medals.
Railway Cottages, Oakley, Bedford. Z2987/B.

HULETT, F. G., Cpl., 2/5th Gloucestershire Regt.
He volunteered in October 1914, and after his training was retained on important duties in England until May 1916. He was then sent to France, but on December 21st, 1916, was unfortunately killed on the Somme by a time-exploding bomb left behind by the Germans in a dug-out which had been captured. He was entitled to the General Service and Victory Medals.
"His life for his Country, his soul to God."
17, Bower Street, Bedford. Z2989/A.

HULL, A. E., Private, 1st Bedfordshire Regiment.
Mobilised at the outbreak of hostilities, he was drafted to France with the First Expeditionary Force, but was unhappily killed in action at Mons on August 22nd, 1914. He was entitled to the Mons Star, and the General Service and Victory Medals.
"A valiant Soldier, with undaunted heart he breasted life's last hill."
Hemmingford Grey, Hunts. Z2990/A

HULL, C. E., Private, R.A.S.C. (M.T.)
He volunteered in the Bedfordshire Regiment in July 1915, but was quickly transferred to the Royal Army Service Corps, and sent to France, where he was engaged on important transport duties in the forward areas during the Battles of the Somme, Arras, Ypres and Cambrai. He did excellent work with his unit and was demobilised in 1919, holding the 1914–15 Star, and the General Service and Victory Medals.
High Street, Cranfield, Beds. Z2992.

HULSTON, T., Corporal, Royal Fusiliers.
Mobilised in August 1914, he was drafted to France five months later, but was wounded at Ypres and admitted to hospital at Boulogne. On his recovery he was sent to the Dardanelles, and took part in the Landing at Cape Helles, and in much severe fighting on Gallipoli. After the Evacuation of the Peninsula, he was transferred to Egypt, but proceeding into Palestine, served with distinction at the Battles of Gaza and the capture of Jerusalem. In March 1918 he was discharged, and holds the 1914–15 Star, and the General Service and Victory Medals. 11, Berrell's Court, Olney, Bucks. Z2993.

HUMPHREY, A. E., Private, 7th Queen's (Royal West Surrey Regiment).
Volunteering in August 1915, he was quickly drafted to the Western Front, but was badly wounded in action at Ypres and invalided home. After protracted hospital treatment at Cambridge, Bedford and in Essex, he was discharged as medically unfit for further service in January 1919, and holds the 1914–15 Star, and the General Service and Victory Medals.
65, Muswell Road, South End, Bedford. Z2999.

HUMPHREY, C. A., Ordinary Seaman, R.N.
He joined in July 1918, and was quickly sent to sea on board H.M.S. "Superb," with which vessel he was engaged on important patrol and escort duties in the Mediterranean. He also served in H.M.T.B. "Wivern," and cruised in the Black Sea. In 1920 he was still in the Royal Navy, and holds the General Service and Victory Medals.
5, Luke Street, Eynesbury, St. Neots, Hunts. Z2997/B.

HUMPHREY, L. T., Pte., Royal Berkshire Regt.
He joined in March 1916, and after his training was engaged on important duties at various home stations until March 1918. He was then drafted to France, but was badly wounded in action in the Cambrai sector during the Retreat in May, and was invalided to Glasgow. On his recovery he was sent to Ireland, where he rendered valuable services until his demobilisation in October 1919. He holds the General Service and Victory Medals.
5, Luke Street, Eynesbury, St. Neots, Hunts. Z2997/A.

HUMPHREY, W., Air Mechanic, Royal Air Force.
Joining in April 1917, he was sent to France in the following September. Whilst on the Western Front he was engaged as a fitter in the aeroplane workshops at Rouen and Etaples, and also did excellent work as a tester in various sectors. He was demobilised in March 1919, and holds the General Service and Victory Medals.
Bow Brickhill, Bletchley, Bucks. Z2998.

HUMPHREYS, F. C., Sergeant, 1/5th Beds. Regt.
Volunteering in August 1914, he was sent to the Dardanelles in the following year, and took a prominent part in heavy fighting on Gallipoli. After the Evacuation of the Peninsula he was drafted to Egypt, but proceeding into Palestine was unfortunately killed in action at the second Battle of Gaza on April 29th, 1917. He was entitled to the 1914–15 Star, and the General Service and Victory Medals.
"He joined the great white company of valiant souls."
1, Hatchway Cottage, Eaton Socon, Beds. Z3000/A.

HUMPHREYS, M. A., Private, 25th King's (Liverpool Regiment).
He joined in August 1917, and on completion of his training was drafted to France in May of the following year. Whilst on the Western Front he saw heavy fighting at Arras, Armentières and on the Lys during the Retreat and Advance of 1918. He was demobilised in November 1919, and holds the General Service and Victory Medals.
Bell End, Brampton, Hunts. TZ3001.

HUMPHREYS, R. H., Private, Northants. Regt.
He volunteered in January 1915, and after a period of training, was engaged on important duties at home stations for two years. He was then drafted to Palestine, where he took part in the Battles of Gaza, the capture of Jerusalem, and in other important engagements during the Advance of General Allenby's Forces. Demobilised in April 1919, he holds the General Service and Victory Medals.
Old Stratford, near Stony Stratford, Bucks. Z2994.

HUMPHREYS, S., Private, Royal Berkshire Regt.
He volunteered in August 1914, and in the following year was drafted to the Western Front, where he took part in the Battles of Hill 60, Ypres, Loos, Vimy Ridge and the Somme. He was seriously wounded in action in July 1916, and unfortunately had his right leg amputated. In March 1917 he was invalided from the Army, and holds the 1914–15 Star, and the General Service and Victory Medals.
52, Gwyn Street, Bedford. X1185/B.

HUMPHRIES, F., Pte., Oxford. and Bucks. L.I.
He volunteered in September 1914, and early in the following year proceeded to the Western Front. Whilst in this seat of war he took part in the heavy fighting at Festubert and Givenchy, where he was wounded and invalided to hospital. On his recovery he was drafted to India and served at Madras and Delhi on important duties attached to the Military Police. He was demobilised in December 1919, and holds the 1914–15 Star, and the General Service and Victory Medals.
3, Northampton Terrace, Newport Pagnell, Bucks. Z2995.

HUMPHRIES, W., Pte., 6th Bedfordshire Regt.
He joined in February 1916, and on completion of his training in the same year was sent to France, where he took part in many engagements in various sectors of the front. He fought at the Battles of Loos, Albert, the Somme, Arras and Cambrai, and was taken prisoner in March 1918. After his release from captivity he was engaged on important duties at home, and rendered good services until demobilised in September 1919, and holds the General Service and Victory Medals.
London Road, Girtford, Sandy. Z2996.

HUNT, E. P. (Miss), Worker, Women's Forestry Corps.
This lady volunteered for work of National importance in August 1917, and was attached to the Forestry Corps. She was engaged on important duties in the forests at Huntingdon, and rendered valuable services until discharged in June 1918. 3, Avenue Road, Huntingdon. Z3003/B.

HUNT, F. E., Driver, Royal Air Force (M.T.)
He joined in 1917, and later in the same year proceeded to France, where he did valuable work in connection with the transport of supplies and ammunition to the forward areas. He served in many important sectors notably those of the Somme, Arras and Cambrai, and was frequently under heavy shell-fire. He was demobilised in August 1919, and holds the General Service and Victory Medals.
Farr's Yard, Blunham, Beds. Z1631/B.

HUNT, G., Sergeant, Royal Engineers.
Mobilised on the declaration of war in August 1914, he was immediately drafted to France, where he rendered excellent services as a despatch-rider. He served with distinction during the Battle of, and in the Retreat from, Mons, and also at the Battles of Ypres, the Somme, Arras and Cambrai. After the cessation of hostilities he proceeded with the Army of Occupation into Germany, and was stationed at Cologne, where he was still serving in 1920. He holds the Mons Star, and the General Service and Victory Medals.
Farr Cottage, Blunham, Sandy, Beds. Z3002/B.

HUNT, H. G., Private, Bedfordshire Regiment.
Volunteering in November 1914, in the Huntingdonshire Cyclist Corps, he completed his training and was engaged on important duties at various stations. Later, in 1917, he was transferred to the Bedfordshire Regiment, and proceeded to France, where he was in action at the Battle of Cambrai. In March 1918 he was taken prisoner and held in captivity until after the conclusion of war. On his return to England he was finally demobilised in April 1919, and holds the General Service and Victory Medals.
West End, Somersham, Hunts. Z1798/B.

HUNT, P., Corporal, Canadian Royal Engineers.
Volunteering in September 1914, he completed his training in the following year and was drafted to France. Whilst on the Western Front he did excellent work as a despatch-rider and served in many important engagements, notably the Battles of Loos, the Somme, Ypres and Cambrai. After the Armistice he went to Germany with the Army of Occupation and served on the Rhine. Returning home he was demobilised in June 1919, and holds the 1914–15 Star, and the General Service and Victory Medals.
Farr Cottage, Blunham, Sandy, Beds. Z3002/A.

HUNTER, J., Sergeant, 6th Gordon Highlanders.
He volunteered in 1914, and on conclusion of his training in the following year, proceeded to the Dardanelles, where he took part in important engagements until September 1915, when he was invalided home. Later he was sent to the Western Front, and was in action during the Somme Offensive and later at the Battle of Arras and was twice wounded—in 1916 and 1917. He made the supreme sacrifice, being killed in action on August 26th, 1918, and was entitled to the 1914–15 Star, and the General Service and Victory Medals.
"His life for his Country, his soul to God."
33, Edward Road, Bedford. Z3004.

HURREN, C., Private, Northumberland Fusiliers.
Joining in February 1916, he completed his training and was drafted overseas. During his service on the Western Front he took an active part in many important engagements. He served at Vimy Ridge and Kemmel Hill, and was wounded, but was later in action at Bapaume and Cambrai. He was demobilised in October 1919, and holds the General Service and Victory Medals.
41, Sandhurst Road, Bedford. Z3005.

HURRY, G., Private, York and Lancaster Regt.
He volunteered at the outbreak of hostilities in August 1914, and in the following year proceeded to France. During his service in this theatre of war he saw much heavy fighting in various sectors He was in action on the Somme, where he was wounded in 1916, and later took part in the Battles of Arras and Ypres. After the conclusion of war he returned home and was demobilised in 1919, holding the 1914–15 Star, and the General Service and Victory Medals.
Pidley, Hunts. Z3006/B.

HURRY, R., Private, Royal Fusiliers.
He joined in 1916, and after completing a period of training was retained on important duties with his unit at Norfolk. Owing to the early cessation of hostilities he was unable to proceed to a theatre of war, but rendered valuable services until demobilised in 1919. Pidley, Hunts. Z3006/A.

HURST, C. W., Private, Queen's Own (Royal West Kent Regiment).
He joined in April 1917, and was quickly drafted to France. During his short period of service on the Western Front, he was in action at the Battles of Messines and Lens, but shortly afterwards was reported missing, and is now presumed to have been killed in action on October 12th, 1917. He was entitled to the General Service and Victory Medals.
"Thinking that remembrance, though unspoken, may reach him where he sleeps."
4, Station Road, Oakley, Bedford. Z3010.

HURST, E., Gunner, Royal Garrison Artillery.
He was serving in Malta at the outbreak of war in August 1914, and was immediately transferred to France, where he took part in the Retreat from Mons and the Battles of the Marne, The Aisne, La Bassée, Ypres and the Somme. In June 1917 he was badly gassed, and as a result invalided to hospital. Returning to the fighting area on his recovery he served through the Retreat and Advance of 1918. He was discharged in February 1919, and holds the Mons Star, and the General Service and Victory Medals.
Priory Street, Newport Pagnell, Bucks. Z3007.

HURST, F. A., Private, R.A.S.C.
He volunteered in 1915, and on conclusion of his training was retained on important duties with his unit in England. Owing to his being medically unfit he was unable to proceed to a theatre of war, but rendered valuable services until discharged in November 1918.
High Street, Somersham, Hunts. Z3008.

HURST, W. J., Private, 6th Bedfordshire Regiment.
When war was declared he was already serving, and at once proceeded to the Western Front, where he fought in the Battle of Mons. He also saw fierce fighting at Ypres, Beaumont-Hamel, Vimy Ridge, Arras, Cambrai and Armentières, and was unhappily killed in action on August 4th, 1918. He was entitled to the Mons Star, and the General Service and Victory Medals.
"Whilst we remember, the sacrifice is not in vain."
Cardington, Bedford. Z3009.

HUTCHESON, A. W., Pte., 2nd Devonshire Regt.
He volunteered in February 1915, and after a course of training at Exeter was drafted overseas four months later. During his service on the Western Front he took an active part in engagements in the Loos and Vimy Ridge sectors, and fell fighting on July 1st, 1916. He was entitled to the 1914–15 Star, and the General Service and Victory Medals.
"A costly sacrifice upon the altar of freedom."
Whaddon Road, Far Bletchley, Bucks. Z2896/B.

HUTCHINGS, F., Private, Bedfordshire Regiment.
He joined in February 1918, but was unable to obtain a transfer to a theatre of war before the cessation of hostilities. After the Armistice he was drafted to Germany and rendered valuable services with the Army of Occupation at Cologne until demobilised in December 1919.
24, Church Walk, Kempston, Beds. X3015/A.

HUTCHINGS, G., Private, Bedfordshire Regiment.
A month after the outbreak of war he volunteered, and in the following year was ordered to Gallipoli. In that theatre of war he saw service in numerous engagements, and fell gloriously on the Field of Battle at Suvla Bay on August 15th, 1915. He was entitled to the 1914–15 Star, and the General Service and Victory Medals.
"A valiant Soldier, with undaunted heart he breasted life's last hill."
30, Canning Street, Bedford. X3014/B.

HUTCHINGS, H., Private, Bedfordshire Regiment.
He volunteered in 1915, and on completion of his training was, in the same year, drafted to Egypt. Subsequently he was sent to Palestine, and on that front experienced fierce fighting in engagements at Gaza, Jerusalem, Haifa and Jaffa. He also served in Damascus, and on his return to England in August 1919 was demobilised, holding the 1914–15 Star, and the General Service and Victory Medals.
24, Church Walk, Kempston, Beds. X3015/C.

HUTCHINGS, J., Private, 2nd Bedfordshire Regt.
Mobilised at the outbreak of hostilities in August 1914, he was at once ordered to the Western Front, where he was in action in the Retreat from Mons. He also took an active part in numerous engagements, and fell fighting at Neuve Chapelle in March 1915. He was entitled to the Mons Star, and the General Service and Victory Medals.
"His life for his Country, his soul to God."
24, Church Walk, Kempston, Beds. X3015/B.

HUTCHINGS, K., Sapper, Royal Engineers.
He volunteered in November 1914, and in the following year proceeded to the Western Front. There he was in action in the Battles of Ypres, the Somme, Arras and Cambrai, and also did good work with a Field Company in the Retreat and Advance of 1918. After the Armistice he advanced into Germany with the Army of Occupation and served at Cologne until demobilised in July 1919, holding the 1914–15 Star, and the General Service and Victory Medals.
25, King's Place, Bedford. X3013.

HUTCHINGS, W., Sergeant, 3rd Bedfordshire Regt.
At the outbreak of hostilities he was already in the Army, but proving to be medically unfit for service overseas, was unsuccessful in his endeavours to obtain a transfer to the war zone. He was stationed at Felixstowe and employed on important clerical work, which he carried out in a very able manner until discharged in March 1917.
85, Woburn Road, Kempston, Beds. X3011.

HUTCHINGS, W., Private, Oxford. and Bucks. L.I.
He joined the Army in August 1918, but owing to the early cessation of hostilities, was unable to obtain a transfer to a theatre of war. He was retained on home defence and served at Dover and Tunbridge Wells, at which stations he fulfilled the duties assigned to him in a highly capable manner. In February 1919 he was demobilised.
12, Buckingham Street, Wolverton, Bucks. Z3012.

HUTCHINGS, W. C., Private, Bedfordshire Regt.
Joining in 1917, he proceeded on completion of his training to the Western Front in the same year. Whilst serving in France he took an active part in severe fighting in the Somme sector, but contracted bronchitis, and unfortunately died on February 1st, 1918. He was entitled to the General Service and Victory Medals.
"Thinking that remembrance, though unspoken, may reach him where he sleeps."
30, Canning Street, Bedford. X3014/A.

HUTCHINS, F., Private, Canadian Overseas Forces.
He volunteered in January 1916, and after a course of training was drafted overseas later in the same year. During his service on the Western Front he was in action at the Battles of the Somme, Arras, Ypres and Cambrai, and saw severe fighting in engagements at Neuve Chapelle and Armentières. Demobilised in February 1919, he holds the General Service and Victory Medals. Wootton, Beds. Z3016.

HUTT, W. G., L/Corporal, Oxford. and Bucks. L.I.
When war was declared in August 1914 he volunteered, and in April of the following year was drafted to the Western Front. After only two weeks' active service he was killed by a sniper at Ploegsteert Wood on April 27th, 1915. He was entitled to the 1914–15 Star, and the General Service and Victory Medals.
"He died the noblest death a man may die,
Fighting for God and right and liberty."
9, North End Square, Buckingham. Z3017/A.

HUTTON, F. C., Stoker, R.N., H.M.S. "Erin."
At the outbreak of hostilities in August 1914 he volunteered, and after completing his training was posted to H.M.S. "Chester." In that ship he took an active part in severe fighting in the Battles of Jutland and Heligoland, and was also engaged on submarine patrol duties in the North and Baltic Seas. He was still serving in the Navy in 1920, and holds the 1914–15 Star, and the General Service and Victory Medals.
1, Dunville Road, Queen's Park, Bedford. Z3018/B.

HUTTON, F. H., Private, Machine Gun Corps.
He joined in December 1917, and after a period of training was in the following year sent to France. On that front he saw severe fighting in the Arras and Cambrai sectors, and was wounded in the Battle of the Somme, which unfortunately resulted in the loss of his left leg. Consequently he was invalided out of the Army in September 1918, holding the General Service and Victory Medals.
1, Dunville Road, Queen's Park, Bedford. Z3018/A.

HYDE, G., Pte., Beds. Regt. and Labour Corps.
He volunteered in September 1914, but owing to ill-health, was unsuccessful in obtaining a transfer to the fighting area. He was retained on home defence, and engaged on important duties with his unit at various stations, and throughout the period of his service performed valuable work. He was eventually demobilised in March 1919.
24, Cobden Street, Bedford. X3021.

HYDE, J., Private, Labour Corps.
Joining in September 1916, he proceeded to the Western Front two months later. During his service in France he was present at fierce fighting in various sectors, and took an active part in operations on the Somme and at Armentières. After the cessation of hostilities he advanced into Germany with the Army of Occupation and served at Cologne until demobilised in May 1919. He holds the General Service and Victory Medals.
33, Foster Street, Bedford. X3022.

HYDE, T. W., Private, Oxford. and Bucks. L.I.
He joined the Army in June 1916, but proved to be medically unfit for service overseas. After performing valuable work with his unit at Cosham and Portsmouth, he was sent to Messrs. Thornycrofts' Munition Works at Southampton. He was employed there until his demobilisation in December 1918, and carried out his duties in a highly satisfactory manner.
19, School Street, New Bradwell, Bucks. Z3019.

HYDE, W. F., Private, 1st Bedfordshire Regiment.
Already serving when war broke out in August 1914, he was immediately ordered to France, and served in the Retreat from Mons. He also experienced fierce fighting in many other engagements, including the Battles of La Bassée, Festubert, the Somme and Arras, but was unhappily killed in action at Oppy Wood on June 28th, 1918. He was entitled to the Mons Star, and the General Service and Victory Medals.
"His life for his Country, his soul to God."
1, Vine Cottages, Bromham, Bedford. Z3020.

HYNES, G. H., Sergeant, Royal Fusiliers.
When war was declared in August 1914 he was serving in India, and in 1915 was drafted to Gallipoli. There he was in action in the Battles of Krithia, Suvla Bay and Chunuk Bair, and was wounded. In 1916 he was transferred to France, where he took a prominent part in engagements at Albert, the Somme, Ypres and Vimy Ridge, and was again wounded. He returned to England in 1918, and rendered valuable services as an Instructor at Hounslow. In 1920 he was still in the Army, and holds the 1914–15 Star, and the General Service and Victory Medals.
59, College Road, Bedford. Z3023.

I

IBBETT, A., Sergeant, R.A.S.C. (M.T.)
He volunteered in August 1914, and in the following year proceeded to the Western Front, where he served in various sectors. He was engaged chiefly in conveying troops to and from the forward areas at Ypres, the Somme, Arras, Cambrai, the Marne and many other places, and was twice wounded in action. He was demobilised in May 1919, and holds the 1914–15 Star, and the General Service and Victory Medals.
4, Foster Street, Bedford. X3046.

IBBETT, A. G., Gunner, R.G.A.
Shortly after joining in 1916 he proceeded to the Western Front, where he saw heavy fighting in various sectors and took part in the Battles of Arras, Messines, Passchendaele and Cambrai, and many other engagements. Severely gassed at Armentières, he unhappily died on April 17th, 1918, and was buried at Etaples. He was entitled to the General Servce and Victory Medals.
"He joined the great white company of valiant souls."
45, Pembroke Street, Bedford. Z3047/B.

IBBETT, F. W., A.B., Royal Navy.
He joined in 1917, and was posted to H.M.S. "Pembroke," on board which vessel he was engaged on various important duties. He was stationed chiefly at Chatham, where he rendered very valuable services until March 1919, when he was demobilised. 45, Pembroke Street, Bedford. Z3047/A.

IBBETT, J., Private, Northants. Regiment.
Joining in August 1916, he was drafted to Egypt on completing a period of training later in that year, and proceeded thence into Palestine. Whilst in this seat of operations he saw much severe fighting, and took part in the Battles of Gaza and the capture of Jaffa and Haifa, and other important engagements. He was demobilised on returning home in February 1919, and holds the General Service and Victory Medals.
Wistow, Hunts. Z3048.

IBBITT, F., Corporal, 4th Bedfordshire Regiment.
He volunteered in 1915, and after a period of training proceeded to the Western Front in the following year, and there saw much severe fighting in various sectors. Mortally wounded in action on the Somme, he unfortunately died on February 9th, 1917. He was entitled to the General Service and Victory Medals.
"A costly sacrifice upon the altar of freedom."
Station Road, Tempsford, near Sandy, Beds. Z2642/B.

IDE, A., Private, Royal Army Service Corps.
Shortly after joining in April 1916 he was sent to the Western Front, where he was engaged on important duties in various sectors. Later, however, he was transferred to Italy and there served on the Piave and the Asiago Plateaux until after the cessation of hostilities. He was demobilised on his return to England in February 1919, and holds the General Service and Victory Medals.
101, London Road, Newport Pagnell, Bucks. Z3049/A.

IDE, C., Private, Northamptonshire Regiment.
He volunteered in May 1915, and later in that year proceeded to the Western Front, where he saw severe fighting in various sectors. He took part in the Battles of Loos, the Somme, Arras, Ypres and Cambrai, and many other important engagements in this theatre of war. He was invalided from the Army in November 1918, suffering from neurasthenia, and holds the 1914–15 Star, and the General Service and Victory Medals. 101, London Rd., Newport Pagnell, Bucks. Z3049/B.

ILLING, L. T., Private, Machine Gun Corps.
He joined in October 1916, and five months later was drafted to the Western Front, where he took part in the Battles of Arras and Vimy Ridge and many other important engagements. He died gloriously on the Field of Battle on the Somme during the Retreat of March 1918. He was entitled to the General Service and Victory Medals.
"The path of duty was the way to glory."
62, St. Mary Street, New Bradwell, Bucks. TZ3050.

INGLEDEW, G. W. E., Private, Essex Regiment.
He joined immediately on attaining military age in July 1918, and shortly afterwards proceeded to the Western Front, where he saw much heavy fighting. He took part in many important engagements during the Advance of 1918, and afterwards served with the Army of Occupation in Germany, where he was stationed at Cologne. He was demobilised on returning home in January 1919, and holds the General Service and Victory Medals. 19, Westbourne Road, Bedford. Z3051.

INGREY, C. R., Sergeant, 8th Bedfordshire Regt.
He volunteered in September 1914, and in August of the following year was drafted to the Western Front, where he took part in the Battles of Loos, Vimy Ridge and the Somme. Invalided home in November 1916, he returned to France, however, in the following month and was again in action in the Battles of Cambrai and the Somme. He was three times wounded whilst overseas, and in 1920 was still with his unit, holding the 1914–15 Star, and the General Service and Victory Medals. Little Stukeley, Hunts. Z3053/B.

INGREY, F. (D.C.M.), Driver, R.A.S.C.
Mobilised in August 1914, he served in the Retreat from Mons and in the Battle of the Marne, and was wounded. Invalided from the Army in December 1914, he re-enlisted, however, and subsequently saw severe fighting in various sectors. He was awarded the D.C.M. for conspicuous bravery, and holds also the Mons Star and the General Service and Victory Medals. 3, Conquest Road, Bedford. Z3052.

INGREY, H. S., Private, Suffolk Regiment.
Joining in March 1916, he was drafted to the Western Front in July of that year, and there took part in many important engagements during the Advance on the Somme. He was unhappily reported missing, and later, killed in action near Loos on October 12th, 1916. He was entitled to the General Service and Victory Medals.
"His memory is cherished with pride."
Little Stukeley, Hunts. Z3053/C.

INGREY, T. H., Private, 8th Bedfordshire Regt.
He volunteered in January 1915, and was retained on important duties in England until July of the following year, when he proceeded to the Western Front. After taking part in the Somme Offensive he was wounded at Oppy Wood in June 1917 and was invalided home, but on his recovery returned to France. He was killed in action at Moeuvres on September 27th 1918. He was entitled to the General Service and Victory Medals.
"His life for his Country, his soul to God."
Little Stukeley, Hunts. Z3053/A.

INNS, H., C.S.M., Bucks. Cyclist Battalion.
Mobilised at the outbreak of war in August 1914, he was immediately drafted to the Western Front, where he fought in the Retreat from Mons. After taking a prominent part also in the Battles of the Marne, the Aisne, La Bassée, Ypres, Hill 60 and Loos, and other engagements, he was transferred in November 1917 to Italy, where he was in action on the Piave. Discharged on returning home in March 1919, he holds the Mons Star, and the General Service and Victory Medals.
8, Lenborough Road, Buckingham. Z3054.

INNS, T. A., Private, 7th Oxford. and Bucks. L.I.
He volunteered in December 1914, and in October of the following year proceeded to the Western Front, where he saw severe fighting. In November 1915, however, he was transferred to Salonika, and there took part in many important engagements on the Doiran and Vardar fronts, and was twice wounded in action. He returned home for demobilisation in March 1919, and holds the 1914–15 Star, and the General Service and Victory Medals. 18, Nelson Street, Buckingham. Z3055.

INSKIP, A. E., Driver, Royal Engineers.
Shortly after volunteering in September 1914 he was drafted to the Western Front, where he served in various sectors. He took an active part in the Battles of Ypres, Festubert, the Somme, Arras and Cambrai, and many other important engagements until the cessation of hostilities, and was for a short time in hospital at Cambridge in 1919, owing to injuries received whilst playing football. Demobilised in February 1919, he holds the 1914–15 Star, and the General Service and Victory Medals. High Road, Clapham, Bedford. Z3056.

INSKIP, P. W., L/Corporal, 2nd London Regiment (Royal Fusiliers).
Volunteering in May 1915, he proceeded to the Western Front in the following August, and there saw severe fighting in various sectors. After taking part in the Battles of Arras and Vimy Ridge and other engagements, he was reported missing in May 1917, but was afterwards discovered to be a prisoner of war in Germany. Released on the cessation of hostilities he was demobilised in December 1919, and holds the 1914–15 Star, and the General Service and Victory Medals.
The Warren, Clapham, Bedford. Z3058.

INSKIP, V., Private, Royal Defence Corps.
Volunteering in January 1916, he was drafted to the Western Front later in the same year and there saw much heavy fighting He took part in the Battles of Albert and the Somme, but after five months' active service was sent home and transferred to the Royal Defence Corps. He was afterwards retained on important duties in England until his demobilisation in 1919, and holds the General Service and Victory Medals.
Keeley Lane, Wootton, Bedford. Z3057.

INSKIP, W. J., Corporal, Royal Engineers.
Volunteering in August 1914, he proceeded to Egypt in the following year and was there engaged on duties of great importance at various stations. He also served in Palestine, where he was present at the Battles of Gaza. He contracted malaria and influenza, and unhappily died in hospital at Alexandria on November 12th, 1918, and was buried at Beyrout. He was entitled to the 1914–15 Star, and the General Service and Victory Medals.
"Steals on the ear the distant triumph song."
43, St. Leonard's Street, Bedford. X1665/A.

INWOOD, A. F., Private, Bedfordshire Regiment.
He volunteered in November 1915, and, after undergoing a period of training, was retained on important pioneer and clerical duties at various stations. He was unable, on account of ill-health, to obtain his transfer to a theatre of war, but, nevertheless, rendered valuable services with his unit until April 1917, when he was invalided from the Army.
63, Albert Street, Bedford. X3059.

INWOOD, B., Rifleman, 21st Rifle Brigade.
He volunteered in May 1915, and in January of the following year was drafted to Egypt, where he was engaged on police and garrison duties at Alexandria, Cairo and other stations. In 1918 he was transferred to India for similar duties at Madras and Delhi, finally returning home in 1919. He was demobilised in December of that year, and holds the General Service and Victory Medals.
60, Priory Street, Newport Pagnell, Bucks. Z3060.

IRELAND, C. G., Pte., 8th Oxford. & Bucks. L.I.
Volunteering in November 1914, he proceeded to the Western Front in September of the following year, and there saw much severe fighting. In January 1916, however, he was transferred to Salonika, where he took part in many important engagements on the Doiran and Vardar fronts until the cessation of hostilities. He was demobilised on his return home in March 1919, and holds the 1914–15 Star, and the General Service and Victory Medals.
Lathbury, Newport Pagnell, Bucks. Z3061.

IRONS, A. A., Sergt., 1st Hunts. Cyclist Battalion and Royal Warwickshire Regiment.
Having enlisted in May 1914, he was already in the Army when war broke out in the following August, and was retained on important duties in England until 1916. He was then drafted to the Western Front, where, after taking part in the Battle of Arras and other engagements, he was wounded and taken prisoner on the Somme in 1917. Held in captivity until after the cessation of hostilities, he was discharged in March 1919, and holds the General Service and Victory Medals.
Berckley Street, Eynesbury, St. Neots, Hunts. Z3062.

ISON, W. G., Sapper, Royal Engineers.
Volunteering in September 1914, he was drafted to the Western Front in the following month, and there served in various sectors. He took an active part in the Battles of La Bassée, Albert, the Somme and Passchendaele and other engagements, and in December 1917 was transferred to Italy. He was three times wounded whilst overseas—at Ypres in May 1915, at Loos in September of that year, and on the Piave in February 1918. He was demobilised in June 1920, and holds the 1914 Star, and the General Service and Victory Medals.
22, Newnham Lane, Goldington Road, Bedford. Z3063/B.

IVES, C., Driver, Royal Engineers.
He volunteered in October 1915, and, after completing a period of training, served at various stations, where he was engaged on duties of great importance. He was not successful in obtaining his transfer to the front on account of ill-health, but, nevertheless, rendered valuable services with his Company until September 1917, when he was invalided from the Army.
146, Bower Street, Bedford. Z2151/B.

IVES, C. G., Private, 2nd Bedfordshire Regiment and Essex Regiment.
He volunteered in November 1915, and in the following year proceeded to Palestine, where he saw much severe fighting. He took part in the entry into Jaffa and Jerusalem, and in many important engagements in this theatre of war, and was twice wounded in action. He holds the General Service and Victory Medals, and in 1920 was still with his unit in India.
54, Wellington Street, Bedford. X3066.

IVES, R., Private, 2nd Bedfordshire Regiment and Hertfordshire Regiment.
Joining in July 1917, he was drafted to the Western Front after three months' training and was there wounded in action near Cambrai in November of the same year. Invalided home, he returned to France, however, on his recovery in June 1918, and saw much severe fighting in the Somme and Cambrai sectors until the cessation of hostilities. He holds the General Service and Victory Medals, and in 1920 was still with his unit on garrison duty in India.
Grange Road, Blunham, Beds. Z2740/C—Z2741/C.

IVES, S. A., Sergeant, Royal Army Service Corps.
He joined in October 1916, and, after undergoing a period of training, was retained at various stations, where he was engaged on duties of a highly important nature. Being medically unfit for active service, he was not successful in obtaining his transfer to a theatre of war, but nevertheless rendered very valuable services until November 1919, when he was demobilised.
21, Gladstone Street, Bedford. X3065.

IVES, W., Private, 13th Hussars.
Already serving in India when war broke out in August 1914, he was shortly afterwards drafted to the Western Front, where he took part in the Battles of Ypres and Festubert, and other engagements. He was afterwards transferred to Mesopotamia, and was there present at the Relief of Kut, the capture of Baghdad, Tekrit and Mosul. He was discharged on returning home in June 1919, and holds the 1914–15 Star, and the General Service and Victory Medals.
7, Chandos Street, Bedford. X3064.

IVES, W. F. (Miss), Despatch Rider, Women's Legion.
Having previously been engaged on munition work at Messrs. Kent's Filling Factory, Luton, for 2½ years, she joined in May 1918. After undergoing a period of training she was retained at various stations, where she was engaged on important duties as a despatch rider attached to the Royal Engineers. She rendered valuable services until her demobilisation in February 1920. Grange Road, Blunham, Beds. Z2740/D—Z2741/D.

IVETT, A. C., Private, Hunts. Cyclist Battalion and Royal Army Veterinary Corps.
He volunteered in 1914, and, after his training, was retained on important duties in England until 1916, when he proceeded to the Western Front. There he saw severe fighting in various sectors and took part in the Battles of the Somme, Arras and Ypres, and other important engagements. He was invalided home in 1918 suffering from trench fever, and was finally demobilised in March of the following year, holding the General Service and Victory Medals. Little Stukeley, Hunts. Z3067/B.

IVETT, H. J., Private, Labour Corps.
He joined in July 1917, and, after serving with the 24th Training Reserve Battalion at various stations, was transferred to the Labour Corps. With this unit he was engaged on important agricultural work in Scotland, where he rendered very valuable services, being unable to obtain his transfer overseas on account of his youth and ill-health. He was demobilised in March 1919. Little Stukeley, Hunts. Z3067/A.

IZZARD, E. L., Driver, R.A.S.C.
He joined in June 1918, and, after a period of training, was retained on important transport duties at various stations. He was unable to obtain his transfer to a theatre of war on account of the early cessation of hostilities, but later proceeded with the Army of Occupation into Germany. He returned home in August 1919, and served in England until March of the following year, when he was demobilised.
The Green, Cardington, Bedford. Z3068.

IZZARD, F., Rifleman, Rifle Brigade.
He joined in November 1916, and was soon drafted to the Western Front, where he played a prominent part in the Battles of Ypres, the Somme (II.), the Aisne (III.) and Bapaume, and in other important engagements during the Retreat and Advance of 1918. He was wounded in action whilst overseas, and was eventually demobilised in November 1919, holding the General Service and Victory Medals.
56, Russell Street, Bedford. X3069/A.

IZZARD, S., Sapper, Royal Engineers.
He volunteered in March 1915 and, proceeding to France in 1917, was engaged on important trench-digging, wiring and tunnelling duties in the Arras, Ypres, Cambrai and Somme sectors. He rendered valuable services with his unit until demobilised in December 1919, and holds the General Service and Victory Medals.
56, Russell Street, Bedford. X3069/B.

J

JACKLIN, W., Private, Machine Gun Corps.
Volunteering in October 1914, he was drafted to France in the following year, and took part in the Battles of Hill 60, Festubert, Loos and the Somme, where he was wounded in action in 1916. In 1917 he was transferred to Palestine, and saw heavy fighting at Gaza and Haifa and throughout the Advance of General Allenby's Forces. He was demobilised in 1919, and holds the 1914–15 Star, and the General Service and Victory Medals. 49, Russell Street, St. Neots, Hunts. Z3071.

JACKLIN, W. F., Corporal, 2nd Beds. Regt.
He volunteered in September 1914, and, after being drafted to France, played a prominent part in the Battles of the Somme, Arras, Ypres and Cambrai, and in heavy fighting at Thièpval, Armentières and Albert. He was twice wounded in action—at Ypres in 1917, and at Albert in the following year—on which occasion he was invalided home. Eventually demobilised in February 1919, he holds the 1914–15 Star, and the General Service and Victory Medals.
Little Raveley, Hunts. Z3070.

JACKMAN, E. G., Pte., Australian Overseas Forces.
Volunteering in Melbourne in August 1914, he landed in France eight months afterwards. Whilst on the Western Front he took part in the Battles of Ypres, the Somme, Arras and Cambrai. Twice wounded in action—on the Somme in 1916, and at Cambrai in 1917—he was invalided home on each occasion. He was eventually demobilised in March 1919, and holds the 1914–15 Star, and the General Service and Victory Medals. Drayton Parslow, Bucks. Z3072/A.

JACKMAN, H. J., Driver, R.A.S.C.
He joined in June 1918, and, after a period of training at Dublin, was sent to France two months later and saw much heavy fighting during the Advance, particularly in the Somme sector. Later he served at Cologne with the Army of Occupation until his return home for demobilisation in February 1920. He holds the General Service and Victory Medals.
Drayton Parslow, Bucks. Z3072/B

JACKSON, A. T., Pte., 5th Oxford. and Bucks. L.I.
Volunteering in December 1914, he was retained in England for some considerable time, but was ultimately sent to France in July 1916. After being twice wounded in action on the Somme he laid down his life for King and Country at the Battle of Ypres (III.) in August 1917. He was entitled to the General Service and Victory Medals.
"He joined the great white company of valiant souls."
Bow Brickhill, near Bletchley, Bucks. Z3075/A.

JACKSON, C., Private, 2nd Bedfordshire Regiment.
Mobilised at the outbreak of war, he was quickly drafted to France and took part in the Retreat from Mons and in other important engagements. Badly wounded in action at the Battle of Hill 60 on April 26th, 1915, he unfortunately died from his wounds the next day. He was entitled to the Mons Star, and the General Service and Victory Medals.
"His life for his Country, his soul to God."
Great Paxton, Hunts. Z3078.

JACKSON, C. J., Pte., 4th Bedfordshire Regiment.
He volunteered in April 1915, and proceeded to France nine months later, but was wounded in action during the Somme Offensive and invalided home. On his recovery he returned to the Western Front, took part in the Battles of Arras, Ypres, Passchendaele and Cambrai, and was wounded on three other occasions. He was eventually demobilised in June 1919, and holds the General Service and Victory Medals.
Station Road, Tempsford, near Sandy, Beds. Z3073/A.

JACKSON D., Pte., 21st West Yorkshire Regt.
He joined in June 1916, and was quickly drafted to France, where he played an important part in the Battles of the Somme, Arras, Ypres and Cambrai, and in the Retreat of 1918. He was badly wounded in action at Amiens in August 1918, and invalided home. After hospital treatment at Dundee he was discharged as medically unfit in February 1919, and holds the General Service and Victory Medals.
Station Road, Warboys, Hunts. Z2823/B.

JACKSON, F. J., Sapper, Royal Engineers.
He volunteered in December 1914, and in the following July was drafted to the Western Front, where he took part in heavy fighting in the Ypres and Somme sectors. In 1916 he was transferred to Egypt, but, proceeding into Palestine, was in action at Gaza. Unfortunately he contracted malarial fever, from which he died on November 12th, 1918. He was entitled to the 1914–15 Star, and the General Service and Victory Medals.
"A costly sacrifice upon the altar of freedom."
Bow Brickhill, near Bletchley, Bucks. Z3075/B.

JACKSON, H., Sapper, Royal Engineers.
Volunteering in August 1914, he was soon drafted to the Western Front, where he took a prominent part in the Battles of Ypres (I.), Loos, the Somme, Arras and Vimy Ridge. He was badly gassed in action at Ypres and invalided home, and, after protracted hospital treatment, was discharged as medically unfit for further service in May 1919. He holds the 1914–15 Star, and the General Service and Victory Medals.
32, Dunville Road, Queen's Park, Bedford. Z3076.

JACKSON, H. T., Sergeant, 2nd Queen's (Royal West Surrey Regiment).
Mobilised at the outbreak of war, he proceeded to France in August 1914, and took part in the Retreat from Mons and the Battles of the Marne, Hill 60 and Festubert. Badly wounded in action at Hill 60, he spent eight months in hospital at Boulogne, but on his recovery rejoined his unit and served with distinction at the Battles of the Somme, Arras, Ypres and Cambrai. He received his discharge in February 1919, and holds the Mons Star, and the General Service and Victory Medals. Warboys, Hunts. Z3079.

JACKSON, S. E., Saddler, M.G.C. (Cavalry).
Volunteering in August 1914, he was first engaged on important duties transporting horses to France. In 1916 he was sent to Mesopotamia, where he saw heavy fighting at Amara and Kut-el-Amara. He afterwards proceeded to India, and served against the Afghans during the risings on the North West Frontier. He was demobilised in October 1919, and holds the 1914–15 Star, and the General Service and Victory Medals, and the India General Service Medal (with Clasp, Afghanistan, North West Frontier, 1919).
4, School Street, New Bradwell, Bucks. Z3074.

JACKSON, S. E., Pte., 2nd R. Warwickshire Regt.
He joined in May 1918, and, proceeding to the Western Front in the following August, took part in heavy fighting on the Somme and at Havrincourt before being badly wounded in action in September and invalided home. On his recovery he was sent to India, and was stationed at Klanspur in 1920. He holds the General Service and Victory Medals.
Station Road, Tempsford, near Sandy, Beds. Z3073/C.

JACKSON, W. A., Pte., 4th Bedfordshire Regt.
He volunteered in December 1915, and, proceeding to France in the following year, was engaged as a transport driver with his unit. Whilst on the Western Front he took an important part in the Battles of the Somme, Arras, Messines, Ypres and Cambrai. He was demobilised in March 1919, and holds the General Service and Victory Medals.
Station Road, Tempsford, near Sandy, Beds. Z3073/B.

JACKSON, W. H., Private, Oxford. & Bucks. L.I.
He joined in July 1918, and two months later was sent to France, where he was engaged with the transport section of his unit and took part in heavy fighting in the Ypres and Cambrai sectors. In 1919 he was sent to Palestine, and was stationed at Damascus until his demobilisation in March 1920, holding the General Service and Victory Medals.
Station Road, Tempsford, near Sandy, Beds. Z3077.

JACOB, A. O., Driver, Royal Horse Artillery.
He volunteered in November 1915, and eight months afterwards was drafted to Egypt. Later he proceeded into Palestine with General Allenby's Forces and took part in the Battles of Gaza and in heavy fighting along the Jordan Valley. Unfortunately he contracted pneumonia and died on February 10th, 1919. He was entitled to the General Service and Victory Medals.
"His memory is cherished with pride."
17, Stukeley Road, Huntingdon. Z3080/A.

JACOB, C. R. W. O., Saddler, R.A.O.C.
He volunteered in August 1914, and, proceeding to France in January 1915, rendered valuable services as a saddler with a travelling workshop in the Somme sector and at Abbeville, Calais and Rouen. He unfortunately contracted influenza, and died in hospital at Le Havre on February 12th, 1919. He was entitled to the 1914–15 Star, and the General Service and Victory Medals.
"Steals on the ear the distant triumph song."
17, Stukeley Road, Huntingdon. Z3080/B.

JACOB, J. C., Sergeant, Gloucestershire Regiment.
He volunteered in the Royal Army Veterinary Corps in November 1915, but, after rendering valuable services as a saddler with this unit, was transferred to the Gloucestershire Regiment. He did not succeed in serving overseas, but did excellent work until August 1918, when he was taken seriously ill. After four months in hospital at Ashington he was discharged as medically unfit in December of the same year.
17, Stukeley Road, Huntingdon. Z3080/C.

JACOB, L. F., Bombardier, R.H.A.
He volunteered in November 1915, and was drafted to France five months later. During his service on the Western Front he played a prominent part with his Battery in the Battles of the Somme, Arras and Cambrai, and in other important engagements. He was demobilised in March 1919, and holds the General Service and Victory Medals.
17, Stukeley Road, Huntingdon. Z3080/D.

JACQUEST, B. M. (Miss), Member, W.R.A.F.
This lady first offered her services to Messrs. Allens, of Bedford, and was engaged on important duties in the aero viewing-room, from 1917 to 1918. She then joined the Women's Royal Air Force, and did excellent work as a lady clerk until her demobilisation in 1918.
Fish Farm, Milton Ernest, Bedford. Z3081/F—Z3082/F.

JACQUEST, E., Private, R.M.L.I.
He joined in August 1918 on attaining military age, and, after a period of training, rendered valuable services at Portsmouth. In 1920 he was still serving with the Bedfordshire Regiment.
Fish Farm, Milton Ernest, Bedford. Z3081/D—Z3082/D.

JACQUEST, G. F., Pte., British Red Cross Society.
Being medically unfit for service in a fighting unit, he joined the No. 3 Detachment of the British Red Cross Society in May 1916, and did excellent work as a night orderly at Bedford Military Hospital until July 1918.
Fish Farm, Milton Ernest, Bedford. Z3081/B—Z3082/B.

JACQUEST, S. C., Sergeant, R.A.V.C.
He volunteered in October 1914, and, proceeding to Egypt in the following year, did excellent work in connection with the treatment of sick and wounded horses. Later he was sent to Palestine, and served at Gaza, Jaffa and Jerusalem. He was demobilised in April 1919, and holds the 1914–15 Star, and the General Service and Victory Medals.
Fish Farm, Milton Ernest, Bedford. Z3081/C—Z3082/C.

JACQUEST, W., L/Cpl., 9th Leicestershire Regt.
He volunteered in September 1914, and was drafted to France on completion of his training. After taking part in the Battles of Festubert and Loos he was badly wounded in action during the Somme Offensive in 1916, and was invalided home. In May 1917 he was discharged as medically unfit for further service, and holds the 1914–15 Star, and the General Service and Victory Medals.
Fish Farm, Milton Ernest, Bedford. Z3081/E—Z3082/E.

JACQUEST, W. H., Private, Hertfordshire Regt.
Volunteering in May 1915, he was sent to France ten months later, but, after being in action at Albert and on the Somme, was invalided home in November 1916. He unfortunately died from pneumonia and pleurisy on July 28th, 1917, and was entitled to the General Service and Victory Medals.
"His memory is cherished with pride."
Fish Farm, Milton Ernest, Bedford. Z3081/A—Z3082/A.

JAKEMAN, W. T., Gunner, Royal Field Artillery.
He volunteered in November 1915, and was drafted to France four months later. Whilst on the Western Front he took part in the Battles of the Somme (I.), Arras, Ypres and the Somme (II.), the Retreat and Advance of 1918, and was gassed in action. He was demobilised in February 1919, and holds the General Service and Victory Medals.
37, Silver Street, Stony Stratford, Bucks. Z3083.

JAKINS, P., Private, 4th Bedfordshire Regiment.
Volunteering in 1914, he was sent to the Western Front after completing his training, and took part in the Battles of the Somme, Arras, Ypres and Cambrai. He was badly wounded in action whilst overseas, and was discharged as medically unfit for further service in March 1918, holding the 1914–15 Star, and the General Service and Victory Medals.
Huntingdon Street, St. Neots, Hunts. Z3084.

JAMES, A., Trooper, Bedfordshire Lancers.
He volunteered in May 1915, and later in the same year was sent to France, where he saw heavy fighting at Loos, Festubert, Arras and Hill 60. In 1917 he was transferred to Palestine, but, after taking part in the Battles of Gaza and the capture of Haifa, returned to the Western Front and saw service there until the cessation of hostilities. He was demobilised in 1919, and holds the 1914–15 Star, and the General Service and Victory Medals.
St. Anne's Road, Godmanchester, Hunts. Z3086/B.

JAMES, C. E., Sergeant, Tank Corps.
He volunteered in August 1914, and was retained on special duties in England until 1916, when he proceeded to France with the Tank Corps. Whilst on the Western Front he served with distinction at the Battles of the Somme, Arras, Ypres and Cambrai, and in other sectors. He was demobilised in March 1919, and holds the General Service and Victory Medals.
27, Commercial Road, Bedford. Z3087.

JAMES, G. O., Rifleman, K.R.R.C.
He volunteered in 1915, and in January 1916 was drafted to the Western Front, where he took part in much severe fighting before being unhappily killed in action during the Somme Offensive on July 23rd, 1916. He was entitled to the General Service and Victory Medals.
"Nobly striving:
He nobly fell that we might live."
Stow Longa, Hunts. Z3085/B.

JAMES, H. G., Private, Royal Welch Fusiliers; and Sapper, Royal Engineers.
Although under military age, he volunteered in the Royal Engineers in September 1914, but was retained on important duties in England for some time. Eventually he was sent to France with the Royal Welch Fusiliers, took part in the Battles of Ypres, Lens, Cambrai and the Somme (II.), and in heavy fighting at Loos and Festubert, and was wounded in action. He was demobilised in February 1919, and holds the General Service and Victory Medals.
Fairfield Cottages, Clapham, Bedford. Z3089.

JAMES, H. W., Private, 2nd Bedfordshire Regiment.
He joined in March 1916, and three months later was drafted to the Western Front, but, after taking part in an engagement at Ypres, was unfortunately killed in action on the Somme on July 23rd, 1916. He was entitled to the General Service and Victory Medals.
"He died the noblest death a man may die,
Fighting for God and right and liberty."
Stow Longa, Hunts. Z3085/A.

JAMES, T. H. P., Private, Bedfordshire Regiment.
He volunteered in October 1915, and in the following year was drafted to France, where he took part in the Battles of the Somme, Arras and Ypres. In 1917 he was invalided home with severe injuries, but on his recovery was transferred to the Labour Corps, and engaged on important agricultural work. He was demobilised in March 1919, and holds the General Service and Victory Medals.
East Street, Godmanchester, Hunts. Z3088.

JAMES, W. A., Guardsman, 1st Grenadier Guards.
A serving soldier, he was drafted to the Western Front in August 1914, and fought through the Retreat from Mons. He also took part in the Battles of La Bassée and Ypres, where he was seriously wounded in action in November 1914. After six months in hospital he was discharged as medically unfit for further service, and holds the Mons Star, and the General Service and Victory Medals.
St. Anne's Road, Godmanchester, Hunts. Z3086/A

JAMIESON, G., Private, Essex Regiment.
He volunteered in September 1914, and, on completion of his training, was retained on special duties at various Home stations. Owing to his being medically unfit he was not drafted to a theatre of war, but did excellent work until his demobilisation in March 1919. Harrold Road, Lavendon, Bucks. Z3090.

JANES, T. W., Private, Bedfordshire Regiment.
He volunteered in the Huntingdonshire Cyclist Battalion in June 1915, but was later transferred to the Bedfordshire Regiment, and sent to France in May 1916. Whilst in this theatre of war he took part in much severe fighting, particularly on the Somme and at Ypres and Lens. He was demobilised in February 1919, and holds the General Service and Victory Medals.
Tilbrook, Hunts. Z3091

JARVIS, A., Guardsman, Grenadier Guards.
Volunteering in February 1915, he was sent to France in the following January, and saw severe fighting in the Givenchy sector. He died gloriously on the Field of Battle during the Somme Offensive on September 25th, 1916, and was entitled to the General Service and Victory Medals.
"Honour to the immortal dead, who gave their youth that the world might grow old in peace."
37, Prebend Street, Bedford. Z3092.

JARVIS, D. G., L/Corporal, Suffolk Regiment.
He volunteered in August 1914, and proceeded to France in the following year. After taking a prominent part in the Battles of Ypres, Festubert, Loos, Vimy Ridge and the Somme he was badly wounded in action at the Battle of Arras in April 1917, and invalided home. He was discharged as medically unfit for further service in February 1918, and holds the 1914–15 Star, and the General Service and Victory Medals.
Wellington Lane, St. Ives, Hunts. Z3095/B.

JARVIS, F. J., Private, 7th Oxford. and Bucks. L.I.
He volunteered in September 1914, but, owing to his being medically unfit for transfer overseas, was retained on special duties at various Home stations on completion of his training. He rendered valuable services with his unit until his demobilisation in February 1919.
99, London Road, Newport Pagnell, Bucks. Z3094/B.

JARVIS, G. F. J. (M.C.), Lieut., 9th W. Yorks. Regt.
He was mobilised with the 5th Reserve of Cavalry in August 1917, and in the following April was drafted to Egypt, where he served in the ranks at Kantara and on the Suez Canal. In May 1916 he returned to England to train for his commission, and was eventually sent to France in March 1917. Whilst on the Western Front he was attached to the West Yorkshire Regiment as transport officer, took part in the Battles of Arras, Ypres and Cambrai, but was unfortunately killed in action near Cambrai on September 28th, 1918. He had been awarded the Military Cross for distinguished bravery and devotion to duty in the Field, and was also entitled to the 1914–15 Star, and the General Service and Victory Medals.
"His life for his Country, his soul to God."
1, West Street, Olney, Bucks. Z3093.

JARVIS, G. W., Sergeant, Oxford. and Bucks. L.I.
He was mobilised in August 1914, and in the following year proceeded to France, where he played a prominent part in the Battles of Loos and the Somme. He suffered from trench feet, and was invalided home, but on his recovery was transferred to Mesopotamia, and again saw much fighting at Kut, Amara, on the Tigris, and at the capture of Baghdad. He returned home and was discharged in March 1919, and holds the 1914–15 Star, and the General Service and Victory Medals.
Wellington Lane, St. Ives, Hunts. Z3095/A.

JARVIS, H., Trooper, Bedfordshire Lancers.
He volunteered in April 1915, and in the following year was drafted to France, where he served for a short time and then proceeded to Egypt. Later he took part in the Advance into Palestine, and saw much fighting at Gaza, Haifa and Jaffa. He returned home and was demobilised in February 1919, holding the General Service and Victory Medals.
99, London Road, Newport Pagnell, Bucks. Z3094/A.

JEEVES, C. A., L/Corporal, 2nd K.O. (Y.L.I.)
He volunteered in September 1914, and in the following July was drafted to France, where he fought at the Battles of Ypres and Loos. He died gloriously on the Field at the Battle of the Somme on July 1st, 1916. He was entitled to the 1914–15 Star, and the General Service and Victory Medals.
"Thinking that remembrance, though unspoken, may reach him where he sleeps."
2, Ewelme Terrace, Chalton, near Sandy, Beds. Z1626/A.

JEEVES, F. A., Private, Queen's (Royal West Surrey Regiment).
He joined in February 1917, and later in the same year was drafted to the East and saw much service in Palestine and Syria. After hostilities ceased he was engaged on various important duties at Cairo and Alexandria, and was employed there until his demobilisation in May 1920. He holds the General Service and Victory Medals.
Ewelme Terrace, near Blunham, Beds. Z3097.

JEEVES, E. C. (M.S.M.), Staff-Sergeant, R.A.M.C.
He volunteered in September 1914, and in the following July proceeded to the Western Front. There he played a distinguished part in the Battles of Loos, the Somme, Ypres, Albert and Cambrai, and was promoted to Staff-Sergeant on the Field. He was awarded the Meritorious Service Medal for conspicuous work and devotion to duty in June 1918. He was demobilised in March 1919, and holds also the 1914–15 Star, and the General Service and Victory Medals.
37, High Street, Bexley, Kent. Z3096/B.

JEEVES, F. W., Private, 11th Suffolk Regiment.
He joined in August 1916, and in the following April was drafted to the Western Front. Whilst in this theatre of war he took part in much heavy fighting at the Battles of Arras, Messines, Ypres, Cambrai and the Somme (II.), and was gassed in March 1918. As a result he was invalided home, but on his recovery returned to France and was again in action until hostilities ceased. He was demobilised in September 1919, and holds the General Service and Victory Medals.
Ivy Cottages, Blunham, Beds. Z3096/A.

JEEVES, H., Private, Royal Army Service Corps.
Volunteering in April 1915, he was drafted overseas in the following year. During his service on the Western Front he was engaged in various sectors on important duties with the Remount Section until he was taken ill. He was discharged in February 1918 as medically unfit for further service, and holds the General Service and Victory Medals.
2, Ewelme Terrace, Chalton, near Sandy, Beds. Z1626/C.

JEEVES, M., Private, Machine Gun Corps.
He joined in February 1916, and in the following year was drafted to Egypt and proceeded thence into Palestine, where he fought at Gaza and Jaffa. He was invalided home, but on his recovery was sent to France and took part in much fighting in the Somme sector. After hostilities ceased he went to Germany with the Army of Occupation and served on the Rhine until his demobilisation in September 1919. He holds the General Service and Victory Medals.
Seddington, near Sandy, Beds. Z3098/A.

JEEVES, S. H., Trooper, Bedfordshire Lancers.
He volunteered in September 1914, but, whilst in training, was discharged in January 1915. He re-enlisted in January 1916 and quickly proceeded to France, where he took part in much fighting in the Somme, Ypres, Arras, Messines and Albert sectors. After the Armistice he went to Germany with the Army of Occupation, and was there attached to Cavalry Headquarters, and served until his demobilisation in May 1919. He holds the General Service and Victory Medals.
Seddington, near Sandy, Beds. Z3098/B.

JEEVES, W. T., Trooper, Essex Dragoons.
He joined in May 1917, and, completing his training in the following year, was drafted to the Western Front. After a few months' heavy fighting he made the supreme sacrifice, being killed during a night raid on June 22nd, 1918. He was entitled to the General Service and Victory Medals.
"He died the noblest death a man may die,
Fighting for God and right and liberty."
5, George Town, Sandy, Beds. Z3099.

JEFFERIES, B., Driver, R.A.S.C.
He joined in February 1917, and later in the same year was drafted to France. In this theatre of war he took an active part in engagements in the Somme and Arras sectors, and during the Retreat and Advance of 1918. After hostilities ceased he went to Germany with the Army of Occupation and served on the Rhine until his demobilisation in 1920. He holds the General Service and Victory Medals.
The Warren, Clapham, Bedford. Z3104/A.

JEFFERIES, F. J., Pioneer, Royal Engineers.
He volunteered in June 1915, and, after a period of training, was engaged at various stations on important duties as a signaller. He was not successful in obtaining a transfer overseas, but rendered valuable services until his demobilisation in November 1919. 64, St. John's, Bedford. Z3100/B.

JEFFERIES, L., Sapper, Royal Engineers.
He volunteered in June 1915, and later in the same year was drafted to the East. In this seat of operations he took part in the Advance into Palestine, and saw much fighting at Gaza, Haifa, Jaffa and the capture of Jericho and Damascus. He was demobilised in September 1919, holding the 1914–15 Star, and the General Service and Victory Medals.
64, St. John's, Bedford. Z3100/A.

JEFFERY, A. J., Gunner Petty Officer, R.N.
He was already in the Royal Navy when war broke out in August 1914, and immediately proceeded to sea on board H.M.S. "Iron Duke." He was engaged with the Grand Fleet in the North Sea, and took part in the Battle of Jutland, but later was sent to Whale Island for a course of gunnery. He then put to sea on board H.M.S. "Winson," in which vessel he saw much service in Russia, and did continuously good work throughout hostilities. In 1920 he was still serving at Portsmouth Harbour, and holds the 1914–15 Star, and the General Service and Victory Medals.
44, Northwood End, Haynes, near Bedford. Z3108/A.

JEFFERY, H. C., L/Corporal, Bedfordshire Regt.
He volunteered in September 1914, and, after a period of training, was engaged at various stations on important duties with his unit. He was unable to obtain a transfer overseas owing to his being medically unfit, but rendered valuable services until his demobilisation in March 1919.
Cold Brayfield, Beds. Z3107.

JEFFERY, J., Sergeant, Royal Marine Artillery.
He was already in the Army when war broke out in August 1914, having previously served in India. He was retained at home in charge of steamboats at Portsmouth, and did continuously good work throughout hostilities, rendering valuable services until his discharge in April 1919.
44, Northwood End, Haynes, near Bedford. Z3108/B.

JEFFREY, H. J., Private, R.A.S.C.
He joined in May 1918, and underwent a period of training prior to his being drafted to Russia. There he saw much active service at Archangel, Murmansk, Bakaritza, Obserskaya and Bolzerska, and was also engaged on various important duties. He was demobilised in September 1919, and holds the General Service and Victory Medals.
10, Denmark Street, Bedford. Z3106.

JEFFRIES, A., Private, 7th Bedfordshire Regt.
He volunteered in 1915, and underwent a period of training prior to his being drafted to the Western Front. There he took part in much heavy fighting in the Arras, Ypres and Somme sectors, and was wounded. He died gloriously on the Field near Beaucourt on September 10th, 1916, and was entitled to the 1914–15 Star, and the General Service and Victory Medals.
"Nobly striving:
He nobly fell that we might live."
Ivel Road, Sandy, Beds. Z3105/B.

JEFFRIES, E. C., Private, Bedfordshire Regiment.
He joined in February 1916, and underwent a period of training prior to his being drafted to France. In this theatre of war he took part in the Battles of Arras, Ypres, Messines, Albert and Cambrai, and was twice wounded in action, being finally invalided home in August 1918. He was demobilised in March 1919, and holds the General Service and Victory Medals.
Park Lane, Blunham, Beds. Z3101.

JEFFRIES, R. (D.C.M.), Sergt., 1st Beds. Regt.
He was already in the Army when war broke out in August 1914, and immediately proceeded to France, where he fought in the Retreat from Mons and at the Battles of the Marne and Festubert. He was badly wounded and invalided home, but on his recovery returned to France, and was again wounded in action and sent to Sheffield Hospital. Later he rejoined his unit, and during heavy fighting captured a German machine-gun which was cutting his men down, for which gallant deed he was awarded the Distinguished Conduct Medal. He was unhappily killed in action on October 23rd, 1918, on the Selle, and was also entitled to the Mons Star, and the General Service and Victory Medals.
"A valiant Soldier, with undaunted heart he breasted life's last hill."
Ivel Road, Sandy, Beds. Z3105/A.

JEFFRIES, S., Private, Middlesex Regiment.
He joined in June 1916, and later in the same year was drafted to France. Whilst in this seat of war he took part in many engagements, including the Battles of the Somme, Ypres and Arras. He was badly wounded in the Somme sector in May 1917, and consequently invalided home. He was finally discharged in December 1918 as medically unfit for further service. He holds the General Service and Victory Medals.
Blunham, Beds. Z3102.

JEFFRIES, W., Bombardier, R.F.A.
He joined in March 1916, and later in the same year proceeded to Mesopotamia, where he took part in engagements at Kut, Amara, and at the capture of Baghdad. He then saw service in Egypt for a time before being transferred to France in April 1918. He saw much heavy fighting, and was wounded in action at Vimy Ridge, and later near Mons on November 10th, 1918. He was demobilised in March 1919, and holds the General Service and Victory Medals.
Wyboston, near St. Neots, Beds. TZ3103.

JEFFRIES, W. C., Private, Machine Gun Corps.
Volunteering in September 1914, he was drafted overseas in the following year. Whilst on the Western Front he took part in many engagements, including the Battles of Ypres, the Somme, Arras, Passchendaele, Cambrai, Loos and Lens. He was taken ill and invalided home, and finally demobilised in December 1919. He holds the 1914–15 Star, and the General Service and Victory Medals.
The Warren, Clapham, Bedford. Z3104/B.

JEFFS, C., Corporal, Royal Army Medical Corps.
He volunteered in September 1915, and, after a short period of training, was drafted to Egypt, whence he proceeded into Palestine and saw much fighting. Later he was transferred to Salonika, and took part in engagements on the Doiran and Struma fronts. He did continuously good work throughout as a stretcher-bearer and in the hospitals, and was demobilised in April 1919. He holds the 1914–15 Star, and the General Service and Victory Medals.
37, High Ash, Great Brickhill, Bucks. Z2919/B.

JEFFS, S., Private, Bedfordshire Regiment.
He was mobilised in August 1914, and immediately drafted to France, where he took part in much heavy fighting in the Battles of Mons and Ypres. He laid down his life for King and Country in 1915, and was entitled to the Mons Star, and the General Service and Victory Medals.
"A costly sacrifice upon the altar of freedom."
6, James Street, Bedford. Z3109/B.

JEFFS, W., Private, Bedfordshire Regiment.
He volunteered in 1914, and underwent a period of training prior to his being drafted to France, where he took part in much heavy fighting, and was wounded at Hill 60. He made the supreme sacrifice, being killed in action in 1916, and was entitled to the 1914–15 Star, and the General Service and Victory Medals.
"Great deeds cannot die:
They with the sun and moon renew their light for ever."
6, James Street, Bedford. Z3109/A.

JELLIE, P., Private, Lancashire Regiment.
He joined in February 1917, and later in the same year was drafted to France. In this theatre of war he took part in much fighting on the Somme and the Aisne, at Bapaume and in the Retreat and Advance of 1918. After hostilities ceased he went to Germany with the Army of Occupation, and served on the Rhine until his demobilisation in January 1920. He holds the General Service and Victory Medals.
Ellington, Hunts. Z3110.

JIGGLES, J., Private, Bedfordshire Regiment.
He volunteered in October 1915, and in the following year proceeded to France, where he saw much fighting in the Arras, Ypres, Somme and Cambrai sectors. He suffered from trench feet and was in hospital for some time, but on his recovery returned to the forward areas, and was engaged in guarding German prisoners. He was demobilised in 1919, and holds the General Service and Victory Medals.
Marston, Beds. TZ3112.

JOHNS, F. T. (M.C.), Captain, Royal Engineers.
He volunteered early in 1915, and later in the same year was sent to the Western Front, where he served with distinction at the Battles of Hill 60, Ypres, Loos and Arras. He was engaged for a time with the Special Gas Section of the Royal Engineers, and was accidentally gassed. For conspicuous gallantry and devotion to duty in bringing a trench-mortar into action in an open field under heavy shell-fire at Boesinghe, he was awarded the Military Cross. He also holds the 1914–15 Star, and the General Service and Victory Medals, and was demobilised in February 1919.
152, Howbury Street, Bedford. Z3114.

JOHNS, P., Corporal, Bedfordshire Regiment.
He volunteered in September 1914 in the Huntingdonshire Cyclist Battalion, but was later transferred to the Bedfordshire Regiment and sent to France. Whilst on the Western Front he took part in the Battles of Loos, Vimy Ridge, the Somme and Arras, and was wounded in August 1916, and again in April 1917, and was evacuated to hospital in England. After a period of hospital treatment he was invalided out of the Army in March 1919, and holds the General Service and Victory Medals. Warboys, Hunts. Z3113.

JOHNSON, A. (Mrs.), Member, V.A.D.
This lady volunteered for work of National importance in 1918, and was engaged as a nurse at Brampton Hospital, where she rendered excellent services in attending to sick and wounded soldiers until the conclusion of the war.
Thrapston Road, Brampton, Hunts. Z3131/E.

JOHNSON, A., Private, South Wales Borderers.
He joined in August 1916, and later in the same year proceeded to France, where he took part in many important engagements in various sectors of the front. He was in action during the Somme Offensive and in the Battles of Arras, Vimy Ridge, Passchendaele, Messines and Cambrai. After the cessation of hostilities he returned home and was demobilised in February 1919, holding the General Service and Victory Medals. Hilton, Hunts. Z3123.

JOHNSON, A. J., Private, Bedfordshire Regiment.
He volunteered in November 1915, and after completing a period of training was sent to France. In the course of his service in this theatre of war he took an active part in the Battles of the Somme and Ypres, and was wounded at Arras in April 1917. As a result he was invalided home and finally discharged as medically unfit for further military service in June 1918. He holds the General Service and Victory Medals.
Wyton, Huntingdonshire. Z3138.

JOHNSON, A. J., Corporal, Royal Engineers.
He volunteered in January 1915, and on conclusion of his training in the following year proceeded to Egypt. During his service in this theatre of war he took an active part in the Advance into Palestine, and was present at the Battles of Gaza and also in the capture of Jaffa and Jerusalem. After the close of war he returned home and was demobilised in July 1919, holding the General Service and Victory Medals.
22, Bedesmans Place, Bedford. X3132.

JOHNSON, B., Private, 3rd Bedfordshire Regt.
He volunteered in September 1914, and early in the following year proceeded to France. Whilst in this seat of hostilities he saw much heavy fighting in various sectors of the front, being in action at the Battles of Hill 60, Festubert, Ypres and Bapaume, and was twice wounded. On the conclusion of war he went with the Army of Occupation into Germany and served at Cologne until returning home for demobilisation in February 1920. He holds the 1914–15 Star, and the General Service and Victory Medals.
Mill Road, Buckden, Hunts. Z3139/A.

JOHNSON, B., Private, Hunts. Cyclist Battalion; and Trooper, Bedfordshire Lancers.
Volunteering in August 1914, he proceeded in the following February to France, where he took part in much heavy fighting in various sectors. He served at Neuve Chapelle, Givenchy, Loos and Albert, and was wounded in February 1916. On his recovery he was in action on the Somme, and later in the Battles of Arras, Ypres and Cambrai, and was also present during the Retreat and Advance of 1918. He was demobilised in February 1919, and holds the 1914–15 Star, and the General Service and Victory Medals.
West End, Somersham, Hunts.
Z3134/G—Z3135/G—Z3136/G.

JOHNSON, C., Sergeant, Oxford. and Bucks. L.I.
Mobilised in August 1914, he was retained at Portsmouth as an Instructor before proceeding to Mesopotamia. Whilst in this theatre of war he served with distinction in many important engagements and was wounded during the heavy fighting at Kut in April 1916. As a result he was sent to England and finally invalided out of the Army in July 1916, and holds the General Service and Victory Medals.
94, Wolverton Road, Stony Stratford, Bucks. Z3124.

JOHNSON, C., Private, 23rd Middlesex Regiment.
He joined in October 1918, and remained at home for a few months. He was then sent to Germany with the Army of Occupation, but returning home in November 1919, he was stationed at various stations in England until his demobilisation in March 1920. 81, Garfield Street, Bedford. Z3129.

JOHNSON, C. S. A., Private, 1st Middlesex Regt.
He joined in January 1917, and two months later landed in France, where he fought in various sectors of the front. He was in action at the Battles of Arras, Ypres and Passchendaele, and was wounded and invalided to the Base. Returning to the fighting area on his recovery he took part in the Battle of Cambrai, and was again wounded. As a result he was sent to England, and after a period of treatment was finally discharged as medically unfit for further service in June 1918, and holds the General Service and Victory Medals.
Renhold Road, Wilden, near Bedford. Z3128.

JOHNSON, D., Sergeant, Bedfordshire Regiment.
He was mobilised at the outbreak of war in August 1914, and immediately drafted to France, where he served with distinction during the Retreat from Mons and the Battles of the Marne, Hill 60 and Festubert, and was wounded at Loos. Later he took part in the heavy fighting at Arras and was again wounded and invalided to England. He was afterwards proved to be medically unfit for military service and was retained in England on important clerical duties until demobilised in February 1919, holding the Mons Star, and the General Service and Victory Medals. Hilton, Hunts. Z3137.

JOHNSON, E., Private, Bedfordshire Regiment.
Volunteering at the outbreak of hostilities in August 1914, he completed a period of training and was sent to Egypt, where he served for a few months. Later he was transferred to the Dardanelles, and took part in the Landing at Suvla Bay, and also in the Evacuation of the Gallipoli Peninsula, but was wounded and invalided to England. After a period of hospital treatment he was discharged as medically unfit for further military service in 1916, and holds the 1914–15 Star, and the General Service and Victory Medals.
West End, Cranfield, Beds. TZ1286/A.

JOHNSON, E. J., Sapper, Royal Engineers.
He volunteered in August 1914 in the Bedfordshire Regiment, and was later drafted to France, where he took part in the Battles of Hill 60, Festubert, and was wounded and invalided home. In 1916 he was transferred to the Royal Engineers, and sent to Egypt. He was in action during the Advance into Palestine, and later took part in the Battles of Gaza and other important engagements until the close of hostilities. He was demobilised in September 1919, and holds the 1914–15 Star, and the General Service and Victory Medals.
Mill Road, Buckden, Hunts. Z3139/B.

JOHNSON, F., Private, Royal Defence Corps.
He volunteered in October 1914, and on the conclusion of his training was retained on important duties with his unit. He was chiefly engaged in escorting prisoners of war from France to England, and also in the guarding of bridges, and rendered valuable services until demobilised in March 1918. He holds the General Service and Victory Medals.
1, Tower Court, Bedford. X3125/A.

JOHNSON, F., Driver, Royal Engineers.
Volunteering in September 1914, he completed his training and proceeded to the Dardanelles. Whilst in this seat of hostilities he saw much heavy fighting, and took part in the Landing in Gallipoli and other important engagements until the Evacuation of the Peninsula. Later he went to Egypt and saw much service, particularly in Palestine at the capture of Jerusalem. In 1917 he was invalided home suffering from fever, and was finally discharged in June 1918, and holds the 1914–15 Star, and the General Service and Victory Medals.
Biddenham, Bedford. Z3119.

JOHNSON, F. C., Pte., 1st Hunts. Volunteer Bn.
He volunteered in 1915, and on completion of his training was retained on important guard and other duties with his unit at various stations. He rendered valuable services throughout the period of hostilities, and was demobilised in 1919.
West End, Somersham, Hunts. Z3134/F—Z3135/F—Z3136/F.

JOHNSON, F. E. (Miss), Worker, Women's Land Army.
Prior to joining the Women's Land Army in July 1918, this lady had rendered valuable services on various farms since 1915. Throughout the war she did excellent work in connection with agriculture, and in 1920 was still engaged in a similar capacity.
West End, Somersham, Hunts. Z3134/C—Z3135/C—Z3136/C.

JOHNSON, F. J., Private, Oxford. and Bucks. L.I.
He was already serving with the Colours at the outbreak of war and was later drafted to France, where he took part in the Battles of Hill 60, Ypres and Loos. In March 1916 he was sent to England, and discharged as time-expired, but he later re-enlisted in the Royal Air Force, and was retained on important duties at various stations. He was demobilised in February 1919, and holds the 1914–15 Star, and the General Service and Victory Medals.
29, Cambridge Street, Wolverton, Bucks. Z3118.

JOHNSON, F. W., Pte., Wiltshire Regt. & R.A.O.C.
He volunteered in November 1915, and in December of the following year proceeded to the Western Front, where he was engaged on transport duties in various sectors. Gassed at Messines, he was invalided home in October 1917, and was afterwards retained in England until his demobilisation in September 1919. he holds the General Service and Victory Medals.
12, Pilcroft Road, Bedford. X3121.

JOHNSON, G., Colour-Sergt., 14th East Surrey Regt.
He rejoined in January 1918, and was retained at various stations, where he was engaged on duties of great importance as an Instructor. He was not successful in his efforts to obtain his transfer to a theatre of war, but nevertheless rendered valuable services with his unit until March 1919, when he was demobilised.
Thrapston Road, Brampton, Hunts. Z3131/F.

JOHNSON, G. V., Private, 3rd Bedfordshire Regt.
Volunteering in September 1914, he was sent to the Western Front in the following year and there saw severe fighting in various sectors. He took part in the Battles of Ypres, Festubert, Loos and Arras, and many minor engagements, and was three times wounded in action—on the Somme in 1916, and on another occasion, and at Albert in 1918. He was invalided from the Army in that year and holds the 1914–15 Star, and the General Service and Victory Medals.
Mill Road, Buckden, Hunts. Z3139/C.

JOHNSON, H., Corporal, Royal Engineers.
Mobilised in August 1914, he was drafted to the Western Front in the following month and there took part in many important engagements until wounded in action near Ypres in December 1914. He was invalided from the Army in June of the following year, but in August 1917, re-enlisted and was retained at various stations in England until finally demobilised in January 1919. He holds the 1914 Star, and the General Service and Victory Medals.
21, Grey Friars Walk, Bedford. X3126.

JOHNSON, H. C., L/Cpl., Northumberland Fusiliers.
Already in the Army when war was declared in August 1914, he was immediately drafted to the Western Front, where, after serving through the Retreat from Mons, he took part in the Battles of Ypres and Festubert. In July 1915 he was transferred to Gallipoli, and there saw severe fighting at Suvla Bay, afterwards proceeding to Salonika, where he served on the Vardar and Doiran fronts. Wounded in action he was sent home and invalided from the Army in June 1917, and holds the Mons Star, and the General Service and Victory Medals. 7, Pilcroft Street, Bedford. X3122.

JOHNSON, J. W., L/Corporal, Norfolk Dragoons (The King's Own Royal Regiment).
Volunteering in August 1914, he was drafted to the Western Front in February of the following year, and there saw much heavy fighting. After taking part in the Battles of Hill 60, Ypres, Loos, the Somme, Arras and Cambrai, and many other important engagements, he was severely wounded in action in July 1918, and admitted to hospital in England. Invalided from the Army in the same year, he holds the 1914–15 Star, and the General Service and Victory Medals.
Somersham, Hunts. Z3134/H—Z3135/H—Z3136/H.

JOHNSON, J. W., Private, R.A.S.C.
He joined in April 1918, and after undergoing a period of training, was retained on important duties at various stations. He was medically unfit for service overseas, and was consequently unable to obtain his transfer to the front, but nevertheless rendered valuable services with his Company until his demobilisation in October 1919.
6, Shakespeare Terrace, Huntingdon. Z3133.

JOHNSON, M. (Miss), Worker, Q.M.A.A.C.
She volunteered in 1915, and after completing a term of training served at various stations, where she was engaged on duties of great importance as a postwoman. She rendered very valuable services during her 4½ years with her unit, and was finally demobilised in 1920.
West End, Somersham, Hunts. Z3134/E—Z3135/E—3136/E.

JOHNSON, M. (Miss), Special War Worker.
For 2½ years during the period of hostilities, this lady was engaged on work of National importance. Employed by the Hammersmith Tramway Corporation as a conductress, she rendered very valuable services until she relinquished her duties in 1919.
West End, Somersham, Hunts. Z3134/D—Z3435/D—Z3136/D.

JOHNSON, P., Private, Bedfordshire Regiment.
Having enlisted in January 1914, he was already in the Army when war broke out in August of that year, and in the following January proceeded to the Western Front, where he took part in the Battles of Neuve Chapelle and Hill 60. He fell fighting at Festubert on August 16th, 1915. He was entitled to the 1914–15 Star, and the General Service and Victory Medals.
"A costly sacrifice upon the altar of freedom."
Thrapston Road, Brampton, Hunts. Z3131/B.

JOHNSON, R., Private, Royal Irish Fusiliers and Royal Army Veterinary Corps.
Mobilised in August 1914, he was drafted to the Western Front in the following year and there saw severe fighting in various sectors. After taking part in the Battles of Ypres, Festubert and Loos, and many minor engagements, he was wounded in action on the Somme in 1916, and invalided home. On his recovery, however, he was retained on important duties with the Royal Army Veterinary Corps, until discharged in April 1919, and holds the 1914–15 Star, and the General Service and Victory Medals. 1, St. Benedict's Court, Huntingdon. Z3115/B.

JOHNSON, S., Driver, R.A.S.C.
Volunteering in May 1915, he was sent to the Western Front in the following September, and was there engaged on important duties with the Remount Section at Le Havre and Dieppe. He was also present at the Battles of Loos and the Somme, and was wounded in January 1916, and at Albert in March of the following year. He was afterwards attached to the Military Foot Police at Wimereux, and later served with the Army of Occupation at Cologne. Returning home in July 1920 he was demobilised in August, and holds the 1914–15 Star, and the General Service and Victory Medals.
West End, Somersham, Hunts. Z3134/B—Z3135/B—Z3136/B.

JOHNSON, S. J., Pte., 1st Royal Berkshire Regt.
He volunteered in December 1914, and in June of the following year proceeded to France, where he saw severe fighting in various sectors of the front. He took part in the Battles of Loos, the Somme, Vimy Ridge and Ypres, and many other important engagements in this theatre of war, and was wounded in action. Demobilised in February 1919, he holds the 1914–15 Star, and the General Service and Victory Medals.
7, Napier Street, Bletchley, Bucks. Z3130.

JOHNSON, T. K., Private, 1/12th Middlesex Regt.
He volunteered in July 1915, and in April of the following year was drafted to the Western Front, where he saw severe fighting in the Ypres sector until invalided home in August 1916, suffering from trench fever. On his recovery, however, he proceeded to the East in H.M.T. "Tyndareus," which struck a mine off Cape Agulhas, fortunately without loss of life. He was afterwards engaged on garrison duties in China and India until his return home in November 1919 for demobilisation in the following month. He holds the General Service and Victory Medals.
Station Grove, Woburn Sands, Beds. Z3117.

JOHNSON, T. W., Private, R.A.V.C.
He joined in May 1916, and after a period of training, was retained at various stations in England until September 1918. He was then drafted to Mesopotamia, where he was engaged in tending the wounded horses and on important clerical duties at Baghdad, Amara, and many other places. He returned home for demobilisation in April 1919, and holds the General Service and Victory Medals.. Park Lane, Sharnbrook, Beds. Z3116.

JOHNSON, W., Private, Royal Warwickshire Regt.
He volunteered in September 1914, and on completing his training in the following year, was drafted to the Western Front. Whilst in this theatre of war he took part in many important engagements, including the Battles of Loos, Albert and Vimy Ridge, and was twice wounded in action on the Somme—in 1916 and in 1918. He was invalided from the Army in March 1918, and holds the 1914–15 Star, and the General Service and Victory Medals. Thrapston Rd., Brampton, Hunts. Z3131/A.

JOHNSON, W., Sergeant, Bedfordshire Regiment.
Having enlisted in March 1913, he was drafted to the Western Front immediately on the outbreak of war in August of the following year, and there fought in the Retreat from Mons. After taking a prominent part also in the Battles of the Aisne, Ypres, Neuve Chapelle, Festubert and Loos, he was wounded in December 1915, and invalided home. On his recovery, however, in October 1916, he returned to France, and attached to the Transport Section served on the Somme and at Arras and Cambrai. Discharged in May 1919, he holds the Mons Star, and the General Service and Victory Medals.
West End, Somersham, Hunts. Z3134/A—Z3135/A—Z3136/A.

JOHNSON, W., Private, 3rd Northants. Regiment.
He volunteered in October 1914, and, after undergoing a period of training, was retained at various stations, where he was engaged on duties of great importance. Unable, owing to ill-health, to obtain his transfer to the front, he nevertheless rendered very valuable services with his unit. He unhappily died of influenza in October 1918.
"His memory is cherished with pride."
128, High Street, Stony Stratford, Bucks. TZ2958/B.

JOHNSON, W. A. (D.C.M.), L/Corporal, Bedfordshire, and Cheshire Regiments.
He volunteered at the outbreak of war in August 1914, and was retained on important duties in England until 1916, and then proceeded to the Western Front, where he took part in the Battles of Albert, the Somme, Arras and Cambrai. He fell in action at Bray on May 23rd, 1918. He had been awarded the Distinguished Conduct Medal for conspicuous bravery displayed in capturing a German gun and taking prisoners in January 1918, and was also entitled to the General Service and Victory Medals.
"And doubtless he went in splendid company."
124, Bower Street, Bedford. Z3120.

JOHNSON, W. S., Private, 1/5th Bedfordshire Regiment and 2/19th London Regiment.
Volunteering in November 1914, he underwent a period of training, but in January of the following year was invalided from the Army. He re-enlisted, however, in 1917, and shortly afterwards proceeded to Egypt and thence took part in the Advance into Palestine, where he was present at the Battles of Gaza, and at the entry into Jaffa. Discharged on his return home in 1919, he holds the General Service and Victory Medals. Church Road, Wilden, near Bedford. Z3127.

JOLLEY, H., Private, Oxford. and Bucks. L.I.
Mobilised in August 1914, he was immediately drafted to the Western Front, where he served through the Retreat from Mons. After taking part also in the Battles of the Marne, the Aisne, Ypres and Loos, he was wounded in action on the Somme in 1916, and invalided home. On his recovery, however, he returned to France in time to fight in the Retreat and Advance of 1918. He was discharged in March 1919, and holds the Mons Star, and the General Service and Victory Medals. 13, Agusta Rd., Stony Stratford, Bucks. TZ3141/B.

JOLLEY, A. G., Private, Bedfordshire Regiment and Hertfordshire Regiment.
He joined in October 1916, and, after completing a period of training, was retained at various stations, where he was engaged on duties of a highly important nature. He was not successful in obtaining his transfer to a theatre of war, but nevertheless rendered valuable services with his unit until November 1919, when he was invalided from the Army.
Church Street, Buckden, Hunts. Z3140.

JOLLEY, H., Gunner, Royal Field Artillery.
He joined in June 1916, and after undergoing a period of training, was engaged on duties of great importance at various stations. He was unable to obtain his transfer to a theatre of war on account of ill-health, but in December 1918 was sent with the Army of Occupation into Germany, where he served at Cologne. He was demobilised on returning home in March 1919. 13, Agusta Road, Stony Stratford, Bucks. TZ3141/A.

JONES, A. (D.C.M.), L/Corporal, 7th Beds. Regt.
He volunteered in August 1914, and in the following year, proceeded to the Western Front, where he took a prominent part in the Battles of Ypres, Vimy Ridge and Messines, and other engagements. In 1917 he was transferred to Egypt, and advancing into Palestine, was present at the entry into Jaffa. He was twice wounded whilst overseas, and was awarded the Distinguished Conduct Medal for conspicuous bravery in rescuing a wounded officer under heavy fire in January 1916. Holding also the 1914–15 Star, and the General Service and Victory Medals, he was demobilised on his return home in March 1919. Bank Houses, Somersham, Hunts. Z3145.

JONES, A. G., Gunner, Royal Garrison Artillery.
He volunteered in November 1914, and was stationed at Yarmouth and Woolwich. He was unhappily taken ill and sent to hospital at Woolwich, where he died of consumption on April 29th, 1915. 6, London Row, Clapham, Bedford. Z3166.

JONES, A. L., Bugle-Major, 2nd Oxford. & Bucks. L.I.
Mobilised in August 1914, he was drafted to France in the following year, and there saw severe fighting in various sectors of the front. He took a distinguished part in the Battles of Ypres, Festubert, Loos, Albert, the Somme, Arras and Cambrai, and many other important engagements until the cessation of hostilities. He was discharged in January 1919, and holds the 1914–15 Star, and the General Service and Victory Medals.
39, Oxford Street, Wolverton, Bucks. Z3158.

JONES, A. W., Private, 6th Oxford. & Bucks. L.I.
He volunteered in September 1914, and in June of the following year was drafted to the Western Front, where he took part in the Battles of Loos and Albert, and many minor engagements. Mortally wounded in action at Ypres, he unhappily died on July 2nd, 1916. He was entitled to the 1914–15 Star, and the General Service and Victory Medals.
"A valiant Soldier, with undaunted heart he breasted life's last hill."
Duck Lake, Maids Moreton, Buckingham. Z3152.

JONES, C., Private, 6th Oxford. and Bucks. L.I.
Volunteering in September 1914, he was sent to the Western Front in March of the following year, and there saw much severe fighting, taking part in the Battle of Ypres and other engagements. He died gloriously on the Field of Battle on the Somme on October 7th, 1916. He was entitled to the 1914–15 Star, and the General Service and Victory Medals.
"Great deeds cannot die:
They with the sun and moon renew their light for ever."
Church Street, Maids Moreton, Buckingham. Z3155.

JONES, E. W., Cpl., 9th Northumberland Fusiliers.
He joined in August 1916, and on completing his training in the following year, proceeded to the Western Front. Whilst in this theatre of war he took part in many important engagements, including the Battles of Arras, Cambrai and the Somme, was gassed and wounded in action and suffered also from dysentery. He was demobilised in November 1919, and holds the General Service and Victory Medals.
33, High Street, Kempston, Bedford. Z3160.

JONES, E. W., Sergeant, Bedfordshire Regiment.
He volunteered in June 1915, and in February of the following year proceeded to the Western Front, where he saw severe fighting in various sectors. He took a prominent part in the Battles of Albert, the Somme, Arras, Vimy Ridge, Ypres, Cambrai, Amiens and Le Cateau, and minor engagements, and served also through the Retreat and Advance of 1918. Demobilised in April 1919, he holds the General Service and Victory Medals.
Stow Brickyard, near Kimbolton, Hunts. Z3144/B.

JONES, F., Pte., Bedfordshire & Hampshire Regts.
He volunteered in August 1914, and in October of the following year was drafted to the East. After taking part in the first landing at Salonika, he served through several important engagements on the Vardar front, and was wounded in action in December 1915. Returning home, he was invalided from the Army in August 1916, and holds the 1914–15 Star, and the General Service and Victory Medals.
3, Millbrook Road, Bedford. Z1949/C.

JONES, F., Private, 1st Bedfordshire Regiment.
He volunteered in 1915, and, on completing his training in the following year, was drafted to the Western Front, where he took part in the Battles of the Somme, Arras, Ypres and Cambrai, and other important engagements. He fell fighting on June 14th, 1918. He was entitled to the General Service and Victory Medals.
"He died the noblest death a man may die,
Fighting for God and right and liberty."
Roxton, Beds. Z3149.

JONES, G., Pte., Hunts. Cyclist Battalion & M.G.C.
After volunteering in August 1914, he was retained in England until August 1916, and was then drafted to India, where he was engaged on garrison duties at various stations. In February 1917 he was transferred to Mesopotamia, and thence, in April of the following year, to Palestine, where he saw much severe fighting. He unhappily died of pneumonia on November 8th, 1918. He was entitled to the General Service and Victory Medals.
"He joined the great white company of valiant souls."
The Green, Great Staughton, Hunts. Z3146/B.

JONES, G. E., Pte. (Signaller), 8th Beds. Regt.
Volunteering in September 1914, he was sent to the Western Front in July of the following year and there took part in the Battle of the Somme and many other important engagements. Mortally wounded in action at Cambrai, he unfortunately died on December 12th, 1917, and was buried at Le Tréport. He was entitled to the 1914–15 Star, and the General Service and Victory Medals.
"Whilst we remember, the sacrifice is not in vain."
15, Shakespeare Place, Huntingdon. Z1084/B.

JONES, G. P., Corporal, 11th (Prince Albert's Own) Hussars.
He was already in the Army when war broke out in August 1914, and was immediately drafted to France, where he fought at the Battle of Mons and in the subsequent Retreat before being badly wounded in action at Neuve Chapelle. As a result he was invalided home, but on his recovery returned to France, and was again in action. He suffered from trench feet and was sent home to hospital, where he remained for about two months. Later he was transferred to the Tank Corps with which he served until his discharge in March 1919. He holds the Mons Star, and the General Service and Victory Medals.
Maids Moreton, Buckingham. Z3154.

JONES, H., Private, Bedfordshire Regiment.
He was mobilised in 1914, and in the following year was drafted to the Dardanelles, where he took part in much severe fighting, including the Landing at Suvla Bay, and was wounded in action. After the Evacuation of the Gallipoli Peninsula, he was engaged on important duties until his discharge in March 1918. He holds the 1914–15 Star, and the General Service and Victory Medals. 9, Farrer Street, Bedford. X3159.

JONES, H., Private, 1st Bedfordshire Regiment.
He was mobilised in August 1914, and quickly proceeded to France, where he took part in the Retreat from Mons, and the Battles of Ypres, Hill 60, Albert, Arras, Passchendaele and Cambrai. Early in 1918 he was transferred to Italy, and took part in much fighting on the Piave. He returned home and was discharged in February 1919, holding the Mons Star, and the General Service and Victory Medals.
59, Albert Street, Bedford. X1692/B.

JONES, H. T., Private, Duke of Cornwall's L.I.
He joined in July 1918, and underwent a period of training prior to his being sent to Ireland, where he was engaged on important duties. In September 1919 he proceeded to India, and served on garrison duties. He then went to Mesopotamia, where in 1920 he was still serving.
4, Brooklands Road, Bletchley, Bucks. Z3143.

JONES, H. W., Bombardier, R.G.A.
He joined the Army in 1912, and when war broke out in August 1914, was serving in India. He was quickly drafted to France and took part in the Battles of Ypres, Loos, the Somme, Arras and Passchendaele. He was invalided home, but on his recovery was engaged on important duties until his discharge in December 1918. He holds the 1914–15 Star, and the General Service and Victory Medals.
Firs Farm Cottage, Old Stratford, Bucks. Z3142.

JONES, J., Bugler, 1st Oxford. and Bucks. L.I.
Volunteering in September 1914, he was drafted overseas after a short period of training. Whilst on the Western Front, he took part in many important engagements, including those in the Ypres, Arras and the Somme sectors. He was invalided home in 1916, but on his recovery proceeded to India, where he served until his demobilisation in August 1919. He holds the 1914–15 Star, and the General Service and Victory Medals.
4, High Street, New Bradwell, Bucks. Z3157.

JONES, J., Private, Machine Gun Corps.
He volunteered in 1915, but was retained at home for some time on various important duties, being medically unfit to proceed overseas until March 1918. Whilst on the Western Front he saw much fighting at Le Cateau, Cambrai and Albert, and was gassed in action. He was demobilised in March 1919, and holds the General Service and Victory Medals.
50, Grey Friars Walk, Bedford. X3148.

JONES, J., Private, Machine Gun Corps (Cavalry).
Volunteering in October 1915, he proceeded to France later in the same year. During his service on the Western Front he took part in engagements in many sectors, including those of Lens, Loos, Ypres, Cambrai, the Somme, Messines and Vimy Ridge. He was discharged in April 1918, and holds the General Service and Victory Medals.
Green End Road, Great Barford, Beds. Z3162.

JONES, J., Private, 8th Bedfordshire Regiment.
He volunteered in March 1915, and two months later was drafted to France. In this seat of war he took part in many engagements, including the Battles of Loos, Ypres and the Somme, and was badly wounded in November 1916. As a result he was invalided home, and finally discharged in November 1917 as medically unfit for further service. He holds the 1914–15 Star, and the General Service and Victory Medals.
77, Grey Friars Walk, Bedford. X3164.

JONES, J. J., Cpl., Royal Army Medical Corps.
He volunteered in December 1914, and in the following April was drafted to the Western Front. There he was engaged as a stretcher-bearer, and took part in the Battles of the Somme (where he was wounded), Arras, Ypres and Cambrai. He did continuously good work, and was demobilised in February 1919, holding the 1914–15 Star, and the General Service and Victory Medals. Wistow, Hunts. Z3163.

JONES, J. J., L/Cpl., R.A.M.C. & Middlesex Regt.
He volunteered in August 1914, and was retained for a time at home stations on important duties. In 1916 he proceeded to France, and took part in engagements at Vimy Ridge, the Ancre and Arras, where he was taken prisoner in April 1917. He was held in captivity in Germany and suffered many hardships during his imprisonment. He was released after the Armistice, returned home, and was demobilised in February 1919. He holds the General Service and Victory Medals.
55, College Road, Bedford. Z3161.

JONES, O. W., Private, 1/5th Suffolk Regiment.
He joined in April 1917, and in the following June was drafted to Egypt. In this seat of operations he took part in the Advance into Palestine, saw much fighting at Gaza, Jaffa and on the Jordan, and was present at the capture of Jerusalem and Jericho. He returned home, and was demobilised in November 1919, holding the General Service and Victory Medals.
4, Albert Street, Bedford. X3147.

JONES, P., Private, Suffolk Regiment.
He joined in June 1918, and underwent a short period of training prior to his being drafted to the Western Front. There he took part in the final engagements of the war in the Somme, Arras and Ypres sectors. He was demobilised in March 1919, and holds the General Service and Victory Medals.
The Green, Great Staughton, Hunts. Z3146/A.

JONES, R., Private, 6th Oxford. and Bucks. L.I.
He volunteered in March 1915, and in the following year proceeded to France, where he took part in the Battle of the Somme and was wounded. As a result he was invalided home, but on his recovery returned to France, and saw much fighting at Ypres, and was again wounded. He was sent home to hospital, and later was engaged on important work at various Home stations until his demobilisation in January 1919. He holds the General Service and Victory Medals.
Maids Moreton, Buckingham. Z3156.

JONES, S. H., Sergeant, Royal Defence Corps.
He volunteered in October 1914, and being over age to proceed to a theatre of war did continuously good work at home. He was engaged on important guard duties at Cranwell Prisoner of War Camp, on agricultural work at Hereford, and various other important duties in Bedford. He was discharged in March 1918. 42, Muswell Road, Bedford. Z3150.

JONES, T., Private, 8th Royal Berkshire Regiment.
He joined in March 1918, and three months later was drafted to France, where he took part in much heavy fighting on the Somme. He died gloriously on the Field of Battle in the Somme sector on September 4th, 1918, and was entitled to the General Service and Victory Medals.
"Honour to the immortal dead, who gave their youth that the world might grow old in peace."
Duck Lake, Maids Moreton, Buckingham. Z3152/B.

JONES, T. (M.M.), Gunner, Royal Field Artillery.
He was mobilised in August 1914, and quickly proceeded to France, where he took part in the Retreat from Mons and the Battle of Ypres. He was then transferred to the Dardanelles, and saw much severe fighting at the Landing at Gallipoli and Suvla Bay. After the Evacuation of this Peninsula he returned to France and played a distinguished part in the Battle of the Somme, and was wounded. He was awarded the Military Medal for conspicuous gallantry and devotion to duty on the Field, but was invalided home and discharged in December 1917 as medically unfit for further service. He holds also the Mons Star, and the General Service and Victory Medals. 12, Derby Street, Bedford. X1864/B.

JONES, W., Sergeant, Oxford. & Bucks. L.I. (T.F.)
He volunteered in September 1914, and in the following March was drafted to France, where he took part in much heavy fighting in many sectors, including that of Ploegsteert Wood. He made the supreme sacrifice, being killed in action at Hébuterne on August 23rd, 1916, and was entitled to the 1914–15 Star, and the General Service and Victory Medals.
"His life for his Country, his soul to God."
Maids Moreton, Buckingham. Z3151.

JONES, W., Driver, R.A.S.C. (M.T.)
He joined in September 1916, and later in the same year proceeded to France. There he served with the Caterpillar Section on important duties in the Somme, Arras, Cambrai and Amiens sectors. He was chiefly employed in taking guns into position at night, and did excellent work throughout. He was demobilised in June 1919, and holds the General Service and Victory Medals.
105, Coventry Road, Bedford. Z3165.

JONES, W., L/Corporal, Machine Gun Corps.
He volunteered in July 1915, and completing his training in the following year, was drafted to France, where he took part in much heavy fighting on the Somme, at St. Eloi and Albert. He was invalided home medically unfit for further service abroad, and served on the land until his demobilisation in March 1919. He holds the General Service and Victory Medals.
Stow Brickyard, near Kimbolton, Hunts. Z3144/A.

JONES, W. B., Private, 1st Gloucestershire Regt.
He joined in March 1917, and after his training served at various stations on important duties. After hostilities ceased he proceeded to Germany with the Army of Occupation, and served on the Rhine for some time. Later he was sent to Ireland, and in 1920 was stationed at Cork.
Maids Moreton, Buckingham. Z3153/A.

JONES, W. J., Private, 2nd Oxford. and Bucks. L.I.
He volunteered in September 1914, and in the following year was drafted to France, where he took part in much heavy fighting at the Battles of Festubert, Hill 60, Loos, the Somme, Vimy Ridge and Beaumont-Hamel. He made the supreme sacrifice, being killed in action on the Ancre front on March 1st, 1917, and was entitled to the 1914–15 Star, and the General Service and Victory Medals.
"A valiant Soldier, with undaunted heart he breasted life's last hill."
Paggs Court, Silver Street, Newport Pagnell, Bucks. Z2727/A.

JONES, W. T., Private, Machine Gun Corps.
He joined in September 1917, and after his training was engaged at various stations on important duties. Later he proceeded to France and took part in much heavy fighting at Cambrai and on the Somme. He holds the General Service and Victory Medals, and in 1920 was still in the Army.
Maids Moreton, Buckingham. Z3153/B.

JORDAN, A., Private, R.A.S.C. (M.T.)
Volunteering in October 1915, he was drafted overseas in the following year. Whilst on the Western Front he served with the Mechanical Transport and saw much fighting in the Arras, Ypres, Neuve Chapelle, the Somme and Cambrai sectors. He was demobilised in August 1919, and holds the General Service and Victory Medals.
2, Cromwell Square, Huntingdon. Z3169.

JORDAN, G., Private, 1st Gordon Highlanders.
He joined in March 1916, and completing his training in three months was drafted to France, where he took part in much severe fighting on the Somme. He died gloriously on the Field near La Bassée on September 12th, 1916, and was entitled to the General Service and Victory Medals.
"Whilst we remember, the sacrifice is not in vain."
8, Ouse Walk, Huntingdon, Hunts. Z3168/A.

JORDAN, R., Private, 5th King's Liverpool Regt.
He was mobilised in August 1914, and was retained on important duties at various Home stations until March 1918, when he was drafted to France. There he took part in several engagements in the La Bassée and Festubert sectors, and was slightly gassed in August 1918. He was demobilised in March 1919, and holds the General Service and Victory Medals.
8, Ouse Walk, Huntington, Hunts. Z3168/B.

JORDAN, S. W., Corporal, Bedfordshire Regiment.
He volunteered in 1914, and in the following year proceeded to France, where he took part in engagements in the Ypres, Arras and Somme sectors, and was wounded. As a result he was invalided home, but on his recovery returned to France. He there saw much fighting at Vimy Ridge, Ypres, Passchendaele and Cambrai, was wounded on two other occasions, and also gassed. He was demobilised in 1919, and holds the 1914–15 Star, and the General Service and Victory Medals.
High Street, Carlton, Beds. Z3167.

JOYCE, G., Corporal, Machine Gun Corps.
He volunteered in November 1914, and after completing his training proceeded to Egypt, thence to the Dardanelles where he saw much fighting at the landing at Gallipoli. Later he returned to Egypt, took part in the Advance into Palestine, and was in action at Gaza, Jaffa and the capture of Jerusalem. He also saw service in Salonika, and was demobilised in July 1919, holding the 1914–15 Star, and the General Service and Victory Medals.
30, Churchville Road, Bedford. Z3170/B.

JOYCE, S., Sapper, Royal Engineers.
He volunteered in September 1914, and on completing his training was drafted to France, where he took part in many engagements, including those at Loos, Delville Wood, Arras, Ypres and Cambrai, and was wounded in 1916. He was unfortunately killed in action at Armentières on April 10th, 1918, and was entitled to the 1914–15 Star, and the General Service and Victory Medals.
"The path of duty was the way to glory."
30, Churchville Road, Bedford. Z3170/A.

JUDD, A. E., Sapper, Royal Engineers.
Volunteering in October 1915, he proceeded to Egypt in the following year. In this theatre of war he was engaged on many important duties in various sectors of the front. Later he was transferred to France and served on the Somme until hostilities ceased. He was demobilised in March 1919, and holds the General Service and Victory Medals.
Chackmore, Buckingham. Z3172.

JUDD, H. M., Private, Queen's Own (Royal West Kent Regiment).
He joined in May 1916, and underwent a period of training prior to his being drafted to France. There he took part in much fighting in the Somme sector, and was badly wounded in August 1918. As a result he was invalided home, and finally discharged in March 1919 as medically unfit for further service. He holds the General Service and Victory Medals.
Great Paxton, St. Neots, Hunts. Z3171/B.

JUDD, P., Sergeant Observer, Royal Air Force.
He joined in June 1918, and on completion of his training was engaged on special duties as an observer on the East Coast and Salisbury Plain. After the cessation of hostilities he rendered valuable services as an Instructor in farming under the Army Education Scheme, and was eventually demobilised in April 1920.
Great Paxton, St. Neots, Hunts. Z3171/A.

JUFFS, A. A., Pte., 2/5th Beds. Regt. and M.G.C.
Volunteering in May 1915, he proceeded to Mesopotamia in the following year. Whilst in this seat of hostilities he saw much heavy fighting with a Lewis gun section at Baghdad and many other places. He was afterwards sent to Egypt, where he was engaged until after the cessation of hostilities. He returned home, and was demobilised in March 1919, holding the General Service and Victory Medals.
Houghton Conquest, near Ampthill, Bedford. Z3173/B.

JUFFS, S. G. W., Private, 7th Bedfordshire Regt.
Volunteering in September 1914, he proceeded overseas in the following July. Whilst on the Western Front he rendered valuable services as a Brigade Runner, and took part in much heavy fighting at the Battles of the Somme, Arras, Ypres, Messines, Passchendaele and Cambrai, and was wounded three times. He was finally invalided home, and later demobilised in March 1919, holding the 1914–15 Star, and the General Service and Victory Medals.
Houghton Conquest, near Ampthill, Beds. Z3173/A.

JUFKINS, C. A., Rifleman, Cameronians (Scottish Rifles).
He joined in January 1917, and completing his training in the following June, was drafted to the Western Front. In this theatre of war he took part in many engagements, including those in the Arras, Vimy Ridge and Cambrai sectors. He was demobilised in July 1919, and holds the General Service and Victory Medals.
Green's Norton, Towcester, Northants. Z3174.

JUSTICE, H. F., Gunner, Royal Field Artillery.
He volunteered in December 1915, and was retained for some time at various Home stations on important duties. In March 1918 he proceeded to France and saw much heavy fighting in the Somme sector until hostilities ceased, when he went to Germany with the Army of Occupation. He served on the Rhine until his demobilisation in October 1919, and holds the General Service and Victory Medals.
Chapel End, Akeley, Buckingham. Z3175.

K

KEDGE, A. J., Cpl., Military Foot Police & R.G.A.
He volunteered in January 1916, but on account of ill-health was not successful in his efforts to obtain a transfer to a theatre of war. Throughout the period of his service he was stationed at Battersfield Park, Darlington, where he did good work with the Military Police. He also served with the Royal Garrison Artillery, and was eventually demobilised in October 1919.
15, Howard Street, Bedford. X3181.

KEDGE, E. F., Private, 2nd Bedfordshire Regt.
A serving man, he proceeded to France in October 1914, and after fighting at La Bassée, was wounded in action at Ypres and again at Hill 60. He also took an active part in the Battles of Festubert, Loos, the Somme and Arras, and whilst engaged in severe fighting at Messines was badly wounded, and unfortunately succumbed on June 8th, 1917. He was entitled to the 1914 Star, and the General Service and Victory Medals.
"A valiant Soldier, with undaunted heart he breasted life's last hill."
27, Union Street, Bedford. X3179—X3180.

KEDGE, F. A., Driver, Royal Engineers.
He volunteered in August 1914, and later in the same year was drafted to the Western Front, where he saw heavy fighting in numerous engagements. He was also employed on important transport work in the Ypres, Festubert, the Somme, Arras, Cambrai and Bapaume sectors. He served in France until February 1919, and was demobilised a month later, holding the 1914 Star, and the General Service and Victory Medals.
42, Pilcroft Street, Bedford. X3178.

KEECH, A., Private, Oxford. and Bucks. L.I.
Volunteering in 1914, he was sent in the following year to Salonika. In that theatre of war he took an active part in numerous important engagements on the Vardar, the Struma, Monastir and the Doiran fronts. Whilst serving there he contracted malaria, and in consequence was discharged as medically unfit for further military duties in January 1918. He holds the 1914–15 Star, and the General Service and Victory Medals. 21, Albert Street, Bedford. X3183.

KEECH, A. E., Private, Oxford. and Bucks. L.I.
A month after the outbreak of war he volunteered, and after serving at Camberly, Blackdown and Salisbury Plain, was drafted to the Western Front in July 1915. He saw heavy fighting in numerous important engagements, and was unfortunately killed in action at Ypres on March 5th, 1916. He was entitled to the 1914–15 Star, and the General Service and Victory Medals.
"His life for his Country."
31, Caldecote Street, Newport Pagnell, Bucks. Z3189/B.

KEECH, A. H., Bombardier, Royal Field Artillery.
He volunteered in 1915, and in the same year embarked for the Western Front. During his service there he was engaged in fierce fighting at the Battles of Festubert, Loos, Albert, the Somme, Ypres and Cambrai, and did good work with his battery until the cessation of hostilities. Demobilised in May 1919, he holds the 1914–15 Star, and the General Service and Victory Medals.
Paggs Court, Silver Street, Newport Pagnell, Bucks. Z3187/C.

KEECH, E. T., Private, Machine Gun Corps.
He volunteered in January 1915, but was retained on important duties in England until January 1918, when he was drafted overseas. Whilst serving on the Western Front he took part in several engagements, and when in action on the Somme in March 1918 was taken prisoner, and sent to Mannheim Camp. In July 1918 he died as a result of the bad treatment he received whilst in captivity, and was entitled to the General Service and Victory Medals.
"The path of duty was the way to glory."
Emberton, Bucks. Z3188.

KEECH, F., Gunner, Royal Field Artillery.
Volunteering in 1915, he was trained at Bedford and Catterick, and in the following year proceeded to the Western Front. There he served for over three years, and during that time saw severe fighting in numerous engagements, including the Battles of Albert, Vimy Ridge, the Somme and Ypres. He was demobilised in December 1919, and holds the General Service and Victory Medals. Potters Cross, Wootton, Beds. Z3185/B.

KEECH, F. O., Sapper, Royal Engineers.
He joined the Army in November 1916, and on completion of his training was two months later drafted to Salonika. During his service in this theatre of war he experienced fierce fighting in numerous important engagements until 1918, when he was transferred to South Russia. There he rendered many valuable services, and was demobilised on his return to England in December 1919. He holds the General Service and Victory Medals. 31, Caldecote St., Newport Pagnell, Bucks. Z3189/A.

KEECH, H., Air Mechanic, Royal Air Force.
Joining in November 1917, he was unable to obtain a transfer overseas before the cessation of hostilities. He was stationed at Halton Camp and Market Drayton, and employed on work requiring exceptional technical knowledge and skill, and carried out his duties with great ability. He was eventually demobilised in February 1919.
31, Caldecote Street, Newport Pagnell, Bucks. Z3189/C.

KEEBLE, H. W., Private, R.A.S.C. (M.T.)
He volunteered in October 1915, and after completing his training was drafted overseas in the following year. Whilst serving on the Western Front he took part in numerous engagements, chiefly in the Ypres and Cambrai sectors. He remained in France until demobilised in July 1919, and holds the General Service and Victory Medals.
19, Bridge Road, Bedford. Z3182.

KEECH, P., Sapper, Royal Engineers.
Joining in February 1917, he received his training at Longmore Camp, and nine months later proceeded to the Western Front. There he saw severe fighting in the Ypres and Lens sectors, and also did good work with his Company in the Battles of Cambrai and the Somme. He also rendered valuable services in the construction of railways, and was demobilised in February 1919, holding the General Service and Victory Medals.
Marston, near Bedford. Z3186.

KEECH, W., Private, 10th Royal Berkshire Regt.
He joined in April 1916, and two months later was ordered to the Western Front. Owing to ill-health he was not sent up to the firing line, but was stationed at Rouen, where he rendered valuable services, loading and unloading shells at the docks. In March 1917 he was invalided to England suffering from heart trouble, and a month later was discharged as medically unfit for further duties. He holds the General Service and Victory Medals. Grove Cottages, Great Linford, Bucks. Z3184.

KEELING, P., Pte., Bedfordshire Regt. and M.G.C.
In November 1916, he joined the Bedfordshire Regiment, and was trained at Ampthill Camp, but on being transferred to the Machine Gun Corps, was drafted overseas in the following year. Whilst on the Western Front, he took part in many engagements, including the Battles of Messines, Ypres, Cambrai, the Somme, the Marne and Havrincourt. He was demobilised in February 1919, and holds the General Service and Victory Medals. Warboys, Hunts. Z3190.

KEEN, T., Sergt., Middlesex Regt. and Labour Corps.
He volunteered in the Middlesex Regiment in August 1914, and in 1915 was sent to France, where he served with distinction at the Battles of Hill 60, Ypres, Loos, the Somme, Arras and Vimy Ridge. In 1917 he was wounded on two occasions, and consequently invalided to England. On his recovery he was transferred to the Labour Corps, and was engaged on important agricultural work at St. Ives until demobilised in January 1919. He holds the 1914–15 Star, and the General Service and Victory Medals.
7, Cumberland Place, Bedford. Z1047/B.

KEENS, A., Corporal, South Wales Borderers.
Joining in March 1916, he received his training at Ampthill and Blundell Sands, and later in the same year proceeded to the scene of activities in Salonika. Throughout the period of his service there he saw much severe fighting particularly on the Doiran, the Struma, and the Vardar fronts, and was gassed. He was demobilised on his return to England in September 1919, and holds the General Service and Victory Medals.
28, Northwood End, Haynes, near Bedford. Z3192.

KEENS, A. G., Private, Devonshire Regiment.
When war was declared in August 1914 he volunteered, and in the following year embarked for the Western Front. In that theatre of war he performed excellent work as a stretcher-bearer at the Battles of Neuve Chapelle, Hill 60, Ypres and Festubert, but was unfortunately killed in action in July 1915. He wa entitled to the 1914–15 Star, and the General Service and Victory Medals.
"A costly sacrifice upon the altar of freedom."
33, Woburn Road, Bedford. X1216/C.

KEENS, E. C., Gunner, Royal Garrison Artillery.
He joined the Army in 1917, and received his training in the Bedfordshire Regiment at Languard. Subsequently he was transferred to the Royal Garrison Artillery, and was engaged on important duties at Derby and also in Ireland. He was unsuccessful in his endeavours to obtain a transfer to the war zone, but, nevertheless, rendered valuable services until demobilised in January 1919. Laburnam Road, Sandy, Bucks. Z3194.

KEENS, E. C., Private, R.A.S.C. (M.T.)
He volunteered in 1915, and, on completion of a period of training, was in the following year drafted overseas. During his service on the Western Front he was present at fierce fighting, chiefly in the Ypres and the Somme sectors, and was also employed in transporting ammunition to the forward areas. He was demobilised in October 1919, and holds the General Service and Victory Medals.
15, Priory Street, Bedford. X3191.

KEENS, P. R., Private, 25th Middlesex Regiment.
He volunteered in August 1914, and after a period of service at Aldershot was discharged in the following year. In 1916, however, he rejoined, and was drafted to China, where he was engaged on important garrison duties at Hong Kong until 1917. He then proceeded to Russia and took part in heavy fighting in several engagements. Returning to England in 1918 he was demobilised in October 1919, holding the General Service and Victory Medals. He was on board the S.S. "Tyndareus" when this ship was mined.
20, Northwood End, Haynes, near Bedford. Z3193.

KEEP, A., Private, Royal Fusiliers.
He volunteered when war broke out in August 1914, but was not able to obtain a transfer overseas before the termination of hostilities. He was retained on home defence, and stationed at Colchester, where he performed valuable work as a shoeing-smith. In 1920 he was still serving in the Army, and was stationed in India. 23, All Hallows Lane, Bedford. X2559/A.

KEEP, A. E., Private, Bedfordshire Regiment.
He joined in 1918, and on conclusion of his training was in the same year ordered to the Western Front, where he served for two years. During that time he was engaged in severe fighting in the Somme sector, and after the close of hostilities was engaged on important duties with his unit. In 1920 he was serving in India, and was stationed at Rawal Pindi.
55, All Hallows Lane, Bedford. X3195.

KEEP, F., Private, Bedfordshire Regiment.
Volunteering in March 1915, he proceeded in the following year to Egypt. After a period of service there he was transferred to Palestine, and on that front took an active part in important engagements at Gaza, Jerusalem, Jaffa and Aleppo. In 1919 he returned to England, and was demobilised in June of that year, holding the General Service and Victory Medals.
40, Bunyan Road, Kempston, Beds. X3197/B.

KEEP, J., Corporal, R.A.S.C. (M.T.)
He joined the Army in 1916, but on completion of his training was unable to secure a transfer to the fighting area. Throughout the period of his service he was stationed at Norwich, where he was employed as a mechanic and carried out his work with the greatest ability until demobilised in August 1919.
33, Iddesleigh Road, Queen's Park, Bedford. Z3196.

KEEP, J., Private, 2nd Bedfordshire Regiment.
Mobilised in August 1914, he at once proceeded to the Western Front, where he fought in the Battles of the Marne and La Bassée, and was wounded at Ypres in October 1914. In 1915 he was drafted to Egypt, and subsequently to Palestine, and on that front took an active part in engagements at Gaza, Jerusalem, Jaffa and Aleppo. He was discharged on his return home in April 1919, and holds the 1914 Star, and the General Service and Victory Medals.
40, Bunyan Road, Kempston, Beds. X3197/A.

KEMP, C. W., A.B., R.N., H.M.T.B. Destroyer "No. 112."
At the declaration of war in August 1914 he was already in the Navy, and during the period of hostilities served in many waters. He was engaged on patrol and escort duties in the North and Baltic Seas, and performed valuable work. Whilst proceeding to Russia in August 1918 his ship was torpedoed, but fortunately he was rescued, and in 1920 was still serving. He holds the 1914–15 Star, and the General Service and Victory Medals. 37, Westbourne Road, Bedford. Z3199/C.

KEMP, F. C., A.B., Mercantile Marine.
When war was declared in August 1914 he was already serving, and during the period of hostilities was engaged in conveying food to France and the Argentine. On several occasions his ship was torpedoed, but fortunately he escaped uninjured. In 1920 he was still in the Merchant Service, and holds the General Service and the Mercantile Marine War Medals.
37, Westbourne Road, Bedford. Z3199/B.

KEMP, G. F., Captain's Cook, R.N., H.M.S. "Marlborough."
Already serving in the Navy when war was declared in August 1914, he saw heavy fighting in various important engagements, including those at the Falkland Islands and in the Dardanelles. He also took part in the bombardment of Ostend and Zeebrugge, and throughout the war performed valuable work. In 1920 he was still serving, and holds the 1914–15 Star, and the General Service and Victory Medals.
37, Westbourne Road, Bedford. Z3199/A.

KEMP, J., Sergeant, Grenadier Guards.
He volunteered in September 1914, and after a period of training was five months later drafted to the Western Front. There he played a conspicuous part in the Battles of Ypres, Loos, the Somme, Arras, Lens and Cambrai, and was wounded on two occasions. In 1917 he returned to England, and performed valuable work as an Instructor in physical training at Chelsea and Caterham. He was demobilised in 1919, and holds the 1914–15 Star, and the General Service and Victory Medals.
Rose Cottages, Clapham, Bedford. Z3198/C.

KEMP, W. G., Sergeant, R.A.V.C.
Mobilised in August 1914, he immediately proceeded to France, where he was in action in the Retreat from Mons. He also took a prominent part in the Battles of the Marne, the Aisne and Ypres, and rendered valuable services attending to sick and wounded horses. He was gassed at Lens, and discharged from the Army in September 1915. On June 6th, 1917, he died from the effects of war service, and was entitled to the Mons Star, and the General Service and Victory Medals.
"Whilst we remember, the sacrifice is not in vain."
26, Tavistock Place, Bedford. Z3200.

KEMPSTER, A., Sapper, Royal Engineers.
He joined in July 1916, and after training at Newark and Chatham, embarked for France in February 1917. During his service on the Western Front he was stationed at Rouen, where he was employed in the quarries. He also did excellent work as a plumber in the various camps. Demobilised in April 1919, he holds the General Service and Victory Medals.
90, Caldecote Street, Newport Pagnell, Bucks. Z3201.

KENT, C., Sapper, Royal Engineers.
Joining in 1916, he was, on conclusion of his training, drafted in the same year to the Western Front. In that theatre of war he was engaged on important clerical duties at Rouen, and carried out his responsible work with the greatest ability. He served in France until demobilised in November 1919, and holds the General Service and Victory Medals.
2, Trinity Road, Queen's Park, Bedford. Z3202.

KENYON, A., Trooper, Bedfordshire Lancers.
He volunteered in April 1915, and, after a period of training, was sent overseas eight months later. Whilst serving on the Western Front he saw heavy fighting in various sectors, and took part in the Battles of the Somme, Arras, Ypres and Cambrai. He was wounded in action at Villers-Bretonneux, and in April 1918 was drafted to Ireland, where he served until demobilised in April 1919. He holds the 1914–15 Star, and the General Service and Victory Medals.
1, Marlborough Road, Bedford. Z2720/B.

KETTLES, P., Cpl., Royal Inniskilling Fusiliers.
When war was declared in August 1914 he was mobilised and was at once sent with the First Expeditionary Force to the Western Front. There he fought in the Battles of Mons, Le Cateau, La Bassée, Ypres, the Somme and Arras, and was in action in numerous important engagements until the close of hostilities. He was discharged in 1919, and holds the Mons Star, and the General Service and Victory Medals.
20, The Grove, Bedford. Z3203.

KETTLES, W., Private, Royal Irish Fusiliers.
He volunteered in August 1914, and after a course of training was discharged three months later suffering from heart disease. In February 1916, however, he re-enlisted, and after a short period of service in Ireland was again discharged as medically unfit for further military duties.
1, Howard Street, Bedford. X3204.

KEY, F. J., Private, Somerset Light Infantry.
In March 1916 he joined the Army, and was engaged on important duties with his unit at Blandford. His health broke down, however, and he was sent home, where he unfortunately died from consumption in June 1917.
"His memory is cherished with pride."
Akeley, Buckingham. Z3205/B.

KEY, H. W., Private, Oxford. and Bucks. L.I.
He joined in February 1918, but was not successful in obtaining a transfer to a theatre of war owing to the early cessation of hostilities. After completing a period of training at Cork, he took an active part in quelling the Sinn Fein disturbances in Ireland, and in 1920 was still serving with his unit at Catterick.
Akeley, Buckingham. Z3205/A.

KIDMAN, E., Private, Suffolk Regiment.
Joining in February 1916, he received his training at Crowborough and Bury-St-Edmunds, and nine months later was drafted to France. On that front he saw fierce fighting in many important engagements in various sectors of the line, and also took part in the Battles of the Ancre and Arras. In 1917 he was invalided to England owing to ill-health, and on his recovery was engaged in guarding prisoners of war until demobilised in September 1919, holding the General Service and Victory Medals.
Robbs Yard, The Waits, St. Ives, Hunts. Z2144/A.

KILBOURN, A. S., Corporal, Cheshire Regiment.
He volunteered in November 1915, and shortly afterwards proceeded to Salonika. In that theatre of war he saw much service and took an active part in severe fighting in important engagements on the Doiran, the Struma and the Vardar fronts. He was demobilised on his return to England in June 1919, and holds the General Service and Victory Medals.
13, Fairfax Road, Bedford. X3206/B.

KILBOURN, H., Private, Cheshire Regiment.
Joining in February 1916, he proceeded later in the same year to the Western Front, where he was in action in the Battles of the Somme, Ypres and Cambrai. In 1917 he was transferred to Italy, and after a short period of service there was drafted back to France. He took part in the Retreat and Advance of 1918, and saw heavy fighting in the final decisive engagements of the war. Demobilised in September 1919, he holds the General Service and Victory Medals.
13, Fairfax Road, Bedford. X3206/A.

KILPIN, W., Private, 4th Bedfordshire Regiment.
He volunteered in December 1915, and seven months later was sent to France, where he fought and was wounded in the Battle of the Somme in July 1916. He was invalided to England, and on his recovery in March 1917 returned to the Western Front. After taking part in engagements at Arras he was mortally wounded at Ypres, and succumbed to his wounds at Etaples hospital on September 16th, 1917. He was entitled to the General Service and Victory Medals.
"His life for his Country, his soul to God."
23, The Crescent, Bury Street, Newport Pagnell, Bucks. Z3208.

KILPIN, W. J., Driver, Royal Field Artillery.
Volunteering in November 1915, he served at various important stations until November 1916 when he was drafted overseas. During his service on the Western Front, he fought at the Battles of the Somme, Arras, Ypres and Cambrai, and after the close of hostilities proceeded into Germany with the Army of Occupation. He served on the Rhine until demobilised in June 1919, holding the General Service and Victory Medals.
Mount Pleasant, Stoke Goldington, Bucks. Z3207.

KILSBY, H., Sapper, Royal Engineers.
He volunteered in November 1915, and on completion of his training was ordered nine months later to the Western Front. There he was in action in the Battles of the Ancre, Vimy Ridge and Messines, and took part in severe fighting in engagements in the Neuve Chapelle and Laventie sectors. He was gassed in August 1918, and was eventually demobilised in January 1919, holding the General Service and Victory Medals.
8, Napier Street, Bletchley, Bucks. Z3209.

KINCH, A. (Miss), Worker, Q.M.A.A.C.
She joined the Q.M.A.A.C. in April 1917, and throughout the period of her service was stationed at the Repatriation Camp, Woking. There she performed excellent work in the officers' mess as a waitress, and carried out her arduous duties in a highly capable manner. She was demobilised in December 1919.
The Kennels, Milton Ernest, near Bedford. Z3212.

KINCH, E. J., Sergeant, Yorkshire Dragoons (Queen's Own).
He volunteered in September 1914, and in July of the following year was drafted to France, where he played a prominent part in the Battles of the Somme, Ypres and Cambrai, and in other important engagements. In 1917 he returned to England, and rendered valuable services as a bombing Instructor. After the Armistice he proceeded to Germany with the Army of Occupation, and served at Cologne until demobilised in June 1919. He holds the 1914–15 Star, and the General Service and Victory Medals.
The Kennels, Milton Ernest, near Bedford. TZ3210.

KINCH, K. (Miss), Worker, Q.M.A.A.C.
She joined in April 1917, and was stationed at the Repatriation Camp, Woking. At that depôt she was employed as a waitress in the officers' mess, and performed very excellent work. After nearly two years' valuable services she was demobilised in December 1918. The Kennels, Milton Ernest, near Beds. Z3211.

KING, A. A. (M.M.), Private, 1st Bedfordshire Regt.
He was mobilised in August 1914, and immediately proceeded to the Western Front, where he fought in the Battle of Mons. He was wounded during the subsequent Retreat and again on the Somme, and also took a prominent part in engagements at Hill 60, Ypres, Albert, Arras and Cambrai. In January 1918 he was awarded the Military Medal for conspicuous gallantry in the Field, and was discharged in March 1919, holding also the Mons Star, and the General Service and Victory Medals. 27, Dane Street, Bedford. X1353/A.

KING, A. C., Private, Labour Corps.
He joined in July 1916, and after a period of training, served in Ireland for a short time. In February 1917he was drafted to the Western Front, where he did excellent work with his unit in connection with the repairing of roads in various sectors. He was demobilised in November 1919, and holds the General Service and Victory Medals.
17, Creed Street, Wolverton, Bucks. Z3228.

KING, A. E., Private, 10th Queen's (Royal West Surrey Regiment).
Joining in April 1916, he was drafted to France in September and took part in the Battles of the Somme, Arras and Vimy Ridge. He died gloriously on the Field at the Battle of Ypres (III.) on July 30th, 1917, and was entitled to the General Service and Victory Medals.
"Great deeds cannot die:
They with the sun and moon renew their light for ever."
15, Thurlow Street, Bedford. X3240/B.

KING, A. T., Private, Oxford. and Bucks. L.I.
After joining in July 1916, he underwent a short period of training, and was sent to France in October of the same year. He took part in the Battles of the Somme and Arras, and was then invalided home with rheumatism. On his recovery he returned to the Western Front, and fought at the Battles of Ypres and Cambrai, and in the Retreat and Advance of 1918. He was demobilised in April 1919, and holds the General Service and Victory Medals.
11, Church Passage, Newport Pagnell, Bucks. Z1707/A.

KING, A. W., Private, R.A.M.C.
Mobilised in August 1914, he was immediately drafted to France, and was engaged on important ambulance work during the Battles of Mons, Ypres, the Somme, Arras and Cambrai. He was twice wounded in action—in March 1916 and in October 1918—and was eventually discharged in April 1919, holding the Mons Star, and the General Service and Victory Medals. 8, Grey Friars Walk, Bedford. X3241.

KING, B. J., Private, 1st Bedfordshire Regiment.
A serving soldier, he was drafted to France at the outbreak of war, and played an important part in the Retreat from Mons and the Battles of Le Cateau and the Aisne. He was taken prisoner in October 1914, and, during his captivity in Germany, suffered many hardships. Repatriated in January 1919 he was then discharged, and holds the Mons Star, and the General Service and Victory Medals.
39, Pembroke Street, Bedford. Z3238/A.

KING, C., Private, Royal Army Service Corps.
Volunteering in August 1914, he was sent to Egypt in the following year, and did excellent work with the 44th Remount Depôt at Cairo. Later he proceeded into Palestine and served at Haifa, Gaza and Jerusalem. He was demobilised on returning to England in March 1919, and holds the 1914–15 Star and the General Service and Victory Medals.
New Town, Kimbolton, Hunts. Z3231/A.

KING, D., Sergeant, 4th Royal Sussex Regiment.
Volunteering in September 1914, he first saw active service in the Dardanelles, where he took part in the Landings at Cape Helles and Suvla Bay. After the Evacuation of the Gallipoli Peninsula he was sent to Egypt, but proceeding to Palestine later, served with distinction at the Battles of Gaza, and at the capture of Haifa and Jaffa. He was finally in action in France, and then went to Germany, where he was stationed near Cologne with the Army of Occupation. Demobilised in October 1919, he holds the 1914–15 Star, and the General Service and Victory Medals.
8, Trinity Road, Queen's Park, Bedford. Z3237.

KING, E., Private, Northamptonshire Regiment.
Already in the Army in August 1914, he proceeded to France with the First Expeditionary Force, and took part in the Battle of, and the Retreat from, Mons. He also served at the Battles of Ypres, Loos and the Somme, but was unfortunately killed in action in July 1917. He was entitled to the Mons Star, and the General Service and Victory Medals.
"And doubtless he went in splendid company."
17, Holme Street, Bedford. X3218/A.

KING, E., Private, Oxford. and Bucks. L.I.
Volunteering in November 1914, he was drafted to France in May 1916, and played a prominent part in many important engagements, including the Battles of the Somme, Ypres and Cambrai. He laid down his life for King and Country on November 2nd, 1918, and was entitled to the General Service and Victory Medals.
"Courage, bright hopes, and a myriad dreams, splendidly given."
Well More, Maids Moreton, Bucks. Z3223.

KING, E., Private, 2nd Northamptonshire Regt.
Volunteering in August 1914, he was sent to France six months later, and took part in the Battles of Ypres, Albert, the Somme, Arras and Cambrai. He was wounded in action in January 1915, and died gloriously on the Field of Battle near Albert on May 12th, 1918. He was entitled to the 1914–15 Star, and the General Service and Victory Medals.
"A valiant Soldier, with undaunted heart he breasted life's last hill."
13, Gratton Road, Queen's Park, Bedford. Z3216/B.

KING, E. C. O., Driver, Royal Engineers.
After volunteering in September 1914, he was retained on important duties at home stations for some time. Eventually he proceeded to Egypt, and was stationed at Cairo, but later advanced into Palestine with General Allenby's Forces, and took part in the Battles of Gaza and the capture of Jerusalem and Tripoli. He was demobilised in May 1919, and holds the General Service and Victory Medals.
8, Denmark Street, Bedford. Z3219/B.

KING, E. D., Private, Royal Warwickshire Regt.
He volunteered in the Huntingdonshire Cyclist Battalion in 1914, but on completion of his training was drafted to France with the Royal Warwickshire Regiment. Whilst on the Western Front, he took part in the Battles of Albert, the Somme, Ypres, Passchendaele and Cambrai. He was demobilised in 1919, and holds the General Service and Victory Medals. Diddington, Hunts. Z3230/C.

KING, E. G., Private, 7th Wiltshire Regiment.
Having volunteered in August 1914, he was sent to France in the following March, and took part in the Battles of Ypres before being transferred to Salonika in September 1915. In the Balkan theatre of war he was in action on the Vardar, Doiran and Struma fronts. Early in 1918 he returned to the Western Front and fought on the Somme, but being wounded in action was invalided home. He was demobilised in March 1919, and holds the 1914–15 Star, and the General Service and Victory Medals.
20, New Street, Stony Stratford, Bucks. Z3215.

KING, F., Private, Queen's Own (Royal West Kent Regiment).
Volunteering in April 1915, he was quickly drafted to France, where he took part in the heavy fighting at the Battles of Hill 60, Festubert and Loos. He made the supreme sacrifice, being killed in action on October 7th, 1915, and was entitled to the 1914–15 Star, and the General Service and Victory Medals.
"Whilst we remember, the sacrifice is not in vain."
16, Hawkins Road, Bedford. TZ3214.

KING, F. G., Driver, Royal Engineers.
He volunteered in August 1914, and, on completion of his training in the following year, was drafet to Egypt. Whilst in the theatre of war he took part in many important engagements. He was later in action during the British Advance into Palestine and took part in the Battles of Rafa and Gaza, and was also present during the capture of Jerusalem. Returning home after the close of war, he was demobilised in June 1919, holding the 1914–15 Star, and the General Service and Victory Medals.
8, Denmark Street, Bedford. Z3219/A.

KING, F. G., Corporal, 1st Bedfordshire Regiment.
Mobilised at the outbreak of war in August 1914, he was immediately sent to France. During his service on the Western Front he did excellent work in various sectors. He fought in the Battle of, and in the Retreat from, Mons and also in the Battles of Ypres, the Somme, Arras and Cambrai, and was twice wounded in action. He was discharged in February 1919, and holds the Mons Star, and the General Service and Victory Medals. 4, Farrer St., Bedford. X3217.

KING, F. W., Private, Bedfordshire Regiment.
He joined in June 1917, and, after completing a period of training, was retained on important duties with his unit at various stations. On March 11th, 1918, he unfortunately died from appendicitis, contracted whilst on military service.
"His memory is cherished with pride."
15, Thurlow Street, Bedford. X3240/A.

KING, G., Corporal, Bedfordshire Regiment.
He volunteered in September 1914, and was retained on important duties until 1916, when he proceeded to the Western Front. During his service in this theatre of war he took part in the Somme Offensive, and later in the heavy fighting at Cambrai, where he was wounded. On his recovery he was engaged on important clerical duties at Calais. He was demobilised in June 1919, and holds the General Service and Victory Medals. 24, Great Northern St., Huntingdon. Z3236.

KING, G., Sapper, Royal Engineers.
Volunteering in 1915, he was quickly drafted to Egypt, where he served for a few months. He was afterwards transferred to the Dardanelles, and took part in the Landing at Suvla Bay. Returning to Egypt he served at many important engagements, and was afterwards in action during heavy fighting in Palestine, particularly at the Battle of Gaza. After the close of war he returned home, and was demobilised in July 1919, holding the 1914–15 Star, and the General Service and Victory Medals. Turvey, Beds. Z3235.

KING, G., Private, Oxford. and Bucks. L.I.
Volunteering in August 1914, he proceeded to the Western Front in January of the following year and there saw severe fighting in various sectors. Later in the same year, however, he was transferred to the East, and after taking part in the first Landing at Salonika, served through many engagements on the Vardar and Doiran fronts. Demobilised on his return home in March 1919, he holds the 1914–15 Star, and the General Service and Victory Medals. Moulsoe, Bucks. Z3229/A.

KING, G., L/Corporal, Wiltshire Regiment.
He joined in April 1916, and after undergoing a period of training, was retained at various stations, where he was engaged on duties of a highly important nature. Owing to ill-health he was unable to obtain his transfer to a theatre of war, but nevertheless rendered valuable services with his unit until March 1919, when he was demobilised.
27, Well Street, Buckingham. Z3224.

KING, G., Private, 1st North Staffordshire Regt.
Shortly after joining in 1916, he proceeded to the Western Front, where he saw much severe fighting and took part in the Battles of the Somme, Arras and Vimy Ridge, and many minor engagements. He died gloriously on the Field of Battle at Cambrai on October 16th, 1918. He was entitled to the General Service and Victory Medals.
"Thinking that remembrance, though unspoken, may reach him where he sleeps."
13, Gratton Road, Queen's Park, Bedford. Z3216/A.

KING, G., Private, 1st North Staffordshire Regt.
He joined in January 1917, and, after a short period of training, was drafted to the Western Front, where he served through the Battles of Arras, Vimy Ridge and Passchendaele, and many other important engagements. He fell fighting at Cambrai in the Retreat of March 1918. He was entitled to the General Service and Victory Medals.
"Courage, bright hopes, and a myriad dreams, splendidly given."
17, Holme Street, Bedford. X3218/B.

KING, H., Private, 6th Queen's Own (Royal West Kent Regiment).
Joining in March 1916, he was drafted to the Western Front in July of that year, and there served in various sectors. He took part in the Battles of the Somme, Arras and Ypres, and many other important engagements, and was also stationed for a time at Boulogne. Engaged later on Grave Registration duties, he did much useful work until his demobilisation in December 1919, and holds the General Service and Victory Medals. Cricket Lane, Goldington, Bedford. Z3239.

KING, H., Private, 3rd Bedfordshire Regiment and Northamptonshire Regiment.
Four months after joining in March 1916, he was drafted to France, where he saw severe fighting in various sectors of that front. He took part in the Battles of the Somme, Arras, Ypres and Passchendaele, and many other important engagements in this theatre of war until the cessation of hostilities. Demobilised in 1919, he holds the General Service and Victory Medals.
Diddington, Hunts. Z3230/A.

KING, H., Private, 53rd Royal Warwickshire Regt.
He joined immediately on attaining military age in August 1918, and after completing a period of training, was retained on important duties with his unit at various stations. Owing to the early cessation of hostilities, he was unable to obtain his transfer to the front, but nevertheless rendered very valuable services until February 1919, when he was demobilised.
Great Brickhill, near Bletchley, Bucks. Z3226.

KING, J. (jun.), Corporal, 4th Bedfordshire Regt.
He volunteered in May 1915, and in January of the following year, proceeded to the Western Front, where he saw much heavy fighting. After taking part in several important engagements, he was severely wounded in action at Arras in April 1916, and was invalided home. He holds the General Service and Victory Medals, and in 1920 was still undergoing treatment in hospital. 17, Holme Street, Bedford. X3218/C.

KING, J., Private, 17th Essex Regiment.
He joined in June 1918, and, on completing a period of training later in that year, was drafted to the Western Front. He was sent thence on the cessation of hostilities into Germany, where he served with the Army of Occupation at various stations. Demobilised on his return home in February 1919, he holds the General Service and Victory Medals.
17, Holme Street, Bedford. X3218/D.

KING, J. C., Sergt., 1st Hampshire Regt. and R.E.
Volunteering in September 1914, he proceeded to the Western Front in January of the following year, and there took a prominent part in the Battles of the Somme, Arras and Ypres, and many other engagements. He was later transferred to the Royal Engineers, and was afterwards engaged on transport duties on the railways in various sectors. Demobilised in March 1919, he holds the 1914–15 Star, and the General Service and Victory Medals. 61, High St., New Bradwell, Bucks. Z3225.

KING, J. F., Private, Labour Corps.
He volunteered in October 1914, and, after undergoing a period of training, was retained at various stations, where he was engaged on duties of great importance. He was unable to obtain his transfer to a theatre of war on account of ill-health, but, nevertheless, rendered valuable services with his unit until February 1919, when he was demobilised.
134, Coventry Road, Queen's Park, Bedford. Z3222.

KING, L. (M.M.), Corporal, Huntingdonshire Cyclist Battalion and 1st Bedfordshire Regt.
He volunteered in 1915, and in July of the following year proceeded to the Western Front. There he saw severe fighting in various sectors, and took part in the Battle of Albert and many other important engagements, being wounded in action on the Somme in August 1916. He was awarded the Military Medal for conspicuous bravery in the Field, and holding also the General Service and Victory Medals, was demobilised in 1919.
Diddington, Hunts. Z3230/B.

KING, L., Trooper, Bedfordshire Lancers.
Volunteering in August 1914, he was drafted to the Western Front in the following year, and there took part in the Battles of Festubert, and Loos, and many other important engagements. He fell in action near Loos on January 27th, 1916. He was entitled to the 1914–15 Star, and the General Service and Victory Medals.
"He passed out of the sight of men by the path of duty and self-sacrifice." Heath Hill, Warboys, Hunts. Z3220.

KING, L., Private, Royal Fusiliers.
Shortly after joining in February 1917, he was drafted to Mesopotamia, where, serving as a stretcher-bearer, he saw much severe fighting. He took part in the capture of Baghdad and Tekrit, and in many other important engagements until the cessation of hostilities, and on his return home in January 1919 was demobilised. He holds the General Service and Victory Medals. Warboys, Hunts. Z3233.

KING, P., Corporal, 2nd Duke of Cornwall's L.I.
He was already serving in China when war broke out in August 1914, and three months later landed in England, whence he proceeded in December to France. After taking part in the Battles of Neuve Chapelle, Hill 60, and Ypres, and other engagements, he was transferred to Salonika, where he was again in action on the Doiran front. On his return home he was for a short time in hospital, suffering from malaria, before being discharged in February 1919, and holds the 1914–15 Star, and the General Service and Victory Medals.
Luke Street, Eynesbury, St. Neots, Hunts. Z3234.

KING, P., Trooper, Bedfordshire Lancers; and Private, King's (Liverpool Regiment).
He joined in June 1916, and in the following year was drafted to the Western Front, where he saw severe fighting in various sectors. After taking part in the Battles of Vimy Ridge, Passchendaele and the Somme, and many other important engagements, he was invalided home on account of injuries caused by a kick from a horse. Discharged as medically unfit for further service in July 1919, he holds the General Service and Victory Medals. Diddington, Hunts. Z3232.

KING, S. H. (M.S.M.), Lieutenant, R.E. (R.O.D.)
He volunteered in May 1915, and was retained in England until January of the following year, when he proceeded to France. There he was engaged on duties of a highly important nature in various sectors of the front, serving chiefly as head storeman, and did much useful work until after the cessation of hostilities. He was awarded the Meritorious Service Medal for continuously good work, and holding also the General Service and Victory Medals, was demobilised in November 1919.
Rose Cottage, Whaddon Road, Far Bletchley, Bucks. Z3213.

KING, S. J., Officer's Steward, Royal Navy.
He volunteered in 1914, and was posted to H.M.S. "Acacia," on board which vessel he served in many waters. Attached to the Grand Fleet in the North Sea, he was engaged chiefly on mine-sweeping duties, afterwards taking part in operations at the Dardanelles, and in the Mediterranean Sea. He was demobilised in 1919, and holds the 1914–15 Star, and the General Service and Victory Medals. 39, Pembroke St., Beds. Z3238/B.

KING, W., Private, 2nd Bedfordshire Regiment.
He joined in September 1918, and after undergoing a period of training, was drafted with the Army of Occupation to Germany, being unable to obtain his transfer to a theatre of war on account of the early cessation of hostilities. There he was stationed at Cologne, but in October 1919 was transferred to India, where he served at Quetta and various other places, and was still with his unit in 1920. 66, Wellington St., Bedford. Z1762/C.

KING, W. G., Gunner, Royal Garrison Artillery.
He volunteered in 1915, and, in September of the following year, proceeded to the Western Front, where he saw much severe fighting, and took part in the Battle of the Somme, and other important engagements in various sectors. Home on leave, he unhappily died of influenza in hospital at Bedford on December 6th, 1918. He was entitled to the General Service and Victory Medals.
"Steals on the ear the distant triumph song."
39, Pembroke Street, Bedford. Z3238/C.

KING, W. H., Private, 9th Cheshire Regiment.
Joining in May 1916, he was sent to the Western Front on completing a period of training later in the same year, and there saw severe fighting in various sectors. He took part in the Battles of the Somme, Arras, Ypres and Cambrai, and many other important engagements, and was wounded in action. He also suffered from trench fever, and in June 1918 was invalided from the Army. He holds the General Service and Victory Medals. 5, Eastville Road, Bedford. TZ3221.

KING, W. H., Private, 2nd Worcestershire Regt.
Three months after joining in July 1918 he was drafted to the Western Front, where he saw much heavy fighting during the Allies' Advance. Severely wounded in action he was invalided home, and was for a time in hospital at Liverpool before being discharged in May 1919 as medically unfit for further service. He holds the General Service and Victory Medals.
51, Great Brickhill, Bucks. Z3227.

KING, W. L., Tpr., Queen's Own Oxford. Hussars.
He joined in June 1917, and after completing a period of training, served at various stations in Ireland, where he was engaged on duties of great importance. Being under age for active service he was unable to obtain his transfer to the front, but in December 1918 was sent to Germany, where he served with the Army of Occupation at Cologne. He was demobilised on his return home in January 1920. Moulsoe, Bucks. Z3229/B.

KINGHAM, W., Private, 4th Bedfordshire Regt.
He volunteered in 1914, and was stationed at Bury St. Edmunds engaged on various duties of an important nature until April 1916, when he was sent to France. There he was in action on the Somme front, but after three months' service overseas was invalided home on account of ill-health. He was eventually discharged in 1916 as unfit for further military duty, and holds the General Service and Victory Medals.
Keysoe, Beds. Z3242.

KINGSTON, A., Private, 3rd Northamptonshire Regiment and Royal Scots.
Volunteering in December 1915, he was drafted a month later to the Western Front. In this theatre of war he took part in heavy fighting on the Loos, Somme, Arras and Ypres fronts, and did good work until he was invalided home on account of ill-health in March 1918. Upon his recovery he was transferred to the Royal Scots, and served in Dublin and Edinburgh until January 1919, when he was demobilised, holding the General Service and Victory Medals.
11, New Row, Pury End, Pauler's Pury, Towcester, Northants. Z3244/A.

KINGSTON, F. J., Rflmn., King's Royal Rifle Corps.
He was serving in India at the outbreak of war in August 1914, and was shortly afterwards drafted to France, where he disembarked in November 1914. He at once participated in heavy fighting, but had only served on the Western Front for two months, when he fell in action at Ypres on January 15th, 1915. He was entitled to the 1914 Star, and the General Service and Victory Medals.
"Whilst we remember, the sacrifice is not in vain."
Caryes Row, Pury End, Pauler's Pury, Towcester, Northants. Z3244/B.

KINGSTON, H., Driver, Royal Field Artillery.
He joined in May 1916, and was employed on various duties of an important nature at Edinburgh, and in Norfolk until August 1917, when he was sent to Palestine. There he was in action at Gaza, Jerusalem, and Jaffa, and performed uniformly good work. Returning home after the signing of the Armistice, he was demobilised in November 1919, and holds the General Service and Victory Medals.
Pury End, Pauler's Pury, Towcester, Northants. Z3030/A.

KINNS, E., Pte., 1/5th Beds. Regt.; & Sapper, R.E.
Called up from the Reserve at the outbreak of war in 1914, he was drafted in the following year to Gallipoli, and was wounded in action at Suvla Bay in August 1915. Upon his recovery he was sent to Egypt, and proceeding later to Palestine took part in further fighting at Gaza and near Jerusalem. He was demobilised on his return home in August 1919, and holds the 1914–15 Star, and the General Service and Victory Medals.
High Street, East End, Cranfield, Beds. Z3243.

KIRBY, A., Sapper, Royal Engineers.
He volunteered in September 1914, and on the completion of his training in the following year was sent to Egypt, where he was stationed for some time. He was drafted later to Palestine, and there was engaged on important duties at Gaza, Jaffa, Haifa, Jerusalem and Damascus. He remained overseas until July 1919, when he returned home for demobilisation. He holds the 1914–15 Star, and the General Service and Victory Medals. The Warren, Clapham, Bedford. Z3245.

KIRBY, B., Private, 1st Bedfordshire Regiment.
Volunteering in January 1915, he was drafted in the following June to the Western Front, and in this theatre of war took part with his unit in many important engagements, including the Battles of Loos, the Somme, Ypres, Arras and Cambrai, and performed consistently good work. Returning home after the Armistice he was demobilised in February 1919, and holds the 1914–15 Star, and the General Service and Victory Medals
Station Road, Tempsford, near Sandy, Beds. Z3246.

KIRBY, F., Private, Queen's (Royal West Surrey Regiment) and Labour Corps.
He joined in March 1917, and a month later proceeded to France and was in action during heavy fighting at Arras and Messines. After two months' service overseas he was invalided home on account of ill-health, but upon his recovery returned to France, and was employed on various duties at a Casualty Clearing Station until he was demobilised in June 1919, holding the General Service and Victory Medals.
Priory Road, St. Ives, Hunts. Z3249/D—Z3250/D.

KIRBY, F., Sergeant, Royal Defence Corps.
He volunteered in 1914, and was stationed at Portsmouth, Bedford, Luton, London and other places, employed on various duties of an important nature, and for some time was engaged on Recruiting for the Bedfordshire Regiment. Unfit for service overseas, he rendered valuable services at home until he was invalided out of the Army on account of ill-health in February 1918. 144, Bower Street, Bedford. Z3247.

KIRBY, H., Sergeant, East Surrey Regiment.
Joining in June 1916, he was drafted in the following September to Salonika. There he played a prominent part in heavy fighting on the Doiran, Vardar and Struma fronts, and performed excellent work. He returned home in September 1919, and was demobilised a month later, holding the General Service and Victory Medals.
Priory Road, St. Ives, Hunts. Z3249/E—Z3250/E.

KIRBY, H., Private, East Surrey Regiment.
He joined in June 1916, and in the following October proceeded to France. During six months' service in this theatre of war he took part in heavy fighting on the Somme front and at Arras, and was badly wounded at Vimy Ridge in April 1917. Invalided home he was sent to hospital at Croydon, where he died on May 6th, 1917, from the effects of his wounds. He was entitled to the General Service and Victory Medals.
"His life for his Country."
Priory Road, St. Ives, Hunts. Z3249/A—Z3250/A.

KIRBY, P., Private, Cheshire Regiment.
Joining in April 1916, he was sent five months later to Salonika. In this theatre of hostilities he participated in strenuous fighting on the Vardar, Doiran and Struma fronts, and did good work. He was for some time in hospital suffering from malaria, but remained overseas until October 1919, and was demobilised on his return home a month later, holding the General Service and Victory Medals.
Priory Road, St. Ives, Hunts. Z3249/C—Z3250/C.

KIRBY, S., Private, 1/5th Bedfordshire Regiment.
He volunteered in January 1915, and six months afterwards proceeded to Gallipoli, where he was in action during the Landing at Suvla Bay, and the subsequent battle. He was later transferred to Palestine, and saw further service before he was killed in action at Gaza on August 26th, 1917. He was entitled to the 1914–15 Star, and the General Service and Victory Medals.
"Great deeds cannot die."
St. Margaret's Cottages, Renhold, near Bedford. Z3248.

KIRBY, S., Private, K.O.(Y.L.I.)
Volunteering in September 1914, he was drafted in the following July to the Western Front, and took part in the Battles of Ypres, Festubert and Loos, where he was wounded. As a result he was invalided home, and after a course of hospital treatment was sent to Salonika, where he was employed on various duties on the Struma front. He was demobilised on his return home in May 1919, and holds the 1914–15 Star, and the General Service and Victory Medals.
Priory Road, St. Ives, Hunts. Z3249/B—Z3250/B.

KIRK, P. B., Sapper, Royal Engineers.
A serving soldier at the outbreak of war in August 1914, he was drafted in the following year to Gallipoli, and was severely wounded whilst taking part in heavy fighting at Suvla Bay in September 1915. As a result he was evacuated to England, and subsequently contracting tuberculosis was eventually invalided out of the Service in September 1918. He holds the 1914–15 Star, and the General Service and Victory Medals.
Upper Dean, Beds. Z3252.

KIRK, W., Private, R.A.V.C.
He joined in September 1916, and was shortly afterwards sent to France. In this theatre of war he did excellent work employed on various veterinary duties in several sectors prior to the Armistice, after which he served in Germany with the Army of Occupation in a similar capacity. He was demobilised in September 1919, and holds the General Service and Victory Medals.
Woodbine Cottage, Drayton Parslow, Bletchley. Z3251.

KIRWAN, W., Corporal, Argyll and Sutherland Highlanders.
Mobilised with the Territorial Force in August 1914, he was stationed at Falkirk and Castle Cary employed on important duties until 1917, when he proceeded to France. There he was in action during the Battles of Arras, Cambrai and the Somme (II.), also in heavy fighting at Vimy Ridge and Lens. He was demobilised in February 1919, and holds the General Service and Victory Medals.
47, Muswell Road, Southend, Bedford. Z3253.

KISBY, C. C., Private, 1/6th Gloucestershire Regt.
He joined in October 1916, and in the following June was drafted to France. After taking part in strenuous fighting at Ypres and Lens, he was transferred to Italy and saw further service on the Piave front. Sent later to Egypt, he afterwards proceeded into Palestine, and was stationed in Jerusalem until invalided home on account of eye trouble. Eventually discharged in November 1919, he holds the General Service and Victory Medals. 61, Coventry Street, Bedford. Z3254.

KITCHENER, A., Private, 1st Bedfordshire Regt.
He volunteered in August 1914, and proceeded to Egypt in the following year. On being transferred to Palestine he saw much severe fighting at Gaza and Jerusalem, and was wounded in action on one occasion. In 1918 he was drafted to the Western Front, where he served in the Retreat and also took part in the final decisive engagements of the war. Demobilised in March 1919, he holds the 1914–15 Star, and the General Service and Victory Medals.
17, Cavendish Street, Bedford. X3255.

KNIBBS, A. H., Air Mechanic, Royal Air Force.
Joining in January 1918, he was not successful in his endeavours to obtain transfer to the fighting area. He was trained at Withnoe, and on being transferred to Norwich was engaged as an air rigger on work which demanded a high degree of technical knowledge and skill. After 14 months' valuable service he was demobilised in March 1919.
25, King's Street, Stony Stratford, Bucks. Z3259/B.

KNIBBS, D., Private, 7th Wiltshire Regiment.
He volunteered in November 1915, and after a period of training on Salisbury Plain was ordered to Salonika. On that front he experienced fierce fighting on the Doiran and the Vardar, and was unhappily killed in action during the Advance on the Doiran on April 24th, 1917. He was entitled to the General Service and Victory Medals.
"His life for his Country, his soul to God."
Akeley, Buckingham. Z3256/B.

KNIBBS, E. R., Private, Oxford. and Bucks. L.I.
He joined in 1916, but was retained on important duties at home until April 1918, when he was drafted to the Western Front. There he was engaged in fierce fighting in the Somme, Amiens and Le Cateau sectors. After the close of hostilities he went into Germany with the Army of Occupation, and served at Cologne until demobilised in March 1919. He holds the General Service and Victory Medals.
The Cottage, Great Brickhill, Bletchley, Bucks. Z3258/A.

KNIBBS, J., Private, 1st Bedfordshire Regiment.
He volunteered in August 1914, and in the following December was drafted to the Western Front, where he took part in the Battles of Ypres (II.), Loos, The Somme and Arras. He died gloriously on the Field of Battle on October 23rd, 1918, during the Advance, and was entitled to the 1914–15 Star, and the General Service and Victory Medals.
"His life for his Country, his soul to God."
Akeley, Bucks. Z3256/A.

KNIBBS, P. H., Private, 7th Oxford. & Bucks. L.I.
Volunteering in September 1914, he proceeded to France 12 months later, but was quickly transferred to Salonika. Whilst in the Balkan theatre of war he took part in heavy fighting on the Struma, Vardar and Doiran fronts. He was demobilised on his return home in March 1919, and holds the 1914–15 Star, and the General Service and Victory Medals.
Chapel End, Akeley, Bucks. Z3257.

KNIBBS, W., Private, Leicestershire Regiment.
Having volunteered in May 1915, he was drafted to France in the following March, and took part in the Battles of Albert, the Somme, Arras, Ypres and Cambrai. He was wounded in action at Ypres in 1917, and was gassed during the Advance in 1918. Demobilised in March 1919, he holds the General Service and Victory Medals.
The Cottage, Great Brickhill, Bletchley, Bucks. Z3258/B.

KNIBBS, W. G., Private, Machine Gun Corps.
He joined in November 1916, and seven months later was drafted to France. During his service on the Western Front he was in action at Kemmel Hill, Ypres and St. Quentin before being taken prisoner in March 1918 during the Retreat. Whilst in captivity he was forced to work in the salt mines, and on his release in March 1919 was discharged as medically unfit for further service. He holds the General Service and Victory Medals.
25, King Street, Stony Stratford, Bucks. Z3259/A.

KNIGHT, B. F., Corporal, Royal Engineers.
He was already in the Army at the outbreak of war in August 1914, and was quickly drafted to France, where he did excellent work as an observer with a Field Survey Company. He served during the Retreat from Mons and also in the Battles of La Bassée, Ypres and the Somme Offensive. Later he was in action during the Retreat and Advance of 1918, and was finally discharged in March 1919. He holds the Mons Star, and the General Service and Victory Medals.
5, Spring Gardens, Newport Pagnell. Z3262.

KNIGHT, C., Private, 1/5th Bedfordshire Regt.
He was already in the Army at the declaration of war in August 1914, and shortly afterwards proceeded to the Dardanelles, where he took part in the Landing at Suvla Bay before being invalided to England. In March 1917 he was sent to Egypt, but was later in action in Palestine, particularly at the Battles of Gaza and in the capture of Jaffa and Jerusalem, and was wounded. He was discharged in July 1919, and holds the 1914–15 Star, and the General Service and Victory Medals.
Montague Street, Eynesbury, St. Neots, Hunts. Z3264.

KNIGHT, E. T., Private, Norfolk Regiment.
Volunteering in April 1915, he proceeded to Egypt in the same year and saw service in various sectors. He was present during the British Advance into Palestine and took part in the Battles of Gaza, and was wounded. On his recovery he was in action at the capture of Jerusalem and other engagements until the close of the war, when he returned to Egypt. In March 1919, after his return home, he was demobilised, and holds the 1914–15 Star, and the General Service and Victory Medals.
7, Carlisle Terrace, St. Ives, Hunts. Z3265.

KNIGHT, E. W., Sapper, Royal Engineers.
He joined in June 1918, and, on completion of his training, was retained on important railway duties in England. On November 17th, 1918, he unfortunately died in Farnham Hospital from influenza.
"His memory is cherished with pride."
51, Spencer Street, New Bradwell, Bucks. Z3261/A.

KNIGHT, F., Private, 3rd Bedfordshire Regiment, and Buffs (East Kent Regiment).
He volunteered in December 1914, and, on conclusion of his training in the following year, proceeded to Mesopotamia. In the course of his service in this seat of war he saw much heavy fighting, and took part in the Battle of Kut-el-Amara. Later he was invalided to India suffering from fever, and, after a period of hospital treatment, was retained there on important duties. On his return to England in March 1919 he was demobilised, and holds the 1914–15 Star, and the General Service and Victory Medals.
Station Road, Tempsford, Bedford. Z3266.

KNIGHT, F. W., Sergeant, R.A.M.C. (T.F.), attached 10th Cavalry Brigade, F.A.
Mobilised at the outbreak of war, he was drafted in the following year to Gallipoli, and took part in the Landing at Suvla Bay. Serving with a Field Ambulance all through the campaign, he was sent to Egypt after the Evacuation, and, attached to the 10th Cavalry Brigade Field Ambulance, took part in the Advance into Palestine at Gaza and Jaffa, the Advance along the Jordan Valley, and in the operations which resulted in the capture of Jerusalem. He was mentioned in Despatches for his splendid work in December 1916. Returning home, he was demobilised in April 1919, and holds the 1914–15 Star, and the General Service and Victory Medals.
4, Spencer Street, New Bradwell, Bucks. Z3260.

KNIGHT, G. A., Private, R.A.V.C.
Volunteering in August 1914, he completed his training in the following year and was sent to Egypt, where he did excellent work attending to the sick and wounded horses. He served during the Advance into Palestine and in the Battles of Gaza and Jaffa. After the cessation of hostilities he returned home and was demobilised in March 1919, holding the 1914–15 Star, and the General Service and Victory Medals.
High Street, Milton Ernest, Bedford. Z3267.

KNIGHT, G. R., Private, 1st Border Regiment.
He was already in the Army at the outbreak of war in August 1914, and later in the following year was drafted to the Dardanelles. Whilst in this seat of hostilities he took part in the Landing in Gallipoli and the Battles of Krithia, in the last of which he was unfortunately killed in action on June 28th, 1918. He was entitled to the 1914–15 Star, and the General Service and Victory Medals.
"Whilst we remember, the sacrifice is not in vain."
51, Spencer Street, New Bradwell, Bucks. Z3261/B.

KNIGHT, H. W., Private, Essex Regiment.
He joined in April 1916, and, later in the same year, was drafted to the Western Front, where he saw much heavy fighting in various sectors. He took part in the Somme Offensive, and in the Battle of Arras was wounded in May 1917. As a result he was invalided home, and, after a period of hospital treatment, was eventually demobilised in September 1919. He holds the General Service and Victory Medals.
Montague Street, Eynesbury, St. Neots, Hunts. Z3269.

KNIGHT, J., Pte., Hertfordshire, and Beds. Regts.
Joining in August 1916, he was quickly sent overseas, and, during his service on the Western Front, took part in many important engagements. In March 1918 he was taken prisoner at the second Battle of the Somme, and suffered many hardships during his period of captivity. He was released after the Armistice and, finally discharged in April 1919, and holds the General Service and Victory Medals.
Berkley Street, Eynesbury, St. Neots, Hunts. Z3270.

KNIGHT, W. A., Private, R.M.L.I.
Joining in August 1917, he completed a period of training, and in the following year proceeded to the Western Front, where he was in action during the heavy fighting in the Somme sector, and was gassed. As a result he was invalided to England and, after a period of treatment, was discharged from hospital. Later he went to India and was engaged on guard duties, attached to the Military Police. He was demobilised in May 1919, after his return home, and holds the General Service and Victory Medals.
22, New Street, Stony Stratford, Bucks. Z3263.

KNIGHT, W. J., Private, R.A.O.C.
He joined in June 1918, and, after completing a period of training, was retained on important duties with his unit at various stations. Owing to the early cessation of hostilities he was not successful in obtaining his transfer to a theatre of war, but, nevertheless, rendered valuable services until demobilised in October 1919.
61, Station Road, Oakley, near Bedford. Z3268.

KNOCK, O., 1st Cl. Stoker, R.N., H.M.S. "Revenge."
He was already in the Navy at the outbreak of war in August 1914, and was posted to H.M.S. "Revenge," in which ship he saw much active service. He was engaged on important patrol duties in the North Sea, and also took part in many raids. After this ship was torpedoed he was transferred to H.M.S. "Sir Thomas Picton," and saw further service, taking part in the operations at the Dardanelles. He served on board this ship throughout the remaining period of hostilities, and was demobilised in March 1919, holding the 1914–15 Star, and the General Service and Victory Medals.
King Street Gardens, Stony Stratford. Z3271.

L

LABRUM, A. E., Private, R.A.S.C.
He joined in February 1917, but owing to ill-health he was not successful in his endeavour to obtain a transfer overseas. Whilst serving at Catford and Camberwell he was engaged on duties of an important nature, and performed excellent work as a carpenter at the workshops in Battersea until demobilised in February 1919. Ravenstone, near Olney, Bucks. Z3272.

LACEY, A., Private, 1st Gordon Highlanders.
Joining in May 1916, he was drafted overseas six months later. During his service on the Western Front he saw heavy fighting in the Somme sector, and also took an active part in the Battles of Arras, Messines, Passchendaele and Cambrai. In 1919 he was sent to Ireland, where he assisted in quelling the Sinn Fein disturbances. He was still serving in 1920, and holds the General Service and Victory Medals.
106, Coventry Road, Queen's Park, Bedford. Z1538/D.

LACEY, J. T., 2nd Lieut., 1st Royal Fusiliers.
He was mobilised in August 1914, and shortly afterwards proceeded to France, where he was in action in the Retreat from Mons. He also took part in the Battles of the Marne, the Aisne, La Bassée and Ypres, and was wounded at Neuve Chapelle in March 1915. On his recovery he returned to the Western Front, served in the Battle of the Somme, and was then transferred to Salonika. On that front he experienced fierce fighting on the Vardar, and on his return to England in March 1919, was discharged, holding the Mons Star, and the General Service and Victory Medals.
The Wharf Inn, Great Linford, Bucks. TZ3273.

LACK, E. T. W., S.M., R.A.S.C. (M.T.)
He joined in February 1916, and later in the same year embarked for Mesopotamia. In that theatre of war he saw fierce fighting in important engagements at Nasiriyeh, Ctesiphon, Basra, Kut, Sanna-i-Yat and Baghdad. Throughout the period of his service he carried out consistently good work, and was demobilised on his return to England in July 1919. He holds the General Service and Victory Medals.
19, Churchville Road, Bedford. Z3274.

LAIRD, A. J., Private, Middlesex Regiment.
Joining in June 1918, he was unable to obtain a transfer to the war zone owing to the early cessation of hostilities. He was stationed at Dover, where he was engaged on important guard duties, and carried out his work in an exemplary manner. He was eventually demobilised in March 1919.
88, Bower Street, Bedford. Z3275/C.

LAIRD, E. G., Private, 2nd Bedfordshire Regt.
At the outbreak of war in August 1914 he was already serving, and immediately proceeded to the Western Front, where he fought in the Battles of the Marne, the Aisne, Ypres, Festubert and Loos. In 1916 he was attached to the Transport Section, and rendered valuable services as a shoeing-smith until the close of hostilities. He was discharged in March 1919, and holds the 1914 Star, and the General Service and Victory Medals
88, Bower Street, Bedford. Z3275/A.

LAIRD, F., Corporal, 2nd Bedfordshire Regiment.
Mobilised at the outbreak of hostilities, he was at once ordered to the scene of activities in France. There he fought in the Battles of the Marne, the Aisne and Ypres, and was unfortunately killed in action in the vicinity of Ypres on December 10th, 1914. He was entitled to the 1914 Star, and the General Service and Victory Medals.
"A valiant Soldier, with undaunted heart he breasted life's last hill."
88, Bower Street, Bedford. Z3275/B.

LAMB, A. E., Private, Labour Corps.
He volunteered in December 1914, and ten months later was drafted to Gallipoli, where he was in action at Suvla Bay. In December 1915 he was transferred to Egypt, and subsequently to Palestine. On that front he saw fierce fighting in engagements at Gaza, Jaffa and Beyrout. He returned to England in February 1919, and a month later was demobilised, holding the 1914–15 Star, and the General Service and Victory Medals.
43, Bletsoe, Bedford. Z3279.

LAMB, D. P., Bombardier, Royal Horse Artillery.
Volunteering in November 1915, he was retained on important duties at Bulford until June 1917, when he was sent to the Western Front. He took an active part in numerous important engagements, principally in the Ypres and Arras sectors, and was present during the triumphal entry into Mons. Demobilised in July 1919, he holds the General Service and Victory Medals.
7, Cromwell Terrace, Huntingdon. Z3278/B.

LAMB, G. F., Sapper, Royal Engineers.
He volunteered in April 1915, and served at Bedford and Borden until May 1918, when he succeeded in obtaining a transfer overseas. During his service on the Western Front he saw much severe fighting in various engagements, and also performed valuable work in connection with the construction of roads in the devastated areas of France. Demobilised in March 1919, he holds the General Service and Victory Medals.
4, Cromwell Terrace, Huntingdon. Z3278/A.

LAMB, G. W., Private, Royal Fusiliers.
Joining in May 1917, he was, on completion of his training, drafted to the Western Front two months later. After taking part in engagements in the Arras, Ypres and Cambrai sectors he fell fighting on the Field of Battle at Mailly on May 24th, 1918. He was entitled to the General Service and Victory Medals.
"Whilst we remember, the sacrifice is not in vain."
9, Gratton Road, Queen's Park, Bedford. Z3276/A.

LAMB, S. P., Private, 7th Lincolnshire Regiment.
He volunteered in August 1914, and, after a period of training, was eleven months later sent to France, where he took part in the Battles of Neuve Chapelle, Ypres, and Vimy Ridge. Whilst engaged in fierce fighting on the Somme he was severely wounded in July 1916, and unfortunately succumbed to his injuries at Netley Hospital on August 19th, 1916. He was entitled to the 1914–15 Star, and the General Service and Victory Medals.
"His life for his Country."
7, Patteshall Street, Bedford. X3277.

LAMBERT, G. H., Air Mechanic, R.A.F.
He joined in May 1918, having been previously engaged on work of National importance. Owing to the early cessation of hostilities he was not successful in obtaining a transfer overseas, but was stationed at Southampton and employed as a rigger in the aeroplane shops. This work, which demands a high degree of technical skill, he carried out until demobilised in April 1919.
27, Wallace Street, New Bradwell, Bucks Z3280/B.

LAMBERT, J. H., Corporal, Royal Engineers.
Volunteering in May 1915, he received his training at Longmore, and in the following September proceeded overseas. During his service on the Western Front he performed consistently good work as a repairer and fitter on the railways in different districts in France and Belgium. After nearly four years' valuable service in the Army he was demobilised in March 1919, holding the 1914–15 Star, and the General Service and Victory Medals.
27, Wallace Street, New Bradwell, Bucks. Z3280/A.

LAMBERT, L., Private, Bedfordshire Regiment.
He volunteered in 1915, and, on completion of his training, was later drafted to the Western Front. There he took an active part in engagements in the Ypres, Vimy Ridge and Arras sectors, and was unhappily killed in action on April 19th, 1917. He was entitled to the General Service and Victory Medals.
"He died the noblest death a man may die,
Fighting for God and right and liberty."
Wootton, Beds. Z3281/B.

LAMBERT, W., Private, Bedfordshire Regiment.
When war was declared he was already serving, and was at once ordered to the Western Front, where he fought in the Battles of Mons and Ypres. He was later transferred to Salonika, and took part in numerous engagements there until sent to Palestine. In that theatre of war he experienced fierce fighting at Gaza, Jaffa and Haifa. He was still in the Army in 1920, and holds the Mons Star, and the General Service and Victory Medals.
Wootton, Bedford. Z1316/B.

LAMBERT, W., L/Cpl., Beds. and Essex Regts.
He joined in September 1916, and later in the same year was drafted to Egypt. Subsequently he was sent to Palestine, where he saw fierce fighting at Gaza and Jaffa until transferred to the Western Front. There he took an active part in important engagements in the Somme, Arras, Ypres and Beaumont-Hamel sectors, and was eventually demobilised in August 1919. He holds the General Service and Victory Medals.
Wootton, Bedford. Z3281/A.

LAMBLE, F., Driver, Royal Horse Artillery.
Previously to the outbreak of war he was in the Territorial Army, and consequently proceeded to France in October 1914. He fought in the Battles of Ypres, Neuve Chapelle, Festubert, Loos, the Somme, Bullecourt and Passchendaele, and was also in action at Givenchy. In October 1917 he was drafted to Italy, but contracted influenza and, after prolonged hospital treatment, unfortunately died in Italy on October 30th, 1918. He was entitled to the 1914 Star, and the General Service and Victory Medals.
95, Church Street, Wolverton, Bucks. Z3283.

LAMBOURNE, J. E., Pte., Royal Berkshire Regt.
He volunteered in July 1915, and, after a period of training at Portsmouth, was in the following year ordered overseas. Whilst serving on the Western Front he took an active part in the Battle of the Somme and was engaged in fierce fighting in the Ypres sector. He was wounded in action on two occasions, and was demobilised in March 1919, holding the General Service and Victory Medals. 11, Bath Lane, Buckingham. Z3282.

LANCASTER, A., L/Cpl., 1st Bedfordshire Regt.
He was mobilised in August 1914, and was at once ordered with the first Expeditionary Force to the Western Front. There he fought in the Battle of Mons and in the subsequent Retreat, and also took an active part in engagements on the Marne, the Aisne, at La Bassée, Ypres, the Somme and Cambrai. He was wounded in action on six occasions, but served in France until the cessation of hostilities. He was discharged in April 1919, and holds the Mons Star, and the General Service and Victory Medals. 34, Mill Street, Newport Pagnell, Bucks. Z3284/A.

LANCASTER, E., Gunner, R.G.A.
He volunteered in 1915, and, after a period of training, was in the following year drafted to France. On that front he saw fierce fighting in various sectors, served in the Battles of the Somme, Ypres and Cambrai, and was wounded in action on one occasion. After the termination of the war he proceeded with the Army of Occupation to Germany, and was stationed there until demobilised in September 1919. He holds the General Service and Victory Medals.
Cranfield, Beds. Z3285/C—Z3286/C.

LANCASTER, H., Private, 16th Queen's (Royal West Surrey Regiment).
Joining in March 1916, he was unable to obtain a transfer overseas owing to ill-health. He was, however, retained on Home Service, and was employed at Cranfield on agricultural work, which duties he performed in a highly efficient manner until demobilised in March 1919.
Cranfield, Beds. Z3285/B—Z3286/B.

LANCASTER, T., Private, 10th Queen's (Royal West Surrey Regiment).
He joined in March 1916, and, on completion of his training, was six months later drafted to the Western Front. During his service there he took part in the Battles of Arras and Ypres, and saw heavy fighting at Cambrai until September 1917, when he was reported missing. Subsequently it was reported that he was killed in action on that date. He was entitled to the General Service and Victory Medals.
"A costly sacrifice upon the altar of freedom."
Cranfield, Beds. Z3285/A—Z3286/A.

LANE, G. P., Private, Oxford. and Bucks. L.I.
In September 1914 he volunteered, and three months later was sent to France, where he fought in the Battles of Neuve Chapelle, Hill 60, Ypres, Festubert and Loos. He gave his life for King and Country on April 9th, 1917, and was entitled to the 1914–15 Star, and the General Service and Victory Medals.
"Nobly striving:
He nobly fell that we might live."
West Perry, near Huntingdon, Hunts. Z2152/B.

LANE, H. J. F., Chief Petty Officer, R.N., H.M.S. "Royal Oak."
When war was declared in August 1914 he was already in the Navy, and throughout the period of hostilities served in H.M.S. "Royal Oak." He took an active part in numerous important engagements in the North and Baltic Seas, and was in action at the Battle of Jutland and the bombardment of Zeebrugge. In 1920 he was still in the Navy, and holds the 1914–15 Star, and the General Service and Victory Medals.
31, Howbury Street, Bedford. Z3288.

LANE, L. A., Private, R.A.M.C.
Volunteering at the outbreak of hostilities in August 1914, he embarked for France shortly afterwards. During his service on the Western Front he experienced fierce fighting in many sectors, and was in action at the Battles of the Somme, Ypres and Cambrai. He was wounded on one occasion, which unfortunately resulted in the loss of his left eye. He was demobilised in July 1920, holding the 1914 Star, and the General Service and Victory Medals.
140, Coventry Road, Queen's Park, Bedford. Z3287.

LANE, P. C., Private, 1st Bedfordshire Regiment.
Mobilised in 1914, he proceeded to France in the following year, and took part in the Battles of Ypres, the Somme, Arras, Vimy Ridge and Cambrai. In 1917 he was transferred to Italy, but, after three months' heavy fighting on the Piave, returned to the Western Front and served throughout the Retreat and Advance of 1918. He was wounded in action whilst overseas, and received his discharge in February 1919, holding the 1914–15 Star, and the General Service and Victory Medals.
48, Cater Street, Kempston, Bedford. Z3289.

LANGCAKE, S. H., Private, Bedfordshire Regt.
He joined in January 1917, and, on conclusion of his training, was three months later sent overseas. Whilst serving on the Western Front he participated in much severe fighting in many important engagements, including the Battles of Arras and Vimy Ridge, but was taken prisoner and kept in captivity in Germany until the close of hostilities. On his release he was demobilised in November 1918, and holds the General Service and Victory Medals.
Bromham Green, near Bedford. Z3290/B.

LANGLEY, C., Driver, Royal Field Artillery.
Joining in February 1918, he received his training on Salisbury Plain, and in the following July embarked for Italy. On that front he was engaged in severe fighting in various sectors, and took an active part in the operations on the Piave. He returned to England and was demobilised in September 1919, holding the General Service and Victory Medals.
33, Queen's Street, Stony Stratford, Bucks. Z3293.

LANGLEY, H., Bugler, 1st Oxford. & Bucks. L.I.
He was mobilised in August 1914, and in January of the following year was drafted to the Western Front. There he fought in the Battles of Neuve Chapelle, Ypres, Festubert and Loos, but was wounded in action on the Somme in March 1916, and invalided to England. Consequently he was discharged as medically unfit for further service in August 1916, and holds the 1914–15 Star, and the General Service and Victory Medals.
3, School Street, New Bradwell, Bucks. Z3291.

LANGLEY, W. J. (D.C.M., M.M.), L/Corporal, Royal Irish Fusiliers.
He volunteered in January 1915, and five months later was drafted to Gallipoli, where he was awarded the Military Medal for conspicuous bravery during the Landing at Suvla Bay. In October 1915 he was sent to Salonika, and played a prominent part in the heavy fighting on the Struma and served through the Retreat from Serbia. He was transferred to Palestine in February 1917, and was in action at the Battles of Gaza and in the Judean Hills. Eventually he served in Russia from March to October 1919, and whilst there was awarded the Distinguished Conduct Medal and the Russian Order of St. George (3rd Class) for great gallantry and devotion to duty against the Bolsheviks. Whilst overseas he was three times wounded in action. In 1920 he was stationed at Constantinople with the Royal Engineers, and also holds the 1914–15 Star, and the General Service and Victory Medals.
8, Prospect Road, Stony Stratford, Bucks. Z3292.

LANSBURY, C. H., Private, 2nd Bedfordshire Regt.
He volunteered in December 1914, and, after completing his training, was ordered to the Western Front in June 1915. Whilst overseas he took an active part in numerous engagements, including those at Festubert, Loos, Givenchy, Arras and Bray. Whilst engaged in physical training he was injured and sent back to England, and consequently discharged as unfit for further service in August 1916. He holds the 1914–15 Star, and the General Service and Victory Medals.
Newton Longville, Bletchley, Bucks. Z3295.

LANSHUTT, M., L/Corporal, West Riding Regt.
Joining in 1916, he was in the following year drafted to the Western Front, where he took part in important engagements in the Passchendaele and Lens sectors. He was unfortunately killed in action in August 1917, and was entitled to the General Service and Victory Medals.
"He died the noblest death a man may die,
Fighting for God and right and liberty."
Bourne End, Cranfield, Beds. Z1447/B.

LARD, H., Private, Oxford. and Bucks. L.I.
He volunteered in January 1915, and later in the same year was drafted to Gallipoli, and served throughout the campaign there. After the Evacuation of the Peninsula he proceeded to Egypt, and was stationed at Alexandria, and also took part in engagements on the Suez Canal. On being transferred to the Western Front he saw heavy fighting on the Somme, where he was wounded in action at Thiepval in September 1916, and invalided to England. He was subsequently discharged as medically unfit for further service in October 1917, and holds the 1914–15 Star, and the General Service and Victory Medals.
16, East Street, Olney, Bucks. Z3296.

LARNER, A. J., Staff-Sergeant, 7th Wiltshire Regiment and Royal Garrison Artillery.
A month after the outbreak of war he volunteered, and in September 1915 was sent to France, where he was in action at Albert. In January 1916 he was transferred to Salonika, and played a conspicuous part in severe fighting on the Doiran and Vardar fronts until invalided home a year later, suffering from malaria and dysentery. On his recovery he returned to the Western Front, and served in engagements at Agincourt, Monchy and Amiens, and was present at the entry into Mons. He was demobilised in May 1919, and holds the 1914–15 Star, and the General Service and Victory Medals.
8, King Street, Stony Stratford, Bucks. Z3298.

LARNER, S., Private, 2nd Northants. Regiment.
At the outbreak of hostilities in August 1914 he was mobilised, and a month later was ordered to the Western Front. After fighting in the Battles of the Marne, La Bassée, Ypres and Neuve Chapelle he was severely wounded in action at Aubers Ridge on May 9th, 1915, and sent back to England. He unfortunately succumbed to his injuries a week later in Exeter Hospital, and was entitled to the 1914 Star, and the General Service and Victory Medals.
"His life for his Country, his soul to God."
19, King Street, Stony Stratford, Bucks. Z3297.

LATHALL, J. E., L/Corporal, R.A.S.C. (M.T.)
He volunteered in September 1914, and, on conclusion of his training on Salisbury Plain in January 1915, embarked for France, where he served for 13 months. During that time he was engaged in severe fighting, principally in the Ypres sector, and in February 1916 was transferred to Salonika. There he saw much service on the Doiran and the Vardar fronts until the close of hostilities. He was demobilised on his return to England in April 1919, and holds the 1914–15 Star, and the General Service and Victory Medals.
25, Mill Street, Newport Pagnell, Bucks. Z3299.

LAUGHTON, E. L., Cook, Royal Navy, H.M.S. "Crescent."
He volunteered in October 1914, and in the following year was posted to H.M.S. "Crescent." In this vessel he proceeded to the Mediterranean Sea, and, during the operations at Gallipoli, served in the Dardanelles. He also took part in the bombardment of Ostend, and served in the Ægean Sea and at Scapa Flow. In 1920 he was still in the Navy, and holds the 1914–15 Star, and the General Service and Victory Medals.
88, George Street, Bedford. Z3300.

LAVENDER, T. W. C., Pte., Bedfordshire Regt.
In January 1916 he volunteered, and was engaged on important duties with his unit at various stations. During an air-raid on Felixstowe in 1917 he sustained serious injuries to his spine, which subsequently caused his death on October 6th, 1919, at Papworth Hall, Huntingdonshire.
"His memory is cherished with pride."
Wennington, Hunts. Z3301/B.

LAVENDER, W. H. D., Private, Bedfordshire and Hertfordshire Regiments.
He volunteered in January 1916, and in the following year proceeded to the Western Front, where he was engaged in severe fighting in the Battles of Arras, Ypres and Cambrai. During the operations on the Somme in 1918 he was gassed, and on his recovery was drafted to India, where he served until 1920. He was demobilised on his return home in October of that year, and holds the General Service and Victory Medals.
Wennington, Hunts. Z3301/A.

LAW, A. V., Pte., Queen's (R. West Surrey Regt.)
He joined the East Kent Regiment in May 1918, and, on being transferred to the Royal West Surrey Regiment, was drafted to France two months later. Whilst on the Western Front he fought in the Battles of Amiens and Cambrai, and took an active part in the final victorious engagements of the war. After the Armistice he served at Cologne with the Army of Occupation until demobilised in November 1919. He holds the General Service and Victory Medals.
Lower Dean, Kimbolton, Hunts. Z3302/D—Z3303/D.

LAW, J., L/Corporal, Bedfordshire Regiment.
Volunteering in February 1915, he received his training at Ampthill and Dovercourt, and in September 1916 proceeded to the Western Front. After only two weeks' service in that theatre of war he died gloriously on the Field of Battle on the Somme on September 25th, 1916. He was entitled to the General Service and Victory Medals.
"He passed out of the sight of men by the path of duty and self-sacrifice."
Lower Dean, Kimbolton, Hunts. Z3302/A—Z3303/A.

LAW, J. J., Private, Machine Gun Corps.
He volunteered in December 1914, and in 1915 was sent to the Western Front, where he was in action in the Battles of Ypres, Festubert, Loos, Albert, the Somme and Arras. In November 1917 he was drafted to Italy, and saw fierce fighting on the Piave and Asiago fronts until March 1918, when he returned to France. He then took part in the Advance on Cambrai and in the final engagements of the war. Demobilised in April 1919, he holds the 1914–15 Star, and the General Service and Victory Medals.
Lower Dean, Kimbolton, Hunts. Z3302/B—Z3303/B.

LAW, L. M., Pte., Middlesex Regt., & Labour Corps.
He joined in December 1917, and four months later was drafted to the Western Front. During his service there he saw much severe fighting in important engagements, including the Battles of Amiens, Cambrai and Le Cateau, and was gassed in August 1918. After the Armistice he proceeded into Germany with the Army of Occupation, and served at Cologne until demobilised in May 1920, holding the General Service and Victory Medals. Lower Dean, Kimbolton, Hunts. Z3302/C—Z3303/C.

LAWES, S., Private, Royal Berkshire Regiment.
When war was declared in August 1914 he was already serving, and was at once ordered to the scene of activities in France. After only six weeks' service there he was wounded in action and invalided to England. Eventually he was discharged as medically unfit for further military duties in January 1916, and holds the 1914 Star, and the General Service and Victory Medals. 20, Eastville Road, South End, Bedford. Z3304.

LAWRENCE, E. C., Sapper, Royal Engineers.
He volunteered in September 1915, and six months later was sent to France, where he served for three years. During that time he saw severe fighting at Gommecourt, and took part in the Battles of the Somme, Arras, Messines and Ypres. He was wounded at Hamel in March 1918 and invalided home, and was subsequently demobilised in February 1919, holding the General Service and Victory Medals.
Duke Street, Aspley Guise, Beds. Z3307.

LAWRENCE, H. S., Gunner, Royal Field Artillery.
Joining in January 1917, he was ordered a year later to France. On that front he was engaged in severe fighting on the Somme, at Armentières and Vimy Ridge, and was gassed in the vicinity of Albert in March 1918. After the close of hostilities he proceeded to Germany with the Army of Occupation, and served on the Rhine until demobilised in October 1919. He holds the General Service and Victory Medals.
8, Bower Street, Bedford. TZ3306.

LAWRENCE, F. J., Gunner, Royal Field Artillery.
He was mobilised in August 1914, and at once ordered to France, where he fought at the Battle of Mons and in the subsequent Retreat. In June 1915 he was transferred to Gallipoli, and was in action at Cape Helles and in numerous other engagements until December 1915, when he was drafted to Mesopotamia. There he took an active part in the Relief of Kut, and on being sent to India, served there until 1918. He then was sent back to the Western Front, and experienced severe fighting in the Retreat and Advance of 1918. He was discharged in March 1920, and holds the Mons Star, and the General Service and Victory Medals.
Chackmore, Buckingham. Z3305.

LAWSON, E., Private, Bedfordshire Regiment.
He volunteered in May 1915, and on completion of his training was in the following year drafted overseas. Whilst serving on the Western Front he saw fierce fighting in engagements in various sectors, and took an active part in the Battles of Arras, Ypres and Cambrai, and was wounded on three occasions. Demobilised in 1919, he holds the General Service and Victory Medals. Barford Cottage, Sandy, Beds. Z3311.

LAWSON, E., A.B., Royal Navy.
Volunteering in 1915, he received his training at the Crystal Palace, and was posted to his ship later in the same year. During the period of hostilities he saw service in various seas, and was engaged on important patrol duties in the North and Baltic Seas. He also served at Gibraltar, and was demobilised in January 1919, holding the 1914–15 Star, and the General Service and Victory Medals.
Ivel Road, Sandy, Beds. Z3310/B.

LAWSON, F. E., L/Corporal, Royal Engineers.
He volunteered in August 1914, but on account of his youth was retained on home defence on the East Coast until 1917. He was then drafted to the Western Front, and employed on special duties in the workshops at the Base. He remained in France until demobilised in June 1919, and holds the General Service and Victory Medals.
17, Hartington Street, Bedford. TX1605/A.

LAWSON, G., Private, Machine Gun Corps.
In May 1917 he joined the Army, and was engaged on important duties with his unit at Grantham. He was not successful in his endeavours to obtain a transfer to a theatre of war, but, nevertheless, rendered many valuable services, particularly in Ireland, and was eventually demobilised in November 1919.
Cambridge Street, St. Neots, Hunts. TZ3309/A.

LAWSON, H. C., Private, 3rd Bedfordshire Regt.
He volunteered in November 1914, and in June of the following year was drafted to the Western Front. There he took an active part in severe fighting at Ypres and Festubert, but after only three months' active service was unfortunately killed in action in the Battle of Loos on September 25th, 1915. He was entitled to the 1914–15 Star, and the General Service and Victory Medals.
"Courage, bright hopes, and a myriad dreams splendidly given."
17, Hartington Street, Bedford. TX1605/B.

LAWSON, W., Private, Royal Warwickshire Regt.
When war broke out he was mobilised with the Huntingdonshire Cyclist Battalion, and served at various home stations until July 1916, when he was transferred to the Royal Warwickshire Regiment and drafted to France. On that front he was in action in the Battles of the Somme, Arras, Ypres, Cambrai and Le Cateau, and saw heavy fighting in the Retreat and Advance of 1918. Discharged in March 1919, he holds the General Service and Victory Medals.
Cambridge Street, St. Neots, Hunts. TZ3309/B.

LAWSON, W. A., Private, 7th Bedfordshire Regt.
A month after the outbreak of war he volunteered, and on completion of his training was sent overseas in 1915. During his service on the Western Front he was engaged in fierce fighting in various sectors, and was wounded on two occasions in the Battle of the Somme. He was invalided to England in 1917, and on his discharge from hospital served at home until demobilised in February 1919. He holds the 1914–15 Star, and the General Service and Victory Medals.
Ivel Road, Sandy, Beds. Z3310/A.

LAWSON, W. J., Rifleman, K.R.R.C.
At the outbreak of hostilities in August 1914 he volunteered, and after a period of training was engaged on duties of an important nature at various stations. He eventually succeeded in obtaining a transfer overseas, and was sent to France on two separate occasions, but each time was invalided home on account of ill-health. He was demobilised in February 1919, and holds the General Service and Victory Medals.
Farrs Yard, Blunham, Beds. Z3308.

LEADEN, J., Driver, Royal Horse Artillery.
He joined in 1916, and on completion of his training on Salisbury Plain was in 1918 ordered to Egypt. After a period of service there he proceeded to Palestine, and in that theatre of war was engaged in severe fighting at Gaza and Jaffa. On his return to England in August 1919 he was demobilised, holding the General Service and Victory Medals.
East Chadley Lane, Godmanchester, Hunts. Z3312/A.

LEE, F. J., Private, 9th Worcestershire Regiment.
He joined in July 1918, but was unable to procure a transfer to the war zone before the cessation of hostilities. In April 1919, however, he proceeded to South Russia, where he saw heavy fighting at Batoum. Whilst in the East he suffered from malaria, and was demobilised on his return to England in November 1919, holding the General Service and Victory Medals. 63, Ledsam Street, Wolverton, Bucks. Z3313.

LEE, H. T., C.S.M., Rifle Brigade.
When war was declared in August 1914 he was already in the Army, but was engaged on important work at Sheerness until 1915, when he was sent to the Western Front. There he played a conspicuous part in many important engagements, including the Battles of Festubert, the Somme, Arras, Lens and Cambrai. In 1918 he was transferred to Egypt, and rendered valuable services as a fire officer. He was still serving in 1920, and holds the 1914–15 Star, and the General Service and Victory Medals. 126, Bower Street, Bedford. Z3314.

LEE, J., Private, Durham Light Infantry.
He joined in November 1916, and in December of the following year was drafted to the Western Front, where he saw much heavy fighting. After taking part in engagements at Ypres and in various other sectors, he was severely wounded in action on the Somme in the Retreat of March 1918, and sent home. He was invalided from the Army in February 1919, and holds the General Service and Victory Medals.
31, Well Street, Buckingham. Z3315.

LEHANE, M., Private, 9th (Queen's Royal) Lancers; and Driver, R.A.S.C.
Volunteering in August 1915, he proceeded to the Western Front, where he saw severe fighting in various sectors. He took part in the Battles of Arras, Bullecourt, Cambrai and the Somme, and many minor engagements, and was wounded whilst carrying despatches at Cambrai in 1918 and on another occasion. He was demobilised in May 1919, and holds the General Service and Victory Medals.
Milton Ernest, Bedford. Z3316.

LEHRLE, A., Corporal, Oxford. and Bucks. L.I.
Mobilised in August 1914, he was retained on important duties in England until 1916, when he was drafted to the Western Front. There he took part in the Battles of the Somme, Arras and Ypres, and many other engagements in various sectors until invalided to hospital in England in 1917. He was discharged in September of that year as medically unfit for further service, and holds the General Service and Victory Medals.
3, Swan Terrace, Stony Stratford, Bucks. TZ3317.

LENTON, W., Rifleman, 21st London Regiment (1st Surrey Rifles).
Joining in March 1917, he was drafted to the Western Front 12 months later, and there saw much heavy fighting. He took part in the Battle of the Somme and many other important engagements in this theatre of war, and was wounded in action at Cambrai in May 1918. Returning home in February 1919, he was demobilised in the following month, and holds the General Service and Victory Medals.
4, George Town, Sandy, Beds. Z3318.

LESTER, S. C., Pte., 5th Royal Sussex Regiment.
Two months after joining in April 1916 he was sent to the Western Front, where he took part in the Battles of the Somme, Vimy Ridge, Ypres and Passchendaele, and many other important engagements. In 1918 he was transferred to Italy, and there saw severe fighting until the cessation of hostilities. He was wounded in action whilst overseas, and was finally demobilised on his return home in November 1919, holding the General Service and Victory Medals.
51, Pilcroft Street, Bedford. X3320.

LESTER, S. T., Sergeant, 5th Bedfordshire Regt. and Labour Corps.
Mobilised in August 1914, he was immediately drafted to the Western Front, where he served through the Retreat from Mons. After taking a prominent part also in the Battle of the Marne and other important engagements, he was wounded in action at Festubert in May 1915 and invalided home. On his recovery he was transferred to the Labour Corps, and retained in England until his discharge in March 1919. He holds the Mons Star, and the General Service and Victory Medals. Warboys, Hunts. Z3319.

LETT, F. W., Private, Labour Corps.
Volunteering in November 1915, he proceeded to France in the following month, and there served at Arras, Ypres and Cambrai, and in various other sectors of the front. He was engaged chiefly in trench-digging and in conveying supplies to the forward areas, and took also an active part in the Retreat and Advance of 1918. He was demobilised in November 1919, and holds the 1914–15 Star, and the General Service and Victory Medals.
32, Castle Lane, Bedford. X3324/A.

LETT, G. E., Private, Royal Berkshire Regiment.
He joined in October 1916, and five months later was drafted to the Western Front, where he saw severe fighting on the Somme and in other sectors. He made the supreme sacrifice, falling in action in August 1917 after only five months' service overseas. He was entitled to the General Service and Victory Medals.
"He died the noblest death a man may die,
Fighting for God and right and liberty."
Prospect Place, Emberton, Bucks. Z3322/B.

LETT, G. R., Rifleman, 5th London Regiment (London Rifle Brigade).
He joined in August 1917, and, on completing his training in March of the following year, was drafted to the Western Front, where he saw much heavy fighting. Severely wounded in action in April 1918, he was invalided home, and was finally discharged in November 1919 as medically unfit for further service. He holds the General Service and Victory Medals.
32, Castle Lane, Bedford. X3324/B.

LETT, H., Sergt., 51st Royal Warwickshire Regt.
He joined in September 1918, and after a period of training, was retained on important duties at various stations. Owing to the early cessation of hostilities, he was unable to obtain his transfer to a theatre of war, but in January 1919 was sent to France and thence into Germany with the Army of Occupation. He was demobilised on his return home in March 1920.
West Street, Olney, Bucks. Z3321.

LETT, H. (D.C.M.), Bombardier, R.F.A.
He volunteered in August 1914, and in January of the following year proceeded to the Western Front. Whilst in this theatre of war he saw severe fighting in various sectors, took part in the Battles of Ypres, the Somme, Arras and Cambrai, and served also through the Retreat and Advance of 1918. He was awarded the Distinguished Conduct Medal for conspicuous bravery displayed in repairing telephone wires under heavy fire near Ypres in March 1917, and, holding also the 1914–15 Star, and the General Service and Victory Medals, was demobilised in March 1919.
Prospect Place, Emberton, Bucks. Z3322 /A.

LETT, H. C., Private, Machine Gun Corps.
Joining in February 1917, he proceeded to the Western Front on completion of a period of training in the following August, and there saw severe fighting in various sectors. He took part in the Battles of Passchendaele, the Somme, Amiens and Epéhy, and many other important engagements until the cessation of hostilities. Returning home in February 1919, he was demobilised in the following month, and holds the General Service and Victory Medals.
37, Warwick Terrace, Olney, Bucks. TZ3323 /A.

LETT, J. T., L/Corporal, 2nd Devonshire Regt.
He joined in October 1916, and in July of the following year was drafted to the Western Front. There, after taking part in the Battle of Ypres and many minor engagements, he was taken prisoner at Passchendaele in November 1917, and was held in captivity in Germany until after the cessation of hostilities. He was demobilised in November 1919, and holds the General Service and Victory Medals.
1, The Mount, Emberton, Bucks. TZ3323 /B.

LETT, W., Drummer, 2nd Essex Regiment.
Already in the Army when war was declared in August 1914, he was immediately drafted to the Western Front, where he served through the Retreat from Mons. He afterwards took part in the Battles of Albert and Bullecourt, and many other important engagements until severely wounded in action at Ypres in 1917, and sent home. He was invalided from the Army in that year, and holds the Mons Star and the General Service and Victory Medals. 14, Dane St., Bedford. X3325.

LETTS, H., Sapper, Royal Engineers.
Volunteering in April 1915, he was drafted to France on completing his training in the following September, and was there engaged on road-making and transport duties. He was also present at the Battles of Loos, the Somme, Arras and Ypres and took an active part in the Retreat and Advance of 1918, being wounded the day before the Armistice was signed. He was for a time in hospital at Southampton and Netley, before being invalided from the Army in April 1919, and holds the 1914–15 Star, and the General Service and Victory Medals.
6, Northampton Terrace, Newport Pagnell, Bucks. Z3326.

LEVITT, F., Rifleman, King's Royal Rifle Corps.
A Territorial, he was mobilised in August 1914, and later in that year proceeded to the Western Front, where he saw much severe fighting in the Ypres sector. Later, however, he was transferred to Salonika, and was there again in action, taking part in many important engagements on the Doiran and Vardar fronts. He returned home for demobilisation in August 1919, and holds the 1914–15 Star, and the General Service and Victory Medals.
46, Spencer Street, Bradwell, Bucks. Z3327.

LEWIN, F. G., Private, 2nd Huntingdon Cyclist Battalion and Royal Berkshire Regiment.
After volunteering in November 1914, he underwent a period of training prior to being drafted to the Western Front in October 1916, and there took part in the Battle of the Somme and minor engagements. He is believed to have been killed in action on the Ancre on March 10th, 1917. He was entitled to the General Service and Victory Medals.
"Great deeds cannot die:
They with the sun and moon renew their light for ever."
Little Stukeley, Hunts. Z3329.

LEWIN, H. V., Private, R.A.M.C.
He joined in June 1917, and, after a short period of training, was engaged on important duties in the hospitals at various stations. Owing to ill-health he was not successful in obtaining his transfer to a theatre of war, but, nevertheless, rendered very valuable services until November 1917, when he was invalided from the Army.
2, St. Anne's Terrace, Godmanchester, Hunts. Z3328.

LEWIS, F., A.B., Royal Navy.
He joined in October 1916, and after serving for a time at the Crystal Palace, was posted to H.M.S. "Neptune," attached to the Grand Fleet in the North Sea. He was engaged on various important duties in these waters, and took part in many actions until the cessation of hostilities. Demobilised in March 1919, he holds the General Service and Victory Medals.
High Street, Somersham, Hunts. Z3331.

LEWIS, W. J., Driver, Royal Engineers.
He volunteered at the outbreak of war in August 1914, and after undergoing a period of training, was retained at various stations, where he was engaged on duties of great importance. He was unable to obtain his transfer overseas, on account of injuries received in an accident, and was finally discharged in October 1917 as medically unfit for further service.
28, Garfield Street, Bedford. X3330.

LIGGINS, C., Private, Royal Berkshire Regiment.
Joining in April 1916, he was drafted to the Western Front in the following October, and there saw much heavy fighting. After taking part in the Battles of the Somme and Arras, he was wounded in action at Oppy Wood in May 1917 and on another occasion, and, as a result, had to have his right arm amputated. He was in hospital in France and at Leeds before being invalided from the Army in June 1918, and holds the General Service and Victory Medals.
18, Tickford St., Newport Pagnell, Bucks. Z3332 /B—Z3333 /B.

LIGGINS, E. J., Private, 1st Northamptonshire Regiment; and Air Mechanic, Royal Air Force.
Having enlisted in December 1913, he proceeded to the Western Front three months after the outbreak of war in August of the following year, and there, after taking part in the Battle of Neuve Chapelle, was wounded at Richburg and invalided home. He returned to France, however, on his recovery in November 1915, and was again in action in the Battles of the Somme, Arras and Ypres. Again sent to hospital in England in 1919, he afterwards served with the Royal Air Force, attached to the Army of Occupation in Germany, and was finally discharged in February 1920. He holds the 1914–15 Star, and the General Service and Victory Medals.
18, Tickford St., Newport Pagnell, Bucks. Z3332 /A—Z3333 /A.

LILLEY, A. G., L/Corporal, Lancashire Fusiliers.
He joined in May 1916, and in the following year proceeded to the Western Front, where he saw much heavy fighting and took part in the Battles of Ypres and the Somme, and other important engagements. Mortally wounded in action near Cambrai in November 1918, he unhappily died on the 29th of that month. He was entitled to the General Service and Victory Medals.
"Whilst we remember, the sacrifice is not in vain."
Bedford Road, Stagsden, Beds. X3335 /C.

LILLEY, C. R., Driver, Royal Engineers.
He joined in February 1916, and in the following year proceeded to the Western Front, where he was engaged on important transport duties in various sectors. He also took an active part in the Battles of Arras, Ypres, Cambrai and Bapaume, and many minor engagements, and was demobilised on his return home in December 1918. He holds the General Service and Victory Medals.
Broad Green, Cranfield, Beds. Z3336.

LILLEY, H., Private, Oxford. and Bucks. L.I.
Shortly after joining in 1917, he proceeded to France, where he saw severe fighting in various sectors of the front. He took part in the Battles of Cambrai and the Somme, and many other important engagements in this theatre of war until the cessation of hostilities. Returning home in 1919, he was demobilised in February of that year, and holds the General Service and Victory Medals.
Bedford Road, Stagsden, Beds. Z3335 /B.

LILLEY, P., Private, Royal Fusiliers.
He volunteered in 1915, and, on completing his training in the following year, was sent to the Western Front. Whilst in this theatre of war he took part in many important engagements, including the Battles of Arras, Messines, Ypres and Cambrai, and was gassed. He was afterwards attached to the Military Police with the Army of Occupation in Germany, returning home for demobilisation in January 1919. He holds the General Service and Victory Medals.
Bedford Road, Stagsden, Beds. Z3335 /A.

LILLEY, S. E., Private, Bedfordshire Regiment and Royal Welch Fusiliers.
He joined in February 1916, and later in that year proceeded to the Western Front, where he was wounded in the Somme Offensive. Invalided home he was afterwards drafted to Mesopotamia in H.M.T. "Cameronia," which was sunk in the Mediterranean in April 1917, but he was fortunately rescued, and afterwards saw severe fighting on the River Tigris. Returning home in February 1919, he was demobilised in the following month, and holds the General Service and Victory Medals.
Manor Farm, Tilbrook, Beds. Z3337.

LILLEY, W. C., Private, Suffolk Regiment.
Joining in February 1916, he was drafted shortly afterwards to the Western Front, where he saw severe fighting in various sectors. He took part in the Battles of Arras, Ypres and Cambrai, and many other important engagements, and was wounded in action on the Somme in July 1916. He afterwards served with the Army of Occupation in Germany, and was demobilised on his return home in October 1919, holding the General Service and Victory Medals.
Kimbolton, Hunts. Z3338.

LILLINGTON, E., Corporal, 6th Bedfordshire Regt.
Volunteering in September 1914, he proceeded to the Western Front in the following year and there took part in the Battles of Loos, Albert, the Somme, Arras and Ypres, and other engagements, and was wounded in action in 1916. He fell fighting at Passchendaele Ridge on October 7th, 1917. He was entitled to the 1914–15 Star, and the General Service and Victory Medals.
"He joined the great white company of valiant souls."
39, Great Brickhill, Bletchley, Bucks. Z3339.

LIMBREY, A. R., Guardsmen, Grenadier Guards.
Having enlisted in March 1910, he was mobilised at the outbreak of war in August 1914, and proceeded to the Western Front in the following month. There he saw much severe fighting and took part in the Battles of the Marne, the Aisne and Ypres, and other engagements until invalided home in November 1917. He was afterwards retained in England until eventually discharged as medically unfit for further service, holding the 1914 Star, and the General Service and Victory Medals. 32, West Street, Olney, Bucks. Z3340/A.

LIMMAGE, C. S., Pte., Royal Warwickshire Regt.
Three months after volunteering in December he was drafted to France, where he saw heavy fighting in various sectors of the front. He took part in the Battles of Neuve Chapelle, Hill 60, Ypres, Loos, the Somme and Arras, and many minor engagements until severely wounded in action in May 1917. He was invalided from the Army in September of that year, and holds the 1914–15 Star, and the General Service and Victory Medals. Piper's Lane, Godmanchester, Hunts. Z3341.

LINCOLN, F. G., Armourer, R.N., H.M.S. "Erebus."
He joined in August 1917, and, posted to H.M.S. "Erebus," was sent to the North Sea, where he was engaged on important patrol duty for over a year. During 1918 he took part in the bombardment of Zeebrugge. After rendering valuable services, he was demobilised in February 1919, and holds the General Service and Victory Medals.
31, Woburn Road, Kempston, Bedford. X3342/A.

LINCOLN, J. W., Gunner, Royal Garrison Artillery.
Ten months after joining in July 1916 he was drafted to France, and took part in the Battles of Messines, Ypres and Cambrai. During the Retreat of 1918 he fought in the second Battle of the Somme, and in the ensuing offensive was gassed. Returning home in January 1919, he was demobilised a month later, and holds the General Service and Victory Medals.
23, Filberts Walk, St. Ives, Hunts. Z3344/A.

LINCOLN, M. F., Bandsman, R.N.D.
Volunteering in November 1914, he was retained at home until 1917, and was then drafted to the Western Front, where he was employed on hospital work at Boulogne and Calais. During the fighting at Ypres, Cambrai and the Somme he did good work as a stretcher-bearer. He was demobilised in March 1919, and holds the General Service and Victory Medals.
10, Hartford Road, Huntingdon, Hunts. Z3346.

LINCOLN, T. W., Private, 3rd and 9th Essex Regt.
He volunteered at the outbreak of war and in the following year embarked for France, where he saw heavy fighting at Festubert, Loos, the Somme, Ypres, Passchendaele Ridge, Cambrai and Albert, and was wounded in August 1918. As well as serving in the Essex Regiment, he was for a time with the Bedfordshire Regiment. Demobilised in March 1919, he holds the 1914–15 Star, and the General Service and Victory Medals. 31, Woburn Road, Kempston, Bedford. X3342/B.

LINCOLN, W., Private, Bedfordshire Regiment.
A time-serving soldier, he was sent to Egypt in 1915 and, attached to the Expeditionary Force, took a prominent part in the Palestine campaign. He fought in the Battles of Gaza, and was in action during the operations leading to the capture of Jaffa, Jerusalem, Tripoli and Aleppo. Returning home he was discharged in March 1919, and holds the 1914–15 Star, and the General Service and Victory Medals.
79, Bunyan Road, Kempston, Bedford. X3343.

LINCOLN, W., Private, Royal Warwickshire Regt.
Volunteering in October 1915, he completed his training and crossed the Channel in the following July. After taking part in the Somme Offensive he was unhappily reported missing and later, killed in action on September 7th, 1916. He was entitled to the General Service and Victory Medals.
"A valiant Soldier, with undaunted heart he breasted life's last hill."
32, Filberts Walk, St. Neots, Hunts. Z3344/B.

LINCOLN, W. A., 2nd Writer, R.N., H.M.S. "Blake."
He joined the Navy in March 1916, and served as a Writer in H.M.S. "Blake" for the remainder of the war. In this vessel he was stationed at Scapa Flow and in the Mediterranean Sea, and rendered valuable services. He was demobilised in June 1919, after his return to shore, and holds the General Service and Victory Medals.
Church Street, St. Neots, Hunts. Z3345.

LINE, B. C., Private, 7th Bedfordshire Regiment.
Volunteering in October 1915, he was drafted to France in the following August, but was wounded in October at Thiepval during the Somme Offensive. After being in hospital in Birmingham for some months, he was eventually invalided out of the Army on account of his wounds in March 1917, and holds the General Service and Victory Medals.
High Street, Sharnbrook, Beds. Z3351/A.

LINE, F. G., Sergeant, 2nd Border Regiment.
A Regular soldier, who was serving at the outbreak of war, he was sent to France in October 1914, but after fighting at La Bassée was severely wounded on October 26th, during the first Battle of Ypres. He unhappily succumbed to his injuries the following day. He was entitled to the 1914 Star, and the General Service and Victory Medals.
"Nobly striving:
He nobly fell that we might live."
54, Oakley, near Bedford. Z3350/A.

LINE, F. W., Private, Oxford. and Bucks. L.I.
He volunteered three months after the declaration of war, and in the following year proceeded to France, where he saw much fighting. On July 19th, 1916, he was reported missing after a heavy engagement on the Somme, and was later presumed killed. He was entitled to the 1914–15 Star, and the General Service and Victory Medals.
"Honour to the immortal dead, who gave their youth that the world might grow old in peace."
High Street, Sharnbrook, Beds. Z3351/B.

LINE, R., Private, 7th Bedfordshire Regiment and Labour Corps.
Volunteering in December 1915, he was sent to France in the following year, and took part in the heavy fighting on that front, including the Somme Offensive, until wounded at Arras on May 3rd, 1917. He was then invalided home and, transferred to the Labour Corps, was employed on the land. After doing good work in that capacity, he was demobilised in March 1919, and holds the General Service and Victory Medals.
Pidley, Hunts. Z3352.

LINE, T. C., Private, 1st Bedfordshire Regiment.
Eight months after volunteering he was sent to France in April 1915, and served on the Arras front. Transferred soon afterwards to the Ypres salient, he was unhappily killed in action during a gas-attack on May 6th, only a few weeks after his arrival in France. He was entitled to the 1914–15 Star, and the General Service and Victory Medals.
"Great deeds cannot die:
They with the sun and moon renew their light for ever."
54, Oakley, near Bedford. Z3350/B.

LINES, F., Stoker, R.N., H.M.S. "Shannon."
He joined the Royal Navy in November 1916, and, after completing his training at Chatham and in Scotland, was sent in H.M.S. "Shannon" to the North Sea, where he served on patrol and escort duties until the Armistice. Returning to shore, he was demobilised in February 1919, and holds the General Service and Victory Medals.
75, Newport Road, New Bradwell, Bucks. TZ3347.

LINES, F. G. (M.M.), Private, R.A.M.C.
Volunteering in September 1915, he proceeded to the Western Front a month later, and was employed as a stretcher-bearer. In this capacity he took part in the Battles of Ypres, the Somme, Arras and Cambrai, and was awarded the Military Medal for great gallantry in rescuing wounded under heavy shell-fire in the Somme sector in 1917. In addition he holds the 1914–15 Star, and the General Service and Victory Medals, and was demobilised in January 1919.
15, Russell Street, Stony Stratford, Bucks. Z3348/A.

LINES, W. H., Private, 1st Worcestershire Regt.; and Corporal, Royal Air Force.
He volunteered in September 1914, and was sent to France in the following March. After taking part in the Battles of Ypres and Loos, he was wounded during the Somme Offensive in 1916, and invalided to hospital at Rouen. On his recovery he rejoined his unit, but in 1917 received a second wound which necessitated his evacuation to England and treatment in hospital for five months. He was then transferred to the Royal Air Force as a corporal and was employed in the shops as a metal worker until March 1919, when he was demobilised, holding the 1914–15 Star, and the General Service and Victory Medals.
15, Russell Street, Stony Stratford, Bucks. Z3348/B.

LINFORD, A., Private, Labour Corps.
Volunteering in July 1915, he completed his training, and in November was sent to France, where he was employed on road construction in the Ypres sector. On September 3rd, 1917, he lost his life owing to a bomb which burst on his dug-out at night. He was entitled to the 1914–15 Star, and the General Service and Victory Medals.
"His life for his Country, his soul to God."
4, Sapley Lane, Hartford, Hunts. Z3349/A.

LINFORD, H., Private, Machine Gun Corps.
A veteran soldier, he was mobilised in August 1914, and, completing his training, was sent to France at the opening of the Somme Offensive, in which he took a prominent part, and was gassed in November. After being in hospital a month he returned to the line and fought at Cambrai and in the Retreat and Advance of 1918. He was discharged in February 1919, and holds the General Service and Victory Medals.
5, Sapley Terrace, Hartford, Hunts. Z3353.

LINFORD, H. G., Bombardier, R.F.A.
He volunteered in August 1914, and in October 1915 was drafted to France, and two months later to Salonika. On that front he served in the Doiran and Struma sectors, and for a time acted as sergeant in charge of a Machine Gun Team. He was demobilised in June 1919 after his return home, and holds the 1914–15 Star, and the General Service and Victory Medals.
14, Duncombe Street, Bletchley, Bucks. Z4380/B—Z4381/B.

LINFORD, W. M., Private, Bedfordshire Regt.
Volunteering in July 1915, he was drafted four months later to the Western Front, where he fought on the Somme and was wounded in January 1917. After two months in hospital at Boulogne, he was again in action, but was taken prisoner at Cambrai in March 1918. Released after the Armistice, he was demobilised in December 1919, and holds the 1914–15 Star, and the General Service and Victory Medals.
4, Sapley Lane, Hartford, Hunts. Z3349/B.

LINGER, S., Private, Royal Sussex Regiment.
He joined in August 1917, but, being unfit for service in a theatre of war, was sent to Ireland later in the year, and served at Sligo and Killarney for 10 months. After rendering valuable services, he returned to England and was demobilised in February 1919. Huntingdon Street, St. Neots, Hunts. Z3354.

LINNELL, A. J. D., Private, 10th Essex Regiment.
He joined in March 1916, and was drafted overseas in 1917. Whilst on the Western Front he served at St. Quentin, but was twice wounded at Albert, losing in consequence his left arm. Invalided home, he was kept for a time in hospital, and in June 1918 was discharged as unfit for further service. He holds the General Service and Victory Medals.
Seven Oaks, Kimbolton, Hunts. Z3355.

LITCHFIELD, A. C., Private, Lincolnshire Regt.
Volunteering in August 1915, he was drafted to the Western Front in the following year, and took part in the Somme Offensive and in the Battles of Ypres and Arras. Wounded at Arras in April 1917, he was evacuated to England, and admitted to hospital at Liverpool for 12 months. He was eventually discharged in February 1919, and holds the General Service and Victory Medals. Hilton, Hunts. Z3356.

LITCHFIELD, C., Private, R.A.M.C.
Already in the Army when war broke out, he was drafted to France in August 1914, and whilst on the Western Front played an important part in the Battles of Ypres, Loos, Festubert, the Somme, Passchendaele and Cambrai. He was wounded and twice gassed in action and was eventually discharged in February 1919, holding the 1914 Star, and the General Service and Victory Medals.
5, Holt Row, Cauldwell Street, Bedford. X3357.

LITCHFIELD, C. C., Private, 52nd Royal Fusiliers.
On attaining military age, he joined the Royal Fusiliers in April 1918, and quickly proceeded to France, where he saw heavy fighting in the Arras, Ypres and Somme sectors. After the cessation of hostilities he served in Germany with the Army of Occupation, and was eventually demobilised in March 1920, holding the General Service and Victory Medals.
94, George Street, Bedford. Z3359.

LITCHFIELD, C. F., Pte., 5th Bedfordshire Regt.
Mobilised in August 1914, he was engaged on important coast defence duties, but owing to his being medically unfit was not drafted overseas. In May 1916 he was transferred to Class W., Army Reserve, and released for work of National importance in a large munition factory, where he rendered valuable services until finally discharged from the Army in January 1919.
6, Holt Row, Bedford. X3361/B.

LITCHFIELD, E., Corporal, 5th Bedfordshire Regt.
Mobilised in August 1914, he underwent his training and was then retained on special medical duties. He was unsuccessful in obtaining his transfer overseas on account of ill-health, but did excellent work until invalided from the Army in March 1918
6, Holt Row, Bedford. X3361/A.

LITCHFIELD, G., Sapper, Royal Engineers.
He volunteered in August 1915, and was quickly drafted to the Western Front, where he took a prominent part in the Battles of Loos, the Somme, Arras, Vimy Ridge, Ypres and Cambrai. He also rendered valuable services during the Retreat and Advance, and was demobilised on his return to England in March 1919, holding the 1914–15 Star, and the General Service and Victory Medals.
17, Muswell Road, South End, Bedford. Z3358.

LITCHFIELD, J., Pte., 2/1st Oxford. & Bucks. L.I.
He volunteered in August 1914, and five months later was drafted to France, where he took part in the Battles of Ypres (II.), Loos and the Somme. He laid down his life for King and Country on September 8th, 1916, during the offensive in the last-named sector. He was entitled to the 1914–15 Star, and the General Service and Victory Medals.
"Courage, bright hopes, and a myriad dreams, splendidly given."
72, Victoria Street, Bletchley, Bucks. Z1859/A.

LITCHFIELD, W. B., Sapper, Royal Engineers.
He joined in February 1917, and later in the same year was drafted to Palestine. Whilst in this theatre of war he was in action at the Battles of Gaza and Jifjaffa and at the capture of Jerusalem and Tripoli. He was demobilised in March 1919, and holds the General Service and Victory Medals.
31, Dunville Road, Queen's Park, Bedford. Z3360/A.

LITCHFIELD, W. F., L/Cpl., Royal Defence Corps.
Owing to the fact that he was overage for service in a fighting unit, he volunteered in the R.D.C. in August 1914, and for nearly three years was engaged in guarding prisoners of war at Brocton Camp, Staffordshire. He did excellent work with his unit until discharged in March 1917.
31, Dunville Road, Queen's Park, Bedford. Z3360/B.

LITTLE, A. C., Gunner, Royal Field Artillery.
He joined in November 1916, and on completion of his training was drafted to the Western Front, where he was in action with his Battery at the Battles of Arras, Ypres, Passchendaele, Cambrai and Le Cateau, and in other important engagements during the Retreat and Advance of 1918. He was demobilised in February 1919, and holds the General Service and Victory Medals. 21, Bedford Street, Wolverton, Bucks. Z3362.

LITTLE, A. J., Driver, R.A.S.C.
Volunteering in November 1915, he was soon drafted to France, where he was engaged on important transport duties in the forward areas at the Battles of the Somme, Arras and Cambrai. He also served throughout the Retreat and Advance of 1918, and received severe injuries as the result of his horse bolting. Demobilised in February 1919, he holds the General Service and Victory Medals.
London Road, Sandy, Beds. Z3363/A

LITTLE, C. H., Rifleman, 21st London Regiment.
He joined in March 1917, and was stationed at Bedford with the 23rd Training Reserve for a time. Proceeding to France later in the same year, he saw much severe fighting at Ypres, Cambrai, Arras and on the Somme. He was demobilised in March 1919, and holds the General Service and Victory Medals.
London Road, Sandy, Beds. Z3363/B.

LITTLE, C. T., L/Cpl., Norfolk Regt. & R.A.M.C.
Joining in 1917, he underwent a period of training before being drafted to the Western Front. After the cessation of hostilities he proceeded into Germany with the Army of Occupation and rendered valuable services on the Rhine until his demobilisation in November 1919, holding the General Service and Victory Medals. 6, Church Road, Willington, Bucks. Z3365.

LITTLE, H., Private, Machine Gun Corps.
He was mobilised in August 1914, but early in the following year was discharged as medically unfit. In September 1917, however, he joined the Machine Gun Corps, and proceeding to France two months later, took part in much severe fighting. On April 10th, 1918, he was reported missing, and is now presumed to have been killed in action near Cambrai on that date. He was entitled to the General Service and Victory Medals.
"His memory is cherished with pride."
Blunham, Sandy, Beds. Z3364.

LITTLEJOHN, T., Private, Oxford. & Bucks. L.I.
Already serving in August 1914, he was sent to France early in the following year, and took part in the Battles of Hill 60, Ypres (II.), Festubert and Loos, where he was gassed in September 1915 and invalided home. On his recovery he proceeded to Mesopotamia, and was in action at Kut and Baghdad and in important engagements along the Tigris. He was demobilised in September 1919, and holds the 1914–15 Star, and the General Service and Victory Medals.
40, Bridge Street, New Bradwell, Bucks. Z3366.

LOCKE, T., Sergeant, R.A.S.C.
Mobilised in August 1914, he was quickly drafted to France, and served with distinction during the Retreat from Mons. He was later engaged on important transport duties in the forward areas during the Battles of the Marne, the Aisne, Ypres, the Somme and Cambrai, and did excellent work. He received his discharge in March 1919, and holds the Mons Star, and the General Service and Victory Medals.
31, Mill Street, Newport Pagnell, Bucks. Z3367.

LONG, A., Sapper, Royal Engineers.
Volunteering in November 1915, he was later sent to Egypt, but after serving for a time at Cairo, proceeded into Palestine and took part in the Advance with General Allenby's Forces. He was in action at Gaza, Jaffa, Jericho, Beyrout and Haifa, and whilst in the East suffered from dysentery and fever. Demobilised in August 1919, he holds the General Service and Victory Medals. 17, Pembroke Street, Bedford. Z3369.

LONG, T., Private, 14th Leicestershire Regiment.
He joined in July 1917, and twelve months later was drafted to the Western Front, where he took part in heavy fighting at La Bassée and Ypres before being invalided home with shell-shock as the result of being buried by a shell explosion. On his recovery he served for a short time in Ireland, and was demobilised in February 1919, holding the General Service and Victory Medals. 2, Elm Street, Buckingham. Z3368.

LONGLAND, A., Pte., North Staffordshire Regt.
He volunteered in the North Staffordshire Regiment in October 1914, but was later transferred to the Northamptonshire Regiment and sent to France, where he took part in the Battles of the Somme, Arras and Bullecourt before being invalided home with trench fever. On his recovery he proceeded to the East, but whilst on the way out the vessel in which he was sailing was torpedoed. He was fortunately rescued and sent on to Mesopotamia and saw heavy fighting at Amara, Baghdad and along the Tigris. In December 1918 he went to South Russia, and served there until his demobilisation in May 1919. Unfortunately he has since died, and was entitled to the General Service and Victory Medals.
"His memory is cherished with pride."
29, West Street, Olney, Bucks. Z3370/B.

LONGLAND, E., Sergeant, Oxford. and Bucks. L.I.; and Sapper, Royal Engineers.
He volunteered in May 1915, and in the following year was sent to France, where he took part in the Battles of Albert, the Somme, Arras, Ypres and Cambrai. In 1917 he was invalided home with trench feet, but later returned to the Western Front, and was gassed in action during the Advance of 1918. Demobilised in January 1919, he holds the General Service and Victory Medals.
29, West Street, Olney, Bucks. Z3370/A.

LONGLAND, H., Private, 5th Devonshire Regt.
He joined in May 1917, and in July of the following year was sent to the Western Front, where he saw heavy fighting in the Cambrai sector during the Advance. After the cessation of hostilities he served at Cologne with the Army of Occupation until his demobilisation in March 1919, holding the General Service and Victory Medals.
30, East Street, Olney, Bucks. Z3371/B.

LONGLAND, J., Private, Oxford. and Bucks. L.I.
He joined in June 1916, and four months later was drafted to the Western Front, where he took part in heavy fighting during the Somme Offensive. He died gloriously on the Field of Battle near St. Quentin in April 1917, and was entitled to the General Service and Victory Medals.
"Nobly striving:
He nobly fell that we might live."
30, East Street, Olney, Bucks. Z3371/A.

LONGLAND, J. S., Private, Bedfordshire Regt.
He volunteered in November 1915, and in the following year was sent to Mesopotamia. Whilst in this theatre of war he was in action at Amara, Basra and Baghdad, and during heavy fighting along the banks of the Tigris. He was demobilised on his return to England in March 1919, and holds the General Service and Victory Medals.
29, West Street, Olney, Bucks. Z3370/C.

LONNON, A. C., Sapper, Royal Engineers.
Volunteering in September 1915, he was quickly drafted to the Western Front, where he rendered valuable services with his unit whilst engaged on important mining, bridge-building and trench-digging duties in the Somme, Arras, Ypres and Cambrai sectors. He was demobilised in August 1919, and holds the 1914–15 Star, and the General Service and Victory Medals.
57, Iddesleigh Road, Bedford. Z3372/A.

LONNON, H., Sergeant, Royal Air Force.
He joined in July 1916, and later in the same year was drafted to the Western Front, where he served with a bombing Squadron, and did excellent work during many raids on enemy positions. He also acted as an Instructor for some time, and was eventually demobilised in March 1919, holding the General Service and Victory Medals.
57, Iddesleigh Road, Bedford. Z3372/B.

LONNON, S. V., Private, 3rd Norfolk Regiment.
He joined in April 1917, and was quickly sent to India for garrison duty, but in December of the same year, was transferred to Salonika. Whilst in the Balkan theatre of war, he took part in heavy ghting on the Doiran and Struma fronts. He was demobilised in March 1919, and holds the General Service and Victory Medals. 57, Iddesleigh Road, Bedford. Z3372/C.

LOOSLEY, A., Private, Queen's Own (Royal West Kent Regiment).
He joined in March 1918, and was drafted to France four months later. During the subsequent Advance of the Allies, he saw heavy fighting in the Cambrai sector before being badly wounded in action in August 1918. He was eventually demobilised in February 1919, and holds the General Service and Victory Medals.
32, St. Leonard's Street, Bedford. X3373/B

LOOSLEY, P. G., L/Corporal, Royal Engineers.
Mobilised in August 1914, he was first retained on important duties of a special nature at various home stations. In March 1918, however, he was sent to France, and was engaged on important transport work during the Retreat and Advance, particularly in the Cambrai and Le Cateau sectors. He was demobilised in June 1919, and holds the General Service and Victory Medals.
32, St. Leonard's Street, Bedford. X3373/A.

LORD, A. E., Private, 1st Bedfordshire Regiment.
He was mobilised in August 1914, and proceeding to France a month later took part in the Battles of the Marne, La Bassée, Ypres and Givenchy. After being wounded in action in 1915, he was engaged as a farrier with the Transport Section of his unit, and did excellent work until May 1916, when he was discharged—time expired. He holds the 1914 Star, and the General Service and Victory Medals.
35, Denmark Street, Fenny Stratford, Bucks. Z3375/A.

LORD, G., Private, Royal Fusiliers; and Driver, Royal Army Service Corps.
Volunteering in January 1916, he proceeded to France with the Royal Fusiliers in the following year, but was later transferred to the Royal Army Service Corps. He was engaged on important transport duties in the Somme, Neuve Chapelle, Arras, Ypres and Cambrai sectors, and did excellent work. Demobilised in March 1919, he holds the General Service and Victory Medals. Chellington, Beds. Z3376/B—Z3377/B.

LORD, S. J., Corporal, R.A.S.C. (M.T.)
He volunteered in May 1915, and in August was drafted to the Western Front, where he was engaged on important transport duties during the Battles of the Somme, Arras, Ypres and Cambrai, and was gassed. He was evacuated to England suffering from appendicitis, and underwent an operation. Demobilised in February 1919, he holds the 1914–15 Star, and the General Service and Victory Medals.
Chellington, Beds. Z3376/A—Z3377/A.

LORD, V. G., Private, 7th Oxford. and Bucks. L.I.
Volunteering in September 1914, he was drafted to France twelve months later, but after a few weeks' service in the Albert sector, was transferred to Salonika, where he took part in heavy fighting on the Vardar and Doiran fronts. He was reported missing on May 9th, 1917, and is now believed to have been killed in action. He was entitled to the 1914–15 Star, and the General Service and Victory Medals.
13, Tavistock Road, Bletchley, Bucks. Z3374/A.

LORD, W., Private, Royal Sussex Regiment.
He joined in June 1918, and after a period of training, was drafted to the Western Front, where he served until the cessation of hostilities. He then proceeded to Germany with the Army of Occupation and remained there until his demobilisation in March 1919, holding the General Service and Victory Medals. Chellington, Beds. Z3376/C—Z3377/C.

LORD, W. G., Driver, R.A.S.C. (H.T.)
He joined the Army in September 1910, and when war broke out in August 1914, was immediately drafted to France. There he was engaged on important duties with the horse transport, and took an active part in engagements at Ypres, Arras, Albert, Cambrai, the Somme and Bapaume. Whilst on leave in July 1918 he was taken ill, and finally discharged in May 1919 as medically unfit for further service. He holds the 1914 Star, and the General Service and Victory Medals.
11, Tavistock Road, Bletchley, Bucks. Z3375/A.

LORD, W. J., Corporal, Oxford. & Bucks. L.I. (T.F.)
He volunteered in December 1914, and in the following June proceeded to the Western Front, where he took part in many engagements, including those at Ypres, Gommecourt, Péronne, Vimy Ridge, Ypres (III.), Passchendaele and Cambrai. He was then transferred to Italy and saw much fighting on the Piave River and Asiago Plateau. After hostilities ceased he saw service in Austria, and was demobilised in February 1919, holding the 1914–15 Star, and the General Service and Victory Medals.
13, Tavistock Road, Bletchley, Bucks. Z3374/B.

LORTON, H. E. S., Pilot, Royal Air Force.
He joined in February 1917, and after completing his training was engaged on important duties at various home stations with his Squadron. He did continuously good work, but was not successful in obtaining a transfer overseas. He was demobilised in June 1919. 17, Churchville Road, Bedford. Z3378/A.

LORTON, R. A., Private, Machine Gun Corps.
He joined in July 1918, and was shortly afterwards sent to Ireland, where he was engaged on important duties as a signaller with his unit. Owing to the early cessation of hostilities, he was unable to obtain a transfer overseas, but rendered valuable services until his demobilisation in February 1919.
17, Churchville Road, Bedford. Z3378/B.

LOVE, F. C., Sergeant, Hunts. Cyclist Battalion.
He volunteered in September 1914, and was retained at various stations, where he was engaged on important duties as an Instructor and also acted as a quartermaster-sergeant. He rendered very valuable services in these capacities, but was unable to obtain his transfer overseas on account of ill-health. After undergoing a serious operation, he was invalided from the Army in October 1918.
6, High Street, Huntingdon. TZ3379.

LOVELL, A. H., Private, 2/6th West Riding Regt.
He joined in March 1916, and underwent a period of training prior to his being drafted to France, where he took part in much severe fighting in the Arras sector. He was reported missing, and is now believed to have been killed in action on May 3rd 1917. He was entitled to the General Service and Victory Medals.
"Thinking that remembrance, though unspoken, may reach him where he sleeps."
Newton Longville, Bucks. Z3387/B.

LOVELL, A. N., Private, 5th Oxford. & Bucks. L.I.
He volunteered in September 1914, and in the following March was drafted to the Western Front, where he took part in many engagements, including those in the Ypres and the Somme sectors, and was wounded in 1915. As a result he was invalided home, but on his recovery returned to France. He is believed to have been killed in action on April 27th, 1916, near Ypres and was entitled to the 1914–15 Star, and the General Service and Victory Medals.
"Great deeds cannot die:
They with the sun and moon renew their light for ever."
Prospect Place, Emberton, Bucks. Z3389/B.

LOVELL, B. F., L/Cpl., King's Royal Rifle Corps.
He volunteered in September 1914, and after completing his training was drafted to France. Whilst in this theatre of war he took part in many important engagements, including those in the Somme, Loos and Ypres sectors, and was badly wounded in action. He was consequently invalided home and discharged in April 1917 as medically unfit for further service. He holds the 1914–15 Star, and the General Service and Victory Medals.
23, St. Martin's Road, Bletchley, Bucks. Z3382/C.

LOVELL, E. J., Private, Middlesex Regiment.
He joined in 1916, and later in the same year was transferred to the King's Own Yorkshire Light Infantry, with which he proceeded to France. In this theatre of war he took part in several engagements, including those at Arras, the Somme, St. Quentin, Ypres and Bapaume, and was gassed in action. He also served with the Labour Corps, and was demobilised in 1919, holding the General Service and Victory Medals.
Wyboston, Beds. Z3381.

LOVELL, F. W., Corporal, 9th Royal Scots.
He volunteered in November 1914, and after completing his training in the following February, proceeded to the Western Front. There he took part in the Battles of Ypres, Festubert, Loos, the Somme (I.), Cambrai and the Somme (II.), and in other important engagements. He was demobilised in February 1919, and holds the 1914–15 Star, and the General Service and Victory Medals.
23, St. Martin's Road, Bletchley, Bucks. Z3382/B

LOVELL, G. A., Private, Middlesex Regiment.
He joined in February 1916, and later in the same year was drafted to France, where he took part in the Battles of the Somme and the Ancre. He was badly wounded and invalided home, but on his recovery returned to France, and was again wounded in action in the Somme sector, and evacuated to England in April 1918. He was demobilised in February 1919, and holds the General Service and Victory Medals.
East End, Wilden, near Bedford. Z2549/A.

LOVELL, G. H. A. N., Pte., 5th Devonshire Regt.
He joined in July 1917, and underwent a period of training prior to his being drafted to France, whence he was sent to Germany with the Army of Occupation in December 1918. There he was engaged on various important duties with the Royal Army Service Corps at Cologne, and did continuously good work until his demobilisation in November 1919. He holds the General Service and Victory Medals.
Prospect Place, Emberton, Bucks. Z3389/C.

LOVELL, H., Private, Bedfordshire Regiment.
He was called up from the Reserve in August 1914, and in the following year was drafted to the Western Front. In this theatre of war he took part in several engagements, including the Battles of Loos, Albert, the Somme, Arras, Ypres, Passchendaele and Amiens, and was wounded in action. He was demobilised in July 1919, and holds the 1914–15 Star, and the General Service and Victory Medals.
6, Nelson Street, Bedford. Z3383.

LOVELL, H. F. T., Cpl., South Staffordshire Regt.
He volunteered in January 1916, and in the following November was drafted to the Western Front. He took part in many engagements, including the Battles of the Somme, Arras, Ypres and Cambrai, and was wounded in action. He was demobilised in February 1919, and holds the General Service and Victory Medals.
23, St. Martin's Road, Bletchley, Bucks. Z3382/A.

LOVELL, H. G., Private, Machine Gun Corps.
He joined in September 1916, and underwent a period of training prior to his being drafted to Egypt. Later he took part in the Advance into Palestine, and served at Gaza, Jerusalem and Aleppo. After the cessation of hostilities he proceeded to India, and in 1920 was stationed at Dinapore. He holds the General Service and Victory Medals.
8, West Lane, Emberton, Bucks. Z3385/A.

LOVELL, J., Sergeant, 1st Bedfordshire Regiment.
Having previously served in India, he rejoined in September 1914, and in the following year was drafted to France. There he took a prominent part in the Battles of the Somme, Ypres, Vimy Ridge, Arras and Cambrai, and was badly wounded. As a result he was invalided home, and after his recovery was retained on important duties until his demobilisation in March 1919. He holds the 1914–15 Star, and the General Service and Victory Medals.
The Avenue, Godmanchester, Hunts. Z3390.

LOVELL, J., Private, 5th Bedfordshire Regiment.
He volunteered in September 1914, and on completing his training in the following year, proceeded to Egypt, but later took part in the Advance into Palestine, and saw much fighting at Gaza, Jaffa and Haifa. He did continuously good work throughout hostilities, and was demobilised in February 1919. Unfortunately he contracted influenza and died of pneumonia on March 10th, 1919. He was entitled to the 1914–15 Star, and the General Service and Victory Medals.
"His memory is cherished with pride."
Tags End, Wootton, Bedford. Z3380/A.

LOVELL, J. J., Private, 5th Bedfordshire Regt.
He was mobilised with the Territorials in August 1914, and retained at home for a time on various important duties before being drafted to France. There he took part in the Battles of Ypres, Arras, Cambrai and the Somme (II.), and in other engagements during the Retreat and Advance of 1918. He was demobilised in March 1919, and holds the General Service and Victory Medals.
3, Castle Hill, Bedford. X3384.

LOVELL, M. L., Trooper, Bedfordshire Lancers.
He volunteered in May 1915, and later in the same year proceeded to France. Whilst in this theatre of war he took part in many important engagements, including those at Ypres, the Somme and Arras. He met with an accident, was invalided home, and on his recovery was discharged in April 1919. He holds the 1914–15 Star, and the General Service and Victory Medals. Church Lane, Emberton, Bucks. Z3386.

LOVELL, J. W. (M.M.), C.S.M., 1st Northants. Regt.
A serving soldier, he was stationed in Egypt in August 1914, but landed in France in time to take part in the closing stages of the Retreat from Mons. He also served with distinction at the Battles of the Marne, the Aisne, La Bassée, Ypres, Hill 60, and other important engagements, particularly during the Retreat and Advance of 1918. He was awarded the Military Medal for conspicuous bravery in capturing seven prisoners single-handed, and also holds the Mons Star, and the General Service and Victory Medals. He received his discharge in August 1919.
Prospect Place, Emberton, Bucks. Z3388/A—Z3389/A.

LOVELL, T., Sergeant, 1/5th Bedfordshire Regt.
Volunteering in August 1914, he was drafted overseas in the following year. Whilst in Egypt he was engaged on important duties in Alexandria, and later played a prominent part in the Advance into Palestine, where he saw much fighting at Gaza, Jaffa and Haifa. He returned home and was demobilised in June 1919, holding the 1914–15 Star, and the General Service and Victory Medals.
Tags End, Wootton, Bedford. Z3380/B.

LOVELL, W. C., Sapper, Royal Engineers.
He joined in July 1918, and underwent a period of training prior to his being drafted to France, where he was engaged on important duties at Boulogne. Later he proceeded to Germany with the Army of Occupation, and served on the Rhine until his demobilisation in March 1919. He holds the General Service and Victory Medals.
8, West Lane, Emberton, Bucks. Z3385/B.

LOVELL, W. C., Private, 1st Oxford. & Bucks. L.I.
Volunteering in December 1915, he proceeded overseas in the following year. Whilst on the Western Front he took part in many engagements, including those on the Somme and at Ypres, where he was badly wounded in August 1917. As a result he was invalided home and discharged in July 1918 as medically unfit for further service. He holds the General Service and Victory Medals.
Newton, Longville Bucks. Z3387/A.

LOVERIDGE, A., Private, 2nd Bedfordshire Regt.
He was mobilised in August 1914, and almost immediately drafted to the Western Front, where he took part in much heavy fighting in the Ypres sector. He made the supreme sacrifice, being killed in action on May 5th, 1915, and was entitled to the 1914–15 Star, and the General Service and Victory Medals.
"Whilst we remember, the sacrifice is not in vain."
20, Church Walk, Kempston, Bedford. X2761/A.

LOVERIDGE, S., Private, Bedfordshire Regiment.
He volunteered in December 1915, and on completing his training in the following year was drafted to France, where he took part in the Battles of Beaumont-Hamel, Arras, Ypres and Passchendaele. He was unfortunately killed in action in the Cambrai sector on April 23rd, 1917, and was entitled to the General Service and Victory Medals.
"A costly sacrifice upon the altar of freedom."
23, All Hallows Lane, Bedford. X2558/A.

LOVESEY, A., Private, 18th Essex Regiment.
He joined in May 1917, and after a period of training was engaged at various stations on important duties with his unit. He was unable to obtain a transfer overseas owing to his being medically unfit, but rendered valuable services until his demobilisation in March 1919.
Mount Pleasant, Aspley Guise, Beds. Z3393/B.

LOVESEY, E., Private, Royal Defence Corps.
He volunteered in April 1915, and after completing his training was engaged at various stations on important duties. He was over age to proceed to a theatre of war, but did continuously good work on the East Coast and on guard duties at Brocton Prison Camp. He was demobilised in April 1919.
22, Queen Street, Bedford. X3392/A.

LOVESEY, H., L/Corporal, R.A.S.C. (M.T.)
He joined in February 1917, and was engaged at various home stations on important duties with the Mechanical Transport. He was not successful in obtaining a transfer overseas, but did consistently good work until his demobilisation in November 1919. 22, Queen Street, Bedford. X3392/B.

LOVESEY, H., L/Corporal, Royal Engineers.
He volunteered in October 1915, and completing his training in the following April, was drafted to Egypt, whence he advanced into Palestine. He then saw much fighting at Gaza, on the River Jordan and at the fall of Jerusalem. He made the supreme sacrifice, being killed in action at Jaffa on November 30th, 1917. He was entitled to the General Service and Victory Medals.
"The path of duty was the way to glory."
Mount Pleasant, Aspley Guise, Beds. Z3393/A.

LOVESY, W. G., Private, Essex Regiment.
Joining in June 1916, he completed his training in the following year, and proceeded to France. During his service on the Western Front he took part in much heavy fighting, but made the supreme sacrifice, being killed in action on July 1st, 1917. He was entitled to the General Service and Victory Medals.
"His life for his Country, his soul to God."
Newton Longville, near Bletchley, Bucks. Z3394.

LOVETT, J., Private, 2nd Bedfordshire Regiment.
He joined in July 1916, and later in the same year proceeded to the Western Front, where he served in various sectors. He was in action during the Battles of Arras, Ypres, Cambrai and the Somme, and after the cessation of hostilities went with the Army of Occupation into Germany and served at Cologne until 1919. Returning home, he was demobilised in March of that year, and holds the General Service and Victory Medals.
Spaldwick, Hunts. Z3395.

LOVETT, J. K., Private, West Yorkshire Regt.
Joining in June 1917, he was retained on important duties at home until April 1918, when he was drafted to France. Whilst in this seat of war he saw much active service and was present during the engagements at Cambrai, St. Quentin, Amiens and others of importance throughout the period of hostilities. He was demobilised in February 1919, and holds the General Service and Victory Medals.
Eaton Ford, St. Neots, Hunts. Z2831/D—Z2833/D.

LOWE, E. J., Sapper, Royal Engineers.
He volunteered in April 1915, and two months later landed in France, where he took part in many important engagements in various sectors of the front. He served at the Battles of Loos, the Somme, Arras and Ypres and later during the fighting at Cambrai, during which he was wounded and was invalided to hospital. On his return home he was demobilised in March 1919, and holds the 1914–15 Star, and the General Service and Victory Medals. 10, Bower Street, Bedford. Z3396.

LOWE, E. J., Sergeant, Bedfordshire Regiment.
He was already in the Army at the outbreak of hostilities in August 1914, and later proceeded to Egypt, where he rendered excellent services throughout the period of hostilities. He served with distinction during the Advance into Palestine, in the Battles of Gaza, Jaffa, and later in the capture of Haifa. On his return to England he was discharged in March 1919, and holds the 1914–15 Star, and the General Service and Victory Medals. Potters Cross, Wootton, Beds. Z3397.

LOWINGS, M. J., Corporal, 6th Northants. Regt.
Volunteering in August 1914, he completed his training in the following year and proceeded to France, where he took part in much heavy fighting in various sectors of the front. He did excellent work at the Battles of Loos, the Somme, Arras, Ypres, where he was wounded, and later at Cambrai and other important engagements until the close of hostilities. In February 1919 he was demobilised, holding the 1914–15 Star, and the General Service and Victory Medals.
Little Raveley, Hunts. Z3398.

LUCAS, E. W., Private, Machine Gun Corps.
He joined in January 1918, and on completion of his training was drafted to France. During his service in this theatre of war he served at various stations in the workshops, where he was chiefly engaged on the repairing of motors, in which capacity he rendered good services until demobilised in October 1919, holding the General Service and Victory Medals.
Stoke Goldington, Bucks. Z3400/B.

LUCAS, R. H., Private, East Yorkshire Regiment.
He joined in March 1916, and after a period of training was engaged on important guard duties in Ireland until April 1918, when he proceeded to France. During his service on the Western Front he took part in the heavy fighting on the Somme, where he was reported missing on May 27th, 1918, and later presumed to have been killed in action on that date. He was entitled to the General Service and Victory Medals.
"Great deeds cannot die."
23, Agusta Road, Stony Stratford, Bucks. TZ3399.

LUCAS, R. H., Private, Royal Berkshire Regiment.
Joining in May 1916, in the Oxfordshire and Buckinghamshire Light Infantry, he was discharged owing to his being under age, but later in the same year was called up, and after a brief period of training was drafted to France in December 1916. Whilst on the Western Front he served at the Battles of Arras and Vimy Ridge, where he was reported missing on May 27th, 1917, and subsequently presumed to have been killed in action on that date. He was entitled to the General Service and Victory Medals.
"Honour to the immortal dead, who gave their youth that the world might grow old in peace."
16, Jubilee Terrace, Stony Stratford, Bucks. Z1064/B.

LUCAS, T., Private, 5th Wiltshire Regiment.
He was already in the Army at the outbreak of war in August 1914, and after a period of training was drafted to Egypt. In the course of his service in the East he took part in the Advance into Palestine and other important engagements. Later he was transferred to Mesopotamia, where he served during the heavy fighting at the relief of Kut and in the capture of Baghdad. He was demobilised on his return to England in November 1919, and holds the 1914–15 Star, and the General Service and Victory Medals.
Stoke Goldington, Bucks. Z3400/A.

LUDDINGTON, F., Pte., 6th Buffs (East Kent Regt.)
He joined in April 1917, and on completion of his training in the same year proceeded to France, where he took part in many important engagements in various sectors of the front. He was in action at the Battles of the Somme, Lens and Amiens, and after the close of hostilities went to Germany with the Army of Occupation, and served on the Rhine. He was demobilised in October 1919, and holds the General Service and Victory Medals.
Great Paxton, St. Neots, Hunts. Z1098/C.

LUDDINGTON, W., Driver, R.A.S.C.
Joining in May 1918 in the Bedfordshire Regiment, he completed his training and was retained on important transport duties attached to the Royal Army Service Corps, and served at various stations. Owing to the early cessation of hostilities he was unable to proceed to a theatre of war, but rendered excellent services until demobilised in May 1920.
Great Paxton, St. Neots, Hunts. Z1098/B

LUDDINGTON, W. M., Sapper, Royal Engineers.
He volunteered at the outbreak of war in August 1914, and on completion of his training in the following year was drafted to the Dardanelles, where he was present during the Landing in Gallipoli, and also took part in other important engagements until the Evacuation of the Peninsula. He was later invalided to England, and after a period of treatment was discharged from hospital and sent to France. In the course of his service in this seat of war he took part in much heavy fighting until the close of hostilities. He was demobilised in March 1919, and holds the 1914–15 Star, and the General Service and Victory Medals.
5, Trinity Road, Queen's Park, Bedford. Z3401.

LUFF, A. C., Private, Cheshire Regiment.
Volunteering at the outbreak of hostilities in August 1914, he was quickly drafted to the Western Front. During his short service in this theatre of war he took part in the heavy fighting at Arras and Vimy Ridge, and was unfortunately killed in action on August 4th, 1915, at Ypres. He was entitled to the 1914–15 Star, and the General Service and Victory Medals.
"The path of duty was the way to glory."
75, Woburn Road, Kempston, Bedford. X3402/B.

LUFF, A. E., Sapper, R.E. (Signal Section).
He volunteered in October 1914, and early in the following year was sent to France, where he was engaged on important duties in connection with the lines of communication. He was present during the heavy fighting at the Battles of Ypres, Loos and the Somme, and later saw service at Cambrai and Amiens. After the conclusion of war he returned home, and was demobilised in March 1919, holding the 1914–15 Star, and the General Service and Victory Medals.
2, Buckley Road, Eynesbury, St. Neots, Hunts.. Z3403/B.

LUFF, A. T., Sergeant, Bedfordshire Regiment.
He volunteered in 1914, and early in the following year proceeded to the Western Front, where he served with distinction in many important engagements in various sectors. He took part in the Battles of Ypres, Albert and the Somme, and was twice wounded, in 1916 and 1917. As a result he was invalided home and finally discharged in November 1917 as medically unfit for further military service. He holds the 1914–15 Star, and the General Service and Victory Medals.
East Street, Kimbolton, Hunts. Z3404.

LUFF, C. W., Corporal, Royal Air Force.
He joined in December 1916, and on conclusion of his training was retained on important duties at various aerodromes in England. He rendered excellent services as a mechanic until demobilised in December 1919.
2, Buckley Road, Eynesbury, St. Neots, Hunts. Z3403/A.

LUFF, J., Private, Northamptonshire Regiment.
Joining in February 1917, he was drafted to France shortly afterwards, and whilst in this theatre of war took part in much heavy fighting in various sectors of the front. He served at the Battles of Arras, Ypres and Cambrai, and others of importance, until the conclusion of hostilities. In February 1919 he was demobilised, and holds the General Service and Victory Medals. 40, Chandos Street, Bedford. X2831/B—X2833/B.

LUFF, J. W., Private, Bedfordshire Regiment.
Already in the Army at the outbreak of war in August 1914, he was immediately drafted to the Western Front, where he took part in the Retreat from Mons, also in the heavy fighting at Hill 60 and Ypres, and was wounded. On his recovery he proceeded to Salonika, and took part in the engagements on the Vardar and Struma fronts. In 1917 he was transferred to Egypt, and was in action during the Advance into Palestine, and later in the Battles of Gaza and Jaffa. After the close of hostilities he returned home, and was engaged on important duties at Chatham, where he was still serving in 1920. He holds the Mons Star, and the General Service and Victory Medals.
10, Cavendish Street, Bedford. X3405.

LUFF, S. C., Private, Royal Berkshire Regiment.
He volunteered in 1915, and on completion of his training proceeded to France. During his service in this theatre of war he took part in much heavy fighting in various sectors of the front. He served at Albert, where he was wounded, Arras and Ypres, and was unfortunately killed in action at Cambrai in December 1917. He was entitled to the General Service and Victory Medals.
"Steals on the ear the distant triumph song."
St. Mary's Street, Eynesbury, St. Neots, Hunts. Z1851/B.

LUFF, W. J., Gunner, Machine Gun Corps.
Volunteering in August 1914, he completed his training and went to France, where he did excellent work in various sectors of the front. He served with his Battery during the heavy fighting at Vimy Ridge, the Somme, Arras and Ypres, and later in the memorable Retreat and Advance of 1918. He was awarded a Divisional Certificate for devotion to duty in the Field, and holds also the 1914–15 Star, and the General Service and Victory Medals being demobilised in March 1919.
75, Woburn Road, Kempston, Bedford. Z3402/A.

LUMBERS, W., Private, Middlesex Regiment.
He joined in 1916, and on completion of his training was drafted to Mesopotamia. Whilst in this seat of war he took part in many important engagements, including the attempted relief of Kut and the capture of Baghdad. Later, in 1918, he was invalided to India, suffering from fever, and after a period of hospital treatment was sent home and demobilised in April 1919, holding the General Service and Victory Medals.
Little Staughton, Hunts. Z3406.

LUMBIS, R. E., L/Corporal, 11th Queen's (Royal West Surrey Regiment).
He volunteered in 1915, but was discharged in the following year as under age. He re-enlisted, however, in July 1917, and in November of that year was drafted to the Western Front. There he took part in the Battle of Kemmel Hill and in many other engagements, and was so severely wounded in action at Ypres in September 1918 as to necessitate the amputation of his right leg. He was invalided from the Army in January 1920, and holds the General Service and Victory Medals.
Silver Street, Great Barford, Beds. Z3407.

LUMLEY, W. H., Private, R.A.M.C.
He volunteered in August 1914, and in the following year was drafted to Gallipoli, where he took part in the Landing at Suvla Bay. He afterwards proceeded to Egypt, and there saw severe fighting on the Suez Canal and at Sollum, and many other places before being transferred in 1918 to the Western Front. Again in action at the Battles of Amiens, Havrincourt, Cambrai and Le Cateau, he was finally demobilised in 1919, and holds the 1914–15 Star, and the General Service and Victory Medals. 8, Gratton Road, Queen's Park, Bedford. Z3408/A.

LUMLEY, F. J., L/Corporal, 4th London Regiment (Royal Fusiliers).
Volunteering at the outbreak of war in August 1914, he was shortly afterwards drafted to Egypt, whence he proceeded in the following year to Gallipoli. There he saw severe fighting, especially at Suvla Bay, and, transferred later to the Western Front, was again in action at the Battles of the Somme, Arras, Ypres and Cambrai. He fell fighting at Passchendaele in January 1918. He was entitled to the 1914–15 Star, and the General Service and Victory Medals.
"His life for his Country, his soul to God."
8, Gratton Road, Queen's Park, Bedford. Z3408/B.

LUSHER, F., Sergeant, Bedfordshire Regiment.
He volunteered in September 1914, and on completing his training in the following year, proceeded to the Western Front. Whilst in this theatre of war he took a prominent part in many important engagements, and was three times wounded in action —at Hill 60, Arras and Passchendaele. He afterwards served as a drill Instructor in England, until his demobilisation in March 1919, and holds the 1914–15 Star, and the General Service and Victory Medals.
38, Ouse Walk, Huntingdon. Z3410.

LUSHER, S. J., Pte., 1/8th R. Warwickshire Regt.
After volunteering in August 1914, he was retained on important duties in England until 1916, and was then sent to the Western Front, where he took part in many important engagements. He died gloriously on the Field of Battle on August 27th, 1916, during the Somme Offensive. He was entitled to the General Service and Victory Medals.
"He passed out of the sight of men by the path of duty and self-sacrifice."
7, Merritt Street, Huntingdon. Z3409.

LYMAN, J., Tpr., 3/1st Royal Bucks. Hussars.
He volunteered in May 1915, and in August of that year proceeded to Egypt, where he saw severe fighting on the Suez Canal. Serving also in Palestine, he took part in the capture of Jerusalem, and in May 1918 was transferred to the Western Front on board H.M.T. "Leasome Castle," which was torpedoed in the Mediterranean. Fortunately rescued, he afterwards took part in the Battle of Ypres and other engagements. Demobilised in March 1919, he holds the 1914–15 Star, and the General Service and Victory Medals.
2, Cottage, Lathbury, Newport Pagnell, Bucks. Z3411.

LYNHAM, F. C., Driver, R.A.S.C.
After volunteering in September 1914, he underwent a period of training prior to being drafted to the Western Front. Whilst in this theatre of war he was engaged on important transport duties in the Cambrai, Somme and various other sectors, and also took an active part in the Retreat and Advance of 1918. He was demobilised in April 1919, and holds the General Service and Victory Medals.
High Street, Great Linford, Bucks. Z3413.

LYNHAM, T., Rifleman, King's Royal Rifle Corps.
Mobilised in August 1914, he procceeded to the Western Front in June of the following year, and there saw much severe fighting. After taking part in the Battle of the Somme, and other engagements, he was gassed near Arras in 1917 and admitted to hospital at Boulogne, but on his recovery rejoined his unit. He was again in action in the Battles of Ypres and Cambrai, and in the Retreat and Advance of 1918, and was finally discharged in June 1919. He holds the 1914–15 Star, and the General Service and Victory Medals.
High Street, Great Linford, Bucks. Z3412.

M

MACE, H., Private, R.A.O.C.
Already in the Army when war was declared in August 1914, he was immediately drafted to the Western Front, where he was engaged on important duties as an armourer in various sectors. He was present also at the Battles of Ypres and the Somme and other engagements, until sent home in February 1918, suffering from shell-shock. Invalided from the Army in May of that year, he holds the 1914 Star, and the General Service and Victory Medals.
London Road, Sandy, Beds. Z3415.

MACE, H., Private, Royal Fusiliers.
Volunteering in May 1915, he proceeded in the following month to France, where he served with an ammunition column in various sectors of the front. He also took part in the Battles of Loos, the Somme, Arras, Vimy Ridge, Ypres and Cambrai, and many other important engagements until the cessation of hostilities.' He was demobilised in February 1919, and holds the 1914–15 Star, and the General Service and Victory Medals.
Church Street, Somersham, Hunts. Z3416/B.

MACE, S. G., Private, 23rd London Regiment.
He volunteered in 1915, and in the following year was drafted to the Western Front. Whilst in this theatre of war he saw severe fighting in various sectors, took part in the Battles of the Somme and Arras, and many other engagements, and, wounded in action, had to have a finger amputated. He was demobilised on his return home in 1919, and holds the General Service and Victory Medals.
High Street, Sandy, Beds. TZ3417.

MACKAY, F. H., Private, R.A.M.C.
Mobilised in August 1914, he was retained in England until November 1916, and was then drafted to the Western Front. There he was engaged as a stretcher-bearer in various sectors, and also took an active part in the Battles of Arras, Vimy Ridge, Messines and Ypres, and was wounded in February 1917. He was reported missing, and later, killed in action at Passchendaele on October 5th, 1917. He was entitled to the General Service and Victory Medals.
"And doubtless he went in splendid company."
20, Bridge Street, New Bradwell, Bucks. Z3418.

MACKERNESS, A. J., Pte., Oxford. & Bucks. L.I.
Shortly after volunteering in February 1915 he was drafted to the Western Front, where, attached to a Trench-mortar Battery he took part in the Battles of Ypres, Loos, Albert and the Somme and other important engagements. He fell fighting at Cambrai on March 21st, 1918, during the Allies' Retreat. He was entitled to the 1914–15 Star, and the General Service and Victory Medals.
"His memory is cherished with pride."
33, The Green, Stony Stratford, Bucks. Z3421/A.

MACKERNESS, P., Private, Machine Gun Corps.
Joining in April 1916, he proceeded to France in December of that year, and was there stationed at Boulogne until January 1917. He was then drafted to Egypt, where he saw much severe fighting before returning to the Western Front in time to take part in the Battles of the Somme and Ypres, and other engagements during the Retreat and Advance of 1918. He was demobilised in January 1919, and holds the General Service and Victory Medals.
17, Russell Street, Stony Stratford, Bucks. Z3419.

MACKERNESS, W., Private, Royal Irish Fusiliers.
Joining in December 1917, he proceeded to the Western Front in April of the following year, and there saw much heavy fighting. After taking part in engagements at Cambrai and many other places, he was severely wounded in action at Amiens in August 1918, and eventually admitted to hospital in England. He was invalided from the Army in May 1919, and holds the General Service and Victory Medals.
33, The Green, Stony Stratford, Bucks. Z3421/B.

MACKNESS, P., Pte., Essex, and Northants. Regts.
He joined in 1916, and, on completing his training in the following year, proceeded to France, where he saw heavy fighting in various sectors of the front. After taking part in many important engagements he was severely wounded in action at Passchendaele in August 1917, and was for a time in hospital in England. He was demobilised in 1919, and holds the General Service and Victory Medals.
West End, Stevington, near Bedford. Z3420.

MADDY, C. H., Driver, Royal Field Artillery.
He joined in 1916, and in January of the following year proceeded to the Western Front, where he took part in the Battles of Vimy Ridge, Messines, Ypres and Passchendaele. In November 1917, however, he was transferred to Italy, but, after fighting on the Piave and Asiago Plateaux, returned to France and was again in action on the Somme and at Amiens and Cambrai, and was wounded in October 1918. He afterwards served with the Army of Occupation at Cologne and Coblenz, and was demobilised on his return home in September 1919, holding the General Service and Victory Medals.
New Town, Hail Weston, St. Neots, Hunts. Z3422.

MAILE, A., Private, 3rd Bedfordshire, and 2nd and 4th Royal Welch Fusiliers.
Volunteering in December 1915, he was shortly afterwards drafted to France, where he saw heavy fighting in various sectors of the Front. After taking part in the Battles of Arras, Ypres and the Somme, and other important engagements he was twice wounded in action on the Somme. He was consequently invalided from the Army in September 1919, and holds the General Service and Victory Medals.
Earith, Hunts. Z3424.

MAILE, J., Private, Queen's Own (Royal West Kent Regiment), and 12th Hampshire Regt.
He volunteered in December 1915, and twelve months later was drafted to Salonika, where he saw much severe fighting. He took part in many important engagements on the Vardar, Doiran and Struma fronts until the cessation of hostilities. Returning home in April 1919, he was demobilised in the following month, and holds the General Service and Victory Medals.
West Perry, near Huntingdon. Z3425.

MAILE, T., Private, Royal Fusiliers.
Volunteering in January 1916, he was sent to the Western Front on completing his training in the following August, and there saw much severe fighting. After taking part in the Battle of the Somme and other important engagements he was invalided home in April 1917, and was afterwards retained at various stations until his demobilisation in February 1919. He holds the General Service and Victory Medals.
10, Royal Oak Passage, Huntingdon. Z3426.

MAILING, G. W., Private, 11th Suffolk Regiment.
Shortly after volunteering in January 1916 he was drafted to the Western Front, where he took part in important engagements in various sectors. He made the supreme sacrifice, being killed in action at Arras on April 7th, 1917. He was entitled to the General Service and Victory Medals.
"Nobly striving:
He nobly fell that we might live."
Cambridge Street, St. Neots, Hunts. Z3427/A.

MAILING, L. A., Pte., 8th North Staffs. Regiment.
Joining in April 1917, he proceeded to the Western Front after four months' training, and there saw severe fighting in various sectors. He took part in the Battles of Ypres, Cambrai and the Somme and many other important engagements until the cessation of hostilities, and was then sent with the Army of Occupation into Germany. Demobilised on his return home in February 1919, he holds the General Service and Victory Medals. Cambridge Street, St. Neots, Hunts. Z3427/B.

MAINDLEY, J., B.S.M., Royal Garrison Artillery.
Having previously served in India and at Cape Town, he was with his Battery in Jamaica when war was declared in August 1914. There he was engaged on duties of a highly important nature for four years, during which period he rendered very valuable services. Returning home in 1918, he was discharged in September of the following year, and holds the General Service and Victory Medals.
Little Staughton, Hunts. Z3428.

MAKEHAM, G. H., Cpl., King's Royal Rifle Corps.
He joined in 1918, and, after undergoing a period of training, was retained on important duties at various stations. Owing to the early cessation of hostilities he was not successful in his efforts to obtain his transfer to the front, but later proceeded with the Army of Occupation to Germany. He was demobilised on his return home in 1919.
147, Bower Street, Bedford. TZ3429.

MAKEPEACE, T. F., Pte, West Yorkshire Regt.
He volunteered in January 1916, and in February of the following year was drafted to Malta, where he served as a bugler until March 1918. He was then transferred to the Western Front, and there took part in the Battles of St. Quentin, Amiens and Cambrai, and other important engagements. He fell in action at Le Cateau on October 11th, 1918. He was entitled to the General Service and Victory Medals.
"Whilst we remember, the sacrifice is not in vain."
4, Stratford Road, Buckingham. Z3430.

MAKS, C., A/Corporal, Hunts. Cyclist Battalion and Bedfordshire Regiment.
Volunteering in 1915, he was sent to the Western Front in July of that year, and there saw much severe fighting at Festubert and elsewhere. He died gloriously on the Field of Battle at Loos on September 4th, 1915, after only two months' active service. He was entitled to the 1914–15 Star, and the General Service and Victory Medals.
"A valiant Soldier, with undaunted heart he breasted life's last hill."
3, St. Mary's Terrace, Godmanchester, Hunts. Z1811/A.

MALES, T., Private, Hunts. Cyclist Battalion and Royal Warwickshire Regiment.
He volunteered in 1915, and in the following year proceeded to the Western Front, where he saw much heavy fighting. He took part in the Battle of Cambrai and many other important engagements, and was twice wounded in action—on the Somme in 1916, and at Ypres in the following year—and was gassed in August 1918. He was invalided from the Army in 1919, and holds the General Service and Victory Medals.
1, School Houses, Godmanchester, Hunts. Z3431.

MALIN, J., Pte., 1/8th Royal Warwickshire Regt.
He was mobilised in August 1914, but was retained on important duties in England until July 1916, when he proceeded to the Western Front. There he took part in many engagements during the Somme Offensive, and, wounded in action in November 1916, was admitted to hospital in England. He was invalided from the Army in April 1917, and holds the General Service and Victory Medals.
Cambridge Street, St. Neots, Hunts. Z3432.

MALIN, W., Private, R.A.S.C.
He volunteered in January 1916, and, after completing a term of training, served at various stations, where he was engaged on important duties with the Forage Section. He was unable to obtain his transfer to a theatre of war on account of ill-health, but nevertheless rendered valuable services with his Company until December 1917, when he was invalided from the Army. Cambridge Street, St. Neots, Hunts. Z3433.

MALLARD, F., L/Corporal, 9th (Queen's Royal) Lancers.
He volunteered in September 1914, and in the following year was drafted to the Western Front. Whilst in this theatre of war he took part in many important engagements, including the Battles of Loos, the Somme, Arras, Vimy Ridge and Cambrai, and was wounded in action in the Retreat of March 1918. He was demobilised in March 1919, and holds the 1914–15 Star, and the General Service and Victory Medals.
32, Coventry Road, Bedford. Z3434.

MALLOWS, A. J., A.B., R.N., H.M.S. "P.63."
He joined the Royal Navy in September 1916, and during the remainder of the war served in H.M.S. "P.63" and in H.M. Submarine "L.10." He was engaged on patrol and escort duties in the English Channel and North Sea and in convoying food ships. Remaining in the Navy until after the Armistice, he was demobilised in May 1919, and holds the General Service and Victory Medals.
9, Howard Avenue, Queen's Park, Bedford. Z3435/A.

MALLOWS, C. D., Private, Royal Fusiliers.
He landed in France in June 1918, after eight months' training and service in England, and took part in the operations during the concluding stages of the Retreat. On July 8th, 1918, however, he was unluckily killed in action on the Cambrai front. He was entitled to the General Service and Victory Medals.
"Great deeds cannot die:
They with the sun and moon renew their light for ever."
9, Howard Avenue, Queen's Park, Bedford. Z3435/B.

MANCHETT, G., A.B., R.N., H.M.S. "Victory."
Volunteering in August 1914, he completed his training and was sent to sea. He served in H.M.S. "Victory" in the North Sea, at Scapa Flow, the Dardanelles, Mudros and Salonika, and took a prominent part in the Battle of Jutland in May 1916. Overtaken by ill-health, he was invalided out of the Service in May 1919, and holds the 1914–15 Star, and the General Service and Victory Medals.
West End, Somersham, Hunts. Z3436.

MANDEVILLE, E., Pte., 5th North Staffs. Regt.
He joined the Army in November 1916, and four months later was drafted to France, where he took part in the third Battle of Ypres, and was taken prisoner in April 1918 on the Somme. Whilst in captivity he unfortunately died as the result of brutal treatment and short rations in Germany. He was entitled to the General Service and Victory Medals.
"His memory is cherished with pride."
Old Stratford, Bucks. Z2717/B.

MANN, C. E., Driver, Royal Engineers.
He joined in February 1916, and, after a period of service in England, was in the following year sent to the Western Front. During about two years' service in France he fought in the Battles of Arras, Vimy Ridge, Ypres, Passchendaele and Bullecourt. In February 1919 he was demobilised, and holds the General Service and Victory Medals.
17, College Road, Bedford. Z3437.

MANN, E. E., L/Corporal, R.A.O.C.
Volunteering in November 1915, he was retained for more than two years in England, and was engaged on various important duties with his Corps. Drafted to France, however, in March 1918, he was employed in the issue of stores and rations to troops proceeding up the line. He was demobilised in February 1919, and holds the General Service and Victory Medals.
7, Dean Street, Goldington Road, Bedford. Z3438.

MANN, H. E., Private, R.A.S.C.
He joined in February 1916, and throughout the period of hostilities he was stationed at Avonmouth and was engaged in the transfer of motor-lorries to France. Though unable to proceed to the firing-line, he rendered valuable services, and was discharged in March 1919, holding the General Service and Victory Medals. 14, Grey Friars Walk, Bedford. X3439/A.

MANN, P., Private, 1st Bedfordshire Regiment.
A time-serving soldier, he was sent to France at the outbreak of war, and fought in the Retreat from Mons. He was also in action in several others of the earlier engagements, but laid down his life for King and Country on September 4th on the Aisne. He was entitled to the Mons Star, and the General Service and Victory Medals.
"A costly sacrifice upon the altar of freedom."
High Street, Blunham, Beds. Z3440/A.

MANN, W. Farrier-Sergt., Royal Gloster Hussars.
He volunteered in October 1914, but was found to be medically unfit for transfer overseas. Whilst in the Army he was stationed at Cirencester and rendered valuable services for over two years as a farrier. In November 1916 he was invalided out owing to the state of his health.
High Street, Blunham, Beds. Z3440/C.

MANN, W., Tpr., Royal Gloucestershire Hussars.
Volunteering in November 1914, he was sent to Egypt in the following August and joined the Palestine Force. He was severely wounded and taken prisoner in April 1916. Unfortunately, on July 26th, 1916, he succumbed to his injuries at Damascus. He was entitled to the 1914–15 Star, and the General Service and Victory Medals.
"Thinking that remembrance, though unspoken, may reach him where he sleeps."
High Street, Blunham, Beds. Z3440/B.

MANNING, C. R., Private, Sherwood Foresters.
He joined in November 1916, and five months later crossed to France, where he served for over a year. He took a prominent part in the Battles of Arras and Vimy Ridge, but made the supreme sacrifice, being killed in action on July 16th, 1917, at Ypres. He was entitled to the General Service and Victory Medals.
"Whilst we remember, the sacrifice is not in vain."
Park Row, Goldington, Bedford. Z3442.

MANNING, R., L/Corporal, 1st Bedfordshire Regt.
Returning from Canada in May 1915, he volunteered in the Bedfordshire Regiment two months later, and served at Ampthill before being sent to France. There he took part in the Battles of Loos, Vimy Ridge and the Somme, but on September 5th, 1916, was reported missing, and later killed in action. He was entitled to the General Service and Victory Medals.
"Nobly striving
He nobly fell that we might live."
Toseland, St. Neots, Hunts. Z3443.

MANNING, W., Private, Royal Sussex Regiment.
He joined in 1916, but was unable to proceed overseas after completing his training. Retained at home, he was stationed at Yarmouth and Gorleston, and was engaged on guard and other duties, in the course of which he rendered valuable services. He was in hospital in Brighton for a short time with fever, and was demobilised in 1919.
Eaton Socon, Beds. Z3444.

MANSELL, H., Sergeant, Military Provost Staff Corps.
Volunteering in September 1914, he completed his training in England with the West Kent Regiment, and was employed in training recruits. Sent to France in July 1915, he served at Ypres and Festubert, but was wounded in the Battle of Loos and invalided home. After hospital treatment he returned to the Western Front in February 1918, and during the Retreat and Advance of that year saw heavy fighting at Cambrai and on the Somme. He was evacuated to England in December 1918 through his wound breaking out, and, after a further period in hospital, was discharged as unfit in the same month, holding the 1914–15 Star, and the General Service and Victory Medals. Lower Dean, Kimbolton, Hunts. Z3445.

MANTON, A. L., Driver, Royal Engineers.
He volunteered in August 1914, and, after the completion of his training, was stationed with his unit at Bedford. Suffering from appendicitis, he was admitted to hospital at Sudbury, but on August 24th he succumbed to the effects of an operation.
"His memory is cherished with pride."
59, Pilcroft Street, Bedford. X3447/D.

MANTON, E. C., Sapper, R.E. (Signal Section).
He volunteered in February 1915, and, after a period of training and service in England, was in 1917 sent to France. There he played an important part in the Battles of Ypres, Arras, Cambrai, Bapaume and Albert, and was employed on special work with his Section. He was demobilised in June 1919, and holds the General Service and Victory Medals.
17, Beaconsfield Street, Bedford. TX3446/A.

MANTON, F. G., Private, 1st Bedfordshire Regt.
Volunteering in August 1914, he was quickly sent to the Western theatre of war, and took part in the Retreat from Mons and several of the early engagements, including the Battle of Hill 60. He also served in the Battle of Loos, but was unhappily killed in action on July 26th, during the Somme Offensive of 1916, at Delville Wood. He was entitled to the Mons Star, and the General Service and Victory Medals.
"His life for his Country, his soul to God."
59, Pilcroft Street, Bedford. X3447/B.

MANTON, F. J., Driver, R.E. (Signal Section).
For 3½ years after volunteering in October 1914 he was retained in England. In June 1918, however, he was sent to France, and took part in the British Offensive, being in action at Cambrai and Le Cateau. Subsequently he served with the Army of Occupation on the Rhine until June 1919, when he was demobilised, holding the General Service and Victory Medals.
17, Beaconsfield Street, Bedford. TX3446/B.

MANTON, H., Sergeant, Queen's Own (Royal West Kent Regiment).
A time-serving soldier, he proceeded to France in August 1914, and fought in the Battles of Mons, the Aisne, Ypres (I.) and Festubert. He was also in action at Loos, the Somme, Arras, Ypres (III.), Cambrai and Albert, and in September 1918 was wounded during the Advance of that year. He was discharged in March 1919, and holds the Mons Star, and the General Service and Victory Medals.
17, Beaconsfield Street, Bedford. TX3446/C

MANTON, H. E., Driver, Royal Engineers.
Mobilised in 1914, he embarked for Egypt in the following year, and, attached to the Expeditionary Force, entered Palestine. There he took part in the Battles of Gaza and in the operations prior to the capture of Jaffa, and for a time acted as officer's servant. Returning home, he was demobilised in September 1919, and holds the 1914–15 Star, and the General Service and Victory Medals. 59, Pilcroft Street, Bedford. X3447/A.

MANTON, W. G., Driver, R.E. (Signal Section).
Volunteering in May 1915, he was sent to the Dardanelles in July, and took part in the Landing at Suvla Bay. After the Evacuation he was sent to Egypt, and served during the Advance through Palestine, being present at the Battles of Gaza and the operations in connection with the capture of Jaffa. After the Armistice he served in Turkey for a time, and, returning home, was demobilised in August 1919. He holds the 1914–15 Star, and the General Service and Victory Medals. 17, Beaconsfield Street, Bedford. TX3446/D.

MANTON, W. H., Private, 1st Dorset Regiment.
He joined in June 1916, and three months later was sent to the Western Front, where he served for nearly two years. During that time he fought at Albert and Amiens, but in July 1918 was severely wounded. Evacuated to England, he was invalided out of the Army shortly afterwards, and holds the General Service and Victory Medals.
59, Pilcroft Street, Bedford. X3447/C.

MANYWEATHER, F., Private, 8th Royal Warwickshire Regiment.
He volunteered in 1915, and in the ensuing year crossed the Channel. Whilst on the Western Front he took part in the Offensive on the Somme and the Battle of Ypres. In 1917 he was sent to Italy, where he fought on the Piave, but, returning to France early in 1918, was in action at Albert and wounded at Cambrai. He was demobilised in February 1919, and holds the General Service and Victory Medals.
8, Bell Court, Bedford. X3451.

MAPLEY, G. F., Pte., 1/5th Lancashire Fusiliers.
He joined in February 1916, and, after training and service in England, was drafted to the Western Front in July 1917. During the third Battle of Ypres he fought at Passchendaele Ridge and St. Julien, but on September 6th of the same year was reported missing, and later killed in action, on that date. He was entitled to the General Service and Victory Medals.
"Great deeds cannot die."
7, St. Paul's Rd., Queen's Park, Bedford. X3449/A—Z3450/A.

MAPLEY, J., Private, R.M.L.I.
After three months' training he was drafted to France in March 1917, and took a prominent part in heavy fighting on the Somme and at Arras, Ypres and Cambrai. Serving in that theatre of war until January 1919, he was demobilised in the following month, and holds the General Service and Victory Medals.
9, Chicheley Street, Newport Pagnell, Bucks. Z3448.

MAPLEY, T. H., Pte., 2nd Beds. Regt. and M.G.C.
Volunteering in September 1914, he underwent a period of training before being sent to France in July 1915. He took part in the Battles of Loos and Ypres, but fell on the Field of Battle during the Somme Offensive on July 7th, 1916. He was entitled to the 1914–15 Star, and the General Service and Victory Medals.
"Honour to the immortal dead who gave their youth that the world might grow old in peace."
14, Beaconsfield Place, Newport Pagnell, Bucks. Z3450/B.

MARDLE, H. A., Signaller, Royal Horse Artillery.
He joined in June 1918, and trained as a gunner and signaller at Woolwich. Though medically unfit for active service, he did valuable work with his Battery until his demobilisation in May 1919.
31, Maitland Street, Bedford. X3452.

MARDLIN, F., Private, 5th Bedfordshire Regt.
Volunteering in September 1914, he proceeded to France in the following July, and fought at Loos, the Somme and Ypres, where he was gassed. Invalided to England and transferred to the Labour Corps, he was sent to Blunham and employed on agricultural work there until March 1919, when he was demobilised, holding the 1914–15 Star, and the General Service and Victory Medals.
Silver Street, Great Barford, Beds. Z3453.

MARDLIN, F., Private, Bedfordshire Regiment.
Volunteering at the outbreak of war, he was sent to Egypt in the next year, and joined the Forces in Palestine. He fought in the Battles of Gaza and in the series of operations which resulted in the capture of Jericho, Jerusalem and Haifa, but contracted malaria and was invalided home. Owing to fever he was discharged as unfit in March 1919, and holds the 1914–15 Star, and the General Service and Victory Medals.
School Lane, Eaton Socon, Beds. Z3454.

MARDON, A. G., A.B., R.N., H.M.S. "Kilderry."
Already in the Royal Navy at the outbreak of war, he was sent to sea in August 1914, and served in H.M.S. "Kilderry" and "Forward." He took part in the Dardanelles campaign, and was subsequently engaged on mine-sweeping and patrol duties in the North Sea, being also present at the Battle of Jutland. He was still serving in 1920, and holds the 1914–15 Star, and the General Service and Victory Medals.
41, Tavistock Place, Bedford. X3455/A.

MARDON, H. W., Private, R.M.L.I.
He volunteered in August 1914, and served in H.M.S. "Agincourt" and "Caryfoot." He was engaged on important duties in the North Sea with the Grand Fleet, and was in H.M.S. "Caryfoot" when she was blown up. He also served in France and Belgium, and was stationed at Dunkirk and Ostend. Demobilised in 1919, he holds the 1914–15 Star, and the General Service and Victory Medals.
41, Tavistock Place, Bedford. X3455/B.

MARDON, H. W., Sapper, Royal Engineers.
Volunteering in February 1915, he served with the Royal Defence Corps at Aldershot and Longmoor, and was engaged in guarding prisoners of war. He also acted as storekeeper whilst attached to the Royal Engineers at Birmingham. After rendering valuable services he was demobilised in December 1918.
41, Tavistock Place, Bedford. X3455/C.

MARKHAM, A., Private, Wiltshire Regiment.
He joined in November 1917, and four months later was drafted to the Western Front, where he was badly wounded in action on the Somme in May 1918. He was invalided to hospital in England and underwent treatment for some time. Eventually demobilised in February 1919, he holds the General Service and Victory Medals.
London Road, Loughton, Bucks. Z3456/B.

MARKHAM, A. J., Sapper, Royal Engineers.
Volunteering in February 1915, he was drafted to France in August, and did much valuable work with his unit until January 1916, when he was invalided home with trench-fever. On his recovery he was sent to Salonika, where he saw heavy fighting on the Doiran and Struma fronts before being transferred to Palestine. He then served at Jaffa and Jerusalem. During hostilities he was chiefly engaged on pioneer duties, and was demobilised in February 1919, holding the 1914–15 Star, and the General Service and Victory Medals.
11, Brooklands Road, Bletchley, Bucks. Z3458.

MARKHAM, A. S., Pte., 1/5th Bedfordshire Regt.
He volunteered in February 1915, and later in the same year was sent to Egypt, but was quickly drafted to the Dardanelles, and was wounded in action during heavy fighting at Gallipoli. After the Evacuation of the Peninsula he was transferred to Palestine, and served at the Battles of Gaza and the capture of Jaffa. He also suffered from malarial fever whilst in the East, and was eventually demobilised in February 1919, holding the 1914–15 Star, and the General Service and Victory Medals.
Luke Street, Eynesbury, St. Neots, Hunts. Z3457.

MARKHAM, E. F., L/Corporal, Bedfordshire Regt.
He enlisted in May 1914, and first saw active service in the Dardanelles, where he unfortunately contracted dysentery, and was invalided home. After some time in hospital he was sent to France in 1917, but, after taking part in much severe fighting in various sectors, was unfortunately killed in action at the Battle of Bapaume on August 25th, 1918. He was entitled to the 1914–15 Star, and the General Service and Victory Medals.
"A costly sacrifice upon the altar of freedom."
Eaton Socon, Beds. Z3461.

MARKHAM, E. G., Private, 29th Canadian Infantry (Canadian Overseas Forces).
Volunteering early in 1915, he was drafted to France later in the same year, and took part in the Battles of the Somme, Arras, Vimy Ridge, Ypres, Passchendaele and Cambrai. He was also in action throughout the Retreat and Advance of 1918, and was demobilised in May 1919, holding the 1914–15 Star, and the General Service and Victory Medals.
34, Albert Street, Bedford. X3460/B.

MARKHAM, F., Leading Seaman, Royal Navy.
Already in the Royal Navy, he proceeded to sea on board H.M.S. "Drake," and took part in the Battles of the Falkland Islands and Jutland and the raid on Zeebrugge. He was also engaged on important patrol and escort duties in the North Sea. Later he cruised in Russian waters, and also served in H.M.S. "Viceroy." He received his discharge in November 1919, holding the 1914–15 Star, and the General Service and Victory Medals.
London Road, Loughton, Bucks. Z3456/A.

MARKHAM, G., Sergeant, Queen's (Royal West Surrey Regiment).
He volunteered in 1914, but, being too old for transfer to a theatre of war, was retained on special duties at various Home stations. He rendered very valuable services as an Instructor throughout the whole period of hostilities, and was demobilised in December 1918.
"The Blue Ball," St. Mary Street, Eynesbury, St. Neots, Hunts. Z3462.

MARKHAM, A. L., Private, 15th Canadian Regt. (Canadian Overseas Forces).
Volunteering in April 1915, he landed in France later in the same year, and took a prominent part in the Battles of Ypres (II.), Loos, Festubert and Arras. He was unhappily killed in action on Vimy Ridge in April 1917, and was entitled to the 1914–15 Star, and the General Service and Victory Medals.
"His life for his Country, his soul to God."
34, Albert Street, Bedford. X3460/C.

MARKHAM, J., Sapper, Royal Engineers.
Volunteering in May 1915, he was soon drafted to Egypt, and was engaged on important wiring and tunnelling operations. Later he proceeded into Palestine, where he took an active part in the Battles of Gaza and the capture of Jerusalem, Jaffa and Aleppo whilst on the lines of communication. He was demobilised in August 1919, and holds the 1914–15 Star, and the General Service and Victory Medals.
34, Albert Street, Bedford. X3460/A.

MARKHAM, J. W., Private, Machine Gun Corps.
He joined in March 1917, and twelve months later proceeded to the Western Front, where he served throughout the Retreat and Advance of 1918. He took part in the Battles of the Somme (II.), Amiens and Cambrai (II.), and was gassed in action in August. Returning home in March 1919, he was demobilised a month later, and holds the General Service and Victory Medals.
Near "The White Lion," Eaton Socon, Hunts. Z3463.

MARKHAM, P., Corporal, Oxford. and Bucks. L.I.
A Reservist, he was called to the Colours in August 1914, and proceeded to France in the following December. Whilst on the Western Front he served with distinction in many important engagements, including the Battles of Loos, the Somme, Arras, Ypres and Cambrai. He was discharged in December 1919, and holds the 1914–15 Star, and the General Service and Victory Medals.
12, Vicarage Road, Old Bradwell, Bucks. Z3459

MARKHAM, W. A., Private, 1/2nd Royal Fusiliers.
Having volunteered in August 1914, he was drafted to the Western Front in July of the following year, but, after taking part in heavy fighting at Arras and Ypres, was taken prisoner during the Somme Offensive in August 1916. Whilst in captivity he suffered many hardships, and, on his repatriation in January 1919, was demobilised, holding the 1914–15 Star, and the General Service and Victory Medals.
"The Crown," Luke Street, Eynesbury, Hunts. Z1204/A.

MARKWELL, W. E., Private, R.A.V.C.
He joined in August 1916, and, on completion of his training, was engaged on important duties in connection with the treatment of sick horses. Owing to medical unfitness he was unsuccessful in obtaining his transfer overseas, but did excellent work with his unit until his discharge in January 1917.
West End, Somersham, Hunts. Z3464.

MARLOW, A., Private, Royal Fusiliers.
He volunteered in April 1915, and later in the same year was sent to the Western Front, where he played an important part in the Battles of Festubert, Loos, the Somme, Arras, Vimy Ridge, Ypres and Cambrai. After the cessation of hostilities he went to Germany with the Army of Occupation, and was stationed on the Rhine until demobilised in June 1919. He holds the 1914–15 Star, and the General Service and Victory Medals. Wistow, Hunts. Z3465.

MARROTT, H., Private, 2nd Argyll & Sutherland Highlanders.
Already in the Army when war was declared, he was immediately drafted to France, where he took part in the Battle of, and the Retreat from, Mons. He was then reported missing, and, as nothing has since been heard of him, he is presumed to have been killed in action. He was entitled to the Mons Star, and the General Service and Victory Medals.
"Courage, bright hopes, and a myriad dreams, splendidly given."
85, Marlborough Road, Bedford. Z3466/D.

MARSHALL, A., Rifleman, 24th Rifle Brigade.
Volunteering in April 1915, he was drafted to India in the following January, and was engaged on important garrison duties at various stations. He also took part in the fighting against the Afghans on the N.W. Frontier, and was eventually demobilised in July 1919. He holds the General Service and Victory Medals, and the India General Service Medal (with Clasp, Afghanistan, N.W. Frontier, 1919).
7, Queen's Row, Bedford. X3473.

MARSHALL, E. A., Pte., 2nd Bedfordshire Regt.
He volunteered in January 1915, and in the following September was drafted to France, where he took part in the Battles of the Somme and Arras. He was unfortunately killed on July 27th, 1917, near Ypres, whilst burying a fallen comrade, and was entitled to the 1914–15 Star, and the General Service and Victory Medals.
"Great deeds cannot die:
They with the sun and moon renew their light for ever."
14, Howbury Street, Bedford. Z3472.

MARSHALL, E. A., Private, 26th Royal Fusiliers.
He volunteered in February 1915, and was eventually drafted to the Western Front, where he took part in the Battles of the Somme and Messines. Seriously wounded in action in June 1917, he was invalided home, and, after a period of hospital treatment, was discharged as medically unfit for further service in December of the same year. He holds the General Service and Victory Medals.
68, Spring Road, Kempston, Bedford. Z3470/A.

MARSHALL, F., Corporal, Bedfordshire Regiment.
He volunteered in July 1915, and was later drafted to the Western Front, where he took part in the Battles of the Somme, Arras, Ypres and Cambrai, and was wounded in action. He was demobilised in 1919, but later re-enlisted and was sent to Mesopotamia, where he was still serving in 1920. He holds the General Service and Victory Medals.
6, St. John's Street, Huntingdon. Z3476.

MARSHALL, G., Private, 2nd East Surrey Regt.
He joined in September 1918, immediately on attaining military age, and, on completion of his training, was sent to the Army of Occupation in Turkey. He rendered valuable services with his unit, and in 1920 was still in the Army.
68, Spring Road, Kempston, Bedford. Z3470/B.

MARSHALL, G., Cpl., 1st Oxford. & Bucks. L.I.
He joined in December 1916, and six months later was sent to India, where he was engaged on important garrison duties. He also did excellent work as a Musketry Instructor at Bangalore, and returned to England in January 1919. In the following March he was demobilised, and holds the General Service and Victory Medals.
9, Wolverton Road, Newport Pagnell, Bucks. Z3471.

MARSHALL, G. M., C.S.M., 1st Bedfordshire Regt.
Volunteering in October 1914, he was drafted overseas in the following year. Whilst on the Western Front he served with distinction at the Battles of Festubert, Loos, the Somme, Ypres and Cambrai (where he was wounded in action), and in other important engagements. He was demobilised in March 1919, but later re-enlisted, and in 1920 was stationed in Ireland. He holds the 1914–15 Star, and the General Service and Victory Medals.
Great Northern Street, Huntingdon. Z3477

MARSHALL, H., Private, R.A.M.C.
Volunteering in January 1915, he was eventually sent to Mesopotamia. Whilst in this theatre of war he rendered valuable services as a Nursing Orderly, attending to the sick and wounded in various hospitals. He returned to England for demobilisation in June 1919, and holds the General Service and Victory Medals.
Goldington, Beds. Z3475.

MARSHALL, J., Private, 1/4th Essex Regiment.
He volunteered in the Bedfordshire Regiment in November 1914, but, on completion of his training, was sent to Egypt with the Essex Regiment in January 1916. After serving in this theatre of war for a time he was transferred to Palestine, where he was unfortunately killed in action at the first Battle of Gaza on March 27th, 1917. He was entitled to the General Service and Victory Medals.
"His life for his Country, his soul to God."
Church Lane, Little Staughton, Hunts. Z3474/A.

MARSHALL, J. M., Pte., 5th Leicestershire Regt.
He volunteered in October 1914, and early in the following year was drafted to the Western Front. There he took part in many important engagements, including Ypres, Lens, Loos and Vimy Ridge, and also participated in heavy fighting during the Retreat and Advance in 1918, being wounded in action at St. Quentin. Returning home after the Armistice, he was demobilised in February 1919, and holds the 1914–15 Star, and the General Service and Victory Medals.
19, Beatrice Street, Kempston, Bedford. Z3469/A.

MARSHALL, K. B., Private, Bedfordshire Regt.
He joined in August 1917, and, after a period of training, proceeded later in the same year to France. In this theatre of war he participated in the Battles of Ypres, Cambrai and Vimy Ridge, and did excellent work. He served in Germany with the Army of Occupation for some time after the cessation of hostilities, and was demobilised in February 1919, holding the General Service and Victory Medals.
Colne, Hunts. Z3467.

MARSHALL, N. O., Pte., 4th North Staffs. Regt.
Volunteering in September 1914, he was stationed for some time afterwards in the Channel Islands, and in 1915 was sent to India. There he was employed with his unit on garrison and other important duties, and performed consistently good work until he contracted fever, from the effects of which he unhappily died on board a hospital ship at Bombay in July 1916. He was entitled to the General Service Medal.
"Thinking that remembrance, though unspoken, may reach him where he sleeps."
19, Beatrice Street, Kempston, Bedford. Z3469/B.

MARSHALL, W., Private, 2nd Bedfordshire Regt.
He joined in January 1917, and in the following September was drafted to the Western Front, where he took part in the Battles of Cambrai and the Somme (II.). Wounded during the fourth Battle of Ypres in September 1918, he was invalided home, and upon his recovery was sent to India, where he was still stationed in 1920. He holds the General Service and Victory Medals.
Church Lane, Little Staughton, Hunts. Z3474 /B.

MARSHALL, W. A., Q.M.S., Bedfordshire Regt.
Volunteering in November 1914, he served at Whitby, employed on various duties of an important nature until 1916, when he was sent to France. There he served with his unit on the Somme front and at Arras and Cambrai, performing exceedingly good work. Demobilised on his return home in March 1919, he holds the General Service and Victory Medals.
6, Princess Street, Huntingdon. Z3468.

MARSHALL, W. C., Sapper, Royal Engineers.
Joining in February 1916, he served at Longmoor Camp for three months, and was then sent to the Western Front. In this theatre of war he served in many sectors with the Railway Operative Department, making and repairing railway lines, and was engaged in this duty during the Retreat and Advance in 1918. He was demobilised in March 1919, holding the General Service and Victory Medals.
Northampton Road, Lavendon, Bucks. Z3478.

MARTIN, A. W., Sapper, Royal Engineers.
He volunteered in August 1914, but was medically unfit for transfer to a theatre of war. Retained at home, he was stationed at various places on the East Coast from 1914 until 1918, engaged on important duties in connection with Coastal Defences, and rendered valuable services. He was subsequently employed on clerical duties at Christchurch until he was demobilised in July 1920.
7, College Street, Kempston, Bedford. Z3481.

MARTIN, C. J., Pte., K.O. (Royal Lancaster Regt.)
Volunteering in November 1914, he was drafted in the following year to Gallipoli, and was wounded whilst taking part in heavy fighting. Invalided home, he was sent to hospital in Thornton Heath, and after his recovery proceeded in 1917 to the Western Front. There he participated in further fighting at Arras, Cambrai and on the Somme front, doing good work until he made the supreme sacrifice, being killed in action on September 25th, 1917, near Ypres. He was buried in the British cemetery, Nine Elms, near Ypres, and was entitled to the 1914–15 Star, and the General Service and Victory Medals.
" Honour to the immortal dead who gave their youth that the world might grow old in peace."
7, Council Cottages, St. Neots Road, Sandy, Beds. Z3483.

MARTIN, E., Private, 2nd Bedfordshire Regiment.
He joined in 1916, and later in the same year proceeded to France. In this theatre of hostilities he took part in strenuous fighting on the Somme front and at Arras and Cambrai, and died gloriously on the Field of Battle at Passchendaele on August 4th, 1917. He was buried in the Ligasenthnek Military Cemetery at Poperinghe, and was entitled to the General Service and Victory Medals.
" Nobly striving :
He nobly fell that we might live."
London Road, Sandy, Beds. Z3484.

MARTIN, F., Rifleman, Rifle Brigade.
He joined in May 1916, and proceeded, on the completion of his training, to the Western Front. There he was in action at Vimy Ridge, Arras, Ypres, Cambrai and on the Somme front, and was twice wounded. After the termination of hostilities he was engaged on transport duties until March 1919, when he was demobilised, holding the General Service and Victory Medals.
11, Church Road, Willington, Beds. Z3489.

MARTIN, F., L/Corporal, 2nd Bedfordshire Regt.
Volunteering in December 1914, he was drafted six months afterwards to France. During his service overseas he participated in strenuous fighting at Loos, Lens, Albert, Arras, Ypres, Cambrai and on the Somme,and was in action in various sectors during the Retreat and Advance of 1918. Returning home after the Armistice, he was demobilised in December 1918, and holds the 1914–15 Star, and the General Service and Victory Medals. Park Lane, Sharnbrook, Beds. Z3485.

MARTIN, F., Private, 1/5th Bedfordshire Regt.
He volunteered in August 1914, and in the following March was sent to France. A month later he proceeded to Gallipoli, and took part in the operations during the Landing. He afterwards served in Egypt and Palestine, and was in action at Gaza and Jerusalem. Returning home in March 1919, he was demobilised, and holds the 1914–15 Star, and the General Service and Victory Medals.
Olney Road, Lavendon, Bucks. Z3479 /A.

MARTIN, F. C., Trooper, Royal Bucks. Hussars.
Volunteering in August 1914, he was retained at home on important duties, stationed in Buckingham, until November 1917, when he was drafted to Italy. After taking part in severe fighting on the Piave front he was sent to Russia, and later proceeded to India. In 1920 he was still serving with the Colours in Mesopotamia, and holds the General Service and Victory Medals.
Bow Brickhill, Bletchley, Bucks. Z3482 /B.

MARTIN, G., Private, 12th Middlesex Regiment.
He volunteered at the outbreak of war in August 1914, and early in the following year proceeded to the Western Front. In this theatre of hostilities he played a prominent part with his unit in the Battles of Festubert, the Somme, Arras, Ypres and Cambrai, and in other important engagements. Returning home after the Armistice, he was demobilised in 1919, and holds the 1914–15 Star, and the General Service and Victory Medals. Church Road, Willington, Bedford. Z3488.

MARTIN, G. W., Corporal, Royal Engineers.
Volunteering in December 1915, he was sent six months later to France. There he was engaged on important duties during the first Battle of the Somme and was wounded. Invalided home, he was admitted to hospital in Rochdale, but returned to France on his recovery, and was employed guarding prisoners of war until the Armistice. Demobilised in March 1919, he holds the 1914–15 Star, and the General Service and Victory Medals. Bow Brickhill, near Bletchley, Bucks. Z3482 /A.

MARTIN, H. C., Pte., R.A.M.C. & R.A.S.C. (M.T.)
He was mobilised in August 1914, and in the following April was drafted to Egypt, where he did good work, serving as stretcher-bearer attached to Field Hospitals. In July 1915 he was sent to Gallipoli and was engaged on similar duties until 1916, when he was sent to Salonika. There he was transferred to the Royal Army Service Corps, and was employed as a motor transport driver on the Vardar, Struma and Doiran fronts. He returned home and was demobilised in March 1919, holding the 1914–15 Star, and the General Service and Victory Medals. 41, Oxford Street, Wolverton, Bucks. Z3480.

MARTIN, S. A., Private, Bedfordshire Regiment.
He volunteered in February 1915, and served in various home stations until May 1916, when he proceeded to France. Wounded in action on the Somme three months later, he returned to England, and for some time was in Edmonton Military Hospital. Upon his recovery he was released from the Colours, and was employed on agricultural work until demobilised in June 1919, holding the General Service and Victory Medals. High Street, Blunham, Beds. Z3486.

MARTIN, W., Private, 7th Northants. Regiment.
Joining in April 1917, he served at Liverpool and Luton during his training. Proceeding to the Western Front in March 1918, he was in action at Ypres and on the Somme, and was taken prisoner after two months' service overseas. He was kept in captivity in Germany up to the Armistice, when he was repatriated and was employed on various duties in home stations until demobilised in November 1919, holding the General Service and Victory Medals.
Olney Road, Lavendon, Bucks. Z3479 /B.

MARTIN, W., Sapper, Royal Engineers.
He volunteered in December 1915, and completed his training at Longmoor Camp. Drafted to France in 1916, he served with his Company on the Arras, Cambrai, Ypres and Somme fronts, and in many sectors during the Retreat and Advance of 1918. He performed consistently good work engaged on various duties of an important nature, and was eventually demobilised in August 1919. He holds the General Service and Victory Medals. London Road, Sandy, Beds. Z3487.

MASH, N. B., Corporal, Royal Horse Artillery.
Mobilised at the outbreak of hostilities in August 1914, he was sent two months later to France. There he participated with his Battery in many important engagements, including the Battles of Ypres, the Somme, Arras and Cambrai, and was wounded on two occasions. During his service overseas he did excellent work, and was still with the Colours in 1920, holding the 1914 Star, and the General Service and Victory Medals.
Stow Longa, Hunts. Z3490.

MASON, F. W., L/Sergt., 1st Grenadier Guards.
He volunteered in August 1914, and early in the following year was drafted to the Western Front. In this theatre of war he took a prominent part with his unit in many severe engagements and participated in the Battles of Festubert, Loos, the Somme, Arras, Ypres and Cambrai, and was wounded. He did good work until he was unfortunately killed in action during the Advance on August 24th, 1918. He was entitled to the 1914–15 Star, and the General Service and Victory Medals.
" Thinking that remembrance, though unspoken, may reach him where he sleeps."
7, Oxford Road, St. Ives, Hunts. Z3491.

MASON, J., Private, 1st Northamptonshire Regt.
Volunteering in November 1914, he was sent to the Western Front on the completion of his training. During his service overseas he took part in severe fighting in many sectors in France and Belgium, and did excellent work until he was badly wounded. Invalided home, he spent a considerable time in hospital at Bristol, and was discharged in August 1916 as unfit for further military duty. He holds the 1914–15 Star, and the General Service and Victory Medals.
Willowdeane, Clapham, Bedford. Z4389 /A.

MASON, J. W., Private, 1st Hertfordshire Regt.
He was mobilised with the Territorial Force in August 1914, and in the following July was drafted to Gallipoli, where he was at once in action at Suvla Bay, and was wounded. In January 1916 he was sent to Mesopotamia, and two months later was again wounded. As a result he was invalided home, and upon his recovery proceeded to France, where he took part in further fighting on the Somme front, also at Ypres, Arras and Cambrai, and fell in action near Amiens on August 24th, 1918. He was entitled to the 1914–15 Star, and the General Service and Victory Medals.
"The path of duty was the way to glory."
Brewery Cottage, Eaton Socon, near St. Neots, Hunts. Z3492.

MASON, W. C. J. (M.M.), Bombardier, R.F.A.
He volunteered in September 1914, and a month later proceeded to France. There he took a prominent part with his Battery in heavy fighting on the Marne, also at Ypres, Neuve Chapelle, Givenchy, Loos and the Somme, where he was wounded in 1916. After his recovery he participated in further fighting, and was again wounded whilst in action at Cambrai. He was awarded the Military Medal for conspicuous bravery and devotion to duty in the Field, and when demobilised in January 1919, was also entitled to the 1914–15 Star, and the General Service and Victory Medals.
29, Ledsam Street, Wolverton, Bucks. Z3493.

MASON, W. H., Gunner, Royal Garrison Artillery.
Joining in March 1916, he was drafted in the following March to the Western Front, and was in action on the Somme, Arras and Ypres fronts. In January 1918 he was invalided home on account of ill-health, but after spending some time in hospital in London, returned to the Western Front, and was again in action at Amiens, Le Cateau and other places during the final Advance. After the signing of the Armistice he was sent to Germany with the Army of Occupation, but whilst stationed in Cologne was admitted to hospital suffering from pneumonia, from the effects of which he unhappily died on April 8th, 1919. He was entitled to the General Service and Victory Medals.
"A costly sacrifice upon the altar of freedom."
Eaton Ford, St. Neots, Hunts. Z2831/C—Z2833/C.

MASSEY, H., Private, Labour Corps.
He joined in January 1916, but was medically unfit for transfer to a theatre of war. Retained at home he was stationed at Ipswich and served with a Cyclist Battalion. He was later transferred to the Labour Corps, and was employed on agricultural work at Thetford and Bletchley, rendering valuable services until he was demobilised in May 1919.
1, Water Eaton, Bletchley, Bucks. Z3494.

MASTERS, J., Private, R.A.S.C. (M.T.)
He joined in June 1916, and was quickly drafted to France, where he was engaged in conveying supplies and ammunition to the forward areas in various sectors of the front. He served during the engagements on the Somme, also at the Battles of Arras, Ypres and Cambrai, and was frequently under heavy shell-fire. He was demobilised on his return to England in August 1920, and holds the General Service and Victory Medals.
56, New Fenlake, Bedford. Z3495.

MASTERS, L. A., Private, 1/5th Bedfordshire Regt.
Mobilised at the outbreak of war in August 1914, he was quickly drafted to France, where he took part in the Retreat from Mons, also the Battles of the Marne and Ypres, and was wounded. Later he saw service at the Battles of Loos and Vimy Ridge, but was again wounded and sent to hospital. On his recovery he was in action at Loos and Cambrai. In December 1918 he was discharged, and holds the Mons Star, and the General Service and Victory Medals.
16, Gladstone Street, Bedford. Z3496/D.

MASTERSON, B., Private, Hunts. Cyclist Battalion and Royal Warwickshire Regiment.
He volunteered in September 1914, and on conclusion of his training in the following year was drafted to France, where he took part in much heavy fighting. He was in action at the Battles of Vimy Ridge and the Somme, where he was wounded, and invalided to England. As a result he was discharged medically unfit for further service in May 1917, holding the 1914–15 Star, and the General Service and Victory Medals.
Nicolas Lane, St. Ives, Hunts. Z3497.

MATHER, W. A., Staff-Sergeant Fitter, R.G.A.
He volunteered in October 1914, and after completing his training was retained on important duties at home. Later in 1916 he proceeded to France, where he did excellent work in various sectors of the front. He served with distinction during the engagements on the Somme, and also at the Battles of Vimy Ridge, Messines, Ypres, Cambrai and St. Quentin. In July 1919 he was demobilised, and holds the General Service and Victory Medals.
29, Woburn Road, Kempston, Bedford. X3498.

MATHERS, F., Private, R.A.S.C. (M.T.)
He volunteered in February 1915, and later in the following year proceeded to France, where he was engaged in conveying supplies and ammunition to the forward areas in various sectors of the front. He served during the engagements on the Somme and also at the Battles of Arras, Ypres and Cambrai. On his return to England, he was demobilised in March 1920, holding the General Service and Victory Medals.
14, Russell Street, Bedford. X3500/B.

MATHERS, G., Driver, Royal Engineers.
Volunteering in September 1914, he completed his training and was drafted to Egypt, where he saw much active service whilst attached to a Field Company. He was present during the Advance into Palestine, and took part in the Battles of Gaza, Jaffa, and in the capture of Jerusalem. Later he saw further service, including the heavy fighting on the River Jordan. He was demobilised on his return home in March 1919, and holds the General Service and Victory Medals.
29, Union Street, Bedford. X3501.

MATHERS, R., 1st Air Mechanic, R.A.F.
He joined in April 1918, and after completing a period of training was retained on important duties as a mechanic. In the course of his service he was chiefly engaged as a fitter in the workshops at Salisbury Plain, where he rendered excellent services until demobilised in July 1919.
14, Russell Street, Bedford. X3500/A.

MATHERS, W. G., Corporal, Royal Air Force.
Volunteering in April 1915, he completed his training and was retained on important duties. He did consistently good work at various aerodromes in England, where he was engaged in the making and repairing of aeroplanes and aero-engines, in which capacity he served until demobilised in February 1919.
84, George Street, Bedford. Z3499.

MATTEN, G. M., Private, 3rd London Regiment (Royal Fusiliers).
He volunteered in March 1915, and on conclusion of his training was sent to France, where he saw much heavy fighting at Arras, Ypres, Cambrai and on the Somme. In 1918 he was severely wounded during heavy fighting at Ypres, and unfortunately died from the effects of his wounds on April 26th, 1918. He was entitled to the General Service and Victory Medals.
"Thinking that remembrance, though unspoken, may reach him where he sleeps."
The Lanes, Houghton, Huntingdon, Hunts. Z3503.

MATTEN, W., Private, Royal Welch Fusiliers.
Volunteering in August 1914, he completed his training and later proceeded to Mesopotamia. During his service in this seat of hostilities he took part in much heavy fighting, including the Battle of Kut-el-Amara, and later in the engagements on the Tigris. He made the supreme sacrifice, being killed in action on January 18th, 1917, and was entitled to the General Service and Victory Medals.
"His life for his Country, his soul to God."
24, Tavistock Place, Bedford. X3502.

MATTHEWS, C., Trooper, Bedfordshire Lancers.
He volunteered at the outbreak of war in August 1914, and early in the following year proceeded to the Western Front, where he took part in the Battles of Ypres, Loos and the Somme. Later he was in action at Arras and Cambrai, and other engagements of importance until the close of hostilities. In 1919 he was sent to Ireland with the 9th (Queen's Royal) Lancers, and was still serving there in 1920. He holds the 1914–15 Star, and the General Service and Victory Medals.
35, Westbourne Road, Bedford. Z3507.

MATTHEWS, F., Driver, Royal Field Artillery.
He joined in August 1917, and on conclusion of his training in the following year was drafted to France. During his service in this theatre of war he served with his Battery in various sectors of the front, and did good work until the close of hostilities. In December 1918 he was demobilised, holding the General Service and Victory Medals.
35, Albert Street, Bletchley, Bucks. Z3506.

MATTHEW, G., Private, 7th London Regiment.
He joined in April 1918, and after a period of training was retained on important duties with his unit at various stations. Owing to his being under age he was unable to proceed to a theatre of war, but, nevertheless, rendered valuable services until demobilised in February 1919.
31, College Road, Bedford. Z3508.

MATTHEWS, H. E., Farrier, R.A.S.C.
He volunteered in November 1914, and during the course of hostilities was engaged on important duties as a farrier at Woolwich, Devonport, Aldershot and Salisbury Plain, where he lost a finger as the result of an accident. He was unsuccessful in obtaining his transfer overseas, but rendered valuable services until his demobilisation in August 1919.
10, Little Grove Place, Bedford. X3504.

MATTHEWS, J., Private, 2nd Bedfordshire Regt.
He was already in the Army at the outbreak of hostilities in August 1914, but was found to be medically unfit for service overseas. He was therefore retained on important duties, and did consistently good work whilst stationed at Felixstowe. On August 25th, 1918, he unfortunately died from the effects of an illness contracted during this period of service.
"His memory is cherished with pride."
80, Cauldwell Street, Bedford. X1761/B.

MATTHEWS, J. W., Sergt., 1st South Staffs. Regt.
Joining in January 1916, he proceeded in the same year to France, where he saw much fighting in various sectors. He was in action during the Somme Offensive and also at the Battles of Arras, Vimy Ridge and Passchendaele, and was wounded in July 1917. On his recovery he was transferred to Italy, and played a prominent part in the engagements on the Piave front. He was awarded an Italian Decoration, and holds also the General Service and Victory Medals. In October 1919 he was demobilised.
18, Cauldwell Street, Bedford. X1761/C.

MATTHEWS, L. F., Sapper, Royal Engineers.
He joined in May 1917, and after a period of training was found to be medically unfit for service overseas. He was therefore retained on important coastal duties, and rendered valuable services until discharged in May 1918.
The Warren, Clapham, Bedford. Z3505.

MAXEY, H., Private, 23rd Middlesex Regiment.
He joined in 1916, and later in the same year was drafted to the Western Front, where he took part in the Battle of Arras and many other important engagements. Mortally wounded in action at Vimy Ridge, he unhappily died on June 12th, 1917. He was entitled to the General Service and Victory Medals.
"He died the noblest death a man may die:
Fighting for God and right and liberty."
2, Derby Street, Bedford. X3523.

MAY, T. A., Private, 2nd Bedfordshire Regiment.
Mobilised at the outbreak of war, he was immediately drafted to France, where he took part in the Retreat from Mons. Later he saw service at the Battles of Arras, Ypres, Cambrai and the Somme, and other important engagements until the close of hostilities. He was discharged in May 1919, and holds the Mons Star, and the General Service and Victory Medals. After he was demobilised he re-enlisted, and served for another period of 12 months.
6, Sloughs Buildings, Huntingdon. Z3509.

MAYES, A. E., Private, Northamptonshire Regt.
He joined in January 1917, and was shortly afterwards drafted to Egypt. During his service in this seat of war he saw much fighting, particularly in Palestine, where he took part in the Battles of Gaza and Jaffa. On November 2nd, 1917, he was reported missing and later presumed to have been killed in action on that date. He was entitled to the General Service and Victory Medals.
"His life for his Country."
The Green, Great Staughton, Hunts. Z3510/B

MAYES, F., Private, South Wales Borderers.
Mobilised at the outbreak of war in August 1914, he was immediately drafted to France, where he was in action at the Battle of, and in the Retreat from, Mons, and also at the Battle of Ypres. He made the supreme sacrifice, being killed on October 21st, 1914, and was entitled to the Mons Star, and the General Service and Victory Medals.
"He died the noblest death a man may die:
Fighting for God and right and liberty."
Berrak Yard, Eynesbury, St. Neots, Hunts. Z3511.

MAYES, G. A., Private, Royal Fusiliers.
He joined in January 1917, and in June was sent to France, where he was wounded in action at the Battle of Ypres two months later. Invalided home, he was in hospital at Bradford, and then returned to the Western Front, but after taking part in the Battles of the Somme and Amiens, was gassed at Cambrai and again evacuated to England. On his recovery he once more returned to France, and served at Le Cateau. After hostilities ceased, he proceeded to Germany with the Army of Occupation and was stationed at Cologne until demobilised in November 1919. He holds the General Service and Victory Medals.
The Green, Great Staughton, Hunts. Z3510/C.

MAYES, H. W., Private, Labour Corps.
Joining in September 1916, he completed his training in the same year, and proceeded to France, where he was engaged on important duties whilst attached to the Graves Registration Department. He saw much service at Arras, Ypres, Cambrai and on the Somme. After the cessation of hostilities he returned home and was demobilised in January 1919, holding the General Service and Victory Medals.
2, Church Road, Willington, Beds. Z3512.

MAYES, J., Corporal, Royal Marine Light Infantry.
Mobilised in August 1914, he was immediately drafted to the Western Front, where he took part in the Defence of Antwerp. In the following year, however, he was transferred to Gallipoli, and there saw much severe fighting at Sedd-el-Bahr, Suvla Bay and Anzac Cove until invalided home suffering from dysentery. He was afterwards engaged on coastal patrol duties, and in 1920 was still serving. He holds the 1914 Star, and the General Service and Victory Medals.
The Green, Great Staughton, Hunts. Z3510/A.

MAYES, J., Private, 1st Hertfordshire Regiment.
Joining in November 1916, he was drafted to the Western Front after four months' training, and there saw severe fighting in various sectors. He took part in the Battles of Arras, Messines, Ypres, Passchendaele and Cambrai, and many other important engagements, and also served through the Retreat and Advance of 1918. He was demobilised in March 1919, and holds the General Service and Victory Medals.
1, St. John's Street, Huntingdon. Z3513.

MAYES, J. G. L., Gunner, Royal Garrison Artillery.
He joined in April 1917, and on completion of a period of training in November of that year proceeded to France. There he saw severe fighting in various sectors of the front, and took part in the Battles of Cambrai and Ypres, and many other important engagements until the cessation of hostilities. Returning home in February 1919, he was demobilised in the following month, and holds the General Service and Victory Medals. 24, King's Place, Bedford. X3514.

MAYES, S. A., Private, 4th Bedfordshire Regiment.
Two months after joining in October 1916 he was drafted to the Western Front, where he saw much heavy fighting. He took part in the Battles of Arras and Ypres, and many other important engagements, and was wounded in action on the Somme in the Retreat of March 1918. Later he served with the Army of Occupation in Germany and was stationed at Cologne until his return home for demobilisation in July 1919. He holds the General Service and Victory Medals.
Wistow, Hunts. Z3515.

MAYES, S. W., Sapper, Royal Engineers.
He volunteered in August 1915, and in the following year was drafted to Egypt, where he served at Alexandria and other stations. Later he proceeded into Palestine, and there took part in the Battles of Gaza and the capture of Jerusalem and Jericho, and was for a time in hospital, suffering from malaria and dysentery. He was invalided from the Army on his return home in 1919, and holds the General Service and Victory Medals. Eaton Socon, Beds. Z3516.

MAYES, W., Private, Royal Marine Light Infantry.
Having enlisted in May 1899, he was mobilised at the outbreak of war in August 1914, and was posted to H.M.S. "Theseus," attached to the Grand Fleet in the North Sea. He also took part in operations at the Dardanelles and later served in Greek, Turkish and Russian waters, being present at many naval actions. He was finally discharged in May 1920, and holds the 1914–15 Star, and the General Service and Victory Medals.
Upper Dean, Beds. Z3517.

MAYHEW, A. A., Air Mechanic, R.A.F.
He joined in June 1918, and after undergoing a period of training, was retained at various stations, where he was engaged on important duties in the workshops. Owing to the early cessation of hostilities, he was not successful in obtaining his transfer to a theatre of war, but nevertheless, rendered valuable services with his Squadron until February 1919, when he was demobilised. Bedford Hill, Great Barford, Beds. Z3518.

MAYHEW, G. H., Private, 9th Argyll & Sutherland Highlanders.
Mobilised in August 1914, he was drafted to the Western Front in February of the following year, and there saw severe fighting in various sectors. He took part in the Battles of Ypres and Cambrai, and many other important engagements, and was twice wounded—at Festubert in May 1915, and on the Ancre in December 1916. He was finally discharged in March 1920, and holds the 1914-15 Star, and the General Service and Victory Medals. 17, Beauchamp Row, Bedford. X3519.

MAYLIN, C. R., Sapper, Royal Engineers.
Volunteering in August 1914, he was drafted to France on completing a term of training in February of the following year, and there saw severe fighting in various sectors of the front. He took part in the Battles of Hill 60, the Somme, Arras and Cambrai, and many other important engagements, and on his return home in March 1919 was demobilised. He holds the 1914–15 Star, and the General Service and Victory Medals. 15, Althorpe Street, Bedford. X3520.

MAYNARD, C. W., Private, Bedfordshire Regt.
He volunteered in September 1914, and in the following year proceeded to the Western Front. Whilst in this theatre of war he took part in many important engagements, including the Battles of Hill 60, Ypres, Arras, Vimy Ridge and Passchendaele, and was wounded in action. He was discharged in February 1918, and holds the 1914–15 Star, and the General Service and Victory Medals. 8, King's Place, Bedford. X3522.

MAYNARD, E., Corporal, 2nd Bedfordshire Regt.
Already in the Army when war was declared in August 1914, he was shortly afterwards drafted to the Western Front, where he served in various sectors. He was engaged on important duties whilst in this theatre of war, and was present at the Battles of Ypres, Loos, the Somme and Arras, and other engagements. He was discharged in March 1919, and holds the 1914 Star, and the General Service and Victory Medals.
91, Bunyan Road, Kempston, Bedford. X3521/A.

MAYNARD, F., Private, Machine Gun Corps.
He was already in the Army when war broke out in August 1914, and was immediately drafted to the Western Front. There, after fighting at Mons, he took part in the Battles of the Marne, Hill 60 and Festubert, and was twice wounded—at Ypres in November 1914 and at Neuve Chapelle in the following year. He was afterwards again in action at Salonika and on the Vardar and Doiran fronts, and on his return home in July 1919 was discharged. He holds the Mons Star, and the General Service and Victory Medals.
91, Bunyan Road, Kempston, Bedford. X3521/C.

MAYNARD, H., Bombardier, Royal Field Artillery.
Shortly after joining in April 1916, he was sent to the Western Front, where he saw severe fighting in various sectors. He took part in the Battles of the Somme, Arras, Ypres and Cambrai, and many other important engagements until the cessation of hostilities and then proceeded with the Army of Occupation to Germany. Demobilised on his return home in October 1919, he holds the General Service and Victory Medals.
91, Bunyan Road, Kempston, Bedford. X3521/D.

MAYNARD, W. (M.M.), Private, 2nd Beds. Regt.
Mobilised in August 1914, he was shortly afterwards drafted to the Western Front, where he served as a stretcher-bearer in various sectors. He took part in the Battles of La Bassée, Ypres, Festubert, Loos, Albert, the Somme and Arras and many minor engagements, and was wounded near Cambrai in 1918. He was awarded the Military Medal for conspicuous bravery in the Field, and holding also the 1914 Star, and the General Service and Victory Medals, was discharged in March 1919. 91, Bunyan Road, Kempston, Bedford. X3521/B.

McDONALD, J. S., Cpl., 4th Gordon Highlanders.
Volunteering in August 1914, he proceeded to the Western Front in March of the following year, and there fought in various sectors. He took part in the Battles of Neuve Chapelle, Hill 60, Ypres and Loos, and many minor engagements, and was twice wounded in action—on the Somme in June 1916, and near Cambrai in 1918. Invalided home, he unhappily died in hospital at Cambridge on July 6th, 1919. He was entitled to the 1914–15 Star, and the General Service and Victory Medals.
"The path of duty was the way to glory."
57, Westbourne Road, Queen's Park, Bedford. Z3414.

MEACE, N., Private, Guards' Machine Gun Regt.
Having enlisted in February 1912, he was drafted to the Western Front 10 months after the outbreak of war, in August 1914, and there saw much severe fighting. He took part in the Battles of Loos, the Somme, Arras, Vimy Ridge, Ypres and Cambrai, and many other engagements, and was gassed and invalided home two days before the signing of the Armistice. He was discharged in February 1919, and holds the 1914–15 Star, and the General Service and Victory Medals.
West End, Somersham, Hunts. Z3524.

MEACHAM, J., Private, 2nd Bedfordshire Regt. and Hertfordshire Regiment.
He joined immediately on attaining military age in January 1918, and after a period of training was retained on important duties at various stations. He was unable to obtain his transfer overseas before the cessation of hostilities, but in September 1919 was drafted to India for garrison duties in the Deccan. He was still with his unit in 1920.
3, Chew Cottages, Little Brickhill, Bucks. Z3525.

MEAD, A., Private, Labour Corps.
He joined in June 1916, and after a short period of training was drafted to the Western Front, where he was engaged on forestry work in various sectors. In 1917 he was sent home and transferred to Class W of the Reserve, was afterwards employed on the construction of mines at Messrs. Vicker's, Ltd., Dartford. He was finally discharged in March 1919, and holds the General Service and Victory Medals.
102, Simpson Road, Fenny Stratford, Bucks. Z3528/B.

MEAD, F., Private, Royal Fusiliers.
He joined immediately on attaining military age in June 1918, and after completing a term of training, was retained on important duties as a despatch-runner at various stations. Owing to the early cessation of hostilities he was unable to obtain his transfer to the front, but in December 1918 was sent with the Army of Occupation to Germany, where he served at Cologne. He was demobilised on his return home in November 1919.
102, Simpson Road, Fenny Stratford, Bucks. Z3528/C.

MEAD, F. H., Private, Royal Warwickshire Regt.
Joining in April 1916, he was drafted to the Western Front in the following August and there took part in the Battles of the Somme, Arras, Vimy Ridge, Bullecourt, Ypres and Cambrai, and many minor engagements. He died gloriously on the Field of Battle on September 7th, 1918. He was entitled to the General Service and Victory Medals
"Great deeds cannot die:
They with the sun and moon renew their light for ever."
3, Vicarage Road, Old Bradwell, Bucks. Z2416/C.

MEAD, G., Private, Oxford. and Bucks. L.I.
He volunteered in April 1915, and 12 months later proceeded to Mesopotamia, where he saw much severe fighting. He took part in the Relief of Kut, the capture of Baghdad, and in many other important engagements, and was twice wounded in action. Returning home in March 1919, he was demobilised in that month, and holds the General Service and Victory Medals. Ravenstone, Bucks. Z3526.

MEAD, G. E., Sapper, Royal Engineers.
He volunteered in September 1914, and in the following March was drafted to France, where he saw much fighting in the Ypres sector. Later he was transferred to Italy and took part in many engagements on the Piave, and was wounded in action. After hostilities ceased he was sent to Germany with the Army of Occupation, and served on the Rhine until he was demobilised in March 1919. He holds the 1914–15 Star, and the General Service and Victory Medals.
26, Church Street, Fenny Stratford, Bucks. Z3527.

MEAD, H. A., Sapper, Royal Engineers.
Volunteering in January 1915, he was drafted overseas in the following August, and whilst on the Western Front was engaged on many important duties, building bridges and trench digging in the Ypres and Somme sectors. He was badly gassed in 1918, and consequently invalided home and discharged in November of that year as medically unfit for further service. He holds the 1914–15 Star, and the General Service and Victory Medals.
102, Simpson Road, Fenny Stratford, Beds. Z3528/A.

MEAD, S. C., Private, R.A.S.C.
He volunteered in June 1915, and in the following year was drafted to Salonika. In this seat of hostilities he was engaged as a blacksmith and did continuously good work until he contracted fever. As a result he was invalided home, and finally discharged in March 1918 as medicaly unfit for further service. He holds the General Service and Victory Medals.
Oakfield, Goldington Road, Bedford. Z3530.

MEAD, T., Sapper, Royal Engineers.
He joined in August 1916, and in the following March was drafted to the Western Front. In this theatre of war he was engaged in repairing trenches, building bridges and various other important duties in the Arras and the Somme sectors. He unfortunately met with an accident on the light railways, and was consequently invalided home. He was demobilised in April 1919, and holds the General Service and Victory Medals. Birds Cottage, Great Linford, Bucks. TZ3529.

MEADS, A., Private, Royal Warwickshire Regt.
He enlisted in May 1916, and four months later was drafted to France, where he took part in many engagements, including those in the Somme, Arras and Ypres sectors. Later he was transferred to Italy, saw much fighting on the Asiago Plateau, and, proceeding to Palestine, served with General Allenby's Forces in the Advance of 1918. He returned home, and was demobilised in November 1919, holding the General Service and Victory Medals.
Radclive Road, Gawcott, Buckingham. Z3534/B.

MEADS, A. T., Private, Machine Gun Corps.
He joined in January 1917, and a few months later was drafted to France, where he took part in many important engagements in the Ypres sector. He died gloriously on the Field of Battle at Ypres in September 1917, and was entitled to the General Service and Victory Medals.
"A costly sacrifice upon the altar of freedom."
Radclive Road, Gawcott, Buckingham. Z3534/C.

MEADS, E., L/Corporal, Royal Berkshire Regt.
He volunteered in the Royal Buckinghamshire Hussars, and was retained at various home stations before proceeding to France in 1917. In this theatre of war he was transferred to the Royal Berkshire Regiment, and took part in much heavy fighting at the Battle of the Somme (II.) and in the Retreat of 1918. He was unfortunately killed in action on September 28th, 1918, and was entitled to the General Service and Victory Medals.
"A valiant Soldier, with undaunted heart he breasted life's last hill."
Radclive Road, Gawcott, Buckingham. Z3534/A

MEADS, G., Private, Machine Gun Corps.
He joined in April 1916, and four months later was drafted to the Western Front. There he took part in many important engagements, including the Battles of the Somme and St. Quentin, where he was made a prisoner of war in March 1918. He was held in captivity in Germany and was forced to work in the stone quarries. Repatriated after the Armistice he returned home and was demobilised in October 1919. He holds the General Service and Victory Medals.
Hill Cottage, Gawcott, Buckingham. Z3533.

MEADS, J. W., L/Corporal, Royal Engineers.
Volunteering in May 1915, he proceeded overseas later in the same year. Whilst on the Western Front he was engaged on many important duties in various sectors, notably at Ypres and Vimy Ridge and on the Somme. He was taken ill and consequently invalided home, being finally discharged in August 1917 as medically unfit for further service. He holds the 1914–15 Star, and the General Serviceand Victory Medals.
2, The Grove, Bedford. Z3531.

MEADS, W., Private, 2nd Worcestershire Regt.
He joined in June 1918, and underwent a period of training prior to his being drafted to France. There he took part in much heavy fighting in the Somme sector, and was severely wounded in action on November 5th, 1918. He unfortunately died of his wounds twelve days later, and was entitled to the General Service and Victory Medals.
"Honour to the immortal dead who gave their youth that the world might grow old in peace."
Main Street, Gawcott, Buckingham. Z3532.

MEARS, J., Private, Oxford. and Bucks. L.I.
He was called up from the Reserve in August 1914, and immediately drafted to the Western Front, where he took part in the Retreat from Mons and the Battles of the Marne, the Aisne and La Bassée. He was unfortunately reported missing about November 23rd, 1914, and is now believed to have been killed in action at Ypres on that date. He was entitled to the Mons Star, and the General Service and Victory Medals.
"Whilst we remember, the sacrifice is not in vain."
5, St. Paul's Terrace, Silver Street, Newport Pagnell, Bucks. Z2621/A.

MEASURES, J. G., Sapper, R.E. (Signal Section).
He joined in August 1916, and in the following March was drafted to France. In this theatre of war he was engaged as a telephone operator, in which capacity he did continuously good work in many sectors of the front. He also served in the wireless section, and was demobilised in January 1919, holding the General Service and Victory Medals.
13, Euston Street, Huntingdon. Z3535.

MEASURES, W. J., Sapper, Royal Engineers.
Volunteering in February 1915, he was drafted overseas three months later, and on the Western Front was engaged on important duties in connection with the railways and transport work in the Ypres, Lens, Arras and Newport sectors. He rendered valuable services, and was demobilised in April 1919, holding the 1914–15 Star, and the General Service and Victory Medals. Abbot's Ripton, Hunts. Z3536.

MEDLOCK, T., Private, R.A.S.C. (M.T.)
He joined in December 1916, and was retained for a time at various home stations before being drafted to France, there he was engaged on important transport and ambulance work in the Ypres, Arras, Albert and Cambrai sectors, and after hostilities ceased proceeded to Germany with the Army of Occupation, and served on the Rhine until his demobilisation in October 1919. He holds the General Service and Victory Medals.
West Perry, near Huntingdon, Hunts. Z3537/A.

MEDLOW, C. W., Private, Middlesex Regiment.
He joined in May 1916, and completing his training in the following August was drafted to the Western Front, where he took part in several engagements. He made the supreme sacrifice, being killed in action on September 26th, 1916, and was entitled to the General Service and Victory Medals.
"Great deeds cannot die:
They with the sun and moon renew their light for ever."
Wyboston, Beds. Z3538/B.

MEDLOW, F., Shoeing-Smith, R.A.V.C.
He volunteered in June 1915, and two months later proceeded to the Western Front, where he did good work as a shoeing-smith. He was engaged in various sectors, including Ypres, Arras and Abbeville, but owing to his being taken ill was sent home and discharged in January 1918 as medically unfit for further service. He holds the 1914–15 Star, and the General Service and Victory Medals.
Wyboston, Beds. Z3538/A.

MEEKS, B. W., Sergeant, 7th Bedfordshire Regt.
He volunteered in August 1914, and in the following May was drafted to France, where he played a prominent part in engagements at Ypres, Loos and Vimy Ridge, and was wounded and gassed in action. He died gloriously on the Field in the Somme sector on November 16th, 1917, and was entitled to the 1914–15 Star, and the General Service and Victory Medals.
"His life for his Country, his soul to God."
14, Adelaide Terrace, Godmanchester, Hunts. Z3539/A.

MEEKS, F., L/Corporal, Suffolk Regiment.
Volunteering in 1915, he was drafted overseas in the following year. Whilst on the Western Front he took part in many engagements, including the Battles of the Somme, Arras and Cambrai, and was twice wounded in action, at Arras in 1917, and on the Somme in 1918. He was demobilised in January 1919, and holds the General Service and Victory Medals.
Croxton, St. Neots, Hunts. Z3541.

MEEKS, G., A.B., Royal Navy.
He volunteered in April 1915, and having undergone a period of training at Harwich proceeded to sea on board one of H.M. Ships, and served with the Grand Fleet. He was engaged off the coasts of Ireland and Belgium on important patrol duties, and did good work throughout. In 1920 he was still at sea on board H.M.S "Verdun," and holds the General Service and Victory Medals.
14, Adelaide Terrace, Godmanchester, Hunts. Z3539/B.

MEEKS, P. L., Driver, Royal Engineers.
He volunteered in May 1915, and underwent a period of training prior to his being drafted to Egypt, thence proceeding into Palestine. There he took part in engagements at Gaza, Jaffa, and in those leading to the fall of Jerusalem. After hostilities ceased he returned home, but unfortunately contracted pneumonia and died from the effects on March 11th, 1919. He was entitled to the General Service and Victory Medals.
"His memory is cherished with pride."
36, Greenhill Street, Bedford. X3540.

MEGEARY, A., Private, Oxford. and Bucks. L.I.
He joined in January 1917, and completing his training four months later was drafted to the Western Front. There he took part in many important engagements, including the Battles of Ypres, Passchendaele, Cambrai, Albert and the Somme (II.), and in the Retreat and Advance of 1918, being slightly gassed and twice wounded. He was demobilised in November 1919, and holds the General Service and Victory Medals.
25, West Street, Olney, Bucks. Z3423.

MEHEW, H. F., Lieutenant, 8th Lincolnshire Regt.
He volunteered in September 1914, and underwent a period of training prior to his being drafted to France. There he played a distinguished part in the Battles of the Somme, Arras, Ypres and Cambrai, and was twice badly wounded in action, being invalided home on each occasion. He was discharged in May 1919, and holds the General Service and Victory Medals.
15, Ouse Walk, Huntingdon, Hunts. Z3542/B.

MEHEW, W. E., Cpl., King's Royal Rifle Corps.
He joined in May 1917, and was retained at various home stations on important duties before proceeding to the Western Front. There he took part in much heavy fighting in many sectors until August 1918, when he was invalided home. He was demobilised in November 1919, and holds the General Service and Victory Medals.
15, Ouse Walk, Huntingdon, Hunts. Z3542/A.

MENDHAM, E., R.S.M., Bedfordshire Regiment.
He was already in the Army when war broke out in August 1914, and was retained at various home stations, where he was engaged on important duties. He was unable to proceed overseas owing to his being medically unfit, but did consistently good work until his discharge in April 1917.
11, Muswell Road, South End, Bedford. TZ3543.

MEPHAM, W. G., Sapper, Royal Engineers.
He volunteered in January 1915, and later in the same year proceeded to France. There he took part in the Battles of Loos, Armentières and the Somme, where he was badly wounded, and invalided home. On his recovery he returned to France, and was again in action on the Somme and at Albert. He was demobilised in February 1919, and holds the 1914–15 Star, and the General Service and Victory Medals.
Mount Pleasant, Wootton, Bedford. TZ3544.

MERRY, A., Sergeant, King's Royal Rifle Corps.
He was mobilised in August 1914, and retained at home on important duties as an Instructor at various stations. He was over age to obtain a transfer overseas, but did consistently good work until he was discharged in October 1916 after 29 years' service with the Colours.
Pipers Lane, Godmanchester, Hunts. Z3545.

MERRY, E., Corporal, Bedfordshire Regiment.
He was mobilised in August 1914, and almost immediately drafted to France, where he took part in much severe fighting in the Battles of the Marne, Ypres, La Bassée and Neuve Chapelle. He was then invalided home and retained as a Musketry Instructor, in which capacity he did continuously good work until his discharge in February 1919. He holds the 1914 Star, and the General Service and Victory Medals.
Pipers Lane, Godmanchester, Hunts. Z3546.

MIDDLETON, A. J., Sapper, Royal Engineers.
He volunteered in July 1915, and in the following January proceeded to Egypt. In this seat of operations he saw much fighting, and later took part in the Advance into Palestine, being in action at Gaza, Jaffa, on the River Jordan, and at the fall of Jerusalem. He suffered from malarial fever, and was in hospital for some time. He returned home and was demobilised in September 1919, holding the General Service and Victory Medals.
1, Little Butts Street, Bedford. X3549.

MIDDLETON, C., Private, 12th Queen's (Royal West Surrey Regiment).
He enlisted in April 1916, and underwent a period of training prior to his being drafted to the Western Front. In this theatre of war he was engaged on important transport work in the Somme and Ypres sectors, and did continuously good service until his demobilisation in October 1919. He holds the General Service and Victory Medals.
1, Little Butts Street, Bedford. X3548.

MIDDLETON, J. W., Gunner, R.F.A.
He volunteered in March 1915, and was retained for a time at various home stations before being drafted to Russia. Later he was transferred to Salonika, where he took part in many engagements on the Vardar and Doiran fronts. After hostilities ceased he returned home, and was demobilised in August 1919, holding the General Service and Victory Medals.
7, Berrells Court, Olney, Bucks. Z3547.

MIDDLETON, S. C., Pte., 2nd Bedfordshire Regt.
He joined in September 1916, and completing his training in the following year, was drafted to the Western Front. There he took part in many important engagements, including the Battles of Arras, Ypres and Cambrai. In 1920 he was still serving in India, and holds the General Service and Victory Medals. 1, Little Butts Street, Bedford. X3550.

MILES, C. J. W., Pte., 1/8th R. Warwickshire Regt.
He volunteered in October 1914, and served on the East Coast for about two years before proceeding to France. There he took part in much heavy fighting in the Somme and Albert sectors and was badly wounded in action. As a result he was invalided home, and on his recovery was engaged with the Labour Corps until his demobilisation in January 1919. He holds the General Service and Victory Medals.
The Avenue, Godmanchester, Hunts. Z3551/A.

MILES, P. W., Sergeant, East Surrey Regiment.
He volunteered in 1915, and later in the same year was drafted to the Dardanelles, where he saw heavy fighting at Suvla Bay. After the Evacuation of the Gallipoli Peninsula he was transferred to Egypt, and thence proceeded to Palestine and fought at Gaza and Jaffa. In 1917 he was sent to France, and played a prominent part in the Battles of Arras, Passchendaele and in the Retreat and Advance of 1918. After hostilities ceased he went to Germany with the Army of Occupation, and served at Cologne until his demobilisation in February 1919. He holds the 1914–15 Star, and the General Service and Victory Medals. 34, Salisbury Street, Bedford. X1158/C.

MILES, W., Gunner (Signaller), R.G.A.
He volunteered in October 1915, and in the following year was sent to Salonika. Proceeding shortly afterwards to Egypt, where he served for a time at Cairo, he took part in the Advance into Palestine and fought at Gaza, and in the operations in connection with the fall of Jaffa. Invalided home with fever, he was discharged in February 1919, but died later. He was entitled to the General Service and Victory Medals.
"Steals on the ear the distant triumph song."
The Avenue, Godmanchester, Hunts. Z3551/B.

MILLARD, A. E., Pte., 2/5th Bedfordshire Regt.
He volunteered in January 1915, and completing his training in the following year was drafted to the Western Front. In this theatre of war he took part in many engagements, including those on the Somme, at Vimy Ridge, Ypres, Cambrai, St. Quentin and Albert, and was wounded in action. He was demobilised in February 1919, and holds the General Service and Victory Medals. 3, Station Road, Sandy, Beds. Z3553.

MILLARD, C. J., Corporal, Oxford. & Bucks. L.I.
He volunteered in December 1914, and underwent a period of training prior to his being drafted to France, where he saw heavy fighting at Laventie and was badly wounded in action. As a result he was invalided home and eventually discharged in June 1917 as medically unfit for further service. He holds the General Service and Victory Medals.
12, Simpson Road, Fenny Stratford, Bucks. Z3552/C.

MILLARD, S. E., Corporal, 21st London Regiment (1st Surrey Rifles).
He joined in September 1917, and early in the following year proceeded to France. Whilst in this theatre of war he took part in many engagements in the Somme, Le Cateau and Mormal Forest sectors. After the Armistice he was engaged on important duties at Etaples until his demobilisation in November 1919. He holds the General Service and Victory Medals.
12, Simpson Road, Fenny Stratford, Bucks. Z3552/B.

MILLARD, W., Private, Bedfordshire Regiment.
He joined the Army in 1905, and when war broke out in August 1914 was quickly drafted to France, where he took part in the Battles of La Bassée and Ypres. There he was badly wounded in action and consequently invalided home. On his recovery he was stationed at Felixstowe until his discharge in April 1916 as medically unfit for further service. He holds the 1914 Star, and the General Service and Victory Medals.
West End, Cranfield, Beds. Z3554.

MILLARD, W. C., Private, Oxford. & Bucks. L.I.
He volunteered in December 1915, and in the following June was drafted to France, where he took part in the Battles of the Somme and Arras, and was badly wounded. As a result he was invalided home, but on his recovery returned to France and fought at Passchendaele, sustaining his second wound. He was again sent home and later retained at various home stations until his discharge in January 1919. He holds the General Service and Victory Medals.
10, Simpson Road, Fenny Stratford, Bucks. Z3552/A.

MILLEN, C., Private, Oxford. and Bucks. L.I.
A month after the outbreak of war he volunteered and in December 1915 proceeded to Salonika. In that theatre of war he took an active part in numerous engagements, and saw severe fighting on the Doiran and the Vardar fronts, and in the Advance into Bulgaria. He was wounded in action on one occasion, and was demobilised on his return home in March 1919, holding the 1914–15 Star, and the General Service and Victory Medals. 38, Caledonian Rd., New Bradwell, Bucks. Z2826/C.

MILLEN, W., Private, Oxford. and Bucks. L.I.
He volunteered in September 1914, and after a period of training at Oxford was ordered overseas in December 1915. During his service in Salonika he was engaged in severe fighting on the Doiran and the Vardar fronts, and took an active part in the Advance into Bulgaria. He was demobilised on his return to England in March 1919, and holds the 1914–15 Star, and the General Service and Victory Medals.
38, Caledonian Road, New Bradwell, Bucks. Z2826/D.

MILLER, E., Pte., Beds. Regt.; and Sapper, R.E.
He joined in April 1917, and on completion of a course of training was 10 months later sent to the Western Front, where he took part in operations in the Somme, Ypres and Cambrai sectors. He was also engaged in mending roads, and rendered very valuable services until his demobilisation in April 1919, holding the General Service and Victory Medals.
51, Newham Street, Bedford. X3556.

MILLER, F. J., Private, R.A.S.C.
He volunteered in the 10th Gloucestershire Regiment in September 1914, and in the following August was sent to France, where he took part in the Battles of Loos, Albert and the Somme, and was badly wounded in action in August 1916. Invalided home, he spent 13 months in hospital, and was then transferred to the Royal Army Service Corps (Remount Section), with which unit he did excellent work until his demobilisation in May 1919. He holds the 1914–15 Star, and the General Service and Victory Medals.
Church End, Sherington, Bucks. Z2925/A.

MILLER, H. V., Cpl., Cambridgeshire Regt. & R.E.
He enlisted in 1912, and after the commencement of hostilities performed valuable work at Bedford with the Military Police. Later he was transferred to the Royal Engineers, and served at Richborough and Holden. In 1915 he proceeded to France, where he experienced fierce fighting in various sectors, and was in action in engagements at Ypres, Dickebusch and the Somme. He was wounded on one occasion and also gassed, and was discharged in February 1919, holding the 1914–15 Star, and the General Service and Victory Medals.
12, Great Butts Street, Bedford. X1734/A.

MILLER, S. B., Private, 1st Beds. Regt. & R.A.V.C.
He was mobilised in August 1914, and was at once ordered to France, where he fought in the Retreat from Mons. He also took part in the Battles of the Marne and La Bassée, but was wounded at Ypres in 1914, and invalided to England. On his discharge from hospital he served at Felixstowe, and in October 1916 was drafted to India. He was then transferred to the Royal Army Veterinary Corps, and rendered valuable services, attending to sick and wounded horses on the North-West Frontier. He was discharged in March 1920, on his return to England, and holds the Mons Star, the General Service and Victory Medals, and the India General Service Medal (with Clasp—Afghanistan, N.W. Frontier, 1919).
4, Tickford Court, Newport Pagnell, Bucks. Z3555.

MILLS, A., Private, Oxford. and Bucks. L.I.
He volunteered in May 1915, and in June of the following year was drafted overseas. Whilst serving on the Western Front he fought in the Battles of the Somme, Arras and Ypres, but contracted trench-fever, and was admitted to hospital. On his recovery he served at Rouen on police duties, but was afterwards sent to the firing-line, where he did good work as a stretcher-bearer in the Albert and Cambrai sectors. Demobilised in March 1919, he holds the General Service and Victory Medals.
Huntingdon Street, St. Neots, Hunts. TZ3567/A.

MILLS, A. J., Corporal, 1st Bedfordshire Regiment.
When war was declared in August 1914 he was already serving, and immediately proceeded to France, where he took part in the Mons Retreat and in the Battles of the Marne, the Aisne, La Bassée, Ypres and Neuve Chapelle. He was wounded in action in November 1914, and on his return to the firing-line was unhappily killed in action at Ypres on May 5th, 1915. He was entitled to the Mons Star, and the General Service and Victory Medals.
"Whilst we remember, the sacrifice is not in vain."
4, Boswell Place, Bedford. X3563/E.

MILLS, F. G., Private, Machine Gun Corps.
He joined in June 1916, and in October of the following year proceeded overseas. After a month's service in France he was transferred to Italy, and was engaged in severe fighting on the Piave and Asiago fronts. In April 1919 he was drafted to Egypt, and was engaged on important duties in Alexandria until sent to England for demobilisation in November 1919. He holds the General Service and Victory Medals.
3, Balsall Street East, Bedford. X3564.

MILLS, G. H., Private, Buffs (East Kent Regt.)
He volunteered in September 1914, and in the following year was drafted to the Western Front, where he saw severe fighting at Festubert and Loos. Whilst in action on the Somme in 1916 he was wounded, and on his recovery took part in the Battles of Arras and Ypres. In March 1918 he was taken prisoner at Cambrai, and kept in captivity until the close of hostilities. Demobilised in February 1919, he holds the 1914–15 Star, and the General Service and Victory Medals.
4, Boswell Place, Bedford. X3563/C.

MILLS, G. W., Corporal, Royal Engineers.
Volunteering in January 1916, he embarked for France in the same year, and served in the Battles of the Somme, Arras, Ypres and Cambrai. He also saw much severe fighting at Nieuport, Armentières and Hamel, and in various other sectors of the front. After the Armistice he proceeded into Germany with the Army of Occupation, and served on the Rhine until demobilised in August 1919, holding the General Service and Victory Medals. 6, Crown Walk, St. Ives, Hunts. Z3565.

MILLS, H., Corporal, Royal Defence Corps.
He volunteered in November 1914, but proved to be medically unfit for service overseas. He was, however, retained on home defence at important stations at Bedford, Maidenhead and in Yorkshire, and carried out his duties in an exemplary manner. He was eventually demobilised in March 1919.
4, Boswell Place, Bedford. X3563/D.

MILLS, J., Private, East Surrey Regiment.
In May 1918 he joined the Army, and on completion of his training was later in the same year drafted to Russia. After rendering valuable services with his unit there he was transferred to India, where he was engaged on important garrison duties at Madras. In 1920 he was still serving, and holds the General Service and Victory Medals.
80, Coventry Road, Queen's Park, Bedford. Z3561/B.

MILLS, M. A., Private, Durham Light Infantry.
He joined in November 1916, and in the following year embarked for France, where he took an active part in the Battles of Arras and Ypres. On being transferred to Italy he saw heavy fighting on the Piave front until January 1918, when he was drafted to Russia. There he performed valuable work with his unit for 13 months, when he was sent to Constantinople. He was still serving in the Army in 1920, and holds the General Service and Victory Medals. Tilbrook, Hunts. Z3566.

MILLS, P., Sapper, Royal Engineers (R.O.D.)
Volunteering in May 1915, he was sent in the following September to the Western Front. There he performed valuable work in connection with railroad making for three months, and was then drafted to Egypt, where he was employed on the same duties. In December 1916 he was invalided to England suffering from Bright's disease, and consequently was discharged as medically unfit in June 1917. He holds the 1914–15 Star and the General Service and Victory Medals.
10, Farrer Street, Bedford. X3560.

MILLS, P., Private, 8th East Surrey Regiment.
He joined in December 1916, and on completion of his training was in the following year sent overseas. During his service on the Western Front he took part in many important engagements in various sectors, and fell fighting at Ypres on October 12th, 1917. He was entitled to the General Service and Victory Medals.
" A valiant Soldier, with undaunted heart he breasted life's last hill."
23, Canning Street, Bedford. X3559.

MILLS, T., Sapper, Royal Engineers.
Volunteering in May 1915, he was engaged on important duties on the East Coast until January 1917, when he was drafted to the Western Front. In that theatre of war he was engaged in severe fighting in various sectors, and was wounded on two occasions—at Ypres in 1917 and again at Cambrai in April 1918. He was demobilised in March 1919, and holds the General Service and Victory Medals.
4, Boswell Place, Bedford. X3563/A.

MILLS, T. A., Private, East Surrey Regiment and Royal Fusiliers.
He joined in January 1918, and after a period of service with the Berkshire Dragoons in Ireland, was drafted in the same year to Russia. In that theatre of war he was engaged on important duties with his unit and rendered very valuable services. In 1919 he returned to England, and was demobilised in December of that year, holding the General Service and Victory Medals. 16, Chandos Street, Bedford. X3557.

MILLS, W., Guardsman, 1st Grenadier Guards.
A Reservist, he was called up when war was declared and at once ordered to the scene of activities in France. There he saw severe fighting at Antwerp, and in the Battles of La Bassée and Ypres, and was severely wounded in action in November 1914. In consequence he was discharged as medically unfit for further service in June 1915, holding the 1914 Star, and the General Service and Victory Medals.
Main Street, Gawcott, Buckingham. Z3558.

MILLS, W., Private, 1/8th Argyll & Sutherland Highlanders.
He volunteered in August 1915, and four months later was drafted to France. On that front he was engaged in severe fighting in the Loos sector, and took an active part in the Battles of the Somme, Arras, Ypres and Cambrai. Owing to ill-health he was discharged as medically unfit for further military service in July 1918, and holds the 1914–15 Star, and the General Service and Victory Medals.
80, Coventry Road, Queen's Park, Bedford. Z3561/A.

MILLS, W. F., Sapper, R.E.; & Pte., Labour Corps.
He volunteered in November 1915, and shortly afterwards was drafted to the Western Front, where he served for over three years. During that time he was engaged in road making in the devastated areas, and also performed excellent work on the railways. On his return to England he was demobilised in May 1919, and holds the 1914–15 Star, and the General Service and Victory Medals. 4, Boswell Place, Bedford. X3563/B.

MILLS, W. G., Sapper, Royal Engineers.
Volunteering in May 1915, he embarked for France two months later. During his service on the Western Front he saw heavy fighting in numerous engagements, and performed excellent work as a signaller in the Battles of the Somme, Arras, Ypres and Cambrai. Whilst in action at Delville Wood he was gassed, and was demobilised in June 1919, holding the 1914–15 Star, and the General Service and Victory Medals.
25, Russell Street, Bedford. X3562.

MILTON, A. D., Corporal, 1/5th Bedfordshire Regiment and 1/4th Dorset Regiment.
He volunteered in August 1914, and in July 1915 was sent to Gallipoli, but was wounded at Suvla Bay a month later. He served on the Peninsula until November 1915, when he was drafted to Egypt, and in January 1916 was invalided to England with malaria. Ten months later he was ordered to Mesopotamia, and fought in engagements at Kut-el-Amara and Baghdad, and was then transferred to Palestine. There he was in action at Gaza and in other battles until February 1918, when he was sent to India, where he was employed on important clerical duties until May 1920. He was demobilised on his return home in July 1920, and holds the 1914–15 Star, and the General Service and Victory Medals.
43, Hitchin Street, Biggleswade, Beds. Z3570/A.

MILTON, H., Private, 1/11th London Regiment (Royal Fusiliers).
He joined the Royal Air Force in January 1917, but was transferred to the Infantry in the following May. Shortly afterwards he was drafted to Palestine, and in that theatre of war was engaged in severe fighting in engagements at Gaza and Jerusalem, and took an active part in the Offensive in 1918. He was demobilised on his return to England in September 1919, and holds the General Service and Victory Medals.
120, Howbury Street, Bedford. Z3571/A.

MILTON, L. F., Private, 1/5th Bedfordshire Regt.
A month after the outbreak of war in August 1914 he volunteered, and after serving at Bury St. Edmunds and Newmarket, in January 1916 embarked for Egypt. Subsequently he was transferred to Palestine, where he took part in numerous important engagements, including those at Gaza. Whilst in the East he suffered from fever, and on his return home was demobilised in June 1919, holding the General Service and Victory Medals. 120, Howbury Street, Bedford. Z3571/B.

MILTON, P. F., Guardsman, Coldstream Guards.
He joined in May 1917, and on completion of his training was later in the same year sent to the Western Front. There he was in action in the Battles of Arras, Ypres, Cambrai and the Somme, took part in severe fighting in the Loos and Givenchy sectors, and was wounded in action at Ypres in 1918. He served in France until demobilised in February 1919, and holds the General Service and Victory Medals.
Wootton, Bedford. Z3568.

MILTON, R. G., Cpl., 5th Beds. Regt. & R.A.S.C. (M.T.)
When war broke out he volunteered, and in 1915 was drafted to Gallipoli, where he served at Suvla Bay and in the subsequent engagements of the campaign. After the Evacuation of the Peninsula he returned to England, but in 1917 proceeded to Palestine. On that front he saw heavy fighting at Gaza and Jaffa, and was engaged on important transport duties. Returning home in May 1919, he was demobilised, holding the 1914–15 Star, and the General Service and Victory Medals.
44, Melbourne Street, Bedford. X3569/B.

MILTON, V. J., Private, 3rd Bedfordshire Regt.
He joined in October 1916, and four months later proceeded overseas. Whilst serving on the Western Front he took an active part in the Battle of Arras in April 1917, and a month later was buried alive at Messines Ridge. Fortunately, however, he was found, but on returning to the firing-line was gassed at Ypres, and was unhappily killed in action at Passchendaele on October 30th, 1917. He was entitled to the General Service and Victory Medals.
" His life for his Country."
43, Hitchin Street, Biggleswade, Beds. Z3570/B.

MILTON, W. J., Private, R.A.S.C. (M.T.)
In October 1916 he joined the Army, and on conclusion of a period of training was three months later drafted to German East Africa. Throughout his service there he was employed on important transport duties at Dar-es-Salaam, and a month after the Armistice returned to England. He was demobilised in October 1919, and holds the General Service and Victory Medals. 44, Melbourne Street, Bedford. X3569/A.

MINGAY, H., Private, Bedfordshire Regiment.
When war was declared in August 1914 he volunteered, and in April 1915 embarked for France. On that front he took an active part in the Battles of Neuve Chapelle and St. Eloi, and was severely wounded in action at Hill 60. After prolonged hospital treatment he was discharged as medically unfit for further military service in January 1917. He holds the 1914–15 Star, and the General Service and Victory Medals.
6, Coventry Road, Bedford. Z3572.

MINNELL, G. A. W., Sergeant, Machine Gun Corps.
He volunteered in November 1915, in the 13th Manchester Regiment, and six months later was sent to Salonika and served on the Doiran front until invalided home with malaria in March 1917. In June 1917 he was drafted to France, where he played a conspicuous part in numerous important engagements and was gassed. After the Armistice he rendered valuable services until demobilised in April 1919, holding the General Service and Victory Medals.
14, Church Cottage, Newport Pagnell, Bucks. Z3573.

MINNEY, S. J., Sergeant, Queen's Own (Royal West Kent Regiment).
He joined in May 1917, and two months later was drafted to the Western Front, where he was engaged in fierce fighting in various sectors. He took a prominent part in the Battles of Arras, Ypres, Cambrai and the Somme, and in the Allied Advance. After the Armistice he proceeded into Germany with the Army of Occupation, and served at Cologne until demobilised in November 1919, holding the General Service and Victory Medals. 44, Muswell Road, Bedford. Z3574.

MINNIS, T. E., L/Corporal, Royal Engineers.
Volunteering in August 1914, he was ordered in the following July to Gallipoli, and after taking part in the engagements at Suvla Bay, was invalided home suffering from dysentery. In July 1916 he embarked for the Western Front, and in that theatre of war saw heavy fighting in the Somme, Arras, Ypres and Cambrai sectors. At the close of hostilities he proceeded with the Army of Occupation to Germany, and served there until demobilised in March 1920. He holds the 1914–15 Star, and the General Service and Victory Medals.
49, Westbourne Road, Queen's Park, Bedford. X3575.

MISSENDEN, F., Private, 2nd Bedfordshire Regt.
When war broke out he was serving in South Africa, and was immediately recalled and sent to France. There he was in action in the Retreat from Mons, and was wounded in the Battle of Ypres in November 1914, and sent back to England. In the following year he returned to the Western Front, but was again wounded at Neuve Chapelle, and in consequence was invalided out of the Army in December 1916, holding the Mons Star, and the General Service and Victory Medals.
West Brook End, Newton Longville, Bucks. Z3577/C.

MISSENDEN, G., Pte., 10th Warwickshire Regt.
He joined in February 1916, but was retained on important work in England until March 1918, when he was drafted overseas. After only a few weeks' service in the Somme sector, he was reported missing on March 28th, 1918, but subsequently it was confirmed that he was killed in action on that date. He was entitled to the General Service and Victory Medals.
"A costly sacrifice upon the altar of freedom."
4, London End, Newton Longville, near Bletchley, Bucks. Z3577/B.

MISSENDEN, J., Private, Oxford. and Bucks. L.I.
Joining in June 1917, he was sent to Ireland, where he was engaged on important duties with his unit. He was not successful in obtaining a transfer overseas before the cessation of hostilities, but after the Armistice he was sent to Germany and served with the Army of Occupation at Cologne until demobilised in February 1919.
4, London End, Newton Longville, near Bletchley, Bucks. Z3577/A.

MITCHELL, G. H., Private, R.A.V.C.
Volunteering in November 1914, he was drafted to Egypt after two months' training, and was there engaged in tending the sick and wounded horses at various stations. Later he proceeded into Palestine, where he was present at the Battles of Gaza and the entry into Jaffa, and other engagements. He was invalided home in March 1918, and was finally demobilised in February 1919, holding the 1914–15 Star, and the General Service and Victory Medals.
High Street, Milton Ernest, Bedford. Z3576.

MITCHELL, H. A., R.S.M., Royal Horse Artillery.
Mobilised in August 1914, he was immediately drafted to the Western Front, where he served through the fighting at Mons. He also took a distinguished part in the Battles of La Bassée, Loos, the Somme, Vimy Ridge and Cambrai, and many other important engagements, and was three times wounded—at Ypres, Festubert and Arras. He was discharged in January 1919, and holds the Mons Star, and the General Service and Victory Medals.
Montague Street, Eynesbury, St. Neots, Hunts. TZ3578.

MOBBS, A., Private, 4th Bedfordshire Regiment.
He volunteered in December 1915, and in August of the following year proceeded to France, where he saw severe fighting in various sectors of the front. He took part in the Battles of the Somme, Arras and Cambrai, and many minor engagements, and, gassed at Ypres in July 1917, was for two months in hospital at the Base. He was demobilised in February 1919, and holds the General Service and Victory Medals.
New Cottages, Stow Longa, Hunts. Z3580/B.

MOBBS, A., Driver, Royal Engineers.
He volunteered in June 1915, and was retained at various stations in England until September of the following year, when he was sent to the Western Front. There he was engaged on important transport duties on the Somme and at Ypres, Passchendaele, Cambrai and many other places until after the cessation of hostilities. Returning home in February 1919, he was demobilised in the following month, and holds the General Service and Victory Medals.
4, Woburn Road, Kempston, Bedford. X3579.

MOBBS, C. W., Private, 5th Royal Fusiliers.
Joining in January 1918, he was drafted to the Western Front on completing his training in the following June, and there saw much severe fighting. After taking part in the Battles of Epéhy, Cambrai and Ypres, and other important engagements, he was wounded in action at Le Cateau in October 1918, and invalided home. He was afterwards retained in England until his demobilisation in May 1919, and holds the General Service and Victory Medals.
Stow Longa, Hunts. Z3581.

MOBBS, F. G., Corporal, 9th Gloucestershire Regt.
Volunteering in September 1914, he proceeded to the Western Front in the following year, and there took part in the Battle of Neuve Chapelle and other important engagements. Transferred later in 1915 to Salonika, he unhappily died there of fever on September 22nd, 1916. He was entitled to the 1914–15 Star, and the General Service and Victory Medals.
"Thinking that remembrance, though unspoken, may reach him where he sleeps."
42, Grey Friars Walk, Bedford. X3582.

MOBBS, H., Corporal, Royal Engineers.
Mobilised in August 1914, he was drafted to the Western Front in December of that year, and was there engaged on transport duties in various sectors. He was also present at the Battles of Neuve Chapelle, Ypres, the Somme and Arras, and other engagements, and, gassed at Cambrai, was for a time in hospital at Trouville. He was discharged in April 1919, and holds the 1914–15 Star, and the General Service and Victory Medals.
7, Marlborough Road, Bedford. Z3585.

MOBBS, H., Private, 8th Bedfordshire Regiment.
He volunteered in March 1915, and in August of the following year proceeded to the Western Front, where he took part in important engagements in various sectors. He made the supreme sacrifice, being killed in action at Arras on April 19th, 1917. He was entitled to the General Service and Victory Medals.
"Nobly striving,
He nobly fell that we might live."
Stow Longa, Hunts. Z3583—Z3584.

MOBBS, H. E., 1st Class Stoker, Royal Navy.
He joined in July 1918, and was posted to H.M.S. "Osea," on board which vessel he was engaged on various important duties off the East Coast. He rendered very valuable services until January 1920, when he was demobilised, and holds the General Service and Victory Medals.
67, Westbourne Road, Queen's Park, Bedford. Z3586.

MOBBS, H. S., Trooper, Bedfordshire Lancers.
Volunteering in May 1915, he proceeded to France in December of that year and there saw heavy fighting in various sectors of the front. He took part in the Battles of the Somme, Messines and Ypres, and many other engagements until wounded in action in 1917 and invalided home. He was afterwards stationed in Ireland and was finally demobilised in April 1919, holding the 1914–15 Star, and the General Service and Victory Medals.
41, Westbourne Road, Queen's Park, Bedford. X3587/B.

MOBBS, J., L/Corporal, Bedfordshire Regiment.
He volunteered in June 1915, and in March of the following year proceeded to the Western Front, where he saw severe fighting at St. Eloi, Albert and the Somme, and was gassed. Invalided home in December 1916, he returned to France however in April 1917, and took part in the Battles of Arras, Vimy Ridge, Ypres, Passchendaele, Cambrai and Amiens. He was demobilised in March 1919, and holds the General Service and Victory Medals. New Cottages, Stow Longa, Hunts. Z3580/A.

MOBBS, R. A., L/Corporal, 1st Bedfordshire Regt.
Volunteering in January 1915, he proceeded to the Western Front in November of that year, and there took part in the Battles of Albert, the Somme, Arras, Ypres and St. Quentin, and was five times wounded in action. He unhappily fell fighting at Cambrai on August 22nd, 1918. He was entitled to the 1914-15 Star, and the General Service and Victory Medals.
"And doubtless he went in splendid company."
41, Westbourne Road, Queen's Park, Bedford. X3587/A.

MOLE, T., Private, Bedfordshire Regiment.
After volunteering in August 1914, he underwent a period of training prior to being drafted to the Western Front in 1916. Whilst in this theatre of war he was engaged on important duties in various sectors, and also took part in the Battles of Arras, Ypres, Cambrai and the Somme, and other engagements. Demobilised on his return home in 1919, he holds the General Service and Victory Medals.
1, Sloughs Buildings, Huntingdon. Z3588.

MOONEY, D., Private, R.A.M.C.
Volunteering in September 1915, he was sent to the Western Front in March of the following year and there saw much heavy fighting in the Somme sector. Buried by the exploding of a shell in July 1916, he was sent home and, admitted to hospital at Keighley, and was finally invalided from the Army in March 1919. He holds the General Service and Victory Medals.
84, London Road, Stony Stratford, Bucks. Z3589/A.

MOONEY, R. E., Bombardier, R.F.A.
Mobilised in August 1914, he was immediately drafted to the Western Front, where he fought in the Battle of Mons and the subsequent Retreat. He afterwards took part in the Battles of the Marne, the Aisne, Ypres, Loos, the Somme and Cambrai, and other engagements until admitted to hospital at Carlisle in 1918, suffering from pneumonia. He was invalided from the Army in November of that year, and holds the Mons Star, and the General Service and Victory Medals.
84, London Road, Stony Stratford, Bucks. Z3589/B.

MOORE, A. C., Private, Argyll and Sutherland Highlanders.
He volunteered in 1914, but after a period of training was discharged as medically unfit for further service. He re-enlisted however, in 1916, and was shortly afterwards drafted to the Western Front, where he took part in engagements at Loos, Albert, Vimy Ridge and Beaucourt and in various other sectors. He was demobilised in March 1919, and holds the General Service and Victory Medals.
Potter's Cross, Wootton, Bedford. Z3590/D—Z3591/D.

MOORE, C., Private, Royal Defence Corps.
He volunteered in January 1915, and after undergoing a period of training was retained at various stations, where he was engaged on duties of a highly important nature. He rendered very valuable services with his unit during the period of hostilities, and was finally discharged in December 1918 as medically unfit for further service on account of rheumatism.
Potter's Cross, Wootton, Bedford. Z3590/A—Z3591/A.

MOORE, E. W., Pte., 1/5th York & Lancaster Regt.
Joining in February 1917, he was drafted to the Western Front after three months' training and there saw severe fighting in various sectors. He took part in the Battles of Arras, Vimy Ridge, Ypres, Cambrai, the Somme and Kemmel Hill and many other important engagements until the cessation of hostilities. He was demobilised in December 1919, and holds the General Service and Victory Medals.
Bank House, Earith, Hunts. Z3592.

MOORE, E. W., Private, 3/5th Bedfordshire Regt.
Three months after joining in March 1916 he proceeded to the Western Front, where he took part in the Battles of the Somme, Vimy Ridge and Ypres, and many minor engagements. He died gloriously on the Field of Battle near Passchendaele on October 22nd, 1917. He was entitled to the General Service and Victory Medals.
"He passed out of the sight of men by the path of duty and self-sacrifice."
Keeley Lane, Wootton, Bedford. Z1580/B.

MOORE, F., Trooper, Bedfordshire Lancers.
He joined in February 1916, and in the following year proceeded to France, where he saw severe fighting in various sectors. He took part in the Battles of Cambrai, the Somme and Bapaume, and many other important engagements in this theatre of war until invalided home in 1918. He was demobilised in February 1919, and holds the General Service and Victory Medals. Rose Cottage, Wootton, Bedford. Z3594/B.

MOORE, F., Sapper, Royal Engineers.
Joining in February 1916, he was drafted to the Western Front on completing a period of training later in the same year, and there served in various sectors. He was engaged on important duties with the signal section whilst in this theatre of war, and was also present at the Battles of the Somme, Arras, Ypres and Cambrai. Demobilised in March 1919, he holds the General Service and Victory Medals. Wootton, Bedford. Z3593.

MOORE, F. J., L/Corporal, 2nd Bedfordshire Regt.
Already in the Army when war was declared in August 1914, he was immediately drafted to the Western Front, where after serving through the Retreat from Mons, he took part in the Battles of La Bassée, Festubert and other engagements. He fell in action near Ypres on June 16th, 1915. He was entitled to the Mons Star, and the General Service and Victory Medals.
"His life for his Country, his soul to God."
Wootton, Bedford. Z1586/C.

MOORE, J., Driver, Royal Engineers.
Shortly after volunteering in September 1914, he proceeded to the Western Front, where he served in various sectors. He was present at the Battles of Ypres, Loos, Arras, Vimy Ridge, the Somme and many other engagements, and was wounded in action. Later he served with the Army of Occupation in Germany, and in 1920 was still with his Company at Aldershot. He holds the 1914-15 Star, and the General Service and Victory Medals. Church End, Wootton, Bedford. TZ3595.

MOORE, J., Q.M.S., 1/5th Bedfordshire Regiment.
He volunteered in September 1914, and in July of the following year proceeded to Egypt, where he served at various stations. Advancing thence into Palestine, he saw much severe fighting in this seat of operations, and unhappily fell in action on September 19th, 1918, during the Offensive under General Allenby. He was entitled to the 1914-15 Star, and the General Service and Victory Medals.
"His memory is cherished with pride."
Rose Cottage, Wootton, Bedford. Z3594/A.

MOORE, J., L/Corporal, Bedfordshire Regt. & R.E.
Already in the Army when war broke out in August 1914, he was immediately drafted to the Western Front, where he fought in the Retreat from Mons. He also took part in the Battles of the Aisne, Hill 60, Ypres and Festubert, and many other important engagements until invalided to hospital at Manchester in 1918. He was discharged in the following year, and holds the Mons Star, and the General Service and Victory Medals.
Potter's Cross, Wootton, Bedford. Z3590/C—Z3591/C.

MOORE, L. G., Corporal, 4th Bedfordshire Regt.
Shortly after volunteering in January 1916 he was drafted to France, where he served at Rouen and Etaples. He also saw severe fighting in various sectors of the front, and took part in the Battles of Albert, Vimy Ridge, the Marne and Le Cateau, and many minor engagements, and was wounded in action. Demobilised in August 1919, he holds the General Service and Victory Medals.
Potter's Cross, Wootton, Bedford. Z3590/B—Z3591/B.

MOORE, S., Private, 2nd Bedfordshire Regiment.
He volunteered in March 1915, and in the following year proceeded to the Western Front, where he took part in the Battles of Albert, Vimy Ridge and the Somme, and many minor engagements. In 1917 he was transferred to Italy, and there saw severe fighting on the Piave and Asiago Plateaux until the cessation of hostilities. He was demobilised in December 1919, and holds the General Service and Victory Medals. Keeley Lane, Wootton, Bedford. Z1580/A.

MORBY, W. J., Private, Oxford. and Bucks. L.I.
He volunteered in September 1915, and on completion of a period of training later in the same year was drafted to India. There he was engaged on important garrison duties at various stations and did much useful work with his unit until his return home for demobilisation in November 1919. He holds the General Service and Victory Medals.
43, Priory Street, Newport Pagnell, Bucks. Z2163/A.

MORGAN, A. T., Private, Royal Defence Corps.
He volunteered in October 1914, and, on account of his age, served with the Royal Defence Corps throughout. After undergoing a period of training, he was retained at various stations, where he was engaged on duties of great importance and did much useful work with his unit. He was demobilised in February 1919. 5, James Street, Bedford. Z3596.

MORGAN, T., Private, Bedfordshire Regiment.
Mobilised in August 1914, he was immediately drafted to the Western Front, where he fought in the Retreat from Mons. He also took part in many minor engagements and, severely wounded in action at Ypres in November 1914, was sent home, and finally invalided from the Army in October of the following year. He holds the Mons Star, and the General Service and Victory Medals.
41, Church Square, Bedford. X3597.

MORLEY, G. H. B., Private, Machine Gun Corps.
He volunteered in August 1914, and in the following year was drafted to the Western Front, where he took part in the Battles of Ypres, Festubert and Loos, and many other important engagements. He died gloriously on the Field of Battle in the Somme sector on February 28th, 1916. He was entitled to the 1914-15 Star, and the General Service and Victory Medals.
"The path of duty was the way to glory."
35, Bury Avenue, Newport Pagnell, Bucks. Z3598.

MORRIS, A. R., Sapper, Royal Engineers.
He volunteered in August 1914, and served at various places on the East Coast until the following December, when he was sent to France. There he was employed repairing bridges and railroads, and did good work until he was invalided home on account of ill-health. He was eventually discharged in May 1915 as unfit for further military service, and holds the 1914–15 Star, and the General Service and Victory Medals.
61, College Road, Bedford. Z3599.

MORRIS, H. G., A.B., R.N., H.M.S. "Lancaster."
He joined in May 1918, and after a period of training at Chatham was posted to H.M.S. "Lancaster," serving in this vessel on various duties of an important nature. After the Armistice he was sent to America as a member of a crew to bring back another vessel. He was demobilised in June 1919, and holds the General Service and Victory Medals.
Harrowden, Bedford. Z3601 /A.

MORRIS, W., Private, Wiltshire Regiment.
Joining in January 1917, he was physically unfit for transfer overseas. He completed his training at Salisbury Plain, and was afterwards employed on garrison and other duties, doing excellent work until he was admitted to hospital suffering from influenza, from which he unhappily died on October 18th, 1918.
"His memory is cherished with pride."
3, Vicarage Walk, Stony Stratford. Z3600 /A.

MORRIS, W., Special War Worker.
Too old for military service, he volunteered for work of National importance, and from January 1917 to December 1918 was employed at the Munition Works, Leighton Buzzard. There he was engaged as carpenter and sawyer, and in these capacities rendered services of a very valuable nature.
3, Vicarage Walk, Stony Stratford. Z3600 /B.

MORRIS, W. T., Private, Royal Berkshire Regt.
He joined in January 1918, and after a brief training was drafted to France. There he participated in strenuous fighting during the Retreat and final Advance, and was wounded at Amiens in August 1918. Evacuated to England, he was sent to hospital at Netley, and later to Whalley, Lancashire, and was eventually invalided out of the Service in April 1920, holding the General Service and Victory Medals.
21, Moggerhanger, near Sandy, Beds. Z3602.

MORTIMER, H., Trooper, Bedfordshire Lancers.
He volunteered in December 1914, and in the following year proceeded to the Western Front. In this theatre of war he took part in the Battles of Neuve Chapelle, Hill 60 and Festubert, and many other important engagements, and fell gloriously on the Field of Battle at Cambrai on November 22nd, 1917. He was entitled to the 1914–15 Star, and the General Service and Victory Medals.
"Whilst we remember, the sacrifice is not in vain."
Bromham, near Bedford. Z3604 /A.

MORTIMER, T., Trooper, Bedfordshire Lancers.
Mobilised in August 1914, he was stationed at Bedford until he proceeded to France in the following year. During his service overseas he participated in strenuous fighting on many fronts, including Ypres, Festubert, Loos, Cambrai and Lens. Returning home after the Armistice, he served in Ireland until he was demobilised in March 1919, holding the 1914–15 Star, and the General Service and Victory Medals.
The Green, Bromham, Bedford. Z3605.

MORTIMER, W. J. (M.M.), C.S.M. 11th Essex Regt.
A Regular soldier, he was drafted to the Western Front immediately after the outbreak of war in August 1914, and fought in the Battle of Mons and the subsequent Retreat. He later played a conspicuous part in the Battles of La Bassée and Festubert, and other engagements, and was awarded the Military Medal for bravery and devotion to duty in the Field. He was taken prisoner on the Somme in 1917, and died whilst in captivity in Germany on May 6th, 1918. He was buried in the Ludfriedhof Cemetery, Cologne, and was entitled to the Mons Star, and the General Service and Victory Medals, in addition to the Military Medal.
"His life for his Country."
Bromham, near Bedford. Z3604 /B.

MORTIMER, W. S., Private, 1st Bedfordshire Regt.
He volunteered in October 1914, and after a brief training proceeded to France. In this theatre of hostilities he took part in the first Battle of Ypres, and was later in action in many other sectors of the front. He later participated in the Battle of the Somme, and fell fighting at Delville Wood on July 27th, 1916. He was entitled to the 1914 Star, and the General Service and Victory Medals.
"Great deeds cannot die."
222, Bedford Road, Kempston, Bedford. X3603.

MORTON, H. J., Private, Royal Naval Division; and A.B., R.N., H.M.S. "Canopus."
He joined the Royal Naval Division in September 1917, and served at Aldershot and Blandford prior to being sent to France in the following January. After taking part in heavy fighting on the Somme front, he was invalided home in March 1918 suffering from fever. Upon his recovery he was transferred to the Royal Navy, and was posted to H.M.S. "Canopus," in which vessel he served as a seaman. He was demobilised in January 1919, holding the General Service and Victory Medals.
32, The Green, Stony Stratford. Z3606 /B.

MOSELEY, A., Sergeant, R.A.V.C.
Volunteering in May 1915, he proceeded in the following October to the Western Front. In this theatre of war he was attached to the Royal Field Artillery, and served on the Ypres, Somme, Arras and Cambrai fronts, performing consistently good work, and being engaged on important veterinary duties. Returning home after the Armistice, he was demobilised in May 1919, and holds the 1914–15 Star, and the General Service and Victory Medals.
41, Union Street, Newport Pagnell. Z3609.

MOSELEY, A. L., Private, 1st Bedfordshire Regt.
A serving soldier, having enlisted in October 1904, he was drafted to France immediately after the outbreak of war in August 1914. He took part in the Battle of Mons and the subsequent Retreat, and later fought at Le Cateau on the Marne and Aisne fronts, and at La Bassée and Givenchy. Wounded in action at Richebourg in October 1914, he was invalided home and sent to hospital in Sunderland, and later to Cambridge. On leaving hospital he served for some time at Felixstowe, but was eventually discharged in September 1916 as unfit for further military duty. He holds the Mons Star, and the General Service and Victory Medals.
13, Park Street, Bletchley, Bucks. Z3607 /A—Z3608 /A.

MOSELEY, E. B., L/Corporal, Royal Engineers.
He joined in March 1917, and a month later was sent to France. There he served with the 239th Light Railway Company, R.O.D., on the Ypres front, and was employed transporting troops and supplies to various sectors. During his service overseas he did excellent work, and was demobilised on returning home in June 1919, holding the General Service and Victory Medals.
13, Park Street, Bletchley, Bucks. Z3607 /C—Z3608 /C.

MOSELEY, W., Driver, Royal Field Artillery.
He was mobilised in August 1914, and two months later proceeded to the Western Front. In this theatre of war he was in action with his Battery at Ypres, Givenchy, Neuve Chapelle, Festubert, Loos, and on the Somme. He was invalided home on account of ill-health in January 1917, and was subsequently discharged in March 1918 as unfit for further service. He holds the 1914 Star, and the General Service and Victory Medals. 14, Cater Street, Kempston, Bedford. X3610.

MOSELEY, W. F., Sapper, Royal Engineers.
Volunteering in October 1915, he was drafted in the following year to France. Whilst overseas he served in the Signal Section of the Royal Engineers on the Somme front and at Albert, Arras, Ypres, and Cambrai, was wounded in 1917, and gassed in 1918 during the final Advance. He returned home after the cessation of hostilities, and was demobilised in July 1919, holding the General Service and Victory Medals.
13, Park Street, Bletchley, Bucks. Z3607 /B—Z3608 /B.

MOULE, T., Private, Labour Corps.
He joined in January 1916, and attached to the Hampshire Regiment, served at Folkestone and Guildford, engaged on various duties of an important nature. He was not successful in obtaining a transfer overseas before the signing of the Armistice, but was sent to Germany in June 1919, and served with the Army of Occupation until February 1920, being demobilised a month later.
St. Ives Road, Somersham, Hunts. Z3611.

MULLEY, J. W., Corporal, 9th Suffolk Regiment.
He volunteered in October 1915, and two months afterwards was sent to France. There he took a prominent part with his unit in heavy fighting at Festubert, Loos and Arras, and rendered excellent service until he was unfortunately killed in action on the Somme on September 16th, 1916. He was entitled to the 1914–15 Star, and the General Service and Victory Medals.
"The path of duty was the way to glory."
Hemingford Grey, Hunts. Z2990 /B.

MUNDAY, C., Colour-Sergeant, Bedfordshire Regt.
Mobilised in August 1914, he was too old for transfer overseas and was consequently retained at home. He rendered valuable services engaged in taking drafts to the Base, and in various other duties of an important nature, and was discharged in October 1918 as unfit for further military duty. He subsequently died at home on September 25th, 1919, from the effects of an injury sustained whilst serving with the Colours.
12, East Street, St. Neots, Hunts. TZ3612 /A.

MUNDAY, C. L., Gunner, Royal Marine Artillery.
He joined in March 1918, and during his training was stationed at Portsmouth. Drafted in the following September to the Western Front, he took part in the second Battle of Cambrai, and was in action in other sectors up to the signing of the Armistice. He remained overseas until June 1919, when he was demobilised, holding the General Service and Victory Medals 96, Simpson Road, Bletchley, Bucks. Z3613 /B.

MUNDAY, F. E., Lieutenant, Royal Navy.
Already in the Royal Navy when war broke out in August 1914, he served in various ships through the whole period of hostilities. He was in action during the Battle of Jutland, also at Heligoland Bight and subsequently served in a destroyer engaged on escort duty. In 1920 he was still serving in the Royal Navy, and holds the 1914-15 Star, and the General Service and Victory Medals. 12, East Street, St. Neots, Hunts. TZ3612/C.

MUNDAY, G. T., Private, Machine Gun Corps.
He joined in November 1916, and in the following February proceeded to France. There he took part in heavy fighting at Vimy Ridge, Arras, Ypres and the Somme, and was twice wounded. During his service overseas he did uniformly good work, and was demobilised on his return home in September 1919. He holds the General Service and Victory Medals.
20, High Street, Fenny Stratford, Bucks. Z3614.

MUNDAY, P., A.B., R.N., H.M.S. "Pembroke."
Joining in May 1918, he served in turn at Chatham, Sheerness and Whale Island. He was not successful in his efforts to proceed to sea before the cessation of hostilities, but, nevertheless, rendered valuable services whilst engaged on important duties until he was demobilised in February 1919.
12, East Street, St. Neots, Hunts. TZ3612/B.

MUNDAY, S. W., Corporal, R.E. (Signal Section).
He volunteered in May 1915, and early in the following year was sent to Egypt. Proceeding later into Palestine, he served at Gaza, Jerusalem, Jaffa and Beyrout, and performed consistently good work whilst engaged with the Signal Section of the Royal Engineers. He returned home for demobilisation in March 1919, and holds the General Service and Victory Medals. 33, Bunyan Road, Kempston, Bedford. X3615/B.

MUNDAY, W. H. (M.M.), Gunner, R.F.A.
He joined in March 1916, and later in the same year was drafted to France. In this theatre of war he was in action with his Battery on the Somme front and at Arras, Passchendaele, Ypres and Cambrai, and in August 1918 was awarded the Military Medal for conspicuous bravery and devotion to duty in the Field. In the same month he was severely wounded near Amiens, and as a result was invalided home and admitted to hospital at Ipswich, where he died on November 9th, 1918, from the effects of his injuries. He was entitled to the General Service and Victory Medals in addition to the Military Medal.
"A costly sacrifice upon the altar of freedom."
96, Simpson Road, Bletchley, Bucks. Z3613/A.

MUNDS, E., Sergeant, Royal Engineers.
Mobilised in October 1914, he proceeded shortly afterwards to the Western Front, and whilst serving at Neuve Chapelle, Givenchy, Albert and Lens, did excellent work whilst engaged on important duties. He was evacuated to England in August 1916, suffering from rheumatism, and was retained at home and employed at various stations until he was demobilised in March 1919, holding the 1914-15 Star, and the General Service and Victory Medals.
8, Honey Hill, Queen's Park, Bedford. Z3616.

MUNN, J. P., Private, Sherwood Foresters.
He volunteered in September 1915, and three months later was sent to France. There he played a prominent part in the Battles of Loos, Albert, Vimy Ridge, the Somme, Arras and Messines, and was wounded at Ypres. He was wounded for the second time and taken prisoner at Cambrai in April 1918, and interned in Germany until the Armistice, after which he was repatriated. He was eventually demobilised in March 1919, and holds the 1914-15 Star, and the General Service and Victory Medals. Mount Pleasant, Aspley Guise, Beds. Z3617.

MUNT, F., Sergeant-Major, Bedfordshire Regiment.
A Regular soldier at the outbreak of war in August 1914, he was stationed at Aldershot and Colchester, and rendered invaluable service training recruits for the New Army until 1916, when he proceeded to France. There he was attached to a Labour Battalion and did excellent work whilst engaged on important duties on the Arras, Cambrai and Somme fronts, until he returned home for demobilisation in February 1919. He holds the General Service and Victory Medals.
16, Stafford Road, Bedford. Z3618/B.

MUNT, R. W., Corporal, Bedfordshire Regiment.
He volunteered in August 1914, and was sent to France early in 1916, but after a short period of service there was sent home owing to his being under age. He was then transferred to the Dorsetshire Regiment, but later rejoined his old unit, and, returning to the Western Front, took part in the Battles of Arras, Vimy Ridge and Ypres, and the Retreat and Advance of 1918. In May 1919 he was demobilised, but a month later rejoined, and in 1920 was stationed in India. He holds the General Service and Victory Medals.
16, Stafford Road, Bedford. Z3618/A.

MURFIN, E. A. G., Private, 3rd Northants. Regt. and Queen's (Royal West Surrey Regiment).
Volunteering in December 1915, he was drafted to France in the following year, but after playing a prominent part in several important engagements, including the Battles of Ypres and Passchendaele, died gloriously on the Field of Battle on September 25th, 1917. He was entitled to the General Service and Victory Medals.
"He joined the great white company of valiant souls."
Montague Street, Eynesbury, St. Neots, Hunts. Z3620/B.

MURFIN, G., Private, 4th Royal Fusiliers.
He volunteered in 1915, and on completion of his training in the following year was drafted to France. Whilst on the Western Front he took part in many important engagements, including the Battles of Arras and Vimy Ridge, and was wounded in action in 1916. Demobilised in 1918, he holds the General Service and Victory Medals.
Eaton Ford, St. Neots, Hunts. Z3619/A.

MURFIN, H., Pte., 14th R. Warwickshire Regt.
He volunteered in November 1915, and eight months later was drafted to the Western Front, where he took part in the Battles of the Somme, Arras, Ypres and Merville, and was wounded early in 1918. Later he saw severe fighting on the Asiago Plateau and the Piave in Italy, and was eventually demobilised in February 1919, holding the General Service and Victory Medals.
Shamrock Cottage, Brook Street, St. Neots, Hunts. Z3621.

MURFIN, W., Private, 9th East Surrey Regiment.
He volunteered in September 1914, and early in the following year was drafted to France, where he took part in the Battles of Festubert and Loos, and other important engagements. He made the supreme sacrifice on December 26th, 1916, and was entitled to the 1914-15 Star, and the General Service and Victory Medals.
"He died the noblest death a man may die:
Fighting for God and right and liberty."
Eaton Ford, Beds. Z3619/B.

MURKETT, H., Private, 18th Lancashire Fusiliers.
He joined in June 1917, and in April of the following year was drafted to France, where he took part in the Battles of St. Quentin, Amiens and Cambrai. He was then taken seriously ill, and unfortunately died on October 30th, 1918. He was entitled to the General Service and Victory Medals.
"Steals on the ear the distant triumph song."
King's Lane, St. Neots, Hunts. Z3622/B.

MURKETT, S., Private, Bedfordshire Regiment.
He volunteered in September 1915, but was retained on important duties at various home stations for some time. Early in 1917, however, he was sent to France, where he took part in the Battles of Arras, Bullecourt, Ypres, Cambrai, Albert and Le Cateau, and was twice wounded in action. Demobilised in February 1919, he holds the General Service and Victory Medals.
King's Lane, St. Neots, Hunts. Z3622/C.

MURPHY, E. T., Bombardier, R.F.A.
He joined in August 1916, and seven months later was sent to India, where he was stationed at Hyderabad on garrison duty for some time. He also served on the North-West Frontier against the Afghans, and saw severe fighting. He was eventually demobilised in December 1919, and holds the General Service and Victory Medals, and the India General Service Medal (with clasp, Afghanistan, N.W. Frontier, 1919).
The Hill, Blunham, Beds. Z3624.

MURPHY, F., Air Mechanic, Royal Air Force.
He volunteered in January 1916, and on completion of his training was engaged in England and Scotland on important duties which demanded a high degree of technical skill. In 1918 he was sent to Russia, where he did excellent work with his Squadron. He was demobilised in November 1919, and holds the General Service and Victory Medals.
11, Euston Street, Huntingdon. Z3623.

MURRETT, F. J., Corporal, Bedfordshire Regt.
Having volunteered in April 1915, he was eventually sent to France, where he played a prominent part in the Battles of the Somme, Arras and Vimy Ridge. In March 1917 he was buried for ten hours as the result of a shell explosion on Vimy Ridge, and two months later was wounded in action. He was invalided home, and after hospital treatment in Yorkshire, was transferred to the Labour Corps. With this unit he did excellent work until demobilised in March 1919, holding the General Service and Victory Medals.
King's Lane, St. Neots, Hunts. Z3622/A.

MUSGROVE, J., Rifleman, 17th Cameronians (Scottish Rifles).
He joined in April 1916, and after completing his training was engaged on special transport work in the River Clyde district. He was unsuccessful in obtaining his transfer overseas, but rendered valuable services with his unit until his demobilisation in March 1919. 32, Coventry Road, Bedford. Z3625

MYERS, A. J., Private, Machine Gun Corps.
He volunteered in the Infantry in December 1914, and was eventually drafted to Salonika in October 1916. Whilst in this theatre of war he did good work with the Machine Gun Corps and took part in much severe fighting on the Doiran, Struma and Vardar fronts, and was present at the recapture of Monastir. He was demobilised in April 1919, and holds the General Service and Victory Medals.
Tilbrook, Kimbolton, Hunts. Z3626/B

MYERS, J. W., Private, 6th Bedfordshire Regt.
He volunteered in September 1914, and 12 months later was drafted to France, where he took part in the Battles of Loos and Albert before being wounded on the Somme in September 1916. After a period of hospital treatment in Birmingham, he returned to the Western Front, and fought at the Battles of Arras, Ypres and Passchendaele. He was unhappily killed in action near Hooge on February 28th, 1918, and was entitled to the 1914–15 Star, and the General Service and Victory Medals.
" A valiant Soldier, with undaunted heart he breasted life's last hill."
Tilbrook, Kimbolton, Hunts. Z3626/A.

MYERS, P., Private, 10th Essex Regiment.
He joined in April 1917, and after a period of training was drafted to the Western Front in the following year. He only served three weeks overseas before being unfortunately killed in action on April 26th, 1918. He was entitled to the General Service and Victory Medals.
" Great deeds cannot die :
They with the sun and moon renew their light for ever."
29, Little Butts Street, Bedford. X3628.

MYERS, S. J. (M.M.), Corporal, 1st Hampshire Regiment and Bedfordshire Regiment.
He volunteered in the Bedfordshire Regiment in November 1914, but after his training was transferred to the Hampshire Regiment, and sent to Salonika in September 1915. He took part in the Retreat from Serbia, and was then invalided home with malarial fever. On his recovery he proceeded to France, where he was in action at the Battles of the Somme, Arras and Ypres, and was wounded in 1917. He was awarded the Military Medal for conspicuous bravery and devotion to duty in the Field, and, also holding the 1914–15 Star, and the General Service and Victory Medals, was demobilised in February 1919.
High Street, Stagsden, Beds. Z3627.

MYNARD, A. E., Private, 8th Oxford. & Bucks. L.I.
He volunteered in November 1914, and in September of the following year was sent to France, but after being in action at Armentières for two months was transferred to Salonika. In the Balkan theatre of war he was engaged on important pioneer duties on the Vardar, Doiran and Struma fronts. He was demobilised in May 1919, and holds the 1914–15 Star, and the General Service and Victory Medals.
The Green, Great Linford, Bucks. Z3630.

MYNARD, W. C., Sergeant, 51st Devonshire Regt.
He joined in May 1918, and on completion of his training was sent to the Army of Occupation in Germany. Whilst stationed at Cologne he did excellent work with his unit and gained rapid promotion. He was demobilised in March 1920.
2, Victoria Row, Olney, Bucks. TZ3629.

N

NASH, A., Private, 52nd Oxford. and Bucks. L.I.
A Reservist, he was called to the Colours in August 1914, and was immediately drafted to the Western Front, where he took part in the fighting at Mons. He also served through the Battles of La Bassée, Ypres, Loos, the Somme, Arras and Cambrai, and many other important engagements until the cessation of hostilities. He was discharged in May 1919, and holds the Mons Star, and the General Service and Victory Medals.
47, Spencer Street, New Bradwell, Bucks. Z3633/A.

NASH, A. W., Private, Durham Light Infantry.
He volunteered in September 1915, and after undergoing a period of training, was retained on important duties at various stations. He was not successful in obtaining his transfer overseas before October 1918, but was then drafted to Russia, where he took part in many important operations. He was demobilised on his return home in September 1919, and holds the General Service and Victory Medals.
47, Spencer Street, New Bradwell, Bucks. Z3633/D.

NASH, B., Private, Worcestershire Regiment.
He joined in March 1917, and after completing a term of training served at various stations, where he was engaged on duties of great importance. He was not successful in obtaining his transfer to a theatre of war, but, nevertheless, rendered valuable services with his unit until June 1919, when he was demobilised.
47, Spencer Street, New Bradwell, Bucks. Z3633/B.

NASH, B. C., Sergeant, Canadian A.S.C.
He joined in June 1916, and proceeded to England, whence he was drafted to France later in the same year. There he served at Boulogne and other stations and engaged on important duties with his Company, rendered very valuable services until his demobilisation in March 1919. He holds the General Service and Victory Medals.
96, Simpson Road, Bletchley, Bucks. Z3613/D.

NASH, C. E., S.S.M., Canadian A.S.C.
He volunteered in February 1915, and proceeding to England with the second Canadian Contingent, was shortly afterwards drafted to France. Whilst in this theatre of war he was engaged on duties of great importance at Boulogne, where he was in charge of the bakeries and did continuously good work. He was demobilised in March 1919, and holds the 1914–15 Star, and the General Service and Victory Medals.
96, Simpson Road, Bletchley Bucks. Z3613/C.

NASH, F., Private, 2nd Wiltshire Regiment.
Volunteering in 1914, he was drafted to the Western Front in November of that year, and there saw heavy fighting in various sectors. He took part in the Battle of Ypres and many other important engagements, and was twice wounded in action, and was sent home in 1918. He was for a considerable period in hospital before being invalided from the Army in March 1919, and holds the 1914 Star, and the General Service and Victory Medals.
2, Church Walk, St. Neots, Hunts. Z3634/A.

NASH, G., Private, 15th Suffolk Regiment.
He volunteered in November 1915, and on completing his training in the following year was sent to Egypt, whence he advanced into Palestine and saw much severe fighting. Transferred to the Western Front in March 1918, he took part in many important engagements, and fell in action on the Somme in October of that year. He was entitled to the General Service and Victory Medals.
" A costly sacrifice upon the altar of freedom."
Sergeant's Yard, Towcester, Northants. Z3631/B

NASH, G. H., Private, Labour Corps.
He volunteered in February 1915, and after his training was retained on important duties in England until August 1918, when he proceeded to the Western Front. There he served in various sectors on important duties on the roads and railways, and did much useful work until his return home for demobilisation in December 1919. He holds the General Service and Victory Medals.
47, Spencer Road, New Bradwell, Bucks. Z3633/C.

NASH, J. F., Corporal, 12th Hampshire Regiment.
He volunteered in November 1915, and twelve months later was drafted to Salonika, where he saw much severe fighting. He took part in many important engagements on the Vardar and Doiran fronts until the cessation of hostilities, and on his return home in May 1919 was demobilised. He holds the General Service and Victory Medals.
Sergeant's Yard, Towcester, Northants. Z3631/A.

NASH, W., Rifleman, King's Royal Rifle Corps.
A Reservist, he was called to the Colours at the outbreak of war in August 1914, and in May 1916 proceeded to the Western Front. Whilst in this theatre of war he took part in many important engagements, including the Battles of the Somme and Arras, and was wounded in action at Ypres in July 1917. He was discharged in July 1919, and holds the General Service and Victory Medals.
61, High Street, New Bradwell, Bucks. Z3632.

NEAL, A., Private, R.A.S.C. (M.T.) & Beds. Regt.
Volunteering in January 1915, he was drafted to the Western Front in the following May, and was there engaged as an ambulance driver in various sectors. He took an active part in the Battles of Ypres, Festubert, Loos and the Somme, and many other important engagements, until sent home in September 1918. He was invalided from the Army in the following month, and holds the 1914–15 Star, and the General Service and Victory Medals.
6, Queen's Row, Bedford. X3636.

NEAL, F. J., Sergt., Royal Warwickshire Regt.
After volunteering in August 1914, he was retained on important duties in England until 1916, and then proceeded to the Western Front, where he saw much severe fighting. He was reported wounded and missing, and is believed to have been killed in action on August 28th, 1916. He was entitled to the General Service and Victory Medals.
" Courage, bright hopes, and a myriad dreams, splendidly given."
Bluntisham, Hunts. Z3637.

NEAL, W. T., Private, 6th Bedfordshire Regiment.
He volunteered in December 1914, and in June of the following year proceeded to the Western Front, where, after seeing severe fighting at La Bassée, Ypres and Festubert, he was wounded at Loos in September 1915. Invalided home, he returned to France, however, in August 1916, and was again in action on the Ancre and at Arras. He was reported missing and later killed in action in April 1917. He was entitled to the 1914–15 Star, and the General Service and Victory Medals.
" His life for his Country, his soul to God."
The Terrace, Wilden, near Bedford. Z3638.

NEEDHAM, D. J., Rflmn., King's Royal Rifle Corps.
He joined in July 1918, and, after undergoing a period of training, served at various stations, where he was engaged on duties of great importance. Owing to the early cessation of hostilities he was unable to obtain his transfer to the front, but later proceeded to Germany with the Army of Occupation. He was demobilised on his return home in March 1920.
7, Raleigh Street, Bedford. Z3639.

NEWELL, S. G., Private, Sherwood Foresters.
He volunteered in May 1915, and in the following year was drafted to the Western Front, where he took part in the Battles of the Somme, Arras, Ypres and Cambrai, and many minor engagements, and was wounded in action. Contracting fever, he unhappily died on January 1st, 1918, and was buried at Boulogne. He was entitled to the General Service and Victory Medals.
"Steals on the ear the distant triumph song."
Piper's Lane, Godmanchester, Hunts. Z3640.

NEWLAND, E. J., Tpr., Bedfordshire Lancers.
Mobilised in August 1914, he was immediately drafted to the Western Front, where he was severely wounded in action in the Retreat from Mons. Invalided home, he was for a considerable period in hospital at Southampton, and unhappily died in Lancashire on January 13th, 1918. He was entitled to the Mons Star, and the General Service and Victory Medals.
"His memory is cherished with pride."
Croft Lane, Brampton, Huuts. Z3641.

NEWMAN, A., Private, Bedfordshire Regiment.
He volunteered at the outbreak of war in August 1914, and after a period of training was retained at various stations, where, attached to the Royal Army Pay Corps, he was engaged on duties of great importance. He was unable to obtain his transfer overseas before the cessation of hostilities, but afterwards served with the Army of Occupation in Germany. He was demobilised on his return home in November 1919.
13, Cavendish Street, Bedford. X3645.

NEWMAN, C., Private, Royal Berkshire Regiment.
He volunteered in July 1915, and in the following year proceeded to the Western Front, where he saw severe fighting in various sectors. He took part in the Battles of the Somme, Arras, Messines, Ypres and Cambrai, and many minor engagements,andalso served through theRetreat and Advance of 1918. Returning home in February 1919, he was demobilised in the following month, and holds the General Service and Victory Medals. 4, New Street, Godmanchester, Hunts. Z3643.

NEWMAN, E. L., Sapper, Royal Engineers.
He volunteered in September 1914, and in July of the following year was drafted to the Western Front, where he took an active part in the Battles of Arras, Vimy Ridge, Ypres and Passchendaele, and also served through the Retreat and Advance of 1918, and was gassed. He unhappily died on November 5th of that year, only six days before the signing of the Armistice. He was entitled to the 1914–15 Star, and the General Service and Victory Medals.
"A costly sacrifice upon the altar of freedom."
4, Ram Yard, Bedford. Z3646.

NEWMAN, F., Private, 1st Wiltshire Regiment.
Volunteering in December 1914, he was sent to the Western Front on completing a period of training in May of the following year and there saw much heavy fighting. Severely wounded in action at Ypres in June 1915, only a month after landing in France, he was eventually invalided from the Army in March 1916. He holds the 1914–15 Star, and the General Service and Victory Medals.
93, Church Street, Wolverton, Bucks. TZ3642.

NEWMAN, G. F., Bombardier, R.F.A.
He volunteered in October 1914, and later in the same year was drafted to France, where he served at Rouen and various other stations. He was engaged on important duties whilst in this theatre of war, and did much useful work with his Battery until his return home in 1919. Demobilised in April of that year, he holds the 1914 Star, and the General Service and Victory Medals. Eaton Ford, Beds. Z3649.

NEWMAN, H., Driver, R.A.S.C.
After volunteering in September 1915, he underwent a period of training prior to being drafted to the Western Front in September 1918. There he was engaged in conveying supplies to the forward areas in various sectors, and served at Arras, Cambrai and Ypres, and many other places. He was afterwards sent with the Army of Occupation to Germany and was stationed at Cologne until his return home for demobilisation in September 1919. He holds the General Service and Victory Medals. 61, Foster Street, Bedford. X3647.

NEWMAN, H., Private, 2nd Bedfordshire Regt.
Volunteering in August 1914, he was drafted to the Western Front on completion of a period of training two months later, and there took part in the Battle of La Bassée. He died gloriously on the Field of Battle at Ypres on October 26th, 1914, only 14 days after landing in France. He was entitled to the 1914 Star, and the General Service and Victory Medals.
"He joined the great white company of valiant souls"
West Perry, near Huntingdon. Z3644.

NEWMAN, M., Pte., 6th South Staffordshire Regt.
He volunteered in August 1914, and in March of the following year was drafted to the Western Front, where he was wounded on the Somme in September 1916. Invalided to hospital at Reading, he returned to France however on his recovery, fought in the Battles of Arras and Cambrai, and in the Retreat and Advance of 1918, and was again wounded at Ypres in August 1917. He was demobilised in February 1919, and holds the General Service and Victory Medals.
Rectory Lane, Somersham, Hunts. TZ3648.

NEWMAN, W., Sapper, Royal Engineers.
He volunteered in December 1915, and after his training was retained on important duties at various stations in England until 1918. He was then drafted to Russia, where, engaged on similar duties, he did much useful work until his return home for demobilisation in August 1919. He holds the General Service and Victory Medals.
23, Cavendish Street, Bedford. X2988/A.

NEWNHAM, C. C., Private, 5th Royal Fusiliers.
He joined in February 1918, and after completing a period of training served at various stations, where, attached to the Signal Section, he was engaged on duties of great importance. He was unable to obtain his transfer overseas, but in December 1918 was transferred to the Machine Gun Corps for duty as a Lewis gunner. He was demobilised in September 1919.
6, Newnham Lane, Bedford. Z3650/C.

NEWNHAM, H., Private, 13th East Surrey Regt.
Joining in April 1917, he proceeded to the Western Front in the following July, and was there wounded in action at Passchendaele in the following month. Invalided home, he returned to France however in January 1918, and was again wounded on the Somme in March of that year. He fell fighting on the Selle on October 16th, 1918. He was entitled to the General Service and Victory Medals.
"The path of duty was the way to glory."
6, Newnham Lane, Bedford. Z3650/B.

NEWNHAM, W. J., Private, Bedfordshire Regiment; and Rifleman, 21st Rifle Brigade.
He joined in February 1916, and after his training was retained on important duties at various stations in England until April of the following year, when he was drafted to Egypt in H.M.T. "Arcadian." He unhappily went down on April 15th, 1917, when this vessel was sunk by a submarine in the Mediterranean, with a loss of nearly 300 lives. He was entitled to the General Service and Victory Medals.
"And doubtless he went in splendid company."
6, Newnham Lane, Bedford. Z3650/A.

NEWTON, A. (M.M.), C.S.M., Bedfordshire Regt. and Essex Regiment.
He volunteered in September 1914, and in June of the following year proceeded to the Western Front, where he was wounded in action at Ypres. Invalided to hospital at Leicester, he was retained in England until 1918, when he returned to France and took a prominent part in the Battle of St. Quentin and other engagements, afterwards serving with the Army of Occupation in Germany. He was awarded the Military Medal for conspicuous bravery in the Field in 1915, and, holding also the 1914–15 Star, and the General Service and Victory Medals, was demobilised in March 1919.
62, Russell Street, St. Neots, Hunts. TZ3651.

NEWTON, C., Corporal, 1st Leinster Regiment.
Having enlisted in September 1911, he was already serving in South Africa when war was declared in August 1914, and in the following April was drafted to Gallipoli, where he took part in the Landing at Cape Helles. He was invalided to Alexandria and thence home, suffering from enteric fever and dysentery, but was afterwards sent to Salonika and fought on the Struma front. He was again sent to Malta and England suffering from dysentery, and was finally discharged in April 1919, holding the 1914–15 Star, and the General Service and Victory Medals.
15, Prospect Row, St. Neots, Hunts. TZ3652.

NICHOLLS, A., Corporal, R.A.M.C. and R.A.S.C.
Mobilised in August 1914, he was immediately drafted to the Western Front, where, after serving through the Retreat from Mons, he took an active part in the Battles of Ypres, Festubert and Loos, and other engagements. In December 1915 he was transferred to Salonika, and was there engaged on transport duties on the Vardar and Doiran fronts until his return home in 1919. He holds the Mons Star, and the General Service and Victory Medals, and in 1920 was still with the Colours.
9, Pilcroft Street, Bedford. X3659.

NICHOLLS, A., Pte., R.A.S.C. (Remount Section).
He joined in May 1916, and after a period of service at various home stations was engaged on important duties transporting remounts from Southampton to France and returning with sick and wounded horses. He did excellent work in this capacity until his demobilisation in October 1919, and holds the General Service and Victory Medals.
Little Brickhill, Bletchley, Bucks. Z3657/A.

NICHOLLS, A., Private, R.A.S.C.
He had already served through the South African campaign and was mobilised in August 1914. Proceeding to France immediately, he was engaged on important transport duties in the forward areas during the Retreat from Mons and the Battles of the Marne, the Aisne and Ypres, and other engagements in various sectors. In 1920 he was still serving, and holds the Queen's and King's South African Medals, the Mons Star, and the General Service and Victory Medals.
Ravenstone, Bucks. Z3655/A.

NICHOLLS, F., Private, 1st Bedfordshire Regt.
Having enlisted in June 1913, he was drafted to France at the outbreak of war, and took part in the Retreat from Mons and the Battles of the Marne, the Aisne and La Bassée, where he was wounded in October 1914. Invalided home, he was in hospital for three months and then returned to the Western Front, but was unfortunately killed in action at the Battle of Neuve Chapelle on March 13th, 1915. He was entitled to the Mons Star, and the General Service and Victory Medals.
"He joined the great white company of valiant souls."
182, Simpson Road, Bletchley, Bucks. Z3653/A.

NICHOLLS, F., Private, Oxford. and Bucks. L.I.
He volunteered in October 1915 and, on completion of his training, was engaged on special duties at Tring. He was found to be medically unfit for transfer overseas, and was then sent on agricultural work near Norwich. He rendered valuable services in this capacity until his demobilisation in January 1919 Ravenstone, near Olney, Bucks. Z3656/B.

NICHOLLS, H. H., Corporal, Royal Engineers.
He joined in August 1916, and, proceeding to France in October, was engaged on special duties with the Railway Operative Department. He was stationed at Andricque, and rendered valuable services as an iron-moulder in the workshops there until March 1919. Demobilised in the same month, he holds the General Service and Victory Medals.
3, Temperance Terrace, Stony Stratford, Bucks Z3658.

NICHOLLS, H. J., Pte., 16th R. Warwickshire Regt.
He joined in February 1917, and eight months later was drafted to the Western Front, but, after a short period of heavy fighting in the Ypres sector, was unhappily killed in action on November 4th, 1917. He was entitled to the General Service and Victory Medals.
"The path of duty was the way to glory."
Ravenstone, near Olney, Bucks. Z3656/A.

NICHOLLS, J., Private, 2nd Oxford. and Bucks. L.I.
He joined in November 1916, and in the following year was sent to India, where he was engaged on important garrison duties at Bangalore for 15 months. He then proceeded to Salonika, and remained there until his demobilisation in November 1919, holding the General Service and Victory Medals.
182, Simpson Road, Bletchley, Bucks. Z3653/B.

NICHOLLS, M. J. (Mrs.), Special War Worker.
For some time during the war this lady was engaged on work of National importance at Messrs. Kent's Munition Factory, Luton. Her duties, which were carried out in a very able manner, were in connection with the manufacture of detonators, and she rendered valuable services until 1918.
Little Brickhill, Bletchley, Bucks. Z3657/B.

NICHOLLS, P., Pte., Oxford. & Bucks. L.I. (T.F.)
Volunteering in June 1915, he was sent to France in March of the following year, and saw severe fighting in the Ypres, Albert and Somme sectors. He was wounded in action in August 1916. In November 1917 he was transferred to Italy, and fought on the Piave and the Asiago Plateaux. Demobilised in April 1919, he holds the General Service and Victory Medals.
182, Simpson Road, Bletchley, Bucks. Z3653/C.

NICHOLLS, W. G., Pte., 1st R. Warwickshire Regt.
He volunteered in January 1916, and, proceeding to France six months later, took part in the Battles of the Somme, Arras, Ypres and Cambrai, where he was wounded in December 1917. After hospital treatment at Boulogne he rejoined his unit, but was badly wounded in action on the Somme in February 1918, and invalided home. He was demobilised in March 1919, and holds the General Service and Victory Medals.
Moulsoe, Bucks. Z3660/B.

NICHOLLS, W. T., Driver, R.A.S.C.
Joining in June 1916, he proceeded to France in November, but, after serving in the Somme sector, was sent to Salonika, where he was engaged on important duties on the Vardar front. In the following year he was transferred to Egypt, and was later engaged on transport work during the Advance through Palestine. He was demobilised in July 1919, and holds the General Service and Victory Medals.
Ravenstone, Bucks. Z3655/B

NICHOLS, A. E., Private, Royal Berkshire Regt.
He joined in June 1916, and later in the same year was drafted to the Western Front, where he was in action at the Battles of the Somme, Arras and Ypres before being taken prisoner in the Cambrai sector in May 1918. He was repatriated in the following December, and then did good work with his unit until his demobilisation in October 1919, holding the General Service and Victory Medals.
2, High Street, Bletchley, Bucks. Z3654/C.

NICHOLS, J. W. E., L/Cpl., 1st Worcestershire Regt.
He volunteered in January 1916, and, proceeding to France six months later, played a prominent part in many important engagements, particularly in the Somme and Arras sectors. He died gloriously on the Field of Battle at Passchendaele on February 13th, 1918, and was entitled to the General Service and Victory Medals.
"His life for his Country, his soul to God."
Moulsoe, Bucks. Z3660/A.

NICHOLS, M. (Miss), Worker, Q.M.A.A.C.
She joined in July 1917, and throughout her service did excellent work at Sydenham and Chatham. She was engaged on important clerical and general duties, and rendered valuable services until her demobilisation in October 1919.
2, High Street, Bletchley, Bucks. Z3654/B

NICHOLS, S., Private, R.A.M.C.
He joined the Devonshire Regiment in April 1918, and, after a period of training, was sent to Ireland, where he was engaged on important duties at various stations. He was unable to obtain his transfer to the front, but in January 1919 proceeded with the R.A.M.C. to Germany, where he served at Cologne. He was demobilised on his return home in April 1920. 2, High Street, Bletchley, Bucks. Z3654/A.

NICHOLSON, H. G., Pte., 2/10th Middlesex Regt.
Volunteering in August 1917, he was drafted to the Dardanelles early in the following year, and, after taking part in the Landing at Cape Helles and in heavy fighting on the Gallipoli Peninsula, was badly wounded in action at Suvla Bay. He was eventually discharged as medically unfit for further service in February 1919, and holds the 1914–15 Star, and the General Service and Victory Medals.
55, Albert Street, Bedford. X3662.

NICKOLSON, F. E. A., Pioneer, Royal Engineers.
He joined in June 1916, and two months later was drafted to the Western Front, where he did excellent work with the Signal Section. He saw heavy fighting in various sectors, including those of the Somme, Ypres, Hill 60, Neuve Eglise and Le Cateau. He was demobilised in February 1919, and holds the General Service and Victory Medals.
148, Howbury Street, Bedford. Z3663.

NOBLE, F., 1st Air Mechanic, R.A.F. (late R.N.A.S.)
He joined in April 1916, and, after his training, was first engaged on important duties with the Staff at Cranwell. In 1917 he was drafted to the Western Front, where he rendered valuable services as a tester of Naval seaplanes. He was eventually demobilised in January 1919, and holds the General Service and Victory Medals.
Carlton, near Sharnbrook, Beds. Z3664.

NOBLE, H., Private, Hunts. Cyclist Battalion.
He volunteered in 1915, and, on completion of his training, rendered valuable services with his unit whilst engaged on important defence duties on the East Coast. In April 1916, however, he was discharged as medically unfit for further military service.
Woolpack Lane, St. Ives, Hunts. Z3665.

NOBLE, J. F., Corporal, R.A.F.
Volunteering in 1915, he completed his training and was then engaged on special duties as a Corporal-mechanic at Farnborough. He later rendered valuable services with his Squadron in Ireland, but, returning to England, was again stationed at Farnborough. He was discharged as medically unfit in February 1918.
8, Oakland Terrace, St. Ives, Hunts. Z3666

NOBLE, J. W., Sergeant, Royal Fusiliers.
Having volunteered in 1915, he was drafted to France in the following year, and whilst on the Western Front served with distinction in many important engagements. He took part in the Battles of the Somme, Arras, Ypres and Cambrai, and was wounded in action. Demobilised in February 1919, he holds the General Service and Victory Medals.
Darwood Place, St. Ives, Hunts. Z3667.

NOBLE, S. W., Corporal, Suffolk Regiment and 7th Northants. Regiment.
He joined in February 1916, and four months later was drafted to France. During his service on the Western Front he played a prominent part in the Battles of the Somme, Arras, Ypres and Cambrai, and in heavy fighting at Loos and Lens. He was demobilised on returning to England in November 1919, and holds the General Service and Victory Medals.
18, Trinity Road, Queen's Park, Bedford. Z3668.

NORMAN, A. J., Private, 1st Bedfordshire Regt.
Already in the Army at the outbreak of hostilities, he was sent to France in August 1914, and took part in the Retreat from Mons and in many of the important engagements at the beginning of the war. Badly wounded in action at the Battle of Festubert in 1915, he was invalided home and eventually discharged as medically unfit for further service in September of the same year. He holds the Mons Star, and the General Service and Victory Medals.
Eaton Ford, Beds. Z3669/A.

NORMAN, E., Private, 1st Bedfordshire Regiment.
He joined in October 1916, and early in the following year was drafted to France, where he played an important part in the Battles of Messines, Ypres and Lens. He gave his life for King and Country at the third Battle of the Aisne on June 1st, 1918, and was entitled to the General Service and Victory Medals.
"A costly sacrifice upon the altar of freedom."
68, Hartington Street, Bedford. TX3671.

NORMAN, E., Private, 2nd Bedfordshire Regiment.
He volunteered in 1915, and in the following year was sent to France, where he took part in the Battles of the Somme, Arras and Ypres, and was badly wounded in action. As a result he was evacuated to England, and in October 1917 was discharged as medically unfit for further service. He holds the General Service and Victory Medals.
Cambridge Street, St. Neots, Hunts. Z3673.

NORMAN, E. J., Private, Labour Corps.
He joined in December 1916, and was quickly drafted to France, where he did excellent work with his unit whilst engaged on pioneer duties in the Albert, Arras, Ypres and Cambrai sectors. In October 1918 he was invalided to hospital at Worcester, suffering from trench fever. He was demobilised in March 1919, and holds the General Service and Victory Medals. Church Path, Sandy, Beds. Z3672.

NORMAN, F., Private, 1st Lincolnshire Regiment.
A Reservist, he was called to the Colours and drafted to France in August 1914. After taking part in the Battles of Mons, the Marne and the Aisne he was unhappily killed in action at the first Battle of Ypres in November of the same year. He was entitled to the Mons Star, and the General Service and Victory Medals.
"Nobly striving:
He nobly fell that we might live."
Bow Brickhill, Bletchley, Bucks. Z3670.

NORMAN, G. A., Private, 12th East Surrey Regt.
He joined in January 1917, and, after his training, was engaged on important agricultural work for four months. He then proceeded to France in July 1917, but after the Battle of Ypres (III.) was reported missing, and is now presumed to have been killed in action, on August 2nd of the same year. He was entitled to the General Service and Victory Medals.
"And doubtless he went in splendid company."
The Gardens, Great Barford, Beds. Z3674.

NORMAN, H. S., Pte., 1st Gloucestershire Regt.
He volunteered in September 1914, and five months later was drafted to France, where he took part in many important engagements. He was unfortunately killed in action on July 18th, 1916, whilst serving as a stretcher-bearer during the Somme Offensive, and was entitled to the 1914–15 Star, and the General Service and Victory Medals.
"He joined the great white company of valiant souls."
Gun Lane, Church End, Sherington, Bucks. Z3765/A.

NORMAN, J., Private, Buffs (East Kent Regt.)
He joined in June 1917, and in March of the following year was drafted to Salonika. Whilst in the Balkan theatre of war he saw much heavy fighting on the Vardar front during the concluding stages of hostilities. He was demobilised in February 1919, and holds the General Service and Victory Medals. Yelling, St. Neots, Hunts. Z3676/B.

NORMAN, J., C.Q.M.S., Royal Engineers.
He was mobilised at the outbreak of war in August 1914, but owing to his being medically unfit for transfer overseas was retained on important defence duties on the East Coast. He rendered valuable services with his unit, and was finally engaged at the Demobilisation Station at Bedford until discharged in April 1920.
105, Marlborough Road, Bedford. Z3675.

NORMAN, P., Private, Bedfordshire Regiment.
Volunteering in November 1914, he proceeded to France early in the following year, and played a prominent part in the Battles of Festubert, Loos, Albert, the Somme, Vimy Ridge, Cambrai, the Marne (II.) and Havrincourt. He was wounded in action on Vimy Ridge in May 1916, and was gassed at Cambrai later. Demobilised in January 1919, he holds the 1914–15 Star, and the General Service and Victory Medals.
Yelling, St. Neots, Hunts. Z3676/A.

NORMAN, W. J., Private, K.O. (Y.L.I.)
He volunteered in 1915, and, on completion of his training, was engaged on important duties in the workshops at Doncaster and Pontefract. He was unsuccessful in obtaining his transfer overseas, but did excellent work until his demobilisation in 1919. Eaton Ford, Beds. Z3669/B.

NORTH, A., Private, Machine Gun Corps.
He volunteered in the Huntingdonshire Cyclist Battalion in September 1914, but was transferred to the Machine Gun Corps and sent to France in 1916. After taking part in the Battles of the Somme, Arras and Vimy Ridge he was invalided home with trench feet. He was in hospital in London for some time, and was discharged as medically unfit in January 1919, holding the General Service and Victory Medals.
26, East Street, Newtown, Huntingdon. Z3677/A.

NORTH, H. W., Gunner, Royal Field Artillery.
He joined in June 1917, and in the following year was sent to India, where he was stationed at Kirkee and Jubbulpore. He also served for a time at Durban and Cape Town, in Africa, but eventually landed at Gaza in Palestine in August 1918. After a month at this place he was invalided home with heart-disease, and in October of the same year was discharged, medically unfit. He holds the General Service and Victory Medals. Drayton Parslow, Bucks. Z3678.

NORTHERN, T., Driver, R.F.A.
Volunteering in June 1915, he was sent to France in December, and was in action with his Battery at Loos, Albert, the Somme, Vimy Ridge, Messines, Bapaume and Cambrai, during which engagements he saw much severe fighting. He was demobilised in January 1919, and holds the 1914–15 Star, and the General Service and Victory Medals.
Church End, Biddenham, Bedford. Z3680.

NORTHFIELD, G. W., Private, Queen's Own (Royal West Kent Regiment).
He joined in June 1916, and, on conclusion of his training, proceeded to the Western Front, where he took part in the Battles of Arras and Vimy Ridge. Later he was invalided to England, and on his recovery was transferred to the Royal Army Service Corps, with which unit he was engaged on important transport duties until demobilised in February 1919. He holds the General Service and Victory Medals.
Southoe, Hunts. Z3681.

NORTHWOOD, F. O., Leading Aircraftsman, Royal Air Force.
Joining in December 1917, he completed a period of training and was sent to Scotland, where he was engaged on important duties as a fitter and repairer of aeroplanes, in which capacity he rendered valuable services until October 1919. He then proceeded to Egypt, where he was still serving in 1920.
Little Butts Street, Bedford. X3683.

NORTHWOOD, R S., Sergeant, M.G.C.
He joined in April 1915, and, after a period of training, was retained on important duties with his unit. Later he contracted an illness, and was finally discharged as medically unfit for further service in April 1917.
32, York Street, Bedford. TZ3682.

NORTON, W. G., Sapper, R.E.; & Private, R.A.S.C.
Called up from the Reserve in August 1914, he was immediately drafted to France, and was wounded during the Retreat from Mons. Early in 1915 he was evacuated to England as the result of an accident, but, after treatment at Liverpool, returned to France and fought at Loos (where he was gassed in action), Albert, Arras, Vimy Ridge and Amiens. In September 1919 he was discharged as medically unfit, but four months later re-enlisted, and was sent to Egypt In 1920 he was serving in Palestine, and holds the Mons Star, and the General Service and Victory Medals
20, Park Road West, Bedford. Z3684.

NOTTAGE, C. W., Private, 5th Bedfordshire Regt.
Volunteering in November 1914, he completed a period of training, but was later found to be medically unfit for service overseas. He was therefore engaged as an Instructor, and did consistently good work until demobilised in May 1919
112, Coventry Road, Queen's Park, Bedford. Z3685.

NOTTINGHAM, O., Private, 2nd London Regt. (Royal Fusiliers).
Mobilised at the outbreak of war in August 1914, he proceeded in the following year to France, where he saw much fighting in various sectors of the front. He took part in the engagements on the Somme, and was also in action at the Battles of Arras and Ypres, where he was twice wounded in 1917. In March 1918 he was taken prisoner at St. Quentin, and held in captivity until after the conclusion of hostilities. Returning home, he was discharged in March 1919, holding the 1914–15 Star, and the General Service and Victory Medals.
21, Cater Street, Kempston, Bedford. X3686.

NUNN, W. J. H., Private, Queen's (Royal West Surrey Regiment).
He volunteered in December 1915, and, on conclusion of his training, was retained on important duties with his unit at various stations. Owing to his being medically unfit he was unsuccessful in obtaining his transfer to a theatre of war, but, nevertheless, rendered valuable services until demobilised in April 1919. 6, Castle Hill Cottages, Bedford. X3687/A.

NUNN, W. W., Private, Essex Regiment.
Volunteering in September 1914, he was later drafted to the Western Front, where he saw much service during the heavy fighting at the Battles of Loos and the Somme, and was wounded at Festubert in July 1917. On his recovery he took part in other important engagements in various sectors until being invalided home with illness and discharged as medically unfit for further service in September 1919. He had been recommended for the Military Medal for devotion to duty in the Field, and holds the 1914–15 Star, and the General Service and Victory Medals.
Station Road, Tempsford, near Sandy, Beds. Z3688.

NUTCHER, F., Private, Machine Gun Corps.
He volunteered in 1915, and, after completing his training, was drafted overseas. During his service on the Western Front he took part in many important engagements in various sectors. He was in action at the Battles of Arras, Ypres, Cambrai, the Somme and the Marne, and was wounded in 1916. In December 1918 he was demobilised, and holds the General Service and Victory Medals.
Cross Hall Ford, Bedfordshire. Z3689/B.

NUTCHER, H. G., Corporal, Machine Gun Corps.
He volunteered in September 1914 in the Bedfordshire Regiment, but was later discharged. Re-enlisting in 1915 in the Machine Gun Corps, he completed a period of training and was drafted to Egypt. Whilst in this seat of hostilities he saw much heavy fighting, particularly in Palestine. He took part in the Battles of Gaza and Jaffa, was present at the capture of Jerusalem, and was later in action during the heavy fighting on the River Jordan. On his return to England he was demobilised in 1919, and holds the General Service and Victory Medals.
Montague Street, Eynesbury, St. Neots. Z3690/A

NUTCHER, W., Private, Bedfordshire Regiment.
Volunteering at the outbreak of hostilities in August 1914, he was drafted to France early in 1915. Whilst in this theatre of war he took part in many important engagements, including the Battles of Festubert, Loos and Albert, where he was wounded and gassed. Later he saw further service, and was present during the heavy fighting at Ypres and Passchendaele. In 1917 he was discharged medically unfit for further service, and holds the 1914–15 Star, and the General Service and Victory Medals.
Cross Hall Ford, Beds. Z3689/A.

NUTT, J., 1st Air Mechanic, Royal Air Force.
Volunteering in 1915, he completed a period of training, but was later found to be medically unfit for service overseas. He was therefore retained on important duties in connection with the repairs of aeroplanes, and did consistently good work until demobilised in April 1919.
7, Castle Hill Cottages, Bedford. X3691.

NUTTING, A. E., Private, R.A.S.C.
He volunteered in October 1914, and later in the same year proceeded to France, where he saw much service as a stretcher-bearer. He took part in the heavy fighting on the Somme, and also at the Battles of Arras, Ypres, Cambrai and the Marne. During the latter part of his service on the Western Front he was engaged as a driver, and did excellent work conveying the sick and wounded to hospital. He was demobilised in March 1919, and holds the 1914–15 Star, and the General Service and Victory Medals. 131, George Street, Bedford. Z3692.

NYE, G. C. S., Private, R.A.S.C. (M.T.)
He volunteered in September 1914, and was quickly drafted to France, where he was engaged on important transport duties and was constantly under heavy shell-fire. He served during many important engagements, including the Battles of Loos, Albert, the Somme, Arras and Ypres, and was twice wounded. After the cessation of hostilities he returned home and was demobilised in May 1919, holding the 1914–15 Star, and the General Service and Victory Medals.
120, George Street, Bedford. Z3693—Z3694.

O

OAKLEY, A., Petty Officer, Royal Navy.
He was mobilised in August 1914, at the outbreak of hostilities, and was posted to H.M. T.B.D. "P.61," with which vessel he saw much service in various waters. He was chiefly engaged on important escort duties and submarine chasing, and rendered excellent services throughout the period of war. In 1920 he was still in the Royal Navy, and holds the 1914–15 Star, and the General Service and Victory Medals.
41, Canning Street, Bedford. X3695/B—X3696/B.

OAKLEY, A., Private, Labour Corps.
Volunteering in May 1915, he completed his training, but was later found to be medically unfit for transfer overseas. He was therefore retained on important guard and other duties with his unit at various stations, and rendered excellent services until demobilised in February 1919.
41, Canning Street, Bedford. X3695/A—X3696/A.

OAKLEY, C., Private, 1st Bedfordshire Regiment.
He was mobilised in August 1914, and was quickly drafted to the Western Front, where he took part in much heavy fighting, particularly at the Battles of La Bassée and Ypres, where he was wounded in November. Later he was in action in other important engagements, but was unfortunately killed on March 17th, 1915. He was entitled to the 1914 Star, and the General Service and Victory Medals.
"The path of duty was the way to glory."
41, Canning Street, Bedford. X3695/E—X3696/E.

OAKLEY, J. F., Private, 2nd Queen's (Royal West Surrey Regiment).
He joined in March 1916, and was later drafted to Egypt, where he saw much heavy fighting. Proceeding to Palestine, he was in action at the Battles of Gaza and Jaffa. In February 1918 he was transferred to the Western Front, and took part in the Battles of the Somme and Cambrai. He returned home and was demobilised in February 1919, holding the General Service and Victory Medals.
41, Canning Street, Bedford. Z3695/B—Z3696/B.

OAKLEY, W. G., Leading Stoker, Royal Navy.
Mobilised at the outbreak of hostilities in August 1914, he was posted to H.M.S. "Forward," in which vessel he saw much service throughout the period of hostilities. He served in various seas on important patrol duties, and also took part in the operations at the Dardanelles. In 1920 he was still serving in H.M. Navy. He holds the 1914–15 Star, and the General Service and Victory Medals.
41, Canning Street, Bedford. X3695/B—X3696/B.

ODELL, A., Driver, Royal Engineers.
He was mobilised with the Territorials in August 1914, and later in the same year drafted to the Western Front. In this theatre of war he took part in many engagements, including the Battles of La Bassée, the Somme, Arras, Cambrai and Kemmel Hill, and was wounded in action in 1914. He was demobilised in July 1919, and holds the 1914–15 Star, and the General Service and Victory Medals.
49, Hassett Street, Bedford. X3699/B.

ODELL, D. W., Leading Stoker, Royal Navy.
He was already in the Navy when war broke out in August 1914, and was serving in China, but immediately proceeded home, and was for a time stationed at Chatham. In 1915 he was sent to the Dardanelles on board H.M.S. "Triumph," which vessel was torpedoed, but fortunately he was rescued. Later he took part in the Battle of Jutland on board H.M.S. "Sapphire," and was afterwards engaged on important duties with the Grand Fleet in the North Sea. He received his discharge in 1919, and holds the 1914–15 Star, and the General Service and Victory Medals.
Marston, near Bedford. Z3700.

ODELL, F., Private, 13th Bedfordshire Regiment.
He joined in January 1917, and, after a period of training, was engaged at various stations on important duties with his unit. He was unable to obtain a transfer overseas owing to his being medically unfit, but rendered valuable services with the Transport Section until his demobilisation in February 1919.
Church Row, Cranfield, Beds. Z3701.

ODELL, F. G., Sapper, Royal Engineers.
Volunteering in August 1914, he proceeded overseas later in the same year, and during his service on the Western Front took part in many engagements, including those at Neuve Chapelle, Loos, Beaumont-Hamel, Ypres, Armentières, Arras, Cambrai and Lille. He was demobilised in December 1918, and holds the 1914–15 Star, and the General Service and Victory Medals.
56, Dudley Street, Bedford. Z3702.

ODELL, G., Pioneer, Royal Engineers.
He joined in March 1918, and was engaged on important transport duties in Kent. Being over age to obtain a transfer to a theatre of war, he rendered valuable services, and was engaged in loading ships for France at Saltpass, near Richborough. He was demobilised in January 1919.
25, Beaconsfield Place, Newport Pagnell, Bucks. Z3703.

ODELL, H. G. (M.M.), Sergeant, 9th Gloucestershire Regiment.
He joined in June 1916, and a few months later proceeded to the Western Front. There he served with distinction in many engagements in the Somme, Ypres and Cambrai sectors, and was awarded the Military Medal for gallantry and devotion to duty in the Field near Cambrai in 1918. He took part in the Retreat and Advance, and after hostilities ceased went into Germany with the Army of Occupation. He was demobilised in September 1920, and holds also the General Service and Victory Medals.
Moulsoe, Bucks. TZ3704.

ODELL, P., Gunner, Royal Garrison Artillery.
He joined in December 1917, and underwent a period of training prior to his being drafted to France. In this theatre of war he took part in several engagements, including those in the Somme, the Marne, Amiens and Cambrai sectors, and was also engaged on various important duties. He was later demobilised in November 1919, and holds the General Service and Victory Medals.
Station Road, Tempsford, near Sandy, Beds. Z3705.

ODELL, S., Private, 1/5th Bedfordshire Regiment.
He volunteered in July 1915, and in the following January was drafted to Egypt, and thence proceeded into Palestine. In this seat of operations he took part in engagements at Gaza, but was reported missing, and is now believed to have been killed in action at Gaza on July 27th, 1917. He was entitled to the General Service and Victory Medals.
"Thinking that remembrance, though unspoken, may reach him where he sleeps."
26, Bridge Street, New Bradwell, Bucks. Z3698.

ODELL, S. C., Private, Labour Corps.
He joined in July 1916, and, after a period of training, was engaged at various home stations on important duties with his unit. He was unable to obtain a transfer overseas owing to his being medically unfit, but rendered valuable services until his demobilisation in December 1918.
Northampton Road, Lavendon, Bucks. Z3697.

ODELL, W. C., Driver, R.E. (Signal Section).
Volunteering in May 1915, he underwent a period of training prior to his being drafted overseas, and whilst on the Western Front took part in many important engagements, including those at Albert, Arras, Passchendaele and Ypres. He served with the Signal Section, and did good work throughout. He was demobilised in February 1919, and holds the General Service and Victory Medals.
49, Hassett Street, Bedford. X3699/A.

ODELL, W. F., Private, Machine Gun Corps.
He volunteered in December 1914, and in the following April was drafted to France. Whilst in this theatre of war he took part in many engagements, including the Battles of Ypres, Festubert, Loos (where he was first wounded) and the Somme. He was again wounded, and consequently invalided home and finally discharged in April 1919 as medically unfit for further service. He holds the 1914–15 Star, and the General Service and Victory Medals. Marston, near Bedford. Z3707.

ODELL, W. J., Private, 6th Bedfordshire Regt.
He was mobilised in August 1914, and immediately drafted to France, where he took part in the Retreat from Mons, the Battles of the Marne, Festubert and the Somme. There he was badly wounded in action, and consequently invalided home to hospital. He eventually had a leg amputated, and was therefore discharged as unfit in 1918, holding the Mons Star, and the General Service and Victory Medals.
High Street, Sandy, Beds. Z3706.

OFFEN, J. E., Private, Royal Defence Corps.
He volunteered in November 1914, and, after a period of training, was engaged at various home stations on important work with his unit. He was employed on guard duties, and rendered valuable services throughout the whole period of hostilities. He was demobilised in January 1919.
8, Nelson Street, Buckingham. Z1767/B.

OLDFIELD, W., Sergeant, 2/4th London Regiment (Royal Fusiliers).
Volunteering in August 1914, he served with the Huntingdonshire Cyclist Battalion during his training in England. Later he proceeded to France, and took part in the Battles of Ypres, Passchendaele, Lens, Cambrai and the Somme (II.), where he was made prisoner of war in March 1918. He was held in captivity in Germany, and suffered many privations. After the Armistice he was repatriated, and demobilised in December 1918, holding the General Service and Victory Medals.
Brampton, Hunts. Z3708.

OLDHAM, H., Sergt., 1/8th R. Warwickshire Regt.
He volunteered in August 1914, and underwent a period of training prior to his being drafted overseas. On the Western Front he played a prominent part in many engagements, including those in the Arras and Ypres sectors, but was unfortunately killed in action on August 27th, 1917. He was entitled to the General Service and Victory Medals.
"Nobly striving:
He nobly fell that we might live."
Church Street, St. Neots, Hunts. Z3709.

OLIFFE, W. H., Sapper, Royal Engineers.
He joined in June 1916, and underwent a short period of training prior to his being drafted to German East Africa. In this seat of hostilities he served at Kilwa and Kissiwani, and was engaged on important duties in connection with telephonic communications. He returned home and was demobilised in September 1919, holding the General Service and Victory Medals. 64, Napier Street, Bletchley, Bucks. Z3710.

OLLIFFE, A., Private, Norfolk Regiment.
He joined in 1918, and later in the same year was drafted to France, where he saw much heavy fighting on the Somme. After hostilities ceased he went to Germany with the Army of Occupation, and served on the Rhine on various important duties until his demobilisation in February 1919. He holds the General Service and Victory Medals.
1, Harford Road, Huntingdon. Z3711.

OLNEY, H. P., Air Mechanic, Royal Air Force.
He joined in May 1918, and, after his training, was engaged at various stations on duties which demanded a high degree of technical skill. Owing to the early cessation of hostilities he was unable to obtain a transfer overseas, but rendered valuable services until his demobilisation in April 1919.
39, St. Giles Street, New Bradwell, Bucks. Z3712.

ORCHARD, W. J., Private, Devonshire Regiment.
He joined in June 1918, and, after undergoing a period of training, served at various stations in Ireland, where he was engaged on duties of great importance. Owing to the early cessation of hostilities he was unable to obtain his transfer to the front, but in February 1919 was drafted to Germany, where he served with the Army of Occupation at Cologne. Returning home in February 1920, he was demobilised in the following month.
31, Brooklands Road, Bletchley, Bucks. Z2892/B.

ORMSTON, B. C., Private, 7th Wiltshire Regiment.
He volunteered in September 1914, and in the following July was drafted to Salonika. In this seat of operations he took part in engagements on the Vardar and Doiran fronts, and was wounded in action. Later he was transferred to France, and took part in the Battle of the Somme (II.), and was again wounded. As a result he was invalided home, and on his recovery demobilised in February 1919, holding the 1914–15 Star, and the General Service and Victory Medals.
6, Coronation Road, Stony Stratford, Bucks. Z3713/A.

ORPIN, F. P., Private, 1st Bedfordshire Regiment.
He volunteered in August 1914 in the Royal Army Service Corps, but in May of the following year was discharged as medically unfit. In July 1916 he rejoined, and two months later proceeded to France, where he took part in the Battles of the Somme, Arras and Ypres. He was unfortunately reported missing during the Advance on October 23rd, 1918, and was afterwards reported killed in action near Cambrai on that date. He was entitled to the General Service and Victory Medals.
"A valiant Soldier, with undaunted heart he breasted life's last hill."
29, Union Street, Bedford. X3714.

ORPIN, L. (M.M.), Pte. (Signaller), 6th Beds. Regt.
He volunteered in 1914, and in the following year proceeded to the Western Front, where he saw severe fighting in various sectors. He took part in the Battles of Neuve Chapelle, Hill 60 and Ypres, and many other important engagements in this theatre of war, and was awarded the Military Medal for conspicuous gallantry on the Somme in 1917. Holding also the 1914–15 Star, and the General Service and Victory Medals, he was demobilised in November 1919.
Bromham Green, near Bedford. Z3290/C.

ORPIN, W., Sergeant, King's Royal Rifle Corps.
Mobilised in August 1914, he was immediately drafted to the Western Front, where, after serving through the Retreat from Mons, he took a prominent part in the Battle of La Bassée and many minor engagements. He died gloriously on the Field of Battle at Hill 60 on April 25th, 1915. He was entitled to the Mons Star, and the General Service and Victory Medals.
"His memory is cherished with pride."
Bromham Green, near Bedford. Z3290/A.

OSBORN, G., Sapper, Royal Engineers.
He joined in May 1916, and, on completing his training later in that year, proceeded to Egypt, where he served at Cairo and other stations, and was also present at the Battle of Rafa. Later he took part in the Advance into Palestine, and there fought in the Battles of Gaza and at the capture of Jerusalem. He was demobilised on returning home in February 1919, and holds the General Service and Victory Medals.
88, Dudley Street, Bedford. Z3715.

OSBORNE, G. H., Squadron Sergeant-Major, 4th (Queen's Own) Hussars.
He was already in the Army when war broke out in August 1914, and was retained at various stations, where he was engaged on important duties as a drill and musketry Instructor. He was unable to obtain his transfer to a theatre of war on account of his age, but, nevertheless, rendered very valuable services with his Squadron until January 1916, when he was discharged, time-expired, after 22 years with the Colours.
Green's Norton, Towcester, Northants. Z3717.

OSBORNE, H., Sapper, Royal Engineers.
He joined in July 1916, and, after completing a term of training, served at various stations, where he was engaged on duties of a highly important nature. Being medically unfit for active service, he was unable to obtain his transfer overseas, but, nevertheless, did useful work with his unit until his demobilisation in March 1919.
46, East Street, St. Neots, Hunts. Z3718.

OSBORNE, T., Corporal, 5th Bedfordshire Regt.
Mobilised in August 1914, he was immediately drafted to the Western Front, where he fought in the Retreat from Mons. He also took part in the Battles of Ypres, Hill 60, Arras, Vimy Ridge, Passchendaele and Cambrai and many minor engagements, and was gassed. He holds the Mons Star, and the General Service and Victory Medals, and in 1920 was still with his unit in India.
22, Beckett Street, Bedford. X3716/A.

OUTEN, G. J., Private, 2nd Monmouthshire Regt.
After volunteering in 1914 he underwent a period of training prior to being drafted to the Western Front in 1917. Whilst in this theatre of war he saw much severe fighting, took part in the Battles of Arras, Ypres, Passchendaele and St. Quentin and other engagements, and was wounded near Cambrai in April 1918. He was demobilised in March 1919, and holds the General Service and Victory Medals.
5, Balsall Street East, Bedford. X3727.

OVERHILL, A. E., Sapper, Royal Engineers.
Three months after volunteering in September 1914 he proceeded to the Western Front, where he took part in severe fighting at Ypres and in other sectors. Mortally wounded in action in the Battle of Neuve Chapelle, he unhappily died in hospital in England on April 22nd, 1915. He was entitled to the 1914–15 Star, and the General Service and Victory Medals.
"Whilst we remember, the sacrifice is not in vain."
92, Iddesleigh Road, Queen's Park, Bedford. TZ3720.

OVERHILL, G. R., Sapper, Royal Engineers.
He joined in April 1917, and in the following year was drafted to France, where he served in various sectors of the front. He was chiefly engaged on construction work at Arras and on the Somme whilst in this theatre of war, and, after the cessation of hostilities, served with the Army of Occupation in Germany. He was demobilised on his return home in September 1919, and holds the General Service and Victory Medals.
10, Littledale Road, Kempston, Bedford. Z3719.

OVERTON, J., A. B., Royal Navy.
He was mobilised at the outbreak of war in August 1914, and was posted to H.M.S. "Virginian," attached to the Portsmouth Division. He was engaged chiefly in escorting troop and food ships in many waters, and was also on patrol duties in the North Sea. He was discharged in January 1919, and holds the 1914–15 Star, and the General Service and Victory Medals.
10, Vernon Terrace, Towcester, Northants. Z3721.

OWEN, A. W., Private, 1st Bedfordshire Regiment and Middlesex Regiment.
Two months after joining in May 1916 he proceeded to the Western Front, where he served in various sectors. He was engaged on important duties behind the lines at Albert, Arras, Cambrai and many other places, being medically unfit for actual fighting, and did much good work until his demobilisation in December 1919. He holds the General Service and Victory Medals.
13, St. Cuthbert's Square, St. Cuthbert's Street, Bedford. X3725.

OWEN, E., Private, 5th Oxford. and Bucks. L.I.
Volunteering in November 1915, he was drafted to the Western Front on completing his training in the following year, and there saw severe fighting in various sectors. He took part in the Battles of the Somme, Ypres and Cambrai and many minor engagements, and was four times wounded in action. He was invalided from the Army in March 1919, and holds the General Service and Victory Medals.
7, Fleece Yard, Buckingham. Z3723.

OWEN, H. W., Pioneer, Royal Engineers.
Joining in December 1916, he was drafted to the Western Front in the following month, and was there engaged on road-making and other important duties, chiefly in the Somme, Cambrai and Ypres sectors. Sent home, he was for over five months in hospital in London before being invalided from the Army in January 1919, and holds the General Service and Victory Medals.
29, Well Street, Buckingham. Z3722.

OWEN, J., Private, South Wales Borderers.
He volunteered in April 1915, and later in the same year was sent to Salonika, where he saw much heavy fighting on the Doiran and Vardar fronts. In 1917 he was transferred to France, and there took part in the Battles of Ypres and Passchendaele, and was severely wounded near Hill 60. He was invalided from the Army in June 1918, and holds the 1914–15 Star, and the General Service and Victory Medals.
4, Cross Keys Yard, Stony Stratford, Bucks. Z3724.

OWEN, J. D., Private, 5th Royal Welch Fusiliers.
He volunteered at the outbreak of war in August 1914, and, after completing a term of training, was retained on important duties at various stations. Being medically unfit for active service, he was unable to obtain his transfer to the front, but, nevertheless, did much useful work with his unit until January 1919, when he was demobilised.
27, Canning Street, Bedford. X3726

P

PACK, F. M., Private, 6th Essex Regiment.
He joined in 1916, and, on completion of his training, was in the same year drafted to Egypt. After a period of service there he proceeded to Palestine, and saw heavy fighting in numerous important engagements at Gaza, Jaffa and Haifa. On his return to England in 1919, he was demobilised, and holds the General Service and Victory Medals.
Spaldwick, Hunts. Z3730.

PACK, F. R., Electrical Artificer, R.N., H.M.S. "Hannibal."
He joined in March 1917, and, on conclusion of his training, was posted to H.M.S. "Hannibal," and proceeded to Egypt in the same year. During his service overseas he was stationed at Alexandria, where he was engaged on work of an important nature in connection with mines. He was demobilised on his return to England in February 1919, and holds the General Service and Victory Medals.
81, Ledsam Street, Wolverton, Bucks. Z3728.

PACK, J., Private, Royal Fusiliers.
Volunteering in November 1915, he received his training at Weymouth, and in the following year was ordered to the Western Front. Owing to ill-health he was not sent to the firing-line, but was stationed at Rouen, where he rendered valuable services guarding prisoners of war. He was demobilised in January 1919, and holds the General Service and Victory Medals.
Grange Cottages, Great Linford, Bucks. Z3729/B.

PAGE, A., Sapper, Royal Engineers.
He joined in March 1916, and in May of the following year embarked for France. On that front he was in action in engagements at Arras and Ypres, and after two months' active service fell fighting on July 23rd, 1917. He was entitled to the General Service and Victory Medals.
"A valiant Soldier, with undaunted heart he breasted life's last hill."
New Street, St. Neots, Hunts. Z3731.

PAGE, C. F., Pte., Hunts. Cyclist Battalion, 8th R. Warwickshire Regt. & Royal Defence Corps.
Having previously served in the Army for four years, he re-enlisted in December 1914, and was retained on important duties at home until July 1916, when he was sent to France. There he fought in the Battle of the Somme and in engagements at Thiepval and Pozières, and was wounded in action in August 1916 and invalided to England. From January to September 1917 he served in Ireland, and in November 1917 was discharged as medically unfit for further military duties. He holds the General Service and Victory Medals.
Hail Weston, St. Neots, Hunts. Z3732.

PAGE, C. H., Corporal, Beds. Lancers and R.F.A.
He volunteered in August 1914, but was not successful in his endeavours to obtain a transfer to a theatre of war. He was retained on home service and stationed at Newcastle, where he performed very valuable work as a saddler and boot-repairer. In March 1917 his health broke down, and he was discharged from the Army as medically unfit for further military duties.
12, Greenhill Street, Bedford. X3733/A.

PAGE, F. N., Private, Queen's Own (Royal West Kent Regiment).
Joining in June 1916, he proceeded in the same year to the scene of activities in Mesopotamia. In that theatre of war he took an active part in engagements at Kut-el-Amara and in the capture of Baghdad. In 1918 he was severely wounded in action, and unfortunately succumbed to his injuries on October 31st, 1918. He was entitled to the General Service and Victory Medals.
"Whilst we remember, the sacrifice is not in vain."
34, Salisbury Street, Bedford. X1158/A.

PAGE, G. F., Telegraphist, R.N., H.M.S. "Flying Fox."
He joined in November 1916, and, on completion of his training, was posted to his ship, and was in action in various seas, rendering valuable services as a telegraphist. He was also engaged in mine-sweeping in the English Channel. In 1919 he transferred to the Royal Air Force, in which he was still serving in 1920, holding the General Service and Victory Medals.
10, Marne Street, Kempston, Beds. Z3734.

PAGE, H. A., Private, Royal Warwickshire Regt.
Joining in May 1917, he received his training at Huntingdon, Bedford and Dover, and in the following year was ordered to France. There he was engaged in severe fighting on the Marne front, but was wounded at Kemmel Hill and sent to hospital in England. Consequently he was invalided out of the Army in September 1918, holding the General Service and Victory Medals.
Montague Street, Eynesbury, St. Neots, Hunts. Z3620/A.

PAGE, R. F., Private, R.A.S.C.
He joined in 1916, and, on conclusion of his training, was in the following year drafted overseas. Whilst serving on the Western Front he took part in the Battles of Ypres and Cambrai, and saw heavy fighting in the Béthune sector. He contracted trench fever, and during the latter period of his service in France was engaged on important clerical work. Demobilised in June 1919, he holds the General Service and Victory Medals.
Earith, Hunts. Z3735.

PAGE, W. G., Gunner, Royal Garrison Artillery.
In October 1916 he joined the Army, but was retained on important work in the repair shops at Prees Heath until March 1918, when he embarked for France. On that front he was in action in the Béthune, the Somme and Le Cateau sectors, and in the final Allied Advance. After the Armistice he served at Namur, and was eventually demobilised in February 1919, holding the General Service and Victory Medals.
Hail Weston, St. Neots, Hunts. Z3736.

PAICE, V., Corporal, Canadian Infantry (Canadian Overseas Forces).
He volunteered in 1915, and in the same year proceeded to the Western Front, where he was engaged in fierce fighting at Neuve Chapelle. He also took an active part in the Battles of Arras, Ypres and Cambrai, and was wounded on two occasions. He was admitted into hospital suffering from tuberculosis, and was demobilised in 1919, holding the 1914–15 Star, and the General Service and Victory Medals.
7, Hawkins Road, Bedford. Z3737/A.

PAICE, W. S., Private, Machine Gun Corps.
Volunteering in 1915, he was unable to obtain a transfer to the fighting area owing to ill-health. He was, however, retained on home defence, and was engaged on important duties at various stations, which he fulfilled with great efficiency. From 1916 to 1917 he was in hospital receiving treatment for tuberculosis, and was eventually demobilised in February 1919.
7, Hawkins Road, Bedford. Z3737/B.

PAIN, A., Private, 10th Bedfordshire Regiment.
He volunteered in November 1915, but proved to be unfit for service overseas. He was therefore retained on important duties at Colchester and Harwich, and performed valuable work until discharged as medically unfit for further military duties in August 1916. 141, Bower Street, Bedford. TZ3738.

PAINE, E., Private, Hunts. Cyclist Battalion and Royal Fusiliers.
He volunteered in 1915, and was employed on important duties at various home stations, but was discharged in the following year as medically unfit for further service. In 1917, however, he rejoined, and in July 1918 was ordered overseas. Whilst on the Western Front he was engaged on transport duties in the Ypres and Albert sectors. Demobilised in November 1919, he holds the General Service and Victory Medals.
13, East Street, Newtown, Huntingdon Z3739.

PAINE, F., Private, 2nd Suffolk Regiment.
When war broke out he was already serving, and was at once ordered to the Western Front, where he saw severe fighting during the Battle of Mons. He was wounded and taken prisoner at Le Cateau in August 1914, and kept in captivity for over four years in Germany. He was released in December 1918, and, returning to England, was discharged in March 1919, holding the Mons Star, and the General Service and Victory Medals. West Street, Moulton, Northants. Z2862/B

PAINTIN, A., Pte., R.A.V.C. & Lancs. Fusiliers.
He volunteered in January 1915, and shortly afterwards proceeded to the Western Front, where he rendered valuable services attending to sick and wounded horses. Later he was transferred to the Lancashire Fusiliers, and took an active part in numerous engagements in various sectors, but was unfortunately killed in action at the Battle of the Somme in April 1918. He was entitled to the 1914-15 Star, and the General Service and Victory Medals.
"His life for his Country, his soul to God."
School Lane, Green's Norton, Towcester, Northants. Z3740.

PALES, A. W. G., Sapper, Royal Engineers and Private, Royal Army Service Corps (M.T.)
At the outbreak of hostilities in August 1914 he volunteered, but was retained on important work at various stations in England. He was unsuccessful in obtaining a transfer overseas before the cessation of hostilities. In December 1918, however, he was drafted to France and stationed at Etaples, where he rendered many valuable services until demobilised in May 1919. Oakley, Bedford. Z3741/A.

PALES, F. C., L/Corporal, Royal Engineers.
When war was declared in August 1914 he was mobilised with the Territorials, but was unable to obtain a transfer to a theatre of war. Nevertheless he performed excellent work with his unit at Landguard, Felixstowe, Wellington and other stations, and rendered valuable services as a despatch rider. He was eventually demobilised in February 1919.
Oakley, Bedford. Z3741/B

PALLITT, C. V., Sapper, Royal Engineers.
He volunteered in June 1915, and, after a period of training in Wales, was eight months later drafted to Mesopotamia. During his service on that front he was engaged in severe fighting at Kut, and was present at the capture of Baghdad. He was demobilised on his return to England in March 1919, and holds the General Service and Victory Medals.
Rivett's Yard, Great Linford, Bucks. Z3742/B

PALLITT, F. G., Driver, Royal Engineers.
Volunteering in August 1914, he received his training a Aldershot, and on being drafted to the Western Front in May 1915, was engaged on important transport duties at Rouen. A month later he was transferred to Italy, where he saw much severe fighting on the Piave front. He was demobilised in March 1919, and holds the 1914-15 Star, and the General Service and Victory Medals.
Rivett's Yard, Great Linford, Bucks. Z3742/A.

PALMER, A. W., 1st Air Mechanic, R.A.F.
He joined in March 1917, but, on completion of his training, was not successful in his endeavours to obtain a transfer to the war zone. Throughout the period of his service he was stationed at Retford and Cranwell, and was engaged on work requiring exceptional technical knowledge and skill. He was demobilised in February 1919.
10, York Road, Stony Stratford, Bucks. Z3743/C—Z3744/C

PALMER, C. F., Corporal, 4th Devonshire Regt.
Joining in June 1916, he was unable to secure a transfer overseas before the cessation of hostilities, but was engaged on important duties with his unit at various stations in Ireland. He was then sent to Germany and served there with the Army of Occupation until demobilised in March 1919.
10, York Road, Stony Stratford, Bucks. Z3743/A—Z3744/A.

PALMER, G. F., L/Cpl., 5th Oxford. & Bucks. L.I.
He joined in August 1916, and four months later embarked for the Western Front. There he took an active part in the Battles of Arras, Messines and Ypres, but was taken prisoner at Flavy in March 1918. He was released from captivity in the following December, and sent back to England. Shortly afterwards he was drafted to Ireland, and served at Cork and Fermoy until demobilised in September 1919, holding the General Service and Victory Medals.
10, York Road, Stony Stratford, Bucks. Z3743/D—Z3744/D.

PALMER, R. W., Tpr., 2/1st Q.O. Ox. Hussars.
He joined the Queen's Own Oxfordshire Hussars in October 1916, and after a course of training was transferred to the 5th Oxfordshire and Buckinghamshire Light Infantry, and in August 1917 was sent to France. On that front he was engaged in fierce fighting in the Messines, Ypres and St. Quentin sectors, but owing to ill-health was sent to the Royal Army Ordnance Corps, and employed on important clerical duties at Abancourt until demobilised in November 1919. He holds the General Service and Victory Medals.
10, York Road, Stony Stratford, Bucks. Z3743/B—Z3744/B.

PALMER, T. W., Private, Labour Corps and Middlesex Regiment.
Joining in March 1916, he was on completion of his training drafted overseas in the same year. During his service on the Western Front he took part in numerous important engagements, including the Battles of the Somme, Ypres and Cambrai. Owing to shell-shock he was discharged as medically unfit for further service in September 1919, and holds the General Service and Victory Medals. Earith, Hunts. Z3746.

PALMER, W. R., Trooper, 6/1st Surrey Lancers (Queen Mary's Regiment).
A month after the outbreak of war he volunteered, and in 1915 proceeded to Egypt, where he served at Cairo and Alexandria, and on the Western Frontier. In 1916 he was transferred to France, and in that theatre of war saw heavy fighting in the Albert sector, and also in the Battles of the Somme, Lens and Cambrai. He was demobilised in February 1919, holding the 1914-15 Star, and the General Service and Victory Medals.
Milton Ernest, near Bedford. Z3745/A.

PANTER, A. E., Private, Oxford. and Bucks. L.I. and Royal Army Ordnance Corps.
He joined the Oxfordshire & Buckinghamshire Light Infantry in August 1916, and four months later embarked for the Western Front. There he took an active part in the operations in the Arras, Messines and Cambrai sectors, and was gassed during the Battle of the Somme in April 1918. On his recovery he was transferred to the Royal Army Ordnance Corps, and performed valuable work at Havre and Rouen. He was demobilised in August 1919, and holds the General Service and Victory Medals. Harrold Road, Lavendon, Bucks. Z3747/B.

PANTER, A. R., Sapper, Royal Engineers.
Volunteering in 1914, he was discharged after twelve months' service, but shortly afterwards rejoined the Army, and in 1915 proceeded overseas. During his service on the Western Front he was in action at the Battles of the Somme, Arras, Ypres and Lens, and was engaged in severe fighting at Albert and Loos. He was gassed on one occasion, and was eventually demobilised in 1919, holding the 1914-15 Star, and the General Service and Victory Medals.
11, Short Street, Queen's Park, Bedford. Z3748/A.

PANTER, C., Private, Bedfordshire Regiment.
He joined in 1918, and on completion of his training was in the same year drafted to the Western Front. After only a short period of active service, he gave his life fo King and Country at the second Battle of Le Cateau on October 23rd, 1918. He was entitled to the General Service and Victory Medals.
"He died the noblest death a man may die:
Fighting for God and right and liberty."
11, Short Street, Queen's Park, Bedford. Z3748/B.

PANTER, F., Private, 2nd East Lancashire Regt.
When war broke out he was serving in Africa, but was immediately recalled and embarked for France in September 1914. He took a prominent part in the Battles of Ypres and Neuve Chapelle, but was unhappily killed in action at St. Eloi on March 14th, 1915. He was entitled to the 1914 Star, and the General Service and Victory Medals.
"A costly sacrifice upon the altar of freedom."
1, Station Road, Oakley, Bedford. Z3749.

PANTER, G. E., Private, R.A.S.C. (M.T.)
He joined the Army in August 1916, and later in the same year proceeded to Egypt. After a period of service there he was drafted to Palestine, where he saw heavy fighting in engagements at Gaza and Jaffa, and performed excellent work as a driver of a motor ambulance. He was demobilised on his return to England in 1920, and holds the General Service and Victory Medals.
4, St. Mary's Terrace, Godmanchester, Hunts. Z3750.

PANTER, J., Trooper, Bedfordshire Lancers.
Volunteering in March 1915, he proceeded nine months later to Egypt, where he was engaged in severe fighting in the Battles of Sollum, El Fasher and Magdhaba. Subsequently he was sent to Palestine, on which front he took an active part in engagements at Gaza and Jerusalem, and was wounded in action in November 1917. On his return to England he was demobilised in April 1919, and holds the 1914–15 Star, and the General Service and Victory Medals.
Harrold Road, Lavendon, Bucks. Z3747/A.

PARGETER, F. E., Pte., 6th Oxford. & Bucks. L.I.
A month after the outbreak of hostilities in August 1914 he volunteered, and received his training at Aldershot. Unfortunately he contracted pneumonia, and died in Connaught Hospital, Aldershot, in April 1915, after only eight months' service in the Army.
"The path of duty was the way to glory."
Maids Moreton, Buckingham. Z3752/B.

PARGETER, G. E., Guardsman, 2nd Grenadier Guards.
When war broke out he was already serving, and was at once ordered overseas. He was in action at the Battle of Mons and in the subsequent Retreat, saw fierce fighting at the Battles of the Marne, the Aisne and La Bassée, and fell gloriously on the Field of Battle at Ypres on November 2nd, 1914. He was entitled to the Mons Star, and the General Service and Victory Medals.
"His life for his Country, his soul to God."
School Terrace, Maids Moreton, Buckingham. Z3751.

PARKER, C., Private, Oxford. and Bucks. L.I.
He volunteered in December 1915, and seven months later was drafted to the Western Front, where he fought and was wounded in the Battle of the Somme in November 1916. In October 1917 he returned to England, and was engaged on important duties in Ireland and at Colchester and Frinton. He was also employed on agricultural work at Bedford until demobilised in April 1919, holding the General Service and Victory Medals.
21, Oakley, near Bedford. Z3753.

PARKER, E., Gunner, Royal Garrison Artillery.
Joining in 1916, he embarked for the Western Front in the following year. He took part in the Battles of Arras, Ypres, Cambrai and the Somme, and was once wounded in action. After the Armistice he proceeded into Germany with the Army of Occupation. He holds the General Service and Victory Medals. Broad Green, Cranfield, Beds. Z3754/A.

PARKER, E. C., Pte., Suffolk Regt. & A.B., R.N.
He was mobilised in August 1914, and in the following January was sent to France, where he fought in the Battles of Neuve Chapelle and Festubert, and was wounded at Ypres in May 1915. He was again wounded at Loos seven months later, and in consequence was invalided out of the Army in January 1916. In January 1917, however, he joined the Navy, but after a period of training at the Crystal Palace, was discharged in December 1917 as medically unfit for further service. He holds the 1914–15 Star, and the General Service and Victory Medals. 4, Shephard's Terrace, Somersham, Hunts. Z3755/B.

PARKER, E. E., Gunner, Royal Field Artillery.
Volunteering in November 1914, he was on conclusion of his training drafted in the following year to France. There he was in action at the Battles of the Somme, Arras, Ypres and Cambrai. He was twice wounded, and was in hospital at Douai. He was demobilised in December 1918, and holds the 1914–15 Star, and the General Service and Victory Medals.
Cross Hall Ford, Beds. Z3689/C.

PARKER, F., Pioneer, Royal Engineers.
He joined in April 1917, and later in the same year was ordered overseas. Whilst on the Western Front he saw much severe fighting in the Arras and Valenciennes sectors, and rendered valuable services in connection with the construction of roads. He served in France until October 1919, when he was demobilised, holding the General Service and Victory Medals.
Church Road, Wootton, Beds. TZ3756.

PARKER, F. C., A.B., Royal Navy.
When war was declared he was already in the Navy, and during the period of hostilities served in H.M.S. "Antrim," "Dragon" and "Swiftsure." He took an active part in engagements in the Suez Canal, the Dardanelles and in the Baltic Sea, and saw heavy fighting at the Battle of Jutland. He was also engaged on important patrol duties in the North Sea, and whilst serving in the Mediterranean was shipwrecked on three occasions, but fortunately escaped unhurt. He was presented with a gold watch and chain by his shipmates on H.M.S. "Swiftsure," in recognition of his bravery in saving the life of a comrade under heavy shell-fire in the Suez Canal in February 1915. He was discharged in August 1919, and holds the 1914–15 Star, and the General Service and Victory Medals.
4, Shephard's Terrace, Somersham, Hunts. Z3755/A.

PARKER, F. L., Sergeant, 2nd Suffolk Regiment.
Mobilised in August 1914, he was immediately ordered to France, where he was in action in the Retreat from Mons. He also fought with distinction at the Battles of Ypres, Loos, the Somme and Arras, but was unhappily killed in action on February 17th, 1917. He was entitled to the Mons Star, and the General Service and Victory Medals.
"Nobly striving:
He nobly fell that we might live."
19, Bunyan Road, South End, Bedford. TZ2616/B.

PARKER, H., Private, Royal Fusiliers.
He joined in 1916, and on completion of a period of training was in the following year drafted to the Western Front. Owing to ill-health he was unable to take part in any actual fighting, but was employed on important clerical duties on the Town Major's Staff at Poperinghe until the close of hostilities. He was discharged as medically unfit for further service in January 1919, and holds the General Service and Victory Medals. High Street, Brampton, Hunts. Z3758.

PARKER, H., Sapper, Royal Engineers.
Joining in February 1916, he proceeded in the following year to the Western Front. There he was engaged in fierce fighting at Neuve Chapelle, and was in action in the Battles of Ypres, Cambrai, the Aisne and the Marne. After the close of hostilities he was sent to Germany with the Army of Occupation, and served on the Rhine until demobilised in September 1919. He holds the General Service and Victory Medals.
Broad Green, Cranfield, Beds. Z3754/B.

PARKER, P. J., Stoker, R.N., H.M.S. "Coventry."
He volunteered in 1915, and after a period of training was posted to H.M.S. "Coventry." In that vessel he took part in various important engagements, including the Battle of Jutland. He also rendered valuable services in the North and Mediterranean Seas, and at Scapa Flow. In 1920 he was still serving in the Navy, and holds the General Service and Victory Medals.
Church Row, Cranfield, Beds. Z3759.

PARKER, S. C., Pte., 16th Royal Welch Fusiliers.
Volunteering in November 1914, he was drafted overseas in January 1915. During his service on the Western Front he took a prominent part in the Battles of Neuve Chapelle, Hill 60 and Loos, but unfortunately fell fighting in the vicinity of Loos on November 9th, 1915. He was entitled to the 1914–15 Star, and the General Service and Victory Medals.
"He passed out of the sight of men by the path of duty and self-sacrifice."
7, Grey Friars Walk, Bedford. X2192/B.

PARKER, T. W., Private, R.A.M.C.
He volunteered in July 1915, and was employed on various duties at home stations until 1917, when he was sent to France. In this theatre of hostilities he served at Arras, Ypres, Albert, on the Somme front and at Cambrai as a stretcher-bearer attached to the 2/3rd West Riding Field Ambulance. He did excellent work until the Armistice, after which he served with the Army of Occupation in Germany until July 1919. Demobilised on his return home in that month, he holds the General Service and Victory Medals.
4, Shephard's Terrace, Somersham, Hunts. Z3755/C.

PARKER, W. H., Sergeant, R.A.V.C.
Volunteering in January 1915, he was drafted four months later to the Western Front. Whilst stationed at Loos, Arras, Ypres, Cambrai and on the Somme front, he performed consistently good work engaged on important veterinary duties. He returned home in January 1919, and was demobilised in the following month, holding the 1914–15 Star, and the General Service and Victory Medals.
19, Oakley, near Bedford. Z3757.

PARKINS, D. C., Private, Queen's Own (Royal West Kent Regiment).
He volunteered in September 1914, and proceeded to France in the following July. During his service overseas he took part in strenuous fighting at Festubert, Loos and Lens, and was badly wounded at Trônes Wood in July 1916, during the first Battle of the Somme. Evacuated to England as a result, he was eventually invalided out of the Service in April 1917, and holds the 1914–15 Star, and the General Service and Victory Medals.
10, Bedford Road, Aspley Guise, Beds. Z3760/A—Z3761/A.

PARKINS, H., Private, R.A.M.C.
He joined in June 1918, but was not successful in obtaining a transfer to a theatre of war before the termination of hostilities. Proceeding to France in January 1919, he served for some time in the British General Hospital, Etaples, and went later to Germany with the Army of Occupation, and was stationed at Cologne, where he was engaged as a Hospital Orderly until demobilised in August 1920.
10, Bedford Road, Aspley Guise, Beds. Z3760/B—Z3761/B

PARRISS, C., Private, Northamptonshire Regt.
Joining in May 1918, he was sent on the completion of his training to the Western Front. There he served in the Arras sector, and afterwards was employed on various duties of an important nature at a prisoner of war camp near Lens. He did good work until he was demobilised in November 1919, holding the General Service and Victory Medals.
High Street, Carlton, Beds. Z3762.

PARROTT, A., Gunner, Royal Field Artillery.
He volunteered in August 1914, and in June of the following year was drafted to France. He played a prominent part with his Battery in many important engagements, including the Battles of Loos, Ypres, the Somme, Albert and Cambrai, and was wounded in August 1918 during the Advance. Invalided home, he was sent to hospital in Stafford, where he remained until demobilised in February 1919. He holds the 1914–15 Star, and the General Service and Victory Medals.
High Street, Milton Ernest, near Bedford. Z3763.

PARROTT, E. J. W., Private, 8th Beds. Regt.
He joined in 1916, and early in the following year proceeded to France. There he was in action at Vermelles, Arras and Cambrai and in many other sectors of the Western Front. As the result of being wounded and gassed in November 1918, he was invalided home and eventually suffered amputation of an arm. After treatment in hospitals at Hendon, Dewsbury and Roehampton, he was discharged in 1919, holding the General Service and Victory Medals.
Silver Street, Stevington, near Bedford. Z3764.

PARROTT, F., Private, R.A.V.C.
He volunteered in October 1915, and was stationed at Blackheath until July 1916, when he was drafted to the Western Front. In this theatre of hostilities he served in veterinary hospitals at Etaples and Rouen, and did excellent work looking after horses evacuated from various sectors. Demobilised on returning home in February 1919, he holds the General Service and Victory Medals.
Church End, Sherington, Bucks. Z3765/B.

PARSONS, A., Private, Royal Berkshire Regt.
Volunteering shortly after the outbreak of war in August 1914, he was unfit for service overseas. Retained at home, he was stationed at Weymouth and did excellent work whilst engaged on guard, patrol and other important duties. His health breaking down, he was admitted to hospital and died on September 11th, 1917, from an illness attributed to his military service
"His memory is cherished with pride."
76, Marlborough Road, Queen's Park, Bedford. Z3676.

PARSONS, C., Private, 2nd Essex Regiment.
He joined in February 1916, and served at various home stations until 1917, when he was sent to France, where he was in action at La Bassée, Arras, on the Somme front and at Bapaume. Early in 1918 he was transferred to Egypt, and later served in Palestine at Jerusalem and Damascus. Returning home in January 1920, he was then demobilised, and holds the General Service and Victory Medals.
38, Salisbury Street, Bedford. Z3767/A.

PARSONS, F., Private, 1/6th Essex Regiment.
He joined in February 1916, and later in the same year proceeded to Egypt. After serving there for some time, during which he was in action near Magdhaba on the Syrian border, he was sent to Palestine, where he was in action at Jerusalem and other places. He did good work whilst overseas, and was demobilised on his return home in August 1919, holding the General Service and Victory Medals.
38, Salisbury Street, Bedford. Z3767/B.

PARSONS, F. A., Private, 26th Royal Fusiliers.
Volunteering in November 1915, he was drafted in the following September to the Western Front. In this theatre of war he took part with his unit in the Battles of the Somme and Arras, also in heavy fighting at Ypres. He was later in action at Messines, where he was unfortunately killed on June 7th, 1917. He was entitled to the General Service and Victory Medals.
"Courage, bright hopes and a myriad dreams, splendidly given."
7, Rich Bell Cottages, Chandos Street, Bedford. X3768.

PARSONS, J., Private, Machine Gun Corps.
He volunteered in December 1914, and five months afterwards was sent to France. There he was in action at Ypres, Festubert, Loos and Arras, and did good work as a range-finder until he was wounded in July 1916 during the Battle of the Somme. Invalided home, he remained some time in hospital at Bury St. Edmunds, and on his recovery served at Grantham. He was later employed on agricultural work at Ramsey and, eventually demobilised in March 1919. He holds the 1914–15 Star, and the General Service and Victory Medals.
Pidley, Hunts. Z3769.

PARSONS, W. G., L/Cpl., 7th Bedfordshire Regt.
Volunteering in September 1914, he was shortly afterwards drafted to the Western Front, where he participated in the final stages of the Retreat from Mons. He later took part in the Battles of the Marne, La Bassée and Ypres (I.), and fell gloriously in action on September 24th, 1916, during the first Battle of the Somme. He was entitled to the Mons Star, and the General Service and Victory Medals.
"And doubtless he went in splendid company."
38, Salisbury Street, Bedford. Z3767/C.

PARTRIDGE, C. H., Private, Royal Irish Fusiliers.
He joined in January 1918, and two months later proceeded to France. In this theatre of hostilities he took part in heavy fighting on the Somme front, and was in action in various sectors during the Retreat and Advance. Wounded at Cambrai in September 1918, he was evacuated to England and sent to hospital in Liverpool, remaining there for six months. He was eventually invalided out of the Service in April 1919, holding the General Service and Victory Medals.
High Street, Lavendon, Bucks. TZ3770.

PARTRIDGE, E., Private, Bedfordshire Regiment.
He volunteered in September 1914, and in the following May was drafted to the Western Front. There he participated in strenuous fighting during the Battles of Loos, Ypres, the Somme, Arras and Cambrai, and also saw service at Abbeville and Albert. He was twice wounded in action on the Somme front in July and August 1916, but remained overseas until April 1919, when he was demobilised. He holds the 1914–15 Star, and the General Service and Victory Medals.
9, Bletsoe, Bedford. Z3771/A.

PARTRIDGE, E. J., Private, M.G.C. & R.A.S.C.
He joined in January 1916, and six months later was sent to France. Shortly afterwards he was wounded in action on the Somme front and, being invalided home, spent four months in hospital at Leeds. On his recovery he was transferred to the Royal Army Service Corps, and returning to France in 1917 was engaged on transport duties on various fronts until January 1919, when he was demobilised, holding the General Service and Victory Medals. 13, Near Town, Olney, Bucks. Z3773/A.

PARTRIDGE, F. W., Gunner, R.G.A.
Joining in May 1916, he proceeded to France in the following September. Whilst overseas he played a prominent part with his Battery in strenuous fighting on the Somme front, and at Albert, Arras, Ypres, Passchendaele and Cambrai. In January 1918 he was severely burned by liquid fire, and as a result was invalided home. Admitted to hospital in London, he was later sent to Ripon, and was subsequently discharged in July 1919, holding the General Service and Victory Medals.
Great Staughton, Hunts. Z3774.

PARTRIDGE, F. W., Private, Royal Irish Fusiliers and Labour Corps.
He joined in June 1916, and after a brief period of training at Bedford was sent to the Western Front. There he served in the Ancre, Arras, Ypres and Cambrai sectors, performing consistently good work whilst employed on various duties of an important nature. He returned home for demobilisation in February 1919, and holds the General Service and Victory Medals. Carlton, Beds. Z3772.

PARTRIDGE, G., Private, Bedfordshire Regiment.
He volunteered in September 1914, and in the following May proceeded to France, where he at once participated in heavy fighting at Ypres and was wounded in the succeeding month. Invalided home, he was subsequently found to be medically unfit for further service overseas, but performed valuable work at home stations whilst engaged on transport and agricultural duties. He was demobilised in April 1919, and holds the 1914–15 Star, and the General Service and Victory Medals.
9, Bletsoe, Bedford. Z3771/B.

PARTRIDGE, J. C., Private, Royal Fusiliers.
An ex-soldier, he re-enlisted in September 1914, and served on the Western Front from May 1915 until December 1918. During this period he played a prominent part in strenuous fighting at Festubert, Ypres, Loos, on the Somme front and at Beaumont-Hamel, and was wounded in action at Arras. He was mentioned in Despatches, whilst stationed in Dunkirk, for devotion to duty during an enemy raid, and was demobilised in January 1919, holding the 1914–15 Star, and the General Service and Victory Medals. 9, Bletsoe, Bedford. Z3775.

PARTRIDGE, W., Private, R.A.M.C.
He joined in 1916, and, after completing his training, was stationed in Bedford until the following year, when he was sent to France. There he was employed on important duties on the Ypres and Cambrai fronts, and after the Armistice served in Germany with the Army of Occupation. He did good work whilst overseas, and was demobilised in September 1919, holding the General Service and Victory Medals.
Near George Bridge, Eaton Socon, Beds. Z3776.

PARTRIDGE, W. J., Sergeant, R.A.M.C.
He volunteered in May 1915, but was medically unfit for transfer to a theatre of hostilities. Retained at home, he was stationed in the Military Hospital at Rednall, Birmingham, and was employed in the operating theatre, and also conducting patients to various convalescent camps. He rendered services of a valuable nature until he was demobilised in August 1919.
13, Near Town, Olney, Bucks. Z3773/B.

PASKELL, P. W., Sapper, Royal Engineers.
Volunteering in July 1915, he served at various home stations, and was engaged on important duties until he was sent to France in September 1917. Whilst overseas he was stationed with his Company on the Arras, Ypres, Albert and Cambrai fronts, and did excellent work. He was invalided home on account of ill-health in July 1918, and was subsequently demobilised in the following December, holding the General Service and Victory Medals.
10, Albert Street, Bedford. X3777.

PATCHING, C. E., Private, Oxford. & Bucks. L.I.
A serving soldier at the outbreak of war in August 1914, he was sent overseas a month later. He took part in the Retreat from Mons and the Battles of La Bassée, Ypres and the Somme, where he was wounded in July 1916. Invalided home, he spent two months in hospital at Croydon and, returning later to France, saw further service at Cambrai, and for some time was employed as a shoeing-smith. He was discharged in June 1920, and holds the Mons Star, and the General Service and Victory Medals.
80, Silver Street, Newport Pagnell. Z3778/A.

PATCHING, W. E., Private, Oxford. & Bucks. L.I.
Mobilised in August 1914, he was drafted in the following June to the Western Front. In this theatre of war he participated with his unit in many important engagements, including the Battles of Ypres, the Somme, Arras and Cambrai, and performed consistently good work. He returned home after the Armistice, and was ultimately demobilised in March 1919, holding the 1914–15 Star, and the General Service and Victory Medals. 80, Silver Street, Newport Pagnell. Z3778/B.

PATEMAN, A. H., Sapper, Royal Engineers.
He volunteered in July 1915, and after completing his training was stationed at Borden Camp, where he was employed as a carpenter, and rendered valuable services. He was sent to France in February 1918, and was similarly employed on the Cambrai front, but was invalided home shortly afterwards suffering from pneumonia, and was eventually discharged in May 1918 as unfit for further service. He holds the General Service and Victory Medals.
High Street, Sherington, Bucks. Z1197/A.

PATEMAN, B. W., Private, 1/5th Beds. Regt.
Volunteering in 1914, he was drafted in the following year to Gallipoli, where he took part in the operations at Suvla Bay. He was later transferred to Egypt, and afterwards proceeded into Palestine. There he took part in heavy fighting at Gaza and near Jerusalem, prior to the capture of that city. Demobilised on his return home in 1919, he holds the 1914–15 Star, and the General Service and Victory Medals.
31, Beatrice Street, Kempston, Beds. Z3781/A.

PATEMAN, R. G., Private, 7th Bedfordshire Regt.
Mobilised at the outbreak of hostilities in August 1914, he was immediately ordered to the Western Front. There he participated in the Battle of Mons and the subsequent Retreat, and also took part in the Battles of the Marne, the Aisne, La Bassée and Ypres, where he fell in action on November 10th, 1914. He was the first Wootton man to make the supreme sacrifice in the war. He was buried at Ypres, and was entitled to the Mons Star, and the General Service and Victory Medals.
"He passed out of the sight of men by the path of duty and self-sacrifice."
Church Cottages, Wootton, Beds. Z3779.

PATEMAN, T., Private, Northamptonshire Regt.
Called up from the Reserve in August 1914, he was later drafted to France. During his service in this theatre of hostilities he took a prominent part with his unit in many important engagements, including the Battles of Loos, Arras, Ypres, Vimy Ridge, the Somme and the Marne, and was wounded in 1917. Returning home after the Armistice, he was discharged in March 1919, and holds the 1914–15 Star, and the General Service and Victory Medals.
73, Coventry Road, Bedford. Z3780.

PATERSON, R., Private, 5th Gordon Highlanders.
He was mobilised in August 1914, and in the following February proceeded to the Western Front. There he was in action at the Battles of Neuve Chapelle, Ypres, Festubert, the Somme and Vimy Ridge. In 1917 he was transferred to Italy, and saw further service on the Piave front. He returned home after the Armistice, and was demobilised in January 1919, holding the 1914–15 Star, and the General Service and Victory Medals.
Harrowden, Bedford. Z3601/B.

PATTERSON, J., Private, 2nd London Regiment (Royal Fusiliers).
Already serving with the Colours, having enlisted in April 1914, he was sent to France in 1915. During his service in this theatre of war he took part in the Battles of Ypres, the Somme and Arras, and in heavy fighting at Cambrai. He was later wounded at Ypres, and invalided home, being eventually discharged in January 1918 as unfit for further service. He holds the 1914–15 Star, and the General Service and Victory Medals. 74, Wellington Street, Bedford. X3783.

PAYNE, A., Private, Labour Corps.
He joined in 1916, and later in the same year was sent to France. There he was employed with his Company on various duties on the Somme and Ypres fronts, but after nine months' service overseas was evacuated to England, and admitted to hospital in London. Upon his recovery he was engaged on agricultural duties in Northamptonshire until February 1919, when he was demobilised. Subsequently he died at Kettering on the 26th of that month from the effects of pneumonia. He was entitled to the General Service and Victory Medals.
"His memory is cherished with pride."
Lower Dean, Kimbolton, Hunts. Z3789/A.

PAYNE, A., Private, 1/5th Bedfordshire Regiment.
He volunteered in September 1914, and in the following July was drafted to Gallipoli, where he took part in severe fighting at Suvla Bay. In December 1915 he was transferred to Egypt, and was later in action in Palestine. He fought at Gaza and was wounded there in April 1917, but afterwards participated in further fighting near Jerusalem. Demobilised on his return home in April 1919, he holds the 1914–15 Star, and the General Service and Victory Medals.
16, Farrer Street, Bedford. X3787.

PAYNE, A. C., Private, Bedfordshire Regiment.
Volunteering in 1915, he was stationed after the completion of his training at Ampthill, Lowestoft and Norwich. He was physically unfit for transfer to a theatre of war, but did good work whilst employed on various duties until he was invalided out of the Service in 1917.
London Road, Sandy, Beds. Z3784/B.

PAYNE, A. C. (jun.), Pte., 7th Bedfordshire Regt.
Mobilised in August 1914, he was at once ordered to France, where he participated in the Retreat from Mons and in the Battles of the Marne, Festubert and the Somme. In 1916 he was transferred to Palestine, and was in action at Jaffa and Haifa. During his service overseas he did excellent work, and was demobilised on his return home in March 1919, holding the Mons Star, and the General Service and Victory Medals.
London Road, Sandy, Beds. Z3784/A.

PAYNE, C. (Miss), Worker, Women's Land Army.
In June 1916 this lady volunteered for work of National importance, and from that time until March 1919 served with the Women's Land Army. She was engaged on agricultural work in the Lower Dean district, and rendered valuable services until she was discharged.
Lower Dean, Kimbolton, Hunts. Z3789/C.

PAYNE, C. H., Private, Canadian Infantry.
He volunteered in 1915, and was drafted to the Western Front in September 1916. In this theatre of war he at once took part in strenuous fighting, but had only served overseas for a few weeks when he made the supreme sacrifice, being killed in action on the Somme front on October 20th, 1916. He was entitled to the 1914–15 Star, and the General Service and Victory Medals.
"Great deeds cannot die."
Lower Dean, Kimbolton, Hunts. Z3789/B.

PAYNE, E., Private, Essex Regiment.
Volunteering in February 1915, he proceeded four months later to France. There he took part with his unit in several important engagements, including, Loos, Albert, Vimy Ridge and the Somme. He was afterwards evacuated to England on account of ill-health, and was eventually discharged in August 1917 as unfit for further service. He holds the 1914–15 Star, and the General Service and Victory Medals.
Oakley, Bedford. Z3785.

PAYNE, F. (M.M.), Sergeant, Bedfordshire Regt. and Suffolk Regiment.
Called up from the Reserve in August 1914, he was sent in the succeeding month to France, where he took part in the Retreat from Mons. He later played a conspicuous part in many severe engagements, including the Battles of La Bassée and Festubert, and was badly wounded at Cambrai in August 1918. Invalided home, he was subsequently discharged in December 1918 as unfit for further military duty. He was awarded the Military Medal in May 1915 for conspicuous bravery in the Field, capturing a German gun and taking the gunner prisoner; and also holds the Mons Star, and the General Service and Victory Medals. Queen's Terrace, Sandy, Beds. Z3786

PAYNE, I. M. (Miss), Worker, Q.M.A.A.C.
She joined Queen Mary's Auxiliary Army Corps in October 1917, and served at Hastings and Bedford, employed on various duties of an important nature. Whilst so engaged she rendered services of a valuable character, and was demobilised in January 1919. Lower Dean, Kimbolton, Hunts. Z3789/D.

PAYNE, M. (Miss), Worker, Q.M.A.A.C.
Joining in November 1916, she was sent in the following year to France. In this theatre of hostilities she was stationed in Rouen, and was employed as waitress and on other duties in the Officers' Club. She performed exceedingly good work until returning home for demobilisation in November 1919, holding the General Service and Victory Medals.
Lower Dean, Kimbolton, Hunts. Z3789/E.

PAYNE, P. W., Private, 2/6th Manchester Regt.
He joined in June 1916, and twelve months afterwards was drafted to the Western Front. There he was in action at Ypres, Passchendaele, Amiens and on the Somme, doing good work until he was wounded and sent to hospital in Rouen, where he unhappily died on March 31st, 1918, from the effects of his injuries. He was buried in St. Stephen's Cemetery, Rouen, and was entitled to the General Service and Victory Medals.
"Nobly striving:
He nobly fell that we might live."
Church Lane, Sharnbrook, Beds. Z3788.

PAYNE, W., Private, 11th Suffolk Regiment.
He volunteered in 1915, and on completing his training in the following year was sent to the Western Front, where he saw severe fighting in various sectors. He took part in the Battles of Albert, the Somme, Vimy Ridge, Messines, Ypres and Cambrai and many other important engagements until the cessation of hostilities. He was demobilised in October 1919, and holds the General Service and Victory Medals.
Eaton Socon, Beds. Z1279/B.

PAYNE, W., Private, King's (Liverpool) Regiment.
He volunteered in March 1915, and after his training was retained on important duties in England until October 1917. He was then drafted to the Western Front, where he took part in the Battles of Passchendaele, the Somme and Armentières, and other engagements, and was wounded in action near Cambrai in September 1918. Invalided home, he was finally demobilised in March 1919, holding the General Service and Victory Medals. Brook Street, St. Neots, Hunts. Z3790.

PEACH, H., Private, 3rd Northants. Regiment.
He volunteered in August 1915, and after undergoing a period of training was retained at various stations in England, where he was engaged on duties of great importance. He was medically unfit for active service and was consequently unable to obtain his transfer overseas, but, nevertheless, did good work with his unit until August 1917, when he was invalided from the Army.
Grange Cottages, Great Linford, Bucks. Z3791.

PEACOCK, A., Sergeant, Machine Gun Corps.
Shortly after volunteering in 1915 he was drafted to the Western Front, where he saw much heavy fighting. He took a prominent part in the Battles of Neuve Chapelle, Hill 60, Ypres, Loos, Albert, the Somme and Vimy Ridge, and many other engagements in various sectors. He was demobilised in February 1919, and holds the 1914–15 Star, and the General Service and Victory Medals.
Preservine Cottages, Clapham, Bedford. Z3792/A.

PEACOCK, A. G., Air Mechanic, Royal Air Force.
Joining in February 1916, he was drafted to the Western Front on completion of a period of training in the following July. Whilst in this theatre of war he was engaged on duties of a highly technical nature in the Somme, Ancre and Arras sectors, and rendered very valuable services with his Squadron. Demobilised in January 1919, he holds the General Service and Victory Medals.
Preservine Cottages, Clapham, Bedford. Z3792/B.

PEACOCK, C., Gunner, Royal Garrison Artillery.
He joined in April 1916, and five months later proceeded to France, where he saw severe fighting in various sectors of the front. He took part in the Battles of the Somme, Arras, Bullecourt, Ypres, Passchendaele, Cambrai, Amiens and Le Cateau and other engagements, and also served through the Retreat and Advance of 1918. He was demobilised in February 1918, and holds the General Service and Victory Medals.
West Perry, near Huntingdon. Z3537/C.

PEACOCK, C. W., Driver, Royal Field Artillery.
He volunteered in January 1915, and later in the same year was drafted to the Western Front. There he served with an ammunition column in various sectors and saw much severe fighting during the period of hostilities. He was demobilised on his return home in June 1919, and holds the 1914–15 Star, and the General Service and Victory Medals.
20, Avenue Road, Huntingdon. Z3793.

PEACOCK, J., Driver, Royal Horse Artillery.
He joined in March 1918, and after a period of training was retained on important duties at various stations. He was unable to obtain his transfer to the front, being under age for active service, but in September 1919 was drafted to Palestine, where he was still serving with his Battery at Jerusalem in 1920. 8, Princess Street, Huntingdon. Z1085/A.

PEACOCK, R. W. (Miss), Member, V.A.D.
She joined in November 1916, and in January of the following year was drafted to the Western Front. There she served for over two years at Le Tréport, where she was engaged on duties of great importance at the 3rd General Hospital, and did much useful work. Returning home in February 1919, she was demobilised in the following month, and holds the General Service and Victory Medals.
West Perry, near Huntingdon. Z3537/B.

PEAK, W., Private, Labour Corps.
He volunteered in May 1915, and after undergoing a period of training served at various stations, where he was engaged on important agricultural work. He was unable, owing to ill-health, to obtain his transfer to the front, but in February 1919 was drafted with the Army of Occupation to Germany, where he was stationed at Cologne. He was demobilised on his return home in September 1919.
Yelling, St. Neots, Hunts. Z3794.

PEAKS, G. C., Pte., Royal Fusiliers, & Sapper, R.E.
Two months after volunteering in October 1915 he proceeded to the Western Front, where he was engaged on bridge-building and repairing and other important duties in various sectors. He was also present at the Battles of Albert, Vimy Ridge, the Somme and Passchendaele and many minor engagements, and on his return home in February 1919 was demobilised. He holds the 1914–15 Star, and the General Service and Victory Medals. Church Street, Somersham, Hunts. Z3416/A.

PEARCE, T. H., Sergeant, Army Cyclist Corps.
He was already serving in India when war was declared in August 1914, and was shortly after drafted to the Western Front, where he took a prominent part in the Battle of Ypres and many other engagements. In 1915 he was transferred to Egypt, whence he proceeded in the following year to Salonika, and saw severe fighting on the Vardar front. He returned to France in 1918, and was finally discharged in November 1919, holding the 1914 Star, and the General Service and Victory Medals. Drayton Parslow, Bucks. Z3797.

PEARCE, W. E., Pte., 7th Oxford. and Bucks. L.I.
Volunteering in September 1914, he was sent to the Western Front twelve months later, and there took part in the Battle of Loos. In November 1915, however, he was transferred to Salonika, where he saw severe fighting on the Doiran front until admitted to hospital at Malta in October 1916. He was also for many months in hospital at Liverpool before being invalided from the Army in October 1917, and holds the 1914–15 Star, and the General Service and Victory Medals.
75, Church Street, Wolverton, Bucks. Z3795.

PEARMAN, F., Private, 2nd Bedfordshire Regt.
Already in the Army when war broke out in August 1914, he was immediately drafted to the Western Front, where he fought in the Retreat from Mons. He also took part in the Battles of the Marne, the Aisne and La Bassée, and was wounded at Ypres in November 1914, and at Neuve Chapelle three months later. In 1916 he was transferred to Egypt, whence he proceeded into Palestine and served through the Battles of Gaza and the entry into Jaffa. He was discharged on his return home in March 1919, and holds the Mons Star, and the General Service and Victory Medals. Biddenham, Beds. Z3796.

PEARSON, C. H., Sergeant, 3rd Hampshire Regt.
A Reservist, he was called to the Colours in August 1914, and was retained on duties of great importance in England until April 1916. He was then drafted to France, where he saw severe fighting in various sectors of the front, and took part in the Battles of the Somme, Vimy Ridge, Ypres and Cambrai, and other engagements. He was discharged in February 1919, and holds the General Service and Victory Medals.
34, Glyn Square, Wolverton, Bucks. Z3798.

PEARSON, H., Private, Bedfordshire Regiment.
Joining in January 1918, he proceeded to the Western Front on completion of a short period of training, and there served through many important engagements during the Allies' Retreat. He made the supreme sacrifice, falling in action at Bapaume in August 1918. He was entitled to the General Service and Victory Medals.
"A valiant Soldier, with undaunted heart, he breasted life's last hill."
9, Lawrence Street, Bedford. Z3800/B

PEARSON, J., Private, Royal Army Service Corps and 11th East Lancashire Regiment.
He volunteered in 1915, and in February of the following year was drafted to the Western Front, where he saw much heavy fighting. After taking part in the Battles of the Somme, Arras and Ypres, and many minor engagements, he was severely wounded in action at Armentières in June 1918, and admitted to hospital at Woolwich. Invalided from the Army in May 1920, he was still undergoing treatment at the end of that year, and holds the General Service and Victory Medals.
Pavenham, near Bedford. Z3801.

PEARSON, R., Sapper, Royal Engineers.
Called up from the Reserve in August 1914, he proceeded to Gallipoli in the following year, and there, after taking part in the landing at Suvla Bay, saw much severe fighting until the Evacuation of the Peninsula. He was then transferred to Egypt, whence he was sent into Palestine and was present at the fall of Jerusalem. He returned home in 1919, and in July of that year was discharged, holding the 1914–15 Star, and the General Service and Victory Medals.
9, Lawrence Street, Bedford. Z3800/A.

PEARSON, T., Air Mechanic, Royal Air Force (late Royal Naval Air Service).
He joined in 1917, and after completing a term of training was retained at various stations, where he was engaged on duties of a highly technical nature. He was not successful in obtaining his transfer to a theatre of war, but, nevertheless, rendered valuable services with his Squadron until his demobilisation in 1919. 139, Bower Street, Bedford. Z3799.

PEASLAND, J. B., Trooper, Northants. Dragoons.
He volunteered in September 1914 at the age of 16 years, but was shortly afterwards discharged on account of his youth. He re-enlisted, however, in January 1916, and was retained in England until February 1918, when he was drafted to the Western Front. There he took part in the Battles of the Somme and Cambrai, and other important engagements, and was wounded in action at Ypres. He was finally demobilised in March 1919, holding the General Service and Victory Medals.
Jubilee Row, Towcester, Northants. Z3802.

PECK, A. E., Private, R.A.M.C.
He joined in October 1916, and in April of the following year was drafted to the Western Front, where he was engaged on important duties in various sectors. He was present at the Battles of the Somme and Amiens, and many other engagements until the cessation of hostilities, and was then sent with the Army of Occupation into Germany. Demobilised on his return home in November 1919, he holds the General Service and Victory Medals.
Berckley Street, Eynesbury, St. Neots, Hunts. Z3804.

PECK, F., Private, 2nd Bedfordshire Regiment and Hertfordshire Regiment.
He joined in May 1918, and after undergoing a period of training was retained at various stations, where he was engaged on duties of great importance, serving first with the Rifle Brigade. He was unable to obtain his transfer overseas before the cessation of hostilities, but in 1919 proceeded to India, where he was with his unit at Secunderabad in 1920.
Station Road, Tempsford, near Sandy, Beds. Z3803.

PEDDAR, A., Private, Bedfordshire Regiment.
Volunteering in 1915, he completed his training in the same year, and proceeded to France, where he saw much active service in various sectors of the front. He took part in the heavy fighting at Arras, Ypres, Cambrai, and on the Somme, and was wounded on two occasions. After the cessation of hostilities, he returned home and was demobilised in 1919, holding the 1914–15 Star, and the General Service and Victory Medals. Upper Shelton, Marston, Beds. TZ3805.

PEDLEY, A., Private, Machine Gun Corps.
He joined in June 1916 in the Bedfordshire Regiment, but was later transferred to the Machine Gun Corps, and proceeded to the Western Front. Whilst in this theatre of war he served with his Battery in the engagements on the Somme, at the Battles of Arras, Cambrai and Albert, and was gassed in August 1918. As a result he was invalided to hospital, and after a period of treatment was finally demobilised in March 1919, holding the General Service and Victory Medals.
Pertenhall, St. Neots, Hunts. Z3807.

PEDLEY, A. J., Private, R.A.S.C. (M.T.)
Joining in June 1916, he completed his training in the following year, and proceeded to France, where he was engaged in conveying supplies and ammunition to the forward areas in various sectors. He did consistently good work and served during many important engagements and was constantly under heavy shell-fire. After the cessation of hostilities, he returned home and was demobilised in December 1919, holding the General Service and Victory Medals.
Pertenhall, St. Neots, Hunts. Z3808/A.

PEDLEY, A. W., Private, Buffs (East Kent Regt.)
He joined in April 1918 on attaining military age, and on conclusion of his training three months later was drafted to Russia. Whilst in this seat of war he took part in much fighting until the close of hostilities. Returning home, he was demobilised in March 1919, and holds the General Service and Victory Medals.
Pertenhall, near St. Neots, Hunts. Z3808/B.

PEDLEY, C., A.B., Royal Navy.
Mobilised in August 1914, he first served on board H.M.S. "Hind," which ship was engaged on important and dangerous patrol and mine-sweeping duties in the North Sea. He also did duty in other vessels in various waters, particularly around the East Indies, and his ship was torpedoed on three occasions. He was discharged in March 1919, and holds the 1914–15 Star, and the General Service and Victory Medals.
Thrapston Road, Crampton, Hunts. Z3131/D.

PEDLEY, E. J., Private, 26th Royal Fusiliers.
He volunteered in June 1915, and was quickly drafted to the Western Front. During his service in this theatre of war he took part in much heavy fighting in the Ypres sector. On June 15th, 1916, he made the supreme sacrifice, being killed in action, and was entitled to the 1914–15 Star, and the General Service and Victory Medals.
"The path of duty was the way to glory."
Pertenhall, St. Neots, Hunts. Z1402/B.

PEDLEY, G., Private, Royal Fusiliers.
He joined in 1916, and after completing a period of training, was retained on important duties with his unit at Dover. Later he was sent to Ireland, where he did consistently good work throughout the remaining period of hostilities. He was discharged as medically unfit for further service in January 1919. Thrapston Road, Brampton, Hunts. Z3131/C.

PEDLEY, J. J., Corporal, Royal Garrison Artillery.
Volunteering at the outbreak of war in August 1914, he completed his training in the following year, and was drafted to Mesopotamia, where he took part in much heavy fighting. He also saw service on the Persian Gulf, and was wounded on two occasions. He was evacuated to England and invalided out in February 1918, holding the 1914–15 Star, and the General Service and Victory Medals.
Piper's Lane, Godmanchester, Hunts. Z3806.

PELL, C. E., Private, Labour Corps.
Joining in June 1916 in the Suffolk Regiment, he completed a period of training, but was later transferred to the Labour Corps. He served at various stations with his unit on important guard and agricultural duties, and did consistently good work until demobilised in October 1919.
Great Staughton, St. Neots, Hunts. Z3810/B.

PELL, C. J., Private, R.A.S.C. (Remounts).
He joined in August 1918, and shortly afterwards proceeded to France, where he was engaged on important transport duties, and also in attending to the horses. After the cessation of hostilities he proceeded with the Army of Occupation into Germany, and served there until returning home for demobilisation in December 1919. He holds the General Service and Victory Medals. Great Staughton, Hunts. Z3810/A.

PELL, C. W., Private, R.A.S.C.
He volunteered in 1915, and on conclusion of his training in the following year proceeded to the Western Front. Whilst in this theatre of war he served in various sectors, where he did good work attending to horses, and was also engaged on important transport duties. Later in 1918 he was invalided home to hospital as the result of a kick, and finally discharged as medically unfit for further service in October 1918, holding the General Service and Victory Medals.
The Green, Great Staughton, Hunts. Z3809.

PELL, F., Pte., 9th Loyal North Lancashire Regt.
He joined in February 1916, and five months later was drafted to the Western Front. After only five weeks' service overseas, during which time he took part in the heavy fighting on the Somme (particularly at Delville Wood), he was unhappily killed in action on September 6th, 1916. He was entitled to the General Service and Victory Medals.
"And doubtless he went in splendid company."
Great Staughton, Hunts. Z3812.

PENWRIGHT, G., Private, Royal Fusiliers.
He joined in June 1916, and proceeding to France in the following year saw heavy fighting at Arras, Vimy Ridge, Ypres and on the Somme before being wounded at Cambrai and evacuated to England. On his recovery he returned to the Western Front and was again in action during the concluding stages of hostilities. He was demobilised in February 1919, and holds the General Service and Victory Medals.
Roxton Road, Great Barford, Beds. Z3813.

PENWRIGHT, L. G., L/Corporal, R.E.
He joined in January 1917, and was shortly afterwards drafted to France. In this theatre of war he was engaged on various important duties in the Somme, Ypres, Arras and Cambrai sectors, and did continuously good work. He returned home after hostilities ceased, but unfortunately contracted pneumonia and died on March 18th, 1919. He was entitled to the General Service and Victory Medals.
"His memory is cherished with pride."
53, Woburn Road, Kempston, Bedford. X3814.

PEPPER, A. W., Private, Royal Welch Fusiliers.
He joined in February 1916, and four months later proceeded to France, where he took part in many important engagements, including the Battles of the Somme, Bullecourt, Albert, Arras, Ypres, Cambrai and Amiens. He also served in the Retreat and Advance of 1918, and was slightly wounded in action. He was demobilised in March 1919, and holds the General Service and Victory Medals.
Dillington, near St. Neots, Hunts. Z3815/B.

PEPPER, B., Private, Queen's Own (Royal West Kent Regiment).
He joined in May 1916, and, completing his training a few weeks later, proceeded to France, where he took part in engagements at Vimy Ridge and the Somme. He made the supreme sacrifice, being killed in action at Beaucourt on September 11th, 1916. He was entitled to the General Service and Victory Medals.
"A valiant Soldier, with undaunted heart he breasted life's last hill."
High Street, Sharnbrook, Beds. Z3816/A.

PEPPER, B. E., Private, Buffs (East Kent Regt.)
He joined in February 1917, and in the following May was drafted to France, where he saw much heavy fighting in the Ypres sector, and was badly gassed. As a result he was invalided home, but on his recovery returned to France. He was unfortunately killed in action during the Retreat on March 23rd, 1918, and was entitled to the General Service and Victory Medals.
"A costly sacrifice upon the altar of freedom."
Dillington, near St. Neots, Hunts. Z3815/A.

PEPPER, H. E., Private, 1/5th Bedfordshire Regt.
He volunteered in September 1914, and in the following year was drafted to the Dardanelles. There he took part in much heavy fighting, including the Landing at Suvla Bay, where he was badly wounded. As a result he was invalided home and finally discharged in March 1916 as medically unfit for further service. He holds the 1914–15 Star, and the General Service and Victory Medals. Marston, near Bedford. Z3817.

PEPPER, S., Petty Officer, Royal Navy.
Already in the Royal Navy in August 1914, he was first employed on the cadet-ship H.M.S. "Carnarvon" off the East Coast. Later he rendered valuable services whilst engaged on important duties in various waters. In 1920 he was still at sea, and holds the 1914–15 Star, and the General Service and Victory Medals. High Street, Sharnbrook, Beds. Z3816/B.

PERKINS, A., Private, 1/5th Bedfordshire Regt.
He volunteered in November 1914, and in the following July proceeded to the Dardanelles, where he saw much heavy fighting at the Landing at Suvla Bay. He was invalided home suffering from dysentery, but on his recovery was drafted to Egypt, took part in the Advance into Palestine, and fought at Gaza and Jaffa He returned home and was demobilised in May 1919. holding the 1914–15 Star, and the General Service and Victory Medals. 48, Melbourne Street, Bedford. X3818.

PERKINS, A., Bandsman, 2nd Bedfordshire Regt.
Volunteering in November 1914, he was retained at various home stations on important duties with his unit. In March 1918 he proceeded to France, where he saw much heavy fighting in the Cambrai, Albert and Le Cateau sectors. He was serving in India in 1920, and holds the General Service and Victory Medals. 48, Melbourne Street, Bedford. X3819.

PERKINS, A., Private, 2nd Essex Regiment.
He joined in June 1916, and early in the following year was drafted to the Western Front. In this seat of war he took part in several engagements, including the Battles of Vimy Ridge, Lens, Cambrai and the Somme (II.). He was demobilised in January 1919, and holds the General Service and Victory Medals. 69, Weston Road, Olney, Bucks. Z3820.

PERKINS, B., Sapper, Royal Engineers.
Volunteering in January 1915, he proceeded overseas after completing his training. Whilst on the Western Front he was engaged on various important duties in connection with the lines of communication in the Ypres and Arras sectors. He did good work throughout, and was demobilised in March 1919, holding the General Service and Victory Medals.
48, Melbourne Street, Bedford. X3821.

PERKINS, C., Private, 1/5th Bedfordshire Regt.
He volunteered in May 1915, and on completing his training in the following February was drafted to the Western Front. There he took part in heavy fighting during the Battle of the Somme, and was badly wounded at Beaumont-Hamel in November 1916. As a result he was invalided home and was in hospital for some considerable time. He was demobilised in March 1919, and holds the General Service and Victory Medals.
12, East Street, Olney, Bucks. Z3822

PERKINS, C. H., Pte., 2/6th Royal Sussex Regt.
He volunteered in October 1914, and was shortly afterwards drafted to India, where he was engaged on the North-West Frontier on important guard duties. He did continuously good work, but owing to a weak heart was invalided home and discharged in June 1919. He holds the General Service and Victory Medals.
Rose Cottage, Milton Ernest, near Bedford. Z3823/A.

PERKINS, G., Bombardier, R.H.A.
He was already in the Army when war broke out in August 1914, and immediately proceeded to France. Whilst on the Western Front he took part in many engagements, including the Battles of Ypres, Loos, the Somme, Vimy Ridge and Cambrai. In 1920 he was serving in India, and holds the Mons Star, and the General Service and Victory Medals.
48, Melbourne Street, Bedford. X3824

PERKINS, H., Sergeant, 9th Essex Regiment.
He volunteered in August 1914, and after a period of training was retained at various home stations as an Instructor. In March 1918 he proceeded to France, and played a prominent part in fighting in the Ypres sector, being twice wounded in action. He was invalided home and finally demobilised in July 1919, holding the General Service and Victory Medals.
48, Melbourne Street, Bedford. X3825.

PERKINS, J. (D.C.M.), Sergeant, Royal Engineers.
He volunteered in January 1915, and underwent a period of training prior to his being drafted to France, where he fought in the Arras and Ypres sectors. Later he was transferred to Italy and played a conspicuous part in the fighting on the Piave, being awarded the Distinguished Conduct Medal for conspicuous gallantry and devotion to duty in the Field. He also holds the General Service and Victory Medals and an Italian decoration, and was demobilised in November 1919.
48, Melbourne Street, Bedford. X3826.

PERKINS, J. G., Private, Queen's (Royal West Surrey Regiment).
He joined in 1916, and later in the same year was drafted to the Western Front. There he took part in much fighting on the Somme and at Arras, Ypres and Cambrai, but unfortunately met with an accident to his knee and was later transferred to the Labour Corps. He did good work connected with the transport of supplies and ammunition, and was demobilised in October 1919. He holds the General Service and Victory Medals. Rose Cottage, Milton Ernest, near Bedford. Z3823/B.

PERKINS, J. J., Gunner, Royal Garrison Artillery.
He volunteered in May 1915, and later in the same year was drafted to France. Whilst in this theatre of war he took part in many engagements, including the Battles of Loos, the Somme, Arras, Ypres, Messines, Albert and Cambrai, where he was wounded in 1917. After hostilities ceased he proceeded to Germany with the Army of Occupation and served at Cologne until his demobilisation in August 1919. He holds the 1914–15 Star, and the General Service and Victory Medals.
Rose Cottage, Milton Ernest, near Bedford. Z3823/C.

PERKINS, S., Private, Bedfordshire Regiment.
He was mobilised in August 1914, and quickly drafted to France, where he took part in the Retreat from Mons and the Battles of the Marne and Hill 60. He was badly wounded in action in 1915, and was consequently invalided home, being in hospital for a considerable time. Later he was engaged on clerical duties at various home stations until his discharge in September 1918, medically unfit for further service. He holds the Mons Star, and the General Service and Victory Medals.
Papworth St. Agnes, Cambridgeshire. Z3827

PERRIN, W. J., Trooper, 1st (King's) Dragoon Guards.
He was mobilised in August 1914, and immediately drafted to France, where he took part in the Battle of Mons and the subsequent Retreat. He was also in action at the Battles of the Marne, the Aisne, La Bassée, Ypres, Hill 60 and Loos, and many other important engagements, particularly during the Retreat and Advance of 1918. He was discharged in February 1919, and holds the Mons Star, and the General Service and Victory Medals. Moulsoe, Bucks. Z3828/A.

PERRY, A. W., Private, 2nd Bedfordshire Regt.
Volunteering in August 1914, he was drafted overseas after a period of training. Whilst on the Western Front he took part in many engagements, including those in the Loos, Somme and Vimy Ridge sectors, and was badly wounded in action. In consequence he was invalided home, and finally discharged in January 1918 as medically unfit for further service. He holds the General Service and Victory Medals.
Maids Moreton, Buckingham, Z3829.

PERRY, C. R., Pte., 9th (Queen's Royal) Lancers.
Having volunteered in August 1914, he was drafted overseas in the following year. Whilst on the Western Front he took part in several engagements, including the Battles of Loos, Vimy Ridge, Arras and Ypres, and was in action during the Retreat and Advance of 1918. He was demobilised in March 1919, and holds the 1914–15 Star, and the General Service and Victory Medals.
16, Albert Street, Bedford. X3834.

PERRY, D. V., Private, Oxford. and Bucks. L.I.
He joined in June 1917, and, completing his training in the following January, proceeded to France. There he took part in much fighting in the Somme and Cambrai sectors, and in the Retreat and Advance of 1918. After hostilities ceased he went to Germany with the Army of Occupation, and served at Cologne until his demobilisation in March 1919. He holds the General Service and Victory Medals.
Newton Longville, Bucks. Z3830.

PERRY, G. J., Private, Royal Defence Corps.
Being over age for service in a fighting unit, he volunteered in November 1914 in the Royal Defence Corps. He did continuously good work throughout, and was engaged in guarding bridges and prisoners of war, and also on agricultural duties. He was discharged in March 1918.
6, Muswell Road, Bedford. Z3833/B.

PERRY, G. J., Pte., Australian Overseas Forces.
He volunteered in October 1914, and in the following June was drafted to the Dardanelles, where he saw much fighting at Anzac Cove and the Landing at Suvla Bay. After the Evacuation of the Gallipoli Peninsula he was transferred to France, and took part in the Battles of the Somme, Ypres, St. Quentin and Cambrai, and was wounded in 1916. He was demobilised in April 1919, and holds the 1914–15 Star, and the General Service and Victory Medals.
6, Muswell Road, Bedford. Z3833/A.

PERRY, J., C.S.M., 7th Bedfordshire Regiment.
Already in the Army when war broke out in August 1914, he was immediately drafted to France, where he took part in the Retreat from Mons, and played a prominent part in the Battles of the Marne, the Aisne, Ypres (where he was wounded), Festubert and Loos. Unfortunately he was killed in action on the Somme on July 7th, 1916, and was entitled to the Mons Star, and the General Service and Victory Medals.
"Whilst we remember, the sacrifice is not in vain."
6, Muswell Road, Bedford. Z3833/C.

PERRY, S. F., Private, 5th Devonshire Regiment.
He joined in July 1917, and after his training saw service in Ireland and at various home stations. After hostilities ceased he went to Germany with the Army of Occupation and served on important duties at Cologne until his demobilisation in April 1920.
110, Victoria Road, Fenny Stratford, Bucks. Z3831.

PERRY, W. W., Private, 1st Northants. Regiment.
He volunteered in September 1914, and after a short period of training was drafted to France. There he took part in many important engagements in the Ypres sector, but was severely wounded in action in December 1914, and consequently invalided home. He unfortunately died from the effects of his wounds on January 7th, 1915, and was entitled to the 1914 Star, and the General Service and Victory Medals.
"The path of duty was the way to glory."
6, Simpson Road, Fenny Stratford, Bucks. Z3832 /A.

PESTELL, C., Private, Bedfordshire Regiment.
Volunteering in February 1915, he was sent to France in April of the following year, and took part in the Battles of the Somme, Vimy Ridge, Messines, Bullecourt, Ypres and Cambrai. He was also in action throughout the Retreat and Advance of 1918, and after the cessation of hostilities served on the Rhine with the Army of Occupation. Demobilised in May 1919, he holds the General Service and Victory Medals.
Huntingdon Street, St. Neots, Hunts. TZ3567 /B.

PETERS, E., Private, Queen's Own (Royal West Kent Regiment).
He joined in 1917, and during the course of that year was sent to France, where he took part in the Battles of Arras, Ypres, Cambrai and the Somme, and was in action throughout the Retreat and Advance of 1918. After the Armistice he proceeded to Germany with the Army of Occupation, and was stationed on the Rhine until his demobilisation in February 1919, holding the General Service and Victory Medals.
5, Oakland Terrace, St. Ives, Hunts. Z3835.

PETTIFER, S., Sapper, Royal Engineers.
Joining in April 1916, he was quickly drafted to France and first rendered valuable services with the Railway Operative Department in the workshops at Audriucque. Later he was transferred to the C.M.E. Branch, and was engaged on special engineering work at Dunkirk and Bray-Dunes. He was demobilised in October 1919, and holds the General Service and Victory Medals.
C3836.

PETTIT, F. W., Private, Bedfordshire Regiment.
He volunteered in May 1915, and, after 18 months' valuable services in England, was sent to France. In January 1917, however, he was invalided home sick, and was in hospital at Sevenoaks until early in 1918. He was then sent to Ireland, where he was engaged on important garrison duties until his demobilisation in February 1919, holding the General Service and Victory Medals.
High Street, Sharnbrook, Beds. Z3839.

PETTIT, H. G., Private, 4th Cambridgeshire Regt.
Having joined in October 1916, he completed his training, and was then engaged on important duties at various home stations. He did excellent work with his unit, but was unsuccessful in obtaining his transfer overseas. On October 30th, 1918, he unfortunately died of fever at Kempston Hospital, Bedford.
"His memory is cherished with pride."
Gayhurst, Newport Pagnell, Bucks. Z3837.

PETTIT, T. W., Sapper, Royal Engineers.
After volunteering in November 1915, he underwent a period of training prior to being drafted to France, where he took an active part in the Battles of the Somme, the Ancre, Arras, Vimy Ridge and Ypres, and in heavy fighting at Combles, Festubert, Loos and Albert. He was demobilised in February 1919, after a period of service at Cologne, and holds the General Service and Victory Medals.
122, Dudley Street, Bedford. Z3838.

PHILLIPS, A. H. D., Pioneer, Royal Engineers.
In August 1917 he joined the Army and was later sent to France, where he was engaged on important wiring, trench-making and bridge-building duties in the Ypres, Arras, Cambrai and Somme sectors. After the termination of hostilities he rendered valuable services with his unit at Cologne on the Rhine, and was eventually demobilised in April 1919, holding the General Service and Victory Medals.
85, Marlborough Road, Bedford. Z3466 /A.

PHILLIPS, E. T., Staff Sergeant-Major, R.A.S.C.
Mobilised in August 1914, he first saw active service in the Dardanelles, where he played a prominent part in the Landing at Cape Helles and in heavy fighting on Gallipoli. On the Evacuation of the Peninsula he proceeded to Egypt, but later advanced into Palestine and served with distinction at Gaza. Early in 1918 he was transferred to the Western Front and was in charge of transports in the Cambrai sector. He was discharged in August 1919, and holds the 1914–15 Star, and the General Service and Victory Medals.
85, Marlborough Road, Bedford. Z3466 /B.

PHILLIPS, H. B., Private, R.M.L.I.
Four months after joining in May 1917 he was drafted to France, and was in action during the Battles of Passchendaele Ridge and Cambrai. In December 1917 he was evacuated to England with trench fever, but returned to the Western Front in November 1918 He was then engaged on important guard duties until his demobilisation in May 1919, and holds the General Service and Victory Medals.
39, Ledsam Street, Wolverton, Bucks. Z3840.

PHILLIPS, J. A., Trooper, 4th (Royal Irish) Dragoon Guards.
Already in the Army at the outbreak of war, he later came from India and landed in France in December 1915. He took part in the Battles of the Somme and Ypres, was twice wounded in action, and was invalided home in 1917. On his recovery he was transferred to the Royal Army Veterinary Corps, and was stationed at Huntingdon. He also served for a time with the Royal Fusiliers and was eventually discharged in 1918, holding the 1914–15 Star, and the General Service and Victory Medals.
8, Princess Street, Huntingdon. Z3841.

PHILLIPS, V. R., Sergeant, R.A.M.C.
He was mobilised in August 1914, and in the following year was drafted to the Dardanelles, where he took part in the Landing at Cape Helles and in heavy fighting on Gallipoli. After the Evacuation of the Peninsula he was sent to Egypt, but proceeding into Palestine, served at Gaza. In 1918 he was transferred to the Western Front, and was in action in the Cambrai sector during the Retreat and Advance. He holds the 1914–15 Star, and the General Service and Victory Medals, and was discharged in August 1919.
85, Marlborough Road, Bedford. Z3466 /C.

PHILLIPS, W., Private, 2nd Bedfordshire Regt.
A serving soldier, he was sent to France shortly after the outbreak of war, and played a prominent part in the Battles of the Marne, La Bassée, Ypres and Loos. He laid down his life for King and Country in December 1915, and was entitled to the 1914 Star, and the General Service and Victory Medals.
"A costly sacrifice upon the altar of freedom."
5, Bardolph's Court, St. Germain Street, Huntingdon. Z1007 /B.

PHILLIPS, W. P., Sergeant, 2nd Yorkshire Regt.
A Reservist, he was called to the Colours in August 1914, and proceeded to France in time to serve through the Retreat from Mons. He also played a prominent part in the Battle of La Bassée, but after an engagement at Ypres, was reported wounded and missing. He is now presumed to have been killed in action on October 22nd, 1914, and was entitled to the Mons Star, and the General Service and Victory Medals.
"Nobly striving:
He nobly fell that we might live."
3, Coronation Road, Stony Stratford, Bucks. Z3842

PICKERING, C., Sapper, Royal Engineers.
He was quickly drafted to France after volunteering in February 1915, and played a prominent part in the Battles of Loos, the Somme, Arras, Vimy Ridge and Ypres. He also served through the Retreat and Advance of 1918, and at the end of hostilities proceeded with the Army of Occupation to Germany, where he was stationed at Cologne. Demobilised in September 1919, he holds the 1914–15 Star, and the General Service and Victory Medals.
52, Russell Street, Bedford. X3845 /B.

PICKERING, F. K., Private, R.A.M.C.
Being already in the Army when war broke out, he was sent to France in August 1914. Whilst on the Western Front he rendered valuable services as a stretcher-bearer during the Battle of, and the Retreat from, Mons, and at the Battles of Ypres, Festubert, Loos, the Somme, Arras and Cambrai. He received his discharge in January 1919, and holds the Mons Star, and the General Service and Victory Medals.
37, High Road, Clapham, Bedford. Z3843.

PICKERING, H., Sapper, Royal Engineers.
He joined in June 1916, and later in the same year proceeded to France. During his service in this theatre of war he was engaged on important duties with the Technical Branch of the Royal Engineers at Audriucque. He did excellent work in connection with the repairing of motors and bridges. Eventually demobilised in 1919, he holds the General Service and Victory Medals. 23, Prebend Street, Bedford. Z3844.

PICKERING, T., Private, Cambridgeshire Regt.
On attaining military age he joined in January 1918, and after six months in training was engaged on important duties at various home stations, and rendered valuable services with his unit. Unfortunately he contracted influenza and was in hospital at Hastings prior to being discharged as medically unfit in November of the same year.
52, Russell Street, Bedford. Z3845 /C.

PICKERING, W., Private, Labour Corps.
He volunteered in February 1915, and a month later was drafted to the Western Front. Whilst in this theatre of war he was engaged on important duties—trench-digging and ammunition and ration carrying in the Ypres, Arras, Somme and Cambrai sectors. He rendered valuable services with his unit until his demobilisation in April 1919, and holds the 1914–15 Star, and the General Service and Victory Medals.
52, Russell Street, Bedford. X3845 /A.

PIERCY, W. G., Sapper, Royal Engineers.
Volunteering in the Royal Warwickshire Regiment in September 1914, he was drafted to France in December and took part in heavy fighting at Ypres, St. Quentin and on the Somme. He also served with the 2nd Bedfordshire Regiment and the 12th Norfolk Regiment before being transferred to the Royal Engineers. Whilst on the Western Front he was twice wounded in action, and was evacuated to England in August 1918. He was demobilised in April 1919, and holds the 1914–15 Star, and the General Service and Victory Medals.
22, Napier Street, Bletchley, Bucks. Z3846.

PIGGOTT, J., Private, Royal Fusiliers.
Mobilised in August 1914, he was sent to France with the first Expeditionary Force and served through the Retreat from Mons. He also took part in the Battles of La Bassée, Ypres, Hill 60, Festubert, the Somme, Arras and Cambrai. Reported missing on March 21st, 1918, he is now presumed to have been unfortunately killed in action on that date. He was entitled to the Mons Star, and the General Service and Victory Medals.
"His life for his Country, his soul to God."
London Road, Girtford, Sandy, Beds. Z3847/A.

PILGRIM, H., Corporal, R.E. and Labour Corps.
He volunteered in August 1914, and was later sent to the Dardanelles, where with the Royal Engineers he took part in the Landing and subsequent fighting. Invalided off the Peninsula owing to ill-health, he later served in France and was employed with the Labour Corps in the repair of roads and work on the railways. He was demobilised in March 1919, and holds the 1914–15 Star, and the General Service and Victory Medals.
33, Muswell Road, South End, Bedford. Z3855.

PILGRIM, P., 2nd Corporal, 483rd Field Coy., R.E.
Volunteering in the early days of the war, he was soon sent to France and fought in the concluding stages of the Retreat from Mons and the famous Battle of the Marne. Later he fought in the Battles of the Aisne, Ypres, Loos and the Somme, and was also in action at Givenchy, Festubert, Ginchy and the Ancre. Demobilised in April 1919, he holds the Mons Star, and the General Service and Victory Medals.
33, Beatrice Street, Kempston, Bedford. Z3856.

PILL, J., Sapper, Royal Engineers.
He volunteered in August 1915, and later in the same year was sent to the Western Front, where he was employed in the repair of roads and duties of a similar nature and served in the Ypres, Festubert, Arras and Cambrai sectors. Owing, however, to his being over age he was sent home and invalided out of the Service in March 1919. He holds the 1914–15 Star, and the General Service and Victory Medals.
14, Beaconsfield Street, Bedford. X3857.

PINCHBECK, C. H., Engine-Room Artificer, R.N., H.M.S. "Marlborough."
He joined the Navy in June 1918, and soon afterwards was sent to sea in H.M.S. "Marlborough." He was present at the surrender of the German High Seas Fleet and its subsequent internment at Scapa Flow, and was engaged on patrol duties in the North and Baltic Seas and off the Russian coast. Demobilised in December 1919, he holds the General Service and Victory Medals. 1, Cromwell Road, Bedford. Z3858.

PINDRED, G. F., Driver, Machine Gun Corps.
Volunteering in October 1915, he was sent to France in 1917, after a period of service in England, and served at Ypres and Arras. Sent to Mesopotamia later in the year, he was drafted to Egypt and fought at Gaza during the Palestine campaign. In March 1918 he returned to the Western Front, and was again in action there. He was demobilised in April 1919, and holds the General Service and Victory Medals.
Berckley Street, Eynesbury, St. Neots, Hunts. Z3859.

PING, A. A., Tpr., Beds. Lancers; and Pte., 19th (Queen Alexandra's Own Royal) Hussars.
He volunteered in June 1915, and after service at Bedford and Colchester was drafted to France in 1916. He took part in the Somme Offensive and fought through the Battles of Arras, Ypres and Cambrai. After about three years' service in that theatre of war he was demobilised in April 1919, and holds the General Service and Victory Medals.
High Street, Cranfield, Beds. Z3860/A.

PING, A. S. E., Private, R.M.L.I.
He joined the Red Marines in March 1917, and was at first stationed at Deal and Plymouth. There he was engaged in H.M.S. "Carnarvon," convoying vessels to Canada and the West Indies, and after the Armistice served off Turkey and Russia, where he received a wound whilst in action. In 1920 he was at Malta, and holds the General Service and Victory Medals. High Street, Cranfield, Beds. Z3860/B.

PIPKIN, J., Private, Labour Corps.
He joined in May 1916, and first served with the Royal Army Service Corps, but was severely injured by a kick from a mule. After hospital treatment he was transferred to the Labour Corps and employed on agricultural duties. He was unsuccessful in obtaining his transfer overseas, but did excellent work until his demobilisation in March 1919.
Simpson, near Bletchley, Bucks. Z3848/A.

PITKIN, S., Private, Buffs (East Kent Regiment).
Having joined in May 1916, he completed his training before being sent overseas in the next year. During his service on the Western Front he was in action on the Somme and at Ypres, Arras and Cambrai, and after the Armistice served at Cologne with the Army of Occupation until April 1920, when he was demobilised, holding the General Service and Victory Medals.
Hilton, Hunts. Z3861.

PITTAM, G. V., Air Mechanic, Royal Air Force.
He volunteered in October 1915, and in the following year was sent to Egypt, where he was stationed at Cairo and Alexandria, and made several flights whilst testing machines. Later he proceeded to Palestine and served with his Squadron as an engine-fitter at Jerusalem. He did excellent work until his demobilisation in October 1919, and holds the General Service and Victory Medals.
Old Stratford, near Stony Stratford, Bucks. Z3849.

PITTS, A. C., L/Corporal, Hampshire Regiment.
He volunteered in December 1914, and after his training rendered valuable services as an Instructor of recruits at a Royal Army Service Corps depôt in Dorsetshire. Later he was transferred to the 3rd Suffolk Regiment, but did not proceed overseas until November 1918, when he was sent to Germany with the Hampshire Regiment and did excellent work whilst with the Army of Occupation. He was demobilised in March 1919. Bedford Road, Great Barford, Beds. Z3851/C.

PITTS, A. E., Private, Sherwood Foresters.
Joining in June 1916, he completed his training and was sent to France in the following February. After taking part in the Battles of Arras, Messines and Ypres he was seriously wounded in action on the Somme and unfortunately suffered the loss of one of his legs. As a result he was invalided from the Army in 1918, and holds the General Service and Victory Medals.
Chalton Terrace, Blunham, Beds. Z3852/B.

PITTS, B., Private, 12th East Surrey Regiment.
He joined in February 1917, and later in the same year was drafted to the Western Front, where he took part in the Battles of Arras, Messines, Ypres and Cambrai, and was wounded in action in July 1917. He died gloriously on the Field of Battle on October 20th, 1918, during the Advance on the Somme, and was entitled to the General Service and Victory Medals.
"He joined the great white company of valiant souls."
Chalton Terrace, Blunham, Beds. Z3852/A.

PITTS, H., Private, South Wales Borderers.
He joined in October 1916, and four months later was sent to France. During his service on the Western Front he took part in the Battles of Arras, Vimy Ridge and Ypres, where he was seriously wounded in action in July 1917. Invalided home a month later, he was in hospital for some time prior to being discharged as medically unfit for further service in April 1919. He holds the General Service and Victory Medals.
Ewelme Terrace, Blunham, Beds. Z3853.

PITTS, W., Driver, Royal Field Artillery.
Four months after joining in April 1916 he was drafted to the Western Front, where he played a prominent part with his Battery in the Battle of the Somme. In December 1916 he was invalided home with nephritis, and after hospital treatment was engaged on special duties at Woolwich and on agricultural work in Northamptonshire. He was demobilised in February 1919, and holds the General Service and Victory Medals.
Ewelme Terrace, Blunham, Beds. Z3850/A.

PITTS, W. C., Private, 6th Bedfordshire Regiment.
He volunteered in March 1915, and later in the same year was drafted to the Western Front, but after taking part in heavy fighting at Arras and Ypres was unfortunately killed in action near Albert on November 16th, 1915. He was entitled to the 1914–15 Star, and the General Service and Victory Medals.
"Honour to the immortal dead, who gave their youth that the world might grow old in peace."
Albert Cottage, Great Barford, Beds. Z3854.

PIXLEY, A., Gunner, Royal Garrison Artillery.
He joined in August 1916, and later in the year was drafted to France. There he served at Ypres and was employed in guarding German prisoners of war. Returning to England in February 1919, he was demobilised in the same month, and holds the General Service and Victory Medals.
45, Hassett Street, Bedford. X2684/B.

POND, E. C., Driver, R.A.S.C. (M.T.)
He volunteered in September 1914, and was stationed at Blackheath, Bridlington and Bath before being drafted to France in 1916. On that front he served in the Amiens district. In the following year he embarked in the "Transylvania" for Egypt, but this vessel being torpedoed without warning in the Gulf of Genoa on May 4th, 1917, he was landed in Italy, after being in the water for about two days. Continuing his voyage, he reached Egypt, and for some time was employed as a despatch-rider with the 906th Company, Motor Transport. He took part in the operations at Gaza, Jaffa, Jerusalem and in the Jordan Valley, and was wounded at Gaza and on the Mount of Olives. Returning home, he was demobilised in July 1919, and holds the General Service and Victory Medals. Park Hall Road, Somersham, Hunts. Z3862.

POOLE, J., Private, Royal Defence Corps.
Volunteering in March 1915, he was retained at home in the Royal Defence Corps, as he was unfit for foreign service. Until 1917 he was engaged in guarding bridges at Clapham, Hendon and Luton, and was afterwards employed on agricultural work at Wootton. He was demobilised in 1919.
Keeley Lane, Wootton, Bedford. Z3863.

POPE, G., Sergeant, 6th Bedfordshire Regiment.
A Regular soldier, he served at Bury St. Edmunds from the outbreak of war until 1915, when he was sent overseas. During about four years on the Western Front he took part in the Battles of Ypres, Hill 60, Festubert, Loos, Lens, the Somme and Cambrai, and in various engagements in the Retreat and Advance of 1918. He was discharged in 1919, and holds the 1914-15 Star, and the General Service and Victory Medals.
67, Muswell Road, South End, Bedford. Z3864/A.

POPE, G., Private, Royal Army Service Corps.
Volunteering in August 1914, he was sent to Egypt in the following year, and took part in the Advance into Palestine. There he fought at Gaza and in the operations which led to the capture of Jaffa and Jerusalem, and was also present at the occupation of Haifa and Aleppo. Returning home, he was demobilised in June 1919, and holds the 1914-15 Star, and the General Service and Victory Medals.
67, Muswell Road, South End, Bedford. Z3864/B.

POPE, H. C., Gunner, Royal Garrison Artillery.
He was mobilised when war broke out, and almost at once proceeded to France, where he took part in the Retreat from Mons and the Battles of La Bassée, Ypres, Neuve Chapelle, Loos, the Somme and Cambrai. During the course of his service he was wounded on two occasions. He was discharged in June 1919, and holds the Mons Star, and the General Service and Victory Medals.
Montague Street, Eynesbury, St. Neots, Hunts. Z3690/B.

POPE, L. A., Private, 8th Bedfordshire Regiment.
He volunteered in September 1914, and was stationed at Shoreham and Aldershot for a few months. Proceeding to the Western Front in August 1915, he was unhappily killed at Ypres on October 21st, after only three months' foreign service. He was entitled to the 1914-15 Star, and the General Service and Victory Medals.

"Nobly striving:
He nobly fell that we might live."

Montague Street, Eynesbury, St. Neots, Hunts. Z3690/C.

POPE, W., Private, Bedfordshire, & Dorset Regts.
Volunteering in September 1914, he proceeded to the Dardanelles in the following year, and took part in the heavy fighting which characterised that campaign. Transferred to Mesopotamia, he again saw fighting, but in spite of a wound received at Baghdad in March 1917, continued his service until 1919. Returning home, he was demobilised in October, and holds the 1914-15 Star, and the General Service and Victory Medals.
Berrick Yard, Eynesbury, St. Neots, Hunts. Z3865.

PORT, T., Corporal, Royal Army Medical Corps and Royal Buckinghamshire Hussars.
He volunteered at the outbreak of war, and in the following March was drafted to Gallipoli with the Royal Army Medical Corps. After taking part in the Landings at Cape Helles and Suvla Bay and the eventual Evacuation of the Peninsula, he was sent to Egypt and, attached to the Royal Buckinghamshire Hussars, served in the Advance into Palestine, being present at the Battle of Gaza, the operations prior to the fall of Jerusalem and the victorious Advance under General Allenby in 1918. Returning home, he was demobilised in March 1919, and holds the 1914-15 Star, and the General Service and Victory Medals.
94, Church Street, Wolverton, Bucks. TZ3866.

PORTWAIN, W., Private, Queen's Own (Royal West Kent Regiment).
A Regular soldier, he was retained at home until November 1915. In that year, however, he was sent to Mesopotamia, but, after seeing fighting there, returned to England in 1916. Early in 1918 he was drafted to Italy, but was sent home again six months afterwards and stationed at Aldershot until his discharge as unfit in September 1918. He holds the 1914-15 Star, and the General Service and Victory Medals.
73, Pilcroft Street, Bedford. X3867/A.

POTTER, F., Sapper, Royal Engineers.
He joined in May 1916, and in the following December was sent to France, where he fought at Messines Ridge and Ypres. During 1917 he saw a brief period of service in Italy, where he was employed on the fortifications, and on his return to the Western Front fought at Bapaume in the Retreat of 1918, and at Ypres and Lille during the subsequent Advance. Demobilised in June 1919, he holds the General Service and Victory Medals.
154, Coventry Road, Queen's Park, Bedford. Z3868.

POTTER, H. J., Private, Sherwood Foresters.
Volunteering in October 1915, he was drafted to France in the following March, and fought in the Somme Offensive and at Merville. He also took a prominent part in the Battles of Ypres, Arras and Cambrai, and was wounded during the Advance of 1918. He continued to serve, however, but in October of that year was invalided home with fever. He was eventually demobilised in February 1919, and holds the General Service and Victory Medals.
Windmill Terrace, St. Neots, Hunts. Z3869.

POTTLE, S. J., Pte., Bedfordshire, & Suffolk Regts.
Volunteering in September 1915, he completed his training, but was unfit for foreign service. He was stationed at various places in England, and was employed as Chaplain's Orderly and in the telegraph office and stores. After rendering valuable services he was discharged owing to rheumatism in June 1917.
23, Marne Street, Kempston, Bedford. Z3870.

PRATT, A. V., Private, 3/9th and 2/10th Middlesex Regiment; and Rifleman, Rifle Brigade.
He volunteered in August 1915, and early in the following year was sent to Egypt, where he joined the Expeditionary Force in Palestine. There he fought at Gaza and in the Jordan Valley, and in the operations leading to the capture of Jerusalem and Bethelehem, but spent some time in hospital. Returning home, he was demobilised in April 1919, and holds the General Service and Victory Medals.
11, Duncombe Street, Bletchley, Bucks. Z3045/B.

PRATT, F. J., Q.M.S., R.E. & Oxford. & Bucks. L.I.
With a record of 21 years' service in the Army, he was stationed at the Gold Coast with the Royal Engineers at the outbreak of war, and at once volunteered for active service. Sent to England, he was transferred to the Oxfordshire and Buckinghamshire Light Infantry, and stationed at Portsmouth, but was unable to obtain a transfer to a theatre of war owing to his age. After the Armistice he was sent back to the Royal Engineers, and in 1920 was serving at the Survey Office at Southampton. He holds the General Service and Long Service and Good Conduct Medals.
2, Spring Gardens, Newport Pagnell, Bucks.
Z1775/B—Z1776/B.

PRATT, F. M. (Mrs.), Worker, Q.M.A.A.C.
She joined in June 1918, and was retained in England during her period of service. Stationed at York, she was employed as a messenger and orderly at the Cavalry Barracks, and rendered valuable services until demobilised in February 1919.
2, Castle Hill Court, Huntingdon. Z3872/B.

PRATT, G. B. H., Private, 4th East Surrey Regt. and Royal Army Medical Corps.
Volunteering in September 1914, he proceeded to the Western Front in February 1915, and fought at Neuve Chapelle, Givenchy and Ypres, but was wounded at Zonnebeke in April. Sent to Egypt in the following October, he served during the Palestine campaign at Gaza, Jerusalem and the Jordan, but was invalided home with malaria. He was eventually transferred to the Royal Army Medical Corps, and employed on hospital duty at Dieppe until demobilised in July 1919. He holds the 1914-15 Star, and the General Service and Victory Medals.
2, Castle Hill Court, Huntingdon. Z3872/A.

PRATT, N. (Mrs.), Special War Worker.
This lady from November 1915 to December 1918 worked as a postwoman at the Newport Pagnell Post Office, delivering letters in all weathers in the surrounding districts, notably the villages of Broughton and Milton Keynes. She rendered very valuable services and relieved a man for service in the Army.
2, Spring Gardens, Newport Pagnell, Bucks.
Z1775/A—Z1776/A.

PRENTICE, W. H. J., Gunner, R.G.A.
A Territorial at the outbreak of war, he served at Bedford until the close of 1914, and was then sent to the Western Front. During about four years' service in that theatre of war he took part in heavy fighting on the Somme and at Arras, Ypres, Loos, Lens, Cambrai and Festubert. Returning home, he was demobilised in February 1919, and holds the 1914-15 Star, and the General Service and Victory Medals.
1, Rabanna Terrace, Clapham, Bedford. Z3873.

PRICE, E., Pte., King's Own (R. Lancaster Regt.)
A time-serving soldier, he was sent to France a month after the outbreak of war, and fought in the Battles of the Marne, the Aisne, Ypres and Neuve Chapelle. Taken prisoner in May 1915, he was made to work in the German mines until November 1918, when he was repatriated. He was discharged in January 1919, and holds the 1914 Star, and the General Service and Victory Medals. 17, Bower Street, Bedford. Z2989/B.

PRICE, W. A., Private, Royal Fusiliers.
He joined in January 1917, and proceeding to the Western Front in April was wounded at Messines a month later. He was subsequently wounded at Cambrai in November 1917 and during the Advance in August 1918, and owing to the latter was invalided home, when his right leg was amputated. He unhappily succumbed to his injuries on November 5th, 1918, and was entitled to the General Service and Victory Medals.

"His memory is cherished with pride."

140, Bower Street, Bedford. Z3874.

PRICKETT, A. W., Pte., 16th (Queen's) Lancers.
Volunteering in August 1914, he was drafted to the Western Front in May of the following year, and there saw severe fighting in various sectors. He took part in the Battles of Ypres, Loos, Albert, the Somme, Arras, Messines, Cambrai and St. Quentin and many minor engagements, and in May 1917 was wounded in action near Epéhy. He was demobilised in February 1919, and holds the 1914–15 Star, and the General Service and Victory Medals. 58, Oakley, Bedford. Z3876/D.

PRICKETT, E. (Miss), Nursing Sister.
She was undergoing training at Ealing Hospital when war broke out in August 1914, and served there during the whole period of hostilities. She was engaged on various important duties, and rendered very valuable services throughout. Contracting pneumonia, she unfortunately died on April 11th, 1919.
"Her memory is cherished with pride."
58, Oakley, Bedford. Z3876/A.

PRICKETT, M. (Miss), Ward Sister.
Having taken up nursing in 1911, she served at Paddington Military Hospital throughout the war, and there, engaged on duties of a highly important nature, rendered very valuable services until after the cessation of hostilities. She unhappily died on April 5th, 1920, of diabetes and the effects of over-work.
"Steals on the ear the distant triumph song."
58, Oakley, Bedford. Z3876/B.

PRICKETT, R. O., Private, R.A.S.C. (M.T.)
Volunteering in May 1915, he was drafted to Egypt in November of that year, and was there engaged on transport duties at various stations until transferred in 1916 to Salonika. After serving on the Vardar, Doiran and Struma fronts, he was invalided home suffering from dysentery, and later in 1917 proceeded to the Western Front, where he was present at the Battles of Ypres, Cambrai and the Somme. He was demobilised in April 1919, and holds the 1914–15 Star, and the General Service and Victory Medals. 58, Oakley, Bedford. Z3876/E.

PRICKETT, T., Sapper, Royal Engineers.
He joined in June 1917, and after five months' training proceeded to the Western Front, where he was engaged on important duties with the Signal Section. He served in various sectors whilst in this theatre of war and took part in the Battles of Cambrai, the Somme and Ypres, and many minor engagements. Returning home in June 1919, he was demobilised in the following month, and holds the General Service and Victory Medals. 3, Little Thurlow Street, Bedford. X3875/C.

PRICKETT, W. E., Sapper, Royal Engineers.
After joining in May 1916 he underwent a period of training prior to being drafted to the Western Front in March 1918. There he served with the Signal Section in various sectors, was present at the Battles of the Somme, Amiens and Cambrai, and other engagements, and took part also in the Retreat and Advance of 1918. He was demobilised in July 1919, and holds the General Service and Victory Medals.
C3876/C.

PRIDMORE, G., C.Q.M.S., Bedfordshire Regt.
A Reservist, he was called to the Colours at the outbreak of war in August 1914, and in June of the following year was drafted to the Western Front. Whilst in this theatre of war he saw severe fighting in various sectors, and took a prominent part in the Battles of Albert, Vimy Ridge, the Somme, Arras, Passchendaele and Cambrai, and other engagements. Invalided home in 1918, he was discharged in May 1919, and holds the 1914–15 Star, and the General Service and Victory Medals.
41, New Fenlake, Bedford Z3877.

PRIME, W. J., L/Corporal, Royal Engineers.
Volunteering in May 1915, he was drafted to France on completing his training in January of the following year, and there served with the Signal Section in various sectors of the front. He was present at the Battles of Arras and Cambrai, and many other important engagements, and took part also in the Retreat and Advance of 1918. Demobilised in May 1919, he holds the General Service and Victory Medals.
22, Brooklands Road, Bletchley, Bucks. Z3878.

PRIOR, B., L/Corporal, Bedfordshire Regiment.
He was mobilised at the outbreak of war in August 1914, and was immediately drafted to the Western Front, where he fought in the Retreat from Mons and also took part in the Battles of the Marne, Festubert and Loos and other engagements. He was reported missing, and is believed to have been killed in action on September 13th, 1916. He was entitled to the Mons Star, and the General Service and Victory Medals.
"A costly sacrifice upon the altar of freedom."
Colne, Hunts. Z3880.

PRIOR, D. L., Private, Machine Gun Corps.
He joined in December 1916, and in July of the following year proceeded to the Western Front, where he saw much severe fighting. After taking part in several engagements, he was wounded in action in October 1917 and, invalided to hospital in Northumberland, was afterwards retained in England. He was demobilised in September 1919, and holds the General Service and Victory Medals.
11, Sapley Lane, Hartford, Hunts. Z3879/B.

PRIOR, G., Air Mechanic, Royal Air Force.
He joined in September 1918, and after undergoing a period of training was retained at various stations, where he was engaged on duties which called for a high degree of technical skill. Unable to obtain his transfer overseas before the cessation of hostilities, he afterwards proceeded, however, to Russia. He was demobilised on his return home in December 1919, and holds the General Service and Victory Medals.
11, Sapley Lane, Hartford, Hunts. Z3879/A.

PRIOR, G., Private, Labour Corps.
He joined in 1917, and shortly afterwards proceeded to the Western Front, where he saw severe fighting in various sectors. Serving with an infantry unit, he took part in the Battles of Arras, Ypres, Cambrai and the Somme and other important engagements, and was afterwards transferred to the Labour Corps and stationed in England. He was demobilised in February 1919, and holds the General Service and Victory Medals. New Town, Kimbolton, Hunts. Z3231/B.

PRIOR, P. G., Sergt., Canadian Overseas Forces.
Volunteering in August 1914, he was drafted to the Western Front in June of the following year, and there saw much heavy fighting. After taking a prominent part in many important engagements, he was severely wounded in action on the Somme in July 1916, and invalided home. On his recovery he was retained on special clerical duties at the War Office until his demobilisation in March 1919, and holds the 1914–15 Star, and the General Service and Victory Medals.
3, Sapley Lane, Hartford, Hunts. Z3881/A.

PRIOR, P. H. A., Gunner, Royal Horse Artillery.
Four months after volunteering in August 1914 he was drafted to France, where he saw severe fighting in various sectors. Invalided to hospital at Woolwich suffering from pleurisy, he returned to the Western Front, however, on his recovery, and was again in action in the Battle of Cambrai and in the Retreat and Advance of 1918. He was demobilised in March 1919, and holds the 1914–15 Star, and the General Service and Victory Medals.
3, Sapley Lane, Hartford, Hunts. Z3881/B.

PROCTOR, G., Private, 2nd Bedfordshire Regiment.
Already in the Army when war was declared in August 1914, he was immediately drafted to the Western Front, where he served through the Retreat from Mons. He also took part in the Battles of La Bassée, Ypres and Neuve Chapelle and many minor engagements until severely wounded in action at Festubert in May 1915. He was invalided from the Army in September 1916, and holds the Mons Star, and the General Service and Victory Medals.
41, Bunyan Road, Kempston, Bedford. X3884.

PROCTOR, R., Private, 10th Lincolnshire Regt.
He joined in May 1916, and after completing four months' training was drafted to the Western Front, where he took part in the Somme Offensive and in other important engagements in various sectors. He died gloriously on the Field of Battle near Ypres on August 26th, 1917. He was entitled to the General Service and Victory Medals.
"Whilst we remember, the sacrifice is not in vain."
Newton Longville, Bucks. Z3883/A.

PROCTOR, T. C., Sgt., Loyal North Lancashire Regt.
He volunteered in July 1915, and was retained on important duties as a drill Instructor at various stations. He was unable to obtain his transfer to a theatre of war, being over age for active service, but, nevertheless, did much useful work with his unit until May 1917, when he was invalided from the Army.
1, Bunyan Road, Kempston, Bedford. X3882.

PROCTOR, T. H., S.Q.M.S., 14th (King's) Hussars.
He was already serving in India when war broke out in August 1914, and in June of the following year was transferred to Mesopotamia. There he saw much severe fighting and took a distinguished part in the relief of Kut, the capture of Amara and Baghdad, and in many other important engagements. He holds the 1914–15 Star, and the General Service and Victory Medals, and in 1920 was still with his Squadron.
Newton Longville, Bucks. Z3883/C.

PROCTOR, W. M., Sergeant, R.F.A.
Already with his Battery in India when war was declared in August 1914, he shortly afterwards proceeded to the Western Front, where he saw much severe fighting and took a prominent part in the Battle of the Somme and many other important engagements. He fell in action near Ypres on August 13th, 1917. He was entitled to the 1914 Star, and the General Service and Victory Medals.
"The path of duty was the way to glory."
Newton Longville, Bucks. Z3883/B.

PULLEY, A., Stoker, Royal Navy.
He volunteered in August 1914, and was posted to H.M.S. "Cyclops," attached to the Devonshire Division. He was engaged chiefly on escort and patrol duties, and saw much active service in the Black and North Seas, and in many other waters. In 1920 he was still at sea on transport duties to and from Australia, and holds the 1914–15 Star, and the General Service and Victory Medals.
Sherington, Newport Pagnell, Bucks. Z3885.

PULLEY, G., Private, R.A.S.C.
He joined in April 1918, and after completing a period of training served at various stations, where he was engaged on important duties with the Remount Section. He was not successful in obtaining his transfer overseas on account of his age, but, nevertheless, rendered valuable services with his Company until May 1919, when he was demobilised.
12, Russell Street, Bedford. X3886.

PULLEY, M. (Miss), Member, V.A.D.
She joined in June 1917, and after a period of training served in the Military Hospitals at Dartford, Warley and various other stations. She was engaged on duties of great importance during the period of hostilities, and rendered very valuable services until July 1920, when she was demobilised.
46, Marlborough Road, Bedford. Z3887.

PUPLETT, J., Private, 1st Bedfordshire Regt.
He volunteered in August 1915, and on completing his training in the following year, proceeded to the Western Front, where he saw heavy fighting in various sectors. He took part in the Battles of the Somme, Arras and Passchendaele, and many minor engagements, and, wounded in action at Ypres in 1917, was sent home and invalided from the Army in the following year. He holds the General Service and Victory Medals.
43, Westbourne Road, Queen's Park, Bedford. X3888/B.

PUPLETT, W., Petty Officer, Royal Navy.
He was already in the Navy when war was declared in August 1914, and afterwards served in H.M.S. "Blanche" in the North and Mediterranean Seas. He was engaged chiefly on patrol duties and took part also in the operations at the Dardanelles and in the Battles of Heligoland Bight and Jutland. He was discharged in January 1919, and holds the 1914–15 Star, and the General Service and Victory Medals.
43, Westbourne Road, Queen's Park, Bedford. X3888/A.

PURSER, H. J., L/Cpl., R.E. & 2nd Welch Regt.
After volunteering in 1915, he underwent a period of training prior to being drafted to the Western Front in the following year, and there took part in the Battles of Passchendaele and Cambrai and many other important engagements. He fell fighting on April 25th, 1918, and was buried at Cambrai. He was entitled to the General Service and Victory Medals.
"His life for his Country, his soul to God."
18, High Street, Pavenham, near Bedford. Z3889/A.

PURSER, S. J., Pte., Beds. & Hertfordshire Regts.
Volunteering in November 1914, he proceeded to France in July of the following year, and there saw severe fighting in various sectors of the front. He took part in the Battles of Albert, the Somme, the Ancre, Arras, Cambrai and the Marne, and many other important engagements until the cessation of hostilities. He was demobilised in March 1919, and holds the 1914–15 Star, and the General Service and Victory Medals.
18, High Street, Pavenham, near Bedford. Z3889/B.

PURSER, W., Sapper, Royal Engineers.
He joined in January 1917, and in November of that year was drafted to Italy. Whilst in this theatre of war he was engaged on various important duties and took an active part in many important engagements on the Piave until the cessation of hostilities. He was demobilised on returning home in November 1919, and holds the General Service and Victory Medals. Church Street, Somersham, Hunts. Z3890.

PURYER, F., Private, 1st Bedfordshire Regiment.
Mobilised in August 1914, he was drafted to the Western Front in the following month, and was there wounded near Ypres in November of the same year. Invalided home, he proceeded to Egypt, however, in January 1916, and was thence sent into Palestine, where he was again wounded in the third Battle of Gaza. He was in hospital at Alexandria, and was afterwards attached to the Northamptonshire Regiment at Port Said until his return home for discharge in March 1919. He holds the 1914 Star, and the General Service and Victory Medals.
28, Mill Street, Newport Pagnell, Bucks. Z3891/A.

PURYER, G., Private, R.M.L.I.
Already in the Navy at the outbreak of war in August 1914, he served in H.M.S. "Zealandia" with the Portsmouth Division, attached to the Grand Fleet in the North Sea. Afterwards transferred to H.M.S. "Privet," he was engaged in escorting transports to and from France and Egypt until after the cessation of hostilities. He holds the 1914–15 Star, and the General Service and Victory Medals, and in 1920 was still serving in H.M.S. "Colombo" in Chinese waters.
28, Mill Street, Newport Pagnell, Bucks. Z3891/B.

PUTMAN, H., Private, Bedfordshire Regiment.
He joined in 1916, and in May of the following year was drafted to the Western Front, where he fought in the Battles of Arras, Bullecourt, Messines and Ypres, and many minor engagements. He was reported missing, and is believed to have been killed in action, in September 1917. He holds the General Service and Victory Medals.
"Thinking that remembrance, though unspoken, may reach him where he sleeps."
103, Church End, Haynes, near Bedford. Z2763/A.

Q

QUARRY, H. G., Sapper, Royal Engineers.
Having enlisted in February 1914, he was already in the Army when war was declared in the following August, and was retained on important duties in England until 1918, being under age for active service. He then proceeded, however, to the Western Front, where he was engaged on bridge building and other duties in the Ypres, Somme and Cambrai sectors. Discharged in April 1919, he holds the General Service and Victory Medals.
44, Dunville Road, Queen's Park, Bedford. Z3892.

R

RADCLIFFE, W. G., A.B., Royal Navy.
He joined in 1916, and was posted to H.M.S. "Renown," with which ship he was engaged on important patrol and escort duties in the North Sea and Baltic. After the cessation of hostilities, he accompanied the Prince of Wales on his world tour, and in 1920 was still serving. He holds the General Service and Victory Medals. 8, Foster Street, Bedford. X3893.

RADFORD, J. S., Rifleman, K.R.R.C.
Joining in 1917, he completed a period of training and was later sent to France. During his service on the Western Front, he was in action during the heavy fighting at St. Quentin. He made the supreme sacrifice, being killed on March 21st, 1918, and was entitled to the General Service and Victory Medals.
"And doubtless he went in splendid company."
Chestnut House, King's Road, St. Ives, Hunts. Z3894.

RAINBOW, A. J., Pte., 5th Oxford. & Bucks. L.I.
He volunteered in September 1914, and three months later was drafted to France. There he played a prominent part in the Battles of Neuve Chapelle and Ypres (II.), and was wounded in action at Givenchy in August 1915. As a result he was invalided home and sent to hospital in Norwich. Returning to France in February 1916, he was in action in various sectors of the Somme front, and was unfortunately killed at Delville Wood on August 24th, 1916. He was entitled to the 1914–15 Star, and the General Service and Victory Medals.
"A costly sacrifice upon the altar of freedom."
The Wheatsheaf, Maids Moreton, Bucks. Z4493/D.

RAINBOW, F., Shoeing-Smith, R. Bucks. Hussars.
Mobilised at the outbreak of hostilities in August 1914, he was shortly afterwards sent to Egypt, and there served with his unit near the Suez Canal. He rendered excellent service as a shoeing-smith until he was admitted to hospital suffering from dysentery, from the effects of which he unhappily died on May 4th, 1915. He was entitled to the 1914–15 Star, and the General Service and Victory Medals.
"His memory is cherished with pride."
The Wheatsheaf, Maids Moreton, Bucks. Z4493/C.

RAINBOW, F. G., Private, 2nd Queen's Own (Royal West Kent Regiment).
Volunteering in August 1914, he completed a period of training, but was later discharged. In August 1915 he re-enlisted in the Oxfordshire and Buckinghamshire Light Infantry, and proceeded to India, where he saw service for a short time. Later he was sent to Mesopotamia, and took part in many important engagements, including those of Kut, and Baghdad. He was afterwards transferred to the Royal West Kent Regiment and returned to India, where he served until returning home for demobilisation in October 1919. He holds the General Service and Victory Medals.
30, Abbey Road, Old Bradwell, Bucks. Z3895.

RAINBOW, J., Private, 1/20th London Regiment.
Joining in September 1917, he completed his training early in the following year, and proceeded to France, where he did consistently good work attached to the Royal West Kent Regiment. He served in many important engagements in various sectors of the front, and was wounded on the Somme in September 1918. As a result he was invalided to England, and after a period of hospital treatment was discharged as medically unfit for further service in May 1919. He holds the General Service and Victory Medals.
High Street, Great Linford, Bucks. Z3897.

RAINBOW, J. G., Sapper, Royal Engineers.
He was called up from the Reserve at the declaration of war in August 1914, and on conclusion of his training proceeded to the Dardanelles, where he took part in the Landing at Suvla Bay and other important engagements until the Evacuation of the Peninsula. He was then invalided home, and after a period of hospital treatment was finally discharged as medically unfit for further service in April 1917. He holds the 1914–15 Star, and the General Service and Victory Medals.
34, Stafford Road, Bedford. Z3896.

RAINBOW, W. G., Gunner, R.G.A.
He joined in April 1917, and after a period of training at Woolwich and Winchester was sent in the same year to France. In this theatre of war he served with his Battery on the Arras, Ypres, Somme and Amiens front, and did good work. After the Armistice he proceeded to Germany and was stationed with the Army of Occupation in Cologne until March 1919, when he was demobilised, holding the General Service and Victory Medals. The Wheatsheaf, Maids Moreton, Bucks. Z4493/A.

RALPH, A. E., B.S.M., Royal Field Artillery.
Already in the Army at the outbreak of war in August 1914, he was retained on important duties at home until February 1917, when he proceeded to France. During his service on the Western Front he served with distinction in many important engagements, including the Battle of Arras. In August 1917 he was transferred to Egypt, but later advanced into Palestine. He played a prominent part in the Battles of Gaza and the capture of Jerusalem. He holds the General Service and Victory Medals, and the Long Service and Good Conduct Medal.
31, Bower Street, Bedford. TZ3898.

RANDALL, B. J., Guardsman, Grenadier Guards.
He volunteered in September 1914, and, after completing a period of training, was retained on important duties with his unit at various stations. Later, in 1916, he was invalided to hospital suffering from pneumonia, and was eventually discharged as medically unfit for further service. He afterwards volunteered for work of National importance, and was engaged on the output of munitions at Coventry, where he rendered valuable services.
Little Brickhill, Bletchley, Bucks. Z3900.

RANDALL, H., Private, 3rd Bedfordshire Regt.
After volunteering in August 1915 he underwent a period of training and proceeded to France. In the course of his service in this theatre of war he took part in the heavy fighting at the Battles of Loos and the Somme. Later in 1916 he was invalided to England, and, after a long period of hospital treatment, was finally discharged as medically unfit for further service in March 1918. He holds the 1914–15 Star, and the General Service and Victory Medals.
Station Road, Tempsford, near Sandy, Beds. Z3899.

RANDALL, W. T., Air Mechanic, R.A.F.
In spite of the fact that he was medically unfit, having been previously rejected three times, he succeeded in joining the Royal Air Force in February 1918, and, after a period of training, was retained on important duties as a fitter, and served at various stations. He rendered valuable services in this capacity until demobilised in March 1919.
Shopyard, Great Linford, Bucks. Z3901.

RAPLEY, J. S., Corporal, Royal Air Force.
Volunteering in September 1915, he completed a period of training with the Royal Naval Air Service, but was later transferred to the Royal Air Force and drafted to France. He served with his Squadron at Dunkirk, and did consistently good work throughout the period of hostilities. In February 1919 he was demobilised, and holds the General Service and Victory Medals.
26, Great Northern Street, Huntingdon. Z3902.

RATCLIFFE, A., Private, 2nd Bedfordshire Regt.
Already in the Army at the outbreak of war, he was immediately drafted to France, and was wounded in action during the Retreat from Mons. He also took part in the Battles of Ypres, Hill 60 and Albert, and other engagements of importance in various sectors. He received his discharge in November 1918, and holds the Mons Star, and the General Service and Victory Medals.
7, Brace Street, Bedford. X3905.

RATCLIFFE, A. J., Signalman, Royal Navy.
He volunteered in November 1914, and later proceeded to sea on board H.M.S. "York," in which ship he saw much service throughout the period of hostilities. He was chiefly engaged on important submarine patrol duties with the Grand Fleet in the North Sea. He was demobilised in March 1919, and holds the General Service and Victory Medals.
Bell End, Brampton, Hunts. Z3903.

RATCLIFFE, C., Private, Royal Naval Division.
He volunteered in June 1915, and, on conclusion of his training in the following year, proceeded to France. During his service in this theatre of war he was in action on the Somme and later at the Battles of Arras and Ypres. In 1917 he was invalided home suffering from trench-fever, but, after a period of treatment, returned to France. Later he took part in the Advance at Cambrai, where he was wounded and sent home. As a result he was discharged as medically unfit for further service in February 1919, and holds the General Service and Victory Medals. Cross Hall Ford, St. Neots, Hunts. Z3904.

RATCLIFFE, T., Private, Oxford. & Bucks. L.I.
In spite of the fact that he was medically unfit for service overseas, he joined in July 1918, and was retained on important duties with his unit at various stations. He did excellent work and rendered valuable services until demobilised in February 1919.
12, Park Road, Stony Stratford, Bucks. Z3906.

RAWLINGS, A. G., Private, Bedfordshire Regt.
After volunteering in December 1915 he completed his training and later proceeded to France. In the course of his service on the Western Front he was in action during the heavy fighting at the Battles of Messines, Ypres, the Somme and the Marne (II.). After the cessation of hostilities he went to Germany with the Army of Occupation, and was stationed at Cologne. He was demobilised in February 1919, holding the General Service and Victory Medals.
West End, Earith, Hunts. Z3910/A.

RAWLINGS, C. W., Driver, R.A.S.C. (M.T.)
Joining in May 1916, he underwent a period of training, but was later found to be medically unfit for service overseas. He was therefore retained on important transport duties and served at various stations, where he did consistently good work until demobilised in September 1919.
Earith, Hunts. Z3911.

RAWLINGS, H. W., Private, Norfolk Regiment.
He joined in June 1918, and was quickly drafted to the Western Front, where he took part in many important engagements throughout the concluding stages of hostilities, particularly on the Somme, the Marne and at Havrincourt. After the close of war he went to Germany with the Army of Occupation, and served at Cologne. He was demobilised on his return home in March 1920, and holds the General Service and Victory Medals. West End, Earith, Hunts. Z3910/B.

RAWLINGS, J., Private, 9th Northants. Regt.
Joining in 1916, he underwent a period of training, and in the following year was drafted to France. During his service in this theatre of war he took part in the heavy fighting at Messines Ridge, Passchendaele and Cambrai. Later in 1918 he was taken prisoner, and suffered many hardships during his period of captivity. On his release after the Armistice he returned home and was finally demobilised in February 1919, holding the General Service and Victory Medals.
Earith, Hunts. Z3909.

RAWLINGS, O. G., Private, 4th Bedfordshire Regt.
Volunteering in November 1915, he completed his training early in the following year and proceeded to the Western Front. In the course of his service in this theatre of war he was in action on the Somme and at the Battle of Vimy Ridge. He was unfortunately killed on April 23rd, 1917, and was entitled to the General Service and Victory Medals.
"A valiant Soldier, with undaunted heart he breasted life's last hill."
Church End, Earith, Hunts. Z3910/C.

RAWLINS, C. J., Private, Norfolk Regiment.
Having joined in March 1918, he was retained on important duties at various stations. Later he was transferred to Ireland, where he was engaged on important guard and other duties. He was not successful in obtaining his transfer to a theatre of war, but, nevertheless, rendered valuable services until demobilised in October 1919.
11, Cople, Bedford. Z3907.

RAWLINS, L. J., Corporal, 1st Norfolk Regiment.
Already in the Army at the outbreak of war in August 1914, he was immediately drafted to the Western Front, where he served with distinction during the Retreat from Mons, and also at the Battles of the Marne, the Aisne, Loos, Festubert and the Somme. He was wounded eight times, and finally sent home and discharged in July 1917. He holds the Mons Star, and the General Service and Victory Medals.
3, Bell Court, Bedford. X3908.

RAY, F., Seaman, Royal Navy.
Joining in May 1918, he was later posted to H.M.S. "Victory," in which vessel he saw much service. He was chiefly engaged on important mine-sweeping duties with the Grand Fleet in the North Sea, and rendered excellent services until discharged in June 1919. He holds the General Service and Victory Medals.
26, Chandos Street, Bedford. X3912/B.

RAY, H., Corporal, Suffolk Regiment.
Volunteering in September 1914, he completed a period of training and was drafted to France. Whilst on the Western Front he took an active part in many important engagements. He fought at the Battles of Loos, Albert, the Somme and the Marne (II.), where he was unfortunately killed in action on July 17th, 1918. He was entitled to the 1914–15 Star, and the General Service and Victory Medals.
"His life for his Country."
9, Church Road, Willington, Bedford. Z3913.

RAY, R., Private, Royal Fusiliers.
After volunteering in October 1915 he underwent a period of training, and later in 1916 proceeded overseas. During his service on the Western Front he was in action on the Somme, where he was wounded. On his recovery he took part in other important engagements, including the heavy fighting at Ypres. He made the supreme sacrifice, being killed in action on August 13th, 1917, and was entitled to the General Service and Victory Medals.
"The path of duty was the way to glory."
26, Chandos Street, Bedford. X3912/A.

RAYSON, D., Private, 1st Northamptonshire Regt.
He volunteered in November 1914, and was immediately drafted to France, where he saw much heavy fighting in various sectors of the front. He took part in the Battles of Givenchy, Festubert and Loos, but was wounded and invalided to hospital in England. Returning to France on his recovery, he saw further service, and was again wounded in action. As a result he was sent home and finally discharged as medically unfit for further service in April 1916. He holds the 1914 Star, and the General Service and Victory Medals.
Pury End, Pauler's Pury, Towcester, Northants. Z3914.

RAYSON, W. T., Private, Machine Gun Corps.
He volunteered in March 1915 in the Northamptonshire Regiment, but, after a period of training, was transferred to the Machine Gun Corps and drafted to France. Whilst in this theatre of war he served in the Somme sector, and was wounded and invalided to hospital. On his recovery in January 1918 he returned to France and took part in the closing operations of the war. He was demobilised in May 1919, and holds the 1914–15 Star, and the General Service and Victory Medals.
Pury End, Pauler's Pury, Towcester, Northants. Z3915/A.

READ, A., Private, Bedfordshire Regiment.
He volunteered in December 1915, and in the following year proceeded overseas. Whilst serving on the Western Front he took part in fierce fighting at Vimy Ridge, but was unfortunately killed in action in the Battle of the Somme on August 9th, 1916. He was entitled to the General Service and Victory Medals.
"A valiant Soldier, with undaunted heart he breasted life's last hill."
Barham, Hunts. Z3920/B.

READ, F. C., Guardsman, 4th Grenadier Guards.
He volunteered in November 1915, and, on conclusion of his training in the following year, proceeded to the Western Front, where he took part in heavy fighting in various sectors. He saw service on the Somme and at the Battles of Arras, Ypres and Cambrai, and was in action during the Retreat and Advance of 1918. He was wounded in 1916. After the close of hostilities he returned home and was demobilised in March 1919, holding the General Service and Victory Medals.
51, Tavistock Street, Fenny Stratford, Bucks. Z3919.

READ, J., Corporal, Oxford. and Bucks. L.I.
Mobilised at the outbreak of war in August 1914, he completed a period of training and proceeded to France. Whilst on the Western Front he served during the heavy fighting at the Battles of Loos, the Somme and Ypres. Later in 1917 he was transferred to Italy, where he took part in the engagements on the Piave front and did excellent work throughout the period of hostilities. He was discharged in March 1919, and holds the 1914–15 Star, and the General Service and Victory Medals.
15, Agusta Road, Stony Stratford. Z3916.

READ, R. G., Sergeant, Military Mounted Police.
He volunteered in November 1915, and three months later proceeded to Salonika, where he served with distinction on the Vardar front. Later he was stationed at Mudros and Alexandria, and was engaged on important police duties. He was eventually demobilised in August 1919, and holds the General Service and Victory Medals.
7, Spring Gardens, Newport Pagnell, Bucks. Z3918.

READ, W. H., Private, East Surrey and Queen's Own (Royal West Surrey) Regiments.
He joined in May 1916, and later in the same year was drafted to the Western Front. There he took an active part in the Battles of the Somme, Ypres and Cambrai, but was severely wounded in action. He was admitted into hospital, and unfortunately succumbed to his injuries on November 13th, 1917. He was entitled to the General Service and Victory Medals.
"A costly sacrifice upon the altar of freedom."
Barham, Hunts. Z3920/A.

READ, W. H., Corporal, Bedfordshire Regiment.
After volunteering in October 1914 in the Huntingdonshire Cyclist Battalion he was later transferred to the Bedfordshire Regiment, and proceeded to France, where he took part in the heavy fighting in the Somme and Arras sectors. In 1917 he was sent to Italy, and was present at the important engagements on the Piave front. Returning to the Western Front, he was in action at the Battles of Bapaume and Cambrai. He was unfortunately killed on September 27th, 1918, and was entitled to the General Service and Victory Medals.
"And doubtless he went in splendid company."
3, St. Germain Street, Huntingdon. Z3917.

READING, A., Pte., 1st Northamptonshire Regt.
He volunteered in May 1915, and, on conclusion of his training, was drafted to France. During his service in this seat of war he was present during the engagements on the Somme, at the Battles of Arras, Ypres and Cambrai, and later in the Retreat and Advance of 1918. After the cessation of hostilities he proceeded with the Army of Occupation into Germany. On his return to England he was demobilised in March 1919, and holds the 1914–15 Star, and the General Service and Victory Medals. Toll Gate House, Great Linford, Bucks. Z3921.

REDFERN, H. J., Corporal, Royal Engineers.
Mobilised in August 1914, he was shortly afterwards drafted to the Western Front, where, after taking part in the Battle of La Bassée, he was wounded at Ypres in October 1914. In 1916 he proceeded to Egypt, and thence into Palestine, where he was again in action in the Battles of Gaza, at the fall of Jaffa and Jerusalem, and on the River Jordan. He was discharged in April 1919, and holds the 1914 Star, and the General Service and Victory Medals.
9, Hartington Street, Bedford. X2789/A.

REDINGTON, L. J., Pte., 7th Bedfordshire Regt.
After volunteering in June 1915 he underwent a period of training prior to being drafted to the Western Front in January 1918. After much severe fighting in this theatre of war he was taken prisoner at Cambrai in the Retreat of March 1918, and was held in captivity until after the cessation of hostilities. He was demobilised in April 1919, and holds the General Service and Victory Medals.
1, Tower Gardens, Bedford. X3922.

REDMAN, A. J., Driver, Royal Engineers.
Volunteering in September 1914, he was drafted to Egypt in February of the following year, and was there engaged as a transport driver at various stations. Proceeding into Palestine, he took an active part in the Battles of Gaza, and was also present at the entry into Jaffa and Jerusalem. Returning home in 1919, he was demobilised in June of that year, and holds the General Service and Victory Medals.
58, Russell Street, Bedford. X3927/A.

REDMAN, H. J., Private, Royal Sussex Regiment.
He joined in March 1918, and, after a short period of training, was drafted to the Western Front, where he saw much severe fighting. He took part in the Battles of the Somme, Cambrai and Ypres and many other important engagements until the cessation of hostilities, and was then sent with the Army of Occupation into Germany. Demobilised on his return home in October 1919, he holds the General Service and Victory Medals. 40, Pembroke Street, Bedford. Z3923/A.

REDMAN, J., Private, 1st Royal Sussex Regiment.
Shortly after volunteering in 1915 he was sent to the Western Front, where he saw heavy fighting in various sectors. He took part in the Battles of Neuve Chapelle, Hill 60, Loos, Albert and Vimy Ridge and many other engagements until 1917, when he was transferred to India. There he was engaged on garrison duties until his return home for demobilisation in November 1919, holding the 1914–15 Star, and the General Service and Victory Medals.
Potter's Cross, Wootton, Bedford. Z3924.

REDMAN, L. W., Sapper, Royal Engineers.
He joined in 1916, and, after completing a term of training, was retained at various stations, where he was engaged on duties of great importance. Being medically unfit for active service, he was unable to obtain his transfer to the front, but, nevertheless, did much useful work with his Company until his demobilisation in 1919. Marston, near Bedford. Z3925.

REDMAN, P. G., Corporal, Royal Engineers.
A month after the outbreak of war in August 1914 he volunteered, and a year later proceeded overseas. He served in Egypt for a short period, and was then drafted to Palestine, where he took an active part in important engagements at Gaza, Jerusalem and Jaffa. He remained in the East until June 1919, and, on his return to England, was demobilised in July of that year, holding the 1914–15 Star, and the General Service and Victory Medals.
22, Great Butts Street, Bedford. X3929/B—Z3928.

REDMAN, W., Private, Royal Sussex Regiment.
He joined in July 1918, but on account of his youth was unable to obtain a transfer overseas before the termination of the war. After the Armistice he was sent to Germany with the Army of Occupation, and was stationed at Cologne. He was eventually demobilised in February 1920.
58, Russell Street, Bedford. X3927/B.

REDMAN, W. H., Private, Royal Fusiliers.
Volunteering in October 1914, he was eventually drafted to Gallipoli, where he served throughout the campaign. After the Evacuation of the Peninsula he proceeded to France, and saw severe fighting at the Battles of Albert, Arras, Ypres and Cambrai, and was wounded in action. Demobilised in February 1919, he holds the 1914–15 Star, and the General Service and Victory Medals.
23, Pembroke Street, Bedford. Z3923/B.

REED, A. E., Guardsman, 4th Grenadier Guards.
Volunteering in November 1914, he was trained at Caterham and Chelsea, and was sent overseas in May 1915. Whilst on the Western Front he was in action in numerous engagements, including the Battle of Ypres, and was severely wounded at Passchendaele. He was admitted into hospital at Boulogne, and unfortunately succumbed to his injuries on August 9th, 1917. He was entitled to the 1914–15 Star, and the General Service and Victory Medals.
"Whilst we remember, the sacrifice is not in vain."
Green's Norton, Towcester, Hunts. Z3025/B.

REED, C. S., Driver, Royal Engineers.
He volunteered in February 1915, and nine months later was drafted to France. After two weeks' service on that front he was transferred to Salonika, where he served for three years. During that time he took an active part in numerous important engagements, and was invalided home in November 1918, suffering from malaria. On his discharge from hospital in February 1919 he was demobilised, and holds the 1914–15 Star, and the General Service and Victory Medals.
Papworth St. Agnes, Cambs. Z3930/B.

REED, H. E., Pte., Q.O. (Royal West Kent Regt.)
He joined in 1916, and in September of that year embarked for France. In that theatre of war he was engaged in severe fighting in various sectors, and was wounded in action at Vimy Ridge and Messines. On his recovery in 1917 he was transferred to Italy, where he took part in engagements on the Piave and Asiago Plateaux. In 1918 he returned to the Western Front, and was again wounded at Albert. He was demobilised in January 1919, and holds the General Service and Victory Medals.
Montague Street, Eynesbury, St. Neots, Hunts. Z3932/B.

REED, J. H., L/Corporal, Hunts. Cyclist Battalion and Bedfordshire Regiment.
He volunteered in January 1915, and, on completion of his training, was drafted to the Western Front, where he saw heavy fighting in various sectors. He was wounded in action in 1916 and sent back to England, and admitted to hospital in Bristol. On his recovery he was engaged on important agricultural work at Hemingford until demobilised in March 1919, holding the General Service and Victory Medals.
Papworth St. Agnes, Cambs. Z3930/A.

REED, T. C., Private, Bedfordshire Regiment.
Volunteering in 1914, he trained at Ampthill, and in June of the following year proceeded to the Western Front. After taking part in numerous important engagements he was severely wounded in action at Loos. He was invalided to Scotland, and, after protracted hospital treatment at Aberdeen, was discharged as medically unfit for further service in 1919. He holds the 1914–15 Star, and the General Service and Victory Medals. Yelling, St. Neots, Hunts. Z3931.

REEDMAN, A. B., Trumpeter, R.F.A.
Volunteering in 1914, he was engaged on important duties with his unit at Bulford until March 1917, when he obtained a transfer to Egypt. He was subsequently drafted to Palestine, where he took part in operations at Gaza, Jerusalem and Haifa. He was demobilised on his return to England in August 1919, and holds the General Service and Victory Medals.
West End, Brampton, Hunts. Z3933.

REEDMAN, O. V., Private, Hunts. Cyclist Battalion. and 24th London Regiment (The Queen's).
When war broke out in August 1914 he volunteered, and, on completion of his training, was drafted overseas in July 1916. Whilst in France he was engaged in fierce fighting in the Battle of the Somme, but was unhappily killed in action on that front on October 8th, 1916. He was entitled to the General Service and Victory Medals.
"His life for his Country, his soul to God."
Little Stukeley, Hunts. Z3934.

REEVE, F. J., Private, R.A.S.C. (M.T.)
He joined in February 1918, but owing to his youth was not successful in his efforts to obtain a transfer overseas. He served at Grove Park, Bulford Camp and Andover, at which stations he was employed in the workshops as a fitter, and carried out his duties with the greatest efficiency. He was demobilised in February 1919.
Green's Norton, Towcester, Northants. Z3935/A.

REEVE, H., Tpr., Northants. Yeomanry; & Spr. R.E.
At the outbreak of hostilities he was already serving, and was ordered to France in August 1914. He saw heavy fighting in the Battles of Ypres and Neuve Chapelle, and, on being transferred to the Royal Engineers, rendered valuable services as fireman on the troop-trains. Whilst taking part in the operations at Cambrai in November 1918 he was wounded and sent to hospital in England. He was discharged in December 1918, and holds the 1914 Star, and the General Service and Victory Medals.
Green's Norton, Towcester, Northants. Z3935/C.

REEVE, J., Rifleman, King's Royal Rifle Corps.
He volunteered in September 1914, and eight months later proceeded to France, where he took part in numerous engagements, chiefly in the Ypres, the Somme and Cambrai sectors. Whilst engaged in severe fighting at Epéhy he was wounded, and in consequence was invalided out of the Army in September 1918, holding the 1914–15 Star, and the General Service and Victory Medals. He was mentioned in Despatches for bravery in attending to the wounded under heavy shell-fire at Arras. Green's Norton, Towcester. Z3935/D.

REEVE, T. A., Private, East Surrey Regiment.
Volunteering in September 1914, he was trained at Devonport, and in February 1915 embarked for France. On that front he saw severe fighting in the Ypres sector, and was wounded at the Battle of Hill 60 in April 1915. He was admitted to hospital in Le Havre, and unfortunately succumbed to his injuries in the following month. He was entitled to the 1914–15 Star, and the General Service and Victory Medals.
"Great deeds cannot die."
Green's Norton, Towcester. Z3935/B.

REEVES, G., A.B., R.N., H.M.S. "Falcon."
At the outbreak of hostilities in August 1914 he was already in the Navy, and took part in the Battles of Heligoland Bight, the Falkland Islands and Jutland. He was present during the bombardment of Zeebrugge, and was also engaged on important patrol duties in the North Sea. During the fighting at Heligoland in 1914 he was wounded, and was discharged in April 1919, holding the 1914–15 Star, and the General Service and Victory Medals.
Little Brickhill, near Bletchley, Bucks. Z3937.

REID, A. C., Trooper, Bedfordshire Lancers.
He joined in January 1916, and in the following year was drafted to the Western Front, where he took part in the Battles of Arras, Vimy Ridge and Ypres. He was wounded and gassed at Cambrai in April 1918, and, after the close of hostilities, was sent with the Army of Occupation to Germany, serving there until demobilised in October 1919. He holds the General Service and Victory Medals.
White Horse Lane, Blunham, Beds. Z3940/A.

REID, H., Gunner, Royal Field Artillery.
Joining in April 1916, he proceeded eleven months later to Salonika, where he served for two years. During that time he was in action in numerous important engagements, and experienced fierce fighting on the Doiran, the Struma and the Vardar fronts. He was invalided home with malaria in March 1919, and was discharged the same month, holding the General Service and Victory Medals.
Park Lane, Blunham, Beds. Z3940/C.

REID, H. A., Sergeant, Royal Engineers.
He volunteered in 1915, and, on crossing to France, played a conspicuous part in the Battles of Festubert, Loos, the Somme, Arras, Ypres and Cambrai. In 1917 he was transferred to Palestine, where he did excellent work with his Company in engagements at Gaza, Jaffa and Haifa, and was wounded on one occasion. He returned to England in 1919, when he signed on for a further period of service, and holds the 1914–15 Star, and the General Service and Victory Medals.
St. Germain Street, Huntingdon. Z3939/C.

REID, H. A. (jun.), Spr., Royal Marine Engineers.
He joined in February 1918, but owing to ill-health was not successful in his efforts to obtain a transfer to a theatre of war. However, he was retained on home defence, and served at Southwick, at which station he did excellent work. He was eventually demobilised in September 1919.
St. Germain Street, Huntingdon. Z3939/A.

REID, J. H., Private, Middlesex Regiment.
A month after the outbreak of war in August 1914 he volunteered, and in the following November was sent to the Western Front, where he served in various sectors. He was engaged in severe fighting at the Battles of the Somme, the Marne, Amiens and Le Cateau, and, on his return to England, was demobilised in April 1919, holding the 1914–15 Star, and the General Service and Victory Medals.
St. Germain Street, Huntingdon. Z3939/B.

REID, J., Private, 2nd Bedfordshire Regiment.
When war broke out he was serving in South Africa, but was immediately recalled and drafted to the Front. There he was engaged in fierce fighting at Antwerp, and was severely wounded in action in the Battle of Ypres in November 1914. He was invalided to England and consequently discharged as medically unfit for further military duties in 1915. He holds the 1914 Star, and the General Service and Victory Medals.
19, Old Ford End, Bedford. Z3938.

REID, W. (M.M.), Sapper, Royal Engineers.
He volunteered in 1915, and in September of that year was drafted overseas. Whilst serving on the Western Front he fought with distinction in the Battles of Loos, Albert, the Somme, Vimy Ridge, Ypres and Cambrai, and was gassed. He was awarded the Military Medal for conspicuous gallantry on the Somme in 1918, and was eventually demobilised in March 1919. He also holds the 1914–15 Star, and the General Service and Victory Medals.
23, York Street, Bedford. Z3941

REID, W. G., Corporal, Royal Field Artillery and Military Mounted Police.
He volunteered in the Royal Field Artillery in March 1915 and later in the same year embarked for France. On that front he saw heavy fighting in the Battles of Festubert, Loos and Ypres, and was gassed during operations on the Somme in 1916. On his recovery he was transferred to the Mounted Military Police, and performed excellent work until demobilised in August 1919, holding the 1914–15 Star, and the General Service and Victory Medals.
White Horse Lane, Blunham, Beds. Z3940/B

REVELL, W., Private, Royal Fusiliers.
Joining in April 1916, he was engaged on important duties at Dover until March 1917, when he was ordered to the Western Front. There he fought in engagements in the Vimy Ridge sector until May 3rd, 1917, when he was reported missing, but it was afterwards presumed that he was killed at Arras on that date. He was entitled to the General Service and Victory Medals.
"The path of duty was the way to glory."
Yelling, St. Neots, Hunts. Z1887/A.

REVELS, H., Corporal, Oxford. and Bucks. L.I.
He volunteered in August 1914, and in March of the following year was drafted to France, where he took an active part in the Battles of Ypres, Loos and Vimy Ridge. Whilst engaged in fierce fighting on the Somme in July 1916 he was severely wounded, and in consequence was discharged as medically unfit for further military service in March 1917. He holds the 1914–15 Star, and the General Service and Victory Medals.
4, Hunter Street, Buckingham. Z3942/A.

REYNOLDS, A., Corporal, R.A.S.C. (M.T.)
Shortly after volunteering in April 1915 he proceeded to France, where he was engaged on transport duties in various sectors of the front. He was present at the Battles of Arras, Ypres, Cambrai and the Somme and many other engagements until the cessation of hostilities, and was then sent with the Army of Occupation to Germany, where he was stationed at Cologne and Bonn. Demobilised on his return home in August 1919, he holds the 1914–15 Star, and the General Service and Victory Medals. Wistow, Hunts. Z3943.

REYNOLDS, F. W., Private, Royal Fusiliers and Labour Corps.
He volunteered in May 1915, and, on completing a period of training later in the same year, proceeded to the Western Front. There he was engaged on important duties with the Labour Corps at Dunkirk, Nieuport and various other stations, and did much useful work. He was invalided from the Army in June 1917, and holds the 1914–15 Star, and the General Service and Victory Medals.
Bridge Cottage, Brampton, Hunts. Z3945.

REYNOLDS, G. A., Sapper, Royal Engineers.
Volunteering in September 1914, he was drafted to the Western Front six months later, and there saw severe fighting in various sectors. He took part in the Battles of the Somme, Arras, Vimy Ridge, Messines and Ypres, and many minor engagements, and was for a considerable period in hospital in France. Invalided from the Army in January 1919, he holds the 1914–15 Star, and the General Service and Victory Medals.
22, Mabel Road, Bedford. TZ3947.

REYNOLDS, H. J., Private, Huntingdonshire Cyclist Battalion and Bedfordshire Regiment.
He volunteered in November 1915, and in the following year was sent to the Western Front. Whilst in this theatre of war he took part in many important engagements, including the Battles of the Somme, Arras and Bapaume, was wounded at Ypres and gassed near Wytschaete, sustained a fractured leg at Albert, and was in hospital at Amiens, suffering from rheumatic fever. He was finally demobilised in January 1919, and holds the General Service and Victory Medals.
5, Oxford Road, St. Ives, Hunts. Z3948.

REYNOLDS, J., Private, Bedfordshire Regiment.
He volunteered in April 1915, and in January 1916 proceeded to the Western Front, where he saw much heavy fighting. After taking part in engagements in the Ypres sector he was severely wounded in action in October 1916, during the Somme Offensive, and was admitted to hospital at Netley, and later at Epsom. He was invalided from the Army in May 1917, and holds the General Service and Victory Medals.
1, Cumberland Place, St. Ives, Hunts. TZ3944.

REYNOLDS, P., Sapper, Royal Engineers (R.O.D.)
Volunteering in July 1915, he was drafted to the Western Front in the following month, and was there engaged on important duties in the railway workshops. He served at various stations whilst in this theatre of war, and did much useful work with his Company until his return home for demobilisation in September 1919. He holds the 1914–15 Star, and the General Service and Victory Medals.
6, Coronation Road, Stony Stratford, Bucks. Z3713/B.

REYNOLDS, P., Private, 1st East Surrey Regt.
Shortly after joining in June 1916 he proceeded to the Western Front, where he saw severe fighting in various sectors. He took part in many important engagements in this theatre of war until taken prisoner in May 1917, and held in captivity at Friedrichsfeld until after the signing of the Armistice. He was demobilised in June 1919, and holds the General Service and Victory Medals. Eaton Ford, Beds. Z2120/B.

REYNOLDS, W. D., Gunner, R.F.A.
He joined in April 1916, and, after a period of training, was drafted in the following year to the Western Front. There he took part in important engagements in various sectors, including the Battle of Arras, and was twice wounded in action—at Ypres and on the Somme. Invalided home, he was in hospital at Ripon for a time, and was finally demobilised in February 1919, holding the General Service and Victory Medals. West Street, St. Ives, Hunts. Z3946.

REYNOLDS, W. G., L/Corporal, Essex Regiment and Middlesex Regiment.
After volunteering in April 1915 he underwent a period of training before proceeding to the Western Front in the following November, and there saw much heavy fighting at Festubert and in various other sectors. He was reported missing, and is believed to have been killed in action at Arras in April 1916. He was entitled to the 1914–15 Star, and the General Service and Victory Medals.
"His life for his Country, his soul to God."
Eaton Socon, Beds. Z3949.

RHODES, H., Private, 2nd Bedfordshire Regiment.
Mobilised in August 1914, he was immediately drafted to the Western Front, where he took part in the fighting at Mons. He also served through the Battles of Ypres, Givenchy, Neuve Chapelle, Hill 60, the Somme, Arras, Vimy Ridge, Cambrai and Lille and many minor engagements, and was wounded at Loos in September 1915. He was discharged in March 1919, and holds the Mons Star, and the General Service and Victory Medals. 7, Eastville Road, Bedford. Z3950.

RICHARDS, T., Private, 7th Bedfordshire Regt.
He volunteered in April 1915, and in January of the following year proceeded to the Western Front, where he took part in the Battles of the Somme, Ypres and Cambrai and many other important engagements. He was unhappily reported wounded and missing, and later, killed in action at St. Quentin on March 23rd, 1918. He was entitled to the General Service and Victory Medals.
"Great deeds cannot die."
5, Tower Court, Bedford. X3952/A.

RICHARDS, W., Private, 3rd Bedfordshire Regt.
He volunteered in March 1915, and, after completing a short period of training, was retained at various stations, where he was engaged on duties of great importance. He was unable, owing to ill-health, to obtain his transfer to the front, and in September 1915 was discharged as medically unfit for further service. 5, Tower Court, Bedford. X3952/B.

RICHARDSON, A., Gdsmn., Gds. Machine Gun Regt.
After volunteering in May 1915 he underwent a period of training prior to being drafted to the Western Front in June of the following year. There he saw severe fighting in various sectors, took part in the Battles of the Somme, Arras, Ypres and Cambrai, and other engagements, and served also through the Retreat and Advance of 1918. Demobilised in February 1919, he holds the General Service and Victory Medals.
Ravenstone, Olney, Bucks. Z3953/A.

RICHARDSON, A. J., Bombardier, R.F.A.
He joined the Army in July 1914, and, when war broke out in the following month, was retained for a period of training before proceeding to France. There he took part in heavy fighting on the Somme, at Arras, Vimy Ridge, Ypres, Beaucourt, Albert, the Ancre, Passchendaele, and in the Retreat and Advance of 1918. After the Armistice he went to Germany with the Army of Occupation, and served there until his discharge in February 1919. He holds the General Service and Victory Medals. 9, Sandhurst Place East, Bedford. Z3966.

RICHARDSON, A. R., Corporal, 8th Beds. Regt.
Having volunteered in September 1914, he underwent a period of training before being drafted to France in the following year. He took part in the Battle of Loos, but was unfortunately killed in action at La Brique on December 20th, 1915. He was entitled to the 1914–15 Star, and the General Service and Victory Medals.
"Whilst we remember, the sacrifice is not in vain."
13, Thurlow Street, Bedford. X3954.

RICHARDSON, A. T., Private, Bedfordshire Regt.
He volunteered in June 1915, and, after a period of training, was engaged at various stations on important duties with his unit. He was unable to obtain a transfer overseas owing to his being medically unfit, but rendered valuable services until his demobilisation in August 1919.
64, St. John's Street, Kempston, Bedford. X3958.

RICHARDSON, C., Pte., 5th Bedfordshire Regt.
He volunteered in November 1914, and underwent a period of training prior to serving at various home stations on important guard duties. He was unable to obtain a transfer overseas owing to medical unfitness, but did good work until his discharge in March 1916. 11, Tower Gardens, Bedford. X3956.

RICHARDSON, E., Pte., 6th Oxford. & Bucks. L.I.
He volunteered in January 1916, and five months later was drafted to France, where he took part in much heavy fighting in the Somme sector. He suffered from trench feet, and was invalided home, but on his recovery returned to France and was taken prisoner near Cambrai on March 21st, 1918. He was held in captivity in Germany, and suffered many hardships. After the Armistice he was repatriated, and returned home for his demobilisation in September 1919. He holds the General Service and Victory Medals.
Preston Road, Cawcott, Buckingham. Z3960/A.

RICHARDSON, E. W., Private, Royal Fusiliers.
Volunteering in July 1915, he was drafted overseas in the following May, and took part in much severe fighting on the Somme before being wounded in action. In consequence he was invalided home, and on his recovery was retained on important duties at Portsmouth until his demobilisation in May 1919. He holds the General Service and Victory Medals.
38, Canning Street, Bedford. X3965.

RICHARDSON, F., Private, 1st Northants. Regt.
Having joined the Army in 1905, he was mobilised in August 1914, and immediately drafted to France. There he took part in the Retreat from Mons and the Battle of the Marne (where he was wounded) and many other engagements throughout the whole period of hostilities. He did continuously good work, and was discharged in February 1919, holding the Mons Star, and the General Service and Victory Medals.
22, Church Street, Stony Stratford, Bucks. TZ3963.

RICHARDSON, F., Private, 20th Hussars.
He joined in April 1917, and underwent a period of training in Ireland prior to his being drafted overseas. Whilst on the Western Front he took part in much fighting in the Somme sector, and also in the Retreat and Advance of 1918. He was demobilised in February 1919, and holds the General Service and Victory Medals.
Preston Road, Gawcott, Buckingham. Z3960/B.

RICHARDSON, F. W. Private, Bedfordshire Regt.
He volunteered in 1915, and trained for a time with the Huntingdonshire Cyclist Battalion before proceeding to France with the Bedfordshire Regiment. He saw much fighting in the Ypres sector, and later was drafted to Italy, where he was in action on the Piave. During his service he was transferred to the 11th West Yorkshire Regiment, and in February 1919 was demobilised, holding the General Service and Victory Medals.
St. Mary's Street, Eynesbury, St. Neots, Hunts. Z3967/A.

RICHARDSON, F. W. P., Pte., East Surrey Regt.
He joined in March 1918, and, completing his training in the following August, was drafted to France, where he took part in heavy fighting in the Amiens and Le Cateau sectors. After hostilities ceased he proceeded to Germany with the Army of Occupation, and served on the Rhine until his demobilisation in November 1919. He holds the General Service and Victory Medals.
Pear Tree House, Ravenstone, near Olney, Bucks. Z3953/B.

RICHARDSON, G. H., Private, Royal Warwickshire Regiment.
He was mobilised in August 1914, and underwent a period of training prior to his being drafted to France, where he took part in many engagements, including the Battles of the Somme, Albert, Vimy Ridge, Arras and Ypres. He acted as a stretcher-bearer, and did continuously good work, but was unfortunately reported missing, and is now believed to have been killed in action at Ypres on August 27th, 1917. He was entitled to the General Service and Victory Medals.
"The path of duty was the way to glory."
Station Road, Warboys, Hunts. Z3968/A.

RICHARDSON, H., Pte., R. Warwickshire Regt.
He joined in December 1917, and, completing his training after the cessation of hostilities, was drafted to East Prussia, and thence to the Rhine. He was attached to the Royal Army Service Corps, and served with the Mechanical Transport on important duties as a wheeler in the workshops at Cologne. In 1920 he was still in the Army.
Preston Road, Gawcott, Buckingham. Z3960/C.

RICHARDSON, H., A.B., Royal Navy.
He volunteered in August 1915, and, after a period of training, proceeded to the North Sea on board H.M.S. "Hilary." Whilst on board this vessel she was torpedoed in 1917, but fortunately he was rescued, and later commissioned to H.M. T.B.D. "Nimrod." He then went to North Russia and Iceland, and in 1920 was serving on board H.M.S. "Wallace." He holds the 1914–15 Star, and the General Service and Victory Medals.
Main Street, Gawcott, Buckingham. Z3959.

RICHARDSON, H., Sapper, Royal Engineers.
He volunteered in January 1915, and in the following July was drafted to the Dardanelles, where he saw much heavy fighting at the Landings at Cape Helles and Suvla Bay. Later he was transferred to Egypt, took part in the Advance into Palestine, and was in action at Gaza and Jaffa. He contracted fever, and unfortunately died through the effects on November 19th, 1918. He was entitled to the 1914–15 Star, and the General Service and Victory Medals.
"Thinking that remembrance, though unspoken, may reach him where he sleeps."
45, Cavendish Street, Bedford. X3957.

RICHARDSON, H. F., Private, Royal Fusiliers.
He joined in November 1917, and in the following June was drafted to the Western Front. There he took part in several engagements, including those in the Arras sector, and was wounded in action. As a result he was invalided home, and finally discharged in August 1920 as medically unfit for further service. He holds the General Service and Victory Medals.
St. Mary's Street, Eynesbury, St. Neots, Hunts. Z3967/B.

RICHARDSON, H. T., Private, 11th (Prince Albert's Own) Hussars.
He joined in February 1918, and, after a period of training, was engaged at various home stations on important duties with his unit. He was unable to obtain a transfer overseas owing to his being medically unfit, but rendered valuable services until his demobilisation in March 1919. He spent a considerable period in hospital at Aldershot, suffering from heart disease.
Moulsoe, Bucks. Z3828/C.

RICHARDSON, J. W., Pte., Lancashire Fusiliers.
Joining in January 1917, he was drafted overseas in the following April. Whilst on the Western Front he took part in many engagements, including the Battles of Arras, Vimy Ridge and Ypres, and was wounded in action. As a result he was invalided home, but on his recovery served on the land, being unfit to return to France. He was demobilised in February 1919, and holds the General Service and Victory Medals.
Station Road, Warboys, Hunts. Z3968/B.

RICHARDSON, R. C., Pte., 2/5th Beds. Regt.
He volunteered in September 1914, and underwent a period of training prior to his being engaged at various home stations on important duties. He was not successful in obtaining a transfer overseas owing to his being medically unfit, but rendered valuable services until his discharge in May 1916.
124, Grey Friars Walk, Bedford. X3955.

RICHARDSON, T. L., Pte., 1st Northants. Regt.
He joined the Army in 1909, and, when war broke out in August 1914, was immediately drafted to France. There he took part in the Battles of Mons, Le Cateau and La Bassée, where he was badly wounded in action. As a result he was invalided home and discharged in August 1915 as medically unfit for further service. He unfortunately died on November 22nd, 1919, through the effects of his wounds, and was entitled to the Mons Star, and the General Service and Victory Medals.
"Great deeds cannot die:
They with the sun and moon renew their light for ever."
152, High Street, Stony Stratford, Bucks. TZ3964.

RICHARDSON, W. J. (D.C.M.), Sergeant, 7th Wiltshire Regiment.
He volunteered in September 1914, and in the following year was drafted to France, where he served at Albert, and was then transferred to Salonika. There he took part in engagements on the Vardar, Struma and Doiran fronts. In 1917 he returned to France and played a conspicuous part in the Battles of Mormal Forest, Amiens and Le Cateau. He was awarded the Distinguished Conduct Medal for conspicuous gallantry and devotion to duty in the Field in October 1918. He was wounded in action, and later demobilised in April 1919. He also holds the 1914–15 Star, and the General Service and Victory Medals.
33, St. Giles Street, New Bradwell, Bucks. Z3961.

RICHES, A. J., Sapper, Royal Engineers.
He volunteered in August 1914, and in the following year was drafted to France. There he took part in many important engagements, including those at Festubert, Ypres, Arras and Delville Wood, and was wounded in action. As a result he was invalided home and discharged in December 1918 as medically unfit for further service. He holds the 1914–15 Star, and the General Service and Victory Medals.
12, Little Grove Place, Bedford. X3951.

RICK, W., Private, R.A.S.C. (M.T.)
He joined in March 1916, and, on completing his training later in that year, was drafted to India. There he was engaged on important garrison duties at Rawal Pindi and various other stations, and also saw active service on the North-West Frontier in 1919. Demobilised on his return home in December of that year, he holds the General Service, Victory, and India General Service Medal (with Clasp, Afghanistan, N.W. Frontier, 1919).
22, Firbank Road, Bedford. TZ3969.

RIDDY, L. C., Private, 4th Bedfordshire Regiment.
Joining in November 1916, he proceeded to the Western Front on completion of a period of training in April of the following year, and there saw severe fighting in various sectors. He took part in the Battles of Arras, Ypres, Passchendaele, Cambrai and the Somme, served also through the Retreat and Advance of 1918, and was wounded in that year. He was demobilised in March 1919, and holds the General Service and Victory Medals.
3, Cater Street, Kempston, Bedford. X3970.

RIDDY, W., Driver, R.A.S.C. (M.T.)
He volunteered in 1915, and in the following year was drafted to Salonika. Whilst in this seat of operations he was engaged on important transport duties, and was present at many engagements on the Macedonian front until the cessation of hostilities. He was demobilised on his return home in December 1918, and holds the General Service and Victory Medals. High Street, Stagsden, Beds. 3971.

RIDEOUT, J. S., Private, 9th Northamptonshire Regiment and Labour Corps.
Having joined early in 1917, he was sent to France later in the same year, and was engaged on important pioneer duties in the Arras, Lens, Cambrai and Passchendaele sectors. He was attached to a Canadian Engineering Company for some time, but in 1918 was invalided home with shell-shock. He was discharged as medically unfit for further service in March 1918, and holds the General Service and Victory Medals.
Pax Cottage, Goldington, Bedford. Z3972.

RIDGWAY, C., Trooper, Royal Bucks. Hussars.
He was mobilised with the Yeomanry when war broke out in August 1914, but was found to be medically unfit for transfer to a theatre of war. Retained on home service, he was stationed in turn at Norwich, King's Lynn, Brentwood and Canterbury, employed on various duties of an important nature, and did excellent work until he was demobilised in May 1919.
"The Wheatsheaf," Maids Moreton, Bucks. Z4493/B.

RIDGWAY, H. J., C.S.M., R. Warwickshire Regt.
Mobilised in August 1914, he was quickly drafted to France, and served with distinction at the Battles of Ypres (I.), Neuve Chapelle and Festubert, where he was seriously wounded in action in May 1915. Invalided to England, he unfortunately died in hospital at Oxford on June 19th, 1915, and was entitled to the 1914 Star, and the General Service and Victory Medals.
"A valiant Soldier, with undaunted heart he breasted life's last hill."
3, Daisy Bank, Akeley, Bucks. Z3973.

RILEY, F., Driver, Royal Army Service Corps.
Volunteering in November 1914, he was drafted to the Western Front in September of the following year, and was engaged on important transport duties in the Ypres, Somme, Arras and Cambrai sectors. He also rendered valuable services with his unit during the Retreat and Advance of 1918, and was eventually demobilised in March 1919, holding the 1914–15 Star, and the General Service and Victory Medals.
Grange Cottages, Great Linford, Bucks. Z3729/A.

RILEY, H., Corporal, Royal Army Service Corps.
Two months after volunteering he proceeded to Mesopotamia in December 1915, and whilst in this theatre of war did excellent work in connection with the transport of supplies during engagements at Amara, Kut, Baghdad and along the Tigris. He also served for a time in Persia, and was demobilised in March 1919, holding the 1914–15 Star, and the General Service and Victory Medals.
46, Church Street, Bletchley, Bucks. Z3974.

RINGROSE, H., Private, Royal Defence Corps.
He had already taken part in the South African campaign, but was medically unfit for service in a fighting unit at the outbreak of war in August 1914. In April 1915, however, he volunteered in the Royal Defence Corps, and was engaged on important guard duties at prisoners of war camps at various stations, and did excellent work until his demobilisation in February 1919. He holds the Queen's and King's South African Medals. 5, Grey Friars Walk, Bedford. X3975.

RINGROSE, T., Sergeant, Gloucestershire Regt.
He joined in July 1916, and in the following December was sent to France, where he took part in the Battles of Arras, Ypres, Cambrai and the Somme. He was gassed in action in 1917, but after hospital treatment behind the line rejoined his unit. At the cessation of hostilities he proceeded to Germany and served with the Army of Occupation at Cologne until his demobilisation in September 1919. He holds the General Service and Victory Medals.
45, Oxford Street, Wolverton, Bucks. Z3976.

RISELEY, A. R., Pioneer, Royal Engineers.
He joined in March 1916, but was retained on important duties at various home stations for two years. In March 1918 he was drafted to the Western Front, where he saw heavy fighting at Flers, Monchy and Cambrai, and was gassed in action during the Advance in September 1918. Demobilised on his return to England in April 1919, he holds the General Service and Victory Medals. 20, Fairfax Road, Bedford. X3977

RISELEY, S., Private, Bedfordshire Regiment.
He volunteered in 1915, and in the following year was drafted to the Western Front, where he took part in heavy fighting at Albert, Vimy Ridge and on the Somme. He was unhappily killed in action on November 16th, 1916, and was entitled to the General Service and Victory Medals.
"A costly sacrifice upon the altar of freedom."
Near The Fox, Carlton, Beds. Z3979.

RISELY, G., Private, R.A.V.C.
He volunteered in January 1916, and on completion of his training was engaged on important duties in connection with the treatment of sick horses at various home depôts. He was not successful in obtaining his transfer overseas owing to medical unfitness, but rendered valuable services until invalided out of the Army in October 1918.
11, Bletsoe, Bedford. Z3978/A.

RISELY, T., Private, R.A.M.C.
He volunteered in June 1915, and later proceeded to Salonika, where he saw much severe fighting during the Balkan campaign. On his return to England in 1919 he was demobilised, but quickly re-enlisted, and in 1920 was serving at Cairo in Egypt. He holds the General Service and Victory Medals.
11, Bletsoe, Bedford. Z3978/B.

RITCHIE, T., Sergeant, Royal Field Artillery.
He volunteered in August 1914, and on completion of his training was engaged on important duties with his Battery in Scotland. In 1916 he was drafted to France and served with distinction at the Battles of the Somme, Arras, Ypres, Passchendaele and Cambrai, before being badly wounded in action. He was invalided home and eventually discharged as medically unfit in June 1918, holding the General Service and Victory Medals. Jubilee Terrace, Eaton Ford, Beds. Z3980.

RIVERS, H. W., A.B., Royal Navy.
Mobilised in August 1914, he was posted to H.M.S. "Inflexible," in which ship he was engaged on important patrol duties in the North Sea. He also took part in the Naval operations at the Dardanelles, and served for a time at Malta and Scapa Flow. Unfortunately he contracted pleurisy and was discharged as medically unfit for further service in January 1918, holding the 1914–15 Star, and the General Service and Victory Medals.
Earith, Hunts. Z3981.

ROACH, A. W., Private, 1st Bedfordshire Regt.
A serving soldier, he proceeded to France with the first Expeditionary Force in August 1914, and took part in the Battles of Mons and Le Cateau and the Retreat from Mons. He was unhappily killed in action near Ypres in October of the same year, and was entitled to the Mons Star, and the General Service and Victory Medals.
"And doubtless he went in splendid company."
72, Westbourne Road, Bedford. X3982/D.

ROACH, F. G., Gunner, Royal Field Artillery.
He was mobilised in August 1914, but owing to his being medically unfit for transfer to a theatre of war, was retained on important garrison duties at various home stations. He did excellent work with his Battery until his demobilisation in April 1919. 72, Westbourne Road, Bedford. X3982/A.

ROACH, R., Driver, Royal Engineers.
Volunteering in December 1914, he was sent to France in the following year. Whilst on the Western Front he took an active part in many important engagements, including the Battle of Ypres, Hill 60, the Somme, Arras, Vimy Ridge and Cambrai. He was demobilised in June 1919, and holds the 1914–15 Star, and the General Service and Victory Medals.
9, Derby Street, Bedford. X3983.

ROACH, R., Driver, Royal Engineers.
He volunteered in August 1914, and five months later was drafted to the Western Front, where he rendered valuable services as a driver with the transport section of his unit in the Somme, Arras, Ypres and Cambrai sectors. He was demobilised on his return to England in May 1919, and holds the 1914–15, Star, and the General Service and Victory Medals.
72, Westbourne Road, Bedford. X3982/C.

ROADNIGHT, J. T., Pte., 7th Gloucestershire Regt.
Having volunteered in October 1915, he was sent to India five months later, but after a period of garrison duty there was transferred to Mesopotamia, where he took part in engagements at Amara, Kut and Baghdad, and was wounded in action. He also served for three months at Baku in the Caucasus before being demobilised in May 1919. He holds the General Service and Victory Medals.
8, Victoria Row, Buckingham. Z3984.

ROBERTS, A., Driver, R.A.S.C.
He joined in March 1916, and three months later was drafted to the Western Front, where he served for three years. During this time he was engaged as a driver of motor transport and ambulances in the Somme, Arras, Vimy Ridge, Passchendaele, Cambrai and Marne sectors. He was demobilised in June 1919, and holds the General Service and Victory Medals.
Biddenham, near Bedford. Z3993.

ROBERTS, A., Corporal, 3/5th Sherwood Foresters.
He joined in March 1916, and was sent to France on completion of his training. Whilst on the Western Front he played a prominent part in the Battles of Arras, Vimy Ridge, Ypres and Cambrai, and in heavy fighting at Loos, Beaumont-Hamel, and Lille. He was demobilised in February 1919, and holds the General Service and Victory Medals.
20, Maryville Road, Bedford. Z3990.

ROBERTS, A., Private, Royal Munster Fusiliers.
Volunteering in December 1914, he was sent to Salonika in the following year, but, after taking part in heavy fighting on the Vardar front, was invalided to Malta with malaria. Later he served at Gaza in Palestine, and at Kut in Mesopotamia, before being transferred to the Western Front, where he fought in the second Battle of the Somme and throughout the Retreat and Advance of 1918. He was demobilised in February 1919, and holds the 1914–15 Star, and the General Service and Victory Medals. 12, Russell Street, Stony Stratford, Bucks. Z3985/B.

ROBERTS, C., Private, 10th Essex Regiment.
He joined in July 1916, and in October was drafted to the Western Front, where he took part in the Battles of the Somme, Arras and Ypres, and in heavy fighting at Albert. He died gloriously on the Field of Battle in the Cambrai sector on March 23rd, 1918. He was entitled to the General Service and Victory Medals.
"His life for his Country, his soul to God."
7, Rich Bell Cottages, Chandos Street, Bedford. X3989/C.

ROBERTS, E. C., Corporal, R.A.M.C.
Mobilised in August 1914, he proceeded to Egypt eight months later and first served as an orderly in hospitals at Cairo and Alexandria. Later he was transferred to Palestine, and was in action as a stretcher-bearer with the 2nd Mounted Field Ambulance Brigade at Gaza and Jerusalem. He was discharged in May 1919, and holds the 1914–15 Star, and the General Service and Victory Medals.
12, Russell Street, Stony Stratford, Bucks. Z3985/A.

ROBERTS, E. P., Pte., Royal Warwickshire Regt.
He joined in March 1918 immediately on attaining military age, but, owing to the early cessation of hostilities, was not drafted overseas. He, however, rendered valuable services with his unit at various stations until his demobilisation in November 1919. Harvey Cottage, High Street, Newport Pagnell, Bucks. Z3987/B.

ROBERTS, G. H., Private, Royal Berkshire Regt.
He volunteered in January 1915, and in the following September was drafted to the Western Front, where he took part in the Battles of the Somme, Ypres and Cambrai, and in important engagements during the Retreat and Advance of 1918. He was twice buried alive by shell explosion, but fortunately escaped unharmed. Demobilised in November 1919, he holds the 1914–15 Star, and the General Service and Victory Medals.
38, Mill Street, Newport Pagnell, Bucks. Z3986.

ROBERTS, H., Sapper, Royal Engineers.
Having volunteered in May 1915, he was drafted to the Western Front in the following year. He took an active part in the Battles of the Somme, Arras, Vimy Ridge, Ypres, Lens and Cambrai, and in heavy fighting at Hill 60 and Loos. As a result of being badly wounded in action, he has lost the use of his left hand. Demobilised in January 1919, he holds the General Service and Victory Medals. 116, Grey Friars Walk, Bedford. X3995.

ROBERTS, H. J. S., Private, Machine Gun Corps.
He volunteered in November 1915, and proceeding to France six months later took part in the Battles of Albert and the Somme, during which he was wounded in action at Beaumont-Hamel in November 1916. After a period of hospital treatment in England, he returned to the Western Front, and fought at Arras, Ypres and St. Quentin. He was demobilised in February 1919, and holds the General Service and Victory Medals. 32, Pilcroft Street, Bedford. X3994/A.

ROBERTS, H. S., Pte., 2nd Oxford. & Bucks. L.I.
He joined in November 1916, and was eventually sent to France in March 1918. He took part in the Battles of the Somme (II.) and the Retreat of 1918, but was unhappily killed in action at Gommecourt on August 23rd of the same year. He was entitled to the General Service and Victory Medals.
"A valiant Soldier, with undaunted heart he breasted life's last hill."
Harvey Cottage, Newport Pagnell, Bucks. Z3987/A.

ROBERTS, J. W., Private, 2nd Bedfordshire Regt.
Mobilised in August 1914, he was drafted to France a month later and took part in the Battles of the Marne, the Aisne, La Bassée, Ypres and Festubert, where he was wounded in action in May 1915. He was invalided home and, after a period of hospital treatment, was discharged as medically unfit for further service in March 1916. He holds the 1914 Star, and the General Service and Victory Medals.
32, Pilcroft Street, Bedford. X3994/B.

ROBERTS, L., Private, 1st Bedfordshire Regt.
A serving soldier, he was drafted to France at the outbreak of war in August 1914, and took part in the Retreat from Mons and the Battles of La Bassée, Hill 60, Ypres and Festubert. He was discharged in 1916—time-expired—and holds the Mons Star, and the General Service and Victory Medals.
Gratton Road, Queen's Park, Bedford. Z3988.

ROBERTS, R., Private, 1/5th Bedfordshire Regt.
He volunteered in August 1914, and, proceeding to the Gallipoli Peninsula, was wounded in action during the Landing at Cape Helles in April 1915. He was evacuated to hospital in Liverpool, and after being under treatment for twelve months was retained on important duties in England until early in 1918. He was then drafted to France, where he was engaged on road-construction work in the Cambrai sector until his demobilisation in March 1919, holding the 1914–15 Star, and the General Service and Victory Medals. 2, Trevor St., Bedford. X3991.

ROBERTS, S., Sergeant, Royal Garrison Artillery.
Already in the Army at the outbreak of war, he was drafted to France in February 1915, and served with distinction at the Battles of Hill 60, Ypres, Festubert, the Somme and Arras, and in other important engagements. After the cessation of hostilities he proceeded to Germany with the Army of Occupation, and was stationed at Cologne until his discharge in 1919. he holds the 1914–15 Star, and the General Service and Victory Medals. Diddington, Hunts. Z3992.

ROBERTSON, J. W. J., Pte., Royal Welch Fusiliers.
He joined in August 1916, but, being medically unfit for transfer to a theatre of war, completed his training, and was then engaged on agricultural work in Wales. In July 1919, however, he was sent to the Army of Occupation, and was stationed at Cologne on the Rhine until his demobilisation in September 1919. 56, Queen's Street, Bedford. X3996.

ROBINS, A., Private, Bedfordshire Regiment.
He volunteered in 1915, and in the same year was drafted to the Western Front, where he took part in the Battles of Loos, the Somme, Arras and Cambrai. He was badly wounded in action in 1917, and as a result lost the sight of his left eye. Demobilised in 1919, he holds the 1914–15 Star, and the General Service and Victory Medals.
Church Street, Sharnbrook, Bedford. Z4000/C.

ROBINS, A., Private, 1st Bedfordshire Regiment.
Volunteering in March 1915, he was sent to France in the following year, and took part in heavy fighting at Givenchy and at the Battles of Arras and Vimy Ridge. In August 1917, he was invalided home suffering severely from trench-fever, and was in hospital at Norwich for some time. He was eventually discharged as medically unfit in April 1920, and holds the General Service and Victory Medals.
Little Staughton, near St. Neots, Hunts. Z3997.

ROBINS, F., Private, 1/5th Bedfordshire Regiment.
He joined in December 1916, and was quickly drafted to Palestine. Whilst serving with General Allenby's Forces he was in action at the Battles of Gaza (where he was wounded) and at the capture of Jaffa and Jerusalem. He was demobilised in April 1919, and holds the General Service and Victory Medals
Little Staughton, near St. Neots, Hunts. Z3998/B.

ROBINS, F. E., Staff-Sergeant, R.A.O.C.
He volunteered early in 1915, and was quickly drafted to France, where he served with distinction at the Battles of Festubert, Loos and Albert. He laid down his life for King and Country at the Battle of the Somme on July 21st, 1916, and was entitled to the 1914–15 Star, and the General Service and Victory Medals. "A costly sacrifice upon the altar of freedom."
Church Street, Sharnbrook, Bedford. Z4000/A.

ROBINS, J., Private, 2nd Bedfordshire Regiment.
Having volunteered in November 1914, he was sent to France in June of the following year. He was unfortunately killed in action near Festubert on June 23rd, 1915, on his first turn of duty in the line, 14 days after landing. He was entitled to the 1914–15 Star, and the General Service and Victory Medals.
"He joined the great white company of valiant souls."
Little Staughton, near St. Neots, Hunts. Z3998/A.

ROBINS, J. C., Pte., 13th North Staffordshire Regt.
He joined in August 1916, and twelve months afterwards was sent to France. Whilst on the Western Front he rendered valuable services with the 798th Labour Battalion in the Somme and Cambrai sectors. He was demobilised on his return home in February 1919, and holds the General Service and Victory Medals. Little Staughton, near St. Neots, Hunts. Z3999.

ROBINS, L. A., Air Mechanic, R.A.F. (R.N.A.S.)
He volunteered in 1915, and on completion of his training was retained on important duties with a Sea-plane Squadron at Felixstowe. He rendered valuable services as a carpenter, but was not successful in obtaining his transfer overseas, and was demobilised in September 1919.
Church Street, Sharnbrook, Bedford. Z4000/B.

ROBINS, L. H., Sapper, Royal Engineers.
Mobilised in August 1914, he proceeded to the Dardanelles in the following April and took part in the Landing at Cape Helles. He was also engaged on important wiring, bridge-building and trench-construction duties. After the Evacuation of the Gallipoli Peninsula, he was transferred to Salonika and saw heavy fighting on the Doiran, Struma and Vardar fronts. He received his discharge in December 1918, and holds the 1914–15 Star, and the General Service and Victory Medals.
High Street, Lavendon, Bucks. Z2676/A.

ROBINSON, A., Private, Labour Corps.
He volunteered in December 1915, and after serving at various stations in England with the Northamptonshire and Manchester Regiments was transferred to the Labour Corps, and drafted to France in 1916. There he was engaged on important duties on the railways in many sectors of the front, and did much good work until his return home for demobilisation in July 1919. He holds the General Service and Victory Medals.
31, Russell Street, St. Neots, Hunts. Z4007/B.

ROBINSON, A., Corporal, Bedfordshire Regiment.
He volunteered in 1915, and was retained on important duties at home until drafted to the Western Front in the following year. Whilst in this theatre of war he took part in many important engagements, including the Battles of Arras, Cambrai and the Somme, and, wounded at Ypres in 1917, was for a time in hospital in France. He was demobilised in March 1919, and holds the General Service and Victory Medals.
Marston, Beds. TZ4004/A.

ROBINSON, A., Private, Royal Fusiliers; and Sapper, Royal Engineers.
He joined in January 1918, and after completing his term of training served at various stations, where he was engaged on duties of a highly important nature with the Signal Section. He was unable to obtain his transfer overseas before the cessation of hostilities, but in January 1919 proceeded to East Prussia, where he was still with his Company in 1920.
2, St. John's Place, Bedford. X4003/B.

ROBINSON, F., Private, Bedfordshire Regiment.
He volunteered at the outbreak of war in August 1914, and after a short period of training was engaged on important duties at various stations. He was medically unfit for active service and was consequently unable to obtain his transfer to a theatre of war, but, nevertheless, rendered valuable services with his unit until invalided from the Army in February 1915.
32, All Hallows Lane, Bedford. X2769/A.

ROBINSON, F., Private, Army Cyclist Corps.
Mobilised in August 1914, he was drafted to Gallipoli in the following year, and there saw severe fighting at Suvla Bay and Anzac Cove. On the Evacuation of the Peninsula, he was transferred to Egypt, whence he proceeded into Palestine and took part in the Battles of Gaza, the entry into Jaffa and Jerusalem, and engagements on the River Jordan. Returning home in January 1919, he was discharged in the following March, and holds the 1914-15 Star, and the General Service and Victory Medals. Station Road, Warboys, Hunts. TZ4017.

ROBINSON, F., Cpl., 11th Somerset Light Infantry.
He joined in May 1917, and was retained on important duties in Ireland until July of the following year, when he was drafted to the Western Front. He saw much severe fighting in this theatre of war, and took part in the Battle of Cambrai and many other engagements during the Advance of 1918. He was demobilised in September 1919, and holds the General Service and Victory Medals.
Castle Road, Lavendon, Bucks. Z4014.

ROBINSON, G., Private, Royal Sussex Regiment.
He joined in February 1917, and, on completing a period of training in September of the same year, was drafted to the Western Front, where he saw much severe fighting. He made the supreme sacrifice, falling in action on the Somme on September 28th, 1917, after only three weeks in France. He was entitled to the General Service and Victory Medals.
"He joined the great white company of valiant souls."
2, Preservine Cottages, Clapham. Z4005.

ROBINSON, H., Pte., 16th (The Queen's) Lancers.
He volunteered in August 1914, and was retained at various stations in Ireland until September 1916, being present in the Rebellion of May of that year. He was then drafted to the Western Front, where, after taking part in the Battle of the Somme and other engagements, he was severely gassed near Cambrai in October 1917. Invalided home, he was discharged in May 1918 as medically unfit for further service, and holds the General Service and Victory Medals.
The Walk, Great Linford, Bucks. Z4013.

ROBINSON, H., Corporal, 11th Suffolk Regiment.
Joining in March 1917, he was sent to the Western Front in the following year, and there saw severe fighting in various sectors. He took part in the Battles of the Somme, Cambrai and Ypres and many other important engagements until the cessation of hostilities, and then proceeded with the Army of Occupation into Germany. He was demobilised on his return home in November 1919, and holds the General Service and Victory Medals. Marston, Beds. TZ4004/B.

ROBINSON, J., Staff-Sergeant, Royal Engineers.
He volunteered in 1915, and in June of the following year proceeded to France, where he was engaged on important duties in various sectors of the front. He played a prominent part in the Battles of the Somme, Arras, Vimy Ridge and Cambrai and many other engagements in this theatre of war. In 1920 he was serving in India on garrison duties, and holds the General Service and Victory Medals.
Potton Cross, Wootton, Bedford. Z1880/C.

ROBINSON, J., Private, 1/5th Bedfordshire Regiment and Royal Army Ordnance Corps.
He volunteered in January 1915, and was retained on important duties in England until May 1916, when he proceeded to Egypt. He was there engaged on important duties at various stations, and, taking part in the Advance into Palestine, was present at the fall of Jerusalem. Returning home in 1919, he was demobilised in March of that year, and holds the General Service and Victory Medals.
The Firs, Goldington Road, Bedford. Z4002.

ROBINSON, R. A., Corporal, Labour Corps.
He volunteered in 1915, and, on completing a term of training in the following year, was drafted to the Western Front. Whilst in this theatre of war he was engaged on important duties with the Military Police in various sectors, and served at Rouen, Ypres, Albert and many other places. He was demobilised in February 1919, and holds the General Service and Victory Medals. Bedford Road, Great Barford, Beds. Z4010.

ROBINSON, S., Private, 6th Bedfordshire Regt.
Volunteering at the outbreak of war in August 1914, he proceeded to the Western Front in April of the following year. After taking part in much severe fighting at Ypres, he was wounded and taken prisoner in May 1915, after only a month's active service and, held in captivity in Germany until the cessation of hostilities, suffered many hardships during this time. Demobilised in March 1919, he holds the 1914-15 Star, and the General Service and Victory Medals.
Sherington, Newport Pagnell, Bucks. Z4009.

ROBINSON, S., Private, Bedfordshire Regiment.
He volunteered in August 1914, and in the following year proceeded to the Western Front. Whilst in this theatre of war he took part in many important engagements, including the Battles of Ypres, Loos and Albert, was wounded in February 1916, and taken prisoner in Jnly of that year. Held in captivity until December 1918, he was demobilised in February 1919, holding the 1914-15 Star, and the General Service and Victory Medals.
Calves' End, Sherington, Newport Pagnell, Bucks. Z4008.

ROBINSON, S. T., Private, East Surrey Regiment.
Two months after joining in March 1918 he was drafted to the Western Front, where he saw much severe fighting, and took part in important engagements in various sectors. He made the supreme sacrifice, being killed in action at Cambrai on October 20th, 1918, and was buried at Bethancourt. He was entitled to the General Service and Victory Medals.
"The path of duty was the way to glory."
2, St. John's Place, Bedford. X4003/A.

ROBINSON, S. W., Cpl., Somerset Light Infantry.
Shortly after joining in April 1916 he was drafted to the Western Front, where he took part in many important engagements. Wounded in action at Arras in 1917, he was invalided home, but on his recovery in the following year returned to France, and was again in action. He afterwards served with the Army of Occupation in Germany, finally returning home for demobilisation in January 1920, holding the General Service and Victory Medals. Green End Rd., Gt. Barford, Beds. Z4001.

ROBINSON, T., L/Corporal, 1st Northants. Regt.
Called up from the Reserve at the outbreak of war in August 1914, he was immediately drafted to the Western Front, where he took part in the fighting at Mons. He also served through many minor engagements, and was wounded in the first Battle of Ypres and twice at Festubert, and as a result had to have a leg amputated. He was invalided from the Army in August 1915, and holds the Mons Star, and the General Service and Victory Medals. 35, Creed Street, Wolverton, Bucks. TZ4011.

ROBINSON, T. G., Private, Machine Gun Corps.
He joined in November 1916, and, on completion of a period of training in the following year, proceeded to Egypt, whence he was sent into Palestine, and took part in the Battles of Gaza. He died gloriously on the Field of Battle near the River Jordan on April 30th, 1917. He was entitled to the General Service and Victory Medals.
"Whilst we remember, the sacrifice is not in vain."
The Gardens, Great Barford, Beds. Z4006.

ROBINSON, W., Private, 1/4th Norfolk Regiment.
Mobilised in August 1914 he was immediately drafted to the Western Front, where he fought in the Retreat from Mons. He also took part in the Battles of the Marne, the Aisne, La Bassée and Neuve Chapelle, and was wounded at Hill 60 in March 1915. Later in that year he was transferred to Egypt, and thence to Palestine, where he was again wounded in the second Battle of Gaza. He returned home in May 1919, and in the following month was demobilised, holding the Mons Star, and the General Service and Victory Medals.
61, Westbourne Road, Queen's Park, Bedford. Z4012.

ROBINSON, W. C., Private, Bedfordshire Regt.
Joining in March 1916, he was drafted to the Western Front two months later, and there saw severe fighting in various sectors. He took part in the Battles of the Somme, Arras, Bullecourt and Ypres and many other important engagements in this theatre of war until the cessation of hostilities. He was demobilised in February 1919, and holds the General Service and Victory Medals. 50, Chandos Street, Bedford. X4015.

ROBINSON, W. W., Bugler, R.H.A.
He volunteered in January 1916 at the age of 15 years, and after undergoing a period of training was retained at various stations, where he was engaged on duties of great importance. He was unable to obtain his transfer to a theatre of war, but, nevertheless, rendered valuable services with his Battery until his demobilisation in 1919.
31, Russell Street, St. Neots, Hunts. Z4007/A.

ROBSON, H. W., Corporal, 13th Middlesex Regt.
He volunteered in August 1914, and in December of the following year was drafted to the Western Front, where, after taking part in the Battles of Ypres and the Somme, he was wounded at Arras in April 1917. Admitted to hospital at Boulogne, he rejoined his unit, however, on his recovery, and, again wounded in action on the Somme in 1918, was invalided to Glasgow. Demobilised in March 1919, he holds the 1914-15 Star, and the General Service and Victory Medals.
Bow Brickhill, near Bletchley, Bucks. Z4018.

RODD, J., Private, 2nd Bedfordshire Regiment.
Having enlisted in August 1907, he was already serving in Africa when war broke out seven years later, and was immediately drafted to the Western Front. There, after fighting in the Retreat from Mons, he took part in the Battles of the Marne, the Aisne and La Bassée, and was severely wounded at Neuve Chapelle, losing his left eye. He was invalided from the Army in September 1917, and holds the Mons Star, and the General Service and Victory Medals.
4, Dunville Road, Queen's Park, Bedford. Z4019.

RODDIS, O. H., Sergeant, R.A.S.C. (M.T.)
Volunteering in 1914, he was drafted to the Western Front in January of the following year, and there served as an ambulance driver in various sectors. He was present at the Battles of Ypres, Festubert, Loos, the Somme and Arras, took part also in the Retreat and Advance of 1918, and was gassed in 1917. He was promoted to the rank of sergeant in the Field and, holding the 1914–15 Star, and the General Service and Victory Medals, was demobilised in August 1919.
Milton Ernest, Bedford. Z4020.

ROE, C. S., Private, 8th Bedfordshire Regiment.
He volunteered in 1915, and after undergoing a period of training was drafted to the Western Front in the following year, and there took part in the Somme Offensive and many minor engagements. He died gloriously on the Field of Battle in February 1917. He was entitled to the General Service and Victory Medals.
"He passed out of the sight of men by the path of duty and self-sacrifice."
7, St. Germain Street, Huntingdon. Z4021/B.

ROE, W., Private, 22nd London Regiment.
After volunteering in 1914 he underwent a period of training prior to being drafted to the Western Front in 1916. After taking part in the Battles of Vimy Ridge and the Somme, he was transferred in the same year to Egypt. Proceeding into Palestine, he fought in the Battles of Gaza and, mortally wounded in action, unhappily died at Kantara in November 1917. He was entitled to the General Service and Victory Medals.
"His memory is cherished with pride."
7, St. Germain Street, Huntingdon. Z4021/A.

ROFFEY, W., Private, Machine Gun Corps.
Shortly after joining in May 1918 he was drafted to the Western Front, where he saw much severe fighting, and took part in the second Battle of the Marne. He made the supreme sacrifice, falling in action on the Somme on July 24th, 1918. He was entitled to the General Service and Victory Medals.
"Courage, bright hopes, and a myriad dreams, splendidly given."
4, Patteshall Street, Bedford. Z4022.

ROFFEY, W. G., Corporal, Bedfordshire Regt.
He volunteered in August 1914, and, on completing his training in the following year, was drafted to the Western Front, where he saw severe fighting in various sectors. He took part in the Battles of Hill 60, Ypres, Loos, Vermelles, Vimy Ridge, the Somme and Passchendaele, fought also in the Retreat and Advance of 1918, and was four times wounded. He was demobilised in February 1919, and holds the 1914–15 Star, and the General Service and Victory Medals.
46, Grey Friars Walk, Bedford. X4023.

ROLLINS, H., Corporal, 1st Northants. Regiment.
Already in the Army when war was declared in August 1914, he was immediately drafted to the Western Front, where, after serving through the Retreat from Mons, he took part in the Battles of the Marne, the Aisne, La Bassée and Ypres. He fell in action in June 1916. He was entitled to the Mons Star, and the General Service and Victory Medals.
"He joined the great white company of valiant souls."
Ravenstone, Olney, Bucks. Z4024.

ROLT, A. V., A.B., R.N.; and Driver, R.F.A.
He joined in 1916 at the age of 15 years, and, shortly afterwards sent to sea, was engaged on important duties in the North and Baltic Seas. Demobilised in January 1919, he enlisted later in the Royal Field Artillery and was drafted to India, where he was still with his Battery in 1920. He holds the General Service and Victory Medals.
Paggs Court, Silver Street, Newport Pagnell, Bucks. Z3187/B.

ROLT, C. H., Private, 3rd (King's Own) Hussars.
He volunteered in 1915 at the age of 16 years, and was retained at various stations until February of the following year, when he was drafted to the Western Front. There he saw severe fighting in various sectors, and took part in the Battles of Vimy Ridge, the Somme, Messines, Cambrai, the Marne and Havrincourt, and many minor engagements. Demobilised in February 1919, he holds the General Service and Victory Medals.
Paggs Court, Silver Street, Newport Pagnell, Bucks. Z3187/A.

ROOK, H. T., Private, Royal Warwickshire Regt.
Volunteering in 1915, he was drafted to the Western Front in the following year, and there saw much heavy fighting. He took part in the Battles of Ypres and Cambrai and many other important engagements, was severely wounded in action at Cambrai, and also suffered from shell-shock. He was consequently invalided from the Army in September 1918, and holds the General Service and Victory Medals.
25, Victoria Terrace, St. Ives, Hunts. Z4027.

ROOK, W., Sapper, Royal Engineers.
Shortly after joining in 1917 he proceeded to Egypt, where he was engaged on important duties at Cairo and various other stations. Taking part in the Advance into Palestine, he saw much severe fighting on the River Jordan and was also present at the fall of Jerusalem. He returned home in 1919, and in January of the following year was demobilised, holding the General Service and Victory Medals.
Station Road, Tempsford, near Sandy, Beds. Z4026.

ROOK, W. J., Private, Bedfordshire Regiment.
He joined in 1916, and after a period of training was drafted to France. In this theatre of war he participated in heavy fighting on various fronts, and was wounded in action on the Somme in March 1918. As a result he was invalided home, and after his recovery served in Ireland, at Dublin, Fermoy and Cork, until he was demobilised in March 1919, holding the General Service and Victory Medals.
25, Victoria Terrace, St. Ives, Hunts. Z4025.

ROOME, C., Private, 3/4th London Regiment (Royal Fusiliers).
He joined in February 1918, and after a short period of training was drafted to the Western Front, where he took part in much severe fighting in various sectors. After serving through many important engagements, he fell in action on August 31st, 1918. He was entitled to the General Service and Victory Medals.
"Honour to the immortal dead who gave their youth that the world might grow old in peace."
16, Honey Hill Road, Queen's Park, Bedford. Z4028.

ROPER, F., Trooper, The Duke of York's Own Loyal Suffolk Hussars.
Joining in 1916, he proceeded in the following year to Palestine, where he played a prominent part with his Squadron in several important engagements. He did good work whilst in action at Gaza, Jaffa and Haifa, and was afterwards evacuated to England on account of ill-health. He was eventually invalided out of the Service in April 1919, and holds the General Service and Victory Medals.
1, New Church Terrace, St. Ives, Hunts. TZ4029.

ROSAMOND, G. M., Cpl., 1st Hunts. Cyclist Battn.
He was mobilised in August 1914, and was stationed at Brentwood before being drafted in 1915 to Gallipoli. There he served at Suvla Bay, and after the Evacuation proceeded to Egypt, where he was employed on various duties at Alexandria, Cairo and Beyrout. He served for some time in Palestine before being invalided home suffering from fever. Eventually discharged in April 1919, he holds the 1914–15 Star, and the General Service and Victory Medals.
The Green, Brampton, Hunts. TZ4030/A.

ROSAMOND, J., Private, Royal Army Medical Corps; and Flying Officer, Royal Air Force.
He volunteered in September 1914, and was stationed at Bedford and Fleet prior to being sent in the following year to Salonika. In this theatre of war he did excellent work employed on important duties on the Doiran and Struma fronts, and was appointed acting-sergeant. In 1916 he returned to England, was granted a commission and attached to the Manchester Regiment, being later transferred to the Royal Air Force. He qualified for his pilot's certificate and rendered very valuable services until he was demobilised in March 1919, holding the 1914–15 Star, and the General Service and Victory Medals. The Green, Brampton, Hunts. TZ4030/B.

ROSE, A., Gunner, Royal Garrison Artillery.
Mobilised at the outbreak of war in August 1914, he was immediately ordered to the Western Front, and served continuously in this theatre of war until after the Armistice. He was in action with his Battery at the Battle of Mons and in the subsequent Retreat, and participated in the Battles of the Marne, the Aisne, La Bassée, Ypres and many other important engagements. During the whole of his service he performed uniformly good work, and was demobilised in March 1919. He holds the Mons Star, and the General Service and Victory Medals. Moulsoe, Bucks. Z3828/B.

ROSE, A. (D.C.M.), Corporal of Horse, 1st Life Gds.
A Regular soldier, he was serving in London when war broke out in August 1914, and was at once drafted to France. There he took part in the Battle of Mons and the Retreat, and also in the Battles of the Marne, the Aisne and La Bassée, before he fell gloriously in action at Ypres in November 1914. He had been awarded the Distinguished Conduct Medal for conspicuous gallantry at Zillebeke, and was also entitled to the Mons Star, and the General Service and Victory Medals.
"Thinking that remembrance, though unspoken, may reach him where he sleeps."
1, Simpson Road, Fenny Stratford, Bucks. Z3832/B.

ROSE, A., Private, 1/8th Manchester Regiment.
He volunteered in February 1915, and, after a period of training at Stockport, proceeded in the same year to the Western Front. He served in the Battles of Ypres and Loos, and was also in action at Albert prior to being transferred in 1916 to Egypt. Proceeding later into Palestine, he saw further service at Gaza and Jerusalem. He was demobilised on returning home in April 1919, and holds the 1914–15 Star, and the General Service and Victory Medals.
94, Tickford Street, Newport Pagnell, Bucks. Z4034/B.

ROSE, A. A., Corporal, 2nd Bedfordshire Regiment.
A serving soldier, he was drafted to France immediately after the outbreak of war in August 1914. In this theatre of hostilities he participated in the Battle of Mons and in the Retreat, and later in many other important engagements, and was twice wounded. Taken prisoner in February 1918, he was interned in Germany until after the Armistice, and was then repatriated. He subsequently served at various stations until May 1920, when he was discharged, holding the Mons Star, and the General Service and Victory Medals.
42, Priory Street, Bedford. X4039.

ROSE, A. J., Private, 7th Oxford. & Bucks. L.I.
He volunteered in November 1914, and early in the following year was sent to the Western Front, where he took part in the Battles of Festubert and Ypres, and was wounded. Invalided home, he spent some time in hospital at Oxford, and upon his recovery proceeded to Palestine. After participating in fighting at Gaza, he was transferred to Salonika and saw further service on the Vardar and Doiran fronts and at Monastir. He returned home for demobilisation in March 1919, and holds the 1914–15 Star, and the General Service and Victory Medals.
94, Tickford Street, Newport Pagnell, Bucks. Z4034/A.

ROSE, C. A., Gunner, Royal Field Artillery.
Mobilised in August 1914, he was drafted a month later to France, and played a prominent part in the Battles of the Marne, La Bassée and Ypres (I.), but was wounded near Ypres in 1915. Invalided home, he spent nine months in hospital in London, and was discharged in January 1916 as unfit for further service. He holds the 1914 Star, and the General Service and Victory Medals.
Water Lane, Sherington, Bucks. Z4033/A.

ROSE, C. H., Private, 1/1st Oxford. & Bucks. L.I.
He volunteered in September 1914, and in the following March proceeded to the Western Front. In this theatre of war he took part in several important engagements, including the Battles of Ypres and the Somme, and in 1916 was invalided home suffering from pleurisy. Sent to hospital in Edinburgh, he was detained there for some time, and was eventually invalided out of the Army in May 1917, holding the 1914–15 Star, and the General Service and Victory Medals.
11, Mill Street, Newport Pagnell. Z4038.

ROSE, C. W., Private, 7th East Kent Regiment.
Volunteering in March 1915, he was sent two months later to France, where he took part in the Battles of Ypres (II.), Festubert, Loos, the Somme, Arras, Ypres (III.), Passchendaele and Cambrai. He performed consistently good work until he was unfortunately killed in action near Cambrai on March 23rd, 1918. He was entitled to the 1914–15 Star, and the General Service and Victory Medals.
"The path of duty was the way to glory."
Station Road, Warboys, Hunts. Z4036/A—Z4037/A.

ROSE, E. E., Private, Royal Berkshire Regiment.
He was mobilised in August 1914, and retained at home on important duties until July 1916, when he proceeded to France. There he took part in severe fighting at Albert and Bullecourt, where he was wounded, and as a result was sent to hospital at Rouen. Upon his recovery he rejoined his unit and participated in further fighting at Vimy Ridge, prior to making the supreme sacrifice, being killed in action on April 16th, 1917, during the Battle of Arras. He was entitled to the General Service and Victory Medals.
"A costly sacrifice upon the altar of freedom."
Station Road, Warboys, Hunts. Z4036/B—Z4037/B.

ROSE, G. H., Private, Royal Berkshire Regiment.
He volunteered in May 1915, and a month later was drafted to the Western Front. Whilst attached to a Labour Battalion he was employed on various duties of an important nature in the Loos, Somme, Arras and Ypres sectors, and did excellent work. He was wounded whilst serving at Poperinghe, and unhappily died from the effects of his injuries on November 1st, 1917. He was entitled to the General Service and Victory Medals.
"His memory is cherished with pride."
5, Railway Terrace, Bletchley, Bucks. Z4032.

ROSE, G. W. (M.M.), L/Corporal, Suffolk Regt.
Volunteering in October 1915, he was drafted in the following June to the Western Front. In this theatre of war he played a prominent part with his unit in strenuous fighting on the Somme front, and at Albert, Vimy Ridge, Arras, Messines, Ypres, Cambrai and Amiens. He performed consistently good work, and in July 1917 was awarded the Military Medal for bravery and devotion to duty during the third Battle of Ypres. Returning home in January 1919, he was demobilised a month later, and holds the General Service and Victory Medals, in addition to the Military Medal.
Station Road, Warboys, Hunts. Z4036/C—Z4037/C.

ROSE, H., Air Mechanic, Royal Air Force.
He joined in May 1918, and after a month's training at Blandford was sent to France. There he was stationed at various aerodromes engaged on important duties which demanded a high degree of technical skill, and rendered valuable services until he returned home for demobilisation in February 1919, holding the General Service and Victory Medals.
33, Clarence Road East, Stony Stratford, Bucks. Z4031/D.

ROSE, J. F., Driver, Royal Field Artillery.
He volunteered in August 1914, and in May of the following year proceeded to France. During his service overseas he took part in the Battles of Ypres, Festubert, Loos and the Somme, and was later in action in many sectors during the Retreat and Advance of 1918. He also participated in the second Battle of Le Cateau, and did excellent work until he was demobilised in May 1919. He holds the 1914–15 Star, and the General Service and Victory Medals.
High Street, Sherington, Bucks. Z4035.

ROSE, J. T., Private, K.O. (Y.L.I.)
Joining in March 1916, he was drafted two months later to France. In the following September he was wounded in action on the Somme, and, invalided home, was sent to hospital at Newton Abbot. Returning to France in March 1917, he took part in heavy fighting at Vimy Ridge, Arras, Messines and Ypres, where he was wounded for the second time. Evacuated to England, he spent some time in hospital at Birmingham, and upon his recovery was once more drafted to France, where he again took part in heavy fighting at Amiens, Epéhy Wood, Ypres and Le Cateau. He was demobilised in January 1919, holding the General Service and Victory Medals.
Station Road, Warboys, Hunts. Z4036/D—Z4037/D.

ROSS, H., Private, Seaforth Highlanders.
Mobilised at the outbreak of war in August 1914, he was at once drafted to France. In this theatre of war he took part in the Battle of Mons and fought through the Retreat. He was subsequently in action at Ypres, Neuve Chapelle and in other engagements, and, later invalided home on account of ill-health, was eventually discharged as time-expired in 1916. He holds the Mons Star, and the General Service and Victory Medals.
29, Albert Street, Bedford. TX4041.

ROSS, W. E., Private, 2nd Essex Regiment.
He joined in May 1916, and in the following October proceeded to the Western Front. There he participated in severe fighting on the Somme front, and also in the Battles of Ypres (III.) and Cambrai. After taking part in several engagements during the Retreat and final Advance, he was unhappily killed in action on October 24th, 1918, near Arras. He was entitled to the General Service and Victory Medals.
"Courage, bright hopes, and a myriad dreams, splendidly given."
32, Great Butts Street, Bedford. X4040.

ROWE, F., Private, 3/5th Bedfordshire Regiment.
He volunteered in November 1915, and during his training was stationed at Holton Park, near Tring. He was later employed on garrison and other important duties, and did good work until February 1916, when he was invalided out of the Army as unfit for further military duty.
9, Tower Court, Bedford. X4042

ROWELL, C. F., Private, Bedfordshire Regiment.
Volunteering in September 1914, he was drafted in the following May to the Western Front. In this theatre of hostilities he at once took part in heavy fighting during the second Battle of Ypres, but had only served overseas for five days when he made the supreme sacrifice, being killed in action on May 6th, 1915. He was entitled to the 1914–15 Star, and the General Service and Victory Medals.
"The path of duty was the way to glory."
Rectory Lane, Somersham, Hunts. Z4043/B.

ROWLES, A., Corporal, 8th Bedfordshire Regt.
He volunteered in August 1914, and later in the same year was sent to France. During his service overseas he played a prominent part with his unit in many important engagements, including the Somme, Arras, Ypres, Cambrai and Beaumont-Hamel, and was wounded in action on the Somme front. Invalided home, he was eventually discharged in January 1918 as unfit for further service, and holds the 1914–15 Star, and the General Service and Victory Medals.
49, Pembroke Street, Bedford. Z4045.

ROWLANDS, A., Corporal, Army Cyclist Corps.
He volunteered in August 1915, and was stationed in turn at Stockport, Bedford and Lowestoft, engaged on important duties until June 1918, when he was sent to France. There he took part in strenuous fighting on the Somme front and at Cambrai and Arras. He performed consistently good work until the Armistice, when he returned home. He was eventually demobilised in February 1919, holding the General Service and Victory Medals.
28, Gladstone Road, Chester. Z4044/A.

ROYSTON, F. F., Corporal, Royal Welch Fusiliers.
Volunteering in September 1914, he was drafted to France in the following May, and a few days later was gassed in action at Ypres. Wounded whilst taking part in heavy fighting at Loos in October 1915, he was invalided home, and sent to hospital at Brockenhurst. Upon his recovery he returned to France, and was in action at Arras, Vimy Ridge, Ypres, and Cambrai, being wounded at Ypres. He subsequently fought in various sectors during the Retreat and Advance of 1918, and was killed in action on August 26th, 1918. He was entitled to the 1914–15 Star, and the General Service and Victory Medals.
"Honour to the immortal dead, who gave their youth that the world might grow old in peace."
Rectory Lane, Somersham, Hunts. Z4043/A.

RUFF, E. (M.M.), Private, 1/5th Bedfordshire Regt.
He joined in December 1916, and three months later was sent to Egypt, proceeding subsequently into Palestine. There he participated in the Battle of Gaza, where he was wounded, and also in several engagements prior to the capture of Jerusalem. He was awarded the Military Medal for bravery and consistent devotion to duty in the Field, and when he was demobilised in August 1919, was also entitled to the General Service and Victory Medals. Keysoe, Beds. Z4046.

RUFF, G. E., Private, 2nd Suffolk Regiment.
He volunteered in November 1914, and after a brief training proceeded to the Western Front. In this theatre of hostilities he played a prominent part with his unit in several of the early engagements of the war, and did excellent work until he fell in action on April 7th, 1915. He was entitled to the 1914–15 Star, and the General Service and Victory Medals.
"He passed out of the sight of men by the path of duty and self-sacrifice."
West End, Somersham, Hunts. Z4047

RUFF, J., Private, 10th Essex Regiment.
Joining in April 1917, he was drafted early in the following year to France, and was in action at Arras, Ypres and on the Somme front, where he was twice wounded. Invalided home in June 1918, he remained for neary two years in hospital, and was eventually discharged in May 1920, holding the General Service and Victory Medals.
West End, Somersham, Hunts. Z4048.

RUFFHEAD, A. E. J., Corporal, 1/8th Essex Regt.
He joined in April 1918, and was at once sent to Ireland. After completing his training in County Clare he served at Sligo and Loos, engaged on various duties of an important nature. He was too young for transfer to a theatre of war, but, nevertheless, rendered valuable services until he was demobilised in September 1919.
40, Glyn Square, Wolverton, Bucks. TZ4049.

RUFFHEAD, J., Corporal, R.A.V.C.
He volunteered in 1914, and after a period of training at Milton Ernest and North Walshingham, proceeded overseas in 1915. He served at Salonika and in Egypt, and in these theatres of war did excellent work whilst engaged on important veterinary duties. Later he served at Gaza and Jaffa in Palestine before returning home for demobilisation in July 1919, holding the 1914–15 Star, and the General Service and Victory Medals.
Church Road, Stevington, near Bedford. Z4050/A.

RUFFHEAD, R., Gunner, R.G.A.
Joining in October 1916, he was drafted in the following year to the Western Front. There he played a prominent part with his Battery in several important engagements, including the Somme, Messines, Ypres and Cambrai. He did good work overseas until the Armistice and subsequently demobilised in February 1919, holds the General Service and Victory Medals.
Church Road, Stevington, near Bedford. Z4050/C.

RUFFHEAD, V. G., Gunner, R.H.A.
A Regular soldier, he was stationed in India at the outbreak of war in August 1914, and in the following year was sent to Mesopotamia. There he participated in actions in various sectors, and took part in the Advance on, and subsequent capture of, Baghdad. In April 1918 he was invalided home suffering from malaria, and sent to hospital in Lewisham, being eventually discharged in February 1919, holding the 1914–15 Star, and the General Service and Victory Medals.
Church Road, Stevington, near Bedford. Z4050/B.

RUSHMER, G. R., Corporal, 1st Bedfordshire Regt.
Serving with the Colours since 1902, he was drafted to France immediately after the outbreak of war in August 1914, and in that theatre of war took part in the Battle of Mons and the subsequent Retreat. He was later in action at Ypres and, reported missing after severe fighting at Hill 60 on April 21st, 1915, was subsequently presumed to have been killed on that day. He was entitled to the Mons Star, and the General Service and Victory Medals.
"Nobly striving :
He nobly fell that we might live."
1, Greenhill Street, Bedford. X4051.

RUSSELL, A. J., Private, 1st Leicestershire Regt.
He enlisted in 1902, and immediately after the outbreak of hostilities in August 1914 proceeded to the Western Front. There he fought in the Battle of Mons and the subsequent Retreat, and also in the first Battle of Ypres. Wounded in 1915, he was evacuated to England, and in the following year was drafted to India, where he was stationed at Lucknow engaged on garrison and other important duties. He returned home for discharge in March 1919, and holds the Mons Star, and the General Service and Victory Medals.
Wootton, near Bedford. X2117/A.

RUSSELL, G., Pte., R.A.S.C. ; and Gunner, R.G.A.
He joined the Royal Army Service Corps in October 1917, and a month later was transferred to the Royal Garrison Artillery. Shortly afterwards he proceeded to France, and was in action at Ypres and on the Somme front, where he was wounded in April 1918. Invalided home as the result, he was discharged in the following August as pyhsically unfit for further military service, and holds the General Service and Victory Medals.
Earith, Hunts. Z4052.

RUSSELL, H., Private, 16th Queen's (Royal West Surrey Regiment).
Joining in February 1916, he completed his training and was then stationed at Bedford, Maidstone, Sutton, Thetford, and Chatham, engaged on various duties of an important nature. He was medically unfit for transfer to a theatre of war, but rendered valuable services at home until he was invalided out of the Army in July 1918 on account of ill-health.
Earith, Hunts. Z4054.

RUSSELL, J., Corporal, 12th Hampshire Regiment.
He joined in June 1916, and later in the same year was sent to Salonika. In the course of his service in this theatre of hostilities he took part in various operations on the Macedonian and Bulgarian fronts, and was wounded. He also served for some time in Rumania, and was then transferred to Egypt and stationed in Alexandria, until he returned home for demobilisation in August 1919. He holds the General Service and Victory Medals. New Street, St. Neots, Hunts. Z4053.

RUSSEN, A. E., L/Corporal, 19th (Queen Alexandra's Own Royal) Hussars.
A Regular soldier, having joined the Army in 1912, he was drafted to France in October 1914. He took part in the Battles of Ypres (I.), Neuve Chapelle, Loos, Vimy Ridge, the Somme, Arras, Passchendaele and Cambrai, where he was severely wounded on October 8th, 1918, unfortunately dying on the following day from the effects of his injuries. He was buried at Doingt near Péronne, and was entitled to the 1914 Star, and the General Service and Victory Medals
"Thinking that remembrance, though unspoken, may reach him where he sleeps."
35, East Street, St. Neots, Hunts. TZ1807/B.

RUST, G., Private, Royal Fusiliers.
He joined in June 1918, and, whilst employed on various duties of an important nature at Newmaket and Bury St. Edmunds, did good work. He was not successful in obtaining a transfer to a theatre of war before the termination of hostilities, but subsequently was sent to India, where he was still serving in 1920. 49, Pilcroft Street, Bedford. X4055/A.

RUST, T., Sapper, Royal Engineers.
He volunteered in August 1914, and was retained at home on important duties until September 1915, when he proceeded to Egypt. There he was stationed with his Company in various places, and was wounded whilst serving at Mersa Matruh in January 1916. Evacuated home as the result, he was subsequently invalided out of the Army in June 1916 as unfit for further service, and holds the 1914–15 Star, and the General Service and Victory Medals.
49, Pilcroft Street, Bedford. X4055/B.

RUTTER, F. H., Gunner, R.G.A.
Joining in June 1916, he proceeded three months later to France, where he was engaged with his Battery in heavy fighting in various sectors. He was in action at Beaumont-Hamel, Thiepval, Ypres, Messines, Passchendaele, Courtrai, Amiens and Le Cateau, and performed consistently good work. He remained overseas until January 1919, and was demobilised in the following month, holding the General Service and Victory Medals. 12, Priory St., Newport Pagnell, Bucks. TZ4056.

S

SABBATELLA, A., Private, R.A.S.C. (M.T.)
He joined in February 1917, and, after his training, was retained in England until drafted in the following year to the East. Engaged on important transport duties, he saw much active service in Mesopotamia, Persia and Salonika until the cessation of hostilities, and afterwards served with the Army of Occupation at Constantinople. He was demobilised on his return home in April 1920, and holds the General Service and Victory Medals.
23, Salisbury Street, Bedford. X4057.

SADDINGTON, C. W., Pte., 7th Bedford. Regt.
Joining in June 1916, he was drafted to the Western Front on completing his training in November of that year, and there took part in many important engagements in the Ancre sector. He died gloriously on the Field of Battle at Arras on May 3rd, 1917. He was entitled to the General Service and Victory Medals.
"Great deeds cannot die:
They with the sun and moon renew their light for ever."
River Terrace, Eynesbury, St. Neots, Hunts. TZ4058.

SADLER, J. A., Corporal, 2nd Scots Guards.
Already in the Army when war was declared in August 1914, he was immediately drafted to the Western Front, where he fought in the Retreat from Mons. He also took part in the Battles of the Marne, the Aisne, La Bassée, Ypres, the Somme, the Ancre and Cambrai, and served through the Retreat and Advance of 1918. He was discharged in February 1919, and holds the Mons Star, and the General Service and Victory Medals. Bow Brickhill, near Bletchley, Bucks. Z4059.

SAINT, A. C., Private, R.A.M.C.
Shortly after volunteering in October 1915 he was drafted to the Western Front, where he was engaged on important duties in various sectors. He was present at the Battles of the Somme, Arras, Ypres and Kemmel Hill, and many other engagements until the cessation of hostilities, and was then sent with the Army of Occupation into Germany. He was demobilised on returning home in July 1919, and holds the 1914–15 Star, and the General Service and Victory Medals.
110, George Street, Bedford. Z4060.

SALE, C. H., Private, Machine Gun Corps.
Volunteering in November 1915, he was sent to the Western Front on completion of a period of training in the following year, and there saw much heavy fighting. He took part in the Battles of Albert, Vimy Ridge, the Somme, Arras, Messines and Cambrai, and many other important engagements in various sectors, and, on his return to England in June 1919, was demobilised. He holds the General Service and Victory Medals. Green End Road, Great Barford, Beds. Z4061.

SALISBURY, R., Gunner, Royal Field Artillery.
He volunteered at the outbreak of war in August 1914, and, on completion of a period of training in the following year, was sent to Salonika. There he saw much severe fighting, and took part in many important engagements on the Vardar and Doiran fronts until the signing of the Armistice. Returning home in 1919, he was demobilised in April of that year, and holds the 1914–15 Star, and the General Service and Victory Medals.
29, Bletsoe, Bedford. Z4062.

SALLOWS, G. E., Gunner, R.G.A.
He joined in February 1916, and later in the same year was drafted to the Western Front, where he saw much heavy fighting. After taking part in many important engagements he was severely wounded in action on the Somme, and, suffering also from shell-shock, was sent home and invalided from the Army in December 1917. He unhappily died at Peterborough on December 6th, 1918. He was entitled to the General Service and Victory Medals.
"Steals on the ear the distant triumph song."
16, Green Street, St. Ives, Hunts. TZ4063.

SALMON, J. E., Private, Suffolk Regiment.
Six months after volunteering in September 1914 he proceeded to the Western Front, where he saw severe fighting in various sectors. He took part in the Battles of Ypres, the Somme and Arras and many other important engagements, and was twice wounded in action. He was demobilised in January 1919, and holds the 1914–15 Star, and the General Service and Victory Medals. 17, Napier Street, Bletchley, Bucks. Z4064.

SAMWELL, H. F., 1st Air Mechanic, R.A.F.
He volunteered in August 1915, and, after undergoing a period of training, was in the following year drafted to Russia. Whilst in this seat of operations he was engaged on duties of a highly technical nature and did much useful work with his Squadron. He was also stationed for a time at Gibraltar, and in 1920 was serving in H.M.S. "Argus," an aeroplane-carrying ship. He holds the General Service and Victory Medals.
85, Tickford Street, Newport Pagnell, Bucks. Z4066/B.

SAMWELL, S., 1st Air Mechanic, R.A.F.
He joined in October 1918, and, after completing a term of training, was retained at various stations, where he was engaged on duties which called for a high degree of technical skill. Owing to the early cessation of hostilities he was unable to obtain his transfer to a theatre of war, but, nevertheless, rendered valuable services with his Squadron until October 1919, when he was demobilised.
85, Tickford Street, Newport Pagnell, Bucks. Z4066/A.

SANDERS, A. E., Sapper, Royal Engineers.
Volunteering at the outbreak of war in August 1914, he was drafted to France in the following year, and there saw much severe fighting, taking part in important engagements in various sectors of the front. He died gloriously on the Field of Battle on July 3rd, 1916. He was entitled to the 1914–15 Star, and the General Service and Victory Medals.
"His memory is cherished with pride."
High Street, Cranfield, Beds. Z4069.

SANDERS, C., Private, Middlesex Regiment.
He volunteered in 1914, and, after completing a period of training, served at various stations, where he was engaged on duties of great importance. He was medically unfit for service overseas, and was consequently unable to obtain his transfer to the front, but did much useful work with his unit until February 1919, when he was demobilised.
Turvey, Beds. Z4071.

SANDERS, E., Private, Northants. Regiment.
He volunteered in August 1915, and, after a short period of training, was retained on important Coastal Defence duties at various stations. He was not successful in his efforts to obtain his transfer to a theatre of war on account of ill-health, but, nevertheless, rendered valuable services with his unit until his demobilisation in December 1918.
23, Tavistock Place, Bedford. X1765/B.

SANDERS, E. T., Private, R.A.S.C. (M.T.)
He joined in June 1917, and, after his training, served at various stations, where he was engaged on important duties as a fitter and turner in the workshops. Although unable to obtain his transfer to a theatre of war, he nevertheless did much useful work with his Company until April 1920, when he was demobilised. High Street, Wootton, Bedford. Z4067/B.

SANDERS, F. G., A.B., Royal Navy.
Already in the Navy when war was declared in August 1914, he afterwards served in H.M.S. "Majestic," and, attached to the Grand Fleet in the North Sea, took part in the Battle of Heligoland Bight. He was also present at operations in the Dardanelles, and in May 1915 his ship was torpedoed and sunk off Cape Helles, but he was fortunately rescued. He was afterwards posted to H.M.S. "Carnarvon," on escort duties to and from America and patrolling home waters. Invalided from the Navy in February 1918, he holds the 1914–15 Star, and the General Service and Victory Medals.
Harrold Road, Lavendon, Bucks. Z4070.

SANDERS, G. W., Bombardier, R.G.A.
Having enlisted in 1908, he was already in the Army when war broke out in August 1914, and was retained on important duties in England until January 1916. He was then drafted to the Western Front, where he took part in the Battles of the Somme, Arras and Ypres and other important engagements, and was wounded in action. He was discharged in March 1920, and holds the General Service and Victory Medals.
Bow Brickhill, near Bletchley, Bucks. Z4068.

SANDERS, P., Sapper, Royal Engineers.
Five months after volunteering in November 1915, he proceeded to France, where he saw severe fighting in various sectors of the front. He took part in the Battles of the Somme, Arras, Vimy Ridge, Lens and Cambrai and many other important engagements until the cessation of hostilities, and, on his return home in April 1919, was demobilised. He holds the General Service and Victory Medals.
High Street, Wootton, Bedford. Z4067/A.

SANDIVER, F., Private, R.A.M.C.
Having enlisted in March 1914, he proceeded to the Western Front immediately on the outbreak of war in the following August, and there served with a Field Ambulance and on ambulance trains in various sectors. He took part in the Retreat from Mons, and was also present at the Battles of Ypres, the Somme and Cambrai, afterwards serving with the Army of Occupation in Germany. Returning home in May 1919, he was discharged in the following month, and holds the Mons Star, and the General Service and Victory Medals.
Eaton Ford, St. Neots, Hunts. TZ4072/A.

SANDIVER, W. T., Corporal, Bedfordshire Yeomanry (Lancers).
Mobilised in August 1914, he was drafted to the Western Front in June of the following year, and there saw much heavy fighting. After taking part in the Battle of Loos and other engagements he was invalided home in July 1916 owing to injuries received in an accident. He returned to France, however, in February 1918, and served in various sectors until his discharge in March 1919. He holds the 1914–15 Star, and the General Service and Victory Medals.
Eaton Ford, St. Neots, Hunts. TZ4072/B.

SANDLEY, W., Private, 2nd Suffolk Regiment.
He volunteered in December 1915, and, on completing his training in the following year, was drafted to the Western Front, where he saw severe fighting in various sectors. He took part in the Battles of the Somme, Arras and Cambrai and many minor engagements, and was wounded in action at Armentières in 1917. He was demobilised in July 1919, and holds the General Service and Victory Medals.
69, Grey Friars Walk, Bedford. TX4073.

SANFORD, C. A., Private, Tank Corps.
Joining in May 1918, he proceeded to the Western Front five months later, and there saw much severe fighting, taking part in the Battle of the Selle and many other engagements until the cessation of hostilities. He was then sent with the Army of Occupation into Germany, where he remained for eight months. Demobilised in November 1919, he holds the General Service and Victory Medals. Graveley, Hunts. Z4074/A.

SANFORD, R. P., Private, Hunts. Cyclist Corps.
He volunteered in January 1915, and, after undergoing a short period of training, was retained at various stations, where he was engaged on duties of great importance. He was unable to obtain his transfer to a theatre of war on account of ill-health, but, nevertheless, rendered valuable services with his unit until September 1915, when he was invalided from the Army. Graveley, Hunts. Z4074 /B.

SANRS, J., Private, Middlesex Regiment; and Air Mechanic, Royal Air Force.
After volunteering in May 1915 he underwent a period of training prior to being sent to Salonika in the following year, and there saw much heavy fighting. He took part in many important engagements on the Macedonian front until invalided home in 1917, suffering from fever. He was afterwards retained in England until his demobilisation in September 1919, and holds the General Service and Victory Medals.
West End, Brampton, Hunts. Z4075.

SAPWELL, A. J., Cpl., 7th Oxford. and Bucks. L.I.
He volunteered in September 1914, and twelve months later proceeded to the Western Front, where he saw much severe fighting. In November 1915, however, he was transferred to Salonika, and there took part in many important engagements on the Vardar front. He was mentioned in Despatches for distinguished service in the Field at Horse Shoe Hill in May 1916, and, holding the 1914–15 Star, and the General Service and Victory Medals, was demobilised on his return home in April 1919. Great Linford, Bucks. Z4076 /B.

SAPWELL, C. L., Private, R.A.V.C.
After volunteering in June 1915 he underwent a period of training, and was later drafted to France. During his service in this theatre of war he did excellent work attending to the sick and wounded horses. Later in 1916 he was invalided to England with pleurisy, and was finally discharged as medically unfit for further service in June 1916. He holds the 1914–15 Star, and the General Service and Victory Medals.
Great Linford, Bucks. Z4076 /D.

SAPWELL, E. B., Private, 2/8th Worcestershire Regiment.
Joining in June 1917, he completed a period of training, and in the following year was drafted overseas. Whilst on the Western Front he saw much heavy fighting, and was in action on the Somme. In March 1918 he was taken prisoner, and held in captivity until after the conclusion of war. He was demobilised in March 1919, and holds the General Service and Victory Medals. Great Linford, Bucks. Z4076 /A.

SAPWELL, W. C., Sergeant, Oxford. & Bucks. L.I.
He volunteered in September 1914, and twelve months later landed in France, where he took an active part in engagements on the Somme. In November 1915 he was transferred to Salonika, and served with distinction during the heavy fighting on the Vardar and Doiran fronts. After the cessation of hostilities he returned home and was demobilised in March 1919, holding the 1914–15 Star, and the General Service and Victory Medals. Great Linford, Bucks. Z4076 /C.

SARGEANT, F., Private, 2nd Bedfordshire Regt.
He joined in February 1917, and, on conclusion of his training in the following year, proceeded to the Western Front, where he took an active part in the heavy fighting at Cambrai and St. Quentin. After the cessation of hostilities he was sent to India, where he was engaged on important garrison duties, and in 1920 was still serving there. He holds the General Service and Victory Medals. 10, Gravel Lane, Bedford. X4078 /B.

SARGEANT, H., Private, Royal Fusiliers.
Having joined in October 1916, he was quickly drafted to the Western Front. During his service in this seat of war he was in action at the Battles of Arras, Passchendaele, Cambrai and Havrincourt. At the conclusion of hostilities he proceeded with the Army of Occupation into Germany, and served at Cologne. He was demobilised in June 1919, holding the General Service and Victory Medals.
10, Gravel Lane, Bedford. X4078 /A.

SARGENT, A. J., Private, Queen's (Royal West Surrey Regiment).
Having joined in June 1918, he completed his training later in the same year. Owing to the early cessation of hostilities he was not successful in obtaining a transfer to a theatre of war, but shortly afterwards proceeded to Germany, where he rendered excellent services with the Army of Occupation at Cologne. He was demobilised in March 1920, and holds the General Service and Victory Medals.
Biddenham, Bedford. Z4079 /B.

SARGENT, B., Private, Lancashire Fusiliers.
Joining in March 1916, he underwent a period of training, and later in the following year was drafted to France. In the course of his service in this seat of hostilities he was in action at the Battle of Messines (where he was gassed), and later took an active part in the engagements at Lens and Cambrai. He was demobilised in March 1919, holding the General Service and Victory Medals.
11, St. Cuthbert's Square, St. Cuthbert's St., Bedford. X4077.

SARGENT, F. G. (M.M.), Gdsmn., Grenadier Guards.
Enlisting in 1911, he proceeded to France in August 1914, and served through the Retreat from Mons. He was also in action at the Battles of the Marne, Givenchy, Loos, Albert, the Somme, Arras and Ypres, where he was badly wounded. Invalided to England, he spent some time in hospital, but, returning to the Western Front on his recovery, served at Cambrai. After the cessation of hostilities he proceeded to Germany with the Army of Occupation, and was stationed at Cologne until his discharge in March 1919. He was awarded the Military Medal for conspicuous bravery in the Field in July 1918, and also holds the Mons Star, and the General Service and Victory Medals.
Bridge Street, Turvey, Beds. Z4080.

SARGENT, W. C., Mechanic, Royal Air Force.
Joining in June 1916, he underwent a period of training, and later in the following year proceeded to Egypt. During his service in this seat of war he did good work as a mechanic, and was attached to Service Flying Squadrons, chiefly at Cairo. Returning home, he was demobilised in November 1919, and holds the General Service and Victory Medals.
Biddenham, Bedford. Z4079.

SAUNDERS, A. E. G., Pte., 4th Devonshire Regt.
On attaining military age he enlisted in June 1918, and was retained on important duties with his unit in Ireland. After the cessation of hostilities he proceeded with the Army of Occupation into Germany, and was stationed at Cologne, where he rendered excellent services. He was demobilised in November 1919.
4, Greenfield Road, Newport Pagnell, Bucks. Z4088.

SAUNDERS, A. S., Air Mechanic, R.A.F.
Having joined in November 1916, he underwent a period of training, and in the following year proceeded to the Western Front, where he acted as a mechanic. He rendered excellent services, particularly in the engagements at Arras, Ypres, Cambrai and on the Somme. After the Armistice he returned home and was demobilised in March 1919, holding the General Service and Victory Medals.
10, Shakespeare Place, Huntingdon. Z4087.

SAUNDERS, C. W., Driver, Royal Engineers.
He joined in April 1916, and, on conclusion of his training in the same year, proceeded to France, where he was engaged on important cable-laying and transport duties. He saw service during the heavy fighting at the Battles of the Somme, Arras, Ypres, Passchendaele and St. Quentin. After the cessation of hostilities he proceeded to Germany with the Army of Occupation. He was demobilised in February 1919, and holds the General Service and Victory Medals.
Prior Cottage, Sandy, Beds. TZ4084.

SAUNDERS, F., Private, R.A.S.C. (M.T.)
Volunteering in April 1915, he completed a period of training in the following year, and was drafted to Salonika, where he was engaged in conveying supplies and ammunition to the forward areas. He took an active part in many engagements on the Vardar and Doiran fronts, and was often under heavy shell-fire. Later he was invalided to hospital, suffering from pneumonia, and unfortunately died on February 2nd, 1919. He was entitled to the General Service and Victory Medals.
"Thinking that remembrance, though unspoken, may reach him where he sleeps."
Park Lane, Stonely, Hunts. Z4083 /A.

SAUNDERS, F., Private, R.A.S.C.
Having joined in June 1917, he underwent a period of training, and was drafted to Mesopotamia, where he saw service at Kut-el-Amara. In 1918 he was transferred to Egypt, and later took part in the Offensive under General Allenby through Palestine. He was demobilised in 1920, and holds the General Service and Victory Medals. Little Staughton, Hunts. Z4081.

SAUNDERS, G., L/Corporal, R.E. (R.O.D.)
Volunteering in 1915, he was later in the same year drafted to Salonika, where he did excellent work attached to the Railway Operative Department. He was present at many important engagements on the Vardar, Doiran and Struma fronts. After the cessation of hostilities he returned home and was demobilised in February 1919, holding the 1914-15 Star, and the General Service and Victory Medals.
King's Ripton, Hunts. Z4089.

SAUNDERS, H., Private, Northants. Regiment.
Volunteering in August 1914, he proceeded to the Western Front six months later, and played a prominent part in the Battles of Ypres, Festubert, Loos, Albert and the Somme, where he was wounded in action in July 1916. He was eventually demobilised in February 1919, and holds the 1914–15 Star, and the General Service and Victory Medals.
Cambridge Street, St. Neots, Hunts. Z1951 /B.

SAUNDERS, H. J., A.B., Royal Navy.
Joining in April 1916, he was later posted to H.M.S. "Delhi," in which vessel he saw much service throughout the period of hostilities. He was engaged on important duties attached to the Grand Fleet in the North Sea, and also saw service in the Baltic Sea and at Scapa Flow. He holds the General Service and Victory Medals, and in 1920 was still serving in H.M. Navy.
Hatchway Cottage, Eaton Socon, Beds. Z3000/B

SAUNDERS, J., Private, 1/5th Bedfordshire Regt.
He volunteered in August 1914, and, after completing his training, was drafted to the Dardanelles, where he took part in the Landing at Cape Helles and Suvla Bay. He was badly wounded and invalided to Malta, and thence home. He unfortunately died from the effects of his service on April 2nd, 1919, and was entitled to the 1914–15 Star, and the General Service and Victory Medals.
"The path of duty was the way to glory."
22, Marne Street, Kempston, Beds. Z4086.

SAUNDERS, J. J. F., Mechanic, Royal Air Force.
He joined in August 1918, and, after a period of training, was drafted to Greece, where he was engaged on many important duties. He later proceeded to Salonika and Malta, and rendered valuable services until his demobilisation in February 1919, and holds the General Service and Victory Medals.
1, Hatchway Cottage, Eaton Socon, Beds. Z3000/C.

SAUNDERS, J. T., Private, 10th Essex Regiment.
Volunteering in November 1915, he was drafted overseas in the following year. Whilst on the Western Front he took part in several engagements, including those at Beaumont-Hamel, Arras, Ypres, and in the Retreat and Advance of 1918, and was wounded in action on the Cambrai front. He was demobilised in February 1919, and holds the General Service and Victory Medals. 50, Russell Street, Bedford. X4082.

SAUNDERS, T. R., Sergeant, 2nd Huntingdonshire and Bedfordshire Regiments.
He volunteered in December 1914, and was retained at various home stations on important duties as a Sergeant Instructor, and did continuously good work. In 1918 he was drafted to France, where he took part in many engagements in various sectors. He was demobilised in January 1919, and holds the General Service and Victory Medals.
3, St. Ann's Terrace, Godmanchester, Hunts. Z4085.

SAVAGE, G., Pte., Northumberland Fusiliers.
He volunteered in January 1915, and was retained for a time at home before being drafted to Mesopotamia. In this seat of operations he took part in fighting near Baghdad, and later proceeded to India for garrison duty, owing to his being medically unfit. He returned home and was demobilised in November 1919, holding the General Service and Victory Medals. 129, High St., Stony Stratford, Bucks. Z4090.

SAVAGE, W. T., Private, Northants. Regiment.
He joined in November 1915, and underwent a period of training prior to his being drafted to France. There he took part in much heavy fighting in the Arras sector, and was badly wounded in May 1917. As a result he was invalided home and finally discharged in November 1917 as medically unfit for further service. He holds the General Service and Victory Medals. Park Road Cottage, Stony Stratford, Bucks. TZ4091.

SAWFORD, C. H., Air Mechanic, Royal Air Force.
He joined in February 1916, and later in the same year proceeded to the Western Front, where he saw fighting in the Arras, Ypres, the Somme and Cambrai sectors. He also saw service in Greece and Mesopotamia, and finally with the Army of Occupation on the Rhine. In 1919 he was demobilised, and holds the General Service and Victory Medals.
Ivy Cottage, Blunham, Beds. Z4092/C.

SAWFORD, E., Air Mechanic, Royal Air Force.
He joined in 1917, and was shortly afterwards drafted to France where he took part in engagements in the Somme, Arras, Cambrai and Loos sectors. After hostilities ceased he proceeded to Germany with the Army of Occupation, and served at Cologne until his demobilisation in 1919. He holds the General Service and Victory Medals.
Ivy Cottage, Blunham, Beds. Z4092/A.

SAWFORD, H., Air Mechanic, Royal Air Force.
Joining in 1917, he was drafted overseas after completing his training. Whilst on the Western Front he saw much fighting in the Somme, Arras and Cambrai sectors, and, after the cessation of hostilities, proceeded to Germany, where he served with the Army of Occupation on the Rhine. He was demobilised in 1919, and holds the General Service and Victory Medals.
Ivy Cottage, Blunham, Beds. Z4092/B.

SAYELL, E., Private, 1/5th Bedfordshire Regt.
He volunteered in June 1915, and four months later was drafted to Egypt. After a short period of service there he proceeded into Palestine, and was in action at the Battles of Gaza and Rafa and at the capture of Jerusalem. He was demobilised in July 1919, and holds the 1914–15 Star, and the General Service and Victory Medals.
44, Spencer Street, New Bradwell, Bucks. Z2962/B.

SAYELL, M., Private, Machine Gun Corps.
He volunteered in September 1915, and in the following year was drafted to the Western Front, where he took part in many engagements in the Somme, Arras and Messines sectors. He made the supreme sacrifice, being killed in action near Messines on June 12th, 1917, and was entitled to the General Service and Victory Medals.
"His life for his Country, his soul to God."
44, Spencer Street, New Bradwell, Bucks. Z2962/C.

SAYER, E., Private, 1st Norfolk Regiment.
He volunteered in November 1914, and in the following year was drafted to France, where he saw much heavy fighting until 1917, when he was transferred to Italy. After a period of service in this seat of hostilities he returned to France. There he was unfortunately killed in action a week later, on April 20th, 1918, and was entitled to the 1914–15 Star, and the General Service and Victory Medals.
"A valiant Soldier, with undaunted heart he breasted life's last hill."
2, Crown Walk, St. Ives, Hunts. Z4093.

SCALES, J., Driver, Royal Army Service Corps; and Private, Labour Corps.
Volunteering in November 1915, he was almost immediately drafted to France, where he was engaged on important transport work in the Ypres, Albert and the Somme sectors. He was invalided home to hospital, suffering from rheumatic fever, and was later transferred to the Labour Corps. He was on agricultural work until his demobilisation in March 1919, and holds the 1914–15 Star, and the General Service and Victory Medals. Upper Dean, Kimbolton, Hunts. Z1071/A.

SCALES, P. A., Private, Middlesex Regiment.
He volunteered in June 1915, and, completing his training in the following year, was drafted to the Western Front. In this theatre of war he took part in the Battles of the Somme, Arras, Ypres, Albert and Passchendaele, and was wounded in action in 1916. After the Armistice he proceeded to Germany with the Army of Occupation, and served on the Rhine until his demobilisation in August 1919. He holds the General Service and Victory Medals. Wistow, Hunts. Z4094.

SCOTT, G., L/Corporal, Military Foot Police.
He volunteered in September 1914, and was shortly afterwards drafted to France, where he saw much heavy fighting and was buried by the explosion of a shell. As a result he was invalided home, but on his recovery returned to France, and was in action at the Battles of Ypres and Hill 60. He was badly gassed, and again sent home suffering from dysentery. Later he served at Felixstowe until his demobilisation in March 1919, and holds the 1914 Star, and the General Service and Victory Medals.
1, Castle Hill Court, Huntingdon, Hunts. Z4097.

SCOTT, J. G., 1st Air Mechanic, R.N.A.S.
He volunteered in May 1915, and was attached to the Plymouth Division. He served for a time in H.M.S. "Ben Machree," and was on board this vessel when she was torpedoed, but was fortunately rescued. He then saw service in Egypt and France, but owing to defective eyesight was invalided home and finally discharged as medically unfit for further duty in February 1918. He holds the General Service and Victory Medals.
86, London Road, Stony Stratford, Bucks. Z4098.

SCOTT, R. P., Private, Buffs (East Kent Regt.)
He joined in 1917, and underwent a short period of training prior to his being drafted to France. In this seat of war he took part in many engagements, including those at Vimy Ridge, Passchendaele, Cambrai, the Marne (II.), and in the Retreat and Advance of 1918. He was demobilised in 1919, and holds the General Service and Victory Medals.
Thrapston Road, Brampton, Hunts. Z4099.

SCOTT, W., Rifleman, King's Royal Rifle Corps.
He joined in January 1917, and was almost immediately drafted to the Western Front. Whilst in this seat of war he took part in heavy fighting in the Somme, Arras, Ypres and Messines sectors, and was twice wounded in action. He was taken prisoner on the Somme, and held in captivity in Germany for about eight months. Repatriated after the Armistice, he returned home and was demobilised in June 1919, holding the General Service and Victory Medals.
45, Bridge Street, New Bradwell, Bucks. Z4095.

SCOTT, W., Corporal, 27th Queen's (Royal West Surrey Regiment).
He joined in March 1917, and was quickly drafted overseas. Whilst on the Western Front he was engaged on important duties constructing railways and roads and conveying supplies to the forward areas in the Arras, Ypres and Somme sectors. He was demobilised in December 1918, and holds the General Service and Victory Medals.
Weston Underwood, Bucks. Z4096.

SCOVELL, J., Private, R.A.S.C. (M.T.)
He joined in March 1916, and, after a period of training, was engaged at various stations on important duties with his unit. He was unable to obtain a transfer overseas owing to his being medically unfit, but rendered valuable services until his demobilisation in October 1919.
4, Abbey Terrace, Newport Pagnell, Bucks. Z4100.

SCRAGG, E., Sapper, Royal Engineers.
He joined in March 1917, and later in the same year was drafted to France. There he was engaged on various important duties, and saw much heavy fighting in the Somme sector. He did continuously good work until his demobilisation in April 1919, and holds the General Service and Victory Medals.
23, Spencer Street, Bradwell, Bucks. Z1850.

SCRIVENER, W., Private, Bedfordshire Regiment.
He was mobilised in August 1914, and immediately drafted to the Western Front. In this theatre of war he acted as a signaller, and took part in the Retreat from Mons, the Battles of La Bassée, Festubert, the Somme, Arras, Vimy Ridge and Cambrai, and was wounded in 1916. He was discharged in March 1919, and holds the Mons Star, and the General Service and Victory Medals. High St., Clapham, Bedford. Z4101.

SCUTTLE, B. C., Private, 1/5th Bedfordshire Regt.
He was mobilised in 1914, and quickly drafted to France, where he took part in the Retreat from Mons and the Battles of La Bassée, Ypres, Hill 60, Vimy Ridge and the Somme. In 1917 he saw service in Italy, and was in action on the Piave. Later he returned to France, and saw much fighting in the Retreat and Advance of 1918. He was discharged in May 1919, and holds the Mons Star, and the General Service and Victory Medals. 19, Union Street, Bedford. X4102.

SEAMARK, G. F., Gunner, R.G.A.
He volunteered in 1914, and in the following year was drafted to the Western Front. There he took part in the Battles of Ypres, Festubert and Loos, where he was wounded and invalided home. On his recovery he returned to France, and fought at Ypres and Passchendaele. He was taken ill and again invalided home, and finally discharged in January 1919 as medically unfit for further service. He holds the 1914–15 Star, and the General Service and Victory Medals.
Alconbury Weston, Hunts. Z4104.

SEAMARK, J., L/Corporal, Royal Fusiliers.
He volunteered in September 1914, and in the following year was drafted to the Dardanelles, where he saw much heavy fighting. After the Evacuation of the Gallipoli Peninsula he was transferred to France, and took part in the Battles of the Somme, Arras and Ypres. He was unfortunately killed in action in the Somme sector on June 17th, 1917, and was entitled to the 1914–15 Star, and the General Service and Victory Medals.
"Whilst we remember, the sacrifice is not in vain."
Sunnyside Cottages, High Street, Cranfield, Beds. Z4103.

SEAMARK, W. J., Private, Essex Regiment.
He joined the Army in September 1911, and, when war broke out in August 1914, was quickly drafted to the Western Front. There he took part in the Retreat from Mons and the Battles of Ypres, the Somme and Arras. He was invalided out of the Service in January 1917 through ill-health, and holds the Mons Star, and the General Service and Victory Medals.
26, Canning Street, Bedford. X4106.

SEAMARK, W. R., Private, Bedfordshire Regt.
He joined in 1916, and underwent a period of training prior to his being drafted to the Western Front. There he saw much heavy fighting in many sectors, and was badly wounded at Le Cateau in 1918. He was invalided home and finally discharged in February 1919 as medically unfit for further service. He holds the General Service and Victory Medals.
Earith, Hunts. Z4105.

SEAR, A. G., Private, Northamptonshire Regiment.
He joined in May 1916 in the Oxfordshire and Buckinghamshire Light Infantry, and, completing his training in the following year, was drafted to France. There he took part in much fighting in the Ypres sector, and was taken prisoner of war, being held in captivity in Germany. After the Armistice he was repatriated, and returned home for his demobilisation. He re-enlisted in the Northamptonshire Regiment, and in 1920 was serving in India, and holds the General Service and Victory Medals. 5, Rumbolds Lane, Buckingham. Z4108.

SEAR, F. C., Corporal, R.A.S.C.
He volunteered in September 1914, and was quickly drafted to France. In this theatre of war he was engaged on important transport duties in the Ypres, Festubert, Loos, the Somme, Arras, Albert and Cambrai sectors, and did continuously good work throughout. He was demobilised in February 1919, and holds the 1914 Star, and the General Service and Victory Medals.
4, St. Mary's Street, New Bradwell, Bucks. Z4107/B.

SEAR, H., Private, 51st Devonshire Regiment.
He joined in April 1917, and, after completing his training, was drafted to France, where he was stationed at Calais, and engaged on important duties. After the cessation of hostilities he proceeded to Germany with the Army of Occupation, and served at Cologne until his demobilisation in February 1920. He holds the General Service and Victory Medals.
45, Creed Street, Wolverton, Bucks. TZ4109.

SEAR, H., Sapper, Royal Engineers.
Volunteering in September 1914, he was retained on important guard and Coastal Defence duties until 1915. He then proceeded to France, and served in various sectors of the front, being chiefly engaged in trench-digging. He was present during the engagements at Loos, the Somme, Arras, Ypres and Cambrai, and those in the Retreat and Advance of 1918, during which he was gassed. In March 1919 he was demobilised, and holds the 1914–15 Star, and the General Service and Victory Medals.
4, St. Mary's Street, New Bradwell, Bucks. Z4107/D.

SEAR, H., Air Mechanic, Royal Air Force.
Having joined in October 1918, he underwent a period of training, and was engaged on important duties with his Squadron at Yarmouth. Later he was invalided to hospital suffering from influenza, but unfortunately died from the effects of his illness on April 2nd, 1919.
"His memory is cherished with pride."
4, St. Mary's Street, New Bradwell, Bucks. Z4107/C.

SEAR, T., Sergeant, 7th Wiltshire Regiment.
Volunteering in September 1914, he completed a period of training, and in the following year was drafted to France, where he served during the fighting at Albert. Later in 1915 he was transferred to Salonika, and took a prominent part in the engagements on the Doiran, Struma and Vardar fronts. He afterwards returned to France, and was present at the Battles of Amiens and Le Cateau (II.), and was gassed in September 1918. In April 1919 he was demobilised, holding the 1914–15 Star, and the General Service and Victory Medals.
4, St. Mary's Street, New Bradwell, Bucks. Z4107/A.

SEARLE, H., Private, 1st Bedfordshire Regiment.
He volunteered in January 1915, and was quickly drafted to the Western Front, where he saw much heavy fighting in various sectors of the front. He was in action at the Battles of Givenchy, Ypres, Festubert, Loos and the Somme, where he was unfortunately killed in action on September 4th, 1916. He was entitled to the 1914–15 Star, and the General Service and Victory Medals.
"His life for his Country, his soul to God."
Windmill Terrace, St. Neots, Hunts. TZ4110.

SEARLE, J., Air Mechanic, Royal Air Force.
Having joined in June 1918, he underwent a period of training, and, after the cessation of hostilities, proceeded with the Army of Occupation into Germany. Whilst on the Rhine he served at various stations, and was chiefly engaged on guard and other important duties until demobilised on his return to England in February 1920.
Eaton Ford, St. Neots, Hunts. Z4111/C.

SEARLE, J., Private, 8th Bedfordshire Regiment.
After volunteering in July 1915, he completed a period of training, and in the following year was drafted overseas. During his service on the Western Front he took part in the Somme Offensive, and later in the Battles of Arras and Vimy Ridge. He made the supreme sacrifice, being killed in action on April 16th, 1917, and was entitled to the General Service and Victory Medals.
"Whilst we remember, the sacrifice is not in vain."
Eaton Ford, St. Neots, Hunts. Z4111/A.

SEARLE, W., Sapper, Royal Engineers.
He volunteered in November 1915, but whilst in training he was unfortunately taken seriously ill, and died in hospital at Chatham on the 21st of the same month, after only three weeks with the Colours.
"Thinking that remembrance, though unspoken, may reach him where he sleeps."
Eaton Ford, St. Neots, Hunts. Z4111/B

SEDGWICK A., Sergeant, Royal Defence Corps.
Although over military age, he volunteered for service in November 1914, and was engaged in guarding German prisoners at various stations. In this capacity he rendered excellent services throughout the period of hostilities, and was demobilised in March 1919.
20, Queen's Street, Bedford. X4112/A.

SEDGWICK, A. E., Cadet, Royal Air Force.
Owing to his being too young he was unable to enlist before September 1918. In that month, however, he joined the Royal Air Force, and was stationed at Andover, where he completed his training and served for a time. He was still with the Royal Air Force in 1920.
20, Queen's Street, Bedford. X4112/C.

SEDGWICK, H. E., Corporal, Suffolk Regiment.
He joined in September 1917, and was quickly drafted to the Western Front, where he took part in much heavy fighting, and was present during the Retreat and Advance of 1918, during which he was wounded. As a result he was invalided to England, and, after a long period in hospital, was eventually demobilised in January 1920. He holds the General Service and Victory Medals.
20, Queen's Street, Bedford. X4112/B.

SEE, W. J. (M.M.), A/Sergeant, M.G.C.
Having joined in 1916, he was quickly drafted to France, where he did excellent work in various sectors of the front. He was in action during the Somme Offensive and also in the Battles of Arras and Ypres, and in July 1917 was awarded the Military Medal for conspicuous bravery and devotion to duty in the Field. Later he returned to England, and was engaged as a Machine-gun Instructor, in which capacity he did good work until demobilised in March 1919. In addition to the Military Medal, he holds the General Service and Victory Medals.
West End, Brampton, Hunts. TZ4113.

SELLERS, J., Private, Machine Gun Corps.
Mobilised at the outbreak of war in August 1914, he was immediately drafted to the Western Front, where he saw much active service. He took part in the Battle of Mons and the subsequent Retreat, also in the Battles of the Marne, the Aisne, Hill 60, Ypres, Festubert, and later in the Somme Offensive. He was also present during the engagements at Arras, Cambrai and throughout the Retreat and Advance of 1918. During this period he was three times wounded—at Ypres in 1914, Hill 60 in 1915, and on the Somme in 1918. In March 1919 he was demobilised, and holds the Mons Star, and the General Service and Victory Medals.
48, High Street, Fenny Stratford, Bucks. Z4114.

SEWELL, A., Private, Royal Fusiliers.
Joining in January 1917, he was shortly afterwards drafted to France, where he saw much heavy fighting. He was in action at the Battles of Messines, Ypres and Passchendaele, and was wounded in August 1917. Later he took part in the Battles of Cambrai and Albert, but, suffering from trench-fever, he was invalided home to hospital, and, after his recovery, was transferred to the Labour Corps, with which he was engaged on important farming duties until demobilised in December 1919. He holds the General Service and Victory Medals.
Toseland, St. Neots, Hunts. Z4115.

SEWELL, A. G., Guardsman, Grenadier Guards.
Volunteering in 1915, he completed his training in the following year, and proceeded to France. In the course of his service in this theatre of war he took an active part in the engagements on the Somme, also in the Battles of Arras, Ypres, Passchendaele and Cambrai, and, after the cessation of hostilities, proceeded to Germany with the Army of Occupation, and served at Cologne. He was demobilised in January 1919, and holds the General Service and Victory Medals.
Croxton, St. Neots, Hunts. Z4116.

SEXTON, C., Private, Bedfordshire Regiment.
Volunteering in September 1914, he proceeded in the following year to France, and whilst in this seat of hostilities took part in much heavy fighting in various sectors of the front, notably in the Battles of Festubert, Loos, Arras, Ypres, Cambrai and the Somme (II.). On conclusion of war he returned home and was demobilised in February 1919, holding the 1914–15 Star, and the General Service and Victory Medals.
West Street, Godmanchester, Hunts. Z4117/B.

SEXTON, T. K., L/Corporal, Hunts. Cyclist Bn.
Although only 16 years of age, he volunteered in 1915, and, on conclusion of his training, in the same year proceeded to France, where he rendered excellent services throughout the period of hostilities. He took part in the Battles of Festubert, Loos, Arras, Ypres and the Retreat and Advance of 1918, and was twice wounded in action—in 1916 and in 1918. On his return home he was demobilised in October 1919, holding the 1914–15 Star, and the General Service and Victory Medals.
West Street, Godmanchester, Hunts. Z4117/A.

SEYMOUR, H., Signalman, R.N., H.M.S. "Renown."
Already serving in the Navy at the outbreak of war in August 1914, he was posted to H.M.S. "Renown," in which vessel he was engaged on important patrol and escort duties in the North Sea. He took part in the Battles of the Falkland Islands and Jutland, where he was wounded. Later he served in the operations at Zeebrugge and Heligoland Bight. He holds the 1914–15 Star, and the General Service and Victory Medals, and in 1920 was still in the Navy.
12, St. Clement's Passage, Huntingdon, Hunts. Z4118/A.

SEYMOUR, J., L/Corporal, Grenadier Guards.
Volunteering in November 1915, he underwent a period of training, and in the following year proceeded to France, where he did excellent work throughout the war. He took part in the engagements on the Somme, and later in the Battles of Arras, Vimy Ridge and Ypres, and was wounded in July 1917 On his recovery he was in action during the Advance of 1918 at Amiens and Cambrai. He was demobilised in April 1919, and holds the General Service and Victory Medals.
Croxton, near St. Neots, Hunts. Z4119.

SEYMOUR, J., Private, Royal Fusiliers.
When war broke out in August 1914 he was serving in India, but was later sent to the Dardanelles, and was present at the Landing at Cape Helles and at Suvla Bay. He was wounded in action, and unfortunately died from the effects of his wounds on August 8th, 1915. He was entitled to the 1914–15 Star, and the General Service and Victory Medals.
"And doubtless he went in splendid company."
12, St. Clement's Passage, Huntingdon. Z4118/B.

SEYMOUR, W., Rflmn., King's Royal Rifle Corps.
Having volunteered in September 1914, he underwent a period of training, and in the following year proceeded to the Western Front. During his service in this theatre of war he took part in the Battles of Ypres, Festubert, Loos, the Somme and Messines. He was reported missing in November 1917, but was later presumed to have been killed in action. He was entitled to the 1914–15 Star, and the General Service and Victory Medals.
"His life for his Country, his soul to God."
12, St. Clement's Passage, Huntingdon. Z4118/C.

SHACKLEFORD, H., Chief Engine Room Artificer, Royal Navy.
Already in the Navy when war broke out in August 1914, he was posted to H.M.S. "Tiger," in which vessel he saw much service throughout the period of hostilities. He took part in the Battles of Dogger Bank and Jutland, and was also present at the surrender of Dar-es-Salaam. Later in 1918 he took part in the bombardment of Ostend. He holds the 1914–15 Star, and the General Service and Victory Medals, and in 1920 was still serving. 52, Spencer Street, Bradwell, Bucks. Z1748/B.

SHACKLETON, C. H., 4th Worcestershire Regt.
Having volunteered in September 1914, he proceeded, on conclusion of his training, to France, where he was present during the Somme Offensive. Later in 1916 he was transferred to Salonika, and took part in the engagements on the Doiran and Struma fronts, and was twice wounded. Returning to France, he was in action on the Cambrai front, and, after the cessation of hostilities, went with the Army of Occupation into Germany and served at Cologne, where in 1920 he was still stationed. He holds the General Service and Victory Medals.
5, Tavistock Street, Fenny Stratford, Bucks. Z4120.

SHADRAKE, L. H., Trooper, Bedfordshire Lancers.
Called up from the Reserve in August 1914, he underwent a period of training, and in the following year was drafted to France. During his service on the Western Front he took part in many important engagements, including the Battles of Hill 60 and Ypres, and was wounded at Loos in October 1915. Later he was present at the Battles of Lens and Cambrai. He was demobilised in 1919, holding the 1914–15 Star, and the General Service and Victory Medals.
5, Lawrence Street, Bedford. Z4121/B.

SHADRAKE, R. E., Corporal, Royal Engineers.
Volunteering in September 1914, he completed his training in the following year and proceeded to Egypt, where he saw much service. Taking part in the Advance into Palestine, he fought in the Battles of Gaza, and later took part in the capture of Jericho and in the Offensive under General Allenby, which included the capture of Damascus. On his return home he was demobilised in July 1919, and holds the 1914–15 Star, and the General Service and Victory Medals.
5, Lawrence Street, Bedford. Z4121/A.

SHARMAN, A., Private, 13th Hussars.
Having joined in November 1916, he underwent a period of training, and in the following year was drafted to India, where he was engaged on important garrison and other duties throughout the period of hostilities. He returned home and was demobilised in 1919, holding the General Service and Victory Medals. River Terrace, Eynesbury, St. Neots, Hunts. Z4125/C.

SHARMAN, G. J., Air Mechanic, Royal Air Force (late Royal Flying Corps).
Having volunteered in December 1914, he completed a period of training, but was medically unfit for service overseas. He was therefore retained on important duties as a mechanic, and served on duties of a highly technical nature at various stations with his Squadron. In February 1918 he was demobilised. 7, St. Paul's Road, Queen's Park, Bedford. X4123.

SHARMAN, H., Guardsman, Grenadier Guards.
Volunteering in September 1914, he completed a period of training, and in the following year proceeded to the Western Front, where he took part in the Battles of Loos, Arras, Vimy Ridge, Cambrai and the Somme. He made the supreme sacrifice, being killed in action on March 27th, 1917, and was entitled to the 1914–15 Star, and the General Service and Victory Medals.
"Whilst we remember, the sacrifice is not in vain."
River Terrace, Eynesbury, St. Neots, Hunts. Z4125/A.

SHARMAN, H., A.B., R.N., H.M.S., "Berwick."
After joining in April 1916 he was posted to H.M.S. "Berwick," and in this vessel saw much service until the conclusion of war. He was cheifly engaged on special duties in connection with the transport of foodstuffs and troops from Canada and America to England. He rendered excellent services until demobilised in December 1918, and holds the General Service and Victory Medals. 40, College Road, Bedford. Z4122.

SHARMAN, T. H., 1/5th Bedfordshire Regiment.
Mobilised from the Reserve at the outbreak of war in August 1914, he completed a period of training, and in the following year proceeded to the Dardanelles, where he took part in the Landing at Suvla Bay. After the Evacuation of the Gallipoli Peninsula he was drafted to Egypt, and during his service in this theatre of war was present at the Advance into Palestine, and also at the Battles of Gaza and the capture of Jerusalem. He was discharged in February 1919, after his return home, and holds the 1914–15 Star, and the General Service and Victory Medals.
St. Mary's Street, Eynesbury, St. Neots, Hunts. Z4124.

SHARMAN, W. (M.M.), Sergt.-Major, R.E. (R.O.D.)
He volunteered in South Africa at the outbreak of hostilities in August 1914, and, after a period of training in England, proceeded to France, where he rendered excellent services. He served with distinction during the Somme Offensive, and later in the Battles of Arras and Cambrai, and in 1917 was awarded the Military Medal for conspicuous bravery and devotion to duty in the Field. Later in 1919 he returned to South Africa for demobilisation, and holds in addition to the Military Medal, the General Service and Victory Medals.
River Terrace, Eynesbury, St. Neots, Hunts. Z4125 /B.

SHARP, A., Private, R.A.M.C.
Already serving in the Army at the outbreak of war in August 1914, he was immediately drafted to France, where he was engaged as a stretcher-bearer, and also on important hospital duties. He was present at the Battle of Mons and the subsequent Retreat, and the Battles of the Marne and Ypres. In September 1915 he was discharged as time-expired, and holds the Mons Star, and the General Service and Victory Medals.
4, Tickford Street, Newport Pagnell, Bucks. Z4127.

SHARP, C., Driver, Royal Field Artillery.
At the outbreak of war he was already serving, and was at once ordered to the scene of activities in France, where he was in action during the Retreat from Mons. He also saw severe fighting in various sectors, took an active part in the Battles of Ypres, the Somme, Bullecourt, Arras and Cambrai, and was wounded. He was discharged in January 1920, and holds the Mons Star, and the General Service and Victory Medals.
3, All Hallows Lane, Bedford. X4129.

SHARP, F., Private, 1st Northants. Regiment.
When war was declared in August 1914 he was already in the Army, and accordingly proceeded to the Western Front with the First Expeditionary Force. Whilst engaged in fierce fighting in the Battle of Mons he was unhappily killed in September 1914. He was entitled to the Mons Star, and the General Service and Victory Medals.
"Whilst we remember, the sacrifice is not in vain."
Spring Gardens, Towcester, Northants. Z4132 /C.

SHARP, J., Private, R.E. and Labour Corps.
He volunteered in August 1915, and shortly afterwards was drafted overseas. During his service on the Western Front he saw heavy fighting in the Loos sector, and was in action in the Battles of the Somme, Arras and Ypres. He was gassed at Cambrai in 1917, and in consequence was discharged as medically unfit for further service in June 1918, holding the 1914–15 Star, and the General Service and Victory Medals.
1, Spring Gardens, Towcester, Northants. Z4132 /B.

SHARP, J., Corporal, Machine Gun Corps.
Volunteering in August 1915, he served with the Huntingdonshire Cyclist Battalion at various important stations until 1917, when he was transferred to the Machine Gun Corps and sent to France. There he took an active part in numerous engagements, including the Battles of Ypres, Cambrai, the Marne and Le Cateau. He was demobilised in February 1919, and holds the General Service and Victory Medals. Hilton, Hunts. Z4131.

SHARP, J., Private, 71st Canadian Infantry.
He volunteered in August 1914, and after a period of training was sent overseas eight months later. Whilst serving on the Western Front he was in action in the Battles of Ypres, the Somme, Arras and Cambrai, and took part in the engagements during the Retreat and Advance of 1918. He was demobilised in March 1919, and holds the 1914–15 Star, and the General Service and Victory Medals.
Church Lane, Emberton, Bucks. Z4126.

SHARP, T., Sergeant, 1st Northamptonshire Regt.
At the outbreak of hostilities he was already serving, and immediately embarked for France. On that front he played a conspicuous part in the Battles of Mons, Ypres (I. and II.), Loos and the Somme, and fell fighting in September 1917. He was entitled to the Mons Star, and the General Service and Victory Medals.
"A valiant Soldier, with undaunted heart he breasted life's last hill."
Spring Gardens, Towcester, Northants. Z4132 /A.

SHARP, W. A., Rifleman, 8th London Regiment (Post Office Rifles).
He volunteered in November 1914, and on completion of his training was drafted to France in July of the following year. Serving on the Western Front he took part in the Battles of Ypres and Festubert, but after only two months' active service gave his life for King and Country at Loos on September 25th, 1915. He was entitled to the 1914–15 Star, and the General Service and Victory Medals.
"A costly sacrifice upon the altar of freedom."
43, Edward Road, Bedford. Z4130.

SHARP, W. S., Private, 3rd Bedfordshire Regiment and 11th Suffolk Regiment.
Volunteering in March 1915, he was trained at Felixstowe, and in June 1916 was drafted to the Western Front. In that theatre of war he performed valuable work as a Lewis gunner in various sectors, and served in the Battles of the Somme, Arras, Ypres and Passchendaele. He was severely wounded in April 1917, and after prolonged hospital treatment in England was invalided out of the Army in August 1918. He holds the General Service and Victory Medals.
Alexandra Road, Goldington, Bedford. Z4128.

SHARPE, F. W., Private, Middlesex Regiment.
He joined in May 1917, but owing to ill-health was not successful in his endeavours to secure a transfer to a theatre of war. Throughout the period of his service he was stationed at Folkestone, where he was engaged on duties of an important nature, which he fulfilled in a highly capable manner. He was eventually demobilised in January 1919.
12, Millbrook Road, Bedford. Z4133.

SHARPE, G., Gunner, Royal Field Artillery.
He volunteered in September 1915, but was retained in England on important duties with his unit at Northampton, Ipswich and Buckingham. He was unable to procure a transfer overseas before the cessation of hostilities, but after the Armistice was sent to Germany with the Army of Occupation, and served at Cologne until demobilised in February 1920.
Hemingford Grey, Hunts. Z4134.

SHARPE, J. J., Private, Bedfordshire Regiment and Labour Corps.
A month after the outbreak of war in August 1914 he volunteered, but was retained on important work in connection with stores at various home stations until 1917, when he obtained a transfer to the Western Front. There he saw heavy fighting in numerous engagements, including the Battles of Cambrai, the Somme and Amiens. He was demobilised in February 1919, and holds the General Service and Victory Medals.
Post Office, Renhold, near Bedford. Z4138

SHARPE, R., Private, Beds. Regt. & Tank Corps.
Volunteering in 1915 he embarked for France in the following year. During his service on the Western Front he was engaged in severe fighting in the Neuve Chapelle and Festubert sectors, and did good work with his unit in the Battles of the Somme, Arras, Ypres and Cambrai, and in the Retreat and Advance of 1918. He was demobilised in 1919, and holds the General Service and Victory Medals.
12, College Road, Bedford. Z4136 /A.

SHARPE, R., Corporal, R.A.O.C.
He volunteered in November 1915, and on completion of his training was in the following year ordered to the Western Front. There he saw much service in various sectors of the line, and took an active part in the Battles of Albert, the Somme, Arras, Ypres, Passchendaele and Cambrai. Demobilised in July 1919, he holds the General Service and Victory Medals. 7, Roise Street, Bedford. X4135.

SHARPE, W., Corporal, Royal Engineers.
When war was declared in August 1914 he volunteered, and in 1915 was drafted to Gallipoli. During the Landing on the Peninsula he was severely wounded and invalided home. On his discharge from hospital he was stationed at Streatham, where he was engaged on important work until June 1917. He was then released from the Army in order to work on munitions, which work he carried out with great efficiency He holds the General Service and Victory Medals.
95, Marlborough Road, Bedford. Z4137.

SHARPE, W., Private, R.A.V.C.
He volunteered in January 1915, and on conclusion of his training was later in the same year sent to Egypt. There he was in action in the Suez Canal engagements, and at Sollum and Magdhaba. Subsequently he proceeded to Palestine and saw severe fighting at Gaza, Jerusalem, Jaffa and Haifa. He was demobilised on his return to England in 1919, and holds the 1914–15 Star, and the General Service and Victory Medals.
12, College Road, Bedford. Z4136 /B.

SHAW, J., Sapper, Royal Engineers.
He joined in October 1918, but owing to the early cessation of hostilities did not succeed in his efforts to obtain a transfer to the war zone. He was, however, retained on home service, and whilst stationed at Longmoor and Bovington performed his various duties in a highly capable manner until demobilised in June 1919. 7, Spencer Street, Bradwell, Bucks. Z1905 /A.

SHAW, R., Sergeant, R.A.V.C.
Volunteering in September 1914, he proceeded in April 1915 to Gallipoli, where he served throughout the campaign. After the Evacuation of the Peninsula he was drafted to Egypt, and was in action during the operations at Magdhaba. Later he was sent to Palestine, and played a prominent part in engagements at Gaza, Jerusalem and Damascus, and in General Allenby's Offensive in 1918. He was demobilised on his return to England in July 1919, and holds the 1914–15 Star, and the General Service and Victory Medals.
The Green, Biddenham, near Bedford. Z4139.

SHEAN, G. W., Private, 1st Oxford. & Bucks. L.I.
When war broke out in August 1914 he volunteered, and in January 1916 embarked for France. In that theatre of war he was engaged in fierce fighting in the Battles of the Somme, Ypres, Cambrai and the Somme (II.), and in the Retreat and Advance of 1918. He was demobilised in February 1919, and holds the General Service and Victory Medals.
32a, The Green, Stony Stratford, Bucks. Z3606 /A.

SHEDDEN, J. M., L/Corporal. R.A.M.C.
He volunteered in August 1914, and eleven months later proceeded to Gallipoli, where he served at Suvla Bay and Anzac. In December 1915 he was invalided home with enteric, and on his recovery was sent to France in 1916. After taking an active part in the Battle of the Somme his health again broke down, and for the remainder of his service he was stationed at Boulogne and Calais, where he performed excellent work until demobilised in April 1920. He holds the 1914–15 Star, and the General Service and Victory Medals.
57, Edward Road, Bedford. Z4140.

SHELLARD, T., Private, Highland Light Infantry.
He enlisted in 1906, and when war was declared in 1914 was serving in India, but was drafted to France in December 1914. Whilst engaged in severe fighting at Ypres he was wounded and taken prisoner in December 1914, and kept in captivity until the close of hostilities. After his release he was discharged from the Army in February 1919, and holds the 1914–15 Star, and the General Service and Victory Medals.
Green's Norton, Towcester, Northants. Z4141/B.

SHELLARD, W. G., Gunner, R.G.A.
He volunteered in March 1915, and after training at Woolwich was shortly afterwards sent to the Western Front. There he took part in numerous important engagements in various sectors and saw heavy fighting in the Battles of Loos, the Somme, Ypres and Cambrai. On his return to England he was demobilised in August 1919, and holds the 1914–15 Star, and the General Service and Victory Medals.
Green's Norton, Towcester, Northants. Z4141/A.

SHELTON, C., Sapper, Royal Engineers.
He joined in 1916, and on completion of his training at Chatham was in the same year drafted to France, where he served for nearly three years. During that period he saw heavy fighting in various sectors, and did good work with his Company in the Battles of the Somme, Arras and Ypres. Demobilised in April 1919, he holds the General Service and Victory Medals.
Little Stukeley, Hunts. Z1637/B.

SHELTON, J., Private, 7th Oxford. & Bucks. L.I.
Volunteering in September 1914, he proceeded eleven months later to Gallipoli, where he was in action at Suvla Bay and in the subsequent engagements of that compaign. After the Evacuation of the Peninsula he was drafted to Salonika, and saw severe fighting on the Doiran and the Vardar fronts. He also served in Russia for a short period, and on his return to England was demobilised in February 1919, holding the 1914–15 Star, and the General Service and Victory Medals.
21, School Street, New Bradwell, Bucks. Z4142.

SHELTON, S., Private, Tank, and Labour Corps.
Joining in July 1917, he proceeded two months later to the Western Front, where he rendered valuable services in connection with the repair of tanks. In March 1918 he returned to England, and was engaged on important duties in the workshops at Dover. Later he was sent to Great Paxton, where he was employed on agricultural duties until demobilised in September 1919. He holds the General Service and Victory Medals. Great Paxton, St. Neots, Hunts. Z4143.

SHEPHERD, A., Private, 3rd Bedfordshire Regt.
He volunteered in January 1915, and trained with the Huntingdonshire Cyclist Battalion, and on being transferred to the 3rd Bedfordshire Regiment was drafted in the same year to France. On that front he was engaged in severe fighting, principally in the Festubert sector, and was wounded in action in 1915 and again in 1918. He was then invalided to England, and after ten months' treatment in Gosport Hospital was demobilised in 1919, holding the 1914–15 Star, and the General Service and Victory Medals.
Papworth St. Agnes, Cambs. Z4145/A.

SHEPHERD, A. W., Trooper, 1/1st Surrey Lancers (Queen Mary's Regiment).
Volunteering in September 1914, he proceeded six months later to Egypt, and after serving at Alexandria and Cairo took part in engagements at Sollum. In March 1916 he was transferred to the Western Front, where he was in action in the Battles of Albert and the Somme, and also experienced fierce fighting in the Amiens, St. Quentin and High Wood sectors. Owing to ill-health he was sent to England in October 1917, and consequently was invalided out of the Army two months later. He holds the 1914–15 Star, and the General Service and Victory Medals. Milton Ernest, Bedford. Z3745/B.

SHEPHERD, H., Private, Royal Marine Light Infantry, H.M.S. "Cleopatra."
He joined in September 1916, and on completion of his training was in the same year posted to H.M.S. "Cleopatra." In that vessel he was engaged on submarine patrol duties in the North Sea, and also rendered valuable services in connection with mine-sweeping. Later he served off the Russian Coast, and on returning to England was discharged in October 1919 as medically unfit for further service. He holds the General Service and Victory Medals.
70, Bower Street, Bedford. Z4144/A.

SHEPHERD, H., Private, Royal Defence Corps.
When war was declared in August 1914, he was already serving in the Army, but was not successful in his endeavours to obtain a transfer to the fighting area. Throughout the period of hostilities he was engaged on important duties with his unit a Sharnbrook and Barrow-on-Sea, and rendered many valuabl services before being discharged in 1919.
70, Bower Street, Bedford. Z4144/B

SHEPHERD, H. V., L/Corporal, M.G.C.
He volunteered in the Huntingdonshire Cyclist Battalion May 1915, but was later transferred to the Machine Gun Corps, and proceeded overseas in 1916. During his service on th Western Front he took an active part in the Battles of Albert, the Somme, Ypres and Cambrai, and was wounded and gassed at Vimy Ridge. He remained in France until demobilised in April 1919, and holds the General Service and Victory Medals.
Papworth St. Agnes, Cambs. Z4145/B

SHERWOOD, J. H. V., Gunner, H.A.C.
Joining in April 1916, he received his training at Catterick, and in the following year was drafted to the Western Front. In that theatre of war he was engaged in severe fighting in various sectors, and served in the Battles of Arras, Messines, Lens and Cambrai. He returned to England in 1918, suffering from shell-shock, and was subsequently demobilised in April 1919, holding the General Service and Victory Medals.
10, Stanley Street, Bedford. Z4146.

SHOEMAKE, W. J., Gunner, Royal Field Artillery.
When war broke out in August 1914 he volunteered, and in October of the following year was drafted to the Western Front, where he saw severe fighting in the Loos sector, and also took an active part in the Battles of the Somme, Arras, Messines, Ypres, Passchendaele and Cambrai, and in the Retreat and Advance of 1918. Demobilised in April 1919, he holds the 1914–15 Star, and the General Service and Victory Medals.
Huntingdon Street, St. Neots, Hunts. Z4147.

SHORLEY, F., Sapper, Royal Engineers.
He volunteered in January 1916, and on completion of his training at Chatham and in Scotland was drafted overseas in 1917. Whilst serving on the Western Front he fought in the Battles of Arras and Cambrai, and took an active part in operations on the Somme. He was gassed on one occasion and admitted into hospital at Rouen. Demobilised in March 1919, he holds the General Service and Victory Medals.
The Old Post Office, Renhold, near Bedford. Z1843/A.

SHORLEY, J., Private, 1st Bedfordshire Regt.
Mobilised in August 1914, he at once proceeded to the Western Front with the first Expeditionary Force, and fought in the Battles of Mons, Festubert and Loos. He was wounded in engagements at Hill 60, the Somme and Ypres, and in November 1917 was transferred to Italy. After serving there for a short period he returned to France in March 1918, and was again wounded at Cambrai. He was discharged in April 1919, and holds the Mons Star, and the General Service and Victory Medals. 1, Tower Court, Bedford X3125/C.

SHORT, H. (M.M.), C.S.M., East Yorkshire Regt.
Already serving in 1914, he proceeded to France immediately on the outbreak of war and served during the Retreat from Mons. He also fought with distinction in the Battles of the Marne, Neuve Chapelle, Festubert and the Somme, and was awarded the Military Medal for conspicuous bravery and devotion to duty in January 1916. Later in the year he was discharged as time-expired, but in October 1916 was called up again, and rendered valuable services as a musketry-instructor in Yorkshire until demobilised in March 1919. He also holds the Mons Star, and the General Service and Victory Medals.
Church Cottages, Wootton, Beds. TZ4148.

SHOTTER, E. E. (M.S.M.), S.-Sgt., R.A.S.C. (M.T.)
He volunteered in September 1914, and three months later proceeded to the Western Front, where he played a conspicuous part in the Battles of Neuve Chapelle, Ypres, Loos, the Somme, Arras and Cambrai. He also saw severe fighting in engagements at Givenchy and Lille, and was awarded the Meritorious Service Medal for gallantry in the Field. Demobilised in April 1919, he also holds the 1914 Star, and the General Service and Victory Medals. 58, St. John's, Bedford. Z4149.

SHOULER, F. E., Pte., 2nd South Wales Borderers.
Volunteering in May 1915, he was drafted three months later to France, and on that front was engaged in fierce fighting in many sectors, notably in the Battles of Loos, the Somme, Arras and Ypres. On the conclusion of hostilities he signed on for a further period of service, and in 1920 was stationed in India. He holds the 1914–15 Star, and the General Service and Victory Medals. 3, Newton Road, Far Bletchley, Bucks. Z4151/B

SHOULER, T., Private, South Wales Borderers.
He volunteered in May 1915, and in the following August was ordered to Gallipoli. There he fought at Suvla Bay and in the subsequent engagements prior to the Evacuation of the Peninsula. In January 1916 he was sent to Mesopotamia, and during his service in that theatre of war was in action at Kut, Baghdad and Mosul. He was demobilised on his return to England in December 1919, and holds the 1914–15 Star, and the General Service and Victory Medals.
3, Newton Road, Far Bletchley, Bucks. Z4151/C.

SHOULER, T. G., Sapper, Royal Engineers.
In May 1915 he volunteered, and four months later proceeded to the Western Front, but only served there for a month before being transferred to Egypt. He was stationed at Cairo, and rendered very valuable services in connection with the railways. He was demobilised on his return to England in April 1919, and holds the 1914–15 Star, and the General Service and Victory Medals. 6, Primrose Road, Old Bradwell, Bucks. Z4150.

SHOULER, W. J., Private, 1st Hampshire Regt.
He joined in December 1917, and after a period of training was three months later sent overseas. During his service on the Western Front he took an active part in the Battle of the Somme, and died gloriously on the Field near Acheux on April 22nd, 1918. He was entitled to the General Service and Victory Medals.

"He died the noblest death a man may die:
Fighting for God and right and liberty."

3, Newton Road, Far Bletchley, Bucks. Z4151/A.

SHREEVES, G., Sapper, Royal Engineers.
Volunteering in June 1915, he received his training at Bedford and Birmingham, and in 1916 embarked for the Western Front. He experienced fierce fighting in the Somme, Ancre, Lens and Cambrai sectors, and was also engaged on special duties with his Company behind the lines. In 1917 he was sent to Italy and served there until March 1919, when he was demobilised, holding the General Service and Victory Medals.
Old Harrowden, near Bedford. Z4153.

SHREEVES, H. J., Private, R.M.L.I.
When war was declared in August 1914 he volunteered, and after a period of training was posted to H.M.S. "Sharon," and took an active part in the Battle of Jutland. He was later transferred to H.M.S. "Faton," in which vessel he was in action off the Belgian and Russian Coasts. He also served in Denmark, Germany and Scotland, and in 1920 was still serving with the Forces, holding the 1914–15 Star, and the General Service and Victory Medals.
31, Beatrice Street, Kempston, Beds. Z3781/B.

SHREEVES, M., Private, Bedfordshire Regiment.
He volunteered in December 1914, and on completion of his training was in the following year ordered to Gallipoli. On that front he was in action in numerous engagements, including those at Suvla Bay, but was unhappily killed in action on August 15th, 1915. He was entitled to the 1914–15 Star, and the General Service and Victory Medals.

"His life for his Country, his soul to God."

34, Beatrice Street, Kempston, Bedford. Z4154/B

SHREEVES, R., Private, R.A.M.C.
Two months after the outbreak of war he volunteered, and in March 1915 proceeded to the Western Front. There he took part in the Battles of Loos, the Somme and the Ancre, but was unfortunately killed on October 1st, 1917, whilst bringing in wounded under heavy shell-fire. He was entitled to the 1914–15 Star, and the General Service and Victory Medals.

"His name liveth for evermore."

Harrowden, near Bedford. Z4152

SHREEVES, T., Sergeant, Leicestershire Regt.
Volunteering in November 1914, he was drafted to the Western Front in February of the following year, and there took part in the Battles of Ypres and Loos, and many minor engagements. Mortally wounded in action on the Somme, he unhappily died in hospital on September 25th, 1916. He was entitled to the 1914–15 Star, and the General Service and Victory Medals.

"His memory is cherished with pride."

34, Beatrice Street, Kempston, Bedford. Z4144/A.

SIBLEY, R. F. (M.M.), Private, R.A.S.C. (M.T.)
Joining in January 1917, he was drafted to the Western Front after two months' training, and there saw much service in the Somme sector. In November of the same year, however, he was transferred to Italy, where he was engaged as an ambulance driver on the Piave, and was wounded. He was awarded the Military Medal for bravery displayed in rescuing the wounded under heavy fire in Italy, and holds also the General Service and Victory Medals. Returning home in November 1919, he was demobilised in the following month.
Simpson, near Bletchley, Bucks. Z4155.

SILLS, A. W., Private, Huntingdonshire Cyclist Battalion, and Bedfordshire Regiment.
He volunteered in January 1915, and was retained on important duties in England until the following year, when he was drafted to the Western Front, and there saw severe fighting in various sectors. He died gloriously on the Field of Battle on the Somme on September 4th, 1916. He was entitled to the General Service and Victory Medals.

"Great deeds cannot die:
They with the sun and moon renew their light for ever."

Hemingford Grey, Hunts. Z4157/A.

SILLS, J. B., Trooper, Herts. Yeomanry (Dragoons).
After joining in September 1916 he underwent a period of training prior to being drafted to the Western Front in the following year. There he took part in the Battles of Ypres, Passchendaele, Cambrai, the Somme and the Marne, and many other important engagements, and fought also in the Retreat and Advance of 1918. Demobilised in January 1919, he holds the General Service and Victory Medals.
Buckworth, Hunts. Z4158.

SIMANTS, A. S., Private, 1st Bedfordshire Regt.
A Reservist, he was called to the Colours at the outbreak of war in August 1914, and was immediately drafted to the Western Front, where, after serving through the Retreat from Mons, he took part in the Battle of the Marne. He unfortunately fell in action at La Bassée on October 22nd, 1914. He was entitled to the Mons Star, and the General Service and Victory Medals.

"A costly sacrifice upon the altar of freedom."

16, Gladstone Street, Bedford. Z3496/A.

SIMANTS, G. H., Sergeant, Bedfordshire Regt.
He was called up from the Reserve when war was declared in August 1914, and was immediately sent to the Western Front, where he took a prominent part in the fighting at Mons. He also served through the Battle of La Bassée and other important engagements, and was wounded at Ypres in November 1914, and at Loos in the following year. In 1916 he was transferred to India for garrison duties, and in 1920 was with his unit at Hong Kong. He holds the Mons Star, and the General Service and Victory Medals.
16, Gladstone Street, Bedford. Z3496/B.

SIMARTS, J., Trooper, 2nd Dragoon Guards (Queen's Bays).
Volunteering in August 1914, he proceeded to France in September of the following year, and there saw severe fighting in various sectors of the Front. He took part in the Battles of Loos, the Somme and Cambrai, and in engagements at Beaumont-Hamel, Lens and many other places. He afterwards served with the Army of Occupation in Germany, and finally returned home for demobilisation in January 1919, holding the 1914–15 Star, and the General Service and Victory Medals. 16, Gladstone Street, Bedford. Z3496/C.

SIMCOE, H. J., Air Mechanic, Royal Air Force.
He joined immediately on attaining military age in August 1918, and after completing a period of training was retained at various stations, where he was engaged on duties of a highly technical nature. Owing to the early cessation of hostilities he was unable to obtain his transfer overseas, but, nevertheless, did much valuable work with his Squadron until February 1919, when he was demobilised.
72, East Street, Olney, Bucks. Z1059/A.

SIMCOE, J., Corporal, Bedfordshire Regiment.
Joining in May 1916, he proceeded to the Western Front in December of the same year, and there saw much severe fighting in the Somme sector and near Vimy Ridge. He made the supreme sacrifice, falling in action at Arras on April 17th, 1917. He was entitled to the General Service and Victory Medals

"He died the noblest death a man may die:
Fighting for God and right and liberty."

River Lane, Roxton, Beds. Z1163/A.

SIMMONS, S., Private, Huntingdonshire Cyclist Battalion and Royal Warwickshire Regiment.
He volunteered in 1915, and after a period of training was retained on important duties in England until April 1917. He was then drafted to the Western Front, where he saw severe fighting in various sectors, and took part in the Battles of Ypres, Cambrai and the Somme, and many other engagements. He was demobilised on his return home in 1919, and holds the General Service and Victory Medals.
Little Staughton, Hunts. Z4159.

SIMMONS, W., Private, 2nd Bedfordshire Regt.
Shortly after volunteering in October 1914 he proceeded to the Western Front, where he took part in the first Battle of Ypres and in many minor engagements in various sectors. He died gloriously on the Field of Battle at Neuve Chapelle on March 12th, 1915. He was entitled to the 1914 Star, and the General Service and Victory Medals.

"A valiant Soldier, with undaunted heart he breasted life's last hill."

5, Tower Gardens, Bedford. X3125/B.

SIMMS, A. C., Private, Royal Sussex Regiment and Labour Corps.
After joining in July 1916 he underwent a period of training prior to being drafted to the Western Front in March 1918. There he was engaged on road-making and other important duties in various sectors, was present at the Battle of Cambrai, and also took an active part in the Allies' Advance. He was demobilised in March 1919, and holds the General Service and Victory Medals. 34, Church Square, Bedford. Z4160.

SIMMS, E., Private, 1st Bedfordshire Regiment.
Mobilised in August 1914, he was retained at various stations, where he was engaged on important coastal defence duties. He was medically unfit for active service, and was consequently unable to obtain his transfer to a theatre of war, but, nevertheless, rendered valuable services with his unit until September 1916, when he was discharged.
6, Pilcroft Street, Bedford. X4163.

SIMMS, E. J., Corporal, 1st Bedfordshire Regt.
He joined in March 1917, and in the following year was drafted to the Western Front. Whilst in this theatre of war he took part in many important engagements, including the Battle of Cambrai, fought also in the Retreat and Advance of 1918, and was wounded in action. He was demobilised in February 1919, and holds the General Service and Victory Medals.
16, Princess Street, Bedford. X2541/B.

SIMMS, F. C., Driver, R.A.S.C.
Two months after volunteering in July 1915, he was drafted to the Western Front, where he served with an ammunition column in various sectors. He was present at the Battles of Loos, the Somme, Arras, Ypres and Cambrai, and many other engagements until the cessation of hostilities, and was then sent with the Army of Occupation into Germany. Demobilised on his return home in July 1919, he holds the 1914–15 Star, and the General Service and Victory Medals.
16, York Street, Bedford. Z4161.

SIMMS, H. F., Sergeant, Border Regiment.
Already in the Army when war broke out in August 1914, he proceeded to the Western Front in the following year, and there saw much heavy fighting. He took a prominent part in the Battles of Hill 60, Ypres and Vimy Ridge, and many other important engagements, and was four times wounded in action. He was invalided from the Army in March 1917, and holds the 1914–15 Star, and the General Service and Victory Medals.
16, Princess Street, Bedford. X2541/A.

SIMMS, W. J., Private, Bedfordshire Regiment.
He joined in July 1917, and after undergoing a short period of training was retained at various stations, where he was engaged on duties of great importance. Being medically unfit for service overseas, he was not successful in obtaining his transfer to the front, but did much good work with his unit until invalided from the Army in December 1917.
High Road, Clapham, Bedford. Z4162.

SIMONS, H. J. (M.M.), Private, Essex Regiment.
Joining in 1916, he proceeded to the Western Front on completing his training in the following year, and there took part in important engagements in various sectors. He fell fighting on August 24th, 1918. He had been awarded the Military Medal for conspicuous bravery in the Field in October 1917, and was also entitled to the General Service and Victory Medals.
"He joined the great white company of valiant souls."
Darwood Place, St. Ives, Hunts. Z4164.

SIMONS, T., Driver, Royal Engineers.
He volunteered in August 1914, and was retained on important duties in England until 1916, when he proceeded to Egypt. There he took part in engagements at Agagia, Sollum and Jifjaffa, and afterwards proceeding into Palestine, fought in the Battles of Gaza and in the operations that led to the fall of Jaffa and Jerusalem. He was demobilised on his return home in 1919, and holds the General Service and Victory Medals. The Green, Clapham, Bedford. Z4165.

SIMS, J. H., Private, 4th Bedfordshire Regiment.
He volunteered in September 1914, and in August of the following year was drafted to France. Whilst in this theatre of war he saw severe fighting in various sectors of the front, and took part in the Battles of Loos, the Somme, Bullecourt, Ypres, Cambrai and Bapaume, and many minor engagements. He was demobilised on returning home in February 1919, and holds the 1914–15 Star, and the General Service and Victory Medals.
Sandy Terrace, London Road, Girtford, Sandy, Beds. Z4167.

SIMS, J. W., Corporal, 6th Bedfordshire Regiment.
Joining in February 1916, he proceeded to the Western Front in December of that year, and there saw heavy fighting in various sectors. After taking part in the Battles of Arras and Ypres, and minor engagements, he was severely wounded at Cambrai in November 1917, and invalided home. He was afterwards retained in England guarding prisoners of war until his demobilisation in August 1919, and holds the General Service and Victory Medals.
Holly Cottage, Park Lane, Blunham, Beds. Z4166.

SINFIELD, A., Private, R.A.S.C.
He joined in June 1917, and after completing a period of training served at various stations, where he was engaged on duties of a highly important nature. He was not successful in his efforts to obtain a transfer to the front, having only one eye, but, nevertheless, rendered valuable services with his Company until his demobilisation in April 1919.
42, Chandos Street, Bedford. X4171/A.

SINFIELD, C. J., A.B., Royal Navy.
He joined in May 1918, and afterwards served in H.M.S. "Penn" and "Cambrian," attached to the Grand Fleet in the North Sea. He was engaged chiefly on patrol duties in these waters, and later was transferred to a monitor, on board which vessel he took part in operations against the Bolsheviks in the Baltic. He holds the General Service and Victory Medals, and in 1920 was still at sea.
Covington's Yard, Turvey, Beds. Z4168/B.

SINFIELD, D. (Miss), Worker, Q.M.A.A.C.
She joined in October 1918, and, after undergoing a period of training, was retained at various stations on duties of great importance. She did excellent work throughout her period of service, and was finally demobilised in October 1919.
42, Chandos Street, Bedford. X4171/B.

SINFIELD, H., Tpr., R. Bucks. Yeomanry (Hussars).
He was mobilised at the outbreak of war in August 1914, and served in England until drafted to Egypt in 1916. He proceeded thence into Palestine, where he saw much severe fighting, taking part in the Battles of Gaza, and was also present at the entry into Jaffa. He fell in action at Beyrout on November 27th, 1917. He was entitled to the General Service and Victory Medals.
"The path of duty was the way to glory."
62, Great Brickhill, Bucks. Z4169/B.

SINFIELD, H. S., Sergeant, R.E. (Postal Section).
Mobilised in August 1914, he was immediately drafted to the Western Front, where he served through the Retreat from Mons. After taking a prominent part also in the Battles of the Marne, Ypres and Givenchy, he was wounded at Loos in 1915 and invalided home. He returned to France, however, in the following year and served on the Postal Staff until the cessation of hostilities, and was afterwards stationed with the Army of Occupation at Cologne. Discharged on his return home in December 1919, he holds the Mons Star, and the General Service and Victory Medals.
30, Western Road, Bletchley, Bucks. Z4172/A.

SINFIELD, T., Rflmn., King's Royal Rifle Corps.
Immediately on the outbreak of war in August 1914 he was mobilised and drafted to the Western Front, where, after fighting in the Retreat from Mons, he took part in the Battles of the Marne and La Bassée, and was twice wounded. He fell fighting at Givenchy on December 7th, 1914. He was entitled to the Mons Star, and the General Service and Victory Medals.
"And doubtless he went in splendid company."
62, Great Brickhill, Bletchley, Bucks. Z4169/C.

SINFIELD, W., Pte., 2/5th Gloucestershire Regt.
He joined in June 1916, and underwent a period of training prior to being drafted to the Western Front in October 1918. He was then sent to the Western Front, where he saw much severe fighting in the Cambrai sector during the last stages of the war. He was afterwards engaged in escorting prisoners of war to Germany, and, demobilised in November 1919, holds the General Service and Victory Medals.
Great Brickhill, near Bletchley, Bucks. Z4170.

SINFIELD, W., Private, R.A.S.C.
He volunteered in January 1915, and was stationed in England until August 1916, when he proceeded to the Western Front. There he was engaged on important transport duties in the Somme and Ypres sectors, and was severely wounded in action near Albert in December 1916. Invalided home, he was afterwards retained in England until his demobilisation in July 1919, and holds the General Service and Victory Medals.
Covington's Yard, Turvey, Beds. Z4168/A.

SINFIELD, W., Chief Stoker, Royal Navy.
Having enlisted in November 1897, he was already in the Navy when war broke out in August 1914, and afterwards served in H.M.S. "Landguard," attached to the Grand Fleet in the North Sea, where he took part in the Battle of Jutland. Later he served in H.M.S. "Theseus" on patrol and escort duties in the Mediterranean and Black Seas. He was finally discharged in March 1920, and holds the 1914–15 Star, and the General Service and Victory Medals.
Pellys Cottage, Great Brickhill, Bucks. Z4169/A.

SINFIELD, W. H., Cpl., R. Warwickshire Regt.
He joined in June 1916, and after completing a period of training was engaged on important clerical duties at various stations. Owing to ill-health he was not successful in obtaining his transfer to a theatre of war, but rendered very valuable services with his unit until January 1919, when he was demobilised. 30, Western Road, Bletchley, Bucks. Z4172/B.

SINGLE, E. (D.C.M.), Sergeant, R.G.A.
A serving soldier, he was drafted to France from Jamaica a few months after the outbreak of war in August 1914. There he took a prominent part in the Battles of Neuve Chapelle, Hill 60, Loos, Albert and the Somme, and other engagements in various sectors of the front, and was wounded. He was killed in action near Arras on April 6th, 1917. He had been awarded the Distinguished Conduct Medal for gallantry in the Field in January 1917, and was also entitled to the 1914–15 Star, and the General Service and Victory Medals.
"His life for his Country, his soul to God."
Rose Cottages, Clapham, Bedford. Z3198/B.

SINGLE, E. M. (M.M.), Private, Royal Sussex Regt.
Volunteering in September 1914, he proceeded to the Western Front in the following year, and there saw severe fighting in various sectors. He took part in the Battles of Neuve Chapelle, Hill 60, Festubert, Loos, Albert and Vimy Ridge, and many minor engagements, and was wounded in action. He was awarded the Military Medal for conspicuous bravery and devotion to duty and, holding also the 1914–15 Star, and the General Service and Victory Medals, was demobilised in 1919.
Rose Cottages, Clapham, Bedford. Z3198/A.

SKERMAN, W., Private, 5th Bedfordshire Regt.
He volunteered in October 1914, and in the following year was drafted to Egypt, where he was engaged on important duties at various stations, and did much useful work with his unit. Contracting fever, he unhappily died at Alexandria on September 22nd, 1915. He was entitled to the 1914–15 Star, and the General Service and Victory Medals.
"Steals on the ear the distant triumph song."
15, Gratton Road, Queen's Park, Bedford. Z4173.

SKEVINGTON, C. E., Private, 4th Beds. Regt.
He volunteered in November 1915, and in September of the following year proceeded to France, where he saw heavy fighting in various sectors of the front. After taking part in many important engagements he was severely wounded in action on the Somme in 1917, and in July of that year was invalided from the Army. He holds the General Service and Victory Medals.
High Street, Carlton, near Sharnbrook, Beds. Z4175/A.

SKEVINGTON, F. W. J., Rflmn., King's Royal Rifles.
Immediately on attaining military age, he joined the Army in November 1918, and on completion of his training was sent to the Army of Occupation in Germany. He rendered valuable services with his unit at Cologne on the Rhine until his demobilisation in October 1919.
High Street, Carlton, near Sharnbrook, Beds. Z4175/B.

SKEVINGTON, P. E., Sapper, Royal Engineers.
He volunteered early in 1915, and was quickly drafted to France, where he was wounded in action at the second Battle of Ypres in May of that year. In 1916 he was taken prisoner, and whilst in captivity in Germany was severely burned as the result of an explosion. Repatriated in 1918, he was eventually demobilised in February 1920, and holds the 1914–15 Star, and the General Service and Victory Medals.
Albert Cottage, Great Barford, Beds. Z4174.

SKINNER, E. W., Private, Norfolk Regiment.
Volunteering in January 1916, he proceeded to France later in the same year. After taking part in the Battles of Arras and Vimy Ridge and in heavy fighting at Ypres, he was unfortunately killed in action at Vimy on May 12th, 1917. He was entitled to the General Service and Victory Medals.
"Nobly striving:
He nobly fell that we might live."
Needingworth Road, St. Ives, Hunts. Z4176/A.

SKINNER, W. E., Private, Lancashire Fusiliers.
He joined in June 1916, and on completion of his training was drafted to France, where he took part in the Battle of the Somme and in heavy fighting at Arras and Ypres. He died gloriously on the Field of Battle at Passchendaele on March 26th, 1917, and was entitled to the General Service and Victory Medals.
"A valiant Soldier, with undaunted heart he breasted life's last hill."
Needingworth Road, St. Ives, Hunts. Z4176/B.

SKINNER, W. J., Stoker, Royal Navy.
He joined in August 1918, and was sent to Chatham for training. On its completion he was engaged on important duties ashore until March 1919, when he was found to be medically unfit for further service and was accordingly discharged.
Cherry Croft, High Street, Sandy, Beds. Z4177.

SLADE, E. H., L/Cpl., Mounted Military Police.
He volunteered in October 1914, and was quickly sent to France, where he was engaged on important traffic-control and other police duties at Le Havre and Rouen. He did excellent work until January 1917, when he was discharged as medically unfit for further service as the result of influenza. He holds the 1914 Star, and the General Service and Victory Medals.
Newton Longville, Bucks. Z4178/B.

SLADE, P. J., Private, 15th Canadian Regiment (Canadian Overseas Forces).
Volunteering in November 1914, he was sent to France early in the following year, and took part in the Battles of Ypres, the Somme, Arras and Cambrai. He laid down his life for King and Country in the Cambrai sector on September 27th, 1918, and was entitled to the 1914–15 Star, and the General Service and Victory Medals.
"A costly sacrifice upon the altar of freedom."
Newton Longville, Bucks. Z4178/A.

SLATER, E. G., Private, 4th Bedfordshire Regt.
He volunteered in January 1915, and later in the same year proceeded to France, where he took part in the Battles of Neuve Chapelle, Ypres, Loos, the Somme, Arras, Lens and Cambrai, and in heavy fighting at Armentières and Lille. He was twice wounded in action—in July 1916, and again in 1918, when he was invalided home. In February 1920 he was discharged as medically unfit for further service, and holds the 1914–15 Star, and the General Service and Victory Medals.
18, Maryville Road, Bedford. Z4181.

SLATER, E. J., Pte., 10th Q.O. (R. West Kent Regt.).
He joined in April 1916, and on completion of his training was retained on important duties at various home stations. In April 1918 he was drafted to France, and after taking part in the Retreat was wounded in action at Passchendaele during the subsequent Advance. He holds the General Service and Victory Medals, and was demobilised in February 1919.
70, St. John's Street, Kempston, Beds. X4180.

SLATER, F., Private, 3rd Bedfordshire Regiment.
He was mobilised in August 1914, but, owing to his being too old for transfer to a theatre of war, was retained on important defence duties on the East Coast. He rendered valuable services with his unit until his demobilisation in March 1919.
18, East Street, Olney, Bucks. Z4179/C.

SLATER, F. F., Gunner, Royal Garrison Artillery.
Stationed in India when war broke out, he landed in France in February 1915, and took part in heavy fighting in the Somme and Ypres sectors. He was seriously wounded in action at Passchendaele in February 1917, when he unfortunately had his nose blown off. Invalided to hospital at Newport (Mon.), he underwent 15 operations, and was eventually discharged in June 1920, holding the 1914–15 Star, and the General Service and Victory Medals.
18, East Street, Olney, Bucks. Z4179/B.

SLATER, W. A., L/Corporal, Royal Sussex Regt.
Having volunteered in February 1915, he was drafted to France five months later, and took part in much severe fighting. Wounded during the Somme Offensive in July 1916, he spent three months in hospital at Manchester, and then returned to the Western Front. He was again in action at the Battles of Ypres and Cambrai, and throughout the Retreat and Advance of 1918. Demobilised on his return to England in November 1919, he holds the 1914–15 Star, and the General Service and Victory Medals.
18, East Street, Olney, Bucks. Z4179/A.

SLAUGHTER, W. H., Sergt., 1/4th R. Sussex Regt.
Volunteering in August 1914, he was retained on special duties in England until July of the following year, when he was sent to Gallipoli. After serving with distinction on the Peninsula for about six weeks, he was unfortunately killed in action on August 14th, 1915. He was entitled to the 1914–15 Star, and the General Service and Victory Medals.
"He joined the great white company of valiant souls."
Earith, Hunts. Z4182.

SLETCHER, C. T., Pte., Queen's (R.W. Surrey Regt.).
He joined in June 1918, but was found to be medically unfit for transfer to a theatre of war. On completion of his training he was therefore retained on important garrison duties with his unit at Sittingbourne, and did excellent work until his demobilisation in January 1919.
47, Hassett Street, Bedford. TX4183/A.

SLETCHER, G. W. H., Corporal, Queen's (Royal West Surrey Regiment).
Joining in February 1917, he was drafted to France later in the same year, and played a prominent part in much severe fighting He was in action at the Battles of Arras, Ypres, Cambrai and the Somme, and in the Retreat and Advance of 1918. He holds the General Service and Victory Medals, and was eventually demobilised in November 1919.
47, Hassett Street, Bedford. TX4183/B

SMART, A. E., Sergeant, 7th Oxford. & Bucks. L.I.
Volunteering in September 1914, he was quickly drafted t France, but after a short period of service in the Ypres secto was transferred to Salonika in February 1915. Whilst in th Balkan theatre of war he played a conspicuous part in heav fighting on the Struma, Doiran and Vardar fronts. Returnin to England in November 1918, he was eventually demobilise in May 1919, holding the 1914–15 Star, and the Genera Service and Victory Medals.
46, Spencer Street, Bradwell, Bucks. Z4186

SMART, C., Corporal, 10th Queen's (Royal Wes Surrey Regiment).
After volunteering in February 1915 he underwent a shor period of training and proceeded to France. Whilst on th Western Front he took part in many important engagement including the Battles of Ypres, the Somme and Cambrai, an was wounded in action on November 11th, 1918, a few hou before the cessation of hostilities. He was in hospital a Northampton for three months before being demobilised i March 1919, and holds the 1914–15 Star, and the Gener Service and Victory Medals.
Pury End, Pauler's Pury, Towcester, Northants. Z4187/

SMART, E. J., Aircraftsman, Royal Air Force.
He joined in September 1918, although under military age, an on completion of his training was engaged on important duti which demanded a high degree of technical skill. He d excellent work at various aerodromes, and in 1920 was st serving. 34, St. Germain Street, Huntingdon. Z418

SMART, F., Private, 1st Northamptonshire Regt
He volunteered in September 1914, and was quickly drafted France, where he took part in much severe fighting, partic larly in the Ypres sector. He was badly wounded in action Vermelles in September 1915, and invalided to hospital Chatham. In March 1916 he was discharged as medical unfit for further service, and holds the 1914–15 Star, and t General Service and Victory Medals.
Church End, Pauler's Pury, Towcester, Northants. Z418

SMART, F., Private, Bedfordshire Regiment.
He volunteered in the Huntingdonshire Cyclist Battalion in August 1914, but on proceeding to France in January 1916 was transferred to the Bedfordshire Regiment. Whilst on the Western Front he took part in the Battles of the Somme, Passchendaele and Le Cateau (II.), where he was wounded in action. Invalided to hospital at Le Havre, he was eventually demobilised in February 1919, and holds the General Service and Victory Medals. Grafham, Hunts. Z4185.

SMART, H., Private, Bedfordshire Regiment.
He joined in August 1916, and six months later was drafted to the Western Front, where he took part in the Battles of Arras, Vimy Ridge, Lens, Cambrai and Le Cateau, and in other engagements of importance in various sectors. He was demobilised in January 1919, and holds the General Service and Victory Medals. Woolley, Hunts. Z4184.

SMART, H. J., Private, 2nd London Regiment (Royal Fusiliers).
He enlisted in April 1914, but was retained on important duties at various home stations until August 1916. He then proceeded to the Western Front, and was in action at Neuve Chapelle and on the Somme before being badly wounded at Passchendaele in July 1917. He was invalided home three months later, and eventually received his discharge in March 1919, holding the General Service and Victory Medals.
9, Holme Street, Bedford. X4190.

SMART, J., Sergeant, R.E. (Signal Section).
He volunteered in September 1914, and in April of the following year proceeded to the Dardanelles, where he took part in the Landing at Cape Helles. After the Evacuation of the Gallipoli Peninsula, however, he was transferred to Egypt, and thence to Palestine, where he served with distinction in the Battles of Gaza. He was demobilised on his return home in September 1919, and holds the 1914–15 Star, and the General Service and Victory Medals.
Pury End, Pauler's Pury, Towcester, Northants. Z4187/B.

SMART, W. J., Private, Bedfordshire Regiment and 1st Hertfordshire Regiment.
A Reservist, he was called to the Colours at the outbreak of war in August 1914, and in January of the following year was drafted to the Western Front, where he saw much heavy fighting. He took part in the Battles of the Somme, the Ancre and Vimy Ridge, and many other engagements, and was wounded at Beaucourt in 1916. He was discharged in February 1919, and holds the 1914–15 Star, and the General Service and Victory Medals.
218, Bedford Road, Kempston, Bedford. X4191.

SMITH, A., Private, Bedfordshire Regiment.
Five months after volunteering in November 1914, he proceeded to the Western Front, where he saw severe fighting in various sectors, and was wounded at Loos in 1915. Invalided home, he returned to France, however, in the following year, and took part in the Battles of the Somme, Arras, Ypres and Cambrai, and was again wounded in action. He was demobilised in February 1919, and holds the 1914–15 Star, and the General Service and Victory Medals.
Luke Street, Eynesbury, St. Neots, Hunts. Z4204.

SMITH, A., Pioneer, Royal Engineers.
Shortly after joining in 1916, he was sent to the Western Front, where he was engaged on duties of great importance in various sectors. He was also present at the Battles of Albert, the Somme, Messines, Ypres and Cambrai, and many other engagements until the cessation of hostilities. He was demobilised on his return home in 1919, and holds the General Service and Victory Medals. Hilton, Hunts. Z4234.

SMITH, A., Private, 1st Bedfordshire Regiment and Labour Corps.
Mobilised in August 1914, he was immediately drafted to the Western Front, where he fought in the Retreat from Mons. He also took part in the Battles of Ypres, Neuve Chapelle, Loos and the Somme, and minor engagements until invalided home in 1916. On his recovery he was retained on agricultural work in England, and was finally discharged in March 1919, holding the Mons Star, and the General Service and Victory Medals. Cambridge Street, St. Neots, Hunts. Z4232/A.

SMITH, A. G., Private, Canadian Overseas Forces.
Volunteering in January 1915, he proceeded to England on completing his training in the following September and in 1916 was drafted to France, where he saw heavy fighting in various sectors of the front. Mortally wounded in action on the Somme, he unhappily died on hospital at Rouen on October 8th, 1916. He was entitled to the 1914–15 Star, and the General Service and Victory Medals.
"Whilst we remember, the sacrifice is not in vain."
15, Clarence Road East, Stony Stratford, Bucks. Z4031/A.

SMITH, A. H., Private, 5th Bedfordshire Regiment.
He volunteered in August 1914, and after a period of training proceeded to Gallipoli, where he saw much heavy fighting. After taking part in several important engagements, he was so severely wounded in action at Suvla Bay in August 1915, as to necessitate the amputation of his right hand. He was invalided from the Army in July 1916, and holds the 1914–15 Star, and the General Service and Victory Medals.
44, St. Leonard's Street, Bedford. X4215/A.

SMITH, A. J., Farrier-Sergeant, R.A.V.C.
He volunteered in 1915, and was retained at various stations, where he was engaged on important duties as an Instructor in shoeing horses. He was not successful in his efforts to obtain his transfer to a theatre of war, but, nevertheless, rendered very valuable services until October 1918, when he was discharged. High Street, Sharnbrook, Bedford. Z4220.

SMITH, A. V., Sergeant, Machine Gun Corps.
Already in the Army when war was declared in August 1914, he was immediately drafted to the Western Front, where he fought in the Retreat from Mons. He also took a prominent part in the Battles of Ypres, Loos, the Somme, Arras, Cambrai and Le Cateau, and many other important engagements, and was twice wounded. He holds the Mons Star, and the General Service and Victory Medals, and in 1920 was serving in Egypt.
2, Grey Friars Walk, Bedford. X4224/A.

SMITH, A. W. (D.C.M.), Company Sergeant-Major, 1st London Regiment (Royal Fusiliers).
Mobilised in August 1914, he was retained on important duties as an Instructor in England until October 1916, and then proceeded to the Western Front, where he was wounded at Arras in June 1917. Invalided home, he returned to France, however, in February 1918, and was unfortunately killed in action at Gommecourt on March 31st of that year. He had been awarded the Distinguished Conduct Medal for conspicuous bravery in the Field at the time of being wounded, and was also entitled to the General Service and Victory Medals.
"His memory is cherished with pride."
34, East Street, St. Neots, Hunts. TZ4231.

SMITH, A. W., Gunner, Royal Field Artillery.
Shortly after joining in June 1917, he proceeded to the Western Front, where he saw much severe fighting, taking part in the second Battle of the Somme and other important engagements. He made the supreme sacrifice, falling in action on May 7th, 1918, and was buried at Mericourt. He was entitled to the General Service and Victory Medals.
"A costly sacrifice upon the altar of freedom."
Hillside, Nash, near Stony Stratford, Bucks. Z4031/C.

SMITH, A. W. (M.M.), Corporal, Royal Engineers.
He joined in 1916, and in May of the following year, proceeded to the Western Front, where he saw severe fighting in various sectors. He took part in the Battles of Arras, Cambrai and the Somme, and many other engagements, and was wounded in action at Hulluch in August 1917. He was awarded the Military Medal for conspicuous gallantry in the Field in the same month, and, holding also the General Service and Victory Medals, was demobilised in February 1919.
35, Bunyan Road, South End, Bedford. Z4217.

SMITH, B. F., Private, 1/1st Essex Regiment.
Two months after joining in April 1916, he proceeded to the Western Front, where he saw much heavy fighting. He served through the Battles of the Somme, Arras and Ypres, and many other important engagements in various sectors, and was wounded in action at Loos and Hill 60. He was demobilised in February 1919, and holds the General Service and Victory Medals. Little Staughton, Hunts. Z4230.

SMITH, C., Driver, Royal Engineers.
After volunteering in June 1915, he underwent a period of training prior to being drafted to the Western Front in 1917. There he was engaged on important duties in various sectors, was present also at the Battles of Arras, Bullecourt, Ypres and Cambrai, and was gassed and wounded in action. He was demobilised in June 1919, and holds the General Service and Victory Medals. 30, All Hallows Lane, Bedford. TX4208.

SMITH, C. A. J., Private, Bedfordshire Regiment.
He volunteered in September 1914, and after undergoing a period of training was retained at various stations, where he was engaged on duties of a highly important nature. Being medically unfit for active service, he was not successful in obtaining his transfer to the front, but, nevertheless, rendered valuable services until May 1919, when he was invalided from the Army. Roxton, Beds. Z4228.

SMITH, C. E. (Miss), Nurse, British Red Cross Soc.
She joined in 1914, and after completing a period of training served in the hospitals at Kimbolton, Romford, and various other stations. Engaged on duties of great importance, she rendered very valuable services throughout the period of hostilities, and was finally demobilised in 1919.
Hail Weston, Hunts. Z4199/B.

SMITH, C. F., L/Corporal, 1st Hertfordshire Regt.
Joining in February 1916, he was drafted to France in December of that year, and there saw heavy fighting in various sectors of the front. He took part in the Battles of Messines, Ypres and Passchendaele, fought also in the Retreat and Advance of 1918, and was wounded near Lens in April 1917, and at Cambrai in October of the following year, sustaining the loss of his left eye. Invalided from the Army in February 1919, he holds the General Service and Victory Medals.
Wyboston, near St. Neots, Hunts. Z4227

SMITH, C. W., Corporal, R.A.S.C.
Three months after joining in May 1916 he proceeded to Salonika, where he was engaged chiefly in conveying supplies to the forward areas. He saw much active service on the Vardar, Doiran and Struma fronts, and was also present at many important engagements until the cessation of hostilities. Demobilised on his return home in August 1919, he holds the General Service and Victory Medals.
Bow Brickhill, near Bletchley, Bucks. Z4194.

SMITH, C. W., Sapper, Royal Engineers.
Volunteering in November 1914, he was sent to the Western Front on completion of a period of training in the following year, and was there engaged on important duties with the Signal Section in various sectors. He was also present at the Battles of Albert, the Somme and Arras, and many other engagements until his return home in 1918. He was demobilised in April 1919, and holds the 1914–15 Star, and the General Service and Victory Medals. Foster Street, Bedford. X4212.

SMITH, C. W. A., Private, 2/22nd London Regt.
He joined in February 1918, and after four months' training proceeded to the Western Front, where he took part in the Battles of Amiens, Bapaume and Cambrai, and many other engagements during the Advance. In August 1919 he was transferred to Egypt, and was there stationed at Alexandria until his return home in April 1920 for demobilisation in the following month. He had served also with the Essex and Norfolk Regiments, and holds the General Service and Victory Medals. 34, Russell Street, Bedford. TX4209.

SMITH, E., Sapper, Royal Engineers.
Mobilised at the outbreak of war in August 1914, he was drafted to Egypt in the following year, and there took part in the capture of Magdhaba and many other engagements. Proceeding into Palestine, he served through the Battles of Gaza and was also present at the fall of Jaffa and Jerusalem. Returning home in 1919, he was demobilised in April of that year, and holds the 1914–15 Star, and the General Service and Victory Medals. 23, St. Leonards Street, Bedford. X4213/B.

SMITH, E., Private, East Lancashire Regiment and 12th Manchester Regiment.
He volunteered in May 1915, and was retained on important duties in England until July of the following year, when he proceeded to the Western Front. After taking part in engagements at Delville Wood, Trônes Wood and many other places in the Somme sector, he was severely wounded in November 1916, and admitted to hospital at Manchester. He was invalided from the Army in October 1917, and holds the General Service and Victory Medals.
1, Club Court, Priory Street, Newport Pagnell, Bucks. Z4206.

SMITH, E., Private, 11th East Surrey Regiment.
Shortly after volunteering in April 1915 he was sent to the Western Front, where he saw much severe fighting. He took part in the Battles of Loos, Arras and Ypres, and many other engagements until invalided home, suffering from shell-shock. He was afterwards retained on agricultural work in England, later serving with the Army of Occupation in Germany until his demobilisation in September 1919. He holds the 1914–15 Star, and the General Service and Victory Medals.
Rectory Lane, Somersham, Hunts. Z4192.

SMITH, E. G., Private, Canadian Overseas Forces.
He volunteered in November 1914, and in the following year proceeded to the Western Front, where he saw heavy fighting in various sectors. He took part in the Battles of Ypres, Festubert, Loos, the Somme, Arras, Vimy Ridge and Passchendaele and many minor engagements, and was severely wounded at Cambrai in November 1917. He was for a time in hospital at Lincoln before being invalided from the Army in 1918, and holds the 1914–15 Star, and the General Service and Victory Medals.
Maltman's Villa, Eaton Socon, St. Neots, Hunts. Z1809/B.

SMITH, F., Sergeant, Royal Field Artillery.
Called up from the Reserve at the outbreak of war in August 1914, he was immediately sent to the Western Front, where he fought at Mons. He also took a prominent part in the Battles of La Bassée, Ypres, Vimy Ridge, the Somme, Arras and Cambrai, and many other engagements until the cessation of hostilities, and then served with the Army of Occupation at Cologne. He was discharged on his return home in June 1919, and holds the Mons Star, and the General Service and Victory Medals.
5, North Street, Newtown, Huntingdon. Z4226.

SMITH, F., Private, Bedfordshire Regiment.
Mobilised in August 1914, he was immediately drafted to the Western Front, where he took part in the fighting at Mons. He also served through the Battles of Ypres and Loos and many other important engagements, was wounded in action, and in 1916 was taken prisoner. Held in captivity until after the cessation of hostilities, he was discharged in March 1919, and holds the Mons Star, and the General Service and Victory Medals.
2, Little Butts Street, Bedford. X1568/C.

SMITH, F., Private, 1st Suffolk Regiment.
Already in the Army when war was declared in August 1914, he was drafted immediately to the Western Front, where he fought in the Retreat from Mons, and also took part in the Battles of Ypres and Loos. In 1917 he was transferred to Egypt, whence he proceeded into Palestine and served through the Battles of Gaza and at the capture of Jerusalem. He was sent to Russia in January 1919, finally returning home in the following year. He holds the Mons Star, and the General Service and Victory Medals, and in 1920 was still with his unit. 2, Grey Friars Walk, Bedford. X4224/B.

SMITH, F. A., Private, Bedfordshire Regiment and Sherwood Foresters.
He joined in 1916, and on completing his training in the following year proceeded to the Western Front. Whilst in this theatre of war he took part in many important engagements, including the Battles of Arras, Messines, Ypres and Cambrai, and was severely wounded in action in 1918. Invalided home, he was for some time in hospital before being demobilised in September 1919, and holds the General Service and Victory Medals. 2, Church Walk, St. Neots, Hunts. Z3634/C.

SMITH, F. C., Private, 2nd Bedfordshire Regiment.
He was mobilised at the outbreak of war in August 1914, and three months later was sent to the Western Front, where he took part in the Battles of Ypres, Neuve Chapelle and Hill 60, and many minor engagements. He died gloriously on the Field of Battle at Festubert in May 1915. He was entitled to the 1914 Star, and the General Service and Victory Medals.
"Whilst we remember, the sacrifice is not in vain."
30, College Street, Kempston, near Bedford. Z4236/A.

SMITH, F. W., Private, 4th Yorkshire Regiment.
He volunteered in December 1915, proceeded to the Western Front after a short period of training, and there saw much severe fighting. After taking part in the Battle of the Somme and other important engagements, he was gassed and three times wounded in action. He was for a considerable period in hospital in England before being invalided from the Army in March 1917, and holds the General Service and Victory Medals.
30, College Street, Kempston, near Bedford. Z4236/B.

SMITH, F. W., Sapper, Royal Engineers.
Volunteering in August 1914, he proceeded to the Western Front in December of that year, and there saw much severe fighting. After taking part in several engagements in this theatre of war he unfortunately fell in action near Neuve Chapelle on January 30th, 1915. He was entitled to the 1914–15 Star, and the General Service and Victory Medals.
"His life for his Country, his soul to God."
Fairfield, High Road, Clapham, Bedford. Z4222.

SMITH, G., Private, 8th Bedfordshire Regiment.
Volunteering in September 1914, he was drafted to the Western Front in February of the following year, and there took part in the Battles of Hill 60, Ypres and Festubert, and was gassed at Loos in September 1915. Invalided home, he returned to France, however, on his recovery in March 1916, and was killed in action on the Somme on July 22nd of that year. He was buried at Vermelles, and was entitled to the 1914–15 Star, and the General Service and Victory Medals.
"The path of duty was the way to glory."
Cambridge Street, St. Neots, Hunts. Z4232/B.

SMITH, G. E., Private, 2nd Yorkshire Regiment.
He volunteered in April 1915, and in May of the following year was drafted to the Western Front, where he saw much severe fighting, taking part in the Advance on the Somme. He was reported missing, and is believed to have been killed in action on the Somme in May 1917. He was entitled to the General Service and Victory Medals.
"Great deeds cannot die:
They with the sun and moon renew thier light for ever."
44, Well Street, Buckingham. Z4202.

SMITH, H. A., Gunner, Tank Corps.
He volunteered in August 1914, and after undergoing a period of training with the 5th Northamptonshire Regiment, was sent to France in May 1915, and there served with the Machine Gun Corps in various sectors. After taking part in the Battles of Ypres and Festubert, he was wounded at Loos in October and invalided home. He returned to France, however, in February 1916, and, transferred to the Tank Corps, fought again on the Somme, at Arras, Messines and Cambrai. He fell in action at Amiens on August 8th, 1918. He was entitled to the 1914–15 Star, and the General Service and Victory Medals.
"A costly sacrifice upon the altar of freedom."
1, Abbey Terrace, Newport Pagnell, Bucks. Z4205.

SMITH, H. D., Private, Middlesex Regiment.
He joined in February 1918, and after completing a period of training was retained on duties of great importance at various stations in Ireland. He was unable to obtain his transfer overseas before the cessation of hostilities, but in February 1919 was drafted with the Army of Occupation to Germany, where he served at Cologne. Returning home in October 1919, he was demobilised in the following month.
17, Park Road, Stony Stratford, Bucks. TZ4210/A.

SMITH, H. G., Private, Royal Fusiliers.
He volunteered in June 1915, and on completion of a term of training in January of the following year proceeded to the Western Front, where he saw severe fighting at Loos and many other places. He died gloriously on the Field of Battle at Albert in April 1916. He was entitled to the General Service and Victory Medals.
"He died the noblest death a man may die:
Fighting for God and right and liberty."
46, Chandos Street, Bedford. X4196.

SMITH, H. J., Sapper, Royal Engineers.
Shortly after volunteering in September 1914, he was drafted to France, where he served in various sectors of the front. He took an active part in the Battles of Ypres, Hill 60, Festubert, Loos, the Somme, Arras, Messines, Cambrai and the Aisne, and many other important engagements until the cessation of hostilities, finally returning home in January 1919. He was demobilised in the following month, and holds the 1914 Star, and the General Service and Victory Medals.
6, Boswell Place, Bedford. X4198.

SMITH, H. J., Private, 9th Suffolk Regiment.
Volunteering in August 1914, he proceeded to the Western Front in June of the following year, and there saw heavy fighting in various sectors. After taking part in the Battles of Loos, the Somme, Ypres and Cambrai, he was severely wounded in action near Mons in October 1918, and was invalided home. He was finally demobilised in February 1919, and holds the 1914–15 Star, and the General Service and Victory Medals.
High Street, Hemingford Grey, Hunts. Z4195.

SMITH, J., Private, Middlesex Regiment.
Having previously been rejected on several occasions, he joined in September 1916, and in the following year was drafted to the Western Front. There he took part in the Battles of Ypres, Cambrai and Le Cateau, and many minor engagements, and fought also in the Retreat and Advance of 1918. He afterwards served with the Army of Occupation at Cologne until his demobilisation in November 1919, and holds the General Service and Victory Medals.
33, The Gardens, Stony Stratford, Bucks. TZ4210/B.

SMITH, J., Private, Bedfordshire Regiment.
Joining in July 1918, he proceeded to the Western Front on completing a short period of training later in the same year and there served in various sectors. He was engaged on duties of great importance whilst in this theatre of war, and did much useful work with his unit until December 1919, when he was demobilised. He holds the General Service and Victory Medals. 23, St. Leonard's Street, Bedford. X4213/C.

SMITH, J., Corporal, 2nd London Regiment (Royal Fusiliers).
He volunteered in August 1914, and was retained for a time at various home stations before proceeding to France in October 1916. He was then in action at the Battles of Arras, Bullecourt and Vimy Ridge, but was taken prisoner of war and held in captivity in Germany, suffering many privations. He was released after the Armistice and returned home for his demobilisation in January 1919. He holds the General Service and Victory Medals.
11, Pilcroft Street, Bedford. X4214.

SMITH, J., Private, 1/5th Bedfordshire Regiment.
He volunteered in June 1915, and early in the following year was drafted to Egypt. In this seat of operations he was engaged on important duties, and later took part in the Advance into Palestine, fighting at Gaza and at the fall of Jerusalem. He returned home and was demobilised in April 1919, holding the General Service and Victory Medals.
10, Grey Friars Walk, Bedford. X4224/D.

SMITH, JOSEPH, Private, Essex Regiment.
He joined in 1916, and in the following year was drafted to France, where he took part in much severe fighting in the Ypres and Arras sectors. He died gloriously on the Field of Battle on the Cambrai front on March 27th, 1918. He was entitled to the General Service and Victory Medals.
"Nobly striving:
He nobly fell that we might live."
2, Grey Friars Walk, Bedford. X4224/C.

SMITH, J., Private, 1st Bedfordshire Regiment.
He was mobilised in 1914, and almost immediately drafted overseas. Whilst on the Western Front he took part in the Mons Retreat, the Battles of Hill 60, Festubert, Loos, Vimy Ridge and Cambrai, and was wounded in action in April 1915. He was discharged in February 1918, and holds the Mons Star, and the General Service and Victory Medals.
58, Chandos Street, Bedford. X4197.

SMITH, J. C., Gunner, Royal Field Artillery.
He joined in May 1917, and early in the following year was drafted to France. There he took part in much fighting in the Cambrai sector, and in the Retreat and Advance of 1918. After hostilities ceased he proceeded to Germany with the Army of Occupation, and served on the Rhine until his demobilisation in November 1919. He holds the General Service and Victory Medals.
121, High Street, Newport Pagnell, Bucks. Z4207.

SMITH, J. F., B.S.M., Royal Field Artillery.
He was already in the Army when war broke out in August 1914 and immediately proceeded to France, where he took part in the Battle of Mons and the subsequent Retreat. He then served at the Battles of the Marne, the Aisne, La Bassée and Ypres, but in April 1915 proceeded to the Dardanelles, and saw much heavy fighting at the Landing at Gallipoli. Later he was sent to Egypt, thence to Palestine, but eventually returned to France, and fought in the Retreat and Advance of 1918. He was once wounded, and served with distinction throughout hostilities. He received his discharge in February 1920, and holds the Mons Star, and the General Service and Victory Medals. Sherington, Bucks. Z4237.

SMITH, J. G., Driver, R.A.S.C.
He joined in May 1917, and after a period of training was engaged at various home stations on important duties with the Mechanical Transport. He was unable to obtain a transfer overseas owing to his being medically unfit, but rendered valuable services until his discharge in November 1917.
6, Paggs Court, Silver St., Newport Pagnell, Bucks. Z1652/B.

SMITH, J. W., L/Corporal, 8th Bedfordshire Regt.
He volunteered in September 1914, and in the following year proceeded to the Western Front. In this theatre of war he took part in many engagements, including those at Loos, the Somme, Ypres and Cambrai, and was badly gassed in May 1918. He was invalided home and demobilised in June 1919, holding the 1914–15 Star, and the General Service and Victory Medals.
30, Pilcroft Street, Bedford. X4221.

SMITH, J. W., Private, Middlesex Regiment.
He joined in April 1917, and two months later was drafted to France, where he took part in much heavy fighting in the Amiens and Somme sectors. In October 1918 he returned home, and was retained on important agricultural work until his demobilisation in March 1919. He holds the General Service and Victory Medals
Little Stukeley, Hunts. Z1637/A.

SMITH, L., Private, 1/5th Bedfordshire Regiment.
He volunteered in June 1915, and in the same year proceeded to Egypt, where he was engaged on important duties. Later he took part in the Advance into Palestine and saw much fighting at Gaza, Jaffa, the fall of Jerusalem and Aleppo. He returned home, and was demobilised in August 1919, holding the 1914–15 Star, and the General Service and Victory Medals.
17, All Hallows Lane, Bedford. X4223.

SMITH, L. T., Bombardier, Royal Field Artillery.
He volunteered in September 1914, and in the following year was drafted to the Dardanelles, where he took part in the Landing at Suvla Bay. After the Evacuation of the Gallipoli Peninsula he was transferred to Egypt, but, proceeding into Palestine, saw much heavy fighting. Later he served in France in the Ypres sector, and was wounded in action. He was eventually discharged in February 1918, holding the 1914–15 Star, and the General Service and Victory Medals.
4, Hunter Street, Buckingham. Z3942/B.

SMITH, P. F., Private, 1st Bedfordshire Regiment.
He volunteered in January 1915, and in the following year was drafted to France, where he took part in many engagements. He made the supreme sacrifice, being killed in action near Arras on April 23rd, 1917, and was entitled to the General Service and Victory Medals.
"Thinking that remembrance, though unspoken, may reach him where he sleeps."
Papworth St. Agnes, Cambridgeshire. Z4235.

SMITH, P. D., Sapper, Royal Engineers.
He was mobilised in 1914, and later in the same year was drafted to France, where he was engaged on important duties in the Ypres, Loos, Festubert, Vimy Ridge and the Somme sectors. He was unfortunately killed at Guinchy on December 23rd, 1915, and was entitled to the 1914–15 Star, and the General Service and Victory Medals.
"His life for his Country, his soul to God."
72, Cauldwell Street, Bedford. X4216.

SMITH, R. P., Private, Lancashire Fusiliers.
Volunteering in May 1915, he was drafted overseas in the following August. Whilst on the Western Front he took part in the Battles of Loos, Vermelles, the Somme and Cambrai. He was demobilised in June 1919, but unfortunately contracted influenza and died on March 27th, 1920. He was entitled to the 1914–15 Star, and the General Service and Victory Medals.
"His memory is cherished with pride."
52, Spencer Street, Bradwell, Bucks. Z1748/A.

SMITH, R. P., Pte., Loyal North Lancashire Regt.
He volunteered in August 1914, and completing his training in the following year was drafted to France. There he took part in much heavy fighting in the Ypres, Somme, Arras and Cambrai sectors, and also in the Retreat and Advance of 1918. He returned from France in May 1919 suffering from pneumonia, and unfortunately died shortly afterwards. He was entitled to the 1914–15 Star, and the General Service and Victory Medals.
"Steals on the ear the distant triumph song."
22, Nelson Street, Buckingham. Z4200/A.

SMITH, S., Private, Royal Warwickshire Regiment.
He joined in 1916, and later in the same year proceeded to France, where he took part in the Battle of the Somme and was wounded in action. As a result he was invalided home, but on his recovery returned to France, and fought at Nieppe Forest, Ypres, Cambrai, the Somme (II.), the Marne (II.) and the Aisne (III.), and was again wounded in action. He was demobilised in February 1919, and holds the General Service and Victory Medals. Eaton Socon, Beds. Z4238.

SMITH, S., Sergeant, Oxford. and Bucks. L.I.
Volunteering in August 1914, he was drafted to France in the following year. In this seat of war he took part in many engagements, including those at Ypres, the Somme, Arras, Vimy Ridge, Passchendaele and Cambrai. He was then sent to Italy, and saw much fighting on the Asiago Plateau and Piave River. He returned home and was demobilised in March 1919, holding the 1914–15 Star and the General Service and Victory Medals. Diddington, Hunts. Z4233.

SMITH, S. A., Private, Royal Naval Division.
He volunteered in April 1915, and, completing his training in the following year, proceeded to France, where he served with the Hawke Battalion. He took part in much fighting in the Somme, Arras, Ypres and Cambrai sectors and was twice wounded in action in 1917. In March 1919 he was demobilised, and holds the General Service and Victory Medals.
Church Street, St. Neots, Hunts. Z4229.

SMITH, S. C., Private, Royal Defence Corps.
He volunteered in June 1915, and after a period of training was engaged at various home stations. He rendered valuable services on guard duties at munition works and bridges in Luton and Hertford, but was discharged in April 1918 as medically unfit. 3, Little Thurlow Street, Bedford. X3875/A.

SMITH, S. H., Corporal, R.A.O.C.
He joined in May 1916, and in the following month proceeded to the Western Front. In this theatre of war he was engaged on various important duties and was stationed at Poperinghe. He rendered valuable services until his demobilisation in November 1919, and holds the General Service and Victory Medals. 28, Canning Street, Bedford. TX4211.

SMITH, S. R., Private, 52nd Devonshire Regiment.
He joined in June 1918 on attaining military age, and underwent a period of training at various home stations. After hostilities ceased he proceeded to Germany with the Army of Occupation, and served on the Rhine until his demobilisation in September 1919.
22, Nelson Street, Buckingham. Z4200/B.

SMITH, T., Private, R.A.S.C.
He joined in October 1916, and, completing his training in the following year, was drafted to India. There he served on important duties on the North-West Frontier, but contracted malaria and was finally invalided home. He was discharged in May 1919 as medically unfit for further service, and holds the General Service and Victory Medals.
56, Priory Street, Newport Pagnell, Bucks. Z1490/B.

SMITH, T. J., Cpl., 8th Beds. Regt. and M.G.C.
Volunteering in the 8th Bedfordshire Regiment in September 1914, he was sent to France in August 1915, but after taking part in the Battle of Loos and being gassed in October, was wounded in action at Ypres in December and invalided home. Returning to the Western Front in April 1916, he was again wounded on the Somme in September and admitted to hospital at Cambridge. On his recovery he was transferred to the Machine Gun Corps, and was drafted to France in March 1917, when he served at Arras and Ypres before proceeding to Italy, where he fought on the Asiago Plateau and the Piave River. He was in hospital at Gènoa for a time with malarial fever, and was eventually demobilised in March 1919, holding the 1914–15 Star, and the General Service and Victory Medals.
Hail Weston, Huntingdon. Z4199/A.

SMITH, T. W., Sergt.-Major, R.A.M.C.
He volunteered in August 1914, and in the following year was drafted to the Dardanelles, where he saw much heavy fighting at Suvla Bay, Krithia and in the Evacuation of the Gallipoli Peninsula. He then proceeded to Egypt, but later took part in the Advance into Palestine, and saw fighting at Gaza, Jaffa and Haifa. He was demobilised in March 1919, and holds the 1914–15 Star, and the General Service and Victory Medals.
13, Hawkins Road, Bedford. Z4219.

SMITH, W., Sergeant, Bedfordshire Regiment.
He was mobilised in August 1914, and in the following year proceeded to Egypt. In this seat of operations he did continuously good work, and later played a prominent part in the Advance into Palestine, being in action at Gaza, Jaffa, the fall of Jerusalem and at Aleppo. He returned home and received his discharge in June 1919, holding the 1914–15 Star, and the General Service and Victory Medals.
23, St. Leonards Street, Bedford. X4213/A.

SMITH, W., Private, Yorkshire Regiment.
He joined in April 1917, and underwent a period of training prior to his being drafted to France. There he took part in the Retreat and Advance of 1918, during which he was in action at Cambrai, St. Quentin and Le Cateau. He was unfortunately killed in action near Mons on November 6th, 1918, and was entitled to the General Service and Victory Medals.
"Honour to the immortal dead who gave their youth that the world might grow old in peace."
12, St. Clement's Passage, Huntingdon. Z4218.

SMITH, W., Driver, Royal Army Service Corps.
He joined in August 1917, and after a period of training was engaged at various home stations on important duties with his unit. He was not successful in obtaining a transfer overseas, but did good work with the transport, and at the docks until his discharge in March 1918.
23, All Hallows Lane, Bedford. X2559/B

SMITH, W. A., Private, Beds. Regt. and M.G.C.
Volunteering in October 1915, he was drafted overseas in the following July. Whilst on the Western Front he took part in several important engagements, including those in the Arras, Ypres and Cambrai sectors. He made the supreme sacrifice, being killed in action on the Somme front on March 21st, 1918. He was entitled to the General Service and Victory Medals.
"The path of duty was the way to glory."
Huntingdon Street, St. Neots, Hunts. Z4203

SMITH, W. C., Corporal, King's Own Scottish Borderers and Military Foot Police.
He was already in the Army when war broke out in August 1914, and was immediately drafted to the Western Front, but was wounded in action and taken prisoner at the Battle of Mons. Whilst in captivity in Germany he suffered many hardships. After hostilities ceased he was repatriated, returned home and in 1920 was still in the Army. He holds the Mons Star, and the General Service and Victory Medals.
3, Little Thurlow Street, Bedford. X3875/B.

SMITH, W. E., A.B., Royal Navy.
He joined in 1916, and after his training proceeded to the North Sea, where he was engaged on important patrol duties with the Grand Fleet, and took part in the Naval operations at Ostend and Zeebrugge. He was on board H.M.S. "Avenger" and "Champagne" when these ships were torpedoed, and in 1920 was serving in H.M.S. "Delhi" in Russian waters. He holds the General Service and Victory Medals.
2, Church Walk, St. Neots, Hunts. Z3634/B.

SMITH, W. G., Corporal, R.A.S.C. (M.T.)
He joined in February 1916, and after a period of service at various home stations was sent to France in November 1917. Whilst on the Western Front he did excellent work in connecton with the transport of supplies in the Somme, Arras, Ypres and Cambrai sectors. He was demobilised in April 1919, and holds the General Service and Victory Medals.
17, Park Road, Stony Stratford, Bucks. TZ4210/C.

SMITH, W. H., Private, R.A.S.C. (M.T.)
He volunteered in September 1914, and in the following year was sent to Mudros in the Eastern Mediterranean, where he was engaged on important transport duties. He also served for a time in the Bedfordshire and Essex Regiments, and did excellent work until invalided home with rheumatic fever. He was discharged as medically unfit in July 1916, and holds the 1914–15 Star, and the General Service and Victory Medals.
44, St. Leonards Street, Bedford. X4215/B.

SMITH, W. H., Private, 1st Bedfordshire Regiment.
Enlisting in June 1911, he proceeded to France shortly after the outbreak of war, and took part in the Retreat from Mons. He was also in action at the Battles of Ypres, Armentières, Loos, the Somme (where he was wounded in August 1916), Arras and Cambrai. He received his discharge in March 1920, and holds the Mons Star, and the General Service and Victory Medals. Church Street, St. Neots, Hunts. Z4193.

SMITH, W. H., L/Corporal, Wiltshire Regiment.
Having volunteered in the Wiltshire Hussars in September 1914, he proceeded to France in the following April with the Wiltshire Regiment, and took part in the Battles of Ypres, Givenchy, Loos, the Somme, Arras and Cambrai. Gassed in action in the Cambrai sector in March 1918, he was invalided to England, and spent several months in hospital at Birmingham. He was discharged as medically unfit for further service in April 1919, and holds the 1914–15 Star, and the General Service and Victory Medals. 17, Moreton Road, Buckingham. Z4201.

SMITH, W. L., Private, R.A.M.C.
Being a Reservist, he was called to the Colours in August 1914, and proceeding to France served through the Retreat from Mons. He later took part in the Battles of the Marne, the Aisne, Ypres, Loos and the Somme as a stretcher-bearer, and also did duty as an orderly in various hospitals. After the cessation of hostilities he went to Germany with the Army of Occupation, and was stationed at Cologne until his discharge in January 1919. He holds the Mons Star, and the General Service and Victory Medals.
15, Clarence Road East, Stony Stratford, Bucks. Z4301/B.

SMITH, W. M., Rifleman, 16th London Regiment.
He joined the Queen's Westminster Rifles in 1917, but owing to his being under age for transfer overseas was retained on important duties at various home stations. He did excellent work with his unit until his demobilisation in 1919.
4, Herbert's Yard, St. Germain Street, Huntingdon. Z4225.

SMITHIES, R. N., Private, R.A.M.C.
Volunteering in August 1914, he proceeded to Gallipoli eight months later, and after taking part in the Landing at Cape Helles, served on the Headquarters' Staff of the 13th Division. In November 1915 he was invalided home with fever, but was eventually sent to France in March 1918. He then participated in the Battle of the Somme (II.) and in the Retreat and Advance. Demobilised in March 1919, he holds the 1914–15 Star, and the General Service and Victory Medals.
"The Grove," Great Linford, Bucks. Z4239.

SNELL, A., Private, Labour Corps.
He volunteered in 1914, but owing to his being medically unfit for service overseas was engaged on important agricultural work at Messrs. Laxton's, Nursery, near Bedford. He rendered valuable services whilst so employed and was eventually demobilised in March 1919.
1, Dean Street, Goldington Road, Bedford. Z4240.

SNOOK, A. H., Gunner, Royal Field Artillery.
He joined in June 1917, and in the following October was drafted to the Western Front. After taking part in heavy fighting at Passchendaele and Cambrai, he was unhappily killed in action on Vimy Ridge in May 1918. He was entitled to the General Service and Victory Medals.
"A costly sacrifice upon the altar of freedom."
Cardington, Bedford. Z4241/B.

SOLESBURY, C., Corporal, R.A.V.C.
He volunteered in May 1915, and on completion of his training was engaged on special duties in connection with the treatment of sick and wounded horses evacuated from various theatres of war. Owing to medical unfitness he was not successful in obtaining his transfer overseas, but did excellent work until invalided from the Army in February 1919.
High Street, Sharnbrook, Beds. Z4242.

SOPER, F. G. R., Cadet, Officers' Training Corps.
He joined the Officers' Training Corps of his school in April 1918, and underwent training for a commission at Cambridge. Unfortunately hostilities ceased before he could obtain his transfer overseas, but he did excellent work until November 1918. 34, Maitland Street, Bedford. X4243/B.

SOPER, G., C.Q.M.S., Royal Engineers.
He volunteered in January 1915, but owing to his being medically unfit for transfer overseas was retained on important duties in England. He rendered valuable services on the clerical staff of the Stores Depôts at Chatham and Bedford prior to being demobilised in October 1919.
34, Maitland Street, Bedford. X4243/A.

SOUSTER, G. L., Private, 1/5th Devonshire Regt.
He joined in July 1918, and after his training was engaged on important garrison duties in Ireland. He was unsuccessful in obtaining his transfer overseas until February 1919, when he was sent to the Army of Occupation in Germany, and was stationed at Cologne on the Rhine until his demobilisation in February 1920.
1, Albert Street, Bletchley, Bucks. Z4244.

SOUTHAM, A. C., Sergeant, R.A.S.C. (M.T.)
Volunteering in October 1914, he was sent to France within a week. Whilst on the Western Front he saw much fighting in the early stages of the war, and later rendered valuable services at Boulogne, where he was engaged as master cook until his demobilisation in April 1919. He holds the 1914 Star, and the General Service and Victory Medals.
16, Oxford Street, Stony Stratford, Bucks. TZ4246.

SOUTHGATE, B., Corporal, Bedfordshire Regt.
He volunteered in December 1915, and proceeded to France in the following year, but was seriously wounded in action during the Somme Offensive. He was invalided home and unfortunately died from his wounds in Folkestone Hospital in October 1916. He was entitled to the General Service and Victory Medals.
"He joined the great white company of valiant souls."
32, Beaconsfield Street, Bedford. X4245/A.

SOUTHGATE, C., Private, Bedfordshire Regiment.
He volunteered in August 1914, but on proceeding to France in the following year, was wounded and taken prisoner near Ypres in 1915. During his captivity in Germany he suffered many hardships, and was eventually repatriated after the cessation of hostilities. He was demobilised in March 1919, and holds the 1914–15 Star, and the General Service and Victory Medals. 32, Beaconsfield Street, Bedford. X4245/B.

SPARKES, G., Private, 1st Bedfordshire Regiment.
Already in the Army at the outbreak of war, he proceeded to France with the first Expeditionary Force and served at the Battle of, and in the Retreat from, Mons. He was also in action on the Marne and the Aisne before being taken prisoner at the Battle of La Bassée in October 1914. Whilst in captivity he suffered many hardships, and had his teeth knocked out by the Germans for refusing to give information. Repatriated after the cessation of hostilities he was discharged in April 1919, holding the Mons Star, and the General Service and Victory Medals.
"The Knoll," Sherington, Newport Pagnell, Bucks. Z4247

SPARKES, W. H. J., Private, 1/5th Bedfordshire Regiment and Royal Fusiliers.
He volunteered in August 1914, and first saw active service on the Gallipoli Peninsula, where he took part in the Landings at Cape Helles and Suvla Bay, and was wounded. Early in 1916 he was evacuated to England with fever, but on his recovery was drafted to the Western Front. He then served at the Battles of the Somme (II.) and the Marne (II.), and was wounded in action on two other occasions. Demobilised in February 1919, he holds the 1914–15 Star, and the General Service and Victory Medals. 5, Raleigh Street, Bedford. Z4248.

SPARKS, A. H., Sergeant, Queen's Own Oxfordshire Hussars.
He enlisted in 1911 and, proceeding to France in September 1914, was in action during the Mons Retreat. He also served with distinction at the Battles of Ypres (I.), Neuve Chapelle, Ypres (II.), Loos, the Somme, Arras, Ypres (III.) and Cambrai, and was wounded at Messines in October 1914. He finally took part in the Retreat and Advance of 1918, and then proceeded to Germany with the Army of Occupation. He holds the Mons Star, and the General Service and Victory Medals, and the Territorial Force Long Service Medal, and was discharged in April 1919.
55, Winsor Street, Bletchley, Bucks. Z4249.

SPARROW, F., Private, Oxford. and Bucks. L.I.
Having volunteered in September 1914, he was sent to France six months later, and served as a bomber during heavy fighting in the Ypres sector. He laid down his life for King and Country at the Battle of Loos in September 1915, and was entitled to the 1914–15 Star, and the General Service and Victory Medals.
"A costly sacrifice upon the altar of freedom."
Emberton, Bucks. Z4250.

SPENCE, J., Petty Officer, Royal Navy.
Already in the Navy when war was declared, he immediately proceeded on active service in August 1914, and did duty on board H.M. Submarine "G.1." This vessel cruised in the North and Baltic Seas and was engaged in chasing German "U" Boats. He was stationed for a time at Scapa Flow, and was still serving in 1920. He holds the 1914–15 Star, and the General Service and Victory Medals.
37 Water Lane, Kempston, Beds. X4251.

SPENCER, A., Driver, Royal Engineers.
He volunteered in August 1914, and proceeded to France on completion of his training. Whilst on the Western Front he played an important part with his unit in the Battles of Neuve Chapelle, Ypres, Loos, the Somme, Arras, Cambrai and Lille. He was demobilised in January 1919, and holds the 1914–15 Star, and the General Service and Victory Medals.
21, Eastville Road, Bedford. TZ4252/B.

SPENCER, A. T., Private, 1/5th Bedfordshire Regt.
Volunteering in October 1914, he was sent to the Dardanelles in the following year and took part in the Landing at Suvla Bay and in heavy fighting on Gallipoli. After the Evacuation of the Peninsula, he proceeded to Egypt, but after serving at Cairo for a time advanced with his unit into Palestine, and was in action at Jerusalem. He was demobilised in June 1919, and holds the 1914–15 Star, and the General Service and Victory Medals. 21, Eastville Road, Bedford. TZ4252/C.

SPENCER, F., Private, 2/5th Bedfordshire Regt.
He volunteered in November 1915, and on completion of his training was engaged on important duties at various home stations. Owing to medical unfitness he was not drafted overseas, but did excellent work with his unit until he was invalided from the Army in August 1917.
21, Eastville Road, Bedford. TZ4252/A.

SPENCER, H., Private, 3rd Bedfordshire Regiment.
He joined in October 1916, but owing to his being too young for transfer to a theatre of war, was retained on special duties in England, and rendered valuable services until his demobilisation in September 1919.
21, Eastville Road, Bedford. TZ4252/E.

SPENCER, R. J., 2nd Corporal, Royal Engineers.
After volunteering in August 1914 he completed his training, and was then sent to France. Whilst in this theatre of war he took an active part in the Battles of Givenchy, Loos, the Somme, Arras, Ypres, Cambrai and Lille, and was twice wounded. Demobilised in May 1919, he holds the 1914–15 Star, and the General Service and Victory Medals.
21, Eastville Road, Bedford. TZ4252/D.

SPENCER, T., Private, 5th Bedfordshire Regiment.
He volunteered in August 1914, and, proceeding to the Dardanelles a few months later, took part in the Landings at Cape Helles and Suvla Bay. After the Evacuation of the Gallipoli Peninsula he was stationed in Egypt for a time before advancing into Palestine, where he was in action at Gaza, Jaffa and Haifa. He was then transferred to the Western Front, and fought at Arras, Ypres and Bullecourt, and in the Retreat and Advance of 1918. Demobilised on his return to England in January 1919, he holds the 1914–15 Star, and the General Service and Victory Medals.
9, Gratton Road, Queen's Park, Bedford. Z3276/B.

SPENDELOW, R. H., Tpr., Bedfordshire Lancers.
He volunteered in September 1914, and early in the following year proceeded to France, where he was attached to the 8th (King's Royal Irish) Hussars. He took part in the Battles of Festubert, Loos, Albert, the Somme, Ypres and Cambrai. After the cessation of hostilities he was sent to Germany with the Army of Occupation, and was stationed at Cologne until his demobilisation in April 1919, holding the 1914–15 Star, and the General Service and Victory Medals.
Great Northern Street, Huntingdon. Z4253.

SPERRING, J. A., Private, Middlesex Regiment.
Joining in February 1916, he proceeded to France later in the same year, and took part in the Battles of Arras, Ypres, Cambrai and the Somme. He was twice wounded in action—at Vimy Ridge in May 1916, and at Delville Wood in April 1918. He holds the General Service and Victory Medals, and was demobilised in August 1919. Easton, Hunts. Z4254.

SPICER, W. A., Bombardier, R.F.A.
Having volunteered in September 1915, he was drafted to the Western Front in the following year and did excellent work with an ammunition column in various sectors, particularly that of Ypres. In May 1918 he met with a serious accident and was invalided home for treatment. He was demobilised in March 1920, and holds the General Service and Victory Medals. 22, Gladstone Street, Bedford. X4255.

SPILLING, E. C., Pte., 2nd Seaforth Highlanders.
After volunteering in January 1915 he underwent a period of training, and was eventually sent to France in August 1916. After two months' heavy fighting in the Somme sector he was invalided home and spent some time in hospital. In March 1918, however, he returned to the Western Front and served through the Retreat and Advance, particularly at Cambrai. He was demobilised in April 1919, and holds the General Service and Victory Medals.
43, Grey Friars Walk, Bedford. X4256.

SPINDLER, W. J., Sergeant, Bedfordshire Regt.
He volunteered in August 1914, and was engaged as an Instructor until drafted to France in 1915. After being in action at Arras he was wounded on the Somme in 1916, and invalided home. On his recovery he again rendered valuable services as a Musketry Instructor, and was eventually demobilised in 1919, holding the 1914–15 Star, and the General Service and Victory Medals. 4, Hawkins Road, Bedford. Z4257.

SPORLE, W., R.S.M., 2/10th London Regiment.
He volunteered in October 1914, and in the following year was drafted to the Western Front, where he served with distinction in many important engagements in various sectors. In 1918 he was invalided home sick, and after hospital treatment in Birmingham was discharged as medically unfit for further service in January 1919. He holds the 1914–15 Star, and the General Service and Victory Medals.
28, Houghton Road, Bedford. Z4258.

SPREADBOROUGH, S., Corporal, R.E.
Mobilised in August 1914, he was sent to France immediately and took part in the Retreat from Mons and the Battle of Ypres. He then did excellent work with his unit on the lines of communication, and was gassed. He was discharged in March 1919 on his return to England, and holds the Mons Star, and the General Service and Victory Medals.
22, Beckett Street, Bedford. X3716/B.

SPRECKLY, F. G., Sapper, Royal Engineers.
He joined in September 1916, and was quickly drafted to the Western Front, where he was engaged on important duties with the Railway Operative Department. He did excellent work as a driver and fireman in the Albert and Somme sectors, and was eventually demobilised in December 1919, holding the General Service and Victory Medals.
126, Honey Hill Road, Queen's Park, Beds. Z4259.

SPRIGGS, F. G., Driver, R.A.S.C.
Two months after volunteering in December 1915 he was sent to France, and whilst in this theatre of war was engaged on important transport duties in the forward areas in the Somme, Ypres and Cambrai sectors. After hostilities ceased he proceeded to Germany with the Army of Occupation, and was stationed at Cologne. He was demobilised in June 1919, and holds the General Service and Victory Medals.
11, Station Terrace, Great Linford, Bucks. Z4260/A.

SPRIGGS, J., Private, 7th Wiltshire Regiment.
Volunteering in September 1914, he was drafted to Mesopotamia twelve months later, and took part in heavy fighting during the Advance to the Relief of Kut. In April 1917 he was reported missing, and is now presumed to have been killed in action. He was entitled to the 1914–15 Star, and the General Service and Victory Medals.
"His life for his Country, his soul to God."
11, Station Terrace, Great Linford, Bucks. Z4260/D.

SPRIGGS, P. A., Private, 9th Gloucestershire Regt.
He joined in April 1916, and four months later landed in Salonika. Whilst in the Balkan theatre of war he took part in heavy fighting on the Doiran and Vardar fronts, and was wounded in action in 1917. He spent some time in hospital at Salonika, but on his recovery rejoined his unit. He was eventually demobilised in March 1919, and holds the General Service and Victory Medals.
Northampton Road, Lavendon, Bucks. Z4261.

SPRIGGS, R. T., Driver, Royal Field Artillery.
Mobilised in August 1914, he immediately proceeded to the Western Front, and took part in the Battle of Mons and in the subsequent Retreat. He also saw severe fighting on the Marne, the Aisne, the Somme and at Ypres, and was wounded on the Somme in May 1918. He was invalided to England, but on his recovery returned to France and served there until discharged in February 1919, holding the Mons Star, and the General Service and Victory Medals.
11, Station Terrace, Great Linford, Bucks. Z4260/C.

SPRIGGS, W. A., Driver, Royal Field Artillery.
When war broke out in August 1914 he was already serving, and was at once ordered to the scene of activities in France. On that front he was in action in various sectors and saw heavy fighting in the Battles of Ypres and the Somme, and in the Retreat and Advance of 1918. After the Armistice he proceeded into Germany with the Army of Occupation, and served at Cologne until discharged in April 1919. He holds the 1914 Star, and the General Service and Victory Medals.
11, Station Terrace, Great Linford, Bucks. Z4260/B.

SPRING, A. S., Private, 1st Northants. Regiment.
Having previously served for seven years in the Army, he was called up from the Reserve at the outbreak of war in August 1914. Three months later he embarked for France, where he was engaged in fierce fighting in the Loos and Ypres sectors, but was unfortunately killed in action at Richebourg on May 13th, 1915. He was entitled to the 1914 Star, and the General Service and Victory Medals.
"Whilst we remember, the sacrifice is not in vain."
8, Railway Terrace, Bletchley, Bucks. Z4262/B.

SPRING, E. G., Sergeant, Bedfordshire Lancers.
He volunteered in October 1914, and rendered valuable services as an Instructor at Bedford and Brentford until 1916, when he was drafted to Palestine. In that theatre of war he fought in engagements at Gaza and Haifa, and in 1918 was transferred to France, where he took a prominent part in severe fighting until the close of hostilities. Demobilised in May 1919, he holds the General Service and Victory Medals.
London Road, Sandy, Beds. Z4263.

SPRING, F. (M.M.), Private, Sherwood Foresters.
He joined in March 1916, and five months later was drafted to the Western Front, where he took part in the Battles of the Somme, Arras and Ypres, and many other important engagements. In August 1917 he was wounded at Ypres, and was awarded the Military Medal for conspicuous bravery at Arras in May 1917. He was taken prisoner at Aveluy Wood in April 1918, and kept in captivity until the cessation of hostilities. On his release he was demobilised in April 1919, and also holds the General Service and Victory Medals.
New Farm, Colesdon, St. Neots, Hunts. Z4264.

SPRING, F. C. (M.M.), L/Sergt., 2nd Beds. Regt.
A month after the outbreak of war he volunteered, and in July 1915 proceeded overseas. During his service on the Western Front he was in action at the Battles of Albert, the Somme, Arras, Ypres and Passchendaele, and also took a prominent part in operations at St. Quentin. He was awarded the Military Medal in August 1917 for great bravery and devotion to duty, and was eventually demobilised in March 1919. He also holds the 1914–15 Star, and the General Service and Victory Medals. Sandy Terrace, London Rd., Sandy, Beds. Z4266.

SPRING, H., Private, Bedfordshire Regiment.
He volunteered in August 1914, and in the following year was drafted to France, where he was engaged in fierce fighting in various sectors. Whilst in action at the Battle of the Somme he was wounded, and on his return to the firing-line took part in the Battles of Arras, Ypres and Cambrai. In 1917 he was transferred to Italy, and served on the Piave and Asiago Plateaux. He was demobilised in March 1919, and holds the 1914–15 Star, and the General Service and Victory Medals.
3, New Street, Godmanchester, Hunts. Z4267.

SPRING, W., Stoker, R.N., H.M.S. "Pembroke."
When war broke out in August 1914 he volunteered, and on conclusion of his training was in the same year posted to H.M.S. "Pembroke." In this ship he took part in the Battle of Jutland and other important engagements, and performed valuable work in the Mediterranean and North Seas. He was demobilised in June 1919, holding the 1914–15 Star, and the General Service and Victory Medals.
Queen's Terrace, London Road, Sandy, Beds. Z4265.

SPRITTLES, A. R., Cpl., 2nd Oxford. & Bucks. L.I.
He volunteered in 1915, and after training at Chelmsford was in the following year sent to France. On that front he fought in various sectors, but was wounded on the Somme in 1917, and invalided to England. He was admitted to hospital in Northumberland, and after protracted treatment there was demobilised in January 1919, holding the General Service and Victory Medals.
11, Mill Lane, Stony Stratford, Bucks. TZ4268/A.

SPRITTLES, D. H., Sergeant, R.A.M.C.
Volunteering in August 1914, he proceeded to Egypt in March 1915. Three months later he was drafted to Gallipoli, and during the campaign there played a conspicuous part in engagements at Suvla Bay and Anzac. After the Evacuation of the Peninsula he was sent to Palestine, where he rendered valuable services at Gaza. He was demobilised on his return to England in July 1919, and holds the 1914–15 Star, and the General Service and Victory Medals.
35, Russell Street Gardens, Stony Stratford, Bucks. TZ4269.

SPRITTLES, F. J., Private, 8th Canadian Infantry (90th Rifles).
He volunteered in 1915, and came over from Canada with the Canadian contingent in 1916, and was then drafted to France. There he fought in the Battles of the Somme, Ypres and Cambrai and many other important engagements, and also served in the Retreat and Advance of 1918. He unfortunately died of nephritis at Boulogne on February 28th, 1919, and was entitled to the General Service and Victory Medals.
"The path of duty was the way to glory."
11, Mill Lane, Stony Stratford, Bucks. TZ4268 /C.

SPRITTLES, J. J., Sergt., 7th Wiltshire Regiment.
Volunteering in September 1914, he proceeded to France in the following year, and, after taking part in severe fighting at Ypres, was transferred to Salonika. There he fought with distinction in numerous engagements on the Vardar and the Doiran fronts until August 1918, when he returned to France, and gave his life for King and Country on October 4th. He was entitled to the 1914–15 Star, and the General Service and Victory Medals.
"Whilst we remember, the sacrifice is not in vain."
11, Mill Lane, Stony Stratford, Bucks. TZ4268 /B.

SPYER, H., A.B., R.N., H.M.S. "Sparrow Hawk."
Having previously served in the Navy, he rejoined in 1916, and, on being posted to H.M.S. "Sparrowhawk," took an active part in the bombardment of Zeebrugge. He also performed excellent work in the North Sea and in connection with coast defence. He was eventually demobilised in July 1919, and holds the General Service and Victory Medals.
4, Featherstone Buildings, Newham Street, Bedford. X4270.

STACEY, A. E., Trooper, 6th Dragoon Guards; and Private, Tank Corps.
He joined in May 1918, but owing to ill-health was unsuccessful in his endeavours to secure a transfer to a theatre of war. Nevertheless, he rendered valuable services, and was engaged on important duties with his unit at various home stations until demobilised in January 1920.
Carter Street, Girtford, Sandy, Beds. Z4271.

STACEY, W. M., Private, Oxford. and Bucks. L.I.
A month after the outbreak of war he volunteered in the Oxfordshire and Buckinghamshire Light Infantry, but was later attached to the Royal Army Medical Corps and drafted to France in September 1915. He performed many valuable services as a doctor's orderly, and on being transferred to the Royal Engineers was engaged on important work as an electrician at Boulogne. He was demobilised in February 1919, and holds the 1914–15 Star, and the General Service and Victory Medals.
78, Queen Anne Street, New Bradwell, Bucks. Z4272.

STAFFERTON, H., Corporal, Bedfordshire Regt.
He was already serving when war was declared in August 1914, and at once proceeded to the Western Front, where he saw heavy fighting at Laventie and Armentières. He also took an active part in the Battles of Mons, the Aisne, Neuve Chapelle and Ypres, and was severely wounded at Festubert, which resulted in the loss of his right arm. In consequence he was discharged as medically unfit in February 1916, holding the Mons Star, and the General Service and Victory Medals.
Queen's Terrace, London Road, Sandy, Beds. Z4274.

STAFFERTON, W., Private, 1/6th Essex Regt.
He volunteered in January 1916, and six months later proceeded to Egypt, where he was engaged in fierce fighting on the Suez Canal and at Mersa Matruh. Subsequently he was transferred to Palestine, in which theatre of war he served in important engagements at Gaza and Jaffa. On his return to England in July 1919 he was demobilised, and holds the General Service and Victory Medals.
Keeley Lane, Wootton, Beds. TZ4273.

STAMFORD, H., Driver, Royal Field Artillery.
Volunteering in 1915, he was on completion of his training ordered overseas in the following year. During his service on the Western Front he took an active part in numerous important engagements, including the Battles of the Somme, Vimy Ridge, Ypres, Passchendaele and Cambrai. He was demobilised in February 1919, and holds the General Service and Victory Medals.
55, Russell Street, St. Neots, Hunts. TZ4277.

STANBRIDGE, H. J., Sergeant, 5th Bedfordshire Regiment and Rifle Brigade.
At the outbreak of war he was serving with the Territorial Forces, but on joining the 5th Bedfordshire Regiment was retained on important duties at Bury St. Edmund's, Newmarket, Southwold and Lowestoft until 1917, when he was drafted to the Western Front. He was then transferred to the Rifle Brigade and played a conspicuous part in the Battles of Arras, Ypres, Cambrai and Havrincourt. Demobilised in March 1919, he holds the General Service and Victory Medals.
Salph End, Renhold, near Bedford. Z4276.

STANBRIDGE, J. T., Private, Essex Regiment.
He joined in April 1916, and after a course of training was in the following year sent to France. On that front he did good work with his unit in various important engagements, and saw much severe fighting at the Battles of Messines, Vimy Ridge, the Somme, the Marne and Bapaume. He remained in France until February 1919, when he was demobilised, holding the General Service and Victory Medals.
8, Featherstone Buildings, Newham Street, Bedford. X4275.

STANFORD, J. W., Private, 12th Suffolk Regt.
He volunteered in August 1915, but was unable to procure a transfer to a theatre of war. He was engaged on important duties with his unit at various stations, but after only seven months' service he developed heart disease, and was discharged from the Army as medically unfit for further military duties in March 1916.
7, Rich Bell Cottages, Chandos Street, Bedford. X3989 /A.

STANFORD, W. P., Private, 10th Suffolk Regt.
Joining in May 1916, he was retained on home defence, and carried out his various duties in a very efficient manner. Unfortunately his health broke down after a short period of service, and he was discharged in August 1916 as physically unfit for further military duties.
7, Rich Bell Cottages, Chandos Street, Bedford. X3989 /B.

STANIFORTH, F., L/Corporal, Sherwood Foresters and Royal Army Service Corps.
A serving soldier, he was sent to the Western Front shortly after the outbreak of war, and fought in the Retreat from Mons. He also took part in the Battles of the Marne, the Aisne, Ypres, Loos and Albert, and saw heavy fighting in numerous other engagements. In 1919 he was transferred to the Royal Army Service Corps, and was engaged on important transport duties at Woolwich. He was still in the Army in 1920, and holds the Mons Star, and the General Service and Victory Medals.
19, Firbank Road, Bedford. Z4278.

STANTON, C. D., Private, Tank Corps.
He volunteered in June 1915, and on completion of his training was in the following year drafted to Egypt, where he was engaged on important duties at Cairo and Alexandria. Subsequently he was sent to Palestine, on which front he participated in much severe fighting at Gaza and Haifa. Returning to England in October 1919, he was demobilised, holding the General Service and Victory Medals.
15, Gawcott Road, Buckingham. Z4283.

STANTON, D., Sergt., 1st R. Warwickshire Regt.
A Reservist, he was called up at the outbreak of war in August 1914, but was retained on important duties in England until 1916, when he obtained a transfer to Egypt. During his service in Palestine he took a prominent part in engagements at Gaza, Jerusalem and Jaffa. Unfortunately his health broke down, and he was discharged from Khartoum in March 1919, holding the Soudan Medal, and the General Service and Victory Medals.
3, North End Square, Buckingham. Z4284 /A.

STANTON, F. P., Pte., 1/7th Warwickshire Regt.
He volunteered in March 1916, and three months later was drafted to the Western Front. After two months' service in the Ypres sector he was transferred to Italy, and whilst engaged in severe fighting in that theatre of war was wounded. On his recovery he was sent in 1917 to Palestine, and took an active part in the capture of Tripoli. He was demobilised on his return to England in September 1919, holding the General Service and Victory Medals.
Dawkes Terrace, Stoke Goldington, Bucks. Z4282 /A.

STANTON, H. J., Sergeant, R.A.V.C.
Volunteering in October 1915, he was on completion of his training drafted overseas in the following year. Whilst serving on the Western Front he experienced fierce fighting in the Battles of the Somme, Lens and Cambrai, and was engaged on important veterinary duties behind the lines. He was demobilised on his return to England in May 1919, and holds the General Service and Victory Medals.
Milton Ernest, Bedford. Z4285.

STANTON, J., Private, Oxford. & Bucks. L.I.
He joined in February 1917, and after a period of training at Canterbury was drafted overseas three months later. He served in the Balkans for four months, and during that time saw heavy fighting in several engagements. In September 1917 he was sent back to Aldershot, where he was engaged on important duties until demobilised in October 1919, holding the General Service and Victory Medals.
3, North End Square, Buckingham. Z4284 /C.

STANTON, J., Private, Royal Welch Fusiliers.
Volunteering in February 1915, he embarked for France in 1916, and fought at St. Eloi, Loos and Albert. In May 1917 he was wounded at Vimy Ridge and invalided to England, and on his discharge from hospital was drafted in November 1917 to Palestine. On that front he was in action in important engagements at Gaza and Jericho, but contracted malaria, and was sent to hospital in England. Subsequently he was discharged as medically unfit for further service in January 1919, and holds the General Service and Victory Medals.
Grafham, Hunts. Z4281.

STANTON, T., Private, Seaforth Highlanders.
He joined in 1917, but owing to his youth was not successful in his endeavours to secure a transfer to the fighting area. He was therefore retained on home defence, and during his service in the Army performed valuable work at Cromarty, until eventually demobilised in December 1919.
3, North End Square, Buckingham. Z4284/B.

STANTON, W. H., Private, Northants. Regiment.
When war was declared in August 1914 he volunteered, and after completing his training at Shoreham was ordered overseas a year later. Whilst serving on the Western Front he took part in numerous important engagements, and performed valuable work as a signaller in the Battles of Loos, Arras, Vimy Ridge, Ypres, Cambrai and the Marne. Demobilised in February 1919, he holds the 1914–15 Star, and the General Service and Victory Medals.
Dawkes Terrace, Stoke Goldington, Bucks. Z4282/B.

STANTON, W. J., Sapper, Royal Engineers.
He volunteered in December 1915, and nine months later embarked for Salonika. In that theatre of war he was engaged on important transport duties on the Vardar and Doiran fronts until 1917, when he was transferred to Palestine. There he saw much service at Gaza and Jerusalem, and on his return to England in January 1919 was demobilised, holding the General Service and Victory Medals.
7, Howard Street, Bedford. X4280.

STANTON, W. T., Private, 6th Oxford. and Bucks. Light Infantry and Machine Gun Corps.
He volunteered in September 1914, and in February of the following year proceeded to France, where he took part in the Battles of Neuve Chapelle, Ypres, Festubert, Loos, the Somme, Arras, Cambrai and Amiens. He was also engaged in fierce fighting at Armentières and in the Retreat and Advance of 1918, but was unhappily killed in action in the vicinity of the Selle on October 1st, 1918. He was entitled to the 1914–15 Star, and the General Service and Victory Medals.
"Nobly striving:
He nobly fell that we might live."
10, Northampton Terrace, Newport Pagnell, Bucks. Z4279.

STAPLETON, C. (M.M.), Sapper, R.E.
Volunteering in August 1914, he embarked in the following year for Gallipoli, and served with distinction throughout the campaign there, being awarded the Military Medal for conspicuous gallantry in the Field. In 1916 he was sent to Egypt, and subsequently to Palestine, on which front he took an active part in important engagements at Gaza and Jerusalem and in General Allenby's Offensive in 1918. He was invalided home with septic poisoning in 1919, and was demobilised in February of that year, also holding the 1914–15 Star, and the General Service and Victory Medals.
6, Bunyan Road, Bedford. Z4286.

STAPLETON, E. C., Pte., 1/5th Beds. Regt.
A month after the outbreak of war he volunteered, and in July 1915 was drafted to Gallipoli. After taking an active part in the Landingat Suvla Bay he contracted dysentery, and unfortunately died on November 4th, 1915, at Malta. He was entitled to the 1914–15 Star, and the General Service and Victory Medals.
"His memory is cherished with pride."
14, Holme Street, Bedford. X4287/B.

STAPLETON, H., Driver, Royal Engineers.
He volunteered in September 1914, and three months later proceeded to the Western Front, where he served for over four years. During that period he was engaged in fierce fighting at the Battles of Ypres, Festubert, the Somme, Arras and Cambrai, and was employed on important transport duties in various sectors. At the close of hostilities he went into Germany with the Army of Occupation, and served at Cologne until demobilised in June 1919. He holds the 1914–15 Star, and the General Service and Victory Medals.
14, Holme Street, Bedford X4287/A.

STAPLETON, H., Trooper, Bedfordshire Lancers.
He joined in August 1916, and served with the Bedfordshire Lancers at Bedford and Colchester until February 1917, when he was transferred to the 19th Hussars and drafted to the Western Front. There he saw fierce fighting in various sectors, and took an active part in the Battles of Arras and Ypres, and in engagements at Albert and St. Quentin. He was demobilised in February 1919, and holds the General Service and Victory Medals.
Covingtons Yard, Turvey, Beds. Z4288.

STARMORE, A. S., Officers' Steward, Royal Navy.
Volunteering in October 1914, he was posted to H.M.S. "Maori," in which vessel he saw much service. He was present at the engagements at Westende, Middlekirke, Ostend, Nieuport and Zeebrugge in 1914, and his ship was instrumental in the sinking of the submarine "U.8" in March 1915. Later in the same year H.M.S. "Maori" was torpedoed, and all the crew were taken prisoners. After the Armistice he was released, and in 1920 was still serving. He holds the 1914–15 Star, and the General Service and Victory Medals.
100, Iddesleigh Road, Bedford. Z4289/E.

STARMORE, E. S., Petty Officer, H.M.S. "Hampshire."
Already serving in the Navy at the outbreak of hostilities in August 1914, he was posted to H.M.S. "Hampshire," in which vessel he was engaged on important patrol duties in the North Sea, the Baltic Sea and the English Channel. Later he took part in the operations at the Battle of Jutland. He was unfortunately drowned on June 5th, 1915, when the "Hampshire" was sunk on the way to Russia. He was entitled to the 1914–15 Star, and the General Service and Victory Medals.
"The path of duty was the way to glory."
100, Iddesleigh Road, Bedford. Z4289/C.

STARMORE, F. H., Gunner, R G.A.
Having joined in February 1916, he underwent a period of training, and in the following year proceeded to France. He was in action during the heavy fighting on the Somme, where he was wounded. He unfortunately died from the effects of his wounds on October 23rd, 1917, and was entitled to the General Service and Victory Medals.
"His life for his country, his soul to God."
100, Iddesleigh Road, Bedford. Z4289/A.

STARMORE, L. S., Gunner, R.G.A.
He joined in August 1916, and on conclusion of his training in the following year proceeded to the Western Front, where he took an active part in the Battles of Arras, Ypres and Passchendaele. On September 22nd, 1917, he was unfortunately killed in action near Ypres, and was entitled to the General Service and Victory Medals.
"He passed out of the sight of men, by the path of duty and self-sacrifice."
100, Iddesleigh Road, Bedford. Z4289/B.

STAUGHTON, W. J., Private, 1/4th Essex Regt.
Volunteering in 1915, he completed his training in the following year, and was drafted to Egypt. During his service in the East he took part in many important engagements, particularly in Palestine, where he was in action at the Battles of Gaza and Jaffa, and in the heavy fighting on the River Jordan. On his return home he was demobilised in March 1919, holding the General Service and Victory Medals.
Near the Church, Moggerhanger, Sandy, Beds. Z4290.

STEELE, A. G., Private, 2nd Bedfordshire Regt.
Mobilised from the Reserve at the outbreak of war in August 1914, he was quickly drafted to the Western Front. During his short service in this theatre of war he took part in heavy fighting at La Bassée and Neuve Chapelle. He made the supreme sacrifice, being killed in action on March 10th, 1915, and was entitled to the 1914 Star, and the General Service and Victory Medals.
"His life for his Country."
Potters Cross, Wootton, Bedford. Z3185/A.

STENNING, F. C., Private, Hampshire Regiment.
Volunteering in August 1914, he completed a period of training in the following year, and proceeded to the Dardanelles, where he was in action during the Landing at Suvla Bay. He made the supreme sacrifice, being killed on November 5th, 1915, and was entitled to the 1914–15 Star, and the General Service and Victory Medals.
"Nobly striving,
He nobly fell that we might live."
100, Iddesleigh Road, Bedford. Z4289/D.

STEPHENSON, W. A., Sapper, R.E. (R.O.D.)
Having joined in February 1917, he underwent a period of training, and in the following year was drafted to France. Whilst in this seat of war he did excellent work attached to the Railway Operative Department, and served during the engagements at Ypres and also in the Retreat and Advance of 1918. He was demobilised in October 1919, holding the General Service and Victory Medals.
7, North Street, New Town, Huntingdon. Z1630/A.

STEVENS, A., Sergeant, 2nd Northants. Regt.
A serving soldier, he was mobilised at the outbreak of hostilities in August 1914, and immediately drafted to France. He served with distinction during the Retreat from Mons and at the Battles of Ypres, Hill 60, Festubert and Loos, where he was unfortunately killed in action in October 1915. He was entitled to the Mons Star, and the General Service and Victory Medals.
"His life for his Country, his soul to God."
12, Haughton Road, Bedford. Z4295/A.

STEVENS, A. G., Private, Bedfordshire Regiment.
Volunteering at the outbreak of hostilities in August 1914, he completed his training and was later drafted to France. In the course of his service in this theatre of war he was in action at the Battles of Arras, Ypres, Cambrai and the Somme. He was discharged as medically unfit for further service in June 1918, and holds the General Service and Victory Medals.
The Quay, St. Ives, Hunts. Z4291/D.

STEVENS, A. W., 1st Class Petty Officer, R.N.
Already serving in the East Indies at the outbreak of war, he was immediately posted to H.M.S. "Swiftsure," and was present during the operations in the Dardanelles. Later he was transferred to H.M.S. "Royal Oak," and took part in the engagements at Jutland and Zeebrugge. He also did good work attached to the Grand Fleet in the North Sea. In 1920 he was discharged, holding the 1914–15 Star, and the General Service and Victory Medals, and the Naval General Service Medal (with clasp, Persian Gulf).
West End, Cranfield, Beds. TZ4296.

STEVENS, C. H., Private, Suffolk Regiment.
Having joined in 1918, he underwent a period of training, but was later found to be medically unfit for service overseas. He was, therefore, engaged on important guard and other duties at Blackpool, where he rendered excellent services until demobilised in 1919.
The Quay, St. Ives, Hunts. Z4291/C.

STEVENS, E., Private, Royal Fusiliers.
Volunteering in 1915, he completed a period of training, and early in the following year proceeded overseas. During his service on the Western Front he was in action at the Battles of Loos, the Somme, Arras, Ypres and Cambrai. After the cessation of hostilities he went with the Army of Occupation into Germany. He was demobilised in 1919, holding the General Service and Victory Medals.
The Quay, St. Ives, Hunts. Z4291/B.

STEVENS, F. A. G., 1st Class Stoker, Royal Navy.
He joined in October 1918, and was afterwards posted to H.M. Mine-sweeper "Cornflower." Using Aden as a base, his vessel was engaged in mine-sweeping in the Mediterranean, and whilst employed in this highly dangerous occupation he did good work. He was still serving in the Royal Navy in 1920. 18, St. Leonard's Street, Bedford. X4294/C.

STEVENS, G., Private, Royal Fusiliers.
Joining in April 1916, he proceeded later in the same year to the Western Front. There he participated in heavy fighting on the Somme front and at Arras, Ypres, Cambrai and Neuve Chapelle. After the Armistice he was sent to Germany, where he served with the Army of Occupation on the Rhine until March 1919, when he was demobilised, holding the General Service and Victory Medals.
Wistow, Hunts. Z4297.

STEVENS, G., Corporal, Bedfordshire Regiment.
He joined in September 1916, and in the following year was drafted to France. In this theatre of war he took part in the Battles of Ypres, Cambrai and the Marne, and also in various engagements during the Retreat and Advance of 1918. He later proceeded to Germany with the Army of Occupation, and was stationed at Cologne until February 1919. He was then demobilised, and holds the General Service and Victory Medals. Warboys, Hunts. Z4292.

STEVENS, R. V., Private, 1st Bedfordshire Regt.
After volunteering in September 1915, he underwent a period of training, and later proceeded to the Western Front, where he took an active part in the Battles of the Somme, Arras and Ypres, and in heavy fighting at Loos. He died gloriously on the Field of Battle on October 11th, 1917, and was entitled to the General Service and Victory Medals.
"A valiant Soldier, with undaunted heart he breasted life's last hill."
The Quay, St. Ives, Hunts. Z4291/A.

STEVENS, S. A. J., Drummer, London Regiment (Royal Fusiliers).
He volunteered in September 1914, and was retained at home on various duties until September 1916, when he was sent to France. There he served with his unit in the Battles of the Somme, Arras, Ypres, Passchendaele and Cambrai, and did good work. He remained in this theatre of hostilities until February 1919, and was demobilised a month later, holding the General Service and Victory Medals.
18, St. Leonard's Street, Bedford. X4294/B.

STEVENS, W., Rifleman, 51st King's Royal Rifle Corps; and Private, Bedfordshire Regiment.
Joining in May 1917, he was stationed at Colchester undergoing training until the following December. He was then drafted to France, where he was in action with his unit at Armentières and on the Somme and Cambrai fronts. He was later employed on important duties in various stations, and did excellent work until he was demobilised in May 1920, holding the General Service and Victory Medals.
12, Houghton Road, Bedford. Z4295/C.

STEVENS, W., Pte., 15th Royal Welch Fusiliers.
He volunteered in January 1915, and, after a brief training, proceeded later in the same year to the Western Front. There he took part with his unit in many important engagements, including those at Armentières, Bullecourt and Cambrai, performing excellent work until the Armistice. He then returned home, was demobilised in March 1919, and holds the 1914–15 Star, and the General Service and Victory Medals.
12, Houghton Road, Bedford. Z4295/B.

STEVENS, W., Gunner, Royal Field Artillery.
He volunteered in August 1915, and, after completing his training, was employed on various duties at home stations until January 1917, when he proceeded to the Western Front. He was medically unfit for service in the front line, and consequently remained at Havre, where he was engaged on important duties at the docks. He did good work until he was invalided home on account of ill-health, and was discharged in December 1918, holding the General Service and Victory Medals.
126, Victoria Road, Fenny Stratford, Bucks. Z4293.

STEVENS, W. J. T., Leading Seaman, R.N., H.M.S. "Coventry."
Already serving at the outbreak of hostilities in August 1914, he was posted to H.M. Torpedo-boat Destroyer "Archer," and served in this vessel on patrol and other important duties in the North Sea and Mediterranean. He performed excellent work, and being later transferred to H.M.S. "Coventry," was still serving in this ship in 1920. He holds the 1914–15 Star, and the General Service and Victory Medals.
18, St. Leonard's Street, Bedford. X4294/A.

STEVENSON, J., Private, Queen's Own Cameron Highlanders.
He volunteered in August 1914, and in the following May was drafted to France. There he was in action at Loos, Vimy Ridge, on the Somme front and at Beaumont-Hamel. In 1917 he was transferred to Salonika, and saw further service on the Vardar and Doiran fronts, and suffered for some time from malaria. After the Armistice he served in Germany with the Army of Occupation, and was eventually discharged in November 1919, holding the 1914–15 Star, and the General Service and Victory Medals.
1, St. Cuthbert's Square, St. Cuthbert's St., Bedford. TX4298.

STEWART, A., Private, 8th Argyll and Sutherland Highlanders.
Volunteering in August 1914, he was sent in May of the following year to the Western Front. In this theatre of war he served with his unit in many engagements, including those at Albert, Ypres, Passchendaele and Arras, where he was wounded. As a result he was evacuated to England and eventually invalided out of the Service in August 1918. He holds the 1914–15 Star, and the General Service and Victory Medals. 7, Roise Street, Bedford. X4301.

STEWART, A. A., Rflmn., 13th Royal Irish Rifles.
Mobilised in August 1914, he proceeded early in the following year to France. There he played a prominent part in heavy fighting on the Ypres, Somme and Cambrai fronts, performing excellent work. He was reported missing after a severe engagement at Cambrai on March 21st, 1918, and was later presumed to have been killed on that day. He was entitled to the 1914–15 Star, and the General Service and Victory Medals.
"His life for his Country."
Dock Cottages, Towcester. Z4300.

STEWART, F., Private, Black Watch.
He was mobilised in August 1914, and three months later was drafted to the Western Front. In this theatre of hostilities he participated in the Battles of Ypres, Arras, Cambrai and many other important engagements in France and Belgium, and did good work. In 1917 he was invalided home on account of ill-health, and on his recovery was released from the Colours in order to work on the land at Easton until he was finally discharged in October 1919. He holds the 1914 Star, and the General Service and Victory Medals.
Easton, Hunts. Z4299.

STIFF, H. G., Private, 8th Bedfordshire Regiment.
He volunteered in April 1915, and, after completing his training, was employed on various duties until he proceeded to France early in 1916. Shortly afterwards he was taken prisoner at Ypres and was interned in Germany until the Armistice. Repatriated in December 1918, he was subsequently demobilised in March 1919, holding the General Service and Victory Medals. Earith, Hunts. Z4302.

STOCK, B. C., Corporal, Royal Engineers.
He joined in April 1916, and five months later was sent to the Western Front. During his service overseas he was employed with his Company on important duties in the Somme, Ancre, and Cambrai sectors, also at Beaumont-Hamel, Arras and Ypres, and was wounded. He performed good work until he returned home for demobilisation in March 1919, and holds the General Service and Victory Medals.
15, Howbury Street, Bedford. Z1022/B.

STOCK, H. G., Sapper, Royal Engineers.
Volunteering in September 1914, he was drafted to Gallipoli in the following July and was engaged on various duties during the operations at Suvla Bay. In December 1915 he was invalided home, suffering from dysentery and rheumatic fever, and on his recovery in the following April was sent to France, where he served for three years, stationed in turn on the Somme front and at Arras, Ypres and Cambrai. Demobilised in May 1919, he holds the 1914–15 Star, and the General Service and Victory Medals. 24, Great Butts Street, Bedford. X1861/A.

STOCK, J., Private, Leicestershire Regiment.
He volunteered in March 1915, and was stationed at Holton Park Camp until the following year, when he proceeded to France. There he did excellent work in action at Loos, Albert, Vimy Ridge, on the Somme front, and also at Arras and Ypres. He was afterwards invalided home on account of ill-health, and was discharged in June 1918 as unfit for further service, holding the General Service and Victory Medals.
High Street, Carlton, Sharnbrook, Beds. Z1340/C.

STOCKER, E. J., Sgt., 1/5th King's (Liverpool Regt.)
Volunteering in August 1915, he was retained at home on important duties until 1917, and was then sent to the Western Front. In this theatre of hostilities he served at Givenchy, La Bassée, Festubert, Albert, Ypres and on the Somme front, being gassed in action at Givenchy and wounded at La Bassée. He was demobilised in February 1919, and holds the General Service and Victory Medals.
Railway Cottages, Needingworth Rd., St. Ives, Hunts. Z4304/B.

STOCKER, F. J., Corporal, R.G.A.
Serving at the outbreak of war in August 1914, he was drafted two months later to France. There he participated with his Battery in the Battles of Ypres, Festubert, Loos, the Somme, Arras and Cambrai, and was twice wounded—on the Somme front in June 1916, and at Arras in October 1918. Returning home in January 1919, he was demobilised in the following month, and holds the 1914 Star, and the General Service and Victory Medals. 20, Cauldwell Street, Bedford. X4303.

STOCKER, J. P., Private, 1st Oxford. & Bucks. L.I.
He volunteered in November 1915, and in the following year proceeded to the Western Front. During his service overseas he was in action on the Somme front, also at Arras, Ypres and Cambrai, and was wounded. He was later transferred to Italy, and saw further service on the Piave front and the Asiago Plateau. Returning home in February 1919, he was then demobilised, and holds the General Service and Victory Medals.
Railway Cottages, Needingworth Road, St. Ives, Hunts.
Z4304/A.

STOCKFORD, F., Pte., Cheshire, & Hampshire Regts.
Mobilised when hostilities broke out in August 1914, he was at once sent to France, where he took part in the Battle of, and Retreat from, Mons, and the Battles of the Marne, Ypres, Neuve Chapelle, Festubert and Loos. Invalided home on account of ill-health in 1916, he spent some time in hospital in London and later returned to France. He was then transferred to the Hampshire Regiment and participated in strenuous fighting at Arras and Passchendaele and in various sectors during the Retreat and Advance of 1918. He was discharged in March 1919, holding the Mons Star, and the General Service and Victory Medals. 30, Bridge St., New Bradwell, Bucks. Z4305.

STOCKWELL, C., Private, East Kent Regiment; and Driver, Tank Corps.
He volunteered in September 1914, and was afterwards drafted to the Western Front, where he was later transferred to the Tank Corps. He was in action on the Neuve Chapelle, Ypres, Somme, Arras and Cambrai fronts, and performed consistently good work. He remained overseas for some time after the Armistice, and was demobilised in July 1919, holding the 1914–15 Star, and the General Service and Victory Medals.
24, Littledale Road, Kempston, Beds. Z4306.

STOKES, A. R., Trooper, Bedfordshire Lancers; and Private, 8th (King's Royal Irish) Hussars.
He was mobilised with the Yeomanry in August 1914, and in the following February proceeded to France. There he was transferred to the 8th Hussars, and served at Ypres, Loos, on the Somme front, and also at Albert, Passchendaele, Amiens and Le Cateau. After the Armistice he was sent to Germany, and served with the Army of Occupation in Cologne until July 1919. He was demobilised a month later, and holds the 1914–15 Star, and the General Service and Victory Medals.
Lodge Drive, Pidley, Hunts. Z4311/B.

STOKES, F. W., Private, Oxford. & Bucks. L.I.
Volunteering in August 1914, he was stationed at Aldershot until July 1915, when he was sent to France. In this theatre of war he took part in many important engagements, including those at Givenchy, Loos, Monchy, Ypres, Arras and Cambrai. He was wounded in June 1918, and, being invalided home, was sent to hospital in Manchester, where he remained until demobilised in April 1919. He holds the 1914–15 Star, and the General Service and Victory Medals.
19, Park Road, Stony Stratford, Bucks. TZ4310.

STOKES, H. W., Pte., Royal Warwickshire Regt.
He volunteered in September 1914, and was employed on various duties in home stations up to July 1916. He was then drafted to France, where he took part in heavy fighting on the Somme front and at Bullecourt and Beaumont-Hamel. In March 1917 he was wounded at Vimy Ridge, and was evacuated to England. On his recovery in November 1917, he was employed on agricultural duties in Lincolnshire until May 1919, when he was demobilised, holding the General Service and Victory Medals. Pidley, Hunts. Z4311/A.

STOKES, S. W., Rifleman, Rifle Brigade.
He joined in May 1917, and served at Winchester and in the Isle of Sheppey until the following August, when he was drafted to France. There he was in action at Lens and Passchendaele, and after only a few months' service overseas made the supreme sacrifice, being killed on December 8th, 1917. He was entitled to the General Service and Victory Medals.
"Great deeds cannot die."
8, Whitbread Avenue, Bedford. Z4308.

STOKES, T., Private, Bedfordshire Regiment.
Volunteering in February 1915, he was shortly afterwards sent to the Western Front. During his service in this theatre of war he was in action at Festubert, Loos, Ypres, Arras, on the Somme and at Cambrai, and was wounded in April 1916 at Ypres. He remained overseas until the cessation of hostilities, and was demobilised in February 1919. He holds the 1914–15 Star, and the General Service and Victory Medals.
Wistow, Hunts. Z4312.

STOKES, W., Private, 6th Northants. Regiment.
He volunteered in September 1914, and proceeded to the Western Front in the following year. There he took part in heavy fighting at Hill 60, Givenchy, Loos, the Somme and Arras, but in July 1917 was severely wounded at Ypres, and in the next month succumbed to his injuries in hospital at Cirencester. He was entitled to the 1914–15 Star, and the General Service and Victory Medals.
"Nobly striving:
He nobly fell that we might live."
14, Prince of Wales Row, Moulton, Northampton. Z4309.

STOKES, W. E., Pte. (Sig.), 7th Wiltshire Regt.
Volunteering in September 1914, he completed a year's training and service in England, and was sent to France, where he served at Albert. In November of the same year he was drafted to Salonika, and served on the Doiran and Vardar fronts, and in Serbia. Returning to the Western Front, he fought at Mormal Forest, Amiens and Le Cateau, and was eventually demobilised in April 1919, holding the 1914–15 Star, and the General Service and Victory Medals.
31, St. Giles Street, New Bradwell, Bucks. Z4307.

STONE, E. F., Sapper, Royal Engineers.
He completed four months' training at Chatham after volunteering, and was in March 1916 sent to Mesopotamia, where he was engaged on duties in his own trade, wood-carving. He rendered valuable services, and, returning home, was demobilised in April 1919, holding the General Service and Victory Medals. Bow Brickhill, near Bletchley, Bucks. Z4313/A.

STONE, J., A.B., R.N., H.M.S. "Courageous."
Volunteering at the outbreak of war, he was posted to H.M.S. "Courageous," and during the war saw service at Scapa Flow, in the North Sea, the Dardanelles and in the Mediterranean. He took part in the Gallipoli and Salonika campaigns, and also fought at Jutland. He was still in the Royal Navy in 1920, and holds the 1914–15 Star, and the General Service and Victory Medals. 63, Caldecote St., Newport Pagnell, Bucks. Z4314.

STONE, T. R., Pte., 52nd Royal Warwickshire Regt.
He joined in March 1916, and after a year's service at different stations in England was sent to France. In that theatre of war he fought at Cambrai, Arras, Beaumont-Hamel and the Somme, and took part in the Retreat and Advance of 1918. He was demobilised in October 1919, and holds the General Service and Victory Medals.
Bow Brickhill, near Bletchley, Bucks. Z4313/B.

STONEBRIDGE, A., Private, Tank Corps.
Volunteering in 1915, he was drafted to the Western Front in the following year, and fought in the Somme Offensive. During 1917 he took part in the Battles of Arras, Messines Ridge and Ypres, but had to spend three months in hospital with shell-shock. During the Retreat and Advance of 1918 he was in action at Cambrai. He was demobilised in February 1919, and holds the General Service and Victory Medals.
6, Rectory Lane, Somersham, Hunts. Z4315/A.

STONEBRIDGE, C. A., Sapper, Royal Engineers.
He volunteered in August 1914, but in February of the next year was discharged as unfit. A year later he was, however, called up again and sent to France a month afterwards. He saw much service there, but was gassed in July 1918 during the Advance in the neighbourhood of Cambrai, and invalided home. He was in consequence again discharged in January 1919, but died from the effects, which brought on consumption, on February 3rd, 1919. He was entitled to the General Service and Victory Medals.
"His life for his Country."
22, Newnham Lane, Goldington Road, Bedford. Z3063/A.

STONEBRIDGE, E. A., Private, Canadian Overseas Forces.
He volunteered in November 1915, and, on completing his training in the following year, proceeded to the Western Front. Whilst in this theatre of war he took part in many important engagements, including the Battles of the Somme, Vimy Ridge, Bullecourt and Cambrai, fought also in the Retreat and Advance of 1918, and was wounded at Ypres in 1917. He was demobilised in May 1919, and holds the General Service and Victory Medals.
6, Rectory Lane, Somersham, Hunts. Z4315/C.

STONEBRIDGE, W. E., Private, Norfolk Regt.
He joined in November 1916, and in September of the following year, was drafted to the Western Front, where he saw severe fighting in various sectors. After taking part in the Battles of Passchendaele and Cambrai, he was invalided home in December 1917, suffering from trench-feet, and was afterwards retained on important duties in England. He was demobilised in May 1919, and holds the General Service and Victory Medals.
6, Rectory Lane, Somersham, Hunts. Z4315/B.

STONESTREET, E., Corporal, R.A.S.C. (M.T.)
Shortly after volunteering in October 1915, he was sent to France, where he was engaged chiefly in conveying supplies to the forward areas. He served on the Somme and at Arras, Ypres and Cambrai, and in various other sectors of the front, and did much good work until his return home for demobilisation in March 1919. He holds the 1914–15 Star, and the General Service and Victory Medals.
34, Beaconsfield Street, Bedford. X4316/A.

STONESTREET, E. W., Corporal, King's (Shropshire Light Infantry).
He joined immediately on attaining military age in January 1918, and after a short period of training was drafted to the Western Front, where he saw much severe fighting, and was wounded in action. Invalided home, he returned to France, however, and was wounded a second time near Cambrai, having fought in the Allies' Retreat and Advance. He holds the General Service and Victory Medals, and in 1920 was with his unit on garrison duties at Aden.
34, Beaconsfield Street, Bedford. X4316/B.

STONESTREET, P., Rifleman, 17th London Regt.
Two months after volunteering in November 1915, he was drafted to the Western Front, where he saw severe fighting in the Somme and Ypres sectors. In June 1916, however, he was transferred to Salonika, and there took part in important engagements on the Vardar front until sent to Egypt in January of the following year. Serving also in Palestine, he was wounded near Jerusalem, and was for a time in hospital at Gaza. Later he returned to France and was again in action in the Retreat and Advance of 1918. Demobilised in December of that year, he holds the General Service and Victory Medals.
34, Beaconsfield Street, Bedford. X4316/C.

STOPP, A. H., Sergeant, Royal Garrison Artillery.
Having enlisted in October 1909, he was already serving in China when war broke out in August 1914, and was then posted for special duty to H.M.S. "Empress of Asia," engaged in chasing the German raider "Emden." Relieved at Aden in January 1915, he returned to China, being finally sent home in November of the following year. Later he served on the Western Front, and there took part inthe Battles of Ypres and the Somme, and other engagements in various sectors. Discharged in February 1919, he holds the 1914–15 Star, and the General Service and Victory Medals.
Duck Lake, Maids Moreton, Buckingham. Z4317/A.

STOPP, A. W., Drummer, 1st Bedfordshire Regt.
A serving soldier, having enlisted in 1908, he was drafted to the Western Front immediately on the outbreak of war in August 1914, and was wounded in action in the Retreat from Mons. Invalided home, he returned to France, however, in July 1917, and took part in the Battles of Ypres, Cambrai and the Somme, and other engagements. He was discharged in February 1919, and holds the Mons Star, and the General Service and Victory Medals. Maids Moreton, Buckingham. Z4320/B.

STOPP, F., Private, Machine Gun Corps.
He volunteered in January 1915, and after training and service in England with the Buckinghamshire Hussars, was in December 1916 sent to Egypt and transferred to the Machine Gun Corps, with which he was in action at Gaza and in the operations which led to the fall of Jericho and Jerusalem. In June 1918 he was drafted to France, and served in the Ypres and Cambrai sectors. He was demobilised in April 1919, and holds the General Service and Victory Medals.
Green's Norton, Towcester, Northants. Z4518.

STOPP, F. C., Private, Oxford. and Bucks. L.I.
Joining in August 1916, he proceeded to the Western Front after four months' training and there saw severe fighting in various sectors. After taking part in the Battles of Arras, Messines and Ypres, and other engagements, he was gassed on the Menin Road in October 1917, and invalided home. He returned to France, however, on his recovery, and was again in action until the cessation of hostilities. Demobilised in February 1919, he holds the General Service and Victory Medals. Maids Moreton, Buckingham. Z4320/A.

STOPP, G. H., C.Q.M.S., 1st Oxford. & Bucks. L.I.
Volunteering in December 1914, he proceeded to the Western Front in June of the following year, and there saw much heavy fighting. He took a prominent part in the Battle of Ypres and other engagements in this theatre of war, and was wounded on the Somme. In December 1917 he was transferred to Italy, and wasagain in action on the Piave and the Asiago Plateaux, finally returning home for demobilisation in January 1919. He holds the 1914–15 Star, and the General Service and Victory Medals. Duck Lake, Maids Moreton, Buckingham. Z4317/B.

STOPP, W. J., Private, 1st Devonshire Regiment.
He joined in February 1917, and in October of that year proceeded to France, whence he was drafted in the following month to Italy. There he saw much severe fighting, taking part in many important engagements on the Piave, Trentino and Asiago Plateaux. He was invalided home in August 1919, suffering from appendicitis, and in the following month was demobilised, holding the General Service and Victory Medals.
Duck Lake, Maids Moreton, Buckingham. Z4319.

STOREY, F. J., Sapper, Royal Engineers.
He joined in August 1918, and, after undergoing a period of training, was retained at various stations, where he was engaged on duties of great importance on the railways. Owing to the early cessation of hostilities he was unable to obtain his transfer to the front, but, nevertheless, rendered valuable services with his unit until August 1919, when he was demobilised. Great Paxton, St. Neots, Hunts. Z4322.

STOREY, H., Sergt., Beds. Yeomanry (Lancers).
He volunteered in September 1914, and was retained on important duties in England until 1917, being transferred from the Bedfordshire Yeomanry to the East Riding Regiment and afterwards to the Royal Army Service Corps. Later, however, he was sent to Egypt and thence into Palestine, where he fought with distinction in the Battles of Gaza and the capture of Haifa. Demobilised on his return home in July 1919, he holds the General Service and Victory Medals.
Offord Cluny, Hunts. Z4323.

STOREY, L., Private, 6th Bedfordshire Regiment.
Volunteering in August 1914, he was drafted to the Western Front in the following year, and there saw heavy fighting in various sectors. After taking part in the Battles of Festubert, Loos, Arras, Vimy Ridge, Cambrai and the Somme and minor engagements, he was wounded in 1918 and admitted to hospital in Cheshire. He was demobilised in February 1919, and holds the 1914–15 Star, and the General Service and Victory Medals.
Offord Cluny, Hunts. Z4324.

STOREY, T., Private, Machine Gun Corps.
Mobilised in August 1914, he was sent to the Western Front in the following month, and there took part in the Battles of the Marne, Ypres, Hill 60 and Loos. In 1916 he was transferred to Egypt and thence advanced into Palestine, where he fought in the Battles of Gaza and on the River Jordan. Returning to France in 1918, he was again in action in the Retreat and Advance, and was gassed and wounded in August of that year. He was discharged in February 1919, and holds the 1914 Star, and the General Service and Victory Medals.
London Road, Godmanchester, Hunts. Z4321/B.

STORTON, A., Sapper, R.E. (Signal Section).
Two months after volunteering in August 1914, he was drafted to France, where he saw severe fighting in various sectors of the front. He took part in the Battles of Ypres, Festubert, Loos, the Somme, Arras and Cambrai and many other important engagements, serving also with the 2nd Bedfordshire Regiment before his demobilisation in June 1919. He holds the 1914 Star, and the General Service and Victory Medals.
41, Bunyan Road, South End, Bedford. Z4325.

STOWE, E. W., Private, Royal Welch Fusiliers.
He volunteered in May 1915, and in the following year was drafted to the Western Front. Whilst in this theatre of war he took part in many important engagements, including the Battles of the Somme, Ypres and Armentières, and was severely wounded in April 1918. Admitted to hospital at Southport, he was afterwards transferred to the Labour Corps, finally being invalided from the Army in March 1919. He holds the General Service and Victory Medals.
Lathbury, Newport Pagnell, Bucks. Z4326/B—Z4327/B.

STOWE, T., Corporal, 6th Oxford. & Bucks. L.I.
He volunteered in September 1914, and in May of the following year was sent to the Western Front, where he took part in the Battles of Ypres, the Somme and Arras, and many minor engagements. Mortally wounded in action at Ypres on August 16th, 1917, he unhappily died on the following day. He was entitled to the 1914–15 Star, and the General Service and Victory Medals.
"Thinking that remembrance, though unspoken, may reach him where he sleeps."
Lathbury, Newport Pagnell, Bucks. Z4326/A—Z4327/A.

STRATTON, A., Private, Machine Gun Corps.
Joining in June 1916, he was drafted to Salonika after five months' training, and there saw much severe fighting. He took part in many important engagements on the Doiran and Struma fronts until the cessation of hostilities, and was then transferred to Russia, where he remained until July 1919. He was demobilised in the following month, and holds the General Service and Victory Medals.
8, Prospect Row, St. Neots, Hunts. Z4329.

STRATTON, E. G., Sapper, Royal Engineers.
He volunteered at the outbreak of war in August 1914, and in the following year was sent to the Dardanelles, where he saw much severe fighting until the Evacuation of the Peninsula. He was then transferred to Egypt, and, proceeding into Palestine, took part in the Offensive under General Allenby. He also served for a time in Mesopotamia, and was present at the capture of Baghdad. Demobilised on returning home in July 1919, he holds the 1914–15 Star, and the General Service and Victory Medals. 49, Garfield Street, Bedford. Z4328.

STREET, A., Trooper, East Riding of Yorkshire Yeomanry (Lancers).
Two months after volunteering in June 1915 he was drafted to Egypt, where he served at various stations in the capacity of a storeman. He afterwards proceeded into Palestine on similar duties, rendering very valuable services until his return to England for demobilisation in March 1919. He holds the 1914–15 Star, and the General Service and Victory Medals. Weston Underwood, near Olney, Bucks. Z4330.

STRETTON, J. H., Private, Oxford. & Bucks. L.I.
He volunteered in August 1914, and in March of the following year proceeded to the Western Front, where he took part in the Battle of Ypres and other important engagements. Afterwards transferred to Italy, he saw severe fighting on the Piave until the cessation of hostilities, and finally returned home for demobilisation in March 1919. He holds the 1914–15 Star, and the General Service and Victory Medals.
32, Greenfield Road, Newport Pagnell, Bucks. Z1825/B.

STRETTON, W., Private, Norfolk Regiment.
Volunteering in August 1914, he was sent to the Western Front on completing his training in the following March, and there saw much heavy fighting. After taking part in the Battles of Ypres and the Somme and other engagements he was severely wounded early in 1917, and was admitted to hospital at Leeds. He was invalided from the Army in August of that year, and holds the 1914–15 Star, and the General Service and Victory Medals. 32, Greenfield Rd., Newport Pagnell, Bucks. Z1825/C.

STRINGER, C., Corporal, Royal Engineers.
He volunteered in August 1914, and underwent a period of training prior to his being drafted to Egypt. There he was engaged on important duties at Cairo and Alexandria, and later took part in the Advance into Palestine through the Sinai Peninsula, and was in action at the fall of Jerusalem. He returned home and was demobilised in March 1919, holding the 1914–15 Star, and the General Service and Victory Medals.
3, Eastville Road, Bedford. Z4331.

STRINGER, F., Private, Bedfordshire Regiment.
He volunteered in January 1915, and in the following year proceeded to Egypt. He took part in the Advance into Palestine, and saw much fighting at Gaza, Haifa and the fall of Jerusalem. Unfortunately he contracted pneumonia, from which he died in Egypt on June 16th, 1919. He was entitled to the General Service and Victory Medals.
"A valiant Soldier, with undaunted heart he breasted life's last hill."
East Chadley Lane, Godmanchester, Hunts. Z3312/B.

STRINGER, F. C., Private, R.A.M.C.
He joined the Army in July 1914, and when war broke out in the following August was immediately drafted to the Western Front. There he took part in many engagements, including the Battles of Mons, Hill 60, Ypres, Festubert and Passchendale, where he was badly wounded in action. In consequence he was invalided home and in hospital for some considerable time. He was discharged in April 1919, and holds the Mons Star, and the General Service and Victory Medals.
20, Marne Street, Kempston, Bedford. Z4333/B.

STRINGER, F. V., Sergeant, Machine Gun Corps.
He volunteered in February 1915, and, completing his training in the following year, was drafted to France. In this theatre of war he played a prominent part in the Battles of the Somme, Arras, Messines and Ypres, and was badly wounded in action. As a result he was invalided home and eventually discharged in June 1918 as medically unfit for further service. He holds the General Service and Victory Medals.
24, Oakley, near Bedford. Z4332/B.

STRINGER, F. W., Sapper, Royal Engineers.
Volunteering in May 1915, he was drafted overseas in the following September. Whilst on the Western Front he took part in many engagements, including the Battles of Loos, the Somme, Arras, Ypres (III.), the Somme (II.) and Ypres (IV.). He was demobilised in August 1919, and holds the 1914–15 Star, and the General Service and Victory Medals.
24, Oakley, near Bedford. Z4332/A.

STRINGER, G. T., Corporal, 1st Bedfordshire Regt.
He was already serving when war broke out in August 1914, and was immediately drafted to France, where he took part in the Retreat from Mons, and was wounded and made prisoner of war. He was held in captivity in Germany, and suffered many privations throughout hostilities. After the Armistice he was released and returned home, and in 1920 was still in the Army. He holds the Mons Star, and the General Service and Victory Medals. 20, Marne St., Kempston, Bedford. Z4333/A.

STRINGER, R., Private, R.A.M.C.
He joined in May 1916, and, after a period of training, was engaged at various home stations on important duties with his unit. He was unable to obtain a transfer overseas owing to his being medically unfit, but rendered valuable services until his demobilisation in February 1919.
24, Oakley, near Bedford. Z4332/C.

STRONG, F., Gunner, Royal Field Artillery.
He volunteered in September 1914, and in the following March was drafted to France, where he saw much fighting at Arras and on the Somme, and was badly wounded in 1916. As a result he was invalided home, but on his recovery returned to France, and took part in engagements at Vimy Ridge. He was again badly wounded and sent home, and remained in hospital for a considerable period. He was demobilised in December 1919, and holds the 1914–15 Star, and the General Service and Victory Medals.
Park Lane, Blunham, near Sandy, Beds. Z2592/B

SUGARS, W. T., L/Corporal, Military Foot Police.
He joined in February 1917, and first saw service in France at Ypres, but was then transferred to Italy. In this seat of operations he took an active part in fighting on the Piave River and the Asiago Plateau. After the Armistice he served with the Army of Occupation in Austria, and later was sent to Egypt for important duties in Cairo. He did good work, and was demobilised in April 1920, holding the General Service and Victory Medals.
25, Cater Street, Kempston, Bedford. X4334.

SUMMERFIELD, C., Private, Bedfordshire Regt.
He volunteered in November 1914, and was retained for some time at various home stations engaged on important duties. Later he proceeded to France and served with the Labour Corps at Dunkirk, where he did good work until his demobilisation in 1919. He holds the General Service and Victory Medals.
7, Dane Street, Bedford. X4335.

SUMMERFIELD, T., Air Mechanic, R.A.F.
He joined in August 1918, and was shortly afterwards drafted to France There he was stationed at Etaples, Calais, Rouen, Arras and Ypres, engaged on important work, which demanded a high degree of technical skill. He was demobilised in March 1919, and holds the General Service and Victory Medals.
47, Pilcroft Street, Bedford. X4336/A.

SUMMERFIELD, T. J., Private, 1/5th Beds. Regt.
He volunteered in August 1914, and underwent a period of training prior to his being drafted to France. In this theatre of war he took part in many engagements, including the Battles of the Somme, Ypres, Passchendaele and Cambrai, and was wounded in action. He was demobilised in April 1919, and holds the General Service and Victory Medals.
47, Pilcroft Street, Bedford. X4336/B.

SUMMERS, F., Private, R.A.M.C.
He was mobilised with the Territorials in August 1914, and in the following year was drafted to Egypt. In this seat of operations he was engaged on important duties at Alexandria until 1916, when he was sent home and discharged, time-expired. Later he re-enlisted and served at various hospitals at home, and did consistently good work. He was demobilised in January 1919, and holds the 1914–15 Star, and the General Service, Victory and Territorial Efficiency Medals.
18, Bridge Street, New Bradwell, Bucks. Z4337.

SUMMERS, P., L/Corporal, Bedfordshire Regt.
He volunteered in September 1914, and underwent a period of training prior to his being drafted to the Western Front. During his service overseas he took part in the Battle of the Somme and various other engagements, and was wounded in action in September 1918. He was demobilised in February 1919, and holds the General Service and Victory Medals.
Ellington, Hunts. Z4338.

SUNDERLAND, F. R., Sapper, Royal Engineers.
He volunteered in January 1916, in the Middlesex Regiment, but was shortly afterwards transferred to the 2/4th Queen's Own (Royal West Kent Regiment), and drafted to Egypt. Whilst in this seat of operations he took part in the Advance into Palestine, and was wounded in action at the Battle of Gaza (II.). As a result he was sent to hospital, and on his recovery transferred to the Royal Engineers, and served with the Field Company at Baghdad and Samarra. He was again wounded, and after his return was demobilised in October 1919, holding the General Service and Victory Medals.
28, Silver Street, Stony Stratford, Bucks. Z4339.

SURRIDGE, J. W., Private, 2nd Bedfordshire Regt.
Volunteering in January 1915, he proceeded overseas later in the same year. Whilst on the Western Front he took part in many engagements, including those at Loos, Arras, the Somme, Ypres and St. Quentin, where he was taken prisoner of war in March 1918. He was held in captivity in Germany and suffered many privations. After the Armistice he was repatriated, returned home and demobilised in March 1919, holding the 1914–15 Star, and the General Service and Victory Medals. Monks Row, Pavenham, near Bedford. Z4340.

SUTCLIFFE, H., L/Corporal, Royal Engineers.
He volunteered in August 1915, and completing his training in the following year was drafted to Egypt. In this seat of operations he was engaged on important duties, and later took part in the Advance into Palestine, being in action at Gaza and Jaffa. He returned home and was demobilised in March 1919, holding the General Service and Victory Medals.
36, Prebend Street, Bedford. Z4341.

SUTER, J., Private, Sherwood Foresters.
He joined in 1916, and underwent a period of training prior to his being drafted to France. There he took part in much heavy fighting in the Somme sector, and was wounded. Whilst being conveyed to hospital he was unfortunately killed by a shell explosion on June 1st, 1917. He was entitled to the General Service and Victory Medals.
"Thinking that remembrance, though unspoken, may reach him where he sleeps."
West End, Brampton, Hunts. Z4342.

SWAIN, D., L/Corporal, Royal Engineers.
He was mobilised in August 1914, and retained at various home stations engaged on important duties until April 1918, when he proceeded to France. There he took part in much heavy fighting in the Cambrai, St. Quentin and Givenchy sectors. He was discharged in March 1919, and holds the General Service and Victory Medals.
36, King's Place, Bedford. X4343.

SWAIN, J., Sergeant, Royal Fusiliers.
Having volunteered in 1914, he was drafted to France in the following year. Whilst on the Western Front he took part in the Battles of Festubert, Ypres and Loos, where he was wounded in action. On his recovery he rejoined his unit, and saw much fighting on the Somme, at Messines and Cambrai. He was demobilised in 1919, and holds the 1914–15 Star, and the General Service and Victory Medals.
Great Staughton, Hunts. Z4344.

WALES, J., Tpr., 1st Beds. Yeomanry (Lancers).
He was mobilised in August 1914, and completing his training in the following March was drafted to the Western Front. There he took part in several engagements, including the Battles of Loos, Festubert, the Somme and Arras. He died gloriously on the Field of Battle at Cambrai on December 4th, 1917, and was entitled to the 1914–15 Star, and the General Service and Victory Medals.
"Great deeds cannot die:
They with the sun and moon renew their light for ever."
28, Patteshall Street, Bedford. X4346/B.

SWALES, S., Sapper, Royal Engineers.
Having volunteered in September 1914, he proceeded to Egypt in the following July. In this seat of operations he was engaged on important duties in connection with the building of bridges, and later proceeded into Palestine. There he saw much fighting at Gaza, Jaffa, and at the fall of Jerusalem. Demobilised in June 1919 on his return home, he holds the 1914–15 Star, and the General Service and Victory Medals.
56, Melbourne Street, Bedford. X4347.

SWALES, T. A., Sapper, Royal Engineers.
He volunteered in September 1914, and after a period of training was drafted overseas in the following year. Whilst in this theatre of war he was engaged on important duties connected with the building of bridges and railways in the Ypres, Somme, Armentières, Cambrai, Loos and Lens sectors. He was demobilised in June 1919, and holds the 1914–15 Star, and the General Service and Victory Medals.
High Road, Clapham. Z4345.

SWANN, J., Sergeant-Major, Royal Engineers.
He was mobilised with the Territorials in August 1914, and in the following year was drafted to the Dardanelles, where he played a prominent part in the Landing at Suvla Bay. After the Evacuation of the Gallipoli Peninsula he proceeded to Egypt and thence to Palestine, and saw much heavy fighting at Gaza and Jerusalem. He was twice mentioned in Despatches for gallantry and devotion to duty in the Field. He returned home and was discharged in August 1919, holding the 1914–15 Star, and the General Service and Victory Medals.
1, St. Margaret's Cottage, Renhold, near Bedford. Z4348.

SWANNELL, A. D. (M.M.), Sergeant, 16th Queen's Lancers.
He was mobilised in August 1914, and immediately drafted to France. There he fought in the Retreat from Mons, and played a prominent part in the Battles of Ypres, the Somme, Arras, Cambrai, Loos and Lens. He was awarded the Military Medal for bravery and devotion to duty in the Field at Ypres. In 1920 he was still serving, and holds also the Mons Star, and the General Service and Victory Medals.
31, Canning Street, Bedford. X4350/B.

SWANNELL, E. R., Private, Tank Corps.
He joined in 1917, and later in the same year was drafted to the Western Front. Whilst in this theatre of war he saw much fighting in the Somme, Cambrai, Ypres and Arras sectors, and did continuously good work until his demobilisation in September 1919. He holds the General Service and Victory Medals.
31, Canning Street, Bedford. X4350/C.

SWANNELL, G. H., Sergeant, 5th (Princess Charlotte of Wales') Dragoon Guards.
He was mobilised in August 1914, and immediately drafted to France, where he played a prominent part in the Battle of Mons and saw much fighting in the Arras sector. He died gloriously in the Field at the Battle of Ypres on May 16th, 1915, and was entitled to the Mons Star, and the General Service and Victory Medals.
"Nobly striving:
He nobly fell that we might live."
31, Canning Street, Bedford. X3450/A.

SWANNELL, W. A., Pte., 1st Bedfordshire Regt.
He joined in March 1916, and, completing his training three months later, was drafted to France, where he took part in the Battles of Arras, Ypres and Cambrai. In December 1917 he was transferred to Italy, and saw much heavy fighting on the Piave. He was invalided home and discharged in August 1918 as medically unfit for further service, and holds the General Service and Victory Medals.
59, Foster Street, Bedford. X4349.

SWIFT, G., Sergeant, Bedfordshire Regiment.
He volunteered in December 1914, and, after training with the Huntingdonshire Cyclist Battalion, proceeded to France. Transferred to the Bedfordshire Regiment, he saw much fighting and played a prominent part in the Battles of the Somme, Arras, Ypres, Messines and Cambrai. He was demobilised in March 1919, and holds the General Service and Victory Medals.
Buckden Road, Brampton, Hunts. Z4351.

SYKES, A., Private, West Riding Regiment.
Volunteering in January 1915, he was drafted overseas later in the same year. Whilst on the Western Front he took part in many engagements, including those at Ypres, Vimy Ridge, the Somme, Arras and Cambrai, and in the Retreat of 1918. In 1920 he was serving in Ireland, and holds the 1914–15 Star, and the General Service and Victory Medals.
28, Bunyan Road, Bedford. Z4352.

SYMES, C., Private, R.A.S.C. (M.T.)
He volunteered in September 1914, and quickly proceeded to the Western Front. In this theatre of war he was engaged with the Mechanical Transport conveying supplies to the forward areas in the Ypres, Arras, Somme, Cambrai and St. Quentin sectors, and was wounded in 1918. He was demobilised in March 1919, and holds the 1914 Star, and the General Service and Victory Medals.
7, Cater Street, Kempston, Bedford. X4353.

SYMONDS, A. (D.C.M.), Pte., Bedfordshire Regt.
He was mobilised in August 1914, and immediately drafted to France, where he took part in the Retreat from Mons and the Battles of the Marne, La Bassée and Neuve Chapelle. He was badly wounded at Ypres in 1915 whilst holding a trench for three days under heavy fire, being the only man left alive. For this gallant deed he was awarded the Distinguished Conduct Medal. He was invalided home and finally discharged in August 1917, and holds also the Mons Star, and the General Service and Victory Medals.
The Gardens, Great Barford, Beds. Z1004/A.

SYRATT, H. T., Pte., 7th Oxford. & Bucks. L.I.
He was mobilised with the Territorials in August 1914, and later in the same year was drafted to France. There he took part in much heavy fighting in the Ypres, Marne, Somme, Arras and Cambrai sectors, and was twice wounded. Eventually invalided home, he was in hospital about six months, and was demobilised in November 1919. He holds the 1914–15 Star, and the General Service and Victory Medals.
54, Spencer Street, Bradwell, Bucks. Z4354/B.

SYRATT, W. E., Private, 2nd Northants. Regt.
He was mobilised with the Territorials in August 1914, and, after a short period of training in Egypt, was drafted to France, where he took part in fighting in the Ypres sector. He made the supreme sacrifice, being killed in action on January 4th, 1915. He was entitled to the 1914–15 Star, and the General Service and Victory Medals.
"The path of duty was the way to glory."
54, Spencer Street, Bradwell, Bucks. Z4354/A.

T

TABBITT, S. A., Corporal, Royal Air Force.
He volunteered in October 1914, and in July of the following year proceeded to the Western Front, where he served with a Flying Squadron in various sectors. He was engaged on important duties on the Somme and at Arras, Poperinghe, Menin and many other places in this theatre of war, and served for a time as acting Technical Quartermaster-Sergeant. He was afterwards sent with the Army of Occupation to Germany, where he was stationed at Cologne until his return home for demobilisation in June 1919. He holds the 1914–15 Star, and the General Service and Victory Medals.
Cemetery Road, St. Ives, Hunts. Z4355.

TANNER, H., Private, 1st Lincolnshire Regiment.
Already in the Army when war was declared in August 1914, he was immediately drafted to the Western Front, where he fought in the Retreat from Mons. He also took part in the Battles of Ypres, Hill 60, Loos, Vimy Ridge and the Somme, and was severely wounded in action on two occasions. He was invalided from the Army in October 1918, and holds the Mons Star, and the General Service and Victory Medals.
19, Tavistock Place, Bedford. TZ4356.

TAPP, G. J. (M.M.), A/Corporal, R.F.A.
Mobilised in August 1914, he was immediately drafted to France, and there served through the Retreat from Mons. He also took a prominent part in the Battles of the Marne, La Bassée, Ypres, Festubert, Arras and Cambrai, and in the Retreat and Advance of 1918, was wounded at Loos in September 1915, and gassed and wounded twelve months later. He was awarded the Military Medal for bravery displayed in rescuing a wounded officer under heavy fire on the Somme in July 1916, and holds also the Mons Star, and the General Service and Victory Medals. He was discharged in January 1919. 2, Bridge Street, New Bradwell, Bucks. Z2183/A.

TAPSTER, E. S., Sapper, Royal Engineers.
A Territorial, he was mobilised in August 1914, and in January of the following year was sent to the Western Front, where he took part in the Battles of Ypres, Vimy Ridge and the Somme. Transferred in 1916 to Salonika, he proceeded thence in the following year to Egypt, and afterwards served in Palestine. There he fought in the Battles of Gaza, and was also present at the capture of Jaffa, Jerusalem, Haifa and Aleppo. He was demobilised on his return home in April 1919, and holds the 1914–15 Star, and the General Service and Victory Medals.
12, Brace Street, Bedford. X4357.

TARBOX, A. C., Private, 1st Devonshire Regiment.
He joined in February 1918, and, after undergoing a period of training, was retained at various stations, where he was engaged on duties of a highly important nature. He was unable to obtain his transfer overseas owing to injuries to the knee, sustained in an accident previous to enlistment, but, nevertheless, did good work with his unit until invalided from the Army in January 1919. 24, Railway Terrace, Bletchley, Bucks. Z4358/B.

TARBOX, A. T., Sapper, R.E. (R.O.D.)
Joining in March 1917, he was drafted to the Western Front in the following month, and was there engaged on important duties on the railways in various sectors. He rendered valuable services with his Company in this theatre of war until the cessation of hostilities, and was then sent with the Army of Occupation to Germany, where he was stationed at Cologne. Demobilised on his return home in November 1919, he holds the General Service and Victory Medals.
8, Railway Terrace, Bletchley, Bucks. Z4262/A.

TARBOX, A. T., Private, 1st Gloucestershire Regt.
Having previously been too young for service with the Colours, he joined immediately on attaining military age in March 1919, and, after completing a period of training, was engaged on important duties at various stations. He rendered very valuable services with his unit, and in 1920 was still serving, having engaged for a period of seven years.
24, Railway Terrace, Bletchley, Bucks. Z4358/A.

TARBOX, G., Corporal, Royal Engineers (R.O.D.)
He joined in February 1917, and in the following year proceeded to France, where he served in various sectors of the front. He was engaged on duties of great importance on the railways whilst in this theatre of war, and did much useful work with his Company until his return home for demobilisation in January 1920. He holds the General Service and Victory Medals. Bow Brickhill, near Bletchley, Bucks. Z4359

TASSELL, N. G. W., Private, Sherwood Foresters.
Volunteering in August 1914, he was drafted to the Western Front early in the following year, and there took part in the Battles of Neuve Chapelle and Hill 60 and many minor engagements. He died gloriously on the Field of Battle near Festubert on July 16th, 1915. He was entitled to the 1914–15 Star, and the General Service and Victory Medals.
"The path of duty was the way to glory."
Russell Street, St. Neots, Hunts. Z4360.

TATMAN, A., Private, Labour Corps.
Shortly after volunteering in May 1915 he proceeded to the Western Front, where he was engaged on road-making and other important duties in various sectors. He was present also at the Battles of Loos, Albert, the Somme, Arras and Ypres and many other engagements until the cessation of hostilities, and on his return home in March 1919 was demobilised. He holds the 1914–15 Star, and the General Service and Victory Medals.
Roxton Road, Great Barford, Beds. Z2928/B.

TATMAN, A. F., Private, Huntingdonshire Cyclist Regiment and 1st Royal Berkshire Regiment.
He volunteered in 1915, and, after his training, was retained on police duties in England until drafted to the Western Front in the following year. There, after taking part in many important engagements, he was mortally wounded in action at Albert, and unhappily died on March 19th, 1917. He was entitled to the General Service and Victory Medals.
"A valiant Soldier, with undaunted heart he breasted life's last hill."
Diddington, Hunts. Z4362.

TATMAN, J., Private, 8th Leicestershire Regiment.
Joining in March 1916, he was drafted to the Western Front on completing his training in the following November, and there saw much severe fighting at Messines and Albert. He was mortally wounded in the Battle of Arras on April 11th, 1917, and died two days later He was entitled to the General Service and Victory Medals.
"Thinking that remembrance, though unspoken, may reach him where he sleeps."
Chalton, near Sandy, Beds. TZ4361.

TATTAM, A., Sapper, Royal Engineers (R.O.D.)
Shortly after joining in January 1917, he proceeded to the Western Front, where he was engaged on important duties in various sectors. He served at Ypres, the Somme and many other places in this theatre of war until severely wounded in action at Cambrai in November 1918, and admitted to hospital at York. He was invalided from the Army in September 1919, and holds the General Service and Victory Medals.
Drayton Parslow, Bucks. Z4363.

TATTAM, C. W., Corporal, 1st Wiltshire Regt.
He joined immediately on attaining military age in June 1918, and after completing a term of training, served at various stations in Ireland, where he was engaged on duties of great importance. Owing to the early cessation of hostilities, he was unable to obtain his transfer to the front, but, nevertheless, rendered valuable services with his unit until October 1919, when he was demobilised.
Drayton Parslow, Bucks. Z4365.

TATTAM, G., Sapper, Royal Engineers (R.O.D.)
Joining in February 1916, he was drafted to the Western Front in the following month. Whilst in this theatre of war he was engaged on transport and other important duties in various sectors, and serving chiefly at Ypres, Cambrai and the Somme, did much useful work with his Company. He was demobilised in October 1919, and holds the General Service and Victory Medals. Drayton Parslow, Bucks. Z4366.

TATTAM, G. W., Sapper, Royal Engineers.
He joined in February 1915, and after his training was retained on important duties in England until the following year, when he proceeded to France. There he was engaged on important duties at Arras, Cambrai and the Somme, and in various other sectors of the front, finally returning home for demobilisation in 1919. He holds the General Service and Victory Medals.
Chestnut Cottage, Drayton Parslow, Bucks. Z4364.

TAYLER, T. G., Sapper, Royal Engineers.
Volunteering in September 1914, he was sent to the Western Front in May of the following year, and there served in various sectors. After taking an active part in the Battles of Ypres, Loos and Albert, he was invalided home in May 1916 suffering from rheumatic fever, and on his recovery was retained on important duties in England. He was discharged in February 1919 as medically unfit for further service, and holds the 1914–15 Star, and the General Service and Victory Medals.
8, St. Paul's Terrace, Newport Pagnell, Bucks. Z4367.

TAYLOR, A. G., Private, Labour Corps.
After volunteering in 1915, he underwent a period of training prior to being drafted to the Western Front in the following year. There he was engaged on road-making and other important duties in various sectors and was present also at the Battles of Arras, Ypres and Cambrai, and other engagements. He was demobilised in September 1919, and holds the General Service and Victory Medals.
5, Slough's Buildings, Huntingdon. Z4368.

TAYLOR, C., Private, Australian Imperial Forces.
He volunteered at the outbreak of war in August 1914, and in January of the following year was sent to the Western Front, where he took part in the Battles of Festubert and Loos and other engagements. Transferred later to Egypt, he proceeded into Palestine, and was there present at the fall of Jerusalem. He afterwards served with the Army of Occupation at Constantinople until his demobilisation in September 1919, and holds the 1914–15 Star, and the General Service and Victory Medals. Rectory Lane, Somersham, Hunts. Z4375.

TAYLOR, C. E., Private, Machine Gun Corps.
Volunteering in August 1914, he proceeded later in the same year to the Western Front, where he took part in the Battles of Armentières, Ypres and Arras. He was afterwards transferred to Egypt, and, advancing into Palestine, fought in the Battles of Gaza, and at the capture of Jaffa and Haifa. He was gassed whilst overseas, and finally returned home for demobilisation in February 1919, holding the 1914–15 Star, and the General Service and Victory Medals.
Cardington, Bedford. Z4382.

TAYLOR, C. G., Private, Royal Fusiliers.
He joined in January 1918, and, on completing a period of training later in the same year, was drafted to the Western Front, where he served in various sectors until the cessation of hostilities. He was then sent to Germany with the Army of Occupation, and was there stationed at Cologne for some months. In September 1919 he proceeded to Mesopotamia, where he was still with his unit in the following year, holding the General Service and Victory Medals.
72, Coventry Road, Queen's Park, Bedford. Z4370.

TAYLOR, J., Private, Labour Corps.
Shortly after volunteering in November 1915, he was drafted to the Western Front, where he was engaged on important duties in various sectors. After taking an active part in the Battles of Arras and Ypres and other engagements, he was sent home and invalided from the Army in June 1917. He unfortunately died of consumption on June 20th, 1918. He was entitled to the 1914–15 Star, and the General Service and Victory Medals.
"Steals on the ear the distant triumph song."
6, Castle Hill Cottages, Bedford. X3687/B.

TAYLOR, F., Private, R.A.S.C.
Six months after joining in October 1916 he proceeded to France, where he was engaged on duties of great importance with the Remount Section. He was stationed chiefly at Rouen, and did much useful work with his Company there until his return home for demobilisation in November 1919. He holds the General Service and Victory Medals.
9, Railway Terrace, Bletchley, Bucks. Z4379.

TAYLOR, G. (M.M.), Private, M.G.C.
Mobilised in August 1914, he was immediately drafted to the Western Front, where he fought in the Retreat from Mons. He also took part in the Battles of Ypres, Hill 60, Loos, Arras, Vimy Ridge, Passchendaele and Cambrai, and many minor engagements, and was wounded in action. He was awarded the Military Medal for conspicuous bravery in the Field, and, holding also the Mons Star, and the General Service and Victory Medals, was discharged in March 1919.
41, All Hallows Lane, Bedford. X4371.

TAYLOR, H., L/Corporal, Royal Engineers.
He joined in February 1917, and, on completing his training in September of that year, was drafted to the Western Front, where, attached to the Signal Section, he was engaged on important clerical duties in various sectors. In January 1918 he was transferred to Italy for similar duties, finally returning home for demobilisation in November 1919. He holds the General Service and Victory Medals.
Green's Norton, Towcester, Northants. Z4377.

TAYLOR, H., Driver, Royal Field Artillery.
He volunteered in October 1915, and in May of the following year proceeded to Salonika, where he saw much severe fighting. He took part in many important engagements on the Vardar, Doiran and Struma fronts whilst in this theatre of war, finally returning home for demobilisation in May 1919. He holds the General Service and Victory Medals.
9, Sergeant's Yard, Towcester, Northants. Z4378/B.

TAYLOR, H., Private, 1/5th Bedfordshire Regt. and King's (Liverpool Regiment).
After volunteering in November 1915 he was retained on important duties in England until August 1917, when he proceeded to the Western Front, and there took part in many engagements. He was reported missing, and later killed in action, on November 20th, 1917. He was entitled to the General Service and Victory Medals.
"He passed out of the sight of men by the path of duty and self-sacrifice."
Mount Pleasant, Milton Ernest, Bedford. Z1646/A.

TAYLOR, J., Private, 4th Worcestershire Regt.
Volunteering in September 1914, he was drafted to Gallipoli in July of the following year, and there saw severe fighting at Suvla Bay and Anzac Cove, and was wounded in October 1915. Invalided to hospital at Malta and thence to England, he proceeded to France, however, in January 1916, fought in the Battles of the Somme, Arras, Vimy Ridge and Ypres, and was again wounded three times. Mortally wounded at Passchendaele, he unhappily died on October 22nd, 1917. He was entitled to the 1914–15 Star, and the General Service and Victory Medals.
"His memory is cherished with pride."
14, Duncombe Street, Bletchley, Bucks. Z4380/A—Z4381/A.

TAYLOR, J. T., Driver, Royal Engineers.
He volunteered at the outbreak of war in August 1914, and, after his training, was retained on important duties in England until February 1916. He was then drafted to Egypt, and, proceeding thence into Palestine, served through the Battles of Gaza and the capture of Jaffa and Haifa. He suffered from malaria whilst in the East, and on his return home in April 1919 was invalided from the Army. He holds the General Service and Victory Medals.
36, Marne Street, Kempston, Bedford. Z4373/B.

TAYLOR, J. W., Gunner, R.G.A.
Four months after volunteering in August 1915 he proceeded to the Western Front, where he saw much severe fighting in the Somme and other sectors. He was afterwards transferred to Italy, and there took part in many important engagements on the Piave, finally returning to England for demobilisation in March 1919. He holds the 1914–15 Star, and the General Service and Victory Medals.
Gayhurst, near Newport Pagnell, Bucks. Z4372.

TAYLOR, S., Private, Huntingdonshire Cyclist Battalion and Labour Corps.
He volunteered in April 1915, and, after completing a period of training, was retained at various stations, where he was engaged on agricultural work and other important duties. Being too old for transfer overseas, he was not successful in obtaining his transfer to the front, but, nevertheless, rendered very valuable services until March 1919, when he was demobilised. Wennington, Hunts. Z4376.

TAYLOR, V. J., Private, R.A.M.C.
Mobilised in August 1914, he was immediately drafted to the Western Front, where he took part in the Battle of Mons and the subsequent Retreat. Acting as a stretcher-bearer, he also served through the Battles of Ypres, Loos, Arras, Vimy Ridge and Cambrai and many other important engagements in various sectors until the cessation of hostilities. He was discharged in February 1919, and holds the Mons Star, and the General Service, Victory, and Long Service and Good Conduct Medals.
11, Holme Street, Bedford. X4369/B.

TAYLOR, W., Sapper, Royal Engineers.
He was mobilised in August 1914, and in January of the following year was drafted to Egypt, where he was engaged on important duties with the Signal Section at Alexandria and Cairo, afterwards proceeding into Palestine. Invalided home in June 1918, he unhappily died of fever in hospital on August 20th of that year. He was entitled to the 1914–15 Star, and the General Service and Victory Medals.
"He joined the great white company of valiant souls."
9, Sergeant's Yard, Towcester, Northants. Z4378/A.

TAYLOR, W. C., Private, Bedfordshire Regiment.
Volunteering in 1915, he proceeded to France on completion of his training in the following year, and there saw heavy fighting in various sectors of the front. He took part in the Battles of Vimy Ridge, the Somme and the Ancre and many minor engagements, and was so severely wounded on the Somme as to necessitate the amputation of his left arm. He was invalided from the Army in November 1917, and holds the General Service and Victory Medals.
36, Marne Street, Kempston, Bedford. Z4373/A.

TAYLOR, W. G., Sapper, Royal Engineers.
Already in the Army when war was declared in August 1914, he was immediately drafted to the Western Front, where he served at Mons, and later took part in the Battles of Ypres, Loos and the Somme, being wounded in February 1915. He was reported missing, and is believed to have been killed in action on November 19th, 1916. He was entitled to the Mons Star, and the General Service and Victory Medals.
"And doubtless he went in splendid company."
11, Holme Street, Bedford. X4369/A.

TAYLOR, W. J., Private, Leicestershire Regt.
He joined in 1916, and in the following year was drafted to the Western Front, where he took part in the Battles of Ypres and Cambrai and many minor engagements. Gassed on the Somme and suffering also from trench feet, he was invalided home in 1918, but on his recovery, however, returned to France in September of that year, and was again in action on the Somme. He was demobilised in 1919, and holds the General Service and Victory Medals.
High Street, Kimbolton, Hunts. Z4374.

TEAGLE, C. S., Sergeant-Bugler, 1st Oxfordshire and Buckinghamshire Light Infantry.
Mobilised in August 1914, he was drafted to the Western Front five months later, and there saw severe fighting in various sectors. After taking a prominent part in the Battles of Neuve Chapelle, Ypres, Festubert, Loos and many other engagements he was sent home and discharged in March 1916, time-expired. He holds the 1914–15 Star, and the General Service and Victory Medals.
12, St. Mary's Street, New Bradwell, Bucks. Z4383.

TEALE, G., Private, R.A.M.C.
He volunteered in September 1915, and was later drafted to the Western Front, where he served as an orderly in a hospital at Rouen, and also as a stretcher-bearer in the Somme, Arras, Ypres and Albert sectors. Invalided to St. Albans suffering from general paralysis, caused through shell-shock, he unfortunately died on September 14th, 1918, and was entitled to the General Service and Victory Medals.
"A costly sacrifice upon the altar of freedom."
108, Tickford Street, Newport Pagnell, Bucks. Z4384.

TEAT, W., L/Corporal, 1/5th Bedfordshire Regt.
He volunteered in January 1915, and, on completion of his training in the following year, proceeded to Egypt. Later he took part in the Advance into Palestine and was in action at the Battles of Gaza and Jaffa. On November 2nd, 1917, he was unfortunately killed, and was buried at the Military Cemetery at Gaza. He was entitled to the General Service and Victory Medals.
"The path of duty was the way to glory."
Abbots Ripton, Hunts. Z4385.

TEMPLE, A., Private, 1st Bedfordshire Regiment.
Mobilised at the outbreak of hostilities in August 1914, he was immediately drafted to the Western Front. In this seat of war he took part in the Retreat from Mons, also in the Battles of the Marne, the Aisne, La Bassée and Ypres. He was later invalided home suffering from nervous debility, and in December 1915 was discharged as medically unfit for further service, holding the Mons Star, and the General Service and Victory Medals. Shop Yard, Great Linford, Bucks. Z4387/A.

TEMPLE, C., Sapper, Royal Engineers.
Having joined in January 1917, he underwent a period of training, but was later found to be medically unfit for service overseas. He was therefore retained on important duties in connection with the building of huts at Chatham, in which capacity he rendered excellent services until demobilised in March 1919.
12, Beaconsfield Place, Newport Pagnell, Bucks. TZ4386.

TEMPLE, H., Pte., Queen's (R. West Surrey Regt.).
After volunteering in August 1915 he completed a period of training in the following year and was drafted to India, where he served at Quetta and later took an active part in the engagements on the Afghanistan Frontier. He was demobilised on his return home in November 1919, holding the General Service and Victory Medals and the India General Service Medal (with Clasp, Afghanistan, N.W. Frontier, 1919).
Shop Yard, Great Linford, Bucks. Z4387/B.

TEMPLE, J. W., Private, 1st Suffolk Regiment.
Already serving with the Colours at the outbreak of war in August 1914, he was immediately drafted to France. Whilst in this theatre of war he took part in the Retreat from Mons, also in the Battles of the Marne, the Aisne, La Bassée, Ypres and the Somme, where he was wounded in 1916. Later he saw much heavy fighting at Cambrai and throughout the Retreat and Advance of 1918. He was discharged in March 1919, holding the Mons Star, and the General Service and Victory Medals. Shop Yard, Great Linford, Bucks. Z4387/C.

TERRY, C. J., Private, Royal Berkshire Regiment.
He volunteered in March 1915, and, after a period of training, was retained on important duties with his unit at various stations. Owing to his being medically unfit he was unable to proceed to a theatre of war, but, nevertheless, rendered excellent services until demobilised in June 1918.
4, Simpson Road, Fenny Stratford, Bucks. Z4388/A.

TERRY, W., A.B., Royal Navy.
At the outbreak of war in August 1914 he was already serving in the Navy, and was on board H.M.S. "Cressy," attached to the Chatham Division. After taking part in the operations at Heligoland Bight his ship was torpedoed off the Hook of Holland, and he was unfortunately drowned, on September 22nd, 1914. He was entitled to the 1914–15 Star, and the General Service and Victory Medals.
"Thinking that remembrance, though unspoken, may reach him where he sleeps."
4, Simpson Road, Fenny Stratford, Bucks. Z4388/B.

THEED, W. H., Private, 4th Bedfordshire Regt.
After joining in February 1916 he underwent a period of training and in the same year was drafted overseas. During his service on the Western Front he took part in many important engagements, including the Battles of Loos, the Somme, Ypres, Cambrai and Lens. He was seriously wounded, and as a result his left arm was amputated, and he was finally discharged in 1919, holding the General Service and Victory Medals.
"Willowdeane," Clapham, Bedford. Z4389/B.

THEOBALD, G., Private, Northamptonshire Regt.
Already in the Army at the outbreak of war in August 1914, he was immediately drafted to the Western Front, and was in action during the Retreat from Mons. He made the supreme sacrifice, being killed on September 17th, 1914, and was entitled to the Mons Star, and the General Service and Victory Medals.
"He died the noblest death a man may die,
Fighting for God and right and liberty."
7, London Road, Clapham, Bedford. Z4390.

THEOBALD, J., Private, 19th Middlesex Regt.
Having joined in May 1918, he completed a period of training later in the same year. Owing to the early cessation of hostilities he was not drafted overseas until February 1919, when he proceeded to Germany, and served with the Army of Occupation on the Rhine. He was demobilised in March 1920.
16, Bedesman's Place, Bedford. X4392.

THEOBALD, W. T. (M.C.), R.S.M., 4th Beds. Regt.
Already in the Army in August 1914, he was first engaged on important duties as an Instructor, but eventually proceeded to France in 1916. He served with distinction at the Battles of Albert, the Somme (I.), the Ancre and Vimy Ridge, and was unhappily killed in action on the Somme on March 25th, 1918. He had been awarded the Military Cross for great gallantry and devotion to duty in the Field on January 1st, 1918, and was also entitled to the General Service and Victory Medals.
"A valiant Soldier, with undaunted heart he breasted life's last hill."
12, Sayer Street, Huntingdon. Z4391.

THOMPKINS, J. S., Pte., South Wales Borderers.
Joining in August 1917, he completed a period of training in the same year and proceeded to France, where he took part in the heavy fighting at the Battles of Ypres, Passchendaele and Cambrai, and was wounded. After the cessation of hostilities he went to Germany and served with the Army of Occupation at Cologne. He was demobilised in December 1919, holding the General Service and Victory Medals.
Warboys, Hunts. Z4394.

THOMPSON, C., Sapper, Royal Engineers.
Volunteering in August 1914, he underwent a period of training, and in the following year was drafted to France, where he served in various sectors of the front. He was engaged on important wiring and trench-digging duties during the engagements on the Somme, at the Battles of Ypres, Arras and Cambrai, and throughout the Retreat and Advance of 1918. In March 1919 he was demobilised, and holds the 1914–15 Star, and the General Service and Victory Medals.
20, Cater Street, Kempston, Beds. X4395.

THOMPSON, F., Private, Machine Gun Corps.
He joined in December 1916, and, on conclusion of his training, was drafted to France, where he saw much service in various sectors of the front. He took part in the Battles of Loos, Beaumont-Hamel, Arras, Ypres and Cambrai and other engagements of importance until the close of the war. In December 1919 he was demobilised, holding the 1914–15 Star, and the General Service and Victory Medals.
44, New Fenlake, Bedford. TZ4397.

THOMPSON, H. P., Private, Essex Regiment.
Having joined in July 1918, he underwent a period of training, and, after the cessation of hostilities, proceeded to Egypt, where he served at various stations as a cook, in which capacity he did excellent work until demobilised in March 1920.
Park Lane, Stonely, Hunts. Z4083/B.

THOMPSON, J. W., Gunner, R.G.A.
After joining in March 1916 he completed his training in the same year, and proceeded overseas. Whilst on the Western Front he was in action in the Somme sector, also at the Battles of Arras, Messines and Ypres, where he was wounded in 1917. On his recovery he took part in other engagements, and served throughout the Retreat and Advance of 1918. He was demobilised in April 1919, holding the General Service and Victory Medals. Forge Cottage, Cople, Bedford. Z4396/A.

THOMPSON, R., Private, Machine Gun Corps.
He joined in June 1916, and four months later landed in France, where he took part in heavy fighting in the Somme, Arras and Ypres sectors. Later in 1917 he was transferred to Italy, and took part in the engagements on the Piave front and the Asiago Plateau. He was demobilised in February 1919, holding the General Service and Victory Medals.
29, Cater Street, Kempston, Bedford. X4398.

THOMPSON, W., Private, 9th Cheshire Regiment.
Having joined in May 1916, he was later in the same year drafted to France and took part in many important engagements, including the Battles of Arras, Cambrai and the Somme. He made the supreme sacrifice, being killed in action on March 25th, 1918, and was entitled to the General Service and Victory Medals.
"Whilst we remember, the sacrifice is not in vain."
12, Farrar Street, Kempston, Bedford. X4399.

THOMPSON, W. J., Rflmn., 9th London Regt.
Having joined in September 1917, he underwent a period of training, and in the following year proceeded to France. Whilst in this theatre of war he took part in much heavy fighting, and was wounded in action at Cambrai. As a result he was invalided home and finally discharged as medically unfit for further service in October 1918. He holds the General Service and Victory Medals.
Forge Cottage, Cople, Bedford. Z4396/B.

THOMPSON, W. J., L/Corporal, R.A.O.C.
Volunteering in October 1915, he underwent a period of training, and later proceeded to France, where he rendered excellent services throughout He was in action during the Battles of Arras, Ypres, Cambrai and the Somme (II.). After the conclusion of war he returned home and was demobilised in February 1919, holding the General Service and Victory Medals. 43, Foster Street, Bedford. X4400.

THORNE, S. A., Ldg. Smn., Royal Naval Division.
He volunteered in October 1915, and on reaching France in 1916 was attached to a Field Ambulance, and performed valuable services as a stretcher-bearer in the Somme and Ypres sectors. Later he was engaged on important duties at a hospital in Rouen, and subsequently was promoted to the rank of bandmaster. He was demobilised in March 1919, holding the General Service and Victory Medals.
Field Cottage, Chawston, St. Neots, Hunts. 2973/B.

THORNTON, W., Sapper, Royal Engineers.
Volunteering in June 1915, he was sent on completion of his training in May 1916 to the Western Front. There he was engaged in severe fighting in the Battles of Albert, the Somme, Arras, Vimy Ridge, Messines, Ypres and Cambrai, and was buried alive on two occasions. After the Armistice he proceeded to Germany with the Army of Occupation, and served on the Rhine until demobilised in August 1919. He holds the General Service and Victory Medals.
5, Victoria Terrace, Cambridge Street, St. Neots, Hunts. Z4403.

THOROGOOD, A. J., Sergeant, 2nd Beds. Regt.
He volunteered in April 1915, and, on completion of his training, was sent overseas in the following year. During his service on the Western Front he played a conspicuous part in many important engagements, and saw fierce fighting in the Battles of the Somme, Ypres and Cambrai. In 1919 he was drafted to Persia, and in 1920 was still serving there, holding the General Service and Victory Medals.
40, Church Square, Bedford. X4401.

THOROGOOD, W., Private, 1/5th Beds. Regt.
At the outbreak of war he volunteered, and in the following year was ordered to Egypt, but, after a period of service there, was drafted to Palestine. On that front he was in action at Gaza until transferred in 1917 to the Western Front. There he took part in the Battles of Arras, Ypres, Passchendaele and Cambrai, and was wounded on two occasions. Consequently he was invalided out of the Army in April 1919, holding the 1914–15 Star, and the General Service and Victory Medals.
24, Church Square, Bedford. X4402.

THORPE, G., Private, 1st Northants. Regiment.
Mobilised in August 1914, he was ordered a month later to the Western Front, where he experienced fierce fighting, chiefly in the Ypres sector. He gave his life for King and Country on May 9th, 1915, and was entitled to the 1914 Star, and the General Service and Victory Medals.
"A valiant Soldier, with undaunted heart he breasted life's last hill."
Branson's Lane, Towcester, Northants. Z4404.

THORPE, H. T., Private, R.A.M.C.
He volunteered in November 1915, and, after completing his training, was in the following year drafted overseas. During his service in Mesopotamia he saw much severe fighting in numerous important engagements, including those at Amara and Kut, and also performed valuable work in the hospitals. He was demobilised on his return to England in November 1919, and holds the General Service and Victory Medals.
31, Muswell Road, South End, Bedford. Z4405.

THORPE, S., Private, Warwickshire Regiment.
When war broke out in August 1914 he volunteered, and in July of the following year was drafted overseas. Whilst serving on the Western Front he was engaged in fierce fighting in various important engagements, including the Battles of Loos, the Somme and Cambrai. He was wounded in action in 1918, and sent back to England, and was eventually demobilised in March 1919, holding the 1914–15 Star, and the General Service and Victory Medals.
2, Shakespeare Place, Huntingdon. Z4407.

THURLEY, A., Sergeant, 1/5th Bedfordshire Regt.
He volunteered in August 1914, and in July of the following year was drafted to Gallipoli, where he served at Suvla Bay and in subsequent engagements until wounded in September 1915. In December of that year he proceeded to Egypt, and later to Palestine, where he took a prominent part in the fighting at Gaza, Jerusalem and Jaffa. He was mentioned in General Allenby's Despatches in 1918, and was demobilised on his return to England in March 1919, holding the 1914–15 Star, and the General Service and Victory Medals.
18, Ampthill Street, Bedford. X4409—X4411/D.

THURLEY, C. E., Drummer, 1/5th Beds. Regt.
He volunteered in August 1914, and, after a period of training, was eleven months later ordered to Gallipoli. There he fought at Suvla Bay and in other important engagements until December 1915, when he was transferred to Egypt. Subsequently he served in Palestine, where he was in action at Gaza and Jerusalem. He was demobilised on his return home in July 1919, holding the 1914–15 Star, and the General Service and Victory Medals. 18, Ampthill St., Bedford. X4411/B.

THURLEY, C. H., Drummer, 2nd Northants. Regt.
When war was declared he was already serving, and shortly afterwards was ordered to France, where he fought in the Battles of the Marne, the Aisne, Ypres, Neuve Chapelle and Loos. He was wounded in action in 1915 at Festubert and Armentières, and again in 1916 at Fleurbaix, when he was invalided to England. After protracted hospital treatment he unfortunately succumbed to his injuries on January 16th, 1919, at Bedford Hospital. He was entitled to the 1914 Star, and the General Service and Victory Medals.
"The path of duty was the way to glory."
Sandy, Beds. Z4410/B.

THURLEY, F., Sergeant, 1/5th Bedfordshire Regt.
He volunteered in August 1914, but on account of his age was not successful in his efforts to obtain a transfer to the war zone. Nevertheless, he rendered valuable services on the East Coast, and performed excellent work as cook and caterer to the Officers' Mess at Halton Camp. He was eventually demobilised in March 1919. 18, Ampthill St., Bedford. X4411/A.

THURLEY, F. W. (M.C.), R.S.M., 2nd Bedfordshire and Hertfordshire Regiments.
Mobilised at the outbreak of hostilities, he proceeded in September 1914 to the Western Front. In that theatre of war he fought with distinction in the Battles of Ypres, Festubert, Loos, Albert, the Somme, Messines and Passchendaele, and was awarded the Military Cross for conspicuous gallantry in the Field and devotion to duty. He was taken prisoner at Cambrai in March 1918, and remained in captivity until the cessation of hostilities. He was still serving in 1920, and also holds the 1914 Star, and the General Service and Victory Medals. 18, Ampthill Street, Bedford. X4411/C.

THURLEY, H. W., Rifleman, 1st Cameronians (Scottish Rifles).
He was already serving at the outbreak of war, and was at once ordered to France, where he fought in the Retreat from Mons and also took an active part in the Battles of Albert, Arras, Ypres and Cambrai. He was wounded in action five times—on the Aisne, at Festubert (twice), Loos and on the Somme. On his return to England he was discharged in February 1919, and holds the Mons Star, and the General Service and Victory Medals. Sandy, Beds. Z4410/A.

THURLEY, L. A., Sergeant, R.A.M.C.
When war broke out in August 1914 he volunteered, but was retained on important duties in the hospital at Woodbridge until January 1917, when he succeeded in obtaining a transfer to the Western Front. There he was stationed at Lille, and rendered many valuable services until the close of hostilities. Demobilised in June 1919, he holds the General Service and Victory Medals. Eaton Socon, Beds. Z4408

THROSSELL, A. E., Private, R.A.S.C. (M.T.)
He volunteered in May 1915, and, after a period of training, was three months later drafted to the Western Front. In that theatre of war he was engaged in transporting ammunition and supplies to the forward areas, and saw much service in the Loos, the Somme, Arras, Ypres and Cambrai sectors, and during the Retreat and Advance of 1918. Demobilised in February 1919, he holds the 1914–15 Star, and the General Service and Victory Medals. Blunham, Sandy, Beds. Z4406

TIBBETTS, A., Pte., 1st Oxford and Bucks L.I. and 7th Warwickshire Regiment.
He joined in June 1916, and three months later embarked for France, where he was engaged in fierce fighting at Péronne, Ypres and Vimy Ridge. In November 1917 he was transferred to Italy, on which front he was in action on the Piav and the Asiago Plateau. After the cessation of hostilities he was drafted to Egypt, and served there for two months, at the end of which time he returned to England and was demobilised in August 1919, holding the General Service and Victory Medals. Akeley, Buckingham. Z4412

TIDMARSH, F., Guardsman, Irish Guards.
He joined the Army in June 1918, but owing to ill health was not successful in obtaining a transfer to the fighting area Throughout the period of his service he was stationed at Caterham and fulfilled his duties in an exemplary manner. After seven months' valuable service he was demobilised in January 1919. 7, Near Town, Olney, Bucks. Z4413

TILBEE, F., Pte., 10th Buffs (East Kent Regt.)
Mobilised in August 1914, he immediately proceeded to the Western Front, and was in action in the Retreat from Mons In July 1916 he was sent to Gallipoli, and saw heavy fighting at Suvla Bay and other important engagements until December 1915, when he was drafted to Egypt. In May 1918 he returned to France and saw service in various sectors, and was wounded on the Somme in September. He was invalided home in February 1919, and discharged shortly afterwards, holding the Mons Star, and the General Service and Victory Medals.
28, Patteshall Street, Bedford. X4346/A.

TIMMS, B. W. J., Private, Royal Fusiliers.
He volunteered in February 1915, and, on conclusion of a period of training, was sent overseas in August of the following year. Whilst serving on the Western Front he took an active part in the Battle of the Somme, and was wounded in action in October 1916. He was invalided to England and discharged as medically unfit for further service in September 1917. He holds the General Service and Victory Medals.
74, Aylesbury Street, Wolverton, Bucks. Z2552/C.

TIMMS, J., Cpl., Queen's Own (R. West Kent Regt.)
Volunteering in January 1915, he proceeded later in the same year to the scene of activities in France. There he fought in the Battles of Festubert, Loos and Vimy Ridge, and was wounded at Messines in June 1917. On his recovery he returned to the firing-line, and was in action in important engagements at Cambrai and the Marne. He was demobilised in February 1919, and holds the 1914–15 Star, and the General Service and Victory Medals. Woolley, Hunts. Z4415.

TIMMS, W. J., Private, 6th Northants. Regiment.
He joined in June 1916, and, after a period of training, was drafted to the Western Front in February 1917. On March 20th, 1917, he was reported missing at St. Léger, and was later presumed to have been killed on that date. He was entitled to the General Service and Victory Medals.
"He died the noblest death a man may die:
Fighting for God and right and liberty"
47, High Street, Kempston, Beds. Z4414.

TIMPSON, S. H., Pte., 1st Loyal North Lancs. Regt.
Joining in May 1916, he was trained at Ampthill, and proceeded overseas eleven months later. During his service on the Western Front he experienced fierce fighting in the Cambrai sector, and was wounded there in November 1917. He was invalided home, but on his recovery returned to France in April 1918, and was in action during the Retreat and Advance. Demobilised in February 1919, he holds the General Service and Victory Medals.
8, Near Town, Olney, Bucks. Z4416/B.

TIMPSON, T. R., L/Cpl., 8th Oxford. & Bucks. L.I.
He joined in January 1917, and in the following July was drafted to the Western Front. There he was engaged in severe fighting in the Somme sector, and was wounded at Arras and sent to hospital in England. On his recovery in October 1918 he was ordered to Palestine, and was engaged on important duties at Jerusalem. He was demobilised on his return home in August 1919, holding the General Service and Victory Medals
8, Near Town, Olney, Bucks. Z4416/A.

TIMS, P. W., Driver, Royal Field Artillery.
In August 1916 he joined the Army, and later in the same year proceeded to the Western Front, where he took part in numerous important engagements in various sectors. He did excellent work with his Battery in the Battles of Ypres, Passchendaele, Cambrai and the Somme, and served in France until the cessation of hostilities. Demobilised in January 1919, he holds the General Service and Victory Medals.
Grafham, Hunts. Z4417.

TINEY, A., Private, Royal Defence Corps.
Owing to ill-health he was ineligible for service overseas, and therefore volunteered in the Royal Defence Corps in January 1915. He was engaged on important duties at Stafford, and carried out his work in a highly efficient manner until demobilised in February 1919. The Warren, Clapham, Beds. Z2694/A.

TINGEY, H., Private, 2nd Suffolk Regiment.
He joined in July 1916, and five months later embarked for France, where he was in action at the Battles of Arras, Ypres, Cambrai and the Somme. He also saw heavy fighting in many other important engagements, and was wounded at La Bassée in 1918. On his return to England in January 1919 he was demobilised, and holds the General Service and Victory Medals.
London Road, Sandy, Beds. Z4418.

TIPLER, S., Private, Northamptonshire Regiment.
At the outbreak of war he was already serving, and accordingly at once proceeded to the Western Front with the first Expeditionary Force. Whilst overseas he was in action in the Retreat from Mons and the Battles of the Marne, the Aisne, La Bassée, Ypres, the Somme, Arras and Cambrai. He also saw much service in the Retreat and Advance of 1918, and was eventually discharged in March 1919, holding the Mons Star, and the General Service and Victory Medals.
2, London Road, Newton Longville, Bucks. Z4419.

TIPPER, J. A., Private, Lancashire Fusiliers.
Mobilised at the outbreak of war, he was immediately ordered to the Western Front. There he took an active part in the Battles of Mons, Ypres, Festubert, Loos, the Somme, Arras and Cambrai, and in many other important engagements until the cessation of hostilities. He served in France until February 1919, and was discharged a month later, holding the Mons Star, and the General Service and Victory Medals.
34, King's Place, Bedford. X4420/B.

TIPPER, W. R., Sergeant, R.A.V.C.
When war was declared in August 1914 he was serving in the Army, but was retained on important work at home until 1915, when he was drafted to Egypt, where he saw much service. Later he was transferred to Palestine, and played a conspicuous part in fierce fighting at Gaza. He also rendered invaluable services to sick and wounded horses until invalided to England in 1919. He unfortunately died from the effects of war service on March 7th, 1919, at Burton-on-Trent Fever Hospital. He was entitled to the 1914–15 Star, and the General Service and Victory Medals.
"The path of duty was the way to glory."
34, King's Place, Bedford. X4420/A.

TIPTON, W., C.S.M., 2nd Bedfordshire Regiment.
He was already serving at the commencement of hostilities, but owing to ill-health was unable to secure his transfer overseas. During the first period of the war he was employed on the important work of training recruits at Felixstowe, and later was transferred to the Convalescent Camp at Eastbourne. There he was engaged on clerical duties, which he fulfilled in a highly efficient manner until discharged in April 1920.
3, College Street, Kempston, Beds. Z4421.

TITCHENER, R., L/Cpl., 5th Wiltshire Regiment.
He volunteered in September 1914, and seven months later proceeded to Gallipoli, taking part in the Landing on the Peninsula and in the subsequent engagements of the campaign. After the Evacuation in January 1916 he was drafted to Mesopotamia, and served on the Kut, Amara and Baghdad fronts. On his return to England he was demobilised in May 1919, and holds the 1914–15 Star, and the General Service and Victory Medals. Church Lane, Emberton, Bucks. Z4422.

TITCHMARCH, S. J., Private, Queen's (Royal West Surrey Regiment).
He volunteered in January 1916, at the age of 17 years, and, after a period of training, was drafted to France. Whilst on the Western Front he played an important part in the Battles of the Somme, Ypres and Cambrai, and in other heavy fighting, and was wounded in action. Demobilised in May 1919, he holds the General Service and Victory Medals.
Hemingford Grey, Hunts Z4423.

TIZARD, W. J., L/Corporal, Royal Engineers.
Volunteering in June 1915, he was later in the same year drafted overseas. During his service on the Western Front he saw severe fighting in the Festubert sector, and took an active part in the Battles of Loos, Vimy Ridge, the Somme and Cambrai. He contracted trench-fever in June 1918, and was invalided to England, and was subsequently demobilised in 1919, holding the 1914–15 Star, and the General Service and Victory Medals. Croxton, Cambs. Z4424.

TOBUTT, M., Sergeant, Huntingdonshire Cyclist Battalion and Bedfordshire Regiment.
A month after the outbreak of war he volunteered, and received his training with the Huntingdonshire Cyclist Battalion in Lincolnshire. On being transferred to the Bedfordshire Regiment he was ordered to the Western Front in 1916, and took a prominent part in the Battles of the Somme, Arras, Ypres and Cambrai. He also saw severe fighting in other important engagements, and was demobilised in January 1919, holding the General Service and Victory Medals.
9, Ambrey Road, Huntingdon. Z4425.

TOKINS, A., Private, Bedfordshire Regiment.
Volunteering in September 1914, he embarked for France early in the following year, and was in action at Ypres, Festubert, Loos and the Somme, where in July 1916 he was wounded. He was invalided home for hospital treatment, but in September of the same year returned to the Western Front and rejoined his unit on the Somme Shortly afterwards he received a severe wound, to which he unhappily succumbed on the 26th of the same month. He was entitled to the 1914–15 Star, and the General Service and Victory Medals.
"Whilst we remember, the sacrifice is not in vain."
St. Mary's Street, Eynesbury, St. Neots, Hunts. Z1606/A.

TOKINS, J., Driver, Royal Field Artillery.
Joining in September 1916, he landed in France in the following February, and was subsequently engaged on important transport duties at Ypres, Péronne and Cambrai. He did excellent work until demobilised in January 1919, and holds the General Service and Victory Medals.
Silver Street, Eynesbury, St. Neots, Hunts. Z4426.

TOLL, H., Air Mechanic, R.A.F.
He joined in June 1918, and at the conclusion of his training was engaged on important duties attached to the Kite Balloon Section. He was not successful in obtaining his transfer overseas before the close of hostilities, but, nevertheless, rendered valuable services until demobilised in January 1919.
73, Pilcroft Street, Beds. X3867/B.

TOLMAN, S. C. J., Air Mechanic, R.A.F.
He joined in January 1918, and five months later proceeded to France, subsequently being engaged as a rigger with his Squadron at Cherbourg. He rendered valuable services until his demobilisation, which took place on his return to England in February 1919, and holds the General Service and Victory Medals. 33, Bridge St., New Bradwell, Bucks. Z4427.

TOLTON, T. B., L/Corporal, 10th King's (Liverpool Scottish Regiment).

Volunteering in May 1915, he was engaged on important home duties until 1918, when he crossed to France. He took part in many of the principal battles during the Retreat and Allied Advance, at the conclusion of which he proceeded with the Army of Occupation to Germany. He was demobilised in May 1919, and holds the General Service and Victory Medals.
34, Napier Street, Bletchley, Bucks. Z4428.

TOMBS, S. F., Private, 52nd Devonshire Regiment.

He joined in May 1918 on attaining military age, and underwent his training at Cromer. He was not successful in obtaining his transfer overseas until February 1919, when he was sent to the Army of Occupation in Germany, and did excellent work with his unit at Cologne prior to his demobilisation in January 1920. 20, Park Street, Stony Stratford, Bucks. TZ4429/B.

TOMBS, W. A., Private, Oxford. and Bucks. L.I.

Nine months after joining in March 1916, he was drafted to Salonika, and whilst in the Balkan theatre of war took part in heavy fighting on the Vardar and Doiran fronts. He was admitted to hospital with malarial fever, and unfortunately died on October 15th, 1918. He was entitled to the General Service and Victory Medals.

"His memory is cherished with pride."

20, Park Street, Stony Stratford, Bucks. TZ4429/A.

TOMPKINS, C., Private, 2nd Northants. Regiment.

Having joined in May 1916, he proceeded to France in September, and went into action at Beaucourt on the Somme. He also took part in the Battles of Arras and Ypres, and was wounded on the Somme in March 1918. He served for a time with the 17th Worcestershire Regiment, and was later attached to the Royal Engineers for special police duties. Demobilised in January 1919, he holds the General Service and Victory Medals. Barker's Lane, Goldington, Bedford. Z4433.

TOMPKINS, C. E., Private, Hampshire Regiment.

He joined in May 1917, and underwent his training with the 7th Reserve of Cavalry. In July 1917 he joined the Hampshire Regiment, but three months later was transferred to the Royal Air Force and proceeded to France. He then served in the Cambrai, Somme, Aisne, Marne, Amiens and Bapaume sectors. Demobilised on his return to England in March 1919, he holds the General Service and Victory Medals.
27, Church Street, Wolverton, Bucks. TZ4432.

TOMPKINS, D. A. (Miss), Nurse.

In January 1917 this lady offered her services and was engaged on important duties at various hospitals. She was awarded the British Red Cross, the Order of St. John of Jerusalem and a Certificate in recognition of the excellent work she rendered for the sick and wounded, and for untiring devotion to duty. She relinquished her services in November 1918.
Whaddon Road, Far Bletchley, Bucks. Z4431/B.

TOMPKINS, F. L., Private, 35th Royal Fusiliers.

He volunteered in April 1915, and twelve months later was drafted to France. During his service in this theatre of war he played a prominent part in heavy fighting in the Ypres, Cambrai and Havrincourt sectors. He was demobilised in February 1919, and holds the General Service and Victory Medals. Whaddon Road, Far Bletchley, Bucks. Z4431/A.

TOMPKINS, H., Air Mechanic, Royal Air Force.

Although under military age he joined the Royal Naval Air Service in January 1917, and first served at Felixstowe. Later he was transferred to the Royal Air Force, and was engaged on important work repairing aero-engines at Uxbridge and Radlett. He was unsuccessful in obtaining his transfer overseas, but rendered valuable services until his demobilisation in 1919. 3, Bunyan Road, Bedford. Z4434/A.

TOMPKINS, J., Pte., Beds. Regt.; and Sapper, R.E.

He volunteered in the Bedfordshire Regiment in 1914, but was discharged from Longmore Camp shortly afterwards owing to a physical deformity. In March 1915, however, he joined the Royal Engineers, and was sent to France, where he rendered valuable services with his unit at Etaples and n the Ypres, Festubert and Cambrai sectors. He was demobilised in 1919, and holds the General Service and Victory Medals.
3, Bunyan Road, Bedford. Z4434/B

TOMPKINS, T., Sapper, Royal Engineers.

A Reservist, he was called up in August 1914, and first served in the Signal Section on the East Coast. In 1915 he was sent to France, where he took an active part in the Battles of the Somme, Arras, Vimy Ridge, Ypres, Cambrai, Lille, Bapaume and the Marne (II.). He was discharged in June 1919, and holds the 1914–15 Star and the General Service and Victory Medals. 79, Garfield Street, Bedford. Z4435.

TOMPKINS, W. A., Gunner, R.F.A.

Having enlisted in January 1913, he was stationed in India at the outbreak of war and proceeded to France early in 1915. After taking part in the Battles of Ypres (II.) and Loos he was sent to Egypt, but later advanced into Palestine and was n action at Gaza. In 1917 he was transferred to Salonika, where he saw heavy fighting on the Doiran front until invalided to England with fever in June 1918. He was discharged in April 1920, and holds the 1914–15 Star, and the General Service and Victory Medals.
19, St. Giles Street, New Bradwell, Bucks. TZ4430.

TOMLIN, G. R., L/Corporal, King's Own Royal Lancaster Regiment.

He volunteered in November 1915, and eight months later was drafted to the Western Front, but after only a fortnight on active service was badly wounded in action at Loos in July 1916 He was invalided to England, and, on his recovery, did excellent work with the Labour Corps until his demobilisation in February 1919, holding the General Service and Victory Medals. 15, Chandos Street, Bedford. X4437.

TOMLIN, S. R., Private, R.A.S.C. (M.T.)

He joined in April 1917, and in the following September was drafted to Salonika, where he was engaged on important duties as a mechanic on the Doiran and Vardar fronts. Whilst on the way home he was taken ill with influenza, and unfortunately died on February 19th, 1920. He was buried near Malta, and was entitled to the General Service and Victory Medals.

"The path of duty was the way to glory."

4, St. Mary's Terrace, Newtown, Hunts. Z4436.

TOMLINSON, C., Private, 1st Bedfordshire Regt.

Mobilised in August 1914, he quickly proceeded to France and took part in the Battles of the Aisne, La Bassée, Ypres (where he was wounded in November), Neuve Chapelle, Hill 60, Festubert, the Somme, Arras and Cambrai. In November 1917 he was transferred to Italy, but, after serving on the Asiago Plateau and the Piave, returned to the Western Front, and was gassed in action in the Nieppe Forest in June 1918. Invalided home, he was finally discharged in May 1920, and holds the 1914 Star, and the General Service and Victory Medals. 42, Westbourne Road, Queen's Park, Bedford. Z4438.

TOMS, E. G., Sapper, Royal Engineers.

He was mobilised in August 1914, and first saw active service in the following July, when he was drafted to the Dardanelles, and took part in the operations at Suvla Bay and Anzac Cove After the Evacuation of the Gallipoli Peninsula he was sent to Egypt, but later proceeded into Palestine and was engaged on important pioneer duties during the heavy fighting at Gaza, Jaffa and Rafa. He was discharged in June 1919, and holds the 1914–15 Star, and the General Service and Victory Medals.
20, Bower Street, Bedford. Z4439.

TOOLEY, R. J., Staff-Sergeant, R.A.S.C. (M.T.)

He volunteered in the Royal Army Medical Corps in October 1914, and, proceeding to Gallipoli in the following August, was wounded in action during the Landing at Suvla Bay, and was invalided home. On his recovery he was transferred to the Royal Army Service Corps (Mechanical Transport), and drafted to France, where he did excellent work whilst engaged in taking supplies and ammunition to the forward areas. He was demobilised in January 1919, and holds the 1914–15 Star, and the General Service and Victory Medals.
9, Russell Street, Stony Stratford, Bucks. Z4440/A

TOOLEY, W. J., Private, 7th Oxford. & Bucks. L.I.

Having volunteered in September 1914, he was sent to France twelve months later, and took part in the Battle of Loos before being transferred to Salonika. He then served on the Doiran and Vardar fronts, and was wounded in August 1916, but on his recovery rejoined his unit in the line. On May 9th, 1917, he was reported missing, and is now presumed to have been killed in action on that date. He was entitled to the 1914–15 Star, and the General Service and Victory Medals.

"A costly sacrifice upon the altar of freedom."

9, Russell Street, Stony Stratford, Bucks. Z4440/B.

TOOTH, A. G., Sapper, Royal Engineers.

He joined in January 1917, and, after his training, was engaged on important duties with the Inland Water Transport. Owing to medical unfitness he was unsuccessful in obtaining his transfer overseas, but did excellent work until his demobilisation in February 1919
Knight's Farm, Great Brickhill, Bletchley, Bucks. Z4442.

TOOTH, R. W., Private, 1st Royal Berkshire Regt.

He joined in February 1916, and was quickly drafted to France, where he took a prominent part in the Battles of the Somme (I.), Arras, Ypres and the Somme (II.). He was invalided home and discharged as medically unfit for further service in November 1918, and holds the General Service and Victory Medals.
15, Railway Terrace, Bletchley, Bucks. Z4441/A.

TOOTH, T. C., Private, Oxford. and Bucks. L.I.

He volunteered in December 1914, but whilst in training at Chelmsford was taken seriously ill with spotted fever and unfortunately died in hospital in March 1915.

"And doubtless he went in splendid company."

15, Railway Terrace, Bletchley, Bucks. Z4441/B.

TOPHAM, E., Gunner, Royal Garrison Artillery.

He joined in August 1916, and six months later landed in France. Whilst on the Western Front he took part in the Battles of Arras, Vimy Ridge, Ypres and the Somme (II.), and was in hospital for some time as the result of a serious illness. He was demobilised in February 1919, and holds the General Service and Victory Medals.
The Green, Toseland, St. Neots, Hunts. Z4443.

TOSELAND, J., Sergeant, Labour Corps.
He volunteered in August 1914, and proceeded to France in June 1916. After rendering valuable services in the Somme, Arras, Messines and Ypres sectors, he was badly wounded in October 1917, and invalided home. He was in hospital in Birmingham for some time, and then did excellent work of a special nature at Leicester until demobilised in February 1919, holding the General Service and Victory Medals.
Pipers Lane, Godmanchester, Hunts. Z4444.

TOTT, G. T. W., Rifleman, Rifle Brigade.
He joined in 1918, but owing to the early cessation of hostilities, was not drafted overseas. Whilst in the Army he rendered valuable services guarding German prisoners of war at Colchester and Ripon, and was eventually demobilised in November 1919. 21, Great Butts Street, Bedford. X2630/B.

TOWNS, T. H., Private, Queen's (Royal West Surrey Regiment).
He joined in July 1916, but was medically unfit for transfer to a theatre of war. Retained at home he was stationed in turn at Crawley, Fenny Stratford and Bedford, and rendered valuable services whilst employed on various duties of an important nature. He was demobilised in March 1919.
78, Grey Friars Walk, Bedford. X4445.

TOWNSEND, A. D., Pte., 2nd Bedfordshire Regt.
He was mobilisedin August 1914, and was immediately drafted to France. There he took part in the Battle of Mons and the subsequent Retreat, and did excellent work until he was unfortunatey killed in action on November 8th, 1914. He was entitled to the Mons Star, and the General Service and Victory Medals.
"Courage, bright hopes, and a myriad dreams, splendidly given."
Wyboston, Beds. Z4447.

TOWNSEND, A. W., Private, 7th Wiltshire Regt.
He volunteered in September 1914, and served at various home stations until August 1915, when he was sent to the Western Front, where he was in action at Ypres. He was later transferred to Salonika, and participated in heavy fighting on the Vardar and Doiran fronts. In May 1918 he returned to France and saw further service, being wounded at Le Cateau in the following October. Admitted to hospital, he was detained there for a month, and was eventually demobilised in February 1919, holding the 1914–15 Star, and the General Service and Victory Medals.
55, High Street, New Bradwell, Bucks. Z4446.

TOWNSEND, F., Air Mechanic, Royal Air Force.
He joined in 1916, but owing to ill-health was not successful in his efforts to obtain a transfer to a theatre of war. Retained at home, he was stationed at Dover, Harrietsham and in other places, and rendered valuable services whilst employed as a carpenter, until he was demobilised in March 1919.
6, Ladysmith Terrace, Eaton Socon, Beds. Z4448.

TOWNSEND, G., Private, East Kent Regiment.
Joining in June 1918, he was sent for training to Dover and remained there until he was drafted to France a few days before the signing of the Armistice. Whilst stationed at Melancourt he was fatally wounded on December 17th, 1918, by the explosion of a bomb, one of a number which were being sorted. He was entitled to the General Service and Victory Medals.
"His memory is cherished with pride."
The Warren, Clapham, Bedford. Z4449.

TRENHOLME, F. G., Private, 1st Welch Regiment.
Volunteering in August 1914, he was drafted in the following March to France. In this theatre of war he took part in heavy fighting at Ypres, and on the Somme, Arras and Cambrai fronts. He was also in action in various sectors during the Retreat and Advance of 1918, and returned to England in January 1919. Later he was sent to India, where he was still serving in 1920, and holds the 1914–15 Star, and the General Service and Victory Medals.
Rivetts Yard, Great Linford, Bucks. Z4451.

TROLLEY, F., Sapper, Royal Engineers.
He volunteered in October 1915, and in the following year proceeded to the Western Front. There he served with his Company on the Somme, Arras, Ypres and Cambrai fronts, engaged on various duties of an important nature, during the course of which he was gassed. He did excellent work until he returned home for demobilisation in March 1919, holding the General Service and Victory Medals.
15, Buckley Road, Eynesbury, St. Neots, Hunts. TZ4450.

TRUEMAN, A., L/Cpl., 1/5th Bedfordshire Regt.
He volunteered in September 1914, and was sent in July of the following year to Gallipoli. There he participated in severe fighting at Suvla Bay, and after the Evacuation was transferred to Egypt. Proceeding later into Palestine, he was in action at Gaza, Jaffa and near Jerusalem prior to the capture of that city. He returned home in February 1919, and was demobilised a month later, holding the 1914–15 Star, and the General Service and Victory Medals.
59, Muswell Road, Southend, Beds. Z4452/B.

TRUEMAN, F., Private, 2nd Queen's Own (Royal West Kent Regiment).
A serving soldier at the outbreak of war in August 1914, he was drafted in the following January to Mesopotamia. In this sphere of hostilities he took part in severe fighting on the Tigris front, and at Kut-el-Amara, Mosul and Baghdad, and was wounded in July 1916. He remained overseas until August 1919, and, being discharged on his return home in the succeeding month, holds the 1914–15 Star, and the General Service and Victory Medals.
59, Muswell Road, Southend, Bedford. Z4452/A.

TRUEMAN, R., Private, 1/5th Bedfordshire Regt.
He was mobilised in August 1914, and retained at home on various duties of an important nature until the following July, when he proceeded to Gallipoli. There he at once participated in severe fighting, but had only served in this theatre of war for a few weeks when he made the supreme sacrifice, being killed in action at Suvla Bay on August 15th, 1915. He was entitled to the 1914–15 Star, and the General Service and Victory Medals.
"Honour to the immortal dead, who gave their youth that the world might grow old in peace."
59, Muswell Road, Southend, Bedford. Z4452/C.

TRUNDLEY, J. T. (D.C.M.), C.S.M., 1st Beds. Regt.
Already serving when war broke out in August 1914, he was employed on important duties with his own unit at Felixstowe, and the Machine Gun Corps at Grantham until April 1916, when he was seut to France. In this theatre of war he took part in strenuous fighting on the Somme front and at Ypres, Vimy Ridge, Messines and Cambrai. He also served in Italy on the Piave front. During his service overseas he was wounded, and was awarded the Distinguished Conduct Medal for conspicuous gallantry and devotion to duty in the Field. He was discharged in May 1919, and also holds the General Service and Victory Medals.
19, St. Germain Street, Huntingdon. Z4453.

TRUSTAM, H., Sapper, Royal Engineers.
He volunteered in November 1914, and proceeded in the following April to the Dardanelles, where he served for five months, during which time he participated in severe fighting at Suvla Bay. Evacuated to England on account of shell-shock, he remained at home until 1917, and was then sent to France. In this theatre of hostilities he was in action at Bullecourt and fought in the Battles of Ypres (III.) and Cambrai, also in several sectors during the Retreat and Advance of 1918. He was demobilised on his return home in March 1919, and holds the 1914–15 Star, and the General Service and Victory Medals. 67, Priory St., Bedford. X4454.

TUCK, D., Private, 8th Northamptonshire Regt.
He joined in March 1916, and during his training was stationed at Sittingbourne and Chatham. Later, found to be medically unfit for further military duty, he was invalided out of the Army in July 1916, after only four months' service.
King's Ripton, Hunts. Z4455.

TUCK, J. W., Corporal, R.E. and Labour Corps.
Volunteering in 1915, he was drafted later in the same year to the Western Front. During the time he was overseas he did excellent work whilst engaged on various duties of an important nature on the Arras, Ypres, Cambrai and Somme fronts. He returned home for demobilisation in 1919, holding the 1914–15 Star, and the General Service and Victory Medals.
King's Ripton, Hunts. Z4456.

TUCK, W., Private, Bedfordshire Regiment.
He joined in March 1916, and four months afterwards proceeded to France. In this theatre of war he participated with his unit in the Battles of the Somme, Ypres (III.), Arras and Cambrai, and was gassed in action at Ypres in July 1917. He remained overseas for some time after the Armistice, and was demobilised in September 1919, holding the General Service and Victory Medals. King's Ripton, Hunts. Z4457.

TUCKER, H. F., Private, 7th Bedfordshire Regt.
Joining in October 1917, he was drafted in the following January to the Western Front. There he took part in heavy fighting at Amiens and in other sectors, but had only been overseas for two months when he fell fighting on the Somme front on March 13th, 1918. He was buried in the British cemetery at Beaumont-Hamel, and was entitled to the General Service and Victory Medals.
"Whilst we remember, the sacrifice is not in vain."
14, Grey Friars Walk, Bedford. X3439/B.

TUCKER, P. A., Private, 7th Oxford. & Bucks. L.I.
He volunteered in September 1914, and was employed at various home stations until September 1915, when he was sent to France. After two months' service there he was transferred to Salonika, where he took a prominent part in many important engagements on the Doiran, Struma and Vardar fronts, also near Monastir, and was wounded on the Vardar front. He was taken prisoner, but after spending three days in captivity, managed to escape and rejoined his unit. Returning home after the Armistice, he was eventually demobilised in March 1919, and holds the 1914–15 Star, and the General Service and Victory Medals. 12, Oxford St., Wolverton, Bucks. Z4458.

TUCKEY, A. S., Pte., 2/4th Oxford. & Bucks. L.I.
He volunteered in March 1915, and whilst training at Catterick, unfortunately sustained internal injuries. He was admitted into St. Thomas' Hospital, Newcastle, and after treatment was discharged as medically unfit for further military service in November 1917. 75, Ledsam St., Wolverton, Bucks. Z4461/A.

TUCKEY, C. W., Private, Suffolk Regiment.
Joining in October 1916, he received his training at Felixstowe, and two months later was drafted to the Western Front. There he was engaged in fierce fighting in the Somme, Albert and Arras sectors, and died gloriously on the Field of Battle at Ypres on September 26th, 1917. He was entitled to the General Service and Victory Medals.
"Courage, bright hopes, and a myriad dreams, splendidly given."
5, Spring Gardens, Towcester, Northants. Z4460.

TUCKEY, E. H., L/Cpl., 2nd Oxford. & Bucks. L.I.
Mobilised in August 1914, he at once proceeded to France, and fought in the Retreat from Mons and in the Battles of the Marne, Ypres, Neuve Chapelle and Festubert. He was wounded at Hill 60 in 1915, and admitted to hospital in Rouen. On his recovery he returned to the firing-line and died gloriously on the Field of Battle at Givenchy on September 25th, 1915. He was entitled to the Mons Star, and the General Service and Victory Medals.
"His life for his Country, his soul to God."
75, Ledsam Street, Wolverton, Bucks. Z4461/B.

TUCKEY, H. G., Private, Oxford. and Bucks. L.I.
He volunteered in April 1915, and was drafted overseas a year later. Whilst on the Western Front he was engaged in fierce fighting in the Battle of the Somme, and was wounded. On rejoining his unit he took part in engagements at Arras and St. Quentin, and was again wounded in May 1917. He also saw much service during the Retreat and Advance of 1918, and was demobilised in January 1919, holding the General Service and Victory Medals.
16, Albert Street, Bletchley, Bucks. Z4459.

TULLETT, J., Gunner, Royal Garrison Artillery.
He joined in June 1916, and on completion of his training at Plymouth was in January 1917 drafted to Salonika. In that theatre of war he did valuable work with the 136th Heavy Battery during the operations on the Doiran front, and experienced fierce fighting in many important engagements. He was demobilised on his return to England in September 1919, and holds the General Service and Victory Medals.
14, Filgrave, near Newport Pagnell, Bucks. Z4462.

TUMEY, E. J., Private, Royal Dublin Fusiliers.
Mobilised on the outbreak of war, he embarked for France shortly afterwards, and was in action in several engagements during the Retreat from Mons. He was wounded and taken prisoner in August 1914, and was held in captivity in Germany until repatriated after the Armistice. He was demobilised in February 1919, and holds the Mons Star, and the General Service and Victory Medals.
Huntingdon Street, St. Neots, Hunts. Z4463.

TURNER, C., Private (Signaller), M.G.C.
He was mobilised when war broke out, and in 1915 proceeded to the Western Front. In the course of his service there he was in action at the Battles of the Somme, Arras, Ypres and Cambrai, and was then drafted to Egypt. Taking part in the British Advance through Palestine, he did good work with his section at Gaza, Jaffa and Haifa, and was present at the entry into Jerusalem. Returning to England on the conclusion of hostilities in 1918, he was discharged on account of service in March 1919, and holds the General Service and Victory Medals. Rectory Lane, Somersham, Hunts. Z4465.

TURNER, G. H., Pte., Beds. & 4th Middlesex Regts.
Volunteering in September 1914, he was drafted to the Western Front on completion of a period of training in the following year, and there took part in important engagements in various sectors. He is believed to have been killed in action on the Somme in 1916. He was entitled to the 1914–15 Star, and the General Service and Victory Medals.
"Whilst we remember, the sacrifice is not in vain."
17, Bunyan Road, Bedford. Z4466.

TURNER, J. W., A.B., Royal Navy.
He joined in July 1916, and after a period of training was posted in the following year to H.M.S. "Leda." On board this vessel he was engaged on mine-sweeping and patrol duties with the Grand Fleet in the North Sea until after the cessation of hostilities, being finally demobilised in May 1919. He holds the General Service and Victory Medals.
20, Spencer Street, New Bradwell, Bucks. Z4467.

TURNER, T., Private, R.A.V.C.
Volunteering in June 1915, he was drafted in the following month to France, where he was engaged in tending sick and wounded horses and on other important duties. He served at Rouen, Boulogne and Etaples and various other stations in this theatre of war, and did much useful work until his return home for demobilisation in February 1919. He holds the 1914–15 Star, and the General Service and Victory Medals.
The Green, Great Linford, Bucks. Z4464/B.

TURNER, W. T. (M.M.), Sergeant, 17th (Duke of Cambridge's Own) Lancers.
Mobilised in August 1914, he was drafted to the Western Front in the following month and there saw much severe fighting, and was wounded on the Somme in 1916. Invalided home, he eturned to France, however, on his recovery and was again in action in the Cambrai sector, taking a prominent part in the Retreat and Advance of 1918. He was awarded the Military Medal for bravery and devotion to duty and the Croix de Guerre for conspicuous gallantry in the Field. Holding also the 1914 Star, and the General Service and Victory Medals, he was discharged in March 1919.
The Green, Great Linford, Bucks. Z4464/A.

TURVEY, C. W., Private, Oxford. & Bucks. L.I.
He volunteered in December 1915. and in May of the following year was sent to Mesopotamia, where he saw much severe fighting. He took part in many important engagements in this seat of operations until sent home and invalided from the Army in April 1918. He holds the General Service and Victory Medals. 95, Tickford Street, Newport Pagnell, Bucks. Z4468.

TURVEY, J., Sapper, Royal Engineers.
Five months after volunteering in August 1915 he was drafted to France, where he was engaged in laying barbed-wire entanglements in various sectors of the front. He was also present at the Battles of Albert, the Somme, Vimy Ridge, Ypres, Passchendaele and Cambrai, and many other engagements until the signing of the Armistice. Demobilised in March 1919, he holds the General Service and Victory Medals.
Warboys, Hunts. Z4469.

TURVEY, R. H., Q.M.S., 5th Lincolnshire Regt.
Volunteering in September 1914, he proceeded to the Western Front in February of the following year, and there saw much heavy fighting. He took a prominent part in the Battles of Loos, Arras and Vimy Ridge, and many other important engagements until sent home in December 1917 in order to take up munition work. He was finally demobilised in March 1919, and holds the 1914–15 Star, and the General Service and Victory Medals.
60, Dudley Street, Bedford. Z4470.

TWEED, S. J., Private, Bedfordshire Regiment.
Shortly after joining in December 1916 he proceeded to France, where he saw severe fighting in various sectors of the front. He took part in the Battles of Arras, Ypres and the Somme, and many other important engagements in this theatre of war until the cessation of hostilities. He was demobilised in May 1919, and holds the General Service and Victory Medals.
85, Howbury Street, Bedford. Z4471.

TWIGDEN, E., L/Corporal, Hunts. Cyclist Bn.
He volunteered in 1914, and on completing his training in the following year was drafted to the Western Front, where he took part in much heavy fighting. He served through the Battles of Ypres, Cambrai and the Somme, and many other engagements in this theatre of war, and was wounded. Demobilised in December 1919, he joined the Arabian Police Force, however, in August of the following year, and holds the 1914–15 Star, and the General Service and Victory Medals.
28, Ouse Walk, Huntingdon. Z4472/B.

TWIGDEN, G., Sapper, Royal Engineers.
He volunteered in March 1915, and in the following year proceeded to the Western Front. Whilst in this theatre of war he saw severe fighting in various sectors and took part in the Battles of the Somme, Arras, Ypres and Cambrai and other important engagements. He afterwards served with the Army of Occupation in Germany, finally returning home for demobilisation in January 1920. He holds the General Service and Victory Medals. 28, Ouse Walk, Huntingdon. Z4472/A.

TWIGDEN, J., Tpr., 3/1st Beds. Yeo. (Lancers).
Having previously volunteered in November 1915 and been discharged in the same month, he re-enlisted in June 1916, and underwent a short period of training. He rendered very valuable services with his Squadron, however, but in August 1916 was finally invalided from the Army.
Huntingdon Street, St. Neots, Hunts. Z4473.

TWIGDEN, P. R., L/Corporal, Queen's (Royal West Surrey Regiment).
He joined in April 1917, and was retained on important duties in England until drafted to the Western Front in the following year. There he took part in many important engagements, including the Battles of the Somme, Cambrai and Ypres, and was severely gassed in action. He was demobilised on his return home in 1919, and holds the General Service and Victory Medals. Huntingdon Street, St. Neots, Hunts. Z4474.

TWIGG, F. G., L/Corporal, Durham Light Infantry.
He mas mobilised in August 1914, and in April of the following year was sent to the Western Front, where he saw severe fighting in various sectors. He took part in the Battles of Ypres and Loos, and many other engagements, and was wounded on the Somme in 1916 and at Ypres in the following year. Invalided home, he was for a time in hospital before being discharged in October 1917 as medically unfit for further service. He holds the 1914–15 Star, and the General Service and Victory Medals. 60, Spencer Street, New Bradwell, Bucks. Z2566/B.

TYLER, H., Private, Royal Fusiliers.
He joined in September 1916, and underwent a period of training prior to being drafted to the Western Front in the following year. There he saw much heavy fighting, and took part in the Battles of Vimy Ridge, Passchendaele, the Somme, Cambrai, Bapaume and Ypres, and many other important engagements in various sectors. Demobilised in January 1919, he holds the General Service and Victory Medals.
Barham, Hunts. Z4475.

TYRRELL, A. J., Pte., 3rd South Staffs. Regt.
Joining in May 1916, he proceeded to France on completing his training in January of the following year, and there saw severe fighting in various sectors of the front. He took part in the Battles of Cambrai and the Somme and many other important engagements, andserved also through the Retreat andAdvance of 1918. He was demobilised in January 1919, and holds the General Service and Victory Medals.
12, Vicarage Walk, Stony Stratford, Bucks. Z4477.

TYRRELL, F W., Gunner, Royal Field Artillery.
Already in the Army when war broke out in August 1914, he proceeded to the Western Front in December of that year and there took part in the Battles of Neuve Chapelle and Ypres and minor engagements, being wounded at Hill 60 in May 1915. He fell fighting at Festubert on July 20th, of that year. He was entitled to the 1914–15 Star, and the General Service and Victory Medals.
"His life for his Country, his soul to God."
9, Houghton Road, Bedford. Z4476/A.

TYRRELL, J., Sapper, Royal Engineers.
Volunteering in September 1914, he proceeded to the Western Front four months later, and there fought in the Battle of Neuve Chapelle. In May 1915 he was invalided home, suffering from trench feet, but returned to France, however, in October of that year and was again in action in the Battles of Loos, the Somme and Cambrai, being wounded at Ypres in 1917. He was demobilised in December 1918, and holds the 1914–15 Star, and the General Service and Victory Medals.
9, Houghton Road, Bedford. Z4476/B.

TYSOE, F. J., Private, 2nd Bedfordshire Regiment.
A serving soldier, he was drafted to the Western Front immediately on the outbreak of war in August 1914, and there fought in the Retreat from Mons, and also took part in the Battles of La Bassée and Ypres. Mortally wounded in action at Neuve Chapelle, he unhappily died in hospital at Boulogne on March 18th, 1915. He was entitled to the Mons Star, and the General Service and Victory Medals.
"He joined the great white company of valiant souls."
18, Greenhill Street, Bedford. X4478/B.

TYSOE, H. H., Private, 2nd Bedfordshire Regt.
Mobilised in August 1914, he was sent to the Western Front in time to take part in the Retreat from Mons, and later fought in the Battles of La Bassée, Ypres and Neuve Chapelle, and many minor engagements. He died gloriously on the Field of Battle at Festubert on May 17th, 1915. He was entitled to the Mons Star, and the General Service and Victory Medals.
"His memory is cherished with pride."
18, Greenhill Street, Bedford. X4478/A.

TYSOE, J. S., Sergeant, Hunts. Cyclist Battalion and Bedfordshire Regiment.
After volunteering in October 1914, he underwent a period of training prior to being drafted to the Western Front in 1916. There he saw much severe fighting, and took part in the Battles of the Somme, Vimy Ridge, Messines and Ypres and many other engagements until invalided home in 1918, suffering from trench feet. Demobilised in December of that year, he holds the General Service and Victory Medals.
High Street, Brampton, Hunts. Z4479.

TYSOE, W., Private, Bedfordshire Regiment.
Volunteering in January 1915, he was drafted to the Western Front in the following November, and there took part in the engagements at Loos, Albert, Beaumont-Hamel and many other places. In 1917 he was transferred to Italy, where he was again in action on the Piave and the Asiago Plateaux. He was twice wounded whilst overseas and was finally discharged on his return home in January 1920, holding the 1914–15 Star, and the General Service and Victory Medals.
4, Leys Cottages, Clapham, Bedford. Z4480.

TYSOE, W. L., 2nd Lieutenant, 22nd London Regt.
He joined in March 1916, and was retained at various stations in England, where he was engaged on duties of a highly important nature until 1918. He then proceeded to France, and there served at Rouen, Calais and many other places, and did much excellent work until his return home for demobilisation in February 1919. He holds the General Service and Victory Medals. 35, Priory Street, Bedford. Z4481.

U

UMNEY, A., Private, Oxford. and Bucks. L.I.
He volunteered in August 1914, and after a short period of training was drafted to France. In this seat of war he took part in many engagements, including those in the Ypres, the Somme, Arras and Cambrai sectors, and was gassed in 1916. He was demobilised in March 1919, and holds the 1914 Star, and the General Service and Victory Medals.
5, Church Passage, Newport Pagnell, Bucks Z2198/A.

UMNEY, B. D., Private, Oxford. & Bucks. L.I.
He volunteered in August 1914, and completing his training in the following year, was drafted to France, where he was badly wounded on the Somme in July 1916. As a result he was invalided home, but on his recovery returned to France, and was unfortunately killed in action in the Arras sector in May 1917. He was entitled to the 1914–15 Star, and the General Service and Victory Medals.
"Whilst we remember, the sacrifice is not in vain."
35, Broad Street, Newport Pagnell, Bucks. Z2199/B.

UMNEY, C. (M.S.M.), Pte., 2nd Ox. & Bucks. L.I.
He volunteered in September 1914, and was quickly drafted to France, where he took part in engagements at Ypres, Festubert, Loos, the Somme, Albert, Cambrai and in the Retreat and Advance of 1918. He was awarded the Meritorious Service Medal for consistently good work and devotion to duty. After the Armistice he served with the Army of Occupation in Germany until his demobilisation in March 1919. He holds also the 1914 Star, and the General Service and Victory Medals.
58, Priory Street, Newport Pagnell, Bucks. Z2200.

UMNEY, F. F., Private, 6th Oxford. and Bucks. L.I.
He volunteered in June 1915, and in the following January was drafted to France. In this theatre of war he took part in many engagements, including those on the Somme, at Arras, Cambrai and in the Retreat and Advance of 1918. He was demobilised in March 1919, and holds the General Service and Victory Medals.
35, Broad Street, Newport Pagnell, Bucks. Z2199/C.

UMNEY, G. E., Private, Royal Scots Fusiliers.
He was already in the Army when war broke out in August 1914, and was drafted to France, where he took part in the Battle of Loos and was wounded. As a result he was invalided home, and on his recovery proceeded to Salonika. There he saw much heavy fighting on the Vardar and Doiran fronts, and was again wounded. He returned home and was discharged in March 1919, holding the 1914 Star, and the General Service and Victory Medals.
35, Broad Street, Newport Pagnell, Bucks. Z2199/A.

UMNEY, H. B. O., Sapper, Royal Engineers.
Volunteering in 1915, he was drafted to France later in the same year. Whilst on the Western Front he was engaged on important duties in the Ypres, Givenchy, Loos and Cambrai sectors. He did continuously good work throughout and was demobilised in March 1919, holding the 1914–15 Star, and the General Service and Victory Medals.
10, The Grove, Bedford. Z2201.

UMNEY, H. E., Private, 6th Oxford. & Bucks. L.I.
He volunteered in September 1914, and in the following March was drafted to the Western Front, where he saw much fighting in the Ypres sector. Later he was transferred to Salonika, and took part in engagements on the Doiran front, being badly wounded in action. As a result he was invalided home and eventually discharged in March 1919. He holds the 1914–15 Star, and the General Service and Victory Medals.
35, Broad Street, Newport Pagnell, Bucks. Z2199/D.

UMNEY, J., L/Cpl., 5th Oxford. and Bucks. L.I.
He volunteered in August 1914, and after a short period of training was drafted to France. There he took part in much heavy fighting in the Marne, La Bassée, Ypres and the Somme sectors. He died gloriously on the Field of Battle at Arras on April 2nd, 1917, and was entitled to the 1914 Star, and the General Service and Victory Medals.
"The path of duty was the way to glory."
5, Church Passage, Newport Pagnell, Bucks. Z2198/B.

UMNEY, J. W., Private, Royal Berkshire Regt.
He joined in 1917, and underwent a period of training prior to his being drafted to France. There he was engaged as a signaller, and took part in many engagements in the Somme and Ypres sectors, and was gassed in action. He also saw fighting near Mons prior to the Armistice, and was demobilised in February 1919, holding the General Service and Victory Medals. 27, Bury Avenue, Newport Pagnell, Bucks. Z2197.

UNDERWOOD, A. G., Private, 1/5th Bedfordshire Regiment and Royal Fusiliers.
He was mobilised in August 1914, and in the following July was drafted to the Dardanelles, where he took part in the Landing at Suvla Bay. He contracted dysentery and was invalided home, but on his recovery proceeded to France and took part in the Battles of Vimy Ridge, Arras and Ypres. He made the supreme sacrifice, being killed in action at Passchendaele on September 20th, 1917, and was entitled to the 1914–15 Star, and the General Service and Victory Medals.
"A costly sacrifice upon the altar of freedom."
26, West Street, Olney, Bucks. Z2795/B.

UNDERWOOD, A. J. (M.M.), Sergeant, Oxfordshire and Buckinghamshire Light Infantry.
He volunteered in February 1915, and, completing his training in the following year, was drafted to France. There he played a distinguished part in the Battles of Arras, Ypres and Cambrai, and was wounded in action. He was awarded the Military Medal for conspicuous bravery in the Field in 1918. He also holds the General Service and Victory Medals, and was demobilised in March 1919.
108, Simpson Road, Bletchley, Bucks. Z4482 /B.

UNDERWOOD, A. W., Pte., Sherwood Foresters.
He joined in September 1917, and in the following year was drafted to Italy. In this seat of operations he served as a machine gunner and took part in many engagements on the Piave and Trentino fronts. He was also employed on various important duties and demobilised in March 1919. He holds the General Service and Victory Medals.
43, Hitchin Street, Biggleswade, Beds. Z3570 /C.

UNDERWOOD, E., Farrier-Sergeant, R.F.A.
Volunteering in September 1914, he was drafted overseas in the following year. During his service on the Western Front he was engaged on important duties in the Loos and Somme sectors. He was unfortunately badly kicked by a horse, which necessitated his being invalided home and eventually discharged in November 1917, as medically unfit for further service. He holds the 1914–15 Star, and the General Service and Victory Medals. 3, Mill Lane, Stony Stratford, Bucks. Z2202.

UNDERWOOD, G., Pte., Oxford. & Bucks. L.I.
He volunteered in September 1914, and was retained for a time at various home stations before being drafted to France in July 1916. There he saw much heavy fighting in the Somme, Albert and Arras sectors, and was buried alive by a shell-explosion. In consequence he was invalided to hospital, but later rejoined his unit. He was unfortunately killed in action on the Ypres front on August 16th, 1917, and was entitled to the General Service and Victory Medals.
"Thinking that remembrance, though unspoken, may reach him where he sleeps."
1, St. Benedict's Court, Huntingdon, Hunts. Z3115 /A.

UNDERWOOD, J. T., Oxford. and Bucks. L.I.
He joined in May 1918, and after two months' training was drafted to France, where he took part in the Advance of that year. After hostilities ceased, he proceeded to Germany with the Army of Occupation and served on the Rhine until his demobilisation in March 1919. He holds the General Service and Victory Medals.
1, Northampton Road, Lavendon, Bucks. TZ2204.

UNDERWOOD, P. A., 1st Class Stoker, R.N.
He joined in 1916, and after a period of training at Chatham proceeded to the North Sea on board H.M.S. "Dominion." He served with the Grand Fleet on important duties and took part in the raid on Zeebrugge. Later he saw service on one of H.M. Torpedo-boat Destroyers in the Baltic and at Scapa Flow, and was eventually demobilised in October 1919, holding the General Service and Victory Medals.
108 Simpson Road, Bletchley, Bucks. Z4482 /A.

UNDERWOOD, W. (M.M.), Private, 1/1st Oxfordshire and Buckinghamshire Light Infantry.
He volunteered in 1914, and was retained on various duties at home before proceeding overseas in 1916. Whilst on the Western Front he took part in the Battles of the Somme, Ypres Passchendaele and Cambrai, and was wounded in the Somme sector and invalided home. In June 1918 he was sent to Italy, where he saw much fighting on the Piave River and Asiago Plateau, being again wounded. He was awarded the Military Medal for conspicuous bravery in the Field when in charge of a Lewis Gun Section on November 2nd, 1918. He returned home and was demobilised in 1919, holding also the General Service and Victory Medals.
Diddington, Hunts. Z2203.

UNDERWOOD, W. T., Sapper, R.E. (R.O.D.)
Volunteering in December 1914, he was quickly drafted to France where he served in various sectors of the front He was engaged on important duties as a plate-layer with the Railway Operative Department, and was wounded by a stray bullet whilst at work. After the conclusion of hostilities he returned home and was demobilised in February 1919, holding the 1914–15 Star and the General Service and Victory Medals.
13 Weston Road Olney Bucks. Z2205.

UNITT, M. J., Sapper, R.E. (R.O.D.)
Having volunteered in June 1915, he underwent a period of training and later in the following year proceeded to France, where he served in various sectors of the front. He was chiefly engaged on important clerical duties at Boulogne and as a guard on trains, in which capacities he rendered excellent services until demobilised in March 1919, holding the General Service and Victory Medals. Green's Norton, Towcester, Northants. Z4483.

UNSWORTH, J., Private, South Wales Borderers.
Volunteering in November 1914, he underwent a period of training and was retained on important coastal defence and other duties with his unit. Owing to his being medically unfit, he was discharged in June 1916, after rendering excellent services. 55, Grey Friars Walk, Bedford. X2206.

UPCHURCH, A. H., Private, King's Own Shropshire Light Infantry.
Having joined in May 1917, he was quickly drafted to France, where he was in action during heavy fighting on the Cambrai front. In April 1918 he was taken prisoner, and held in captivity until the cessation of hostilities. After his release he returned home, and was demobilised in April 1919, holding the General Service and Victory Medals.
Sapley Lane, Hartford, Hunts. Z2208 /C.

UPCHURCH, E., Private, Labour Corps.
Having joined in June 1917, he completed his training and served at various stations in England, Scotland and Ireland. He was chiefly engaged on important transport duties, and also in the docks, where he rendered excellent services until demobilised in July 1919.
4, St. Benedict's Court, Huntingdon. Z2207.

UPCHURCH, F., Corporal, Army Cyclist Corps.
Mobilised at the outbreak of war in August 1914, he was quickly drafted to France, where he served in various sectors of the front as a despatch-rider. He was also attached to the Royal Engineers, and did excellent work in connection with trench-making and cable-laying, particularly during the Retreat and Advance of 1918. In March 1919 he was discharged, holding the 1914–15 Star, and the General Service and Victory Medals.
Walnut Tree Cottage, Hartford, Hunts. Z2208 /A.

UPCHURCH, W., Private, 1st Bedfordshire Regt.
After volunteering in October 1914, he underwent a period of training, and later proceeded to France, where he took part in heavy fighting on the Somme and also in the Battles of Arras, Ypres and Cambrai. Later in 1917 he was transferred to Italy and took part in the engagements on the Piave front. Returning to France, he was in action during the Retreat and Advance of 1918. He was demobilised in April 1919, holding the General Service and Victory Medals.
Walnut Tree Cottage, Hartford, Hunts. Z2208 /B.

USHER, A., Private, 2/5th Bedfordshire Regiment.
Volunteering in September 1914, he underwent a period of training, and in the following year proceeded to the Western Front, where he took part in the heavy fighting at Vimy Ridge. He was taken prisoner in 1917, and held in captivity until the cessation of hostilities. On his return home he was demobilised in January 1919, holding the 1914–15 Star, and the General Service and Victory Medals.
Eaton Socon, Beds. Z2213 /C.

USHER, A., Trooper, Bedfordshire Lancers.
Volunteering in September 1914, he completed a period of training and was later engaged on important duties at various stations until 1917. He then proceeded to the East, and saw much service, particularly in Palestine, where he took part in the Battles of Gaza, Jaffa and the capture of Jerusalem. Returning home, he was demobilised in 1919, holding the General Service and Victory Medals.
25, Salisbury Street, Bedford. X2209.

USHER, A. H., L/Corporal, 1/5th Buffs (East Kent Regiment).
After volunteering in September 1914, he was quickly drafted to India, where he rendered excellent services as corporal in charge of hospital orderlies, and also took part in engagements on the Frontier in 1916. After the cessation of hostilities he returned home and was demobilised in February 1919, holding the General Service and Victory Medals.
2, Christchurch Road, Ashford, Kent. Z2211 /A.

USHER, A. V., L/Corporal, 26th Royal Fusiliers.
Volunteering in December 1915, he saw active service in France, where he took part in the Battles of the Somme, Ypres and Passchendaele. Badly wounded in action in 1917, he was invalided to England, and on his recovery was engaged on important duties in Ireland and Somerset. He was demobilised in May 1919, and holds the General Service and Victory Medals. 1, Baker's Lane, Tempsford, near Sandy, Beds. Z2214.

USHER, E. G., Private, 1/5th Bedfordshire Regt.
Volunteering in September 1914, he was sent to the Dardanelles and saw heavy fighting in Gallipoli. After the Evacuation of the Peninsula, he was transferred to the 7th Bedfordshire Regiment, and drafted to France, where he took part in many important engagements, including the Battle of the Somme. He was demobilised in July 1919, and holds the 1914–15 Star, and the General Service and Victory Medals.
Eaton Socon, Beds. Z2213 /A.

USHER, F. W., Private, 5th Norfolk Regiment.
He volunteered in September 1914, and proceeded to Egypt in the following year, but after a period of service there advanced with General Allenby's Forces into Palestine and took part in the Battles of Gaza and Haifa, and the capture of Jerusalem and Jericho. Whilst in the East he was in hospital for a time with enteric fever. He was demobilised in January 1919, and holds the 1914–15 Star, and the General Service and Victory Medals. Cambridge Street, St. Neots, Hunts. Z2212

USHER, H. A., Staff-Sergeant, R.A.S.C.
Having volunteered in September 1914, he was drafted to German East Africa in December 1916, and was engaged on important transport duties during the Advance in that theatre of war. He rendered valuable services with his unit until his demobilisation in February 1919, and holds the General Service and Victory Medals. Laburnum Rd., Sandy, Beds. Z2211/B.

USHER, T. B, Drummer, 3/5th Bedfordshire Regt.
He volunteered in June 1915, and after his training was retained on important duties at various home stations. Owing to his being under age he was not drafted overseas, but did excellent work until his demobilisation in March 1919. Two months later he joined the Royal Navy, and in 1920 was serving on board H.M.S. "Dragon." Eaton Socon, Beds. Z2213/B.

V

VALE, F. T., L/Corporal, Machine Gun Corps.
After volunteering in 1915 he underwent his training, and was sent to France in the following year. He took part in the Battles of the Somme, Arras, Ypres and Cambrai, and in heavy fighting at Neuve Chapelle. At the cessation of hostilities, he proceeded into Germany with the Army of Occupation, and served on the Rhine until demobilised in November 1919, holding the General Service and Victory Medals. Turvey, Beds. Z2215.

VARNEY, C. G., Sapper, Royal Engineers.
After volunteering in June 1915 he underwent a period of training prior to being drafted to the Western Front in 1918. Whilst in this theatre of war he was engaged on important clerical duties in various sectors, and unfortunately suffered from septic poisoning. He was demobilised in March 1919, and holds the General Service and Victory Medals.
135, Tickford Street, Newport Pagnell, Bucks. Z2216/B.

VARNEY, G. F. (Miss), Worker, Q.M.A.A.C.
She joined in May 1917, and after completing a term of training was retained at various stations, where she was engaged on duties of a highly important nature. She did excellent work throughout her period of service, and was finally demobilised in November 1918.
17, Brooklands Road, Bletchley, Bucks. Z4484/B.

VARNEY, J. T., Air Mechanic, Royal Air Force.
He joined in March 1918, and after his training served at various stations, where he was engaged on important duties which called for a high degree of technical skill. Owing to the early cessation of hostilities he was unable to obtain his transfer overseas, but, nevertheless, rendered valuable services with his Squadron until November 1919, when he was demobilised.
17, Brooklands Road, Bletchley, Bucks. Z4484/A.

VARNEY, R. T., 1st Class Boy, Royal Navy.
He volunteered in April 1915, and was posted to H.M.S. "Black Prince," attached to the Grand Fleet in the North Sea, where, engaged on various duties, he also took part in many Naval actions. He unhappily lost his life when his ship was sunk at the Battle of Jutland on May 31st, 1916. He was entitled to the General Service and Victory Medals.
"And doubtless he went in splendid company."
135, Tickford Street, Newport Pagnell, Bucks. Z2216/A.

VARNHAM, W. (D.C.M.), L/Corporal, 7th Northamptonshire Regiment.
Volunteering in September 1914, he proceeded to the Western Front in the following year, and there took part in the Battles of Ypres, Loos and Passchendaele, and many minor engagements. He fell fighting at St. Quentin on March 21st, 1918. He had been awarded the Distinguished Conduct Medal for conspicuous gallantry in the Field, and was also entitled to the 1914–15 Star, and the General Service and Victory Medals.
"A costly sacrifice upon the altar of freedom."
Abbots Ripton, Hunts. Z2217.

VAUGHAN, F. J., Aircraftsman, Royal Air Force.
He volunteered in May 1915, and after his training was retained on duties of a highly technical nature in England until 1918. He was then drafted to France, where he served with the Mechanical Transport Section at Rouen until his return home for demobilisation in December 1919. He holds the General Service and Victory Medals.
8, Hawkins Road, Bedford. Z2218/A.

VAUGHAN, S. G., Gunner, R.G.A.
Volunteering in August 1914, he was drafted to the Western Front in January of the following year, and there saw severe fighting in various sectors. He took part in the Battles of Arras and Cambrai, and minor engagements, was twice wounded on the Somme, and also suffered from shell-shock. He was finally demobilised in January 1919, and holds the 1914–15 Star, and the General Service and Victory Medals.
8, Hawkins Road, Bedford. Z2218/B.

VICKERY, S. B., Pte., 2nd Royal Sussex Regt.
He volunteered in October 1914, and in June of the following year was drafted to the Western Front, where he saw severe fighting in various sectors. After taking part in the Battles of Loos and the Somme and engagements at Ypres, Festubert and many other places, he was transferred in November 1916 to Class W of the Reserve for important munition work at home. He was finally demobilised in February 1919, and holds the 1914–15 Star, and the General Service and Victory Medals.
37, Muswell Road, Bedford. Z2219.

VIGORS, E., Private, Bedfordshire Regiment.
After volunteering in 1915 he underwent a period of training prior to being drafted to the Western Front in the following year. There he saw much heavy fighting, took part in the Battles of Albert and Arras and other engagements, and was severely wounded in action on the Somme and on another occasion. Admitted to hospital in London in 1917, he was invalided from the Army in December of the following year, and holds the General Service and Victory Medals.
Cambridge Road, Sandy, Beds. Z2220.

VINTER, R. E., Corporal, R.A.S.C. (M.T.)
Four months after volunteering in February 1915 he proceeded to the Western Front, where he served in various sectors. He was present at the Battles of Albert, the Somme, Arras and Ypres, and many other important engagements, and was for a time in hospital in France, suffering from trench feet. He afterwards served with the Army of Occupation at Cologne and other stations in Germany, finally returning home for demobilisation in October 1919. He holds the 1914–15 Star, and the General Service and Victory Medals.
5, High Street, Huntingdon. TZ2221.

VINTINER, F. W., Private, 1st Bedfordshire Regt.
Joining in June 1916, he was drafted to the Western Front in the following December, and there took part in severe fighting at Ypres, Festubert and Loos, and was wounded at Arras in April 1917. Invalided home, the ship on which he sailed, H.M.H.S. "Donegal," was torpedoed in the Channel, but he was fortunately rescued. In November 1917 he was sent to Italy, where he fought on the Piave and the Asiago Plateaux. Returning later to France, he was again wounded at Merville in June 1918. He was finally demobilised in February 1919, and holds the General Service and Victory Medals
8, Albert Street, Bedford. X2222.

VINTNER, A., Corporal, Military Mounted Police.
He joined in June 1916, and after four months' training proceeded to the Western Front. Whilst in this theatre of war he was engaged on duties of great importance in various sectors, and was also present at the Battles of Arras, Ypres and Cambrai and many other engagements, until the cessation of hostilities. He was demobilised in April 1920, and holds the General Service and Victory Medals. 39, Newham St., Bedford. X2225.

VINTNER, A., Private, 1st Northants. Regiment.
He joined in May 1916, and after his training was retained on important duties in England until June of the following year, when he was drafted to the Western Front. There he saw severe fighting in various sectors, and took part in the Battles of Arras, Passchendaele and Amiens, and many minor engagements. He was demobilised in April 1919, and holds the General Service and Victory Medals.
18, Great Butts Street, Bedford. X2223.

VINTNER, J., Private, 2nd Norfolk Regiment.
He joined in April 1916, and on completion of a period of training in the following year was drafted to Mesopotamia, where he saw much severe fighting. He took part in many important engagements in this seat of operations, and also saw active service in Salonika and Egypt before being invalided home in April 1919. He was demobilised in September of that year, and holds the General Service and Victory Medals.
17, The Grove, Bedford. X2224.

VIRGIN, G. W., Private, West Riding Regiment.
Joining in March 1916, he was sent to the Western Front in the following year, and there took part in the Battles of Arras, Ypres, Cambrai and the Somme, and other important engagements in various sectors. He died gloriously on the Field of Battle on August 25th, 1918, and was buried near Bapaume. He was entitled to the General Service and Victory Medals.
"Whilst we remember, the sacrifice is not in vain."
Ivel Road, Sandy, Beds. Z2226.

VYNE, A., Private, East Surrey Regiment.
Having joined in October 1916, he underwent a period of training, and in the following year proceeded to Salonika. During his service in this seat of war he did good work and took part in the recapture of Monastir and in engagements on the Doiran and Vardar fronts. On his return home he was demobilised in May 1919, and holds the General Service and Victory Medals. 25, Edward Road, Bedford. Z2210.

W

WABY, W. A., Private, Labour Corps.
He joined in November 1916, but on account of his being unfit for service overseas was retained on special duties at Chatham. He, nevertheless, did consistently good work until the cessation of hostilities, and was demobilised in September 1919.
24, Cater Street, Kempston, Bedford. X2245.

WADE, C., Corporal, R.A.S.C. (M.T.)
He volunteered in 1915, and after a period of service in London proceeded to the Eastern theatre of war, where he was engaged on important transport duties in Egypt, Palestine and the Balkans. Whilst in the East he was employed in carrying up food and ammunition to forward areas during the advance on Baghdad, and also saw service in Salonika. He returned to England suffering from shell-shock, and was demobilised in March 1919, holding the General Service and Victory Medals.
30, Stafford Road, Bedford. Z2246.

WADSWORTH, A. J. S., Private, M.G.C.
Volunteering in December 1915, he completed a period of training at Ampthill Park, and was drafted to France in July of the following year. He took part in many important engagements, including the Battles of the Somme (I. and II.), Arras and Cambrai, and was gassed during the Retreat of 1918. Admitted into hospital at Rouen, he unfortunately died from the effects of gas-poisoning on April 8th, 1918, and was entitled to the General Service and Victory Medals.
"He joined the great white company of valiant souls."
Bow Brickhill, near Bletchley, Bucks. Z2247/B.

WADSWORTH, R. H., Pte., 1st Worcestershire Regiment.
He joined in May 1916, and two months later proceeded to the Western Front, where he saw much heavy fighting in various sectors, including the Somme and Ypres, and rendered valuable services until he made the supreme sacrifice at Messines, being killed in action on the Ridge on September 2nd, 1917. He was buried at Underhill Cemetery, Ploegsteert. He was entitled to the General Service and Victory Medals.
"His life for his Country, his soul to God."
Bow Brickhill, near Bletchley, Bucks. Z2247/A.

WAGSTAFF, A., Corporal, R.A.S.C. (M.T.)
Six months after joining in March 1916, he was drafted to Salonika, where he was engaged on important transport duties on the Vardar front. He did consistently good work throughout many engagements in this theatre of war until December 1918. He was then sent to Turkey, and did duty at Constantinople until his return to England for demobilisation in November 1919. He holds the General Service and Victory Medals. Pertenhall, Beds. Z2250/C.

WAGSTAFF, A., Sergeant, R.G.A.
He was already serving with the Colours at the outbreak of war in August 1914, and was shortly afterwards sent to the Western Front. He fought with distinction at the Battles of the Aisne, Ypres and Neuve Chapelle and was wounded in July 1915. He was invalided to England in consequence, and after his recovery was drafted to India, where in 1920 he was still serving He holds the 1914 Star, and the General Service and Victory Medals.
Sandy Terrace, London Road, Sandy, Beds. Z2248/D.

WAGSTAFF, C. E., Rifleman, 16th London Regiment (Queen's Westminster Rifles).
He volunteered in February 1915, and after a period of training was sent to France in the following September. In this theatre of war he took part in many important engagements, and saw heavy fighting on the Somme, but was unfortunately killed in action during the Offensive of 1916, and was buried at the British cemetery at Gommecourt. He was entitled to the 1914–15 Star, and the General Service and Victory Medals.
"Whilst we remember, the sacrifice is not in vain."
Pertenhall, Beds. Z2250/B.

WAGSTAFF, F. H., Private, Machine Gun Corps.
Joining in July 1917, he completed a period of training at various camps and was drafted to France in July of the following year. He was engaged in much heavy fighting on the Cambrai front, and also took part in the Advance of 1918. After the Armistice he proceeded to Germany, and did duty with the Army of Occupation on the Rhine until his demobilisation in April 1920. He holds the General Service and Victory Medals. Pertenhall, Beds. Z2250/A.

WAGSTAFF, H., L/Cpl., 1/5th Lancashire Fusiliers.
He joined in January 1916, and after completing his training was drafted to the Western Front in the following July. He took part in heavy fighting at Vimy Ridge, the Somme, Arras and Messines, but was wounded on September 9th, 1917, at the Battle of Ypres, and died in hospital the same day. He was entitled to the General Service and Victory Medals.
"His memory is cherished with pride."
2, Caldecote Road, Upper Caldecote, Beds. Z2251.

WAGSTAFF, J. (D.S.M.), Chief Petty Officer, R.N.
He was already in His Majesty's Navy at the outbreak of war in August 1914, having served since a boy, and immediately proceeded to sea in H.M.S. "Princess Royal." He took part in the Battle of the Falkland Isles in 1914, and was also in action at Jutland in May 1916. He later saw service in the North Sea, and was awarded the Distinguished Service Medal for conspicuous gallantry in action. He also holds the 1914–15 Star, and the General Service and Victory Medals, and in 1920 was still serving in the Navy.
Weston Underwood, Bucks. Z2249.

WAGSTAFF, R. B., Private, 2nd Bedfordshire Regt.
Volunteering in May 1915, he completed a period of training, and was drafted to the Western Front in March of the following year. There he was in action in many important sectors, and took part in the Battles of Albert and Bullecourt. He was severely wounded on the Somme, and unfortunately died in hospital after the amputation of a leg on December 6th, 1916. He was entitled to the General Service and Victory Medals.
"The path of duty was the way to glory."
Sandy Terrace, London Road, Sandy, Beds. Z2248/A.

WAGSTAFF, V. H., Pte., 7th Bedfordshire Regt.
He volunteered in September 1914, and after completing his training was sent to France in the following July. In this theatre of war he took part in many important engagements, including the Battles of the Somme and Beaumont-Hamel, and was wounded in October 1916 near Albert. He was invalided to England, and was ultimately discharged in April 1917 as physically unfit for further service. He holds the 1914–15 Star, and the General Service and Victory Medals.
Sandy Terrace, London Road, Sandy, Beds Z2248/B.

WAGSTAFF, W. G., Sergeant, 1st (King's) Dragoon Guards.
Serving in India at the outbreak of war in August 1914, he was immediately drafted to France and played a distinguished part in many important engagements. He was in action at the Battles of Ypres, Loos, Festubert, the Somme and Messines, but in 1917 was again sent to India, where he was engaged on important garrison duties. Returning to England, he was discharged in December 1919, and holds the 1914 Star, and the General Service and Victory Medals.
Sandy Terrace, London Road, Sandy, Beds. Z2248/C.

WAIN, T. W., Gunner, Royal Field Artillery.
Four months after joining in July 1916, he proceeded to the Western Front, where he took part in many important engagements, and saw heavy fighting in various sectors. He was in action with his Battery at Ypres, Messines, Arras and Passchendaele and made the supreme sacrifice on August 22nd, 1917, being killed in action on the Somme. He was entitled to the General Service and Victory Medals.
"Great deeds cannot die."
74, Marlborough Road, Queen's Park, Bedford. Z2252.

WAINE, H. (M.S.M.), R.Q.M.S., M.G.C.
Mobilised at the outbreak of war in August 1914, he was retained in England until April of the following year, and was then drafted to the Western Front, where he played a distinguished part in several engagements. Later, transferred to Italy in November 1917, he saw service on the Piave, and was awarded the Meritorious Service Medal for conspicuous bravery and was mentioned in Despatches. He was demobilised in March 1919, and holds the 1914–15 Star, and the General Service and Victory Medals.
54, Wolverton Road, Stony Stratford, Bucks. Z2253.

WAITE, C. H., Private, Queen's (Royal West Surrey Regiment) and Manchester Regiment.
Joining in 1916, and, completing his training at Colchester, he was sent to the Western Front in April of the following year, and took part in many engagements. He was in action at the Battles of Arras, Ypres, Lens and Cambrai, and also saw service during the Retreat and Advance of 1918. He was eventually demobilised in February 1919, and holds the General Service and Victory Medals.
Kimbolton, Hunts. Z2255.

WAITE, D., Private, Oxford. and Bucks. L.I.
He joined in March 1916, and after undergoing the necessary training at Oxford, was drafted to France in 1917. He took part in many important engagements, and was invalided to England through wounds sustained on the Somme. Returning to the Western Front, he saw further severe fighting in various sectors, and was wounded on two later occasions at Cambrai. Demobilised in March 1919, he holds the General Service and Victory Medals.
49, High Street, New Bradwell, Bucks. Z2254.

WAITE, R., Corporal, Royal Engineers.
He volunteered in June 1915, and five months later proceeded to France, where he was engaged on important work on the Somme. Transferred to Egypt in December 1917, he served at Jaffa and did duty as an engine driver. He returned to England and was demobilised in November 1919, holding the 1914–15 Star, and the General Service and Victory Medals.
44, Napier Street, Bletchley, Bucks. Z1386/A.

WAKEFIELD, F., Private, R.A.V.C.
Volunteering in December 1915, he was sent to the Western Front in January 1916, and was engaged on the important duties of attending sick and wounded horses. He rendered valuable services in this theatre of war, and was invalided home suffering from shell-shock in July 1916. He was discharged in consequence in the following month, and holds the General Service and Victory Medals
The Green, Cardington, Bedford Z2256

WALDOCK, A. M., Driver, R.A.S.C.
He joined in February 1917, and was drafted to France later in the same year. There he was engaged on important duties in connection with the transport of food and ammunition to forward areas, but after serving with the Royal Fusiliers and Leicestershire Regiment on various fronts he was unfortunately killed on October 28th, 1917. He was entitled to the General Service and Victory Medals.
"And doubtless he went in splendid company."
Montague Street, Eynesbury, St. Neots. Z3932/A.

WALDOCK, W. E., Rifleman, Rifle Brigade.
He joined in July 1917, and later in the same year proceeded to France, where he took part in many important engagements, including the Battles of Ypres and Cambrai. He was taken prisoner on the Somme in April 1918 during the great Retreat, and after the Armistice was repatriated and eventually demobilised in December 1919. He holds the General Service and Victory Medals. 2, Albert Terrace, St. Neots, Hunts. Z1319/B.

WALDUCK, A., L/Cpl., 6th Bedfordshire Regt.
He volunteered in August 1914, and after training at Ampthill was drafted to the Western Front in July 1915. In this theatre of war he took part in many important engagements, and saw heavy fighting at Ypres and on the Somme. On April 11th, 1916, he made the supreme sacrifice, being killed in action at Monchy. He was entitled to the 1914–15 Star, and the General Service and Victory Medals.
"A valiant Soldier, with undaunted heart he breasted life's last hill."
Drayton Parslow, Bucks. Z2038/B.

WALDUCK, A. W., Pte., 2nd Oxford. & Bucks. L.I.
He was mobilised in August 1914, but owing to his being too old for active service in a theatre of war, was retained on special duties on the East Coast of England and at Oswestry He, nevertheless, rendered valuable services during the period of hostilities, and was demobilised in March 1919.
7, Aylesbury Street, Fenny Stratford, Bucks. Z2257/B.

WALDUCK, S. A., Lieut., 2nd Oxford. & Bucks. L.I.
He was mobilised in August 1914, and was drafted to France in August of the following year. He first served as a private, but owing to his splendid work in various sectors of the front he was gazetted to commissioned rank He played a distinguished part in the Battles of Ypres, the Somme, Arras and Cambrai, and rendered valuable services during the Retreat and Advance of 1918. He was wounded in October of that year, and was invalided to England, where he remained until his demobilisation in March 1919. He holds the 1914–15 Star, and the General Service and Victory Medals.
7, Aylesbury Street, Fenny Stratford, Bucks. Z2257/A.

WALE, W. J., L/Corporal, 2nd Bedfordshire Regt.
He was already serving in the Army at the outbreak of war in August 1914, and was immediately drafted to the Western Front, where he took part in the Retreat from Mons and the Battles of La Bassée and Festubert. He was unhappily reported wounded and missing after severe fighting at Givenchy and was later presumed to have been killed in action there on June 15th, 1915. He was entitled to the Mons Star, and the General Service and Victory Medals.
"Great deeds cannot die."
Cambridge Road, Sandy, Beds. Z2258.

WALKER, A., Private, 2nd Cheshire Regiment.
He joined in June 1916, and after training on the East Coast was drafted to Salonika in the following November. In this theatre of war he took part in many important engagements on the Doiran front and rendered valuable services until the cessation of hostilities. He then returned to England and was demobilised in June 1919, holding the General Service and Victory Medals. 3, Church Walk, St. Neots, Hunts. Z2266.

WALKER, A., Private, Bedfordshire Regiment.
Volunteering in January 1915, he was drafted to France in the following May and took part in many important engagements, including the Battles of Loos, the Somme, Arras and Cambrai, and was wounded. He returned to England in 1916, and was again wounded during an air raid at Felixstowe. In 1919 he embarked for India, and in 1920 was engaged on important garrison duties at Landi Kotal. He holds the 1914–15 Star, and the General Service and Victory Medals.
106, Coventry Street, Queen's Park, Bedford. Z1538/C.

WALKER, A., Sergeant, 1st Wiltshire Regiment.
He volunteered in January 1915, and in the following July proceeded to the Western Front, where he fought with distinction in many engagements. He was in action at the Battles of Loos and the Somme, and was invalided home through wounds. He returned to France and was wounded on the Somme in 1916. Later he did duty in Ireland, where he acted as a Machine Gun Instructor until his demobilisation in March 1919. He holds the 1914–15 Star, and the General Service and Victory Medals
Berkley Cottages, Stoke Goldington Bucks. Z2260/A.

WALKER, A., Private, 5th Northants. Regiment.
He volunteered in September 1914, and after training at Shorncliffe was drafted to the Western Front in May 1915. There he took part in many important engagements, including those on the Ypres, Somme, Arras and Cambrai fronts, and later was in action during the Retreat and Advance of 1918. He holds the 1914–15 Star, and the General Service and Victory Medals, and was demobilised in March 1919
Berkley Cottages, Stoke Goldington, Bucks. Z2260/B.

WALKER, A. C., Private, 1/5th Bedfordshire Regt.
Volunteering in November 1914, he completed his training and was sent to the Dardanelles in July of the following year. There he took part in much heavy fighting during the Landing at Suvla Bay, and after the Evacuation in 1916 proceeded to Egypt. He also saw service in Palestine, taking part in engagements at Gaza and Jaffa. He suffered from pneumonia in 1918, and later returned to England and was demobilised in April 1919, holding the 1914–15 Star, and the General Service and Victory Medals. 8, Woburn Rd., Kempston, Bedford. X2261/B.

WALKER, E., Pte., 2nd Beds. Regt. & R.A.S.C.
Already serving with the Colours at the outbreak of war in August 1914, he was shortly afterwards drafted to France, and took part in heavy fighting at La Bassée, Ypres, Loos, Vimy Ridge and the Somme, and was wounded on three occasions. He finally returned to England in April 1917, and was engaged on important transport duty until his discharge in March 1919. He holds the 1914 Star, and the General Service and Victory Medals. 8, Woburn Road, Kempston, Bedford. X2261/C.

WALKER, E., Sergeant, Royal Field Artillery.
Mobilised at the outbreak of war in August 1914, he immediately proceeded to the Western Front, and fought with distinction in the Retreat from Mons. He was also in action with his Battery at numerous other engagements, including the Battles of the Marne, the Aisne, La Bassée, Hill 60, Festubert, Ypres and Loos, and made the supreme sacrifice on February 13th, 1916, being killed in action on the Somme. He was entitled to the Mons Star, and the General Service and Victory Medals.
"Great deeds cannot die."
8, Woburn Road, Kempston, Bedford. X2261/A.

WALKER, F., Sapper, Royal Engineers.
He was mobilised in August 1914, and after completing a course of training was drafted to the Dardanelles early in the following year. There he took part in many important engagements on the Gallipoli Peninsula, and was later transferred to the Egyptian and Palestine theatres of war. He did consistently good work at Cairo, Gaza, Jerusalem and Aleppo as a signaller on the lines of communication, and after his return home was eventually demobilised in June 1919, holding the 1914–15 Star, and the General Service and Victory Medals.
10, St. Leonard's Street, Bedford. X2259.

WALKER, G. A., Sergeant, East Yorkshire Regt.
Mobilised at the outbreak of war in August 1914, he was sent to France in September and played a distinguished part in the Battle of the Aisne, during which he was wounded. He was invalided to England, and after spending three months in hospital was transferred to the Royal Air Force, and performed good work at various important aerodromes. He holds the 1914 Star, and the General Service and Victory Medals, and was demobilised in March 1919.
41, Beaconsfield Place, Newport Pagnell. Z2262.

WALKER, H., Private, 7th Northants. Regiment.
He volunteered in September 1914, and after training at Southwick was drafted to the Western Front in March 1915. There he took part in many important engagements, including the Battles of Ypres, Loos, and was wounded in the latter sector in September 1915. He was invalided home, and after the cessation of hostilities proceeded to Mesopotamia in September 1920, where he was in 1921 still serving. He holds the 1914–15 Star, and the General Service and Victory Medals.
Berkley Cottages, Stoke Goldington, Bucks Z2260/C.

WALKER, H., Corporal, 2nd Northants. Regt.
He was already serving in the Army in India at the outbreak of war in August 1914, and immediately embarked for France. In this theatre of war he played a prominent part in several engagements, including the Battles of Ypres and Neuve Chapelle, and made the supreme sacrifice at the latter place, being killed in action on March 15th, 1915. He was entitled to the 1914 Star, and the General Service and Victory Medals.
"A costly sacrifice upon the altar of freedom."
Berkley Cottages, Stoke Goldington, Bucks. Z2260/D.

WALKER, H. J., Private, R.A.S.C.
He joined in 1916, and after a period of training served with the Royal Guernsey Light Infantry for twelve months. He was then transferred to the Royal Army Service Corps, and drafted to France in March 1917, did consistently good work in the Remount Section. In June 1917 he returned to England, having been found unfit for overseas service, and was employed in attending horses until his demobilisation in July 1919. He holds the General Service and Victory Medals.
24, Ledsam Street, Wolverton, Bucks. Z2264.

WALKER, P., L/Cpl., 8th Oxford. & Bucks. L.I.
He volunteered in September 1914, and, completing, his training was drafted a year later to the Western Front, where he served in the Albert and Somme sectors. He was transferred to Salonika two months later, and took part in much heavy fighting on the Doiran and Vardar fronts. After rendering valuable services, he returned to England, and was demobilised in June 1919, holding the 1914–15 Star, and the General Service and Victory Medals. 26, Water Eaton, Bletchley, Bucks. Z2265.

WALKER, R. B., Pioneer, Royal Engineers.
He joined in May 1916, and later in the same year was drafted to France. There he took part in many important engagements, and was present at the Battles of Arras, Vimy Ridge and Bullecourt. In 1917 he was transferred to Italy, and after seeing service on the Piave, returned to the Western Front, and was in action on the Somme during the Retreat and Advance of 1918. He holds the General Service and Victory Medals, and was demobilised in June 1919.
Mount Pleasant, Wootton, Beds. Z2263.

WALLACE, C. B., L/Corporal, 1st Queen's (Royal West Surrey Regiment).
Joining in October 1917, he was drafted to France in the following April, and took part in the Advance of 1918, serving through the fighting on the Somme and at Cambrai, Epéhy, Ypres (IV.), Amiens and Le Cateau (II.), and rendered valuable services until the cessation of hostilities. He was demobilised in February 1919, and holds the General Service and Victory Medals. 10, Station Road, Warboys, Hunts. Z2267/B.

WALLACE, F. H., Rifleman, 2/21st London Regiment (1st Surrey Rifles).
Mobilised at the outbreak of war in August 1914, he was at first retained at various important stations in England, but in June 1916 was drafted to France, where he served on the Somme until the end of the year. He was then transferred to Salonika, and was in action on the Doiran front. He later fought in Palestine, rendering valuable services at Gaza (III.), Jaffa, Jerusalem and on the River Jordan. He holds the General Service and Victory Medals, and was demobilised in March 1919. 10, Station Road, Warboys, Hunts. Z2267/A.

WALLER, A., Sapper, Royal Engineers.
He volunteered in October 1915, and after a period of training was drafted to Egypt in April 1916. He also served in Palestine and did consistently good work on the Gaza front, where he was employed on the construction of light railways. He was sent home and discharged in April 1919 as medically unfit, holding the General Service and Victory Medals.
85, Priory Street, Bedford. X2268/A.

WALLER, F. G., Pte., 4th Royal Welch Fusiliers.
Joining in January 1916, he was drafted to the Western Front six months later, and took part in heavy fighting in various sectors, including Ypres and Arras. He was wounded in action at Bullecourt, but continued his service until the cessation of hostilities. He was discharged in November 1919, and holds the General Service and Victory Medals.
85, Priory Street, Bedford. X2268/B.

WALLINGER, B., Private, 1st Northants. Regt.
He was mobilised in August 1914, and was immediately drafted to the Western Front. In this theatre of war he took part in many important engagements, and fought at Ypres, Neuve Chapelle, St. Eloi, Festubert and Loos. He was also in action at Vimy Ridge and on the Somme, and made the supreme sacrifice in July 1917 at the Battle of the Dunes. He was entitled to the 1914 Star, and the General Service and Victory Medals.
"Great deeds cannot die."
39, Warwick Terrace, Olney, Bucks. Z2269.

WALLINGER, G. A., Private, R.A.S.C. (M.T.)
Volunteering in November 1914, he was drafted to France in March of the following year, and was engaged on important transport duties in forward areas, including those of Ypres and the Somme. He was wounded in 1915 near Ypres when taking up supplies, and was invalided to England and finally demobilised in March 1919, after a period of service at home. He holds the 1914–15 Star, and the General Service and Victory Medals. 40, High Street, Bedford. Z2270/B.

WALLINGER, H. J., Pte., 2nd Bedfordshire Regt.
He was already serving in South Africa at the outbreak of war in August 1914, and was immediately drafted to France, where he took part in many important engagements. He rendered valuable services on the Marne and the Aisne, but was unfortunately killed in action in the Ypres salient on October 26th, 1914, and was entitled to the 1914 Star, and the General Service and Victory Medals.
"He died the noblest death a man may die."
40, High Street, Fenny Stratford, Bucks. Z2270/A.

WALLIS, L., Private, Middlesex Regiment.
He volunteered in August 1914, and after a period of service at important stations in England was drafted to the Western Front in 1917. There he took part in many of the concluding engagements on the Somme and at Ypres and Cambrai, and was severely gassed. He also did duty for a time with the Y.M.C.A. in forward areas, and holds the General Service and Victory Medals. He was demobilised in February 1919.
Huntingdon Street, St. Neots, Hunts. Z2271.

WALTERS, A., Private, 7th Wiltshire Regiment.
He was mobilised in August 1914, and after training at Marlborough, was drafted to Mesopotamia in September 1915. There he took part in many important engagements during the Advance on Kut and Baghdad, and in February 1918 was transferred to France. He saw much heavy fighting in this theatre of war, and rendered valuable services during the Retreat and Advance of that year. Demobilised in December 1918, he holds the 1914–15 Star, and the General Service and Victory Medals.
17, Station Terrace, Great Linford, Bucks. Z2272.

WALTERS, A. J., Private, Northants. Regiment.
He joined in April 1918, and five months later proceeded to the Western Front, where he was in time to take part in the Advance of that year. He rendered valuable services at Amiens and Le Cateau, and after the Armistice advanced into Germany, where he did duty with the Army of Occupation on the Rhine. He was eventually demobilised in October 1919, and holds the General Service and Victory Medals.
9, St. Mary's Street, New Bradwell, Bucks Z2273.

WALTERS, H. C., Bandsman, 7th Wiltshire Regt.
He volunteered in September 1914, and after a period of training was sent to the Western Front in September of the following year. He saw active service on the Somme, but in November 1915 was transferred to Salonika, where he took part in much severe fighting on the Doiran and Vardar fronts. In May 1918 he returned to France, and after being in action during the Retreat, met with a serious accident which necessitated his return home and final discharge in September 1919. He holds the 1914–15 Star, and the General Service and Victory Medals.
9, Alexandria Court, Old Bradwell, Bucks. Z2744/B.

WALTERS, P. J., Pte., 2nd Northamptonshire Regt.
Volunteering in 1915, he was drafted to France later in the same year, and was in action at the Battles of Ypres, Festubert, Loos, the Somme and Albert. He also took part in much severe fighting in various other sectors, and made the supreme sacrifice on March 4th, 1917, being killed in action at Vimy Ridge. He was entitled to the 1914–15 Star, and the General Service and Victory Medals.
"A costly sacrifice upon the altar of freedom."
9, Alexandria Court, Old Bradwell, Bucks. Z2744/A.

WALTON, A. E., Sapper, Royal Engineers.
He joined in June 1917, and was first engaged on the construction of Army huts in various parts of England. Just prior to the cessation of hostilities he was drafted to France, where he worked at his own trade as a carpenter at Audriucq, Lille, Ypres and Dixmude. He rendered valuable services, and was demobilised in March 1919, holding the General Service and Victory Medals.
23, Beaconsfield Place, Newport Pagnell, Bucks. Z2274.

WALTON, E., Private, 5th Bedfordshire Regiment.
He volunteered in 1914, and was retained on special duties in various parts of England. He was unable to obtain his transfer to a theatre of war during the period of hostilities, but, nevertheless, rendered valuable services until his demobilisation in March 1919. 18, The Grove, Bedford. Z2276/C.

WALTON, F. G. (M.M.), C.S.M., 1st Northants. Regt
He was already serving with the Colours in August 1914, and two months later proceeded to France, where he fought with distinction at numerous engagements, and was wounded on three occasions. He was in action at the Battles of La Bassée, Ypres, Festubert, Loos, Albert, the Somme, Vimy Ridge, Arras and Ypres (III.), and was invalided home four times through wounds. He was awarded the Military Medal for conspicuous bravery and devotion to duty during the Advance of 1918, and also holds the 1914 Star, and the General Service and Victory Medals. He was discharged in May 1919.
5, Cobbs Cottages, High Street, Olney, Bucks. Z2275/A.

WALTON, J., Private, Somerset Light Infantry.
Joining in February 1917, he completed a course of training and was drafted to the Western Front in August. There he took part in many important engagements, and saw much severe fighting during the short time he was in France. After serving at the Battle of Ypres he made the supreme sacrifice on October 4th, 1917, being killed in action at Passchendaele. He was entitled to the General Service and Victory Medals.
"His memory is cherished with pride."
5, Cobbs Cottages, High Street, Olney, Bucks. Z2275/B.

WALTON, L. E., L/Corporal, M.G.C.
He volunteered in 1915, and later in the same year proceeded to France, where he took part in many important engagements. He was in action at the Battles of Ypres, Festubert, Loos, the Somme and Vimy Ridge and rendered valuable services until the cessation of hostilities. In 1919 he embarked for India, and in 1920 was serving at Rawal Pindi. He holds the 1914–15 Star, and the General Service and Victory Medals.
18, The Grove, Bedford. Z2276/B.

WALTON, W. C., L/Corporal, Military Police.
He was already serving in the Army at the outbreak of war in August 1914, and in the following year proceeded to France, where he was present at the Battles of Ypres and Neuve Chapelle. In 1915 he was transferred to the Dardanelles, and took part in the Landing at Suvla Bay and other engagements of importance until the Evacuation of the Gallipoli Peninsula in December 1915. He also saw service in Palestine until the cessation of hostilities, and holds the 1914–15 Star, and the General Service and Victory Medals. In 1920 he was serving in India. 18, The Grove, Bedford. Z2276/A.

WALTZER, T., Private, 1st Hertfordshire Regt.
He volunteered in June 1915, and after doing consistently good work at various important stations in England, was drafted to the Western Front in October 1917. There he was in action at many engagements of importance, and was wounded at Ypres in the following month. He was again wounded in March 1918 at Cambrai, during the Retreat, and, returning to England, was eventually demobilised in April 1919, holding the General Service and Victory Medals.
1, Tower Gardens, Bedford. X2277.

WARD, A. H., Sapper, Royal Engineers.
He volunteered in November 1915, and after completing his training was drafted to the Western Front, where he saw much severe fighting at Ypres, Arras and on the Somme. He was taken prisoner on March 3rd, 1917, and after the Armistice was repatriated and eventually demobilised in December 1919, holding the General Service and Victory Medals.
9, Fairfax Road, Bedford. X2289.

WARD, B. J., Private, 1/5th Bedfordshire Regt.
Volunteering in May 1915, he underwent a period of training and was drafted to the Western Front in January of the following year. There he took part in fierce fighting, but was unfortunately killed in action on the Ypres front in April 1916, after only three months' service in France. He was entitled to the General Service and Victory Medals.
"A valiant Soldier, with undaunted heart he breasted life's last hill."
Orchard Cottages, Olney, Bucks. Z2279.

WARD, B. W., Driver, Royal Engineers.
He volunteered in May 1915, and after consistently good work at various stations in England was drafted to France in 1917. He did duty on the Arras, Vimy Ridge, Passchendaele, Somme and Cambrai fronts, and rendered valuable services whilst engaged in transport work during the period of hostilities. He holds the General Service and Victory Medals, and was demobilised in July 1919.
20, Greenhill Street, Bedford. X2284/B.

WARD, C. W., L/Cpl., 2nd Bedfordshire Regt.
He volunteered in September 1914, and, after training at Colchester and Aldershot, was drafted to the Western Front in the following year. There he took part in many engagements of importance and was in action at the Battles of the Somme, Loos, Lens, Arras and Cambrai. He rendered valuable services until the cessation of hostilities, and was demobilised in March 1919, holding the 1914–15 Star, and the General Service and Victory Medals. High Street, Sharnbrook, Beds. Z2287.

WARD, C. W., L/Cpl., 7th Bedfordshire Regt.
Four months after joining in July 1916, he was sent to France, and took part in the severe fighting in many sectors. He rendered valuable services on the Ypres front, but was unfortunately killed in action on October 22nd, 1917, and was entitled to the General Service and Victory Medals.
"He passed out of the sight of men by the path of duty and self-sacrifice."
Brook Street, St. Neots, Hunts. Z2283.

WARD, F. G., Private, 2nd London Regiment (Royal Fusiliers).
He joined in October 1916, and after undergoing a period of training was sent to the Western Front in the following year. In this theatre of war he took part in many engagements of importance, including those at Ypres, Albert, the Somme, Arras, Cambrai and Le Cateau, and was slightly gassed during the Advance of 1918. He holds the General Service and Victory Medals, and was demobilised in March 1919.
16, Prospect Row, St. Neots, Hunts. Z2285/B.

WARD, G. W., Private, 7th Northants. Regiment.
Volunteering in September 1914, he proceeded to France after a period of training, and was in action at the Battles of Loos, the Somme, Arras and Cambrai. He also did duty in connection with the transport of food and ammunition to forward areas and rendered valuable services during the Retreat and Advance of 1918. Demobilised in March 1919, he holds the 1914–15 Star, and the General Service and Victory Medals.
Olney Road, Lavendon, Bucks. Z2288.

WARD, H. R., Sapper, Royal Engineers (Signals).
He volunteered in April 1915, and after doing consistently good work in England was drafted to France in March 1917. There he was engaged on important duties on the lines of communication and served with distinction on the Ypres, Arras, Albert and Cambrai fronts. He holds the General Service and Victory Medals, and was demobilised in July 1919.
2, Derwent Place, Bedford. Z2280.

WARD, J. J. H., Private, 4th Devonshire Regt.
He joined in June 1918, and was retained on special duties at important stations in Ireland. He was not successful in obtaining his transfer to a theatre of war, but, nevertheless, rendered valuable services in connection with garrison work until his demobilisation in March 1919.
2, Railway Terrace, Bletchley, Bucks. TZ4485.

WARD, W., Rifleman, Rifle Brigade.
Joining in June 1918, he was retained on important duties, at various stations in England until the cessation of hostilities. He was then sent to Germany, where he was engaged on guard and other duties with the Army of Occupation on the Rhine. He eventually returned home and was discharged in November 1919, no longer physically fit for military services.
16, Prospect Row, St. Neots, Hunts. Z2285/A.

WARD, W. G., Private, 2nd East Surrey Regiment.
He volunteered in October 1914, and after a period of training was drafted to France in January of the following year. There he took part in many important engagements, including the Battles of Neuve Chapelle and Vimy Ridge, and made the supreme sacrifice on May 9th, 1915, being killed in action at Ypres. He was entitled to the 1914–15 Star, and the General Service and Victory Medals.
"Whilst we remember, the sacrifice is not in vain."
Cromwell Cottages, East Chadley Lane, Godmanchester, Hunts Z2286.

WARD, W. H., Private, 2nd London Regiment (Royal Fusiliers).
He joined in February 1917, and in the following month was drafted to France, where he was in action at numerous engagements. He saw much severe fighting at Arras and Vimy Ridge and was gassed in action before being taken prisoner in April 1917. Repatriated after the Armistice, he was eventually demobilised in March 1919, and holds the General Service and Victory Medals.
20, All Hallows Lane, Bedford. X2284/A.

WARNER, T. H., Private, Bedfordshire Regiment.
Volunteering in June 1915, he was sent to France later in the same year, and took part in much heavy fighting on the Arras, Ypres and Cambrai fronts. He also rendered valuable services during the Retreat and the initial stages of the Advance, but was unfortunately killed in action near Albert in August 1918. He was entitled to the 1914–15 Star, and the General Service and Victory Medals.
"He died the noblest death a man may die."
48, Chandos Street, Bedford. X2291/A.

WARNER, W., Private, Royal Defence Corps.
He volunteered in December 1914, and being over military age was retained on important duties in England. He rendered valuable services guarding prisoners of war, railway bridges and important munition factories at Coventry until his discharge in August 1918. 48, Chandos Street, Bedford. X2291/B.

WARR, R. J., Private, Machine Gun Corps (New Zealand Overseas Forces).
He volunteered in June 1915, and was drafted from New Zealand to France shortly afterwards. In this theatre of war he was in action at many important engagements, and saw much heavy fighting on the Ypres and Somme fronts. He was unfortunately killed at Passchendaele Ridge on October 12th, 1917, and was entitled to the 1914–15 Star, and the General Service and Victory Medals.
"His memory is cherished with pride."
10, Woodbine Terrace, Fenny Stratford, Bucks. Z2281.

WARR, W. T., Private, R.M.L.I.
Volunteering in December 1915, he was engaged on guard duties at Deal and Gosport after completing his training, and in 1916 was drafted to France. There he took part in many engagements of importance on the Somme, Arras and Ypres fronts, and was wounded and invalided to England. He was eventually discharged in October 1918 as medically unfit for further service, and holds the General Service and Victory Medals. 20, North End Square, Buckingham, Bucks. Z2290.

WARREN, A., Private, Duke of Cornwall's L.I.
Five months after volunteering in March 1915 he was drafted to the Western Front, and was attached to a Labour Company. He did good work whilst engaged on the important duties of trench-digging and the carrying of rations to forward areas on the Ypres, Arras and Cambrai fronts, and was wounded. He holds the 1914–15 Star, and the General Service and Victory Medals, and was discharged in March 1918.
53, Priory Street, Bedford. X2282.

WARREN, C. A., Private, 2nd Bedfordshire Regt.
He joined in January 1916, and in the following November was sent to France, where he took part in many engagements, including those at Ypres, Arras, the Somme and Cambrai. He suffered from gas-poisoning, and was wounded on two occasions whilst in action. He rendered valuable services, and was eventually demobilised in May 1919, holding the General Service and Victory Medals.
The Lanes, Houghton, Huntingdon, Hunts. Z2294/B.

WARREN, E., Driver, Royal Field Artillery.
Volunteering in the Royal Army Veterinary Corps in April 1915, he underwent training at Woolwich, and was later transferred to the Royal Field Artillery at Aldershot. He was drafted to France later in the same year, and was in action with his Battery in the Ypres, Somme and Cambrai sectors before making the supreme sacrifice on September 25th, 1918, being killed in action near Péronne during the Advance. He was entitled to the 1914–15 Star, and the General Service and Victory Medals.
"Fighting for God and right and liberty."
High Street Stoke Goldington, Bucks. Z2292/B.

WARREN, G. H., Private, Queen's (Royal West Surrey Regiment) and Royal Defence Corps.
He volunteered in November 1915, and was retained on important duties in various parts of England and Scotland. He was unable to obtain his transfer to a theatre of war owing to medical unfitness, but, nevertheless, did consistently good work with the Royal Defence Corps until his demobilisation in March 1919.
Water Lane, Sherington, Newport Pagnell, Bucks. Z2293/B.

WARREN, G. W., Private, Royal Berkshire Regt.
He joined in May 1917, but being medically unfit for service in a theatre of war, was retained on special duties at various important stations in England. He, nevertheless, rendered valuable services until October 1917, when he was discharged from the Army.
High Street, Stoke Goldington, Bucks. Z2292/A.

WARREN, J. H., Colour-Sergeant, R.M.L.I.
Mobilised at the outbreak of war in August 1914, he was stationed at Plymouth during the first part of his service, and was afterwards posted to H.M.S. "King Alfred," in which ship he did duty with the Atlantic Fleet, patrolling the West Coast of Africa. In 1917 he was transferred to Greenwich, where he was engaged on the training of young officers, and in 1918–19 was attached to the Plymouth Division. He holds the 1914–15 Star, the General Service and Victory Medals, and the Long Service and Good Conduct Medal, and was discharged in May 1919. Mill Street, Houghton, Hunts. Z2295.

WARREN, J. H., Private, 1st Bedfordshire Regt.
Volunteering in May 1915, he completed a period of training, and was drafted to France in 1916. There he took part in many engagements of importance, including the Battles of Ypres, the Somme, Arras and Cambrai, and rendered valuable services. He made the supreme sacrifice on April 16th, 1917, being killed in action in the Vimy Ridge sector, and was entitled to the General Service and Victory Medals.
"Great deeds cannot die."
The Lanes, Houghton, Huntingdon, Hunts. Z2294/A.

WARREN, J. H., Ordinary Seaman, Royal Navy.
He joined in October 1917, and did duty in H.M.S. "Pembroke" patrolling the North Sea and escorting merchant vessels in the war zone. He also saw service in the Baltic and took part in operations at Zeebrugge in 1918. Demobilised in August 1919, he holds the General Service and Victory Medals.
Water Lane, Sherington, Newport Pagnell, Bucks. Z2293/A.

WARREN, S., Private, 2nd Bedfordshire Regiment.
He joined in February 1918, and was retained on special duties at the Tower of London. He was unable to obtain his transfer overseas on account of age, but, nevertheless, rendered valuable services until the cessation of hostilities. He was still serving in the Army in 1920. 46, High St., Kempston, Beds. X2296.

WARRINGTON, A., Trooper, 3rd Beds. Lancers.
He volunteered in June 1915, and after a period of training was drafted to the Western Front, where he took part in many important engagements. He was in action at Neuve Chapelle, Ypres, the Somme, Arras and Cambrai, and after the Armistice proceeded to Germany, where he did duty with the Army of Occupation on the Rhine. He was demobilised in March 1919, and holds the General Service and Victory Medals.
Bedford Road, Sandy, Beds. Z2297.

WARWICK, G. (Miss), Corporal, W.R.A.F.
After being engaged on the highly dangerous work of shell-filling with T.N.T. at a munition works at Hayes, Middlesex, for over two years, she joined the Women's Royal Air Force in May 1917, and did consistently good work in the capacity of clerk, stationed at Milton, Buckinghamshire, until April 1919, when she was demobilised.
The Grove, Great Linford, Bucks. Z1778/C.

WATSON, A. (sen.), Pte., 13th Royal Fusiliers.
Joining in November 1916, he underwent a period of training, and was drafted to the Western Front in the following year. There he took part in many important engagements, including the Battles of Messines and the Somme, and was wounded in action in 1918. He was invalided to England, and finally discharged in May 1919 as physically unfit for further service, holding the General Service and Victory Medals.
Montague Street, Eynesbury, St. Neots, Hunts. Z2305/A

WATSON, A. (jun.), Private, R.A.M.C.
He volunteered in 1915, and did consistently good work at Cambridge during the first part of his service. In January 1918 he was sent to France, but, owing to being under military age, was claimed out of the Army. He, nevertheless, rejoined in March 1920, and in 1921 was serving with the R.A.S.C. (M.T.). He holds the General Service and Victory Medals.
Montague Street, Eynesbury, St. Neots, Hunts. Z2305/B.

WATSON, G. H., Private, 4th Bedfordshire Regt.
Volunteering in September 1914, he was sent to the Western Front in the following year, and was in action at Festubert and Loos. He was also engaged in much fierce fighting in other sectors, and was wounded and gassed on the Somme in 1916. Invalided to England, he was detained in hospital for 18 months, and was eventually discharged in May 1918 as physically unfit for further service. He holds the 1914–15 Star, and the General Service and Victory Medals.
Bell End, Brampton, Hunts. Z2299.

WATSON, G. W., Private, Manchester Regiment.
He volunteered in April 1915, but, after training with the Royal Army Veterinary Corps, was transferred to the Manchester Regiment and drafted to France in June 1916. In this theatre of war he took part in many engagements of importance, including the Battles of Ypres, the Somme, Arras and Cambrai, and after the Armistice proceeded to Germany. There he was engaged on important garrison duties, and was demobilised in May 1919, holding the General Service and Victory Medals. High Street, Sharnbrook, Beds. Z2302.

WATSON, P., Private, 2nd Bedfordshire Regiment.
He was already serving in the Army at the outbreak of war in August 1914, and was shortly afterwards drafted to the Western Front. There he took part in much heavy fighting in various sectors, and was in action at the Battles of Ypres (II.) and Festubert. He made the supreme sacrifice on May 18th, 1915, being killed in action at Festubert on that date. He was entitled to the 1914–15 Star, and the General Service and Victory Medals.
"And doubtless he went in splendid company."
Montague Street, Eynesbury, St. Neots, Hunts. Z2305/C.

WATSON, P. L., Private, 12th Lancers.
Volunteering in September 1914, he was drafted to France in the following year, and saw much heavy fighting in various sectors. He was in action at the Battles of the Somme, Albert, Ypres, Passchendaele, Messines and Vimy Ridge, and was wounded during the Advance from Cambrai in June 1918. After the Armistice he proceeded to Germany, and did duty with the Army of Occupation. He was eventually demobilised in May 1919, holding the 1914–15 Star, and the General Service and Victory Medals.
1, Dilleys Yard, Huntingdon, Hunts. Z2304/A.

WATSON, T., Private, Royal Fusiliers.
He volunteered in January 1915, and, completing his training, was drafted to France in February 1916. In this theatre of war he took part in many important engagements, including those at Ypres, Loos and the Somme, and was wounded at Givenchy in December 1916. He rendered valuable services until the cessation of hostilities, and was demobilised in March 1919, holding the General Service and Victory Medals.
Alconbury Weston, Hunts. Z2301.

WATSON, W., Private, R.A.M.C.
He joined in 1916, and was retained on special duties with his Corps at various important stations in England. He was not successful in obtaining his transfer overseas, but, nevertheless, did consistently good work until the cessation of hostilities. He was demobilised in August 1919.
Hemingford Abbot, Hunts. Z2300.

WATSON, W. E., Rifleman, Rifle Brigade.
He joined in March 1918, but was unsuccessful in obtaining his transfer overseas during hostilities. In February 1919, however, he was sent to Germany, where he rendered valuable services with the Army of Occupation on the Rhine until November of the same year. He then returned to England for demobilisation. 1, Dilleys Yard, Huntingdon. Z2304/B.

WATSON, W. F., Private, R.A.O.C.
He joined in January 1917, and after training with the Royal Field Artillery at various stations, was transferred to the Royal Army Ordnance Corps in June 1918, and did consistently good work. He was not successful in obtaining his transfer overseas on account of physical unfitness, and was eventually demobilised in March 1919. 19, High St., Buckingham, Bucks. Z2298.

WATSON, W. H., Gunner, R.G.A.
He volunteered in November 1915, but being medically unfit for service in a theatre of war was retained on important duties in connection with anti-aircraft work in London and Birmingham. He rendered valuable services, and was demobilised in January 1919.
Luke Street, Eynesbury, St. Neots, Hunts. Z2303.

WATTS, A., Driver, Canadian Field Artillery.
He volunteered in Canada in 1915, and was first sent to England. In July of the same year he proceeded to the Western Front, where he was in action with his Battery on the Somme, at Ypres, Arras and Cambrai, and suffered from gas-poisoning. He was invalided to England in 1918, and was eventually demobilised in April 1919, holding the 1914–15 Star, and the General Service and Victory Medals.
60, Russell Street, St. Neots, Hunts. TZ2309.

WATTS, A. J., Private, 2nd Oxford. and Bucks. L.I.
He joined in February 1916, and in the following November was drafted to the Western Front, where he was in action at numerous important engagements. He saw much heavy fighting on the Somme, Ypres and Arras fronts, and made the supreme sacrifice on April 28th, 1917, being killed in action at Oppy Wood. He was entitled to the General Service and Victory Medals.
"Courage, bright hopes, and a myriad dreams, splendidly given."
Castle Road, Lavendon, Bucks. Z2306.

WATTS, C. J. P., Sapper, Royal Engineers.
He volunteered in October 1915, and in the following March was drafted to France and did consistently good work as a coach-builder at Rouen and Calais. He also served in forward areas of the Western Front, where he was engaged on the construction of pontoon bridges. He rendered valuable services until the cessation of hostilities. He holds the General Service and Victory Medals, and was demobilised in December 1919.
35, Broad Street, Newport Pagnell. Z2308.

WATTS, F., Private, 4th Bedfordshire Regiment.
He joined in January 1916, and four months later proceeded to the Western Front, where he was in action during the Somme Offensive, and was wounded at Albert in July 1916. He was invalided to England, but returned to France in 1917 and served on the Ypres front until December of the following year. He holds the General Service and Victory Medals, and was demobilised in February 1919.
High Street, Carlton, near Sharnbrook, Beds. Z2317.

WATTS, F., Private, Royal Warwickshire Regt.
Volunteering in September 1914, he did duty at various stations in England during the first part of his service, and was drafted to the Western Front in July 1916. There he took part in much heavy fighting on the Somme, and was wounded and taken prisoner in March 1918 near Cambrai, during the Retreat of that year. He was released after the Armistice, and eventually demobilised in March 1919, holding the General Service and Victory Medals.
Main Street, Hartford. Z2318 /C.

WATTS, F. W., Gunner, Royal Field Artillery.
He volunteered in December 1914, and after training at Woolwich was drafted to France in July of the following year. He was in action with his Battery on the Ypres, Somme and Cambrai fronts, and rendered valuable services during the Retreat and Advance of 1918. He holds the 1914–15 Star, and the General Service and Victory Medals, and was demobilised in May 1919.
Water Side, Sherington, Newport Pagnell. Z4033 /C

WATTS, G., Corporal, Royal Warwickshire Regt.
Volunteering in November 1914, he went into training at Filey and Scarborough with the Huntingdonshire Cyclists, but was transferred to the Royal Warwickshire Regiment, and drafted to France in June 1916. He took part in much heavy fighting on the Somme, where he was wounded and was reported missing. He is now presumed killed in action in July 1916, and was entitled to the General Service and Victory Medals.
"His memory is cherished with pride."
Main Street, Hartford. Z2318 /A.

WATTS, G., L/Corporal, East Surrey Regiment.
He joined in March 1917, and was drafted to France later in the same year after training at Dover. He took part in many important engagements, and saw much heavy fighting at Amiens and Bapaume before making the supreme sacrifice on October 18th, 1918, at Cambrai, being killed in action during the Advance of that year. He was entitled to the General Service and Victory Medals.
"A costly sacrifice upon the altar of freedom."
40, Oxford Street, Wolverton, Bucks. Z2307 /A.

WATTS, H., Private, 32nd Royal Fusiliers.
Volunteering in September 1914, he underwent a period of training and duty in England during the first part of his service, but in September 1916 was sent to France. There he took part in many important engagements, including the Battles of the Somme and Bullecourt, and was seriously wounded at Messines on June 7th, 1917. He unhappily died on the following day, and was entitled to the General Service and Victory Medals.
"He died the noblest death a man may die."
29, Stanmore Road, Watford. X2312.

WATTS, H. J., Sergt., 7th Oxford. & Bucks. L.I.
He joined in February 1916, and after training in Dorset was drafted to Salonika in August of the same year. During the Balkan campaign he was in action in the Struma and Monastir sectors, and was wounded in the Advance on the Vardar. Returning to England he was demobilised in June 1919, and holds the General Service and Victory Medals.
40, Oxford Street, Wolverton, Bucks. Z2307 /B.

WATTS, J., Private, 9th Hampshire Regiment.
Joining in July 1916, he was drafted to India in the following month. There he was engaged on important garrison duties with the Dorset Regiment, but was later transferred to the Hampshires, and sent to Russia in 1918. He rendered valuable services at Omsk, Eketteringburg and Vladivostok, and remained in Siberia until his return to England for demobilisation in December 1919. He holds the General Service and Victory Medals.
Gawcott Road, Buckingham, Bucks. Z2313.

WATTS, J., Private, 1st Northamptonshire Regt.
Mobilised at the outbreak of war in August 1914, he was immediately drafted to the Western Front, where he took part in the Battle of Mons and the subsequent Retreat. He was wounded on the Aisne, and was invalided to England, but on his recovery proceeded to the Dardanelles and took part in the heavy fighting during the Landing on the Gallipoli Peninsula. He also saw service on the Gaza front in Palestine, and in 1917 returned to France, where he rendered valuable services in the Ypres and Somme sectors. He holds the Mons Star, and the General Service and Victory Medals, and was discharged in February 1919. 17, Silver Street, Stony Stratford. TZ2314.

WATTS, J., Private, 2nd Northants. Regiment.
He volunteered in October 1914, and after training at Weybridge was drafted to the Western Front in January 1915. There he took part in many engagements of importance in the Ypres and Neuve Chapelle sectors, and made the supreme sacrifice on March 12th, 1915, being killed in action at Neuve Chapelle. He was entitled to the 1914–15 Star, and the General Service and Victory Medals.
"The path of duty was the way to glory."
2, Swan Terrace, Stony Stratford. TZ2315.

WATTS, J. H., Sapper, Royal Engineers (R.O.D.)
He was already serving in the Army at the outbreak of war in August 1914, and after training with the Bedfordshire Yeomanry was transferred to the Royal Engineers. Proceeding to France in June 1915, he did consistently good work on the Somme, Ypres and Arras fronts, whilst engaged as an engine driver on ambulance, troop and supply trains. He holds the 1914–15 Star, and the General Service and Victory Medals, and was discharged iu April 1919.
Main Street, Hartford. Z2318 /B.

WATTS, L., Private, R.A.S.C.
Joining in October 1917, he was engaged on important duties in England for a time and then proceeded to France in January 1918. He did consistently good work at Calais, where he was employed at a Field Bakery, and after the Armistice served with the Army of Occupation on the Rhine. He holds the General Service and Victory Medals, and was demobilised in December 1919. Main Street, Gawcott, Buckingham. Z2316.

WATTS, P. G., Trooper, Bedfordshire Lancers.
He volunteered in October 1915, and after a period of training was drafted to France in August 1916. In this theatre of war he took part in much heavy fighting in various sectors, and was in action on the Somme, at Arras and Cambrai. He was wounded in November 1917, but after recovery rejoined his unit and rendered valuable services in the Retreat and Advance of 1918. Demobilised in May 1919, he holds the General Service and Victory Medals.
Waterside, Sherington, Newport Pagnell. Z4033 /B.

WATTS, W., Rifleman, Rifle Brigade.
He joined in May 1916, and four months later proceeded to the Western Front, where he took part in many important engagements. He was invalided home in December 1916, but in February of the following year returned to France, and was in action with a Lewis gun section at Arras, Ypres and Cambrai. He was demobilised in January 1919, and holds the General Service and Victory Medals.
Rectory Lane, Houghton Conquest, near Bedford. Z2310.

WATTS, W. H., Private, Bedfordshire Regiment.
Joining in July 1916, he was retained on special duties at various stations in England owing to his being unfit for service overseas. He, nevertheless, rendered valuable services until the cessation of hostilities, and was demobilised in January 1919. Laws Row, Eaton Socon, Beds. Z2311.

WAYMAN, C., Private, Bedfordshire Regiment.
Volunteering in August 1914, he underwent a period of training, and in September 1915 proceeded to the Western Front, where he took part in heavy fighting at Festubert, Loos, Albert and the Somme Offensive of 1916. In August of that year he was transferred to Palestine and was in action at the Battles of Gaza and Jaffa. Sent to the Western Front in September 1918 he finally saw service during the latter part of the Advance of that year, and was demobilised in January 1919. He holds the 1914–15 Star, and the General Service and Victory Medals.
Mill Road, Buckden, Hunts. Z2549 /B

WEASER, W., Private, R.A.M.C.
He volunteered in May 1915, and drafted to France three months later, took part in engagements on the Loos front. He saw service in this theatre of war for only two months, and was then transferred to the Dardanelles, where he was present at the Landing at Suvla Bay. He also did consistently good work in Egypt and Palestine, serving at Cairo, Jaffa and Jerusalem, and was invalided home suffering from gas-poisoning and discharged in December 1918 as unfit for further service. He holds the 1914–15 Star, and the General Service and Victory Medals. 44, St. Germain Street, Huntingdon. Z2319.

WEATHERLEY, B., L/Cpl., 1st Ox. & Bucks. L.I.
He volunteered in September 1914, and after completing his training was drafted to Mesopotamia in December of the following year. He was in action during the attempted relief of Kut and rendered valuable services in the Advance on Baghdad, taking part in much heavy fighting in this theatre of war. He was eventually demobilised in April 1919 after his return home, and holds the General Service and Victory Medals.
81, Aylesbury Street, Wolverton, Bucks. Z232

WEBB, A. W., Sergeant, 1st Bedfordshire Regiment and 4th Nigra, West African Regiment.
Volunteering in September 1914, he did consistently good work at various important stations in England during the first portion of his service and in 1917 proceeded to France. There he played a distinguished part in many engagements, notably the Battles of Ypres, Lens, Passchendaele and Cambrai, and suffered from gas-poisoning. After being invalided home he was drafted to West Africa in August 1918, and did garrison duty at Lagos with Frontier Forces. He returned to England and was demobilised in September 1919, holding the General Service and Victory Medals.
2, Railway Cottage, Oakley, Bedford. Z2324.

WEBB, E. J., Cpl., 1/6th Royal Welch Fusiliers.
He volunteered in August 1914, and after serving at various stations in England was drafted to the Dardanelles in July 1915. In this theatre of war he took a prominent part in the heavy fighting at Suvla Bay, and was wounded in action on August 11th, 1915. He unhappily died on board H.M.H.S. "Salta" on his way to hospital at Malta, four days later, and was buried at sea. He was entitled to the 1914–15 Star, and the General Service and Victory Medals.
"His memory is cherished with pride."
Well More, Maids Moreton, Buckingham. Z2323.

WEBB, F. A., Sapper, Royal Engineers.
Volunteering in November 1915, he completed a course of training and was drafted to the Eastern theatre of war in March 1916. He saw service in both Egypt and Palestine and was in action at Gaza, Jerusalem, Jaffa and Aleppo, where he was engaged on the lines of communication. He was demobilised in August 1919, on his return to England, and holds the General Service and Victory Medals.
46, Hassett Street, Bedford. X2326.

WEBB, G., Private, 8th Bedfordshire Regiment.
He volunteered in 1915, and later in the same year was drafted to France, where he took part in much heavy fighting in many sectors, and was in action at the Battles of Arras, Ypres and Cambrai. He made the supreme sacrifice, being killed in January 1916 in the Ypres salient, and was entitled to the 1914–15 Star, and the General Service and Victory Medals.
"Nobly striving :
He nobly fell that we might live."
Cambridge Road, Sandy Beds. Z2327.

WEBB, G., Pte., Queen's (Royal West Surrey Regt).
He joined in June 1918, and after a period of training was drafted to the Western Front, where he took part in many important engagements, including those at Cambrai and Ypres during the Advance of 1918. He rendered valuable services and was demobilised in September 1919, holding the General Service and Victory Medals.
39, West End, Haynes, near Bedford. Z2321/B.

WEBB, G., Corporal, 1st Royal Berkshire Regt.
He volunteered in March 1915, and after a period of training and service on the East Coast was drafted to France in June 1916. There as a Lewis gunner he played a prominent part in many engagements, and was in action during the Retreat and Advance of 1918. He also served with the Army of Occupation on the Rhine, and returning to England was demobilised in March 1919, holding the General Service and Victory Medals.
Main Street, Hartford. Z2325.

WEBB, R., Private, Royal Warwickshire Regiment.
He joined in 1916 and later in the same year was drafted to the Western Front, where he took part in many important engagements, including those at Ypres and on the Somme. He only served for a brief period in France before he made the supreme sacrifice, being killed in action on October 23rd, 1916. He was entitled to the General Service and Victory Medals.
"And doubtless he went in splendid company."
31, Willington Street, Bedford. Z2328.

WEBB, W., L/Corporal, Bedfordshire Regiment.
He volunteered in May 1915, and after training at various stations in England was drafted to the Western Front in 1916. After taking part in many important engagements, including those at Vimy Ridge, the Somme and the Ancre, he was invalided home later in the same year, but returned to France in 1917, and was unfortunately killed in action during heavy fighting on the Somme. He was entitled to the General Service and Victory Medals.
"Great deeds cannot die."
39, West End, Haynes, Beds. Z2321/A.

WEBB, W. A. G., Private, Oxford. and Bucks. L.I.
Volunteering in November 1914, he was undergoing a period of training on Salisbury Plain preparatory to being drafted overseas, when he unhappily contracted diphtheria and scarlet fever, and died in hospital on July 17th, 1915.
"Whilst we remember, the sacrifice is not in vain."
3, Elm Street, Buckingham. Z2322/A.

WEBB, W. J., Gunner, Royal Garrison Artillery.
He enlisted in January 1919, and during his training was stationed at Plymouth. He was subsequently sent to Dublin, and in 1920 was still serving in Ireland.
15, Elm Street, Buckingham, Bucks. Z2322/B.

WEBBER, J. L., Private, R.A.M.C.
Volunteering in November 1915, at Guildford, he was sent to Eastbourne, but less than three weeks later was discharged as physically unfit for further service.
King Street, Somersham, Hunts. Z2329

WEBBER, W. J., Rfn., 1/17th London Regt. (Rifles).
He enlisted in 1912, and at the outbreak of war in August 1914 went through a final course of training, and was drafted to the Western Front in March 1915. In this theatre of war he was engaged in much heavy fighting, being in action at the Battles of Festubert, Givenchy and Loos, and was wounded. He was invalided to England in July 1916, and was discharged in June 1917 as unfit for further military service. He holds the 1914–15 Star, and the General Service and Victory Medals.
Piper's Lane, Godmanchester. Z2330.

WEED, W. T., Trooper, Bedfordshire Lancers.
He volunteered in May 1915, and later in the same year proceeded to France, where he was in action at many important engagements, including the Battles of the Somme, Arras and Bullecourt, and was wounded at Fricourt. He rendered valuable services until the cessation of hostilities, and was discharged in April 1919, holding the 1914–15 Star, and the General Service and Victory Medals.
Mill Green, Turvey, Beds. Z2331.

WELCH, B., Private, 1/5th Bedfordshire Regiment.
Mobilised at the outbreak of war in August 1914, he was drafted to the Dardanelles in July 1915, and took part in the heavy fighting at Suvla Bay, and was wounded. He proceeded to Egypt, and later to Palestine after the Evacuation of the Gallipoli Peninsula, and was in action at the Battles of Gaza (where he was wounded), and the taking of Jerusalem and Jaffa. He eventually returned to England and was demobilised in June 1919, holding the 1914–15 Star, and the General Service and Victory Medals.
65, Westbourne Road, Queen's Park, Bedford. Z2332.

WELHAM, W., Corporal, Machine Gun Corps.
He volunteered in August 1914, and after a period of training was drafted to the Dardanelles in April 1915. He played a prominent part in the fighting during the Landing on the Gallipoli Peninsula, and after the Evacuation proceeded to Mesopotamia. He rendered valuable services at Kut-el-Amara, and returning to England was demobilised in May 1919, holding the General Service and Victory Medals.
28, Westbourne Road, Bedford. Z2834/B.

WELLER, W. T., Cpl., 7th R. Warwickshire Regt.
He was mobilised at the outbreak of war in August 1914, and was shortly afterwards drafted to France, where he played an important part in the fighting during the Retreat from Mons. He was also in action in the Battles of the Marne, the Aisne, Ypres, the Somme and Cambrai, and was wounded. He was in consequence invalided to England and eventually discharged in March 1919 as medically unfit. He holds the Mons Star and the General Service and Victory Medals.
Newton Longville, Bucks. Z2333.

WELLS, C., L/Corporal, 2nd Bedfordshire Regt.
He joined in July 1917, and after a period of training was drafted to the Western Front in April of the following year. He took part in many of the concluding Battles of the war during the Advance of 1918, notably those at Cambrai, Albert and Kemmel Hill, and was wounded at Cambrai on September 29th, 1918. Upon recovery he was sent to India, where in 1920 he was still serving. He holds the General Service and Victory Medals.
Oddfellows Cottages, London Road, Sandy, Beds. Z2334.

WELLS, C. A., Trooper, Bedfordshire Lancers.
He volunteered in September 1914, and after a period of service at various stations in England and Ireland was drafted to the Eastern theatre of war in January 1916. There he saw service both in Egypt and Palestine until he was sent to France in February 1918. He then took part in the final engagements of the war during the Retreat and Advance of 1918, and was demobilised in March 1919, holding the General Service and Victory Medals. Main Street, Hartford. Z2335/A.

WELLS, H. M., Private, 5th Battalion Canadian Overseas Forces.
He joined in June 1916, and four months later proceeded to the Western Front after completing his training. He took part in much heavy fighting in various sectors, and was reported missing and later presumed killed in action near Passchendaele on August 16th, 1917. He was entitled to the General Service and Victory Medals.
"And doubtless he went in splendid company."
Main Street, Hartford. Z2335/B.

WELLS, H. V., Private, East Surrey Regiment.
He volunteered in August 1914, and in the following month was drafted to France, where he saw much heavy fighting. After being in action at the Battles of Ypres and on the Somme he made the supreme sacrifice, being killed at Messines Ridge on March 2nd, 1916. He was entitled to the 1914 Star, and the General Service and Victory Medals.
"He died the noblest death a man may die."
Main Street, Hartford. Z2335/C.

WELLS, M., Private, East Surrey Regiment.
He volunteered in August 1914, and in the following month proceeded to the Western Front, where he took part in many important engagements, including those at Ypres, Loos and the Somme, and was wounded in July 1916. He was invalided to the Isle of Wight, and on recovery from his wounds returned to France, and fought on the Arras front. Rejoining his unit after having been wounded a second time, he was in action in the Cambrai sector, where he was again wounded and gassed. He was demobilised in March 1919 after a short period of service in Ireland, and holds the 1914 Star, and the General Service and Victory Medals. Main Street, Hartford. Z2335 /D.

WENMAN, A. J., Private, Machine Gun Corps.
Volunteering in April 1915, he underwent a period of training, and was drafted to France in June 1916. There he was in action at many important engagements on the Ypres, Somme and Cambrai fronts, and rendered valuable services during the course of hostilities. He holds the General Service and Victory Medals, and was demobilised in March 1919.
Drayton Parslow, Bucks. Z2336.

WESLEY, G., Private, Royal Defence Corps.
Volunteering in October 1914, he was engaged on the important duties of guarding bridges and prisoners of war in various parts of England. He did consistently good work throughout the period of hostilities, and was demobilised in February 1919.
24, North End Square, Buckingham. Z2339.

WESLEY, G., Sergeant, Royal Dragoons.
He was already in the Army at the outbreak of war in August 1914, and was immediately drafted to France, where he took part in the Retreat from Mons. He also played a distinguished part in subsequent engagements, including the Battles of La Bassée, Festubert, Amiens, Ypres, the Somme, Arras and Cambrai, and was wounded at Ypres in 1915. He was discharged in June 1919, and holds the Mons Star, and the General Service and Victory Medals.
54, Canton Street, Poplar, E.14. Z2337 /C.

WESLEY, J., Corporal, 1st Grenadier Guards.
Mobilised at the outbreak of war in August 1914, he was shortly afterwards drafted to the Western Front, where he played a distinguished part in the heavy fighting during the Retreat from Mons. He was also in action at the Battles of the Marne, the Aisne, La Bassée and Ypres, but was unfortunately killed during heavy fighting at Neuve Chapelle on March 13th, 1915. He was entitled to the Mons Star, and the General Service and Victory Medals.
"A valiant Soldier, with undaunted heart he breasted life's last hill."
Covington's Yard, Turvey, Beds. Z2337 /B.

WESLEY, W., Guardsman, Grenadier Guards.
Mobilised from the Reserve in August 1914, he was immediately drafted to France, and took part in the Retreat from Mons. He was also in action at subsequent engagements, including the Battles of the Marne, La Bassée and Ypres, but was taken prisoner at the end of 1914. He suffered many hardships in captivity and was eventually repatriated and discharged in December 1918. He holds the Mons Star, and the General Service and Victory Medals.
23, Pleasant Street, New Brighton. Z2337 /A.

WESLEY, W. G., Driver, Royal Field Artillery.
Already serving with the Colours at the outbreak of war in August 1914, he was immediately sent to France, where he was in action with his Battery during the Retreat from Mons. He also rendered valuable services at many subsequent engagements, including the Battles of Ypres, the Somme, Hill 60, Vimy Ridge and Cambrai, and later the Retreat and Advance of 1918. He was discharged in February 1919, and holds the Mons Star, and the General Service and Victory Medals.
1, All Hallows Lane, Bedford. X2338.

WEST, A., Private, Oxford. and Bucks. L.I.
He volunteered in September 1914, and, completing his training, was sent to the Western Front in July of the following year. There he took part in many important engagements, including the Battles of Ypres, Neuve Chapelle, Loos and Armentières, and was wounded. He was invalided to England, and on recovery was transferred to a Labour Corps and drafted to France, where he did consistently good work on the Cambrai front, and at Bapaume, Amiens and Le Cateau, and was again wounded just before the Armistice. He holds the 1914–15 Star, and the General Service and Victory Medals, and was demobilised in April 1919.
109, High Street, Newport Pagnell, Bucks. Z2347.

WEST, A. J., Sapper, Royal Engineers.
He joined in 1916, and after undergoing a period of training, was drafted to France in the following year. He was engaged on important duties in this theatre of war, and saw service at Ypres, Arras and Cambrai, but lost a leg at Lille during the Advance of 1918. He was in consequence discharged in May 1919, and holds the General Service and Victory Medals.
53, Albert Street, Bedford. X2342.

WEST, A. W., Private, Royal Fusiliers.
Joining in July 1917, after being engaged on work of National importance, he was drafted to France in the following December and took part in engagements on the Cambrai front. He also saw heavy fighting during the Retreat and Advance of 1918, and was demobilised in March 1919, holding the General Service and Victory Medals.
20a, Mill Street, Newport Pagnell, Bucks. Z1463 /B.

WEST, F., Corporal, Royal Engineers.
He joined in February 1917, and after completing his training was drafted to the Eastern theatre of war. He saw service in both Egypt and Palestine, and did good work on railroad construction at Gaza and other sectors of importance. He returned to England, and was demobilised in January 1920, holding the General Service and Victory Medals.
Bow Brickhill, near Bletchley, Bucks. Z2341 /B.

WEST, G., Air Mechanic, Royal Air Force.
He joined in March 1918 on attaining military age, and was engaged on work which required a high degree of technical skill. He rendered valuable services, but was not successful in obtaining his transfer to a theatre of war before the cessation of hostilities, and was demobilised in April 1919.
3, Beaconsfield Place, Newport Pagnell, Bucks. Z2343 /B.

WEST, G. H., Private, 4th Royal Welch Fusiliers.
He volunteered in 1914, and after a period of training with the Bedfordshire Regiment was transferred to the Royal Welch Fusiliers, and proceeded to France in the following year. There he took part in the Battles of the Somme, Albert, Festubert, Loos, Ypres and Cambrai, and was wounded. He eventually returned to England, and was demobilised in 1919, holding the 1914–15 Star, and the General Service and Victory Medals. Bluntisham, Hunts. Z2344.

WEST, H., Private, R.A.M.C.
He was mobilised in August 1914, but owing to ill-health was discharged in the following November. He was called up again in September 1916, and acted as stretcher-bearer and hospital orderly on his arrival in France in April 1917. He did consistently good work until August of the same year, when he was again discharged as no longer fit for military service. He holds the General Service and Victory Medals.
Goldington Green, Bedford. Z2348.

WEST, H. C., Sapper, Royal Engineers.
He joined in April 1916, and after a period of training was sent to France early in 1917. There he was engaged on important engineering duties in the Ypres and Cambrai sectors, and did consistently good work until the cessation of hostilities. He holds the General Service and Victory Medals, and was demobilised in March 1919.
3, Beaconsfield Place, Newport Pagnell, Beds. Z2343 /A.

WEST, J., Private, 2nd Hampshire Regiment.
He volunteered in September 1914, and after training at various stations, was drafted to the Dardanelles early in the following year. There he took part in many important engagements, including the Landing at Suvla Bay, and was wounded at Chocolate Hill on August 6th, 1915. After undergoing several operations in hospital he eventually lost a leg through amputation, and was discharged in December 1917 as unfit for further service. He holds the General Service and Victory Medals. 9, West Lane, Emberton, Bucks. Z2349 /A.

WEST, J., Sapper, Royal Engineers.
He volunteered in November 1915, and was stationed at Maidenhead and Bethnal Green, attached to the Fire Brigade for air-raid duties. After the Armistice he was sent to Germany, where he served with the Army of Occupation on the Rhine. He was demobilised in September 1919 on his return to England.
Bow Brickhill, near Bletchley, Bucks. Z2341 /A.

WEST, J. B., Private, 1/5th Bedfordshire Regt.
Volunteering in January 1915, he was sent to France after 12 months' training and served on the Somme and in the Ypres salient. He was wounded at Ypres in October 1916, after serving in many engagements, and was invalided to England and ultimately discharged in April 1917 as physically unfit for further service. He holds the General Service and Victory Medals. 2, The Mount, Emberton, Beds. Z2349 /B.

WEST, P., Private, Oxford. and Bucks. L.I.
He volunteered in November 1914, and after a period of service in England was drafted to the Western Front in 1916. There he was present at many important engagements on the Somme and at Péronne, Ypres and Vimy Ridge. He was sent to Italy in 1917, and saw service on the Piave and the Asiago Plateaux. He holds the General Service and Victory Medals, and was demobilised in February 1919.
Broughton, Hunts. TZ2340.

WEST, P., Private, 2nd Highland Light Infantry.
At the outbreak of war in August 1914, he was serving in India, and embarked for France immediately afterwards. He took part in much severe fighting in this theatre of war, and was in action at La Bassée and Ypres, but made the supreme sacrifice at the Battle of Neuve Chapelle, being killed in March 1915. He was entitled to the 1914 Star, and the General Service and Victory Medals.
"His life for his Country, his soul to God."
High Street, Stoke Goldington. Z2346.

WEST, P. (M.M.), Corporal, Royal Field Artillery.
Mobilised at the outbreak of war in August 1914, he was immediately drafted to the Western Front, and was in action with his Battery during the Retreat from Mons. He also played a prominent part in the Battles of La Bassée, the Somme and Arras, and was wounded towards the end of 1917 near Cambrai. He was awarded the Military Medal for conspicuous bravery and devotion to duty on the Field. After being invalided home he was demobilised in August 1919, and holds, in addition to the Military Medal, the Mons Star, and the General Service and Victory Medals.
20a, Mill Street, Newport Pagnell, Bucks. Z1463/A.

WEST, P. J., Private, Queen's (Royal West Surrey Regiment).
He joined in January 1918, on attaining military age, and was drafted to France in the following June. There he took part in many of the final engagements of the war, including those on the Cambrai front, and later in the Retreat and Advance of 1918. He holds the General Service and Victory Medals, and was demobilised in November 1919.
Ford End Cottages, Bedford. Z2350.

WEST, R., Private, 8th King's Own (Royal Lancaster Regiment).
He volunteered in November 1915, and after a period of training was drafted to France in the following March. There he took part in much heavy fighting in various sectors, including engagements on the Ypres, Somme and Arras fronts, but was unhappily killed in action at Monchy on May 12th, 1917. He was entitled to the General Service and Victory Medals.
"He died the noblest death a man may die."
20a, Mill Street, Newport Pagnell, Bucks. Z1463/C.

WEST, R., Air Mechanic, R.A.F. (late R.N.A.S.)
He joined in March 1918, on attaining military age, and was engaged on special duties at Yarmouth whilst attached to seaplane and motor-boat Squadrons. He did consistently good work until the cessation of hostilities, but was not successful in obtaining his transfer to a theatre of war.
3, Beaconsfield Place, Newport Pagnell, Bucks. Z2343/C.

WEST, S. A., Private, Hunts. Cyclist Battalion.
He volunteered in August 1914, but after a short period of service was discharged as unfit on account of defective eyesight He was, however, called up in 1917, and later in the same year was drafted to the East, where he saw service in Egypt and Palestine. He took part in heavy fighting in this theatre of war and was wounded in action. Returning to England, he was demobilised in June 1919, and holds the General Service and Victory Medals.
9, St. Clement's Passage, Huntingdon. Z2345.

WEST, W. (M.M.), Cpl., 7th Northants. Regiment.
He volunteered in September 1914, and was drafted to France in March 1915. There he played a prominent part in many engagements of importance, including the heavy fighting in the Ypres sector, and was wounded in action in July 1917. He was invalided to England, but unhappily died of wounds on November 3rd. He was awarded the Military Medal for conspicuous bravery in the Field, and was also entitled to the 1914–15 Star, and the General Service and Victory Medals.
"Great deeds cannot die."
Ravenstone, Bucks. Z3655/C.

WEST, W. L., Driver, Royal Field Artillery.
Volunteering in October 1915, he underwent a period of training at Luton, and, after being retained for some time at home stations, was drafted to the Western Front in April 1918. He was in action with his Battery at many important engagements in the Ypres sector, and took part in the Retreat and Advance of 1918. He was demobilised in May 1918, and holds the General Service and Victory Medals.
The Tower, Emberton, Bucks. Z2349/C.

WESTIN, A. S., Private, 25th Canadian Forestry Corps.
He joined in February 1916, and later in the same year was drafted to the Western Front, where he did good work on the Somme and at Ypres, Passchendaele and Cambrai, and was wounded in action in 1917. He was invalided home and eventually discharged in July 1918 as physically unfit for further service. He holds the General Service and Victory Medals.
Aspley Hill, Woburn Sands, Beds. Z2351.

WESTON, A. (M.M.), Corporal, Royal Engineers.
He volunteered in September 1914, and, after completing a period of training, was drafted to the Western Front in August of the following year. He rendered valuable services whilst engaged on the important duties of trench-digging and pontoon-building, and saw service at Festubert, Loos, the Somme, Vermelles, Bullecourt, Ypres and Cambrai. He was awarded the Military Medal for conspicuous bravery and devotion to duty at Neuve Chapelle in 1916. He was transferred to Italy in November 1917, and was in action on the Asiago and Piave fronts. In addition to the Military Medal, he holds the 1914–15 Star, and the General Service and Victory Medals, and was demobilised in March 1919.
51, Greenfield Road, Newport Pagnell, Bucks. Z2352.

WHARTON, F. C., Private, 3/5th Beds. Regt.
Volunteering in October 1914, he underwent a period of training, and was retained on special duties at important stations in England. Owing to his being unfit for service overseas he was unable to obtain his transfer to a theatre of war, but, nevertheless, rendered valuable services until his discharge in June 1918, after doing consistently good work whilst attached to the Royal Engineers at Folkestone.
23, Cater Street, Kempston, Bucks. X2353.

WHATTON, C. D., Private, 5th Northants. Regt.
He volunteered in August 1914, and, after a period of training, was drafted to the Western Front in January of the following year. In this theatre of war he took part in much heavy fighting in the Ypres and Loos sectors, and was wounded. Invalided to England, he spent 15 months in hospital, and was afterwards discharged as unfit for further service in October 1918. He holds the 1914–15 Star, and the General Service and Victory Medals.
Prospect Place, Emberton, Bucks. Z2354.

WHEATLEY, J., Private, 2nd Bedfordshire Regt
He joined in 1916, and, after undergoing a period of training, was drafted to France in the following year. There he took part in many engagements of importance, including the Battles of Ypres, Albert, St. Quentin and Cambrai, but fell in action on July 3rd, 1918, during the Retreat of that year. He was entitled to the General Service and Victory Medals.
"The path of duty was the way to glory."
Grange Road, Blunham, Beds. Z2356.

WHEATLEY, J. R., L/Cpl., 11th Lancs. Fusiliers.
Mobilised at the outbreak of war in August 1914, he did consistently good work at various stations in England during the first part of his service, and was drafted to France in September 1916. He took part in several important engagements, including those on the Somme and at Ypres and Arras, and was taken prisoner at Cambrai during the Retreat of 1918. He was repatriated after the Armistice, and eventually demobilised in April 1919, holding the General Service and Victory Medals.
14, Pilcroft Street, Bedford. X2355.

WHEATLEY, R., Private, R.A.S.C.
He joined in 1916, and later in the same year proceeded to the Western Front, where he was engaged on important duties in connection with Remounts. He saw service at Arras, the Somme, Vimy Ridge, Passchendaele and Cambrai, and was also employed on the transport of food and ammunition to forward areas. Demobilised in February 1919, he holds the General Service and Victory Medals.
London Road, Girtford, Sandy, Beds. Z3847/B.

WHEELER, A. J., Sergeant, R.A.S.C.
Volunteering in September 1914, he was at first retained at Aldershot and engaged in instructing recruits. In the autumn of 1915 he was drafted to France, and served at Amiens and Cappy. Later sent to Salonika, he was in action on the Vardar, but in September 1918 was wounded on the Doiran front. Invalided home, he spent some time in hospital, and was eventually discharged as unfit in May 1919, holding the 1914–15 Star, and the General Service and Victory Medals.
8, Coronation Road, Stony Stratford, Bucks. Z2358.

WHEELER, F., A.B., R.N., H.M.S. "Orion."
He was already serving in the Navy at the outbreak of war in August 1914, and immediately proceeded to the North Sea, where he was engaged on important convoy and patrol duties. He rendered valuable services in H.M.S. "Orion," and took part in operations at Zeebrugge and Ostend. He holds the General Service and Victory Medals, and was demobilised in January 1919. 11, Patteshall Street, Bedford. X2357.

WHEELER, F., Farrier, R.A.S.C.
He volunteered in September 1915, and was sent to the Dardanelles shortly afterwards. After the Evacuation of the Peninsula he proceeded to Egypt and served at Alexandria for a time before joining the Forces operating in Palestine, where he was in action at Gaza, Jaffa and Haifa. He subsequently saw service at Salonika, and, returning home, was demobilised in January 1919. He holds the 1914–15 Star, and the General Service and Victory Medals. Cople, Bedford. TZ2359.

WHIFFIN, E., Sapper, Royal Engineers.
Volunteering in 1915, he was drafted to the Eastern theatre of war later in the same year, and saw service on the Gallipoli Peninsula and in Egypt and Palestine. He took part in numerous engagements, and was present at the Battles of Rafa, Gaza and Jaffa. Returning to England, he was demobilised in 1919, and holds the 1914–15 Star, and the General Service and Victory Medals.
31, Bunyan Road, South End, Bedford. Z2360.

WHITBREAD, J., Driver, Royal Engineers.
He volunteered in September 1914, and was drafted to the East in February 1916, after a period of training and service in England. He did excellent work in many places, notably at Gaza and Jerusalem in Palestine. Returning to England after the Armistice, he was demobilised in July 1919, and holds the General Service and Victory Medals.
7, Russell Street, Bedford. X2397

WHITBY, A. J., Private, 12th Norfolk Regiment.
He joined in April 1917, and, after a period of training, was drafted to the Western Front in April of the following year. There he took part in many engagements of importance, including the Battles of Albert, the Somme and Cambrai, but was unfortunately killed in action on August 18th, 1918, during the Advance of that year. He was entitled to the General Service and Victory Medals.
"His life for his Country, his soul to God."
Longfields Road, Sandy, Beds. Z2361/B.

WHITBY, G., C.Q.M.S., Bedfordshire Regiment.
Already in the Army at the outbreak of war in August 1914, he was retained at important stations in England until 1917, when he was drafted to France. There he was employed at Headquarters on the Arras front, and rendered valuable services until November 1919, when he was demobilised. He holds the General Service and Victory Medals.
70, Bunyan Road, Kempston, Bedford. X2362.

WHITBY, G. H., Private, 1/5th Bedfordshire Regt.
He volunteered in June 1915, and after a period of training was drafted to the Eastern Front in January of the following year. During his service in Egypt and Palestine he was in action at Gaza and Beyrout, and rendered valuable services until the cessation of hostilities. Returning home in July 1919, he was demobilised in the following month, and holds the General Service and Victory Medals.
Longfields Road, Sandy, Beds. Z2361/A.

WHITE, A., Chief Petty Officer, Royal Navy.
He was already serving in H.M. Navy at the outbreak of war in August 1914, and immediately afterwards was sent to the North Sea in H.M.S. "Diligence" on mine-sweeping operations. He also did good work on patrol and escort duties in the Channel, and was discharged in February 1919, time-expired. He holds the 1914–15 Star, and the General Service and Victory Medals.
4, St. Leonard's Street, Bedford. X2373/A.

WHITE, A., Corporal, Hampshire Regiment.
Joining in 1917, he was drafted to Mesopotamia later in the same year, and played a prominent part in engagements in this theatre of war. He was afterwards transferred to Egypt, and later to Palestine, where he remained until the cessation of hostilities. After the Armistice he did duty with the Army of Occupation in Egypt and the Soudan. He holds the General Service and Victory Medals, and was demobilised in March 1920. Cranfield, Beds. Z2366.

WHITE, A., Private, 1/5th Bedfordshire Regiment.
He joined in November 1916, and after undergoing a period of training, was drafted in March 1917 to the Eastern theatre of war, where he saw service in Palestine and Egypt. He took part in many important engagements, and was in action at the Battles of Gaza and the taking of Jerusalem. He returned to England and was eventually demobilised in June 1919, holding the General Service and Victory Medals.
14, College Street, Kempston. Z2370/B.

WHITE, A., Private, 5th Bedfordshire Regiment.
He volunteered in September 1915, and later in the same year was drafted first to Egypt and then to Palestine. There he saw much service, and was in action at the Battles of Gaza, the entry into Jerusalem, and the capture of Aleppo. Returning to England after the Armistice, he was demobilised in March 1919, and holds the General Service and Victory Medals.
8, Marlborough Road, Bedford. Z1122/D.

WHITE, C., Rifleman, King's Royal Rifle Corps.
Volunteering in October 1914, he completed his training and was drafted to France, where he took part in many important engagements, including the Battles of Ypres, Loos, Albert, Vimy Ridge and the Somme. Wounded in December 1916 on the Ancre front, he was invalided home, and on recovery served at Colchester until his demobilisation in February 1919. He holds the 1914–15 Star, and the General Service and Victory Medals. 26, Bletsoe, Bedford. Z2379.

WHITE, C., C.S.M., Machine Gun Corps.
He volunteered in September 1914, and after a period of service in England was drafted to the Western Front in August 1915. In this theatre of war he played a distinguished part in the heavy fighting in many sectors, and was in action at the Battles of Loos and Ypres, and in many other engagements of importance until the cessation of hostilities. He proceeded to Germany after the Armistice and served with the Army of Occupation on the Rhine until his demobilisation in May 1919. He holds the 1914–15 Star, and the General Service and Victory Medals. Buckden, Hunts. Z2376.

WHITE, E. W., Sapper, Royal Engineers.
He joined in 1916, but owing to his being physically unfit for service in a theatre of war, was retained on special duties in connection with the air-raid service in London. He, nevertheless, rendered valuable services until the cessation of hostilities, and was demobilised in March 1919.
Cranfield, Beds. Z2367.

WHITE, F., Private, Suffolk Regiment.
He volunteered in 1915, and was retained on special duties on the East Coast of England. He was unable to obtain his transfer to a theatre of war owing to physical unfitness, but, nevertheless, rendered valuable services, and was discharged through deafness in 1917. Cranfield, Beds. Z2368.

WHITE, F. B., Cadet, R.N.V.R.
He enlisted in June 1918 on attaining military age, and proceeded to the Crystal Palace for a course of training. He was about to be drafted overseas when the Armistice was signed, and his services no longer being required, he was demobilised in December 1918.
8, Brooklands Road, Bletchley, Bucks. TZ4486/C.

WHITE, F. E., Private, Royal Sussex Regiment.
Mobilised at the outbreak of war in August 1914, he was retained at various stations in England during the first part of his service, and was drafted to France in July 1916. He saw much active service in various sectors, including the Battles of the Somme and Ypres, and was reported missing and afterwards presumed killed in action near Lens on August 4th, 1917. He was entitled to the General Service and Victory Medals.
"Whilst we remember, the sacrifice is not in vain."
3, Little Butts Street, Bedford. X2374.

WHITE, F. W., Private, 1/5th Bedfordshire Regt.
He volunteered in August 1914, and after a period of training was drafted early in 1915 to the Dardanelles, where he took part in fighting on the Gallipoli Peninsula, and was wounded. Transferred to Egypt after the Evacuation in December 1915, he was stationed at Cairo, and later served at the Battles of Gaza, and other engagements of importance during the Palestine campaign. He returned to England after the Armistice, and was demobilised in April 1919, holding the 1914–15 Star, and the General Service and Victory Medals.
Houghton Conquest, near Ampthill, Beds. Z2378/A.

WHITE, G., Sergeant, Grenadier Guards.
Mobilised at the outbreak of war in August 1914, he was immediately drafted to France, and played a distinguished part in the fighting during the Retreat from Mons. He was also in action at the Battles of the Marne, Festubert and Hill 60, and other engagements of importance, but was accidentally killed at Rouen on March 24th, 1916. He was entitled to the Mons Star, and the General Service and Victory Medals.
"His memory is cherished with pride."
Church Street, Buckden, Hunts. Z2377.

WHITE, G., Gunner, Royal Garrison Artillery.
Already serving in the Army at the outbreak of war in August 1914, he was drafted in January 1915 to France, where he was in action with his Battery at numerous engagements of importance, and was wounded on the Arras front in the following April. He was invalided to England, but, returning to the Western Front in October 1917, served in the Ypres and Cambrai sectors, and was wounded and gassed in May 1918 during the Retreat. He holds the 1914–15 Star, and the General Service and Victory Medals, and in 1920 was serving at Peshawar in India. 25, High St., Buckingham. Z2083/B.

WHITE, G., Corporal, Royal Engineers.
He volunteered in September 1914, and after a period of training was drafted to the Western Front in March 1915. After playing a prominent part in many engagements, particularly in the Ypres, Arras and Somme sectors, he was recalled to England in August 1916, and was engaged on work of National importance in connection with munitions of war until the cessation of hostilities. He holds the 1914–15 Star, and the General Service and Victory Medals.
8, Marlborough Road, Bedford. Z1122/C.

WHITE, G., Gunner, R.N., H.M.S. "Venerable."
He was already serving in H.M. Navy at the outbreak of war in August 1914, and proceeded to sea in H.M.S. "Venerable." He rendered valuable services patrolling the North Sea, the Baltic and the Atlantic Ocean, and was also engaged in the bombardment of the Dardanelles in 1915. He was at first reported missing, and was later reported killed in action in 1917. He was entitled to the 1914–15 Star, and the General Service and Victory Medals.
"His life for his Country, his soul to God."
14, College Street, Kempston, Beds. Z2370/A.

WHITE, G., Private, Bedfordshire Regiment.
He joined in June 1916, and after a period of training was drafted to France in the following year. He took part in heavy fighting in various sectors, including the Battles of Arras and Vimy Ridge, and was wounded in action at Messines in June 1917. He was invalided home, and on recovery was employed at various camps in England until his discharge, as unfit for further service, in 1919. He holds the General Service and Victory Medals.
Sunnyside Cottage, West End, Cranfield, Beds. Z2365/B.

WHITE, H., Private, 19th Lancashire Fusiliers.
Volunteering in October 1914, he completed a period of training and service in England, and was drafted in October 1916 to France, where he took part in numerous important engagements, including those on the Somme and at Hill 60, Ypres, Arras and Cambrai, and was tiwce wounded. He was also in action during the Retreat and Advance of 1918. He holds the General Service and Victory Medals, and was demobilised in June 1919. The Haven, Blunham, Beds. Z2363.

WHITE, H., Private, Bedfordshire Regiment.
Mobilised from the Reserve in August 1914, he went through his training at various camps in England, and was drafted to the Western Front in the following year. In this theatre of war he took part in heavy fighting in various sectors, and was in action at the Battles of Hill 60, Ypres and Festubert. Wounded in 1916 he was invalided home, but returned to France, and was engaged on the Somme and at Arras and Cambrai, and was wounded on three further occasions. After treatment at hospitals in France he was eventually discharged in February 1919, and holds the 1914–15 Star, and the General Service and Victory Medals.
Sunnyside Cottage, West End, Cranfield, Beds. Z2365/C.

WHITE, J., L/Corporal, 2/5th East Surrey Regt.
He volunteered in September 1914, and was retained on special duties at various stations in England. He was not successful in obtaining his transfer to a theatre of war before the cessation of hostilities owing to his special qualifications, but, nevertheless, rendered valuable services until his demobilisation in January 1919. Moulsoe, Bucks. Z2372.

WHITE, J., Sapper, Royal Engineers.
He was mobilised at the outbreak of war in August 1914, and during the first part of his service was for a time stationed at Darlington. He was, however, drafted to France in 1916, and served on the Somme and at Cambrai, and later, during the Retreat of 1918. He holds the General Service and Victory Medals, and was eventually demobilised in February 1919.
8, Marlborough Road, Bedford. Z1122/E.

WHITE, M., Corporal, 2nd Bedfordshire Regiment.
Mobilised in August 1914, he was retained at various stations in England during the first part of his service, and was drafted to the Western Front in January 1916. There he played a prominent part in many engagements, including the Somme Offensive of 1916, and was wounded and invalided to England. He returned to France in due course, but was unhappily killed in action on the Menin Road in December 1917. He was entitled to the General Service and Victory Medals.
"A valiant Soldier, with undaunted heart he breasted life's last hill."
67, Ford End Road, Bedford. TZ2364/A.

WHITE, O. A., Pte., 1/1st London Regt. (R. Fus.)
He joined in April 1918, and, after undergoing a period of training, was drafted to Egypt in February 1919, and was sationed at Alexandria and Cairo. He was engaged on important garrison duties, and, returning to England in 1920, was demobilised in April of that year. 37, Bletsoe, Bedford. Z2371.

WHITE, P., Pte., 8th (King's Royal Irish) Hussars.
He was already serving in the Army at the outbreak of war in August 1914, and was immediately sent to the Western Front, where he took part in many important engagements in various sectors. He was in action at the Battles of Ypres, Arras, Vimy Ridge, the Somme and Cambrai, and after the cessation of hostilities proceeded to Germany, where he served with the Army of Occupation on the Rhine. He returned to England for discharge in March 1919, and holds the 1914 Star, and the General Service and Victory Medals.
67, Ford End Road, Bedford. TZ2364/B.

WHITE, P. R., Private, 2/5th Bedfordshire Regt.
He volunteered in 1915, and, after a period of training, was drafted to the Eastern theatre of war in the following year. There he was in action at many important engagements, both in Egypt and Palestine, and was present at the taking of Jerusalem and Jaffa, and was wounded. He holds the General Service and Victory Medals, and was demobilised in April 1919, after his return home.
Houghton Conquest, near Ampthill, Beds. Z2378/B.

WHITE, R., Air Mechanic, Royal Air Force.
He joined in May 1917, but owing to his being medically unfit for service in a theatre of war was retained on special duties at important aerodromes in England. He, nevertheless, rendered valuable services until the cessation of hostilities, and was demobilised in November 1919.
4, St. Leonard's Street, Bedford. X2373/B.

WHITE, R. E., Gunner (Signaller), R.G.A.
Joining in October 1916, he was sent to France in June 1917, after a period of training, and was in action with his Battery at many important engagements. He took part in much heavy fighting in various sectors, including Ypres, Passchendaele and Arras, and rendered valuable services during the Advance of 1918. He proceeded to Germany after the Armistice, and did duty with the Army of Occupation on the Rhine. Demobilised in November 1919, he holds the General Service and Victory Medals.
8, Brooklands Road, Bletchley, Bucks. TZ4486/B.

WHITE, S. W., Private, 7th Wiltshire Regiment.
He volunteered in August 1914, and, after undergoing a period of training, was drafted to the Western Front in September 1915. He saw much heavy fighting on the Somme before being transferred to Salonika in the following month. He then served on the Vardar and Doiran fronts, but was reported missing, and later presumed killed in action, on April 24/25th, 1917. He was entitled to the 1914–15 Star, and the General Service and Victory Medals.
"His memory is cherished with pride."
8, Brooklands Road, Bletchley, Bucks. TZ4486/A.

WHITE, T., Corporal, Royal Fusiliers.
He volunteered in August 1914, and, after a course of training, and service in England, was drafted to the Western Front in 1916. In this theatre of war he played a prominent part in many important engagements, including those on the Somme and at Ypres. He was missing after heavy fighting at St. Eloi in March 1917, and was later officially reported killed in action. He was entitled to the General Service and Victory Medals.
"Whilst we remember, the sacrifice is not in vain."
14, College Street, Kempston, Beds. Z2370/C.

WHITE, W., Private, Bedfordshire Regiment.
Volunteering in August 1914, he underwent a period of training at Bedford and Bury St. Edmunds, but unfortunately contracted an illness, from the effects of which he unhappily died on January 15th, 1915.
"His memory is cherished with pride."
Sunnyside Cottage, West End, Cranfield, Beds. Z2365/A.

WHITE, W., Engine-room Artificer, Royal Navy.
He joined in January 1918, and was engaged on patrol duties on board H.M. T.B.D. "Starfish" in the North Sea, where he served for three months. He was subsequently stationed at Harwich, and did good work on the repair of ships damaged in action. He holds the General Service and Victory Medals, and was demobilised in July 1919.
15, Coventry Road, Bedford. X2369.

WHITE, W. A., Private, Beds. and Suffolk Regts.
Mobilised at the outbreak of war in August 1914, he was immediately drafted to France, where he took part in the Retreat from Mons. He was also in action at numerous subsequent engagements, and saw much heavy fighting at Ypres, Hill 60, Albert, the Somme, Arras, Passchendaele and Cambrai. He continued his service until the cessation of hostilities, and was discharged in December 1918, holding the Mons Star, and the General Service and Victory Medals.
12, Swiss Cottage, Castle Lane, Bedford. X2375.

WHITEHEAD, J., Private, Oxford. & Bucks. L.I.
Joining in March 1916, he was later drafted to the Western Front, and took part in much heavy fighting in various sectors. He served on the Somme, Arras and Ypres fronts until 1918, when he was taken seriously ill in November and sent into hospital at Rouen. He was eventually invalided to England, and was demobilised in March 1919, holding the General Service and Victory Medals.
19, Chalk Lane, Marefair, Northampton. TZ2381/A.

WHITEHEAD, J. C., Private, 7th Wiltshire Regt.
He volunteered in August 1914, and, after a period of training, was drafted to France in September of the following year. There he was engaged as a driver in the Transport Section of his unit, and did good work on the Albert front in 1915. He was transferred to Salonika in November 1915, and served on the Doiran and Vardar fronts. Returning to France in May 1918, he was present at the heavy fighting at Amiens, Le Cateau and Normal Forest during the final Advance in this theatre of war, and holds the 1914–15 Star, and the General Service and Victory Medals. He was demobilised in April 1919.
19, Park Road, Stony Stratford, Bucks. TZ2381/B.

WHITEHOUSE, R. A., Air Mechanic, R.A.F.
He joined in December 1916, and, after a course of training on Salisbury Plain, was drafted to France in June 1917. There he did much good work as a fitter and rigger in the aeroplane shops at Lyons, Calais and Nancy, and, returning to England, was demobilised in March 1919, holding the General Service and Victory Medals.
Main Street, Hartford. Z2587/A—Z2588/A.

WHITEMAN, A. G. (M.M.), Company Sergeant-Major, Royal Sussex Regiment.
He volunteered in September 1914, and, after being employed at various stations in England during the first portion of his service, was drafted to the Western Front in 1916. There he took a distinguished part in the heavy fighting at Ypres, Arras and Cambrai, and was awarded the Military Medal for conspicuous bravery and devotion to duty in the Field on September 27th, 1916, at Tower Hamlets. He also holds the General Service and Victory Medals, and was demobilised in February 1919. High Street, Blunham, Beds. Z2382.

WHITEMAN, C. C., Private, 1/4th Essex Regt.
He volunteered in 1915, and, after a period of training, was drafted to the Eastern theatre of war in June 1916. He saw much active service in Egypt and Palestine, and took part in many important engagements, including the Battles of Gaza, the capture of Jerusalem and Jaffa, and was wounded. He holds the General Service and Victory Medals, and was demobilised in July 1919, after his return home.
10, Bell Court, Bedford. X2383.

WHITEMAN, J., Sapper, Royal Engineers.
He joined in February 1916, and later in the same year was sent to France, where he was engaged on special duties in various sectors of the front. He did good work on the Somme and at Ypres, Arras, Passchendaele and Cambrai, and served during the Retreat and Advance of 1918. He holds the General Service and Victory Medals, and was demobilised in September 1919. 32, Salisbury Street, Bedford. X2384.

WHITEMAN, W. (sen.), Private, Northants. Regt.
Volunteering in August 1914, he underwent a period of training and was drafted to the Western Front in September of the following year. Unhappily, after taking part in many important engagements in various sectors, he made the supreme sacrifice on September 27th, 1915, being killed in action at the Battle of Loos. He was entitled to the 1914–15 Star, and the General Service and Victory Medals.
"A costly sacrifice upon the altar of freedom."
Lower Dean, Kimbolton, Hunts. Z2380/A.

WHITEMAN, W. (jun.), Pte., Buffs (East Kent Regt).
He joined in 1916, and, completing his training, was drafted to the Western Front in the following year. In this theatre of war he took part in numerous engagements, notably in much heavy fighting on the Somme and at Arras, Ypres and Cambrai, but was on March 26th, 1918, unhappily killed in action during the Retreat of that year. He was entitled to the General Service and Victory Medals.
"Great deeds cannot die."
Lower Dean, Kimbolton, Hunts. Z2380/B.

WHITFIELD, E. E., Pte., 1st Oxford. & Bucks. L.I.
He was called up from the Reserve at the outbreak of war in August 1914, and was drafted to France in April 1915 after a course of training. There he took part in much heavy fighting at Hill 60 and in the Ypres salient, but was reported missing after an engagement at Ypres, and later officially declared killed in action on May 5th, 1915. He was entitled to the 1914–15 Star, and the General Service and Victory Medals.
"His memory is cherished with pride."
23, School Street, New Bradwell, Bucks. Z2385.

WHITING, A., Private, 3rd Devonshire Regiment.
He joined in June 1918, but owing to his being medically unfit for service overseas, was retained on special duties with his unit at important stations in England. He suffered from a serious illness, and after six months' treatment in hospital was eventually demobilised in April 1919.
High Street, Stoke Goldington, Bucks. Z1330/A.

WHITING, A. J., Private, Bedfordshire Regiment.
He volunteered in August 1914, and after a period of training was drafted to France in the following year. In this theatre of war he saw heavy fighting at Loos, Arras and on the Somme, and in 1917 was transferred to Italy, where he was in action on the Piave and Asiago fronts. Returning to England he was demobilised in March 1919, and holds the 1914–15 Star, and the General Service and Victory Medals.
44, St. Paul's Road, Bedford. Z2386.

WHITING, E. A., Private, 2nd Bedfordshire Regt.
Volunteering in December 1915, he completed his training at Bedford, and was drafted to France in March 1916. In this theatre of war he took part in many important engagements, including the Battles of the Somme, Ypres and Cambrai, and was wounded and taken prisoner in March 1918 during the Retreat. He was repatriated after the Armistice, and was eventually demobilised in March 1919, holding the General Service and Victory Medals.
88, Wolverton Road, Stony Stratford. Z2631/B.

WHITING, F. J., Private, Royal Fusiliers.
Mobilised at the outbreak of war in August 1914, he was immediately drafted to France, and took part in the Battle of Mons. He was also in action at numerous subsequent engagements, including the Battles of the Marne and La Bassée, and was wounded at Ypres. He was invalided home, but was in October 1915 drafted to Salonika, where he saw service on the Vardar and Doiran fronts. He returned to the Western Front in October 1918, and took part in the concluding stages of the great Advance. He holds the Mons Star, and the General Service and Victory Medals, and was discharged in March 1919.
13, Greenfield Road, Newport Pagnell, Bucks. Z2389.

WHITING, F. W., L/Corporal, Northants Regt.
He volunteered in September 1914, and was shortly afterwards drafted to the Western Front, where he took part in many engagements of importance. He was in action in the Ypres, Somme and Cambrai sectors, and was wounded, but later served during the Retreat and Advance of 1918. He proceeded to Germany after the cessation of hostilities, and did duty with the Army of Occupation until his return to England for demobilisation in March 1919. He holds the 1914 Star, and the General Service and Victory Medals.
The Fields, Stoke Goldington, Bucks. Z2390/B.

WHITING, H. W., Private, Oxford. & Bucks. L.I.
He joined in January 1916, and six months later was drafted to France, where he took part in many important engagements. He saw heavy fighting on the Somme and at Arras and Cambrai, and made the supreme sacrifice on October 25th, 1918, being killed in action during the Advance of that year. He was entitled to the General Service and Victory Medals.
"He died the noblest death a man may die."
The Fields, Stoke Goldington, Bucks Z2390/C.

WHITING, J. W., Gunner, R.G.A.
Joining in July 1916 he underwent a period of training and proceeded to Gibraltar in September of the following year. There he was engaged on important garrison and other duties for six months, and finally returned to England, and was demobilised in February 1919, holding the General Service Medal. Gayhurst, Newport Pagnell, Bucks. Z2387.

WHITING, T. G., Private, Oxford. & Bucks. L.I.
He joined in March 1916, and after a period of training was drafted to France in July of the same year. He took part in many severe engagements on the Somme, and was badly wounded in 1916. He was invalided to England and underwent five operations during the 12 months he was confined to hospital. He was eventually discharged from hospital, and until his demobilisation in March 1919, was employed in driving steam ploughs. He holds the General Service and Victory Medals. The Fields, Stoke Goldington, Bucks. Z2390/A.

WHITING, W. J., Private, Royal Berkshire Regt.
He volunteered in October 1915, and after completing a period of training, was drafted to France in March of the following year. After taking part in heavy fighting in various sectors of the front, including the Ypres salient, he was unhappily killed in action on November 30th, 1917, at the Battle of Cambrai. He was entitled to the General Service and Victory Medals.
"Fighting for God and right and liberty."
Dawkes Terrace, Stoke Goldington, Bucks. Z2388.

WHITING, W. P., Stoker Petty Officer, R.N.
He was already serving in the Royal Navy at the outbreak of war in August 1914, and did duty in H.M. Ships "Russell" and "Garth." He took part in operations at the Dardanelles, and was engaged in the landing of troops on the Gallipoli Peninsula in 1915. He was also employed on mine-sweeping duties in the North and Baltic Seas, and in March 1920 was discharged. He holds the 1914–15 Star, and the General Service and Victory Medals.
14, Gratton Road, Queen's Park, Bedford. Z2391.

WHITLOCK, C., Private, Somerset Light Infantry.
Joining in June 1917, he completed his training, and was drafted to France six months later. There he took part in many important engagements, and saw much heavy fighting on the Somme and Cambrai fronts, but was unhappily killed in August 1918 whilst in action on the Somme during the Advance of that year. He was entitled to the General Service and Victory Medals.
"The path of duty was the way to glory."
9, Beaconsfield Place, Newport Pagnell. Z1851/B.

WHITLOCK, E. A., Sergeant, 2/1st London Regiment (Royal Fusiliers).
He volunteered in January 1915, and later in the same year was drafted to the Western Front, where he played a distinguished part in the fighting in many sectors, particularly at the Battles of the Somme, Ypres, Arras and Cambrai, and was wounded in action and gassed. He was demobilised in March 1919, and holds the 1914–15 Star, and the General Service and Victory Medals. Turvey, Beds. Z2393/C.

WHITLOCK, E. R., Private, 5th Bedfordshire Regiment and Royal Fusiliers.
Volunteering in February 1915, he completed a period of training, and was drafted to France in the following year. There he was in action in many engagements of importance, including the Battles of Ypres, the Somme, Vimy Ridge, Passchendaele and Cambrai, and suffered from gas-poisoning. He holds the General Service and Victory Medals, and was demobilised in February 1919.
Near George Bridge, Eaton Socon, Beds. Z2392.

WHITLOCK, F. B., Farrier, 15th Hussars.
He volunteered in 1915, and after completing a period of training was sent to France in the following year. He did good work in this theatre of war as a shoeing-smith, and was stationed for the greater part of his service at Rouen. After the Armistice, however, he proceeded to Germany, where he did duty with the Army of Occupation on the Rhine, and was demobilised in March 1920, holding the General Service and Victory Medals. Turvey, Beds. Z2393/B.

WHITLOCK, G. H. (M.M.), Corporal, 4th Middlesex Regiment.
Mobilised at the outbreak of war in August 1914, he was immediately drafted to the Western Front, and played a prominent part in the Battle of Mons. He was taken prisoner on August 28th, 1914, but after suffering many hardships in captivity, escaped after 3½ years' confinement. He was awarded the Military Medal for conspicuous bravery, and holds also the Mons Star, and the General Service and Victory Medals. He was discharged in 1919. Turvey, Beds. Z2393/A.

WHITLOCK, H., Pioneer, Royal Engineers.
He joined in September 1916, and after training at Colchester and Sittingbourne, was drafted to the Western Front in March 1917. He was present at many engagements of importance, and rendered valuable services in various sectors until the cessation of hostilities. He was demobilised in February 1919, and holds the General Service and Victory Medals.
Dock Cottage, Towcester, Northants. Z4487/B.

WHITLOCK, T., Private, Labour Corps.
Joining in June 1916, he was retained on special agricultural work in various parts of the country, but owing to physical unfitness was not successful in obtaining his transfer to a theatre of war. He, nevertheless, rendered valuable services, and was demobilised in February 1919.
Dock Cottages, Towcester, Northants. Z4487/A.

WHITMEE, E., Bombardier, R.F.A.
He volunteered in August 1914, and after completing a period of training on Salisbury Plain, was drafted to the Western Front in 1916. He rendered valuable services in this theatre of war, and was in action with his Battery on the Somme and Ancre, and also at the Battles of Messines and Lens. He was demobilised in March 1919, and holds the General Service and Victory Medals.
West End, Brampton, Hunts. TZ2394/A.

WHITMEE, H. R., Sergeant, Machine Gun Corps.
He joined in 1916, and served in the Balkans, where he was in action with the armoured cars on the Vardar and other fronts. He also saw service in Mesopotamia and Russia with the Armoured Car Section. Returning home, he was demobilised in February 1919, and holds the General Service and Victory Medals. West End, Brampton, Hunts. TZ2394/B.

WHITMORE, B. S., Private, 1st Norfolk Regt.
Mobilised from the Reserve in October 1914, he first served with his unit at important stations in England, and was not drafted to France until 1917. There he took part in many important engagements, including Arras and Passchendaele, and was badly wounded at Bazencourt. He unfortunately died at the 56th Casualty Clearing Station Hospital on August 23rd, 1918, from his injuries. He was entitled to the General Service and Victory Medals.
"His memory is cherished with pride."
31, Gladstone Street, Bedford. X2395.

WHITMORE, T., Private, R.A.S.C.
He joined in July 1916, and was drafted to France in the following year. There he was engaged on important transport duties, particularly in taking supplies to forward areas in various sectors, notably Ypres, the Somme, Arras and Cambrai. He was demobilised in April 1919, and holds the General Service and Victory Medals. 35, Chandos Street, Bedford. X2396.

WHITMORE, W. T., Private, 11th Essex Regiment.
Volunteering in December 1915, he completed a period of training, and was drafted to the Western Front in the following year. In this theatre of war he took part in many important engagements, including the Battles of St. Quentin, Loos, La Bassée and Bullecourt, and was wounded at Vaux in February 1918. He was also injured by an aeroplane bomb. He was demobilised in January 1919, and holds the General Service and Victory Medals.
10, Leys Cottages, Clapham, Bedford. Z2398.

WHITTEMORE, A. V., Private, 16th (The Queen's) Lancers.
Mobilised at the outbreak of war in August 1914, he was immediately drafted to the Western Front, where he took part in the Battle of Mons. He was also in action at numerous subsequent engagements, including the Battles of Loos, Festubert, the Somme, Ypres, Arras and Cambrai. He rendered valuable services during the course of hostilities, and was discharged in April 1919, holding the Mons Star, and the General Service and Victory Medals.
Luke Street, Eynesbury, St. Neots, Hunts. Z2399/B.

WHITTEMORE, G. J., Corporal, Bedfordshire Regt.
He joined in May 1916, and was drafted to France after a period of training. In this theatre of war he played a prominent part in the fighting in important sectors, was in action at the Battles of the Somme, Ypres, Lens and Cambrai, and was wounded at St. Quentin in 1916. He holds the General Service and Victory Medals, and in 1920 was serving with his unit in India.
The Grovage, Park Hall Road, Somersham, Hunts. Z1596/A.

WHITTEMORE, R., Private, Essex Regiment.
Joining in October 1916, he was retained on special duties at various camps in England owing to his being medically unfit for service in a theatre of war. He, nevertheless, did consistently good work in guarding prisoners, and later was employed on the land at Boxted. He was demobilised in September 1919.
Luke Street, Eynesbury, St. Neots, Hunts. Z2399/A.

WHITTINGTON, H., Gunner, R.G.A.
He joined in 1917, and later in the same year was drafted to France, where he was in action with his Battery at Ypres and Cambrai and in many important engagements until the cessation of hostilities. He then proceeded to Germany, and did duty with the Army of Occupation on the Rhine until his return to England for demobilisation in 1919. He holds the General Service and Victory Medals. Marston, Beds. Z2400.

WHITWORTH, H. J., Air Mechanic, R.A.F.
He joined in July 1917, and later in the same year was sent to France, where he was engaged on important duties which called for a high degree of technical skill. He rendered valuable services in workshops behind the line until the cessation of hostilities, and was demobilised in January 1920, holding the General Service and Victory Medals.
33, Marlborough Road, Queen's Park, Bedford. Z2401/B.

WHITWORTH, R., Corporal, Royal Engineers.
He volunteered in January 1915, and six months later proceeded to the Western Front, where he was attached to the Signalling Section and played a prominent part in many engagements. He saw active service at Loos, the Somme, Ypres, Arras and Cambrai, and did consistently good work on the lines of communication. Demobilised in June 1919, he holds the 1914–15 Star, and the General Service and Victory Medals.
33, Marlborough Road, Queen's Park, Bedford. Z2401/A.

WHORNE, H., Sergeant, Bedfordshire Regiment.
He was already serving with the Colours at the outbreak of war in August 1914, and was immediately sent to the Western Front, where he played a distinguished part in the Battle of Mons and many subsequent engagements of importance. He was invalided to England in March 1916, suffering from gas-poisoning, and on recovery did consistently good work training recruits and carrying out guard duties at prisoners of war camps in England. He was discharged in March 1919, and holds the Mons Star, and the General Service and Victory Medals.
2, Castle Street, Bedford. X1981/B.

WHYTON, F. W., Pte., 7th Gloucestershire Regt.
Volunteering in October 1915, he completed a period of training and was sent to Mesopotamia in March 1916. He took part in many important engagements prior to the Relief of Kut, and saw much subsequent fighting in this theatre of war. He returned to England suffering from sunstroke, and was eventually discharged in October 1916 as unfit for further service, holding the General Service and Victory Medals.
Hill Cottage, Gawcott, Buckingham. Z2402.

WICKHAM, W. J. W., Cpl., 9th Rifle Brigade.
Mobilised at the outbreak of war in August 1914, he underwent a period of training and was drafted to the Western Front in May of the following year. There he played a prominent part in the heavy fighting at Ypres, and made the supreme sacrifice on August 2nd, 1915, being killed in action at Hooge He was entitled to the 1914–15 Star, and the General Service and Victory Medals.
"Thinking that remembrance, though unspoken, may reach him where he sleeps."
24, Althorp Street, Bedford. X2403.

WILDER, C., Sapper, Royal Engineers.
He volunteered in February 1915, but, being unfit for service in a theatre of war, was unable to obtain his transfer overseas. He, nevertheless, did consistently good work at various stations in England whilst attached to a Field and Signalling Company, and was demobilised in March 1919.
9, White Hart Road, Slough, Bucks. X2404.

WILDMAN, C., Trooper, 1st Bedfordshire Lancers and Private, Machine Gun Corps.
Volunteering in September 1914, he underwent a period of training, and was drafted to the Western Front in June 1915. There he took part in many important engagements, including those of the Somme and the Battles of Ypres, Arras and Cambrai. He also rendered valuable services during the Retreat and Advance of 1918, and after the Armistice proceeded to Germany, where he did duty with the Army of Occupation on the Rhine. He was demobilised in March 1919, and holds the 1914–15 Star, and the General Service and Victory Medals.
High Street, Pavenham, Bedford. Z2405/B.

WILDMAN, H. G., Staff-Sergeant, R.G.A.
He volunteered in August 1914, and did consistently good work at various camps in England during the first part of his service, but was drafted to France in September 1917. He was soon in action at Ypres, and, after much severe fighting, was taken prisoner at Cambrai on November 30th, 1917. He was repatriated after the Armistice and eventually demobilised in December 1918, holding the General Service and Victory Medals.
2, Tavistock Place, Bedford. X2408.

WILDMAN, J. H., Private, 5th Bedfordshire Regt.
Volunteering in November 1914, he completed a period of training, and was drafted to France in August of the following year. There he saw much severe fighting in various sectors, and was in action at the Battle of Loos before being wounded in October 1915 He was invalided home, and eventually discharged in 1916 as unfit for further service, and holds the 1914–15 Star, and the General Service and Victory Medals.
High Street, Pavenham, near Bedford. Z2405/A.

WILDMAN, P. E., Private, 5th Bedfordshire Regt.
Mobilised at the outbreak of war in August 1914, he was attached to the Cyclist Battalion of the 5th Bedfordshire Regiment and was drafted to France, where he took part in many important engagements. He was transferred to the Dardanelles in 1915, and saw much heavy fighting on the Gallipoli Peninsula, including the Landing at Suvla Bay. He also saw service in Palestine in 1917, and was in action at the Battles of Gaza and at the entry into Jerusalem and Damascus. He holds the 1914–15 Star, and the General Service and Victory Medals, and was demobilised in June 1919.
40, Cavendish Street, Bedford. X2406.

WILDMAN, W. E., Sapper, Royal Engineers.
He volunteered in October 1914, and, completing a period of training, was drafted to France in the following year. He was present at engagements at Festubert, Loos, Vimy Ridge and Ypres, and was wounded and gassed at Delville Wood in May 1916, when he was invalided to England and discharged in March 1917 as unfit for further service. He holds the 1914–15 Star, and the General Service and Victory Medals.
13, Little Thurlow Street, Bedford. X2407.

WILES, A., Pte., 1/5th Royal Warwickshire Regt.
He joined in 1916, and, after undergoing a period of training, was drafted to France in the following year. He was, however, sent to Italy shortly afterwards, and, being taken ill with influenza, died in hospital in that theatre of war on October 15th, 1918. He was entitled to the General Service and Victory Medals.
"His memory is cherished with pride."
High Street, Sandy, Beds. Z2409.

WILES, A., Drummer, 1/5th Bedfordshire Regt.
He volunteered in August 1914, and, after a period of training, was drafted to the Dardanelles in July 1915. He was in action at the Landing at Suvla Bay, and was invalided to England with dysentery. Recovering, he was sent to the Eastern theatre of war, and saw much service in Egypt and Palestine, and took part in the fighting at Gaza and on the Jordan. He holds the 1914–15 Star, and the General Service and Victory Medals, being demobilised in May 1919.
Longfield, St. Neots Road, Sandy, Beds. Z2410/A.

WILES, E. J., Private, Manchester Regiment.
Joining in February 1916, he completed a period of training before being sent to India in January of the following year, and was engaged on important garrison duties. Later he did duty in China and Russia and rendered valuable services until his return to England for demobilisation in December 1919. He holds the General Service and Victory Medals.
Longfield Road, Sandy, Beds. Z2412/B.

WILES, F., Gunner, Royal Field Artillery.
Mobilised in August 1914, he did consistently good work with his Battery during the early part of hostilities, and in 1916 was drafted to Salonika. There he was in action on the Struma and the Doiran and Vardar fronts, and rendered valuable services. He was, however, invalided home with malaria, and discharged in February 1919, holding the General Service and Victory Medals.
Longfield, St. Neots Road, Sandy, Beds. Z2410/B.

WILES, G. W., Private, Lancashire Fusiliers.
He joined in January 1917, and proceeded to France later in the same year. In this theatre of war he took part in many important engagements, including those at Ypres, the Somme, Arras and Cambrai, and was wounded. He also rendered valuable services as a stretcher-bearer, and suffered from trench feet. Demobilised in January 1919, he holds the General Service and Victory Medals. Cross Hall Ford, Beds. Z2411.

WILES, H., Private, 2/1st Norfolk Regiment.
He joined in 1917, and on completion of his training was retained on important duties with his unit at various stations in Ireland. He rendered valuable services, but was not successful in obtaining his transfer to a theatre of war, and was demobilised in November 1919.
Longfields Road, Sandy, Beds. Z2412/A.

WILKINS, C. C., Private, R.A.O.C.
He volunteered in October 1915, and was drafted to France in May of the following year. He did consistently good work in the Ypres and Somme sectors, and was transferred to Italy in November 1917. After serving on the Piave he returned to the Western Front in February 1918, and again saw service on the Somme. In 1920 he was still in the Army, and holds the General Service and Victory Medals.
6, South Terrace, Green's Norton, Towcester. Z4488/B.

WILKINS, J., Rifleman, 1st Cameronians (Scottish Rifles).
He enlisted in 1912, and at the outbreak of war in August 1914, was immediately drafted to the Western Front, where he was in action at Mons and during the subsequent Retreat. He also took part in the Battles of the Marne, La Bassée, Ypres, Festubert, the Somme and Passchendaele, and made the supreme sacrifice on May 25th, 1917, being killed in action at Arras. He was entitled to the Mons Star and the General Service and Victory Medals.
"And doubtless he went in splendid company."
6, South Terrace, Green's Norton, Towcester. Z4488/A.

WILKINSON, G., R.Q.M.S., Middlesex Regiment.
He enlisted in October 1900, and at the outbreak of war in August 1914 was immediately sent to France, where he played a distinguished part in the fighting during the Retreat from Mons. He later rendered valuable services at the Battles of the Somme, Arras, Passchendaele and Cambrai, serving with the Third Division from November 1915, and was wounded on two occasions. He was discharged in February 1920, and holds the Mons Star, and the General Service and Victory Medals.
56, New Fenlake, Bedford. Z2414.

WILKINSON, G. A., Private, Cheshire Regiment.
Mobilised at the outbreak of war in August 1914, he was at once drafted to France and took part in the Battle of Mons. He was also in action at Ypres, Festubert, Loos, Vimy Ridge, the Somme and Cambrai, and was reported missing during the Retreat of 1918, and presumed killed in action in March of that year. He was entitled to the General Service and Victory Medals.
"A valiant Soldier, with undaunted heart he breasted life's last hill."
6, Little Cuthbert's Square, Bedford. TX2413.

WILKINSON, H. H., Private, East Surrey Regt.
He volunteered in August 1914, and, after training at Devonport, was drafted to the Western Front in March 1915. He took part in much severe fighting in various sectors, and served at Ypres and on the Somme, where he was wounded in August 1916. He unfortunately died of his wounds in hospital at Abbeville in the following month, and was entitled to the 1914–15 Star, and the General Service and Victory Medals.
"His memory is cherished with pride."
7, South Terrace, Green's Norton, Towcester. Z4489

WILLETT, A., Private, Oxford. and Bucks. L.I.
He joined in June 1916, and later in the same year was drafted to France, where he was engaged in much heavy fighting on the Somme, Arras, Ypres and Cambrai fronts, and made the supreme sacrifice on October 23rd, 1918, being killed in action during the Advance of that year. He was entitled to the General Service and Victory Medals.
"He died the noblest death a man may die:
Fighting for God and right and liberty."
5, Vicarage Road, Old Bradwell, Bucks. Z2416/A.

WILLETT, F. F., Private, Devonshire Regiment.
He volunteered in February 1915, and after a period of training on Salisbury Plain was drafted to France in the following June. There he saw much heavy fighting on the Ypres, Somme and Arras fronts, and was attached to the transport section of his unit. He rendered valuable services, and was demobilised in March 1919, holding the 1914–15 Star, and the General Service and Victory Medals.
Marsh Farm, Great Linford. Z2415/A.

WILLETT, H. G., Sapper, Royal Engineers.
Joining in June 1917, he did consistently good work at various stations in England before proceeding to the Western Front in November 1918. He took part in the concluding engagements on the Cambrai front, and at one time served as a despatch rider. After the Armistice he was sent to Germany and did duty with the Army of Occupation on the Rhine. Demobilised in February 1920, he holds the General Service and Victory Medals.
Marsh Farm, Great Linford, Bucks. Z2415/B.

WILLETT, J., Private, Oxford. and Bucks. L.I.
He joined in June 1916, but, being medically unfit for service overseas, was retained on special duties in connection with agriculture. He, nevertheless, did consistently good work, and was demobilised in February 1916.
5, Vicarage Street, Old Bradwell, Bucks. Z2416/B.

WILLEY, T. W., Gunner, Royal Field Artillery.
He volunteered in December 1914, and, completing a period of training, was drafted to the Western Front in the following year. There he was in action with his Battery at the Battles of Ypres and Loos. In February 1916 he was transferred to the East, and saw service in Palestine. He was engaged in much severe fighting during the Advance in this theatre of war, taking part in the Battles of Gaza and Jaffa, and was then sent to Salonika, where he rendered valuable services on the Vardar and Bulgarian frontier in 1917. Returning to France in April 1918, he was in action during the Retreat, and was wounded in the Advance of that year. He holds the 1914–15 Star, and the General Service and Victory Medals, and was demobilised in May, 1919. 2, Church Street, Olney, Bucks. Z2417.

WILLIAMS, A., Private, 5th Bedfordshire Regt.
He volunteered in August 1914, but owing to physical unfitness was retained on special guard duties on the East Coast. He, nevertheless, rendered valuable services, and was discharged in December 1914 as unfit for military duties.
31, Pilcroft Street, Bedford. X2624/B.

WILLIAMS, F. (Miss), Special War Worker.
This lady volunteered her services in November 1915, and was engaged on special agricultural duties in Bedford. She did consistently good work until June 1917, when she relinquished the duties which she had carried out in a highly commendable manner. 31, Pilcroft Street, Bedford. X2624/E.

WILLIAMS, F. C., Corporal, R.A.M.C.
Volunteering in August 1914, he was quickly drafted to France, and first did consistently good work in a military hospital at Rouen. He later took an active part in heavy fighting on the Somme, Arras, Ypres and Cambrai fronts, and was wounded in action at Valenciennes. Demobilised in April 1919, he holds the 1914 Star, and the General Service and Victory Medals.
22, Great Butts Street, Bedford. X3929/A.

WILLIAMS, G. H., Private, Machine Gun Corps.
He joined in July 1916, and, after undergoing a period of training, was drafted to France in March of the following year. Whilst on the Western Front he took part in several important engagements, including those in the Arras, Ypres and Cambrai sectors, and was severely wounded in December 1917. As a result he was invalided from the Service in January 1918, and holds the General Service and Victory Medals.
11, King Street, Stony Stratford, Bucks. Z2418.

WILLIAMS, H., Sergeant, Norfolk Regiment.
He volunteered in July 1915, and was drafted to France in October of the following year. There he fought with distinction at the Battles of the Somme, Albert, Arras, Ypres and Passchendaele, and was wounded in February 1918. He was invalided to Scotland, and until his demobilisation in December 1919 did consistently good work as a Musketry Instructor and as a Provost Sergeant. He holds the General Service and Victory Medals.
Shepherds Lane, Towcester, Northants. Z4490.

WILLIAMS, H. S., Gunner, Tank Corps.
He volunteered in April 1915, and in the following year was drafted to France after a period of training as a Tank Gunner. He rendered valuable services in many sectors and served on the Somme and at Arras, Ypres and Cambrai, and was wounded. He also suffered from shell-shock, and was detained in hospital for 12 months before being eventually demobilised in January 1919. He holds the General Service and Victory Medals.
4, St. Ann's Terrace, Godmanchester, Hunts. Z2421.

WILLIAMS, O. R., Stoker, Royal Navy.
He volunteered in August 1914, and served on board H.M.S. "Express" in many waters. He rendered valuable services as a stoker throughout the period of hostilities, and was demobilised in 1919, holding the 1914–15 Star, and the General Service and Victory Medals.
Park Lane, Sharnbrook, Bedford. Z2629/B.

WILLIAMS, P., Private, Sherwood Foresters.
He volunteered in August 1914, and in the following year was drafted to the Western Front. There he took part in many important engagements, including the Battles of Ypres, Arras, the Somme and Cambrai, and was wounded at Hill 60. He also served on the Piave in Italy, to which theatre of war he was transferred in March 1918. He was demobilised in February 1919, holding the 1914–15 Star, and the General Service and Victory Medals. 31, Pilcroft, Bedford. X2624/C.

WILLIAMS, R., Private, Royal Defence Corps.
He volunteered in September 1915, and for 3½ years rendered valuable services with his unit. He was chiefly engaged on important guard duties at the prisoners of war camps at Sharnbrook, Radwell and Hunstanton, and was eventually demobilised in February 1919. 31, Pilcroft Street, Bedford. X2624/A.

WILLIAMS, S. E., Private, R.A.M.C.
Mobilised at the outbreak of war in August 1914, he was immediately drafted to France, where he took part in the Battle of Mons. He also rendered valuable services as a stretcher-bearer at subsequent engagements, including the Battles of the Marne, the Aisne and Ypres, and was present during much heavy fighting throughout the period of hostilities. He was demobilised in January 1919, and holds the Mons Star, and the General Service and Victory Medals.
36, Aylesbury Street, Wolverton, Bucks. Z2419.

WILLIAMS, W. E., Corporal, M.G.C.
Volunteering in February 1915, he underwent a period of training, and was drafted to France in the following year. There he took a prominent part in many engagements, including the Battles of the Somme, Ypres, Arras and Cambrai, and made the supreme sacrifice on April 16th, 1918, being killed in action at Hill 60. He was entitled to the General Service and Victory Medals.
"He joined the great white company of valiant souls."
Post Office, Cardington, Bedford. Z4241/A.

WILLIAMS, W. J., Corporal, M.G.C.
Joining in July 1916, he proceeded to France in the following year and played a prominent part in the fighting at numerous engagements. He was in action at the Battles of Ypres, Arras, Cambrai and Béthune, and rendered valuable services during the Retreat and Advance of 1918. He was sent to Germany after the Armistice, and did duty at Cologne with the Army of Occupation until his demobilisation in March 1920, holding the General Service and Victory Medals. Biddenham, Beds. Z2420.

WILLIAMSON, F., Private, 2nd Yorkshire Regt.
He joined in June 1917, and in April of the following year was sent to France, but, after heavy fighting in the Cambrai and Somme sectors, was wounded and taken prisoner during the Retreat in June 1918. He was repatriated in December, and demobilised in October 1919, holding the General Service and Victory Medals Bedford Rd., Great Barford, Beds. Z3851/B.

WILLIAMSON, G., Private, 2nd Bedfordshire Regiment and Hertfordshire Regiment.
He joined in July 1917, and, completing a period of training, was drafted to the Western Front in April 1918. He rendered valuable services at Cambrai and on the Somme, and, after the Armistice, proceeded to India, where he was in 1920 engaged on important garrison duties. He holds the General Service and Victory Medals.
Bedford Road, Great Barford, Beds. Z3851/A.

WILLIS, E., Private, Middlesex Regiment.
He volunteered in 1915, and, after a period of training, was drafted to the Western Front, where he took part in many engagements of importance, including the Battles of Hill 60, the Somme, Albert, Arras and Cambrai, and was wounded in action. He rendered valuable services, but was discharged in December 1918 as unfit for further military duties, and holds the 1914–15 Star, and the General Service and Victory Medals.
260, Bedford Road, Kempston, Bedford. X2422.

WILLIS, G., Driver, Royal Field Artillery.
He joined in October 1917, and, completing his training, was sent to France in April of the following year. There he was in action with his Battery at numerous engagements, including the Battle of Cambrai (II.) and the Retreat and Advance of 1918, during which he did consistently good work until the cessation of hostilities. He also served with the Army of Occupation on the Rhine, and was demobilised in July 1919, holding the General Service and Victory Medals.
8, Mount Pleasant, Fenny Stratford, Bucks. Z2425/B.

WILLIS, J., Sergeant, 2nd Bedfordshire Regiment.
Three months after volunteering in April 1915 he was drafted to the Western Front, and served with distinction at numerous engagements. He was in action at Ypres and during the Somme Offensive of 1916, and was badly wounded. He was invalided to England in consequence, and, after doing consistently good work until September 1919, embarked for India, where in 1920 he was still serving. He holds the 1914–15 Star, and the General Service and Victory Medals.
8, Mount Pleasant, Fenny Stratford, Bucks. Z2425/A

WILLIS, W., Private, Oxford. and Bucks. L.I.
He volunteered in November 1915, and, completing his training, was drafted to France in the following year. After taking part in various important engagements he was wounded at Vimy Ridge in 1917, but on his recovery proceeded to Salonika. There he was again in action, serving on the Vardar and Doiran fronts until 1918, when he was transferred to Egypt and Palestine. Returning to England, he was demobilised in October 1919, and holds the General Service and Victory Medals. Drayton Parslow, Bletchley, Bucks. Z4491.

WILLOWS, A., Shoeing-Smith, R.F.A.
He volunteered in May 1915, and in the following month proceeded to France, where he did consistently good work. He served on many fronts, including those of Festubert, Ypres and Loos, and was invalided to England on account of accidental injuries sustained whilst on transport work. Before his discharge in December 1917, he rendered valuable services in Ireland as a shoeing-smith. He holds the 1914–15 Star, and the General Service and Victory Medals.
17, St. Benedict's Court, Huntingdon. Z2423/A.

WILLOWS, E., Private, Army Cyclist Corps.
He volunteered in September 1914, and, after a period of training, was drafted to the Eastern theatre of war and saw service in Palestine. He was in action at the Battles of Gaza and Jaffa and in engagements on the Jordan until May 1918, when he was transferred to France. There he took part in much heavy fighting during the Advance of 1918, and was sent to Ireland at the cessation of hostilities. He was demobilised in February 1919, and holds the 1914–15 Star, and the General Service and Victory Medals.
17, St. Benedict's Court, Huntingdon. Z2423/B.

WILLOWS, E., Private, Army Cyclist Corps; and Trooper, 21st North Somerset Yeomanry.
He volunteered in August 1914, and, after completing his training, was drafted to the Dardanelles in March 1915. There he took part in much heavy fighting on the Gallipoli Peninsula, and, after the Evacuation, proceeded to Egypt in January 1916. He also saw service in Palestine, and was wounded near Gaza in 1917, but again went into action on recovery. He holds the 1914–15 Star, and the General Service and Victory Medals, and was demobilised in February 1919.
7, Royal Oak Passage, Huntingdon. Z2424

WILLS, A. C., Pte., 3rd Somerset Light Infantry.
He joined in July 1918, and, after a period of training, was drafted to France, where he served on the Somme during the Advance of that year. He was wounded in action, and in consequence was invalided home in October, and, after five months in hospital, served with the Military Foot Police in Ireland. He holds the General Service and Victory Medals, and was demobilised in September 1919.
Weston Underwood, Bucks. Z2427.

WILLS, J. G., Rifleman, King's Royal Rifle Corps.
He volunteered in October 1915, and, after doing consistently good work at various stations in England, was drafted to France in March 1918. There he took part in much heavy fighting during the Retreat and Advance of that year, and was severely wounded. He returned to England and was eventually discharged in April 1919 unfit for further service, having lost a leg by amputation. He holds the General Service and Victory Medals. Offord D'Arcy, Hunts. Z2426.

WILMOT, W. A., Private, 9th Northants. Regt.
Joining in October 1916, he was retained on special duties at important stations in England owing to his being unfit for service in a theatre of war. He, nevertheless, did consistently good work until the cessation of hostilities, and was demobilised in March 1919.
Fir Tree Cottage, Cardington, Bedford. Z2428.

WILSHER, W., Private, Bedfordshire Regiment.
Mobilised at the outbreak of war in August 1914, he proceeded to France in the following year, and took part in many important engagements, including the Battles of Ypres, Neuve Chapelle, the Somme, Arras and Cambrai. He later did good work in connection with the transport of food and ammunition, and was discharged time-expired in March 1918. He holds the 1914–15 Star, and the General Service and Victory Medals.
Bedford Road, Sandy, Beds. Z2429.

WILSON, A., Private, Middlesex Regiment.
Volunteering in 1915, he was retained with his unit on special duties at important stations in England. Owing to his being unfit for service overseas he was unable to obtain his transfer to a theatre of war, but, nevertheless, rendered valuable services until his demobilisation in February 1919.
Wyboston, Beds. Z1921/A.

WILSON, A., Private, Oxford. & Bucks. L.I.
Mobilised at the outbreak of war in August 1914, he was at once sent to the Western Front, where he took part in the Retreat from Mons. He was also in action at the Battles of the Marne, Festubert and Loos, and was wounded. He was evacuated to England, and after losing the sight of an eye as the result of his wounds, was discharged as physically unfit in October 1917. He holds the Mons Star, and the General Service and Victory Medals.
Hemingford Grey, Hunts. Z4157/B.

WILSON, A. D., Private, Machine Gun Corps.
He joined in June 1918, and three months later proceeded to France, where he was unfortunately badly wounded in October 1918, the first time he went into action. He was invalided home, and after hospital treatment in Nottingham, was discharged in 1919, holding the General Service and Victory Medals. Huntingdon Street, St. Neots, Hunts. Z2430/A.

WILSON, A. G., Guardsman, Grenadier Guards.
He was mobilised at the outbreak of war in August 1914, and after doing consistently good work as an orderly in England during the first part of his service, was drafted to France in September 1916. There he took part in much heavy fighting on the Somme before making the supreme sacrifice on November 16th, 1916, being killed in action at Trones Wood. He was entitled to the General Service and Victory Medals.
"And doubtless he went in splendid company."
Shop Yard, Great Linford, Bucks. Z4387/D.

WILSON, A. L., Private, King's Own Scottish Borderers.
He was already serving with the Colours in August 1914, and in the following year proceeded to the Western Front. There he took part in many important engagements, including the Battles of Ypres, Hill 60 and Arras, and was wounded at Delville Wood. He rendered valuable services, but on December 3rd, 1917, made the supreme sacrifice, being killed in action at Passchendaele. He was entitled to the 1914–15 Star, and the General Service and Victory Medals.
"Great deeds cannot die."
15, Muswell Road, South End, Bedford. Z2431/A.

WILSON, C., Drummer, 2nd Suffolk Regiment.
He was already serving in Ireland at the outbreak of war in August 1914, and was immediately drafted to France, where he took part in the Battle of Mons. He was also in action at La Bassée and Ypres, and was gassed during the Somme Offensive of 1916. He was sent to England for treatment, and was discharged as unfit in April 1917, but unhappily died on March 21st of the following year. He was entitled to the Mons Star, and the General Service and Victory Medals.
"His memory is cherished with pride."
Wyboston, Beds. Z2432.

WILSON, C., Sergeant, Canadian Overseas Forces.
He volunteered in January 1915, and, after a period of training, was drafted to France in February 1916. He served with distinction in various important sectors, and was in action at the Battles of Vimy Ridge, Ypres, Passchendaele and Cambrai. He rendered valuable services on the Western Front until 1918, when he returned to England, and was demobilised in March 1920, holding the General Service and Victory Medals.
14, Gravel Lane, Bedford. X2433.

WILSON, F., Corporal, Royal Fusiliers.
Mobilised at the outbreak of war in August 1914, he was drafted to the Western Front in the following year, and played a prominent part in many engagements of importance. He saw much heavy fighting in various sectors, and took part in the Battles of Ypres, Givenchy, Loos, the Somme, Bullecourt, Arras, Messines and Cambrai, and was slightly wounded in 1917. He was also in action during the Retreat and Advance of 1918, and was discharged in March 1919, holding the 1914–15 Star, and the General Service and Victory Medals.
Huntingdon Street, St. Neots, Hunts. Z2430/B.

WILSON, G., Private, Royal Defence Corps.
He volunteered in January 1916, but being unfit for service in a theatre of war was retained on special agricultural work in various parts of the country. He, nevertheless, rendered valuable services during the course of hostilities, and was demobilised in March 1919.
10, West Street, Olney, Bucks. TZ2434.

WILSON, G., Private, Dorsetshire Regiment.
He volunteered in September 1914, and after a period of training, was drafted to France in the following year. There he took part in many engagements of importance, and saw much heavy fighting in various sectors of the front. He rendered valuable services, and on October 12th, 1917, made the supreme sacrifice, being killed in action at Cambrai. He was entitled to the 1914–15 Star, and the General Service and Victory Medals.
"A costly sacrifice upon the altar of freedom."
224, Bedford Road, Kempston, Bedford. X2435.

WILSON, J., Private, Machine Gun Corps.
Volunteering in September 1914, he was shortly afterwards discharged as unfit, but re-enlisted in February 1915, and proceeded to France. He took part in many important engagements, including the Battles of Neuve Chapelle, Ypres, Festubert, the Somme and Givenchy, and later the Retreat and Advance of 1918. He rendered valuable services, and was transferred to the Army Reserve in 1919, holding the 1914–15 Star, and the General Service and Victory Medals.
24, West Street, Olney, Bucks. Z2436.

WILSON, J., Private, Bedfordshire Regiment.
He volunteered in June 1915, and was retained on special duties at important stations on the coast and elsewhere in England. Owing to being medically unfit, he was unable to obtain his transfer to a theatre of war, but, nevertheless, rendered valuable services until his discharge in March 1919.
3, Wellington Street, St. Ives, Hunts. Z2437.

WILSON, J. F., Gunner, Royal Field Artillery.
Volunteering in May 1916, he completed a course of training, and was drafted to the Western Front in December 1917. In this theatre of war he was in action with his Battery at many important engagements, including the Battles of Vimy Ridge, Ypres (III.), Arras and Passchendaele, and rendered valuable services. Demobilised in 1919, he holds the General Service and Victory Medals.
15, Muswell Road, South End, Bedford. Z2431/B.

WILSON, J. W., Pte., Australian Overseas Forces.
Volunteering in 1915, he proceeded to England from Australia, and was eventually drafted to France in December 1916. In this theatre of war he took part in much heavy fighting in various sectors, including those of Albert, the Somme, Ypres and Arras, but was unfortunately killed in action at Passchendaele on September 26th, 1917. He was entitled to the General Service and Victory Medals.
"His life for his Country, his soul to God."
17, Church Street, Olney, Bucks. Z3340/B.

WILSON, M., Air Mechanic, Royal Air Force.
He joined in August 1918, and was retained on special duties at various aerodromes in England. He was unable to obtain his transfer to a theatre of war on account of being over age, but nevertheless, did consistently good work until his demobilisation in February 1919.
13, Foster Street, Bedford. X2438.

WILSON, R. C., Private, Bedfordshire Regiment.
Joining in March 1916, he completed his training, and was drafted to France with the Bedfordshire Regiment in October 1916. There he took part in much heavy fighting on the Somme, Arras and Messines fronts, and was wounded at Ypres in September 1917. He was invalided home, and later was posted to the Royal Air Force, but again went into hospital on account of his wounds, and unhappily died on October 28th, 1918, after undergoing an operation. He was buried with full military honours at St. Neots, and was entitled to the General Service and Victory Medals.
"His memory is cherished with pride."
Huntingdon Street, St. Neots, Hunts. Z2430/C.

WILSON, T., Private, R.A.V.C.
He joined in May 1916, but owing to his being medically unfit for service overseas was retained on important duties in the care of horses at various camps in England. He, nevertheless, did consistently good work during the course of hostilities, and was demobilised in August 1919.
16, Duke Street, Aspley Guise, Beds. Z2439.

WINDER, H., Private, Army Cyclist Corps.
He was serving in India at the outbreak of war in August 1914, and immediately embarked for France. He took part in numerous engagements on his arrival on the Western Front, and was in action at the Battles of Ypres, Neuve Chapelle, Hill 60, Loos, the Somme, Arras, Passchendaele and Cambrai, and was taken prisoner during the Advance of 1918. He was repatriated after the cessation of hostilities, and finally discharged in January 1919, holding the 1914 Star, and the General Service and Victory Medals.
Cromwell Cottages, East Chadley Lane, Godmanchester, Hunts. Z2440.

WINFIELD, J. A., Private, Machine Gun Corps.
He volunteered in 1915, and was drafted to France after a period of training. From 1916 until the cessation of hostilities he saw much service in the Western theatre of war, and was in action with his unit at the Battles of Ypres, the Somme, Arras and Cambrai, and rendered valuable services. Demobilised in August 1919, he holds the General Service and Victory Medals. 8, St. Germain Street, Huntingdon. Z2441.

WINSOR, E. W., Rifleman, 1st Rifle Brigade.
He was called up from the Reserve in August 1914, and was immediately drafted to the Western Front, where he was in action at the Battle of Mons. After being wounded at Le Cateau he was taken prisoner in September 1914, and held in captivity for 3 years, 12 months of which were spent in Switzerland. He was eventually discharged in January 1918, and holds the Mons Star, and the General Service and Victory Medals. Whaddon Road, Bletchley, Bucks. Z4492.

WINTER, A. T., Private, Middlesex Regiment.
Volunteering in September 1915, he completed a period of training, and was drafted to Salonika in the following year. In this theatre of war he took part in many engagements on the Doiran and Struma fronts, and was wounded in action. He was invalided to France, and after a period in hospital at Le Havre, was in action during the Retreat and Advance of 1918. He holds the General Service and Victory Medals, and was demobilised in March 1919. Warboys, Hunts. Z2442.

WISE, H. E. C., Private, Oxford. and Bucks. L.I.
He volunteered in September 1914, and, completing his training, was drafted to France in September 1915, and served in the Loos sector until the end of the year. He was then transferred to Salonika and took part in important engagements on the Doiran front until July 1917, when he went into hospital. In July 1918 he was transferred to the Royal Irish Regiment, and rendered valuable services during the Advance in this theatre of war. He returned to England in January 1920, and was demobilised in March of that year, holding the 1914–15 Star, and the General Service and Victory Medals.
8, Oxford Street, Wolverton, Bucks. Z2445.

WISE, W., Private, 2/4th Oxford. and Bucks. L.I.
He volunteered in October 1915, and was drafted to France three months later. There he took part in many important engagements on the Somme, and at Ypres, Arras, Cambrai and St. Quentin, but was wounded and taken prisoner during the Retreat of March 1918. He was repatriated after the cessation of hostilities, and eventually demobilised in February 1919, holding the General Service and Victory Medals.
Chackmore, Buckingham. Z2443.

WOOD, H., Corporal, Royal Engineers.
He joined in April 1916, and two months later was drafted to France, where he was attached to the Railway Operative Department, and was engaged on important duties in connection with railroad construction. He did consistently good work on the Western Front for three years, and, returning to England, was demobilised in April 1919. He holds the General Service and Victory Medals.
44, Ledsam Street, Wolverton, Bucks. Z2446.

WOOD, T. W., Pte., Queen's (R. West Surrey Regt).
Volunteering in March 1915, he underwent a period of training, and was sent to France in January 1916. He fought in many engagements, and was wounded during the Offensive on the Somme in 1916 and sent to hospital. Recovering within six months, he was drafted to Mesopotamia, and served in the Advance on Baghdad. He suffered from fever in June 1918, and, after a further period in hospital, returned to England and was discharged in December 1918 as medically unfit. He holds the General Service and Victory Medals.
69, Caldecote Street, Newport Pagnell. Z2448.

WOOD, V. G., Pte., Queen's (R. West Surrey Regt).
He joined in April 1916, and trained at various camps in England before proceeding to the Western Front in February 1917. He was in action at the Battles of Ypres, the Somme, Arras, Lens and Bullecourt, but, owing to failing eyesight, was transferred to a Labour Battalion, and did consistently good work until his demobilisation in October 1919. He holds the General Service and Victory Medals.
43, College Road, Bedford. Z2447.

WOODCOCK, A., Private, 1st Bedfordshire Regt.
He was already serving with the Colours at the outbreak of war in August 1914, and was immediately drafted to the Western Front, where he took part in the Retreat from Mons. He was also in action at subsequent engagements of importance, including the Battles of Ypres and Arras, and made the supreme sacrifice on September 7th, 1915, being killed in action on the Somme front. He was entitled to the Mons Star, and the General Service and Victory Medals.
"Great deeds cannot die."
44, Russell Street, Bedford. X2449

WOODCROFT, A., Private, Bedfordshire Regt.
He volunteered in April 1915, and, after completing his training, was drafted to the Western Front, where he took part in many important engagements. He saw much heavy fighting in various sectors, and was in action at the Battles of Ypres, the Somme, Arras and Cambrai, and was wounded on three occasions—at Loos, during the Somme Offensive, and at Cambrai. He was eventually demobilised in January 1919, and holds the 1914–15 Star, and the General Service and Victory Medals. 35, Howbury Street, Bedford. Z2450.

WOODGATE, H. W., Corporal, Royal Engineers.
He volunteered in September 1914, and, completing his training, was drafted to the Western Front in the following December. He played an important part in engagements on various fronts, particularly at Neuve Chapelle, Loos, Albert, Amiens, Bapaume and on the Marne, but was invalided home through illness in October 1918. He holds the 1914–15 Star, and the General Service and Victory Medals, and was demobilised in February 1919. 51, Coventry Rd., Bedford. Z2451.

WOODHAM, C., Private, 2nd London Regiment (Royal Fusiliers).
Volunteering in September 1914, he did duty for a time at various stations in England, and was drafted to France in August 1916. He served through much heavy fighting on the Somme and at Beaumont-Hamel, Arras, Messines, Ypres and Lens, and was wounded in August 1917. He was invalided to England, and, after a period in hospital, was eventually discharged in August 1918 as unfit for further service. He holds the General Service and Victory Medals.
Stow Longa, Hunts. Z2454.

WOODHAM, F., Private, Bedfordshire Regiment.
He volunteered in May 1915, and was drafted to France in 1916 after a period of training. There he took part in many important engagements, and was in action on the Somme, Arras and Ypres fronts. He suffered from gas-poisoning, and later was invalided home with trench fever. On his recovery he was transferred to the Labour Corps, and did good work on agricultural duties until his demobilisation in March 1919. He hold sthe General Service and Victory Medals Melchbourne, Beds. Z2452.

WOODHAM, S. F., Private, Border Regiment.
Four months after joining in May 1916 he was drafted to Salonika, and saw much active service on the Struma and Doiran fronts, and took part in many important engagements during the Offensive in this theatre of war. He proceeded to Constantinople after the signing of the Armistice, and did duty with the Army of Occupation until his return to England for demobilisation in October 1919. He holds the General Service and Victory Medals. Tilbrook, Kimbolton, Hunts. Z2453.

WOODHAM, W., Private, Bedfordshire Regiment.
He volunteered in February 1915, and, after a period of training, was drafted to the Western Front in January 1916 In this theatre of war he took part in much severe fighting, and rendered valuable services on the Somme and at Loos and St. Eloi. He made the supreme sacrifice on October 18th, 1916, being killed in action at Albert. He was entitled to the General Service and Victory Medals.
"The path of duty was the way to glory."
Church Lane, Spaldwick, Hunts. Z2455.

WOODING, A. L., Pte., 8th Oxford. & Bucks. L.I.
Volunteering in September 1914, he underwent a course of training, and was sent to Salonika in September of the following year. There he was engaged on important transport duties, and did consistently good work on the Vardar and Doiran fronts until the cessation of hostilities. He returned to England and was demobilised in March 1919, holding the 1914–15 Star, and the General Service and Victory Medals.
Harrold Road, Lavendon, Bucks. Z2457.

WOODING, C. H. (M.M.), Private, King's Own Scottish Borderers.
He was mobilised at the outbreak of war in August 1914, and was immediately drafted to the Western Front, where he took part in the Retreat from Mons. He was also in action at the Battles of La Bassée, Festubert, Loos, Messines and Cambrai, and was wounded on the Somme and at Ypres. He was awarded the Military Medal for conspicuous bravery and devotion to duty, and was discharged in April 1919, holding also the Mons Star, and the General Service and Victory Medals.
25, Union Street, Bedford. X2456.

WOODING, G., Private, 53rd Royal Sussex Regt.
He joined in September 1918, and, after undergoing a period of training, was sent to Germany, where he was engaged on garrison and other duties with the Army of Occupation at Cologne from January 1919 until February 1920. He returned to England and was demobilised in March of the latter year. 36, Grey Friars Walk, Bedford. X2461.

WOODING, J., Private, Machine Gun Corps.
He volunteered in October 1915, and, after a period of training with the Bedfordshire Regiment, was drafted to the Western Front in July of the following year. There he rendered valuable services with the Machine Gun Corps, saw much heavy fighting at Ypres, Vimy Ridge, the Somme and Bapaume, and was wounded in action at Arras in April 1917. He holds the General Service and Victory Medals, and was demobilised in June 1919.
Taggs End, Wootton, Bedford. Z2458.

WOODING, J. H., Private, 11th Royal Fusiliers.
He joined in 1916, and, after training at Tring, was drafted to France later in the same year. He took part in much heavy fighting in various sectors, was in action at the Battles of the Ancre, Arras, Messines and Ypres, and was wounded at Albert during the Somme Offensive. He was invalided home an discharged as unfit for further service in March 1917, and holds the General Service and Victory Medals.
Rectory Lane, Houghton Conquest, near Bedford. Z2462.

WOODING, W., Sapper, Royal Engineers.
He volunteered in May 1915, and was drafted to the Western Front in the following year. In this theatre of war he rendered valuable services, and did consistently good work on the Somme and at Neuve Chapelle, Ypres, Arras and Albert until the cessation of hostilities. Demobilised in September 1919, he holds the General Service and Victory Medals.
25, Salisbury Street, Bedford. X2459.

WOODING, W. H., Pte., 4th Oxford. & Bucks. L.I.
Joining in October 1916, he completed a course of training, and was sent to the Western Front in March 1917. There he took part in the heavy fighting in many sectors, and rendered valuable services at Arras and the third Battle of Ypres. He made the supreme sacrifice on September 29th, 1917, being killed in action at Messines. He was entitled to the General Service and Victory Medals.
"His life for his Country, his soul to God."
Olney Road, Lavendon, Bucks. Z2460.

WOODLAND, R., Private, Bedfordshire Regiment.
He joined in February 1916, and did consistently good work at various stations in England until December, when he was drafted to India. There he was engaged on important garrison and other duties for nearly three years, and rendered valuable services with his unit. Returning to England in 1919, he was demobilised in December of that year, and holds the General Service and Victory Medals. Wootton, Bedford. Z2463.

WOODRUFF, J. H. T., Pte., 1/5th Beds. Regt.
He was mobilised at the outbreak of war in August 1914, and after serving in England for a time, was drafted to the East, where he saw service in Egypt. He took part in much heavy fighting, but owing to ill-health was invalided to England in December 1915, and was discharged in April 1917 as unfit for further service. He holds the General Service and Victory Medals. 76, Westbourne Road, Bedford. X2464.

WOODRUFF, W. M., Sergeant, R.A.V.C.
He volunteered in December 1915, and was retained on important duties in connection with the care of sick and wounded horses until November 1918, when he was sent to France. He rendered valuable services whilst stationed at Rouen, Harfleur and Bray, and afterwards returned to England, and was demobilised in April 1919, holding the General Service and Victory Medals. 14, Sapley Lane, Hartford. Z2473.

WOODS, A. V. (M.M.), Sergeant, R.E.
Volunteering in April 1915, he proceeded to France later in the same year, and played a distinguished part in many important engagements on the Somme and in the Ypres salient. He was awarded the Military Medal for conspicuous bravery and devotion to duty in the Field in 1917, and also holds the 1914–15 Star, and the General Service and Victory Medals. He was discharged in September 1918. Hemingford Grey, Hunts. Z2467/A.

WOODS, C., Trooper, 4th (Royal Irish) Dragoon Guards.
He joined in June 1918 on attaining military age, and was retained on important duties at various stations in England. He was unable to obtain his transfer overseas before the cessation of hostilities, but, nevertheless, rendered valuable services, and in 1920 was still serving with his unit.
55, Union Street, Bedford. X2470.

WOODS, C. T., Private, R.A.V.C.
He volunteered in August 1914, and after a course of training was drafted to the East, where he served in Egypt and Palestine. He did consistently good work in connection with the care of sick and wounded horses at Jerusalem, Gaza and Jaffa, and returning to England in 1919, was demobilised in June of that year. He holds the 1914–15 Star, and the General Service and Victory Medals.
High Street, Milton Ernest, Bedford. Z2465/A.

WOODS, E. D., A.B., Royal Navy.
He was already serving in H.M. Navy at the outbreak of war in August 1914, and at once proceeded to sea in H.M. T.B.D. "Woolston." He was engaged on important duties whilst attached to the Grand Fleet in the North Sea, and was present at the Battle of Jutland in May 1916. He also did duty in the Baltic, and in 1920 was still in the Service. He holds the 1914–15 Star, and the General Service and Victory Medals.
44, Chandos Street, Bedford. X2468.

WOODS, E. F., Sapper, Royal Engineers.
He volunteered in 1914, and after training at various important stations, was drafted to the Dardanelles in the following year. In this theatre of war he took part in much heavy fighting on the Gallipoli Peninsula, and made the supreme sacrifice, being killed in action on September 2nd, 1915. He was entitled to the 1914–15 Star, and the General Service and Victory Medals.
"Nobly striving,
He nobly fell that we might live."
11, Trinity Road, Bedford. Z4044/B.

WOODS, E. H., Private, 4th Suffolk Regiment.
He joined in October 1917, and after a period of service in England, was drafted to France in January 1918, and rendered valuable services whilst attached to a Trench Mortar Battery. He took part in many important engagements, including those at Ypres and the Menin Road, and was also in action during the Advance of 1918. Demobilised in November 1919, he holds the General Service and Victory Medals.
44, Marlborough Road, Bedford. Z2471/A.

WOODS, E. R., Sergeant, Royal Air Force.
Volunteering in September 1914, he was sent to the Dardanelles in the following year, and served with distinction during many engagements on the Gallipoli Peninsula, including the Landing at Suvla Bay, whilst attached to a Flying Squadron. In 1916 he was transferred to Mesopotamia, but was unfortunately taken ill after a few months and sent to India. He returned to England, but in 1918 saw service in Palestine with General Allenby's troops. He was awarded the Medaille d'honeur for gallantry in rescuing a machine from the sea under difficult circumstances. He also holds the 1914–15 Star, and the General Service and Victory Medals, and was demobilised in March 1919. Hemingford Grey, Hunts. Z2467/B.

WOODS, F. J., 2nd Corporal, Royal Engineers.
He volunteered in August 1914, and four months later proceeded to the Western Front, where he played a prominent part in the fighting in various sectors. He rendered valuable services on the Somme and at La Bassée, and made the supreme sacrifice at Delville Wood, being killed in action on August 5th, 1916. He was entitled to the 1914–15 Star, and the General Service and Victory Medals.
"Great deeds cannot die."
44, Marlborough Road, Bedford. Z2471/B.

WOODS, I. M., Private, 53rd Royal Fusiliers.
He joined in September 1918, and was retained on important duties with his unit. He was unable to obtain his transfer overseas owing to his not having completed his training when hostilities ceased. He, nevertheless, did good work, and was demobilised in February 1919.
Old Court Hall, London Street, Godmanchester, Hunts. Z2472.

WOODS, J., Private, Labour Corps.
Joining in August 1917, he underwent a period of training and was later posted to a Labour Battalion. He was engaged on important agricultural duties in various parts of the country, and did consistently good work until September 1919, when he was demobilised.
1, Osbourne Villas, Rumbolds Lane, Buckingham. Z2466.

WOODS, J., Private, 1/5th Bedfordshire Regiment.
Mobilised in August 1914, he was stationed at Bury St. Edmunds, and shortly afterwards contracted typhoid fever. He unhappily fell a victim to the disease and died in the military hospital there on November 29th of the same year.
"His memory is cherished with pride."
3, Maitland Street, Bedford. X2710/B.

WOODS, T., 1st Class Stoker, Royal Navy.
He joined in January 1917, and did duty with the Grand Fleet in the North Sea. He rendered valuable services on board H.M.S. "Orion," and was engaged on important patrol and escort work until the termination of hostilities. He holds the General Service and Victory Medals, and was demobilised in May 1919. 2, Balsall Street, East Bedford. X2469.

WOODS, W., Private, Bedfordshire Regiment.
He volunteered in August 1914, and after a period of training and duty at Filey and Flamborough, was drafted to the Western Front in January 1916. He took part in heavy fighting on the Somme and was severely wounded in July 1916. Invalided to England, he was eventually discharged in June 1918, after two years in hospital, as physically unfit for further service, and holds the General Service and Victory Medals.
3, Avenue Road, Huntingdon. Z3003/A.

WOODS, W., Shoeing-Smith, R.A.V.C.
Volunteering in August 1914, he was drafted to Egypt in the following year. Later he did consistently good work in Palestine, where he was engaged on the important duties of attending sick and wounded horses. He rendered valuable services at Gaza, Jaffa and Jerusalem, and returning to England was demobilised in June 1919, holding the 1914–15 Star, and the General Service and Victory Medals.
High Street, Milton Ernest, Bedford. Z2465/B.

WOOLERSON, A. E., L/Corporal, R.E.
He was mobilised at the outbreak of war in August 1914, and proceeded to France in October. There he was engaged on important mining operations in many sectors of the front, and did consistently good work of various kinds at La Bassée, Ypres, Loos, Vimy Ridge, Festubert, the Somme, Cambrai, Arras, St. Quentin and Armentières. He was demobilised in March 1919, and holds the 1914 Star, and the General Service and Victory Medals. 5, Queen's Row, Bedford. X2474.

WOOLLARD, E. S., Private, Hunts. Cyclist Bn.
He joined in 1916, and after completing his training was drafted to France later in the same year. There he took part in many important engagements, including the Battles of the Somme, Ypres and Cambrai, and was wounded on two occasions. He was eventually invalided to England and discharged in February 1919 as unfit for further service. He holds the General Service and Victory Medals.
6, Avenue Road, Huntingdon. Z2718/A.

WOOTTON, A., Pte., 4th Q.O. (R. West Kent Regt.)
He volunteered in April 1915, and was drafted to Mesopotamia in February 1916, and took part in numerous engagements in this theatre of war. In November 1917 he was transferred to India, and after doing important garrison duty, was engaged in quelling the rising of the native tribesmen on the North-Western Frontier. He was demobilised in November 1919, and holds the India General Service Medal (with clasp, "Afghanistan, N.W. Frontier, 1919"), and the General Service and Victory Medals. 59, Westbourne Rd., Queen's Park, Bedford. Z2475/C.

WOOTTON, A. L., Pte., 1/5th Bedfordshire Regt.
Volunteering in January 1915, he completed a period of training and was drafted to the Eastern theatre of war in January ot the following year. He took part in many engagements in Palestine, and rendered valuable services at the Battles of Gaza, the entry into Jerusalem and the taking of Jaffa and Jericho. He returned to England for demobilisation in June 1919, and holds the General Service and Victory Medals.
8, Chandos Street, Bedford. X2477.

WOOTTON, F., Sapper, Royal Engineers.
He volunteered in March 1915, and in the following October was sent to France, where he was employed on important duties as a telegraphist. In this capacity he served in many sectors of the Western Front, and did excellent work. He was demobilised in March 1919, and holds the 1914–15 Star, and the General Service and Victory Medals.
Pauler's Pury End, Towcester. Z3915/B.

WOOTTON, G., Pte., 9th (Queen's Royal) Lancers.
He volunteered in May 1915, and proceeded to France in the following December. In this theatre of war he was in action at numerous engagements of importance and fought at the Battles of Ypres, Arras, Albert, the Somme and Cambrai, before being wounded in December 1917. He rendered valuable services during the course of hostilities, and was demobilised in March 1919, holding the 1914–15 Star, and the General Service and Victory Medals. 59, Westbourne Rd., Bedford. Z2475/A.

WOOTTON, L., Sapper, Royal Engineers.
Volunteering in September 1914, he was drafted to the Dardanelles in July of the following year, and did good work during the Landing at Suvla Bay and other engagements of importance. He proceeded to the Western Front after the Evacuation of the Peninsula, and was present at the Battles of Ypres, Arras, the Somme and Cambrai. Returning to England, he was demobilised in July 1919, and holds the 1914–15 Star, and the General Service and Victory Medals.
59, Westbourne Road, Bedford. Z2475/B.

WOOTTON, S. A., Private, 6th Bedfordshire Regt.
He joined in May 1916, and after a period of training was drafted to the Western Front, where he took part in many important engagements. He saw much heavy fighting in various sectors, including those of Ypres, Arras and Messines, and was wounded at Cambrai in May 1918 during the Retreat. He was eventually discharged in October 1918 as unfit for further service, and holds the General Service and Victory Medals. 8, Chandos Street, Bedford. X2478.

WOOTTON, T. F., Corporal, Bedfordshire Regt.
Mobilised at the outbreak of war in August 1914, he was immediately drafted to the Western Front, where he played a prominent part during the fighting in the Retreat from Mons. He was also in action at numerous other engagements of importance, including the Battles of Ypres, Hill 60, Vimy Ridge, Arras and Cambrai, and rendered valuable services during the Retreat and Advance of 1918. He holds the Mons Star, and the General Service and Victory Medals, and was discharged in March 1919. 58, Queen's St., Bedford. X2476/A.

WOOTTON, W., Gunner, Royal Field Artillery.
He was already in the Army at the outbreak of war in August 1914, and, proceeding to the Western Front, took part in the Retreat from Mons. He was also in action with his Battery at the Battles of Ypres and the Somme, but in 1916, after being stationed at Malta for a short time, was drafted to the Balkans in September of that year, and rendered valuable services in Salonika. He was discharged in February 1919, on his return to England, and holds the Mons Star, and the General Service and Victory Medals. 7, Canning Street, Bedford. X2479.

WOOTTON, W. H., Private, R.A.M.C.
Already serving with the Colours in August 1914, he immediately proceeded to the Western Front, and rendered valuable services during the Retreat from Mons. He also did consistently good work at the Battles of Ypres, the Somme, Albert, Loos, Lens, Arras, Passchendaele and Cambrai, and was discharged in March 1919, holding the Mons Star, and the General Service and Victory Medals.
2, Farrar Street, Kempston, Bedford. X1892/B.

WOOTTON, W. H., Corporal, Royal Engineers.
Two months after volunteering in June 1915, he proceeded to the Dardanelles and played a prominent part in heavy fighting during the Landing at Suvla Bay in August 1915, when he was wounded. He also did consistently good work at many subsequent engagements, and after the Evacuation of the Gallipoli Peninsula, was sent to Egypt, where he rendered valuable services until his return to England for demobilisation in February 1919. He holds the 1914–15 Star, and the General Service and Victory Medals.
58, Queen's Street, Bedford. X2476/B.

WORKER, C., Corporal, R.A.S.C.
He was mobilised in August 1914, and quickly drafted to France, where he was engaged on important transport duties with an ammunition column. He rendered valuable services at Mons, Ypres, Arras and Cambrai, taking troops and rations to forward areas, and suffered from gas-poisoning. Discharged in May 1918, he holds the Mons Star, and the General Service and Victory Medals. 6, Beckett Street, Bedford. X2480.

WORKER, P., Private, Bedfordshire Regiment.
He joined in February 1918, and after completing his training was sent to the Eastern theatre of war later in the same year and was stationed at Port Said, Egypt, where he was engaged on important garrison and other duties. He rendered valuable services, and in 1920 was still serving in the Army, and holds the General Service and Victory Medals.
288, Bedford Road, Kempston, Beds. X2481.

WORLEDGE, G., Pte., Royal Warwickshire Regt.
Volunteering in November 1915, he underwent a period of training and was drafted to the Western Front in July of the following year. After being in action on the Somme and at Arras and Messines, he was wounded at Ypres in August 1917, and was in consequence invalided home, but returned to France in March 1918, and served during the Advance of that year. Demobilised in January 1919, he holds the General Service and Victory Medals.
London Road, Godmanchester. Z4321/A.

WORRALL, A., Corporal, Royal Engineers.
Volunteering in August 1914, he completed a period of training and was drafted to the East in the following year. He took a prominent part in operations in Egypt and Palestine and did consistently good work at the Battles of Gaza and the taking of Jerusalem, and was promoted on the Field to the rank of Corporal for devotion to duty. He holds the 1914–15 Star, and the General Service and Victory Medals, and in 1920 was still serving in the Army.
7, Derwent Place, Bedford. Z2485/C.

WORRALL, A. J., L/Corporal, Bedfordshire Regt.
He volunteered in November 1914, and after a period of training was drafted to France in June 1915. In this theatre of war he took part in many engagements, including those at Festubert, Loos and Delville Wood, and was wounded during the Somme Offensive of 1916. He was later unfortunately killed in action at Cambrai. He was entitled to the 1914–15 Star, and the General Service and Victory Medals.
"The path of duty was the way to glory."
6, Cople, Bedford. Z2483/C—Z2484/C.

WORRALL, F. H., Corporal, 6th Bedfordshire Regt.
He joined in March 1916, and four months later proceeded to France, where he played a prominent part in many important engagements. He was in action on the Somme and at Cambrai, and later rendered valuable services during the Retreat and Advance of 1918. He was eventually demobilised in September 1919, and holds the General Service and Victory Medals.
33, Bunyan Road, Kempston. X3615/A.

WORRALL, L., Private, 1st Essex Regiment.
He joined in June 1918, and completing his training was drafted to the Western Front in October. There he took part in the Advance, and was engaged in much heavy fighting until the cessation of hostilities. He was demobilised in March 1919, and holds the General Service and Victory Medals.
6, Cople, Bedford. Z2483/A—Z2484/A.

WORRALL, P. J., Sergeant, Bedfordshire Regt.
Already serving in the Army at the outbreak of war in August 1914, he was drafted to France in the following year and played a distinguished part in many engagements until he was wounded on the Somme in 1916. Returning to England, he was in hospital for some time, and later obtained his release for work on munitions of war. He afterwards rejoined his unit, and in 1920 was serving in India. He was promoted on the Field to the rank of sergeant for consistently good work, and holds the 1914–15 Star, and the General Service and Victory Medals. 7, Derwent Place, Bedford. Z2485/A.

WORRALL, R. (M.M.), Sgt., 4th (R. Irish) Drag. Gds.
He was already serving with the Colours at the outbreak of war in August 1914, and shortly afterwards proceeded to the Western Front, where he was wounded in action on two occasions. He fought with distinction in many important engagements, and was promoted on the Field to the rank of sergeant for consistently good work. He was awarded the Military Medal for conspicuous bravery and devotion to duty, and in 1920 was serving with the Army of Occupation on the Rhine. In addition to the Military Medal, he holds the Mons Star, and the General Service and Victory Medals.
7, Derwent Place, Bedford. Z2485 /B.

WORRALL, R. S., 1st Air Mechanic, R.A.F.
He joined in May 1918, on attaining military age, and was stationed with his Squadron at various aerodromes in England. He was unable to obtain his transfer overseas before the cessation of hostilities, but after the Armistice, proceeded to Germany, where he did duty with the Army of Occupation on the Rhine. Returning to England, he was demobilised in February 1920. 12, Hartington Street, Bedford. X2482.

WORRALL, W., Private, 2nd Bedfordshire Regiment and Labour Corps.
He joined in March 1916, and later in the same year was drafted to the Western Front, where he took part in the Battles of the Somme and Arras and other engagements of importance. He also served during the Retreat and Advance of 1918, and after the Armistice proceeded to Germany, where he performed good work at a telephone exchange in Cologne. He holds the General Service and Victory Medals, and was demobilised in March 1919. 6, Cople, Bedford. Z2483 /B—Z2484 /B.

WORSLEY, A. R., Sergeant, 7th Bedfordshire Regt.
Volunteering in September 1914, he proceeded to France in the following June and fought with distinction at the Battles of Ypres, Arras, Vimy Ridge, Messines, Passchendaele, Albert and Cambrai. He suffered from gas-poisoning whilst overseas, but served through the Retreat and Advance of 1918. He returned to England, and was demobilised in February 1919, holding the 1914–15 Star, and the General Service and Victory Medals. 19, Ampthill Street, Bedford. X2486 /A.

WORSLEY, F. W. A., Corporal, 7th Beds. Regt.
He volunteered in September 1915, and completing a period of training, was drafted in 1916 to the Western Front, where he played a prominent part in the fighting in various sectors. He was in action at the Battles of Vimy Ridge, Bullecourt, Arras, Ypres and Cambrai, and served right on until the cessation of hostilities. In October 1919 he was sent to India, and was in 1920 still serving with his unit. He holds the General Service and Victory Medals. 19, Ampthill Street, Bedford. X2486 /C.

WORSLEY, H. P. R., Bandsman, 2nd Beds. Regt.
He joined in September 1917, and was retained on special duties with his Battalion at various important stations in England. He was unable to obtain his transfer overseas before the cessation of hostilities, but in October 1919 proceeded to India, where in 1920 he was still serving.
19, Ampthill Street, Bedford. X2486 /B.

WREN, W., Private, Royal Fusiliers.
He volunteered in August 1914, and was retained at various stations in England during the first part of his service. In 1916, however, he was drafted to the Western Front, and after taking part in important engagements on the Somme and at Arras, was wounded at Ypres. He holds the General Service and Victory Medals, and was demobilised in February 1919.
Church Street, St. Neots, Hunts. Z1054 /A.

WRENCH, H. A., L/Corporal, Royal Engineers.
Volunteering in September 1914, he was shortly afterwards sent to the Western Front, and took part in much heavy fighting in various sectors. He was in action at the Battles of Ypres, Neuve Chapelle, Loos, the Somme, Lens, Beaumont-Hamel, Arras and Cambrai. He also saw service for a time in Russia, and in 1920 was serving with his unit in England. He holds the 1914–15 Star, and the General Service and Victory Medals.
128, Dudley Street, Bedford. Z2487.

WRIGHT, A. E., Pte., 8th Beds. Regt. & M.G.C.
He volunteered in August 1915, and in due course proceeded to the Western Front, where he was in action with his unit at many important engagements. He saw much service in this theatre of war whilst attached to a Machine Gun Corps, and took part in the Battles of Vimy Ridge, Ypres and Arras, but was invalided home with trench fever in 1918. Demobilised in February 1919, he holds the 1914–15 Star, the General Service and Victory Medals. 14, Garfield Street, Bedford. X2500.

WRIGHT, A. S., A.B., Royal Navy.
He volunteered in September 1914, and at once proceeded to the North Sea in H.M.S. "Calliope." He was in action at the Battle of Jutland in May 1916, and lost the sight of one eye whilst in action. He also did consistently good work in the Baltic, and after the cessation of hostilities was demobilised in July 1919, holding the 1914–15 Star, and the General Service and Victory Medals. 45, Canning Street, Bedford. X2497.

WRIGHT, A. V., A.B., Royal Navy.
He volunteered in January 1915, and was stationed at Osea Island during the first period of his service. He also did duty at Scapa Flow and in the North Sea, where he was engaged on important patrol and escort work during the progress of hostilities. He holds the 1914–15 Star, and the General Service and Victory Medals, and was demobilised in March 1919. 34, Mill Street, Newport Pagnell. Z3284 /B.

WRIGHT, C. F., Private, 3rd Bedfordshire Regt.
Volunteering in February 1915, he was drafted to France later in the same year, and served on the Ypres front. In the early part of 1916 he embarked for Russia, but after a period of service in that theatre of war was transferred to Mesopotamia in 1918, and took part in heavy fighting until his return to England. He holds the General Service and Victory Medals, and in 1920 was still serving.
Church End, Sherington, Newport Pagnell, Bucks. Z2923 /E.

WRIGHT, C. S., Private, Queen's (Royal West Surrey Regiment).
He joined in 1916, and in the following April was drafted to France, where he took part in much heavy fighting in many engagements. He was gassed at Passchendaele Ridge and, invalided to England for treatment, was eventually discharged in February 1919, suffering from shell-shock. He holds the General Service and Victory Medals. Southoe, Hunts. Z2499 /B.

WRIGHT, C. V., Leading Stoker, Royal Navy.
He was already serving in H.M. Navy at the outbreak of war in August 1914, and immediately proceeded in H.M.S. "Derwent" to the North Sea, where he was engaged on important patrol and escort duties. He also rendered valuable services escorting troops to France, and was unfortunately drowned in the English Channel on May 2nd, 1917, when his vessel foundered. He was entitled to the 1914–15 Star, and the General Service and Victory Medals.
"The path of duty was the way to glory."
33, Beaconsfield Street, Bedford. X2488 /A.

WRIGHT, C. W., Corporal, Oxford. & Bucks. L.I.
Mobilised at the outbreak of war in August 1914, he was drafted to France in March 1915, after a course of training. He saw service in many sectors, and took a prominent part in the Battles of Ypres, the Somme and Cambrai. He was unfortunately killed in action near Ypres on August 22nd, 1917, and was entitled to the 1914–15 Star, and the General Service and Victory Medals.
"His life for his Country."
Church End, Sherington, Newport Pagnell. Z2923 /C.

WRIGHT, C. W., Private, Bedfordshire Regiment.
Already serving with the Colours at the outbreak of war in August 1914, he was at once drafted to the Western Front, and took part in the Retreat from Mons. He was also in action on the Marne and at Ypres, Neuve Chapelle, Hill 60, and Festubert, and was wounded in 1915. He was invalided to hospital in England, and after recovery did duty on the East Coast until his discharge in 1918. He holds the Mons Star, and the General Service and Victory Medals.
Balls Yard, London Street, Godmanchester, Hunts. Z1725 /C.

WRIGHT, E. A., A.B., Royal Navy.
He joined in January 1917, and did duty in H.M.S. "Inimitable" and "General Wolfe," and in patrol boats and monitors during the course of hostilities. He was attached to the Grand Fleet, and rendered valuable services in the North Sea, but unfortunately contracted influenza and died in hospital at Chatham Naval Barracks on October 20th, 1918. He was entitled to the General Service and Victory Medals.
"His memory is cherished with pride."
Wilden, near Bedford. Z2492.

WRIGHT, F., Private, Bedfordshire Regiment.
He was mobilised in August 1914, and immediately drafted to the Western Front. There he took part in the Retreat from Mons and many subsequent engagements, including the Battles of Ypres, Loos, Vimy Ridge and Cambrai, and later during the Retreat and Advance of 1918. He was wounded in action and invalided to England, where in 1920 he was still in hospital suffering from his injuries. He holds the Mons Star, and the General Service and Victory Medals.
19, Cavendish Street, Bedford. X2496 /A.

WRIGHT, F. E., Gunner, Royal Field Artillery.
He volunteered in 1914, and after a period of training was sent to France in June 1915. There he took part with his Battery in many important engagements, including the Battles of Ypres, Loos and the Somme, and in 1917 was transferred to Italy, where he saw service on the Piave. Eventually returning to the Western Front before the cessation of hostilities, he was in action at Amiens and Cambrai in 1918. He holds the 1914–15 Star, and the General Service and Victory Medals, and was demobilised in June 1919. Southoe, Hunts. Z2499 /A.

WRIGHT, F. J., Sapper, Royal Engineers.
He volunteered in January 1915, and later in the same year proceeded to Egypt, where he joined the forces operating in Palestine. He was present at the Battles of Gaza and the taking of Jerusalem and Jaffa, and rendered valuable services until the cessation of hostilities. He eventually returned to England, and was demobilised in January 1919, holding the 914–15 Star, and the General Service and Victory Medals.
19, Cavendish Street, Bedford. X2496 /C.

WRIGHT, G., Private, 11th West Yorkshire Regt.
He volunteered in January 1915, and six months later was drafted to the Western Front, where he took part in many important engagements. He served on the Ypres and Somme fronts, and was wounded during the Somme Offensive of 1916. Invalided to England, he was discharged in January 1917, and holds the 1914–15 Star, and the General Service and Victory Medals.
Church End, Sherington, Newport Pagnell, Bucks. Z2923/D.

WRIGHT, H. W., Shoeing-Smith, R.A.S.C.
Volunteering in March 1915, he was retained on special duties at Shirehampton, where he was attached to the Remount Depôt. He did consistently good work during the course of hostilities, but was not successful in obtaining a transfer overseas owing to his being medically unfit. He was demobilised in September. 1919. Abbotts Ripton, Hunts. Z2490.

WRIGHT, J. E., Corporal, 1/1st Welch Regiment.
He enlisted in May 1913, and at the outbreak of war in August 1914 was employed as an Instructor of recruits. In 1916 he was drafted to France, but after playing a prominent part in the fighting at Ypres, Lens, Loos, Albert, Hill 60, the Somme and Cambrai, was wounded on April 25th, 1918, during the great Retreat. He was invalided to England, and was eventually discharged in March 1920, holding the General Service and Victory Medals.
13, Farrar Street, Kempston, Bedford. X2495.

WRIGHT, J. E., Private, 2nd Bedfordshire Regt.
Mobilised at the outbreak of war in August 1914, he was immediately drafted to France, and was in action during the Retreat from Mons. He also took part in much subsequent fighting in various sectors, including the Battles of Festubert and Loos, and was invalided out of the Army in 1916. He afterwards re-enlisted in the Royal Air Force, and was demobilised in 1919, after doing good work, and holds the Mons Star, and the General Service and Victory Medals.
Free Church Passage, St. Ives, Hunts. Z2491.

WRIGHT, L. J. L., A.B., R.N., H.M.S. "Europa."
He joined the Navy in July 1917, and whilst in the Navy served in the Eastern part of the Mediterranean Sea, notably at the Dardanelles and Salonika and in Grecian and Turkish waters. He was employed largely on patrol and escort duties and served in H.M.S. "Europa," and H.M.M.L. "K.5" and "K.59." Returning to shore, he was demobilised in September 1919, and holds the General Service and Victory Medals.
33, Beaconsfield Street, Bedford. X2488/A.

WRIGHT, M. R. (Miss), Worker, Q.M.A.A.C.
She joined in May 1918, and during the latter period of hostilities was engaged on special duties whilst attached to the Q.M.A.A.C. She was employed as a cook at various important stations in England, and did good service until she was demobilised in October 1919.
33, Beaconsfield Street, Bedford. X2488/C.

WRIGHT, N. (Mrs.), Forewoman, Q.M.A.A.C.
She joined in 1916, and was immediately engaged on special duties at Haines Park during the course of hostilities. She rendered valuable service with her unit, and was demobilised in July 1918. 48, Denmark Street, Bedford. Z2503/B.

WRIGHT, P. H., Private, 7th Bedfordshire Regt.
He joined in March 1916, and after a short period of training was drafted to France, where he served on the Somme. He was unfortunately killed in action on September 27th, 1916, during his first engagement, and was entitled to the General Service and Victory Medals.
"Honour to the immortal dead who gave their youth that the world might grow old in peace."
Pyms Cottages, Bedford Road, Sandy, Beds. Z2501.

WRIGHT, P. W., Private, 11th Middlesex Regt.
Joining in March 1916, he trained at Reading and was drafted to France three months later. In this theatre of war he took part in many engagements of importance, including those on the Somme, and was wounded in November 1916. He was invalided home, and after nearly two years in hospital was finally discharged in December 1918 as no longer physically fit for further service. He holds the General Service and Victory Medals.
Church End, Sherington, Newport Pagnell. Z2923/B.

WRIGHT, R. L., Private, 6th Bedfordshire Regt.
Volunteering in June 1915, he underwent a period of training, and was drafted to the Western Front later in the same year. There he took part in much heavy fighting in many sectors, and was in action at the Battles of Loos, the Somme, Vimy Ridge and Ypres, but unfortunately lost his left leg through sustaining serious wounds in 1917. He was discharged in 1917, and holds the 1914–15 Star, and the General Service and Victory Medals.
28, Cobden Street, Bedford. X2489.

WRIGHT, S., Sapper, Royal Engineers.
He volunteered in August 1914, but owing to his being medically unfit for transfer overseas, was retained on important duties with his unit at various stations in England. He, nevertheless, did consistently good work until the cessation of hostilities, and was discharged in 1918.
48, Denmark Street, Bedford. Z2503/A.

WRIGHT, S., Stoker Petty Officer, Royal Navy.
He was already in H M. Navy at the outbreak of war in August 1914, and served on board H.M.S. "Glasgow" in the North Sea, Mediterranean and Baltic. He was engaged on important patrol and escort duties, and was in action on H.M.S. "Birkenhead" at the Battle of Jutland in May 1916. He rendered valuable services during the course of hostilities, and in 1920 was still in the Navy. He holds the 1914–15 Star, and the General Service and Victory Medals.
Maltmans Gardens, Eaton Socon, Beds. Z2494.

WRIGHT, S. G., Pte., 1st Duke of Cornwall's L.I.
Mobilised at the outbreak of war in August 1914, he was immediately drafted to France, and took part in the Battle of Mons. During the subsequent Retreat he was taken prisoner at Douai and held in captivity in Germany. He was later transferred to Switzerland through illness, and was repatriated and eventually discharged in March 1917 as unfit for further service. He holds the Mons Star, and the General Service and Victory Medals.
Maids Moreton, Buckingham. Z3752/A.

WRIGHT, W., Private, 4th Bedfordshire Regiment.
He joined in February 1917, and was drafted to France later in the same year, after undergoing a course of training. In this theatre of war he took part in many important engagements in various sectors of the front, and was wounded. He was reported missing after the Battle of Passchendaele in October 1917, and was later presumed killed in action. He was entitled to the General Service and Victory Medals.
"His memory is cherished with pride."
Duck End, Biddenham, Bedford. Z2502.

WRIGHT, W., Gunner, Royal Field Artillery.
He volunteered in January 1915 and, after training at Portsmouth and other important stations, was drafted to the Dardanelles in the following April. There he was in action with his Battery at the Landing on the Gallipoli Peninsula and saw further fighting until the Evacuation in December 1915. He was then transferred to the East, and did good service in Egypt and Salonika. After being in action on the Doiran front and other engagements, he returned to England and was demobilised in July 1919. He holds the 1914–15 Star, and the General Service and Victory Medals.
Lathbury, near Newport Pagnell, Bucks. Z2498.

WRIGHT, W., Trooper, Bedfordshire Yeomanry.
Volunteering in September 1914, he completed a period of training, and was sent to France in June 1915. There he saw much heavy fighting in various sectors, and was in action on the Somme and at Arras, Ypres, Loos, Festubert, Albert, Amiens, Péronne, Passchendaele and Cambrai. He continued his service until after the cessation of hostilities, and was demobilised in March 1919, holding the 1914–15 Star, and the General Service and Victory Medals.
7, Cowpers Place, St. Mary Street, Huntingdon. Z2493.

WRIGHT, W. H., Private, R.A.S.C. (M.T.)
He joined in April 1916, but owing to his being medically unfit for transfer to a theatre of war was retained on important transport duties in London. He, nevertheless, rendered valuable services until September 1917, when he was discharged as no longer physically fit for further service.
19, Cavendish Street, Bedford. X2496/B.

WRIGHTON, F., Gunner, Royal Garrison Artillery.
Joining in June 1916, he underwent a period of training and was drafted to the Western Front in the following year. There he was in action with his Battery in many important engagements, including those at Ypres and Passchendaele, and also took part in the Retreat and Advance of 1918. He holds the General Service and Victory Medals, and was demobilised in February 1919. Old Stratford, Bucks. Z1065/B.

WYATT, E. L., Cpl., 5th Oxford. and Bucks. L.I.
He volunteered in December 1915, and after training at Bovington Camp was drafted to France in June of the following year. He played a prominent part in many important engagements, including those on the Somme and at Ypres, Arras and St. Quentin, and was wounded. He was also in action during the Retreat and Advance of 1918, and was eventually demobilised in March 1919, holding the General Service and Victory Medals. Akeley, Buckingham. Z2444.

WYKES, A. E., Sapper, Royal Engineers.
Mobilised at the outbreak of war in August 1914, he landed at the Dardanelles in July of the following year, and took part in many engagements on the Gallipoli Peninsula, including Suvla Bay. After the Evacuation he proceeded to Egypt, and thence to Palestine, where he was present at the Battles of Gaza and Jaffa. Discharged in August 1919 after his return home, he holds the 1914–15 Star, and the General Service and Victory Medals. 88, Bower Street, Bedford. Z2504.

Y

YATES, P. A., Corporal, 15th Hussars.
He enlisted in 1906, and at the outbreak of war in August 1914 was immediately drafted to the Western Front, where he was in action at the Battle of Mons. He also took a prominent part in the fighting at numerous subsequent engagements, including the Battles of La Bassée, Ypres, the Somme, Vimy Ridge and Cambrai, and was wounded on two occasions, the first in 1914 at Ypres and finally during the Retreat of 1918. He holds the Mons Star, and the General Service and Victory Medals, and was demobilised in June 1919.
Little Stukeley, Hunts. Z2506.

YATES, W., Sergeant, R.A.S.C.
He joined in March 1917, and was retained on important transport and forage duties in Huntingdon, Lincoln and Cambridge. He was not successful in obtaining his transfer to a theatre of war before the cessation of hostilities, but, nevertheless, rendered valuable services until his demobilisation in May 1919. St. Mary's Street, Eynesbury, St. Neots. Z2505.

YEOMANS, C. S., Private, 1st Bedfordshire Regt.
Volunteering in April 1915, he was drafted to France in the following year, and took part in the Battles of the Somme, Bullecourt, Ypres and Cambrai. He was transferred to Italy in 1917, and after serving on the Piave returned to the Western Front. He made the supreme sacrifice on September 30th, 1918, being killed in action near Arras. He was entitled to the General Service and Victory Medals.
"Great deeds cannot die."
12, Greenhill Street, Bedford. X3733/B.

YERRELL, S., Sergeant, Bedfordshire Regiment.
Volunteering at the age of 17 in April 1915, he was stationed with the 2/1st Huntingdonshire Cyclist Battalion on the East Coast until July 1916, when he was sent to France. There he took part in the Somme offensive, but, wounded at Vimy Ridge in the following April, was sent to hospital. On his recovery he was drafted to Italy and served on the Piave and Asiago fronts. Returning to France in April 1918, he was in action at Achiet-le-Grand, Bapaume, Cambrai and other places. Demobilised in May 1919, he holds the General Service and Victory Medals. Warboys, Hunts. Z2508.

YORK, G. W., Sapper, Royal Engineers.
Volunteering in November 1915, he underwent a period of training and was drafted to France in January of the following year. There he did consistently good work on the Somme and in the Ypres sectors, and was engaged chiefly on the building of pontoon bridges. He also saw service on the Piave in Italy, to which theatre of war he was transferred in 1917. Returning to England he was demobilised in February 1919, and holds the General Service and Victory Medals.
18, Farrer Street, Bedford. X2510.

YORK, W. G., Air Mechanic, R.A.F.; and Private, Bedfordshire Regiment.
He volunteered in August 1914, and was stationed at Felixstowe until August 1915, when he was sent to France. There he was in action on the Somme and at Arras and Ypres, and was wounded on three occasions. He was invalided to England, but after ten months in hospital returned to the Western Front and was transferred to the Royal Air Force, with which he did excellent work in the repair shops until demobilised in January 1919. He holds the 1914–15 Star, and the General Service and Victory Medals.
Little Brickhill, Bucks. Z2509.

YORK, W. F., Private, Machine Gun Corps.
He volunteered in November 1914, and, completing his training, was drafted to the Western Front in February 1915. He was in action at Neuve Chapelle, Festubert, Loos, the Somme, Ypres and Cambrai, and rendered valuable services during the Retreat and Advance of 1918. Demobilised in July 1919, he holds the 1914–15 Star, and the General Service and Victory Medals. 10, Beauchamp Row, Bedford. X2511.

YOUNG, C., Private, 3rd Bedfordshire Regiment.
He volunteered in September 1914, but was not successful in obtaining his transfer to a theatre of war on account of being over military age. He, nevertheless, did consistently good work with his unit at various important stations, and was eventually discharged in July 1916.
66a, Pilcroft Street, Bedford. X2519.

YOUNG, F. A., Private, Bedfordshire Regiment.
He was mobilised at the outbreak of war in August 1914, and was at once drafted to the Western Front, where he took part in the Retreat from Mons, and saw heavy fighting in subsequent engagements. He was in action at the Battles of the Marne, the Somme and Cambrai, and was so seriously wounded in action that he was invalided home and finally discharged in December 1917, as no longer physically fit for further service. He holds the Mons Star, and the General Service and Victory Medals.
130, Honey Hill Road, Queen's Park, Bedford Z2515.

YOUNG, F. C., Gunner, Royal Garrison Artillery.
He joined in August 1916, but owing to his being medically unfit for service overseas, was retained on special duties with an anti-aircraft section, and was stationed at New Holland, Hull. He did consistently good work, and was discharged in November 1918 after a long illness.
Pavenham, near Bedford. Z2520.

YOUNG, G., Private, 8th Bedfordshire Regiment.
He volunteered in September 1914, and in the following year was drafted to the Western Front. There he took part in numerous engagements of importance, including the Battles of Loos, the Somme, Ypres, Arras, Messines, Passchendaele and Albert, and was gassed at Cambrai in March 1918. He was invalided home in consequence, and was eventually demobilised in March 1919, holding the 1914–15 Star, and the General Service and Victory Medals.
London Road, Sandy, Beds. Z2518/B.

YOUNG, G. W., Private, 1st Essex Regiment.
Joining in July 1916, he was drafted to France four months later and took part in many important engagements. He was in action on the Somme, and at Ypres and Arras, but was invalided home suffering from neuphritis and nervous breakdown. He was in consequence discharged, in January 1918 as unfit for further service, and holds the General Service and Victory Medals. 3, Boswell Place, Bedford. X2512.

YOUNG, H. J., Private, 9th Essex Regiment.
He joined in April 1917, and two months later proceeded to the Western Front, where he took part in heavy fighting. He was in action during the Battles of Messines, Ypres and Albert, and made the supreme sacrifice at Cambrai during the Retreat of 1918 on May 28th, 1918, dying of wounds and gas-poisoning. He was entitled to the General Service and Victory Medals.
"His life for his Country, his soul to God."
London Road, Sandy, Beds. Z2518/C.

YOUNG, J. H., Rifleman, King's Royal Rifle Corps; and Private, Labour Corps.
Volunteering in November 1915, he underwent a period of training, but owing to his being medically unfit for service in a theatre of war, was retained on special duties with a Labour Corps at Reading. He, nevertheless, did consistently good work until the cessation of hostilities, and was eventually demobilised in May 1919
52, Great Brickhill, Bletchley, Bucks. Z2516.

YOUNG, W., Private, 7th East Surrey Regiment and Labour Corps.
Three months after volunteering in September 1915, he was drafted to France, and took part in heavy fighting at Arras and Cambrai, and in other engagements of importance on the Western Front. He was later transferred to the Labour Corps, and did consistently good work on road-making and bridge-building during the course of hostilities He was demobilised in March 1919, and holds the 1914–15 Star, and the General Service and Victory Medals.
9, Tower Court, Bedford. X2521.

YOUNG, W. C., Private, 8th Suffolk Regiment.
He volunteered in September 1914, and after a period of training and duty in England during the first part of his service, was drafted to the Western Front in September 1916. He took part in much heavy fighting in this theatre of war, and was in action at the Battles of the Somme, Albert, Vimy Ridge, Messines and Arras, and was wounded at Ypres in October 1917, and at Passchendaele a month later. He was invalided home, and was eventually demobilised in March 1919, holding the General Service and Victory Medals.
Queen's Terrace, London Road, Sandy, Beds. Z2518/D.

YOURIN, S., Corporal, Lancers.
Volunteering in January 1915, he completed a period of training and was drafted to France in the following year. There he took part in much heavy fighting in various sectors, being in action at the Battles of the Somme, the Ancre, Ypres, Lens and Cambrai, and suffered from gas-poisoning. He returned to England after the Armistice, and was demobilised in December 1918, holding the General Service and Victory Medals.
Silver Lane, Haynes, near Bedford. Z2514.

THE NATIONAL ROLL OF THE GREAT WAR 1914 1918

SECTION XII.

PART II.

A

ABBEY, E. (Mrs.), Member, V.A.D.
She volunteered in September 1914 in the British Red Cross Society, and after undergoing a period of training served at the Northampton General Hospital and at Abington Avenue V.A.D. Hospital. There engaged on duties of great importance, she rendered valuable services until December 1920, when she was demobilised. 37, Bostock Avenue, Northampton. Z2040.

ABBEY, J., Private, 2nd Northants. Regiment.
Mobilised at the outbreak of war, he at once proceeded to the Western Front, where he fought in the Retreat from Mons and the Battle of La Bassée, but was wounded in action in November 1914 and invalided home. He returned to France shortly afterwards, took part in severe fighting at Ypres and Festubert, and fell gloriously on the Field of Battle on Aubers Ridge on May 9th, 1915. He was entitled to the Mons Star, and the General Service and Victory Medals.
"Whilst we remember, the sacrifice is not in vain"
38, Gladstone Terrace, Northampton. Z1152/B.

ABBOTT, C., Gunner, Royal Garrison Artillery.
He volunteered in February 1915, and in the following year was drafted overseas. Whilst serving in Salonika he took an active part in numerous engagements on the Struma and the Vardar fronts, and did good work with his Battery in various other sectors until the close of hostilities. He suffered from malaria whilst overseas, and was demobilised on his return to England in August 1919, holding the General Service and Victory Medals. 5, Cooper Street, Northampton. Z1001/C.

ABBOTT, T., Private, 7th Norfolk Regiment.
Joining in November 1917, he embarked for the Western Front in June of the following year, and was engaged in fierce fighting in the Arras, Somme and Cambrai sectors. He was severely wounded at the Battle of Amiens in August 1918, and sent to hospital in Southampton, whence he was discharged as medically unfit for further service in January 1919. He holds the General Service and Victory Medals.
5, Cooper Street, Northampton. Z1001/A.

ADAMS, A., Bombardier, Royal Field Artillery.
Shortly after volunteering in April 1915, he was drafted to the Western Front, where he took part in the Battles of Loos, the Somme, Arras and Vimy Ridge, and other engagements. He was wounded in action at St. Eloi in September 1916, and severely gassed in April 1918, was admitted to hospital in London. He was finally demobilised in April 1919, and holds the 1914–15 Star, and the General Service and Victory Medals.
5, Pine Street, Northampton. Z1355/A.

ADAMS, A., Private, R.A.O.C.
He joined in September 1916, and in February of the following year was drafted to the Western Front, where he was engaged on important duties at St. Omer and other stations. He was also present at the Battle of Ypres, and took an active part in the Retreat and Advance of 1918. He was demobilised in July 1920, and holds the General Service and Victory Medals
48, Southampton Road, Northampton. Z3213.

ADAMS, A., Sapper, Royal Engineers (R.O.D.)
Shortly after joining in February 1917, he was sent to the Western Front, where he was engaged on important duties on the railways in various sectors. He was also present at the Battles of Ypres, Cambrai, the Somme, Amiens and Le Cateau, and served through the final Advance of 1918. Demobilised in November 1919, he holds the General Service and Victory Medals. Main Road, Bugbrooke, Northants. Z3210/A.

ADAMS, A. E., Air Mechanic, Royal Air Force.
He joined immediately on attaining military age in 1918, and after undergoing a period of training, was retained at various stations, where he was engaged on duties of a technical nature. He was unable to obtain his transfer overseas, but, nevertheless, rendered valuable services with his Squadron until demobilised in 1919.
The Bungalow, St. Leonard's Road, Far Cotton, Northampton. Z2930.

ADAMS, A. E., Pte., 8th Royal Berkshire Regt.
Called up from the Reserve in August 1914, he was retained on important duties in England until July 1916, and then proceeded to the Western Front. After taking part in the Battles of the Somme, Arras, Ypres and Cambrai, he was taken prisoner in May 1918, and unhappily died whilst still in captivity in Germany on August 22nd of that year. He was entitled to the General Service and Victory Medals.
"His memory is cherished with pride."
Church Villa, Church Lane, Mursley, near Winslow, Bucks. Z3211.

ADAMS, A. W., Gunner, R.G.A.
Having volunteered in September 1915, he embarked for the Western Front in the following March. In this seat of operations he was in action with his Battery at the Battles of the Somme, Bullecourt and Arras, and was wounded at Albert in September and at Armentières in November 1917. On his recovery he was present at the second Battle of the Somme and in the Retreat and Advance of 1918. Discharged in November 1920, he holds the General Service and Victory Medals.
34, Baring Road, Northampton. Z2550/A.

ADAMS, B. F., Private, 1st Bedfordshire Regt.
He volunteered in November 1915, and on completion of his training was ordered overseas early in the following year. Serving on the Western Front, he was in action in many engagements of note, including the Battles of the Somme and Ypres, and was wounded at Cambrai in 1917. He remained in France until June 1919, when he was demobilised, holding the General Service and Victory Medals.
22, Silver Street, Northampton. Z1002.

ADAMS, C. E., Private, Royal Sussex Regiment.
Having joined in March 1916, he completed a period of training, and in the following year proceeded to France, where he was in action on the Somme before being wounded in October 1917. Invalided to England, he underwent a period of treatment, and on his recovery rejoined his unit on the Somme front. He fell in action on July 4th, 1918, and was entitled to the General Service and Victory Medals.
"A costly sacrifice upon the altar of freedom."
34, Baring Road, Northampton. Z2550/B.

ADAMS, F., Corporal, 6th Northants. Regiment.
Volunteering in June 1915, he embarked later in the same year for the Western Front, where he took part in many important engagements. He was in action at the Battles of Loos, Vimy Ridge, the Somme, Arras, and Cambrai, and also in the Retreat and Advance of 1918. Whilst overseas he was three times wounded, and in February 1919 was demobilised, holding the General Service and Victory Medals.
29, Devonshire Street, St. James' End, Northampton. Z2551.

ADAMS, F. G., Private, R.A.S.C.
Two months after volunteering in November 1915, he was drafted to Egypt, where he was engaged on duties of great importance Serving at various places he did much good work with his Company, and was for a time in hospital suffering from malaria. He returned home for demobilisation in August 1919, and holds the General Service and Victory Medals. High Street, West Haddon, near Rugby. Z3212.

ADAMS, J. C. W., L/Cpl., 1st Manchester Regt.
Volunteering in January 1915, he was sent to the Western Front in the following June, and there took part in the Battle of Loos and minor engagements until January 1916. He was then transferred to Mesopotamia, where he was present at the Relief of Kut and the capture of Baghdad, and was severely wounded in October 1918, and sent home. He was invalided from the Army in December of that year, and holds the 1914–15 Star, and the General Service and Victory Medals.
71, Cedar Road, Northampton. Z2041.

ADAMS, J. W., Sapper, Royal Engineers.
Joining in February 1917, he was drafted to France in the following month, and was there stationed at Dunkirk. He was engaged chiefly on important clerical duties and rendered very valuable services with his Company until his return home for demobilisation in November 1919. He holds the General Service and Victory Medals.
27, Alton Street, Far Cotton, Northampton. Z2929.

ADAMS, O., L/Corporal, R.A.M.C.
He volunteered in November 1915, and was retained for a time on important duties at various home stations before proceeding to Salonika in June 1917. In this seat of operations he saw much fighting on the Vardar front, and later served as hospital orderly, but contracting malaria, was eventually invalided home, and discharged in March 1919. He holds the General Service and Victory Medals.
14, Orchard Street, Northampton. Z2329.

ADAMS, S., Private, Duke of Cornwall's L.I.
A Reservist, he was called up at the declaration of war, and at once ordered to France, where he was present during the fighting at Mons. He was also in action at the Battles of the Marne, the Aisne, La Bassée, Ypres, Neuve Chapelle, Festubert, Loos and Armentières. In April 1916, however, his health broke down, and in consequence he was invalided out of the Army five months later, holding the Mons Star, and the General Service and Victory Medals.
6, Doddridge Square, Northampton. Z1003.

ADDICOTT, F., Corporal, R.A.S.C. (M.T.)
A month after war broke out he volunteered, and in May 1915 crossed to France. On that front he took an active part in the Battles of the Somme, Ypres, Cambrai and the Marne, saw heavy fighting in the Armentières sector, and rendered valuable services conveying food and ammunition to the forward areas. Demobilised in June 1919, he holds the 1914–15 Star, and the General Service and Victory Medals.
61, Compton Street, Northampton. Z1004.

ADDINGTON, C., Sapper, Royal Engineers.
He joined in January 1917, and after his training was retained on important duties in England until April of the following year and then proceeded to the Western Front, where he saw severe fighting at Ypres. He died gloriously on the Field of Battle in June 1918, and was entitled to the General Service and Victory Medals.
"He nobly fell that we might live."
13, Lea Road, Northampton. Z2042.

ADKIN, F. E. (M.M.), 2nd Lieutenant, 2nd Royal Sussex Regiment.
Having previously served in the Boer War, he rejoined in the ranks in September 1914, and proceeded to France in the following year. He played a prominent part in many important engagements, and was awarded the Military Medal for conspicuous bravery under heavy shell-fire. After being granted a commission he saw further severe fighting, but was unhappily killed in action at St. Quentin in 1918. He had already held the Queen's and King's South African Medals, and was also entitled to the 1914–15 Star, and the General Service and Victory Medals.
"His name liveth for evermore."
101, Adam's Avenue, Northampton. Z2330.

ADKINS, G. W., Gunner, Royal Field Artillery.
He volunteered in January 1915, and later in the same year was drafted to Salonika, where he saw much fighting on the Vardar and Doiran fronts. Later he proceeded to Egypt, thence to Palestine, and took part in several engagements, including those of Jaffa and the capture of Jerusalem, and was gassed. Demobilised in March 1919, he holds the 1914–15 Star, and the General Service and Victory Medals.
Milton, Northampton. Z2331.

AFFORD, S. A., Sapper, Royal Engineers.
He enlisted in April 1916, and four months later was drafted to France. Whilst in this theatre of war he served with the Field Survey Company, and saw much fighting at Armentières, Messines, Bullecourt and Dickebusch, and was gassed. He also met with an accident in November 1917, and was invalided home, and on his recovery was retained at home. Eventually demobilised in January 1919, he holds the General Service and Victory Medals.
124, Wycliffe Road, Northampton. Z2332.

AGER, J., Sergeant, 4th Bedfordshire Regiment.
Volunteering in October 1915, he was drafted overseas in the following year. Whilst on the Western Front he played a prominent part in engagements on the Somme and at Arras, where he was badly wounded in April 1917. In consequence he was invalided home, but on his recovery returned to France, and was again in action in the Cambrai and Le Cateau sectors. Demobilised in February 1919, he holds the General Service and Victory Medals. 25, Cecil Road, Northampton. Z2333.

AGER, W. G., Private, R.A.M.C.
He volunteered in October 1915, and five months later was drafted to the Western Front, where he served in various sectors. He was present at the Battles of Arras, Vimy Ridge, Bullecourt, Ypres, Cambrai and Bapaume and many other engagements, and also took part in the Retreat and Advance of 1918. Demobilised in January 1919, he holds the General Service and Victory Medals.
24, Ashburnham Road, Northampton. Z2043.

AINGE, A. A., Private, 2/5th Manchester Regt.
Three months after joining in March 1917 he proceeded to France, where he saw severe fighting in various sectors and took part in many important engagements. He made the supreme sacrifice, falling in action on March 21st, 1918, in the second Battle of the Somme. He was entitled to the General Service and Victory Medals.
"He died the noblest death a man may die,
Fighting for God and right and liberty."
40, Gray Street, Northampton. Z1356.

ALCOCK, J. W., Private, 7th Northants. Regt.
He volunteered in October 1915, and five months later proceeded overseas. Serving on the Western Front, he took an active part in the Battles of the Somme, Arras, Vimy Ridge, Messines, Ypres and Cambrai, and in many other engagements of note. He remained in France until January 1919, when he was demobilised, holding the General Service and Victory Medals. 54, Vernon Street, Northampton. Z1837.

ALDERMAN, F. W., Corporal, R.G.A.
He volunteered in November 1915, and, after a period of training, ten months later proceeded to the Western Front. There he fought in the Battles of the Somme, Ypres and Cambrai and many other important engagements, and was wounded in action on two occasions. He was demobilised in July 1919, and holds the General Service and Victory Medals.
32, Adelaide Street, Northampton. Z1005.

ALDRIDGE, H., Private, 6th Northants. Regt.
Called up from the Reserve in August 1914, he was drafted to France in the following year, and there saw severe fighting in various sectors of the front. He took part in the Battles of Loos, the Somme, Arras, Ypres and Cambrai, fought also in the Retreat and Advance of 1918, and was three times wounded. He served also with the Northamptonshire Dragoons and the Royal Flying Corps before being discharged in February 1919, and holds the 1914–15 Star, and the General Service and Victory Medals.
48, Wilby Street, Northampton. Z2044.

ALIBONE, A. V., Private, 2nd Northants Regt.
He volunteered in March 1915, and, completing his training in the following year, was drafted to France. In this theatre of war he took part in several engagements, including those in the Ypres, Somme, Arras, St. Eloi, Passchendaele and Cambrai sectors, and was wounded in action in March 1918. As a result he was invalided home and eventually demobilised in February 1919. He holds the General Service and Victory Medals. 107, Semilong Road, Northampton. Z2334.

ALLARD, J. W., Private, 2nd Northants. Regt.
When war broke out in August 1914 he was serving in Egypt, but was recalled and drafted to the Western Front in November 1914. Whilst overseas he was engaged in severe fighting in the Battles of Ypres and Neuve Chapelle, but was wounded at Ypres on April 7th, 1916, and unhappily succumbed to his injuries a day later. He was entitled to the 1914 Star, and the General Service and Victory Medals.
"A costly sacrifice upon the altar of freedom."
41, Adelaide Street, Northampton. Z1006.

ALLARD, T., Guardsman, Grenadier Guards.
Mobilised in August 1914, he was ordered to France three months later, and fought in the Battles of Ypres, Neuve Chapelle, Festubert and Loos, and was wounded at the Somme in 1916. On returning to the firing-line he was in action at Arras, Passchendaele and Cambrai, and did good work with his unit in operations during the Retreat and Advance of 1918. He was discharged in April 1919, and holds the 1914 Star, and the General Service and Victory Medals.
23, Manor Road, Kingsthorpe, Northampton. Z1007.

ALLBRIGHT, A. G., Private, 2nd Northants. Regt.
He volunteered in July 1915, and in September of the following year was drafted to the Western Front, where he took part in the Battle of Arras and many other important engagements. He made the supreme sacrifice, falling in action on May 2nd, 1917, and was buried at Villers-Guislain. He was entitled to the General Service and Victory Medals.
"Whilst we remember, the sacrifice is not in vain."
76, Henry Street, Northampton. Z2045.

ALLBRIGHT, J., Private, Yorkshire Regiment.
Joining in April 1916, he was attached to the Suffolk Regiment, and embarked for France in the following September. Shortly afterwards he was transferred to the Yorkshire Regiment and fought in the Battles of the Somme, Arras, Vimy Ridge, Messines and Cambrai, and also did good work with his unit during the Retreat and Advance of 1918. He was demobilised in March 1919, and holds the General Service and Victory Medals. 27, Hervey Street, Northampton. Z1840.

ALLEN, A., Driver, R.A.S.C.
Volunteering in November 1915, he was drafted four months later to the Western Front. There he was engaged on important transport duties in the Somme, Arras, Ypres, Cambrai, Lys, Bailleul and Ménil sectors, rendering valuable services until the cessation of hostilities. After the Armistice he advanced into Germany with the Army of Occupation, and was stationed at Cologne until demobilised in July 1919. He holds the General Service and Victory Medals.
9, Liz Street, Northampton. Z1009.

ALLEN, A., Sergeant, R.A.S.C. (M.T.)
He volunteered in September 1914, and in March of the following year was drafted to Egypt, where he was engaged on important transport duties at Alexandria and Cairo until October 1915. He was then transferred to Salonika, where he served on the Struma and Doiran fronts and at Monastir, and contracted malaria. Sent home in May 1918, he was invalided from the Army in November, and holds the 1914–15 Star, and the General Service and Victory Medals.
111, Market Street, Northampton. Z2046.

ALLEN, G., Gunner, Royal Navy.
He joined in June 1916, and was posted to H.M.S. "Princess Thyra," on board which vessel he was engaged on patrol and other duties in the English Channel until November 1918. Unfortunately taken ill, he was admitted to hospital at Brighton, where he died of influenza on November 16th, 1919. He was entitled to the General Service and Victory Medals.
"Steals on the ear the distant triumph song."
4, West View, Long Buckby, Northants. Z3216/B.

ALLEN, H., Pte., Princess Patricia's Canadian L.I.
Called up from the Reserve in August 1914, he was shortly afterwards sent to England, and thence proceeded to the Western Front in 1915. Severely wounded in action at Ypres in that year, he was invalided to hospital at Bromley, where he was for a considerable period undergoing treatment. Discharged in May 1919, he holds the 1914–15 Star, and the General Service and Victory Medals.
The Green, Lower Heyford, Northants. Z3214/A.

ALLEN, H. J., Pte., The Buffs (East Kent Regt.)
He joined the Middlesex Regiment in January 1917, and in April of the following year was sent to France, where he took part in severe fighting, chiefly in the Ypres and Armentières sectors. In March 1919 he was invalided to England, and on his recovery was transferred to the Buffs, and served at Shorncliffe until demobilised in October 1919, holding the General Service and Victory Medals.
32, Althorp Street, Northampton. Z1010/A.

ALLEN, I. H., Sergt., 16th R. Warwickshire Regt.
A Reservist, he was called to the Colours in August 1914, and in the following year proceeded to the Western Front, where he took part in many important engagements, including the Battles of Ypres and the Somme. He was reported missing, and is believed to have been killed in action near Ypres on October 9th, 1917. He was entitled to the 1914–15 Star, and the General Service and Victory Medals.
"A costly sacrifice upon the altar of freedom."
The Green, Lower Heyford, Northants. Z3214/B.

ALLEN, J., Air Mechanic, Royal Air Force.
He joined in August 1917, and after undergoing a period of training was retained at Croydon Aerodrome on duties of a highly technical nature as a rigger. He was unable to obtain his transfer overseas before the cessation of hostilities, but in December 1918 proceeded with the Army of Occupation to Cologne. He was demobilised on returning home in May 1919.
The Green, Lower Heyford, Northants. Z3214/C.

ALLEN, J., Private, 7th Northants. Regiment.
He joined in March 1917, and in April of the following year was sent to the Western Front, where he saw severe fighting in various sectors. He took part in the Battle of Cambrai and many other important engagements during the Retreat and Advance of 1918, and was demobilised on returning home in September 1919. He holds the General Service and Victory Medals. West Street, Long Buckby, Northants. Z3215.

ALLEN, J., Private, R.A.M.C.
Volunteering in October 1915, he completed his training and proceeded overseas in the early part of 1916. Whilst on the Western Front he rendered valuable services as a stretcher-bearer, particularly in the Somme sector, until invalided home with trench fever. On his recovery he was retained on home defence, and was engaged on duties of an important nature at various stations until demobilised in February 1919. He holds the General Service and Victory Medals.
32, Althorp Street, Northampton. Z1010/B.

ALLEN, J., Private, 1st Northamptonshire Regt.
He volunteered in August 1915, and, on conclusion of his training ten months later, embarked for France. On that front he was in action in many engagements, including the Battles of the Somme and Ypres, but was taken prisoner in July 1917 and held in captivity until the cessation of hostilities. On his release he returned to England and was demobilised in January 1919, holding the General Service and Victory Medals.
15, Herbert Street, Northampton. Z1008.

ALLEN, L. G., Private, R.A.S.C.
He volunteered in November 1915, and was immediately drafted to France. Whilst overseas he served with the Transport, and was engaged on important duties in the forward areas during heavy fighting at Béthune, Arras, Armentières, Albert, the Somme, Cambrai, St. Quentin, and in the Retreat and Advance of 1918. Demobilised in January 1919, he holds the 1914–15 Star, and the General Service and Victory Medals.
Forest View, Hartwell, Northampton. Z2335/A.

ALLEN, T., Gunner, Royal Marine Artillery.
He joined in June 1918, and was retained on special duties at Portsmouth. Owing to his being under age he was unsuccessful in obtaining his transfer overseas, but rendered valuable services. In 1921 he was still in the Army, having signed on for twelve years with the Colours.
Forest View, Hartwell, Northampton. Z2335/B.

ALLEN, T., L/Corporal, King's Own (Royal Lancaster Regiment).
Shortly after volunteering in December 1914 he was sent to France, where he took part in the Battles of Hill 60 and Ypres, afterwards being transferred to the Dardanelles. There he served with the 4th Northamptonshire Regiment at the Landing at Suvla Bay, later returning to France, where, after fighting in the Battles of Vimy Ridge, the Somme and Passchendaele, he was severely wounded at Amiens in 1918 and invalided home. Demobilised in December 1919, he holds the 1914–15 Star, and the General Service and Victory Medals.
98, Clarke Road, Northampton. Z2047/A.

ALLEN, W. G., Gunner, R.G.A.
Joining in November 1917, he proceeded to the Western Front in April of the following year, and there fought in the Battles of the Somme, St. Quentin and Cambrai, and many other engagements in the Retreat and Advance of 1918. He was afterwards sent with the Army of Occupation to Cologne, finally being demobilised in November 1919, holding the General Service and Victory Medals.
Camp Hill, Bugbrooke, Northants. Z3217.

ALLIBONE, A., Private, 1st Hertfordshire Regt.
Having previously served in the South African campaign, he joined the Army in March 1917, and rendered valuable services in training recruits at various stations. In January 1918 he was drafted to the Western Front, but was taken ill shortly afterwards and died on March 10th, 1918. He had held the Queen's and King's South African Medals, and was entitled to the General Service and Victory Medals.
"His memory is cherished with pride."
12, Melbourne Street, Northampton. Z1838.

ALLIBONE, W. G. H., A/Sergeant, R.E.
He joined in May 1916, but was not successful in obtaining a transfer to a theatre of war. During the period of his service he was engaged on work of an important nature in the Army Surveyor's Office, and fulfilled his duties with the greatest ability. After nearly three years' valuable service he was demobilised in March 1919. 63, Denmark Rd., Northampton. Z1839.

ALLISON, S. F., Corporal, 9th King's Own (Royal Lancaster Regiment).
He joined in June 1916, and three months later proceeded to Salonika. There he saw heavy fighting on the Vardar, the Struma and the Doiran fronts until drafted in 1918 to Russia. After taking an active part in operations there he was sent back to Ireland, where he served until demobilised in August 1919. He holds the General Service and Victory Medals.
74, Stanley Street, Northampton. Z1011.

AMOS, C. J., A.B., Royal Naval Division.
He joined immediately on attaining 18 years of age in 1917, and was shortly afterwards drafted with the Drake Battalion to the Western Front, where he took part in the Battles of Ypres, Passchendaele and Cambrai and other engagements. He fell in action on August 23rd, 1918, and was entitled to the General Service and Victory Medals.
"Whilst we remember, the sacrifice is not in vain."
Church Street, Northampton. Z3218.

AMOS, S. G., Private, 1/4th Northants Regiment.
He was called up from the Reserve in August 1914, and in the following year drafted to the Dardanelles, where he saw much heavy fighting at the Landing at Cape Helles, but, contracting dysentery, was invalided home. On his recovery he proceeded to Egypt, thence to Palestine and took part in the Battles of Rafa and Gaza, later serving with General Allenby's Forces in the final Advance to Aleppo. Demobilised in May 1919, he holds the 1914–15 Star, and the General Service and Victory Medals. 22, Stanley Road, Northampton Z2336.

ANDERSON, W., Private, 2nd Northants Regt.
A serving soldier, he was drafted to the Western Front in August 1914, and there fought in the Battle of, and the Retreat from, Mons. He also took part in the Battles of the Marne, the Aisne, La Bassée and Ypres, was wounded and also suffered from frost bite. Transferred later to Egypt, he proceeded into Palestine, where he fought in the Battles of Gaza. Discharged on returning home in November 1919, he holds the Mons Star, and the General Service and Victory Medals.
9, Albert Place, Northampton. Z3220/C

ANDREW, S. J., Private, R.A.S.C. (M.T.)
He volunteered for active service in October 1915, but owing to ill-health was not successful in his endeavours to secure a transfer to the fighting area. Nevertheless, he performed very valuable work at various stations, but was unfortunately discharged from the Army as medically unfit for further military duties in December 1916
30, Alexandra Road, Northampton. Z3841.

ANDREWS, A., Private, Devonshire Regiment.
He volunteered in January 1915, and twelve months later was sent to the Western Front. Whilst in this theatre of war he took part in many important engagements, including the Battles of Arras, Vimy Ridge, Ypres and Cambrai, and was gassed. He was demobilised in January 1919, and holds the General Service and Victory Medals.
78, Cloutsham Street, Northampton. Z1357.

ANDREWS, C., Private, 19th Queen's (Royal West Surrey Regiment), and Labour Corps.
He joined in June 1918, and was engaged on duties of an important nature at Lowestoft and Sutton. In September 1918, however, his health broke down, and in consequence he was discharged from the Army as medically unfit for further military duties, after only three months' service.
2, Moat Street, Northampton. Z1012.

ANDREWS, S. C., Sapper, Royal Engineers.
Having joined in June 1916 in the Royal Fusiliers, he was later transferred to the Royal Engineers, and in the following December embarked for the Western Front. Whilst in this theatre of war he was engaged on important bridge-building and road-construction duties, and was present during heavy fighting in the Somme, Ypres and Cambrai sectors. He also served during the Retreat and Advance of 1918, and in February 1919 was demobilised, holding the General Service and Victory Medals.
Rectory Cottage, Wootton, Northants. Z2553.

ANDREWS, T. H., Gunner, R.G.A.
Two months after volunteering in January 1916, he proceeded to the Western Front, where he saw much heavy fighting. He took part in the Battles of the Somme, Arras and Ypres, and many other important engagements, and fought also in the Retreat and Advance of 1918. He was demobilised in February 1919, and holds the General Service and Victory Medals.
Church Street, Long Buckby, Northants. Z3219.

APPLETON, C., Private, Machine Gun Corps.
Joining in January 1917, he was drafted to the Western Front in the following month, and there saw much heavy fighting. After taking part in the Battles of Arras, Ypres, Passchendaele, St. Quentin, and the Somme, and many minor engagements in various sectors, he was wounded at Ypres in March 1918. Demobilised in August 1919, he holds the General Service and Victory Medals.
11, Duke Street, Northampton. Z1358/B.

APPLETON, F., Private, 7th Suffolk Regiment.
Volunteering in December 1915, he completed a period of training before being transferred to France. Whilst on the Western Front he took part in heavy fighting on the Somme, where he was wounded in November 1916. As a result he was invalided to hospital in England, and thence to Ireland, but on his recovery rejoined his unit in France. He was in action at Cambrai before being wounded and taken prisoner in November 1917. After being released from captivity in May 1918 he returned home, and in the following September was invalided out of the Army, holding the General Service and Victory Medals. 11 Duke Street, Northampton Z1358/A.

ARCH, F W., Private, 2nd Essex Regiment.
Having volunteered in September 1914, he underwent a period of training, and in February 1916 embarked for India, where he first served on important duties at several stations. From March 1917 until the close of hostilities he was engaged in escorting prisoners of war from Mesopotamia to India, where he afterwards remained until his return home for demobilisation in April 1919, holding the General Service and Victory Medals. 26, Cattle Market Street, Northampton. Z2554.

ARCHER, A., Private, 1st Northants. Regiment.
Shortly after volunteering in August 1914, he was drafted to the Western Front, when he saw much severe fighting, and took part in the Battle of La Bassée and other engagements. He died gloriously on the Field of Battle there on January 20th, 1915, and was entitled to the 1914 Star, and the General Service and Victory Medals.
"He nobly fell that we might live.
near Bridge, Kislingbury, Northants. Z3221/B

ARCHER, H., Rifleman, 9th London Regiment (Queen Victoria's Rifles).
After volunteering in August 1914, he underwent a period of training prior to being drafted to the Western Front in 1916. There he took part in many engagements, including the Battles of the Somme (I. and II.), Arras and Cambrai, fought also in the Retreat and Advance of 1918, and was twice wounded. He was demobilised in March 1919, and holds the General Service and Victory Medals.
near Bridge, Kislingbury, Northants. Z3221/A.

ARCHER, W. A., Sapper, Royal Engineers.
Shortly after volunteering in August 1915, he was drafted to the Western Front, where, transferred to the Labour Corps, he was engaged in making roads, railroads and trenches. He served chiefly in the Somme, Ypres and Cambrai sectors, and took part in the Retreat and Advance of 1918. Demobilised in February 1919, he holds the 1914–15 Star, and the General Service and Victory Medals.
near Bridge, Kislingbury, Northants. Z3221/C.

ARNOLD, A. W., Private, 4th Northants. Regt.
After volunteering in September 1914 he was retained on important duties in England until 1917, and was then drafted to the Western Front, where he saw severe fighting in the Somme and Cambrai sectors. Mortally wounded in action, he unhappily died at the 53rd Casualty Clearing Station on November 13th, 1917, and was buried at Bailleul. He was entitled to the General Service and Victory Medals.
"The path of duty was the way to glory."
22, Perry Street, Northampton. Z2048/A.

ARNOLD, F. A., Private, 3/4th Northants. Regt.
Volunteering in October 1915, he received his training at Tring, but on account of ill-health was not transferred to a theatre of war. He was engaged on important duties at various stations, and carried out his work in a highly efficient manner until invalided from the Army in October 1916.
8, Brunswick Place, Northampton. Z1843/A

ARNOLD, G., Private, 2/7th Manchester Regt.
Joining in February 1917, he proceeded to the Western Front in October of that year, and there saw severe fighting in various sectors. After taking part in the Battles of Passchendaele and Cambrai and minor engagements, he was taken prisoner in the Retreat of March 1918, and held in captivity until January 1919. Demobilised in the following month, he holds the General Service and Victory Medals.
85, Stimpson's Avenue, Northampton. Z2049.

ARNOLD H. M., Private, 2nd Northants. Regt.
He volunteered in December 1915, and eleven months later was ordered to the Western Front, where he was in action in engagements on the Somme. In March 1917 he was taken ill and sent to England, returning later in the year to France. He there took part in severe fighting at Arras and in the Advance of 1918. Demobilised in March 1919, he holds the General Service and Victory Medals.
2, Carey Street, Northampton. Z1844/A.

ARNSBY, F. W., Pte., 3rd & 7th Northants. Regt.
Volunteering in May 1915, he proceeded to France in April of the following year and fought in the Battle of the Somme. He was invalided home in 1917 with trench fever, but on his recovery in March 1918 was again drafted to the Western Front, and a few weeks later was wounded on the Somme and sent to hospital in Edinburgh. On his discharge thence he was retained on home service until demobilised in January 1919, and holds the General Service and Victory Medals.
18, Victoria Street, Northampton. Z1845.

ASHBY, A. E., Trooper, Northants. Dragoons.
He volunteered in September 1914, and whilst in training met with an accident, but later proceeded to France in September 1915. Whilst overseas he took part in many engagements, including the Battles of Monchy, Beaumont-Hamel and Arras, and on being transferred to the Northamptonshire Regiment was wounded during the Retreat in March 1918. Demobilised in April 1919, he holds the General Service and Victory Medals. 11, Hazelwood Road, Northampton Z2337/A.

ASHBY, A. J., Private, Norfolk Regiment.
Joining in January 1918 he was drafted to the Western Front on completion of his training later in the same year, and there saw much heavy fighting. He took part in the Battle of Le Cateau and minor engagements until, severely wounded, he was admitted to hospital in England He was invalided from the Army in January 1919 and holds the General Service and Victory Medals 22, Mill Road, Northampton. Z3222/B

ASHBY, F., Private Royal Fusiliers.
He enlisted in April 1916, and later in the same year was drafted to France. There he served with the Labour Battalion, and was engaged on important work in connection with road-making and trench-digging in the Somme, Ypres, Cambrai and Lille sectors. Owing to medical unfitness he was unable to proceed to the firing-line, but rendered valuable services until his demobilisation in June 1919. He holds the General Service and Victory Medals. The Willows Milton, Northants. Z2338/B

ASHBY, F., Private, 1/4th Northants. Regiment.
He attested under the Derby Scheme in 1915, but owing to the important nature of his civilian occupation was exempt from military service until called up early in 1917. Whilst sailing for Egypt in the S.S. "Transylvania" his ship was torpedoed and he was unhappily drowned on May 4th, 1917. He was entitled to the General Service and Victory Medals.
"Thinking that remembrance, though unspoken, may reach him where he sleeps"
20, Raymond Road, St. James, Northampton. Z2555.

ASHBY, F., Private, R.A.S.C.
Called up from the Reserve in August 1914, he was retained on important duties in England until December of the following year, and was then drafted to Salonika. There he was engaged on various fronts and was present at much of the fighting on the Struma before returning home for discharge in June 1919. He holds the 1914–15 Star, and the General Service and Victory Medals. 16, Spencer Street, Northampton Z2931/A

ASHBY, G., Gunner, Royal Field Artillery.
Mobilised in August 1914, he was immediately drafted to France, where, after fighting in the Battle of, and Retreat from, Mons, he took part in the Battles of the Marne, the Aisne, La Bassée, Neuve Chapelle, St. Eloi, Hill 60, Ypres and Festubert. Transferred in January 1916 to Salonika, he was again in action on the Struma front, and contracted malaria. He was discharged on returning home in March 1919, and holds the Mons Star, and the General Service and Victory Medals.
16, Spencer Street, Northampton. Z2931/B.

ASHBY, G., Private, Royal Defence Corps.
Having previously served with the 16th Northamptonshire Regiment, he re-enlisted in the Royal Defence Corps in May 1915, and was retained on important duties at various stations. Contracting pneumonia, he unhappily died on May 16th, 1916, after 15 years' combined service
"Steals on the ear the distant triumph song."
22, Mill Road, Northampton. Z3222/A.

ASHBY, H., Private, Northumberland Fusiliers.
He joined in October 1917, and, on completing his training in April of the following year, was drafted to the Western Front, where he saw severe fighting in various sectors. After taking part in engagements in the Somme and Ypres sectors he was severely gassed and invalided home. Finally demobilised in December 1918, he holds the General Service and Victory Medals. The Willows, Milton, Northants. Z2338/A.

ASHBY, H. G., Private, Machine Gun Corps.
Joining in October 1918, he was unable to obtain a transfer overseas before the cessation of hostilities. On completion of his training at St, Albans he was drafted to Germany in April 1919, and served with the Army of Occupation at Cologne, where he did valuable work until sent to England for demobilisation in April 1920.
10, Upper Harding Street, Northampton. Z1013.

ASHBY, J., Private, Royal Defence Corps.
He was called up from the Reserve in August 1914 for home service, and was engaged with the Royal Defence Corps at various stations on important duties. He was chiefly employed on guard duties, and rendered valuable services until his discharge in 1917 as medically unfit for further duty.
6, Pine Street, Northampton. Z1359/A.

ASHBY, J. W., Private, 1st Northants. Regiment.
Volunteering in December 1914, he proceeded in the following March to France. Serving on the Western Front, he took part in many important engagements in various sectors. He was in action with his unit at the Battles of Neuve Chapelle, Hill 60, Ypres, Loos, Albert and Vimy Ridge, before being taken prisoner in June 1916. After the cessation of hostilities, he was released from captivity, and demobilised in February 1919, holding the 1914–15 Star, and the General Service and Victory Medals.
8, Gregory Street, Northampton. Z2556.

ASHBY, W. H., Private, Middlesex Regiment.
Joining in May 1916, he was drafted to the Western Front in the following December, and took part in the Battles of the Ancre, Arras, Vimy Ridge, Bullecourt, Messines, Ypres, Passchendaele, Cambrai and the Somme, and minor engagements. He fell fighting near Ypres on August 24th, 1918, and was entitled to the General Service and Victory Medals.
"Whilst we remember, the sacrifice is not in vain."
16, Spencer Street, Northampton. Z2931/C.

ASHTON, G., Trooper, Northants. Dragoons.
He volunteered in May 1915, and three months later embarked for France, where he was in action in the Battles of Loos, Albert, Vimy Ridge and the Somme. He was wounded at Arras in 1917, and invalided to England, but on his discharge from hospital was sent back to the Western Front. Being transferred to the 2nd Dragoon Guards, he was engaged on important duties in the Somme and Ypres sectors until hostilities ceased. Demobilised in April 1919, he holds the 1914–15 Star, and the General Service and Victory Medals.
14, East Street, Northampton. Z1846/A.

ASHTON, P. R., Sergeant, Military Mounted Police.
Volunteering in November 1915 he proceeded to Egypt in February of the following year, but was shortly afterwards transferred to Salonika. Invalided later to Egypt, he proceeded on his recovery into Palestine, and there took a prominent part in the capture of Jaffa and Jerusalem, and was wounded at Gaza in March 1917. He was mentioned in Despatches for distinguished services, and in March 1919 was demobilised, holding the General Service and Victory Medals.
45, Louise Road, Northampton. Z2932.

ASHTON, T., Private, 3rd Northants. Regiment.
When war was declared in August 1914 he was already serving and, proceeding to France with the first Expeditionary Force, was in action in the Retreat from Mons. He was also engaged in fierce fighting in the Battles of the Marne, the Aisne, La Bassée and Ypres, and was wounded on four occasions. He was discharged as medically unfit in August 1917, holding the Mons Star, and the General Service and Victory Medals.
8, Cromwell Street Northampton. Z1014.

ASHTON, W. C., Private, 2nd Northants Regt.
Volunteering in September 1914, he was sent to the Western Front in April of the following year, and there saw much severe fighting. He made the supreme sacrifice, being killed in action at Aubers Ridge on May 9th, 1915, only a few weeks after landing in France. He was entitled to the 1914–15 Star, and the General Service and Victory Medals.
"His life for his Country, his soul to God."
11, Florence Road, Northampton. Z2050

ATKINS, B., Private, 1st Northants. Regiment.
He volunteered in August 1914, and after a period of training was drafted overseas in the following November During his service on the Western Front he took an active part in heavy fighting in the Ypres sector, but was unhappily killed in action at La Bassée on January 6th, 1915. He was entitled to the 1914 Star, and the General Service and Victory Medals.
"A valiant Soldier, with undaunted heart he breasted life's last hill."
74, Scarletwell Street, Northampton Z1015.

ATKINS, G. W., Private, 2nd Battalion Canadian Overseas Forces.
Volunteering in December 1915, he completed his training prior to being drafted to France. In this theatre of war he fought in the Battles of Arras, Vimy Ridge, Ypres, Passchendaele and Cambrai, where he was wounded in November 1917. Invalided to hospital at Liverpool, he underwent a period of treatment, and in the following year returned to the Western Front, where he took part in the Retreat and Advance of 1918. Returning to Canada, he was demobilised in April 1919, holding the General Service and Victory Medals.
9, Gas Street, Northampton. Z2557

ATKINSON, F. J., Rifleman, Rifle Brigade.
He joined in October 1918, and on completion of his training at Falmouth was engaged on duties of an important nature at various home stations Owing to the early cessation of hostilities he was unable to obtain a transfer to a theatre of war, but, nevertheless, did valuable work with his unit until demobilised in February 1919. 42, Castle Street, Northampton. Z1016.

ATKINSON, H., Stoker, R.N., H.M.S. "Repulse."
Volunteering in October 1915, he completed his training, and was then posted to H.M.S. "Repulse" On board this vessel he was engaged in fierce fighting in the Battles of Jutland and Heligoland, and took an active part in various minor engagements in the North Sea. His ship was also present at Scapa Flow during the surrender of the German Fleet. Demobilised in January 1919, he holds the 1914–15 Star, and the General Service and Victory Medals.
32, Louise Road, Northampton. Z1265/A.

ATKINSON, P., Private, 1st Norfolk Regiment.
At the outbreak of war in August 1914 he was serving in Ireland, and was at once ordered to France. On that front he was in action at the Battles of Mons, the Marne, Ypres, Neuve Chapelle, Festubert, Loos and the Somme, and gave his life for King and Country at Delville Wood on July 17th, 1916. He was entitled to the Mons Star, and the General Service and Victory Medals.
"His life for his Country, his soul to God."
32, Louise Road, Northampton. Z1265/B.

ATTWOOD, A., Private, 1st Northants. Regiment.
Volunteering in July 1915, he was drafted overseas in December of the following year, and whilst serving on the Western Front took part in the Battles of Arras, Vimy Ridge and Messines. He gave his life for King and Country at Ypres on July 10th, 1917, and was entitled to the General Service and Victory Medals.
"Thinking that remembrance, though unspoken, may reach him where he sleeps."
64, Melbourne Street, Northampton. Z1847.

AUSTIN, A., Sergeant, 6th Northants. Regiment.
Shortly after volunteering in September 1914, he proceeded to the Western Front, where he saw much heavy fighting. He took a prominent part in the Battles of Ypres, Neuve Chapelle, Loos, Vimy Ridge, the Somme, Arras and Cambrai, and many other engagements, and was severely wounded in 1918. Demobilised in 1919, he holds the 1914 Star, and the General Service and Victory Medals. 55, Clarke Road, Northampton. Z2051/A.

AUSTIN, F., Private, 2nd Northants. Regiment.
He volunteered in September 1914, and in January of the following year was drafted to the Western Front, where he fought at Aubers Ridge, and was wounded at Ypres in May 1915. Invalided home, he returned to France, however, in March 1916, but, again wounded at St. Eloi, was again sent to England, where he was retained until demobilised in February 1920. He holds the 1914–15 Star, and the General Service and Victory Medals. Spratton, Northants. Z2933/B.

AUSTIN, J. A., Gunner, Royal Garrison Artillery.
He joined in June 1916 and three months later was drafted to France, where he was in action in many engagements in the Somme and Arras sectors. He died gloriously on the Field of Battle at Arras on April 9th, 1917, and was entitled to the General Service and Victory Medals.
"A costly sacrifice upon the altar of freedom."
81, Cambridge Street, Northampton. Z1017.

AUSTIN, T., Driver, Royal Engineers.
He volunteered in August 1914, and after his training was retained on important duties in England until 1917, and then proceeded to the Western Front. There he saw severe fighting in various sectors, taking part in the Battle of Ypres and other important engagements, and afterwards served with the Army of Occupation in Germany. Demobilised on returning home in 1919, he holds the General Service and Victory Medals.
55, Clarke Road, Northampton. Z2051 /B.

AUSTIN, W., Private, Royal Fusiliers.
He joined in July 1918, immediately on attaining military age, and after undergoing a period of training was retained on important duties at various stations. He was unable to obtain his transfer overseas before the cessation of hostilities, but later proceeded with the Army of Occupation to Germany. He was demobilised on his return home in 1920.
55, Clarke Road, Northampton. Z2051 /C.

AUSTIN, W., 3rd Air Mechanic, Royal Air Force.
He joined in June 1918, but being over age for active service, was unable to secure his transfer overseas Whilst in the Royal Air Force he served at Plymouth and Blandford, at which stations he was chiefly engaged in the construction of aeroplane sheds. After eight months valuable work he was demobilised in February 1919.
10, Stockley Street, Northampton. Z1848 /B.

AUSTIN, W. A., C.S.M., Machine Gun Corps.
Volunteering in February 1915, he was drafted to France later in the same year, and played a conspicuous part in engagements in the Somme and other sectors. In March 1916 he was taken prisoner, and was held in captivity until December 1918, when he was sent back to England. Shortly afterwards he proceeded to Turkey, rendering valuable services at Constantinople until his return home for demobilisation in November 1919. He holds the 1914–15 Star, and the General Service and Victory Medals. 10, Stockley Street, Northampton. Z1848 /A.

AUSTIN, W. H., Sergeant, 6th Bedfordshire Regt.
Volunteering in August 1914, he proceeded to the Western front in July of the following year, and there saw much heavy fighting. After taking a prominent part in several engagements he was severely wounded in November 1915, and was admitted to hospital at Leicester. He was finally invalided from the Army in September 1918, and holds the 1914–15 Star, and the General Service and Victory Medals.
Spratton, Northants. Z2933 /A.

AXFORD, W., Private, R.A.M.C.
He volunteered in June 1915, and in the following year was sent to Salonika, where he was engaged on important duties on the Macedonian front. He was also present at many engagements in this theatre of war until invalided home, suffering from dysentery in December 1918. He was demobilised in March 1919, and holds the General Service and Victory Medals.
22, Thursby Road, Northampton. Z2339.

AYRES, H., Private, East Surrey Regiment.
Joining in March 1916, he proceeded to Salonika on completing his training in the following July, and there, attached to the Machine Gun Corps as a gunner, saw much severe fighting. He took part in many engagements on the Vardar, Struma and Doiran fronts, and finally returned home for demobilisation in March 1919. He holds the General Service and Victory Medals. Kislingbury, Northants. Z3225 /A.

AYRES, J. J., Cpl., 8th (King's Royal Irish) Hussars.
He was serving in India when war was declared, and was quickly drafted to the Western Front, where he saw much heavy fighting. After taking part in the Battles of Hill 60, Ypres, the Somme and Arras, he was taken prisoner on the Somme in March 1918, and was forced to work on the land whilst in captivity. Released in December 1918, he was discharged in the following April, and holds the 1914–15 Star, and the General Service and Victory Medals.
77, Somerset Street, Northampton. Z3224.

AYRES, T. P., Private, 1st Northants. Regiment.
He volunteered in October 1915, and after his training was retained in England until 1917, when he proceeded to the Western Front. There he was so severely wounded on the Somme in March of that year as to necessitate the amputation of his left leg. He was invalided from the Army in October 1918, and holds the General Service and Victory Medals.
The Green, Kislingbury, Northants. Z3225 /B.

AYRES, W., Petty Officer, Royal Navy.
He re-enlisted in April 1915, and afterwards served in H.M.S. "Aurora" and "Victory," and other vessels attached to the Grand Fleet in the North Sea. He was engaged chiefly on minesweeping and patrol duty, and also served in the Baltic Sea. Invalided from the Navy in December 1915, suffering from neurasthenia he holds the 1914–15 Star, and the General Service and Victory Medals.
George Row, Kilsby, Northants. Z3223.

AYRES, W., Private, 1/4th Northants Regiment.
Three months after joining in April 1917, he was drafted to Egypt with the Machine Gun Corps, and was later transferred to the Royal Sussex Regiment. Proceeding into Palestine, he took part in the third Battle of Gaza and in the capture of Jerusalem and Aleppo, afterwards serving at Alexandria and Cairo. Demobilised on returning home in April 1920, he holds the General Service and Victory Medals.
Kislingbury, Northants. Z3225 /C.

B

BABBINGTON, J., Private, Bedfordshire Regt.
He joined in March 1918, but owing to ill-health was unsuccessful in his efforts to obtain a transfer to a theatre of war. After completing his training, he served at various home stations, where he carried out the duties assigned to him in a highly efficient manner until demobilised in November 1919.
27, Brunswick Place, Northampton. Z1849.

BAILEY, A. E., Driver, R.A.S.C.
He volunteered in November 1914, and in the following year was drafted to Salonika. In this seat of operations he served with the transport, and was engaged in conveying ammunition and supplies to the forward areas. He contracted malaria and was eventually sent home and discharged in March 1919, holding the 1914–15 Star, and the General Service and Victory Medals. 88, Milton Street, Northampton. Z1266 /B.

BAILEY, A. G., Saddler, Royal Field Artillery.
Volunteering in August 1914, he was drafted overseas in the following year. Whilst on the Western Front he was engaged on important duties as a saddler, and also took part in several battles, including those of Ypres and the Somme. He was demobilised in March 1919, and holds the 1914–15 Star, and the General Service and Victory Medals.
88, Milton Street, Northampton. Z1266 /A.

BAILEY, C., Private, Northants. Regiment.
He volunteered in August 1914, and underwent a period of training prior to his being drafted to France, where he took part in several engagements. He made the supreme sacrifice, being killed in action on the Somme in July 1916, and was entitled to the 1914–15 Star, and the General Service and Victory Medals.

"A valiant Soldier, with undaunted heart he breasted life's last hill."

11, St. Andrew's Place, Northampton. Z1020 /A.

BAILEY, C. G., Corporal, R.A.M.C.
Volunteering in April 1915, he was sent to the Western Front in the following August, and there served in various sectors until transferred in 1916 to Salonika, where he did good work at several hospitals. He contracted malaria and unhappily died on December 3rd, 1917, being entitled to the 1914–15 Star, and the General Service and Victory Medals.

"His memory is cherished with pride"

91, Lutterworth Road, Northampton. Z2052.

BAILEY, F., A.B., Royal Navy.
He was already in the Royal Navy when war broke out in August 1914, and immediately put to sea on board H.M.S. "Natal." He first saw much service in the North Sea, and was engaged on important duties, but later proceeded to the Mediterranean. He unfortunately lost his life when H.M.S. "Natal" was blown up on December 31st, 1915, in Cromarty Firth by an internal explosion. He was entitled to the 1914–15 Star, and the General Service and Victory Medals,

"The path of duty was the way to glory."

11, St. Andrew's Place, Northampton. Z1020 /B.

BAILEY, H. D., Private, 5th Northants. Regt.
Volunteering in October 1915, he completed his training and proceeded overseas in February 1916. During his service on the Western Front he saw heavy fighting in various sectors, took part in the Battles of Albert, the Somme, the Ancre, Vimy Ridge, Bullecourt, Epéhy and the Scarpe, and was wounded in action in August 1918. He was demobilised in April 1919, and holds the General Service and Victory Medals.
50, Queen's Road, Northampton. Z1850.

BAILEY, S. J., Private, Sherwood Foresters.
He volunteered in September 1915, and completing his training in the following July was drafted to the Western Front, where he took part in several engagements. He died gloriously on the Field of Battle on the Somme front in October 1916, and was entitled to the General Service and Victory Medals.

"He died the noblest death a man may die:
Fighting for God and right and liberty."

11, St. Andrew's Place, Northampton. Z1020 /C.

BAILEY, W., Driver, St. John Ambulance Assoc.
Having previously been rejected three times for service overseas, he volunteered in St. John Ambulance Corps in June 1915. He did continuously good work as a motor driver conveying wounded to various hospitals, and was also engaged on other important duties. He was demobilised in March 1919.
21, St Mary's Street, Northampton. Z1018 /F—Z1019 /F.

BAILEY, W., Gunner, Royal Garrison Artillery.
Joining in May 1917, he was sent to the Western Front in November of the same year and saw severe fighting in various sectors. He took part in the Battle of Ypres and many other important engagements in the Retreat and Advance of 1918, and was wounded in May of that year. Demobilisedin January 1919, he holds the General Service and Victory Medals.
90, Euston Road, Northampton. Z2934.

BAINES, A., Private, 7th Royal Sussex Regiment.
Joining in March 1916, he proceeded to France and took part in the Battles of Messines, Cambrai and the Somme (II.). During the Retreat in June 1918 he became separated from his Regiment, but, after six days, succeeded in rejoining, and was admitted to hospital in France as a result of his privations. On his recovery he acted as a postman in a prisoner of war camp, and was eventually demobilised in September 1919, holding the General Service and Victory Medals.
1, Thomas Street, Northampton. Z1360.

BAINES, J. T. A., Sapper, R.E. (R.O.D.)
He joined in March 1916, and in the following month was drafted to France, where he served in various sectors of the front. He was engaged chiefly in conveying supplies to the forward areas whilst in this theatre of war, and was injured in an accident near Ypres. Demobilised in February 1920, he holds the General Service and Victory Medals.
124, Southampton Road, Northampton. Z2935/A.

BAINES, W. C., A.B., Royal Naval Division.
He joined in May 1917, and, after undergoing a period of training in H.M.S. "Victory," was drafted to the Western Front in March of the following year. After taking part in the Battle of the Somme and other important engagements in the Retreat and Advance of 1918, he was wounded and taken prisoner at Achiet-le-Grand, and was held in captivity until the cessation of hostilities. Demobilised in October 1919, he holds the General Service and Victory Medals.
124, Southampton Road, Northampton. Z2935/B.

BAKER, C., Private, 6th Northants. Regiment.
Already in the Army when war broke out in August 1914, he was immediately drafted to France, where he fought in the Battle of Mons, and was wounded. As a result he was invalided home, but on his recovery returned to France, and took part in much fighting in the Somme and Ypres sectors. He was unfortunately killed in action on February 17th, 1917, and was entitled to the Mons Star, and the General Service and Victory Medals.
"Thinking that remembrance, though unspoken, may reach him where he sleeps."
39, Gladstone Terrace, Northampton. TZ1022/B.

BAKER, C. C., Private, 1st Suffolk Regiment.
He volunteered in November 1915, and after completing a period of training served at various stations, where he was engaged on duties of a highly important nature. He was not successful in obtaining his transfer to a theatre of war, but, nevertheless, rendered valuable services with his unit until demobilised in April 1919.
39, Ambush Street, St. James, Northampton. Z2340.

BAKER, E., Private, East Yorkshire Regiment.
Volunteering in November 1915, he was drafted overseas in the following year. During his service on the Western Front he took part in several engagements, including the Battles of the Somme and Beaumont-Hamel. Wounded in action in 1917 he was consequently invalided home, and eventually discharged in July 1918, holding the General Service and Victory Medals.
39, Gladstone Terrace, Northampton. TZ1022/A.

BAKER, E., Pte., Royal Warwickshire Regiment.
Joining in February 1917 in the Northamptonshire Regiment, he was later transferred to the Royal Warwickshire Regiment, and in the following year was drafted overseas. Whilst on the Western Front he took part in many important engagements in various sectors. He fell in action during heavy fighting at Ypres on September 27th, 1918, and was entitled to the General Service and Victory Medals.
"His life for his Country, his soul to God"
30, Abbey Street, Daventry, Northants. TZ2558/A.

BAKER, F., Private, 6th Northants. Regiment.
He volunteered in September 1914, and in the following July was drafted to the Western Front. In this theatre of war he took part in several engagements, including the Battles of the Somme, Arras, Ypres, Cambrai, St. Quentin and in the Retreat of 1918, and was twice wounded in action. He was demobilised in March 1919, and holds the 1914–15 Star, and the General Service and Victory Medals.
39, Gladstone Terrace, Northampton. Z1021/A.

BAKER, G. W., Private, Royal Defence Corps.
He volunteered in August 1914, and underwent a period of training prior to his being engaged at various stations on important duties with his unit. He did continuously good work in guarding bridges, viaducts and prisoners of war until his discharge in February 1918.
84, Moore Street, Kingsley, Northampton. Z1023.

BAKER, R. V., Gunner, Royal Horse Artillery.
He joined in May 1916, and in September of the following year proceeded to the Western Front, whence he was transferred to Italy two months later. There he saw much severe fighting, taking part in important engagements on the Piave, Trentino and Asiago Plateau until the cessation of hostilities. Demobilised in March 1919, he holds the General Service and Victory Medals.
The Green, Hartwell, Northants. Z2341/D.

BAKER, W., Private, Suffolk Regiment.
He joined in August 1918, and after a period of training was engaged at various stations on important duties with his unit. Owing to his being medically unfit he was unable to proceed overseas, but rendered valuable services until his demobilisation in November 1919.
39, Gladstone Terrace, Northampton. Z1021/B.

BAKER, W. J., Private, South Staffordshire Regt.
Volunteering at the outbreak of hostilities he was first engaged on important duties with his unit at Grantham. Proceeding to the Dardanelles in June 1915, he took part in the Gallipoli campaign. He was reported missing in August 1915, and was later presumed to have been killed in action. He was entitled to the 1914–15 Star, and the General Service and Victory Medals.
"And doubtless he went in splendid company."
30, Abbey Street, Daventry, Northants. TZ2558/B.

BALDERSON, A., Saddler, Machine Gun Corps.
He volunteered in October 1915, and, completing his training in the following year, was drafted to Mesopotamia, where he served in the Amara and Kut sectors of the front. Later he was transferred to Egypt, proceeded into Palestine, and saw much fighting at the Battles of Gaza. He returned home, and was demobilised in July 1919, holding the General Service and Victory Medals.
12, Lower Harding Street, Northampton. Z1024.

BALDERSON, B. H., Sergt., 1/4th Northants. Regt.
He volunteered in August 1915, and was retained on important duties in England until January 1917, when he was drafted to Egypt. He proceeded thence into Palestine, where he took a prominent part in the Battles of Rafa and Gaza, and the capture of Jerusalem, Jericho, Tripoli and Aleppo. Demobilised on returning home in July 1919, he holds the General Service and Victory Medals.
School Road, Spratton, Northants. Z2936/A.

BALDERSON, F. C. (M.M.), Sergeant, 14th Gloucestershire Regiment.
Two months after volunteering in August 1914, he was drafted to the Western Front, where he played a distinguished part in the Battles of Arras, Vimy Ridge, Messines and Ypres, and other engagements. He died gloriously on the Field of Battle on October 22nd, 1917. He had been awarded the Military Medal for conspicuous bravery in the Field, and was also entitled to the 1914 Star, and the General Service and Victory Medals.
"His memory is cherished with pride."
School Road, Spratton, Northants. Z2936/C.

BALDWIN, A. C., Private, Sherwood Foresters.
He enlisted in January 1917, and three months later was drafted to France. There he took part in engagements at Arras, Passchendaele and Cambrai, and was twice wounded in action. As a result he was invalided home, but on his recovery served on important duties until his demobilisation in February 1919. He holds the General Service and Victory Medals.
31, Brunswick Street, Northampton. Z1361.

BALDWIN, G., Private, 20th Hussars.
Volunteering in February 1915, he was sent to the Western Front in the following November with the Bedfordshire Lancers, and was there transferred to the 20th Hussars. He took part in the Battles of the Somme, Arras, Ypres and Cambrai and many minor engagements, was gassed, and afterwards served with the Army of Occupation at Cologne. He was demobilised in August 1919, and holds the 1914–15 Star, and the General Service and Victory Medals.
Milton, Northants. Z2342/A.

BALDWIN, J. T., Driver, Royal Field Artillery.
Shortly after joining in February 1916 he was drafted to the Western Front, where he saw much heavy fighting. He took part in the Battles of the Somme, Ypres, Arras and Cambrai, and many other important engagements, and later proceeded with the Army of Occupation into Germany, where he was stationed at Cologne and Bonn. Demobilised in September 1919, he holds the General Service and Victory Medals.
Milton, Northants. Z2342/B.

BALDWIN, W. J., Stoker Petty Officer, R.N.
He enlisted in May 1904, and, after the outbreak of war in August 1914, served in H.M.S. "Zealandia" and H.M.T.B.D. "Boxer." He was engaged chiefly on escort and patrol duties in the English Channel, and did much good work until invalided from the Navy in March 1917. He holds the 1914–15 Star, and the General Service and Victory Medals.
Milton, Northants. Z2342/C.

BALL, A. W., Private, 2/4th Northants. Regt.
He volunteered in October 1914, and, after completing his training, was engaged at various stations on important duties with his unit. Owing to his being medically unfit he was unable to obtain a transfer overseas, but rendered valuable services until he was taken ill and sent to hospital. He was eventually discharged in February 1916.
46, King Street, Northampton. Z1267.

BALL, W. J., Pte., Queen's (Royal West Surrey Regt.)
He joined in March 1918 on attaining military age, and after his training was engaged at various home stations on important transport duties with his unit. Owing to the early cessation of hostilities he was unable to proceed overseas, but rendered valuable services until his demobilisation in April 1919.
48, Essex Street, Northampton. Z1025.

BAMFORD, A. C., L/Corporal, Northants. Regt.
Volunteering in May 1915, he proceeded overseas in the following month. Whilst on the Western Front he took part in several engagements, including those at Loos, St. Eloi, Albert, Vermelles Ploegsteert, Vimy Ridge, the Somme, Arras, Lens and Cambrai, and was wounded and gassed in action. He was demobilised in February 1919, and holds the 1914–15 Star, and the General Service and Victory Medals.
8, Deal Street, Northampton. Z1362.

BANDY, J. F., Private, 7th Northants. Regiment.
Having volunteered in June 1915, he was drafted overseas later in the same year. Whilst on the Western Front he took part in many engagements, including those at Loos, St. Eloi, Albert, Vermelles, Ploegsteert, Vimy Ridge, the Somme, Arras, Bullecourt, Ypres, Lens and Cambrai, and was gassed in action. Demobilised in January 1919, he holds the 1914–15 Star, and the General Service and Victory Medals.
12, Kettering Gardens, Northampton. Z3226.

BANKS, W. F., Private, 9th Royal Fusiliers.
He joined in February 1918, and, after four months' training was ordered to France. On that front he was engaged in fierce fighting in the Somme sector, at Albert and elsewhere, and was wounded in action in August 1918, and invalided home. After prolonged hospital treatment, he was demobilised in July 1919, holding the General Service and Victory Medals.
3, Dunster Street, Northampton. Z1851.

BARBER, F. A., Corporal, Royal Defence Corps.
Having previously served in the Zulu War, he volunteered in the Royal Defence Corps in November 1914, and was engaged on various important duties. He served chiefly on guarding railways and munition dumps, and did continuously good work throughout hostilities. He was demobilised in February 1919, and holds the Zulu War Medal.
39, Herbert Street, Northampton. Z1026/C—Z1027/C.

BARBER, H., Driver, Royal Field Artillery.
He volunteered in October 1915, and on completion of his training later in the same year was ordered to India. After a period of service there he was transferred to Mesopotamia, in which theatre of war he was in action in numerous engagements, and did good work with his Battery during operations at Kut and Baghdad. On his return to England he was demobilised in October 1919, holding the General Service and Victory Medals. 165, St. Edmund's Road, Northampton. Z1852.

BARBER, J., Private, 2/5th Manchester Regt.
He volunteered in October 1915, and was retained for a time on important duties before proceeding to France in May 1917. There he took part in the Battles of Ypres, Passchendaele and St. Quentin, where he was wounded and taken prisoner in March 1918. Repatriated after the Armistice he returned home, and was demobilised in April 1919, holding the General Service and Victory Medals.
33, Cleveland Road, Northampton. Z1364.

BARBER, N., Driver, R.A.S.C.
After volunteering in March 1915, he completed his training in the same year, and proceeded to France, where he took part in many engagements in various sectors of the front. He was engaged on important transport duties during the Battles of Loos, Albert, Ypres, Cambrai, Bapaume and Armentières. Demobilised in July 1919, he holds the 1914–15 Star, and the General Service and Victory Medals.
61, Hood Street, Northamptonshire. TZ1363.

BARBER, T. W., Driver, Royal Field Artillery.
Joining in April 1916, he proceeded later in the same year to Salonika, where he saw much service. He was in action during heavy fighting on the Doiran, Struma, Monastir and Vardar fronts, and also saw much active service in Serbia and Roumania. On his return home in September 1919 he was demobilised, holding the General Service and Victory Medals.
36, St. James Street, Northampton. Z2559.

BARBER, W., Sapper, Royal Engineers.
He joined in May 1916, and in the following year was drafted to Mesopotamia, where he was engaged on electrical and other important duties. Stationed at Basra and various other places, he rendered valuable services with his Company until his return home for demobilisation in April 1919. He holds the General Service and Victory Medals.
25, Wilby Street, Northampton. Z2053.

BARBER, W. J., Private, 2nd Queen's (Royal West Surrey Regiment).
He volunteered in November 1915, and in the following July was drafted to France, where he took part in the Battles of the Somme, Arras and Ypres. Later he was transferred to Italy, and saw much fighting on the Piave River and the Asiago Plateau. He returned home, and was discharged in October 1918, and holds the General Service and Victory Medals.
39, Herbert Street, Northampton. Z1026/B—Z1027/B.

BARDEN, W., Sergeant, 7th Northants. Regiment.
Having previously served during the South African campaign, he was called up in August 1914, and shortly afterwards drafted to France, where he served with distinction at the Battles of La Bassée, Ypres, St. Eloi and Loos, before being wounded in November 1915. Returning to France on his recovery he took part in various engagements, and also in the Retreat and Advance of 1918. He was discharged in February 1919, and holds the Queen's and King's South African Medals, the 1914–15 Star, and the General Service and Victory Medals.
27, North Street, Daventry, Northampton. Z2560.

BARFORD, J., Private, 1st Northants. Regiment.
Shortly after joining in May 1918 he was drafted to the Western Front, where he saw severe fighting in various sectors. He took part in many important engagements in the final stages of the war, and was wounded in action before returning home for demobilisation in February 1919. He holds the General Service and Victory Medals. Pitsford, Northants. Z2937/C.

BARFORD, W., Private, 3rd Northants. Regiment.
He volunteered in January 1916, and after a period of training was sent to the Western Front, where, after taking part in many important engagements, he was wounded and gassed. On his recovery he was transferred to the Lancashire Fusiliers and was again in action until the cessation of hostilities. He was demobilised in December 1918, and holds the General Service and Victory Medals. Pitsford, Northants. Z2937/B.

BARKER, A. J., Gunner, Motor M.G.C.
He volunteered in December 1915, and twelve months later was sent to German East Africa, where he served with the armoured cars in many engagements. Returning home in 1917 he was retained on important duties in England until his demobilisation in March 1919, and holds the General Service and Victory Medals.
9, Monks Park Road, Northampton. Z2055.

BARKER, C. A., L/Corporal, Royal Fusiliers.
He was called up from the Reserve in August 1914, and retained for a time at various home stations, engaged on special work. In February 1916 he proceeded to France, and took part in the Battles of the Somme, Albert, Vimy Ridge and Arras, where he was severely gassed in April 1917. As a result he was invalided home, but unfortunately died through the effects of gas-poisoning on May 24th, 1917. He was entitled to the General Service and Victory Medals.

"Nobly striving:
He nobly fell that we might live."

49, Regent Street, Northampton. Z1029/B.

BARKER, E. C., Private, 2nd Northants. Regt.
He joined the Army in 1909, and when war broke out in August 1914, was serving in Egypt, but was immediately drafted to France. There he took part in the Retreat from Mons and the Battles of La Bassée and Neuve Chapelle. He made the supreme sacrifice, being killed in action on January 23rd, 1915, and was entitled to the Mons Star, and the General Service and Victory Medals.

"Whilst we remember, the sacrifice is not in vain."

31, Oakley Street, Northampton. Z1268.

BARKER, P. W., Gunner, Royal Field Artillery.
He joined in June 1916, and on completing his training in the following year was sent to the Western Front, where he saw much severe fighting. He took part in the Battles of Messines, Passchendaele, Cambrai, the Somme and Havrincourt, fought also in the Retreat and Advance of 1918, and was wounded in that year. He was demobilised in February 1919, and holds the General Service and Victory Medals.
57, Clarke Road, Northampton. Z2054.

BARKER, T. G., Private, Royal Fusiliers.
He joined in February 1916, and later in the same year was drafted to the Western Front. In this theatre of war he took part in many engagements, including those on the Ancre front, and was wounded in action at the Battle of Arras in 1917. On his recovery he was stationed at Etaples on garrison duties until his demobilisation in October 1919. He holds the General Service and Victory Medals.
11, Leicester Street, Northampton. Z1269.

BARKER, W., Private, Buffs (East Kent Regt.)
He joined in March 1917, and underwent a period of training prior to his being drafted overseas the following May. During his service on the Western Front he saw much heavy fighting in the Ypres sector, and was severely wounded near Cambrai. He was invalided to hospital in Rouen, where he unfortunately died of wounds in September 1917, and was entitled to the General Service and Victory Medals.

"He joined the great white company of valiant souls."

19, Bristol Street, Northampton. Z1028.

BARKER, W., Private, Labour Corps.
Volunteering in July 1915, he was drafted overseas later in the same year. Whilst on the Western Front he was engaged on important duties in the Somme sector. He was unfortunately killed by a shell while digging a trench on the Ypres front in October 1917, and was entitled to the General Service and Victory Medals.
"His life for his Country, his soul to God."
4, Windsor Terrace, Northampton. Z1030.

BARKER, W. J., Pte., 2nd Northants. Regiment.
Having volunteered in September 1914, he proceeded to France, where he took part in many important engagements, including those in the Somme and Ypres sectors, and was wounded. He was also in action during the Retreat of 1918, when he was taken prisoner at St Quentin, and held in captivity until the cessation of hostilities. Returning home he was eventually demobilised in March 1919, and holds the 1914–15 Star, and the General Service and Victory Medals.
12, Ulcombe Road, Northampton. Z1365.

BARKWOOD, W. C., Driver, R.F.A.
After volunteering in August 1914, he underwent a period of training prior to being drafted to France in November of the following year. There he took part in the Battles of Vimy Ridge, the Somme, Arras, Ypres and Passchendaele before being transferred in November 1917 to Italy, where he fought on the Piave. Returning to France, he served through the Retreat and Advance of 1918, and was finally demobilised in March 1919, holding the 1914–15 Star, and the General Service and Victory Medals.
6, St. James' Terrace, St. James' St., Northampton. Z2938/D.

BARNARD, G., Corporal, 5th Northants. Regt.
Mobilised with the Royal Field Artillery in August 1914, he was discharged shortly afterwards as medically unfit, but in September of the same year re-enlisted in the Northamptonshire Regiment, and proceeded to France in the following May. In this seat of war he took part in the Battles of the Somme, Ypres and Messines, and was gassed and twice wounded in action. Later he saw six months' service in Russia, and was finally demobilised in April 1920, holding the 1914–15 Star, and the General Service and Victory Medals.
55, Compton Street, Northampton. Z1031/A.

BARNARD, J., Private, Durham Light Infantry.
He joined in June 1916, and completing his training in the following year, was drafted to the Western Front. There he took part in the Battle of Cambrai and in the Retreat of 1918, during which he was reported missing. Later he was unfortunately reported killed in action about June 29th, 1918, and was entitled to the General Service and Victory Medals.
"Honour to the immortal dead who gave their youth that the world might grow old in peace."
5, Cooper Street, Northampton. Z1001/B.

BARNARD, J. T., Sergeant, Machine Gun Corps.
He volunteered in August 1915 in the Civil Service Rifles, but later was transferred to the Machine Gun Corps, and in January 1917 was drafted to France. In this seat of war he played a prominent part in several engagements, including the Battles of Ypres, Messines, Cambrai and the Somme (II.), being twice wounded in action. Demobilised in August 1919, he holds the General Service and Victory Medals.
55, Compton Street, Northampton. Z1031/B.

BARNES, E. W., Private, R.A.S.C.
Shortly after volunteering in May 1915, he was sent to the Western Front, where he was engaged on important duties in various sectors. He was also present at the Battles of Loos, the Somme and Ypres, took part in the Retreat and Advance of 1918, and afterwards served with the Army of Occupation at Cologne. He was demobilised in November 1919, and holds the 1914–15 Star, and the General Service and Victory Medals.
Camp Hill, Bugbrooke, Northants. Z2939/D.

BARNES, F. E., Private, R.A.S.C.
He volunteered in November 1915, and on completing a period of training in the following year was drafted to India, whence he proceeded later to Mesopotamia. Whilst in this theatre of operations he was engaged on important duties at Amara, Kut, Baghdad and other stations, finally returning home for demobilisation in June 1919. He holds the General Service and Victory Medals.
Camp Hill, Bugbrooke, Northants. Z2939/B.

BARNES, H. J., Private, Machine Gun Corps.
He joined in February 1916, and after a period of training was transferred to the Tank Corps, and drafted to the Western Front in the following year. There he took part in important engagements in various sectors, including the Battles of Arras, Ypres and Cambrai, and fought also in the Retreat and Advance of 1918. Demobilised in February 1919, he holds the General Service and Victory Medals.
Camp Hill, Bugbrooke, Northants. Z2939/A.

BARNES, J. E., Private, 11th (Prince Albert's Own) Hussars.
A Reservist, he was called to the Colours in August 1914, and was immediately drafted to the Western Front, where after fighting in the Retreat from Mons, he took part in the Battles of the Marne, the Aisne, La Bassée and Neuve Chapelle. He fell in action at Ypres on May 24th, 1915, and was entitled to the Mons Star, and the General Service and Victory Medals.
"A costly sacrifice upon the altar of freedom."
Camp Hill, Bugbrooke, Northants. Z2939/C.

BARNES, R. W., Stoker, R.N.V.R.
Called up from the Reserve in August 1914, he was quickly drafted to France, where he took part in the Defence of Antwerp, and was taken prisoner of war. He was held in captivity in Germany, and was forced to work in the mines and on the land throughout hostilities, during which time he suffered many hardships. Repatriated after the Armistice, he was discharged in January 1919, and holds the 1914 Star, and the General Service and Victory Medals.
31, Clare Street, Northampton. Z3227.

BARNES, W., Sapper, Royal Engineers.
Having joined in January 1917, he completed his training at Chatham, and in the following September embarked for the Western Front. Whilst in this theatre of war he was engaged on very important duties and served in various sectors. He did consistently good work until demobilised in February 1919, holding the General Service and Victory Medals.
40, Oxford Street, Daventry, Northampton. Z2561.

BARR, E., Private, 7th Cheshire Regiment.
He volunteered in October 1914, and in the following July was drafted to the Dardanelles, where he fought at Suvla Bay, Chocolate Hill, Anzac Cove, and in the Evacuation of the Gallipoli Peninsula. He was then sent to Egypt, thence to Palestine, taking part in much fighting at Jaffa, Gaza and Jerusalem. In 1918 he proceeded to France, and was in action in many engagements during the Advance of 1918. Demobilised in March 1919, he holds the 1914–15 Star, and the General Service and Victory Medals.
Vine Cottage, Bugbrooke, Northants. Z3228.

BARRATT, F., Pte., 2nd R. Warwickshire Regt.
Having enlisted in October 1903, he was serving at Malta at the outbreak of war, and was immediately drafted to the Western Front, where he took part in the Battles of Mons, the Marne and La Bassée. He unfortunately fell in action at Ypres on October 20th, 1914, and was entitled to the Mons Star, and the General Service and Victory Medals.
"His memory is cherished with pride."
26, Market Street, Northampton. Z2056/A.

BARRATT, J. T., Rifleman, 18th K.R.R.C.
He joined in September 1917, and, after completing a period of training, was retained on important duties at various stations. He was unable to obtain his transfer to the front, but later proceeded with the Army of Occupation to Germany, where he served at Cologne until his return home for demobilisation in October 1919.
26, Market Street, Northampton. Z2056/B.

BARRATT, W. G., Leading Seaman, Royal Navy.
He was already in the Royal Navy when war broke out in August 1914, and quickly proceeded to the North Sea on board H.M.S. "Iron Duke." He was engaged on important patrol and escort duties, and took part in the Battles of Heligoland Bight and Jutland. Throughout the war he did continuously good work and received his discharge in March 1919. He holds the 1914–15 Star, and the General Service and Victory Medals. 3, Bath Gardens, Northampton. Z1032/A.

BARRINGER, T., Sergeant, 1st Northants. Regt.
Having enlisted in November 1911, he was sent to France immediately on the outbreak of war, and there took a prominent part in the Battle of Mons and the subsequent Retreat. He also fought in the Battles of the Marne, La Bassée, Vimy Ridge and Messines, was wounded on the Aisne in September 1914, and at Contalmaison in June 1916, and was taken prisoner in July 1917. Released on the cessation of hostilities, he was discharged in March 1919, and holds the Mons Star, and the General Service and Victory Medals.
13, Steene Street, Northampton. Z2343.

BARRITT, E., Private, 1st Cambridgeshire Regt.
Four months after joining in June 1916 he was drafted to the Western Front, where he saw heavy fighting in various sectors. After taking part in the first Battle of the Somme he was severely wounded in January 1917, and was treated in hospital at Le Havre and Glasgow. He also served with the Royal Engineers before being invalided from the Army in January 1919, and holds the General Service and Victory Medals.
Church Street, Brixworth, Northants. Z2940.

BARRON, L., Private, 7th Northants. Regiment.
Joining in October 1915, he embarked for France in the following March. Whilst in this seat of operations he was in action in many important engagements, including the Battle of Messines, where he was gassed and invalided home. On his recovery he rejoined his unit on the Western Front and served through the Retreat and Advance of 1918. Demobilised in May 1919, he holds the General Service and Victory Medals.
39, Abbey Street, Northampton. Z2562.

BARTON, A. W., Pte., Royal Inniskilling Fusiliers.
Volunteering in August 1914, he was drafted to the Western Front in January of the following year, and there saw much heavy fighting. He took part in the Battles of Neuve Chapelle, St. Eloi, Ypres, the Somme, Arras and Cambrai, served also through the Retreat and Advance of 1918, and was wounded. He was demobilised in April 1919, and holds the 1914–15 Star, and the General Service and Victory Medals.
136, Southampton Road, Northampton. Z2941 /D.

BARTON, E. T., Private, Northants. Regiment.
Called up from the Reserve in August 1914, he was immediately sent to the Western Front, where he was taken prisoner in the Retreat from Mons. He was held in captivity in Germany until after the cessation of hostilities, suffering many hardships during this period, and was discharged on his release in January 1919. He holds the Mons Star, and the General Service and Victory Medals.
136, Southampton Road, Northampton. Z2941 /A.

BARTON, R. J., Private, Sherwood Foresters.
He volunteered in September 1914, and in the following February was drafted to the Western Front, where he took part in several important engagements, including the Battles of Neuve Chapelle and Ypres. He fell fighting at Loos in September 1915, and was entitled to the 1914–15 Star, and the General Service and Victory Medals.
"Whilst we remember, the sacrifice is not in vain."
136, Southampton Road, Northampton. Z2941 /C.

BASELEY, C. F., Pte., 1st Bedfordshire Regiment.
Called up from the Reserve in August 1914, he quickly proceeded to the Western Front, where he took part in the Battle of the Marne and many minor engagements. He died gloriously on the Field of Battle at Ypres on November 7th, 1914, and was entitled to the 1914 Star, and the General Service and Victory Medals.
"A costly sacrifice upon the altar of freedom."
27, Ambush Street, St. James', Northampton. Z2344 /B.

BASELEY, F. C., Private, 13th Queen's (Royal West Surrey Regiment).
Two months after joining in March 1917 he proceeded to the Western Front, where he saw severe fighting in various sectors. After taking part in the Battles of Messines, Ypres, Passchendaele and Cambrai and minor engagements, he was wounded at Ypres in October 1918, and invalided home. Demobilised in January 1919, he holds the General Service and Victory Medals. 27, Ambush St., St. James, Northampton. Z2344 /A.

BASON, A., Private, R.A.M.C.
He volunteered in October 1915, and in March of the following year proceeded to France, where he served with a Field Ambulance at Ypres and Arras. Transferred in March 1917 to Salonika, he was engaged on important duties on the Struma and Vardar fronts and at Monastir. He was demobilised on returning home in May 1919, and holds the General Service and Victory Medals. 45, Stanhope Rd., Northampton. Z2345.

BASS, A. S. J., Private, Machine Gun Corps.
He volunteered in March 1915, and was retained at various home stations before being drafted to France in February 1918. Whilst overseas he took part in the Retreat and Advance of the Allies, and, after the cessation of hostilities, proceeded to Germany with the Army of Occupation. He served on the Rhine, but, contracting influenza, unfortunately died through the effects in February 1919, and was entitled to the General Service and Victory Medals.
"His memory is cherished with pride."
Bugbrooke, Northants. Z3229 /A.

BASS, G. W., Private, R.A.S.C.
He volunteered in October 1914, and was retained for a time on transport duties with the Royal Army Service Corps. In May 1917 he was transferred to the 14th Royal Irish Rifles and drafted to France, where he took part in much fighting in the Ypres sector, and was badly wounded. As a result he was invalided home and eventually discharged medically unfit in August 1918. He holds the General Service and Victory Medals. Bugbrooke, Northants. Z3229 /B.

BASS, J. H. D., Private, Machine Gun Corps.
He volunteered in March 1915 in the Northamptonshire Dragoons, and, after serving at various home stations, was transferred to the Machine Gun Corps and drafted to France. There he took part in the Retreat and Advance of 1918, and, after hostilities ceased, proceeded to Germany with the Army of Occupation. Demobilised in November 1919, he unfortunately contracted influenza, and died on October 22nd, 1920, and was entitled to the General Service and Victory Medals.
"He joined the great white company of valiant souls."
Bugbrooke, Northants. Z3229 /C.

BASSETT, W. H., Ordinary Seaman, R.N.V.R.
He joined in October 1917, and, after a period of training, proceeded to Italy on board H.M.S. "Weymouth." Whilst in this seat of operations he was engaged on important duties with the Kite Balloon and Submarine Sections until 1919, when he returned home. He was demobilised in April 1919, and holds the General Service and Victory Medals.
18, Little Cross Street, Northampton. Z1033

BATCHELOR, C. L., Private, 1st Northants. Regt.
Four months after volunteering in January 1916 he was sent to the Western Front, where he took part in many important engagements. He made the Supreme Sacrifice, being killed in action on the Somme on July 1st, 1916, and was entitled to the General Service and Victory Medals.
"Courage, bright hopes, and a myriad dreams, splendidly given."
18, Roseholme Road, Northampton. Z2057.

BATCHELOR, G. H., Sergt., 5th Northants. Regt.
He volunteered in September 1914, and in the following August was drafted to France, where he took part in much fighting at Loos, but, suffering from frost-bite, was consequently invalided home. On his recovery he returned to France and served with distinction at Vermelles and on the Somme. In November 1916 he was again invalided home, suffering from blood-poisoning. Later he again proceeded to France, and fought in the Battles of Arras, Cambrai and in the Retreat and Advance of 1918. He holds the 1914–15 Star, and the General Service and Victory Medals, and was demobilised in February 1919.
83, Delapre Street, Far Cotton, Northampton. Z3230 /B.

BATES, A., Private, Suffolk Regiment.
Shortly after joining in 1916 he proceeded to France, where he saw much heavy fighting. He took part in the Battles of Albert, Ypres, Passchendaele and Cambrai, and many other engagements until gassed and severely wounded in 1918 and invalided home. He was finally demobilised in 1919, and holds the General Service and Victory Medals.
106, Adam's Avenue, Northampton Z2058.

BATES, A., Private, 1/4th Northants. Regiment.
Mobilised in August 1914, he was drafted to the Dardanelles, where he saw much heavy fighting at the Landing at Suvla Bay and was also in action at Anzac Cove and Chocolate Hill. After the Evacuation of the Gallipoli Peninsula he was sent to Egypt, and later proceeded to Palestine. There he fought in the Battles of Gaza, the capture of Jerusalem and engagements on the River Jordan. He returned home and was demobilised in June 1919, holding the 1914–15 Star, and the General Service and Victory Medals.
46, Regent Street, Northampton. Z1034 /A.

BATES, A., L/Corporal, 5th Northants. Regt.
He volunteered in August 1914, and, completing his training in the following May, was drafted to France. In this theatre of war he took part in many engagements, including the Battles of Ypres, the Somme, Arras, Cambrai, Armentières and the Somme (II.), and was twice wounded in action. He was demobilised in March 1919, and holds the 1914–15 Star, and the General Service and Victory Medals.
20, Shelley Street, Kingsley, Northampton. Z1036.

BATES, G., Private, Royal Defence Corps.
He volunteered in June 1915, and, after a period of training, was engaged at various home stations on important duties with his unit. He was employed chiefly in guarding bridges, and was also on guard duties in a prisoner of war camp. He did continuously good work throughout his service, and was demobilised in March 1919.
46, Regent Street, Northampton. Z1034 /B.

BATES, J., Rifleman, Rifle Brigade.
Volunteering in September 1915, he was retained on home service until 1917, when he was drafted overseas. Whilst on the Western Front he was in action in many engagements of note, including the Battles of Arras, Ypres and Cambrai, and was actively engaged in the Retreat and Advance of 1918. He also served in the Queen's (Royal West Surrey Regiment), and was demobilised in January 1919, holding the General Service & Victory Medals. 69, Perry St., Northampton. Z1853 /B

BATES, W. J., Private, 1st Northants. Regiment.
Having enlisted in 1909, he was drafted to France in August 1914, and fought in the Retreat from Mons. He was also in action in the Battles of the Marne, the Aisne, La Bassée, Ypres, Neuve Chapelle, Loos, the Somme and Arras, and was severely wounded in November 1917 and invalided to England. In consequence he was discharged as medically unfit for further service in June 1918, holding the Mons Star, and the General Service and Victory Medals.
70, Melbourne Street, Northampton. Z1854

BATTAMS, P., Gunner, Royal Garrison Artillery
He volunteered in November 1915, and, after two months training, was drafted to the Western Front, where he saw much heavy fighting. He took part in the Battles of Albert, the Somme, Arras and Ypres and other engagements, and fought also in the Retreat and Advance of 1918. He was demobilised in March 1919, and holds the General Service and Victory Medals. 21, West Street, Northampton. Z2059

BATTERSHILL, G. W., Sapper, R.E.
Volunteering in November 1915, he underwent a period of training prior to his being drafted to France. In this seat of war he served with the transport of his unit, and was engaged on important duties in the Ypres, Cambrai and the Somme sectors. He was demobilised in February 1919, and holds the General Service and Victory Medals.
14, Little Cross Street, Kingsthorpe, Northampton. Z1035 /.

BATTISON, A. V., Private, 23rd Royal Fusiliers.
He joined in June 1918, and, after undergoing a period of training, was retained on important duties at various stations, where he rendered valuable services with his unit. Owing to the early cessation of hostilities he was unable to obtain his transfer to the front, but in February 1919 was sent with the Army of Occupation to Germany. He was demobilised on returning home in January 1920.
34, Byfield Road, St. James, Northampton. Z2346.

BATTISON, C. T., Private, 7th Northants. Regt.
He volunteered in May 1915, and later in the same year was drafted to the Western Front. Whilst overseas he took part in many engagements, including those in the Ypres and Somme sectors, and was badly wounded in action in 1916. As a result he was invalided home and eventually discharged in March 1918 as medically unfit for further service. He holds the 1914–15 Star, and the General Service and Victory Medals.
4, Compton Street, Northampton. Z1037.

BATTISON, T. (M.M.), Sergeant, 2nd and 1st Northamptonshire Regiment.
Mobilised in August 1914, he was quickly drafted to France. There he played a distinguished part in the Battles of Mons, the Marne, the Aisne, Ypres, Neuve Chapelle, Loos and the Somme, where he was badly wounded in action. He was awarded the Military Medal and Médaille Militaire in 1915 for great gallantry and devotion to duty in the Field, and also holds the Mons Star, and the General Service and Victory Medals. He was discharged in February 1919.
Brayfield, Rose Cottage, Northampton. Z3231.

BATTISSON, A., Private, K.O. (Y.L.I.)
Volunteering in September 1914, he proceeded to the Western Front in April of the following year and saw heavy fighting in various sectors. He took part in many important engagements in this theatre of war, and was wounded at Aubers Ridge in May 1915, and on the Somme in September 1916. Invalided home, he was then retained in Ireland until demobilised in February 1919, holding the 1914–15 Star, and the General Service and Victory Medals.
Rothersthorpe, Northants. Z2942.

BATTISSON, J., Corporal, 1/4th Northants. Regt.
Volunteering in August 1914, he was drafted to Gallipoli in April of the following year and there, after taking part in the Landing at Cape Helles, fought in the Battles of Krithia and Suvla Bay. He was afterwards transferred to Egypt and thence to Palestine, where, after much severe fighting, he fell in action at the third Battle of Gaza in November 1917. He was entitled to the 1914–15 Star, and the General Service and Victory Medals.
"His memory is cherished with pride."
43, Wycliffe Road, Northampton. Z2347.

BAUCUTT, D., Private, Middlesex Regiment.
He joined in July 1916, and later in the same year was drafted to Mesopotamia, where he took part in much heavy fighting at Amara, Kut, the capture of Baghdad and engagements on the Tigris. Later he saw service in India, being stationed in the Punjab on important duties. He returned home and was demobilised in February 1920, holding the General Service and Victory Medals.
42, Arthur St., Kingsthorpe Hollow, Northampton. Z1270/A.

BAUCUTT, J., Private, Royal Army Medical Corps.
Shortly after volunteering in June 1915 he was drafted to the Western Front, where he served as a stretcher-bearer in various sectors. He was present at the Battles of the Somme, Arras, Ypres and Cambrai and many other engagements, and was finally demobilised on his return home in March 1919. He holds the 1914–15 Star, and the General Service and Victory Medals. 4, Alpha Street, Northampton. Z1271.

BAUCUTT, W. J., Private, 1st Northants. Regt.
Having previously fought in the South African War, he was called up from the Reserve in August 1914, and was quickly sent to France, where he fought in the Retreat from Mons. He also took part in the Battles of the Aisne, Ypres, Loos, Albert, the Somme and Cambrai and other engagements, and was twice wounded. Discharged in March 1919, he holds the Queen's and King's South African Medals, the Mons Star, and the General Service and Victory Medals.
37, Arthur St., Kingsthorpe Hollow, Northampton. Z1272/A.

BAWCUTT, H., Trooper, Northants. Dragoons.
He volunteered in January 1915, and in May of the following year proceeded to the Western Front, where he saw severe fighting in various sectors. He took part in the Battles of the Somme, Vimy Ridge, Bullecourt, Messines, Passchendaele, Cambrai, the Lys, the Aisne, the Marne and Amiens, and was gassed and twice wounded. Demobilised in May 1919, he holds the General Service and Victory Medals.
5, Crambrook Street, Northampton. Z2348.

BAYES, C. W. (M.M.), Private, Duke of Cornwall's Light Infantry.
A Reservist, he was called to the Colours in August 1914, and in October of the following year proceeded to France, where he took part in many important engagements in various sectors of the front. He was awarded the Military Medal for conspicuous gallantry in the Field at Flers, and, holding also the 1914–15 Star, and the General Service and Victory Medals, was discharged in March 1919.
34, Overstone Road, Northampton. Z2943.

BAYES, F. (Mrs.), Special War Worker.
For nearly three years of the war this lady was engaged on work of National importance with the Advance Motor Co., where she was employed on responsible duties in connection with the manufacture of shell-cases. She rendered very valuable services until the cessation of hostilities.
17, St. Andrew's Gardens, Northampton. Z1040/B.

BAYES, G. H., Private, 4th Yorkshire Regiment.
Volunteering in November 1914, he proceeded to the Western Front on completing his training in the following April, and there saw much severe fighting. He took part in the Battles of Ypres, Loos, the Somme, Arras and Cambrai and other engagements until the cessation of hostilities, and was demobilised on his return home in February 1919. He holds the 1914–15 Star, and the General Service and Victory Medals.
17, St. Andrew's Gardens, Northampton. Z1040/A.

BAYES, W. H., A/Sergeant, R.M.L.I.
When war broke out he was serving in H.M.S. "Prince George," in which ship he was engaged on important patrol and transport duties in the North Sea. He also did duty on H.M.S. "Blenheim," "Europa," "Egmont" and "Barham," and was stationed for a time at Mudros and Malta, where he performed valuable work on the printing staff. He was invalided out of the Service in April 1920, holding the 1914–15 Star, and the General Service and Victory Medals.
36, Denmark Road, Northampton. Z1855.

BAYLISS, C. E., Private, 6th Northants. Regt.
He volunteered in September 1914, and in the following year was drafted to the Western Front, where he saw much severe fighting. After taking part in several important engagements he died gloriously on the Field of Battle in 1916. He was entitled to the 1914–15 Star, and the General Service and Victory Medals.
"He nobly fell that we might live."
105, St. Leonard's Road, Northampton. Z2944/B.

BAYLISS, W. F., Private, Labour Corps.
After joining in March 1917 he underwent a period of training with the East Surrey Regiment prior to being drafted to the Western Front in April of the following year. There he was present at many important engagements in the Advance of 1918, and was twice wounded on the Somme—in April and July of that year. He unhappily died of pneumonia on November 14th, 1918. He was entitled to the General Service and Victory Medals.
"Steals on the ear the distant triumph song."
4, Doddridge Square, Northampton. Z1038/B.

BAYLISS, W. F., Private, Royal Sussex Regiment.
Shortly after joining in 1917 he was sent to the Western Front, where he saw severe fighting in various sectors and took part in the Battles of Ypres, Cambrai and Lille and other engagements. Invalided home on account of exposure, he unhappily died in hospital in 1918. He was entitled to the General Service and Victory Medals.
"Steals on the ear the distant triumph song."
105, St. Leonard's Road, Northampton. Z2944/A.

BAZELEY, A., Private, R.A.M.C.
He volunteered in October 1915, and, on conclusion of his training in June 1917, was drafted to France, where he served with a Field Ambulance in various sectors of the front. He was present at the Battles of Ypres, Passchendaele, Cambrai, Havrincourt and the Sambre, and, after the cessation of hostilities, proceeded with the Army of Occupation to Germany. Demobilised in June 1919, he holds the General Service and Victory Medals. 5, Foundry St., Northampton. Z2563/B.

BAZELEY, A. E., Private, Royal Fusiliers.
He joined in July 1916 in the Royal Fusiliers, and in the following year was drafted to France. In this theatre of war he saw much heavy fighting in the Somme, Arras and Monchy sectors, was gassed and wounded in action and buried by a shell explosion in 1917. He was also attached to the Royal Army Veterinary Corps, and served at No. 8 Veterinary Hospital, and was demobilised in February 1919, holding the General Service and Victory Medals.
20, Bath Street, Northampton. Z1039/A.

BAZELEY, F., Sergeant, R.A.S.C. (M.T.)
Joining in October 1916, he underwent a period of training, and in the following year was drafted to Egypt. Later he saw much fighting in Palestine, particularly at the Battles of Gaza and Rafa, where he rendered excellent services. In May 1918 he was transferred to Salonika, and, attached to an Ammunition Column, took part in the engagements on the Doiran and Struma fronts. He did continuously good work throughout hostilities, and in November 1919 was demobilised, holding the General Service and Victory Medals.
75, Earl Street, Northampton. Z1367.

BEAKEN, R. P., L/Cpl., Royal Sussex Regiment.
He volunteered in December 1915, and in the following year embarked for Salonika with the 1st Leinster Regiment, and there saw heavy fighting on the Struma front. In 1917 he was transferred to Egypt, and subsequently to Palestine, in which theatre of war he took an active part in engagements at Gaza, Beersheba and Jerusalem. He was demobilised on his return to England in February 1919, and holds the General Service and Victory Medals. 69, Perry St., Northampton. Z1853/A.

BEAL, J., Private, 10th Essex Regiment.
Six months after volunteering in December 1915 he was drafted to the Western Front, where he saw heavy fighting in various sectors. After taking part in many important engagements he was severely wounded on the Ancre, and, admitted to hospital at Nottingham, was afterwards retained in England. Invalided from the Army in February 1918, he holds the General Service and Victory Medals.
76, Salisbury Street, Northampton. TZ1041.

BEAN, A. A., Private, R.A.S.C. (M.T.)
He enlisted in July 1917, and was shortly afterwards drafted to France. In this theatre of war he served with the Mechanical Transport Section, and was engaged in driving a motor-lorry in the forward areas of various sectors. He was demobilised in March 1920, and holds the General Service and Victory Medals. 70, Purser Road, Northampton. Z2060/C.

BEAN, W. F., Private, 6th Northants. Regiment.
He volunteered in September 1914, and later in the same year was drafted to the Western Front, where he took part in much heavy fighting in various sectors. He made the supreme sacrifice, being killed in action in March 1916, and was entitled to the 1914–15 Star, and the General Service and Victory Medals.

"Great deeds cannot die:
They with the sun and moon renew their light for ever."

70, Purser Road, Northampton. Z2060/B.

BEARD, H., Rflmn., Canadian Queen Victoria's Rfls.
He was in Canada when war broke out in August 1914, and, having previously served in the Royal Navy, volunteered in the following March and was sent to Montreal for training After three months' service he was discharged as medically unfit for further duty in June 1915.
54, West Street, Northampton. Z2061.

BEASLEY, A., Private, 5th Northants. Regiment.
He volunteered in September 1914, and three months later was drafted to France, where he took part in the Battles of Neuve Chapelle, Ypres and Loos, and was wounded in action. As a result he was invalided home, but on his recovery proceeded to Salonika and saw much heavy fighting on the Struma and Monastir fronts. He contracted malaria, and was eventually discharged in January 1919, and holds the 1914–15 Star, and the General Service and Victory Medals.
75, Delapre Street, Northampton. Z3232/B.

BEASLEY, E. H., Sergeant, Herts. Dragoons.
He re-enlisted in August 1914, and, after training with the Northamptonshire Regiment, was retained on important duties in England until October 1917, when he proceeded to Mesopotamia with the Hertfordshire Dragoons. There he took a prominent part in many important engagements, including that at Khan Baghdadie and the occupation of Mosul. Demobilised on returning home in July 1919, he holds the Queen's and King's South African Medals, and the General Service and Victory Medals.
5, St. James' Square, St. James' St., Northampton. Z2945.

BEASLEY, F., Private, Hampshire Regiment.
He volunteered in August 1914, and in the following year was drafted to France There he took part in many engagements on the Somme, at Ypres, Arras, Cambrai and in the Retreat of 1918. Later he was transferred to Salonika and served there until his demobilisation in May 1919. He holds the 1914–15 Star, and the General Service and Victory Medals.
Crick, Northants. Z3233/B.

BEASLEY, F. A., Bombardier, R.G.A.
He volunteered in August 1914, but, after a short period of training, was discharged as medically unfit. Later he rejoined in the Royal Garrison Artillery and proceeded to France, where he took part in many engagements in the Somme and Ypres sectors. He was invalided home owing to ill-health, and eventually discharged in November 1918. He holds the General Service and Victory Medals.
Crick, Northants. Z3233/A.

BEASLEY, G., Rifleman, Rifle Brigade.
He volunteered in August 1914, and, after a period of training, was drafted to the Western Front, where he took part in several engagements, including the Battle of Neuve Chapelle. He made the supreme sacrifice, being killed in action at Ypres in May 1917, and was entitled to the 1914–15 Star, and the General Service and Victory Medals.

"The path of duty was the way to glory."

Derry Lane, Crick, Northants. Z3234.

BEASLEY, J. C., Private, 2nd Northants. Regt.
Having previously served in the South African campaign, he re-enlisted at the outbreak of war and was retained on important duties as a cook at Northampton Barracks. He was unable to obtain his transfer to a theatre of war owing to his being over age, but, nevertheless, rendered very valuable services until demobilised in January 1919, holding the Queen's and King's South African Medals.
4, Adnitt Place, Northampton. Z2564.

BEDFORD, C. L., Corporal, Royal Engineers.
Volunteering in May 1915, he later in the same year proceeded to France. Whilst in this theatre of war he took an active part in many important engagements, including the Battles of Loos, Vimy Ridge, the Somme, Arras, Ypres, Passchendaele and Cambrai. He was also present at many engagements in the Retreat and Advance of 1918, and in March 1919 was demobilised, holding the 1914–15 Star, and the General Service and Victory Medals.
Cogenhoe, Northants. Z3235/D.

BEDFORD, E. A., Sergeant, R.A.M.C.
Mobilised at the outbreak of hostilities, he was immediately drafted to the Western Front, where he served with distinction at the Battle of, and in the Retreat from, Mons. He was afterwards stationed at the 39th General Hospital, Le Havre, and did continuously good work whilst attending to the sick and wounded. After the cessation of hostilities he was transferred to the Army Reserve in May 1919, and holds the Mons Star, and the General Service and Victory Medals.
Cogenhoe, Northants. Z3235/C.

BEDFORD, H. W., Pioneer, Royal Engineers.
Joining in October 1916, he was first engaged on important duties with his unit in England and Scotland. Proceeding to France in the following May, he served through fierce fighting on the Arras and Ypres fronts. He died gloriously on the Field of Battle on April 1st, 1918, and was entitled to the General Service and Victory Medals.

"A costly sacrifice upon the altar of freedom."

Cogenhoe, Northants. Z3235/A.

BEDFORD, R. T., Private, 53rd Bedfordshire Regt.
He joined in July 1917, and in the following year was drafted to the Western Front. Whilst in this theatre of war he saw much fighting in various sectors and took part in the Battle of the Somme and other engagements, afterwards serving with the Army of Occupation at Cologne. Demobilised on returning home in October 1919, he holds the General Service and Victory Medals.
22, Hampton Street, Northampton. Z1042.

BEDFORD, T. E., Private, Royal Fusiliers.
Joining in May 1918, he was retained on important duties with his unit at various stations. Owing to the early cessation of hostilities he was unsuccessful in taking part in operations in a theatre of war. He, however, proceeded to Germany with the Army of Occupation, and was stationed at Cologne, where he was engaged on guard and other important duties until demobilised in March 1920.
Cogenhoe, Northants. Z3235/B.

BEDINGFIELD, A., Private, Labour Corps.
Volunteering in March 1915 in the Royal Fusiliers, he was shortly afterwards drafted to the Dardanelles. In this theatre of war he took part in the Landing at Suvla Bay, but was later invalided to hospital, suffering from frost-bite. On his recovery he was transferred to the Western Front, and, after a short period of service there, was evacuated to England and finally discharged as medically unfit in May 1916. He holds the 1914–15 Star, and the General Service and Victory Medals.
17, Portland Street, Northampton. Z1368.

BEEBY, A., Rifleman, King's Royal Rifle Corps.
Joining in April 1917, he first served with a Training Reserve Battalion attached to the Loyal North Lancashire Regiment, but was later transferred to the King's Royal Rifle Corps and proceeded to France in January 1918. Whilst on the Western Front he was transferred to another unit and took part in the Battles of Arras, Ypres, Passchendaele, Cambrai and Amiens. He was wounded in February 1918, and in November 1919 was demobilised, holding the General Service and Victory Medals. 34, St. James' Street, Northampton. Z2565.

BEEBY, G. R., Private, Queen's Own (Royal West Kent Regiment).
Joining in June 1918, he shortly afterwards proceeded overseas. During his service on the Western Front he took part in the final operations of the war. He later contracted an illness, and as a result was invalided home to hospital, and, after a period of treatment, was demobilised in October 1919, holding the General Service and Victory Medals.
48, Rothersthorpe Road, Northampton. Z3236.

BELLAMY, C., Private, 1st Northants. Regiment.
Volunteering in April 1915, he underwent a period of training, and twelve months later embarked for the Western Front. Whilst in this seat of operations he took part in heavy fighting at Arras and also in the Battles of Vimy Ridge and the Somme, where he fell in action on November 24th, 1916. He was entitled to the General Service and Victory Medals.

"A valiant Soldier, with undaunted heart he breasted life's last hill."

6 House, 3 Court, Brook Street, Daventry, Northants. Z2568/A.

BELLAMY, E., Driver, Royal Field Artillery.
Volunteering at the outbreak of war, he was drafted in the following year to France. Serving on the Western Front he was in action with his Battery at the Battles of Hill 60, Festubert, Loos, the Somme, Arras, Ypres, Passchendaele and Cambrai, and also in the Retreat and Advance of 1918. He returned home for demobilisation in January 1919, and holds the 1914–15 Star, and the General Service and Victory Medals.
18, Orchard Street, Daventry, Northants. Z2566.

BELLAMY, E. C. (M.M.), Gunner, R.G.A.
Volunteering in June 1915, he served on important duties at home before proceeding to the Western Front in August 1917. In this theatre of war he was in action with his Battery in many important engagements in various sectors. He was unfortunately killed in May 1918 near Albert. Awarded the Military Medal for conspicuous bravery and devotion to duty in the Field, he was also entitled to the General Service and Victory Medals. "His life for his Country."
6, West View, Daventry, Northants. Z2567.

BELLAMY, F. J. (M.M.), Cpl, 1st Northants. Regt.
Already serving in the Army, he was mobilised in August 1914, and immediately drafted to France. There he served with distinction in the Battle of, and Retreat from, Mons and also in the Battles of the Marne, the Aisne, Vimy Ridge, the Somme, Arras and St. Quentin, where he was unhappily killed in action in October 1918. He had been awarded the Military Medal for conspicuous bravery in the Field, and was also entitled to the 1914–15 Star, and the General Service and Victory Medals.
"Great deeds cannot die."
14, Brook Street, Daventry, Northants. Z2568/B.

BELLAMY, S., Corporal, 9th East Surrey Regt.
He joined immediately on attaining military age in August 1918, and, after completing a period of training, was retained on important duties at various stations. Owing to the early cessation of hostilities he was unable to obtain his transfer to the front, but in March 1919 was sent with the Army of Occupation to Cologne. He was demobilised on his return home twelvemonthslater. 11,KinburnPlace,Northampton. Z1043/A.

BELLAMY, W. H., Private, Royal Welch Fusiliers.
Having joined in February 1917, he landed in France two months later, and whilst in this theatre of war was engaged on important duties as a stretcher-bearer during heavy fighting on the Ypres front. He was reported missing on October 23rd, 1917, and was later presumed to have been killed in action on that date, and was entitled to the General Service and Victory Medals.
"Steals on the ear the distant triumph song."
11, St. James' Street, Daventry, Northants. Z2569.

BELLHAM, A., Sergeant, 4th Northants. Regt.
He was serving in Egypt at the outbreak of war, but was quickly drafted to France, where he played a prominent part in the Retreat from Mons and also in the Battles of Le Cateau, La Bassée and Neuve Chapelle and many minor engagements. Proceeding to Egypt in 1917, he later advanced into Palestine, wherehe servedwith General Allenby's Forces on various fronts. Whilst overseas he was wounded, and, on returning home in January 1919, was discharged, holding the 1914–15 Star, and the General Service and Victory Medals.
53, Devonshire Street, Northampton. Z2570.

BELLHAM, A. E., Air Mechanic, Royal Air Force.
After volunteering in August 1914 he underwent a period of training prior to being drafted to the Western Front in 1916. There he was engaged on duties of a highly technical nature, being present at the Battles of Vimy Ridge, the Somme, Arras, Ypres and Cambrai, and was afterwards sent with the Army of Occupation into Germany. He was demobilised in February 1919, and holds the General Service and Victory Medals.
43, Lorne Road, Northampton. Z1273

BENNETT, F., Private, 108th Canadian Infantry.
He joined in April 1916, was trained in Canada and later in the same year was drafted to the Western Front. There he fought in numerous important engagements in various sectors, but was unhappily killed in action in May 1918. He was entitled to the General Service and Victory Medals.
"He died the noblest death a man may die,
Fighting for God and right and liberty."
31, New Town Road, Northampton. Z1856.

BENNETT, I., Private, East Surrey Regiment.
Joining in 1916, he embarked later in the same year for Salonika. Whilst in this theatre of war he saw much severe fighting and was present in engagements on the Doiran and Struma fronts. He contracted malarial fever, and as a result was invalided home, and was eventually demobilised in January 1919, holding the General Service and Victory Medals.
10, St. Peter's Street, Northampton. Z2571.

BENSON, T., Private, 4th Northants. Regiment.
A Territorial, he was mobilised in August 1914, and afterwards served at various stations, where he was engaged on duties of great importance. Being over age for active service, he was not successful in obtaining his transfer overseas, but rendered valuable services with his unit until his discharge in February 1919. 9, Moat Street, Northampton. Z1044/A.

BENSON, T., Driver, Royal Engineers.
After volunteering in August 1915, he was retained on important duties in England until February 1917, and was then sent to the Western Front. There he took an active part in the Battles of Arras and Cambrai and other engagements until severely wounded in action and admitted to hospital at Cambridge. He was invalided from the Army in February 1918, and holds the General Service and Victory Medals.
9, Moat Street, Northampton. Z1044/B.

BENT, C., Private, Royal Army Medical Corps.
Shortly after volunteering in October 1915 he proceeded to France, where he served as a stretcher-bearer in various sectors until transferred to Salonika in 1917, and thence to Egypt in April of that year. Returning to the Western Front in 1918, he was present at the Battles of the Somme, Cambrai and Ypres and other engagements, and was awarded the Divisional Scrip Certificate for conspicuous bravery in the Field. Holding also the 1914–15 Star, and the General Service and Victory Medals, he was demobilised in 1919.
82, Balmoral Road, Northampton. Z2349.

BENT, S., Cpl., Mounted Military Police.
Called up from the Reserve with the 1st Life Guards in August 1914, he was later transferred and drafted to France. Whilst in this theatre of war he did consistently good work and took an active part in engagements in the Somme, Arras and Cambrai sectors. After the cessation of hostilities he proceeded to Germany, where he served with the Army of Occupation. Returning home, he was discharged in August 1920, and holds the 1914–15 Star, and the General Service and Victory Medals.
West Street, Long Buckby. Z3237.

BENTLEY, J., Private, 3/4th Northants. Regt.
After volunteering in January 1916 he underwent a period of training prior to being drafted to the Western Front in 1918. There he saw much severe fighting, and, being taken prisoner near Soissons, suffered many hardships until released on the cessation of hostilities. He unhappily died as a result of his ill-treatment early in 1920, and was entitled to the General Service and Victory Medals.
"He joined the great white company of valiant souls."
Pitsford, Northants. Z2946.

BENTLEY, S., Driver, Royal Field Artillery.
He volunteered in October 1914, and was retained for a time at various home stations before proceeding to France in 1916. Whilst overseas he took part in various engagements, including those in the Somme, Arras, Vimy Ridge, Messines and Ypres sectors, and in the Retreat and Advance of 1918. Demobilised in May 1919, he holds the General Service and Victory Medals. 37, Cedar Road, Northampton. Z2062.

BENTON, C. E., Private, 1st Northants. Regiment.
He joined in July 1916, and in June of the following year was drafted to the Western Front, where he saw much heavy fighting. He took part in the Battles of Ypres, Passchendaele and Cambrai and other engagements, served also through the Retreat of 1918, and was severely wounded during the Advance in October of that year. Invalided from the Army in February 1919, he holds the General Service and Victory Medals.
110, Wycliffe Road, Northampton. Z2350.

BENTON, T., Private, Labour Corps.
In spite of the fact that he was over age for military service, he joined in April 1917, and, after a period of training, was retained on important guard and other duties at Felixstowe. He did continuously good work, and in March 1919 was demobilised. 13, Spencer Road, Northampton. Z1369/B.

BERWICK, A., Private, Northants. Regiment.
Mobilised from the Reserve at the outbreak of hostilities, he was immediately drafted to the Western Front, where he took part in the Battle of, and the Retreat from, Mons and the Battle of La Bassée. In November of that year he was invalided home, suffering from rheumatism, but on his recovery rejoined his unit in France and was in action at Loos. Later, however, he was evacuated to England and eventually discharged as medically unfit for further service in September 1916. He holds the Mons Star, and the General Service and Victory Medals. 6, Thomas Street, Northampton. Z1370.

BETTS, W. J., Gunner, Royal Field Artillery.
Three months after joining in October 1916, he proceeded to France, where he saw severe fighting in various sectors of the Front. He took part in the Battles of Arras and the Somme and many other engagements until invalided home in April 1918, suffering from shell-shock. He was finally demobilised in February 1919, and holds the General Service and Victory Medals. 55, Lorne Road, Northampton. Z1274.

BEX, J. R., Cpl., 18th (Queen Mary's Own) Hussars.
A Reservist, he was called to the Colours in August 1914, and was immediately drafted to France, where he fought in the Retreat from Mons. He also took part in the Battles of the Marne, the Aisne, La Bassée, Ypres, the Somme and St. Quentin, and served through the Retreat and Advance of 1918, later proceeding with the Army of Occupation to Cologne. Discharged in March 1919, he holds the Mons Star, and the General Service and Victory Medals.
16, Adelaide Street, Northampton. Z1045/B—Z1046/B.

BICKERSTAFF, F., Air Mechanic, R.A.F.
Having joined in January 1917, he landed in France two months later. Whilst on the Western Front he was engaged on important duties which demanded a high degree of technical skill, and served during the Battles of Arras, Ypres and Cambrai and in the Retreat and Advance of 1918. He was demobilised in February 1919, and holds the General Service and Victory Medals. 39, Symington Street, Northampton. Z2572.

BIGGS, E., Driver, Royal Army Service Corps.
Having previously served for 21 years, he re-enlisted in September 1914, and was later drafted to Salonika. During his service overseas he was engaged in conveying foodstuffs and supplies to the forward areas on various fronts. He was wounded, and as a result was invalided home and eventually discharged as medically unfit for further service in October 1916. He holds the 1914–15 Star, and the General Service and Victory Medals. 24, Augustin Rd., Northampton. Z2573/B.

BIGGS, H., Gunner, Royal Horse Artillery.
Although only 16 years of age, he joined in November 1918, but owing to his being under age was unable to proceed overseas. He was therefore retained on important duties with his Battery at various stations, and rendered very valuable services until demobilised in March 1920.
24, Augustin Street, Northampton. Z2573/C.

BIGGS, W., Ordinary Seaman, Royal Navy.
Joining in February 1917, he was immediately posted to H.M.S. "Carmichael," in which vessel he was on important mine-sweeping duties with the Grand Fleet in the North Sea. He was also engaged in patrolling these waters until demobilised in February 1919, holding the General Service and Victory Medals. Later in the same year he enlisted in the 19th Hussars, and in 1921 was serving in India.
24, Augustin Street, Northampton. Z2573/A.

BIGNELL, A. R., Private, 1/4th Northants. Regt.
Volunteering in November 1914, he proceeded in the following year to the Dardanelles, where he took part in the Gallipoli campaign. After the Evacuation of the Peninsula he saw service in Egypt, and later advanced into Palestine and was in action in various engagements, including the Battle of Gaza. He was badly wounded, and unhappily died from the effects of his wounds on December 2nd, 1917, and was entitled to the 1914–15 Star, and the General Service and Victory Medals.
"His life for his Country, his soul to God."
54, Abbey Road, Northampton. Z3238.

BIGNELL, A. W., L/Corporal, Royal Engineers.
He attested in November 1915, and in January 1917 was called to the Colours. In the following month he was drafted to the Western Front, where he was engaged on important duties in various sectors and was present also at the Battles of Ypres, the Somme and Lille. He was demobilised on his return home in April 1919, and holds the General Service and Victory Medals. 3, Euston Road, Far Cotton, Northampton. Z2947.

BIGNELL, H., Bombardier, R.G.A.
He volunteered in October 1915, and in the following year was drafted to the Western Front, where he took part in several engagements in various sectors. He made the Supreme Sacrifice, being killed in action at Passchendaele in November 1917, and was entitled to the General Service and Victory Medals.
"A costly sacrifice upon the altar of freedom."
77, Purser Road, Northampton. Z2063/A.

BIGNELL, J., Private, Volunteer Training Corps.
He volunteered in January 1915, and, after his training, was engaged at various stations on important duties with his unit. He was unable to obtain a transfer overseas owing to the loss of three fingers, but rendered valuable services until his discharge in January 1918. 1, Collingwood Street, Northampton. Z2064.

BILLETT, C., Private, R.A.O.C.
Joining in June 1916, he received his training at Woolwich and Chatham, and in the following year proceeded to Salonika. After taking part in severe fighting on that front he was transferred to South Russia, and was engaged on important duties at Batoum. On his return to England he was invalided out of the Army, suffering from malaria, in September 1919, and holds the General Service and Victory Medals.
81, Perry Street, Northampton. Z1857

BILLING, J., L/Corporal, Labour Corps.
Joining in June 1917, he was sent to the Western Front in the following month, and was there engaged on important duties in the Somme, Ypres and various other sectors. He died gloriously on the Field of Battle on the Somme on March 22nd, 1918, during the Retreat, and was buried at Arras. He was entitled to the General Service and Victory Medals.
"His life for his Country, his soul to God."
20, Scarlet Well Street, Northampton. Z1047.

BILLING, T. H., Private, Queen's Own (Royal West Surrey Regiment).
Four months after joining in May 1916 he proceeded to the Western Front, where, after taking part in many engagements, he was wounded at Cambrai in 1917. On his recovery he saw severe fighting in the Somme sector, and contracted dysentery. He was finally demobilised in September 1919, and holds the General Service and Victory Medals
Spratton, Northants. Z2948.

BILLINGHAM, A., Private, 4th Northants. Regt.
Volunteering in May 1915, he underwent a period of training prior to being drafted to Egypt in the following year, where he served on important duties with his unit, and on proceeding into Palestine took part in many important engagements, including the Battles of Gaza and Jaffa. Demobilised on returning home in July 1919, he holds the General Service and Victory Medals.
9, Abbey Street, Daventry, Northants. Z2575/C.

BILLINGHAM, A., Private, Northants. Regiment.
Mobilised when war broke out, he immediately proceeded to France and took part in the actions at Mons. He also saw heavy fighting in the Battles of Le Cateau, the Marne, the Aisne, La Bassée, Ypres and Festubert, and was wounded at Loos in September 1915. On his return to the firing-line he was again wounded and sent to England, and in consequence was invalided out of the Army in November 1916, holding the Mons Star, and the General Service and Victory Medals.
6, Alexandra Road, Northampton. Z1858.

BILLINGHAM, A., Private, Royal Fusiliers.
He joined in August 1918, and underwent a period of training at various stations. He was not successful in obtaining his transfer to a theatre of war on account of the early cessation of hostilities, but nevertheless rendered valuable services with his unit until his demobilisation in February 1919.
10, Salisbury Street, Northampton. Z1048/B.

BILLINGHAM, A. H., Rflmn., 16th London Regt. (Queen's Westminster Rifles).
Joining in February 1917, he later in the same year landed in France. Whilst on the Western Front he was in action during heavy fighting at Ypres. He made the Supreme Sacrifice, being killed in action at Passchendaele on October 28th, 1917, and was entitled to the General Service and Victory Medals.
"He died the noblest death a man may die,
Fighting for God and right and liberty."
Orchard View, Kislingbury, Northants. Z3239/B.

BILLINGHAM, A. R., Pte., 1/4th Northants. Regt.
He volunteered in October 1914, and, proceeding to the Western Front in the following year, took part in many important engagements in various sectors. Later he was transferred to Gallipoli, but contracted dysentery and was invalided to England in 1916. Consequently he was discharged as medically unfit for further service in April 1917, and holds the 1914–15 Star, and the General Service and Victory Medals.
28, Bouverie Street, Northampton. Z1859/C.

BILLINGHAM, C., Sapper, Royal Engineers.
Although under age, he joined in January 1918, but, on conclusion of his training, was retained on important guard and other duties at various stations. He was unsuccessful in obtaining his transfer to a theatre of war owing to his being medically unfit, but, nevertheless, rendered very valuable services until demobilised in December 1919.
Orchard View, Kislingbury. Z3239/C.

BILLINGHAM, E., Corporal, Royal Engineers.
He volunteered in January 1916, and, completing his training later in the same year, was drafted to Mesopotamia. In this seat of operations he was engaged on various important duties, but contracted malarial fever and was eventually sent home. He was demobilised in November 1919, and holds the General Service and Victory Medals.
9, Abbey Street, Daventry, Northants. Z2575/B.

BILLINGHAM, F., Private, 4th and 6th Northamptonshire Regiment.
He volunteered in August 1914, and in the following year was drafted to the Dardanelles, where he saw much heavy fighting, but, contracting dysentery and rheumatism, was invalided home. On his recovery he was sent to France, took part in the Battle of Arras, and was badly wounded. As a result he was sent home and invalided out of the Army in October 1917. He holds the 1914–15 Star, and the General Service and Victory Medals. 22, Waterloo, Daventry, Northants. Z2574.

BILLINGHAM, F., Pte., 11th Royal Sussex Regt.
Having joined in February 1917, he was shortly afterwards drafted to France. Whilst in this seat of operations he took part in much heavy fighting, and was in action on the Ypres front. He died gloriously on the Field of Battle on December 7th, 1917, and was entitled to the General Service and Victory Medals.
"Whilst we remember, the sacrifice is not in vain."
The Green, Kislingbury. Z3240/A.

BILLINGHAM, H., Private, 2/5th Yorkshire Regt.
He joined in September 1916, but on account of his age was not successful in his efforts to obtain a transfer to a theatre of war. During the period of his service he was retained on home defence at Catterick, Blackpool and Chelmsford, at which stations he carried out his duties with great ability, until demobilised in March 1919.
The Green, Kislingbury, Northants. Z3240/B.

BILLINGHAM, H. F., Pte., 1st Northants. Regt.
Volunteering in September 1914, he was retained on important work at home until 1916, when he was sent to the Western Front. There he was in action in many engagements, including the Battle of the Somme, but was taken prisoner whilst fighting at the Dunes. On his release from captivity he was demobilised in January 1919, holding the General Service and Victory Medals. The Green, Kislingbury, Northants. Z3240/C.

BILLINGHAM, J. C., Pte., 1/5th Suffolk Regt.
Volunteering in November 1914, he was drafted to Salonika in 1916, and served at the Landing and on the Doiran and Monastir fronts. In October 1917 he was transferred to Palestine, where he fought in numerous engagements, including the capture of Aleppo. After the Armistice he was stationed at Alexandria until sent to England for demobilisation in August 1919. He holds the General Service and Victory Medals. 28, Bouverie Street, Northampton. Z1859/B.

BILLINGHAM, J. G., Private, East Surrey Regt.
He joined in February 1917, and later in the same year was drafted to the Western Front, where he was actively engaged in the Battles of Ypres, Cambrai and the Somme. After taking part in the Retreat of 1918 his health broke down and he was invalided to England, and when discharged from hospital was retained on home service until demobilised in February 1919. He holds the General Service and Victory Medals.
9, Weston Terrace, Kislingbury, Northants. Z3240/D.

BILLINGHAM, O. G., Private, Manchester Regt.
Joining the Norfolk Regiment in April 1917 he was sent overseas later in the same year on completion of his training. During his service on the Western Front he was engaged on important signalling duties in various sectors, and whilst in action on the Somme in March 1918 was taken prisoner, and held in captivity until the following December. Demobilised in January 1919, he holds the General Service and Victory Medals. Orchard View, Kislingbury, Northants. Z3239/A.

BILLINGHAM, R., Private, 1/4th Northants. Regt.
A Reservist, he was called up when war broke out in August 1914, and engaged on important work at St. Albans until drafted to Egypt in 1916. Subsequently he was sent to Palestine, on which front he was engaged in fierce fighting at Gaza, Jerusalem and Jaffa. He was discharged on his return to England in May 1919, and holds the General Service and Victory Medals.
5, Blue Row, Kislingbury, Northants. Z3240/E.

BILLINGHAM, T., Sergeant, 7th Northants. Regt.
Having volunteered in September 1914, he was drafted overseas later in the same year. During his service on the Western Front he played a prominent part in many engagements in various sectors, and did continuously good work throughout hostilities. He was demobilised in February 1919, and holds the 1914 Star, and the General Service and Victory Medals.
9, Abbey Street, Daventry, Northants. Z2575/A.

BILLINGTON, T., Private, Royal Defence Corps.
He volunteered in October 1914, and after a period of training, was engaged at various stations on important guard duties. He was unable to obtain a transfer overseas owing to his being over age, but rendered valuable services until his demobilisation in March 1919.
66, Brook Street, Daventry, Northants. Z2576.

BILLINGHAM, W., Private, Royal Sussex Regt.
Joining in January 1918, he was drafted to France after four months' training and there saw severe fighting in various sectors. He took part in the Battle of Lille and many other important engagements during the Advance, and was afterwards stationed at Ypres until his demobilisation in November 1919. He had also served with the Royal Fusiliers, and holds the General Service and Victory Medals.
10, Salisbury Street, Northampton. Z1048/A.

BILLINGHAM, W., Pte., 1/4th Northants. Regt.
He volunteered in April 1915, and in the following January was drafted to Egypt. In this seat of operations, he took part in several engagements, and also saw fighting in Palestine with General Allenby's Forces. He returned home, and was demobilised in June 1919, holding the General Service and Victory Medals.
58, Market Street, Northampton. Z2065

BILLINGHAM, W., Gunner, R.G.A.
He joined in February 1917, and embarking for the Western Front shortly afterwards, was engaged on important signalling duties at the Battles of Arras, Ypres, Cambrai and the Somme. He also did good work with his Battery in the operations during the German Offensive and Allied Advance of 1918. On his return home he was demobilised in February 1919, holding the General Service and Victory Medals.
Starmers Lane, Kislingbury, Northants. Z3241.

BILLINGHAM, W., Private, 51st Queen's (Royal West Surrey Regiment).
On attaining military age he joined in August 1918, but owing to the early cessation of hostilities was unable to secure a transfer to the fighting area. He was retained on home defence at various stations, and carried out his duties with great efficiency until demobilised in February 1919. Subsequently he enlisted in the Merchant Service, and in 1921 was still serving. 63, Oxford Street, Northampton. Z3242.

BILLINGHAM, W. P., Private, East Yorks. Regt.
Three months after volunteering in October 1915, he proceeded to the Western Front, where he saw heavy fighting in various sectors. He took part in the Battles of the Somme, Arras, Ypres and Cambrai, and many other important engagements, and was twice wounded in action. He was demobilised in February 1919, and holds the General Service and Victory Medals. 55, St. Andrew's Street, Northampton. Z1049.

BILLINGHAM, W. R., Driver, R.A.S.C.
He volunteered in November 1914, but was retained on important duties at home until November 1916, when he was drafted to Salonika. There he was engaged in fierce fighting on the Doiran and Struma fronts, and was wounded in action at Monastir in May 1918. He was demobilised on his return to England in April 1919, and holds the General Service and Victory Medals. 28, Bouverie Street, Northampton. Z1859/A.

BILLSON, A. C., Trooper, 11th (Prince Albert's Own) Hussars.
Having already served in the Army since 1910, he was mobilised at the outbreak of hostilities, and immediately drafted to France. Whilst in this seat of operations he took part in the Retreat from Mons and the Battles of the Marne, the Aisne, Ypres, Loos, the Somme, Arras, Messines, Lens and Cambrai. He was wounded in March 1918, and invalided to England, and after a period of hospital treatment, was discharged as medically unfit in October 1918. He holds the Mons Star, and the General Service and Victory Medals.
18, Monarch Road, Northampton. Z1371.

BILLSON, W., Leading Seaman, Royal Navy.
A serving sailor, he was on board H.M.S. "Fearless" in August 1914, and in this vessel took part in the Battles of Heligoland Bight and Jutland, and in the raid on Cuxhaven. He was also engaged in experimenting with mines at Portsmouth and later served in Russian waters. He was awarded a decoration for bravery displayed during operations against the Bolsheviks, and, holding also the 1914–15 Star, and the General Service and Victory Medals, was still at sea in 1920. 84, Hunter Street, Northampton. Z1372.

BIRCH, E., Rifleman, King's Royal Rifle Corps.
He joined in May 1918, but was unsuccessful in obtaining a transfer overseas before the cessation of hostilities. He was engaged on work of an important nature at various home stations until December 1918, when he was drafted to Germany, serving with the Army of Occupation at Cologne until sent home for demobilisation in March 1919.
Church Street, Long Buckby, Northants. Z3243/B.

BIRCH, G. Mc., Special Constable.
Joining in 1915, during the war he was engaged on important duties as a special constable. He rendered valuable services, carrying out his work in a most reliable manner, but contracting fever in August 1917, was in hospital for some time, and eventually invalided out in January 1918.
87, Holly Road, Northampton. Z2066.

BIRCH, H., Private, Royal Naval Division.
Volunteering in November 1915, he proceeded to the Western Front with the "Hawke" Battalion in October of the following year. Whilst overseas he saw heavy fighting in the Arras, Bullecourt, Ypres and Lens sectors, and took part in the Battles of Cambrai and the Somme, and in the engagements during the Retreat and Advance of 1918. Serving in France until demobilised in May 1919, he holds the General Service and Victory Medals.
Church Street, Long Buckby, Northants. Z3243/A.

BIRCH, R., Private, Machine Gun Corps.
He joined in September 1917, but whilst in training at Rugeley, was admitted to hospital suffering from infleunza and rheumatism. On November 4th, 1917, he unfortunately died after only two months' service in the Army.
"His memory is cherished with pride."
2, Portland Street, Northampton. Z1373/B.

BIRCH, W., Private, 2nd Northants. Regiment.
Called up with the Reserve at the outbreak of war, he was shortly afterwards drafted to France. During his service in this seat of operations, he took part in fierce fighting at Ypres, and was badly wounded. He unfortunately died from the effects of his wounds on February 17th, 1915, and was entitled to the 1914–15 Star, and the General Service and Victory Medals.
"Thinking that remembrance, though unspoken, may reach him where he sleeps."
24, Poole Street, Northampton. Z1374.

BIRCH, W. H., Private, 1/2nd Warwickshire Regt.
Volunteering in February 1915, he was retained on important duties at various stations before proceeding to India, where he saw much service. Later, however, he was transferred to Mesopotamia, and was present at the engagements on the Tigris and at the capture of Baghdad. Returning home he was demobilised in June 1919, holding the General Service and Victory Medals.
2, House, 2 Block, Bective Road, Kingsthorpe, Northampton. Z1375.

BIRD, A. J., Private, 1/5th West Riding Regt.
He joined in March 1917, having been rejected in 1915, and was quickly drafted to France, where he first served with the Labour Corps, but was later transferred to a fighting unit. He took part in several engagements in the Ypres sector, and was afterwards engaged in guarding prisoners of war and on salvage duties. He was for six months in hospital, suffering from neurasthenia, before being demobilised in July 1920. He holds the General Service and Victory Medals.
13, Union Street, Northampton. Z2067/A.

BIRD, E., Corporal, Machine Gun Corps.
He joined in December 1916, and after three months' training with the Tank Corps was sent with the Machine Gun Corps to the Western Front. Whilst in this theatre of war he saw much severe fighting, and took part in the Battles of Ypres, Cambrai and the Somme, and minor engagements. Demobilised in February 1919, he holds the General Service and Victory Medals. 29, Fort Street, Northampton. Z1050.

BIRD, F., Private, Royal Sussex Regiment.
He joined in August 1918, and after completing a period of training was retained on important duties at various stations. Owing to the early cessation of hostilities, he was unable to obtain his transfer to the front, but in December 1918 was sent with the Army of Occupation to Germany. He was discharged on his return home in April 1920.
5, Bull Head Lane, Northampton. Z1051.

BIRD, F. C., Corporal, 2nd South Wales Borderers.
Two months after joining in January 1917, he was sent to the Western Front, where he fought in the Battles of Arras, Vimy Ridge, Ypres, Passchendaele, Lens and Cambrai. He was wounded in the latter engagement, but on his recovery returned to the firing line, and was in action in the Retreat and Advance of 1918. After the Armistice he proceeded to Germany with the Army of Occupation, serving at Cologne until demobilised in July 1919, holding the General Service and Victory Medals. 50, Hervey Street, Northampton. Z3244.

BIRD, G., Private, 1/4th Northants. Regiment.
He volunteered in August 1915, and was retained for a time at various home stations before proceeding to France in 1917. Whilst in this theatre of war he was transferred to the 1/7th Northamptonshire Regiment, and took part in several engagements, including the Retreat and Advance of 1918. Demobilised in February 1919, he holds the General Service and Victory Medals.
91, Stanley Road, Northampton. Z2577.

BIRD, G. R., Private, 18th (Queen Mary's Own) Hussars.
Already in the Army when war broke out in August 1914, he was immediately drafted to France, where he took part in the Battles of Mons and Le Cateau, being badly wounded and taken prisoner. He was at first in hospital behind the German lines, but on his recovery sent to Cologne and held in captivity, suffering many hardships. After the Armistice he escaped and walked 90 miles into Holland, whence he was sent home. Discharged in April 1919, he holds the Mons Star, and the General Service and Victory Medals.
13, Union Street, Northampton. Z2067/B.

BIRD, H. T., Company Sergeant-Major, M.G.C.
He enlisted in November 1904, and after the outbreak of war, was retained in England until April 1915. He was then sent to Gallipoli, where, after taking a prominent part in the Landing at Cape Helles, he fought in the Battles of Krithia, later proceeding to Egypt, whence he advanced into Palestine. He served through the Battles of Gaza and other engagements, and was twice mentioned in Despatches for distinguished service. Holding the 1914–15 Star, and the General Service and Victory Medals, he was discharged on returning home in March 1919.
9, Leslie Terrace, Northampton. Z1052.

BIRD, W., Private, 7th Northamptonshire Regt.
After volunteering in November 1914, he underwent a period of training prior to being drafted to the Western Front in 1916, and there took part in the Battles of Vimy Ridge and the Somme, and many minor engagements. Mortally wounded in action on the Ancre, he unhappily died in hospital at St. Omer on February 1st, 1917. He was entitled to the General Service and Victory Medals.
"The path of duty was the way to glory."
32, Ambush Street, St. James, Northampton. Z2351/A.

BIRD, W., Private, 1/4th Northants. Regiment.
He volunteered in September 1915, and in April of the following year proceeded to Egypt, whence he advanced into Palestine. There he took part in engagements at Haifa, Beyrout and many other places, and, being wounded in the third Battle of Gaza, was for a time in hospital at Cairo. He was invalided from the Army in January 1920 owing to injuries received in a railway accident, and holds the General Service and Victory Medals.
5, Bull Head Lane, Northampton. Z1053.

BIRD, W., Driver, Royal Field Artillery.
He volunteered in December 1914, and completing his training in the following September was drafted to France. There he took part in the Battles of Ypres and Loos, but later was sent for duty to Le Havre, where he served with the Royal Horse Artillery. In 1918 he returned to the firing line, and was in action in the Advance at Cambrai. Demobilised in March 1919, he holds the 1914–15 Star, and the General Service and Victory Medals. 35, Florence Road, Northampton. Z2068.

BIRD, W., Sapper, Royal Engineers.
Joining in June 1916 he underwent a period of training, and was drafted to France, where he was attached to a Field Company and engaged on important duties in connection with the building of bridges. He was present during engagements on the Arras, Ypres and Cambrai fronts, and also in the Retreat and Advance of 1918, being wounded in April 1918. Demobilised on his return home in February 1919, he holds the General Service and Victory Medals.
Virginia Cottage, Roade, Northants. Z2069.

BISEKER, C. W., Private, 12th Suffolk Regiment (Bantam Battalion).
He volunteered in October 1915, and in the following year was drafted to the Western Front. There he took part in many engagements, including those in the Loos, Somme and Cambrai sectors, and was badly wounded at Villers-Guislain in 1917. Invalided home to hospital he did excellent work with the 581st Labour Company on his recovery, and was eventually demobilised in January 1919, holding the General Service and Victory Medals. 7, Gas Street, Northampton. Z2578.

BLACKWELL, T. H., A/Corporal, R.A.F.
He joined in October 1917, and after his training was retained at various stations on duties of a highly technical nature. He was unable to obtain his transfer overseas before the cessation of hostilities, but in February 1919 was sent to France, where he served at St. Omer. He was afterwards stationed with the Army of Occupation at Cologne until his demobilisation in November 1919.
33, Scarlet Well Street, Northampton. Z1054.

BLAKE, B., Private, Royal Marines.
Mobilised in August 1914, he embarked for France and served with the Royal Naval Division at Antwerp. He was sent to Gallipoli in 1915, and saw heavy fighting at Suvla Bay, and in the subsequent engagements of the campaign. After the Evacuation he returned to the Western Front, and took part in many notable battles, including the one at Vimy Ridge. He was discharged in May 1919, and holds the 1914 Star, and the General Service and Victory Medals.
77, Delapre Street, Northampton. Z3245/B.

BLAKEMAN, H., Private, 7th Northants. Regt.
He volunteered in September 1914, and in the following year proceeded to the Western Front, where he took part in the Battles of Loos and the Somme, and was wounded at Kemmel in 1916. Invalided home he returned to France, however, in the following year, and was again in action serving through the Retreat and Advance of 1918. Demobilised in January 1919, he holds the 1914–15 Star, and the General Service and Victory Medals. 18, St John's Place, Northampton. Z2949/A.

BLAKEMAN, W., Corporal, 1st (Royal) Dragoons.
Called up from the Reserve in August 1914, he was at once drafted to the Western Front, where after fighting in the Retreat from Mons, he took part in the Battles of the Marne, the Aisne, Ypres, Loos and the Somme. Transferred in 1918 to Italy, he returned to France, however, with the Royal Warwickshire Regiment, and fell in action on the Somme on April 12th, 1918. He was entitled to the Mons Star, and the General Service and Victory Medals.
"His life for his Country, his soul to God."
18, St. John's Place, Northampton Z2949/B.

BLAND, A. E., Private, 1/4th Northants. Regt.
He volunteered in May 1915, and completing his training in the following year, was drafted to Egypt. Later he took part in the Advance into Palestine, during which he saw much heavy fighting. He was unfortunately reported missing at the first Battle of Gaza in April 1917, and is now believed to have been killed in action. He was entitled to the General Service and Victory Medals.
"A costly sacrifice upon the altar of freedom."
Hardingstone, Northants. Z2579.

BLAND, H. B. S., Private, 9th East Surrey Regt.
He joined in July 1918, but owing to the early cessation of hostilities was not successful in his efforts to obtain a transfer overseas before the Armistice. In March 1919, however, he was drafted to Germany and was engaged on duties of an important nature at Cologne, until sent to England for demobilisation in April 1920. 42, Vernon Street, Northampton Z1860.

BLAND, W. W., Air Mechanic, Royal Air Force.
He joined in December 1916, and twelve months later was drafted to the Western Front, where he was engaged on duties of great importance at the 54th Wing Headquarters. He saw much active service on the Somme, and was also stationed at Boulogne before his return home for demobilisation in December 1919. He holds the General Service and Victory Medals.
18, Bull Head Lane, Northampton. Z1055/A—Z1056/A.

BLASON, A. H., Sergeant, R.A.S.C. (M.T.)
He volunteered in June 1915, and, transferred to the 1/4th Dorsetshire Regiment, was drafted to India in the following year. There he served again with the Royal Army Service Corps on important garrison duties at various stations, and also on the Afghan frontier. Demobilised on returning home in April 1920, he holds the General Service, Victory, and India General Service Medals (with clasp, "Afghanistan, N.W. Frontier, 1919). Newland, Brixworth, Northants. Z2950.

BLASON, F. E., Pioneer, Royal Engineers.
Called up from the Reserve in August 1914, he was immediately drafted to France, where he was engaged on mine-laying, bridge-building and other important duties. After serving through the Retreat from Mons, he was present at the Battles of the Marne, Ypres, Loos, the Somme, Arras, Messines and Cambrai, and was gassed in the Advance of 1918. Discharged in April 1919, he holds the Mons Star, and the General Service and Victory Medals. 27, Regent St., Northampton. Z1057/A.

BLENCOWE, W., Corporal, 2nd Northants. Regt.
He volunteered in October 1915, and in September of the following year proceeded to France, where he took part in the Battle of the Somme, and many minor engagements until wounded at Ypres in August 1917. Invalided home he was then retained in England until drafted later to India, where he was still serving on the Afghan frontier in 1920. He holds the General Service, Victory and India General Service Medals (with clasp, "Afghanistan, N.W. Frontier, 1919.)
16, Kinburn Place, Northampton. Z1058.

BLINCOW, A., Gunner, Royal Garrison Artillery.
Mobilised with the Reserve at the outbreak of war he was immediately drafted to France, where he was in action with his Battery during the Retreat from Mons, and also at the Battles of the Marne, the Aisne, Ypres, Neuve Chapelle, Festubert, Loos and the Somme before being invalided to hospital. On his recovery he took part in heavy fighting at Arras, Passchendaele, Cambrai and the Retreat of 1918. He was twice wounded, and as a result was invalided home and discharged as medically unfit for further service in October 1918, holding the Mons Star, and the General Service and Victory Medals.
"The Layes," Roade, Northants. Z2070.

BLOXHAM, H., Private, R.A.V.C.
Shortly after joining in April 1916, he was drafted to the Western Front, where he was engaged in tending the sick and wounded horses near Neuve Chapelle and in other sectors. Transferred to Italy in 1917 he later returned to France, however, and was there stationed at Boulogne until invalided from the Army in October 1918. He holds the General Service and Victory Medals.
9, Connaught Street, Northampton. Z1275.

BLUNT, A., Private, Northumberland Fusiliers.
After volunteering in August 1915, he underwent a period of training with the Royal Engineers, prior to being sent to the Western Front in November of the following year. There he saw severe fighting in various sectors, and took part in the Battles of Arras, Ypres, Cambrai and the Somme, and minor engagements. He was demobilised in May 1919, and holds the General Service and Victory Medals.
48, Alliston Gardens, Northampton. Z1059.

BLUNT, G., Sergeant, 1/4th Northants. Regiment.
Volunteering in August 1914, he proceeded to Gallipoli in July of the following year, and was there wounded at Suvla Bay in November 1915 and invalided home. In March 1917, however, he was sent to the Western Front with the Labour Corps, and was there engaged on important duties in the Ypres sector, finally returning home for demobilisation in February 1919. He holds the 1914–15 Star, and the General Service and Victory Medals.
2 House, 3 Block, Naseby Street, Northampton. Z1276.

BLUNT, M. (Miss), Worker, Q.M.A.A.C.
She joined in April 1918, and in the following month, was drafted to the Western Front. Whilst in this theatre of war, she was stationed at Etaples and St. Pol, where, engaged on duties of great importance, she rendered very valuable services. She was demobilised on her return home in April 1920, and holds the General Service and Victory Medals.
8, Buckingham Street, Wolverton, Northants. Z2352.

BODDINGTON, E. E. E. (M.M.), Corporal, 1/4th Northamptonshire Regiment.
Called up with the Territorials in August 1914, he underwent a period of training prior to being drafted to the Western Front. Whilst in this seat of operations he did consistently good work with his unit, and took part in the Battles of the Somme, Beaumont-Hamel, Arras, Messines, Ypres, Passchendaele and Cambrai. He was awarded the Military Medal for conspicuous bravery and devotion to duty in the Field, and, demobilised in March 1919, he also holds the General Service and Victory Medals. 103, Market Street, Northants. Z2071.

BODDINGTON, T., Gunner, Royal Field Artillery.
After volunteering in March 1915, he underwent a period of training, and was retained on important duties with his unit before proceeding to France in March 1918. Whilst n this theatre of war he took part in the Retreat and Advance, and after the cessation of hostilities he went with the Army of Occupation into Germany and served at Cologne. He did continuously good work, and in February 1919 was demobilised, holding the General Service and Victory Medals.
18, Alcombe Road, Northants. Z1376.

BODILY, A., Private, Royal Defence Corps.
He joined in October 1917, and after undergoing a period of training with the Queen's Own (Royal West Kent Regiment), was transferred to the Royal Defence Corps. He was then engaged on duties of great importance at various stations in Ireland, where he did much useful work until his demobilisation in May 1919. 3, Todds Lane, Northampton. Z1060.

BODILY, F., Guardsman, Coldstream Guards.
Mobilised in August 1914, he was immediately drafted to the Western Front, where he fought in the Retreat from Mons. He also took part in the Battles of the Marne, the Aisne, Ypres and the Somme, and other engagements until gassed in April 1918, and invalided home. He was finally discharged in March 1919, and holds the Mons Star, and the General Service and Victory Medals.
117, Harborough Road, Kingsthorpe, Northampton. Z1061/A.

BODILY, J., Private, 15th Manchester Regiment.
Shortly after joining in April 1917, he proceeded to the Western Front, where he saw severe fighting in various sectors. He took part in the Battles of Ypres, Cambrai and the Somme, and many other engagements until admitted to hospital at Preston in December 1918, suffering from trench fever. He was invalided from the Army in March 1919, and holds the General Service and Victory Medals.
117, Harborough Road, Kingsthorpe, Northampton. Z1061/B.

BODSWORTH, F. C., Private, Labour Corps.
Volunteering in the Northamptonshire Regiment in October 1914, he was later transferred to the Essex Regiment, and in June 1916 embarked for France. On that front he saw much severe fighting, chiefly in the Somme sector, until wounded in action in October 1916 He was sent to hospital in England, and on his recovery was transferred to the Labour Corps, being engaged on various important duties until invalided out of the Army in November 1917, holding the General Service and Victory Medals. 35, Hervey Street, Northampton. Z1861.

BODSWORTH, J. (M.M.), Private, R.A.M.C.
Three months after volunteering in October 1915, he proceeded to the Western Front where, engaged on various important duties, he was present at the Battles of the Somme, Arras, Ypres, Kemmel Hill and Amiens, and other engagements. He was awarded the Military Medal for conspicuous bravery in the Field, and, holding also the General Service and Victory Medals, was demobilised in August 1919.
33, Bell Barn Street, Northampton. Z1062.

BOLGER, J., Private, Northants. Regiment.
He volunteered in September 1914, and proceeding to Gallipoli in 1915 served at Suvla Bay and Anzac, and in the subsequent engagements of the campaign. In 1916 he was drafted to France, where he was in action in the Battles of the Somme and Arras and was severely wounded at Ypres in July 1917. He was invalided to London, and unhappily succumbed to his injuries at King George's Hospital on August 17th, 1917. He was entitled to the 1914–15 Star, and the General Service and Victory Medals.
"Whilst we remember, the sacrifice is not in vain."
43, Francis Street, Northampton. Z1063.

BOLT, G., Sapper, Royal Engineers.
Volunteering in May 1915 in the Northamptonshire Dragoons, he was drafted to the Western Front in September 1916. Later he was transferred to the Royal Engineers, and was engaged on important duties on the ammunition and troop trains. He also saw heavy fighting in the Ypres sector, and did good work at Boulogne and Dunkirk. Demobilised in May 1919, he holds the General Service and Victory Medals.
79, Lower Hester Street, Northampton. Z1064.

BOND, J. H., Sergeant, 2nd Northants. Regiment.
A Reservist, he was called up at the declaration of war in August 1914, and eight months later was drafted overseas. During his service on the Western Front he played a conspicuous part in the Battles of Festubert, Loos and the Somme, but was unhappily killed in action at Ypres on November 23rd, 1917. He was entitled to the 1914–15 Star, and the General Service and Victory Medals.
"Whilst we remember, the sacrifice is not in vain."
9, Maycocks Road, Bridge Street, Northampton. Z2951.

BONE, A. E., Captain, Royal Field Artillery.
Mobilised in August 1914, he was at once ordered to the Western Front, and served in the Retreat from Mons. He also fought with distinction at the Battles of the Marne, the Aisne, La Bassée, Ypres, Neuve Chapelle and the Somme, and was mentioned in Despatches for good work in the Field in 1917. He was gassed in the vicinity of Cambrai in 1917, and unhappily succumbed to the effects on November 3rd, 1918. He had been granted his commission in September 1915, and was entitled to the Mons Star, and the General Service and Victory Medals.
"He nobly died that we might live."
The Green, Lower Heyford, Northants. Z3246.

BONHAM, C., Pte., Northants. Regiment (T.F.)
Volunteering in August 1914, he completed a period of training before proceeding to the Western Front, where he took part in many engagements. He was in action duiing heavy fighting on the Somme, and was wounded, and as a result he unfortunately lost the sight of an eye. On his recovery he served with his unit until demobilised in March 1919, and holds the 1914–15 Star, and the General Service and Victory Medals.
49, Cloutsham Street, Northampton. Z1377/C.

BONHAM, G., Air Mechanic, Royal Air Force.
Having previously served during the South African campaign, he re-enlisted in May 1915 in the Volunteer Training Corps, and was first engaged in guarding prisoners of war at various stations. Later he served with the Labour Corps, but was afterwards transferred to the Royal Air Force and engaged on important duties in Scotland. Returning to Rugby, he served there until demobilised in January 1919, and holds the Queen's and King's South African Medals.
49, Cloutsham Street, Northampton. Z1377/A.

BONHAM, H., Private, 2nd Northants. Regiment.
Mobilised from the Reserve in August 1914, he was immediately drafted overseas. Whilst on the Western Front he took part in many important engagements in various sectors, and did consistently good work with his unit. He made the supreme sacrifice, being killed in action on May 6th, 1917, and was entitled to the 1914 Star, and the General Service and Victory Medals. "His life for his Country, his soul to God."
49, Cloutsham Street, Northampton. Z1377/B.

BONHAM, M., Private, Queen's (Royal West Surrey Regiment).
Joining in August 1918, he proceeded to France later in the same year. Whilst in this seat of operations he took part in many engagements until the close of hostilities, and was wounded. On his recovery he rejoined his unit, and did continuously good work until demobilised in January 1919. He holds the General Service and Victory Medals.
49, Cloutsham Street, Northampton. Z1377/D

BONHAM, W. J. I., Driver, R.A.S.C.
Volunteering in November 1914, he was retained on important work at Norwich until 1916, when he was drafted to Salonika. On that front he saw much service in operations on the Vardar and the Doiran, but contracted malaria and was invalided to England in 1918. On his discharge from hospital he was stationed at Park Royal until demobilised in February 1919, holding the General Service and Victory Medals.
Church Street, Kislingbury, Northants. Z3247.

BOOKER, F. E., Sergeant, R.A.V.C.
Volunteering in January 1915, he completed his training, and later in the same year proceeded to the Western Front, where he served for four years. During that time he was engaged on important duties, and rendered valuable services to sick and wounded horses. He remained in France until May 1919, when he was sent home for demobilisation, and holds the 1914–15 Star, and the General Service and Victory Medals.
Broad Street, Brixworth, Northants. Z2952.

BORSBERRY, C. H., Corporal, 1st Essex Regt.
Called up from the Reserve in August 1914, he proceeded to Egypt about twelve months later. In this seat of operations he saw much fighting, and took part in the Advance into Palestine, being in action at Rafa, Gaza (I., II. and III.) and at the capture of Jerusalem. He returned home and was demobilised in February 1919, holding the 1914–15 Star, and the General Service and Victory Medals.
105, Green Street, Northampton. Z2580.

BOSWORTH, A. C., Trooper, Northants. Dragoons.
He volunteered in April 1915 and in the following year was ordered to Egypt, where he served in numerous engagements until transferred to the Western Front in November 1917. Whilst in France he saw heavy fighting at Péronne, and did good work with his unit in operations during the Retreat and Advance of 1918. He was demobilised in April 1919, and holds the General Service and Victory Medals.
7, Melbourne Street, Northampton. Z1862.

BOSWORTH, T., Private, 18th Manchester Regt.
He joined in April 1917, and in the following June was sent to the Western Front. There he took an active part in the operations in the Ypres sector, and after only one month's active service, died gloriously on the Field of Battle on July 26th, 1917. He was entitled to the General Service and Victory Medals.
"He died the noblest death a man may die:
Fighting for God and right and liberty."
63, Castle Street, Northampton. Z1065.

BOSWORTH, T. H., Private, 7th Suffolk Regt.
After joining in December 1916, he underwent a period of training and in the following year was drafted to France, where he took part in heavy fighting at Amiens, Havrincourt and Cambrai, before being wounded in November 1917. As a result he was evacuated to England and eventually discharged in May 1918, holding the General Service and Victory Medals.
18, Somerset Street, Northampton. Z1378.

BOSWELL, V. R., Pte., Q.O. (R. West Kent Regt.)
He volunteered at the age of 17 years in 1914, and after completing a period of training, was drafted to India, where he served at various stations. He also saw active service on the North West frontier, and suffered from malaria whilst overseas. Demobilised on his return home in 1920, he holds the General Service and Victory, and India General Service (with clasp, "Afghanistan, N.W. Frontier, 1919") Medals.
29, Adam's Avenue, Northampton. Z2353.

BOTT, A. B., Corporal, 2nd Northants. Regiment.
At the outbreak of war in August 1914, he was serving in Egypt, but was shortly afterwards transferred to the Western Front, where he was in action at the Battles of Neuve Chapelle and the Somme, before being wounded in September 1916. On his recovery in the following year he returned to France in time to take part in the Battles of Arras and Cambrai (II.). He did consistently good work, and in May 1919 was discharged, holding the 1914 Star, and the General Service and Victory Medals.
69, Stanhope Road, Northampton. Z1379.

BOTTERILL, H. T., Driver, R.F.A.
Joining in April 1916, he proceeded to Mesopotamia in September of the same year, and there saw much severe fighting. He took part in the relief of Kut and the capture of Baghdad, and in many other important engagements, and on returning home, served for a few weeks at Marsailles. He was demobilised in December 1919, and holds the General Service and Victory Medals. 25, Cecil Road, Northampton. Z2354.

BOTTERILL, W., Private, 3rd Northants. Regt.
He enlisted in March 1918, and four months later was drafted to the Western Front, where he was engaged on important duties at the base. After hostilities ceased he proceeded to Germany with the Army of Occupation, and served on the Rhine until his demobilisation in October 1919. He holds the General Service and Victory Medals.
6, Weston Row, Northampton. Z2581.

BOTTERILL, W. T., Private, 4th Royal Fusiliers.
Having joined in June 1916, he completed his training at Shoreham, and proceeded to France, where he took part in various important engagements, including the Battle of Passchendaele, before being wounded and invalided home. On his recovery he returned to France, and was in action during the Retreat and Advance of 1918. He died gloriously on the Field of Battle at Cambrai on September 27th, and was entitled to the General Service and Victory Medals.
"His life for his Country."
144, Adnitt Road, Northampton. Z2072.

BOTWOOD, G., Leading Seaman, Royal Navy.
When war was declared in August 1914, he was already in the Navy, and served with the Grand Fleet in the North Sea for two years, taking an active part in the Battles of Heligoland and Jutland. In 1916 he was transferred to the submarine service, and was engaged on important patrol duties in the North Sea and English Channel until the close of hostilities. He was discharged in April 1919, and holds the 1914–15 Star, and the General Service and Victory Medals.
3, Compton Street, Northampton. Z1066.

BOULTER, A., Private, 1st Northants. Regiment.
Having joined in August 1917 he completed a period of training, but owing to the early cessation of hostilities he was unable to take part in operations in a theatre of war. After the conclution of hostilities, however, he proceeded with the Army of Occupation into Germany, and was engaged on important guard and other duties. In 1921 he was serving in Ireland.
51, Market Street, Northampton. Z2073/A.

BOULTER, F., L/Corporal, 1st Northants. Regt.
A serving soldier, he was mobilised in August 1914, and immediately proceeded to the Western Front, where he took part in the Battle of, and the Retreat from, Mons. He also fought in the Battles of the Marne, the Aisne, La Bassée, Neuve Chapelle, St. Eloi, Hill 60 and Ypres. He made the supreme sacrifice, being killed in action on May 9th, 1915, and was entitled to the Mons Star, and the General Service and Victory Medals. "The path of duty was the way to glory."
51, Market Street, Northampton. Z2073/C.

BOULTER, F. J., Private, 4th Northants. Regt.
Joining in August 1916, he was immediately drafted to Egypt, where he took part in the Battle of Romani and the capture of Magdhaba. He then proceeded to Palestine, and was in action at the Battles of Rafa, Gaza, and the capture of Jerusalem and Jericho. Later, in 1918, he contracted malarial fever and was invalided to hospital at Alexandria, and eventually demobilised in August 1919, holding the General Service and Victory Medals. 51, Market Street, Northampton. Z2073/D

BOULTER, W. C., Private, 4th Northants. Regt.
He joined in September 1916, and three months later was drafted to Egypt, where he fought at Magdhaba. Proceeding into Palestine, he was in action at Siwa, Rafa and Gaza (I.) but after the second Battle of Gaza was reported missing. He is now presumed to have been unfortunately killed in April 1917, and was entitled to the General Service and Victory Medals. "Great deeds cannot die."
51, Market Street, Northampton. Z2073/B

BOUNDS, A., Private, Machine Gun Corps.
He joined the 4th Northamptonshire Regiment in November 1916, and after a course of training was transferred to the Machine Gun Corps, and ordered to France in July 1917 Whilst on the Western Front he fought in the Battles of Ypres, Passchendaele, Lens, Cambrai and the Somme, and did good work with his unit in the Retreat and Advance of 1918, being gassed on one occasion. Demobilised in February 1919, he holds the General Service and Victory Medals.
Clarks Yard, West Street, Long Buckby, Northants. Z3248 /A

BOUNDS, B., Sergeant, 6th Northants. Regiment.
Volunteering in August 1914, he embarked in May 1916 for the scene of activities in France. On that front he played a prominent part in the Battles of the Somme, Beaumont-Hamel, Vimy Ridge, Ypres, Passchendaele and Cambrai, and fell fighting in January 1918. He was entitled to the General Service and Victory Medals.
"A valiant Soldier, with undaunted heart he breasted life's last hill."
Clarks Yard, West Street, Long Buckby, Northants. Z3248 /C.

BOUNDS, F., Private, Lancashire Fusiliers.
He joined in February 1917, and four months later was drafted to the Western Front, where he did good work with his unit at the Battles of Ypres, Passchendaele and Cambrai. In December 1917 he was wounded and invalided home, and on his discharge from hospital was engaged on important duties in England until demobilised in February 1919. He holds the General Service and Victory Medals.
Clarks Yard, West Street, Long Buckby, Northants. Z3248 /B.

BOUNDS, G., Private, 2nd Northants. Regiment.
He volunteered in September 1914, and was retained at Chatham for a time before being drafted to France in April 1917. After three months' fighting in the Ypres sector, he unhappily fell in action on the Menin Road on July 31st 1917. He was entitled to the General Service and Victory Medals.
"Whilst we remember, the sacrifice is not in vain."
25, Abbey Street, Northampton. Z2582 /B.

BOUNDS, G., Private, Royal Berkshire Regiment.
He volunteered in September 1914, and in the following August was drafted to France, where he took part in several engagements. In November 1915 he was sent to Salonika, but owing to ill-health was unable to join his unit in the firing-line. He spent a considerable time in hospital, and being later evacuated to England, was invalided out of the Army in January 1918, holding the 1914–15 Star, and the General Service and Victory Medals. Clarks Yard, West Street, Long Buckby. Z3248 /D.

BOUNDS, R. W., Private, 5th Northants. Regt.
He joined the Northamptonshire Regiment in 1916, but was later transferred to the Northumberland Fusiliers, and drafted to France. There he was in action in many engagements and was wounded on one occasion. On being transferred to the Shropshire Light Infantry he was ordered to Mesopotamia, where he saw fighting in various sectors and contracted malaria. Demobilised on his return home in March 1919, he holds the General Service and Victory Medals.
Cank Farm, Church Brampton, Northants. Z2953.

BOURNE, J. F., Private, R.A.S.C. (M.T.)
Shortly after volunteering in January 1916, he embarked for the Western Front, where he was engaged on duties of an important nature with his unit. For the greater period of his service overseas he was employed as an electrician at Armentières, Neuve Eglise, Poperinghe and Brussels, and various other places, and did much valuable work. He was demobilised in August 1919, and holds the General Service and Victory Medals. 23, Kingswell Terrace, Northampton. Z2954.

BOWERS, J., Corporal, Northants. Dragoons.
He volunteered in September 1914, and shortly afterwards was sent to France, where he fought in the Battles of Ypres, Neuve Chapelle, Hill 60, and Festubert. In 1916 he was transferred to Italy, in which theatre of war he saw much service in engagements on the Piave front and Asiago Plateau until the cessation of hostilities. He was demobilised in February 1919, and holds the 1914 Star, and the General Service and Victory Medals.
Spring Gardens, Spratton, Northants. Z2955.

BOWERS, J. J., Sergeant, M.G.C. (Motor Section).
He joined in May 1916, and later in the same year embarked for India. He was afterwards sent to Mesopotamia, where he was employed driving armoured cars near Kut, Baghdad and on other fronts. He was severely wounded when his car was hit by a shell, being the only member of the crew to escape alive. Demobilised on returning home in December 1919, he holds the General Service and Victory Medals.
Wards Lodge, Bugbrooke, Northants. Z3249.

BOYES, E., Private, 1/4th Norfolk Regiment.
He volunteered in March 1915, and first saw active service in Egypt, to which theatre of war he was sent early in 1916. Advancing into Palestine with General Allenby's Forces, he saw much severe fighting, particularly on the Gaza and Jerusalem fronts. He was ultimately demobilised in April 1919, and holds the General Service and Victory Medals.
9, New Buildings, Blisworth, Northants. Z2074 /A.

BOYES, G. H., Sapper, Royal Engineers.
Joining in March 1917, he completed his training at Borden before proceeding overseas. Whilst on the Western Front he served with the Railway Operative Department in various sectors, and did consistently good work during heavy fighting on the Arras and Cambrai fronts. Returning home for demobilisation in November 1919, he holds the General Service and Victory Medals. 2, New Buildings, Blisworth, Northants. Z2074 /B.

BOYES, P. J., Sapper, Royal Engineers.
Joining in March 1916, he trained at Chatham, and five months later embarked for France. On that front he was engaged in severe fighting in the Battles of the Somme, Arras and Ypres, but was unhappily killed in action at Cambrai on February 17th 1918. He was entitled to the General Service and Victory Medals.
"Nobly striving:
He nobly fell that we might live."
103, Byron Street, Kingsley Park, Northampton. Z1067 /B.

BOYES, R. A., Pte., Norfolk Regt. & Labour Corps.
Volunteering in January 1916, he was drafted overseas on completion of his training in the following July. During his service in France he took an active part in the Battles of the Somme, Arras, and Ypres, but unfortunately his health broke down, and he was invalided to England in September 1917. On his recovery he was retained on important duties at Sutton until demobilised in March 1919, holding the General Service and Victory Medals.
103, Byron Street, Kingsley Park, Northampton. Z1067 /A.

BOYSON, A., Private, 1/4th Northants. Regiment.
Volunteering in November 1915, he was trained at Sheringham, and in the following year was drafted to Egypt. After a period of service there he was sent to Palestine, but was wounded in the Battle of Gaza in April 1917. On his discharge from hospital he returned to the firing-line and fought in numerous engagements until the termination of the war. He was demobilised on his return home in March 1919, holding the General Service and Victory Medals.
Church Street, Rothersthorpe, Northants. Z2957 /B

BOYSON, E. T., Corporal, New Zealand Rifles.
When war broke out he was in New Zealand, and joining the Army in July 1916, proceeded to England and was drafted to the Western Front in 1917. Whilst overseas he was engaged on important duties at Etaples, but unfortunately his health broke down, and he was discharged as medically unfit for further service in November 1917. He holds the General Service and Victory Medals.
New Cottages, Rothersthorpe, Northants. Z2956 /C.

BOYSON, F., Private, 16th Manchester Regiment.
He joined in April 1917, and after a period of training proceeded overseas later in the same year. Whilst serving on the Western Front he was engaged in fierce fighting, chiefly in the Ypres sector, but was severely wounded and unhappily succumbed to his injuries on September 29th, 1917. He was entitled to the General Service and Victory Medals.
"A costly sacrifice upon the altar of freedom."
Church Street, Rothersthorpe, Northants. Z2957 /A.

BOYSON, F. G., Private, 4th Northants. Regiment.
Volunteering in May 1915, he sailed for Gallipoli two months later, and took part in the Suvla Bay Landing and in the subsequent engagements of the campaign. After the Evacuation he was drafted to France, on which front he was actively engaged in various actions until taken prisoner in July 1917 at the Dunes. He was repatriated in December 1918, and three months later was demobilised, holding the 1914–15 Star, and the General Service and Victory Medals.
New Cottages, Rothersthorpe, Northants. Z2956 /A.

BOYSON, F. J., Private, Tank Corps.
He joined in October 1916, and, embarking for the Western Front in December of the following year, fought in the Battle of the Somme and other important engagements. In 1918 he was wounded at Morlincourt, but on his recovery returned to the firing-line, and was almost continuously in action until the close of hostilities. He was demobilised in February 1919, and holds the General Service and Victory Medals.
New Cottages, Rothersthorpe, Northants. Z2956 /D.

BOYSON, H. B., Cpl., New Zealand Imperial Forces.
Volunteering in the 6th Wellington Mounted Rifles in December 1914, he was sent to Cairo with the New Zealand Contingent in March 1915 for a course of training. Five months later he was ordered to Gallipoli, but after a short period of service there died gloriously on the Field of Battle at Achi Baba on August 27th, 1915. He was entitled to the 1914–15 Star, and the General Service and Victory Medals.
"His life for his Country, his soul to God."
New Cottages, Rothersthorpe, Northants. Z2956 /E.

BOYSON, J. F., Lieutenant, Border Regiment.
Having volunteered in January 1915, he proceeded to France in the following year. In this theatre of war he took a prominent part in many important engagements in various sectors of the front. He was in action at the Battles of Vimy Ridge, Arras, Ypres, Cambrai, and, after the cessation of hostilities, went to Germany and served with the Army of Occupation. Demobilised in 1919, he holds the General Service and Victory Medals. 2, Collins Street, Northampton. Z2075.

BOYSON, R., A.B., Royal Naval Volunteer Reserve.
He joined in September 1918, on attaining the age of 18, but owing to the early cessation of hostilities was not successful in his endeavours to be posted to sea before the Armistice. Throughout the period of his service he was stationed at the Crystal Palace, where he fulfilled his duties with great ability, until demobilised in January 1918.
52, Clinton Road, Far Cotton, Northants. Z2958/A.

BOYSON, T. E., R.Q.M.S., 1st Northants. Regt.
Mobilised at the outbreak of war, he was at once ordered to the Western Front, and served in the Retreat from Mons. He also fought in the Battles of the Marne, the Aisne, La Bassée, Ypres, the Somme and Cambrai, and was wounded on three occasions. During the Retreat and Advance of 1918, he rendered valuable services, and was discharged in March 1919, holding the Mons Star, and the General Service and Victory Medals. New Cottages, Rothersthorpe, Northants. Z2956/B.

BRADBURY, A. (M.M.), Pte., York & Lancs. Regt.
A Reservist, he was called up in August 1914, and proceeding to France, served in the Retreat from Mons. He was also in action at the Battles of the Marne, the Aisne, Ypres, Neuve Chapelle, Festubert and Loos, and was severely wounded at the Somme in 1916, consequently being invalided out of the Army in January 1918. He was awarded the Military Medal for conspicuous bravery in capturing 50 German prisoners single-handed, and also holds the Mons Star, and the General Service and Victory Medals. Town Yard, Hanslope Bucks Z2959/A.

BRADSHAW, F. W., Private, 3rd Canadian Infantry (Toronto).
Mobilised in August 1914 with the Territorial Forces, he was trained in Toronto, and drafted to France in February 1915. After taking part in severe fighting in the Ypres sector, he gave his life for the freedom of England on April 24th, 1915. He was entitled to the 1914-15 Star, and the General Service and Victory Medals. "Great deeds cannot die:
They with the sun and moon renew their light for ever."
170, Harborough Road, Kingsthorpe, Northampton. TZ1068.

BRADSHAW, R. A., Pte., 3rd East Surrey Regt.
He joined the Northamptonshire Regiment in April 1916, and after a period of training, embarked for the Western Front with the East Surrey Regiment. There he was in action in numerous important engagements, including the Battles of the Somme, Arras, Ypres and Cambrai, saw heavy fighting in the Retreat of 1918, and was wounded on three occasions. He was invalided to England, eventually being demobilised in March 1919, holding the General Service and Victory Medals.
21, Melbourne Street, Northampton. Z1864.

BRADSHAW, T., Saddler, Royal Field Artillery.
He volunteered in October 1915, and was sent to France early in the following year. He was attached to the 15th Divisional Ammunition Column, and whilst employed as a saddler, served at Loos, Arras, the Somme, Ypres, Cambrai, Soissons and Vimy Ridge. He performed consistently good work until he returned home for demobilisation in July 1919, and holds the General Service and Victory Medals.
35, Horseshoe Street, Northampton. Z3250.

BRADSHAW, T. D., Private, 29th Middlesex Regt.
Having previously been engaged on work of National importance for nearly two years, he joined the Colours in November 1916, but, after completing his training, was found to be medically unfit for transfer overseas. He was therefore retained on important duties with his unit at various stations, and rendered excellent services until demobilised in February 1919.
103, Adnitt Road, Northampton. Z2076.

BRAGG, S. C., Private, 3rd Buffs (East Kent Regt.)
Joining in February 1918, he was trained at Dover, and six months later was drafted to France. On that front he was in action in various sectors, and took part in the Battles of Bapaume, Havrincourt, Cambrai, Ypres and Le Cateau. After the Armistice he contracted typhoid, and on his recovery was demobilised in November 1919, holding the General Service and Victory Medals. 6, Brunswick St., Northampton. Z1865.

BRAMFITT, A., Private, Labour Corps.
Volunteering in October 1914, he served in turn with the 2/4th Northamptonshire Regiment, the Queen's (Royal West Surrey Regiment) and the Labour Corps. He was stationed in various home depôts until June 1916, when he was sent to France, where he served at Ypres, Poperinghe, Passchendaele and Lens, and in several sectors during the Retreat and Advance of 1918. He was demobilised in April 1919, holding the General Service and Victory Medals.
9, Weedon Road, Northampton. Z3251.

BRAMLEY, W., Private, 2nd Northants. Regt.
Having enlisted in 1908, he was serving in Egypt at the declaration of war, but was immediately transferred to the Western Front. He took part in the Retreat from Mons, and the Battles of Ypres (I. and II.) and Neuve Chapelle. He died gloriously on the Field of Battle at Aubers Ridge on May 9th, 1915, and was entitled to the Mons Star, and the General Service and Victory Medals.
"A costly sacrifice upon the altar of freedom.'
7, Brunswick Street, Northampton. Z1380/A.

BRANSON, A. G., Pte., 7th Northants. Regiment.
Joining in 1916 he completed his training, and n the following year embarked for France. Whilst on the Western Front he took part in various engagements, particularly during the Retreat and Advance of 1918, before being wounded. Invalided to England he underwent a period of hospital treatment, and was eventually discharged in November 1919, holding the General Service and Victory Medals.
106, Lloyd Road, Northampton. Z2077.

BRANSON, E., L/Corporal, R.A.M.C.
Called up from the Reserve in August 1914, he was immediately drafted to the Western Front, where he served at Mons. He was also present at the Battles of Ypres, the Somme, and Messines, was gassed on the Somme in 1916, and in 1918 was admitted to hospital at Le Havre, suffering from influenza. Discharged in February 1919, he holds the Mons Star, and the General Service and Victory Medals.
76, Colwyn Road, Northampton. Z1382.

BRANSON, M. I. (Miss), Worker, Q.M.A.A.C.
She joined in June 1918, and after a short period of training was retained at Rugeley, Clipston, Catterick and various other stations. There in the capacity of senior clerk she was engaged on duties of a highly important nature, and rendered valuable services until her demobilisation in December 1919.
4, Dover Street, Northampton. Z1381.

BRANSON, W. E., Private, 7th Northants. Regt.
He volunteered in February 1915, and, on conclusion of his training in the following year, was drafted to France. In this seat of operations he took part in heavy fighting in the Somme and Arras sectors before being badly wounded in April 1917. As a result he was invalided home, and, after a period of treatment in hospital, was discharged in December 1919, holding the General Service and Victory Medals.
34, Roseholme Street, Northampton. Z2078.

BRAUNSTON, O., Private, 1st Northants. Regt.
Having first joined in June 1906 and served in India, he was called up from the Reserve in August 1914, and, proceeding to France, fought in the Battle of the Marne before being badly wounded on the Aisne in September. After hospital treatment at Aldershot he was discharged as medically unfit for further service in March 1915, and holds the 1914 Star, and the General Service and Victory Medals.
No. 4, Court 3, Brook Street, Daventry, Northants. Z2583.

BRAY, A. E., Private, 7th Northants. Regiment.
He volunteered in January 1916, and, on completion of his training, was sent overseas in the following May. During his service on the Western Front he was engaged in fierce fighting on the Somme, but was reported missing on August 18th, 1916, and was subsequently presumed to have been killed on that date. He was entitled to the General Service and Victory Medals.
"He nobly died that we might live."
Church Street, Brixworth, Northants. Z2960.

BRAY, C. D., Private, Machine Gun Corps.
He volunteered in January 1916, but was retained on important duties at home until January 1917, when he was drafted to the Western Front. After only three months' active service he gave his life for King and Country at the Battle of Arras on April 17th, 1917. He was entitled to the General Service and Victory Medals.
"A valiant Soldier, with undaunted heart he breasted life's last hill."
Newland Street, Brixworth, Northants. Z2962.

BRAY, C. H., Private, 9th Northants. Regiment.
Joining in April 1916, he received his training at Shoreham, and was then engaged on various duties of an important nature at different stations in England. Owing to physical unfitness he was not successful in his endeavours to obtain a transfer to the fighting area, but, nevertheless, rendered valuable services before being demobilised in April 1919.
Woofs Cottages, Newland St., Brixworth, Northants. Z2963.

BRAY, F., Private, 1st Northants. Regiment.
He volunteered in December 1915, and, proceeding to the Western Front in the following year, took an active part in numerous engagements of note in various sectors. Whilst fighting on the Somme in 1917 he was wounded, and again at Ypres in the following year, and also gassed. On his return to England he was discharged as medically unfit in April 1919, holding the General Service and Victory Medals.
Northampton Road, Brixworth, Northants. Z2961.

BRAY, J. E., Sapper, Royal Engineers.
Joining in April 1917, he was drafted a month later to the Western Front, and served there for nearly two years. During that time he was engaged on important pioneer work in the Somme, Arras, Amiens and Havrincourt sectors, and also carried out important duties on various railways. He was demobilised on his return home in April 1919, and holds the General Service and Victory Medals.
Church Street, Brixworth, Northants. Z2964/A.

BREAVINGTON, G. C., Rifleman, K.R.R.C.
He joined in August 1917, and, on completion of his training, was engaged on important duties with his unit at Northampton. Owing to ill-health he was not successful in his endeavours to obtain a transfer to the fighting area, but, nevertheless, rendered many valuable services before being demobilised in July 1919.
37, Arthur St., Kingsthorpe Hollow, Northampton. Z1272/B.

BREE, G. W., Private, Northants. Regiment.
He joined on attaining military age in July 1918, but was not successful in obtaining a transfer overseas owing to the termination of hostilities. After completing his training at Oswestry he did good work whilst employed on various duties of an important character until July 1919, when he was demobilised.
Harbridges Lane, Long Buckby, Northants. Z3252.

BREE, H., Private, Northamptonshire Regiment.
He volunteered in September 1914, and early in the following year was drafted to the Western Front. Shortly afterwards he was severely wounded in action at Aubers Ridge and was invalided home. The nature of his wound rendered him unfit for further service overseas, and he was employed on various important duties until he was demobilised in February 1919, holding the 1914–15 Star, and the General Service and Victory Medals. Harbridges Lane, Long Buckby, Northants. Z3253.

BREWSTER, F. H., Private, 15th Essex Regiment.
He joined in June 1916, and, after undergoing a period of training, served at various stations, where he was engaged on important duties for two years, afterwards being transferred to the Royal Army Pay Corps for clerical work. Owing to ill-health he was unable to obtain his transfer overseas, but, nevertheless, rendered valuable services until his demobilisation in March 1919. 28, Gray Street, Northampton. Z1383.

BRICE, J. T., Rifleman, Royal Irish Rifles.
Joining in 1916, he was drafted overseas later in the same year. During his service on the Western Front he took part in many engagements, including those in the Loos, Vimy Ridge, the Somme, Ypres and Cambrai sectors, and in the Retreat and Advance of 1918, being five times wounded in action and finally invalided home. He was demobilised in 1919, and holds the General Service and Victory Medals.
19, Alma Street, Northampton. Z2584/A.

BRICE, R. J., Private, Bedfordshire Regiment.
He enlisted in 1917, and, on completing his training later in the same year, was drafted to France. In this seat of war he took part in much heavy fighting in the Loos, Ypres, Passchendaele and Amiens sectors, and was gassed and wounded in action He was demobilised in 1919, and holds the General Service and Victory Medals.
19, Alma Street, Northampton. Z2584/B.

BRICKWOOD, A., Private, 9th Royal Fusiliers.
Having previously served in the South African War, he volunteered in June 1915 and quickly proceeded to France, where he fought at Ypres and on the Somme. He was gassed and contracted trench fever, which resulted in his being invalided home, but on his recovery he returned to France and took part in the Retreat and Advance of 1918. Discharged in January 1919, he holds the Queen's and King's South African Medals, the 1914–15 Star, and the General Service and Victory Medals.
Water Lane, Wootton, Northants. Z2585.

BRIGGS, W., Private, 3rd (King's Own) Hussars.
A Reservist, he was called to the Colours in August 1914, and in the following month proceeded to the Western Front, where he saw much severe fighting until February 1915. He was then sent to Ireland, where he was retained on various important duties until April 1919, when he was demobilised, holding the 1914 Star, and the General Service and Victory Medals. He re-enlisted later in the Royal Army Service Corps, and in 1920 was serving with the Army of Occupation at Cologne.
7, Brunswick Street, Northampton. Z1380/B.

BRIGHTMAN, A., Private, K.O. (Yorkshire L.I.)
He joined in 1917, and was shortly afterwards drafted to the Western Front. Whilst in this theatre of war he took part in many engagements, including the Battles of Ypres, Passchendaele, Lens, Cambrai, the Somme (II.) and the final engagements of the campaign. He was demobilised in 1920, and holds the General Service and Victory Medals.
7, Freeschool Street, Northampton. Z2586.

BRIGHTWELL, W. (M.M.), Corporal, 26th Royal Fusiliers.
He volunteered in August 1914, but was retained on important duties at home until June 1917, when he was drafted to France. There he fought with distinction in the Battles of Ypres, Passchendaele and Cambrai, and was awarded the Military Medal in August 1917 for conspicuous bravery in attending to wounded under heavy shell-fire. In October 1917 he was transferred to Italy, but six months later returned to the Western Front, where he was awarded a bar to his Military Medal for gallantry in the Field in October 1918. After the Armistice he proceeded into Germany with the Army of Occupation, serving there until demobilised in May 1919. He also holds the General Service and Victory Medals.
53, Lorne Road, Northampton. Z1277.

BRINKLOW, E., L/Corporal, R.A.M.C.
He volunteered in October 1914, and, after a period of training, was ordered overseas in the following year. Whilst serving on the Western Front he did valuable work with a Field Ambulance in the Ypres, the Somme and Arras sectors, and in the Retreat and Advance of 1918. He was also engaged on important duties at the Base hospitals, and was eventually demobilised in October 1919, holding the 1914–15 Star, and the General Service and Victory Medals.
127, Euston Road, Northampton. Z2965/B.

BRINKLOW, H., Driver, 62nd R.F.A.
Volunteering in January 1915, he embarked in March of the following year for Salonika. In that theatre of war he was in action in numerous engagements on the Doiran and the Vardar fronts, but contracted pneumonia, to which he unfortunately succumbed on August 26th, 1916. He was entitled to the General Service and Victory Medals.
"The path of duty was the way to glory."
127, Euston Road, Northampton. Z2965/A.

BRIODY, T. C. (D.C.M.), C.S.M., 1/4th Northamptonshire Regiment.
Mobilised with the Territorials in August 1914, he was drafted to the Dardanelles in the following year. In this seat of operations he saw much heavy fighting until November 1915, when he was sent to Egypt. During the Advance into Palestine he played a prominent part in many engagements, and was badly wounded at Gaza, where he was awarded the Distinguished Conduct Medal for great gallantry in the Field in April 1917. Demobilised in April 1920, he also holds the 1914–15 Star, and the General Service and Victory Medals.
27, Abbey Street, Northampton. Z2587.

BRITTAIN, W., Corporal, Royal Engineers.
Volunteering in August 1914 in the Northamptonshire Regiment, he was sent to France in the following December, but was wounded a month later and invalided out of the Army in September 1915. In the following month, however, he re-enlisted in the Royal Engineers, and, proceeding to the Western Front in December 1915, was engaged on important duties in connection with the railways until the close of hostilities. He was demobilised in March 1919, and holds the 1914–15 Star, and the General Service and Victory Medals.
36, Parkwood Street, Northampton. Z2409/B.

BRITTEN, C. R., Private, 1st Northamptonshire Regiment and 53rd Bedfordshire Regiment.
Joining in December 1917, he was trained at Crowborough, and three months later was ordered overseas. Whilst serving in France he was in action on the Somme, Cambrai, St. Quentin and Armentières fronts, and took an active part in severe fighting in the final engagements of the war. After the Armistice he advanced into Germany with the Army of Occupation, and served at Cologne until demobilised in October 1919, holding the General Service and Victory Medals.
20, Carlton Road, Northampton. Z1278/A.

BRITTEN, E., Private, 3rd Essex Regiment.
At the outbreak of war he was mobilised, and, proceeding to France in September 1914, fought in the Retreat from Mons, and was wounded. On his recovery he was in action at the Battles of the Marne, the Aisne, Hill 60, Ypres, Festubert, Loos, Vimy Ridge and the Somme, and also did good work with his unit during the Retreat and Advance of 1918. Serving in France until discharged in August 1919, he holds the Mons Star, and the General Service and Victory Medals.
87, Euston Road, Far Cotton, Northampton. Z2966.

BRITTEN, J. W., Rifleman, K.R.R.C.
He volunteered in June 1915, and in the early part of 1916 embarked for the Western Front. Whilst taking part in the Battle of the Somme he was wounded and invalided home. On his recovery he returned to France, but, after fighting in numerous important engagements in the Cambrai sector, he was gassed and sent to England for treatment. He was demobilised in March 1919, and holds the General Service and Victory Medals. 20, Carlton Road, Northampton. Z1278/B

BRITTEN, R., Private, East Yorkshire Regiment.
He volunteered in June 1915, and in August of the following year was sent to France, where he fought in the Battles of Arras, Bullecourt and Ypres, and was wounded at Passchendaele in 1917. On his return to the firing-line he was again wounded, but on his recovery was in action in the Retreat and Advance of 1918. He was demobilised in March 1919, and holds the General Service and Victory Medals.
62, Wellington Street, Northampton. Z1866/A—Z1938/A.

BRITTEN, W. J., Private, R.A.O.C.
Joining in March 1916, he proceeded to France early in the following year on the completion of his training. Being medically unfit for actual fighting, he was stationed at Calais, where he was engaged on important duties, which he fulfilled in a highly efficient manner. He was demobilised on his return to England in September 1919, and holds the General Service and Victory Medals.
20, Carlton Road, Northampton. Z1278/C.

BROCK, W. J., Private, 7th Northants. Regiment.
Four months after volunteering in October 1915 he was drafted to the Western Front, where, after much severe fighting, he was wounded in April 1917. Rejoining, his unit on his recovery, he was again in action in the Battle of Vimy Ridge, and died gloriously on the Somme in August 1916. Buried at Guillemont, he was entitled to the General Service and Victory Medals.
"He nobly fell that we might live."
25, Sunderland Street, Northampton. Z2356.

BROMAGE, H., Corporal, 1st Northants. Regt.
Mobilised in August 1914, he was at once ordered to the Western Front, where he took part in the fighting at Mons. He was also in action at the Battles of the Marne, the Aisne, La Bassée, Ypres and Hill 60, and died gloriously on the Field of Battle at Neuve Chapelle in March 1915. He was entitled to the Mons Star, and the General Service and Victory Medals.
"A valiant Soldier, with undaunted heart he breasted life's last hill."
6, Maple Street, Northampton. Z1279/A.

BROMWICH, A., Bombardier, R.G.A.
At the outbreak of war he was already in the Army, and immediately proceeded overseas. Serving on the Western Front, he fought in the Battles of La Bassée, Ypres, Loos, the Somme, Vimy Ridge and Passchendaele and other engagements of note, and took an active part in the operations during the Retreat and Advance of 1918. He was discharged in February 1919, and holds the 1914 Star, and the General Service and Victory Medals.
10, Cranstown Street, Northampton. Z1280.

BROOKS, E., Private, 6th Northants. Regiment.
When war was declared in August 1914 he was mobilised, and in March of the following year was sent to the Western Front. There he experienced fierce fighting in many sectors, took an active part in the Battles of Ypres, the Somme and Arras, and was reported missing in the vicinity of Arras on May 3rd, 1917. He was subsequently presumed to have been killed on that date, and was entitled to the 1914–15 Star, and the General Service and Victory Medals.
"Great deeds cannot die."
32, Spring Lane, Northampton. Z1069/B.

BROOKS, J., Private, 7th Middlesex Regiment.
He joined in February 1917, and, after three months' training, proceeded to the Western Front, where he saw much severe fighting. He was unhappily reported missing, and is presumed to have been killed in action at the Battle of Messines in June 1917, after only a month's service in France. He was entitled to the General Service and Victory Medals.
"A costly sacrifice upon the altar of freedom."
32, Ambush Street, St. James, Northampton. Z2351/B.

BROOME, W. E., Private, R.A.M.C.
He joined in July 1917, but owing to physical disability was unable to obtain a transfer to a theatre of war. After his training he was engaged on important duties in hospitals at Lichfield and Bentley, and also rendered valuable services on the hospital trains conveying the wounded from the various ports. He was eventually demobilised in October 1919.
Squirrel Lane, Old Duston. Z2967/A.

BROUGHTON, A., Private, Machine Gun Corps.
He joined in July 1917, and, on completion of his training at Grantham, was, five months later, drafted overseas. During his service on the Western Front he saw heavy fighting in various sectors, and took an active part in important engagements on the Somme and at Ypres and St. Quentin. After the Armistice he returned to England, and was invalided out of the Army in February 1919, holding the General Service and Victory Medals. 33, Francis St., Northampton. Z1071/C.

BROUGHTON, W., Private, Highland L.I.
Mobilised in August 1914, he was at once ordered to the Western Front, where he served in the Battle of Mons and the subsequent Retreat. After taking part in engagements on the Marne and the Aisne he gave his life for King and Country whilst fighting at Ypres on October 23rd, 1914. He was entitled to the Mons Star, and the General Service and Victory Medals.
"His life for his Country, his soul to God."
22, Regent Street, Northampton. Z1070/C.

BROWETT, J., Private, 5th Northants. Regiment.
He volunteered in April 1915, and, after at period of training at Gillingham, was drafted overseas in the following year. During his service on the Western Front he was in action in numerous important engagements in various sectors, and fought in the Battles of the Somme, Arras, Ypres and Cambrai. Demobilised in March 1919, he holds the 1914–15 Star, and the General Service and Victory Medals.
37, Castle Street, Northampton. Z1072.

BROWN, A., Private, 23rd Queen's (Royal West Surrey Regiment).
He attested in November 1915, and was called up in February 1917, and shortly afterwards proceeded to France. On that front he took an active part in the Battles of Ypres, Passchendaele, the Somme, Amiens, Bapaume, Havrincourt, Cambrai and Ypres, and was almost continuously in action until the cessation of hostilities. He was demobilised in March 1919, and holds the General Service and Victory Medals.
10, Lorne Road, Northampton. Z1281.

BROWN, A. J., Corporal, 1st Northants. Regt.
When war was declared in August 1914 he was mobilised, and at once ordered to the Western Front with the first Expeditionary Force. He took part in the Retreat from Mons and the Battles of the Marne, the Aisne, La Bassée, Ypres, Neuve Chapelle, the Somme, Arras and Cambrai, and many other engagements of note, and was wounded on three occasions. He was discharged in February 1919, and holds the Mons Star, and the General Service and Victory Medals.
7, Stockley Street, Northampton. Z1868/A.

BROWN, C. E., Private, Machine Gun Corps.
Having joined in July 1916, he completed his training in the same year and proceeded to Salonika. Whilst in this seat of operations he took part in heavy fighting on the Doiran and Vardar fronts. In August 1918 he was transferred to France, where he took part in the final Advance. He returned home for demobilisation in November 1919, and holds the General Service and Victory Medals.
68, Great Russell Street, Northampton. Z2079.

BROWN, E., Rifleman, 1st King's Royal Rifles.
Joining in June 1917, he completed his training at Margate and crossed to France three months later. After taking an active part in fierce fighting in various sectors, he was severely wounded during the Battle of the Somme in March 1918. He was invalided to England, and consequently discharged as medically unfit for further service in September 1918, holding the General Service and Victory Medals.
68, Moore Street, Kingsley, Northants. Z1073.

BROWN, E. G., C.Q.M.S., Royal Scots Fusiliers.
Already in the Army when war was declared, he immediately proceeded to France and served with distinction at the Battles of the Marne and Aisne. He gave his life for King and Country at the first Battle of Ypres on November 11th, 1914, being posthumously mentioned in Despatches for conspicuous work during this engagement. He was entitled to the 1914–15 Star, and the General Service and Victory Medals.
"His name liveth for evermore."
8, Vernon Terrace, Northampton. Z2081.

BROWN, E. O., Pte., R.N.D. (Anson Battalion).
Joining in July 1917, he was ordered overseas on the completion of his training nine months later. During his service on the Western Front he fought in numerous engagements in the German Offensive and Allied Advance of 1918, and was wounded in action in November of that year. On his discharge from hospital in Rouen he returned to England and was demobilised in January 1919, holding the General Service and Victory Medals.
27, Clinton Road, Far Cotton, Northampton. Z2968/C.

BROWN, G., Corporal, 1st Leicestershire Regiment.
Called up from the Reserve in August 1914, he was sent a month later to France. He participated in the Battles of the Marne, the Aisne, Ypres (II.), the Somme, the Aisne (III.) and Ypres (IV.), and was three times wounded—at Armentières in October 1914, and at Ypres in March 1915 and October 1918. He was discharged in February 1919, and holds the 1914 Star, and the General Service and Victory Medals.
15, Letts Road, Far Cotton, Northants. Z3254.

BROWN, H., L/Corporal, Northants. Regiment.
He volunteered in October 1915, and after a period of training was drafted overseas in February of the following year. Whilst serving on the Western Front he was engaged in severe fighting at Villers-Bretonneux, and also took an active part in the Battles of Albert, the Somme and Ypres. In 1917 he was sent back to England, where he was employed on important duties at Northampton until demobilised in March 1920. He holds the General Service and Victory Medals.
7, Johnson's Row, Northampton. Z1074.

BROWN, H., Private, 21st Canadian Infantry.
Volunteering in November 1914, he came over with the first Canadian Contingent, and was drafted to France in September 1915. Whilst on the Western Front he was in action in many engagements of note, including the Battles of Albert, Arras, Vimy Ridge, Messines, Ypres, Passchendaele, Cambrai and Amiens. He served in France until February 1919, and was demobilised a month later, holding the 1914–15 Star, and the General Service and Victory Medals.
19, Althorp Street, Northampton. Z1075/A.

BROWN, H., Aircraftsman, Royal Air Force.
He volunteered in January 1915, and after a period of training was engaged at various home stations on duties which demanded a high degree of technical skill. He was unable to obtain a transfer overseas, but rendered valuable services until his demobilisation in August 1919.
25, Tanner Street, Northampton. Z2588.

BROWN, H., Driver, Royal Field Artillery.
Mobilised in August 1914, he was at once ordered to the Western Front, and served in the Retreat from Mons. Whilst in France he fought in numerous engagements, including the Battles of Ypres, Passchendaele, Cambrai, the Somme and Bapaume, and was gassed on one occasion. In 1918 he proceeded to Italy and took an active part in the Piave Offensive. He was discharged in 1919, holding the Mons Star, and the General Service and Victory Medals.
20, St. Peter Street, Northampton. Z2970.

BROWN, H. A., Private, 1st Northants. Regiment.
Already in the Army in August 1914, he was at once drafted to France and fought at Mons. He also played a prominent part in the Battles of the Marne, the Aisne, La Bassée and Ypres, but being badly wounded in action was invalided home. He was eventually discharged as medically unfit for further service in May 1917, and holds the Mons Star, and the General Service and Victory Medals. 1, Albert Place, Northampton. Z3365.

BROWN, H. C., Trooper, Northants. Dragoons.
He volunteered for active service in December 1914, but during his training was taken ill with appendicitis, to which he unfortunately succumbed in Cambridge Hospital on May 19th, 1915.
"His memory is cherished with pride."
27, Clinton Road, Far Cotton, Northampton. Z2968/A.

BROWN, J., Sergeant, Royal Field Artillery.
Having enlisted at the age of 17 years, he was serving in India in August 1914, and was immediately drafted to France, where he saw much heavy fighting. He took a prominent part in the Battles of La Bassée and Ypres, and other engagements, and was wounded and gassed. Discharged in March 1919, he holds the 1914 Star, and the General Service and Victory Medals. 25, Spencer Road, Northampton. Z1384.

BROWN, J., Private, Machine Gun Corps.
He joined in 1917, and in the same year crossed to France, where he took part in the Battles of Ypres, Passchendaele and Cambrai. His health breaking down he was invalided to England, and on his return to the Western Front was almost continuously in action until the close of hostilities. After the Armistice he served with the Army of Occupation in Germany until demobilised in 1919, and holds the General Service and Victory Medals.
157, St. Edmund's Road, Northampton. Z1867.

BROWN, J., Private, 1/4th Northants. Regiment.
He volunteered in May 1915, and having completed his training in the following year was drafted to Egypt. Later he took part in the Advance into Palestine and saw much fighting at the Battles of Gaza. He made the Supreme Sacrifice, being killed in action near Jaffa on September 19th, 1918, and was entitled to the General Service and Victory Medals.
"Thinking that remembrance, though unspoken, may reach him where he sleeps."
Crown Inn, Hardingstone, Northants. Z2589/A.

BROWN, P. H., Private, Queen's (Royal West Surrey Regiment).
He joined the East Surrey Regiment in October 1917, was later transferred to the Hertfordshire Dragoons, and drafted to France in August 1918. He took part in heavy fighting at Kemmel Hill, and after the Armistice was transferred to the Queen's (Royal West Surrey Regiment), proceeding with this unit into Germany. He served with the Army of Occupation in Cologne until November 1919, and was then demobilised, holding the General Service and Victory Medals.
38, Holly Road, Northants. Z3255.

BROWN, R. P., Private, 6th Northants. Regiment.
Shortly after joining in January 1917, he was sent to the Western Front, where, after taking part in the Battles of Ypres, Passchendaele and Cambrai, he was wounded and invalided home. He returned to France, however, in time to fight in the Retreat and Advance of 1918, and was finally demobilised in March 1919. He holds the General Service and Victory Medals. 107, Hunter Street, Northampton. Z1385.

BROWN, S. A., Private, 1st Northants. Regiment.
Mobilised at the declaration of war, he at once proceeded to the Western Front, where he served in the Retreat from Mons, and also fought in the Battle of Ypres and other important engagements. He gave his life for the freedom of England at Aubers Ridge on May 9th, 1915, and was entitled to the Mons Star, and the General Service and Victory Medals.
"A costly sacrifice upon the altar of freedom."
23, Kerr Street, Northampton. Z1869.

BROWN, T., Sapper, Royal Engineers.
Joining in April 1916, he completed his training and two months later proceeded overseas. Whilst serving on the Western Front he was engaged in fierce fighting in various sectors, but unfortunately his health broke down and he was invalided to England in September 1916. After receiving hospital treatment he was discharged as medically unfit for further service in January 1917, holding the General Service and Victory Medals.
69, Euston Road, Far Cotton, Northampton. Z2969.

BROWN, T. F., Private, R.A.M.C.
Joining in February 1917, he proceeded in the following year to France, where he served as a stretcher-bearer on the Somme and Ypres fronts, and in several engagements during the Retreat and Advance of 1918. After the Armistice he proceeded to Germany and served with the Army of Occupation in Cologne until September 1919, when he was demobilised, holding the General Service and Victory Medals.
Barley Mow Cottages, Kislingbury, Northants. Z3256.

BROWN, T. W., Private, 1st Northants. Regiment.
Mobilised with the Reserve at the declaration of war, he immediately proceeded to the Western Front, where he was in action during the Retreat from Mons, and also at the Battles of the Marne, the Aisne, La Bassée and Ypres, before being wounded and invalided home. On his recovery he rejoined his unit in France, and took part in engagements on the Somme and Cambrai fronts, and also in the Retreat and Advance of 1918. Discharged in 1919, he holds the Mons Star, and the General Service and Victory Medals.
7, New Buildings, Blisworth, Northampton. Z2080/A.

BROWN, W., Private, 1st Northants. Regiment.
Having enlisted in June 1901, he proceeded to France three months after the outbreak of war, and there saw much severe fighting until March 1916. He was then transferred to Egypt and thence to Palestine, where he took part in many important engagements. He was also in action in Salonika before his return home in 1918, and in 1920 was still with his unit. He holds the 1914 Star, and the General Service and Victory Medals. 8, Third Square, Nelson Street, Northampton. Z1386.

BROWN, W., Gunner, Royal Garrison Artillery.
He was mobilised in August 1914, and was drafted to France in the following year. During his service in that theatre of war he took part with his Battery in heavy fighting at Loos, Ypres and on the Somme front, also at Arras and in many sectors during the Retreat and Advance of 1918. He returned home for demobilisation in January 1919, and holds the 1914–15 Star, and the General Service and Victory Medals.
1, Alton Terrace, Far Cotton, Northants. Z3257.

BROWN, W. J., Private, 8th East Yorkshire Regt.
He volunteered in September 1915, and 11 months later embarked for the scene of activities in France. On that front he fought in numerous notable engagements, including the Battles of the Somme and Ypres, but was unhappily killed in action during operations at Zonnebeke on September 26th, 1917. He was entitled to the General Service and Victory Medals.
"He nobly died that we might live."
27, Clinton, Far Cotton, Northampton. Z2968/B.

BRUCE, H. E., Private, Machine Gun Corps.
Joining in July 1917, he was drafted to the Western Front in the following year, and did valuable work with his unit during operations in the Retreat and Advance of 1918. After the Armistice he proceeded to Germany with the Army of Occupation, and was engaged on duties of an important nature. In October 1919 he was sent to India, where in 1920 he was still serving, holding the General Service and Victory Medals.
126, Southampton Road, Northampton. Z2971.

BRUDENELL, M. E. (Miss), Nursing Sister.
Already a qualified nurse when war was declared in August 1914, she immediately volunteered for active service, and after doing much good work at Southampton was drafted to France. There she was engaged on duties of great importance at the Base Hospital at Le Havre and was later sent to India, where in 1921 she was serving as ward sister near the Khyber Pass.
36, Bostock Avenue, Northampton. Z2082.

BRUMHILL, A., L/Cpl., 1st Northants. Regiment.
Volunteering in September 1914 at the age of 17, he was shortly afterwards sent to France, where he was engaged on important duties at the Base until May 1915. He was then sent up to the firing line, and fought in the Battles of Ypres, Festubert, Loos and Vermelles, being severely wounded on the Somme in July 1916. In consequence he was invalided out of the Army in February 1918, holding the 1914 Star, and the General Service and Victory Medals. 36, Lawrence St., Northampton. Z1282.

BRUMHILL, S. C., L/Cpl., 1/4th Northants. Regt.
At the declaration of war in August 1914 he volunteered, and early in the following year was sent to Egypt. After a period of service there, he was transferred to Palestine, where he saw heavy fighting at Gaza, and in many other engagements of note, until the cessation of hostilities. He was demobilised on his return to England in March 1919, and holds the 1914–15 Star, and the General Service and Victory Medals.
3, Althorp Street, Northampton. Z1076/B.

BRUMHILL, W. J., Sergt., 1/4th Northants. Regt.
He volunteered in August 1914, but was retained on important work in England until 1917, when he was drafted to the Western Front. There he played a conspicuous part in numerous engagements until severely wounded in action in October 1917. After prolonged hospital treatment he was discharged as medically unfit for further service in January 1919, and holds the General Service and Victory Medals.
10, First Square, Northampton. Z1283

BRYAN, H. J., Cook's Mate, R.N., H.M.S. "Pembroke."
He joined the Navy in January 1918, but was not successful in being posted to sea before the close of hostilities. During the period of his service he was stationed at Chatham in H.M.S. "Pembroke," and carried out the various duties assigned to him in a highly capable manner. After 14 months' valuable work, he was demobilised in March 1919.
4, Vernon Street, Northampton. Z1870.

BUBB, C., Corporal, Australian Imperial Forces.
He volunteered in Australia in October 1914, and was drafted to France in July of the following year. Whilst on the Western Front he took part in severe fighting in the Battles of Ypres, Loos, Albert, the Somme and Cambrai, and in the Retreat and Advance of 1918. He was wounded in 1915, and again in 1917, being sent to England for treatment on each occasion. Demobilised in December 1919, he holds the 1914–15 Star, and the General Service and Victory Medals.
Camp Hill, Bugbrooke, Northants. Z2972/B.

BUBB, E., Pte., 10th (Prince of Wales' Own) Hussars.
Volunteering in August 1914, he proceeded to France in the following July, and saw heavy fighting in the Ypres sector. He was transferred to the 2nd Gloucestershire Regiment in November 1915, and was drafted to Salonika, where he was in action on the Doiran and the Vardar fronts. On December 9th, 1916, he was severely wounded and unhappily succumbed to his injuries three days later. He was entitled to the 1914–15 Star, and the General Service and Victory Medals.
"Great deeds cannot die."
Camp Hill, Bugbrooke, Northants. Z2972/A.

BUBB, H., Pte., 10th (Prince of Wales' Own) Hussars.
He volunteered in August 1914, and 11 months later was sent to France, where he fought in engagements at Ypres. On being transferred to the 2nd Gloucestershire Regiment he was drafted to Salonika, where he took part in fierce fighting on the Struma, the Doiran and the Vardar fronts. He was demobilised on his return to England in July 1919, and holds the 1914–15 Star, and the General Service and Victory Medals.
Camp Hill, Bugbrooke, Northants. Z2972/C.

BUCKBY, R. H. H., Air Mechanic, R.A.F.
He volunteered in June 1915, but was not successful in his endeavours to secure a transfer to a theatre of war. After completing his training at Blandford he was stationed at various depôts, where he was engaged on duties of an important nature in the workshops, carrying out his work with the utmost skill and efficiency until demobilised in March 1919.
Station Road, Spratton. Z2973.

BUFFHAM, J. W. (M.S.M.), Sergeant, 5th South Staffordshire Regiment.
Volunteering in September 1914, he was sent to France in March of the following year and there took a prominent part in the Battles of Neuve Chapelle, Hill 60, and Ypres and minor engagements until transferred to Egypt in January 1916. Returning to the Western Front in the following April, he was again in action at Vermelles, the Somme, the Ancre, Lens and St. Quentin, serving also with the Machine Gun Corps. He was awarded the Meritorious Service Medal for continuously good work, and, holding also the 1914–15 Star, and the General Service and Victory Medals, was demobilised in January 1919.
18, Hazelwood Road, Northampton. Z2357.

BULL, A. J., Pte., Queen's (R. West Surrey Regt.)
Joining in March 1917, he was drafted overseas a month later. Serving on the Western Front, he was engaged on important duties at the Base for some time, but on being sent up the line was engaged in fierce fighting in the Ypres, Cambrai and Béthune sectors. He remained in France until March 1919, when he was demobilised, holding the General Service and Victory Medals. 43, Essex Street, Northampton. Z1284/A.

BULL, E. J., Private, Suffolk Regiment.
He enlisted in March 1916, and three months later was drafted to France. Whilst on the Western Front he took part in several engagements, including the Battles of the Somme (I.), Arras, Vimy Ridge, Bullecourt, Ypres (III.), Passchendaele, Cambrai and the Somme (II.), where he was badly wounded. As as result he was invalided home and later demobilised in February 1919, holding the General Service and Victory Medals. 38, Raymond Road, St. James, Northampton. Z2590.

BULL, H. V., Private, Royal Fusiliers.
Joining in January 1917 he underwent a period of training at Dover prior to being drafted to France. In this seat of operations he took part in many important engagements, including the Battles of Passchendaele, Cambrai and the Retreat and Advance of 1918, being wounded in action at Cambrai in September. Evacuated to England he underwent a period of hospital treatment, and on his recovery was engaged in guarding prisoners of war until demobilised in Nomember 1919. He holds the General Service and Victory Medals.
Roade, Northampton. Z2083/A.

BULL, J. C., Corporal, Machine Gun Corps.
Already in India at the outbreak of war, he landed in France in December 1914, but after being wounded during heavy fighting in the Ypres sectors in 1915, was transferred to Salonika. There he was in action on the Doiran, Struma and Vardar fronts, and did good work with his unit. Discharged in March 1919, he holds the 1914–15 Star, and the General Service and Victory Medals. Stoke Road, Blisworth, Northampton. Z2084.

BULL, R. J., Private, Royal Army Medical Corps.
Volunteering in February 1915, he was drafted overseas later in the same year. Whilst on the Western Front he acted as a stretcher-bearer, and took part in the fighting in the Ypres, Loos, Albert, the Somme, Cambrai and Amiens sectors. Contracting rheumatic fever he was invalided home, and was demobilised in July 1919. Later he unfortunately died through the effects of his war service, and was entitled to the 1914–15 Star, and the General Service and Victory Medals.
"Great deeds cannot die:
They with the sun and moon renew their light for ever."
Castlethorpe, Stony Stratford, Bucks. Z2592.

BULL, W. F., Private, 2nd Northants. Regiment.
Already in the Army at the outbreak of war, he was immediately drafted to France. There he took part in the Retreat from Mons, the Battles of the Marne, the Aisne, La Bassée and Ypres, and was twice wounded in action. He unhappily fell in action at the Battle of the Somme on August 13th, 1916, and was entitled to the Mons Star, and the General Service and Victory Medals.
"He died the noblest death a man may die:
Fighting for God and right and liberty."
Sutton Street, Flore, Northants. Z2591.

BULLIMORE, A. W., Private, R.A.S.C. (M.T.)
He volunteered in May 1915, and in the following year was drafted to Egypt, where he first saw service at Alexandria and Cairo. Later he proceeded into Palestine, and was engaged on important work with the Secret Service on the Gaza, Rafa and Haifa fronts, and at Jerusalem. He did continuously good work, and was demobilised in July 1919, holding the General Service and Victory Medals.
Bliss Lane, Flore, Northants. Z2593.

BUNGARD, S. G., 1st Air Mechanic, R.A.F.
Two months after joining in September 1916, he was sent to France, where he served at St. Omer, Lille and various other stations on duties of a highly technical nature. He was also atached to the B.A.S.D. at Paris for 12 months, and in March 1919 was transferred to Egypt, where he was engaged as a fitter at Cairo. Demobilised on returning home in November 1919, he holds the General Service and Victory Medals.
19, Seymour Street, Northampton. Z2358.

BURGE, G., Private, Royal Army Service Corps.
He volunteered in October 1914, and 12 months later was drafted to Salonika, where he was engaged on duties of great importance. He was also present at many engagements on the Macedonian front until sent home and invalided from the Army in August 1916. He holds the 1914–15 Star, and the General Service and Victory Medals.
101, Great Russell Street, Northampton. Z1387.

BURNELL, G., Private, 4th Northants. Regiment.
At the declaration of war in August 1914 he volunteered, and throughout the period of his service was engaged on work of national importance, which he carried out in a very able manner. Owing to medical unfitness he was unable to secure his transfer to the war zone, but, nevertheless, rendered valuable services in various capacities until demobilised in 1919.
12, Oxford Street, Northampton. Z2974.

BURNELL, H. M., Private, 2nd Northants. Regt.
Volunteering in September 1915, he completed his training and was drafted overseas a year later. Serving on the Western Front he was in action in the Battles of the Somme, Beaumont-Hamel and Arras, and was wounded at Ypres in July 1917, and invalided to England. In March 1918 he returned to France, saw heavy fighting during the Retreat and Advance of that year, and was present during the entry into Mons. Demobilised in June 1920, he holds the General Service and Victory Medals. 59, West Street, Northampton. Z1871.

BURNELL, W., Private, Northants. Regiment.
He volunteered in August 1914, and completing his training in the following May, was drafted to the Western Front. In this theatre of war he took part in much fighting at Ypres, Armentières, Loos, Albert, the Somme, Arras, Béthune and Cambrai, and in the Retreat and Advance of 1918. Demobilised in March 1919, he holds the 1914–15 Star, and the General Service and Victory Medals.
Castlethorpe, Stony Stratford, Bucks. Z2594.

BURNS, A., Private, 5th Lancashire Fusiliers.
Volunteering in January 1916, he was sent to the Western Front in the following April, and there saw heavy fighting in various sectors. After taking part in many important engagements, he was severely wounded in action at Ypres in 1917, and admitted to hospital in England. He was invalided from the Army in February 1919, and holds the General Service and Victory Medals.
162, Semilong Road, Northampton. Z2359.

BURNS, F. G., Private, Northamptonshire Regt.
He joined in July 1916, and five months later was sent to the Western Front, where he was in action in many engagements before being wounded at Arras in April 1917. On returning to the firing-line he saw heavy fighting on the Somme, and during the Retreat of 1918 was again wounded at Cambrai. He was invalided to England, and was subsequently demobilised in January 1919, holding the General Service and Victory Medals. 19, Melbourne Street, Northampton. Z1872 /C.

BURNS, H. W., Private, 7th Northants. Regiment.
Joining in July 1916, he embarked five months later for the Western Front. There he took part in many engagements, including the Battle of the Somme, until invalided home with typhoid in January 1917. In the following August he returned to France, saw heavy fighting at Hargicourt, and was so severely wounded at Cambrai in November 1917 as to necessitate the amputation of his left leg. After protracted hospital treatment he was discharged in December 1919, holding the General Service and Victory Medals.
19, Melbourne Street, Northampton. Z1872 /A.

BURNS, T., Driver, Royal Field Artillery.
When war was declared in August 1914 he was called up from the Reserve, and in the following year proceeded to France, where he was in action in the Ypres sector. In 1916 he was transferred to Mesopotamia, on which front he was engaged in severe fighting at Kut and Amara. On his return to England he unfortunately contracted influenza, to which he succumbed at Catterick Hospital in June 1918. He was entitled to the 1914–15 Star, and the General Service and Victory Medals.
"The path of duty was the way to glory."
4, Kinburn Place, Northampton. Z1077 /B.

BURNS, W. J., Private, Welch Regiment.
He volunteered in January 1915, and in the following May was ordered overseas. During his service on the Western Front he took part in severe fighting in many engagements of note, including the Battle of Ypres, but was gassed during the Retreat of 1918, and sent to hospital in England. On his recovery he was retained on home service until demobilised in September 1919, holding the 1914–15 Star, and the General Service and Victory Medals.
18, Melbourne Street. Northampton. Z1872 /B.

BURROWS, A., Private, R.A.M.C.
He volunteered in July 1915, but was engaged on important work in England until March 1917, when he was drafted to the Western Front. In the following October he was wounded in action and invalided home, but, returning to France in March 1918, served with the South African Overseas Forces in numerous battles of note until hostilities ceased. He also served in Germany with the Army of Occupation before being demobilised in April 1920, and holds the General Service and Victory Medals. 50, Roe Road, Northampton. Z2976.

BURROWS, E. W., Private, 1st Queen's (Royal West Surrey Regiment).
He enlisted in October 1916, and was shortly afterwards drafted to France. In this seat of war he took part in much fighting in the Ypres and Cambrai sectors, and in the Retreat and Advance of 1918, being badly wounded in October of that year. Invalided home to hospital, he afterwards proceeded to Russia, and served there until his demobilisation in December 1919. He holds the General Service and Victory Medals. 45, St. James' Street, Northampton. Z2596.

BURROWS, F. C., Private, 8th Bedfordshire Regt.
Shortly after joining in March 1916, he was drafted to the Western Front, where he took part in engagements at Ploegsteert Wood, Thiépval and many other places. He was unfortunately reported missing, and is presumed to have been killed in action on the Somme on September 25th, 1916. He was entitled to the General Service and Victory Medals.
"Whilst we remember, the sacrifice is not in vain."
1, Orchard Street, Northampton. Z2360 /C.

BURROWS, H., Gunner, Royal Field Artillery.
Joining in February 1916, he was sent in May of the following year to the Western Front. There he fought in the Battles of Arras, Ypres and Passchendaele and other important engagements, and did good work with his Battery during the Retreat of 1918. He was gassed in July 1918, and sent to hospital in Manchester, eventually being demobilised in March 1919, holding the General Service and Victory Medals.
23, Mayorhold, Northampton. Z1873.

BURROWS, T., Private, 2nd Northants. Regiment.
When war was declared in August 1914 he volunteered, and after a period of training was drafted overseas in January of the following year. Serving on the Western Front, he fought in the Battles of Neuve Chapelle and other notable engagements, but was unhappily killed in action at Aubers Ridge on May 9th, 1915. He was entitled to the 1914–15 Star, and the General Service and Victory Medals.
"He joined the great white company of valiant souls."
75, St. John's Street, Northampton. Z2975 /B.

BURROWS, T., Private, Manchester Regiment.
Joining in April 1917, he was sent to the Western Front two months later and there saw much heavy fighting. After taking part in many important engagements, he was severely gassed in March 1918 during the Allies' Retreat and was admitted to hospital in England. He was invalided from the Army in April 1918, and holds the General Service and Victory Medals.
1, Orchard Street, Northampton. Z2360 /B.

BURT, A., Private, East Yorkshire Regiment.
A Reservist, he was called up at the outbreak of war and was drafted to France in August 1915. He did good work with his unit in the Battles of Loos, Albert, the Somme, Arras, Ypres and Cambrai, saw heavy fighting at Givenchy and in the Retreat and Advance of 1918, and was wounded in action. Returning to England in January 1919, he was demobilised, and holds the 1914–15 Star, and the General Service and Victory Medals.
26, St. Mary's Street, Northampton. Z1078 /B.

BURT, A. E., Private, 2nd Northants. Regiment.
Called up from the Reserve in August 1914, he was at once ordered to the Western Front, where he served in the Retreat from Mons. He also fought in the Battles of the Aisne, Ypres, Neuve Chapelle, Festubert, Loos, the Somme and Arras, and was wounded on three occasions. He was invalided to England in 1917, and in consequence was discharged as unfit for further service in October of that year. He holds the Mons Star, and the General Service and Victory Medals.
No. 4, No. 1 Court, St. Mary's Street, Northampton. Z1079.

BURT, W. (Mrs.), Special War Worker.
For 15 months this lady devoted her time to nursing and other important work at the Duston War Hospital. Throughout the period of her service she carried out her duties with untiring energy, and proved to be of invaluable assistance, her work being greatly appreciated.
26, St. Mary's Street, Northampton. Z1078 /A.

BURTON, R. L. D., Special War Worker
He attested in 1915, but owing to defective eyesight was not called to the Colours. From February 1916, however, he was engaged on work of National importance at Messrs, Armstrong and Whitworth's, Newcastle-on-Tyne, where, employed on responsible duties in connection with the construction of Hotchkiss guns, he rendered valuable services until December 1918.
18, William Street, Northampton. Z1388.

BUSBY, C. W., Private, 3rd Northants. Regiment.
He joined in February 1916, and was sent for training to Chatham. Three months later he was admitted to Fort Pitt Hospital, Chatham, suffering from fever, from the effects of which he unhappily died on May 15th, 1916. He was buried at Rochester Cemetery, Chatham.
"His memory is cherished with pride."
Mill Lane, Cogenhoe, Northants. Z3258 /A.

BUSBY, G. E., Sergeant, R.F.A. and R.G.A.
He volunteered in October 1915, and was sent to France in July 1916. During his service overseas he was in action at Arras, Ypres, Passchendaele, Cambrai, on the Somme and at Amiens. He later served in various sectors during the Retreat and Advance of 1918, and after the Armistice proceeded to Germany, where he remained with the Army of Occupation until he was demobilised in January 1920, holding the General Service and Victory Medals.
Mill Lane, Cogenhoe, Northants. Z3258 /B.

BUSBY, H. G., Private, R.A.S.C.
When called up in June 1916 he was rejected on medical grounds, but on joining in January 1917 was retained on home defence. He was not successful in obtaining a transfer overseas, but was engaged on important duties at Aldershot and Avonmouth, and carried out his work in a highly efficient manner until demobilised in March 1919.
59, Denmark Road, Northampton. Z1875.

BUSHELL, S., Corporal, 1st Northants. Regiment.
He volunteered in August 1914, and, proceeding to the Western Front in February 1916, took part in the Battles of Albert and the Somme. In November 1916, however, his health broke down and he was invalided to England, and transferred to the Royal Air Force. He was then stationed at Tring, where he was employed on work of a highly technical nature until demobilised in February 1919, holding the General Service and Victory Medals.
9, Priory Terrace, Northampton. Z1080 /A.

BUSHELL, S. P., Drummer, 2nd Northants. Regt.
He joined in September 1918, and on completion of his training was engaged on important duties at Northampton and Colchester. Owing to the early cessation of hostilities he was unable to obtain a transfer to a theatre of war, but in 1919, however, was drafted to India, where in 1920 he was still serving. 9, Priory Terrace, Northampton. Z1080 /B.

BUSS, F. C., Sergeant, Royal Engineers.
Volunteering in August 1914, he was quickly drafted to France, where he served as a despatch rider, and took part in the Retreat from Mons. Later he played a prominent part in the Battles of the Marne, Ypres and several other engagements, but was badly wounded in 1917. As a result he was invalided home, and on his recovery was retained on important work until his demobilisation in March 1919. He holds the Mons Star, and the General Service and Victory Medals.
New Street, Lower Weedon, Northants. Z2586.

BUSTIN, W. H., Private, 2nd Royal Warwickshire Regiment.
Mobilised in August 1914, he was immediately drafted to the Western Front, where after fighting at Mons he took part in the Battles of the Marne, the Aisne, La Bassée, Ypres, Neuve Chapelle, St. Eloi, Hill 60 and Loos. He fell in action on July 15th, 1916, in the Somme Offensive. He was entitled to the Mons Star, and the General Service and Victory Medals.
"A costly sacrifice upon the altar of freedom."
48, Cloutsham Street, Northampton. Z1389.

BUSWELL, G. C., Private, 1/4th Northants. Regt.
Shortly after volunteering in May 1915, he was ordered to Egypt, and took an active part in numerous important engagements. Subsequently he was transferred to the Royal Army Service Corps, and did valuable work with that Corps until sent home in 1919. He was then drafted to Ireland, where he rendered valuable services until demobilised in April 1920, holding the 1914–15 Star, and the General Service and Victory Medals.
Clay Hill, Brixworth, Northants. Z2977.

BUSWELL, W., Corporal, 4th Northants Regt.
Volunteering in June 1915, he embarked in the following January for Egypt, and later proceeded to Palestine. He participated in heavy fighting at Gaza and near Jerusalem prior to the capture of that city, and was afterwards present at the capture of Jericho and Tripoli. He was demobilised on returning home in June 1919, and holds the General Service and Victory Medals.
School Road, Spratton, Northants. Z3259.

BUSWELL, W., A.B., Royal Naval Division.
He volunteered in November 1915, and in the following July was drafted to France. In this theatre of war he took part in the Battles of the Somme, Arras and Cambrai, and was gassed in March 1918. Rejoining his unit when he recovered, he participated in further fighting, and was unhappily killed in action on September 3rd, 1918. He was entitled to the General Service and Victory Medals.
"Great deeds cannot die."
8, West View Terrace, Long Buckby. Z3260.

BUTCHER, R., Private, 1st Northants. Regiment.
He volunteered in January 1915, and on completion of his training at Chatham 12 months later embarked for France. On that front he was in action chiefly in the Somme sector until wounded and invalided home. On his recovery he returned to the firing-line, and fell fighting on March 1st, 1918. He was entitled to the General Service and Victory Medals.
"His life for his Country, his soul to God."
14, Mount Gardens, Northampton. Z1876.

BUTLER, A., Private, 6th Northants. Regiment.
He enlisted in February 1916, and after his training was drafted overseas three months later. Whilst on the Western Front he took part in many engagements, including the Battles of Arras, Ypres, Cambrai and the Somme (II.), and was wounded in 1918. As a result he was invalided home and eventually demobilised in January 1919, holding the General Service and Victory Medals.
9, Dickens Terrace, Northampton. Z2599.

BUTLER, W. G., Sergeant, R.A.O.C.
Joining in March 1917, he was drafted to Mesopotamia in September of the same year, and there served at Basra and various other stations. He was engaged on duties of great importance whilst in this seat of operations, and rendered valuable services until his return home for demobilisation in February 1920. He holds the General Service and Victory Medals.
35, Grove Road, Northampton. Z1390.

BUTLIN, G. J., Gunner, Royal Garrison Artillery.
Having volunteered in October 1915, he was drafted overseas in the following May. Whilst on the Western Front he took part in many important engagements, including the Battles of the Somme, Arras, Ypres, Passchendaele, Cambrai, Amiens and in the Retreat and Advance of 1918. He was demobilised in June 1919, and holds the General Service and Victory Medals.
3, Drayton Place, Daventry, Northants. Z2600/C.

BUTLIN, H. E., Gunner, Royal Field Artillery.
He volunteered in October 1915, and after a period of training was engaged at various stations on important duties with his unit. He was unable to obtain a transfer overseas, but rendered valuable services until his demobilisation in July 1919. He also served with the Dorsetshire Regiment.
3, Drayton Place, Daventry, Northants. Z2600/B.

BUTLIN, J. H., L/Corporal, Durham L.I.
He enlisted in April 1916, and later in the same year was drafted to France, where he took part in many engagements, including the Battles of Arras and Ypres. He was unfortunately reported missing, and is now believed to have been killed in action on July 12th, 1917. He was entitled to the General Service and Victory Medals.
"Steals on the ear the distant triumph song."
3, Drayton Place, Daventry, Northants. Z2600/A.

BUTT, C. (M.M.), Sergeant, 4th King's Own (Royal Lancaster Regiment).
Joining in March 1917, he was drafted to France later in the same year, and served with distinction at the Battles of Ypres and Cambrai, and in heavy fighting during the Retreat and Advance of 1918, particularly at Givenchy and La Bassée. He was awarded the Military Medal for conspicuous bravery in capturing six prisoners single-handed at La Bassée in August 1918, and was demobilised in August 1919, holding also the General Service and Victory Medals.
78, Great Russell Street, Northampton. Z1877/A—Z1878/A.

BUTT, G., Pte., 23rd Queen's (R. W. Surrey Regt.)
He joined in March 1917, and shortly afterwards proceeded to France. There he took part in various engagements, including the Battles of Bullecourt, Messines, Ypres and Cambrai, and was in action during the Retreat and Advance of 1918. After the Armistice he served for some time at Namur, and was eventually demobilised in October 1920, holding the General Service and Victory Medals.
19, Swan Street, Northampton. Z3261.

BUTT, S. G., Private, 6th Northants. Regiment.
He joined in 1916, and, crossing to France in the same year, was in action at the Battles of the Somme, the Marne and Amiens. He was also engaged in fierce fighting in operations in the Retreat and Advance of 1918, but unfortunately contracted pneumonia, and died that year. He was entitled to the General Service and Victory Medals.
"His memory is cherished with pride."
5, Narrow Toe Lane, near the Green, Northampton. Z2978.

BUTTERY, C. W., Private, 1st Northants. Regt.
A serving soldier, he was immediately drafted to France in August 1914, and fought in the Retreat from Mons. He also took part in the Battles of the Marne, the Aisne, La Bassée, Ypres and Loos, and minor engagements until severely wounded at Passchendaele in November 1917, and sent home. Invalided from the Army in October 1918, he holds the Mons Star, and the General Service and Victory Medals.
5, Spencer Road, Northampton. Z1391/A.

BYRNE, A. H., L/Sergeant, 7th Canadian Infantry.
He volunteered in August 1915, and came to England with the Canadian Contingent, being drafted to the Western Front in March 1916. After taking a prominent part in engagements in the Ypres and the Somme sectors, he died gloriously on the Field of Battle at Hill 60 in September 1916. He was entitled to the General Service and Victory Medals.
"He passed out of the sight of men by the path of duty and self-sacrifice."
28, Herbert Street, Northampton. Z1081.

BYRNE, J. T., Sergt.-Major, 1/4th Northants. Regt.
Having previously served for 18 years with the Colours, he re-enlisted in August 1914, and in July of the following year proceeded to Egypt, where he served for a time at Alexandria. Advancing into Palestine, he took a prominent part in the Battles of Siwa, Rafa, Gaza, and others before returning home in February 1919. He was discharged in February 1919, and holds the 1914–15 Star, and the General Service and Victory Medals.
29, Dover Street, Northampton. Z1392.

C

CADD, E. A., Sergeant, 1st Northants. Regiment.
Called up from the Reserve in August 1914, he was immediately drafted to France, where he fought in the Retreat from Mons. After taking a prominent part also in the Battle of the Marne, he was severely wounded on the Aisne in September 1914, and was admitted to hospital at Torquay. He was finally invalided from the Army in August 1917, and holds the Mons Star, and the General Service and Victory Medals.
Clare Terrace, Wootton, Northants. Z2602.

CAIGER, E. C., Private, 5th Northants. Regiment.
He volunteered in September 1914, and in the following year was drafted to the Western Front, where he took part in the Battles of Ypres, Loos, the Somme, Arras and Passchendaele, and minor engagements. He died gloriously on the Field of Battle at Cambrai on November 30th, 1917, and was entitled to the 1914–15 Star, and the General Service and Victory Medals.
"And doubtless he went in splendid company."
8, Bath Square, Northampton. Z1082.

CAIRNS, G. J., Battery Sergeant-Major, R.G.A.
A serving soldier, he proceeded to France in August 1914, and fought at Mons. After taking part also in the Battles of the Marne, the Aisne, La Bassée, Neuve Chapelle, St. Eloi, Hill 60, Loos and the Somme, he was wounded at Beaumont-Hamel in March 1917, and sent home. He returned to France, however, in July and fought at Ypres. Discharged in April 1919, he holds the Mons Star, and the General Service and Victory Medals. 42, Monks Pond Street, Northampton. Z1083.

CANHAM, C. H., Sapper, Royal Engineers.
Joining in May 1916, he was drafted overseas in November of the same year, and saw heavy fighting in many parts of the Western Front. Invalided home in 1917, he underwent a period of hospital treatment and on his recovery was transferred to Mesopotamia. There he took an active part in many important engagements before contracting malarial fever. As a result he was evacuated to England and eventually demobilised in May 1919, holding the General Service and Victory Medals. 40, Market Street, Northampton. Z2085.

CAPELL, G., Private, 2nd Northants. Regiment.
When war broke out he was already serving, and was at once ordered to the Western Front, where he was in action in the Retreat from Mons. He was also engaged in fierce fighting in various important battles in different sectors, but was invalided out of the Army through frost-bite in 1917. He holds the Mons Star, and the General Service and Victory Medals.
11, Queen's Road, Northampton. Z1879.

CARDWELL, T., Private, R.A.S.C. (M.T.)
Joining in April 1918, he proceeded to the Western Front in the following month and there served in various sectors. Engaged chiefly in conveying ammunition and supplies to the forward areas, he was also for a time on ambulance work, and rendered very valuable services until his return home for demobilisation in May 1919. He holds the General Service and Victory Medals. 10, Argyle Street, Northampton. Z2601.

CARE, A., Seaman, Royal Navy.
He joined in May 1917, and after completing a period of training was posted to H.M.S. "Gibraltar," attached to the Grand Fleet in the North Sea. He was engaged on patrol and other important duties in these waters and at Scapa Flow until August 1919, when he was demobilised. He holds the General Service and Victory Medals.
77, Hervey Street, Northampton. Z1393/B.

CARE, W. G., Gunner, Royal Field Artillery.
He joined in May 1916, and in March of the following year was sent to the Western Front, where he took part in important engagements in various sectors. Mortally wounded in action, he unhappily died three days later at Le Tréport on August 17th, 1918. He was entitled to the General Service and Victory Medals.
"Whilst we remember, the sacrifice is not in vain."
77, Hervey Street, Northampton. Z1393/A.

CARPENTER, J., Pte., 2nd Bedfordshire Regiment.
Joining in March 1917, he proceeded to the Western Front two months later, but was gassed at Ypres in July and, after being in hospital at Rouen, was invalided home. He returned to France, however, in February 1918, and was wounded and taken prisoner in the following month. Released by exchange in October 1918, he was discharged in that month, and holds the General Service and Victory Medals.
1b, Salisbury Street, Northampton. Z1084.

CARR, C. W., Gunner, Royal Garrison Artillery.
He joined in April 1916, and after a period of training was ordered overseas in the following September. Serving on the Western Front, he was in action at the Battles of the Somme, Arras and Cambrai, and in many minor engagements until hostilities ceased. After the Armistice he advanced into Germany wth the Army of Occupation, and was stationed at Cologne until demobilised in September 1919, holding the General Service and Victory Medals. 89, Stanhope Rd., Northampton. Z2362.

CARR, J. H., Gunner, Royal Field Artillery.
A Reservist, he was called up at the outbreak of war in August 1914, and was engaged on duties of an important nature at Shrewsbury. In September 1914 he was injured in an accident and sent to hospital at Cambridge. After prolonged treatment he was discharged as medically unfit for further military service in May 1915. 45, Queen's Rd., Northampton. Z1880.

CARR, R., Corporal, Royal Engineers.
He volunteered in February 1915, and was shortly afterwards drafted to France, where he took part in numerous engagements, including those at Ypres and Passchendaele. He also did excellent work in laying railways on various fronts. He remained in this area until March 1919, when he returned home and was demobilised in March 1919, holding the 1914–15 Star, and the General Service and Victory Medals.
22, Oxford Street, Northampton. Z3262.

CARR, W., Sapper, Royal Engineers.
Joining in March 1916, he proceeded to France in the following September, and there served in various sectors. He was present at the Battles of Arras, Vimy Ridge, Bullecourt, Messines, Ypres, Passchendaele, Cambrai, the Somme, Bapaume and Le Cateau, took part also in the Retreat and Advance of 1918, and then served with the Army of Occupation in Germany. Demobilised in September 1919, he holds the General Service and Victory Medals. 8, Snakespeare Rd., Northampton. Z1394.

CARTER, A. L., Pte., 5th Buffs (East Kent Regt.)
He joined in August 1917, and two months later was drafted to India, where he was engaged on important garrison duties at Bangalore until the cessation of hostilities. After the Armistice he was sent to Salonika, rendered valuable services there and also in Bulgaria. On his return to England he signed on for a further period of two years, and holds the General Service Medal. 17, Ambush Street, St. James Northampton. Z2361.

CARTER, C. R., Bombardier, Royal Field Artillery.
Having previously served in the Army, he volunteered in March 1915, and in the following November was sent to the Western Front and saw heavy fighting. He was in action at the Battles of the Somme, Vimy Ridge and Cambrai, and many other engagements of note, and was wounded on one occasion. Returning home he was demobilised in January 1919, holding the 1914–15 Star, and the General Service and Victory Medals. 19, Oxford Street, Daventry, Northants. Z2979.

CARTER, E., L/Corporal, 4th Northants. Regt.
Having previously served in India and in the South African campaign, he volunteered in May 1915, but was retained on duties of an important nature at various stations in England. He fulfilled his duties in a very exemplary manner, and was discharged as medically unfit for further military service in October 1917. He holds the India General Service Medal with Bar, and the Queen's and King's South African Medals.
43 Parkwood Street, Northampton. Z2363.

CARTER, S., L/Corporal, Royal Engineers.
Volunteering in December 1915, he embarked for France in March of the following year, and was engaged on important duties with the Special Signal Staff in connection with the construction of telephone routes from General Headquarters. He rendered valuable services in the Ypres, Somme and Arras sectors, and was ultimately demobilised in August 1919, holding the General Service and Victory Medals.
98, Adnitt Road, Northampton. Z2086.

CARTER, W. (M.C.), R.S.M., 7th Northants. Regt.
At the outbreak of war he was serving in Egypt, but was recalled and ordered to France in August 1915. He played a distinguished part in many notable engagements, including the Battles of Loos and the Somme, and was awarded the Military Cross for conspicuous gallantry in the Field. After 29 years' valuable service he was discharged in October 1919, and also holds the 1914–15 Star, the General Service and Victory Medals, and the Long Service and Good Conduct Medal.
14, Semilong Road, Northampton. Z2365.

CARTER, W. A., Private, 18th Middlesex Regt.
On attaining military age he joined in January 1917, and embarking for the Western Front in June of the following year, was engaged in heavy fighting in the Arras and Vimy Ridge sectors. He was also in action at the Battles of Ypres and Cambrai, and did good work in the Advance of 1918. Demobilised in November 1919, he holds the General Service and Victory Medals.
9, Ambush Street, St. James' End, Northampton. Z2364/A.

CARTER, W. G., Corporal, Northants. Dragoons.
He volunteered in 1914, and in the following year was drafted to France, where he fought at Ypres, the Somme and Arras. He afterwards proceeded to Italy, where he was in action on the Piave, and also took part in the Offensive of October 1918. He remained in this area until 1919, when he returned home and was demobilised, holding the 1914–15 Star, and the General Service and Victory Medals.
88, Rothersthorpe Road, Northampton. Z3263.

CARTER, W. J., Private, 7th Northants. Regiment.
He joined in June 1916, and after a course of training was sent overseas six months later. During his service on the Western Front he fought in numerous engagements, including the Battles of the Somme, Bullecourt and Ypres, and was wounded at Passchendaele in 1917. After his discharge from hospital in England he was retained on home service until demobilised in June 1919, holding the General Service and Victory Medals.
39, Clinton Road, Far Cotton, Northampton. Z2980.

CARTWRIGHT, H. T., Private, R.A.S.C.
Shortly after joining in 1916 he was drafted to the Western Front, where, engaged on important transport duties in various sectors, he was present at many actions. Mortally wounded in 1917, he unfortunately died, after 18 months' active service. He was entitled to the General Service and Victory Medals.
"Nobly striving,
He nobly fell that we might live."
84, Robert Street, Northampton. Z1412.

CARWELL, W. G., Pte., 1st Monmouthshire Regt.
Volunteering in February 1915, he was drafted in the following year to the Western Front, where he saw much severe fighting. He took part in the Battles of the Somme, Arras, Ypres and Cambrai, fought also in the Retreat and Advance of 1918, and was twice wounded and gassed. He afterwards served with the Military Foot Police in Germany, and was demobilised in October 1919, holding the General Service and Victory Medals.
1, Abbey Terrace, Northampton. Z2603.

CASSON, L., Private, R.A.S.C. (M.T.)
Volunteering in September 1914, he received his training at Preston, and in the following year embarked for France. On that front he saw much service at Ypres and in many other notable engagements, being almost continuously in action until the cessation of hostilities. He remained in France until June 1919, when he was demobilised, holding the 1914–15 Star, and the General Service and Victory Medals.
22, London Road, Daventry, Northants. Z2918

CATTELL, A., Private, 6th Bedfordshire Regiment.
Two months after joining in January 1917 he was drafted to the Western Front, where he took part in many important engagements, including the Battles of Arras, Ypres, Passchendaele and the Somme. Suffering from trench feet, he was transferred to the Labour Corps in March 1918, and was then engaged in guarding prisoners of war at Boulogne. He was demobilised in October 1919, and holds the General Service and Victory Medals. 70, Byron Street, Northampton. Z1085/C.

CATTELL, A., Leading Aircraftsman, R.A.F.
He joined in February 1916, and was engaged on work of a highly technical nature in connection with the manufacture of aeroplane parts at Felixstowe. Unsuccessful in his endeavours to secure a transfer to a theatre of war, he, nevertheless, rendered invaluable services during the most critical moments of the war, eventually being demobilised in May 1919.
11, Crambrook Road, Northampton. Z2366/B.

CATTELL, E. G., Private, 2nd Northants. Regt.
Volunteering in April 1915, he was sent to Gallipoli in the following September, and there fought at Suvla Bay and Chocolate Hill. He was afterwards transferred to the Western Front, where he took part in the Battle of the Somme and many other engagements, and was three times wounded at Ypres. Invalided from the Army in March 1918, he holds the 1914–15 Star, and the General Service and Victory Medals.
176, Harborough Road, Kingsthorpe, Northampton. TZ1086.

CATTELL, T. W., Private, Queen's (Royal West Surrey Regiment).
Joining in May 1916, he proceeded overseas on completion of his training in the following October. After only one month's service on the Western Front he died gloriously on the Field of Battle on the Ancre on November 19th, 1916. He was entitled to the General Service and Victory Medals.
"Honour to the immortal dead, who gave their youth that the world might grow old in peace."
11, Crambrook Road, Northampton. Z2366/A.

CATTELL, W., Corporal, R.A.M.C.
Mobilised in August 1914, he was immediately drafted to the Western Front, where he was engaged on important duties at No. 4 Casualty Clearing Station until June 1918. He was then transferred to Egypt, where he was stationed at Alexandria, and also served in Palestine. He was discharged on his return home in March 1919, and holds the Mons Star, and the General Service and Victory Medals.
195, Harborough Road, Kingsthorpe, Northampton. TZ1087.

CAUDWELL, O., Driver, Royal Field Artillery.
He joined in May 1917, and after a period of training embarked for the scene of activities in France. On that front he fought in the Battle of the Somme, and numerous other important engagements, and did excellent work with his Battery during operations in the Retreat and Advance of 1918. He remained in France until January 1919, when he was demobilised, holding the General Service and Victory Medals.
25, Orchard Street, Northampton. Z2367.

CAVE, B. G., Pte., 1st Buffs (East Kent Regt.)
He joined in December 1916, and shortly afterwards proceeded to the Western Front. Whilst in this theatre of war he took part in many important engagements, including the Battles of Arras, Vimy Ridge, Ypres, Cambrai, the Somme, the Aisne, the Marne, Bapaume and Le Cateau, and afterwards served with the Army of Occupation in Germany. He holds the General Service and Victory Medals, and in 1920 was still serving.
43, Deal Street Northampton. Z1395/A.

CAVE, C. W., Private, R.M.L.I.
Already serving at Portsmouth in August 1914, he was afterwards posted to H.M.S. "Heron," and in January of the following year was sent to Egyptian waters. He served also in the Ægean Sea on patrol and convoy duties, and in 1921 was still at sea. He holds the 1914–15 Star, and the General Service and Victory Medals.
43, Deal Street, Northampton. Z1395/C.

CAVE, E., L/Corporal, 11th Northumberland Fusiliers.
Mobilised in August 1914, he was retained on important duties at home until June 1916, when he was drafted to France. There he was in action at the Battles of the Somme, Messines and Passchendaele, and in 1917 was transferred to Italy. On that front he saw heavy fighting on the Asiago Plateau, and was wounded during the Piave offensive in 1918. He was discharged as a time-expired man in July 1920, and holds the General Service and Victory Medals.
35, Tanner Street, Northampton. Z2982/A.

CAVE, F., Private, 4th North Staffs. Regiment.
He joined in November 1916, and, after his training, was retained on important duties in England until April 1918, and was then drafted to the Western Front, where he saw severe fighting on the Somme and at Cambrai. He fell gallantly in action on September 29th, 1918, and was entitled to the General Service and Victory Medals.
"Great deeds cannot die :
They with the sun and moon renew their light for ever"
38, King Street, Northampton. Z1285/B.

CAVE, G. H., Private, 5th Northants. Regiment.
After volunteering in December 1914 he underwent a period of training prior to being drafted to the Western Front in October 1916. There he took part in the Battles of Ypres and Armentières and other engagements until wounded at Fleurbaix in January 1918 and admitted to hospital at Brighton. He was invalided from the Army in September 1918, and holds the General Service and Victory Medals.
6, Francis Street, Northampton. Z1088.

CAVE, J. T., Private, 1/4th Northants. Regiment.
Mobilised with the Territorials in August 1914, he was drafted in January of the following year to Egypt, where he served at various stations. Advancing into Palestine, he took part in the Battles of Siwa, Rafa and Gaza and the capture of Jerusalem, and was later in hospital at Alexandria, suffering from malaria. Demobilised on returning home in June 1919, he holds the 1914–15 Star, and the General Service and Victory Medals. 43, Deal Street, Northampton. Z1395/B.

CAVE, M. W., Gunner, Royal Field Artillery.
He volunteered in April 1915, and in December of that year proceeded to the Western Front. There he took part in many important engagements, including the Battles of Ypres, Cambrai and the Somme, fought also in the Retreat and Advance of 1918, and was gassed. Demobilised on returning home in February 1919, he holds the 1914–15 Star, and the General Service and Victory Medals.
34, Tanner Street, Northampton. Z2604.

CAVE, W., Private, Machine Gun Corps.
He volunteered in October 1915, and, after a period of training, proceeded to Mesopotamia two years later. There he served at Kut, Baghdad, Amara and various other places, but was unfortunately drowned whilst crossing the River Tigris on October 25th, 1918. He was entitled to the General Service and Victory Medals.
"He joined the great white company of valiant souls."
38, King Street, Northampton. Z1285/C.

CHADWICK, A. J. (M.M.), Sergeant, Rifle Brigade.
Volunteering in August 1914, he was drafted to France in March of the following year and was in action at Neuve Chapelle, Hill 60, Ypres, Loos, Arras, Vimy Ridge, Passchendaele and Cambrai, and also served in the Retreat and Advance of 1918. He was awarded the Military Medal for conspicuous gallantry on the Field, and also holds the 1914–15 Star, and the General Service and Victory Medals. He was demobilised in March 1919. North View, Kilsby, Rugby. Z3264.

CHALLONER, T., Private, 2nd Suffolk Regiment.
Six months after joining in January 1917 he was drafted to the Western Front, where he was wounded in action at Ypres in the same year and invalided home. He returned to France, however, on his recovery, and saw much heavy fighting in various sectors of the front. He was demobilised in February 1919, and holds the General Service and Victory Medals.
22, Spring Lane, Northampton. Z1089/A.

CHAMBERLAIN, A. J., Pte., 2nd Northants. Regt.
Already in the Army, he was mobilised at the outbreak of hostilities, and shortly afterwards landed in France. In this seat of operations he was engaged in heavy fighting at the Battles of Neuve Chapelle, St. Eloi, Hill 60 and Festubert. He was unhappily killed in action in May 1915, and was entitled to the 1914–15 Star, and the General Service and Victory Medals.
"His life for his Country, his soul to God."
63, Market Street, Northampton. Z2087/B.

CHAMBERLAIN, T., Guardsman, Grenadier Gds.
He volunteered in August 1914, and, proceeding to the Western Front in the following year, took part in numerous engagements with the Guards Division, and was twice wounded. He was invalided home, but on his recovery returned to France, where he remained until the cessation of hostilities. He was demobilised in April 1919, and holds the 1914–15 Star, and the General Service and Victory Medals.
10, Margaret Street, Northampton. Z3265/B.

CHAMBERS, A., Corporal, 16th (The Queen's) Lancers.
He volunteered in December 1915, and was retained on important duties at home until 1917, when he was sent to the Western Front. There he took part in the Battles of Ypres, Cambrai and the Somme and many other engagements until wounded at Villers-Brettoneux in August 1918 and admitted to hospital at Glasgow. He was demobilised in March 1919, and holds the General Service and Victory Medals.
19, Uppingham Street, Northampton. Z1090/A.

CHAMBERS, J. T. T., Pte., 1st Northants. Regt.
He joined in 1916, and shortly afterwards was sent to France, where he fought at Vimy Ridge and the Somme. He was later transferred to Salonika, where he took part in numerous engagements. Later he did excellent service in Egypt, but contracted malaria and jaundice. He was demobilised in 1919, and holds the General Service and Victory Medals.
47, Richard Street, Northampton. Z3266.

CHAMBERS, R., Rifleman, King's Royal Rifles.
Called up from the Reserve in August 1914, he was immediately drafted to the Western Front, where he fought in the Retreat from Mons. After taking part also in the Battles of the Marne, the Aisne and La Bassée, he was taken prisoner at Ypres in November 1914, and whilst in captivity in Germany was employed on agricultural work. Released in December 1918, he was discharged in the following April, and holds the Mons Star, and the General Service and Victory Medals.
19, Uppingham Street, Northampton. Z1090/B.

CHAMBERS, S., Pte., 6th Bedfordshire Regiment.
Joining in August 1916, he was sent to the Western Front in the following month, and there, after taking part in the Battle of the Somme, was wounded at Arras in April 1917. Invalided home, he returned to France, however, on his recovery, and was again in action in many engagements during the Retreat and Advance of 1918. Demobilised in October 1919, he holds the General Service and Victory Medals.
High Street, Hardingstone, Northants. Z2608.

CHAMBERS, W. C., Private, Machine Gun Corps.
He joined in July 1916, and, after six months' training with the Royal Sussex Regiment, was drafted to France with the Machine Gun Corps. There, after much heavy fighting, he was severely wounded at Arras in April 1917, and was sent to hospital in England. He was ultimately invalided from the Army in January 1920, and holds the General Service and Victory Medals. 2, St. James' Street, Northampton. Z2605.

CHANDLER, H. L., Private, 8th East Surrey Regt.
He joined in October 1916, and, after a month's training at Felixstowe, was drafted overseas. Whilst serving on the Western Front he took part in numerous important engagements in various sectors, being almost continuously in action until the cessation of hostilities. He remained in France until March 1919, when he was demobilised, and holds the General Service and Victory Medals.
2, Mount Gardens, Northampton. Z1881.

CHANDLER, R. J., Corporal, 2nd Northants. Regt.
Mobilised in August 1914, he quickly proceeded to France, where he fought in the Retreat from Mons. He also took part in the Battles of the Marne, the Aisne, La Bassée, Ypres, Neuve Chapelle and Festubert, and was severely gassed at Loos in September 1915. Admitted to hospital at Huddersfield, he was invalided from the Army in August 1916, suffering from chronic bronchitis, and holds the Mons Star, and the General Service and VictoryMedals.
14, Doddridge Square, Northampton. Z1091.

CHAPLIN, A., Trooper, Hampshire Dragoons (Carabiniers).
Volunteering in September 1914, he underwent a period of training, but was later found to be medically unfit for transfer overseas. He was, therefore, retained on special duties with his unit, and served in England, Scotland and Ireland, where he did excellent work until demobilised in March 1919.
2, Orchard Row, Roade, Northants. Z2088/C—Z2089/C.

CHAPLIN, C., Bombardier, R.G.A.
He joined in May 1916, and, on conclusion of his training in the same year, was drafted overseas. Serving with his Battery on the Western Front, he took part in many important engagements, particularly in the Somme, Arras, Ypres and Cambrai sectors. He was also present during the Retreat and Advance of 1918, and did consistently good work throughout the period of hostilities. Demobilised in January 1919, he holds the General Service and Victory Medals.
2, Orchard Row, Roade, Northampton, Z2088/D—Z2089/D.

CHAPLIN, F., Private, 1st Northants. Regiment.
Two months after joining in March 1916 he was drafted to the Western Front, where he saw severe fighting in various sectors. He took part in the Battles of the Somme and Arras and many other engagements, and was wounded at Givenchy. Discharged in August 1918 as medically unfit for further service, he holds the General Service and Victory Medals.
14, Regent Street, Northampton. Z1092.

CHAPLIN, H., Private, R.M.L.I.
Volunteering at the outbreak of war, he completed his training at Chatham, prior to being drafted to the Dardanelles, where he took part in the Landings at Cape Helles and Suvla Bay and in other important engagements. After the Evacuation of the Peninsula he was transferred to France, and was in action on the Somme front. He was unhappily killed on November 16th, 1916, and was entitled to the 1914–15 Star, and the General Service and Victory Medals.
"Whilst we remember, the sacrifice is not in vain."
2, Orchard Row, Roade, Northampton. Z2088/A—Z2089/A.

CHAPLIN, P., Driver, R.A.S.C.
Volunteering in November 1915, he was quickly drafted to France. Whilst in this theatre of war he was engaged on important transport duties during heavy fighting on the Armentières, Albert, the Somme, Arras, Ypres, Cambrai, Amiens and Le Cateau (II.) fronts. He did continuously good work, and in April 1919 was demobilised, holding the 1914–15 Star, and the General Service and Victory Medals.
"The Layes," Roade, Northants. Z2088/E—Z2089/E.

CHAPLIN, T., Private, 2nd Northants. Regiment.
Mobilised in August 1914, he was quickly drafted to France, where he took part in the Battles of Ypres, Neuve Chapelle, Aubers Ridge, Festubert, Loos, Albert, the Somme and Arras. He made the supreme sacrifice, being killed in action near Ypres on August 12th, 1917, and was entitled to the Mons Star, and the General Service and Victory Medals.
"A valiant Soldier, with undaunted heart he breasted life's last hill."
2, Orchard Row, Roade, Northampton. Z2088/B—Z2089/B.

CHAPMAN, A., Private, East Lancashire Regt.
Having enlisted in August 1906, he was drafted to France on the outbreak of war in August 1914, and fought at Mons. Wounded and taken prisoner at Le Cateau, he was held in captivity at Doberitz and other German camps, where he suffered many hardships, finally being released on the cessation of hostilities. Discharged in March 1919, he holds the Mons Star, and the General Service and Victory Medals.
25, Monarch Road, Northampton. Z1286.

CHAPMAN, A. G., Driver, Royal Engineers.
He volunteered in August 1915, and, after serving for a time in England proceeded in July 1917 to the Western Front. Whilst in this theatre of war he was engaged on important duties with the Pontoon Section in various sectors, and served at Arras, Ypres, Cambrai and the Somme. He was demobilised in February 1919, and holds the General Service and Victory Medals. 30, Alliston Gardens, Northampton Z1093.

CHAPMAN, B., Sergeant, 7th Northants. Regt.
He volunteered in September 1914, and twelve months later proceeded to the Western Front, where he took a prominent part in the Battles of Loos, Albert, the Somme and Arras, and was wounded at Ypres in July 1917. He fell fighting on August 8th of the following month, and was entitled to the 1914–15 Star, and the General Service and Victory Medals.
"A costly sacrifice upon the altar of freedom."
4, Bristol Street, Northampton. Z1094/A.

CHAPMAN, E. G. (M.M.), Private, King's Shropshire Light Infantry.
He joined in September 1917, and four months later was drafted to France. In this theatre of war he took part in many engagements, including those in the Ypres and Somme sectors, and in the Advance of 1918, being wounded in action. He was awarded the Military Medal for conspicuous bravery in rescuing wounded under heavy shell-fire. Invalided home to hospital, he was eventually discharged in November 1919, and holds also the General Service and Victory Medals.
Rose Cottage, Roade, Northampton. Z2090/B.

CHAPMAN, F., Private, East Surrey Regiment.
He volunteered in October 1914, and in September of the following year proceeded to France, where he saw much severe fighting and took part in the Battles of Loos and Albert. He made the supreme sacrifice, falling in action on the Somme in August 1916. He was entitled to the 1914–15 Star, and the General Service and Victory Medals.
"The path of duty was the way to glory."
4, Bristol Street, Northampton. Z1094/D.

CHAPMAN, F. E., Private, 1st Northants. Regt.
Volunteering in June 1915, he was drafted to the Western Front six months later and served at the Battle of Loos. In March 1916 his health broke down, and he was sent to England, but returned to France in the following June and was severely wounded during the Battle of the Somme in August 1916, and in consequence was invalided out of the Army in May 1917. He holds the 1914–15 Star, and the General Service and Victory Medals. 16, Wimbledon Street, Northampton. Z2368.

CHAPMAN, F. W., Private, 7th Northants. Regt.
He enlisted in March 1916, and later in the same year was drafted to France, where he served as a machine-gunner in the Somme, Ypres, Arras, Cambrai and Albert sectors. After hostilities ceased he proceeded to Germany with the Army of Occupation, and was engaged as a signaller on the Rhine. In 1921 he was still serving, and holds the General Service and Victory Medals.
Rose Cottage, Roade, Northampton. Z2090/A.

CHAPMAN, G. A., Private, 1/6th Essex Regt.
He joined in August 1916, and, on completion of his training, was drafted in the following February to Egypt. After a period of service there he was sent to Palestine, where he was engaged in fierce fighting at Gaza and Jaffa and in the Offensive under General Allenby. He was demobilised on his return to England in November 1919, and holds the General Service and Victory Medals. 26, Semilong Rd., Northampton. Z2369.

CHAPMAN, J., Corporal, Labour Corps.
He volunteered in September 1915, and was quickly sent to France, where he served in numerous engagements, including those at Amiens and Arras. He also took part in the Retreat and Advance of 1918. He remained in this area till February 1919, when he returned home and was demobilised, holding the General Service and Victory Medals.
80, Euston Road, Northampton. Z3267.

CHAPMAN, L., Private, 1st Northants. Regiment.
Enlisting in April 1905, he was at once drafted to the Western Front, where he was engaged in fierce fighting at Mons. He was also in action in the Battles of the Marne, the Aisne, Vermelles, the Somme, Arras and Amiens, and in the Retreat and Advance of 1918, and was wounded on three occasions. After the Armistice he served with the Army of Occupation until discharged in March 1919, holding the Mons Star, and the General Service and Victory Medals
12, Wimbledon Street, Northampton. Z2370.

CHAPMAN, L., Private, R.A.M.C.
He joined the Queen's (Royal West Surrey Regiment) in September 1918, but owing to the early cessation of hostilities was unable to secure a transfer overseas before the Armistice. He was engaged on important duties at various home stations until April 1919, when he was drafted to Germany and transferred to the Royal Army Medical Corps, serving with the Army of Occupation until demobilised in May 1920.
47, Clinton Road, Far Cotton, Northampton. Z2984.

CHAPMAN, P., Private, R.A.V.C.
Volunteering in April 1915, he received his training at Aldershot, and eight months later proceeded to the Western Front. There he rendered invaluable services at Abbeville, Le Havre and Etaples attending to sick and wounded horses, and also acted in a similar capacity in the Arras and Ypres sectors. He was invalided to hospital in England in October 1918, and discharged as medically unfit two months later, holding the General Service and Victory Medals.
Osborn Cottages, Hanslope, Bucks. Z2985 /A.

CHAPMAN, P. P., Private, R.A.S.C. (M.T.)
A month after joining in July 1916 he embarked for the scene of activities in France, where he was engaged on important transport duties on the Somme, Ypres, Arras and Cambrai fronts. He also did valuable work with his unit during the Retreat and Advance of 1918, and after the Armistice proceeded with the Army of Occupation to Germany, serving there until demobilised in February 1920. He holds the General Service and Victory Medals.
Osborn Cottages, Hanslope, Bucks. Z2985 /B.

CHAPMAN, S., Private, Royal Irish Fusiliers.
He enlisted in April 1914, and, drafted to France with the Bedfordshire Regiment immediately on the outbreak of war, fought in the Battle of, and Retreat from, Mons and in the Battle of Ypres. Transferred in November 1915 to Salonika, he served on the Vardar and Doiran fronts with the Royal Irish Fusiliers before proceeding to Egypt and thence into Palestine, where he fought at Gaza, Jerusalem and on the Jordan, and was twice wounded. Discharged in April 1920, he holds the Mons Star, and the General Service and Victory Medals
4, Bristol Street, Northampton. Z1094 /C.

CHAPMAN, T., Corporal, East Surrey Regiment.
He joined in May 1918, and, after a short period of training, served at various stations on duties of great importance. Unable to obtain his transfer overseas before the cessation of hostilities, he proceeded in August 1919, however, to Germany, where he served with the Army of Occupation until November of that year. He then returned home for demobilisation.
4, Bristol Street, Northampton. Z1094 /B.

CHAPMAN, W., Private, 1/10th Manchester Regt.
Three months after joining in March 1917 he proceeded to the Western Front. Whilst in this theatre of war he fought in the Battle of Ypres and other notable engagements, and was twice wounded when in action on the Somme in 1918. He was invalided to England in October of that year, and, on his discharge from hospital, was demobilised in March 1919, holding the General Service and Victory Medals.
68, Whitworth Road, Northampton. Z1882.

CHAPMAN, W. F., Driver, R.F.A.
He enlisted in May 1916, and, after a period of training, was drafted to the Western Front. Whilst in this seat of war he took part in the Battles of Vimy Ridge, Messines, Ypres, Passchendaele, Cambrai and the Somme, and in the Retreat and Advance of 1918. After the Armistice he proceeded to Germany with the Army of Occupation, and served there until his demobilisation in September 1919. He holds the General Service and Victory Medals.
36, Roe Road, Northampton. Z2091.

CHAPPELL, J., Private, 2/4th Northants. Regt.
He volunteered in October 1914, and, after his training, was retained on important duties in England until 1916, when he was sent to the Western Front. After taking part in many engagements he was gassed and taken prisoner on the Somme during the Retreat of March 1918, and was held in captivity until the cessation of hostilities. Demobilised in May 1919, he holds the General Service and Victory Medals.
6, Abbey Street, Daventry, Northants. Z2606 /A.

CHARVILL, E. G., Driver, Royal Horse Artillery.
Volunteering in August 1915, he proceeded to France later in the same year and fought at Loos, Albert, Armentières, the Somme, Arras, St. Quentin, Ypres and Cambrai. He also served in the Retreat and Advance of 1918. He returned home and was demobilised in March 1919, holding the 1914–15 Star, and the General Service and Victory Medals.
Lower Heyford, Weedon, Northants. Z3268 /A.

CHARVILL, H. G., Sergeant, R.F.A.
A serving soldier at the outbreak of war, he was at once drafted to France. He fought in the Retreat from Mons and at Ypres, Neuve Chapelle, Loos, the Somme, Albert, St. Quentin and Cambrai, and was wounded. He was unfortunately killed in action on August 22nd, 1918, and was entitled to the Mons Star, and the General Service and Victory Medals.
"The path of duty was the way to glory."
Lower Heyford, Weedon, Northants. Z3268 /B.

CHATER, T. L., Private, Queen's Own (Royal West Kent Regiment).
He volunteered in December 1915, and five months later was sent to France, where he saw much heavy fighting. After taking part in the Battles of Arras and Ypres he was severely gassed at Kemmel Hill in September 1915, and invalided home. He was finally demobilised in February 1919, and holds the General Service and Victory Medals.
26, Arthur St., Kingsthorpe Hollow, Northampton. Z1397.

CHATER, H. W., Private, 5th Northants. Regt.
Volunteering in August 1914, he proceeded to France in the following May, and there took part in the Battles of the Somme, Arras and Messines, and was wounded at Cambrai and sent to hospital at Wimereux. Rejoining his unit, he was again in action in the Advance of 1918, and was finally demobilised in February 1919. He holds the 1914–15 Star, and the General Service and Victory Medals.
50, Hunter Street, Northampton. Z1396.

CHATTERS, P. J., Private, 7th Northants. Regt.
He volunteered in August 1915, and, after completing his training, was drafted to France, where he took part in many important engagements. He died gloriously on the Field of Battle in January 1917, and was entitled to the 1914–15 Star, and the General Service and Victory Medals.
"Thinking that remembrance, though unspoken, may reach him where he sleeps."
55, Roe Road, Northampton. Z2093.

CHECKLEY, W. D., Private, 6th Northants. Regt.
He joined in March 1917, and, after two months' training, was drafted overseas. Whilst serving on the Western Front he took part in many important engagements, principally in the Ypres sector, until wounded in October 1917 and sent to hospital in England. On his recovery he was retained on home service until demobilised in January 1919. He holds the General Service and Victory Medals.
19, Freehold Street, Northampton. Z1883.

CHEETHAM, C. J., Gunner, R.G.A.
Joining in May 1916, he was sent to France in the following September and was actively engaged in the Battles of the Somme, Arras, Ypres and Cambrai. He also did excellent work as a gunner in the Retreat and Advance of 1918, and, after the cessation of hostilities, proceeded into Germany with the Army of Occupation. Serving at Cologne until demobilised in September 1919, he holds the General Service and Victory Medals. 7, Grey Friars Street, Northampton. Z1884.

CHENEY, J. W., Corporal, 1st Northants. Regt.
He joined the Royal Sussex Regiment in March 1918, and in the following December was drafted to France, and thence to the Army of Occupation in Germany. In October 1919 he proceeded to India, and was transferred to the 1st Northamptonshire Regiment and was stationed at Rawal Pindi. In February 1921 he was serving in Ireland.
The Green, Lower Heyford, Northants. Z3269

CHEVERTON, M. A., Sapper, Royal Engineers.
He joined the Queen's (Royal West Surrey Regiment) in September 1917, but, after his training, was engaged with his unit on important duties at various stations, and was later transferred to the Royal Engineers. He rendered valuable services, but was not successful in obtaining his transfer overseas before the cessation of hostilities. He was demobilised in October 1919. 32, Alton Street, Northampton. Z3270.

CHICK, T. W., Private, 10th East Yorks. Regt.
He volunteered in October 1915, and in the following August proceeded to France, but, after taking part in the Somme offensive, was invalided home in November 1916, suffering from dysentery. He returned to the Western Front, however, in June 1917, and fought in the Battles of Ypres, the Somme and Armentières, and also in the Retreat and Advance of 1918. He was demobilised in April 1919, and holds the General Service and Victory Medals. 49, Charles St., Northampton. Z1287.

CHILDS, G., Chief Stoker, Royal Navy.
Already in the Royal Navy when war broke out in August 1914, he quickly proceeded to sea on board H.M.S. "Glasgow." He took part in the Battles of the Falkland Islands and Jutland, and was engaged on important escort duties within the area of activities. He also served on board H.M.S. "Nyth," and did continuously good work throughout hostilities. In 1921 he was still in the Navy, and holds the 1914–15 Star, and the General Service and Victory Medals.
21, Clarke Road, Northampton. Z2094.

CHOWN, J. W. H., Corporal, 2nd London Regt. (Royal Fusiliers).
He volunteered in December 1914, and in the following year proceeded to Gallipoli, where he saw severe fighting at Suvla Bay until invalided home suffering from frost-bite. He was afterwards drafted to France, and there took part in engagements on the Somme, where he was gassed. He was demobilised in May 1919, and holds the 1914–15 Star, and the General Service and Victory Medals.
61, Sheaf Street, Daventry, Northants. Z2607.

CHURCH, A. E., Private, 2nd Northants. Regt.
A Reservist, he was called to the Colours in August 1914, and in March of the following year proceeded to the Western Front, where he served as a stretcher-bearer in various sectors. He took part in the Battles of Ypres and Cambrai, fought also in the Retreat and Advance of 1918, and was gassed on the Somme in 1916. He was discharged in February 1919, and holds the 1914–15 Star, and the General Service and Victory Medals. 1, Alpha Street, Northampton. Z1288.

CHURCH, J. T., Private, Machine Gun Corps.
Two months after joining in February 1916 he was drafted to France, where he took part in important engagements in various sectors of the front. Transferred later to Mesopotamia, he was again in action until sent home and admitted to hospital at Brighton, suffering from malaria. He was invalided from the Army in November 1919, and holds the General Service and Victory Medals.
Nene Cottage, Cattle Market Road, Northampton. Z2609.

CHURCHMAN, E. A., Private, 4th Suffolk Regt.
Two months after joining in January 1917 he was drafted to the Western Front, where he took part in the Battle of Arras. Invalided to hospital in England in May 1917, however, he was afterwards retained on important duties at home until demobilised in February 1919. He holds the General Service and Victory Medals.
54, Poole Street, Northampton. Z1398/B.

CHURCHMAN, W., Private, 2nd King's Own (Royal Lancaster Regiment).
He volunteered in August 1914, and, after a period of training with the 1st Northamptonshire Regiment, was drafted to the Western Front, where he took part in many engagements, and was wounded. Afterwards transferred to Salonika, he was again in action on the Macedonian front, and in 1920 was with his unit in India. He holds the 1914 Star, and the General Service and Victory Medals.
24, Nelson Street, Northampton. Z1289/B.

CHURCHMAN, W. O., Pte., 1/4th Northants. Regt.
He joined in August 1916, and four months later proceeded to France, but, after taking part in much fighting, was wounded in March 1917 and invalided home. He was drafted to Egypt, however, in July of that year, and advanced thence into Palestine. He fell fighting in the third Battle of Gaza on November 2nd, 1917, and was entitled to the General Service and Victory Medals.
"His life for his Country, his soul to God."
54, Poole Street, Northampton. Z1398/A.

CIVIL, J., Private, 1st Northants. Regiment.
Having enlisted in April 1913, he proceeded to France with the first Expeditionary Force at the declaration of war, and took part in the fighting at Mons. After only two months' active service he died gloriously on the Field of Battle on October 22nd, 1914. He was entitled to the Mons Star, and the General Service and Victory Medals.
"He nobly fell that we might live."
16, Wellington Street, Northampton. Z1885.

CIVIL, W., Sergeant, 1/4th Northants. Regiment.
Mobilised with the Territorials in August 1914, he was drafted to the Dardanelles in July of the following year, and there, after the Landing at Suvla Bay, took a prominent part in much severe fighting. Sent home on the Evacuation of the Peninsula, he was discharged in October 1916, suffering from debility, and holds the 1914–15 Star, and the General Service and Victory Medals. 51, Lorne Road, Northampton. Z1290.

CLAGUE, W. E., Pte., 16th R. Warwickshire Regt.
He volunteered in September 1914, was sent to France in the following year, and took part in numerous engagements, including those on the Somme. He died gloriously on the Field of Battle at Albert on July 27th, 1916, and was entitled to the 1914–15 Star, and the General Service and Victory Medals.
"A valiant Soldier, with undaunted heart he breasted life's last hill."
34, Rothersthorpe Road, Northampton. Z3271.

CLARE, C., A.B., Royal Navy.
He volunteered in April 1915, and, after training in Scotland, was posted to H.M.S. "Birkenhead," attached to the Grand Fleet in the North Sea, where he took part in the Battle of Jutland and minor actions. He afterwards served in H.M.S. "Europa" in the Ægean Sea, and was finally demobilised in April 1920, holding the General Service and Victory Medals.
7, Gordon Street, Northampton. Z1291.

CLARK, C. G., Private, 2nd Royal Berks. Regt.
Volunteering in January 1915, he was shortly afterwards drafted to France, where, after a few months' heavy fighting in the Ypres sector, he was unfortunately reported missing. He was afterwards presumed to have been killed in action at the Battle of Loos in September 1915, and was entitled to the 1914–15 Star, and the General Service and Victory Medals.
"The path of duty was the way to glory."
near Chapel, Blisworth, Northampton. Z2095/B.

CLARK, F. W., Gunner, Royal Marine Artillery.
He was already in the Marine Artillery when war broke out in August 1914, and quickly proceeded to sea on board H.M.S. "Warspite." He served in the North Sea and took part in the Battle of Jutland and many minor operations, and was wounded in action. Several attempts were made to torpedo the "Warspite," but fortunately she escaped serious damage. He was also engaged at Scapa Flow on patrol duty. Invalided out of the Service in August 1920, he holds the 1914–15 Star, and the General Service and Victory Medals.
96, Oliver Street, Northampton. Z1399

CLARK, G., Guardsman, Coldstream Guards.
He volunteered in December 1915, and, after a period of training, was in the following October sent overseas. Whilst serving on the Western Front he took part in many engagements, saw heavy fighting in the Cambrai sector, and was unhappily killed in action in March 1917. He was entitled to the General Service and Victory Medals.
"He died the noblest death a man may die,
Fighting for God and right and liberty."
47, Roe Road, Northampton. Z2462/A—Z2371/A.

CLARK, G. H., Private, Manchester Regiment.
He joined in October 1916, and in the following September was drafted to France, where he took part in the Battle of Cambrai. Later he was transferred to Italy, and saw much heavy fighting there until the cessation of hostilities. He then proceeded to Egypt, where he was engaged on important duties before returning home for his demobilisation in May 1920. He holds the General Service and Victory Medals.
27, East Street, Northampton. Z2098.

CLARK, S., Private, 34th Royal Fusiliers.
He enlisted in March 1916, and later in the same year was drafted to France. Being unfit for the firing-line, he served with a Labour Battalion, and was engaged on important duties in connection with making roads and rail-roads in the Somme and Ypres sectors. Demobilised in September 1919, he holds the General Service and Victory Medals.
10, New Buildings, Blisworth, Northants. Z2095/A.

CLARK, W. A., 2nd Corporal, Royal Engineers.
Mobilised with the Territorials in August 1914, he was sent to Egypt in the following February, but two months later was discharged time-expired. In May 1915, however, he rejoined, and proceeded to France, where he took part in the Battles of Loos, Vimy Ridge, the Somme, Arras, Ypres and Cambrai, and was twice wounded. Invalided home in March 1918, he was demobilised in February 1919, and holds the 1914–15 Star, and the General Service and Victory Medals.
Blyths Wood, Weedon Road, St. James, Northampton. Z3462.

CLARKE, A., Pte., 7th Oxford. and Bucks. L.I.
Shortly after volunteering in September 1915 he was drafted to France, whence he proceeded in November of that year to Salonika There he took part in many important engagements on the Doiran and Vardar fronts until severely wounded in 1918 and sent to hospital in England. He was invalided from the Army in November 1919, and holds the 1914–15 Star, and the General Service and Victory Medals.
Halfway Houses, Hanslope, Bucks. Z2614/A.

CLARKE, A., Gunner, Royal Field Artillery.
He joined in January 1917, and underwent a period of training prior to being drafted to the Western Front in October of the following year. After much severe fighting he proceeded with the Army of Occupation into Germany, where he was stationed at Cologne until his return home for demobilisation in April 1920. He holds the General Service and Victory Medals.
18, Waterloo, Daventry, Northants. Z2611.

CLARKE, A. E., Air Mechanic, R.A.F.
He joined in November 1917, and, after completing a period of training, was retained at Plymouth, where he was engaged on important duties as a rigger, and was also for a time in hospital suffering from appendicitis. He was unable to obtain his transfer overseas, but, nevertheless, rendered valuable services with his Squadron until demobilised in October 1919.
Halfway Houses, Hanslope, Bucks. Z2614/C.

CLARKE, B., Private, 6th Buffs (East Kent Regt.)
He joined in July 1917, and twelve months later proceeded to the Western Front, where, after seeing much severe fighting in the Somme sector, he was badly wounded at Morlancourt in August 1918. He was admitted to hospital at Shrewsbury, and was finally invalided from the Army in January 1919. He holds the General Service and Victory Medals.
7, Crispin Street, Northampton. Z1097/A.

CLARKE, C. H., Private, 1st Northants. Regt.
When war broke out he was already serving, and was at once ordered to the Western Front, where he fought in the Retreat from Mons. After taking an active part in the Battles of the Marne, La Bassée, Neuve Chapelle, Ypres and Festubert, he was severely wounded at Loos in December 1915, and invalided home. In consequence he was discharged as medically unfit in October 1916, and holds the Mons Star, and the General Service and Victory Medals.
Forest View, Hartwell, Northants. Z2372/B.

CLARKE, C. W., Private, Suffolk Regiment.
He volunteered in November 1915, and, after completing a period of training, served at various stations, where he was engaged on duties of great importance, afterwards being transferred to the Labour Corps. Owing to ill-health he was unable to obtain his transfer overseas but, nevertheless, did much good work until demobilised in July 1919.
44, Monk's Pond Street, Northampton. Z1100/D.

CLARKE, E. E., Sergeant, King's Own (Royal Lancaster Regiment).
He was already serving in India when war was declared in August 1914, and in January of the following year was drafted to France. There he took a prominent part in many important engagements, including the Battles of Ypres, Loos, the Somme and Cambrai, and was wounded on the Somme in June 1918. Discharged in March 1919, he holds the 1914–15 Star, and the General Service and Victory Medals.
46, Monk's Pond Street, Northampton. Z1100/C.

CLARKE, E., Sergeant, Royal Field Artillery.
Shortly after volunteering in August 1914 he was drafted to Egypt, but, after a period of service there, contracted malaria and was admitted to hospital. On his recovery he rejoined his unit and was ordered to Salonika, on which front he played a prominent part in many engagements of note. He was demobilised on his return home in February 1919, and holds the 1914–15 Star, and the General Service and Victory Medals.
38, West Street, Weedon, Northants. Z2987/B.

CLARKE, E. M., Sapper, Royal Engineers.
He joined in 1918, and, after completing his training, was engaged at various stations on important duties with his unit. He rendered valuable services, but was not successful in obtaining his transfer overseas before the cessation of hostilities. He was demobilised in February 1920.
10, Chapel Gardens, Northampton. Z3275.

CLARKE, F., L/Corporal, 4th Northants. Regt.
Mobilised in August 1914, he proceeded to Gallipoli a year afterwards and served at Suvla Bay. In October 1915 he was sent to Egypt, but eight months later was drafted to Mesopotamia, on which front he was engaged in fierce fighting at Kut, Baghdad and Deli Abbas. He was transferred to India in April 1918, serving there until sent home to be discharged in December 1919. He holds the Long Service and Good Conduct Medal, the 1914–15 Star, and the General Service and Victory Medals.
33, Gregory Street, Northampton. Z2988/A.

CLARKE, F., Private, 5th Northants. Regiment.
He joined in October 1916, and in the following February was drafted to France. There he took part in several engagements, including those at Arras and Monchy, where he was wounded. On his recovery he rejoined his unit and was taken prisoner at Cambrai in November 1917. Released after the Armistice, he returned home and was demobilised in October 1919. He holds the General Service and Victory Medals.
53, Hood Street, Northampton. Z1400.

CLARKE, F., Private, 6th Northants. Regiment.
He joined in May 1916, and in the following September was drafted to France, where he took part in heavy fighting on the Somme, and was wounded and taken prisoner at Thiépval in February 1917. He was held in captivity in Germany and suffered many hardships. Repatriated after the Armistice, he returned home and was demobilised in March 1919, holding the General Service and Victory Medals.
The Grove, Roade, Northampton. Z2096.

CLARKE, F. L., Private, 6th Suffolk Regiment.
He joined in March 1917, and after a period of training with the 6th Suffolk Regiment was drafted to France with the 6th Wiltshire Regiment in May of the following year. There he saw much severe fighting at Ypres and in other sectors, and in June 1919 was transferred to Egypt, where he served at Cairo and Port Said. Demobilised on returning home in January 1920, he holds the General Service and Victory Medals.
4, Fife Street, St. James' End, Northampton. Z2613/A.

CLARKE, F. W., L/Corporal, Royal Engineers.
He volunteered in August 1915, and after a period of training was engaged at various stations on important duties with his unit. Owing to his being medically unfit he was unable to obtain a transfer overseas, but rendered valuable services until his demobilisation in January 1919.
102, Lea Road, Northampton. Z2097.

CLARKE, G., 2nd Corporal, Royal Engineers.
He volunteered in May 1915, and on conclusion of his training was drafted overseas in January of the following year. During his service on the Western Front he saw heavy fighting in the Battle of Vimy Ridge, and took an active part in numerous engagements of note in various sectors. He remained in France until demobilised in January 1919, holding the General Service and Victory Medals.
38, West Street, Weedon, Northants. Z2987/A.

CLARKE, G., Private, Suffolk Regiment.
He joined in March 1916, and six months later was drafted to the Western Front, where he took part in much severe fighting, particularly in the Somme, Arras and Cambrai sectors. He did excellent work with his unit throughout hostilities, and was twice wounded in action. Demobilised in December 1919, he holds the General Service and Victory Medals.
4, Chaucer Street, Kingsley Park, Northampton. Z1095/A.

CLARKE, G., Corporal, 99th Training Reserve, Northamptonshire Regiment.
He volunteered in August 1914, and for over four years was engaged on special duties with the 39th and 99th Training Reserve Battalions of the Northamptonshire Regiment. During this time he rendered valuable services and did excellent work as a machine-gun Instructor. He was not successful in obtaining his transfer overseas, and was demobilised in March 1919.
47, Lawrence Street, Northampton. Z1292.

CLARKE, G. A., Driver, Royal Engineers.
He volunteered in January 1915, but was retained on special duties in England until March 1917. Proceeding to France in that month, he played a prominent part in the Battles of Ypres, Rheims, the Somme (II.) and Bapaume, where he was badly wounded and invalided home. He was discharged as medically unfit for further military service in January 1919, and holds the General Service and Victory Medals.
46, Salisbury Street, Northampton. Z1099.

CLARKE, H., Corporal, Machine Gun Corps.
He joined the Royal Army Service Corps in September 1916, and after completing his training was transferred to the Machine Gun Corps. He was drafted to France in July 1917, fought at St. Quentin and Ypres, and also took part in the Retreat and Advance of 1918. He was demobilised in October 1919, and holds the General Service and Victory Medals.
11, Weston Row, Northants. Z3274.

CLARKE, H. E., Rifleman, 17th K.R.R.C.
Volunteering in October 1915, he was drafted to the Western Front in June 1917, and took part in numerous important engagements in various sectors. He saw much service in the Battles of Ypres, Passchendaele and the Somme, and was wounded at Cambrai in September 1918. Invalided to hospital in England, he was eventually demobilised in January 1919, and holds the General Service and Victory Medals.
33, Gregory Street, Northampton. Z2988/B.

CLARKE, H. S., Private, 5th Oxford. & Bucks. L.I.
Volunteering in November 1914, he was shortly afterwards drafted to the Western Front, where he saw heavy fighting in various sectors. After taking part in the Battles of Ypres, Festubert, Loos, the Somme and Arras, he was wounded in 1916 and again in the following year, and was sent to hospital at Southport in 1917. Invalided from the Army in July 1918, he holds the 1914–15 Star, and the General Service and Victory Medals.
Halfway Houses, Hanslope, Bucks. Z2614/B.

CLARKE, J., Seaman-Gunner, Royal Navy.
He joined in September 1917, and served on board H.M.S. "Canada" in the North Sea on convoy duties. He took part in the attack on Zeebrugge and in numerous other important operations, and was accidentally injured. He was demobilised in March 1919, and holds the General Service and Victory Medals.
36, Hervey Street, Northampton. Z3273.

CLARKE, J. D., Private, South Wales Borderers.
He joined in January 1917, and on conclusion of his training was drafted overseas shortly afterwards. Serving on the Western Front, he saw heavy fighting in various sectors, took part in the Battles of Arras and Vimy Ridge, and was wounded at Monchy in 1917. After 17 months' treatment in hospital in England he was demobilised in 1919, holding the General Service and Victory Medals.
81, St. Edmund's Road, Northampton. Z1886.

CLARKE, J. J., Private, 1st Suffolk Regiment.
He joined in March 1918, and proceeded to France four months later. During the final Advance of the Allies he took part in much severe fighting, particularly in the Ypres sector, and did excellent work with his unit. He was demobilised in May 1919, and holds the General Service and Victory Medals.
61, Bath Street, Northampton. Z1098/B.

CLARKE, J. T., Trooper, Bedfordshire Lancers.
Volunteering in December 1915, he proceeded to Egypt in the following year and, advancing into Palestine, took part in the Battles of Rafa and Gaza. Transferred in October 1917 to France, he was again in action at Cambrai and Amiens and in other engagements in the Retreat and Advance of 1918. He afterwards served with the Army of Occupation in Germany, and was demobilised in February 1919, holding the General Service and Victory Medals.
114, Green Street, Northampton. Z2610.

CLARKE, J. W., L/Corporal, Royal Sussex Regt.
He joined in March 1916, and later in the same year embarked for the Western Front. There he was in action at the Battles of the Somme, Arras, Vimy Ridge, Messines, Ypres and Cambrai and other notable engagements, and also fought in the Retreat and Advance of 1918. After the Armistice he advanced into Germany with the Army of Occupation and served at Cologne until demobilised in April 1919, holding the General Service and Victory Medals.
47, Euston Road, Northampton. Z2986.

CLARKE, L., Private, Bedfordshire Regiment.
On attaining military age he joined in April 1918, but owing to his youth was not successful in obtaining a transfer to a theatre of war before the cessation of hostilities. After the Armistice he was drafted to Germany, where he did consistently good work with the Army of Occupation until sent home for demobilisation in March 1920.
44, Denmark Road, Northampton. Z1889/B.

CLARKE, L., Private, K.O. (Yorkshire L.I.)
He enlisted in September 1916, and in the following January was drafted to the Western Front, where he took part in much severe fighting in the Ypres sector. He made the supreme sacrifice, being killed in action in May 1917, and was entitled to the General Service and Victory Medals.
"Great deeds cannot die:
They with the sun and moon renew their light for ever."
136, Abington Avenue, Northampton. Z2099.

CLARKE, L. J., A/Sergeant, Royal Engineers.
He volunteered in May 1915, but was retained on important instructional duties in England until March 1918, when he succeeded in securing a transfer to India. There he rendered very valuable services at Manora and Karachi until after the close of hostilities. He was demobilised on his return to England in December 1919, and holds the General Service and Victory Medals.
100, St. Leonard's Road, Far Cotton, Northampton. Z1887.

CLARKE, M. W., Private, 1st Northants. Regt.
Mobilised at the outbreak of war he was at once sent to France, where he fought in the Retreat from Mons, and at the Battles of the Marne, the Aisne, Ypres, Aubers Ridge, Festubert, Loos and Albert. He was unfortunately killed in action on the Somme on July 19th, 1916, and was entitled to the Mons Star, and the General Service and Victory Medals.
"Whilst we remember, the sacrifice is not in vain."
Bugbrooke, Northants. Z3272/B.

CLARKE, R. H., Private, 1/4th Northants. Regt.
Volunteering in May 1915 he completed his training, and 11 months later was ordered to Egypt. After rendering valuable services on that front he was sent to Palestine, and died gloriously on the Field of Battle at Gaza on April 19th, 1917. He was entitled to the General Service and Victory Medals.
"He passed out of the sight of men by the path of duty and self-sacrifice."
Forest View, Hartwell, Northants. Z2372/A.

CLARKE, R. W. T., Private, 4th Northants. Regt.
After volunteering in October 1915, he underwent a period of training prior to being sent to the Western Front in January 1917. There after taking part in much severe fighting at Béthune and various other places, he fell fighting at Arras on August 23rd, 1917. He was entitled to the General Service and Victory Medals.
"Whilst we remember, the sacrifice is not in vain."
4, Fife Street, St. James' End, Northampton. Z2613/B.

CLARKE, S. A., Private, 1/4th Northants. Regt.
A Reservist, he was called up at the outbreak of war, and in July 1915 was drafted to Gallipoli. There he was in action at Suvla Bay, Anzac and Chocolate Hill, and after the Evacuation of the Peninsula served in Egypt. In 1917 he proceeded to Palestine, and fought in engagements at Gaza, Jerusalem, Jaffa and on the Jordan. He was discharged on his return home in June 1919, and holds the 1914–15 Star, and the General Service and Victory Medals.
Forest View, Hartwell, Northants. Z2373/B.

CLARKE, S. W., Sergeant, 5th Northants. Regt.
He volunteered in August 1914, and nine months later was drafted overseas. Serving on the Western Front he saw heavy fighting at Armentières, took a prominent part in the Battles of Loos, Albert, Arras, Ypres and Cambrai, and was wounded at Epéhy in September 1918. After protracted hospital treatment in London he was demobilised in August 1920, and holds the 1914–15 Star, and the General Service and Victory Medals.
Forest View, Hartwell, Northants. Z2372/C.

CLARKE, T., Private, Essex Regiment.
Shortly after joining in June 1916, he was drafted to the Western Front, where he saw severe fighting in various sectors. He took part in many important engagements until badly wounded on the Somme and invalided home. He was then transferred to the Royal Army Medical Corps, and retained in England until demobilised in August 1919, holding the General Service and Victory Medals.
25, Pytchley Street, Northampton. Z1888.

CLARKE, W., Private, Tank Corps.
Joining in September 1916, he first served with the Suffolk Regiment, but was later transferred to the Tank Corps. He did excellent work in connection with the repairing and manufacture of tanks at Birmingham, but was unsuccessful in serving in a theatre of war. He was demobilised in January 1919.
7, Shelley Street, Kingston Road, Northampton. Z1096/A.

CLARKE, W., Private, 6th Northants. Regiment.
He volunteered in January 1916, and in the following August was drafted to the Western Front, where he took part in the Battles of the Somme, Ypres and Passchendaele. He laid down his life for King and Country in the last-named sector on January 13th, 1918, and was entitled to the General Service and Victory Medals.
"His memory is cherished with pride."
61, Bath Street, Northampton. Z1098/A.

CLARKE, W. H., Sergeant, Northants. Regiment.
Volunteering at the outbreak of war he proceeded to the Western Front in 1915, and played a prominent part in the Battles of Neuve Chapelle, Hill 60, and Ypres. He was wounded at Loos in 1916, and after his discharge from hospital in England was retained on important instructional duties at various home stations. In 1920 he was still serving, and holds the 1914–15 Star, and the General Service and Victory Medals. 53, Charles Street, Northampton. Z2989.

CLARKE, W. J., Private, 1st Northants. Regiment.
Mobilised from the Reserve when war was declared, he proceeded to France in August 1914, and fought in the Retreat from Mons, and the Battles of the Marne, the Aisne and La Bassée. He gave his life for the freedom of England at Ypres on October 29th, 1914, and was entitled to the Mons Star, and the General Service and Victory Medals.
"Whilst we remember, the sacrifice is not in vain."
Bugbrooke, Northants. Z3272/C.

CLARKE, W. T., Pte., 1st South Staffordshire Regt.
Joining in January 1917, he proceeded to the Western Front in the following September and there saw much severe fighting. He was unfortunately reported missing and is presumed to have been killed in action at Ypres on October 26th, 1917, after only a few weeks in the firing-line. He was entitled to the General Service and Victory Medals.
"His life for his Country, his soul to God."
44, Denmark Road, Northampton. Z1889/A.

CLAYDON, A. T., Private, Oxford. & Bucks. L.I.
When war broke out he was called up from the Reserve, and was at once ordered to France, where he served in the Retreat from Mons. After fighting in the Battle of La Bassée, he gave his life for King and Country at Ypres in November 1914. He was entitled to the Mons Star, and the General Service and Victory Medals.
"He died the noblest death a man may die:
Fighting for God and right and liberty."
12, Euston Road, Northampton. Z2990/B—Z2991/B.

CLAYDON, F., Drummer, 52nd Queen's (Royal West Surrey Regiment).
He enlisted in October 1916, and completing his training shortly afterwards was drafted to France. There he took part in many important engagements, and was wounded in action. Later he was transferred to the Royal Fusiliers and served in various sectors until hostilities ceased. He was demobilised in September 1919, holding the General Service and Victory Medals. 106, Purser Road, Northampton. Z2100.

CLAYDON, H., Private, R.A.M.C.
Volunteering in November 1914, he was drafted to the Western Front in April of the following year. Whilst in France he was engaged in severe fighting at the Battles of Festubert, St. Eloi, Albert, Vimy Ridge, the Somme, Beaumont-Hamel, Bullecourt, Lens and Cambrai, and was present during the entry into Mons. Demobilised on his return home in March 1919, he holds the 1914–15 Star, and the General Service and Victory Medals.
12, Euston Road, Northampton. Z2990/A—Z2991/A.

CLAYDON, J. E., Corporal, R.A.S.C.
Joining in January 1917, he was drafted to the Western Front in the following month, and was there engaged as a driver and on other important duties at Le Havre and elsewhere. After the cessation of hostilities he served with the Army of Occupation at Cologne, finally returning home for demobilisation in October 1919. He holds the General Service and Victory Medals. 8, Baring Road, Northampton. Z2615/B.

CLAYDON, W., L/Corporal, Bedfordshire Regt.
On attaining military age he joined in December 1916, and after a period of training was engaged on duties of an important nature at various home stations. He was also employed in conducting prisoners of war from France to the camps in England, and rendered valuable services until demobilised in June 1919, holding the General Service and Victory Medals.
12, Euston Road, Northampton Z2990/C—Z2991/C.

CLAYSON, A., Private, Royal Sussex Regiment.
He joined in March 1918, and was engaged on work of an important nature at various stations in England. Owing to his youth he was not successful in obtaining a transfer to a theatre of war, but, nevertheless, performed valuable work, carrying out the various duties assigned to him in a highly capable manner, until demobilised in February 1919.
45, Spencer Street, Northampton. Z2992/D.

CLAYSON, A., Private, Middlesex Regiment and Labour Corps.
Volunteering in May 1915 he completed his training, and eight months later was sent overseas. Serving on the Western Front he was actively engaged in numerous notable battles, but was wounded at the Battle of Ypres and invalided to England. On his discharge from hospital at Norwich he was demobilised in March 1919, holding the General Service and Victory Medals.
45, Spencer Street, Northampton. Z2992/B.

CLAYSON, H., Gunner, Royal Field Artillery.
He enlisted in March 1916, and completing his training early in the following year was drafted to France. In this seat of war he took part in many engagements, including the Battles of Arras, Vimy Ridge, Ypres, Passchendaele and the Somme (II.). After hostilities ceased he proceeded to Germany with the Army of Occupation, and served there until his demobilisation in October 1919. He holds the General Service and Victory Medals. 45, Spencer Street, Northampton. Z2992/A.

CLAYSON, J., Private, 1st Northants. Regiment.
Having volunteered in August 1914, he was sent to France early in the following year, and took part in the Battles of Ypres (II.) and Loos, where he was severely wounded in action in September 1915. Invalided to Wandsworth Hospital, he unfortunately had to suffer amputation of his left arm, and was discharged as medically unfit in March 1916. He holds the 1914–15 Star, and the General Service and Victory Medals.
8, Grafton Street, Northampton. Z1101/A.

CLAYSON, W., Private, Canadian Overseas Forces.
He volunteered in December 1914, and in the following month proceeded to France. Whilst on the Western Front he saw much heavy fighting, and took part in the Battle of Vimy Ridge. In December 1917 he was invalided home, suffering from neurasthenia, and discharged as medically unfit for further service. He holds the 1914–15 Star, and the General Service and Victory Medals.
45, Spencer Street, Northampton. Z2992/C.

CLAYSON, W. C., Gunner, R.G.A.
Joining in May 1917, he was drafted overseas in the following August. Whilst on the Western Front he took part in several engagements, including the Battles of Ypres, Amiens, Havrincourt, Epéhy, Cambrai (II.), Le Cateau (II.) and the Sambre. He was demobilised in February 1919, and holds the General Service and Victory Medals.
76, East Street, Northampton. Z2101.

CLEAVER, J. (Miss), British Red Cross Society.
She volunteered in the British Red Cross Society in March 1915, and throughout hostilities was engaged on important duties making bandages and pneumonia coats. She carried out her duties in a highly commendable manner, and rendered valuable services. In December 1918 she was demobilised.
119, Holley Road, Northampton. Z2102/B.

CLIFTON, C., Private, Labour Corps.
He joined in June 1916, and within a month was drafted to France. During his service on the Western Front he was engaged on special duties with his unit in various sectors, and did excellent work. He was eventually demobilised in January 1919, and holds the General Service and Victory Medals.
45, Lawrence Street, Northampton. Z1293.

CLIFTON, H., Private, 2nd Northants. Regiment.
A Territorial, he was mobilised in August 1914, and was drafted to Egypt in 1916. Whilst overseas he was in action at Jifjaffa, Katia, El Fasher, Romani, Magdhaba, Rafa and Siwa. He also fought in the three Battles of Gaza in the Jordan Valley and at the capture of Jerusalem, and at the end of the Palestine campaign was sent to India, where he was still serving in 1921. He holds the General Service and Victory Medals.
Mill Hill, Long Buckby, Northants. Z3276.

CLIPSTON, A. J., Gunner, R.G.A.
He enlisted in May 1917, and in September of the same year was drafted to France. There he took part in many engagements, including the Battles of Passchendaele and Kemmel Hill, and fought also in the Retreat and Advance of 1918. He did good work throughout his service, and was demobilised in January 1919, holding the General Service and Victory Medals. 1, Spring Garden Terrace, Northampton. Z2993.

CLOUT, A. W., Pte., 3rd (King's Own) Hussars.
He was called up from the Reserve in August 1914, and immediately drafted to France. Whilst in this theatre of war he took part in several engagements, including the Battles of Mons, the Somme, Arras, Ypres and Amiens, and was slightly wounded in action in 1918. He served overseas for 4½ years and received his discharge in March 1919, holding the Mons Star, and the General Service and Victory Medals.
1, Pine Street, Northampton. Z1401.

CLUES, G., Private, 4th Northants. Regiment.
A Reservist, he was called to the Colours in August 1914, and was retained on special duties in England for a time. In July 1915 he was drafted to the Gallipoli Peninsula, and after taking part in the Landing at Suvla Bay, was unfortunately killed in action on October 6th of the same year. He was entitled to the 1914–15 Star, and the General Service and Victory Medals.
"His name liveth for evermore."
13, Priory Square, Northampton. Z1102/B.

CLOWES, A., Sapper, Royal Engineers.
Volunteering in August 1915, he was sent overseas later in the same year on completion of his training. Whilst serving on the Western Front he was in action in many engagements in various sectors, and was employed on special duties with his Company until the cessation of hostilities. He was demobilised in March 1919, holding the 1914–15 Star, and the General Service and Victory Medals.
93, St. James' Park Road, Northampton. Z2374/A.

CLOWES, J., A.B., Royal Navy.
At the outbreak of war in August 1914 he was already in the Navy, and during the period of hostilities was engaged on important duties in many waters. He lost his life whilst serving on Submarine "K 5" when she was sunk at the approach to the English Channel in January 1921. He was entitled to the 1914–15 Star and the General Service and Victory Medals.
"His life for his Country, his soul to God"
93, St. James' Park Road, Northampton. Z2374/B.

COBB, H. G., Private, 9th Essex Regiment.
Volunteering in October 1915 he was sent to France in the following July, and after taking part in heavy fighting at Albert and during the Somme Offensive, was badly wounded in action at the Battle of Arras in April 1917. He was invalided home to hospital in Stockport and on his recovery was transferred to the Royal Air Force, with which unit he did excellent work as an armourer. He holds the General Service and Victory Medals, and was demobilised in April 1920.
29, Regent Street, Northampton. Z1103.

COCKERELL, H., Private, Sherwood Foresters.
Joining in 1916, he was drafted overseas after a period of training. Whilst on the Western Front he took part in many important engagements, including those in the Vimy Ridge, Somme and Cambrai sectors. In 1918 he was discharged in order to do work of National importance, and holds the General Service and Victory Medals.
91, St. Leonard's Road, Northampton. Z2994/B

COCKERELL, J. T. (M.M.), Sergt., Middlesex Regt.
He enlisted in 1916, and later in the same year was drafted to France, where he played a prominent part in the Battles of Vimy Ridge, Ypres, Cambrai, and Amiens, and other important engagements. He was mentioned in Despatches and awarded the Military Medal for gallantry and devotion to duty in the Field. Demobilised in 1919, he holds also the General Service and Victory Medals.
91, St. Leonard's Road, Northampton. Z2994/C.

COCKERILL, A. A., Gunner, R.G.A.
He enlisted in 1916, and later in the same year was drafted to France. In this theatre of war he took part in much heavy fighting at Vimy Ridge, the Lys and Cambrai (II.), and was present at the entry into Mons on Armistice Day. He was demobilised in 1919, and holds the General Service and Victory Medals. 98, Clarke Road, Northampton. Z2047/B.

COCKERILL, D. A., Private 1st Northants. Regt.
He volunteered in April 1915, and was sent to the Western Front in the following November. In the course of his service overseas he was in action in several sectors, performing valuable work in the firing-line in many engagements. Wounded near Béthune on June 7th, 1916, he died of his injuries the following day, and was entitled to the 1914–15 Star, and the General Service and Victory Medals.
"Great deeds cannot die."
14, York Place, Weston Street, Northampton. Z3277

COCKING, J. W., Q.M.S., Royal Field Artillery.
He volunteered in 1915, and was retained at home for a time before proceeding to France in 1917. Whilst on the Western Front he played a prominent part in much heavy fighting in the Battles of Bullecourt and Cambrai, and was badly wounded in action. As a result he was invalided home, and was eventually demobilised in March 1919, holding the General Service and Victory Medals.
12, Clarke Road, Northampton. Z2103.

COE, C. T., Gunner, Royal Horse Artillery.
He joined in February 1917, and in June was sent to France, where he took part in the Battles of Ypres and the Somme (II.). He was also in action with his Battery during the Retreat and Advance of 1918, and was at Mons on Armistice Day. After the cessation of hostilities he served at Cologne with the Army of Occupation until demobilised in November 1919, holding the General Service and Victory Medals.
8, Alpha Street, Northampton. Z1294.

COLEMAN, A. J., Sergeant, R.A.S.C.
He volunteered in March 1915, but on account of ill-health was unsuccessful in his repeated endeavours to obtain a transfer to a theatre of war. Throughout the period of his service he was engaged on important clerical duties which he fulfilled with the utmost ability until demobilised in January 1919. 57, Adams Avenue, Northampton. Z2375/A.

COLEMAN, A. W., L/Corporal, 2nd Queen's (Royal West Surrey Regiment).
Volunteering in April 1915, he crossed to France in August 1916, and took part in heavy fighting at Bapaume, Beaumont-Hamel, Pozières and was wounded on March 14th, 1917. After treatment at Boulogne he was evacuated to England and admitted to Norwich Thorpe Hospital, and on recovery served at Sittingbourne and Sutton until discharged on medical grounds in May 1918. He holds the General Service and Victory Medals. High Street, Long Buckby, Northants. Z3278.

COLEMAN, C. G., A.B., Royal Navy.
He volunteered in June 1915, and after a period of training was commissioned to H.M.S. "Malay" for service with the Portsmouth Division in the North Sea. He was engaged on important patrol duties, and took part in the Battle of Jutland, where he was unfortunately killed in action on May 31st, 1916. He was entitled to the General Service and Victory Medals.
"Thinking that remembrance, though unspoken, may reach him where he sleeps."
27, St. John's Street, Northampton. Z2995/B.

COLEMAN, W., Sergt., South Staffordshire Regt.
Volunteering in August 1914, he was sent to Gallipoli in the following year, and, after taking a prominent part in the Landing at Cape Helles, was severely wounded in August 1915. He was sent to hospital at Alexandria and thence home, where, on his recovery, he was retained on munition work until finally invalided from the Army in 1917. He holds the 1914–15 Star, and the General Service and Victory Medals.
New Street, Lower Weedon, Northants. Z2616.

COLES, E. F., Bombardier, R.G.A.
He volunteered in October 1915, and four months later proceeded to the Western Front, where he did excellent work with his Battery at the Battles of the Somme, Ypres and Cambrai, and throughout the Retreat and Advance of 1918. He was gassed in action on the Somme, and after hostilities ceased was stationed on the Rhine with the Army of Occupation. Demobilised in April 1919, he holds the General Service and Victory Medals. 51, Spring Lane, Northampton. Z1104.

COLES, F. L., Private, 3rd Northants. Regiment.
He volunteered at the commencement of hostilities in August 1914, and on completion of his training served with his Battalion at various depôts in the South of England. Engaged as a boot-repairer he rendered valuable services, but was unable to obtain his transfer to a theatre of war before hostilities ceased, and was demobilised in December 1918.
4, Saunders Terrace, Long Buckby, Northants. Z3279.

COLES, G. B. H., Private, 9th Cheshire Regiment.
He volunteered in October 1915, and seven months later was drafted to France, where he took part in much severe fighting on the Somme, and was gassed in 1917. Later he was severely wounded on March 27th, 1918, and unhappily died on the following day. He was entitled to the General Service and Victory Medals.
"He passed out of the sight of men by the path of duty and self-sacrifice."
41, East Street, Northampton. Z2996/B.

COLES, J., Private, Royal Defence Corps.
He volunteered in May 1915, and underwent a period of training before being engaged at various stations on important guard duties. He rendered excellent services, but owing to ill-health was discharged in August 1916 as medically unfit for further duty.
41, East Street, Northampton. Z2996/A.

COLES, R., Rifleman, 8th London Regiment (Post Office Rifles).
He volunteered in September 1915, and in March of the following year proceeded to the Western Front, where he saw much heavy fighting. After taking part in the Battle of Vimy Ridge, he was wounded and buried for 24 hours at High Wood in September 1916, during the Somme Offensive. Admitted to hospital in England he was invalided from the Army in November 1917, and holds the General Service and Victory Medals. 56, Denmark Road, Northampton Z1890.

COLES, T. E., Private, 7th Northants. Regiment.
He volunteered in April 1915, and in September of that year was drafted to the Western Front, where he saw severe fighting in various sectors. He took part in the Battles of Loos, Vimy Ridge, the Somme, Arras and Ypres and many other important engagements until the cessation of hostilities. Demobilised in April 1919, he holds the 1914–15 Star, and the General Service and Victory Medals.
6, Mount Pleasant, Daventry, Northants. Z2617.

COLLAR, D. A., Trooper, Northants. Dragoons.
Two months after volunteering in September 1914 he embarked for the Western Front, where he was in action in many engagements, including the Battles of Ypres, the Somme and Arras, until drafted to Italy in November 1917. He took an active part in severe fighting on the Piave front and Asiago Plateau, and was wounded in November 1918. Demobilised in March 1919, he holds the 1914 Star, and the General Service and Victory Medals. The Green, Milton, Northants. Z2376/C.

COLLAR, F., L/Corporal, Royal Engineers.
He joined in August 1917, and was retained on home defence throughout the period of his service. He was stationed at Longmoor, where he was engaged on duties of an important nature and performed them in a highly capable manner. Owing to ill-health he was unable to secure a transfer overseas, but did much valuable work until demobilised in August 1919.
The Green, Milton, Northants. Z2376/A.

COLLAR, J. W., Private, 12th (Prince of Wales' Royal) Lancers.
When war was declared in August 1914 he was mobilised, and immediately proceeded to the Western Front with the First Expeditionary Force. Shortly after landing in France he was unhappily killed in action whilst fighting in the Battle of Mons. He was entitled to the Mons Star, and the General Service and Victory Medals.
"Great deeds cannot die:
They with the sun and moon renew their light for ever."
The Green, Milton, Northants. Z2376/B.

COLLAR, T. H., Corporal, 6th Northants. Regiment.
He volunteered in September 1914, and in 1916 was drafted to France, where he fought in the Battle of the Somme, and was wounded in July of that year. On his discharge from hospital in England he returned to the Western Front, and did valuable work with the Military Police until the Armistice. He was then sent to Palestine, and in 1920 was serving at Haifa, holding the General Service and Victory Medals.
The Green, Milton, Northants. Z2376/D.

COLLIER, C., Private, 2nd Bedfordshire Regiment.
Joining in February 1917, he was sent to France in the following July, and there saw much heavy fighting. He took part in the Battles of Arras, Ypres, Cambrai, the Somme and Le Cateau, and minor engagements, fought also in the Retreat and Advance of 1918, and later was sent with the Army of Occupation to Cologne. Demobilised in December 1919, he holds the General Service and Victory Medals.
6, Hervey Street, Northampton. Z1891.

COLLIER, F. R., Sapper, Royal Engineers.
Volunteering in 1915, he embarked for the Western Front in the following year, and served there until the close of the war. During this period he did excellent work with his section in the forward areas, and was present at the Battles of Vimy Ridge, the Somme, Ypres, Cambrai and during the Retreat and Advance of 1918. He was demobilised in 1919, and holds the General Service and Victory Medals.
44, Oxford Street, Northampton. Z3280.

COLLIER, J. H., Private, Machine Gun Corps.
He joined in June 1916, after having been employed on munitions for a considerable period, and sailed for France three months later. Serving in various parts of the line he was gassed in September 1917, but, rejoining his unit after treatment at Boulogne, took an active part in operations until the Armistice. He holds the General Service and Victory Medals, and was demobilised in January 1919.
Stone House, West Haddon, Northants. Z3281/B.

COLLIER, T. S., Pte., Duke of Cornwall's L.I.
He was mobilised in August 1914, and immediately drafted to the Western Front. There he took part in many engagements, including the Battles of Mons, the Marne and the Aisne, fought also in the defence of Antwerp, and was wounded. As a result he was invalided home, and later received his discharge—time expired—in 1916. He holds the Mons Star, and the General Service and Victory Medals.
7, Maple Street, Northampton. Z1402.

COLLIER, W. D., Private, 6th Welch Regiment.
Joining in October 1916, he was ordered a year later to the Western Front, where he served for two years. During that time he fought in the Battles of Ypres, Passchendaele, Lens, Cambrai, the Somme and Bapaume, and was wounded and gassed at Cambrai in October 1918. He was invalided to England, and was eventually demobilised in December 1919, holding the General Service and Victory Medals.
61, Stanley Road, Northampton. Z2377.

COLLIER, W. F. D., Corporal, Coldstream Guards.
He volunteered in January 1916, was trained at Caterham, and in June 1917 landed on the Western Front. There he was engaged in fierce fighting in the Ypres salient and was severely wounded. Invalided to Sheffield for hospital treatment he was eventually demobilised in December 1918, and holds the General Service and Victory Medals.
Stone House, West Haddon, Northants. Z3281 /A.

COLLIER, W. P., Sergeant, 2nd Northants. Regt.
He joined in March 1917, and gaining rapid promotion to Sergeant was sent to France in June. After taking part in strenuous fighting at Ypres, he was badly wounded on August 1st of the same year, and died the following day. He was entitled to the General Service and Victory Medals.
"A valiant Soldier, with undaunted heart he breasted life's last hill."
2, Monk's Pond Street, Northampton. Z1105.

COLLINS, A. C., Private, Royal Naval Division.
Joining in May 1917, he was drafted to France in April of the following year and served with the "Hood" Battalion, 2nd Naval Brigade. After taking part in heavy fighting on the Somme, he was badly wounded in action in May 1918, and invalided to hospital in Chatham. He was discharged as medically unfit for further service in February 1919, and holds the General Service and Victory Medals.
4, Castle Gardens, Northampton. Z1106 /B.

COLLINS, C., Private, 1st King's (Liverpool Regt.)
Joining in May 1916, he was stationed in Ireland for a time, and proceeded to France in the following year. Whilst on the Western Front he was in action in several engagements, including those during the Retreat and Advance of 1918, and was reported missing at Arras in August 1918. He was later presumed to have been killed in action near Arras, and was entitled to the General Service and Victory Medals.
"His memory is cherished with pride."
New Cottage, Kislingbury, Northants. Z3283 /A.

COLLINS, H., Private, 1st Hertfordshire Regt.
Mobilised in August 1914, he was drafted to the Western Front two months later and saw much heavy fighting. He took part in the Battles of Ypres, Neuve Chapelle, Hill 60, Loos, Arras, Passchendaele, Cambrai, the Somme, Amiens and Bapaume, and fought also in the Retreat and Advance of 1918. He was demobilised in February 1919, and holds the 1914 Star, and the General Service and Victory Medals.
31, Norton Road, Daventry, Northants. Z2618.

COLLINS, H., Private, 1st Northants. Regiment.
Volunteering in September 1914, he was drafted to the Western Front in the following March, and fought in several engagements in the Ypres salient. He was severely wounded at Aubers Ridge in May 1915, and, being sent home on account of his injuries, received protracted hospital treatment. He was invalided out of the service in May 1916, and holds the 1914–15 Star, and the General Service and Victory Medals.
New Cottage, Kislingbury, Northants. Z3283 /B.

COLLINS, P., Gunner, Royal Garrison Artillery.
He volunteered in August 1914, and proceeding to France in the following year served in various parts of the British Front until the conclusion of hostilities. During this period he was engaged in strenuous fighting in the Ypres salient, on the Somme, at Arras and Cambrai and in the Retreat and Advance of 1918. Returning to England for demobilisation in March 1919, he holds the 1914–15 Star, and the General Service and Victory Medals.
The Green, Lower Heyford, Northants. Z3284 /D.

COLLINS, S. J., Guardsman, Coldstream Guards.
A Regular, he crossed to the Western Front on the outbreak of war in August 1914, and was in almost continuous action in the Retreat from Mons and at the Battles of the Marne, the Aisne, La Bassée and Ypres. He also took part in the Battles of Loos, the Somme, Cambrai, those of the German Offensive, and in the subsequent Allied Advance of 1918. Discharged on his return to England in March 1919, he holds the Mons Star, and the General Service and Victory Medals.
The Green, Lower Heyford, Northants. Z3284 /C.

COLLINS, W. (jun.), Gunner, R.F.A.
He joined in August 1916, and embarking for France in the following year fought in several important engagements, notably those at Ypres, Cambrai and on the Somme. Taking an active part in operations during the Retreat, he was also in action in the final Allied Advance of 1918, after which he served with the Army of Occupation in Germany. He returned from Cologne for demobilisation in October 1920, and holds the General Service and Victory Medals.
near Red Lion, Kislingbury, Northants. Z3282 /A.

COLLINS, W. (sen.), Pte., 1/4th Northants. Regt.
A Reservist, he was mobilised on the declaration of war, and after completing his training served with his Battalion at various stations. He was engaged on important coastal defence work and rendered valuable services, but owing to being over military age was unsuccessful in securing his transfer overseas before the termination of the war, and was demobilised in January 1919. near Red Lion, Kislingbury, Northants. Z3282B.

COLLINS, W. C., Private, Machine Gun Corps.
Joining in January 1917, he sailed for the Western Front in the same year and did good work with his section in the Battles of Ypres, Passchendaele, Cambrai and the Somme. He was wounded in March 1918, and after treatment returned to the firing-line to take part in operations during the final stages of the war. Returning to England he was demobilised in February 1919, and holds the General Service and Victory Medals.
The Green, Lower Heyford, Northants. Z3284 /A.

COLLINS, W. E., Gunner, R.G.A.
Volunteering in July 1915, he proceeded overseas in the following year and saw active service in France and Flanders. He was engaged with his Battery at the Battles of the Somme, Arras, Ypres and Cambrai, and was wounded in 1918 in the second Battle of the Somme. On recovery he rejoined his Battery and served in engagements until the close of the war. He holds the General Service and Victory Medals, and was demobilised in February 1919.
The Green, Lower Heyford, Northants. Z3284 /B.

COLLINS, W. J., Private, Royal Fusiliers.
Shortly after volunteering in 1915 he was sent to the Western Front with the Royal Army Service Corps (M.T.), afterwards being transferred to the Royal Fusiliers. There he took part in many important engagements in various sectors and was wounded in action. He was demobilised on returning home in 1919, and holds the 1914–15 Star, and the General Service and Victory Medals. 37, Church St., Weedon, Northants. Z2619.

COLLINTON, H. W., Pte., 6th Bedfordshire Regt.
He joined in January 1917, and after a few months' training was drafted to France, where he took part in the Battles of Vimy Ridge, Arras, Messines and Ypres. He made the supreme sacrifice, being killed in action on August 6th, 1917, and was entitled to the General Service and Victory Medals.
"The path of duty was the way to glory."
28, Arthur Street, Kingsthorpe, Hollow, Northampton. Z1403

COLLIS, G. W., Corporal, R.A.S.C.
He volunteered in August 1914, and was drafted to the Western Front in the following July. Engaged on important transport work, his duties led him into the forward areas, and he was often exposed to heavy fire. He was wounded in the course of operations, but returning to his unit on recovery continued performing his duties until the Armistice, when he returned to England. He was demobilised in March 1919, and holds the 1914–15 Star, and the General Service and Victory Medals.
88, Delapore Street, Northants. Z3285.

COLLYER, W. J., L/Corporal, Machine Gun Corps.
He joined in 1916, and after a period of training at Dover was drafted overseas in 1917. Whilst serving on the Western Front he took part in numerous engagements, including the Battles of Arras and Ypres, and did good work with his unit during the German Offensive and Allied Advance of 1918. He was demobilised on his return home in 1919, and holds the General Service and Victory Medals. 108, Balmoral Rd., Northampton. Z2378.

COMPTON, J., Sergeant, 7th Northants. Regiment.
He joined in February 1916, and in September of the same year was drafted to France. There he played a distinguished part in several engagements, including the Battles of Cambrai and the Somme and in the Retreat and Advance of 1918. After the cessation of hostilities he proceeded to Germany with the Army of Occupation, and served there until his demobilisation in January 1920. He holds the General Service and Victory Medals. 29, Florence Road, Northampton. Z2104.

CONIE, A., Driver, Royal Horse Artillery.
Having enlisted in September 1911, he was drafted to France immediately on the outbreak of war and fought in the Battle of, and the Retreat from, Mons. After taking part also in the Battles of the Marne, the Aisne, La Bassée, Ypres, Neuve Chapelle and Loos, he was severely wounded at Cambrai in November 1917. Mentioned in Despatches for distinguished services in October 1914, he holds the Mons Star, and the General Service and Victory Medals, and in October 1918 was invalided from the Army.
King's Lane, Flore, near Weedon, Northants. Z2620.

CONSTABLE, F. W., Corporal, 1st Northants. Regt.
He volunteered in June 1915 and on completing his training later in that year was drafted to the Western Front, where he saw much severe fighting at Ypres and in various other sectors. He died gloriously on the Field of Battle on the Somme in July 1916, and was entitled to the 1914–15 Star, and the General Service and Victory Medals.
"Whilst we remember, the sacrifice is not in vain."
Berry Lane, Wootton, Northants. Z2621 /D.

CONSTABLE, G., Corporal, Rifle Brigade.
A serving soldier, he was sent to the Western Front in August 1914, and there fought in the Retreat from Mons, and also took part in the Battles of the Marne, the Aisne and La Bassée. He was four times wounded—at Ypres in November 1914, Aubers Ridge in 1915, the Somme in the following year and Arras in 1917—and on each occasion was invalided home. Discharged in September 1918 as medically unfit for further service, he holds the Mons Star, and the General Service and Victory Medals. Berry Lane, Wootton, Northants. Z2621 /B.

CONSTABLE, W. J., Driver, R.E. (R.O.D.)
He volunteered in April 1915, and in the following year was drafted to the Western Front, where he served as an engine driver in various sectors. He was also present at many important engagements, until injured in an accident on the Somme in July 1916, when his engine overturned. He was for a time in hospital at Le Havre, and was finally demobilised in October 1919, holding the General Service and Victory Medals.
30, Albert Street, Northampton. Z1892.

COLTON, T., Driver, R.A.S.C.
Volunteering in February 1915, he was sent to Egypt in the same year, and then to Gallipoli, where he did good work during the Landing at Suvla Bay. After the Evacuation his unit was transferred to Salonika and was employed on duties in connection with the transport of ammunition and supplies during several engagements in the Balkans. Demobilised in 1919, he holds the 1914–15 Star, and the General Service and Victory Medals. Mill Hill, near Buckby, Northants. Z3286.

COOK, A. E. (Miss), Worker, Q.M.A.A.C.
Joining in October 1917, she was drafted to France in the following month and there served at Dièppe. Engaged on duties of great importance whilst in this theatre of war she rendered very valuable services throughout, and finally returned home in February 1919. She was demobilised in the following month, and holds the General Service and Victory Medals.
Newport Road, Hanslope, Bucks. Z2624 /A.

COOK, C., Private, 2nd Northants. Regiment.
Enlisting in 1903 he crossed to France in August 1914 and fought in the Retreat from Mons and the Battles of Ypres, Festubert and Loos. He also took part in the Somme Offentive, the Battles of Arras, Ypres, Passchendaele and Cambrai, and those at Amiens and Dickebusch. He was twice wounded in the course of operations, and was discharged in 1919, after upwards of five years' service overseas. He holds the Mons Star, and the General Service and Victory Medals.
Salem, Long Buckby, Northants. Z3287.

COOK, C. W., Private, 10th Royal Fusiliers.
Joining in March 1917 he proceeded two months later to the Western Front, where he took part in the Battles of Messines, Ypres and Passchendaele, and minor engagements. He was unhappily reported missing, and later presumed to have been killed in action on September 1st, 1917. He was entitled to the General Service and Victory Medals.
"A costly sacrifice upon the altar of freedom."
30, East Street, Northampton. Z1893.

COOPER, F., Private, 1st Northants. Regiment.
He volunteered in September 1914, and four months later embarked for the Western Front, where he was in action at Festubert and Loos. Wounded in 1915 he returned to France in the following year, and whilst taking part in the Somme Offensive was again wounded on July 1st, 1916. Evacuated to England, he was treated at Bristol Hospital, and ultimately discharged, as medically unfit in March 1918, holding the 1914–15 Star, and the General Service and Victory Medals.
Station Road, Long Buckby, Northants. Z3288.

COOK, F. W., Private, 4th Northants. Regiment.
He volunteered in October 1915, and in September of the following year was drafted to the Western Front. After only two months' active service he was severely wounded at Beaumont-Hamel, and was admitted to hospital at Leicester. He was finally invalided from the Army in September 1917, and holds the General Service and Victory Medals.
42, Baring Road, Northampton. Z2625.

COOK, G. W., Private, North Staffordshire Regt.
He volunteered in February 1915, and completing his training in the following year was drafted to France. There he took part in many important engagements, particularly during the Retreat of 1918, when he was wounded in action in March 1918. As a result he was invalided home to hospital and eventually discharged in March 1919. He holds the General Service and Victory Medals. Sutton Street, Flore, Northants. Z2623.

COOK, H. A., Air Mechanic, Royal Air Force.
He enlisted in January 1918, and after a period of training was stationed at the Orkney Islands, where he was engaged on work of a highly technical nature in connection with repairing seaplanes. Owing to the early cessation of hostilities he was unable to proceed to a theatre of war, but rendered valuable services as a fitter until his demobilisation in May 1919.
Newport Road, Hanslope, Bucks. Z2624 /B.

COOPER, J. F., Shoeing-Smith, R.F.A.
Volunteering in October 1915, he proceeded to France a month later and in the folowing January was drafted to Salonika. In the Balkans he did excellent work during engagements on the Struma, Doiran and Vardar fronts, and was present at the capture of Monastir. In January 1919 he was sent into Russia with his Battery, but returned to England for demobilisation in May 1919. He holds the 1914–15 Star, and the General Service and Victory Medals.
Little Haughton, Northants. Z3289.

COOK, J. H., Private, 2nd Norfolk Regiment.
Having volunteered in January 1916, he proceeded to Mesopotamia six months later. In this seat of operations he took part in many engagements on the Tigris, and later was sent to India, where he served on garrison duty at various stations. He returned home, and was demobilised in August 1919, holding the General Service and Victory Medals.
Spratton, Northants. Z2998 /B.

COOK, J. H., Private, 1st Northants. Regiment.
Volunteering in November 1914, he was drafted overseas in May of the following year. During his service on the Western Front he took part in many engagements, including those in the Ypres and Loos sectors, before being wounded in October 1915. Invalided home he was afterwards retained on important duties at various stations until demobilised in February 1919. He holds the 1914–15 Star, and the General Service and Victory Medals. Silver Street, Brixworth, Northants. Z2997.

COOK, T. A., Private, 2nd Bedfordshire Regiment.
He enlisted in March 1916, and completing his training in October of the same year was drafted to France, where he took part in many engagements in the Vimy Ridge, Messines, Ypres and Passchendaele sectors. He made the supreme sacrifice, being killed in action at Arras on September 20th, 1917, and was entitled to the General Service and Victory Medals.
"His life for his Country, his soul to God."
Spratton, Northants. Z2998 /A.

COOK, W., Private, 6th Northants. Regiment.
After volunteering in September 1914, he was sent to France ten months later. Whilst on the Western Front he took part in many important engagements, including the Battles of the Somme, Arras, Ypres, Passchendaele, St. Quentin, Albert and Armentières. He was demobilised in March 1919, and holds the 1914–15 Star, and the General Service and Victory Medals.
67, Washington Street, Kingsthorpe, Northampton. Z1107 /A.

COOKE, A., Rifleman, Rifle Brigade.
Already serving in India at the outbreak of war he returned home, and in 1915 was drafted to France, where he took part in several engagements in the Ypres sector and was wounded. As a result he was invalided home, but on his recovery returned to France, and was again in action. He was badly wounded at Delville Wood and sent home, was discharged in November 1916, being totally blind. In 1921 he was still at St. Dunstan's Hostel, and holds the 1914–15 Star, and the General Service and Victory Medals.
90, Spencer Road, Northampton. Z2999 /A.

COOKE, A. F., Sergeant, 1/4th Northants. Regt.
He volunteered in June 1915, and completing his training in the following year, was drafted to France. In this seat of war he played a prominent part in engagements at St. Eloi and Arras, where he contracted trench fever, and was consequently invalided home. On his recovery he was transferred to the Dublin Fusiliers and returned to France. He saw much fighting at Messines, Passchendaele and Cambrai, and was wounded in action. Demobilised in February 1919, he holds the General Service and Victory Medals.
18, Allen Road, Northampton. Z2105 /B.

COOKE, G., Corporal, R.A.S.C. (M.T.)
Joining in June 1916, he was drafted to the Western Front on completing his training in October of that year and there served in various sectors. He took an active part in the Battles of the Somme, Arras, Vimy Ridge, Messines, Ypres, Passchendaele and Cambrai and many other engagements, and also fought in the Retreat and Advance of 1918, afterwards serving with the Army of Occupation in Germany. Demobilised in August 1919, he holds the General Service and Victory Medals. 15, Wood Street, Northampton. Z1894.

COOKE, J., Driver, Royal Engineers.
He volunteered in August 1915, and was retained at home for a time before being drafted to France in January 1917. Whilst overseas he saw heavy fighting at Ypres and Passchendaele, but six months later was transferred to Italy and fought on the Piave. Returning to France he took part in the Retreat of 1918, when he was wounded, and as a result was invalided home, and eventually discharged in January 1919 as medically unfit for further service. He holds the General Service and Victory Medals. 90, Spencer Bridge Road, Northampton. Z2999 /B.

COOKE, J. O., Gunner, Royal Garrison Artillery.
He volunteered in November 1915, and in the following May was drafted to France. There he took part in many important engagements, including the Battles of Ypres, the Somme, Arras, Lens, Albert, Cambrai and in the Advance of 1918. After hostilities ceased he proceeded to Germany with the Army of Occupation, and served there until his demobilisation in October 1919. He holds the General Service and Victory Medals. 8, Abbey Terrace, Northampton. Z2622.

COOKE, W. H., Gunner, Royal Field Artillery.
He volunteered in June 1915, and later in the same year was sent to France, where he fought in the Battles of Ypres, the Somme, Arras, Vimy Ridge and Cambrai. During the German Offensive of March 1918 he was gassed and invalided home, but returned to the Western Front in the following October, and served in the final decisive engagements of the war. Advancing into Germany he served at Cologne until demobilised in May 1919, holding the 1914–15 Star, and the General Service and Victory Medals. 53, Edinburgh Rd., Northampton. Z2380.

COOKSON, J. H., Gunner, Royal Horse Artillery.
Already in the Army when war broke out in August 1914, he was quickly drafted to the Western Front. In this theatre of war he took part in many important engagements in various sectors, and was three times wounded in action. In 1921 he was still serving, and holds the Queen's and King's South African Medals, the Mons Star, and the General Service and Victory Medals. 10, Queen Street, Weedon, Northants. Z2626.

COOMBES, J. W., Private, Manchester Regiment.
Joining early in 1917, he completed his training and in May of that year was ordered to France. On that front he was engaged in fierce fighting in numerous battles in various sectors until severely wounded at Nieuport in August 1917. He was invalided home and unfortunately had to have his left leg amputated, eventually being discharged in April 1919, holding the General Service and Victory Medals.
5, Marlborough Road, Northampton. Z2381.

COOMBES, W. B., Private, 2/5th Manchester Regt.
Three months after joining in March 1916 he was drafted to France and was in action at Nieuport, Vimy Ridge and Ypres, before being taken prisoner at St. Quentin in March 1917. He was released from captivity in December 1918, and in the following month was demobilised, holding the General Service and Victory Medals. 38, Craven Street, Northampton. Z1295.

COOPER, F., Private, 1st Royal Fusiliers.
He enlisted in November 1916, and completing his training in the following May was drafted to France. In this seat of war he took part in several minor engagements, and was wounded in action and consequently invalided home. On his recovery he returned to France, and was in action in the Advance of 1918, but contracting trench fever, was again invalided home, to hospital. He was demobilised in January 1919, and holds the General Service and Victory Medals.
39, Gray Street, Northampton. Z1404.

COOPER, G., Private, 1st Northants. Regiment.
Mobilised in August 1914, he was quickly drafted to France. There he took part in the Retreat from Mons, the Battles of Neuve Chapelle, Hill 60, Ypres, and saw much severe fighting in 1918 before being badly wounded in action. As a result he was invalided home, but on his recovery returned to France, and was again in action. Discharged in February 1919, he holds the Mons Star, and the General Service and Victory Medals. 23, Lawrence Street, Northampton. Z1405.

COOPER, J. W., Private, North Staffordshire Regt.
Volunteering in August 1914, he first saw active service in Gallipoli, where he took part in the Landing at Suvla Bay and in other important engagements until the Evacuation of the Peninsula in January 1916. He then proceeded to France, but after heavy fighting at Vimy Ridge, Cambrai and on the Somme was unfortunately killed in action on October 3rd, 1918. He was buried at St. Quentin, and was entitled to the 1914–15 Star, and the General Service and Victory Medals.
"Greater love hath no man than this."
5, Pine Street, Northampton. Z1296.

COOPER, W., Private, 4th Northants. Regiment.
A Regular, he was mobilised when war was declared and was retained on home service duties at Sheringham and other stations. Engaged in the boot-repairing shop of his Battalion, he performed valuable work, but owing to being over military age was unable to secure his transfer to a theatre of war, and was discharged—time-expired—in February 1919.
4, West View, Long Buckby, Northants. Z3216/A.

COOPER, W. G., Private, 4th East Surrey Regt.
He enlisted in January 1918, but shortly afterwards was transferred to the Machine Gun Corps, and in the May of that year was drafted to France. There he took part in important engagements during the Retreat and Advance, particularly at Ypres and Cambrai. After hostilities ceased he proceeded to Germany with the Army of Occupation, and served at Cologne until his demobilisation in September 1919. He holds the General Service and Victory Medals.
28, York Place, Northampton. Z2627.

COPP, A. E., A.B., Royal Navy.
He volunteered in May 1915 at the age of 15 years, and, after training on board H.M.S. "Impregnable," was commissioned to H.M.S. "Benbow," and did duty in the North Sea. He took part in the Battle of Jutland, and was also engaged on important duties throughout hostilities. In 1921 he was serving on board H.M.S. "Warspite," and holds the General Service and Victory Medals. 30, Roe Road, Northampton. Z2106/B.

COPP, A. S., Private, Royal Warwickshire Regt.
He volunteered in the Royal Army Service Corps in June 1915, and underwent a period of training at Woolwich, being afterwards transferred to the Royal Warwickshire Regiment. He was engaged at various home stations on important duties, and rendered valuable services until his demobilisation in January 1919. 30, Roe Road, Northampton. Z2106/A.

COPPIN, B. J. H., Corporal, Worcestershire Regt.
Already serving when war broke out in August 1914, he was drafted to the Dardanelles in the following year. He took part in much severe fighting at the Landing at Gallipoli, and was wounded in action. Later he was drafted to Egypt, thence to France, where he fought on the Somme and was again wounded and invalided home. He returned to France in 1918, and was in action in the Retreat and Advance of 1918, being eventually demobilised in February 1919. He holds the 1914–15 Star, and the General Service and Victory Medals.
12, Oakley Street, Northampton. Z1406/B.

COPSON, H. O., Pioneer, Royal Engineers.
He volunteered in November 1914 in the 4th Northamptonshire Regiment, and in the following March was drafted to France, where he was transferred to the Royal Engineers and took part in the Battles of the Somme, Arras and Vimy Ridge. He died gloriously on the Field of Battle in the Cambrai sector on September 15th, 1917, and was entitled to the 1914–15 Star, and the General Service and Victory Medals.
"He nobly fell that we might live."
School Road, Spratton, Northants. Z3000.

CORBY, H., 1st Air Mechanic, Royal Air Force.
He joined in June 1917, and, after a period of training, was engaged at various stations on important duties with his unit. He was unable to obtain a transfer overseas owing to his being too old, but rendered valuable services until his demobilisation in March 1919. 41, Adnitt Road, Northampton. Z2107/A.

CORCORAN, R., Private, 4th Northants. Regt.
He volunteered in October 1914, and was retained for a time at home before being drafted to Egypt. Later he proceeded into Palestine and took part in the Battles of Gaza (where he was wounded in 1917), and afterwards served with General Allenby's Forces in the Advance of 1918. He was then transferred to Salonika, and eventually returned home and was demobilised in April 1919, holding the General Service and Victory Medals. 21, Devonshire St., Northampton. Z2628.

CORNELIUS, J. E., Private, 7th Northants. Regt.
He volunteered in January 1915, and in September of the same year was drafted to France. In this theatre of war he took part in much heavy fighting at Loos and Lens, and was wounded in action. He was taken prisoner in April 1917, and was held in captivity in Germany, where he suffered many hardships. Repatriated after the Armistice, he was demobilised in January 1919, and holds the 1914–15 Star, and the General Service and Victory Medals.
10, Main Road, Northampton. Z3001.

CORSBY, H. G., Private, Norfolk Regiment.
He joined in December 1917, and proceeded to France early in 1918. During the Retreat and Advance of that year he saw much severe fighting in various sectors, particularly in those of Ypres and the Somme. He was demobilised in April 1919, and holds the General Service and Victory Medals.
42, Silver Street, Northampton. Z1108/B.

CORSBY, J. C., Gunner, Royal Field Artillery.
He joined in April 1917, and later in the same year was drafted to France, where he played a prominent part with his Battery in heavy fighting at Arras, Vimy Ridge and on the Somme. He made the supreme sacrifice on August 31st, 1918, and was entitled to the General Service and Victory Medals.
"His life for his Country, his soul to God."
42, Silver Street, Northampton. Z1108/A.

CORY, W. S., Gunner, Royal Garrison Artillery.
He enlisted in October 1917, and, completing his training in the following March, was drafted to France, where he acted as a signaller and took part in many engagements in the Advance of 1918. After hostilities ceased he proceeded to Germany, and served on the Rhine until his demobilisation in February 1919. He holds the General Service and Victory Medals.
5, Newcombe Road, Northampton. Z2629.

COSFORD, A., Private, Royal Naval Division.
He joined the Drake Battalion of the Royal Naval Division in June 1916, and, after a period of training, was sent to the Western Front, where he took part in heavy fighting in the Somme and Ypres sectors. Severely wounded in action in January 1917, he was invalided home, and was finally demobilised in February 1919. He holds the General Service and Victory Medals. 9, Stockley Street, Northampton. Z1895/A

COSFORD, F., Private, 2/20th London Regiment.
He volunteered in February 1915, and in September was sent to France, but, after being wounded in action at Ypres, was transferred to Salonika in August 1916. He then fought on the Vardar front before being sent to Palestine in March 1917. He was again wounded in action at the third Battle of Gaza, but later took part in further engagements. Demobilised in April 1919, he holds the 1914–15 Star, and the General Service and Victory Medals.
33, Upper Harding Street, Northampton. Z1109

COSFORD, J., Sergeant, 1st Northants. Regiment
He volunteered in November 1915, and in September of the following year was sent to France. After serving with distinction on the Somme he was invalided home in February 1917, but in October returned to the Western Front and played a prominent part in the Battle of Cambrai and the Retreat and Advance of 1918. Proceeding to Germany with the Army of Occupation, he served at Cologne until demobilised in February 1919, and holds the General Service and Victory Medals.
58, Craven Street, Northampton. Z1297

COSFORD, W. B., Private, 6th Northants. Regt.
He joined in January 1918, and, on completing his training six months later, was drafted to the Western Front, where he saw much severe fighting. He made the supreme sacrifice, being killed in action at Cambrai in September 1918, and was entitled to the General Service and Victory Medals.
"Thinking that remembrance, though unspoken, may reach him where he sleeps."
9, Stockley Street, Northampton. Z1895/B.

COTCHIN, H., Corporal, R.A.S.C.
He joined in December 1916, and, after training at Aldershot, St. Albans and Bath, was drafted to France in September 1917. On the Western Front he rendered valuable services as a clerk in supply depôts at various stations. After hostilities ceased he went to Germany with the Army of Occupation, and remained there until demobilised in September 1919, holding the General Service and Victory Medals.
30, Louise Road, Northampton. Z1298.

COTTON, W., Private, 10th Royal Fusiliers.
He enlisted in March 1917, and two months later was drafted to the Western Front, where he took part in several engagements, including the Battle of Ypres (III.). He died gloriously on the Field of Battle at Hamel on October 6th, 1917, and was entitled to the General Service and Victory Medals.
"A costly sacrifice upon the altar of freedom."
49, Brunswick Street, Northampton. Z1407.

COTTON, W. H., L/Corporal, Tank Corps.
Volunteering in the Infantry in August 1914, he was sent to France in October, and took part in the Battles of Ypres, Aubers Ridge, Loos, Albert, the Somme (during which he was wounded in action at Pozières in July 1916) and Cambrai. Severely wounded at Villers-Brétonneux in August 1918, he was invalided to hospital in England, and unfortunately had to have his left leg amputated. He was discharged in July 1919, and holds the 1914 Star and the General Service and Victory Medals. 72, Moore St., Kingsley, Northampton. Z1110.

COULSON, E. J., Private, R.A.M.C.
He volunteered in the Royal Army Medical Corps in October 1915, and in August 1916 was sent to France, where he rendered valuable services as a stretcher-bearer at the Battles of the Somme, Arras and Ypres. Wounded in action in September 1917, he was invalided home, but on his recovery was transferred to the 1/4th Northamptonshire Regiment and went to Palestine, where he served at Jerusalem and Jaffa. He was demobilised in August 1919, and holds the General Service and Victory Medals. 11, Pike Lane, Northampton. Z1135/B.

COULSON, FREDERIC, Sergeant, 1/4th Northamptonshire Regiment.
Called up from the Reserve in August 1914, he proceeded to the Dardanelles in July 1915, and served at the Landing at Suvla Bay and in further heavy fighting until the Evacuation of the Gallipoli Peninsula in January 1916. He was then sent to Egypt, but, advancing into Palestine, fought at Gaza (I., II. and III.) before being badly wounded in action near Jerusalem on November 27th, 1917. He unfortunately died the following day, and was entitled to the 1914–15 Star, and the General Service and Victory Medals.
"A costly sacrifice upon the altar of freedom."
3, Cooper Street, Northampton. Z1111/D.

COULSON, F., Private, Royal Defence Corps.
He volunteered in October 1914, and during the whole period of hostilities rendered valuable services in Derbyshire, Yorkshire and Northamptonshire. He was chiefly engaged in guarding railways, bridges and German prisoners of war, and did good work until demobilised in March 1919.
3, Cooper Street, Northampton. Z1111/A.

COULSON, F., Private, Royal Berkshire Regt.
He volunteered in the Northamptonshire Regiment in August 1914, and, proceeding to France early in 1915, took part in heavy fighting at Aubers Ridge, Festubert, Ypres and Loos, where he was wounded in January 1916. Returning to the Western Front after hospital treatment at Lincoln, he served with the Royal Berkshire Regiment, and was unhappily killed in action on November 15th, 1916. He was entitled to the 1914–15 Star, and the General Service and Victory Medals.
"Nobly striving:
He nobly fell that we might live."
3, Cooper Street, Northampton. Z1111/B.

COULSON, G. H., Private, 23rd Middlesex Regt.
He joined in October 1918, and underwent a period of training before proceeding overseas. In January 1919 he was sent to Germany, and served on various important duties with the Army of Occupation on the Rhine. He returned home, and was demobilised in April 1920.
77, Great Russell Street, Northampton. Z1408.

COULSON, H., Driver, Royal Field Artillery.
He volunteered in October 1915, and three months later landed in France, where he served for three years. During this time he was in action with his Battery at Ypres, Arras, Cambrai and on the Somme, and saw much severe fighting. Demobilised in March 1919, he holds the General Service and Victory Medals.
3, Cooper Street, Northampton. Z1111/C.

COULTON, F. W., Corporal, 10th Essex Regiment.
He joined in March 1917, and, drafted overseas in the following year, saw active service on the Western Front. He took part in fierce fighting in the German Offensive and at Albert and other places in the subsequent Allied Advance until wounded at Bray in August 1918. Invalided to England, he received hospital treatment, and on recovery served on light duties. He was demobilised in January 1919, and holds the General Service and Victory Medals.
1, Meacock's Row, Bridge Street, Northampton. Z3290.

COUSINS, H., Private, 2nd Northants. Regiment.
He was already serving in Egypt when war was declared in August 1914, and was shortly afterwards sent to France, where he took part in the Battles of Neuve Chapelle, St. Eloi and Hill 60 and many minor engagements. He fell fighting at Ypres on May 9th, 1915, and was entitled to the 1914–15 Star and the General Service and Victory Medals.
"The path of duty was the way to glory."
40, East Street, Northampton. Z1896.

COUSNER, A. R., Corporal, M.G.C. (Infantry).
He joined in February 1917, and in the following June embarked for France, where he saw heavy fighting in the Arras sector. After taking part in the Battles of Messines and Ypres he was gassed at Wytschaete in August 1917, and invalided home. On his discharge from hospital he was retained on important duties in England until demobilised in January 1919, holding the General Service and Victory Medals.
17, Edinburgh Road, Northampton. Z2382.

COWELL, H. J., Cpl., Royal Warwickshire Regt.
Called up from the Reserve in August 1914, he was drafted to France twelve months later. Whilst on the Western Front he took part in engagements in various sectors until 1917, when he proceeded to Italy. Later he returned to France and was in action in the Advance of 1918, serving also with the 11th Hussars and the Royal Army Veterinary Corps. He received his discharge in November of that year, and holds the 1914–15 Star, and the General Service and Victory Medals.
124, St. Leonard's Road, Far Cotton, Northampton. Z3002.

COWLING, A. G., Private, 1/4th Northants. Regt.
Joining in June 1916, he underwent a period of training prior to his being engaged at various stations on important duties with his unit. He was not successful in obtaining a transfer overseas, but rendered valuable services until his discharge in December 1917. 61, Abington Avenue, Northampton. Z2108.

COX, A. (M.M.), Wheeler, Royal Field Artillery.
When war was declared he was serving in Egypt, but was recalled and drafted to France in October 1914. He took a prominent part in the Battles of Ypres, Neuve Chapelle, the Somme, Arras, Messines, Vimy Ridge and Cambrai, and in the operations in the Retreat and Advance of 1918, being awarded the Military Medal for conspicuous gallantry at Delville Wood in 1916. Discharged in February 1919, after nine years' service, he also holds the 1914 Star, and the General Service and Victory Medals. 12, Cecil Road, Northampton Z2383.

COX, A., Rifleman, 2nd King's Royal Rifle Corps.
He joined in January 1917, and, after serving in England for 16 months, proceeded to France. Whilst on the Western Front he took part in heavy fighting at Albert, Amiens and St. Quentin, during the Retreat and Advance, and was wounded in September 1918. Invalided home, he was in hospital at Burnley for some time before being demobilised in January 1919, holding the General Service and Victory Medals.
2, Leicester Street, Northampton. Z1299.

COX, A., Private, 5th Northants. Regiment.
Having volunteered in October 1915, he was drafted to France five months afterwards and played an important part in heavy fighting in the Somme, Arras, Vimy Ridge, Ypres and Cambrai sectors. He was demobilised on his return home in March 1919, and holds the General Service and Victory Medals.
34, Crispin Street, Northampton. Z1112/B

COX, A. J., Leading Seaman, Royal Navy.
Already in the Navy when war broke out in August 1914, he quickly proceeded to sea on board H.M.S. "Wessex." He first saw service in the Mediterranean, and later was engaged on patrol, escort and dangerous mine-sweeping duties in the Dardanelles, being wounded on one occasion. Whilst serving in H.M.S. "Cornwallis" this vessel was sunk by a submarine on January 11th, 1917, but fortunately he was rescued. Later he was engaged on patrol duties in the Atlantic Ocean and Baltic Sea, and did continuously good work throughout. In 1920 he was still in the Navy, and holds the 1914–15 Star, and the General Service and Victory Medals.
75, Alcombe Road, Northampton. Z1409.

COX, B., Private, Royal Fusiliers.
Joining in March 1917, he was quickly drafted to France, where he took part in the Battles of Messines, Ypres, Cambrai and the Somme, and was twice buried by exploding shells. Evacuated to England with trench fever, he was on board H.M.S. "Warhilda" when that ship was torpedoed in August 1918. Fortunately he was rescued and admitted to hospital in Portsmouth, whence he was demobilised in February 1919, holding the General Service and Victory Medals.
31, St. Mary's Street, Northampton. Z1113/B.

COX, E. (Miss), Worker, Q.M.A.A.C.
She joined in April 1918, and was stationed at Eastbourne, where she was engaged as a cook for the troops and also in the Officers' Mess. She rendered valuable services for twelve months, and was demobilised in April 1919.
38, Silver Street, Northampton. Z1114.

COX, F., Private, Northants. Regiment.
He enlisted in July 1918, and underwent a few months' training prior to his being drafted to France, where he took part in the Advance of that year. After the cessation of hostilities he proceeded to Germany with the Army of Occupation, and served there until his demobilisation in March 1920. He holds the General Service and Victory Medals.
12, Weedon Road, Northampton. Z2631.

COX, H., L/Corporal, 1/4th Berkshire Regiment.
Joining in March 1917, he was drafted overseas three months later. Whilst on the Western Front he took part in much heavy fighting in the Ypres sector before being wounded in action in August of that year. As a result he was invalided home to hospital, and on his recovery was transferred to the Royal Army Ordnance Corps, being retained at Aldershot until his demobilisation in January 1919. He holds the General Service and Victory Medals.
36, Newcombe Road, Northampton. Z2630.

COX, H., Private, 6th Northants. Regiment.
He joined in October 1917, and six months later proceeded to France, where he was in action at Albert and on the Somme before being wounded and taken prisoner at Combles in August 1918. Whilst in captivity he was forced to work, and was severely injured by falling trucks. After his release he was sent to Ireland, where he was still serving in 1920, and holds the General Service and Victory Medals.
34, Crispin Street, Northampton. Z1112/A.

COX, T., Private, Middlesex Regiment.
Volunteering in July 1915, he underwent a period of training, and in the following year was drafted overseas. In the course of his service on the Western Front he took part in many important engagements, particularly in the Somme and Cambrai sectors. He was wounded and taken prisoner in November 1917, and held in captivity until after the conclusion of hostilities. Returning home, he was demobilised in March 1919, and holds the General Service and Victory Medals.
20, Upper Harding Street, Northampton. Z1116/B.

COX, W., Private, 3rd Northants. Regiment.
Volunteering in August 1914, he was drafted to France after three months' training, and there saw much heavy fighting. He took part in the Battles of Loos, Ploegsteert Wood, Vimy Ridge and the Somme and minor engagements, and was wounded in May 1916, and again in November 1918. He was demobilised in February 1919, and holds the 1914–15 Star, and the General Service and Victory Medals.
54, Broad Street, Northampton. Z1897.

COX, W. D., Private, 7th Middlesex Regiment.
He joined in January 1917, and, after a period of training, was engaged at various home stations on important duties with his unit. He was not successful in obtaining a transfer overseas owing to his being medically unfit, but rendered valuable services until his demobilisation in January 1919.
5 of Court, Brook Street, Daventry, Northants. Z2632.

COX, W. H., Guardsman, Coldstream Guards.
After volunteering in September 1915 he completed his training and proceeded to the Western Front. During his service in this seat of operations he took part in fierce fighting at Ypres and on the Somme. He made the supreme sacrifice, being killed in action in September 1916, and was entitled to the General Service and Victory Medals.
"And doubtless he went in splendid company."
7, Cooper Street, Northampton. Z1117/B.

COX, W. J., Private, Machine Gun Corps.
Having volunteered in January 1915, he was shortly afterwards drafted to France, where he took an active part in many important engagements in the Somme and Ypres sectors. He later contracted trench fever, and was invalided to England, and, after a period of hospital treatment, was eventually demobilised in March 1919, holding the 1914–15 Star, and the General Service and Victory Medals.
4, Spring Lane, Northampton. Z1115

COXFORD, J., Rifleman, 13th Royal Irish Rifles.
Joining in July 1916, he underwent a period of training, and early in the following year was drafted to the Western Front, where he took part in the heavy fighting at Ypres. He died gloriously on the Field of Battle on June 4th, 1917, and was entitled to the General Service and Victory Medals.
"Thinking that remembrance, though unspoken, may reach him where he sleeps."
7, Union Court, Northampton. Z1118/A.

COXFORD, W., Corporal, 1st Northants. Regt.
Having enlisted in April 1911, he was sent to France in August 1914, and served at the Battle of Mons and in the Retreat before being wounded on the Aisne and invalided home in October. On his recovery he returned to France in June 1916 but, after being in action at Loos, was badly wounded at Pozières in August, during the Somme Offensive. After hospital treatment in Manchester he rendered valuable services as a signalling instructor until his discharge in April 1919, holding the Mons Star, and the General Service and Victory Medals. 7, Union Court, Northampton. Z1118/B.

COZENER, W., Private, 4th Royal Sussex Regt.
After joining in February 1916 he underwent a period of training, but was later found to be medically unfit for service overseas. He was, therefore, retained on important guard and other duties with his unit at various stations, and rendered excellent services until demobilised in March 1919.
85, Lower Hester Street, Northampton. Z1119.

CRANE, W. A., L/Corporal, Machine Gun Corps.
Enlisting in December 1911, he was drafted to the Gallipoli Peninsula in July 1915, and took part in severe fighting there until the Evacuation. He then proceeded to Egypt, but later advanced into Palestine and played a prominent part in the Battles of Gaza and the capture of Beyrout and Damascus. Returning to England, he received his discharge in December 1919, and holds the 1914–15 Star, and the General Service and Victory Medals. 80, Salisbury Street, Northampton. Z1120.

CRAPPER, A. T., Private, 76th Canadian Regt. (Canadian Overseas Forces).
Volunteering in February 1915, he underwent a period of training in Canada, and later embarked for the Western Front. Whilst in this theatre of war he saw service at Armentières, Albert, the Somme and Vimy Ridge. He made the supreme sacrifice, being killed in action on April 9th, 1917, and was entitled to the General Service and Victory Medals.
"His life for his Country, his soul to God."
19, Althorp Street, Northampton. Z1121/B.

CRAWFORD, F., Corporal, 4th London Regt. (Royal Fusiliers).
He volunteered in September 1914, and in the following year was drafted to Gallipoli, where, after taking part in the Landing at Suvla Bay, he saw much severe fighting. Transferred later to France, he fought in the Battles of Arras, Ypres, Passchendaele and Cambrai, and was wounded and gassed. He was invalided from the Army in October 1918, and holds the 1914–15 Star, and the General Service and Victory Medals.
9, Althorp Road, Northampton. Z2384.

CRICK, F. A., Private, 3rd Northants. Regiment.
Volunteering in November 1915, he was drafted overseas in the following year. Whilst in France he took part in several important engagements, including that of Bapaume, where he was badly wounded in February 1917, and consequently invalided home. He was eventually discharged in October 1917 as medically unfit for further service, and holds the General Service and Victory Medals.
25, Vernon Terrace, Northampton. Z1410/A.

CRISP, A., Private, West Yorkshire Regiment.
He volunteered in August 1915, and was engaged on important duties connected with coastal defence. He rendered valuable services during several air-raids, but was unable to proceed overseas owing to his being medically unfit. He was demobilised in 1918. 8, Collins Street, Northampton. Z2109.

CROFTS, E. R., Private, 2/19th London Regiment.
He joined in November 1917, and underwent a period of training prior to his being drafted to Egypt. In this seat of operations he saw much fighting, and took part in the Advance into Palestine, where he was in action at Haifa. He was also engaged on important duties until he returned home and was demobilised in March 1920. He holds the General Service and Victory Medals.
69, Great Russell Street, Northampton. Z1411.

CROFTS, J., Trooper, Northants. Dragoons.
Volunteering in May 1915, he was drafted overseas in the following year. Whilst in France he took part in the Battles of the Somme, Arras, Ypres and Cambrai. Later he proceeded to Italy, where he saw much heavy fighting on the Piave and in other important engagements. He returned home and was demobilised in February 1919, holding the General Service and Victory Medals.
9, Henry Street, Northampton. Z2110.

CROSS, J., Corporal, Royal Defence Corps.
Having volunteered in December 1914, he completed his training and was retained on important guard duties over bridges in Northamptonshire. He was also engaged in guarding prisoners of war, in which capacity he rendered excellent services until demobilised in March 1919.
13, Fort Street, Northampton. Z1122/B.

CROSS, O. F., Sapper, Royal Engineers.
He enlisted in November 1916, and underwent a period of training prior to being drafted to France in April 1917. During his service overseas he took part in several engagements in the Ypres sector, but was later engaged on garrison duties at Marseilles until his return home for demobilisation in May 1919. He holds the General Service and Victory Medals.
32, Euston Road, Northampton. Z3003.

CROSS, R. H., Private, 12th Royal Sussex Regt.
Three months after joining in March 1916 he was drafted to the Western Front, where, acting as runner to his Battalion, he was present at many important engagements. He died gloriously on the Field of Battle on October 18th, 1916, during the Advance on the Somme, and was entitled to the General Service and Victory Medals.
"Whilst we remember, the sacrifice is not in vain."
16, Mount Gardens, Northampton. Z1898.

CROSS, W. J., Private, 5th Northants. Regiment.
Volunteering in August 1914, he completed a period of training, and in the following year proceeded overseas. In the course of his service on the Western Front he was in action at the Battles of Neuve Chapelle, Ypres, Givenchy and Loos. He died gloriously on the Field of Battle on October 13th, 1915, and was entitled to the 1914–15 Star, and the General Service and Victory Medals.
"Whilst we remember, the sacrifice is not in vain."
13, Fort Street, Northampton. Z1122/A.

CROSS, W., Pte., 1st Northants. Regt. and M.G.C.
He enlisted in October 1913, and, sent to France on the outbreak of war in August 1914, fought in the Retreat from Mons and the Battles of the Marne, the Aisne, La Bassée, Neuve Chapelle and Loos, and was twice wounded. He was later in action at Vermelles, Ploegsteert Wood, the Somme and in the German Offensive, and was wounded on the Marne in the subsequent Allied Advance. He was discharged in May 1920, and holds the Mons Star, and the General Service and Victory Medals. 20, Mill Road, Northampton. Z3291.

CROSSMAN, A., Private, 7th Northants. Regt.
He volunteered in September 1914, and, completing his training in the following year, was drafted to France. Whilst in this theatre of war he took part in many important engagements, including the Battle of Loos. He was twice wounded in action, and finally evacuated to England. Invalided out of the Service in September 1910, he holds the 1914–15 Star, and the General Service and Victory Medals.
101, Overstone Road, Northampton. Z1413/A.

CROSSMAN, G., Private, Bedfordshire Regiment.
He joined in March 1920, and, after a period of training, was engaged at various stations on important duties with his unit. Later he proceeded to Ireland, where in 1921 he was still serving.
101, Overstone Road, Northampton. Z1413/B.

CROSSMAN, H., Private, East Yorkshire Regt.
He volunteered in October 1915, and, on conclusion of his training in the following year, was drafted to the Western Front, where he took part in heavy fighting on the Somme and at Bullecourt before being gassed in December 1917. As a result he was invalided home, and eventually discharged as medically unfit for further service in January 1917. He holds the 1914–15 Star, and the General Service and Victory Medals.
13, Doddridge Square, Northampton. Z1123/B.

CROSSMAN, H. W., Private, R.A.S.C.
After volunteering in October 1915 he was quickly drafted to Salonika, where he was engaged on important transport duties. He served during the engagements on the Vardar and Doiran fronts, and was frequently under heavy shell-fire. In March 1916 he contracted bronchitis and rheumatism, and was invalided to hospital at Alexandria, and thence to England. In the following month he was discharged as medically unfit for further service, holding the 1914–15 Star, and the General Service and Victory Medals.
13, Doddridge Square, Northampton. Z1123/A.

CROSSMAN, S., Private, 3rd (King's Own) Hussars.
He joined the Army in 1908, and, when war broke out in August 1914, was immediately drafted to France. Whilst overseas he took part in many important engagements, and was wounded in action in November 1914. He served in France throughout hostilities, and was discharged in September 1920, time-expired. He holds the 1914 Star, and the General Service and Victory Medals.
101, Overstone Road, Northampton. Z1413/C.

CROWLEY, H., Private, Machine Gun Corps.
He volunteered in October 1914, but was retained on important work at home until 1916, when he was drafted to Egypt. Serving there for eight months, he did valuable work with his unit until transferred to the Western Front. There he saw heavy fighting in various sectors, and after the cessation of hostilities was demobilised in March 1919, holding the General Service and Victory Medals.
15, Robert Street, Northampton. Z1414.

CROXFORD, W. J., Private, Royal Sussex Regt.
He joined in July 1918, having been previously engaged on work of National importance, but whilst in training contracted pneumonia and pleurisy, and was in hospital at Newhaven. On his recovery he proceeded to Germany, and rendered valuable services with the Army of Occupation until demobilised in February 1920.
High Street, West Haddon, Northants. Z3292

CRUMP, C., Corporal, Royal Garrison Artillery.
He volunteered in October 1915, and in July of the following year proceeded to the Western Front, where he took part in many important engagements during the Somme Offensive. Severely wounded in action on the Ancre, he was admitted to hospital in England, where he was retained on his recovery. Demobilised in February 1919, he holds the General Service and Victory Medals.
16, Brunswick Place, Northampton. Z1899.

CRUTCHLEY, A. E., Private, 4th Northants. Regt.
He volunteered in April 1915, and in the following December was drafted to France, where he took part in many engagements and was wounded in action. He was taken prisoner at the Battle of the Dunes in 1917, and was held in captivity in Germany, suffering many hardships. Repatriated after the Armistice, he was demobilised in June 1919, holding the 1914–15 Star, and the General Service and Victory Medals.
150, St. Leonard's Road, Far Cotton, Northampton. Z3004/A.

CRUTCHLEY, A. B., Private, Queen's (Royal West Surrey Regiment).
Joining in July 1918, he proceeded two months later to the Western Front, where he was engaged in fierce fighting on the Somme. He was wounded in action in October 1918, and invalided to England. On his discharge from hospital at Brighton he was employed on important duties at Bedford until demobilised in March 1919, holding the General Service and Victory Medals.
42, Duke Street, Northampton. Z1415/A.

CRUTCHLEY, W. G., Corporal, 4th Northants. Regiment and Royal Army Service Corps.
A Reservist, he was called up at the outbreak of war, and in April 1915 was drafted to Gallipoli, and served during the Landing on the Peninsula. Shortly afterwards he contracted malaria, and was admitted to hospital in Malta, subsequently being sent to England. In 1918 he proceeded to France, where he was engaged on important transport duties in the Somme and Cambrai sectors. He was discharged in May 1919, and holds the 1914–15 Star, and the General Service and Victory Medals.
42, Duke Street, Northampton. Z1415/B.

CUFAUDE, E. H., Private, 9th Suffolk Regiment.
He joined the Northamptonshire Regiment in April 1916, and afterwards was transferred to the Suffolk Regiment. In September 1916 he proceeded to France and fought gallantly at Arras, Ypres and Passchendaele. He fell fighting for King and Country on September 22nd, 1917, and was entitled to the General Service and Victory Medals.
"He died the noblest death a man may die,
Fighting for God and right and liberty."
Corner of High Street, Crick, Northants. Z3353.

CULVERHOUSE, T. H., Pte., 7th Northants. Regt.
Volunteering in May 1915, he completed a period of training, and in the same year proceeded overseas. Whilst on the Western Front he was in action at the Battles of Loos and the Somme. He made the supreme sacrifice, being killed on December 10th, 1916, and was entitled to the 1914–15 Star, and the General Service and Victory Medals.
"He joined the great white company of valiant souls."
100, Scarletwell Street, Northampton. Z1124/A.

CUMBERPATCH, F., Private, 1/4th Northants. Regiment and Royal Army Service Corps.
Mobilised in August 1914, he proceeded in the following year to India, and subsequently to Mesopotamia, on which front he was engaged in transport duties at Kut, Baghdad and the Tigris. In 1917 he was transferred to Palestine, and took an active part in severe fighting at Gaza, Jerusalem, Jaffa and the Jordan. Whilst in the East he suffered from malaria, and was discharged on his return to England in August 1919. He holds the 1914–15 Star, and the General Service and Victory Medals.
26, Poole Street, Northampton. Z1416/B.

CUMBERPATCH, H. J. (sen.), Pte., 1st Northants. Regiment.
After volunteering in November 1914 he underwent a period of training, and in the following year was drafted to France, where he saw service in various sectors of the front. He took part in the fighting at Ypres, Vermelles and Lens, and was later invalided home, suffering from tuberculosis. As a result he was discharged as medically unfit for further service in March 1916, holding the 1914–15 Star, and the General Service and Victory Medals.
13, Doddridge Street, Northampton. Z1125/A.

CUMBERPATCH, H. J. (jun.), Gunner, R.F.A.
Having joined the Marines in October 1918, he completed his training and was retained on important duties at Liverpool until demobilised in February 1919. He re-enlisted in May 1919 in the Royal Field Artillery, and was drafted to India, where in 1920 he was still serving.
13, Doddridge Street, Northampton. Z1125/C.

CUMBERPATCH, J. H., Rifleman, Cameronians (Scottish Rifles).
Mobilised from the Reserve at the outbreak of war in August 1914, he was immediately drafted to the Western Front, where he took part in the Battle of, and in the Retreat from, Mons, also the Battles of the Marne, the Aisne and La Bassée. He died gloriously on the Field of Battle on October 22nd, 1914, and was entitled to the Mons Star, and the General Service and Victory Medals.
"A costly sacrifice upon the altar of freedom."
13, Doddridge Street, Northants.

CURREY, H., Private, Royal Fusiliers.
He enlisted in 1917, and later in the same year was drafted to the Western Front, where he took part in much heavy fighting in various sectors. He made the supreme sacrifice, being killed in action in 1918, and was entitled to the General Service and Victory Medals.
"He died the noblest death a man may die,
Fighting for God and right and liberty."
4, St. Peter's Terrace, Northampton. Z2633.

CURRIN, T., Private, Northamptonshire Regiment.
He volunteered in 1915, and in the same year embarked for the Western Front. There he took an active part in numerous important engagements, including the Battles of Ypres, Festubert, Loos and the Somme, and was severely wounded in action in 1916. He was invalided to England, and consequently discharged as medically unfit for further service in 1917, holding the 1914–15 Star, and the General Service and Victory Medals. 59, Portland Street, Northampton. Z1417.

CURTIS, G. A., Private, 5th Bedfordshire Regt.
Volunteering in March 1915, he completed his training at Felixstowe, and embarking for Egypt in 1916, served in numerous important engagements. On being sent to Palestine he did good work with his unit in the operations at Gaza and in other battles of note. He was demobilised on his return to England in September 1919, and holds the General Service and Victory Medals.
7, Spencer Road, Northampton. Z1418/B.

CURTIS, G. F., Private, 1/4th Yorkshire Regt.
Volunteering in April 1915 in the Northamptonshire Regiment, he completed his training, but was later transferred to the Yorkshire Regiment and drafted to France. Whilst in this theatre of war he took part in engagements in the Somme and Arras sectors, and was wounded in May 1917. As a result he was evacuated to England and eventually invalided out of the Army in February 1918, holding the 1914–15 Star, and the General Service and Victory Medals.
8, St. Mary's Street, Nortnampton. Z1126/A.

CURTIS, H. T., Sapper, Royal Engineers.
He enlisted in May 1916, and two months later was drafted to France. Whilst in this theatre of war he served with the Railway Operative Department, and was engaged on important duties at Audruicq, Rouen and Etaples. He returned home and was demobilised in May 1919, holding the General Service and Victory Medals. Roade, Northampton. Z2111/A.

CURTIS, J. R., Private, 10th Battalion, Canadian Overseas Forces.
He volunteered in August 1914, and, completing his training in the following February, was drafted to France, where he took part in much heavy fighting at Neuve Chapelle. He made the supreme sacrifice, being killed in action near Ypres on April 22nd, 1915, and was entitled to the 1914–15 Star, and the General Service and Victory Medals.
"He nobly fell that we might live."
Roade, Northampton. Z2111/B.

CURTIS, M. H., Cpl., Queen's (Royal W. Surrey Regt)
Having been rejected three times, he joined in February 1917, and in April of the same year was drafted to France. In this seat of war he took part in many engagements, including those in the Arras and Ypres sectors. Later he was transferred to the Labour Corps on account of ill-health, and served on important duties until his demobilisation in February 1920. He holds the General Service and Victory Medals.
43, New Town Road, Northampton. Z3005.

CURTIS, T., Private, 1st Northants. Regiment.
He volunteered at the outbreak of hostilities in August 1914, and, on conclusion of his training in the following year, was drafted overseas. In the course of his service on the Western Front he took part in fierce fighting at Loos, where he was badly gassed and invalided to hospital. After a period of treatment he was evacuated to England, and eventually discharged as medically unfit for further service in February 1918. He holds the 1914–15 Star, and the General Service and Victory Medals.
1, St. Andrew's Gardens, Northampton. Z1127.

CURTIS, T. W., Private, 4th Northants. Regiment.
He volunteered in March 1915, and in the following October was drafted to the Dardanelles, where he saw much heavy fighting. Later he proceeded to Egypt and thence to Palestine, and there took part in the Battles of Gaza, afterwards serving with General Allenby's Forces in the Advance of 1918. He returned home and was demobilised in April 1919, holding the 1914–15 Star, and the General Service and Victory Medals.
15, Spencer Street, Northampton. Z3006.

CURTIS, W., Private, 1st Northants. Regiment.
He volunteered in August 1914, and in April of the following year was ordered to Gallipoli, where he was in action during the Landing on the Peninsula and in the subsequent engagements of the campaign. In January 1916 he was sent to England suffering from malaria, and on his recovery eleven months later was drafted to France. After taking an active part in operations on the Somme he was taken prisoner in July 1917, and unhappily died in captivity in Germany in December 1918. He was entitled to the 1914–15 Star, and the General Service and Victory Medals.
"He joined the great white company of valiant souls."
7, Spencer Road, Northampton. Z1418/A.

CURTIS, W. E., Sgt., 10th Canadian Overseas Forces.
He volunteered in August 1914, and was drafted in the following year to France. In this theatre of war he played a prominent part in many engagements, including the Battles of Neuve Chapelle, Ypres, Loos, the Somme, Arras, Cambrai, and in the Retreat and Advance of 1918. Demobilised in February 1919, he holds the 1914–15 Star, and the General Service and Victory Medals.
Roade, Northampton. Z2111/C.

CUTLER, F., Sapper, Royal Engineers.
He joined in January 1917, and underwent a period of training at various home stations, and later was engaged on important duties. Owing to his being medically unfit he was unable to obtain a transfer overseas, but rendered valuable services until his discharge in October 1917.
164, Lutterworth Road, Northampton. Z2112.

D

DADLEY, W., C.S.M., 1/4th Northants. Regt.
Mobilised with the Territorials in August 1914, he was quickly drafted to Egypt, where he served for some time. He later advanced into Palestine, but after playing a prominent part in the Battles of Jaffa and Gaza (I., II. and III.), was seriously wounded in action and unhappily died at Port Said in January 1918. He had already held the Queen's and King's South African, and the Long Service and Good Conduct Medals, and was entitled to the 1914–15 Star, and the General Service and Victory Medals.
"His name liveth for evermore."
42, Oxford Street, Daventry, Northants. Z2634.

DADSWELL, H. C., Sgt., 16th West Yorks. Regt.
He volunteered in September 1914, and, completing his training in the following year, was drafted to Egypt, where he was engaged on important duties. Early in 1916 he was transferred to France, and played a prominent part in the Battle of the Somme. He died gloriously on the Field of Battle at Ovillers on July 1st, 1916, and was entitled to the 1914–15 Star, and the General Service and Victory Medals.
"The path of duty was the way to glory."
46, Watkins Terrace, Northampton. Z1300.

DALLEY, H. D., Ordinary Seaman, Royal Navy.
He enlisted in October 1918, and, after a period of training, was commissioned to H.M.S. "Eaglet," in which vessel he was engaged on important patrol work and in conveying supplies to the Grand Fleet at Scapa Flow. He was present at the surrender of the German Fleet, and was eventually demobilised in October 1919, holding the General Service and Victory Medals. 62, Clinton Road, Northampton. Z3007/B.

DALLEY, H. T., Sapper, Royal Engineers.
He enlisted in February 1917, and, after completing his training, was drafted to the Western Front. In this theatre of war he took part in many engagements, including those in the Somme, Cambrai and Bapaume sectors, and in the Retreat and Advance of 1918. He remained in France until his demobilisation in December 1919, and holds the General Service and Victory Medals. 62, Clinton Road, Northampton. Z3007/A.

DANIELS, H., Private, East Surrey Regiment.
He joined in June 1917, and was shortly afterwards drafted to Mesopotamia. In this seat of operations he was engaged on important duties, and took part in the capture of Baghdad and the occupation of Mosul. Contracting yellow jaundice, he was eventually invalided home, and on his recovery demobilised in November 1919. He holds the General Service and Victory Medals. 33, Margaret St., Northampton. Z1301/A.

DARLOW, W. L., L/Corporal, Worcestershire and Suffolk Regiments.
Volunteering in October 1915, he was ordered four months later to Salonika. Whilst serving there he was in action in numerous important engagements, including those on the Struma, Monastir and the Doiran fronts. Contracting malaria, he was admitted to hospital, and unfortunately died from the effects in October 1918. He was entitled to the General Service and Victory Medals.
"His memory is cherished with pride."
28, Park Street, Northampton. Z1419.

DARNELL, J., Private, 4th Northants. Regiment.
A Reservist, he was mobilised at the outbreak of war in August 1914, but was not successful in obtaining a transfer overseas. He served with the Royal Defence Corps at Peterborough and at various other places in England on guard and defence duties, and rendered valuable services throughout. He was demobilised in February 1919.
13, Kettering Gardens, Northampton. Z3293/B.

DARNELL, W., Private, 2nd Northants. Regiment.
Joining in May 1916, he was sent in April of the following year to France, and was in action in the Battle of Ypres and in many minor engagements in that sector. Unfortunately he was wounded, and, invalided home, was drafted on his recovery to Germany, where he served with the Army of Occupation. He was later engaged on garrison duties in India, but returned home for discharge in March 1920, holding the General Service and Victory Medals.
13, Kettering Gardens, Northampton. Z3293/A.

DARTNELL, G. W., C.S.M., R.A.S.C. (M.T.)
Joining in April 1916, he was later in the same year drafted to Mesopotamia. Whilst in this theatre of war he served at Baghdad, where he was engaged in the workshops on very important duties which demanded a high degree of technical skill. He did continuously good work, and in December 1919 was demobilised, holding the General Service and Victory Medals. 4, Church Hill, Wootton, Northants. Z2635.

DAVERSON, H. G., Pte., 1/4th Northants. Regt.
He volunteered in May 1915, and underwent a period of training prior to his being drafted to Egypt in the following year. In this seat of operations he was engaged on important duties, and later took part in the Advance into Palestine, where he fought at Gaza (I. II. and III.), and in many other engagements. He was recommended for a decoration, holds the General Service and Victory Medals, and was demobilised in July 1919. 14, Herbert Street, Northampton. Z1128.

DAVIES, D., L/Cpl., York and Lancaster Regt.
He volunteered in September 1914, and in the September following was drafted to France. There he took part in several engagements, including those in the Loos, Albert, the Somme and Arras sectors, and was wounded in action in April 1917. On his recovery he rejoined his unit and fought at Passchendaele and Cambrai, but was again wounded in the Advance of 1918. Demobilised in January 1919, he holds the 1914–15 Star, and the General Service and Victory Medals.
Yew Tree Cottages, Roade, Northampton. Z2113/B.

DAVIES, L. J., 1st Lieut., 6th R. Warwickshire Regt.
He joined the Officers' Training Corps in October 1914, and obtained his commission in the following April in the Royal Warwickshire Regiment, but was retained on important work in England until May 1917. Proceeding to the Western Front, he played a conspicuous part in the Battles of Messines, Vimy Ridge, Bullecourt and Cambrai, fought with distinction in the Retreat and Advance of 1918, and was wounded on two occasions. He was demobilised in February 1919, and holds the General Service and Victory Medals.
69, Bostock Avenue, Northampton. Z2114.

DAVIS, A. O., Private, Border Regiment.
He volunteered in September 1914, and was retained at various stations before proceeding to France. There he took part in several engagements, including the Battles of the Somme, Ypres and Cambrai, where he was badly wounded. As a result he was invalided to the Base, and later demobilised in January 1919, holding the General Service and Victory Medals.
28, St. Paul's Road, Northampton. Z1302.

DAVIS, C. H., Private, 1st East Yorkshire Regt.
A serving soldier, he was drafted to the Western Front immediately on the outbreak of war in August 1914, fought in the Retreat from Mons, and also took part in many other important engagements. He died gloriously on the Field of Battle at Hooge on September 21st, 1915, and was buried at St. Jean. He was entitled to the Mons Star, and the General Service and Victory Medals.
"A costly sacrifice upon the altar of freedom."
66, Abington Avenue, Northampton. Z2385—Z2386.

DAVIS, D., Private, 8th East Surrey Regiment.
Having joined in March 1916, he shortly afterwards embarked for the Western Front, where he took part in many important engagements in the Somme and Ypres sectors before being wounded in September 1917. On his recovery he was stationed at various prisoner of war camps, where he was engaged on important guard duties until demobilised in October 1919, holding the General Service and Victory Medals.
16, Abbey Street, Northampton. Z2636.

DAVIS, E. C., Corporal, 5th Royal Welch Fusiliers.
Mobilised in August 1914, he was retained for a time on special duties before proceeding to France. Whilst on the Western Front he took part in many engagements, including the Battles of Loos, Ypres and the Somme, where he was badly gassed. As a result he was discharged in December 1916 as medically unfit for further service. He holds the 1914–15 Star, and the General Service and Victory Medals.
6, Cartwright Road, Northampton. Z1303.

DAVIS, F., Private, The Queen's Own Worcestershire Hussars.
He joined in 1917 on attaining military age, and early in the following year crossed to France. During the course of his service in this theatre of war, he fought in the Battles of Ypres and in many other engagements of note until the conclusion of the war. He holds the General Service and Victory Medals, and in 1920 was still in the Army.
86, Rothersthorpe Road, Northampton. Z3294/B.

DAVIS, J., Private, 2nd Royal Sussex Regiment.
He joined in January 1917, and having completed his training later in the same year was drafted to France. Whilst in this theatre of war he took part in several engagements, including those in the Monchy, Ypres, the Somme and Cambrai sectors. In 1920 he was still serving and holds the General Service and Victory Medals. 31, Bath Street, Northampton. Z1129/B.

DAVIS, W. A., Driver, M.G.C. (Cavalry).
He joined in March 1917, and in the following month proceeded overseas. Serving on the Western Front, he took part in various engagements, including those in the Ypres and Cambrai sectors. He was also in action during the Retreat of 1918, during which he was unfortunately killed on April 5th, and was entitled to the General Service and Victory Medals.
"His life for his Country."
4, Abbey Street, Northampton. Z2637.

DAVIS, W. J., Private, 11th Suffolk Regiment.
Volunteering in January 1915, he was drafted overseas in the following year. During his service on the Western Front he took part in much heavy fighting on the Somme, where he was badly wounded in action. As a result he was evacuated to England, his right leg having to be amputated, and in May 1917 he was invalided out of the Service. He holds the General Service and Victory Medals. 1, Castle Gardens, Northampton. Z1130.

DAVIS, W. L., Pte., 2nd Northumberland Fusiliers.
Although only 15 years of age he volunteered in November 1914 in the Royal Field Artillery, and shortly afterwards proceeded to France and served at Rouen. Later in the same year he returned home, and was discharged in April 1916 owing to his being under age. Re-enlisting in April 1917, he was retained on important duties with his unit at Newcastle, where he rendered excellent services until demobilised in March 1919, holding the 1914–15 Star, and the General Service and Victory Medals. 33, Argyle Street, Northampton. Z2638.

DAWE, F., Sergeant, Royal Field Artillery.
Volunteering in March 1915, he was drafted shortly afterwards to Egypt, where he served for six months before proceeding to the Western Front. In this seat of operations he played a prominent part in many engagements, particularly in the Somme, Arras and Cambrai sectors prior to being wounded in March 1918. Invalided to England he was engaged on important duties until he was drafted to Ireland, where he was still serving in 1921. He holds the General Service and Victory Medals. 49, Brook Street, Daventry, Northampton. Z2639.

DAWES, G., Sergeant, Duke of Cornwall's L.I.
Mobilised in August 1914, he was quickly drafted to France, took part in several engagements, and served with distinction at the Battle of Hill 60, where he was promoted to the rank of sergeant. Later he was badly wounded at Arras and consequently invalided home, being discharged in May 1916 as medically unfit for further service. He holds the 1914 Star, and the General Service and Victory Medals.
50, Lincoln Street, Kingsthorp, Northampton. Z1131.

DAWKINS, H., Private, Lancashire Fusiliers.
He joined the Middlesex Regiment in June 1916, and in January of the following year embarked for the Western Front. Transferred to the Lancashire Fusiliers he fought in the engagements at Arras and Vimy Ridge, and was blown up by the explosion of a shell in March 1917. Suffering from shell-shock he was invalided home, and was subsequently discharged in April 1918. He holds the General Service and Victory Medals. 25, Oxford Street, Northampton. 3295.

DAWSON, G., Private, 11th Royal Sussex Regt.
He volunteered in May 1915, and later in the same year was drafted to France, but shortly afterwards proceeded to Egypt. Later he took part in the Advance into Palestine, and was gassed in action, but on his recovery was sent back to France, where he saw much fighting, and was wounded three times. After hostilities ceased he went to Germany with the Army of Occupation, and served on the Rhine until his demobilisation in January 1919. He holds the 1914–15 Star, and the General Service and Victory Medals.
6, Lower Harding Street, Northampton. Z1132/C.

DAWSON, W. D., Petty Officer, Royal Navy.
He volunteered in August 1914, and was posted to H.M.S. "King George V.," attached to the Grand Fleet for patrol duties in the North Sea. He also served in H.M. Submarine "D.7" in the Irish Sea, and took part in the Battles of Heligoland Bight and Jutland, and the bombardment of Ostend. Demobilised, he later joined the Merchant Service, and in 1921 was serving in S.S. "Poona." He holds the 1914–15 Star, and the General Service and Victory Medals.
37, Park Street, Northampton. Z1900.

DAY, A. V., Private, Northants. Regiment.
He volunteered in August 1914, and after a period of training was engaged at various stations on important duties with his unit. He was unable to obtain a transfer overseas owing to his being medically unfit, but rendered valuable services until his discharge in September 1916. 46, King St., Northampton. Z1304.

DAY, E. A., Private, 1st Northants. Regiment.
He volunteered in January 1916, and in the following May was drafted to the Western Front. There he took part in the Battle of the Somme, but contracted trench feet, and was consequently invalided home. On his recovery he served at various home stations until his demobilisation in June 1919, and holds the General Service and Victory Medals
74, Milton Street, Northampton. Z1305.

DAY, S. J. S., Private, Northants. Regiment.
Volunteering in September 1914, he proceeded overseas shortly afterwards, and whilst in France saw much heavy fighting. He was in action at St. Eloi, Hill 60, Ypres, Festubert, Vermelles, Ploegsteert Wood, the Somme and Arras, and on three different occasions was wounded. He was eventually demobilised in February 1919, and holds the 1914–15 Star, and the General Service and Victory Medals.
4, Letts Road, Far Cotton, Northampton. Z3296.

DAY, W., Pte., 7th Queen's (R. West Surrey Regt.)
Having attested under the Derby Scheme, he was called to the Colours in July 1917. Proceeding to France in April 1918, he was in action during heavy fighting in the Somme sector, and also at the Battles of Amiens and Epéhy. Whilst overseas he was twice wounded, and as a result was invalided home in 1918, and eventually discharged in March 1919, holding the General Service and Victory Medals.
11, York Place, Northampton. Z2640/A.

DAY, W. H., Trooper, Northants. Dragoons.
Volunteering in March 1915, he was stationed at Towcester, where he was in training and engaged on important duties with his unit. He was later found to be medically unfit, and was therefore discharged in June 1915, after rendering valuable services. 11, York Place, Northampton. Z2640/B.

DAZELEY, F., Private, Middlesex Regiment.
He joined in 1917, and on completion of his training was in the same year drafted overseas. Serving on the Western Front he fought in the Battle of Ypres, but was wounded at Passchendaele and invalided home. On his recovery he returned to the firing-line, was engaged in fierce fighting in various sectors, and was gassed. He was demobilised in 1919, and holds the General Service and Victory Medals.
86, Adams Avenue, Northampton. Z2115/C.

DAZELEY, HERBERT, Corporal, R.A.O.C.
When war broke out in 1914 he volunteered, and on completion of a period of training proceeded overseas. He served at Limnos and Mudros for three years, during which time he was engaged on important duties which he carried out with great ability. He also did valuable work in Egypt, and on his return to England was demobilised in 1919, holding the General Service and Victory Medals. 86, Adams Avenue, Northampton. Z2115/B.

DAZELEY, H., Gunner, Royal Garrison Artillery.
Volunteering in 1915, he was ordered overseas in the same year on completion of his training. During his service on the Western Front he fought in many engagements, and did excellent work as a gunner at the Battles of Ypres, Loos, Vimy Ridge, the Somme, Passchendaele, Cambrai and Amiens. He was demobilised in 1919, and holds the 1914–15 Star, and the General Service and Victory Medals.
86, Adams Avenue, Northampton. Z2115/A.

DAZELEY, J., Gunner, Royal Garrison Artillery.
He volunteered in 1915 and after a period of training was ordered to the Western Front, where he served for nearly four years. During that time he was engaged in much severe fighting in various sectors, and did good work with his Battery in the Battles of Loos, Vimy Ridge, the Somme, Ypres, Passchendaele, Cambrai and Amiens. Demobilised in 1919, he holds the 1914–15 Star, and the General Service and Victory Medals.
86, Adams Avenue, Northampton. Z2115/D.

DEACON, A. E., Private, 2nd Welch Regiment.
He joined the Army in July 1914, and when war broke out in the following month was immediately drafted to France, where he took part in the Battles of Mons, the Aisne and Ypres. He made the supreme sacrifice, being killed in action at Loos on October 21st, 1915. He was entitled to the Mons Star, and the General Service and Victory Medals.
"A valiant Soldier, with undaunted heart he breasted life's last hill."
20, Gladstone Terrace, Northampton. Z1306/B.

DEAN, J. C. (M.M.), Private, Queen's Own (Royal West Kent Regiment).
Joining in 1916 he proceeded overseas later in the same year. Whilst on the Western Front he saw much heavy fighting in various sectors, and was in action at the Battles of Ypres, Passchendaele and Cambrai, where he was taken prisoner and held in captivity until after the conclusion of hostilities. He was awarded the Military Medal for conspicuous bravery and devotion to duty in the Field, and in 1919 was demobilised, holding also the General Service and Victory Medals.
16, St. Peter's Street, Northampton. Z2641.

DENIS, G. A., Corporal, 7th Manchester Regiment.
Joining in October 1917, he received his training at Southend and Colchester, and two months later crossed to France. On that front he was in action in numerous engagements, chiefly in the Somme and Ypres sectors, until wounded and taken prisoner in 1918. On his release he returned to England and was demobilised in December 1919, holding the General Service and Victory Medals.
152, Adnitt Road, Northampton. Z2116.

DENNINGTON, J. P., Gunner, R.F.A.
Called up from the Reserve in August 1914, he was immediately sent to France, where he fought in the Battles of Mons and the subsequent Retreat. He also took part in the Battles of Le Cateau, the Marne, the Aisne, La Bassée, Ypres, Neuve Chapelle, Festubert, the Somme, Arras, Cambrai and Amiens, and was wounded. Discharged in February 1919, he holds the Mons Star, and the General Service and Victory Medals.
14, Freehold Street, Northampton. Z1901.

DENNY, G., Private, 5th Northants. Regiment.
Volunteering in August 1914, he landed in France in the following May. In this theatre of war he was in action at the Battles of Vimy Ridge, the Somme, Arras, Bullecourt, Cambrai, and in the Retreat and Advance. Wounded in September 1918 he was invalided to hospital in England, and eventually demobilised in February 1919, holding the 1914–15 Star, and the General Service and Victory Medals.
36, West Street, Lower Weedon, Northants. Z2642/C.

DENNY, R., L/Corporal, Queen's Own (Royal West Kent Regiment).
Volunteering in May 1915 in the Royal Army Ordnance Corps, he proceeded to France with the Royal West Kent Regiment in November 1917, but was quickly transferred to Italy. He was at once admitted to hospital, and was under treatment for four months. On his recovery he returned to the Western Front, and was killed in action on the Somme in March 1918. He was entitled to the General Service and Victory Medals.
"He nobly fell that we might live."
36, West Street, Lower Weedon, Northants. Z2642/B.

DENNY, W., Pte., Queen's (R.W. Surrey Regt.)
Joining in October 1917, he was drafted overseas in the following year. Serving on the Western Front he was in action in various engagements in the Somme sector before being wounded in June 1918. Invalided to England he underwent a period of hospital treatment, and on his recovery was retained on important duties. He was demobilised in February 1919, and holds the General Service and Victory Medals.
36, West Street, Lower Weedon, Northants. Z2642/A.

DENTON, A. A., Corporal, Royal Fusiliers.
He joined in October 1918, but owing to the early cessation of hostilities was unable to secure a transfer overseas before the Armistice. In March 1919, however, he was drafted to Germany, and was engaged on important work with the Army of Occupation at Cologne. He was invalided home in May 1919, and was demobilised six months later, after rendering valuable services. 149, Lutterworth Rd., Northampton. Z2117.

DENTON, H., Corporal, Royal Air Force.
He volunteered in the 1/4th, Northamptonshire Regiment in November 1914, and the following July was drafted to the Dardanelles, where he fought at the Landing at Suvla Bay and Anzac Cove, and was wounded in action. Later he proceeded to Egypt, thence to Palestine, where he took part in several engagements until July 1916, when he was transferred to the Royal Air Force, and served at Alexandria on important duties. He was demobilised in February 1921, and holds the 1914–15 Star, and the General Service and Victory Medals.
52, Regent Street, Northampton. Z1134.

DENTON, S. H., Rifleman, Royal Irish Rifles.
He joined in February 1916, and shortly afterwards was ordered overseas. During his service on the Western Front, he was in action in many notable engagements, including the Battles of St. Eloi, Ploegsteert Wood and Vimy Ridge, and was wounded on one occasion. After the Armistice he proceeded with the Army of Occupation to Germany, serving there until demobilised in September 1919, holding the General Service and Victory Medals.
63, Market Street, Northampton. Z2087/A.

DENTON, W. A., Private, 7th Northants. Regt.
Volunteering in September 1914, he was drafted overseas in the following year. Whilst on the Western Front he took part in several engagements, including the Battle of Loos, where he was badly wounded. As a result he was invalided home, and eventually discharged in June 1916 as medically unfit for further service. He holds the 1914–15 Star, and the General Service and Victory Medals.
11, Alpha Street, Northampton. Z1307/A.

DENTON, W. S., Private, 1/5th Devonshire Regt.
He volunteered in January 1916, and after completing his training was drafted to Egypt, where he saw much fighting and later took part in the Advance into Palestine. He was in action at Gaza, the fall of Jerusalem and on the River Jordan In June 1918 he was transferred to France, and served with distinction at Arras and on the Marne, being wounded and mentioned in Despatches in July 1918 for good work on the Field. He was serving in Ireland in 1920, and holds the General Service and Victory Medals.
67, Gladstone Terrace, Northampton. Z1133/A.

DERHAM, B. D. (Miss), Nursing Sister.
Already a qualified nurse when war broke out she was afterwards engaged on important duties at Duston War Hospital, where she did excellent work throughout the period of hostilities. She was mentioned in Despatches for distinguished services and devotion to duty, and in 1921 was still at the hospital. 5, Symington Street, Northampton. Z2643/B.

DERHAM, D. V., Private, 1/4th Northants. Regt.
He joined in March 1916, and four months later landed in France. During his short period of service on the Western Front he fought in engagements on the Somme. He made the supreme sacrifice, being killed in action on September 9th, 1916, and was entitled to the General Service and Victory Medals.
"A valiant Soldier, with undaunted heart he breasted life's last hill."
5, Symington Street, Northampton. Z2643/A.

DESBURGH, F., Private, 2nd Northants. Regt.
Volunteering in November 1914, he was sent to the Western Front in the following month and was gassed at Loos and wounded in 1916. After taking part in the Battle of Neuve Chapelle and many other important engagements, he was again wounded and taken prisoner on the Somme in March 1918, and unhappily died whilst still in captivity on June 13th of that year. He was entitled to the 1914–15 Star, and the General Service and Victory Medals.
"His memory is cherished with pride."
81, Stanhope Road, Northampton. Z2387.

DEXTER, H. D., C.Q.M.S., R.E. (R.O.D.)
He volunteered in November 1915, and in the following June was drafted to France. There he served in the Ypres sector, and was engaged in the Transport Section, organizing the distribution of supplies. He did continuously good work throughout his service, and was demobilised in August 1919. He holds the General Service and Victory Medals.
11, Pike Lane, Northampton. Z1135/A.

DICKENS, F. C., Pte., Buffs (East Kent Regt.)
He joined in February 1918, and after four months' training was sent to the Western Front, where he saw severe fighting in various sectors during the Allies' Advance, and was wounded on the Somme in September 1918. He afterwards proceeded with the Army of Occupation to Germany, where he was stationed at Cologne until his return home for demobilisation in November 1919. He holds the General Service and Victory Medals. Forest View, Hartwell, Northants. Z2373/A.

DICKENSON, D. J., Pte., Middlesex Regiment.
He joined in June 1917, and underwent a period of training prior to his being drafted overseas two months later. Whilst on the Western Front he took part in many engagements in the Ypres and Armentières sectors, and was also employed on various duties. He was demobilised in January 1919, and holds the General Service and Victory Medals.
40, Northcote Street, Northampton. Z1136.

DICKERSON, F. A., Corporal, 53rd Rifle Brigade.
He joined in August 1918, but was not successful in his efforts to obtain a transfer overseas before the cessation of hostilities. He was engaged on duties of an important nature at various stations in England until March 1919, when he was sent to Germany. Serving there with the Army of Occupation he did valuable work until demobilised in March 1920.
44, Wilby Street, Northampton. Z1118.

DICKERSON, T., Private, 1st Northants. Regt.
He volunteered in September 1914, and five months later was drafted to the Western Front, where he took part in much heavy fighting at Neuve Chapelle, St Eloi and Hill 60. He made the supreme sacrifice, being killed in action at Aubers Ridge on May 9th, 1915, and was entitled to the 1914–15 Star, and the General Service and Victory Medals.
"Whilst we remember, the sacrifice is not in vain."
School Road, Spratton, Northants. Z3008.

DICKS, H. C., Gunner, Royal Field Artillery.
Joining in May 1916, he was drafted to France later in the same year. Whilst on the Western Front he took part in several engagements, including those on the Somme, at Cambrai and in the Retreat of 1918, and was badly wounded in October of that year. As a result he was invalided home, and eventually discharged in December 1919. He holds the General Service and Victory Medals.
Squirrel Lane, Old Duston, Northants. Z3009/A.

DICKS, S., L/Corporal, 2nd Northants. Regiment.
He joined in August 1916, and having completed his training in the following year was drafted to the Western Front. There he took part in many important engagements, including those in the Somme, Ypres and Epéhy Wood sectors, and was three times wounded in action, being finally invalided home. Discharged in May 1919, he holds the General Service and Victory Medals. Squirrel Lane, Old Duston, Northants. Z3009/B.

DICKS, W. A., Bombardier, R.F.A.
Volunteering in October 1915, he proceeded overseas in the following January. During his service in France he took part in the Battles of the Somme, Ypres and Cambrai, and in the Retreat and Advance of 1918. After hostilities ceased he was sent to Germany with the Army of Occupation, and served on the Rhine until his demobilisation in July 1919. He holds the General Service and Victory Medals.
Squirrel Lane, Old Duston, Northants. Z3009/C.

DIGBY, A. C., L/Corporal, 1st Northants. Regt.
A Reservist, he was called to the Colours in August 1914, and two months later proceeded to France, where he took part in the Battles of Ypres and Neuve Chapelle, and other engagements. Severely gassed at Loos in September 1915 he was admitted to hospital at Leicester, and was finally invalided from the Army in April 1918. He unhappily died of gas-poisoning in September of that year, and was entitled to the Mons Star, and the General Service and Victory Medals.
"Steals on the ear the distant triumph song."
High Street, Gayton, Northants Z2388/B.

DILLEY, W. J., Trooper, Northants. Dragoons.
He volunteered in March 1915, and, transferred to the Leicestershire Regiment, proceeded to France, where he took an active part in many important engagements. He was seriously wounded at Epéhy Wood in December 1917, and in the same month unhappily died from the effects of his injuries. He was entitled to the General Service and Victory Medals.
"His life for his Country."
47, Purser Road, Northampton. Z3297.

DIMMOCK, A. S., Sapper, Royal Engineers.
Having joined in March 1917, he completed his training later in the same year, and proceeded to France. Whilst in this theatre of war he served with the Railway Operative Department in the forward areas in various sectors of the front. He did continuously good work during the period of hostilities and in November 1919 was demobilised, holding the General Service and Victory Medals.
34, Sharman Road, Northampton. Z2644.

DIPPER, J. G., Private, R.A.V.C.
He volunteered in April 1915, and later in the same year embarked for the Western Front. Whilst in this theatre of war he was engaged in attending to the sick and wounded horses, and served during heavy fighting at the Battles of Vimy Ridge, the Somme, Arras, Ypres, Passchendaele, Cambrai and also in the Retreat and Advance of 1918. Demobilised in January 1919, he holds the 1914–15 Star, and the General Service and Victory Medals. 8, Waterloo, Daventry, Northants. Z2645.

DIVINE, J. (M.M.), Cpl., 1st Northants. Regiment.
Mobilised in August 1914, he was shortly afterwards drafted to France, where he took part in the Battles of Ypres and Festubert, and was badly wounded. As a result he was invalided home, but on his recovery returned to France and served with distinction in the La Bassée sector, being awarded the Military Medal for great gallantry and devotion to duty in the Field. Later he saw service in Russia, and received the Order of St. George (3rd Class) for bravery in the Field. He was discharged in July 1920, and also holds the 1914–15 Star, and the General Service and Victory Medals.
43, Allistons Gardens, Northampton. Z1137

DIX, A., Pte., 5th Northamptonshire Regiment.
He volunteered in August 1914, and in May of the following year proceeded to the Western Front, where he took part in the Battle of Loos. Invalided home in October 1915, suffering from rheumatism, he returned to France, however, in November of the following year, and fought in the Battles of Arras, Cambrai, the Somme and Armentières. Demobilised in April 1919, he holds the 1914–15 Star, and the General Service and Victory Medals. 16, Upper Harding Street, Northampton. Z1138.

DIX, W., Pte., Queen's Own (R. West Kent Regt.)
He enlisted in July 1916, and underwent a period of training prior to being drafted in the following December to France, where he took part in many important engagements. He was unfortunately killed in action on February 10th, 1917, and was entitled to the General Service and Victory Medals.
"He joined the great white company of valiant souls."
Silver Street, Brixworth, Northants.
Z3110/C—Z3111/C—Z3112/C.

DIYMENT, F., Private, M.G.C. (Cavalry).
Volunteering in August 1914, he underwent a period of training and in the following year was drafted to France, where he took part in many important engagements in various sectors of the front. He was in action at the Battles of Loos, the Somme, Ypres and Cambrai. Prior to his being drafted to France he was attached to the Monmouthshire Regiment. Demobilised in January 1919, he holds the 1914–15 Star, and the General Service and Victory Medals.
46, Monks Ponds Street, Northampton. Z1100/A.

DOBSON, A., Private, Middlesex Regiment.
Joining in February 1917, he was drafted to the Western Front in the following month, and after taking part in the Battle of Messines, was gassed and wounded and sent to hospital at the Base. Transferred to the Labour Corps, he was later engaged in guarding prisoners of war at Rouen, and was finally demobilised in January 1919. He holds the General Service and Victory Medals. 12, West Street, Northampton. Z1902.

DODD, J., Private, 3rd Durham Light Infantry.
Mobilised at the outbreak of war in August 1914, he was immediately drafted to France, where he served throughout the Retreat from Mons, and also at the Battles of the Marne, the Aisne and Ypres, where he was wounded in December 1914. Evacuated to England, he underwent a period of hospital treatment, and was eventually discharged. Later, however, he was recalled in June 1916, and transferred to the Royal Defence Corps, and was retained at Northampton on important guard duties. Afterwards he went to South Wales, where he was engaged in a similar capacity. He was demobilised in January 1919, and holds the Mons Star, and the General Service and Victory Medals.
49, Regent Street, Northampton. Z1139.

DODMAN, C. E., Bombardier, R.G.A.
A Reservist, he was called up at the outbreak of war, and at once ordered to France, where he took part in the actions at Mons. He also fought in the Battles of the Marne, the Aisne, Ypres, Neuve Chapelle, Hill 60, and Loos, and was wounded on one occasion. In 1916 he returned home, and after being transferred to the 2nd Life Guards, served at various important stations in England until discharged in March 1919. He holds the Mons Star, and the General Service and Victory Medals.
5, Florence Road, Northampton. Z2119.

DONALDSON, S. H., 1st Class Petty Officer, R.N.
He enlisted in April 1911, and after the outbreak of war in August 1914, served in H.M.S. "Marlborough," attached to the Grand Fleet in the North Sea. In these waters he was engaged on patrol and coastal defence duties, and also took part in the Battle of Jutland and minor actions. He holds the 1914–15 Star, and the General Service and Victory Medals, and in 1920 was still at sea.
19, Knightly Road, Northampton. Z1308.

DORR, G., Private, Labour Corps.
He joined in June 1916, and after a short period of training with the Northamptonshire Regiment proceeded to France with the Labour Corps, and was engaged on road-making duties in the Somme, Arras, Ypres and Cambrai sectors. Severely gassed in the Advance of 1918, he was invalided from the Army in March 1919. He unhappily died of consumption on May 16th, 1920, and was entitled to the General Service and Victory Medals.
"Steals on the ear the distant triumph song."
47, St. Mary's Street, Northampton. Z1140.

DOUCE, A., Rifleman, Rifle Brigade.
A Reservist, he was called to the Colours in August 1914 and quickly drafted to France, where he fought in the Retreat from Mons. He also took part in the Battles of the Marne, the Aisne, La Bassée, Ploegsteert Wood and the Somme, and many other engagements, and was finally discharged on his return home in March 1919. He holds the Mons Star, and the General Service and Victory Medals.
19, Vernon Terrace, Northampton. Z1903.

DOUGLAS, C., Private, 1st Northants. Regiment.
A Reservist, he was mobilised at the declaration of war, and was drafted with the First Expeditionary Force to France, where he fought at Mons and in the subsequent engagements. He was also in action at Ypres and St Quentin and in various other sectors of the front, and was twice wounded. He was discharged in June 1918 as medically unfit for further service, and holds the Mons Star, and the General Service and Victory Medals. 14, Henley Street, Far Cotton, Northampton. Z3299.

DOUGLAS, R., Private, Yorkshire Regiment.
He joined in July 1916, and on completion of his training was sent to the Western Front. During his service there he fought in the engagements at Ypres, Passchendaele and the Somme, and, attached to the 50th Division, did excellent work as a signaller. He was gassed at Ham and sent into hospital at Rouen and later came to England, where he was retained with the Royal Defence Corps. He was ultimately demobilised in November 1919, and holds the General Service and Victory Medals.
8, Southampton Road, Far Cotton, Northampton. Z3300.

DOUGLAS, S. A H., Private, Northants. Regt.
Two months after volunteering in August 1914, he was sent to the Western Front, where he took part in the Battles of Ypres, Festubert, Loos, Albert, the Somme and Arras. Four times wounded and severely gassed, he was invalided home in 1916, but on his recovery in the following year returned to France with the Royal Engineers for transport duty. He was demobilised in March 1919, and holds the 1914 Star, and the General Service and Victory Medals. Hartwell, Northants. Z2389.

DOUGLAS, S. W., Air Mechanic, R.A.F.
He volunteered in 1915, at the age of 16 years, and after having completed a course of training served at various aerodromes on duties which required a high degree of technical skill. He was unable to secure a transfer overseas on account of being under military age, but, nevertheless, rendered very valuable services until demobilised in 1919.
39, Richard Street, Northampton. Z3298.

DOVE, C., Private, 2nd Northants. Regiment.
Volunteering in June 1915, he was sent to the Western Front in the following October and there fought in various sectors. After taking part in the Battles of the Somme, Arras and Ypres, and other engagements, he was wounded and taken prisoner in the Retreat of March 1918, and held in captivity until the cessation of hostilities. Demobilised in December 1918, he holds the 1914–15 Star, and the General Service and Victory Medals. 47, West Street, Northampton. Z1905.

DOVE, T. G., Guardsman, 3rd Grenadier Guards.
He volunteered in January 1915, and 12 months later proceeded to the Western Front. Whilst in this theatre of war he took part in many important engagements, including the Battles of the Somme, Arras, Vimy Ridge, Messines and Ypres, fought also in the Retreat and Advance of 1918, and was wounded. He was demobilised in January 1919, and holds the General Service and Victory Medals.
70, Melbourne Street, Northampton. Z1904.

DOVEY, F. H., Private, R.M.L.I.
At the outbreak of war he was called up from the Reserve, and immediately proceeded to the Western Front. There he was engaged in fierce fighting at Antwerp, but was unfortunately taken prisoner in October 1914, and held in captivity in Germany. After enduring many hardships, he was repatriated in January 1919, and demobilised two months later, holding the 1914 Star, and the General Service and Victory Medals.
94, Lower Thrift Street, Northampton. Z2120.

DOWDEN, F. J. W., L/Corporal, 14th London Regiment (London Scottish).
He volunteered in November 1915, and in April of the following year was drafted to the Western Front, where he took part in the Battles of Arras and Ypres, and many other engagements. He fell nobly on the Field of Battle on October 9th, 1917, and was entitled to the General Service and Victory Medals.
"The path of duty was the way to glory."
23, Hervey Street, Northampton. Z1906.

DOWDY, A., Ordinary Seaman, R.N.V.R.
Joining in August 1918, he underwent a period of training, but owing to the early cessation of hostilities, was unable to obtain his transfer to a theatre of war. He was therefore retained on important duties at Crystal Palace, where he rendered very valuable services until demobilised in January 1919.
50, Baring Road, Northampton. Z2646.

DOWNING, F., Private, 6th Northants. Regiment.
Volunteering in August 1914, he completed his training and proceeded overseas in the following year. Serving on the Western Front he was in action in numerous engagements of note, was wounded on two occasions, and also suffered from trench fever. In 1918 he was transferred to the Motor Transport Section and drafted to Ireland, where he served until demobilised in June 1920, holding the 1914–15 Star, and the General Service and Victory Medals.
77, Purser Road, Northampton. Z2063/C.

DOWNING, T., Private, 1st Northants. Regiment.
When war was declared in August 1914, he volunteered, and on completion of his training in the following year embarked for the Western Front. There he fought in numerous important engagements in various sectors, was almost continuously in action until the close of hostilities, and was gassed on one occasion. Serving in France until demobilised in December 1919, he holds the 1914–15 Star, and the General Service and Victory Medals. 77, Purser Road, Northampton. Z2063/B.

DOWSON, A., Private, Yorkshire Regiment.
He volunteered in September 1914, and in the following year was drafted to France. There he took part in much heavy fighting in the Ypres, Festubert and Loos sectors, and was wounded in action in September 1915. As a result he was invalided home, and on his recovery was transferred to the Labour Corps, engaged on various important duties until his demobilisation in February 1919. He holds the 1914–15 Star, and the General Service and Victory Medals.
Bubgrooke, Northants. Z3010/A.

DRAGE, A. (jun.), Private, Bedfordshire Regiment.
Joining in July 1918, in the Northamptonshire Regiment, he underwent a period of training, and in the following January proceeded to Germany. Whilst there he was transferred to the Bedfordshire Regiment, and served with the Army of Occupation at Cologne, where he rendered very valuable services until demobilised in October 1919.
35, Gregory Street, Northampton. Z2647/A

DRAGE, A., Gunner, Royal Garrison Artillery.
Joining in September 1916, he completed a period of training before being drafted overseas in the following June. During his short service on the Western Front he took part in heavy fighting at Ypres. He died gloriously on the Field of Battle on July 31st, 1917, and was entitled to the General Service and Victory Medals.
"Thinking that remembrance, though unspoken, may reach him where he sleeps."
35, Gregory Street, Northampton. Z2647/B.

DRAGE, C. E., Private, Royal Fusiliers.
Joining in August 1916, he embarked early in the following year for the Western Front. During his service there, he was in action on the Menin Road, at Passchendaele and Cambrai, and was wounded and gassed, and on each occasion invalided home. Rejoining his unit on his recovery he fought in the Allied Advance of 1918, and returning home in February 1919 was demobilised, holding the General Service and Victory Medals. West Haddon, Northants. Z3301/A.

DRAGE, E. S., Sergt., Queen's (R.W. Surrey Regt.)
He joined in May 1916, and three months later landed in France, and there fought at Messines, Beaumont-Hamel and Bullecourt, and in many other important battles. He was unfortunately wounded in August 1917, and, invalided home, received medical treatment at Scurbank Hospital. On recovery he served as an Instructor at various stations, and was eventually demobilised in September 1919, holding the General Service and Victory Medals.
West Haddon, Northants. Z3301/B.

DRAGE, F., Private, 10th London Regiment.
He joined in November 1917, and in June of the following year was drafted overseas. Serving on the Western Front he was engaged in fierce fighting during the Retreat of 1918, and also took an active part in the final decisive engagements of the war. After the Armistice he advanced into Germany with the Army of Occupation, and was stationed at Cologne until demobilised in November 1919. He holds the General Service and Victory Medals.
29, Somerset Street, Northampton. Z1420/A.

DRAGE, J., Private, 1/4th Northants. Regiment.
At the outbreak of war he volunteered, and proceeding to Egypt in July 1915, rendered valuable services there until 1917, when he was sent to Palestine. On that front he was wounded in the Battle of Gaza, but on his recovery experienced fierce fighting at Jerusalem and Jericho, being almost continuously in action until the close of hostilities. Demobilised on his return home in April 1919, he holds the 1914–15 Star, and the General Service and Victory Medals.
29, Somerset Street, Northampton. Z1420/C.

DRAGE, P., L/Corporal, 6th Northants. Regiment.
He volunteered in August 1914, and in 1916 embarked for the scene of activities in France, but was wounded shortly after going up the line. Whilst overseas he fought in the Battles of the Somme, Arras, Vimy Ridge Ypres and Cambrai, but was again wounded during the Retreat of 1918, and invalided to England. Consequently he was discharged as unfit for further service in January 1919, and holds the General Service and Victory Medals. 29, Somerset Street, Northampton. Z1420/B.

DRAGE, W., Private, Royal Naval Division.
He joined in July 1917, and four months later crossed to France, where he served with the Hawke Battalion in various engagements. He was unhappily killed in action by the explosion of a shell in December 1917, and was entitled to the General Service and Victory Medals.
"A costly sacrifice upon the altar of freedom."
10, Margaret Street, Northampton. Z3265/A.

DRAPER, C., Private, 1st Black Watch.
He volunteered in October 1915, and in May of the following year was drafted to the Western Front, where he took part in the Battles of Albert and the Somme. He was invalided home in December 1916, suffering from trench feet, but returned to France in time to fight in the Advance of 1918. Demobilised in March 1919, he holds the General Service and Victory Medals. 43, Lower Harding Street, Northampton. Z1141.

DRINKWATER, J. (M.M.), Sergeant, 12th East Surrey Regiment.
Mobilised with the Territorials in August 1914 he was retained for a time at various home stations before proceeding to France. There he played a prominent part in many engagements in the Vimy Ridge, Messines, Passchendaele and Somme sectors and afterwards saw service in Italy. He was awarded the Military Medal for conspicuous bravery and devotion to duty in the Field, and holding also the General Service and Victory Medals, was demobilised in February 1919.
85, West Street, Weedon, Northants. Z3011/A.

DRIVER, C. E., Private, Bedfordshire Regiment.
He joined the Northamptonshire Regiment in March 1916, and nine months later proceeded to the Western Front. Whilst overseas he was in action at the Battles of Arras, Ypres, Cambrai and the Somme, and did good work with his unit during the Advance of 1918. After the Armistice he was transferred to the Bedfordshire Regiment, and served with the Army of Occupation in Germany until demobilised in August 1919, holding the General Service and Victory Medals.
82, Market Street, Northampton. Z2121.

DUDLEY, B. W. (Miss), Member, V.A.D.
She joined in December 1917, having previously served in St. John Ambulance Association, and during her service did continuously good work at Barry Road Hospital, Northampton. She carried out her duties in a highly commendable manner, rendering valuable services until her demobilisation in May 1919. 28, Euston Road, Northampton. Z3012/B.

DUDLEY, E., L/Corporal, R.A.M.C.
He volunteered in October 1915, and five months later proceeded to the Western Front, where he played a prominent part in the heavy fighting on the Somme. He unfortunately contracted pneumonia and died on September 15th, 1916, after rendering valuable services with his unit. He was entitled to the General Service and Victory Medals.
"The path of duty was the way to glory."
28, Euston Road, Far Cotton, Northampton. Z3012/D.

DUDLEY, H. E. A., L/Corporal, Royal Engineers.
He joined in February 1917, and was quickly drafted to the Western Front, where he rendered valuable services with his unit in many important engagements, particularly in the Somme sector. He remained overseas until March 1919, when he was demobilised, holding the General Service and Victory Medals.
28, Euston Road, Far Cotton, Northampton. Z3012/C.

DUDLEY, R., Private, Bedfordshire Regiment.
He joined in February 1918, and after serving with the Norfolk and Essex Regiments, proceeded to France with the Bedfordshire Regiment, and took part in the Battles of the Somme (II.), Epéhy and Cambrai, and in other engagements during the Retreat and Advance of 1918. After hostilities ceased he served at Cologne with the Army of Occupation, and was demobilised in August 1919, holding the General Service and Victory Medals.
28, Euston Road, Far Cotton, Northampton. Z3012/A.

DUGAN, P. J. (D.C.M.), 2nd Lieutenant, R.G.A.
Already in the Ranks in August 1914, he was sent to France in 1915, and served with distinction at the Battles of Neuve Chapelle, the Somme and Cambrai. Transferred to Italy, he unfortunately broke his leg, and was invalided home to hospital in Netley. In June 1918 he was granted a commission, and in 1921 was stationed at Cologne with the Army of Occupation. He was awarded the Distinguished Conduct Medal and the Croix de Guerre for conspicuous bravery at Neuve Chapelle, when he stuck to his gun and repaired it under heavy shell-fire, and also holds the 1914–15 Star, and the General Service and Victory Medals.
59, Oxford Street, Daventry, Northants. Z3013.

DUMAYNE, G. H., Private, 1st London Regiment (Royal Fusiliers).
Two months after joining in March 1917, he was sent to the Western Front, where he took part in the Battles of Messines, Ypres and the Somme, and many other engagements. He fought also in the Retreat and Advance of 1918, and was so severely wounded at Le Cateau in October as to necessitate the amputation of his leg. He was invalided from the Army in October 1919, and holds the General Service and Victory Medals. 37, Hervey Street, Northampton. Z1907.

DUNKLEY, A., Private, 2nd Northants. Regiment.
Joining in April 1917, he proceeded in the following July to France, whence after one month's service he was transferred to Italy. In this theatre of war he was in action in numerous engagements on the Piave, and in October 1918 was wounded. On recovery he returned to his unit, and landing in England was demobilised in January 1919, holding the General Service and Victory Medals.
103, Abbey Road, Far Cotton, Northampton. Z3304.

DUNKLEY, A., C.S.M., Royal Irish Fusiliers.
Already serving in India when war was declared, he was drafted to the Western Front in December 1914, and there saw severe fighting in various sectors. After taking a prominent part in the Battles of Ypres, the Somme and Arras, and minor engagements, he was invalided home in 1917, and retained as an Instructor at Dublin until his discharge in March 1919. He holds the 1914–15 Star, and the General Service and Victory Medals.
31, Moore Street, Kingsley Park, Northampton. Z1142.

DUNKLEY, A., Private, Northants. Regiment.
Having joined in September 1916, he underwent a period of training and was afterwards found to be medically unfit for service overseas. He was therefore engaged on important hay baleing duties in Kent, and later served with the Military Police at Richmond, where he rendered very valuable services until demobilised in November 1919.
King's Lane, Flore, Northampton. Z2648.

DUNKLEY, A., Private, Northants. Regiment.
Four months after joining in January 1917, he was drafted to the Western Front, where, after taking part in the Battle of Arras and many minor engagements, he was severely wounded at Ypres in June 1917. Admitted to hospital at Sheffield he was finally discharged in December of the same year as medically unfit for further service. He holds the General Service and Victory Medals.
41, St. Andrew's Street, Northampton. Z1143.

DUNKLEY, A. A., Tpr., Beds. Yeomanry (Lancers).
He volunteered in November 1915, and after a period of training was drafted to Egypt, and, proceeding into Palestine with the Machine Gun Corps, took part in many important engagements. He unhappily contracted dysentery, and died on October 6th, 1918, being entitled to the General Service and Victory Medals.
"Courage, bright hopes and a myriad dreams, splendidly given."
65, Dunster Street, Northampton. Z1908.

DUNKLEY, A. T., Private, Machine Gun Corps.
At the outbreak of war in August 1914 he volunteered, and served for a time with the Oxfordshire and Buckinghamshire Light Infantry. Transferred to the Machine Gun Corps, he was drafted to India in November 1917, and there carried out important garrison duties until his return home for demobilisation in January 1920. He holds the General Service and Victory Medals. Kilsby, Northants. Z3306.

DUNKLEY, F., Private, 7th Northants. Regt.
He volunteered in February 1915, and in September proceeded to France, where he took part in the Battles of Loos, the Somme, Arras, Vimy Ridge, Ypres, Passchendaele and Cambrai. He was also in action during the Retreat and Advance, and was gassed in November 1918. Demobilised in July 1919, he holds the 1914–15 Star, and the General Service and Victory Medals.
School Road, Spratton, Northants. Z3014.

DUNKLEY, F. G., Private, 26th Royal Fusiliers.
Joining in June 1916 he proceeded to the Western Front in the following December and fought in the Battles of Arras, Messines Ypres and Passchendaele. Transferred later to Italy, he served on the Piave until his return to France in time to take part in the Retreat and Advance of 1918. He was severely wounded in October of that year, and was finally invalided from the Army in January 1919, holding the General Service and Victory Medals.
45, Ethel Street, Northampton. Z1909.

DUNKLEY, G., Private, 19th Middlesex Regiment.
Joining in August 1917, he proceeded to Italy in the following November and there saw severe fighting on the Piave and the Asiago Plateaux. Transferred to France in March 1918, he took part in the Battles of the Somme and Cambrai, and other engagements in the Retreat and Advance, and later served with the Army of Occupation at Cologne. Demobilised in March 1919, he holds the General Service and Victory Medals.
26, Monks Pond Street, Northampton. Z1144.

DUNKLEY, H., L/Corporal, M.G.C. (Cavalry).
He volunteered in March 1915, and on completing his training was drafted overseas nine months later. Whilst serving on the Western Front he saw heavy fighting in various sectors, and took an active part in the Battles of the Somme, Arras, Bullecourt and Cambrai, and other engagements of note. He was demobilised in April 1919, and holds the 1914–15 Star, and the General Service and Victory Medals.
113, Great Russell Street, Northampton. Z1422.

DUNKLEY, J., Private, 1st Dorsetshire Regiment.
A Reservist, he was called up at the declaration of war, and at once ordered to the Western Front, where he fought in the Battle of Mons, and was wounded. On his return to the firing-line he was in action in numerous important engagements until the cessation of hostilities, and was wounded on two occasions. He was discharged in March 1919, and holds the Mons Star, and the General Service and Victory Medals.
75, Melville Street, Northampton. Z2122.

DUNKLEY, J., Special War Worker.
Owing to his age he was exempted from military service, but prior to the outbreak of hostilities he had been in the Army for 12 years. For two years during the war he was engaged on important work in connection with the manufacture of lasts for boots for the Army, at the British-American Last Works, and carried out his duties with great efficiency, to the entire satisfaction of his firm
27, Market Street, Northampton. Z2123.

DUNKLEY, J. H., Air Mechanic, R.A.F.
After volunteering in August 1915, he underwent a period of training prior to being drafted to the Western Front in August 1917. There he was engaged on important duties as a rigger in the Somme, Ypres, Cambrai and Arras sectors, finally returning home for demobilisation in April 1919. He holds the General Service and Victory Medals.
14, Todd's Lane, Northampton. Z1145.

DUNKLEY, R. W., Rifleman, Royal Irish Rifles.
He joined in September 1916, and after a period of training was four months later sent to the Western Front. There he saw heavy fighting on the Somme and was in action in the Battle of Ypres and other engagements until invalided home in October 1917. Subsequently he was drafted to Ireland, where he was attached to the Royal Engineers and engaged on important clerical work until demobilised in January 1919, holding the General Service and Victory Medals.
31, Wilby Street, Northampton. Z2124.

DUNKLEY, S. (D.C.M.), Driver, R.F.A.
Volunteering in October 1915, he embarked in February of the following year for France, and took part in the heavy fighting during the Somme Offensive. He also served in the Ypres sector and at Dickebusch and High Wood, and in many other notable engagements, including those in the Retreat and Advance of 1918. He was awarded the Distinguished Conduct Medal for conspicuous bravery in saving a man and horses under heavy shell-fire in November 1918, and also holds the General Service and Victory Medals. He was demobilised on his return to England in June 1919.
Station Road, Long Buckby, Northants. Z3302.

DUNKLEY, S., Private, 7th Lincolnshire Regt.
Enlisting in March 1917, he was drafted overseas twelve months later. Whilst on the Western Front he took part in much heavy fighting during the Retreat of 1918, being badly wounded in action in April of that year and invalided home. As a result he was discharged as medically unfit for further service in July 1919, and holds the General Service and Victory Medals.
52, Clinton Road, Northampton. Z2958/B.

DUNKLEY, W. E. J., 1st Air Mechanic, R.A.F.
He volunteered in January 1916, and after completing a term of training, was retained at various stations, where, in the capacity of rigger, he was engaged on duties of a highly technical nature. Unable, on account of ill-health, to obtain his transfer overseas, he, nevertheless, rendered valuable services with his Squadron until February 1919, when he was demobilised.
20, Gladstone Terrace, Northampton. Z1306/A.

DUNKLEY, W. R., Private, R.A.V.C.
He volunteered in June 1915, and after a period of training, crossed to the Western Front, and saw service in many sectors. Throughout he rendered valuable services in tending the sick and wounded horses, and after the Armistice proceeded to Germany, where he was stationed with the Army of Occupation on the Rhine. Returning home in March 1919 he was demobilised, holding the 1914–15 Star, and the General Service and Victory Medals. Crick, Northants. Z3305.

DUNLOP, W. H., Gunner, Royal Field Artillery.
Volunteering in October 1915, he was drafted to Egypt in the following year and shortly afterwards to Salonika. In that theatre of war he did valuable work with his Battery on the Doiran and Vardar fronts, and took part in severe fighting in various sectors until hostilities ceased. Whilst in the East he suffered from malaria, and was demobilised on his return to England in 1919, holding the General Service and Victory Medals. 1, Portland Street, Northampton. Z1421.

DUNMORE, G., Private, 1st Northants. Regt.
Already serving in Egypt in August 1914, he was immediately drafted to the Western Front, where he fought in the Retreat from Mons. After taking part also in the Battles of the Marne, the Aisne, La Bassée, Ypres and the Somme, he was wounded and taken prisoner at Nieuport in July 1917, and held in captivity until the cessation of hostilities. Discharged in March 1919, he holds the Mons Star, and the General Service and Victory Medals.
36, Shelley Street, Kingsley, Northampton. Z1146.

DUNMORE, H. J., Private, R.A.S.C. (M.T.)
Joining in May 1916, he proceeded shortly afterwards to France and whilst there rendered excellent services in the Somme sector. He was unhappily killed in action whilst conveying ammunition and supplies to the forward areas on July 3rd, 1916, and was entitled to the General Service and Victory Medals.
"The path of duty was the way to glory."
Mill Lane, Kislingbury, Northants. Z3307/B.

DUNN, H. R., Gunner, Royal Garrison Artillery.
Volunteering in November 1915, he was drafted overseas in May of the following year on the completion of his training. Whilst serving on the Western Front he was engaged in fierce fighting in the Battles of the Somme, Vimy Ridge, Messines and Ypres, and was almost continuously in action with the 91st Siege Battery until the termination of the war. He was demobilised in August 1919, and holds the General Service and Victory Medals. 38, Abington Avenue, Northampton. Z2125/B.

DUNN, W. A., Corporal, Royal Field Artillery.
He volunteered in November 1915, and four months later embarked for the Western Front, where he was in action in various sectors. He fought in engagements at Loos, Arras, Vimy Ridge and Cambrai, and did good work with his Battery in operations during the Advance of 1918. After the Armistice he proceeded to Germany with the Army of Occupation, and being demobilised in April 1919, holds the General Service and Victory Medals.
38, Abington Avenue, Northampton. Z2125/A.

DURDEN, R. C., Sergeant, 1st Northants. Regt.
A serving soldier, he proceeded to the Western Front immediately on the outbreak of war in August 1914, and there, after fighting at Mons, took a prominent part in the Battles of the Marne and the Aisne. He died gloriously on the field of Battle at Ypres on November 11th, 1914. He was entitled to the Mons Star, and the General Service and Victory Medals.
"His memory is cherished with pride."
4, Northcote Street, Northampton. Z1147/A.

DYER, J. F., Driver, R.A.S.C. (H.T.)
He joined in December 1916, and after undergoing a period of training was retained on duties of great importance at various stations and was also engaged in conveying horses to and from France. Unable to obtain his transfer to the front, he, nevertheless, rendered valuable services with his Company until his demobilisation in June 1919. He holds the General Service and Victory Medals.
39, Edinburgh Road, Northampton. Z2390.

E

EAGLE, A. G., Private, Queen's Own (Royal West Kent Regiment).
Volunteering in June 1915, he was first engaged on important duties with his unit. Proceeding to France in January 1917, he was later transferred to the Labour Corps, and served in many important engagements in various sectors of the front. He was evacuated to England in the following year and was stationed at Salisbury Plain, where he was engaged as a shoemaker. Demobilised in January 1919, he holds the General Service and Victory Medals.
13, York Place, Northampton. Z2649.

EAGLE, W., Sapper, Royal Engineers.
Having volunteered in June 1915, he was drafted overseas four months later. Whilst in France he took part in many important engagements in the Arras sector, and was badly wounded in action in 1916. As a result he was invalided home, and eventually discharged in January 1919 as medically unfit for further service. He holds the 1914–15 Star, and the General Service and Victory Medals.
81, Roe Road, Northampton. Z3015.

EAKINS, E. S., Private, 2nd Northants. Regiment.
He volunteered in August 1914, and six months later was drafted to the Western Front, where he took part in much severe fighting. He laid down his life for King and Country at the Battle of Neuve Chapelle on March 12th, 1915, being only 17 years of age. He was entitled to the 1914–15 Star, and the General Service and Victory Medals.
"A costly sacrifice upon the altar of freedom."
8, Dickens Terrace, Northampton. Z3311.

EALES, A. A., Sapper, Royal Engineers.
He volunteered in June 1915, and in September was drafted to the Eastern theatre of war. After serving in Egypt for a time he was transferred to Palestine, and was engaged on special railway work during the operations at Gaza, Jerusalem, Jaffa and along the Jordan. He was demobilised in April 1919, and holds the 1914–15 Star, and the General Service and Victory Medals. Church End, Bugbrooke, Northants. Z3308/B.

EALES, A. E., Private, 12th Manchester Regiment.
Three months after joining in March 1917, he was sent to France where he took part in the Battles of Ypres, Bapaume, Gouzeaucourt, Havrincourt and Le Cateau, and other engagements during the Retreat and Advance. Badly wounded in action in November 1918, he was invalided home, and was eventually discharged as medically unfit in July 1919, holding the General Service and Victory Medals.
King Street, Long Buckby, Northants. Z3310.

EALES, G. W., Driver, Royal Field Artillery.
Called up from the Reserve in August 1914, he was at once ordered to the Western Front, where he served during the fighting at Mons. He was also in action at the Battles of the Marne, Neuve Chapelle, Loos, the Somme and Cambrai, and was wounded and gassed in 1918. On his recovery he returned to the firing-line, and took part in the final Advance. He was discharged in March 1919, holding the Mons Star, and the General Service and Victory Medals.
43, Duke Street, Northampton. Z1423.

EALES, H., Bombardier, Royal Field Artillery.
Already in the Army in August 1914, he was immediately drafted to France, and was severely wounded and taken prisoner during the Retreat from Mons. After hospital treatment in Potsdam he was sent to Switzerland, whence he was repatriated in 1917. He was discharged as medically unfit in the same year owing to the loss of his left eye, and holds the Mons Star, and the General Service and Victory Medals.
King Street, Long Buckby, Northants. Z3309/A.

EALES, R., Sergt., 2nd K.O. (R. Lancaster Regt.)
Having enlisted in April 1907, he proceeded to the Western Front shortly after the outbreak of war, and there took a prominent part in the Battles of Ypres, Hill 60, Loos and Passchendaele, and other engagements. He was transferred in 1918 to Salonika, and there fought on the Struma and Doiran fronts, and contracted malaria. He was wounded whilst overseas, and was discharged on returning home in April 1919, holding the 1914 Star, and the General Service and Victory Medals.
145, St. Edmund's Road, Northampton. Z1910.

EALES, R. B., Private, Royal Sussex Regiment.
He joined immediately on attaining military age in July 1918, but was unsuccessful in obtaining his transfer overseas until after the cessation of hostilities. He then rendered valuable services with the Army of Occupation at Cologne until his demobilisation in February 1920.
King Street, Long Buckby, Northants. Z3309/B.

EALES, W. T., Sergeant, Royal Air Force.
A Territorial, he was mobilised in August 1914 with the Northamptonshire Regiment, and in June of the following year proceeded to Gallipoli, where he fought at Suvla Bay. Later, transferred to Egypt, he advanced into Palestine, and took a prominent part in the Battles of Gaza and the capture of Jerusalem. He afterwards served as a Sergeant-Instructor in the Royal Air Force, until discharged in March 1919, and holds the 1914–15 Star, and the General Service and Victory Medals. 24, Gladstone Terrace, Northampton. Z1148.

EARL, W., Sapper, Royal Engineers.
He volunteered in February 1915, and two months later sailed for France. Whilst on the Western Front he rendered valuable services with his unit on railway construction work in various sectors. In April 1918 he was invalided home with heart trouble, and was ultimately demobilised in March 1919, holding the 1914–15 Star, and the General Service and Victory Medals.
59, Abbey Road, Far Cotton, Northampton. Z3312.

EARLS, W., Bombardier, Royal Field Artillery.
Mobilised with the 3rd North Staffordshire Regiment (T.F.) at the outbreak of war he was later transferred to the Royal Field Artillery, and proceeded to France in February 1915. Whilst on the Western Front he was in action with his Battery during heavy fighting at Ypres, before being invalided home with shell-shock. After a period of hospital treatment, he was retained on important duties at Ripon. He was discharged in February 1919, and holds the 1914–15 Star, and the General Service and Victory Medals.
18, New Street, Weedon, Northants. Z2650.

EASON, A., Sapper, Royal Engineers.
Volunteering at the declaration of war, he was, in the following year, drafted to the Western Front, where he served during the Battles of Hill 60, Ypres, Festubert, Loos, Albert, Ploegsteert Wood, Vimy Ridge, the Somme and Arras before being wounded in April 1917 and invalided home. On his recovery he proceeded to Palestine, and was engaged on the lines of communication during the offensive under General Allenby. Demobilised in May 1919, he holds the 1914–15 Star, and the General Service and Victory Medals.
18, Countess Road, Northampton. Z2651.

EAST, E. W., 1st Class Stoker, Royal Navy.
He enlisted in 1913, and after the outbreak of war in August of the following year, served in H.M.S. "Venerable," attached to the Grand Fleet in the North Sea. Whilst in these waters he took part in the Battle of Jutland, the raid on Zeebrugge and many minor actions, afterwards serving off Constantinople. He holds the 1914–15 Star, and the General Service and Victory Medals, and in 1920 was still at sea.
19, Althorp Road, Northampton. Z2391

EAST, J., Driver, Royal Army Service Corps.
He volunteered in November 1915, and in the following year was drafted to Salonika, where he took an active part in numerous engagements on the Struma and the Vardar fronts. He rendered valuable services conveying rations to the forward areas, and was demobilised on his return to England in April 1919, holding the General Service and Victory Medals.
62, Hervey Street, Northampton. Z1424.

EASTLEIGH, A. E., Private, R.A.M.C.
Volunteering in January 1916, he received his training at Blackpool and Dover, but being medically unfit for active service was unable to obtain a transfer to the fighting area. Nevertheless, he did much valuable work fulfilling his duties as hospital Orderly at Lewisham and Bermondsey with the greatest ability. He was eventually demobilised in January 1919. Yew Cottages, Roade, Northants. Z2113/A.

EASTMENT, W., Private, Royal Defence Corps.
He volunteered in the Northamptonshire Regiment in September 1914, he was transferred to the East Surrey, the Royal West Surrey, the Middlesex and the Labour Corps, with which last-named unit he proceeded to France in October 1916, and did excellent work in various sectors for fourteen months. In January 1918 he was sent home to the Royal Defence Corps, and in the following October was discharged as medically unfit, holding the General Service and Victory Medals.
4, Gas Street, Northampton. Z2652.

EATON, A. H., Private, King's (Liverpool) Regt.
Three months after volunteering in April 1915, he was sent to the Western Front, where he was wounded at Loos in September and invalided home. He returned to France, however, in 1916, and took part in the Battles of the Somme, Arras, Ypres and Cambrai, and in the Retreat and Advance of 1918. He also served in the Middlesex and Manchester Regiments, and was demobilised in January 1919, holding the 1914–15 Star, and the General Service and Victory Medals.
60, Ethel Street, Northampton. Z1911.

EDGLEY, H., Private, 1st K.O. (Y.L.I.)
He joined in July 1916, and in the following January was ordered to Salonika, on which front he was engaged in severe fighting on the Doiran and the Struma. Contracting malaria, he was admitted to hospital, and on his recovery was transferred to the Royal Army Service Corps and drafted to France in June 1918. He was then attached to the Life Guards, and saw much service until the Armistice. Demobilised in August 1919, he holds the General Service and Victory Medals.
40, Manfield Road, Northampton. Z2126.

EDWARDS, A., Driver, Royal Engineers.
He volunteered in August 1915, but was retained at home for two years. Proceeding to the Western Front in September 1917, he saw heavy fighting at Lens, Cambrai, the Somme, Bullecourt, Béthune, Bapaume, the Scarpe, Havrincourt and Mons. After hostilities ceased he was sent to Germany with the Army of Occupation, and was eventually demobilised in May 1919, holding the General Service and Victory Medals.
39, Devonshire Street, St. James' End, Northampton. Z2654/C.

EDWARDS, D. (Miss), Member, V.A.D.
This lady volunteered her services to the V.A.D. in March 1918, and for twelve months was engaged on important duties at Catterick. During that time she performed very valuable work, and carried out her various duties in a highly efficient and satisfactory manner.
15, William Street, Northampton. Z1425.

EDWARDS, E., Private, Northamptonshire Regt.
Although only 18 years of age he volunteered in August 1914, and four months later embarked for the Western Front. Whilst in this theatre of war he was in action during fierce fighting at Ypres. He made the supreme sacrifice, being killed in action on January 6th, 1915, and was entitled to the 1914 Star and the General Service and Victory Medals.
"Honour to the immortal dead who gave their youth that the world might grow old in peace."
43, Abbey Road, Northampton. Z2653/B.

EDWARDS, F. J., Private, 2nd Northants. Regt.
Enlisting in 1908, he was stationed in Egypt in August 1914, but was immediately drafted to France and fought at Mons. He also took part in the Battles of the Marne, the Aisne, Ypres (I.) and (II.), before being unfortunately killed in action in the Loos sector on June 19th, 1915. He was entitled to the Mons Star, and the General Service and Victory Medals.
"A valiant Soldier, with undaunted heart he breasted life's last hill."
13, Brunswick Street, Northampton. Z3314.

EDWARDS, O., Private, Queen's (Royal West Surrey Regiment).
He joined in February 1917, and was quickly sent to France, where he rendered valuable services with the Labour Battalion of his unit whilst engaged on special pioneer work at Cambrai, and throughout the Retreat and Advance of 1918. After hostilities ceased he went to Germany with the Army of Occupation, and was ultimately demobilised in March 1919, holding the General Service and Victory Medals.
5, Weedon Road, Northampton. Z3313.

EDWARDS, W., Driver, Royal Field Artillery.
Volunteering in October 1915, he proceeded to France in the following year. Whilst in this theatre of war he was in action with his Battery during heavy fighting at La Bassée, Neuve Chapelle and Ploegsteert Wood. He also took part in the Battles of the Somme, Beaumont-Hamel, Vimy Ridge, Messines, Ypres (where he was gassed), Passchendaele, and the Retreat and Advance of 1918. Demobilised in March 1919, he holds the General Service and Victory Medals.
29, Devonshire Street, Northampton. Z2654/A.

EDWARDS, W., Gunner, Royal Field Artillery.
Having volunteered in October 1915, he landed in France in the following year. Whilst on the Western Front he saw much heavy fighting in the Somme and Ypres sectors. In November 1917 he was transferred to Italy, where he was in action on the Piave and Asiago Plateaux. Returning home for demobilisation in February 1919, he holds the General Service and Victory Medals. 39, Devonshire Street, Northants. Z2654/A.

EGAN, A. S. T. S., Gunner, R.G.A.
He joined in May 1917, and six months later was sent to France, where he was in action with his Battery at the Battles of Cambrai, the Somme (II.), Amiens, the Menin Road, Ypres and other important engagements during the Retreat and Advance of 1918. He was demobilised on his return home in February 1919, and holds the General Service and Victory Medals.
Kilsby, Northants. Z3315.

ELEY, W., Corporal, Royal Engineers.
He volunteered in August 1915, and after his training was retained on important duties in England until May 1918, and was then drafted to the Western Front. There he took an active part in the Battles of Cambrai and Le Cateau and other engagements in the Advance, and was awarded the Divisional Certificate for conspicuous bravery in the Field. Holding also the General Service and Victory Medals, he was demobilised in November 1919.
8, Little Cross Street, Northampton. Z1149.

ELLARD, J., Private, 1st Northants. Regiment.
Joining in May 1916, he embarked for the Western Front in the following September, and took part in heavy fighting in the Somme sector before being invalided home in March 1917. Returning to France later in the same year he was in action at the Battle of Ypres and Passchendaele. He died gloriously on the Field of Battle on November 15th, 1917, and was entitled to the General Service and Victory Medals.
"Whilst we remember, the sacrifice is not in vain."
13, Orchard Street, Drayton, Daventry, Northants. Z2655/B.

ELLIOTT, A., Private, R.A.M.C.
He volunteered in August 1914, and completing his training in the September of the following year was drafted to France. There he took part in several engagements, including the Battles of Loos, the Somme, Arras and Cambrai, and saw much fighting during the Retreat and Advance of 1918. He returned home and was demobilised in January 1919, holding the 1914–15 Star, and the General Service and Victory Medals.
83, Euston Road, Far Cotton, Northampton. Z3016/A.

ELLIOTT, A. G., Private, 4th Northants. Regt.
Having volunteered in October 1914, he was retained on important duties with his unit until April 1917. Proceeding to the Western Front he was in action at the Battles of Messines and Ypres, before being invalided home with trench fever. On his recovery he was transferred to Ireland and served with the Royal Defence Corps. Demobilised in January 1919, he holds the General Service and Victory Medals.
16, Orchard St., Drayton, near Daventry, Northants. Z2656.

ELLIOTT, G., Gunner, Royal Garrison Artillery.
He enlisted in 1917 and underwent a period of training prior to his being drafted to France. In this theatre of war he took part in many engagements, including those in the Ypres, Albert and Cambrai sectors, and in the Retreat and Advance of 1918. He also saw service at Poperinghe, and was eventually demobilised in March 1919, holding the General Service and Victory Medals. Gladstone Terrace, Gold St., Hanslope, Bucks. Z3017.

ELLIOTT, G. H. L., Gunner, R.G.A.
Volunteering in October 1915, he was sent to France after three months' training, and there saw severe fighting in various sectors. He took part in the Battles of the Somme, Arras and Ypres, and many other important engagements, and was gassed. He was demobilised on his return home in January 1919, and holds the General Service and Victory Medals.
9, Currie Road, Northampton. Z1309.

ELLIS, A., Private, Royal Inniskilling Fusiliers.
Joining in November 1916, he proceeded to France two months later, but after serving in the Somme sector, was sent to Salonika in March 1917, and fought on the Struma front. At the end of the year he was transferred to Palestine, where he was in action at Gaza and Beersheba before returning to France in June 1918. He was wounded at the second Battle of Cambrai in October and invalided to Brighton Hospital, whence he was discharged in February 1919, holding the General Service and Victory Medals.
32, Sand Hill Road, St. James, Northampton. Z2657.

ELLIS, A., Gunner, Royal Garrison Artillery.
Volunteering in August 1914, he was quickly drafted to France. Whilst on the Western Front he was in action with his Battery at the Battles of Ypres (I.), Festubert, and during fierce fighting at Loos. Transferred to Mesopotamia in February 1917 he took part in the capture of Baghdad, and also in the Occupation of Mosul. He was demobilised in August 1920, and holds the 1914 Star, and the General Service and Victory Medals.
60, Green Street, Northampton. Z2658.

ELLIS, G., Pte., 11th (Prince Albert's Own) Hussars.
Mobilised in August 1914, he was at once ordered to the Western Front and served in the Retreat from Mons. He also took an active part in the Battles of the Marne, the Aisne, Ypres, Neuve Chapelle, Vimy Ridge and the Somme, and did excellent work during the Retreat and Advance of 1918. Returning to England in January 1919, he was still serving in 1920, and holds the Mons Star, and the General Service and Victory Medals. 31, Vernon Terrace, Northampton. Z2127.

ELLIS, J. W. F., Private, Machine Gun Corps.
He joined in April 1916, and completing his training in the following year was drafted to France, where he took part in many engagements, including those at Ypres, Passchendaele, and on the Somme. Contracting trench fever he was invalided home, but on his recovery returned to France, whence he proceeded to Italy, and remained there until his demobilisation in February 1919. He holds the General Service and Victory Medals. Church Street, Brixworth, Northants. Z3018.

ELLIS, R. H., Private, 1/4th Northants. Regiment.
Mobilised with the Territorials in August 1914, he was retained at various stations, where he was engaged on duties of great importance. He was unable to obtain his transfer overseas, but, nevertheless, did much useful work with his unit until demobilised in February 1919. He re-enlisted, however, in the following June and was employed on exhumation duties in France until finally demobilised in July 1920.
33, Gladstone Terrace, Northampton. TZ1150.

ELMS, A., Driver, Royal Field Artillery.
Joining in March 1916, he proceeded to the scene of activities in France in the following year. During his service on the Western Front he fought in numerous notable engagements, including the Battle of the Somme, and was also in action in the German Offensive and Allied Advance of 1918. He remained in France until February 1919 when he was demobilised, holding the General Service and Victory Medals.
95, Cedar Road, Northampton. Z2128.

ELSTON, F. K. (Miss), Worker, Q.M.A.A.C.
She joined in November 1917, and shortly afterwards was sent to France, where she was stationed at Le Havre for two years. During that time she was engaged on important duties which she carried out with the utmost efficiency, and rendered valuable services until demobilised in November 1919. She holds the General Service and Victory Medals.
5, Market Street, Northampton. Z2129/B.

ELSTON, T. (jun.), Pte., R. Warwickshire Regt.
Volunteering in January 1915 he received his training in Ireland, and was drafted overseas in February 1916. Serving on the Western Front he saw severe fighting in the Loos and Albert sectors, and took an active part in the Battles of Arras, Vimy Ridge, Messines, Ypres, Cambrai, the Somme, the Aisne, Havrincourt, Epéhy and the Sambre. He was demobilised in February 1919, and holds the General Service and Victory Medals. 5, Market Street, Northampton. Z2129/A.

ELSTON, T., Private, 6th Northants. Regiment.
When war was declared in August 1914 he volunteered, and in the following January embarked for France. On that front he was engaged in fierce fighting at the Battles of Neuve Chapelle, St. Eloi, Hill 60, Ypres, Festubert, Loos, Albert, Vimy Ridge, Ploegsteert Wood, the Somme, Beaumont-Hamel, Arras, Cambrai, the Aisne, the Marne, Amiens and Havrincourt. Serving in France until January 1919, he was demobilised ten months later, holding the 1914–15 Star, and the General Service and Victory Medals. 5, Market St., Northampton. Z2129/C.

EMERTON, R. N., Private, Royal Defence Corps.
Unable to serve in a combatant unit he volunteered in the Royal Defence Corps in April 1915, and for nearly two years was engaged on special guard duties in various parts of England. He rendered valuable services until March 1917, when he was discharged. 3, Newcombe Road, Northampton. Z2659/B.

EMERTON, W. T., Pte., 10th King's Liverpool Regt.
Volunteering in April 1915 in the Northamptonshire Dragoons, he proceeded in the following year to France, where he took part in many engagements in various sectors of the front. Evacuated to England, he was transferred to the Liverpool Scottish, returned to France on his recovery, and was in action in the Ypres sector. He was unhappily killed on January 5th, 1918, and was entitled to the General Service and Victory Medals. "His life for his Country, his soul to God."
3, Newcombe Street, Northants. Z2659/A.

EMERY, J. G., Rifleman, Royal Irish Rifles.
He joined in October 1916, and three months later was drafted to France, where he was in action at the Battles of Bullecourt, Messines and Ypres (III.). Badly wounded in August 1917, he was in hospital in England for twelve months, and on his recovery served in Ireland until his demobilisation in March 1919, holding the General Service and Victory Medals.
18, Horse Shoe Street, Northampton. Z3376/C.

EMERY, W. C., C.S.M., Tank Corps.
He was serving in India at the outbreak of war, but was quickly drafted to the Western Front, and was first engaged on important secret service duties. He afterwards played a prominent part in the Battles of Albert, Arras, Vimy Ridge, Bullecourt, Messines, Ypres, Béthune and in the Retreat and Advance of 1918, and was wounded in action. Discharged in January 1919, he holds the 1914–15 Star, and the General Service and Victory Medals. 19, Tanner Street, Northampton. Z2660.

EMERY, W. P., Private, 7th Northants. Regiment.
He enlisted in the 4th Northamptonshire Regiment in 1913, and at the outbreak of war was retained for a time at various home stations before proceeding with the 7th Battalion to France in 1916. He took part in many engagements, including the Battles of the Somme, Arras, Vimy Ridge, Ypres, Messines and Cambrai, and also saw heavy fighting in the Retreat and Advance of 1918. Discharged in March 1919, he holds the General Service and Victory Medals.
1, Tanner Row, Northampton. Z3019.

ENFIELD, I. (Mrs.), Special War Worker.
For nearly 3½ years of the war this lady was engaged on work of National importance at the Northampton Post Office Employed as a post-woman, she thereby released a man for service with the Colours, and did much good work until her discharge in September 1919.
18, Fort Street, Northampton. Z1151/A.

ENFIELD, S., Gunner, Royal Field Artillery.
He volunteered in November 1915, and five months later was ordered to the Western Front. There he did good work with his Battery in the Armentières sector, and was gassed at Delville Wood and again at Ypres in 1917. He was invalided to England, and on his discharge from hospital was retained on home service until demobilised in April 1919, holding the General Service and Victory Medals.
18, Fort Street, Northampton Z1151/B.

ENGLAND, A. (jun.), Sergt., 1/4th Northants. Regt.
At the outbreak of war he volunteered, and embarking for Gallipoli, in April 1915, was wounded during the Landing on the Peninsula. He was sent to hospital in Alexandria, and on his recovery served in Egypt until drafted to Palestine. There he played a conspicuous part in engagements at Gaza, Jerusalem, Jaffa and Haifa. He was demobilised on his return to England in May 1919, and holds the 1914–15 Star, and the General Service and Victory Medals.
39, Essex Street, Northampton. Z1310/A.

ENGLAND, A. (sen.), Pte., 6th Northants. Regt.
He was called up from the Reserve in August 1914, and in July of the following year crossed to France. On that front he fought in the Battles of the Somme, Arras, Ypres, Cambrai, St. Quentin, Amiens and Mons, and did good work with his unit in the operations during the Retreat and Advance of 1918. After the Armistice he served with the Army of Occupation on the Rhine, until discharged in March 1919, holding the 1914–15 Star, and the General Service and Victory Medals.
39, Essex Street, Northampton. Z1310/B.

ENGLAND, O. C., L/Cpl., 1/4th Northants. Regt.
He volunteered in May 1915, and in April of the following year proceeded to Egypt and advanced thence into Palestine. There he took part in the capture of Haifa and in other engagements, and also fought in General Allenby's Offensive of September 1918, and contracted malaria. He was demobilised on returning home in July 1919, and holds the General Service and Victory Medals. 31, Vernon Street, Northampton. Z1912.

ENTWISTLE, E., Sergeant, 1/4th Northants. Regt.
Volunteering in October 1914, he was first engaged as an Instructor of recruits. Later he attained the rank of Quartermaster-sergeant, but afterwards reverted to sergeant in order to give lectures on the use of gas in modern warfare. He rendered valuable services in this capacity at Newmarket, and was eventually demobilised in February 1919.
West End Street, West Haddon, Northants. Z3317.

ESPINER, F., Private, 12th Lancers.
Already in the Army in August 1914, he at once proceeded to France and fought at Mons. He was also in action at the Battles of the Marne, the Aisne, Ypres, Neuve Chapelle and Cambrai, before being sent to Ireland in January 1918. He remained there on important duty for three years, and received his discharge in January 1921, after 18 years with the Colours. He holds the Mons Star, and the General Service and Victory Medals. King's Lane, Flore, Northants. Z2661

ESSAM, A. H., 1st Class Stoker, Royal Navy.
He joined in May 1918, and on completion of his training was sent to H.M.S. "Myrtle," in which ship he was engaged in minesweeping duties in Russian waters. Acting in a similar capacity in the North Sea in H.M.S. "Carnation," he rendered valuable services until discharged as medically unfit in December 1919. He holds the General Service and Victory Medals.
4, Balfour Road, Northampton. Z1311/A.

ESSAM, B., Private, 4th Yorkshire Regiment.
Joining in May 1916, he underwent a period of training, and in the following year embarked for the Western Front. In the course of his service in this theatre of war he took part in the Battles of Cambrai (I.), the Somme (II.) and the Aisne (III.). He made the supreme sacrifice, being killed in action in May 1918, and was entitled to the General Service and Victory Medals.
"A valiant Soldier, with undaunted heart he breasted life's last hill."
6, Bristol Street, Northampton. Z1666/D.

ESSAM, G., Private, Royal Sussex Regiment.
He joined in August 1916, and after training at Colchester, was drafted to the Western Front a year later. After only about a month's active service, he was killed in action in September 1917 during heavy fighting around Lens. He was entitled to the General Service and Victory Medals.
"Thinking that remembrance, though unspoken, may reach him where he sleeps."
6, Bristol Street, Northampton. Z1666/B.

ESSAM, R., Private, Suffolk Regiment.
After joining in February 1916, he completed a period of training and in the same year was drafted to France. Whilst in this seat of operations he was in action with his unit on the Somme and Ancre fronts. He was unfortunately killed on November 1st, 1916, and was entitled to the General Service and Victory Medals.
"The path of duty was the way to glory."
6, Bristol Street, Northampton. Z1666/C.

ESSAM, W., Sergeant, Rifle Brigade.
Volunteering in October 1914, he was engaged in the important work of training recruits at Northampton for over two years. Owing to his age he was unable to take part in actual fighting, but rendered valuable services conducting drafts to the Western Front until May 1918, when he was discharged. He holds the General Service and Victory Medals.
4, Balfour Road, Northampton. Z1311/B.

ETTE, A., Rifleman, Rifle Brigade.
He joined in May 1918, and four months later was drafted to the Western Front, but owing to his age did not participate in any actual fighting. During his 12 months' service overseas, however, he was engaged on duties of an important nature at various prisoner of war camps in France, and performed much valuable work until demobilised in September 1919. He holds the General Service and Victory Medals.
42, Somerset Street, Northampton. Z1426/A.

EVANS, C. H., Trooper, Northants. Dragoons.
Volunteering in November 1914, he was retained on important duties with his unit before being drafted to France in January 1916. In this seat of operations he was in action at the Battles of Ploegsteert Wood, Vermelles, Vimy Ridge, Ypres, Lens, Cambrai, and in the Retreat and Advance of 1918. Whilst overseas he also served with the 7th Northamptonshire Regiment, was three times wounded—in March, August and November 1918, and in March 1919 was demobilised, holding the General Service and Victory Medals.
18, York Place, Northants. Z2663.

EVANS, F. A., Driver, Royal Field Artillery.
Volunteering in October 1915, he underwent a period of training before being drafted to France. Whilst in this theatre of war he took part in many important engagements in various sectors of the front. He was in action with his Battery at the Battles of Arras, Ypres, Cambrai, the Somme, and also in the Retreat and Advance of 1918. Demobilised in February 1919, he holds the General Service and Victory Medals.
37, Melbourne Street, Northampton. Z1913.

EVANS, H., R.S.M., Middlesex Regiment.
Already in the Army in August 1914, he was immediately drafted to the Western Front, where he served with distinction at the Battle of, and in the Retreat from, Mons, and also at the Battles of Le Cateau, the Marne, La Bassée and Ypres. He was then sent to England, and engaged as an Instructor, in which capacity he rendered excellent services until discharged in 1920, holding the Mons Star, and the General Service and Victory Medals. 14, Alma Street, Northants. Z2665.

EVANS, W. C., Private, 2/1st Oxfordshire and Buckinghamshire Light Infantry (T.F.)
Having volunteered in November 1915, he underwent a period of training, and in the following year proceeded to France, where he saw much heavy fighting. He was in action with his unit on the Armentières, the Somme, Arras and Ypres fronts, and died gloriously on the Field of Battle on August 23rd, 1917. He was entitled to the General Service and Victory Medals.
"And doubtless he went in splendid company."
Park Road, Hanslope, Bucks. Z2664.

EVANS, W. G., Private, Leicester Regiment.
Volunteering in January 1915, he was sent to France twelve months later, and whilst on the Western Front was in action with his unit in many important engagements. Badly gassed in February 1917 he was invalided home, and unfortunately died from the effects of gas-poisoning in February 1920. He was entitled to the General Service and Victory Medals.
"His name liveth for evermore."
7, Freeschool Street, Northampton. Z2662.

EVERITE, S. H., Cpl., 1st & 6th Northants. Regt.
He joined in April 1916, and after a period of training was drafted to the Western Front, where he experienced severe fighting in various sectors of the line. He took a prominent part in the operations on the Somme and in other engagements of note, and was wounded in action on four occasions. Demobilised in March 1920, he holds the General Service and Victory Medals. 35, Gladstone Terrace, Northampton. Z1152/A.

EYERS, W., Pioneer, Royal Engineers.
Volunteering in August 1914, he embarked a year later for Gallipoli, where he served at Suvla Bay, Chocolate Hill, and in the subsequent engagements of the campaign. After the Evacuation he was sent to Palestine, but was wounded at Gaza in April 1917, and invalided to England. On his recovery he was drafted to France in August 1918, and took an active part in the Advance at Amiens and Ypres. Demobilised in April 1919, he holds the 1914–15 Star, and the General Service and Victory Medals.
17, Lower Harding Street, Northampton. Z1153.

EYLES, C., Driver, Royal Army Service Corps.
Mobilised at the declaration of war, he crossed to France in September 1914 and fought in the Retreat from Mons. He was also present at the Battles of the Marne, the Aisne and Ypres, and gave his life for the freedom of England on the Somme on October 22nd, 1918. He was entitled to the Mons Star, and the General Service and Victory Medals.
"A costly sacrifice upon the altar of freedom."
23, Lower Priory Street, Northampton. Z1154/B.

EYLES, O., Private, Royal Fusiliers.
He joined in February 1917, and after two months' training was drafted to the Western Front, where he saw severe fighting in various sectors. He took part in the Battles of Arras, Vimy Ridge, Messines, Ypres and the Somme, and other engagements, and also served through the Retreat and Advance of 1918. Demobilised in March 1919, he holds the General Service and Victory Medals.
18, Marlborough Road, Northampton. Z2392.

EYRE, J. T., Private, Bedfordshire Regiment.
He volunteered in the Royal Army Service Corps in November 1915, and on being transferred to the Bedfordshire Regiment was drafted overseas in September 1917. Serving on the Western Front, he was in action at the Battles of Cambrai and the Somme, and gave his life for King and Country at Amiens on August 14th, 1918. He was entitled to the General Service and Victory Medals.
"His memory is cherished with pride."
25, Deal Street, Northampton Z1427/A.

F

FACER, C. W., 2nd Lieutenant, Manchester Regt.
Volunteering in the Ranks in August 1914, he first saw heavy fighting in German West Africa, but was sent to France in November 1916. After taking a prominent part in many important engagements in various sectors, he came to England for his commission and rendered valuable services until he returned to Africa for his demobilisation in April 1919, holding the 1914–15 Star, and the General Service and Victory Medals.
Prospect Place, Long Buckby, Northampton. Z3318.

FACER, E. C., Private, Royal Army Medical Corps.
He volunteered in September 1914, and early in the following year was sent to France, where he took part in the Battles of St. Eloi, Albert, Vimy Ridge, Ploegsteert Wood, the Somme, Arras and other important engagements, before being badly wounded in action. He was invalided to hospital in Kent, and was eventually demobilised in February 1919, holding the 1914–15 Star, and the General Service and Victory Medals.
7, Kettering Gardens, Northampton. Z3319.

FACER, P. W., L/Corporal, 7th Northants. Regt.
After volunteering in September 1915, he was ordered to the Western Front, where he served for over three years. During that time he fought in the Battles of Vermelles, Vimy Ridge, the Somme, Messines, Ypres, Passchendaele, Amiens and Bapaume, and did good work with his unit during the Retreat and Advance of 1918. He was demobilised in February 1919, and holds the 1914–15 Star, and the General Service and Victory Medals
29, Wantage Road, Northampton. Z2130.

FAIRBROTHER, H. E., Pte., 6th Leicester Regt.
He joined in July 1916, and in the following year was drafted to the Western Front, where he took part in the Battles of Ypres, Cambrai and the Somme (II.). In 1917 he was wounded in action, but after a period of hospital treatment, returned to the line and saw further heavy fighting. He was demobilised in February 1919, and holds the General Service and Victory Medals.
Church Hill, Wootton, Northants. Z2666/B.

FAIRBROTHER, J. F., L/Corporal, R.E. (R.O.D.)
Joining in March 1916, he was drafted to the Western Front later in the same year, and rendered valuable services with the Railway Operative Department. He was chiefly engaged in the construction of railways and bridges in various sectors. Demobilised on returning home in April 1919, he holds the General Service and Victory Medals.
Water Lane, Wootton, Northants. Z2666/A.

FAIREY, C. H., Trooper, 2nd Northants. Dragoons.
Having volunteered in November 1914, he underwent a period of training, and was then engaged on important duties at Towcester. He did excellent work with his unit until March 1915, when he was found to be medically unfit for further military service, and was accordingly discharged.
31, Newcombe Road, Northampton. Z2667.

FAIRY, J. W., Private, R.N.D. (Hood Battalion).
Volunteering in October 1914 he proceeded to Egypt four months later and took part in engagements on the Suez Canal. In April 1915, he was sent to Gallipoli, where he was in action at Krithia and Achi-Baba, serving on the Peninsula until the Evacuation. In April 1916, he was drafted to France, and after fighting in the Battles of the Ancre and Havrincourt, was wounded and taken prisoner at Ypres. He was released from captivity in December 1918, and three months later was demobilised, holding the 1914–15 Star, and the General Service and Victory Medals.
25, Leicester Street, Northampton. Z1312/B.

FALKNER, P. J., Private, 7th Northants. Regt.
He volunteered in August 1914, and in September of the following year embarked for the Western Front. There he was in action at Loos, St. Eloi, Albert, Vermelles, Ploegsteert Wood, Vimy Ridge and the Somme, but was unhappily killed at Messines on June 17th, 1916. He was entitled to the 1914–15 Star, and the General Service and Victory Medals.
"Whilst we remember, the sacrifice is not in vain."
32, Collingwood Street, Northampton. Z2131.

FARMER, A. S., Private, 4th Sussex Regiment.
He enlisted in March 1917, and having completed his training later in the same year, was drafted to France, where he saw much heavy fighting in the Ypres and Somme sectors, and was badly wounded in October 1917. As a result he was invalided home to hospital, and later retained on important duties until his demobilisation in February 1919. He holds the General Service and Victory Medals.
Main Road, Old Duston, Northants. Z3022/A.

FARMER, E. W., Private, K.O. (Y.L.I.)
Having joined in January 1917, he was drafted overseas later in the same year. During his service on the Western Front he took part in much heavy fighting in the Somme and Cambrai sectors, and was badly wounded in August 1918. In consequence he was invalided home, and on his recovery retained at various stations until his demobilisation in January 1919. He holds the General Service and Victory Medals.
Main Road, Old Duston, Northants. Z3022/B.

FARMER, F. W., L/Cpl., 1st Seaforth Highlanders.
Already serving in India in August 1914, he proceeded to France in October, and wounded at La Bassée in the following month, was sent to hospital at Boulogne and later at Gravesend. Returning to the Western Front in March 1915, he was again wounded at Serre in October and a third time at Beaumont-Hamel in July 1916, when, having sustained the loss of a leg, he lay for eight days before being discovered. Invalided from the Army in February 1918, he holds the 1914 Star, and the General Service and Victory Medals.
49, Ambush Street, St. James, Northampton. Z2393.

FARMER, H. C., Gunner, Royal Field Artillery.
He volunteered shortly after the outbreak of war in August 1914, and on completion of a period of training in September of the following year was drafted to the Western Front, where he saw much severe fighting. He fell in action in October 1915, only a month after landing in France, and was entitled to the 1914–15 Star, and the General Service and Victory Medals.
"His life for his Country, his soul to God."
9, Lincoln Road, Northampton. Z3320/B.

FARMER, H. F., L/Cpl., 4th Worcestershire Regt.
Volunteering in September 1914, he proceeded to Gallipoli in the following June and saw severe fighting at Achi-Baba and Chocolate Hill. Transferred later to Egypt, he was sent thence to France, where after taking part in the Battles of the Somme and Ypres, he served with the Royal Engineers (R.O.D.) at various stations. He was demobilised in May 1919, and holds the 1914–15 Star, and the General Service and Victory Medals.
9, Lincoln Road, Northampton. Z3320/C.

FARMER, J., Private, Northants. Regiment.
Called up from the Reserve in August 1914, he was immediately sent to the Western Front, where after fighting in the Battle of, and the Retreat from, Mons, he took part in the Battles of the Marne, the Aisne, La Bassée, Ypres and Neuve Chapelle. He fell in action at Nieuport on June 26th, 1916, and was entitled to the Mons Star, and the General Service and Victory Medals.
"He nobly fell that we might live"
9, Lincoln Road, Northampton. Z3320/A.

FARMER, W., Private, Worcestershire Regiment.
He volunteered in the Leicester Regiment in July 1915, and proceeding to France, saw much severe fighting until wounded in action. On his recovery he was sent to Egypt, but after a period of service there was transferred to Italy with the Worcester Regiment, and took part in important engagements on the River Piave front. He was demobilised in May 1919, and holds the General Service and Victory Medals.
11, North Street, Daventry, Northants. Z2668.

FARROW, H. S., Private, 6th Northants. Regt.
He enlisted in May 1916, and was quickly drafted to France, where he took part in much heavy fighting and was wounded in action. As a result he was invalided home, but on his recovery returned to France, and was again in action. Later he was severely wounded and invalided to Rouen, where he unfortunately died on April 16th, 1917. He was entitled to the General Service and Victory Medals.
"A valiant Soldier, with undaunted heart he breasted life's last hill."
171, Southampton Road, Far Cotton, Northampton. Z3023/B.

FARROW, R., Rifleman, Rifle Brigade.
Having joined in May 1917, he underwent a period of training prior to his being drafted to France in April 1918. In this theatre of war he took part in much heavy fighting in the Vimy Ridge, Havrincourt and Cambrai sectors. He did good work throughout his service, and was demobilised in November 1919, holding the General Service and Victory Medals.
171, Southampton Road, Far Cotton, Northampton. Z3023/A.

FAULKNER, B., Private, East Yorkshire Regt.
He volunteered in November 1915, and, proceeding to the Western Front in September of the following year, saw severe fighting at Poperinghe. He was also in action in the Battles of the Ancre, Arras and Cambrai, and in many other engagements of note. After the Armistice he proceeded into Germany with the Army of Occupation, serving at Duren until demobilised in August 1919, and holds the General Service and Victory Medals. 30, Gladstone Terrace, Northampton. TZ1156.

FAULKNER, E. (Miss), Worker, Q.M.A.A.C.
She joined in August 1917, and after a period of service at Hastings was drafted to France later in the same year. Whilst overseas she was engaged on important clerical duties, which she fulfilled with the greatest ability. She remained in France until May 1919, when she was demobilised, holding the General Service and Victory Medals.
11, Purser Road, Northampton. Z2132/C.

FAULKNER, G., Private, 5th Northants. Regt.
He volunteered in September 1914, and early in 1915 was drafted to France. Whilst in this theatre of war he took part in many engagements, including those in the Ypres, Hill 60, Loos, the Somme and Arras sectors, and in the Advance of 1918. He was slightly wounded in action and eventually demobilised in April 1919. He holds the 1914–15 Star, and the General Service and Victory Medals.
Church Street, Brixworth, Northampton. Z3024.

FAULKNER, G., Sergt., 1st D. of Cornwall's L.I.
A Reservist, he was called to the Colours in August 1914, and played a prominent part in the Battles of the Marne, the Aisne and other important engagements. He was transferred to Italy in November 1917, but two months later returned to France, and after serving through the Retreat, was unhappily killed in action near Albert at the commencement of the Advance, on August 21st, 1918. He was entitled to the 1914 Star, and the General Service and Victory Medals.
"His name liveth for evermore."
12, York Place, Weston Street, Northampton. Z2669.

FAULKNER, H., Private, 2nd Suffolk Regiment.
Joining in June 1916, he completed his training at Felixstowe, and crossed to France four months later. Whilst serving on the Western Front he was engaged in severe fighting in the Ypres sector, and was wounded on the Somme in 1917. He was invalided to England, and on his discharge from hospital at Derby was retained on home service until demobilised in March 1919. He holds the General Service and Victory Medals.
2, Kinburn Place, Northampton. Z1043/B.

FAULKNER, J., Private, 4th Northants. Regt.
He volunteered in June 1915, and was retained on special duties at various home stations. Unable to obtain his transfer overseas owing to medical unfitness, he rendered valuable services with his unit, but after a period of hospital treatment at Sutton was invalided from the Army in March 1918.
50, Stanley Road, Northampton. Z2670.

FAULKNER, J. G., Private, 36th Royal Fusiliers.
He joined in June 1916, and shortly afterwards proceeded to the Western Front, where he was engaged on various duties, including trench-digging and road-making. During his service in France he also took part in the Battles of the Somme, Ypres and Cambrai, and fought in the Retreat of 1918. He was demobilised on his return to England in September 1919, and holds the General Service and Victory Medals.
Stoke Road, Blisworth, Northampton. Z2133.

FAULKNER, S. O. R., Private, 33rd Royal Fusiliers
He volunteered in January 1916, and after a period of training was ordered overseas in the following April. During his service in France he did good work with his unit in many important engagements, including the Battles of the Somme, Arras, Vimy Ridge and Lens. On his return to England he was demobilised in September 1919, and holds the General Service and Victory Medals. 10, Mill Road, Semilong, Northampton. Z1157

FAULKNER, T., Private, 12th Royal Fusiliers.
Volunteering in September 1914, he proceeded to France 11 months later, and took part in the Battles of Loos, the Somme, Messines, Ypres and Cambrai. He was admitted to hospital at Oxford suffering from heart trouble and was ultimately discharged after a period of convalescence in March 1919, holding the 1914–15 Star, and the General Service and Victory Medals. 51, Sand Hill Road, Northampton. Z2671.

FAULKNER, W. S., Private, Machine Gun Corps.
He volunteered in the Royal Army Service Corps in January 1915, and on being transferred to the Rifle Brigade was sent to France in September 1915, and served at Le Havre, Ypres and Cambrai. Subsequently he was attached to the Machine Gun Corps, and after taking an active part in operations on the Somme, was gassed and invalided to England. He was discharged as medically unfit for further service in January 1919, and holds the 1914–15 Star, and the General Service and Victory Medals.
5, Chaucer Street, Kingsley Park, Northampton. Z1155.

FAVELL, H. G., Corporal, 5th Northants. Regt.
At the outbreak of war in August 1914 he volunteered, and in the following year embarked for France. On that front he saw heavy fighting in the Armentières sector, and took an active part in the Battles of Ypres, Festubert, Loos, the Somme, Arras, Passchendaele and Cambrai, and was gassed in 1917. Demobilised in March 1919, he holds the 1914–15 Star, and the General Service and Victory Medals.
15, Alliston's Gardens, Northampton. Z1158.

FEAREY, P. E., Gunner, Royal Garrison Artillery.
He volunteered in November 1914, and on completion of his training was ordered in the following year to the Western Front. There he was in action in the Battles of the Somme, Arras, Ypres and Cambrai, and many other engagements, and did excellent work as a gunner in the Retreat and Advance of 1918. He was demobilised in March 1919, and holds the 1914–15 Star, and the General Service and Victory Medals.
15, Stanley Street, Northampton. Z1159/C.

FELCE, R. E., Private, Machine Gun Corps.
He joined in June 1917, and in December was drafted to the Western Front, where he took part in heavy fighting at Ypres, and was wounded. He was reported missing during the second Battle of the Somme in March 1918, and is now presumed to have been killed in action. He was entitled to the General Service and Victory Medals.
"A costly sacrifice upon the altar of freedom."
16, Baring Road, Northampton. Z2672.

FELL, M. F., Sister, Territorial Force Nursing Service.
Having previously been trained as a nurse, she was called up at the outbreak of war, and was retained in London until December 1915, when she proceeded to Malta. After three months' service there she was transferred to France, where she did excellent work in various sectors until the cessation of hostilities. Demobilised in July 1919, she holds the Royal Red Cross, awarded for devotion to duty, and the General Service and Victory Medals.
Old Manor House, Kilsby, Northants. Z3321/B.

FELLS, B. N., Lieut., 5th Worcestershire Regt.
Joining in 1917, he proceeded to the Western Front later in the same year, and there saw severe fighting in various sectors. He took a distinguished part in the Battles of Ypres and Passchendaele and other engagements, and was wounded. Granted a commission for distinguished services in the Field, he holds the General Service and Victory Medals, and was demobilised in 1920. 4, Park View, Northampton. Z3322/C.

FELLS, H. J., Private, 13th London Regiment.
He volunteered in May 1915, and, after a period of training, proceeded to Egypt, whence he advanced into Palestine. There he took part in the Battles of Gaza and the capture of Jerusalem, and also saw severe fighting in General Allenby's Offensive of September 1918. He contracted malaria, and on returning home in 1919 was demobilised, holding the General Service and Victory Medals.
4, Park View, Northampton. Z3322/B.

FELLS, W. J. F., Sergeant, 13th London Regt.
Volunteering in July 1915, he afterwards proceeded to France, but, after seeing much severe fighting, was transferred to Salonika and thence to Egypt. Proceeding into Palestine, he took a prominent part in many important engagements, serving under General Allenby. Demobilised on his return home in 1919, he holds the General Service and Victory Medals.
4, Park View, Northampton. Z3322/A.

FENN, J. A. (M.M.), Cpl., 9th Norfolk Regiment.
Joining in January 1916, he completed a period of training and was retained on important duties with his unit at various stations before proceeding to the Western Front in March 1918. In this theatre of war he did consistently good work, and was in action in the Somme sector before being wounded and invalided home. He was awarded the Military Medal for distinguished bravery and devotion to duty in the Field, and was demobilised in December 1919, also holding the General Service and Victory Medals.
22, Thenford Street, Northampton. Z1914.

FENN, L. W., L/Corporal, Royal Field Artillery.
Having attested under the Derby Scheme, he was called to the Colours in January 1917, and, after completing a period of training, was transferred to the Royal Army Ordnance Corps, and drafted to Salonika in July 1917. Whilst in this seat of operations he took part in many important engagements until the cessation of hostilities, and was in hospital at Monastir with malaria. He then proceeded to Russia, thence to Constantinople, where he was engaged on important duties. Demobilised in December 1919, he holds the General Service and Victory Medals. 14, Whitworth Road, Northampton. Z1915/A.

FENN, R. A., Air Mechanic, Royal Air Force.
Having previously been rejected four times, he joined in March 1918, and completed a period of training before proceeding to Egypt. In this theatre of war he was engaged on important duties with his Squadron, and served at various stations. He did continuously good work, and in January 1920 was demobilised, holding the General Service and Victory Medals.
14, Whitworth Road, Northampton. Z1915/B.

FIDDY, A. E. (M.S.M.), Q.M.S., 1st Northants. Regt.
A serving soldier, he proceeded to France in August 1914, and fought at Mons. After taking a prominent part also in the Battle of the Marne, and minor engagements, he was severely wounded on the Aisne, and admitted to hospital at Newcastle. He was afterwards retained as Orderly Room Clerk at Northampton until his discharge in June 1920. He was awarded the Meritorious Service Medal for continuously good work, and holds also the Queen's and King's South African Medals, the Mons Star, and the General Service, Victory and Long Service, and Good Conduct Medals.
10, Wimbledon Street, Northampton. Z2394.

FIELD, G. L., Private, 1/4th Northants. Regiment.
Mobilised with the Territorials in August 1914, he was sent to the Dardanelles in June of the following year, but unfortunately suffered from frost-bite. He was later transferred to Egypt and thence to Palestine, where he was severely wounded in the Battle of Gaza and contracted dysentery. He unhappily died on November 27th, 1917, and was entitled to the 1914–15 Star, and the General Service and Victory Medals.
"The path of duty was the way to glory."
5, Chapel Gardens, Northampton. Z3323.

FIELD, J. G., Private, 5th Northants. Regiment.
Volunteering in September 1914, he proceeded to the Western Front in May of the following year and there, after taking part in the Battles of Ypres, Loos, the Somme, Arras and Cambrai, he was wounded in April 1918, and sent to hospital at Etaples. Returning to the line, however, he was again in action until invalided home on account of an accident in August 1918. Demobilised in February 1919, he holds the 1914–15 Star, and the General Service and Victory Medals.
109, Euston Road, Northampton. Z3025.

FIELD, T., Private, 22nd Manchester Regiment.
Joining in June 1917, he was sent to France in the following September, and fought in the Battles of Cambrai (I.), the Somme (II.) and the Aisne (III.). In March 1918 he was drafted to Italy, but after serving on the Piave front his health broke down, and he was invalided home, where he unfortunately died on March 8th, 1920. He was entitled to the General Service and Victory Medals.
"His memory is cherished with pride."
49, Market Street, Northampton. Z2134/A.

FIELDING, J., Driver, R.A.S.C.
Shortly after volunteering in November 1914, he crossed to the Western Front, and saw heavy fighting in various sectors. He was principally engaged in conveying supplies and ammunition to the Somme, Arras, Ypres, Passchendaele and Cambrai fronts. On the cessation of hostilities he passed into Germany with the Army of Occupation, and was eventually demobilised in January 1919, holding the 1914–15 Star, and the General Service and Victory Medals.
5, Knight's Lane, Kingsthorpe, Northampton. Z1160.

FINCH, J. F., Private, Machine Gun Corps.
He joined in 1917, and was soon drafted to India, where he rendered valuable services with his unit whilst engaged on important garrison duties at various stations. He suffered from malarial fever during his stay in the East, and was eventually demobilised in 1919, holding the General Service and Victory Medals. 29, Alma Street, Northampton. Z2673.

FINEDON, J. W., Private, 4th Beds. Regiment.
He joined in March 1917, trained at Felixstowe, and two months later was sent to the Western Front. After fighting in numerous engagements in the Somme sector, he died gloriously on the Field of Battle at Arras in August 1918. He was entitled to the General Service and Victory Medals.
"A valiant Soldier, with undaunted heart he breasted life's last hill."
118, Scarletwell Street, Northampton. Z1161.

FISHER, A. H., Private, 1/4th Northants. Regt.
He volunteered in October 1914, but was retained on special duties in England for 15 months. In January 1916, he was sent to Egypt, and later advanced into Palestine, where he was in action at the Battles of Rafa and Gaza, and during the Offensive of General Allenby's Forces. He was demobilised in July 1919, and holds the General Service and Victory Medals.
17, Devonshire Street, St. James' End, Northampton. Z2674.

FISHER, A. T., Private, 7th Northants. Regiment
He volunteered in September 1914, and 12 months later was drafted to France. There he took part in the Battles of Loos, the Somme, Vimy Ridge, Messines and Ypres (III.), where he was wounded in 1917. On his recovery he was transferred to the 25th King's Royal Rifle Corps (Pioneer Battalion), with which Regiment he served until his demobilisation in January 1919. He holds the 1914–15 Star, and the General Service and Victory Medals.
60, Abbey Road, Far Cotton, Northampton. Z3324/A.

FISHER, C. J., Rifleman, King's Royal Rifles.
Having volunteered in May 1915, in the Royal Army Service Corps, he completed his training and was retained on important duties with his unit. Later, however, he was transferred to the King's Royal Rifle Corps, and proceeded to the Western Front, where he was in action at the Battles of the Somme (II.), Havrincourt, Epéhy, Cambrai (II.) and Ypres (IV.). He did continuously good work, and in February 1919 was demobilised, holding the General Service and Victory Medals.
2, East Street, Northampton. Z1916.

FISHER, E. G., Pte., Royal Army Service Corps.
He volunteered in August 1914, and after a period of training was retained on special duties at various home stations. He was unsuccessful in obtaining his transfer overseas, but rendered valuable services as a baker until October 1919, when he was taken seriously ill and died at his home in Dallington.
"His memory is cherished with pride."
8, Baring Road, Northampton. Z2615/A.

FISHER, M., Private, M.G.C. (Cavalry).
He volunteered in the Bedfordshire Lancers in November 1915, but was later transferred to the City of London Lancers, serving in Ireland until 1916, when he was drafted to Egypt. Later he was sent to Palestine, and after taking part in engagements at Gaza, Jerusalem and Jericho, was ordered to France. On that front he was transferred to the Machine Gun Corps, and fought in the Retreat and Advance of 1918. Demobilised in February 1919, he holds the General Service and Victory Medals. 42, Alcombe Road, Northampton. Z1428/A.

FISHER, W., Private, 2nd Northants. Regt.
He enlisted in November 1916, and in the following January was drafted to France. In this theatre of war he took part in many engagements, including the Battles of the Somme and Passchendaele, where he was badly wounded. As a result he was invalided home to hospital, and finally discharged in August 1918 as medically unfit for further service. He holds the General Service and Victory Medals.
60, Abbey Road, Far Cotton, Northampton. Z3324/B.

FISHER, W. E., Private, Machine Gun Corps.
Joining in November 1916, he proceeded a year later to the Western Front, and there saw heavy fighting in various sectors. Whilst in action in the Retreat of 1918 he was severely wounded and taken prisoner, and unhappily succumbed to his injuries whilst in captivity on May 3rd, 1918. He was entitled to the General Service and Victory Medals.
"Whilst we remember, the sacrifice is not in vain."
42, Alcombe Road, Northampton. Z1428/B.

FITCHETT, H. S., Pte., 4th Northants. Regiment.
He joined in July 1916, and in the following December embarked for France. On that Front he was engaged in fierce fighting in the Armentières, Arras and Ypres sectors, but was reported missing on July 10th, 1917, and was subsequently presumed to have been killed on that date. He was entitled to the General Service and Victory Medals.
"His life for his Country, his soul to God."
54, St. Mary's Street, Northampton. Z1162/A.

FITCHETT, J., Pte., 1/4th Northants. Regiment.
Volunteering in September 1914, he completed his training, and, proceeding to Gallipoli, was in action at Suvla Bay. Later he contracted malaria, and was sent to Alexandria, and when returning to England was on H M.H.S. "King George" when she was torpedoed in the Mediterranean, but fortunately was rescued. In 1917 he was drafted to France, and fought in the Battles of Ypres and Cambrai, and in the Retreat and Advance of 1918. Unfortunately he contracted pneumonia, to which he succumbed on November 9th, 1918. He was entitled to the 1914–15 Star, and the General Service and Victory Medals.
"The path of duty was the way to glory."
54, St. Mary's Street, Northampton. Z1162/C.

FITCHETT, J. W., Sergeant, 170th Overseas Battalion, Canadian Forces.
He volunteered in Canada in May 1915, and on his arrival in England five months later was stationed at Regents Park and employed on important postal duties. In July 1916 he was drafted to the Western Front, where he was employed in a similar capacity in the Rouen, Arras and Ypres sectors until the close of hostilities. After rendering invaluable services he wa demobilised in March 1919, holding the General Service and Victory Medals.
54, St. Mary's Street, Northampton. Z1162/B.

FITZHUGH, E., Sapper, Royal Engineers.
Volunteering in August 1915, he completed his training, and was then employed as a musketry Instructor at Maidenhead until sent to France in March 1917. Whilst on the Western Front he was engaged in severe fighting at Monchy, Arras, Vimy Ridge, Ypres, Zillebeke and Cambrai, but was seriously wounded at Gouzeaucourt in February 1918, which unhappily resulted in the loss of his left arm and leg. He was sent to England for treatment, and invalided out of the Army in March 1919, holding the General Service and Victory Medals.
28, Monk's Pond Street, Northampton. Z1313.

FITZHUGH, G. T., Private, Northants. Regiment.
He volunteered in the Northamptonshire Regiment in July 1915, but owing to ill-health was not successful in obtaining a transfer overseas. On the completion of his training he was transferred to the Royal Air Force, and engaged on duties of an important nature as an air mechanic at various stations, until discharged as medically unfit for further service in September 1917. 6, Arthur St., Kingsthorpe Hollow, Northampton. Z1314.

FITZHUGH, G. W., Sapper, Royal Engineers.
He enlisted in January 1916, and after a period of training was engaged at various stations in England and Ireland on important duties with his unit. He was unable to obtain a transfer overseas owing to his being medically unfit, but rendered valuable services until his demobilisation in September 1919.
Cogenhoe, Northants. Z3325/B.

FLANAGAN, W., Private, 4th Northants. Regt.
He volunteered in 1914, and was ultimately sent to France, where he saw much severe fighting. He was in action at the Battles of the Somme, Arras and Ypres, and rendered valuable services as a signaller, but was unfortunately killed at Cambrai in 1918. He was entitled to the General Service and Victory Medals.
"Great deeds cannot die."
35, Alma Street, Northampton. Z2675.

FLAVELL, C. F., Corporal, 3rd Grenadier Guards.
Called up from the Reserve in August 1914, he was retained in England until 1916, and engaged on important duties. Whilst on the Western Front he took part in many engagements, including that of Ypres, where he was badly wounded in January 1917. As a result he was invalided home and eventually discharged in 1919, holding the General Service and Victory Medals. 18, The Banks, Long Buckby, Northants. Z3326.

FLEMING, J. F., Corporal, Royal Engineers.
Having previously served in the South African War, he volunteered in March 1915, and three months later was drafted to France, where he was engaged as a mining-engineer on important duties in the Ypres, Loos, Festubert and Givenchy sectors. He was unhappily killed by the explosion of a German mine on July 1st, 1916, and was entitled to the 1914–15 Star, and the General Service and Victory Medals.
"He nobly fell that we might live."
Rosetree Cottage, Bugbrooke, Northants. Z3272/A.

FLETCHER, C. P., Rifleman, 8th London Regt. (Post Office Rifles).
He volunteered in September 1915, and six months later was sent to the Western Front, where he served in various sectors. After taking part in the Battles of Vimy Ridge and the Somme, he was wounded at Flers in September 1916, and invalided to England. In consequence he was discharged as medically unfit for further service in May 1917, and holds the General Service and Victory Medals. 89, Ivy Road, Northampton. Z2135.

FLETCHER, H., Trooper, 4th Dragoon Guards.
He volunteered in September 1914, and was quickly drafted to France, where he took part in the Battles of Ypres and Hill 60, but, contracting an illness, was consequently invalided home. In 1916 he returned to France and served on the Somme, but was again sent home. Later he was transferred to the Royal Engineers, and engaged on important duties in France until his demobilisation in May 1919. He holds the 1914–15 Star, and the General Service and Victory Medals.
Counsel Cottage, Kilsby, Northants. Z3327.

FLIPPANCE, G., Pte., 7th Wiltshire Regiment.
When war broke out he volunteered, and in 1915 was drafted to France, and there fought in the Battles of Vimy Ridge, the Somme, Arras, Bullecourt and Lens. In 1917 he was transferred to Salonika, on which front he was in action on the Doiran and the Vardar, until sent back to the Western theatre of war in 1918. After taking part in engagements at Amiens, he was wounded at Cambrai and admitted to hospital in Rouen. He was demobilised in March 1919, and holds the 1914–15 Star, and the General Service and Victory Medals. 9, Pine St., Northants. Z1315.

FLOWER, W., Pte., 2nd Dragoons (R. Scots Greys).
He joined in May 1916, and underwent a period of training prior to his being drafted to France in the following December. He took part in many engagements, but was unfortunately killed in action near Ypres on October 22nd, 1917. He was entitled to the General Service and Victory Medals.
"A valiant Soldier, with undaunted heart he breasted life's last hill."
14, Henley Street, Far Cotton, Northampton. Z3328.

FLYNN, H. P., Private, 12th (Prince of Wales' Own Royal) Lancers.
Mobilised in August 1914, he at once proceeded to the Western Front, and took part in the fighting at Mons. He was also in action at the Battles of the Marne, the Aisne, La Bassée, Ypres, Neuve Chapelle, Loos, the Somme, Passchendaele and Cambrai, did good work with his unit during the Retreat and Advance of 1918, and was wounded on one occasion. After the Armistice he proceeded into Germany with the Army of Occupation, serving at Cologne until discharged in March 1919. He holds the Mons Star, and the General Service and Victory Medals.
73, Essex Street, Northampton. Z1316.

FOLWELL, A., Private, 53rd Bedfordshire Regt.
He joined immediately on attaining military age in September 1918, and after a period of training was retained on important duties at various stations. He was unable to obtain his transfer overseas before the cessation of hostilities, but in March 1919 was sent with the Army of Occupation to Germany. He was demobilised on returning home in April 1920.
90, Spencer Bridge Road, St. James, Northampton. Z2999/C.

FOLWELL, F. G., Private, 1st Northants. Regt.
At the outbreak of war he was already serving, and was at once ordered to the scene of activities in France. On that front he took an active part in severe fighting, and died gloriously on the Field of Battle at Moulins on September 17th, 1914. He was entitled to the 1914 Star, and the General Service and Victory Medals.
" He died the noblest death a man may die:
Fighting for God and right and liberty."
6, Pine Street, Northampton. Z1359/B.

FORBES, A. E., Private, 1st Bedfordshire Regt.
Mobilised at the declaration of war, he was drafted to the Western Front with the first Expeditionary Force, and fought in the Retreat from Mons. After taking an active part in the Battles of the Marne and the Aisne he gave his life for the freedom of England at the Battle of Ypres in November 1914. He was entitled to the Mons Star, and the General Service and Victory Medals.
" Nobly striving:
He nobly fell that we might live."
19, Kinburn Place, Northampton. Z1163/B.

FORD, W. T., Private, 9th Suffolk Regiment.
He volunteered in January 1915, and after completing a course of training was sent to the Western Front in August 1916. After only a month's active service he was unhappily killed whilst engaged in severe fighting on the Somme. He was entitled to the General Service and Victory Medals.
" Honour to the immortal dead who gave their youth that the world might grow old in peace."
11, Francis Street, Northampton. Z1164/A.

FORREST, R. G., Driver, Royal Field Artillery.
He joined in November 1916, and in April of the following year was drafted to the Western Front, where he took part in the Battles of Arras, Vimy Ridge and Ypres, and minor engagements. He was sent home in July 1917 suffering from nephritis, and in February of the following year was invalided from the Army. He holds the General Service and Victory Medals.
135, Adnitt Road, Northampton. Z2395.

FORSKITT, H., Corporal, 2nd Northants. Regt.
Volunteering in March 1915, he embarked for the Western Front in the following year and fought in engagements at Armentières. He was also in action at the Battles of the Somme, Arras, Vimy Ridge, Ypres and Cambrai, and in the Retreat and Advance of 1918 Serving in France until demobilised in March 1919, he holds the General Service and Victory Medals.
87, Perry Street, Northampton. Z2136.

FOSTER, A., Private, 4th Yorkshire Regiment.
He volunteered in September 1914, and a year later was drafted overseas. Whilst serving on the Western Front he was engaged in fierce fighting in many engagements, including the Battle of the Somme, and was wounded and gassed. In May 1918 he was taken prisoner and held in captivity until hostilities ceased. On his release he returned home, and was demobilised in January 1919, holding the 1914–15 Star, and the General Service and Victory Medals.
47, East Street, Northampton. Z2137/B.

FOSTER, A. E., Corporal, 11th Cheshire Regt.
A month after the outbreak of war he volunteered, and in September 1915 embarked for the Western Front. There he was in action in numerous important engagements, including the Battles of the Somme, Arras, Vimy Ridge and Messines, but was severely wounded at Ypres in July 1917. In consequence he was invalided out of the Army five months later, holding the 1914–15 Star, and the General Service and Victory Medals. 36, Craven Street, Northampton. Z1317.

FOSTER, C., Sapper, Royal Engineers.
He enlisted in April 1916, and later in the same year was drafted to the Western Front. There he was engaged on important duties in connection with bridge-building and mine-laying in the Somme, Ypres and Cambrai sectors, and in the Retreat of 1918. He did excellent work, and was demobilised in February 1919, holding the General Service and Victory Medals.
School House Lane, Lower Heyford, Northants. Z3329/B.

FOSTER, G. H. P., Private, Army Cyclist Corps.
He volunteered in the Northamptonshire Regiment in September 1914, but was later transferred to the Army Cyclist Corps and drafted to Gallipoli. There he was in action at Suvla Bay and in the subsequent engagements of the campaign. After the Evacuation he proceeded to Egypt, and after serving on the Suez Canal, was sent to Palestine, where he saw heavy fighting until the close of hostilities. He was demobilised on his return to England in June 1919, and holds the 1914–15 Star, and the General Service and Victory Medals.
36, Craven Street, Northampton. Z1318.

FOSTER, J., Rifleman, Rifle Brigade; and Trooper, East Riding of Yorkshire Lancers.
He joined in August 1917, and after completing a period of training in Norfolk was drafted to Ireland, where he was engaged on duties of an important nature, which he fulfilled in a very able manner. He was not successful in obtaining a transfer to a theatre of war, but, nevertheless, rendered valuable services until demobilised in December 1919.
32, Leicester Street, Northampton. Z1319/D.

FOSTER, W., Private, Middlesex Regiment.
Joining in September 1918, he was unsuccessful in obtaining a transfer to the war zone before the Armistice, owing to the early cessation of hostilities. In November 1918, however, he was ordered to France, and advanced into Germany with the Army of Occupation, rendering valuable services until sent to England for demobilisation in December 1919.
47, East Street, Northampton. Z2137/A.

FOSTER, W. C., Private, 1/4th Northants. Regt.
Four months after joining in August 1916 he was drafted to Egypt, but later advanced in Palestine, and after serving at Rafa, Gaza and Jerusalem, was taken prisoner by the Turks in 1917. Whilst in captivity he was forced to work on the railways, and was in hospital for some time owing to severe attacks of dysentery. In September 1918 he was released as an exchanged prisoner, and was demobilised in February 1919, holding the General Service and Victory Medals.
52, Sand Hill Road, Northampton. Z2676.

FOUNTAIN, C. J., Driver, R.A.S.C.
He volunteered in November 1915, and was almost immediately drafted to France. During his service on the Western Front he was engaged on important duties with the transport conveying supplies to the forward areas. He was slightly wounded on one occasion, and demobilised in August 1919, holding the 1914–15 Star, and the General Service and Victory Medals.
West Haddon, Rugby, Northants. Z3330/A.

FRADLEY, W. H., Private, 21st Middlesex Regt.
He joined in July 1917, and on completion of his training was drafted to the Western Front in the following November. Shortly afterwards he was severely wounded whilst fighting in the Battle of Cambrai, and unhappily succumbed to his injuries on November 29th, 1917. He was entitled to the General Service and Victory Medals.
" His life for his Country, his soul to God."
18, Allen Road, Northampton. Z2105/A.

FRANKLIN, A., Private, Duke of Cornwall's L.I.
Mobilised when war was declared in August 1914, he immediately embarked for the Western Front, and served in the engagements at Mons. He also experienced fierce fighting at the Battle of the Aisne, but was unhappily killed in action at La Bassée on October 21st, 1914. He was entitled to the Mons Star, and the General Service and Victory Medals.
" Thinking that remembrance, though unspoken, may reach him where he sleeps."
22 Adelaide Street, Northampton. Z1165/A.

FRANKPITT, A., Private, 7th Northants. Regt.
Volunteering in September 1914, he underwent a period of training before being drafted to the Western Front, where he saw heavy fighting in various sectors. He was in action with his unit at the Battles of Ploegsteert Wood and at Guillemont, on the Somme, where he was unfortunately killed on August 17th, 1916. He was entitled to the 1914–15 Star, and the General Service and Victory Medals.
" Whilst we remember, the sacrifice is not in vain."
8, Brunswick Place, Northampton Z1843/B.

FREEMAN, A., Private, Royal Fusiliers.
Joining in September 1916, he was trained at Dover, and six months later embarked for the Western Front. There he was in action in numerous engagements, but was reported missing on May 3rd, 1917, and subsequently was presumed to have been killed in action on that date. He was entitled to the General Service and Victory Medals.
" He nobly died that we might live."
7, Roe Road, Northampton. Z2138.

FREEMAN, A. C. (Miss), Special War Worker.
This lady joined the Land Army in April 1915, and was engaged on important agricultural work in various parts of England. Throughout the period of her service she performed valuable work, and carried out her responsible and arduous duties in a highly efficient manner. She was demobilised in March 1919. 1, Nelson Street, Northampton. Z1320.

FREEMAN, C. E., Sapper, Royal Engineers.
He volunteered in January 1916, and a month later proceeded to France, where he was engaged on important work in the engineering shops. In 1918, however, his health broke down, and he was invalided to England, but on his recovery, rendered valuable services with the Railway Operative Department at Longmore until demobilised in November 1919. He holds the General Service and Victory Medals.
23, Brunswick Street, Northampton. Z1429

FREEMAN, E. H., Bombardier, R.G.A.
Joining in April 1916, he was engaged on important work at home until May 1918, when he obtained a transfer overseas. During his service on the Western Front he did good work with his Battery in the operations during the Retreat and Advance, and was gassed in November 1918. He was admitted to hospital at Le Havre, and on his recovery returned to England, and was demobilised in February 1919, holding the General Service and Victory Medals.
30, Clare Street, Northampton. Z1431/A.

FREEMAN, F., Corporal, Royal Engineers.
When war broke out he was stationed in Malta, having enlisted in September 1908, but was recalled and drafted to the Western Front in November 1914. He took an active part in numerous important engagements in various sectors, and was wounded in action on one occasion. He also did good work with his Battery in Italy, and after the cessation of hostilities was ordered to India, where in 1920 he was still serving. He holds the 1914 Star, and the General Service and Victory Medals.
79, Cloutsham Street, Northampton. Z1430/A.

FREEMAN, F., Corporal, 1st Northants. Regt.
Enlisting in January 1911, he was mobilised in August 1914, and immediately proceeded to the scene of activities in France. On that front he was in action in several engagements, and died gloriously on the Field of Battle on the Aisne in September 1914. He was entitled to the 1914 Star, and the General Service and Victory Medals.
"Whilst we remember, the sacrifice is not in vain."
79, Cloutsham Street, Northampton. Z1430/B.

FREEMAN, G., Private, 7th Bedfordshire Regt.
Mobilised in August 1914, he was drafted to the Western Front a month later, and served in the Battles of the Marne, Ypres, Neuve Chapelle, Loos and Albert. He was wounded whilst engaged in fierce fighting on the Somme in July 1916, and again at Thiepval two months later. In consequence he was invalided out of the Army in May 1917, and holds the 1914 Star, and the General Service and Victory Medals.
13, Lower Harding Street, Northampton. Z1166.

FREEMAN, H. J. G., Driver, R.A.S.C.
He volunteered in November 1915, and in August of the following year was drafted to Salonika. In that theatre of war he was in action in numerous important engagements, and saw heavy fighting on the Doiran, the Vardar, the Struma and Monastir fronts. In 1918 he contracted malaria, and on his recovery was sent to Russia, where he served at Batoum until sent home for demobilisation in September 1919. He holds the General Service and Victory Medals.
9, Whitworth Road, Northampton. Z2139/B—Z2140/B.

FREEMAN, J. E., Private, 1st Northants. Regt.
Mobilised in August 1914, he was immediately ordered to France and fought in the Retreat from Mons. He was also in action at the Battles of the Marne, Ypres and Loos, and was wounded on the Somme in 1916, and invalided to England. On his recovery he returned to the Western Front, and took an active part in operations at Arras and Cambrai, and in the Retreat and Advance of 1918. He was still serving in 1920, and holds the Mons Star, and the General Service and Victory Medals. Roade, Northants. Z2141.

FREEMAN, P., Sapper, Royal Engineers.
At the outbreak of war he was mobilised, and immediately proceeded to the Western Front with the first Expeditionary Force. Whilst engaged in severe fighting in the Battle of Mons he was wounded, and subsequently taken prisoner. During his captivity he was very badly treated owing to the fact that he refused to make munitions for the enemy. On his release he was discharged in March 1919, and holds the Mons Star, and the General Service and Victory Medals.
9, Whitworth Road, Northampton. Z2139/A—Z2140/A.

FREEMAN, R., 2nd Lieut., Northants. Regiment.
Volunteering in June 1915 he proceeded to France in September and played a prominent part in the Battles of Loos, the Somme, Vimy Ridge, Messines and Ypres (III.). He also served with distinction at St. Elci and Hooge, and in March 1918 returned home for his commission. He was eventually demobilised in January 1919, and holds the 1914–15 Star and the General Service and Victory Medals.
18, Raymond Road, St. James, Northampton. Z2677.

FREEMAN, T., Private, R.A.S.C.
Volunteering in November 1914, he was drafted to France four months later, and rendered valuable services with the Remount Section. He was engaged on important duties at Albert, Arras and on the Somme, before proceeding to Italy, where he served on the Piave, and at various other places. Demobilised in February 1919, he holds the 1914–15 Star, and the General Service and Victory Medals.
109, Green Street, Northampton. Z2678.

FREER, A. W., Private, 1st Northants. Regiment.
When war was declared in August 1914 he was mobilised from the Reserve, and at once proceeded overseas with the first Expeditionary Force. Whilst on the Western Front he fought in the Retreat from Mons, and the Battle of the Marne, but was unhappily killed in action on the Aisne in September 1914. He was entitled to the Mons Star, and the General Service and Victory Medals.
"A costly sacrifice upon the altar of freedom."
60, Craven Street, Northampton. Z1321/B.

FREESTONE, A. E., Cpl., R. Warwickshire Regt.
Mobilised in August 1914, he was stationed at Chatham, and employed on important instructional duties until June 1917, when he secured a transfer overseas. Serving on the Western Front, he was in action in many engagements in the Ypres and Poperinghe sectors, and was wounded at Ypres in November 1917. He was discharged in March 1919, and holds the General Service and Victory Medals.
3, House, 2, Court, Chalk Lane, Northampton. Z1167

FREESTONE, T., Private, 7th Northants. Regt.
Having previously served in the Grenadier Guards before the war, he re-enlisted in August 1914, and, proceeding to the Western Front in 1915, was wounded in action at Loos. On his return to the firing-line he took part in many engagements, and gave his life for King and Country at the Battle of the Somme on November 7th, 1916. He was entitled to the 1914–15 Star, and the General Service and Victory Medals.
"Great deeds cannot die."
7, Pine Street, Northampton. Z1322/B.

FROST, A. E., Sergeant, 4th Northants. Regt.
Volunteering in April 1915, he was drafted overseas in the following year. Whilst on the Western Front he played a prominent part in many engagements, including those in the Somme, Beaumont-Hamel and Messines sectors. Later he rendered valuable services with the Chinese Labour Corps, and was eventually discharged in August 1919 as medically unfit for further duty. He holds the General Service and Victory Medals. 47, Abbey Rd., Far Cotton, Northampton. Z3332/A.

FROST, B. J., Corporal, 1st Northants. Regiment.
Already in the Army at the outbreak of war, he was quickly drafted to France, where he took part in the Retreat from Mons and the Battles of the Marne, the Aisne, Neuve Chapelle and Festubert. He made the supreme sacrifice, being killed in action at Aubers Ridge on May 9th, 1915, and was entitled to the Mons Star, and the General Service and Victory Medals.
"His life for his Country, his soul to God."
47, Abbey Road, Far Cotton, Northampton. Z3332/B.

FROST, E., Private, 4th Northants. Regiment.
Mobilised in August 1914, he was quickly drafted to the Western Front, where he saw much heavy fighting for nearly three years. He took part in the Battles of the Somme, Arras and Ypres, but was unhappily killed in action on July 31st, 1917. He was entitled to the 1914–15 Star, and the General Service and Victory Medals.
"And doubtless he went in splendid company."
33, Brook Street, Daventry, Northants. Z2679.

FROST, J. H., Sapper, Royal Engineers.
He enlisted in June 1916, and, completing his training in the following November, was drafted to France. In this theatre of war he did continuously good work with the Royal Engineers, and took part in the Battles of Ypres, Passchendaele and Cambrai. After the Armistice he proceeded to Germany, and served with the Army of Occupation until his demobilisation in April 1919. He holds the General Service and Victory Medals.
22, Purcer Road, Northampton. Z3331.

FROST, W. J., Private, R.A.S.C. (M.T.)
Volunteering in May 1915, he completed his training, and later in the same year crossed to France. In that theatre of war he saw much service in the Somme, Arras, Ypres and Cambrai sectors, and was engaged on important transport duties on various fronts. He was demobilised in March 1919, and holds the 1914–15 Star, and the General Service and Victory Medals.
23, Little Cross Street, Northampton. Z1168.

FRYER, J., Private, Machine Gun Corps.
He volunteered in the 12th York and Lancaster Regiment in May 1915, but later was transferred to the Machine Gun Corps and drafted to France in January 1916, and was wounded in the Battle of the Somme six months later. On his recovery he was sent to Mesopotamia, on which front he took an active part in many engagements of note, until hostilities ceased. He was demobilised on his return to England in December 1919, and holds the General Service and Victory Medals.
24, Chalk Lane, Northampton. Z1169.

FULLON, M., Pte., 10th York and Lancaster Regt.
He joined in January 1917, and on conclusion of his training in the following September was ordered to the Western Front. There he saw much service in various sectors, and was wounded at Ypres in October 1917. On his recovery he returned to the firing-line, fought in the Battle of the Somme and other important engagements, until the termination of the war. Demobilised in November 1919, he holds the General Service and Victory Medals.
20, Upper Harding Street, Northampton. Z1116/A.

FULTON, R. E. C., Air Mechanic, R.A.F.
Joining in January 1917, he was engaged on duties of a highly technical nature at various home stations. He was unable to secure a transfer overseas before the close of hostilities, but in 1919 was drafted to France, where he served at St. Omer. Subsequently he proceeded to Germany, and did valuable work with the Army of Occupation until demobilised in January 1920.
39, Bective Road, Kingsthorpe, Northampton. Z1170.

G

GADSBY, W., Seaman, Mercantile Marine Reserve.
He joined in November 1917, and during hostilities rendered valuable services. He was engaged on dangerous mine-sweeping duties in the North Sea, in the Gun-boat "N.E. 52," on special work with the "Q" Mystery Ship "Hydrabad," and also on transport duties in the "London Bell" to North Russia, Alexandria, Gibraltar and New York. Demobilised in February 1919, he holds the General Service and Mercantile Marine War Medals. Water Lane, Wootton, Northants. Z2682 A.

GADSBY, W. A., Private, 1st Northants. Regiment.
Already in the Army in August 1914, he quickly proceeded to France and fought in the Battles of the Aisne, La Bassée and Ypres (I.). In February 1915 he was invalided home with trench feet, but in August returned to France, and served at Loos before being transferred to the Royal Air Force. He was then engaged as a millwright at Farnborough until discharged in December 1919, holding the 1914 Star, and the General Service and Victory Medals.
Water Lane, Wootton, Northants. Z2682/B.

GADSBY, W. J., Private, 1/4th Northants. Regt.
Volunteering in August 1914, he was sent to Gallipoli in the following April and saw heavy fighting at the Cape Helles and Suvla Bay Landings. After the Evacuation of the Peninsula he proceeded to Egypt, but, advancing into Palestine, was in action at Gaza and Jaffa. He was demobilised in March 1919, and holds the 1914–15 Star, and the General Service and Victory Medals. Water Lane, Wootton, Northants. Z2682/C.

GAMBLE, J., Private, East Surrey Regiment.
He volunteered in November 1915, and in the following year proceeded to France, where he took part in several engagements, including the Battles of Ypres, Passchendaele and Cambrai. Later he was transferred to Italy and saw much fighting on the Piave, and was wounded in action. He returned home, and was demobilised in March 1919, holding the General Service and Victory Medals. 3, Hunter Street, Northampton. Z1432.

GAMMAGE, E. A., Private, Northants. Regiment.
He volunteered in August 1914, and, completing his training in the following January, was drafted to France. There he took part in much fighting at Neuve Chapelle, Aubers Ridge, Loos, the Somme and Trônes Wood, where he was wounded in action in August 1916. He was eventually discharged in July 1918, and holds the 1914–15 Star, and the General Service and Victory Medals. 48, Silver Street, Northampton. Z1171/A.

GAMMAGE, J., Private, Black Watch.
Volunteering in 1915, he proceeded to France on the completion of his training and fought in numerous engagements until taken prisoner during the German Offensive of March 1918. He unfortunately died whilst in captivity on the following November 18th, and was entitled to the General Service and Victory Medals.
"His memory is cherished with pride."
Kilsby, Northants. Z3333.

GAMMAGE, S., Private, 2nd Suffolk Regiment.
He joined in May 1916, and underwent a period of training prior to his being drafted to France. In this seat of war he took part in engagements at Bullecourt, Ypres and Arras, where he was taken prisoner. He was held in captivity behind the German lines, being forced to work on labour duties. Released after the Armistice he returned home, and was demobilised in March 1919, holding the General Service and Victory Medals.
91, Baker Street, Northampton. Z1172.

GAMMAGE, T. F., Private, 51st Royal Fusiliers.
He joined in July 1918, immediately on attaining military age, and after a period of training was awaiting to be drafted overseas when the Armistice was signed. He did excellent work with his unit until February 1919, when he was demobilised in order to take up his studies.
68, Harlestone Road, St. James, Northampton. Z2683.

GAMMONS, W., Private, 1st Northants. Regiment.
Mobilised in August 1914, he was quickly drafted to France, where he first served with the Royal Army Service Corps. He was engaged on important transport work, conveying supplies and ammunition to the forward areas throughout hostilities. Later he was transferred to the 1st Northamptonshire Regiment, and in 1921 was still serving. He holds the Mons Star, and the General Service and Victory Medals.
20, Bath Street, Northampton. Z1039/B.

GARDINER, T. B., Driver, Royal Engineers.
He volunteered in September 1914, and was drafted to Egypt in the following February. He was in action at Mersa Matruh, Agagia, Sollum, Jifjaffa, Katia and El Fasher, and in September 1916 was invalided home. Subsequently he was discharged in January 1918, and holds the General Service and Victory Medals. Blythewood, Weedon Road, Northampton. Z3465.

GARDNER, E. D., Private, 7th Middlesex Regt.
He enlisted in February 1917, and three months later was drafted to France, where he took part in the Battles of Arras and Bullecourt, before being wounded in 1917. As a result he was invalided home, but on his recovery proceeded to Salonika, and saw much fighting on the Vardar front. Demobilised in July 1919, he holds the General Service and Victory Medals.
46, Colwyn Road, Northampton. Z1434.

GARDNER, F., Private, 1st Northants. Regiment.
He was called up from the Reserve in August 1914, and immediately drafted to the Western Front, where he fought in the Battle of, and the Retreat from, Mons, and the Battle of the Marne. He died gloriously on the Field of Battle on the Aisne on September 14th, 1914, and was entitled to the Mons Star, and the General Service and Victory Medals.
"A valiant Soldier, with undaunted heart he breasted life's last hill."
13, Alpha Street, Northampton. Z1323.

GARDNER, F., Private, 7th Lincolnshire Regt.
He enlisted in February 1917, and later in the same year was drafted to the Western Front. In this theatre of war he took part in several engagements, including the Battles of the Somme, Ypres, Albert and Mericourt Wood, being twice wounded in action. He was demobilised in May 1919, and holds the General Service and Victory Medals.
8, Kinburn Place, Northampton. Z1173/A.

GARDNER, H., Sapper, R.E. (R.O.D.)
Joining in August 1916, he was drafted to the Western Front in the same year and served at Albert, the Somme, Arras, Ypres and Cambrai. He also took part in the Retreat and Advance of 1918, and returning to England was demobilised in March of the following year, holding the General Service and Victory Medals.
Church End, Bugbrooke, Northants. Z3334.

GARDNER, J., Staff-Sergeant, R.A.M.C.
He volunteered in October 1914, but was retained on important work at home until March 1916, when he was sent to France. There he rendered valuable services in the Ypres and Albert sectors, but was himself wounded whilst bringing in the wounded under heavy shell-fire, and unfortunately succumbed to his injuries on September 4th, 1916. He was entitled to the General Service and Victory Medals.
"Great deeds cannot die."
15, Artizan Road, Northampton. Z2142/C.

GARDNER, P. G. T., Pte., East Yorkshire Regt.
He volunteered in August 1914, and in the following year was drafted to France, where he took part in several engagements, including the Battles of Loos, the Somme and Ypres (III.). He made the supreme sacrifice, being killed in action on August 1st, 1917, and was entitled to the 1914–15 Star, and the General Service and Victory Medals.
"Whilst we remember, the sacrifice is not in vain."
8, Kinburn Place, Northampton. Z1173/C.

GARDNER, R. J., Private, 7th Middlesex Regt.
He joined in February 1917, and was quickly drafted to France. In this theatre of war he took part in several engagements, including the Battles of Vimy Ridge, Passchendaele and the Somme (II.), but contracting trench fever in July 1918 was invalided to hospital at Rouen. Demobilised in 1919, he holds the General Service and Victory Medals.
46, Colwyn Road, Northampton. Z1433.

GARDNER, S. A., Driver, Royal Field Artillery.
Joining in March 1917, he was drafted overseas three months later. During his service on the Western Front he took part in much fighting at Ypres, Vimy Ridge, Passchendaele, Cambrai and in the Advance of 1918. After the cessation of hostilities he proceeded to Germany with the Army of Occupation and served on the Rhine until his demobilisation in October 1919. He holds the General Service and Victory Medals.
8, Norfolk Street, Northampton. Z1324.

GARDNER, T. A., Leading Seaman, Royal Navy.
When war was declared in August 1914, he was already serving, and proceeding to the North Sea was in action in several engagements. He was serving with his ship off the coast of Cromarty when she was sunk by a submarine with all hands on board on December 30th, 1915. He was entitled to the 1914–15 Star, and the General Service and Victory Medals.
"Thinking that remembrance, though unspoken, may reach him where he sleeps."
15, Artizan Road, Northampton. Z2142/B.

GARDNER, W., Private, 4th Northants. Regiment.
Volunteering in May 1915, he received his training at Wellington and Peterborough, but before he could obtain his transfer overseas he was taken ill and admitted to hospital in Northampton. After only eight months' service he unfortunately died on January 15th, 1916.
"His memory is cherished with pride."
15, Artizan Road, Northampton Z2142/A.

GARDNER, W., Rifleman, Rifle Brigade.
He joined in September 1918 on attaining military age, and underwent a period of training at Northampton and Aldershot. After hostilities ceased he was drafted to India, and whilst stationed at Quetta, was engaged on important garrison duties. In 1921 he was still serving.
8, Kinbnrn Place, Northampton. Z1173/B.

GARDNER, W., Private, 1st Northants. Regiment,
Already in the Army in August 1914, he was soon sent to France and fought at Mons. He also took part in the Battles of the Marne, the Aisne and Ypres, where he was wounded in November. After hospital treatment in England he returned to the Western Front, but after being in action at Loos and on the Somme, was buried alive and wounded. As a result he was again sent home, and ultimately discharged as medically unfit in April 1917, holding the Mons Star, and the General Service and Victory Medals.
Eve's Cottage, Wootton, Northants. Z2684.

GARDNER, W. H. (M.M.), Gunner, R.G.A.
He volunteered in May 1915, and in September 1916 was drafted overseas. Serving on the Western Front he fought in the Battles of Arras, Messines, Ypres, Passchendaele, Cambrai and the Somme, and did good work as a gunner in the Retreat and Advance of 1918. He was awarded the Military Medal in that year for conspicuous bravery in carrying Despatches under heavy shell-fire. Demobilised in December 1919, he also holds the General Service and Victory Medals.
41, Henry Street, Northampton. Z2143.

GARDNER, W. J., Sapper, R.E. (R.O.D.)
Joining in January 1917, he proceeded to the Western Front in the following month and was there engaged on important duties on the rail-roads in various sectors. He was present also at the Battles of Cambrai and Amiens and other engagements, and served through the Retreat and Advance of 1918. He was demobilised in March 1919, holding the General Service and Victory Medals. Camp Hill, Bugbrooke, Northants. Z3026/B.

GARLICK, J. G., Private, 1st Northants. Regt.
He volunteered in December 1914, and in the following year was drafted to France. Whilst in this theatre of war he took part in many important engagements, including the Battle of Loos, where he was wounded in action. As a result he was invalided home, and eventually discharged in August 1916, as medically unfit for further service. He holds the 1914–15 Star and the General Service and Victory Medals.
20, Stanley Road, Northampton. Z1174.

GARLICK, S. H., Bombardier, R.G.A.
He volunteered in November 1915, and drafted to France in the following May, took part in the engagements on the Somme and at Arras, Cambrai and Ypres. In June 1918 he was severely gassed and invalided home to hospital. On recovery he served on important duties at various depôts until February 1919, when he was demobilised, holding the General Service and Victory Medals.
1, Sanders Terrace, Long Buckby, Northants. Z3335.

GARNER, A., Pte., Queen's Own (Royal West Kent Regiment).
He joined in March 1917, and two months later was drafted to the Western Front, where he took part in several engagements, including the Battles of Ypres and Passchendaele. He made the supreme sacrifice, being killed in action at Armentières on March 17th, 1918, and was entitled to the General Service and Victory Medals.
"Honour to the immortal dead who gave their youth that the world might grow old in peace."
16, Fort Street, Northampton. Z1194/B.

GARNER, C. E. J., Gunner, R.F.A.
He joined in September 1916, and after undergoing a period of training was retained at various stations in Ireland, where he was engaged on duties of great importance. He was not successful in obtaining his transfer to the front, but did good work with his Battery until invalided from the Army in November 1918, suffering from heart-trouble.
3, Gardner Cottage, Weedon, Northants. Z3028.

GARNER, H., Private, 8th (King's Royal Irish) Hussars.
After volunteering in September 1914, he underwent a period of training prior to being drafted to the Western Front in December 1916, and there took part in the Battles of Arras, Vimy Ridge, Messines, Ypres, Passchendaele, Cambrai and the Somme. He was unhappily drowned accidentally on May 22nd, 1918, and was entitled to the General Service and Victory Medals.
"Steals on the ear the distant triumph song"
15, St. James' Square, St. James' St, Northampton. Z3027.

GARNER, S., Pte., Queen's (R.W. Surrey Regt.)
Immediately on attaining military age he joined in June 1918, but was not successful in being transferred overseas. He did excellent work with his unit at Tonbridge, Sittingbourne and Aldershot, and also rendered valuable services with the 13th Hussars before being demobilised in November 1919.
Water Lane, Wootton, Northants. Z2685/B.

GARNER, W., Private, 1st Northants. Regiment.
Volunteering in August 1915, he was drafted overseas in the following year. Whilst on the Western Front he took part in several engagements, including heavy fighting on the Somme, where he was badly wounded and consequently invalided home. He was discharged in October 1917 as medically unfit for further service and holds the General Service and Victory Medals. 53, Fort Street, Northampton. Z1175.

GARRATT, F. O., Corporal, Northants. Yeomanry (Dragoons).
He volunteered in November 1914, and was retained for some time at various stations on important duties before proceeding to France with the 2nd Dragoon Guards. There he took part in the Battle of the Somme (II.) and in the Retreat and Advance of 1918. After the Armistice he went to Germany with the Army of Occupation, and served there until his demobilisation in January 1919. He holds the General Service and Victory Medals.
45, Beaconsfield Terrace, Northampton. Z1435.

GARRATT, R., Pte., 7th Oxford. & Bucks. L.I.
He volunteered in September 1914, and twelve months later was drafted to France, but after a short period at Albert was transferred to Salonika. In the Balkan theatre of war he saw heavy fighting on the Doiran and Vardar fronts, and was wounded in 1917. After hospital treatment in Malta, he returned to Salonika, and served there until his demobilisation in April 1919, holding the 1914–15 Star, and the General Service and Victory Medals.
2, Osborn Cottages, Hanslope, Bucks. Z2686/A.

GARRATT, R. D. (Mrs.), Member, W.R.A.F.
She joined in January 1917, and during her service did excellent work whilst engaged on important clerical duties. She was stationed at the aerodromes at Oxford, Bicester and Ruislip, and was eventually demobilised in September 1919.
2, Osborn Cottages, Hanslope, Bucks. Z2686/B.

GARRETT, A., Private, 3rd London Regiment (Royal Fusiliers).
He volunteered in September 1914, and in the following year proceeded to Salonika, where he saw severe fighting on the Doiran and Vardar Fronts. Invalided home suffering from malaria in April 1918, he was drafted to France in the following October. There he fell fighting on November 8th, 1918, and was entitled to the 1914–15 Star, and the General Service and Victory Medals.
"Whilst we remember, the sacrifice is not in vain."
High Street, Hanslope, Bucks. Z3029/A.

GARRETT, F. C. H., Private, Machine Gun Corps.
He volunteered in May 1915, and after his training was retained on important duties in England until June 1917, when he proceeded to the Western Front. There he took part in many engagements, including the Battles of Ypres, Cambrai, Amiens and Le Cateau, fought also in the Retreat and Advance of 1918, and was gassed in May of that year. He was demobilised in February 1919, and holds the General Service and Victory Medals.
Malt Mill Lane, Hanslope, Bucks. Z3029/B

GARRETT, H. W., Pte., 2/5th Lancashire Regt.
He joined the Northamptonshire Regiment in June 1916 and underwent a period of training prior to his being drafted to the Western Front. After only seven weeks' heavy fighting in the Ypres sector, he was unfortunately killed in action on August 3rd, 1917. He was entitled to the General Service and Victory Medals.
"His life for his Country, his soul to God."
32, Lorne Road, Northampton. Z1325/B.

GARRETT, J. C., Sapper, R.E. (R.O.D.)
Joining in December 1917, he proceeded to France in the following year, and was engaged on important duties on the railways in the Somme area. He returned home, and was demobilised in March 1919, and holds the General Service and Victory Medals.
Mill Lane, Kislingbury, Northants. Z3307/A.

GARRETT, R. C., Private, 6th Norfolk Regiment.
He joined in November 1916, and after a period of training was engaged at various home stations, and in Ireland, on important duties with his unit. He was not successful in obtaining a transfer to a theatre of war, but rendered valuable services until his demobilisation in January 1919.
32, Lorne Road, Northampton. Z1325/A.

GARRETT, T. W., Gunner, R.G.A.
Joining in May 1916, he was drafted to France in the following July, and took part in the engagements on the Somme and at Arras, Ypres, Cambrai and St. Quentin. In March 1918, during the Retreat, he was gassed, but on recovery served in the Advance, and after the Armistice was stationed at Cologne until August 1919, when he was demobilised, holding the General Service and Victory Medals.
Lower Heyford, Weedon, Northants. Z3336.

GARWOOD, E. J., Sergeant, 1st Essex Regiment.
He joined the Army in June 1904, and, when war broke out in August 1914, was serving in India, but immediately proceeded to France. There he played a prominent part in the Battles of the Aisne, Ypres, Ploegsteert, the Somme, Delville Wood and in the Retreat and Advance of 1918, being three times wounded in action and once invalided home. He received his discharge in March 1920, and holds the 1914 Star, and the General Service and Victory Medals. 43, Brunswick St., Northampton. Z1436.

GASCOYNE, E. M., Private, 1st Northants. Regt.
Joining in February 1916, he embarked for the Western Front a month later, and took part in several important engagements. After only four months' active service he died gloriously on the Field of Battle on the Somme on July 10th, 1916. He was entitled to the General Service and Victory Medals.
"He died the noblest death a man may die:
Fighting for God and right and liberty."
19, Lea Road, Northampton. Z2144/B.

GASCOYNE, S. A., Special War Worker.
After repeated endeavours to join the Army he was called up in June 1917, and after only one day's service was discharged as medically unfit. From that time until the termination of the war he was engaged on important work in connection with the manufacture of Army boots, which he carried out with the utmost ability. 19, Lea Road, Northampton. Z2144/A.

GASSON, E., Rifleman, King's Royal Rifle Corps.
He was called up from the Reserve in August 1914, and immediately drafted to France, where he took part in the Battle of, and Retreat from, Mons, and the Battles of the Marne and the Aisne. He died gloriously on the Field of Battle at La Bassée in October 1914, and was entitled to the Mons Star, and the General Service and Victory Medals.
"He died the noblest death a man may die:
Fighting for God and right and liberty."
11, Liz Street, Northampton. Z1176.

GASSON, T. W., Pte., Queen's Own (Royal West Kent Regiment).
He enlisted in June 1916, and later in the same year was drafted to France, where he took part in the Battle of the Somme and was wounded in action. As a result he was invalided to hospital in Boulogne, and on his recovery was transferred to Egypt. Later he saw much fighting during the Advance into Palestine. He made the supreme sacrifice, being killed in action at the third Battle of Gaza in November 1917, and was entitled to the General Service and Victory Medals.
"Thinking that remembrance, though unspoken, may reach him where he sleeps."
34, Leicester Street, Northampton. Z1326.

GATEHOUSE, H. E., Private, 19th Hussars.
Called up from the Reserve in August, he was quickly drafted to the Western Front, where he fought in the Retreat from Mons, and was severely injured in an accident. He was admitted to hospital at Southend in January 1915, and in May of that year was invalided from the Army. He holds the Mons Star, and the General Service and Victory Medals.
41, West Street, Weedon, Northants. Z3030.

GATES, A. R., L/Corporal, 2nd Norfolk Regiment.
Already serving in India when war broke out in August 1914, he was drafted to Mesopotamia in the following year. In this seat of operations he took part in much heavy fighting until late in 1915, when he returned to India and served as a telegraphist until his discharge in October 1919. He holds the 1914–15 Star, and the General Service and Victory Medals
54, Overstone Road, Northampton. Z1437/A.

GATES, W. J., Trooper, 1st Life Guards.
He volunteered in October 1915, and, completing his training in the following year, was drafted to the Western Front, where he took part in several engagements. He died gloriously on the Field of Battle in October 1917, and was entitled to the General Service and Victory Medals.
"Nobly striving:
He nobly fell that we might live."
54, Overstone Road, Northampton. Z1437/B.

GAYTON, A., Private, R.A.M.C.
He volunteered in November 1915, and in September of the following year proceeded to the Western Front, where he served with a Field Ambulance at Dunkirk, Rouen and elsewhere, and was also present at the Battles of Arras, Messines and Ypres. He also served in Italy, and later, with the Army of Occupation at Cologne. Demobilised in March 1919, he holds the General Service and Victory Medals.
63, Grove Road, Northampton. Z3031.

GEE, I. J., Gunner, Royal Garrison Artillery.
Shortly after joining in May 1916, he was sent to France, where he saw severe fighting in various sectors, took part in the Battles of the Somme, Arras, Vimy Ridge and Ypres, and was wounded in March 1917. Contracting pneumonia, he unhappily died in hospital in October 1918, and was buried near Cambrai. He was entitled to the General Service and Victory Medals.
"His life for his Country, his soul to God."
19, Sharman Road, Northampton. Z2396.

GEORGE, G. (M.M.), Pte., 1st and 2nd Northants. Regiment.
Six months after volunteering in September 1914, he was sent to France, where he played a prominent part in the Battles of Neuve Chapelle and Festubert, and was wounded in action at Aubers Ridge in May 1915. After hospital treatment at Sunderland, he returned to the Western Front and fought at Ypres and Villers-Bretonneux, where he was awarded the Military Medal for great gallantry in April 1918. He was demobilised in March 1919, and also holds the 1914–15 Star, and the General Service and Victory Medals.
27, Devonshire St., St. James' End, Northampton. Z2687/A.

GEORGE, S., Gunner, Royal Garrison Artillery.
He joined in May 1916, and in the following year proceeded to France, where he was in action at Arras, Ypres, Passchendaele and Cambrai. He also served in the Retreat and Advance of 1918, and after the Armistice was stationed with the Army of Occupation on the Rhine. He returned to England, and was demobilised in October 1919, and holds the General Service and Victory Medals. Bugbrooke, Weedon, Northants. Z3337.

GEORGE, W. H., Private, 2nd Northants. Regt.
He volunteered in September 1915, and in December of the following year proceeded to the Western Front, where he took part in the Battles of Messines and Passchendaele and other engagements. He was unhappily reported missing, and is now presumed to have been killed in action on the Somme on March 25th, 1918. He was entitled to the General Service and Victory Medals.
"His life for his Country, his soul to God."
35, Tanner Street, Northampton. Z2982/B.

GIBBARD, G., Driver, Royal Field Artillery.
Volunteering in September 1914, he proceeded to the Western Front in the following January and there saw much heavy fighting. After taking part in the Battles of Festubert and Loos and many other engagements, he was severely wounded in action and admitted to hospital at Brighton. Invalided from the Army in September 1916, he later re-enlisted in the Royal Army Service Corps, and holds the 1914–15 Star, and the General Service and Victory Medals.
45, Parkwood Street, Northampton. Z2397.

GIBBINS, A., Sapper, Royal Engineers.
He volunteered in August 1915, and in February of the follow-year was drafted to Egypt, where he served at various stations. He also took part in the Battles of Gaza and other important engagements in Palestine, before being admitted to hospital at Alexandria suffering from malaria. He unhappily died there in August 1918, and was entitled to the General Service and Victory Medals.
"He joined the great white company of valiant souls."
12, Spring Lane Terrace, Northampton. Z1177/A.

GIBBINS, E. R., Private, Royal Fusiliers.
He joined in June 1917, and after three months' training was sent to the Western Front, where he took part in many important engagements in the Ypres sector. Mortally wounded in action, he unfortunately died on December 15th, 1917, at the Canadian Casualty Clearing Station at Poperinghe. He was entitled to the General Service and Victory Medals.
"The path of duty was the way to glory."
48, High Street, Kingsthorpe, Northampton. TZ1178.

GIBBINS, F. A., Private, Essex Regiment.
He volunteered in December 1915, and, after undergoing a period of training, was retained at various stations on duties of great importance, afterwards being transferred to the Labour Corps. He was unable, on account of ill-health, to obtain his transfer overseas, but nevertheless, rendered very valuable services until his demobilisation in September 1919.
50, Arthur Street, Kingsthorpe Hollow, Northampton. Z1327.

GIBBINS, J. W., A.B., Royal Naval Division.
He joined in June 1916, and after his training was retained on important duties in England until April 1917, and was then drafted to the Western Front, where he saw severe fighting in the Ypres sector. He died gloriously on the Field of Battle on May 25th, 1917, after only a few weeks' active service, and was entitled to the General Service and Victory Medals.
"Steals on the ear the distant triumph song."
34, Upper Harding Street, Northampton. Z1180/B.

GIBBINS, R. C., Corporal, Royal Engineers.
He volunteered in August 1915, and on conclusion of his training in the following year was drafted overseas. Whilst on the Western Front he was engaged on important pioneer work, and served during the Somme Offensive, at the Battles of Arras and Ypres, and in the Retreat and Advance of 1918. He was wounded and gassed on one occasion, and in May 1919 was demobilised, holding the General Service and Victory Medals. 12, Brunswick Place, Northampton. Z1918.

GIBBINS, T. H., Driver, R.A.S.C.
A Territorial, he was mobilised in August 1914, and in November of that year proceeded to the Western Front, where he was engaged on important duties in various sectors. He was also present at the Battles of Ypres, Loos, the Somme, Arras and Cambrai, and was finally discharged on returning home in June 1919. He holds the 1914 Star, and the General Service and Victory Medals.
34, Upper Harding Street, Northampton. Z1180/A.

GIBBINS, W., Private, Machine Gun Corps.
He volunteered in September 1914, and after his training served with the Royal Army Service Corps at various stations until February 1918, when he was transferred to the Machine Gun Corps and drafted to France. After taking part in many engagements during the Retreat and Advance he fell fighting on October 14th, 1918. He was entitled to the General Service and Victory Medals.
"Courage, bright hopes, and a myriad dreams, splendidly given."
36, King Street, Northampton. Z1328/A.

GIBBINS, W. E., L/Corporal, 5th Northants. Regt.
Volunteering in September 1914, he was sent to France in April of the following year and there saw much heavy fighting. He took part in the Battles of Ypres, the Somme and Arras, and many other engagements, and was wounded at Vermelles in June 1916, and at Cambrai in November 1917. Demobilised in March 1919, he holds the 1914–15 Star, and the General Service and Victory Medals.
69, Byron Street, Kingsley, Northampton. Z1179.

GIBBONS, G. H., Corporal, 13th London Regt.
He joined in May 1917, and was quickly sent to Palestine, where he played a prominent part in the Battles of Gaza and the taking of Jerusalem, Beersheba and Bethlehem. He also served throughout General Allenby's Offensive, was stationed at Alexandria, Cairo and in Turkey, and was with the Royal West Kent Regiment for some time. He was ultimately demobilised in December 1920, and holds the General Service and Victory Medals.
27, Morton Road, Daventry, Northants. Z2688.

GIBBS, A. J., Pte., Queen's (R.W. Surrey Regt.)
Joining in March 1917, he was drafted to the Western Front in the following month, and there saw severe fighting in various sectors. After taking part in the Battles of Ypres, the Somme and St. Quentin and many other engagements, he was sent home, and finally invalided from the Army in April 1919, suffering from neurasthenia. He holds the General Service and Victory Medals. 96, Stanley Street, Northampton. Z1182.

GIBBS, F., A.B., Royal Navy.
He volunteered in 1915, and later in the same year was sent to Mesopotamia, where he served with the land forces of the Royal Navy. He played a prominent part in the Relief of Kut and the Capture of Baghdad. Whilst in the East he suffered severely from malaria and dysentery and was eventually demobilised in 1919, holding the 1914–15 Star, and the General Service and Victory Medals.
46, Lawrence Street, Northampton. Z2549.

GIBBS, G., Engine-room Artificer, Royal Navy.
He volunteered in November 1915, and was posted to H.M.S. "Tormentor," attached to the Harwich Division. He also served in H.M.S. "Satyr" on patrol duties in the North Sea, and was on board H.M.T.B. "4" when she was torpedoed off Ramsgate. Demobilised in March 1919, he holds the General Service and Victory Medals.
89, Stanley Street, Northampton. Z1181/B.

GIBBS, G., Private, 7th Northants. Regiment.
At the outbreak of war he volunteered, but after three months' service was discharged as medically unfit. In October 1915, however, he volunteered again, and, crossing to France in the following March, fought in the Battles of the Somme, Messines, Ypres, Passchendaele, Lens and Cambrai, and was wounded at Thiepval in 1916. He was also in action during the Retreat and Advance of 1918, and was demobilised in March 1919, holding the General Service and Victory Medals.
74, East Street, Northampton. Z2145.

GIBSON, A A., Private, Northants. Regiment.
He volunteered in May 1915, and in January of the following year proceeded to Egypt, where he was engaged on duties of great importance at various stations and saw much active service. Invalided home, he unhappily died of poisoning in hospital at Manchester in October 1917. He was entitled to the General Service and Victory Medals.
"His memory is cherished with pride."
65, High Street, Kingsthorpe, Northampton. Z1183/C.

GIBSON, A. V., Private, Queen's Own (Royal West Kent Regiment).
Joining in February 1917, he was sent to France in the following June, and took part in severe fighting at Ypres, Passchendaele and Cambrai. He was twice wounded, and in April 1918 was invalided home. Subsequently he was discharged in March 1919, holding the General Service and Victory Medals.
Cogenhoe, Northants. Z3338.

GIBSON, B., Private, R.M.L.I.
He volunteered in September 1914, and after undergoing training at Dover, was posted to a unit of the Grand Fleet for service in the North Sea, where he took part in the Battle of Jutland. He was also engaged on various duties off the coast of South Africa, and in 1921 was serving in Ireland. He holds the 1914–15 Star, and the General Service and Victory Medals.
65, High Street, Kingsthorpe, Northampton. Z1183/A.

GIBSON, E. E., Driver, Royal Field Artillery.
Mobilised with the Territorials at the outbreak of hostilities, he underwent a period of training prior to being drafted overseas in December 1916. Whilst in Salonika he was in action with his Battery on the Doiran and Struma fronts. He later contracted malarial fever, and as a result was invalided home to hospital. On his recovery, in November 1918, he was drafted to France, where he was engaged on important salvage work until June 1919. Returning home he was demobilised in that month, and holds the General Service and Victory Medals.
48, Denmark Road, Northampton. Z1919.

GIBSON, E. F., Private, East Yorkshire Regiment.
He volunteered in June 1915 in the Northamptonshire Regiment, and in September of the following year was drafted with the East Yorkshire Regiment to the Western Front, where he saw much severe fighting. He made the supreme sacrifice, falling in action on the Somme on November 17th, 1916, and was entitled to the General Service and Victory Medals.
"Great deeds cannot die:
They with the sun and moon renew their light for ever."
65, High Street, Kingsthorpe, Northampton. Z1183/B.

GIBSON, S. P., Private, 7th Royal Fusiliers.
Four months after volunteering in November 1915, he proceeded to the Western Front, where he took part in many important engagements, including the Battles of Vimy Ridge, the Somme, Arras, Ypres, Passchendaele and Cambrai. Mortally wounded at Valenciennes in the Advance, he died on November 11th, 1918. He was entitled to the General Service and Victory Medals.
"His life for his Country, his soul to God."
14, Dover Street, Northampton. Z1439.

GILBERT, H., Private, 5th Northants. Regiment.
He volunteered in October 1915, and in May of the following year was sent to the Western Front, where, after taking part in the Battles of Arras, Bullecourt and Ypres, he was gassed at Cambrai in 1917, and sent to hospital at Rouen. Afterwards transferred to the Labour Corps, he did much good work until demobilised in March 1919, holding the General Service and Victory Medals.
68, Semilong Road, Northampton. Z2398.

GILBERT, H., Pte., Queen's (R.W. Surrey Regt.)
Joining in May 1916, he proceeded to France in December, and after taking part in the Battles of Arras, Vimy Ridge, Bullecourt, Ypres, Lens and Cambrai, was wounded and invalided home. On his recovery he rejoined his unit on the Western Front, but was again admitted to hospital in Birmingham owing to an illness. He returned to the Western Front a third time and remained there until demobilised in January 1919, holding the General Service and Victory Medals.
10, Adnitt Place, Northampton. Z2690.

GILBERT, J., Private, 1/4th Northants. Regt.
Having enlisted in January 1911, he was drafted to the Western Front immediately on the outbreak of war and fought in the Retreat from Mons. In 1915, however, he was transferred to Gallipoli, where he saw much severe fighting, afterwards serving in Egypt and Palestine, where he took part in the Battles of Gaza and Jaffa. He was wounded whilst overseas, and on his return home in August 1919 was discharged, holding the Mons Star, and the General Service and Victory Medals.
92, Gordon Street, Northampton. Z1329.

GILBERT, J W., Sergeant, 7th Northants. Regt.
Volunteering in January 1915, he was drafted to the Western Front in the following September, and was there severely gassed and wounded at Loos in the same month. Invalided to hospital at Dublin he was afterwards retained on clerical duties at home until his demobilisation in February 1919. He holds the 1914–15 Star, and the General Service and Victory Medals. 11, Cleveland Road, Northampton. Z1440.

GILHAM, A. H., Corporal, Royal Air Force.
He volunteered in August 1915, at the age of 17 years, and after undergoing a period of training was retained at various stations, where, in the capacity of first air-mechanic, he was engaged on duties of a highly technical nature. He was unable to obtain his transfer overseas, but, nevertheless, rendered valuable services with his Squadron, until demobilised in July 1919.
16, Semilong Road, Northampton. Z2399.

GILLHAM, H., Private, 27th Middlesex Regiment.
He volunteered in June 1915, and early in the following year was sent to France, where he saw severe fighting in various sectors of the front. He took part in the Battles of the Somme, Ypres and Cambrai and many other important engagements until the cessation of hostilities, and was demobilised in March 1919. He holds the General Service and Victory Medals.
3, Kinburn Place, Northampton. Z1184.

GILTROW, W. R., Air Mechanic, Royal Air Force.
Called up from the Reserve in August 1914, he quickly proceeded to France with the Northamptonshire Regiment and fought in the Retreat from Mons. After taking part also in the Battles of the Aisne, Ypres, Neuve Chapelle and Loos, he was wounded on the Somme in 1916, and sent to hospital at Bristol. Returning to France in 1917 with the Royal Air Force, he remained there until discharged in February 1919, holding the Mons Star, and the General Service and Victory Medals. 19, St. Mary's Street, Northampton. Z1185.

GINNS, H., Corporal, Mounted Military Police.
Two months after volunteering he proceeded to Egypt in January 1916, but was quickly transferred to Salonika, where he rendered valuable service, whilst engaged in regulating transport during the heavy fighting on the Doiran and Struma fronts. He returned home for demobilisation in April 1919, and holds the General Service and Victory Medals.
8, Countess Road, St. James, Northampton. Z2691.

GLANISTER, E. A., Private, Machine Gun Corps.
He joined in October 1916, and proceeded to France in the following year on completing his training at Grantham. After taking part in the Battles of Ypres, Cambrai (I.) and the Somme (II.), he laid down his life for King and Country at the second Battle of Cambrai on September 5th, 1918, and was entitled to the General Service and Victory Medals.
"A valiant Soldier, with undaunted heart he breasted life's last hill."
Bank, Hardingstone, Northants. Z2692/A.

GLANISTER, E. A., Pte., R. Warwickshire Regt.
Volunteering in December 1915, he proceeded to France in the following year and served in the Somme, Ypres and Cambrai sectors, being attached to the Machine Gun Corps as a signaller. He was unfortunately killed in action at Cambrai on September 4th, 1918, and was entitled to the General Service and Victory Medals.
"Steals on the ear the distant triumph song."
School House Lane, Lower Heyford, Northants. Z3329/A.

GLANISTER, E. J., Gunner, R.F.A.
He volunteered in August 1914, and was drafted overseas in the following year. Whilst on the Western Front he was in action with his Battery at the Battles of Ypres, the Somme and Cambrai, where he was badly wounded in November 1917. Invalided home, he was discharged early in 1918 as medically unfit for further service, and holds the 1914–15 Star, and the General Service and Victory Medals.
Bank, Hardingstone, Northants. Z2692/B.

GLANISTER, R. H. P., Pte., Middlesex Regiment.
He joined in April 1916, and in the following year crossed to France, where he was engaged on important duties in the Somme and Ypres sectors with the Labour Company. After rendering most valuable services he returned to England and was demobilised in January 1919, holding the General Service and Victory Medals.
36, Alton Street, Northampton. Z3339.

GLASPELL, A. E., Private, R.A.S.C.
He joined in October 1917, and after a period of training was engaged on important duties with the Royal Field Artillery at various stations, later being transferred to the Royal Army Service Corps. Unable on account of ill-health to obtain his transfer overseas, he, nevertheless, rendered very valuable services until his demobilisation in October 1919.
70, Byron Street, Kingsley, Northampton. Z1085/B.

GLASPOLL, A. T., Private, 8th (King's Royal Irish) Hussars.
Mobilised in August 1914, he was immediately drafted to the Western Front, where he fought in the Retreat from Mons with the 4th (Queen's Own) Hussars. He also took part in the Battles of La Bassée, Ypres, Festubert, Loos, the Somme Cambrai and St. Quentin, and was wounded whilst carrying despatches on the Aisne in September 1914. Discharged in January 1920, he holds the Mons Star, and the General Service and Victory Medals.
70, Byron Street, Kingsley, Northampton. Z1085/A.

GLAZEBROOK, B., Private, 1st Wiltshire Regt.
He joined in March 1917, and after his training was retained on important duties in England until April of the following year, when he was sent to the Western Front. There he was taken prisoner during severe fighting on the Somme in the same month, and unhappily died on May 11th, 1918, whilst in captivity. He was entitled to the General Service and Victory Medals.
"His memory is cherished with pride."
111, Harborough Road, Kingsthorpe, Northampton. Z1186.

GLEAVE, P. G., Private, Manchester Regiment.
Volunteering in 1914, he was drafted overseas on completion of his training, and took part in numerous engagements on the Western Front. He then proceeded to Italy, where he fought on the Piave in the campaign against the Austrians. He returned home and was demobilised in 1919, and holds the General Service and Victory Medals.
32, Oxford Street, Northampton. Z3340.

GLEED, A. A., Sergeant, Manchester Regiment.
He was serving at the outbreak of war, and immediately proceeded to France, where he took part in the fighting at Mons. He was unfortunately wounded in this memorable engagement and fell into the hands of the enemy. Sent to Germany, he unhappily died there whilst in captivity in January 1915. He was entitled to the Mons Star, and the General Service and Victory Medals. Little Houghton, Northants. Z3341/B.

GLEED, H. T., Private, R.A.S.C.
Joining in September 1916, he was engaged on important duties with his unit at various stations. He was not successful in obtaining his transfer overseas prior to the cessation of hostilities, but, nevertheless, rendered valuable services until demobilised in September 1919.
Little Houghton, Northants. Z3341/A.

GLENN, F., 1st Class Stoker, Royal Navy.
Joining in August 1916, he received his training in H.M.S. "Victory" at Portsmouth, and was later posted to H.M.S "Lucia." On board this ship he was engaged on important patrol and escort duties in the North Sea, and subsequently proceeded to Russia, where he rendered valuable services at Archangel. He was demobilised on his return home in August 1919, and holds the General Service and Victory Medals.
Wright's Yard, Roade, Northants. Z2146.

GLENN, W. C., Sapper, Royal Engineers.
Joining in September 1916, he was drafted to France in February of the following year and there served in various sectors. He was present at the Battles of Messines, Ypres and Passchendaele, and other engagements until severely gassed and wounded at Cambrai in February 1918 and sent home. He was invalided from the Army in September of that year and unhappily died on November 26th, 1920. He was entitled to the General Service and Victory Medals.
"Steals on the ear the distant triumph song."
25, Alton Street, Northampton. Z3032/B.

GOFF, A., Sergeant, 6th Northants. Regiment.
Volunteering in September 1914, he was sent to the Western Front in the following year and took a prominent part in important engagements in various sectors. He made the supreme sacrifice, falling in action at Meautte in 1915, after six months' service in France. He was entitled to the 1914–15 Star, and the General Service and Victory Medals.
"He joined the great white company of valiant souls."
25, Melbourne Street, Northampton. Z2400.

GOFF, F. (D.C.M.), Sergeant, Machine Gun Corps.
Volunteering in August 1914, he proceeded to Gallipoli twelve months later, and was transferred thence to Egypt in December 1915. Advancing into Palestine, he took a prominent part in the Battles of Rafa and Siwa, was wounded in the third Battle of Gaza and fought also in General Allenby's Offensive. Awarded the Distinguished Conduct Medal for conspicuous bravery in the Field, he holds also the 1914–15 Star, and the General Service and Victory Medals, and was demobilised on returning home in March 1919.
22, Stanley Road, Northampton. Z2401.

GOFF, W. H., Pte., Royal Sussex Regt. and M.G.C.
Joining in February 1917, he was sent to France in the following June, and took part in the Battles of Ypres and Cambrai. He also served in the Retreat and Advance of 1918, and after the Armistice was stationed with the Army of Occupation in Germany until October 1919, when he returned to England and was demobilised, holding the General Service and Victory Medals.
9, Sanders Terrace, Long Buckby, Northants. Z3342.

GOLDSMITH, W. E., Private, 7th Northants. Regt.
Joining in June 1916, he was drafted to the Western Front in the following December, where he saw severe fighting in various sectors. He was also engaged for a time on important duties at Rouen, Calais and other stations until invalided home. He was finally demobilised in September 1919, and holds the General Service and Victory Medals.
23, Brunswick Street, Northampton. Z1441.

GOODE, A. E. (M.M.), Pte., Royal Dublin Fusiliers.
He joined in 1916, and in April of the following year proceeded to the Western Front, but, wounded at Ypres, was invalided home in July 1917. He returned to France, however, four months later, took part in the Battle of the Somme and was again wounded at Cambrai in September 1918, and sent to England. Awarded the Military Medal for conspicuous bravery in the Field, he holds also the General Service and Victory Medals, and in February 1919 was demobilised.
3, Fort Street, Northampton. Z1190.

GOODE, A. E., Private, 1st Northants. Regiment.
Volunteering in September 1914, he was sent to France in July of the following year, and there took part in the Battles of the Somme, Ypres and Cambrai and other engagements in various sectors. He was mortally wounded in action at Aubigny and unhappily died at a casualty clearing station on September 6th, 1918. He was entitled to the 1914–15 Star, and the General Service and Victory Medals.
"Whilst we remember, the sacrifice is not in vain."
7, Bristol Street, Northampton. Z1187/A.

GOODE, B. J., A.B., Royal Naval Division.
He joined in March 1916, at the age of 16, and after a period of training was drafted overseas later in the same year. Whilst serving with the Anson Battalion on the Western Front he took part in the Battles of the Somme, Ypres and Cambrai, but was wounded at the Somme in July 1918, and unhappily succumbed to his injuries. He was entitled to the General Service and Victory Medals.
"He nobly died that we might live."
6, New Buildings, Blisworth, Northants. Z2147/A—Z2148/A.

GOODE, J., Sergeant, 4th Northants. Regiment.
Called up from the Reserve in August 1914, he proceeded to Gallipoli in the following year and took part in numerous engagements until the Evacuation. He was then drafted to Egypt and served in the Palestine campaign, being in action at Gaza, Jerusalem and Jericho. He was severely wounded during the Offensive of 1918, and was invalided home and ultimately was discharged in November of that year, holding the 1914–15 Star, and the General Service and Victory Medals.
High Street, Long Buckby, Northants. Z3343.

GOODE, P. A., Private, 23rd Royal Fusiliers.
Joining in January 1918, he was sent to France after four months' training in Ireland and there took part in many important engagements. He made the supreme sacrifice, falling in action on the Somme on July 21st, 1918. He was entitled to the General Service and Victory Medals.
"He died the noblest death a man may die:
Fighting for God and right and liberty."
7, Bristol Street, Northampton. Z1187/B.

GOODE, T. (M.M.), C.S.M., 4th Northants. Regt.
He volunteered in August 1914, and twelve months later proceeded to Gallipoli, where he took part in the Landing at Suvla Bay. He was later transferred to Egypt, and thence to Palestine, where he fought with distinction and was wounded in the second Battle of Gaza, afterwards being admitted to hospital at Alexandria. He was awarded the Military Medal for conspicuous bravery in the Field in Palestine and, holding also the 1914–15 Star, and the General Service and Victory Medals, was demobilised in December 1919.
100, Harborough Road, Kingsthorpe, Northampton. Z1189.

GOODE, W., L/Cpl., 2nd Sherwood Foresters.
He joined in February 1917, and after his training served at various stations with several units, including the Queen's Own (Royal West Kent Regiment), the Buffs (East Kent Regiment) and the Royal Fusiliers. Being too young for active service, he was unable to obtain his transfer to the front, but in August 1919 proceeded to Egypt, where he was serving as a signalling Instructor at Alexandria in 1921.
4, Cambridge Street, Northampton. Z1188.

GOODE, W. J., Private, Machine Gun Corps.
Shortly after volunteering in January 1915, he proceeded to Egypt, whence he advanced into Palestine, and took part in the Battles of Gaza and the capture of Jerusalem and Jericho. Transferred in March 1918 to France, he was again in action in the Retreat and Advance of that year, finally being demobilised in March 1919. He holds the 1914–15 Star, and the General Service and Victory Medals.
21, Alton Street, Northampton. Z3032/A.

GOODMAN, A., Private, 8th Queen's (Royal West Surrey Regiment).
He joined in September 1917, and in March of the following year proceeded to the Western Front, where he saw severe fighting in various sectors. He took part in the Battle of the Somme and other engagements, and was wounded at Cambrai in July 1918, afterwards serving with the Army of Occupation at Cologne. Demobilised in October 1919, he holds the General Service and Victory Medals.
20, Lower Harding Street, Northampton. Z1191/A.

GOODMAN, F., Private, 1st Norfolk Regiment.
After volunteering in January 1915, he underwent a period of training prior to being drafted to the Western Front early in 1917. He took part in the Battle of Ypres and other engagements, before being transferred to Italy, where he fought on the Piave, returning to France in 1918. He was wounded at Cambrai and was finally demobilised in January 1919, holding the General Service and Victory Medals.
63, Lower Hester Street, Northampton. Z1192.

GOODMAN, G. A., Private, R.A.S.C. (M.T.)
Volunteering in April 1915, he was drafted to France in August of that year and was there engaged on various important duties. He served in the Somme and other sectors of the Western Front and did much useful work until his return home for demobilisation in July 1919. He holds the 1914–15 Star, and the General Service and Victory Medals.
17, Lower Hester Street, Northampton. Z1193/B.

GOODMAN, J. A., Sapper, Royal Engineers.
He joined in March 1916, and in February of the following year proceeded to the Western Front, where he was engaged on pontoon-building, trench-digging and other important duties in the Ypres and Somme sectors. Severely gassed and wounded on the Somme in June 1918, he unhappily died in hospital at Canterbury in February of the following year. He was entitled to the General Service and Victory Medals.
"Steals on the ear the distant triumph song."
17, Lower Hester Street, Northampton. Z1193/A.

GOODMAN, T. E., Gunner, Royal Field Artillery.
Volunteering in November 1915, he was retained on special duties in England before proceeding to Palestine in 1917. He was chiefly engaged on an ammunition dump, but took part in the third Battle of Gaza, the Offensive under General Allenby and was present at the capture of Tripoli and Aleppo. Demobilised in February 1919, he holds the General Service and Victory Medals. 62, Stanley Road, Northampton. Z2693.

GOODMAN, W. A., Private, 10th Essex Regiment.
Joining in May 1917, he completed his training, and in March of the following year embarked for France. On that front he was in action in engagements at Amiens, Albert and Méricourt, but was taken prisoner in August 1918, and during his captivity was employed in making roads. He was repatriated in January 1919, and demobilised 10 months later, holding the General Service and Victory Medals.
42, Roseholme Road, Northampton. Z2149.

GOODRICH, A., A.B., Royal Naval Division.
He volunteered in October 1915, and five months later was sent to the Western Front with the Nelson Battalion of the Royal Naval Division, and saw severe fighting in various sectors. He died gloriously on the Field of Battle at Arras on April 24th, 1917, and was entitled to the General Service and Victory Medals.
"Thinking that remembrance, though unspoken, may reach him where he sleeps."
19, Cleveland Road, Northampton. Z1442.

GOODRIDGE, W. E., Gunner, R.F.A.
When war broke out he volunteered, and on completion of his training was ordered to the Western Front in 1915. Whilst overseas he was engaged in severe fighting in the Ypres sector, and was wounded at the Battle of the Somme in July 1916. He was invalided to England, subsequently being discharged as medically unfit for further service in December 1917, and holds the 1914–15 Star and the General Service and Victory Medals. 25, New Buildings, Blisworth Northants. Z2150.

GOODSON, H. A., Corporal, Royal Field Artillery.
Two months after joining in February 1917 he was drafted to France, where he saw heavy fighting in various sectors. He took part in the Battles of Arras, Cambrai, and the Marne and many other important engagements, serving also through the Retreat and Advance of 1918. Demobilised in October 1919, he holds the General Service and Victory Medals.
7, Cleveland Road, Northampton. Z1443.

GOOM, T. R., Sapper, Royal Engineers.
He volunteered in May 1915, and in February of the following year proceeded to the Western Front, but was invalided home three months later suffering from gastritis. Returning to France, he served with the signal section until again sent to England in April 1917, in order to work on munitions. Demobilised in December 1918, he holds the General Service and Victory Medals. The Green, Milton, Northants. Z2402/A.

GOODWIN, E. J., Cpl., 2nd Monmouthshire Regt.
Having enlisted in 1912, he was sent to France with the first Expeditionary Force, and served through the Retreat from Mons. He also played a prominent part in the Battles of La Bassée, Ypres (I.), Beaumont-Hamel (during the Somme Offensive), Ypres (III.) and Cambrai, and in other engagements of importance. After four years' service overseas he was invalided home with trench fever in 1918, and received his discharge in 1919, holding the Mons Star, and the General Service and Victory Medals. 19, Robert St., Northampton. Z1444.

GOOSEY, G., Rifleman, Rifle Brigade.
Already serving in August 1914, he immediately proceeded to France and fought at the Battle of, and in the Retreat from, Mons. He was wounded in 1914, but on his recovery rejoined his unit, and was unfortunately killed in action on September 14th, 1915. He was entitled to the Mons Star, and the General Service and Victory Medals.
"A valiant Soldier, with undaunted heart he breasted life's last hill."
27, Park Street, Northampton. Z1445.

GORDON, E. A., Private, 7th Northants. Regt.
He volunteered in September 1914, and in October of the following year was drafted to the Western Front, where he saw much heavy fighting. Severely wounded in action at Loos in December 1915, he was sent home and was finally invalided from the Army in October 1916. He holds the 1914–15 Star, and the General Service and Victory Medals.
81, Cecil Road, Northampton. Z2403.

GORDON, W., Private, 2nd Gordon Highlanders.
He joined the Bedford Regiment in March 1918, and after his training at Hastings and Felixstowe, and service in Ireland, volunteered for duty in Russia. He did much valuable service with the Gordon Highlanders at Vladivostock and on the Dvinsk, and was also stationed for a time at Constantinople. After his return home he was demobilised in March 1921.
Gouard Cottage, Bugbrooke, Weedon, Northants. Z3344.

GORE, R. R., Pte., The Buffs (East Kent Regt.)
He joined in March 1917, and 11 months later proceeded to the Western Front, where he saw heavy fighting in various sectors, and fought in engagements at Ypres. He was taken prisoner at Albert, and held in captivity for six months. After his release he was drafted to India, where in 1920 he was serving with the 2nd Northamptonshire Regiment, holding the General Service and Victory Medals.
82, Lutterworth Road, Northampton. Z2151.

GOSLING, W., C.S.M., 5th Northants. Regiment.
Called up from the Reserve in August 1914, he served at various stations as a Drill Instructor before proceeding to France 12 months later. Whilst in this seat of operations he played a prominent part at the Battles of Arras, Vimy Ridge and Monchy, where he was wounded in August 1918. Invalided to England, he underwent a period of hospital treatment, and on his recovery was engaged on important duties until discharged in April 1919, holding the 1914–15 Star, and the General Service and Victory Medals.
5, Stockley Street, Northampton. Z1868/B.

GOUDE, W. W., Private, R.A.M.C.
After volunteering in October 1915, he underwent a period of training prior to being drafted to Mesopotamia, where he served at Basra and also during heavy fighting at Kut-el-Amara before being invalided to hospital with dysentery. On his recovery he was transferred to East Africa and was engaged as an orderly in the British Base Hospital at Mombasa until demobilised in November 1919. He holds the General Service and Victory Medals.
77, Market Street, Northampton. Z1920.

GOUGH, C. J., Private, Northants. Regiment.
Joining in October 1916, he passed through his course of training at Chatham, and in January 1917 proceeded to France, where he was in action at Arras, and was taken prisoner at Bullecourt. After his repatriation in January 1919, he did good service in Ireland till September 1919, when he was demobilised. He holds the General Service and Victory Medals. 108, Southampton Road, Northampton. Z3345/A.

GOWEN, A., Rifleman, 16th King's Royal Rifles.
Joining in June 1917, he was ordered to France on the completion of his training 10 months later. He did good work with his unit during fierce fighting at Ypres and Cambrai and was wounded in the latter engagement. He was invalided to England, and after protracted hospital treatment was demobilised in January 1919, holding the General Service and Victory Medals. 14, Manfield Road, Northampton. Z2152/A.

GOWEN, H., Pte., 7th Northants. Regiment.
He volunteered in May 1915, and in the following November was drafted to France, on which front he took part in the Battles of Messines, Vimy Ridge, Ypres and Passchendaele. In September 1917 he was severely wounded and gassed at Hooge and eventually was invalided home. On his recovery he was transferred to the Labour Corps, and served at Dover until demobilised in February 1919, holding the General Service and Victory Medals.
14, Manfield Road, Northampton. Z2152/B.

GOWEN, J. T., Corporal, 1st Northants. Regiment.
He volunteered in June 1915, and, proceeding to France, was in charge of the signallers of his Company. He rendered valuable services at Loos, Givenchy, Peronne, Messines, Passchendaele, Arras and St. Quentin and on the Somme before being wounded in action in October 1918. He was demobilised in March 1919, and holds the General Service and Victory Medals.
16, Fort Street, Northampton. Z1194/A.

GOWING, S. G., Driver, Royal Field Artillery.
Having previously served for 15 years, he was called from the Reserve in August 1914 and sent to France, where he was in action with his Battery at the Battles of Mons, the Marne, the Aisne, Ypres, Neuve Chapelle and other engagements before being badly wounded in 1916. Invalided home, he underwent treatment in London, and was then retained at various home stations until his discharge in January 1919, holding the Mons Star, and the General Service and Victory Medals.
5, Argyle Street, St. James' End, Northampton. Z2694.

GRAHAM, W., C.S.M., 5th Middlesex Regiment.
At the outbreak of hostilities he volunteered, and in 1915 was ordered overseas. Serving on the Western Front, he played a prominent part in the Battles of Ypres, Loos, the Somme, Arras and Cambrai, did excellent work during the Retreat and Advance of 1918, and was wounded on four occasions. He was demobilised in June 1919, and holds the 1914–15 Star, and the General Service and Victory Medals.
13, New Buildings, Blisworth, Northants. Z2153.

GRANT, J. R. J., Private, Royal Fusiliers.
He joined in July 1917, and in April of the following year was sent to France, where he saw severe fighting in various sectors of the front. He took part in the Battles of Amiens and Ypres and many other engagements during the Allied Offensive, and was demobilised on returning home in March 1919. He holds the General Service and Victory Medals.
Camp Hill, Bugbrooke, Northants. Z3033.

GRAY, A. E., Private, 20th London Regiment.
Having previously been rejected for military service in 1914, he joined in June 1917, and three months later was sent to the Western Front. There he was in action in the Battles of Cambrai, the Somme, Bapaume and Ypres, and also fought in the Retreat and Advance of 1918. After the Armistice he advanced into Germany with the Army of Occupation and served at Cologne until demobilised in March 1919. He holds the General Service and Victory Medals.
30, Lutterworth Road, Northampton. Z2154.

GRAY, C., Private, 2nd Northants. Regiment.
Stationed in Egypt in August 1914, he immediately proceeded to France and fought in the Mons Retreat. He also took part in the Battles of the Aisne, Ypres (I. and II.), Neuve Chapelle, Loos, the Somme, Arras and Passchendaele, was five times wounded, and invalided home on each occasion. He was unfortunately killed in action on May 11th, 1918, and was entitled to the Mons Star, and the General Service and Victory Medals.
"His name liveth for evermore."
35, Doddridge Street, Northampton. Z1195/B.

GRAY, J., Air Mechanic, Royal Air Force.
He joined in December 1917, and on completion of his training was engaged on duties demanding a high degree of technical skill. He was not drafted overseas owing to medical unfitness, but rendered valuable services as a rigger in various workshops until his demobilisation in January 1919.
17, Stanley Street, Northampton. Z1196.

GRAY, W. A. V., Private, 16th Manchester Regt.
He joined in April 1917, and was sent to France in June. Whilst on the Western Front he was in action at Ypres, Messines, Zillebeke and the Menin Road before being invalided home owing to being buried by a shell. On his recovery he was transferred to the Royal Army Service Corps, returned to France, and served at Monchy, Arras, Cambrai, Valenciennes, Mons and other important places. Demobilised in January 1920, he holds the General Service and Victory Medals.
47, Hood Street, Northampton. Z1446.

GRAY, W. J., L/Corporal, Essex Regiment.
He joined in February 1916, and on the conclusion of his training was drafted to the Western Front. He took an active part in the Battles of Ypres, Passchendaele and Cambrai, and in many important engagements of the Offensive of 1918, until wounded in the eye near Monchy in September. After being invalided home he was demobilised in April 1919, and holds the General Service and Victory Medals.
Station Road, Cogenhoe, Northants. Z3346.

GREAVES, A., 1st Northamptonshire Special Constabulary.
In 1914 he offered his services as a special constable and throughout the whole period of hostilities, did excellent work with the 1st Borough Police Reserve. He was chiefly engaged on night duties during air-raids, and on being demobilised in 1919, was awarded the Long Service Certificate.
7, King Street, Northampton. Z1330/C.

GREAVES, A. E., Driver, Australian R.E.
Volunteering in August 1914, he saw heavy fighting at Anzac Cove and Suvla Bay during the Gallipoli campaign. Transferred to France when the Peninsula was evacuated in January 1916, he served with the 7th Field Company on the Somme, at Arras, Ypres and Cambrai, and in the Retreat and Advance of 1918. He holds the 1914–15 Star, and the General Service and Victory Medals, and was demobilised in February 1919.
7, King Street, Northampton. Z1330/D.

GREAVES, G. T., L/Corporal, 3rd Northants. Regt.
Volunteering in August 1914, he was under age for transfer to a theatre of war, and was therefore retained on important duties in England until January 1918. He then proceeded to France, and rendered valuable services in the Retreat, but was wounded in April 1918. Invalided home through illness in August, he was in hospital at Colchester before being demobilised in April 1919, and holds the General Service and Victory Medals. 7, King Street, Northampton. Z1330/A.

GREEN, A., Gunner, Royal Field Artillery.
He joined in May 1916, and underwent a period of training at Woolwich, where he did much good work with his Battery. He was unfortunately gassed accidentally, and after being for a considerable period in hospital was discharged in May 1918, as medically unfit for further service.
Rothersthorpe, Northants. Z3034.

GREEN, A. M., Private, R.A.M.C.
He joined in April 1916, and was soon drafted to France, where he rendered valuable services attending to the wounded in various hospitals and advanced dressing stations. He saw severe fighting in several sectors of the Western Front and returned home suffering from bronchitis in December 1920. He was then discharged as medically unfit, and holds the General Service and Victory Medals.
11, Tanners Street, Northampton. Z2696

GREEN, A. T., Private, Tank Corps.
Joining in 1917, he proceeded to France later in the same year and took part in many important engagements. He was in action at the Battles of Arras, Messines, Ypres, Passchendaele, Lens, Cambrai and the Somme, and in the Retreat and Advance of 1918. He also entered Mons, and after the conclusion of hostilities proceeded with the Army of Occupation to Germany. Demobilised in 1919, he holds the General Service and Victory Medals. 97, St. Edmund's Road, Northampton. Z1921.

GREEN, B. (Mrs.), Member, V.A.D.
This lady volunteered her services as a nurse in the St. John Ambulance Brigade at the outbreak of war. Throughout the period of hostilities she was engaged in nursing the sick and wounded at various hospitals, and rendered valuable services during air-raids. She was demobilised in November 1918, and was awarded a medal in recognition of her excellent work.
103, Holly Road, Northampton. Z2158/B.

GREEN, C., Private, 1st Northants. Regiment.
After volunteering in October 1914, he was trained at Weymouth, and in March 1915 proceeded to the Western Front. Shortly after his arrival he went into action at Aubers Ridge and was unhappily killed in that area on May 9th, 1915. He was entitled to the 1914–15 Star, and the General Service and Victory Medals.
"His life for his Country, his soul to God."
Market Square, Long Buckby, Northants. Z3347.

GREEN, C., Q.M.S., University Training Corps.
He volunteered in 1915, but in spite of repeated endeavours to secure a transfer to a fighting unit he was retained on home service until the cessation of hostilities. Stationed at Northampton, he was engaged on important transport and guard duties, and performed excellent work during air-raids. After three years' valuable work he was demobilised in December 1918. 103, Holly Road, Northampton. Z2158/A.

GREEN, C. J., Private, 2/4th Northants. Regt.
Volunteering in March 1915, he proceeded to the Western Front in August of the following year. He took part in many notable engagements, including those at Vermelles, but was severely wounded at Albert in April 1917, and invalided to England. On his discharge from hospital he was transferred to the Royal Fusiliers and drafted to Ireland, where he served until demobilised in March 1919. He holds the General Service and Victory Medals.
17, St. Edmund's Street, Northampton. Z2157.

GREEN, E. B., L/Corporal, R.A.M.C.
Volunteering in February 1915, he was sent to France in May 1916, and from that date until the close of hostilities rendered valuable services as a stretcher-bearer in many engagements of great importance, including those in the Somme, Ypres and Arras sectors. After his return to England he was demobilised in April 1919, and holds the General Service and Victory Medals.
24, St. James' Park Road, Northampton. Z3348.

GREEN, E. W., Pte., R.A.S.C. and Northants. Regt.
He joined in March 1917, and on completion of his training was employed on important clerical duties at Northampton. Subsequently he worked in the Woolwich Records Office, where he rendered valuable services. He was not successful in his efforts to secure a transfer to the fighting area, but, nevertheless, did much excellent work until demobilised in March 1919. 145, Lutterworth Road, Northampton. Z2155.

GREEN, F., Armourer Sergeant-Major, R.A.O.C.
Enlisting in April 1897, he was attached to the Grenadier Guards at Warley in August 1914, but proceeding to Gallipoli a year later, served at Suvla Bay and in other engagements. After the Evacuation of the Peninsula he was sent to Egypt, but advancing into Palestine saw heavy fighting at the three Battles of Gaza, and was present at the capture of Jaffa, Jerusalem, Beyrout and Tripoli. He rendered valuable services with the 9th and 21st Corps, and was discharged in July 1920, holding the 1914–15 Star, and the General Service, Victory and the Long Service and Good Conduct Medals.
Sutton Street, Flore, Northants. Z2695.

GREEN, J. B., Private, 53rd Bedfordshire Regt.
On attaining military age he joined in May 1918, but was unsuccessful in obtaining his transfer to a theatre of hostilities. He did excellent work with his unit at various stations until September 1919, when he was discharged as medically unfit for further service owing to his suffering from neurasthenia.
12, Augustin Street, Northampton. Z2698/B.

GREEN, J. W., Pioneer, Royal Engineers.
He volunteered in August 1915, and was soon drafted to France, where he rendered valuable services with his Company at the Battles of Vermelles, Albert, the Somme, Arras, Messines, Ypres, Lens and Cambrai, and throughout the Retreat and Advance of 1918. He was demobilised on his return home in March 1919, and holds the 1914–15 Star, and the General Service and Victory Medals.
12, Augustin Street, Northampton. Z2698/A.

GREEN, W. H., Private, 9th West Riding Regt.
Joining in August 1917, he was not drafted overseas until September 1918, but then proceeded to France, and after severe fighting in several minor engagements was badly wounded at the Foret du Mormal and invalided home. He was in hospital at Liverpool for some time before being discharged as medically unfit in August 1919, and holds the General Service and Victory Medals.
Sutton Street, Flore, Northants. Z2697.

GREGORY, H., Private, 5th Northants. Regiment.
Volunteering in August 1914, he proceeded to the Western Front in the following May, and there served as a driver with the Transport Section. He was present also at the Battles of Ypres, Loos, the Somme, Arras, Vimy Ridge, Bullecourt, Passchendaele and Cambrai, and took part in the Retreat and Advance of 1918. Demobilised in April 1919, he holds the 1914–15 Star, and the General Service and Victory Medals.
Church Street, Brixworth, Northants. Z3035.

GRESHAM, C. P. (M.M.), Pioneer, R.E.
He was serving with the Colours when war broke out and was at once drafted to France, where he took part in the Retreat from Mons and the Battles of Ypres and the Somme. He also served with distinction in many engagements in the Retreat and Advance of 1918, and was present at the entry into Mons at the Armistice. He was awarded the Military Medal for his conspicuous bravery in the Field, and also holds the Mons Star, and the General Service and Victory Medals. He was discharged in 1919.
69, St. Leonard's Road, Far Cotton, Northampton. Z3349.

GREY, J. W., Rifleman, Royal Irish Rifles.
He joined in October 1916, and proceeding to France three months later was in action at numerous important engagements. He laid down his life for King and Country at the opening of the Retreat on March 28th, 1918, and was entitled to the General Service and Victory Medals.
"His name liveth for evermore."
Waterloo, Daventry, Northants. Z2699.

GRIBBLE, H., Pte., 2nd R. Inniskilling Fusiliers.
He joined in April 1917, and in March of the following year was sent to the Western Front, where he fought in various sectors. After taking part in engagements at Messines, Armentières, Neuve Chapelle and La Bassée, he was severely wounded at Ypres in October 1918, and sent home. He was invalided from the Army in June 1919, and holds the General Service and Victory Medals. 44, Adelaide Street, Northampton. Z3036.

GRIBBLE, H., Private, Northumberland Fusiliers.
Already in the Northamptonshire Regiment in August 1914, he was discharged in January 1915. In July, however, he rejoined in the Norfolk Regiment and proceeded to India, where he was transferred to the Northumberland Fusiliers. He was sent to Mesopotamia in June 1917, and rendered valuable services whilst engaged on pioneer duties. He holds the General Service and Victory Medals, and was demobilised in November 1919
9, Spring Lane Terrace, Northampton. Z1197

GRIFFIN, A., Private, Royal Army Medical Corps.
Joining in August 1917, he was soon drafted to Italy. Whilst in this theatre of war he rendered valuable services in various hospitals, where he was engaged in attending the sick and wounded. He returned to England for demobilisation in March 1919, and holds the General Service and Victory Medals.
7, Charles Street, Northampton. Z1332/B.

GRIFFIN, C. E., A.B., Royal Naval Division.
He joined in July 1917, and after the completion of his training at Blandford and Aldershot proceeded to the Western Front in March 1918. After valuable service at Albert, Amiens and other operations in the earlier Offensives of that year he was accidentally injured in June, and being invalided home was discharged in October as medically unfit for further service. He holds the General Service and Victory Medals.
Little Houghton, Northants. Z3350.

GRIFFIN, E., Private, 1st Northants. Regiment
He volunteered in May 1915, and proceeding to France on completion of his training, took part in heavy fighting at Loos, the Somme, Arras, Vimy Ridge, and Ypres before being unhappily killed in action on the Dunes on July 10th, 1917. He was entitled to the General Service and Victory Medals.
"A costly sacrifice upon the altar of freedom."
7, Charles Street, Northampton. Z1332/C.

GRIFFIN, J. A., Private, Labour Corps.
Joining in February 1917, he was sent to the Western Front in October of that year, and was there engaged in road-making and on other important duties in various sectors. He took an active part in the Battles of the Somme, Péronne and Valenciennes, and also served through the Retreat and Advance of 1918. Demobilised in January 1919, he holds the General Service and Victory Medals.
High Street, Gayton, Northants. Z2404.

GRIFFIN, J. W., Private, 13th Royal Sussex Regt.
Joining in February 1917, he was drafted overseas seven months later on completion of his training. Whilst serving in France he fought in engagements at Ypres and Passchendaele, but was severely wounded on the Menin Road in November 1917 and sent to hospital in England. In consequence he was discharged as medically unfit for further service in August 1918, and holds the General Service and Victory Medals.
15, Market Street, Northampton. Z2156.

GRIFFIN, T., Private, R.A.O.C.
He volunteered in December 1915, and was quickly drafted to France, where he was engaged on special duties in the workshops at Calais. In October of the same year he was invalided home with gastritis, and, after hospital treatment at Ipswich and Eastbourne, was discharged as medically unfit in October 1918. He holds the General Service and Victory Medals.
70, Charles Street, Northampton. Z1331/B.

GRIFFIN, W., L/Corporal, 1st Northants. Regt.
He joined in March 1916, and in July was drafted to France, but, after taking part in the Battle of the Somme, was sent to Calais for special duty. Later he rendered valuable services on an ammunition dump near Dunkirk, and was eventually demobilised in January 1920, holding the General Service and Victory Medals. 70, Charles Street, Northampton. Z1332/A.

GRIFFITH, F. H., Private, Labour Corps.
He volunteered in November 1915, and in the following January was drafted to Egypt. Joining the Palestine Forces, he served at Gaza, and was wounded in the second Battle at that place. He unfortunately became seriously ill during the later stages of the Advance and unhappily died in hospital at Damascus in November 1918. He was entitled to the General Service and Victory Medals.
"The path of duty was the way to glory."
Kilsby, Northants. Z3351.

GRIFFITHS, H., Sapper, Royal Engineers.
Shortly after volunteering in August 1915, he proceeded to France, where he served in various sectors. He was present at the Battles of Albert, Arras, Messines, Ypres and Passchendaele and in many other engagements, was wounded at Vimy Ridge in 1916, and gassed at Cambrai. He was consequently invalided from the Army in August 1918, and holds the 1914–15 Star and the General Service and Victory Medals.
7, Ambush Street, St. James, Northampton. Z2405.

GRIFFITHS, O., Pte., 1st Monmouthshire Regt.
A Reservist, he was called to the Colours in August 1914, and, proceeding to France, rendered valuable services as a driver with the transport of his unit at Mons, the Aisne, the Marne, Ypres, Neuve Chapelle, Givenchy, Loos and Lens. He was discharged—time-expired—in February 1916, and holds the Mons Star, and the General Service and Victory Medals.
35, Lower Harding Street, Northampton. Z1199.

GRIFFITHS, W. C., A.B., Royal Navy.
He volunteered in November 1914, and whilst on board H.M.S. "Gipsy" was attached to the Dover Patrol. Later he was engaged on patrol and convoy work in the North Sea and the Atlantic, and took part in the Naval operations off the Belgian coast. His ship was instrumental in sinking five German submarines, and, during an engagement with the "U.48," he was wounded. Discharged as a result in December 1918, he holds the General Service and Victory Medals.
20, Kinburn Place, Northampton. Z1198.

GRIGG, A. P. G., Private, 2nd Bedfordshire Regt.
He volunteered in October 1915, and in December of the following year was sent to France, where he was engaged in fierce fighting on the Somme and the Ancre fronts. He was wounded at Vimy Ridge in April 1917, and invalided home, but on his recovery returned to the Western Front and served there until the close of hostilities. Demobilised in 1919, he holds the General Service and Victory Medals.
97, Upper Thrift Street, Northampton. Z2159/A.

GRIGG, L. G. A., Private, Sherwood Foresters.
Joining in January 1917, he received his training at Chatham, and in the following March embarked for the Western Front. He was in action in various important engagements, but, after two months' active service, was unhappily killed in action on May 18th, 1917. He was entitled to the General Service and Victory Medals.
"A valiant Soldier, with undaunted heart he breasted life's last hill."
97, Upper Thrift Street, Northampton. Z2159/B.

GRIPTON, W. H., Private, 5th Northants. Regt.
He volunteered in September 1914, and eight months later proceeded to the Western Front. There he took part in many engagements of note, including the Battles of Ypres and Vimy Ridge, and was wounded on the Somme in September 1916. He was invalided to Scotland, but, after his discharge from hospital, contracted influenza, to which he unfortunately succumbed on November 9th, 1918. He was entitled to the 1914–15 Star, and the General Service and Victory Medals.
"The path of duty was the way to glory."
19, Allen Road, Northampton. Z2160.

GROOM, B. (Mrs.), Special War Worker.
In June 1917 this lady offered her services at Messrs. Hanwell's Munition Factory, where, engaged on various responsible duties, she did much excellent work. She was afterwards employed at Messrs. Smith's Timber Yard as a cutter, in which capacity she rendered valuable services until December 1919. 4, St. James' Square, Northampton. Z3038/B.

GROOM, H., Pte., 11th (Prince Albert's Own) Hussars.
A Reservist, he was mobilised in August 1914, and immediately drafted to France, where he was wounded in the Retreat from Mons. After lying for four days undiscovered, he was taken prisoner, and held in captivity in Germany until November 1916, when he was sent into Switzerland. Finally released, he was discharged in December 1919, holding the Mons Star, and the General Service and Victory Medals.
4, St. James' Square, Northampton. Z3038/A.

GROOM, W., 1st Class Wireman, Royal Navy.
Joining in January 1917 he was retained on important duties at various ports on the South Coast, where he was engaged in fixing depth charges on ships proceeding to sea. He also rendered valuable services at Scapa Flow but was ultimately discharged as medically unfit in February 1919, owing to consumption contracted whilst in the Navy.
Long Street, Hanslope, Bucks. Z2700.

GROVE, T. H., Sapper, Royal Engineers.
Joining in May 1916, he was drafted to the Western Front in the following month, and first served as a despatch-rider with a Field Survey Company. Later he was attached to the Canadian Artillery as an observer for counter battery work, and saw severe fighting at Armentières, Ploegsteert Wood, and Messines, and other engagements. Demobilised on returning home in February 1919, he holds the General Service and Victory Medals.
23, Sandringham Road, Northampton. Z2406.

GROVES, F., Private, 5th Northants. Regiment.
Volunteering in August 1914, he completed his training and proceeded to France in 1915. He took an active part in the Battles of Loos, the Somme, Vermelles, Ploegsteert Wood, Arras, Lens, Cambrai, and of the Somme, Amiens and Epéhy in the Offensive of 1918. He was present at the entry into Mons on Armistice Day, and after his return home was demobilised in 1919, holding the 1914–15 Star, and the General Service and Victory Medals.
West Street, Long Buckby, Northants. Z3352.

GROVES, G. H. (M.M.), Sapper, Royal Engineers.
He volunteered in October 1914 at the age of 18, and after completing his training proceeded to France, where he rendered valuable services as a stretcher-bearer at the Battles of Hill 60, Ypres, the Somme and other engagements of importance, up to the cessation of hostilities. He was awarded the Military Medal for conspicuous gallantry in the Field, and also holds the 1914–15 Star, and the General Service and Victory Medals. He was demobilised in 1919 after four years' service overseas.
86, Rothersthorpe Road, Far Cotton, Northampton. Z3294/A.

GUARE, W. C., Private, R.A.S.C.
He volunteered in February 1915, but, owing to a physical infirmity, was retained on special clerical duties at the supply depôts at Bath, Colchester, Thetford and Purfleet. He rendered valuable services until his demobilisation in January 1919.
21, Oak Street, Northampton. Z1447.

GUTTERIDGE, W. T., Gunner, R.F.A.
Having enlisted in February 1910, he was serving in Africa at the outbreak of war, but was quickly transferred to the Western Front. In this seat of operations he was in action with his Battery at the Battles of Ypres (I.), Neuve Chapelle, Givenchy, Ypres (II.), Festubert and Loos. In November 1917 he was drafted to Italy, where he served with the 7th Division on the Piave front. Discharged in February 1919, he holds the 1914 Star, and the General Service and Victory Medals. 67, Lower Thrift Street, Northampton. Z1922.

H

HACKETT, D., Private, 4th Northants. Regiment.
Volunteering in November 1915, he completed a period of training and was then attached to the Royal Engineers, with which unit he was retained on important duties at various stations. During his service he fractured his knee, and as a result was discharged as medically unfit in September 1917, after nearly two years' excellent work.
16, Letts Road, Far Cotton, Northampton. Z3354/B.

HACKETT, T. E., Private, Royal Fusiliers.
Joining in March 1916, he was first engaged on important duties with his unit at various stations. Proceeding to the Western Front in February 1918, he took part in many engagements, including the Battles of the Aisne (III.), the Marne (II.), Amiens, Bapaume, Havrincourt, Epéhy and Cambrai (II.), where he unfortunately fell in action on September 29th, 1918, and was entitled to the General Service and Victory Medals.
"His life for his Country, his soul to God."
16, Letts Road, Far Cotton, Northampton. Z3354/A.

HADDON, C. A., Trooper, Northants. Dragoons.
Mobilised in August 1914, he proceeded to France in November, and, after taking part in the Battle of Ypres (I.), was invalided home with frost-bite. Returning to France later he fought at Vermelles, Vimy Ridge, the Somme and Arras before being transferred to Italy, where he was in action on the Piave front. He returned home to be demobilised in May 1919, and holds the 1914 Star, and the General Service, Victory and Territorial Force Efficiency Medals.
1, Delapre Street, Far Cotton, Northants. Z3355.

HADDON, F. W., Private, Queen's Own (Royal West Kent Regiment).
Joining in May 1916, he underwent a period of training and proceeded to the Western Front, where he took part in the engagements on the Somme and also in the Battles of Arras and Vimy Ridge. He was reported missing on May 3rd, 1917, and was later presumed to have been killed in action on that date. He was entitled to the General Service and Victory Medals.
"Whilst we remember, the sacrifice is not in vain."
59, Poole Street, Northampton. Z1448.

HADDON, T. T., Private, 1st Northants. Regiment.
He volunteered in September 1914, and was shortly afterwards drafted to France, where he took part in engagements at Ypres and Givenchy, but owing to illness was sent home. In April 1915 he rejoined his unit and fought at Aubers Ridge, where he was gassed and again invalided home. On his recovery he proceeded to Egypt, and served there until January 1916, when he contracted fever and returned to England. Later he was sent to France, was transferred to the Royal Army Medical Corps, and engaged on an ambulance train until returning home in May 1918. Demobilised in February 1919, he holds the 1914–15 Star, and the General Service and Victory Medals.
28, Gas Street, Northampton. Z2701.

HADLEY, R. C., Sick Berth Steward, R.N.
He joined the Royal Navy in 1903, and when war broke out quickly proceeded to the North Sea on board H.M.S. "Invincible." He served with the Grand Fleet and took part in the Battles of Heligoland Bight, the Falkland Islands and the Dogger Bank. He unfortunately lost his life when H.M.S. "Invincible" was sunk at the Battle of Jutland on May 31st, 1916, and was entitled to the 1914–15 Star, and the General Service and Victory Medals.
"Thinking that remembrance, though unspoken, may reach him where he sleeps."
37, Dundee Street, Northampton. Z2702.

HAFFORD, A. C., Sergeant, Royal Berks. Regt.
He joined in 1916, and later in the same year was drafted to France. In this theatre of war he took part in many important engagements, including the Battles of Vimy Ridge and the Somme. Later, he saw much severe fighting at Amiens, and was present at the Entry into Mons on Armistice Day. Demobilised in 1919, he holds the General Service and Victory Medals. 32, Dundee Street, Northampton. Z2703.

HAKES, J., Private, Northants. Regiment.
Having enlisted in March 1910, he was serving in Egypt on the declaration of war, but was quickly transferred to France, where he took part in the Battles of Neuve Chapelle, Loos, Vermelles and the Somme. He was twice badly wounded, and as a result was invalided home in 1916. On his recovery he proceeded to Russia in 1918, and served there until discharged in September 1919. He holds the 1914 Star, and the General Service and Victory Medals.
37, East Street, Northampton. Z1923.

HALEY, J., L/Corporal, Machine Gun Corps.
He enlisted in 1916, and, having completed his training, later in the same year was drafted to France. There he took part in the Battles of the Somme and Passchendaele and saw much heavy fighting in various other sectors, being wounded in action. After the Armistice he proceeded to Germany with the Army of Occupation and served there until his demobilisation in 1919. He holds the General Service and Victory Medals.
25, Alma Street, Northampton. Z2704.

HALL, C. W. (D.S.O., D.C.M.), 2nd Lieut., R.F.A.
Enlisting in 1900, he was retained on special duties at home until 1916, when he was sent to Salonika as a Battery Sergeant-major. He served with distinction in important engagements, and was awarded the Distinguished Conduct Medal for conspicuous bravery under heavy fire, at the same time being granted a commission. Transferred to France early in 1918, he was unhappily killed in action on August 11th of that year, after having been awarded the Distinguished Service Order for great gallantry. He was also entitled to the General Service and Victory Medals.
"His name liveth for evermore."
150, St. Leonard's Road, Far Cotton, Northampton. Z3004/B.

HALL, W. F., Private, Training Reserve Bn.
After joining in March 1917, he proceeded to Dover, but on completing a period of training was found to be medically unfit for service overseas, and was therefore discharged in October of that year; 21, Craven Street, Northampton. Z1333.

HAMBIDGE, W., Private, 3rd Northants. Regt.
Called up from the Reserve in August 1914, he proceeded to the Western Front early in the following year and took part in the Battles of Loos and the Somme, and other engagements. Invalided home in December 1916 suffering from trench feet, he returned to France on his recovery and fell in action near Arras on July 23rd, 1917. He held the Queen's and King's South African Medals, and was entitled to the 1914–15 Star, and the General Service and Victory Medals.
"Whilst we remember, the sacrifice is not in vain."
18, Spencer Road, Northampton. Z1449.

HAMER, F., Private, Tank Corps.
He volunteered in May 1915, and, after training with the Royal Field Artillery, proceeded to France in the following August with the Machine Gun Corps, and was later transferred to the Tank Corps. There he took part in the Battles of the Somme, the Ancre, Arras, Ypres and Cambrai and in minor engagements until severely wounded on the Somme in March 1918, and invalided home. He afterwards served as a Tank Instructor in England until demobilised in February 1919, holding the 1914–15 Star, and the General Service and Victory Medals.
29, Monarch Road, Northampton. Z3039.

HAMES, A. E. W., Driver, R.A.S.C.
Having volunteered in October 1914, he was retained on important transport duties at home before being transferred to France. Whilst on the Western Front he served in a similar capacity during the Retreat and Advance of 1918. After the cessation of hostilities he proceeded to Germany with the Army of Occupation, and was stationed at Cologne. He was demobilised in July 1919, and holds the General Service and Victory Medals. 14, Craven Street, Northampton. Z1450.

HAMMETT, G., Private, 1st Northants. Regiment.
Volunteering in September 1914, he underwent a period of training, but, owing to his being over age, was unable to proceed overseas. He was therefore retained at home and was engaged in training recruits, in which capacity he rendered excellent services until demobilised in January 1919.
5, Bell Barn Street, Northampton. Z1200.

HAMMONDS, A., Private, 5th Bedfordshire Regt.
He joined in March 1917, and early in the following year was drafted to the Western Front. There he was transferred to the 7th Norfolk Regiment, and took part in many engagements in the Advance of 1918, and was twice wounded in action on the Somme. Invalided to hospital, he was eventually demobilised in January 1919, and holds the General Service and Victory Medals.
51, Newcombe Road, Northampton. Z2705.

HAMSON, A. J., Private, Machine Gun Corps.
Volunteering in 1915, he later in the same year embarked for France, where he took part in many important engagements, including the Battles of Ypres and Festubert, before being badly wounded. On his recovery he was in action at the Battles of Ypres, Passchendaele, Lens, the Somme (II.) and Cambrai. After the cessation of hostilities he returned home for demobilisation in 1919, and holds the 1914–15 Star, and the General Service and Victory Medals.
5, Rickard Street, Far Cotton, Northampton. Z3356.

HAMSON, F. A., Corporal, Royal Engineers.
He volunteered in August 1915, and on completion of his training was retained on important duties with his unit at various stations. Proceeding to France in January 1917, he took an active part in the Battles of Ypres, Passchendaele, Cambrai, the Somme (II.) and also in the Retreat and Advance of 1918. Demobilised in February 1919, he holds the General Service and Victory Medals.
7, Euston Road, Northampton. Z3357.

HAMSON, H. A., Corporal, Royal Engineers.
Volunteering in August 1915, he completed his training and proceeded overseas. Whilst on the Western Front he did consistently good work, and took part in many important engagements, including the Battles of Ypres, Passchendaele, Cambrai and the Somme. He was also present during the Retreat and Advance of 1918, and in February 1919 was demobilised, holding the General Service and Victory Medals.
21, Oxford Street, Northampton. Z3358.

HANCOCK, A. T., Corporal, R.A.S.C. (M.T.)
He enlisted in December 1916, and in the following month was drafted to France. Whilst in this theatre of war he served with the Mechanical Transport as a lorry-driver, conveying ammunition to the forward areas in the Arras, Vimy Ridge, Somme, Passchendaele and Cambrai sectors, and in the Retreat and Advance of 1918, being wounded in action. Demobilised in November 1919, he holds the General Service and Victory Medals.
44, Brook Street, Daventry, Northants. Z2706/A.

HANCOCK, G., Private, 4th Northants. Regiment.
He was mobilised in August 1914, and retained at various home stations on special duties with his unit. He rendered valuable services whilst engaged as a shoe-maker, and on other work of importance, before his discharge in April 1917—time-expired.
44, Brook Street, Daventry, Northants. Z2706/B.

HANCOCK, T. R., Private, R.A.V.C.
Joining in September 1916, he was immediately drafted to France, where he did continuously good work whilst attending to the sick and wounded horses. He served at Abbeville, and was also present during heavy fighting at Arras and St. Quentin. After the conclusion of the war he proceeded to Germany and served with the Army of Occupation at Cologne. He was demobilised in August 1919, and holds the General Service and Victory Medals.
9, St. Mary's Street, Northampton. Z1201.

HAND, W. (sen.), Special War Worker.
From June 1917 until the close of hostilities he was engaged on work of National importance at Bicester. During that time he was chiefly employed as a carpenter in making aeroplane sheds and also the wooden aeroplane parts, which work he carried out with the greatest skill and efficiency until December 1918, when he relinquished his position.
27, Florence Road, Northampton. Z2161/A.

HAND, W. T. (jun.), Special War Worker.
He joined the Church Lads' Brigade in June 1918, at the age of 16, and from that time until October 1919 rendered valuable services to the wounded at Abingdon. In recognition of his excellent work and untiring energy he was presented with a certificate. 27, Florence Road, Northampton. Z2161/B.

HANNAFORD, W. H., Private, R.A.M.C.
Volunteering in 1915, he proceeded to France with the Welsh Field Ambulance, and rendered valuable services attending to sick and wounded on ambulance and troop trains. Later he was transferred to Italy for work of a similar nature, and after the Armistice was stationed in Germany with the Army of Occupation. He was demobilised in 1919, and holds the General Service and Victory Medals.
84, Adams Avenue, Northampton. Z2162/A.

HARBAGE, G. F., Private, Suffolk Regiment.
He joined in March 1916, and proceeded to France later in the same year. During his service in this theatre of war he fought in engagements on the Arras and Ypres fronts. On November 13th, 1916, he was reported missing, and is now presumed to have been killed in action near Albert on that date. He was entitled to the General Service and Victory Medals.
"A valiant Soldier, with undaunted heart he breasted life's last hill."
"The Layes," Roade, Northants. Z2163.

HARDING, J. W., Gunner, R.H.A.
After joining in February 1917 he underwent a period of training, but was later found to be medically unfit for service overseas, and was therefore retained on important duties with his Battery. Later, however, he was thrown from his horse, and as a result was invalided to hospital and eventually discharged as unfit for further service in October 1918.
2nd House, 5th Block, Naseby Street, Northampton. Z1334.

HARDWICK, J. H., Sapper, Royal Engineers.
Volunteering in June 1915, he completed a period of training prior to being drafted to Italy. Whilst in this theatre of war he served at various stations as a carpenter, and did continuously good work throughout hostilities. In May 1919 he was demobilised, and holds the General Service and Victory Medals. 40, Ruskin Road, Northampton. Z1842.

HARDY, F., Private, 1st Northants. Regiment.
He was already serving at the outbreak of hostilities and was at once drafted to France. Whilst on the Western Front he was in action with his unit at the Battles of Ypres, Loos, the Somme, Arras, Vimy Ridge, Bullecourt, Messines and Cambrai. He also took part in the Retreat and Advance of 1918, and in December 1918 was discharged, holding the 1914 Star, and the General Service and Victory Medals.
13, Leicester Street, Northampton. Z3359.

HARLEY, G., Private, 2nd Northants. Regiment.
Mobilised in August 1914, he was immediately drafted to the Western Front, where he fought at the Battles of the Marne, the Aisne, La Bassée and Ypres. He was reported missing in March 1915, and is now presumed to have been unfortunately killed in action at Aubers Ridge. He was entitled to the 1914 Star, and the General Service and Victory Medals.
"And doubtless he went in splendid company."
Near Bridge, Kislingbury, Northants. Z3360/B.

HARLEY, T. P., Private, Labour Corps.
Having previously been rejected three times, he joined in February 1917, and was immediately drafted to France. In this theatre of war he was engaged on important duties in connection with the construction of railways and roads, and was present during heavy fighting in the Ypres sector. He was demobilised in January 1919, and holds the General Service and Victory Medals. Near Bridge, Kislingbury, Northants. Z3360/A.

HARLEY, W., Private, Royal Fusiliers.
Volunteering in August 1914, he underwent a period of training and was retained on important duties with his unit at Hounslow Barracks. He was later found to be medically unfit for further service, and was therefore discharged in December 1915.
Near Bridge, Kislingbury, Northants. Z3360/C.

HARLOW, V., Guardsman, 1st Grenadier Guards.
Mobilised in August 1914, he was immediately drafted to the Western Front, where he fought in the Battle of and Retreat from Mons. He also took part in the Battles of the Marne and the Aisne and, severely wounded at Ypres in November 1914, was admitted to hospital at Birmingham. Invalided from the Army in December 1917, he holds the Mons Star, and the General Service and Victory Medals.
1, Sunderland Street, Northampton. Z2407.

HARNWELL, E. A. (M.S.M.), L/Corporal, R.E.
Having volunteered in December 1915, he underwent a period of training prior to being drafted overseas in August 1916. Whilst on the Western Front he was engaged on important duties with his unit and served during heavy fighting at Albert, Thiépval and Courcellette in the Somme sector. He did consistently good work, and was awarded the Meritorious Service Medal for devotion to duty in the Field. After the cessation of hostilities, he served with the Army of Occupation at Bonn. Demobilised in April 1919, he also holds the General Service and Victory Medals. Roade, Northants. Z2164.

HARRIS, A., Private, 7th Northants. Regiment.
Volunteering in May 1915, he completed his training in the same year, and was drafted overseas. Whilst on the Western Front he took part in heavy fighting in the Ypres and Somme sectors before being badly wounded in May 1916. He unfortunately died from the effects of his wounds shortly afterwards, and was entitled to the 1914-15 Star, and the General Service and Victory Medals.
"The path of duty was the way to glory."
11, Phœnix Street, Northampton. Z1202.

HARRIS, A. G., Private, 6th Northants. Regt.
Volunteering in August 1914, he was sent to the Western Front in the following year, and there saw much heavy fighting. After taking part in the Battles of Ypres and Loos he was severely wounded and gassed on the Somme in July 1916, and invalided home. He was afterwards engaged on farm work until demobilised in February 1919, holding the 1914-15 Star, and the General Service and Victory Medals.
High Street, Gayton, Northants. Z2408.

HARRIS, C. L., Driver, Royal Field Artillery.
He volunteered in October 1915, and in June of the following year was drafted to the Western Front, where he saw severe fighting in various sectors. He took part in the Battles of the Somme, Arras, Vimy Ridge, Bullecourt, Ypres and Cambrai, fought also in the Retreat and Advance of 1918 and afterwards served with the Army of Occupation in Germany. Demobilised in June 1920, he holds the General Service and Victory Medals. 85, Greenwood Road, Northampton. Z2410/A.

HARRIS, E. K., Rifleman, Rifle Brigade.
Serving in India in August 1914, he was quickly drafted to the Western Front, where he took part in the Battles of Neuve Chapelle and Hill 60, and in minor engagements. He died gloriously on the Field of Battle at Ypres on May 10th, 1915, and was entitled to the 1914-15 Star, and the General Service and Victory Medals.
"Steals on the ear the distant triumph song."
85, Greenwood Road, Northampton. Z2410/B.

HARRIS, F., Private, 10th Suffolk Regiment.
He joined in April 1916, and after a period of training was retained on duties of an important nature at Felixstowe, rendering valuable services during air raids over that town. Unfortunately his health broke down, and he was discharged as medically unfit for further military duties in May 1917, after 13 months' excellent work in the Army.
17, Weedon Road, Northampton. Z3361.

HARRIS, F., Private, 11th (Prince Albert's Own) Hussars.
He enlisted in 1917, and after a period of training was engaged at Aldershot on important duties with his unit. Owing to his being over age he was unable to proceed to a theatre of war, but rendered valuable services until his demobilisation in 1919.
66, Abbey Street, Northampton. Z2708.

HARRIS, F. A. J., Bombardier, R.F.A.
Having joined in January 1917, he was drafted overseas later in the same year. During his service in France he took part in many important engagements, and was gassed in action. After hostilities ceased he proceeded to Germany with the Army of Occupation and served there until his demobilisation in September 1919. He holds the General Service and Victory Medals.
18, Melbourne Road, St. James' End, Northampton. Z2707.

HARRIS, G., L/Cpl., 1/4th Northants. Regiment.
He volunteered in August 1914, and in the following July was drafted to the Dardanelles, where he saw much heavy fighting. Later he was sent to Egypt, thence to Palestine, and took part in the Battles of Rafa and Gaza and in the fall of Jerusalem. Contracting malaria, he was invalided home and eventually demobilised in March 1919, holding the General Service and Victory Medals. 36, Parkwood Street, Northampton. Z2409/A.

HARRIS, G. F. W., Sergeant, 14th Royal Warwickshire Regiment.
Volunteering in December 1915, he first served with the 12th Lancers during the Irish Rebellion in April 1916. In the following December he proceeded to France and played a prominent part in the Battles of Arras, Vimy Ridge, Messines, Ypres and Passchendaele. Transferred to the Royal Warwickshire Regiment, he was sent to Italy and fought on the Piave and the Asiago Plateau before returning to the Western Front, where, after being gassed at Nieppe Forest and fighting at Amiens, he died gloriously on the Field of Battle at Gouzeaucourt on September 15th, 1918. He was entitled to the General Service and Victory Medals.
"A costly sacrifice upon the altar of freedom."
43, Poole Street, Northampton. Z2166/B.

HARRIS, H., Private, Suffolk Regiment.
Joining in March 1916, he underwent a period of training and in the following year was drafted to France, where he took part in much fighting on the Ypres and Cambrai fronts. On November 30th, 1917, he was reported missing, and is now presumed to have been killed in action on that date. He was entitled to the General Service and Victory Medals.
"And doubtless he went in splendid company."
12, Fitzroy Terrace, Northampton. Z1203.

HARRIS, J. F., Private, M.G.C. (Infantry).
Mobilised from the Reserve at the outbreak of war in August 1914, he was immediately drafted to the Western Front, where he took part in the Retreat from Mons and also in the Battles of the Marne, the Aisne, La Bassée, Ypres, Neuve Chapelle, Loos and the Somme. Later, however, he contracted an illness and was evacuated to England, and after a period of hospital treatment was invalided out of the Army in August 1918. He holds the Mons Star, and the General Service and Victory Medals. 65, Duke Street, Northampton. Z1451/A.

HARRIS, J. G., Private, Royal Fusiliers.
After joining in 1918 he completed a period of training, but, owing to the early cessation of hostilities, was unable to take part in operations in a theatre of war. He was, however, drafted to India in 1919 for important garrison duties with his unit, and was still serving there in 1920.
3, First Square, Nelson Street, Northampton. Z1335.

HARRIS, J. S., Private, Northants. Regiment.
Volunteering in August 1914, he completed his training in the following year, and proceeded overseas. During his service on the Western Front he took part in many important engagements in various sectors, particularly during heavy fighting at Givenchy, Loos, the Somme and Ypres. Later he was invalided to England, and in August 1917 was discharged as medically unfit for further service, holding the 1914–15 Star, and the General Service and Victory Medals.
14, Little Cross Street, Northampton. Z1035/B.

HARRIS, M. E. (Miss), Worker, Q.M.A.A.C.
She joined in June 1916, and, after a short period of training, served at Portsmouth and, later, at Winchester. There she was engaged on important duties as a cook, and in this capacity rendered very valuable services until March 1919, when she was demobilised. 27, St. John's Street, Northampton. Z2995/C

HARRIS, S., Private, 1st Northants. Regiment.
Called up with the Reserve in August 1914, he was immediately drafted to France, where he took part in the Retreat from Mons and the Battles of the Marne, the Aisne and Ypres before being wounded and invalided home. Returning to France on his recovery, he was in action on the Somme, Ypres and Cambrai fronts, and also during the Retreat and Advance of 1918. He was discharged in February 1919, and holds the Mons Star, and the General Service and Victory Medals.
51, Monks Park Road, Northampton. Z2167.

HARRIS, T., Private, 1st Bedfordshire Regiment.
He joined in April 1917, and after completing a period of training was retained on important duties at various stations. He was unable to obtain his transfer overseas before the cessation of hostilities, but in December 1918 was sent to Cologne with the Army of Occupation. Returning home for demobilisation in 1919, he re-enlisted in the Royal Army Service Corps, and in 1920 proceeded to India, and thence to Mesopotamia, where he was serving at Basra in 1921.
27, St. John's Street, Northampton. Z2995/A.

HARRIS, T. F., Signalman, R.N.V.R.
He joined in April 1917, and, after his training, was posted to S.S. "Kilchrenan" for escort duties to Port Said, returning to Dundee in S.S. "Moora." He was also engaged on important duties in S.S. "Kilham," "Vigo" and other vessels in the North and Mediterranean Seas, finally being demobilised in January 1919. He holds the General Service and Victory Medals. 36, Rothersthorpe Road, Northampton. Z3040.

HARRISON, A., Private, R.A.M.C.
He volunteered in November 1915, and in the following year was drafted to France. There he served as a stretcher-bearer, and took part in much heavy fighting in the Somme, Ypres and Arras sectors. After hostilities ceased he proceeded to Germany with the Army of Occupation and served on the Rhine until his demobilisation in March 1919. He holds the General Service and Victory Medals.
The Green, Milton, Northants. Z2411.

HARRISON, A. E., Private, 1/4th Northants. Regt.
He volunteered in June 1915, and in the following August was sent to Egypt. After serving in this theatre of war for some time he advanced into Palestine, where he saw much severe fighting with General Allenby's Forces, and was in action in the Battles of Gaza and at the capture of Jerusalem. Demobilised in July 1919, he holds the 1914–15 Star, and the General Service and Victory Medals.
Vine Cottage, Union Court, St. Andrew's Street, Northampton. Z1205.

HARRISON, A. G., Private, R.M.L.I.
He joined in May 1918, and underwent a period of training at Chatham and Deal. After the cessation of hostilities he was commissioned to H.M.S. "Barham," and proceeded to sea. In 1921 he was still serving in foreign waters.
7, Stenson Street, Northampton. Z2709/D.

HARRISON, F. C., Pte., 2/8th Lancs. Fusiliers.
Volunteering in April 1915, he was retained on important duties at various stations before proceeding overseas in 1917. Whilst on the Western Front he took part in engagements in the Ypres, the Somme and Givenchy sectors, and was badly wounded on the Somme in March 1918. In consequence he was invalided home and discharged as medically unfit in September 1918. He holds the General Service and Victory Medals. The Green, Milton, Northants. Z2412/A.

HARRISON, H., Private, Queen's Own (Royal West Kent Regiment).
Joining in October 1917, he was quickly drafted to the Western Front, where he took part in many engagements, including the Battles of Cambrai, the Somme (II.) and Amiens, and was wounded in August 1918. As a result he was evacuated to hospital in Wales, and, after a period of treatment, was demobilised in February 1919. He holds the General Service and Victory Medals. 13, Althorp Street, Northampton. Z1204.

HARRISON, J., Corporal, Queen's Own (Royal West Kent Regiment).
When war broke out he was serving in the Territorial Forces, and was stationed at various depôts in England until 1917, when he obtained a transfer to France. On that front he was engaged in fierce fighting, chiefly in the Ypres sector, until the cessation of hostilities. He was demobilised on his return to England in March 1919, and holds the General Service and Victory Medals. 77, Delapre Street, Northampton. Z3245/A.

HARRISON, L. J., Sergeant, Tank Corps.
He enlisted in February 1917 and, having completed his training in the following January, was drafted to France. In this theatre of war he took a prominent part in much heavy fighting, but, contracting trench fever, was invalided home. On his recovery he was retained on important duties until his demobilisation in October 1919, and holds the General Service and Victory Medals. The Green, Milton, Northants. Z2412/B.

HARRISON, P., L/Cpl., Leicester Hussars.
He joined as a private in February 1914 in the Royal Army Service Corps, and, after the outbreak of war, was transferred to the Leicester Hussars and drafted to France in January 1916. In this theatre of war he took part in the Battles of St. Eloi, Albert, the Somme, Beaumont-Hamel, Arras and Cambrai, and was wounded in July 1916. After the Armistice he proceeded with the Army of Occupation to Germany, where he served until his discharge in March 1920. He holds the General Service and Victory Medals.
7, Stenson Street, Northampton. Z2709/A.

HARRISON, S. (Mrs.), Driver, American Red Cross.
She joined in November 1917, and for over two years was engaged as a driver of a Red Cross Ambulance at the Statten Island Hospital, New York, U.S.A. She rendered very valuable services in this capacity until March 1920, when she was discharged owing to a breakdown in health.
Sportsman's Arms, Bath Street, Northampton. Z2709/C.

HARRISON, T. S., Pte., 13th Middlesex Regiment.
Shortly after joining in February 1916 he was drafted to the Western Front, where he saw much heavy fighting. After taking part in several important engagements, he was severely wounded in the Somme Offensive of the same year, and was admitted to hospital at Edmonton. He was finally invalided from the Army in October 1918, and holds the General Service and Victory Medals.
Squirrel Lane, Old Duston, Northants. Z3041.

HARRISON, W., Private, Middlesex Regiment.
At the outbreak of hostilities in August 1914 he volunteered, and in April of the following year proceeded overseas. Serving on the Western Front, he took part in numerous engagements, including the Battles of Ypres and Festubert, but was unhappily killed in action in August 1915. He was entitled to the 1914–15 Star, and the General Service and Victory Medals.
"Whilst we remember, the sacrifice is not in vain."
108, Southampton Road, Northampton. Z3345/B.

HART, A. J., Corporal, R.A.S.C. (M.T.)
Joining in June 1916, he underwent a period of training and in the following October proceeded to Mesopotamia. In this seat of operations he was engaged in conveying ammunition and foodstuffs to the forward areas and served during heavy fighting at Baghdad. He also did continuously good work in attending to the sick and wounded, and in December 1919 was demobilised, holding the General Service and Victory Medals.
57, Stimpson Avenue, Northampton. Z2168.

HART, C. S., Ordinary Seaman, Royal Navy.
He joined in October 1918, at the age of 17 years, and after completing a short period of training was posted to H.M.S. "Eaglet." On board this vessel he was engaged chiefly in guarding the German Fleet at Scapa Flow, and rendered very valuable services until finally demobilised in October 1919.
72, Rothersthorpe Road, Northampton. Z3042.

HART, C. S., Private, 10th Queen's (Royal West Surrey Regiment).
He joined in February 1916, and, proceeding to France in the following September, saw heavy fighting at Dickebusch and the Somme. His health breaking down he was invalided home, but on his recovery he returned to the Western Front, and was transferred to the Royal Army Service Corps and stationed at Boulogne. Unfortunately he was again taken ill and admitted to hospital in Boulogne, and on his return home was demobilised in May 1919, holding the General Service and Victory Medals.
5, Southampton Road, Far Cotton, Northampton. Z3362.

HART, F., Gunner, Royal Garrison Artillery.
He enlisted in 1916, and after a period of training was drafted later in the same year to India. There he was engaged at various stations on important garrison duties and did good work throughout his service. He was in hospital for a time suffering from malaria, and was eventually demobilised in December 1919, holding the General Service and Victory Medals. 17, Chapel Lane, Daventry, Northants. Z2710.

HART, F. W., Sapper, Royal Engineers.
He volunteered in October 1915, and proceeding to France, first served as a signaller with the Royal Field Artillery at the Battles of Ypres, Passchendaele and Cambrai, and in the Retreat of 1918. Badly wounded in action at the Battle of Bapaume at the beginning of the Advance in August, he was evacuated to England after seven weeks' in hospital at Trouville. On his recovery he was stationed at Plymouth until his demobilisation in February 1919, holding the General Service and Victory Medals.
57, Stimpson's Avenue, Northampton. Z2169.

HART, H., Private, Royal Fusiliers.
He volunteered in September 1915, and on conclusion of his training in the following year was drafted to France. Whilst on the Western Front he served in various sectors, and was in action at the Battles of the Somme, Arras, Ypres and Cambrai. He did consistently good work throughout the period of hostilities, and was wounded and gassed. Demobilised in June 1919, he holds the General Service and Victory Medals.
23, Fort Street, Northampton. Z1206.

HARTLEY, G., Private, R.A.V.C.
He volunteered in October 1915, and being drafted to France early in the following year was engaged on special duties with his unit in the Somme, Arras, Ypres and Cambrai sectors. He also rendered valuable services during the Retreat and Advance of 1918, and was demobilised in November 1919, holding the General Service and Victory Medals.
55, Alcombe Road, Northampton. Z1924.

HARTWELL, G. S. B., Tpr., Northants. Dragoons.
Volunteering in October 1914, he was drafted in the following year to France, where he was in action at the Battles of Hill 60 and Ypres, and other notable engagements. In 1917 he was transferred to Italy, where he saw heavy fighting on the Piave and Asiago fronts, until he contracted pneumonia, to which he unhappily succumbed on October 24th, 1918. He was entitled to the 1914–15 Star, and the General Service and Victory Medals.
"His memory is cherished with pride."
2, St. Giles Terrace, Northampton. Z3363/A.

HARVEY, G. H., A/Corporal, R.N.D.
He joined in September 1916, and in August of the following year was sent to France, where he was in action with the Hood Battalion at Arras, Aveluy Wood, Miraumont, Beaumont-Hamel, Ypres, Passchendaele, St. Quentin, Marcoing, Bapaume, Havrincourt, Valenciennes and Mons. He was also stationed at Calais, and was demobilised in February 1919, holding the General Service and Victory Medals.
66, Hood Street, Northampton. Z1452.

HARVEY, J., Private, 1/4th Northants. Regt.
Called up from the Reserve in August 1914, he was sent to the Dardanelles in April 1915 and saw much severe fighting there until the Evacuation of the Gallipoli Peninsula. He then proceeded to Egypt, but being wounded in action in September 1916, was invalided home. After hospital treatment in York he rejoined his unit in Palestine and fought at Gaza. Discharged in March 1919, he holds the 1914–15 Star, and the General Service and Victory Medals.
23, Spencer Road, Northampton. Z1453/A.

HASDELL, E. W., Sergeant, Royal Engineers.
He was mobilised with the Territorials in August 1914, and in the following month was drafted to France, where he played a prominent part in the Battles of the Marne, La Bassée and Ypres, and was wounded. As a result he was invalided home, but on his recovery returned to France, and was in action at Albert, Ploegsteert, Vimy Ridge, the Somme, Arras, Ypres, Cambrai and in the Retreat and Advance of 1918. Discharged in July 1919, he holds the 1914 Star, and the General Service and Victory Medals.
98, Adnitt Road, Northampton. Z2413.

HASKER, A., Rifleman, Rifle Brigade.
After joining in October 1918, he underwent a period of training, but owing to the early cessation of hostilities, was unable to take part in operations in a theatre of war. He proceeded to Germany, however, and served with the Army of Occupation at Cologne, where he was engaged on important guard duties until demobilised in March 1920.
15, Regent Street, Northampton. Z1207.

HASLER, W. A., Bandsman, 12th Manchester Regt.
Joining in March 1917, he was shortly afterwards drafted to the Western Front, where he took part in many important engagements. He saw much fighting at Ypres, and was wounded at Péronne in March 1918. As a result he was evacuated to hospital in England, but on his recovery rejoined his unit in France and was in action on the Somme before being wounded again. Returning home he was demobilised in May 1919, holding the General Service and Victory Medals.
43, Hampton Street, Northampton. Z1208/A.

HASLOP, W., Leading Seaman, Royal Navy.
Already in the Navy at the outbreak of war, he quickly proceeded to the North Sea on board H.M.S. "Revenge." He took part in the Battles of Heligoland Bight, the Dogger Bank and Jutland, and was also engaged on important patrol and convoy duties. Later he was present at the surrender of the German Fleet at Scapa Flow, and in 1921 was stationed in the West Indies. He holds the 1914–15 Star, and the General Service and Victory Medals.
2, Abbey Terrace, Abbey Street, Northampton. Z2711.

HASTINGS, A., Private, 2nd Northants. Regt.
He joined in June 1916, and crossing to France in the following November fought in the Battles of the Ancre and Beaumont-Hamel, and was wounded at Ypres in 1917. On his return to the firing line he was in action during the Retreat of 1918, but was again wounded at Amiens. On rejoining his unit in May 1918 he was wounded and taken prisoner and held in captivity until the Armistice. Demobilised in December 1918, he holds the General Service and Victory Medals.
Brayfield on the Green, Northants. Z3366.

HATTON, P. F., Trooper, Northants. Dragoons.
Joining in February 1916, he was sent overseas in January of the following year. Serving on the Western Front he fought in engagements on the Somme and in the Ypres sector, but was taken prisoner at the Dunes in July 1917. He was released from captivity in December 1918, and demobilised a month later, holding the General Service and Victory Medals.
99, Abbey Road, Far Cotton, Northampton. Z3367/B.

HATTON, W. D., Private, 2/2nd London Regiment (Royal Fusiliers).
Four months after joining in March 1917 he embarked for France, on which front he took part in numerous engagements of note. Whilst fighting on the Somme in March 1918 he was taken prisoner and held in captivity in Saxony. Unfortunately his health broke down and he died in December 1918, and was entitled to the General Service and Victory Medals.
"The path of duty was the way to glory."
99, Abbey Road, Far Cotton, Northampton. Z3367/A.

HAWKER, T. P., Private, 11th (Prince Albert's Own) Hussars.
He was mobilised at the outbreak of war in August 1914, and shortly afterwards was drafted to France, where he fought through the Retreat from Mons. He later took part in many important engagements on various fronts, doing excellent work, and was wounded on two occasions, his second wound necessitating his evacuation to England. Eventually invalided out of the service in January 1918, he holds the Mons Star, and the General Service and Victory Medals, and the Delhi Durbar Medals. 99, Overstone Road, Northampton. Z1454.

HAWKINS, C., Corporal, R.A.M.C.
Mobilised in August 1914, he was immediately drafted to the Western Front, where after serving at Mons, he was present at the Battles of Ypres and Neuve Chapelle. Transferred in October 1915 to Salonika he was there engaged on important duties on the Vardar and Struma fronts, before returning home in February 1919. He was discharged in November 1919, and holds the Mons Star, and the General Service and Victory Medals. 61, Denmark Road, Northampton. Z3043/B.

HAWKINS, F. P., Corporal, 4th Northants Regt.
He volunteered in the Middlesex Regiment in August 1914, but on completing his training in the following December was invalided from the Army. He re-enlisted, however, in October 1915, and was retained on important duties at various stations, being unable to obtain his transfer overseas on account of ill-health. He was discharged in March 1917 as medically unfit for further service.
69, Denmark Road, Northampton. Z3043/A.

HAWKINS, J., Cpl., 8th Lincolnshire Regiment.
He joined in January 1917, and completing his training later in the same year was drafted to France. Whilst in this theatre of war he took part in much heavy fighting in the Ypres and Lys sectors, and was twice wounded in action—in 1917 and 1918. He was demobilised in October 1919, and holds the General Service and Victory Medals.
37, Greenwood Road, Northampton. Z2712/B.

HAWKINS, S. A. V., Gunner, R.G.A.
He enlisted in 1917, and underwent a period of training prior to his being drafted to France. In this theatre of war he took part in the Retreat and Advance f 1918, being in action at Albert, and Le Cateau, and after the cessation of hostilities proceeded to Germany. He served with the Army of Occupation at Cologne until his demobilisation in October 1919, holding the General Service and Victory Medals.
32, Cecil Road, Northampton. Z2414.

HAWKINS, W. (M.S.M.), Driver, R.A.S.C. (M.T.)
He volunteered in October 1915, and was quickly drafted to France. In this theatre of war he was engaged on important transport duties, and served during heavy fighting at Armentières, and also at the Battles of Vimy Ridge, the Somme, Messines, Ypres, Bapaume and Le Cateau (II.). He was awarded the Meritorious Service Medal for gallantry and devotion to duty in the Field, and in June 1919 was demobilised, holding also the 1914–15 Star, and the General Service and Victory Medals.
39, Roseholme Road, Northampton. Z2170.

HAYMAN, W. J., Pte., 1st Leicestershire Regiment.
Mobilised in August 1914, he proceeded in the following February to the Western Front, where he participated in the Battles of Neuve Chapelle, St. Eloi, Hill 60, Ypres, Festubert, Loos, the Somme and Arras. He performed good work during his service overseas, and was unhappily killed in action on March 21st, 1918, during the second Battle of the Somme. He was entitled to the 1914–15 Star, and the General Service and Victory Medals.
"A valiant Soldier, with undaunted heart he breasted life's last hill."
37, Ash Street, Northampton. Z1336.

HAYNES, C. M. (M.M.), Private, Northants. Regt.
Mobilised in August 1914, he proceeded to France and fought in the Battle of, and the Retreat from, Mons, the Battles of the Marne, the Aisne and Ypres (I.), where he was wounded and invalided home. On his recovery he was discharged after 17 years' service, but re-enlisted in January 1916, again proceeded to France, and was awarded the Military Medal for conspicuous bravery on the Somme. Badly wounded in July 1916 he was evacuated to England, but in June 1917 returned to France for the third time with the Royal Army Service Corps (M.T.), and did splendid work with a supply column until demobilised in March 1919, also holding the Mons Star, and the General Service and Victory Medals.
6, Little Cross Street, Northampton. Z1209.

HAYNES, F. C., L/Corporal, 7th Northants. Regt.
Joining in January 1916, he shortly afterwards landed in France. In this seat of operations he took part in many important engagements in various sectors of the front, and was gassed. He did continuously good work until 1918, when he was invalided home suffering from trench fever. On his recovery he was engaged on important duties until demobilised in November 1919, and holds the General Service and Victory Medals. 22, Brunswick Street, Northampton. Z1925.

HAYNES, G. J., Pte., 4th Northants. Regiment.
He volunteered in October 1914, and underwent a period of training prior to his being drafted to France in the following year. Whilst on the Western Front he took part in several engagements in the Ypres sector until 1916, when he was invalided home. Later he was retained on important duties, and was eventually demobilised in February 1919. He holds the 1914–15 Star, and the General Service and Victory Medals.
18, Abbey Street, Daventry, Northants. Z2606/C.

HAYNES, H., L/Corporal, 4th Royal Fusiliers.
He enlisted in February 1918, and three months later was drafted to France, where he took part in many engagements on the Somme and Amiens fronts and in the Advance of 1918. After the cessation of hostilities he returned home, but later proceeded to Mesopotamia, where in 1921 he was still serving. He holds the General Service and Victory Medals.
18, Abbey Street, Daventry, Northampton. Z2606/B.

HAYNES, W., Private, 4th Northants. Regiment.
He volunteered in January 1915, and twelve months later was sent to Egypt, where he was in action at Romani and El Arish. Later proceeding into Palestine, he took part in the Battles of Gaza (being wounded during the third engagement), and was taken prisoner in the Advance on Jerusalem. He was released after the Armistice, and was demobilised in April 1919, holding the General Service and Victory Medals.
50, Castle Street, Northampton. Z1210.

HAYTER, F. L., Driver, Royal Field Artillery.
Joining in April 1917, he was sent to India on completion of a period of training in the following October. There he was engaged on important garrison duties at Quetta, Poona and Rawal Pindi, and rendered valuable services with his Battery. He was demobilised on his return home in April 1919 and holds the General Service and Victory Medals.
Spratton, Northants. Z3044.

HAYWOOD, C. H., Private, 1/4th Northants. Regt.
After volunteering in April 1915 in the Royal Army Service Corps, he underwent a period of training and proceeded to Egypt, where he saw much service. Whilst in this seat of operations he was transferred to the Northamptonshire Regiment, and later served with General Allenby's Forces in Palestine, being in action at many important engagements. He returned home for demobilisation in June 1919, and holds the General Service and Victory Medals.
112, Lloyd Road, Northampton. Z2172.

HAZLEWOOD, J., Gunner, Royal Field Artillery.
He joined in February 1917, and after a period of training proceeded in the following May to France. In this theatre of war, he was in action with his Battery in several important engagements including the Battles of Ypres, Cambrai and the Somme. Returning home after the Armistice, he was ultimately demobilised in July 1919, and holds the General Service and Victory Medals.
51, Brook Street, Northampton. Z1211.

HEADLAND, W., Trooper, Northamptonshire Dragoons.
He volunteered in October 1915, and in the following August was drafted to the Western Front. After taking part in strenuous fighting on the Ypres front, he was sent to Le Havre, where he was employed on guard and other duties at a prisoner of war camp, doing good work until he was demobilised in March 1919, holding the General Service and Victory Medals. He also served with the 3rd Cheshire Regiment.
20, Spring Lane, Northampton. Z1212.

HEALEY, E. W. A., Private, Machine Gun Corps.
He joined in December 1916, and in the following year was drafted to India, thence to Mesopotamia. In this seat of operations he took part in the capture of Baghdad and the occupation of Mosul. Later he returned to India, where he served on the North West Frontier at Kurdistan. Demobilised in February 1920, he holds the General Service, Victory, and the India General Service Medals (with Clasp, Afghanistan, N.W. Frontier, 1919). School Lane, Bletchley, Bucks. Z2714.

HEARD, E. D. T., Private, 16th (The Queen's) Lancers.
Mobilised at the outbreak of hostilities, he was immediately drafted to France, where he took part in the Battle of, and the Retreat from, Mons, and the Battles of the Marne, the Aisne, Ypres (I.), Neuve Chapelle, Hill 60, Ypres (II.), Loos, the Somme, Vimy Ridge, Arras and Ypres (III.). He was afterwards engaged on important duties at the Base, and rendered excellent services until discharged in June 1919, holding the Mons Star, and the General Service and Victory Medals.
22, Freehold Street, Northampton. Z1926

HEDGE, F., Bombardier, Royal Garrison Artillery.
Joining in May 1916, he was sent in February of the following year to France, where he served with a Howitzer Battery in severe actions on various fronts, and was also employed for some time in conveying supplies to the front line. He performed consistently good work during his service overseas, and was demobilised in September 1919, holding the General Service and Victory Medals.
60, Oliver Street, Northampton. Z1337/A.

HEDGE, F., Private, Royal Army Service Corps.
He volunteered in October 1915, but was too old for transfer to a theatre of war. Retained at home, he was employed on various duties in the bakery section of the Royal Army Service Corps, and was stationed at Salisbury Plain and Northampton. He rendered excellent service until he was demobilised in March 1919.
51, Poole Street, Northampton. Z1455/A.

HEDGE, F. W., Private, Royal Fusiliers.
He joined in August 1918, but was not successful in obtaining a transfer to a theatre of war owing to the termination of hostilities. During his training he served with the Royal Fusiliers at Newmarket, and was later transferred to the Royal Engineers, and proceeded to Mildenhall Signal School. In February 1919 he was sent to Germany, and served with the Army of Occupation until he was demobilised in October 1919.
51, Poole Street, Northampton. Z1455/B.

HEEL, H., Private, Machine Gun Corps.
Six months after joining in March 1916 he was drafted to Mesopotamia, where he saw much heavy fighting. After taking part in several engagements he was severely wounded at the capture of Baghdad in March 1917, sustaining the loss of the sight of his right eye. He was afterwards engaged on garrison duties in India until his return home for demobilisation in April 1919, and holds the General Service and Victory Medals. 5, Euston Road, Northampton. Z3045.

HEFFORD, A., Private, R.A.M.C.
Joining the Middlesex Regiment in February 1917, he proceeded two months later to France, where he participated in the Battles of Arras and Messines, and was wounded at the latter place in June 1917. As a result he was invalided home, and having later transferred to the Royal Army Medical Corps, returned to France in March 1918. Whilst employed in the 53rd General Hospital, Wimereux, on various duties, he rendered excellent service, and was demobilised in October 1919, holding the General Service and Victory Medals.
11, Oakley Street, Northampton. Z1338.

HEFFORD, A. H., Pte., 1st Northants. Regiment.
He volunteered in August 1914, and later in the same year was drafted to France, where he took part in many important engagements in various sectors. He made the supreme sacrifice, being killed in action at Aubers Ridge on May 9th, 1915, and was entitled to the 1914 Star, and the General Service and Victory Medals.
"A valiant Soldier, with undaunted heart he breasted life's last hill."
11a, First Square, Northampton. Z3046.

HEFFORD, F., Private, 2/5th Manchester Regt.
He joined in March 1916, and after a brief training was drafted to the Western Front. During his service overseas he was in action with his unit on the Somme and Ypres fronts, and was wounded at Passchendaele in September 1918, being invalided home in consequence. After a course of hospital treatment he was ultimately demobilised in April 1919, and holds the General Service and Victory Medals.
112, Scarletwell Street, Northampton. Z1213.

HELL, J. W., Rifleman, 18th London Irish Rifles.
He joined in February 1916, and three months later was drafted to the Western Front, where he took part in much heavy fighting in the Somme and Ypres sectors, and was wounded in 1916. He made the supreme sacrifice, being killed in action on the Aisne in May 1918, and was entitled to the General Service and Victory Medals.
"A valiant Soldier, with undaunted heart he breasted life's last hill."
Gayton, Northampton. Z2388/A.

HELMS, C. W., Lieut., 7th King's (Liverpool Regt.)
He joined the Ranks in September 1914, and on conclusion of his training in the following July proceeded overseas. Serving on the Western Front, he took part in heavy fighting at Ypres, Messines and Loos, before being invalided home with rheumatism. On his recovery he was granted a commission and returned to France, where he played a prominent part in many important engagements, particularly in the Somme sector, but was wounded at Festubert in April 1918 and evacuated to England. He was once more sent to France, and was gassed near Tournai, and yet again invalided home. Demobilised in September 1919, he holds the 1914–15 Star, and the General Service and Victory Medals. 41, Abington Road, Northampton. Z2173.

HENMAN, F. G., Private, Cheshire Regiment.
He joined in November 1916, and proceeding to the Western Front a month later, saw much service in the Ypres sector. He was also in action in numerous important engagements during the Retreat and Advance of 1918, and was wounded on three occasions. After the cessation of hostilities he advanced with the Army of Occupation into Germany, serving there until demobilised in January 1919. He holds the General Service and Victory Medals. Denton, Northants. Z3368.

HENMAN, W., Sapper, Royal Engineers.
Volunteering in August 1915, he completed his training and was retained on important duties as a blacksmith and general engineering work at various stations. Later in 1918 he was drafted to Russia, where he served at Archangel, the Murman Coast, and other stations on important duties until demobilised in August 1919, holding the General Service and Victory Medals.
"Rose Cottage," Roade, Northampton. Z2090/C.

HENRY, M., Worker, Q.M.A.A.C.
She joined Queen Mary's Auxiliary Army Corps in 1917, and during the period of her engagement was employed on various duties in the Gunnery School at Lydd and in London. She performed consistently good work until she was demobilised in 1919. 24, Earl Street, Northampton. Z1456.

HENSHAW, F. W., Sergeant, R.A.S.C. (M.T.)
Joining in November 1916, he was not successful in his endeavours to secure a transfer to a theatre of war. Throughout the period of his service he was engaged on important inspection duties in connection with the manufacture of munitions, which work demanded a high degree of technical knowledge. He carried out his duties with the utmost efficiency and was eventually demobilised in September 1919.
44, Abbey Street, Northampton. Z3369

HEPPEL, W. J. B. (M.M.), Cpl., 7th Beds. Regt.
He volunteered in November 1914, and on conclusion of his training was drafted overseas. Whilst on the Western Front he did consistently good work with his unit and took part in many important engagements in various sectors. He was awarded the Military Medal for conspicuous bravery and devotion to duty in the Field at Westhoek Ridge. In February 1919 he was demobilised, holding also the 1914–15 Star, and the General Service and Victory Medals.
8, Cloutsham Street, Northampton. Z1927.

HERBERT, W., Pte., 7th Oxford. and Bucks. L.I.
He volunteered in September 1914, and twelve months later was drafted to France, where he took part in engagements in the Albert sector. Later he was transferred to Salonika, and saw much fighting on the Vardar and Doiran fronts before being wounded in May 1917 and invalided to hospital. He afterwards rejoined his unit, and was eventually demobilised in May 1919, holding the 1914–15 Star, and the General Service and Victory Medals. Long Street, Hanslope, Bucks. Z2716.

HERBERT. W. C., Cpl., 3rd Somersetshire L.I.
He enlisted in June 1916, and three months later was drafted to France, where he fought on the Somme, at Arras and Ypres, and was wounded in September 1917. Invalided home, he later returned to his unit, and took part in the Advance of 1918, being gassed in action and again invalided home. On his recovery he proceeded to Ireland and served there until his demobilisation in August 1919. He holds the General Service and Victory Medals. Hartwell, Northants. Z2715.

HERITAGE, C. W. A., Private, R.A.S.C.
Owing to ill-health he was rejected for military service on two occasions, but ultimately joined in December 1916. He was retained on home service and engaged on clerical and other duties of an important nature at various stations, carrying out his responsible work with great ability until demobilised in September 1919.
65, Lower Thrift Street, Northampton. Z3370—Z2174.

HEWITT, G., Sergeant, Northamptonshire Regt.
A Regular soldier, he was stationed in Egypt at the outbreak of hostilities in August 1914, and was at once drafted to France. There he took part in the Retreat from Mons and in the Battles of the Marne, the Aisne, La Bassée, Ypres and the Somme, doing good work until he fell fighting near Arras on April 17th, 1917. He was entitled to the Mons Star and the General Service and Victory Medals.
"His life for his Country."
33, Francis Street, Northampton. Z1071/A.

HIAMS, C., Private, East Surrey Regiment.
He volunteered in June 1915, and in the following January proceeded to France, where he was in action on the Arras and Somme fronts, and was wounded. He was later sent to Italy, but after a few months' service on the Piave front returned to France in March 1918, and in the same month was taken prisoner on the Somme front. Repatriated after the Armistice, he was demobilised in March 1919, and holds the General Service and Victory Medals.
52, Gladstone Terrace, Northampton. Z1214.

HICKMAN, F. E., Private, 17th Royal Fusiliers.
Volunteering in July 1915, he was sent twelve months later to France. There he took part in the Battles of the Somme, Arras, Ypres and Cambrai, was wounded in April 1918, and invalided home in the following August as the result of being gassed. After spending some time in hospital in Kent, he was eventually demobilised in March 1919, holding the General Service and Victory Medals.
43, Arthur Street, Kingsthorpe Hollow, Northants. Z1339.

HICKMAN, H. L., Driver, R.A.S.C.
He volunteered in November 1915, and in the following June was drafted to France, where he served as a driver on a train conveying supplies and ammunition to the forward areas in the Somme and Arras sectors. After the Armistice he proceeded to Germany and served with the Army of Occupation until his demobilisation in 1919. He afterwards rejoined for three years and first saw service in Egypt, and in 1921 was serving in Ireland. He holds the General Service and Victory Medals.
31, Brook Street, Daventry, Northants. Z2717/B.

HICKMAN, J. W., Private, 1st Bedfordshire Regt.
Already in South Africa at the outbreak of war, he was immediately drafted to France and took part in the Battles of the Marne and the Aisne. He died gloriously on the Field of Battle at Ypres on November 24th, 1914, and was entitled to the 1914 Star, and the General Service and Victory Medals.
"A valiant Soldier, with undaunted heart he breasted life's last hill."
31, Brook Street, Daventry, Northants. Z2717/A.

HICKS, J., Driver, Royal Field Artillery.
He volunteered in 1914, and later in that year was sent to France. He took part with his Battery in several of the earlier engagements of the war, and later served in the Battles of the Somme and Vimy Ridge, and in various actions during the Retreat and Allied Advance in 1918. Returning home after the Armistice, he was demobilised in 1919, and holds the 1914–15 Star, and the General Service and Victory Medals.
60, Lawrence Street, Northampton. Z1340.

HIGGINBOTTOM, J. T., Pte., 7th Northants. Regt.
Volunteering in January 1915, he was drafted to the Western Front in the following September, and was engaged in severe fighting at Loos and Armentières. He also took part in the Battles of Albert, the Somme, Arras, Vimy Ridge and Cambrai, and did good work with his unit in operations during the Retreat and Advance of 1918. Serving in France until February 1919, he was demobilised a month later, holding the 1914–15 Star, and the General Service and Victory Medals.
Hazelwood, Bugbrooke, Northants. Z3371.

HIGGINS, C., Private, 4th Northants. Regiment.
He volunteered in November 1914, but was discharged shortly afterwards as medically unfit. In 1916, however, he re-enlisted in the 3rd Welch Regiment, and after a period of training was transferred to the Royal Army Veterinary Corps. He rendered valuable services, but owing to his being accidentally gassed, he was eventually discharged in February 1918.
3, St. Leonard's Road, Northampton. Z3047/B.

HIGGINS, T. D., Sergeant, V.A.D.
He volunteered in August 1914, and was retained at Northampton and various other stations on duties of a highly important nature. He rendered very valuable services throughout the period of hostilities, and was finally demobilised in February 1919, holding the Long Service Medal with two bars. He was also awarded the Royal Humane Society's Medal for bravery in saving life.
3, St. Leonard's Road, Northampton. Z3047/A.

HIGGS, J. W. S., L/Corporal, K.R.R.C.
He joined on attaining military age in March 1918, but was not successful in obtaining a transfer overseas before the termination of hostilities. During his training he was stationed in Colchester, and was later employed on garrison and other duties. For some time prior to being demobilised in October 1919 he did good work as an instructor in physical training.
25, Herbert Street, Northampton. Z1215.

HILL, A. R., Private, 11th Suffolk Regiment.
He joined in January 1918, and was posted to the Bedfordshire Regiment, being later transferred to the 11th Suffolk Regiment. After a period of training at Brocton Camp and Norwich, he was sent to France in August 1918, was employed at the Base for some time, and then sent to a convalescent camp on the Somme. He remained overseas until 1919, and was eventually demobilised in January 1920, holding the General Service and Victory Medals. 10, Oak Street, Northampton. Z1457/A.

HILL, B. T., Driver, Royal Engineers.
Called up from the Reserve in August 1914, he was immediately drafted to France. There he took part in the Battles of Mons, the Marne, the Aisne, the Somme, Ypres, and saw much heavy fighting in the Advance of 1918, being gassed and twice wounded in action. Discharged in February 1919, he holds the Mons Star, and the General Service and Victory Medals.
1, Richmond Terrace, Northampton. Z2416.

HILL, C. A., Private, 5th Northamptonshire Regt.
He volunteered in August 1914, and in the following May was drafted to France. In this theatre of war he took part in many important engagements, including the Battles of Ypres, the Somme, Arras and Cambrai, and various actions during the Retreat and Advance of 1918. Returning home after the Armistice, he was demobilised in February 1920, and holds the 1914–15 Star, and the General Service and Victory Medals.
14, Kinburn Place, Northampton. Z1163/A.

HILL, E. A., Private, 1st Northants. Regiment.
Already in the Army at the outbreak of war, he was at once drafted to France, and was in action at Mons. After taking part in further heavy fighting he was badly wounded at the end of 1914, and invalided to England. On his recovery he was retained on special duties at various home stations and did excellent work until his discharge in 1919, holding the Mons Star, and the General Service and Victory Medals.
105, St. Leonard's Road, Far Cotton, Northampton. Z3048.

HILL, F. W., Air Mechanic, Royal Air Force.
Joining in March 1917, he underwent a period of training, and was retained on important duties at Roehampton, where he was chiefly engaged as an Instructor in Chemistry. Owing to his being medically unfit as the result of an accident, he was unsuccessful in obtaining his transfer to a theatre of war, but, nevertheless, rendered very valuable services until demobilised in March 1919.
12, Stimpson Avenue, Northampton. Z2175.

HILL, G. H., Sapper, Royal Engineers.
He joined in October 1916, and on conclusion of his training was drafted to the Western Front. Whilst in this theatre of war he took an active part in many important engagements, including the Battles of Arras, Ypres, Passchendaele, Cambrai and the Somme (II.). He was also present at the Entry of Mons at dawn on Armistice Day, and after the conclusion of hostilities proceeded to Germany with the Army of Occupation. Demobilised in 1920, he holds the General Service and Victory Medals.
6, Clarke Road, Northampton. Z2176.

HILL, H. H., Private, 1/4th Northants. Regiment.
He had served in the Territorial Force previous to volunteering in August 1914, and in the following July was sent to Gallipoli, where he was engaged during the various operations. After the Evacuation he was transferred to France, and took part in several important engagements before he was unhappily killed in action near Bapaume on March 4th, 1917. He was buried at Bouchavesnes Wood, near Bapaume, and was entitled to the 1914–15 Star, and the General Service and Victory Medals.
"Whilst we remember, the sacrifice is not in vain."
10, Oak Street, Northampton. Z1457/B.

HILL, R. V., Aircraftsman, Royal Air Force.
He enlisted in May 1918, and after a period of training was engaged in Cornwall on important clerical duties. Owing to the early cessation of hostilities he was unable to obtain a transfer overseas, but rendered valuable services until his demobilisation in March 1919.
15, Sandringham Road, Northampton. Z2417.

HILL, T. S., Sergeant, Royal Field Artillery.
Already in the Army when war broke out in August 1914, he was drafted to India. There he served on the North West Frontier, and saw much fighting against the Afghans. He did continuously good work throughout hostilities, and in 1919 proceeded to Germany with the Army of Occupation, and in 1921 was still serving. He holds the General Service and Victory, and the India General Service Medals (with clasp, Afghanistan, N.W. Frontier, 1919).
3, Parkwood Street, Northampton. Z2418/B.

HILL, W., Private, 1/4th Northants. Regiment.
He volunteered in June 1915, and four months later was drafted to Egypt, where he took part in the engagements on the Suez Canal. In 1916 he was sent home owing to his being under military age, but in March 1918 he proceeded to France and fought on the Somme and in the Retreat and Advance of 1918. Being wounded in action, he was discharged in January 1919, and holds the 1914–15 Star, and the General Service and Victory Medals.
3, Parkwood Street, Northampton. Z2418/A.

HILL, W., Private, Labour Corps.
Joining the Queen's Own (Royal West Kent Regiment) in July 1916, he was shortly afterwards transferred to the Labour Corps and sent to France. During his service overseas he did good work whilst engaged in road-making and digging trenches, but in June 1918 was invalided home on account of ill-health. After a course of treatment in hospital at Croydon he was discharged in September 1918, and holds the General Service and Victory Medals. 34, King Street, Northampton. Z1341/B.

HILL, W. E., Private, 1/4th Northants. Regiment.
Having volunteered in July 1915, he was retained for a time at various home stations before proceeding to France in November 1917. In this theatre of war he took part in much severe fighting in the Ypres and Cambrai sectors, and was badly gassed. As a result he was invalided home and discharged in August 1918, as medically unfit for further service. He holds the General Service and Victory Medals.
103, Abington Avenue, Northampton. Z2419.

HILL, W. G., Q.M.S., R.A.M.C.
Having previously tried to enlist and been rejected, he was called to the Colours in October 1916, and classed as fit for home service only. He was first engaged on clerical duties at Bath, but later did excellent work on the embarkation staff at Southampton, where he remained until his demobilisation in November 1919. 18, Manfield Road, Northampton. Z2177.

HILLERY, R., Driver, R.H.A. and R.F.A.
Having joined the Army in 1900, he was immediately drafted to France, where he took part in the Retreat from Mons and the Battle of the Marne before being badly wounded in action. As a result he was invalided home, and on his recovery was retained on important duties, training recruits at various home stations until his discharge in July 1917. He holds the Mons Star, and the General Service and Victory Medals.
7, Alma Street, Northampton. Z2718.

HILLSON, A. E., Driver, Royal Field Artillery.
He enlisted in October 1917, and having completed his training in the following February was drafted to France. In this theatre of war he took part in many engagements, including those in the Somme and Ypres sectors, and in the Retreat and Advance of 1918. Demobilised in February 1919, he holds the General Service and Victory Medals.
The Green, Hardingstone, Northants. Z2719.

HILLYARD, H. G., Private, 2/19th London Regt.
He enlisted in January 1917, and a few months later was drafted to Egypt. Proceeding into Palestine, he saw much heavy fighting at the Battles of Gaza, and later took part in the Advance to Aleppo with General Allenby's Forces. He returned home and was demobilised in 1920, holding the General Service and Victory Medals. 15, Alma Street, Northampton. Z2720/A.

HILLYARD, R., Rifleman, Rifle Brigade.
He joined in September 1918 on attaining military age, and underwent a few months' training. After hostilities ceased he proceeded to Germany, where he served with the Army of Occupation on various important duties and rendered valuable services. He returned home for his demobilisation in March 1920. 15, Alma Street, Northampton. Z2720/B.

HILLYER, T., Private, Oxford & Bucks. L.I.
Joining in October 1917, he was drafted overseas in the following February. Whilst on the Italian front he took part in several engagements on the Piave River, but owing to the important nature of his previous work was recalled to England, where he was engaged on special duties at Wolverton Carriage Works until his demobilisation in December 1918. He holds the General Service and Victory Medals.
Long Street, Hanslope, Bucks. Z2721/C.

HILLYER, J., L/Cpl., King's Royal Rifle Corps.
He volunteered in August 1914, and in the following May was drafted to France, where he took part in much heavy fighting at Ypres, Festubert, Loos and on the Somme before being wounded in August 1916. He made the supreme sacrifice, being killed in action at Ypres on September 11th, 1917, and was entitled to the 1914–15 Star, and the General Service and Victory Medals.
"The path of duty was the way to glory."
Long Street, Hanslope, Bucks. Z2721/B.

HILLYER, W. G., Gunner, R.F.A.
Having volunteered in August 1914, he was drafted overseas in the following year. Whilst on the Western Front he took part in several engagements, including those at Loos, Albert, Armentières, the Somme, Ypres, Cambrai and in the Retreat and Advance of 1918. He was in hospital for a time suffering from shell-shock, and was eventually demobilised in February 1919, holding the 1914-15 Star, and the General Service and Victory Medals.
Long Street, Hanslope, Bucks. Z2721/A.

HILTON, F., Private, 2nd Bedfordshire Regiment.
He joined the Army in October 1911, and when war broke out in August 1914 was quickly drafted to France. There he took part in the Retreat from Mons and the Battles of the Marne, the Aisne and Ypres, where he was wounded and taken prisoner. Whilst held in captivity in Germany he suffered many hardships. He was released in January 1918, returned home and was eventually discharged from hospital in May 1918. He holds the Mons Star, and the General Service and Victory Medals. 14, West Street, Northampton. Z1928.

HIRONS, S., Rifleman, Rifle Brigade.
He volunteered in September 1914, and in the following May crossed to the Western Front, and whilst there fought in the Battles of Loos and Ypres. He was unfortunately wounded in August 1915, and after receiving hospital treatment was discharged as medically unfit in June 1916. He holds the 1914-15 Star, and the General Service and Victory Medals.
Kilsby, Northampton. Z3372.

HOBBS, A. E., Sapper, Royal Engineers.
He volunteered in December 1915, but was rejected owing to the important nature of his work. In April 1917, however, he joined, and a month later proceeded to France, where he served in many sectors and did valuable work in repairing the railway tracks in preparation for the Advance of 1918. After the Armistice he was sent with the Army of Occupation into Germany and served at Cologne. He was demobilised in October 1919, and holds the General Service and Victory Medals. 65, Ethel Street, Northampton. Z3373.

HOBBS, F. J., Private, York and Lancaster Regt.
Volunteering in 1915, he proceeded in the same year to France, where he fought and was wounded at the Battle of Loos. Returning to the Western Front on his recovery, he took an active part in the fighting throughout the remaining period of war, and after hostilities ended proceeded with the Army of Occupation into Germany. He holds the 1914-15 Star, and the General Service and Victory Medals, and in 1920 was serving in Mesopotamia.
22, Mill Road, Northampton. Z3222/C.

HOBBS, J., Gunner, Royal Garrison Artillery.
Volunteering in September 1914, he was drafted overseas early in the following year. During his service on the Western Front he fought at Ypres, the Somme, Cambrai and in the heavy fighting in many other engagements of note, particularly in the Retreat and Advance of 1918, and was gassed. After his return to England he was demobilised in March 1919, and holds the 1914-15 Star, and the General Service and Victory Medals.
The Green, Lower Heyford, Northampton. Z3374/B.

HOBBS, S., Driver, R.A.S.C. (H.T.)
He volunteered in October 1915, and in the following month proceeded to the Western Front. There he was engaged in conveying ammunition to the forward areas in the Loos, Ploegsteert, Vimy Ridge, the Somme, Arras, Messines, Ypres, Passchendaele, Cambrai and Bapaume sectors, and in the Retreat and Advance of 1918. He was gassed in June 1917, and demobilised in March 1919, holding the 1914-15 Star, and the General Service and Victory Medals.
22, Ruskin Road, Northampton. Z1929.

HOCKENHULL, J., Private, Labour Corps.
Having previously been rejected six times on medical grounds, he joined in June 1916, and after completing a period of training was retained on important agricultural duties with his unit. Owing to his being unfit he was unable to obtain his transfer to a theatre of war, but rendered valuable services until demobilised in November 1918.
13, Portland Street, Northampton. Z2178/B.

HOCKENHULL, T., Pte., North Staffordshire Regt.
Already in the Army in August 1914, he was immediately drafted to France, where he took part in the Retreat from Mons and the Battles of the Marne, the Aisne and La Bassée. He was afterwards drafted to the Dardanelles, and was in action at the Landing at Suvla Bay, before being twice wounded and invalided home. On his recovery he was engaged on important duties attached to the Military Police until discharged in 1919. He holds the Mons Star, and the General Service and Victory Medals. 13, Portland Street, Northampton. Z2178/C.

HOCKENHULL, W., Sergt., Lancashire Fusiliers.
Volunteering in 1915, he landed in Egypt later in the same year. Whilst in this seat of operations he took part in the engagements on the Suez Canal. He afterwards proceeded to France, and served with distinction on the Somme and Ypres fronts before being severely wounded in 1917. As a result he was invalided home and eventually demobilised in 1918, holding the 1914-15 Star, and the General Service and Victory Medals.
13, Portland Street, Northampton. Z2178/A.

HODBY, W., Private, Middlesex Regiment.
He joined in February 1917, and on completion of his training was drafted overseas in the following May. During his service on the Western Front he was in action in many notable engagements, and died gloriously on the Field of Battle on December 26th, 1917. He was entitled to the General Service and Victory Medals.

"He died the noblest death a man may die:
Fighting for God and right and liberty."

7, Hut, Abington Park, Northampton. Z3375.

HODGES, A., Gunner, Royal Garrison Artillery.
He enlisted in August 1916, and was retained for a time at various home stations before proceeding to France in February 1918. In this theatre of war he took part in many engagements, including the Battles of the Somme (II.), Amiens, Bapaume, Havrincourt, Cambrai (II.) and Ypres (IV.). He was demobilised in February 1919, and holds the General Service and Victory Medals.
5, St. James' Terrace, St. James' Street, Northampton. Z3040.

HODGES, R. R., 2nd Lieutenant, Royal Air Force.
He volunteered in September 1914, and after passing the necessary tests was sent to France in January 1915. Whilst on the Western Front he rendered valuable services with his Squadron in many engagements, particularly at the Battles of Loos and Ypres. He was demobilised on returning to England in March 1919, and holds the 1914-15 Star, and the General Service and Victory Medals.
8, Vernon Terrace, Northampton. Z2179.

HODGSON, E. E., Sergeant, Coldstream Guards.
A Reservist, he was mobilised in August 1914, and immediately drafted to France. He fought in the Battle of Mons and the Retreat, and also in the Battles of Le Cateau, the Marne, the Aisne, La Bassée, Ypres, Neuve Chapelle, St. Eloi, Hill 60 and Ypres (II). Invalided home as the result of being wounded, he returned to France upon his recovery and was shortly afterwards killed in action on July 31st, 1917. He was entitled to the Mons Star, and the General Service and Victory Medals.

"His life for his Country."

2, Deal Street, Northampton. Z1458.

HODSON, J. W., Private, 2nd Monmouthshire Regt.
He was mobilised with the Territorial Force in August 1914, and was retained at home until early in 1916, when he proceeded to France. During his service overseas he was employed on various duties on the Somme front, and did good work up to the time he was invalided home on account of ill-health, eventually dying in May 1918 from the effects of consumption. He was entitled to the General Service and Victory Medals.

"Great deeds cannot die."

16, Spring Lane Terrace, Northampton. Z1216.

HOLDEN, C. L., Private, R.A.M.C.
He enlisted in April 1917, and having completed his training in the following year was drafted to France. There he was engaged on important duties at Rouen and St. Omer, and whilst in the latter place was buried alive during an air raid. Later he was taken ill and consequently invalided home. Discharged in May 1918, he holds the General Service and Victory Medals.
56, St. Leonard's Road, Far Cotton, Northampton. Z3050.

HOLDEN, J. A., Pte., 2/5th Sherwood Foresters.
He enlisted in the Buffs in March 1917, and after a period of training was drafted to France, where he was transferred to the Sherwood Foresters. He took part in many engagements, including those in the Kemmel Hill and Vimy Ridge sectors, and was wounded in action. As a result he was invalided home, and on his recovery served with the Royal Army Ordnance Corps until demobilised in October 1919, holding the General Service and Victory Medals.
56, St. Leonard's Road, Far Cotton, Northampton. Z3051.

HOLDER, H. W., Driver, R.H.A.
He joined in February 1917, and three months later was drafted to the Western Front. There he took part in the Battles of Ypres, Lens, the Somme, Cambrai and the Aisne, and after the Armistice served in Germany with the Army of Occupation. He returned home in 1919, and was demobilised in October of that year, holding the General Service and Victory Medals.
1 House, 2 Block, Naseby Street, Northampton. Z1342.

HOLDING, F., Private, 6th Middlesex Regiment.
Joining in March 1916, he completed a period of training at Felixstowe before proceeding to France in the same year. During his service overseas he took part in heavy fighting in the Somme, Ypres and Cambrai sectors before being wounded and invalided to hospital at Boulogne in January 1918. On his recovery he rejoined his unit, and was in action during the Retreat and Advance of 1918. He was demobilised in October 1919, and holds the General Service and Victory Medals.
6, New Buildings, Blisworth, Northants. Z2147/B—Z2148/B

HOLDING, G. B., Private, East Surrey Regiment.
Having joined in March 1916, he underwent a period of training and in the same year was drafted to the Western Front, where he took part in the Somme Offensive before being badly gassed and evacuated to England. Returning to France on his recovery, he took part in engagements in the Ypres and Cambrai sectors, but was again wounded in October 1918. Invalided to England, he was eventually discharged in March 1919, and holds the General Service and Victory Medals.
8, New Buildings, Blisworth, Northampton. Z2180.

HOLDSWORTH, T., Private, 1st Northants. Regt.
Called up from the Reserve in August 1914, he was at once sent to France, where he fought in the Battle of and Retreat from Mons, and at the Battles of the Marne, the Aisne, La Bassée and Ypres. He was severely wounded on July 18th, 1916, during the Battle of the Somme, and unhappily died on the same day from the effects of his injuries. He was entitled to the Mons Star, and the General Service and Victory Medals.
"His memory is cherished with pride."
70, Lower Adelaide Street, Northampton. Z1217/B.

HOLLAND, A. E., Private, 1st Northants. Regt.
He volunteered in June 1915, and after a period of training at Wendover embarked for Gallipoli. He took part in heavy fighting at Suvla Bay, where he was wounded and as a result sent to hospital in Egypt. On his recovery he was drafted to France and participated in further fighting, being wounded for the second time whilst in action on the Somme front. He was demobilised in March 1919, and holds the 1914–15 Star, and the General Service and Victory Medals.
15, Gladstone Terrace, Northampton. Z1219.

HOLLAND, C., L/Corporal, King's Shropshire L.I.
At the outbreak of war he was serving in India, but was at once recalled and drafted to the Western Front, where he fought in the operations following the Retreat from Mons. He was also actively engaged in many notable battles in various sectors, until severely wounded and invalided home. After protracted hospital treatment he was discharged as medically unfit in June 1919, and holds the 1914 Star, and the General Service and Victory Medals. West Haddon, Northants. Z3376.

HOLLAND, F., Private, Buffs (East Kent Regt.).
Joining in May 1918, he underwent a period of training at Dover prior to being drafted to the Western Front. Whilst in this seat of operations he took part in heavy fighting in the Somme and Cambrai sectors, but was invalided home with trench fever. On his recovery he was engaged on important duties in Ireland until demobilised in September 1919, holding the General Service and Victory Medals.
Stoke Road, Blisworth, Northants. Z2181/B.

HOLLAND, G. L., Corporal, R.A.M.C.
Volunteering in August 1914, he completed a period of training and was retained at Peterborough Hospital as an orderly. He did consistently good work whilst attending to the sick and wounded, but owing to the important nature of his duties he was unable to secure his transfer to a theatre of war. He, nevertheless, rendered valuable services until demobilised in May 1919. Stoke Road, Blisworth, Northampton. Z2181/A.

HOLLAND, J., L/Cpl., Guards Machine Gun Regt.
He enlisted in June 1913 in the Grenadier Guards, and in June 1915 was drafted to the Western Front. There he participated in the Battle of Loos, and was wounded in action at Hulloch, being invalided home as the result. After a course of treatment in various hospitals he was transferred to the Guards Machine Gun Regiment and served in London and at Epsom until his discharge in July 1917. He holds the 1914–15 Star, and the General Service and Victory Medals.
60, Cambridge Street, Northampton. Z1343.

HOLLAND, P., Private, 1st Bedfordshire Regt.
Joining in May 1917, he proceeded to France in the same year, and took part in the first Battle of Cambrai, after which he was transferred to Italy and saw further service on the Piave front. He returned to France in 1918, and was in action in various sectors during the Retreat and final Advance. He was demobilised in February 1919, and holds the General Service and Victory Medals. 15, Duke Street, Northampton. Z1459.

HOLLAND, T., Private, 1st Northants. Regiment.
He joined in November 1917, and four months later was drafted to France. In this theatre of war he participated in severe engagements on the Somme, Cambrai and Ypres fronts. After the Armistice he proceeded into Germany and served with the Army of Occupation in Bonn until March 1920, when he was demobilised, holding the General Service and Victory Medals.
15, Gladstone Terrace Northampton. Z1218.

HOLLIDAY, H., Private, R.A.M.C.
He volunteered in June 1915, and in the following year was drafted to Mesopotamia, where he was engaged on special laboratory work for a short time. Later he proceeded to India and served in a similar capacity at Poona, Bombay, Secunderabad and Dolali. He returned home and was demobilised in November 1919, holding the General Service and Victory Medals. 35, Euston Road, Northampton Z3052/B.

HOLLIS, A., Private, 5th Northants. Regiment.
Volunteering in August 1914, he proceeded in the following May to France, and shortly afterwards was wounded during the second Battle of Ypres. Evacuated to England for hospital treatment, he returned to France on his recovery, and took part in further fighting on the Somme front and at Ypres, Arras and Cambrai. He was again wounded at St. Quentin in 1918, and invalided home, being eventually demobilised in January 1919. He holds the 1914–15 Star, and the General Service and Victory Medals. 19, Alpha Street Northampton. Z1344.

HOLLIS, F., A.B., Royal Naval Division.
Joining in September 1917, he was trained at Blandford and, embarking for the Western Front seven months later, saw heavy fighting in numerous minor engagements. He saw much service at Achiet-le-Petit, the Canal du Nord, St. Quentin, Cambrai and in the Retreat and Advance of 1918, being almost continuously in action until the cessation of hostilities. On his return to England he was demobilised in April 1919, holding the General Service and Victory Medals.
Mill Hill, Long Buckby, Rugby. Z3377/B.

HOLLOWAY, F., Sergeant, 21st (Empress of India's) Lancers.
A Regular soldier, he was stationed at Meerut at the outbreak of hostilities in August 1914, and during the whole period of the war he remained in India. He was employed with his unit on garrison and other duties of an important nature, and for some time served on the frontier. Discharged on his return home in November 1919, he holds the General Service and Victory Medals. 16, Adelaide St., Northants. Z1045/A—Z1046/A.

HOLLOWELL, E., Driver, R.A.S.C.
He volunteered in November 1915, and a month later was drafted to France, where he served in the Loos and Ypres sectors. In November 1917 he was transferred to Italy and served on the Piave front until he was sent to hospital at Bordighera suffering from injuries caused by a kick from a horse. He returned home and was demobilised in February 1919, holding the 1914–15 Star, and the General Service and Victory Medals. 3, Currie Road, Northampton. Z1345.

HOLLOWELL, E., Private, Machine Gun Corps.
He volunteered in January 1915, and three months later proceeded to France. There he took part in heavy fighting on the Somme front and at Vimy Ridge, Arras, Bullecourt and Cambrai, and was twice wounded. He was also in action during the Retreat and Advance of 1918, and after the Armistice served with the Army of Occupation in Germany until January 1919, when he was demobilised, holding the 1914–15 Star, and the General Service and Victory Medals.
Brafield-on-the-Green, Northants. Z3378.

HOLLOWELL, J. T., Driver, R.F.A.
Volunteering in January 1915, he crossed to France in the following August and did excellent work whilst engaged on transport duties on the Ypres, Somme and Cambrai fronts. He remained in this theatre of war until the cessation of hostilities, and was demobilised on his return home in March 1919. He holds the 1914–15 Star, and the General Service and Victory Medals. 3, Althorp Street, Northampton. Z1220.

HOLME, G., Private, Honourable Artillery Coy.
Having attested under the Derby Scheme, he was called to the Colours in May 1917, and shortly afterwards drafted to France, thence to Italy. In this seat of operations he served as a runner and did good work with the Honourable Artillery Company during heavy fighting on the Piave River and Asiago Plateaux. He was awarded an Italian decoration, holds also the General Service and Victory Medals, and was demobilised in February 1919. 33, Raymond Road, St. James', Northampton. Z2722.

HOLMES, H. R. B., Sergeant, 12th (Prince of Wales' Royal) Lancers.
Already in the Army at the outbreak of war, he was immediately drafted to France. There he took part in the Retreat from Mons, served with distinction at the Battles of the Marne and the Aisne and in many engagements throughout hostilities, and was twice wounded in action. After the Armistice he proceeded to Germany with the Army of Occupation and served on the Rhine, and was afterwards sent to Ireland until he received his discharge in June 1920, having completed 21 years' service. He holds the Queen's and King's South African Medals, and the Mons Star, and the General Service and Victory Medals. Pitsford, Northants. Z3053.

HOLTON, T., Gunner, Royal Field Artillery.
He volunteered in December 1915, and having completed, his training in the following year, was drafted to the Western Front. In this theatre of war he took part in several engagements, including the Battles of the Somme, Cambrai, and in the Retreat and Advance of 1918. Demobilised in March 1919, he holds the General Service and Victory Medals.
7, Castle Terrace, Northampton. Z1221/A.

HOOLEY, W. G., Private, Durham Light Infantry.
Called up from the Reserve in August 1914, he served with the Northamptonshire Regiment for about twelve months before proceeding to France. There he was transferred to the Durham Light Infantry, and took part in engagements in the Ypres Loos and the Somme sectors. Badly wounded in 1917, he was invalided home and eventually discharged in October of the same year as medically unfit. He holds the 1914–15 Star, and the General Service and Victory Medals.
Rothersthorpe, Northants. Z3054.

HOPE, F., L/Corporal, 1st Northants. Regiment.
He enlisted in August 1916, and three months later was drafted to France, where he saw much fighting at the Battles of Ypres and Passchendaele, and was wounded on the Somme in March 1918. In consequence he was invalided home, but on his recovery proceeded to Germany with the Army of Occupation, and serv d there until his demobilisation in February 1919. He holds the General Service and Victory Medals.
33, Bath Street, Northampton. Z1222/B.

HOPE, G., Driver, Royal Field Artillery.
He enlisted in May 1917, and having completed his training in the following September, was drafted to Mesopotamia. In this seat of operations he took part in many engagements, including those at Kut and at the capture of Baghdad. He returned home, and was demobilised in January 1919, holding the General Service and Victory Medals.
24, Stanley Road, Northampton. Z2420/D.

HOPE, H., A.B., Royal Navy.
Already in the Royal Navy when war broke out in August 1914, he immediately proceeded to the North Sea on board H.M.S. "Queen Mary," and took part in the Battles of Heligoland Bight, the Falkland Islands and in several minor operations. He unfortunately lost his life when H.M.S. "Queen Mary" was sunk at the Battle of Jutland on May 31st, 1916. He was entitled to the 1914–15 Star, and the General Service and Victory Medals.
"His life for his Country, his soul to God."
33, Bath Street, Northampton. Z1222/A.

HOPE, J., Private, Tank Corps.
He joined in February 1917, and underwent a period of training prior to his being drafted to the Western Front. In this seat of war he took part in much fighting in the Somme, Albert, Arras, Cambrai and Bapaume sectors. He was demobilised in February 1919 on his return home, and holds the General Service and Victory Medals.
9, Doddridge Street, Northampton. Z1223.

HORN, W. J., Pte., Queen's (R. West Surrey Regt.)
He enlisted in December 1916, and completing his training in the following June, was drafted to the Western Front, where he took part in many engagements, including those at Ypres and Passchendaele. He was unfortunately reported missing on August 10th, 1917, and is now believed to have been killed in action. He was entitled to the General Service and Victory Medals.
"Thinking that remembrance, though unspoken, may reach him where he sleeps."
Court I, 6, Brook Street, Daventry, Northants. Z2723.

HORNE, A. C., A.B., Royal Navy.
He enlisted in February 1916, and after four months' training was commissioned to H.M.S. "Spey." Whilst on patrol work he took part in minor operations in the North Sea, off the Belgium coast and in the Adriatic. Later he was transferred to H.M.D. "Routter," in which vessel he served until his demobilisation in May 1919. He holds the General Service and Victory Medals. Spratton, Northants. Z3057.

HORNE, A. J., Gunner, Royal Field Artillery.
He joined in April 1916, and in the following month was drafted to France, where he took part in several engagements, including those at Ypres and on the Somme, and was wounded. As a result he was invalided home, but on his recovery returned to France and fought in the Retreat and Advance of 1918, being again wounded and sent home. He was eventually demobilised in September 1919, and holds the General Service and Victory Medals. Court I, 4, Brook St., Daventry, Northants. TZ2724.

HORNE, L., Private, 8th East Yorkshire Regiment.
He volunteered in June 1915, and having completed his training in August of the following year, was drafted to the Western Front, where he took part in many engagements. He was unfortunately reported missing at Vimy Ridge about May 3rd, 1917, and is now believed to have been killed in action. He was entitled to the General Service and Victory Medals.
"Thinking that remembrance, though unspoken, may reach him where he sleeps."
Near Hall, Spratton Northants. Z3056.

HORNE, T., Private, 1st Northants. Regiment.
Called up from the Reserve in August 1914, he was quickly drafted to France, where he fought at Mons and Ypres, and was wounded in action. As a result he was invalided home, but on his recovery returned to France, and took part in engagements in the Loos Aubers Ridge and Cambrai sectors. Discharged in January 1918, he holds the Mons Star, and the General Service and Victory Medals.
near Hall, Spratton, Northants. Z3055/A.

HORSLEY, C. J., Private, 5th Royal Fusiliers.
He enlisted in February 1916, on attaining military age, and in the following year was drafted to the Western Front. In this theatre of war he took part in several engagements, including those in the Somme and Bullecourt sectors, and was wounded in action. Invalided home, he was afterwards retained at various stations until his demobilisation in November 1919, and holds the General Service and Victory Medals.
89, Euston Road, Far Cotton, Northampton. Z3058.

HOUGHTON, H. W., Private, Royal Fusiliers
Joining in November 1916, he proceeded overseas in the following year. Whilst on the Western Front he took part in several engagements, including those in the Lens and Cambrai sectors, before being wounded in February 1918. He was eventually discharged in January 1919, and holds the General Service and Victory Medals.
40, Brook Street, Northampton. Z1224.

HOUGHTON, J., Private, 1st Bedfordshire Regt.
Having previously served for four years, he rejoined in August 1914, and was immediately drafted to France. There he took part in the Battles of Mons, the Marne, the Aisne, Ypres, Neuve Chapelle, Givenchy, Loos, Festubert and the Somme, before being wounded in action. As a result he was invalided home, and on his recovery proceeded to Mesopotamia, but owing to ill-health was sent home and discharged in August 1917. He holds the Mons Star, and the General Service and Victory Medals. 10, Gas Street, Northampton. Z2725.

HOUGHTON, W. R., Rifleman, K.R.R.C.
He enlisted in 1916 in the Northamptonshire Dragoons, but after six months' training was claimed out on account of his age. In 1917 he re-enlisted in the King's Royal Rifle Corps, proceeded to France, and took part in much fighting in the Ypres, Passchendaele, Cambrai, the Aisne and the Marne sectors, and was wounded. As a result he was invalided home, but on his recovery returned to France and served until his demobilisation in October 1919. He holds the General Service and Victory Medals. 75, Stanley Road, Northampton. Z2421.

HOWARD, E., Pte., 4th Queen's (R. W. Surrey Regt.)
He joined in March 1916, and was shortly afterwards drafted to France. There he took part in much heavy fighting in the Ypres, Messines and Passchendaele sectors, but was taken ill with appendicitis and invalided home. On his recovery he rejoined his unit and was eventually demobilised in March 1919, holding the General Service and Victory Medals.
59, Ambush Street, St. James, Northampton. Z2422/B.

HOWARD, F. W., Gunner, R.F.A.
He volunteered in March 1915, and in the following September was drafted to Mesopotamia. In this seat of hostilities he took part in several engagements, including the capture of Baghdad. After the Armistice he returned home, but contracted influenza, and was in hospital for some time. Demobilised in March 1919, he holds the 1914–15 Star, and the General Service and Victory Medals.
59, Ambush Street, St. James, Northampton. Z2422/A.

HOWARD, G., Gunner, Royal Garrison Artillery.
He joined in July 1916, and after a period of training at Woolwich was drafted to France. In this theatre of war he participated in several severe engagements, and was unfortunately killed in action near Arras on August 20th, 1917. He was entitled to the General Service and Victory Medals.
"Whilst we remember, the sacrifice is not in vain."
1, Church Street, Kislingbury, Northants. Z3380/B.

HOWARD, P. G., Sapper, R.E. (R.O.D.)
Volunteering in February 1915, he was sent in the following May to France, where he served with the Railway Operative Division, Royal Engineers. He was employed with his Company laying rail-roads and on various duties in connection with railway transport on the Ypres, Loos, Somme, Arras and Cambrai fronts. Returning home in March 1919, he was demobilised a month later, and holds the 1914–15 Star, and the General Service and Victory Medals.
Bugbrooke, near Weedon, Northants. Z3379

HOWARD, W., Private, 1/4th Northants. Regt.
Called up from the Reserve in August 1914, he embarked in the following April for Gallipoli, where he took part in the various operations. After the Evacuation, he was sent to Egypt, and later, in Palestine, participated in heavy fighting at Gaza, Jerusalem, Jaffa and Aleppo. Returning home in March 1919, he was demobilised, holding the 1914–15 Star, and the General Service and Victory Medals.
1, Church Street, Kislingbury, Northants. Z3380/C.

HOWES, A., Rflmn., Cameronians (Scottish Rifles).
Already in the Army when war broke out in August 1914, he was immediately drafted to France. There he took part in the Retreat from Mons, the Battles of Loos, Vermelles, Ploegsteert and Arras, and was wounded on three occasions. He was eventually discharged in March 1919 as medically unfit for further service, and holds the 1914–15 Star, and the General Service and Victory Medals.
28, Kerr Street, Northampton. Z1930.

HOWES, F., Rifleman, 8th London Regiment (Post Office Rifles).
He joined in May 1917, and served in various home stations until April 1918 when he was sent to France. During his service overseas he was in action in many sectors in the Retreat and Advance of 1918, participating in heavy fighting at Epéhy and Cambrai. He returned to England, and was demobilised in January 1919, and holds the General Service and Victory Medals.
38, Symington Street, Northampton. Z3381.

HOWLETT, H. J., Gunner, Royal Field Artillery.
Called up from the Reserve in August 1914, he was immediately drafted to France, where he took part in the Retreat from Mons and the Battles of the Aisne and Ypres. Later he was transferred to Egypt, and after much fighting on the Suez Canal proceeded into Palestine, where he was in action at Gaza, Jaffa and the capture of Jerusalem. He returned home and was demobilised in July 1919, holding the Mons Star, and the General Service and Victory Medals.
56, Regent Street, Northampton. Z1226/B.

HOWLETT, P., Private, 1st Northants. Regiment.
He volunteered in August 1914, and after a short period of training was drafted to France, where he took part in the Battle of Ypres, Neuve Chapelle and Hill 60. He gave his life for King and Country at Aubers Ridge on May 9th, 1915, and was entitled to the 1914–15 Star, and the General Service and Victory Medals.
"He joined the great white company of valiant souls."
81, Chaucer Street, Kingsley, Northampton. Z1225/B.

HOWLETT, W., Gunner, Royal Garrison Artillery.
Volunteering in December 1915, he was drafted overseas in the following year. During his service on the Western Front he took part in several engagements, including the Battles of the Somme, Arras and Ypres. Invalided home on account of ill-health, he was eventually discharged in September 1917 as medically unfit for further service. He holds the General Service and Victory Medals.
81, Chaucer Street, Kingsley, Northampton. Z1225/A.

HOWLETT, Wm., Driver, Royal Field Artillery.
He joined the Army in October 1909, and when war broke out in August 1914 was immediately drafted to France. There he took part in much heavy fighting in many sectors, including the Retreat from Mons, the Battles of Ypres, Loos, the Somme, Arras, Armentières, Passchendaele and Cambrai, and did continuously good work throughout. He received his discharge in May 1920, and holds the Mons Star, and the General Service and Victory Medals.
81, Chaucer Street, Kingsley, Northampton. Z1225/C.

HOWS, S., Corporal, Northamptonshire Regiment.
He volunteered in March 1915, and was engaged at various home stations on important duties with his unit. He was unable to obtain a transfer overseas before the cessation of hostilities owing to medical unfitness, but rendered valuable services. After the Armistice he proceeded to France, where he was employed on exhumation duties until his demobilisation in May 1920.
24, Adelaide Street, Northampton. Z1227.

HUGHES, A. A., Sapper, Royal Engineers.
He joined in December 1916, and was quickly drafted to France. Whilst in this theatre of war he served as an engine-driver, and was engaged in various sectors of the front conveying ammunition and supplies to the forward areas. He was once wounded in action and later demobilised in February 1919. He holds the General Service and Victory Medals.
4, Park Street, Northampton. Z1460/B.

HUGHES, E. A., Mechanic, Royal Air Force.
He joined in January 1918, and after a period of training was engaged at various home stations on important duties which demanded a high degree of technical skill. Owing to the early cessation of hostilities he was unable to obtain a transfer over seas, but rendered valuable services until his demobilisation in January 1919. 4, Park Street, Northampton. Z1460/A.

HUGHES, H. E., Private, 2nd Northants. Regt.
He enlisted in July 1918, and after completing his training was sent to Germany with the Army of Occupation and served on the Rhine until October 1919. He was then drafted to India, and was engaged on important garrison duties at Rawal Pindi. Later he came home and proceeded to Ireland, where in 1921 he was still serving.
10, Compton Street, Northampton. Z1229/B.

HUGHES, H. M., Corporal, South Wales Borderers.
He volunteered in June 1915, and in the following year was drafted to France, where he took part in the Battle of the Somme. Later he was transferred to Salonika, and saw much fighting on the Vardar front before being wounded, but on his recovery he was again in action. He returned home and was demobilised in March 1919, holding the General Service and Victory Medals. 10, Compton Street, Northampton. Z1229/A.

HUGHES, J., Corporal, 12th (Prince of Wales' Royal) Lancers.
Already in the Army when war broke out in August 1914, he was immediately drafted to France. There he took part in the Retreat from Mons, the Battles of the Marne, the Aisne, La Bassée, Ypres, the Somme, Arras and Cambrai. After hostilities ceased he proceeded to Germany with the Army of Occupation, and served on the Rhine until his discharge in March 1919. He holds the Mons Star, and the General Service and Victory Medals. 48, Compton Street, Northampton. Z1228/A.

HUGHES, J., R.S.M., 1st Royal Dublin Fusiliers.
Already serving in Ireland in August 1914, he was retained on important duties at home until June 1916, and was then drafted to France, where he took a distinguished part in the Battles of the Somme, Arras and Ypres. He was reported missing, and is believed to have been killed in action in March 1918. He was entitled to the General Service and Victory Medals.
"A costly sacrifice upon the altar of freedom."
48, Compton Street, Northampton. Z1228/B.

HULL, A., Driver, Royal Field Artillery.
Volunteering in September 1914, he was drafted overseas in the following June. During his service on the Western Front he saw much heavy fighting in the Loos, Forres, Somme, Arras, Monchy, Cambrai, Ovillers and Poizières sectors. He did continuously good work and was finally demobilised in May 1919, holding the 1914–15 Star, and the General Service and Victory Medals. 22, Countess Road, Northampton. Z2727.

HULTGREN, H. A. (D.S.M.), Chief Yeoman of Signals, Royal Navy.
Already serving in the Royal Navy, he was mobilised in August 1914 and posted to H.M.S. "Cornwall," in which vessel he took part in the Battle of the Falkland Isles. He afterwards proceeded to the Dardanelles, where he played a prominent part in the Naval operations during the Gallipoli campaign. After the Evacuation of the Peninsula he served on board H.M.S. "Hinde" and H.M.T.B.D. "Lochinvar," being engaged on important submarine-chasing and escort duties in the English Channel. Later he saw service in the China Sea, and was awarded the Distinguished Service Medal for conspicuous bravery. Discharged in March 1919, he also holds the 1914–15 Star, and the General Service and Victory Medals.
Roade, Northants. Z2183/A.

HUMPHREY, A., Pte., Loyal North Lancs. Regt.
He volunteered in June 1915, and in the following year was drafted to the Western Front, where he took part in many important engagements, including the Battles of Albert, the Somme and Arras. Mortally wounded in action at Ypres, he unhappily died on September 23rd, 1917. He was entitled to the General Service and Victory Medals.
"His life for his Country, his soul to God."
40, Francis Street, Northampton. Z1230.

HUMPHREY, A., Sergeant, 6th Northants. Regt.
He re-enlisted in September 1914, and was retained at various stations, where he was engaged on important duties as a Drill Instructor, Sergeant Cook and Provost Sergeant. Being over age for active service, he was unable to obtain his transfer to the front, but, nevertheless, rendered very valuable services with his unit. He was discharged in September 1918, after 34 years with the Colours.
72, Stanley Street, Northampton. Z1231/A.

HUMPHREY, A. H., Drmr., 1st Northants. Regt.
A serving soldier, he proceeded to France in August 1914, and, after serving through the Retreat from Mons, took part in the Battles of the Marne, the Aisne, La Bassée, Ypres and the Somme. Mortally wounded at Ypres in June 1917, he unhappily died in hospital at Colchester on November 26th of that year. He was entitled to the Mons Star, and the General Service and Victory Medals.
"He joined the great white company of valiant souls."
72, Stanley Street, Northampton. Z1231/B.

HUMPHREY, F., Private, R.A.S.C. (M.T.)
He enlisted in December 1916, and was immediately drafted to Salonika. In this theatre of war he served with the Mechanical Transport, and was chiefly engaged in driving cars. He rendered valuable services throughout, and was finally demobilised in March 1919, holding the General Service and Victory Medals.
56, St. James' Park Road, Northampton. Z2423.

HUMPHREY, F. G., Trooper, Northants. Dragoons.
Having volunteered in August 1914, he underwent a period of training and was retained on important duties with his unit at Towcester and Luton. He was later found to be medically unfit for transfer overseas, and was therefore discharged in March 1917, after rendering valuable services.
Roade, Northants. Z2184/B.

HUMPHREY, G. F., Sergeant-Drummer, 1st Northamptonshire Regiment.
Called up from the Reserve in August 1914, he was immediately drafted to France, where he fought in the Retreat from Mons. After taking a prominent part also in the Battles of the Marne, the Aisne, La Bassée and Ypres, he was wounded in May 1915, and admitted to hospital at Liverpool. He was finally discharged in March 1919, and holds the Mons Star, and the General Service and Victory Medals.
72, Stanley Street, Northampton. Z1231/E.

HUMPHREY, R. C., L/Corporal, Military Mounted Police.
He joined in May 1918, and after undergoing a period of training was retained on important duties at various stations. He was unable to obtain his transfer overseas before the cessation of hostilities, but in April 1919 was drafted with the Army of Occupation to Germany. There he was stationed at Cologne until his return home for demobilisation in March 1920.
89, Baker Street, Northampton. Z1232.

HUMPHREY, T. H., Farrier-Sergeant, R.A.V.C.
Volunteering in February 1915, he shortly afterwards landed in Egypt. Whilst in this theatre of hostilities he saw much heavy fighting, and proceeding to Palestine, was present at the Battles of Gaza and Jaffa, and also during the operations at Jerusalem and on the River Jordan. He did consistently good work as a farrier, and in May 1919 was demobilised, holding the 1914–15 Star, and the General Service and Victory Medals.
Roade, Northants. Z2184/A.

HUMPHREY, W. J., Private, Machine Gun Corps.
Joining in March 1917, he completed his training in the same year, and was drafted overseas. Whilst on the Western Front he served as a gunner and a shoeing-smith, and was in action at the Battle of Lens and also during the Retreat and Advance of 1918. He did consistently good work, and in January 1919 was demobilised, holding the General Service and Victory Medals. Roade, Northants. Z2184/C.

HUMPHREYS, A. J., Private, 7th Northants. Regt.
A Reservist, he was called to the Colours in August 1914, but was retained on important duties in England until June 1916, when he proceeded to the Western Front. After taking part in the Battle of the Somme and minor engagements, he fell fighting at Messines on June 7th, 1917. He was entitled to the General Service and Victory Medals.
"His life for his Country, his soul to God."
72, Stanley Street, Northampton. Z1231/C.

HUMPHREYS, F. W., Gunner, R.F.A.
He joined in October 1916, and on completing his training in the following year was sent to the Western Front, where he saw severe fighting in various sectors. He took part in the Battles of Ypres and St. Quentin and engagements at Albert, Péronne and many other places until the cessation of hostilities. Demobilised in November 1919, he holds the General Service and Victory Medals.
72, Stanley Street, Northampton. Z1231/D.

HUMPHREYS, J., Sergeant, 4th Northants. Regt.
Mobilised in August 1914, he was retained on important duties as a Drill Instructor in England until February 1916, when he proceeded to the Western Front. There he took a prominent part in the Battle of the Somme—where he was wounded in October 1916—and in other engagements until taken prisoner in September 1918. Released on the cessation of hostilities, he was discharged in June 1919, holding the General Service and Victory Medals.
6, Gladstone Terrace, Northampton. Z1346.

HUMPHREYS, T. W., Gunner, R.F.A.
A serving soldier, he was drafted to the Western Front in August 1914, and fought in the Retreat from Mons. He also took part in the Battles of Ypres, Festubert, Loos, the Somme, Arras, Vimy Ridge and Cambrai, and many other important engagements, and was discharged on his return home in February 1919. He holds the Mons Star, and the General Service and Victory Medals. 7, Pine Street, Northampton. Z1322/A.

HUMPHRIES, A., Private, 2nd Northants. Regt.
Mobilised in August 1914, he quickly proceeded to the Western Front, where, after fighting in the Retreat from Mons, he took part in the Battles of the Marne, the Aisne and La Bassée. He made the supreme sacrifice, falling in action at Ypres on November 1st, 1914, after 14 years' service. He was entitled to the Mons Star, and the General Service and Victory Medals.
"His memory is cherished with pride."
44, Alcombe Road, Northampton. Z1461/C.

HUMPHRIES, D. A., Pte., 7th Ox. & Bucks. L.I.
He volunteered in September 1914, and twelve months later was drafted to France, where he took part in the Battle of Loos. Later he was transferred to Salonika, and saw much fighting on the Vardar, Doiran and Struma fronts. Contracting malaria, he was invalided to Malta, and eventually demobilised in March 1919. He holds the 1914–15 Star, and the General Service and Victory Medals. Long Street, Hanslope, Bucks. Z2728/A.

HUMPHRIES, H. C., Private, Cheshire Regiment.
He volunteered in September 1915, and in the following year was drafted to the Western Front, where he served in various sectors. He was engaged chiefly in guarding prisoners of war, and did much useful work until June 1917, when he was discharged as medically unfit for further service. He holds the General Service and Victory Medals.
44, Alcombe Road, Northampton. Z1461/D.

HUMPHRIES, P. A., Private, Army Cyclist Corps.
He volunteered in October 1915, and in the following year proceeded to Salonika, where he saw much severe fighting. He took part in many important engagements on the Doiran and Vardar fronts until the cessation of hostilities, and was then transferred to Sonth Russia. Demobilised on his return home in November 1919, he holds the General Service and Victory Medals.
44, Alcombe Road, Northampton. Z1461/A.

HUMPHRIES, R. W., Private, Norfolk Regiment.
Shortly after joining in 1917 he was drafted to France, where he saw heavy fighting in various sectors of the front. After taking part in many engagements in the Retreat and Advance of 1918, he was severely gassed, and, admitted to hospital in England, was finally invalided from the Army in 1919. He holds the General Service and Victory Medals.
44, Alcombe Road, Northampton. Z1461/B.

HUMPHRIES, W. G., Pte., 7th Ox. & Bucks. L.I.
He volunteered in April 1915, and six months later was drafted to France, where he fought at Loos, Albert, the Somme, Arras and Ypres, and was wounded three times. Later he proceeded to Italy, and took part in engagements on the Piave River and Asiago Plateaux. In 1921 he was serving in India, and holds the 1914–15 Star, and the General Service and Victory Medals.
Long Street, Hanslope, Bucks. Z2728/B.

HUNNIBELL, F. C., Bombardier, R.F.A.
He volunteered in August 1915, and twelve months later proceeded to the Western Front, where he took part in much severe fighting during the Advance on the Somme. He died gloriously on the Field of Battle there on September 21st, 1916, after only a few weeks' active service, and was entitled to the General Service and Victory Medals.
"The path of duty was the way to glory."
21, Beaconsfield Terrace, Northampton. Z1462/A.

HUNT, T., L/Sergeant, 15th Gloucestershire Regt.
He volunteered in August 1914, and in July of the following year proceeded to the Western Front, where, after taking a prominent part in the Battles of Loos and the Somme, he was wounded at Cambrai in November 1917. Invalided home he returned to France, however, in February 1918, and unhappily fell in action on November 4th of that year. He was entitled to the 1914–15 Star, and the General Service and Victory Medals.
"A costly sacrifice upon the altar of freedom."
4, Althorp Street, Northampton. Z1233.

HUNTER, H., Sapper, Royal Engineers (R.O.D.).
He volunteered in May 1915, and in the following October proceeded overseas. After serving for two months in France he was sent to Egypt, where he remained until the termination of hostilities. Attached to the Railway Operating Division, Royal Engineers, he was employed as a platelayer and did excellent work. Demobilised on his return home in March 1919, he holds the 1914–15 Star, and the General Service and Victory Medals. 3, Henley Street, Northampton. Z3382.

HURLEY, H., Corporal, Northants. Cyclist Corps.
Volunteering in September 1914, he was drafted to the Western Front in May of the following year, and there saw much heavy fighting. After taking part in the Battles of Ypres, Loos, the Somme, and Vimy Ridge and minor engagements, he was severely wounded in March 1917, and admitted to hospital at Manchester. He was invalided from the Army in October 1918, and holds the 1914–15 Star, and the General Service and Victory Medals.
9, Arthur Street, Kingsthorpe Hollow, Northampton. Z1347/A.

HURLEY, J. W., A.B., R.N.V.R.
He joined in September 1917, and in April of the following year proceeded to France with the Royal Naval Division, and there took part in heavy fighting on the Somme. Severely wounded in May 1918, he was sent to hospital in England, and was finally invalided from the Service in April 1919. He holds the General Service and Victory Medals.
9, Arthur Street, Kingsthorpe Hollow, Northampton. Z1347/B.

HURST, J., Private, 1st Northants. Regiment.
He volunteered in August 1914, and after his training was sent to the Western Front, where he fought in various sectors and took part in the second Battle of Ypres, where he was gassed. Invalided home, he returned to France, however, and fought in the Battles of Loos, the Somme and Arras. He was demobilised in February 1919, and holds the 1914–15 Star, and the General Service and Victory Medals.
44, Silver Street, Northampton. Z1235/B.

HURST, W. G., Private, 2nd Northants. Regiment.
Called up from the Reserve in August 1914, he proceeded quickly to the Western Front, where he fought in the Retreat from Mons. He also took part in the Battles of the Marne and the Aisne and other engagements until severely wounded near Ypres, and sent to hospital in England, but returned later to France. He was discharged in August 1917, and holds the Mons Star, and the General Sevtice and Victory Medals.
1, Windsor Terrace, Northampton. Z1234.

HUTCHINGS, E. A., Gunner, Royal Field Artillery.
Already in the Army at the outbreak of hostilities, he quickly proceeded to France. In this theatre of war he took part in many engagements, including those in the Ypres, the Somme and Passchendaele sectors, and was wounded in action. He did continuously good work and received his discharge in December 1919 after six years' service, holding the Mons Star, and the General Service and Victory Medals.
8, Newcombe Road, Northampton. Z2729.

HUTCHINS, F., Sergeant, Labour Corps.
He joined in May 1916, and after his training was retained on important duties with the Royal Army Service Corps in England. In March 1918, however, he was drafted with the Labour Corps to the Western Front, where he served in various sectors and did much excellent work until discharged in October 1918. He holds the General Service and Victory Medals. 87, Adelaide Street, Northampton. Z1236/B.

HUTT, A. V., Bombardier, Royal Field Artillery.
He joined in June 1917, and after completing a period of training was retained at various stations, where he was engaged on duties of a highly important nature. Owing to ill-health he was unable to obtain his transfer to a theatre of war, but, nevertheless, rendered valuable services with his Battery until demobilised in February 1919. 30, Stanley St., Northampton. Z1237/B.

HYDE, J., Private, R.A.S.C. (Remounts).
Joining in May 1916, he was stationed at Swathling, and rendered excellent service whilst engaged on various veterinary duties. He made a number of trips with horses to and from the Western Front, and was eventually demobilised in July 1919, holding the General Service and Victory Medals.
73, Ivy Road, Northampton. Z3383.

I

ILIFFE, A. C., Private, Machine Gun Corps.
He volunteered in February 1915 in the Northamptonshire Dragoons, but was later transferred to the Machine Gun Corps. He served in various stations in England until the Armistice, after which he was sent to France, and later proceeded into Germany. He served for a short period with the Army of Occupation in Cologne prior to being invalided home, suffering from dysentery, and was ultimately demobilised in January 1919. 11, Southampton Road, Far Cotton, Northants. Z3384.

ILIFFE, J. H., Private, R.A.S.C. (M.T.)
Volunteering in April 1915, he was drafted overseas later in the same year. Whilst on the Western Front he served with the Mechanical Transport, being engaged in conveying supplies to the forward areas in the Vimy Ridge, the Somme, Arras, Messines, Cambrai and several other sectors. Demobilised in February 1919, he holds the General Service and Victory Medals. 20, Vernon Street, Northampton. Z1931.

ILLING, B., Private, 16th Middlesex Regiment.
Shortly after joining in March 1917, he was drafted to the Western Front, where he saw severe fighting in various sectors. After taking part in engagements at Ypres and the Somme, he was so severely wounded in action at Cambrai in December 1917 as to necessitate the amputation of his left leg. He was invalided from the Army in December 1919, and holds the General Service and Victory Medals.
The Green, Wootton, Northants. Z2730.

INGRAM, A. R., 1st Air Mechanic, R.A.F.
He enlisted in the Royal Navy in June 1917, but, after training at the Crystal Palace, was transferred to the Royal Air Force (late Royal Naval Air Service), and rendered valuable services as a fitter on important duties in connection with aero-engines. He was not drafted overseas, but did excellent work until demobilised in November 1919.
65, Northcote Street, Northampton. Z1238.

INGRAM, H., Gunner, Royal Garrison Artillery.
Volunteering in October 1915, he was sent to France three months later, and took part in many engagements with his Battery. He was in action at the Battles of the Somme, Ypres and Cambrai, and was wounded. Demobilised in February 1919, he holds the General Service and Victory Medals.
10, Byron Street, Kingsley, Northampton. Z1239/B.

INGRAM, J., Private, 6th Bedfordshire Regiment.
He joined in January 1917, and in March was drafted overseas. During his service on the Western Front he saw heavy fighting at Arras and Ypres, but being badly wounded in action at Passchendaele in October 1917, was invalided to hospital in Reading. He was discharged, medically unfit, in May 1918, and holds the General Service and Victory Medals.
20, Byron Street, Kingsley, Northampton. Z1239/A.

INGRAM, J., Guardsman, Coldstream Guards.
He volunteered in January 1915, and six months later was drafted to the Western Front. Whilst in this theatre of war he took part in several engagements, including the Battles of Ypres, Loos, the Somme, Arras, Ypres (III.), Passchendaele, Cambrai and the Somme (II.), and was twice wounded in action. He was demobilised in March 1919, and holds the 1914–15 Star, and the General Service and Victory Medals.
6, Freehold Street, Northampton. Z1932.

INNS, G. H., Gunner, Royal Field Artillery.
He enlisted in February 1918, and two months later was drafted to France. Whilst overseas he took part in many important engagements, including those in the Passchendaele sector, and in the Retreat and Advance of 1918. Remaining in France until January 1919, he returned home and was demobilised, holding the General Service and Victory Medals.
Newland Street, Brixworth, Northants. Z3059.

INNS, P. R. H., Private, East Surrey Regiment.
He joined in January 1917, and after a period of training was engaged at Dover on important duties with his unit. Owing to his being under military age he was unable to obtain a transfer overseas, but rendered valuable services. He was unfortunately taken ill and died in hospital through the effects of pneumonia on April 1st, 1918.
"He joined the great white company of valiant souls."
93, Semilong Road, Northampton. Z2424.

INNS, W. G., Private, Cheshire Regiment.
Volunteering in October 1914, he was drafted to France in the following year, and took part in the Battle of Ypres (II.) and in several other important engagements. In 1917 he was transferred to Italy, where he participated in heavy fighting on the Piave front. He served overseas for more than four years, was once wounded, and was eventually demobilised in 1919, holding the 1914–15 Star, and the General Service and Victory Medals. 32, Oxford Street, Northampton. Z3385.

INWOOD, A., Driver (Saddler), R.F.A.
He volunteered in August 1915, and in the following year was drafted to the Western Front, where he saw much heavy fighting. He took part in many important engagements on the Vardar, Struma and Doiran fronts until sent home in December 1918 suffering from malaria. After undergoing treatment in hospital at Birmingham, he was invalided from the Army in March 1919, and holds the General Service and Victory Medals.
Hardingstone, Northants. Z2731/A.

INWOOD, C. H., Private, 4th Northants. Regiment.
He volunteered in September 1915, and having completed his training, was engaged at various stations on important duties with his unit. Owing to his being medically unfit he was unable to obtain a transfer overseas, but rendered valuable services until his discharge in August 1916.
11, Stanley Road, Northampton. Z2425.

INWOOD, C. W., Private, 2nd Lincolnshire Regt.
He volunteered in January 1916, and later in the same year was sent to the Western Front. There he saw severe fighting in various sectors, and after taking part in the Battle of Ypres and other engagements, was taken prisoner on the Somme on May 22nd, 1918. Released in December of that year, he was demobilised in February 1919, and holds the General Service and Victory Medals. Hardingstone, Northants. Z2731/B.

INWOOD, H., Private, Yorkshire Regiment.
Having volunteered in June 1915, he proceeded to France in October and played a prominent part in heavy fighting during the Somme Offensive. He died gloriously on the Field of Battle at Arras on April 23rd, 1917, and was entitled to the 1914–15 Star, and the General Service and Victory Medals.
"Whilst we remember, the sacrifice is not in vain."
20, Northcote Street, Northampton. Z1240/A.

INWOOD, R., Private, 6th Northants. Regiment.
Volunteering in September 1914, he was drafted to France in July of the following year. After taking part in much severe fighting in various sectors, he was badly wounded in action at Fricourt during the Somme Offensive in 1916, and was invalided to hospital at Taplow. He was discharged as medically unfit in July 1916, and holds the 1914–15 Star, and the General Service and Victory Medals. 9, Gordon St., Northampton. Z1348.

INWOOD, W., Private, Yorkshire Regiment.
He volunteered in August 1915, and was drafted to France in October of the following year, but after being in action during the Somme Offensive, gave his life for King and Country at the Battle of Arras on April 23rd, 1917. He was entitled to the General Service and Victory Medals.
"Nobly striving:
He nobly fell that we might live."
20, Northcote Street, Northampton. Z1240/B.

INWOOD, W. (sen.), Private, R.A.O.C.
He volunteered in October 1914, but owing to his being too old for transfer to a theatre of war was retained on important duties at Darlington, Northampton and Peterborough. He rendered valuable services at his own trade of boot repairer until his discharge in March 1918.
20, Northcote Street, Northampton. Z1240/C.

IRONS, F., Corporal, 6th East Yorkshire Regiment.
Volunteering in August 1915, he proceeded to Gallipoli in November, but a month later was wounded at Chocolate Hill. Evacuated to hospital in Alexandria, he was sent to France on his recovery in July 1916, but was badly wounded on the Somme in November of the same year. He was invalided to England, and after protracted hospital treatment at Cheltenham, was discharged as medically unfit in March 1918, holding the 1914–15 Star, and the General Service and Victory Medals. 25, Castle Street, Northampton. Z1241.

ISAAC, W. E., Private, R.A.S.C. (M.T.)
He joined in March 1916, but whilst engaged on important transport duties at Woolwich was taken seriously ill, and died from heart disease in the Military Hospital there in May of the same year.
"His memory is cherished with pride."
39, Herbert Street, Northampton. Z1026/A—Z1027/A.

IZZARD, H., Private, 10th Royal Sussex Regiment.
After joining in May 1916, he underwent a period of training prior to being drafted to Salonika in the following year, and there took part in many important engagements on various fronts. Invalided home suffering from malaria and dysentery, he unhappily died at Manchester in February 1919. He was entitled to the General Service and Victory Medals.
"His memory is cherished with pride."
3, South Street, Weedon, Northants. Z2732/B

IZZARD, R., Cpl., 8th London Regt. (P.O. Rifles).
Shortly after volunteering in January 1916 he proceeded to the Western Front, where he saw severe fighting in various sectors. He took part in many important engagements in this theatre of war and was wounded in action at Havrincourt and on another occasion. Demobilised in February 1919, he holds the General Service and Victory Medals.
3, South Street, Weedon, Northants. Z2732/A.

J

JACKMAN, A. E., Gunner, R.G.A.
He volunteered in 1915, and in the following year was drafted to France. There he served as a signaller, took part in many engagements in the Passchendaele sector, and was severely gassed in action. In consequence he was invalided home, and later saw service in Ireland until his demobilisation in 1919. He holds the General Service and Victory Medals.
74, Rothersthorpe Road, Northampton. Z2983.

JACKSON, E. C., Pte., Loyal North Lancs. Regt.
Joining in May 1916, he landed in France later in the same year. Whilst in this seat of operations he took part in many important engagements, including the Battles of the Somme, Arras and Ypres. He was also in action during the Retreat of 1918, but was unhappily killed on May 22nd, 1918. He was entitled to the General Service and Victory Medals.
"The path of duty was the way to glory."
49, Melbourne Street, Northampton. Z2185/B.

JACKSON, E. E., Private, Suffolk Regiment.
He joined in February 1918, but, owing to his being medically unfit for transfer to a theatre of war, was retained on important duties at Queensborough and Sheerness. He rendered valuable services with his unit until demobilised in March 1919.
93, Adelaide Street, Northampton. Z1243.

JACKSON, J., Private, 1/4th Northants. Regt.
He volunteered in September 1914, and first saw active service in Gallipoli, where he took part in the Landing at Suvla Bay and the Evacuation of the Peninsula, during which he was blown up by a shell. Invalided to Malta, he was later sent on leave to England, and was then transferred to the Machine Gun Corps. Proceeding to Mesopotamia, he was in action at Kut and Baghdad before returning home to be demobilised in April 1919. He holds the 1914–15 Star, and the General Service and Victory Medals. 5, Craven Street, Northampton. Z1349.

JACKSON, R. (D.C.M.), C.S.M., 6th Northants. Regiment.
Mobilised from the Reserve in August 1914, he served with distinction at the Suvla Bay Landing, at Chocolate Hill, and in the Evacuation of the Gallipoli Peninsula. Proceeding to France in 1916, he played a prominent part in the Battles of the Somme, Albert, Arras, Vimy Ridge, Ypres and Cambrai, and was awarded the Distinguished Conduct Medal for great gallantry and devotion to duty. He also holds the 1914–15 Star, and the General Service and Victory Medals, and was discharged in January 1919.
12, Upper Harding Street, Northampton. Z1242.

JACKSON, T. F., C.S.M., 2nd Northants. Regt.
Having enlisted in 1900, he was serving in Egypt when war was declared, and in November 1914 proceeded to France, where he was wounded at Neuve Chapelle four months later. Invalided home, he was afterwards transferred to the Machine Gun Corps for service as an Instructor, and was finally discharged in April 1921, time-expired. He holds the Queen's and King's South African Medals, the 1914 Star, and the General Service and Victory Medals.
49, Melbourne Street, Northampton. Z2185/A.

JACKSON, W., Private, Machine Gun Corps.
Joining in January 1917, he proceeded to France in the same year, and took part in the Battles of Ypres, Passchendaele, Lens, the Somme (II.), the Retreat and Advance of 1918, and the entry into Mons. After hostilities ceased he served in Germany with the Army of Occupation until demobilised in January 1919, and holds the General Service and Victory Medals. 9, Lawrence Street, Northampton. Z1350.

JAMES, A., L/Corporal, Northants. Dragoons.
He joined in November 1917, but was not successful in obtaining a transfer overseas before the termination of hostilities. Whilst serving in various home stations he was employed on different duties of an important character, and did excellent work until he was demobilised in March 1919.
55, Oxford Street, Northampton. Z3386/C.

JAMES, A. H., Driver, R.A.S.C.
A Reservist, he was called up in August 1914, and immediately drafted to France, but after taking part in the Battle of Mons, was badly wounded during the subsequent Retreat and invalided home. He spent four months in hospital in Birmingham, and was then discharged as medically unfit in December 1914, holding the Mons Star, and the General Service and Victory Medals.
91, Junction Road, Kingsley Park, Northampton. Z1244.

JAMES, A. T., L/Corporal, R.A.M.C.
He attested in 1915, but was not called to the Colours until August 1917. After a period of training he was engaged on important duties on the Headquarters Staff at various stations, where he rendered very valuable services, not being successful in his efforts to obtain his transfer to the front. He was demobilised in February 1919. 1, Cedar Rd., Northants. Z2186.

JAMES, A. W., Private, 1st Cameron Highlanders.
He joined in December 1917, and proceeded to the Western Front four months later, but, after taking part in the heavy fighting in the Somme and Cambrai sectors, was badly gassed in action at St. Quentin, and invalided home to hospital in Blackpool in September 1918. He was demobilised in February 1919, and holds the General Service and Victory Medals.
24, Monk's Pond Street, Northampton. Z1245.

JAMES, B., Private, 3rd Suffolk Regiment.
Joining in January 1917, he was drafted to France in March and took part in heavy fighting on the Somme and at Ypres before being badly wounded in April 1918. He was invalided to hospital in Gloucester, and was eventually demobilised in September 1919, holding the General Service and Victory Medals. 35, Compton Street, Northampton. TZ1246.

JAMES, C. H. B., Pte., Canadian Overseas Forces.
He volunteered in September 1914, and was drafted to France in 1916, but shortly afterwards was sent to England and discharged owing to his being under age. In 1917, however, he re-enlisted in the Royal Navy, and rendered valuable services as a stoker on board H.M.S. "Dublin." He was still serving in 1921, and holds the General Service and Victory Medals.
4, Castle Farm, Rothersthorpe, Northants. Z3062/B.

JAMES, F., Private, Northants. Regiment.
Volunteering in September 1914, he proceeded to France in the following January. In this theatre of war he saw much heavy fighting, was in action at the Battles of Neuve Chapelle, the Somme, Vimy Ridge, Ypres, Passchendaele, Cambrai, and also in the Retreat and Advance of 1918. Whilst overseas he was four times wounded, and in December 1918 was demobilised, holding the 1914–15 Star, and the General Service and Victory Medals. 55, Oxford Street, Northampton. Z3386/B.

JAMES, F. T. W., Flight Cadet, Royal Air Force.
He joined in April 1918, and was retained at Hastings, Uxbridge and various other stations, where he underwent training as a pilot. He did much excellent work during his period of service, but owing to the early cessation of hostilities was unable to complete his training. He was demobilised in January 1919. 32, Baring Road, Northampton. Z2735.

JAMES, G., S.S.M., Royal Army Service Corps.
Four months after volunteering in February 1915 he was drafted to Egypt, where he served at Alexandria, Kantara and various other stations. Engaged on duties of a highly important nature, he rendered very valuable services during his four years overseas, and was mentioned in Despatches for good work in the Field in February 1918. Demobilised in July 1919, he holds the 1914–15 Star, and the General Service and Victory Medals.
Drayton Lane, Daventry, Northants Z2734.

JAMES, G., Private, R.A.M.C.
Having previously served in the St. John Ambulance Corps, he volunteered in September 1914, and after completing a period of training was retained on important duties with his unit. Owing to his being over age he was unable to obtain his transfer to a theatre of war, and was eventually discharged in December 1916. He was afterwards engaged on important duties at the Ministry of Munitions, where he was still employed in 1921. 55, Oxford Street, Northampton. Z3386/A.

JAMES, H., Private, 1st Northants. Regiment.
Called up from the Reserve in August 1914, he was immediately drafted to France, where he took part in the Retreat from Mons and the Battle of the Marne. He was severely wounded at the Battle of the Aisne on September 27th, 1914, and was consequently invalided home. He unhappily died through the effects of his wounds on October 1st, 1914, and was entitled to the Mons Star, and the General Service and Victory Medals.
"His life for his Country, his soul to God."
Church Street, Rothersthorpe, Northants. Z3061.

JAMES, J., Driver, Royal Field Artillery.
Shortly after volunteering in August 1915, he was drafted to France, where he saw severe fighting in various sectors of the front. He took part in many important engagements in this theatre of war until the cessation of hostilities, and was finally demobilised on his return home in July 1919. He holds the 1914–15 Star, and the General Service and Victory Medals.
65, Melville Street, Northampton. Z2187.

JAMES, R. W., Private, 1st South Staffs. Regt.
He enlisted in January 1917, and in the October following was drafted to the Western Front, where he took part in much heavy fighting in the Ypres sector, and was severely wounded in action. He unfortunately died on November 11th, 1917, and was entitled to the General Service and Victory Medals.
"A valiant Soldier, with undaunted heart he breasted life's last hill."
Pitsford, Northants. Z3060.

JAMES, T., Private, 2nd Northants. Regiment.
Shortly after volunteering in 1915, he proceeded to the Western Front, where he saw heavy fighting in various sectors. After taking part in many important engagements in this theatre of war, particularly during the Retreat and Advance of 1918, he was severely wounded in action and sent home. Finally invalided from the Army in November 1920, he holds the General Service and Victory Medals.
3, Palmerston Terrace, Northampton. Z2733.

JAMES, W., Private, 6th Northants. Regiment.
Volunteering in September 1914, he was sent to the Western Front in August of the following year, and there took part in severe fighting at Loos, St. Eloi, Albert and Ploegsteert Wood. He was unhappily reported missing and is presumed to have been killed in action on the Somme on July 14th, 1916. He was entitled to the 1914–15 Star, and the General Service and Victory Medals.
138, Market Street, Northampton. Z2188.

JAMES, W. E., Private, East Yorkshire Regiment.
He volunteered in October 1915, and completing his training in the following year, was drafted to France. There he took part in much heavy fighting on the Somme, and was wounded in July 1916. He made the supreme sacrifice, being killed in action near Cambrai in October 1917, and was entitled to the General Service and Victory Medals.
"He died the noblest death a man may die:
Fighting for God and right and liberty."
4, Castle Farm, Rothersthorpe, Northants. Z3062/A.

JARMAN, C. V., Gunner, Royal Field Artillery.
He volunteered in August 1914, and in the November of the following year was drafted to France, where he took part in the Battles of Vimy Ridge, Ploegsteert, Ypres and the Somme. He died gloriously on the Field of Battle on November 10th, 1916, and was entitled to the 1914–15 Star, and the General Service and Victory Medals.
"The path of duty was the way to glory."
9, Orchard Street, Northampton Z3063/B

JARMAN, J. H., Private, K.O. (Y.L.I.)
Having volunteered in October 1915, he proceeded twelve months later to France, where he took part in many engagements, including those at Vimy Ridge and Ploegsteert Wood. He was unfortunately killed in action on October 4th, 1917, and was entitled to the General Service and Victory Medals.
"Whilst we remember, the sacrifice is not in vain."
9, Orchard Street, Northampton. Z3063/A.

JARRETT, J. H., Private, Machine Gun Corps.
He volunteered in September 1914, and proceeding to France in December 1917, served with the Cavalry Section of the Machine Gun Corps. During the Retreat and Advance of 1918 he took part in the Battles of the Somme (II.), Amiens, Cambrai (II.) and Ypres (IV.). He returned home for demobilisation in April 1919, and holds the General Service and Victory Medals.
4, Doddridge Street, Northampton. Z1247.

JARRETT, R. H., Rifleman, K.R.R.C.
He joined in 1917, but was not successful in his endeavours to secure a transfer to a theatre of war before the cessation of hostilities. He was engaged on duties of an important nature at various stations until drafted to Germany in 1918. Serving with the Army of Occupation at Cologne, he did valuable work until demobilised in 1919.
32, Maple Street, Northampton. Z1463.

JARVIS, A. E., Private, Suffolk Regiment.
Volunteering in March 1915, he proceeded five months later to the Western Front, and after serving in various sectors was invalided home with trench fever in November 1915. On his return to France he fought in the Battles of the Somme, Arras, Ypres and Cambrai, but was wounded on the Somme in October 1918, and was discharged as unfit for further military duties in January 1919. He holds the 1914–15 Star, and the General Service and Victory Medals.
31, Adelaide Street, Northampton. Z1248.

JEFFCOTT, W. H., Bombardier, R.G.A.
He joined in May 1917, and in the following September was drafted to France. In this seat of war he took part in much fighting at Nieuport, Cambrai, Amiens, Ypres and Le Cateau during the Retreat and Advance of 1918. After hostilities ceased he proceeded to Germany with the Army of Occupation and served there until his demobilisation in February 1919. He holds the General Service and Victory Medals.
2, Alexandra Road, Northampton. Z1933.

JEFFERY, F., L/Corporal, R.E. (R.O.D.)
He enlisted in February 1917, and was shortly afterwards drafted to France. In this theatre of war he was engaged on important duties in connection with the making of railways in the Somme, Ypres and Cambrai sectors. He was demobilised in March 1919, and holds the General Service and Victory Medals. Rothersthorpe, Northants. Z3064.

JEFFERY, H. T. W., Pte., Queen's (Royal West Surrey Regiment).
Volunteering in December 1915, he first served on important duties with his unit at Northampton. Proceeding to France in March 1917, he was chiefly engaged in digging gun-pits, and was present during heavy fighting in the Ypres sector. He contracted neuritis, and as a result was invalided to England, where he was transferred to the Labour Corps and retained on important duties. Demobilised in January 1919, he holds the General Service and Victory Medals.
18, Mill Road, Northampton. Z3387.

JEFFS, F., Private, 1st Buffs (East Kent Regt.)
Joining in February 1917, he was drafted to the Western Front after three months' training, and there took part in the Battles of Arras, Vimy Ridge, Messines, Ypres and Cambrai, and fought also in the Retreat of 1918. He fell in action near St. Quentin on September 18th of that year, and was entitled to the General Service and Victory Medals.
"The path of duty was the way to glory."
15, Cedar Road, Northampton. Z2189.

JEFFS, F., Private, 1/4th Northants. Regiment.
He volunteered in September 1914, but on completing his training in the following January was invalided from the Army. He re-enlisted, however, in June 1915, and was retained with the Labour Corps at various stations, where he was engaged on important coastal defence duties and as a blacksmith, and did much useful work. He was demobilised in April 1919.
Newport Road, Hanslope, Bucks. Z2737.

JEFFS, H., Private, Royal Fusiliers.
Joining in June 1916, he landed in France in the following month. Whilst in this theatre of war he served with the Labour Corps on important road-making and trench-digging duties in various sectors of the front. He was present at the Battles of Albert, the Somme, Ypres and Cambrai before being invalided home with influenza in February 1919. Finally demobilised in April 1919, he holds the General Service and Victory Medals. Bugbrooke, Northants. Z3390.

JEFFS, H., Private, Royal Welch Fusiliers.
He volunteered in January 1915, and later in the same year embarked for the Western Front, where he took part in engagements in the Ypres and Somme sectors. He was gassed in 1916, and as a result was invalided to hospital, and on his recovery proceeded to Ireland, where he served until demobilised in February 1919. He holds the 1914–15 Star, and the General Service and Victory Medals.
Near Bridge, Kislingbury, Northants. Z3388.

JEFFS, J., Gunner, Royal Garrison Artillery.
He joined in May 1916, and after four months' training was sent to the Western Front, where he saw much heavy fighting. He took part in the Battles of Arras, Messines, Ypres and Cambrai, and many other engagements, and also fought in the Retreat and Advance of 1918. He was demobilised in October 1919, and holds the General Service and Victory Medals.
2, Church Walk, Daventry, Northants. Z2736.

JEFFS, R., Private, 4th Yorkshire Regiment.
Having volunteered in November 1915, he completed his training, and in the following August was drafted overseas. Serving on the Western Front, he fought in engagements in the Somme and Arras sectors. He unhappily fell in action on April 23rd, 1917, and was entitled to the General Service and Victory Medals.
"Whilst we remember, the sacrifice is not in vain."
Church Street, Kislingbury, Northants. Z3389.

JEFFS, W. J., Private, 4th Bedfordshire Regiment.
Volunteering in January 1915, he was drafted overseas in the following year. During his service on the Western Front he took part in several engagements, including those at St. Eloi, Albert, Vimy Ridge, the Somme, Arras, Messines, Ypres (III.), Cambrai and the Somme (II.). He was unfortunately killed in action on March 13th, 1918, and was entitled to the General Service and Victory Medals.
"His life for his Country, his soul to God."
36, East Street, Northampton. Z1934.

JELLIS, J., Gunner, Royal Field Artillery.
Already serving in India when war broke out, he was quickly drafted to France, where he took part in the Battles of St. Eloi, Ypres (II.), Armentières and the Somme. Later he was transferred to Salonika, and saw much fighting on the Struma and Doiran fronts. After the Armistice he proceeded to Russia, and remained there until his discharge after 11 years' service in May 1919. He holds the 1914–15 Star, and the General Service and Victory Medals.
Silver Street, Brixworth, Northants. Z3065.

JENNINGS, A., Trooper, Northants. Dragoons.
He volunteered in May 1915, and having completed his training in the following January, was drafted to France, where he took part in much heavy fighting in the Arras sector. He was unfortunately killed in action in April 1917, and was entitled to the General Service and Victory Medals.
"He died the noblest death a man may die:
Fighting for God and right and liberty."
8, Cecil Road, Northampton. Z2426/C

JENNINGS, H. H., Lieut., 6th Leicestershire Regt.
He volunteered in August 1914, and in the following July was drafted to France. There he took a prominent part in several engagements, including the Battles of Arras, Bullecourt, Messines, Vimy Ridge, Ypres, the Somme (II.), where he was wounded early in 1918. On his recovery he rejoined his unit and fought in the Retreat and Advance of 1918. He did continuously good work and consequently obtained his commission. Demobilised in July 1919, he holds the 1914-15 Star, and the General Service and Victory Medals.
8, Cecil Road, Northampton. Z2426/B.

JENNINGS, W., Private, 6th Northants. Regiment.
Volunteering in August 1914, he was drafted overseas in the following July. Whilst on the Western Front he took part in several engagements, including the Battle of Loos, and in heavy fighting on the Somme, where he was wounded in action. As a result he was invalided home and finally discharged in May 1916 as medically unfit for further service. He holds the 1914-15 Star, and the General Service and Victory Medals.
8, Cecil Road, Northampton. Z2426/A.

JEYES, A. E., Sapper, Royal Engineers (R.O.D.)
Joining in December 1917, he proceeded to France in the following year. Whilst in this theatre of war he was engaged on important duties in connection with the construction of railways and roads. He was present during engagements on the Arras, Ypres, Cambrai and Somme fronts, and also served throughout the Retreat and Advance of 1918. Demobilised in April 1919, he holds the General Service and Victory Medals.
Bugbrooke, Northants. Z3392.

JEYES, A. T., Corporal, Royal Engineers.
He joined in May 1916, and, crossing to France in the following November, took an active part in many engagements of note, including the Battles of Arras, Vimy Ridge, Bullecourt, Messines, Ypres and Cambrai. After the cessation of hostilities he proceeded to Germany with the Army of Occupation, serving there until demobilised in September 1919, holding the General Service and Victory Medals.
36, Cleveland Road, Northampton. Z1464.

JEYES, J., Corporal, King's Royal Rifle Corps.
At the outbreak of war he was already serving, and at once proceeded overseas with the first Expeditionary Force. Whilst on the Western Front he was in action at the Battles of Mons, the Marne and Ypres, but was seriously wounded at La Bassée in June 1915. After protracted hospital treatment in England he was invalided out of the Army in April 1918, and holds the Mons Star, and the General Service and Victory Medals.
8, Fitzroy Terrace, Northampton. Z1249.

JEYES, J. W., Gunner, Royal Garrison Artillery.
After joining in March 1916 he was soon drafted to France, where he was attached to a Mobile Section, and was engaged in conveying ammunition to the forward areas. He was present at the Battles of Albert, the Somme, Arras, Ypres, Cambrai, and also during the Retreat and Advance of 1918. Returning home for demobilisation in March 1919, he holds the General Service and Victory Medals.
Bugbrooke, Northants. Z3391.

JOHNSON, A., Driver, Royal Field Artillery.
He volunteered in November 1915, and was retained at various home stations before proceeding to France in March 1918. Whilst overseas he took part in the Retreat and Advance of 1918, during which he saw fighting at Amiens, Villers-Bretonneux, Mericourt and Albert. Demobilised in March 1919, he holds the General Service aod Victory Medals.
24, Wellington Street, Northampton. Z1935.

JOHNSON, A., Air Mechanic, R.A.F.
He joined in 1917, and, after completing a term of training, was retained at various stations, where he was engaged on duties of a highly technical nature. Owing to ill-health he was not successful in obtaining his transfer overseas, but, nevertheless, rendered valuable services with his Squadron until demobilised in 1919.
1, St. Peter's Terrace, Northampton. Z2742.

JOHNSON, A. T., Private, Royal Fusiliers.
He joined in December 1917, and six months later proceeded to the Western Front, where he took part in many important engagements in the Somme sector. He died gloriously on the Field of Battle at Albert on August 25th, 1918, and was entitled to the General Service and Victory Medals.
"A valiant Soldier, with undaunted heart he breasted life's last hill."
Bank, Hardingstone, Northants. Z2739.

JOHNSON, A. T., Corporal, 1/4th Northants. Regt.
He volunteered in August 1914, and in July 1915 was drafted to Gallipoli, where he was in action at Suvla Bay, Chocolate Hill and the subsequent engagements of the campaign. After the Evacuation he proceeded to Egypt, and later to Palestine, on which front he took part in heavy fighting at Gaza, Jaffa and Beirut. In August 1918 he was sent to Salonika, where he served on the Struma front until hostilities ceased. He was demobilised on his return to England in March 1919, and holds the 1914-15 Star, and the General Service and Victory Medals. 9, Cooper Street, Northampton. Z1255.

JOHNSON, B. T., Driver, Machine Gun Corps.
He joined in May 1917, and in April of the following year was sent to the Western Front, where he was engaged on transport duties in various sectors. He also took part in many engagements on the Somme and elsewhere during the Retreat and Advance of 1918, and afterwards served with the Army of Occupation at Cologne. Demobilised in March 1920, he holds the General Service and Victory Medals.
Hardingstone, Northants. Z2740.

JOHNSON, B. W. A., Corporal, 4th Suffolk Regt.
He volunteered in January 1915, and later in that year was drafted to the Western Front, where he saw heavy fighting in various sectors. After taking part in the Battles of Ypres and the Somme and many other important engagements, he was taken prisoner in 1917 and held in captivity until after the cessation of hostilities. Demobilised in March 1919, he holds the 1914-15 Star, and the General Service and Victory Medals.
Bank, Hardingstone, Northants. Z2741/B.

JOHNSON, C. W., Cpl., Mounted Military Police.
Volunteering in April 1915 in the Northamptonshire Regiment, he completed his training and proceeded five months later to Gallipoli. There he saw heavy fighting on the Anzac front, and, after the Evacuation of the Peninsula, was sent to Egypt. He was then transferred to the Mounted Military Police, and in February 1917 was drafted to Palestine and took part in engagements at Gaza and Jerusalem. On his return to England he was demobilised, and holds the 1914-15 Star, and the General Service and Victory Medals.
57, Gladstone Terrace, Northampton. Z1251.

JOHNSON, E., C.S.M., 1st Northants. Regiment.
Called up from the Reserve in August 1914, he was retained on important duties in England until drafted to France in the following year. There he played a distinguished part in the Battles of Ypres, Albert, the Somme, Arras and Cambrai, fought also in the Retreat and Advance of 1918, and was wounded. He holds the 1914-15 Star, and the General Service and Victory Medals, and in 1921 was still with his unit in Ireland. Bank, Hardingstone, Northants. Z2741/D.

JOHNSON, F. M., L/Cpl., 17th Royal Sussex Regt.
He joined in June 1918, and, on conclusion of his training at Lowestoft, was drafted overseas in the following November, shortly before the close of hostilities. Whilst in France he was engaged on important garrison duties at Lille, Barlin and Dunkirk, until transferred in May 1919 to Egypt, serving there until sent to England for demobilisation in April 1920. He holds the General Service and Victory Medals.
5, Bullhead Lane, Northampton. Z1252.

JOHNSON, F.O.G., Corporal, Rifle Brigade.
A serving soldier, he was sent to the Western Front in August 1914, and there, after fighting in the Retreat from Mons, took part in the Battles of the Marne and the Aisne and minor engagements. He fell in action at Ypres in May 1915, and was entitled to the Mons Star, and the General Service and Victory Medals.
"He nobly fell that we might live."
Bank, Hardingstone, Northants. Z2741/C.

JOHNSON, F. S., Private, Machine Gun Corps.
Volunteering in August 1915, he proceeded in the following year to Egypt and saw much service. He later advanced into Palestine, where he was in action at the Battles of Gaza, the capture of Jerusalem and Jericho, and also took part in heavy fighting on the Jordan and in Syria. Demobilised on his return home in April 1919, he holds the General Service and Victory Medals. Murcott, Long Buckby. Z3395.

JOHNSON, F. W. (Miss), Worker, Forage Corps.
She joined in May 1918, and, after a short period of training, was attached to the Royal Army Service Corps on important duties on the baling machines at Bedford. She afterwards served at other stations on various duties, and did much excellent work until October 1919, when she was demobilised.
41, Symington Street, Northampton. Z2738/B.

JOHNSON, G. C., Driver, Royal Field Artillery.
Joining in October 1917, he was drafted overseas on completion of his training in April of the following year. Serving on the Western Front, he was engaged in fierce fighting in the Somme Offensive, but was wounded at Merville in August 1918, and invalided to England. On his discharge from hospital he was demobilised in February 1919, holding the General Service and Victory Medals. 25, Regent Street, Northampton. Z1253/B.

JOHNSON, H. T., Corporal, Northants. V.T.C.
He joined the Volunteers in December 1914, and, after undergoing a period of training, was engaged on various important duties with his unit. He did much excellent work during his period of service, being promoted to the rank of corporal, and was finally discharged in October 1917, for private reasons.
41, Symington Street, Northampton. Z2738/C.

JOHNSON, H. T., Gunner, R.G.A.
Volunteering in February 1915, he was drafted overseas in the following May. Whilst on the Western Front he took part in many important engagements in various sectors, particularly during the Retreat and Advance of 1918. He did continuously good work, and was demobilised in April 1919, holding the General Service and Victory Medals.
136, Southampton Road, Northampton. Z2941/B.

JOHNSON, J., Gunner, Royal Garrison Artillery.
He joined in April 1917, and four months later embarked for France. On that front he did excellent work as a gunner in numerous engagements, including the Battles of Ypres, Passchendaele and Cambrai, but was wounded at Erquinghen and invalided to England. On his discharge from hospital he was engaged on important duties at Ripon until demobilised in April 1919, holding the General Service and Victory Medals.
11, Leslie Road, Northampton. Z1250.

JOHNSON, J. W., 1st Air Mechanic, Royal Air Force (late Royal Naval Air Service).
Joining in August 1916, he underwent a period of training and was retained on important duties which demanded a high degree of technical skill. He was unable to obtain his transfer to a theatre of war, but, nevertheless, rendered very valuable services at various aerodromes until demobilised in March 1919.
36, Southampton Road, Northampton. Z3391.

JOHNSON, M., Private, R.A.S.C.
He volunteered in October 1915, and underwent a short period of training prior to his being drafted to France. There he first saw service at Le Havre and Abbeville, but later proceeded to the forward areas, where he was engaged on transport duties. He was demobilised in February 1919, and holds the General Service and Victory Medals.
9, Demand Road, Northampton. Z1936.

JOHNSON, N. (Mrs.), Special War Worker.
This lady volunteered for work of National importance, and during the period of hostilities was engaged on important agricultural duties on various farms. She rendered very valuable services until relinquishing her work in 1919.
15, Main Road, Northampton. Z3393/A.

JOHNSON, R. H., Private, Labour Corps.
He volunteered in the Royal Army Medical Corps in November 1915, but in May of the following year was transferred to the 18th London Regiment, and in the following month to the Royal Defence Corps. Transferred again to the London Irish Rifles, he proceeded to Egypt in December 1917, and thence to Palestine, where he took part in the capture of Jericho and fighting on the Jordan. Admitted to hospital in 1918, he was later posted to the 1st Leinster Regiment, and fought under General Allenby until again sent to hospital in September 1918. He was afterwards transferred to the Labour Corps, and served at Damascus until his return home for demobilisation in May 1919, holding the General Service and Victory Medals.
41, Symington Street, Northampton. Z2738/A.

JOHNSON, T., Sapper, Royal Engineers.
Having previously served in the South African campaign, he volunteered in August 1915, and eleven months later proceeded to France. Whilst serving there he was in action at the Battles of Ypres, Passchendaele and Cambrai, and did good work during the Retreat and Advance of 1918. He was gassed when fighting on the Somme in June 1918, and was demobilised in January 1919, holding the Queen's and King's South African Medals and the General Service and Victory Medals.
9, Arthur Street, Kingsthorpe Hollow, Northampton. Z1347/C.

JOHNSON, W., Private, Royal Defence Corps.
Being ineligible for service with the Colours on account of his age, he joined the Royal Defence Corps in February 1915. He was engaged on important duties at various stations and did splendid work with his unit until discharged in December 1917. Having previously served in the South African War, he holds the Queen's South African Medal and the Long Service and Good Conduct Medals. 46, Silver St., Northampton. Z1171/B.

JOHNSON, W., Special War Worker.
Having been rejected for military service owing to his being over age, he volunteered for work of National importance, and throughout the period of hostilities was engaged on important agricultural duties on the farms at Briar Hill. During this period he did much good work, and rendered very valuable services until 1919. 15, Main Road, Northampton. Z3393/B.

JOHNSON, W. H., Private, 1/4th Northants. Regt.
Mobilised at the outbreak of war in August 1914, he was ordered a month later to the Western Front. There he was engaged in fierce fighting at the Battles of La Bassée, Ypres, Loos, the Somme, Arras and Cambrai, and many other important engagements, and was wounded in action. He was discharged in July 1919, and holds the 1914 Star, and the General Service and Victory Medals.
19, Bell Barn Street, Northampton. Z1254.

JOHNSTON, J., Corporal, Royal Field Artillery.
Already serving in India at the outbreak of war, he was quickly drafted to France, where he took part in the Battles of Ypres, Festubert and Loos, and was gassed in action. In December 1915 he was discharged time-expired, but re-enlisted in August 1916, and was sent to Mesopotamia. There he served at Baghdad, Kut and on the River Tigris, and later was transferred to Egypt, thence to Palestine. He saw much fighting at Jaffa and Jerusalem, and was eventually discharged in February 1919. He holds the 1914–15 Star, and the General Service and Victory Medals.
75, St. John's Street, Northampton. Z2975/A.

JOLL, E. S., B.Q.M.S., Royal Field Artillery.
He volunteered in September 1914, and was retained on important duties in England and Ireland until 1916, and then proceeded to Salonika. There he played a distinguished part in many engagements on the Doiran and Vardar fronts, seeing much severe fighting until the cessation of hostilities. Demobilised on returning home in May 1919, he holds the General Service and Victory Medals.
22, Perry Street, Northampton. Z2048/B.

JOLLEY, J., Rifleman, 24th Rifle Brigade.
He volunteered at the outbreak of hostilities in August 1914, and, after a period of training, was in August 1915 drafted to India. There he was engaged on important garrison duties at Agra, rendering valuable services until invalided to England with consumption, to which he unhappily succumbed in February 1919. He was entitled to the General Service and Victory Medals.
"His memory is cherished with pride."
46, Compton Street, Northampton. Z1256.

JOLLY, B. J., Private, R.A.S.C. (M.T.)
He joined in August 1916, and in the following October was drafted overseas. During his service on the Western Front he did excellent work with an ammunition column in many engagements in the Somme and Arras sectors, and died gloriously on the Field of Battle in April 1917. He was entitled to the General Service and Victory Medals.
"A valiant Soldier, with undaunted heart he breasted life's last hill."
90, Bath Street, Northampton. Z1257/B.

JOLLY, J., 2nd Air Mechanic, Royal Air Force.
Joining in January 1917, he was not successful in his endeavours to obtain a transfer overseas on account of physical disability. Throughout the period of his service he was engaged on the construction of aircraft at various stations, which work he carried out with the greatest efficiency and skill. He was eventually demobilised in March 1919.
65, Duke Street, Northampton. TZ1451/B.

JONES, A., Private, 28th Canadian Infantry.
He volunteered in October 1914, and came to England with the Canadian Contingent in 1915, being drafted to France in September of that year. Whilst overseas he was in action in numerous engagements in the Ypres sector, but was taken prisoner there in June 1916, and held in captivity until hostilities ceased. He was repatriated in December 1918, and demobilised four months later, holding the 1914–15 Star, and the General Service and Victory Medals.
4, Junction Road, Kingsley, Northampton. Z1260.

JONES, A. E., Private, R.A.M.C.
When war was declared in August 1914 he was mobilised, and at once ordered to the scene of activities in France. On that front he rendered valuable services as a stretcher-bearer, and saw heavy fighting at the Battles of Mons, the Marne, the Aisne, Ypres, the Somme and Cambrai. He was discharged in March 1919, and holds the Mons Star, and the General Service and Victory Medals.
74, Gladstone Terrace, Northampton. Z1258/A.

JONES, A. E., Capt. & Q.M.S., Northants. Regt.
He enlisted in 1893, and prior to the outbreak of war in August 1914 had served in the Tirah Expedition and the South African campaign. Proceeding to the Western Front as a Regimental Quartermaster-Sergeant, he rendered valuable services whilst engaged on supply work at the Base. Granted a commission in 1915, he was sent to Egypt and thence to Salonika, where he did excellent work of a similar nature, and was twice mentioned in Despatches. In 1919 he was invalided home with malaria and eventually retired in March 1920. He holds the India General Service Medal (1895 with three Clasps), the Queen's South African Medal (with two Clasps), the 1914–15 Star, and the General Service and Victory Medals, and several Army Educational Certificates.
46, Wood Street, Northampton. Z1937.

JONES, C., Private, 1/4th Suffolk Regiment.
He volunteered in November 1915, and on completing his training was sent overseas eight months later. During his service on the Western Front he was engaged in fierce fighting in the Battle of the Somme and other engagements of note, and was taken prisoner at Arras in April 1917. He was held in captivity until December 1918, and when repatriated was demobilised in March 1919, holding the General Service and Victory Medals.
25, Althorp Street, Northampton. Z1262/C.

JONES, C. E., Private, 2nd Northants. Regiment.
Joining in January 1917, he trained at Chatham, and two months later embarked for the Western Front. After taking an active part in the Battles of Arras, Vimy Ridge, Messines, Ypres and Cambrai, he was wounded in action in April 1918, and invalided to England. On his discharge from hospital in Sheffield he was demobilised in 1919, and holds the General Service and Victory Medals.
3, Pine Street, Northampton. Z1465.

JONES, D., Gunner, Royal Garrison Artillery.
At the outbreak of war he volunteered, and in December 1915 was drafted to the Western Front. Whilst serving there he took an active part in many engagements of note, did good work with his Battery in the Battles of Arras, Vimy Ridge, Bullecourt, Messines, Ypres, Passchendaele and Lens, and was wounded in action on 14 occasions. He was demobilised in December 1919, and holds the 1914-15 Star, and the General Service and Victory Medals.
39, Ash Street, Northampton. Z1351/B—Z1352/B.

JONES, F., Private, R.A.M.C.
He volunteered in November 1915, and was retained at various stations on important duties before proceeding to France. There he took part in much fighting at Cambrai, the Somme, Amiens, Ypres and Arras. After hostilities ceased he proceeded to Germany, where he served with the Army of Occupation until his demobilisation in March 1919. He holds the General Service and Victory Medals.
82, Whitworth Road, Northampton. Z1939.

JONES, F., Rifleman, 24th Rifle Brigade.
After volunteering in November 1914, he underwent a period of training prior to being drafted to India in January 1916. There he was engaged on important garrison duties at Agra, Lahore and various other stations, was present at the Amritsar riots, and was for seven months in hospital suffering from malaria. Returning home in May 1919, he was demobilised in the following month, and holds the General Service and Victory Medals. 15, Horse Shoe Street, Northampton. Z2743.

JONES, F. (M.M.), Private, 5th Northants. Regt.
He was mobilised in August 1914, and in May of the following year was drafted to the Western Front, where he saw much severe fighting. He took part in the Battles of Loos and Arras and many minor engagements, and fought also in the Retreat and Advance of 1918. Awarded the Military Medal for conspicuous bravery in the Field at Gouzeaucourt in September 1918, he holds also the 1914-15 Star, and the General Service and Victory Medals, and was discharged in January 1919.
23, Devonshire Street, St. James, Northampton. Z2744.

JONES, F., Private, Middlesex Regiment.
Shortly after joining in 1916, he was sent to France, where he saw severe fighting in various sectors of the front. He took part in engagements at St. Eloi, Albert and many other places in this theatre of war and served also with the 19th London Regiment and other units. Demobilised in 1919, he holds the General Service and Victory Medals.
38, Alma Street, Northampton. Z2745.

JONES, G., 1st Air Mechanic, Royal Air Force.
Joining in October 1916 in the Devonshire Regiment, he underwent a period of training, and was later transferred to the Royal Air Force, with which unit he was engaged on important duties as a carpenter in the Wireless Section at various aerodromes. He was unsuccessful in obtaining his transfer to a theatre of war owing to his being medically unfit, but rendered very valuable services until demobilised in March 1919.
Lower Heyford, Northants. Z3396.

JONES, G. A., Private, 4th Yorkshire Regiment and Labour Corps.
He volunteered in October 1915, and in September of the following year proceeded to France, but was wounded whilst fighting on the Somme shortly afterwards and invalided to England. On his recovery he returned to the Western Front in June 1917, and served in the Battles of Ypres and Passchendaele and other engagements until the close of hostilities. Demobilised in May 1919, he holds the General Service and Victory Medals.
18, Knightly Road, Northampton. Z1353.

JONES, G. H., Driver, R.A.S.C. (M.T.)
He enlisted in November 1916, and two months later was drafted to the Western Front. Whilst in this theatre of war he was engaged in driving a motor ambulance, and did continuously good work in the Albert, Somme, Bullecourt and Cambrai sectors and in the Retreat and Advance of 1918. Demobilised in March 1919, he holds the General Service and Victory Medals.
63, Clinton Road, Far Cotton, Northampton. Z3066.

JONES, G. J., Corporal, Sherwood Foresters.
Joining in March 1916, he crossed to France later in the year on completion of his training, and served in various engagements on the Somme and Ypres fronts. Whilst fighting in the second Battle of the Somme in March 1918 he was taken prisoner and held in captivity until 1919. On his release he was demobilised in September of that year, holding the General Service and Victory Medals.
23, Spencer Road, Northampton. Z1453/B.

JONES, G. L., Private, R.A.M.C.
He volunteered in 1915, and later in the same year was drafted to Salonika. In this seat of operations he was engaged on responsible duties as an orderly in the hospitals, and in this capacity did excellent work throughout his service. He suffered from malaria and was eventually demobilised in 1919, holding the 1914-15 Star, and the General Service and Victory Medals. 101, St. Leonard's Road, Northampton. Z3067.

JONES, G. T., L/Corporal, Military Foot Police.
Volunteering in August 1915, he served in the Duke of Cornwall's Light Infantry, the Royal Dublin Fusiliers and the Worcestershire Regiment before being transferred to the Military Police and drafted to Salonika. Whilst in this seat of operations he took an active part in many important engagements in various sectors. He later contracted malarial fever and was evacuated to England, but after a period of treatment was transferred to France, where he was present at the Battles of Cambrai, the Somme and the Lys. Early in 1919 he was invalided to hospital suffering from bronchial pneumonia, and unfortunately died from the effects on February 20th, 1919. He was entitled to the 1914-15 Star, and the General Service and Victory Medals.
"His memory is cherished with pride."
24, Park Street, Northampton. Z1466.

JONES, G. T., Gunner, Royal Field Artillery.
Joining in November 1916, he underwent a period of training and in the following year proceeded to France. Whilst in this seat of operations he was in action with his Battery at the Battles of Arras, Ypres, Passchendaele and Cambrai. He died gloriously on the Field of Battle on March 19th, 1918, and was entitled to the General Service and Victory Medals.
"His life for his Country, his soul to God."
33, Althorp Street, Northants. Z1261/B.

JONES, H., Sergeant, Royal Garrison Artillery.
When war broke out in August 1914 he was serving in India, but was shortly afterwards drafted to Mesopotamia. In the course of his service in this theatre of war he took part in heavy fighting at Kut and did continuously good work. He was taken prisoner, and during his captivity suffered many hardships, and unfortunately died from starvation on July 30th, 1916. He was entitled to the 1914-15 Star, and the General Service and Victory Medals.
"The path of duty was the way to glory."
14, Moore Street, Kingsley, Northants. Z1259.

JONES, H., Sapper, Royal Engineers (Field Coy.)
Volunteering in July 1915, he underwent a period of training, but was found to be medically unfit for service overseas. He was therefore retained on important duties in connection with the building of aeroplanes, in which capacity he rendered excellent services until demobilised in March 1919.
74, Gladstone Terrace, Northampton. Z1258/B.

JONES, H. S., Sergeant, R.A.S.C. (M.T.)
Volunteering in May 1915, he was retained for a time on important duties before being drafted to France. There he served with the Mechanical Transport and did continuously good work in the forward areas, and was gassed in action. As a result he contracted consumption, and was eventually discharged in January 1919. He holds the 1914-15 Star, and the General Service and Victory Medals.
80, Ruskin Road, Northampton. Z1940.

JONES, J. H., Private, 6th Northants. Regiment.
He enlisted in November 1916, and two months later was drafted to France. Whilst in this theatre of war he took part in many engagements, including the Battle of Arras, where he was wounded and consequently invalided to the Base. On his recovery he rejoined his unit and saw much heavy fighting on the Somme, at Ypres, and in the Retreat and Advance of 1918. He was demobilised in February 1919, and holds the General Service and Victory Medals.
62, Marlborough Road, Northampton. Z2427.

JONES, R., Driver, Royal Field Artillery.
He volunteered in January 1915, and ten months later was ordered overseas. Whilst serving on the Western Front he fought in many engagements, including the Battles of the Somme, Ypres and Cambrai, and did good work with his Battery during the operations in the Retreat and Advance of 1918. He was still serving in 1920, and holds the 1914-15 Star, and the General Service and Victory Medals.
23, Spencer Road, Northampton. Z1453/C.

JONES, W., Corporal, 11th Manchester Regiment.
He enlisted in March 1916, and in the following month was drafted to France. In this theatre of war he took part in several engagements, including the Battles of Ypres and Passchendaele, and in the Retreat and Advance of 1918, being wounded in action in July 1917. Demobilised in February 1919, he holds the General Service and Victory Medals. 29, Vernon Terrace, Northampton. Z1941.

JONES, W. H., Private, 2nd Northants. Regiment.
When war broke out he was serving in Egypt, but was at once recalled and drafted to France, where he was in action during the Mons Retreat. After fighting in the Battles of the Marne, the Aisne and La Bassée, he was wounded at Loos and again at Ypres in 1915. In consequence he was invalided out of the Army in September 1916, and holds the Mons Star, and the General Service and Victory Medals.
14, Spring Lane Terrace, Northampton. Z117/B.

JONES, W. J., Private, 8th East Yorkshire Regt.
He volunteered in November 1915, and in September of the following year was drafted overseas. During his service on the Western Front he was engaged in fierce fighting at Beaumont-Hamel, but was wounded there and invalided to England. Unhappily he succumbed to his injuries on December 25th, 1916, at Leeds, and was entitled to the General Service and Victory Medals.
"His life for his Country, his soul to God."
42, Burleigh Road, Northampton. Z1354.

JOYCE, L., Bombardier, Royal Garrison Artillery.
Volunteering in October 1915, he was first engaged on important duties at Plymouth. Proceeding to France in February 1917, he took part in many important engagements, including the Battles of Ypres, Passchendaele and Cambrai, and in the heavy fighting during the Retreat and Advance of 1918. In February 1919 he was demobilised, and holds the General Service and Victory Medals. Denton, Northants. Z3397.

JOYCE, R., Private, R.A.M.C.
He volunteered in December 1915, and after his training was retained on important duties in England until January 1917, when he proceeded to the Western Front. There he served as a stretcher-bearer at the Battles of Arras, Bullecourt, Ypres, Passchendaele, the Somme, Amiens, Bapaume and Havrincourt, and was afterwards sent with the Army of Occupation to Germany. He was demobilised on returning home in January 1919, and holds the General Service and Victory Medals.
25, Fife Street, St. James, Northampton. Z2746.

JOYNES, J., Pioneer, Royal Engineers.
He joined in March 1916, and served in the Northamptonshire, Hertfordshire and Essex Regiments, until finally posted to the Royal Engineers and drafted to the Western Front in January 1918. Whilst in France he was engaged on special duties with his Company in the Ypres, Vimy Ridge and Cambrai sectors, rendering many valuable services until demobilised in September 1919. He holds the General Service and Victory Medals.
16, Todds Lane, Northampton. Z1263.

JUDD, J. A. V., Gunner, Royal Garrison Artillery.
He volunteered at the declaration of war, but was retained on duties of an important nature in Ireland until 1916, when he embarked for France. On that front he was in action in many important engagements, including those at Loos, Albert, Arras, Ypres and Cambrai, and was wounded on three occasions. He also served with the Northamptonshire Regiment, and was demobilised in March 1919, holding the General Service and Victory Medals. 10, Cromwell Street, Northampton. Z1264.

JUDGE, W., Pte., 7/8th Royal Inniskilling Fusiliers.
He volunteered in September 1915, and completing his training in the following year was drafted to France, where he took part in the Battle of the Somme. He was wounded near Cambrai in 1916, and was consequently invalided home, but on his recovery returned to France. He died gloriously on the Field of Battle at Cambrai (II.) on September 1st, 1918, and was entitled to the General Service and Victory Medals.
"He died the noblest death a man may die:
Fighting for God and right and liberty."
2, Carey Street, Northampton. Z1844/B.

JUDGE, W. A., Private, 4th Northants. Regiment.
Having volunteered in March 1915, he was drafted to Mesopotamia later in the same year. In this seat of operations he saw much heavy fighting in various sectors and did continuously good work. He also saw service in India, and was eventually demobilised in April 1920, holding the 1914–15 Star, and the General Service and Victory Medals.
Newland Street, Brixworth, Northants. Z3068.

JUETT, G. H., Shoeing-Smith, R.H.A.
Already serving in India when war was declared, he was drafted to the Western Front in 1914, and saw severe fighting in various sectors. He took part in many important engagements and was wounded in action in this theatre of war, finally being discharged in February 1919, having completed 21 years' service. He holds the 1914 Star, and the General Service and Victory Medals.
21, West Street, Weedon, Northants. Z2747.

JUFFKINS, W. H., Sergeant, R.A.M.C.
He volunteered in August 1915, and in January of the following year proceeded to the Western Front, where he served with a Field Ambulance in the Ypres and Arras sectors. Severely injured in an accident, he was invalided home, but returned to France on his recovery in 1918, and was engaged on important duties on hospital barges, Demobilised in January 1919, he holds the General Service and Victory Medals.
43, Newcombe Road, Northampton. Z2748.

K

KEEBER, A. F., Private, 11th Welch Regiment.
He joined in December 1916, and after a period of training was drafted to Salonika. In this seat of operations he took part in much heavy fighting on the Vardar and Doiran fronts, and was wounded in action on three occasions. After hostilities ceased he returned home, and was discharged in January 1919 as medically unfit for further service. He holds the General Service and Victory Medals.
42, Somerset Street, Northampton. Z1426/B

KEEBER, F. J., Cpl., South Staffordshire Regt.
He volunteered in August 1914, and in the following June was drafted to the Dardanelles, where he saw much heavy fighting. Later he proceeded to France, and took part in many engagements in the Somme sector. He was unhappily killed in action in September 1916, and was entitled to the General Service and Victory Medals.
"A costly sacrifice upon the altar of freedom."
Church Street, Brixworth, Northants. Z3069/A.

KEEBER, H., Pte., 1/7th Manchester Regiment.
Volunteering in 1915, he later in the same year proceeded overseas. Serving on the Western Front he was in action in many important engagements in the Somme, Arras, and Ypres sectors before being wounded and invalided home. On his recovery he returned to France and fought at the Battle of Cambrai (II.), where he was unhappily killed in action on September 26th, 1918, and was entitled to the 1914–15 Star, and the General Service and Victory Medals.
"He nobly fell that we might live."
Newland Street, Brixworth, Northants. Z3070.

KEEDLE, J., Private, 19th Middlesex Regiment.
Volunteering in December 1915, he proceeded to France in the following June and fought on the Somme and at Ypres and Arras. He was then sent to Italy in November 1917, and was engaged on the Piave and Trentino fronts. In March 1918 he returned to France, and was wounded during the Retreat on the Somme. After treatment at a hospital in England, he again returned to the front, and went with the Army of Occupation to the Rhine, where he remained until his demobilisation in May 1919. He holds the General Service and Victory Medals.
16, Monks Pond Street, Northampton. Z1467.

KEEVES, A. D., Pte., 2/1st Oxford. & Bucks. L.I.
Having volunteered in March 1915, he proceeded to France in the following October and took part in the Battles of Loos, Albert and the Somme before being badly wounded in September 1916. Invalided home, he underwent a period of hospital treatment and on his recovery was transferred to the Labour Corps and retained on important agricultural duties until demobilised in April 1919. He holds the 1914–15 Star, and the General Service and Victory Medals.
Market Square, Hanslope, Bucks. Z3071/C.

KEEVES, F. J., Pte., 2/1st Oxford. & Bucks. L.I.
Having volunteered in March 1915, he completed his training in the same year and embarked for the Western Front. In this theatre of war he was in action during heavy fighting at Loos and also at the Battles of Albert, the Somme, Arras, Ypres and Cambrai. He was taken prisoner in March 1918, and held in captivity until after the cessation of hostilities. Returning home for demobilisation in May 1919, he holds the 1914–15 Star, and the General Service and Victory Medals.
Market Square, Hanslope, Bucks. Z3071/A.

KEEVES, G. H., Private, R.A.S.C. (Remounts).
Mobilised in August 1914, he was immediately drafted to the Western Front. In this seat of operations he did excellent work in attending to the sick and wounded horses, and served during the Retreat from Mons, and the Battles of the Aisne, Ypres, Loos, the Somme and Cambrai. He was taken prisoner in March 1918, and whilst in captivity he suffered many hardships, and unhappily died in the same year. He was entitled to the Mons Star, and the General Service and Victory Medals.
"A costly sacrifice upon the altar of freedom."
Market Square, Hanslope, Bucks. Z3071/D.

KEEVES, G. H., Private, Somerset Light Infantry.
After volunteering in March 1915 in the Royal Army Service Corps, he was retained on important duties with his unit at Southampton. Early in 1918 he was transferred to the Somerset Light Infantry and proceeded to France, where he fought during the Retreat of that year. He made the supreme sacrifice, being killed in action on July 4th, 1918, and was entitled to the General Service and Victory Medals.
"His life for his Country, his soul to God."
Town Yard, Hanslope, Bucks. Z2959/B.

KEEVES, M. (Miss), Member, V.A.D.
This lady volunteered in 1915, and after a period of training was stationed at Basingstoke and Duston War Hospitals, where she did consistently good work whilst attending to the sick and wounded. She rendered very valuable services throughout the period of hostilities, and in 1921 was still at Duston War Hospital. Market Square, Hanslope, Bucks. Z3071/B.

KENCH, E. C., Signalman, Royal Navy.
Joining in June 1918, he was posted to H.M.S. "Diadem," in which vessel he was engaged on important duties at Portsmouth. Owing to the early cessation of hostilities he saw no active service, but, nevertheless, did consistently good work until demobilised in January 1919.
Spratton, Northants, Z3072.

KENDALL, R. C., Private, 7th Northants. Regt.
Volunteering in September 1914, he completed his training and was drafted in the next year to the Western Front, where he saw much heavy fighting in the Ypres and Somme sectors, also at St. Eloi. He served all through the Retreat and Advance of 1918, acting chiefly as a stretcher-bearer, until the Armistice. Demobilised in March 1919, he holds the 1914–15 Star, and the General Service and Victory Medals.
41, Cloatsham Street, Northampton. Z1468.

KENT, B., Private, 1st Northants. Regiment.
Already in the Army when war broke out in August 1914, he was immediately drafted to France. There he took part in several engagements, including the Battles of the Marne, Ypres, Loos, Vimy Ridge and the Somme, where he was badly wounded. As a result he was invalided home and discharged as medically unfit for further service. He holds the 1914 Star, and the General Service and Victory Medals.
19, Albert Street, Northampton. Z1942.

KENT, T., Sergeant, 1st Bedfordshire Regiment.
Mobilised in August 1914, he was immediately drafted to France, where he took part in the Battles of Mons, the Marne and Ypres. He was badly wounded at Hill 60, and consequently invalided home, being eventually discharged in May 1917 as medically unfit for further service. He unfortunately died on June 24th, 1920, as a result of his wounds, and was entitled to the Mons Star, and the General Service and Victory Medals.
"His memory is cherished with pride."
13, St. Andrew's Gardens, Northampton. Z1040/C.

KENT, W., Sergeant, 11th Cameron Highlanders.
He volunteered in December 1915, and was drafted to France in June 1916 with the Royal Fusiliers as Sergeant-major. He was then transferred to the Cameron Highlanders, and did good service in actions in the Somme and Ypres sectors, and at Albert and Cambrai. He served with distinction through the final stages of the war and, demobilised in March 1919 holds the General Service and Victory Medals
42, Lower Harding Street, Northampton. Z1469.

KETTLE, F. W., Trooper, Royal Horse Guards.
He volunteered in August 1914, and proceeded overseas in the following April. During his service on the Western Front he took part in several engagements, including the Battles of Ypres, Loos, Vimy Ridge, the Somme, Arras, Ypres (III.), Passchendaele, Cambrai, Amiens and the Advance of 1918, and was wounded in action. In 1921 he was still with his Regiment, and holds the 1914–15 Star, and the General Service and Victory Medals.
5, Sunderland Street, Northampton. Z2428.

KIBBLER, H. J., Private, Royal Welch Fusiliers.
He joined in May 1917, and in the following year was drafted to the Western Front, where he saw severe fighting in various sectors. He took part in many important engagements in the Retreat and Advance of 1918, and was twice wounded in action. He holds the General Service and Victory Medals, and in 1921 was with his unit on garrison duties at Lucknow.
Berry Lane, Wootton, Northants. Z2621/A.

KIBBLER, J. W., Corporal, Royal Welch Fusiliers.
A serving soldier, he proceeded to France in August 1914, and after fighting in the Retreat from Mons, took part in the Battles of the Marne and the Aisne. He was four times wounded in action—at Ypres in January and Loos in September 1915, on the Somme in 1916 and on one other occasion, sustaining the loss of his right eye—and was invalided home on each occasion. Discharged in February 1919, he holds the Mons Star, and the General Service and Victory Medals.
Berry Lane, Wootton, Northants. Z2621/C.

KIDGER, A., Sergeant, Royal Garrison Artillery.
Having previously served for six years, he was mobilised in August 1914, and first took part in the Gallipoli campaign. After the Evacuation of the Peninsula, he saw service in Egypt prior to being drafted to France, where he played a prominent part in engagements in the Somme and Ypres sectors. Later, in 1917, he was transferred to Italy, and saw severe fighting on the Piave front before being wounded in October 1918. He was invalided home and finally discharged in January 1919, holding the 1914–15 Star, and the General Service and Victory Medals. 50, Clinton Road, Northampton. Z3073.

KIDSLEY, E. A., Sergeant, 4th Leicestershire Regt.
Volunteering in November 1915, he was drafted overseas after completing his training. Whilst on the Western Front he played a prominent part in the Battles of Messines, Passchendaele and saw much fighting in various sectors, being wounded in action. Demobilised in October 1919, he holds the General Service and Victory Medals.
77, St. Edmund's Road, Northampton. Z1943/B.

KIDSLEY, H. W., Guardsman, Coldstream Guards.
Having volunteered soon after the outbreak of hostilities, he was drafted to France in November 1914, and fought in many engagements of that critical period of the war, including Ypres, La Bassée and La Gorge. He was twice wounded at Givenchy in December of the same year and invalided to hospital in England. On recovery he returned to France in October 1915, and was engaged at Ypres and Loos, but developing heart trouble he was discharged in June 1916 as unfit for further service, and holds the 1914–15 Star, and the General Service and Victory Medals.
82, Shelley Street, Kingsley, Northampton. Z1470.

KIDSLEY, W., Private, 16th Manchester Regt.
He joined in April 1917, and later in the same year was drafted to France. Whilst overseas he took part in many engagements, including those in the Ypres, Passchendaele, Lens, Messines, Cambrai and Ypres sectors, and was taken prisoner in 1918. He was held in captivity in Germany for several months, but after the Armistice was repatriated. He was demobilised in February 1919, and holds the General Service and Victory Medals.
77, St. Edmund's Road, Northampton. Z1943/A.

KIGHTLEY, E., Gunner, Royal Field Artillery.
Called up from the Reserve in August 1914, he was drafted to France in the following May. Whilst on the Western Front he took part in many engagements, including those in the Ypres and Somme sectors. In 1917 he was severely gassed, which resulted in his being invalided home, where he unfortunately died of gas-poisoning on June 6th, 1919. He was entitled to the 1914–15 Star, and the General Service and Victory Medals.
"A valiant Soldier, with undaunted heart he breasted life's last hill."
11, Kinburn Place, Northampton. Z1042/C.

KIGHTLEY, F. C., Private, R.A.M.C.
He volunteered in May 1915, and after a period of training was drafted to Salonika, where he served as a stretcher-bearer, and took part in engagements on the Struma front. Later he was attached to the Royal Field Artillery and transferred to Egypt, whence he proceeded into Palestine and fought in the capture of Jerusalem. He returned home and was demobilised in September 1919, holding the General Service and Victory Medals.
49, Derby Road, Northampton. Z1944.

KIGHTLEY, W., Rifleman, 1st Cameronians (Scottish Rifles).
Mobilised from the Reserve in August 1914, he was immediately drafted to the Western Front, where he served through the Retreat from Mons and also took part in the Battles of the Marne and the Aisne. He fell fighting at La Bassée in October 1914, and was entitled to the Mons Star, and the General Service and Victory Medals.
"His memory is cherished with pride."
5, Abbey Street, Northampton. Z2749.

KILBORN, J. R., Private, 7th Northants. Regt.
He volunteered in May 1915, and later in the same year was drafted to France, where he took part in engagements on the Somme. He was then transferred to the Machine Gun Corps, and fought at Ypres, Passchendaele, Cambrai, and in the Retreat and Advance of 1918, and was gassed at Messines in 1916. Demobilised in March 1919, he holds the 1914–15 Star, and the General Service and Victory Medals.
14, Brunswick Place, Northampton. Z1945.

KILBY, H. R. C., Private, 1/4th Northants. Regt.
Mobilised at the outbreak of hostilities, he was sent for training in England, and proceeded in April 1915 to Gallipoli, where he took part in the famous Landing, and was wounded. After being invalided to hospital in England he was on his recovery retained on home service until his demobilisation in March 1919. He holds the 1914–15 Star, and the General Service and Victory Medals. 14, Liz Street, Northampton. Z1471.

KILBY, W., Seaman, Merchant Service.
He joined in July 1917, and was first engaged in home waters on board the S.S. "Eaglet," carrying supplies to various ports. Later he served on the Staff at Portsmouth Barracks, but eventually joined S.S. "Cullan" on auxiliary work in the North Sea. He finally served with the Northamptonshire Regiment in India, and was demobilised in February 1919, holding the General Service, Mercantile Marine War and Victory Medals.
145, Southampton Road, Northampton. Z3398.

KILLE, B. H., Sergeant, Royal Horse Artillery.
Having enlisted in 1904, he was drafted to France immediately on the outbreak of war, and there saw severe fighting in various sectors. He took a prominent part in the Battles of Ypres and Hill 60, and other engagements, and was three times wounded in action. He holds the 1914 Star, and the General Service and Victory Medals, and in 1921 was still with his Battery.
45, New Street, Weedon, Northants. Z2750.

KILPIN, G., Trooper, Northants Dragoons.
Volunteering in April 1915, he was sent to France in the following December, and did service there for two years, seeing fighting on the Somme, in the Ypres and Arras sectors, at Passchendaele Ridge and Cambrai. In December 1917 he was transferred to Italy, and was in action on the Asiago Plateau. Completing his service on that front, he was demobilised in March 1919, and holds the 1914–15 Star, and the General Service and Victory Medals.
53, Lawrence Street, Northampton. Z1472.

KILSBY, A. R., Pte., 1st Buffs (East Kent Regt.)
He joined in August 1917, and in January of the following year was sent to the Western Front. Whilst in this theatre of war he took part in many important engagements, including the Battles of Bapaume, Havrincourt and Ypres, and was wounded at Cambrai in October 1918, and sent to hospital at Chichester. He was demobilised in October 1919, and holds the General Service and Victory Medals.
64, Brook Street, Daventry, Northants. Z2751.

KILSBY, R. J., Private, Royal Irish Fusiliers.
Four months after joining in November 1916 he proceeded to the Western Front, but after taking part in the Battles of Messines, Ypres and Passchendaele, he was injured in an accident and invalided home. He returned to France, however, in time to fight in the Retreat of March 1918, where he was wounded and gassed at St. Quentin and again sent to England. He rejoined his unit again in France and was finally demobilised in February 1919, holding the General Service and Victory Medals. 19, Brook Street, Daventry, Northants. Z2752.

KINCH, W., Private, 2/5th North Staffs. Regt.
Joining in January 1917, he received training in Scotland, and also did duty as clerk with the Royal Army Service Corps on Salisbury Plain. He was drafted to France in September of the same year, and was in action in the Ypres and Arras sectors, but at the commencement of the Retreat on March 21st, 1918, he was reported missing on the Somme, and later officially presumed killed. He was entitled to the General Service and Victory Medals.
"His life for his Country."
109, Lower Adelaide Street, Northampton. Z1473.

KING, A. E., Private, Northants. Regiment.
Joining in August 1918, he completed his training, and although unsuccessful in obtaining his transfer overseas before the cessation of hostilities, was sent after the Armistice to the Army of Occupation on the Rhine, and remained with it until November 1919. He was still serving at Northampton in 1920.
86, Shelley Street, Kingsley, Northampton. Z1474 /A.

KING, F., Private, 7th Northants. Regiment.
He volunteered in January 1916, and later in the same year was drafted to the Western Front, where he took part in the Battles of Arras, Vimy Ridge and Bullecourt. He made the supreme sacrifice, being killed in action at Messines on June 18th, 1917, and was entitled to the General Service and Victory Medals.
"A valiant Soldier, with undaunted heart he breasted life's last hill."
7, Thenford Street, Northampton. Z1946.

KING, G. J. R., L/Corporal, Royal Fusiliers.
He volunteered in August 1914, and in November of the following year was drafted to the Western Front, where he saw much heavy fighting. After taking part in many important engagements he was severely wounded in action in January 1917, sustaining the loss of a leg. Admitted to hospital in England, he was finally invalided from the Army in August 1918, and holds the 1914–15 Star, and the General Service and Victory Medals.
4, Lea Road, Northampton. Z2190.

KING, H., Private, Royal Fusiliers.
Shortly after joining in November 1916 he was sent to Salonika, where with the Leinster Regiment he took part in important engagements on the Struma front and at Monastir. Transferred later to Egypt, he served also in Palestine and, being wounded at Gaza, was admitted to hospital at Alexandria, suffering also from malaria. He served also with the Gloucestershire Regiment, and was demobilised on returning home in February 1919, holding the General Service and Victory Medals.
128, Market Street, Northampton. Z2191.

KING, J. W., Private, R.M.L.I.
Having enlisted in May 1913, he was serving at the outbreak of hostilities on coastal defence in the South of England. In April 1915 he was drafted to the Dardanelles, and on May 3rd gave his life for his Country during the second Krithia Battle on the Gallipoli Peninsula. He was entitled to the 1914–15 Star, and the General Service and Victory Medals.
"He nobly fell that we might live."
86, Shelley Street, Kingsley, Northampton. Z1474 /B.

KINGSTON, A., Private, 7th Northants. Regiment.
He joined in February 1916, and later in the same year was drafted to the Western Front, where he took part in much severe fighting in the Somme and Ypres sectors. He made the supreme sacrifice, being killed in action on April 13th, 1917, and was entitled to the General Service and Victory Medals.
"His life for his Country, his soul to God."
Milton, Northants. Z2431 /B.

KINGSTON, A., Driver, Royal Field Artillery.
Called up from the Reserve in August 1914, he was immediately drafted to the Western Front. There he was in action with his Battery at the Battle of and in the Retreat from Mons, and also at the Battles of the Marne, the Aisne, Ypres, Hill 60, Vimy Ridge, Arras, Bullecourt, Passchendaele and Cambrai. He also served with the Royal Army Ordnance Corps and the Labour Corps, and in April 1919 was discharged, holding the Mons Star, and the General Service and Victory Medals.
Church Street, Brixworth, Northants. Z3075.

KINGSTON, B. J., Corporal, R.G.A.
He volunteered in October 1915, and, after completing his training, proceeded to the Western Front. Whilst in this theatre of war he did consistently good work and was in action with his Battery in the Somme, Ypres and Cambrai sectors. He also took part in the Retreat and Advance of 1918, and in March 1919 was demobilised, holding the General Service and Victory Medals.
The Green, Lower Heyford, Northants. Z3374 /A.

KINGSTON, H. J., Sapper, Royal Engineers.
He joined in January 1917, and quickly proceeded to France, where he was engaged on important duties in connection with the building of permanent ways in the Somme and Ypres sectors. He also served at Abbeville and throughout the Retreat and Advance of 1918, and did excellent work with his unit. Demobilised in January 1920, he holds the General Service and Victory Medals.
High Street, Gayton, Northants. Z2429.

KINGSTON, J. P., Gunner, R.G.A.
Volunteering in October 1915, he embarked in the following April for France. Whilst in this theatre of war he took part in many important engagements in various sectors of the front, and was in action with the 80th Siege Battery at the Battles of the Somme, Arras, Messines, Ypres and St. Quentin. Returning home for demobilisation in February 1919, he holds the General Service and Victory Medals.
"Crispin Arms," St. James' St., Daventry, Northants. Z3074.

KINGSTON, T. W., Private, Royal Fusiliers.
He enlisted in February 1916, and completing his training later in the same year was drafted to France. Whilst overseas he took part in many engagements, including the Battles of the Somme, Ypres, Arras and Cambrai, where he was wounded in 1917, and consequently invalided to hospital. On his recovery he returned to France and saw much fighting in the Retreat and Advance of 1918. Demobilised in March 1919, he holds the General Service and Victory Meda
Milton, Northants. Z2431 /A.

KINGSTON, W. C., Private, R.A.V.C.
He volunteered in May 1915, and was immediately drafted to France. In this seat of war he rendered valuable services whilst engaged in attending to sick and wounded horses at Abbeville and also in the Ypres, Loos, the Somme, Albert and Cambrai sectors. He was discharged in April 1917, and holds the 1914–15 Star, and the General Service and Victory Medals.
Park Row, Hartwell, Northants. Z2430.

KIRK, D. J., Private, Bedfordshire Regiment.
He joined the Bedfordshire Regiment in April 1918, and served with his unit at various places in the United Kingdom. He was not successful in obtaining his transfer overseas before the cessation of hostilities, but after transfer to the Royal Army Service Corps did good work as a clerk until finally demobilised in February 1920.
68, Charles Street, Northampton. Z1475 /C.

KIRK, J., Sapper, Royal Engineers.
Volunteering in August 1915, he completed his training and was then engaged on special work in the North-east and East of England. He rendered valuable services with his unit until August 24th, 1916, when he was accidentally drowned whilst on duty at Saltfleet, in Lincolnshire.
"His memory is cherished with pride."
68, Charles Street, Northampton. Z1475 /B.

KIRK, J., Sergeant, Tank Corps.
Joining in June 1916, he shortly afterwards landed in France. Whilst on the Western Front he took part in the Battles of the Somme, Arras, Ypres and Cambrai, and many minor engagements. After the cessation of hostilities he proceeded to Germany and served with the Army of Occupation at Cologne. Demobilised on his return home in 1919, he holds the General Service and Victory Medals.
Kenil Terrace, Brixworth, Northants. Z3076.

KIRK, T., Sergeant, R.A.S.C.
Mobilised in August 1914, he was immediately sent to France, where he served with distinction at Le Cateau and Antwerp (attached to the Royal Naval Division). Later he was stationed at Rouen and Abbeville, where he did excellent work whilst engaged as a clerk at the Supplies Office and on the lines of communication. Discharged in June 1919, he holds the 1914 Star, and the General Service and Victory Medals.
68, Charles Street, Northampton. Z1475 /A.

KNIBB, W., Private, 4th Northants. Regiment.
He volunteered in August 1914, and served after his training with his unit at various places in the United Kingdom. He rendered valuable services, but was not successful in obtaining his transfer overseas owing to a physical disability, and after doing good work was discharged in 1917 as unfit for further duty. 36, Scarletwell Street, Northampton. Z1476.

KNIGHT, A., Private, 4th Suffolk Regiment.
He joined in January 1917, and was drafted to France in the following March. He saw heavy fighting at the third Battle of Ypres, at Passchendaele Ridge, St. Quentin and in the Retreat on the Somme in 1918. Continuing his service all through the final stages of the campaign, he was eventually demobilised in October 1919, and holds the General Service and Victory Medals.
93, Baker Street, Northampton. Z1477/A.

KNIGHT, A. E., Private, Norfolk Regiment.
Volunteering in February 1915, he proceeded to Mesopotamia in the following May, and was present at the capture of Amara, and also in action later at Kut-el-Amara in December of the same year. He afterwards took part in the capture of Baghdad and many other engagements. After completing his service on that front he returned to England in February 1919, and was then sent to Ireland, from which country he was finally demobilised in December of that year. He holds the 1914–15 Star, and the General Service and Victory Medals.
10, Oakley Street, Northampton. Z1478/A.

KNIGHT, C. A., Driver, R.A.S.C. (M.T.)
Volunteering in August 1914, he underwent a period of training and was retained on important transport and other duties at Clipston. He was unsuccessful in obtaining his transfer to a theatre of war, but, nevertheless, rendered very valuable services until demobilised in October 1919.
Denton, Northants. Z3399.

KNIGHT, E., Private, 6th Middlesex Regiment.
Joining in March 1917, he was drafted to France in the following June and fought in the Ypres sector, on the Somme and at Passchendaele Ridge and Cambrai. He also served through the Retreat and Advance of 1918 until the Armistice, and was not demobilised until November 1919. He holds the General Service and Victory Medals.
93, Baker Street, Northampton. Z1477/B.

KNIGHT, F. G., Private, 7th Northants. Regt.
Volunteering in September 1915, he later in the same year embarked for France. Whilst on the Western Front he took part in many important engagements, including those in the Somme, Ypres and Cambrai sectors, and was badly wounded. In February 1919 he was demobilised, and holds the 1914–15 Star, and the General Service and Victory Medals.
22, Alton Street, Far Cotton, Northants. Z3400.

KNIGHT, G., Private, 2nd Northants. Regiment.
Volunteering in September 1914, he proceeded to France in March of the following year, and there saw much severe fighting. He took part in the Battles of Neuve Chapelle, Ypres, Loos, the Somme, Vimy Ridge and Cambrai, and fought also in the Retreat and Advance of 1918. He was awarded the Croix de Guerre for conspicuous bravery in the Field in May 1918, and holding also the 1914–15 Star, and the General Service and Victory Medals, was demobilised in February 1919.
6, Court Road, Northampton. Z2753.

KNIGHT, J., Gunner, Royal Field Artillery.
Three months after volunteering in October 1915 he proceeded to the Western Front, where he took part in the Battles of Vimy Ridge, the Somme, Arras, Messines, Ypres, Passchendaele, Cambrai, Amiens and Bapaume and minor engagements. Severely gassed at Ypres in 1918, he was sent to hospital at Edinburgh, finally being demobilised in February 1919. He holds the General Service and Victory Medals.
33, Florence Road, Northampton. Z2192/A.

KNIGHT, L. S., Sergeant, Royal Engineers.
Already in the Army when war broke out in August 1914, he was retained as an Instructor of Recruits for ten months, but then proceeded to France. There he fought with distinction at Ypres, but was later transferred to Mesopotamia, and played a prominent part in the fighting at Kut, Baghdad and Mosul. In 1921 he was still serving, and holds the 1914–15 Star, and the General Service and Victory Medals.
60, Abington Avenue, Northampton. Z2432.

KNIGHT, M. (Miss), Nursing Sister, V.A.D.
This lady volunteered in August 1914, and first served at Barry Road Hospital, where she was engaged as a nursing sister, and did excellent work whilst attending to the sick and wounded. She also attended to the sick at Messrs. Adnitt Bros. and Messrs. John Lewis' in London, with which firms she rendered very valuable services until demobilised in November 1918. Spencer Parade, Northampton. Z3077.

KNIGHT, T., Trooper, Bedfordshire Lancers.
He volunteered in November 1915, and in July of the following year was drafted to Egypt and thence into Palestine, where he saw much severe fighting. Transferred in March 1918 to the Western Front, he took part in many engagements in the Retreat and Advance, finally being demobilised in May 1919. He holds the General Service and Victory Medals.
33, Florence Road, Northampton. Z2192/B.

KNIGHT, T., Private, 9th East Surrey Regiment.
Joining in October 1917, he proceeded to France in the following February, and was in action near Lens and at other points in the line during the Retreat and Advance of 1918. In November of that year he was seized with illness and invalided to England. After treatment in hospital near London he was demobilised in March 1919, and holds the General Service and Victory Medals.
10, Oakley Street, Northampton. Z1478/B.

KNIGHTON, J. H., Private, Royal Sussex Regt.
He joined in May 1916, and four months later was drafted to India. There he saw much fighting on the North West Frontier and was also engaged on garrison duties. He did good work throughout and also saw service with the Rifle Brigade. In December 1919 he returned home and was demobilised, holding the General Service, Victory and India General Service Medals (with clasp, Afghanistan, N.W. Frontier, 1919).
11, Sunderland Street, Northampton. Z2433.

L

LABRUM, F., Private, 2nd Northants. Regiment.
He volunteered in April 1915, and two months later was drafted to the Western Front, where he took part in several engagements, including the Battles of Hill 60, Ypres and Loos. He died gloriously on the Field of Battle on the Somme on October 27th, 1916, and was entitled to the 1914–15 Star, and the General Service and Victory Medals.
"A costly sacrifice upon the altar of freedom."
4, Northcote Street, Northampton. Z1147/B.

LABRUM, H., Sergeant, 1st Northants. Regiment.
Mobilised from the Reserve in August 1914, he was immediately drafted to France and served with distinction during the operations at Mons and at the Battles of the Marne, the Aisne, Ypres, Neuve Chapelle, Aubers Ridge, Festubert and Loos, where he was severely wounded in September 1915. Invalided to England, he unfortunately suffered amputation of his right leg whilst in Lincoln Hospital. As a result he was discharged in January 1917, holding the Mons Star, and the General Service and Victory Medals.
40, Lower Harding Street, Northampton. Z1480.

LABRUM, H., L/Corporal, Royal Fusiliers.
He joined in April 1916, and after a period of training was drafted overseas three months later. During his service on the Western Front he was in action in numerous engagements of note, including the Battles of Arras, Ypres and Cambrai, and was wounded in September 1918. He also served with the Royal West Surrey Regiment and remained in France until April 1919, when he was demobilised, holding the General Service and Victory Medals.
2, Meacocks Row, Bridge Street, Northampton. Z3402.

LABRUM, J., Private, 1/4th Northants. Regt.
Volunteering in May 1915, he was sent for training to Windsor and Tring, before being drafted to Egypt in April 1916. Here he served on the Palestine and Gaza fronts, and in the course of the second Battle of Gaza was reported missing and afterwards officially presumed killed in April 1917, thus giving his life in the cause of freedom. He was entitled to the General Service and Victory Medals.
"The path of duty was the way to glory."
104, Scarlet Well Street, Northampton. Z1479/A.

LABRUM, J. C., Private, Royal Fusiliers.
He joined in June 1916, and was quickly drafted to the Western Front, where he rendered valuable services whilst engaged as a stretcher-bearer and in the digging of trenches in the Somme, Ypres and Cambrai sectors. He also took part in the Retreat and Advance of 1918, and was demobilised in March 1919, holding the General Service and Victory Medals.
104, Scarlet Well Street, Northampton. Z1479/B.

LABRUM, M. R., Private, 17th Royal Fusiliers.
Joining in May 1917, he completed his training and later in the same year proceeded to the Western Front. There he took part in severe fighting at the Battles of Ypres, Cambrai and the Somme, and other notable engagements, but was taken prisoner at Cambrai in March 1918. Unfortunately he died on October 2nd, 1918, whilst in captivity, as the result of ill-treatment, and was entitled to the General Service and Victory Medals.
"His memory is cherished with pride."
Near "Red Lion," Kislingbury, Northants. Z3401.

LABRUM, S. B., Rifleman, 1st K.R.R.C.
Having attested in 1916, he was called to the Colours in September 1917 on attaining military age, and after a period of training was drafted to France. There he took part in several engagements, including those at Amiens, Bapaume, Havrincourt and Cambrai (II.), where he was badly wounded in action. As a result he was invalided home and eventually demobilised in January 1919, holding the General Service and Victory Medals. 48, Wood Street, Northampton. Z1947.

LAMBERT, F. T., Bombardier, R.F.A.
When war was declared in August 1914 he volunteered, and was engaged on important duties with his Battery at Chelmsford. Unfortunately he was severely injured in an accident with his horses, and after prolonged hospital treatment at Rugby was discharged as medically unfit for further military service in August 1915. Kilsby, Northants. Z3403.

LAMBLEY, A. P., Rifleman, Rifle Brigade.
When war broke out he was serving in India, but was at once recalled and drafted to the Western Front, where he fought in the Retreat from Mons. He was also in action in the Battles of the Marne, the Aisne and La Bassée, and gave his life for the freedom of England at Ypres in May 1915. He was entitled to the Mons Star, and the General Service and Victory Medals.
"Whilst we remember, the sacrifice is not in vain."
80, Great Russell Street, Northampton. Z1948/C.

LAMBLEY, E. W., Driver, Royal Field Artillery.
Mobilised in August 1914, he immediately proceeded to France with the first Expeditionary Force, and served in the Retreat from Mons. He was also in action in the Battles of the Marne, the Aisne, La Bassée, Ypres, Neuve Chapelle, the Somme and Cambrai, saw heavy fighting during the Retreat and Advance of 1918, and was wounded on one occasion. After the Armistice he proceeded into Germany with the Army of Occupation, serving on the Rhine until discharged in September 1919. He holds the Mons Star, and the General Service and Victory Medals. 80, Great Russell Street, Northampton. Z1948/A.

LAMBLEY, F. J., Bombardier, R.H.A.
Serving in Egypt at the outbreak of war, he was recalled and drafted to France in October 1914. He fought in the Battles of La Bassée, Neuve Chapelle, Festubert, Bullecourt and Cambrai, and other notable engagements, and did good work with his Battery during the Retreat and Advance of 1918. At the close of hostilities he proceeded to Germany with the Army of Occupation, and served on the Rhine until discharged in March 1919, holding the Mons Star, and the General Service and Victory Medals. 82, Great Russell Street, Northampton. Z1948/D.

LAMBLEY, J. C., Sergeant, Royal Scots Fusiliers.
At the outbreak of war he was already serving, and immediately proceeded to the Western Front, where he took part in the engagements at Mons. He was also in action in the Battles of the Marne, the Aisne, Neuve Chapelle, Ypres, the Somme and Cambrai, and did excellent work with his unit in the Retreat and Advance of 1918. After the Armistice he was engaged on important duties with the Army of Occupation on the Rhine. He was still serving in 1920, and holds the Queen's and King's South African Medals, the Mons Star, and the General Service and Victory Medals.
80, Great Russell Street, Northampton. Z1948/B.

LANCASTER, G., Sergeant, Royal Field Artillery.
He volunteered in October 1915, and, embarking for the Western Front ten months later, saw much service in various sectors of the line. He took a prominent part in the Battles of the Somme and Ypres and other notable engagements, and did good work with his Battery at Givenchy. He was demobilised on his return to England in July 1919, and holds the General Service and Victory Medals. Weston Favell, Northampton. Z3404.

LANE, A., Private, 19th Manchester Regiment.
Joining in February 1917, he proceeded to the Western Front in the following June and there saw much severe fighting in the Ypres sector. He died gloriously on the Field of Battle at Zillebeke on July 31st, 1917, after only a few weeks' active service, and was entitled to the General Service and Victory Medals.
"Whilst we remember, the sacrifice is not in vain."
28, Market Street, Northants. Z2193.

LANE, F. J., Private, Northamptonshire Regt.
He volunteered in August 1914, but was retained on important duties at home until April 1916, when he was drafted to France. On that front he was engaged in fierce fighting in the Albert and the Somme sectors, until invalided to Cardiff suffering from shell-shock in August 1916. On his recovery he was transferred to the Labour Corps and employed on agricultural work in Yorkshire until demobilised in August 1919, holding the General Service and Victory Medals.
19, Althorp Street, Northampton. Z1121/A.

LANE, W., Private, Machine Gun Corps.
Volunteering in November 1915, he proceeded to France in the next year, and fought at Vermelles, Vimy Ridge and other places. Later he took part in hard fighting in the Ypres sector and at Cambrai, where he was severely wounded and was invalided to England. After some months' treatment in hospital he was discharged as unfit for further service in April 1919. He holds the General Service and Victory Medals.
49, Portland Street, Northampton. Z1481.

LANGLEY, F. W. W., Lieutenant, Middlesex Regt.
He volunteered in 1915, and in the following year was sent to France with the 9th London Regiment (Queen Victoria's Rifles), and there saw severe fighting in various sectors of the front. He played a prominent part in the Battles of the Somme, Ypres and Cambrai, and was wounded and gassed. Engaged afterwards as a Lewis-gun Instructor, he was finally demobilised in 1919, holding the General Service and Victory Medals.
80, Adams Avenue, Northampton. Z2194.

LANGLEY, P., Bombardier, R.G.A.
He volunteered in 1915, and in February of the following year was sent to the Western Front, where he saw heavy fighting in various sectors. After taking part in several important engagements he was severely wounded on the Somme in 1916, and was for nearly two years in hospital in England. He was invalided from the Army in May 1918, and holds the General Service and Victory Medals.
16, Garrick Road, Northampton. Z2434.

LANTSBERY, C. J., Pte., 15th Suffolk Yeomanry.
He volunteered in January 1915, and early in the following year was drafted to Egypt, and proceeding to Palestine, fought at Gaza. In August 1917 he was transferred to the Western Front, where he took part in several engagements on the Somme, and was badly wounded in September 1918. After hospital treatment in Aberdeen he was discharged as medically unfit in February 1920, and holds the General Service and Victory Medals.
2, Stanley Street, Northampton. Z1482.

LAPWORTH, F. J., Private, R.A.S.C.
Volunteering in November 1915, he was sent to France in the next month, and did good service in the transport of supplies of all kinds, being engaged near Albert, Ypres, on the Somme, at Arras, Armentières and Cambrai. He carried on his difficult and often dangerous duties until the Armistice and, demobilised in August 1919, holds the 1914–15 Star, and the General Service and Victory Medals.
5, Fort Street, Northampton. Z1483.

LAPWORTH, F. T. S., Private, R.D.C.
He volunteered in February 1915, and rendered valuable services in guarding bridges and prisoners of war, being ineligible for service overseas. He was engaged at a German prisoners of war camp when he unfortunately contracted a serious illness, from which he died on February 7th, 1917, at Duston War Hospital.
"He passed out the sight of men by the path of duty and self-sacrifice."
9, Fort Street, Northampton. Z1484/A.

LAPWORTH, O. V (Miss), Worker, Land Army.
This lady volunteered in 1918 for work of National importance, and rendered valuable services in the Women's Land Army, taking the place of men who had gone to the front. She carried out all kinds of agricultural work in Northamptonshire for a year, and was discharged in March 1919.
9, Fort Street, Northampton. Z1484/B.

LARKIN, S., Air Mechanic, Royal Air Force.
Volunteering in January 1916, he was sent for training to Felixstowe for three months, and to France in the following April. He did good work at aerodromes in the forward areas, notably on the Somme, at St. Eloi and Vimy. In 1917 he contracted trench fever and was admitted to a Base hospital, but returned to duty and was finally demobilised in March 1919. He holds the General Service and Victory Medals.
52, Colwyn Road, Northampton. Z1485.

LARKMAN, A. C., Trooper, Northants. Dragoons.
Volunteering in October 1914, he completed his training and was sent overseas in the following year. During his service on the Western Front he fought in many engagements of note in various sectors, and was wounded on two occasions. He was almost continuously in action until the close of hostilities, and served in France until demobilised in February 1919, holding the 1914–15 Star, and the General Service and Victory Medals.
51, Dunster Street, Northampton. Z1949/A.

LARKMAN, F., Private, 1st Northants. Regiment.
Having enlisted in 1912, he was ordered to the Western Front shortly after the outbreak of war, and was wounded at the Battle of the Aisne and again at Aubers Ridge. During his service in France he experienced much severe fighting in many important engagements, and did good work with his unit until the termination of the war. He was discharged in February 1919, and holds the 1914 Star, and the General Service and Victory Medals.
51, Dunster Street, Northampton. Z1949/B.

LARKMAN, H., Private, 2nd Yorkshire Regiment.
At the declaration of war in August 1914 he was already in the Army and was at once ordered to the Western Front with the first Expeditionary Force. Whilst overseas he saw much service in various sectors, fought in numerous notable engagements, and was wounded on two occasions. He was discharged in February 1919, and holds the 1914 Star, and the General Service and Victory Medals.
51, Dunster Street, Northampton. Z1949/D.

LARKMAN, W. A., Pte., 16th (Queen's) Lancers.
He joined the Royal Air Force in September 1917, but after three months' valuable work was discharged. Shortly afterwards, however, he rejoined in the 16th Lancers, and was drafted to Ireland, where he rendered valuable services. In 1919 he proceeded to Egypt, and was engaged on important duties with his unit until invalided home and discharged as medically unfit for further service in June 1920.
51, Dunster Street, Northampton. Z1949/C.

LAW, A., Private, Machine Gun Corps.
He joined in April 1917, and in March of the following year was sent to the Western Front, where he saw much severe fighting. He took part in engagements at Albert, Péronne and many other places, and also served through the Retreat and Advance of 1918. Demobilised in March 1919, he holds the General Service and Victory Medals.
31, Marlborough Road, Northampton. Z2435.

LAW, A. (Miss), Worker, Land Army.
She joined the Land Army in June 1916, and after undergoing a period of training was engaged on important duties at various stations. She served for twelve months with the Forage Corps at Bedford on hay-baling duties, and rendered very valuable services until her demobilisation.
128, Market Street, Northampton. Z2195/A.

LAW, A., Private, 1st Essex Regiment.
Volunteering in September 1914, he proceeded to Egypt in the following April and served on garrison duty at Kantara, Cairo, Port Said, Alexandria and other places. He carried out this work and rendered valuable services until his demobilisation in March 1919, and holds the 1914–15 Star, and the General Service and Victory Medals.
48, Crontsham Street, Northampton. Z1486.

LAW, E., Private, 1st Cheshire Regiment.
He volunteered in October 1915, and after training at Birkenhead proceeded to France in the following February and served at Poperinghe and in the Ypres sector. In November 1917 he was transferred to Italy and fought on the Piave and the Asiago Plateau. Later he returned to France and was in action at Merville, where he was wounded in June 1918, and on the Somme in the Retreat of that year. He was in the Advance to Mons in November, and, demobilised in April 1919, holds the General Service and Victory Medals.
33, Regent Street, Northampton. Z1487.

LAW, F., Private, Bedfordshire Regiment.
Joining in February 1916, he received his training at Felixstowe and later in the year embarked for the Western Front. There he was engaged in fierce fighting in many important battles in various sectors, and was wounded on one occasion. Later he contracted trench fever and in consequence was discharged as medically unfit for further military duties in October 1917. He holds the General Service and Victory Medals.
53, Dunster Street, Northampton. Z1950.

LAW, H. W., Rifleman, 5th London Regiment (London Rifle Brigade).
Volunteering in February 1916, he was drafted to France in the following May and was in the trenches in the Ypres sector, where he contracted frost-bite and trench fever, and was invalided to England. On recovery he returned to the front, and was captured on the Somme in the Retreat of 1918. On his repatriation he was demobilised in May 1919, but re-enlisted in the Rifle Brigade, and was still serving in 1920. He holds the General Service and Victory Medals.
38, Hood Street, Northampton. Z1488.

LAW, W. J., Guardsman, Grenadier Guards.
He joined in 1917, and served at various stations in the South of England. He rendered valuable services, but was not successful in obtaining his transfer overseas before the cessation of hostilities. After doing good work on guard and other duties he was demobilised in January 1919.
38, Lower Harding Street, Northampton. Z1506/B.

LAWRENCE, A., Trooper, Bedfordshire Lancers.
Volunteering in November 1915, he was drafted to France in the following year, and was in action at Vermelles, Vimy Ridge and on the Somme. After much heavy fighting he was severely wounded at Cambrai, and invalided to hospital in England, where he underwent treatment until finally demobilised in 1919. He holds the General Service and Victory Medals.
13, Margaret Street, Northampton. Z1489/A.

LAWRENCE, A., Gunner, R.G.A.
Joining in May 1917, he was drafted to the Western Front in the following November, and was engaged in fierce fighting at the Battles of Ypres, Cambrai and the Somme. He also took part in the operations during the Retreat and Advance of 1918, and after the cessation of hostilities advanced into Germany with the Army of Occupation, serving at Cologne until demobilised in October 1919. He holds the General Service and Victory Medals.
East View, Kislingbury, Northants. Z3239/D.

LAWRENCE, A. E., Gunner, R.M.A.
A veteran soldier who enlisted in 1897 and had served on seven different ships before the war, he was in H.M.S. "Zealandia" in August 1914, and remained aboard this ship until October 1917. He was then transferred to the Siege Guns on the Belgian front, where he rendered valuable services. After this fine record he was discharged in February 1919, and holds, in addition to the Long Service and Good Conduct Medal, the 1914–15 Star, and the General Service and Victory Medals.
14, Norfolk Street, Northampton. Z1490.

LAWRENCE, A. H. (M.M.), Sgt., Northants. Regt.
Volunteering in August 1914, he proceeded to France in the following May, and there took a prominent part in the Battles of Loos, Albert, the Somme and Arras, and was wounded in 1915. He was awarded the Military Medal for conspicuous bravery, and was twice mentioned in Despatches in 1915 and in April of the following year for good work in the Field. He fell in action at Ypres on August 11th, 1917, and was entitled also to the 1914–15 Star, and the General Service and Victory Medals.
"He nobly fell that we might live."
Church View Cottage, Hartwell, Northants. Z2436/A.

LAWRENCE, F., Sergeant, 1st Northants. Regt.
Mobilised at the outbreak of war, he proceeded to France with the first Expeditionary Force and fought in the Retreat from Mons and in all the important battles which followed it. In 1915, in an action near Aubers Ridge, he died gloriously on the Field of Battle, and was entitled to the Mons Star, and the General Service and Victory Medals.
"His life for his Country, his soul to God."
13, Margaret Street, Northampton. Z1489/C.

LAWRENCE, F. G., Private, N. Stafford. Regt.
He joined in January 1917, and was sent to France two months afterwards. He saw service in the Somme and Ypres sectors, being in action at different places in the line. He then unfortunately developed trench fever, which resulted in his being invalided to hospital in England. He was discharged in September 1918 as unfit for further service, and holds the General Service and Victory Medals.
95, Lower Adelaide Street, Northampton. Z1491.

LAWRENCE, G., Private, R.A.S.C.
Volunteering in 1915, he was sent to France in the same year and did good service in connection with engagements at Ypres and Loos, and later at Vimy Ridge and on the Somme in 1916. He continued to carry out supply duties at the Battle of Messines Ridge and many other actions, and, serving right through until the Armistice, was demobilised in May 1919. He holds the 1914–15 Star, and the General Service and Victory Medals. 13, Margaret Street, Northampton. Z1489/B.

LAWRENCE, G. C., Rifleman, Rifle Brigade.
He volunteered in June 1915, and in April of the following year proceeded to France, where he was wounded on the Somme in September 1916, and invalided home. On his recovery he was transferred to the Royal Engineers, and, returning to the Western Front, served as a signaller in the Ypres sector. He was demobilised in May 1919, and holds the General Service and Victory Medals.
Church View Cottage, Hartwell, Northants. Z2436/B.

LAWRENCE, G. H., L/Corporal, R.E.
He volunteered in October 1915, and after three months' training was drafted to Egypt, where he served at Kantara and also on the Suez Canal. Attached throughout to the Cable Section, he was engaged on various important duties and rendered valuable services until his return home for demobilisation in January 1919. He holds the General Service and Victory Medals. 73, Lutterworth Road, Northampton. Z2196.

LAWRENCE, H. C., Private, 4th Northants. Regt.
Having attested under the Derby Scheme in 1915, he was called to the Colours in January 1917, and in October proceeded to France with the 17th Royal Fusiliers. He was wounded in action at the first Battle of Cambrai, but on his recovery rejoined his unit and later proceeded into Germany with the Army of Occupation. Returning home in October 1919, he was demobilised, and holds the General Service and Victory Medals. 9, St. Leonard's Road, Northampton. Z3080.

LAWRENCE, J., Sergeant, 1st Essex Regiment.
Having previously served for five years, he was mobilised in August 1914 and quickly drafted to France, where he was in action at the Battle of the Aisne before being wounded and invalided home. On his recovery he proceeded to the Dardanelles and served with distinction throughout the Gallipoli campaign. After the Evacuation of the Peninsula he returned to England, and was retained on important duties until discharged in May 1918, holding the 1914 Star, and the General Service and Victory Medals.
113, Euston Road, Northampton. Z3079.

LAWRENCE, J. S., Sapper, Royal Engineers.
He volunteered in November 1914, and in April of the following year was drafted to France. On that front he was in action in numerous important engagements, including the Battles of the Somme, Arras, Vimy Ridge, Bullecourt, Ypres, Passchendaele, Cambrai, Amiens and Bapaume, and saw much service during the German Offensive of 1918. He was demobilised in March 1919, and holds the 1914–15 Star, and the General Service and Victory Medals. 34, Swan Street, Northampton. Z3405.

LAWSON, R. G., Gunner, Royal Garrison Artillery.
Joining in November 1916, he was ordered overseas a month later, on the completion of a period of training. Throughout the period of his service he was stationed at Malta, where he was engaged on important garrison duties, carrying out his work in a highly capable manner. On his return to England he was demobilised in March 1920, holding the General Service and Victory Medals. Little Houghton, Northants. Z3416/A.

LEA, A. H., Private, R.A.S.C. (M.T.)
A few months after joining in June 1917 he was sent to Italy, where he was engaged on duties of a highly important nature. Stationed at Taranto and various other places, he rendered very valuable services with his Company, serving also in Albania before his return home in 1919. He was demobilised in May of the following year, and holds the General Service and Victory Medals. 50, Florence Road, Northampton. Z2197/B.

LEA, G. A., Battery Sergeant-Major, R.F.A.
A serving soldier, he was drafted to the Western Front in August 1914, and there fought in the Retreat from Mons. He also took a prominent part in the Battle of the Somme and many minor engagements, and, severely wounded in action in 1916, was invalided home. There he unhappily died of wounds in 1919, entitled to the Mons Star, and the General Service and Victory Medals.
"Steals on the ear the distant triumph song."
9, Althorp Road, Northampton. Z2437.

LEA, S. W., L/Corporal, 21st (Empress of India's) Lancers.
After volunteering in November 1915 he underwent a period of training prior to being drafted to the Western Front in February 1917. There he took part in many important engagements, including the Battles of Ypres and Cambrai, fought also in the Retreat and Advance of 1918, and was gassed in November of that year. Demobilised in March 1919, he holds the General Service and Victory Medals.
50, Florence Road, Northampton. Z2197/A.

LEACH, W. H., Private, R.A.M.C.
Joining in May 1917, he proceeded to France in the same year, and rendered valuable services on sanitary work round Trouville and Boulogne, and also as a hospital orderly. Owing to his being in a low category he was not sent up into the forward areas, but carried out the duties assigned to him with diligence and care. He holds the General Service and Victory Medals.
31, Oakley Street, Northampton. Z1492.

LEATHERLAND, H. W., Private, 5th Northants. Regiment and Tank Corps.
He volunteered in September 1914, and eight months later proceeded to the Western Front. Whilst overseas he took part in fierce fighting in many notable engagements, including the Battles of Ypres, Festubert, the Somme, Arras and Messines, and gave his life for King and Country in June 1917. He was entitled to the 1914–15 Star, and the General Service and Victory Medals.
"A costly sacrifice upon the altar of freedom."
101, St. James' Park Road, Northampton. Z3406/B.

LEATHERLAND, J., Private, 7th Northants. Regt.
Volunteering in September 1914, he was sent overseas in August of the following year on the completion of his training. Serving on the Western Front, he was engaged in fierce fighting in many battles of note, but was unhappily killed in action at Loos in October 1915. He was entitled to the 1914–15 Star, and the General Service and Victory Medals.
"Whilst we remember, the sacrifice is not in vain."
101, St. James' Park Road, Northampton. Z3406/A.

LEATHERLAND, W., Leading Aircraftsman, Royal Air Force.
Joining in May 1917, he was quickly drafted to France. Whilst in this theatre of war he was engaged in the workshops at St. Omer on duties which demanded a high degree of technical skill, and rendered very valuable services. He afterwards served with the Army of Occupation at Cologne, and in April 1917 was demobilised, holding the General Service and Victory Medals. High Street, Spratton, Northants. Z3081.

LEATON, W. (D.C.M.), Staff Sergeant-Major, 6th (Inniskilling) Dragoons.
At the outbreak of war he was serving in India, but was at once recalled and drafted to France. He was in action at the Battles of the Marne, the Aisne, Ypres, Neuve Chapelle, Loos, the Somme and Arras, and in the Retreat and Advance of 1918, being awarded the Distinguished Conduct Medal for conspicuout bravery in the Field. After the Armistice he proceeded to Germany, and was stationed at Cologne with the Army of Occupation. He was serving in England with the Northamptonshire Dragoons in 1920, and also holds the 1914 Star, and the General Service and Victory Medals, and the Long Service and Good Conduct Medal.
King Street, Long Buckby, Northants. Z3407.

LEE, F., Private, Royal Army Medical Corps.
He volunteered in September 1914, and after his training was retained on important duties in England until May 1917, and was then sent to Salonika, where he served at various stations. Invalided home in March 1918, suffering from malaria, he was afterwards stationed at Ripon until his demobilisation in January 1919. He holds the General Service and Victory Medals. 94, Purser Road, Northants. Z2198/A.

LEE, F. J., 2nd Air Mechanic, Royal Air Force.
He joined the Royal Air Force in December 1917, and after a period of training at Aldershot was ordered overseas in the following January. Whilst serving in France he was engaged on various duties of an important nature at Etaples, being physically unfit to participate in actual fighting. After 13 months' valuable work he returned home for demobilisation in February 1919, and holds the General Service and Victory Medals.
Clark's Yard, James Street, Long Buckby, Northants. Z3408.

LEE, G., Gunner, Royal Field Artillery.
Mobilised at the outbreak of war, he was sent with his Battery to France in the first Expeditionary Force and served through the Mons Retreat and the Battles of the Marne and Ypres (I. and II.). Later he was in action at Vimy Ridge and on the Somme, and was severely wounded. After treatment at a hospital in Oxford he was on his recovery transferred to India in 1916, and, contracting malaria there, was finally discharged in April 1919. He holds the Mons Star, and the General Service and Victory Medals. 55, Charles Street, Northampton. Z1493.

LEE, T. W., Private, R.A.M.C.
He volunteered in April 1915, and in July was sent to the Dardanelles, where he took part in the Landing at Suvla Bay. After the Evacuation of the Gallipoli Peninsula he was transferred to Egypt and Palestine, and rendered valuable services as an orderly in various hospitals. Demobilised in March 1919, he holds the 1914–15 Star, and the General Service and Victory Medals. 2, Lower Harding St., Northampton. Z1496.

LEE, W., Private, 4th Northamptonshire Regt.
Volunteering in June 1915, he was drafted in the following January to Egypt, and later saw fighting in various engagements on the Palestine front, including the second and third Gaza Battles and the Offensive under General Allenby in September 1918. Completing his service in that area of the campaign, he was demobilised in April 1919, and holds the General Service and Victory Medals.
12, Alcombe Road, Northampton. Z1494.

LEE, W. J., Private, Worcestershire Regiment.
He joined in November 1916, and after training was drafted to France in the next year, and served with his Battalion in various parts of the line. He fought in many important battles, and after the Retreat and Advance of 1918, in which he also took part, went into Germany with the Army of Occupation and served there for over a year. He was demobilised in January 1920, and holds the General Service and Victory Medals.
17, Lawrence Street, Northampton. Z1495.

LEEDON, W. H., Private, Devonshire Regiment.
He volunteered in May 1915, and in the following year was drafted to the Western Front, where he saw severe fighting in various sectors. He took part in the Battles of the Somme, Arras, Ypres and Cambrai, and many minor engagements, was wounded and gassed in 1917, and also suffered from shell-shock. Demobilised in February 1919, he holds the General Service and Victory Medals.
Milton, Northants. Z2438/A.

LEESON, M. G., L/Corporal, Royal Irish Regt.
He joined the Royal Field Artillery in May 1916, but was later transferred to the Royal Irish Regiment, and embarked for France in April 1917. Whilst on the Western Front he fought in the Battles of Arras, Ypres and Passchendaele, and was wounded in September 1917. On his return to the firing-line he served in the Retreat of 1918, but was again wounded at Bapaume and invalided home. Demobilised in February 1919, he holds the General Service and Victory Medals.
31, Sunderland Street, Northampton. Z3409.

LEIGHTON, F., Driver, R.A.S.C.
A Reservist, he was mobilised at the outbreak of war and sent for training to Northampton and Salisbury. He proceeded to France in January 1915, and did good service at many places in the forward areas, including Beaumont-Hamel, Thiépval, La Bassée, Armentières, Kemmel and Messines Ridge. Later he met with a serious accident, and was sent to a Base hospital, and thence to England. On his recovery he was transferred to the Royal Field Artillery, and, returning to France, served there until he was demobilised in June 1919. He holds the 1914–15 Star, and the General Service and Victory Medals.
35, Hood Street, Northampton. Z1497.

LEMON, S., Driver, Royal Field Artillery.
An old soldier with 22 years' previous service, he volunteered in September 1914, and was sent to the Western Front in the following February. He was in action at Neuve Chapelle, Hill 60, Ypres (II.), Loos, Albert and many other places. In July 1916 he sustained an injury to his leg by being thrown from his horse, and after some months' treatment in hospital in England, was retained on home service until his demobilisation in January 1919. He holds the Queen's and King's South African Medals, the 1914–15 Star, and the General Service and Victory Medals, and the Long Service and Good Conduct Medal. 48, Shakespeare Road, Northampton. Z1498/B.

LENTON, R. A., A.B., Merchant Service.
Joining in March 1916, he was posted to H.M.T. "Tyndareus," and was engaged in conveying troops and supplies of all kinds from England to China, Japan, India, Java and America. Whilst employed on this duty his ship was mined on its way to China in February 1917, but he was fortunately rescued, and was still serving in 1920. He holds the General Service and Mercantile Marine War Medals. 42, Francis St., Northampton. Z1500.

LENTON, S. R., Private, R.A.M.C.
Mobilised from the Reserve at the outbreak of war, he proceeded to France in August 1914, and served in the Mons Retreat and also in the Battles of Ypres (I.), Loos, Somme (I.), Ypres (III.) and Cambrai, doing duty with the Field Ambulance as a stretcher-bearer. During the Retreat and Advance of 1918 he rendered valuable services at Kemmel Hill and on the Marne. Demobilised in April 1919, he holds the Mons Star, and the General Service and Victory Medals.
42, Francis Street, Northampton. Z1501.

LEONARD, G., Rifleman, Royal Irish Rifles.
Volunteering in May 1915, he passed through his training and after a considerable period of service in England was drafted to France in March 1918. He saw much heavy fighting in the Retreat and Advance of 1918, especially in the Ypres sector, and, reaching Lille in the victorious operations of that autumn, was demobilised in January 1919. He holds the General Service and Victory Medals. 33, Lawrence St., Northampton. Z1499

LESLIE, F. E. H. (M.M.), Cpl., 1st Life Guards.
Mobilised in August 1914, he proceeded to France in August 1914, and fought in the Battles of Mons, the Marne, the Aisne, Ypres (I.) and Festubert before being wounded and gassed at Hill 60 in May 1915. After hospital treatment in England he returned to the Western Front and played a prominent part in the Battles of Loos, Vimy Ridge, the Somme (I.), Arras, Messines, Ypres (III.), Passchendaele, Cambrai, the Somme (II.), Amiens, Bapaume, Havrincourt and Le Cateau, being again wounded at Flers in September 1917. He was awarded the Military Medal for conspicuous bravery in saving the life of a comrade on the Somme in 1916, and also holds the Mons Star, and the General Service and Victory Medals. He received his discharge in November 1920.
31, Park St., Northampton. Z1502.

LESTER, H., Pioneer, Royal Engineers.
Shortly after volunteering in September 1915 he proceeded to the Western Front, and saw much severe fighting at the Battles of the Somme, Ypres, Cambrai, and Bapaume. He also did good work with his company during the Retreat of 1918, and served in France until hostilities ceased. Unfortunately his health broke down, and he died in Northampton Hospital on October 23rd, 1919, being entitled to the 1914–15 Star, and the General Service and Victory Medals.
"His memory is cherished with pride."
Church Street, Kislingbury, Northants. Z3410.

LETTS, F. R., Private, 1st Northants. Regiment.
Mobilised at the outbreak of hostilities, he was sent for training to Weymouth, and embarked for France in April 1915. He was in action in the Albert sector,and gave his life in the great cause of freedom at Aubers Ridge on May 9th of the same year. He was entitled to the 1914–15 Star, and the General Service and Victory Medals. "His name liveth for evermore."
70, Gladstone Terrace, Northampton. Z1503.

LETTS, F. W., L/Corporal, Suffolk Regiment.
He joined in June 1916, and, after training, embarked for France in the early part of 1917. He served at Ypres and Passchendaele, and was then invalided to Ampthill Hospital with frost-bite. On recovery he was sent to Italy and fought on the Piave and Asiago Plateau. In March 1918 he returned to France, and, serving through all the final operations of the campaign, was eventually demobilised in October 1919. He holds the General Service and Victory Medals.
27, Newington Road, Kingsthorpe, Northampton. Z1504.

LETTS, H., Private, King's (Liverpool Regiment).
He joined in April 1916, and was engaged on important duties with a special Battalion at Liverpool Docks, where he rendered valuable services loading and unloading ships until June 1918. He was then discharged as medically unfit, but in the following October re-enlisted in the Royal Air Force and did excellent work at Blandford and Uxbridge before being finally demobilised in February 1919.
45, Lower Harding Street, Northampton. Z1505.

LETTS, J., Sergeant, Northamptonshire Regiment.
Mobilised at the outbreak of war, he at once proceeded to the Western Front, and was in action during the engagements at Mons. He also played a conspicuous part in the Battles of the Marne, the Aisne, Ypres, Neuve Chapelle and Hill 60, and fell fighting at Aubers Ridge on May 9th, 1915. He was entitled to the Mons Star, and the General Service and Victory Medals.
"A costly sacrifice upon the altar of freedom."
25, Deal Street, Northampton. Z1427/B.

LETTS, W. J., Private, 7th Northants. Regiment.
Joining in January 1917, he embarked for the Western Front in the following October, and was engaged on important signalling duties in various sectors. He fought in the Battles of Cambrai and the Somme and in the Retreat and Advance of 1918, but was wounded in September of that year. Invalided to England, he was demobilised on his discharge from hospital in December 1918, and holds the General Service and Victory Medals. Harbidges Lane, Long Buckby, Northants. Z3411.

LETTS, W. T., Private, 2nd Yorkshire Regiment.
A Reservist, he was called up at the outbreak of hostilities, and, immediately proceeding to the Western Front with the First Expeditionary Force, fought in the engagements at Mons. He was severely wounded in October 1914, which unhappily resulted in the loss of an arm, and after hospital treatment in England he was invalided out of the Army in February 1915. holding the Mons Star, and the General Service and Victory Medals. 75, Delapre Street, Northampton. Z3232/A.

LEWIN, W. T., Private, Royal Berkshire Regt.
He volunteered in November 1915, and on completion of his training was drafted overseas eight months later. Serving on the Western Front, he took an active part in the Battle of the Somme and other engagements of note, but was unhappily killed in action in November 1916. He was entitled to the General Service and Victory Medals.
"A valiant Soldier, with undaunted heart he breasted life's last hill."
54, Turner Street, Northampton. Z1951.

LEWIS, E., Signalman, Royal Navy.
When war broke out in August 1914 he was mobilised, and during the period of hostilities served on H.M.S. "Princess Royal," "Lion," "Nicator" and "Impregnable." He took an active part in the Battles of Jutland and Dogger Bank, and saw heavy fighting in various minor engagements in the North Sea. He also served in Italy and Austria, and was discharged on his return home in November 1919, holding the 1914–15 Star, and the General Service and Victory Medals.
3, Weedon Road, Northampton. Z3412.

LEWIS, B., Private, 1/4th Northants. Regiment.
A Reservist, he was mobilised at the outbreak of war, and drafted to Gallipoli in the following July. He was engaged in the Suvla Bay Landing, and shortly afterwards fell fighting in action at Chocolate Hill, giving his life for King and Country on September 7th, 1915. He was entitled to the 1914–15 Star, and the General Service and Victory Medals.
"He passed out of the sight of men by the path of duty and self-sacrifice."
38, Lower Harding Street, Northampton. Z1506/A.

LEWIS, B. M., L/Corporal, Northants. Dragoons.
Volunteering in October 1915, he was sent for training to Towcester and Luton, and embarked for France in the next year. On arrival there he was transferred to the King's Own Royal Lancaster Regiment and fought through many severe actions right on to the end of the war. Demobilised in February 1919, he holds the General Service and Victory Medals.
2, Nelson Street, Northampton. Z1508.

LEWIS, F. W., Pte., 4th Buffs (East Kent Regt.).
Joining in August 1917, he underwent training and was sent in October 1918 to Russia, where he took part in the operations at Archangel, being chiefly engaged working at the Ordnance Stores. After valuable services in that region he returned to England and, demobilised in September 1919, holds the General Service and Victory Medals.
16, Clare Street, Northampton. Z1507.

LEWIS, J., Trooper, Northants. Dragoons.
After volunteering in November 1914 he was sent for training to Towcester and drafted to France in April of the next year. He was in action in the Ypres, Arras and Somme sectors, and in November 1917 was transferred to Italy, where he fought on the Piave and Asiago Plateau. Concluding his service on that front, he was demobilised in February 1919, and holds the 1914–15 Star, and the General Service and Victory Medals.
61, Cambridge Street, Northampton. Z1509.

LIDDINGTON, G., Rifleman, Rifle Brigade.
When war broke out he was mobilised and at once ordered to the Western Front with the first Expeditionary Force. He was actively engaged in fierce fighting at the Battles of Mons, the Marne, the Aisne, Ypres, Loos, the Somme and Cambrai, and gave his life for King and Country on March 21st, 1918. He was entitled to the Mons Star, and the General Service and Victory Medals.
"He nobly fell that we might live."
19, Norton Road, Daventry, Northants. Z2755.

LIDDINGTON, J. T., Private, 7th Northants. Regt.
He volunteered in September 1914, but was retained on important duties at home until August 1916, when he was sent to France. On that front he saw heavy fighting in numerous notable engagements, including the Battles of Ypres, Passchendaele, Lens and Cambrai. During the German Retreat of 1918 he was wounded and admitted to hospital at Boulogne. Demobilised in February 1919, he holds the General Service and Victory Medals.
The Bank, Denton, near Northampton. Z3413.

LIDDINGTON, P. J., Private, 1st Northants.Regt.
Having enlisted in March 1914, he embarked for France with the Expeditionary Force in August, and fought in the Retreat from Mons and in the Battles of the Marne, the Aisne, La Bassée, Ypres (I.) and Neuve Chapelle. On May 9th, 1915, he was severely wounded in action at Aubers Ridge, and died of his wounds on the next day in Béthune Hospital. He was entitled to the Mons Star, and the General Service and Victory Medals.
"He joined the great white company of valiant souls."
30, King Street, Northampton. Z1510/A.

LIDDINGTON, W. J. J., A.B., R.N.D.
He joined in August 1917, and after being sent for training to Blandford, proceeded to France in April 1918, and served on the Somme and at Cambrai in the Retreat and Advance of that year, seeing much heavy fighting. He continued his service right through the final operations until the Armistice and, demobilised in February 1919, holds the General Service and Victory Medals.
30, King Street, Northampton. Z1510/B.

LIGHTWOOD, F. P., Private, 2nd Northants. Regt.
He was serving in Egypt when war broke out, but was at once recalled and drafted to France in September 1914, and took part in the Retreat from Mons. He also fought in the Battles of the Marne and Neuve Chapelle, and was wounded. On his return to the firing-line he was in action in various engagements, but was unhappily killed on the Somme on October 25th, 1916. He was entitled to the Mons Star, and the General Service and Victory Medals.
"His life for his Country."
8, Weston Row, Northampton. Z2764.

LILFORD, B., Sapper, Royal Engineers.
He joined in April 1918, and was stationed at Chatham, where he carried out his various duties in a highly capable and efficient manner. He proved to be unsuccessful in his endeavours to secure a transfer to a theatre of war, but, nevertheless, rendered valuable services before being demobilised in February 1919. 7, King Street, Northampton. Z1330/B.

LILFORD, F. O., Pte., 1st Bedfordshire Regiment.
Joining in July 1917, he completed his period of training, and in the following December was ordered to India, where he served for nearly twelve months. During that time he was engaged on important garrison duties at Delhi and Agra, and did consistently good work until sent to England for demobilisation in December 1919. He holds the General Service Medal. 43, Bouverie Street, Northampton. Z1952.

LILFORD, W. F., Driver, Royal Engineers.
He volunteered in August 1915, but was engaged on duties of an important nature in England until August 1917, when he was drafted to the Western Front. After fighting in various engagements in the Somme sector, he died gloriously on the Field of Battle at Gouzeaucourt in October 1917. He was entitled to the General Service and Victory Medals.
"His life for his Country, his soul to God."
24, Melbourne Street, Northampton. Z1953/B.

LILFORD, W. J., Private, 1st Northants. Regiment.
He volunteered in March 1915, and in January of the following year was drafted to Egypt. Subsequently he was sent to Palestine, in which theatre of war he saw much severe fighting in numerous engagements, including those at Gaza and Aleppo. After the Armistice he served in Egypt until sent to England for demobilisation in April 1919, and holds the General Service and Victory Medals. 24, Melbourne Road, Northampton. Z1953/A.

LILLYMAN, W., 1st Class Air Mechanic, R.A.F.
He volunteered in December 1915, and was sent to France after twelve months' training. He did good service in an observation balloon section near Arras, Ypres, Lens and Cambrai. Later he served through the Retreat and Advance of 1918, carrying on his observer's duties at Amiens, Bapaume, Havrincourt Wood and Epéhy, and was present at the entry of Mons on Armistice Day. Demobilised in March 1919, he holds the General Service and Victory Medals.
95, Hunter Street, Northampton. Z1511.

LINAKER, F., L/Corporal, 2nd Northants. Regt.
Six months after volunteering in September 1914, he proceeded to the Western Front and fought in the Battles of Neuve Chapelle, Hill 60, Ypres, Loos, Vimy Ridge and the Somme. He was gassed in the latter engagement, and on returning to the firing-line served in the Retreat of 1918, being wounded and taken prisoner at Lens. On his release from captivity he returned to England and was demobilised in January 1919, holding the 1914–15 Star, and the General Service and Victory Medals.
The Lane, Denton, near Northampton. Z3414—Z3415.

LINDSAY, E. A. (Mrs.), Special War Worker.
During the period of hostilities this lady offered her services to the Canadian Convalescent Home at Sturrey, where she served as an assistant cook. She was afterwards engaged on important duties in the wards at Duston War Hospital, where she rendered valuable services until April 1918.
24, Parkwood Street, Northampton. Z2439/A.

LINDSAY, J. C., Rifleman, Cameronians (Scottish Rifles).
He volunteered in July 1915 in the Highland Light Infantry, and in the following November was drafted to the Western Front. There he took part in the Battles of Vermelles, Vimy Ridge, the Somme, Arras, Ypres and Lille, fought also in the Retreat and Advance of 1918, and was wounded in July and November 1916, and in September 1917. He afterwards served with the Army of Occupation in Germany and, demobilised in February 1919, holds the General Service and Victory Medals. 24, Parkwood Street, Northampton. Z2439/B.

LINE, A., Private, Northamptonshire Regiment.
When war broke out he was mobilised, and, proceeding to France, took part in the Battles of Mons, Le Cateau, the Marne and the Aisne, and was wounded at Ypres in 1914. On his recovery he was again wounded at Festubert in 1915, and, on returning to the firing-line, fought in engagements at Loos, Vermelles, Vimy Ridge, the Somme, Passchendaele, Bapaume, Le Cateau and the Sambre. After the close of hostilities he proceeded into Germany with the Army of Occupation, and in 1920 was still serving, holding the Mons Star, and the General Service and Victory Medals.
5, Shakespeare Road, Northampton. Z1954.

LINES, W., Sapper, Royal Engineers (R.O.D.)
He volunteered in June 1915, and after a short period of training embarked a month later for France. On that front he was engaged on important work in connection with the railways and various other duties, principally at Ypres and Poperinghe, until the cessation of hostilities. He served in France until April 1919, when he was sent home for demobilisation, and holds the 1914–15 Star, and the General Service and Victory Medals.
156, St. Leonard's Road, Far Cotton, Northampton. Z3082.

LINES, W., L/Corporal, 5th Northants. Regt.
Mobilised in August 1914, he was at once ordered to France, and fought in the actions at Mons. He also took part in the Battles of the Marne, the Aisne, La Bassée, Neuve Chapelle, St. Eloi, Hill 60, Ypres, Festubert and Loos, but was severely wounded in an explosion, and unhappily succumbed to his injuries in September 1915 after 20 years' service. He was entitled to the Mons Star, and the General Service and Victory Medals.
"His life for his Country."
12, Spencer Street, Northampton. Z3083.

LINNELL, F. (D.C.M.), C.S.M., 7th Northamptonshire Regiment.
Mobilised from the Reserve in August 1914, he quickly proceeded to France, and was in action at Mons. He later served with distinction at the Battles of the Aisne, La Bassée, Ypres (I.), Neuve Chapelle, Aubers Ridge (where he was wounded in May 1915), Festubert, the Somme, Arras, Passchendaele and Cambrai. Badly wounded in October 1918 at Cambrai (II.), he was invalided to Colchester for treatment. He was awarded the Distinguished Conduct Medal for conspicuous gallantry in holding up the enemy at Rosières in March 1918, and also holds the Mons Star, and the General Service and Victory Medals. He was discharged as medically unfit through his wounds in March 1920.
47, Lower Harding Street, Northampton. Z1513.

LITTLEMORE, J., Private, 1st Northants. Regt.
He volunteered in September 1914, and in the following year embarked for France. On that front he fought in the Battles of Neuve Chapelle, Hill 60, Loos, the Somme, Arras, Vimy Ridge and Cambrai, and did good work with his unit during the Retreat and Advance of 1918. After the Armistice he proceeded to Germany with the Army of Occupation, serving at Cologne until demobilised in March 1919. He holds the 1914–15 Star, and the General Service and Victory Medals.
14, Grey Friars Street, Northampton. Z1955.

LITTLER, H., Trooper, Northants. Dragoons.
Volunteering in November 1914, he was drafted overseas in February of the following year. Serving on the Western Front, he was in action at the Battles of Neuve Chapelle and Loos, fought in engagements at Aubers Ridge and was wounded at Monchy in April 1916. He was invalided home, and on his recovery served in England until demobilised in January 1919, holding the 1914–15 Star, and the General Service and Victory Medals.
83, Delapre Street, Far Cotton, Northampton. Z3230/A.

LLOYD, F. W., Private, 17th Middlesex Regiment.
Joining in February 1917, he embarked for France in the following May, and was in action near Festubert and at Passchendaele Ridge. In January 1918 he was unfortunately wounded and taken prisoner at Cambrai, and after a year's captivity in Germany was, on repatriation, demobilised in April 1919. He holds the General Service and Victory Medals. 63, High St., Kingsthorpe, Northampton. Z1514/A.

LOAKES, C., Private, West Yorkshire Regiment.
Joining in May 1917, at the age of 17, he was sent overseas on completion of his training in the following year. Whilst on the Western Front he was engaged in fierce fighting, but after only 14 days' active service he gave his life for King and Country. He was entitled to the General Service and Victory Medals.
"He nobly fell that we might live."
3 Collins Street, Northampton. Z1956/C.

LOAKES, C., Private, Northumberland Fusiliers.
Shortly after volunteering in 1915 he was sent to the Western Front, where he saw heavy fighting in various sectors. After taking part in the Battles of Hill 60 and Ypres, and many other engagements, he was severely wounded in action and admitted to hospital in England. He was invalided from the Army in September 1916, and holds the 1914–15 Star, and the General Service and Victory Medals.
1, Wycliffe Road, Northampton. Z2440/A—Z2441/A.

LOAKES, F. (M.M.), Sergeant, R.A.M.C.
He volunteered in September 1915, and in the following year was sent to the Western Front, where he served in various sectors, being present at the Battles of Vimy Ridge, the Somme, Ypres and Passchendaele and other engagements. He was awarded the Military Medal for conspicuous bravery in rescuing the wounded under heavy fire, and, holding also the General Service and Victory Medals, was demobilised in February 1919.
88, Adams Avenue, Northampton. Z2200.

LOAKES, H., Sergeant, 1st Northants. Regiment.
Called up from the Reserve in August 1914, he was at once drafted to France, where he fought in the Retreat from Mons, took a prominent part also in the Battles of the Marne, the Aisne, Ypres, the Somme, Arras and Cambrai, and was wounded in 1915. He fell fighting on August 5th, 1918, during the Allies' Advance, and was entitled to the Mons Star, and the General Service and Victory Medals.
"His memory is cherished with pride."
1, Wycliffe Road, Northampton. Z2440/B—Z2441/B.

LOAKES, H., Private, Northants. Regiment.
Mobilised at the outbreak of war, he at once proceeded to France with the first Expeditionary Force, and was in action in the Retreat from Mons. He also served with distinction as a sniper in numerous notable engagements, and died gloriously on the Field of Battle at Loos in September 1915. He was entitled to the Mons Star, and the General Service and Victory Medals.
"Thinking that remembrance, though unspoken, may reach him where he sleeps."
3, Collins Street, Northampton. Z1956/B.

LOAKES, T. H., A.B., Royal Naval Division.
Volunteering in October 1915, he was sent for training to Chatham and Blandford, and sailed for the Eastern Mediterranean in February of the next year. After a few months' service at Mudros, he was transferred to France, and was in action in the Albert and Somme sectors. Later he developed tuberculosis, and being invalided to England, was discharged as unfit for further service in April 1917. He holds the General Service and Victory Medals.
4, Seymour Place, Kingsthorpe, Northampton. Z1515/C.

LOAKES, W., Corporal, 1/4th Northants. Regt.
He volunteered in June 1915, and shortly afterwards was drafted to Gallipoli and fought at Suvla Bay and in the subsequent engagements of the campaign. After the Evacuation he was sent to Palestine, on which front he took part in the three Battles of Gaza, but was unhappily killed in action at Jerusalem on November 27th, 1917. He was entitled to the 1914–15 Star, and the General Service and Victory Medals.
"Great deeds cannot die."
3, Collins Street, Northampton. Z1956/A.

LOCKETT, H. W., Private, 17th Royal Fusiliers.
Volunteering in December 1914, he was sent for training to Salisbury Plain and Worthing, and embarked for France in the following July. He served in the Ypres sector and on the Somme, where he was wounded in 1916, but remained with his unit. On November 13th of the same year he died a valiant soldier's death at Beaumont-Hamel, and was entitled to the 1914–15 Star, and the General Service and Victory Medals.
"He nobly fell that we might live."
34, Adelaide Street, Northampton. Z1516/C.

LOCKETT, W., Sergeant, 1st Northants. Regt.
Mobilised in August 1914, he immediately proceeded to France and fought in the Battles of Mons, the Aisne, Ypres and Loos. He was badly wounded in the last-named sector in February 1916 and invalided to Scotland, but on his recovery was retained on special duties at Hounslow until his discharge as medically unfit in May 1918. He then took up work of National importance on munitions at Messrs. J. Main & Co., Ltd., of Paisley, but unfortunately sustained serious injuries in a crane accident, and died in hospital on October 23rd, 1918. He was entitled to the Mons Star, and the General Service and Victory Medals.
"His memory is cherished with pride."
41, Gladstone Terrace, Northampton. Z1517/B.

LOE, F. W., Private, 1st Northants. Regiment.
Already in the Army in August 1914, he at once proceeded to France and served at the Battle of, and in the Retreat from, Mons. He also took part in the Battles of the Marne, the Aisne, Ypres and Loos before giving his life for King and Country in the last-named sector on October 13th, 1915. He was entitled to the Mons Star, and the General Service and Victory Medals.
"The path of duty was the way to glory."
19, Lincoln Street, Kingsthorpe, Northampton. Z1518/A.

LOE, J. (M.M.), Sergeant, Royal Field Artillery.
Having enlisted in August 1913, he was immediately sent to France at the outbreak of war, and served with distinction in the Battle of Mons. After taking part in the subsequent Retreat, he fought in the Battles of the Marne, Ypres, the Somme, the Ancre, Bourlon Wood and Cambrai. He was awarded the Military Medal for conspicuous bravery at Bourlon Wood, being wounded in action at the same time. Receiving his discharge in August 1919, he holds also the Mons Star, and the General Service and Victory Medals.
19, Lincoln Street, Kingsthorpe, Northampton. Z1518/B.

LONG, C. J., C.S.M., 3/4th Northants. Regiment.
He volunteered in January 1916, but, before being drafted to France in December 1917 was transferred to the Army Gymnastic Staff and engaged as a Physical Training Instructor. On proceeding to the Western Front he rendered valuable services in a similar capacity at various places behind the line, and was eventually demobilised in February 1919, holding the General Service and Victory Medals.
42, Hunter Street, Northampton. Z1519/A.

LONG, F. W., Corporal, 3/10th London Regiment.
He joined the King's Royal Rifle Corps in July 1916, but was later transferred to the London Regiment and sent to Egypt. Proceeding into Palestine, he fought in the Battles of Siwa, Rafa, Gaza (I., II. and III.) and other important engagements culminating in the capture of Jerusalem, being once wounded in action. He was demobilised in February 1919, and holds the General Service and Victory Medals.
42, Hunter Street, Northampton. Z1519/B.

LONGLAND, E., Private, 6th Northants. Regt.
He volunteered in May 1915, but was retained on special duties with his unit at Tring until January 1917, when he embarked for France. On that front he was engaged in fierce fighting at the Battles of Arras, Vimy Ridge and Bullecourt, but was unhappily killed in action on May 3rd, 1917. He was entitled to the General Service and Victory Medals.
"His life for his Country, his soul to God."
Little Houghton, Northants. Z3416/B.

LOVE, J. E., Leading Aircraftsman, R.A.F.
He volunteered in November 1915, and was engaged on work of a highly technical nature at Montrose, Leeds, Tring, Aldershot and Edinburgh. Unsuccessful in his efforts to secure a transfer to the fighting area, he, nevertheless, rendered many valuable services, and fulfilled his duties with the greatest ability until demobilised in November 1919.
28, Victoria Street, Northampton. Z1957/A—Z1958/A.

LOVE, L. L., Private, 2nd West Riding Regiment.
Joining in November 1917, he was drafted to the Western Front in the following March and saw much heavy fighting in the Ypres sector, during which he was severely wounded by shrapnel. After treatment in hospital at Brighton he was, on his recovery, retained on home service with the Reserve Battalion of his Regiment until his demobilisation in October 1919. He holds the General Service and Victory Medals.
34, Hunter Street, Northampton. Z1520.

LOVE, P., Gunner, Royal Field Artillery.
Volunteering in February 1916, he proceeded with his Battery to France in the following October. He was in action in the Ypres and Somme sectors, and was slightly gassed. Later he fought in the Battle of Cambrai and through the Retreat and Advance of 1918, rendering valuable service with the guns. Demobilised in October 1919, he holds the General Service and Victory Medals. 14, Oak Street, Northampton. Z1521.

LOVE, W. F., A.B., Royal Naval Division.
On attaining military age in July 1917, he joined the Royal Naval Division, and later in the same year was drafted to the Western Front. There he saw heavy fighting, chiefly in the Ypres sector, and did good work during operations in the Retreat and Advance of 1918. He was gassed on one occasion, and in February 1919 was discharged as medically unfit for further service, holding the General Service and Victory Medals.
28, Victoria Street, Northampton. Z1957/B—Z1958/B.

LOVELL, G. F., Private, 7th Middlesex Regiment.
Joining in March 1916, he was sent for training to Purfleet and Dover, and sailed for France in the following October. After doing good service in the Ypres sector he unfortunately developed serious illness, and, being invalided to King's College Hospital in London, was discharged as medically unfit for further service in August 1917. He holds the General Service and Victory Medals.
6, Seymour Place, King Street, Northampton. Z1524/B.

LOVELL, G. H., Driver, R.A.S.C. (H.T.)
He volunteered in October 1914, but was retained on important duties in England until August 1917, when he was drafted to the Western Front. There he was engaged in fierce fighting at Arras, Ypres, Cambrai and Valenciennes, and did good work with his unit in the final victorious engagements of the war. He was accidentally wounded in April 1918, and was demobilised in March 1919, holding the General Service and Victory Medals.
38, Euston Rd., Far Cotton, Northampton. Z3084/A—Z3085/A.

LOVELL, L. C., Private, 19th London Regiment.
Volunteering in November 1915, he was trained at Eastbourne and proceeded overseas seven months later. During his service on the Western Front he was in action in numerous engagements of note, but unfortunately contracted trench fever and was invalided to England. On his discharge from hospital he was retained on home service until demobilised in February 1919, holding the General Service and Victory Medals.
38, Euston Rd., Far Cotton, Northampton. Z3084/B—Z3085/B.

LOVELL, P., Sergeant, 7th Northants. Regiment.
Volunteering in August 1914, he was sent to France twelve months later and served with distinction at the Battles of Loos, the Somme, Albert, Arras and Ypres. He was also in action during the Retreat and Advance of 1918, and was wounded and buried by a shell explosion. Demobilised in February 1919, he holds the 1914–15 Star, and the General Service and Victory Medals.
6, Seymour Place, King Street, Northampton. Z1524/A.

LOVELL, S., Private, Royal Army Medical Corps.
He joined in July 1917, and during his two years' service was engaged on special duties in various hospital ships bringing sick and wounded from France, Egypt and China to England. He did consistently good work throughout, and was demobilised in July 1919, holding the General Service and Victory Medals. 8, Arnold Road, Northampton. Z1523.

LOVELL, W., Private, 2/5th Manchester Regiment.
He joined in January 1917, and was drafted to France in the following May. He served at Nieuport, Passchendaele Ridge and the Somme, and saw heavy fighting all through the final stages of the war, both in the Retreat and Advance of 1918. He was demobilised in October 1919, and holds the General Service and Victory Medals.
55, Gordon Street, Northampton. Z1522.

LOVELL, W. C., Corporal, Military Mounted Police.
He volunteered in the Northamptonshire Dragoons in November 1914, and in May 1916 was sent to the Western Front. There he was in action in numerous important engagements, including those at Mauberge and Cambrai, and was subsequently transferred to the Military Mounted Police. He advanced into Germany with the Army of Occupation after the Armistice, and was demobilised in July 1919, holding the General Service and Victory Medals.
38, Euston Road, Far Cotton, Northampton.
Z3084/C—Z3085/C.

LOVELL, W. E., L/Cpl., Military Mounted Police
He volunteered in November 1915, and three months later proceeded to the Western Front, where he saw heavy fighting in the Somme sector, and was wounded in July 1916. Whilst in France he was also in action at the Battles of Arras, Ypres, Passchendaele, Cambrai and Amiens, and in the final engagements of the war. Advancing into Germany with the Army of Occupation, he served at Bonn until demobilised in July 1919, holding the General Service and Victory Medals.
73, Ethel Street, Northampton. Z3417.

LOVITT, A., Sergeant-Major, R.A.M.C.
He volunteered in November 1915, and was retained at various stations, where he was engaged on duties of great importance as an Instructor and Lecturer. He was not successful in his efforts to obtain his transfer to the front, but, nevertheless, rendered valuable services with his unit until demobilised in December 1918.
73, Abington Avenue, Northampton. Z2201/A.

LOVITT, W., Signalman, Royal Navy.
He volunteered in May 1915, and was posted to H.M.S. "Alsatian," which ship was engaged on blockade duties off Greenland. He was later transferred to H.M.S. "Dundee" for service in the Mediterranean Sea, and was on board this vessel when she was torpedoed in the English Channel, but he was picked up by an American destroyer. He afterwards served in H.M.S. "Opossum" until demobilised in January 1920, and holds the General Service and Victory Medals.
73, Abington Avenue, Northampton. Z2201/B.

LOW, B., Private, 4th Northants. Regiment.
Volunteering in September 1915, he was sent for training to Tring and sailed for Egypt in April 1916. He saw much heavy fighting on the Palestine front, being in action at the Gaza Battles, in the capture of Jerusalem, and the operations in the Jordan Valley. Continuing his service in this theatre of war, he fought all through the final stages of the campaign, and was demobilised in December 1919. He holds the General Service and Victory Medals.
60, Gladstone Terrace, Northampton. Z1525.

LOWE, T. W., Sergeant, Sherwood Foresters.
Already in the Army when war was declared, he was retained on special duties as a Drill Instructor until August 1915. He then proceeded to France, where he served with distinction at the Battles of the Somme (I.), Ypres, Cambrai and the Somme (II.). After rendering valuable services he unfortunately died from heart disease at Nottingham on June 26th, 1920, and was entitled to the 1914–15 Star, and the General Service and Victory Medals.
"His memory is cherished with pride."
9, Kenburn Place, Northampton. Z1526.

LUCAS, C. O., Trooper, Northants. Dragoons.
He volunteered in October 1915, and, after his training, proceeded to France, where he was stationed at Le Havre until transferred to Italy. There he saw much severe fighting, taking part in many important engagements on the Piave and the Asiago Plateaux. Demobilised on returning home in April 1919, he holds the General Service and Victory Medals.
67, Ivy Road, Northampton Z2202.

LUCK, A., Gunner, Royal Garrison Artillery.
Having joined the Territorials in 1908, he served for four years with the Northamptonshire Yeomanry, and was then discharged as medically unfit. He rejoined in November 1917, and was engaged at various stations on important duties with his unit. Unable to obtain a transfer overseas, he rendered valuable services until his demobilisation in February 1920.
75, Melville Street, Northampton. Z2203.

LUCK, A. B., Private, 23rd Middlesex Regiment.
He joined in August 1917, but owing to his youth was unable to obtain a transfer overseas before the cessation of hostilities. In December 1918, however, he was drafted to Germany, where he did consistently good work with the Army of Occupation at Cologne until sent to England for demobilisation in November 1919.
11, Francis Street, Northampton. Z1164/B.

LUCK, A. J., Private, York and Lancaster Regt.
He joined in March 1916, and five months later was sent to France, where he played a prominent part in the Battles of the Somme, Bullecourt, Messines and Ypres. He laid down his life for King and Country at Passchendaele on October 29th, 1917, and was entitled to the General Service and Victory Medals.
"His name liveth for evermore."
70, Hunter Street, Northampton. Z1527.

LUCK, W. J., Private, 1/4th Northants. Regt.
Volunteering in April 1915, he received his training at Tring, and in January of the following year was drafted to Egypt. Whilst serving there he was stationed at Cairo and Alexandria, where he was engaged on various duties of an important nature, which he fulfilled in a highly efficient manner. He was demobilised on his return to England in July 1919, and holds the General Service and Victory Medals.
4, St. John's Place, Northampton. Z3086.

LUCY, R., Staff Sergeant-Major, R.A.S.C.
He volunteered in May 1915, and in September 1916 was ordered to Egypt, but a month later was transferred to Salonika. In that theatre of war he took a prominent part in engagements on the Doiran and the Vardar fronts, and was mentioned in Despatches. He also saw much service in Bulgaria and Russia, and was demobilised on his return to England in December 1920, holding the General Service and Victory Medals.
Sydney Cottage, Weedon, Northants. Z3087.

LUKER, E. R., Private, 5th Northants. Regiment.
Volunteering in November 1914, he was ordered to the Western Front in the following March. Whilst in France he served in the Battles of Ypres, Loos, Ploegsteert Wood, Arras, Messines, Vimy Ridge and Lens, and was twice wounded, being sent home for treatment on each occasion. He also saw heavy fighting with the 2nd Scottish Rifles in the final decisive engagements of the war, and was demobilised in February 1919, holding the 1914–15 Star, and the General Service and Victory Medals.
51, Thirlestone Road, Far Cotton, Northampton. Z3418/C.

LYMAN, A. G., Gunner, Royal Field Artillery.
He joined in February 1918, and in June was drafted to France, where he rendered valuable services with a Trench-mortar Battery on the Somme and at Cambrai. Gassed in action, he was in hospital in France, but returned to the line later. He was demobilised in March 1919, and holds the General Service and Victory Medals.
66, Salisbury Street, Northampton. TZ1528.

LYMAN, G., Private, 1/4th Northants. Regiment.
Shortly after volunteering in March 1915 he was drafted to Egypt, where he was in action in various engagements. Proceeding to Palestine, he fought in the three Battles of Gaza, and was twice wounded. On his return to the firing-line he took part in operations at Jerusalem and in the Offensive of 1918. Returning home, he was demobilised in May 1919, and holds the 1914–15 Star, and the General Service and Victory Medals.
7, Lincoln Road, Northampton. Z3419/B.

LYMAN, H., Private, 13th Middlesex Regiment.
Volunteering in November 1915, he received his training at Chatham and, embarking for the Western Front in July 1917, took an active part in the Battle of Ypres. After three months' active service he was injured in an explosion and invalided to England. On his discharge from hospital he was engaged on important duties with the Royal Defence Corps until demobilised in February 1919. He holds the General Service and Victory Medals. Cogenhoe, Northants. Z3420.

LYMAN, J., Private, 4th Northamptonshire Regt.
He volunteered in June 1915, and later in the same year was drafted to Egypt, where he saw much service until transferred to Palestine. In that theatre of war he was engaged in fierce fighting at Gaza and Jerusalem, did good work with his unit during General Allenby's Offensive, and was wounded in action. He was demobilised on his return home in 1919, and holds the 1914–15 Star, and the General Service and Victory Medals.
7, Lincoln Road, Northampton. Z3419/C

LYMAN, P., Private, 2nd Northants. Regiment.
On attaining military age he joined the Army in July 1918, but owing to the early cessation of hostilities was unable to secure a transfer overseas before the Armistice. In 1918 he was drafted to India, where he was engaged on various duties of an important nature, which he fulfilled in a very able manner. He was demobilised on his return to England in March 1921. 7, Lincoln Road, Northampton. Z3419/A.

LYON, A. W., Private, 1/4th Northants. Regiment.
Volunteering in September 1914, he proceeded to Gallipoli in July 1915, and fought at Suvla Bay and other engagements. Later he was sent to Egypt, where he served at Jifjaffa and on the Suez Canal. Subsequently he was drafted to Palestine, on which front he was in action at Gaza (I., II. and III.) and other notable battles,and was wounded at Jerusalem in December 1917. He was demobilised on his return to England in July 1919, and holds the 1914–15 Star, and the General Service and Victory Medals.
40, Euston Road, Far Cotton, Northampton. Z3088/B.

LYON, C., Private, Northamptonshire Regiment.
He joined in 1916, and underwent a period of training prior to his being drafted to Egypt. In this seat of operations he was engaged on various important duties on the lines of communication. Contracting malarial fever, he was in hospital for a time. He returned home and was demobilised in 1919, holding the General Service and Victory Medals.
24, Clarke Road, Northampton. Z2204.

LYON, G., L/Corporal, 19th Middlesex Regiment.
On attaining military age he joined the Buffs in August 1918, but was later transferred to the Middlesex Regiment. Owing to the early cessation of hostilities he was unable to obtain a transfer overseas before the Armistice, but in April 1919 proceeded to Germany with the Army of Occupation. He rendered valuable services at Cologne until sent home for demobilisation in March 1920. 34, Gregory Street, Northampton. Z3021.

LYON, H. S., Driver, Royal Field Artillery.
He joined in May 1916, and embarking for the Western Front in August of the following year did good work with his Battery at the Battles of Cambrai, Bapaume, Havrincourt, the Scarpe and Ypres. He was also in action in the final engagements of the war, and after the Armistice advanced into Germany with the Army of Occupation. Serving at Cologne until demobilised in September 1919, he holds the General Service and Victory Medals. 40, Euston Rd., Far Cotton, Northampton. Z3088/A.

LYON, W., Private, North Staffordshire Regiment.
He volunteered in November 1915, and after a period of training was six months later drafted overseas. During his service on the Western Front he was in action at the Battles of the Somme and Ypres and other important engagements, and saw heavy fighting in various sectors of the line. Subsequently he did good work with the Military Police at Boulogne and Marseilles, and was demobilised in December 1919, holding the General Service and Victory Medals.
4, Castle Gardens, Northampton. Z1106/A.

M

MACHIN, R., Private, Royal Scots.
A serving soldier in India on the outbreak of war, he sailed for France in December 1914, and fought at Neuve Chapelle, where he was gassed, but continued to serve. In the second Battle of Ypres, on May 4th, 1915, he gave his life for the freedom of England, and was entitled to the 1914–15 Star, and the General Service and Victory Medals
"A valiant Soldier, with undaunted heart he breasted life's last hill."
36, Poole Street, Northampton. Z1530/A.

MACKAY, R. T. (M.M.), Pte., 5th Northants. Regt.
Volunteering in August 1914, he went through his training in Kent, and embarked for France in the following April. He saw much heavy fighting at Aubers Ridge, Ypres, Givenchy and Loos, and during these actions was awarded the Military Medal for conspicuous bravery in carrying a wounded officer from the Field under heavy fire. Later he was twice wounded on the Somme in the Retreat of 1918, and was invalided to hospital at Doncaster. Demobilised in March 1919, he also holds the 1914–15 Star, and the General Service and Victory Medals. 52, Regent Street, Northampton. Z1531.

MACKLEY, A. E., Private, 1st Northants. Regt.
When war broke out in August 1914 he was already serving, and immediately embarked for the Western Front with the First Expeditionary Force. After fighting in the Battle of Mons he was unhappily killed during the subsequent Retreat on September 17th, 1914. He was entitled to the Mons Star, and the General Service and Victory Medals.
"He passed out of the sight of men by the path of duty and self-sacrifice."
43, Essex Street, Northampton. Z1284/B.

MACREADY, G., Rifleman, K.R.R.C.
He joined in February 1917, and was engaged on important duties with his unit at St. Albans and Harwich. Owing to his youth he was not successful in securing his transfer overseas before the close of hostilities, but in January 1919 was sent to Germany with the Army of Occupation. He served at Cologne until his return to England for demobilisation in November 1919. 6, Lower Harding Street, Northampton. Z1132/A.

MACREADY, H., Private, 5th Northants. Regt.
Volunteering in August 1914, he proceeded overseas in May of the following year. Serving on the Western Front, he was in action in numerous engagements, including the Battles of the Somme and Ypres, and was wounded at Epéhy. He was invalided to England, and on his discharge from hospital was retained on home service until demobilised in March 1919, holding the 1914–15 Star, and the General Service and Victory Medals. 6, Lower Harding Street, Northampton. Z1132/B.

MAGINN, W. C., Pte., 15th Royal Welch Fusiliers.
He volunteered in February 1915, and the following month was drafted to the Western Front. In this theatre of war he took part in many engagements, including the Battles of Givenchy, Guillemont, Arras, Albert and Delville Wood, and was wounded in action on four occasions. He was demobilised in January 1919, and holds the 1914–15 Star, and the General Service and Victory Medals.
19, Lea Road, Northampton. Z2205.

MAINS, H. V., Private, Machine Gun Corps.
He volunteered in September 1914, in the 2/4th Northamptonshire Regiment, but was transferred to the Machine Gun Corps, and drafted to Salonika in October 1916. In this seat of operations he took part in engagements on the Doiran front, and was later sent to France. There he saw much fighting until hostilities ceased, and was eventually demobilised in April 1919, holding the General Service and Victory Medals.
87, Uppper Thrift Street, Northampton. Z2206.

MAJOR, G. (M.M.), Sergeant, Machine Gun Corps.
Called up from the Reserve in August 1914, he proceeded to France with the first Expeditionary Force and served with distinction at Mons. He was also in action in nearly all the important engagements until the cessation of hostilities, and was wounded. For conspicuous bravery and devotion to duty in the Field he was awarded the Military Medal, and was discharged in 1919, also holding the Mons Star, and the General Service and Victory Medals.
27, Lawrence Street, Northampton. Z1535.

MAJOR, H., L/Corporal, Royal Fusiliers.
Joining in March 1917, he was sent for training to Tunbridge Wells, and sailed for France in the May following. He was in action at Arras and in the Battle of Messines Ridge, in which he was severely wounded in June 1917, and sent to hospital in England. On recovery he was detained on home service until his demobilisation in April 1919. He holds the General Service and Victory Medals.
2, Uppingham Street, Northampton. Z1534.

MALABON, T. O., Private, West Riding Regiment.
Joining in April 1917, he was drafted to the Western Front five months later, and saw heavy fighting in the Passchendaele sector. He also served in numerous notable engagements, including the Battle of Havrincourt, and was wounded in action. He was awarded a Certificate for submitting to transfusion of blood to save a comrade's life, and was demobilised in February 1919, holding the General Service and Victory Medals. 56, Church Street, Weedon, Northants. Z3078.

MALCHER, D. E., Corporal, V.A.D.
He joined in November 1914, and after a period of training served in the hospitals at Dallington and various other stations, where he was engaged on duties of a highly important nature. He rendered very valuable services throughout and was finally demobilised in June 1919.
33, Sharman Road, Northampton. Z2442.

MALIN, A. J., Private, 9th Northants. Regiment.
He enlisted in June 1916, and underwent a period of training at Sheringham, Salthouse and on the East Coast. He was unable to obtain a transfer overseas owing to fever, which he contracted whilst in training, and was for a time in hospital before being discharged as medically unfit for further service in June 1917. Kilsby, Northampton. Z3421.

MALIN, F. C., Private, Royal Fusiliers.
He volunteered in January 1915, and proceeding to the Western Front in the same year,took part in much heavy fighting in the Ypres, Loos, the Somme, Arras, Passchendaele Ridge and Cambrai sectors, being wounded twice in action. He served through the Retreat and Advance of 1918 until the Armistice, after which he sailed for the East, and was still serving on garrison duty at Aden in 1920. He holds the 1914–15 Star, and the General Service and Victory Medals.
13, St. Mary's Street, Northampton. Z1536/A.

MALIN, G., Private, 24th Royal Fusiliers.
Joining in June 1916, he was sent to the Western Front in January of the following year, and there saw heavy fighting in various sectors. After taking part in the Battles of Arras, Vimy Ridge, Ypres and Cambrai he was severely wounded in January 1918, and admitted to hospital in London. He was invalided from the Army in September of that year, and holds the General Service and Victory Medals.
Bliss Lane, Flore, Northampton. Z2769.

MALIN, H., Private, Royal Army Medical Corps.
He joined in June 1918, and after training at Blackpool was sent to France in August of that year. He did consistently good work with his Corps in the victorious Advance, and after the Armistice went with the Army of Occupation to Cologne. He was demobilised in September 1919, and unhappily died at home on November 28th, 1920. He was entitled to the General Service and Victory Medals.
"Whilst we remember, the sacrifice is not in vain."
13, St. Mary's Street, Northampton. Z1536/B.

MALIN, R. (M.M.), Corporal, 11th Royal Fusiliers.
He joined in March 1916, and two months later was drafted to the Western Front, where he took part in the Battles of the Somme, Messines, Ypres and Passchendaele. Contracting trench fever, he was invalided home, but on his recovery in 1918 returned to France and served with distinction at Bray, Albert and Villers-Bretonneux. He was awarded the Military Medal for conspicuous bravery in the Field whilst in charge of a Lewis Gun Team. Demobilised in February 1919, he also holds the General Service and Victory Medals.
Ivy Cottage, Crick, Northants. Z3422.

MALLARD, A. J. J., Private, Suffolk Regiment.
He joined in April 1916, and was stationed with his unit at various places in the United Kingdom. He rendered valuable services, but owing to medical unfitness was not successful in obtaining his transfer overseas, and after doing work in the Labour Corps at Luton, and being discharged as unfit, re-enlisted and did duty at many places on the East Coast until finally discharged in October 1918.
42, King Street, Northampton. Z1537/B.

MALLARD, F., Private, 3rd Northants. Regiment.
He joined in November 1916, and after a period of training was drafted to France, where he took part in much fighting on the Ypres front. He was later sent home and discharged in November 1917, owing to the important nature of his previous work, and was retained on munitions until the cessation of hostilities. He holds the General Service and Victory Medals.
Stoke Road, Blisworth. Z2207.

MALLARD, H., Private, 7th Leicestershire Regt.
Having previously served for a short time with the Royal Engineers, he re-enlisted in October 1914, and underwent a period of training at Aldershot, where he did much good work with his unit. After only three months' service, however, he was invalided from the Army, and was afterwards engaged on important work for the Government.
13, Newcombe Road, Northampton. Z2771.

MALLARD, T., Private, R.A.V.C.
He volunteered in December 1915, and shortly afterwards embarked for France. On that front he saw much service in various sectors, and did invaluable work attending to sick and wounded horses. In November 1917 he was transferred to Italy, in which theatre of war he was employed in a similar capacity until discharged from the Army in May 1918. He holds the 1914–15 Star, and the General Service and Victory Medals. 46, Monks Pond Street, Northampton. Z1100/B.

MALLARD, W., Private, 1st Cheshire Regiment.
He volunteered in March 1915, and after his training proceeded to the Western Front, where he saw severe fighting in various sectors before being transferred to Italy. There he was admitted to hospital at Genoa, where he unfortunately died in March 1918. He was entitled to the General Service and Victory Medals.
"He joined the great white company of valiant souls."
1, Woodford Street, Northampton. Z2443.

MALLARD, W. H., Air Mechanic, Royal Air Force (late Royal Naval Air Service).
He joined in November 1917, at the age of 17 years, and after a period of training was stationed at Scapa Flow, where he was retained on duties of a highly technical nature, and was also in action with enemy submarines. He was later engaged in conveying mails to and from Germany, and in 1921 was still serving, holding the General Service and Victory Medals.
14, Newcombe Road, Northampton. Z2770.

MALPAS, C. E., Driver, Royal Engineers.
Volunteering in August 1915, he completed his training, and, not being of age to proceed overseas, did service in England until April 1918, when he was sent to France, and took part in various engagements on the Somme, at Epéhy and Le Cateau during the Retreat and Advance of that year. Returning to England not long after the Armistice, he was demobilised in June 1919, and holds the General Service and Victory Medals.
56, Hunter Street, Northampton. Z1538.

MALPAS, H., Gunner, Royal Field Artillery.
Three months after volunteering in October 1915 he was sent to the Western Front, where he saw severe fighting in various sectors. He took part in the Battles of Ploegsteert Wood, the Somme, Arras, Vimy Ridge, Messines and Amiens, and many other engagements, and was twice gassed. Demobilised in January 1919, he holds the General Service and Victory Medals. 5, Orchard Street, Northampton. Z2444/C.

MALPAS, H., Driver, Royal Army Service Corps.
He joined the 53rd Bedfordshire Regiment in August 1918, and after undergoing a period of training served with the Royal Army Service Corps at various stations. Owing to the early cessation of hostilities he was unable to obtain his transfer to the front, but in March 1919 was sent with the Army of Occupation to Germany. He also served in Ireland before being demobilised in March 1920.
5, Orchard Street, Northampton. Z2444/A.

MALPAS, H. J., Sergt., Duke of Cornwall's L.I.
A Reservist, he was called up at the outbreak of war and at once ordered to the Western Front. There he played a conspicuous part in the Battles of Mons, Le Cateau, the Marne, the Aisne and La Bassée. In February 1915, he was invalided to England owing to ill-health, and on his discharge from hospital was engaged on important duties at various home stations until demobilised in March 1919. He holds the Mons Star, and the General Service and Victory Medals.
34, Park Street, Northampton. Z1959.

MALPAS, L C., Driver, Royal Field Artillery.
He volunteered in October 1915, and in July of the following year was sent to the Western Front, where he took part in many important engagements on the Somme. He made the supreme sacrifice, falling in action at High Wood on November 20th, 1916, and was entitled to the General Service and Victory Medals.
"A costly sacrifice upon the altar of freedom."
5, Orchard Street, Northampton. Z2444/B.

MALPAS, R. G., Private, 5th Northants. Regiment.
Volunteering in July 1915, he was sent to France in the following December, and there saw much heavy fighting. He took part in the Battles of Vermelles, Ploegsteert Wood, the Somme, Arras, Vimy Ridge, Messines, Ypres and Amiens and other engagements, and suffered from trench fever. He was demobilised in July 1919, and holds the 1914–15 Star, and the General Service and Victory Medals.
5, Orchard Street, Northampton. Z2444/D.

MALPASS, H., Private, 1st Northants. Regiment.
A Reservist, he was called up at the outbreak of war and at once ordered to the Western Front, where he fought in the Retreat from Mons. He was also actively engaged at the Battles of the Marne and the Aisne, but was unhappily killed in action at Ypres on October 22nd, 1914. He was entitled to the Mons Star, and the General Service and Victory Medals.
"A valiant Soldier with undaunted heart he breasted life's last hill."
8, Maycocks Road, Bridge Street, Northampton. Z3089.

MANDLEY, W., Sergeant, 2nd Northants. Regt.
Having enlisted in August 1912, he was drafted to France in November 1914, and served with distinction at the Battles of Neuve Chapelle and Loos before being wounded on Vimy Ridge in May 1916. After hospital treatment at Rouen he rejoined his unit, but was badly wounded shortly afterwards during the Somme Offensive. Invalided to England, he was again under treatment for some considerable time in London, and was finally discharged in March 1919, holding the 1914 Star, and the General Service and Victory Medals.
8, Salisbury Street, Northampton. Z1539.

MANN, A. C., Private, 16th Middlesex Regiment.
He enlisted in March 1916, and four months later was drafted to France. In this theatre of war he took part in many engagements, including those at Ypres, the Somme, Arras, Messines, Passchendaele and Langemarck, and was taken prisoner at Cambrai in November 1917. He was held in captivity in Westphalia for 12 months, and was demobilised in September 1919, holding the General Service and Victory Medals.
Station Road, Cogenhoe, Northants. Z3423—1960.

MANN, F. H., Private, Royal Army Medical Corps.
Volunteering in October 1915, he completed his training and five months later proceeded to the scene of activities in France. On that front he rendered valuable services as a stretcher-bearer in the Somme, Arras, Ypres and Cambrai sectors, did good work during the Retreat and Advance of 1918, and was gassed on one occasion. He was demobilised in February 1919, and holds the General Service and Victory Medals.
60, Oliver Street, Northampton. Z1337/B.

MANN, H., Sergt., 6th (Inniskilling) Dragoons.
He was called up from the Reserve in August 1914, and immediately proceeding to France, fought in the engagements at Mons. After taking a prominent part in the Battles of Le Cateau and the Marne, he was severely wounded at Ypres in May 1915, and sent to hospital in England. On his recovery he was retained on important duties at Greenwich until discharged in April 1919, holding the Mons Star, and the General Service and Victory Medals.
3, St. Edmund's Street, Northampton. Z1961.

MANN, R., L/Corporal, Royal Engineers.
Having volunteered in June 1915, he was drafted overseas after completing his training. Whilst on the Western Front he took part in several engagements, including the Battles of Armentières, Messines, Cambrai and the Somme (II.). He was also employed on important duties and finally demobilised in May 1919. He holds the General Service and Victory Medals. 10, Bostock Road, Northampton. Z2208.

MANN, R. C., Gunner, Royal Field Artillery.
He joined in March 1916, and was retained for a time at various home stations prior to his being drafted to France in May 1918. Whilst in this theatre of war he took part in many engagements in the Somme and other sectors during the Advance of 1918. He was demobilised in August 1919, and holds the General Service and Victory Medals.
Station Road, Cogenhoe, Northants. Z3424.

MANN, W., Private, Northamptonshire Regiment.
Called up from the Reserve in August 1914, he was found to be medically unfit for transfer overseas. He was therefore retained on special guard duties, and rendered valuable services on the East Coast Defences. In December 1915 he was discharged as medically unfit.
48, Adelaide Street, Northampton. Z1540/B.

MANN, W. J. J., Private, 6th Suffolk Regiment.
Volunteering in January 1916, he was sent for training to Saxmundham, and embarked for France in 1917. He served on the Somme (where he was gassed) and at Arras, and in the Ypres sector. Later he fought through the Retreat and Advance of 1918 until the Armistice and, returning to England shortly afterwards, was demobilised in March 1919, holding the General Service and Victory Medals.
48, Adelaide Street, Northampton. Z1540/A.

MANNING, G., Corporal, Northants. Regiment.
He volunteered in August 1914, and in the following year was drafted to France, where he took part in several engagements, but owing to ill-health was sent home and discharged. Later he re-enlisted and, again proceeding to France, saw much heavy fighting on the Somme, the Marne and at Amiens. Demobilised in April 1919, he holds the 1914–15 Star, and the General Service and Victory Medals.
144, Market Street, Northampton. Z2209/C.

MANNING, G. W., Sergeant, 4th Northants. Regt.
Volunteering in January 1915, he proceeded to Gallipol six months later and fought at Suvla Bay and in the subsequent engagements of the campaign. After the Evacuation of the Peninsula he served in Egypt for a time and, when transferred to Palestine, took an active part in the three Battles of Gaza and in the capture of Tripoli. Demobilised on his return home in July 1919, he holds the 1914–15 Star, and the General Service and Victory Medals. Spratton, Northants. Z3090.

MANNING, H., Gunner, Royal Field Artillery.
Volunteering in 1915, he was drafted overseas in the following year. During his service on the Western Front he took part in several engagements, including those in the Somme, Vimy Ridge, Arras and Amiens sectors, and was badly wounded. As a result he was invalided home and eventually discharged in November 1919. He holds the General Service and Victory Medals. 144, Market Street, Northampton. Z2209/A.

MANNING, H. S., Sapper, Royal Engineers.
Five months after volunteering in January 1915 he was drafted to the Western Front, where he was engaged on various duties. He was in action at the Battles of Loos, St. Eloi, Albert, Ypres, Passchendaele, Cambrai, Amiens, Havrincourt and Le Cateau, and did good work with his Company during the German Offensive of 1918. Serving in France until demobilised in February 1919, he holds the 1914–15 Star, and the General Service and Victory Medals.
Clay Hill, Brixworth, Northants. Z3091.

MANNING, J., Private, 1st Northants. Regiment.
Already in the Army when war broke out in August 1914, he was immediately drafted to France, where he fought at the Battles of Mons, the Marne, the Aisne and La Bassée, and was wounded in action. As a result he was invalided home, but on his recovery returned to France and saw much heavy fighting at Ypres, Festubert and Loos. Unfortunately he was reported missing, but later reported killed in action, on October 13th, 1915. He was entitled to the Mons Star, and the General Service and Victory Medals.
"A valiant Soldier, with undaunted heart he breasted life's last hill."
144, Market Street, Northampton. Z2209/B.

MANNING, L. J., A.B., Royal Navy.
A serving sailor on the outbreak of war, he was attached to the Portsmouth Division and served on H.M.S. "P. 52," doing patrol and convoy duties in the North Sea and the English Channel. He also took part in many raids, and in the course of them helped to sink two German submarines. He was still serving on H.M.S. "Windsor" in 1920, and holds the 1914–15 Star, and the General Service and Victory Medals.
94, Milton Street, Northampton. Z1541.

MANNING, S., Saddler, R.A.S.C. (M.T.)
He volunteered in May 1915, and two months later embarked for Salonika, taking part in the Landing there and in numerous engagements on the Vardar and the Struma fronts. In February 1916 he was transferred to Egypt and subsequently to Palestine, on which front he saw severe fighting at Gaza, Jerusalem and in other battles of note. He was demobilised on his return home in June 1919, and holds the 1914–15 Star, and the General Service and Victory Medals.
Spratton, Northants. Z3092.

MANSFIELD, A., Private, 4th Northants. Regt.
He volunteered in October 1914, and, after completing a period of training, served at various stations, where he was engaged on duties of great importance. He was unable to obtain his transfer to a theatre of war on account of his age but, transferred to the Royal Defence Corps, did good work with his unit until demobilised in March 1919.
4, Tanner Row, Tanner Street, Northampton. Z2772/B.

MANSFIELD, C. W., Driver, Royal Field Artillery.
Volunteering in November 1915, he was sent with his Battery to France in 1916, and did good service on the Somme, and later in actions at Arras, Passchendaele and Cambrai. In 1917 he was wounded near Ypres, but served on to the end of the campaign in France, and then proceeded to India and Mesopotamia, where he was still doing duty in 1920. He holds the General Service and Victory Medals.
4, Scarletwell Terrace, Northampton. Z1542.

MARDLE, E. L. T., 1st Air Mechanic, R.A.F.
He joined in May 1918 at the age of 16 years, and after a period of training was engaged at various stations on work which demanded a high degree of technical skill. Owing to the early cessation of hostilities he was unable to proceed overseas, but, nevertheless, rendered valuable services, and in 1921 was still with his Squadron.
15, Weedon Road, Northampton. Z3425.

MARIS, H., Corporal, Royal Air Force.
Volunteering in July 1915, he was sent for training with the Oxfordshire and Buckinghamshire Light Infantry, and was then transferred to the Royal Air Force, in which he served at Acton and Farnborough. In November 1917 he sailed for Egypt, and his ship, H.M.T. "Aragon," was torpedoed on the way. He was fortunately rescued and reached Alexandria, where he rendered valuable services as an Instructor in aeroplane workshops until demobilised in March 1919. He holds the General Service and Victory Medals.
38, Bath Street, Northampton. Z1543.

MARKS, N., Private, 4th Northants. Regiment.
Volunteering in January 1915, he was retained on various duties of an important nature at home stations, and carried out his work with the greatest ability. He was not successful in his endeavours to obtain a transfer to a theatre of war owing to his age, but, nevertheless, rendered valuable services until demobilised in March 1919.
Newland Street, Brixworth, Northants. Z3093.

MARLOW, A., Private, 1/4th Northants. Regt.
Volunteering in August 1914, he completed his training at Colchester, and in the following year was sent to Gallipoli. On that front he was in action in numerous engagements of note, and died gloriously on the Field of Battle on October 4th, 1915. He was entitled to the 1914–15 Star, and the General Service and Victory Medals.
"He passed out of the sight of men by the path of duty and self-sacrifice."
92, Gordon Street, Northampton. Z3094.

MARLOW, G., Pte., Queen's (R.W. Surrey Regt.).
He joined in October 1916, and after a period of training was in November of the following year drafted overseas. Whilst on the Western Front he took an active part in many engagements, including the Battles of Ypres and Passchendaele, and in June 1918 was invalided home through illness. He was eventually demobilised in March 1919, and holds the General Service and Victory Medals.
33, Vernon Terrace, Northampton. Z1962.

MARRIOTT, A. (D.C.M.), Gunner, R.F.A.
He volunteered in October 1915, and in the following April proceeded to France. There he played a prominent part in the Battles of the Somme (I.), Vimy Ridge, Ypres, Messines and the Somme (II.), where he was badly wounded and eventually invalided to England. He was awarded the Distinguished Conduct Medal for gallantry and devotion to duty in the Field in 1918. On his recovery he was retained at home on important work until his demobilisation in February 1919. He also holds the General Service and Victory Medals.
53, Abington Avenue, Northampton. Z2210.

MARRIOTT, A. J., Private, Tank Corps.
Volunteering in September 1914, he served with the Northamptonshire Regiment at Penzance and Weymouth for training and guard duties, but was discharged as unfit in March 1915. In August 1917 he re-enlisted, and joined the Tank Corps, in which he did duty at St. Albans, Dover and the Repairs Depôt in Dorset until his demobilisation in February 1919. 14, Harding Terrace, Northampton. Z1546.

MARRIOTT, A. T., Private, Labour Corps.
Joining in April 1916, he received his training at Dovercourt, and shortly afterwards proceeded to the Western Front. There he was engaged on various duties with the 103rd Labour Company, including trench-digging and road-repairing, and was engaged in severe fighting in the Battles of the Somme, Arras, Ypres and Cambrai. He was demobilised in March 1919, and holds the General Service and Victory Medals.
67, Washington Street, Kingsthorpe, Northampton. Z1107B.

MARRIOTT, C. W., 2nd Lieut., Royal Berks. Regt.
He volunteered in September 1914, and twelve months later proceeded to the Western Front, where he was wounded at Loos and invalided home in October 1915. Returning to France in March 1916, he took a prominent part in the Battles of the Somme and Arras, and was sent home in October 1917 to train for a commission. Again returning to France, he was in action until the cessation of hostilities and, demobilised in January 1919, holds the 1914–15 Star, and the General Service and Victory Medals. 77, Cecil Road, Northampton. Z2445.

MARRIOTT, E. F., Gunner, R.G.A.
He enlisted in May 1916, and, completing his training in the following March, was drafted to France. In this theatre of war he took part in much heavy fighting at the Battles of Arras, Ypres and Cambrai. After hostilities ceased he proceeded to Germany with the Army of Occupation, and served on the Rhine until his demobilisation in October 1919. He holds the General Service and Victory Medals.
10, Whitworth Road, Northampton. Z2211.

MARRIOTT, F., Private, 5th Northants. Regiment.
Five months after volunteering in October 1915 he was sent to the Western Front, where he saw severe fighting in various sectors. He took part in the Battles of Albert, Vimy Ridge, the Somme, Arras, Messines, Ypres, Passchendaele, Cambrai and Amiens and minor engagements, and fought also in the Retreat and Advance of 1918. Demobilised in March 1919, he holds the General Service and Victory Medals.
34, Norton Road, Daventry, Northants. Z2774.

MARRIOTT, F., Private, 1st Northants. Regiment.
Called up from the Reserve in August 1914, he was drafted overseas in the following January. Whilst on the Western Front he took part in many engagements, including the Battle of Loos, and was badly wounded on the Somme in July 1916. As a result he was invalided home and eventually discharged in April 1918 as medically unfit. He holds the 1914–15 Star, and the General Service and Victory Medals.
7, Dickens Terrace, Northampton. Z3426.

MARRIOTT, H., Private, 4th Northants. Regt.
Having previously served through the Boer War, he re-enlisted in August 1914, and was retained on important duties at various stations, afterwards being transferred to the Royal Defence Corps. Owing to ill-health he was unable to obtain his transfer overseas, and after rendering valuable services with his unit was invalided from the Army. He holds the Queen's and King's South African Medals.
35, Brook Street, Daventry, Northants. Z2773.

MARRIOTT, H., Private, West Riding Regiment.
Joining in March 1917, he proceeded to France in the next month and was in engagements at Arras, Ypres, Cambrai, St. Quentin and in the Retreat of 1918. He also served through the final operations of the campaign until the Armistice, after which he returned to England and was demobilised in March 1919. He holds the General Service and Victory Medals
16, Kinburn Place, Northampton. Z1545.

MARRIOTT, J., Corporal, 1st Northants. Regt.
Already serving in Egypt when war broke out, he left for France, and arrived in time to fight in the Retreat from Mons. He was also in action at the Battles of the Aisne, La Bassée, Ypres, Hill 60, the Somme and Cambrai, and was three times wounded —on the Aisne, at Hill 60 and on the Somme. He received his discharge in September 1919, and holds the Mons Star, and the General Service and Victory Medals.
5, Todd's Lane, Northampton. Z1544.

MARRIOTT, J., Trooper, Bedfordshire Lancers.
He volunteered in November 1915, and was retained for a time at various home stations before proceeding to France in 1917. Whilst overseas he took part in the Battles of Ypres and Cambrai, and in the Retreat of 1918, being wounded in action in April. As a result he was invalided home and eventually demobilised in February 1919. He had also served in the 17th Lancers, and holds the General Service and Victory Medals. 53, Abington Avenue, Northampton. Z2212.

MARRIOTT, J. S., Rifleman, K.R.R.C.
He joined in July 1917, and was stationed at Colchester, where he carried out his duties with great ability. On account of his youth he was unable to secure his transfer overseas before the cessation of hostilities, but in December 1918 was sent to Germany, and served at Cologne with the Army of Occupation until demobilised in March 1919.
53, Perry Street, Northampton. Z1963/A.

MARRIOTT, R. L., Private, 10th E. Yorks. Regt.
At the outbreak of war he volunteered in the Northamptonshire Regiment, and in 1915 was drafted to Gallipoli, where he saw heavy fighting at Suvla Bay and in other engagements. Invalided home with dysentery, he proceeded in June 1916 to France, and after taking part in many battles was wounded on the Somme in 1918. On returning to the firing-line he was unhappily killed in action at Ypres on September 28th, 1918. He was entitled to the 1914–15 Star, and the General Service and Victory Medals.
"Great deeds cannot die."
4, London Road, Daventry, Northants. Z3096.

MARRIOTT, T., Sapper, Royal Engineers.
He enlisted in June 1917, and after a period of training was engaged at various stations on important duties with his unit. He was unable to obtain a transfer overseas owing to his being too old, but rendered valuable services until his demobilisation in February 1919.
High Street, Blisworth, Northampton. Z2213.

MARRIOTT, W., Private, 32nd Royal Fusiliers.
He volunteered in June 1915, but was retained on important duties at home until September of the following year, when he was ordered overseas. Serving on the Western Front, he was in action at the Battles of Arras and Vimy Ridge, and gave his life for the freedom of England on June 7th, 1917, at Ypres. He was entitled to the General Service and Victory Medals.
"Whilst we remember, the sacrifice is not in vain."
6, St. James Street, Daventry, Northants. Z3095.

MARRIOTT, W., Pte., Queen's (R.W. Surrey Regt.)
Joining in February 1917, he was ordered to the Western Front in the following August, and experienced fierce fighting in the Somme, Ypres and Cambrai sectors. In 1918 he was gassed and admitted to hospital in Rouen, and on his recovery did good work with the Machine Gun Corps in operations during the Retreat and Advance of 1918. He was demobilised in October 1919, and holds the General Service and Victory Medals.
68, Ethel Street, Northampton. Z1964.

MARRIOTT, W., Private, 1st Norfolk Regiment.
Mobilised in August 1914, he sailed for France in the next month, and served with the Northamptonshire Regiment in the Ypres sector until December, when he was invalided home suffering from rheumatic fever. After a year's treatment in hospital he was sent to India and stationed at Karachi, where he remained until his demobilisation in December 1919. He holds the 1914 Star, and the General Service and Victory Medals. 21, Cooper Street, Northampton. Z1547.

MARSH, W., Private, R.A.V.C.
Volunteering in February 1915, he proceeded to the Western Front in the following April and was engaged in tending the sick and wounded horses in various sectors. He was also present at the Battles of Loos, Vimy Ridge, the Somme, Arras, Ypres and Passchendaele and minor engagements, finally returning home for demobilisation in November 1919. He holds the 1914–15 Star, and the General Service and Victory Medals.
83, Green Street, Northampton. Z2775.

MARSHALL, A., Pte., 16th (The Queen's) Lancers.
Serving in Ireland on the outbreak of war, he was sent at once to France and fought in the Retreat from Mons, and also in the Battles of the Marne, the Aisne and Ypres (I.). Later he took part in the Somme Offensive of 1916 and many other engagements. On November 3rd, 1917, in an action on the Somme front, he gave his life for King and Country. He was entitled to the Mons Star, and the General Service and Victory Medals. His body lies in the British cemetery at Hargicourt.
"He nobly fell that we might live."
22, Silver Street, Northampton. Z1558/A.

MARSHALL, H., Sergeant, 4th Northants. Regt.
Having previously served in the Army, he re-enlisted in September 1914 in the 4th Northamptonshire Regiment, and was attached to the Military Mounted Police until discharged in January 1915. In the following month he joined the Royal Defence Corps and, engaged in guarding prisoners of war, did excellent work during hostilities. Demobilised in January 1919, he holds the Egyptian Medal, with clasp, Tel-el-Kebir, and the Khedive's Bronze Star. Bugbrooke, Northants. Z3427.

MARSHALL, J. F., Gunner, R.G.A.
Joining in August 1916, he was drafted overseas in October of the following year. Whilst on the Western Front he took part in the Battles of Ypres and Passchendaele, and, badly wounded at Kemmel Hill in March 1918, was invalided to hospital at Boulogne, but later rejoined his Battery. Shortly afterwards he was sent to Le Havre, and was eventually demobilised in February 1919, holding the General Service and Victory Medals.
Church Street, Kislingbury, Northants. Z3428

MARSHALL, W., Sapper, Royal Engineers.
He volunteered in August 1914 in the Royal Field Artillery, and was retained at home for some time before being drafted to France in September 1916. He was then transferred to the Royal Engineers, and, engaged on important duties in connection with the railways in the Arras, Ypres and Cambrai sectors, was slightly gassed in July 1917. Demobilised in June 1919, he holds the General Service and Victory Medals.
6, Purser Road, Northampton. Z3429.

MARSHALL, W. E., Corporal, R.A.S.C. (M.T.)
He joined in March 1917, and was quickly drafted to the Western Front, where he rendered valuable services whilst engaged on special duties as a wheelwright in the Royal Army Service Corps workshops in the Ypres sector. Returning to England in May 1919, he was then demobilised, and holds the General Service and Victory Medals.
65, Baker Street, Northampton Z1548.

MARSTON, J. P., Driver, R.A.S.C. (M.T.)
Joining in June 1916, he embarked for Salonika in the following September, and in that theatre of hostilities did good work whilst employed as a motor-transport driver on various fronts. He remained overseas until January 1919, when he was invalided home owing to ill-health and, after a course of hospital treatment, was eventually discharged in July 1919. He holds the General Service and Victory Medals.
11, Thinford Street, Northampton. Z1965.

MARTIN, A. V., Sergeant, 6th Northants. Regt.
He joined in June 1916, and four months later was sent to the Western Front, where he served with distinction in heavy fighting in the Albert, Somme, Passchendaele and Cambrai sectors, and during the Retreat and Advance of 1918. He was demobilised in September 1919, and holds the General Service and Victory Medals.
3, Stanley Street, Northampton. Z1549/A.

MARTIN, F., Gunner, Royal Field Artillery.
Having volunteered in November 1915, he was drafted in the following month to France. There he saw much heavy fighting and took part in the Battle of the Somme and other engagements, being badly wounded in action at Passchendaele. As a result he was invalided out of the Army in April 1918, and holds the 1914-15 Star, and the General Service and Victory Medals.
11, Hut, Abington Park, Northampton. Z3430.

MARTIN, G. A. E., Gunner, R.G.A.
Joining in April 1917, he was sent for training to Rugeley Camp and Catterick, and sailed for France in the following August. He did good service in actions on the Ypres and Arras fronts and in the Battle of Cambrai. Serving all through the final operations until the Armistice, he was demobilised in July 1919, and holds the General Service and Victory Medals.
71, Earl Street, Northampton. Z1550.

MARTIN, H., Sergeant, 5th Northants. Regiment.
Called up from the Reserve in August 1914, he was drafted to France early in the following year and played a conspicuous part in the Battles of Ypres, the Somme (I.) (where he was gassed in 1916), Arras, Cambrai and the Somme (II.). He also fought throughout the Retreat and Advance of 1918. He was discharged in February 1919, and holds the 1914-15 Star, and the General Service and Victory Medals.
3, Stanley Street, Northampton. Z1549/C.

MARTIN, J., Pte., 12th York and Lancaster Regt.
Shortly after joining in June 1916 he was drafted to the Western Front, where he saw much severe fighting during the Advance on the Somme. Contracting pneumonia, he unhappily died in hospital near Albert in November 1916, and was entitled to the General Service and Victory Medals.
"Steals on the ear the distant triumph song."
Water Lane, Wootton, Northants. Z2776/B.

MARTIN, L., Gunner, Royal Field Artillery.
He joined in June 1917, and, proceeding to France later in the same year, was in action with his Battery at the Battles of Ypres, Cambrai, the Somme (II.), in heavy fighting at Arras, and during the Retreat and Advance of 1918. He was demobilised in November 1919, and holds the General Service and Victory Medals. 3, Stanley Street, Northampton. Z1549/A.

MARTIN, P., Gunner, Royal Garrison Artillery.
Volunteering in October 1915, he was sent for training to Yarmouth, and sailed for France in the following January. He did good service with a Trench-mortar Battery in the Lys sector. On March 3rd, 1916, in an action at Armentières, he died a valiant soldier's death in the Field, and was entitled to the General Service and Victory Medals. His body lies in the cemetery at Bois Grenier, near Armentières.
"His memory is cherished with pride."
3, Stanley Street, Northampton. Z1549/B.

MARTIN, P., Pte., 3rd Queen's (R.W. Surrey Regt.)
He attested in December 1915, and when called up five months afterwards joined the Labour Corps, later serving with the 4th Northamptonshire Regiment at various stations. Owing to ill-health he was unable to secure a transfer to the fighting area, but throughout the period of his service carried out his various important duties with the utmost efficiency, eventually being demobilised in September 1919.
36, Towcester Road, Far Cotton, Northampton. Z3097.

MARTIN, W. A., Private, 2nd London Regiment (Royal Fusiliers).
He joined in May 1916, and later in that year proceeded to the Western Front, where he saw severe fighting in various sectors. He was unfortunately reported missing, and is now presumed to have been killed in action, near Ypres on May 11th, 1917. He was entitled to the General Service and Victory Medals.
"His life for his Country, his soul to God"
Berry Lane, Wootton, Northants. Z2776/A.

MARTYN, F. L., Private, 1/19th London Regt.
He joined in May 1917, and after training at Sittingbourne was sent to the Western Front in April 1918. During the Retreat and Advance of that year he saw much severe fighting, particularly on the Somme, the Lys, the Aisne and at Lille, and did excellent work with his unit. Demobilised in February 1919, he holds the General Service and Victory Medals.
90, Upper Thrift Street, Northampton. Z2214/A.

MARTYN, R. S., Private, 2nd Bedfordshire Regt.
He volunteered in February 1915, and was shortly afterwards drafted to India, where he served at various stations on important garrison duties and also on the Afghan frontier. He contracted malarial fever, but on his recovery was transferred to Egypt, being at Alexandria for a time and eventually invalided home. He was discharged in April 1920, and holds the General Service and Victory Medals and the India General Service Medal (with clasp, Afghanistan, N.W. Frontier, 1919).
90, Upper Thrift Street, Northampton. Z2214/B.

MASH, A. E., Sergeant, R.A.S.C. (M.T.)
He joined in July 1917, and after a period of training was ordered to Egypt a month later. After rendering valuable services at Alexandria he proceeded to Palestine, where he was engaged on important transport duties, conveying food and ammunition to the troops in the fighting areas. After nearly three years' excellent work in the East he returned home for demobilisation in April 1920, and holds the General Service and Victory Medals.
67, Abbey Road, Far Cotton, Northampton. Z3098/B.

MASH, S. R., Private, 1/4th Northants. Regiment.
At the outbreak of war he volunteered and, proceeding to Egypt in February 1915, was in action on the Suez Canal and in other important engagements. On being transferred to Palestine, he took part in the Battles of Gaza and in the Offensive under General Allenby, and was wounded on one occasion. Demobilised on his return to England in February 1920, he holds the 1914-15 Star, and the General Service and Victory Medals.
67, Abbey Road, Far Cotton, Northampton. Z3098/A.

MASON, A. W., Sergeant, 2nd Queen's (Royal West Surrey Regiment).
He volunteered in November 1915, and two months later proceeded to the Western Front. In this theatre of war he played a prominent part with his unit in the Battles of the Somme, Ypres, Arras and Cambrai, and was wounded on the Somme front in March 1918. He was afterwards in action in various sectors during the Retreat and Advance of 1918, and was demobilised in February 1919, holding the General Service and Victory Medals.
4, Stockley Street, Northampton. Z1967/A.

MASON, C. A., Private, 2nd Northants. Regiment.
Volunteering in July 1915, he was sent to France in September of the following year, and took part in many important engagements, including those at Hooge, Equancourt, Fins, Sorel, Hendicourt, Gouzeaucourt, Dessart and Gauche Woods, Villers-Guislain, Gonnelieu, Westhoek Ridge and Armentières. He was unfortunately killed in action on April 25th, 1918, and was entitled to the General Service and Victory Medals.
"His life for his Country, his soul to God."
30, Artizan Road, Northampton. Z2215.

MASON, G., Driver, Royal Field Artillery.
Mobilised as a Reservist at the outbreak of hostilities, he served at Norwich and Northampton, doing cook-house duties until 1916, when he was sent to Egypt. Later he saw service on the Palestine front, being in action at Jifjaffa and the Gaza Battles, also in the capture of Jerusalem. He remained on this front until the end of the campaign and, being demobilised in April 1919, holds the General Service and Victory Medals.
9, Watkin Place, Northampton. Z1551.

MASON, G. F., Staff Q.M.S., R.A.O.C.
Called up from the Reserve in August 1914, he proceeded to Gallipoli in June of the following year, and there fought with distinction at Suvla Bay. He was afterwards transferred to Egypt, where he was stationed at Cairo and Alexandria, and unhappily died of heart disease on July 25th, 1918. He was entitled to the 1914-15 Star, and the General Service and Victory Medals.
"His memory is cherished with pride."
1, Stanhope Road, Northampton. Z2446.

MASON, T. W., Private, 9th Royal Sussex Regt.
He joined when he attained the age of 18 in June 1917, and in the following February was sent to France. There he took part in several engagements in the Loos sector, but in June 1918 was admitted to hospital at Wimereux, having injured his knee. He was later evacuated to England, and served at Rugeley Camp until he was demobilised in October 1919, holding the General Service and Victory Medals.
25, Leicester Street, Northampton. Z1312/A.

MASON, W., Private, 1/4th Northants. Regiment.
Volunteering in September 1914, he was sent to the Dardanelles in July of the following year, but, contracting dysentery, was admitted to hospital at Alexandria and later invalided home. On his recovery he proceeded to France, and took part in the Battles of Arras, Passchendaele and Cambrai. Demobilised in February 1919, he holds the 1914-15 Star, and the General Service and Victory Medals.
8, Byfield Road, St. James', Northampton. Z2447.

MASTERS, C. S., Sergeant, Bedford. Regiment.
He enlisted in January 1913, and was drafted to France immediately after the outbreak of war in August 1914. He took part in the Battle of, and the Retreat from, Mons, and was later in action at the Battles of the Marne, the Aisne and Ypres, where he was wounded in November 1914. Sent to hospital at Glasgow, he was retained at home until 1918, when he embarked for India, and there served at Peshawar, Delhi and Mooltan on garrison and other duties. He was afterwards invalided home on account of ill-health, and was discharged in May 1920 as unfit for further service. He also served with the Hertfordshire Regiment, and holds the Mons Star, and the General Service and Victory Medals.
44, Silver Street, Northampton. Z1235/A.

MASTERS, G. W., Sergeant, Leicestershire Regt.
Called up from the Reserve in August 1914, he was sent a month later to France, and fought in the Retreat from Mons. Wounded in action in 1915, he was invalided home and admitted to hospital, returning to France in December 1916. He then took part in further fighting, doing good work until he was gassed shortly before the Armistice. Again invalided home, he was eventually discharged in June 1919, holding the Mons Star, and the General Service and Victory Medals.
20, Brunswick Street, Northampton. Z1968.

MASTERS, T., Private, 7th Northants. Regiment.
He volunteered in September 1914, and proceeded to France twelve months later, but after only three weeks' active service was wounded at the Battle of Loos in September 1915. Invalided home, he was in hospital at Stafford, but on his recovery returned to the Western Front, and was in action in the Ypres sector. In April 1916 he was evacuated to England through illness, but again proceeded to France and fought at Loos and Vimy Ridge and in the Retreat and Advance of 1918. He was demobilised in February 1919, and holds the 1914–15 Star, and the General Service and Victory Medals.
52, St. Mary's Street, Northampton. Z1552.

MASTERS, W. T., Sergeant, 4th Northants. Regt.
At the outbreak of war he was already serving, and in 1915 was drafted to Gallipoli. There he took part in numerous important engagements, until severely wounded and invalided to England. After receiving hospital treatment in London he was discharged as medically unfit for further service in July 1916, holding the 1914–15 Star, and the General Service and Victory Medals.
22, Norton Road, Daventry, Northants. Z2777.

MASTON, H. W., Sergeant, R.A.S.C.
Volunteering in August 1914, he was first engaged on important duties in England and Ireland. He later proceeded to Salonika, where he rendered valuable services in many important engagements, including those on the Struma front. Whilst overseas he contracted malarial fever, and in June 1919 was demobilised, holding the 1914–15 Star, and the General Service and Victory Medals.
19, Cloutsham Street, Northampton. Z3099.

MATCHAM, E., Guardsman, Grenadier Guards.
Called up from the Reserve in August 1914, he was immediately drafted to France, where he took part in the Battles of Mons, the Marne, the Aisne, La Bassée and Ypres. He died gloriously on the Field of Battle on October 24th, 1914, and was entitled to the Mons Star, and the General Service and Victory Medals.
"He died the noblest death a man may die :
Fighting for God and right and liberty."
91, Market Street, Northampton. Z2216.

MATTHEWS, B. H. (M.M.), Corporal, R.G.A.
He volunteered in December 1915, and after a period of training was drafted in May 1917 to France. There he took part in the Battles of Messines, Ypres, Passchendaele and Cambrai and many engagements during the Advance of 1918. He was promoted to the rank of corporal in the Field, and was awarded the Military Medal for conspicuous bravery and devotion to duty in the Field. After hostilities ceased he proceeded to Germany with the Army of Occupation. Demobilised in October 1919, he also holds the General Service and Victory Medals. 18, Lincoln Road, Northampton. Z3432.

MATTHEWS, J. E., Shoeing-Smith, R.A.S.C.
He volunteered in 1914, and was later drafted to Salonika. In this seat of operations he was engaged on important duties with the Royal Army Service Corps, and saw much fighting on the Struma and Monastir fronts. He contracted malaria and was in hospital for some time before being demobilised on returning home in 1919. He holds the General Service and Victory Medals.
37, Rickards Street, Northampton. Z3431.

MATTHEWS, J. W., Corporal, N.Z. Engineers.
Volunteering in October 1914, he was sent to Salisbury Plain for training and sailed for Gallipoli in the following April. He saw heavy fighting in the Landing at Cape Helles, but was badly wounded by a sniper on July 17th. Removed to the hospital ship "Sicilia," he died from his wounds eight days afterwards, and was entitled to the 1914–15 Star, and the General Service and Victory Medals.
"His life for his Country, his soul to God."
8, Monarch Road, Northampton. TZ1553.

MATTOCK, P. A., Gunner, R.G.A.
He volunteered in November 1915, and after training at Sheerness embarked for France in the following March, and did good service on the Somme, in the Ypres and Arras sectors and at Bullecourt. Near this place he was wounded in March 1918, but after treatment at a Base hospital returned to the front and served through the Advance until the Armistice. He was demobilised in February 1919, and holds the General Service and Victory Medals.
41, Shelley Street, Kingsley, Northampton. Z1554.

MATTOCK, W. G., Air Mechanic, R.A.F.
He joined in August 1917, and after completing a period of training was retained at various stations, where he was engaged on duties of a highly technical nature as a rigger. He was unable to obtain his transfer overseas, but, nevertheless, rendered valuable services with his Squadron until demobilised in May 1919.
144, Abington Avenue, Northampton. Z2217.

MAUDE, F. G., Gunner, Royal Horse Artillery.
Volunteering in October 1915, he underwent a period of training and in the following January proceeded to Mesopotamia. Whilst in this theatre of war he saw much heavy fighting, and took part in engagements at Sanna-i-Yat, the Tigris, Ramadieh and Khan Baghdadie, and was also present at the relief of Kut, the capture of Baghdad and Tekrit, and the occupation of Mosul. Demobilised in April 1919, he holds the General Service and Victory Medals.
20, Euston Road, Northampton. Z3100.

MAULE, A. H., Private, Royal Sussex Regiment.
Joining in June 1918, he saw service with the Royal Sussex and Queen's Own (Royal West Kent Regiment), and in the following November was sent to France. There he was engaged on important transport duties at Calais, Boulogne and Etaples until sent to Germany with the Army of Occupation. He was stationed at Cologne until sent home for demobilisation in September 1919, and holds the General Service and Victory Medals.
Water Lane, Wootton, Northants. Z2778/A—Z2779/A.

MAULE, E. W., Private, R.A.S.C.
He joined in September 1916, and after a period of training at Reading was engaged on important agricultural work, which he carried out with great ability. Unsuccessful in obtaining a transfer overseas owing to ill-health, he, nevertheless, rendered valuable services until demobilised in October 1919.
Water Lane, Wootton, Northants. Z2778/B—Z2779/B.

MAWBY, A. W., Private, Suffolk Regiment.
Joining in February 1917, he was drafted in the following April to the Western Front, where he saw hard fighting at Arras, Ypres and on the Somme. In the victorious Advance of the autumn of 1918 he was seriously wounded at Cambrai on October 23rd, and, being removed to hospital, died of his wound five days later. He was entitled to the General Service and Victory Medals.
"Thinking that remembrance, though unspoken, may reach him where he sleeps."
5, Monarch Road, Northampton. Z1555/A.

MAWBY, W. E., Sergeant, 1/4th Northants. Regt.
Mobilised with the Territorials in August 1914, he was retained for a short time at various home stations and later proceeded to the Dardanelles, where he saw much heavy fighting at Suvla Bay. After the Evacuation of the Gallipoli Peninsula he was sent to Egypt, and thence home, being discharged in April 1916, time-expired. He holds the 1914–15 Star, and the General Service and Victory Medals.
Clark's Yard, West Street, Long Buckby, Northants. Z3433.

MAY, C. W., Private, R.A.S.C. (M.T.)
Joining in March 1916, he was drafted to East Africa, on completing a period of training, in the following July. He was there engaged on important transport duties at Dar-es-Salaam and other stations, and did much good work with his unit until his return home for demobilisation in September 1919. He holds the General Service and Victory Medals.
86, Perry Street, Northampton. Z2218/C.

MAY, J. J., Private, R.A.S.C. (M.T.)
Four months after joining in March 1916 he was sent to the Western Front, where he served with the Caterpillar Section on transport duties in various sectors. He was present at the Battles of the Somme and Arras and many other engagements in this theatre of war, finally being demobilised in August 1919. He holds the General Service and Victory Medals.
86, Perry Street, Northampton. Z2218/B.

MAYCOCK, G., Sapper, Royal Engineers.
After volunteering in 1915 he was retained on important duties in England until drafted to France in the following year. There he took part in the Battles of the Somme, Arras, Vimy Ridge, Ypres and other engagements until severely wounded in September 1917, and sent home. He was invalided from the Army in April 1918, and holds the General Service and Victory Medals.
26, Wilby Street, Northampton. Z2219.

MAYCOCK, P. A., Sergeant, 6th Northants. Regt.
He joined in May 1917 on attaining military age, and after completing his training about twelve months later was drafted to France. Here he served with distinction at Albert, on the Somme and in the Retreat of 1918, and was promoted to the rank of sergeant. He was unfortunately killed in action at Cambrai in September 1918, and was entitled to the General Service and Victory Medals.
"A valiant Soldier, with undaunted heart he breasted life's last hill."
West Street, Long Buckby, Northants. Z3434/B.

MAYCOCK, S., Private, Oxford. and Bucks. L.I.
He volunteered in August 1914, and three months later was drafted to France, where he took part in several engagements, including the Battles of Loos, and was wounded. As a result he was invalided home, but on his recovery proceeded to Mesopotamia, and served with the Kut relieving forces at Um-el-Hannah. He made the supreme sacrifice, being killed in action on April 6th, 1916, and was entitled to the 1914 Star, and the General Service and Victory Medals.
"Whilst we remember, the sacrifice is not in vain."
West Street, Long Buckby, Northants. Z3434/A.

MAYES, C., Q.M.S., 2nd Northants. Regiment.
Already in the Army at the outbreak of war, he was quickly drafted to France. Whilst in this theatre of war he played a prominent part in many engagements, including the Battles of the Marne, the Aisne, Neuve Chapelle, Ypres, Loos and the Somme. In 1918 he was severely wounded in action, and unhappily died through the effects of his wounds a few days later. He was entitled to the 1914 Star, and the General Service and Victory Medals.
"A costly sacrifice upon the altar of freedom."
Stanhope Road, Northampton. Z3435.

McGIBBON, W. A., Private, 9th Cheshire Regt.
Volunteering in August 1914, he was sent to Liverpool for training, and drafted to France in the next year. He saw heavy fighting in the Ypres sector and on the Somme, where he was badly wounded in July 1916. Evacuated to the French Military Hospital at Farnham in Surrey, he unfortunately succumbed to his wounds on July 12th, 1916. He was entitled to the 1914–15 Star, and the General Service and Victory Medals.
"His life for his Country."
3, Lower Harding Street, Northampton. Z1529.

McLAUCHLAN, E. W., Private, 2/7th Royal Warwickshire Regiment.
He volunteered in February 1915, and was sent for training into Essex and to Bristol. He was then transferred to the Royal Flying Corps, and sailed for France in August 1916. He served at an aerodrome near Rouen for a year doing repairs as a first-class air mechanic, and was blown up by the explosion of an engine. He then returned to England, and was engaged on home duties until his demobilisation in January 1919. He holds the General Service and Victory Medals.
29, Louise Road, Northampton. Z1532.

McNAMARA, W. A., Rflmn., 16th London Regt.
Joining in September 1917, he was sent for training to Dover, Northampton and Colchester, and sailed for France in April 1918. He saw much heavy fighting at Lens, Cambrai and Valenciennes in the victorious Advance, and after the Armistice marched back with his unit, by way of Doullens and Abbeville, to Dieppe. Continuing his service after his return to England, he was not demobilised until January 1920, and holds the General Service and Victory Medals.
70, Salisbury Street, Northampton. Z1533.

MEACHAM, G. L., 1st Air Mechanic, R.A.F.
Joining in August 1916, he was drafted to France with the Royal Naval Air Service in March of the following year, and there served at Dunkirk, the Somme, Amiens and Bapaume and in other sectors as an observer. He was later stationed at Cologne with the Army of Occupation, finally returning home for demobilisation in June 1919. He holds the General Service and Victory Medals.
31, Thursby Road, Northampton. Z2448.

MEACOCK, H. R., Lieut., 3rd West Yorks. Regt.
He volunteered in the ranks in 1915, and later in the same year embarked for France. Whilst in this theatre of war he was granted a commission and served with distinction in many important engagements in various sectors of the front. He did consistently good work, and was once wounded in action. Demobilised in 1919, he holds the 1914–15 Star, and the General Service and Victory Medals.
103, St. Leonard's Road, Northampton. Z3101.

MEASURES, J., Gunner, Royal Field Artillery.
Shortly after volunteering in 1915 he was sent to Mesopotamia, where he saw much severe fighting, taking part in the relief of Kut, the capture of Baghdad and the occupation of Mosul. He afterwards served in India, and whilst in the East contracted dysentery. Demobilised on returning home in 1919, he holds the 1914–15 Star, and the General Service and Victory Medals. 75, Adams Avenue, Northampton. Z2449.

MERRICK, F., A.B., Royal Naval Division.
He joined in July 1917, and nine months later was drafted to the Western Front, but after a short period of heavy fighting during the Retreat on the Somme was taken prisoner in May 1918. Repatriated in the following November, he was demobilised in January 1919, and holds the General Service and Victory Medals.
62, St. John's Street, Northampton. Z3102/A.

MERRICK, W. J., Private, Machine Gun Corps.
Volunteering in October 1915, in the Bedfordshire Lancers, he was first engaged on important duties with his unit in England and Ireland. He was later transferred to the Machine Gun Corps and, proceeding to France in 1917, saw much heavy fighting on the Albert, Ypres and Cambrai fronts. He was also in action during the Retreat and Advance of 1918, and afterwards served with the Army of Occupation at Cologne. Demobilised in January 1919, he holds the General Service and Victory Medals.
62, St. John's Street, Northampton. Z3102/B.

MERRICKS, H., Corporal, 8th London Regiment.
Volunteering in the Post Office Rifles in August 1915, he was sent in the following January to France. In this theatre of war he was in action with his unit at Loos, Albert, Vermelles, Vimy Ridge and on the Somme front, where he was severely wounded in September 1916. Invalided home, he spent a considerable time in hospitals at Guildford, Seaford and Blackdown, and was eventually discharged in December 1917 as unfit for further service. He holds the General Service and Victory Medals.
32, Denmark Road, Northampton. Z1970.

METCALF, W. E., Sergeant, R.G.A.
He volunteered in August 1915, and in January of the following year was drafted to the Western Front, where he saw severe fighting in various sectors. He took a prominent part in many important engagements, including the Battles of the Somme, Arras, Ypres and Cambrai, and served also through the Retreat and Advance of 1918. Demobilised in February 1919, he holds the General Service and Victory Medals.
16, Cedar Road, Northampton. Z2221.

MICKLEY, W., Private, 2/5th Durham L.I.
He joined in February 1917, and twelve months later proceeded to the Western Front, where he saw severe fighting in various sectors. He took part in many engagements during the Retreat and Advance of 1918, and was afterwards stationed at Calais until his return home for demobilisation in October 1919. He holds the General Service and Victory Medals.
38, Market Street, Northampton. Z2222.

MIDDLETON, A., Private, 2nd Northants. Regt.
Having previously served in India and South Africa, he re-enlisted in September 1914, and in the following July was drafted to Gallipoli, where he saw much severe fighting. He was later transferred to Egypt, where he was stationed at Alexandria and also on the Suez Canal. Demobilised on returning home in July 1919, he holds the Queen's and King's South African Medals, the 1914–15 Star, and the General Service and Victory Medals.
62, Stanhope Road, Northampton. Z2450.

MIDDLETON, C. (Mrs.), Special War Worker.
Throughout the period of hostilities this lady was engaged on work of National importance on the land. Employed by the local farmers, she rendered very valuable services thrashing, hoeing and on various other duties until October 1920.
7, New Buildings, Blisworth, Northants. Z2080/B.

MIDDLETON, W. H., Private, 2/4th Northants. Regiment.
Having volunteered in August 1915, he completed a period of training and in the following year proceeded overseas. Whilst on the Western Front he took part in many important engagements in various sectors, and was wounded and gassed. He did continuously good work, and in 1919 was demobilised, holding the General Service and Victory Medals.
Bakers Lane, Spratton, Northants. Z3103.

MIDGLEY, P., Driver, Royal Field Artillery.
Mobilised on the outbreak of war, he was retained on special duties at various stations in England until January 1917, when he was sent to France, and was in action at Vimy Ridge, Arras, Ypres and Passchendaele. He was then invalided home with trench feet, and on his recovery proceeded to India, where he remained doing garrison duty until demobilised in November 1919. He holds the General Service and Victory Medals.
46, High Street, Kingsley, Northampton. Z1556.

MILLER, A., Private, 1st Northants. Regiment.
Prior to the outbreak of hostilities he had served in the Territorial Force, and in July 1916 joined the Northamptonshire Regiment. Four months later he was drafted to France, where he saw heavy fighting in the Somme sector. During an engagement on the Dunes he was wounded and taken prisoner in July 1917, being held in captivity until the Armistice. He was demobilised in December 1919, and holds the General Service and Victory Medals.
14, Gas Street, Northampton. Z2780.

MILLER, A. E., Pte., Queen's Own (Royal West Kent Regiment).
Having previously fought in the South African campaign, he rejoined in 1916, and, after a period of training, was retained at various stations on duties of great importance. Unable to obtain his transfer overseas, he, nevertheless, rendered very valuable services with his unit until his demobilisation in 1919. He holds the Medal of St. John of Jerusalem, awarded for special services, and the Queen's South African Medal.
50, Clarke Road, Northampton. Z2223.

MILLER, C. F., Gunner, Royal Garrison Artillery.
Volunteering in September 1915, he was drafted to France five months later, and was in action with his Battery at Arras, Ypres, Amiens and throughout the Retreat and Advance of 1918. In January 1919 he was invalided home suffering from muscular rheumatism, and, after a short period of hospital treatment, was demobilised, holding the General Service and Victory Medals.
52, Edith Street, Northampton. Z1971.

MILLER, G., Private, Royal Army Medical Corps.
He joined in January 1917, and being drafted to France at the end of the same year, rendered valuable services attending the sick and wounded in the 41st General Hospital near Amiens and also at Poperinghe and other places. After hostilities ceased he was stationed at Cologne with the Army of Occupation, and was ultimately demobilised in September 1919, holding the General Service and Victory Medals.
12, Harvey Street, Northampton. Z1974/B.

MILLER, G. T., Trooper, Northants. Dragoons.
Volunteering in September 1914, he was sent for training to Tidworth, and afterwards drafted to France in 1916. He saw fighting in many different engagements, but was then transferred to Italy, where he fought on the Piave and was badly wounded. After hospital treatment he returned to England and was demobilised in February 1919. He holds the General Service and Victory Medals.
2, Overstone Road, Northampton. Z1557.

MILLER, H., Rifleman, Royal Irish Rifles.
Having volunteered in October 1915, he completed his training before being drafted to the Western Front, where he saw much service in various sectors. He took part in the Battles of Bullecourt, Ypres, Cambrai and also in the Retreat and Advance of 1918. Demobilised in March 1919, he holds the General Service and Victory Medals.
12, Harvey Street, Northampton. Z1973/A.

MILLER, T. A., Private, 7th Northants. Regiment.
Volunteering in February 1915, he landed in France four months later. In this seat of operations he took part in many important engagements, particularly in the Somme sector, before being wounded and invalided home. On his recovery he rejoined his unit on the Western Front, and was in action at the Battle of Arras. He died gloriously on the Field of Battle on April 12th, 1917, and was entitled to the 1914–15 Star, and the General Service and Victory Medals.
"Whilst we remember, the sacrifice is not in vain."
12, Harvey Street, Northampton. Z1973/B.

MILLER, T. S., Leading Aircraftsman, R.A.F.
He joined in March 1918, and after undergoing a period of training was retained at various stations, where he was engaged on duties of great importance with the Kite Balloon Section. He was not successful in obtaining his transfer overseas, but, nevertheless, did much good work with his Squadron until February 1919, when he was demobilised.
17, Henry Street, Northampton. Z2224.

MILLER, W. J., A.B., Royal Naval Division.
After joining in September 1917, he underwent a period of training prior to being drafted overseas. Whilst on the Western Front he took part in many important engagements in various sectors. He was gassed and later contracted trench fever, as a result of which he was invalided home and eventually demobilised in January 1919, holding the General Service and Victory Medals.
33, New Town Road, Northampton. Z1972.

MILLER, W. O., Pte., Queen's (R.W. Surrey Regt.)
He joined in March 1917, and on conclusion of his training in the following year was drafted to the Western Front. Whilst in this seat of operations he took part in many important engagements, including the Battles of the Somme (II.), Amiens, Havrincourt and Le Cateau (II.). He was wounded on two occasions, and after the conclusion of war was transferred to Ireland, where he was engaged as a bootmaker until demobilised in September 1919, holding the General Service and Victory Medals.
12, Harvey Street, Northampton. Z1974/A.

MILLS, A. R., Private, 1st Northants. Regiment.
A Reservist, he was in South America when war broke out, but being mobilised returned immediately to England, and was sent to France in January 1915. Whilst in this seat of hostilities he took part in many important engagements in various sectors of the front. He made the supreme sacrifice, being killed in action at the Battle of the Dunes on July 10th, 1917, and was entitled to the 1914–15 Star, and the General Service and Victory Medals.
"The path of duty was the way to glory."
19a, Crispin Street, Northampton. Z1097/B.

MILLS, C., Private, 1/4th Leicestershire Regiment.
Volunteering at the outbreak of hostilities, he underwent a period of training, and in April of the following year landed in France, where he took part in the Battle of Ypres (II.) before being wounded and invalided home. Returning to France on his recovery, he rejoined his unit, and was in action during the Somme Offensive. He died gloriously on the Field of Battle on July 14th, 1916, and was entitled to the 1914–15 Star, and the General Service and Victory Medals.
"Thinking that remembrance, though unspoken, may reach him where he sleeps."
25, Brunswick Place, Northampton. Z1976.

MILLS, F., Gunner, Royal Garrison Artillery.
Joining in March 1916, he was quickly drafted to the Western Front, where he saw much service in various sectors. He was in action with the 139th Battery at the Battles of Vimy Ridge, the Somme, Arras, Messines, Ypres, Passchendaele and many other important engagements until the close of hostilities. Returning home, he was demobilised in March 1919, and holds the General Service and Victory Medals.
76, Whitworth Road, Northampton. Z1975.

MILLS, J. H. C., Private, Middlesex Regiment.
He joined in September 1916, but owing to ill-health was not successful in his endeavours to secure a transfer to a theatre of war. He was retained on home service and was engaged on duties of an important nature at Reading and various other stations under the Southern Command. After rendering consistently good services he was demobilised in December 1919. Church Road, Hanslope, Bucks. Z2781.

MILLS, T., Sergeant, Northamptonshire Regiment.
When war broke out in August 1914 he was serving with the Territorial Force, and for a considerable period was engaged on important instructional duties at various home stations. Subsequently he succeeded in obtaining a transfer to the Western Front, and did valuable work with the Army Cyclist Corps until sent to England for demobilisation in March 1919. He holds the General Service and Victory Medals.
25, Norton Road, Daventry, Northants. Z2782.

MILLS, W., Private, 6th Northants. Regiment.
Volunteering in August 1914, he completed his training and in January of the following year proceeded to France. Whilst in this seat of operations he took part in the Battles of Albert, the Somme, Ypres, Cambrai and Le Cateau (II.). He did consistently good work, and in March 1919 was demobilised, holding the 1914–15 Star, and the General Service and Victory Medals. 7, Crispin Street, Northampton. Z1097/C.

MINNARDS, A. R., Private, 2nd Northants. Regt.
He volunteered in August 1914, and early in the following year was drafted overseas. Serving on the Western Front he was engaged in severe fighting in the Battle of Ypres, and was wounded in action at Neuve Chapelle and invalided home in 1915. After prolonged hospital treatment he was discharged as medically unfit in December 1917, holding the 1914–15 Star, and the General Service and Victory Medals.
Water Lane, Wootton, Northants. Z2685/A.

MINNEY, C., Private, R.A.S.C. (M.T.)
He volunteered in January 1916, and was sent in the same year to the Western Front, where he rendered valuable services with a supply column during engagements on the Somme and in the Ypres and Arras sectors, being chiefly engaged in taking ammunition and foodstuffs to the front line. He carried on this important and often dangerous duty until the end of the war, and, being demobilised in March 1919, holds the General Service and Victory Medals.
22, Silver Street, Northampton. Z1558/B.

MITCHELL, A. T., Corporal, Royal Field Artillery
He enlisted in February 1914, and when war broke out six months later was quickly drafted to France, where he took part in the Retreat from Mons and in the Battles of the Marne, Ypres, Armentières and Hill 60. Later he was transferred to Salonika and saw much fighting on various fronts. He returned home and was demobilised in February 1919, holding the Mons Star, and the General Service and Victory Medals.
3, King Street, Long Buckby, Northants. Z3436.

MITCHELL, B., Private, 4th Yorkshire Regiment.
Called up from the Reserve at the outbreak of hostilities, he underwent a period of training prior to being drafted to France. Whilst on the Western Front he took part in engagements in the Somme and Ypres sectors before being taken prisoner in May 1918. During his captivity he contracted pneumonia, and unfortunately died from the effects on October 16th, 1918. He had been awarded a Divisional Scrip Certificate for distinguished service, and was also entitled to the 1914–15 Star, and the General Service and Victory Medals.
"A valiant Soldier, with undaunted heart he breasted life's last hill."
4, Grafton Street, Northampton. Z1101/B.

MITCHELL, E. T., Sapper, Canadian Engineers.
Joining in January 1917, he was sent for training to Witley Camp, and sailed for France in March of the following year. He rendered valuable services during the Retreat andAdvance of 1918, being principally engaged in building bridges and other constructive work. He was both gassed and suffered from trench fever, but did not leave France until just before his demobilisation in June 1919. He holds the General Service and Victory Medals.
50, Watkin Terrace, Northampton. Z1559.

MITCHELL, H. F., Private, 1st Northants. Regt.
Volunteering in August 1914, he went through a period of training and service in England, and was drafted to France in September 1915. He was in action at Loos, Ypres, Hill 60 and Neuve Chapelle, and was wounded in December 1917. During the German Advance on the Somme in March 1918 he was unfortunately taken prisoner, and after his repatriation was demobilised in April 1919, holding the General Service and Victory Medals.
19, Military Road, Northampton. Z1560.

MITCHELL, H. M., Private, 1st Northants. Regt.
Volunteering in August 1914, he proceeded to France in the same year, and took part in heavy fighting at La Bassée. On December 21st, 1914, he was taken prisoner, and whilst in captivity suffered many hardships and privations, being made to work in the mines, and also on the land. After the cessation of hostilities he was released and eventually demobilised in January 1919, holding the 1914 Star, and the General Service and Victory Medals.
12, Albert Street, Northampton. Z1978/B—Z1979/B.

MITCHELL, H. W., Capt., 9th Leicestershire Regt.
When war broke out he was in Russia, but returned to England and volunteered in January 1915. In July 1916 he was sent to France, where he fought in the Battle of the Somme, and was wounded at the capture of Bazentin-le-Petit. Invalided home, he was retained on important duties until June 1918, when he volunteered for service in Russia, and took part in heavy fighting there for eight months. Demobilised in January 1921, he holds the 1914–15 Star, and the General Service and Victory Medals. 3, Glasgow Street, Northampton. Z2783.

MITCHELL, J., Sergeant-Major, R.F.A.
He joined the Army in 1900, and at the outbreak of war was immediately drafted to France. There he served with distinction in many engagements, including the Battles of Mons, Ypres, Neuve Chapelle, Loos, the Somme and Arras, and fought also in the Retreat and Advance of 1918. After hostilities ceased he proceeded to Germany with the Army of Occupation, remaining until November 1919, when he returned home. He received his discharge, time-expired, in February 1921, and holds the India General Service Medal, the Mons Star, and the General Service, Victory and Long Service and Good Conduct Medals.
5, West View Terrace, Long Buckby, Northants. Z3437.

MITCHELL, J. H., Trooper, Northamptonshire Yeomanry (Dragoons).
Volunteering in April 1915, he completed a period of training before being drafted to France in the following year. In the course of his active service he took part in various engagements, particularly in the Somme and Ypres sectors. Later in 1917 he contracted trench fever, and as a result was invalided to hospital at Le Havre, thence to England. Demobilised in 1919, he holds the General Service and Victory Medals. He later rejoined the Army, and was still serving in 1921.
12, Albert Street, Northampton. Z1978/A—Z1979/A.

MOBBS, A., Sapper, Royal Engineers (R.O.D.)
He joined in November 1917, and a month later proceeded to the Western Front. Whilst overseas he rendered valuable services constructing roads and railways through the devastated areas, and also was engaged in fierce fighting in the Battles of the Somme, Cambrai and Ypres. He was demobilised on his return home in March 1919, and holds the General Service and Victory Medals.
Berry Lane, Wootton, Northants. Z2784/B.

MOBBS, H., Sapper, Royal Engineers (R.O.D.)
Volunteering in February 1915, he received his training at Longmoor, and in the following year embarked for France. On that front he was principally engaged in the construction of railways and bridges, and also did valuable work with his Company in operations during the Retreat of 1918. He was demobilised in March 1919, and holds the General Service and Victory Medals. The Green, Wootton, Northants. Z2784/A.

MOBBS, J., Corporal, Northamptonshire Regiment.
He volunteered in September 1914, and crossing to France early in the following year took part in the Battles of Ypres, the Somme, Arras and Cambrai. He also fought in engagements in the Retreat of 1918, and whilst overseas was wounded on three occasions, returning to England for treatment each time. Demobilised in March 1919, he holds the 1914–15 Star, and the General Service and Victory Medals.
Water Lane, Wootton, Northants. Z2784/C.

MOLCHER, H. A., 1st Air Mechanic, R.A.F.
Two months after joining in June 1917 he was sent to the Western Front, where he was engaged on important duties as a fitter with the 64th Squadron in the Arras sector. He took part also in the Advance of 1918, and afterwards served with the Army of Occupation at Cologne, finally returning home for demobilisation in July 1919. He holds the General Service and Victory Medals.
Yew Tree Cottages, Roade, Northants. Z2225.

MONK, H. J A., Pte., Queen's (R.W. Surrey Regt.)
He volunteered in August 1914, and on completing his training in the following year was drafted to the Western Front, where he saw much heavy fighting. After taking part in the Battles of Ypres, the Somme and Arras and other engagements, he was severely gassed in 1917, and admitted to hospital at Aberdeen. Finally demobilised in February 1919, he holds the 1914–15 Star, and the General Service and Victory Medals.
Chapel Hill, Blisworth, Northants. Z2226.

MONTGOMERY, F., Private, R.A.M.C.
He volunteered in June 1915, and, receiving his training at Blackpool, was sent to France in 1916. He served in the Somme, Ypres and Arras sectors, and also at Cambrai, doing duty as a stretcher-bearer in the Field and as an orderly in hospital. He did excellent work with his unit, and was demobilised in March 1919, holding the General Service and Victory Medals. 27, Kinburn Place, Northampton. Z1561/A.

MONTGOMERY, J., Corporal, Queen's (Royal West Surrey Regiment).
After joining in April 1916, he completed his training and in the same year proceeded overseas. Whilst on the Western Front he did consistently good work, and saw much heavy fighting, particularly in the Somme, Ypres and Arras sectors. Invalided to England in 1918 owing to an illness, he underwent a period of hospital treatment, but returned to France and was engaged on important duties until demobilised in October 1919, holding the General Service and Victory Medals.
53, Perry Street, Northampton. Z1963/B.

MONTGOMERY, W., Private, 1st Northants. Regt.
Already in the Army when war was declared, he proceeded to France with the first Expeditionary Force and fought through the Retreat from Mons. He was also in action at the Battles of the Marne, the Aisne, La Bassée and Ypres, but died gloriously on the Field at Neuve Chapelle on March 11th, 1915. He was entitled to the Mons Star, and the General Service and Victory Medals.
"His name liveth for evermore."
27, Kinburn Place, Northampton. Z1561/B.

MOORE, A. T., Leading Seaman, Royal Navy.
Already in the Royal Navy, he was mobilised in August 1914 and posted to H.M.S. "Prince of Wales," in which vessel he was engaged on patrol duties in the English Channel. In 1915 he proceeded to the Dardanelles, where he took part in the operations at Gallipoli until after the Evacuation of the Peninsula. He was afterwards transferred to H.M.T.B.D. "116," and was engaged on important patrol and escort duties between Portsmouth and Smyrna. After the Armistice he served on board H.M.S. "Galatea" on special duties in Russian waters. Discharged in September 1920, he holds the 1914–15 Star, and the General Service and Victory Medals.
67, Vernon Street, Northampton. Z1980.

MOORE, B., Sergeant, 1/4th Northants. Regiment.
He was already in the Army when war broke out, and in February 1915 was drafted to Egypt, where he saw much fighting on the Suez Canal. Later he proceeded into Palestine, and played a prominent part in the first Battle of Gaza. He was unfortunately killed in action there in April 1917, and was entitled to the 1914–15 Star, and the General Service and Victory Medals.
"Great deeds cannot die:
They with the sun and moon renew their light for ever."
1, King Street, Long Buckby, Northants. Z3438/B—Z3439/B.

MOORE, E., Private, Royal Sussex Regiment.
Joining in February 1916, he proceeded to France in the following June, but was wounded whilst fighting on the Somme a month later. On his return to the firing-line he was in action in the Battles of Arras, Ypres, Passchendaele, Cambrai and Amiens, and whilst taking part in the Advance of 1918 was buried by the explosion of a shell. He was eventually demobilised in January 1919, and holds the General Service and Victory Medals. 89, Green Street, Northampton. Z2785.

MOORE, E. C., Gunner, Royal Field Artillery.
Volunteering in August 1914, he quickly proceeded to the Western Front, but after taking part with his Battery in the Battles of Ypres, Neuve Chapelle, St. Eloi and Hill 60 and other important engagements was badly wounded in action and invalided home. He was discharged as medically unfit for further service in February 1918, and holds the 1914 Star, and the General Service and Victory Medals.
22, Freeschool Street, Northampton. Z3140

MOORE, H. J., Sergeant, 1/4th Northants. Regt.
Already serving at the outbreak of war, he proceeded in 1915 to the Dardanelles, where he took part in much heavy fighting. After the Evacuation of the Gallipoli Peninsula he returned home, owing to ill-health, and did excellent work at various stations. He was unable to obtain his transfer overseas a second time owing to heart trouble, and was eventually discharged in February 1919, holding the 1914–15 Star, and the General Service and Victory Medals.
1, King Street, Long Buckby, Northants. Z3438/D—Z3439/D.

MOORE, J., Bombardier, Royal Horse Artillery.
At the outbreak of war he volunteered, and after a course of training was ordered overseas in May 1915. During his service on the Western Front he was in action in numerous notable engagements, and was wounded in 1916 and again in 1917, returning to England for hospital treatment on each occasion. He was demobilised in March 1919, and holds the 1914–15 Star, and the General Service and Victory Medals.
18, Oxford Street, Daventry, Northants. Z2786/A.

MOORE, J., Private, Royal Scots.
A Reservist, he was called up in August 1914, and at once ordered to France, and fought in the Battles of Mons, the Marne, the Aisne, Neuve Chapelle, Ypres, Festubert, St. Eloi, Loos, Albert and Cambrai. He also took part in the Retreat and Advance of 1918, but was gassed in May of that year, and invalided to England. On his recovery he was retained on home service until discharged in February 1919, holding the Mons Star, and the General Service and Victory Medals.
26, Freeschool Street, Northampton. Z2787.

MOORE, J., Bombardier, Royal Field Artillery.
He volunteered in October 1915, and completing his training in the following February was drafted to Egypt, where he saw much fighting at Sollum, Jifjaffa and El Fasher. Later he proceeded into Palestine, and took part in the Battles of Gaza and the capture of Jericho, Tripoli and Aleppo. He returned home and was demobilised in July 1919, holding the 1914–15 Star, and the General Service and Victory Medals.
King Street, Long Buckby, Northants. Z3438/A—Z3439/A.

MOORE, J. C., Pte., Queen's (R. West Surrey Regt.)
He joined in April 1917, and was stationed with his unit at Sittingbourne. He rendered valuable services, but, owing to medical unfitness, was not successful in obtaining his transfer overseas, and after being admitted to hospital at Gravesend was discharged on that account in December of the same year.
28, Gladstone Terrace, Northampton. Z1562.

MOORE, M. (Mrs.), Worker, Q.M.A.A.C.
She joined in October 1917, and on completion of her training was engaged on important duties in the hospitals at Bristol, Bulford, Boscombe and Christchurch. Throughout the period of her service she performed the various duties assigned to her in a highly capable and efficient manner, and was eventually demobilised in January 1919.
18, Oxford Street, Daventry, Northants. Z2786/B.

MOORE, P. J., Sergeant, 4th Suffolk Regiment.
He joined in March 1916, and after training at Halton Camp near Tring, was drafted to France in January 1917, and saw heavy fighting on the Somme, and at Arras, Nieuport, Ypres and Passchendaele. During the Retreat and Advance of 1918 he was in action at St. Quentin, Amiens, Villers-Bretonneux, Valenciennes and Tournai, and after the Armistice served with the Army of Occupation on the Rhine. Demobilised in September 1919, he holds the General Service and Victory Medals.
44, Francis Street, Northampton. Z1563.

MOORE, R., L/Cpl., 2nd K.O. Scottish Borderers.
He joined in September 1913, and at the outbreak of war was immediately drafted to France. In this seat of operations he took part in the Battles of Mons, the Marne, the Aisne, La Bassée, Ypres, St. Eloi, Hill 60, the Somme, Vimy Ridge and Cambrai. Later he proceeded to Italy, but shortly afterwards returned to France and fought in the final engagements until the Armistice. In September 1920 he was placed on the Reserve, and holds the Mons Star, and the General Service and Victory Medals.
King Street, Long Buckby, Northampton Z3438/C—Z3439/C.

MOORE, R. R., 2nd Corporal, Royal Engineers.
Mobilised in August 1914, he was sent to the Western Front in the following month, and there served in various sectors. He took an active part in the Battles of the Aisne, La Bassée, Ypres, Neuve Chapelle and Festubert and other engagements until severely gassed at Loos in September 1915, and invalided home. He was afterwards retained in England until discharged in March 1919, holding the 1914 Star, and the General Service and Victory Medals. 155, Adnitt Road, Northampton. Z2227.

MOORES, T., Shoeing-Smith, 12th Lancers.
A serving soldier, he was drafted to the Western Front in August 1914, and there fought in the Retreat from Mons. He also took part in the Battles of the Marne, the Aisne, Ypres, the Somme, Passchendaele and Cambrai, and many other engagements, and served through the Retreat and Advance of 1918. He was discharged in February 1919, and holds the Mons Star, and the General Service and Victory Medals.
86, Perry Street, Northampton. Z2218/A.

MORGAN, G., Gunner, Royal Field Artillery.
Volunteering in October 1915, he proceeded to France with his Battery a month later, and was shortly afterwards transferred to Mesopotamia, where he rendered valuable services with his Battery during the Kut and Baghdad operations. In August 1918 he was sent to Russia, and served on that front until his demobilisation in June 1919. He holds the 1914–15 Star, and the General Service and Victory Medals.
8, Moat Street, Northampton. Z1564.

MORING, S. T. (M.M.), Pte., 1/4th Northants. Regt.
Volunteering in August 1915, he was drafted to Egypt in the following April, and was in action at Romani. Later he advanced into Palestine and fought in the second Battle of Gaza, where he gained the Military Medal for conspicuous gallantry in carrying despatches under heavy fire, and was severely wounded. Evacuated to hospital at Alexandria, he remained under treatment until the cessation of hostilities, and was finally demobilised in August 1919. He holds the General Service and Victory Medals.
20, Oak Street, Northampton. Z1565.

MORRIS, H. E., Corporal (Drummer), 8th Queen's Own (Royal West Kent Regiment).
Having enlisted in 1898, he was drafted to the Western Front immediately on the outbreak of war, and fought in the Battle of Mons. He also took part in the Battles of La Bassée, Ypres, Loos, Vimy Ridge and Ploegsteert Wood before being gassed and invalided home in 1918. He was discharged in 1919, and holds the Queen's and King's South African Medals, the Mons Star, and the General Service and Victory Medals.
16, Freeschool Street, Northampton. Z3105.

MORRIS, J. J., L/Corporal, 4th Northants. Regt.
He enlisted in November 1916, and three months later was drafted to Egypt and thence to Palestine. Whilst in this theatre of operations he took part in the Battles of Gaza and the capture of Jerusalem, and fought in the Advance with General Allenby's Forces to Tripoli and Aleppo. Demobilised on returning home in February 1919, he holds the General Service and Victory Medals.
Little Houghton, Northants. Z3440.

MORRIS, W. S., Sergeant, 3rd Northants. Regt.
Having previously served for 16 years with the Colours, he re-enlisted in 1916, and later in the same year was drafted to France, where he took a prominent part in many important engagements. Transferred to Italy, he proceeded later to Egypt where he was again in action, finally being invalided home in 1919. Demobilised in April of that year, he holds the General Service and Victory Medals.
86, Market Street, Northampton. Z2228.

MORRIS, W. T., Lieut., 1st Bedfordshire Regiment.
Called up from the Reserve in August 1914, he quickly proceeded to France, where he took a prominent part in the Battles of Ypres, Neuve Chapelle and the Somme, and was wounded at Ypres in October 1914, at Festubert in May 1915 and at Armentières in September 1916. He also served in Italy on the Piave, but returned to France in time to take part in the Retreat and Advance of 1918, and was a fourth time wounded at Havrincourt. Later he served with the Army of Occupation in Germany, and was demobilised in October 1919, holding the 1914 Star, and the General Service and Victory Medals.
17, Stanhope Road, Northampton Z2451.

MORTIMER, F., Corporal, Northants. Dragoons.
Mobilised with the Territorials in August 1914, he proceeded to France in September of the following year, and there took part in the Battles of Vimy Ridge, the Somme, Arras, Ypres and Passchendaele, and minor engagements. Returning home in September 1917, he was transferred to the Cheshire Regiment, and retained in England as an Instructor until his discharge in March 1919. He holds the 1914–15 Star, and the General Service and Victory Medals.
32, Wantage Road, Northampton. Z2229.

MORTIBOYS, A. L., Gunner, Royal Field Artillery.
Shortly after volunteering in September 1919, he proceeded to France, and took part in the Battles of La Bassée, Ypres and Loos. In 1915 he was transferred to Salonika, on which front he was in action in numerous engagements of note in various sectors, and was wounded in February 1916. He was demobilised on his return to England in February 1919, and holds the 1914–15 Star, and the General Service and Victory Medals.
9, North Street, Daventry, Northants. Z2788.

MORTIMER, H. F., Private, M.G.C.
Volunteering in November 1915, he completed his training in England and embarked for France early in 1917. After doing good service on the Western Front he was transferred to Palestine, and was in action at the Gaza battles, at the capture of Jerusalem, and in the later operations under General Allenby. In 1918 he returned to France in time to take part in the Advance and the entry into Mons on Armistice Day. Demobilised in April 1919, he holds the General Service and Victory Medals.
7, Hunter Street, Northampton. Z1566

MORTON, F. W., Private, Royal Fusiliers.
He joined in June 1916, and after training at Falmouth and Dover was drafted to France. Whilst in this seat of war he took part in many important engagements in the Somme and Ypres sectors before being wounded and invalided to hospital. On his recovery he was transferred to the Labour Corps and served on the Cambrai front. He returned home for demobilisation in December 1919, and holds the General Service and Victory Medals.
19, Stockley Street, Northampton. Z1981.

MORTON, R. J., Private, 7th Suffolk Regiment.
Joining in June 1916, he was drafted to the Western Front in the following October, and took part in much severe fighting on the Somme. He was unhappily reported wounded and missing, and is believed to have been killed in action at Arras in April 1917. He was entitled to the General Service and Victory Medals.
"Whilst we remember, the sacrifice is not in vain."
The Green, Milton, Northants. Z2452.

MOSELEY, A., Private, 2nd Northants. Regiment.
Volunteering in August 1914, he was shortly afterwards drafted to the Western Front, where he took part in many important engagements. He died gloriously on the Field of Battle at Aubers Ridge on May 9th, 1915, and was entitled to the 1914–15 Star, and the General Service and Victory Medals.
"A valiant Soldier, with undaunted heart he breasted life's last hill."
158, Semilong Road, Northampton. Z2453.

MOSELEY, H., Gunner, Royal Garrison Artillery.
After joining in September 1916 he underwent a period of training prior to being drafted to the Western Front in May 1918. There he saw much severe fighting in the Ypres sector until he contracted trench feet, and was admitted to hospital at the Base. He was demobilised in February 1919, and holds the General Service and Victory Medals.
156, Semilong Road, Northampton. Z2454.

MOSELEY, P. H., Trooper, Northants. Dragoons.
He volunteered in January 1915, and was stationed with his unit at Scarborough, where he was engaged on transport duties. He rendered valuable services, but was not successful in obtaining his transfer overseas owing to an unfortunate fall from a waggon, causing a serious injury to his leg. This resulted in his removal to hospital and his discharge in July 1917. 47, Gladstone Terrace, Northampton. Z1567.

MOSS, H. S., Private, 85th Battalion Canadian Overseas Forces.
He enlisted in the Royal Navy in November 1913, and rendered valuable services on board H.M.S. "Cumberland" until September 1916. He then transferred to the Canadian Infantry and proceeded to France four months later, but after taking part in the Battles of Arras, Ypres, Cambrai, the Somme (II.) and the Retreat, was unhappily killed in action at the commencement of the Advance on September 2nd, 1918. He was entitled to the 1914–15 Star, and the General Service and Victory Medals.
"The path of duty was the way to glory."
74, Shelley Street, Kingsley Park, Northampton. Z1568/B.

MOSS, J. A., Sapper, Royal Engineers.
He joined in November 1916, and in July of the following year was drafted to the Western Front, where he served in various sectors. He was engaged chiefly in repairing the lines of communication, and rendered very valuable services with his Company until his return home for demobilisation in August 1919. He holds the General Service and Victory Medals.
26, Kingswell Street, Northampton. Z3106.

MOSS, M. A. S. (Miss), Worker, Women's Land Army.
This lady joined the Women's Land Army in July 1918, and was engaged on special hay-baling work with the Forage Corps in various parts of Northamptonshire. She rendered valuable services for nearly a year, and was demobilised in June 1919.
74, Shelley Street, Kingsley Park, Northampton. Z1568/A.

MOTT, J. L., Private, Machine Gun Corps.
He joined in March 1917, and was eventually drafted to France in the following February. After only a short period of active service, during which he saw heavy fighting at Cambrai and on the Somme, he laid down his life for King and Country on May 27th, 1918. He was entitled to the General Service and Victory Medals.
"A costly sacrifice upon the altar of freedom."
15, Lower Harding Street, Northampton. Z1569/A.

MOTT, W. H., Private, Royal Army Medical Corps.
He volunteered in November 1915, but owing to his being medically unfit for transfer overseas was retained on special duties as a nursing orderly and on the staff of the Base Medical Stores. He rendered valuable services at various stations and was ultimately demobilised in April 1919.
15, Lower Harding Street, Northampton. Z1569/B.

MOULD, W. T., Private, 6th Northants. Regiment.
Joining in May 1917, he completed a period of training at Gillingham prior to being drafted to France in the same year. In this seat of operations he was in action at the Battles of Ypres, Passchendaele, Cambrai and the Retreat of 1918, during which he was badly wounded. As a result he was invalided to hospital at Camberwell, and unfortunately died from the effects of his wounds on July 28th, 1918. He was entitled to the General Service and Victory Medals.
"Steals on the ear the distant triumph song."
8, St. Mary's Street, Northampton. Z1126/B.

MOULDING, G. V. (M.M.), Corporal, R.G.A.
Volunteering in October 1915, he was drafted to France in the following year and played a prominent part with his Battery in the Battles of Ypres, Cambrai and Amiens, and in the Retreat and Advance of 1918. He was awarded the Military Medal for conspicuous gallantry in the Field in 1918, but, being badly gassed in action, was sent to hospital in Northampton, where he unfortunately died on June 8th, 1920. He was also entitled to the General Service and Victory Medals.
"His life for his Country, his soul to God."
69, Charles Street, Northampton. Z1570.

MOULES, F., Private, Machine Gun Corps.
After joining in 1916 he proceeded in the same year to Egypt, where he took part in many important engagements before being invalided home with malarial fever and dysentery. On his recovery he was transferred to France, and took part in heavy fighting on the Vimy Ridge, Cambrai, Amiens and Ypres fronts. He was demobilised in February 1919, and holds the General Service and Victory Medals.
85, Dunster Street, Northampton. Z1982.

MUDDIMAN, A., Private, Machine Gun Corps.
On attaining military age he joined in June 1917, and in May of the following year was ordered overseas. During his service on the Western Front he fought in the Battles of the Somme and Ypres, did valuable work in the Retreat and Advance of 1918, and was wounded in action in September of that year. Returning home, he was demobilised in January 1919, and holds the General Service and Victory Medals.
95, Stanley Road, Northampton. Z2789.

MUDDIMAN, W., Sergt., 7th Northants. Regt.
He volunteered in September 1914, and after a period of training was drafted to France, where he played a distinguished part in many engagements, including the Battles of Festubert and Loos. He was severely wounded in action at Guillemont in 1916, and unhappily died through the effects of his wounds shortly afterwards. He was entitled to the 1914–15 Star, and the General Service and Victory Medals.
"The path of duty was the way to glory."
Mill Hill, Long Buckby, Northants. Z3441.

MUDDIMAN, W. G., Gunner, R.G.A.
He enlisted in 1917, and later in the same year was drafted to France. In this theatre of war he took part in several engagements, including the Battles of Ypres, Passchendaele and Cambrai, and was badly gassed in action. After the cessation of hostilities he returned home and was demobilised in 1920, holding the General Service and Victory Medals.
Mill Hill, Long Buckby, Northants. Z3442.

MUDDIMAN, W. J., Private, 1st Northants. Regt.
Joining in August 1917, he embarked for France in January 1918, and served in the Retreat and Advance of that year, being in action at St. Quentin and other places. After the Armistice he was blown up in an accidental explosion on December 24th, and after removal to a Base Hospital and thence to Southampton, was discharged immediately afterwards. He holds the General Service and Victory Medals.
47, Lawrence Street, Northampton. Z1571.

MUDDIMAN, W. J., Rifleman, Rifle Brigade.
Having enlisted in July 1917, he underwent a period of training before being drafted to France in June 1918. Whilst overseas he took part in several engagements in various sectors during the Advance of the Allies, and was wounded in action. He was demobilised in April 1919, and holds the General Service and Victory Medals. High St., Long Buckby, Northants. Z3443.

MULLARD, A., Private, 52nd Royal Fusiliers.
Joining in April 1918, he was sent for his training to Newmarket, and served with his unit in England. He was not successful in obtaining his transfer overseas before the cessation of hostilities, but in March 1919 was sent to the Army of Occupation on the Rhine, and did duty there until his demobilisation in April 1920.
14, Francis Street, Northampton. Z1572.

MULVANEY, F. J. (D.C.M.), Sergeant, 2nd Canadian Machine Gun Corps.
He volunteered in Ottowa in February 1915, and landed in France in the following January, after a period of training in England. Whilst on the Western Front he played a prominent part in the Battles of the Somme, Arras, Vimy Ridge, Ypres, Passchendaele, Lens and Cambrai, and in the Retreat and Advance of 1918. He was awarded the Distinguished Conduct Medal for conspicuous bravery at Ypres in 1916, and after hostilities ceased served at Cologne with the Army of Occupation. Demobilised in May 1919, he also holds the General Service and Victory Medals.
88, Shelley Street, Kingsley, Northampton. Z1573

MUNDAY, W. T., L/Corporal, R.A.O.C.
Joining in August 1916, he proceeded to France in the following November, and whilst stationed at Calais in the Stores Department was engaged in loading up ammunition and supplies for conveyance to the forward areas. He also carried out similar duties on the Somme front and rendered valuable services until he was demobilised in October 1919. He holds the General Service and Victory Medals.
94, Lower Adelaide Street, Northampton. Z1574.

MUNNS, A., Private, 4th East Yorkshire Regt.
After volunteering in June 1915 he was sent for training to Windsor, and drafted to France in the next year. He was in action on the Somme, at Albert and St. Quentin, and was wounded at Mametz Wood in 1917, but after a month in hospital in France returned to the fighting line and served through the rest of the campaign. Demobilised in March 1919, he holds the General Service and Victory Medals.
15, Spencer Road, Northampton. Z1575.

MUNNS, W., Private, Royal Marine Light Infantry.
He joined in May 1918, and served with his unit at a Southern station in England. He rendered valuable services, but was not successful in obtaining his transfer overseas before the cessation of hostilities owing to medical unfitness, and after doing good work as cook in barracks was demobilised in January 1919. 1, Leslie Terrace, Northampton. Z1576.

MUNROE, A. E., L/Corporal, 7th Northants. Regt.
Volunteering in September 1914, he underwent a period of training before being drafted overseas in the following year. Whilst on the Western Front he was in action during fierce fighting at Loos. He made the supreme sacrifice, being killed on February 23rd, 1916, and was entitled to the 1914–15 Star, and the General Service and Victory Medals.
"He nobly fell that we might live."
21, Freehold Street, Northampton. Z1983/E.

MUNROE, F., Corporal, Northants. Dragoons.
Volunteering in May 1915, he was drafted to France in August 1916, and was engaged on special duties at a prisoner of war camp at Le Havre for twelve months. He then returned to England and rendered valuable services as an Instructor with the Tank Corps and the Cheshire Regiment until his demobilisation in February 1919, holding the General Service and Victory Medals.
56, Harvey Street, Northampton. Z1577.

MUNROE, W., Private, 1st Northants. Regiment.
Volunteering in March 1915, he underwent a period of training at Chatham prior to being drafted overseas. Whilst on the Western Front he served with a Tunnelling Company of the Royal Engineers, and was present during heavy fighting at Loos, where he was badly gassed and unfortunately died from the effects on May 23rd, 1916. He was entitled to the General Service and Victory Medals.
"Whilst we remember, the sacrifice is not in vain."
21, Freehold Street, Northampton. Z1983/D.

MUNTON, J. C., Air Mechanic, R.A.F.
Shortly after joining in January 1917, he was sent to France, where he served in various sectors of the front. He was engaged on duties of great importance whilst in this theatre of war, and rendered valuable services with his Squadron until his demobilisation in February 1919. He holds the General Service and Victory Medals.
Chapel Yard, Gayton, Northants. Z2455.

MURDIN, F. V., Private, 1st Northants. Regt.
Mobilised at the declaration of war, he at once proceeded to France, and fought in the Retreat from Mons. He was also in action in the Battles of the Marne and the Aisne, and was wounded at La Bassée in October 1914. On his return to the firing-line he took part in engagements at Ypres, but was unhappily killed in action at La Bassée on January 28th, 1915. He was entitled to the Mons Star, and the General Service and Victory Medals.
"Great deeds cannot die."
47, Warwick Street, Daventry, Northants. Z2791.

MURDIN, J., Private, 4th Northants. Regiment.
Volunteering in August 1914, he was drafted to Gallipoli in July 1915, and served at Suvla Bay and in subsequent engagements of the campaign. In December 1915 he was sent to Egypt and subsequently to Palestine, where he was engaged in fierce fighting at Gaza. Owing to ill-health he was invalided home in September 1918, and was demobilised in March of the following year, holding the 1914–15 Star, and the General Service and Victory Medals.
27, New Street, Daventry, Northants. Z2790.

MURRAY, J. A., Private, Royal Fusiliers.
Joining in February 1917, he was sent to the Western Front in October of the same year, and was there very severely wounded in action at Cambrai in the following month. Admitted to hospital at Le Tréport, he was afterwards invalided home and unhappily died in hospital at Totnes on March 17th, 1918. He was entitled to the General Service and Victory Medals.
"His memory is cherished with pride."
41, Artisan Road, Northampton. Z2230.

MURTON, A. J., Sapper, Royal Engineers.
He joined in 1916, but owing to ill-health was not successful in his endeavours to secure a transfer to a fighting area. He was, however, retained on home service, and was engaged in the dockyards on duties of an important nature, which he carried out in a highly efficient manner. After two years' valuable work he was demobilised in 1918.
38, Gregory Street, Northampton. Z2792.

MUSCUTT, G., Corporal, 1st Grenadier Guards.
He enlisted in April 1917, and having completed his training in the following year was drafted to France. During his service overseas he took part in the Advance of 1918, and after the cessation of hostilities proceeded to Germany, where he served with the Army of Occupation at Cologne. He returned home in 1919, and was engaged on important duties until demobilised in May 1920. He holds the General Service and Victory Medals.
Skin Yard Lane, Long Buckby, Northants. Z3444.

MUSCUTT, R. G., Private, 10th Bedford. Regt.
He enlisted in June 1916, and in November of the same year was drafted to France. There he took part in several engagements, including the Battle of Arras, where he was wounded in action. As a result he was invalided home, and on his recovery served at various stations until his demobilisation in March 1919. He holds the General Service and Victory Medals. Knutsford Lane, Long Buckby, Northants. Z3345.

MUSGROVE, F., Private, Essex Regiment.
He volunteered in 1915, and after undergoing a period of training was drafted to India, where he was engaged on important garrison duties at various stations, serving also with the Middlesex Regiment. Contracting malaria, he unhappily died of heart disease as a result in 1919, and was entitled to the General Service and Victory Medals.
"His memory is cherished with pride."
6, Oxford Street, Northampton. Z3107.

MUSGROVE, W. F., Drmr., 1/10th Middlesex Regt.
He volunteered in 1915, and in the following year was drafted to India, where he took part in engagements on the North-West Frontier. Later he saw much service in China and, contracting malaria, was in hospital for some time, being eventually sent home. Demobilised in 1919, he holds the General Service and Victory Medals.
105, St. Leonard's Road, Far Cotton, Northampton. Z3446.

MYNARD, G. R., Sapper, Royal Engineers.
Shortly after joining in February 1918 he was drafted to the Western Front, where he served in various sectors. He was present at the Battles of the Somme, Havrincourt, Epéhy and Cambrai and other engagements during the Retreat and Advance of 1918, and was gassed. He was demobilised in February 1919, and holds the General Service and Victory Medals.
1, Albert Place, Northampton. Z3364.

N

NASEBY, R., Private, 2nd Northants. Regiment.
He was serving at Malta at the outbreak of war, and was immediately drafted to France, where, after fighting in the Retreat from Mons and the Battle of La Bassée, he was wounded at Neuve Chapelle. Invalided home, he returned to the Western Front, however, and three months later was taken prisoner at Ploegsteert Wood. He was eventually released and in March 1919 was discharged, holding the Mons Star, and the General Service and Victory Medals.
High Street, West Haddon, near Rugby, Northants. Z3330/B.

NASH, A., Private, 3rd Suffolk Regiment.
He joined in May 1916, and after training at Dovercourt and Felixstowe embarked for France in January 1917. He was in action at Arras, Ypres and Passchendaele in that year, but unfortunately developed rheumatism and trench feet, and being invalided to England was discharged as unfit for further service in February 1918. He holds the General Service and Victory Medals. 74, Moore St., Kingsley, Northampton. Z1578.

NASH, C., Private, 11th Suffolk Regiment.
Joining in February 1916, he underwent a period of training and in the same year proceeded to France. In this theatre of war he took part in heavy fighting on the Arras front before being wounded and invalided home. He was unfortunately killed during an air-raid on Felixstowe on July 19th, 1917, and was entitled to the General Service and Victory Medals.
"His memory is cherished with pride."
11, Stockley Street, Northampton. Z1984/B.

NASH, H., Private, 1st Northants. Regiment.
Having enlisted in September 1905, he proceeded to France immediately on the outbreak of war, and fought in the Battle of and Retreat from Mons. He also took part in the Battle of the Marne before being wounded on the Aisne and invalided home. Returning to France in 1917, he was again in action and was gassed near Arras. He was consequently invalided from the Army in January 1918, and holds the Mons Star, and the General Service and Victory Medals.
West Haddon, near Rugby, Northants. Z3447.

NASH, J. A., Private, 11th Suffolk Regiment.
Mobilised from the Reserve at the outbreak of war, he completed a period of training at Felixstowe before proceeding to France in 1916. Whilst in this seat of operations he took part in many important engagements before being taken prisoner at Arras in April 1917. He was held in captivity until after the cessation of hostilities and, returning home, was demobilised in March 1919, holding the General Service and Victory Medals.
11, Stockley Street, Northampton. Z1984/A.

NAYLOR, T. S., L/Cpl., Royal Inniskilling Fus.
He joined in November 1916, and in January of the following year was sent to the Western Front, where he saw heavy fighting in the Somme sector. In April 1917 he was wounded at Savy Wood, and invalided home, and on his recovery was drafted to Ireland in March 1918. After a period of service there he was discharged as medically unfit for further military duties in October 1918, holding the General Service and Victory Medals.
9, Dundee Street, Northampton. Z2793.

NEAL, A. H., Private, 4th Northants. Regiment.
Joining in May 1917, he completed his training, and eight months later embarked for France. On that front he fought in the Battle of the Somme, and was severely wounded at St. Quentin in March 1918. He unfortunately succumbed to his injuries in hospital at Rouen in the following month, and was entitled to the General Service and Victory Medals.
"Whilst we remember, the sacrifice is not in vain."
24, Brook Street, Daventry, Northants. Z2794.

NEAL, F., L/Cpl., 16th (The Queen's) Lancers.
Joining in February 1916, he was drafted to the Western Front in the following November, and there saw much severe fighting. He took part in the Battles of Arras, Bullecourt and Cambrai and minor engagements, fought also in the Retreat and Advance of 1918, and afterwards served with the Army of Occupation in Germany. Demobilised on returning home in February 1919, he holds the General Service and Victory Medals.
116, Abington Avenue, Northampton. Z2231—Z2232.

NEALE, G. J., Private, R.A.M.C.
He volunteered in October 1915, and in December of the following year was drafted to Mesopotamia. Whilst in this seat of operations he was engaged on duties of great importance at Basra and various other stations, and rendered very valuable services with his Company. Demobilised on returning home in November 1919, he holds the General Service and Victory Medals. 59, Wycliffe Road, Northampton. Z2233/A.

NEALE, W., Telegraphist, R.N.V.R.
He joined in January 1917, and after undergoing a period of training was retained at various wireless stations, where he was engaged on duties of great importance. Although unable to obtain his transfer to a unit of the Fleet, he rendered very valuable services until his demobilisation in August 1919.
59, Wycliffe Road, Northampton. Z2233/B.

NEEDHAM, J. H., Sapper, Royal Engineers.
He volunteered in 1915, and in the following year was sent to the Western Front. There he was present at the Battles of Vimy Ridge, the Somme and Cambrai and other engagements, took part also in the Retreat and Advance of 1918, and was severely gassed and suffered from trench fever. He was demobilised in 1919, and holds the General Service and Victory Medals.
42, Oxford Street, Northampton. Z3448.

NEEDHAM, R. A., Private, R.A.O.C.
Four months after joining in November 1916 he was sent to the Western Front, where he was engaged on duties of a highly technical nature in the Arras, Ypres and Somme sectors. Unfortunately injured in an accident, he was invalided home and was afterwards retained in England until his demobilisation in October 1919. He holds the General Service and Victory Medals. 6, Main Road, Northampton. Z3108.

NEIL, B. W., Driver, Royal Field Artillery.
Volunteering in April 1915, he was drafted to France in the following September, and saw service in the Arras sector. Found to be too young for service overseas, he was sent back to England in 1916, and discharged, but re-enlisted in 1918 and served with his unit at Newcastle-on-Tyne until his demobilisation in April 1919. He holds the 1914–15 Star, and the General Service and Victory Medals.
100, Earl Street, Northampton. Z1579/B.

NEIL, W., C.S.M., 7th Northamptonshire Regt.
Having already served in the Boer War, he was mobilised in August 1914, and retained on special duties as an Instructor of Recruits until early in the following year. He then proceeded to France, but after serving with distinction in the Ypres sector, died gloriously on the Field of Battle at Loos in September 1915. He already held the Queen's and King's South African Medals, and was entitled to the 1914–15 Star, and the General Service and Victory Medals.
"His name liveth for evermore."
100, Earl Street, Northampton. Z1579/A.

NEVILLE, W. G. (jun.), A.B., Royal Navy.
He volunteered in August 1914, and after training in H.M.S. "Vivid" served in H.M. submarines "C 11," "C 5" and "K 11"; H.M.S. "Dolphin" and various other vessels in many waters. He was on board S.S. "Baynyassa" when she was attacked by a submarine in the Atlantic in July 1917, but fortunately he was rescued by a British trawler and served afterwards in S.S. "Anchoria" until she was torpedoed in March 1918. He was later serving as a gunner in S.S. "War Council" when she was sunk in October 1918, and he was wounded. Demobilised in February 1919, he holds the 1914–15 Star, and the General Service and Victory Medals.
38, Hazelwood Road, Northampton. Z2456/B.

NEVILLE, W. G. (M.V.O.), Trooper, Royal Horse Guards.
Called up from the Reserve in August 1914, he was immediately drafted to the Western Front, where he took part in the Battles of Mons, the Marne and the Aisne. Transferred in 1915 to the Dardanelles, he saw much severe fighting in Gallipoli, afterwards serving on the Staff in Egypt. He was wounded whilst overseas and was discharged on returning home in November 1915. He was awarded the Royal Victorian Order for distinguished services, rendered prior to the war, and holds also the Mons Star, and the General Service and Victory Medals.
38, Hazelwood Road, Northampton. Z2456/A.

NEWBROOK, A. L., Stoker, Royal Navy.
He volunteered in August 1914, and after training at Devonport was posted to a light cruiser for patrol duties in African and other waters. He was afterwards transferred to H.M.S. "Lion," on board which vessel he was still serving at Scapa Flow in 1921. He holds the 1914–15 Star, and the General Service and Victory Medals.
9, Sunderland Street, Northampton. Z2457/C.

NEWBROOK, H., Corporal, 1st Northants. Regt.
Mobilised in August 1914, he was quickly drafted to the Western Front, where he served through the Battle of Mons and also took part in the Battles of the Marne, the Aisne and Ypres. Invalided home suffering from frost-bite, he proceeded to West Africa in October 1915, and later saw service in East Africa. He holds the Mons Star, and the General Service and Victory Medals, and in 1921 was serving as a Colour-Sergeant with a Nigerian Regiment.
9, Sunderland Street, Northampton. Z2457/A.

NEWBROOK, J. H. A., Private, 5th Northants. Regiment.
Volunteering in August 1914, he was sent to France in the following year, and there saw much heavy fighting, and was gassed in 1916. He took part in the Battles of Ypres, Loos, the Somme, Arras, Vimy Ridge, Passchendaele, Cambrai, Amiens and Bapaume and other engagements, and fought also in the Advance of 1918. Demobilised in February 1919, he holds the 1914–15 Star, and the General Service and Victory Medals.
9, Sunderland Street, Northampton. Z2457/D.

NEWBROOK, R. W., Gunner, R.G.A.
Four months after joining in March 1916 he was drafted to the Western Front, where he saw severe fighting in various sectors. He took part in the Battles of the Somme, Arras, Messines, Ypres, Passchendaele, Cambrai and Kemmel Hill, and many minor engagements, serving also through the Retreat and Advance of 1918. He was demobilised in June 1919, and holds the General Service and Victory Medals.
9, Sunderland Street, Northampton. Z2457/B.

NEWBURY, W. G., Trumpeter, 1/2nd Northants. Dragoons.
He volunteered in September 1914, and on completion of a term of training proceeded to the Western Front. Whilst in this theatre of war he served in various sectors with the Military Mounted Police, and, engaged chiefly in guarding prisoners of war did much good work with his unit. Demobilised late in 1918, he holds the 1914–15 Star, and the General Service and Victory Medals.
The Bungalow, St. Leonard's Road, Far Cotton, Northampton. Z3109.

NEWCOMEN, E. J., Private, 2/7th Durham L.I.
He volunteered in October 1914, and after a period of training was retained on important duties in England with the 4th Northamptonshire Regiment, and afterwards with the 18th Yorkshire Regiment until October 1918. He was then drafted to North Russia, where he took part in operations at Archangel, finally returning home for demobilisation in August 1919. He holds the General Service and Victory Medals.
100, Roe Road, Northampton. Z2234.

NEWELL, H. W., Private, 5th Northants. Regt.
He volunteered in April 1915, and crossing to France seven months later fought in the Battles of Arras, Bullecourt and Ypres, and was gassed in November 1917. He was sent to hospital in England, and on his recovery returned to the Western Front and took part in the final decisive engagements of the war. Demobilised in January 1919, he holds the 1914–15 Star, and the General Service and Victory Medals.
19–21, Cross Street, Drayton, near Daventry, Northants. Z2795/A.

NEWELL, R. S., Private, 6th Royal Fusiliers.
Joining in January 1918, he was drafted to Ireland to receive his training, but unfortunately his health broke down, and he was discharged as medically unfit for further military duties in March 1918, after only two months' service in the Army.
19, Cross St., Drayton, near Daventry, Northants. Z2795/B.

NEWICK, T. E., Private, R.A.S.C. (M.T.)
He volunteered in June 1915, and on completing a period of training proceeded to the Western Front, where he was engaged in conveying supplies and ammunition to the forward areas. He died gloriously on the Field of Battle in June 1916, and was entitled to the General Service and Victory Medals.
"Whilst we remember, the sacrifice is not in vain."
2, St. Giles' Terrace, Northampton. Z3363/B.

NEWITT, A., Private, Worcestershire Regiment.
Joining in February 1917, he proceeded in the same month to the Western Front, and served in the Ypres and Arras sectors as a stretcher-bearer. In the following August he was badly gassed near Ypres and, being invalided to hospital in Manchester, remained under treatment until his demobilisation in July 1919. He holds the General Service and Victory Medals.
9, Grafton Place, Northampton. Z1580.

NEWMAN, A., A.B., Royal Naval Division.
He joined in September 1917, and was sent for training to Blandford. After twelve months' service in England he was drafted to France, and fought in the Advance of 1918, on the Somme and at Cambrai, where he was severely wounded in September. Evacuated to a hospital in London, he was discharged in March 1919 as unfit for further service, and holds the General Service and Victory Medals.
45, Ambush Street, Northampton. Z1581.

NEWMAN, B. A., Private, 4th Northants. Regt.
Joining in January 1917, he completed a period of training, and was retained on important guard and other duties with his unit at various stations. Owing to his being medically unfit he was unable to take part in operations overseas, and was eventually discharged in January 1918.
15, Mounts Gardens, Northampton. Z1985.

NEWTON, C. H., Private, 7th Northants. Regt.
Volunteering in February 1915, he was sent to France in the following September, and there served with the Transport Section in various sectors. He took part also in the Battles of Loos, Vimy Ridge, the Somme, Arras, Messines, Ypres, Cambrai, Amiens and Bapaume, and served through the Retreat and Advance of 1918. He was demobilised in February 1919, and holds the 1914–15 Star, and the General Service and Victory Medals.
Silver Street, Brixworth, Northants.
Z3110/A—Z3111/A—Z3112/A.

NEWTON, F., Rifleman, 8th K.R.R.C.
He joined in March 1917, and three months later proceeded to the Western Front, where he saw much severe fighting. After taking part in the Battle of Passchendaele and minor engagements, he was taken prisoner at St. Quentin in March 1918, and was held in captivity at Doberitz and other camps in Germany. Released on the cessation of hostilities, he also served with the 2/13th London Regiment before being demobilised in June 1919, and holds the General Service and Victory Medals.
Silver Street, Brixworth, Northants.
Z3110/B—Z3111/B—Z3112/B.

NICHOLLS, C. H., Special War Worker.
Being medically unfit for service with the Colours, he was engaged during the period of hostilities on work of National importance. Employed on various responsible duties in connection with the construction of aeroplanes, he rendered very valuable services throughout.
73, St. Leonard's Road, Far Cotton, Northants. Z3132/B.

NICHOLLS, T., Private, Machine Gun Corps.
Joining the Middlesex Regiment in August 1917, he did his training at Chatham, and was then transferred to the Machine Gun Corps at Grantham. Drafted to France in December of the same year, he saw much heavy fighting in the Somme and Ypres sectors, and later in the victorious Advance, on the Aisne and at Amiens. On September 20th, 1918, he fell fighting on the Field of Battle, and was entitled to the General Service and Victory Medals.
"A costly sacrifice upon the altar of freedom."
16, Monarch Road, Northampton. Z1582/B.

NICHOLLS, T. A., Private, 1/2nd Middlesex Regt.
He joined in August 1917, and on conclusion of his training in the same year was drafted overseas. Whilst on the Western Front he did consistently good work as a Lewis gunner, and was in action during engagements in the Somme and Ypres sectors. He made the supreme sacrifice, being killed in action in September 1918, and was entitled to the General Service and Victory Medals.
"And doubtless he went in splendid company."
80, Great Russell Street, Northampton. Z1986/B.

NICHOLS, W. G., Sapper, Royal Engineers.
He joined the Royal Engineers in June 1916, and, later transferred to the Loyal North Lancashire Regiment, embarked for the Western Front in the following December, and took part in numerous minor engagements in the Ypres sector. He was wounded in action at Messines in June 1917, and after his discharge from hospital in England was transferred to the Royal Air Force in 1918. After rendering valuable services at various home stations he was demobilised in January 1919, holding the General Service and Victory Medals.
3, Fife Street, St. James, Northampton. Z2796.

NICKERSON, J., Sapper, Royal Engineers.
Two months after volunteering in March 1915 he was drafted to the Western Front, where he was engaged on important duties on the railways in various sectors. He was present also at the Battles of Arras, Ypres and Cambrai and many other engagements, finally returning home for demobilisation in May 1919. He holds the 1914–15 Star, and the General Service and Victory Medals.
High Street, Long Buckby, Northants. Z3449.

NIGHTINGALE, A., Pte., Oxford. and Bucks. L.I.
He joined in June 1918, and after undergoing a period of training was retained at Dover, where he was engaged on duties of great importance. Owing to the early cessation of hostilities he was not successful in obtaining his transfer overseas, but, nevertheless, did good work with his unit until demobilised in February 1919.
Bugbrooke, Northants. Z3113/B.

NIGHTINGALE, F., Sergeant, M.G.C.
He volunteered in the Northamptonshire Regiment in October 1914, and after his training was retained on important duties in England until February 1917, and then proceeded to France, where he took a prominent part in the Battles of Arras, Vimy Ridge and Ypres. He fell fighting at Cambrai on November 30th, 1917, and was entitled to the General Service and Victory Medals.
"The path of duty was the way to glory."
Bugbrooke, Northants. Z3113/A.

NIGHTINGALE, P., Sapper, R.E. (R.O.D.)
Volunteering in November 1914, he proceeded to the Western Front in February of the following year, and was there engaged on transport and other duties on the railways. He served chiefly in the Ypres, Loos, Somme, Arras and Cambrai sectors, and also took an active part in the Retreat and Advance of 1918. Demobilised in March 1919, he holds the 1914–15 Star, and the General Service and Victory Medals.
Bugbrooke, Northants. Z3451/A.

NIGHTINGALE, T. W., Pte., 1/4th Northants. Regiment.
He joined in June 1916, and in March of the following year was sent to Egypt and thence into Palestine, where he served as a signaller. He made the supreme sacrifice, falling in action in the second Battle of Gaza in April 1917, only a month after landing in the East. He was entitled to the General Service and Victory Medals.
"His life for his Country, his soul to God."
13, Symington Street, St. James, Northampton. Z3450.

NIGHTINGALE, W. P., L/Cpl., M.G.C.
He volunteered in October 1914, and in June of the following year proceeded to Gallipoli with the 11th London Regiment, and there served at Suvla Bay. Invalided home suffering from enteric fever, he was later transferred to the Machine Gun Corps and sent to France, where he was wounded and taken prisoner on the Dunes in June 1917. He was released in February 1918, and in August of that year was discharged as medically unfit for further service. He holds the 1914–15 Star, and the General Service and Victory Medals.
Bugbrooke, Northants. Z3451/B.

NIND, R., Private, 10th Royal Fusiliers.
Joining in March 1917, he was drafted two months later to the Western Front, where he fought in numerous important engagements, including the Battle of Ypres. Whilst in action on the Somme he gave his life for King and Country on January 7th, 1918, and was entitled to the General Service and Victory Medals.
"A valiant Soldier, with undaunted heart he breasted life's last hill."
23, Abbey Street, Northampton. Z2797.

NOBBS, J. G., Driver, R.A.S.C. (H.T.)
He volunteered in November 1915, and after completing a term of training served at various stations, where he was engaged on transport and other important duties. He was unable to obtain his transfer to a theatre of war, but, nevertheless, rendered valuable services with his Company until demobilised in October 1919.
37, Parkwood Street, Northampton. Z2458.

NORRIS, A. E., Seaman-Gunner, Royal Navy.
He enlisted in 1903, and after the outbreak of war in August 1914 served in H.M.S. "Monarch," attached to the Grand Fleet in the North Sea. He took part in the Battle of Jutland and many minor actions in these waters, and was also present at the surrender of the German Fleet. Discharged in February 1919, he holds the 1914–15 Star, and the General Service and Victory Medals.
15, Wilby Street, Northampton. Z2235/B.

NORTH, T. C., Private, Royal Sussex Regiment.
He joined in June 1917, and after his training was engaged on duties of great importance at various stations. He was unable to obtain his transfer overseas before the cessation of hostilities, but in December 1918 was sent to France, whence he proceeded in the following month to Germany. There he served with the Army of Occupation at Cologne until his return home for demobilisation in September 1919.
Rothersthorpe, Northants. Z3114/B.

NORTH, W. A., Private, Machine Gun Corps.
He volunteered in November 1915, and, after training with the Bedfordshire Lancers, proceeded to Egypt in 1916, and was then transferred to the City of London Lancers (Rough Riders). Advancing into Palestine, he took part in the Battles of Gaza before being drafted in 1918 to France, where he was in action on the Somme and was gassed in October. He was invalided from the Army in February 1919, and holds the General Service and Victory Medals.
Rothersthorpe, Northants. Z3114/A.

NORTHOVER, E., Private, Sherwood Foresters.
Three months after joining in September 1917, he was drafted to the Western Front, where he saw heavy fighting in various sectors. He took part in the Battle of the Somme and other engagements in the Retreat and the early stages of the Advance of 1918 before being wounded in September of that year. He was sent home and finally invalided from the Army in February 1919, holding the General Service and Victory Medals.
32, Southampton Road, Northampton. Z3115/B.

NORTHOVER, F. A., Private, 6th Beds. Regiment.
He joined the Northamptonshire Regiment in September 1916, and, transferred to the 6th Bedfordshire Regiment, proceeded to the Western Front in the following December, and there saw much severe fighting. He died gloriously on the Field of Battle at Arras on April 10th, 1917, and was entitled to the General Service and Victory Medals.
"Whilst we remember, the sacrifice is not in vain."
32, Southampton Road, Northampton. Z3115/A.

NOTTON, A. T., Private, Highland Light Infantry.
After volunteering in February 1916, he completed a period of training and proceeded to Ireland, where he took part in the Irish Rebellion and was wounded. As a result he was invalided home and discharged as medically unfit for further service in October 1917.
27, Regent Street, Northampton. Z1253/A.

NOTTON, J., Private, 8th Northants. Regiment.
He volunteered in December 1915, and, after a period of training with the Northamptonshire Regiment, was transferred to the Labour Corps, and retained on important duties at various stations. He was unable to obtain his transfer overseas, but, nevertheless, rendered valuable services with his unit until March 1919, when he was demobilised.
Cogenhoe, Northants. Z3452.

NUTT, J., Gunner, Royal Garrison Artillery.
Volunteering in October 1915, he went for his training to Yarmouth and Newbury, and embarked for France in the following year. After being in action in the Somme and Ypres sectors he was transferred to Italy, and fought on the Piave and in other actions on that front. Completing his service in that country, he was demobilised in March 1919, and holds the General Service and Victory Medals.
30, Liz Street, Northampton. Z1583.

O

OAKENFULL, S., Sergt., Duke of Cornwall's L.I.
Serving in China at the outbreak of war, he embarked at once for France, and fought in the Battles of the Marne, the Aisne, La Bassée and Ypres (I.). Later, in 1915, he was severely wounded near Ypres, and sent into hospital at Brighton, where he suffered the loss of an eye, and was eventually discharged, after 17 years' service, in October 1919. He holds the 1914 Star, and the General Service and Victory Medals.
26, Upper Harding Street, Northampton. Z1584.

ODAMS, J., L/Corporal, 2nd Northants. Regt.
He volunteered in December 1915, and after a period of training was drafted to France in November 1916. He took part in the later stages of the Somme Offensive, but in March 1917 was severely wounded near Albert. After treatment at various hospitals in England and Wales, he was finally discharged as unfit for further service in May 1918. He holds the General Service and Victory Medals.
42, Gray Street, Northampton. Z1585.

ODEA, J. J., Gunner, Royal Garrison Artillery.
Having joined in 1916, he proceeded to France in the same year, where he took part in many important engagements. He was in action with his Battery at the Battles of Vimy Ridge, the Somme, Ypres, Cambrai and many minor engagements. After the cessation of hostilities he returned home, and was demobilised in March 1919, holding the General Service and Victory Medals.
167, St. Edmund's Road, Northampton. Z1987.

OGDEN, A. G., Private, 23rd Middlesex Regiment.
Volunteering in January 1916, he proceeded to France in the following month, and saw heavy fighting in the Ypres sector, where he was severely wounded in April. After being invalided to a hospital in Stoke, he remained under treatment for nine months, and was eventually discharged as unfit for further service in May 1918. He holds the General Service and Victory Medals.
30, Herbert Street, Northampton. Z1586.

OGDEN, L. H., Gunner, Royal Garrison Artillery.
He joined in August 1917, and after undergoing a period of training was retained at various stations on important duties on the anti-aircraft guns. He was not successful in obtaining his transfer overseas, but, nevertheless, did much useful work with his Battery until August 1919, when he was demobilised.
15, Hazelwood Road, Northampton. Z2459.

OLIVER, B., Private, Cheshire Regiment.
After volunteering in September 1914, he underwent a period of training prior to being drafted to the Western Front. There he took part in the Battles of the Somme and Cambrai and many other engagements before being transferred to Italy, where he was again in action. He was wounded whilst overseas, and was demobilised on his return home in 1919, holding the General Service and Victory Medals.
24, Alma Street, Northampton. Z3116.

OLIVER, G., Guardsman, Grenadier Guards.
He joined in March 1917, and after being sent for training to Lowestoft, was drafted to France in August 1918, and saw much heavy fighting during the victorious Advance of that Autumn. On October 10th he gave his life for King and Country, dying a soldier's death in the Field. He was entitled to the General Service and Victory Medals.
"And doubtless he went in splendid company."
50, Crispin Street, Northampton. Z1587/A.

OLIVER, G. T., Private, 7th Northants. Regiment.
He volunteered in October 1914, at the age of 15 years, and after his training was retained on important duties in England until February 1918, and then proceeded to the Western Front, where he saw much severe fighting on the Somme. He was unhappily killed whilst carrying a message to Headquarters on March 21st, 1918, after only a few weeks' active service. He was entitled to the General Service and Victory Medals.
"Honour to the immortal dead who gave their youth that the world might grow old in peace."
29, Sunderland Street, Northampton. Z2460.

OLIVER, J. T., Private, 7th Northants. Regiment.
He joined in May 1916, and after training at Dovercourt, proceeded to France in June 1917. He at once saw heavy fighting on the Somme front, and died a valiant soldier's death in that region in the month of July. He was entitled to the General Service and Victory Medals.
"Whilst we remember, the sacrifice is not in vain."
50, Crispin Street, Northampton. Z1587/D.

OLIVER, O. J. C., Driver, R.A.S.C. (M.T.)
He volunteered in October 1915, and, after a short training at Aldershot, was sent to France in December, and did good work whilst engaged on supply duties in the Ypres, Loos and Arras sectors, conveying ammunition and foodstuffs to the front line. He carried on this important and often dangerous duty throughout the rest of the campaign, and, demobilised in March 1919, holds the 1914–15 Star, and the General Service and Victory Medals.
50, Crispin Street, Northampton. Z1587/B.

OLIVER, P. O., Gunner, Royal Horse Artillery.
Joining in February 1917, he was drafted to Egypt in the same month, and saw service on the Palestine front, being in action at the Gaza battles, in the victorious Advance to Jerusalem, the capture of Jericho, and the Offensive under General Allenby. Completing his service on that front, he was finally demobilised in September 1919, and holds the General Service and Victory Medals. 50, Crispin Street, Northampton. Z1587/C.

OLIVER, W., Private, 4th Northants. Regiment.
Having previously served for 12 years with the Territorial Forces, he was mobilised in August 1914, but was retained on important duties at home until 1917, when he was sent to France. There he was in action in the Somme and at Albert, but was taken prisoner whilst fighting at the Dunes in July 1917. He was invalided out of the Army when released from captivity in May 1919, and holds the General Service and Victory Medals. 5, Abbey Street, Northampton. Z2798.

OLIVER, W. E., Pte., Queen's (R.W. Surrey Regt.)
He attested under the Derby Scheme in 1915, but was retained on important work on the railways until called up in April 1918. In October of that year he proceeded to France, where he fought in the final stages of the Advance, and was later sent with the Army of Occupation to Cologne. He was demobilised on returning home in March 1919, and holds the General Service and Victory Medals.
Lower Heyford, Weedon, Northants. Z3453.

ONLEY, F., L/Corporal, Northants. Regiment.
Mobilised from the Reserve at the outbreak of war, he embarked for France early in September 1914, and fought in the last stages of the Retreat from Mons and the Battles of the Marne, the Aisne and Ypres (I.). In this last action he was severely wounded, and, after being admitted to hospital at Oxford, was finally discharged on account of his wounds in October 1915. He holds the Mons Star, and the General Service and Victory Medals.
7, Oakley Street, Northampton. Z1588.

ONLEY, W. H., Private, R.A.O.C.
Joining in September 1916, he received training at Tidworth on Salisbury Plain, and in August 1917 was sent to Mesopotamia, where he rendered valuable services at the advance Base at Baghdad as storeman for the remainder of the campaign. Continuing his duties at that place, he was not demobilised until April 1920, and holds the General Service and Victory Medals.
5, Monarch Road, Northampton. Z1555/B.

ORME, A. W., Private, R.A.O.C.
Four months after joining in April 1917 he was drafted to the Western Front, where he rendered valuable services at the Ordnance Depôt, Calais, for a year. He was then sent to Arquata in Italy, and did splendid work there until he returned home for demobilisation in July 1919. He holds the General Service and Victory Medals.
39, Gordon Street, Northampton. Z1589.

ORTON, J., Private, 10th Queen's Own (Royal West Kent Regiment).
Joining in December 1917, he was sent for his training to Felixstowe, and drafted to France in the following April. He was repeatedly in action during the Advance of 1918, notably at St. Quentin and Amiens, and was wounded on October 25th, shortly before the Armistice, but was not sent to England until February 1919. Demobilised in the next month, he holds the General Service and Victory Medals.
7, Bath Square, Northampton. Z1590.

OSBORN, J. (jun.), Private, 10th Hants. Regiment.
Volunteering in August 1914, he was drafted to Gallipoli in April of the following year, and there, after taking part in the landing at Cape Helles, saw much severe fighting, especially at Suvla Bay. He was afterwards transferred to Salonika, but, severely wounded in 1916, was sent home, and in September of that year invalided from the Army. He holds the 1914–15 Star, and the General Service and Victory Medals.
53, Melbourne Street, Northampton. Z2236/A.

OSBORN, T., Corporal, Northants. Regiment.
Volunteering in August 1914 in the 3rd Bedfordshire Regiment, he was retained in England on important duties as a Drill Instructor until 1916, and then proceeded to France. There he took part in many important engagements, including the Battle of the Somme, until sent home in 1918 suffering from shell-shock. He was invalided from the Army in May of that year, and holds the General Service and Victory Medals.
53, Melbourne Street, Northampton. Z2236/C.

OSBORN, J. (sen.), Private, Machine Gun Corps.
He volunteered in November 1915, and after his training served at various stations, where he was engaged on important duties with the 3rd Bedfordshire Regiment, and later the Machine Gun Corps. He was unable to obtain his transfer to a theatre of war, but, nevertheless, rendered valuable services until his demobilisation in December 1919.
53, Melbourne Street, Northampton. Z2236/B.

OSBORN, W., Private, 23rd Middlesex Regiment.
He joined in February 1917, and three months later proceeded to France, but in June of the same year was wounded at Messines and invalided home. After a period of hospital treatment, he returned to the Western Front, and gave his life for King and Country at Ypres on March 8th, 1918. He was entitled to the General Service and Victory Medals.
"A costly sacrifice upon the altar of freedom."
11, William Street, Northampton. Z1593.

OSBORN, W., Pioneer, Royal Engineers.
He joined the Royal Engineers in June 1916, but was transferred to the 1/4th South Lancashire Regiment, and in December of that year drafted to the Western Front. There he took part in the Battles of Ypres, Passchendaele, Cambrai, the Somme and Armentières and other engagements, and fought also in the Retreat and Advance of 1918. Demobilised in February 1919, he holds the General Service and Victory Medals.
The Wharf, Bugbrooke, Northants. Z3454.

OSBORN, W. A., Private, 4th Middlesex Regiment.
Volunteering in February 1916, he sailed for France in the next month, and saw heavy fighting on the Somme and Ypres fronts, being wounded near Messines in June of that year. In March 1917 he made the great sacrifice in the cause of freedom, dying gloriously in the Field at Ypres, and was entitled to the General Service and Victory Medals.
"His life for his Country."
90, Milton Street, Northampton. Z1591/B.

OSBORNE, A., Rifleman, Rifle Brigade.
Joining in May 1916, he completed a period of training, but was later found to be medically unfit for transfer overseas. He was therefore retained on important guard and other duties with his unit, and rendered excellent services until demobilised in September 1919.
59, Derby Street, Northampton. Z1988.

OSBORNE, A. H., C.S.M., K.O. (Y.L.I.)
Mobilised in August 1914, he quickly proceeded to France, and fought at Mons. He also served with distinction at the Battles of the Marne, the Aisne, La Bassée, Ypres, Hill 60, Loos, the Somme, Arras, Messines and Cambrai, and was twice wounded. Wounded for the third time in March 1918, he was then taken prisoner and interned on the Baltic coast. He was repatriated and discharged in 1919, holding the Mons Star, and the General Service and Victory Medals.
10, Dover Street, Northampton. Z1592/A.

OSBORNE, H. G., Private, 2nd Beds. Regiment.
Already serving in the Army, he was mobilised at the outbreak of hostilities and immediately drafted to the Western Front, where he took part in the Retreat from Mons, and also in the Battles of Ypres and Loos. He was wounded in August 1916, and as a result was invalided home and eventually discharged as medically unfit for further service in August 1917, holding the Mons Star, and the General Service and Victory Medals.
100, Scarletwell Street, Northampton. Z1124/B.

OSBORNE, W., L/Corporal, 8th Somerset L.I.
He volunteered in November 1915, and early in the following year was drafted to the Western Front. Whilst overseas he took part in the Battles of Ypres, Cambrai and the Somme, and other notable engagements, but was unhappily killed during a bombing raid on Cambrai on October 8th, 1918. He was entitled to the General Service and Victory Medals.
"A costly sacrifice upon the altar of freedom."
Chapel Yard, Wootton, Northants. Z2799.

OST, H., Private, Northamptonshire Regiment.
He volunteered in August 1914, and, after training with the Royal Army Service Corps, was drafted in 1916 to the Western Front with the Machine Gun Corps. There he took part in important engagements in the Somme and other sectors, was wounded in 1916, and was later gassed and invalided home. He was then retained in England with the Northamptonsnire Regiment until demobilised in March 1919, holding the General Service and Victory Medals.
66, Great Russell Street, Northampton. Z3455.

OUGHTON, T., Private, 2nd Northants. Regiment.
Joining in February 1916, he was drafted to the Western Front in August of that year, and there saw severe fighting in various sectors. He took part in the Battles of the Somme, Arras, Ypres and Cambrai, and many minor engagements and served also through the Retreat and Advance of 1918. He was demobilised in October 1919, and holds the General Service and Victory Medals.
83, Delapré Street, Northampton. Z3230/C.

OWEN, A. W., Private, Devonshire Regiment.
He volunteered in the Devonshire Regiment in September 1915, and, after a course of training, was ordered to the Western Front in the following year. Being medically unfit for actual fighting, he was transferred to the Labour Corps and engaged on important duties behind the lines, rendering valuable services in the postal section and in the construction of roads until the cessation of hostilities. Demobilised in August 1919, he holds the General Service and Victory Medals.
Castlethorpe, Stony Stratford, Bucks. Z2800.

OWEN, W. A., Private, 6th Northants. Regiment.
Volunteering in November 1914, he was sent to Tring for training, and embarked for France in the following February. He served on the Ypres, Loos, Somme and Arras fronts, but was wounded and taken prisoner in November 1917 at Cambrai. After a year's captivity in Germany he was, on repatriation, demobilised in May 1919, and holds the 1914–15 Star, and the General Service and Victory Medals.
1st House, 4th Block, Naseby Street, Northampton. Z1594

P

PACEY, B., Air Mechanic, Royal Air Force.
He joined in May 1916, and after completing a term of training was retained at various stations, where he was engaged on important transport duties. Being medically unfit for active service, he was unable to obtain his transfer overseas, but, nevertheless, rendered valuable services with his Squadron until his demobilisation in March 1919.
Stoke Road, Blisworth. Z2237/B.

PACEY, B. L., Private, Middlesex Regiment.
Shortly after joining in June 1916, he was sent to France, where he saw severe fighting in various sectors of the front. He took part in the Battle of the Somme and many minor engagements until sent home in 1917, and transferred to Class W of the Reserve. He was then engaged on munition work until demobilised in March 1919, and holds the General Service and Victory Medals. Near Chapel, Blisworth. Z2237/C.

PACEY, W., Air Mechanic, Royal Air Force.
He joined in September 1918, and after a period of training was engaged on important transport duties at various stations. He was not successful in obtaining his transfer to a theatre of war on account of his age, but did much useful work with his Squadron until January 1919, when he was demobilised.
Stoke Road, Blisworth. Z2237/A.

PACKE, A. E., A.B., Royal Naval Division.
He joined in January 1917, and in February of the following year was drafted to the Western Front with the "Hood" Battalion of the Royal Naval Division. There, after taking part in the Battles of the Somme and Cambrai and other engagements, he was severely wounded and gassed, and sent home in September 1918. He was demobilised in February 1919, and holds the General Service and Victory Medals.
34, Spencer Street, Northampton. Z3117.

PACKER, C., Gunner, Royal Garrison Artillery.
He joined in November 1916, and in June of the following year was drafted to the Western Front, where he saw much heavy fighting. After taking part in the Battles of Passchendaele, Lens and Cambrai, he was sent home in November 1917, suffering from shell-shock, and was finally invalided from the Army in September of the following year. He holds the General Service and Victory Medals.
Murcott, Long Buckby, Northants. Z3456/A.

PACKER, H., Private, Northants. Regiment.
He joined in June 1917, and in March of the following year proceeded to France, where he saw severe fighting in various sectors of the front. He took part in the second Battle of the Somme and many other engagements in the Retreat and Advance of 1918, and was gassed and wounded at Cambrai in October of that year. Demobilised in November 1919, he holds the General Service and Victory Medals.
Murcott, Long Buckby, Northants. Z3456/B.

PAGE, J., Sergeant, 6th Northants. Regiment.
Volunteering in September 1914, he was drafted to France in January of the following year, and there saw heavy fighting in various sectors of the front. After taking a prominent part in many important engagements, he was severely wounded at Trônes Wood in the Somme Offensive of July 1917, and admitted to hospital at Chatham. Invalided from the Army in June 1917, he holds the 1914–15 Star, and the General Service and Victory Medals.
24, Leicester Street, Northampton. Z1595.

PAGE, J. J., L/Corporal, East Yorkshire Regt.
He volunteered in November 1915, and, completing his training in the following year, was drafted to France, where he saw much fighting in the Ypres and Cambrai sectors. After being twice wounded he was invalided home, but on his recovery returned to France, and took part in engagements at Cambrai, Havrincourt and in the Advance of 1918. Demobilised in February 1919, he holds the General Service and Victory Medals.
26, Hunter Street, Northampton. Z2310/B.

PAINTER, H. G., Corporal, Queen's (Royal West Surrey Regiment).
He joined on attaining military age in September 1917, and in April of the following year was sent to the Western Front, where he saw much heavy fighting. After taking part in many important engagements he was invalided home in September 1918, suffering from trench fever, and was retained in England until his demobilisation in October 1919. He holds the General Service and Victory Medals.
Mill Hill, Long Buckby, Northants. Z3377/C.

PAINTER, S. F. (M.M.), 2nd Lieutenant, R.F.A.
He volunteered in the Ranks in January 1916, and in the following August proceeded to the Western Front, where he fought with distinction in the Battles of Arras, Vimy Ridge, Messines and St. Quentin, and many other engagements, and was gassed. He returned home in May 1918 in order to train for a commission. He was awarded the Military Medal for conspicuous bravery in carrying a message under heavy fire at Ypres, and, holding also the General Service and Victory Medals, was demobilised in January 1919.
Mill Hill, Long Buckby, Northants. Z3377/A.

PALLETT, A. I., Driver, Royal Field Artillery.
After joining in May 1917 he landed in France two months later, and took part in many important engagements. He was in action with his Battery during heavy fighting on the Ypres, Passchendaele and Cambrai fronts. Invalided to hospital in London, he underwent a period of treatment, and was discharged in May 1918. On March 24th, 1919, he unfortunately died from the effects of his service, and was entitled to the General Service and Victory Medals.
"Steals on the ear the distant triumph song."
27, Regent's Street, Northampton. Z1057/B.

PALLETT, W. C., Private, R.A.S.C.
He volunteered in 1914, and after undergoing a period of training was retained at various stations, where he was engaged on duties of great importance. Owing to ill-health he was unable to obtain his transfer overseas, but, nevertheless, rendered valuable services until finally demobilised late in 1918.
2, Henley Street, Far Cotton, Northampton. Z3457.

PALMER, J. A., Stoker, Royal Navy.
Already in the Navy when war was declared in August 1914, he afterwards served in H.M.S. "Defence," attached to the Grand Fleet in the North Sea on patrol and convoy duties, and also took part in actions with the "Goeben" in the Mediterranean. He unhappily lost his life when his ship was sunk in the Battle of Jutland on May 31st, 1916. He was entitled to the 1914–15 Star, and the General Service and Victory Medals.
"His life for his Country, his soul to God."
41, Essex Street, Northampton. Z1596.

PALMER, H., Private, 1st Northants. Regiment.
Called up from the Reserve in August 1914, he was immediately drafted to the Western Front, where he fought in the Retreat from Mons. He also took part in the Battles of the Marne, the Aisne, Ypres, the Somme and Cambrai, served through the Retreat and Advance of 1918, and was twice wounded. He holds the Mons Star, and the General Service and Victory Medals, and in 1921 was serving in Ireland.
6, Alpha Street, Northampton. Z1597/B.

PANCOUST, A., Guardsman, Coldstream Guards.
Three months after volunteering in August 1914 he was sent to the Western Front, but, wounded in action in December 1914, was admitted to hospital in England. Returning to France in September of the following year, he took part in the Battles of Loos, the Somme, Arras, Vimy Ridge and Cambrai, and was again wounded in November 1917, and sent home. Finally demobilised in March 1919, he holds the 1914 Star, and the General Service and Victory Medals.
36, Marlborough Road, Northampton. Z2461/C.

PANCOUST, ELSIE, Special War Worker.
During the period of hostilities this lady offered her services to the Y.M.C.A. at Northampton, where she was employed on very responsible work, rendering valuable services until her discharge in August 1917. She was afterwards engaged on other work of National importance until June of the following year. 47, Roe Road, Northampton. Z2462—2371/C.

PANCOUST, H. S., Corporal, Coldstream Guards.
He volunteered in April 1915, and in June of the following year was drafted to the Western Front, where he saw much severe fighting in the Arras sector. He made the supreme sacrifice, falling in action at Ginchy in September 1916, and was entitled to the General Service and Victory Medals.
"A valiant Soldier, with undaunted heart he breasted life's last hill."
47, Roe Road, Northampton. Z2462—2371/B.

PANCOUST, J., Private, 1st Northants. Regiment.
He joined the Army in 1913, and when war broke out in August 1914 was immediately drafted to France, where he took part in the Retreat from Mons and the Battles of the Marne, the Aisne and La Bassée. He made the supreme sacrifice, being killed in action at the Battle of Ypres in November 1914, and was entitled to the Mons Star and the General Service and Victory Medals.
"A costly sacrifice upon the altar of freedom."
36, Marlborough Road, Northampton. Z2461/B.

PANKHURST, W. W., Private, Northants. Regt.
Volunteering in November 1914, he later proceeded to Egypt, but eventually advanced into Palestine. There he was in action at the three Battles of Gaza, and was present at the capture of Jerusalem and other important engagements with General Allenby's Forces. He was wounded on two occasions, and in May 1919 was demobilised, holding the 1914–15 Star, and the General Service and Victory Medals.
6, Portland Street, Northampton. Z1373/A.

PANTER, A., Corporal, 7th Northants. Regiment.
Six months after volunteering in May 1915 he proceeded to the scene of activities in France. On that front he saw much service in the Battles of Loos, the Somme and Ypres, and gave his life for the freedom of England on April 17th, 1917, at Arras. He was entitled to the 1914–15 Star, and the General Service and Victory Medals.
"He passed out of the sight of men by the path of duty and self-sacrifice."
43, Abbey Street, Northampton. Z2653/A.

PANTER, W. J., Private, 2nd Northants. Regt.
He volunteered in December 1914, and, completing his training in the following January, was drafted to France. Whilst in this theatre of war he took part in much heavy fighting in the Ypres, Arras and Vimy Ridge sectors, and was wounded in action. As a result he was invalided home, but, on his recovery, he was retained at various stations on important duties. Demobilised in January 1919, he holds the 1914–15 Star, and the General Service and Victory Medals.
63, Byfield Road, Northampton. Z2463.

PANTLING, J., Private, 2nd Northants. Regiment.
Mobilised in August 1914, he quickly proceeded to France, where he took part in the Battle of Mons and the subsequent Retreat. He also fought in the Battles of the Marne, the Aisne and La Bassée, and other engagements, was three times wounded—at Ypres in November 1914, on the Somme in March 1916, and in April of the following year—and was gassed on the Somme in March 1918. Discharged in March 1919, he holds the Mons Star, and the General Service and Victory Medals.
13, Lower Cross Street, Northampton. Z1598.

PANTLING, J. S., Private, 3rd Northants. Regt.
Mobilised in August 1914, he was immediately drafted to France, where he played a distinguished part in the Battles of Mons, Ypres, La Bassée, Loos, the Somme, Arras and Cambrai, and was wounded three times. He was mentioned in Despatches for good work on the Field, and was eventually discharged in February 1919. He holds the Mons Star, and the General Service and Victory Medals.
11, St. Andrew's Place, Northampton. Z1020/D.

PARBERY, D., Private, 7th Oxford. & Bucks. L.I.
He volunteered in September 1914, and in the following year was drafted to Salonika, where he saw much severe fighting. He took part in many important engagements on the Macedonian front, and whilst in this seat of operations sustained a broken leg. He was finally demobilised on returning home in March 1919, and holds the 1914–15 Star, and the General Service and Victory Medals.
32, Leicester Street, Northampton. Z1319/A.

PARBERY, E., Private, 3rd Northants. Regt.
Having volunteered in June 1915, he was drafted overseas in the following year. Whilst on the Egyptian front he took part in several important engagements, and was also employed on special duties. After hostilities ceased he returned home and was demobilised in August 1919, holding the General Service and Victory Medals.
32, Leicester Street, Northampton. Z1319/B.

PARBERY, J., Private, 1/5th King's Own (Royal Lancaster Regiment).
He joined in May 1916, and after a period of training with the 10th Royal Sussex Regiment was drafted in January of the following year to the Western Front, and there took part in the Battle of Arras. He died gloriously on the Field of Battle at Ypres on August 3rd, 1917, and was entitled to the General Service and Victory Medals.
"Whilst we remember, the sacrifice is not in vain."
37, Bective Road, Kingsthorpe, Northampton. Z1599.

PARISH, A. J., Private, 53rd Queen's (Royal West Surrey Regiment).
He enlisted in June 1918, and underwent a period of training at Cromer. After the cessation of hostilities he proceeded to Germany with the Army of Occupation, and rendered valuable services at Cologne whilst engaged on important duties until his demobilisation in March 1920.
17, Artizan Road, Northampton. Z2238.

PARISH, E. G., Private, Northants. Dragoons.
He volunteered in October 1914, and in the following April was drafted to France, where he took part in several engagements, including the Battles of Ypres, Festubert, Loos, the Somme and Arras. Later he proceeded to Italy, and saw much fighting on the Piave River and Asiago Plateaux. He returned home and was demobilised in March 1919, holding the 1914–15 Star, and the General Service and Victory Medals.
Roade, Northampton. Z2183/B.

PARISH, F., Private, Bedfordshire Regiment.
He enlisted in March 1917, and after a period of training was drafted to France, where he took part in many engagements, and was wounded in action. On his recovery he was sent to Italy, and there saw much heavy fighting until the cessation of hostilities. Demobilised in September 1919, he holds the General Service and Victory Medals.
13, New Town Road, Northampton. Z1989.

PARISH, F. W., Private, Labour Corps.
He joined the Royal Fusiliers in April 1916, and a month later was sent to France, and subsequently transferred to the Labour Corps. Whilst on the Western Front he was present at the Battles of the Somme, Arras and Cambrai, served in the Retreat and Advance of 1918, and was gassed on one occasion. He was demobilised on his return to England in March 1919, and holds the General Service and Victory Medals.
3, St. James' Place, Northampton. Z2801.

PARKER, E. C., Private, 1/4th Northants. Regt.
He volunteered in August 1915, and in March of the following year was sent to Palestine, where he saw much severe fighting. He took part in the Battles of Siwa, Rafa and Gaza, and many other important engagements, was present also at the fall of Jerusalem, and was twice wounded. Demobilised on returning home in September 1919, he holds the General Service and Victory Medals. 50, Castle Street, Northampton. Z1601.

PARKER, E. T., Private, 1st Northants. Regiment.
Mobilised in August 1914, he was retained on important duties in England until November of the following year, when he was drafted to France. After taking part in the Battles of the Somme, Arras and Passchendaele he was sent home, suffering from trench fever, but rejoined his unit, however, later in 1917 and fought at Ypres. Invalided from the Army in March 1919, he holds the 1914–15 Star, and the General Service and Victory Medals.
35, Upper Harding Street, Northampton. Z1602.

PARKER, F. E., Private, 5th Northants. Regt.
He volunteered in August 1914, and in May of the following year proceeded to the Western Front, where, after taking part in the Battles of Ypres and Loos, he was wounded at Givenchy in December 1915, and sent home. Returning to France on his recovery, he was again wounded and gassed at Guillemont in July 1916, and admitted to hospital at Birmingham. He was invalided from the Army in March 1917, and holds the 1914–15 Star, and the General Service and Victory Medals.
4, Todd's Lane, Northampton. Z1600.

PARKER, H. C., Pte., 6th Oxford. and Bucks. L.I.
Volunteering in September 1914, he was sent to the Western Front in July of the following year and there fought in various sectors. After taking part in the Battles of Loos, the Somme and Ypres, he was wounded at Langemarck in September 1917, and sent to hospital at the Base. In January of the following year he was transferred to the Royal Air Force, and was finally demobilised in April 1919, holding the 1914–15 Star, and the General Service and Victory Medals.
4, St. Katherine's Street, Northampton. Z3458.

PARKER, J. W., Petty Officer, Royal Navy.
He joined the Royal Navy in July 1909, and when war broke out in August 1914 quickly proceeded to the North Sea on board H.M.S. "Cochrane." He took part in the Battle of Jutland, in several minor operations, and also saw much service in other waters throughout hostilities. In 1921 he was still at sea completing twelve years' service, and holds the 1914–15 Star, and the General Service and Victory Medals.
70, Purser Road, Northampton. Z2060/A.

PARKINSON, H., Bombardier, R.G.A.
Five months after volunteering in October 1915 he proceeded to France, where he saw severe fighting in various sectors of the front. He took part in the Battles of Albert, the Somme, Arras, Messines, Ypres, Passchendaele, Cambrai and Le Cateau, and many other engagements, and fought also in the Retreat and Advance of 1918. Demobilised in July 1919, he holds the General Service and Victory Medals.
Lower Heyford, Weedon, Northants. Z3459/A.

PARKINSON, T., Private, 7th Leicestershire Regt.
Joining the 3rd Northamptonshire Regiment in April 1917, he was drafted to the Western Front with the 7th Leicestershire Regiment in March of the following year, and there took part in the Battle of the Somme and minor engagements in the final Retreat. He died gloriously on the Field of Battle on May 26th, 1918, after only two months' active service, and was entitled to the General Service and Victory Medals.
"He nobly fell that we might live."
Lower Heyford, Weedon, Northampton. Z3459/B.

PARRISH, H. J., Pioneer, Royal Engineers.
Mobilised in August 1914, he served with the Northamptonshire Regiment, but was later transferred to the Royal Engineers, and was retained on important duties at home until drafted to France in 1917. He was engaged in fierce fighting in the Ypres sector, and was gassed at Passchendaele in 1918, and sent to hospital in England. In November 1918 he was invalided out of the Army, holding the General Service and Victory Medals.
Water Lane, Wootton, Northants. Z2802.

PARRY, S., Private, 7th Northants. Regiment.
He joined in April 1916, and twelve months later proceeded to the Western Front, where he served as a signaller in various sectors and took part in the Battles of Ypres and St. Quentin, and other engagements. He fell fighting on March 27th, 1918, during the Allies' Retreat, and was entitled to the General Service and Victory Medals.
"He nobly fell that we might live."
35, Gray Street, Northampton. Z1603.

PARSONS, C., Sergeant, R.A.S.C.
He volunteered in February 1915, and in the following month proceeded to the Western Front, where he served with a Supply Column in various sectors. He was present at the Battles of Ypres, Loos, Vimy Ridge, the Somme, Arras, Bullecourt, Messines and Cambrai, and minor engagements until transferred in November 1917 to Italy, where he served on the Piave and Asiago Plateaux. Demobilised in February 1919, he holds the 1914–15 Star, and the General Service and Victory Medals. 90, Cyril Street, Northampton. Z3460.

PARTRIDGE, B. C., Private, 1st Northants. Regt.
Having previously served in the Army for 18 years, he volunteered in April 1915, and was engaged at Weymouth during his training. He unfortunately strained his heart, and as a result was discharged in September 1915. He died through the effects of his service on May 5th, 1916.
"His memory is cherished with pride."
42, Arthur Street, Kingsthorpe Hollow, Northampton.
Z1270/B.

PARTRIDGE, H., Rifleman, K.R.R.C.
He joined in May 1917, and in March of the following year proceeded to the Western Front, where he saw much heavy fighting. After taking part in many important engagements, he was severely wounded at Ypres in October 1918, and admitted to hospital in England. He was finally invalided from the Army in June 1920, and holds the General Service and Victory Medals. West Street, Long Buckby, Northants. Z3463.

PARTRIDGE, W., L/Corporal, 18th K.R.R.C.
Mobilised in August 1914, he was quickly drafted with the Royal Army Service Corps to the Western Front, where he fought in the Battle of Mons. He also took part in the Battles of the Marne, the Aisne and Ypres, and other engagements until transferred to Italy in January 1918. Returning to France in the following month, he was taken prisoner during the Retreat and, released on the cessation of hostilities, was discharged in January 1919, holding the Mons Star, and the General Service and Victory Medals.
23, Henley Street, Northampton. Z3461.

PARTRIDGE, W. J., Gunner, R.G.A.
Mobilised in August 1914, he proceeded a month later to France, and fought in the Retreat from Mons. He was wounded at the Battle of the Marne, and on his recovery was in action in engagements at Loos, the Somme, Arras and Cambrai. During the Retreat in March 1918 he was again wounded and invalided to England. He was still serving in 1920, and holds the Mons Star, and the General Service and Victory Medals.
12, Adnitt Place, Northampton. Z2803.

PASCOE, E. J. (M.M.), Sergeant, 1/4th Northants. Regiment.
Volunteering in September 1914, he proceeded to Gallipoli in July of the following year and was wounded at the Landing at Suvla Bay. After the Evacuation of the Peninsula he was transferred to Egypt, whence he advanced into Palestine and was again wounded in the second and third Battles of Gaza. He was awarded the Military Medal for conspicuous bravery in the Field there in November 1917, and, holding also the 1914–15 Star, and the General Service and Victory Medals, was invalided from the Army in May 1918.
16, St. John's Place, Northampton. Z3118.

PASSMORE, C. P., Staff-Sergeant, 1st Northants. Regiment.
He was mobilised with the Territorials in August 1914, and, completing his training in the following year, was drafted to Salonika. In this seat of operations he took a prominent part in several engagements on the Vardar, Struma and Doiran fronts. He returned home and was demobilised in February 1919, holding the General Service and Victory Medals.
22, Adelaide Street, Northampton. Z1165/B.

PATCHING, F., Bombardier, R.F.A.
He enlisted in May 1914, and twelve months later proceeded to the Western Front, where he took part in the Battle of Loos, before being transferred to Salonika. There he saw much severe fighting on the Doiran front, where he was wounded in September 1917, but in 1918 returned to France in time to serve through the Retreat and Advance. He was discharged in May 1919, and holds the 1914–15 Star, and the General Service and Victory Medals.
11, St. James' Square, Northampton. Z3119.

PATEMAN, B. I., Guardsman, 4th Grenadier Gds.
Shortly after volunteering in September 1914 he proceeded to the Western Front, where he saw severe fighting in various sectors. He took part in the Battles of La Bassée, Ypres, Loos, Vimy Ridge, the Somme and Cambrai, and many other engagements, and was wounded in action. Demobilised in September 1920, he holds the 1914 Star, and the General Service and Victory Medals.
Newland Street, Brixworth, Northants. Z3120.

PATEMAN, E. A., Private, R.A.S.C. (H.T.)
He volunteered in November 1915, and, after completing a brief term of training, was retained at various stations on important duties as a shoeing-smith, in which capacity he did much useful work. Owing to ill-health, however, he was discharged in February 1916, as medically unfit for further service.
Spratton, Northants. Z3121.

PATRICK, F. W., Private, 1st Northants. Regt.
He joined in September 1917, and after undergoing a period of training was retained at various stations on duties of a highly important nature. Unable on account of ill-health to obtain his transfer to a theatre of war, he, nevertheless, rendered valuable services with his unit until his demobilisation in September 1919.
118, Scarletwell Street, Northampton. Z1604.

PATTISON, F., Pte., 16th (The Queen's) Lancers.
Volunteering in November 1915, he was retained for a time on important duties before proceeding to France in November 1917. In this theatre of war he took part in much heavy fighting at Cambrai, Bourlon Wood and in the Advance of 1918. He also served with the Tank Corps and Bedfordshire Lancers, and was eventually demobilised in January 1919. He holds the General Service and Victory Medals.
39, Monks Park Road, Northampton. Z2239.

PATTISON, G. I. B., Private, 4th Northants. Regt.
He volunteered in October 1914, but was retained on important duties at home until August 1916, when he obtained a transfer overseas. After only two months' service on the Western Front he gave his life for King and Country, and was entitled to the General Service and Victory Medals.
"He died the noblest death a man may die,
Fighting for God and right and liberty."
40, Baring Road, Northampton. Z2804.

PAXTON, A. G., Private, 5th Royal Inniskilling Fusiliers.
He volunteered in August 1914 at the age of 17, and after completing his training in May 1916, was drafted to France, where he took part in much fighting on the Somme, and was wounded. As a result he was invalided home, but on his recovery was transferred to Salonika, and was in action on the Struma front. Later he proceeded to Egypt, thence into Palestine, and in 1918 returned to France. He fought at Cambrai, but was again wounded and invalided home, being eventually discharged on account of wounds in January 1919. He holds the General Service and Victory Medals.
High Street, Blisworth, Northampton. Z2240.

PAXTON, W. J., Gunner, Royal Garrison Artillery.
Joining in May 1916, he proceeded to the Western Front in the following August, and there took part in the Battles of the Somme, Arras, Vimy Ridge and Ypres, and minor engagements. Invalided from the Army suffering from tuberculosis in November 1917, he unhappily died on February 11th, 1918, and was entitled to the General Service and Victory Medals.
"Steals on the ear the distant triumph song."
Church End, Bugbrooke, Northants. Z3308/A

PAYNE, A. M., Private, Suffolk Regiment.
He enlisted in April 1916, and early in the following year was drafted to Egypt, thence into Palestine, where he took part in the Battles of Gaza, the fall of Jerusalem and Beersheba. Later he was transferred to France, and was badly wounded in action at the fourth Battle of Ypres in September 1918. As a result he was invalided home, and eventually demobilised in September 1919, holding the General Service and Victory Medals. 114, Abington Avenue, Northampton. Z2241.

PAYNE, C., Private, 1st Northants. Regt. and Royal Army Medical Corps.
He volunteered in April 1915, and two months later was drafted to France, where he fought at La Bassée and Loos, but owing to ill-health was invalided home. On his recovery he returned to France, took part in the Battle of the Somme, and, being wounded in action, was again sent home. In 1917 he once more proceeded to France, and saw much fighting at Arras and Monchy, where he was gassed, and eventually sent to England for treatment. Discharged in May 1919 as medically unfit, he holds the 1914–15 Star, and the General Service and Victory Medals.
47, Adnitt Road, Northampton. Z2242.

PAYNE, E., Private, 1/5th Suffolk Regiment.
Joining in December 1917, he was drafted to Egypt in March of the following year. Subsequently he was sent to Palestine, and whilst serving at Gaza was injured in an accident, and sent to hospital at Alexandria. On his recovery he rejoined his unit, and took part in numerous battles until hostilities ceased. He was demobilised on his return to England in August 1919, and holds the General Service and Victory Medals.
45, Glasgow Road, St. James', Northampton. Z2805.

PAYNE, F. G., Private, Royal Army Medical Corps.
Having enlisted in May 1908, he was serving in Egypt at the outbreak of war, and was immediately drafted to France, where he took part in the Retreat from Mons. He also served through many other important engagements in this theatre of war, and was twice wounded in action. He was discharged in May 1919, holding the Mons Star, and the General Service and Victory Medals.
15, London Road, Daventry, Northants. Z3122.

PAYNE, G. O., Corporal, R.A.S.C. (M.T.)
He volunteered in September 1914, and was immediately drafted to France. In this seat of war he served with the Mechanical Transport Section, and was engaged on important duties in the Ypres, Somme and Arras sectors. He was chiefly employed in driving officers to and from the forward areas and did continuously good work throughout. Demobilised in May 1919, he holds the 1914 Star, and the General Service and Victory Medals.
21, Beaconsfield Terrace, Northampton. Z1462/B

PAYNE, H., Private, 2/4th Queen's (Royal West Surrey Regiment).
He joined in February 1917, and in March of the following year was drafted to Egypt, where he was stationed at Kantara. He also served in Palestine before being transferred in June 1918 to the Western Front, where he saw much severe fighting in the Ypres sector. He afterwards served with the Army of Occupation at Cologne until his demobilisation in September 1919, and holds the General Service and Victory Medals.
7, High Street, Kingsthorpe, Northampton. Z1605

PAYNE, P. G., Gunner, Royal Garrison Artillery.
He volunteered in October 1915, and in the following February was drafted to the Western Front, where he took part in many engagements, including the Battles of Messines, Ypres and Passchendaele. He was reported missing, but later killed in action, on May 27th, 1918, and was entitled to the General Service and Victory Medals.
"His life for his Country, his soul to God."
39, Ash Street, Northampton. Z1351/A—Z1352/A.

PEACOCK, W. S., Private, 1/4th Northants. Regt.
Mobilised in August 1914, he was retained for a time at home before being drafted to France in January 1916. In this theatre of war he took part in the Battles of Ypres and the Somme. Later he was transferred to Salonika, and saw much fighting on the Doiran front, where he was wounded in action. Invalided home, he was eventually discharged in July 1917 as medically unfit for further service, and holds the General Service and Victory Medals. 3, Bath Gardens, Northampton. Z1032/B.

PEARSON, A., Stoker, Royal Navy.
A Reservist, he was called up in August 1914, and was posted to H.M.S. "Leviathan," on board which vessel he was engaged on various important duties. He served chiefly in the Mediterranean Sea, but also cruised off the coasts of Africa and India and in the Persian Gulf. Discharged in February 1919, he holds the 1914–15 Star, and the General Service and Victory Medals. 42, Roe Road, Northampton. Z3123/B.

PEARSON, B. E., Sapper, Royal Engineers.
Volunteering in October 1915, he underwent a period of training and in the same year was drafted to France. Whilst in this seat of operations he took an active part in many important engagements in various sectors of the front and, severely injured in an accident, sustained the loss of a finger. He did consistently good work until discharged in June 1919, holding the 1914–15 Star, and the Genera Service and Victory Medals.
8, Chapel Brampton, Northants. Z3124/A.

PEARSON, E., Stoker, Royal Navy.
Mobilised from the Reserve at the outbreak of war, he was posted to H.M.S. "Dreadnought," in which vessel he saw much active service in the North Sea. He was present at the Battle of Heligoland Bight and later took part in the engagements at the Falkland Islands and the Dogger Bank. He did consistently good work until discharged in March 1919, and holds the 1914–15 Star, and the General Service and Victory Medals. 42, Roe Road, Northampton. Z3123/C.

PEARSON, F., Private, 5th Northants. Regiment.
Volunteering in August 1914, he received his training at Colchester and in the following year was sent to the Western Front There he was in action in numerous important engagements, including the Battles of Ypres, Albert, the Somme, Arras and Cambrai, and was wounded in April 1917 and again in 1918. He was demobilised on his return home in February 1919, and holds the 1914–15 Star, and the General Service and Victory Medals. 18, Castle Street, Northampton. Z2806.

PEARSON, F. H., Sergeant, 6th Northants. Regt.
Volunteering in September 1914, he was first engaged on important duties as a Drill Instructor. Proceeding to France in 1915, he served with distinction in many important engagements in various sectors before being wounded. He was unhappily killed in action in August 1917, near Ypres, and was entitled to the 1914–15 Star, and the General Service and Victory Medals.
"Whilst we remember, the sacrifice is not in vain."
8, Chapel Brampton, Northants. Z3124/B.

PEARSON, J., Private, Norfolk Regiment.
He joined in 1916, and after completing a term of training served at various stations, where he was engaged on duties of great importance. He was medically unfit for active service and was consequently unable to obtain his transfer to the front, but, nevertheless, did useful work with his unit until his demobilisation in 1919.
33, Lower Harding Street, Northampton. Z1608/B.

PEARSON, J., Private, 4th Bedfordshire Regiment.
Shortly after joining in January 1917, he was sent to the Western Fronf, where he saw heavy fighting in various sectors. He took part in the Battles of Cambrai and the Somme and many minor engagements until severely wounded in March 1918, and admitted to hospital at Norwich. He was invalided from the Army in February 1919, and holds the General Service and Victory Medals. 6, Uppingham Street, Northampton. Z1607.

PEARSON, P. G., Private, 1st Bedfordshire Regt.
Having volunteered in April 1915, he was retained in England on important duties with his unit before being drafted to France in the following February. Serving on the Western Front, he was present during heavy fighting in the Ypres and Somme sectors. He made the supreme sacrifice, being killed in action in October 1916, and was entitled to the General Service and Victory Medals.
"His life for his Country, his soul to God."
42, Roe Road, Northampton. Z3123/D.

PEARSON, R. S., Trooper, Bedfordshire Lancers.
Having volunteered in October 1915, he was engaged on important duties in Ireland prior to being drafted to France in July 1916. In this theatre of war he saw much heavy fighting in various sectors. He afterwards proceeded to Egypt, where he took part in several engagements, but later in 1917 returned to the Western Front, where he served until demobilised in March 1919. He holds the General Service and Victory Medals.
42, Roe Road, Northampton. Z3123/A.

PEARSON, R. T., Private, Duke of Cornwall's L.I.
A Reservist, he was called to the Colours in August 1914, and was immediately drafted to the Western Front, where, after serving through the Retreat from Mons, he took part in the Battles of the Marne and the Aisne. He fell in action at La Bassée on October 22nd, 1914, and was entitled to the Mons Star, and the General Service and Victory Medals.
"Whilst we remember, the sacrifice is not in vain."
33, Lower Harding Street, Northampton. Z1608/A.

PEARSON, T., Private, 4th Yorkshire Regiment.
He volunteered in September 1914, and after his training was retained in England until December 1917, when he proceeded to France with the Royal Field Artillery. There he took part in the Battle of the Somme and many minor engagements until severely wounded at Bullecourt and sent home. He served also with the Royal Army Service Corps and Royal Army Veterinary Corps before being invalided from the Army in May 1918, and holds the General Service and Victory Medals.
7, Lincoln Street, Kingsthorpe, Northampton. TZ1606.

PECK, J. W., Private, 1st East Yorkshire Regiment.
He volunteered in May 1915, in the Northamptonshire Regiment, but was later transferred to the East Yorkshire Regiment and proceeded to France. Whilst in this seat of operations he took part in many important engagements, including the Battles of the Somme, Arras, Messines, Ypres and Cambrai. He was also in action in the Retreat of 1918, when he was taken prisoner and held in captivity until January 1919. Demobilised in the following month, he holds the General Service and Victory Medals.
35, Euston Road, Northampton. Z3052/A.

PELL, C. J., Corporal, 13th Yorkshire Regiment.
Called up from the Reserve in August 1914, he quickly proceeded to France, where he fought in the Retreat from Mons, and, after taking part also in the Battles of the Marne, the Aisne and Ypres, was wounded at Givenchy in January 1915. Invalided home, he returned to France, however, in December, and was again wounded on the Somme in July 1916, and sent to England. He afterwards served in North Russia until his discharge in August 1919, and holds the Mons Star, and the General Service and Victory Medals.
18, Monks Pond Street, Northampton. Z1610/C.

PELL, H., Private, 1/4th Northants. Regiment.
Volunteering in October 1914, he was drafted to Gallipoli in April of the following year, and there, after taking part in the Landing at Cape Helles, fought at Chocolate Hill and Suvla Bay. He was afterwards transferred to Egypt and thence to Palestine, where he served in the capture of Jerusalem and was blown up and buried by an explosion in the third Battle of Gaza, and as a result suffered from shell-shock. Demobilised in June 1919, he holds the 1914–15 Star, and the General Service and Victory Medals.
18, Monks Pond Street, Northampton. Z1610/A.

PELL, H. A., Private, 10th Royal Fusiliers.
He volunteered in December 1915, and underwent a period of training prior to being drafted to the Western Front in May 1917. There he took part in the Battles of Arras and Ypres and many other important engagements, and was finally invalided home suffering from dysentery. He also served with the Labour Corps, and in April 1919 was discharged as medically unfit for further service, holding the General Service and Victory Medals. 18, Adelaide St., Northampton. Z1609.

PELL, O. W., Trooper, Northants. Dragoons.
He volunteered in November 1914, and in the following year was drafted to France, where he took part in much fighting in the Ypres and Somme sectors. Later he was transferred to Italy, and was in action on the Piave River and Asiago Plateaux. He was invalided home and eventually discharged in May 1919 as medically unfit, holding the 1914–15 Star, and the General Service and Victory Medals.
The Green, Milton, Northants. Z2464.

PELL, W. G., Private, Queen's (R.W. Surrey Regt.)
He enlisted in February 1917, and later in the same year was drafted overseas. Whilst on the Western Front he took part in several engagements, including the Battles of Cambrai (I.), the Somme (II.), Ypres (IV.) and in heavy fighting during the Retreat and Advance of 1918. He was demobilised in April 1919, and holds the General Service and Victory Medals.
Anchor Terrace, Milton, Northants. Z2465.

PENDERED, T. A., Pte., 1/4th Northants. Regt.
He volunteered in September 1914, and in the following year was drafted to Gallipoli, where he took part in the Landing at Suvla Bay and was severely wounded in action. Sent to hospital at Gibraltar and thence home, he was finally invalided from the Army in April 1917. He holds the 1914–15 Star, and the General Service and Victory Medals.
12, Adelaide Street, Northampton. Z1611/B—Z1612/B.

PENDERED, W., Private, 1/4th Northants. Regt.
He volunteered in July 1915, and in November of the following year proceeded to France, where he saw severe fighting at Loos and in other sectors. Invalided home in 1917, he was drafted in November of that year to Egypt and thence to Palestine, where he took part in the Battles of Jaffa and Haifa. He was demobilised in August 1919, and holds the General Service and Victory Medals.
12, Adelaide Street, Northampton. Z1611/A—Z1612/A.

PENN, A. E., Private, 2nd East Lancashire Regt.
Joining in March 1917, he was sent to France after two months' training and there took part in important engagements in various sectors and was wounded at Ypres in October 1917. He died gloriously on the Field of Battle at Rheims on May 27th, 1918, and was entitled to the General Service and Victory Medals.
"The path of duty was the way to glory."
20, Military Road, Northampton. Z1614.

PENN, C. A., Private, 1/4th Northants. Regiment.
Mobilised from the Reserve in August 1914, he underwent a period of training before proceeding to the Dardanelles. Whilst in this seat of operations he took part in the Landing at Suvla Bay, where he was wounded and evacuated to England. On his recovery he was transferred to France, and was in action in many engagements before being taken prisoner in July 1917. After the conclusion of hostilities he was released from captivity and eventually discharged in August 1919, holding the General Service and Victory Medals.
37, Stanley Street, Northampton. Z1613/A.

PENN, F. G., Private, 3rd Hampshire Regiment.
He enlisted in June 1916, and after completing his training was drafted to France. In this theatre of war he served with his unit in many engagements, and saw much heavy fighting in the Arras, Vimy Ridge and Ypres sectors. He returned home and was demobilised in February 1919, holding the General Service and Victory Medals.
13, Sharman Road, Northampton. Z2466/A.

PENN, G., Rifleman, King's Royal Rifle Corps.
Mobilised at the outbreak of war in August 1914, he was immediately drafted to France, where he was in action during the Retreat from Mons and also at the Battle of Ypres before being wounded. He unfortunately died from the effects of his wounds on November 23rd, 1914, and was entitled to the Mons Star, and the General Service and Victory Medals.
"His life for his Country, his soul to God."
15, Lower Cross Street, Northampton Z1615.

PENN, G. H., Armourer, Royal Air Force.
He joined in June 1917, and underwent a period of training at Blandford before proceeding to France. There he rendered valuable services with his Squadron as an armourer and was engaged on important work examining machine-guns in the Arras, Vimy Ridge and Ypres sectors. Demobilised in December 1919, he holds the General Service and Victory Medals. 13, Sharman Road, Northampton. Z2466/B.

PENN, H., A/Bombardier, Royal Field Artillery.
He joined in September 1916, and after completing a term of training was retained at various stations on duties of a highly important nature. He was not successful in obtaining his transfer to the front on account of ill-health, and was ultimately discharged in December 1917 as medically unfit for further service. Little Houghton, Northants. Z3466.

PENN, J., Private, 13th Essex Regiment.
He joined in June 1918, and on completion of a period of training was drafted to the Western Front shortly after the Armistice was signed in November 1918. Whilst in France he was engaged on various duties of an important nature, which he carried out in a highly efficient manner. Returning to England, he was demobilised in March 1919, after nine months' valuable service. 15, York Place, Northampton. Z2808.

PENN, J. C. W., Private, 4th West Riding Regt.
He joined on attaining military age in August 1918, and after a period of training in Ireland was retained on important duties at various stations. He was unable to obtain his transfer overseas before the cessation of hostilities, but in June 1919 was sent with the 20th Hussars to Egypt, where he served at Tel-el-Kebir. He was demobilised on returning home in May 1920. 55, Thirlestane Rd., Far Cotton, Northampton. Z3464.

PENN, W., Corporal, Rifle Brigade.
Called up from the Reserve at the declaration of war, he was quickly drafted overseas. Serving on the Western Front, he was in action at the Battles of Ypres, Neuve Chapelle, St. Eloi, Loos, Vimy Ridge, Beaumont-Hamel and Arras. He died gloriously on the Field of Battle in August 1917, and was entitled to the 1914–15 Star, and the General Service and Victory Medals.
"And doubtless he went in splendid company."
7, St. James' Place, Northampton. Z3126.

PENN, W. J., Corporal, Royal Army Medical Corps.
Joining in April 1917, he was drafted in July of the same year to Salonika. Whilst in this theatre of war he was engaged on important duties during heavy fighting on the Struma Front. He contracted malarial fever, and as a result was invalided to hospital in Egypt, and thence to England. Finally demobilised in March 1920, he holds the General Service and Victory Medals.
73, Hood Street, Northampton. Z3125.

PENNELL, E., Sergeant, Northants. Regiment.
He enlisted in October 1891, and prior to the outbreak of war in August 1914 he had served in India for ten years. Owing to his being over age for service in a fighting area he was retained on important duties at various stations, and did continuously good work until discharged in March 1917.
6, Military Road, Northampton. Z1616.

PENNY, P., A.B., Royal Navy.
He joined the Royal Navy in 1902, and at the outbreak of war was posted to H.M. submarine "E 42," in which vessel he saw much service in the North Sea, where he was engaged on important patrol duties. Later in 1917 he took part in the destroyer action off Dover, and did continuously good work until discharged in April 1919, holding the 1914–15 Star, and the General Service and Victory Medals.
69, Spencer Street, Northampton. Z3127.

PERCIVAL, J. A., Trooper, Royal Horse Guards.
Volunteering in September 1915, he was drafted overseas on completing a period of training in July of the following year. Whilst on the Western Front he took part in many engagements, including the Battles of Arras, Vimy Ridge, Bullecourt and Cambrai, and also fought in the Retreat and Advance of 1918. He was demobilised in March 1919, and holds the General Service and Victory Medals.
62, Wellington Street, Northampton. Z1938—1866/B.

PERCIVAL, W., Private, 5th Royal Warwick. Regt.
After joining in May 1916 he underwent a period of training at Salisbury Plain, but was later found to be medically unfit for military service. He was therefore discharged in the following August, after serving for only three months with the Colours.
46, Grey Street, Northampton. Z1617.

PERKINS, A. E., Air Mechanic, Royal Air Force.
He enlisted in August 1917, and after a period of training was engaged at Blandford on important duties which demanded a high degree of technical skill. He was not successful in obtaining a transfer overseas, but rendered valuable services until his demobilisation in November 1919.
7, Semilong Road, Northampton. Z2468.

PERKINS, A. J., Stretcher-Bearer, V.A.D.
Already serving with the St. John Ambulance Brigade when war broke out, he was afterwards attached to the V.A.D. at Northampton, where he was engaged on important duties with the Railway Section, rendering very valuable services throughout the period of hostilities. He was awarded the Order of St. John of Jerusalem with twelve bars for his good work, and in 1921 was still serving.
24, Parkwood Street, Northampton. Z2467.

PERKINS, F., Pte., Queen's Own (Royal West Kent Regiment).
Joining in May 1916, he was drafted to France five months later, and there served as a stretcher-bearer in various sectors. He took part in the Battles of the Somme, Arras, Ypres and Cambrai and many other important engagements, and was wounded during the Advance of 1918. Demobilised in February 1919, he holds the General Service and Victory Medals. Wards Lodge, Bugbrooke, Northants. Z3468.

PERKINS, F. J., Gunner, Royal Horse Artillery.
He enlisted in February 1916, and in the following August was drafted to Egypt. In this seat of operations he saw much fighting and, advancing into Palestine, took part in the Battles of Rafa, Gaza and the capture of Jerusalem. He was in hospital with malaria for a time, but was eventually demobilised in March 1919, holding the General Service and Victory Medals. 32, Byfield Road, St. James, Northampton. Z2469

PERKINS, G. H., Private, 2nd Northants. Regt.
Having volunteered in September 1914, he completed a period of training and in the following year was drafted overseas. Whilst on the Western Front he took part in the Battle of Neuve Chapelle, where he was unfortunately killed in action on March 12th, 1915. He was entitled to the 1914–15 Star, and the General Service and Victory Medals.
"Whilst we remember, the sacrifice is not in vain."
21, Alliston Gardens, Northampton. Z1618.

PERKINS, G. M., Corporal, 13th Hussars.
Already in the Army in August 1914, he proceeded in February 1915 to the Western Front, where he took part in heavy fighting at Neuve Chapelle, Givenchy and Ypres. He was afterwards transferred to Mesopotamia, and served at Kut, during the engagements on the Tigris, at Amara and the capture of Baghdad. Later, however, in 1917 he proceeded to India, where he was engaged on garrison duties on the Afghanistan Frontier. He did consistently good work, and in May 1919 was discharged, holding the 1914–15 Star, and the General Service and Victory Medals.
5, Grafton Place, Northampton. Z1620

PERKINS, G. W., Private, Highland Light Infantry.
Volunteering in March 1915, he underwent a period of training and proceeded to France. During his service in this theatre of war he took part in much fighting at Ypres before being wounded and evacuated to England. On his recovery he returned to the Western Front, and was engaged on important duties at Calais. After the conclusion of war he was transferred to Ireland with the 1st Northamptonshire Regiment, and in 1920 was still serving there. He holds the General Service and Victory Medals. 50, Silver Street, Northampton. Z1619.

PERKINS, H. G. D., A.B., Royal Naval Division.
He volunteered in June 1915, and after a period of training was drafted to France, where he served with the Nelson Battalion, and took part in heavy fighting in the Ypres, the Somme and Arras sectors. He made the supreme sacrifice, being killed in action on the Arras front on April 23rd, 1917, and was entitled to the 1914–15 Star, and the General Service and Victory Medals.
"The path of duty was the way to glory."
Near Chapel, Blisworth, Northampton. Z2243.

PERKINS, H. H., Private, Essex Regiment.
He joined the Norfolk Regiment in June 1918, and in the following September was drafted to France, where he was transferred to the Essex Regiment, and took part in the final operations of the Advance. After hostilities ceased he proceeded to Germany with the Army of Occupation, and served at Cologne until his demobilisation in May 1919. He holds the General Service and Victory Medals.
57, Edinburgh Road, Northampton. Z2415.

PERKINS, P., Private, Buffs (East Kent Regt.)
Joining in May 1918, he was drafted to the Western Front on completion of a period of training four months later, and there saw much severe fighting at Cambrai. He made the supreme sacrifice, falling in action at Péronne on September 24th, 1918, only 14 days after landing in France. He was entitled to the General Service and Victory Medals.
"His memory is cherished with pride."
Ward's Lodge, Bugbrooke, Northants. Z3467.

PERKINS, W. H., Private, R.A.S.C.
Volunteering in November 1915, he was quickly drafted to the Western Front, where he took part in many important engagements until transferred in 1916 to Salonika. Proceeding to Egypt, he afterwards advanced into Palestine, and was present at several engagements. Contracting malarial fever, he underwent a period of treatment in hospital at Cairo, and on returning home in August 1919 was demobilised, holding the 1914–15 Star, and the General Service and Victory Medals.
55, St. James' Street, Daventry, Northants. Z3128.

PERRETT, A., Gunner, Royal Garrison Artillery.
He volunteered in October 1915, and, on conclusion of his training in the following year, proceeded overseas. In the course of his service on the Western Front he took part in many important engagements, including the Battles of Vimy Ridge, Messines, Arras, Passchendaele and Cambrai. He also served during the Advance of 1918, and was demobilised in July 1919, holding the General Service and Victory Medals.
64, Hood Street, Northampton. Z1621.

PERRIN, W., Private, 6th Northants. Regiment.
After volunteering in March 1915, he was quickly drafted to France, where he took part in heavy fighting at Ypres, Givenchy, Loos, Albert and the Somme. He was unfortunately killed by a sniper on December 8th, 1916, and was entitled to the 1914–15 Star, and the General Service and Victory Medals.
"He passed out of the sight of men by the path of duty and self-sacrifice."
15, Alliston Gardens, Northamptonshire. Z1622.

PERRY, W., Sergeant, Royal Field Artillery.
Volunteering in October 1915, he was retained for a time on important duties before proceeding to France in 1917. There he played a prominent part in many engagements, including the Battles of Ypres, Passchendaele and Cambrai, and saw much fighting on the Somme and at Le Cateau and Mons. Demobilised in 1919, he holds the General Service and Victory Medals.
39, Althorp Road, Northampton. Z2470.

PERRY, W., Sergeant, Royal Field Artillery.
Volunteering in February 1915, he completed his training and, proceeding to Ireland, fought during the Rebellion there. Early in 1917 he was drafted to the Western Front, where he took part in the Battles of Arras and Ypres, and did good work with his Battery during the Retreat and Advance of 1918. He was demobilised in May 1919, and holds the General Service and Victory Medals.
7, Stenson Street, Northampton. Z2709/B.

PESCOW, A., Private, 6th Northants. Regiment.
Having volunteered in May 1915, he completed a period of training and proceeded to France. In this seat of operations he saw much service in various sectors of the front, and took part in heavy fighting at St. Eloi, Ypres and Arras, before being invalided home with bronchitis. Returning to France on his recovery he was in action at Cambrai and St. Quentin, where he was wounded. As a result he was evacuated to England, and eventually discharged in August 1919, holding the 1914–15 Star, and the General Service and Victory Medals.
31, Arthur Street, Kingsthorpe Hollow, Northampton. TZ1623.

PETTIFER, T. J., Private, South Wales Borderers
He enlisted in January 1917, and in the following month was drafted to the Western Front. There he took part in much heavy fighting in the Arras, Vimy Ridge, Messines and Ypres sectors, and was wounded. On his recovery he rejoined his unit and was in action in the Retreat of 1918, being again wounded and taken prisoner. He was held in captivity in Germany for several months. Repatriated after the Armistice, he returned home, and was demobilised in September 1919, holding the General Service and Victory Medals.
44, Marlborough Road, Northampton. Z2471.

PETTIT, A., Private, Manchester Regiment.
Joining in April 1916, he was shortly afterwards drafted to France, where he took part in the Battle of Beaumont-Hamel before being wounded and evacuated to England. On his recovery he rejoined his unit in France, and was in action at the Battles of Ypres, Cambrai, Amiens, and also in the Retreat and Advance of 1918. He was demobilised in March 1919, and holds the General Service and Victory Medals.
28, Oakley Street, Northampton. Z1625.

PETTIT, E. G., Private, East Surrey Regiment.
He joined in October 1916, and in June of the following year was drafted to the Western Front. Whilst in this theatre of war he saw severe fighting in various sectors, took part in the Battles of Ypres and Amiens and other important engagements, and was wounded in June 1917. He was demobilised in February 1919, and holds the General Service and Victory Medals. Great Billing, Northants. Z3469.

PETTIT, E. R., Private, Sherwood Foresters.
He enlisted in January 1917, and, completing his training later in the same year, was drafted to France, where he took part in several engagements, including the Battles of Ypres and Passchendaele. He made the supreme sacrifice, being killed in action on the Somme on March 21st, 1918, and was entitled to the General Service and Victory Medals.
"He died the noblest death a man may die,
Fighting for God and right and liberty."
43, Hampton Street, Northampton. Z1208/B.

PETTIT, J. E., Private, Machine Gun Corps.
Joining in February 1917, he underwent a period of training before being drafted to Egypt. Whilst in this seat of operations he saw much service, and, proceeding to Palestine, fought at the Battles of Gaza. Later, in May 1918, he was transferred to France, and served there until he contracted an illness, and was invalided to hospital at Taplow. He was eventually demobilised in February 1919, and holds the General Service and Victory Medals.
163, Harborough Road, Kingsthorpe, Northants. Z1624/B.

PETTITT, A. E., Private, 7th Northants. Regiment.
Volunteering in November 1914, he underwent a period of training, and in the following year was drafted to France. Whilst in this theatre of war he served on the Somme front before being wounded in August 1916. As a result he was invalided to hospital at Newport, and eventually discharged as medically unfit for further service in March 1917. He holds the 1914–15 Star, and the General Service and Victory Medals.
11, Upper Harding Street, Northampton. Z1627/A.

PETTITT, F. A., Private, 7th Northants. Regt.
Volunteering in September 1914, he completed his training in the following year and proceeded to France. In the course of his service in this seat of operations he was in action at the Battles of Loos, the Somme and Arras. He made the supreme sacrifice, being killed on April 9th, 1917, and was entitled to the 1914–15 Star, and the General Service and Victory Medals.
"The path of duty was the way to glory."
11, Upper Harding Street, Northampton. Z1627/B.

PETTITT, W., Private, Suffolk Regiment.
Having volunteered in September 1915, he underwent a period of training before being drafted to France. Whilst in this theatre of war he took part in the Battles of Albert and the Somme. Later in 1916 he was taken prisoner and held in captivity until after the cessation of hostilities. He was demobilised in September 1919, and holds the General Service and Victory Medals.
14, Fitzroy Terrace, Northampton. Z1626/A.

PHILLIPS, A., Private, Duke of Cornwall's L.I.
A Reservist, he was called up in August 1914, and at once ordered to France, where he fought in the Battles of Mons, the Marne, the Aisne, La Bassée, Ypres, Neuve Chapelle and Hill 60. He was invalided home in 1915, on account of ill-health, and in the following year was sent to Salonika. There he took part in many notable engagements, and was wounded on one occasion. Returning to England, he was discharged in February 1919, holding the Mons Star, and the General Service and Victory Medals.
12, Augustin Street, Northampton. Z2809.

PHILLIPS, C. J., Pte., 10th Royal Warwickshire Regiment.
He enlisted in 1917, and was shortly afterwards drafted to France, where he saw much heavy fighting in the Dickebusch sector and was badly wounded in action. As a result he was invalided to hospital, but, on his recovery, proceeded to Germany with the Army of Occupation and served there until his demobilisation in October 1919. He holds the General Service and Victory Medals.
93, Adams Avenue, Northampton. Z2472.

PHILLIPS, H., Private, Royal Sussex Regiment.
He joined in March 1917, and two months later proceeded to France. In this theatre of war he was in action in the Menin Road and Ypres sectors, and was wounded. As a result he was invalided home, and on his recovery was retained at various home stations on important duties. He also served with the Royal Fusiliers, and was finally discharged in April 1918 as medically unfit for further service. He holds the General Service and Victory Medals.
175, Adnitt Road, Northampton. Z2244/B.

PHILLIPS, J. L., Private, 24th Training Reserve.
He joined in March 1917, and after a period of training was transferred to the Labour Corps, and engaged at various home stations on important duties with his unit. He was unable to obtain a transfer overseas owing to his being medically unfit, but rendered valuable services until his discharge in June 1919. 70, Charles Street, Northampton. Z1331/A.

PHILLPOTT, F. A., Sergeant, 4th Northants. Regt.
Having served in the Army since June 1905, he was retained on special duties after the outbreak of war, and, owing to the important nature of his work, was not drafted overseas. He rendered valuable services until January 1915, when he was discharged. 40, Louise Road, Northampton. Z1628.

PHILPOT, H. R., Corporal, Royal Engineers.
He volunteered in February 1915, and in the April of the following year was drafted to France. Whilst in this seat of war he took part in several engagements, including the Battle of the Somme, where he was badly wounded in July 1916. As a result he was invalided home, and on his recovery was retained at various home stations on important duties. Demobilised in April 1919, he holds the General Service and Victory Medals. 95, Cedar Road, Northampton. Z2245.

PHIPPEN, L., Private, R.A.M.C.
Having volunteered in September 1915, he was drafted overseas in the following March. Whilst on the Western Front he served with the 132nd Field Ambulance, and took part in several engagements, including the Battles of the Somme, Beaumont-Hamel, Ypres and Passchendaele, and was in action throughout the Retreat and Advance of 1918. He was demobilised in July 1919, and holds the General Service and Victory Medals.
82, Lea Road, Northampton. Z2246.

PHIPPS, A., Sergeant, Machine Gun Corps.
Already in the Army when war broke out in August 1914, he was immediately drafted to France. There he played a prominent part in many engagements, including the Battles of Mons, the Marne, Ypres, Festubert, Loos, the Somme, Arras, Cambrai and in the Retreat and Advance of 1918. He received his discharge in January 1920, and holds the Mons Star, and the General Service and Victory Medals.
35, Poole Street, Northampton. Z2247/B.

PHIPPS, ALBERT, Private, 1/4th Northants. Regiment.
Mobilised with the Territorials in August 1914, he was drafted to the Dardanelles in the following year. In this seat of operations he took part in the heavy fighting at Suvla Bay, Anzac Cove and Chocolate Hill. After the Evacuation of the Gallipoli Peninsula, he proceeded to Egypt, but owing to defective hearing was invalided home and discharged in August 1917 as medically unfit for further service. He holds the 1914–15 Star, and the General Service and Victory Medals.
35, Poole Street, Northampton. Z2247/A.

PHIPPS, A., Sergeant, Machine Gun Corps.
He enlisted in March 1913 in the Cameronians (Scottish Rifles), and at the outbreak of war proceeded to France. There he played an important part in the Retreat from Mons and the Battles of the Marne, the Aisne, La Bassée, Ypres, Loos, the Somme (I. and II.) and Passchendaele. Whilst overseas he also served with the Machine Gun Corps, and in April 1919 was discharged, holding the Mons Star, and the General Service and Victory Medals.
69, Spencer Street, Northampton. Z3129.

PHIPPS, C., L/Corporal, Machine Gun Corps.
He volunteered in August 1915, and underwent a period of training prior to his being drafted to France in the following year. In this seat of war he took part in many engagements, including those in the Somme, Ypres, Arras, Passchendaele and Cambrai sectors, and in the Retreat and Advance of 1918. He was demobilised in February 1919, and holds the General Service and Victory Medals.
35, Poole Street, Northampton. Z2247/C.

PICKERING, F. L., Private, 5th Northants. Regt.
Having volunteered in May 1915, he was drafted overseas in the following January. Whilst on the Western Front, he took part in many engagements in the Somme and Arras sectors, where he was badly wounded in May 1917. As a result he was invalided home, and was eventually demobilised in January 1919, holding the General Service and Victory Medals.
30, Kerr Street, Northampton. Z1990.

PICKERING, F. T., Private, Manchester Regt.
Joining in 1917, he was drafted to France in the same year, and fought in the Battles of Vimy Ridge and Ypres, and was wounded. On his discharge from hospital in England he returned to the Western Front, and was in action in engagements at the Somme, the Marne and Cambrai. Invalided home with shell-shock in 1918, he was eventually demobilised in 1919, holding the General Service and Victory Medals.
5, St. Peter Gardens, Northampton. Z2310.

PICKERSGILL, A., Sapper, Royal Engineers.
He joined in March 1917, and in February of the following year was sent to France, where he was stationed at Cherbourg until transferred to Italy. He proceeded thence to Egypt and, serving also in Palestine, was stationed at Port Said and Jerusalem with the Postal Section. Demobilised on returning home in September 1919, he holds the General Service and Victory Medals. 40, Ethel Street, Northampton. Z1991.

PICKFORD, A., Private, Queen's Own (Cameron Highlanders).
Already in the Army, he was mobilised at the outbreak of war and immediately drafted to France. Whilst on the Western Front he was in action during the Retreat from Mons, and also at the Battles of the Marne, Ypres, Loos and Arras, and was twice wounded. As a result he was evacuated to England and eventually discharged as medically unfit for further service in December 1917, holding the Mons Star, and the General Service and Victory Medals.
25, Chalk Lane, Northampton. Z1630/B.

PICKFORD, C., Private, 1/4th Northants. Regt.
Volunteering in February 1915, he completed his training in the following year and proceeded to Egypt, where he saw much service at Katia and El Fasher, and was afterwards in action in Palestine. He took part in the Battles of Rafa, Gaza, and also in the capture of Jerusalem, and did continuously good work until demobilised in June 1919, holding the General Service and Victory Medals. 24, Chalk Lane, Northampton. Z1629/C.

PICKFORD, C. F., L/Cpl., 2nd Northants. Regt.
A serving soldier, he was drafted to the Western Front in August 1914, and after taking part in the fighting at Mons, served through the Battles of the Marne, La Bassée and Ypres and minor engagements. He fell in action in May 1915, and was entitled to the Mons Star, and the General Service and Victory Medals.
"His life for his Country, his soul to God."
25, Chalk Lane, Northampton. Z1630/A.

PICKFORD, J., Corporal, 8th East Surrey Regt.
Volunteering in September 1914, he was drafted to France in July of the following year, and there saw much heavy fighting. After taking part in the Battles of Loos, Vimy Ridge, the Somme, Arras and Ypres, he was severely wounded at Passchendaele in 1917, and admitted to hospital at Brighton. He was invalided from the Army in May 1918, and holds the 1914–15 Star, and the General Service and Victory Medals.
24, Chalk Lane, Northampton. Z1629/A.

PICKFORD, L., Private, Northants. Regiment.
Two months after volunteering in February 1915, he proceeded to the Western Front, where he saw severe fighting in various sectors. He took part in the Battles of Ypres, Loos, the Somme, Arras and Cambrai, and many minor engagements, and was twice wounded. Demobilised in February 1919, he holds the 1914–15 Star, and the General Service and Victory Medals.
25, Chalk Lane, Northampton. Z1630/C.

PICKFORD, W., Private, 6th Northants. Regt.
He volunteered in September 1914, and in October of the following year was sent to the Western Front, where he took part in many important engagements, including the Battles of Loos, Albert and Vimy Ridge. He died gloriously on the Field of Battle on the Somme in July 1916, and was entitled to the 1914–15 Star, and the General Service and Victory Medals.
"A costly sacrifice upon the altar of freedom."
32, Castle Street, Northampton. Z1629/B.

PICKFORD, W. H., Private, 2nd Highland L.I.
He enlisted in May 1916, and after completing his training in the following October was drafted to the Western Front, where he saw much heavy fighting in the Neuve Chapelle sector, but was unfortunately reported missing, and later presumed killed in action on November 13th, 1916. He was entitled to the General Service and Victory Medals.
"He died the noblest death a man may die :
Fighting for God and right and liberty."
Roe Road, Monk's Park, Northampton. Z2248.

PILSBURY, A. E., Private, 2nd Duke of Cornwall's Light Infantry.
Volunteering in August 1914, he was drafted to France three months later, and there took part in the first Battle of Ypres and in minor engagements in various sectors. He made the supreme sacrifice, falling in action at Ypres on April 23rd, 1915, and was entitled to the 1914 Star, and the General Service and Victory Medals.
"He joined the great white company of valiant souls."
22, Semilong Road South, Northampton. Z1632.

PILSBURY, F., Corporal, 2nd Duke of Cornwall's Light Infantry.
He volunteered in August 1914, and in November of that year proceeded to France, where, after taking part in the Battle of Neuve Chapelle, he was wounded at Hill 60, and admitted to hospital at Bristol. In April 1916 however, he rejoined his unit, and fought in the Battles of Vimy Ridge and the Somme. He was injured in January 1919, whilst working on an ammunition dump, and was again in hospital before being demobilised in May 1920. He holds the 1914–15 Star, and the General Service and Victory Medals.
22, Semilong Road South, Northampton. Z1631.

PINCKARD, W., Private, Wiltshire Regiment.
Having previously served in the South African campaign, he was mobilised in August 1914, and at once ordered to the Western Front with the first Expeditionary Force. After taking part in fierce fighting in the Retreat from Mons and other important engagements, he was severely wounded and invalided home in 1914. After protracted hospital treatment he was discharged as medically unfit in 1916, holding the Queen's and King's South African Medals, the Mons Star, and the General Service and Victory Medals.
37, Alma Street, Northampton. Z2811.

PINFIELD, H. F., Private, Worcestershire Regt.
He was called up from the Reserve in August 1914, and underwent a period of training at Woolwich before proceeding to India in July of the following year. There he was engaged at various stations on important garrison duties, and did continuously good work throughout, serving also with the Royal Field Artillery. In 1921 he was still in India, and holds the General Service and Victory Medals.
7, Spencer Road, Northampton. Z1418/C.

PINKARD, A., Private, 1st East Surrey Regt.
Joining in February 1917, he was drafted to the Western Front three months later, and there saw much heavy fighting. He took part in the Battle of Ypres and many other engagements, was wounded in 1917, and gassed in 1918, and was for two months in hospital at Le Havre. He fell fighting on September 23rd, 1918, during the Advance, and was entitled to the General Service and Victory Medals.
"He nobly fell that we might live."
31, Brunswick Street, Northampton. Z1633.

PINKARD, A., Sergeant, Royal Fusiliers.
Already serving in India when war was declared, he shortly afterwards proceeded to the Western Front, where he saw much heavy fighting. He took a prominent part in the Battles of Ypres, Neuve Chapelle, Hill 60, Loos, the Somme and Arras, and minor engagements until sent home suffering from frost-bite and malaria. He was invalided from the Army in October 1917, and holds the 1914 Star, and the General Service and Victory Medals. 96, Euston Road, Northampton. Z3470/B.

PINKARD, P., Sergeant, Highland L.I.
He was serving in India at the outbreak of war, and was quickly drafted to the Western Front, where he took a distinguished part in the first Battle of Ypres and minor engagements. Mortally wounded in action at Neuve Chapelle, he unhappily died on April 23rd, 1915, and was entitled to the 1914 Star, and the General Service and Victory Medals.
"The path of duty was the way to glory."
96, Euston Road, Northampton. Z3470/A.

PIPER, W. E., Rifleman, Rifle Brigade.
He volunteered in October 1915, and saw service with the Rifle Brigade and Royal Fusiliers. He was sent to the Western Front in 1916, and took part in heavy fighting in various sectors, being in action at the Battles of Albert, the Somme and Arras, and was invalided home in 1917. In April 1918 he returned to France, but after a month's service there was sent to England, and discharged as medically unfit in August 1918. He holds the General Service and Victory Medals.
Church End, Hanslope, Bucks. 2812.

PITT, A. W., Private, Lancashire Fusiliers.
He volunteered in December 1915, and in the following year was drafted to Salonika, where he took part in much fighting on the Doiran and Struma fronts. Contracting malaria and dysentery, he was invalided home, but on his recovery was transferred to France. There he was in action at Arras, Ypres, Cambrai and the Somme before being taken prisoner of war in March 1918. Repatriated after the Armistice, he returned home and was demobilised in March 1919, holding the General Service and Victory Medals.
35, Castle Street, Northampton. Z1634/A.

PITT, F., Mechanic, Royal Air Force.
He joined in December 1917, and underwent a period of training prior to his being drafted to France. There he was engaged on work of a highly technical nature and later was employed on guard duties in a prisoner of war camp. Invalided home with pneumonia in December 1918, he was eventually demobilised in November 1919, holding the General Service and Victory Medals.
35, Castle Street, Northampton. Z1634/B.

PITTAM, B., L/Corporal, Machine Gun Corps.
He volunteered in August 1914, and in the following July was drafted to the Dardanelles, where he saw much heavy fighting, but, contracting dysentery, was invalided home. On his recovery he was sent to France, and took part in many engagements, including the Battle of Messines, Ypres, Passchendaele, the Somme (II.), the Aisne (III.), the Marne (II.), Amiens, Bapaume, Epèhy and Cambrai. Demobilised in February 1919, he holds the 1914–15 Star, and the General Service and Victory Medals. 14, Hunter Street, Northampton. Z1635.

PITTAM, E., Corporal, Royal Army Service Corps.
Volunteering in April 1915, he embarked a month later for the Western Front, where he served for nearly four years. During that time he was engaged on important transport and other duties at Rouen, and also rendered valuable services at Amiens and St. Quentin. He remained in France until February 1919, when he was sent to England for demobilisation, and holds the 1914–15 Star, and the General Service and Victory Medals. Castlethorpe, Bucks. Z2813.

PITTAM, H. J., L/Corporal, 1st K.R.R.C.
Having previously enlisted on two occasions, but been reclaimed on account of his youth, he joined the King's Royal Rifle Corps in September 1917, and after a period of training was drafted to France. There he took part in much heavy fighting at Monchy, where he was severely gassed, and suffering also from trench fever, was invalided home. He was eventually demobilised in February 1919, and holds the General Service and Victory Medals. 10, Brunswick Street, Northampton. Z1992.

PITTAM, W. B., Private, Northants. Regiment.
Already in the Army when war broke out in August 1914, he was immediately drafted to the Western Front. Whilst overseas he took part in many engagements, including the Battles of Mons, the Somme, Messines, Ypres and Cambrai, and was wounded in action on three occasions. He received his discharge in April 1919, and holds the Mons Star, and the General Service and Victory Medals.
90, Bath Street, Northampton. Z1257/A.

PITTS, F., Private, Royal Naval Division.
He joined in March 1916, and in the following August was drafted to the Western Front. In this theatre of war he took part in several engagements, including the Battles of the Somme, Arras, Ypres and Cambrai. He was demobilised in April 1919, but re-enlisted in January 1920 for six years' service, and holds the General Service and Victory Medals.
29, Crispin Street, Northampton. Z1636/D—Z1637/D.

PLACKETT, J., Private, Queen's (Royal West Surrey Regiment).
He joined in June 1917, and in the following October was drafted to France. Whilst in this theatre of war he took part in many engagements, including those at Ypres, on the Somme, at Cambrai and in the Retreat and Advance of 1918. After hostilities ceased he proceeded to Germany, but was taken ill and invalided home. He was eventually discharged in August 1919, and holds the General Service and Victory Medals.
4, Greyhound Yard, Milton, Northants. Z2473.

PLAWRIGHT, J. G., L/Cpl., 1st Manchester Regt.
Joining in June 1917, he proceeded later in the same year to France, where he took part in many important engagements in various sectors. He was afterwards transferred to Italy, and took part in heavy fighting on the Piave front. Returning home for demobilisation in October 1919, he holds the General Service and Victory Medals.
45, Euston Road, Far Cotton, Northampton. Z3130.

PLOWMAN, A., Corporal, 2nd Northants. Regt.
A serving soldier, he was sent to France in August 1914, and there fought in the Battle of, and Retreat from, Mons. After taking part also in the Battles of the Marne, the Aisne, La Bassée and Ypres, he was invalided home suffering from frost-bite, but later returned to France and fought in the Somme Offensive. He fell in action at High Wood on September 9th, 1916, and was entitled to the Mons Star, and the General Service and Victory Medals.
"He nobly fell that we might live."
9, Albert Place, Northampton. Z3220/A.

PLOWMAN, B. H., Gunner, R.G.A.
He volunteered in October 1915, and in the following year was drafted to India, where he was engaged on important garrison duties, but, contracting dysentery, was invalided home in 1917. On his recovery he was sent to France, and took part in the Advance of 1918, at Cambrai. Demobilised in June 1919, he holds the General Service and Victory Medals.
61, Whitworth Road, Northampton. Z2249.

PLOWMAN, J., Private, 6th Northants. Regiment.
He joined in 1916, and on completion of a period of training, was drafted to the Western Front, where he saw much severe fighting. After taking part in the Battle of Arras and other engagements, he was sent home and discharged in 1917, in order to do work of National importance. He holds the General Service and Victory Medals.
32, Rickard Street, Far Cotton, Northampton. Z3471.

PLOWMAN, W. (D.C.M.), Pte., 6th Northants. Regt.
Volunteering in August 1914, he proceeded to the Western Front in the following year, and there took part in the Battles of Neuve Chapelle, St. Eloi, Hill 60, Ypres, Festubert and Loos and minor engagements until wounded in action. He was awarded the Distinguished Conduct Medal for conspicuous gallantry in rescuing an officer under heavy shell-fire, although himself badly wounded, in September 1915, and holds also the 1914–15 Star, and the General Service and Victory Medals. He was for a considerable period in hospital before being invalided from the Army in March 1917.
9, Albert Place, Northampton. Z3220/B.

PLUNKETT, E., Sergeant, 1st Northants. Regt.
He volunteered in August 1914, and was shortly afterwards drafted to France, where he played a distinguished part in much fighting at Neuve Chapelle. He made the supreme sacrifice, being killed in action at Ypres on January 29th, 1915, and was entitled to the 1914 Star, and the General Service and Victory Medals.
"A valiant Soldier, with undaunted heart he breasted life's last hill."
35, Norfolk Street, Northampton. Z1638/A.

PLUNKETT, F. E. G., A.B., Royal Navy.
Already in the Royal Navy when war broke out in August 1914, he was attached to the Portsmouth Division and quickly proceeded to Scapa Flow, where he served on board H.M.S. "Monarch." He was chiefly engaged on patrol and convoy duties and did continuously good work throughout hostilities. Owing to an accident during manœuvres, he was discharged in March 1920 as medically unfit for further service. He holds the 1914–15 Star, and the General Service and Victory Medals.
35, Norfolk Street, Northampton. Z1638/B.

PLUNKETT, V. R., A.B., Royal Navy.
He was already serving when war broke out in August 1914, and was engaged throughout hostilities on board H.M.S. "Rapid," "Hindustan" and "Glory." He was chiefly employed on important patrol and convoy duties in the North Sea, and did continuously good work. In 1920 he was still serving, and holds the 1914–15 Star, and the General Service and Victory Medals.
35, Norfolk Street, Northampton. Z1638/C.

POLLARD, A. H., Gunner, R.G.A.
He joined in July 1916, and on completing his training in the following year was drafted to France. There he took part in much heavy fighting in the Vimy Ridge, Messines, Passchendaele, Béthune and Aubers Ridge sectors. Contracting trench fever, he was invalided home and eventually discharged in January 1919, holding the General Service and Victory Medals. 127, Lutterworth Road, Northampton. Z2250.

POLLARD, S., Private, 18th Yorkshire Regiment.
Called up with the National Reserves in August 1914 (having previously served 21 years with the Volunteers), he was first engaged on important duties at various home stations, but after the Armistice proceeded to Russia. There he was employed on guard and police duty, and did continuously good work throughout. He was discharged in August 1919, holding the General Service and Victory Medals.
175, Adnitt Road, Northampton. Z2244/A.

POLLARD, W., Private, 2/8th Worcester. Regt.
He joined in January 1917, and, completing his training in the following June, was drafted to the Western Front, where he took part in much heavy fighting and was severely wounded in action in August 1917. He unfortunately died the next day through the effects of his wounds, and was entitled to the General Service and Victory Medals.
"He nobly fell that we might live."
6, Leicester Street, Northampton. Z1639/B.

POOLE, A. J., L/Corporal, R.A.S.C. (M.T.)
Volunteering in May 1915, he proceeded overseas two months later. During his service on the Western Front, he was engaged with the Mechanical Transport on important duties in the Loos, Arras and Somme sectors, and in the Retreat and Advance of 1918. He was demobilised in June 1919, and holds the 1914–15 Star, and the General Service and Victory Medals. 39, Craven Street, Northampton. Z1640/B.

POOLE, A. T., C.S.M., Cameronians (Scottish Rifles).
He volunteered in August 1914, and was retained for a time at various home stations as a Gymnastic Instructor. In 1917 he proceeded to France and did continuously good work in the same capacity at Army Headquarters. He returned home in 1918, and in 1921 was serving in Ireland. He holds the General Service and Victory Medals.
39, Craven Street, Northampton. Z1640/A.

POOLE, D. W., Private, 6th Northants. Regiment.
He joined in May 1916, and two months later was drafted overseas. Whilst serving on the Western Front he was in action in numerous engagements, and was wounded in March 1917, and invalided home. On his recovery he returned to France, was attached to the North Staffordshire Regiment, and saw heavy fighting at Arras, Vimy Ridge and Cambrai, and in the Retreat and Advance of 1918. Demobilised in September 1919, he holds the General Service and Victory Medals. King's Lane, Flore, Northants. Z2814.

POOLE, E. W., A/Sergeant, 2nd Northants. Regt.
Having enlisted in 1906, he was mobilised in August 1914, and immediately drafted to France. There he played a prominent part in the Retreat from Mons, the Battles of the Marne, the Aisne, Ypres (I. and II.), Festubert and Loos, and was wounded at Neuve Chapelle in 1915. He was afterwards transferred to the Gloucestershire Regiment, and was in action on the Armentières and the Somme fronts. He was unhappily killed on July 29th, 1916, and was entitled to the Mons Star, and the General Service and Victory Medals.
"A costly sacrifice upon the altar of freedom."
Bugbrooke, Northants. Z3131.

POOLE, H. R., Air Mechanic, Royal Air Force.
He joined in September 1918, immediately on attaining military age, and on completion of his training was employed as a rigger in the workshops and aeroplane sheds at various aerodromes. Although not sent overseas he, nevertheless, did splendid work for six months, and was demobilised in March 1919. Breach Lane, Roade, Northants. Z2251.

POPE, G. H. (D.C.M.), Sergeant, 3/4th Northants. Regiment.
He volunteered in May 1915, and after a period of training was drafted to France in March 1917. In this theatre of war he played a prominent part in the Battles of Arras and Passchendaele and, before being taken prisoner at Cambrai in November 1917, was awarded the Distinguished Conduct Medal for conspicuous bravery displayed in attempting to hold the line against heavy odds in this engagement. Repatriated after the Armistice, he was demobilised in April 1919, also holding the General Service and Victory Medals.
15, St. Edmund's Street, Northampton. Z1993/A.

POPE, J. J., Private, Royal Army Service Corps.
He volunteered in November 1915, and was immediately drafted to France. Whilst on the Western Front, he was engaged on important transport work in the Somme, Ypres, Passchendaele and Cambrai sectors. After hostilities ceased he returned home and was demobilised in March 1919, holding the 1914–15 Star, and the General Service and Victory Medals.
15, St. Edmund's Street, Northampton. Z1993/B.

POULTON, J., Private, Durham Light Infantry.
He enlisted in June 1916, and underwent a period of training prior to his being drafted to France. In this seat of war he took part in several engagements, including the Battles of Arras, Ypres, Cambrai and the Somme (II.), and was gassed in action. He was demobilised in April 1919, and holds the General Service and Victory Medals.
72, Castle Street, Northampton. Z1641.

POWELL, H., Private, Essex Regiment.
Shortly after volunteering in 1915, he was drafted to Gallipoli, where he saw much severe fighting, particularly at Suvla Bay. He was later transferred to Egypt and thence to Palestine, where he was again in action, taking part in many engagements. He also served in Montenegro before returning home for demobilisation in 1919, and holds the 1914–15 Star, and the General Service and Victory Medals.
49, Rickard Street, Far Cotton, Northampton. Z3472/B.

POWELL, H. C., Private, 1st Northants. Regt.
Mobilised in August 1914, he was immediately drafted to the Western Front, where he fought in the Retreat from Mons and many minor engagements. He fell gloriously on the Field of Battle on the Aisne in September 1914, and was entitled to the Mons Star, and the General Service and Victory Medals.
"Whilst we remember, the sacrifice is not in vain."
49, Rickard Street, Far Cotton, Northampton. Z3472/A.

POWELL, P., Private, Royal Naval Division.
On attaining military age he joined in 1918, and after completing his training was retained on important duties at various stations. Owing to the early cessation of hostilities, he was unsuccessful in obtaining his transfer to a theatre of war, but, nevertheless, rendered very valuable services until demobilised in 1919.
7, St. Leonard's Road, Far Cotton, Northampton. Z3132/A.

POWELL, W., A.B., Royal Naval Division.
He volunteered in October 1915, and served with the Anson Battalion at Blandford on important duties. He was unable to obtain a transfer overseas owing to his being medically unfit, but rendered valuable services until his discharge in December 1917.
11, Wimbledon Street, St. James, Northampton. Z2475.

POWER, C. P., Bombardier, Royal Field Artillery.
Volunteering in October 1915, he was drafted overseas in the following year. Whilst on the Western Front, he took part in much heavy fighting during the Battles of the Somme, Ypres, St. Quentin and the Retreat and Advance of 1918. Demobilised in June 1919, he holds the General Service and Victory Medals.
90, Milton Street, Northampton. Z1591/A.

PRAGNELL, W. J., Corporal, 1st Buffs (East Kent Regiment).
Joining in November 1916, he was trained at Luton, and two months later was ordered to France. On that front he was in action at the Battles of Arras, Ypres, Cambrai and the Somme, and other important engagements, but was wounded at Kemmel in November 1918, and sent to hospital in England. On his discharge from hospital he was demobilised in January 1919, holding the General Service and Victory Medals.
3, Sunnyside, Wootton, Northants. Z2815.

PRATT, A. H., Private, 15th (The King's) Hussars.
He joined in February 1918, but, after a period of training, was transferred to the Machine Gun Corps and drafted to France, where he took part in the final engagements of the war. After hostilities ceased, he proceeded to Germany with the Army of Occupation and served on the Rhine until his demobilisation in November 1919. He holds the General Service and Victory Medals.
4, Seymour Place, King Street, Northampton. Z1515/A.

PRATT, C., Private, East Surrey Regiment.
He volunteered in November 1915, and, after a period of training, was drafted overseas in August of the following year. Serving on the Western Front, he was in action in numerous important engagements, including the Battles of Arras and Vimy Ridge, but was severely wounded in April 1917. In consequence he was invalided out of the Army in November 1917, holding the General Service and Victory Medals.
31, New Street, Daventry, Northants. Z2816.

PRATT, E. W., L/Corporal, Royal Inniskilling Fusiliers.
He joined in November 1916, and in the following January was drafted to Egypt. Later he proceeded into Palestine, and took part in the Battles of Gaza, Jaffa, and in engagements on the River Jordan. He was unfortunately killed in action near Jerusalem on March 26th, 1918, and was entitled to the General Service and Victory Medals.
"His life for his Country, his soul to God."
4, Seymour Place, King Street, Northampton. Z1515/B.

PRATT, F., Private, Royal Army Medical Corps.
He volunteered in May 1915, and, after undergoing a period of training, was retained at various places, where he was engaged on important duties as a stretcher-bearer and orderly on ambulance trains. He was unable to obtain his transfer overseas, but, nevertheless, did good work with his Company until demobilised in March 1919.
27, Abbey Road, Far Cotton, Northampton. Z3473/A.

PRATT, G., Sergeant, Q.M.A.A.C.
She joined immediately on the formation of the Q.M.A.A.C. and was among the first to be drafted to the Western Front. There she was stationed chiefly at Etaples on responsible duties as a chief cook, and rendered very valuable services, being mentioned in Despatches for her good work. After being for a time in hospital in France, she was sent home and discharged in July 1919, suffering from neurasthenia. She holds the General Service and Victory Medals.
27, Abbey Road, Far Cotton, Northampton. Z3473/B.

PREECE, E. C., Private, Oxford and Bucks. L.I.
Volunteering in November 1915, he completed his training, and six months later proceeded to Mesopotamia. On that front he fought in the Battles of the Tigris, Kut-el-Amara, Ramadieh and Khan Baghadie, and also took part in numerous minor engagements until the close of hostilities. He was demobilised on his return to England in November 1919, and holds the General Service and Victory Medals.
20, Raymond Road, St. James, Northampton. Z2817.

PREECE, W. J. C., Private, 2nd Northants. Regt.
He volunteered in August 1914, and was shortly afterwards drafted to France, where he took part in the Battles of Ypres, Hill 60, Neuve Chapelle, Loos, Vimy Ridge, the Somme and Arras. He died gloriously on the Field of Battle at Ypres on July 31st, 1917, and was entitled to the 1914 Star, and the General Service and Victory Medals.
"Whilst we remember, the sacrifice is not in vain."
70, Hunter Street, Northampton. Z1642.

PRESTON, W. W., Gunner, Royal Field Artillery.
Mobilised at the outbreak of war, he immediately proceeded to the Western Front, and served in the fighting at Mons. He was also in action at the Battles of the Marne, the Aisne and Ypres, was wounded at Neuve Chapelle in March 1915, and later was gassed there. After taking part in many other notable engagements, he was invalided home in November 1918, and eventually discharged in January 1919, holding the Mons Star, and the General Service and Victory Medals.
21, North Street, Daventry, Northants. Z2818.

PRICE, W. E., Gunner, Royal Garrison Artillery.
He volunteered in October 1915, and, completing his training in the following March, was drafted to France, where he took part in the Battle of the Somme. Later he proceeded to Italy, and saw much fighting on the Piave, but shortly afterwards was sent back to France. There he fought in the Somme and Cambrai sectors, and, after hostilities ceased, went to Germany with the Army of Occupation, and served there until his demobilisation in February 1919. He holds the General Service and Victory Medals.
42, Compton Street, Northampton. Z1643.

PRICKETT, W., L/Corporal, 1st Northants. Regt.
Volunteering in June 1915, he proceeded overseas in the following year. During his service on the Western Front, he saw much heavy fighting in the Somme and Ypres sectors, being badly wounded in action in 1917. Invalided home, he returned to France on his recovery, and was in action in the Advance of 1918. He was demobilised in March 1919, and holds the General Service and Victory Medals.
2, St. Andrew's Gardens, Northampton. Z1644.

PRITCHARD, H., Sergt., 6th Leicestershire Regt.
Volunteering in September 1914, he was shortly afterwards drafted overseas. Serving on the Western Front, he fought in many important engagements, and played a prominent part in the Battles of Ypres, Hill 60, Loos and Albert. He fell in action on September 26th, 1916, and was entitled to the 1914–15 Star, and the General Service and Victory Medals.
"He died the noblest death a man may die,
Fighting for God and right and liberty."
Rose Cottages, Silver Street, Brixworth, Northants. Z3133/A.

PRUDAN, J. W., Private, 19th London Regiment.
He joined in January 1917, and in the following year was drafted to France, where he took part in much fighting in the Cambrai sector. He was gassed at the Battle of the Somme (II.), and taken prisoner of war, being held in captivity in Germany at Gristrow Camp. Repatriated after the Armistice, he was demobilised in October 1919, holding the General Service and Victory Medals.
36, Earl Street, Northampton. Z1645.

PULLEY, E., Guardsman, Grenadier Guards.
At the outbreak of war he was called up from the Reserve, and in November 1914 was ordered overseas. During his service on the Western Front, he was engaged in fierce fighting in the Ypres sector, but was severely wounded in action in December 1914. Invalided to England, he was subsequently discharged as medically unfit for further military duties in May 1917, holding the 1914 Star, and the General Service and Victory Medals. Hardingstone, Northants. Z2819.

PULLEY, F., Private, 8th Northants. Regiment.
He joined in June 1916, and three months later was drafted to the Western Front, where he took part in the Battles of the Somme, Arras and Cambrai. Subsequently he was transferred to the Royal Fusiliers, and was engaged on important duties at Boulogne until sent to England for demobilisation in January 1919. He holds the General Service and Victory Medals. The Green, Wootton, Northants. Z2820.

PULLEY, F. H., Private, Northants. Regiment.
He joined in April 1916, and later in the same year was drafted to France. Whilst in this theatre of war he was stationed at Calais, where he was engaged on various important duties. Owing to medical unfitness, he was unable to proceed to the firing-line, but rendered valuable services until his demobilisation in February 1919. He holds the General Service and Victory Medals. 175, Adnitt Road, Northampton. Z2244/C.

PULLEY, J. H., Gunner, Royal Field Artillery.
Already in India when war broke out in August 1914, having had 15 years' service with the Colours, he was sent to Mesopotamia in 1915. There he took part in many important engagements, including the capture of Baghdad, and the Battle of Ramadieh. After hostilities ceased he returned home, and received his discharge in February 1919. He holds the 1914–15 Star, and the General Service and Victory Medals.
5, Denmark Road, Northampton. Z1994.

PURSER, J., Private, 1/4th Northants. Regiment.
Joining in March 1917, he was trained at Tring, and shortly afterwards embarked for the scene of activities in France. On that front he fought in various notable engagements, and died gloriously on the Field of Battle at Ypres in August 1917. He was entitled to the General Service and Victory Medals.
"He passed out of the sight of men by the path of duty and self-sacrifice."
20, Muscott Street, Northampton. Z2821.

PUTSEY, J. E., Sergeant, Rifle Brigade.
He volunteered in 1915, and later in the same year was drafted to France. In this theatre of war he played a prominent part in much heavy fighting at the Battles of Vimy Ridge and the Somme. After hostilities ceased he proceeded to Germany with the Army of Occupation and was engaged there on important duties. He also served with the King's Royal Rifle Corps, and was finally demobilised in 1920, holding the 1914–15 Star, and the General Service and Victory Medals.
108, Adams Avenue, Northampton. Z2252.

Q

QUARTERMAN, G., Corporal, 5th Tank Corps.
He went to France in March 1915, as a voluntary Red Cross worker and motor mechanic with a private car, and rendered valuable services to the wounded at Hill 60. Later he joined the Field Ambulance Union, and did excellent work evacuating a district of typhoid cases. In October 1916 he obtained a transfer to the Tank Corps, and took a prominent part in many engagements of note, being mentioned in Despatches in October 1918. After nearly four years' splendid work, he was unhappily killed in action at Bohain on October 11th, 1918. He was entitled to the 1914–15 Star, and the General Service and Victory Medals.
"Great deeds cannot die:
They with the sun and moon renew their light for ever."
51, Beaconsfield Terrace, Northampton. Z1646.

QUENNELL, F., Private, 1/5th Suffolk Regiment.
He joined in May 1916, but on completion of his training was retained on important duties at various home stations. He was not successful in his efforts to secure a transfer overseas before the cessation of hostilities, but in February 1919 he was drafted to Egypt. There he did valuable work with the Military Police until sent home for demobilisation in February 1920.
Crown Inn, Hardingstone, Northants. Z2589/B.

QUINNEY, J. J., Bombardier, R.F.A.
Volunteering in January 1915, he proceeded to the Western Front in December of that year, and there saw much heavy fighting. After taking part in the Battles of Vimy Ridge, the Somme, Arras, Ypres, Passchendaele and Cambrai and other engagements, he was severely wounded at Ypres in July 1918, and sent home. He was invalided from the Army in December of that year, and holds the 1914–15 Star, and the General Service and Victory Medals.
107, Bridge Street, Northampton. Z3474.

R

RABBITT, J., Air Mechanic, Royal Air Force.
He joined in October 1917, and, proceeding to the Western Front two months later, served as a rigger with No. 1 Kite Balloon Section. He did excellent work until illness led to his evacuation to England for treatment, after which he was employed on important duties with his Squadron at various aerodromes, and was demobilised in January 1919. He holds the General Service and Victory Medals.
Station Road, Long Buckby, Northants. Z3475.

RACE, G., Private, 4th Northants. Regiment.
Joining in July 1916, he completed his training and was engaged on important duties with his Battalion at various depôts. He rendered valuable services, but was unsuccessful in securing his transfer to a theatre of war before the conclusion of hostilities, owing to medical unfitness for general service, and was demobilised in February 1919.
11, Foxes Yard, Bridge Street, Northampton. Z3476.

RAINBOW, C. G., Private, 7th Bedfordshire Regt.
He joined in July 1917, and was drafted overseas in the following March. Serving in various parts of the line in France, he was engaged in heavy fighting at Albert and other places during the Retreat and Advance of 1918, in September of which year he returned to England. Transferred to the Royal Army Service Corps, he was employed on home service duties until demobilised in February 1920, and holds the General Service and Victory Medals.
"Shoulder of Mutton," Crick Road, Crick, Northants. Z3477.

RAINBOW, F., Driver, Royal Field Artillery.
Having volunteered in August 1915 in the Royal Army Veterinary Corps, he was later transferred to the Royal Field Artillery, and in the following January proceeded to France. Whilst in this theatre of war, he was in action with his Battery at the Battles of the Somme, Arras, Vimy Ridge, Ypres and Cambrai. He also took part in the Retreat and Advance of 1918, and, after the cessation of hostilities, served with the Army of Occupation at Cologne. Demobilised in July 1919, he holds the General Service and Victory Medals.
43, Delapre Street, Far Cotton, Northampton. Z3020.

RAINBOW, G. W. J., Private, Northants. Regt.
Volunteering in October 1914, he proceeded to the Dardanelles in April 1915, and took part in the Landings at Cape Helles and Suvla Bay and the three Battles of Krithia. After the Evacuation of Gallipoli, he was in hospital at Malta and in England with dysentery, but in June 1916 was sent to France. He then served at the Battles of the Somme, Arras and Ypres, but was later reported missing, and is now presumed to have been killed in action cn August 22nd, 1918. He was entitled to the 1914–15 Star, and the General Service and Victory Medals.
"His name liveth for evermore."
44, Countess Road, St. James', Northampton. Z2822.

RAINES, F., Private, 6th Northamptonshire Regt.
When war was declared in August 1914 he volunteered, and eleven months later proceeded overseas. Whilst in France he saw heavy fighting at Givenchy and Armentières, and was in action at the Battles of Loos, the Somme, Arras, Ypres, Passchendaele and Cambrai, but was unfortunately killed on April 5th, 1918. He was entitled to the 1914–15 Star, and the General Service and Victory Medals.
"Whilst we remember, the sacrifice is not in vain."
15, Althorp Street, Northampton. Z1647/A.

RAINES, F. W., Private, Middlesex Regiment.
He joined in September 1917, and in March of the following year was drafted to France, where he was engaged in fierce fighting in various sectors. Whilst taking part in operations on the Somme in April 1918, he was taken prisoner, and held in captivity until the close of hostilities. He was repatriated in December 1918, and employed on important duties at a prisoner of war camp until demobilised in November 1919, holding the General Service and Victory Medals.
15, Althorp Street, Northampton. Z1647/B.

RALLEY, E., Private, 1st Northamptonshire Regiment and Labour Corps.
Volunteering in August 1915, he embarked eight months later for France, and saw heavy fighting in the Loos sector. He was wounded during the Battle of the Somme in August 1916, and invalided to England. On his recovery he returned to the Western Front in February 1917, and was engaged on making roads in the devastated areas until demobilised in June 1919. He holds the General Service and Victory Medals.
86, Shelley Street, Kingsley, Northampton. Z1648.

RANDALL, C. J., Private, 5th Northants. Regt.
Having been rejected three times owing to defective eyesight, he finally enlisted in June 1916, and in the following year was drafted to France. There he took part in much severe fighting on the Somme, where he was seriously wounded on April 6th, 1918, and unhappily died the same day through the effects of his wounds. He was entitled to the General Service and Victory Medals.
"Great deeds cannot die:
They with the sun and moon renew their light for ever."
62, Countess Road, St. James', Northampton. Z2823—1649/A.

RANDALL, W. C., Corporal 7th Northants. Regt.
A month after the outbreak of war he volunteered, and in October 1915 crossed to France. On that front he fought in various engagements in different sectors, served at the Battles of the Somme, Vimy Ridge, Arras, Messines and Cambrai, and was wounded in action on two occasions. He returned to England in November 1918, and three months later was demobilised, holding the 1914–15 Star, and the General Service and Victory Medals.
44, Clare Terrace, Northampton. Z1649/B.

RANDS, C., A.B., Royal Navy.
He volunteered as a private in the 3/4th Northamptonshire Regiment in August 1915, but when under orders for Egypt was reclaimed from the Army in July 1916 as under age. He then undertook work of National importance until December 1917, when he joined the Royal Navy. After his training he was engaged on dangerous mine-sweeping duties in the North Sea, his vessel being badly damaged by enemy shell-fire. Later he was transferred to H.M.S. "Hercules," and on board this ship sailed through the Kiel Canal after the Armistice, having been in action at Heligoland in 1918. Demobilised in May 1919, he holds the General Service and Victory Medals.
29, Brunswick Place, Northampton. Z1995.

RANSBEY, F., Private, Yorkshire Regiment.
He enlisted in May 1917, and, completing his training in the following year, was drafted to France. In this theatre of war he took part in the Advance on the Somme in 1918, but owing to ill-health was invalided home to hospital. Later he was transferred to the Labour Corps, and retained in Buckinghamshire until his demobilisation in 1919. He holds the General Service and Victory Medals.
The Green, Hanslope, Bucks. Z2824.

RATCLIFFE, J. G., 7th Oxford. and Bucks. L.I.
He volunteered in September 1914, and in November of the following year was drafted to Salonika. In this seat of operations he took part in many important engagements, including those on the Doiran front, and was badly wounded in action. As a result he was invalided home and eventually discharged in March 1917 as medically unfit for further service. He holds the 1914–15 Star, and the General Service and Victory Medals.
67, Palmerston Road, Northampton. Z1996.

RATE, J. A. (D.C.M.), Sergeant, Royal Engineers.
He enlisted in January 1910, and at the outbreak of war was immediately drafted to the Western Front. There he served with distinction during the Retreat from Mons, and also at the Battles of the Marne, the Aisne, Ypres (I., II., III. and IV.), Vimy Ridge and the Somme. He was badly gassed in the Retreat of 1918, and on his recovery took part in the final Advance, afterwards serving with the Army of Occupation at Cologne. He was mentioned in Despatches and was awarded the Distinguished Conduct Medal for conspicuous bravery in the Field, and, holding also the Mons Star, and the General Service and Victory Medals, was discharged in February 1919.
3, Abbey Street, Northampton. Z3134.

RAWLINGS, H., Guardsman, 3rd Coldstream Gds.
Having previously served in the South African campaign, he was mobilised at the declaration of war and immediately drafted to France. There he was in action during the Retreat from Mons, and also at the Battles of Loos, the Somme, Arras and Ypres. He was later invalided home and finally discharged as medically unfit for further service in September 1917. He holds the Queen's and King's South African Medals, the Mons Star, and the General Service and Victory Medals.
81, Green Street, Northampton. Z3137.

RAWLINGS, J., Private, Royal Defence Corps.
Although over military age, he volunteered in November 1914, and, after completing a period of training, was retained on guard and other important duties at various stations. He did consistently good work during the period of hostilities, and rendered very valuable services until demobilised in March 1919. 80, Green Street, Northampton. Z3136.

RAYBOULD, G. W., Private, R.A.S.C.
Volunteering in September 1914, he was quickly drafted to France, where he saw much service in various sectors of the front. He was in action during heavy fighting at La Bassée, and whilst overseas was twice wounded. Returning home for demobilisation in February 1919, he holds the 1914–15 Star, and the General Service and Victory Medals.
7, London Road, Daventry, Northants. Z3138.

RAYSON, G., Sapper, Royal Engineers.
He volunteered in May 1915, and was engaged on home defence duties with his Company, and attached for a time to the 8th Royal Sussex Regiment. Sent to the Western Front in December 1917, he was employed with a Tunnelling Company in the forward areas, and performed valuable work until the close of hostilities, when he returned to England. Demobilised in February 1919, he holds the General Service and Victory Medals. 13a, Main Road, Northampton. Z3478.

REDLEY, H., Private, Queen's Own (Royal West Surrey Regiment).
He enlisted in May 1916, and, completing his training in the following August, was drafted to the Western Front, where he took part in several engagements, including those in the Somme and Ypres sectors. He made the supreme sacrifice, being killed in action on March 29th, 1917, and was entitled to the General Service and Victory Medals.
"Whilst we remember, the sacrifice is not in vain."
30, Clare Street, Northampton. Z1431/C.

REDLEY, W. M., Private, 2nd Devonshire Regt.
He enlisted in March 1917, and, completing his training in April of the following year, was drafted to France. There he took part in the Retreat and Advance of 1918, and, severely wounded in action, was invalided home. Demobilised in October 1919, he unfortunately died later from the effects of his war service. He was entitled to the General Service and Victory Medals, and was also recommended for a decoration for bravery.
"The path of duty was the way to glory."
30, Clare Street, Northampton. Z1431/B.

REED, W. F., 1st Air Mechanic, R.A.F.
He volunteered in September 1914 in the Northamptonshire Regiment, and in the following year was drafted to France, where he took part in several engagements, and was wounded in action. Later he was transferred to the Royal Air Force, and served in the workshops in various sectors. Demobilised in January 1919, he holds the 1914–15 Star, and the General Service and Victory Medals.
34, Melbourne Street, Northampton. Z1997/A.

REEVE, G. (M.C., M.M.), Lieutenant, 1st Royal Irish Fusiliers.
Having enlisted in 1901, he proceeded to France in August 1914, and, after serving through the Retreat from Mons, took a distinguished part in the Battles of the Aisne, La Bassée, Ypres, Neuve Chapelle, Festubert, Loos, the Somme, Arras and Cambrai, and was four times wounded. Sent home in April 1918, he unhappily died of injuries received in an accident on October 15th of that year. He had been awarded the Military Medal for bravery in the Field and the Military Cross for conspicuous gallantry in 1917, and was mentioned in Despatches in November 1915. He was also entitled to the Mons Star, and the General Service and Victory Medals.
"His memory is cherished with pride."
15, King Street, Northampton. Z2476/C.

REEVE, G., Staff-Sergeant, 1st Northants. Regt.
Called from the Reserve in August 1914, he was immediately drafted to France. There he played a prominent part in the Battles of Mons, Le Cateau, the Marne, the Aisne and Ypres, and was also in action at Landrecies and St. Quentin, but, contracting fever, was invalided home, and later retained at various stations on important duties as a Physical Training Instructor. In 1921 he was serving in Egypt, and holds the Mons Star, and the General Service and Victory Medals.
31, Devonshire Street, St. James' End, Northampton. Z2826.

REEVE, H., Private, 1st Northants. Regiment.
Volunteering in August 1914, he crossed to France a month later, and took part in several engagements, including those at Ypres. He was severely wounded at Aubers Ridge in May 1915, and had a leg amputated in consequence. Invalided home to hospital, he was discharged as physically unfit for further service in September 1915, and holds the 1914 Star, and the General Service and Victory Medals.
17, John Place, Northampton. Z3480/C.

REEVE, H., Trooper, 6th Northants. Dragoons.
He volunteered in September 1914, and, embarking for the Western Front in the following June, was in action at the Battles of Loos, Vimy Ridge, the Somme, Beaumont-Hamel, Arras, Bullecourt, Ypres, Passchendaele and Cambrai. He also fought in the Allied Retreat, and made the supreme sacrifice in the final Advance, being killed in action on September 28th, 1918. He was entitled to the 1914–15 Star, and the General Service and Victory Medals.
"His life for his Country."
38, Southampton Road, Northampton. Z3480/B.

REEVE, H. S., Gunner, Royal Field Artillery.
Mobilised with the Territorials on the outbreak of war, he sailed for Egypt in February 1915, and fought at Messa Matruh, Agayia, Sollum, Jifjaffa, Katia and El Fasher. He was also in action in General Allenby's Advance through Palestine, and served through the Battles of Rafa, Siwa and Gaza, at the fall of Jerusalem and the capture of Jericho, Tripoli and Aleppo. Returning to England for demobilisation in August 1919, he holds the 1914–15 Star, and the General Service and Victory Medals.
38, Southampton Road, Northampton. Z3480/A.

REEVE, R. H., Sergeant, Queen's (Royal West Surrey Regiment).
Volunteering in September 1914, he completed his training, and was retained on important duties at Bury St. Edmunds, Hertford, Northampton and various other stations, where he was engaged as a Gymnastic Instructor. In this capacity he rendered very valuable services until demobilised in February 1919. 15, King Street, Northampton. Z2476/A.

REEVE, S., Private, 7th Northamptonshire Regt.
Volunteering in October 1914, he completed a period of training prior to being drafted overseas. Whilst on the Western Front he was in action with his unit at the Battles of Ypres, Festubert, Loos and the Somme. He died gloriously on the Field of Battle on August 17th, 1916, and was entitled to the 1914–15 Star, and the General Service and Victory Medals.
"A costly sacrifice upon the altar of freedom."
15, King Street, Northampton. Z2476/B

REEVE, S. P., Private, 8th East Surrey Regiment.
Joining in January 1918, he was immediately drafted overseas Serving on the Western Front, he took part in many important engagements in various sectors, and was in action with his unit in the Retreat of 1918, during which he was badly wounded He unhappily died from the effects of his wounds on May 19th, 1918, and was entitled to the General Service and Victory Medals.
"His life for his Country, his soul to God."
15, King Street, Northampton. Z2476/D.

REEVE, W. D., Gunner, Royal Field Artillery.
Volunteering in October 1915, he proceeded to Mesopotamia in the following May, and took part in operations for the Relief of Kut. He did good work in engagements leading to the capture of Baghdad and the Battle of Ramadieh, and fought also on the Tigris. Malaria caused his evacuation to India for treatment, after which he returned to England, and was eventually demobilised in November 1919. He holds the General Service and Victory Medals.
Knutsford Lane, Long Buckby, Northamptonshire. Z3479.

REILLY, T., Saddler, Royal Army Service Corps.
He volunteered in October 1915, and, after a period of training, was engaged at various home stations on important duties with his unit. Unable to obtain a transfer overseas owing to the special nature of his work, he, nevertheless, rendered valuable services until his demobilisation in April 1919.
28, Augustin Street, Northampton. Z2825.

RENDALL, L., Private, Machine Gun Corps.
He enlisted in August 1916, and underwent a period of training prior to his being drafted to France. There he took part in many important engagements, particularly on the Lys, where he was wounded in action. After hostilities ceased he returned home and was demobilised in January 1919, holding the General Service and Victory Medals.
16, Pytchley Street, Northampton. Z2253.

REUBEN, W., Private, Middlesex Regiment.
Having joined in April 1916, he completed his training, and in the same year was drafted to France. In this theatre of war he took part in many important engagements in various sectors of the front. He made the supreme sacrifice, being killed in action, and was entitled to the General Service and Victory Medals.
"A valiant Soldier, with undaunted heart he breasted life's last hill."
102, Purser Road, Northampton. Z2254.

REYNOLDS, J. H., Sergeant, R.E. (R.O.D.)
Volunteering in September 1914, he was drafted to the Western Front in the following year, and there served with distinction in the Ypres, Somme and Arras sectors, and in the Retreat of March 1918, being gassed at Ypres. He was awarded the Divisional Scrip Certificate for devotion to duty in handling parties of men engaged in repairing the lines under heavy shell-fire, and holds also the 1914–15 Star, and the General Service and Victory Medals. He also served with the 2nd Northamptonshire Regiment before being demobilised in March 1919.
3, Sunny Side, Wootton, Northants. Z2827.

REYNOLDS, W., Private, Norfolk Regiment.
Volunteering in January 1916, he received his training at Colchester and Parkstone, and four months later was ordered to Mesopotamia, where he served for over three years. During that time he fought in many engagements, and did good work with his Unit during operations on the Tigris and at Shamrunbend. He was demobilised on his return to England in December 1919, and holds the General Service and Victory Medals. 4, Union Court, Northampton. Z1650.

RHODES, C. G., Trooper, Northants. Dragoons.
He volunteered in August 1914, and in the same year landed in France. Serving on the Western Front, he took part in many engagements, including the Battles of Ypres (I. and II.), Neuve Chapelle, Hill 60, Loos, Vimy Ridge, the Somme and Arras. Transferred to Italy in November 1917, he served on the Piave front and, returning home for demobilisation in February 1919, holds the 1914 Star, and the General Service and Victory Medals. 13, Florence Road, Northampton. Z2255/B.

RHODES, T. H., Corporal, 4th Northants. Regt.
He joined in March 1916, but, on completion of his training, was retained on special duties at various home stations for two years, during which time he rendered valuable services. Proceeding to France, he saw heavy fighting at Ypres, and in April 1918—a month after landing—was badly wounded and evacuated to England. He was discharged as medically unfit for further service in October of the same year, and holds the General Service and Victory Medals.
13, Florence Road, Northampton. Z2255/A.

RICE, J., Private, 2nd Leinster Regiment.
Already in the Army when war broke out in August 1914, he was immediately drafted to France. There he took part in the Retreat from Mons and the Battles of the Marne, the Aisne and La Bassée, where he was wounded and consequently invalided home. On his recovery he returned to France and fought in the Vimy Ridge sector, being again wounded, sustaining the loss of two fingers. He was discharged in December 1917 as medically unfit for further service, and holds the Mons Star, and the General Service and Victory Medals.
24, Shakespeare Road, Northampton. Z1998.

RICE, O. L., Private, 28th Royal Fusiliers.
Having joined in April 1916, he underwent a period of training before being drafted to Salonika in September. In this seat of operations he took part in heavy fighting on the Doiran and Struma fronts. He later contracted malarial fever, and, as a result, was invalided to hospital in Birmingham. On his recovery he was retained on important duties until demobilised in January 1919, holding the General Service and Victory Medals. 24, Hazelwood Road, Northampton. Z2477.

RICH, C., Corporal, 10th Royal Sussex Regiment.
Although only 17½ years of age, he volunteered in 1915, and, after completing a period of training, was retained on important duties with his unit. He did consistently good work, but was unable to obtain his transfer overseas owing to his being medically unfit, and was therefore discharged in 1916.
40, Aithorp Road, Northampton. Z2478.

RICHARDS, E., Cpl., 1st Monmouthshire Regt.
Volunteering in September 1914, he first saw active service in Egypt, but, proceeding to France in May 1916, played a prominent part in heavy fighting at Loos, Ypres, on the Somme and during the Retreat and Advance. He was badly wounded near St. Quentin in October 1918, and was invalided to hospital in Birmingham. In January 1919 he was demobilised, and holds the 1914–15 Star, and the General Service and Victory Medals. 24, Byfield Road, St. James, Northampton. Z2479.

RICHARDSON, B., Driver, Royal Engineers.
He volunteered in August 1915, and, on completion of his training, was retained on special duties with his Unit at Doncaster, Harrogate, Worksop, Southampton and Thetford. Later he proceeded to Russia with Army remounts, and rendered valuable services until his demobilisation in August 1919, holding the General Service and Victory Medals.
51, Louise Road, Northampton. Z1652/A.

RICHARDSON, C., Private, 16th Cheshire Regt.
Having volunteered in August 1915, he underwent a period of training prior to being drafted overseas. Whilst on the Western Front he took part in many important engagements in the Somme and Ypres sectors On October 22nd, 1917, he was reported missing, and was later presumed to have been killed in action on that date. He was entitled to the General Service and Victory Medals.
"His life for his Country."
70, Perry Street, Northampton. Z2256.

RICHARDSON, F. E., Private, Labour Corps.
Joining in March 1917, he was at once drafted to France and, transferred to the Loyal North Lancashire Regiment three months later, fought in several battles, including those during the Retreat and Advance of 1918. Reported missing on August 29th, 1918, he was later presumed to have been killed in action on that date, and was entitled to the General Service and Victory Medals.
"He nobly fell that we might live."
Boughton, Northants. Z3481.

RICHARDSON, H., Private, 5th Northants. Regt.
Joining in May 1918, he shortly afterwards embarked for the Western Front. Whilst in this seat of operations, he took part in several important engagements, including the Battle of Epéhy. After the conclusion of the war, he was transferred to the Royal Engineers and served in the workshops, finally returning home for demobilisation in September 1919. He holds the General Service and Victory Medals.
83, Euston Road, Far Cotton, Northants. Z3016/B.

RICHARDSON, P. J., Private, 11th Border Regt.
Joining in October 1916, he proceeded to France in January of the following year. Serving on the Western Front, he saw much heavy fighting and was in action in engagements in the Arras, Ypres, Cambrai and Somme sectors. He also took part in the Retreat and Advance of 1918, and was twice wounded. As a result he was invalided home and discharged in December 1918 as medically unfit for further service, holding the General Service and Victory Medals.
Station Road, Spratton, Northants. Z3139.

RICHARDSON, S., L/Corporal, Northants. Regt.
He volunteered in May 1915, and, later in the same year, was drafted to France, where he took part in many important engagements in various sectors. He gave his life for King and Country, falling in action in April 1915, and was entitled to the General Service and Victory Medals.
"Thinking that remembrance, though unspoken, may reach him where he sleeps."
65, Dunster Street, Northampton. Z1999/B.

RICHARDSON, W. C., Private, R.A.M.C.
He volunteered in September 1915, and in the following year was drafted to the Western Front, where he did excellent work with his Unit on the Somme, at Ypres, Arras, Givenchy, Delville Wood, Vimy Ridge, and throughout the Retreat and Advance of 1918, during which he saw heavy fighting in the Cambrai sector. He was demobilised in May 1919, and holds the General Service and Victory Medals. 51, Louise Road, Northants. Z1652/B.

RICHARDSON, W. T., L/Cpl., Northants. Regt.
He enlisted in February 1916, and, after a period of training, was engaged at various home stations on important duties with his Unit. Later he was transferred to the Middlesex Regimen but, owing to medical unfitness, was unable toproceed overseas. He rendered valuable services, and was invalided from the Army in February 1919.
65, Dunster Street, Northampton. Z1999/A.

RICHMOND, A., Private, 1st Bedfordshire Regt.
Mobilised at the outbreak of war, he at once proceeded to the Western Front, and served in the Retreat from Mons. He also took part in the Battles of the Marne, the Aisne, La Bassée, Ypres, Neuve Chapelle, the Somme and Cambrai, and was engaged in much severe fighting during the Retreat and Advance of 1918. He was discharged in March 1919, and holds the Mons Star, and the General Service and Victory Medals.
30, Brook Street, Northampton. Z1654.

RICKARD, D. (Mrs., *née* Miss D. Tack), Worker, Queen Mary's Army Auxiliary Corps.
In May 1917 she joined the Women's Army Auxiliary Corps, and was sent to Whittington Barracks, Lichfield. For 15 months she carried out her duties in a very capable manner and rendered valuable services. She was demobilised in July 1918.
Milton, Northampton. Z2438/C.

RICKARD, W. H., Private, Machine Gun Corps.
Joining in May 1917, he underwent a period of training at Grantham prior to being drafted to Italy. In this seat of operations he was in action on the Piave and Asiago Plateaux fronts, and was twice wounded. After the conclusion of hostilities he proceeded to Egypt, where he served at Alexandria and Cairo. He returned home for demobilisation in February 1920, and holds the General Service and Victory Medals. Milton, Northamptonshire. Z2438/B.

RICKERD, G. D., Private, R.A.M.C.
He volunteered in November 1915, and was retained for a time on important duties before being drafted to France in April 1917. In this seat of war he served as a stretcher-bearer at St. Omer, and later proceeded to the Arras and Cambrai fronts, and rendered valuable services. He was gassed in action and was demobilised in April 1919, holding the General Service and Victory Medals.
13, Verulum Buildings, Northampton. Z2828.

RIDDLE, J., Sergt., Northants. Regt. and M.G.C.
At the outbreak of war he was already serving, and was engaged on important instructional duties at Weymouth and Gillingham. He was not successful in his endeavours to secure a transfer to a theatre of war, but, nevertheless, performed most valuable work until his health broke down. Unhappily he died of consumption at Mansfield Hospital on May 18th, 1917.
"His memory is cherished with pride."
41, Gladstone Terrace, Northampton. Z1517/A.

RIGBY, C. E., Private, 1/4th Northants. Regiment.
He volunteered in August 1914, and, on completion of his training at Northampton, was ordered to Egypt in the following year. Subsequently he was drafted to Palestine, where he was engaged in fierce fighting, and died gloriously on the Field of Battle at Gaza in April 1917. He was entitled to the 1914-15 Star, and the General Service and Victory Medals.
"His life for his Country, his soul to God."
17, Herbert Street, Northampton. Z1655/A.

RIGBY, T., Private, 2/10th London Regiment.
When war broke out in August 1914 he volunteered, and in the following year was drafted overseas. Serving on the Western Front, he was in action in many important engagements, including the Battles of the Somme and Ypres, and gave his life for King and Country at Cambrai in September 1917. He was entitled to the 1914-15 Star, and the General Service and Victory Medals.
"He nobly died that we might live."
17, Herbert Street, Northampton. Z1655/B.

RIBGY, T. H., L/Corporal, Royal Engineers.
Although only 17½ years of age, he volunteered in July 1915, and on conclusion of his training was drafted overseas. Whilst on the Western Front, he was engaged on important duties as a draughtsman, and served with the Headquarters Staff of the 1st Army at Rouen and Bergecourt. He did consistently good work, and in April 1919 was demobilised, holding the General Service and Victory Medals.
32, Florence Road, Northampton. Z2257.

RILEY, A., Corporal, West Riding Regiment.
He joined in March 1916, and shortly afterwards was drafted to the Western Front, where he was wounded during the Battle of the Somme in July 1916, and invalided to England. In 1917 he returned to France, took part in numerous engagements, and was unhappily killed in action at Cambrai on September 18th, 1918. He was entitled to the General Service and Victory Medals.
"The path of duty was the way to glory."
22, Herbert Street, Northampton. Z1656.

RIMMER, W., L/Corporal, 5th Welch Regiment.
Volunteering in August 1914, he completed his training, and in the following year was drafted to the Dardanelles. Shortly after landing in Gallipoli he contracted enteric fever, and, as a result, was invalided home. On his recovery he proceeded to Egypt, where he was engaged on important duties. He afterwards served with General Allenby's Forces in Palestine, and was present at the Battles of Gaza, the capture of Jerusalem, and in the Advance to Damascus. Returning home for demobilisation in June 1919, he holds the 1914-15 Star, and the General Service and Victory Medals.
11, Florence Road, Northampton. Z2258.

RINGROSE, G., L/Corporal, R.A.S.C.
Volunteering in September 1915, he was shortly afterwards drafted to France, and engaged on important transport duties in the forward areas. He saw much service during the Battles of the Somme, Arras, Ypres, Cambrai and Amiens, and in the Retreat and Advance of 1918. He remained in France until March 1919, when he was demobilised, holding the 1914-15 Star, and the General Service and Victory Medals.
43, Charles Street, Northampton. Z1658.

RIVETT, B., Private, Royal Defence Corps.
Unable to serve in a combatant Unit, he volunteered in the Royal Defence Corps in August 1914, and during the whole period of hostilities did excellent work. He was chiefly engaged in guarding the railways and bridges at various important points in England, and was eventually demobilised in March 1919. Bliss Lane, Flore, Northants. Z2829.

RIXSON, P. T., Private, 1st Northants. Regiment.
Mobilised in August 1914, he proceeded to France with the first Expeditionary Force and fought in the Retreat from Mons. He was also in action at the Battles of the Aisne, La Bassée, Ypres (I.), Neuve Chapelle, Albert, Givenchy, Loos, the Somme, Arras, Passchendaele, Cambrai and Ypres (IV.), and was wounded on three occasions. After the Armistice, he went into Germany with the Army of Occupation, serving on the Rhine until discharged in January 1921. He holds the Mons Star, and the General Service and Victory Medals.
42, King Street, Northampton. Z1537/A.

ROAN, H. J., Private, 2/4th Gloucestershire Regt.
Mobilised in August 1914, he was immediately drafted to France. In this theatre of war he took part in the Retreat from Mons, and the Battles of the Marne, the Aisne, La Bassée, Ypres, the Somme, Arras and Cambrai, fought also in the Retreat and Advance of 1918, and was wounded in action on three occasions. Discharged in March 1919, he holds the Mons Star, and the General Service and Victory Medals.
23, Lower Priory Street, Northampton. Z1154/A.

ROBERTS, A. B., Gunner, R.F.A.
Enlisting in 1912, he was sent to the Western Front when war was declared in August 1914, and was in almost continuous action in the Retreat from Mons, and the Battles of the Marne and the Aisne. He gave his life for King and Country on September 16th, 1914, and was entitled to the Mons Star, and the General Service and Victory Medals.
"A valiant Soldier, with undaunted heart he breasted life's last hill."
Brayfield-on-the-Green, Northants. Z3483/B.

ROBERTS, A. W., L/Cpl., 1st Northants. Regt.
He volunteered in August 1914, and, crossing to France in the following January, participated in the Battle of Neuve Chapelle, and was wounded in March 1915. After treatment at Leeds, he returned to his Unit and fought at Messines and Passchendaele, and was again wounded in August 1916, and sent home, after which he served at Arras, Cambrai and St. Quentin, and was wounded for the third time at St. Quentin. He was demobilised in March 1919, and holds the 1914-15 Star, and the General Service and Victory Medals.
Brayfield-on-the-Green, Northants. Z3483/A.

ROBERTS, C. A., Cpl.-Shoeing-Smith, R.F.A.
Mobilised at the outbreak of war, he was at once ordered to the Western Front, and took an active part in many engagements of note, until discharged as a time-expired man in November 1915. In July 1916 he rejoined, and, proceeding to France in the following April, was in action in severe fighting on the Somme and Ypres fronts. He was demobilised in May 1919, and holds the 1914 Star, and the General Service and Victory Medals. 63, Compton Street, Northampton. TZ1660.

ROBERTS, C. S., Gunner, Royal Garrison Artillery.
Joining in 1916, he underwent a period of training, and in the same year proceeded overseas. Serving on the Western Front, he was in action with his Battery at the Battles of Arras, Vimy Ridge, Bullecourt, Messines, Ypres, Lens and Cambrai, and was gassed. Invalided home to hospital owing to an illness, he was eventually demobilised in January 1919, and holds the General Service and Victory Medals.
144, Market Street, Northampton. Z2209/D.

ROBERTS, F., Private, 2nd Northants. Regiment.
Volunteering in 1915, he embarked for the Western Front later in the same year, and took part in the Battle of Neuve Chapelle and several other important engagements. He saw heavy fighting during the Somme Offensive, and gave his life for the freedom of England in 1916. He was entitled to the 1914-15 Star, and the General Service and Victory Medals.
"Whilst we remember, the sacrifice is not in vain."
74, Oxford Street, Far Cotton, Northampton. Z3482.

ROBERTS, F., Private, 1st Hertfordshire Regt.
He joined in August 1916, and, after service at various home depôts, sailed for France in December 1917. Whilst on the Western Front he was in action in several engagements in the final stages of the war, and was wounded at Ypres. On recovery he fought at Bapaume, Havrincourt, Cambrai and Gouzeaucourt, and was gassed and wounded. He was discharged in February 1919, and holds the General Service and Victory Medals.
High Street, Long Buckby, Northants. Z3485.

ROBERTS, G. J., Gunner, Royal Field Artillery.
He enlisted in 1911, and was stationed in India when war broke out. Proceeding to Mesopotamia, he served with the forces under General Townsend, and took part in operations in the advance to Baghdad. Wounded during the siege of Kut in 1916, he was removed to hospital and died of his injuries on February 14th of that year. He was entitled to the 1914-15 Star, and the General Service and Victory Medals.
"Great deeds cannot die."
Brayfield-on-the-Green, Northants. Z3484.

ROBERTS, H., Private, 5th Northants. Regiment.
He volunteered in November 1915, and 13 months later was sent to the Western Front. There he took an active part in many important engagements in various sectors until taken prisoner near Nieuport. He was held in captivity until January 1919, and, when repatriated, was demobilised in the following month, holding the General Service and Victory Medals. 11, Cowper Street, Northampton. Z1661.

ROBERTS, H. C. (M.M.), Bombardier, R.G.A.
After volunteering in October 1915, he landed in France early in the following year. In the course of his active service he was in action with his Battery at the Battles of Albert and the Somme, before being wounded and invalided home. Returning to the Western Front on his recovery, he rejoined his Battery, and took part in the Retreat and Advance of 1918. He was awarded the Military Medal for great gallantry and devotion to duty in the Field, and in February 1919 was demobilised, holding also the General Service and Victory Medals. 48, Manfield Road, Northampton. Z2259.

ROBERTS, H. C., Pte., 2nd R. Warwickshire Regt.
Having joined in August 1916, he underwent a period of training prior to being drafted overseas. Whilst on the Western Front, he took part in various engagements, including the Battles of Arras and Bullecourt. He made the supreme sacrifice, being killed in action on May 4th, 1917, and was entitled to the General Service and Victory Medals.
"Steals on the ear the distant triumph song."
15, Wilby Street, Northampton. Z2235/A.

ROBERTS, I., Private, 1/4th Royal Welch Fusiliers.
He volunteered in August 1914, and three months later was drafted to France, where he took part in many engagements, including the Battles of Neuve Chapelle, Festubert, Loos, the Somme, Arras and Ypres. He was unfortunately killed in action in the Retreat on March 23rd, 1918, and was entitled to the 1914-15 Star, and the General Service and Victory Medals.
"He nobly fell that we might live."
14, Mount Gardens, Northampton. Z4000.

ROBERTS, J. H. F., Private, R.A.S.C. (M.T.), and Royal Welch Regiment.
He joined the Royal Army Service Corps in January 1917, but was later transferred to the Welch Regiment, and in June 1917 proceeded overseas. Whilst serving on the Western Front, he fought in the Battles of Messines, Ypres, Passchendaele, Lens, Havrincourt and Le Cateau, was gassed on one occasion and also blown up by an explosion. Demobilised in September 1919, he holds the General Service and Victory Medals.
72, Charles Street, Northampton. Z1659.

ROBERTS, M. (Miss), Member, British Red Cross Society.
She volunteered in March 1915, and was employed making comforts for the soldiers, and also in the manufacture of ammunition until October of that year. She was afterwards engaged on important nursing duties at Barry Road Hospital, and, throughout the period of hostilities, rendered excellent services. 119, Holly Road, Northampton. Z2102/A.

ROBERTS, O., L/Cpl., Royal Dublin Fusiliers.
Joining in February 1916, he completed his training, and in the following year was drafted to the Western Front, where he was in action at the Battles of Messines, Ypres and Cambrai before being invalided home with appendicitis. On his recovery he was transferred to Ireland, where he was engaged as a Musketry Instructor, in which capacity he rendered valuable services until demobilised in March 1919, holding the General Service and Victory Medals.
57, Ambush Street, St. James, Northampton. Z2480.

ROBERTS, W., Bombardier, R.G.A.
Volunteering in October 1915, he was drafted to France two months later, and, after fighting in various engagements, was wounded in the Battle of the Somme. On his return to the firing-line he was again wounded at Vimy Ridge, and invalided to England in November 1916. In March 1918 he returned to France, and saw much service in the Ypres, Albert, Cambrai and Amiens sectors. He was demobilised in January 1919, and holds the 1914-15 Star, and the General Service and Victory Medals. 23, Uppingham St., Northampton. Z1662.

ROBERTSON, A. V., Guardsman, Coldstream Gds.
A Regular, he was mobilised and sent to France in August 1914, and, fighting in the Retreat from Mons, was wounded in the following September. After treatment at Aldershot, he returned to the Western Front in May 1915, and was in action at the Battles of Ypres, Festubert, Loos, Albert, the Somme, Arras and Cambrai, and in the Retreat and Advance of 1918. He was discharged in January 1919, and holds the Mons Star, and the General Service and Victory Medals.
Lower Heyford, Weedon, Northants. Z3486.

ROBERTSON, W., Private, Norfolk Regiment.
He volunteered in December 1914, and, crossing to the Western Front a month later, served in various sectors until the close of the war. During this period he took part in the Battles of the Somme, Arras, Vimy Ridge, Ypres and Messines, and those of the German Offensive and the subsequent Allied Advance of 1918. He returned to England for demobilisation in April 1919, and holds the 1914-15 Star, and the General Service and Victory Medals. Denton, Northants. Z3487/B.

ROBERTSON, W. G., Driver, Canadian F.A.
He volunteered in 1915 in Canada, and shortly afterwards embarked for the Western Front. In this seat of operations he took part in many important engagements, particularly in the Somme, Ypres and Cambrai sectors. He was gassed during heavy fighting in the Retreat of 1918, and, as a result, was invalided to England. On his recovery he returned to Canada for demobilisation in May 1919, and holds the General Service and Victory Medals. Chapel Yard, Gayton, Northants. Z2481.

ROBERTSON, W. H., Private, 3rd Northants. Regt.
Volunteering in December 1914, he passed through a course of training, and, stationed in the South of England, was engaged on important duties with his Battalion. He rendered valuable services, but was not sent overseas owing to medical unfitness for general service, and was discharged in consequence in April 1915. Denton, Northants. Z3487/A.

ROBBINS, A. G., Private, Northants. Regiment.
Joining in February 1916, he was trained at Gillingham, and drafted to the Western Front four months later. Whilst in France he was engaged in severe fighting in various sectors, but was taken prisoner in March 1917, and held in captivity in Poland, unfortunately dying there of starvation in October 1918. He was entitled to the General Service and Victory Medals. "The path of duty was the way to glory."
17, Denmark Road, Northampton. Z3140.

ROBINS, D., Private, 1st Northants. Regiment.
He volunteered in January 1916, and in the following July was drafted to France and fought on the Somme, where he was blown up by shell explosion and consequently invalided to Le Havre. Returning to his unit shortly afterwards, he was unfortunately killed in action on the Somme on July 23rd, 1916. He was entitled to the General Service and Victory Medals.
"A costly sacrifice upon the altar of freedom."
6, Newcombe Road, Northampton. Z2830/A.

ROBINS, H. W., Tpr., 2/1st Scottish Horse (Dgns.)
He joined in July 1916, and, after a period of training, was engaged at various home stations on important duties with his Unit. He was not successful in obtaining a transfer overseas, but rendered valuable services until his demobilisation in November 1919. 6, Newcombe Rd., Northampton. Z2830/B.

ROBINS, W. J., Private, R.A.M.C.
He volunteered in August 1915, and in the following December was ordered to France, where he rendered valuable services as a stretcher-bearer on the Somme and Armentières fronts. In November 1917 he was invalided to England suffering from nephritis, but, on his discharge from hospital, was drafted to Palestine in January 1918, and saw heavy fighting at Jaffa. He was demobilised on his return home in March 1919, and holds the 1914-15 Star, and the General Service and Victory Medals. 58, Bath Street, Northampton. Z1663.

ROBINS, W. J., Private, 1/4th Northants. Regt.
Called up from the Reserve in August 1914, he embarked for Gallipoli in July 1915, and saw heavy fighting at Suvla Bay, Chocolate Hill and Anzac. After the Evacuation, he was drafted to Egypt and subsequently to Palestine, on which front he was in action at Gaza, Jaffa, Jerusalem and Aleppo. In October 1918 he was transferred to Salonika, and served there for two months. He was discharged on his return to England in March 1919, holding the 1914-15 Star, and the General Service and Victory Medals.
43, Regent Street, Northampton. Z1664.

ROBINSON, A. C., Corporal, Lancashire Fusiliers.
He joined in 1917, and, after a period of training at Norwich, was ordered overseas in the same year. Serving on the Western Front, he fought in the Battles of Ypres and the Somme, and other engagements of note, but was unhappily kill..d in action in June 1918. He was entitled to the General Service and Victory Medals.
"He died the noblest death a man may die,
Fighting for God and right and liberty."
22, Stanley Street, Northampton. Z1665/B.

ROBINSON, A. J., Private, 2nd Northants. Regt.
A month after the outbreak of war he volunteered, and in January 1915 embarked for France. On that front he was engaged in severe fighting, chiefly in the Ypres sector, and died gloriously on the Field of Battle at Neuve Chapelle in March 1915. He was entitled to the 1914-15 Star, and the General Service and Victory Medals.
"Honour to the immortal dead who gave their youth that the world might grow old in peace."
22, Stanley Street, Northampton. Z1665/A.

ROBINSON, A. J. (sen.), Bandsman, 1/4th Northamptonshire Regiment.
He volunteered in August 1915, and was engaged on duties of an important naturr at Newmarket. He was not successful in obtaining a transfer to a theatre of war on account of his age, but, nevertheless, rendered valuable services until discharged in March 1916.
22, Stanley Street, Northampton. Z1665/C.

ROBINSON, C., Driver, R.A.S.C.
Joining in May 1916, he completed a period of training at Ripon, but was later found to be medically unfit for transfer overseas. He was therefore retained on important transport duties in Yorkshire, where he rendered very valuable services until demobilised in September 1919.
Milton, Northants. Z2482/A.

ROBINSON, E., Private, Northumberland Fusiliers.
Volunteering in August 1914, he was retained on home service until 1916, when he proceeded to India and was engaged on important garrison duties at various stations, including Poona. He was also engaged in fierce fighting in various engagements on the North-West Frontier. On his return to England he was demobilised in November 1919, holding the General Service and Victory Medals, and the India General Service Medal (with clasp, Afghanistan, N.W. Frontier, 1919).
2, Althorp Street, Northampton. Z1668.

ROBINSON, E. D., Private, Bedfordshire Regt.
Joining in August 1918, he was shortly afterwards drafted to the Western Front, where he took part in the final Advance. After the cessation of hostilities, he proceeded with the Army of Occupation to Germany, and was stationed at Cologne, where he was engaged on important guard and other duties until demobilised in August 1920. He holds the General Service and Victory Medals. Milton, Northampton. Z2482/B.

ROBINSON, E. S., L/Cpl., 8th Northants. Regt.
Volunteering in October 1914, he was first engaged on important duties with his Unit at Weymouth. Proceeding to France in January 1916, he was in action on the Somme, where he was reported missing on July 11th, 1916, and later presumed to have been killed on that date. He was entitled to the General Service and Victory Medals.
"He nobly fell that we might live."
11, Hazelwood Road, Northampton. Z2337/B.

ROBINSON, G., Gunner, Royal Field Artillery.
He was called up from the Reserve in August 1914, and immediately drafted to France. There he took part in the Retreat from Mons and the Battles of the Marne, Ypres, Armentières, Loos, the Somme, Arras, Ypres (III.), Passchendaele and Cambrai, fought also in the Advance of 1918, and was wounded in action. As a result he was invalided home and eventually discharged in February 1919 as medically unfit for further service. He holds the Mons Star, and the General Service and Victory Medals. 36, King Street, Northampton. Z1328/B.

ROBINSON, G. C., Private, 1st Northants. Regt.
Eight months after volunteering in April 1915, he was ordered to the Western Front, where he was in action in numerous important engagements and did good work with his Unit in the Battles of the Somme, Arras, Ypres, Cambrai and La Bassée. He served in France until February 1919, when he was demobilised, holding the 1914–15 Star, and the General Service and Victory Medals. 6, Bristol Street, Northampton. Z1666/A.

ROBINSON, G. E., Private, 4th Northants. Regt.
He volunteered in 1915, and, sailing for France in the following year, was in action in the Somme Offensive and in the Battles of Ypres, Passchendaele, Lens, and Cambrai. He also fought in the Retreat and Advance of 1918, and, after the Armistice, was stationed in Germany with the Army of Occupation for several months. Demobilised on his return to England in August 1919, he holds the General Service and Victory Medals.
Brayfield-on-the-Green, Northants. Z3490.

ROBINSON, J. M., Private, R.A.M.C.
Volunteering in October 1915, he completed his training and embarked for the Western Front in the following year. In this theatre of war he did consistently good work as a stretcher-bearer and served during heavy fighting in the Somme, Arras and Ypres sectors. He was unhappily killed whilst conveying the wounded to a Casualty Clearing Station on August 6th, 1917, and was entitled to the General Service and Victory Medals.
"A costly sacrifice upon the altar of freedom."
85, Military Road, Northampton. Z2261.

ROBINSON, L. G., Trooper, Northants. Dragoons.
Volunteering in October 1914, he landed on the Western Front in the following March, and took part in heavy fighting on the Somme and in the Ypres salient. He was seriously wounded in the Battle of Arras in May 1917, and, sent to England, was admitted to Cambridge Hospital, Aldershot, for treatment, after which he was invalided out of the Service in September 1917. He holds the 1914–15 Star, and the General Service and Victory Medals. Kilsby, Northants. Z3491.

ROBINSON, P. J., Private, 7th Suffolk Regiment.
Having joined in January 1917, he was drafted overseas three months later. Whilst on the Western Front he took part in much heavy fighting at Cambrai. He was taken prisoner and held in captivity in Germany, where he was forced to work as a coal-heaver, and suffered many hardships. Repatriated after the Armistice, he was discharged in May 1919 as medically unfit for further service, and holds the General Service and Victory Medals. 20, Sandhill Road, St. James, Northampton. Z2831.

ROBINSON, S. J., Private, R.A.S.C. (M.T.)
He volunteered in 1915, and, on conclusion of his training in the following year, proceeded to France, where he was engaged on important transport duties. He took an active part in many important engagements, particularly in the Ypres sector, and was also present at the entry of Mons at dawn on Armistice Day. After the cessation of hostilities, he served with the Army of Occupation in Germany. Demobilised in 1919, he holds the General Service and Victory Medals.
75, Edmund's Road, Northampton. Z2260.

ROBINSON, W., Corporal, 1st Northants. Regt.
Already in the Army when war broke out in August 1914, he was immediately drafted to France. In this seat of war he took part in the Retreat from Mons, and in the Battles of the Aisne, La Bassée, Ypres, Aubers Ridge, Loos, the Somme, Arras, Passchendaele and Cambrai, served also in the Advance of 1918, and was wounded on four occasions. In 1921 he was serving in Ireland, and holds the Mons Star, and the General Service and Victory Medals.
49, Regent Street, Northampton. Z1029/A.

ROBINSON, W., Sapper, Royal Engineers.
Joining in April 1917, he landed in France a month later. Whilst in this seat of operations, he was engaged on important duties with the Railway Operative Department, and served during heavy fighting in the Ypres and Cambrai sectors. He also took an active part in the Retreat and Advance of 1918, and in February 1919 was demobilised, holding the General Service and Victory Medals.
3, Ivor Terrace, Roade, Northampton. Z2262.

ROBINSON, W., Private, 3rd Bedfordshire Regt.
Joining in February 1917, he proceeded to France two months later and was in action in several engagements in the Somme sector. He was wounded near St. Quentin during the Battle of the Somme in March 1918, and was sent to hospital in Scotland. On his recovery in July 1919, he was drafted with the Army of Occupation to Germany and was stationed at Cologne. He served also with the Machine Gun Corps, and was demobilised in the following October, holding the General Service and Victory Medals.
49, The Lane, Denton, Northants. Z3489.

ROBINSON, W. B., Pioneer, Royal Engineers.
He joined in April 1917, and was retained on home service duties until November 1918, when he crossed to the Western Front. There he was employed with his Section on bridge and pontoon building, and did excellent work at a Base for several months. Illness led to his evacuation to England, where he was eventually demobilised in March 1919. He holds the General Service and Victory Medals.
The Lane, Denton, Northants. Z3488.

ROBINSON, W. W., Private, Machine Gun Corps.
Joining in January 1918, he was drafted to the Western Front in August of that year, and saw severe fighting in various sectors, taking part in the Battle of Le Cateau and other engagements. Severely injured in an accident, he was in hospital in France, before being invalided home, and was finally demobilised in November 1920. He holds the General Service and Victory Medals. 43, Hood Street, Northampton. Z1667.

ROCKINGHAM, F., Cpl., 4th Northants. Regt.
He volunteered in April 1915, and, after a period of training, was engaged at various stations on important sanitary inspection duties. Owing to his being over age, he was unable to obtain a transfer to a theatre of war, but rendered valuable services until his demobilisation in January 1919.
29, Warwick Street, Daventry, Northants. Z2832.

RODDIS, A., Private, 9th Cheshire Regiment.
He volunteered in October 1915, and later in the same year was drafted to France, where he took part in many engagements, including those at Monchy, Messines, Vimy Ridge and the Somme, and was gassed in 1917. Invalided home, he returned to France, however, and was wounded and again gassed at Cambrai in March 1918. He was finally demobilised in February 1919, and holds the 1914–15 Star, and the General Service and Victory Medals.
111, St. Michael's Street, Northampton. Z2001.

RODDIS, C. H., Lieutenant, R.N.V.R.
He volunteered in Canada in 1915, and, proceeding to England, was posted to his ship and rendered valuable services mine-sweeping in the North Sea. He was wounded in action in April 1916, and was awarded the Humane Society's Medal for saving the life of a fisherman. Demobilised in February 1919, after four years' excellent work, he also holds the General Service and Victory Medals.
35, Denmark Road, Northampton. Z3141/B.

RODDIS, W. S., Sapper, Royal Engineers.
Volunteering in April 1915, he embarked for Egypt two months later and was engaged on important wireless and signalling duties at Alexandria and Cairo, and in the Desert. Proceeding to Palestine, he saw heavy fighting at Gaza, Haifa and Jaffa, but was transferred to Italy in 1917, and took part in engagements on the Piave front. Shortly afterwards he returned to Egypt, serving there until sent home for demobilisation in August 1919, and holds the 1914–15 Star, and the General Service and Victory Medals.
35, Denmark Road, Northampton. Z3141/A.

RODHOUS, A., Corporal, R.A.S.C.
He joined in 1916, and later in the same year was drafted to France. In this theatre of war he was engaged with the transport, conveying supplies to the forward areas during heavy fighting in various sectors. He did good work throughout, and was demobilised in 1919, holding the General Service and Victory Medals.
22, Alma Street, Northampton. Z2833.

ROE, C. E., Private, 1st Northants. Regiment.
Volunteering in August 1915, he was drafted overseas in the following February. Whilst on the Western Front he took part in several important engagements, including those in the Ypres, Somme and Arras sectors. He was wounded in action and taken prisoner of war in August 1918, being held in captivity in Germany for four months. Repatriated after the Armistice, he returned home and was demobilised in January 1919. He holds the General Service and Victory Medals
11, Weston Row, Northampton. Z2835.

ROE, J., Sapper, Royal Engineers.
He joined in July 1917, and, on completing a period of training in January of the following year, proceeded to France. There he was engaged on duties of great importance at Calais, and various other stations and did much useful work until his return home for demobilisation in February 1919. He holds the General Service and Victory Medals.
29, Burleigh Road, Northampton. Z1669.

ROE, J. W., Private, 16th Lancashire Fusiliers.
He joined in November 1917, and, in the following March was drafted to France. Whilst on the Western Front he took part in engagements on the Somme, at Ypres, Messines and Arras, where he was gassed and badly wounded. As a result he was invalided home and was later demobilised in January 1919. He holds the General Service and Victory Medals.
22, Queen's Road, Northampton. Z2002.

ROFF, H., Private, 14th Leicestershire Regiment.
He joined in November 1915 and, crossing to France in June of the following year, was in action in the Battle of the Somme and other notable engagements, and was wounded. Invalided home with appendicitis in April 1917, he returned to the Western Front in July 1918, and rendered valuable services there until demobilised in June 1919, holding the General Service and Victory Medals. 28, Spencer Street, Northampton. Z3142/A.

ROFF, W. G., Private, 2/4th Northants. Regt.
A month after the outbreak of war in August 1914, he volunteered, and was engaged on duties of an important nature at Northampton. Unfortunately his health broke down, and he was discharged as medically unfit for further military service in December 1914.
28, Spencer Street, Northampton. Z3142/B.

ROGERS, G. H., Sergeant, Royal Field Artillery.
Shortly after volunteering in 1915, he was sent to the Western Front, where he was engaged in fierce fighting in the Battles of the Somme, Arras, Bullecourt, Messines, Ypres and Cambrai. He also did excellent work with his Battery during the German Offensive and subsequent Allied Advance of 1918. Serving in France until sent home for demobilisation in February 1919, he holds the 1914–15 Star, and the General Service and Victory Medals.
21, Clinton Road, Far Cotton, Northampton. Z3143/A.

ROGERS, H. (M.M. and Bar), Corporal, 1st Royal Warwickshire Regiment.
Enlisting in April 1914, he proceeded to the Western Front in March of the following year, but was wounded at Ypres two months later and invalided home. Returning to France on his recovery, however, he was again wounded on the Somme in 1916, and sent to England. He rejoined his unit a second time in January 1917, and took part in the Battles of Arras, Vimy Ridge, Passchendaele and the Somme, and in the Retreat and Advance of 1918. He was awarded the Military Medal for conspicuous gallantry in the Field in 1916, and a Bar for bravery and devotion to duty in the following year. Holding also the 1914–15 Star, and the General Service and Victory Medals, he was discharged in February 1919.
High Street, Flore, Northants. Z2835.

ROGERS, W., 1st Air Mechanic, Royal Air Force.
He joined in 1918, and was engaged on important duties in the Motor Transport Section at various stations in England. Owing to the early cessation of hostilities, he was unable to secure a transfer to a theatre of war, but, nevertheless, rendered valuable services until discharged as medically unfit for further duty in June 1920.
21, Clinton Street, Far Cotton, Northampton. Z3143/B.

ROLFE, J. W., Private, Royal Army Medical Corps.
He volunteered in August 1914, and about 12 months later was drafted to Mudros, thence to Palestine. In this seat of operations he was attached to the 1st and 2nd East Anglian Field Ambulance, and took part in the Battle of Gaza, the capture of Jerusalem, and the Advance of 1918 with General Allenby's Forces. Demobilised in April 1919, he holds the 1914–15 Star, and the General Service and Victory Medals.
64, Countess Road, St. James, Northampton. Z2836.

ROOK, H., Private, 5th Royal Inniskilling Fusiliers.
Joining in November 1916, he was drafted to Salonika early in the following year. Whilst in this theatre of war he took part in much heavy fighting. Later in the same year he was transferred to Egypt, and saw service there before proceeding to Palestine, where he was in action at the Battles of Gaza and Beersheba. He was afterwards drafted to the Western Front, and was present at engagements during the Retreat and Advance of 1918, before being gassed at Le Cateau in October. Evacuated to England, he was eventually discharged in September 1919, and holds the General Service and Victory Medals.
High Street, Gayton, Northampton. Z2483.

ROSE, F., L/Corporal, 12th Gloucestershire Regt. and 5th Bedfordshire Regiment.
Joining in 1917, he completed his training, and in the same year embarked for the scene of activities in France. On that front he was in action in the Battles of Ypres, Passchendaele and Cambrai, and in numerous other engagements of note, and was gassed in 1918. He was present during the triumphal entry into Mons, eventually being demobilised in March 1919, holding the General Service and Victory Medals.
Newland Street, Brixworth, Northampton. Z3145.

ROSE, J., Private, Royal Army Ordnance Corps.
Joining in August 1916, after having been twice rejected, he underwent a course of training, and was employed on important duties with his Unit at Didcot and other depôts. He rendered valuable services, but, owing to medical unfitness, was unable to secure his transfer overseas. Sent to Ireland, however, he did work of a useful nature, and was demobilised in August 1919. 6 House, Court 3, Wellington Street, Northants. Z3492.

ROSE, T., Private, 10th and 12th Hampshire Regt.
He volunteered in May 1915, and, after a period of training, was drafted to Salonika in October of the following year. Whilst overseas he took an active part in numerous notable engagements on the Vardar and the Doiran fronts, until invalided home with malaria in November 1918. On his recovery he was retained on home service until demobilised in August 1919, holding the General Service and Victory Medals.
Newland Street, Brixworth, Northants. Z3144.

ROUGHTON, E. (Mrs.), Member, V.A.D.
She joined the V.A.D. in 1918, and was stationed at Barry Road Hospital, Northampton, for six months. During this period she was engaged on important duties, and did much excellent work, her services being very highly valued, until her discharge.
84, Euston Road, Northampton. Z3135/A.

ROUGHTON, F., Rifleman, 17th London Regt.
In August 1915 he volunteered in the Royal Army Medical Corps, but, before proceeding to France in 1916, was transferred to the London Regiment. After six months' heavy fighting on the Western Front, he was sent to Salonika, where he was in action on the Doiran. At the end of 1916 he was transferred to Egypt, and, advancing into Palestine, took part in the three Battles of Gaza. He was unfortunately killed in action near Jerusalem on December 8th, 1917, and was entitled to the General Service and Victory Medals.
"His name liveth for evermore."
31, Marlborough Road, Northampton. Z2484/A—3146.

ROUGHTON, W., Private, R.A.M.C.
Joining in June 1918, he completed his training, but owing to the early cessation of hostilities, was unable to take part in operations in a fighting area. He was therefore engaged on important duties in connection with the Dispersal Staff at Connaught Hospital, where he rendered very valuable services until demobilised in January 1919.
31, Marlborough Road, Northampton. Z2484/B.

ROUGHTON, W. H., Private, R.A.M.C.
He volunteered in September 1914, and in the following year embarked for the Western Front. Whilst in this seat of operations he served during heavy fighting on the Somme, where he was wounded in 1916. On his recovery he took part in the Battles of Arras, Vimy Ridge, Ypres, Passchendaele, Cambrai, and also in the Retreat and Advance of 1918. He was demobilised in February 1919, and holds the 1914–15 Star, and the General Service and Victory Medals.
84, Euston Road, Northampton. Z3135/B.

ROWE, F. B., Air Mechanic, Royal Air Force.
He joined in May 1918, and in the following October was drafted to the Western Front. There he served as a despatch-rider, and was engaged on important duties in various sectors of the front. He remained overseas until after hostilities ceased, and was eventually demobilised in February 1919. He holds the General Service and Victory Medals.
115, Lower Thrift Street, Northampton. Z2003.

ROWE, J. A., Sapper, Royal Engineers.
Having attested in 1915, he was called to the Colours in November 1916, and was retained on important duties with his Unit before proceeding to France in March 1918. In this theatre of war he was engaged on important wiring and trench digging, and was present during heavy fighting at the Battles of Amiens, Bapaume and Cambrai. He was gassed during this period, and in September 1919 was demobilised, holding the General Service and Victory Medals.
107, Cecil Road, Northampton. Z2485.

ROWLANDS, J. W., Driver, R.A.S.C.
He volunteered in August 1914, and, after a period of training, was retained on important duties in England until January 1917, when he proceeded to Salonika. There he saw much severe fighting on the Doiran and Vardar fronts, and was for a time in hospital in July 1917, suffering from malaria. He was demobilised on his return home in July 1919, and holds the General Service and Victory Medals.
28, Victoria Street, Northampton. Z1957/C—Z1958/C.

ROYCE, H., Private, 1/4th Northants. Regiment.
Already serving in India in August 1914, he proceeded to Mesopotamia in the following year, and there took part in the capture of Amara and engagements at Kut, where he was wounded, sustaining the loss of his left eye. Invalided home, he was for a considerable period in hospital before being discharged in January 1918 as medically unfit for further service, and holds the 1914–15 Star, and the General Service and Victory Medals. 41, Bailiff Street, Northampton. Z1670.

RUFF, F., Private, 1st Northants. Regiment.
He enlisted in May 1898, and at the outbreak of war was quickly drafted to France, where he took part in the Retreat from Mons, and was wounded during the Battle of the Aisne. As a result he was invalided home, and on his recovery retained at Aldershot before being transferred to the Leicestershire Regiment and again sent to France. He was in action during the Advance of 1918, and eventually received his discharge in June 1919. He holds the Queen's and King's South African Medals, the Mons Star, General Service, Victory and Long Service and Good Conduct Medals.
12, Argyle Street, St. James, Northampton. Z2837.

RUFF, R. F., Corporal, Royal Garrison Artillery.
Joining in May 1916, he proceeded to France with the 266th Siege Battery in February 1917, and played a prominent part in the Battles of Arras, Bullecourt, Messines, Ypres (III.) and Cambrai. During the Retreat and Advance of 1918 he was in action at Henin, Agny, Ficheux, Moyenville, Ervillers, Mory, Noreuil, Quéant, Pronville, Hermies, Demiecourt, Noyelles and other places, and was twice gassed. He was demobilised in March 1919, and holds the General Service and Victory Medals. 27, Symington Street, Northampton. Z2839.

RUFUS, W., Private, 2nd Royal Sussex Regiment.
He volunteered in June 1915, and was drafted overseas on the completion of his training six months later. During his service on the Western Front, he was engaged in severe fighting at Hill 60 and in various sectors, and gave his life for King and Country at the Battle of the Somme on September 9th, 1916. He was entitled to the 1914–15 Star, and the General Service and Victory Medals.
"A costly sacrifice upon the altar of freedom."
10, Rose Court, St. James' Street, Daventry, Northants. Z3147.

RUSSELL, C., Private, 1st Bedfordshire Regiment.
Called up from the Reserve in August 1914, he was immediately drafted to France, where he fought in the Retreat from Mons, and also took part in the Battles of the Marne, the Aisne and Ypres. Invalided home in December 1914, he was transferred to the Royal Irish Fusiliers and sent to Salonika, where he served on the Struma front, afterwards proceeding to Palestine. There he took part in the Battle of Gaza and the entry into Jaffa and Jerusalem, finally being discharged in January 1919. He holds the Queen's and King's South African Medals, and the Mons Star, and the General Service and Victory Medals.
25, Arthur Street, Northampton. Z1671.

RUSSELL, F., Private, Royal Army Service Corps.
Shortly after volunteering in October 1915, he was drafted to France, where he was engaged on duties of great importance on the docks and the railways. He was stationed at Boulogne, Calais and various other places, and did much useful work until his return home for demobilisation in November 1919. He holds the 1914–15 Star, and the General Service and Victory Medals. 37, Spring Lane, Northampton. Z1672.

RUSSELL, H., Private, R.A.O.C.
Joining in July 1916, he was drafted to France in the following month. Whilst in this theatre of war he rendered very valuable services as a boot-repairer and was stationed at Calais, Rouen and Le Havre. He did continuously good work throughout hostilities, and in December 1919 was demobilised, holding the General Service and Victory Medals.
7, Semilong Road, Northampton. Z2486.

RUSSELL, H., Private, Royal Defence Corps.
He was mobilised at the outbreak of war in August 1914, and served afterwards at various stations in Ireland and Wales, where he was engaged on duties of a highly important nature. He rendered very valuable services with his Unit until March 1919, when he was demobilised.
22, Spring Lane, Northampton. Z1089/B.

RUSSELL, H. T., Sapper, Royal Engineers.
Volunteering in August 1915, he underwent a period of training at Maidenhead prior to being drafted to France. He first served on important duties with his Unit at Rouen, but afterwards took an active part in the Battles of Loos, the Somme, Amiens, Bapaume and Havrincourt. After the cessation of hostilities he proceeded to Germany with the Army of Occupation. Returning home for demobilisation in March 1919, he holds the General Service and Victory Medals.
100, Upper Thrift Street, Northampton. Z2263.

RUSSELL, W., Private, 1st Northants. Regiment.
Shortly after volunteering in August 1914, he was sent to the Western Front, where he saw severe fighting in various sectors and took part in the Battles of La Bassée and Ypres, and many minor engagements. He was unhappily reported missing, and is believed to have been killed in action at Aubers Ridge on May 9th, 1915. He was entitled to the 1914 Star, and the General Service and Victory Medals.
"His life for his Country, his soul to God."
21, Scarletwell Street, Northampton. Z1673/A—1075/B.

RUSSELL, W. G., Driver, Royal Field Artillery.
He volunteered in October 1915, and, drafted to India in the following July, was stationed there for a year. Sent to Mesopotamia in July 1917, he took part in the capture of Tekrit and in various other operations until the conclusion of hostilities, when he returned to India for a further period of service, during which he was engaged in quelling disturbance in the Punjab. Demobilised on his return to England in September 1919, he holds the General Service and Victory Medals.
44, Clare Terrace, Northampton. Z1649/C.

RYAN, J. W., L/Corporal, Sherwood Foresters.
Already serving in India in August 1914, he returned home two months later, and in November was drafted to the Western Front, where he took part in the first Battle of Ypres and minor engagements. He was reported missing, and, later, killed in action at Neuve Chapelle on March 13th, 1915. He was entitled to the 1914 Star, and the General Service and Victory Medals.
"His memory is cherished with pride."
10, Lorne Road, Northampton. Z1674.

S

SABIN, W. J., Driver, Royal Field Artillery.
He joined in 1916, and, after completing a period of training, was drafted to the Western Front, where he saw severe fighting in various sectors. He took part in many important engagements in this theatre of war until the cessation of hostilities, and was demobilised on returning home in February 1919. He holds the General Service and Victory Medals.
4, Lutterworth Road, Daventry, Northants. Z2838.

SADD, T. H., Pte., Queen's (R.W. Surrey Regt.)
Joining in 1916, he completed his training, and the same year landed in France. In this theatre of war he took part in many important engagements in various sectors of the front. He was badly wounded in action, and as a result was invalided home and eventually discharged as medically unfit for further service in 1918. He holds the General Service and Victory Medals.
41, Portland Street, Northampton. Z2264.

SADLER, B., Wheeler, Royal Field Artillery.
Volunteering in February 1915, he was sent to France in the following July, and there saw severe fighting in various sectors of the front. He took part in the Battles of the Somme, Arras, Vimy Ridge, Ypres and Passchendaele, and served also through the Retreat and Advance of 1918. He was demobilised in September 1919, and holds the 1914–15 Star, and the General Service and Victory Medals.
9, Grove Road, Northampton. Z1675.

SADLER, J., Private, 6th Northants. Regiment.
Joining in February 1916, he was drafted to the Western Front in July of that year, and took part in the Battles of the Somme, the Ancre and Vimy Ridge and other engagements. Severely wounded and taken prisoner at Lens, he unhappily died in hospital on August 17th, 1917, whilst in captivity. He was entitled to the General Service and Victory Medals.
"His life for his Country, his soul to God."
27, Devonshire St., St. James' End, Northampton. Z2687/B.

SALE, H., Driver, Royal Field Artillery.
Joining in April 1917, he was drafted overseas in the same year. Serving with his Battery on the Western Front, he took part in many important engagements, particularly during the Retreat and Advance of 1918. After the conclusion of hostilities, he proceeded with the Army of Occupation into Germany. Returning home for demobilisation in January 1919, he holds the General Service and Victory Medals.
79, Semilong Road, Northants. Z2487.

SALEM, A., Private, Cheshire Regiment.
After volunteering in 1914, he underwent a period of training prior to being drafted to the Western Front in the following year. There he took part in the Battles of Hill 60, Loos, Arras, Vimy Ridge, Cambrai and the Marne, and many other important engagements, and was twice wounded in action. Demobilised in 1920, he holds the 1914–15 Star, and the General Service and Victory Medals.
21, Alma Street, Northampton. Z2840.

SALLOWS, C. P., Trooper, Northants. Dragoons.
Volunteering in November 1914, he was engaged on important duties with his Unit at various home stations prior to being drafted to France in July 1916. In this seat of operations he took part in heavy fighting at Arras. Transferred to Italy in November 1917, he was in action on the Piave and Asiago Plateaux. He did consistently good work, and in May 1919 was demobilised, holding the General Service and Victory Medals. 97, Greenwood Road, Northampton. Z2488.

SALMONS, W. C., Gunner, R.G.A.
He joined in 1916, and after completing a course of training, served with the Anti-Aircraft Section at various stations on coastal defence duties. He was not able to secure a transfer overseas on medical grounds, but, nevertheless, rendered valuable services until demobilised in 1919.
68, Rothersthorpe Road, Far Cotton, Northampton. Z3493.

SALT, E., Sergeant, Tank Corps.
He volunteered in January 1915, and, after his training, was retained on important duties in England until August 1917, when he proceeded to France. There he took a prominent part in severe fighting at Arras, where he was wounded in the following month, and was sent to hospital at Boulogne. He afterwards fought in the Advance of 1918, and was finally demobilised in January 1919, holding the General Service and Victory Medals.
Sutton Street, Flore, Northants. Z2841.

SAMWELL, H., Corporal, Machine Gun Corps.
Although only 16 years of age, he volunteered in September 1914, but was discharged on account of his youth in June 1915. Re-enlisting in May 1916, he underwent a period of training, and was retained on important duties with the Machine Gun Corps at various stations. He was later transferred to the 10th Hussars, and in 1921 he was still serving.
50, East Street, Northampton. Z2265/B.

SANDERSON, J. M., Gunner, R.G.A.
Called up from the Reserve in August 1914, he proceeded to France in March of the following year, and there took part in many important engagements until wounded. Invalided home, he returned to the Western Front, however, and, again in action, was gassed, and again sent home. He was retained in England until his discharge in February 1919, and holds the 1914-15 Star, and the General Service and Victory Medals.
21, Freehold Street, Northampton. Z1983/C.

SANDERSON, H. C., Gunner, R.G.A.
A Reservist, he was called to the Colours in August 1914, and immediately proceeded to France, where he fought in the Battle of, and Retreat from, Mons. He also took part in the Battles of the Marne, the Aisne, La Bassée, Ypres, Festubert, Loos, the Somme, Arras and Cambrai, and many other engagements, and was three times gassed. He was discharged in March 1919, and holds the Mons Star, and the General Service and Victory Medals.
21, Freehold Street, Northampton. Z1983/B.

SAPWELL, T. E., Private, 2/4th Oxfordshire and Buckinghamshire Light Infantry.
Joining in July 1916, he received his training at Oxford, and was ordered overseas seven months later. Serving on the Western Front, he fought in the Battles of Arras, Ypres and Cambrai, and other important engagements, did good work with his Unit during operations in the Retreat and Advance of 1918, and suffered from shell-shock. He was demobilised in February 1919, and holds the General Service and Victory Medals.
Gladstone Terrace, Gold Street, Hanslope, Bucks. Z3148.

SARGEANT, T. J., Private, R.A.M.C.
He volunteered in November 1915, and after his training was retained on important duties in England until March 1917, when he proceeded to Mesopotamia. There he took part in the capture of Baghdad, and in severe fighting on the Tigris, and was stationed also at Kut, Amara and Mosul. He also served on the Afghan frontier before returning home for demobilisation in June 1919, and holds the General Service and Victory Medals.
40, Poole Street, Northampton. Z1676.

SARGENT, A. J., Private, 15th Essex Regiment.
Joining in March 1917, he underwent a period of training before proceeding to the Western Front. Whilst in this theatre of war he took an active part in the fighting at Amiens, Arras, Armentières, and in many other engagements during the later stages of the war, being present at the final entry into Mons. He was demobilised in November 1919, and holds the General Service and Victory Medals.
Kilsby, Northampton. Z3495.

SARGENT, E. J. T., L/Corporal, R.A.M.C.
Joining in November 1916, he crossed early in the following year to the Western Front, where he acted as a stretcher-bearer throughout the course of his service. He was present during the Battles of Arras, Ypres, Albert, Cambrai and in the Retreat and Advance of 1918, and was slightly gassed. Later he proceeded with the Army of Occupation into Germany, and, returning home in October 1919, was demobilised, holding the General Service and Victory Medals.
Lower Heyford, Weedon, Northampton. Z3494/A.

SARGENT, R., Private, Northants. Regiment.
He joined in June 1918, on attaining military age, and, after having completed his training, was engaged on important guard duties at various stations. He rendered valuable services, but was unsuccessful in obtaining a transfer overseas before hostilities ceased. Afterwards he was drafted to India, where in 1921 he was still serving.
Lower Heyford, Weedon, Northampton. Z3494/B.

SARGENT, W. H., Private, Labour Corps.
Volunteering in August 1914, he proceeded to France with the Northamptonshire Regiment in March of the following year, and there took part in the Battles of Neuve Chapelle and Festubert. Wounded in September 1915, he was invalided home and afterwards served with the Labour Corps in England. He was demobilised in February 1919, and holds the 1914-15 Star, and the General Service and Victory Medals.
54, Craven Street, Northampton. Z1677.

SAUNDERS, W., Private, 7th Northants. Regt.
Volunteering in October 1914, he was sent to the Western Front on completion of a period of training in the following March, and there took part in the Battle of Ypres and many other engagements. Severely wounded in the Somme Offensive of 1916, he was invalided home, and later served with the Royal Army Medical Corps in London until his demobilisation in June 1919. He holds the 1914-15 Star, and the General Service and Victory Medals.
30, Spring Lane, Northampton. Z1069/A.

SAUNDERS, W., Private, Northants. Regiment.
He volunteered in May 1915, and after undergoing a period of training, was retained at various stations, where he was engaged on duties of great importance. Being over age for active service, he was unable to obtain his transfer to the front, but, nevertheless, did much good work with his Unit until November 1918, when he was invalided from the Army.
14, Gladstone Terrace, Northampton. Z1678.

SAVAGE, J. B., Private, Labour Corps.
He was called up from the Reserve in August 1914, and was retained at various stations on duties of great importance with the Northamptonshire Regiment, afterwards being transferred to the Labour Corps. Being medically unfit for active service, he was unable to obtain his transfer to the front, but, nevertheless, did good work with his Company until demobilised in March 1919.
13, Priory Square, Northampton. Z1102/C.

SAVAGE, S. G., Private, 4th Northants. Regiment.
He volunteered in November 1914, but, after a period of training, was retained on important duties at various stations, being unable to obtain his transfer overseas on account of ill-health. After rendering valuable services with his Unit, he was invalided from the Army in October 1916. He re-enlisted, however, in August 1919 in the Royal Air Force, but in April of the following year was again discharged as medically unfit for further service.
13, Priory Square, Northampton. Z1102 A.

SCARSBROOK, W., Sapper, Royal Engineers.
Volunteering in the Bedfordshire Regiment in August 1914, he was later transferred to the Royal Engineers, and drafted to France 11 months later. He was engaged on important work on the railways in the Ypres and Loos sectors until injured in an explosion and invalided home. Returning to the Western Front in August 1916, he saw much service in the Battles of the Somme, Arras, Ypres and Cambrai. Demobilised in March 1919, he holds the 1914-15 Star, and the General Service and Victory Medals.
3, Gladstone Terrace, Gold Street, Hanslope, Bucks. Z3149.

SCOTT, C. J., Private, Leicestershire Regiment.
Having joined in March 1917, he underwent a period of training, and in the following year was drafted to France. Whilst on the Western Front, he was in action at the Battles of the Somme (II.), the Aisne (III.), the Marne (II.), Amiens, Bapaume, Havrincourt, Epéhy, Ypres (IV.), and Le Cateau (II.). He was twice wounded, and also gassed, and after the cessation of hostilities, was transferred to Ireland, where he was still serving in 1921. He holds the General Service and Victory Medals.
43, Collingwood Road, Northampton. Z2490.

SCOTT, F., 1st Class Stoker, Royal Navy.
He volunteered in November 1915, and was posted to H.M.S. "Agamemnon," in which ship he did excellent work whilst engaged in operations in the Eastern Mediterranean. Early in 1918 he was transferred to a torpedo-boat destroyer, and was based on Gibraltar. Demobilised in March 1919, he holds the General Service and Victory Medals.
95, Stanhope Road, Northampton. Z2489.

SCOTT, J. E., Private, R.A.M.C.
Volunteering at the outbreak of hostilities, he proceeded in the following January to France. Whilst in this seat of operations he was engaged on important duties as a nursing orderly, and did consistently good work until April 1916. He then contracted pneumonia, and unfortunately died from the effects on April 11th, 1916. He was entitled to the 1914-15 Star, and the General Service and Victory Medals.
"His memory is cherished with pride."
151, Wycliffe Road, Northampton. Z2266.

SCOTT, L. W. (M.M.), Sergeant, 6th Northants. Regiment.
Having volunteered in September 1914, he landed in France 12 months later. Whilst in this theatre of war he served with distinction at St. Eloi, Albert, Ploegsteert Wood, the Somme, and in many other important engagements, being wounded and gassed in action. He was awarded the Military Medal for conspicuous bravery and devotion to duty in the Field. Demobilised in January 1919, he holds also the 1914-15 Star, and the General Service and Victory Medals.
43, Collingwood Road, Northampton. Z2490/B.

SCOTT, T. A., Pte., 25th York & Lancaster Regt.
Volunteering in July 1915, he underwent a period of training, and first served on important duties at Margate. Later he was transferred to Ireland, where he was engaged as a Regimental shoemaker and cook. He was unable to take part in operations in a fighting area, but, nevertheless, rendered valuable services until demobilised in March 1919.
21, Wimbledon Street, Northampton. Z2491.

SCOTT, W., Private, Labour Corps.
At the declaration of war he was mobilised with the Territorials, and in March of the following year proceeded to France, where he took part in the severe fighting at Ypres and was wounded. Invalided home, he received medical treatment, and, on recovery, returned to the Western Front, but, suffering from severe shell-shock, was sent to England and was subsequently discharged in May 1916. He holds the 1914–15 Star, and the General Service and Victory Medals.
14, Hut, Abington Park, Northampton. Z3496.

SCOTT, W. E., Pte., Volunteer Training Corps.
Owing to the fact that he was over age for service in the fighting forces, he volunteered in the Training Corps in August 1914, and for twelve months rendered valuable services. He was chiefly engaged in guarding important bridges, and also did excellent work during air raids. He was discharged in August 1915.
43, Collingwood Road, Northampton. Z2490/A.

SCOUSE, A., Private, Bedfordshire Regiment.
Shortly after volunteering in August 1914, he was sent to the Western Front, where he saw severe fighting in various sectors. He took part in many important engagements in this theatre of war, and was three times wounded in action—at Ypres, the Somme and Arras. He was demobilised in February 1919, and holds the 1914 Star, and the General Service and Victory Medals. 21, Pytchley Street, Northampton. Z2005.

SCOUSE, S. A., Driver, Royal Field Artillery.
Four months after joining in May 1916, he was drafted to the Western Front, where, after taking part in the Battles of Vimy Ridge and Messines, he was wounded at Ypres in July 1917. Invalided home, he returned to France, however, in January 1918, and served in the Somme sector and at Bailleul, afterwards proceeding with the Army of Occupation to Cologne. He served also with the 2nd Leinster Regiment before being demobilised in February 1919, and holds the General Service and Victory Medals. 42, Ruskin Road, Northampton. Z2004.

SCREEN, W., Private, 1st Northants. Regiment.
He volunteered at the outbreak of war in August 1914, and, in November 1916, was sent to the Western Front, where he saw severe fighting at Delville Wood and many other places. Invalided to hospital at Rouen, he unhappily died there on March 9th, 1917, and was entitled to the General Service and Victory Medals.
"He joined the great white company of valiant souls."
9, Orchard St., Drayton, near Daventry, Northants. Z2655/A.

SEABY, G., Private, 7th Suffolk Regiment.
Three months after joining in December 1916, he proceeded to the Western Front, where he saw much heavy fighting. After taking part in the Battles of Ypres, Cambrai and the Somme, and other engagements, he was severely wounded in October 1918, and admitted to hospital at Rouen, and later at Leicester. Demobilised in August 1919, he holds the General Service and Victory Medals. 35, Monarch Road, Northampton. Z1679.

SEAL, T., Private, 3rd Northamptonshire Regt.
After volunteering in August 1915, he underwent a period of training prior to being drafted to the Western Front in September 1917. There he took part in the Battle of Cambrai and many other important engagements in the Retreat and Advance of 1918, and afterwards served with the Army of Occupation at Cologne. He was demobilised on returning home in June 1919, and holds the General Service and Victory Medals.
44, Herbert Street, Northampton. Z1680.

SEARCY, C., Private, Training Reserve Battalion.
He joined in October 1917, and was sent to Rugeley Camp, where, during the course of his training, he contracted pneumonia, as a result of which he unhappily died on December 16th, 1917.
"His memory is cherished with pride."
Church Street, Kislingbury, Northampton. Z3380/A.

SEVILLE, G. E., Private, 10th Queen's (Royal West Surrey Regiment).
He joined immediately on attaining military age in June 1918, and, after completing a period of training, served at various stations on duties of great importance. He was unable to obtain his transfer overseas before the cessation of hostilities, but in January 1919, proceeded with the Army of Occupation to Germany. He was demobilised on returning home in November 1919. 64, Louise Road, Northampton. Z1681.

SHALLARD, B., Private, 1st Northamptonshire Regiment and Machine Gun Corps.
At the declaration of war in August 1914, he was mobilised and quickly drafted to France, where he fought in the Retreat from Mons. He was also in action at the Battles of La Bassée, Ypres, Neuve Chapelle, St. Eloi, Hill 60, Loos, Vimy Ridge, the Somme, Arras, Bullecourt, Cambrai and in many other engagements, including the Retreat and Advance of 1918. He holds the Mons Star, and the General Service and Victory Medals, and in 1921 was still serving.
18, Horseshoe Street, Northampton. Z3316/A.

SHALLARD, J. E., Corporal, King's Own (Royal Lancaster Regiment).
He was already in the Army and on Indian service when war broke out in August 1914, and in January of the following year proceeded to France. There he fought at Hill 60 and Neuve Chapelle, but owing to ill-health was invalided home. He returned, on his recovery, to the Western Front, but was unhappily killed in action at Aubers Ridge on May 8th, 1915, and was entitled to the 1914–15 Star, and the General Service and Victory Medals.
"His life for his Country, his soul to God."
18, Horseshoe Street, Northampton. Z3316/B.

SHARMAN, A., Private, 3rd Northants. Regt.
Shortly after joining in 1916, he was drafted to the Western Front, where he saw severe fighting in various sectors. He took part in the Battles of the Somme, Messines, Passchendaele and Cambrai, and many other important engagements, and was demobilised on his return home in 1919. He holds the General Service and Victory Medals.
19, Robert Street, Northampton. Z1682/C

SHARMAN, G. H., Private, 8th Lincolnshire Regt.
Joining in December 1916 he proceeded in the following May to the Western Front, where he fought and was wounded at Messines. Invalided to hospital, he was later transferred to the Royal Air Force, with which he returned to France. He was then engaged on important clerical duties until demobilised in April 1919, and holds the General Service and Victory Medals. 2, St. Giles' Terrace, Northampton. Z3363/D

SHARMAN, H. J., Private, 4th Northants. Regt.
Mobilised from the Reserve at the outbreak of war, he was unable to obtain a transfer to a theatre of hostilities on account of being over military age. He, nevertheless, rendered very valuable services with the Royal Defence Corps at Newport and various other places until demobilised in 1919.
2, St. Giles' Terrace, Northampton. Z3363/C.

SHARMAN, H. J., Pte., Australian Imp. Forces.
Shortly after volunteering in 1915, he was drafted to Egypt and thence to the Dardanelles, where he took part in much of the fierce fighting. He was unhappily killed in action on August 6th, 1915, and was entitled to the 1914–15 Star, and the General Service and Victory Medals.
"He passed out of the sight of men by the path of duty and self-sacrifice."
2, St. Giles' Terrace, Northampton. Z3363/E.

SHARMAN, P., Private, Middlesex Regiment.
He joined in 1917, and, on completion of a period of training, was drafted to the Western Front, where he saw much heavy fighting. After taking part in several engagements, he was so severely wounded in action near Ypres as to necessitate the amputation of a leg. He was invalided from the Army in 1919, and holds the General Service and Victory Medals.
19, Robert Street, Northampton. Z1682/B.

SHARMAN, W. G., R.S.M., 1st Northants. Regt.
Shortly after volunteering in 1915, he was sent to the Dardanelles, where, after taking a prominent part in the Landing at Suvla Bay, he saw much severe fighting. Later he served in Egypt on the Suez Canal, and, proceeding into Palestine, served in many important engagements, and was wounded at Gaza. Demobilised on returning home in August 1919, he holds the 1914–15 Star, and the General Service and Victory Medals.
19, Robert Street, Northampton. Z1682/A.

SHARMAN, W. H., Corporal, Royal Marines.
Already serving at the outbreak of hostilities in August 1914, he proceeded to the North Sea in H.M.S. "Canada," on board which ship he was engaged on important patrol and convoy duties. He took part in severe fighting in the Battle of Jutland, and was also in action in other engagements in the North Sea. He was discharged as medically unfit in June 1920, and holds the General Service and Victory Medals.
64, Earl Street, Northampton. Z3150.

SHARP, E. J. (Mrs.), Worker, Land Army.
She joined in August 1915, and, after undergoing a period of training, was stationed at Flore, where she was engaged on general duties as a farm hand and did much excellent work during her four years' service. She was demobilised in November 1919, and was awarded the Good Conduct Badge.
Sutton Street, Flore, Northants. TZ2842.

SHARP, F. J. (D.C.M.), Pte., 2nd Highland L.I.
Having enlisted in August 1911, he was serving in India when war broke out, and in May 1915 was drafted to France. There he took part in the Battles of Albert, the Somme, Arras, Vimy Ridge and Cambrai, and minor engagements, and fought also in the Retreat and Advance of 1918. He was awarded the Distinguished Conduct Medal for conspicuous gallantry on the Somme in July 1916, and, holding also the 1914–15 Star, and the General Service and Victory Medals, was discharged in April 1919.
78, Shelley Street, Kingsley Northampton. Z1683/A.

SHARP, G., Private, 14th (King's) Hussars.
He enlisted in 1913, and, drafted to France immediately on the outbreak of war in August 1914, took part in the Retreat from Mons and in the Battles of the Marne and Ypres, and was wounded at Neuve Chapelle in March 1915. In 1916 he was sent to Mesopotamia, where he took part in the relief of Kut. Discharged on returning home in August 1920, he holds the Mons Star, and the General Service and Victory Medals.
78, Shelley Street, Kingsley, Northampton. Z1683/B.

SHARP, W. H., Gunner, Royal Garrison Artillery.
Joining in October 1917, he crossed in June of the following year to France, where he experienced much heavy fighting. He was in action at Amiens, St. Quentin and in the Retreat and Advance of 1918, and was wounded in October of that year. After receiving medical treatment, he was demobilised in December 1918, and holds the General Service and Victory Medals. Baker Crick, Northampton. Z3497.

SHARPE, E. W., Private, 2/5th Manchester Regt.
Two months after joining in March 1916, he proceeded to the Western Front, but, after taking part in engagements at Ypres and Passchendaele, was invalided home in June 1917, suffering from trench fever. Returning to France twelve months later, he took part in the Battle of Amiens, and in September 1918 was again sent to England with heart trouble. Demobilised in February 1919, he holds the General Service and Victory Medals. 42, Sand Hill Rd., St. James, Northampton. Z2843.

SHAW, A., Private, 5th Northants. Regiment and Royal Welch Fusiliers.
He volunteered in September 1914, and, embarking for the Western Front in 1915, fought in the Battles of Neuve Chapelle, St. Eloi, Hill 60, Ypres, Festubert and Loos. He was wounded in 1916 and invalided to England, but on his recovery returned to France, and was in action in numerous important engagements during the Retreat and Advance of 1918. Demobilised in February 1919, he holds the 1914–15 Star, and the General Service and Victory Medals.
24, Spencer Street, Northampton. Z3151/A.

SHAW, A. A., Private, Northants. Regiment.
Three months after volunteering in September 1914, he was drafted to the Western Front, where he took part in important engagements in various sectors, including the Battles of Ypres and Loos. He died gloriously on the Field of Battle in the Somme Offensive of July 1916. He was entitled to the 1914–15 Star, and the General Service and Victory Medals.
"A valiant Soldier, with undaunted heart he breasted life's last hill."
77, Northcote Street, Northampton. Z1685/B.

SHAW, A. E., Private, Royal Army Medical Corps.
Prior to joining in December 1915, he had voluntarily served at St. John's Auxiliary Hospital, Guilsborough. Proceeding in April 1917 to France, he did excellent work with his unit in the Béthune sector, and was present in many other engagements of note. During the Advance of 1918, he was badly gassed at Vermand in September of that year, and was subsequently demobilised in February 1919. He holds the General Service and Victory Medals.
79, Abbey Road, Far Cotton, Northampton. Z3498.

SHAW, B., Corporal, K.O.S.B.
Volunteering in the Northamptonshire Regiment in September 1914 at the age of 15, he proceeded to France in the following year and fought in the Battles of Ypres and Loos. Owing to his youth he was sent home in 1916, but returned to the Western Front in 1917, and was severely wounded, which unhappily resulted in the loss of his left leg. He was invalided out of the Army in August 1920, holding the 1914–15 Star, and the General Service and Victory Medals.
24, Spencer Street, Northampton. Z3151/B.

SHAW, F. K., Private, 1/4th Northants. Regt.
He volunteered in June 1915, and, in January of the following year, proceeded to Egypt, where he served with a Trench Mortar Battery. Advancing into Palestine, he took part in the Battles of Gaza, the entry into Jaffa and in fighting on the River Jordan, finally returning home in June 1919. Demobilised in the following month, he holds the General Service and Victory Medals.
33, Bective Road, Kingsthorpe, Northampton. Z1684/A.

SHAW, F. S., Private, Royal Marine Light Infantry.
He joined in September 1918, and, after undergoing a period of training, was retained on important duties at various stations. Owing to the early cessation of hostilities, he was unable to obtain his transfer to a theatre of war, but later was drafted to India, and was still serving at Calcutta in 1921.
77, Northcote Street, Northampton. Z1685/A.

SHAW, M. A., Private, 16th Cheshire Regiment.
He volunteered in October 1915, and, after training with the Royal Engineers, was drafted with the Cheshire Regiment to France in November of the following year, and there took part in the Battles of Arras, Vimy Ridge and Ypres. He fell fighting at Passchendaele on October 22nd, 1917, and was entitled to the General Service and Victory Medals.
"Steals on the ear the distant triumph song."
33, Bective Road Kingsthorpe, Northampton. Z1684/C.

SHAW, R. L., A.B., Royal Naval Division.
Joining in June 1917, he completed his training and in the following April was drafted to France. In the course of his active service, he took part in several engagements on the Hindenburg Line before being wounded and invalided to hospital. On his recovery he was in action during the Advance of 1918. He returned home for demobilisation in June 1919, and holds the General Service and Victory Medals.
29, Monks Park Road, Northampton. Z2267.

SHAW, W. E., Private, 11th Suffolk Regiment.
He joined in June 1917, and in February of the following year proceeded to the Western Front, where he took part in the Battle of the Somme and many other important engagements in the Retreat of 1918. Gassed and wounded in June of that year, he was afterwards engaged in guarding prisoners of war until his demobilisation in November 1919. He holds the General Service and Victory Medals.
33, Bective Road, Kingsthorpe, Northampton. Z1684/B.

SHEATHER, F., Private, Royal Fusiliers.
Volunteering in November 1915, he underwent a period of training and early in the following year landed in France Whilst on the Western Front he took part in heavy fighting at Ploegsteert and on the Somme before being wounded in July 1916. On his recovery, he rejoined his unit and was in action at the Battle of Bullecourt. He was unhappily killed on May 12th, 1917, and was entitled to the General Service and Victory Medals.
"And doubtless he went in splendid Company."
5, Hazelwood Road, Northampton. Z2492/A.

SHEATHER, G., Private, Wiltshire Regiment.
He volunteered in August 1914, and in December was sent to France, but, after taking part in much severe fighting, was very badly wounded at Ypres in June 1915. Invalided to England, he was in hospital for over three years, and was discharged as medically unfit in September 1918, holding the 1914–15 Star, and the General Service and Victory Medals.
5, Hazelwood Road, Northampton. Z2492/B.

SHEFFIELD, C. H., Private, R.A.S.C. (M.T.)
Joining in April 1917, he was drafted to German East Africa in the following month, and there took part in important operations at various places. He was engaged chiefly in conveying ammunition and supplies to the forward areas and did much useful work until his return home for demobilisation in September 1919. He holds the General Service and Victory Medals. 5, Vernon Street, Northampton. Z2006.

SHELLARD, H., Sapper, Royal Engineers.
He was mobilised when war was declared in August 1914, quickly proceeded to France, and served throughout the Retreat from Mons and the subsequent engagements. He gave his life for the freedom of England at the Battle of Ypres on November 6th, 1914, and was entitled to the Mons Star, and the General Service and Victory Medals.
"His life for his Country, his soul to God."
Denton, Northampton. Z3499.

SHEPHERD, W., Private, Bedfordshire Regt.
He joined in 1917, but was not successful in obtaining a transfer to a fighting unit on account of ill-health. Transferred to a Labour Battalion, he did work of National importance at various stations, and also rendered valuable services on coastal defence duties until demobilised in 1918.
86, Oxford Street, Northampton. Z3500.

SHERIFF, W. A., Corporal, R.G.A.
After volunteering in August 1914 he underwent a period of training prior to being drafted to the Western Front in January 1916. There, after taking part in the Battle of Vimy Ridge and many engagements during the Somme Offensive, he fell fighting in that sector in January 1917. He was entitled to the General Service and Victory Medals
"Whilst we remember, the sacrifice is not in vain."
5, Pine Street, Northampton. Z1355/B.

SHERRY, W., Private, 12th Royal Fusiliers.
He joined in 1917, and after a period of training was sent overseas in the same year. During his service on the Western Front, he took an active part in several engagements of note, including the Battles of Ypres and Passchendaele, but was unhappily killed in action in 1917. He was entitled to the General Service and Victory Medals.
"He died the noblest death a man may die:
Fighting for God and right and liberty."
68, Rothersthorpe Road, Northampton. Z3152.

SHIRLEY, J. H., Private, 4th Northants. Regt.
He volunteered in February 1915, and in September of the following year was sent to France, where he took part in the Battles of Vimy Ridge and Cambrai and other engagements. Wounded at Ribecourt in December 1917, and at Landricourt in March 1918, he was taken prisoner on the Somme in that month, and was held in captivity until after the cessation of hostilities. He was demobilised in March 1919, and holds the General Service and Victory Medals.
7, Weston Place, Northampton. Z2844.

SHORT, J., Private, 2nd Bedfordshire Regiment.
A serving soldier, he proceeded to France in October 1914, and was there taken prisoner at the first Battle of Ypres in the same month. Held at captivity in Germany until after the cessation of hostilities, he was forced, during this period, to work in the fields and sugar factories, and suffered from dysentery and influenza. Discharged in March 1919, he holds the 1914 Star, and the General Service and Victory Medals.
31, Shakespeare Road, Northampton. Z1686.

SHORT, J. G., Private, 4th Northants. Regiment.
Volunteering in August 1914, he first saw service in the Dardanelles, where he took part in the Battles of Krithia. After the Evacuation of the Gallipoli Peninsula he was drafted to Egypt, but, proceeding into Palestine, was in action at the Battles of Gaza and other important engagements. Whilst overseas he was four times wounded and also contracted malaria fever. Demobilised in March 1919, he holds the 1914–15 Star, and the General Service and Victory Medals.
28, Market Street, Northampton. Z2195/B.

SHORTLAND, G., L/Corporal, R.A.O.C.
Two months after joining in November 1916, he was drafted to the Western Front, where he served at Dunkirk and many other places. Attached to the Labour Corps, he was engaged on duties of great importance at various ammunition dumps, and rendered valuable services until his demobilisation in June 1919. He holds the General Service and Victory Medals.
32, Gray Street, Northampton. Z1687.

SHRIVES, A., Lieutenant (Observer), Royal Air Force (late Royal Flying Corps).
He joined in February 1917, and, in April of the following year, was drafted to the Western Front, where he served in various sectors. There he took a prominent part in many bombing raids, was engaged also on photographic duties, and was brought down and wounded at Bailleul in July 1918. Demobilised in February 1919, he holds the General Service and Victory Medals. 26, Freehold Street, Northampton. Z2007.

SIBLEY, F. W., Rifleman, Royal Irish Rifles.
Joining in October 1916, he was drafted to France after three months' training with the Northamptonshire Regiment and there saw much severe fighting. He took part in the Battles of Ypres, Cambrai and the Somme, and other engagements, and was wounded. Demobilised in February 1919, he re-enlisted, however, in September, in the Royal Air Force, and in 1921 was still with his Squadron. He holds the General Service and Victory Medals.
55, Northcote Street, Northampton. Z1688/A.

SIBLEY, P. H., Private, Machine Gun Corps.
Joining in January 1917, he was shortly afterwards drafted to France, where he saw much fighting at the Battles of Arras, Vimy Ridge, Messines, Ypres and Cambrai, and the Retreat of 1918. In July of that year he was taken prisoner at Soissons, and held in captivity until after the cessation of hostilities. Returning home for demobilisation in March 1919, he holds the General Service and Victory Medals.
56, Stimpson Avenue, Northampton. Z2268.

SIBLEY, S. H., Private, 4th Norfolk Regiment.
He joined in March 1917, and, on completing his training in the following November, was drafted to Egypt. He proceeded thence into Palestine, and there saw much severe fighting on the River Jordan, and took part in the capture of Haifa, and in other important engagements. Demobilised on his return home in April 1919, he holds the General Service and Victory Medals.
55, Northcote Street, Northampton. Z1688/B.

SIBLEY, S. R., L/Corporal, 7th Northants. Regt.
He volunteered in September 1914, and in the following year was drafted to France, where he first saw much fighting at the Battle of Loos, and was badly wounded. As a result he was invalided home, but, on his recovery, returned to France and was again in action on the Somme, at Arras, Ypres, Passchendaele, Cambrai, Bapaume, Amiens and Albert, being again wounded in action and consequently invalided home. He was discharged in February 1919, and holds the 1914–15 Star, and the General Service and Victory Medals.
31, Charles Street, Northampton. Z1689.

SIMMONDS, G., A.B., Royal Navy.
Already in the Navy when war broke out in August 1914, he afterwards served in H.M.S. "Indefatigable," attached to the Devonport Division, on patrol and convoy duties in the North Sea. He unfortunately lost his life when his ship was sunk at the Battle of Jutland on May 31st, 1916, and was entitled to the 1914–15 Star, and the General Service and Victory Medals.
"A costly sacrifice upon the altar of freedom."
17, Lower Hester Street, Northampton. Z1193/C.

SIMMONDS, R. W., Gunner, R.G.A.
Joining in May 1916, he landed in France later in the same year. Whilst with his Battery on the Western Front, he was in action during heavy fighting in the Somme sector. He made the supreme sacrifice, being killed near Combles on February 28th, 1917, and was entitled to the General Service and Victory Medals.
"Thinking that remembrance, though unspoken, may reach him where he sleeps."
14, Albany Road, Northampton. Z2493.

SIMONS, H. J., Private, 1/4th Northants. Regt.
He volunteered in April 1915 at the age of 17 years, and four months later proceeded to Gallipoli, where he saw much severe fighting until invalided home in December 1915. In April 1917, however, he was drafted to France with the 7th Northamptonshire Regiment, but was shortly afterwards admitted to hospital at Bristol, suffering from trench fever. He later returned to his Unit, and was again in action until the cessation of hostilities, finally being demobilised in March 1919. He holds the 1914–15 Star, and the General Service and Victory Medals. 44, Gray Street, Northampton. Z1690.

SIMPSON, A. E., Private, Royal Berkshire Regt.
A serving soldier, he was retained on important duties in England until 1916, and was then drafted to the Western Front, where he was wounded during the Somme Offensive of the same year. Invalided to hospital at Bath, he was finally discharged in March 1919, holding the General Service and Victory Medals.
Church Hill, Wootton, Northants. Z2845/A—Z2846/A.

SIMPSON, J., Sergeant, 1/4th Northants. Regt.
A Territorial, he was mobilised in August 1914, and in the following year was drafted to the Dardanelles, where he saw much fighting. Later he was transferred to Egypt and played a prominent part in several engagements, but was shortly afterwards discharged, time-expired. He re-enlisted and proceeded to France, but was taken prisoner and held in captivity in Germany several months. Released after the Armistice, he returned home and was demobilised in March 1920, holding the 1914–15 Star, and the General Service and Victory Medals.
31, Ash Street, Northampton. Z1691.

SIMPSON, J. T., L/Corporal, Royal Fusiliers.
Joining in March 1916, he proceeded to France after two months' training and there saw much heavy fighting. He took part in the Battles of Albert, the Somme, Arras, Ypres, Passchendaele and Cambrai and minor engagements, fought also in the Retreat and Advance of 1918, and later served with the Army of Occupation at Cologne. Demobilised in November 1919, he holds the General Service and Victory Medals.
7, Cooper Street, Northampton. Z1117/A.

SIMPSON, T., Trooper, 2nd Life Guards.
He volunteered in November 1914, and was first engaged on important duties at various home stations with his Unit. Proceeding to the Western Front in July 1916, he took part in heavy fighting at the Battles of Albert, the Somme, Bullecourt, Ypres and Cambrai, before being wounded and invalided home. Returning to France on his recovery, he was in action during the Retreat and Advance of 1918. Demobilised in February 1919, he holds the General Service and Victory Medals. 35, Wycliffe Road, Northampton. Z2494.

SKELTON, A. C., A.B., Royal Naval Division.
Joining in 1917, he completed his training, and, crossing to France in the same year, was actively engaged in the Battles of Lens, Cambrai and the Somme. He also did valuable work with his Unit in operations during the Retreat and Advance of 1918, serving during the triumphal entry into Mons. He was demobilised on his return home in 1919, and holds the General Service and Victory Medals.
6, Freeschool Street, Northampton. Z3153.

SKETCHLEY, J., Gunner, Royal Field Artillery.
Three months after joining in January 1918, he was drafted to the Western Front, where he saw severe fighting in various sectors. He took part in the Battles of the Somme, Amiens and Cambrai and many other engagements in the Retreat and Advance of the Allies, and, on returning home in February 1919, was demobilised. He holds the General Service and Victory Medals. 31, Bath Street, Northampton. Z1129/A.

SKILLMAN, E., Cpl., 2nd Monmouthshire Regt.
Volunteering in September 1914, he was drafted to the Western Front two months later and took part in the Battles of Ypres (I.), Neuve Chapelle, St. Eloi and Hill 60, and minor engagements. He fell in action at Ypres on May 8th, 1915, and was entitled to the 1914 Star, and the General Service and Victory Medals.
"Whilst we remember, the sacrifice is not in vain."
19, Horseshoe Street, Northampton. Z2847/A.

SKILLMAN, F. (jun.), Pte., South Wales Borderers.
He joined immediately on attaining military age in March 1918, and, after a period of training, was retained on important duties at various stations. He was unable to obtain his transfer overseas, but, nevertheless, rendered valuable services with his unit until December 1918, when he was released in order to return to his civil occupation as a miner.
19, Horseshoe Street, Northampton. Z2847/B.

SKINNER, E. M. (Miss), Special War Worker.
For a considerable period this lady volunteered her services at the Duston War Hospital, where her untiring energy and skill in nursing did much to alleviate the sufferings of the wounded troops from the different theatres of war. In 1920 she was still rendering valuable services as a nurse.
50, Clarke Road, Northampton. Z2269.

SLATER, D., Private, Middlesex Regiment.
He volunteered in 1915, but being under age for active service, was not successful in his endeavours to secure a transfer to a theatre of war. Throughout the period of hostilities he was retained on important duties at various home stations serving also with the Bedfordshire Regiment, and carried out his work in a very able manner until demobilised in 1919.
95, Clarke Road, Northampton. Z2495/B.

SLATER, E., Private, 1st Northants. Regiment.
Volunteering at the outbreak of war in August 1914, he was shortly afterwards drafted to the Western Front and took part in the Battle of Mons. He was also in action in many other engagements, and died gloriously on the Field of Battle at La Bassée in January 1915, at the early age of 17. He was entitled to the Mons Star, and the General Service and Victory Medals.
"Great deeds cannot die."
95, Clarke Road, Northampton. Z2495/A.

SLEET, H., L/Corporal, Queen's Own (Royal West Kent Regiment).
He came from America to England in December 1914 in order to enlist, but was rejected on account of defective teeth. Attesting in 1915, he was called up, however, in April 1917, and two months later proceeded to India, where he was stationed at Jubbulpore, and was for a time in hospital, suffering from malaria. He also served in Mesopotamia and Salonika before returning home for demobilisation in March 1919, and holds the General Service and Victory Medals.
26, Raymond Road, St. James, Northampton. Z2848.

SLINN, F., Driver, Royal Garrison Artillery.
He joined in August 1917 in the Royal Field Artillery, and shortly afterwards was transferred to the Royal Garrison Artillery and embarked for France. On that front he was in action in engagements at Arras, Ypres, Passchendaele, Cambrai and the Somme, and did good work with his Battery in operations during the Retreat and Advance of 1918. He was demobilised on his return to England in February 1919, and holds the General Service and Victory Medals.
107, Stanhope Road, Northampton. Z2496.

SLINN, F. H., Private, 2nd Northants. Regiment.
He was called up from the Reserve in August 1914, and retained for a time at various home stations before being drafted to France in June 1915. There he took part in the Battles of Festubert, Loos, the Somme, Albert, Arras, Ypres, Passchendaele and Cambrai, and was severely wounded in action on March 8th, 1918. He unfortunately died of wounds six days later, and was buried at Wimereaux. He was entitled to the 1914–15 Star, and the General Service and Victory Medals.
"His life for his Country, his soul to God."
26, Regent Street, Northampton. Z1692/A.

SLINN, R., A.B., Royal Naval Division.
He volunteered in October 1915, and in January of the following year crossed to France and served with the "Hawke" Battalion in various sectors. He fought at Vimy Ridge, and on the Somme, and died gloriously on the Field of Battle at Arras on April 23rd, 1917. He was entitled to the General Service and Victory Medals.
"Great deeds cannot die."
13, Somerset Street, Northampton. Z3501.

SLINN, T. D., Private, 1st Northants. Regiment.
Volunteering in September 1914, he was drafted overseas in the following year. Whilst on the Western Front he took part in several engagements, including the Battles of Ypres, Festubert, Loos, the Somme, Arras and Cambrai. Contracting trench feet he was invalided home, but, on his recovery, returned to France and served in the Advance of 1918. In 1920 he was engaged on duties in Ireland, and holds the 1914–15 Star, and the General Service and Victory Medals.
26, Regent Street, Northampton. Z1692/C.

SLINN, W. C., Private, 7th Royal Fusiliers.
He joined in May 1918, and completing his training in the following July was drafted to France, where he took part in much heavy fighting in the Advance. He made the supreme sacrifice, being killed in action on August 22nd, 1918, and was entitled to the General Service and Victory Medals.
"He died the noblest death a man may die:
Fighting for God and right and liberty."
26, Regent Street, Northampton. Z1692/B.

SLYNE, D., Private, 3rd Northants. Regiment.
Volunteering in November 1915, he underwent a period of training at Chatham, and was afterwards transferred to the Royal Munster Fusiliers. Proceeding to France in May 1917, he was engaged on important duties in different sectors of the front until demobilised in February 1919, and holds the General Service and Victory Medals.
Station Road, Long Buckby, Northampton. Z3303.

SMART, A., Trumpeter, 20th Hussars.
Having enlisted in July 1911, he proceeded to the Western Front in August 1914, and there fought in the Retreat from Mons. He also took part in the Battles of the Marne, the Aisne, Ypres, Loos, the Somme, Arras and Cambrai and in the Retreat and Advance of 1918, and was wounded. He afterwards served with the Army of Occupation in Germany until November 1919, and was discharged in July of the following year, holding the Mons Star, and the General Service and Victory Medals. 24, West Street, Northampton. Z2008.

SMART, E., Corporal, 1/4th Northants. Regiment.
He volunteered in August 1915, and was shortly afterwards drafted to the Dardanelles, where he took part in heavy fighting at Suvla Bay and in the Evacuation of the Gallipoli Peninsula. Later he was transferred to Egypt, thence to Palestine, and fought at the Battle of Gaza, the fall of Jerusalem and on the River Jordan. He returned home and was demobilised in July 1919, holding the 1914–15 Star, and the General Service and Victory Medals.
1st House, 1st Block, Naseby Street, Northampton. Z1693.

SMART, G. F., Rifleman, K.R.R.C.
He joined in July 1918, on attaining military age, and after a period of training was engaged at various stations on important duties with his Unit. Owing to the early cessation of hostilities, he was unable to obtain a transfer overseas, but rendered valuable service until his demobilisation in October 1919.
4, Knightley Road, Northampton. Z1694.

SMART, H., Private, 16th Cheshire Regiment.
Volunteering in the Royal Engineers in August 1915, he was subsequently transferred to the 16th Cheshire Regiment, and ordered to France in September 1916. Whilst overseas he fought in the Battles of Arras and Ypres and other notable engagements, but was unhappily killed in action at Ypres on October 25th, 1918. He was entitled to the General Service and Victory Medals.
"Whilst we remember, the sacrifice is not in vain."
160, Semilong Road, Northampton. Z2497

SMART, J. W., Private, R.A.S.C. (M.T.)
He joined in November 1916, and in August of the following year was drafted to Egypt and served at Alexandria and Cairo for a time. He also saw service at Gaza, Haifa, Jaffa and other important engagements with General Allenby's Forces in Palestine, and was present at the entry into Jerusalem. Returning home, he was demobilised in December 1919, and holds the General Service and Victory Medals.
Mill Lane, Cogenhoe, Northampton. Z3325/A.

SMART, W. F., Private, Machine Gun Corps.
He joined in December 1917, and underwent a period of training prior to his being drafted to France, where he was stationed at Armentières. After hostilities ceased he proceeded to Germany with the Army of Occupation and served on the Rhine until his demobilisation in March 1919. He holds the General Service and Victory Medals.
33, Lincoln Street, Kingsthorpe, Northampton. Z1695.

SMART, W. S., Private, 1/4th Northants. Regt.
He volunteered in November 1914, and, after a period of training, was drafted to Egypt, where he took part in much fighting at Magdhaba and was wounded in action. On his recovery he rejoined his Unit in Palestine and was in action at the Battles of Gaza and the fall of Jerusalem. He returned home and was demobilised in February 1919, holding the General Service and Victory Medals.
16, Monarch Road, Northampton. TZ1582/A.

SMEDLEY, H. V., Private, Sherwood Foresters.
When war broke out he was already serving, and in March 1915 proceeded overseas. Whilst on the Western Front, he was in action in many engagements of note, including the Battles of St. Eloi, Hill 60 and Ypres, and was wounded on three occasions. He was invalided to England in 1917, and on his discharge from hospital was retained on home defence until discharged in March 1919. He holds the 1914–15 Star, and the General Service and Victory Medals.
4, Muscott Street, St. James', Northampton. Z2498/C.

SMEDLEY, P. W., Private, 11th (Prince Albert's Own) Hussars.
Already serving in August 1914, he was at once ordered to France, and saw much fighting in the Battles of Mons, Ypres, Loos, Vimy Ridge, Cambrai and Amiens. He was admitted to hospital in Rouen, suffering from frost bite, and later was injured in an accident and invalided to England. He was discharged in February 1919, and holds the Mons Star, and the General Service and Victory Medals.
4, Muscott Street, St. James', Northampton. Z2498/B.

SMITH, A., Private, 4th Northants. Regiment.
Having attested under the Derby scheme in 1915, he was called up in March 1917, and engaged at various home stations on important duties with his Unit. Owing to his being medically unfit, he was unable to obtain a transfer overseas, but rendered valuable services until his discharge in May 1919.
3, Seymour Place, King Street, Northampton. Z1696.

SMITH, A., Private, South Wales Borderers.
Joining in January 1917, he was sent to the Western Front on completion of a period of training two months later, and there saw much severe fighting in the Arras sector. He was unhappily reported wounded and missing, and is now believed to have been killed in action at Monchy on April 23rd, 1917. He was entitled to the General Service and Victory Medals.
"The path of duty was the way to glory."
80, Great Russell Street, Northampton. Z1986/A.

SMITH, A., Gunner, Royal Garrison Artillery.
Volunteering in the Royal Garrison Artillery in October 1915, he proceeded to France six months later, and did good work with his Battery in various sectors. Whilst fighting in the Battle of the Somme, he was gassed and sent to hospital in Rouen, subsequently being invalided to England. On his discharge from hospital, he was transferred to the Labour Corps, and did much valuable work until demobilised in February 1919. He holds the General Service and Victory Medals.
144, Semilong Road, Northampton. Z2499.

SMITH, A., Private, Machine Gun Corps.
Volunteering in February 1915, he was retained on important duties at various stations in England with the Northamptonshire Dragoons until February 1918, when he secured a transfer overseas with the Machine Gun Corps. During his service on the Western Front, he took part in many notable engagements in various sectors, and fought in the Battle of Amiens. Remaining in France until demobilised in January 1919, he holds the General Service and Victory Medals.
3, Byfield Road, St. James, Northampton. Z2500.

SMITH, A., Private, 17th (Duke of Cambridge's Own) Lancers.
Having enlisted in 1910, he was serving in India when war broke out, and in November 1914 proceeded to France. Whilst in this theatre of war he took part in important engagements in various sectors, including the Battles of Neuve Chapelle, Ypres, Bullecourt and Cambrai, and was wounded. He was discharged in 1919, and holds the 1914 Star, and the General Service and Victory Medals.
29, Alma Street, Northampton. Z2849.

SMITH, A., Private, 1st Northants. Regiment.
A Reservist, he was called up at the outbreak of war in August 1914, and a month later was drafted overseas. Whilst serving on the Western Front, he was in action in numerous engagements of note, including the Battle of Ypres, and was wounded on one occasion. He was invalided to England, and, after protracted hospital treatment, was discharged in February 1919, holding the 1914 Star, and the General Service and Victory Medals. Near Hall Spratton, Northants. Z3154.

SMITH, A. C. (M.M.), Gunner, Royal Field Artillery.
Already in the Army when war broke out in August 1914, he was immediately drafted to France. There he played a distinguished part in the Battles of Mons, Ypres, Givenchy, Neuve Chapelle, Loos, the Somme, Ypres, Passchendaele, Cambrai, and in the Retreat and Advance of 1918, and was wounded in action. He was awarded the Military Medal in July 1916 for conspicuous gallantry and devotion to duty in the Field. Discharged in July 1919, he holds also the Mons Star, and the General Service and Victory Medals.
81, Milton Street, Kingsley, Northampton. Z1697.

SMITH, A. C., Private, 4th Northants. Regiment.
Volunteering in May 1915, he was drafted overseas in the following year. Whilst on the Western Front he took part in several engagements, including the Battles of the Somme, Ypres and Cambrai. He contracted trench fever, and was invalided home, being eventually discharged in June 1919. He holds the General Service and Victory Medals.
17, Todds Lane, Northampton. Z1698.

SMITH, A. C., Private, 1st Northants. Regiment.
A Reservist, he was called to the Colours in August 1914, and in the same month proceeded to the Western Front, where he saw much severe fighting. He made the supreme sacrifice, falling in action at the first Battle of the Aisne in September 1914, and was entitled to the 1914 Star, and the General Service and Victory Medals.
"A valiant Soldier, with undaunted heart he breasted life's last hill."
4, Tanner Row, Tanner Street, Northampton. Z2772/A.

SMITH, A. D., Corporal, R.G.A.
Volunteering in May 1915, he was retained on important duties at various home stations before proceeding overseas. Serving on the Western Front, he was in action with his Battery at the Battles of Bullecourt, Messines and Cambrai, where he was burnt by liquid fire in November 1917, and invalided to Netley Hospital. He was eventually demobilised in January 1919, holding the General Service and Victory Medals.
31, Whitworth Road, Northampton. Z2270.

SMITH, A. E., Private, 1st London Regiment (Royal Fusiliers).
He joined the Essex Regiment in March 1917, and after two months' training was sent to the Western Front with the Royal Fusiliers, and there took part in the Battle of Messines and minor engagements. He died gloriously on the Field of Battle at Ypres on July 31st, 1917, and was entitled to the General Service and Victory Medals.
"Whilst we remember, the sacrifice is not in vain."
66, Countess Road, St. James, Northampton. Z2850.

SMITH, A. H., L/Cpl., 11th Lancashire Fusiliers.
He joined in February 1916, and, landing in France four months later, took part in the heavy fighting in the Somme sector, where he was gassed. Rejoining his Unit later, he was unfortunately severely wounded near Albert in August 1916, necessitating the amputation of an arm. He was eventually discharged as physically unfit in June 1917, and holds the General Service and Victory Medals.
Brayfield-on-the-Green, Northampton. Z3506.

SMITH, A. H., Driver, Royal Field Artillery.
He volunteered in December 1915, but was retained on important duties at home until March 1917, when he was sent to the Western Front. There he saw heavy fighting in various sectors, took part in the Battles of Bullecourt, Passchendaele and Cambrai, and was wounded in the last-named engagement. Invalided home with trench fever in September 1918, he was eventually demobilised six months later, holding the General Service and Victory Medals.
46, Military Road, Northampton. Z3156.

SMITH, A. J., Sergeant, 1/4th Devonshire Regt.
Volunteering in March 1915, he was drafted to Gallipoli in November of that year, but, on the Evacuation of the Peninsula in the following month, was transferred to Egypt. He was invalided home in 1916, but, in December of the same year, proceeded to India, where he was engaged on garrison duties at various stations. He was wounded whilst overseas, and on returning home in December 1919, was demobilised, holding the 1914–15 Star, and the General Service and Victory Medals.
High Street, Flore, Northants. Z2851.

SMITH, A. T., Private, Buffs (East Kent Regt.)
He joined in 1916, and, after a period of training, was drafted to the Western Front, where he saw severe fighting in various sectors. He took part in the Battles of Arras, Ypres, Passchendaele and Amiens, and other engagements, fought also in the Retreat and Advance of 1918, and afterwards served with the Army of Occupation in Germany. Demobilised on returning home in 1919, he holds the General Service and Victory Medals. 4, St. Peter's Street, Northampton. Z2852.

SMITH, A. W., A/Corporal, 1st Border Regiment.
Mobilised in August 1914, he embarked for Gallipoli in April 1915, and took part in the Landing at Cape Helles, and in the Battles of Krithia. He was wounded in October 1915, and two months later was drafted to France. There he was engaged in fierce fighting at Neuve Chapelle, Ypres, and the Somme, and in the Retreat and Advance of 1918, and was wounded at Bullecourt, Albert and Fricourt. He was discharged in February 1919, and holds the 1914–15 Star, and the General Service and Victory Medals.
55, Wycliffe Road, Northampton. Z2501/A.

SMITH, B., Private, 2nd Northants. Regiment.
He joined in December 1916, and, completing his training in the following year, was drafted to France, where he took part in many important engagements in various sectors. He made the supreme sacrifice, being killed in action in April 1918, and was entitled to the General Service and Victory Medals.
"Honour to the immortal dead, who gave their youth that the world might grow old in peace."
47, Cloutsham Street, Northampton. Z1703.

SMITH, B. H., Private, 53rd Bedfordshire Regt.
On attaining military age he joined in September 1918, and, after completing a period of training, was retained on important duties with his Unit. He later proceeded to Germany, where he served with the Army of Occupation until demobilised in July 1919. 40, Wantage Road, Northampton. Z2271.

SMITH, C., L/Corporal, 1st Northants. Regiment.
Called up from the Reserve in August 1914, he quickly proceeded to the Western Front, where he took part in the Retreat from Mons, the Battles of the Marne, the Aisne, La Bassée and Ypres. He died gloriously on the Field of Battle on the Somme in August 1916, and was entitled to the Mons Star, and the General Service and Victory Medals.
"A valiant Soldier, with undaunted heart he breasted life's last hill."
6, Alpha Street, Northampton. Z1597/A.

SMITH, C., Private, 2nd Norfolk Regiment.
Joining in June 1916, he proceeded in the following December to Mesopotamia. There he fought in important engagements, and was severely wounded on February 24th, 1917, and unhappily died from the effects of his injuries a day later. He was entitled to the General Service and Victory Medals.
"He died the noblest death a man may die:
Fighting for God and right and liberty."
55, Delapre Street, Northampton. Z3504.

SMITH, C. A., Sapper, Royal Engineers.
Joining in June 1916, he completed a period of training at Chatham, and was drafted to Salonika. In this seat of operations he was attached to a Field Company and engaged on important bridge-building duties during heavy fighting on the Doiran and Vardar fronts. Demobilised in July 1919, he holds the General Service and Victory Medals.
55, Adnitt Road, Northampton. Z2272.

SMITH, C. E. J., Gunner, R.G.A.
He volunteered in October 1915, and, on completion of a period of training at Plymouth, was drafted to West Africa, where he was engaged on important coast defence duties at Sierra Leone. He also did much valuable work in British East Africa, and whilst overseas suffered from malaria. On his return to England in February 1919, he was demobilised, holding the General Service and Victory Medals.
7, Sharman Road, St. James' End, Northampton. Z2503.

SMITH, C. F., Private, Gloucestershire Regiment.
Joining in June 1916, he proceeded to the Western Front in the following year, on the conclusion of his training. After taking part in numerous important engagements, he was taken prisoner during the German Offensive, but unhappily died from starvation whilst held in captivity on June 29th, 1918. He was entitled to the General Service and Victory Medals.
"His memory is cherished with pride."
Rose Cottage, Silver St., Brixworth, Northampton. Z3133/B.

SMITH, E., Private, Middlesex Regiment.
Joining in February 1917, he completed his training and in the following May was drafted to the Western Front. After only one month's service in that theatre of war, he was severely wounded in the Battle of Messines in June 1917, and was invalided to England. Transferred to the Labour Corps, he was subsequently discharged as medically unfit for further service in June 1918, and holds the General Service and Victory Medals. 8, Orchard Street, Northampton. Z2502.

SMITH, E., Private, 4th Northants. Regiment.
He volunteered in June 1915, and, after completing a course of training, served at various stations on important duties with his Unit. He was unsuccessful in obtaining a transfer to a fighting area prior to the termination of hostilities, but rendered valuable services until demobilised in February 1919.
52, Abbey Road, Northampton. Z3503.

SMITH, E. L., Private, 12th West Yorks. Regt.
Volunteering in June 1915, he embarked for the Western Front early in the following year. Whilst in this theatre of war, he took an active part in the fighting at Ypres, the Somme and Arras, and gave his life for the freedom of England at the Battle of Cambrai in November 1917. He was entitled to the General Service and Victory Medals.
"Steals on the ear the distant triumph song."
Church Street, Kislingbury, Northampton. Z3508.

SMITH, F., Private, Norfolk Regiment.
He enlisted in May 1918, and, after a period of training, was engaged at various stations on important duties with his Unit. He was under age to obtain a transfer overseas, but rendered valuable services until his demobilisation in November 1919.
68, Castle Street, Northampton. Z1699/C.

SMITH, F. C., L/Corporal, 3rd Northants. Regt.
Volunteering in May 1915, he underwent a period of training and proceeded to the Western Front, where he did continuously good work. He took part in heavy fighting on the Somme and also in the Retreat and Advance of 1918 before being wounded. As a result he was invalided home and eventually discharged as medically unfit for further service in August 1919. He holds the General Service and Victory Medals.
27, Leicester Street, Northamptonshire. Z1701/A.

SMITH, F. D., Sergeant, R.A.S.C. (M.T.)
Having enlisted in 1900, he at once proceeded to the Western Front with the first Expeditionary Force at the outbreak of hostilities in August 1914. Whilst in France he did valuable work in the Transport Section, conveying food and ammunition to the troops in the forward areas until the termination of the war. He was still serving in 1920, and holds the 1914 Star, and the General Service and Victory Medals.
Newland, Brixworth, Northants. Z3155.

SMITH, F. T., Q.M.S., 1/4th Northants. Regiment.
Volunteering in August 1914, he was drafted to Egypt in the following year, and was there engaged on important duties at various stations. Proceeding into Palestine, he took a prominent part in the Battles of Gaza, in the capture of Jerusalem and Jericho, and in General Allenby's Offensive. Demobilised on returning home in June 1919, he holds the 1914–15 Star, and the General Service and Victory Medals.
35, Hervey Street, Northampton. Z2009/A.

SMITH, G., Private, Sherwood Foresters.
A serving soldier, he was mobilised at the outbreak of war in August 1914, and immediately drafted to the Western Front. In this theatre of war he took part in the Retreat from Mons, and also in the Battles of the Marne, the Aisne, La Bassée and Ypres. He died gloriously on the Field of Battle on January 27th, 1915, and was entitled to the Mons Star, and the General Service and Victory Medals.
"And doubtless he went in splendid company."
67, Scarletwell Street, Northampton. Z1700.

SMITH, G., Private, 1st Northants. Regiment.
Volunteering in August 1914, he completed a period of training and was drafted to France, where he took part in many important engagements, including the Battles of Ypres and Neuve Chapelle. He was wounded in March 1915, and invalided home, and was eventually discharged as medically unfit for further service in May 1916. He unfortunately died from the effects in March 1919, and was entitled to the 1914–15 Star, and the General Service and Victory Medals.
"His memory is cherished with pride."
68, Castle Street, Northamptonshire. Z1699/B.

SMITH, G., Private, Oxford. and Bucks. L.I.
Having volunteered in September 1915, he completed a period of training and was drafted to India. Whilst in this seat of war, he was engaged on very important duties with his unit at Cawnpore, Secunderabad, Dicorn and various other stations. During his service he contracted malaria fever, and in February 1920 was demobilised, holding the General Service and Victory Medals. 126, Market Street, Northampton. Z2273.

SMITH, G., Pte., 5th Oxford. and Bucks. L.I.
Joining in June 1916, he proceeded to the Western Front in the following November and there saw much heavy fighting. After taking part in the Battles of the Somme, Arras and Ypres, and other engagements, he was severely wounded in the Retreat of March 1918, and was sent to hospital at Abbeville and thence home, where he was retained on farm work until the following November. He then returned to France, finally being demobilised in March 1919, holding the General Service and Victory Medals. Long Street, Hanslope, Bucks. Z2853/B.

SMITH, G., Private, Northamptonshire Regiment.
He joined in 1917, and, after having completed his training, was drafted to Ireland, where he carried out various important duties. He was unable to secure a transfer to a theatre of war on medical grounds, but, nevertheless, rendered very valuable services until his demobilisation in September 1919.
Brayfield-on-the-Green, Northampton. Z3502.

SMITH, G. E., Pte., 13th Queen's (R.W. Surrey Regt.)
Joining in July 1916, he landed in France in the following month. Whilst on the Western Front he was engaged on important transport duties, and was present at the Battles of the Somme, Arras, Ypres and St. Quentin. Later, in 1918, he was transferred to the Labour Corps, but remained with a transport column during the Retreat and Advance of 1918. Demobilised in February 1919, he holds the General Service and Victory Medals. 39, Poole St., Northampton. Z2166/A.

SMITH, G. E., Sapper, Royal Engineers.
Two months after volunteering in December 1915, he was drafted to France, where he served with the Cable Section in various sectors of the front. He was also present at the Battles of Arras, Vimy Ridge, Ypres and Cambrai, and many other important engagements, and finally returned home for demobilisation in July 1919. He holds the General Service and Victory Medals. 40, Brook St., Daventry, Northants. Z2854.

SMITH, G. E., Private, 4th Bedfordshire Regiment.
Joining in July 1916, he proceeded later in the same year to the Western Front, and served in the Somme sector. Whilst going into action, he was unhappily killed near Albert in January 1917, and was entitled to the General Service and Victory Medals.
"Whilst we remember, the sacrifice is not in vain."
Kilsby, Northampton. Z3509.

SMITH, G. H., Member, British Red Cross Society.
Soon after the outbreak of war he joined the V.A.D., and during his spare time rendered valuable services conveying wounded from the ambulance trains to various hospitals. From April 1918 until the following December he devoted the whole of his time to similar work with the British Red Cross Society, and on relinquishing his duties was awarded the Certificate of the British Red Cross Society and the Order of St. John of Jerusalem for his excellent services.
169, Adnitt Road, Northampton. Z2274/B.

SMITH, G. S., Private, 1st Northants. Regiment.
A Reservist, he was called to the Colours in August 1914, and was immediately drafted to the Western Front, where he fought in the Retreat from Mons, and also took part in the Battles of the Marne, the Aisne, La Bassée, Ypres and Neuve Chapelle. He fell in action at Hill 60 on May 4th, 1915, and was entitled to the Mons Star, and the General Service and Victory Medals.
"He nobly fell that we might live."
35, Hervey Street, Northampton. Z2009/B.

SMITH, H., Driver, Royal Army Service Corps.
After joining in May 1918, he was immediately drafted to Egypt, where he did continuously good work as a transport driver. He served at many important enngagements in various sectors of the front, and was frequently under heavy shell-fire. Demobilised on his return home in April 1919, he holds the General Service and Victory Medals.
29, Crispin Street, Northampton. Z1636/C—Z1637/C.

SMITH, H., Private, Royal Scots Fusiliers.
At the declaration of war in August 1914 he was mobilised and at once ordered to the Western Front, where he fought in the Retreat from Mons. He was also actively engaged in the Battles of the Marne, the Aisne, La Bassée, Neuve Chapelle, Festubert, Loos, the Somme, Messines, Ypres and Passchendaele, and in the Retreat and Advance of 1918, and was twice wounded. Discharged in January 1921, he holds the Mons Star, and the General Service and Victory Medals.
94, Roe Road, Northampton. Z3158/A.

SMITH, H. C., Private, Royal Army Medical Corps.
Volunteering in 1915, he was shortly afterwards drafted to France, where he was engaged on important duties as a stretcher-bearer. He saw much heavy fighting in various sectors, and was in action at the Battles of Neuve Chapelle, Hill 60, Festubert, Cambrai, and also in the Retreat and Advance of 1918. Whilst overseas he was wounded and gassed, and in 1920 was demobilised, holding the 1914–15 Star, and the General Service and Victory Medals.
11, Portland Street, Northampton. Z2275/A.

SMITH, H. S., Able Seaman, Royal Naval Division.
He joined in July 1916, and, after a period of training at Blandford, was later in the same year ordered overseas. Whilst serving on the Western Front, he took part in numerous important engagements in various sectors, and was gassed. He remained in France until January 1919, when he was demobilised, holding the General Service and Victory Medals.
27, Sharman Road, Northampton. Z2504.

SMITH, H. W., L/Corporal, 1/4th Northamptonshire Regiment (T.F.)
Mobilised with the Territorials at the outbreak of war in August 1914, he was shortly afterwards drafted to Egypt. Later, however, he proceeded into Palestine, where he made the supreme sacrifice, being killed in action on April 19th, 1917. He was entitled to the 1914–15 Star, and the General Service and Victory Medals.
"A valiant Soldier, with undaunted heart he breasted life's last hill."
27, Leicester Street, Northampton. Z1701/B.

SMITH, J., Private, Royal Defence Corps.
Volunteering in September 1915 in the Royal Army Medical Corps, he was engaged on important duties at Ripon Hospital. He also served with the 2/17th County of London Regiment before being transferred to the Labour Corps, in which regiment he was engaged on important guard duties until discharged in December 1917.
36, Crispin Street, Northampton. Z1706.

SMITH, J. (M.M.), Sergt., 2nd Northants. Regt.
A serving soldier, he proceeded to France in October 1914, and there took a prominent part in the Battles of Ypres, Neuve Chapelle, Loos, the Somme, Arras, Passchendaele and Cambrai, and minor engagements. After being wounded, he was taken prisoner in May 1918, and held in captivity until the following December. He was awarded the Divisional Certificate for holding the lines of communication at Westhoek in July 1917, was mentioned in Despatches for distinguished service in November of that year and was awarded the Military Medal for conspicuous bravery in the Field. He also holds the 1914 Star, and the General Service and Victory Medals, and was discharged in February 1919.
19, Alliston Gardens, Northampton. Z1705.

SMITH, J., Tpr., Northants. Dragoons (Yeomanry).
After volunteering in October 1915, he underwent a period of training and proceeded overseas. During his service on the Western Front, he took part in many important engagements, including the Battle of Arras. He was later transferred to Italy, where he served on the Piave front and did continuously good work until demobilised in February 1919, holding the General Service and Victory Medals.
68, Castle Street, Northamptonshire. Z1699/A.

SMITH, J., Private, 1/4th Northants. Regiment.
Volunteering in August 1914, he embarked in the following year for Gallipoli, and served throughout the campaign there. After the Evacuation of the Peninsula, he was sent to Egypt, and, after taking part in heavy fighting, was drafted to Palestine. On that front he was in action in engagements at Gaza and Jaffa, but contracted dysentery and was admitted to hospital. Demobilised on his return home in April 1919, he holds the 1914–15 Star, and the General Service and Victory Medals.
4, St. James' Street, Daventry, Northants. TZ3161.

SMITH, J., Private, 1st Northants. Regiment.
When war broke out in August 1914, he was called up from the Reserve, and, embarking for the Western Front a month later, served in the Retreat from Mons. He also fought in the Battles of the Marne and the Aisne, but was reported missing in October 1914, and subsequently reported killed on November 2nd, 1914. He was entitled to the Mons Star, and the General Service and Victory Medals.
"His life for his Country, his soul to God."
Near Hall Spratton, Northants. Z3160.

SMITH, J. B., Driver, Royal Field Artillery.
Volunteering in August 1914, he proceeded to Gallipoli in July 1915, and served at Suvla Bay and Anzac Cove. After the Evacuation of the Peninsula he was sent to Egypt, but, advancing into Palestine, fought at Gaza and Jaffa, and was wounded. Transferred to France in October 1917, he was badly gassed during the Retreat in May 1918 and invalided home. He was demobilised in February 1919, but unfortunately died from the effects of gas-poisoning on May 30th, 1920, and was entitled to the 1914–15 Star, and the General Service and Victory Medals.
"His memory is cherished with pride."
Lower Heyford, Weedon, Northants. Z3268/C.

SMITH, J. C., Sergeant, Northants. Regiment.
Shortly after joining in April 1917, he was sent to the Western Front, where he saw severe fighting in various sectors. He played a prominent part in the Battles of Ypres and the Somme and many other important engagements until the cessation of hostilities, and in 1920 was with his Unit in Ireland. He holds the General Service and Victory Medals.
69, Perry Street, Northampton. Z1853/C.

SMITH, J. H., Private, 3rd Northants. Regiment.
Called up from the Reserve in August 1914, he was immediately drafted to the Western Front, where he served through the Retreat from Mons, and took part also in the Battles of the Marne, the Aisne, La Bassée, Ypres, the Somme and Cambrai, and other engagements. He unhappily died of heart failure on April 26th, 1920, and was entitled to the Mons Star, and the General Service and Victory Medals.
"His memory is cherished with pride."
39, Herbert Street, Northampton. Z1026/D—Z1027/D.

SMITH, J. H., Driver, Royal Field Artillery.
Joining in March 1916, he was sent to Salonika three months later, and served with an ammunition column in important engagements on various fronts. Transferred in June 1917 to Egypt, he was again in action in this seat of operations, finally returning to England for demobilisation in December 1919. He holds the General Service and Victory Medals.
3, Weston Place, Northampton. Z2856.

SMITH, J. H., Private, 7th Northants. Regiment.
Volunteering in September 1914, he was drafted to France twelve months later, and saw heavy fighting in various sectors of the front. After taking part in the Battles of Loos, Albert, Vermelles and Vimy Ridge, he was severely wounded on the Somme in July 1916, and invalided to hospital at Edmonton. There he unhappily died on October 17th of the same year, entitled to the 1914–15 Star, and the General Service and Victory Medals.
"His memory is cherished with pride.'
34, Countess Road, St. James, Northampton. Z2855.

SMITH, J. J., Private, Labour Corps.
Joining in December 1917, he was drafted overseas in March of the following year. During his service on the Western Front, he saw much heavy fighting, and did excellent work in various sectors until returning home for demobilisation in February 1919. He holds the General Service and Victory Medals.
51, Thirlestone Road, Far Cotton, Northampton. Z3418/B.

SMITH, J. S. (M.M.), Private, R.A.M.C.
After volunteering in 1915, he proceeded to France later in the same year. He did continuously good work as a stretcher-bearer and served during many important engagements in various sectors of the front, and was awarded the Military Medal for conspicuous bravery and devotion to duty under heavy shell-fire. Demobilised in 1919, he holds also the 1914–15 Star, and the General Service and Victory Medals.
11, Portland Street, Northampton. Z2275/B.

SMITH, J. T., Private, 1st Northants. Regiment.
Joining in May 1918, he completed a period of training and was drafted to the Western Front. Whilst in this seat of operations, he was in action at Ypres and Cambrai, where he was unfortunately killed in October 1918. He was entitled to the General Service and Victory Medals.
"Whilst we remember, the sacrifice is not in vain."
27, Crispin Street, Northamptonshire. Z1636/B—Z1637/B.

SMITH, J. T., Private, 1/4th Northants. Regiment.
Volunteering in August 1915, he embarked four months later for Egypt, and was in action in engagements at Sollum, Jifjaffa, Katia, El Fasher, Romani and Magdhaba. In 1917 he proceeded to Palestine, and after serving at Rafa and Siwa, was wounded whilst fighting in the second Battle of Gaza. He afterwards served with the Labour Corps, and when hostilities ceased returned to England and was demobilised in July 1919, holding the 1914–15 Star, and the General Service and Victory Medals. 79, Roe Road, Northampton. Z2505.

SMITH, J. T., Private, 12th Staffordshire Regt.
He joined in May 1917, and, after a period of training was sent overseas in the following year. Whilst serving on the Western Front, he took an active part in the Somme Offensive, and saw fierce fighting in the final decisive engagements of the war, being wounded on one occasion. After the Armistice, he advanced into Germany with the Army of Occupation, serving at Cologne until demobilised in November 1919, holding the General Service and Victory Medals.
New Cottages, Rothersthorpe, Northants. Z3159.

SMITH, J. W., Rifleman, Royal Irish Rifles.
Already serving in the Army, he was mobilised at the outbreak of war in August 1914, and immediately drafted to France. In the course of his service, he was in action during the Retreat from Mons and also at the Battle of La Bassée. He died gloriously on the Field of Battle in October 1914, and was entitled to the Mons Star, and the General Service and Victory Medals.
"A costly sacrifice upon the altar of freedom."
29, Crispin Street, Northampton. Z1636/A—Z1637/A.

SMITH, J. W., Private, Machine Gun Corps.
He joined in September 1917, and, in February of the following year, was sent to the Western Front, where he was taken prisoner near St. Quentin in the Retreat of March 1918. He was held in captivity until December of that year, and was finally demobilised in March 1919. He holds the General Service and Victory Medals.
33, Alfred Street, Northampton. Z2010.

SMITH, J. W., Rifleman, 1st Rifle Brigade.
On attaining military age he joined in October 1918, but, owing to the early cessation of hostilities, was unable to secure a transfer overseas before the Armistice. He was retained on duties of an important nature at various home stations until September 1919, when he was drafted to Mesopotamia, where in 1921 he was still serving.
54, Stanhope Road, Northampton. Z2506.

SMITH, J. W., Private, 1st Northants. Regiment.
Mobilised in August 1914, he was at once drafted to the Western Front and fought in the Retreat from Mons. After serving in the Battles of Le Cateau, the Marne and the Aisne, he was reported missing at La Bassée in October 1914, and was subsequently presumed to have been killed. He was entitled to the Mons Star, and the General Service and Victory Medals.
"He nobly died that we might live."
Spring Gardens, Spratton, Northants. Z3157.

SMITH, M., Private, Royal Fusiliers.
Joining in June 1916, he was shortly afterwards drafted to France, where he took part in many important engagements. He saw much heavy fighting in the Somme and Ypres sectors before being wounded and taken prisoner in February 1917. After the cessation of hostilities, he was released from captivity and eventually demobilised in August 1920. He holds the General Service and Victory Medals.
25, Castle Street, Northampton. Z1708.

SMITH, M., Private, 2/6th Royal Warwick. Regt.
He joined in August 1917, and in March of the following year was sent to the Western Front, where he took part in many important engagements during the Retreat and the earlier stages of the Allied Advance. He fell fighting on September 4th, 1918, and was buried near Hazebrouck. He was entitled to the General Service and Victory Medals.
"He nobly fell that we might live."
Long Street, Hanslope, Bucks. Z2853/A.

SMITH, M., Corporal, 4th Northamptonshire Regt. and Leicestershire Regiment.
Volunteering in 1915, he received his training at Tring, and in the following year crossed to France. On that front he was in action in many notable engagements, including the Battle of Arras, and was wounded at Ypres in 1917. He was invalided to England, and, after hospital treatment in Leicester, was discharged as medically unfit in September 1918, holding the General Service and Victory Medals.
Church Street, Brixworth, Northants. Z3069/B.

SMITH, P. H., Private (Signaller), Essex Regiment.
Having previously served for 12 months in the V.A.D., he joined the Colours in March 1918 on attaining military age. After a period of training, he was transferred to the Labour Corps and drafted to France, where he was engaged on important duties with his Unit in various sectors of the front. He was demobilised in January 1919, and holds the General Service and Victory Medals.
169, Adnitt Road, Northampton. Z2274/A.

SMITH, R., Private, 10th Canadian Regiment.
After volunteering in September 1914, he completed a period of training in Canada, and embarked for France. Whilst in this theatre of war he took part in many important engagements, including those in the Ypres sector, and was twice wounded. As a result he was invalided home, and eventually discharged as medically unfit for further service in December 1916. He holds the 1914-15 Star, and the General Service and Victory Medals.
14, Manor Road, Kingsthorpe, Northampton. Z1707.

SMITH, R. C., Private, Machine Gun Corps.
Shortly after joining in 1916, he was drafted to the Western Front, where he fought in the Battles of Ypres and Passchendaele and many other engagements of note. He also did good work with his Unit during the Retreat and Advance of 1918, and was present at the entry into Mons. After the Armistice, he proceeded to Germany with the Army of Occupation, and on his return home in 1919 was demobilised, holding the General Service and Victory Medals.
99, Adams Avenue, Northampton. Z2507.

SMITH, R. H., Private, Queen's Own (Royal West Kent Regiment).
Joining in February 1917, he sailed a year later for France, and whilst there experienced much severe fighting. He was in action at Cambrai and throughout the Retreat and Advance of 1918, and, returning home in November 1919, was demobilised, holding the General Service and Victory Medals.
51, Thirlestone Road, Far Cotton, Northampton. Z3418/A.

SMITH, R. W., Private, Training Reserve Battn.
On attaining military age he joined in January 1918, but, after a few months' training at Purfleet, his health broke down and he was admitted to hospital. Subsequently he was discharged as medically unfit for further military duties in June 1918, after only five months' service in the Army.
55, Wycliffe Road, Northampton. Z2501/B.

SMITH, S. A., L/Cpl., 6th York and Lancaster Regt.
Six months after joining in September 1916, he was sent to the Western Front, where he took part in the Battles of the Somme, Vimy Ridge and Amiens, fought also in the Retreat of 1918, and was wounded in July 1917. He unhappily fell in action on September 29th, 1918, and was entitled to the General Service and Victory Medals.
"The path of duty was the way to glory."
30, Brook Street, Daventry, Northants. Z2857.

SMITH, S. M., Private, 1st Northants. Regiment.
Mobilised at the outbreak of war, he was ordered to the Western Front and fought in the Retreat from Mons. He was also engaged in fierce fighting in the Battles of the Marne, the Aisne and Ypres, and was twice wounded, but was unhappily killed in action on the Dunes on July 10th, 1917. He was entitled to the Mons Star, and the General Service and Victory Medals.
"A costly sacrifice upon the altar of freedom."
The Green, Hartwell, Northants. Z2341/B.

SMITH, S. R., Private, Royal Naval Division.
Joining in 1917, he was shortly afterwards drafted to France, and, whilst on the Western Front, took part in many important engagements, including the Battles of Vimy Ridge, Ypres and Cambrai. He did continuously good work, and in May 1919 was demobilised, holding the General Service and Victory Medals.
11, Portland Street, Northampton. Z2275/C.

SMITH, T., Private, Labour Corps.
Joining in July 1917, he completed a period of training, and served with the Training Reserve before being transferred to the Labour Corps. He was afterwards engaged on important agricultural work, in which capacity he rendered excellent services until demobilised in February 1919.
6, Todds Lane, Northampton. Z1709.

SMITH, T. B. S., Corporal, Royal Engineers.
Volunteering in August 1915, he was drafted to France in June 1917, and, whilst in this theatre of war, rendered valuable services in various sectors of the front. He was present at the severe fighting at Passchendaele and Cambrai, and served for a time with the York and Lancaster Regiment. In June 1918 he rejoined the Royal Engineers, and served with them until demobilised in August 1919. He holds the General Service and Victory Medals.
38, Delapre Street, Northampton. Z3505.

SMITH, W., Private, Northamptonshire Regiment.
He enlisted in March 1909, and, at the outbreak of war, was immediately drafted to the Western Front, where he saw much service in various sectors. He was in action at Neuve Chapelle, Loos, Armentières and Arras, before being wounded in April 1917. As a result he was invalided to hospital in England, and, after a period of treatment, was eventually discharged as medically unfit for further service in September 1918. He holds the 1914-15 Star, and the General Service and Victory Medals. 65, Lorne Road, Northampton. Z1704.

SMITH, W. (M.M.), Sergeant, Suffolk Regiment.
Joining in June 1916, he was shortly afterwards drafted to the Western Front, where he served with distinction in many important engagements, including those in the Somme, Ypres, and Cambrai sectors. He was awarded the Military Medal for conspicuous bravery and devotion to duty in the field. Later, in 1918, he was taken prisoner and held in captivity until the conclusion of war. Demobilised in October 1919, he holds also the General Service and Victory Medals.
14, Fitzroy Terrace, Northampton. Z1626/B.

SMITH, W., Gunner, Royal Garrison Artillery.
Volunteering in August 1915, he underwent a period of training, and in the following year proceeded to the Western Front. Whilst in this seat of operations he was in action with his Battery during the fighting at Ypres, Arras, Lens and the Somme before being gassed and invalided home in October 1917. On his recovery he was retained on important duties at various stations until demobilised in November 1919, holding the General Service and Victory Medals.
70, Castle Street, Northampton. Z1710.

SMITH, W., Driver, Royal Horse Artillery.
Shortly after volunteering in June 1915, he was sent to the Western Front, where he saw much heavy fighting. He took part in the Battles of Ypres, Loos, Albert, Arras and Cambrai, and other engagements, and also fought in the Retreat and Advance of 1918. He was later sent to the East, and, after serving in Egypt, Mesopotamia and India, was, in 1921, with his Battery in Persia. He holds the 1914-15 Star, and the General Service and Victory Medals.
34, King Street, Northampton. Z1341/A.

SMITH, W., Private, Seaforth Highlanders.
He volunteered in February 1915, and, in August of the following year, was drafted to the Western Front, where, serving also with the Canadian Scottish, he took part in many important engagements. He died gloriously on the Field of Battle on the Somme on November 13th, 1916, and was entitled to the General Service and Victory Medals.
"He nobly fell that we might live."
The Green, Hartwell, Northants. Z2341/C.

SMITH, W., Rifleman, Canadian Mounted Rifles.
Volunteering in Canada in February 1915, he was drafted to the Western Front nine months later and saw heavy fighting in various sectors. He took an active part in the Battles of Albert, the Somme, Arras, Vimy Ridge, Ypres and Cambrai, was wounded on three occasions, and also gassed. He was demobilised in April 1919, and holds the 1914–15 Star, and the General Service and Victory Medals.
The Green, Hartwell, Northants. Z2341/A.

SMITH, W. C., Private, 5th Northants. Regiment.
Volunteering at the outbreak of war, he was later drafted to the Western Front. In this seat of operations he took part in many important engagements, including the Battles of Loos, the Somme, Ypres, Messines and Cambrai. Whilst overseas he was twice wounded, and in March 1919 was demobilised, holding the 1914–15 Star, and the General Service and Victory Medals. 140, Market Street, Northampton. Z2276.

SMITH, W. E., Corporal, 1st Northants. Regiment.
Having enlisted in 1913, he proceeded to the Western Front in August of the following year, and there fought in the Retreat from Mons. He also took part in the Battles of the Marne, the Aisne, Ypres, Neuve Chapelle, Loos, the Somme, Arras, Cambrai, and in the Retreat and Advance of 1918, and later served with the Army of Occupation at Cologne. Discharged in March 1919, he holds the Mons Star, and the General Service and Victory Medals.
18, Grey Friars Street, Northampton. Z2011.

SMITH, W. E., L/Sergeant, 1st Northants. Regt.
He volunteered in November 1915, and, in August of the following year, proceeded to France, where he was severely wounded in the Somme Offensive at High Wood, after only a month's active service. Invalided home, he was retained on important duties in England until his demobilisation in February 1919. He holds the General Service and Victory Medals. 13, Dundee Street, Northampton. Z2858.

SMITH, W. H., Driver, Royal Army Service Corps.
Twelve months after volunteering in October 1914 he was drafted to Salonika, where he served on various fronts. He was engaged chiefly in conveying ammunition and supplies to the forward areas, and was for a considerable period in hospital, suffering from malaria. He was demobilised on his return home in February 1919, and holds the General Service and Victory Medals.
9, Weston Row, Northampton. Z2859.

SMITH, W. H., Private, Buffs (East Kent Regt.)
Joining in June 1916, he proceeded to France after four months' training, and there saw much severe fighting. After taking part in the Battles of the Somme, Vimy Ridge and Ypres, and many other important engagements, he was invalided home in July 1918, and was then retained in England until his demobilisation in February 1919. He holds the General Service and Victory Medals.
33, New Street, Daventry, Northants. Z2860.

SMITH, W. J., Pte., Queen's (R.W. Surrey Regt.)
He joined in April 1916, and three months later proceeded to the Western Front, where he saw heavy fighting in various sectors. After serving in the Battles of the Somme, Messines, Ypres and Passchendaele, he gave his life for the freedom of England at Villers-Bretonneux in April 1918. He was entitled to the General Service and Victory Medals.
"Whilst we remember, the sacrifice is not in vain."
94, Roe Road, Monk's Park, Northampton. Z3158/B.

SMITH, W. R. S., Sapper, Royal Engineers.
After volunteering in January 1915, he completed his training, but was later found to be medically unfit for service overseas. He was therefore retained on important guard and other duties with his Unit at Maidenhead, and rendered excellent services until demobilised in 1918.
21, Scarletwell Street, Northampton. Z1673/B.

SMITH, W. W., Saddler, Royal Field Artillery.
He volunteered in October 1915, and five months later was drafted to France. There he participated in the Battle of the Somme, the capture of Bullecourt and the Battle of Cambrai, and was gassed and blown up on the Somme. In September 1918, he was sent to Italy, where he was in action on the Piave front. Invalided home in the following December owing to ill-health, he was ultimately discharged in January 1919, holding the General Service and Victory Medals.
37, Greenwood Street, Northampton. Z2712/A.

SNEDKER, C. G., Private, Royal Sussex Regiment.
He joined in May 1916, and in the following February embarked for Egypt, proceeding later to Palestine. In this theatre of war he took part in heavy fighting at Jaffa and Haifa, and was unhappily killed in action at the third Battle of Gaza on November 6th, 1917. He was entitled to the General Service and Victory Medals.
"Whilst we remember, the sacrifice is not in vain."
4, Drayton Place, Daventry, Northants. Z2861/A.

SNEDKER, I., Driver, Royal Field Artillery.
Mobilised in August 1914, he was at once sent to France, where he was in action during the Retreat from Mons, and at the Battles of the Marne, the Aisne, Ypres, Neuve Chapelle, Hill 60, Ypres (II.), Loos, the Somme, Arras, Ypres (III.), and Cambrai. He later served in various sectors during the Retreat and Advance of 1918, and was discharged on returning home in 1919. He holds the Mons Star, and the General Service and Victory Medals.
4, Drayton Place, Daventry, Northants. Z2861/B.

SNEDKER, W., Private, 27th Middlesex Regiment.
Volunteering in April 1915, he was drafted in June of the following year to France, where he took part in the Battles of the Somme, Arras and Ypres. He was severely wounded in May 1917, and was invalided home to hospital at Folkestone. After recovering, he was employed on various duties in home stations until he was demobilised in November 1919, holding the General Service and Victory Medals.
4, Drayton Place, Daventry, Northants. Z2861/C.

SNEDKER, W. H., 2nd Air Mechanic, R.A.F.
He joined in November 1917, and throughout the period of his service was engaged on important duties in the Technical Department in London. Unsuccessful in his endeavours to obtain a transfer to a theatre of war, he, nevertheless, rendered many valuable services in connection with research work until demobilised in January 1919.
Spratton, Northants. Z3162.

SNOW, T., Private, 1st Northants. Regiment.
At the declaration of war in August 1914 he was already serving, and immediately proceeded to France, where he was in action in the Retreat from Mons. He also fought in the Battles of La Bassée, Ypres (I.), Neuve Chapelle, Ypres (II.), Loos, Vermelles, Vimy Ridge, Beaumont-Hamel, Arras, Ypres (III.), Passchendaele, Cambrai, the Somme and Bapaume, and was wounded on three occasions and also gassed. He was discharged in January 1919, holding the Mons Star, and the General Service and Victory Medals.
16, Oxford Street, Far Cotton, Northampton. Z3163.

SOAMES, J., Private, Machine Gun Corps.
He volunteered in September 1914, joined the Northamptonshire Yeomanry, and was later transferred to the Machine Gun Corps. He served on the Western Front from October 1915 until after the Armistice, and was in action at Loos, on the Somme, and at Arras, Bullecourt, Ypres, Bapaume and Cambrai, being wounded on one occasion. He was demobilised on his return home in May 1919, and holds the 1914–15 Star, and the General Service and Victory Medals.
22, St. James' Street, Northampton. Z2762/A.

SOUSTER, G., Private, R.A.M.C.
Volunteering in October 1915, he underwent a period of training and was drafted to the Western Front, where he served with the 102nd Field Ambulance as a stretcher-bearer. He took an active part in the Battles of Albert, Arras, Péronne, Cambrai and other engagements. Later he contracted rheumatism, was invalided home, and discharged as medically unfit for further service in February 1918, holding the General Service and Victory Medals.
39, Francis Street, Northampton. Z1711/A.

SOUSTER, G., Air Mechanic, Royal Air Force.
In spite of the fact that he was under age, he joined in September 1918, and after a period of training was retained at Nottingham, where he rendered excellent services as a fitter-engineer. Later he was transferred to the Royal Army Service Corps, and was stationed at Bulford, where he was still serving in 1920.
39, Francis Street, Northampton. Z1711/B.

SOUTHALL, F. P. (M.M.), Driver, R.F.A.
He was serving in India in August 1914, and was afterwards drafted to France, where he fought in the Battles of Ypres, Loos and Festubert, and was awarded the Military Medal for conspicuous bravery and devotion to duty in the Field. He later served at Gaza in Palestine, and also in Mesopotamia, where he was in action near Baghdad. Returning to France in 1918, he fought in the final Advance, and was eventually discharged in October 1919, holding also the 1914–15 Star, and the General Service and Victory Medals.
Spring Lane, Flore, Northampton. Z2862.

SOUTHCLIFFE, C. W., Private, 22nd R. Fusiliers.
He joined in June 1916, and in the following November proceeded to France. In this theatre of war he served at Vimy Ridge, Arras and Bapaume, and was unhappily killed in action at Petit-Miraumont on February 17th, 1917. He was entitled to the General Service and Victory Medals.
"He passed out of the sight of men by the path of duty and self-sacrifice."
34, Brook Street, Daventry, Northampton. Z2863.

SPANTON, H., L/Corporal, 5th Northants. Regt.
Volunteering in August 1914, he was sent to the Western Front in the following February, and took part in the Battles of Neuve Chapelle, Hill 60, Ypres, Albert, Vimy Ridge, the Somme, and Arras, and minor engagements. He fell fighting on the Somme on March 27th, 1918, and was entitled to the 1914–15 Star, and the General Service and Victory Medals.
"The path of duty was the way to glory."
9 Ambush Street, St. James, Northampton. Z2364/B.

SPATCHER, W., Private, 1/4th Northants. Regt.
He volunteered in October 1915, and in the following March was drafted to Egypt. In this seat of operations he was engaged on important duties, and later took part in the Advance into Palestine, fighting at Gaza, Jaffa and at the fall of Jerusalem. He was demobilised in September 1919, and holds the General Service and Victory Medals.
38, King Street, Northampton. Z1285/A.

SPEAR, C., Private, 19th Manchester Regiment.
Having volunteered in January 1915, he completed a period of training, but was later found to be medically unfit for service overseas. He was therefore retained on important duties with his unit, and rendered excellent services until discharged in the following June.
29, Naseby Street, Northampton. Z1702/A.

SPEAR, D. T., Armourer Staff-Sergeant, R.A.O.C.
Joining in July 1917, he was quickly drafted overseas. Whilst on the Western Front, he took part in many important engagements in various sectors. In March 1918 he was transferred to Italy, where he did continuously good work, and was awarded an Italian decoration for gallantry in repairing the guns under heavy shell-fire. After the conclusion of war, he was drafted to Mesopotamia, where in 1921 he was still serving. He holds also the General Service and Victory Medals.
29, Naseby Street, Northampton. Z1702/B.

SPENCE, E. F., Gunner, Royal Field Artillery.
He volunteered in October 1915, and in the following year was drafted to France, where he took part in the Battles of the Somme, Arras, Vimy Ridge, Messines, Ypres, Cambrai and Armentières, and was gassed and wounded in action. He was demobilised on his recovery in February 1919, and holds the General Service and Victory Medals.
8, Cranstown Street, Northampton. Z1712/A.

SPENCE, J. E. K., Private, North Staffs. Regt.
He joined in November 1916, and eight months later was drafted to France, where he took part in the Battles of Ypres, Lens, Cambrai, the Somme (II.), Amiens, Bapaume and Havrincourt, and was unfortunately killed in action near Mons in November 1918. He was entitled to the General Service and Victory Medals.
"His memory is cherished with pride."
8, Cranstown Street, Northampton. Z1712/B.

SPENCE, M. V., Private, Durham Light Infantry.
Having previously been rejected on seven occasions, he joined in 1917, and, after a period of training, was retained at various stations, where, attached to the Red Cross, he was engaged on duties of great importance. He was unable to obtain his transfer overseas, but, nevertheless, rendered valuable services until his demobilisation in 1919.
57, Adam's Avenue, Northampton. Z2375/B.

SPENCER, G., Private, 5th Northants. Regiment.
Volunteering in August 1914, he was drafted to France in March 1915, and served in this theatre of war throughout hostilities. He took part in the Battles of Ypres (II.), the Somme, Arras and Cambrai, and the Retreat and Advance of 1918, and was mentioned in Despatches for bravery in the Field. He holds the 1914–15 Star, and the General Service and Victory Medals, and was demobilised in March 1919.
56, Scarletwell Street, Northampton. Z1713.

SPENCER, H., Sapper, Royal Engineers.
He volunteered in June 1915, and seven months later was sent to Egypt, but, in July 1916, was transferred to the Western Front. He there rendered valuable services with a Field Company in the Somme, Arras and Cambrai sectors until September 1917, when he was discharged. He holds the General Service and Victory Medals.
13, Washington Street, Kingsthorpe, Northampton. TZ1714.

SPENCER, T. H., Private, 6th Northants. Regt.
He volunteered in February 1915, but was retained on important duties in England for three years. He then proceeded to France, and, after taking part in the Retreat, was twice wounded in action on the Somme during the Advance—in August and October 1918. Demobilised in October 1919, he holds the General Service and Victory Medals.
14, Scarletwell Street, Northampton. Z1715.

SPENCER, W. T., Private, 1/5th Bedford. Regt.
He volunteered in June 1915, but, owing to his being medically unfit for transfer overseas, was retained on special guard duties at Dovercourt. He rendered valuable services until July 1916, when he was invalided from the Army suffering from heart disease. 37, Stanley Street, Northampton. Z1613/B.

SPICE, F. G., Rifleman, 13th K.R.R.C.
He joined in March 1918, but, owing to his being under age for transfer to a theatre of war, was retained on important duties at home until March 1919. He was then sent to the Army of Occupation in Germany, and rendered valuable services with his Unit at Cologne until demobilised twelve months later.
50, Lower Hester Street, Northampton. Z1716.

SPILLER, A., Private, Northamptonshire Regt.
He volunteered in September 1914, and in the following January proceeded to France, where he was in action at Albert, Ypres, the Somme and Cambrai. He unfortunately contracted an illness, but, after receiving hospital treatment, rejoined his unit and fought in various engagements during the Retreat and Advance of 1918. He was ultimately demobilised in January 1919, and holds the 1914–15 Star, and the General Service and Victory Medals.
9, Southampton Road, Far Cotton, Northampton. Z3510.

SPRIGGS, F., A.B., Royal Navy.
Volunteering in August 1914, he was later posted to H.M.S. "Castor," and in this vessel served with the Grand Fleet in the North Sea. He was present at the Battle of Jutland and during various operations off Zeebrugge and Ostend, and was afterwards engaged on important duties in the Mediterranean. He was demobilised in August 1920, holding the 1914–15 Star, and the General Service and Victory Medals.
36, Brook Street, Daventry, Northampton. Z2864.

SPRIGGS, W. J., L/Cpl., Oxford. and Bucks. L.I.
He volunteered in September 1914, and in October of the following year proceeded to Salonika, where he was transferred for duty to the Military Foot Police. Invalided to Alexandria and later to Malta suffering from dysentery, he was afterwards sent to France in 1918, and there served at Rouen and other stations. He was demobilised in July 1919, and holds the 1914–15 Star, and the General Service and Victory Medals.
Hartwell, Northants. Z2508.

SPRING, E., Private, 1/4th Cheshire Regiment.
Called up from the Reserve in August 1914, he quickly proceeded to France, where he was wounded at Mons and invalided home. Returning to the Western Front, he was again wounded and admitted to hospital in England, but was again sent to France on his recovery. He was transferred thence to Egypt, but returned to the Western Front in June 1918, and there fell in action on the Marne on July 23rd of that year. He was entitled to the Mons Star, and the General Service and Victory Medals.
"His life for his Country, his soul to God."
10, Brunswick Place, Northampton. Z2012.

SPRINGWELL, T., Private, Northants. Regiment.
Volunteering in September 1914, he underwent a period of training before proceeding to France, where he took part in the Battles of Ypres, Festubert, Loos and the Somme prior to being wounded and invalided home in July 1916. On his recovery he was transferred to the Royal Engineers and drafted to Egypt, where he saw much service. He later advanced into Palestine and fought at the Battles of Gaza, Jaffa and the capture of Jerusalem. Invalided home with malaria fever, he was eventually demobilised in April 1919, holding the 1914–15 Star, and the General Service and Victory Medals.
Roade, Northants. Z2277.

SPROSTON, C., Driver, Royal Field Artillery.
Mobilised at the outbreak of hostilities, he was immediately drafted to the Western Front, and was in action with his Battery at the Battle of, and in the Retreat from, Mons. He then saw much heavy fighting in various sectors before being unfortunately killed in September 1918. He was entitled to the Mons Star, and the General Service and Victory Medals.
"Whilst we remember, the sacrifice is not in vain."
54, Clarke Road, Northampton. Z2278.

SPROSTON, F. S., Private, Northamptonshire Regiment and Machine Gun Corps.
He joined in July 1916, and, embarking for France four months later, served there for a short time before proceeding to Egypt. Later he returned to the Western Front, and saw heavy fighting at Nieuport and Ypres until invalided home in November 1917. Subsequently he was drafted back to France, and took part in engagements at Comines and Espierres. Demobilised in February 1919, he holds the General Service and Victory Medals. 43, Spencer Street, Northampton. Z3164.

SPROSTON, W. E., Driver, R.F.A.
He enlisted in August 1919 at the age of 18 years, was drafted to Ireland and underwent a period of training, and was then engaged on important garrison duties. He rendered valuable services, but, owing to medical unfitness, was eventually discharged in August 1920.
34, Melbourne Street, Northampton. Z1997/B.

SQUIRES, A. E., Private, 7th Northants. Regt.
He joined in January 1916, and in the following July was drafted to the Western Front. After taking part in several important engagements in various sectors, he died gloriously on the Field of Battle at High Wood on September 1st, 1916 He was entitled to the General Service and Victory Medals.
"He died the noblest death a man may die:
Fighting for God and right and liberty."
49, East Street, Northampton. Z2013/B

SQUIRES, E., Sergeant, 7th Northants. Regiment.
A month after the outbreak of war he volunteered, and on completion of his training was drafted overseas. Serving on the Western Front, he played a prominent part in many engagements, including the Battles of Ypres, Festubert and Loos, but unfortunately contracted dysentery and died in September 1916. He was entitled to the 1914 Star, and the General Service and Victory Medals.
"His memory is cherished with pride."
49, East Street, Northampton. Z2013/A

STAMP, J. E., Private, Wiltshire Regiment.
At the outbreak of war he volunteered, and in 1916 embarked for France and fought in the Battles of Albert, the Somme, Arras, Vimy Ridge and Ypres. In 1917 he was gassed and invalided to England, but, on his recovery, returned to the Western Front in February 1918. He then served in the Retreat and Advance of that year, and was demobilised in April 1919, holding the General Service and Victory Medals.
35, Doddridge Street, Northampton. Z1195/A.

STAMPS, L. J., Bandsman, 2nd Northants. Regt.
He joined in September 1916, but was retained on duties of an important nature at various home stations until the cessation of hostilities. After the Armistice he was sent to Belgium, where he did valuable work until transferred to India, where in 1920 he was still serving.
4, Chaucer Street, Kingsley, Northants. Z1095/C.

STAMPS, T., Private, Cheshire Regiment.
Volunteering in the Royal Engineers in August 1915, he was later transferred to the Cheshire Regiment and ordered overseas in December 1916. During his service on the Western Front, he was engaged in severe fighting on the Somme, took part in numerous battles and was wounded at Cambrai. He served in France until January 1919, when he was demobilised, holding the General Service and Victory Medals.
4, Chaucer Street, Kingsley Park, Northampton. Z1091/B.

STANLEY, W. H., L/Corporal, 1st Northants. Regt.
At the outbreak of war he was already serving, having enlisted in January 1907, and was at once ordered to the Western Front, where he was in action in various parts of the line. He fought in numerous notable engagements, but was wounded in the Battle of the Somme in July 1916. On his recovery, he was almost continuously in action until the cessation of hostilities. He was discharged in March 1919, and holds the 1914 Star, and the General Service and Victory Medals.
24, Nelson Street, Northants. Z1289/A.

STANTON, H., Air Mechanic, Royal Air Force.
He joined in January 1918, and, after completing his training, served at various aerodromes on duties which demanded a high degree of technical skill. He was unable to secure a transfer overseas on account of being under military age, but, nevertheless, rendered valuable services until demobilised in February 1920.
1, Henley Street, Northampton. Z3511.

STAPLETON, W., Air Mechanic, R.A.F.
He joined the Flying Corps in January 1918, and, after completing his training, was engaged on special duties with his Squadron in the Orkney Islands. In spite of his not being drafted overseas, he rendered valuable services until his demobilisation in February 1919.
129, Lutterworth Road, Northampton. Z2279.

STARMER, C. S., Private, Leinster Regiment.
Volunteering in October 1915, he proceeded to France seven months later, but, after heavy fighting on the Somme, was transferred to Salonika, where he was in action on the Doiran and Struma fronts. In June 1917 he was sent to Palestine, and took part in the Battle of Gaza and the capture of Jerusalem. Whilst overseas he suffered from malaria and trench feet, and was demobilised in June 1919, holding the General Service and Victory Medals.
20, Monk's Pond Street, Northampton. Z1717.

STARMER, F. C., Private, Essex Regiment.
He joined in June 1918, and, after a period of training, proceeded overseas early in the following November. Serving on the Western Front, he was engaged in fierce fighting in the Battle of the Sambre, and, after the Armistice was signed, did valuable work with his Unit in France until sent to England for demobilisation in January 1919. He holds the General Service and Victory Medals.
67, Edith Street, Northampton. Z2014.

STARMER, F. W., Private, Labour Corps.
He volunteered in the Royal Army Service Corps in February 1915, and was transferred to the Royal Scots. He proceeded to France in 1917, where he took part in important operations and was disabled at Ypres. He was then sent to the Labour Corps, with which he served until April 1919, when he was demobilised, holding the General Service and Victory Medals.
Muircott, Long Buckby, Northants. Z3512.

STAUGHTON, P. H., Corporal, R.A.S.C. (M.T.)
Volunteering in November 1915, he was engaged on duties of an important nature in England until October 1917, when he secured a transfer to France. There he was stationed at Cherbourg, and placed in charge of a workshop, rendering valuable services until the termination of the war. He was demobilised on his return home in August 1919, and holds the General Service and Victory Medals.
13, St. Edmund's Street, Northampton. Z2015.

STEEL, A., Private, Machine Gun Corps.
He joined the Norfolk Regiment in January 1917, and four months later was sent to the Western Front, where he took part in the Battles of Lens and Cambrai. In March 1918 he was transferred to the Machine Gun Corps, and shortly afterwards was taken prisoner whilst fighting on the Somme, and held in captivity until the Armistice. When released, he served in France until demobilised in September 1919, holding the General Service and Victory Medals.
5, St. James' Place, Northampton. Z2865.

STEEL, J. T., Private, 2/4th Northants. Regiment.
He volunteered in October 1914, and in 1916 was sent to France, on which front he was in action at the Battles of the Somme, Vimy Ridge, Ypres, Lens and Cambrai, and was wounded at Loos in 1917. On his return to the firing-line he saw heavy fighting at Havrincourt and Le Cateau, and was present during the entry into Mons. Demobilised in March 1919, he holds the General Service and Victory Medals.
82, Dunster Street, Northampton. Z2016.

STEELE, A. W. C., Corporal, Northants. Regt.
Shortly after volunteering in January 1915, he was ordered to the Western Front, where he saw heavy fighting in various sectors. He took an active part in the Battles of Ypres, Festubert, Loos, Albert, the Somme and Arras, and was severely wounded at Ypres in 1917 and invalided to England. Consequently he was discharged as medically unfit for further military service in July 1918, and holds the 1914–15 Star, and the General Service and Victory Medals.
33, Althorp Street, Northampton. Z1261/A.

STEELE, W. H., Corporal, Labour Corps.
He volunteered in the Northamptonshire Regiment in November 1915, and was stationed at various places in England. In April 1917 he met with an accident which rendered him physically unfit for transfer overseas. He was transferred to the Labour Corps, and did excellent work at Nottingham until demobilised in February 1919.
12, Cranstown Street, Northampton. Z1718.

STENNETT, J. G., Corporal, 1st Northants. Regt.
Already in the Army in August 1914, he immediately proceeded to France, but, after taking part in the Battle of Mons and the subsequent Retreat, and also the Battle of the Marne, was badly wounded in action and invalided home. He was in hospital at Chatham and Maidstone, and on his recovery was retained on home service. In 1920 he was serving in Mesopotamia, and holds the Mons Star, and the General Service and Victory Medals. 13, Ash Street, Northampton. Z1719.

STENT, H., Private, Norfolk Regiment.
He joined in January 1918, but, on account of his youth, was not successful in his efforts to obtain a transfer to the fighting area. Throughout the period of his service, he was engaged on important coastal defence duties at Hastings and other stations, and carried out his work with great efficiency until demobilised in March 1919.
18, Bull Head Lane, Northampton. Z1055/B—Z1056/B.

STENT, W. D., Private, 2nd Northants. Regiment.
Volunteering in October 1914, he was trained at Newmarket, and, proceeding to France in the early part of 1916, fought in the Battles of the Somme and Ypres and other engagements of note. During the second Battle of the Somme, he was wounded and reported missing on April 24th 1918, and subsequently was presumed to have been killed on that date. He was entitled to the General Service and Victory Medals.
"A costly sacrifice upon the altar of freedom."
18, Bull Head Lane, Northampton. Z1055/C—Z1056/C.

STEPHENS, T. A., Private, 10th Queen's (Royal West Surrey Regiment).
He joined in May 1916, and, proceeding to France in September, fought at Ypres, La Bassée, St. Eloi, the Somme, Hill 60, Messines and Cambrai. Transferred to Italy, he was in action on the Piave, but, after being in hospital owing to a bad knee, returned to the Western Front. At the cessation of hostilities, he advanced with the Army of Occupation into Germany, where he served until demobilised in April 1919, holding the General Service and Victory Medals.
15, Manfield Road, Northampton. Z2280.

STEVENS, A., Private, 1st Northants. Regiment.
When war broke out in August 1914 he volunteered, and during the period of his service was stationed at Tunbridge Wells, Newmarket and Ipswich, where he was engaged on duties of an important nature. Owing to ill-health, he was unsuccessful in securing a transfer to the war zone, but, nevertheless, did valuable work in various capacities until demobilised in March 1919.
Squirrel Lane, Old Duston, Northants. Z3165/A.

STEVENS, A. H., L/Cpl., 2nd Northants. Regt.
Volunteering in November 1914, he was sent to France in August 1916, and took part in the Battles of the Somme and Ypres, where he was badly wounded in August 1917 and invalided home. After hospital treatment in Leicester, he was transferred to the Royal Defence Corps and sent to Ireland, where he was engaged on important duties, guarding railway bridges. Demobilised in February 1919, he holds the General Service and Victory Medals.
138, Stanhope Road, Northampton. Z1720/A.

STEVENS, F. (M.M.), Private, 2nd Northants. Regt.
Mobilised in August 1914, he immediately proceeded to France and played a prominent part in the Battles of Mons, La Bassée, Ypres (I.), Neuve Chapelle, St. Eloi, Hill 60, Ypres (II.), Festubert, Loos, Albert, Vimy Ridge, the Somme, Arras, Bullecourt and Cambrai. He was wounded and taken prisoner after having been awarded the Military Medal for great gallantry in rescuing a wounded officer under heavy shell-fire. Repatriated after the Armistice, he was discharged in December 1919, and also holds the Mons Star, and the General Service and Victory Medals.
83, Market Street, Northampton. Z2281.

STEVENS, J., Sergeant, 7th Northants. Regiment.
A month after the outbreak of war he volunteered, and in September 1915 embarked for the Western Front. There he fought with distinction in the Battles of Loos, the Somme and Arras, and gave his life for King and Country at Ypres in July 1917. He was entitled to the 1914–15 Star, and the General Service and Victory Medals.
"He died the noblest death a many may die,
Fighting for God and right and liberty."
67, Gladstone Terrace, Northampton. Z1133/B.

STEVENS, S. E., Private, 7th Royal Fusiliers.
He joined in June 1916, but was retained on important duties on Salisbury Plain until April 1918. Proceeding then to France, he was in action on the Somme and at St. Quentin, Cambrai, Amiens and Villers-Bretonneux before being killed in action on September 27th, 1918. He was entitled to the General Service and Victory Medals.
"His name liveth for evermore."
5, Fort Street, Northampton. Z1721

STEVENS, S. J., Sergeant, 1/4th Leicester. Regt.
Volunteering in December 1915, he was drafted to France four months later and served with distinction at Arras, Lens, St. Quentin and on the Somme. Badly gassed in action in October 1918, he was in hospital at Swindon until demobilised in February 1919. He holds the General Service and Victory Medals. 120, Lower Adelaide Street, Northampton. Z1722.

STEVENS, W. H., Private, 2nd Northants. Regt.
He joined in February 1917, and in May was sent to France, where he took part in heavy fighting at Arras, Ypres and High Wood, and was wounded in action in August 1917. Invalided to Dalmeny Hospital, Edinburgh, with gastritis, he returned to France in February 1918, and was taken prisoner during the Retreat in May, after being again wounded. He was released and demobilised in February 1919, holding the General Service and Victory Medals.
9, Poole Street, Northampton. Z1720/B.

STEVENSON, A. H., Private, R.A.O.C.
He joined in April 1918, and, after a period of training with an infantry Unit, served at various stations on important duties with the Royal Army Ordnance Corps. He was unable to obtain his transfer overseas before the cessation of hostilities, but in September 1919 was drafted to France, where he was stationed at Calais until his return home for demobilisation three months later.
The Green, Milton, Northampton. Z2402/B.

STEVENSON, A. W., 2nd Lieutenant, Sherwood Foresters.
He joined in April 1917, and, on conclusion of his training later in the same year, was ordered overseas. During his service on the Western Front, he played a conspicuous part in many notable engagements, and fought with distinction in the Battles of the Somme and Ypres. On his return to England he was demobilised in May 1919, and holds the General Service and Victory Medals.
49, Perry Street, Northampton. Z2017/B.

STEVENSON, G. J., Private, Tank Corps.
Joining in March 1917, he was shortly afterwards drafted to France. He was engaged as a driver and took part in numerous engagements, including those at Albert and the Somme, and was later employed as a Tank Instructor and rendered valuable services. He returned home and was discharged in March 1920 as medically unfit for further service, and holds the General Service and Victory Medals.
33, Oxford Street, Far Cotton, Northants. Z3513.

STEVENSON, J., Cpl., Military Mounted Police.
Volunteering in December 1914, he completed his training and performed valuable work at various important home stations until 1918, when he succeeded in securing a transfer to Salonika. In that theatre of war he fought in numerous engagements on the Vardar front, and also saw service in Bulgaria. He was demobilised on his return to England in July 1919, and holds the General Service and Victory Medals.
49, Perry Street, Northampton. Z2017/C.

STEVENSON, J. G., Trooper, Northants. Dragoons.
He volunteered in January 1915, and was engaged on important duties with his unit until February 1918, when he was drafted to France, but after two weeks returned home. Later he was sent to Russia on secret service and served at Vladivostok before proceeding to China, Japan and Canada. He was demobilised in March 1919, and holds the General Service and Victory Medals. Church End, Bugbrooke, Northants. Z3514.

STEVENSON, R. C. S., Gunner, R.H.A.
He volunteered in September 1914, and, in the following January, was sent to France, where he fought in engagements at Neuve Chapelle and Ypres. In March 1916 he was transferred to Egypt, but, after two months' service in Alexandria, was drafted back to the Western Front. There he took part in the Battles of the Somme, Arras, Cambrai, Béthune and Armentières, and was demobilised in January 1919, holding the 1914–15 Star, and the General Service and Victory Medals.
49, Perry Street, Northampton. Z2017/A.

STEVENSON, W. A. A., Private, 1st Northants. Regiment.
Mobilised in August 1914, he was sent to the Western Front in November, but, being badly wounded near Neuve Chapelle in January 1915, was invalided to hospital at Netley. Five months later he returned to France and took part in the Battles of Loos, Hulloch, the Somme and the Dunes, where he was taken prisoner in July 1917. He was released from captivity in Bavaria and discharged in April 1919, holding the 1914 Star, and the General Service and Victory Medals.
50, Castle Street, Northampton. Z1723.

STEWART, J. W., Rifleman, 3rd Royal Irish Rifles.
He volunteered in October 1915, and proceeded to France in the following year, but was badly wounded during the Somme Offensive and evacuated to England. Returning to the Western Front on his recovery, he was again wounded at Cambrai and sent home. After hospital treatment, he was sent to France once more, but was wounded for the third time at Ypres and yet again invalided home. He was then retained on important duties until his demobilisation in September 1919, and holds the General Service and Victory Medals.
Stoke Road, Blisworth, Northants. Z2282.

STINN, G., Corporal, Royal Army Service Corps.
He enlisted in 1917, and, after a period of training, was engaged at various home stations on important duties as a driver. He was not successful in obtaining a transfer overseas, but rendered valuable services until his demobilisation in 1919.
51, Clarke Road, Northampton. Z2283/A.

STINN, J., Private, Essex Regiment.
Having volunteered in 1915, he was drafted to Egypt in 1917. Whilst in this seat of operations, he took part in several engagements, and, advancing later into Palestine, was in action at the three Battles of Gaza and the fall of Jerusalem. He served with General Allenby's forces during the Offensive and was wounded. He returned home and was demobilised in 1919, holding the General Service and Victory Medals.
51, Clarke Road, Northampton. Z2283/B.

STOCKWELL, P. (M.M.) Private, 1st Northants. Regiment.
Mobilised when war was declared in August 1914, he immediately proceeded to the Western Front with the first Expeditionary Force. Whilst overseas he fought with distinction in numerous engagements of note, was wounded in action on four occasions, and was awarded the Military Medal for conspicuous gallantry in the Field. He was discharged in March 1920, and also holds the 1914 Star, and the General Service and Victory Medals.
32, Leicester Street, Northampton. Z1319/C.

STOCKWELL, R., Private, 1st Northants. Regt.
A Reservist, he was called up in August 1914, proceeded to France a month later, and fought in the Battles of the Marne, La Bassée and Ypres before being wounded and invalided home in February 1915. Nine months afterwards, he returned to France and served as a stretcher-bearer in the Loos, Albert, Somme, Arras, Passchendaele and Cambrai sectors. He was discharged in January 1919, and holds the 1914 Star, and the General Service and Victory Medals.
45, Lower Harding Street, Northampton. Z1724.

STOCKWIN, A., Private, Machine Gun Corps.
He joined the Northamptonshire Regiment in July 1916, and was afterwards transferred to the Machine Gun Corps and drafted to France, thence to Egypt. On the voyage his vessel was torpedoed, and he was adrift four days on a raft before being rescued. He was eventually landed in Palestine, where he served in important engagements. He was demobilised in August 1919, and holds the General Service and Victory Medals.
17, Main Road, Far Cotton, Northants. Z3515/B.

STOCKWIN, F. (Mrs.), Special War Worker.
This lady was engaged at the Filling Factory at Ross, near Hereford, from August 1917 until August 1918. She was employed in filling 9.2 and 12-inch shells and also gas bombs. Her duties, which were of a dangerous and important nature, were carried out with great care and efficiency, and she rendered valuable services.
17, Main Road, Far Cotton, Northants. Z3515/A.

STORY, W., Sergeant, Royal Army Medical Corps.
Volunteering in September 1914, he proceeded to the Western Front a year later, and rendered valuable services as a stretcher-bearer at Loos, Albert, Armentières, the Somme, Arras and Ypres. He was wounded in 1916 and again in the following year, in consequence of which he was invalided out of the Army in April 1918. He unfortunately died from the effects of war service at Malta on April 5th, 1920, and was entitled to the 1914–15 Star, and the General Service and Victory Medals.
"His memory is cherished with pride."
Long Street, Hanslope, Bucks. Z2866.

STOW, A. A. E., A.B., Merchant Service.
Already in the Mercantile Marine at the outbreak of war, he did excellent work throughout hostilities whilst engaged on the transport of troops and supplies to various theatres of operations. He served principally in the North Sea, the Southern Pacific and the Atlantic, and in 1921 was on board the S.S. "Hildebrand." He holds the General Service and Mercantile Marine War Medals.
163, Harborough Road, Kingsthorpe, Northampton. Z1624/A.

STOW, F. C. (D.C.M.), Sergt., 2nd E. Surrey Regt.
Mobilised in August 1914, he proceeded to France in October and played a prominent part in the Battles of the Marne, Ypres, Festubert, the Somme (where he was wounded in 1916), Arras, Vimy Ridge and Passchendaele. He was wounded and taken prisoner at Cambrai in November 1917, and held in captivity until December 1918. Whilst overseas he was awarded the Distinguished Conduct Medal for great gallantry and devotion to duty. In 1919 he served in Russia and Ireland, and in 1921 was stationed at Aldershot, holding also the 1914 Star, and the General Service and Victory Medals.
163, Harborough Road, Kingsthorpe, Northampton. Z1624/C.

STOWE, W., Private, 1/4th Northants. Regiment.
He volunteered in June 1915, and, after a period of training, embarked for Egypt ten months later, and was engaged in much severe fighting. Subsequently he was sent to Palestine, and was in action at Rafa and in the three Battles of Gaza and other important engagements. On his return to England in August 1919 he was demobilised, holding the General Service and Victory Medals.
34, Albert Street, Northampton. Z2018.

STRATFORD, J. A., Private, 23rd Middlesex Regt.
Joining in February 1916, he proceeded to the Western Front in the following April, and took part in the Battles of Arras, Ypres, Passchendaele and Cambrai, and many minor engagements. Transferred later to Italy, he fought on the Piave, and was afterwards sent with the Army of Occupation to Cologne. Demobilised on returning home in September 1919, he holds the General Service and Victory Medals.
41, Stanhope Road, Northampton. Z2509.

STREET, G. F. L., Special War Worker.
After being rejected for the Army, he was engaged on work of National importance on the London and North Western Railway. Whilst employed as a bricklayer, he carried out his duties with great efficiency and rendered valuable services during the war.
19, Main Road, Far Cotton, Northants. Z3516.

STRETTON, C., Gunner, R.G.A.
Three months after joining, he proceeded to France in August 1917, and was in action with his Battery at Zillebeke, St. Quentin, Cambrai and throughout the Retreat and Advance of 1918. After hostilities ceased, he served at Cologne with the Army of Occupation until demobilised in February 1919, and holds the General Service and Victory Medals.
36, Essex Street, Northampton. Z1725.

STURGESS, B., Private, Labour Corps.
He joined in 1917, and, after a period of training, was drafted in the same year to the Western Front, where he served for two years. During that time he took an active part in numerous engagements of note in various sectors of the line, and did good work with his Unit in operations during the Retreat and Advance of 1918. He was demobilised in December 1919, and holds the General Service and Victory Medals.
8, St. Peter's Terrace, Northampton. Z2867.

STURGESS, F., Private, 1st Northants. Regiment.
Mobilised in August 1914, he was drafted to France a month later, and there fought in the Battles of La Bassée, Neuve Chapelle, Hill 60, Ypres, Arras and Vimy Ridge, and was wounded on four occasions, being twice invalided home. In June 1917 he was taken prisoner, and held in captivity in Germany until hostilities ceased. On his release he was proceeding home, but was taken ill with influenza at Calais, and unfortunately died on January 5th, 1919. He was entitled to the 1914 Star, and the General Service and Victory Medals.
"The path of duty was the way to glory."
14, East Street, Northampton. Z1846/A.

STURGESS, J., Private, 1/4th Northants. Regt.
He volunteered in March 1915 at the age of 16, and in February 1916 embarked for Egypt. After taking part in several engagements there, he was sent to Palestine, and died gloriously on the Field of Battle at Gaza on April 19th, 1917. He was entitled to the General Service and Victory Medals.
"Honour to the immortal dead who gave their youth that the world might grow old in peace."
14, East Street, Northampton. Z1846/B.

STURGESS, W. J. O., Gunner, R.G.A.
He volunteered in October 1915, and underwent a period of training before proceeding to France in January 1916. Whilst overseas he served with the anti-aircraft guns, and was engaged on this important work in various sectors. Later he was transferred to Italy, and saw severe fighting on the Piave until the cessation of hostilities. Demobilised on returning home in March 1919, he holds the General Service and Victory Medals.
28, Roe Road, Northampton. Z2284.

SULLIVAN, W. (M.M.), Sergeant, 6th Northants. Regiment.
Called up from the Reserve when war broke out, he immediately proceeded to France, and served through the Retreat from Mons. He was also in action at the Battles of the Aisne, Ypres (I.), Neuve Chapelle, Aubers Ridge (where he was wounded in May 1915), Ypres (II.) and Loos, but laid down his life for the freedom of England on the Somme on September 16th, 1916. He had been awarded the Military Medal for conspicuous bravery at Trônes Wood six days before his death, and was also entitled to the Mons Star, and the General Service and Victory Medals.
"He nobly fell that we might live."
46, Francis Street, Northampton. Z1726/A.

SUMMERFIELD, F., Private, 1st Northants. Regt.
Already serving at the declaration of war in August 1914, he was at once ordered to the Western Front with the first Expeditionary Force, and fought in the engagements at Mons. Whilst in action in the Battle of Ypres he was severely wounded, which unhappily resulted in the loss of his eyesight. After hospital treatment in England, he was invalided out of the Army in February 1915, and holds the Mons Star, and the General Service and Victory Medals.
90, Green Street, Northampton. Z3167.

SUMMERFIELD, J., Private, R.A.M.C.
When war was declared in August 1914 he volunteered, and was engaged on important duties at Ipswich for twelve months. Whilst proceeding to Gallipoli on the "Royal Edward" he unhappily lost his life when this ship was torpedoed in the Ægean Sea on August 17th, 1915. He was entitled to the General Service and Victory Medals.
"Thinking that remembrance, though unspoken, may reach him where he sleeps."
Silver Street, Brixworth, Northants. Z3166.

SURRIDGE, C., Private, 7th Northants. Regiment.
Volunteering in April 1915, he was sent to France in July, and played a prominent part in the Battles of the Somme, Arras (where he was wounded in action in April 1917), Ypres and Cambrai. He was demobilised on his return to England in February 1919, and holds the 1914–15 Star, and the General Service and Victory Medals.
53, Francis Street, Northampton. Z1727/A.

SURRIDGE, W. T., Private, 1/4th Suffolk Regt.
He joined in March 1916, and five months later was drafted to the Western Front, where he took part in the heavy fighting in the Somme, Ypres and Cambrai sectors, and was gassed in action at Ypres. Demobilised in February 1919, he holds the General Service and Victory Medals.
53, Francis Street, Northampton. Z1727/B.

SWAIN, C., A.B., Royal Navy.
He joined the Royal Navy in November 1917, and served in H.M.S. "Mona's Isle." He was sent to the North Sea, where he was engaged on mine-laying and other important duties, and rendered valuable services. He remained in this area till March 1919, when he was demobilised, holding the General Service and Victory Medals.
19a, Oxford Street, Far Cotton, Northants. Z3517/B.

SWAIN, E., Private, 15th Lancashire Fusiliers.
Joining in June 1917, he proceeded to the Western Front in the following October, and saw much heavy fighting. He took part in the Battles of Cambrai, the Somme, Amiens, Bapaume and Ypres, and many other engagements during the Retreat and Advance of 1918, and was gassed. He afterwards served with the Army of Occupation in Germany, and was demobilised on his return home in November 1919, holding the General Service and Victory Medals.
191, Adnitt Road, Northampton. Z2285/B.

SWAIN, E. J., Private, Northants. Regiment.
He volunteered in September 1914, and proceeded to France twelve months later, but, after being in action at the Battle of Loos, was taken prisoner in October 1915. Whilst in captivity, he was forced to work on the roads, suffered harsh treatment at the hands of his captors, and had both his legs broken. He was repatriated and demobilised in February 1919, holding the 1914–15 Star, and the General Service and Victory Medals.
191, Adnitt Road, Northampton. Z2285/A.

SWAIN, F. W., Private, 1st Northants. Regiment.
A serving soldier at the outbreak of war, he was at once sent to France, where he took part in the Retreat from Mons and the Battles of the Marne, the Aisne, La Bassée, Ypres and Vimy Ridge, and was wounded. He was killed in action on the Somme on August 16th, 1916, and was entitled to the Mons Star, and the General Service and Victory Medals.
"Whilst we remember, the sacrifice is not in vain."
19a, Oxford Street, Far Cotton, Northants. Z3517/A.

SWALLOW, J. E., Private, 2nd Leinster Regiment.
He joined in May 1916, and in August was drafted to France, after training in Ireland. Whilst on the Western Front, he took part in the Battles of Beaumont-Hamel, Arras, Vimy Ridge, Bullecourt and Messines, but was killed in action at the third Battle of Ypres on July 31st, 1917, having been previously reported missing. He was entitled to the General Service and Victory Medals.
"His name liveth for evermore."
48, Shakespeare Road, Northampton. Z1498/A.

SWANN, A. R., Sergeant, 1/4th Northants. Regt.
At the outbreak of war he was mobilised with the Territorials, and in July 1915 proceeded to Gallipoli. There he saw fierce fighting in the Suvla Bay Landing and other important engagements, but contracted dysentery and was invalided home. He unfortunately died at Nottingham Hospital on December 12th, 1915, and was entitled to the 1914–15 Star, and the General Service and Victory Medals.
"The path of duty was the way to glory."
124, Green Street, Northampton. Z2868/A.

SWANN, A. S., L/Corporal, 2nd Northants. Regt.
A serving soldier at the outbreak of war, he was drafted to France in the following November, and fought at Ypres, Neuve Chapelle and Aubers Ridge, where he was wounded. He was invalided home, but, returning to France, was engaged at Arras and Vimy Ridge. He was unhappily killed in action on the Somme in August 1917, and was entitled to the 1914 Star, and the General Service and Victory Medals.
"And doubtless he went in splendid company."
2, Foxes Yard, Bridge Street, Northants. Z3518/A.

SWANN, H. W., Corporal, 1/4th Northants. Regt.
A Territorial, he was mobilised at the outbreak of hostilities in August 1914, and 11 months later was sent to Egypt. On that front he was in action in many engagements, including the Battle of Rafa, but, on proceeding to Palestine, was unhappily killed in action at Gaza on April 19th, 1917. He was entitled to the 1914–15 Star, and the General Service and Victory Medals.
"His life for his Country, his soul to God."
124, Green Street, Northampton. Z2868/B.

SWANN, W. F., Private, 1st Northants. Regiment.
He was serving at the outbreak of war, and was immediately sent to France, where he took part in the Retreat from Mons and in the fighting at the Marne, the Aisne and La Bassée. He gave his life for the freedom of England at the Battle of Ypres on November 3rd, 1914, and was entitled to the Mons Star, and the General Service and Victory Medals.
"Great deeds cannot die."
2, Foxes Yard, Bridge Street, Northants. Z3518/B.

SWANN, W. J., Gunner, Royal Garrison Artillery.
Volunteering in October 1915, he crossed to France in the following year, and fought in numerous engagements, including the Battles of the Somme and Arras. He also did excellent work as a gunner during the German Offensive and Allied Advance of 1918. After the Armistice he returned to England and was demobilised in January 1919, holding the General Service and Victory Medals.
12, Oakley Street, Northampton. Z1406/A.

SWANNELL, J., Sergeant, 7th Northants. Regt.
When war broke out he was called up from the Reserve and, embarking for France, served in the Retreat from Mons. He also took a prominent part in the Battles of the Marne, Ypres, Loos, the Somme and Arras, and was gassed in May 1915 and wounded at Ypres in July 1917. He was invalided to England, but returned to the Western Front five months later, and was engaged on important duties behind the line until discharged in February 1919. He holds the Mons Star, and the General Service and Victory Medals.
26, Poole Street, Northampton. Z1416/A.

SWAYSLAND, E. G. C., Private, 27th Royal Fusiliers and Machine Gun Corps.
He volunteered in 1915, and, after a period of training, was drafted overseas in the following year. Serving on the Western Front, he fought in the Battles of the Somme, Arras, Vimy Ridge and Ypres, but was gassed in August 1917. He was invalided home in March 1918, and admitted to hospital in Plymouth, eventually being demobilised in February 1919. He holds the General Service and Victory Medals.
66, Glasgow Street, St. James, Northampton. Z2869.

SWAYSLAND, E. J. C., Flight-Sergeant, R.A.F.
He volunteered in October 1915, and, after two years' valuable services at various aerodromes in England, was sent to France. He was there engaged on important duties which called for a high degree of technical skill with the 65th Squadron, and saw heavy fighting in the Ypres, Somme and Dunkirk sectors. Demobilised in October 1919, he holds the General Service and Victory Medals.
49, Beaconsfield Terrace, Northampton. Z1728/B.

SWAYSLAND, W. H. C., Private, M.G.C.
On attaining military age he joined in October 1917, was sent to France four months later, and played a prominent part in many minor engagements in the Ypres sector. After the cessation of hostilities, he proceeded to Germany with the Army of Occupation and served there until his demobilisation in November 1919. He holds the General Service and Victory Medals. 49, Beaconsfield Terrace, Northampton. Z1728/A.

SYMONDS, T. W., Private, 1st Northants. Regt.
He enlisted in May 1914 in the Royal Army Service Corps, but, after a period of service in England, was discharged as medically unfit. In August 1916, however, he joined the 1st Northamptonshire Regiment, and four months later proceeded to the Western Front, where he was chiefly engaged in making roads in various areas. In July 1917 he was sent to Egypt, and was there employed on duties of an important nature until sent to England for demobilisation in July 1919. He holds the General Service and Victory Medals.
5, Brunswick Place, Northampton. Z2019.

SYMONS, W., Pte, 9th Royal Warwickshire Regt.
He enlisted in October 1916, and in the following year was drafted to Mesopotamia, where he took part in many engagements in various sectors of the front, but, contracting malaria, was in hospital for some time. After the Armistice he proceeded to Russia, and served there until his demobilisation in March 1919. He holds the General Service and Victory Medals. 10, St. Edmund's Terrace, Northampton. Z2286.

T

TABANOR, J., Private, 2nd Northants. Regiment.
Joining in September 1917, he was drafted overseas in May of the following year on completion of his training. During his service on the Western Front, he was engaged in fierce fighting at the Battle of the Aisne, but was taken prisoner and held in captivity until the cessation of hostilities. On his release he returned to England, and was demobilised in September 1919, holding the General Service and Victory Medals.
35, Horseshoe Street, Northampton. Z2870.

TALBOT, F. S., Private, 13th York and Lancaster Regiment.
He joined in May 1916, and later in the same year was drafted to the Western Front. In this theatre of war he took part in much heavy fighting on the Somme, at Arras, Vimy Ridge, St. Quentin and Armentières, before being wounded in October 1918. He was demobilised in June 1919, and holds the General Service and Victory Medals.
70, Moore Street, Kingsley Park, Northampton. Z1729.

TALBOT, J. R., Private, 2nd Northants. Regt.
He was called up from the Reserve in August 1914 and immedately drafted to France. There he took part in the Retreat from Mons, the Battles of the Marne, the Aisne, La Bassée, Ypres and the Somme. He was severely wounded in action on March 14th, 1917, and unfortunately died through the effects of his wounds four days later. He was entitled to the Mons Star, and the General Service and Victory Medals.
"He joined the great white company of valiant souls."
30, Essex Street, Northampton. Z1730.

TALLETT, C. F. W., Private, 2nd Northants. Regt.
He volunteered in August 1914, and, completing his training in the following July, was drafted to France, where he took part in the Battle of Loos. He died gloriously on the Field of Battle during the Somme Offensive in July 1916, and was entitled to the 1914–15 Star, and the General Service and Victory Medals.
"Great deeds cannot die:
They with the sun and moon renew their light for ever."
3, Vernon Terrace, Northampton. Z2287/A.

TALLETT, F. G. C., Driver, R.F.A.
He volunteered in October 1915, and, after a period of training, was engaged at various home stations on important duties with his Unit. He was unable to obtain a transfer overseas owing to defective hearing, but rendered valuable services until he was invalided from the Army in August 1916.
3, Vernon Terrace, Northampton. Z2287/B.

TALMAGE, P. A., A.B., Royal Navy.
He joined in June 1917, and, after a period of training at the Crystal Palace and Devonport, was commissioned to H.M.S. "Cedric." In this vessel he served as a signalman, and was engaged on important convoy work between England, America, Canada and France. Demobilised in January 1919, he holds the General Service and Victory Medals.
5, Parkwood Street, Northampton. Z3168.

TANDY, F., Gunner, Royal Garrison Artillery.
He volunteered in October 1915, and in the following year was drafted to France. Whilst on the Western Front, he took part in several engagements, including the Battles of Ypres, Arras and Messines. He was also engaged on important duties, and was demobilised in July 1919, holding the General Service and Victory Medals.
87, Adelaide Street, Northampton. Z1236/A.

TANSER, A. T., Private, R.A.S.C.
He volunteered in August 1914, and, after completing his training, was drafted to France. In this theatre of war he served with the Supply Column in various sectors, and was wounded at Loos in 1915 and invalided home. On his recovery he returned to France, thence to Italy, and did good work with his Unit until his demobilisation in January 1919. He holds the 1914 Star, and the General Service and Victory Medals.
57, Cloutsham Street, Northampton. Z3169.

TAPP, A. J., Private, 1st Northants. Regiment.
He volunteered in August 1914, and, after a period of training, was engaged at various stations on important duties with his Unit. He was not successful in obtaining a transfer overseas, but rendered valuable services until his discharge in February 1916 as medically unfit for further service.
18, Bath Street, Northampton. Z1731/C.

TAPP, E. C., Private, Bedfordshire Regiment.
He joined in 1916, and later in the same year was drafted to France. Whilst overseas he took part in many engagements, including those on the Somme, at Arras, Albert, Ypres and Passchendaele, before being badly wounded in 1918. As a result, he was invalided home and eventually discharged in October 1918, as medically unfit for further service. He holds the General Service and Victory Medals.
16, Bath Street, Northampton. Z1731/B.

TAPP, G. H., Private, King's (Liverpool Regt.)
Mobilised in August 1914, he was quickly drafted to France, where he took part in several engagements, including the Mons Retreat and the Battles of the Marne, the Aisne, Ypres and Neuve Chapelle. He made the Supreme Sacrifice, being killed in action on April 5th, 1915, and was entitled to the Mons Star, and the General Service and Victory Medals.
"He nobly fell that we might live."
16, Bath Street, Northampton. Z1731/A.

TARRY, A., Private, 1st Northants. Regiment.
Called up from the Reserve in August 1914, he was quickly drafted to France, where he took part in the Battle of Ypres and was badly wounded. As a result he was invalided home, but, on his recovery, returned to France and fought at Neuve Chapelle and Aubers Ridge, where in May 1915 he was gassed and again sent home. Later he was placed on the Reserve, but in March 1918 was recalled and again proceeded to France. He was discharged in January 1919, and holds the 1914 Star, and the General Service and Victory Medals.
111, Euston Road, Northampton. Z3170/A.

TARRY, E. A., Corporal, Royal Army Pay Corps.
Volunteering in January 1916, he underwent a period of training, and was then engaged on important duties in the Pay Office at Blackheath. Owing to his being medically unfit, he was unable to obtain a transfer overseas, but rendered valuable services until his demobilisation in March 1920.
47, Adnitt Road, Northampton. Z2107/B.

TARRY, F., Private, Norfolk Regiment.
He volunteered in January 1915, and four months later was drafted to India, where he served on the North-West Frontier. Later he was transferred to Mesopotamia, and took part in much fighting at Kut, Baghdad, and on the River Tigris. He returned home and was demobilised in March 1919, holding the 1914–15 Star, and the General Service and Victory Medals.
Bugbrooke, Northants. Z3010/B.

TARRY, G., A.B., R.N.V.R.
He joined in July 1917, and underwent several months' training at the Crystal Palace prior to his being sent to sea. He served on board H.M.S. "Cornelius" and "Carrol," in the Mediterranean, where these vessels were engaged on important patrol and convoy duties. Demobilised in September 1919, he holds the General Service and Victory Medals.
111, Euston Road, Northampton. Z3170/B.

TASSELL, C. W., Private, 11th Bedfordshire Regt.
He joined in May 1916, and, after his training, was engaged at various stations on important duties with his Unit. He was unable to obtain a transfer overseas owing to his being medically unfit, but rendered valuable services until his demobilisation in March 1919. 66, Oliver Street, Northampton. Z1732.

TATE, H., Private, 5th Northamptonshire Regt.
Volunteering in September 1914, he completed his training, and in May of the following year was sent to the Western Front. After taking part in severe fighting in the Battles of Ypres and Festubert, he was wounded in action at Loos, and unfortunately succumbed to his injuries on October 13th, 1915. He was entitled to the 1914–15 Star, and the General Service and Victory Medals.
"Whilst we remember, the sacrifice is not in vain."
4, Chapel Gardens, Northampton. Z3519

TATE, J. W., Private, 6th Lincolnshire Regiment.
He volunteered in August 1915, and in the following year proceeded to Gallipoli, where, after taking part in the Landing at Cape Helles, he saw much severe fighting, and was twice wounded. Later, transferred to Egypt, he fought also in Palestine, and was sent to France in time to serve through the Retreat and Advance of 1918, being again wounded. He was mentioned in Despatches in November 1918 for distinguished service, and, holding the 1914–15 Star, and the General Service and Victory Medals, was demobilised in February 1919.
27, Stanley Road, Northampton. Z2510.

TAYLER, G. F., Private, M.G.C. (Infantry).
When war broke out he was working on the railway, and volunteering for service overseas, was sent to France in 1917, and was engaged on important duties on the railway at Cherbourg. Subsequently he returned to England, and joined the Machine Gun Corps in October 1918. Whilst serving with this Corps, he did valuable work at various home stations, eventually being demobilised in February 1919.
23, Alton Street, Far Cotton, Northampton. Z3520.

TAYLOR, A. C., Private, 8th Royal Fusiliers.
Volunteering in the Queen's Own (Royal West Kent Regiment) in December 1915, he was ordered in the following October to the Western Front. There he was in action in various important engagements, including the Battle of Arras. He was wounded at Cambrai in November 1917, and invalided to England, subsequently being discharged as medically unfit for further service in August 1918. He holds the General Service and Victory Medals.
39, Warwick Street, Daventry, Northants. Z2873.

TAYLOR, A. C. H., Private, Northants. Regiment.
Having volunteered in November 1915, he was drafted overseas in the following year. Whilst on the Western Front, he took part in several engagements, including those in the Arras, Bullecourt and Somme sectors, and was wounded in March 1918. Later he proceeded to Italy, and served on the Piave River and Asiago Plateaux. He returned home, and was demobilised in March 1919, holding the General Service and Victory Medals. Spratton, Northants. Z3172.

TAYLOR, G. W. P., Private, 4th Northants. Regt.
He volunteered in January 1915, and six months later was drafted to the Dardanelles, where he saw much heavy fighting at Suvla Bay and in the Evacuation of the Gallipoli Peninsula. Later he proceeded to Egypt, thence to Palestine, and took part in the Battles of Gaza (I., II. and III.). He returned home and was demobilised in April 1919, holding the 1914–15 Star, and the General Service and Victory Medals.
Spratton, Northants. Z3171.

TAYLOR, J., Private, 1/4th Northants. Regiment.
Mobilised in August 1914, he proceeded to Gallipoli in July 1915, and fought at Suvla Bay and in subsequent engagements of the campaign. After the Evacuation he was sent to Egypt, and later to Mesopotamia, where he was in action at Sanna-i-yat, Baghdad and on the Tigris, and was wounded. In January 1919 he was ordered to India, serving on the North-West Frontier until sent home to be discharged in January 1920. He holds the 1914–15 Star, and the General Service and Victory Medals, and the India General Service Medal (with Clasp, Afghanistan, N.W. Frontier, 1919).
4, Francis Street, Northampton. Z1733.

TAYLOR, J., Private, Northants. Regiment.
He volunteered in August 1914, and in the following March was drafted to Egypt. In this seat of operations, he took part in engagements at Agayia, Romani and the occupation of Sollum. He then proceeded into Palestine and fought at the Battles of Gaza. He was unfortunately killed in action on November 27th, 1917, and was entitled to the 1914–15 Star, and the General Service and Victory Medals.
"Thinking that remembrance, though unspoken, may reach him where he sleeps."
7, Purser Road, Northampton. Z2288.

TAYLOR, J., Staff-Sergeant, R.A.S.C.
He was called up from the Reserve in August 1914, and in the following year was drafted to the Dardanelles, where he played a prominent part in much fighting at the Landing at Gallipoli. Later he was sent to Egypt, thence to Palestine, but contracted malaria, and was invalided to Alexandria Hospital. He unfortunately died on October 20th, 1919, from the effects of malaria, and was entitled to the 1914–15 Star, and the General Service and Victory Medals.
"His memory is cherished with pride."
13, Spencer Road, Northampton. Z1369/A.

TAYLOR, J., Corporal, York and Lancaster Regt.
He enlisted in December 1917, and underwent a short period of training prior to his being drafted to France. In this theatre of war he took part in many engagements in the Somme and Cambrai sectors. He was gassed during the Advance of 1918, and was eventually demobilised in March 1919, holding the General Service and Victory Medals.
Squirrel Lane, Old Duston, Northants. Z3165/B.

TAYLOR, L., Bombardier, Royal Field Artillery.
Mobilised when war broke out, he proceeded to the Western Front in September 1914, and fought in the Battles of the Marne, the Aisne, Neuve Chapelle, Ypres, Vermelles, the Somme, the Ancre, Beaumont-Hamel, Bullecourt, Lens and Cambrai. He also did good work with his Battery in the Retreat and Advance of 1918, and was eventually discharged in March 1920, holding the 1914 Star, and the General Service and Victory Medals.
34, Parkwood Street, Northampton. Z2872/A.

TAYLOR, W., Private, South Staffordshire Regt.
He volunteered in January 1916, and, crossing to France five months later, did excellent work as a Lewis gunner at the Battles of the Somme, Arras, Ypres, Lens and Cambrai. In March 1918 he was taken prisoner and held in captivity until the following December. On his release, he returned to England and was demobilised in December 1919, holding the General Service and Victory Medals.
34, Parkwood Street, Northampton. Z2872/B.

TAYLOR, W., Driver, Royal Army Service Corps.
A month after volunteering in October 1914, he was drafted to the scene of activities in France. On that front he was engaged on important transport duties, conveying food and ammunition to the troops in the Albert, the Somme, Arras, Messines and Ypres sectors. He also did good work with his Unit during the Retreat and Advance of 1918, and was gassed. Demobilised in April 1919, he holds the 1914–15 Star, and the General Service and Victory Medals.
19, York Place, Northampton. Z2871.

TEAR, A. E., Private, Royal Army Medical Corps.
Having previously served in the South African Campaign, he volunteered in 1915, and in the following year was drafted to France, where he took part in several engagements. Later he was transferred to Salonika, and saw much fighting in the Balkans. He contracted malaria, and was in hospital for some time. Demobilised in July 1919, he holds the Queen's and King's South African Medals, and the General Service and Victory Medals. 34, Lawrence Street, Northampton. Z1734.

TEAR, E., Private, 8th Norfolk Regiment.
He joined in January 1917, and three months later was drafted to France, where he served with the 258th Tunnelling Company. Whilst conveying supplies up to Havrincourt Wood, he was unfortunately killed on July 21st, 1917. He was entitled to the General Service and Victory Medals.
"His life for his Country, his soul to God."
21, Cowper Street, Northampton. Z1735.

TEAR, W., L/Corporal, 11th Middlesex Regiment.
He enlisted in April 1916, and underwent a period of training prior to his being drafted to the Western Front. There he took part in several engagements, including those in the Somme and Arras sectors. He died gloriously on the Field of Battle at Arras on April 10th, 1917, and was entitled to the General Service and Victory Medals.
"A costly sacrifice upon the altar of freedom."
37, Bell Barn Street, Northampton. Z1736.

TEBBUTT, A. F., Corporal, 1st Volunteer Battn., Northamptonshire Regiment.
He joined the Volunteers in October 1916, and, after undergoing a period of training, was engaged on important coastal defence duties in Norfolk. Attached to the Welch Regiment, he served as a full-time soldier and did much excellent work with his Unit until his demobilisation in October 1919.
58, Denmark Road, Northampton. Z2020.

TEBBUTT, H. H., Private, Labour Corps.
He joined in January 1918, and, after a short period of training, was drafted overseas. Whilst on the Western Front he was engaged on important duties in the forward areas during the Retreat and Advance of 1918, and in the Ypres sector. After the Armistice he served in France until his discharge in April 1920 as medically unfit for further service. He holds the General Service and Victory Medals.
14, Alcombe Road, Northampton. Z1737.

TEBBUTT, J., Sapper, Royal Engineers.
He joined the Royal Engineers in October 1917, and was engaged on special duties at Bristol. He was then transferred to the 1st Norfolk Regiment, but, after being stationed in Yorkshire and at Chepstow, was sent back to the Royal Engineers for important work in the shipbuilding yards. He was unsuccessful in obtaining his transfer overseas, but rendered valuable services until demobilised in December 1918.
3, Whitworth Road, Northampton. Z2289.

TEBBUTT, T., Private, 6th Northants. Regiment.
He volunteered in September 1914, and in the following July was drafted to the Western Front, where he took part in the Battles of Ypres and Loos. He was severely wounded in action at the Battle of the Somme and unfortunately died through the effects in July 1916. He was entitled to the 1914–15 Star, and the General Service and Victory Medals.
"He died the noblest death a man may die:
Fighting for God and right and liberty."
4, Kinburn Place, Northampton. Z1077/A.

TEE, G. A., Private, 10th (Prince of Wales' Own Royal) Hussars.
A serving soldier, he was quickly drafted to the Western Front, where he fought in the Retreat from Mons. After taking part also in the Battles of Ypres and Hill 60 and other engagements, he was severely wounded at Ypres in May 1915, and sent to hospital at Birmingham. He was invalided from the Army in September 1915, and holds the Mons Star, and the General Service and Victory Medals.
86, Stanhope Road, Northampton. Z2512.

TEE, W. H., Gunner, Royal Field Artillery.
He volunteered in September 1914, and was retained at Shorncliffe on important duties before being drafted to France. Whilst in this theatre of war he served with the Labour Corps during heavy fighting in various sectors, and was wounded in action. On his recovery he was attached to the Military Police, and was engaged on special work until his demobilisation in February 1919. He holds the General Service and Victory Medals. 18, Margaret Street, Northampton. Z1738.

TEMPLEMAN, C. H., Private, R.A.S.C. (M.T.)
Shortly after volunteering in September 1915, he was drafted to the Western Front, and was engaged in fierce fighting in the Battles of the Somme, Beaumont-Hamel, Vimy Ridge, Ypres and Cambrai. He also did valuable work conveying ammunition and food supplies to the forward areas. After the Armistice, he served at Cologne with the Army of Occupation until demobilised in January 1919, holding the 1914–15 Star, and the General Service and Victory Medals.
52, Vernon Street, Northampton. Z2021.

TENCH, S. A., Sergt., Royal Army Medical Corps.
He volunteered in January 1916, and, completing his training in the following year, was drafted to France. Whilst on the Western Front, he was engaged on special sanitary work, and rendered valuable services in the Ypres and Armentières sectors. Demobilised in September 1919, he holds the General Service and Victory Medals.
83, Perry Street, Northampton. Z2290.

TENNET, T., Private, Royal Army Service Corps.
Volunteering in March 1915, he was drafted overseas with an infantry Unit later in the same year. Whilst on the Western Front, he took part in much heavy fighting in the Ypres sector, and was wounded in action and contracted trench feet. As a result he was invalided home, but, on his recovery, was transferred to the Royal Army Service Corps, with which Corps he served until his demobilisation in February 1919. He holds the 1914–15 Star, and the General Service and Victory Medals.
6, Maple Street, Northampton. Z1279/B.

TERO, A., Private, East Surrey Regiment.
He volunteered in June 1915, and, after a period of training, was retained at various home stations before proceeding to France in January 1918. There he took part in engagements in the Somme and Ypres sectors, and was wounded in action in April. As a result he was invalided home, but, on his recovery, returned to France and served there until his demobilisation in February 1919, holding the General Service and Victory Medals. 99, Scarletwell Street, Northampton. Z1739.

TERO, H. G., Private, 4th Northants. Regiment.
Volunteering in September 1914, he was sent in the following year to Gallipoli, but, after two months' severe fighting, was wounded in August 1915, and invalided to Egypt and thence home. On his recovery, however, he proceeded to France and there took part in many engagements and served also with the Labour Corps. Demobilised in April 1919, he holds the 1914–15 Star, and the General Service and Victory Medals.
20, Nelson Street, Northampton. Z1740.

TEW, A. S., Private, Queen's (R.W. Surrey Regt.)
He enlisted in February 1917, and later in the same year was drafted to the Western Front. Whilst in this theatre of war, he took part in many engagements, including the Battles of Ypres, Passchendaele, Cambrai and the Somme (II.). He was demobilised in November 1919, and holds the General Service and Victory Medals.
12, Collins Street, Northampton. Z2291

TEW, H., Private, 1st Northamptonshire Regt.
He volunteered in August 1914, and in the following year was drafted to France, where he took part in much fighting in the Battle of Neuve Chapelle. He made the Supreme Sacrifice being killed in action at Aubers Ridge on May 9th, 1915, and was entitled to the 1914–15 Star, and the General Service and Victory Medals.
"His life for his Country, his soul to God."
159, Bridge Street, Northampton. Z3173

TEW, J. E., Private, 1st Cambridgeshire Regiment.
Joining in April 1917, he was drafted overseas on completion of his training nine months later. Serving on the Western Front, he was engaged in fierce fighting in the St. Quentin Amiens, Vermelles and Ypres sectors, and took an active part in the final victorious operations of the war. He remained in France until March 1919, when he was demobilised, holding the General Service and Victory Medals.
5, Lutterworth Street, Daventry, Northants. Z2874

THEOBALD, J. W., Private, Northants. Regiment.
A Reservist, he was called up at the outbreak of war, and, proceeding to France, fought in the Retreat from Mons. He served in many other engagements, until wounded in 1916 and invalided to England. On his recovery, he returned to the Western Front, and was in action in various sectors until taken prisoner. On his release from captivity, he returned home and was discharged in February 1919, holding the Mons Star, and the General Service and Victory Medals.
60, Craven Street, Northampton. Z1321/A.

THEOBALD, W. E., C.Q.M.S., 1st Northants. Regt.
He enlisted in 1900, and, when war broke out in August 1914, was at once ordered to France. On that front he was engaged in fierce fighting in the Mons Retreat, and played a conspicuous part in the Battles of the Marne and the Aisne. In 1915 he was sent to England and retained on duties of an important nature until the close of hostilities. He was still serving in 1920, and holds the Queen's and King's South African Medals (with five bars), the Mons Star, and the General Service and Victory Medals. 68, Louise Street, Northampton. Z1741/A.

THOMAS, E., Sapper, Royal Engineers.
He joined in March 1918, and prior to that time was employed in the mines and therefore exempted from military service. Proceeding to Chatham, he was engaged on important duties there, but was unsuccessful in obtaining a transfer overseas. Nevertheless, he did much valuable work until demobilised in December 1918.
3, Burns Street, Northampton. Z1743.

THOMAS, J., Private, Royal Army Medical Corps.
Volunteering in October 1915, he was trained at Eastbourne and a year later was sent to the Western Front. There he rendered valuable services to the wounded in the Somme sector until September 1917, when he was drafted to Italy. He did excellent work on the Piave front until the close of hostilities, when he proceeded to Belgium, serving there until demobilised in March 1919. He holds the General Service and Victory Medals. 58, Compton Street, Northampton. Z1742.

THOMAS, J. E. P., Sergeant, 16th (The Queen's) Lancers and Royal Field Artillery.
At the outbreak of war he was serving in Russia, but was recalled and sent to Ireland for a time before proceeding to the Western Front in May 1916. Whilst in France he took a prominent part in the Battles of the Somme, Arras, Ypres, Passchendaele and Cambrai, and was gassed in January 1918. Invalided to hospital in England, he was eventually discharged in January 1919, and holds the General Service and Victory Medals.
14, Saunders Terrace, Long Buckby, Northants. Z3521.

THOMAS, W., Bombardier, Royal Field Artillery.
He joined in December 1916, and, in September of the following year, embarked for Egypt, where he was engaged on important duties at Alexandria until transferred to Palestine. In that theatre of war he did good work with his Battery in many engagements, including those at Gaza, Jaffa and Jerusalem. He was demobilised on his return to England in July 1919, and holds the General Service and Victory Medals.
5, Pike Lane, Northampton. Z1744/A.

THOMAS, W. E., Signalman, R.N.V.R.
He joined in February 1915, and was sent to Chatham for training, and subsequently to Portsmouth, where he served in H.M.S. "Victory." Owing to the early cessation of hostilities, he was not successful in his efforts to be posted to sea, but, nevertheless, rendered valuable services before being demobilised in March 1919.
5, Pike Lane, Northampton. Z1744/B.

THOMASON, J., Private, 11th Queen's (Royal West Surrey Regiment).
Joining in May 1916, he completed his training, and in the following December crossed to France. On that front he was engaged in severe fighting in the Somme and Ypres sectors, and gave his life for King and Country at Vimy Ridge on September 22nd, 1917. He was entitled to the General Service and Victory Medals.
"He died the noblest death a man may die,
Fighting for God and right and liberty."
63, High Street, Kingsthorpe, Northampton. Z1514/B.

THOMASON, J. W., Private, R.A.M.C.
Volunteering in August 1915, he landed in France in January of the following year. Whilst on the Western Front, he did continuously good work with the 103rd Field Ambulance, and served during heavy fighting in the Arras and Ypres sectors before being severely gassed in March 1918. On his recovery he took part in various important engagements until the conclusion of hostilities. Demobilised in January 1919, he holds the General Sevrice and Victory Medals.
43, Newcombe Road, Northampton. Z2875.

THOMPSON, A., Corporal, 2nd Northants. Regt.
When war broke out in August 1914 he was serving in Egypt, but was shortly afterwards drafted to France. In this seat of operations he did consistently good work, and was in action at the Battles of Ypres, Neuve Chapelle, Loos, the Somme and Arras. He was wounded and gassed in 1917, and, as a result, was invalided home and discharged as medically unfit for further service in August 1917, holding the 1914 Star, and the General Service and Victory Medals.
47, Abbey Street, Northampton. Z2876.

THOMPSON, C. H., Gunner, R.G.A.
He volunteered in December 1915, and five months later embarked for the scene of activities in France. On that front he was actively engaged in the Battles of the Somme, Arras, Vimy Ridge and Messines, and fell fighting at Ypres in September 1917. He was entitled to the General Service and Victory Medals.
"A valiant Soldier, with undaunted heart he breasted life's last hill."
Little Houghton, Northants. Z3522.

THOMPSON, F. (jun.), L/Corporal, K.O.S.B.
Volunteering in November 1915, he underwent a period of training, and in July of the following year embarked for the Western Front, where he took part in various important engagements. He made the supreme sacrifice, being killed in action at the Battle of Arras on May 3rd, 1917, and was entitled to the General Service and Victory Medals.
"He nobly fell that we might live."
24, Stanley Street, Northampton. Z2420/B.

THOMPSON, F., Private, R.A.S.C.
He volunteered in November 1915, and in January of the following year landed in France. Whilst in this theatre of war, he was chiefly engaged in conveying ammunition to various sectors, and served at Boulogne, Calais, Rouen and Abbeville before being invalided home. On his recovery in May 1917, he returned to France, and served in a similar capacity until October 1917, when he was transferred to Ireland. Discharged in January 1918 as medically unfit for further service, he holds the General Service and Victory Medals.
24, Stanley Road, Northampton. Z2420/C.

THOMPSON, J., Rifleman, 15th London Regiment (Civil Service Rifles).
He enlisted in June 1917, and, completing his training in the following March, was drafted to France. Whilst on the Western Front he took part in the Retreat of 1918, being badly wounded in May, and consequently invalided home. He was demobilised in January 1919, and holds the General Service and Victory Medals.
88, Bostock Avenue, Northampton. Z3174.

THOMPSON, J., Private, 7th Northants. Regiment.
He volunteered in October 1914, and in the following January was drafted to France. There he took part in many important engagements, including those in the Ypres, Somme and Arras sectors, and was badly wounded in 1917. As a result he was invalided home and eventually discharged in December 1918 as medically unfit. He holds the 1914–15 Star, and the General Service and Victory Medals.
10, Maycocks Road, Cattle Market Rd., Northampton. Z3175.

THOMPSON, M., Private, Machine Gun Corps.
Having joined in September 1918, he proceeded to Clipstone. Whilst in training there he contracted an illness, and as a result was invalided to hospital. He was later found to be medically unfit for military service, and was therefore discharged in December 1918.
7, West View, Daventry, Northants. Z2877.

THOMPSON, R., Private, 2nd Northants. Regt.
Already serving in the Army, he was mobilised at the declaration of war, and was quickly drafted overseas. Serving on the Western Front, he fought at the Battle of Ypres, where he laid down his life for his King and Country on February 5th, 1915. He was entitled to the 1914–15 Star, and the General Service and Victory Medals.
"Whilst we remember, the sacrifice is not in vain."
24, Stanley Road, Northampton. Z2420/A.

THOMPSON, W., A.B., Royal Naval Division.
Joining in September 1917, he underwent a period of training and in April of the following year was drafted to France. Whilst in this seat of hostilities, he served with the Anson Battalion during the Retreat and Advance of 1918. He was gassed in October 1918, and, as a result, was invalided to hospital and thence to England, where he was demobilised in January 1919, holding the General Service and Victory Medals.
85, Semilong Road, Northampton. Z2513.

THOMPSON, W. F., Corporal, 3rd Northants. Regt.
Having previously served in the South African War, he volunteered in November 1915, but, being medically unfit for service overseas, was stationed at Chatham, where he was engaged as an Instructor in musketry and drill. Later he was transferred to the Royal Engineers, and was chiefly employed in building gun-pits. After performing much valuable work, he was demobilised in February 1919, holding the Queen's and King's South African Medals.
4, Stockley Street, Northampton. Z1967/B.

THOMPSON, W. J., Cpl., 1/7th Warwickshire Regt.
He joined in March 1917, and, six months later, proceeded to France, and fought in the Ypres sector. In November 1917 he was transferred to Italy, and took an active part in engagements on the Piave and Asiago Plateau. After the close of hostilities, he was drafted to Egypt, serving at Alexandria until January 1920, when he was sent to England and demobilised two months later. He holds the General Service and Victory Medals. 6, Priory Terrace, Northampton. Z1745.

THOMSON, C. S., Private, 5th Bedfordshire Regt.
Joining in January 1917, he received his training at Wendover, and in the following May was drafted overseas. During his service on the Western Front, he saw heavy fighting in engagements in the Messines sector, and died gloriously on the Field of Battle at Ypres on October 9th, 1917. He was entitled to the General Service and Victory Medals.
"His life for his Country, his soul to God."
Syers Green Lane, Long Buckby, Northants. Z3523.

THORNEYCROFT, W., Leading Stoker, R.N.
Having already served prior to the outbreak of war, he proceeded to sea in August 1914 on board H.M.S. "Active." He took part in the Battle of Heligoland Bight, and was also present during the engagements off the Belgian coast, serving in the bombardments of Zeebrugge and Ostend. He did continuously good work throughout in the North and Baltic Seas, and in 1921 was still serving, holding the 1914–15 Star, and the General Service and Victory Medals.
49, Ambush Street, St. James, Northampton. Z2514.

THORNLEY, A. H., Rifleman, 8th London Regt.
Volunteering in September 1915, he was drafted six months later to the Western Front. There he was in action in many engagements, including the Battles of Vimy Ridge and the Somme. In November 1916 he was invalided home with trench fever, and on his recovery was transferred to the Royal Engineers, and sent to Egypt in February 1918, rendering very valuable services with the Postal Section until discharged as medically unfit for further military duties in September 1919. He holds the General Service and Victory Medals. 63, Vernon Street, Northampton. Z2022.

THORNTON, E. W. L., Private, Queen's (Royal West Surrey Regiment).
Joining in July 1918, he underwent a period of training, but, owing to the early cessation of hostilities, he was unable to obtain his transfer overseas, and was therefore retained on important duties at various stations until demobilised in February 1919. Re-enlisting in the Royal Field Artillery, he proceeded to Russia, where he served at Murmansk until drafted to India in 1920. Shortly afterwards, he was invalided to hospital and thence to England, where he was discharged in October 1920, holding the General Service and Victory Medals. 23, Sunderland Street, Northampton. Z2515.

THORNTON, H. H., Gunner, Royal Field Artillery.
He joined in October 1916, and in the following year was drafted to the Western Front, where he saw much heavy fighting during several engagements. He was unhappily killed in action at Nieuport on August 5th, 1917, and was entitled to the General Service and Victory Medals.
"Great deeds cannot die:
They with the sun and moon renew their light for ever."
117, Euston Road, Northampton. Z3176.

TIBBS, A., A.B., Royal Naval Division.
Joining in August 1917, he received his training at Blandford and Aldershot, and in August 1918 was drafted overseas. During his service on the Western Front, he was in action in various sectors, and was engaged in fierce fighting in the final decisive engagements of the war. He was demobilised in March 1919, and holds the General Service aud Victory Medals.
28, Park Street, Northampton. Z1785/B.

TILLEY, E. J., Private, 1/4th Northants. Regt.
A Territorial, he was mobilised in August 1914, and in July of the following year proceeded to the Dardanelles, where he took part in the Landing at Suvla Bay. After seeing much heavy fighting, he was severely wounded in November 1915 and, sent home, was admitted to hospital at Leicester. He was invalided from the Army in December 1916, and holds the 1914–15 Star, and the General Service and Victory Medals.
1, Castle Hill, Northampton. Z1746/A.

TILLEY, H. F., Private, 6th Queen's (Royal West Surrey Regiment).
Joining in July 1917, he was drafted overseas later in the same year. During his service on the Western Front, he saw much heavy fighting in the Cambrai sector, but, contracting trench fever, was admitted into Base hospitals at Boulogne and Calais. Evacuated to England, he underwent further treatment at Stoke and Stone in Staffordshire and was eventually discharged in March 1919, holding the General Service and Victory Medals.
144, Adnitt Road, Northampton. Z2292.

TILLEY, W. G., Private, R.A.S.C.
He volunteered in December 1915, and, after completing a term of training, was retained at various stations on duties of great importance. Unable on account of ill-health to obtain his transfer overseas, he, nevertheless, rendered valuable services with his Company until February 1919, when he was demobilised. 42, Hervey Street, Northampton. Z1747.

TILLEY, W. J., Gunner (Fitter), R.G.A.
Joining in August 1916, he proceeded to the Western Front in the following month, and there took part in the Battles of the Somme, Vimy Ridge, Ypres, Passchendaele, Cambrai and the Somme (II.), and other engagements. He fell fighting near Arras on April 26th, 1918, and was buried at Bullecourt. He was entitled to the General Service and Victory Medals.
"The path of duty was the way to glory."
23, St. Mary's Street, Northampton. Z1113/A.

TILLEY, W. J., Private, 1st London Regiment (Royal Fusiliers).
Volunteering in November 1915, he completed his training in the 4th Royal Sussex Regiment, and proceeded to France in May 1917. Shortly afterwards he was transferred to the Royal Fusiliers, and was in action with his Unit at the Battles of Messines and Ypres, before being badly gassed in August 1917. As a result he was invalided to hospital and thence to England, where he underwent a period of treatment at various hospitals. He was eventually discharged in February 1919, and holds the General Service and Victory Medals.
11, Ambush Street, St. James' End, Northants. Z2516.

TILSON, J. E., Air Mechanic, Royal Air Force.
He joined in March 1917, and, after a period of training with the Royal Field Artillery, was transferred to the Royal Air Force, and in November of the same year was drafted to France. There he was engaged on duties of a highly technical nature as a fitter in the aeroplane shops at various stations, and did good work with his Squadron until March 1919, when he was demobilised. He holds the General Service and Victory Medals. 2, Windsor Terrace, Northampton. Z1748.

TIMMS, A., Rifleman, 1st Cameronians (Scottish Rifles).
Already in the Army in August 1914, he was immediately drafted to the Western Front, where he took part in the Battle of Mons and the subsequent Retreat, and in many minor engagements. He died gloriously on the Field of Battle at Ypres on October 22nd, 1914, and was entitled to the Mons Star, and the General Service and Victory Medals.
"His name liveth for evermore."
49, Gladstone Terrace, Northampton. Z1517/C.

TIPLER, W. S., R.Q.M.S., 1/4th Northants. Regt.
Volunteering in April 1915, he was drafted to Gallipoli in the following September, and there saw severe fighting until the Evacuation of the Peninsula. He was then transferred to Egypt and thence to Palestine, where he took a distinguished part in the Battles of Rafa and Gaza, and the capture of Jerusalem. Demobilised on returning home in August 1919, he holds the 1914–15 Star, and the General Service and Victory Medals.
6, Somerset Street, Northampton. Z1749.

TIPPING, A. C., Rifleman, K.R.R.C.
He was already serving at the declaration of war, and was immediately drafted overseas. Whilst on the Western Front, he was in action in the Battle of, and Retreat from, Mons, and also at the Battle of the Aisne. He died gloriously on the Field on September 14th, 1914, and was entitled to the Mons Star, and the General Service and Victory Medals.
"A costly sacrifice upon the altar of freedom."
30, Abbey Street, Northampton. Z2878/A.

TIPPING, G., Private, 2nd Northants. Regiment.
Volunteering at the outbreak of hostilities, he underwent a period of training prior to being drafted to France in the following March. Serving on the Western Front, he fought at the Battles of Neuve Chapelle, Hill 60, and Aubers Ridge, where he fell in action on May 9th, 1915. He was entitled to the 1914–15 Star, and the General Service and Victory Medals.
"Thinking that remembrance, though unspoken, may reach him where he sleeps."
30, Abbey Street, Northampton. Z2878/B.

TIPPING, R. H., Private, R.A.M.C.
He joined in August 1917, and, after undergoing a period of training, served at various stations, where he was engaged on duties of great importance. He was medically unfit for active service, and was consequently unable to obtain his transfer overseas, but, nevertheless, did much useful work with his Company until demobilised in January 1919.
36, Poole Street, Northampton. Z1530/B.

TIPPING, W. J., Driver, R.A.S.C. (M.T.)
Two months after volunteering in May 1915, he proceeded to the Western Front, where he was present at the Battles of Loos, Albert, Vermelles, Vimy Ridge and the Somme, and other engagements until November 1917. He was then transferred to Italy, where he served on the Piave and the Asiago Plateaux until his return home for demobilisation in March 1919. He holds the 1914–15 Star, and the General Service and Victory Medals. 20, Thomas Street, Northampton. Z1750.

TITE, A., Private, 7th Northamptonshire Regt.
Volunteering at the declaration of war, he proceeded to France in February 1915, and in this seat of operations took part in many important engagements in various sectors of the front, and was wounded in 1915. He was unhappily killed in action in 1916, and was entitled to the 1914–15 Star, and the General Service and Victory Medals.
"He died the noblest death a man may die:
Fighting for God and right and liberty."
20, Garrick Road, Northampton. Z2517/B.

TITE, G., Private, Royal Welch Fusiliers.
Joining in 1916, he landed in France later in the same year, and there took part in many important engagements with his Unit in various sectors before being wounded. In March 1918 he was taken prisoner, and held in captivity until the following year. Demobilised on his return home in 1919, he holds the General Service and Victory Medals.
20, Garrick Road, Northampton. Z2517/A.

TITE, W. E., Private, Royal Marine Light Infantry.
Having served for two years prior to the outbreak of war, he proceeded to sea in August 1914, and was in action in the Battle of the Falkland Islands. He did continuously good work throughout the period of hostilities, and took part in many important engagements. Whilst serving at Plymouth he contracted influenza, and unfortunately died from the effects on March 4th, 1919. He was entitled to the 1914–15 Star, and the General Service and Victory Medals.
"His memory is cherished with pride."
20, Garrick Road, Northampton. Z2517/C.

TITMAN, J. T., Private, 6th Bedfordshire Regt.
Having joined in February 1916, he proceeded overseas later in the same year. Whilst in France he took part in many engagements, including those in the Somme sector, and was severely wounded. As a result he was invalided home and eventually discharged in December 1916 as medically unfit for further service. He holds the General Service and Victory Medals. Clay Hill, Newland St., Brixworth, Northants. Z3177.

TOBIN, D. G., Private, 1/4th Northants. Regiment.
Called up from the Reserve in August 1914, he was retained on important duties with his Unit until July 1915. Proceeding to the Dardanelles, he took part in the Landing at Suvla Bay, where he was wounded in November. He was unhappily killed in action during the Evacuation of the Gallipoli Peninsula on December 6th, 1915, and was entitled to the 1914–15 Star, and the General Service and Victory Medals.
"A valiant Soldier, with undaunted heart he breasted life's last hill."
Bank, Hardingstone, Northants. Z2879/A.

TOBIN, F. J., Private, 7th Northants. Regiment.
He volunteered in August 1914, and, on conclusion of his training in the following August, embarked for France. Whilst in this theatre of war, he was engaged on important duties as a cook, and served in many engagements on the Somme, Ypres and Cambrai fronts. He did continuously good work, and in February 1919 was demobilised, holding the 1914–15 Star, and the General Service and Victory Medals.
Bank, Hardingstone, Northants. Z2879/B.

TOBIN, W. H., Private, Welch Regiment.
Joining in May 1916, he proceeded in the following year to France. In this seat of operations he took part in many important engagements, particularly in the Somme, Ypres and Arras sectors. He was also in action during the Retreat and Advance of 1918, and, after the cessation of hostilities, served with the Army of Occupation at Cologne. Returning home for demobilisation in October 1919, he holds the General Service and Victory Medals. Bank, Hardingstone, Northants. Z2879/C.

TOCOCK, J., Driver, R.A.S.C.
Shortly after volunteering in January 1915, he was drafted to the Western Front, where he was engaged on important duties in various sectors. He took an active part in the Battles of Ypres, Loos, the Somme, Arras, Cambrai and the Aisne, and other engagements, and was finally demobilised in April 1919. He holds the 1914–15 Star, and the General Service and Victory Medals. 9, Cartwright Road, Northampton. Z1751.

TOMALIN, A. J., Driver, R.A.S.C.
Volunteering in January 1915, he landed in France seven months later. In this theatre of war he was engaged on important transport duties and served in various sectors of the front. He was present during heavy fighting in the Somme, Arras, Ypres and Cambrai sectors and, after the cessation of hostilities, proceeded with the Army of Occupation to Germany. Demobilised on his return home in May 1919, he holds the 1914–15 Star and the General Service and Victory Medals.
Gayton, Northampton. Z2518.

TOMKINS, J., Private, 1st Northants. Regiment.
Having enlisted in March 1905, he proceeded to France in August 1914, and there took part in the fighting at Mons. After taking part also in the Battles of the Marne, the Aisne, Ypres, Aubers Ridge and Loos, he was severely wounded in action and admitted to hospital in England. He was discharged in April 1920, and holds the Mons Star, and the General Service and Victory Medals.
34, Burleigh Road, Northampton. Z1752.

TOMLINSON, G., Private, 1/4th Northants. Regt.
Called up from the Reserve in August 1914, he was drafted to the Dardanelles, but, after taking part in the Landings at Cape Helles and Suvla Bay, laid down his life for King and Country in October 1915. He was entitled to the 1914–15 Star, and the General Service and Victory Medals.
"A valiant Soldier, with undaunted heart he breasted life's last hill."
49, Market Street, Northampton. Z2134/B.

TOMPKINS, B. M., Gunner, American Artillery.
Joining in May 1917, he was drafted to the Western Front in the following October and there saw severe fighting in various sectors. He took part in the Battle of Ypres and many other important engagements during the Retreat and Advance of 1918, and was finally demobilised in January 1919. He holds the General Service and Victory Medals.
35, Arthur Street, Kingsthorpe Hollow, Northants. Z1753/A.

TOMPKINS, C. H., Sergeant, Royal Field Artillery.
Having enlisted in 1901, he was sent to the Western Front immediately on the outbreak of war, and there fought in the Retreat from Mons, and also took a prominent part in the Battles of the Marne, the Aisne, Ypres and Neuve Chapelle. Mortally wounded at Aubers Ridge, he unhappily died in hospital at Boulogne on May 10th, 1915, and was entitled to the Mons Star, and the General Service and Victory Medals.
"A costly sacrifice upon the altar of freedom."
35, Arthur Street, Kingsthorpe Hollow, Northants. Z1753/B.

TOMPKINS, F. J., Private, Oxford. & Bucks. L.I.
Mobilised from the Reserve at the outbreak of hostilities, he was first engaged on important duties at Chelmsford. Proceeding to the Western Front in February 1915, he was in action at the Battles of Ypres, Festubert and Loos, and in other engagements. Returning to England, he was discharged, time-expired, in March 1916, and holds the 1914–15 Star, and the General Service and Victory Medals.
Church End, Hanslope, Bucks. Z2881.

TOMPKINS, G. H., Cpl., 5th Oxford. &. Bucks. L.I.
He volunteered in August 1914 and in July of the following year proceeded to the Western Front, where he was wounded at Loos and admitted to hospital at Etaples. On rejoining his Unit he was again wounded near Ypres in February 1916, and was invalided home. He returned to France, however, and, mortally wounded at Ypres, died on October 23rd, 1917. He was entitled to the 1914–15 Star, and the General Service and Victory Medals.
"His name liveth for evermore."
70, Hood Street, Northampton. Z1754.

TOMPKINS, V., Private, Royal Scots.
Volunteering in January 1915, he proceeded in the same year to France, where he was in action during heavy fighting at Ypres and Loos. He was afterwards transferred to Salonika, and there took part in many important engagements on the Doiran and Vardar fronts. After the conclusion of hostilities, he was drafted to Russia, where he was engaged on important duties until his return home in August 1919. Demobilised in the same month, he holds the General Service and Victory Medals. 40, Tanner Street, Northampton. Z2880.

TORNBERG, E., Private, 7th Northants. Regiment.
He volunteered in September 1914, and, after a period of training, was ordered to the Western Front twelve months later. Whilst serving in France, he took part in numerous engagements of note, including the Battles of Loos, Arras and Ypres, and was gassed during heavy fighting on the Somme in August 1918. He was demobilised on his return to England in February 1919, and holds the 1914–15 Star, and the General Service and Victory Medals. 10, Raglan Street, Northampton. Z3524.

TOSELAND, A., Private, 3/4th Northants. Regt.
He volunteered in September 1915, and twelve months later proceeded to the Western Front, where he saw much heavy fighting. He took part in the Battle of the Somme and other important engagements, and, severely wounded in October 1916, was invalided home. He was afterwards retained in England with the Royal Defence Corps until discharged in March 1919, and holds the General Service and Victory Medals.
55, Gladstone Terrace, Northampton. TZ1755/B.

TOSELAND, W., Private, Buffs (East Kent Regt.)
He joined in May 1918, and, after completing a term of training, served at various stations, where he was engaged on duties of great importance, afterwards being transferred to the Labour Corps. Unable to obtain his transfer overseas on account of ill-health, he, nevertheless, did good work with his Unit until his demobilisation in June 1919.
55, Gladstone Terrace, Northampton. TZ1755/A.

TOSELAND, W., Private, 3rd Essex Regiment.
He joined in August 1917, and, on completion of his training, was stationed at Felixstowe throughout the period of his service, and fulfilled the various duties assigned to him in a highly capable manner. Unsuccessful in his endeavours to secure a transfer to a theatre of war, he, nevertheless, did much valuable work until demobilised in January 1919.
30, Kerr Street, Northampton. Z2023.

TOWELL, A. J., Gunner, R.G.A.
He volunteered in November 1915, and, after a short period of training, was drafted to Aden, whence he proceeded in October 1916 to Mesopotamia. There he was engaged on important duties at Baghdad and various other places, finally returning home for demobilisation in March 1919. He holds the General Service and Victory Medals.
57, Compton Street, Northampton. Z1756.

TOWELL, J. H., Private, Bedfordshire Regiment.
Mobilised from the Reserve in August 1914, he was afterwards retained on important duties in England until 1916, and then proceeded to the Western Front. There he took part in the Battles of the Somme, Arras and Ypres and other engagements, and, twice wounded, was sent to hospital in Scotland. He was finally discharged in April 1919, holding the General Service and Victory Medals.
36, Althorp Street, Northampton. Z1757.

TOWERS, S. A. W., Sergeant, 1st Northants. Regt.
He enlisted in 1900, and, immediately on the outbreak of war in August 1914, proceeded to France, where he took a prominent part in the Battle of Mons. He also fought in the Battles of La Bassée, Ypres, Neuve Chapelle, Hill 60, Festubert and Loos and minor engagements until wounded at Aubers Ridge and invalided home. He afterwards served as an Instructor, and in 1921 was still with his Unit, holding the Mons Star, and the General Service and Victory Medals.
33, Margaret Street, Northampton. Z1301/B.

TOWNING, F., Gunner, Royal Field Artillery.
He volunteered in August 1914, and in the following January was drafted to France. In this theatre of war he took part in many engagements in the Ypres sector, and was badly wounded. As a result he was invalided home to hospital, and eventually discharged in February 1916 as medically unfit for further service. He holds the 1914–15 Star, and the General Service and Victory Medals.
38, Bruce Street, Northampton. Z3178/D.

TOWNING, H., Private, 3rd Lincolnshire Regt.
Called up from the Reserve in August 1914, he was immediately drafted to the Western Front, where he took part in the Battle of Mons and the subsequent Retreat. He made the supreme sacrifice, being killed in action in September 1914, and was entitled to the Mons Star, and the General Service and Victory Medals.
"A costly sacrifice upon the altar of freedom."
38, Bruce Street, Northampton. Z3178/C.

TOWNING, R., Sapper, Royal Engineers.
He joined in 1916, and, on completion of a period of training, was drafted to the Western Front, where he served with the Inland Water Transport Section. Engaged on important duties, he did much excellent work in various sectors, finally returning home for demobilisation in 1919. He holds the General Service and Victory Medals.
38, Bruce Street, Northampton. Z3178/A.

TOWNING, T. H., Driver, Royal Field Artillery.
A Reservist, he was called to the Colours in August 1914 and quickly proceeded to France, where he fought in the Retreat from Mons. He also took part in the Battles of La Bassée, Ypres, Loos, Vermelles, Ploegsteert Wood, Vimy Ridge, the Somme, Arras, Bullecourt, Messines and Passchendaele and many minor engagements. Discharged in 1918 time-expired, he holds the Mons Star, and the General Service and Victory Medals. 38, Bruce Street, Northampton. Z3178/B.

TOWNSEND, F., Private, 1st Northants. Regt.
Volunteering in September 1914, he proceeded to the Western Front on completion of his training at Weymouth in the following February. He was in action at the Battle of Neuve Chapelle and other important engagements, and gave his life for King and Country at Aubers Ridge on May 9th, 1915. He was entitled to the 1914–15 Star, and the General Service and Victory Medals.
"He nobly died that we might live."
High Street, Long Buckby, Northants. Z3525/B.

TOWNSEND, S., Private, 1st Northants. Regiment.
A month after the outbreak of war in August 1914 he volunteered, and in February of the following year was drafted overseas. During his service on the Western Front, he saw fierce fighting in the Battles of Neuve Chapelle and other notable engagements, but was unhappily killed in action at Aubers Ridge on May 9th, 1915. He was entitled to the 1914–15 Star, and the General Service and Victory Medals.
"He died the noblest death a man may die."
High Street, Long Buckby, Northants. Z3525/A.

TRASLER, W. J., Sapper, Royal Engineers.
He volunteered in August 1918, and in December of the following year was drafted to the Western Front with the Cheshire Regiment. There he saw much heavy fighting, and, after taking part in several engagements, was severely wounded and taken prisoner at Arras in April 1917. He unhappily died in captivity in Germany in June of that year, and was entitled to the General Service and Victory Medals.
"He joined the great white company of valiant souls."
38, Monarch Road, Northampton. Z1758.

TRAVELL, B. M. (Mrs.), Corporal, Q.M.A.A.C.
She joined in May 1917, and after a period of training proceeded to Bristol and later to Wales. There she was engaged on many important duties as a cook and rendered valuable services. She also saw service at Winchester and Wareham, but, owing to ill-health, was discharged in August 1919.
1, Hunter Street, Northampton. Z1759/A.

TRAVELL, F. E., Private, 1/4th Northants. Regt.
Mobilised in August 1914, he was drafted to the Dardanelles in the following year, and there took part in the Landing at Cape Helles, and was wounded. After the Evacuation of the Peninsula, he was transferred to Egypt, and later advanced into Palestine, where he was in action at the Battles of Gaza and the capture of Jerusalem. Invalided home in 1918, he unhappily died from the effects of wounds on May 3rd, 1918, and was entitled to the 1914–15 Star, and the General Service and Victory Medals.
"And doubtless he went in splendid company."
34, Abbey Street, Northampton. Z2883/A.

TRAVELL, P. G., Driver, Tank Corps.
He volunteered in December 1915 in the Royal Air Force, but, during his training, was transferred to the Tank Corps, and later proceeded to France. In this theatre of war he saw much heavy fighting at Cambrai but, contracting trench fever, was invalided home. On his recovery, he served at home on important duties until his demobilisation in September 1919. He holds the General Service and Victory Medals.
1, Hunter Street, Northampton. Z1759/C.

TRAVELL, R. T., Air Mechanic, R.A.F.
He joined in November 1917, and, after a period of training, was engaged at various stations on important duties which demanded a high degree of technical skill. He was not successful in obtaining a transfer overseas, but rendered valuable services until his demobilisation in March 1919.
1, Hunter Street, Northampton. Z1759/B.

TRAVILL, W., Private, 1st Northants. Regiment.
Mobilised in August 1914, he was at once drafted to France and fought at Mons. He also played a prominent part in the Battles of the Marne, the Aisne, Loos and the Somme, and was wounded in action before being taken prisoner on the Dunes in July 1916. After harsh treatment whilst in captivity, he was repatriated and discharged in May 1919, holding the Mons Star, and the General Service and Victory Medals.
78, Great Russell Street, Northampton. Z1877/B—Z1878/B.

TRAVILL, W. T. (M.C.), Regimental Sergeant-Major, 4th Northumberland Fusiliers.
He was already serving at the outbreak of war, and was first engaged on important duties in England. Proceeding to France in July 1915, he was in action in many important engagements, served with distinction at the Battles of the Somme and Arras, and was also in action during the Retreat and Advance of 1918. Awarded the Military Cross for distinguished bravery and devotion to duty in the Field, he was discharged in November 1920, holding also the 1914–15 Star, and the General Service and Victory Medals.
13, St. James' Street, Northampton. Z2884.

TRAVILL, W. T. E., Private, 1/4th Northants. Regiment.
Volunteering in August 1914, he first saw active service in Egypt, but in 1916 was invalided home suffering from fever. On his recovery he was drafted to the Western Front, and took part in much severe fighting. He was reported missing on July 31st, 1917, and is now presumed to have been killed in action on that date. He was entitled to the 1914–15 Star, and the General Service and Victory Medals.
"A costly sacrifice upon the altar of freedom."
78, Great Russell Street, Northampton. Z1877/C—Z1878/C.

TREADGOLD, S. G., Private, 5th Northants. Regt.
Volunteering in March 1915, he embarked five months later for France, where he was engaged on important signalling duties at Headquarters. He also took an active part in the Battles of Vimy Ridge, the Somme, Arras, Ypres and Passchendaele, but was unhappily killed in the vicinity of Cambrai on December 3rd, 1917. He was entitled to the 1914–15 Star, and the General Service and Victory Medals.
"His life for his Country, his soul to God."
26, Shakespeare Road, Northampton. Z2024/B.

TREADGOLD, W. H. C., A/Sergeant, R.F.A.
He joined in April 1916, and later in the same year was drafted to Salonika, where he served for three years. During that time he played a prominent part in numerous engagements, did good work with his Battery on the Doiran and Vardar fronts, and was for six months in hospital at Malta, suffering from malaria. After the Armistice, he signed on for a further period of four years. He holds the General Service and Victory Medals. 26, Shakespeare Road, Northampton. Z2024/A.

TREDWELL, T. W., Signalman, Royal Navy.
He joined in June 1918, and, after a period of training, was engaged at Portsmouth on important duties as a signalman. Owing to his being under age, he did not proceed to sea, but rendered valuable services until his demobilisation in January 1919. 20, Lower Harding Street, Northampton. Z1191/B.

TRESSLER, F. J., Private, 6th Northants. Regt.
He enlisted in March 1916, and later in the same year was drafted to the Western Front. In this theatre of war he took part in several engagements, including the Battles of the Somme, Ypres and Arras, where he was badly gassed. As a result, he was invalided home and eventually discharged in December 1917 as medically unfit for further service. He holds the General Service and Victory Medals.
16, Essex Street, Northampton. Z1760.

TRIPP, H., R.Q.M.S., 1st Northants. Regiment.
Having joined the Army in 1896 and served in India until 1911, he was retained at home when war broke out in August 1914, and did continuously good work throughout hostilities. He was engaged on special duties at various stations in England and Ireland, and was eventually discharged in November 1919, after 23 years' exemplary service.
68, Louise Road, Northampton. Z1741/B.

TRUSLER, H., Private, 1st Northants. Regiment.
He volunteered in August 1914, and early in the following year was drafted to France. There he took part in many engagements, including the Battles of Neuve Chapelle and Loos, where he was badly wounded. As a result he was invalided home and eventually discharged as medically unfit for further service in January 1918. He holds the 1914–15 Star, and the General Service and Victory Medals.
4, Northcote Street, Northampton. Z1147/C.

TRUSLER, W., Private, 6th Northants. Regiment.
Three months after joining in May 1917, he was sent to the Western Front, where he saw severe fighting in various sectors. He took part in the Battles of Ypres, Cambrai and Armentières and other engagements, served also through the Retreat and Advance of 1918, and suffered from trench feet. He was demobilised in February 1919, and holds the General Service and Victory Medals.
65, St. John's Street, Northampton. Z3179.

TUBB, H. D., A.B., Royal Navy.
When war broke out in August 1914 he volunteered, and, during the period of his service, did duty in H.M.S. "Victory," "Superb" and "Termagant." He took an active part in several engagements of note, including the Battle of Jutland, and was also engaged on important patrol work in the North Sea. He was demobilised on his return home in April 1919, and holds the 1914–15 Star, and the General Service and Victory Medals.
9, Fox's Yard, Bridge Street, Northampton. Z3526.

TULL, A. D. E., Sapper, Royal Engineers.
Joining in June 1917, he completed his training in the following March and proceeded overseas. Whilst on the Western Front, he was attached to a Field Survey Company and served at Etaples and other places in various sectors of the front. He did consistently good work, and in May 1919 was demobilised, holding the General Service and Victory Medals.
43, St. James' Street, Northampton. Z2885/A.

TULL, H., Corporal, Royal Army Service Corps.
Volunteering in March 1915, he underwent a period of training and was retained on important duties at various stations, where he did continuously good work breaking in horses. He was unable to obtain his transfer to a theatre of war owing to his being medically unfit, and was therefore discharged in March 1917.
43, St. James' Street, Northampton. Z2885/B.

TULLY, W. B., Gunner, Royal Horse Artillery.
Having previously served in the South African Campaign, he was mobilised in August 1914, and, crossing to France, fought in the Mons Retreat. He was also in action in numerous other engagements, including the Battles of Ypres, and was wounded at Passchendaele. In 1917 he was gassed at Cambrai, and unfortunately succumbed to the effects shortly afterwards. He had already held the Queen's and King's South African Medals, and was entitled to the Mons Star, and the General Service and Victory Medals.
"Great deeds cannot die."
10, Homefield Terrace, Long Buckby, Northants. Z3527.

TURLAND, C., Private, Northamptonshire Regt.
He volunteered in September 1914, and twelve months later proceeded to the Western Front, where he saw much severe fighting. He was unfortunately reported missing, and is now believed to have been killed in action at Loos on September 27th, 1915, less than four weeks after landing in France. He was entitled to the 1914–15 Star, and the General Service and Victory Medals.
"His life for his Country, his soul to God."
Camp Hill, Bugbrooke, Northants. Z3181/A.

TURLAND, E. W., Sapper, Royal Engineers.
He joined in April 1916, and, after a course of training, was drafted in the following September to Egypt. After a period of service there, he was sent to Palestine, in which theatre of war he was engaged in severe fighting in many important battles until the cessation of hostilities. He was demobilised on his return to England in February 1919 and holds the General Service and Victory Medals.
7, Delapre Street, Far Cotton, Northampton. Z3528.

TURLAND, F. H., Pte., 2nd South Wales Borderers.
Joining in January 1917, he completed his training and, two months later, embarked for the scene of activities in France. On that front he was in action chiefly in the Arras sector, and, after a few weeks' active service, was unhappily killed at Monchy on April 23rd, 1917. He was entitled to the General Service and Victory Medals.
"A costly sacrifice upon the altar of freedom."
44, Abbey Road, Far Cotton, Northampton. Z3529.

TURLAND, L. W., Private, Queen's (Royal West Surrey Regiment).
Volunteering in December 1915, he was retained on important duties at home until April 1917, when he crossed to France. On that front he saw heavy fighting at Arras and Kemmel, and was wounded in the Battle of Ypres in 1917. On his recovery he returned to the firing-line, but, gassed at Ypres in May 1918, was invalided to England. He was demobilised in February 1919, holding the General Service and Victory Medals.
14, Edith Street, Northampton. Z2025.

TURLAND, P., Gunner, Royal Field Artillery.
Shortly after volunteering in September 1915, he was drafted to the Western Front, where he saw severe fighting in various sectors. After taking part in the Battles of Loos, the Somme, Arras, Ypres and Cambrai, he was invalided home in 1918 suffering from frost-bite, and was for a considerable period in hospital. He was demobilised in February 1919, holding the 1914–15 Star, and the General Service and Victory Medals.
Camp Hill, Bugbrooke, Northants. Z3181/B.

TURLAND, T., L/Corporal, R.A.S.C.
He volunteered in January 1915, and in July of the following year was sent to Salonika, where he was engaged chiefly in conveying supplies to the forward areas on the Struma, Vardar and Doiran fronts. In December 1918 he was transferred to South Russia for transport duties and, returning home in August 1919, was demobilised in the following month. He holds the General Service and Victory Medals.
Bugbrooke, Northants. Z3180.

TURNBULL, J., Gunner, Royal Garrison Artillery.
After five unsuccessful attempts to enlist, he was finally accepted for military service in December 1915, but, owing to defective eyesight, was unable to obtain a transfer overseas. He was stationed on the East Coast and attached to the Anti-Aircraft Mobile Section, and did valuable work in many air-raids. Unfortunately his health broke down, and he was invalided out of the Army in September 1918.
8, The Drapery, Northampton. Z3530.

TURNER, E. (Miss), Special War Worker.
For four years this lady was engaged on work of National importance at Messrs. Hanwell, Northampton. During that time, she was chiefly employed in making munitions, which responsible work she carried out with great efficiency. She was also engaged in the manufacture of aeroplane parts, and rendered valuable services before being discharged in August 1920. 25, Henley Street, Far Cotton Northampton. Z3531.

TURNER, F., A.B., Royal Naval Division.
He volunteered in May 1915, and two months later proceeded with the Hawke Battalion to the Dardanelles, where he saw much severe fighting until the Evacuation of the Gallipoli Peninsula. He was then drafted to France, and there, after fighting at Arras, was wounded at Gavrelle and was in hospital at Boulogne and Etaples. He later rejoined his Battalion and in February 1919 was demobilised, holding the 1914–15 Star, and the General Service and Victory Medals.
52, St. Leonard's Road, Far Cotton, Northampton Z3183.

TURNER, F. G. (D.C.M.), Sergt., 2nd Northants. Regiment.
Joining in July 1916, he shortly afterwards proceeded to the Western Front, where, after taking a prominent part in many important engagements, he was severely gassed. Sent home, he was promoted to the rank of Sergeant and drafted to India for garrison duties at various stations. He was awarded the Distinguished Conduct Medal for conspicuous bravery in the Field and, holding also the General Service and Victory Medals, was still with his Unit in 1921.
Pitsford, Northants. Z3182.

TURNER, F. J., Private, Royal Fusiliers.
Joining in February 1918, he underwent a period of training prior to being drafted overseas. Serving with his Unit on the Western Front, he was in action at Arras during the final Advance, and made the supreme sacrifice, being killed on August 23rd, 1918. He was entitled to the General Service and Victory Medals.
"He nobly fell that we might live."
Milton, Northampton. Z2520.

TURNER, J., Corporal, 1/4th Northants. Regt.
Volunteering in October 1914, he completed his training and was retained on important duties with his Unit at various stations. Later he was in charge of a Machine Gun Section attached to the 4th Welch Regiment, and, engaged on coastal defence duties, rendered very valuable services until demobilised in February 1919.
26, Thursby Road, Northampton. Z2519.

TURNER, T. W. F., Driver, Royal Engineers.
Volunteering in August 1915, he was drafted overseas after completing his training. Whilst on the Western Front, he took part in several engagements, including the Battles of Ypres, Cambrai and Lens. After hostilities ceased, he proceeded to Germany with the Army of Occupation, and served on the Rhine until his demobilisation in April 1919. He holds the General Service and Victory Medals.
36, Burleigh Road, Northampton. Z1761.

TURNER, V. G., Private, Northants. Regiment.
Joining in May 1918, he was drafted to the Western Front on completing a term of training in the following September, and there saw much heavy fighting. After taking part in the Battles of Le Cateau and minor engagements, he was wounded early in November 1918, and admitted to hospital at Eastleigh. He was demobilised in February 1919, and holds the General Service and Victory Medals. Roade, Northants. Z2083/B.

TURNOCK, H. W., Petty Officer, R.N.B.
Mobilised in August 1914, he was posted to H.M.S. "Carrigan Head," on board which vessel he was engaged on important duties as Sick Berth Petty Officer in many waters. He took part in the Dardanelles campaign, serving also in the Mediterranean Sea and at the Royal Naval Brigade Hospital at Malta. He holds the 1914–15 Star, and the General Service and Victory and Long Service and General Service Medals, and in 1921 was serving at Portsmouth.
76, High Street, Daventry, Northants. Z3184.

TURNOCK, J. S., Private, 4th Northants. Regt.
A Territorial, he was mobilised in August 1914, and in the following year was sent to the Dardanelles, where he saw much heavy fighting. Mortally wounded in action, he unhappily died in hospital on September 4th, 1915, and was buried at Gibraltar. He was entitled to the 1914–15 Star, and the General Service and Victory Medals.
"His life for his Country, his soul to God."
32, Market Street, Northampton. Z2294.

TURVEY, A., Private, 7th Suffolk Regiment.
He volunteered in November 1915, and was retained for a time at home before proceeding to France. In this seat of war he took part in several engagements, including those in the Cambrai and St. Quentin sectors, and was badly wounded in action. As a result he was invalided home and eventually discharged in January 1919. He holds the General Service and Victory Medals.
42, Moore Street, Kingsley, Northampton. Z1762.

TWELFTREE, T. H., Private, Bedfordshire Regt.
Joining in June 1917, he received his training at Felixstowe and was ordered overseas four months later. Serving on the Western Front, he took part in many notable engagements, and was almost continuously in action until the close of hostilities. In 1919 he contracted influenza, and, on his discharge from hospital in England, was retained on home service until demobilised in February 1920. He holds the General Service and Victory Medals. Brayfield, Northants. Z3532.

TWIGG, H., Corporal, 1st Northants. Regiment.
He joined in February 1916, and, proceeding to France three months later, fought in the Battles of Albert, Vimy Ridge, Ypres and Passchendaele. In 1917 he was wounded and gassed and sent to hospital in England, but, on his recovery, returned to the Western Front, where he was in action during the Retreat and Advance of 1918. After the Armistice, he served with the Army of Occupation in Germany until demobilised in April 1919, holding the General Service and Victory Medals. 3, House, 3, Court, Wellington St., Northampton. Z2026.

TWISELTON, A., Sapper, Royal Engineers.
Joining in December 1916, he landed in France a month later. Whilst in this theatre of war, he was engaged on important bridge-building and trench-digging duties, and, present at many engagements, served during heavy fighting in the Somme, Ypres and Cambrai sectors. Demobilised on his return home in November 1919, he holds the General Service and Victory Medals.
The Green, Milton, Northamptonshire. Z2521/B.

TWISELTON, G., Sergeant, R.A.S.C. (M.T.)
Having joined in June 1916, he completed a period of training and was retained on important transport duties at various stations. He did consistently good work and rendered very valuable services until he contracted pneumonia and unhappily died from the effects on March 9th, 1919.
"Thinking that remembrance, though unspoken, may reach him where he sleeps."
Anchor Terrace, Milton, Northampton. Z2521/A.

TWITE, S. T., Lieutenant, 20th Hussars.
Mobilised in August 1914, he at once proceeded to the Western Front and served in the actions at Mons. He also played a conspicuous part in the Battles of the Marne, the Aisne, La Bassée, Ypres, Neuve Chapelle, Hill 60, Festubert, Loos, Vimy Ridge, the Somme, Arras, Messines, Lens, Cambrai and Amiens and many other engagements, and was wounded at Zillebeke in 1917. He was discharged in December 1918, holding the Mons Star, and the General Service and Victory Medals. Manor House, Kilsby. Z3321/A.

TYE, A. C., Wireless Operator, Royal Navy.
He joined on attaining the age of 18 in January 1918, and, on completing his training in the following September was posted to H.M.S. "Snowden." Attached to the Grand Fleet in the North Sea, he was engaged on important mine-sweeping duties in these waters until demobilised in February 1919. He holds the General Service and Victory Medals.
161, Adnitt Road, Northampton. Z2295.

TYRELL, W. H., Private, 6th Northants. Regt.
Volunteering in May 1915, he proceeded to the Western Front in the following December, and there, after fighting at Albert, was wounded at Trônes Wood in July 1916. Invalided home, he returned to France, however, in November, took part in the Battles of Arras, Messines, Ypres and Passchendaele, and was again wounded in March 1918. Again sent to England, he was discharged in October of that year as medically unfit for further service, and holds the 1914–15 Star, and the General Service and Victory Medals.
Hazelbeach Grange, Hazelbeach, Northampton. Z3185.

TYRRELL, E. (Mrs.), Special War Worker.
During the war this lady was engaged at the Northampton Machinery Company, Ltd., on work of National importance. She rendered valuable services and carried out her difficult work in a highly commendable manner for over two years.
48, Lower Harding Street, Northampton. Z1763/B.

TYRRELL, H. E., Engineer, Merchant Service.
He volunteered in 1914, and quickly proceeded to sea. He was engaged on various ships in many waters, chiefly employed in conveying troops, guns and ammunition to different theatres of war, and was torpedoed on three occasions. He did continuously good work, and in 1921 was still serving. He holds the General Service and Mercantile Marine War Medals.
39, Robert Street, Northampton. Z1764.

TYRRELL, J. S., Private, 18th Manchester Regt.
He enlisted in May 1916, and later in the same year was drafted to France, where he took part in much heavy fighting in the Arras and Ypres sectors, and in July 1917 was badly wounded. In consequence he was invalided home and eventually discharged in March 1918 as medically unfit for further service. He holds the General Service and Victory Medals.
48, Lower Harding Street, Northampton. Z1763/A.

TYSOE, F. A. A., Private, 6th Northants. Regt.
At the declaration of war in August 1914 he volunteered, and in the following year crossed to France. In that theatre of war he saw heavy fighting at Fricourt and in many other important engagements, until severely wounded in the Battle of the Somme. In consequence he was invalided out of the Army in August 1916, holding the 1914–15 Star, and the General Service and Victory Medals.
15, Oxford Street, Far Cotton, Northampton. Z3533.

TYSON, H., Private, 1st Northamptonshire Regt.
Volunteering in November 1914, he was retained on important duties in England after his training. Proceeding to the Western Front in January 1916, he took part in engagements at Ypres and Passchendaele, and was wounded before being taken prisoner in July of the same year. After the conclusion of hostilities, he was released from captivity and returned home for demobilisation in March 1919. He holds the General Service and Victory Medals.
46, Stanhope Road, Northampton. Z2522.

U

UNDERWOOD, F., L/Corporal, Royal Engineers.
He volunteered in August 1915, and, on completion of a period of training, proceeded to the Western Front with the 16th Cheshire Regiment, and there took part in important engagements in various sectors. He died gloriously on the Field of Battle in October 1917, and was entitled to the General Service and Victory Medals.
"Whilst we remember, the sacrifice is not in vain."
37, Melville Street, Northampton. Z2296.

UNDERWOOD, G., Wireless Operator, R.N.
He joined in March 1918, and was shortly afterwards commissioned to H.M.S. "Orion," attached to the Grand Fleet in the North Sea. Engaged as a wireless operator, he took part in important operations in these waters, finally being demobilised in January 1919. He holds the General Service and Victory Medals.
11, Purser Road, Northampton. Z2132/A.

UNDERWOOD, J., Corporal, 10th Hussars.
Having enlisted in 1906, he was serving in South Africa when war broke out and quickly proceeded to the Western Front, where he was severely wounded in the second Battle of Ypres. Invalided home, he was afterwards retained in England on important duties until the cessation of hostilities, when he was sent with the Army of Occupation to Germany. Discharged on returning home in April 1919, he holds the Delhi Durbar Medal, the 1914 Star, and the General Service and Victory Medals. 115, Market Street, Northampton. Z2297.

UNDERWOOD, J. W., Pte., 5th Northants. Regt.
He volunteered in September 1914, and underwent a period of training prior to his being drafted to the Western Front. Whilst overseas he took part in several engagements, including the Battles of Ypres, the Somme, St. Quentin, Cambrai, and in the Retreat and Advance of 1918. Demobilised in February 1919, he holds the 1914–15 Star, and the General Service and Victory Medals.
5, Spencer Road, Northampton. Z1391/B.

UNDERWOOD, R., Sergt., Leicestershire Hussars.
Shortly after volunteering in August 1914, he was drafted to France, where he saw severe fighting in various sectors of the front. He played a prominent part in many important engagements in this theatre of war, and finally returned home for demobilisation in April 1919. He holds the 1914 Star, and the General Service and Victory Medals.
11, Purser Road, Northampton. Z2132/B.

V

VALENTINE, E. A., Private, 4th Suffolk Regt.
He volunteered in January 1916, and, after six months' training, was drafted to the Western Front, where he saw much severe fighting. Mortally wounded in action on the Somme, he unhappily died in hospital on August 22nd, 1916, and was buried at Albert. He was entitled to the General Service and Victory Medals.
"A costly sacrifice upon the altar of freedom."
29, Spencer Street, Northampton. Z3186/B.

VALENTINE, F., Private, 3rd Northants. Regt.
Volunteering in August 1914, he was sent to the Western Front in January of the following year, and there saw severe fighting in various sectors. He took part in the Battles of Neuve Chapelle, St. Eloi, Hill 60, Ypres, Festubert and Loos, and other engagements, and was three times wounded in action. Demobilised in January 1919, he holds the 1914–15 Star, and the General Service and Victory Medals.
29, Spencer Street, Northampton. Z3186/A.

VALENTINE, G. H., L/Cpl., West Yorks. Regt.
He joined in August 1916, and, after a short period of training, was drafted to the Western Front, where he took part in the Battles of the Ancre, Arras and Vimy Ridge, and minor engagements. He was unfortunately reported missing, and is now believed to have been killed in action on May 3rd, 1917. He was entitled to the General Service and Victory Medals.
"His life for his Country, his soul to God."
29, Spencer Street, Northampton. Z3186/C.

VALENTINE, G. H., Driver, R.A.S.C. (M.T.)
He volunteered in September 1914, and, proceeding to France shortly afterwards, did valuable work conveying food and ammunition to the forward areas. After seeing much service in the Battles of Neuve Chapelle, Hill 60, Ypres and Loos, he was transferred in March 1917 to East Africa. There he was engaged on important duties with his Unit until sent home for demobilisation in March 1919. He holds the 1914 Star, and the General Service and Victory Medals.
Little Houghton, Northants. Z3534/B.

VALENTINE, R. E., L/Cpl., Royal Welch Fusiliers.
Volunteering in October 1915, he was drafted to the Western Front in the following year, and saw heavy fighting in various sectors. He was in action at the Battles of Ploegsteert Wood, Vimy Ridge, Bullecourt, Passchendaele and Cambrai, and in many other engagements until the termination of the war. Serving in France until demobilised in January 1919, he holds the General Service and Victory Medals.
Little Houghton, Northants. Z3534/A.

VARNSVERRY, W. J., Private, 1st Cambridgeshire Regiment.
Volunteering in October 1915, he was retained at home for a time and engaged on important duties. In 1917 he proceeded to France, where he took part in much heavy fighting in the Ypres sector, but, contracting trench feet, was invalided home. As a result he had eight toes amputated, and was eventually invalided out of the Service in June 1918. He holds the General Service and Victory Medals.
30, Stanley Street, Northampton. Z1237/A.

VAUGHAN, G. L., Private, R.A.M.C.
Volunteering in October 1915, he was engaged on important duties with his Unit before being drafted to Mesopotamia in January 1917. Whilst in this seat of operations, he was stationed at the 31st British Stationary Hospital at Baghdad, where he rendered very valuable services as a Hospital Orderly. He returned home for demobilisation in October 1919, and holds the General Service and Victory Medals.
5, Queen's Street, Northampton. Z2886.

VERNON, J., Private, 25th Machine Gun Corps.
Joining in March 1916, he proceeded overseas later in the same year. During his service on the Western Front, he took part in several engagements, including those in the Ypres, Somme, Fleurs and Le Cateau sectors, and was gassed and wounded in action. He was demobilised in January 1919, and holds the General Service and Victory Medals.
37, Fort Street, Northampton. Z1765/A.

VERNON, J., Private, 17th Royal Fusiliers.
He joined in February 1917, and served in Colchester until January 1918, when he was sent to France. Medically unfit for service in the front-line, he was stationed at Calais and engaged on various duties of an important nature, doing good work until he returned home and was demobilised in March 1919, holding the General Service and Victory Medals.
37, Fort Street, Northampton. Z1765/B.

VERNON, L. B., Gunner, R.H.A.
Already serving at the outbreak of war, he immediately proceeded to France, where he did consistently good work throughout the period of hostilities. He was in action with his Battery at the Battles of the Marne, the Aisne, La Bassée, Neuve Chapelle, Ypres, Loos, Vimy Ridge, Arras and Cambrai, and many minor engagements. Discharged in November 1919, having completed 21 years' service, he holds the 1914 Star, and the General Service and Victory Medals.
Sutton Street, Flore, Northants. Z2887.

VERRALL, M. A. (Miss), Nurse, V.A.D.
This lady joined the V.A.D. when war was declared in August 1914, and, throughout the period of hostilities, was engaged in nursing the wounded at various important hospitals in England. She carried out her arduous duties with untiring energy and skill, and rendered very valuable services during air-raids. She was demobilised in November 1918.
4, Victoria Street, Northampton. Z2027.

VERRECCHIA, D., Gunner, R.F.A.
He volunteered in September 1914, and early in the following year proceeded to France, where he was in action with his Battery in many important engagements, including the Battles of Ypres and the Somme, and was gassed. In November 1917 he was transferred to Italy and saw further service on the Piave front. Returning home after the Armistice, he was demobilised in March 1920, and holds the 1914–15 Star, and the General Service and Victory Medals.
25, Cooper Street, Northampton. Z1766/A.

VERRECCHIA, M., Pte., R. Warwickshire Regt.
Volunteering in January 1915, he was stationed during his training at Bedford, after which he was employed on various duties until early in 1917, when he embarked for Egypt. Whilst on the voyage to the East, he was unfortunately drowned when the vessel he was in was torpedoed and sunk in April 1917. He was entitled to the General Service and Victory Medals.
"His memory is cherished with pride."
25, Cooper Street, Northampton. Z1766/B.

VOKE, J., Rifleman, 12th Rifle Brigade.
Shortly after volunteering in November 1914, he proceeded to France, where he saw severe fighting in various sectors of the front. He took part in the Battles of Ypres, Amiens and Bapaume, and many other engagements in this theatre of war, and also served for a time as a batman. Demobilised in January 1919, he holds the 1914–15 Star, and the General Service and Victory Medals.
School Road, Spratton, Northants. Z2936/B.

VORLEY, B., Private, R.A.M.C.
He volunteered in October 1915, and in November of the following year was sent to the Western Front, where he was engaged on important duties in various sectors. He was also present at the Battles of Arras, Vimy Ridge and Passchendaele, and was gassed at Amiens in August 1918. Demobilised in March 1919, he holds the General Service and Victory Medals. 58, Holly Road, Northampton. Z2298.

VOSS, O., Pte., Queen's (Royal West Surrey Regt.)
He joined in July 1918, but was not successful in obtaining a transfer to a theatre of war before the termination of hostilities. In April 1919 he was sent to Germany, and served with the Army of Occupation in Cologne, being engaged on postal duties until April 1920, when he returned home and was demobilised.
6, Hopes Place, Kingsthorpe, Northampton. Z1767.

W

WADDELOW, F. T., Electrician, Royal Navy.
He joined in July 1916, and was posted to H.M.S. "Renown," subsequently serving in various other ships, including H.M.S. "Dublin," "Caledon," "Galatea" and "New Zealand." He took an active part in the fighting at Heligoland in November 1917, and was engaged on important duties in the North Sea with the Grand Fleet. He was serving at Scapa Flow during the surrender of the German Fleet, and was demobilised in March 1919, holding the General Service and Victory Medals.
55, Abbey Road, Far Cotton, Northampton. Z3535.

WADE, G., Sergeant, Machine Gun Corps.
Volunteering in the Hampshire Regiment in August 1915, he was later transferred to the Machine Gun Corps and embarked for India. There he did continuously good work, and served with his Unit in many important engagements on the Afghanistan Frontier. He returned home for demobilisation in December 1920, and holds the General Service, Victory and India General Service Medal (with Clasp, Afghanistan, N.W. Frontier, 1919).
26, Marlborough Road, Northampton. Z2461/A.

WADSWORTH, R., Sapper, Royal Engineers.
Volunteering in August 1915, he proceeded to the Western Front in the following month, and there served in various sectors. After taking part in the Battle of the Somme and engagements near Ypres, he was severely gassed and was invalided home, suffering also from shell-shock. He was discharged in January 1917 as medically unfit for further service, and holds the 1914-15 Star, and the General Service and Victory Medals. Squirrel Lane, Old Duston, Northants. Z2967/B.

WAITE, E. G., Private, 1st Suffolk Regiment.
Joining in March 1918, he was engaged with his Unit at many different stations on the East Coast. He rendered valuable services, but was not successful in obtaining his transfer overseas before the cessation of hostilities. Having contracted severe bronchitis during his service at Lowestoft, he was discharged on that account in March 1919.
10, Dover Street, Northampton. Z1592/B.

WALDEN, E. A., Private, Tank Corps.
Having joined in December 1916, he underwent a period of training and was retained on important duties at Lincoln and other stations. He was unsuccessful in obtaining his transfer overseas, but, nevertheless, rendered very valuable services until demobilised in October 1919.
18, Spencer Bridge Road, Northampton. Z2523.

WALDEN, H., Corporal, Northants. Dragoons.
He volunteered in December 1914, and, after his training, was retained on important duties in England until 1917, and was then drafted to France with the Military Mounted Police. He was transferred later to Italy, and proceeded thence to Salonika, finally returning home for demobilisation in June 1919. He holds the General Service and Victory Medals.
Pitsford, Northants. Z2937/A.

WALDEN, W., Sapper, Royal Engineers.
Joining in August 1917, he embarked for France in the following month. In this theatre of war he served with the Railway Operative Department during many important engagements in various sectors of the front, where he was chiefly engaged in repairing the railway lines. Demobilised in February 1919, he holds the General Service and Victory Medals.
42, Parkwood Street, Northampton. Z2524.

WALDING, A., Gunner, Royal Field Artillery.
He volunteered in August 1915, and in the following January embarked for Mesopotamia. In this theatre of war he played a prominent part with his Battery in strenuous fighting at Kut-el-Amara and on the Tigris front, and also participated in the capture of Baghdad. He was demobilised on his return to England in June 1919, and holds the General Service and Victory Medals.
12, Cartwright Road, Northampton. Z1770.

WALDING, A. E., Pte., 53rd Royal Sussex Regt.
Joining in October 1917, he was employed on important duties in home stations until December 1918, when he proceeded to Germany. There he served with the Army of Occupation on the Rhine, doing good work in various ways. He was eventually discharged on account of service in October 1919.
17, Bullhead Lane, Northampton. Z1768.

WALDING, H., Private, Labour Corps.
He joined the Queen's (Royal West Surrey Regiment) in March 1917, and shortly afterwards was drafted to France, where he was transferred to the Labour Corps. During his service overseas, he was employed on important duties on the Ypres, Armentières, Albert and Somme fronts, and in May 1918 was invalided home on account of ill-health. After a course of hospital treatment at Redhill, Leicester and Northampton, he was ultimately discharged in June 1918, holding the General Service and Victory Medals.
31, Arthur Street, Kingsthorpe Hollow, Northampton. Z1769.

WALDING, P., Private, Machine Gun Corps.
After volunteering in August 1915, he underwent a period of training prior to being drafted to the Western Front. There he saw severe fighting in various sectors, took part in the Battles of the Somme and Ypres, and other engagements, and also served through the Retreat and Advance of 1918. Demobilised in February 1919, he holds the General Service and Victory Medals.
6, Cedar Road, Northampton. Z2299/B.

WALDING, W., Private, R.A.M.C.
Shortly after volunteering in November 1915, he was sent to the Western Front, where he was present at the Battle of Ypres and other engagements before being invalided home in 1917 suffering from trench fever. Returning to France in 1918, he served on the Somme and at Havrincourt, and afterwards proceeded with the Army of Occupation to Cologne. He was demobilised in June 1919, and holds the General Service and Victory Medals.
6, Cedar Road, Northampton. Z2299/A.

WALKER, A., Private, Suffolk Regiment.
He joined in June 1916, and, on completing his training later in the same year, proceeded to the Western Front, where he took part in the Battles of the Somme, Ypres and Cambrai and many other engagements. He was invalided home in 1918 suffering from trench fever and dysentery, and was finally demobilised in February 1919, holding the General Service and Victory Medals.
Roade, Northants. Z2301/B.

WALKER, A., Pte., 5th R. Inniskilling Fusiliers.
He joined in October 1916, and shortly afterwards was sent to Salonika, where he took part in numerous engagements before being transferred to Egypt. After two years' service there, during which time he saw fierce fighting, he was drafted to the Western Front, remaining there until sent to England for demobilisation in October 1919. He holds the General Service and Victory Medals.
52, New Town Road, Northampton. Z2028.

WALKER, A., Sapper, Royal Engineers.
Volunteering in October 1915, he completed his training, and in the following April was drafted to France, where he was engaged on important wiring and mining duties in various sectors of the front. He was present during the Retreat and Advance of 1918, and, after the conclusion of hostilities, served with the Army of Occupation in Germany. Demobilised in March 1919, he holds the General Service and Victory Medals. 18, Garrick Road, Northampton. Z2525.

WALKER, F., L/Corporal, Royal Engineers.
He joined in July 1917, and, after undergoing a period of training, was retained at various stations, where he was engaged on important defence duties on the searchlights. He was not successful in obtaining his transfer overseas, but, nevertheless rendered valuable services with his Company until demobilised in November 1919.
Roade, Northants. Z2301/A.

WALKER, F. W., Private, 1/4th Northants. Regt.
He volunteered in October 1914, and in the following year was drafted to the Dardanelles, where, after taking part in the Landing at Cape Helles, he saw severe fighting until the Evacuation. He was then transferred to Egypt, where he was again in action until sent home and discharged in 1918 for work of National importance. He holds the 1914-15 Star, and the General Service and Victory Medals.
South View, Brixworth, Northants. Z3187.

WALKER, H. E., Rifleman, K.R.R.C.
He joined in August 1918, but, owing to the early cessation of hostilities, was unable to secure a transfer overseas before the Armistice. Subsequently he was drafted to Germany with the Army of Occupation, and was engaged on duties of an important nature at Cologne and various other stations until sent home for demobilisation in February 1920.
4, St. Katherine's Street, Northampton. Z3536.

WALKER, J., Sapper, Royal Engineers.
He joined in July 1918, and, after a short period of training, was retained on important duties at various stations. Owing to the early cessation of hostilities, he was unable to obtain his transfer to a theatre of war, but in January 1919 proceeded with the Army of Occupation to Germany. There he was stationed at Cologne until his return home for demobilisation in April 1920.
72, Gladstone Terrace, Northampton. Z1771/B.

WALKER, R. L., 1st Air Mechanic, R.A.F.
He joined in February 1916, and, after conpleting a term of training, served at various stations, where he was engaged on duties of a highly technical nature. Being medically unfit for active service, he was unable to obtain his transfer overseas, but, nevertheless, did useful work with his Squadron until demobilised in February 1919.
Roade, Northants. Z2301/C.

WALKER, S. T., Private, 7th Northants. Regt.
At the outbreak of war he volunteered, and in June 1915 was drafted to the Western Front, where he saw heavy fighting in various sectors. Whilst in action at the Battle of Loos, he was severely wounded and invalided home, consequently being discharged as medically unfit for further military service in September 1915. He holds the 1914-15 Star, and the General Service and Victory Medals.
53, Allen Road, Northampton. Z2300.

WALKER, W., Sergeant, 2nd Northants. Regt.
Mobilised in August 1914, he was drafted to the Western Front in March of the following year, and saw much severe fighting. After only six days' active service, he died gloriously on the Field of Battle at Neuve Chapelle on March 11th, 1915. He was entitled to the 1914-15 Star, and the General Service and Victory Medals.
"Thinking that remembrance, though unspoken, may reach him where he sleeps."
72, Gladstone Terrace, Northampton. Z1771/A.

WALKER, W. (M.M.), Corporal, M.G.C.
He volunteered in October 1915, and in February of the following year proceeded to the Western Front, where he took a prominent part in the Battles of Albert, the Somme, Arras, Ypres and Cambrai and other engagements. He was unhappily reported wounded and missing, and later, killed in action on March 28th, 1918. He had been awarded the Military Medal for conspicuous bravery in the Field at Arras, and was entitled also to the General Service and Victory Medals.
"His memory is cherished with pride."
191, Knox Road, Wellingboro', Northants. Z1772.

WALLINGTON, J., Gunner, R.G.A.
Joining in May 1917, he was ordered overseas later in the same year on the conclusion of his training. During his service on the Western Front, he fought in the Battles of Ypres, Cambrai and the Somme, and did valuable work with his Battery in operations during the Retreat and Advance of 1918. He was demobilised in March 1919, and holds the General Service and Victory Medals.
Barley Mow, Kislingbury, Northants. Z3537.

WALLIS, F., Gunner, Royal Garrison Artillery.
Volunteering in October 1915, he proceeded to France in the following June, and, after taking part in heavy fighting at Ypres, was wounded in February 1917. On his return to the firing-line, he was in action at Cambrai and in the Retreat of 1918, but was gassed at Arras and invalided home. In November 1918 he returned to the Western Front and was engaged on important duties at St. Pol until demobilised in June 1919, holding the General Service and Victory Medals.
51, Melbourne Street, Northampton. Z2302/B.

WALLIS, H., Private, Essex Regiment.
Having previously served in the South African campaign, he volunteered in April 1915 at the age of 50 years, and was four months later drafted to Egypt and thence to Palestine. Whilst in this seat of operations he served under General Allenby at Jerusalem and other stations, where he was engaged on important garrison duties. He did consistently good work and rendered very valuable services until demobilised in March 1919, holding the Queen's and King's South African Medals, the 1914–15 Star, and the General Service and Victory Medals.
73, Stanley Road, Northampton. Z2526.

WALLIS, W., Private, 23rd Royal Fusiliers.
He joined immediately on attaining military age in April 1918, and, proceeding to France in the following October, took part in the final engagements of the Advance. After hostilities ceased, he did excellent work with the Army of Occupation at Cologne, and was eventually demobilised in April 1920, holding the General Service and Victory Medals.
51, Melbourne Street, Northampton. Z2302/A.

WALMSLEY, H. J., Private, 1st Northants. Regt.
He volunteered in September 1914, and in March of the following year was drafted to the Western Front, where he saw severe fighting in various sectors, taking part in the Battles of Ypres and the Somme, and other engagements. He unfortunately died of fever in hospital at Le Havre on August 21st, 1917, and was entitled to the 1914–15 Star, and the General Service and Victory Medals.
"He joined the great white company of valiant souls"
6, Castle Terrace, Northampton. Z1221/B.

WALPOLE, J., Private, R.A.S.C.
When war was declared he volunteered, and, after a period of training, was drafted overseas in June 1916. Whilst on the Western Front, he did valuable work conveying ammunition and food supplies to the troops in the Somme, Arras, Bullecourt, Ypres and Bapaume sectors, and also served with his Unit during the Retreat and Advance of 1918. He was demobilised in April 1919, and holds the General Service and Victory Medals.
24, Stimpsons Avenue, Northampton. Z2303.

WALTER, C., Corporal, 1/4th Northants. Regt.
Re-enlisting in July 1915, he was drafted to Gallipoli two months later, but, after the Evacuation of the Peninsula, was transferred to Egypt. Advancing thence into Palestine, he there took part in the Battles of Gaza and other engagements, and, mortally wounded in action, unhappily died in hospital on November 1st, 1917. He had held the Queen's and King's South African Medals, and was also entitled to the 1914–15 Star, and the General Service and Victory Medals.
"The path of duty was the way to glory."
7, Maycocks Row, Northampton. Z3188

WALTERS, W. H., Sapper, Royal Engineers.
He volunteered in the 2nd Monmouthshire Regiment in August 1914, and three months later embarked for the Western Front, where he saw heavy fighting in various sectors. Transferred to the Royal Engineers in August 1916, he took an active part in the Battles of Cambrai, the Somme and Havrincourt, and in the operations during the Retreat and Advance of 1918. Whilst in France he suffered from trench fever, and was demobilised in March 1919, holding the 1914 Star, and the General Service and Victory Medals.
28, Roe Road, Northampton. Z2304.

WALTON, R., Driver, Royal Engineers.
After volunteering in August 1915, he underwent a period of training prior to being drafted to France in October 1917, and proceeded thence to Italy in the following month. There he saw much active service on the Asiago Plateaux, the Piave and Trentino, engaged chiefly on the transport of supplies. Returning home in March 1919, he was demobilised in April, holding the General Service and Victory Medals.
36, Arthur St., Kingsthorpe Hollow, Northampton. Z1773/A.

WALTON, W., Driver, Royal Engineers.
Two months after volunteering in August 1915, he proceeded to the Western Front, where he was engaged on transport duties in various sectors until November 1917. He was then transferred to Italy, where he served on the Piave, the Asiago Plateaux and the Trentino until his return home in March 1919 for demobilisation in the following month. He holds the 1914–15 Star, and the General Service and Victory Medals.
43, Alma Street, St. James' End, Northampton. Z1773/B.

WALTON, W., Driver, Royal Engineers.
Volunteering in 1915, he was drafted later in the same year to France, and whilst in this seat of operations took part in much heavy fighting in various sectors. He was later transferred to Italy, where he did continuously good work during the engagements on the Piave front. Demobilised in 1919, he holds the 1914–15 Star, and the General Service and Victory Medals. 43, Alma Street, Northampton. Z2889.

WAPLES, O. C., Corporal, 7th Northants. Regt.
Volunteering in September 1914, he embarked for France a year later and, after serving in engagements at Loos and Guillemont, was wounded and invalided home. On returning to the Western Front, he was again wounded at Passchendaele and sent to hospital in London. In 1918 he was drafted back to France and fought in the Retreat and Advance of that year. Demobilised in March 1919, he holds the 1914–15 Star, and the General Service and Victory Medals.
2?, Freehold Street, Northampton. Z1983/A.

WARD, A. T., Private, Suffolk Regiment.
He joined in October 1916, and in the following year proceeded to Egypt, whence he advanced into Palestine. There he saw much severe fighting until wounded in the third Battle of Gaza in November 1917, and admitted to hospital in Egypt. Returning to England in February 1919, he was drafted to India in December of that year for garrison duties, and was finally sent home in February 1921. He holds the General Service and Victory Medals. 13, Craven St., Northampton. Z1775/A.

WARD, B., Corporal, Royal Engineers.
A Reservist, he was called to the Colours in August 1914, but was retained at various stations on duties of a highly important nature. Owing to ill-health, he was unable to obtain his transfer to the front, but, nevertheless, rendered valuable services until invalided from the Army in November 1915. He holds the India General Service Medal (with Clasp, Tirah), and the Queen's and King's South African Medals with seven Bars for previous campaigns.
55, Duke Street, Northampton. Z1776/B.

WARD, B. H., Private, Royal Fusiliers.
He joined in January 1918, immediately on attaining military age, and in the following July was drafted to the Western Front. After much heavy fighting, he was severely wounded on the Somme in the following month, and, admitted to hospital at Manchester, was afterwards retained in England with the Royal Army Medical Corps. He was demobilised in October 1919, and holds the General Service and Victory Medals.
55, Duke Street, Northampton. Z1776/A.

WARD, C., L/Corporal, 6th Northants. Regiment.
Mobilised in August 1914, he was immediately drafted to the Western Front, where he fought in the Retreat from Mons. After taking part also in the Battles of the Marne and the Aisne and minor engagements, he was severely wounded at Ypres in November 1914 and sent home. He was finally invalided from the Army in July 1917, and holds the Mons Star, and the General Service and Victory Medals.
33, Alliston Gardens, Northampton. Z1782.

WARD, C., Private, 4th Northants. Regiment.
Called up from the Reserve in August 1914, he proceeded to Gallipoli in August of the following year, and there, after taking part in the Landing at Suvla Bay, saw much severe fighting. Transferred later to Palestine, he served through the three Battles of Gaza and other engagements, and also fought in General Allenby's Offensive of September 1918. Discharged on returning home in August 1919, he holds the 1914–15 Star, and the General Service and Victory Medals.
42, Leicester Street, Northampton. Z1774.

WARD, G., Private, 2nd Northants. Regiment.
Volunteering in August 1914, he was sent to the Western Front in April of the following year, and there saw much severe fighting in the Ypres sector. He made the Supreme Sacrifice, falling in action at Aubers Ridge on May 9th, 1915, after only a few weeks' overseas service. He was entitled to the 1914–15 Star, and the General Service and Victory Medals.
"His life for his Country, his soul to God."
19a, Crispin Street, Northampton. Z1780/A.

WARD, G. E., Gunner, Royal Horse Artillery.
Volunteering in August 1915, he was ordered to France 10 months later, and fought in the Battles of Arras, Ypres and Lens, and many other engagements of note. He also did valuable work during the German Offensive and Allied Advance of 1918, until invalided home with blood poisoning in October of that year. On his discharge from hospital, he was demobilised in January 1919, and holds the General Service and Victory Medals.
161, Wycliffe Road, Northampton. Z2305.

WARD, G. O., Sergeant, 12th (Prince of Wales' Royal) Lancers.
A Reservist, he was in South Africa when war broke out, but returned to England and was drafted to the Western Front in March 1915. Whilst overseas he took a prominent part in numerous notable engagements until 1917, when he was sent to Rouen. There he was engaged on important duties at a prisoners of war camp until discharged in February 1919, holding the 1914–15 Star, and the General Service and Victory Medals.
Knutsford Terrace, Long Buckby, Northants. Z3539/B.

WARD, H., Private, 2/5th Manchester Regiment.
Two Months after joining in March 1917, he was sent to the Western Front, where he saw severe fighting in various sectors. After taking part in the Battle of Ypres and minor engagements, he was taken prisoner at St. Quentin and held in captivity until 1919. He was demobilised in March of that year, and holds the General Service and Victory Medals.
33, Brunswick Street, Northampton. Z1778.

WARD, H. W., Private, 7th Northants. Regiment.
Volunteering in August 1914, he was drafted to the Western Front 12 months later, and there saw much severe fighting. He made the Supreme Sacrifice, falling in action at Loos on September 27th, 1915, after only three days in the trenches. He was entitled to the 1914–15 Star, and the General Service and Victory Medals.
"He nobly fell that we might live."
13, Craven Street, Northampton. Z1775/B.

WARD, J., Private, R.M.L.I.
At the outbreak of war in August 1914 he was mobilised and posted to H.M.S. "Carisford." On board this vessel he saw fierce fighting in numerous minor engagements, and served with the Grand Fleet in the North Sea, carrying out important patrol and escort work until the cessation of hostilities. He was discharged in July 1920, and holds the 1914–15 Star, and the General Service and Victory Medals.
12, Alton Street, Far Cotton, Northampton. Z3538.

WARD, J. E., Private, 1/3rd London Regiment (Royal Fusiliers).
He volunteered in October 1914, and, after a period of training, was ordered to Gallipoli, where he saw heavy fighting until the Evacuation of the Peninsula. After a short period of service in Egypt, he was drafted to France, on which front he was in action in the Battles of Albert, Vermelles, Ploegsteert and the Somme, and gave his life for the freedom of England at Arras in April 1917. He was entitled to the 1914–15 Star, and the General Service and Victory Medals.
"He nobly fell that we might live."
10, Edith Street, Northampton. Z2029.

WARD, R., Private, 13th R. Warwickshire Regt.
He joined in March 1916, and was employed in various home stations until April 1918, when he was drafted to France. After only two days' service in the firing-line, he was wounded and taken prisoner, and was interned in Germany until after the Armistice. He was then repatriated and eventually demobilised in January 1919, holding the General Service and Victory Medals.
Knutsford Terrace, Long Buckby, Northants. Z3539/A.

WARD, R. J., Private, 52nd Royal Sussex Regt.
Joining in May 1918, he completed a period of training, and was retained on important coastal defence duties at various stations. Owing to his being medically unfit, he was unable to obtain his transfer overseas, but rendered very valuable services until invalided out of the Army in July 1919.
28, Sunderland Street, Northampton. Z2527.

WARD, P. E., Private, R.A.M.C.
He volunteered in September 1915, and four months later was drafted to the Western Front, where he was present at important engagements in various sectors. He died nobly on the Field of Battle at Ypres on July 4th, 1917, and was entitled to the General Service and Victory Medals.
"Thinking that remembrance, though unspoken, may reach him where he sleeps."
16, Thomas Street, Northampton. Z1777.

WARD, S., Private, 5th Northants. Regiment.
He volunteered in July 1915, and, in February of the following year, proceeded to the Western Front, where, after taking part in the Battles of Albert, the Somme, Arras and Ypres, he was twice wounded and gassed. Invalided home, suffering also from shell-shock, he returned to France, however, in time to fight in the Retreat and Advance of 1918. Demobilised in March 1919, he unhappily died on August 3rd, 1920. He was entitled to the General Service and Victory Medals.
"His memory is cherished with pride."
1, St. Mary's Street, Northampton. Z1781.

WARD, T. H., L/Corporal, 1st Northants. Regt.
Having enlisted in January 1913, he was sent to France in August of the following year, and fought at Mons. He also took part in the Battles of Ypres, Loos, the Somme, Arras and Cambrai and other engagements, and was wounded on the Somme in March 1918. He holds the Mons Star, and the General Service and Victory Medals, and in 1921 was still serving in Ireland.
38, Crispin Street, Northampton. Z1780/B.

WARD, V., Corporal, Suffolk Regiment.
Joining the Suffolk Regiment in February 1917, he was later transferred to the Bedfordshire Regiment, and was stationed for some time at Weybridge. He afterwards served at Sutton, Surrey, with the Labour Corps, and performed good work. Owing to ill-health he was unable to obtain a transfer overseas, and was finally invalided out of the Army in August 1918.
Knutsford Terrace, Long Buckby, Northants. Z3539/C.

WARD, W., Corporal, 21st Cheshire Regiment.
Joining in April 1916, he underwent a period of training, and proceeded overseas. In the course of his service on the Western Front, he took part in many important engagements with a Trench Mortar Battery in various sectors. He did consistently good work during heavy fighting at Armentières, Lille and Roubaix, and in July 1919 was demobilised, holding the General Service and Victory Medals.
54, Poole Street, Northampton. Z1398/C.

WARD, W. G., Wireless Telegraphist, Royal Navy.
He joined in February 1917, and, after a period of training at Devonport and Shotley, was posted to H.M.S. "Ambrose" in December 1917. On board this ship, he was engaged on important wireless duties on the Clyde, and later proceeded to Bantry Bay, where he was employed in a similar capacity. He was still serving in 1920.
98, Roe Road, Northampton. Z2306.

WARDEN, A. E., Private, 1/6th Welch Regiment.
Having joined in March 1917 in the Norfolk Regiment, he completed a period of training, but was later transferred to the Welch Regiment and drafted to France. Whilst in this seat of operations, he took part in the engagements on the Arras, Ypres, the Somme and Cambrai fronts. After the cessation of hostilities, he proceeded to Germany and served with the Army of Occupation at Cologne. Demobilised in September 1919, he holds the General Service and Victory Medals.
25, Castle Street, Northampton. Z1783.

WARDEN, J. B., Gunner, R.G.A.
After volunteering in July 1915, he underwent a period of training prior to being drafted to the Western Front in October of the same year. In the course of his service, he was in action during the heavy fighting at Loos and St. Eloi, and also in the Battles of Albert, Vermelles, Ploegsteert Wood, Vimy Ridge, Messines, Ypres, Passchendaele, the Somme, Amiens, Bapaume and the Scarpe. He was demobilised in July 1919, holding the 1914–15 Star, and the General Service and Victory Medals.
27, Fife Street, St. James, Northampton. Z2890.

WAREING, A., Corporal, Royal Air Force.
He volunteered in May 1915, and served for some time in the King's Royal Rifle Corps prior to being transferred to the Royal Air Force. Proceeding to France in January 1916, he was employed on important duties on the Ypres, Somme, Cambrai and Arras fronts, and rendered excellent service. He was demobilised on his return to England in February 1919, and holds the General Service and Victory Medals.
Station Road, Long Buckby, Northants. Z3540.

WARNER, A., Private, 7th Northants. Regiment.
A month after the outbreak of war he volunteered, and, proceeding to the Western Front on completion of his training, saw much service in different parts of the line. He took part in the Battle of the Somme, but was wounded at Ypres in June 1917, and invalided home. On his recovery, he was engaged on agricultural work at Northampton until demobilised in March 1919, holding the 1914–15 Star, and the General Service and Victory Medals.
Chapel Lane, Blisworth, Northampton. Z2307/A.

WARNER, D., Private, Royal Sussex Regiment.
Volunteering in August 1915, he underwent a period of training, and in the following year was drafted to France. During his service in this theatre of war, he took part in many important engagements, particularly in the Ypres sector, where he was wounded in October 1917. As a result he was invalided to hospital at Liverpool, and eventually discharged as medically unfit for further service in August 1918. He holds the General Service and Victory Medals.
91, Stanley Street, Northampton. Z1784.

WARNER, E., L/Corporal, 7th Northants. Regt.
He volunteered in September 1914, and, after a period of training, was drafted overseas in the following year. During his service on the Western Front, he was engaged in severe fighting, chiefly in the Ypres sector, and was accidentally killed when leaving the trenches on January 21st, 1916. He was entitled to the 1914–15 Star, and the General Service and Victory Medals.
"His memory is cherished with pride."
Chapel Lane, Blisworth, Northampton. Z2307/C.

WARNER, E. H., Private, 4th Northants. Regt.
He joined in May 1917, and in the following August was drafted to the Western Front, where he was in action at Ypres and Vimy Ridge. In November 1917 he was admitted to a Base hospital owing to ill-health, and, later evacuated to England, spent some time in hospital in London. After his recovery, he served in home stations until he was demobilised in January 1919, holding the General Service and Victory Medals.
24, The Banks, Long Buckby, Northants. Z3541.

WARNER, F., Private, Middlesex Regiment and Labour Corps.
Joining in October 1917, he was unable to obtain a transfer to the war zone owing to ill-health. On completion of his training, he served at Oxford and Chatham, at which stations he was engaged in the construction of huts and aeroplane sheds, which work he carried out in a highly efficient and satisfactory manner, He was eventually demobilised in March 1919.
Chapel Lane, Blisworth, Northampton. Z2307/B.

WARNER, G. A., Sergeant, 7th Northants. Regt.
Volunteering in January 1915, he proceeded to the Western Front in the following October. There he played a distinguished part in important engagements in various sectors, including the Battles of Loos, the Somme, Arras, Vimy Ridge, Ypres and Cambrai, and fought also in the Retreat and Advance of 1918. He was demobilised in February 1919, and holds the 1914–15 Star, and the General Service and Victory Medals.
25, Abbey Street, Northampton. Z2582/A.

WARNER, L., Rifleman, K.R.R.C.
He joined in March 1918 on attaining military age, but was not successful in his efforts to secure a transfer overseas before the cessation of hostilities. After a period of training he was engaged on important guard duties, and subsequently was employed on agricultural work, which he performed in a highly capable manner until demobilised in December 1920.
Chapel Lane, Blisworth, Northampton. Z2307/D.

WARNER, M. A. (Mrs., née M. A. Ling), Private, Forage Corps (attached R.A.S.C.)
Joining in June 1916 in the Forage Corps, she underwent a period of training and served with the Royal Army Service Corps in Suffolk, Norfolk, Hampshire and various other stations. Her duties chiefly consisted in baling hay, and she rendered very valuable services until discharged in November 1918. 1, Althorp Street, Northampton. Z1512/A.

WARNER, T. F., Bombardier, R.F.A.
Mobilised from the Reserve in August 1914, he was immediately drafted to the Western Front, where he did continuously good work with his Battery. He took part in the Retreat from Mons, and also in the Battles of the Marne, La Bassée and Ypres. In 1915 he was transferred to Salonika, and served on the Vardar and Doiran fronts before proceeding to Egypt. Later he saw much fighting in Palestine, particularly at the Battles of Gaza, Rafa, and in the capture of Jerusalem. Returning home, he was discharged in May 1920, as time-expired. He holds the Mons Star, and the General Service and Victory Medals. 1, Althorp Street, Northampton. Z1512/B.

WARNES, H., Private, 1/4th Norfolk Regiment.
Joining in October 1916, he completed his training, and in the following year proceeded to Palestine. He was in action at the Battles of Gaza, Jaffa, and also at the capture of Jerusalem. After the close of hostilities, he served with the Army of Occupation at Alexandria. Demobilised on his return home in February 1920, he holds the General Service and Victory Medals.
25, Althorp Street, Northampton. Z1262/B.

WARNES, W., L/Corporal, Machine Gun Corps.
After joining in August 1916, he underwent a period of training before proceeding to France. Whilst in this seat of operations, he did continuously good work with his Unit and took part in heavy fighting in the Arras, Ypres, Cambrai and Somme sectors. Demobilised in February 1919, he holds the General Service and Victory Medals.
25, Althorp Street, Northampton. Z1262/A.

WARNES, W., Private, 7th Oxford. & Bucks. L.I.
At the outbreak of war he volunteered and, after a period of training, served on the Western Front and in Salonika. In each of these theatres of war he took an active part in numerous engagements of note in various sectors, serving also with the Royal Army Service Corps. His health broke down in 1918, and he was invalided home from Salonika, being in hospital until demobilised in March 1919, holding the General Service and Victory Medals.
1, Mount Gardens, Northampton. Z2030.

WARREN, A. E. V., Pte., 1st Northants. Regt.
Mobilised from the Reserve in August 1914, he was immediately drafted to the Western Front, where he was in action during the Retreat from Mons and also at the Battles of the Marne, the Aisne and Ypres. He died gloriously on the Field of Battle at Aubers Ridge on May 9th, 1915, and was entitled to the Mons Star, and the General Service and Victory Medals.
"And doubtless he went in splendid company."
11, Alpha Street, Northampton. Z1307/B.

WARREN, A. W., Private, 2nd Norfolk Regiment.
Volunteering in December 1915, he underwent a period of training, and in the following year was drafted to Mesopotamia. Whilst in this seat of operations, he took part in much fighting at Kut and also in the engagements on the Tigris before being wounded in 1917. As a result he was invalided to hospital in India and thence to England, eventually being discharged in September 1919. He holds the General Service and Victory Medals.
23, Earl Street, Northampton. Z1787/A.

WARREN, E., Private, 7th Northants. Regiment.
Having joined in August 1916, he was shortly afterwards drafted to the Western Front, where he was in action in the Ancre and Arras sectors. He made the Supreme Sacrifice, being killed at Vimy Ridge on April 13th, 1917, and was entitled to the General Service and Victory Medals.
"Thinking that remembrance, though unspoken, may reach him where he sleeps."
23, Earl Street, Northampton. Z1787/B.

WARREN, H., Private, 7th Northants. Regiment.
Shortly after volunteering in May 1915 he was ordered to the scene of activities in France, and fought in numerous engagements at Ypres and Armetières. He was severely wounded during the Battle of the Somme in September 1916, and invalided home, subsequently being discharged as medically unfit for further service in August 1917. He holds the 1914–15 Star, and the General Service and Victory Medals.
High Street, Blisworth, Northants. Z2308.

WARREN, S. R., Chief Engine Room Stoker, R.N.
Already in the Royal Navy, he was mobilised at the outbreak of war and posted to H.M.S. "Speedwell," in which vessel he saw much service. He was chiefly engaged on dangerous mine-sweeping duties in the North Sea, where he did consistently good work. In January 1917 he was invalided home suffering from a diseased spine, and was discharged later in that month. Entitled to the 1914–15 Star, and the General Service and Victory Medals, he unfortunately died on January 8th, 1920, and was buried at the General Cemetery, Northampton.
"His name liveth for evermore."
28, Park Street, Northants. Z1785/A.

WARREN, T., Bombardier, Royal Field Artillery.
Called up from the Reserve in August 1914, he was at once drafted to France and fought in the Battle of and Retreat from Mons. He later took part in heavy fighting at Ypres, and early in 1915 was wounded, being invalided home as the result. He subsequently served in various home depôts, and in 1920 was still with the Colours, stationed in Glasgow. He holds the Mons Star, and the General Service and Victory Medals.
2, Main Road, Far Cotton, Northants. Z3542.

WARREN, T. J., Cpl., 3rd (King's Own) Hussars.
Volunteering in August 1914, he proceeded to the Dardanelles in July 1915 and took part in the Gallipoli campaign, and was wounded before being invalided home with dysentery. On his recovery he was transferred to France, where he saw much heavy fighting, particularly in the Somme sector, and was twice wounded. He also served with the Royal Fusiliers, and in June 1919 was discharged, holding the 1914–15 Star, and the General Service and Victory Medals.
76, St. James' Road, Northampton. Z2891.

WARREN, T. W., Private, Essex Regiment.
After joining in June 1917, he underwent a period of training and later in the same year was drafted to India. Whilst in this seat of operations, he did continuously good work and was engaged on important garrison duties with his Unit at various stations. Demobilised on his return home in December 1920 he holds the General Service and Victory Medals.
34, Great Russell Street, Northampton. Z1786.

WARREN, T. W., Saddler, R.G.A.
Joining in January 1916, he shortly afterwards proceeded to Salonika. Whilst in this seat of operations he saw much service and took an active part in engagements on the Vardar, Struma and Monastir fronts. He did consistently good work and, on his return home in February 1919, was demobilised, holding the General Service and Victory Medals.
34, Abbey Street, Northampton. Z2883/B.

WARREN, W., L/Corporal, Royal Engineers.
Having volunteered in August 1915, he was first engaged on important duties with his Company at various stations. Proceeding to the Western Front in June 1917, he served with the Railway Operative Department, and was engaged on the construction of rail-roads in the Arras sector, where he rendered very valuable services. Demobilised in July 1919, he holds the General Service and Victory Medals.
28, Sand Hill Road, St. James, Northampton. Z2892.

WARREN, W. P., Private, Queen's Own (Royal West Kent Regiment).
Joining in October 1917, he completed a period of training before proceeding to the Western Front, where he took part in engagements in the Somme and Ypres sectors, and was also in action during the Retreat and Advance of 1918. After the conclusion of hostilities, he served with the Army of Occupation at Cologne. Demobilised in March 1919, he holds the General Service and Victory Medals.
89, Stanley Street, Northampton Z1181/A.

WARRIOR, A. E., Corporal, 2nd Northants. Regt.
Having previously served in the South African campaign, he was stationed in Egypt at the outbreak of war, but was immediately drafted to France. He took part in the Battles of Ypres (I.), Neuve Chapelle, Givenchy, Loos and the Somme, and was twice wounded. As a result he was invalided home, and, after a period of hospital treatment, was discharged as medically unfit for further service in October 1917. He holds the Queen's and King's South African Medals, the 1914 Star, and the General Service and Victory Medals.
12, Doddridge Square, Northampton. Z1788.

WARWICK, E., Sergeant, Royal Engineers.
Mobilised from the Reserve at the outbreak of war, he was immediately drafted to France. In this theatre of hostilities he served with distinction in the Battle of, and Retreat from, Mons, and also in the Battles of the Marne, the Aisne, La Bassée, Ypres, the Somme and Cambrai, and was three times wounded. He holds the Mons Star, and the General Service and Victory Medals, and in 1921 was serving at Chatham.
Hardingstone, Northants. Z2893/B.

WARWICK, E. C., Corporal, Royal Sussex Regt.
Joining in March 1916, he proceeded to the Western Front later in the same year, and served in many notable engagements, including the Battles of the Somme and Ypres. He was wounded in the vicinity of Cambrai in September 1917, was invalided to England, and in consequence was discharged as medically unfit for further military duties in May 1918, holding the General Service and Victory Medals.
Near Chapel, Blisworth, Northants. Z2309/A.

WARWICK, E. P., Private, 17th Royal Fusiliers.
Joining in February 1917, he was shortly afterwards drafted to the Western Front, where he served with the Labour Corps on important duties in connection with the construction of railways and roads. He was present at many important engagements, particularly in the Somme sector, and, after the conclusion of hostilities, proceeded with the Army of Occupation to Germany. Demobilised in October 1919, he holds the General Service and Victory Medals.
Chapel Yard, Wootton, Northants. Z2894/A.

WARWICK, E. V., Pte., 52nd Sherwood Foresters.
He joined in June 1917, but was retained on important duties at various home stations until the cessation of hostilities. In December 1918 he was drafted to Germany, and rendered valuable services with the Army of Occupation at Cologne until transferred to Ireland in June 1919. He was stationed at Dublin, and was actively engaged in quelling the attacks of the Sinn Feiners until his demobilisation.
Chapel Hill, Blisworth, Northants. Z2309/B.

WARWICK, J. C., Corporal, 1st Life Guards.
He volunteered in September 1915, and was retained on important duties in England until November of the following year, and was then drafted to the Western Front, where he saw much severe fighting. He fell in action on October 7th, 1917, and was entitled to the General Service and Victory Medals.
"Steals on the ear the distant triumph song."
Goodes Lane, Church Street, Brixworth, Northants. Z2964/B.

WARWICK, J. W., Private, 1st Northants. Regt.
Called up from the Reserve at the declaration of war, he was immediately drafted to France, where he was in action in the Battle of, and Retreat from, Mons, and also at the Battles of the Marne, the Aisne, La Bassée and Ypres, before being invalided home with trench fever. On his recovery he returned to France, and fought at the Battle of Aubers Ridge, where he fell in action on May 9th, 1915, and was entitled to the Mons Star, and the General Service and Victory Medals.
"Whilst we remember, the sacrifice is not in vain."
Hardingstone, Northants. Z2893/A.

WARWICK, L., Driver, R.A.S.C.
He enlisted in June 1914, and was drafted to the Western Front two months after the outbreak of hostilities. He had only served overseas for two weeks when he made the Supreme Sacrifice, being killed in action at Ypres in October 1914. He was buried where he fell, and was entitled to the 1914 Star, and the General Service and Victory Medals.
"He nobly fell that we might live."
27, Swan Street, Northampton. Z3543.

WARWICK, S. G., Sapper, R.E. (R.O.D.)
He volunteered in July 1915, and, after training with the Queen's (Royal West Surrey Regiment), was drafted in the following year to Salonika, where he was transferred to the Royal Engineers. Whilst in this seat of operations, he was engaged on various important duties on the railways on the Doiran and Vardar fronts, finally returning home for demobilisation in March 1919. He holds the General Service and Victory Medals.
Camp Hill, Bugbrooke, Northants. Z3189.

WARWICK, T. H. R., Private, 16th (The Queen's) Lancers.
A serving soldier, he was sent to France immediately after the outbreak of war in August 1914, and took part in the Retreat from Mons. He was afterwards in action at Ypres, Hill 60 and Passchendaele, and in many other important engagements, and was wounded. Discharged on his return home in March 1919, he holds the Mons Star, and the General Service and Victory Medals.
19, Delapre Street, Northampton. Z3544.

WARWICK, W. G., Private, R.A.S.C. (M.T.)
Volunteering at the age of 49 in August 1915, he was quickly drafted to France and was stationed at St. Omer, where he was engaged in the workshops as a fitter and repairer of engines. He did consistently good work during the period of hostilities, and in February 1919 was demobilised, holding the 1914–15 Star, and the General Service and Victory Medals.
Water Lane, Wootton, Northants. Z2894/B.

WARWICKS, W. A., Pte., 6th Bedfordshire Regt.
He volunteered in July 1915, and, in December of the following year, was drafted to the Western Front, where he saw much heavy fighting. After taking part in engagements at Loos, Arras and Vimy Ridge, he was severely wounded on the Somme in March 1917, and was sent home. He was invalided from the Army in December of that year, and holds the General Service and Victory Medals.
Spratton, Northants. Z3190.

WATERFIELD, T. W., Private, 6th Buffs (East Kent Regiment).
He joined in February 1917, and, proceeding to the Western Front in the following June, was engaged in fierce fighting at Monchy, Cambrai, Bazancourt and Morlancourt. He was also in action at the Battles of Vimy Ridge and Epéhy, and did good work with his Unit in operations during the Retreat and Advance of 1918, being wounded on two occasions. Demobilised in February 1919, he holds the General Service and Victory Medals. 31, Brunswick Place, Northampton. Z2031.

WATKIN, C. W., Private, 1st Northants. Regt.
Volunteering in March 1915, he embarked for the Western Front later in the same year, and fought in the Battles of Ypres and Loos. He was wounded in action in January 1916, and, on his return to the firing-line, took part in engagements at the Somme, Arras and Ypres, and in the Retreat and Advance of 1918. After the Armistice, he advanced into Germany with the Army of Occupation, and was stationed at Bonn until demobilised in March 1919, holding the 1914–15 Star, and the General Service and Victory Medals.
26, Hunter Street, Northampton. Z2310/A.

WATKIN, E. A., Private, 5th Northants. Regt.
At the declaration of war he volunteered, and in May 1915 was ordered to France, where he was engaged in severe fighting in various parts of the front. After serving in the Battles of Ypres, Loos and Albert, he gave his life for King and Country at Aveluy on August 2nd, 1916. He was entitled to the 1914–15 Star, and the General Service and Victory Medals.
"A valiant Soldier, with undaunted heart he breasted life's last hill."
26, Hunter Street, Northampton. Z2310/C.

WATKINS, J. E., Private, 2nd Northants. Regt.
After joining in 1917, he was drafted to France later in the same year. Serving on the Western Front, he was in action at the Battles of Vimy Ridge and Passchendaele before being invalided to hospital, but, on his recovery, was present during heavy fighting at Armentières and elsewhere. Demobilised on his return home in October 1919, he holds the General Service and Victory Medals.
5, Althorp Road, Northampton. Z2528.

WATSON, A., Private, 8th Queen's (Royal West Surrey Regiment).
He joined in August 1917, and in the following April proceeded to the Western Front, where he participated in strenuous fighting in many sectors, including Cambrai and the Somme. In October 1918 he was invalided home, having been severely burned by liquid fire, and was in hospital at Northampton until March 1919, when he was demobilised, holding the General Service and Victory Medals.
Mount Pleasant, Bugbrooke, Northants. Z3545.

WATSON, G. H., Rifleman, London Regiment (Queen Victoria's Rifles).
Joining in July 1917, he was sent later in the same year to France. There he took part in the Battles of the Somme (II.), Cambrai (II.), and Ypres (IV.), and in many other engagements during the Retreat and Advance of 1918. He returned home after the Armistice, and was demobilised in February 1919, holding the General Service and Victory Medals.
Near Bridge, Kislingbury, Northants. Z3221/D.

WATSON, J. W., Rifleman, Rifle Brigade.
He volunteered in the Royal Army Service Corps in March 1915, but was later transferred to the Rifle Brigade and drafted to France. On that front he was in action in many engagements, including the Battle of Cambrai, but was badly wounded and taken prisoner on December 1st, 1917, and unhappily succumbed to his injuries two days later. He was entitled to the General Service and Victory Medals.
"Whilst we remember, the sacrifice is not in vain."
26, Ashburnham Road, Northampton. Z2311.

WATSON, T. M., Corporal, 1/4th Northants. Regt.
A Reservist, he was called to the Colours in August 1914, but was retained on important duties in England until December 1916. He was then drafted to the Western Front, where he saw much severe fighting, and took part in the Battles of Vimy Ridge, Bullecourt and Cambrai and other engagements. Discharged in September 1919, he holds the General Service and Victory Medals.
29, Oxford Street, Daventry, Northants. Z3191.

WATSON, W., Bombardier, Royal Field Artillery.
Volunteering in October 1914, he proceeded to the Western Front in the following year, and was in action at the Battles of Ypres, Loos, Vimy Ridge and the Somme. He was severely wounded at Arras in April 1917, and sent to hospital in Birmingham. On his recovery, he was retained on home service until demobilised in February 1919, and holds the 1914–15 Star, and the General Service and Victory Medals.
108, Lutterworth Road, Northampton. Z2312.

WATT, W., Sergeant, Royal Scots Greys.
Having enlisted in September 1899, he was mobilised when war was declared in August 1914, and immediately proceeded to the Western Front with the first Expeditionary Force. On reaching Le Havre, he was found to be medically unfit for further service, and was invalided out of the Army in November 1914, after 15 years' valuable service. He holds the 1914 Star, and the General Service and Victory Medals.
49, Monk's Park Road, Northampton. Z2313.

WATTS, A. G., Private, Loyal North Lancs. Regt.
Joining in June 1916, he was drafted to France in the following December, and there took part in many important engagements in the Somme sector. Mortally wounded in action, he unhappily died in hospital at Wimereux on April 28th, 1918, and was entitled to the General Service and Victory Medals.
"He nobly fell that we might live."
147, Euston Road, Northampton. Z3193.

WATTS, F. A., Driver, Royal Field Artillery.
He joined in January 1917, and, after a period of training, was sent overseas 10 months later. Serving on the Western Front, he took an active part in the Battle of Ypres and many other engagements of note, until his health broke down in September 1918, and he was invalided to England. On his discharge from hospital, he was demobilised in January 1919, and holds the General Service and Victory Medals.
15, East Street, Northampton. Z2265/A.

WATTS, F. C., Gunner, R.G.A. (183rd Siege Bty.)
Joining in November 1916, he was drafted four months later to the Western Front, where he was in action at the Battles of Arras, Bullecourt, Ypres and Cambrai. He also saw heavy fighting at Nieuport and Ayette, and was severely wounded in November 1918. After protracted hospital treatment in England, he was discharged as medically unfit for further service in February 1920, holding the General Service and Victory Medals.
149, Wycliffe Road, Northampton. Z2314.

WATTS, G., Corporal, Bedfordshire Lancers.
He volunteered in the Northamptonshire Dragoons in August 1914, but in the following January was discharged as medically unfit. In January 1916 he rejoined, and, after his training, was drafted to France in February 1917. Whilst overseas, he saw much fighting at Arras, Vimy Ridge, Péronne, Ypres, Passchendaele, Cambrai and the Somme (II.), but, contracting dysentery, was invalided home. On his recovery, he served in Ireland until his demobilisation in January 1919. He holds the General Service and Victory Medals.
55, Ardington Road, Northampton. Z2529.

WATTS, H. S., Private, Duke of Cornwall's L.I.
He volunteered in May 1915, and in July of the following year was drafted to Salonika, where he saw much severe fighting. He took part in many important engagements on the Doiran and Vardar fronts until the cessation of hostilities, and finally returned home for demobilisation in February 1919. He holds the General Service and Victory Medals.
8, Church Street, Lower Weedon, Northants. Z3192.

WATTS, L. A., Sergeant, Tank Corps.
A serving soldier, he was drafted to the Dardanelles 12 months after the outbreak of war, and there, after taking part in the Landing at Suvla Bay, was wounded in action. He was invalided home, and, on his recovery, was retained in England as an Instructor. He holds the 1914–15 Star, and the General Service and Victory Medals, and in 1921 was still serving.
91, St. Leonard's Road, Northampton. Z2994/A.

WATTS, L. F., Private, Monmouthshire Regiment.
He volunteered in November 1914, and, after a brief training, embarked for France. In this theatre of war he took part in heavy fighting at Ypres, on the Somme and at Arras and Vimy Ridge, and was badly gassed in 1917. Evacuated to England, he was sent to hospital and was eventually invalided out of the Army in December 1918, holding the 1914–15 Star, and the General Service and Victory Medals.
109, Bridge Street, Northampton. Z3546.

WATTS, S. C. T., Private, Sherwood Foresters.
Having joined in January 1917 in the Northamptonshire Regiment, he was later transferred to the Sherwood Foresters, and drafted to the Western Front. In this seat of operations, he was in action at the Battles of Arras, Vimy Ridge and Bullecourt. He made the Supreme Sacrifice, being killed on May 15th, 1917, and was entitled to the General Service and Victory Medals.
"His life for his Country, his soul to God."
8, Ash Street, Northamptonshire. Z1789.

WEARN, C. H., Private, R.A.M.C.
Joining in June 1918, he underwent a period of training, and was drafted overseas. Whilst on the Western Front, he did continuously good work as a stretcher-bearer at various Casualty Clearing Stations. He was present during engagements at La Bassée, Passchendaele, Loos and Dunkirk. After the conclusion of war, he was engaged on special duties until demobilised in February 1919, holding the General Service and Victory Medals.
26, Deal Street, Northampton. Z1791.

WEATHERALL, A. J., Private, Lancs. Fusiliers.
He joined the Royal Engineers in April 1917, but was later transferred to the Lancashire Fusiliers and drafted to France. He participated in several severe engagements on the Ypres, Somme and Albert fronts, and was wounded in June 1918. Sent home for treatment, he spent some time in hospital at Glasgow and Duston prior to being demobilised in February 1919, holding the General Service and Victory Medals.
The Wharf, Bugbrooke, Northants. Z3547.

WEBB, A. H., Private, 2nd East Surrey Regiment.
He enlisted in April 1917, and underwent a period of training prior to his being drafted to France in the following February. Fighting in the Retreat of 1918, he was wounded and taken prisoner in March of that year, and was held in captivity in Germany until September 1918. He then proceeded to Switzerland and thence home, being demobilised in November 1919. He holds the General Service and Victory Medals.
83, Stanley Road, Northampton. Z2530.

WEBB, C. E., Private, 1st Northamptonshire Regt.
Mobilised in August 1914, he was immediately drafted to France, where he took part in the Battle of, and the Retreat from, Mons, and several other engagements before being wounded. On his recovery, he was in action during heavy fighting at Albert, and was taken prisoner. Whilst in captivity, he suffered many hardships, and unhappily died in 1919, when on his way to England. He was entitled to the Mons Star, and the General Service and Victory Medals.
"A valiant Soldier, with undaunted heart he breasted life's last hill."
27, Rickard Street, Far Cotton, Northampton. Z3549/A.

WEBB, F., Private, 2nd Bedfordshire Regiment.
He volunteered in August 1915, and, on conclusion of his training in the following March, was drafted overseas. Serving on the Western Front, he was in action at the Battles of the Somme, Arras, Vimy Ridge, Bullecourt, Ypres and Passchendaele, before being wounded and invalided home in October 1917. On his recovery, he returned to France, and took part in the Retreat and Advance of 1918, and was gassed. Demobilised in January 1919, he holds the General Service and Victory Medals. 83, Stanley Road, Northampton. Z2895.

WEBB, F. J., Private, 2nd Gloucestershire Regt.
Already serving in the Army, he was mobilised at the declaration of war and immediately proceeded overseas. Whilst on the Western Front, he was in action during the Retreat from Mons, and also in several other engagements. He made the Supreme Sacrifice, being killed at the Battle of Hill 60 in May 1915, and was entitled to the Mons Star, and the General Service and Victory Medals.
"Whilst we remember, the sacrifice is not in vain."
27, Oxford Street, Far Cotton, Northampton. Z3549/B.

WEBB, G., Trooper, Northants. Dragoons.
Volunteering in October 1915, he completed his training prior to being drafted overseas in February 1917. Whilst on the Western Front, he served as a shoeing-smith, and was present in many important engagements in various sectors. He was later transferred to Italy, where he was engaged in a similar capacity on the Piave front. Returning home for demobilisation in February 1919, he holds the General Service and Victory Medals. 13, Newcombe Road, Northampton. Z2896.

WEBB, G. T., A.B., R.N.V.R.
He joined in November 1916, and was posted to H.M.S. "President," on board which vessel he was engaged on important coastal defence duties at Chatham. He served chiefly on the searchlights and anti-aircraft guns, and rendered valuable services until February 1919, when he was demobilised. 43, Clinton Road, Far Cotton, Northampton. Z3194.

WEBB, G. W., Private, Training Reserve.
Having joined in March 1918, he proceeded to Dover, but whilst in training contracted an illness, and as a result was admitted to hospital there and in London, where he was discharged as medically unfit for further service in December 1918. 1, Althorp Street, Northampton. Z1512/C.

WEBB, H. E., Sapper, R.E. (Signals).
Joining in March 1916, he underwent a short period of training before proceeding overseas in June. Whilst on the Western Front, he took an active part in engagements in the Somme and Ypres sectors, but in November 1916 was badly wounded. As a result, he was invalided home and eventually discharged as medically unfit for further service in March 1917. He holds the General Service and Victory Medals.
34, Adelaide Street, Northamptonshire. Z1516/A.

WEBB, J. R., Pte., Queen's (R.W. Surrey Regt.)
Joining in August 1916, he landed in Salonika two months later, and in this theatre of war saw much severe fighting, being in action on the Vardar and Struma fronts. He contracted malaria fever, and as a result was invalided to hospital and thence to England, where he underwent a period of treatment, and was finally demobilised in March 1919, holding the General Service and Victory Medals.
24, Glasgow Street, St. James, Northampton. Z2897.

WEBB, R., L/Corporal, Royal Scots.
Already in the Army in August 1914, he at once proceeded to France, and was in action at Mons. He also took part in many other important engagements, including the Battle of Ypres, and was gassed. After fighting throughout the Retreat and Advance of 1918, he returned to England, and was discharged in 1919, holding the Mons Star, and the General Service and Victory Medals.
38, Rickard Street, Far Cotton, Northampton. Z3548.

WEBB, T., Private, 2nd Northamptonshire Regt.
Volunteering in September 1914, he completed his training, and in the following year was drafted to France. Whilst in this theatre of war he was in action at Neuve Chapelle and Aubers Ridge, where he was wounded in April 1915. Evacuated to hospital at Bristol, he was eventually invalided out of the Army in November 1915. He holds the 1914–15 Star, and the General Service and Victory Medals.
46, Francis Street, Northampton. Z1726/B.

WEBB, T., Wireless Operator, Royal Navy.
Although only 17 years of age he joined the Royal Navy in 1917, and, throughout the remaining period of hostilities, saw much service on board various vessels in the North Sea. He served for some time in H.M.S. "Duncan," in which ship he was engaged on important duties. In 1919 he was demobilised, holding the General Service and Victory Medals.
36, Oxford Street, Far Cotton, Northampton. Z3350/B.

WEBB, W., Gunner, Royal Garrison Artillery.
Volunteering in October 1915, he was drafted 12 months later to Egypt, where he served before proceeding to Palestine. In this theatre of war he took part in various engagements, including the Battles of Gaza, and, contracting malaria fever, was invalided to hospital. On his recovery, he rejoined his Battery, and remained in Palestine. Finally returning home for discharge in September 1919, he holds the General Service and Victory Medals.
29, North Street, Daventry, Northants. Z2898.

WEBB, W. G., Air Mechanic, Royal Air Force.
Volunteering in 1915, he proceeded in the following year to France, where he took part in many important engagements in various sectors of the front. He was in action during heavy fighting at Ypres, and also at the Battles of Passchendaele and the Somme. Whilst overseas he was three times wounded, and in 1918 returned to England, where he was in training for a commission. Finally demobilised in 1919, he holds the General Service and Victory Medals.
36, Oxford Street, Far Cotton, Northampton. Z3550/A.

WEBB, W. H., Private, Northamptonshire Regt.
He volunteered in December 1914, and in the following year was drafted to the Western Front, where he took part in the Battle of Ypres, and was twice wounded on the Somme in 1916. He was later transferred to Egypt, and was engaged on bridge-building and other duties with the Royal Engineers. Demobilised on returning home in February 1919, he holds the 1914–15 Star, and the General Service and Victory Medals.
Gough's Cottages, Old Duston, Northants. Z3195.

WEBSTER, C., A.B., Royal Naval Division.
He joined in August 1917, and, after completing a period of training, was retained at various stations, where he was engaged on duties of great importance. He was unable to obtain his transfer overseas, but, nevertheless, did much excellent work. In March 1919 he re-engaged in the 2nd Northamptonshire Regiment, and was later drafted to India, where he was still serving in 1921.
6, St. James' Terrace, St. James' Street, Northampton. Z2938/B.

WEBSTER, D., Driver, Royal Field Artillery.
Joining in November 1916, he completed his training, and in the following year proceeded to France. Whilst in this seat of operations, he was in action with his Battery at the Battles of Arras, Ypres, Passchendaele, Cambrai and the Somme (II.). He was also present during the Retreat and Advance of 1918, and, after the cessation of hostilities, served with the Army of Occupation in Germany. Demobilised in November 1919, he holds the General Service and Victory Medals.
6, St. James' Terrace, St. James' Street, Northants. Z2938/A.

WEBSTER, G., A.B., Royal Navy.
Already in the Royal Navy when war was declared, he first served on board H.M. T.B.D. "81" on important patrol and escort duties in the North Sea, and was in action at the Battle of Heligoland Bight. Later he was transferred to Submarine "E.22," and was unfortunately drowned when this vessel was sunk on April 16th, 1916. He was entitled to the 1914–15 Star, and the General Service and Victory Medals.
"His name liveth for evermore."
6, St. James' Terrace, St. James' Street, Northampton. Z2938/C.

WEBSTER, W., Private, 21st (Empress of India's) Lancers.
Called up from the Reserve in August 1914, he first served in Ireland. Proceeding in April 1915 to India, he was engaged on important garrison duties at various stations, and also saw active service on the Afghan frontier. He did continuously good work, and, on his return home in December 1919, was discharged, holding the General Service, Victory and India General Service Medals (with Clasp, Afghanistan, N.W. Frontier, 1919). 33, Bowden Road, Northampton. Z2899.

WELCH, W., H., L/Cpl., 9th (Queen's R.) Lancers.
He volunteered in December 1914, and in the following year embarked for France, where he served as a Wireless Operator with the 21st Lancers in many important engagements in various sectors. Afterwards he was transferred to the Queen's Own (Royal West Kent Regiment), and was in action during heavy fighting on the Ypres and Somme fronts, and was wounded. Demobilised in December 1918, he holds the 1914–15 Star, and the General Service and Victory Medals.
Kennell Terrace, Brixworth, Northants. Z3196.

WELFORD, O. H., Corporal, R.F.A.
Having volunteered in July 1915, he landed in France in the following month, and was there in action with his Battery during heavy fighting at Armentières and Ypres before being wounded and invalided home. Returning to the Western Front on his recovery, he took part in the Battles of the Somme (II.), Havrincourt, Epéhy and Cambrai. He was demobilised in March 1919, and holds the 1914–15 Star, and the General Service and Victory Medals.
31, Bowden Road, Northampton. Z2900.

WELLS, F., Private, 1/4th Northants. Regiment.
He volunteered in May 1915, and, on conclusion of his training 12 months later, was drafted to Egypt. Advancing into Palestine, he was in action at the Battles of Gaza, where he was twice wounded, and in November 1917 was invalided to hospital at El-Arish. On his recovery, he rejoined his Unit and took part in the capture of Jerusalem and Jericho. Demobilised on his return home in August 1919, he holds the General Service and Victory Medals. 22, Brook St., Daventry, Northants. Z2901.

WELLS, G., Private, 1st Cheshire Regiment.
Mobilised from the Reserve in August 1914, he was quickly drafted to France. During his service in this seat of war, he took part in the Retreat from Mons and also in the Battle of La Bassée, where he was taken prisoner in October 1914. Whilst in captivity, he suffered many hardships, and had both his legs amputated. He was released from Germany and discharged in May 1916, but unfortunately died as a result of his harsh treatment on October 2nd, 1918. He was entitled to the 1914 Star, and the General Service and Victory Medals.
"And doubtless he went in splendid company."
1, Salisbury Street, Northampton. TZ1790.

WELTON, T. P., Rifleman, K.R.R.C.
Volunteering in August 1914, he proceeded overseas in the following March. Serving on the Western Front, he took part in many important engagements, particularly in the Ypres and Somme sectors. He was badly wounded in 1916, and as a result was invalided home, and, on his recovery, was retained on important duties in England. Demobilised in March 1919, he holds the 1914–15 Star, and the General Service and Victory Medals. 5, St. Leonard's Road, Northampton. Z3197.

WESLEY, A. E., Private, 19th Manchester Regt.
When war broke out, he came over from Canada and rendered valuable services at a munition factory until February 1917, when he joined the Army. Six months later he was drafted to the Western Front, where he took part in heavy fighting in the Retreat of 1918. During the Allied Advance of that year, he was wounded and sent to hospital in Manchester, eventually being demobilised in August 1919, holding the General Service and Victory Medals.
5, Mount Gardens, Northampton. Z2032.

WESLEY, G. T., Sergeant, 12th (Prince of Wales' Royal) Lancers.
Already serving in August 1914, he was immediately drafted to the Western Front. There he took part in the Retreat from Mons, and the Battles of Ypres, the Somme, Arras, Bullecourt, Passchendaele and Cambrai. He was wounded in March 1918 during the Retreat, and as a result was invalided to England. On his recovery, he was engaged on important duties in Ireland. Discharged in February 1920, he holds the Mons Star, and the General Service and Victory Medals.
6, St. James' Street, Daventry, Northants. TZ3198.

WEST, J. H., Private, Royal Defence Corps.
Volunteering in October 1914, he completed a period of training and was retained on important guard duties over railway bridges and viaducts. He was also engaged in guarding prisoners of war in Lincolnshire and Yorkshire, and rendered excellent services until demobilised in March 1919.
11, Chaucer Street, Kingsley, Northampton. Z1792/B.

WEST, J. W., Gunner, Royal Field Artillery.
Having volunteered in November 1915, he underwent a period of training, but was retained on important duties as a bootmaker and repairer, and served at various stations. Owing to the importance of the work in which he was engaged, he was unable to proceed to a theatre of war, but, nevertheless, rendered excellent services until demobilised in February 1919.
25, Chaucer Street, Kingsley, Northampton. Z1792/A.

WEST, T. G., A.B., Royal Navy.
He was already in the Royal Navy, and, immediately on the declaration of war in August 1914, was posted to H.M.S. "Monarch," in which vessel he was engaged on important patrol and escort duties attached to the Grand Fleet in the North Sea. Later, in 1916, he was invalided home suffering from tuberculosis and unfortunately died from the effects on October 5th, 1917. He was entitled to the 1914–15 Star, and the General Service and Victory Medals.
"Steals on the ear the distant triumph song."
11, Chaucer Street, Kingsley, Northampton. Z1792/C.

WEST, W., Corporal, Essex Regiment.
He volunteered in January 1916, and two months later was drafted to Egypt. In this seat of operations he took part in several engagements, and advanced into Palestine, where he was in action at Siwa and Gaza, and with General Allenby's forces in the Offensive of September 1918. He returned home and was demobilised in August 1919, holding the General Service and Victory Medals.
49, Stanley Road, Northampton. Z2531.

WESTBURY, F., Private, 1st Northants. Regt.
A Reservist, he was called to the Colours at the outbreak of war, and proceeded to France with the first Expeditionary Force. After taking part in the Battle of Mons, he was reported missing during the subsequent Retreat, and is now presumed to have been killed in action some time in August 1914. He was entitled to the Mons Star, and the General Service and Victory Medals.
"His name liveth for evermore."
18, Bective Road, Kingsthorpe, Northampton. Z1793/C.

WESTBURY, W. H., Sapper, Royal Engineers.
Joining in August 1916, he proceeded in the following year to France. There he served on the Ypres, Arras, Cambrai and Somme fronts, being employed with his Company digging trenches and erecting pontoon bridges. In June 1918 he was gassed on the Somme front, and, evacuated to England, spent some time in hospital in Birmingham prior to being discharged in October 1918. He holds the General Service and Victory Medals.
18, Bective Road, Kingsthorpe, Northampton. Z1793/B.

WESTBURY, W. T., 1st Air Mechanic, R.A.F.
He joined in April 1918, but was not successful in obtaining a transfer overseas owing to the termination of hostilities. After the conclusion of his training, he was stationed at various aerodromes, and was engaged on important duties which demanded a high degree of technical skill. He rendered excellent service until he was demobilised in July 1920.
18, Bective Road, Kingsthorpe, Northampton. Z1793/A.

WESTLEY, A. H., Private, Queen's (Royal West Surrey Regiment).
Joining in January 1917, he underwent a period of training, and was retained on important duties at various stations. He was unable to obtain his transfer to a theatre of war owing to his being medically unfit, but, nevertheless, rendered very valuable services until discharged in March 1919.
19, Abbey Street, Northampton. Z2902.

WESTLEY, E., Private, R.A.M.C.
After volunteering in November 1914, he underwent a period of training prior to being drafted to the Western Front in March 1917. There he took an active part in the Battles of Arras, Bullecourt, Ypres, Passchendaele and Cambrai and served also through the Retreat and Advance of 1918. He was demobilised in March 1919, and holds the General Service and Victory Medals.
104, Wycliffe Road, Northampton. Z2532.

WESTLEY, F., Private, Queen's Own (Royal West Kent Regiment).
Joining in March 1917, he was shortly afterwards drafted to the Western Front, where he took part in many important engagements, including the Battles of Ypres, Passchendaele, the Somme and Kemmel Hill. He was badly gassed in action and was in hospital for some time. In September 1919 he was demobilised, and holds the General Service and Victory Medals.
18, Spencer Street, Northampton. Z3199.

WESTLEY, G. E., Sergt., 2nd Northants. Regt.
Already serving at the outbreak of war in August 1914, he was immediately sent to France, where he fought in the Battle of Mons and the subsequent Retreat. He later took part in the Battle of Ypres and many other important engagements, and was wounded on three occasions. Taken prisoner in March 1918, he was interned in Germany until after the Armistice, when he was repatriated and eventually discharged in April 1919, holding the Mons Star, and the General Service and Victory Medals.
6, Leicester Street, Northampton. Z1639/A.

WESTLEY, H., Private, 1st Northants. Regiment.
A serving soldier, he proceeded to France in August 1914, and fought in the Retreat from Mons and in minor engagements. He was taken prisoner in September 1914 at the Battle of the Marne, was held in captivity in Germany until the cessation of hostilities, and suffered many hardships during this period. He afterwards served in Ireland until discharged in August 1920, time-expired, and holds the Mons Star, and the General Service and Victory Medals.
73, Greenwood Road, Northampton. Z2533.

WESTLEY, W., Trooper, Berkshire Dragoons.
He volunteered in October 1915, and served with the Northamptonshire Dragoons at various stations. He was later transferred to the Berkshire Dragoons, and in 1917 embarked for Egypt. On the voyage to the East, he was saved when the ship was torpedoed and sunk. After a brief period of service in Egypt, he was sent to France, and took part in various actions during the Allied Advance. Demobilised in July 1919, he holds the General Service and Victory Medals.
80, Louise Road, Northampton. Z1794.

WESTON, G. W., Bandsman, 2nd Northants. Regt.
He joined in March 1916, but, being too young for transfer overseas, served in Northampton and Gillingham until October 1918, when he was sent to France with the band of his Regiment. He took part in the Advance to Germany, and served with the Army of Occupation on the Rhine until 1919. He was stationed in India in 1921, and holds the General Service and Victory Medals.
63, Poole Street, Northampton. Z1795/C.

WESTON, J., C.S.M., Northamptonshire Regt.
He had taken part in the South African campaign, and had completed 24 years' Colour service prior to the outbreak of war in August 1914, when he re-enlisted. Unfit for transfer overseas, he rendered valuable services training recruits at Northampton during the whole period of hostilities. He was demobilised in February 1919, holding the Queen's and King's South African Medals and the Long Service and Good Conduct Medal. 63, Poole Street, Northampton. Z1795/B.

WESTON, J. H., Gunner, Royal Garrison Artillery.
He joined in October 1917, and, on completing his training in September of the following year, was sent to the Western Front. Whilst in this theatre of war, he served as a signaller in various sectors, and saw much severe fighting until the cessation of hostilities. Demobilised in March 1919, he holds the General Service and Victory Medals. Z2535.

WESTON, J. W., Private, 6th Northants. Regiment.
He volunteered in September 1915, and three months later proceeded to France. There he took part in heavy fighting in the Loos sector, but was wounded at Trônes Wood in July 1916 during the Battle of the Somme and was invalided home. After a protracted period of hospital treatment, he was transferred to the Labour Corps, and served in Kent until his demobilisation in February 1919. He holds the 1914–15 Star, and the General Service and Victory Medals.
63, Poole Street, Northampton. Z1795/A.

WESTON, V. R., Private, Machine Gun Corps.
Shortly after volunteering in 1915, he proceeded to the Western Front, where he saw severe fighting in various sectors. He took part in the Battles of Loos, Vimy Ridge and Ypres and many other engagements, was gassed, and was among the troops to enter Mons at dawn of Armistice Day. He holds the 1914–15 Star, and the General Service and Victory Medals and in 1921 was still with his Unit.
65, Adam's Avenue, Northampton. Z2534.

WHALE, H., Private, 3rd Northants. Regiment.
He was mobilised in August 1914, but found to be medically unfit for transfer to a theatre of war. Retained at home, he served in turn at Weymouth, Colchester and Shorncliffe, and did excellent work whilst engaged on garrison and other important duties. He was invalided out of the Army in April 1915.
25, Upper Harding Street, Northampton. Z1796/B.

WHALE, W., Private, 5th South Staffordshire Regt.
He volunteered in 1915, and, after a period of training, was sent to Ireland. Whilst stationed in Dublin, he did good work engaged on important duties, and early in 1916 was drafted to France. There he took part in heavy fighting in various sectors, and was reported missing after a strenuous action. He was later presumed to have been killed in the same year, and was entitled to the General Service and Victory Medals.
"The path of duty was the way to glory."
Barrow Street, West Bromwich. Z1796/A.

WHAPPLES, W., 2nd Lieutenant, 1/5th Lincolnshire Regiment.
He volunteered in February 1915 and, on completion of his training in the following year, was sent overseas. Serving on the Western Front, he took a conspicuous part in numerous important engagements, fought with distinction in the Battles of Vimy Ridge, the Somme, Ypres and Passchendaele, and was gassed on two occasions. Contracting trench fever in October 1918, he was invalided to Portsmouth, and on his discharge from hospital was demobilised in January 1919, holding the General Service and Victory Medals.
19, Princess Street, Northampton. Z2033.

WHEELER, P. E., Gunner, Royal Field Artillery.
He volunteered in September 1914, and in the following year was drafted to the Dardanelles, where he took part in the Landings at Cape Helles and Suvla Bay and in the Evacuation of the Gallipoli Peninsula. Later he was sent to France and, transferred to the Royal Engineers, saw much fighting on the Somme, at Ypres, Cambrai and in the Advance of 1918, being eventually demobilised in January 1919. He holds the 1914–15 Star, and the General Service and Victory Medals.
Woodbine Cottage, Kilsby, Northants. Z3551.

WHEELER, W., Rifleman, Rifle Brigade.
Mobilised with the Reserve at the declaration of war, he was immediately drafted to France. There he was in action in the Battle of and Retreat from Mons, and also at the Battles of Ypres (II. and III.), Loos and Arras. He was wounded in July 1917, and as a result sustained the loss of the sight of an eye, and was afterwards invalided home. Discharged in March 1919, he holds the Mons Star, and the General Service and Victory Medals.
67, Green Street, Northampton. Z2903.

WHISTON, P. S., Corporal, 6th Northants. Regt.
Having volunteered in May 1915, he was drafted in August of the same year to France, where he took part in important engagements in various sectors. He was in action at the Battles of the Somme, Arras, Ypres and Passchendaele, and also in the Retreat and Advance of 1918. He did consistently good work, and in March 1919, was demobilised, holding the 1914–15 Star, and the General Service and Victory Medals.
9, Cambridge Street, Northampton. Z2904.

WHITBREAD, P., Private, Northants. Regiment.
Mobilised in August 1914, he was immediately drafted to the Western Front, where he was in action in the Battle of and Retreat from Mons, and also at the Battles of Le Cateau (I.), La Bassée, Ypres, Neuve Chapelle and Loos. He was three times wounded and on each occasion was invalided home. Later, transferred to the Labour Corps, he was retained on important duties at Chatham until discharged in August 1917, holding the Mons Star, and the General Service and Victory Medals. 5, Adelaide Place, Northampton. Z2905.

WHITE, A., Driver, Royal Garrison Artillery.
Volunteering in October 1915, he proceeded to the Western Front six months later. In that theatre of war he served with his Battery in several important engagements, performing consistently good work until he was unfortunately killed at Arras on May 3rd, 1917, whilst employed conveying ammunition to the firing-line. He was entitled to the General Service and Victory Medals.
"Whilst we remember, the sacrifice is not in vain."
7, Shakespeare Road, Northampton. Z1797.

WHITE, A. C., Private, Manchester Regiment.
Having volunteered in March 1915, he was drafted overseas three months later. Whilst on the Western Front, he took part in many engagements, including the Battles of the Somme, Ypres, Cambrai and in the Retreat and Advance of 1918. He was slightly wounded in action and eventually demobilised in January 1919, holding the 1914–15 Star, and the General Service and Victory Medals.
11, Denton, Northants. Z3553.

WHITE, A. J., Sergeant, Royal Field Artillery.
Joining in February 1917, he was shortly afterwards drafted to France. Whilst on the Western Front, he played a prominent part in many important engagements, particularly in the Somme, Ypres and Cambrai sectors. He was also present during the Retreat and Advance of 1918, and, after the Armistice, served with the Army of Occupation in Germany. Returning home for demobilisation in August 1919, he holds the General Service and Victory Medals.
Chapel Yard, Wootton, Northants. Z2906/B.

WHITE, C., Private, 7th Worcestershire Regt.
He attested in 1915, and was called up for service in 1917, crossing later in the same year to France. After serving for a short period on the Western Front, he was transferred to Italy, where he took part with his Unit in numerous engagements on the Piave front. He returned home after the Armistice and was demobilised in February 1919, holding the General Service and Victory Medals.
49, Duke Street, Northampton. Z1798.

WHITE, E. T., Seaman, Mercantile Marine Reserve.
He joined in February 1918, and, after a period of training, was engaged at the Liverpool Docks on important duties, rendering valuable services until his demobilisation in January 1919. In the following April he re-enlisted for six years as a driver in the Royal Field Artillery, and proceeded to Mesopotamia, where he saw some fighting near Baghdad. In 1921 he was still serving there.
7, Alton Terrace, Far Cotton, Northampton. Z3552.

WHITE, G., Private, Machine Gun Corps.
He volunteered in August 1915, and served with the Northamptonshire Regiment until the following November, when he was discharged as under age. He rejoined in January 1917, was stationed in Grantham until February 1918, and was then sent to France. There he participated in severe fighting on various fronts, and was later invalided home suffering from dysentery. After a period of treatment at Croydon, he was eventually demobilised in January 1919, and holds the General Service and Victory Medals.
18, Arthur Street, Kingsthorpe Hollow, Northampton. Z1800.

WHITE, H., Private, 3rd Essex Regiment.
He was called up from the Reserve in August 1914 and, as he was physically unfit for transfer overseas, was retained on home service and employed on various duties at Shorncliffe. He rendered excellent service until he was admitted to hospital at Tottenham, and died there in March 1918 from consumption.
"His memory is cherished with pride."
2, Alpha Street, Northampton. Z1801.

WHITE, J. H., Private, 6th Northants. Regiment.
Volunteering in September 1914, he proceeded in the following year to France. There he took part with his Unit in several severe engagements, including the Somme, High Wood and Ypres, and in 1916 was wounded. He was wounded for the second time in 1917, and, evacuated to England, where he remained in hospital at Edmonton until he was invalided out of the Service in August 1917, holding the 1914–15 Star, and the General Service and Victory Medals.
9, Duke Street, Northampton. Z1799.

WHITE, M. O., Private, East Surrey Regiment.
Having joined in February 1917, he was quickly drafted overseas. During his short service on the Western Front, he was in action with his Unit during heavy fighting at Arras. He made the Supreme Sacrifice, being killed in action in September 1917, and was entitled to the General Service and Victory Medals.
"He died the noblest death a man may die,
Fighting for God and right and liberty."
Chapel Yard, Wootton, Northants. Z2906/A.

WHITE, P. T., Private, 2nd Leicestershire Regt.
Having enlisted in September 1908, he was stationed in India in August 1914, but, proceeding to France, fought at the Battles of La Bassée, Neuve Chapelle and Aubers Ridge with a Signal Section of the Royal Engineers. Transferred to Egypt in November 1915, he was sent to Mesopotamia in December and was in action at Samara, Kut, Baghdad and on the Tigris. After hospital treatment at Amara for dysentery and malaria, he proceeded to Palestine and served under General Allenby. He was transferred to the Reserve in February 1919, and holds the 1914 Star, and the General Service and Victory Medals.
4, Doddridge Square, Northampton. Z1038/A.

WHITE, T. W., Private, 1/5th Essex Regiment.
Two months after joining in January 1917, he was drafted to Egypt, whence he proceeded into Palestine. There he saw much severe fighting and took part in the three Battles of Gaza, the capture of Jerusalem and other engagements. Invalided home suffering from malaria, he was finally demobilised in October 1919, and holds the General Service and Victory Medals.
10, Muscott Street, St. James, Northampton. Z2536

WHITEHALL, W., Private, Royal Defence Corps.
He volunteered in March 1915 and, being too old for active service, was retained with the Royal Defence Corps at various home stations. There, engaged on duties of great importance, he rendered very valuable services until finally demobilised in 1919. 15, Althorp Road, Northampton. Z2537.

WHITEHEAD, R. W., Pte., 9th R. Sussex Regt.
He volunteered in February 1915, and was later drafted to France. Serving on the Western Front, he was in action during fierce fighting at Loos, where he was taken prisoner, and was held in captivity until after the conclusion of the war. Returning home for demobilisation in January 1919, he holds the 1914–15 Star, and the General Service and Victory Medals.
25, Chapel Lane, Daventry, Northants. Z2907.

WHITEMAN, E. R., Private, 1st Northamptonshire and Bedfordshire Regiments.
Volunteering in December 1915, he was discharged as medically unfit in the following September, and was then engaged on work of National importance at Messrs. Diver's, Ltd., Northampton. In July 1918 he re-enlisted and, proceeding to France two months later, saw heavy fighting during the closing stages of hostilities. After the Armistice, he served with the Army of Occupation in Germany, and was eventually demobilised in September 1919, holding the General Service and Victory Medals. 2, Adelaide Place, Northampton. Z3200.

WHITING, A. A., Leading Seaman, Royal Navy.
Already in the Navy in August 1914, he afterwards served in various vessels attached to the Grand Fleet in the North Sea on patrol and convoy duties, and also in the Dardanelles, where he was wounded. He was on board H.M.S. "Zulu" when she was severely damaged in the Straits of Dover in October 1916, and succeeded in saving the papers of H.M.S. "Albemarle" when her crew were forced to abandon her, and was for ten hours in the water. He also served in H.M.S. "Minotaur," and in 1921 was still at sea, holding the 1914–15 Star, and the General Service and Victory Medals.
The Green, Milton, Northants. Z2539.

WHITING, B., Pte., 22nd Northumberland Fusiliers.
He volunteered in November 1915, and in the following September proceeded to France. There he played a prominent part with his Unit in many important engagements, including the Battles of the Somme and Ypres. He was wounded at Wancourt, and, being invalided home, was for a considerable time in hospital at Canterbury and in Cambridge prior to being discharged in May 1919. He holds the General Service and Victory Medals.
44, Burleigh Road, Northampton. Z1802.

WHITING, C. A., Pte., Buffs (East Kent Regt.)
Having volunteered in June 1915, he completed a period of training and in the following year was drafted to the Western Front. Whilst in this theatre of war, he fought in many important engagements, particularly in the Somme and Arras sectors. He died gloriously on the Field of Battle in April 1917, and was entitled to the General Service and Victory Medals.
"His life for his Country, his soul to God."
Church Hill, Wootton, Northants. Z2485/B—Z2486/B.

WHITING, F. T., Sergeant, R.A.M.C.
He volunteered in August 1914, and in September of the following year was drafted to France, where he was engaged on important duties on an ambulance train in the Arras, Ypres, Cambrai, Somme and Amiens sectors. Transferred in 1917 to Italy, he was on similar duties on the Piave until his return home for demobilisation in February 1919. He holds the 1914–15 Star, and the General Service and Victory Medals.
78, Balmoral Road, Northampton. Z2538/B.

WHITING, G. T., Private, Essex Regiment.
Joining in January 1916, he proceeded later in the same year to France. Serving on the Western Front, he was in action in many engagements in the Somme, Ypres and Cambrai sectors, was wounded in November 1917, and as a result was invalided to England and eventually discharged as medically unfit for further service in February 1918. He holds the General Service and Victory Medals.
Church Hill, Wootton, Northants. Z2845/C—Z2846/C.

WHITING, H., Corporal, 1/4th Northants. Regt.
Mobilised in August 1914, he embarked in the following June for the Dardanelles, where he was in action at Suvla Bay and during the various operations until the Evacuation. He was then sent to Palestine and took part in further fighting at Gaza, Jerusalem and on the Jordan. Three times wounded during his service overseas, he was discharged on returning home in March 1919, and holds the 1914–15 Star, and the General Service and Victory Medals.
7, Shelley Street, Kingsley Park, Northampton. Z1096/B.

WHITING, H. E., (M.M.), L/Corporal, 7/11th Queen's (Royal West Surrey Regiment).
He joined in September 1917, and in April of the following year was drafted to the Western Front, where he saw much heavy fighting, taking part in the Battles of the Somme and Cambrai and many other engagements in the Retreat and Advance of 1918. He afterwards served with the Army of Occupation at Cologne, finally returning home for demobilisation in December 1919. He was awarded the Military Medal for conspicuous bravery in the Field near Le Cateau in September 1918, and holds also the General Service and Victory Medals.
78, Balmoral Road, Northampton. Z2538/A.

WHITING, T. W. E., Corporal, K.R.R.C.
Joining in April 1917, he was first engaged on important duties with his Unit in England. Proceeding to France in the following year, he took part in heavy fighting on the Somme, but, invalided to England in 1918 with pneumonia, underwent a period of hospital treatment. He was eventually demobilised in March 1919, holding the General Service and Victory Medals.
Bank, Hardingstone, Northants. Z2741/A.

WHITING, W. G., Private, 3rd Suffolk Regiment.
He volunteered in September 1915, but was retained on important duties at home until September 1917, when he was sent to France. There he was engaged on telephone duties at Ypres and Passchendaele, and was wounded whilst fighting at Béthune in June 1918. He was invalided home and subsequently demobilised in May 1919, holding the General Service and Victory Medals.
37, Vernon Street, Northampton. Z2315.

WHITLOCK, G., Sergeant, 1st Northamptonshire and Norfolk Regiments.
Enlisting in January 1912, he was in action throughout the Retreat from Mons and the Battles of the Marne, the Aisne and La Bassée. Wounded at Ypres in November, he was invalided home, but, in September 1915, was drafted to Mesopotamia and served with distinction at Sanna-i-yat (where he was wounded), Kut and Baghdad. In December 1917 he was transferred to Palestine and fought at Jerusalem, but, returning to Mesopotamia, was wounded at Hit and Mosul. He was finally in action on the North-West Frontier of India, and eventually received his discharge in May 1920, holding the Mons Star, the General Service and Victory Medals, and the India General Service Medal (with Clasp, Afghanistan, N.W. Frontier, 1919). "The Leyes," Roade, Northants. Z2316/A.

WHITLOCK, H., Sergeant, Northants. Regiment.
Having enlisted in June 1912, he fought through the Retreat from Mons, and was wounded during the Battle of the Aisne in September 1914. After hospital treatment at Paris and in England, he returned to France, served with distinction at Aubers Ridge, Ypres, Festubert, Loos, the Somme, Arras and Cambrai, and in the Retreat and Advance of 1918, being again wounded in 1916 and 1917. He was discharged in August 1919, and holds the Mons Star, and the General Service and Victory Medals. "The Leyes," Roade, Northants. Z2316/B.

WHITLOCK, S., Private, Northants. Regiment.
He volunteered in May 1915, and, whilst in training at Colchester, had a finger accidentally blown off, which rendered him unfit for active service. Stationed at Woolwich, he was engaged on duties of an important nature with the Labour Corps, and rendered valuable services until demobilised in February 1919. "The Leyes," Roade, Northampton. Z2316/C.

WHITWORTH, A., Private, 1st Northants. Regt.
Mobilised in August 1914, he was immediately drafted to the Western Front, where he took part in the fighting at Mons and also served through the Battles of the Marne, Neuve Chapelle and Festubert. Mortally wounded in action, he unfortunately died on August 18th, 1915, and was entitled to the Mons Star, and the General Service and Victory Medals.
"His life for his Country, his soul to God."
32, Bath Street, Northampton. Z1803.

WHITWORTH, F., Sergeant, 2nd Northants. Regt.
Mobilised in August 1914, he was retained on important duties in England until March 1916, and then proceeded to the Western Front. After taking a prominent part in many engagements on the Somme, he was severely wounded at Vermelles in August 1916, and was sent home. He was invalided from the Army in December 1918, and holds the General Service and Victory Medals.
45, Alliston Gardens, Northampton. Z1804.

WHITWORTH, F., Leading Seaman, Royal Navy.
Having enlisted in April 1903, he immediately proceeded to the North Sea on board H.M.S. "Monarch" in August 1914, and took part in the Battle of Heligoland Bight. He was also engaged on important patrol duties and in the operations off the Belgian Coast. Badly wounded in action during a cruiser engagement in November 1915, he was admitted to hospital in Southend, and was discharged as medically unfit in April 1916. He holds the 1914–15 Star, and the General Service and Victory Medals.
"The Fox and Hounds," High Street, Flore, Northants. Z2908.

WHITWORTH, W. A., Private, Royal Fusiliers.
After volunteering in September 1914, he underwent a period of training prior to being drafted to the Western Front early in 1916. There he took part in many important engagements, including the Battles of the Somme, Arras and Ypres, and, wounded in 1917, was invalided home. He returned to France and fought on the Somme, finally being demobilised in March 1919, holding the General Service and Victory Medals. 8, Johnson's Row, Northampton. Z1805.

WHITWORTH, W. E., Private, 6th Royal Fusiliers.
He joined in March 1916, and proceeded to France later in the same year. After taking part in several important engagements in various sectors, he was invalided home with badly frost-bitten feet, and on his recovery was transferred to the Royal Air Force. He then rendered valuable services with his Squadron at Winchester until his demobilisation in October 1919, and holds the General Service and Victory Medals.
16, Sharman Road, Northampton. Z2909.

WHYMAN, W. C. (M.M.), Gunner, R.G.A.
He volunteered in October 1915, and in the following March was drafted to the Western Front. There he served as a signaller and took part in several engagements, including the Battles of the Somme, Arras, Ypres, Passchendaele and Cambrai, and was wounded in 1917. He was awarded the Military Medal for gallantry and devotion to duty in the Field on November 6th, 1917. Demobilised in January 1919, he holds also the General Service and Victory Medals.
Denton, Northants. Z3554.

WICKHAM, G., Trooper, 1st Northants. Dragoons.
He volunteered in May 1915, and in the following year proceeded to the Western Front, where he took part in the Battles of the Somme and Ypres and many minor engagements. He was transferred in 1917 to Italy, and was there again in action on the Piave and the Asiago Plateaux. Demobilised on returning home in February 1919, he holds the General Service and Victory Medals. Gayton, Northants. Z2540.

WICKHAM, J., Gunner, Royal Field Artillery.
Having attested in 1915, he was called up for service in February 1917, and was sent to France in time to take part in heavy fighting during the Retreat and Advance of 1918. He was in action with his Battery at the Battles of the Somme (II.), the Marne (II.) and Ypres (IV.) and, after hostilities ceased, proceeded to Germany. He served with the Army of Occupation at Cologne until demobilised in September 1919, and holds the General Service and Victory Medals.
16, York Place, Weston Street, Northampton. Z2910.

WIGGINS, A., Sapper, Royal Engineers.
Shortly after joining in March 1916, he proceeded to France, where he was engaged on bridge-building and other important duties in various sectors. He was present at the Battles of the Somme, Arras, Ypres, Passchendaele and Cambrai and minor engagements, and was wounded at Ypres in August 1917. Demobilised in February 1919, he holds the General Service and Victory Medals.
21, St. Mary's Street, Northampton. Z1018/E—Z1019/E.

WIGGINS, A. J., Private, 1st Northants. Regiment.
He enlisted in May 1918, and four months later was drafted to the Western Front. Whilst in this theatre of war, he took part in several engagements in the Cambrai sector, and was badly wounded in action. As a result, he was invalided home and eventually discharged in February 1920, holding the General Service and Victory Medals.
Weston Favell, Northampton. Z3555.

WIGGINS, C., Private, Labour Corps.
He joined in April 1916 and, after completing a period of training, was retained on duties of great importance at various stations. Owing to ill-health, he was not successful in obtaining his transfer to a theatre of war, and in December 1918 was discharged as medically unfit for further service.
21, St. Mary's Street, Northampton. Z1018/B—Z1019/B.

WIGGINS, H. S., Rifleman, 15th London Regiment.
Joining the Civil Service Rifles in February 1917, he was drafted to France in December after being transferred to the Machine Gun Corps. Whilst on the Western Front, he saw heavy fighting at Arras and during the Retreat. He was gassed in March 1918, and two months later was invalided home with trench fever. He holds the General Service and Victory Medals, and was demobilised in February 1919.
15, Symington Street, Northampton. Z2911.

WIGGINS, J., Private, 1st Northants. Regiment.
He volunteered in May 1915, and in July of the following year was sent to the Western Front, where he saw severe fighting in various sectors. He took part in the Battles of the Somme, Arras, Ypres, Passchendaele, Cambrai and Amiens and minor engagements, and was wounded in October 1918. He was demobilised in May 1919, and holds the General Service and Victory Medals.
21, St. Mary's Street, Northampton. Z1018/A—Z1019/A.

WIGGINS, J., Private (Signaller), 1st Northants. Regiment.
He volunteered in May 1915, and, in February of the following year, was drafted to the Western Front. Whilst in this theatre of war, he took part in many engagements, including the Battles of Albert, the Somme, Arras, Vimy Ridge, Ypres and Cambrai, and was wounded in 1918. He afterwards served with the Army of Occupation at Cologne until his demobilisation in June 1919, and holds the General Service and Victory Medals.
21, St. Mary's Street, Northampton. Z1018/D—Z1019/D.

WIGGINS, R., Private, Bedfordshire Regiment.
He joined in September 1918, and, after his training, was engaged on important duties at various stations. He was unable to obtain his transfer to a theatre of war on account of his youth, but in February 1919 was sent with the Army of Occupation to Germany. There he served at Cologne until his return home for demobilisation in March 1920.
21, St. Mary's Street, Northampton. Z1018/C—Z1019/C.

WIGGINS, R., Gunner (Signaller), R.G.A.
He joined in 1917, but was retained in England until October of the following year, when he was drafted to the Western Front. There he took part in engagements at Lille, the Somme and many other places until the cessation of hostilities, finally being demobilised in March 1919. He holds the General Service and Victory Medals.
2, Liz Street, Northampton. Z1806.

WILBY, J. F., Private, 7th Northants. Regiment.
Three months after joining in August 1916, he proceeded to the Western Front, where he saw severe fighting in various sectors. After taking part in several engagements, he was wounded in action in November 1916 and, admitted to hospital at Glasgow, was afterwards retained in England. He was demobilised in November 1919, and holds the General Service and Victory Medals. 74, Baker Street, Northampton. Z1807.

WILCOX, F. J., L/Corporal, 1st Northants. Regt.
A Reservist, he was called to the Colours in August 1914, and, early in the following year, was sent to the Western Front, where he took part in the Battle of Ypres and minor engagements. He was reported missing, and is believed to have been killed in action at Aubers Ridge in May 1915. He was entitled to the 1914–15 Star, and the General Service and Victory Medals.
"His memory is cherished with pride."
15, Stanley Street, Northampton. Z1159/B.

WILCOX, H. R., Private, 2nd Northants. Regt.
He volunteered in November 1914 and, after a short period of training, proceeded to the Western Front, where he saw much severe fighting in the Ypres sector. He was unfortunately reported missing, and is believed to have been killed in action at Aubers Ridge on May 9th, 1915. He was entitled to the 1914–15 Star, and the General Service and Victory Medals.
"He nobly fell that we might live."
15, Stanley Street, Northampton. Z1159/A.

WILCOX, J., Gunner, Royal Marine Artillery.
He volunteered in September 1914 and, on completion of a period of training in the following year, was drafted to German East Africa, where he took part in important operations at various places. He unhappily died of fever on March 27th, 1917, and was entitled to the 1914–15 Star, and the General Service and Victory Medals.
"Steals on the ear the distant triumph song."
58, Regent Street, Northampton. Z1226/C.

WILCOX, T. E., Gunner, Royal Marine Artillery.
After volunteering in September 1914, he underwent a period of training at Portsmouth and Scapa Flow before being drafted to France in April 1918. There he took part in the Battles of the Somme, Arras, Ypres and Cambrai and other engagements in various sectors. He was demobilised in March 1919, and holds the General Service and Victory Medals.
58, Regent Street, Northampton. Z1226/B.

WILCOX, W., Private, 2nd Northants. Regiment.
He volunteered in October 1914, and seven months later proceeded to the Western Front. There he took part in many important engagements, including the Battles of Ypres, Loos, Albert, the Somme, Arras, Passchendaele and Cambrai, fought also in the Retreat and Advance of 1918, and was wounded at Ypres in August 1917. He was demobilised in March 1919, and holds the 1914–15 Star, and the General Service and Victory Medals.
58, Regent Street, Northampton. Z1226/A.

WILKES, C. W., Staff-Sergeant, R.A.O.C.
He volunteered in September 1914, and was sent to France in the following year. During his service on the Western Front, he did excellent work as an Armourer Staff-Sergeant in various parts of the line, and was wounded and gassed. Returning to England in March 1920, he was then demobilised, and holds the General Service and Victory Medals.
23, New Street, Weedon, Northants. Z2912.

WILKINS, A. M., Private, 10th Sherwood Foresters.
Joining in January 1917, he was trained at Chatham, and two months later was drafted overseas. During his service in France, he was engaged in severe fighting at the Battles of Arras, Vimy Ridge and Ypres, but was gassed in the last-named engagement, and invalided home. Subsequently he was discharged as medically unfit for further service in July 1917, and holds the General Service and Victory Medals.
33, Roseholme Road, Northampton. Z2317.

WILKINS, F. G., Private, 51st Bedfordshire Regt.
He joined in April 1918 and, after a period of training, was retained on important duties at various stations. Owing to the early cessation of hostilities, he was unable to obtain his transfer to a theatre of war, but in March 1919 was sent to Germany. There he served with the Army of Occupation near Cologne until his return home for demobilisation in October 1919. 18, Monk's Pond Street, Northampton. Z1610/B.

WILKINS, H., Private, 7th Royal Fusiliers.
He joined in December 1917, and, in July of the following year, was drafted to the Western Front, where he took part in the Battle of Amiens and minor engagements. He died gloriously on the Field of Battle at Bapaume on August 21st, 1918, after only five weeks' active service. He was entitled to the General Service and Victory Medals.
"The path of duty was the way to glory."
2 House, 2 Court, Chalk Lane, Northampton. Z1809/B.

WILKINS, J. M., Aircraftsman, Royal Air Force.
He joined in August 1918, and, after completing a term of training, served at various stations, where he was engaged on duties of great importance. Owing to ill-health, he was unable to obtain his transfer overseas, but, nevertheless, rendered valuable services with his Squadron until February 1919, when he was demobilised.
2 House, 2 Court, Chalk Lane, Northampton. Z1809/A.

WILKINS, J. W., Private, R.A.M.C.
Four months after volunteering in October 1915, he was drafted to the Western Front, where he served with the 35th Field Ambulance in various sectors. He was present at the Battles of the Somme, Vimy Ridge, Messines, Ypres and Cambrai, and other engagements, and was finally demobilised on returning home in July 1919. He holds the General Service and Victory Medals.
2 House, 2 Court, Chalk Lane, Northampton. Z1809/D.

WILKINS, W. T., Pte., 2/8th Worcestershire Regt.
He volunteered in December 1915 in the Royal Sussex Regiment, but, after six months' training, was invalided from the Army. He re-enlisted, however, in December 1917, and in the following month proceeded to France, where he saw severe fighting at Cambrai, and was wounded at La Bassée in May 1918, and invalided home. He had served with the Gloucestershire and Hampshire Regiments and the Labour Corps, but in June 1919 was sent with the Worcestershire Regiment to Egypt, where he was still serving in 1921. He holds the General Service and Victory Medals.
2 House, 2 Court, Chalk Lane, Northampton. Z1809/C.

WILLARS, J. T., Private, 1/4th Northants. Regt.
He volunteered in June 1915, and in February of the following year was drafted to Egypt, whence he proceeded later into Palestine. There he took part in many important engagements, including the three Battles of Gaza, and finally returned to England for demobilisation in July 1919. He holds the General Service and Victory Medals.
66, Lower Adelaide Street, Northampton. Z1217/A.

WILLETT, E. A., Corporal, 2nd Bedfordshire Regt.
He volunteered in January 1916, and in the following December was drafted to the Western Front, where he was in action at the Battle of Arras. He also took part in many engagements in the Ypres sector until wounded and taken prisoner at Ham in March 1918. After his release from captivity, he returned to England and was demobilised in September 1919, holding the General Service and Victory Medals.
62, Manfield Road, Northampton. Z2318/B.

WILLETT, R. E., Pte., 8th Q. (R. W. Surrey Regt.)
Joining in July 1917, he was ordered overseas in the following April. Whilst on the Western Front he was in action at the Battles of the Somme, Bapaume, the Scarpe, Havrincourt and Le Cateau, and was present during the entry into Mons. After the Armistice, he advanced with the Army of Occupation into Germany, where he served until demobilised in October 1919. He holds the General Service and Victory Medals.
62, Manfield Road, Northampton. Z2318/A.

WILLFORD, A. E., Private, 1/4th Northants Regt.
He joined the Northamptonshire Regiment in September 1917, and in July of the following year was drafted to France with the Essex Yeomanry (Dragoons), and there, transferred to the Essex Regiment, fought in various sectors. After taking part in several engagements, he was wounded at Achiet-le-Grand, and invalided home. He was finally demobilised in February 1919, and holds the General Service and Victory Medals.
81, Cambridge Street, Northampton. Z1810/B.

WILLFORD, G., Private, 6th Lancashire Fusiliers.
Called up from the Reserve in August 1914, he proceeded to Gallipoli 12 months later, and there saw much fighting at Suvla Bay. He afterwards served in Egypt, but in May 1916 was sent home and discharged, time-expired. Re-enlisting in February 1917, he was drafted to France, and, after being wounded in June of that year and at Ypres in October, he was taken prisoner near Amiens in March 1918, and held in captivity until the cessation of hostilities. Demobilised in March 1919, he holds the 1914–15 Star, and the General Service and Victory Medals. 14, Norfolk Street, Northampton. Z1811.

WILLFORD, J. R., Private, 6th Bedfordshire Regt.
Four months after joining in August 1916, he was sent to the Western Front, where he took part in many important engagements in the Ancre sector. He made the Supreme Sacrifice, falling in action at Arras on May 22nd, 1917, and was entitled to the General Service and Victory Medals.
"He died the noblest death a man may die,
Fighting for God and right and liberty."
81, Cambridge Street, Northampton. Z1810/A.

WILLIAMS, A., Corporal, Royal Engineers.
He volunteered in September 1915, and three months later proceeded to Egypt, serving at Alexandria until March 1916, when he was drafted to Salonika. There he did valuable work as a despatch rider on the Doiran, the Struma, the Vardar and Monastir fronts until the cessation of hostilities. He was demobilised on his return to England in May 1919, and holds the 1914–15 Star, and the General Service and Victory Medals.
12, Vernon Terrace, Northampton. Z2319.

WILLIAMS, A. I., Private, South Wales Borderers.
He enlisted in February 1917, and was quickly drafted to the Western Front, but after only a short period of active service, during which time he took part in heavy fighting, he laid down his life for King and Country at Pilkem Ridge in July of the same year. He was entitled to the General Service and Victory Medals.
"His name liveth for evermore."
18, New Street, Weedon, Northants. Z2914/B.

WILLIAMS, A. O., Private, 3/4th and 1st Northamptonshire Regiment.
Volunteering in October 1915, he completed his training and shortly afterwards crossed to France. On that front he fought in many engagements, and was twice wounded in action at the Dunes. In July 1917 he was taken prisoner and held in captivity in Germany for 18 months. On his return home, he was discharged as unfit for further service in March 1919, and holds the General Service and Victory Medals.
13, Turner Street, Northampton. Z2034.

WILLIAMS, C., Corporal, South Wales Borderers.
When war was declared in August 1914 he volunteered, and was engaged on the important work of training recruits at various home stations. He was not successful in securing a transfer to a theatre of war, and, after rendering valuable services, was discharged in February 1915.
105, St. Edmund's Road, Northampton. Z2320.

WILLIAMS, C., Sergeant, 1st Northants. Regt.
He volunteered in August 1914, and three months later was drafted to France, where he played a prominent part in the Battles of Ypres, Neuve Chapelle, Hill 60, Festubert, Loos and Vimy Ridge. He made the Supreme Sacrifice, being killed in action on the Somme in July 1916, and was entitled to the 1914 Star, and the General Service and Victory Medals.
"His life for his Country, his soul to God."
Church Street, Brixworth, Northants. Z3202/A.

WILLIAMS, C. G., Q.M.S., Queen's (Royal West Surrey Regiment).
Shortly after joining in February 1917, he was drafted to the Western Front, where he saw severe fighting in various sectors. He took a prominent part in many important engagements in this theatre of war, and was wounded in action. He finally returned home for demobilisation in October 1919, and holds the General Service and Victory Medals.
60, Overstone Road, Northampton. Z1814.

WILLIAMS, C. H., 1st Air Mechanic, R.A.F.
He joined in June 1917, and, after a period of training, was engaged with the 116th Squadron at various stations on important duties which demanded a high degree of technical skill. He was not successful in obtaining a transfer overseas, but rendered valuable services until his demobilisation in March 1919.
59, Stanley Street, Northampton. Z1812.

WILLIAMS, E. A., Sapper, Royal Engineers.
He joined in September 1916, and in April of the following year embarked for the Western Front. There he was actively engaged in the Battles of Arras, Bullecourt and Ypres, and was severely wounded at Passchendaele in 1916. He was invalided to England, and, after his discharge from hospital, was engaged on important duties in Ireland until demobilised in October 1919, holding the General Service and Victory Medals.
29, Ashburnham Road, Northampton. Z2321.

WILLIAMS, F. A., Private, 6th Buffs (East Kent Regiment).
Two months after joining in April 1917, he was drafted to the Western Front, where he took part in important engagements in various sectors. He died gloriously on the Field of Battle near Albert on April 5th, 1918, and was entitled to the General Service and Victory Medals.
"He died the noblest death a man may die,
Fighting for God and right and liberty."
1, Orchard Street, Northampton. Z2360/A.

WILLIAMS, F. E., Private, Northants. Regiment.
Volunteering in August 1915, he was drafted overseas later in the same year. Whilst on the Western Front, he took part in many engagements, including those in the Somme, Cambrai and Ypres sectors, and was wounded in action, which resulted in his being invalided home. He was discharged in June 1918 as medically unfit for further service, and holds the 1914–15 Star, and the General Service and Victory Medals.
22, Regent Street, Northampton. Z1070/B.

WILLIAMS, G., Private, Cambridgeshire Regt.
He enlisted in March 1916, and, after a period of training, was engaged at various stations on important duties with his Unit. He was not successful in obtaining a transfer overseas, but rendered valuable services whilst engaged on important agricultural duties until his demobilisation in June 1919.
Silver Street, Brixworth, Northants. Z3202 /B.

WILLIAMS, G. H., Private, 4th Northumberland Fusiliers.
He joined in May 1917 at the age of 18 years, and in July was sent to France. Whilst in this theatre of war, he took part in the Battles of Ypres (III.), Passchendaele and Cambrai, but was badly wounded in action at Monchy in November of the same year. Invalided home, he spent some time in hospital before being discharged as medically unfit in May 1919, holding the General Service and Victory Medals.
13, St. James' Street, Northampton. Z2913.

WILLIAMS, H., Corporal, Royal Welch Fusiliers.
Volunteering in September 1914, he was engaged on duties of an important nature at various home stations until June 1917, when he was ordered to France. On that front he took part in many engagements, including the Battles of Bullecourt and Cambrai, but was gassed and sustained severe shell-shock, and in consequence was invalided out of the Army in February 1918. He holds the General Service and Victory Medals.
120, Upper Thrift Street, Northampton. Z2322.

WILLIAMS, H., Gunner, Royal Field Artillery.
He volunteered at the commencement of hostilities, and, proceeding to France shortly afterwards, fought in the Retreat from Mons and the first Battle of Ypres. He was also engaged in heavy fighting in several other engagements until invalided home owing to shell-shock and gas-poisoning sustained at Passchendaele. On recovery he was employed on special duties at various depôts, and was demobilised in February 1919. He holds the Mons Star, and the General Service and Victory Medals.
4, Gardeners' Cottages, Weedon, Northants. Z3011 /B.

WILLIAMS, J. E., Private, Canadian M.G.C.
Having volunteered in September 1914, he was quickly drafted to France. Whilst on the Western Front he saw much heavy fighting in various sectors, including those of St. Quentin, Ypres, Loos, Le Cateau, Landrecies and Mons, being wounded in action. As a result he was invalided home and eventually demobilised in April 1919, holding the 1914–15 Star, and the General Service and Victory Medals.
25, Hood Street, Northampton. Z1813.

WILLIAMS, J. H., Private, 2nd Bedfordshire Regt.
He joined in March 1918, and, after a period of training, was engaged at various stations on important duties with his Unit. Owing to the early cessation of hostilities, he was unable to proceed overseas before the Armistice, but rendered valuable services. In 1921 he was serving in India.
22, Regent Street, Northampton. Z1070 /A.

WILLIAMS, R., Private, 2nd Norfolk Regiment.
He joined in 1917, and, after a period of training at Felixstowe, was drafted overseas. During his service on the Western Front, he took part in much severe fighting, but was invalided home with trench fever. On his recovery, he served with the Cambridgeshire Regiment until his demobilisation in March 1919, and holds the General Service and Victory Medals.
18, New Street, Weedon, Northants. Z2914 /A.

WILLIAMS, V., Air Mechanic, Royal Air Force.
Prior to joining the Royal Air Force in 1917, he was employed on work of National importance, having been rejected for military service on three occasions owing to ill-health. Whilst with the Colours he was engaged on duties of a highly technical nature, and fulfilled them in a very able manner. After two years' valuable service he was demobilised in 1919.
17, Collins Street, Northampton. Z2035.

WILLIAMSON, L., Driver, Royal Field Artillery.
Volunteering in October 1915, he was sent to France four months later, and was first engaged on important duties on the 16th Divisional Staff. Later, however, he was in action at Ploegsteert and the Battles of Ypres (III.), the Somme (II.), and Ypres (IV.), where he was badly wounded in October 1918. After hospital treatment in Bradford, he was demobilised in February 1919, holding the General Service and Victory Medals.
28, Raymond Road, St. James, Northampton. Z2915.

WILLIAMSON, S. H., 2nd London Regiment (Royal Fusiliers).
He joined in February 1916, and, on completion of his training, was drafted overseas in December 1917. During his service on the Western Front, he was engaged on duties of a special nature, but was knocked down by a motor lorry and unfortunately succumbed to his injuries on October 25th, 1919. He was entitled to the General Service and Victory Medals.
"His memory is cherished with pride."
19, Collingwood Road, Northampton. Z2323.

WILLINGHAM, H., Cpl., 2/1st Ox. & Bucks. L.I.
Volunteering in October 1915, he was sent to France in the following year, and played a prominent part in the Battles of the Somme, Arras and Ypres. Badly wounded in action in August 1917, he was invalided home, and, on his recovery, rendered valuable services whilst engaged on important clerical duties in Northumberland. He holds the General Service and Victory Medals, and was demobilised in April 1919. Barnwell's Buildings, Hanslope, Bucks. Z2916

WILLIS, F., Private, Suffolk Regiment.
He joined in May 1916, and, drafted to the Western Front in the following April, took part in heavy fighting on the Somme and in the Ypres salient. He was severely wounded at Albert, and had his left leg amputated as a result of his injuries. Evacuated to England, he received hospital treatment at Leeds, and was eventually discharged as physically unfit in March 1919. He holds the General Service and Victory Medals.
17, Pike Row, Weston Favell, Northampton. Z3556 /A.

WILLIS, F. T., Private, Oxford. & Bucks. L.I.
He volunteered in November 1915, and two months later was drafted to the Western Front, but, after taking part in much severe fighting, was unfortunately killed in action on July 19th, 1916, shortly after the opening of the Somme Offensive. He was entitled to the General Service and Victory Medals.
"A costly sacrifice upon the altar of freedom."
High Street, Hanslope, Bucks. Z2917.

WILLIS, T., Corporal, Manchester Regiment.
Volunteering in August 1914, he was retained on home defence duties until 1917, when he was sent to Italy. In that theatre of war he took part in various operations, doing good work in the firing-line in heavy fighting on the Asiago Plateau, and was wounded. Returning to England on the conclusion of hostilities, he was demobilised in August 1919, and holds the General Service and Victory Medals.
17, Pike Row, Weston Favell, Northampton. Z3556 /B.

WILLMORE, D. V., Rifleman, K.R.R.C.
On attaining military age, he joined the Army in June 1918, but was unable to secure his transfer overseas before the cessation of hostilities. In March 1919 he proceeded to Germany, and did consistently good work with the Army of Occupation until sent to England for demobilisation in February 1920.
153, Adnitt Road, Northampton. Z2324.

WILLOUGHBY, H., Pte., 2nd Middlesex Regt.
He joined in March 1917, and two months later was drafted overseas. Whilst on the Western Front he took part in much fighting in the Ypres, Bullecourt, Cambrai and the Somme sectors. He was wounded and taken prisoner of war in July 1917, being held in captivity in Germany, and was forced to work in the salt mines. Repatriated after the Armistice, he was demobilised in April 1919, and holds the General Service and Victory Medals.
4, Military Road, Northampton. Z1410 /B.

WILLS, A. E., Sergeant, Cheshire Regiment.
Already serving in India in August 1914, he proceeded to France in the following year, and there took part in the Battle of Hill 60, and was wounded at Ypres in May 1915. Invalided home, he was later drafted to Gallipoli, whence he was sent, on the Evacuation, to Egypt, where he served on the Suez Canal. He was afterwards transferred to Mesopotamia, and, after serving at the Relief of Kut, was wounded at the capture of Baghdad. Invalided to India, he later returned to Mesopotamia, but proceeded to the Afghan Frontier in 1919. He was transferred to the Reserve in November 1920, and holds the 1914–15 Star, the General Service and Victory Medals, and the India General Service Medal (with Clasp, Afghanistan, N.W. Frontier, 1919). 81, Duke Street, Northampton. Z1815.

WILLS, A. H., Gunner, Royal Garrison Artillery.
He joined in May 1916, and in the following year was drafted to the Western Front. In this theatre of war he took part in several important engagements in the Ypres, Cambrai and Lens sectors. He was badly gassed during the Retreat in 1918, and consequently invalided home. Demobilised in April 1919, he holds the General Service and Victory Medals.
15, Upper Priory Street, Northampton. Z1816.

WILLS, A. L., Private, 3rd Northants. Regiment.
Joining in June 1918, he completed his training, and was engaged on important duties with his Battalion at Sheerness, where he did excellent work. Contracting influenza, he was removed to hospital, but unfortunately died in November 1918.
"His memory is cherished with pride."
Newland, Brixworth, Northants. Z3203.

WILLS, C., Guardsman, 2nd Grenadier Guards.
Mobilised in August 1914, he was immediately drafted to the Western Front, where he fought in the Retreat from Mons, and also took part in the Battles of the Marne, the Aisne, La Bassée, Ypres and Neuve Chapelle. He fell fighting at Ypres on May 19th, 1915, and was entitled to the Mons Star, and the General Service and Victory Medals.
"A costly sacrifice upon the altar of freedom."
13, Marlborough Road, Northampton. Z2542 /A.

WILLS, J., Private, 6th Northants. Regiment.
Volunteering in January 1915, he was sent to the Western Front on completion of his training in the following July, and there saw severe fighting in various sectors. He made the Supreme Sacrifice, falling in action at Trônes Wood on July 14th, 1916, and was entitled to the 1914–15 Star, and the General Service and Victory Medals.
"His memory is cherished with pride."
26, Stanley Road, Northampton. Z2541.

WILLS, T., Sergeant, 2/4th Northants. Regiment.
He volunteered in September 1914 and, after his training, was retained on important duties in England until 1918, when he was drafted to France. There, after taking a prominent part in many engagements, he was severely wounded in August of that year, and admitted to hospital at Manchester. He was invalided from the Army in January 1920, and holds the General Service and Victory Medals.
13, Marlborough Road, Northampton. Z2542/B.

WILMER, A., Sergeant, 2nd Northants. Regiment.
He joined the Army in January 1906, and, when war broke out in August 1914, was already serving in Egypt, but was quickly transferred to France. There he played a prominent part during much heavy fighting in various sectors, and was badly wounded at Ypres. He received his discharge in March 1919, and holds the 1914 Star, and the General Service and Victory Medals.
11, 3rd Square, Nelson Street, Northampton. Z1817.

WILSON, A., Private, 1/3rd London Regiment (Royal Fusiliers).
He joined the Queen's (Royal West Surrey Regiment) in February 1917, but was later transferred to the London Regiment and drafted overseas in January 1918. During his service on the Western Front he took part in engagements at Albert, Armentières and the Somme, and was wounded in action in August 1918. Returning to the firing-line on his recovery, he was in action until hostilities ceased, and was demobilised in May 1919, holding the General Service and Victory Medals.
48, Wellington Street, Northampton. Z2036.

WILSON, C., Private, 8th Bedfordshire Regiment.
Having volunteered in August 1915, he was drafted overseas in the following year. During his service in France, he was engaged on important duties and saw much heavy fighting on the Somme, where he was badly wounded in 1916. Invalided home, he was eventually discharged in March 1919 as medically unfit for further service. He holds the General Service and Victory Medals.
89, Scarletwell Street, Northampton. Z1479/C.

WILSON, E. G., Private, 9th Manchester Regiment.
Joining in May 1916, he was sent to France after 15 months in England, and saw heavy fighting at Arras, Vimy Ridge, Ypres, Bullecourt, Passchendaele, Havrincourt, Cambrai, the Sambre and Vermelles, and was wounded in action. After hostilities ceased, he re-enlisted for a further period in the 2/1st East Lancashire Regiment, and in 1920 was stationed in Ireland. He holds the General Service and Victory Medals.
5, Foundry Street, Northampton. Z2563/A.

WILSON, E. R., Private, R.A.M.C.
He joined in November 1917, and early in the following year was drafted to Salonika. In this seat of operations he served as a stretcher-bearer, and took part in engagements on the Vardar front. He rendered valuable services, and was demobilised in March 1919. He holds the General Service and Victory Medals.
9, Johnson's Row, Northampton. Z1818/A.

WILSON, E. R. (sen.), Mechanic, R.A.F.
He volunteered in January 1915, and, after a period of training, was engaged at various stations on duties which demanded a high degree of technical skill. Owing to his being over age, he was unable to obtain a transfer overseas, but rendered valuable services until his demobilisation in March 1919.
9, Johnson's Row, Northampton. Z1818/B.

WILSON, H., Gunner, Royal Garrison Artillery.
Joining in 1916, he proceeded to France in the following year and was in action with his Battery at the Battles of Arras, Messines, Ypres, Cambrai, the Somme (II.) and throughout the Retreat and Advance of 1918. After hostilities ceased, he served at Cologne with the Army of Occupation until he was demobilised in September 1919, holding the General Service and Victory Medals.
53, Devonshire Street, Northampton. Z2918.

WILSON, J., Sergeant, Royal Naval Division.
He volunteered in December 1914, and in the following May proceeded to Gallipoli with the Anson Battalion, Royal Naval Division. He served with distinction at Suvla Bay and in heavy fighting until the Evacuation of the Peninsula. Transferred to France, he was in action at the Battles of the Somme (I.), Arras, Vimy Ridge, Ypres, Cambrai, the Somme (II.) and in the Retreat and Advance of 1918. He was demobilised in June 1919, and holds the 1914–15 Star, and the General Service and Victory Medals.
The Forge, Hardingstone, Northants. Z2919.

WILSON, W. (M.M.), Corporal, 3rd Northants. Regt.
A Reservist, he was mobilised and sent to France when war broke out and, taking part in the Retreat from Mons, was wounded. Rejoining his Unit after treatment in England, he did excellent work at Loos and in several subsequent battles, including those of the German Offensive and the subsequent Allied Advance, and was awarded the Military Medal in August 1918 for conspicuous gallantry in the Field. He also holds the Mons Star, and the General Service and Victory Medals, and was discharged in February 1919, after serving with the Army of Occupation in Germany.
Church Street, Brixworth, Northants. Z3204.

WINGROVE, G., Private, Buffs (East Kent Regt.)
Having joined in March 1917, he proceeded overseas two months later. Whilst on the Western Front, he took part in many engagements, including the Battles of Ypres, Cambrai and the Somme (II.), where he was taken prisoner. He was held in captivity in Germany for several months, but, after the Armistice, was repatriated and returned home. Demobilised in November 1919, he holds the General Service and Victory Medals. 2 House, 2 Block, Naseby St., Northampton. Z1819.

WINTERBONE, V. C., Sapper, Royal Engineers.
He joined in June 1918 on attaining military age, and was engaged on important duties with his Unit at various home stations. Owing to the early cessation of hostilities, he was not successful in obtaining a transfer overseas before the Armistice, but in March 1919 was sent to Germany, where he served with the Army of Occupation until demobilised in February 1920.
132, Ashburnham Road, Northampton. Z2325.

WISEMAN, B., Sergeant, 25th King's (Liverpool Regiment).
Mobilised from the Reserve on the outbreak of war, he completed his training, and was employed on home service duties until February 1918, when he crossed to the Western Front. There he took a prominent part in engagements in the Somme, Ypres and Cambrai sectors during the Retreat and Advance, and was mentioned in Sir Douglas Haig's Despatches for good work in the Field. He was demobilised in March 1919, and holds the General Service and Victory Medals.
Church View, Bugbrooke, Northants. Z3210/B.

WOOD, A., Sapper, Royal Engineers.
Having volunteered in November 1915, he underwent a period of training prior to his being drafted to France 12 months later. Whilst in this theatre of war, he took part in engagements at Arras, Ypres, Passchendaele and in the Retreat and Advance of 1918. After the Armistice, he proceeded to Germany with the Army of Occupation, and served there until his demobilisation in April 1919. He holds the General Service and Victory Medals. 15, Stenson Street, Northampton. Z2920.

WOOD, C. H., Private, King's (Liverpool Regt.)
He joined in May 1917, and later in the same year was drafted to Salonika, where he saw much fighting on the Vardar and Doiran fronts. In June 1918 he was transferred to France and took part in the Retreat and Advance of 1918, being wounded at Le Cateau. He was demobilised in December 1919, and holds the General Service and Victory Medals.
5, Military Road, Northampton. Z1820.

WOOD, G. W., 2nd Lieutenant, Royal Air Force.
He volunteered in the Northamptonshire Dragoons in 1914, and, after his training, proceeded to the Western Front, where he fought in the Battle of the Somme and minor engagements. Transferred in 1918 to Mesopotamia, he there took a prominent part in much severe fighting and contracted malaria. He was twice wounded whilst overseas and, granted a commission in the Royal Air Force, finally returned home for demobilisation in 1920. He holds the General Service and Victory Medals.
67, Adams Avenue, Northampton. Z2543.

WOODFORD, F., Private, R.A.M.C.
He volunteered in August 1915, and a year later embarked for France. Whilst in this theatre of war he was engaged on important duties with his Unit at various hospitals, and performed valuable work attending to the sick and wounded brought in from the forward areas. He returned to England for demobilisation in May 1919, and holds the General Service and Victory Medals. 23, Albion Place, Northampton. Z3205.

WOODHAMS, J. W., L/Corporal, 9th (Queen's Royal) Lancers.
Having previously served with the Colours, he re-enlisted in August 1914, and was retained on important duties in England and Ireland until May 1917. He then proceeded to France with the Military Police, and served at Calais and other stations until his return home in October 1918. Invalided from the Army in that month, he holds the General Service and Victory Medals.
4, Muscott Street, St. James, Northampton. Z2498/A.

WOODING, H., Private, Northamptonshire Regt.
Mobilised from the Reserve in August 1914, he underwent a period of training, but was later found to be medically unfit for transfer overseas. He was therefore retained on important duties with his Unit at various stations, and rendered excellent services until discharged in October 1916.
44, Lower Harding Street, Northampton. Z1821.

WOODWARD, H., Private, Machine Gun Corps.
Joining in November 1916, he proceeded to the Western Front in the following year and fought in the Battles of Arras, Ypres, Cambrai and the Somme. He also did good work with his Unit during the Retreat and Advance of 1918, and was gassed. After the close of hostilities, he advanced into Germany with the Army of Occupation and served at Cologne until demobilised in February 1919. He holds the General Service and Victory Medals. 42, Palmerston Road, Northampton. Z2037.

WOOLSTON, W. H., Private, National Reserve.
Engaged on work of National importance, his duties led to his exemption from military service. He joined the National Reserve, however, in November 1916, and, until demobilised in October 1919, did excellent work on guard and other duties carried out by that body during the war.
46, Southampton Road, Northampton. Z3557.

WOOTTON, A., Private, R.A.M.C.
Volunteering in August 1915, he underwent a period of training, and in the following year was drafted to France. Whilst in this theatre of war he served as a stretcher-bearer, and was present at many important engagements, including those at Albert, Arras and Ypres, before being invalided home. Returning to France, he served on the ambulance trains on important duties until November 1917. Evacuated to England, he underwent an operation, and was eventually demobilised in June 1919, holding the General Service and Victory Medals.
8, Harding Terrace, Northampton. Z1822.

WOOTTON, G. W., Corporal, 3rd Bedfordshire Regt.
He volunteered in January 1915, and in the following year was drafted to France, where he took part in many engagements, including the Battles of the Somme (I.), Ypres (III.) and Cambrai. He made the Supreme Sacrifice, being killed in action on the Somme in August 1918, and was entitled to the General Service and Victory Medals.
"A valiant Soldier, with undaunted heart he breasted life's last hill."
High Street, Hardingstone, Northants. Z2921/B.

WOOTTON, S., Private, R.A.S.C. (M.T.)
Called up from the Reserve in August 1914, he was quickly drafted to France, where he served with the Mechanical Transport and was engaged in conveying supplies to the forward areas. He was injured in an accident, which necessitated his being invalided home, and on his recovery he was sent to Ireland, but later returned to France. Discharged in March 1919, he holds the Mons Star, and the General Service and Victory Medals.
High Street, Hardingstone, Northants. Z2921/C.

WOOTTON, T., Private, 3rd Northants. Regiment.
He joined in June 1916, and later in the same year was drafted to the Western Front, where he took part in much heavy fighting on the Somme, and was wounded in action. Suffering from trench feet, he was invalided home to hospital, and unhappily died from blood poisoning in July 1917. He was entitled to the General Service and Victory Medals.
"His memory is cherished with pride."
High Street, Hardingstone, Northants. Z2921/A.

WOOTTON, W. J., Private, 4th Northants. Regt.
He volunteered in September 1914, and in the July following was drafted to the Dardanelles. In this seat of operations he took part in the heavy fighting at the Landing at Suvla Bay, and was badly wounded in action. As a result he was invalided home and finally discharged in June 1916 as medically unfit for further service. He holds the 1914–15 Star, and the General Service and Victory Medals.
High Street, Hardingstone, Northants. Z2922.

WRIGHT, G. E., Private, 3/5th Bedfordshire Regt.
Having volunteered in December 1915, he was drafted overseas in May 1917. Whilst on the Western Front, he took part in many engagements, including those in the Ypres, Dickebusch, Passchendaele and St. Quentin sectors, and was wounded. As a result he was invalided home, but returned to France in July 1918, and was again wounded a month later at Achiet-le-Petit. He was sent home and eventually discharged in January 1919, holding the General Service and Victory Medals.
Long Street, Hanslope, Bucks. Z2923.

WORTH, A. J., A.B., Royal Naval Division.
Joining in August 1917, he completed his training before being drafted to France. In the course of his service in this theatre of war, he took part in heavy fighting on the Albert and Somme fronts. He made the Supreme Sacrifice, being killed in action on May 18th, 1918, and was entitled to the General Service and Victory Medals.
"His life for his Country, his soul to God."
13, Arundel Street, Northampton. Z1823/A.

WORTH, F. F., Private, R.A.M.C.
Volunteering in October 1915, he completed a period of training and in the following year proceeded to France, where he did continuously good work as a stretcher-bearer. He was present during heavy fighting on the Somme and also at the Battles of Ypres, Passchendaele, Lens and Cambrai, and was wounded and gassed in 1917. Demobilised in January 1919, he holds the General Service and Victory Medals.
13, Arundel Street, Northampton. Z1823/B.

WORTH, J. G. A., Rifleman, Rifle Brigade.
Joining in August 1917, he received his training at Aldershot and Northampton, and in March 1918 embarked for France. On that front he fought in the Battle of the Somme and served in the Retreat and Advance of 1918, but was unhappily killed in action on August 24th, 1918. He was entitled to the General Service and Victory Medals.
"His life for his Country, his soul to God."
35, Wantage Road, Northampton. Z2198/B.

WORTH, W., C.S.M., 16th Worcestershire Regt.
Mobilised as soon as war was declared, he proceeded to France and fought in the Retreat from Mons and the Battles of Le Cateau and the Marne and other engagements. He was wounded at Ypres in November 1914, and, after treatment at Boulogne and Paignton, Devon, served as an Instructor and in conducting drafts to the Western Front. He was discharged in March 1919, and holds the Mons Star, and the General Service, Victory and Delhi Durbar Medals.
28, Henby Street, Far Cotton, Northampton. Z3558.

WRIGHT, A., Private, R.A.M.C.
Volunteering in April 1915, he underwent a period of training and proceeded to Egypt, where he served as a hospital orderly. He also did continuously good work as a stretcher-bearer in Palestine, and was present at many important engagements, particularly at the Battles of Gaza, Jaffa and the capture of Jerusalem. Demobilised in June 1919, he holds the 1914–15 Star, and the General Service and Victory Medals.
46, High Street, Kingsthorpe, Northants. Z1828/A.

WRIGHT, A. G., Private, 3rd Northants. Regt.
He volunteered in June 1915 and, drafted to Egypt in the following January, fought at Messa Matruh, Agayia, Sollum, Jifjaffa and other places. Sent to Salonika in June 1916, he served on various fronts in the Balkans, and returned to Egypt in 1917 to take part in the Advance through Palestine. He was in action in the three Battles of Gaza and in operations which led to the capture of Jerusalem. Demobilised in March 1919, he holds the General Service and Victory Medals.
Little Houghton, Northampton. Z3559.

WRIGHT, E., Private, Suffolk Regiment.
Joining in January 1917, he landed in France two months later. Whilst on the Western Front he was in action with his Unit at the Battle of Arras, where he was wounded in June 1917. As a result he was invalided to hospital at Brighton, and was eventually discharged as medically unfit for further service in August 1918, and holds the General Service and Victory Medals.
18, Orchard Street, Northampton. Z2544.

WRIGHT, E. (Miss), Worker, Land Army.
Joining in January 1917, she underwent a course of training and, for upwards of three years, was employed on farms at various places in England. Engaged in hay-making and baling, she rendered very valuable services throughout her period with the Land Army. 12, Mill Road, Northampton. Z3206/A.

WRIGHT, G., Pte., Queen's (R. W. Surrey Regt.)
Volunteering in October 1915, he completed his training, and in the following year was drafted to France. Whilst in this theatre of war, he took part in heavy fighting on the Somme, where he made the Supreme Sacrifice, being killed in action on September 15th, 1916. He was entitled to the General Service and Victory Medals.
"Whilst we remember, the sacrifice is not in vain."
2, Todds Lane, Northampton. Z1827.

WRIGHT, H., Bombardier, Royal Field Artillery.
Joining in April 1917, he underwent a period of training and was drafted overseas. During his service on the Western Front, he took part in the Battles of Arras, Vimy Ridge and Bullecourt. He died gloriously on the Field of Battle on April 29th, 1917, and was entitled to the General Service and Victory Medals.
"He nobly fell that we might live."
46, High Street, Kingsthorpe, Northampton. Z1828/B.

WRIGHT, H., Private, 2/19th London Regiment.
He volunteered in October 1915, and, embarking for France in June 1916, saw heavy fighting in the St. Eloi sector. Six months later he was transferred to Salonika, where he served on the Doiran and Vardar fronts. In May 1917 he was sent to Egypt, and subsequently to Palestine, where he was in action in important engagements at Gaza, Jerusalem and Jericho. Returning to England, he was demobilised in July 1919, and holds the General Service and Victory Medals.
32, Queen's Road, Northampton. Z2038/B.

WRIGHT, H., Private, 1st Northants. Regiment.
He joined in April 1916, and later in the same year was drafted to the scene of activities in France. There he fought in the Battles of the Somme and Vimy Ridge and other notable engagements, but was taken prisoner at Nieuport in 1917 and held in captivity for 18 months. When released, he returned to England, and was demobilised in August 1919, holding the General Service and Victory Medals.
76, Clarke Street, Northampton. Z2326.

WRIGHT, H., Private, Machine Gun Corps.
He joined in March 1917, and was sent overseas in the following December. Serving on the Western Front, he saw heavy fighting in the Ypres, Passchendaele and Cambrai sectors, during the Retreat and Advance of 1918, and in January 1919 embarked for Egypt, where he was employed on garrison duties until his return to England for demobilisation in April 1919. He holds the General Service and Victory Medals.
Church Street, Brixworth, Northants. Z3207.

WRIGHT, J., Private, Bedfordshire Regiment.
Having previously served in the South African war, he was mobilised in 1914, and quickly drafted to France. There he saw much severe fighting in the Retreat from Mons and many other engagements. In 1918 he was taken prisoner of war, and, whilst in captivity in Germany, suffered many privations. Repatriated after the Armistice, he returned home and was demobilised in 1919, holding the Queen's and King's South African Medals, the Mons Star, and the General Service and Victory Medals.
41, Alma Street, Northampton. Z2924.

WRIGHT, J., Sergeant, Suffolk Regiment.
Joining in October 1916, he sailed for Egypt in the following June, and did good work with the forces operating in Palestine, where he contracted malaria. In that theatre of war he was in action in many engagements, notably the three Battles of Gaza, and performed consistently good work until the conclusion of hostilities. Demobilised on returning to England in October 1919, he holds the General Service and Victory Medals.
12, Mill Road, Northampton. Z3206/B.

WRIGHT, J. P., Gunner, Royal Garrison Artillery.
He joined in March 1918, and, landing in France two months later, took part in operations in the latter stages of the German Offensive. His Battery was also engaged in the final Allied Advance, in the course of which he fought in the Battles of Albert, Amiens, Cambrai, Ypres and Le Cateau. He holds the General Service and Victory Medals, and was demobilised in February 1919.
Camp Hill, Bugbrooke, Northants. Z3026/A.

WRIGHT, J. W., Armourer Staff-Sergt., R.A.O.C.
Having volunteered in 1915, he embarked for the Western Front later in the same year. Whilst in France he rendered valuable services supervising the repair of guns which had been damaged in action, and was stationed at Calais. He carried out his responsible duties in a very efficient manner, and was demobilised in 1919, holding the 1914–15 Star, and the General Service and Victory Medals.
3, Cranstown Street, Northampton. Z1824.

WRIGHT, J. W., Private, West Yorkshire Regt.
Volunteering in November 1915, he proceeded overseas in August of the following year. Whilst serving on the Western Front, he was engaged in heavy fighting on the Somme, and was so severely wounded in November 1916 as to necessitate the amputation of his right leg. He was discharged as medically unfit for further service in February 1918, holding the General Service and Victory Medals.
50, Marlborough Road, Northampton. Z2545.

WRIGHT, O. W., Gunner, R.G.A.
Joining in March 1916, he proceeded to the Western Front in the following July, and was almost immediately in action in the Somme Offensive. He was also engaged in fierce fighting in the Battles of Ypres, Cambrai and the Somme (II.), and during the Retreat and Advance of 1918. Returning to England, he was demobilised in March 1919, and holds the General Service and Victory Medals.
The Green, Lower Heyford, Northants. Z3560/A.

WRIGHT, S. J., Lieutenant, 4th Northants. Regt.
He volunteered in November 1915, and in the following year was drafted to the Western Front, where he played a distinguished part in the Battles of the Somme, Arras, Ypres, Passchendaele and Cambrai. He was unfortunately killed in action at Foncquevillers on August 23rd, 1918, and was entitled to the General Service and Victory Medals.
"The path of duty was the way to glory."
Bliss Lane, Flore, Northampton. Z2925.

WRIGHT, T., Private, Northants. Regiment.
He volunteered in September 1914, and four months later was drafted to France, where he took part in the Battles of St. Eloi, Ypres and Vimy Ridge, and many other important engagements. He was blown up and buried by an explosion on the Somme in July 1916, and, being invalided home, afterwards contracted rheumatic fever. He was discharged in August 1917 as medically unfit for further service, and holds the 1914–15 Star, and the General Service and Victory Medals.
17, St. James' Street, Northampton. Z2926.

WRIGHT, W., Private, 1/4th Northants. Regt.
He volunteered in April 1915, and, after a short period of training, was drafted to the Dardanelles. There he took part in the Landing at Suvla Bay and the Evacuation of the Gallipoli Peninsula. Later he proceeded to Egypt, thence to Palestine, and was in action at the Battles of Gaza, the capture of Jerusalem, and the Advance of 1918 under General Allenby. Demobilised in 1919, he holds the 1914–15 Star, and the General Service and Victory Medals.
21, Alma Street, Northampton. Z2927.

WRIGHT, W., Private, 2/19th London Regiment.
Volunteering in October 1915, he proceeded to France eight months later, and served at St. Eloi. In December 1916 he was drafted to Salonika, where he saw heavy fighting on the Doiran and Vardar fronts before being transferred to Egypt in May 1917. Subsequently he was ordered to Palestine, and, after taking part in the Battles of Gaza, Jerusalem and Jericho, was unhappily killed in action on September 19th, 1918. He was entitled to the General Service and Victory Medals.
"A costly sacrifice upon the altar of freedom."
32, Queen's Road, Northampton. Z2038/A.

WRIGHT, W. A., Private, Labour Corps.
Joining in June 1916, he underwent a period of training, but was later found to be medically unfit for service overseas. He was therefore retained on important agricultural duties with his Unit, and served at various stations, where he rendered valuable services until discharged in September 1918.
53, Upper Harding Street, Northampton. Z1826.

WRIGHT, W. J., Corporal, R.A.S.C.
Mobilised in August 1914, he was drafted to France shortly afterwards, and served in the Retreat from Mons and the Battles of the Marne, and the Aisne. Engaged on transport work, his duties led him into the forward areas, and, wounded and sustaining shell-shock in 1916, he was invalided to England for treatment. He was discharged as medically unfit in 1917, and holds the Mons Star, and the General Service and Victory Medals.
The Green, Lower Heyford, Northants. Z3560/B.

WRIGLEY, F., Private, 2nd Bedfordshire Regt.
A Reservist, he was called up at the outbreak of war, and proceeded to the Western Front with the first Expeditionary Force. After taking an active part in severe fighting, he was wounded, and unhappily succumbed to his injuries on November 29th, 1914. He was entitled to the 1914 Star, and the General Service and Victory Medals.
"He nobly died that we might live."
61, Wycliffe Road, Northampton. Z2327.

WRIGLEY, T. E., Trooper, Northants. Yeomanry (Dragoons).
After volunteering in April 1915, he completed his training in the same year, and proceeded to France. Whilst in this theatre of war, he took part in heavy fighting on the Somme, Ancre, Arras and Ypres fronts. In November 1917 he was transferred to Italy, and served on the Piave and Asiago Plateaux. Demobilised in April 1919, he holds the 1914–15 Star, and the General Service and Victory Medals.
16, Monarch Road, Northampton. TZ1582/C.

WRIGLEY, T., Sergeant, Royal Garrison Artillery.
He was serving in Africa at the outbreak of war in August 1914, but was shortly afterwards drafted to the Western Front. In this theatre of war he served with distinction at many important engagements, particularly in the Ypres, Somme, and Cambrai sectors, and was twice wounded in 1918. After the cessation of hostilities, he proceeded to Ireland, where he was still serving in 1920. He holds the 1914–15 Star, and the General Service and Victory Medals.
13, Compton Street, Northampton. Z1825.

WYANT, F., Private, R.A.M.C.
He volunteered in October 1915, and, sent to the Western Front in the following May, served as a nursing orderly, and later with a Field Ambulance at Ypres. Drafted to Italy in December 1917, he saw service on the Piave, and, returning to France three months later, went through the Retreat and Advance of 1918, and was wounded at Bapaume. He holds the General Service and Victory Medals, and in 1921 was serving in England.
65, Abbey Road, Far Cotton, Northampton. Z3208.

WYKES, C., Corporal, Northamptonshire Regt.
Already serving at the outbreak of hostilities, he was immediately drafted to the Western Front, where he took part in the Retreat from Mons, and also in the Battles of the Marne, the Aisne and La Bassée, before being wounded and invalided home. On his recovery he returned to France, and did continuously good work in the Somme sector, but was again wounded. Evacuated to England, he underwent a period of hospital treatment, and was eventually discharged as medically unfit for further service in June 1918. He holds the Mons Star, and the General Service and Victory Medals.
32, Gladstone Terrace, Northamptonshire. Z1829.

WYKES, E. J., Private, 51st Royal Sussex Regt.
He joined in July 1918, and, on completion of his training, was employed on important duties with his Battalion at various depôts. Owing to being under age, he was unsuccessful in his efforts to secure his transfer to a theatre of war before hostilities were concluded, but rendered valuable services until demobilised in March 1919. Spratton, Northants. Z3209.

WYKES, J., Private, 1st Northamptonshire Regt.
Mobilised from the Reserve in August 1914, he was immediately drafted overseas. Whilst on the Western Front, he was in action during the Retreat from Mons, and also at the Battles of the Marne, the Aisne and La Bassée. He made the Supreme Sacrifice, being killed in action on January 9th, 1915, and was entitled to the Mons Star, and the General Service and Victory Medals.
"Thinking that remembrance, though unspoken, may reach him where he sleeps."
3, Althorp Street, Northampton. Z1076/A.

WYKES, L. J., Private, 4th Northants. Regiment.
Volunteering in August 1914, he sailed for Gallipoli in the following April, and took part in operations from the first Landing to the Evacuation of the Peninsula. Sent then to Egypt, he took part in the British Advance through Palestine, during which he was in action at Gaza and the capture of Jerusalem. He returned to England for demobilisation in August 1919, and holds the 1914–15 Star, and the General Service and Victory Medals.
Church Street, Long Buckby, Northants. Z3561.

WYKES, W., Corporal, Royal Berkshire Regiment.
A Reservist, he was mobilised on the declaration of war, and was employed on home service duties until his embarkation for France in 1916. Serving in various parts of the line, he did excellent work in many important engagements until wounded and invalided home. His injuries resulted in the amputation of a finger, and, discharged as physically unfit in May 1918, he holds the General Service and Victory Medals.
Near Hall, Spratton, Northants. Z3055/B.

WYMAN, G., A.B., Royal Naval Division.
Joining in August 1916, he shortly afterwards proceeded overseas, and, whilst on the Western Front, took part in the Battle of Arras before being invalided home with trench feet. On his recovery, in April 1917, he rejoined his Unit and was in action on the Somme and also during the Retreat and Advance of 1918. Wounded in November, he was invalided to England and eventually demobilised in September 1919, holding the General Service and Victory Medals.
29, Wimbledon Street, Northampton. Z2546.

WYMAN, P. G., L/Corporal, 6th Northants. Regt.
He volunteered in September 1914, and in the March following was drafted to the Western Front. There he took part in many important engagements, including the Battles of Hill 60, Festubert and the Somme. He was unhappily killed in action at Thiepval in September 1916, and was entitled to the 1914–15 Star, and the General Service and Victory Medals.
"He died the noblest death a man may die,
Fighting for God and right and liberty."
100, Greenwood Road, Northampton. Z2928.

Y

YATES, A., Private, Buffs (East Kent Regiment).
Having joined in March 1917, he completed a period of training, and was drafted to France. Whilst in this seat of operations he took part in heavy fighting on the Cambrai front. He was reported missing on November 30th, 1917, and is now presumed to have been killed in action on that date. He was entitled to the General Service and Victory Medals.
"The path of duty was the way to glory."
33, Francis Street, Northampton. Z1071/B.

YATES, F. G., Private, R.A.S.C. (M.T.)
Volunteering in April 1915, he proceeded to France in the following year. In this seat of operations he was engaged on important transport duties in various sectors, and was present during heavy fighting on the Somme, Ypres and Cambrai fronts. Invalided to hospital with influenza, he unhappily died from the effects in January 1919, and was entitled to the General Service and Victory Medals.
"And doubtless he went in splendid company."
Eagle Terrace, Milton, Northampton. Z2547/B.

YATES, H. A., Private, Middlesex Regiment.
Joining in April 1917, he underwent a period of training, but was later found to be medically unfit for service overseas. He was therefore retained as a Drummer and on other important duties with his Unit at York, where he rendered very valuable services until demobilised in March 1919.
Eagle Terrace, Milton, Northampton. Z2547/C.

YATES, R. C., Trooper, Bedfordshire Lancers.
Having volunteered in October 1915, he was drafted to France in February of the following year. Whilst in this theatre of war, he took part in the Battle of Albert, and also in other engagements in the Somme sector. Returning to England in May 1917, he was retained on important duties in connection with the output of ammunition, until discharged in December 1918. He holds the General Service and Victory Medals.
Eagle Terrace, Milton, Northampton. Z2547/A.

YATES, T. W., Bombardier, R.F.A.
Already serving at the declaration of war, he was immediately drafted to the Western Front. In this seat of operations, he was in action with his Battery during the Retreat from Mons, and also at the Battles of the Marne, the Aisne, La Bassée, Ypres (I., II., III.), Festubert, Loos, the Somme, Arras, St. Quentin and Cambrai, and many minor engagements. He did continuously good work throughout the period of hostilities and in February 1919, was discharged, holding the Mons Star, and the General Service and Victory Medals.
Eagle Terrace, Milton, Northampton. Z2548

YATES, W. J., L/Corporal, 6th Queen's (Royal West Surrey Regiment).
He volunteered in June 1915, and in the following August was drafted to France, where he saw much heavy fighting in many engagements, particularly at the Battles of the Somme, Ypres and Arras. He made the Supreme Sacrifice, being killed in action at Albert in June 1918, and was entitled to the 1914–15 Star, and the General Service and Victory Medals.
"Whilst we remember, the sacrifice is not in vain."
1, Castle Hill, Northampton. Z1746/B.

YEOMAN, A. F., Private, R.A.M.C.
He volunteered in 1915, and in the following year was drafted to the Western Front with the Welsh Field Ambulance. Whilst overseas he saw heavy fighting in numerous engagements, including the Battles of Vermelles, Vimy Ridge, the Somme, the Marne, Amiens and Ypres. After the Armistice he advanced into Germany with the Army of Occupation, and served there until demobilised in May 1919, holding the General Service and Victory Medals.
84, Adams Avenue, Northampton. Z2162/B.

YORK, A., Private, 5th Northants. Regiment.
Having volunteered in April 1915, he was drafted overseas after completing his training. Whilst in France he took part in many important engagements, including the Battles of Arras and the Somme (II.), where he was badly wounded and consequently invalided home. He was discharged in March 1919 as medically unfit for further service, and holds the 1914–15 Star, and the General Service and Victory Medals.
34, Crispin Street, Northampton. Z1830.

YORK, C., Private, 37th Royal Fusiliers.
He enlisted in June 1916, and in the following month was drafted to the Western Front. In this theatre of war he was engaged on important duties making and repairing roads in the Somme, Péronne, Arras and Cambrai sectors. He was demobilised in February 1919, and holds the General Service and Victory Medals.
4, Little Cross Street, Northampton. Z1831.

YORK, E., S.Q.M.S., Royal Army Service Corps.
He volunteered in April 1915, and a month later embarked for Gallipoli, where he was in action at Suvla Bay and in other engagements. After the Evacuation he was sent to Egypt, and was engaged on important duties at Alexandria and Ismailia, before proceeding to Palestine. On that front he played a conspicuous part in the Battles of Gaza, Jerusalem and Aleppo, and was demobilised on his return home in August 1920, holding the 1914–15 Star, and the General Service and Victory Medals. 33, Brunswick Place, Northampton. Z2039.

YORK, F. C., Gunner, Royal Field Artillery.
He volunteered in the Royal Army Veterinary Corps in May 1915, and was engaged on important duties at Woolwich and other stations for upwards of three years. Transferred to the Royal Field Artillery, he landed on the Western Front in April 1918 and, retained at a Base, was employed on duties of an important nature until his return to England for demobilisation in March 1919. He holds the General Service and Victory Medals. West Street, Long Buckby, Northants. Z3562.

YORK, F. W., Gunner, Royal Garrison Artillery.
He joined in May 1918, and was engaged on important signalling duties at Portsmouth and Winchester and various other stations in England. Unsuccessful in his endeavours to obtain a transfer to the fighting area, he, nevertheless, did much valuable work with his Battery until demobilised in January 1919.
1, Whitworth Road, Northampton. Z2328.

YORK, H., Driver, Royal Field Artillery.
Volunteering in January 1916, he carried out various duties with his Battery at several home depôts, and in March 1918 proceeded to France. There he was stationed at Le Havre, and did good work in the Band for a year. Demobilised on his return to England in March 1919, he holds the General Service and Victory Medals.
West Street, Long Buckby, Northants. Z3563.

YORK, J. B., L/Corporal, 5th Northants Regiment.
He volunteered in August 1914, and early in the following year was drafted to France. Whilst on the Western Front he took part in several engagements, including the Battles of Ypres, the Somme (I. and II.), and Cambrai, before being badly gassed at Fleurbaix in 1918. As a result he was invalided home and later demobilised in March 1919, holding the 1914–15 Star, and the General Service and Victory Medals.
6, Lower Harding Street, Northampton. Z1132/D.

ADDENDA

ABBOTT, E., Private, K.O. (Y.L.I.)
Joining in 1916, he underwent a period of training, but was retained on important guard and other duties with his Unit at various stations. He was also engaged for a time on agricultural work, and rendered very valuable services during the period of hostilities. Owing to his being medically unfit, he was unable to obtain his transfer overseas, and was finally demobilised in March 1919.
50, Russell Street, St. Neots, Hunts. Z1006/A.

ADAIR, J. K., Driver, Royal Field Artillery.
Volunteering in August 1915, he was in the following March drafted to Egypt, where he served before proceeding to Palestine. There he was in action with his Battery at the Battles of Gaza and Jaffa, and during heavy fighting in Syria. He did consistently good work, and in June 1919 was demobilised, holding the General Service and Victory Medals.
13, Union Street, Kilmarnock, Scotland. X1025.

ATKINS, L. G., Air Mechanic, Royal Air Force.
Having joined in February 1918, he landed in France in the following month. There he was stationed at Calais, and engaged in repairing and making parts of aeroplanes. During this period he did much good work and, returning to England, was demobilised in February 1920, holding the General Service and Victory Medals.
67, High Street, New Bradwell, Bucks. Z1111/A.

BEAL, S., Private, Bedfordshire Regiment.
He volunteered in 1914, and during the war saw much active service in France, Egypt and Palestine. Whilst in the last-named theatre of hostilities he was in action at Gaza, Jaffa and Haifa, and was wounded. He was eventually discharged as medically unfit, and holds the 1914–15 Star, and the General Service and Victory Medals.
Potter's Cross, Wootton, Beds. Z1552/C.

BEAL, W., Private, Bedfordshire Regiment.
He joined in 1916, and shortly afterwards landed in France, where he took part in much heavy fighting in various sectors. He was in action with his Unit at the Battles of Albert, Vimy Ridge, the Somme, Messines, Passchendaele, Lens, Cambrai and Amiens. Whilst overseas he was wounded, and in 1919 was demobilised, holding the General Service and Victory Medals. Potter's Cross, Wootton, Bedford. Z1552/A.

BENNETT, A. J., Gunner, R.G.A.
Joining in May 1918, he later in the same year proceeded to France. There he served with his Battery in several engagements on the Cambrai front, where he did much good work during the final decisive operations. Returning to England after the conclusion of war, he was eventually demobilised in September 1919, holding the General Service and Victory Medals. 39, Spencer Street, Bradwell, Bucks. Z1262.

BUCK, A., Private, North Staffordshire Regiment.
He joined in May 1917, and quickly proceeded to the Western Front, where he took part in heavy fighting at Arras and Bullecourt. He also fought at the Battles of Passchendaele and Cambrai, before being invalided home with trench fever in August 1918. On his recovery he served in Ireland until discharged in August 1919, holding the General Service and Victory Medals. 14, Derby Street, Bedford. X1486/B.

BUCK, C., Private, 2nd Northamptonshire Regt.
He was already in the Army at the declaration of war in August 1914, and quickly proceeded to France. There he was in action throughout the Mons Retreat, and also at the Battle of Ypres, and was severely wounded. He unfortunately died of his wounds on February 22nd, 1915, and was entitled to the Mons Star, and the General Service and Victory Medals.
"Whilst we remember, the sacrifice is not in vain."
14, Derby Street, Bedford. X1486/A.

BURNAGE, H., Driver, R.A.S.C.
Volunteering in October 1914, he was retained on important duties at Grantham until 1917. He then proceeded to the Western Front, where he took an active part in heavy fighting in the Ypres sector, and was badly wounded and taken prisoner. Whilst in captivity, he unfortunately had to have one of his legs amputated. After the cessation of hostilities, he was released and finally discharged in February 1920, holding the General Service and Victory Medals.
4, The Grove, Bedford. Z1523/A.

BURNAGE, T. C., Pte., 5th Bedfordshire Regiment.
An old soldier, he re-joined the Army in April 1915, and, after completing a period of training, was retained in England, where he served at various stations guarding prisoners of war. He was unable to obtain his transfer overseas, owing to his being medically unfit, and was therefore discharged in October 1917, holding the Egyptian and Soudan Medals.
4, The Grove, Bedford. Z1523/B.

BUTLER, T. W. R., Sergeant, Bedfordshire Regt.
Volunteering at the declaration of war, he was first engaged on important duties in England. Proceeding to the Dardanelles, he played a prominent part at the Landing of Suvla Bay, where he unfortunately fell in action on August 6th, 1915. He was entitled to the 1914–15 Star, and the General Service and Victory Medals.
"A costly sacrifice upon the altar of freedom."
Potter's Cross, Wootton, Bedford. Z1552/B.

CHILLERY, H. K., Private, 2nd Suffolk Regiment.
He joined in May 1916, and later in the same year was sent to France, where he took part in the Battles of Arras and Ypres. Badly wounded in August 1917, he was invalided home, but eight months later returned to the Western Front. After being in action at the Somme, Lille and Cambrai, he was unhappily killed on October 1st, 1918, and was entitled to the General Service and Victory Medals.
"His name liveth for evermore."
1, Eastville Road, Southend, Bedford. Z1647/A.

COLE, B., Private, Sherwood Foresters.
He joined in February 1916, and in the following year was drafted to the Western Front. In this theatre of war he took part in heavy fighting at Arras, Ypres, on the Somme and Cambrai fronts, and also during the Retreat and Advance of 1918. Returning home after the termination of hostilities, he was demobilised in 1919, and holds the General Service and Victory Medals.
1, Bridge Terrace, Fenstanton, Hunts. Z1742/C.

COLE, H. J., Private, Middlesex Regiment.
He volunteered in September 1915, and five months later was drafted to France, where he took part in engagements at Albert and on the Somme. Later he proceeded to Salonika, and served on the Doiran and Struma fronts, but, suffering from malaria, was invalided home. On his recovery he embarked on board H.M.T. "Aragon" for Egypt, but unhappily lost his life when this vessel was sunk off Alexandria on December 30th, 1917. He was entitled to the 1914–15 Star, and the General Service and Victory Medals.
"Thinking that remembrance, though unspoken, may reach him where he sleeps."
1, Bridge Terrace, Fenstanton, Hunts. Z1742/D.

COLE, M., Sergeant, Essex Regiment.
He volunteered in the Huntingdonshire Cyclists' Battalion in August 1914, but was later transferred to the Essex Regiment, and retained at various stations on important duties as an Instructor of Signals. In 1917 he was drafted to France, took part in much fighting in the Arras, Ypres, the Somme and Cambrai sectors, and was wounded in action. Demobilised in 1919, he holds the General Service and Victory Medals.
1, Bridge Terrace, Fenstanton, Hunts. Z1742/A.

COLE, R. M., Pte., 8th Australian Overseas Forces.
He volunteered in January 1915, and two months later was drafted to Egypt, thence to the Dardanelles, where he saw much heavy fighting at Anzac Cove, Suvla Bay, and in the Evacuation of the Gallipoli Peninsula. He was then transferred to France, and was in action on the Somme. He made the Supreme Sacrifice, being killed in action at Pozières on July 20th, 1916, and was entitled to the 1914–15 Star, and the General Service and Victory Medals.
"The path of duty was the way to glory."
1, Bridge Terrace, Fenstanton, Hunts. Z1742/B.

COLE, V., Sergeant, Essex Regiment.
Having volunteered in August 1914 in the Huntingdonshire Cyclist Battalion, he was shortly afterwards transferred to the Essex Regiment, and retained on the East Coast as a Signal Instructor. Later he was drafted to the Western Front, and saw much fighting in the Arras, Ypres, Cambrai and the Somme sectors. In 1921 he was still serving, and holds the General Service and Victory Medals.
1, Bridge Terrace, Fenstanton, Hunts. Z1742/E.

CORBETT, J., Sergeant, Royal Field Artillery.
Volunteering in September 1914, he was retained on important duties in England until July of the following year, and then proceeded to the Dardanelles, where he took a prominent part in the Landing at Suvla Bay. He died gloriously on the Field of Battle there on August 18th, 1915, and was entitled to the 1914–15 Star, and the General Service and Victory Medals.
"Whilst we remember, the sacrifice is not in vain."
St. Mary's Street, Eynesbury, St. Neots, Hunts. Z1808.

CROUCH, W. J., Private, 1/5th Bedfordshire Regt.
Already serving in August 1914, he was drafted to Gallipoli in July of the following year, but, severely wounded in the Landing at Suvla Bay, was invalided home. In March 1918, however, he proceeded to Egypt and thence into Palestine, where he was stationed at Jaffa and Jerusalem. Returning home in May 1919, he was discharged in the following month, holding the 1914–15 Star, and the General Service and Victory Medals. 5, Hassett Street, Bedford. X1875.

DALRYMPLE, J., Corporal, R.G.A.
He volunteered in August 1914, and in the following year was drafted to France, where, after fighting in the Battles of Ypres, Loos and the Somme, he was wounded at Vimy Ridge in March 1917. Invalided home in H.M.H.S. "Donegal," he was fortunately rescued when this ship was torpedoed, and, later in the same year returned to France, where he served with the Chinese Labour Corps until gassed in June 1918. He was invalided from the Army in October of that year, and holds the 1914–15 Star, and the General Service and Victory Medals. 5, Gratton Road, Queen's Park, Bedford. Z1899.

DARLOW, B., Sergeant, Royal Engineers.
He volunteered in January 1915, and was retained at home on various duties of an important nature until 1916, when he was sent to France. There he served with his Company on the Ypres, Arras and Somme fronts, performing excellent work. He was gassed at Arras in 1917, but remained overseas until after the Armistice, and was demobilised in April 1919, holding the General Service and Victory Medals.
20, Beatrice Street, Kempston, Beds. Z1915.

DARRINGTON, A. T., Pte., 4th Bedfordshire Regt.
Volunteering in January 1915, he was sent to the Western Front in the following year, but was very severely wounded in action shortly afterwards. Invalided home, he unhappily died in hospital on February 21st, 1916, and was entitled to the General Service and Victory Medals.
"He died the noblest death a man may die,
Fighting for God and right and liberty."
Wyboston, Beds. Z1921/B.

DARRINGTON, G., Pte., 2nd Bedfordshire Regt.
He volunteered in November 1914, and, in June of the following year, was drafted to the Western Front, where he saw heavy fighting in various sectors. After taking part in the Battles of Loos and the Somme, and many other engagements, he was invalided home in 1917, and was retained in England until demobilised in 1919. He holds the 1914–15 Star, and the General Service and Victory Medals. Roxton, Beds. Z1922/A.

DARRINGTON, J. H., Pte., Warwickshire Regt.
He volunteered in the Hunts Cyclist Battalion in October 1914, and, after a period of training, was retained on important duties at various stations, serving also with the Royal Warwickshire Regiment and the Essex Regiment. Early in November 1918, however, he proceeded to the Western Front, where he was engaged in guarding prisoners of war. Demobilised in February 1919, he holds the General Service and Victory Medals.
Eaton Socon, Beds. Z1925.

DOD, C. F., Staff-Sergt., Canadian Overseas Forces.
He volunteered in August 1914, and shortly afterwards proceeded to the Western Front, where he saw severe fighting in various sectors. He took a prominent part in the Battles of Hill 60, Ypres, Loos, the Somme, Arras and Cambrai, and many other engagements, and afterwards served with the Army of Occupation in Germany. Demobilised in August 1919, he holds the 1914–15 Star, and the General Service and Victory Medals. 19, Dalmeny Avenue, Norbury, Surrey. Z4494.

FAVELL, O., Private, The Queen's Regiment.
He joined in 1918, and, after completing a term of training, was retained at various stations, where he was engaged on duties of great importance. He was unable to obtain his transfer to a theatre of war, but, nevertheless, rendered valuable services with his Unit until his demobilisation in 1919. Hemingford Grey, Hunts. Z2142.

FOUNTAIN, J. W., Sapper, Royal Engineers.
Shortly after joining in 1916, he was drafted to the Western Front, where he was engaged on road-making, bridge-building, and other important duties. He served in various sectors, and was present at the Battles of Arras, Vimy Ridge, Ypres and the Somme, and other engagements. He was demobilised in February 1919, and holds the General Service and Victory Medals. 1, Eastville Road, Southend, Bedford. Z1647/B.

GOODGER, R. H., Pte., 2/1st R. Bucks. Hussars.
Joining in March 1917, he was drafted to France in the following December, and there saw much heavy fighting. He took part in many important engagements in this theatre of war, including the Battle of St. Quentin, but in April 1918 was severely wounded at Laventie. Admitted to hospital in England, he was invalided from the Army in February 1919, holding the General Service and Victory Medals.
16, The Green, Stony Stratford, Bucks. Z3567.

HARRIS, G., Private, 1st Bedfordshire Regiment.
Shortly after volunteering in March 1915, he proceeded to the Western Front, where he saw severe fighting at Neuve Chapelle and elsewhere, and was wounded at Ypres and Givenchy. He was unfortunately reported missing, and is believed to have been killed in action at Loos early in September 1915. He was entitled to the 1914–15 Star, and the General Service and Victory Medals.
"A costly sacrifice upon the altar of freedom."
Mount Pleasant, Wootton, Bedford. Z2768/B.

HODGEMAN, W. G., Private, R.M.L.I. and R.A.V.C.; and Gunner, R.F.A.
Serving when war broke out in August 1914, he was at once drafted to the Western Front, where he took part in the operations at Antwerp. He was later sent to East Africa, and served there until October 1916, when he returned to France and was transferred to the Royal Army Veterinary Corps. Employed looking after invalid horses, he did good work until the following year, when he was transferred to the Royal Field Artillery, and sent to Salonika. There he was in action with his Battery on the Vardar, Doiran and Struma fronts. He was still serving with the Colours in 1920, and holds the 1914 Star, and the General Service and Victory Medals.
32, Pilcroft Street, Bedford. X2905.

HOLLAND, C. J., Pte., 4th Worcestershire Regt.
Five months after joining in December 1916, he was drafted to the Western Front, where he saw much heavy fighting. After taking part in the Battle of Ypres and other engagements, he was severely wounded in action and admitted to hospital at Newcastle, where he remained for seven months. Invalided from the Army in March 1918, he holds the General Service and Victory Medals. 67, High St., New Bradwell, Bucks. Z1111/B.

HOLLAND, C. J., Pte., 4th Worcestershire Regt.
Volunteering in December 1915, he proceeded to the Western Front in May of the following year, and there saw much severe fighting. After taking part in engagements in the Somme, Arras and Ypres sectors, he was badly wounded in August 1916, and sent to hospital at Gosport. He was discharged in March 1917 as medically unfit for further service, and holds the General Service and Victory Medals.
Laura Cottage, Mill Lane, Stony Stratford, Bucks. Z2910.

HOLT, J. H. T., Private, Bedfordshire Regiment.
He volunteered in September 1914, and in July of the following year proceeded to Gallipoli, where, after taking part in the Landing at Suvla Bay, he fought in the capture of Chunuk Bair, and was wounded in October 1915. Admitted to hospital in England, he was finally invalided from the Army in January 1918, and holds the 1914–15 Star, and the General Service and Victory Medals.
52, Priory Street, Newport Pagnell, Bucks. Z3566/B.

HOLT, T. W., Private, Oxford. & Bucks. L.I.
Already in the Army at the outbreak of war, he was immediately drafted to France, where he took part in the Retreat from Mons and the Battles of the Marne, Ypres, Neuve Chapelle and Hill 60. He died gloriously on the Field of Battle at Ypres on May 17th, 1915, and was entitled to the Mons Star, and the General Service and Victory Medals.
"A valiant Soldier, with undaunted heart he breasted life's last hill."
52, Priory Street, Newport Pagnell, Bucks. Z3566/C.

HOLT, W. C., Private, Oxford. & Bucks. L.I.
He volunteered in August 1914, and two months later was drafted to the Western Front, where he fought in the Battles of Ypres, Neuve Chapelle, Festubert, Loos, Lens and Albert. He was unhappily killed in action on the Somme on October 21st, 1916, and was entitled to the 1914 Star, and the General Service and Victory Medals.
"His life for his Country, his soul to God."
52, Priory Street, Newport Pagnell, Bucks. Z3566/D.

HUCKLE, W., Private, 4th East Surrey Regt.
He joined in July 1916, and later in the same year was drafted to France, where he took part in much fighting on the Somme, and was wounded. He was reported missing on September 15th, 1918, and is now believed to have been killed in action on that date. He was entitled to the General Service and Victory Medals.
"Honour to the immortal dead who gave their youth that the world might grow old in peace."
Colne, Hunts. Z2980.

JAKES, F., Private, 1st Warwickshire Regiment.
He volunteered in the Huntingdonshire Cyclist Battalion in November 1915, and, completing his training in the following July, was drafted to France, where he saw much heavy fighting on the Somme. He was unhappily reported missing on August 27th, 1916, and is now believed to have been killed in action on that date. He was entitled to the General Service and Victory Medals.
"He died the noblest death a man may die,
Fighting for God and right and liberty."
50, Russell Street, St. Neots, Hunts. Z1006/B.

LANCASTER, F. R., Private, 1st Northants. Regt.
Volunteering in September 1914, he proceeded to France three months later, and there participated in the Battles of Neuve Chapelle, Hill 60, Ypres, Loos and Passchendaele. He was twice invalided home on account of wounds, and was also in hospital suffering from enteric. He was eventually demobilised in March 1919, holding the 1914–15 Star, and the General Service and Victory Medals. Sutton Street, Flore, Northants. Z2754.

LANDERYOU, F. H., Chief Petty Officer, R.N.
Mobilised from the Reserve at the outbreak of war, he first served on board H.M.S. "Research." He was later stationed at Portland, where he was engaged on responsible duties at the Signal Stations, and rendered very valuable services during the period of hostilities. Discharged in May 1919, he holds the General Service, Victory and Long Service and Good Conduct Medals. 44, Spencer Bridge Road, Northampton. Z2756.

LANGRIDGE, N., Pte., R. D.C. and Beds. Regt.
Volunteering in November 1914, he was retained on important duties with his Unit at home until March 1916, when he was drafted overseas. Whilst on the Western Front, he took part in the fighting at Festubert, the Ancre and Givenchy. He was wounded in action at Ypres in July 1917, and invalided to England, where he remained until demobilised in April 1919, holding the General Service and Victory Medals.
Aspley Hill, Woburn Sands, Beds. Z3294.

LAWTON, A. E., Private, K.O. (Y.L.I.)
Mobilised at the outbreak of war in August 1914, he was drafted to France in the following year, and took part in heavy fighting on the Ypres, Loos, Vimy Ridge, Somme, Arras and Cambrai fronts. He was severely wounded in 1917 and, invalided home, was admitted to hospital at Salisbury, being eventually discharged in April 1918 as unfit for further service. He holds the 1914–15 Star, and the General Service and Victory Medals. Sutton Street, Flore, Northants. Z2757/A.

LAWTON, H., Corporal, K.O. (Y.L.I.), & M.G.C.
Mobilised in August 1914, he proceeded to France eight months later and fought in the Battles of Ypres (II.), Loos, the Somme, Arras, Vimy Ridge, Ypres (III.), and Cambrai before being wounded and taken prisoner in March 1918. After nine months in captivity he was repatriated, and received his discharge in March 1919, holding the 1914–15 Star, and the General Service and Victory Medals.
Sutton Street, Flore, Northants. Z2757/B.

LEA, F. K. (Mrs.), Special War Worker.
In August 1916 this lady undertook work of National importance at the Barracks, Northampton, where she was engaged as a supervisor of all the clerks. She carried out her responsible duties in an able manner, and rendered valuable services until August 1917. 53, Symington St., Northampton. Z2758/B.

LEA, F. T., Sergeant, Northants. Regiment.
Mobilised from the Reserve in August 1914, he was drafted to West Africa at once, and served with distinction during heavy fighting in the Cameroons, where he was wounded in May 1915. On his recovery he rejoined his Unit, but contracted malaria and was invalided home. He was discharged, medically unfit, in March 1918, and holds the 1914–15 Star, and the General Service and Victory Medals.
53, Symington Street, Northampton. Z2758/A.

LEACH, A. C., Bombardier, R.F.A.
Mobilised at the outbreak of war, he quickly proceeded to France, and served with distinction with his Battery at the Battles of the Marne, Ypres, the Somme, Arras and Cambrai, and throughout the Retreat and Advance of 1918. He had previously served in the Boer War and in India for four years, and was discharged in February 1919, holding the Queen's and King's South African Medals, the 1914 Star, and the General Service and Victory Medals.
1, Dundee Street, Northampton. Z2760.

LEACH, F. F., Private, 4th Northamptonshire Regiment and Yorkshire Regiment.
He volunteered in 1915, and in the following year was drafted to the Western Front, where he fought in the Battles of the Somme, Arras and Ypres. In 1917 he was gassed and invalided home, and, on returning to France, served in engagements at Passchendaele and the Somme. He was severely wounded in February 1918, and in consequence was discharged as medically unfit five months later, holding the 1914–15 Star, and the General Service and Victory Medals.
1, Drayton Place, Daventry, Northants. Z2761.

LEACH, W. M., Private, 1/4th Northants. Regt.
He volunteered in December 1914, and in the following year was drafted to Egypt, where he saw much service until transferred to Palestine. On that front he took an active part in the Battles of Gaza, and was wounded, and, on his return to the firing-line, was engaged in fierce fighting at Jaffa and Haifa. He was demobilised on his return to England in July 1919, and holds the 1914–15 Star, and the General Service and Victory Medals. 34, Brook St., Daventry, Northants. Z2759.

LETTS, J. J. C., Private, 3rd Bedfordshire Regt.
He joined in February 1918, but, owing to ill-health, was unsuccessful in his endeavours to obtain a transfer to the war zone. He was retained on home service at various important centres, and fulfilled the various duties allotted to him in a highly efficient manner. Unfortunately his health broke down, and he was invalided out of the Army in October 1919.
22, St. James' Street, Northampton. Z2762/B.

LIGHTFOOT, B., Corporal, Queen's (Royal West Surrey Regiment).
Being under age, he did not enlist until April 1918, but, after serving for a time at Bury St. Edmunds, was sent to Germany, where he joined the Army of Occupation at Cologne. After remaining on the Rhine for nearly 10 months, he was demobilised in November 1919. 22, Gwyn St., Bedford. X3334/B.

LIGHTFOOT, W. C., Cpl., Royal Berkshire Regt.
Volunteering in August 1914, he served in England with the Bedfordshire Regiment, but was transferred to the 2/1st Oxfordshire and Buckinghamshire Light Infantry, and drafted to France in March 1916. He was in action at Albert, on the Somme, at Arras, Vimy Ridge and Ypres, and was wounded at St. Quentin in April 1917, and sent to hospital. Joining the Royal Berkshire Regiment on his recovery, he was wounded in August during the Advance of 1918. Demobilised in March 1919, he holds the General Service and Victory Medals.
22, Gwyn Street, Bedford. X3334/A.

LONG, H., Private, 4th Suffolk Regiment.
He joined in April 1916, and in the following August embarked for the Western Front, where he was in action in many engagements of note in various sectors. Whilst fighting on the Somme, he was severely wounded, and unhappily succumbed to his injuries on December 22nd, 1916, at Rouen. He was entitled to the General Service and Victory Medals.
"A costly sacrifice upon the altar of freedom."
3, Greenwood Road, Northampton. Z2765.

LONG, T., Private, Oxford. and Bucks. L.I.
Already in the Army at the outbreak of war in August 1914, he was quickly drafted to France. In this theatre of war he took part in the Retreat from Mons, the Battles of the Marne and Festubert, but, owing to ill-health, and having completed 12 years with the Colours, was invalided home, and eventually discharged in 1915. He holds the Mons Star, and the General Service and Victory Medals.
3, St. Neots Road, Sandy, Beds. Z3568.

LOVE, P. G., Private, 4th Royal Fusiliers.
Joining in June 1916, he proceeded to the Western Front three months later, and fought in numerous engagements in the Ypres sector. He was wounded in December 1916, and invalided home, and on his recovery returned to France, but was reported wounded and missing in May 1917, and was subsequently presumed to have been killed. He was entitled to the General Service and Victory Medals.
"His life for his Country."
10, Orchard Street, Drayton, Northants. Z2766.

LOVE, W., A.B., Royal Naval Division.
He volunteered in 1915, and in the following year was sent to the Western Front. There he was engaged in fierce fighting at the Battles of St. Eloi, Albert, Ploegsteert Wood, Vimy Ridge, the Ancre and Cambrai. Unfortunately his health broke down, and he was admitted to hospital, subsequently being invalided out of the Service in 1918. He holds the General Service and Victory Medals.
40, Alma Street, Northampton. Z2767.

LOVELL, A. T., Trooper, Bedfordshire Lancers.
Volunteering in January 1916, he received his training at Bedford and Colchester, and proceeded overseas in June 1917. Serving on the Western Front, he was in action at the Battle of Ypres, and saw heavy fighting at Arras, but was thrown from his horse, and sustained severe injuries. In consequence he was discharged as medically unfit in February 1918, holding the General Service and Victory Medals.
81, Green Street, Northampton. Z2768.

LOVERIDGE, L. B., 2nd Lieutenant, 6th (Reserve) Dragoon Guards.
From April 1915 for two years he served with the St. John Ambulance (V.A.D.), at Towcester and other places in Northamptonshire, but, in April 1917, joined the 1st Life Guards as a Trooper, and was stationed at Knightsbridge. Recommended for a commission, he proceeded in June 1918 to a Cadet training centre at Kildare, where he remained until gazetted as a 2nd Lieutenant in April 1919. He was, however, demobilised in the same month. 40, York Street, Bedford. Z3391.

MANN, R., Sapper, Royal Engineers.
He joined in 1916 and, completing his training, embarked for France. After taking part in the Battles of the Somme, Ypres and Passchendaele, he was sent to the Italian theatre of war, and was in action on the River Piave and the Asiago Plateau. Returning home, he was demobilised in 1919, and holds the General Service and Victory Medals.
22, Avenue Road, Huntingdon. Z3441.

NASH, G. H., Captain, 2/4th Queen's (Royal West Surrey Regiment).
Mobilised at the outbreak of war, he at once proceeded to France as a Sergeant, and took a distinguished part in the fighting during the Retreat from Mons. He was also in action at the great Battles of the Marne, Festubert, Ypres, the Somme, Arras and Cambrai, and was wounded. Promoted to commissioned rank, he quickly gained his Captaincy, and served in Germany with the Army of Occupation at Cologne. Returning home, he was discharged in April 1919, and holds the Mons Star, and the General Service and Victory Medals.
High Street, Sharnbrook, Bedford. Z3635.

NICHOLS, A. G. H., Sapper, Royal Engineers.
He joined in May 1918, and within a month was sent to France, where he rendered valuable services with the Railway Operative Department at Audruicq, Boulogne and Lille, and in the Cambrai sector. He was demobilised in November 1919, and holds the General Service and Victory Medals.
66, Clarence Road, Stony Stratford, Bucks. Z3661.

PANTER, A., 2/Corporal, Royal Engineers.
He volunteered in August 1914, but was unable to obtain his transfer overseas before the end of the war, and was stationed at various places in England. In December 1918, however, he was sent to Salonika, and served with the Signal Section on the Doiran and Vardar. He was demobilised in April 1919, after his return to England. 27, Bunyan Road, Bedford. Z3782.

PELL, E. J., L/Corporal, 1st Queen's (Royal West Surrey Regiment).
Volunteering in February 1915, he proceeded to France six months later, and fought at Festubert, Loos and Lens. Severely wounded on the Somme in 1916, he was invalided home, but later returned to the front and served on until 1919. In 1920 he was stationed at Lifford Camp in Ireland, and holds the 1914–15 Star, and the General Service and Victory Medals.
Colne, Hunts. Z3811.

POWELL, A. E., Pte., 1st R. Warwickshire Regt.
He volunteered in April 1915, and in July was sent to France, where he was wounded during the Battle of Loos After being in hospital for six months, he returned to the Western Front and fought in the Cambrai sector. In November 1917 he was unhappily reported missing, and is now presumed to have been killed in action He was entitled to the 1914–15 Star, and the General Service and Victory Medals.
"Thinking that remembrance, though unspoken, may reach him where he sleeps."
21, Russell Street, Stony Stratford, Bucks. Z3871/B.

REEVE, A., Sapper, Royal Engineers.
He joined in March 1916, and in August was sent to Salonika, where he fought on the Doiran, Vardar and Struma fronts, and suffered from repeated attacks of malaria. In April 1919 he returned home, and in the following November was demobilised. He holds the General Service and Victory Medals.
Erning Street, Godmanchester, Hunts. Z3936/B.

REEVE, C., Rifleman, Royal Irish Rifles.
When war was declared in August 1914 he volunteered, and two months later was ordered to France. In that theatre of war he saw much service in various sectors, and took an active part in the Battles of Festubert, Loos, Albert, the Somme, Arras and Ypres. He was wounded on one occasion, and was eventually demobilised in 1919, holding the 1914 Star, and the General Service and Victory Medals.
Erning Street, Godmanchester, Hunts. Z3936/A.

RICHARDSON, A. G., Pte., Middlesex Regt.; and Rflmn., 9th London Regt. (Q. Victoria's Rifles).
He joined in May 1916, and in the following July was drafted to the Western Front. In that theatre of war he took part in the Battles of the Somme (where he was wounded), and, after his return to the trenches, of Cambrai and in the Retreat and Advance of 1918. He also served for a time in Germany with the Army of Occupation, and was eventually demobilised in September 1919, holding the General Service and Victory Medals. 1, Tavistock Place, Bedford. X3962.

ROBINSON, C., Sapper, R.E. (Signal Section).
He joined in February 1917, and in the succeeding month was sent to France, where he went into action in the Battle of Arras. On August 3rd, 1917, he laid down his life for the great cause at the third Battle of Ypres. He was entitled to the General Service and Victory Medals.
"Thinking that remembrance, though unspoken, may reach him where he sleeps."
Near Elms, Elstow, Beds. Z4016/A.

ROBINSON, P. A., Private, Queen's (Royal West Surrey Regiment).
Owing to his being under age, he was unable to join the Army before May 1918. He, however, completed a period of training and service in England, and in November 1918 was sent to France, whence with the Army of Occupation he proceeded to Germany. He was eventually demobilised in March 1920 after his return to England. Near Elms, Elstow, Beds. Z4016/B.

RUSSELL, A. G., Private, 3rd Beds. & Herts. Regt.
He enlisted in June 1917, and, after a period of training, was engaged at various home stations, but was unable to obtain a transfer overseas before the cessation of hostilities. In 1919 he was drafted to India, and served on important garrison duties at Secunderabad and Trimulgherry. He was still serving in 1921. Mount Pleasant, Wootton, Bedford. Z2768/A.

SALTER, L. F., Bombardier, R.F.A.
Mobilised at the outbreak of war, he was not sent to the Western Front until September 1917. He there took part in the Battles of Passchendaele and Cambrai, and, drafted to Italy two months afterwards, saw fighting on the Piave and Asiago fronts. Returning to France in May 1918, he was gassed at Arras, but served through the General Advance of that year, and was not demobilised until June 1919. He holds the General Service and Victory Medals.
28, Trefethick Street, Merthyr Tydvil, South Wales. Z4065.

SILK, T., Sergeant, 1st Buffs (East Kent Regt.)
He joined in November 1916, and in the following year was drafted to India, where he served on the North-West Frontier. He was stationed at different places there, and was employed as an Instructor, in which capacity he did good service. Returning home, he was demobilised in December 1919, and holds the General Service Medal.
Croft House, Pidley, Hunts. Z4156.

STEWART, J. T., Private, Royal Defence Corps.
He volunteered in November 1914, and after a period of training was engaged at various stations on important duties guarding German prisoners of war. He rendered valuable services, but, owing to his being medically unfit, was discharged in November 1915. 52, Priory Street, Newport Pagnell, Bucks. Z3566/A.

STYLES, F. W., Private, R.A.M.C. (1/2nd South Midland Brigade, Field Ambulance).
Having served with his Unit since April 1908, he was sent to Gallipoli in April 1915, and took part in the Landing at Suvla Bay and the heavy fighting at Krithia. After the Evacuation he was sent home, and in April 1916 was discharged as time-expired. He holds the 1914–15 Star, and the General Service and Victory Medals.
3, King Street, Stony Stratford, Bucks. Z3871/A.

THOMAS, A. L., Sergeant, Royal Engineers.
He joined in April 1917, and, whilst on his way to Egypt was torpedoed in the "Aragon" off Alexandria on December 30th, 1917. Rescued after some time in the water, he did good service at Alexandria and in Palestine. Returning home, he was eventually demobilised in January 1920, and holds the General Service and Victory Medals.
3, Radcliffe Street, Wolverton, Bucks. Z4393.

VYNE, J. S., Private, Royal Welch Fusiliers.
Volunteering in March 1915, he was shortly afterwards drafted to the Western Front, where he took part in the Battles of Loos, the Somme, Bullecourt and Ypres, and was badly wounded. He unfortunately died from the effects of his injuries on September 29th, 1917, and was entitled to the 1914–15 Star, and the General Service and Victory Medals.
"And doubtless he went in splendid company."
7, Pilcroft Street, Bedford. X2228.

YEARRELL, A. W., Sergeant, 4th Beds. Regt.
He volunteered in August 1914, and in the following year proceeded to France, where he took a distinguished part in the fighting at Festubert, Loos, Arras, Albert and on the Somme, and was wounded in 1916. After returning to the Western Front, he made the Supreme Sacrifice in April 1917, being killed in action. He was buried at Point-du-Goun Military Cemetery No. 1, and was entitled to the 1914–15 Star, and the General Service and Victory Medals.
"Great deeds cannot die."
High Street, Offord D'Arcy, Hunts. Z2507/A.

YEARRELL, H., Private, Norfolk Regiment.
Joining in 1917, he was drafted to France later in the same year, and took part in several of the concluding engagements of the war. He was in action on the Somme and at Ypres and Cambrai, and later rendered valuable services during the Retreat and Advance of 1918. He proceeded to Germany after the cessation of hostilities, and did duty on the Rhine with the Army of Occupation. Demobilised in November 1919, he holds the General Service and Victory Medals.
High Street, Offord D'Arcy, Hunts. Z2507/B.

YEARRELL, S., Private, Tank Corps.
He joined in 1917, and, on completion of his training, was drafted to France later in the same year. In this theatre of war he played an important part in many engagements, and rendered valuable services at the Battles of Vimy Ridge, the Somme, Ypres, Cambrai and Amiens, and later, during the Retreat and Advance of 1918. He holds the General Service and Victory Medals, and was demobilised in 1919.
High Street, Offord D'Arcy, Hunts. Z2507/C.

YORK, J. T., Gunner, Royal Field Artillery.
A serving soldier, he was stationed in Ireland when war broke out and was drafted to the Western Front in October 1914. He was almost immediately engaged in heavy fighting at La Bassée, and also served in the Battles of Ypres and Neuve Chapelle. He died gloriously on the Field of Battle on May 3rd, 1915, and was entitled to the 1914 Star, and the General Service and Victory Medals.
"Great deeds cannot die."
Murcott, Long Buckby, Northants. Z3564/A.

YORK, R. H., L/Corporal, R.A.S.C.
He was mobilised in August 1914, and, crossing to France at once, served in the Retreat from Mons, and was wounded. On his recovery he was engaged on important transport duties in the Battles of Ypres, Arras, Vimy Ridge and Bullecourt, and was gassed. Evacuated to England for treatment, he was invalided out of the Army in 1917, and holds the Mons Star, and the General Service and Victory Medals.
Barrack Row, West Street, Long Buckby, Northants. Z3565.

YORK, W., Private, Middlesex Regiment.
He volunteered in September 1914, and underwent a period of training, but, owing to ill-health, was discharged in November 1916. Later he re-enlisted in the Labour Corps, and was engaged at various home stations on important duties. He rendered valuable services, and was demobilised in February 1919.
1, House, 5th Block, Naseby Street, Northampton. Z1832.

YORK, W. F., Private, Princess Patricia's Canadian Light Infantry.
Volunteering in Canada in August 1914, he was sent to England and thence to France in the same year. Whilst on the Western Front, he fought in several engagements until wounded at Ypres in May 1915. After treatment in England, he returned to France, and, owing to medical unfitness for service in the trenches, was employed on duties at Staff Headquarters. Demobilised in February 1919, he holds the 1914 Star, and the General Service and Victory Medals.
Murcott, Long Buckby, Northants. Z3564/B.

YORK, W. S., Private, Army Cyclist Corps.
He volunteered in December 1915, and, after a period of training, was engaged at various stations on important duties with his Unit. Owing to his being over age, he was unable to obtain a transfer overseas, but rendered valuable services until his demobilisation in February 1919.
55, Charles Street, Northampton. Z1833.

YOUNG, A., Private, 2nd Bedfordshire Regt.
Mobilised from the Reserve in August 1914, he was immediately drafted to France, and was in action at the Battle of Mons. He also took part in much heavy fighting on the Marne and at Neuve Chapelle, but was unfortunately killed by a sniper at Hill 60, in April 1915. He was entitled to the Mons Star and the General Service and Victory Medals.
"His memory is cherished with pride."
71, Wellington Street, Bedford. X2517/B.

YOUNG, B., Air Mechanic, Royal Air Force.
He volunteered in the Northamptonshire Yeomanry and underwent a period of training, but was later transferred to the Royal Air Force, and engaged on duties which demanded a high degree of technical skill. He served on board a motor patrol-boat in the North Sea and off the Belgian and French Coasts. He did continuously good work throughout hostilities, holds the General Service and Victory Medals, and was demobilised in February 1920.
31, Beaconsfield Terrace, Northampton. Z1834.

YOUNG, E., Private, Cameronians (Scottish Rifles); and Sapper, Royal Engineers.
Mobilised from the Reserve at the outbreak of war in August 1914, he was quickly drafted to the Western Front, and took part in the Battle of Mons. He was also in action on the Marne and in other engagements of importance, including those at Ypres, Hill 60, Festubert, Cambrai and on the Ancre. After the cessation of hostilities, he served at a base depôt near Boulogne, and was finally discharged in April 1919. He holds the Mons Star, and the General Service and Victory Medals.
71, Wellington Street, Bedford. X2517/A.

YOUNG, T., 1st Class Petty Officer, R.N.R.
He was already in H.M. Navy at the outbreak of war in August 1914, and did duty in H.M. Ships "Lord Nelson" and "Hawke." He rendered valuable services, but, unfortunately, lost his life when H.M.S. "Hawke" was torpedoed on October 15th, 1914, in the North Sea. He was entitled to the 1914–15 Star, and the General Service and Victory Medals.
"And doubtless he went in splendid company."
71, Wellington Street, Bedford. X2517/C.

YOUNG, W., Private, Middlesex Regiment and Labour Corps.
He joined in September 1916, and later in the same year proceeded to France, where he took part in many engagements of importance. He was in action at the Battles of the Somme, Ypres, Loos, Bullecourt and Arras, and, on his transfer to the Labour Corps, did salvage work behind the lines. He was demobilised in April 1919, and holds the General Service and Victory Medals.
71, Wellington Street, Bedford. X2517/D.

YOUNG, W. H., Private, 7th Royal Fusiliers.
He joined in February 1917, and later in the same year was drafted to the Western Front. There he took part in several important engagements, including the Battles of the Somme and Cambrai, but, contracting trench feet in 1918, was invalided home. Demobilised in June 1919, he holds the General Service and Victory Medals.
18, Carlton Road, Northampton. Z1835.

YOUNG, W. H., L/Corporal, R.E. (Signal Section).
Volunteering in October 1915, he was retained at various home stations and engaged on important duties before proceeding to France in May 1918. There he served with the Signal Section, and took part in many engagements in various sectors during the Retreat and Advance. He was demobilised in March 1919, and holds the General Service and Victory Medals.
7, Cambridge Street, Northampton. Z1836.

Printed at Intype London Ltd

Printed in the United Kingdom
by Lightning Source UK Ltd.
127377UK00002B/35-100/A